WHITAKER'S CONCISE ALMANACK 2002

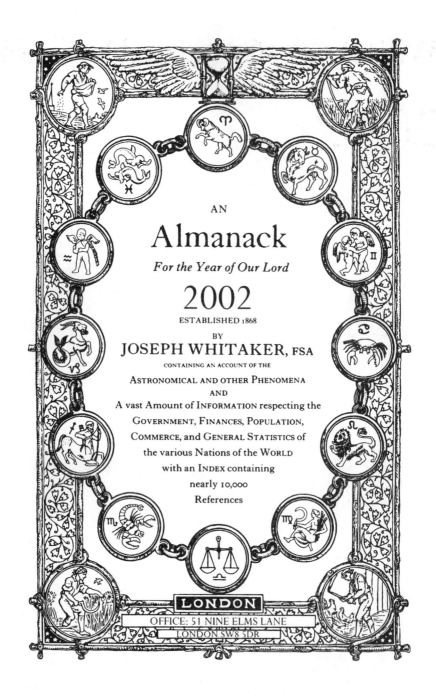

AN

Almanack

For the Year of Our Lord

2002

ESTABLISHED 1868

BY

JOSEPH WHITAKER, FSA

CONTAINING AN ACCOUNT OF THE

ASTRONOMICAL AND OTHER PHENOMENA

AND

A vast Amount of INFORMATION respecting the
GOVERNMENT, FINANCES, POPULATION,
COMMERCE, and GENERAL STATISTICS of
the various Nations of the WORLD
with an INDEX containing
nearly 10,000
References

LONDON

OFFICE: 51 NINE ELMS LANE
LONDON SW8 5DR

The traditional design of the title page for Whitaker's Almanack which has appeared in each edition since 1868

Whitaker's Concise Almanack

2002

LONDON
THE STATIONERY OFFICE

THE STATIONERY OFFICE LTD

51 Nine Elms Lane, London SW8 5DR

Whitaker's Almanack published annually since 1868

© 134th edition The Stationery Office Ltd 2001

Concise Almanack
0 11 702278 0

Designed by Douglas Martin
Jacket designed by Compendium
Jacket photographs: PA Photos, Ltd
Typeset in Great Britain by Tradespools Ltd, Frome, Somerset
Printed in Great Britian by The Stationery Office Ltd,
Parliamentary Press, London.
Bound by William Clowes Ltd, Beccles, Suffolk.

EDITORIAL CONSULTANTS
Gyles Brandreth
Rupert Pennant-Rea

EDITORIAL STAFF
Publisher: Tim Probart
Editor: Vanessa White
Development Editor: Inna Ward
Assistant Editors: Chris Sadowski, Tom Brundle, Sharon Taylor
Editorial Assistant: Debbie Paola

EDITORIAL CONTACT DETAILS
Tel: 020-7873 8442
Fax: 020-7873 8723
Email: whitakers.almanack@theso.co.uk
Web: www.whitakers-almanack.co.uk or
        www.thestationeryoffice.com
        www.clicktso.com

Published by The Stationery Office and available from:

The Publications Centre
(mail, telephone and fax orders only)
PO Box 276, London SW8 5DT
General enquiries/Telephone orders 0870-600 5522
Fax orders 0870-600 5533

The Stationery Office Bookshops
123 Kingsway, London WC2B 6PQ
020-7242 6393   Fax 020-7242 6394
16 Arthur Street, Belfast BTI 4GD
028-9023 8451   Fax 020-9023 5401
68-69 Bull Street, Birmingham B4 6AD
0121-236 9696   Fax 0121-236-9699
33 Wine Street, Cardiff CF1 2BZ
0117-926 4306   Fax 0117-929 4515
The Stationery Office Oriel Bookshop
18-19 High Street, Cardiff CF1 2BZ
029-2039 5548   Fax 029-2038 4347
71 Lothian Road, Edinburgh EH3 9AZ
0870-606 5566   Fax 0870-606 5588
9-21 Princess Street, Manchester M60 8AS
0161-834 7201   Fax 0161-833 0634

The Stationery Office's Accredited Agents
(see Yellow Pages)
and through good booksellers

Contents

AVAILABLE IN WHITAKER'S ALMANACK
(hardback, £40)

FINANCE

British currency, banking, mutual societies, national savings,
insurance, financial regulation, Stock Exchange, stamp
duties, taxation

LEGAL NOTES

Consumer law, wills, divorce

MEDIA

Broadcasting, the press, book publishers, annual reference
books

ORGANISATIONS

Trade and employers' associations, trade unions, national
academies of scholarship, research councils and associations,
sports bodies, clubs, societies and institutions

INTERNATIONAL ORGANISATIONS

European Union, the Commonwealth, CIS, United Nations

COUNTRIES OF THE WORLD

Countries A–Z, UK Overseas Territories

THE YEAR 2000–1

Archaeology, architecture, broadcasting, conservation and
heritage, dance, film, literature, opera, Parliament, acts of
parliament, white papers, science, sports results and records,
theatre, weather

Preface

Welcome to the new edition of Whitaker's Concise Almanack. I had hoped that this edition would have its primary focus on the June 2001 general election. An election year is always an important one in the compilation of Whitaker's Almanack as so many of our sections are totally revised to reflect the changes in parliament and government in general. This edition includes all the information you would expect to find including a fully updated list of MPs, comprehensive election results and details of all the new cabinet and shadow cabinet posts.

However, the terrorist attack on the World Trade Centre twin towers in New York City on the 11 September 2001 has highlighted a greater need than ever for understanding and information to help us come to terms with such an all encompassing 'world changing' event. The attack has sent enormous shock waves around the world. The media has quite rightly flooded us with news, commentary and analysis of this event, examining both its impact on future events and the factors that may have caused it. However, such media coverage can sometimes leave us wanting to know more of the background and, to expand our knowledge of certain regions and peoples of the world. Whitaker's Almanack can help to provide answers to some of the many questions that may arise over the weeks and months to come and tries to live up to its descriptive by-line of offering 'information for a changing world'. (*A brief summary of the media coverage of the attack on the twin towers is given in the Stop Press section at the back of this edition.*)

To those who are familiar with Whitaker's Almanack, the breadth of its coverage is no doubt one of the key motivations for its usage. I have always been in awe of the diversity of its content and would like to take this opportunity to draw perhaps newer readers to the events of the year section, a detailed chronological summary of news events both in the UK and around the world.

This edition of Whitaker's Almanack has also seen a change in editorship. I took over the compilation of the Whitaker's Almanack series in January of this year and hope to have done it justice in this short time. As always we are grateful to hear readers comments and suggestions. My warmest thanks go to my team and the many contributors who made this edition possible. Thank you also to the many individuals and organisations who assisted with our research.

WHITAKER'S ALMANACK
THE STATIONERY OFFICE
51 Nine Elms Lane, London SW8 5DR
TEL: 020-7873 8442
FAX: 020-7873 8723
E-MAIL: whitakers.almanack@theso.co.uk
Web: www.whitakers-almanack.co.uk
    www.thestationeryoffice.com
    www.clicktso.com

VANESSA WHITE
Editor

The Year 2002

CHRONOLOGICAL CYCLES AND ERAS

Dominical Letter	F
Golden Number (Lunar Cycle)	VIII
Julian Period	6715
Roman Indiction	10
Solar Cycle	23

	Beginning
Japanese year Heisei 14	1 January
Chinese year of the Horse	12 February
Regnal year 51	6 February
Hindu new year	13 April
Indian (Saka) year 1924	22 March
Muslim year AH 1423	15 March
Sikh new year	13 April
Jewish year AM 5763	7 September
Roman year 2755 AUC	

RELIGIOUS CALENDARS

CHRISTIAN

Epiphany	6 January
Presentation of Christ in the Temple	2 February
Ash Wednesday	13 February
The Annunciation	25 March
Maundy Thursday	28 March
Good Friday	29 March
Easter Day (western churches)	31 March
Easter Day (Eastern Orthodox)	5 May
Rogation Sunday	5 May
Ascension Day	9 May
Pentecost (Whit Sunday)	19 May
Trinity Sunday	26 May
Corpus Christi	30 May
All Saints' Day	1 November
Advent Sunday	1 December
Christmas Day	25 December

HINDU

Makara Sankranti	14 January
Vasant Panchami (Sarasvati-puja)	17 February
Mahashivaratri	12 March
Holi	28 March
Chaitra (Hindu new year)	13 April
Ramanavami	21 April
Raksha-bandhan	22 August
Janmashtami	30 August
Ganesh Chaturthi, first day	10 September
Ganesh festival, last day	20 September
Durga-puja	7 October
Navaratri festival, first day	7 October
Sarasvati-puja	12 October
Dasara	15 October
Diwali, first day	2 November
Diwali, last day	6 November

JEWISH

Purim,	26 February
Passover, first day	28 March
Feast of Weeks, first day	17 May
Jewish new year, first day	7 September
Yom Kippur (Day of Atonement)	16 September
Feast of Tabernacles, first day	21 September
Chanucah, first day	30 November

MUSLIM

Muslim new year	15 March
Ramadan, first day	6 November

SIKH

Birthday of Guru Gobind Singh Ji	5 January
Baisakhi Mela (Sikh new year)	13 April
Martyrdom of Guru Arjan Dev Ji	16 June
Birthday of Guru Nanak Dev Ji	11 November
Martyrdom of Guru Tegh Bahadur Ji	24 November

CIVIL CALENDAR

Accession of Queen Elizabeth II	6 February
Duke of York's birthday	19 February
St David's Day	1 March
Earl of Wessex birthday	10 March
Commonwealth Day	11 March
St Patrick's Day	17 March
Birthday of Queen Elizabeth II	21 April
St George's Day	23 April
Europe Day	9 May
Coronation of Queen Elizabeth II	2 June
Duke of Edinburgh's birthday	10 June
The Queen's Official Birthday	15 June
Queen Elizabeth the Queen Mother's birthday	4 August
Princess Royal's birthday	15 August
Princess Margaret's birthday	21 August
Lord Mayor's Day	9 November
Remembrance Sunday	10 November
Prince of Wales's birthday	14 November
Wedding Day of Queen Elizabeth II	20 November
St Andrew's Day	30 November

LEGAL CALENDAR

LAW TERMS

Hilary Term	11 January to 27 March
Easter Term	9 April to 31 May
Trinity Term	18 June to 31 July
Michaelmas Term	1 October to 21 December

QUARTER DAYS

England, Wales and Northern Ireland

Lady	25 March
Midsummer	24 June
Michaelmas	29 September
Christmas	25 December

TERM DAYS

Scotland

Candlemas	28 February
Whitsunday	28 May
Lammas	28 August
Martinmas	28 November
Removal Terms	28 May, 28 November

2002

JANUARY

Sunday	6	13	20	27
Monday	7	14	21	28
Tuesday	1	8	15	22	29
Wednesday	2	9	16	23	30
Thursday	3	10	17	24	31
Friday	4	11	18	25
Saturday	5	12	19	26

FEBRUARY

Sunday	3	10	17	24
Monday	4	11	18	25
Tuesday	5	12	19	26
Wednesday	6	13	20	27
Thursday	7	14	21	28
Friday	1	8	15	22
Saturday	2	9	16	23

MARCH

Sunday	3	10	17	24	31
Monday	4	11	18	25
Tuesday	5	12	19	26
Wednesday	6	13	20	27
Thursday	7	14	21	28
Friday	1	8	15	22	29
Saturday	2	9	16	23	30

APRIL

Sunday	7	14	21	28
Monday	1	8	15	22	29
Tuesday	2	9	16	23	30
Wednesday	3	10	17	24
Thursday	4	11	18	25
Friday	5	12	19	26
Saturday	6	13	20	27

MAY

Sunday	5	12	19	26
Monday	6	13	20	27
Tuesday	7	14	21	28
Wednesday	1	8	15	22	29
Thursday	2	9	16	23	30
Friday	3	10	17	24	31
Saturday	4	11	18	25

JUNE

Sunday	2	9	16	23	30
Monday	3	10	17	24
Tuesday	4	11	18	25
Wednesday	5	12	19	26
Thursday	6	13	20	27
Friday	7	14	21	28
Saturday	1	8	15	22	29

JULY

Sunday	7	14	21	28
Monday	1	8	15	22	29
Tuesday	2	9	16	23	30
Wednesday	3	10	17	24	31
Thursday	4	11	18	25
Friday	5	12	19	26
Saturday	6	13	20	27

AUGUST

Sunday	4	11	18	25
Monday	5	12	19	26
Tuesday	6	13	20	27
Wednesday	7	14	21	28
Thursday	1	8	15	22	29
Friday	2	9	16	23	30
Saturday	3	10	17	24	31

SEPTEMBER

Sunday	1	8	15	22	29
Monday	2	9	16	23	30
Tuesday	3	10	17	24
Wednesday	4	11	18	25
Thursday	5	12	19	26
Friday	6	13	20	27
Saturday	7	14	21	28

OCTOBER

Sunday	6	13	20	27
Monday	7	14	21	28
Tuesday	1	8	15	22	29
Wednesday	2	9	16	23	30
Thursday	3	10	17	24	31
Friday	4	11	18	25
Saturday	5	12	19	26

NOVEMBER

Sunday	3	10	17	24
Monday	4	11	18	25
Tuesday	5	12	19	26
Wednesday	6	13	20	27
Thursday	7	14	21	28
Friday	1	8	15	22	29
Saturday	2	9	16	23	30

DECEMBER

Sunday	1	8	15	22	29
Monday	2	9	16	23	30
Tuesday	3	10	17	24	31
Wednesday	4	11	18	25
Thursday	5	12	19	26
Friday	6	13	20	27
Saturday	7	14	21	28

PUBLIC HOLIDAYS

	England and Wales	Scotland	Northern Ireland
New Year	†1 January	1, †2 January	†1 January
St Patrick's Day	–	–	‡18 March
*Good Friday	29 March	29 March	29 March
Easter Monday	1 April	–	1 April
Early May	†6 May	6 May	†6 May
Golden Jubilee	3 June	3 June	3 June
Spring	4 June	†4 June	4 June
Battle of the Boyne	–	–	‡12 July
Summer	26 August	5 August	26 August
*Christmas	25, 26 December	25, †26 December	25, 26 December

*In England, Wales and Northern Ireland, Christmas Day and Good Friday are common law holidays
In the Channel Islands, Liberation Day is a bank and public holiday
† Subject to royal proclamation
‡ Subject to proclamation by the Secretary of State for Northern Ireland

2003

JANUARY					
Sunday		5	12	19	26
Monday		6	13	20	27
Tuesday		7	14	21	28
Wednesday	1	8	15	22	29
Thursday	2	9	16	23	30
Friday	3	10	17	24	31
Saturday	4	11	18	25	

FEBRUARY					
Sunday		2	9	16	23
Monday		3	10	17	24
Tuesday		4	11	18	25
Wednesday		5	12	19	26
Thursday		6	13	20	27
Friday		7	14	21	28
Saturday	1	8	15	22	

MARCH						
Sunday		2	9	16	23	30
Monday		3	10	17	24	31
Tuesday		4	11	18	25	
Wednesday		5	12	19	26	
Thursday		6	13	20	27	
Friday		7	14	21	28	
Saturday	1	8	15	22	29	

APRIL					
Sunday		6	13	20	27
Monday		7	14	21	28
Tuesday	1	8	15	22	29
Wednesday	2	9	16	23	30
Thursday	3	10	17	24	
Friday	4	11	18	25	
Saturday	5	12	19	26	

MAY					
Sunday		4	11	18	25
Monday		5	12	19	26
Tuesday		6	13	20	27
Wednesday		7	14	21	28
Thursday	1	8	15	22	29
Friday	2	9	16	23	30
Saturday	3	10	17	24	31

JUNE					
Sunday	1	8	15	22	29
Monday	2	9	16	23	30
Tuesday	3	10	17	24	
Wednesday	4	11	18	25	
Thursday	5	12	19	26	
Friday	6	13	20	27	
Saturday	7	14	21	28	

JULY					
Sunday		6	13	20	27
Monday		7	14	21	28
Tuesday	1	8	15	22	29
Wednesday	2	9	16	23	30
Thursday	3	10	17	24	31
Friday	4	11	18	25	
Saturday	5	12	19	26	

AUGUST					
Sunday		3	10	17	24	31
Monday		4	11	18	25
Tuesday		5	12	19	26
Wednesday		6	13	20	27
Thursday		7	14	21	28
Friday	1	8	15	22	29
Saturday	2	9	16	23	30

SEPTEMBER					
Sunday		7	14	21	28
Monday	1	8	15	22	29
Tuesday	2	9	16	23	30
Wednesday	3	10	17	24	
Thursday	4	11	18	25	
Friday	5	12	19	26	
Saturday	6	13	20	27	

OCTOBER					
Sunday		5	12	19	26
Monday		6	13	20	27
Tuesday		7	14	21	28
Wednesday	1	8	15	22	29
Thursday	2	9	16	23	30
Friday	3	10	17	24	31
Saturday	4	11	18	25	

NOVEMBER					
Sunday		2	9	16	23	30
Monday		3	10	17	24
Tuesday		4	11	18	25
Wednesday		5	12	19	26
Thursday		6	13	20	27
Friday		7	14	21	28
Saturday	1	8	15	22	29

DECEMBER					
Sunday		7	14	21	28
Monday	1	8	15	22	29
Tuesday	2	9	16	23	30
Wednesday	3	10	17	24	31
Thursday	4	11	18	25	
Friday	5	12	19	26	
Saturday	6	13	20	27	

PUBLIC HOLIDAYS	*England and Wales*	*Scotland*	*Northern Ireland*
New Year	†1 January	1, †2 January	†1 January
St Patrick's Day	—	—	‡17 March
*Good Friday	18 April	18 April	18 April
Easter Monday	21 April	—	21 April
Early May	†5 May	5 May	†5 May
Spring	26 May	†26 May	26 May
Battle of the Boyne	—	—	‡14 July
Summer	25 August	4 August	25 August
*Christmas	25, 26 December	25, †26 December	25, 26 December

*In England, Wales and Northern Ireland, Christmas Day and Good Friday are common law holidays
In the Channel Islands, Liberation Day is a bank and public holiday
† Subject to royal proclamation
‡ Subject to proclamation by the Secretary of State for Northern Ireland

FORTHCOMING EVENTS 2002

*Provisional dates

JANUARY
12–27   London International Mime Festival
16–20   Art 2002, Business Design Centre, London

FEBRUARY
1–3   Labour Party Conference, Cardiff Indoor Arena
18–19 May   American Sublime, Tate Britain

MARCH
2–10   Bath Literature Festival
6–1 April   Ideal Home Exhibition, Earls Court
7–10   Crufts Dog Show, NEC Birmingham
8–10   Liberal-Democrat Party Conference, MICC Manchester
8–17   National Science Week
17–19   London Book Fair

APRIL
14   London Marathon

MAY
17–2 June   Bath International Music Festival
18–19   London Tattoo, Wembley Arena
23–24   Chelsea Flower Show, Royal Hospital, Chelsea
31–9 June   The Hay Festival, Hay on Wye

JUNE
6–15   Hampton Court Palace Music Festival
7–23   The Aldeburgh Festival
8   Trooping the Colour – the Queen's Birthday Parade, Horse Guards Palace
11–9 August Royal Academy Summer Exhibition
25–27   Wisley Flower Show, RHS Garden, Woking
25–11 July   City of London Festival
29–14 July   Cheltenham International Festival of Music
29–24 August Kenwood House – Lakeside Concerts, Hampstead

JULY
1–4   The Royal Show, National Agricultural Centre, Stoneleigh Park
2–7   Hampton Court Palace Flower Show
*6–15 July   York Early Music Festival
11–21   Buxton Festival
18–27   The Welsh Proms, St David's Hall, Cardiff
19–14 September BBC Promenade Concerts, Royal Albert Hall

AUGUST
2–24 August Edinburgh Military Tattoo
13–2 September Edinburgh International Festival
*4–11   National Eisteddfod of Wales
*17–23   Three Choirs Festival, Hereford
20–22   Wisley Flower Show, RHS Garden, Woking
25–16   Notting Hill Carnival, London
30–3 November Blackpool Illuminations

SEPTEMBER
7   Braemar Royal Highland Gathering
*14–23   Southampton International Boat Show

OCTOBER
7–10   Conservative Party Conference, BIC Bournemouth
*8–8 December Glyndebourne Festival Opera Season

NOVEMBER
3   London to Brighton Veteran Car Run
10   Lord Mayor's Procession and Show, London
20 November– Huddersfield Contemporary Music
1 December   Festival
*7–22   London Film Festival, NFT and Odeon West End Cinema

SPORTS EVENTS

ATHLETICS
1–3 March   European Indoor Championships, Vienna
25 July–24 August Commonwealth Games, Manchester

CRICKET
Test Matches
16–20 May   England v. Sri Lanka, 1st, Lord's
30 May–3 June England v. Sri Lanka, 2nd, Edgbaston
13–17 June   England v. Sri Lanka, 3rd, Old Trafford
25–29 July   England v. India, 1st, Lord's
8–12 August England v. India, 2nd, Trent Bridge
22–26 August England v. India, 3rd, Headingley
5–9 September England v. India, 4th, Oval

NatWest Series
27 June   England v. Sri Lanka, Headingly
29 June   England v. India, Lord's
30 June   India v. England, Oval
2 July   England v. Sri Lanka, Headingly
4 July   England v. India, Durham
7 July   England v. Sri Lanka, Old Trafford
9 July   England v. India, Oval
13 July   The Final

CURLING
5–14 April   World Championships, Bismark, ND, USA

EQUESTRIAN EVENTS
2–5 May   The Mitsubishi Motors Badminton Horse Trials, Badminton
15–19 May   Royal Windsor Horse Show, Home Park, Windsor
29 August–1 Burghley Horse Trials, Stamford
September
5–8 September Blenheim Horse Trials
*26–30 September Horse of the Year Show, Wembley Arena, London
18–22 December International Show Jumping Championships, Olympia

FOOTBALL
24 February	Worthington Cup Final
4 May	FA Cup Final, Millennium Stadium, Cardiff
4 May	Scottish FA Cup Final, Hampden Park, Glasgow
4 May	Welsh FA Cup Final, Millennium Stadium, Cardiff
8 May	UEFA Cup Final
15 May	UEFA Champions League Final
31 May–30 June	FIFA World Cup Finals, Japan and South Korea

GOLF
3–8 June	Royal Porthcawl GC/Pyle and Kenfig GC
11–14 July	Loch Lomond Invitational
18–21 July	The Open, The Honourable Company of Edinburgh Golfers, Muirfield
28–30 September	Ryder Cup, The Belfry

HORSERACING
15 March	Cheltenham Gold Cup
4–6 April	The Martell Grant National, Aintree
20 April	Stakis Casinos Scottish Grand National, Ayr
27 April	Whitbread Gold Cup, Sandown Park
29 April–12 August	Windsor Evening Race Meeting Season
4–6 May	1000 Guineas, Newmarket
8 June	The Vodaphone Derby, Epsom
18–21 June	Royal Ascot
9–11 July	Newmarket July
27 July	King George VI and Queen Elizabeth Diamond Stakes, Ascot
30 July–3 August	Glorious Goodwood
11–14 September	St Leger, Doncaster
3 November	Hennessy Cognac Gold Cup, Newbury

MOTOR SPORTS
12–14 July	Formula 1: The British Grand Prix, Silverstone
1–7 June	Motorcycles: TT Races, Isle of Man

OLYMPICS
8–24 February	Winter Olympic Games, Salt Lake
7–16 March	Winter Paralympic Games, Salt Lake

ROWING AND YACHTING
3–13	48th London Boat Show
3–7 July	Henley Royal Regatta
24 March	The Oxford and Cambridge Boat Race

RUGBY LEAGUE
27 April	Challenge Cup Final, Murrayfield, Edinburgh

RUGBY UNION SIX NATIONS
2 February	Scotland v. England, Murrayfield
3 February	Ireland v. Wales, Lansdowne Road
16 February	Italy v. Scotland, Rome; Wales v. France, Cardiff; England v. Ireland, Twickenham
2 March	Ireland v. Scotland, Lansdowne Road; Wales v. Italy, Cardiff; France v. England, Paris
23 March	Ireland v. Italy, Lansdowne Road; Scotland v. France, Murrayfield; England v. Wales, Twickenham
6 April	Wales v. Scotland, Cardiff; France v. Ireland, Paris
7 April	Italy v. England, Rome

SHOOTING
29 June–13 July	Imperial Meeting, Bisley
25 July–3 August	Commonwealth Games, Bisley

SNOOKER
3–10 February	Benson & Hedges Masters, Wembley Conference Centre, London
20 April–6 May	Embassy World Championship, Crucible Theatre, Sheffield

TENNIS
10–16 June	Stella Artois Tournament, Queens Club
24 June–7 July	The All-England Championships, Wimbledon, London
4–8 December	Honda Challenge, Royal Albert Hall

CENTENARIES OF 2002

1602
14 February   Francesco Cavalli, Italian composer, born

1702
8 March   William III Orange, Dutch King 1689–1702, died

1802
26 February   Victor Hugo, French novelist and poet, born

6 March   Sir Edwin Landseer, painter and sculptor, born

18 April   Erasmus Darwin, physician, free-thinker, poet and grandfather of Charles Darwin, died

12 June   Harriet Martineau, essayist and novelist, born

24 July   Alexandre Dumas, French novelist and playwright, born

15 November   George Romney, painter, died

1902
5 January   Stella Gibbons, novelist, journalist and poet, born

31 January   Tallulah Bankhead, American actress, born

4 February   Charles Lindbergh, American aviator, born

27 February   John Steinbeck, American novelist, born

16 March   Dame Lucie Rie, Austrian-British potter, born

17 March   Bobby Jones, American golfer, born

26 March   Cecil Rhodes, colonialist, founder of Rhodesia, died

28 March   Dame Flora Robson, actress, born

29 March   Sir William Walton, composer, born

23 April   Halldor Laxness, Icelandic writer and Nobel literature laureate 1995, born

6 June   Lord Kings Norton Cox, aeronautical engineer, industrialist, chancellor of Cranfield University 1969-97, born

18 June   Samuel Butler, novelist, essayist and critic, died

28 June   Richard Rodgers, American composer, born

28 July   Sir Karl Popper, Austrian-British philosopher of natural and social science, born

31 July   Sir George Allen, cricketer, born

16 August   Georgette Heyer, novelist, born

19 August   Ogden Nash, American humorous poet, born

20 September   Florence Smith, poet, born

21 September   Sir Allen Lane, pioneer of paperback publishing, born

29 September   Émile Zola, French novelist, died

29 October   Susie Cooper, potter, born

9 December   R. A. Butler, Conservative politician, born

19 December   Sir Ralph Richardson, actor, born

CENTENARIES OF 2003

1503
14 December   Nostradamus, astrologer, physician and seer, born

11 January   Girolamo Mazzola, painter, born

1603
24 March   Elizabeth I, Tudor Queen of England 1558-1603, died

1703
15/16 May   Charles Perrault, poet, prose writer and storyteller; wrote 'Tales of Mother Goose', died

26 May   Samuel Pepys, diarist, died

17 June   John Wesley, co-founder of the Methodist movement, born

5 October   Jonathan Edwards, theologian and metaphysician, born

1803
3 March   Alexandre Gabriel Decamps, painter, of the Romantic school, born

25 May   Edward Bulwer Lytton, novelist, playwright, poet, essayist and politician, born

25 May   Ralph Waldo, Emerson, lecturer, poet and essayist, born

5 July   George Borrow, writer and traveller, born

16 October   Robert Stephenson, engineer, born

29 November   Christian Doppler, physicist, developed 'Doppler's Principle', born

11 December   Hector Berlioz, composer, born

21 December   Sir Joseph Whitworth, engineer, born

1903
10 January   Dame Barbara Hepworth, sculptor, born

11 January   Alan Paton, novelist, born

19 January   Sir Alfred Beit, financier and philanthropist, born

13 February   Georges Simenon, novelist, born

22 February   Hugo Wolf, composer, died

24 March   Malcolm Muggeridge, television broadcaster, born

2 May   Dr Benjamin Spock, paediatrician and child psychologist, born

8 May   Paul Gauguin, post-Impressionist painter, died

12 May   Sir Lennox Berkeley, composer, born

29 May   Bob Hope, actor, born

6 June   Aram Ilich Khachaturian, composer, born

19 June   Walter Hammond, cricketer, born

25 June   George Orwell, author, born

1 July   Amy Johnson, aviator, born

2 July   Lord Home of the Hirsel, Alec Douglas-Home, Prime Minister 1963-4, born

17 July   James M. Whistler, painter, died

18 August   Marcel Carne, film director, born

24 August   Graham Sutherland, painter, born

25 September   Mark Rothko, painter, born

28 October   Evelyn Waugh, novelist, born

13 November   Camille Pissarro, painter, died

4 December   Alfred Leslie Rowse, historian, born

13 December   John Piper, painter, born

28 December   George Gissing, novelist, died

Astronomy

The following pages give astronomical data for each month of the year 2002. There are four pages of data for each month. All data are given for 0h Greenwich Mean Time (GMT), i.e. at the midnight at the beginning of the day named. This applies also to data for the months when British Summer Time is in operation (for dates, *see* below).

The astronomical data are given in a form suitable for observation with the naked eye or with a small telescope. These data do not attempt to replace the *Astronomical Almanac* for professional astronomers.

A fuller explanation of how to use the astronomical data is given on pages 71–3.

CALENDAR FOR EACH MONTH

The calendar for each month shows dates of religious, civil and legal significance for the year 2002.

The days in bold type are the principal holy days and the festivals and greater holy days of the Church of England as set out in the calendar authorized for use from 1997. Observance of certain festivals and greater holy days is transferred if the day falls on a principal holy day. The calendar shows the date on which holy days and festivals are to be observed in 2002.

The days in small capitals are dates of significance in the calendars of non-Anglican denominations and non-Christian religions.

The days in italic type are dates of civil and legal significance. The royal anniversaries shown in italic type are the days on which the Union flag is to be flown.

The rest of the calendar comprises days of general interest and the dates of birth or death of well-known people.

Fuller explanations of the various calendars can be found under Time Measurement and Calendars (pages 81–9).

The zodiacal signs through which the Sun is passing during each month are illustrated. The date of transition from one sign to the next, to the nearest hour, is given under Astronomical Phenomena.

JULIAN DATE

The Julian date on 2002 January 0.0 is 2452274.5. To find the Julian date for any other date in 2002 (at 0h GMT), add the day-of-the-year number on the extreme right of the calendar for each month to the Julian date for January 0.0.

SEASONS

The seasons are defined astronomically as follows:

Spring from the vernal equinox to the summer solstice
Summer from the summer solstice to the autumnal equinox
Autumn from the autumnal equinox to the winter solstice
Winter from the winter solstice to the vernal equinox

The seasons in 2002 are:

Northern hemisphere

Vernal equinox	March 20d 19h GMT
Summer solstice	June 21d 13h GMT
Autumnal equinox	September 23d 05h GMT
Winter solstice	December 22d 01h GMT

Southern hemisphere

Autumnal equinox	March 20d 19h GMT
Winter solstice	June 21d 13h GMT
Vernal equinox	September 23d 05h GMT
Summer solstice	December 22d 01h GMT

The longest day of the year, measured from sunrise to sunset, is at the summer solstice. The longest day in the United Kingdom will fall on 21 June in 2002. *See also* page 81.

The shortest day of the year is at the winter solstice. The shortest day in the United Kingdom will fall on 22 December in 2002. *See also* page 81.

The equinox is the point at which day and night are of equal length all over the world. *See also* page 81.

In popular parlance, the seasons in the northern hemisphere comprise the following months:

Spring	March, April, May
Summer	June, July, August
Autumn	September, October, November
Winter	December, January, February

BRITISH SUMMER TIME

British Summer Time is the legal time for general purposes during the period in which it is in operation (*see also* page 75). During this period, clocks are kept one hour ahead of Greenwich Mean Time. The hour of changeover is 01h Greenwich Mean Time. The duration of Summer Time in 2002 is from March 31 01h GMT to October 27 01h GMT.

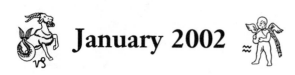

January 2002

FIRST MONTH, 31 DAYS. *Janus*, god of the portal, facing two ways, past and future

1	*Tuesday*	**Naming and Circumcision of Jesus.** *Bank Holiday in UK.*	1
2	*Wednesday*	*Bank Holiday in Scotland.* Alexander William Kinglake d. 1891	2
3	*Thursday*	Bill Travers b. 1922. Jeremiah Horrocks d. 1641	3
4	*Friday*	Augustus John b. 1878. Donald Campbell d. 1967	4
5	*Saturday*	Stella Gibbons b. 1902. Queen Catherine de Medici d. 1589	5
6	*Sunday*	**The Epiphany. 2nd S. of Christmas.**	6
7	*Monday*	Hirohito Michinomiya d. 1989.	*week 1 day* 7
8	*Tuesday*	Dennis Wheatley b. 1897. En-lai Chou d. 1976	8
9	*Wednesday*	Richard Nixon b. 1913. Metropolitan Line, Paddington to Holborn Hill, first underground trains in operation (journey took 20 mins) 1863	9
10	*Thursday*	Lucila Godoy de Alcayaga d. 1957. Penny Post introduced 1840	10
11	*Friday*	*Hilary Law Sittings begin.* Louis François Roubillac d.1762	11
12	*Saturday*	Charles Perrault b. 1628.	12
13	*Sunday*	**1st S. of Epiphany.** Independent Labour Party founded 1893	13
14	*Monday*	Albert Schweitzer b. 1875. Jean Ingres d. 1867	*week 2 day* 14
15	*Tuesday*	Ivor Novello b. 1893. Rosa Luxemburg d. 1919	15
16	*Wednesday*	Léo Delibes d. 1891. Start of Prohibition in the USA 1920	16
17	*Thursday*	David Lloyd George b. 1963. George Bancroft d. 1891	17
18	*Friday*	A. A. Milne b. 1882. Captain Scott reaches the South Pole 1912	18
19	*Saturday*	Sir Alfred Beit b. 1903. William Congreve d. 1729	19
20	*Sunday*	**2nd S. of Epiphany.** First assembly of the House of Commons 1265	20
21	*Monday*	King Louis XVI d. 1793. Concorde entered service 1976	*week 3 day* 21
22	*Tuesday*	Capture of Tobruk 1941	22
23	*Wednesday*	Sergey Eisenstein b. 1898. Charles Kingsley d. 1875	23
24	*Thursday*	William Congreve b. 1670. Amedeo Modigliani d. 1920	24
25	*Friday*	**Conversion of St Paul.** Virginia Woolf b. 1882	25
26	*Saturday*	Sir Henry Cotton b. 1907. Edward G. Robinson d. 1973	26
27	*Sunday*	**9th S. before Easter.** Johann Gottlieb Fichte d. 1814	27
28	*Monday*	Sir Henry Stanley b. 1841. Joseph Alexandrovich Brodsky d. 1996	*week 4 day* 28
29	*Tuesday*	Robert Lee Frost d. 1963. Institution of the V.C. 1856	29
30	*Wednesday*	Charles Bradlaugh d. 1891. Hitler formed Nazi government in Germany 1933	30
31	*Thursday*	Jean Simmons b. 1929. Jean Giraudoux d. 1944	31

ASTRONOMICAL PHENOMENA

d	h	
1	06	Jupiter at opposition
2	15	Earth at perihelion (147 million km)
12	00	Mercury at greatest elongation E.19°
13	13	Venus in conjunction with Moon. Venus 1° N.
14	12	Venus in superior conjunction
15	05	Mercury in conjunction with Moon. Mercury 4° N.
18	21	Mercury at stationary point
19	03	Mars in conjunction with Moon. Mars 5° N.
20	06	Sun's longitude 300° ≈≈
24	16	Saturn in conjunction with Moon. Saturn 0°.06 S.
26	12	Venus in conjunction with Mercury. Venus 4° S.
26	19	Jupiter in conjunction with Moon. Jupiter 0°.9 S.
27	19	Mercury in inferior conjunction
28	14	Neptune in conjunction

MINIMA OF ALGOL

d	h	d	h	d	h
1	23.6	13	10.9	24	22.2
4	20.5	16	07.8	27	19.0
7	17.3	19	04.6	30	15.9
10	14.1	22	01.4		

CONSTELLATIONS

The following constellations are near the meridian at

	d	h		d	h
December	1	24	January	16	21
December	16	23	February	1	20
January	1	22	February	15	19

Draco (below the Pole), Ursa Minor (below the Pole), Camelopardus, Perseus, Auriga, Taurus, Orion, Eridanus and Lepus

THE MOON

Phases, Apsides and Node	d	h	m
☾ Last Quarter	6	03	55
● New Moon	13	13	29
☽ First Quarter	21	17	46
○ Full Moon	28	22	50

	d	h	m
Perigee (365,384km)	2	07	21
Apogee (405,538km)	18	08	55
Perigee (359,983km)	30	09	06

Mean longitude of ascending node on January 1, 86°

THE SUN   S.D 16'.1

Day	Right Ascension	Dec. −	Equation of Time	Rise 52°	Rise 56°	Transit	Set 52°	Set 56°	Sidereal time	Transit of First Point of Aries
	h m s	° ′	m s	h m	h m	h m	h m	h m	h m s	h m s
1	18 45 10	23 02	− 3 17	8 08	8 31	12 04	15 59	15 36	6 41 53	17 15 17
2	18 49 35	22 57	− 3 46	8 08	8 31	12 04	16 00	15 37	6 45 50	17 11 21
3	18 54 00	22 52	− 4 13	8 08	8 31	12 04	16 01	15 39	6 49 46	17 07 25
4	18 58 24	22 46	− 4 41	8 08	8 30	12 05	16 02	15 40	6 53 43	17 03 29
5	19 02 47	22 39	− 5 08	8 07	8 30	12 05	16 04	15 41	6 57 39	16 59 33
6	19 07 11	22 32	− 5 35	8 07	8 29	12 06	16 05	15 43	7 01 36	16 55 37
7	19 11 34	22 25	− 6 01	8 07	8 29	12 06	16 06	15 44	7 05 32	16 51 41
8	19 15 56	22 18	− 6 27	8 06	8 28	12 07	16 08	15 46	7 09 29	16 47 45
9	19 20 18	22 09	− 6 52	8 06	8 27	12 07	16 09	15 47	7 13 26	16 43 49
10	19 24 39	22 01	− 7 17	8 05	8 26	12 07	16 10	15 49	7 17 22	16 39 54
11	19 29 00	21 52	− 7 41	8 04	8 26	12 08	16 12	15 51	7 21 19	16 35 58
12	19 33 20	21 42	− 8 05	8 04	8 25	12 08	16 13	15 52	7 25 15	16 32 02
13	19 37 40	21 33	− 8 28	8 03	8 24	12 09	16 15	15 54	7 29 12	16 28 06
14	19 41 59	21 22	− 8 51	8 02	8 23	12 09	16 16	15 56	7 33 08	16 24 10
15	19 46 18	21 12	− 9 13	8 01	8 21	12 09	16 18	15 58	7 37 05	16 20 14
16	19 50 35	21 01	− 9 34	8 00	8 20	12 10	16 19	16 00	7 41 02	16 16 18
17	19 54 53	20 49	− 9 54	7 59	8 19	12 10	16 21	16 02	7 44 58	16 12 22
18	19 59 09	20 37	−10 14	7 59	8 18	12 10	16 23	16 03	7 48 55	16 08 26
19	20 03 24	20 25	−10 33	7 57	8 17	12 11	16 24	16 05	7 52 51	16 04 30
20	20 07 39	20 12	−10 52	7 56	8 15	12 11	16 26	16 07	7 56 48	16 00 34
21	20 11 53	19 59	−11 09	7 55	8 14	12 11	16 28	16 09	8 00 44	15 56 39
22	20 16 07	19 46	−11 26	7 54	8 12	12 12	16 30	16 11	8 04 41	15 52 43
23	20 20 19	19 32	−11 42	7 53	8 11	12 12	16 31	16 14	8 08 37	15 48 47
24	20 24 31	19 18	−11 57	7 52	8 09	12 12	16 33	16 16	8 12 34	15 44 51
25	20 28 42	19 03	−12 12	7 50	8 08	12 12	16 35	16 18	8 16 31	15 40 55
26	20 32 52	18 49	−12 25	7 49	8 06	12 13	16 37	16 20	8 20 27	15 36 59
27	20 37 02	18 33	−12 38	7 48	8 04	12 13	16 38	16 22	8 24 24	15 33 03
28	20 41 10	18 18	−12 50	7 46	8 03	12 13	16 40	16 24	8 28 20	15 29 07
29	20 45 18	18 02	−13 01	7 45	8 01	12 13	16 42	16 26	8 32 17	15 25 11
30	20 49 25	17 46	−13 11	7 43	7 59	12 13	16 44	16 28	8 36 13	15 21 15
31	20 53 31	17 29	−13 21	7 42	7 57	12 13	16 46	16 30	8 40 10	15 17 19

DURATION OF TWILIGHT (in minutes)

Latitude	52°	56°	52°	56°	52°	56°	52°	56°
	1 January		11 January		21 January		31 January	
Civil	41	47	40	45	38	43	37	41
Nautical	84	96	82	93	80	90	78	87
Astronomical	125	141	123	138	120	134	117	130

THE NIGHT SKY

Mercury is at greatest eastern elongation on the 11th, and is visible for the first three weeks of the month. During this period it is an evening object, its magnitude fading from − 0.7 to + 1.0. Mercury is visible for a short while at the end of evening civil twilight, low in the south-western sky. After becoming lost in the evening twilight it passes through inferior conjunction on the 27th. On the evening of the 15th the thin crescent Moon, 2 days old, is 9 degrees to the left of Mercury, low above the south-western horizon, though this will require very good conditions for successful observation.

Venus passes through superior conjunction on the 14th and is therefore unsuitably placed for observation throughout the month.

Mars, magnitude +0.9, is visible in the south-western sky in the evenings. During the month the planet will be seen moving eastwards, south of the Square of Pegasus.

Unusually, it can be said that for the whole month, for the whole of mainland Britain, it is visible until about 21h 30m L.M.T. (i.e. when it has reached an altitude of 5 degrees in the western sky). The crescent Moon will be seen 7 degrees south of the planet on the evening of the 18th, while it will be about 10 degrees to the left of it on the following evening.

Jupiter, magnitude −2.7, is at opposition on the 1st and is therefore visible throughout the hours of darkness. Jupiter is retrograding slowly in the western part of the constellation of Gemini. On the early evening of the 26th Jupiter will be seen only about 0.1 degrees from the lower limb of the gibbous Moon.

Saturn, magnitude −0.2, is an evening object and visible in the southern and south-western sky for the greater part of the night. Saturn is moving slowly westwards in the constellation of Taurus, north of the Hyades. The gibbous Moon will be seen near the planet on the evening of the 24th.

THE MOON

Day	RA	Dec.	Hor. par.	Semi-diam	Sun's co-long.	PA of Bright Limb	Phase	Age	Rise 52°	Rise 56°	Transit	Set 52°	Set 56°
	h m	°	'	'	°	°	%	d	h m	h m	h m	h m	h m
1	8 16	+22.8	59.8	16.3	113	95	97	17.1	18 24	18 02	1 38	10 00	10 23
2	9 17	+19.9	60.0	16.3	125	102	91	18.1	19 49	19 33	2 38	10 35	10 52
3	10 16	+15.8	60.0	16.3	138	107	84	19.1	21 14	21 04	3 34	11 01	11 13
4	11 12	+10.7	59.8	16.3	150	110	74	20.1	22 38	22 33	4 28	11 23	11 30
5	12 05	+ 5.2	59.4	16.2	162	112	63	21.1	23 59	—	5 18	11 42	11 44
6	12 57	- 0.6	59.0	16.1	174	113	52	22.1	—	0 00	6 07	12 00	11 57
7	13 48	- 6.3	58.5	15.9	186	112	41	23.1	1 20	1 26	6 56	12 19	12 11
8	14 39	-11.5	58.0	15.8	198	109	30	24.1	2 39	2 51	7 45	12 39	12 27
9	15 31	-16.1	57.5	15.7	210	106	21	25.1	3 58	4 15	8 36	13 04	12 46
10	16 25	-19.9	57.0	15.5	223	101	13	26.1	5 14	5 36	9 28	13 34	13 12
11	17 20	-22.5	56.5	15.4	235	95	7	27.1	6 25	6 51	10 21	14 13	13 46
12	18 16	-24.0	56.1	15.3	247	87	2	28.1	7 28	7 56	11 15	15 01	14 33
13	19 11	-24.2	55.6	15.1	259	68	0	29.1	8 19	8 46	12 08	15 59	15 32
14	20 05	-23.1	55.2	15.0	271	287	0	0.4	8 59	9 23	12 59	17 04	16 40
15	20 58	-21.0	54.8	14.9	284	266	2	1.4	9 30	9 50	13 47	18 12	17 53
16	21 47	-17.9	54.4	14.8	296	259	6	2.4	9 54	10 09	14 33	19 21	19 07
17	22 35	-14.2	54.2	14.8	308	254	11	3.4	10 13	10 24	15 16	20 29	20 20
18	23 20	- 9.9	54.1	14.7	320	251	18	4.4	10 30	10 37	15 57	21 37	21 32
19	0 04	- 5.3	54.1	14.7	332	249	25	5.4	10 45	10 48	16 38	22 44	22 43
20	0 47	- 0.5	54.3	14.8	344	249	34	6.4	10 59	10 58	17 19	23 51	23 55
21	1 30	+ 4.4	54.6	14.9	357	249	43	7.4	11 15	11 09	18 0	—	—
22	2 15	+ 9.2	55.1	15.0	9	250	53	8.4	11 31	11 22	18 44	1 01	1 09
23	3 02	+13.7	55.8	15.2	21	253	62	9.4	11 52	11 37	19 31	2 12	2 25
24	3 52	+17.8	56.6	15.4	33	257	72	10.4	12 17	11 58	20 22	3 26	3 44
25	4 46	+21.1	57.5	15.7	45	262	81	11.4	12 52	12 28	21 17	4 41	5 04
26	5 44	+23.4	58.5	15.9	57	268	89	12.4	13 38	13 11	22 17	5 53	6 20
27	6 46	+24.3	59.3	16.2	69	277	95	13.4	14 40	14 12	23 19	6 58	7 25
28	7 49	+23.6	60.1	16.4	82	291	99	14.4	15 55	15 31	—	7 50	8 15
29	8 52	+21.3	60.6	16.5	94	26	100	15.4	17 21	17 02	0 21	8 31	8 50
30	9 53	+17.5	60.9	16.6	106	94	98	16.4	18 49	18 37	1 20	9 01	9 16
31	10 52	+12.5	60.9	16.6	118	104	94	17.4	20 17	20 11	2 17	9 26	9 35

MERCURY

Day	RA	Dec.	Diam.	Phase	Transit	5° high 52°	5° high 56°
	h m	°	"	%	h m	h m	h m
1	19 52	-23.0	5	87	13 11	16 17	15 42
3	20 05	-22.3	6	84	13 16	16 28	15 56
5	20 17	-21.5	6	79	13 21	16 39	16 09
7	20 29	-20.6	6	75	13 24	16 50	16 22
9	20 39	-19.7	6	69	13 27	16 59	16 33
11	20 49	-18.7	7	62	13 28	17 07	16 43
13	20 57	-17.7	7	54	13 27	17 13	16 51
15	21 02	-16.8	7	45	13 24	17 17	16 56
17	21 06	-16.0	8	35	13 19	17 16	16 57
19	21 06	-15.4	8	25	13 11	17 12	16 53
21	21 04	-14.9	9	16	13 00	17 03	16 45
23	20 58	-14.7	9	9	12 46	16 49	16 31
25	20 50	-14.7	10	4	12 29	16 32	16 14
27	20 41	-14.9	10	1	12 12	16 13	15 54
29	20 30	-15.3	10	1	11 54	7 55	8 14
31	20 21	-15.8	10	4	11 36	7 41	8 01

VENUS

Day	RA	Dec.	Diam.	Phase	Transit	5° high 52°	5° high 56°
	h m	°	"	%	h m	h m	h m
1	18 31	-23.6	10	100	11 50	14 48	14 11
6	18 59	-23.3	10	100	11 58	14 59	14 22
11	19 26	-22.7	10	100	12 05	15 12	14 38
16	19 53	-21.9	10	100	12 13	15 27	14 55
21	20 19	-20.7	10	100	12 19	15 43	15 15
26	20 45	-19.3	10	100	12 26	16 01	15 35
31	21 11	-17.6	10	100	12 31	16 18	15 56

MARS

Day	RA	Dec.	Diam.	Phase	Transit	5° high 52°	5° high 56°
1	23 13	- 5.8	6	89	16 30	21 28	21 20
6	23 26	- 4.3	6	89	16 24	21 30	21 23
11	23 39	- 2.8	6	90	16 17	21 31	21 26
16	23 53	- 1.2	6	90	16 11	21 33	21 29
21	0 06	+ 0.3	6	90	16 04	21 34	21 32
26	0 19	+ 1.8	6	91	15 58	21 36	21 34
31	0 32	+ 3.3	5	91	15 51	21 37	21 37

SUNRISE AND SUNSET

	London 0°05′ 51°30′		Bristol 2°35′ 51°28′		Birmingham 1°55′ 52°28′		Manchester 2°15′ 53°28′		Newcastle 1°37′ 54°59′		Glasgow 4°14′ 55°52′		Belfast 5°56′ 54°35′	
	h m	h m	h m	h m	h m	h m	h m	h m	h m	h m	h m	h m	h m	h m
1	8 06	16 02	8 16	16 12	8 18	16 04	8 25	16 00	8 31	15 49	8 47	15 54	8 46	16 09
2	8 06	16 03	8 16	16 13	8 18	16 05	8 25	16 01	8 31	15 50	8 47	15 55	8 46	16 10
3	8 06	16 04	8 16	16 14	8 18	16 07	8 25	16 03	8 31	15 51	8 47	15 56	8 46	16 11
4	8 05	16 05	8 15	16 15	8 18	16 08	8 24	16 04	8 30	15 53	8 46	15 58	8 45	16 12
5	8 05	16 06	8 15	16 17	8 17	16 09	8 24	16 05	8 30	15 54	8 46	15 59	8 45	16 14
6	8 05	16 08	8 15	16 18	8 17	16 10	8 23	16 06	8 29	15 55	8 45	16 00	8 44	16 15
7	8 04	16 09	8 14	16 19	8 17	16 12	8 23	16 08	8 29	15 57	8 45	16 02	8 44	16 16
8	8 04	16 10	8 14	16 20	8 16	16 13	8 22	16 09	8 28	15 58	8 44	16 04	8 43	16 18
9	8 04	16 12	8 13	16 22	8 15	16 14	8 22	16 11	8 28	16 00	8 43	16 05	8 43	16 19
10	8 03	16 13	8 13	16 23	8 15	16 16	8 21	16 12	8 27	16 01	8 42	16 07	8 42	16 21
11	8 02	16 14	8 12	16 25	8 14	16 17	8 20	16 14	8 26	16 03	8 42	16 08	8 41	16 23
12	8 02	16 16	8 12	16 26	8 14	16 19	8 20	16 15	8 25	16 05	8 41	16 10	8 40	16 24
13	8 01	16 17	8 11	16 28	8 13	16 20	8 19	16 17	8 24	16 06	8 40	16 12	8 39	16 26
14	8 00	16 19	8 10	16 29	8 12	16 22	8 18	16 18	8 23	16 08	8 39	16 14	8 38	16 28
15	7 59	16 20	8 09	16 31	8 11	16 23	8 17	16 20	8 22	16 10	8 38	16 16	8 37	16 29
16	7 59	16 22	8 08	16 32	8 10	16 25	8 16	16 22	8 21	16 12	8 36	16 17	8 36	16 31
17	7 58	16 24	8 08	16 34	8 09	16 27	8 15	16 23	8 20	16 13	8 35	16 19	8 35	16 33
18	7 57	16 25	8 07	16 35	8 08	16 28	8 14	16 25	8 19	16 15	8 34	16 21	8 34	16 35
19	7 56	16 27	8 06	16 37	8 07	16 30	8 13	16 27	8 18	16 17	8 33	16 23	8 33	16 36
20	7 55	16 28	8 05	16 39	8 06	16 32	8 12	16 29	8 16	16 19	8 31	16 25	8 32	16 38
21	7 54	16 30	8 03	16 40	8 05	16 34	8 11	16 31	8 15	16 21	8 30	16 27	8 30	16 40
22	7 52	16 32	8 02	16 42	8 04	16 35	8 09	16 32	8 14	16 23	8 28	16 29	8 29	16 42
23	7 51	16 34	8 01	16 44	8 02	16 37	8 08	16 34	8 12	16 25	8 27	16 31	8 28	16 44
24	7 50	16 35	8 00	16 45	8 01	16 39	8 07	16 36	8 11	16 27	8 25	16 33	8 26	16 46
25	7 49	16 37	7 59	16 47	8 00	16 41	8 05	16 38	8 09	16 29	8 24	16 35	8 25	16 48
26	7 48	16 39	7 57	16 49	7 58	16 42	8 04	16 40	8 08	16 31	8 22	16 37	8 23	16 50
27	7 46	16 41	7 56	16 51	7 57	16 44	8 02	16 42	8 06	16 33	8 21	16 39	8 22	16 52
28	7 45	16 42	7 55	16 52	7 56	16 46	8 01	16 44	8 05	16 35	8 19	16 42	8 20	16 54
29	7 43	16 44	7 53	16 54	7 54	16 48	7 59	16 46	8 03	16 37	8 17	16 44	8 18	16 56
30	7 42	16 46	7 52	16 56	7 53	16 50	7 58	16 48	8 01	16 39	8 15	16 46	8 17	16 58
31	7 40	16 48	7 50	16 58	7 51	16 52	7 56	16 49	7 59	16 41	8 13	16 48	8 15	17 00

JUPITER

Day	RA		Dec.		Transit		5° high			
							52°		56°	
	h	m	°	′	h	m	h	m	h	m
1	6	46.4	+23	01	0	04	7	35	7	53
11	6	40.6	+23	08	23	15	6	51	7	09
21	6	35.2	+23	14	22	30	6	07	6	25
31	6	30.7	+23	19	21	47	5	23	5	42

Diameters – equatorial 47″ polar 44″

SATURN

Day	RA		Dec.		Transit		5° high			
							52°		56°	
	h	m	°	′	h	m	h	m	h	m
1	4	31.7	+20	04	21	46	5	03	5	17
11	4	29.3	+20	01	21	04	4	21	4	35
21	4	27.5	+19	59	20	23	3	40	3	54
31	4	26.5	+19	59	19	43	2	59	3	13

Diameters – equatorial 20″ polar 18″
Rings – major axis 45″ minor axis 20″

URANUS

Day	RA		Dec.		Transit		10° high			
							52°		56°	
	h	m	°	′	h	m	h	m	h	m
1	21	40.2	-14	41	14	56	18	20	17	55
11	21	42.1	-14	32	14	19	17	44	17	19
21	21	44.2	-14	21	13	41	17	08	16	43
31	21	46.3	-14	10	13	04	16	32	16	08

Diameter 4″

NEPTUNE

Day	RA		Dec.		Transit		10° high			
							52°		56°	
	h	m	°	′	h	m	h	m	h	m
1	20	39.3	-18	18	13	55	16	50	16	15
11	20	40.7	-18	13	13	17	16	13	15	39
21	20	42.3	-18	07	12	40	15	36	15	02
31	20	43.8	-18	02	12	02	14	59	14	25

Diameter 2″

February 2002

SECOND MONTH, 28 or 29 DAYS. *Februa*, Roman festival of Purification

1	*Friday*	Clark Gable b. 1901. Piet Mondrian d. 1944	32
2	*Saturday*	**The Presentation of Christ in the Temple (Candlemas).**	33
3	*Sunday*	**8th S. before Easter.** Elizabeth Blackwell b. 1821	34
4	*Monday*	Pierre Marivaux b. 1688. RNLI founded 1824	*week 5 day* 35
5	*Tuesday*	William S. Burroughs b. 1914. Sir Robert Peel b. 1788	36
6	*Wednesday*	*Queen's Accession 1952.* Christopher Marlowe b. 1564	37
7	*Thursday*	Sir Thomas More b. 1478. Joseph Sheridan Le Fanu d. 1873	38
8	*Friday*	Sir Giles Gilbert Scott d. 1960. Rt. Hon. Enoch Powell d. 1998	39
9	*Saturday*	Edward Carson b. 1854. Yuri Andropov d. 1984	40
10	*Sunday*	**7th S. before Easter.** PAYE introduced 1944	41
11	*Monday*	Sir Vivian Fuchs b. 1908. Sergey Eisenstein d. 1948	*week 6 day* 42
12	*Tuesday*	Shrove Tuesday. *Chinese Year of the Horse*	43
13	*Wednesday*	**Ash Wednesday.** Queen Catherine Howard d. 1542	44
14	*Thursday*	St Valentines Day. William Sherman d. 1891	45
15	*Friday*	Henry Hunt d. 1835. Introduction of decimal currency in Britain 1971	46
16	*Saturday*	Angela Carter d. 1992. Giosue Carducci d. 1907	47
17	*Sunday*	**1st S. in Lent.** Sir John Jones b. 1923	48
18	*Monday*	Queen Mary I Tudor b. 1516. Fra Angelico d. 1455	*week 7 day* 49
19	*Tuesday*	*Duke of York b. 1960.* Luigi Boccherini b. 1743	50
20	*Wednesday*	Honoré Daumier b. 1808. Joseph Hume d. 1855	51
21	*Thursday*	Léo Delibes b. 1836. Battle of Verdun 1915	52
22	*Friday*	Sir John Mills b. 1908. Oskar Kokoschka d. 1980	53
23	*Saturday*	George Watts b. 1817. Stefan Zweig d. 1942	54
24	*Sunday*	**2nd S. in Lent.** Nikolai Bukharin (Bulganin) d. 1975	55
25	*Monday*	Sir John Tenniel d. 1914. Tennessee Williams d. 1983	*week 8 day* 56
26	*Tuesday*	John Philip Kemble b. 1823. First issue of £1 and £2 notes 1797	57
27	*Wednesday*	Antoinette Sibley b. 1939. Ivan Pavlov d. 1936	58
28	*Thursday*	Sir John Tenniel b. 1820. Albert Lippert d. 1998	59

ASTRONOMICAL PHENOMENA

d	h	
8	02	Saturn at stationary point
8	17	Mercury at stationary point
10	07	Mercury in conjunction with Moon. Mercury 5° N.
12	23	Venus in conjunction with Moon. Venus 3° N.
13	17	Uranus in conjunction
17	04	Mars in conjunction with Moon. Mars 5° N.
18	20	Sun's longitude 330° ♓
21	00	Saturn in conjunction with Moon. Saturn 0°.2 S.
21	16	Mercury at greatest elongation W.27°
23	02	Jupiter in conjunction with Moon. Jupiter 0°.9 S.

MINIMA OF ALGOL

d	h	d	h	d	h
2	12.7	14	00.0	25	11.3
5	09.5	16	20.8	28	08.1
8	06.3	19	17.6		
11	03.1	22	14.4		

CONSTELLATIONS

The following constellations are near the meridian at

	d	h		d	h
January	1	24	February	15	21
January	16	23	March	1	20
February	1	22	March	16	19

Draco (below the Pole), Camelopardus, Auriga, Taurus, Gemini, Orion, Canis Minor, Monoceros, Lepus, Canis Major and Puppis

THE MOON

Phases, Apsides and Node	d	h	m
☾ Last Quarter	4	13	33
● New Moon	12	07	41
☽ First Quarter	20	12	02
○ Full Moon	27	09	17
Apogee (406,382km)	14	22	32
Perigee (356,893km)	27	19	50

Mean longitude of ascending node on February 1, 85°

THE SUN   S.D 16'.1

Day	Right Ascension h m s	Dec. – ° '	Equation of Time m s	Rise 52° h m	Rise 56° h m	Transit h m	Set 52° h m	Set 56° h m	Sidereal time h m s	Transit of First Point of Aries h m s
1	20 57 36	17 13	−13 30	7 40	7 55	12 14	16 47	16 33	8 44 06	15 13 24
2	21 01 41	16 56	−13 38	7 39	7 53	12 14	16 49	16 35	8 48 03	15 09 28
3	21 05 44	16 38	−13 45	7 37	7 51	12 14	16 51	16 37	8 52 00	15 05 32
4	21 09 47	16 20	−13 51	7 35	7 49	12 14	16 53	16 39	8 55 56	15 01 36
5	21 13 49	16 02	−13 57	7 34	7 47	12 14	16 55	16 41	8 59 53	14 57 40
6	21 17 51	15 44	−14 01	7 32	7 45	12 14	16 57	16 44	9 03 49	14 53 44
7	21 21 51	15 26	−14 05	7 30	7 43	12 14	16 59	16 46	9 07 46	14 49 48
8	21 25 51	15 07	−14 09	7 29	7 41	12 14	17 01	16 48	9 11 42	14 45 52
9	21 29 50	14 48	−14 11	7 27	7 39	12 14	17 02	16 50	9 15 39	14 41 56
10	21 33 48	14 29	−14 13	7 25	7 37	12 14	17 04	16 52	9 19 35	14 38 00
11	21 37 45	14 09	−14 13	7 23	7 35	12 14	17 06	16 55	9 23 32	14 34 04
12	21 41 42	13 49	−14 14	7 21	7 33	12 14	17 08	16 57	9 27 29	14 30 09
13	21 45 38	13 29	−14 13	7 19	7 30	12 14	17 10	16 59	9 31 25	14 26 13
14	21 49 33	13 09	−14 11	7 17	7 28	12 14	17 12	17 01	9 35 22	14 22 17
15	21 53 27	12 49	−14 09	7 15	7 26	12 14	17 14	17 03	9 39 18	14 18 21
16	21 57 21	12 28	−14 06	7 14	7 24	12 14	17 15	17 06	9 43 15	14 14 25
17	22 01 14	12 07	−14 03	7 12	7 21	12 14	17 17	17 08	9 47 11	14 10 29
18	22 05 06	11 46	−13 58	7 10	7 19	12 14	17 19	17 10	9 51 08	14 06 33
19	22 08 58	11 25	−13 53	7 08	7 17	12 14	17 21	17 12	9 55 04	14 02 37
20	22 12 49	11 04	−13 48	7 05	7 14	12 14	17 23	17 14	9 59 01	13 58 41
21	22 16 39	10 42	−13 41	7 03	7 12	12 14	17 25	17 16	10 02 58	13 54 45
22	22 20 28	10 20	−13 34	7 01	7 09	12 14	17 27	17 19	10 06 54	13 50 49
23	22 24 17	9 58	−13 26	6 59	7 07	12 13	17 28	17 21	10 10 51	13 46 54
24	22 28 05	9 36	−13 18	6 57	7 04	12 13	17 30	17 23	10 14 47	13 42 58
25	22 31 53	9 14	−13 09	6 55	7 02	12 13	17 32	17 25	10 18 44	13 39 02
26	22 35 40	8 52	−12 59	6 53	7 00	12 13	17 34	17 27	10 22 40	13 35 06
27	22 39 26	8 29	−12 49	6 51	6 57	12 13	17 36	17 29	10 26 37	13 31 10
28	22 43 12	8 07	−12 38	6 49	6 55	12 13	17 37	17 32	10 30 33	13 27 14

DURATION OF TWILIGHT (in minutes)

Latitude	52°	56°	52°	56°	52°	56°	52°	56°
	1 February		11 February		21 February		28 February	
Civil	37	41	35	39	34	38	34	37
Nautical	77	86	75	83	74	81	73	80
Astronomical	117	130	114	126	113	124	112	124

THE NIGHT SKY

Mercury, although it attains greatest western elongation on the 21st, is unsuitably placed for observation from these latitudes.

Venus is too close to the Sun for observation during the first half of the month but then becomes visible as an evening object, magnitude -3.9, low above the west-south-western horizon for a short while after sunset.

Mars, magnitude +1.2, continues to be visible as an evening object in the south-western sky. Mars is in the constellation of Pisces but enters Aries at the very end of the month. The crescent Moon will be seen passing about 7 degrees below the planet on the evening of the 16th.

Jupiter is a conspicuous evening object in the southern skies, magnitude -2.5. It is almost stationary in the western part of Gemini. On the evenings of the 22nd and 23rd the gibbous Moon is in the vicinity of the planet. The four Galilean satellites are readily observable with a small telescope or even a good pair of binoculars provided that they are held rigidly.

Saturn, magnitude 0.0, continues to be visible in the southern and south-western part of the sky in the evenings. It reaches its second stationary point on the 8th, in Taurus, resuming its direct motion. The Moon, near First Quarter, is near the planet on the evenings of the 20th and 21st.

Zodiacal Light. The evening cone may be observed stretching up from the western horizon, along the ecliptic, after the end of twilight, from the beginning of the month up to the 13th. This faint phenomenon is only visible under good conditions and in the absence of both moonlight and artificial lighting.

THE MOON

Day	RA h m	Dec. °	Hor. par. '	Semi-diam '	Sun's co-long. °	PA of Bright Limb °	Phase %	Age d	Rise 52° h m	Rise 56° h m	Transit h m	Set 52° h m	Set 56° h m
1	11 48	+ 6.9	60.6	16.5	130	108	87	18.4	21 43	21 42	3 11	9 46	9 50
2	12 42	+ 0.9	60.0	16.4	142	110	78	19.4	23 06	23 11	4 02	10 05	10 04
3	13 35	- 5.0	59.4	16.2	154	110	67	20.4	—	—	4 52	10 24	10 18
4	14 27	-10.5	58.6	16.0	167	108	56	21.4	0 28	0 38	5 42	10 44	10 33
5	15 19	-15.3	57.9	15.8	179	105	45	22.4	1 48	2 03	6 33	11 07	10 51
6	16 13	-19.3	57.2	15.6	191	101	35	23.4	3 05	3 26	7 24	11 36	11 15
7	17 07	-22.1	56.5	15.4	203	96	25	24.4	4 18	4 42	8 17	12 11	11 46
8	18 02	-23.8	55.9	15.2	215	89	17	25.4	5 22	5 50	9 10	12 56	12 28
9	18 57	-24.3	55.4	15.1	227	82	10	26.4	6 16	6 44	10 02	13 50	13 23
10	19 51	-23.5	55.0	15.0	240	74	5	27.4	6 59	7 24	10 54	14 53	14 28
11	20 43	-21.7	54.7	14.9	252	62	2	28.4	7 32	7 53	11 43	16 00	15 39
12	21 33	-18.8	54.4	14.8	264	22	0	29.4	7 58	8 15	12 29	17 09	16 53
13	22 21	-15.2	54.1	14.8	276	280	1	0.7	8 19	8 31	13 13	18 17	18 06
14	23 07	-11.1	54.0	14.7	288	262	3	1.7	8 36	8 44	13 55	19 25	19 19
15	23 51	- 6.5	54.0	14.7	301	255	7	2.7	8 51	8 55	14 36	20 33	20 30
16	0 34	- 1.7	54.0	14.7	313	253	12	3.7	9 05	9 05	15 16	21 40	21 42
17	1 17	+ 3.2	54.2	14.8	325	252	19	4.7	9 20	9 16	15 57	22 48	22 54
18	2 01	+ 8.0	54.5	14.9	337	252	27	5.7	9 36	9 27	16 39	23 57	—
19	2 47	+12.6	55.0	15.0	349	254	35	6.7	9 54	9 41	17 23	—	0 08
20	3 35	+16.7	55.7	15.2	1	257	45	7.7	10 16	9 59	18 11	1 09	1 25
21	4 26	+20.2	56.4	15.4	14	261	55	8.7	10 45	10 23	19 03	2 21	2 43
22	5 21	+22.8	57.3	15.6	26	266	65	9.7	11 24	10 58	19 59	3 33	3 59
23	6 19	+24.2	58.3	15.9	38	272	75	10.7	12 17	11 49	20 58	4 40	5 08
24	7 20	+24.2	59.3	16.2	50	280	84	11.7	13 24	12 58	21 59	5 37	6 04
25	8 23	+22.6	60.2	16.4	62	288	92	12.7	14 45	14 23	23 00	6 22	6 45
26	9 25	+19.4	60.9	16.6	74	299	97	13.7	16 13	15 57	23 59	6 57	7 15
27	10 25	+14.9	61.3	16.7	87	331	100	14.7	17 44	17 34	—	7 25	7 36
28	11 24	+ 9.3	61.4	16.7	99	84	99	15.7	19 13	19 10	0 55	7 47	7 53

MERCURY

Day	RA h m	Dec. °	Diam. "	Phase %	Transit h m	5° high 52° h m	5° high 56° h m
1	20 16	-16.1	10	6	11 28	7 35	7 55
3	20 09	-16.6	10	12	11 14	7 23	7 44
5	20 04	-17.1	10	18	11 01	7 14	7 36
7	20 01	-17.6	9	24	10 51	7 07	7 30
9	20 01	-18.0	9	30	10 44	7 02	7 25
11	20 02	-18.3	8	36	10 38	6 58	7 22
13	20 06	-18.6	8	41	10 34	6 56	7 20
15	20 11	-18.7	8	46	10 31	6 54	7 18
17	20 17	-18.8	8	51	10 29	6 52	7 17
19	20 24	-18.8	7	55	10 29	6 52	7 16
21	20 32	-18.7	7	58	10 29	6 51	7 16
23	20 40	-18.5	7	61	10 30	6 50	7 15
25	20 50	-18.2	7	64	10 31	6 50	7 13
27	20 59	-17.9	6	67	10 33	6 49	7 12
29	21 10	-17.4	6	70	10 36	6 48	7 10
31	21 20	-16.9	6	72	10 39	6 47	7 09

VENUS

Day	RA h m	Dec. °	Diam. "	Phase %	Transit h m	5° high 52° h m	5° high 56° h m
1	21 16	-17.3	10	100	12 32	16 22	16 00
6	21 41	-15.4	10	100	12 38	16 40	16 21
11	22 05	-13.3	10	99	12 42	16 58	16 42
16	22 29	-11.1	10	99	12 46	17 16	17 02
21	22 53	- 8.7	10	99	12 50	17 33	17 22
26	23 16	- 6.3	10	99	12 54	17 50	17 42
31	23 39	- 3.8	10	98	12 57	18 07	18 01

MARS

Day	RA h m	Dec. °	Diam. "	Phase %	Transit h m	5° high 52° h m	5° high 56° h m
1	0 35	+ 3.6	5	91	15 50	21 37	21 37
6	0 48	+ 5.1	5	92	15 44	21 38	21 39
11	1 02	+ 6.6	5	92	15 37	21 39	21 42
16	1 15	+ 8.0	5	92	15 31	21 40	21 44
21	1 28	+ 9.4	5	93	15 24	21 41	21 46
26	1 42	+10.8	5	93	15 18	21 42	21 47
31	1 55	+12.1	5	93	15 12	21 42	21 49

SUNRISE AND SUNSET

	London 0°05′ 51°30′		Bristol 2°35′ 51°28′		Birmingham 1°55′ 52°28′		Manchester 2°15′ 53°28′		Newcastle 1°37′ 54°59′		Glasgow 4°14′ 55°52′		Belfast 5°56′ 54°35′	
	h m	h m	h m	h m	h m	h m	h m	h m	h m	h m	h m	h m	h m	h m
1	7 39	16 49	7 49	17 00	7 50	16 54	7 54	16 51	7 58	16 43	8 12	16 50	8 13	17 02
2	7 37	16 51	7 47	17 01	7 48	16 55	7 53	16 53	7 56	16 45	8 10	16 52	8 11	17 04
3	7 36	16 53	7 46	17 03	7 46	16 57	7 51	16 55	7 54	16 47	8 08	16 54	8 10	17 06
4	7 34	16 55	7 44	17 05	7 45	16 59	7 49	16 57	7 52	16 49	8 06	16 57	8 08	17 08
5	7 33	16 57	7 42	17 07	7 43	17 01	7 47	16 59	7 50	16 52	8 04	16 59	8 06	17 10
6	7 31	16 59	7 41	17 09	7 41	17 03	7 46	17 01	7 48	16 54	8 02	17 01	8 04	17 12
7	7 29	7 00	7 39	17 11	7 39	17 05	7 44	17 03	7 46	16 56	8 00	17 03	8 02	17 14
8	7 27	17 02	7 37	17 12	7 38	17 07	7 42	17 05	7 44	16 58	7 58	17 05	8 00	17 16
9	7 26	17 04	7 36	17 14	7 36	17 09	7 40	17 07	7 42	17 00	7 56	17 08	7 58	17 19
10	7 24	17 06	7 34	17 16	7 34	17 11	7 38	17 09	7 40	17 02	7 53	17 10	7 56	17 21
11	7 22	17 08	7 32	17 18	7 32	17 13	7 36	17 11	7 38	17 04	7 51	17 12	7 54	17 23
12	7 20	17 10	7 30	17 20	7 30	17 14	7 34	17 13	7 36	17 06	7 49	17 14	7 52	17 25
13	7 18	17 11	7 28	17 21	7 28	17 16	7 32	17 15	7 34	17 08	7 47	17 16	7 50	17 27
14	7 17	17 13	7 26	17 23	7 26	17 18	7 30	17 17	7 32	17 11	7 45	17 19	7 48	17 29
15	7 15	17 15	7 25	17 25	7 24	17 20	7 28	17 19	7 29	17 13	7 42	17 21	7 46	17 31
16	7 13	17 17	7 23	17 27	7 22	17 22	7 26	17 21	7 27	17 15	7 40	17 23	7 43	17 33
17	7 11	17 19	7 21	17 29	7 20	17 24	7 24	17 23	7 25	17 17	7 38	17 25	7 41	17 35
18	7 09	17 21	7 19	17 31	7 18	17 26	7 22	17 25	7 23	17 19	7 35	17 27	7 39	17 37
19	7 07	17 22	7 17	17 32	7 16	17 28	7 20	17 27	7 20	17 21	7 33	17 29	7 37	17 39
20	7 05	17 24	7 15	17 34	7 14	17 30	7 17	17 29	7 18	17 23	7 31	17 32	7 35	17 41
21	7 03	17 26	7 13	17 36	7 12	17 31	7 15	17 31	7 16	17 25	7 28	17 34	7 32	17 43
22	7 01	17 28	7 11	17 38	7 10	17 33	7 13	17 33	7 14	17 27	7 26	17 36	7 30	17 45
23	6 59	17 30	7 09	17 40	7 08	17 35	7 11	17 35	7 11	17 29	7 24	17 38	7 28	17 47
24	6 57	17 31	7 07	17 41	7 06	17 37	7 09	17 37	7 09	17 31	7 21	17 40	7 25	17 49
25	6 55	17 33	7 04	17 43	7 03	17 39	7 06	17 39	7 07	17 33	7 19	17 42	7 23	17 51
26	6 52	17 35	7 02	17 45	7 01	17 41	7 04	17 41	7 04	17 36	7 16	17 44	7 21	17 53
27	6 50	17 37	7 00	17 47	6 59	17 43	7 02	17 42	7 02	17 38	7 14	17 47	7 18	17 56
28	6 48	17 38	6 58	17 49	6 57	17 44	7 00	17 44	6 59	17 40	7 11	17 49	7 16	17 58

JUPITER

Day	RA		Dec.		Transit		5° high			
							52°		56°	
	h	m	°	′	h	m	h	m	h	m
1	6	30.3	+23	20	21	42	5	19	5	37
11	6	27.0	+23	23	21	00	4	37	4	55
21	6	25.1	+23	26	20	19	3	56	4	14
31	6	24.5	+23	27	19	39	3	16	3	35

Diameters – equatorial 44″ polar 41″

SATURN

Day	RA		Dec.		Transit		5° high			
							52°		56°	
	h	m	°	′	h	m	h	m	h	m
1	4	26.4	+19	59	19	39	2	55	3	09
11	4	26.2	+20	02	19	00	2	16	2	30
21	4	26.8	+20	06	18	21	1	38	1	52
31	4	28.2	+20	11	17	43	1	00	1	15

Diameters – equatorial 19″ polar 17″
Rings – major axis 43″ minor axis 19″

URANUS

Day	RA		Dec.		Transit		10° high			
							52°		56°	
	h	m	°	′	h	m	h	m	h	m
1	21	46.5	−14	09	13	00	9	32	9	57
11	21	48.8	−13	57	12	23	8	54	9	18
21	21	51.0	−13	46	11	46	8	15	8	39
31	21	53.2	−13	34	11	09	7	37	8	00

Diameter 4″

NEPTUNE

Day	RA		Dec.		Transit		10° high			
							52°		56°	
	h	m	°	′	h	m	h	m	h	m
1	20	44.0	−18	01	11	58	9	00	9	34
11	20	45.5	−17	55	11	20	8	22	8	55
21	20	47.0	−17	50	10	42	7	43	8	16
31	20	48.4	−17	44	10	04	7	04	7	37

Diameter 2″

March 2002

THIRD MONTH, 31 DAYS. *Mars*, Roman god of battle

1	*Friday*	**St David's Day**. Girolamo Frescobaldi d. 1643	60
2	*Saturday*	Ivar Kreuger b. 1880. Cardinal Archbishop Hume b. 1923	61
3	*Sunday*	**3rd S. in Lent.** Abolition of Serfdom in Russia 1861	62
4	*Monday*	Bernard Haitink b. 1929	*week 9 day* 63
5	*Tuesday*	Gerardus Mercator b. 1512. Franz Mesmer d. 1815	64
6	*Wednesday*	Frankie Howerd b. 1922. Melina Mercouri d. 1994	65
7	*Thursday*	1st Earl of Snowdon, Antony Armstrong Jones. b. 1930. Anstide Briand d. 1932	66
8	*Friday*	Lynn Seymour b. 1939. Count Ferdinand von Zeppelin d. 1917	67
9	*Saturday*	Comte de Mirabeau Honoré Riqueti b. 1749. Jules Mazarin d. 1661	68
10	*Sunday*	**4th S. in Lent.** Mothering Sunday. *Earl of Wessex b. 1964.*	69
11	*Monday*	Commonwealth Day. Harold Wilson b. 1916	*week 10 day* 70
12	*Tuesday*	Bishop George Berkeley b. 1685. Saint Gregory d. 604	71
13	*Wednesday*	Odette Hallowes d. 1995. First submarine telephone lines laid 1891	72
14	*Thursday*	Jim Clark b. 1936. Busby Berkeley d. 1976	73
15	*Friday*	MUSLIM NEW YEAR. Andrew Jackson b. 1767	74
16	*Saturday*	George Ohm b. 1787. William Beveridge d. 1963	75
17	*Sunday*	**5th S. in Lent.** Ronnie Kray d. 1995	76
18	*Monday*	St Patrick's Day. *Bank Holiday in Northern Ireland.*	*week 11 day* 77
19	*Tuesday*	**St Joseph of Nazareth.** Sir John Jones d. 1998	78
20	*Wednesday*	Sir Michael Redgrave b. 1908. Beverley Cross d. 1998	79
21	*Thursday*	Paul Tortelier b. 1914. Sir Michael Redgrave d. 1985	80
22	*Friday*	Stephen Sondheim b. 1930. Jonathan Edwards d. 1758	81
23	*Saturday*	Princess Eugenie of York b. 1990. Sir Roger Bannister b. 1929	82
24	*Sunday*	**Palm Sunday.** E. H. Shepard d. 1976	83
25	*Monday*	**The Annunciation.** Achille-Claude Debussy d. 1918	*week 12 day* 84
26	*Tuesday*	William Hague b. 1961. Robert Lee Frost b. 1874	85
27	*Wednesday*	*Hilary Law Sittings end.* Mstislav Rostropovich b. 1927	86
28	*Thursday*	**Maundy Thursday.** PASSOVER begins.	87
29	*Friday*	**Good Friday.** *Bank Holiday in UK.*	88
30	*Saturday*	Easter Eve. James Cagney d. 1986	89
31	*Sunday*	**Easter Day.** Robert Bunsen b. 1811	90

ASTRONOMICAL PHENOMENA

d	h	
1	15	Jupiter at stationary point
12	03	Mercury in conjunction with Moon. Mercury 3° N.
15	10	Venus in conjunction with Moon. Venus 4° N.
18	03	Mars in conjunction with Moon. Mars 4° N.
20	10	Saturn in conjunction with Moon. Saturn 0.4° S
20	15	Pluto at stationary point
20	19	Sun's longitude 0° ♈
22	12	Jupiter in conjunction with Moon. Jupiter 1° S

MINIMA OF ALGOL

d	h	d	h	d	h
3	04.9	14	16.2	26	03.5
6	01.7	17	13.0	29	00.3
8	22.5	20	09.8	31	21.1
11	19.4	23	06.6		

CONSTELLATIONS

The following constellations are near the meridian at

	d	h		d	h
February	1	24	March	16	21
February	15	23	April	1	20
March	1	22	April	15	19

Cepheus (below the Pole), Camelopardus, Lynx, Gemini, Cancer, Leo, Canis Minor, Hydra, Monoceros, Canis Major and Puppis

THE MOON

Phases, Apsides and Node	d	h	m
☾ Last Quarter	6	01	24
● New Moon	14	02	02
☽ First Quarter	22	02	28
○ Full Moon	28	18	25
Apogee (406,707km)	14	01	25
Perigee (357,013km)	28	07	48

Mean longitude of ascending node on March 1, 83°

THE SUN   S.D 16'.1

Day	Right Ascension	Dec.	Equation of Time	Rise 52°	Rise 56°	Transit	Set 52°	Set 56°	Sidereal time	Transit of First Point of Aries
	h m s	° '	m s	h m	h m	h m	h m	h m	h m s	h m s
1	22 46 57	− 7 44	−12 27	6 46	6 52	12 12	17 39	17 34	10 34 30	13 23 18
2	22 50 42	− 7 21	−12 15	6 44	6 50	12 12	17 41	17 36	10 38 26	13 19 22
3	22 54 26	− 6 58	12 03	6 42	6 47	12 12	17 43	17 38	10 42 23	13 15 26
4	22 58 10	− 6 35	−11 50	6 40	6 45	12 12	17 45	17 40	10 46 20	13 11 30
5	23 01 53	− 6 12	−11 37	6 38	6 42	12 12	17 46	17 42	10 50 16	13 07 34
6	23 05 36	− 5 49	−11 24	6 35	6 39	12 11	17 48	17 44	10 54 13	13 03 39
7	23 09 19	− 5 26	−11 10	6 33	6 37	12 11	17 50	17 46	10 58 09	12 59 43
8	23 13 01	− 5 03	−10 55	6 31	6 34	12 11	17 52	17 48	11 02 06	12 55 47
9	23 16 43	− 4 39	−10 41	6 29	6 32	12 11	17 54	17 51	11 06 02	12 51 51
10	23 20 25	− 4 16	−10 26	6 26	6 29	12 10	17 55	17 53	11 09 59	12 47 55
11	23 24 06	− 3 52	−10 10	6 24	6 26	12 10	17 57	17 55	11 13 55	12 43 59
12	23 27 47	− 3 29	− 9 55	6 22	6 24	12 10	17 59	17 57	11 17 52	12 40 03
13	23 31 27	− 3 05	− 9 39	6 19	6 21	12 10	18 01	17 59	11 21 49	12 36 07
14	23 35 07	− 2 41	− 9 22	6 17	6 19	12 09	18 02	18 01	11 25 45	12 32 11
15	23 38 47	− 2 18	− 9 06	6 15	6 16	12 09	18 04	18 03	11 29 42	12 28 15
16	23 42 27	− 1 54	− 8 49	6 13	6 13	12 09	18 06	18 05	11 33 38	12 24 19
17	23 46 07	− 1 30	− 8 32	6 10	6 11	12 08	18 08	18 07	11 37 35	12 20 24
18	23 49 46	− 1 07	− 8 15	6 08	6 08	12 08	18 09	18 09	11 41 31	12 16 28
19	23 53 25	− 0 43	− 7 57	6 06	6 06	12 08	18 11	18 11	11 45 28	12 12 32
20	23 57 04	− 0 19	− 7 40	6 03	6 03	12 08	18 13	18 13	11 49 24	12 08 36
21	0 00 43	+ 0 05	− 7 22	6 01	6 00	12 07	18 14	18 15	11 53 21	12 04 40
22	0 04 22	+ 0 28	− 7 04	5 59	5 58	12 07	18 16	18 17	11 57 18	12 00 44
23	0 08 00	+ 0 52	− 6 46	5 56	5 55	12 07	18 18	18 19	12 01 14	11 56 48
24	0 11 39	+ 1 16	− 6 28	5 54	5 52	12 06	18 20	18 21	12 05 11	11 52 52
25	0 15 17	+ 1 39	− 6 10	5 52	5 50	12 06	18 21	18 24	12 09 07	11 48 56
26	0 18 55	+ 2 03	− 5 52	5 49	5 47	12 06	18 23	18 26	12 13 04	11 45 00
27	0 22 34	+ 2 26	− 5 33	5 47	5 44	12 05	18 25	18 28	12 17 00	11 41 05
28	0 26 12	+ 2 50	− 5 15	5 45	5 42	12 05	18 27	18 30	12 20 57	11 37 09
29	0 29 50	+ 3 13	− 4 57	5 42	5 39	12 05	18 28	18 32	12 24 53	11 33 13
30	0 33 29	+ 3 37	− 4 39	5 40	5 37	12 04	18 30	18 34	12 28 50	11 29 17
31	0 37 07	+ 4 00	− 4 20	5 38	5 34	12 04	18 32	18 36	12 32 47	11 25 21

DURATION OF TWILIGHT (in minutes)

Latitude	52°	56°	52°	56°	52°	56°	52°	56°
	1 March		11 March		21 March		31 March	
Civil	34	37	34	37	34	37	34	38
Nautical	73	80	73	80	74	81	75	84
Astronomical	112	124	113	125	115	128	120	135

THE NIGHT SKY

Mercury, remains too close to the Sun for observation throughout the month.

Venus, magnitude -3.9, is visible as an evening object, low in the western sky after sunset. The thin crescent Moon, only 1.7 days old, will be seen about 5 degrees to the left of Venus on the evening of the 15th.

Mars continues to be visible in the south-western sky in the early evenings, magnitude +1.4. Its slightly reddish appearance is an aid to its identification. Mars is in the constellation of Aries. The crescent Moon will be seen passing about 6 degrees below Mars on the evening of the 17th.

Jupiter, magnitude -2.3, continues to be visible as a conspicuous evening object in the south-western quadrant of the sky from shortly after sunset until well after midnight. Jupiter reaches its second stationary point in the western part of Gemini on the 1st and then resumes its direct motion. On the evenings of the 21st and 22nd the Moon, near First Quarter, is near the planet.

Saturn is still an evening object in the western sky but before the end of the month it will be too low in the sky to be visible after midnight. Its magnitude is +0.1. The crescent Moon is in the vicinity of Saturn on the evenings of the 19th and 20th. On the last day of the month Saturn is 4 degrees north of Aldebaran. The rings of Saturn present a beautiful spectacle to the observer with a small telescope. The Earth passed through the ring plane twice in 1995 and since then the rings have been slowly opening up: the diameter of the minor axis is now 20 arcseconds, marginally greater than the polar diameter of the planet itself. The rings will not be at their maximum opening until early next year.

Zodiacal Light. The evening cone may be observed, stretching up from the western horizon, along the ecliptic, after the end of twilight, from the beginning of the month up to the 15th.

THE MOON

Day	RA h m	Dec. °	Hor. par. '	Semi-diam '	Sun's co-long. °	PA of Bright Limb °	Phase %	Age d	Rise 52° h m	Rise 56° h m	Transit h m	Set 52° h m	Set 56° h m
1	12 20	+ 3.2	61.2	16.7	111	102	96	16.7	20 41	20 43	1 49	8 07	8 08
2	13 15	− 3.0	60.7	16.5	123	106	90	17.7	22 08	22 15	2 42	8 27	8 22
3	14 09	− 8.9	59.9	16.3	135	107	82	18.7	23 32	23 45	3 34	8 47	8 37
4	15 03	−14.2	59.1	16.1	147	105	72	19.7	—	—	4 26	9 09	8 54
5	15 58	−18.5	58.1	15.8	159	101	61	20.7	0 53	1 12	5 19	9 36	9 16
6	16 53	−21.8	57.2	15.6	172	97	51	21.7	2 09	2 33	6 12	10 10	9 45
7	17 49	−23.8	56.4	15.4	184	91	40	22.7	3 17	3 45	7 06	10 52	10 24
8	18 44	−24.5	55.7	15.2	196	85	31	23.7	4 15	4 43	7 59	11 44	11 16
9	19 39	−24.0	55.1	15.0	208	79	22	24.7	5 01	5 27	8 51	12 44	12 18
10	20 31	−22.3	54.7	14.9	220	73	15	25.7	5 36	5 59	9 40	13 50	13 28
11	21 21	−19.7	54.3	14.8	233	66	9	26.7	6 03	6 22	10 27	14 58	14 41
12	22 09	−16.2	54.1	14.7	245	59	4	27.7	6 25	6 39	11 11	16 07	15 55
13	22 55	−12.2	54.0	14.7	257	45	1	28.7	6 43	6 52	11 54	17 16	17 08
14	23 40	− 7.6	53.9	14.7	269	347	0	29.7	6 58	7 03	12 35	18 23	18 20
15	0 23	− 2.8	54.0	14.7	281	272	1	0.9	7 13	7 14	13 15	19 31	19 32
16	1 06	+ 2.1	54.1	14.7	294	259	3	1.9	7 27	7 24	13 55	20 39	20 44
17	1 50	+ 7.0	54.3	14.8	306	256	8	2.9	7 42	7 34	14 37	21 48	21 58
18	2 35	+11.7	54.6	14.9	318	255	13	3.9	7 58	7 47	15 20	22 58	23 13
19	3 22	+15.9	55.1	15.0	330	257	21	4.9	8 19	8 02	16 06	—	—
20	4 11	+19.6	55.6	15.2	342	260	29	5.9	8 44	8 23	16 56	0 10	0 30
21	5 04	+22.4	56.3	15.3	355	265	39	6.9	9 18	8 53	17 49	1 21	1 45
22	6 00	+24.2	57.1	15.6	7	270	49	7.9	10 03	9 35	18 45	2 28	2 56
23	6 58	+24.6	58.0	15.8	19	276	60	8.9	11 02	10 34	19 43	3 27	3 56
24	7 58	+23.6	58.9	16.1	31	283	70	9.9	12 15	11 50	20 42	4 16	4 41
25	8 59	+21.1	59.8	16.3	43	289	80	10.9	13 38	13 19	21 40	4 54	5 14
26	9 59	+17.2	60.6	16.5	55	296	89	11.9	15 06	14 53	22 37	5 24	5 38
27	10 57	+12.1	61.1	16.7	68	303	95	12.9	16 36	16 29	23 32	5 48	5 57
28	11 54	+ 6.1	61.4	16.7	80	318	99	13.9	18 06	18 05	—	6 08	6 12
29	12 49	− 0.2	61.3	16.7	92	58	100	14.9	19 35	19 40	0 25	6 27	6 26
30	13 45	− 6.5	60.9	16.6	104	98	98	15.9	21 03	21 14	1 19	6 47	6 40
31	14 40	−12.3	60.3	16.4	116	103	93	16.9	22 30	22 46	2 12	7 08	6 56

MERCURY

Day	RA h m	Dec. °	Diam. ''	Phase %	Transit h m	5° high 52° h m	5° high 56° h m
1	21 10	−17.4	6	70	10 36	6 48	7 10
3	21 20	−16.9	6	72	10 39	6 47	7 09
5	21 31	−16.2	6	74	10 42	6 46	7 06
7	21 42	−15.5	6	76	10 45	6 45	7 04
9	21 54	−14.7	6	78	10 49	6 43	7 01
11	22 05	−13.8	6	80	10 52	6 41	6 58
13	22 17	−12.9	6	82	10 56	6 39	6 55
15	22 29	−11.8	5	84	11 01	6 37	6 51
17	22 42	−10.7	5	85	11 05	6 34	6 47
19	22 54	− 9.5	5	87	11 10	6 32	6 44
21	23 07	− 8.2	5	89	11 14	6 29	6 40
23	23 19	− 6.8	5	90	11 19	6 26	6 36
25	23 32	− 5.4	5	92	11 24	6 24	6 31
27	23 45	− 3.8	5	94	11 30	6 21	6 27
29	23 59	− 2.3	5	95	11 35	6 18	6 23
31	0 13	− 0.6	5	97	11 41	6 15	6 19

VENUS

Day	RA h m	Dec. °	Diam. ''	Phase %	Transit h m	5° high 52° h m	5° high 56° h m
1	23 30	− 4.8	10	98	12 56	18 00	17 53
6	23 53	− 2.2	10	98	12 59	18 17	18 12
11	0 15	+ 0.3	10	97	13 02	18 33	18 30
16	0 38	+ 2.9	10	97	13 05	18 49	18 49
21	1 01	+ 5.5	10	96	13 08	19 05	19 07
26	1 23	+ 7.9	10	96	13 11	19 21	19 25
31	1 46	+10.4	10	95	13 14	19 37	19 43

MARS

Day	RA h m	Dec. °	Diam. ''	Phase %	Transit h m	5° high 52° h m	5° high 56° h m
1	1 50	+11.6	5	93	15 14	21 42	21 48
6	2 03	+12.8	5	94	15 08	21 43	21 50
11	2 17	+14.1	5	94	15 02	21 43	21 52
16	2 30	+15.3	5	94	14 56	21 43	21 53
21	2 44	+16.4	5	95	14 50	21 44	21 54
26	2 58	+17.5	4	95	14 44	21 44	21 56
31	3 12	+18.4	4	95	14 38	21 44	21 56

SUNRISE AND SUNSET

	London 0°05′ 51°30′ h m h m	Bristol 2°35′ 51°28′ h m h m	Birmingham 1°55′ 52°28′ h m h m	Manchester 2°15′ 53°28′ h m h m	Newcastle 1°37′ 54°59′ h m h m	Glasgow 4°14′ 55°52′ h m h m	Belfast 5°56′ 54°35′ h m h m
1	6 46 17 40	6 56 17 50	6 55 17 46	6 57 17 46	6 57 17 42	7 09 17 51	7 14 18 00
2	6 44 17 42	6 54 17 52	6 52 17 48	6 55 17 48	6 55 17 44	7 06 17 53	7 11 18 02
3	6 42 17 44	6 52 17 54	6 50 17 50	6 53 17 50	6 52 17 46	7 04 17 55	7 09 18 04
4	6 40 17 45	6 49 17 56	6 48 17 52	6 50 17 52	6 50 17 48	7 01 17 57	7 06 18 06
5	6 37 17 47	6 47 17 57	6 46 17 54	6 48 17 54	6 47 17 50	6 59 17 59	7 04 18 08
6	6 35 17 49	6 45 17 59	6 43 17 55	6 46 17 56	6 45 17 52	6 56 18 01	7 02 18 09
7	6 33 17 51	6 43 18 01	6 41 17 57	6 43 17 57	6 42 17 54	6 54 18 03	6 59 18 11
8	6 31 17 52	6 41 18 03	6 39 17 59	6 41 18 00	6 40 17 56	6 51 18 06	6 57 18 13
9	6 29 17 54	6 38 18 04	6 37 18 01	6 39 18 02	6 37 17 58	6 48 18 08	6 54 18 15
10	6 26 17 56	6 36 18 06	6 34 18 03	6 36 18 03	6 35 18 00	6 46 18 10	6 52 18 17
11	6 24 17 58	6 34 18 08	6 32 18 04	6 34 18 05	6 32 18 02	6 43 18 12	6 49 18 19
12	6 22 17 59	6 32 18 09	6 30 18 06	6 31 18 07	6 30 18 04	6 41 18 14	6 47 18 21
13	6 20 18 01	6 30 18 11	6 27 18 08	6 29 18 09	6 27 18 06	6 38 18 16	6 44 18 23
14	6 17 18 03	6 27 18 13	6 25 18 10	6 27 18 11	6 25 18 08	6 36 18 18	6 42 18 25
15	6 15 18 05	6 25 18 15	6 23 18 12	6 24 18 13	6 22 18 10	6 33 18 20	6 39 18 27
16	6 13 18 06	6 23 18 16	6 20 18 13	6 22 18 15	6 20 18 12	6 30 18 22	6 37 18 29
17	6 10 18 08	6 20 18 18	6 18 18 15	6 19 18 16	6 17 18 14	6 28 18 24	6 34 18 31
18	6 08 18 10	6 18 18 20	6 16 18 17	6 17 18 18	6 15 18 16	6 25 18 26	6 32 18 33
19	6 06 18 11	6 16 18 21	6 13 18 19	6 15 18 20	6 12 18 18	6 22 18 28	6 29 18 35
20	6 04 18 13	6 14 18 23	6 11 18 20	6 12 18 22	6 09 18 20	6 20 18 30	6 27 18 37
21	6 01 18 15	6 11 18 25	6 09 18 22	6 10 18 24	6 07 18 22	6 17 18 32	6 24 18 39
22	5 59 18 16	6 09 18 26	6 06 18 24	6 07 18 26	6 04 18 24	6 15 18 34	6 22 18 41
23	5 57 18 18	6 07 18 28	6 04 18 26	6 05 18 27	6 02 18 25	6 12 18 36	6 19 18 43
24	5 55 18 20	6 05 18 30	6 01 18 28	6 02 18 29	5 59 18 27	6 09 18 38	6 17 18 45
25	5 52 18 21	6 02 18 31	5 59 18 29	6 00 18 31	5 57 18 29	6 07 18 40	6 14 18 46
26	5 50 18 23	6 00 18 33	5 57 18 31	5 58 18 33	5 54 18 31	6 04 18 42	6 12 18 48
27	5 48 18 25	5 58 18 35	5 54 18 33	5 55 18 35	5 52 18 33	6 01 18 44	6 09 18 50
28	5 45 18 27	5 55 18 36	5 52 18 35	5 53 18 37	5 49 18 35	5 59 18 46	6 07 18 52
29	5 43 18 28	5 53 18 38	5 50 18 36	5 50 18 38	5 47 18 37	5 56 18 48	6 04 18 54
30	5 41 18 30	5 51 18 40	5 47 18 38	5 48 18 40	5 44 18 39	5 54 18 51	6 02 18 56
31	5 39 18 32	5 49 18 42	5 45 18 40	5 45 18 42	5 41 18 41	5 51 18 53	5 59 18 58

JUPITER

Day	RA	Dec.	Transit	5° high 52°	56°
	h m	° ′	h m	h m	h m
1	6 24.5	+23 27	19 47	3 24	3 42
11	6 25.2	+23 27	19 08	2 45	3 04
21	6 27.2	+23 27	18 31	2 08	2 26
31	6 30.5	+23 26	17 55	1 32	1 50

Diameters – equatorial 40″ polar 38″

SATURN

Day	RA	Dec.	Transit	5° high 52°	56°
	h m	° ′	h m	h m	h m
1	4 27.9	+20 10	17 51	1 08	1 22
11	4 29.8	+20 17	17 13	0 31	0 46
21	4 32.5	+20 25	16 37	23 52	0 10
31	4 35.8	+20 34	16 01	23 16	23 31

Diameters – equatorial 18″ polar 16″
Rings – major axis 41″ minor axis 18″

URANUS

Day	RA	Dec.	Transit	10° high 52°	56°
	h m	° ′	h m	h m	h m
1	21 52.8	−13 37	11 17	7 45	8 08
11	21 54.9	−13 25	10 39	7 06	7 29
21	21 57.0	−13 15	10 02	6 28	6 50
31	21 58.8	−13 05	9 25	5 49	6 11

Diameter 4″

NEPTUNE

Day	RA	Dec.	Transit	10° high 52°	56°
	h m	° ′	h m	h m	h m
1	20 48.1	−17 45	10 12	7 12	7 45
11	20 49.4	−17 40	9 34	6 33	7 06
21	20 50.6	−17 36	8 56	5 55	6 27
31	20 51.6	−17 32	8 17	5 16	5 48

Diameter 2″

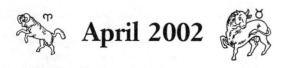

April 2002

FOURTH MONTH, 30 DAYS. *Aperire*, to open; Earth opens to receive seed

1	Monday	Bank Holiday in England, Wales and Northern Ireland.	*week* 13 *day* 91
2	Tuesday	Sir Alec Guinness b. 1914. Comte de Mirabeau Honoré Riqueti d. 1791	92
3	Wednesday	Leslie Howard b. 1893. Richard D'Oyly Carte d. 1901	93
4	Thursday	Maurice de Vlaminck b. 1876. Zulfikar Ali Bhutto d. 1979	94
5	Friday	Jean-Honoré Fragonard b. 1732. Chiang Kai-Shek d. 1975	95
6	Saturday	Alexander Herzen b. 1812. Modern Olympic Games revived at Athens 1896	96
7	Sunday	**1st S. after Easter.** Dick Turpin d. 1739	97
8	Monday	General Omar Bradley d. 1981. Entente Cordiale signed 1904	*week* 14 *day* 98
9	Tuesday	*Easter Law Sittings begin.* François Rabelais d. 1553	99
10	Wednesday	Antonia White d. 1980. Battle of Toulouse 1814	100
11	Thursday	Masaru Ibuka b. 1908. Francis Durbridge d. 1998	101
12	Friday	Beverley Cross b. 1931. First manned space flight by Yuri Gagarin in Vostok 1 1961	102
13	Saturday	HINDU NEW YEAR. SIKH NEW YEAR	103
14	Sunday	**2nd S. after Easter.** Abraham Lincoln shot 1865	104
15	Monday	Il-sung Kim b. 1912. Jean Genet d. 1986	*week* 15 *day* 105
16	Tuesday	Francisco de Goya y Lucientes d. 1828. Battle of Culloden 1746	106
17	Wednesday	Thornton Wilder b. 1897. Rhodesia became Zimbabwe 1980	107
18	Thursday	Louis-Adolphe Thiers b. 1797. San Francisco earthquake 1906	108
19	Friday	b. Frankie Howerd d. 1992. Battle of Lexington 1775	109
20	Saturday	Johann Agricola b. 1494. Adolf Hitler b. 1889	110
21	Sunday	**3rd S. after Easter.** *Queen Elizabeth II b. 1926.*	111
22	Monday	Madame de Stael Anne Necker b. 1766. Richard Nixon d. 1994	*week* 16 *day* 112
23	Tuesday	**St George.** Paulette Goddard d. 1990	113
24	Wednesday	Marshal Philippe Pétain b. 1856. Bill Edrich d. 1986	114
25	Thursday	**St Mark.** Vladimir Nemirovich-Danchenko d. 1943	115
26	Friday	Rudolf Hess b. 1894. Sid James d. 1976	116
27	Saturday	Mary Wollstonecraft Godwin b. 1759. William Macready d. 1873	117
28	Sunday	**4th S. after Easter.** The League of Nations founded 1919	118
29	Monday	Sir Thomas Beecham b. 1870	*week* 17 *day* 119
30	Tuesday	Sir Henry Bishop d. 1855. George Washington inaugurated as the first President of the USA 1789	120

ASTRONOMICAL PHENOMENA

d	h	
7	09	Mercury in superior conjunction
13	10	Mercury in conjunction with Moon. Mercury 4° N.
14	19	Venus in conjunction with Moon. Venus 3° N.
16	00	Mars in conjunction with Moon. Mars 2° N.
16	20	Saturn in conjunction with Moon. Saturn 0°.8 S.
18	23	Jupiter in conjunction with Moon. Jupiter 2° S.
20	06	Sun's longitude 30° ♉

MINIMA OF ALGOL

d	h	d	h	d	h
3	17.9	15	05.2	26	16.5
6	14.7	18	02.0	29	13.3
9	11.6	20	22.8		
12	08.4	23	19.7		

CONSTELLATIONS

The following constellations are near the meridian at

	d	h		d	h
March	1	24	April	15	21
March	16	23	May	1	20
April	1	22	May	16	19

Cepheus (below the Pole), Cassiopeia (below the Pole), Ursa Major, Leo Minor, Leo, Sextans, Hydra and Crater

THE MOON

Phases, Apsides and Node	d	h	m
☾ Last Quarter	.4	15	29
● New Moon	12	19	21
☽ First Quarter	20	12	48
○ Full Moon	27	03	00
Apogee (406,390km)	10	05	41
Perigee (360,096km)	25	16	31

Mean longitude of ascending node on April 1, 82°

THE SUN   S.D 16'.1

Day	Right Ascension	Dec. +	Equation of Time	Rise 52°	Rise 56°	Transit	Set 52°	Set 56°	Sidereal time	Transit of First Point of Aries
	h m s	° '	m s	h m	h m	h m	h m	h m	h m s	h m s
1	0 40 46	4 23	− 4 02	5 36	5 31	12 04	18 33	18 38	12 36 43	11 21 25
2	0 44 24	4 46	− 3 45	5 33	5 29	12 04	18 35	18 40	12 40 40	11 17 29
3	0 48 03	5 09	− 3 27	5 31	5 26	12 03	18 37	18 42	12 44 36	11 13 33
4	0 51 42	5 32	− 3 09	5 29	5 23	12 03	18 38	18 44	12 48 33	11 09 37
5	0 55 21	5 55	− 2 52	5 26	5 21	12 03	18 40	18 46	12 52 29	11 05 41
6	0 59 00	6 18	− 2 34	5 24	5 18	12 02	18 42	18 48	12 56 26	11 01 45
7	1 02 40	6 41	− 2 17	5 22	5 16	12 02	18 44	18 50	13 00 22	10 57 50
8	1 06 20	7 03	− 2 01	5 20	5 13	12 02	18 45	18 52	13 04 19	10 53 54
9	1 09 59	7 26	− 1 44	5 17	5 10	12 02	18 47	18 54	13 08 16	10 49 58
10	1 13 40	7 48	− 1 28	5 15	5 08	12 01	18 49	18 56	13 12 12	10 46 02
11	1 17 20	8 10	− 1 12	5 13	5 05	12 01	18 50	18 58	13 16 09	10 42 06
12	1 21 01	8 32	− 0 56	5 11	5 03	12 01	18 52	19 00	13 20 05	10 38 10
13	1 24 42	8 54	− 0 40	5 08	5 00	12 01	18 54	19 02	13 24 02	10 34 14
14	1 28 23	9 16	− 0 25	5 06	4 58	12 00	18 56	19 04	13 27 58	10 30 18
15	1 32 05	9 37	− 0 10	5 04	4 55	12 00	18 57	19 06	13 31 55	10 26 22
16	1 35 47	9 59	+ 0 04	5 02	4 53	12 00	18 59	19 08	13 35 51	10 22 26
17	1 39 30	10 20	+ 0 18	5 00	4 50	12 00	19 01	19 10	13 39 48	10 18 30
18	1 43 12	10 41	+ 0 32	4 57	4 48	11 59	19 02	19 12	13 43 44	10 14 35
19	1 46 56	11 02	+ 0 45	4 55	4 45	11 59	19 04	19 14	13 47 41	10 10 39
20	1 50 39	11 23	+ 0 58	4 53	4 43	11 59	19 06	19 17	13 51 38	10 06 43
21	1 54 23	11 43	+ 1 11	4 51	4 40	11 59	19 08	19 19	13 55 34	10 02 47
22	1 58 08	12 04	+ 1 23	4 49	4 38	11 59	19 09	19 21	13 59 31	9 58 51
23	2 01 52	12 24	+ 1 35	4 47	4 35	11 58	19 11	19 23	14 03 27	9 54 55
24	2 05 38	12 44	+ 1 46	4 45	4 33	11 58	19 13	19 25	14 07 24	9 50 59
25	2 09 23	13 04	+ 1 57	4 43	4 31	11 58	19 14	19 27	14 11 20	9 47 03
26	2 13 09	13 23	+ 2 08	4 41	4 28	11 58	19 16	19 29	14 15 17	9 43 07
27	2 16 56	13 42	+ 2 17	4 39	4 26	11 58	19 18	19 31	14 19 13	9 39 11
28	2 20 43	14 02	+ 2 27	4 37	4 24	11 57	19 19	19 33	14 23 10	9 35 15
29	2 24 31	14 20	+ 2 36	4 35	4 21	11 57	19 21	19 35	14 27 07	9 31 20
30	2 28 19	14 39	+ 2 44	4 33	4 19	11 57	19 23	19 37	14 31 03	9 27 24

DURATION OF TWILIGHT (in minutes)

Latitude	52°	56°	52°	56°	52°	56°	52°	56°
	1 April		11 April		21 April		30 April	
Civil	34	38	35	39	37	42	39	44
Nautical	76	84	79	89	83	96	89	106
Astronomical	120	136	127	147	137	165	152	204

THE NIGHT SKY

Mercury passes through superior conjunction on the 7th and about ten days later becomes visible as an evening object, low above the west- north-western horizon for a short while, around the end of evening civil twilight. During this period its magnitude fades from -1.2 to 0.0. This is the most favourable evening apparition of the year for observers in the latitudes of the British Isles.

Venus continues to be visible for a short time in the evenings, low in the western sky after sunset. Its magnitude is -3.9. The crescent Moon, only 2 days old, will be seen about 3 degrees below and to the left of the planet, on the evening of the 14th.

Mars, magnitude +1.6, is visible for a short while low above the western horizon in the evenings. Early in the month Mars moves from Aries eastwards into Taurus, passing between the two open clusters, the Pleiades and the Hyades. Mars passes 6 degrees north of Aldebaran on

the 29th. On the evening of the 15th the crescent Moon, three days old, passes 4 degrees below the planet.

Jupiter is an evening object, magnitude -2.1, visible in the south-western sky until midnight. The crescent Moon will be seen only 2 degrees to the right of Jupiter on the evening of the 18th.

Saturn, magnitude +0.1, is still an evening object in the western sky, though continuing to draw closer to the Sun. By the end of the month it will be too low to be detected two hours after sunset. On the evening of the 16th the crescent Moon will occult Saturn (see page 67 for details).

THE MOON

Day	RA	Dec.	Hor. par.	Semi-diam	Sun's co-long.	PA of Bright Limb	Phase	Age	Rise 52°	Rise 56°	Transit	Set 52°	Set 56°
	h m	°	'	'	°	°	%	d	h m	h m	h m	h m	h m
1	15 37	−17.2	59.4	16.2	128	101	85	17.9	23 52	—	3 07	7 34	7 16
2	16 34	−21.0	58.5	15.9	141	98	77	18.9	—	0 14	4 02	8 05	7 42
3	17 31	−23.6	57.5	15.7	153	93	67	19.9	1 07	1 34	4 58	8 45	8 18
4	18 28	−24.7	56.6	15.4	165	87	57	20.9	2 10	2 39	5 53	9 35	9 06
5	19 24	−24.5	55.8	15.2	177	82	47	21.9	3 01	3 29	6 46	10 34	10 06
6	20 18	−23.1	55.1	15.0	189	76	37	22.9	3 40	4 04	7 37	11 39	11 15
7	21 09	−20.6	54.6	14.9	201	71	28	23.9	4 09	4 29	8 25	12 48	12 29
8	21 58	−17.3	54.3	14.8	214	66	20	24.9	4 32	4 48	9 10	13 57	13 43
9	22 44	−13.4	54.0	14.7	226	62	13	25.9	4 51	5 02	9 53	15 05	14 56
10	23 29	− 8.9	54.0	14.7	238	58	7	26.9	5 06	5 13	10 34	16 13	16 08
11	0 12	− 4.1	54.0	14.7	250	53	3	27.9	5 21	5 23	11 14	17 21	17 21
12	0 55	+ 0.9	54.1	14.7	263	40	1	28.9	5 34	5 33	11 55	18 29	18 33
13	1 39	+ 5.8	54.3	14.8	275	311	0	0.2	5 49	5 43	12 36	19 38	19 47
14	2 23	+10.7	54.6	14.9	287	265	1	1.2	6 05	5 54	13 19	20 49	21 03
15	3 10	+15.1	55.0	15.0	299	260	5	2.2	6 23	6 09	14 04	22 01	22 20
16	3 59	+19.0	55.4	15.1	311	261	9	3.2	6 47	6 27	14 53	23 13	23 37
17	4 51	+22.1	55.9	15.2	324	264	16	4.2	7 17	6 53	15 44	—	—
18	5 46	+24.1	56.5	15.4	336	268	24	5.2	7 58	7 30	16 39	0 22	0 49
19	6 43	+24.9	57.1	15.6	348	274	34	6.2	8 51	8 22	17 35	1 23	1 52
20	7 42	+24.3	57.8	15.8	0	279	44	7.2	9 58	9 31	18 32	2 14	2 41
21	8 40	+22.3	58.6	16.0	12	285	55	8.2	11 15	10 53	19 29	2 54	3 17
22	9 38	+18.9	59.3	16.2	25	291	66	9.2	12 38	12 22	20 24	3 25	3 43
23	10 35	+14.3	60.0	16.3	37	295	77	10.2	14 05	13 55	21 18	3 50	4 02
24	11 31	+ 8.8	60.5	16.5	49	299	86	11.2	15 32	15 28	22 10	4 11	4 17
25	12 25	+ 2.6	60.8	16.6	61	302	93	12.2	17 00	17 02	23 03	4 30	4 31
26	13 20	− 3.7	60.9	16.6	73	307	98	13.2	18 29	18 36	23 56	4 48	4 44
27	14 15	− 9.8	60.6	16.5	86	353	100	14.2	19 57	20 11	—	5 08	4 58
28	15 11	−15.2	60.1	16.4	98	94	99	15.2	21 24	21 44	0 50	5 31	5 16
29	16 09	−19.7	59.4	16.2	110	98	95	16.2	22 45	23 11	1 46	5 59	5 38
30	17 08	−22.9	58.5	16.0	122	95	89	17.2	23 57	—	2 43	6 36	6 10

MERCURY

Day	RA	Dec.	Diam.	Phase	Transit	5° high 52°	5° high 56°
	h m	°	"	%	h m	h m	h m
1	0 19	+ 0.3	5	98	11 44	6 14	6 17
3	0 34	+ 2.0	5	99	11 51	6 11	6 12
5	0 48	+ 3.8	5	100	11 57	6 08	6 08
7	1 03	+ 5.6	5	100	12 04	18 05	18 07
9	1 18	+ 7.5	5	100	12 11	18 22	18 25
11	1 33	+ 9.3	5	99	12 19	18 39	18 44
13	1 48	+11.2	5	97	12 26	18 56	19 02
15	2 04	+13.0	5	94	12 34	19 13	19 21
17	2 19	+14.7	5	90	12 41	19 30	19 39
19	2 34	+16.3	6	85	12 49	19 45	19 57
21	2 49	+17.8	6	79	12 55	20 00	20 13
23	3 03	+19.1	6	73	13 02	20 14	20 28
25	3 17	+20.3	6	66	13 07	20 26	20 41
27	3 30	+21.3	7	60	13 12	20 36	20 53
29	3 42	+22.2	7	53	13 16	20 45	21 02
31	3 53	+22.9	7	47	13 18	20 51	21 09

VENUS

Day	RA	Dec.	Diam.	Phase	Transit	5° high 52°	5° high 56°
	h m	°	"	%	h m	h m	h m
1	1 51	+10.8	10	95	13 15	19 40	19 46
6	2 15	+13.1	11	94	13 18	19 56	20 04
11	2 38	+15.3	11	93	13 23	20 12	20 22
16	3 02	+17.3	11	93	13 27	20 27	20 39
21	3 27	+19.1	11	92	13 32	20 42	20 56
26	3 52	+20.7	11	91	13 37	20 57	21 13
31	4 18	+22.1	11	90	13 43	21 11	21 28

MARS

Day	RA	Dec.	Diam.	Phase	Transit	5° high 52°	5° high 56°
1	3 15	+18.6	4	95	14 37	21 43	21 57
6	3 29	+19.6	4	96	14 32	21 43	21 57
11	3 43	+20.4	4	96	14 26	21 42	21 57
16	3 57	+21.2	4	96	14 21	21 42	21 57
21	4 11	+21.9	4	97	14 15	21 40	21 57
26	4 26	+22.5	4	97	14 10	21 39	21 56
31	4 40	+23.0	4	97	14 05	21 37	21 55

SUNRISE AND SUNSET

	London 0°05′ 51°30′ h m	h m	Bristol 2°35′ 51°28′ h m	h m	Birmingham 1°55′ 52°28′ h m	h m	Manchester 2°15′ 53°28′ h m	h m	Newcastle 1°37′ 54°59′ h m	h m	Glasgow 4°14′ 55°52′ h m	h m	Belfast 5°56′ 54°35′ h m	h m
1	5 36	18 33	5 46	18 43	5 43	18 42	5 43	18 44	5 39	18 43	5 48	18 55	5 57	19 00
2	5 34	18 35	5 44	18 45	5 40	18 43	5 41	18 46	5 36	18 45	5 46	18 57	5 54	19 02
3	5 32	18 37	5 42	18 47	5 38	18 45	5 38	18 48	5 34	18 47	5 43	18 59	5 52	19 04
4	5 30	18 38	5 40	18 48	5 36	18 47	5 36	18 49	5 31	18 49	5 41	19 01	5 49	19 06
5	5 27	18 40	5 37	18 50	5 33	18 48	5 33	18 51	5 29	18 51	5 38	19 03	5 47	19 08
6	5 25	18 42	5 35	18 52	5 31	18 50	5 31	18 53	5 26	18 53	5 35	19 05	5 44	19 09
7	5 23	18 43	5 33	18 53	5 29	18 52	5 29	18 55	5 24	18 55	5 33	19 07	5 42	19 11
8	5 21	18 45	5 31	18 55	5 26	18 54	5 26	18 57	5 21	18 57	5 30	19 09	5 39	19 13
9	5 18	18 47	5 28	18 57	5 24	18 55	5 24	18 58	5 19	18 59	5 28	19 11	5 37	19 15
10	5 16	18 48	5 26	18 58	5 22	18 57	5 22	19 00	5 16	19 01	5 25	19 13	5 34	19 17
11	5 14	18 50	5 24	19 00	5 20	18 59	5 19	19 02	5 14	19 03	5 23	19 15	5 32	19 19
12	5 12	18 52	5 22	19 02	5 17	19 01	5 17	19 04	5 11	19 04	5 20	19 17	5 29	19 21
13	5 10	18 53	5 20	19 03	5 15	19 02	5 15	19 06	5 09	19 06	5 17	19 19	5 27	19 23
14	5 07	18 55	5 17	19 05	5 13	19 04	5 12	19 08	5 06	19 08	5 15	19 21	5 25	19 25
15	5 05	18 57	5 15	19 07	5 11	19 06	5 10	19 09	5 04	19 10	5 12	19 23	5 22	19 27
16	5 03	18 58	5 13	19 08	5 08	19 08	5 08	19 11	5 02	19 12	5 10	19 25	5 20	19 29
17	5 01	19 00	5 11	19 10	5 06	19 09	5 05	19 13	4 59	19 14	5 07	19 27	5 17	19 30
18	4 59	19 02	5 09	19 12	5 04	19 11	5 03	19 15	4 57	19 16	5 05	19 29	5 15	19 32
19	4 57	19 03	5 07	19 13	5 02	19 13	5 01	19 17	4 54	19 18	5 02	19 31	5 13	19 34
20	4 55	19 05	5 05	19 15	5 00	19 15	4 59	19 19	4 52	19 20	5 00	19 33	5 10	19 36
21	4 53	19 07	5 03	19 17	4 58	19 16	4 56	19 20	4 50	19 22	4 58	19 35	5 08	19 38
22	4 50	19 08	5 01	19 18	4 55	19 18	4 54	19 22	4 47	19 24	4 55	19 37	5 06	19 40
23	4 48	19 10	4 59	19 20	4 53	19 20	4 52	19 24	4 45	19 26	4 53	19 39	5 03	19 42
24	4 46	19 12	4 56	19 22	4 51	19 22	4 50	19 26	4 43	19 28	4 50	19 41	5 01	19 44
25	4 44	19 13	4 54	19 23	4 49	19 23	4 48	19 28	4 40	19 30	4 48	19 43	4 59	19 46
26	4 42	19 15	4 52	19 25	4 47	19 25	4 45	19 29	4 38	19 32	4 46	19 45	4 57	19 48
27	4 40	19 17	4 50	19 27	4 45	19 27	4 43	19 31	4 36	19 34	4 43	19 47	4 54	19 50
28	4 38	19 18	4 49	19 28	4 43	19 28	4 41	19 33	4 34	19 36	4 41	19 49	4 52	19 51
29	4 37	19 20	4 47	19 30	4 41	19 30	4 39	19 35	4 31	19 38	4 39	19 51	4 50	19 53
30	4 35	19 22	4 45	19 31	4 39	19 32	4 37	19 37	4 29	19 39	4 36	19 53	4 48	19 55

JUPITER

Day	RA h m	Dec. ° ′	Transit h m	5° high 52° h m	56° h m
1	6 30.9	+23 25	17 52	1 28	1 47
11	6 35.5	+23 23	17 17	0 53	1 12
21	6 41.1	+23 18	16 43	0 19	0 37
31	6 47.6	+23 12	16 10	23 42	0 04

Diameters — equatorial 36″ polar 34″

SATURN

Day	RA h m	Dec. ° ′	Transit h m	5° high 52° h m	56° h m
1	4 36.1	+20 35	15 57	23 13	23 28
11	4 40.0	+20 44	15 22	22 39	22 54
21	4 44.4	+20 54	14 47	22 05	22 20
31	4 49.2	+21 04	14 12	21 31	21 46

Diameters — equatorial 17″ polar 15″
Rings — major axis 39″ minor axis 17″

URANUS

Day	RA h m	Dec. ° ′	Transit h m	10° high 52° h m	56° h m
1	21 59.0	-13 04	9 21	5 45	6 07
11	22 00.7	-12 56	8 43	5 06	5 29
21	22 02.1	-12 48	8 05	4 28	4 50
31	22 03.2	-12 43	7 27	3 49	4 11

Diameter 4″

NEPTUNE

Day	RA h m	Dec. ° ′	Transit h m	10° high 52° h m	56° h m
1	20 51.7	-17 31	8 14	5 12	5 44
11	20 52.5	-17 28	7 35	4 33	5 05
21	20 53.1	-17 26	6 56	3 54	4 26
31	20 53.5	-17 24	6 17	3 15	3 47

Diameter 2″

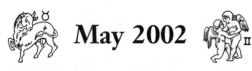

May 2002

FIFTH MONTH, 31 DAYS, *Maia*, goddess of growth and increase

1	*Wednesday*	**SS. Philip and James.** Great Exhibition opened 1851	
2	*Thursday*	Senator Joseph McCarthy d. 1957. Berlin surrendered to Russian troops 1945	122
3	*Friday*	Richard D'Oyly Carte b. 1844. Opening of Festival of Britain 1951	123
4	*Saturday*	Joseph Whitaker b. 1820. Marshal Josip Tito d. 1980	124
5	*Sunday*	**5th S. after Easter.** EASTER DAY (Eastern Orthodox)	125
6	*Monday*	*Bank Holiday in UK.* Tony Blair b. 1953.	*week 18 day* 126
7	*Tuesday*	Caspar Friedrich d. 1840. Lusitania torpedoed 1915	127
8	*Wednesday*	Harry Truman b. 1884. Restoration of the British Monarchy 1660	128
9	*Thursday*	**Ascension Day.** John Brown b. 1800	129
10	*Friday*	Owen Brannigan d. 1973. Resignation of Chamberlain 1940	130
11	*Saturday*	Irving Berlin b. 1888. Prime Minister Spencer Perceval assassinated 1812	131
12	*Sunday*	**S. after Ascension (6th after Easter).** Coronation of George VI and Queen Elizabeth 1937	132
13	*Monday*	John Nash d. 1835. Gary Cooper d. 1961	*week 19 day* 133
14	*Tuesday*	**St Matthias.** Thomas Gainsborough b. 1727	134
15	*Wednesday*	Edwin Muir b. 1887. Charles Perrault d. 1703	135
16	*Thursday*	Sir John Hare b. 1844. Russian spacecraft Venus 5 touched down on Venus 1969	136
17	*Friday*	FEAST OF WEEKS begins. Summer Time Act came into force 1916	137
18	*Saturday*	Pope John Paul II b. 1920. Napoleon proclaimed Emperor of the French 1804	138
19	*Sunday*	**Pentecost (Whit Sunday).** Nathaniel Hawthorne d. 1864	139
20	*Monday*	Mary Lamb d. 1847. First solo transatlantic flight by a woman completed by Amelia Earhart 1932	*week 20 day* 140
21	*Tuesday*	Andrey Sakharov b. 1921. Christopher Columbus d. 1506	141
22	*Wednesday*	Elizabeth David d. 1992. Blackwall Tunnel opened 1897	142
23	*Thursday*	Heinrich Himmler d. 1945. Coalition Ministry dissolved 1945	143
24	*Friday*	Joseph Alexandrovich Brodsky b. 1940. Field Marshall 1st Earl Archibald Percival Wavell d. 1950	144
25	*Saturday*	Robert Capa d. 1954. Consecration of re-built Coventry Cathedral 1962	145
26	*Sunday*	**Trinity Sunday.** Saint Augustine d. 604/5	146
27	*Monday*	Arnold Bennett b. 1867. Habeus Corpus Act passed 1679	*week 21 day* 147
28	*Tuesday*	Patrick White b. 1912. Jean Muir d. 1995	148
29	*Wednesday*	Erich Honecker d. 1994. Oak Apple Day - Restoration of Charles II 1660	149
30	*Thursday*	**Corpus Christi.** Christopher Marlowe d. 1593	150
31	*Friday*	**Visit of the Virgin Mary to Elizabeth.** *Easter Law Sittings end.*	151

ASTRONOMICAL PHENOMENA

d	h	
4	04	Mercury at greatest elongation E.21°
4	06	Saturn in conjunction with Mars. Saturn 2° S.
7	12	Saturn in conjunction with Venus. Saturn 2° S.
10	20	Mars in conjunction with Venus. Mars 0°3 S.
13	12	Neptune at stationary point
13	22	Mercury in conjunction with Moon. Mercury 2° N.
14	08	Saturn in conjunction with Moon. Saturn 1° S.
14	19	Mars in conjunction with Moon. Mars 0°6 N.
14	23	Venus in conjunction with Moon. Venus 0°8 N.
15	19	Mercury at stationary point
16	12	Jupiter in conjunction with Moon. Jupiter 2° S.
21	05	Sun's longitude 60°Ⅱ
27	07	Mercury in inferior conjunction

MINIMA OF ALGOL

Algol is inconveniently situated for observation during May

CONSTELLATIONS

The following constellations are near the meridian at

d	h		d	h
April 1	24	May	16	21
April 15	23	June	1	20
May 1	22	June	15	19

Cepheus (below the Pole), Cassiopeia (below the Pole), Ursa Minor, Ursa Major, Canes Venatici, Coma Berenices, Bootes, Leo, Virgo, Crater, Corvus and Hydra

THE MOON

Phases, Apsides and Node	d	h	m
☾ Last Quarter	4	07	16
● New Moon	12	10	45
☽ First Quarter	19	19	42
○ Full Moon	26	11	51
Apogee (405,452km)	7	19	20
Perigee (365,006km)	23	15	40

Mean longitude of ascending node on May 1, 80°

THE SUN   S.D 16′.1

Day	Right Ascension	Dec. +	Equation of Time	Rise 52°	Rise 56°	Transit	Set 52°	Set 56°	Sidereal time	Transit of First Point of Aries
	h m s	° ′	m s	h m	h m	h m	h m	h m	h m s	h m s
1	2 32 08	14 57	+ 2 52	4 31	4 17	11 57	19 24	19 39	14 35 00	9 23 28
2	2 35 57	15 15	+ 2 59	4 29	4 14	11 57	19 26	19 41	14 38 56	9 19 32
3	2 39 47	15 33	+ 3 06	4 27	4 12	11 57	19 28	19 43	14 42 53	9 15 36
4	2 43 37	15 51	+ 3 12	4 25	4 10	11 57	19 29	19 45	14 46 49	9 11 40
5	2 47 28	16 08	+ 3 18	4 23	4 08	11 57	19 31	19 47	14 50 46	9 07 44
6	2 51 20	16 25	+ 3 23	4 22	4 06	11 57	19 33	19 49	14 54 42	9 03 48
7	2 55 12	16 42	+ 3 27	4 20	4 04	11 57	19 34	19 51	14 58 39	8 59 52
8	2 59 04	16 59	+ 3 31	4 18	4 01	11 56	19 36	19 53	15 02 36	8 55 56
9	3 02 58	17 15	+ 3 34	4 16	3 59	11 56	19 38	19 55	15 06 32	8 52 00
10	3 06 52	17 31	+ 3 37	4 15	3 57	11 56	19 39	19 57	15 10 29	8 48 05
11	3 10 46	17 47	+ 3 39	4 13	3 55	11 56	19 41	19 59	15 14 25	8 44 09
12	3 14 41	18 02	+ 3 41	4 11	3 53	11 56	19 42	20 01	15 18 22	8 40 13
13	3 18 37	18 17	+ 3 42	4 10	3 51	11 56	19 44	20 02	15 22 18	8 36 17
14	3 22 33	18 32	+ 3 42	4 08	3 50	11 56	19 46	20 04	15 26 15	8 32 21
15	3 26 30	18 46	+ 3 42	4 06	3 48	11 56	19 47	20 06	15 30 11	8 28 25
16	3 30 27	19 00	+ 3 41	4 05	3 46	11 56	19 49	20 08	15 34 08	8 24 29
17	3 34 25	19 14	+ 3 40	4 04	3 44	11 56	19 50	20 10	15 38 05	8 20 33
18	3 38 23	19 28	+ 3 38	4 02	3 42	11 56	19 52	20 12	15 42 01	8 16 37
19	3 42 22	19 41	+ 3 36	4 01	3 40	11 56	19 53	20 14	15 45 58	8 12 41
20	3 46 21	19 54	+ 3 33	3 59	3 39	11 57	19 55	20 15	15 49 54	8 08 45
21	3 50 21	20 06	+ 3 29	3 58	3 37	11 57	19 56	20 17	15 53 51	8 04 50
22	3 54 22	20 18	+ 3 25	3 57	3 36	11 57	19 57	20 19	15 57 47	8 00 54
23	3 58 23	20 30	+ 3 21	3 55	3 34	11 57	19 59	20 20	16 01 44	7 56 58
24	4 02 24	20 42	+ 3 16	3 54	3 32	11 57	20 00	20 22	16 05 40	7 53 02
25	4 06 26	20 53	+ 3 11	3 53	3 31	11 57	20 02	20 24	16 09 37	7 49 06
26	4 10 29	21 03	+ 3 05	3 52	3 30	11 57	20 03	20 25	16 13 34	7 45 10
27	4 14 32	21 14	+ 2 58	3 51	3 28	11 57	20 04	20 27	16 17 30	7 41 14
28	4 18 35	21 24	+ 2 51	3 50	3 27	11 57	20 05	20 28	16 21 27	7 37 18
29	4 22 39	21 33	+ 2 44	3 49	3 26	11 57	20 07	20 30	16 25 23	7 33 22
30	4 26 44	21 43	+ 2 36	3 48	3 24	11 57	20 08	20 31	16 29 20	7 29 26
31	4 30 48	21 51	+ 2 28	3 47	3 23	11 58	20 09	20 33	16 33 16	7 25 30

DURATION OF TWILIGHT (in minutes)

Latitude	52°	56°	52°	56°	52°	56°	52°	56°
	1 May		11 May		21 May		31 May	
Civil	39	44	41	48	44	53	46	57
Nautical	89	106	97	120	106	141	115	187
Astronomical	152	204	176	TAN	TAN	TAN	TAN	TAN

THE NIGHT SKY

Mercury, its magnitude fading from 0.0 to +1.0, is visible as an evening object for the first week of the month, low above the west-north-western horizon for a short while around the end of evening civil twilight. Thereafter it is too close to the Sun for observation, passing through inferior conjunction on the 27th.

The Moon and the planets on the evening of the 14th.
On this occasion the Moon and the planets Venus, Mars Jupiter and Saturn will all be within 20 degrees of each other. At the end of evening civil twilight Jupiter should be clearly visible, almost due west, with Venus about 20 degrees to its right. The crescent Moon, only 2.4 days old, will be 2 or 3 degrees below Venus. Mars, the faintest of these planets, will be about 2 degrees below and to the right of Venus. Saturn will also be difficult to detect since it will be 7 degrees below and 4 degrees to the right of Venus.

Venus, magnitude −3.9, is visible as a brilliant object in the western sky for nearly two hours after sunset. Venus is moving eastwards at a rate of over 1 degree per day, passing

both Saturn and Mars. It passes Saturn at midday on the 7th and in the evening will be seen about 2.5 degrees above this planet. On the evening of the 10th Venus passes 0.3 degrees north of Mars and this close conjunction should help observers to locate the fainter planet. Venus is 6 degrees north of Aldebaran on the 4th.

Mars, magnitude +1.7, continues to be visible as an evening object low above the west-north-western horizon for a short while after dusk. Early in the month Mars and Saturn are close together and on the 4th Mars passes 2 degrees north of Saturn, the latter being several times brighter and therefore a useful guide to locating Mars. Mars is coming towards the end of its evening apparition and will be lost to view shortly before the end of the month.

Jupiter, magnitude −1.9, is still visible as an evening object, in the south-western sky, though by the end of the month it is only visible for about two hours after sunset.

Saturn, magnitude +0.1, becomes increasingly difficult to detect low in the western sky in the gathering evening twilight and is unlikely to be seen after the middle of the month.

THE MOON

Day	RA h m	Dec. °	Hor. par. '	Semi-diam '	Sun's co-long. °	PA of Bright Limb °	Phase %	Age d	Rise 52° h m	Rise 56° h m	Transit h m	Set 52° h m	Set 56° h m
1	18 07	−24.6	57.6	15.7	134	90	81	18.2	—	0 26	3 41	7 22	6 53
2	19 05	−24.9	56.7	15.5	146	85	73	19.2	0 55	1 25	4 37	8 19	7 50
3	20 01	−23.9	55.9	15.2	159	79	63	20.2	1 40	2 06	5 30	9 24	8 58
4	20 54	−21.7	55.2	15.0	171	74	53	21.2	2 13	2 35	6 20	10 34	10 12
5	21 44	−18.5	54.7	14.9	183	70	43	22.2	2 38	2 56	7 07	11 44	11 27
6	22 31	−14.7	54.3	14.8	195	67	34	23.2	2 58	3 11	7 50	12 53	12 42
7	23 17	−10.3	54.1	14.7	207	64	25	24.2	3 14	3 23	8 32	14 01	13 55
8	0 00	− 5.6	54.1	14.7	220	62	18	25.2	3 29	3 33	9 13	15 09	15 07
9	0 43	− 0.6	54.2	14.8	232	61	11	26.2	3 42	3 42	9 53	16 17	16 20
10	1 27	+ 4.4	54.4	14.8	244	60	6	27.2	3 56	3 52	10 34	17 26	17 33
11	2 11	+ 9.3	54.7	14.9	256	58	2	28.2	4 11	4 03	11 16	18 37	18 49
12	2 57	+14.0	55.1	15.0	269	45	0	29.2	4 29	4 16	12 01	19 50	20 07
13	3 46	+18.1	55.5	15.1	281	273	0	0.6	4 51	4 32	12 49	21 03	21 25
14	4 38	+21.5	56.0	15.3	293	264	2	1.6	5 19	4 56	13 40	22 14	22 41
15	5 33	+23.8	56.5	15.4	305	266	7	2.6	5 56	5 29	14 35	23 19	23 49
16	6 30	+25.0	57.0	15.5	318	271	13	3.6	6 45	6 16	15 31	—	—
17	7 28	+24.7	57.5	15.7	330	277	21	4.6	7 48	7 20	16 28	0 14	0 42
18	8 27	+23.0	58.0	15.8	342	282	30	5.6	9 01	8 38	17 24	0 57	1 22
19	9 24	+20.0	58.6	16.0	354	287	41	6.6	10 22	10 04	18 18	1 30	1 49
20	10 20	+15.8	59.0	16.1	7	291	52	7.6	11 46	11 33	19 11	1 56	2 10
21	11 14	+10.6	59.5	16.2	19	295	64	8.6	13 10	13 04	20 02	2 17	2 25
22	12 07	+ 4.8	59.8	16.3	31	296	74	9.6	14 35	14 34	20 52	2 35	2 38
23	13 00	− 1.3	60.0	16.4	43	297	84	10.6	16 00	16 05	21 43	2 53	2 51
24	13 53	− 7.4	60.1	16.4	55	296	92	11.6	17 26	17 37	22 35	3 11	3 04
25	14 48	−13.1	59.9	16.3	68	295	97	12.6	18 53	19 10	23 30	3 31	3 19
26	15 45	−18.0	59.5	16.2	80	298	100	13.6	20 18	20 41	—	3 56	3 38
27	16 43	−21.7	58.9	16.1	92	93	100	14.6	21 36	22 04	0 27	4 28	4 04
28	17 43	−24.1	58.2	15.9	104	94	97	15.6	22 42	23 12	1 25	5 10	4 41
29	18 42	−25.0	57.4	15.7	116	89	92	16.6	23 34	—	2 22	6 03	5 33
30	19 40	−24.5	56.7	15.4	128	83	86	17.6	—	0 02	3 18	7 06	6 38
31	20 36	−22.7	55.9	15.2	141	78	78	18.6	0 13	0 37	4 11	8 15	7 52

MERCURY

Day	RA h m	Dec. °	Diam. "	Phase %	Transit h m	5° high 52° h m	5° high 56° h m
1	3 53	+22.9	7	47	13 18	20 51	21 09
3	4 02	+23.4	8	41	13 20	20 55	21 13
5	4 11	+23.7	8	35	13 20	20 57	21 16
7	4 18	+24.0	9	30	13 19	20 56	21 15
9	4 24	+24.0	9	25	13 16	20 54	21 13
11	4 28	+24.0	9	20	13 12	20 49	21 08
13	4 31	+23.8	10	16	13 07	20 42	21 00
15	4 32	+23.4	10	12	13 00	20 32	20 50
17	4 32	+23.0	11	9	12 52	20 21	20 38
19	4 31	+22.5	11	6	12 43	20 08	20 25
21	4 29	+21.8	12	3	12 32	19 53	20 09
23	4 26	+21.1	12	2	12 21	19 38	19 53
25	4 22	+20.4	12	1	12 09	19 21	19 36
27	4 18	+19.6	12	0	11 57	4 48	4 34
29	4 13	+18.9	12	0	11 45	4 40	4 27
31	4 09	+18.2	12	1	11 33	4 32	4 20

VENUS

Day	RA h m	Dec. °	Diam. "	Phase %	Transit h m	5° high 52° h m	5° high 56° h m
1	4 18	+22.1	11	90	13 43	21 11	21 28
6	4 43	+23.3	12	88	13 49	21 24	21 43
11	5 10	+24.1	12	87	13 56	21 36	21 55
16	5 36	+24.7	12	86	14 03	21 46	22 06
21	6 02	+25.0	12	85	14 09	21 54	22 15
26	6 29	+25.0	12	83	14 16	22 01	22 21
31	6 55	+24.7	13	82	14 22	22 05	22 25

MARS

Day	RA h m	Dec. °	Diam. "	Phase %	Transit h m	5° high 52° h m	5° high 56° h m
1	4 40	+23.0	4	97	14 05	21 37	21 55
6	4 55	+23.5	4	97	13 59	21 34	21 53
11	5 09	+23.8	4	98	13 54	21 31	21 50
16	5 24	+24.1	4	98	13 49	21 28	21 47
21	5 38	+24.3	4	98	13 44	21 24	21 43
26	5 53	+24.4	4	98	13 39	21 19	21 39
31	6 07	+24.4	4	99	13 33	21 14	21 33

SUNSET AND SUNRISE

Day	London 0°05' 51°30'		Bristol 2°35' 51°28'		Birmingham 1°55' 52°28'		Manchester 2°15' 53°28'		Newcastle 1°37' 54°59'		Glasgow 4°14' 55°52'		Belfast 5°56' 54°35'	
	h m	h m	h m	h m	h m	h m	h m	h m	h m	h m	h m	h m	h m	h m
1	4 33	19 23	4 43	19 33	4 37	19 34	4 35	19 38	4 27	19 41	4 34	19 55	4 46	19 57
2	4 31	19 25	4 41	19 35	4 35	19 35	4 33	19 40	4 25	19 43	4 32	19 57	4 44	19 59
3	4 29	19 26	4 39	19 36	4 33	19 37	4 31	19 42	4 23	19 45	4 30	19 59	4 42	20 01
4	4 27	19 28	4 37	19 38	4 31	19 39	4 29	19 44	4 21	19 47	4 27	20 01	4 39	20 03
5	4 25	19 30	4 35	19 40	4 29	19 40	4 27	19 45	4 19	19 49	4 25	20 03	4 37	20 05
6	4 24	19 31	4 34	19 41	4 27	19 42	4 25	19 47	4 16	19 51	4 23	20 05	4 35	20 06
7	4 22	19 33	4 32	19 43	4 26	19 44	4 23	19 49	4 14	19 53	4 21	20 07	4 33	20 08
8	4 20	19 34	4 30	19 44	4 24	19 45	4 21	19 51	4 12	19 55	4 19	20 09	4 31	20 10
9	4 18	19 36	4 29	19 46	4 22	19 47	4 19	19 52	4 10	19 56	4 17	20 11	4 29	20 12
10	4 17	19 38	4 27	19 48	4 20	19 49	4 18	19 54	4 09	19 58	4 15	20 13	4 28	20 14
11	4 15	19 39	4 25	19 49	4 19	19 50	4 16	19 56	4 07	20 00	4 13	20 15	4 26	20 16
12	4 14	19 41	4 24	19 51	4 17	19 52	4 14	19 58	4 05	20 02	4 11	20 17	4 24	20 17
13	4 12	19 42	4 22	19 52	4 15	19 54	4 12	19 59	4 03	20 04	4 09	20 19	4 22	20 19
14	4 10	19 44	4 21	19 54	4 14	19 55	4 11	20 01	4 01	20 06	4 07	20 21	4 20	20 21
15	4 09	19 45	4 19	19 55	4 12	19 57	4 09	20 03	3 59	20 07	4 05	20 22	4 19	20 23
16	4 07	19 47	4 18	19 57	4 11	19 58	4 07	20 04	3 58	20 09	4 03	20 24	4 17	20 24
17	4 06	19 48	4 16	19 58	4 09	20 00	4 06	20 06	3 56	20 11	4 02	20 26	4 15	20 26
18	4 05	19 50	4 15	20 00	4 08	20 01	4 04	20 07	3 54	20 13	4 00	20 28	4 14	20 28
19	4 03	19 51	4 13	20 01	4 06	20 03	4 03	20 09	3 53	20 14	3 58	20 30	4 12	20 29
20	4 02	19 53	4 12	20 03	4 05	20 04	4 01	20 11	3 51	20 16	3 56	20 32	4 10	20 31
21	4 01	19 54	4 11	20 04	4 03	20 06	4 00	20 12	3 49	20 18	3 55	20 33	4 09	20 33
22	3 59	19 55	4 09	20 05	4 02	20 07	3 59	20 14	3 48	20 19	3 53	20 35	4 07	20 34
23	3 58	19 57	4 08	20 07	4 01	20 09	3 57	20 15	3 46	20 21	3 52	20 37	4 06	20 36
24	3 57	19 58	4 07	20 08	4 00	20 10	3 56	20 17	3 45	20 22	3 50	20 38	4 05	20 37
25	3 56	19 59	4 06	20 09	3 58	20 12	3 55	20 18	3 44	20 24	3 49	20 40	4 03	20 39
26	3 55	20 01	4 05	20 11	3 57	20 13	3 53	20 19	3 42	20 26	3 47	20 41	4 02	20 40
27	3 54	20 02	4 04	20 12	3 56	20 14	3 52	20 21	3 41	20 27	3 46	20 43	4 01	20 42
28	3 53	20 03	4 03	20 13	3 55	20 15	3 51	20 22	3 40	20 28	3 45	20 45	3 59	20 43
29	3 52	20 04	4 02	20 14	3 54	20 17	3 50	20 23	3 39	20 30	3 43	20 46	3 58	20 45
30	3 51	20 06	4 01	20 15	3 53	20 18	3 49	20 25	3 38	20 31	3 42	20 47	3 57	20 46
31	3 50	20 07	4 00	20 17	3 52	20 19	3 48	20 26	3 36	20 33	3 41	20 49	3 56	20 47

JUPITER

Day	RA		Dec.		Transit		5° high 52°		5° high 56°	
	h	m	°	'	h	m	h	m	h	m
1	6	47.6	+23	12	16	10	23	42	0	04
11	6	54.9	+23	04	15	38	23	09	23	27
21	7	02.8	+22	54	15	07	22	37	22	55
31	7	11.2	+22	41	14	36	22	05	22	22

Diameters – equatorial 34″ polar 32″

SATURN

Day	RA		Dec.		Transit		5° high 52°		5° high 56°	
	h	m	°	'	h	m	h	m	h	m
1	4	49.2	+21	04	14	12	21	31	21	46
11	4	54.2	+21	14	13	38	20	58	21	13
21	4	59.5	+21	23	13	04	20	25	20	40
31	5	05.0	+21	32	12	30	19	52	20	08

Diameters – equatorial 17″ polar 15″
Rings – major axis 38″ minor axis 17″

URANUS

Day	RA		Dec.		Transit		10° high 52°		10° high 56°	
	h	m	°	'	h	m	h	m	h	m
1	22	03.2	-12	43	7	27	3	49	4	11
11	22	04.1	-12	38	6	49	3	10	3	31
21	22	04.7	-12	36	6	10	2	31	2	52
31	22	04.9	-12	35	5	31	1	52	2	13

Diameter 4″

NEPTUNE

Day	RA		Dec.		Transit		10° high 52°		10° high 56°	
	h	m	°	'	h	m	h	m	h	m
1	20	53.5	-17	24	6	17	3	15	3	47
11	20	53.6	-17	24	5	38	2	35	3	07
21	20	53.6	-17	24	4	59	1	56	2	28
31	20	53.3	-17	25	4	19	1	17	1	49

Diameter 2″

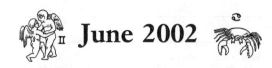

June 2002

SIXTH MONTH, 30 DAYS. *Junius*, Roman *gens* (family)

1	*Saturday*	Leslie Howard d. 1943. Battle of Glorious First of June 1794	152
2	*Sunday*	**1st S. after Trinity.** *Coronation Day 1953.*	153
3	*Monday*	*Golden Jubilee Bank Holiday in UK.* Elisabeth Powell d. 1995	*week 22 day* 154
4	*Tuesday*	*Bank Holiday in UK.* Lord Thorneycroft George Thorneycroft d. 1994	155
5	*Wednesday*	David Hare b. 1947. William Sidney Porter d. 1910	156
6	*Thursday*	Dame Ninette de Valois b. 1898. Robert Francis Kennedy d. 1968	157
7	*Friday*	Beau Brummell b. 1778. Dorothy Parker d. 1967	158
8	*Saturday*	Frink Lloyd Wright b. 1969. Andrew Jackson d. 1845	159
9	*Sunday*	**2nd S. after Trinity.** Saint Columba d. 597	160
10	*Monday*	*Duke of Edinburgh b. 1921.* Sir Henry Coward d. 1944	*week 23 day* 161
11	*Tuesday*	**St. Barnabus.** Dame Millicent Fawcett b. 1847	162
12	*Wednesday*	Charles Kingsley b. 1819. John Ireland d. 1962	163
13	*Thursday*	Fanny Burney b. 1752. Boxer Rebellion broke out 1900	164
14	*Friday*	Sam Wanamaker b. 1919. Battle of Naseby 1645	165
15	*Saturday*	*Queen's Official Birthday.* First non-stop transatlantic flight 1919	166
16	*Sunday*	**3rd S. after Trinity.** Imre Nagy d. 1958	167
17	*Monday*	Beryl Reid b. 1920. Joseph Addison d. 1719	*week 24 day* 168
18	*Tuesday*	*Trinity Law Sittings begin.* Samuel Butler d. 1902	169
19	*Wednesday*	James I b. 1566. Sir Joseph Banks d. 1820	170
20	*Thursday*	Jacques Offenbach b. 1819. Willem Barents d. 1597	171
21	*Friday*	Prince William of Wales b. 1982. King Edward III d. 1377	172
22	*Saturday*	Darius Milhaud d. 1974. Coronation of George V 1911	173
23	*Sunday*	**4th S. after Trinity.** Cecil James Sharp d. 1924	174
24	*Monday*	**John the Baptist.** Marie François Carnot d. 1894	*week 25 day* 175
25	*Tuesday*	Antonio Gaudí b. 1852. Colonel George Custer d. 1876	176
26	*Wednesday*	Francisco Pizarro d. 1541. UN Charter signed at San Francisco 1945	177
27	*Thursday*	Charles Stewart Parnell b. 1846. Joseph Smith d. 1844	178
28	*Friday*	Luigi Pirandello b. 1867. Coronation of Queen Victoria 1838	179
29	*Saturday*	**SS. Peter and Paul.** Paul Klee d. 1940	180
30	*Sunday*	**5th S. after Trinity.** Margery Allingham d. 1966	181

ASTRONOMICAL PHENOMENA

d	h	
3	00	Uranus at stationary point
3	23	Jupiter in conjunction with Venus. Jupiter 2° S.
7	05	Pluto at opposition
8	15	Mercury at stationary point
9	11	Saturn in conjunction
9	13	Mercury in conjunction with Moon. Mercury 3° S.
10	21	Saturn in conjunction with Moon. Saturn 1° S.
11	00	Annular eclipse of Sun (see page 66)
12	12	Mars in conjunction with Moon. Mars 0°.9 S.
13	04	Jupiter in conjunction with Moon. Jupiter 2° S.
13	22	Venus in conjunction with Moon. Venus 1° S.
21	13	Sun's longitude 90°♋
21	14	Mercury at greatest elongation W.23°

MINIMA OF ALGOL

Algol is inconveniently situated for observation during June

CONSTELLATIONS

	d	h		d	h
May	1	24	June	15	21
May	16	23	July	1	20
June	1	22	July	16	19

Cassiopeia (below the Pole), Ursa Minor, Draco, Ursa Major, Canes Venatici, Bootes, Corona, Serpens, Virgo and Libra

THE MOON

Phases, Apsides and Node	d	h	m
☾ Last Quarter	3	00	05
● New Moon	10	23	46
☽ First Quarter	18	00	29
○ Full Moon	24	21	42
Apogee (404,484km)	4	13	00
Perigee (369,343km)	19	07	36

Mean longitude of ascending node on June 1, 78

THE SUN

S.D 16′.1

Day	Right Ascension h m s	Dec. + ° ′	Equation of Time m s	Rise 52° h m	Rise 56° h m	Transit h m	Set 52° h m	Set 56° h m	Sidereal time h m s	Transit of First Point of Aries h m s
1	4 34 54	22 00	+ 2 19	3 46	3 22	11 58	20 10	20 34	16 37 13	7 21 35
2	4 38 59	22 08	+ 2 10	3 45	3 21	11 58	20 11	20 35	16 41 10	7 17 39
3	4 43 06	22 16	+ 2 01	3 45	3 20	11 58	20 12	20 37	16 45 06	7 13 43
4	4 47 12	22 23	+ 1 51	3 44	3 19	11 58	20 13	20 38	16 49 03	7 09 47
5	4 51 19	22 30	+ 1 40	3 43	3 18	11 58	20 14	20 39	16 52 59	7 05 51
6	4 55 26	22 37	+ 1 30	3 43	3 18	11 59	20 15	20 40	16 56 56	7 01 55
7	4 59 34	22 43	+ 1 19	3 42	3 17	11 59	20 16	20 41	17 00 52	6 57 59
8	5 03 41	22 49	+ 1 07	3 42	3 16	11 59	20 17	20 42	17 04 49	6 54 03
9	5 07 50	22 54	+ 0 56	3 41	3 15	11 59	20 18	20 43	17 08 45	6 50 07
10	5 11 58	22 59	+ 0 44	3 41	3 15	11 59	20 18	20 44	17 12 42	6 46 11
11	5 16 07	23 03	+ 0 32	3 40	3 14	12 00	20 19	20 45	17 16 39	6 42 15
12	5 20 15	23 08	+ 0 20	3 40	3 14	12 00	20 20	20 46	17 20 35	6 38 19
13	5 24 25	23 11	+ 0 07	3 40	3 14	12 00	20 21	20 47	17 24 32	6 34 24
14	5 28 34	23 15	− 0 06	3 40	3 13	12 00	20 21	20 47	17 28 28	6 30 28
15	5 32 43	23 17	− 0 18	3 39	3 13	12 00	20 22	20 48	17 32 25	6 26 32
16	5 36 53	23 20	− 0 31	3 39	3 13	12 01	20 22	20 49	17 36 21	6 22 36
17	5 41 02	23 22	− 0 44	3 39	3 13	12 01	20 23	20 49	17 40 18	6 18 40
18	5 45 12	23 24	− 0 57	3 39	3 13	12 01	20 23	20 50	17 44 14	6 14 44
19	5 49 21	23 25	− 1 10	3 39	3 13	12 01	20 23	20 50	17 48 11	6 10 48
20	5 53 31	23 26	− 1 23	3 39	3 13	12 01	20 24	20 50	17 52 08	6 06 52
21	5 57 40	23 26	− 1 36	3 40	3 13	12 02	20 24	20 50	17 56 04	6 02 56
22	6 01 50	23 26	− 1 49	3 40	3 13	12 02	20 24	20 51	18 00 01	5 59 00
23	6 05 59	23 26	− 2 02	3 40	3 14	12 02	20 24	20 51	18 03 57	5 55 04
24	6 10 09	23 25	− 2 15	3 40	3 14	12 02	20 24	20 51	18 07 54	5 51 09
25	6 14 18	23 24	− 2 28	3 41	3 14	12 03	20 24	20 51	18 11 50	5 47 13
26	6 18 27	23 22	− 2 41	3 41	3 15	12 03	20 24	20 51	18 15 47	5 43 17
27	6 22 37	23 20	− 2 53	3 42	3 15	12 03	20 24	20 50	18 19 43	5 39 21
28	6 26 46	23 18	− 3 06	3 42	3 16	12 03	20 24	20 50	18 23 40	5 35 25
29	6 30 54	23 15	− 3 18	3 43	3 17	12 03	20 24	20 50	18 27 37	5 31 29
30	6 35 03	23 12	− 3 30	3 43	3 17	12 04	20 23	20 49	18 31 33	5 27 33

DURATION OF TWILIGHT (in minutes)

Latitude	52°	56°	52°	56°	52°	56°	52°	56°
	1 June		11 June		21 June		31 June	
Civil	46	58	48	61	49	63	48	61
Nautical	116	TAN	124	TAN	127	TAN	124	TAN
Astronomical	TAN	TAN	TAN	TAN	TAN	TAN	TAN	TAN

THE NIGHT SKY

Mercury, is at greatest western elongation on the 21st, but the long duration of twilight renders observation impossible.

Venus, magnitude -4.0, is visible as a brilliant object in the western sky in the evenings. Although it is continuing to increase its eastern elongation from the Sun, the period available for observation actually decreases slightly during the month because it is moving southwards in declination and also because the Sun is setting about a quarter of an hour later at the end of the month than it is at the beginning. On the evening of the 3rd Venus passes 1.6 degrees north of Jupiter, while on the 9th it passes 5 degrees south of Pollux.

Mars is too close to the Sun for observation.

Jupiter, magnitude -1.9, is coming towards the end of its period of visibility and will only be detected during the first half of the month, low in the western sky for a diminishing period after sunset. The waxing crescent Moon is near Jupiter on the evenings of the 12th and 13th.

Saturn passes through conjunction on the 9th and thus remains too close to the Sun for observation throughout the month.

THE MOON

Day	RA	Dec.	Hor. par.	Semi-diam	Sun's co-long.	PA of Bright Limb	Phase	Age	Rise 52°	Rise 56°	Transit	Set 52°	Set 56°
	h m	°	'	'	°	°	%	d	h m	h m	h m	h m	h m
1	21 28	−19.8	55.3	15.1	153	74	69	19.6	0 42	1 01	5 00	9 27	9 08
2	22 16	−16.1	54.8	14.9	165	70	60	20.6	1 04	1 18	5 46	10 38	10 24
3	23 03	−11.8	54.4	14.8	177	67	50	21.6	1 21	1 31	6 28	11 47	11 38
4	23 47	− 7.1	54.2	14.8	189	65	41	22.6	1 36	1 42	7 10	12 55	12 51
5	0 30	− 2.2	54.2	14.8	202	65	32	23.6	1 50	1 52	7 50	14 03	14 03
6	1 13	+ 2.8	54.4	14.8	214	65	23	24.6	2 03	2 01	8 30	15 11	15 16
7	1 57	+ 7.8	54.7	14.9	226	66	16	25.6	2 18	2 11	9 12	16 21	16 31
8	2 43	+12.5	55.1	15.0	238	68	9	26.6	2 34	2 23	9 56	17 34	17 49
9	3 31	+16.9	55.6	15.1	251	71	4	27.6	2 54	2 38	10 43	18 48	19 08
10	4 22	+20.5	56.1	15.3	263	76	1	28.6	3 19	2 58	11 33	20 01	20 26
11	5 16	+23.3	56.7	15.5	275	203	0	0.0	3 53	3 28	12 27	21 10	21 39
12	6 14	+24.8	57.3	15.6	287	265	1	1.0	4 39	4 10	13 24	22 10	22 39
13	7 13	+24.9	57.8	15.7	300	272	5	2.0	5 38	5 10	14 22	22 57	23 23
14	8 13	+23.6	58.2	15.9	312	278	10	3.0	6 50	6 25	15 19	23 34	23 55
15	9 11	+20.8	58.6	16.0	324	284	18	4.0	8 10	7 50	16 15	—	—
16	10 08	+16.8	58.9	16.0	336	288	28	5.0	9 33	9 19	17 08	0 01	0 17
17	11 02	+11.9	59.1	16.1	349	291	38	6.0	10 57	10 48	17 59	0 24	0 34
18	11 55	+ 6.2	59.3	16.2	1	294	50	7.0	12 20	12 17	18 48	0 42	0 47
19	12 46	+ 0.3	59.4	16.2	13	294	61	8.0	13 43	13 45	19 37	0 59	0 59
20	13 38	− 5.7	59.3	16.2	25	293	72	9.0	15 06	15 15	20 28	1 17	1 12
21	14 31	−11.4	59.2	16.1	37	291	82	10.0	16 30	16 45	21 20	1 35	1 25
22	15 25	−16.4	59.0	16.1	50	287	90	11.0	17 54	18 14	22 14	1 58	1 42
23	16 22	−20.5	58.6	16.0	62	282	96	12.0	19 14	19 40	23 11	2 25	2 04
24	17 20	−23.4	58.1	15.8	74	273	99	13.0	20 25	20 55	—	3 02	2 35
25	18 20	−24.9	57.6	15.7	86	140	100	14.0	21 24	21 53	0 08	3 49	3 20
26	19 18	−24.9	56.9	15.5	98	93	99	15.0	22 09	22 35	1 05	4 48	4 19
27	20 15	−23.5	56.3	15.3	111	85	95	16.0	22 42	23 04	2 00	5 56	5 30
28	21 09	−20.9	55.7	15.2	123	79	90	17.0	23 07	23 23	2 51	7 08	6 47
29	21 59	−17.5	55.1	15.0	135	74	83	18.0	23 26	23 38	3 39	8 20	8 04
30	22 47	−13.3	54.7	14.9	147	71	75	19.0	23 42	23 50	4 23	9 31	9 20

MERCURY

Day	RA	Dec.	Diam.	Phase	Transit	5° high 52°	5° high 56°
	h m	°	"	%	h m	h m	h m
1	4 08	+17.9	12	2	11 28	4 28	4 16
3	4 04	+17.3	12	4	11 17	4 20	4 09
5	4 02	+16.9	12	6	11 07	4 13	4 02
7	4 01	+16.6	11	9	10 58	4 05	3 54
9	4 00	+16.4	11	12	10 50	3 58	3 47
11	4 01	+16.4	10	16	10 43	3 51	3 41
13	4 03	+16.5	10	19	10 38	3 45	3 34
15	4 07	+16.7	9	23	10 33	3 39	3 28
17	4 11	+17.1	9	27	10 30	3 34	3 22
19	4 17	+17.5	9	31	10 28	3 29	3 17
21	4 23	+18.0	8	35	10 27	3 25	3 13
23	4 31	+18.6	8	40	10 27	3 22	3 09
25	4 40	+19.2	8	45	10 28	3 19	3 05
27	4 50	+19.9	7	49	10 31	3 17	3 03
29	5 01	+20.5	7	55	10 34	3 17	3 02
31	5 13	+21.2	7	60	10 39	3 17	3 01

VENUS

Day	RA	Dec.	Diam.	Phase	Transit	5° high 52°	5° high 56°
	h m	°	"	%	h m	h m	h m
1	7 00	+24.6	13	82	14 24	22 05	22 25
6	7 26	+23.9	13	80	14 30	22 07	22 25
11	7 51	+23.0	14	79	14 35	22 06	22 24
16	8 16	+21.8	14	77	14 40	22 04	22 20
21	8 40	+20.4	14	75	14 45	21 59	22 14
26	9 04	+18.7	15	74	14 49	21 53	22 06
31	9 27	+16.9	15	72	14 52	21 46	21 57

MARS

Day	RA	Dec.	Diam.	Phase	Transit	5° high 52°	5° high 56°
	h m	°	"	%	h m	h m	h m
1	6 10	+24.4	4	99	13 32	21 13	21 32
6	6 25	+24.3	4	99	13 27	21 07	21 26
11	6 39	+24.2	4	99	13 22	21 00	21 20
16	6 53	+23.9	4	99	13 16	20 53	21 12
21	7 07	+23.6	4	99	13 11	20 45	21 04
26	7 21	+23.2	4	99	13 05	20 37	20 55
31	7 35	+22.7	4	100	12 59	20 28	20 46

SUNSET AND SUNRISE

	London 0°05' 51°30'		Bristol 2°35' 51°28'		Birmingham 1°55' 52°28'		Manchester 2°15' 53°28'		Newcastle 1°37' 54°59'		Glasgow 4°14' 55°52'		Belfast 5°56' 54°35'	
	h m	h m	h m	h m	h m	h m	h m	h m	h m	h m	h m	h m	h m	h m
1	3 49	20 08	3 59	20 18	3 51	20 20	3 47	20 27	3 35	20 34	3 40	20 50	3 55	20 49
2	3 48	20 09	3 58	20 19	3 50	20 21	3 46	20 28	3 34	20 35	3 39	20 52	3 54	20 50
3	3 47	20 10	3 58	20 20	3 50	20 22	3 45	20 29	3 33	20 36	3 38	20 53	3 53	20 51
4	3 47	20 11	3 57	20 21	3 49	20 23	3 45	20 31	3 33	20 38	3 37	20 54	3 52	20 52
5	3 46	20 12	3 56	20 22	3 48	20 24	3 44	20 32	3 32	20 39	3 36	20 55	3 52	20 53
6	3 46	20 13	3 56	20 23	3 48	20 25	3 43	20 33	3 31	20 40	3 35	20 56	3 51	20 54
7	3 45	20 14	3 55	20 23	3 47	20 26	3 43	20 34	3 30	20 41	3 35	20 57	3 50	20 55
8	3 45	20 14	3 55	20 24	3 47	20 27	3 42	20 34	3 30	20 42	3 34	20 58	3 50	20 56
9	3 44	20 15	3 54	20 25	3 46	20 28	3 41	20 35	3 29	20 43	3 33	20 59	3 49	20 57
10	3 44	20 16	3 54	20 26	3 46	20 29	3 41	20 36	3 29	20 43	3 33	21 00	3 49	20 58
11	3 43	20 17	3 54	20 27	3 45	20 30	3 41	20 37	3 28	20 44	3 32	21 01	3 48	20 59
12	3 43	20 17	3 53	20 27	3 45	20 30	3 40	20 38	3 28	20 45	3 32	21 02	3 48	21 00
13	3 43	20 18	3 53	20 28	3 45	20 31	3 40	20 38	3 27	20 46	3 32	21 03	3 47	21 00
14	3 43	20 19	3 53	20 28	3 45	20 31	3 40	20 39	3 27	20 46	3 31	21 03	3 47	21 01
15	3 43	20 19	3 53	20 29	3 44	20 32	3 40	20 39	3 27	20 47	3 31	21 04	3 47	21 02
16	3 42	20 20	3 53	20 29	3 44	20 33	3 40	20 40	3 27	20 48	3 31	21 05	3 47	21 02
17	3 42	20 20	3 53	20 30	3 44	20 33	3 39	20 40	3 27	20 48	3 31	21 05	3 47	21 03
18	3 42	20 20	3 53	20 30	3 44	20 33	3 39	20 41	3 27	20 48	3 31	21 05	3 47	21 03
19	3 43	20 21	3 53	20 31	3 44	20 34	3 39	20 41	3 27	20 49	3 31	21 06	3 47	21 03
20	3 43	20 21	3 53	20 31	3 44	20 34	3 40	20 41	3 27	20 49	3 31	21 06	3 47	21 04
21	3 43	20 21	3 53	20 31	3 45	20 34	3 40	20 42	3 27	20 49	3 31	21 06	3 47	21 04
22	3 43	20 21	3 53	20 31	3 45	20 34	3 40	20 42	3 27	20 50	3 31	21 06	3 47	21 04
23	3 43	20 22	3 54	20 31	3 45	20 34	3 40	20 42	3 28	20 50	3 32	21 07	3 48	21 04
24	3 44	20 22	3 54	20 31	3 45	20 35	3 41	20 42	3 28	20 50	3 32	21 07	3 48	21 04
25	3 44	20 22	3 54	20 31	3 46	20 35	3 41	20 42	3 28	20 50	3 32	21 07	3 48	21 04
26	3 44	20 22	3 55	20 31	3 46	20 35	3 41	20 42	3 29	20 50	3 33	21 06	3 49	21 04
27	3 45	20 22	3 55	20 31	3 47	20 34	3 42	20 42	3 29	20 49	3 33	21 06	3 49	21 04
28	3 45	20 21	3 56	20 31	3 47	20 34	3 42	20 42	3 30	20 49	3 34	21 06	3 50	21 04
29	3 46	20 21	3 56	20 31	3 48	20 34	3 43	20 41	3 30	20 49	3 35	21 06	3 51	21 03
30	3 47	20 21	3 57	20 31	3 48	20 34	3 44	20 41	3 31	20 49	3 35	21 05	3 51	21 03

JUPITER

Day	RA		Dec.		Transit		5° high			
							52°		56°	
	h	m	°	'	h	m	h	m	h	m
1	7	12.0	+22	39	14	33	22	01	22	19
11	7	20.8	+22	24	14	02	21	29	21	46
21	7	30.0	+22	06	13	32	20	57	21	14
31	7	39.3	+21	46	13	02	20	25	20	41

Diameters – equatorial 32 polar 30″

SATURN

Day	RA		Dec.		Transit		5° high			
							52°		56°	
	h	m	°	'	h	m	h	m	h	m
1	5	05.6	+21	33	12	27	5	05	4	49
11	5	11.1	+21	40	11	53	4	30	4	14
21	5	16.7	+21	47	11	19	3	56	3	40
31	5	22.2	+21	53	10	45	3	21	3	05

Diameters – equatorial 16″ polar 15″
Rings – major axis 37″ minor axis 17″

URANUS

Day	RA		Dec.		Transit		10° high			
							52°		56°	
	h	m	°	'	h	m	h	m	h	m
1	22	05.0	−12	35	5	27	1	48	2	09
11	22	04.9	−12	35	4	47	1	08	1	30
21	22	04.5	−12	38	4	08	0	29	0	51
31	22	03.8	−12	42	3	28	23	45	0	11

Diameter 4″

NEPTUNE

Day	RA		Dec.		Transit		10° high			
							52°		56°	
	h	m	°	'	h	m	h	m	h	m
1	20	53.3	−17	25	4	15	1	13	1	45
11	20	52.8	−17	27	3	36	0	33	1	05
21	20	52.1	−17	30	2	56	23	50	0	26
31	20	51.3	−17	34	2	15	23	10	23	42

Diameter 2″

July 2002

SEVENTH MONTH, 31 DAYS, *Julius* Caesar, formerly *Quintilis*, fifth month of Roman pre-Julian calendar

1	*Monday*	Robert Mitchum d. 1997. Battle of the Boyne 1690	*week 26 day* 182
2	*Tuesday*	Sir Robert Peel d. 1850. Battle of Marston Moor 1644	183
3	*Wednesday*	**St Thomas.** Ken Russell b. 1927	184
4	*Thursday*	Nathaniel Hawthorne b. 1804. James Monroe d. 1831	185
5	*Friday*	George Borrow b. 1803. Walter Gropius d. 1969	186
6	*Saturday*	George W Bush b. 1946. Aneurin Bevan d. 1960	187
7	*Sunday*	**6th S. after Trinity.** Georg S. Ohm d. 1854	188
8	*Monday*	Count Ferdinand von Zeppelin b. 1838. Il-sung Kim d. 1994	*week 27 day* 189
9	*Tuesday*	David Hockney b. 1937. Jan Van Eyck d. 1441	190
10	*Wednesday*	Marcel Proust b. 1871. George Stubbs d. 1806	191
11	*Thursday*	King Robert I b. 1274. Lord Laurence Olivier d. 1989	192
12	*Friday*	Amedeo Modigliani b. 1884. Kenneth More d. 1982	193
13	*Saturday*	Sir Reginald Goodall b. 1901. Titus Oates d. 1705	194
14	*Sunday*	**7th S. after Trinity.** Madame de Stael Anne Necker d. 1817	195
15	*Monday*	Sir Harrison Birtwistle b. 1934. Royal Society received its charter 1662	*week 28 day* 196
16	*Tuesday*	Baroness Llewelyn-Davies of Hastoe b. 1915. Sir Stephen Spender d. 1995	197
17	*Wednesday*	Jean Muir b. 1928. Adam Smith d. 1790	198
18	*Thursday*	William Makepeace Thackeray b. 1811. Spanish Civil War began 1936	199
19	*Friday*	Sir James Goldsmith d. 1997. *Mary Rose* sank 1545	200
20	*Saturday*	Elisabeth Powell b. 1901. Andrew Lang d. 1912	201
21	*Sunday*	**8th S. after Trinity.** Salvator Rosa b. 1615	202
22	*Monday*	**Mary Magdalene.** Michael Denison d. 1998	*week 29 day* 203
23	*Tuesday*	Raymond Chandler b. 1888. Marshal Philippe Pétain d. 1951	204
24	*Wednesday*	E. F. Benson b. 1867. Isaac Bashevis Singer d. 1991	205
25	*Thursday*	**St James.** First cross-channel flight by Bleriot 1909	206
26	*Friday*	Lord Thorneycroft b. 1909. George Bernard Shaw b. 1856	207
27	*Saturday*	James Mason d. 1984. Sealing of charter establishing the Bank of England 1694	208
28	*Sunday*	**9th S. after Trinity.** Sir Garfield Sobers b. 1936	209
29	*Monday*	Benito Mussolini b. 1883. Frans Hals d. 1666	*week 30 day* 210
30	*Tuesday*	Emily Brontë b. 1818. Claudette Colbert d. 1996	211
31	*Wednesday*	*Trinity Law Sittings end.* Saint Ignatius Loyola d. 1556	212

ASTRONOMICAL PHENOMENA

d h
2 12 Saturn in conjunction with Mercury. Saturn 0°2 N.
3 13 Jupiter in conjunction with Mars. Jupiter 0°8 S.
6 04 Earth at aphelion (152 million km.)
8 12 Saturn in conjunction with Moon. Saturn 2° S.
9 09 Mercury in conjunction with Moon. Mercury 2° S.
10 23 Jupiter in conjunction with Moon. Jupiter 3° S.
11 04 Mars in conjunction with Moon. Mars 2° S.
13 15 Venus in conjunction with Moon. Venus 4° S.
20 01 Jupiter in conjunction
20 16 Jupiter in conjunction with Mercury. Jupiter 1° S.
21 02 Mercury in superior conjunction
23 00 Sun's longitude 120°♌
25 15 Mars in conjunction with Mercury. Mars 0°6 S.

MINIMA OF ALGOL

d	h	d	h	d	h
1	15.2	13	02.5	24	13.7
4	12.0	15	23.3	27	10.5
7	08.8	18	20.1	30	07.3
10	05.6	21	16.9		

CONSTELLATIONS

The following constellations are near the meridian at

d	h		d	h
June	1	24	July	16	21
June	15	23	August	1	20
July	1	22	August	16	19

Ursa Minor, Draco, Corona, Hercules, Lyra, Serpens, Ophiuchus, Libra, Scorpius and Sagittarius

THE MOON

Phases, Apsides and Node	d	h	m
☾ Last Quarter	2	17	19
● New Moon	10	10	26
☽ First Quarter	17	04	47
○ Full Moon	24	09	07
Apogee (404,171km)	2	07	34
Perigee (367,876km)	14	13	12
Apogee (404,707km)	30	01	39

Mean longitude of ascending node on July 1, 77°

THE SUN   S.D 16'.1

Day	Right Ascension	Dec. +	Equation of Time	Rise 52°	Rise 56°	Transit	Set 52°	Set 56°	Sidereal time	Transit of First Point of Aries
	h m s	° '	m s	h m	h m	h m	h m	h m	h m s	h m s
1	6 39 11	23 08	− 3 42	3 44	3 18	12 04	20 23	20 49	18 35 30	5 23 37
2	6 43 19	23 04	− 3 53	3 45	3 19	12 04	20 23	20 49	18 39 26	5 19 41
3	6 47 27	22 59	− 4 04	3 46	3 20	12 04	20 22	20 48	18 43 23	5 15 45
4	6 51 35	22 55	− 4 16	3 46	3 21	12 04	20 22	20 47	18 47 19	5 11 49
5	6 55 42	22 49	− 4 26	3 47	3 22	12 05	20 21	20 47	18 51 16	5 07 54
6	6 59 49	22 44	− 4 37	3 48	3 23	12 05	20 21	20 46	18 55 12	5 03 58
7	7 03 56	22 38	− 4 47	3 49	3 24	12 05	20 20	20 45	18 59 09	5 00 02
8	7 08 02	22 31	− 4 57	3 50	3 25	12 05	20 20	20 44	19 03 06	4 56 06
9	7 12 08	22 24	− 5 06	3 51	3 26	12 05	20 19	20 43	19 07 02	4 52 10
10	7 16 14	22 17	− 5 15	3 52	3 28	12 05	20 18	20 42	19 10 59	4 48 14
11	7 20 19	22 09	− 5 24	3 53	3 29	12 05	20 17	20 41	19 14 55	4 44 18
12	7 24 24	22 01	− 5 32	3 54	3 30	12 06	20 16	20 40	19 18 52	4 40 22
13	7 28 28	21 53	− 5 39	3 55	3 32	12 06	20 15	20 39	19 22 48	4 36 26
14	7 32 31	21 44	− 5 47	3 56	3 33	12 06	20 15	20 38	19 26 45	4 32 30
15	7 36 35	21 35	− 5 53	3 58	3 34	12 06	20 14	20 36	19 30 41	4 28 34
16	7 40 37	21 26	− 5 59	3 59	3 36	12 06	20 12	20 35	19 34 38	4 24 38
17	7 44 40	21 16	− 6 05	4 00	3 37	12 06	20 11	20 34	19 38 35	4 20 43
18	7 48 41	21 06	− 6 10	4 01	3 39	12 06	20 10	20 32	19 42 31	4 16 47
19	7 52 42	20 55	− 6 15	4 03	3 41	12 06	20 09	20 31	19 46 28	4 12 51
20	7 56 43	20 44	− 6 18	4 04	3 42	12 06	20 08	20 29	19 50 24	4 08 55
21	8 00 43	20 33	− 6 22	4 05	3 44	12 06	20 07	20 28	19 54 21	4 04 59
22	8 04 42	20 21	− 6 25	4 07	3 46	12 06	20 05	20 26	19 58 17	4 01 03
23	8 08 41	20 09	− 6 27	4 08	3 47	12 06	20 04	20 25	20 02 14	3 57 07
24	8 12 39	19 57	− 6 29	4 09	3 49	12 06	20 03	20 23	20 06 11	3 53 11
25	8 16 37	19 44	− 6 30	4 11	3 51	12 07	20 01	20 21	20 10 07	3 49 15
26	8 20 34	19 31	− 6 30	4 12	3 52	12 07	20 00	20 19	20 14 04	3 45 19
27	8 24 30	19 18	− 6 30	4 14	3 54	12 07	19 58	20 18	20 18 00	3 41 23
28	8 28 26	19 04	− 6 29	4 15	3 56	12 06	19 57	20 16	20 21 57	3 37 28
29	8 32 21	18 50	− 6 28	4 17	3 58	12 06	19 55	20 14	20 25 53	3 33 32
30	8 36 16	18 36	− 6 26	4 18	4 00	12 06	19 54	20 12	20 29 50	3 29 36
31	8 40 10	18 22	− 6 24	4 20	4 02	12 06	19 52	20 10	20 33 46	3 25 40

DURATION OF TWILIGHT (in minutes)

Latitude	52°	56°	52°	56°	52°	56°	52°	56°
	1 July		11 July		21 July		31 July	
Civil	48	61	47	58	44	53	42	49
Nautical	124	TAN	117	TAN	107	146	98	123
Astronomical	TAN	TAN	TAN	TAN	TAN	TAN	182	TAN

THE NIGHT SKY

Mercury passes through superior conjunction on the 21st and therefore is unsuitably placed for observation throughout the month.

Venus continues to be visible as a brilliant object in the western sky after sunset. Its magnitude is -4.1. The crescent Moon, 3 days old, passes within 4 degrees of Venus on the evening of the 13th. On the 10th Venus passes 1 degree north of Regulus.

Mars continues to be unsuitably placed for observation.

Jupiter passes through conjunction on the 20th and is therefore too close to the Sun for observation.

Saturn is too close to the Sun for observation at first but as it slowly emerges from the morning twilight it may be detected by the middle of the month, low above the eastern horizon, for a short while before the brightening sky inhibits observation. Its magnitude is +0.1.

Twilight. Reference to the section above shows that astronomical twilight lasts all night for a period around the summer solstice (i.e. in June and July), even in southern England. Under these conditions the sky never gets completely dark as the Sun is always less than 18 degrees below the horizon.

THE MOON

Day	RA	Dec.	Hor. par.	Semi-diam.	Sun's co-long.	PA of Bright Limb	Phase	Age	Rise 52°	Rise 56°	Transit	Set 52°	Set 56°
	h m	°	′	′	°	°	%	d	h m	h m	h m	h m	h m
1	23 32	− 8.7	54.4	14.8	159	68	66	20.0	23 56	—	5 05	10 40	10 34
2	0 16	− 3.8	54.3	14.8	172	67	57	21.0	—	0 00	5 46	11 48	11 46
3	0 59	+ 1.2	54.3	14.8	184	67	47	22.0	0 10	0 09	6 26	12 56	12 59
4	1 42	+ 6.1	54.5	14.8	196	68	38	23.0	0 24	0 19	7 06	14 04	14 12
5	2 27	+11.0	54.9	14.9	208	70	29	24.0	0 39	0 29	7 49	15 15	15 28
6	3 13	+15.4	55.4	15.1	221	73	20	25.0	0 57	0 43	8 34	16 28	16 46
7	4 03	+19.3	56.0	15.3	233	77	13	26.0	1 20	1 01	9 23	17 42	18 05
8	4 57	+22.4	56.7	15.4	245	83	7	27.0	1 50	1 26	10 16	18 54	19 21
9	5 54	+24.4	57.4	15.6	257	92	2	28.0	2 30	2 02	11 12	19 58	20 28
10	6 53	+25.0	58.1	15.8	270	116	0	29.0	3 25	2 56	12 11	20 52	21 19
11	7 54	+24.1	58.6	16.0	282	257	0	0.6	4 34	4 07	13 10	21 33	21 56
12	8 54	+21.7	59.1	16.1	294	275	3	1.6	5 53	5 31	14 08	22 05	22 22
13	9 53	+17.9	59.4	16.2	306	283	9	2.6	7 18	7 02	15 03	22 29	22 41
14	10 49	+13.1	59.6	16.2	319	288	16	3.6	8 43	8 33	15 55	22 49	22 55
15	11 43	+ 7.5	59.6	16.2	331	291	26	4.6	10 07	10 03	16 46	23 06	23 08
16	12 35	+ 1.6	59.5	16.2	343	292	36	5.6	11 31	11 32	17 35	23 23	23 20
17	13 26	− 4.4	59.3	16.1	355	292	48	6.6	12 54	13 00	18 25	23 41	23 33
18	14 18	−10.2	59.0	16.1	8	290	59	7.6	14 17	14 29	19 15	—	23 48
19	15 11	−15.3	58.6	16.0	20	287	70	8.6	15 39	15 57	20 08	0 02	—
20	16 06	−19.6	58.2	15.9	32	282	80	9.6	16 59	17 23	21 02	0 27	0 07
21	17 03	−22.8	57.8	15.7	44	276	88	10.6	18 12	18 41	21 58	0 59	0 35
22	18 01	−24.6	57.3	15.6	56	268	94	11.6	19 15	19 45	22 55	1 42	1 13
23	19 00	−25.0	56.8	15.5	69	256	98	12.6	20 04	20 32	23 50	2 36	2 06
24	19 56	−24.1	56.3	15.3	81	223	100	13.6	20 41	21 05	—	3 40	3 12
25	20 51	−21.9	55.7	15.2	93	103	99	14.6	21 09	21 28	0 42	4 50	4 27
26	21 43	−18.7	55.3	15.1	105	84	97	15.6	21 30	21 44	1 31	6 03	5 45
27	22 31	−14.7	54.8	14.9	117	77	93	16.6	21 47	21 57	2 17	7 15	7 02
28	23 17	−10.2	54.5	14.8	130	73	87	17.6	22 02	22 07	3 00	8 25	8 17
29	0 01	− 5.3	54.3	14.8	142	70	80	18.6	22 16	22 16	3 41	9 33	9 30
30	0 44	− 0.3	54.2	14.8	154	69	72	19.6	22 29	22 26	4 2	10 41	10 43
31	1 27	+ 4.7	54.2	14.8	166	69	64	20.6	22 44	22 36	5 02	11 49	11 55

MERCURY

Day	RA	Dec.	Diam.	Phase	Transit	5° high 52°	5° high 56°
	h m	°	″	%	h m	h m	h m
1	5 13	+21.2	7	60	10 39	3 17	3 01
3	5 27	+21.8	6	66	10 45	3 19	3 02
5	5 41	+22.4	6	71	10 51	3 22	3 05
7	5 56	+22.9	6	77	10 59	3 27	3 09
9	6 13	+23.3	6	83	11 08	3 33	3 15
11	6 30	+23.5	5	88	11 17	3 41	3 23
13	6 48	+23.6	5	92	11 28	3 51	3 32
15	7 06	+23.5	5	96	11 38	4 02	3 43
17	7 25	+23.2	5	98	11 49	4 15	3 56
19	7 43	+22.7	5	99	12 00	19 30	19 47
21	8 02	+22.1	5	100	12 10	19 36	19 52
23	8 20	+21.3	5	99	12 20	19 40	19 56
25	8 37	+20.4	5	98	12 29	19 44	19 58
27	8 54	+19.3	5	97	12 38	19 46	19 59
29	9 10	+18.2	5	95	12 46	19 47	19 59
31	9 25	+17.0	5	93	12 53	19 47	19 58

VENUS

Day	RA	Dec.	Diam.	Phase	Transit	5° high 52°	5° high 56°
	h m	°	″	%	h m	h m	h m
1	9 27	+16.9	15	72	14 52	21 46	21 57
6	9 49	+14.9	16	70	14 54	21 37	21 46
11	10 11	+12.8	16	68	14 56	21 28	21 35
16	10 32	+10.6	17	66	14 58	21 17	21 22
21	10 52	+ 8.2	18	64	14 58	21 06	21 09
26	11 12	+ 5.8	18	62	14 58	20 53	20 54
31	11 32	+ 3.4	19	60	14 58	20 40	20 39

MARS

Day	RA	Dec.	Diam.	Phase	Transit	5° high 52°	5° high 56°
1	7 35	+22.7	4	100	12 59	20 28	20 46
6	7 49	+22.2	4	100	12 53	20 19	20 36
11	8 03	+21.6	4	100	12 47	20 09	20 25
16	8 16	+20.9	4	100	12 41	19 59	20 14
21	8 29	+20.2	4	100	12 34	19 48	20 02
26	8 43	+19.4	4	100	12 28	19 37	19 50
31	8 56	+18.5	4	100	12 21	19 25	19 38

SUNRISE AND SUNSET

	London 0°05' 51°30' h m	h m	Bristol 2°35' 51°28' h m	h m	Birmingham 1°55' 52°28' h m	h m	Manchester 2°15' 53°28' h m	h m	Newcastle 1°37' 54°59' h m	h m	Glasgow 4°14' 55°52' h m	h m	Belfast 5°56' 54°35' h m	h m
1	3 47	20 21	3 57	20 30	3 49	20 33	3 44	20 41	3 32	20 48	3 36	21 05	3 52	21 03
2	3 48	20 20	3 58	20 30	3 50	20 33	3 45	20 40	3 33	20 48	3 37	21 04	3 53	21 02
3	3 49	20 20	3 59	20 30	3 51	20 33	3 46	20 40	3 34	20 47	3 38	21 04	3 54	21 02
4	3 49	20 20	4 00	20 29	3 51	20 32	3 47	20 39	3 34	20 47	3 39	21 03	3 54	21 01
5	3 50	20 19	4 00	20 29	3 52	20 32	3 48	20 39	3 35	20 46	3 40	21 03	3 55	21 01
6	3 51	20 18	4 01	20 28	3 53	20 31	3 49	20 38	3 36	20 45	3 41	21 02	3 56	21 00
7	3 52	20 18	4 02	20 28	3 54	20 30	3 50	20 38	3 37	20 45	3 42	21 01	3 57	20 59
8	3 53	20 17	4 03	20 27	3 55	20 30	3 51	20 37	3 39	20 44	3 43	21 00	3 58	20 58
9	3 54	20 17	4 04	20 26	3 56	20 29	3 52	20 36	3 40	20 43	3 44	20 59	4 00	20 58
10	3 55	20 16	4 05	20 26	3 57	20 28	3 53	20 35	3 41	20 42	3 45	20 58	4 01	20 57
11	3 56	20 15	4 06	20 25	3 58	20 27	3 54	20 34	3 42	20 41	3 47	20 57	4 02	20 56
12	3 57	20 14	4 07	20 24	3 59	20 27	3 55	20 33	3 43	20 40	3 48	20 56	4 03	20 55
13	3 58	20 13	4 08	20 23	4 00	20 26	3 56	20 32	3 45	20 39	3 49	20 55	4 04	20 54
14	3 59	20 12	4 09	20 22	4 02	20 25	3 58	20 31	3 46	20 38	3 51	20 54	4 06	20 52
15	4 00	20 11	4 11	20 21	4 03	20 24	3 59	20 30	3 47	20 36	3 52	20 53	4 07	20 51
16	4 02	20 10	4 12	20 20	4 04	20 23	4 00	20 29	3 49	20 35	3 54	20 51	4 08	20 50
17	4 03	20 09	4 13	20 19	4 05	20 21	4 01	20 28	3 50	20 34	3 55	20 50	4 10	20 49
18	4 04	20 08	4 14	20 18	4 07	20 20	4 03	20 27	3 52	20 33	3 57	20 48	4 11	20 48
19	4 05	20 07	4 16	20 17	4 08	20 19	4 04	20 25	3 53	20 31	3 58	20 47	4 13	20 46
20	4 07	20 06	4 17	20 16	4 09	20 18	4 06	20 24	3 55	20 30	4 00	20 45	4 14	20 45
21	4 08	20 05	4 18	20 14	4 11	20 16	4 07	20 23	3 56	20 28	4 02	20 44	4 16	20 43
22	4 09	20 03	4 19	20 13	4 12	20 15	4 09	20 21	3 58	20 27	4 03	20 42	4 17	20 42
23	4 11	20 02	4 21	20 12	4 14	20 14	4 10	20 20	3 59	20 25	4 05	20 41	4 19	20 40
24	4 12	20 01	4 22	20 11	4 15	20 12	4 12	20 18	4 01	20 24	4 07	20 39	4 21	20 39
25	4 13	19 59	4 24	20 09	4 16	20 11	4 13	20 17	4 03	20 22	4 08	20 37	4 22	20 37
26	4 15	19 58	4 25	20 08	4 18	20 09	4 15	20 15	4 04	20 20	4 10	20 36	4 24	20 36
27	4 16	19 56	4 26	20 06	4 19	20 08	4 16	20 14	4 06	20 19	4 12	20 34	4 25	20 34
28	4 18	19 55	4 28	20 05	4 21	20 06	4 18	20 12	4 08	20 17	4 14	20 32	4 27	20 32
29	4 19	19 53	4 29	20 03	4 22	20 05	4 19	20 10	4 10	20 15	4 16	20 30	4 29	20 30
30	4 21	19 52	4 31	20 02	4 24	20 03	4 21	20 09	4 11	20 13	4 17	20 28	4 31	20 29
31	4 22	19 50	4 32	20 00	4 26	20 01	4 23	20 07	4 13	20 11	4 19	20 26	4 32	20 27

JUPITER

Day	RA h m	Dec. ° '	Transit h m	5° high 52° h m	56° h m
1	7 39.3	+21 46	13 02	20 25	20 41
11	7 48.7	+21 24	12 32	19 53	20 09
21	7 58.1	+20 59	12 02	19 20	19 36
31	8 07.4	+20 33	11 32	18 48	19 03

Diameters – equatorial 31 polar 30″

SATURN

Day	RA h m	Dec. ° '	Transit h m	5° high 52° h m	56° h m
1	5 22.2	+21 53	10 45	3 21	3 05
11	5 27.5	+21 58	10 11	2 47	2 30
21	5 32.6	+22 02	9 37	2 12	1 56
31	5 37.4	+22 04	9 02	1 37	1 21

Diameters – equatorial 17″ polar 15″
Rings – major axis 38″ minor axis 17″

URANUS

Day	RA h m	Dec. ° '	Transit h m	10° high 52° h m	56° h m
1	22 03.8	–12 42	3 28	23 45	0 11
11	22 02.9	–12 47	2 47	23 06	23 28
21	22 01.7	–12 54	2 07	22 26	22 48
31	22 00.4	–13 01	1 26	21 46	22 09

Diameter 4″

NEPTUNE

Day	RA h m	Dec. ° '	Transit h m	10° high 52° h m	56° h m
1	20 51.3	–17 34	2 15	23 10	23 42
11	20 50.4	–17 37	1 35	22 30	23 03
21	20 49.3	–17 42	0 55	21 50	22 23
31	20 48.2	–17 46	0 14	21 11	21 44

Diameter 2″

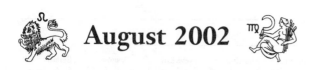

August 2002

EIGHTH MONTH, 31 DAYS, *Augustus*, formerly *Sextilis*, sixth month of Roman pre-Julian calendar

1	*Thursday*	Richard Wilson b. 1714. Battle of the Nile (Aboukir Bay) 1798	213
2	*Friday*	William II d. 1100. King William II Normandy d. 1100	214
3	*Saturday*	1st Earl Baldwin of Bewdley Stanley Baldwin b. 1867. Ida Lupino d. 1995	215
4	*Sunday*	**10th S. after Trinity.** *Queen Elizabeth the Queen Mother b. 1900.*	216
5	*Monday*	*Bank Holiday in Scotland.* Thomas Newcomen d. 1729	*week 31 day* 217
6	*Tuesday*	**The Transfiguration.** Anne Hathaway d. 1623	218
7	*Wednesday*	Oliver Hardy d. 1957. Konstantin Stanislavsky d. 1938	219
8	*Thursday*	Princess Beatrice of York b. 1988. Nixon resigned over Watergate scandal 1974	220
9	*Friday*	Joe Mercer d. 1990. Second atomic bomb dropped, Nagasaki 1945	221
10	*Saturday*	Sir Charles Napier b. 1782	222
11	*Sunday*	**11th S. after Trinity.** Edith Wharton d. 1937	223
12	*Monday*	William Blake d. 1827. Glorious Twelfth - start of grouse shooting season	*week 32 day* 224
13	*Tuesday*	Ben Hogan b. 1912. Sir Basil Spence b. 1907	225
14	*Wednesday*	Ira Sankey d. 1908. William Randolph Hearst d. 1951	226
15	*Thursday*	**Blessed Virgin Mary.** *Princess Royal b. 1950.*	227
16	*Friday*	Ted Hughes b. 1930. Stewart Granger d. 1993	228
17	*Saturday*	Wilfred Scawen Blunt b. 1840. Ludwig Mies van der Rohe d. 1969	229
18	*Sunday*	**12th S. after Trinity.** Guido Reni d. 1642	230
19	*Monday*	John Flamsteed b. 1646. Julius Marx d. 1977	*week 33 day* 231
20	*Tuesday*	Gen. William Booth d. 1912. George Adamson d. 1989	232
21	*Wednesday*	*Princess Margaret b. 1930.* Leon Trotsky d. 1940	233
22	*Thursday*	Achille-Claude Debussy b. 1862. Jean-Honoré Fragonard d. 1806	234
23	*Friday*	King Louis XVI b. 1754. 1st Duke of Buckingham George Villiers d. 1628	235
24	*Saturday*	**St Bartholomew.** Cardinal Cormac Murphy O'Connor b. 1932.	236
25	*Sunday*	**13th S. after Trinity.** Erich Honecker b. 1912	237
26	*Monday*	*Bank Holiday in England, Wales and Northern Ireland.* Charles Boyer d. 1978	*week 34 day* 238
27	*Tuesday*	Tiziano Vecellio Titian d. 1576. Battle of Dresden 1813	239
28	*Wednesday*	1st Duke of Buckingham. George Villiers b. 1592. John Huston d. 1987	240
29	*Thursday*	Jean Ingres b. 1780. Joseph Wright d. 1797	241
30	*Friday*	Mary Wollenstonecraft Shelly b. 1797. Denis Healy b. 1917	242
31	*Saturday*	Clive Lloyd b. 1944. John Bunyan d. 1688	243

ASTRONOMICAL PHENOMENA

d	h	
2	01	Neptune at opposition
5	03	Saturn in conjunction with Moon. Saturn 2° S.
7	19	Jupiter in conjunction with Moon. Jupiter 3° S.
8	20	Mars in conjunction with Moon. Mars 3° S.
10	04	Mercury in conjunction with Moon. Mercury 4° S.
10	22	Mars in conjunction
12	03	Venus in conjunction with Moon. Venus 6° S.
20	01	Uranus at opposition
22	13	Venus at greatest elongation E.46°
23	07	Sun's longitude 150°♍
26	11	Pluto at stationary point

MINIMA OF ALGOL

d	h	d	h	d	h
2	04.1	13	15.4	25	02.6
5	00.9	16	12.2	27	23.4
7	21.7	19	09.0	30	20.2
10	18.6	22	05.8		

CONSTELLATIONS

The following constellations are near the meridian at

	d	h		d	h
July	1	24	August	16	21
July	16	23	September	1	20
August	1	22	September	15	19

Draco, Hercules, Lyra, Cygnus, Sagitta, Ophiuchus, Serpens, Aquila and Sagittarius

THE MOON

Phases, Apsides and Node	d	h	m
☾ Last Quarter	1	10	22
● New Moon	8	19	15
☽ First Quarter	15	10	12
○ Full Moon	22	22	29
☾ Last Quarter	31	02	31
Perigee (362,945km)	10	23	22
Apogee (405,669km)	26	17	33

Mean longitude of ascending node on August 1, 75°

THE SUN   S.D 16'.1

Day	Right Ascension h m s	Dec. + ° '	Equation of Time m s	Rise 52° h m	Rise 56° h m	Transit h m	Set 52° h m	Set 56° h m	Sidereal time h m s	Transit of First Point of Aries h m s
1	8 44 03	18 07	− 6 20	4 21	4 03	12 06	19 50	20 08	20 37 43	3 21 44
2	8 47 56	17 52	− 6 17	4 23	4 05	12 06	19 49	20 06	20 41 40	3 17 48
3	8 51 49	17 36	− 6 13	4 24	4 07	12 06	19 47	20 04	20 45 36	3 13 52
4	8 55 40	17 21	− 6 08	4 26	4 09	12 06	19 45	20 02	20 49 33	3 09 56
5	8 59 31	17 05	− 6 02	4 28	4 11	12 06	19 43	20 00	20 53 29	3 06 00
6	9 03 22	16 48	− 5 56	4 29	4 13	12 06	19 42	19 58	20 57 26	3 02 04
7	9 07 12	16 32	− 5 50	4 31	4 15	12 06	19 40	19 55	21 01 22	2 58 08
8	9 11 01	16 15	− 5 43	4 32	4 17	12 06	19 38	19 53	21 05 19	2 54 13
9	9 14 50	15 58	− 5 35	4 34	4 19	12 06	19 36	19 51	21 09 15	2 50 17
10	9 18 38	15 41	− 5 26	4 35	4 21	12 05	19 34	19 49	21 13 12	2 46 21
11	9 22 26	15 23	− 5 17	4 37	4 23	12 05	19 32	19 47	21 17 09	2 42 25
12	9 26 13	15 05	− 5 08	4 39	4 24	12 05	19 30	19 44	21 21 05	2 38 29
13	9 29 59	14 47	− 4 58	4 40	4 26	12 05	19 28	19 42	21 25 02	2 34 33
14	9 33 45	14 29	− 4 47	4 42	4 28	12 05	19 26	19 40	21 28 58	2 30 37
15	9 37 31	14 10	− 4 36	4 44	4 30	12 05	19 24	19 37	21 32 55	2 26 41
16	9 41 15	13 52	− 4 24	4 45	4 32	12 04	19 22	19 35	21 36 51	2 22 45
17	9 45 00	13 33	− 4 12	4 47	4 34	12 04	19 20	19 33	21 40 48	2 18 49
18	9 48 43	13 13	− 3 59	4 48	4 36	12 04	19 18	19 30	21 44 44	2 14 53
19	9 52 27	12 54	− 3 46	4 50	4 38	12 04	19 16	19 28	21 48 41	2 10 58
20	9 56 09	12 34	− 3 32	4 52	4 40	12 03	19 14	19 25	21 52 38	2 07 02
21	9 59 51	12 15	− 3 17	4 53	4 42	12 03	19 12	19 23	21 56 34	2 03 06
22	10 03 33	11 55	− 3 02	4 55	4 44	12 03	19 10	19 20	22 00 31	1 59 10
23	10 07 14	11 34	− 2 47	4 57	4 46	12 03	19 08	19 18	22 04 27	1 55 14
24	10 10 55	11 14	− 2 31	4 58	4 48	12 02	19 05	19 15	22 08 24	1 51 18
25	10 14 35	10 54	− 2 15	5 00	4 50	12 02	19 03	19 13	22 12 20	1 47 22
26	10 18 15	10 33	− 1 59	5 01	4 52	12 02	19 01	19 10	22 16 17	1 43 26
27	10 21 55	10 12	− 1 42	5 03	4 54	12 02	18 59	19 08	22 20 13	1 39 30
28	10 25 34	9 51	− 1 24	5 05	4 56	12 01	18 57	19 05	22 24 10	1 35 34
29	10 29 13	9 30	− 1 06	5 06	4 58	12 01	18 54	19 03	22 28 06	1 31 38
30	10 32 51	9 08	− 0 48	5 08	5 00	12 01	18 52	19 00	22 32 03	1 27 43
31	10 36 30	8 47	− 0 30	5 10	5 02	12 00	18 50	18 58	22 36 00	1 23 47

DURATION OF TWILIGHT (in minutes)

Latitude	52°	56°	52°	56°	52°	56°	52°	56°
	1 August		11 August		21 August		31 August	
Civil	41	49	39	45	37	42	35	40
Nautical	97	121	90	107	84	97	79	90
Astronomical	179	TAN	154	210	139	168	128	148

THE NIGHT SKY

Mercury remains too close to the Sun for observation throughout the month.

Venus, magnitude -4.3, is visible low in the western sky in the evenings after sunset. Although greatest eastern elongation (46°) occurs on the 22nd, Venus is only visible for a short time after sunset. On the evenings of the 11th and 12th the crescent Moon is near the planet.

Mars remains too close to the Sun for observation, as it passes through conjunction on the 10th.

Jupiter, after the first week or ten days of the month, becomes visible as a morning object, low above the eastern horizon for a short while before sunrise, magnitude -1.8. Jupiter is in the constellation of Cancer.

Saturn continues to be visible as a morning object, magnitude +0.1. By the end of the month it is visible low above the eastern horizon at midnight. During the early hours of the 5th the old crescent Moon will be seen 1 degree above Saturn.

Uranus is at opposition on the 20th, on the boundary between Capricornus and Aquarius. Uranus is barely visible to the naked eye as its magnitude is +5.7, but it is readily located with only small optical aid.

Neptune is at opposition on the 2nd, in Capricornus. It is not visible to the naked eye since its magnitude is +7.8.

Meteors. The maximum of the famous Perseid meteor shower occurs on the night of the 12th-13th. Conditions are favourable since the 4-day old crescent Moon sets in the late evening, before the radiant has reached an altitude of about 30 degrees.

THE MOON

Day	RA h m	Dec. °	Hor. par. '	Semi-diam '	Sun's co-long. °	PA of Bright Limb °	Phase %	Age d	Rise 52° h m	Rise 56° h m	Transit h m	Set 52° h m	Set 56° h m
1	2 11	+ 9.5	54.5	14.8	178	71	54	21.6	23 00	22 48	5 43	12 58	13 09
2	2 57	+14.1	54.9	15.0	191	73	45	22.6	23 20	23 03	6 26	14 09	14 25
3	3 45	+18.1	55.5	15.1	203	77	35	23.6	23 46	23 24	7 13	15 22	15 43
4	4 36	+21.5	56.2	15.3	215	82	26	24.6	—	23 55	8 03	16 34	17 00
5	5 31	+23.9	57.0	15.5	227	88	17	25.6	0 21	—	8 58	17 42	18 11
6	6 29	+25.0	57.8	15.8	240	95	10	26.6	1 09	0 40	9 55	18 41	19 10
7	7 30	+24.7	58.6	16.0	252	105	4	27.6	2 12	1 43	10 55	19 28	19 53
8	8 31	+22.8	59.4	16.2	264	123	1	28.6	3 28	3 03	11 54	20 03	20 23
9	9 31	+19.4	59.9	16.3	276	229	0	0.2	4 53	4 34	12 52	20 31	20 45
10	10 30	+14.8	60.3	16.4	288	275	2	1.2	6 21	6 08	13 47	20 53	21 01
11	11 26	+ 9.2	60.4	16.5	301	285	7	2.2	7 49	7 42	14 3	21 11	21 15
12	12 20	+ 3.1	60.3	16.4	313	288	14	3.2	9 15	9 15	15 30	21 29	21 27
13	13 13	- 3.1	60.0	16.3	325	290	24	4.2	10 40	10 45	16 21	21 47	21 40
14	14 06	- 9.0	59.5	16.2	337	289	34	5.2	12 05	12 16	17 12	22 07	21 54
15	14 59	-14.4	58.9	16.1	350	286	45	6.2	13 28	13 45	18 04	22 30	22 12
16	15 54	-18.9	58.3	15.9	2	282	57	7.2	14 49	15 12	18 58	23 00	22 36
17	16 50	-22.3	57.7	15.7	14	277	67	8.2	16 04	16 32	19 53	23 39	23 11
18	17 47	-24.4	57.1	15.6	26	271	77	9.2	17 09	17 39	20 49	—	23 58
19	18 45	-25.2	56.6	15.4	39	263	85	10.2	18 02	18 31	21 44	0 28	—
20	19 41	-24.5	56.1	15.3	51	256	92	11.2	18 42	19 07	22 37	1 29	1 00
21	20 36	-22.6	55.6	15.1	63	246	96	12.2	19 12	19 33	23 26	2 37	2 12
22	21 28	-19.7	55.2	15.0	75	229	99	13.2	19 35	19 50	—	3 49	3 29
23	22 17	-15.9	54.8	14.9	87	151	100	14.2	19 53	20 04	0 13	5 01	4 47
24	23 04	-11.5	54.5	14.8	99	90	99	15.2	20 08	20 15	0 57	6 12	6 02
25	23 48	- 6.7	54.2	14.8	112	78	96	16.2	20 22	20 24	1 38	7 21	7 16
26	0 31	- 1.7	54.1	14.7	124	74	91	17.2	20 35	20 33	2 19	8 29	8 29
27	1 14	+ 3.4	54.1	14.7	136	72	85	18.2	20 49	20 43	2 59	9 37	9 41
28	1 57	+ 8.3	54.2	14.8	148	72	78	19.2	21 04	20 53	3 39	10 45	10 54
29	2 42	+12.9	54.4	14.8	160	74	70	20.2	21 22	21 07	4 21	11 55	12 09
30	3 29	+17.1	54.8	14.9	173	76	61	21.2	21 45	21 24	5 06	13 06	13 25
31	4 18	+20.7	55.4	15.1	185	80	51	22.2	22 15	21 50	5 54	14 17	14 41

MERCURY

Day	RA h m	Dec. °	Diam. "	Phase %	Transit h m	5° high 52° h m	5° high 56° h m
1	9 33	+16.3	5	92	12 57	19 47	19 57
3	9 47	+15.0	5	90	13 03	19 46	19 55
5	10 01	+13.6	5	87	13 09	19 45	19 52
7	10 14	+12.3	5	85	13 14	19 42	19 48
9	10 27	+10.8	5	83	13 19	19 39	19 44
11	10 39	+ 9.4	6	81	13 23	19 36	19 40
13	10 50	+ 8.0	6	79	13 26	19 32	19 35
15	11 01	+ 6.6	6	76	13 29	19 28	19 29
17	11 12	+ 5.2	6	74	13 32	19 23	19 24
19	11 22	+ 3.8	6	72	13 34	19 18	19 18
21	11 32	+ 2.4	6	70	13 36	19 13	19 11
23	11 41	+ 1.1	6	67	13 37	19 07	19 05
25	11 50	- 0.2	6	65	13 38	19 02	18 58
27	11 58	- 1.4	7	62	13 38	18 55	18 51
29	12 06	- 2.6	7	60	13 38	18 49	18 43
31	12 13	- 3.8	7	57	13 37	18 42	18 35

VENUS

Day	RA h m	Dec. °	Diam. "	Phase %	Transit h m	5° high 52° h m	5° high 56° h m
1	11 36	+ 2.9	20	59	14 58	20 38	20 36
6	11 54	+ 0.4	20	57	14 57	20 24	20 21
11	12 13	- 2.1	22	55	14 55	20 10	20 04
16	12 31	- 4.5	23	52	14 54	19 55	19 47
21	12 48	- 6.9	24	50	14 51	19 39	19 30
26	13 05	- 9.3	25	47	14 48	19 23	19 11
31	13 21	-11.5	27	44	14 45	19 07	18 52

MARS

Day	RA h m	Dec. °	Diam. "	Phase %	Transit h m	5° high 52° h m	5° high 56° h m
1	8 58	+18.4	4	100	12 20	5 16	5 04
6	9 11	+17.4	4	100	12 13	5 15	5 03
11	9 24	+16.5	4	100	12 06	5 13	5 03
16	9 36	+15.5	4	100	11 59	5 12	5 02
21	9 49	+14.4	4	100	11 52	5 10	5 01
26	10 01	+13.3	4	100	11 44	5 08	5 01
31	10 13	+12.2	4	100	11 37	5 07	5 00

SUNRISE AND SUNSET

	London 0°05' 51°30' h m	h m	Bristol 2°35' 51°28' h m	h m	Birmingham 1°55' 52°28' h m	h m	Manchester 2°15' 53°28' h m	h m	Newcastle 1°37' 54°59' h m	h m	Glasgow 4°14' 55°52' h m	h m	Belfast 5°56' 54°35' h m	h m
1	4 24	19 49	4 34	19 59	4 27	20 00	4 24	20 05	4 15	20 10	4 21	20 24	4 34	20 25
2	4 25	19 47	4 35	19 57	4 29	19 58	4 26	20 03	4 17	20 08	4 23	20 22	4 36	20 23
3	4 27	19 45	4 37	19 55	4 30	19 56	4 28	20 02	4 18	20 06	4 25	20 20	4 37	20 21
4	4 28	19 44	4 38	19 54	4 32	19 55	4 29	20 00	4 20	20 04	4 27	20 18	4 39	20 19
5	4 30	19 42	4 40	19 52	4 33	19 53	4 31	19 58	4 22	20 02	4 29	20 16	4 41	20 17
6	4 31	19 40	4 41	19 50	4 35	19 51	4 33	19 56	4 24	20 00	4 30	20 14	4 43	20 15
7	4 33	19 38	4 43	19 48	4 37	19 49	4 34	19 54	4 26	19 58	4 32	20 12	4 45	20 13
8	4 34	19 37	4 44	19 46	4 38	19 47	4 36	19 52	4 27	19 55	4 34	20 10	4 46	20 11
9	4 36	19 35	4 46	19 45	4 40	19 45	4 38	19 50	4 29	19 53	4 36	20 07	4 48	20 09
10	4 37	19 33	4 48	19 43	4 42	19 43	4 39	19 48	4 31	19 51	4 38	20 05	4 50	20 07
11	4 39	19 31	4 49	19 41	4 43	19 41	4 41	19 46	4 33	19 49	4 40	20 03	4 52	20 05
12	4 41	19 29	4 51	19 39	4 45	19 39	4 43	19 44	4 35	19 47	4 42	20 01	4 54	20 03
13	4 42	19 27	4 52	19 37	4 47	19 37	4 45	19 42	4 37	19 45	4 44	19 58	4 55	20 00
14	4 44	19 25	4 54	19 35	4 48	19 35	4 46	19 40	4 39	19 42	4 46	19 56	4 57	19 58
15	4 45	19 23	4 55	19 33	4 50	19 33	4 48	19 38	4 40	19 40	4 48	19 54	4 59	19 56
16	4 47	19 21	4 57	19 31	4 52	19 31	4 50	19 36	4 42	19 38	4 50	19 51	5 01	19 54
17	4 49	19 19	4 59	19 29	4 53	19 29	4 52	19 33	4 44	19 36	4 52	19 49	5 03	19 52
18	4 50	19 17	5 00	19 27	4 55	19 27	4 53	19 31	4 46	19 33	4 54	19 47	5 05	19 49
19	4 52	19 15	5 02	19 25	4 56	19 25	4 55	19 29	4 48	19 31	4 56	19 44	5 06	19 47
20	4 53	19 13	5 03	19 23	4 58	19 23	4 57	19 27	4 50	19 29	4 58	19 42	5 08	19 45
21	4 55	19 11	5 05	19 21	5 00	19 21	4 58	19 25	4 52	19 26	4 59	19 39	5 10	19 42
22	4 57	19 09	5 07	19 19	5 01	19 19	5 00	19 22	4 54	19 24	5 01	19 37	5 12	19 40
23	4 58	19 07	5 08	19 17	5 03	19 16	5 02	19 20	4 55	19 22	5 03	19 34	5 14	19 38
24	5 00	19 05	5 10	19 15	5 05	19 14	5 04	19 18	4 57	19 19	5 05	19 32	5 16	19 35
25	5 01	19 03	5 11	19 12	5 06	19 12	5 05	19 16	4 59	19 17	5 07	19 29	5 17	19 33
26	5 03	19 00	5 13	19 10	5 08	19 10	5 07	19 13	5 01	19 14	5 09	19 27	5 19	19 31
27	5 04	18 58	5 15	19 08	5 10	19 07	5 09	19 11	5 03	19 12	5 11	19 24	5 21	19 28
28	5 06	18 56	5 16	19 06	5 11	19 05	5 11	19 09	5 05	19 09	5 13	19 22	5 23	19 26
29	5 08	18 54	5 18	19 04	5 13	19 03	5 12	19 06	5 07	19 07	5 15	19 19	5 25	19 23
30	5 09	18 52	5 19	19 02	5 15	19 01	5 14	19 04	5 09	19 04	5 17	19 17	5 27	19 21
31	5 11	18 49	5 21	18 59	5 16	18 58	5 16	19 02	5 10	19 02	5 19	19 14	5 28	19 18

JUPITER

Day	RA h m	Dec. ° '	Transit h m	5° high 52° h m	5° high 56° h m
1	8 08.4	+20 31	11 29	4 14	3 59
11	8 17.5	+20 03	10 59	3 46	3 32
21	8 26.5	+19 34	10 29	3 19	3 05
31	8 35.1	+19 04	9 58	2 51	2 37

Diameters - equatorial 32" polar 30"

SATURN

Day	RA h m	Dec. ° '	Transit h m	5° high 52° h m	5° high 56° h m
1	5 37.8	+22 05	8 59	1 34	1 17
11	5 42.2	+22 07	8 24	0 59	0 42
21	5 46.1	+22 08	7 48	0 23	0 06
31	5 49.4	+22 08	7 12	23 44	23 27

Diameters - equatorial 17" polar 16"
Rings - major axis 39" minor axis 18"

URANUS

Day	RA h m	Dec. ° '	Transit h m	10° high 52° h m	10° high 56° h m
1	22 00.2	−13 02	1 22	21 42	22 05
11	21 58.8	−13 10	0 42	21 02	21 25
21	21 57.2	−13 18	0 01	20 23	20 45
31	21 55.7	−13 26	23 16	19 43	20 06

Diameter 4"

NEPTUNE

Day	RA h m	Dec. ° '	Transit h m	10° high 52° h m	10° high 56° h m
1	20 48.1	−17 47	0 10	3 10	2 37
11	20 47.0	−17 51	23 26	2 29	1 56
21	20 46.0	−17 55	22 46	1 48	1 14
31	20 45.0	−17 59	22 05	1 07	0 33

Diameter 2"

September 2002

NINTH MONTH, 30 DAYS, *Septem* (seven), seventh month of Roman pre-Julian calendar

1	*Sunday*	**14th S. after Trinity.** James Corbett b. 1866	244
2	*Monday*	John Howard b. 1726. Formal surrender of Japan (aboard USS Missouri) and end of World War II 1945	*week 35 day* 245
3	*Tuesday*	Oliver Cromwell d. 1658. Battle of Dunbar 1650	246
4	*Wednesday*	Darius Milhaud b. 1892. Forth Road Bridge opened 1964	247
5	*Thursday*	King Louis XIV b. 1638. Jean Rook d. 1991	248
6	*Friday*	Austin Reed b. 1873. Gertrude Lawrence d. 1952	249
7	*Saturday*	JEWISH NEW YEAR. Queen Catherine Parr d. 1548	250
8	*Sunday*	**15th S. after Trinity.** Peter Sellers b. 1925	251
9	*Monday*	John Curry b. 1949. Burgess Meredith d. 1997	*week 36 day* 252
10	*Tuesday*	Arnold Palmer b. 1929. Wilfred Scawen Blunt d. 1922	253
11	*Wednesday*	O. Henry b. 1862. Battle of Malplaquet 1709	254
12	*Thursday*	Louis MacNeice b. 1907. Jean-Philippe Rameau d. 1764	255
13	*Friday*	Claudette Colbert b. 1903. Andrea Mantegna d. 1506	256
14	*Saturday*	**Holy Cross Day.** Augustus Pugin d. 1852	257
15	*Sunday*	**16th S. after Trinity.** Prince Henry of Wales b. 1984.	258
16	*Monday*	YOM KIPPUR. Marc Bolan d. 1977	*week 37 day* 259
17	*Tuesday*	Hildegard of Bingen d. 1179. Constitution of the USA was signed 1787	260
18	*Wednesday*	Dr. Samuel Johnson b. 1709. Jimi Hendrix d. 1970	261
19	*Thursday*	Zandra Rhodes b. 1940. Hermes Pan d. 1990	262
20	*Friday*	Kenneth More b. 1914. Battle of the Alma 1854	263
21	*Saturday*	**St Matthew.** FEAST OF TABERNACLES.	264
22	*Sunday*	**17th S. after Trinity.** Queen Anne of Cleves b. 1515	265
23	*Monday*	Aldo Moro b. 1916. Dorothy Lamour d. 1996	*week 38 day* 266
24	*Tuesday*	Theophrastus von Hohenheim d. 1541. George Cross introduced 1940	267
25	*Wednesday*	Dmitry Shostakovich b. 1906. Battle of Stamford Bridge 1066	268
26	*Thursday*	Ivan Pavlov b. 1849. Hugh Lofting d. 1947	269
27	*Friday*	Professor R. V. Jones b. 1911. Sylvia Pankhurst d. 1960	270
28	*Saturday*	Georges Clemenceau b. 1841. Leslie Crowther d. 1996	271
29	*Sunday*	**St Michael and All Angels. 18th S. after Trinity.**	272
30	*Monday*	Truman Capote b. 1924. George Whitefield d. 1770	*week 39 day* 273

ASTRONOMICAL PHENOMENA

d	h	
1	10	Mercury at greatest elongation E.27°
1	17	Saturn in conjunction with Moon. Saturn 2° S.
4	15	Jupiter in conjunction with Moon. Jupiter 4° S.
6	12	Mars in conjunction with Moon. Mars 4° S.
8	22	Mercury in conjunction with Moon. Mercury 8° S.
10	07	Venus in conjunction with Moon. Venus 7° S.
14	20	Mercury at stationary point
23	05	Sun's longitude 180°♎
26	11	Venus at greatest brilliancy
27	19	Mercury in inferior conjunction
29	03	Saturn in conjunction with Moon. Saturn 3° S.

MINIMA OF ALGOL

d	h	d	h	d	h
2	17.0	14	04.3	25	15.5
5	13.8	17	01.1	28	12.3
8	10.6	19	21.9		
11	07.5	22	18.7		

CONSTELLATIONS

The following constellations are near the meridian at

	d	h		d	h
August	1	24	September	15	21
August	16	23	October	1	20
September	1	22	October	16	19

Draco, Cepheus, Lyra, Cygnus, Vulpecula, Sagitta, Delphinus, Equuleus, Aquila, Aquarius and Capricornus

THE MOON

Phases, Apsides and Node	d	h	m
●New Moon	7	03	10
☽ First Quarter	13	18	08
○Full Moon	21	13	59
☾ Last Quarter	29	17	03
Perigee (358,754km)	8	03	11
Apogee (406,341km)	23	03	11

Mean longitude of ascending node on September 1, 73°

THE SUN   S.D 16'.1

Day	Right Ascension	Dec.	Equation of Time	Rise 52°	Rise 56°	Transit	Set 52°	Set 56°	Sidereal time	Transit of First Point of Aries
	h m s	° '	m s	h m	h m	h m	h m	h m	h m s	h m s
1	10 40 08	+ 8 25	− 0 11	5 11	5 04	12 00	18 48	18 55	22 39 56	1 19 51
2	10 43 45	+ 8 04	+ 0 08	5 13	5 06	12 00	18 45	18 52	22 43 53	1 15 55
3	10 47 22	+ 7 42	+ 0 27	5 15	5 08	11 59	18 43	18 50	22 47 49	1 11 59
4	10 50 59	+ 7 20	+ 0 46	5 16	5 10	11 59	18 41	18 47	22 51 46	1 08 03
5	10 54 36	+ 6 57	+ 1 06	5 18	5 11	11 59	18 39	18 45	22 55 42	1 04 07
6	10 58 13	+ 6 35	+ 1 26	5 19	5 13	11 58	18 36	18 42	22 59 39	1 00 11
7	11 01 49	+ 6 13	+ 1 46	5 21	5 15	11 58	18 34	18 39	23 03 35	0 56 15
8	11 05 25	+ 5 50	+ 2 07	5 23	5 17	11 58	18 32	18 37	23 07 32	0 52 19
9	11 09 01	+ 5 28	+ 2 27	5 24	5 19	11 57	18 29	18 34	23 11 29	0 48 23
10	11 12 37	+ 5 05	+ 2 48	5 26	5 21	11 57	18 27	18 32	23 15 25	0 44 28
11	11 16 13	+ 4 42	+ 3 09	5 28	5 23	11 57	18 25	18 29	23 19 22	0 40 32
12	11 19 48	+ 4 20	+ 3 30	5 29	5 25	11 56	18 22	18 26	23 23 18	0 36 36
13	11 23 24	+ 3 57	+ 3 51	5 31	5 27	11 56	18 20	18 24	23 27 15	0 32 40
14	11 26 59	+ 3 34	+ 4 12	5 32	5 29	11 56	18 18	18 21	23 31 11	0 28 44
15	11 30 34	+ 3 11	+ 4 34	5 34	5 31	11 55	18 15	18 18	23 35 08	0 24 48
16	11 34 09	+ 2 48	+ 4 55	5 36	5 33	11 55	18 13	18 16	23 39 04	0 20 52
17	11 37 45	+ 2 24	+ 5 16	5 37	5 35	11 55	18 11	18 13	23 43 01	0 16 56
18	11 41 20	+ 2 01	+ 5 38	5 39	5 37	11 54	18 08	18 10	23 46 58	0 13 00
19	11 44 55	+ 1 38	+ 5 59	5 41	5 39	11 54	18 06	18 08	23 50 54	0 09 04
20	11 48 30	+ 1 15	+ 6 21	5 42	5 41	11 53	18 04	18 05	23 54 51	0 05 08
21	11 52 05	+ 0 51	+ 6 42	5 44	5 43	11 53	18 01	18 02	23 58 47	{ 0 01 13 / 23 57 17 }
22	11 55 40	+ 0 28	+ 7 03	5 45	5 45	11 53	17 59	18 00	0 02 44	23 53 21
23	11 59 16	+ 0 05	+ 7 25	5 47	5 47	11 52	17 57	17 57	0 06 40	23 49 25
24	12 02 51	− 0 19	+ 7 46	5 49	5 49	11 52	17 54	17 54	0 10 37	23 45 29
25	12 06 27	− 0 42	+ 8 07	5 50	5 51	11 52	17 52	17 52	0 14 33	23 41 33
26	12 10 02	− 1 05	+ 8 28	5 52	5 53	11 51	17 50	17 49	0 18 30	23 37 37
27	12 13 38	− 1 29	+ 8 48	5 54	5 54	11 51	17 47	17 46	0 22 27	23 33 41
28	12 17 15	− 1 52	+ 9 08	5 55	5 56	11 51	17 45	17 44	0 26 23	23 29 45
29	12 20 51	− 2 15	+ 9 29	5 57	5 58	11 50	17 43	17 41	0 30 20	23 25 49
30	12 24 28	− 2 39	+ 9 49	5 59	6 00	11 50	17 40	17 39	0 34 16	23 21 54

DURATION OF TWILIGHT (in minutes)

Latitude	52°	56°	52°	56°	52°	56°	52°	56°
	1 September		11 September		21 September		30 September	
Civil	35	39	34	38	34	37	34	37
Nautical	79	89	76	85	74	82	73	80
Astronomical	127	147	120	136	116	129	113	125

THE NIGHT SKY

Mercury is at greatest eastern elongation on the 1st and passes through inferior conjunction on the 27th, but continues to remain too close to the Sun for observation.

Venus, magnitude −4.5, is a magnificent object in the south-western sky in the early evenings for a very short time after sunset. Venus passes 0.9 degrees south of Spica on the 1st. The planet is gradually drawing closer to the Sun and being well south of the equator is unlikely to be seen from the latitudes of the British Isles after the first fortnight in September. Only observers much farther south will be able to see the planet at its greatest brilliancy on the 26th.

Mars is too close to the Sun for observation at first but during the last few days of the month it may be glimpsed as a difficult morning object, low above the eastern horizon for a short while before twilight inhibits observation. Mars, magnitude +1.8, is in the constellation of Leo.

Jupiter, magnitude −1.9, continues to be visible as a conspicuous morning object in the south-eastern quadrant of the sky. Jupiter is moving eastwards in Cancer. On the morning of the 4th the old crescent Moon will be seen approaching the planet.

Saturn, magnitude +0.1, is still a morning object, now visible in the eastern sky well before midnight. The old crescent Moon is near the planet on the mornings of the 1st and 2nd, and again on the 29th. Also on the 1st, Venus passes only 0.9 degrees south of Spica.

Zodiacal Light. The morning cone may be seen reaching up from the eastern horizon along the ecliptic, before the beginning of morning twilight, from the 6th to the 19th.

THE MOON

Day	RA	Dec.	Hor. par.	Semi-diam	Sun's co-long.	PA of Bright Limb	Phase	Age	Rise 52°	Rise 56°	Transit	Set 52°	Set 56°
	h m	°	'	'	°	°	%	d	h m	h m	h m	h m	h m
1	5 11	+23.4	56.1	15.3	197	85	41	23.2	22 55	22 27	6 45	15 26	15 54
2	6 07	+25.0	57.0	15.5	209	91	31	24.2	23 50	23 20	7 40	16 28	16 58
3	7 05	+25.2	57.9	15.8	221	98	22	25.2	—	—	8 38	17 19	17 47
4	8 05	+23.9	58.8	16.0	234	106	13	26.2	1 00	0 32	9 36	17 59	18 22
5	9 06	+21.1	59.7	16.3	246	114	7	27.2	2 21	1 59	10 35	18 30	18 47
6	10 05	+16.9	60.4	16.5	258	127	2	28.2	3 48	3 33	11 31	18 54	19 05
7	11 03	+11.6	60.9	16.6	270	182	0	29.2	5 18	5 09	12 26	19 14	19 20
8	11 59	+ 5.4	61.1	16.7	283	272	1	0.9	6 48	6 45	13 19	19 32	19 32
9	12 53	- 1.0	61.0	16.6	295	284	5	1.9	8 17	8 20	14 12	19 50	19 45
10	13 48	- 7.3	60.6	16.5	307	287	12	2.9	9 45	9 54	15 04	20 10	19 59
11	14 43	-13.1	60.0	16.3	319	286	21	3.9	11 12	11 27	15 58	20 32	20 16
12	15 39	-18.0	59.2	16.1	332	283	31	4.9	12 37	12 58	16 53	21 00	20 38
13	16 36	-21.8	58.4	15.9	344	278	42	5.9	13 56	14 23	17 49	21 36	21 09
14	17 34	-24.3	57.6	15.7	356	273	53	6.9	15 05	15 36	18 45	22 23	21 53
15	18 32	-25.3	56.9	15.5	8	266	63	7.9	16 02	16 32	19 40	23 21	22 51
16	19 29	-25.0	56.2	15.3	20	260	73	8.9	16 45	17 12	20 33	—	—
17	20 24	-23.3	55.6	15.1	33	253	81	9.9	17 17	17 39	21 24	0 27	0 01
18	21 16	-20.6	55.1	15.0	45	247	88	10.9	17 41	17 58	22 11	1 38	1 16
19	22 05	-17.0	54.7	14.9	57	241	94	11.9	18 00	18 13	22 55	2 49	2 34
20	22 52	-12.7	54.4	14.8	69	232	98	12.9	18 16	18 24	23 37	4 01	3 50
21	23 36	- 7.9	54.2	14.8	81	209	100	13.9	18 30	18 33	—	5 10	5 04
22	0 20	- 2.9	54.0	14.7	93	112	100	14.9	18 43	18 42	0 18	6 19	6 17
23	1 03	+ 2.2	54.0	14.7	106	82	98	15.9	18 56	18 51	0 57	7 26	7 30
24	1 46	+ 7.2	54.0	14.7	118	76	95	16.9	19 10	19 00	1 38	8 35	8 43
25	2 30	+11.9	54.1	14.8	130	75	90	17.9	19 26	19 12	2 19	9 44	9 57
26	3 15	+16.3	54.4	14.8	142	76	83	18.9	19 47	19 28	3 02	10 55	11 12
27	4 03	+20.0	54.8	14.9	154	79	76	19.9	20 13	19 49	3 48	12 05	12 28
28	4 54	+22.9	55.3	15.1	166	83	67	20.9	20 48	20 20	4 37	13 14	13 42
29	5 48	+24.9	56.0	15.3	179	89	57	21.9	21 36	21 05	5 30	14 18	14 48
30	6 45	+25.5	56.8	15.5	191	95	47	22.9	22 37	22 08	6 25	15 12	15 42

MERCURY

Day	RA	Dec.	Diam.	Phase	Transit	5° high 52°	5° high 56°
	h m	°	"	%	h m	h m	h m
1	12 17	- 4.3	7	55	13 36	18 39	18 32
3	12 23	- 5.3	7	52	13 35	18 32	18 24
5	12 29	- 6.2	8	48	13 32	18 24	18 15
7	12 33	- 7.1	8	45	13 29	18 17	18 07
9	12 37	- 7.8	8	41	13 25	18 09	17 59
11	12 40	- 8.3	8	36	13 19	18 01	17 50
13	12 42	- 8.7	9	31	13 13	17 52	17 41
15	12 42	- 8.9	9	26	13 05	17 44	17 32
17	12 41	- 8.9	9	21	12 56	17 35	17 24
19	12 39	- 8.6	10	16	12 45	17 26	17 15
21	12 35	- 8.0	10	11	12 32	17 17	17 07
23	12 29	- 7.1	10	6	12 19	17 09	17 00
25	12 22	- 6.0	10	3	12 04	17 01	16 52
27	12 15	- 4.7	10	1	11 49	6 47	6 54
29	12 08	- 3.3	10	1	11 34	6 24	6 30
31	12 02	- 1.9	10	3	11 20	6 03	6 08

VENUS

Day	RA	Dec.	Diam.	Phase	Transit	5° high 52°	5° high 56°
	h m	°	"	%	h m	h m	h m
1	13 24	-12.0	27	43	14 44	19 03	18 48
6	13 40	-14.1	29	40	14 40	18 46	18 28
11	13 54	-16.1	31	37	14 34	18 28	18 07
16	14 08	-17.9	34	34	14 28	18 09	17 46
21	14 20	-19.5	36	30	14 20	17 49	17 23
26	14 30	-20.9	39	26	14 10	17 29	16 59
31	14 37	-22.0	43	22	13 58	17 08	16 35

MARS

Day	RA	Dec.	Diam.	Phase	Transit	5° high 52°	5° high 56°
1	10 16	+12.0	4	100	11 35	5 07	5 00
6	10 28	+10.9	4	100	11 28	5 05	4 59
11	10 40	+ 9.7	4	100	11 20	5 03	4 59
16	10 52	+ 8.5	4	100	11 12	5 02	4 58
21	11 04	+ 7.2	4	100	11 04	5 00	4 58
26	11 15	+ 6.0	4	99	10 56	4 59	4 57
31	11 27	+ 4.7	4	99	10 48	4 57	4 57

SUNRISE AND SUNSET

	London 0°05′ 51°30′ h m h m	Bristol 2°35′ 51°28′ h m h m	Birmingham 1°55′ 52°28′ h m h m	Manchester 2°15′ 53°28′ h m h m	Newcastle 1°37′ 54°59′ h m h m	Glasgow 4°14′ 55°52′ h m h m	Belfast 5°56′ 54°35′ h m h m
1	5 12 18 47	5 22 18 57	5 18 18 56	5 18 18 59	5 12 18 59	5 21 19 12	5 30 19 16
2	5 14 18 45	5 24 18 55	5 20 18 54	5 19 18 57	5 14 18 57	5 23 19 09	5 32 19 14
3	5 16 18 43	5 26 18 53	5 21 18 52	5 21 18 54	5 16 18 54	5 25 19 07	5 34 19 11
4	5 17 18 40	5 27 18 50	5 23 18 49	5 23 18 52	5 18 18 52	5 27 19 04	5 36 19 09
5	5 19 18 38	5 29 18 48	5 25 18 47	5 25 18 50	5 20 18 49	5 29 19 01	5 38 19 06
6	5 20 18 36	5 30 18 46	5 26 18 45	5 26 18 47	5 22 18 47	5 31 18 59	5 39 19 04
7	5 22 18 34	5 32 18 44	5 28 18 42	5 28 18 45	5 23 18 44	5 33 18 56	5 41 19 01
8	5 24 18 31	5 34 18 41	5 30 18 40	5 30 18 42	5 25 18 42	5 35 18 54	5 43 18 59
9	5 25 18 29	5 35 18 39	5 31 18 38	5 32 18 40	5 27 18 39	5 36 18 51	5 45 18 56
10	5 27 18 27	5 37 18 37	5 33 18 35	5 33 18 38	5 29 18 37	5 38 18 48	5 47 18 54
11	5 28 18 25	5 38 18 35	5 35 18 33	5 35 18 35	5 31 18 34	5 40 18 46	5 49 18 51
12	5 30 18 22	5 40 18 32	5 36 18 30	5 37 18 33	5 33 18 32	5 42 18 43	5 50 18 48
13	5 32 18 20	5 42 18 30	5 38 18 28	5 39 18 30	5 35 18 29	5 44 18 40	5 52 18 46
14	5 33 18 18	5 43 18 28	5 40 18 26	5 40 18 28	5 36 18 27	5 46 18 38	5 54 18 43
15	5 35 18 15	5 45 18 25	5 41 18 23	5 42 18 25	5 38 18 24	5 48 18 35	5 56 18 41
16	5 36 18 13	5 46 18 23	5 43 18 21	5 44 18 23	5 40 18 21	5 50 18 32	5 58 18 38
17	5 38 18 11	5 48 18 21	5 45 18 19	5 46 18 20	5 42 18 19	5 52 18 30	6 00 18 36
18	5 40 18 08	5 50 18 18	5 46 18 16	5 47 18 18	5 44 18 16	5 54 18 27	6 01 18 33
19	5 41 18 06	5 51 18 16	5 48 18 14	5 49 18 16	5 46 18 14	5 56 18 25	6 03 18 31
20	5 43 18 04	5 53 18 14	5 50 18 11	5 51 18 13	5 48 18 11	5 58 18 22	6 05 18 28
21	5 44 18 02	5 54 18 12	5 51 18 09	5 52 18 11	5 49 18 09	6 00 18 19	6 07 18 26
22	5 46 17 59	5 56 18 09	5 53 18 07	5 54 18 08	5 51 18 06	6 02 18 17	6 09 18 23
23	5 48 17 57	5 58 18 07	5 55 18 04	5 56 18 06	5 53 18 03	6 04 18 14	6 11 18 21
24	5 49 17 55	5 59 18 05	5 56 18 02	5 58 18 03	5 55 18 01	6 06 18 11	6 12 18 18
25	5 51 17 52	6 01 18 02	5 58 18 00	5 59 18 01	5 57 17 58	6 07 18 09	6 14 18 16
26	5 52 17 50	6 02 18 00	6 00 17 57	6 01 17 58	5 59 17 56	6 09 18 06	6 16 18 13
27	5 54 17 48	6 04 17 58	6 02 17 55	6 03 17 56	6 01 17 53	6 11 18 03	6 18 18 10
28	5 56 17 45	6 06 17 55	6 03 17 53	6 05 17 54	6 03 17 51	6 13 18 01	6 20 18 08
29	5 57 17 43	6 07 17 53	6 05 17 50	6 07 17 51	6 05 17 48	6 15 17 58	6 22 18 05
30	5 59 17 41	6 09 17 51	6 07 17 48	6 08 17 49	6 06 17 45	6 17 17 55	6 24 18 03

JUPITER

Day	RA h m	Dec. ° ′	Transit h m	5° high 52° h m	5° high 56° h m
1	8 35.9	+19 01	9 55	2 48	2 35
11	8 44.1	+18 32	9 24	2 19	2 07
21	8 51.8	+18 03	8 52	1 51	1 38
31	8 58.9	+17 36	8 20	1 21	1 09

Diameters - equatorial 33″ polar 31″

SATURN

Day	RA h m	Dec. ° ′	Transit h m	5° high 52° h m	5° high 56° h m
1	5 49.7	+22 08	7 09	23 40	23 23
11	5 52.4	+22 08	6 32	23 03	22 46
21	5 54.4	+22 08	5 55	22 26	22 09
31	5 55.6	+22 08	5 17	21 48	21 31

Diameters - equatorial 18″ polar 17″
Rings- major axis 41″ minor axis 18″

URANUS

Day	RA h m	Dec. ° ′	Transit h m	10° high 52° h m	10° high 56° h m
1	21 55.6	−13 27	23 12	2 49	2 26
11	21 54.1	−13 35	22 31	2 07	1 44
21	21 52.8	−13 42	21 50	1 26	1 02
31	21 51.7	−13 47	21 10	0 45	0 21

Diameter 4″

NEPTUNE

Day	RA h m	Dec. ° ′	Transit h m	10° high 52° h m	10° high 56° h m
1	20 44.9	−18 00	22 01	1 03	0 29
11	20 44.0	−18 03	21 21	0 22	23 44
21	20 43.3	−18 06	20 41	23 38	23 04
31	20 42.8	−18 08	20 01	22 58	22 24

Diameter 2″

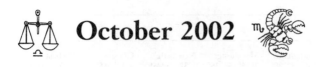

October 2002

TENTH MONTH, 31 DAYS. *Octo* (eighth), eighth month of Roman pre-Julian calendar

1	*Tuesday*	Michaelmas Law Sittings begin. People's Republic of China formally proclaimed 1949	274
2	*Wednesday*	Julius Marx b. 1890. Dr Marie Stopes d. 1958	275
3	*Thursday*	Jean Anouilh d. 1987. 1st British Atomic Bomb tested off north west coast of Australia 1952	276
4	*Friday*	Sir Arthur Whitten Brown d. 1948. Printing of first English (Coverdale) Bible 1535	277
5	*Saturday*	Jonathan Edwards b. 1703. *R101* disaster 1930	278
6	*Sunday*	**19th S. after Trinity.** William Tyndale d. 1536	279
7	*Monday*	Archbishop William Laud b. 1573. Cyril Cusack d. 1993	*week* 40 *day* 280
8	*Tuesday*	Clement Attlee d. 1967. Great Fire of Chicago 1871	281
9	*Wednesday*	André Maurois d. 1967. Breathalyser tests came into force 1967	282
10	*Thursday*	Fridtjof Nansen b. 1861. Viscount Nuffield b. 1877	283
11	*Friday*	Johann Albert Fabricius b. 1668. Andy Stewart d. 1993	284
12	*Saturday*	Ramsay Macdonald b. 1866. Anatole France d. 1924	285
13	*Sunday*	**20th S. after Trinity.** Prince of Wales Edward b. 1453	286
14	*Monday*	Hon. George Grenville b. 1712. Erwin Rommel d. 1944	*week* 41 *day* 287
15	*Tuesday*	Dr Marie Stopes b. 1880. First manned balloon flight (Jean de Rozier) 1783	288
16	*Wednesday*	Günter Grass b. 1927. Nicholas Ridley d. 1555	289
17	*Thursday*	Sir Philip Sidney b. 1586. Arthur Miller b. 1915	290
18	*Friday*	**St Luke.** Viscount Palmerston d. 1865	291
19	*Saturday*	Jonathan Swift d. 1745. Surrender of British Troops, American War of Independence 1781	292
20	*Sunday*	**21st S. after Trinity.** Arthur Rimbaud b. 1854	293
21	*Monday*	Geoffrey Boycott b. 1940. Arthur Schnitzler d. 1931	*week* 42 *day* 294
22	*Tuesday*	Joan Fontaine b. 1917. Thomas Sheraton d. 1806	295
23	*Wednesday*	Pierre Larousse b. 1817. Zane Grey d. 1939	296
24	*Thursday*	1st Baron Gladwyn Gladwyn Jebb d. 1996. United Nations formally came into existence 1945	297
25	*Friday*	Johann Strauss b. 1825. Battle of Agincourt 1415	298
26	*Saturday*	Alma Cogan d. 1966. Founding of Royal Marines 1664	299
27	*Sunday*	**9th S. before Christmas. Last Sunday after Trinity**	300
28	*Monday*	**SS Simon and Jude.** John Locke d. 1704	*week* 43 *day* 301
29	*Tuesday*	Sir Walter Raleigh d. 1618. International Red Cross founded 1863	302
30	*Wednesday*	Louis Malle b. 1932. Dame Rose Macaulay d. 1958	303
31	*Thursday*	Kai-Shek Chiang b. 1887. Mrs Indira Gandhi d. 1984	304

ASTRONOMICAL PHENOMENA

d	h	
2	09	Jupiter in conjunction with Moon. Jupiter 4° S.
5	04	Mars in conjunction with Moon. Mars 4° S.
5	12	Mercury in conjunction with Moon. Mercury 5° S.
6	19	Mercury at stationary point
8	15	Venus in conjunction with Moon. Venus 9° S.
10	19	Venus at stationary point
11	13	Saturn at stationary point
13	07	Mercury at greatest elongation W.18°
20	14	Neptune at stationary point
23	14	Sun's longitude 210°♏
26	09	Saturn in conjunction with Moon. Saturn 3° S.
30	00	Jupiter in conjunction with Moon. Jupiter 4° S.
31	12	Venus in inferior conjunction

MINIMA OF ALGOL

d	h	d	h	d	h
1	09.1	12	20.4	24	07.6
4	05.9	15	17.2	27	04.4
7	02.8	18	14.0	30	01.3
9	23.6	21	10.8		

CONSTELLATIONS

The following constellations are near the meridian at

	d	h		d	h
September	1	24	October	16	21
September	15	23	November	1	20
October	1	22	November	15	19

Ursa Major (below the Pole), Cepheus, Cassiopeia, Cygnus, Lacerta, Andromeda, Pegasus, Capricornus, Aquarius and Piscis Austrinus

THE MOON

Phases, Apsides and Node	d	h	m
● New Moon	6	11	18
☽ First Quarter	13	05	33
○ Full Moon	21	07	20
☾ Last Quarter	29	05	28
Perigee (356,918km)	6	13	10
Apogee (406,369km)	20	04	24

Mean longitude of ascending node on October 1, 72°

THE SUN   S.D 16'.1

Day	Right Ascension	Dec. –	Equation of Time	Rise 52°	Rise 56°	Transit	Set 52°	Set 56°	Sidereal time	Transit of First Point of Aries
	h m s	° ′	m s	h m	h m	h m	h m	h m	h m s	h m s
1	12 28 05	3 02	+10 08	6 00	6 02	11 50	17 38	17 36	0 38 13	23 17 58
2	12 31 42	3 25	+10 27	6 02	6 04	11 49	17 36	17 33	0 42 09	23 14 02
3	12 35 19	3 48	+10 46	6 04	6 06	11 49	17 33	17 31	0 46 06	23 10 06
4	12 38 57	4 12	+11 05	6 05	6 08	11 49	17 31	17 28	0 50 02	23 06 10
5	12 42 36	4 35	+11 23	6 07	6 10	11 48	17 29	17 25	0 53 59	23 02 14
6	12 46 14	4 58	+11 41	6 09	6 12	11 48	17 27	17 23	0 57 56	22 58 18
7	12 49 53	5 21	+11 59	6 11	6 14	11 48	17 24	17 20	1 01 52	22 54 22
8	12 53 33	5 44	+12 16	6 12	6 16	11 48	17 22	17 18	1 05 49	22 50 26
9	12 57 12	6 07	+12 33	6 14	6 18	11 47	17 20	17 15	1 09 45	22 46 30
10	13 00 53	6 30	+12 49	6 16	6 20	11 47	17 18	17 13	1 13 42	22 42 34
11	13 04 33	6 52	+13 05	6 17	6 23	11 47	17 15	17 10	1 17 38	22 38 39
12	13 08 14	7 15	+13 21	6 19	6 25	11 47	17 13	17 07	1 21 35	22 34 43
13	13 11 56	7 37	+13 35	6 21	6 27	11 46	17 11	17 05	1 25 31	22 30 47
14	13 15 38	8 00	+13 50	6 23	6 29	11 46	17 09	17 02	1 29 28	22 26 51
15	13 19 21	8 22	+14 04	6 24	6 31	11 46	17 06	17 00	1 33 25	22 22 55
16	13 23 04	8 44	+14 17	6 26	6 33	11 46	17 04	16 57	1 37 21	22 18 59
17	13 26 48	9 06	+14 30	6 28	6 35	11 45	17 02	16 55	1 41 18	22 15 03
18	13 30 32	9 28	+14 42	6 29	6 37	11 45	17 00	16 52	1 45 14	22 11 07
19	13 34 17	9 50	+14 54	6 31	6 39	11 45	16 58	16 50	1 49 11	22 07 11
20	13 38 02	10 12	+15 05	6 33	6 41	11 45	16 56	16 48	1 53 07	22 03 15
21	13 41 48	10 33	+15 16	6 35	6 43	11 45	16 54	16 45	1 57 04	21 59 19
22	13 45 35	10 55	+15 25	6 37	6 45	11 44	16 52	16 43	2 01 00	21 55 24
23	13 49 23	11 16	+15 34	6 38	6 47	11 44	16 50	16 40	2 04 57	21 51 28
24	13 53 11	11 37	+15 43	6 40	6 49	11 44	16 48	16 38	2 08 53	21 47 32
25	13 56 59	11 58	+15 51	6 42	6 52	11 44	16 46	16 36	2 12 50	21 43 36
26	14 00 49	12 18	+15 58	6 44	6 54	11 44	16 44	16 33	2 16 47	21 39 40
27	14 04 39	12 39	+16 04	6 45	6 56	11 44	16 42	16 31	2 20 43	21 35 44
28	14 08 30	12 59	+16 09	6 47	6 58	11 44	16 40	16 29	2 24 40	21 31 48
29	14 12 22	13 19	+16 14	6 49	7 00	11 44	16 38	16 27	2 28 36	21 27 52
30	14 16 15	13 39	+16 18	6 51	7 02	11 44	16 36	16 24	2 32 33	21 23 56
31	14 20 08	13 59	+16 21	6 53	7 04	11 44	16 34	16 22	2 36 29	21 20 00

DURATION OF TWILIGHT (in minutes)

Latitude	52°	56°	52°	56°	52°	56°	52°	56°
	1 October		11 October		21 October		31 October	
Civil	34	37	34	37	34	38	35	39
Nautical	73	80	73	80	74	81	75	83
Astronomical	113	125	112	124	113	124	114	126

THE NIGHT SKY

Mercury reaches greatest western elongation (18°) on the 13th and is visible as a morning object after the first week of the month, low above the east-south-eastern horizon around the time of morning civil twilight. During the last week of the month it is getting too close to the Sun to be detected, even though its magnitude has brightened to -1.0. This is the most favourable morning apparition of the year for observers in the latitudes of the British Isles. For some days around the 10th Mercury will only be a few degrees east of Mars.

Venus is unsuitably placed for observation throughout October. Although it is still 37 degrees from the Sun at the beginning of the month, its declination of -23 degrees completely nullifies this apparently favourable elongation, as seen from the latitudes of the British Isles. Venus passes rapidly through inferior conjunction on the last day of the month, becoming visible early in November.

Mars, magnitude +1.8, continues to be visible in the pre-dawn sky, low above the east-south-eastern horizon. Early in the month Mars moves eastwards from Leo into Virgo. Under good conditions on the morning of the 5th, about 1 hour before sunrise, the old Moon, less than 2 days before New, may be seen about 4 degrees to the left of the planet.

Jupiter, is a conspicuous object in the south-eastern quadrant of the sky in the mornings until twilight inhibits observation. By the end of the month the planet is visible low above the eastern horizon by midnight. The Moon is near Jupiter on the mornings of the 2nd and the 30th.

The four Galilean satellites are readily observable with a small telescope or even a good pair of binoculars provided that they are held rigidly.

Saturn continues to be visible as a morning object, magnitude -0.1. It reaches its first stationary point on the 11th, in the constellation of Orion, just south of the Taurus-Gemini border, some 15 degrees north of Betelgeuse. On the morning of the 26th the gibbous Moon passes 2 degrees north of Saturn.

THE MOON

Day	RA	Dec.	Hor. par.	Semi-diam	Sun's co-long.	PA of Bright Limb	Phase	Age	Rise 52°	Rise 56°	Transit	Set 52°	Set 56°
	h m	°	'	'	°	°	%	d	h m	h m	h m	h m	h m
1	7 43	+24.8	57.7	15.7	203	101	37	23.9	23 51	23 26	7 22	15 55	16 21
2	8 42	+22.6	58.6	16.0	215	107	26	24.9	—	—	8 18	16 29	16 49
3	9 40	+19.0	59.6	16.2	227	113	17	25.9	1 15	0 56	9 15	16 55	17 09
4	10 37	+14.2	60.4	16.5	240	119	9	26.9	2 43	2 30	10 09	17 16	17 24
5	11 33	+ 8.3	61.0	16.6	252	126	4	27.9	4 12	4 06	11 03	17 35	17 37
6	12 29	+ 1.9	61.4	16.7	264	147	1	28.9	5 42	5 42	11 56	17 52	17 50
7	13 24	− 4.7	61.4	16.7	276	265	1	0.5	7 13	7 19	12 50	18 11	18 03
8	14 20	−10.9	61.1	16.6	289	282	4	1.5	8 44	8 56	13 44	18 32	18 18
9	15 17	−16.5	60.5	16.5	301	283	9	2.5	10 13	10 32	14 41	18 58	18 38
10	16 16	−20.9	59.7	16.3	313	280	17	3.5	11 39	12 04	15 38	19 31	19 05
11	17 16	−23.9	58.7	16.0	325	275	27	4.5	12 56	13 25	16 37	20 15	19 45
12	18 15	−25.4	57.8	15.7	337	269	37	5.5	13 59	14 30	17 34	21 11	20 39
13	19 14	−25.4	56.9	15.5	350	263	48	6.5	14 47	15 16	18 29	22 16	21 47
14	20 10	−24.1	56.1	15.3	2	257	58	7.5	15 22	15 46	19 21	23 26	23 03
15	21 04	−21.5	55.4	15.1	14	252	68	8.5	15 48	16 07	20 09	—	—
16	21 54	−18.1	54.9	15.0	26	247	76	9.5	16 08	16 22	20 54	0 39	0 21
17	22 41	−13.9	54.5	14.8	38	243	84	10.5	16 24	16 34	21 36	1 50	1 38
18	23 26	− 9.2	54.2	14.8	51	240	90	11.5	16 38	16 43	22 17	3 00	2 52
19	0 09	− 4.3	54.0	14.7	63	236	95	12.5	16 51	16 52	22 57	4 09	4 06
20	0 52	+ 0.9	54.0	14.7	75	231	98	13.5	17 04	17 00	23 37	5 17	5 18
21	1 35	+ 5.9	54.0	14.7	87	201	100	14.5	17 17	17 09	—	6 25	6 31
22	2 18	+10.8	54.1	14.7	99	91	100	15.5	17 33	17 20	0 18	7 34	7 46
23	3 04	+15.4	54.3	14.8	111	80	97	16.5	17 51	17 34	1 01	8 45	9 01
24	3 51	+19.3	54.6	14.9	123	79	94	17.5	18 15	17 53	1 46	9 56	10 18
25	4 42	+22.5	55.0	15.0	136	82	88	18.5	18 47	18 19	2 34	11 07	11 33
26	5 35	+24.7	55.4	15.1	148	86	81	19.5	19 29	18 59	3 25	12 12	12 42
27	6 30	+25.7	56.0	15.3	160	92	73	20.5	20 24	19 54	4 18	13 09	13 39
28	7 26	+25.4	56.7	15.4	172	98	63	21.5	21 32	21 05	5 13	13 55	14 22
29	8 24	+23.7	57.5	15.7	184	103	53	22.5	22 50	22 28	6 08	14 30	14 53
30	9 20	+20.6	58.3	15.9	196	109	42	23.5	—	23 58	7 03	14 57	15 14
31	10 16	+16.3	59.1	16.1	209	113	31	24.5	0 13	—	7 56	15 19	15 31

MERCURY

Day	RA	Dec.	Diam.	Phase	Transit	5° high 52°	5° high 56°
	h m	°	''	%	h m	h m	h m
1	12 02	− 1.9	10	3	11 20	6 03	6 08
3	11 57	− 0.7	9	8	11 08	5 45	5 49
5	11 55	+0.3	9	15	10 59	5 30	5 33
7	11 54	+ 1.0	8	23	10 51	5 19	5 22
9	11 57	+ 1.3	8	33	10 46	5 12	5 15
11	12 01	+ 1.3	7	42	10 43	5 10	5 12
13	12 08	+0.9	7	52	10 42	5 11	5 13
15	12 16	+ 0.2	7	61	10 43	5 15	5 18
17	12 26	− 0.6	6	69	10 45	5 21	5 25
19	12 36	− 1.7	6	75	10 48	5 30	5 34
21	12 47	− 2.9	6	81	10 51	5 39	5 45
23	12 59	− 4.2	6	85	10 55	5 50	5 57
25	13 11	− 5.5	5	89	10 59	6 01	6 09
27	13 23	− 6.9	5	92	11 03	6 13	6 22
29	13 35	− 8.2	5	94	11 08	6 25	6 36
31	13 48	− 9.6	5	96	11 12	6 37	6 50

VENUS

Day	RA	Dec.	Diam.	Phase	Transit	5° high 52°	5° high 56°
	h m	°	''	%	h m	h m	h m
1	14 37	− 22.0	43	22	13 58	17 08	16 35
6	14 42	− 22.9	46	17	13 42	16 46	16 11
11	14 44	− 23.3	50	13	13 24	16 24	15 48
16	14 41	− 23.2	54	8	13 01	16 02	15 27
21	14 35	− 22.6	58	5	12 35	15 42	15 09
26	14 26	− 21.4	60	2	12 06	15 24	14 54
31	14 15	− 19.7	62	1	11 36	15 07	14 41

MARS

Day	RA	Dec.	Diam.	Phase	Transit	5° high 52°	5° high 56°
1	11 27	+ 4.7	4	99	10 48	4 57	4 57
6	11 39	+ 3.5	4	99	10 40	4 56	4 56
11	11 51	+ 2.2	4	99	10 32	4 54	4 56
16	12 02	+ 0.9	4	99	10 24	4 53	4 55
21	12 14	− 0.4	4	99	10 16	4 51	4 55
26	12 26	− 1.6	4	98	10 08	4 50	4 55
31	12 37	− 2.9	4	98	10 00	4 49	4 55

SUNRISE AND SUNSET

	London 0°05' 51°30' h m / h m		Bristol 2°35' 51°28' h m / h m		Birmingham 1°55' 52°28' h m / h m		Manchester 2°15' 53°28' h m / h m		Newcastle 1°37' 54°59' h m / h m		Glasgow 4°14' 55°52' h m / h m		Belfast 5°56' 54°35' h m / h m	
1	6 01	17 39	6 11	17 49	6 08	17 45	6 10	17 46	6 08	17 43	6 19	17 53	6 25	18 00
2	6 02	17 36	6 12	17 46	6 10	17 43	6 12	17 44	6 10	17 40	6 21	17 50	6 27	17 58
3	6 04	17 34	6 14	17 44	6 12	17 41	6 14	17 41	6 12	17 38	6 23	17 48	6 29	17 55
4	6 05	17 32	6 15	17 42	6 13	17 38	6 15	17 39	6 14	17 35	6 25	17 45	6 31	17 53
5	6 07	17 30	6 17	17 40	6 15	17 36	6 17	17 37	6 16	17 33	6 27	17 42	6 33	17 50
6	6 09	17 27	6 19	17 37	6 17	17 34	6 19	17 34	6 18	17 30	6 29	17 40	6 35	17 48
7	6 10	17 25	6 20	17 35	6 19	17 32	6 21	17 32	6 20	17 28	6 31	17 37	6 37	17 45
8	6 12	17 23	6 22	17 33	6 20	17 29	6 23	17 30	6 22	17 25	6 33	17 35	6 39	17 43
9	6 14	17 21	6 24	17 31	6 22	17 27	6 24	17 27	6 24	17 23	6 35	17 32	6 41	17 41
10	6 15	17 18	6 25	17 28	6 24	17 25	6 26	17 25	6 26	17 20	6 37	17 30	6 42	17 38
11	6 17	17 16	6 27	17 26	6 26	17 22	6 28	17 22	6 28	17 18	6 39	17 27	6 44	17 36
12	6 19	17 14	6 29	17 24	6 27	17 20	6 30	17 20	6 30	17 15	6 41	17 25	6 46	17 33
13	6 20	17 12	6 30	17 22	6 29	17 18	6 32	17 18	6 31	17 13	6 43	17 22	6 48	17 31
14	6 22	17 10	6 32	17 20	6 31	17 16	6 34	17 16	6 33	17 11	6 45	17 20	6 50	17 28
15	6 24	17 08	6 34	17 18	6 33	17 13	6 35	17 13	6 35	17 08	6 47	17 17	6 52	17 26
16	6 26	17 05	6 35	17 15	6 34	17 11	6 37	17 11	6 37	17 06	6 49	17 15	6 54	17 24
17	6 27	17 03	6 37	17 13	6 36	17 09	6 39	17 09	6 39	17 03	6 52	17 12	6 56	17 21
18	6 29	17 01	6 39	17 11	6 38	17 07	6 41	17 06	6 41	17 01	6 54	17 10	6 58	17 19
19	6 31	16 59	6 41	17 09	6 40	17 05	6 43	17 04	6 43	16 59	6 56	17 07	7 00	17 17
20	6 32	16 57	6 42	17 07	6 42	17 03	6 45	17 02	6 45	16 56	6 58	17 05	7 02	17 14
21	6 34	16 55	6 44	17 05	6 43	17 00	6 47	17 00	6 47	16 54	7 00	17 02	7 04	17 12
22	6 36	16 53	6 46	17 03	6 45	16 58	6 49	16 58	6 49	16 52	7 02	17 00	7 06	17 10
23	6 38	16 51	6 48	17 01	6 47	16 56	6 50	16 55	6 51	16 49	7 04	16 58	7 08	17 08
24	6 39	16 49	6 49	16 59	6 49	16 54	6 52	16 53	6 53	16 47	7 06	16 55	7 10	17 05
25	6 41	16 47	6 51	16 57	6 51	16 52	6 54	16 51	6 55	16 45	7 08	16 53	7 12	17 03
26	6 43	16 45	6 53	16 55	6 52	16 50	6 56	16 49	6 57	16 43	7 10	16 51	7 14	17 01
27	6 45	16 43	6 55	16 53	6 54	16 48	6 58	16 47	6 59	16 40	7 12	16 48	7 16	16 59
28	6 46	16 41	6 56	16 51	6 56	16 46	7 00	16 45	7 01	16 38	7 14	16 46	7 18	16 57
29	6 48	16 39	6 58	16 49	6 58	16 44	7 02	16 43	7 04	16 36	7 17	16 44	7 20	16 54
30	6 50	16 37	7 00	16 47	7 00	16 42	7 04	16 41	7 06	16 34	7 19	16 42	7 22	16 52
31	6 52	16 36	7 02	16 46	7 01	16 40	7 06	16 39	7 08	16 32	7 21	16 39	7 24	16 50

JUPITER

Day	RA		Dec.		Transit		5° high 52°		56°	
	h	m	°	'	h	m	h	m	h	m
1	8	58.9	+17	36	8	20	1	21	1	09
11	9	05.3	+17	11	7	47	0	50	0	39
21	9	10.8	+16	48	7	13	0	18	0	08
31	9	15.5	+16	29	6	38	23	42	23	32

Diameters – equatorial 35″ polar 33″

SATURN

Day	RA		Dec.		Transit		5° high 52°		56°	
	h	m	°	'	h	m	h	m	h	m
1	5	55.6	+22	08	5	17	21	48	21	31
11	5	56.1	+22	07	4	38	21	09	20	52
21	5	55.7	+22	07	3	58	20	29	20	12
31	5	54.6	+22	06	3	18	19	49	19	32

Diameters – equatorial 19″ polar 18″
Rings – major axis 44″ minor axis 19″

URANUS

Day	RA		Dec.		Transit		10° high 52°		56°	
	h	m	°	'	h	m	h	m	h	m
1	21	51.7	−13	47	21	10	0	45	0	21
11	21	50.8	−13	52	20	30	0	04	23	36
21	21	50.1	−13	54	19	50	23	20	22	56
31	21	49.8	−13	56	19	10	22	40	22	16

Diameter 4″

NEPTUNE

Day	RA		Dec.		Transit		10° high 52°		56°	
	h	m	°	'	h	m	h	m	h	m
1	20	42.8	−18	08	20	01	22	58	22	24
11	20	42.5	−18	09	19	22	22	18	21	44
21	20	42.4	−18	10	18	42	21	39	21	04
31	20	42.5	−18	10	18	03	21	00	20	25

Diameter 2″

November 2002

ELEVENTH MONTH, 30 DAYS, *Novem* (nine), ninth month of Roman pre-Julian calendar

1	*Friday*	**All Saints' Day.** Michael Denison b. 1915	305
2	*Saturday*	Queen Marie Antoinette b. 1755. Jenny Lind d. 1887	306
3	*Sunday*	**4th S. before Advent.** First dog launched into space in Sputnik II 1957	307
4	*Monday*	Guido Reni b. 1575. Russian troops invaded Budapest 1956	*week 44 day* 308
5	*Tuesday*	Jacques Tati d. 1982. Battle of Inkerman 1854	309
6	*Wednesday*	RAMADAN begins. Abraham Lincoln elected 16th President of the USA 1860	310
7	*Thursday*	Joan Sutherland b. 1926. Gene Tunney d. 1978	311
8	*Friday*	Bram Stoker b. 1847. Anya Seton d. 1990	312
9	*Saturday*	King Edward VII Saxe-Coburg and Gotha b. 1841. Ramsay Macdonald d. 1937	313
10	*Sunday*	**3rd S. before Advent.** Remembrance Sunday.	314
11	*Monday*	Ned Kelly d. 1880. Armistice Day 1918	*week 45 day* 315
12	*Tuesday*	Auguste Rodin b. 1840. Harry R. Haldeman d. 1993	316
13	*Wednesday*	Dr George Carey b. 1935. King Edward III b. 1312	317
14	*Thursday*	*Prince of Wales b. 1948.* Gottfried Leibniz d. 1716	318
15	*Friday*	Daniel Barenboim b. 1942. Aneurin Bevan b. 1897	319
16	*Saturday*	Burgess Meredith b. 1907. Lucia Popp d. 1993	320
17	*Sunday*	**2nd S. before Advent.** Auguste Rodin d. 1917	321
18	*Monday*	Marcel Proust d. 1922. Consecration of St Peter's Church, Rome 1626	*week 46 day* 322
19	*Tuesday*	Nicolas Poussin d. 1665. Gettysburg Address by Lincoln 1863	323
20	*Wednesday*	*Queen's Wedding Day 1947.* Thomas Chatterton b. 1752	324
21	*Thursday*	Malcolm Williamson b. 1931. Edward Bawden d. 1989	325
22	*Friday*	Sir Peter Hall b. 1930. Mae West d. 1981	326
23	*Saturday*	Michael Gough b. 1917. Louis Malle d. 1995	327
24	*Sunday*	**S. next before Advent.** Georges Clemenceau d. 1929	328
25	*Monday*	Francis Durbridge b. 1912. Upton Sinclair d. 1968	*week 47 day* 329
26	*Tuesday*	Sir Henry Coward b. 1849. John McAdam d. 1836	330
27	*Wednesday*	Alexander Dubcek b. 1921. Eugene O'Neill d. 1953	331
28	*Thursday*	Friedrich Engels b. 1820. Kenneth Connor d. 1993	332
29	*Friday*	Christian Doppler b. 1803. Claudio Monteverdi d. 1643	333
30	*Saturday*	**St Andrew.** CHANUCAH.	334

ASTRONOMICAL PHENOMENA

d	h	
2	20	Mars in conjunction with Moon. Mars 3° S.
4	06	Uranus at stationary point
4	08	Venus in conjunction with Mercury. Venus 6° S.
4	10	Venus in conjunction with Moon. Venus 8° S.
4	10	Mercury in conjunction with Moon. Mercury 2° S.
14	05	Mercury in superior conjunction
21	07	Venus at stationary point
22	12	Sun's longitude 240°♐
22	12	Saturn in conjunction with Moon. Saturn 3° S.
26	10	Jupiter in conjunction with Moon. Jupiter 4° S.

MINIMA OF ALGOL

d	h	d	h	d	h
1	22.1	13	09.3	24	20.6
4	18.9	16	06.1	27	17.4
7	15.7	19	03.0	30	14.2
10	12.5	21	23.8		

CONSTELLATIONS

The following constellations are near the meridian at

	d	h		d	h
October	1	24	November	15	21
October	16	23	December	1	20
November	1	22	December	16	19

Ursa Major (below the Pole), Cepheus, Cassiopeia, Andromeda, Pegasus, Pisces, Aquarius and Cetus

THE MOON

Phases, Apsides and Node	d	h	m
●New Moon	4	20	34
☽ First Quarter	11	20	52
○Full Moon	20	01	34
☾ Last Quarter	27	15	46
Perigee (358,146km)	4	00	40
Apogee (405,823km)	16	11	20

Mean longitude of ascending node on November 1, 70°

THE SUN   S.D 16'.1

Day	Right Ascension	Dec. −	Equation of Time	Rise 52°	Rise 56°	Transit	Set 52°	Set 56°	Sidereal time	Transit of First Point of Aries
	h m s	° ′	m s	h m	h m	h m	h m	h m	h m s	h m s
1	14 24 02	14 18	+16 23	6 54	7 06	11 44	16 32	16 20	2 40 26	21 16 04
2	14 27 57	14 37	+16 25	6 56	7 09	11 44	16 30	16 18	2 44 22	21 12 09
3	14 31 53	14 56	+16 26	6 58	7 11	11 44	16 28	16 16	2 48 19	21 08 13
4	14 35 50	15 15	+16 26	7 00	7 13	11 44	16 27	16 13	2 52 16	21 04 17
5	14 39 47	15 33	+16 25	7 02	7 15	11 44	16 25	16 11	2 56 12	21 00 21
6	14 43 46	15 52	+16 23	7 03	7 17	11 44	16 23	16 09	3 00 09	20 56 25
7	14 47 45	16 10	+16 20	7 05	7 19	11 44	16 21	16 07	3 04 05	20 52 29
8	14 51 45	16 27	+16 17	7 07	7 21	11 44	16 20	16 05	3 08 02	20 48 33
9	14 55 46	16 45	+16 13	7 09	7 23	11 44	16 18	16 03	3 11 58	20 44 37
10	14 59 47	17 02	+16 08	7 11	7 26	11 44	16 17	16 02	3 15 55	20 40 41
11	15 03 50	17 19	+16 02	7 12	7 28	11 44	16 15	16 00	3 19 51	20 36 45
12	15 07 53	17 35	+15 55	7 14	7 30	11 44	16 13	15 58	3 23 48	20 32 49
13	15 11 57	17 51	+15 48	7 16	7 32	11 44	16 12	15 56	3 27 45	20 28 54
14	15 16 02	18 07	+15 39	7 18	7 34	11 44	16 11	15 54	3 31 41	20 24 58
15	15 20 08	18 23	+15 30	7 19	7 36	11 45	16 09	15 52	3 35 38	20 21 02
16	15 24 14	18 38	+15 20	7 21	7 38	11 45	16 08	15 51	3 39 34	20 17 06
17	15 28 22	18 53	+15 09	7 23	7 40	11 45	16 06	15 49	3 43 31	20 13 10
18	15 32 30	19 08	+14 57	7 25	7 42	11 45	16 05	15 48	3 47 27	20 09 14
19	15 36 39	19 22	+14 45	7 26	7 44	11 45	16 04	15 46	3 51 24	20 05 18
20	15 40 49	19 36	+14 31	7 28	7 46	11 46	16 03	15 44	3 55 20	20 01 22
21	15 45 00	19 49	+14 17	7 30	7 48	11 46	16 01	15 43	3 59 17	19 57 26
22	15 49 11	20 03	+14 02	7 31	7 50	11 46	16 00	15 42	4 03 14	19 53 30
23	15 53 24	20 15	+13 47	7 33	7 52	11 46	15 59	15 40	4 07 10	19 49 34
24	15 57 37	20 28	+13 30	7 35	7 54	11 47	15 58	15 39	4 11 07	19 45 39
25	16 01 51	20 40	+13 13	7 36	7 56	11 47	15 57	15 38	4 15 03	19 41 43
26	16 06 05	20 52	+12 54	7 38	7 58	11 47	15 56	15 36	4 19 00	19 37 47
27	16 10 21	21 03	+12 36	7 39	7 59	11 48	15 55	15 35	4 22 56	19 33 51
28	16 14 37	21 14	+12 16	7 41	8 01	11 48	15 55	15 34	4 26 53	19 29 55
29	16 18 54	21 24	+11 55	7 42	8 03	11 48	15 54	15 33	4 30 50	19 25 59
30	16 23 12	21 35	+11 34	7 44	8 05	11 49	15 53	15 32	4 34 46	19 22 03

DURATION OF TWILIGHT (in minutes)

Latitude	52°	56°	52°	56°	52°	56°	52°	56°
	1 November		11 November		21 November		30 November	
Civil	36	40	37	41	38	43	40	45
Nautical	75	84	78	87	80	90	82	93
Astronomical	115	127	117	130	120	134	123	138

THE NIGHT SKY

Mercury passes through superior conjunction on the 14th and thus remains too close to the Sun for observation throughout the month.

Venus, magnitude -4.4, becomes visible as a morning object after the first week of the month. It is then visible above the south-eastern horizon before dawn. Venus is now moving rapidly away from the Sun and by the end of the month can be detected low above the horizon nearly three hours before sunrise.

Mars is still a morning object, magnitude +1.8, moving steadily eastwards in the constellation of Virgo, passing 3 degrees north of Spica on the 20th. The old crescent Moon will be seen near Mars on the mornings of the 2nd and 3rd.

Jupiter, magnitude -2.2, continues to be visible as a conspicuous morning object, though now visible well before midnight. At the very beginning of the month the planet moves eastwards from Cancer into Leo. The gibbous Moon will be near Jupiter on the morning of the 26th.

Saturn is now visible for the greater part of the night as it approaches opposition next month, magnitude -0.3. The gibbous Moon is near the planet on the 22nd and 23rd. The rings of Saturn present a beautiful spectacle to the observer with a small telescope. The Earth passed through the ring plane twice in 1995 and since then the rings have been slowly opening up: the diameter of the minor axis is now 20 arcseconds, marginally greater than the polar diameter of the planet itself. The rings will not be at their maximum opening until early next year.

Meteors. The Leonid meteor shower, associated with Comet Tempel-Tuttle, does not usually provide a very noticeable display to the casual observer, but on rare occasions spectacular displays of short duration have been observed. There is a possibility of such a display in the early morning hours of the 18th, though the gibbous Moon will create interference.

THE MOON

Day	RA h m	Dec. °	Hor. par. '	Semi-diam '	Sun's co-long. °	PA of Bright Limb °	Phase %	Age d	Rise 52° h m	Rise 56° h m	Transit h m	Set 52° h m	Set 56° h m
1	11 10	+10.9	59.9	16.3	221	117	21	25.5	1 39	1 30	8 48	15 38	15 44
2	12 04	+ 4.9	60.6	16.5	233	119	12	26.5	3 07	3 04	9 40	15 55	15 55
3	12 58	- 1.6	61.1	16.6	245	121	5	27.5	4 36	4 38	10 32	16 12	16 07
4	13 54	- 8.1	61.2	16.7	257	126	1	28.5	6 06	6 15	11 26	16 31	16 21
5	14 50	-14.1	61.1	16.6	270	240	0	0.1	7 38	7 53	12 22	16 55	16 37
6	15 49	-19.2	60.6	16.5	282	279	2	1.1	9 08	9 31	13 21	17 24	17 01
7	16 50	-23.0	59.9	16.3	294	278	7	2.1	10 33	11 01	14 21	18 04	17 35
8	17 52	-25.2	59.0	16.1	306	273	13	3.1	11 46	12 17	15 21	18 56	18 24
9	18 54	-25.8	58.0	15.8	318	267	22	4.1	12 42	13 13	16 19	19 59	19 29
10	19 53	-24.8	57.1	15.6	331	261	31	5.1	13 24	13 50	17 14	21 11	20 45
11	20 48	-22.6	56.2	15.3	343	255	41	6.1	13 53	14 14	18 05	22 24	22 04
12	21 40	-19.3	55.5	15.1	355	251	51	7.1	14 15	14 31	18 51	23 37	23 23
13	22 28	-15.2	54.9	15.0	7	247	61	8.1	14 33	14 43	19 35	—	—
14	23 14	-10.6	54.5	14.8	19	245	70	9.1	14 47	14 53	20 16	0 48	0 39
15	23 58	- 5.7	54.2	14.8	31	243	78	10.1	15 00	15 02	20 56	1 57	1 53
16	0 40	- 0.6	54.0	14.7	44	242	86	11.1	15 12	15 10	21 36	3 06	3 06
17	1 23	+ 4.5	54.0	14.7	56	242	92	12.1	15 25	15 19	22 16	4 14	4 18
18	2 07	+ 9.5	54.2	14.8	68	243	96	13.1	15 40	15 29	22 58	5 23	5 32
19	2 52	+14.2	54.4	14.8	80	243	99	14.1	15 57	15 41	23 43	6 34	6 48
20	3 39	+18.4	54.7	14.9	92	201	100	15.1	16 19	15 58	—	7 46	8 06
21	4 29	+21.8	55.0	15.0	104	81	99	16.1	16 48	16 22	0 31	8 57	9 23
22	5 22	+24.3	55.4	15.1	116	83	96	17.1	17 27	16 57	1 21	10 05	10 35
23	6 17	+25.6	55.9	15.2	129	88	92	18.1	18 18	17 47	2 14	1 06	1 37
24	7 13	+25.6	56.4	15.4	141	94	85	19.1	19 22	18 53	3 09	11 55	12 24
25	8 10	+24.3	56.9	15.5	153	100	77	20.1	20 36	20 13	4 04	12 33	12 58
26	9 06	+21.6	57.5	15.7	165	105	68	21.1	21 56	21 38	4 58	13 02	13 21
27	10 01	+17.6	58.1	15.8	177	110	57	22.1	23 19	23 07	5 50	13 25	13 38
28	10 54	+12.7	58.8	16.0	189	113	46	23.1	—	—	6 41	13 44	13 52
29	11 46	+ 7.0	59.4	16.2	202	115	35	24.1	0 43	0 37	7 31	14 00	14 03
30	12 38	+ 0.9	59.9	16.3	214	116	25	25.1	2 07	2 07	8 20	14 16	14 14

MERCURY

Day	RA h m	Dec. °	Diam. "	Phase %	Transit h m	5° high 52° h m	5° high 56° h m
1	13 54	-10.3	5	97	11 14	6 43	6 57
3	14 06	-11.6	5	98	11 19	6 56	7 11
5	14 19	-12.9	5	99	11 24	7 08	7 25
7	14 31	-14.2	5	99	11 28	7 21	7 39
9	14 44	-15.4	5	100	11 33	7 34	7 53
11	14 56	-16.5	5	100	11 38	7 46	8 07
13	15 09	-17.7	5	100	11 43	7 59	8 22
15	15 22	-18.7	5	100	11 47	8 11	8 36
17	15 35	-19.7	5	100	11 52	8 23	8 50
19	15 48	-20.6	5	100	11 57	8 35	9 05
21	16 01	-21.5	5	100	12 03	15 17	14 45
23	16 14	-22.3	5	99	12 08	15 16	14 42
25	16 27	-23.0	5	99	12 13	15 15	14 39
27	16 40	-23.6	5	98	12 19	15 15	14 37
29	16 53	-24.2	5	98	12 24	15 15	14 35
31	17 07	-24.6	5	97	12 30	15 17	14 35

VENUS

Day	RA h m	Dec. °	Diam. "	Phase %	Transit h m	5° high 52° h m	5° high 56° h m
1	14 13	-19.3	62	1	11 30	7 57	8 22
6	14 03	-17.3	61	1	11 00	7 13	7 35
11	13 56	-15.3	59	4	10 33	6 33	6 51
16	13 51	-13.5	55	8	10 10	5 58	6 15
21	13 51	-12.2	52	12	9 50	5 30	5 45
26	13 54	-11.4	48	17	9 34	5 09	5 23
31	14 00	-11.0	44	21	9 21	4 54	5 08

MARS

Day	RA h m	Dec. °	Diam. "	Phase %	Transit h m	5° high 52° h m	5° high 56° h m
1	12 40	- 3.2	4	98	9 59	4 48	4 54
6	12 52	- 4.4	4	98	9 51	4 47	4 54
11	13 03	- 5.7	4	98	9 43	4 46	4 54
16	13 15	- 6.9	4	97	9 35	4 45	4 55
21	13 27	- 8.1	4	97	9 27	4 44	4 55
26	13 39	- 9.3	4	97	9 20	4 43	4 55
31	13 51	-10.5	4	96	9 12	4 42	4 55

SUNRISE AND SUNSET

	London 0°05' 51°30' h m h m		Bristol 2°35' 51°28' h m h m		Birmingham 1°55' 52°28' h m h m		Manchester 2°15' 53°28' h m h m		Newcastle 1°37' 54°59' h m h m		Glasgow 4°14' 55°52' h m h m		Belfast 5°56' 54°35' h m h m	
1	6 53	16 34	7 03	16 44	7 03	16 38	7 08	16 37	7 10	16 30	7 23	16 37	7 26	16 48
2	6 55	16 32	7 05	16 42	7 05	16 37	7 09	16 35	7 12	16 28	7 25	16 35	7 28	16 46
3	6 57	16 30	7 07	16 40	7 07	16 35	7 11	16 33	7 14	16 26	7 27	16 33	7 30	16 44
4	6 59	16 28	7 09	16 38	7 09	16 33	7 13	16 31	7 16	16 24	7 29	16 31	7 32	16 42
5	7 00	16 27	7 10	16 37	7 11	16 31	7 15	16 29	7 18	16 22	7 31	16 29	7 34	16 40
6	7 02	16 25	7 12	16 35	7 13	16 29	7 17	16 27	7 20	16 20	7 34	16 27	7 36	16 38
7	7 04	16 23	7 14	16 33	7 14	16 28	7 19	16 26	7 22	16 18	7 36	16 25	7 38	16 36
8	7 06	16 22	7 16	16 32	7 16	16 26	7 21	16 24	7 24	16 16	7 38	16 23	7 40	16 35
9	7 08	16 20	7 17	16 30	7 18	16 24	7 23	16 22	7 26	16 14	7 40	16 21	7 42	16 33
10	7 09	16 19	7 19	16 29	7 20	16 23	7 25	16 20	7 28	16 12	7 42	16 19	7 44	16 31
11	7 11	16 17	7 21	16 27	7 22	16 21	7 27	16 19	7 30	16 10	7 44	16 17	7 46	16 29
12	7 13	16 16	7 23	16 26	7 23	16 19	7 29	16 17	7 32	16 09	7 46	16 15	7 48	16 27
13	7 14	16 14	7 24	16 24	7 25	16 18	7 30	16 16	7 34	16 07	7 48	16 13	7 50	16 26
14	7 16	16 13	7 26	16 23	7 27	16 16	7 32	16 14	7 36	16 05	7 50	16 12	7 52	16 24
15	7 18	16 11	7 28	16 21	7 29	16 15	7 34	16 12	7 38	16 04	7 52	16 10	7 53	16 23
16	7 20	16 10	7 30	16 20	7 31	16 14	7 36	16 11	7 40	16 02	7 54	16 08	7 55	16 21
17	7 21	16 09	7 31	16 19	7 32	16 12	7 38	16 09	7 42	16 00	7 56	16 07	7 57	16 19
18	7 23	16 07	7 33	16 18	7 34	16 11	7 40	16 08	7 44	15 59	7 58	16 05	7 59	16 18
19	7 25	16 06	7 35	16 16	7 36	16 10	7 41	16 07	7 46	15 57	8 00	16 04	8 01	16 16
20	7 26	16 05	7 36	16 15	7 38	16 08	7 43	16 05	7 48	15 56	8 02	16 02	8 03	16 15
21	7 28	16 04	7 38	16 14	7 39	16 07	7 45	16 04	7 50	15 55	8 04	16 01	8 05	16 14
22	7 30	16 03	7 39	16 13	7 41	16 06	7 47	16 03	7 51	15 53	8 06	15 59	8 07	16 12
23	7 31	16 02	7 41	16 12	7 43	16 05	7 48	16 02	7 53	15 52	8 08	15 58	8 09	16 11
24	7 33	16 01	7 43	16 11	7 44	16 04	7 50	16 01	7 55	15 51	8 10	15 56	8 10	16 10
25	7 34	16 00	7 44	16 10	7 46	16 03	7 52	16 00	7 57	15 49	8 12	15 55	8 12	16 09
26	7 36	15 59	7 46	16 09	7 48	16 02	7 54	15 59	7 59	15 48	8 14	15 54	8 14	16 08
27	7 37	15 58	7 47	16 08	7 49	16 01	7 55	15 58	8 00	15 47	8 16	15 53	8 16	16 07
28	7 39	15 57	7 49	16 07	7 51	16 00	7 57	15 57	8 02	15 46	8 17	15 52	8 17	16 06
29	7 40	15 56	7 50	16 07	7 52	15 59	7 58	15 56	8 04	15 45	8 19	15 51	8 19	16 05
30	7 42	15 56	7 52	16 06	7 54	15 58	8 00	15 55	8 05	15 44	8 21	15 50	8 21	16 04

JUPITER

Day	RA		Dec.		Transit		5° high			
							52°		56°	
	h	m	°	'	h	m	h	m	h	m
1	9	15.9	+16	28	6	34	23	39	23	28
11	9	19.4	+16	14	5	59	23	04	22	54
21	9	21.8	+16	05	5	22	22	28	22	18
31	9	22.9	+16	02	4	43	21	50	21	40

Diameters - equatorial 39" polar 36"

SATURN

Day	RA		Dec.		Transit		5° high			
							52°		56°	
	h	m	°	'	h	m	h	m	h	m
1	5	54.4	+22	06	3	13	19	44	19	28
11	5	52.5	+22	05	2	32	19	03	18	47
21	5	49.9	+22	05	1	50	18	21	18	05
31	5	46.8	+22	04	1	08	17	39	17	22

Diameters - equatorial 20" polar 18"
Rings- major axis 46" minor axis 20"

URANUS

Day	RA		Dec.		Transit		10° high			
							52°		56°	
	h	m	°	'	h	m	h	m	h	m
1	21	49.8	–13	56	19	06	22	36	22	12
11	21	49.9	–13	55	18	27	21	57	21	33
21	21	50.3	–13	53	17	48	21	18	20	54
31	21	51.0	–13	49	17	10	20	40	20	16

Diameter 4"

NEPTUNE

Day	RA		Dec.		Transit		10° high			
							52°		56°	
	h	m	°	'	h	m	h	m	h	m
1	20	42.6	–18	09	17	59	20	56	20	21
11	20	42.9	–18	08	17	20	20	17	19	43
21	20	43.5	–18	06	16	42	19	39	19	04
31	20	44.3	–18	03	16	03	19	00	18	26

Diameter 2"

December 2002

TWELFTH MONTH, 31 DAYS. *Decem* (ten), tenth month of Roman pre-Julian calendar

1	*Sunday*	**Advent Sunday.** Samuel Courtauld d. 1947	335
2	*Monday*	Georges Seurat b. 1859. Hernan Cortés d. 1547	*week* 48 *day* 336
3	*Tuesday*	Hernando Cortés d. 1894. Battle of Austerlitz 1805	337
4	*Wednesday*	Edith Cavell b. 1865. Luigi Galvani d. 1798	338
5	*Thursday*	Fritz Lang b. 1890. Sir Henry Wotton d. 1639	339
6	*Friday*	George Chisholm d. 1997. Finland declared its independence 1917	340
7	*Saturday*	Ferdinand de Lesseps d. 1894. Thornton Wilder d. 1975	341
8	*Sunday*	**2nd S. of Advent.** Jean Sibelius b. 1865	342
9	*Monday*	Douglas Fairbanks Junior b. 1909. R. A. Butler b. 1902	*week* 49 *day* 343
10	*Tuesday*	Paolo Uccello d. 1475. Nobel Prizes awarded for the first time 1901	344
11	*Wednesday*	Colley Cibber d. 1757. Abdication of Edward VIII and accession of George VI 1936	345
12	*Thursday*	Edward G. Robinson b. 1893. Frank Sinatra b. 1915	346
13	*Friday*	Glen Byam Shaw b. 1904. L. P. Hartley d. 1972	347
14	*Saturday*	Pierre Puvis de Chavannes b. 1824. 1st Earl Baldwin of Bewdley Stanley Baldwin d. 1947	348
15	*Sunday*	**3rd S. of Advent.** Sir George Cayley d. 1857	349
16	*Monday*	Quentin Bell d. 1996. Cromwell becomes Lord Protector 1653	*week* 50 *day* 350
17	*Tuesday*	Professor R. V. Jones d. 1997. First flight by Wright Brothers 1903	351
18	*Wednesday*	Paul Klee b. 1879. Abolition of Slavery in USA 1865	352
19	*Thursday*	Jean Genet b. 1910. Leonid Brezhnev b. 1906	353
20	*Friday*	Artur Rubinstein d. 1982	354
21	*Saturday*	*Michaelmas Law Sittings end.* Mayflower Pilgrims land at Plymouth Rock 1620	355
22	*Sunday*	**4th S. of Advent.** Sir Henry Cotton d. 1987	356
23	*Monday*	Richard Arkwright b. 1732. Thomas Malthus d. 1834	*week* 51 *day* 357
24	*Tuesday*	Saint Ignatius Loyola b. 1491. William Makepeace Thackeray d. 1863	358
25	*Wednesday*	**Christmas Day.** *Bank Holiday in UK.*	359
26	*Thursday*	**St Stephen.** Boxing Day. *Bank Holiday in UK.*	360
27	*Friday*	**St John.** Sergei Esenin d. 1925	361
28	*Saturday*	**Holy Innocents.** Dame Maggie Smith b. 1934	362
29	*Sunday*	**1st S. of Christmas.** Rainer Maria Rilke d. 1926	363
30	*Monday*	L. P. Hartley b. 1895. Irving Lazar d. 1993	*week* 52 *day* 364
31	*Tuesday*	John Denver b. 1943. The farthing ceased to be legal tender 1960	365

ASTRONOMICAL PHENOMENA

d	h	
1	11	Mars in conjunction with Moon. Mars 2° S.
1	15	Venus in conjunction with Moon. Venus 2° S.
4	08	Total eclipse of Sun (see page 66)
4	12	Jupiter at stationary point
5	04	Mercury in conjunction with Moon. Mercury 0°6 S.
7	01	Venus at greatest brilliancy
9	17	Pluto in conjunction
17	17	Saturn at opposition
19	15	Saturn in conjunction with Moon. Saturn 3° S.
22	01	Sun's longitude 270°♐
23	14	Jupiter in conjunction with Moon. Jupiter 4° S.
26	05	Mercury at greatest elongation E.20°
30	01	Mars in conjunction with Moon. Mars 1° S.
30	08	Venus in conjunction with Moon. Venus 2° N.

MINIMA OF ALGOL

d	h	d	h	d	h
3	11.0	14	22.3	26	09.6
6	07.9	17	19.1	29	06.4
9	04.7	20	15.9		
12	01.5	23	12.8		

CONSTELLATIONS

The following constellations are near the meridian at

d	h		d	h
November	1	24	December	16	21
November	15	23	January	1	20
December	1	22	January	16	19

Ursa Major (below the Pole), Ursa Minor (below the Pole), Cassiopeia, Andromeda, Perseus, Triangulum, Aries, Taurus, Cetus and Eridanus

THE MOON

Phases, Apsides and Node	d	h	m
●New Moon	4	07	34
☽ First Quarter	11	15	49
○Full Moon	19	19	10
☾ Last Quarter	27	00	31
Perigee (362,272km)	2	08	43
Apogee (404,950km)	14	03	52
Perigee (367,874km)	30	00	57

Mean longitude of ascending node on December 1, 69°

THE SUN   S.D 16'.1

Day	Right Ascension	Dec.	Equation of Time	Rise 52°	Rise 56°	Transit	Set 52°	Set 56°	Sidereal time	Transit of First Point of Aries
	h m s	° ′	m s	h m	h m	h m	h m	h m	h m s	h m s
1	16 27 30	21 44	+11 13	7 45	8 06	11 49	15 52	15 31	4 38 43	19 18 07
2	16 31 49	21 54	+10 50	7 47	8 08	11 49	15 52	15 30	4 42 39	19 14 11
3	16 36 09	22 02	+10 27	7 48	8 10	11 50	15 51	15 29	4 46 36	19 10 15
4	16 40 29	22 11	+10 03	7 49	8 11	11 50	15 51	15 29	4 50 32	19 06 19
5	16 44 50	22 19	+ 9 39	7 51	8 13	11 51	15 50	15 28	4 54 29	19 02 23
6	16 49 11	22 27	+ 9 14	7 52	8 14	11 51	15 50	15 27	4 58 25	18 58 28
7	16 53 33	22 34	+ 8 49	7 53	8 16	11 51	15 49	15 27	5 02 22	18 54 32
8	16 57 56	22 40	+ 8 23	7 54	8 17	11 52	15 49	15 26	5 06 19	18 50 36
9	17 02 19	22 47	+ 7 56	7 56	8 18	11 52	15 49	15 26	5 10 15	18 46 40
10	17 06 42	22 52	+ 7 29	7 57	8 20	11 53	15 49	15 26	5 14 12	18 42 44
11	17 11 06	22 58	+ 7 02	7 58	8 21	11 53	15 48	15 25	5 18 08	18 38 48
12	17 15 30	23 03	+ 6 35	7 59	8 22	11 54	15 48	15 25	5 22 05	18 34 52
13	17 19 55	23 07	+ 6 07	8 00	8 23	11 54	15 48	15 25	5 26 01	18 30 56
14	17 24 20	23 11	+ 5 38	8 01	8 24	11 55	15 48	15 25	5 29 58	18 27 00
15	17 28 45	23 15	+ 5 10	8 02	8 25	11 55	15 48	15 25	5 33 54	18 23 04
16	17 33 10	23 18	+ 4 41	8 02	8 26	11 56	15 49	15 25	5 37 51	18 19 08
17	17 37 36	23 20	+ 4 12	8 03	8 27	11 56	15 49	15 25	5 41 48	18 15 13
18	17 42 01	23 23	+ 3 43	8 04	8 28	11 57	15 49	15 25	5 45 44	18 11 17
19	17 46 27	23 24	+ 3 13	8 05	8 28	11 57	15 49	15 26	5 49 41	18 07 21
20	17 50 54	23 25	+ 2 44	8 05	8 29	11 58	15 50	15 26	5 53 37	18 03 25
21	17 55 20	23 26	+ 2 14	8 06	8 30	11 58	15 50	15 26	5 57 34	17 59 29
22	17 59 46	23 26	+ 1 44	8 06	8 30	11 59	15 51	15 27	6 01 30	17 55 33
23	18 04 12	23 26	+ 1 15	8 07	8 30	11 59	15 51	15 28	6 05 27	17 51 37
24	18 08 39	23 25	+ 0 45	8 07	8 31	12 00	15 52	15 28	6 09 23	17 47 41
25	18 13 05	23 24	+ 0 15	8 07	8 31	12 00	15 53	15 29	6 13 20	17 43 45
26	18 17 31	23 23	− 0 15	8 08	8 31	12 00	15 53	15 30	6 17 17	17 39 49
27	18 21 58	23 21	− 0 44	8 08	8 32	12 01	15 54	15 30	6 21 13	17 35 53
28	18 26 24	23 18	− 1 14	8 08	8 32	12 01	15 55	15 31	6 25 10	17 31 57
29	18 30 50	23 15	− 1 43	8 08	8 32	12 02	15 56	15 32	6 29 06	17 28 02
30	18 35 15	23 12	− 2 13	8 08	8 32	12 02	15 57	15 33	6 33 03	17 24 06
31	18 39 41	23 08	− 2 42	8 08	8 32	12 03	15 58	15 35	6 36 59	17 20 10

DURATION OF TWILIGHT (in minutes)

Latitude	52°	56°	52°	56°	52°	56°	52°	56°
	1 December		11 December		21 December		31 December	
Civil	40	45	41	47	41	47	41	47
Nautical	82	93	84	96	85	97	84	96
Astronomical	123	138	125	141	126	142	125	141

THE NIGHT SKY

Mercury remains too close to the Sun for most of December. However, for the last week of the month it may be detected low above the south-western horizon around the end of evening civil twilight. During this period its magnitude fades from -0.5 to +0.2.

Venus is a magnificent object in the early mornings, attaining its greatest brilliancy (magnitude -4.7) on the 7th. It completely dominates the south-eastern sky for several hours before sunrise. Venus is only a few degrees east of Mars. The old crescent Moon will be seen approaching Venus on the morning of the 1st and again on the 30th. These dates are favourable for locating Venus in daylight, if the observer keeps in shadow, say 1 hour after sunrise. On the first occasion Venus will be found about 3.6 degrees to the left and below the Moon, while on the second occasion it will be 3 degrees above the Moon.

Mars, magnitude +1.6, continues to be visible for several hours in the south-eastern sky in the early mornings. The old crescent Moon is close to Mars on the mornings of the 1st and 30th.

Jupiter, magnitude -2.4, is still a prominent morning object in the southern sky, but already visible in the east in the late evening. Jupiter reaches its first stationary point on the 4th, commencing its retrograde motion and returning from Leo back into Cancer. The gibbous Moon is near Jupiter on the morning of the 23rd.

Saturn, magnitude -0.5, reaches opposition on the 17th and is therefore visible throughout the hours of darkness. Saturn is moving slowly retrograde in the constellation of Taurus. The Full Moon is near Saturn on the 19th.

Meteors. The maximum of the well-known Geminid meteor shower occurs on the night of the 13th-14th. Conditions are not favourable before about 02h since the bright gibbous Moon will be above the horizon until then.

THE MOON

Day	RA h m	Dec. °	Hor. par. '	Semi-diam '	Sun's co-long. °	PA of Bright Limb °	Phase %	Age d	Rise 52° h m	Rise 56° h m	Transit h m	Set 52° h m	Set 56° h m
1	13 31	− 5.5	60.3	16.4	226	115	15	26.1	3 34	3 39	9 11	14 34	14 26
2	14 25	−11.5	60.5	16.5	238	113	8	27.1	5 02	5 14	10 05	14 54	14 40
3	15 22	−17.0	60.5	16.5	250	109	2	28.1	6 32	6 51	11 01	15 19	14 59
4	16 22	−21.4	60.2	16.4	262	101	0	29.1	8 01	8 26	12 01	15 53	15 27
5	17 24	−24.4	59.6	16.3	275	281	1	0.7	9 22	9 52	13 02	16 39	16 08
6	18 27	−25.7	58.9	16.1	287	273	4	1.7	10 28	11 00	14 03	17 38	17 07
7	19 29	−25.4	58.1	15.8	299	266	9	2.7	11 18	11 47	15 01	18 48	18 20
8	20 27	−23.6	57.2	15.6	311	260	16	3.7	11 54	12 17	15 55	20 04	19 41
9	21 22	−20.6	56.4	15.4	323	255	25	4.7	12 19	12 37	16 44	21 19	21 02
10	22 12	−16.7	55.6	15.2	336	251	34	5.7	12 38	12 51	17 30	22 33	22 21
11	23 00	−12.2	55.0	15.0	348	248	44	6.7	12 54	13 02	18 13	23 43	23 37
12	23 44	− 7.3	54.5	14.9	360	246	53	7.7	13 07	13 11	18 53	—	—
13	0 28	− 2.2	54.3	14.8	12	245	63	8.7	13 20	13 19	19 33	0 52	0 50
14	1 10	+ 3.0	54.1	14.8	24	246	72	9.7	13 33	13 28	20 13	2 00	2 03
15	1 53	+ 8.0	54.2	14.8	36	247	80	10.7	13 46	13 37	20 54	3 09	3 16
16	2 38	+12.8	54.4	14.8	49	249	87	11.7	14 02	13 48	21 38	4 19	4 31
17	3 24	+17.2	54.7	14.9	61	253	93	12.7	14 22	14 03	22 25	5 30	5 48
18	4 13	+20.9	55.1	15.0	73	259	97	13.7	14 49	14 24	23 15	6 43	7 06
19	5 06	+23.7	55.6	15.1	85	270	99	14.7	15 24	14 55	—	7 54	8 22
20	6 01	+25.4	56.1	15.3	97	51	100	15.7	16 12	15 41	0 08	8 58	9 29
21	6 58	+25.8	56.6	15.4	109	84	98	16.7	17 13	16 43	1 03	9 52	10 23
22	7 56	+24.7	57.1	15.5	121	93	95	17.7	18 25	18 00	1 59	10 35	11 01
23	8 53	+22.3	57.5	15.7	133	100	89	18.7	19 45	19 25	2 54	11 07	11 27
24	9 49	+18.6	58.0	15.8	146	106	81	19.7	21 07	20 53	3 47	11 31	11 46
25	10 42	+13.9	58.4	15.9	158	110	72	20.7	22 29	22 22	4 38	11 51	12 00
26	11 34	+ 8.4	58.7	16.0	170	112	62	21.7	23 52	23 50	5 27	12 07	12 12
27	12 25	+ 2.4	59.1	16.1	182	113	50	22.7	—	—	6 16	12 23	12 22
28	13 16	− 3.7	59.3	16.2	194	113	39	23.7	1 15	1 18	7 05	12 39	12 33
29	14 08	− 9.7	59.5	16.2	206	111	28	24.7	2 39	2 49	7 55	12 57	12 46
30	15 02	−15.2	59.6	16.2	219	108	18	25.7	4 06	4 22	8 48	13 19	13 02
31	15 59	−19.9	59.5	16.2	231	102	10	26.7	5 33	5 55	9 45	13 48	13 24

MERCURY

Day	RA h m	Dec. °	Diam. "	Phase %	Transit h m	5° high 52° h m	5° high 56° h m
1	17 07	−24.6	5	97	12 30	15 17	14 35
3	17 20	−25.0	5	96	12 35	15 19	14 35
5	17 34	−25.3	5	95	12 41	15 22	14 36
7	17 47	−25.5	5	94	12 47	15 26	14 39
9	18 01	−25.6	5	92	12 52	15 31	14 43
11	18 15	−25.7	5	91	12 58	15 36	14 49
13	18 28	−25.6	5	88	13 03	15 43	14 57
15	18 41	−25.4	5	86	13 09	15 50	15 05
17	18 54	−25.1	6	83	13 13	15 58	15 15
19	19 06	−24.7	6	80	13 18	16 07	15 25
21	19 18	−24.3	6	76	13 22	16 15	15 36
23	19 29	−23.7	6	71	13 25	16 23	15 46
25	19 39	−23.1	7	65	13 26	16 31	15 56
27	19 48	−22.4	7	58	13 27	16 37	16 04
29	19 55	−21.7	7	50	13 25	16 41	16 10
31	20 00	−21.1	8	41	13 22	16 43	16 13

VENUS

Day	RA h m	Dec. °	Diam. "	Phase %	Transit h m	5° high 52° h m	5° high 56° h m
1	14 00	−11.0	44	21	9 21	4 54	5 08
6	14 10	−11.1	41	26	9 11	4 44	4 58
11	14 21	−11.5	38	30	9 03	4 38	4 53
16	14 35	−12.1	35	34	8 57	4 36	4 51
21	14 50	−13.0	32	37	8 52	4 37	4 53
26	15 07	−14.0	30	41	8 50	4 41	4 58
31	15 25	−15.0	28	44	8 48	4 46	5 04

MARS

Day	RA h m	Dec. °	Diam. "	Phase %	Transit h m	5° high 52° h m	5° high 56° h m
1	13 51	−10.5	4	96	9 12	4 42	4 55
6	14 04	−11.6	4	96	9 05	4 42	4 56
11	14 16	−12.7	4	96	8 57	4 41	4 57
16	14 29	−13.8	4	95	8 50	4 40	4 57
21	14 41	−14.9	4	95	8 43	4 40	4 58
26	14 54	−15.8	4	95	8 36	4 39	4 59
31	15 07	−16.8	5	94	8 29	4 39	5 00

SUNRISE AND SUNSET

	London 0°05′ 51°30′ h m	51°30′ h m	Bristol 2°35′ 51°28′ h m	51°28′ h m	Birmingham 1°55′ 52°28′ h m	52°28′ h m	Manchester 2°15′ 53°28′ h m	53°28′ h m	Newcastle 1°37′ 54°59′ h m	54°59′ h m	Glasgow 4°14′ 55°52′ h m	55°52′ h m	Belfast 5°56′ 54°35′ h m	54°35′ h m
1	7 43	15 55	7 53	16 05	7 55	15 58	8 01	15 54	8 07	15 43	8 23	15 49	8 22	16 03
2	7 45	15 54	7 55	16 05	7 57	15 57	8 03	15 53	8 09	15 43	8 24	15 48	8 24	16 02
3	7 46	15 54	7 56	16 04	7 58	15 57	8 04	15 53	8 10	15 42	8 26	15 47	8 25	16 01
4	7 47	15 53	7 57	16 03	7 59	15 56	8 06	15 52	8 12	15 41	8 27	15 46	8 27	16 01
5	7 49	15 53	7 58	16 03	8 01	15 55	8 07	15 52	8 13	15 41	8 29	15 46	8 28	16 00
6	7 50	15 52	8 00	16 03	8 02	15 55	8 09	15 51	8 15	15 40	8 30	15 45	8 29	16 00
7	7 51	15 52	8 01	16 02	8 03	15 55	8 10	15 51	8 16	15 40	8 32	15 45	8 31	15 59
8	7 52	15 52	8 02	16 02	8 04	15 54	8 11	15 50	8 17	15 39	8 33	15 44	8 32	15 59
9	7 53	15 52	8 03	16 02	8 06	15 54	8 12	15 50	8 18	15 39	8 34	15 44	8 33	15 58
10	7 55	15 51	8 04	16 02	8 07	15 54	8 13	15 50	8 20	15 39	8 36	15 43	8 35	15 58
11	7 56	15 51	8 05	16 01	8 08	15 54	8 15	15 50	8 21	15 38	8 37	15 43	8 36	15 58
12	7 57	15 51	8 06	16 01	8 09	15 54	8 16	15 50	8 22	15 38	8 38	15 43	8 37	15 58
13	7 58	15 51	8 07	16 01	8 10	15 54	8 17	15 49	8 23	15 38	8 39	15 43	8 38	15 58
14	7 58	15 51	8 08	16 01	8 11	15 54	8 18	15 49	8 24	15 38	8 40	15 43	8 39	15 58
15	7 59	15 51	8 09	16 02	8 12	15 54	8 18	15 50	8 25	15 38	8 41	15 43	8 40	15 58
16	8 00	15 52	8 10	16 02	8 12	15 54	8 19	15 50	8 26	15 38	8 42	15 43	8 41	15 58
17	8 01	15 52	8 11	16 02	8 13	15 54	8 20	15 50	8 27	15 38	8 43	15 43	8 41	15 58
18	8 02	15 52	8 11	16 02	8 14	15 54	8 21	15 50	8 27	15 38	8 44	15 43	8 42	15 58
19	8 02	15 52	8 12	16 03	8 15	15 55	8 22	15 50	8 28	15 39	8 44	15 43	8 43	15 59
20	8 03	15 53	8 13	16 03	8 15	15 55	8 22	15 51	8 29	15 39	8 45	15 44	8 44	15 59
21	8 03	15 53	8 13	16 03	8 16	15 55	8 23	15 51	8 29	15 40	8 46	15 44	8 44	15 59
22	8 04	15 54	8 14	16 04	8 16	15 56	8 23	15 52	8 30	15 40	8 46	15 45	8 45	16 00
23	8 04	15 54	8 14	16 04	8 17	15 57	8 24	15 52	8 30	15 41	8 47	15 45	8 45	16 00
24	8 05	15 55	8 15	16 05	8 17	15 57	8 24	15 53	8 31	15 41	8 47	15 46	8 45	16 01
25	8 05	15 56	8 15	16 06	8 18	15 58	8 24	15 54	8 31	15 42	8 47	15 47	8 46	16 02
26	8 05	15 56	8 15	16 06	8 18	15 59	8 25	15 54	8 31	15 43	8 47	15 47	8 46	16 03
27	8 06	15 57	8 15	16 07	8 18	15 59	8 25	15 55	8 31	15 44	8 48	15 48	8 46	16 03
28	8 06	15 58	8 16	16 08	8 18	16 00	8 25	15 56	8 32	15 45	8 48	15 49	8 46	16 04
29	8 06	15 59	8 16	16 09	8 18	16 01	8 25	15 57	8 32	15 45	8 48	15 50	8 46	16 05
30	8 06	16 00	8 16	16 10	8 18	16 02	8 25	15 58	8 32	15 46	8 48	15 51	8 46	16 06
31	8 06	16 01	8 16	16 11	8 18	16 03	8 25	15 59	8 31	15 48	8 48	15 52	8 46	16 07

JUPITER

Day	RA h m	Dec. ° ′	Transit h m	5° high 52° h m	56° h m
1	9 22.9	+16 02	4 43	21 50	21 40
11	9 22.8	+16 05	4 04	21 10	21 00
21	9 21.3	+16 14	3 23	20 28	20 18
31	9 18.7	+16 29	2 41	19 45	19 34

Diameters - equatorial 42″ polar 40″

SATURN

Day	RA h m	Dec. ° ′	Transit h m	5° high 52° h m	56° h m
1	5 46.8	+22 04	1 08	8 33	8 49
11	5 43.4	+22 04	0 25	7 50	8 06
21	5 39.8	+22 03	23 38	7 07	7 23
31	5 36.4	+22 02	22 55	6 24	6 41

Diameters - equatorial 21″ polar 19″
Rings- major axis 47″ minor axis 21″

URANUS

Day	RA h m	Dec. ° ′	Transit h m	10° high 52° h m	56° h m
1	21 51.0	−13 49	17 10	20 40	20 16
11	21 52.0	−13 43	16 31	20 02	19 39
21	21 53.3	−13 36	15 53	19 25	19 02
31	21 54.8	−13 27	15 15	18 49	18 26

Diameter 4″

NEPTUNE

Day	RA h m	Dec. ° ′	Transit h m	10° high 52° h m	56° h m
1	20 44.3	−18 03	16 03	19 00	18 26
11	20 45.4	−17 59	15 25	18 23	17 49
21	20 46.5	−17 55	14 47	17 45	17 12
31	20 47.8	−17 50	14 09	17 08	16 35

Diameter 2″

RISING AND SETTING TIMES

TABLE 1. SEMI-DIURNAL ARCS (HOUR ANGLES AT RISING/SETTING)

Dec.	0°	10°	20°	30°	40°	45°	50°	52°	54°	56°	58°	60°	Dec.
	h m	h m	h m	h m	h m	h m	h m	h m	h m	h m	h m	h m	
0°	6 00	6 00	6 00	6 00	6 00	6 00	6 00	6 00	6 00	6 00	6 00	6 00	0°
1°	6 00	6 01	6 01	6 02	6 03	6 04	6 05	6 05	6 06	6 06	6 06	6 07	1°
2°	6 00	6 01	6 03	6 05	6 07	6 08	6 10	6 10	6 11	6 12	6 13	6 14	2°
3°	6 00	6 02	6 04	6 07	6 10	6 12	6 14	6 15	6 17	6 18	6 19	6 21	3°
4°	6 00	6 03	6 06	6 09	6 13	6 16	6 19	6 21	6 22	6 24	6 26	6 28	4°
5°	6 00	6 04	6 07	6 12	6 17	6 20	6 24	6 26	6 28	6 30	6 32	6 35	5°
6°	6 00	6 04	6 09	6 14	6 20	6 24	6 29	6 31	6 33	6 36	6 39	6 42	6°
7°	6 00	6 05	6 10	6 16	6 24	6 28	6 34	6 36	6 39	6 42	6 45	6 49	7°
8°	6 00	6 06	6 12	6 19	6 27	6 32	6 39	6 41	6 45	6 48	6 52	6 56	8°
9°	6 00	6 06	6 13	6 21	6 31	6 36	6 44	6 47	6 50	6 54	6 59	7 04	9°
10°	6 00	6 07	6 15	6 23	6 34	6 41	6 49	6 52	6 56	7 01	7 06	7 11	10°
11°	6 00	6 08	6 16	6 26	6 38	6 45	6 54	6 58	7 02	7 07	7 12	7 19	11°
12°	6 00	6 09	6 18	6 28	6 41	6 49	6 59	7 03	7 08	7 13	7 20	7 26	12°
13°	6 00	6 09	6 19	6 31	6 45	6 53	7 04	7 09	7 14	7 20	7 27	7 34	13°
14°	6 00	6 10	6 21	6 33	6 48	6 58	7 09	7 14	7 20	7 27	7 34	7 42	14°
15°	6 00	6 11	6 22	6 36	6 52	7 02	7 14	7 20	7 27	7 34	7 42	7 51	15°
16°	6 00	6 12	6 24	6 38	6 56	7 07	7 20	7 26	7 33	7 41	7 49	7 59	16°
17°	6 00	6 12	6 26	6 41	6 59	7 11	7 25	7 32	7 40	7 48	7 57	8 08	17°
18°	6 00	6 13	6 27	6 43	7 03	7 16	7 31	7 38	7 46	7 55	8 05	8 17	18°
19°	6 00	6 14	6 29	6 46	7 07	7 21	7 37	7 45	7 53	8 03	8 14	8 26	19°
20°	6 00	6 15	6 30	6 49	7 11	7 25	7 43	7 51	8 00	8 11	8 22	8 36	20°
21°	6 00	6 16	6 32	6 51	7 15	7 30	7 49	7 58	8 08	8 19	8 32	8 47	21°
22°	6 00	6 16	6 34	6 54	7 19	7 35	7 55	8 05	8 15	8 27	8 41	8 58	22°
23°	6 00	6 17	6 36	6 57	7 23	7 40	8 02	8 12	8 23	8 36	8 51	9 09	23°
24°	6 00	6 18	6 37	7 00	7 28	7 46	8 08	8 19	8 31	8 45	9 02	9 22	24°
25°	6 00	6 19	6 39	7 02	7 32	7 51	8 15	8 27	8 40	8 55	9 13	9 35	25°
26°	6 00	6 20	6 41	7 05	7 37	7 57	8 22	8 35	8 49	9 05	9 25	9 51	26°
27°	6 00	6 21	6 43	7 08	7 41	8 03	8 30	8 43	8 58	9 16	9 39	10 08	27°
28°	6 00	6 22	6 45	7 12	7 46	8 08	8 37	8 52	9 08	9 28	9 53	10 28	28°
29°	6 00	6 22	6 47	7 15	7 51	8 15	8 45	9 01	9 19	9 41	10 10	10 55	29°
30°	6 00	6 23	6 49	7 18	7 56	8 21	8 54	9 11	9 30	9 55	10 30	12 00	30°
35°	6 00	6 28	6 59	7 39	8 24	8 58	9 46	10 15	10 58	12 00	12 00	12 00	35°
40°	6 00	6 34	7 11	7 56	8 59	9 48	12 00	12 00	12 00	12 00	12 00	12 00	40°
45°	6 00	6 41	7 25	8 21	9 48	12 00	12 00	12 00	12 00	12 00	12 00	12 00	45°
50°	6 00	6 49	7 43	8 54	12 00	12 00	12 00	12 00	12 00	12 00	12 00	12 00	50°
55°	6 00	6 58	8 05	9 42	12 00	12 00	12 00	12 00	12 00	12 00	12 00	12 00	55°
60°	6 00	7 11	8 36	12 00	12 00	12 00	12 00	12 00	12 00	12 00	12 00	12 00	60°
65°	6 00	7 29	9 25	12 00	12 00	12 00	12 00	12 00	12 00	12 00	12 00	12 00	65°
70°	6 00	7 56	12 00	12 00	12 00	12 00	12 00	12 00	12 00	12 00	12 00	12 00	70°
75°	6 00	8 45	12 00	12 00	12 00	12 00	12 00	12 00	12 00	12 00	12 00	12 00	75°
80°	6 00	12 00	12 00	12 00	12 00	12 00	12 00	12 00	12 00	12 00	12 00	12 00	80°

TABLE 2. CORRECTION FOR REFRACTION AND SEMI-DIAMETER

	m	m	m	m	m	m	m	m	m	m	m	m	
0°	3	3	4	4	4	5	5	5	6	6	6	7	0°
10°	3	3	4	4	4	5	5	6	6	6	7	7	10°
20°	4	4	4	4	5	5	6	7	7	8	8	9	20°
25°	4	4	4	4	5	6	7	8	8	9	11	13	25°
30°	4	4	4	5	6	7	8	9	11	14	21	—	30°

NB: Regarding Table 1. If latitude and declination are of the same sign, take out the respondent directly. If they are of opposite signs, subtract the respondent from 12h.
Example:

Table 1 gives the complete range of declinations in case any user wishes to calculate semi-diurnal arcs for bodies other than the Sun and Moon.

Lat.	Dec.	Semi-diurnal arc
+52°	+20°	7h 51m
+52°	−20°	4h 09m

SUNRISE AND SUNSET

The local mean time of sunrise or sunset may be found by obtaining the hour angle from Table 1 and applying it to the time of transit. The hour angle is negative for sunrise and positive for sunset. A small correction to the hour angle, which always has the effect of increasing it numerically, is necessary to allow for the Sun's semi-diameter (16′) and for refraction (34′); it is obtained from Table 2. The resulting local mean time may be converted into the standard time of the country by taking the difference between the longitude of the standard meridian of the country and that of the place, adding it to the local mean time if the place is west of the standard meridian, and subtracting it if the place is east.

Example – Required the New Zealand Mean Time (12h fast on GMT) of sunset on May 23 at Auckland, latitude 36° 50′ S. (or minus), longitude 11h 39m E. Taking the declination as +20°.6 (page 33), we find:

		h	m
New Zealand Standard Time		+ 12	00
Longitude		– 11	39
Longitudinal Correction		+ 0	21
Tabular entry for Lat. 30° and Dec. 20°, opposite signs		+ 5	11
Proportional part for 6° 50′ of Lat.		–	15
Proportional part for 0°.6 of Dec.		–	2
Correction (Table 2)		+	5
Hour angle		4	58
Sun transits (page 33)		11	57
Longitudinal correction		+	21
New Zealand Mean Time		17	16

MOONRISE AND MOONSET

It is possible to calculate the times of moonrise and moonset using Table 1, though the method is more complicated because the apparent motion of the Moon is much more rapid and also more variable than that of the Sun.

TABLE 3. LONGITUDE CORRECTION

X A h	40m	45m	50m	55m	60m	65m	70m
	m	m	m	m	m	m	m
1	2	2	2	2	3	3	3
2	3	4	4	5	5	5	6
3	5	6	6	7	8	8	9
4	7	8	8	9	10	11	12
5	8	9	10	11	13	14	15
6	10	11	13	14	15	16	18
7	12	13	15	16	18	19	20
8	13	15	17	18	20	22	23
9	15	17	19	21	23	24	26
10	17	19	21	23	25	27	29
11	18	21	23	25	28	30	32
12	20	23	25	28	30	33	35
13	22	24	27	30	33	35	38
14	23	26	29	32	35	38	41
15	25	28	31	34	38	41	44
16	27	30	33	37	40	43	47
17	28	32	35	39	43	46	50
18	30	34	38	41	45	49	53
19	32	36	40	44	48	51	55
20	33	38	42	46	50	54	58
21	35	39	44	48	53	57	61
22	37	41	46	50	55	60	64
23	38	43	48	53	58	62	67
24	40	45	50	55	60	65	70

The parallax of the Moon, about 57′, is near to the sum of the semi-diameter and refraction but has the opposite effect on these times. It is thus convenient to neglect all three quantities in the method outlined below.

Notation

ϕ	= latitude of observer
λ	= longitude of observer (measured positively towards the west)
T_{-1}	= time of transit of Moon on previous day
T_0	= time of transit of Moon on day in question
T_1	= time of transit of Moon on following day
δ_0	= approximate declination of Moon
δ_R	= declination of Moon at moonrise
δ_S	= declination of Moon at moonset
h_0	= approximate hour angle of Moon
h_R	= hour angle of Moon at moonrise
h_S	= hour angle of Moon at moonset
t_R	= time of moonrise
t_S	= time of moonset

Method

1. With arguments ϕ, δ_0 enter Table 1 on page 64 to determine h_0 where h_0 is negative for moonrise and positive for moonset.

2. Form approximate times from
$$t_R = T_0 + \lambda + h_0$$
$$t_S = T_0 + \lambda + h_0$$

3. Determine δ_R, δ_S for times t_R, t_S respectively.

4. Re-enter Table 1 on page 64 with
   (*a*) arguments ϕ, δ_R to determine h_R
   (*b*) arguments ϕ, δ_S to determine h_S

5. Form $t_R = T_0 + \lambda + h_R + AX$
   $t_S = T_0 + \lambda + h_S + AX$

   where $A = (\lambda + h)$

   and $X = (T_0 - T_{-1})$ if $(\lambda + h)$ is negative
   $X = (T_1 - T_0)$ if $(\lambda + h)$ is positive

   AX is the respondent in Table 3.

Example – To find the times of moonrise and moonset at Vancouver (ϕ = +49°, λ = +8h 12m) on 2002 March 11. The starting data (page 26) are:

T_{-1}	= 9h 40m
T_0	= 10h 27m
T_1	= 11h 11m
δ_0	= −19°

1. h_0 = 4h 26m
2. Approximate values
   t_R = 11d 10h 27m + 8h 12m + (-4h 26m)
   = 11d 14h 13m
   t_S = 11d 10h 27m + 8h 12m + (+4h 26m)
   = 11d 23h 05m
3. δ_R = −17°.6
   δ_S = −16°.3
4. h_R = −4h 34m
   h_S = +4h 41m
5. t_R = 11d 10h 27m + 8h 12m + (-4h 34m) + 7m
   = 11d 14h 12m
   t_S = 11d 10h 27m + 8h 12m + (+4h 41m) + 23m
   = 11d 23h 43m

To get the LMT of the phenomenon the longitude is subtracted from the GMT thus:

Moonrise = 11d 14h 12m - 8h 12m = 11d 06h 00m
Moonset = 11d 23h 43m - 8h 12m = 11d 15h 31m

ECLIPSES AND OCCULTATIONS 2002

ECLIPSES

During 2002 there will be two eclipses, both of the Sun. (Penumbral eclipses are not mentioned in this section as they are so difficult to observe).

1. An annular eclipse of the sun on June 10-11 is visible as a partial eclipse from western Asia, Indonesia, the Philippine Islands, northern Australia, the Pacific Ocean and most of North America (except the north-east and southern Mexico). The eclipse begins at 20h 52m and ends at 02h 37m. The track of annularity starts in the Celebes Sea, crosses the Pacific Ocean, and then passes just south of Lower California and ends on the west coast of Mexico, south-west of Guadalajara. Annularity begins at 21h 54m and ends at 01h 35m. The maximum duration is 23s.

2. A total eclipse of the Sun on December 4 is visible as a partial eclipse from the south-east Atlantic Ocean, Africa, Madagascar, part of Antarctica, the Indian Ocean, Australia (except the extreme east) and Indonesia. The partial phase begins at 04h 51m and ends at 10h 11m. The track of totality starts in the south-west Atlantic and crosses Angola, Zambia, extreme north-east Namibia, northern Botswana, southern Zimbabwe and extreme north-east of South Africa and Mozambique. It then crosses the southern Indian Ocean before ending in south-eastern Australia. The total phase begins at 05h 50m and ends at 09h 12m. The maximum duration is 2m 04s.

LUNAR OCCULTATIONS

Observations of the times of occultations are made by both amateur and professional astronomers. Such observations are later analysed to yield accurate positions of the Moon; this is one method of determining the difference between ephemeris time and universal time.

Many of the observations made by amateurs are obtained with the use of a stop-watch which is compared with a time-signal immediately after the observation. Thus an accuracy of about one-fifth of a second is obtainable, though the observer's personal equation may amount to one-third or one-half of a second.

The list on page 67 includes most of the occultations visible under favourable conditions in the British Isles. No occultation is included unless the star is at least 10° above the horizon and the Sun sufficiently far below the horizon to permit the star to be seen with the naked eye or with a small telescope. The altitude limit is reduced from 10° to 2° for stars and planets brighter than magnitude 2.0 and such occultations are also predicted in daylight.

The column Phase shows (i) whether a disappearance (D) or reappearance (R) is to be observed; and (ii) whether it is at the dark limb (D) or bright limb (B). The column headed 'El. of Moon' gives the elongation of the Moon from the Sun, in degrees. The elongation increases from 0° at New Moon to 180° at Full Moon and on to 360° (or 0°) at New Moon again. Times and position angles (P), reckoned from the north point in the direction north, east, south, west, are given for Greenwich (lat. 51° 30', long. 0°) and Edinburgh (lat. 56° 00', long. 3° 12' west).

The coefficients a and b are the variations in the GMT for each degree of longitude (positive to the west) and latitude (positive to the north) respectively; they enable approximate times (to within about 1m generally) to be found for any point in the British Isles. If the point of observation is $\Delta\lambda$ degrees west and $\Delta\phi$ degrees north, the approximate time is found by adding $a.\Delta\lambda + b.\Delta\phi$ to the given GMT.

Example: the disappearance of ZC5 on October 18 at Coventry, found from both Greenwich and Edinburgh.

	Greenwich	Edinburgh
	°	°
Longitude	0.0	+3.2
Long. of Coventry	+1.5	+1.5
$\Delta\lambda$	+1.5	−1.7
Latitude	+51.5	+56.0
Lat. of Coventry	+52.4	+52.4
$\Delta\phi$	+0.9	−3.6

	h m	h m
GMT	21 06.1	21 02.2
$a.\Delta\lambda$	− 3.6	+ 2.7
$b.\Delta\phi$	+ 0.2	− 2.9
	21 02.7	21 02.0

If the occultation is given for one station but not the other, the reason for the suppression is given by the following code:

N = star not occulted
A = star's altitude less than 10° (2° for bright stars and planets)
S = Sun not sufficiently below the horizon
G = occultation is of very short duration

In some cases the coefficients a and b are not given; this is because the occultation is so short that prediction for other places by means of these coefficients would not be reliable.

LUNAR OCCULTATIONS 2002

		ZCNo.	Mag.	Phase	El. of Moon	GREENWICH UT	a	b	P	EDINBURGH UT	a	b	P
						h m	m	m	°	h m	m	m	°
January	17	3396	7.9	D.D.	46	17 32.9	−1.2	−0.7	73	17 27.2	−0.9	−0.3	60
	21	303	6.6	D.D.	90	18 31.9	−0.8	+1.9	24	18 40.5	−0.2	+2.9	4
	21	322	5.7	D.D.	92	23 00.1	−0.4	+1.0	21	23 09.3	G		351
	24	691	6.6	D.D.	125	18 28.8	−1.5	+0.7	95	18 29.4	−1.1	+1.2	81
	25	828	6.5	D.D.	137	17 20.0	−0.3	+2.2	49	17 30.2	−0.1	+2.5	35
	25	861	6.5	D.D.	140	23 20.4	−1.1	−2.6	128	23 07.4	−1.2	−1.6	111
	31	1702	4.2	R.D.	222	22 23.8	−0.4	+1.3	276	22 27.7	−0.3	+1.0	290
February	21	766	6.0	D.D.	105	17 44.5	−1.6	+0.2	102	S			
	21	784	6.2	D.D.	107	22 12.6	−1.2	+0.1	53	22 10.7	−1.2	+0.9	37
	21	792	5.1	D.D.	108	24 01.5	−0.2	−2.1	112	23 51.6	−0.4	−1.9	102
	22	923	6.9	D.D.	117	18 09.5	−1.1	+1.6	68	18 14.6	−0.8	+2.1	52
	22	956	6.3	D.D.	120	23 32.8	−0.9	−0.9	77	23 26.1	−1.0	−0.6	66
March	2	1921	5.9	R.D.	220	4 49.5	−1.1	−1.3	294	4 40.6	−1.0	−1.2	296
	2	1924	5.8	R.D.	221	5 34.7	−1.0	−1.4	282	5 25.4	−1.0	−1.3	284
	17	352	7.3	D.D.	41	19 15.8	−0.6	0.0	43	19 15.3	−0.5	+0.6	26
	19	593	5.8	D.D.	63	19 56.1	G		160	19 28.6	−0.9	−3.2	124
	21	887	7.1	D.D.	87	21 08.1	−0.7	−2.4	121	20 56.0	−0.8	−1.9	109
	22	1041	8.0	D.D.	99	20 01.8	−1.6	+0.7	58	20 02.4	−1.5	+1.9	41
	22	1052	6.8	D.D.	101	23 12.8	−1.0	−0.3	50	23 08.9	−1.3	+0.3	39
April	16	Saturn	0.2	D.D.	46	21 00.2	G		147	20 46.6	+0.2	−3.0	131
	16	Saturn	0.2	R B.	46	21 26.0	G		200	21 26.0	−0.4	−0.1	214
	18	1019	6.7	D.D.	70	22 59.2	G		25	N			
	22	1535	7.1	D.D.	121	20 59.1	−1.7	−0.2	86	20 54.3	−1.6	+0.3	77
	23	1659	6.8	D.D.	135	21 46.3	−1.8	0.0	83	21 41.7	−1.7	+0.4	75
May	14	Saturn	0.1	D.D.	21	6 44.4	G		161	6 41.7	G		137
	14	Saturn	0.1	R.D.	21	6 47.1	G		167	7 06.2	G		191
June	19	1941	4.8	D.D.	115	21 56.5	G		196	21 44.8	G		192
	22	2337	6.4	D.D.	154	21 30.5	−0.9	−0.5	147	S	G		22
July	20	2434	5.6	D.D.	137	21 07.0	G		31	21 08.1	G		22
	28	3536	4.7	R.D.	233	23 53.5	−1.0	+1.4	288	23 57.1	−0.9	+1.5	294
September	13	2500	3.4	D.D.	91	19 09.4	−1.5	−1.0	128	19 01.2	−1.3	−0.7	125
	14	2657	6.7	D.D.	103	19 21.2	−1.6	−0.1	69	A			
	18	3227	6.4	D.D.	150	22 22.4	−1.2	+0.6	44	22 22.0	−0.9	+0.7	35
	19	3349	4.2	D.D.	161	22 28.7	−1.1	+1.1	39	22 30.4	−0.9	+1.1	30
	23	249	4.7	R.D.	205	20 25.7	G		169	20 39.3	G		180
	24	354	5.5	R.D.	216	20 47.9	−0.2	+1.7	268	20 55.1	−0.2	+1.8	273
October	12	2750	2.1	D.D.	83	15 21.5	−1.9	+2.0	39	A			
	12	2750	2.1	R.B.	83	16 06.0	−1.0	−0.2	327	A			
	15	3178	6.2	D.D.	119	18 05.6	−1.2	+1.6	33	A			
	18	3536	4.7	D.D.	152	18 36.9	−0.8	+1.9	62	18 43.2	−0.7	+1.9	58
	18	5	4.7	D.D.	153	21 06.1	−2.4	+0.2	109	21 02.2	−1.6	+0.8	97
November	9	2862	8.0	D.D.	65	17 20.7	G		19	A			
	11	3141	6.0	D.D.	88	17 15.9	−1.8	+0.4	98	17 13.0	−1.4	+0.6	92
	12	3276	7.4	D.D.	101	19 24.1	−1.1	+0.6	42	19 23.7	−0.8	+0.6	32
	13	3396	7.9	D.D.	112	20 52.6	−0.1	+1.7	6	DB			
	24	1117	5.1	R.D.	228	5 25.3	−1.2	−1.4	280	5 15.3	−1.0	−1.5	290
December	8	3087	7.7	D.D.	57	17 52.0	−1.4	−1.0	91	A			
	10	3343	5.8	D.D.	80	17 33.0	−1.0	+0.9	36	17 34.5	−0.7	+1.0	26
	11	3480	7.3	D.D.	92	19 36.2	−0.8	+0.7	36	19 37.7	−0.5	+0.9	21
	11	3484	6.8	D.D.	92	20 57.5	−1.2	−1.0	80	20 50.6	−0.9	−0.6	65
	13	150	6.2	D.D.	114	20 12.6	−2.9	−2.0	115	20 01.2	−1.8	−0.3	94
	21	1170	3.7	R.D.	204	18 36.5	+0.2	+1.0	285	18 41.6	+0.1	+1.0	296
	26	1702	4.2	R.D.	260	5 53.3	−0.5	−2.1	344	5 42.4	−0.3	−2.2	351

MEAN PLACES OF STARS 2002.5

Name	Mag.	RA h m	Dec. ° '	Spectrum
α And *Alpheratz*	2.1	0 08.5	+29 06	A0p
β Cassiopeiae *Caph*	2.3	0 09.3	+59 10	F5
γ Pegasi *Algenib*	2.8	0 13.4	+15 12	B2
β Mensae	2.9	0 25.9	−77 14	G0
α Phoenicis	2.4	0 26.4	−42 18	K0
α Cassiopeiae *Schedar*	2.2	0 40.7	+56 33	K0
β Ceti *Diphda*	2.0	0 43.7	−17 58	K0
γ Cassiopeiae*	Var.	0 56.9	+60 44	B0p
β Andromedae *Mirach*	2.1	1 09.9	+35 38	M0
δ Cassiopeiae	2.7	1 26.0	+60 15	A5
α Eridani *Achernar*	0.5	1 37.8	−57 13	B5
β Arietis *Sheratan*	2.6	1 54.8	+20 49	A5
γ Andromedae *Almak*	2.3	2 04.1	+42 21	K0
α Arietis *Hamal*	2.0	2 07.3	+23 28	K2
α Ursae Minoris *Polaris*	2.0	2 34.7	+89 17	F8
β Persei *Algol**	Var.	3 08.3	+40 58	B8
α Persei *Mirfak*	1.8	3 24.5	+49 52	F5
η Tauri *Alcyone*	2.9	3 47.6	+24 07	B5p
α Tauri *Aldebaran*	0.9	4 36.1	+16 31	K5
β Orionis *Rigel*	0.1	5 14.7	−8 12	B8p
α Aurigae *Capella*	0.1	5 16.9	+46 00	G0
γ Orionis *Bellatrix*	1.6	5 25.3	+6 21	B2
β Tauri *Elnath*	1.7	5 26.5	+28 37	B8
δ Orionis	2.2	5 32.1	−0 18	B0
α Leporis	2.6	5 32.8	−17 49	F0
ε Orionis	1.7	5 36.3	−1 12	B0
ζ Orionis	1.8	5 40.9	−1 56	B0
κ Orionis	2.1	5 47.9	−9 40	B0
α Orionis *Betelgeuse**	Var.	5 55.3	+7 24	M0
β Aurigae *Menkalinan*	1.9	5 59.7	+44 57	A0p
β CMa *Mirzam*	2.0	6 22.8	−17 57	B1
α Carinae *Canopus*	−0.7	6 24.0	−52 42	F0
γ Geminorum *Alhena*	1.9	6 37.9	+16 24	A0
α Canis Majoris *Sirius*	−1.5	6 45.3	−16 43	A0
ε Canis Majoris	1.5	6 58.7	−28 59	B1
δ Canis Majoris	1.9	7 08.5	−26 24	F8p
α Geminorum *Castor*	1.6	7 34.8	+31 53	A0
α CMi *Procyon*	0.4	7 39.4	+5 13	F5
β Geminorum *Pollux*	1.1	7 45.5	+28 01	K0
ζ Puppis	2.3	8 03.7	−40 01	Od
γ Velorum	1.8	8 09.6	−47 21	Oap
ε Carinae	1.9	8 22.6	−59 31	K0
δ Velorum	2.0	8 44.8	−54 43	A0
λ Velorum *Suhail*	2.2	9 08.1	−43 27	K5
β Carinae	1.7	9 13.2	−69 44	A0
ι Carinae	2.2	9 17.2	−59 17	F0
κ Velorum	2.6	9 22.2	−55 01	B3
α Hydrae *Alphard*	2.0	9 27.7	−8 40	K2
α Leonis *Regulus*	1.3	10 08.5	+11 57	B8
γ Leonis *Algeiba*	1.9	10 20.1	+19 50	K0
β Ursae Majoris *Merak*	2.4	11 02.0	+56 22	A0
α Ursae Majoris *Dubhe*	1.8	11 03.9	+61 44	K0
δ Leonis	2.6	11 14.2	+20 31	A3
β Leonis *Denebola*	2.1	11 49.2	+14 33	A2
γ Ursae Majoris *Phecda*	2.4	11 54.0	+53 41	A0
γ Corvi	2.6	12 15.9	−17 33	B8
α Crucis	1.0	12 26.7	−63 07	B1
γ Crucis	1.6	12 31.3	−57 08	M3
γ Centauri	2.2	12 41.7	−48 58	A0
γ Virginis	2.7	12 41.8	−1 28	F0
β Crucis	1.3	12 47.9	−59 42	B1
ε Ursae Majoris *Alioth*	1.8	12 54.1	+55 57	A0p
α Canum Venaticorum	2.9	12 56.1	+38 18	A0p
ζ Ursae Majoris *Mizar*	2.1	13 24.0	+54 55	A2p
α Virginis *Spica*	1.0	13 25.3	−11 10	B2
ε Centauri	2.6	13 40.0	−53 29	B1
η Ursae Majoris *Alkaid*	1.9	13 47.6	+49 18	B3
β Centauri *Hadar*	0.6	14 04.0	−60 23	B1
θ Centauri	2.1	14 06.8	−36 23	K0
α Bootis *Arcturus*	0.0	14 15.8	+19 10	K0
α Centauri *Rigil Kent*	0.1	14 39.8	−60 51	G0
ε Bootis	2.4	14 45.1	+27 04	K0
β UMi *Kochab*	2.1	14 50.7	+74 09	K5
γ Ursae Minoris	3.1	15 20.7	+71 50	A2
α CrB *Alphecca*	2.2	15 34.8	+26 42	A0
β Trianguli Australis	3.0	15 55.4	−63 26	F0
δ Scorpii	2.3	16 00.5	−22 38	B0
β Scorpii	2.6	16 05.6	−19 49	B1
α Scorpii *Antares*	1.0	16 29.6	−26 26	M0
α Trianguli Australis	1.9	16 48.9	−69 02	K2
ε Scorpii	2.3	16 50.3	−34 18	K0
α Herculis†	Var.	17 14.8	+14 23	M3
λ Scorpii	1.6	17 33.8	−37 06	B2
α Ophiuchi *Rasalhague*	2.1	17 35.1	+12 34	A5
θ Scorpii	1.9	17 37.5	−43 00	F0
κ Scorpii	2.4	17 42.7	−39 02	B2
γ Draconis	2.2	17 56.7	+51 29	K5
ε Sgr Kaus *Australis*	1.9	18 24.3	−34 23	A0
α Lyrae *Vega*	0.0	18 37.0	+38 47	A0
σ Sagittarii	2.0	18 55.4	−26 18	B3
β Cygni *Albireo*	3.1	19 30.8	+27 58	K0
α Aquilae *Altair*	0.8	19 50.9	+8 52	A5
α Capricorni	3.8	20 18.2	−12 32	G5
γ Cygni	2.2	20 22.3	+40 16	F8p
α Pavonis	1.9	20 25.8	−56 44	B3
α Cygni *Deneb*	1.3	20 41.5	+45 17	A2p
α Cephei *Alderamin*	2.4	21 18.6	+62 36	A5
ε Pegasi	2.4	21 44.3	+9 53	K0
δ Capricorni	2.9	21 47.2	−16 07	A5
α Gruis	1.7	22 08.4	−46 57	B5
δ Cephei†	3.7	22 29.3	+58 26	†
β Gruis	2.1	22 42.8	−46 52	M3
α PsA *Fomalhaut*	1.2	22 57.8	−29 37	A3
β Pegasi *Scheat*	2.4	23 03.9	+28 06	M0
α Pegasi *Markab*	2.5	23 04.9	+15 13	A0

*γ Cassiopeiae, 2000 mag. 2.2. β Persei, mag. 2.1 to 3.4.
α Orionis, mag. 0.1 to 1.2.
†α Herculis, mag. 3.1 to 3.9. δ Cephei, mag. 3.7 to 4.4,
spectrum F5 to G0.

The positions of heavenly bodies on the celestial sphere are defined by two co-ordinates, right ascension and declination, which are analogous to longitude and latitude on the surface of the Earth. If we imagine the plane of the terrestrial equator extended indefinitely, it will cut the celestial sphere in a great circle known as the celestial equator. Similarly the plane of the Earth's orbit, when extended, cuts in the great circle called the ecliptic. The two intersections of these circles are known as the First Point of Aries and the First Point of Libra. If from any star a perpendicular be drawn to the celestial equator, the length of this perpendicular is the star's declination. The arc, measured eastwards along the equator from the First Point of Aries to the foot of this perpendicular, is the right ascension. An alternative definition of right ascension is that it is the angle at the celestial pole (where the Earth's axis, if prolonged, would meet the sphere) between the great circles to the First Point of Aries and to the star.

The plane of the Earth's equator has a slow movement, so that our reference system for right ascension and declination is not fixed. The consequent alteration in these quantities from year to year is called precession. In right ascension it is an increase of about 3 seconds a year for equatorial stars, and larger or smaller changes in either direction for stars near the poles, depending on the right ascension of the star. In declination it varies between +20″ and −20″ according to the right ascension of the star.

A star or other body crosses the meridian when the sidereal time is equal to its right ascension. The altitude is then a maximum, and may be deduced by remembering that the altitude of the elevated pole is numerically equal to the latitude, while that of the equator at its intersection with the meridian is equal to the co-latitude, or complement of the latitude.

Thus in London (lat. 51° 30′) the meridian altitude of Sirius is found as follows:

	°	′
Altitude of equator	38	30
Declination south	16	43
Difference	21	47

The altitude of Capella (Dec. +46° 00′) at lower transit is:

	°	′
Altitude of pole	51	30
Polar distance of star	44	00
Difference	7	30

The brightness of a heavenly body is denoted by its magnitude. Omitting the exceptionally bright stars Sirius and Canopus, the twenty brightest stars are of the first magnitude, while the faintest stars visible to the naked eye are of the sixth magnitude. The magnitude scale is a precise one, as a difference of five magnitudes represents a ratio of 100 to 1 in brightness. Typical second magnitude stars are Polaris and the stars in the belt of Orion. The scale is most easily fixed in memory by comparing the stars with Norton's *Star Atlas* (*see* page 71). The stars Sirius and Canopus and the planets Venus and Jupiter are so bright that their magnitudes are expressed by negative numbers. A small telescope will show stars down to the ninth or tenth magnitude, while stars fainter than the twentieth magnitude may be photographed by long exposures with the largest telescopes.

MEAN AND SIDEREAL TIME

Acceleration						Retardation					
h	m	s	m	s	s	h	m	s	m	s	s
1	0	10	0	00	0	1	0	10	0	00	0
2	0	20	3	02	1	2	0	20	3	03	1
3	0	30	9	07	2	3	0	29	9	09	2
4	0	39	15	13	3	4	0	39	15	15	3
5	0	49	21	18	4	5	0	49	21	21	4
6	0	59	27	23	5	6	0	59	27	28	5
7	1	09	33	28	6	7	1	09	33	34	6
8	1	19	39	34	7	8	1	19	39	40	7
9	1	29	45	39	8	9	1	28	45	46	8
10	1	39	51	44	9	10	1	38	51	53	9
11	1	48	57	49	10	11	1	48	57	59	10
12	1	58	60	00		12	1	58	60	00	
13	2	08				13	2	08			
14	2	18				14	2	18			
15	2	28				15	2	27			
16	2	38				16	2	37			
17	2	48				17	2	47			
18	2	57				18	2	57			
19	3	07				19	3	07			
20	3	17				20	3	17			
21	3	27				21	3	26			
22	3	37				22	3	36			
23	3	47				23	3	46			
24	3	57				24	3	56			

The length of a sidereal day in mean time is 23h 56m 04s.09. Hence 1h MT = 1h+9s.86 ST and 1h ST = 1h−9s.83 MT.

To convert an interval of mean time to the corresponding interval of sidereal time, enter the acceleration table with the given mean time (taking the hours and the minutes and seconds separately) and add the acceleration obtained to the given mean time. To convert an interval of sidereal time to the corresponding interval of mean time, take out the retardation for the given sidereal time and subtract.

The columns for the minutes and seconds of the argument are in the form known as critical tables. To use these tables, find in the appropriate left-hand column the two entries between which the given number of minutes and seconds lies; the quantity in the right-hand column between these two entries is the required acceleration or retardation. Thus the acceleration for 11m 26s (which lies between the entries 9m 07s and 15m 13s) is 2s. If the given number of minutes and seconds is a tabular entry, the required acceleration or retardation is the entry in the right-hand column above the given tabular entry, e.g. the retardation for 45m 46s is 7s.

Example – Convert 14h 27m 35s from ST to MT

	h	m	s
Given ST	14	27	35
Retardation for 14h		2	18
Retardation for 27m 35s			5
Corresponding MT	14	25	12

For further explanation, *see* pages 73–74.

ECLIPSES AND SHADOW TRANSITS OF JUPITER'S SATELLITES 2002

GMT			Sat.	Phen.
d	h	m		
JANUARY				
2	19	18	II	Sh.E
4	04	32	I	Sh.I
5	03	23	III	Ec.R
5	04	07	I	Ec.R
5	20	58	IV	Ec.R
5	23	01	I	Sh.I
6	01	16	I	Sh.E
6	05	48	II	Sh.I
6	22	36	I	Ec.R
7	19	44	I	Sh.E
8	02	49	II	Ec.R
9	19	06	II	Sh.I
9	21	55	II	Sh.E
13	00	55	I	Sh.I
13	03	10	I	Sh.E
14	00	31	I	Ec.R
14	04	59	IV	Sh.I
14	19	24	I	Sh.I
14	21	39	I	Sh.E
15	18	17	III	Sh.I
15	18	59	I	Ec.R
15	21	21	III	Sh.E
16	21	43	II	Sh.I
17	00	32	II	Sh.E
18	18	43	II	Ec.R
20	02	50	I	Sh.I
21	02	26	I	Ec.R
21	21	18	I	Sh.I
21	23	33	I	Sh.E
22	20	54	I	Ec.R
22	22	16	III	Sh.I
23	01	21	III	Sh.E
24	00	20	II	Sh.I
24	03	08	II	Sh.E
25	21	19	II	Ec.R
28	04	21	I	Ec.R
28	23	13	I	Sh.I
29	01	28	I	Sh.E
29	22	49	I	Ec.R
30	02	15	III	Sh.I
30	19	57	I	Sh.E
30	23	00	IV	Sh.I
31	02	02	IV	Sh.E
31	02	57	II	Sh.I
FEBRUARY				
1	23	55	II	Ec.R
2	19	26	III	Ec.R
3	19	03	II	Sh.E
5	01	08	I	Sh.I
5	03	23	I	Sh.E
6	00	44	I	Ec.R
6	19	37	I	Sh.I
6	21	52	I	Sh.E
7	19	13	I	Ec.R
9	02	31	II	Ec.R
9	20	18	III	Ec.D
9	23	27	III	Ec.R
10	18	52	II	Sh.I
10	21	40	II	Sh.E
12	03	03	I	Sh.I
13	02	39	I	Ec.R
13	21	32	I	Sh.I
13	23	47	I	Sh.E
14	21	08	I	Ec.R
16	20	13	IV	Sh.E
17	00	18	III	Ec.D
17	21	28	II	Sh.I
18	00	16	II	Sh.E
20	23	27	I	Sh.I
21	01	42	I	Sh.E
21	23	03	I	Ec.R
22	20	10	I	Sh.E
25	00	05	II	Sh.I
25	00	17	IV	Ec.D
26	21	03	II	Ec.R
27	21	24	III	Sh.E
28	01	22	I	Sh.I
MARCH				
1	00	59	I	Ec.R
1	19	51	I	Sh.I
1	22	06	I	Sh.E
2	19	27	I	Ec.R
5	23	40	II	Ec.R
6	22	15	III	Sh.I
7	01	25	III	Sh.E
8	21	44	I	Sh.I
9	00	01	I	Sh.E
9	21	23	I	Ec.R
13	21	48	IV	Ec.R
14	21	23	II	Sh.E
15	23	41	II	Sh.I
16	23	18	I	Ec.R
17	20	25	I	Sh.E
21	21	12	II	Sh.I
21	23	59	II	Sh.E
24	20	06	I	Sh.I
24	20	18	III	Ec.D
24	22	21	I	Sh.E
24	23	33	III	Ec.R
28	23	47	II	Sh.I
30	20	52	II	Ec.R
31	22	01	I	Sh.I
APRIL				
1	21	37	I	Ec.R
6	23	30	II	Ec.R
7	23	09	IV	Sh.I
8	23	32	I	Ec.R
9	20	41	I	Sh.E
11	21	29	III	Sh.E
15	21	04	II	Sh.E
16	22	37	I	Sh.E
18	22	16	III	Sh.I
22	20	52	II	Sh.I
23	22	17	I	Sh.I
24	21	51	I	Ec.R
SEPTEMBER				
16	03	46	I	Sh.E
23	03	23	I	Sh.I
27	03	56	III	Ec.D
OCTOBER				
5	03	18	II	Ec.D
8	04	16	I	Ec.D

GMT			Sat.	Phen.
d	h	m		
9	03	55	I	Sh.E
14	02	55	II	Sh.E
16	03	32	I	Sh.I
21	02	39	II	Sh.I
23	05	25	I	Sh.I
24	02	32	I	Ec.D
25	02	10	I	Sh.E
26	03	52	IV	Sh.E
28	05	14	II	Sh.I
31	04	25	I	Ec.D
NOVEMBER				
1	01	47	I	Sh.I
1	04	03	I	Sh.E
2	03	20	III	Ec.R
6	02	52	II	Sh.E
8	03	40	I	Sh.I
8	05	56	I	Sh.E
9	03	44	III	Ec.D
13	05	25	II	Ec.D
15	02	35	II	Sh.E
15	05	33	I	Sh.I
16	02	41	I	Ec.D
17	02	17	I	Sh.E
20	00	44	IV	Ec.D
20	01	16	III	Sh.E
20	05	31	IV	Ec.R
22	02	18	II	Sh.I
22	05	10	II	Sh.E
23	04	34	I	Ec.D
24	01	54	I	Sh.I
24	04	10	I	Sh.E
27	01	41	III	Sh.I
27	05	13	III	Sh.E
29	04	53	II	Sh.I
30	23	49	II	Ec.D
DECEMBER				
1	03	47	I	Sh.I
1	06	03	I	Sh.E
2	00	56	I	Ec.D
3	00	32	I	Sh.E
4	05	38	III	Sh.I
6	23	33	IV	Ec.R
7	23	14	III	Ec.R
8	02	22	II	Ec.D
8	05	40	I	Sh.I
9	02	50	I	Ec.D
9	23	41	II	Sh.E
10	00	09	I	Sh.I
10	02	25	I	Sh.E
14	23	35	III	Ec.D
15	03	12	III	Ec.R
15	04	55	II	Ec.D
15	05	08	IV	Sh.I
16	04	44	I	Ec.D
16	23	23	II	Sh.I
17	02	02	I	Sh.I
17	02	17	II	Sh.E
17	04	18	I	Sh.E
17	23	12	I	Ec.D
18	22	46	I	Sh.E
22	03	33	III	Ec.D
23	06	38	I	Ec.D
24	01	59	II	Sh.I
24	03	55	I	Sh.I
24	04	53	II	Sh.E
24	06	11	I	Sh.E
25	01	06	I	Ec.D
25	22	23	I	Sh.I
26	00	40	I	Sh.E
31	04	35	II	Sh.I
31	05	48	I	Sh.I
31	23	06	IV	Sh.I

Jupiter's satellites transit across the disk from east to west, and pass behind the disk from west to east. The shadows that they cast also transit across the disk. With the exception at times of Satellite IV, the satellites also pass through the shadow of the planet, i.e. they are eclipsed. Just before opposition the satellite disappears in the shadow to the west of the planet and reappears from occultation on the east limb. Immediately after opposition the satellite is occulted at the west limb and reappears from eclipse to the east of the planet. At times approximately two to four months before and after opposition, both phases of eclipses of Satellite III may be seen. When Satellite IV is eclipsed, both phases may be seen.

The times given refer to the centre of the satellite. As the satellite is of considerable size, the immersion and emersion phases are not instantaneous. Even when the satellite enters or leaves the shadow along a radius of the shadow, the phase can last for several minutes. With Satellite IV, grazing phenomena can occur so that the light from the satellite may fade and brighten again without a complete eclipse taking place.

The list of phenomena gives most of the eclipses and shadow transits visible in the British Isles under favourable conditions.

Ec. = Eclipse   R. = Reappearance
Sh. = Shadow transit   I. = Ingress
D. = Disappearance   E. = Egress

EXPLANATION OF ASTRONOMICAL DATA

Positions of the heavenly bodies are given only to the degree of accuracy required by amateur astronomers for setting telescopes, or for plotting on celestial globes or star atlases. Where intermediate positions are required, linear interpolation may be employed.

Definitions of the terms used cannot be given here. They must be sought in astronomical literature and textbooks. Probably the best source for the amateur is Norton's *Star Atlas and Reference Handbook* (Longman, 18th edition, 1989; £26.99), which contains an introduction to observational astronomy, and a series of star maps showing stars visible to the naked eye. Certain more extended ephemerides are available in the British Astronomical Association Handbook, an annual popular among amateur astronomers (Secretary: Burlington House, Piccadilly, London W1J 0DU).

A special feature has been made of the times when the various heavenly bodies are visible in the British Isles. Since two columns, calculated for latitudes 52° and 56°, are devoted to risings and settings, the range 50° to 58° can be covered by interpolation and extrapolation. The times given in these columns are Greenwich Mean Times for the meridian of Greenwich. An observer west of this meridian must add his/her longitude (in time) and vice versa.

In accordance with the usual convention in astronomy, + and − indicate respectively north and south latitudes or declinations.

All data are, unless otherwise stated, for 0h Greenwich Mean Time (GMT), i.e. at the midnight at the beginning of the day named. Allowance must be made for British Summer Time during the period that this is in operation (*see* pages 15 and 75).

PAGE ONE OF EACH MONTH

The calendar for each month is explained on page 15.

Under the heading Astronomical Phenomena will be found particulars of the more important conjunctions of the Sun, Moon and planets with each other, and also the dates of other astronomical phenomena of special interest.

Times of Minima of Algol are approximate times of the middle of the period of diminished light.

The Constellations listed each month are those that are near the meridian at the beginning of the month at 22h local mean time. Allowance must be made for British Summer Time if necessary. The fact that any star crosses the meridian 4m earlier each night or 2h earlier each month may be used, in conjunction with the lists given each month, to find what constellations are favourably placed at any moment. The table preceding the list of constellations may be extended indefinitely at the rate just quoted.

The principal phases of the Moon are the GMTs when the difference between the longitude of the Moon and that of the Sun is 0°, 90°, 180° or 270°. The times of perigee and apogee are those when the Moon is nearest to, and farthest from, the Earth, respectively. The nodes or points of intersection of the Moon's orbit and the ecliptic make a complete retrograde circuit of the ecliptic in about 19 years. From a knowledge of the longitude of the ascending node and the inclination, whose value does not vary much from 5°, the path of the Moon among the stars may be plotted on a celestial globe or star atlas.

PAGE TWO OF EACH MONTH

The Sun's semi-diameter, in arc, is given once a month.

The right ascension and declination (Dec.) is that of the true Sun. The right ascension of the mean Sun is obtained by applying the equation of time, with the sign given, to the right ascension of the true Sun, or, more easily, by applying 12h to the Sidereal Time. The direction in which the equation of time has to be applied in different problems is a frequent source of confusion and error. Apparent Solar Time is equal to the Mean Solar Time plus the Equation of Time. For example, at noon on August 8 the Equation of Time is −5m 39s and thus at 12h Mean Time on that day the Apparent Time is 12h −5m 39s = 11h 54m 21s.

The Greenwich Sidereal Time at 0h and the Transit of the First Point of Aries (which is really the mean time when the sidereal time is 0h) are used for converting mean time to sidereal time and vice versa.

The GMT of transit of the Sun at Greenwich may also be taken as the local mean time (LMT) of transit in any longitude. It is independent of latitude. The GMT of transit in any longitude is obtained by adding the longitude to the time given if west, and vice versa.

LIGHTING-UP TIME

The legal importance of sunrise and sunset is that the Road Vehicles Lighting Regulations 1989 (SI 1989 No. 1796) make the use of front and rear position lamps on vehicles compulsory during the period between sunset and sunrise. Headlamps on vehicles are required to be used during the hours of darkness on unlit roads or whenever visibility is seriously reduced. The hours of darkness are defined in these regulations as the period between half an hour after sunset and half an hour before sunrise.

In all laws and regulations 'sunset' refers to the local sunset, i.e. the time at which the Sun sets at the place in question. This common-sense interpretation has been upheld by legal tribunals. Thus the necessity for providing for different latitudes and longitudes, as already described, is evident.

SUNRISE AND SUNSET

The times of sunrise and sunset are those when the Sun's upper limb, as affected by refraction, is on the true horizon of an observer at sea-level. Assuming the mean refraction to be 34′, and the Sun's semi-diameter to be 16′, the time given is that when the true zenith distance of the Sun's centre is 90°+34′+16′ or 90° 50′, or, in other words, when the depression of the Sun's centre below the true horizon is 50′. The upper limb is then 34′ below the true horizon, but is brought there by refraction. An observer on a ship might see the Sun for a minute or so longer, because of the dip of the horizon, while another viewing the sunset over hills or mountains would record an earlier time. Nevertheless, the moment when the true zenith distance of the Sun's centre is 90° 50′ is a precise time dependent only on the latitude and longitude of the place, and independent of its altitude above sea-level, the contour of its horizon, the vagaries of refraction or the small seasonal change in the Sun's semi-diameter; this moment is suitable in every way as a definition of sunset (or sunrise) for all statutory purposes. (For further information, *see* footnote on page 72.)

TWILIGHT

Light reaches us before sunrise and continues to reach us for some time after sunset. The interval between darkness and sunrise or sunset and darkness is called twilight. Astronomically speaking, twilight is considered to begin or end when the Sun's centre is 18° below the horizon, as no light from the Sun can then reach the observer. As thus defined twilight may last several hours; in high latitudes at the summer solstice the depression of 18° is not reached, and twilight lasts from sunset to sunrise.

The need for some sub-division of twilight is met by dividing the gathering darkness into four stages.

(1) *Sunrise or Sunset*, defined as above
(2) *Civil twilight*, which begins or ends when the Sun's centre is 6° below the horizon. This marks the time when operations requiring daylight may commence or must cease. In England it varies from about 30 to 60 minutes after sunset and the same interval before sunrise
(3) *Nautical twilight*, which begins or ends when the Sun's centre is 12° below the horizon. This marks the time when it is, to all intents and purposes, completely dark
(4) *Astronomical twilight*, which begins or ends when the Sun's centre is 18° below the horizon. This marks theoretical perfect darkness. It is of little practical importance, especially if nautical twilight is tabulated

To assist observers the durations of civil, nautical and astronomical twilights are given at intervals of ten days. The beginning of a particular twilight is found by subtracting the duration from the time of sunrise, while the end is found by adding the duration to the time of sunset. Thus the beginning of astronomical twilight in latitude 52°, on the Greenwich meridian, on March 11 is found as 06h 24m–1 13m = 04h 31m and similarly the end of civil twilight as 17h 57m+34m = 18h 31m. The letters TAN (twilight all night) are printed when twilight lasts all night.

Under the heading The Night Sky will be found notes describing the position and visibility of the planets and other phenomena.

PAGE THREE OF EACH MONTH

The Moon moves so rapidly among the stars that its position is given only to the degree of accuracy that permits linear interpolation. The right ascension (RA) and declination (Dec.) are geocentric, i.e. for an imaginary observer at the centre of the Earth. To an observer on the surface of the Earth the position is always different, as the altitude is always less on account of parallax, which may reach 1°.

The lunar terminator is the line separating the bright from the dark part of the Moon's disk. Apart from irregularities of the lunar surface, the terminator is elliptical, because it is a circle seen in projection. It becomes the full circle forming the limb, or edge, of the Moon at New and Full Moon. The selenographic longitude of the terminator is measured from the mean centre of the visible disk, which may differ from the visible centre by as much as 8°, because of libration.

Instead of the longitude of the terminator the Sun's selenographic co-longitude (Sun's co-long.) is tabulated. It is numerically equal to the selenographic longitude of the morning terminator, measured eastwards from the mean centre of the disk. Thus its value is approximately 270° at New Moon, 360° at First Quarter, 90° at Full Moon and 180° at Last Quarter.

The Position Angle (PA) of the Bright Limb is the position angle of the midpoint of the illuminated limb, measured eastwards from the north point on the disk. The Phase column shows the percentage of the area of the Moon's disk illuminated; this is also the illuminated percentage of the diameter at right angles to the line of cusps. The terminator is a semi-ellipse whose major axis is the line of cusps, and whose semi-minor axis is determined by the tabulated percentage; from New Moon to Full Moon the east limb is dark, and vice versa.

The times given as moonrise and moonset are those when the upper limb of the Moon is on the horizon of an observer at sea-level. The Sun's horizontal parallax (Hor. par.) is about 9″, and is negligible when considering sunrise and sunset, but that of the Moon averages about 57′. Hence the computed time represents the moment when the true zenith distance of the Moon is 90° 50′ (as for the Sun) minus the horizontal parallax. The time required for the Sun or Moon to rise or set is about four minutes (except in high latitudes). *See also* page 65 and footnote below.

The GMT of transit of the Moon over the meridian of Greenwich is given; these times are independent of latitude but must be corrected for longitude. For places in the British Isles it suffices to add the longitude if west, and vice versa. For other places a further correction is necessary because of the rapid movement of the Moon relative to the stars. The entire correction is conveniently determined by first finding the west longitude λ of the place. If the place is in west longitude, λ is the ordinary west longitude; if the place is in east longitude λ is the complement to 24h (or 360°) of the longitude and will be greater than 12h (or 180°). The correction then consists of two positive portions, namely λ and the fraction $\lambda/24$ (or $\lambda°/360$) multiplied by the difference between consecutive transits. Thus for Christchurch, New Zealand, the longitude is 11h 31m east, so λ=12h 29m and the fraction $\lambda/24$ is 0.52. The transit on the local date 2002 September 1 is found as follows:

		d	h	m
GMT of transit at Greenwich	August	31	05	54
λ			12	29
$0.52 \times (5h 54m - 5h 06m)$				25
GMT of transit at Christchurch		31	18	48
Corr. to NZ Standard Time			12	00
Local standard time of transit	September	1	06	48

As is evident, for any given place the quantities λ and the correction to local standard time may be combined permanently, being here 24h 29m.

Positions of Mercury are given for every second day, and those of Venus and Mars for every fifth day; they may be interpolated linearly. The diameter (Diam.) is given in seconds of arc. The phase is the illuminated percentage of the disk. In the case of the inner planets this approaches 100 at superior conjunction and 0 at inferior conjunction. When the phase is less than 50 the planet is crescent-shaped or horned; for greater phases it is gibbous. In the case of the exterior planet Mars, the phase approaches 100 at conjunction and opposition, and is a minimum at the quadratures.

Since the planets cannot be seen when on the horizon, the actual times of rising and setting are not given; instead, the time when the planet has an apparent altitude of 5° has been tabulated. If the time of transit is between 00h and 12h the time refers to an altitude of 5° above the eastern horizon; if between 12h and 24h, to the western horizon. The phenomenon tabulated is the one that occurs between

SUNRISE, SUNSET AND MOONRISE, MOONSET

The tables have been constructed for the meridian of Greenwich and for latitudes 52° and 56°. They give Greenwich Mean Time (GMT) throughout the year. To obtain the GMT of the phenomenon as seen from any other latitude and longitude in the British Isles, first interpolate or extrapolate for latitude by the usual rules of proportion. To the time thus found, the longitude (expressed in time) is to be added if west (as it usually is in Great Britain) or subtracted if east. If the longitude is expressed in degrees and minutes of arc, it must be converted to time at the rate of 1°=4m and 15′=1m.

A method of calculating rise and set times for other places in the world is given on pages 64 and 65.

sunset and sunrise. The times given may be interpolated for latitude and corrected for longitude, as in the case of the Sun and Moon.

The GMT at which the planet transits the Greenwich meridian is also given. The times of transit are to be corrected to local meridians in the usual way, as already described.

PAGE FOUR OF EACH MONTH

The GMTs of sunrise and sunset for seven cities, whose adopted positions in longitude (W.) and latitude (N.) are given immediately below the name, may be used not only for these phenomena, but also for lighting-up times (*see* page 71 for a fuller explanation).

The particulars for the four outer planets resemble those for the planets on Page Three of each month, except that, under Uranus and Neptune, times when the planet is 10° high instead of 5° high are given; this is because of the inferior brightness of these planets. The diameters given for the rings of Saturn are those of the major axis (in the plane of the planet's equator) and the minor axis respectively. The former has a small seasonal change due to the slightly varying distance of the Earth from Saturn, but the latter varies from zero when the Earth passes through the ring plane every 15 years to its maximum opening half-way between these periods. The rings were last open at their widest extent (and Saturn at its brightest) in 1988; this will occur again in 2002. The Earth passed through the ring plane in 1995–6 and will do so again in 2009.

TIME

From the earliest ages, the natural division of time into recurring periods of day and night has provided the practical time-scale for the everyday activities of the human race. Indeed, if any alternative means of time measurement is adopted, it must be capable of adjustment so as to remain in general agreement with the natural time-scale defined by the diurnal rotation of the Earth on its axis. Ideally the rotation should be measured against a fixed frame of reference; in practice it must be measured against the background provided by the celestial bodies. If the Sun is chosen as the reference point, we obtain Apparent Solar Time, which is the time indicated by a sundial. It is not a uniform time but is subject to variations which amount to as much as a quarter of an hour in each direction. Such wide variations cannot be tolerated in a practical time-scale, and this has led to the concept of Mean Solar Time in which all the days are exactly the same length and equal to the average length of the Apparent Solar Day.

The positions of the stars in the sky are specified in relation to a fictitious reference point in the sky known as the First Point of Aries (or the Vernal Equinox). It is therefore convenient to adopt this same reference point when considering the rotation of the Earth against the background of the stars. The time-scale so obtained is known as Apparent Sidereal Time.

GREENWICH MEAN TIME

The daily rotation of the Earth on its axis causes the Sun and the other heavenly bodies to appear to cross the sky from east to west. It is convenient to represent this relative motion as if the Sun really performed a daily circuit around a fixed Earth. Noon in Apparent Solar Time may then be defined as the time at which the Sun transits across the observer's meridian. In Mean Solar Time, noon is similarly defined by the meridian transit of a fictitious Mean Sun moving uniformly in the sky with the same average speed as the true Sun. Mean Solar Time observed on the meridian of the transit circle telescope of the Old Royal Observatory at Greenwich is called Greenwich Mean Time (GMT). The mean solar day is divided into 24 hours and, for astronomical and other scientific purposes, these are numbered 0 to 23, commencing at midnight. Civil time is usually reckoned in two periods of 12 hours, designated a.m. (*ante meridiem*, i.e. before noon) and p.m. (*post meridiem*, i.e. after noon).

UNIVERSAL TIME

Before 1925 January 1, GMT was reckoned in 24 hours commencing at noon; since that date it has been reckoned from midnight. To avoid confusion in the use of the designation GMT before and after 1925, since 1928 astronomers have tended to use the term Universal Time (UT) or Weltzeit (WZ) to denote GMT measured from Greenwich Mean Midnight.

In precision work it is necessary to take account of small variations in Universal Time. These arise from small irregularities in the rotation of the Earth. Observed astronomical time is designated UT0. Observed time corrected for the effects of the motion of the poles (giving rise to a 'wandering' in longitude) is designated UT1. There is also a seasonal fluctuation in the rate of rotation of the Earth arising from meteorological causes, often called the annual fluctuation. UT1 corrected for this effect is designated UT2 and provides a time-scale free from short-period fluctuations. It is still subject to small secular and irregular changes.

APPARENT SOLAR TIME

As mentioned above, the time shown by a sundial is called Apparent Solar Time. It differs from Mean Solar Time by an amount known as the Equation of Time, which is the total effect of two causes which make the length of the apparent solar day non-uniform. One cause of variation is that the orbit of the Earth is not a circle but an ellipse, having the Sun at one focus. As a consequence, the angular speed of the Earth in its orbit is not constant; it is greatest at the beginning of January when the Earth is nearest the Sun.

The other cause is due to the obliquity of the ecliptic; the plane of the equator (which is at right angles to the axis of rotation of the Earth) does not coincide with the ecliptic (the plane defined by the apparent annual motion of the Sun around the celestial sphere) but is inclined to it at an angle of 23° 26'. As a result, the apparent solar day is shorter than average at the equinoxes and longer at the solstices. From the combined effects of the components due to obliquity and eccentricity, the equation of time reaches its maximum values in February (−14 minutes) and early November (+16 minutes). It has a zero value on four dates during the year, and it is only on these dates (approximately April 15, June 14, September 1 and December 25) that a sundial shows Mean Solar Time.

SIDEREAL TIME

A sidereal day is the duration of a complete rotation of the Earth with reference to the First Point of Aries. The term sidereal (or 'star') time is a little misleading since the time-scale so defined is not exactly the same as that which would be defined by successive transits of a selected star, as there is a small progressive motion between the stars and the First Point of Aries due to the precession of the Earth's axis. This makes the length of the sidereal day shorter than the true period of rotation by 0.008 seconds. Superimposed on this steady precessional motion are small oscillations (nutation), giving rise to fluctuations in apparent sidereal time amounting to as much as 1.2 seconds. It is therefore customary to employ Mean Sidereal Time, from which these fluctuations have been removed. The conversion of GMT to Greenwich sidereal time (GST) may be performed by adding the value of the GST at 0h on the day in question (Page Two of each month) to the GMT converted to sidereal time using the table on page 069.

Example – To find the GST at August 8d 02h 41m 11s GMT

	h	m	s
GST at 0h	21	05	19
GMT	2	41	11
Acceleration for 2h			20
Acceleration for 41m 11s			7
Sum = GST =	23	46	57

If the observer is not on the Greenwich meridian then his/her longitude, measured positively westwards from Greenwich, must be subtracted from the GST to obtain Local Sidereal Time (LST). Thus, in the above example, an observer 5h east of Greenwich, or 19h west, would find the LST as 4h 46m 57s.

EPHEMERIS TIME

An analysis of observations of the positions of the Sun, Moon and planets taken over an extended period is used in preparing ephemerides. (An ephemeris is a table giving the apparent position of a heavenly body at regular intervals of time, e.g. one day or ten days, and may be used to compare current observations with tabulated positions.) Discrepancies between the positions of heavenly bodies observed over a 300-year period and their predicted positions arose because the time-scale to which the observations were related was based on the assumption that the rate of rotation of the Earth is uniform. It is now known that this rate of rotation is variable. A revised time-scale, Ephemeris Time (ET), was devised to bring the ephemerides into agreement with the observations.

The second of ET is defined in terms of the annual motion of the Earth in its orbit around the Sun(1/ 31556925.9747 of the tropical year for 1900 January 0d 12h ET). The precise determination of ET from astronomical observations is a lengthy process as the requisite standard of accuracy can only be achieved by averaging over a number of years.

In 1976 the International Astronomical Union adopted Terrestrial Dynamical Time (TDT), a new dynamical time-scale for general use whose scale unit is the SI second (*see* Atomic Time). TDT was renamed Terrestrial Time (TT) in 1991. ET is now of little more than historical interest.

TERRESTRIAL TIME

The uniform time system used in computing the ephemerides of the solar system is Terrestrial Time (TT), which has replaced ET for this purpose. Except for the most rigorous astronomical calculations, it may be assumed to be the same as ET. During 2002 the estimated difference TT–UT is about 67 seconds.

ATOMIC TIME

The fundamental standards of time and frequency must be defined in terms of a periodic motion adequately uniform, enduring and measurable. Progress has made it possible to use natural standards, such as atomic or molecular oscillations. Continuous oscillations are generated in an electrical circuit, the frequency of which is then compared or brought into coincidence with the frequency characteristic of the absorption or emission by the atoms or molecules when they change between two selected energy levels. The National Physical Laboratory (NPL) routinely uses clocks of high stability produced by locking a quartz oscillator to the frequencies defined by caesium or hydrogen atoms.

International Atomic Time (TAI), established through international collaboration, is formed by combining the readings of many caesium clocks and was set close to the astronomically-based Universal Time (UT) near the beginning of 1958. It was formally recognized in 1971 and since 1988 January 1 has been maintained by the International Bureau of Weights and Measures (BIPM). The second markers are generated according to the International System (SI) definition adopted in 1967 at the 13th General Conference of Weights and Measures: 'The second is the duration of 9 192 631 770 periods of the radiation corresponding to the transition between the two hyperfine levels of the ground state of the caesium-133 atom.'

Civil time in almost all countries is now based on Co-ordinated Universal Time (UTC), which was adopted for scientific purposes on 1972 January 1. UTC differs from TAI by an integer number of seconds (determined from studies of the rate of rotation of the Earth) and was designed to make both atomic time and UT accessible with accuracies appropriate for most users. The UTC time-scale is adjusted by the insertion (or, in principle, omission) of leap seconds in order to keep it within ±0.9 s of UT. These leap seconds are introduced, when necessary, at the same instant throughout the world, either at the end of December or at the end of June. So, for example, the 22nd leap second occurred at 0h UTC on 1999 January 1. All leap seconds so far have been positive, with 61 seconds in the final minute of the UTC month. The time 23h 59m 60s UTC is followed one second later by 0h 0m 00s of the first day of the following month. Notices concerning the insertion of leap seconds are issued by the International Earth Rotation Service (IERS) at the Observatoire de Paris.

RADIO TIME-SIGNALS

UTC is made generally available through time-signals and standard frequency broadcasts such as MSF in the UK, CHU in Canada and WWV and WWVH in the USA. These are based on national time-scales that are maintained in close agreement with UTC and provide traceability to the national time-scale and to UTC. The markers of seconds in the UTC scale coincide with those of TAI.

To disseminate the national time-scale in the UK, special signals are broadcast on behalf of the National Physical Laboratory from the BT radio station at Rugby (call-sign MSF). The signals are controlled from a caesium beam atomic frequency standard and consist of a precise frequency carrier of 60 kHz which is switched off, after being on for at least half a second, to mark every second. The first second of the minute begins with a period of 500 ms with the carrier switched off, to serve as a minute marker. In the other seconds the carrier is always off for at least one tenth of a second at the start and then it carries an on-off code giving the British clock time and date, together with information identifying the start of the next minute. Changes to and from summer time are made following government announcements. Leap seconds are inserted as announced by the IERS and information provided by them on the difference between UTC and UT is also signalled. Other broadcast signals in the UK include the BBC six pips signal, the BT Timeline ('speaking clock'), the NPL

Truetime service for computers, and a coded time-signal on the BBC 198 kHz transmitters which is used for timing in the electricity supply industry. From 1972 January 1 the six pips on the BBC have consisted of five short pips from second 55 to second 59 (six pips in the case of a leap second) followed by one lengthened pip, the start of which indicates the exact minute. From 1990 February 5 these signals have been controlled by the BBC with seconds markers referenced to the satellite-based US navigation system GPS (Global Positioning System) and time and day referenced to the MSF transmitter. Formerly they were generated by the Royal Greenwich Observatory. The BT Timeline is compared daily with the National Physical Laboratory caesium beam atomic frequency standard at the Rugby radio station. The NPL Truetime service is directly connected to the national time scale.

Accurate timing may also be obtained from the signals of international navigation systems such as the ground-based Omega, or the satellite-based American GPS or Russian GLONASS systems.

STANDARD TIME

Since 1880 the standard time in Britain has been Greenwich Mean Time (GMT); a statute that year enacted that the word 'time' when used in any legal document relating to Britain meant, unless otherwise specifically stated, the mean time of the Greenwich meridian. Greenwich was adopted as the universal meridian on 13 October 1884. A system of standard time by zones is used world-wide, standard time in each zone differing from that of the Greenwich meridian by an integral number of hours, either fast or slow. The large territories of the USA and Canada are divided into zones approximately 7.5° on either side of central meridians. (For time zones of countries of the world, see Index.)

Variations from the standard time of some countries occur during part of the year; they are decided annually and are usually referred to as Summer Time or Daylight Saving Time.

At the 180th meridian the time can be either 12 hours fast on Greenwich Mean Time or 12 hours slow, and a change of date occurs. The internationally recognized date or calendar line is a modification of the 180th meridian, drawn so as to include islands of any one group on the same side of the line, or for political reasons. The line is indicated by joining up the following co-ordinates:

Lat.	Long.	Lat.	Long.
60° S.	180°	48° N.	180°
51° S.	180°	53° N.	170° E.
45° S.	172.5° W.	65.5° N.	169° W.
15° S.	172.5° W.	75° N.	180°
5° S.	180°		

Changes to the date line would require an international conference.

BRITISH SUMMER TIME

In 1916 an Act ordained that during a defined period of that year the legal time for general purposes in Great Britain should be one hour in advance of Greenwich Mean Time. The Summer Time Acts 1922 and 1925 defined the period during which Summer Time was to be in force, stabilizing practice until the Second World War.

During the war the duration of Summer Time was extended and in the years 1941 to 1945 and in 1947 Double Summer Time (two hours in advance of Greenwich Mean Time) was in force. After the war, Summer Time was extended each year in 1948–52 and in 1961–4 by Order in Council.

Between 1968 October 27 and 1971 October 31 clocks were kept one hour ahead of Greenwich Mean Time throughout the year. This was known as British Standard Time.

The most recent legislation is the Summer Time Act 1972, which enacted that 'the period of summer time for the purposes of this Act is the period beginning at two o'clock, Greenwich mean time, in the morning of the day after the third Saturday in March or, if that day is Easter Day, the day after the second Saturday in March, and ending at two o'clock, Greenwich mean time, in the morning of the day after the fourth Saturday in October.'

The duration of Summer Time can be varied by Order in Council and in recent years alterations have been made to bring the operation of Summer Time in Britain closer to similar provisions in other countries of the European Union; for instance, since 1981 the hour of changeover has been 01h Greenwich Mean Time.

The duration of Summer Time in 2002 is:

March 31 01h GMT to October 27 01h GMT

MEAN REFRACTION

Alt.	Ref.		Alt.	Ref.		Alt.	Ref.	
°	′	′	°	′	′	°	′	′
1	20		3	12		7	54	
1	30	21	3	34	13	9	27	6
1	41	20	4	00	12	11	39	5
1	52	19	4	30	11	15	00	4
2	05	18	5	06	10	20	42	3
2	19	17	5	50	9	32	20	2
2	35	16	6	44	8	62	17	1
2	52	15	7	54	7	90	00	0
3	12	14						

The refraction table is in the form of a critical table (see page 69)

ASTRONOMICAL CONSTANTS

Solar parallax	8″.794
Astronomical unit	149597870 km
Precession for the year 2002	50″.291
Precession in right ascension	3s.075
Precession in declination	20″.043
Constant of nutation	9″.202
Constant of aberration	20″.496
Mean obliquity of ecliptic (2002)	23° 26′ 21″
Moon's equatorial hor. parallax	57′ 02″.70
Velocity of light in vacuo per second	299792.5 km
Solar motion per second	20.0 km
Equatorial radius of the Earth	6378.140 km
Polar radius of the Earth	6356.755 km
North galactic pole (IAU standard)	
RA 12h 49m (1950.0). Dec. +27°.4 N.	
Solar apex	RA 18h 06m Dec.+30°

Length of year (in mean solar days)

Tropical	365.24219
Sidereal	365.25636
Anomalistic (perihelion to perihelion)	365.25964
Eclipse	346.62000

Length of month (mean values)	d	h	m	s
New Moon to New	29	12	44	02.9
Sidereal	27	07	43	11.5
Anomalistic (perigee to perigee)	27	13	18	33.2

ELEMENTS OF THE SOLAR SYSTEM

Orb	Mean distance from Sun (Earth = 1)	km 10⁶	Sidereal period days	Synodic period days	Incl. of orbit to ecliptic ° '	Diameter km	Mass (Earth = 1)	Period of rotation on axis days
Sun	—	—	—	—	—	1,392,530	332,946	25–35*
Mercury	0.39	58	88.0	116	7 00	4,879	0.0553	58.646
Venus	0.72	108	224.7	584	3 24	12,104	0.8150	243.019r
Earth	1.00	150	365.3	—	—	12,756e	1.0000	0.997
Mars	1.52	228	687.0	780	1 51	6,794e	0.1074	1.026
Jupiter	5.20	778	4,332.6	399	1 18	142,984e / 133,708p	317.89	0.410e /
Saturn	9.54	1427	10,759.2	378	2 29	120,536e / 108,728p	95.18	0.426e /
Uranus	19.18	2870	30,684.6	370	0 46	51,118e	14.54	0.718r
Neptune	30.06	4497	60,191.0	367	1 46	49,528e	17.15	0.671
Pluto	39.80	5954	91,708.2	367	17 09	2,302	0.002	6.387

e equatorial, *p* polar, *r* retrograde, * depending on latitude

THE SATELLITES

Name	Star mag.	Mean distance from primary km	Sidereal period of revolution d
EARTH			
I Moon	—	384,400	27.322
MARS			
I Phobos	12	9,378	0.319
II Deimos	13	23,459	1.262
JUPITER			
XVI Metis	17	127,960	0.295
XV Adrastea	19	128,980	0.298
V Amalthea	14	181,300	0.498
XIV Thebe	16	221,900	0.675
I Io	5	421,600	1.769
II Europa	5	670,900	3.552
III Ganymede	5	1,070,000	7.155
IV Callisto	6	1,883,000	16.689
XIII Leda	20	11,094,000	239
VI Himalia	15	11,480,000	251
X Lysithea	18	11,720,000	259
VII Elara	17	11,737,000	260
XII Ananke	19	21,200,000	631r
XI Carme	18	22,600,000	692r
VIII Pasiphae	17	23,500,000	735r
IX Sinope	18	23,700,000	758r
199JI	—	23,960,000	719
SATURN			
XVIII Pan	—	133,583	0.575
XV Atlas	18	137,640	0.602
XVI Prometheus	16	139,353	0.613
XVII Pandora	16	141,700	0.629
XI Epimetheus	15	151,422	0.695
X Janus	14	151,472	0.695
I Mimas	13	185,520	0.942
II Enceladus	12	238,020	1.370
III Tethys	10	294,660	1.888
XIII Telesto	19	294,660	1.888
XIV Calypso	19	294,660	1.888
IV Dione	10	377,400	2.737
XII Helene	18	377,400	2.737
V Rhea	10	527,040	4.518

Name	Star mag.	Mean distance from primary km	Sidereal period of revolution d
SATURN			
VI Titan	8	1,221,850	15.945
VII Hyperion	14	1,481,100	21.277
VIII Iapetus	11	3,561,300	79.330
IX Pheobe	16	12,952,000	550.48r
URANUS			
VI Cordelia	–	49,750	0.335
VII Orphelia	–	53,760	0,376
VIII Bianca	–	59,170	0.435
IX Cressida	–	61,780	0.464
X Desdemona	–	62,660	0.474
XI Juliet	–	64,360	0.493
XII Portia	–	66,100	0.513
XIII Rosalind	–	69,930	0.558
XIV Belinda	–	75,260	0.624
S/1986U10	–	76,420	0.638
XV Puck	–	86,000	0.762
V Miranda	17	129,800	1.413
I Ariel	14	191,200	2.520
II Umbriel	15	266,000	4.144
III Titania	14	435,800	8.706
IV Oberon	14	583,600	13.463
XVI Caliban	–	7,164,600	579.4
XX Stephano	–	9,608,400	900
XVII Sycorax	–	12,174,700	1,283.7
XVIII Prospero	–	16,668,000	2056
XIX Setebos	–	18,288,000	2363
NEPTUNE			
III Naiad	25	48,230	0.294
IV Thalassa	24	50,070	0.311
V Despina	23	52,530	0.335
VI Galatea	22	61,950	0.429
VII Larissa	22	73,550	0.555
VIII Proteus	20	117,650	1.122
I Triton	13	354,760	5.877
II Nereid	19	5,513,400	360.136
PLUTO			
I Charon	17	19,600	6.387

THE EARTH

The shape of the Earth is that of an oblate spheroid or solid of revolution whose meridian sections are ellipses not differing much from circles, whilst the sections at right angles are circles. The length of the equatorial axis is about 12,756 km, and that of the polar axis is 12,714 km. The mean density of the Earth is 5.5 times that of water, although that of the surface layer is less. The Earth and Moon revolve about their common centre of gravity in a lunar month; this centre in turn revolves round the Sun in a plane known as the ecliptic, that passes through the Sun's centre. The Earth's equator is inclined to this plane at an angle of 23.4°. This tilt is the cause of the seasons. In mid-latitudes, and when the Sun is high above the Equator, not only does the high noon altitude make the days longer, but the Sun's rays fall more directly on the Earth's surface; these effects combine to produce summer. In equatorial regions the noon altitude is large throughout the year, and there is little variation in the length of the day. In higher latitudes the noon altitude is lower, and the days in summer are appreciably longer than those in winter.

The average velocity of the Earth in its orbit is 30 km a second. It makes a complete rotation on its axis in about 23h 56m of mean time, which is the sidereal day. Because of its annual revolution round the Sun, the rotation with respect to the Sun, or the solar day, is more than this by about four minutes (see page 73). The extremity of the axis of rotation, or the North Pole of the Earth, is not rigidly fixed, but wanders over an area roughly 20 metres in diameter.

TERRESTRIAL MAGNETISM

The Earth's main magnetic field corresponds approximately to that of a very strong small bar magnet near the centre of the Earth, but with appreciable smooth spatial departures. The origin of the main field is not fully understood but is generally ascribed to electric currents associated with fluid motions in the Earth's core. As a result not only does the main field vary in strength and direction from place to place, but also with time. Superimposed on the main field are local and regional anomalies whose magnitudes may in places approach that of the main field; these are due to the influence of mineral deposits in the Earth's crust. A small proportion of the field is of external origin, mostly associated with electric currents in the ionosphere. The configuration of the external field and the ionisation of the atmosphere depend on the incident particle and radiation flux from the Sun. There are, therefore, short-term and non-periodic as well as diurnal, 27-day, seasonal and 11-year periodic changes in the magnetic field, dependent upon the position of the Sun and the degree of solar activity.

A magnetic compass points along the horizontal component of a magnetic line of force. These lines of force converge on the 'magnetic dip-poles', the places where the Earth's magnetic field is vertical. These poles move with time, and their present approximate adopted mean positions are 81°.4 N., 111°.0 W. and 64°.6 S., 138°.2 E.

There is also a 'magnetic equator', at all points of which the vertical component of the Earth's magnetic field is zero and a magnetised needle remains horizontal. This line runs between 2° and 12° north of the geographical equator in Asia and Africa, turns sharply south off the west African coast, and crosses South America through Brazil, Bolivia and Peru; it recrosses the geographical equator in mid-Pacific.

Reference has already been made to secular changes in the Earth's field. The following table indicates the changes in magnetic declination (or variation of the compass). Declination is the angle in the horizontal plane between the direction of true north and that in which a magnetic compass points. Similar, though much smaller, changes have occurred in 'dip' or magnetic inclination. Secular changes differ throughout the world. Although the London observations suggest a cycle with a period of several hundred years, an exact repetition is unlikely.

London				Greenwich			
1580	11°	15'	E.	1900	16°	29'	W.
1622	5°	56'	E.	1925	13°	10'	W.
1665	1°	22'	W.	1950	9°	07'	W.
1730	13°	00'	W.	1975	6°	39'	W.
1773	21°	09'	W.	1998	3°	32'	W.
1850	22°	24'	W.				

In order that up-to-date information on declination may be available, many governments publish magnetic charts on which there are lines (isogonic lines) passing through all places at which specified values of declination will be found at the date of the chart.

In the British Isles, isogonic lines now run approximately north-east to south-west. Though there are considerable local deviations due to geological causes, a rough value of magnetic declination may be obtained by assuming that at 50° N. on the meridian of Greenwich, the value in 2002 is 2°19' west and allowing an increase of 13' for each degree of latitude northwards and one of 27' for each degree of longitude westwards. For example, at 53° N., 5° W., declination will be about 2°19'+39'+135', i.e. 5°13' west. The average annual change at the present time is about 12' decrease.

The number of magnetic observatories is about 180, irregularly distributed over the globe. There are three in Great Britain, run by the British Geological Survey: at Hartland, north Devon; at Eskdalemuir, Dumfries and Galloway; and at Lerwick, Shetland Islands. The following are some recent annual mean values of the magnetic elements for Hartland.

Year	Declination West		Dip or inclination		Horizontal force	Vertical force
	°	'	°	'	gauss	gauss
1960	9	59	66	44	0.1871	0.4350
1965	9	30	66	34	0.1887	0.4354
1970	9	06	66	26	0.1903	0.4364
1975	8	32	66	17	0.1921	0.4373
1980	7	44	66	10	0.1933	0.4377
1985	6	56	66	08	0.1938	0.4380
1990	6	15	66	10	0.1939	0.4388
1995	5	33	66	07	0.1946	0.4395
2000	4	44	66	07	0.1951	0.4405

As well as navigation at sea, in the air and on land by compass the oil industry depends on the Earth's magnetic field as a directional reference. They use magnetic survey tools when drilling well-bores and require accurate estimates of the local magnetic field, taking into account the crustal and external fields.

MAGNETIC STORMS

Occasionally, sometimes with great suddenness, the Earth's magnetic field is subject for several hours to marked disturbance. During a severe storm in 1989 the declination at Lerwick changed by almost 8° in less than an hour. In many instances such disturbances are accompanied by widespread displays of aurorae, marked changes in the incidence of cosmic rays, an increase in the reception of 'noise' from the Sun at radio frequencies, and rapid changes in the ionosphere and induced electric currents within the Earth which adversely affect satellite operations, telecommunications and electric power transmission systems. The disturbances are caused by changes in the stream of ionised particles which emanates from the Sun and through which the Earth is continuously passing. Some of these changes are associated with visible eruptions on the Sun, usually in the region of sun-spots. There is a marked tendency for disturbances to recur after intervals of about 27 days, the apparent period of rotation of the Sun on its axis, which is consistent with the sources being located on particular areas of the Sun.

ARTIFICIAL SATELLITES

To consider the orbit of an artificial satellite, it is best to imagine that one is looking at the Earth from a distant point in space. The Earth would then be seen to be rotating about its axis inside the orbit described by the rapidly revolving satellite. The inclination of a satellite orbit to the Earth's equator (which generally remains almost constant throughout the satellite's lifetime) gives at once the maximum range of latitudes over which the satellite passes. Thus a satellite whose orbit has an inclination of 53° will pass overhead all latitudes between 53° S. and 53° N., but would never be seen in the zenith of any place nearer the poles than these latitudes. If we consider a particular place on the earth, whose latitude is less than the inclination of the satellite's orbit, then the Earth's rotation carries this place first under the northbound part of the orbit and then under the southbound portion of the orbit, these two occurrences being always less than 12 hours apart for satellites moving in direct orbits (i.e. to the east). (For satellites in retrograde orbits, the words 'northbound' and 'southbound' should be interchanged in the preceding statement.) As the value of the latitude of the observer increases and approaches the value of the inclination of the orbit, so this interval gets shorter until (when the latitude is equal to the inclination) only one overhead passage occurs each day.

OBSERVATION OF SATELLITES

The regression of the orbit around the Earth causes alternate periods of visibility and invisibility, though this is of little concern to the radio or radar observer. To the visual observer the following cycle of events normally occurs (though the cycle may start in any position): invisibility, morning observations before dawn, invisibility, evening observations after dusk, invisibility, morning observations before dawn, and so on. With reasonably high satellites and for observers in high latitudes around the summer solstice, the evening observations follow the morning observations without interruption as sunlight passing over the polar regions can still illuminate satellites which are passing over temperate latitudes at local midnight. At the moment all satellites rely on sunlight to make them visible, though a satellite with a flashing light has been suggested for a future launching. The observer must be in darkness or twilight in order to make any useful observations. (For durations of twilight, and sunrise and sunset times, *see* Page Two of each month.)

Some of the satellites are visible to the naked eye and much interest has been aroused by the spectacle of a bright satellite disappearing into the Earth's shadow. The event is even more interesting telescopically as the disappearance occurs gradually as the satellite traverses the Earth's penumbral shadow, and during the last few seconds before the eclipse is complete the satellite may change colour (in suitable atmospheric conditions) from yellow to red. This is because the last rays of sunlight are refracted through the denser layers of our atmosphere before striking the satellite.

Some satellites rotate about one or more axes so that a periodic variation in brightness is observed. This was particularly noticeable in several of the Soviet satellites.

Satellite research has provided some interesting results, including a revised value of the Earth's oblateness (1/298.2), and the discovery of the Van Allen radiation belts.

LAUNCHINGS

Apart from their names, e.g. Cosmos 6 Rocket, the satellites are also classified according to their date of launch. Thus 1961 α refers to the first satellite launching of 1961. A number following the Greek letter indicated the relative brightness of the satellites put in orbit. From the beginning of 1963 the Greek letters were replaced by numbers and the numbers by roman letters e.g. 1963–01A. For all satellites successfully injected into orbit following table gives the designation and names of the main objects, the launch date and some initial orbital data. These are the inclination to the equator (i), the nodal period of revolution (P), and the apogee and perigee heights.

Although most of the satellites launched are injected into orbits less than 1,000 km high, there are an increasing number of satellites in geostationary orbits, i.e. where the orbital inclination is zero, the eccentricity close to zero, and the period of revolution is 1436.1 minutes. Thus the satellite is permanently situated over the equator at one selected longitude at a mean height of 35,786 km. This geostationary band is crowded. In one case there are four television satellites (Astra 1A, Astra 1B, Astra 1C and Astra 1D) orbiting within a few tens of kilometres of each other. In the sky they appear to be separated by only a few arc minutes.

In 1997 a number of *Iridium* satellites were launched into high inclination orbits. These are owned by the mobile telephone company Cellnet. For visual observers, these satellites have the interesting characteristic that the large aeriels they carry can, when in exactly the right orientation with respect to the Sun and the observer, give off a 'flare' in brightness which can on occasion attain a magnitude of –6, much brighter than Venus. The flare can be visible to the naked eye for nearly a minute.

The Russian Space Station, Mir, 1986-17A, which was launched in 1986 was successfully de-orbited on March 23 2001. The re-entry was carried out in several stages, the first small burn to lower the orbit occurring at 00h 33m. The main de-orbit burn began at 05h 07m, which lowered the perigee height to 80km. The new International Space Station ISS, 1998-67A, is currently being assembled in an orbit of similar size and inclination to Mir. It will become even brighter as more parts are added to it. When passing over Britain it can appear to be almost as bright as Jupiter on favourable transits, though only visible for four or five minutes on each pass.

ARTIFICIAL SATELLITE LAUNCHES 2000–2001

Desig-nation	Satellite	Launch date	P	i	Apogee height	Perigee height
2000–			m	°	km	km
011	Garuda 1, rocket	February 12	908.0	10.2	36007	13380
012	Superbird 4, rocket	February 18	1417.9	0.2	35792	35088
013	Express 6A, rocket, platform, rocket	March 12	1432.5	0.3	35752	35702
014	MTI, rocket	March 12	96.6	97.4	614	577
015	Fregat Rocket /Cluster II	March 20	320.4	64.7	18033	256
016	Asiastar, Insat 3B, Sylda 5,rocket	March 21	636.6	7.0	35694	598
017	Image, rocket, rocket	March 25	856.3	90.0	46005	1000
018	Soyuz TM-30, rocket	April 4	91.1	51.7	340	339
019	Sesat	April 17	1449.8	0.1	36083	36046
020	Galaxy IVR	April 19	1435.9	0.1	35803	35784
021	Progress M-2	April 25	91.2	51.7	344	340
022	GOES-L, rocket	May 3	999.0	5.9	42242	11219
023	Cosmos 2370, Soyuz rocket	May 3	90.0	64.8	316	254
024	USA 149 DSP, rocket, rocket	May 8	(No elements available)			
025	USA 150 Navstar 47, rocket, rocket	May 11	356.9	39.2	20410	189
026	Dummysat-01, Dummysat-02, rocket	May 16	95.7	86.4	571	556
027	STS-101 Atlantis F21	May 19	91.5	51.6	365	353
028	Eutelsat W4, rocket	May 24	835.4	20.0	45789	243
029	Gorizont 33, rocket, tank	June 6	619.0	48.8	35001	382
030	TSX-5, rocket	June 7	106.3	69.0	1717	416
031	Express 3A, rocket, platform, rocket	June 24	637.5	48.7	36076	260
032	Unknown, rocket	June 25	1438.3	1.1	35871	35808
033	Nadezhda, Tzinghua 1,Snap 1,rocket	June 28	98.7	98.2	721	696
034	TDRS-8, rocket	June 30	480.9	27.1	27683	249
035	Sirius-1, rocket, platform, rocket	June 30	995.2	63.4	47127	6177
036	Cosmos 2371,rocket, platform, rocket	July 5	633.9	48.7	35890	265
037	Zvezda, rocket	July 12	91.0	51.6	367	299
038	Echostar 6, rocket	July 14	673.9	26.7	38027	162
039	Ruben, Champ/Mita, rocket	July 15	93.6	87.3	489	435
040	GPS Navstar 48, rocket, rocket	July 16	357.9	39.0	20465	197
041	Cluster II/FM7 & FM6, rocket	July 16	321.4	64.7	18085	263
042	Mightysat II.1, rocket	July 19	96.0	97.9	598	561
043	Pas-9, rocket	July 28	1427.4	0.1	35798	35456
044	Progress M1-3, rocket	August 6	89.2	51.4	259	227
045	Cluster II/FM-5 Rumba, FM-4 Tango, rocket	August 9	597.3	65.0	33998	254
046	Nilesat, rocket	August	1005.8	0.4	35744	18012
047	Lacrosse 4 USA 152 Onyx, rocket	August 17	98.4	68.1	704	676
048	DM-F3, rocket	August 23	361.0	27.7	20654	200
049	Raduga 1–5, rocket, platform	August 28	1472.5	2.3	36595	36420
050	PRC 44 ZY-2, rocket	September 1	94.3	97.5	505	487
051	Sirius-2, rocket, platform, rocket	September 5	994.5	63.4	47070	6205
052	Eutelsat W1, rocket	September 6	633.0	7.0	35783	324
053	STS-106 Atlantis F22	September 8	90.7	51.6	344	292
054	Astra 2B, GE-7, rocket, platform	September 14	1318.8	0.4	35774	31166
055	NOAA 16, rocket	September 21	102.1	98.8	877	861
056	Cosmos 2372, rocket	September 25	90.0	64.8	344	223
057	Tiungsat-1, Megsat, Unisat, Saudisat-1A, Saudisat-1B, rocket	September 26	97.5	64.6	656	647
058	Cosmos 2373, rocket	September 29	89.4	70.4	290	223
059	GE-1A, rocket, platform, rocket	October 1	630.2	48.6	35733	229
060	Nsat-110, rocket	October 6	1430.6	0.0	35753	35610

ARTIFICIAL SATELLITE LAUNCHES 2000–2001

Desig-nation	Satellite	Launch date	P	i	Apogee height	Perigee height
2000–			m	°	km	km
061	Hete-2, rocket	October 9	97.1	2.0	649	608
062	STS-92 Discovery F-18	October 11	92.2	51.6	393	387
063	Cosmos 2374–6, platform, rocket, rocket	October 13	675.6	64.9	19140	19136
064	Progress M-43, rocket	October 16	88.8	51.7	245	201
065	DSCS-III B-11 USA-153, rocket, IUS	October 20	(No elements available)			
066	Thuraya-1, rocket	October 21	632.2	6.4	35821	243
067	GE-6, rocket, platform, rocket, platform	October 21	746.2	18.7	35785	5985
068	Europe *star FM-1, rocket	October 29	655.7	7.0	36981	288
069	Abeidou-1 (Navsat), rocket	October 30	753.2	25.0	41901	208
070	Soyuz TM-31, rocket	October 31	89.7	51.6	282	260
071	GPS Navstar 49 USA-154, rocket, PAM-D	November 10	724.3	55.1	20510	20191
072	PAS-1R. Amsat P3D, Oscar 40, STRV-1C, STRV-1D, rocket, Sylda, ASAP	November 16	704.2	6.5	39077	627
073	Progress M1–4, rocket	November 16	89.9	51.6	281	274
074	Quickbird 1 (Cosmos Rocket)	November 20	91.5	65.8	614	81
075	EO-1, SAC-C, Munin, rocket, DPAF	November 21	98.8	98.3	721	704
076	Anik F1, rocket	November 21	864.8	3.0	41232	6169
077	Sirius 3, rocket, platform, rocket	November 30	1141.9	63.4	47085	12539
078	STS-97	December 1	89.8	51.6	335	218
079	Eros A-1, rocket	December 5	94.7	97.4	520	504
080	USA-155, rocket	December 6	(No elements available)			
081	Astra 2D, GE-8, LDREX, rocket, Sylda	December 20	630.3	2.0	35746	224
082	Beidou 1B, rocket	December 20	752.7	25.0	41882	203
2001–						
001	SZ-2, rocket	January 9	91.2	42.6	346	341
002	Turksat 2A, rocket	January 10	1428.4	0.2	35748	35547
003	Progress M1–5, rocket	January 24	90.5	51.7	319	297
004	GPS Navstar 50 = USA-156, rocket, PAM-D	January 30	356.6	39.2	20410	173
005	Sicral 1, Skynet 4F, rocket, Spelda	February 7	840.5	2.4	35763	10508
006	STS-98 Atlantis F23	February 7	91.7	51.6	376	363
007	Odin, rocket	February 20	97.1	97.9	634	624
008	Progress M1–44, rocket	February 26	90.0	51.6	295	278
009	Milstar DFS-4, rocket	February 27	(No elements available)			
010	STS-102 Discovery F19	March 8	89.6	51.6	286	246

Time Measurement and Calendars

MEASUREMENTS OF TIME

Measurements of time are based on the time taken by the earth to rotate on its axis (day); by the moon to revolve round the earth (month); and by the earth to revolve round the sun (year). From these, which are not commensurable, certain average or mean intervals have been adopted for ordinary use.

THE DAY

The day begins at midnight and is divided into 24 hours of 60 minutes, each of 60 seconds. The hours are counted from midnight up to 12 noon (when the sun crosses the meridian), and these hours are designated a.m. (*ante meridiem*); and again from noon up to 12 midnight, which hours are designated p.m. (*post meridiem*), except when the 24-hour reckoning is employed. The 24-hour reckoning ignores a.m. and p.m., numbering the hours 0 to 23 from midnight.

Colloquially the 24 hours are divided into day and night, day being the time while the sun is above the horizon (including the four stages of twilight defined on page 72). Day is subdivided into morning, the early part of daytime, ending at noon; afternoon, from noon to about 6 p.m.; and evening, which may be said to extend from 6 p.m. until midnight. Night, the dark period between day and day, begins at the close of astronomical twilight (*see* page 72) and extends beyond midnight to sunrise the next day.

The names of the days are derived from Old English translations or adaptations of the Roman titles.

Sunday	Sun	Sol
Monday	Moon	Luna
Tuesday	Tiw/Tyr (god of war)	Mars
Wednesday	Woden/Odin	Mercury
Thursday	Thor	Jupiter
Friday	Frigga/Freyja (goddess of love)	Venus
Saturday	Saeternes	Saturn

THE MONTH

The month in the ordinary calendar is approximately the twelfth part of a year, but the lengths of the different months vary from 28 (or 29) days to 31.

THE YEAR

The equinoctial or tropical year is the time that the earth takes to revolve round the sun from equinox to equinox, i.e. 365.24219 mean solar days, or 365 days 5 hours 48 minutes and 45 seconds.

The calendar year usually consists of 365 days but a year containing 366 days is called bissextile (*see* Roman calendar, page 89) or leap year, one day being added to the month of February so that a date 'leaps over' a day of the week. In the Roman calendar the day that was repeated was the sixth day before the beginning of March, the equivalent of 24 February.

A year is a leap year if the date of the year is divisible by four without remainder, unless it is the last year of the century. The last year of a century is a leap year only if its number is divisible by 400 without remainder, e.g. the years 1800 and 1900 had only 365 days but the year 2000 has 366 days.

THE SOLSTICE

A solstice is the point in the tropical year at which the sun attains its greatest distance, north or south, from the Equator. In the northern hemisphere the furthest point north of the Equator marks the summer solstice and the furthest point south the winter solstice.

The date of the solstice varies according to locality. For example, if the summer solstice falls on 21 June late in the day by Greenwich time, that day will be the longest of the year at Greenwich though it may be by only a second, but it will fall on 22 June, local date, in Japan, and so 22 June will be the longest day there. The date of the solstice is also affected by the length of the tropical year, which is 365 days 6 hours less about 11 minutes 15 seconds. If a solstice happens late on 21 June in one year, it will be nearly six hours later in the next (unless the next year is a leap year), i.e. early on 22 June, and that will be the longest day.

This delay of the solstice does not continue because the extra day in leap year brings it back a day in the calendar. However, because of the 11 minutes 15 seconds mentioned above, the additional day in leap year brings the solstice back too far by 45 minutes, and the time of the solstice in the calendar is earlier, in a four-year pattern, as the century progresses. The last year of a century is in most cases not a leap year, and the omission of the extra day puts the date of the solstice later by about six hours too much. Compensation for this is made by the fourth centennial year being a leap year. The solstice has become earlier in date throughout this century and, because the year 2000 is a leap year, the solstice will get earlier still throughout the 21st century.

The date of the winter solstice, the shortest day of the year, is affected by the same factors as the longest day.

At Greenwich the sun sets at its earliest by the clock about ten days before the shortest day. The daily change in the time of sunset is due in the first place to the sun's movement southwards at this time of the year, which diminishes the interval between the sun's transit and its setting. However, the daily decrease of the Equation of Time causes the time of apparent noon to be continuously later day by day, which to some extent counteracts the first effect. The rates of the change of these two quantities are not equal or uniform; their combination causes the date of earliest sunset to be 12 or 13 December at Greenwich. In more southerly latitudes the effect of the movement of the sun is less, and the change in the time of sunset depends on that of the Equation of Time to a greater degree, and the date of earliest sunset is earlier than it is at Greenwich, e.g. on the Equator it is about 1 November.

THE EQUINOX

The equinox is the point at which the sun crosses the Equator and day and night are of equal length all over the world. This occurs in March and September.

DOG DAYS

The days about the heliacal rising of the Dog Star, noted from ancient times as the hottest period of the year in the northern hemisphere, are called the Dog Days. Their incidence has been variously calculated as depending on the Greater or Lesser Dog Star (Sirius or Procyon) and their duration has been reckoned as from 30 to 54 days. A generally accepted period is from 3 July to 15 August.

CHRISTIAN CALENDAR

In the Christian chronological system the years are distinguished by cardinal numbers before or after the birth of Christ, the period being denoted by the letters BC (Before Christ) or, more rarely, AC (*Ante Christum*), and AD (*Anno Domini* – In the Year of Our Lord). The correlative dates of the epoch are the fourth year of the 194th Olympiad, the 753rd year from the foundation of Rome, AM 3761 in Jewish chronology, and the 4714th year of the Julian period. The actual date of the birth of Christ is somewhat uncertain.

The system was introduced into Italy in the sixth century. Though first used in France in the seventh century, it was not universally established there until about the eighth century. It has been said that the system was introduced into England by St Augustine (AD 596), but it was probably not generally used until some centuries later. It was ordered to be used by the Bishops at the Council of Chelsea (AD 816).

THE JULIAN CALENDAR

In the Julian calendar (adopted by the Roman Empire in 45 BC, *see* page 89) all the centennial years were leap years, and for this reason towards the close of the 16th century there was a difference of ten days between the tropical and calendar years; the equinox fell on 11 March of the calendar, whereas at the time of the Council of Nicaea (AD 325), it had fallen on 21 March. In 1582 Pope Gregory ordained that 5 October should be called 15 October and that of the end-century years only the fourth should be a leap year (*see* page 81).

THE GREGORIAN CALENDAR

The Gregorian calendar was adopted by Italy, France, Spain and Portugal in 1582, by Prussia, the Roman Catholic German states, Switzerland, Holland and Flanders on 1 January 1583, by Poland in 1586, Hungary in 1587, the Protestant German and Netherland states and Denmark in 1700, and by Great Britain and Dominions (including the North American colonies) in 1752, by the omission of eleven days (3 September being reckoned as 14 September). Sweden omitted the leap day in 1700 but observed leap days in 1704 and 1708, and reverted to the Julian calendar by having two leap days in 1712; the Gregorian calendar was adopted in 1753 by the omission of eleven days (18 February being reckoned as 1 March). Japan adopted the calendar in 1872, China in 1912, Bulgaria in 1915, Turkey and Soviet Russia in 1918, Yugoslavia and Romania in 1919, and Greece in 1923.

In the same year that the change was made in England from the Julian to the Gregorian calendar, the beginning of the new year was also changed from 25 March to 1 January (*see* page 86).

THE ORTHODOX CHURCHES

Some Orthodox Churches still use the Julian reckoning but the majority of Greek Orthodox Churches and the Romanian Orthodox Church have adopted a modified 'New Calendar', observing the Gregorian calendar for fixed feasts and the Julian for movable feasts.

The Orthodox Church year begins on 1 September. There are four fast periods and, in addition to Pascha (Easter), twelve great feasts, as well as numerous commemorations of the saints of the Old and New Testaments throughout the year.

THE DOMINICAL LETTER

The dominical letter is one of the letters A–G which are used to denote the Sundays in successive years. If the first day of the year is a Sunday the letter is A; if the second, B; the third, C; and so on. A leap year requires two letters, the first for 1 January to 29 February, the second for 1 March to 31 December (*see* page 84).

EPIPHANY

The feast of the Epiphany, commemorating the manifestation of Christ, later became associated with the offering of gifts by the Magi. The day was of great importance from the time of the Council of Nicaea (AD 325), as the primate of Alexandria was charged at every Epiphany feast with the announcement in a letter to the churches of the date of the forthcoming Easter. The day was also of importance in Britain as it influenced dates, ecclesiastical and lay, e.g. Plough Monday, when work was resumed in the fields, fell on the Monday in the first full week after Epiphany.

LENT

The Teutonic word *Lent*, which denotes the fast preceding Easter, originally meant no more than the spring season; but from Anglo-Saxon times at least it has been used as the equivalent of the more significant Latin term Quadragesima, meaning the 'forty days' or, more literally, the fortieth day. Ash Wednesday is the first day of Lent, which ends at midnight before Easter Day.

PALM SUNDAY

Palm Sunday, the Sunday before Easter and the beginning of Holy Week, commemorates the triumphal entry of Christ into Jerusalem and is celebrated in Britain (when palm is not available) by branches of willow gathered for use in the decoration of churches on that day.

MAUNDY THURSDAY

Maundy Thursday is the day before Good Friday, the name itself being a corruption of *dies mandati* (day of the mandate) when Christ washed the feet of the disciples and gave them the mandate to love one another.

EASTER DAY

Easter Day is the first Sunday after the full moon which happens on, or next after, the 21st day of March; if the full moon happens on a Sunday, Easter Day is the Sunday after.

This definition is contained in an Act of Parliament (24 Geo. II c. 23) and explanation is given in the preamble to the Act that the day of full moon depends on certain tables that have been prepared. These tables are summarized in the early pages of the Book of Common Prayer. The moon referred to is not the real moon of the heavens, but a hypothetical moon on whose 'full' the date of Easter depends, and the lunations of this 'calendar' moon consist of twenty-nine and thirty days alternately, with certain necessary modifications to make the date of its full agree as nearly as possible with that of the real moon, which is known as the Paschal Full Moon.

A FIXED EASTER

In 1928 the House of Commons agreed to a motion for the third reading of a bill proposing that Easter Day shall, in the calendar year next but one after the commencement of the Act and in all subsequent years, be the first Sunday after the second Saturday in April. Easter would thus fall on the second or third Sunday in April, i.e. between 9 and 15 April (inclusive). A clause in the Bill provided that before it shall come into operation, regard shall be had to any opinion expressed officially by the various Christian churches. Efforts by the World Council of Churches to secure a unanimous choice of date for Easter by its member churches have so far been unsuccessful.

ROGATION DAYS

Rogation Days are the Monday, Tuesday and Wednesday preceding Ascension Day and from the fifth century were observed as public fasts with solemn processions and supplications. The processions were discontinued as religious observances at the Reformation, but survive in the ceremony known as 'beating the parish bounds'. Rogation Sunday is the Sunday before Ascension Day.

EMBER DAYS

The Ember Days at the four seasons are the Wednesday, Friday and Saturday (*a*) before the third Sunday in Advent, (*b*) before the second Sunday in Lent, and (*c*) before the Sundays nearest to the festivals of St Peter and of St Michael and All Angels.

TRINITY SUNDAY

Trinity Sunday is eight weeks after Easter Day, on the Sunday following Pentecost (Whit Sunday). Subsequent Sundays are reckoned in the Book of Common Prayer calendar of the Church of England as 'after Trinity'. Thomas Becket (1118–70) was consecrated Archbishop of Canterbury on the Sunday after Whit Sunday and his first act was to ordain that the day of his consecration should be held as a new festival in honour of the Holy Trinity. This observance spread from Canterbury throughout the whole of Christendom.

MOVABLE FEASTS TO THE YEAR 2035

Year	Ash Wednesday	Easter	Ascension	Pentecost (Whit Sunday)	Advent Sunday
2002	13 February	31 March	9 May	19 May	1 December
2003	5 March	20 April	29 May	8 June	30 November
2004	25 February	11 April	20 May	30 May	28 November
2005	9 February	27 March	5 May	15 May	27 November
2006	1 March	16 April	25 May	4 June	3 December
2007	21 February	8 April	17 May	27 May	2 December
2008	6 February	23 March	1 May	11 May	30 November
2009	25 February	12 April	21 May	31 May	29 November
2010	17 February	4 April	13 May	23 May	28 November
2011	9 March	24 April	2 June	12 June	27 November
2012	22 February	8 April	17 May	27 May	2 December
2013	13 February	31 March	9 May	19 May	1 December
2014	5 March	20 April	29 May	8 June	30 November
2015	18 February	5 April	14 May	24 May	29 November
2016	10 February	27 March	5 May	15 May	27 November
2017	1 March	16 April	25 May	4 June	3 December
2018	14 February	1 April	10 May	20 May	2 December
2019	6 March	21 April	30 May	9 June	1 December
2020	26 February	12 April	21 May	31 May	29 November
2021	17 February	4 April	13 May	23 May	28 November
2022	2 March	17 April	26 May	5 June	27 November
2023	22 February	9 April	18 May	28 May	3 December
2024	14 February	31 March	9 May	19 May	1 December
2025	5 March	20 April	29 May	8 June	30 November
2026	18 February	5 April	14 May	24 May	29 November
2027	10 February	28 March	6 May	16 May	28 November
2028	1 March	16 April	25 May	4 June	3 December
2029	14 February	1 April	10 May	20 May	2 December
2030	6 March	21 April	30 May	9 June	1 December
2031	26 February	13 April	22 May	1 June	30 November
2032	11 February	28 March	6 May	16 May	28 November
2033	2 March	17 April	26 May	5 June	27 November
2034	22 February	9 April	18 May	28 May	3 December
2035	7 February	25 March	3 May	13 May	2 December

NOTES

Ash Wednesday (first day in Lent) can fall at earliest on 4 February and at latest on 10 March
Mothering Sunday (fourth Sunday in Lent) can fall at earliest on 1 March and at latest on 4 April
Easter Day can fall at earliest on 22 March and at latest on 25 April
Ascension Day is forty days after Easter Day and can fall at earliest on 30 April and at latest on 3 June

Pentecost (Whit Sunday) is seven weeks after Easter and can fall at earliest on 10 May and at latest on 13 June
Trinity Sunday is the Sunday after Whit Sunday
Corpus Christi falls on the Thursday after Trinity Sunday
Sundays after Pentecost – there are not less than 18 and not more than 23
Advent Sunday is the Sunday nearest to 30 November

EASTER DAYS AND DOMINICAL LETTERS 1500 TO 2035

Dates up to and including 1752 are according to the Julian calendar. For dominical letters in leap years, *see* page 82

	1500–1599	1600–1699	1700–1799	1800–1899	1900–1999	2000–2035
March						
d	22 1573	1668	1761	1818		
e	23 1505/16	1600	1788	1845/56	1913	2008
f	24	1611/95	1706/99		1940	
g	25 1543/54	1627/38/49	1722/33/44	1883/94	1951	2035
A	26 1559/70/81/92	1654/65/76	1749/58/69/80	1815/26/37	1967/78/89	
b	27 1502/13/24/97	1608/87/92	1785/96	1842/53/64	1910/21/32	2005/16
c	28 1529/35/40	1619/24/30	1703/14/25	1869/75/80	1937/48	2027/32
d	29 1551/62	1635/46/57	1719/30/41/52	1807/12/91	1959/64/70	
e	30 1567/78/89	1651/62/73/84	1746/55/66/77	1823/34	1902/75/86/97	
f	31 1510/21/32/83/94	1605/16/78/89	1700/71/82/93	1839/50/61/72	1907/18/29/91	2002/13/24
April						
g	1 1526/37/48	1621/32	1711/16	1804/66/77/88	1923/34/45/56	2018/29
A	2 1553/64	1643/48	1727/38	1809/20/93/99	1961/72	
b	3 1575/80/86	1659/70/81	1743/63/68/74	1825/31/36	1904/83/88/94	
c	4 1507/18/91	1602/13/75/86/97	1708/79/90	1847/58	1915/20/26/99	2010/21
d	5 1523/34/45/56	1607/18/29/40	1702/13/24/95	1801/63/74/85/96	1931/42/53	2015/26
e	6 1539/50/61/72	1634/45/56	1729/35/40/60	1806/17/28/90	1947/58/69/80	
f	7 1504/77/88	1667/72	1751/65/76	1822/33/44	1901/12/85/96	
g	8 1509/15/20/99	1604/10/83/94	1705/87/92/98	1849/55/60	1917/28	2007/12
A	9 1531/42	1615/26/37/99	1710/21/32	1871/82	1939/44/50	2023/34
b	10 1547/58/69	1631/42/53/64	1726/37/48/57	1803/14/87/98	1955/66/77	
c	11 1501/12/63/74/85/96	1658/69/80	1762/73/84	1819/30/41/52	1909/71/82/93	2004
d	12 1506/17/28	1601/12/91/96	1789	1846/57/68	1903/14/25/36/98	2009/20
e	13 1533/44	1623/28	1707/18	1800/73/79/84	1941/52	2031
f	14 1555/60/66	1639/50/61	1723/34/45/54	1805/11/16/95	1963/68/74	
g	15 1571/82/93	1655/66/77/88	1750/59/70/81	1827/38	1900/06/79/90	2001
A	16 1503/14/25/36/87/98	1609/20/82/93	1704/75/86/97	1843/54/65/76	1911/22/33/95	2006/17/28
b	17 1530/41/52	1625/36	1715/20	1808/70/81/92	1927/38/49/60	2022/33
c	18 1557/68	1647/52	1731/42/56	1802/13/24/97	1954/65/76	
d	19 1500/79/84/90	1663/74/85	1747/67/72/78	1829/35/40	1908/81/87/92	
e	20 1511/22/95	1606/17/79/90	1701/12/83/94	1851/62	1919/24/30	2003/14/25
f	21 1527/38/49	1622/33/44	1717/28	1867/78/89	1935/46/57	2019/30
g	22 1565/76	1660	1739/53/64	1810/21/32	1962/73/84	
A	23 1508	1671		1848	1905/16	2000
b	24 1519	1603/14/98	1709/91	1859		2011
c	25 1546	1641	1736	1886	1943	

HINDU CALENDAR

The Hindu calendar is a luni-solar calendar of twelve months, each containing 29 days, 12 hours. Each month is divided into a light fortnight (Shukla or Shuddha) and a dark fortnight (Krishna or Vadya) based on the waxing and waning of the moon. In most parts of India the month starts with the light fortnight, i.e. the day after the new moon, although in some regions it begins with the dark fortnight, i.e. the day after the full moon.

The new year begins in the month of Chaitra (March/April) and ends in the month of Phalgun (March). The twelve months, Chaitra, Vaishakh, Jyeshtha, Ashadh, Shravan, Bhadrapad, Ashvin, Kartik, Margashirsh, Paush, Magh and Phalgun, have Sanskrit names derived from twelve asterisms (constellations). There are regional variations to the names of the months but the Sanskrit names are understood throughout India.

Every lunar month must have a solar transit and is termed pure (shuddha). The lunar month without a solar transit is impure (mala) and called an intercalary month. An intercalary month occurs approximately every 32 lunar months, whenever the difference between the Hindu year of 360 lunar days (354 days 8 hours solar time) and the 365 days 6 hours of the solar year reaches the length of one Hindu lunar month (29 days 12 hours).

The leap month may be added at any point in the Hindu year. The name given to the month varies according to when it occurs but is taken from the month immediately following it. There is no leap month in 2002.

The days of the week are called Raviwar (Sunday), Somawar (Monday), Mangalwar (Tuesday), Budhawar (Wednesday), Guruwar (Thursday), Shukrawar (Friday) and Shaniwar (Saturday). The names are derived from the Sanskrit names of the Sun, the Moon and five planets, Mars, Mercury, Jupiter, Venus and Saturn.

Most fasts and festivals are based on the lunar calendar but a few are determined by the apparent movement of the Sun, e.g. Sankranti and Pongal (in southern India), which are celebrated on 14/15 January to mark the start of the Sun's apparent journey northwards and a change of season.

Festivals celebrated throughout India are Chaitra (the New Year), Raksha-bandhan (the renewal of the kinship bond between brothers and sisters), Navaratri (a nine-night festival dedicated to the goddess Parvati), Dasara (the victory of Rama over the demon army), Diwali (a festival of lights), Makara Sankranti, Shivaratri (dedicated to Shiva), and Holi (a spring festival).

Regional festivals are Durga-puja (dedicated to the goddess Durga (Parvati)), Sarasvati-puja (dedicated to the goddess Sarasvati), Ganesh Chaturthi (worship of Ganesh on the fourth day (Chaturthi) of the light half of Bhadrapad), Ramanavami (the birth festival of the god Rama) and Janmashtami (the birth festival of the god Krishna).

The main festivals celebrated in Britain are Navaratri, Dasara, Durga-puja, Diwali, Holi, Sarasvati-puja, Ganesh Chaturthi, Raksha-bandhan, Ramanavami and Janmashtami.

For dates of the main festivals in 2002, *see* page 9.

JEWISH CALENDAR

The story of the Flood in the Book of Genesis indicates the use of a calendar of some kind and that the writers recognized thirty days as the length of a lunation. However, after the diaspora, Jewish communities were left in considerable doubt as to the times of fasts and festivals. This led to the formation of the Jewish calendar as used today. It is said that this was done in AD 358 by Rabbi Hillel II, though some assert that it did not happen until much later.

The calendar is luni-solar, and is based on the lengths of the lunation and of the tropical year as found by Hipparchus (*c.*120 BC), which differ little from those adopted at the present day. The year AM 5762 (2000–2001) is the 5th year of the 304th Metonic (Minor or Lunar) cycle of 19 years and the 22st year of the 206th Solar (or Major) cycle of 28 years since the Era of the Creation. Jews hold that the Creation occurred at the time of the autumnal equinox in the year known in the Christian calendar as 3760 BC (954 of the Julian period). The epoch or starting point of Jewish chronology corresponds to 7 October 3761 BC. At the beginning of each solar cycle, the Tekufah of Nisan (the vernal equinox) returns to the same day and to the same hour.

The hour is divided into 1080 minims, and the month between one new moon and the next is reckoned as 29 days, 12 hours, 793 minims. The normal calendar year, called a Regular Common year, consists of 12 months of 30 days and 29 days alternately. Since 12 months such as these comprise only 354 days, in order that each of them shall not diverge greatly from an average place in the solar year, a 13th month is occasionally added after the fifth month of the civil year (which commences on the first day of the month Tishri), or as the penultimate month of the ecclesiastical year (which commences on the first day of the month Nisan). The years when this happens are called Embolismic or leap years.

Of the 19 years that form a Metonic cycle, seven are leap years; they occur at places in the cycle indicated by the numbers 3, 6, 8, 11, 14, 17 and 19, these places being chosen so that the accumulated excesses of the solar years should be as small as possible.

A Jewish year is of one of the following six types:

Minimal Common	353 days
Regular Common	354 days
Full Common	355 days
Minimal Leap	383 days
Regular Leap	384 days
Full Leap	385 days

The Regular year has alternate months of 30 and 29 days. In a Full year, whether common or leap, Marcheshvan, the second month of the civil year, has 30 days instead of 29; in Minimal years Kislev, the third month, has 29 instead of 30. The additional month in leap years is called Adar I and precedes the month called Adar in Common years. Adar II is called Adar Sheni in leap years, and the usual Adar festivals are kept in Adar Sheni. Adar I and Adar II always have 30 days, but neither this, nor the other variations mentioned, is allowed to change the number of days in the other months, which still follow the alternation of the normal twelve.

These are the main features of the Jewish calendar, which must be considered permanent because as a Jewish law it cannot be altered except by a great Sanhedrin.

The Jewish day begins between sunset and nightfall. The time used is that of the meridian of Jerusalem, which is 2h 21m in advance of Greenwich Mean Time. Rules for the beginning of sabbaths and festivals were laid down for the latitude of London in the 18th century and hours for nightfall are now fixed annually by the Chief Rabbi.

JEWISH CALENDAR 5762–3

AM 5762 (762) is a Regular Common year of 12 months, 50 sabbaths and 354 days. AM 5763 (763) is a Full leap year of 13 months, 55 sabbaths and 385 days.

Month (first day)	AM 5762	AM 5763
Tishri 1	18 September 2001	7 September 2002
Marcheshvan 1	18 October	7 October
Kislev 1	16 November	6 November
Tebet 1	16 December	6 December
Shebat 1	14 January 2002	4 January 2003
*Adar 1	13 February	3 February
†Adar II		5 March
Nisan 1	14 March	3 April
Iyar 1	13 April	3 May
Sivan 1	12 May	1 June
Tammuz 1	11 June	1 July
Ab 1	10 July	30 July
Elul 1	9 August	29 August

*Known as Adar Rishon in leap years
†Known as Adar Sheni in leap years

JEWISH FASTS AND FESTIVALS

For dates of principal festivals in 2002, *see* page 9.

Tishri 1–2	Rosh Hashanah (New Year)
Tishri 3	*Fast of Gedaliah
Tishri 10	Yom Kippur (Day of Atonement)
Tishri 15–21	Succoth (Feast of Tabernacles)
Tishri 21	Hoshana Rabba
Tishri 22	Shemini Atseret (Solemn Assembly)
Tishri 23	Simchat Torah (Rejoicing of the Law)
Kislev 25	Chanucah (Dedication of the Temple) begins
Tebet 10	Fast of Tebet
†*Adar* 13	§Fast of Esther
†*Adar* 14	Purim
†*Adar* 15	Shushan Purim
Nisan 15–22	Pesach (Passover)
Sivan 6–7	Shavuot (Feast of Weeks)
Tammuz 17	*Fast of Tammuz
Ab 9	*Fast of Ab

*If these dates fall on the sabbath the fast is kept on the following day
†Adar Sheni in leap years
§This fast is observed on Adar 11 (or Adar Sheni 11 in leap years) if Adar 13 falls on a sabbath

THE MUSLIM CALENDAR

The Muslim era is dated from the *Hijrah*, or flight of the Prophet Muhammad from Mecca to Medina, the corresponding date of which in the Julian calendar is 16 July AD 622. The lunar *hijri* calendar is used principally in Iran, Egypt, Malaysia, Pakistan, Mauritania, various Arab states and certain parts of India. Iran uses the solar *hijri* calendar as well as the lunar *hijri* calendar. The dating system was adopted about AD 639, commencing with the first day of the month Muharram.

The lunar calendar consists of twelve months containing an alternate sequence of 30 and 29 days, with the intercalation of one day at the end of the twelfth month at stated intervals in each cycle of 30 years. The object of the intercalation is to reconcile the date of the first day of the month with the date of the actual new moon.

Some adherents still take the date of the evening of the first physical sighting of the crescent of the new moon as that of the first of the month. If cloud obscures the moon the present month may be extended to 30 days, after which the new month will begin automatically regardless of whether the moon has been seen. (Under religious law a month must have less than 31 days.) This means that the beginning of a new month and the date of religious festivals can vary from the published calendars.

In each cycle of 30 years, 19 years are common and contain 354 days, and 11 years are intercalary (leap years) of 355 days, the latter being called *kabisah*. The mean length of the Hijrah years is 354 days 8 hours 48 minutes and the period of mean lunation is 29 days 12 hours 44 minutes.

To ascertain if a year is common or kabisah, divide it by 30: the quotient gives the number of completed cycles and the remainder shows the place of the year in the current cycle. If the remainder is 2, 5, 7, 10, 13, 16, 18, 21, 24, 26 or 29, the year is kabisah and consists of 355 days.

MUSLIM CALENDAR 1422-23

Hijrah year 1422 AH (remainder 12) is a common year, 1423 AH (remainder 13) is a kabisah year.

Month (length)	1423 (1422) AH
Dhû'l-Qa'da (30)	(15 January)
Dhû'l-Hijjah (29 or 30)	(15 February)
Muharram (30)	15 March
Safar (29)	14 April
Rabi' I (30)	14 May
Rabi' II (29)	12 June
Jumada I (30)	12 July
Jumada II (29)	10 August
Rajab (30)	9 September
Sha'ban (29)	8 October
Ramadân (30)	6 November
Shawwâl (29)	6 December

MUSLIM FESTIVALS

Ramadan is a month of fasting for all Muslims because it is the month in which the revelation of the *Qur'an* (Koran) began. During Ramadan Muslims abstain from food, drink and sexual pleasure from dawn until after sunset throughout the month.

The two major festivals are *Id al-Fitr* and *Id al-Adha*. Id al-Fitr marks the end of the Ramadan fast and is celebrated on the day after the sighting of the new moon of the following month. Id al-Adha, the festival of sacrifice (also known as the great festival), celebrates the submission of the Prophet Ibrahim (Abraham) to God. Id al-Adha falls on the tenth day of Dhul-Hijjah, coinciding with the day when those on *hajj* (pilgrimage to Mecca) sacrifice animals. Other days accorded special recognition are:

Muharram 1	New Year's Day
Muharram 10	Ashura (the day Prophet Noah left the Ark and Prophet Moses was saved from Pharaoh (Sunni), the death of the Prophet's grandson Husain (Shi'ite))
Rabi'u-l-Awwal (Rabi' I) 12	Mawlid al-Nabi (birthday of the Prophet Muhammad)
Rajab 27	Laylat al-Isra' wa'l-Mi'raj (The Night of Journey and Ascension)
Ramadân One of the odd-numbered nights in the last 10 of the month	Laylat al-Qadr (Night of Power)
Dhû'l-Hijjah 10	Id al-Adha (Festival of Sacrifice)

THE SIKH CALENDAR

The Sikh calendar is a lunar calendar of 365 days divided into 12 months. The length of the months varies between 29 and 32 days.

There are no prescribed feast days and no fasting periods. The main celebrations are Baisakhi Mela (the new year and the anniversary of the founding of the Khalsa), Diwali Mela (festival of light), Hola Mohalla Mela (a spring festival held in the Punjab), and the Gurpurbs (anniversaries associated with the ten Gurus).

For dates of the major celebrations in 2002, *see* page 9.

CIVIL AND LEGAL CALENDAR

THE HISTORICAL YEAR

Before 1752, two calendar systems were used in England. The civil or legal year began on 25 March and the historical year on 1 January. Thus the civil or legal date 24 March 1658 was the same day as the historical date 24 March 1659; a date in that portion of the year is written as 24 March 165⅞, the lower figure showing the historical year.

THE NEW YEAR

In England in the seventh century, and as late as the 13th, the year was reckoned from Christmas Day, but in the 12th century the Church in England began the year with the feast of the Annunciation of the Blessed Virgin ('Lady Day') on 25 March and this practice was adopted generally in the 14th century. The civil or legal year in the British Dominions (exclusive of Scotland) began with Lady Day until 1751. But in and since 1752 the civil year has begun with 1 January. New Year's Day in Scotland was changed from 25 March to 1 January in 1600.

Elsewhere in Europe, 1 January was adopted as the first day of the year by Venice in 1522, German states in 1544, Spain, Portugal and the Roman Catholic Netherlands in 1556, Prussia, Denmark and Sweden in 1559, France in 1564, Lorraine in 1579, the Protestant Netherlands in 1583, Russia in 1725, and Tuscany in 1751.

REGNAL YEARS

Regnal years are the years of a sovereign's reign and each begins on the anniversary of his or her accession, e.g. regnal year 51 of the present Queen begins on 6 February 2002.

The system was used for dating Acts of Parliament until 1962. The Summer Time Act 1925, for example, is quoted as 15 and 16 Geo. V c. 64, because it became law in the parliamentary session which extended over part of both of these regnal years. Acts of a parliamentary session during which a sovereign died were usually given two year numbers, the regnal year of the deceased sovereign and the regnal year of his or her successor, e.g. those passed in 1952 were dated 16 Geo. VI and 1 Elizabeth II. Since 1962 Acts of Parliament have been dated by the calendar year.

QUARTER AND TERM DAYS

Holy days and saints days were the usual means in early times for setting the dates of future and recurrent appointments. The quarter days in England and Wales are the feast of the Nativity (25 December), the feast of the Annunciation (25 March), the feast of St John the Baptist (24 June) and the feast of St Michael and All Angels (29 September).

The term days in Scotland are Candlemas (the feast of the Purification), Whitsunday, Lammas (Loaf Mass), and Martinmas (St Martin's Day). These fell on 2 February, 15 May, 1 August and 11 November respectively. However, by the Term and Quarter Days (Scotland) Act 1990, the dates of the term days were changed to 28 February (Candlemas), 28 May (Whitsunday), 28 August (Lammas) and 28 November (Martinmas).

RED-LETTER DAYS

Red-letter days were originally the holy days and saints days indicated in early ecclesiastical calendars by letters printed in red ink. The days to be distinguished in this way were approved at the Council of Nicaea in AD 325.

These days still have a legal significance, as judges of the Queen's Bench Division wear scarlet robes on red-letter days falling during the law sittings. The days designated as red-letter days for this purpose are:

Holy and saints days
The Conversion of St Paul, the Purification, Ash Wednesday, the Annunciation, the Ascension, the feasts of St Mark, SS Philip and James, St Matthias, St Barnabas, St John the Baptist, St Peter, St Thomas, St James, St Luke, SS Simon and Jude, All Saints, St Andrew

Civil calendar (for dates, *see* page 9)
The anniversaries of The Queen's accession, The Queen's birthday and The Queen's coronation, The Queen's official birthday, the birthday of the Duke of Edinburgh, the birthday of Queen Elizabeth the Queen Mother, the birthday of the Prince of Wales, St David's Day and Lord Mayor's Day

PUBLIC HOLIDAYS

Public holidays are divided into two categories, common law and statutory. Common law holidays are holidays 'by habit and custom'; in England, Wales and Northern Ireland these are Good Friday and Christmas Day.

Statutory public holidays, known as bank holidays, were first established by the Bank Holidays Act 1871. They were, literally, days on which the banks (and other public institutions) were closed and financial obligations due on that day were payable the following day. The legislation currently governing public holidays in the UK, which is the Banking and Financial Dealings Act 1971, stipulates the days that are to be public holidays in England, Wales, Scotland and Northern Ireland.

Certain holidays (indicated by * below) are granted annually by royal proclamation, either throughout the UK or in any place in the UK. The public holidays are:

England and Wales
*New Year's Day
Easter Monday
*The first Monday in May
The last Monday in May
The last Monday in August
26 December, if it is not a Sunday
27 December when 25 or 26 December is a Sunday

Scotland

New Year's Day, or if it is a Sunday, 2 January
2 January, or if it is a Sunday, 3 January
Good Friday
The first Monday in May
*The last Monday in May
The first Monday in August
Christmas Day, or if it is a Sunday, 26 December
*Boxing Day – if Christmas Day falls on a Sunday, 26 December is given in lieu and an alternative day is given for Boxing Day

Northern Ireland

New Year's Day
7 March, or if it is a Sunday, 18 March
Easter Monday
*The first Monday in May
The last Monday in May
*12 July, or if it is a Sunday, 13 July
The last Monday in August
26 December, if it is not a Sunday
27 December if 25 or 26 December is a Sunday
For dates of public holidays in 2002 and 2003, *see* pages 10–11.

CHRONOLOGICAL CYCLES AND ERAS

SOLAR (OR MAJOR) CYCLE

The solar cycle is a period of twenty-eight years in any corresponding year of which the days of the week recur on the same day of the month.

METONIC (LUNAR, OR MINOR) CYCLE

In 432 BC, Meton, an Athenian astronomer, found that 235 lunations are very nearly, though not exactly, equal in duration to 19 solar years and so after 19 years the phases of the Moon recur on the same days of the month (nearly). The dates of full moon in a cycle of 19 years were inscribed in figures of gold on public monuments in Athens, and the number showing the position of a year in the cycle is called the golden number of that year.

JULIAN PERIOD

The Julian period was proposed by Joseph Scaliger in 1582. The period is 7980 Julian years, and its first year coincides with the year 4713 BC. The figure of 7980 is the product of the number of years in the solar cycle, the Metonic cycle and the cycle of the Roman indiction (28 × 19 × 15).

ROMAN INDICTION

The Roman indiction is a period of fifteen years, instituted for fiscal purposes about AD 300.

EPACT

The epact is the age of the calendar Moon, diminished by one day, on 1 January, in the ecclesiastical lunar calendar.

CHINESE CALENDAR

A lunar calendar was the sole calendar in use in China until 1911, when the government adopted the new (Gregorian) calendar for official and most business activities. The Chinese tend to follow both calendars, the lunar calendar playing an important part in personal life, e.g. birth celebrations, festivals, marriages; and in rural villages the lunar calendar dictates the cycle of activities, denoting the change of weather and farming activities.

The lunar calendar is used in Hong Kong, Singapore, Malaysia, Tibet and elsewhere in south-east Asia. The calendar has a cycle of 60 years. The new year begins at the first new moon after the sun enters the sign of Aquarius, i.e. the new year falls between 21 January and 19 February in the Gregorian calendar.

Each year in the Chinese calendar is associated with one of 12 animals: the rat, the ox, the tiger, the rabbit, the dragon, the snake, the horse, the goat or sheep, the monkey, the chicken or rooster, the dog, and the pig.

The date of the Chinese new year and the astrological sign for the years 2001–2005 are:

2001	24 January	Snake
2002	12 February	Horse
2003	1 February	Goat or Sheep
2004	22 January	Monkey
2005	9 February	Chicken or Rooster

COPTIC CALENDAR

In the Coptic calendar, which is used in parts of Egypt and Ethiopia, the year is made up of 12 months of 30 days each, followed, in general, by five complementary days. Every fourth year is an intercalary or leap year and in these years there are six complementary days. The intercalary year of the Coptic calendar immediately precedes the leap year of the Julian calendar. The era is that of Diocletian or the Martyrs, the origin of which is fixed at 29 August AD 284 (Julian date).

INDIAN ERAS

In addition to the Muslim reckoning, other eras are used in India. The Saka era of southern India, dating from 3 March AD 78, was declared the national calendar of the Republic of India with effect from 22 March 1957, to be used concurrently with the Gregorian calendar. As revised, the year of the new Saka era begins at the spring equinox, with five successive months of 31 days and seven of 30 days in ordinary years, and six months of each length in leap years. The year AD 2002 is 1924 of the revised Saka era.

The year AD 2002 corresponds to the following years in other eras:

Year 2059 of the Vikram Samvat era
Year 1409 of the Bengali San era
Year 1178 of the Kollam era
Vedanga Jyotisa year 3 of the five-yearly cycle (385th cycle of Paitamah Siddhanta)
Year 6003 of the Kaliyuga era
Year 2546 of the Buddha Nirvana era

JAPANESE CALENDAR

The Japanese calendar is essentially the same as the Gregorian calendar, the years, months and weeks being of the same length and beginning on the same days as those of the Gregorian calendar. The numeration of the years is different, based on a system of epochs or periods each of which begins at the accession of an Emperor or other important occurrence. The method is not unlike the British system of regnal years, except that each year of a period closes on 31 December. The Japanese chronology begins about AD 650 and the three latest epochs are defined by the reigns of Emperors, whose actual names are not necessarily used:

Epoch
Taishō 1 August 1912 to 25 December 1926
Shōwa 26 December 1926 to 7 January 1989
Heisei 8 January 1989

The year Heisei 14 begins on 1 January 2002.

The months are known as First Month, Second Month, etc., First Month being equivalent to January. The days of the week are Nichiyōbi (Sun-day), Getsuyōbi (Moon-day), Kayōbi (Fire-day), Suiyōbi (Water-day), Mokuyōbi (Wood-day), Kinyōbi (Metal-day), Doyōbi (Earth-day).

THE MASONIC YEAR

Two dates are quoted in warrants, dispensations, etc., issued by the United Grand Lodge of England, those for the current year being expressed as *Anno Domini* 2000 – *Anno Lucis* 6000. This *Anno Lucis* (year of light) is based on the Book of Genesis 1:3, the 4000-year difference being derived, in modified form, from *Ussher's Notation*, published in 1654, which places the Creation of the World in 4004 BC.

OLYMPIADS

Ancient Greek chronology was reckoned in Olympiads, cycles of four years corresponding with the periodic Olympic Games held on the plain of Olympia in Elis once every four years. The intervening years were the first, second, etc., of the Olympiad, which received the name of the victor at the Games. The first recorded Olympiad is that of Choroebus, 776 BC.

ZOROASTRIAN CALENDAR

Zoroastrians, followers of the Iranian prophet Zarathush-tra (known to the Greeks as Zoroaster) are mostly to be found in Iran and in India, where they are known as Parsees.

The Zoroastrian era dates from the coronation of the last Zoroastrian Sasanian king in AD 631. The Zoroastrian calendar is divided into twelve months, each comprising 30 days, followed by five holy days of the Gathas at the end of each year to make the year consist of 365 days.

In order to synchronize the calendar with the solar year of 365 days, an extra month was intercalated once every 120 years. However, this intercalation ceased in the 12th century and the New Year, which had fallen in the spring, slipped back to August. Because intercalation ceased at different times in Iran and India, there was one month's difference between the calendar followed in Iran (Kadmi calendar) and that followed by the Parsees (Shenshai calendar). In 1906 a group of Zoroastrians decided to bring the calendar back in line with the seasons again and restore the New Year to 21 March each year (Fasli calendar).

The Shenshai calendar (New Year in August) is mainly used by Parsees. The Fasli calendar (New Year, 21 March) is mainly used by Zoroastrians living in Iran, in the Indian subcontinent, or away from Iran.

THE ROMAN CALENDAR

Roman historians adopted as an epoch the foundation of Rome, which is believed to have happened in the year 753 BC. The ordinal number of the years in Roman reckoning is followed by the letters AUC (*ab urbe condita*), so that the year 2002 is 2755 AUC (MMDCCLV). The calendar that we know has developed from one said to have been established by Romulus using a year of 304 days divided into ten months, beginning with March. To this Numa added January and February, making the year consist of 12 months of 30 and 29 days alternately, with an additional day so that the total was 355. It is also said that Numa ordered an intercalary month of 22 or 23 days in alternate years, making 90 days in eight years, to be inserted after 23 February.

However, there is some doubt as to the origination and the details of the intercalation in the Roman calendar. It is certain that some scheme of this kind was inaugurated and not fully carried out, for in the year 46 BC Julius Caesar found that the calendar had been allowed to fall into some confusion. He sought the help of the Egyptian astronomer Sosigenes, which led to the construction and adoption (45 BC) of the Julian calendar, and, by a slight alteration, to the Gregorian calendar now in use. The year 46 BC was made to consist of 445 days and is called the Year of Confusion.

In the Roman (Julian) calendar the days of the month were counted backwards from three fixed points, or days, and an intervening day was said to be so many days before the next coming point, the first and last being counted. These three points were the Kalends, the Nones, and the Ides. Their positions in the months and the method of counting from them will be seen in the table below. The year containing 366 days was called *bissextilis annus*, as it had a doubled sixth day (*bissextus dies*) before the March Kalends on 24 February – *ante diem sextum Kalendas Martias*, or a.d. VI Kal. Mart.

Present days of the month	*March, May, July, October have thirty-one days*		*January, August, December have thirty-one day*		*April, June, September, November have thirty day*		*February has twenty-eight days, and in leap year twenty-nine*	
1	Kalendis		Kalendis		Kalendis		Kalendis	
2	VI		IV	ante Nonas	IV	ante Nonas	IV	ante Nonas
3	V	ante Nonas	III		III		III	
4	IV		pridie Nonas		pridie Nonas		pridie Nonas	
5	III		Nonis		Nonis		Nonis	
6	pridie Nonas		VIII		VIII		VIII	
7	Nonis		VII		VII		VII	
8	VIII		VI	ante Idus	VI	ante Idus	VI	ante Idus
9	VII		V		V		V	
10	VI	ante Idus	IV		IV		IV	
11	V		III		III		III	
12	IV		pridie Idus		pridie Idus		pridie Idus	
13	III		Idibus		Idibus		Idibus	
14	pridie Idus		XIX		XVIII		XVI	
15	Idibus		XVIII		XVII		XV	
16	XVII		XVII		XVI		XIV	
17	XVI		XVI		XV		XIII	
18	XV		XV		XIV		XII	
19	XIV		XIV		XIII		XI	
20	XIII		XIII		XII	ante Kalendas (of the month following)	X	ante Kalendas Martias
21	XII		XII	ante Kalendas (of the month following)	XI		IX	
22	XI	ante Kalendas (of the month following)	XI		X		VIII	
23	X		X		IX		VII	
24	IX		IX		VIII		*VI	
25	VIII		VIII		VII		V	
26	VII		VII		VI		IV	
27	VI		VI		VI		III	
28	V		V		V		pridie Kalendas	
29	IV		IV		IV			
30	III		III		III			
31	pridie Kalendas (Aprilis, Iunias, Sextilis, Novembris)		pridie Kalendas (Februarias, Septembris, Ianuarias)		pridie Kalendas (Maias, Quinctilis, Octobris, Decembris)		* (repeated in leap year)	

Calendar for Any Year 1780–2040

To select the correct calendar for any year between 1780 and 2040, consult the index below
* leap year

Year		Year		Year		Year		Year		Year		Year		Year	
1780	N*	1813	K	1846	I	1879	G	1912	D*	1945	C	1978	A	2011	M
1781	C	1814	M	1847	K	1880	J*	1913	G	1946	E	1979	C	2012	B*
1782	E	1815	A	1848	N*	1881	M	1914	I	1947	G	1980	F*	2013	E
1783	G	1816	D*	1849	C	1882	A	1915	K	1948	J*	1981	I	2014	G
1784	J*	1817	G	1850	E	1883	C	1916	N*	1949	M	1982	K	2015	I
1785	M	1818	I	1851	G	1884	F*	1917	C	1950	A	1983	M	2016	L*
1786	A	1819	K	1852	J*	1885	I	1918	E	1951	C	1984	B*	2017	A
1787	C	1820	N*	1853	M	1886	K	1919	G	1952	F*	1985	E	2018	C
1788	F*	1821	C	1854	A	1887	M	1920	J*	1953	I	1986	G	2019	E
1789	I	1822	E	1855	C	1888	B*	1921	M	1954	K	1987	I	2020	H*
1790	K	1823	G	1856	F*	1889	E	1922	A	1955	M	1988	L*	2021	K
1791	M	1824	J*	1857	I	1890	G	1923	C	1956	B*	1989	A	2022	M
1792	B*	1825	M	1858	K	1891	I	1924	F*	1957	E	1990	C	2023	A
1793	E	1826	A	1859	M	1892	L*	1925	I	1958	G	1991	E	2024	D*
1794	G	1827	C	1860	B*	1893	A	1926	K	1959	I	1992	H*	2025	G
1795	I	1828	F*	1861	E	1894	C	1927	M	1960	L*	1993	K	2026	I
1796	L*	1829	I	1862	G	1895	E	1928	B*	1961	A	1994	M	2027	K
1797	A	1830	K	1863	I	1896	H*	1929	E	1962	C	1995	A	2028	N*
1798	C	1831	M	1864	L*	1897	K	1930	G	1963	E	1996	D*	2029	C
1799	E	1832	B*	1865	A	1898	M	1931	I	1964	H*	1997	G	2030	E
1800	G	1833	E	1866	C	1899	A	1932	L*	1965	K	1998	I	2031	G
1801	I	1834	G	1867	E	1900	C	1933	A	1966	M	1999	K	2032	J*
1802	K	1835	I	1868	H*	1901	E	1934	C	1967	A	2000	N*	2033	M
1803	M	1836	L*	1869	K	1902	G	1935	E	1968	D*	2001	C	2034	A
1804	B*	1837	A	1870	M	1903	I	1936	H*	1969	G	2002	E	2035	C
1805	E	1838	C	1871	A	1904	L*	1937	K	1970	I	2003	G	2036	F*
1806	G	1839	E	1872	D*	1905	A	1938	M	1971	K	2004	J*	2037	I
1807	I	1840	H*	1873	G	1906	C	1939	A	1972	N*	2005	M	2038	K
1808	L*	1841	K	1874	I	1907	E	1940	D*	1973	C	2006	A	2039	M
1809	A	1842	M	1875	K	1908	H*	1941	G	1974	E	2007	C	2040	B*
1810	C	1843	A	1876	N*	1909	K	1942	I	1975	G	2008	F*		
1811	E	1844	D*	1877	C	1910	M	1943	K	1976	J*	2009	I		
1812	H*	1845	G	1878	E	1911	A	1944	N*	1977	M	2010	K		

A

	January	February	March
Sun.	1 8 15 22 29	5 12 19 26	5 12 19 26
Mon.	2 9 16 23 30	6 13 20 27	6 13 20 27
Tue.	3 10 17 24 31	7 14 21 28	7 14 21 28
Wed.	4 11 18 25	1 8 15 22	1 8 15 22 29
Thur.	5 12 19 26	2 9 16 23	2 9 16 23 30
Fri.	6 13 20 27	3 10 17 24	3 10 17 24 31
Sat.	7 14 21 28	4 11 18 25	4 11 18 25

	April	May	June
Sun.	2 9 16 23 30	7 14 21 28	4 11 18 25
Mon.	3 10 17 24	1 8 15 22 29	5 12 19 26
Tue.	4 11 18 25	2 9 16 23 30	6 13 20 27
Wed.	5 12 19 26	3 10 17 24 31	7 14 21 28
Thur.	6 13 20 27	4 11 18 25	1 8 15 22 29
Fri.	7 14 21 28	5 12 19 26	2 9 16 23 30
Sat.	1 8 15 22 29	6 13 20 27	3 10 17 24

	July	August	September
Sun.	2 9 16 23 30	6 13 20 27	3 10 17 24
Mon.	3 10 17 24 31	7 14 21 28	4 11 18 25
Tue.	4 11 18 25	1 8 15 22 29	5 12 19 26
Wed.	5 12 19 26	2 9 16 23 30	6 13 20 27
Thur.	6 13 20 27	3 10 17 24 31	7 14 21 28
Fri.	7 14 21 28	4 11 18 25	1 8 15 22 29
Sat.	1 8 15 22 29	5 12 19 26	2 9 16 23 30

	October	November	December
Sun.	1 8 15 22 29	5 12 19 26	3 10 17 24 31
Mon.	2 9 16 23 30	6 13 20 27	4 11 18 25
Tue.	3 10 17 24 31	7 14 21 28	5 12 19 26
Wed.	4 11 18 25	1 8 15 22 29	6 13 20 27
Thur.	5 12 19 26	2 9 16 23 30	7 14 21 28
Fri.	6 13 20 27	3 10 17 24	1 8 15 22 29
Sat.	7 14 21 28	4 11 18 25	2 9 16 23 30

EASTER DAYS
March 26 1815, 1826, 1837, 1967, 1978, 1989
April 2 1809, 1893, 1899, 1961
April 9 1871, 1882, 1939, 1950, 2023, 2034
April 16 1786, 1797, 1843, 1854, 1865, 1911, 1922, 1933, 1995, 2006, 2017
April 23 1905

B (LEAP YEAR)

	January	February	March
Sun.	1 8 15 22 29	5 12 19 26	4 11 18 25
Mon.	2 9 16 23 30	6 13 20 27	5 12 19 26
Tue.	3 10 17 24 31	7 14 21 28	6 13 20 27
Wed.	4 11 18 25	1 8 15 22 29	7 14 21 28
Thur.	5 12 19 26	2 9 16 23	1 8 15 22 29
Fri.	6 13 20 27	3 10 17 24	2 9 16 23 30
Sat.	7 14 21 28	4 11 18 25	3 10 17 24 31

	April	May	June
Sun.	1 8 15 22 29	6 13 20 27	3 10 17 24
Mon.	2 9 16 23 30	7 14 21 28	4 11 18 25
Tue.	3 10 17 24	1 8 15 22 29	5 12 19 26
Wed.	4 11 18 25	2 9 16 23 30	6 13 20 27
Thur.	5 12 19 26	3 10 17 24 31	7 14 21 28
Fri.	6 13 20 27	4 11 18 25	1 8 15 22 29
Sat.	7 14 21 28	5 12 19 26	2 9 16 23 30

	July	August	September
Sun.	1 8 15 22 29	5 12 19 26	2 9 16 23 30
Mon.	2 9 16 23 30	6 13 20 27	3 10 17 24
Tue.	3 10 17 24 31	7 14 21 28	4 11 18 25
Wed.	4 11 18 25	1 8 15 22 29	5 12 19 26
Thur.	5 12 19 26	2 9 16 23 30	6 13 20 27
Fri.	6 13 20 27	3 10 17 24 31	7 14 21 28
Sat.	7 14 21 28	4 11 18 25	1 8 15 22 29

	October	November	December
Sun.	7 14 21 28	4 11 18 25	2 9 16 23 30
Mon.	1 8 15 22 29	5 12 19 26	3 10 17 24 31
Tue.	2 9 16 23 30	6 13 20 27	4 11 18 25
Wed.	3 10 17 24 31	7 14 21 28	5 12 19 26
Thur.	4 11 18 25	1 8 15 22 29	6 13 20 27
Fri.	5 12 19 26	2 9 16 23 30	7 14 21 28
Sat.	6 13 20 27	3 10 17 24	1 8 15 22 29

EASTER DAYS
April 1 1804, 1888, 1956, 2040
April 8 1792, 1860, 1928, 2012
April 22 1832, 1984

C

	January	February	March
Sun.	7 14 21 28	4 11 18 25	4 11 18 25
Mon.	1 8 15 22 29	5 12 19 26	5 12 19 26
Tue.	2 9 16 23 30	6 13 20 27	6 13 20 27
Wed.	3 10 17 24 31	7 14 21 28	7 14 21 28
Thur.	4 11 18 25	1 8 15 22	1 8 15 22 29
Fri.	5 12 19 26	2 9 16 23	2 9 16 23 30
Sat.	6 13 20 27	3 10 17 24	3 10 17 24 31

	April	May	June
Sun.	1 8 15 22 29	6 13 20 27	3 10 17 24
Mon.	2 9 16 23 30	7 14 21 28	4 11 18 25
Tue.	3 10 17 24	1 8 15 22 29	5 12 19 26
Wed.	4 11 18 25	2 9 16 23 30	6 13 20 27
Thur.	5 12 19 26	3 10 17 24 31	7 14 21 28
Fri.	6 13 20 27	4 11 18 25	1 8 15 22 29
Sat.	7 14 21 28	5 12 19 26	2 9 16 23 30

	July	August	September
Sun.	1 8 15 22 29	5 12 19 26	2 9 16 23 30
Mon.	2 9 16 23 30	6 13 20 27	3 10 17 24
Tue.	3 10 17 24 31	7 14 21 28	4 11 18 25
Wed.	4 11 18 25	1 8 15 22 29	5 12 19 26
Thur.	5 12 19 26	2 9 16 23 30	6 13 20 27
Fri.	6 13 20 27	3 10 17 24 31	7 14 21 28
Sat.	7 14 21 28	4 11 18 25	1 8 15 22 29

	October	November	December
Sun.	7 14 21 28	4 11 18 25	2 9 16 23 30
Mon.	1 8 15 22 29	5 12 19 26	3 10 17 24 31
Tue.	2 9 16 23 30	6 13 20 27	4 11 18 25
Wed.	3 10 17 24 31	7 14 21 28	5 12 19 26
Thur.	4 11 18 25	1 8 15 22 29	6 13 20 27
Fri.	5 12 19 26	2 9 16 23 30	7 14 21 28
Sat.	6 13 20 27	3 10 17 24	1 8 15 22 29

EASTER DAYS
March 25   1883, 1894, 1951, 2035
April 1   1866, 1877, 1923, 1934, 1945, 2018, 2029
April 8   1787, 1798, 1849, 1855, 1917, 2007
April 15   1781, 1827, 1838, 1900, 1906, 1979, 1990, 2001
April 22   1810, 1821, 1962, 1973

E

	January	February	March
Sun.	6 13 20 27	3 10 17 24	3 10 17 24 31
Mon.	7 14 21 28	4 11 18 25	4 11 18 25
Tue.	1 8 15 22 29	5 12 19 26	5 12 19 26
Wed.	2 9 16 23 30	6 13 20 27	6 13 20 27
Thur.	3 10 17 24 31	7 14 21 28	7 14 21 28
Fri.	4 11 18 25	1 8 15 22	1 8 15 22 29
Sat.	5 12 19 26	2 9 16 23	2 9 16 23 30

	April	May	June
Sun.	7 14 21 28	5 12 19 26	2 9 16 23 30
Mon.	1 8 15 22 29	6 13 20 27	3 10 17 24
Tue.	2 9 16 23 30	7 14 21 28	4 11 18 25
Wed.	3 10 17 24	1 8 15 22 29	5 12 19 26
Thur.	4 11 18 25	2 9 16 23 30	6 13 20 27
Fri.	5 12 19 26	3 10 17 24 31	7 14 21 28
Sat.	6 13 20 27	4 11 18 25	1 8 15 22 29

	July	August	September
Sun.	7 14 21 28	4 11 18 25	1 8 15 22 29
Mon.	1 8 15 22 29	5 12 19 26	2 9 16 23 30
Tue.	2 9 16 23 30	6 13 20 27	3 10 17 24
Wed.	3 10 17 24 31	7 14 21 28	4 11 18 25
Thur.	4 11 18 25	1 8 15 22 29	5 12 19 26
Fri.	5 12 19 26	2 9 16 23 30	6 13 20 27
Sat.	6 13 20 27	3 10 17 24 31	7 14 21 28

	October	November	December
Sun.	6 13 20 27	3 10 17 24	1 8 15 22 29
Mon.	7 14 21 28	4 11 18 25	2 9 16 23 30
Tue.	1 8 15 22 29	5 12 19 26	3 10 17 24 31
Wed.	2 9 16 23 30	6 13 20 27	4 11 18 25
Thur.	3 10 17 24 31	7 14 21 28	5 12 19 26
Fri.	4 11 18 25	1 8 15 22 29	6 13 20 27
Sat.	5 12 19 26	2 9 16 23 30	7 14 21 28

EASTER DAYS
March 24   1799
March 31   1782, 1793, 1839, 1850, 1861, 1907, 1918, 1929, 1991, 2002, 2013
April 7   1822, 1833, 1901, 1985
April 14   1805, 1811, 1895, 1963, 1974
April 21   1867, 1878, 1889, 1935, 1946, 1957, 2019, 2030

D (LEAP YEAR)

	January	February	March
Sun.	7 14 21 28	4 11 18 25	3 10 17 24 31
Mon.	1 8 15 22 29	5 12 19 26	4 11 18 25
Tue.	2 9 16 23 30	6 13 20 27	5 12 19 26
Wed.	3 10 17 24 31	7 14 21 28	6 13 20 27
Thur.	4 11 18 25	1 8 15 22 29	7 14 21 28
Fri.	5 12 19 26	2 9 16 23	1 8 15 22 29
Sat.	6 13 20 27	3 10 17 24	2 9 16 23 30

	April	May	June
Sun.	7 14 21 28	5 12 19 26	2 9 16 23 30
Mon.	1 8 15 22 29	6 13 20 27	3 10 17 24
Tue.	2 9 16 23 30	7 14 21 28	4 11 18 25
Wed.	3 10 17 24	1 8 15 22 29	5 12 19 26
Thur.	4 11 18 25	2 9 16 23 30	6 13 20 27
Fri.	5 12 19 26	3 10 17 24 31	7 14 21 28
Sat.	6 13 20 27	4 11 18 25	1 8 15 22 29

	July	August	September
Sun.	7 14 21 28	4 11 18 25	1 8 15 22 29
Mon.	1 8 15 22 29	5 12 19 26	2 9 16 23 30
Tue.	2 9 16 23 30	6 13 20 27	3 10 17 24
Wed.	3 10 17 24 31	7 14 21 28	4 11 18 25
Thur.	4 11 18 25	1 8 15 22 29	5 12 19 26
Fri.	5 12 19 26	2 9 16 23 30	6 13 20 27
Sat.	6 13 20 27	3 10 17 24 31	7 14 21 28

	October	November	December
Sun.	6 13 20 27	3 10 17 24	1 8 15 22 29
Mon.	7 14 21 28	4 11 18 25	2 9 16 23 30
Tue.	1 8 15 22 29	5 12 19 26	3 10 17 24 31
Wed.	2 9 16 23 30	6 13 20 27	4 11 18 25
Thur.	3 10 17 24 31	7 14 21 28	5 12 19 26
Fri.	4 11 18 25	1 8 15 22 29	6 13 20 27
Sat.	5 12 19 26	2 9 16 23 30	7 14 21 28

EASTER DAYS
March 24   1940
March 31   1872, 2024
April 7   1844, 1912, 1996
April 14   1816, 1968

F (LEAP YEAR)

	January	February	March
Sun.	6 13 20 27	3 10 17 24	2 9 16 23 30
Mon.	7 14 21 28	4 11 18 25	3 10 17 24 31
Tue.	1 8 15 22 29	5 12 19 26	4 11 18 25
Wed.	2 9 16 23 30	6 13 20 27	5 12 19 26
Thur.	3 10 17 24 31	7 14 21 28	6 13 20 27
Fri.	4 11 18 25	1 8 15 22 29	7 14 21 28
Sat.	5 12 19 26	2 9 16 23	1 8 15 22 29

	April	May	June
Sun.	6 13 20 27	4 11 18 25	1 8 15 22 29
Mon.	7 14 21 28	5 12 19 26	2 9 16 23 30
Tue.	1 8 15 22 29	6 13 20 27	3 10 17 24
Wed.	2 9 16 23 30	7 14 21 28	4 11 18 25
Thur.	3 10 17 24	1 8 15 22 29	5 12 19 26
Fri.	4 11 18 25	2 9 16 23 30	6 13 20 27
Sat.	5 12 19 26	3 10 17 24 31	7 14 21

	July	August	September
Sun.	6 13 20 27	3 10 17 24 31	7 14 21 28
Mon.	7 14 21 28	4 11 18 25	1 8 15 22 29
Tue.	1 8 15 22 29	5 12 19 26	2 9 16 23 30
Wed.	2 9 16 23 30	6 13 20 27	3 10 17 24
Thur.	3 10 17 24 31	7 14 21 28	4 11 18 25
Fri.	4 11 18 25	1 8 15 22 29	5 12 19 26
Sat.	5 12 19 26	2 9 16 23 30	6 13 20 27

	October	November	December
Sun.	5 12 19 26	2 9 16 23 30	7 14 21 28
Mon.	6 13 20 27	3 10 17 24	1 8 15 22 29
Tue.	7 14 21 28	4 11 18 25	2 9 16 23 30
Wed.	1 8 15 22 29	5 12 19 26	3 10 17 24 31
Thur.	2 9 16 23 30	6 13 20 27	4 11 18 25
Fri.	3 10 17 24 31	7 14 21 28	5 12 19 26
Sat.	4 11 18 25	1 8 15 22 29	6 13 20 27

EASTER DAYS
March 23   1788, 1856, 2008
April 6   1828, 1980
April 13   1884, 1952, 2036
April 20   1924

G

	January	February	March
Sun.	5 12 19 26	2 9 16 23	2 9 16 23 30
Mon.	6 13 20 27	3 10 17 24	3 10 17 24 31
Tue.	7 14 21 28	4 11 18 25	4 11 18 25
Wed.	1 8 15 22 29	5 12 19 26	5 12 19 26
Thur.	2 9 16 23 30	6 13 20 27	6 13 20 27
Fri.	3 10 17 24 31	7 14 21 28	7 14 21 28
Sat.	4 11 18 25	1 8 15 22	1 8 15 22 29
	April	**May**	**June**
Sun.	6 13 20 27	4 11 18 25	1 8 15 22 29
Mon.	7 14 21 28	5 12 19 26	2 9 16 23 30
Tue.	1 8 15 22 29	6 13 20 27	3 10 17 24
Wed.	2 9 16 23 30	7 14 21 28	4 11 18 25
Thur.	3 10 17 24	1 8 15 22 29	5 12 19 26
Fri.	4 11 18 25	2 9 16 23 30	6 13 20 27
Sat.	5 12 19 26	3 10 17 24 31	7 14 21 28
	July	**August**	**September**
Sun.	6 13 20 27	3 10 17 24 31	7 14 21 28
Mon.	7 14 21 28	4 11 18 25	1 8 15 22 29
Tue.	1 8 15 22 29	5 12 19 26	2 9 16 23 30
Wed.	2 9 16 23 30	6 13 20 27	3 10 17 24
Thur.	3 10 17 24 31	7 14 21 28	4 11 18 25
Fri.	4 11 18 25	1 8 15 22 29	5 12 19 26
Sat.	5 12 19 26	2 9 16 23 30	6 13 20 27
	October	**November**	**December**
Sun.	5 12 19 26	2 9 16 23 30	7 14 21 28
Mon.	6 13 20 27	3 10 17 24	1 8 15 22 29
Tue.	7 14 21 28	4 11 18 25	2 9 16 23 30
Wed.	1 8 15 22 29	5 12 19 26	3 10 17 24 31
Thur.	2 9 16 23 30	6 13 20 27	4 11 18 25
Fri.	3 10 17 24 31	7 14 21 28	5 12 19 26
Sat.	4 11 18 25	1 8 15 22 29	6 13 20 27

EASTER DAYS
March 23 1845, 1913
March 30 1823, 1834, 1902, 1975, 1986, 1997
April 6 1806, 1817, 1890, 1947, 1958, 1969
April 13 1800, 1873, 1879, 1941, 2031
April 20 1783, 1794, 1851, 1862, 1919, 1930, 2003, 2014, 2025

I

	January	February	March
Sun.	4 11 18 25	1 8 15 22	1 8 15 22 29
Mon.	5 12 19 26	2 9 16 23	2 9 16 23 30
Tue.	6 13 20 27	3 10 17 24	3 10 17 24 31
Wed.	7 14 21 28	4 11 18 25	4 11 18 25
Thur.	1 8 15 22 29	5 12 19 26	5 12 19 26
Fri.	2 9 16 23 30	6 13 20 27	6 13 20 27
Sat.	3 10 17 24 31	7 14 21 28	7 14 21 28
	April	**May**	**June**
Sun.	5 12 19 26	3 10 17 24 31	7 14 21 28
Mon.	6 13 20 27	4 11 18 25	1 8 15 22 29
Tue.	7 14 21 28	5 12 19 26	2 9 16 23 30
Wed.	1 8 15 22 29	6 13 20 27	3 10 17 24
Thur.	2 9 16 23 30	7 14 21 28	4 11 18 25
Fri.	3 10 17 24	1 8 15 22 29	5 12 19 26
Sat.	4 11 18 25	2 9 16 23 30	6 13 20 27
	July	**August**	**September**
Sun.	5 12 19 26	2 9 16 23 30	6 13 20 27
Mon.	6 13 20 27	3 10 17 24 31	7 14 21 28
Tue.	7 14 21 28	4 11 18 25	1 8 15 22 29
Wed.	1 8 15 22 29	5 12 19 26	2 9 16 23 30
Thur.	2 9 16 23 30	6 13 20 27	3 10 17 24
Fri.	3 10 17 24	7 14 21 28	4 11 18 25
Sat.	4 11 18 25	1 8 15 22 29	5 12 19 26
	October	**November**	**December**
Sun.	4 11 18 25	1 8 15 22 29	6 13 20 27
Mon.	5 12 19 26	2 9 16 23 30	7 14 21 28
Tue.	6 13 20 27	3 10 17 24	1 8 15 22 29
Wed.	7 14 21 28	4 11 18 25	2 9 16 23 30
Thur.	1 8 15 22 29	5 12 19 26	3 10 17 24 31
Fri.	2 9 16 23 30	6 13 20 27	4 11 18 25
Sat.	3 10 17 24 31	7 14 21 28	5 12 19 26

EASTER DAYS
March 22 1818
March 29 1807, 1891, 1959, 1970
April 5 1795, 1801, 1863, 1874, 1885, 1931, 1942, 1953, 2015, 2026, 2037
April 12 1789, 1846, 1857, 1903, 1914, 1925, 1998, 2009
April 19 1829, 1835, 1981, 1987

H (LEAP YEAR)

	January	February	March
Sun.	5 12 19 26	2 9 16 23	1 8 15 22 29
Mon.	6 13 20 27	3 10 17 24	2 9 16 23 30
Tue.	7 14 21 28	4 11 18 25	3 10 17 24 31
Wed.	1 8 15 22 29	5 12 19 26	4 11 18 25
Thur.	2 9 16 23 30	6 13 20 27	5 12 19 26
Fri.	3 10 17 24 31	7 14 21 28	6 13 20 27
Sat.	4 11 18 25	1 8 15 22 29	7 14 21 28
	April	**May**	**June**
Sun.	5 12 19 26	3 10 17 24 31	7 14 21 28
Mon.	6 13 20 27	4 11 18 25	1 8 15 22 29
Tue.	7 14 21 28	5 12 19 26	2 9 16 23 30
Wed.	1 8 15 22 29	6 13 20 27	3 10 17 24
Thur.	2 9 16 23 30	7 14 21 28	4 11 18 25
Fri.	3 10 17 24	1 8 15 22 29	5 12 19 26
Sat.	4 11 18 25	2 9 16 23 30	6 13 20 27
	July	**August**	**September**
Sun.	5 12 19 26	2 9 16 23 30	6 13 20 27
Mon.	6 13 20 27	3 10 17 24 31	7 14 21 28
Tue.	7 14 21 28	4 11 18 25	1 8 15 22 29
Wed.	1 8 15 22 29	5 12 19 26	2 9 16 23 30
Thur.	2 9 16 23 30	6 13 20 27	3 10 17 24
Fri.	3 10 17 24 31	7 14 21 28	4 11 18 25
Sat.	4 11 18 25	1 8 15 22 29	5 12 19 26
	October	**November**	**December**
Sun.	4 11 18 25	1 8 15 22 29	6 13 20 27
Mon.	5 12 19 26	2 9 16 23 30	7 14 21 28
Tue.	6 13 20 27	3 10 17 24	1 8 15 22 29
Wed.	7 14 21 28	4 11 18 25	2 9 16 23 30
Thur.	1 8 15 22 29	5 12 19 26	3 10 17 24 31
Fri.	2 9 16 23 30	6 13 20 27	4 11 18 25
Sat.	3 10 17 24 31	7 14 21 28	5 12 19 26

EASTER DAYS
March 29 1812, 1964
April 5 1896
April 12 1868, 1936, 2020
April 19 1840, 1908, 1992

J (LEAP YEAR)

	January	February	March
Sun.	4 11 18 25	1 8 15 22 29	7 14 21 28
Mon.	5 12 19 26	2 9 16 23	1 8 15 22 29
Tue.	6 13 20 27	3 10 17 24	2 9 16 23 30
Wed.	7 14 21 28	4 11 18 25	3 10 17 24 31
Thur.	1 8 15 22 29	5 12 19 26	4 11 18 25
Fri.	2 9 16 23 30	6 13 20 27	5 12 19 26
Sat.	3 10 17 24 31	7 14 21 28	6 13 20 27
	April	**May**	**June**
Sun.	4 11 18 25	2 9 16 23 30	6 13 20 27
Mon.	5 12 19 26	3 10 17 24 31	7 14 21 28
Tue.	6 13 20 27	4 11 18 25	1 8 15 22 29
Wed.	7 14 21 28	5 12 19 26	2 9 16 23 30
Thur.	1 8 15 22 29	6 13 20 27	3 10 17 24
Fri.	2 9 16 23 30	7 14 21 28	4 11 18 25
Sat.	3 10 17 24	1 8 15 22 29	5 12 19 26
	July	**August**	**September**
Sun.	4 11 18 25	1 8 15 22 29	5 12 19 26
Mon.	5 12 19 26	2 9 16 23 30	6 13 20 27
Tue.	6 13 20 27	3 10 17 24 31	7 14 21 28
Wed.	7 14 21 28	4 11 18 25	1 8 15 22 29
Thur.	1 8 15 22 29	5 12 19 26	2 9 16 23 30
Fri.	2 9 16 23 30	6 13 20 27	3 10 17 24
Sat.	3 10 17 24 31	7 14 21 28	4 11 18 25
	October	**November**	**December**
Sun.	3 10 17 24 31	7 14 21 28	5 12 19 26
Mon.	4 11 18 25	1 8 15 22 29	6 13 20 27
Tue.	5 12 19 26	2 9 16 23 30	7 14 21 28
Wed.	6 13 20 27	3 10 17 24	1 8 15 22 29
Thur.	7 14 21 28	4 11 18 25	2 9 16 23 30
Fri.	1 8 15 22 29	5 12 19 26	3 10 17 24 31
Sat.	2 9 16 23 30	6 13 20 27	4 11 18 25

EASTER DAYS
March 28 1880, 1948, 2032
April 4 1920
April 11 1784, 1852, 2004
April 18 1824, 1976

K

	January	February	March
Sun.	3 10 17 24 31	7 14 21 28	7 14 21 28
Mon.	4 11 18 25	1 8 15 22	1 8 15 22 29
Tue.	5 12 19 26	2 9 16 23	2 9 16 23 30
Wed.	6 13 20 27	3 10 17 24	3 10 17 24 31
Thur.	7 14 21 28	4 11 18 25	4 11 18 25
Fri.	1 8 15 22 29	5 12 19 26	5 12 19 26
Sat.	2 9 16 23 30	6 13 20 27	6 13 20 27

	April	May	June
Sun.	4 11 18 25	2 9 16 23 30	6 13 20 27
Mon.	5 12 19 26	3 10 17 24 31	7 14 21 28
Tue.	6 13 20 27	4 11 18 25	1 8 15 22 29
Wed.	7 14 21 28	5 12 19 26	2 9 16 23 30
Thur.	1 8 15 22 29	6 13 20 27	3 10 17 24
Fri.	2 9 16 23 30	7 14 21 28	4 11 18 25
Sat.	3 10 17 24	1 8 15 22 29	5 12 19 26

	July	August	September
Sun.	4 11 18 25	1 8 15 22 29	5 12 19 26
Mon.	5 12 19 26	2 9 16 23 30	6 13 20 27
Tue.	6 13 20 27	3 10 17 24 31	7 14 21 28
Wed.	7 14 21 28	4 11 18 25	1 8 15 22 29
Thur.	1 8 15 22 29	5 12 19 26	2 9 16 23 30
Fri.	2 9 16 23 30	6 13 20 27	3 10 17 24
Sat.	3 10 17 24 31	7 14 21 28	4 11 18 25

	October	November	December
Sun.	3 10 17 24 31	7 14 21 28	5 12 19 26
Mon.	4 11 18 25	1 8 15 22 29	6 13 20 27
Tue.	5 12 19 26	2 9 16 23 30	7 14 21 28
Wed.	6 13 20 27	3 10 17 24	1 8 15 22 29
Thur.	7 14 21 28	4 11 18 25	2 9 16 23 30
Fri.	1 8 15 22 29	5 12 19 26	3 10 17 24 31
Sat.	2 9 16 23 30	6 13 20 27	4 11 18 25

EASTER DAYS
March 28   1869, 1875, 1937, 2027
April 4   1790, 1847, 1858, 1915, 1926, 1999, 2010, 2021
April 11   1819, 1830, 1841, 1909, 1971, 1982, 1993
April 18   1802, 1813, 1897, 1954, 1965
April 25   1886, 1943, 2038

M

	January	February	March
Sun.	2 9 16 23 30	6 13 20 27	6 13 20 27
Mon.	3 10 17 24 31	7 14 21 28	7 14 21 28
Tue.	4 11 18 25	1 8 15 22	1 8 15 22 29
Wed.	5 12 19 26	2 9 16 23	2 9 16 23 30
Thur.	6 13 20 27	3 10 17 24	3 10 17 24 31
Fri.	7 14 21 28	4 11 18 25	4 11 18 25
Sat.	1 8 15 22 29	5 12 19 26	5 12 19 26

	April	May	June
Sun.	3 10 17 24	1 8 15 22 29	5 12 19 26
Mon.	4 11 18 25	2 9 16 23 30	6 13 20 27
Tue.	5 12 19 26	3 10 17 24 31	7 14 21 28
Wed.	6 13 20 27	4 11 18 25	1 8 15 22 29
Thur.	7 14 21 28	5 12 19 26	2 9 16 23 30
Fri.	1 8 15 22 29	6 13 20 27	3 10 17 24
Sat.	2 9 16 23 30	7 14 21 28	4 11 18 25

	July	August	September
Sun.	3 10 17 24 31	7 14 21 28	4 11 18 25
Mon.	4 11 18 25	1 8 15 22 29	5 12 19 26
Tue.	5 12 19 26	2 9 16 23 30	6 13 20 27
Wed.	6 13 20 27	3 10 17 24 31	7 14 21 28
Thur.	7 14 21 28	4 11 18 25	1 8 15 22 29
Fri.	1 8 15 22 29	5 12 19 26	2 9 16 23 30
Sat.	2 9 16 23 30	6 13 20 27	3 10 17 24

	October	November	December
Sun.	2 9 16 23 30	6 13 20 27	4 11 18 25
Mon.	3 10 17 24 31	7 14 21 28	5 12 19 26
Tue.	4 11 18 25	1 8 15 22 29	6 13 20 27
Wed.	5 12 19 26	2 9 16 23 30	7 14 21 28
Thur.	6 13 20 27	3 10 17 24	1 8 15 22 29
Fri.	7 14 21 28	4 11 18 25	2 9 16 23 30
Sat.	1 8 15 22 29	5 12 19 26	3 10 17 24 31

EASTER DAYS
March 27   1785, 1842, 1853, 1910, 1921, 2005
April 3   1825, 1831, 1983, 1994
April 10   1803, 1814, 1887, 1898, 1955, 1966, 1977, 2039
April 17   1870, 1881, 1927, 1938, 1949, 2022, 2033
April 24   1791, 1859, 2011

L (LEAP YEAR)

	January	February	March
Sun.	3 10 17 24 31	7 14 21 28	6 13 20 27
Mon.	4 11 18 25	1 8 15 22 29	7 14 21 28
Tue.	5 12 19 26	2 9 16 23	1 8 15 22 29
Wed.	6 13 20 27	3 10 17 24	2 9 16 23 30
Thur.	7 14 21 28	4 11 18 25	3 10 17 24 31
Fri.	1 8 15 22 29	5 12 19 26	4 11 18 25
Sat.	2 9 16 23 30	6 13 20 27	5 12 19 26

	April	May	June
Sun.	3 10 17 24	1 8 15 22 29	5 12 19 26
Mon.	4 11 18 25	2 9 16 23 30	6 13 20 27
Tue.	5 12 19 26	3 10 17 24 31	7 14 21 28
Wed.	6 13 20 27	4 11 18 25	1 8 15 22 29
Thur.	7 14 21 28	5 12 19 26	2 9 16 23 30
Fri.	1 8 15 22 29	6 13 20 27	3 10 17 24
Sat.	2 9 16 23 30	7 14 21 28	4 11 18 25

	July	August	September
Sun.	3 10 17 24 31	7 14 21 28	4 11 18 25
Mon.	4 11 18 25	1 8 15 22 29	5 12 19 26
Tue.	5 12 19 26	2 9 16 23 30	6 13 20 27
Wed.	6 13 20 27	3 10 17 24 31	7 14 21 28
Thur.	7 14 21 28	4 11 18 25	1 8 15 22 29
Fri.	1 8 15 22 29	5 12 19 26	2 9 16 23 30
Sat.	2 9 16 23 30	6 13 20 27	3 10 17 24

	October	November	December
Sun.	2 9 16 23 30	6 13 20 27	4 11 18 25
Mon.	3 10 17 24 31	7 14 21 28	5 12 19 26
Tue.	4 11 18 25	1 8 15 22 29	6 13 20 27
Wed.	5 12 19 26	2 9 16 23 30	7 14 21 28
Thur.	6 13 20 27	3 10 17 24	1 8 15 22 29
Fri.	7 14 21 28	4 11 18 25	2 9 16 23 30
Sat.	1 8 15 22 29	5 12 19 26	3 10 17 24 31

EASTER DAYS
March 27   1796, 1864, 1932, 2016
April 3   1836, 1904, 1988
April 17   1808, 1892, 1960

N (LEAP YEAR)

	January	February	March
Sun.	2 9 16 23 30	6 13 20 27	5 12 19 26
Mon.	3 10 17 24 31	7 14 21 28	6 13 20 27
Tue.	4 11 18 25	1 8 15 22 29	7 14 21 28
Wed.	5 12 19 26	2 9 16 23	1 8 15 22 29
Thur.	6 13 20 27	3 10 17 24	2 9 16 23 30
Fri.	7 14 21 28	4 11 18 25	3 10 17 24 31
Sat.	1 8 15 22 29	5 12 19 26	4 11 18 25

	April	May	June
Sun.	2 9 16 23 30	7 14 21 28	4 11 18 25
Mon.	3 10 17 24	1 8 15 22 29	5 12 19 26
Tue.	4 11 18 25	2 9 16 23 30	6 13 20 27
Wed.	5 12 19 26	3 10 17 24 31	7 14 21 28
Thur.	6 13 20 27	4 11 18 25	1 8 15 22 29
Fri.	7 14 21 28	5 12 19 26	2 9 16 23 30
Sat.	1 8 15 22 29	6 13 20 27	3 10 17 24

	July	August	September
Sun.	2 9 16 23 30	6 13 20 27	3 10 17 24
Mon.	3 10 17 24 31	7 14 21 28	4 11 18 25
Tue.	4 11 18 25	1 8 15 22 29	5 12 19 26
Wed.	5 12 19 26	2 9 16 23 30	6 13 20 27
Thur.	6 13 20 27	3 10 17 24 31	7 14 21 28
Fri.	7 14 21 28	4 11 18 25	1 8 15 22 29
Sat.	1 8 15 22 29	5 12 19 26	2 9 16 23 30

	October	November	December
Sun.	1 8 15 22 29	5 12 19 26	3 10 17 24 31
Mon.	2 9 16 23 30	6 13 20 27	4 11 18 25
Tue.	3 10 17 24 31	7 14 21 28	5 12 19 26
Wed.	4 11 18 25	1 8 15 22 29	6 13 20 27
Thur.	5 12 19 26	2 9 16 23 30	7 14 21 28
Fri.	6 13 20 27	3 10 17 24	1 8 15 22 29
Sat.	7 14 21 28	4 11 18 25	2 9 16 23 30

EASTER DAYS
March 26   1780
April 2   1820, 1972
April 9   1944
April 16   2028
April 23   1848, 1916, 2000

GEOLOGICAL TIME

The earth is thought to have come into existence approximately 4,600 million years ago, but for nearly half this time, the Archean era, it was uninhabited. Life is generally believed to have emerged in the succeeding Proterozoic era. The Archean and the Proterozoic eras are often together referred to as the Precambrian.

Although primitive forms of life, e.g. algae and bacteria, existed during the Proterozoic era, it is not until the strata of Palaeozoic rocks is reached that abundant fossilised remains appear.

Since the Precambrian, there have been three great geological eras:

PALAEOZOIC ('ancient life')
c.570–c.245 million years ago

Cambrian – Mainly sandstones, slate and shales; limestones in Scotland. Shelled fossils and invertebrates, e.g. trilobites and brachiopods appear
Ordovician – Mainly shales and mudstones, e.g. in north Wales; limestones in Scotland. First fishes
Silurian – Shales, mudstones and some limestones, found mostly in Wales and southern Scotland
Devonian – Old red sandstone, shale, limestone and slate, e.g. in south Wales and the West Country
Carboniferous – Coal-bearing rocks, millstone grit, limestone and shale. First traces of land-living life
Permian – Marls, sandstones and clays. First reptile fossils

There were two great phases of mountain building in the Palaeozoic era: the Caledonian, characterised in Britain by NE–SW lines of hills and valleys; and the later Hercyian, widespread in west Germany and adjacent areas, and in Britain exemplified in E.–W. lines of hills and valleys.

The end of the Palaeozoic era was marked by the extensive glaciations of the Permian period in the southern continents and the decline of amphibians. It was succeeded by an era of warm conditions.

MESOZOIC ('middle forms of life')
c. 245–c.65 million years ago

Triassic – Mostly sandstone, e.g. in the West Midlands
Jurassic – Mainly limestones and clays, typically displayed in the Jura mountains, and in England in a NE–SW belt from Lincolnshire and the Wash to the Severn and the Dorset coast
Cretaceous – Mainly chalk, clay and sands, e.g. in Kent and Sussex

Giant reptiles were dominant during the Mesozoic era, but it was at this time that marsupial mammals first appeared, as well as *Archaeopteryx lithographica*, the earliest known species of bird. Coniferous trees and flowering plants also developed during the era and, with the birds and the mammals, were the main species to survive into the Cenozoic era. The giant reptiles became extinct.

CENOZOIC ('recent life')
from c. 65 million years ago

Palaeocene } The emergence of new forms of life,
Eocene   } including existing species

Oligocene – Fossils of a few still existing species
Miocene – Fossil remains show a balance of existing and extinct species
Pliocene – Fossil remains show a majority of still existing species

Pleistocene – The majority of remains are those of still existing species
Holocene – The present, post-glacial period. Existing species only, except for a few exterminated by man

In the last 25 million years, from the Miocene through the Pliocene periods, the Alpine-Himalayan and the circum-Pacific phases of mountain building reached their climax. During the Pleistocene period ice-sheets repeatedly locked up masses of water as land ice; its weight depressed the land, but the locking-up of the water lowered the sea-level by 100–200 metres. The glaciations and interglacials of the Ice Age are difficult to date and classify, but recent scientific opinion considers the Pleistocene period to have begun approximately 1.64 million years ago. The last glacial retreat, merging into the Holocene period, was 10,000 years ago.

HUMAN DEVELOPMENT

Any consideration of the history of mankind must start with the fact that all members of the human race belong to one species of animal, i.e. *Homo sapiens*, the definition of a species being in biological terms that all its members can interbreed. As a species of mammal it is possible to group man with other similar types, known as the primates. Amongst these is found a sub-group, the apes, which includes, in addition to man, the chimpanzees, gorillas, orang-utans and gibbons. All lack a tail, have shoulder blades at the back, and a Y-shaped chewing pattern on the surface of their molars, as well as showing the more general primate characteristics of four incisors, a thumb which is able to touch the fingers of the same hand, and finger and toe nails instead of claws. The factors available to scientific study suggest that human beings have chimpanzees and gorillas as their nearest relatives in the animal world. However, there remains the possibility that there once lived creatures, now extinct, which were closer to modern man than the chimpanzees and gorillas, and which shared with modern man the characteristics of having flat faces (i.e. the absence of a pronounced muzzle), being bipedal, and possessing large brains.

There are two broad groups of extinct apes recognised by specialists. The ramapithecines, the remains of which, mainly jaw fragments, have been found in east Africa, Asia, and Turkey. They lived about 14 to 8 million years ago, and from the evidence of their teeth it seems they chewed more in the manner of modern man than the other presently living apes. The second group, the australopithecines, have left more numerous remains amongst which sub-groups may be detected, although the geographic spread is limited to south and east Africa. Living between 5 and 1.5 million years ago, they were closer relatives of modern man to the extent that they walked upright, did not have an extensive muzzle and had similar types of pre-molars. The first australopithecine remains were recognised at Taung in South Africa in 1924 and subsequent discoveries include those at the Olduvai Gorge in Tanzania. The most impressive discovery was made at Hadar, Ethiopia, in 1974 when about half a skeleton, known as 'Lucy', was found.

Also in east Africa, between 2 million and 1.5 million years ago, lived a hominid group which not only walked upright, had a flat face, and a large brain case, but also made simple pebble and flake stone tools. On present evidence these habilines seem to have been the first people to make tools, however crude. This facility is related to the larger brain size and human beings are the only animals to

GEOLOGICAL TIME

Era	Period	Epoch	Date began*	Evolutionary stages
Cenozoic	Quaternary	Holocene	0.01	Man
		Pleistocene	1.64	
	Tertiary	Pliocene	5.2	
		Miocene	23.3	
		Oligocene	35.4	
		Eocene	56.5	
		Palaeocene	65.0	
Mesozoic	Cretaceous		145.6	
	Jurassic		208.0	First birds
	Triassic		245.0	First Mammals
Palaeozoic	Permian		290.0	First Reptiles
	Carboniferous		362.5	First amphibians and insects
	Devonian		408.5	
	Silurian		439.0	
	Ordovician		510.0	First fishes
	Cambrian		570.0	First invertebrates
Precambrian			4,600.0	First primitive life forms, e.g. algae and bacteria

* millions of years ago

make implements to be used in other processes. These early pebble tool users, because of their distinctive characteristics, have been grouped as a separate sub-species, now extinct, of the genus *Homo* and are known as *Homo habilis*.

The use of fire, again a human characteristic, is associated with another group of extinct hominids whose remains, about a million years old, are found in south and east Africa, China, Indonesia, north Africa and Europe. Mastery of the techniques of making fire probably helped the colonisation of the colder northern areas and in this respect the site of Vertesszollos in Hungary is of particular importance. *Homo erectus* is the name given to this group of fossils and it includes a number of famous individual discoveries, e.g. Solo Man, Heidelberg Man, and especially Peking Man who lived at the cave site at Choukoutien which has yielded evidence of fire and burnt bone.

The well-known group Neanderthal Man, or *Homo sapiens neandertalensis*, is an extinct form of modern man who lived between about 100,000 and 40,000 years ago, thus spanning the last Ice Age. Indeed, its ability to adapt to the cold climate on the edge of the ice-sheets is one of its characteristic features, the remains being found only in Europe, Asia and the Middle East. Complete neanderthal skeletons were found during excavations at Tabun in Israel, together with evidence of tool-making and the use of fire. Distinguished by very large brains, it seems that neanderthal man was the first to develop recognisable social customs, especially deliberate burial rites. Why the neanderthalers became extinct is not clear but it may be connected with the climatic changes at the end of the Ice Ages, which would have seriously affected their food supplies; possibly they became too specialised for their own good.

The Swanscombe skull is the only known human fossil remains found in England. Some specialists see Swanscombe Man (or, more probably, woman) as a neanderthaler. Others group these remains together with the Steinheim skull from Germany, seeing both as a separate sub-species. There is too little evidence as yet on which to form a final judgement.

Modern Man, *Homo sapiens sapiens*, the surviving sub-species of *Homo sapiens*, had evolved to our present physical condition and had colonised much of the world by about 30,000 years ago. There are many previously distin-guished individual specimens, e.g. Cromagnon Man, which may now be grouped together as *Homo sapiens sapiens*. It was modern man who spread to the American continent by crossing the landbridge between Siberia and Alaska and thence moved south through North America and into South America. Equally it is modern man who over the last 30,000 years has been responsible for the major developments in technology, art and civilisation generally.

One of the problems for those studying fossil man is the lack in many cases of sufficient quantities of fossil bone for analysis. It is important that theories should be tested against evidence, rather than the evidence being made to fit the theory. The Piltdown hoax is a well-known example of 'fossils' being forged to fit what was seen in some quarters as the correct theory of man's evolution.

CULTURAL DEVELOPMENT

The Eurocentric bias of early archaeologists meant that the search for a starting point for the development and transmission of cultural ideas, especially by migration, trade and warfare, concentrated unduly on Europe and the Near East. The Three Age system, whereby pre-history was divided into a Stone Age, a Bronze Age and an Iron Age, was devised by Christian Thomsen, curator of the National Museum of Denmark in the early 19th century, to facilitate the classification of the museum's collections. The descriptive adjectives referred to the materials from which the implements and weapons were made and came to be regarded as the dominant features of the societies to which they related. The refinement of the Three Age system once dominated archaeological thought and remains a generally accepted concept in the popular mind. However, it is now seen by archaeologists as an inadequate model for human development.

Common sense suggests that there were no complete breaks between one so-called Age and another, any more than contemporaries would have regarded 1485 as a complete break between medieval and modern English history. Nor can the Three Age system be applied universally. In some areas it is necessary to insert a Copper Age, while in Africa south of the Sahara there would seem to be no Bronze Age at all; in Australia, Old Stone Age societies survived, while in South America, New Stone Age communities existed into modern times. The civilisations in other parts of the world clearly invalidate a Eurocentric theory of human development.

The concept of the 'Neolithic revolution', associated with the domestication of plants and animals, was a development of particular importance in the human cultural pattern. It reflected change from the primitive hunter/gatherer economies to a more settled agricultural way of life and therefore, so the argument goes, made possible the development of urban civilisation. However, it can no longer be argued that this 'revolution' took place only in one area from which all development stemmed. Though it appears that the cultivation of wheat and barley was first undertaken, together with the domestication of cattle and goats/sheep in the Fertile Crescent (the area bounded by the rivers Tigris and Euphrates), there is evidence that rice was first deliberately planted and pigs domesticated in south-east Asia, maize first cultivated in Central America and llamas first domesticated in South America. It has been recognised in recent years that cultural changes can take place independently of each other in different parts of the world at different rates and different times. There is no need for a general diffusionist theory.

Although scholars will continue to study the particular societies which interest them, it may be possible to obtain a reliable chronological framework, in absolute terms of years, against which the cultural development of any particular area may be set. The development and refinement of radio-carbon dating and other scientific methods of producing absolute chronologies is enabling the cross-referencing of societies to be undertaken. As the techniques of dating become more rigorous in application and the number of scientifically obtained dates increases, the attainment of an absolute chronology for prehistoric societies throughout the world comes closer to being achieved.

Tidal Tables

CONSTANTS

The constant tidal difference may be used in conjunction with the time of high water at a standard port shown in the predictions data (pages 98–103) to find the time of high water at any of the ports or places listed below.

These tidal differences are very approximate and should be used only as a guide to the time of high water at the places below. More precise local data should be obtained for navigational and other nautical purposes.

All data allow high water time to be found in Greenwich Mean Time; this applies to data for the months when British Summer Time is in operation and the hour's time difference should be allowed for. Ports marked * are in a different time zone and the standard time zone difference also needs to be added/subtracted to give local time.

EXAMPLE

Required time of high water at Stranraer at 2 January 2002
Appropriate time of high water at Greenock

	Afternoon tide 2 January	1423hrs
Tidal difference		−0020hrs
High water at Stranraer		1403hrs

The columns headed 'Springs' and 'Neaps' show the height, in metres, of the tide above datum for mean high water springs and mean high water neaps respectively.

Port		Diff. h m	Springs m	Neaps m
Aberdeen	Leith	−1 19	4.4	3.4
*Antwerp (Prosperpolder)	London	+0 50	5.8	4.8
Ardrossan	Greenock	−0 15	3.2	2.6
Avonmouth	London	−6 45	12.2	9.8
Ayr	Greenock	−0 25	3.0	2.5
Barrow (Docks)	Liverpool	0 00	9.3	7.1
Belfast	London	−2 47	3.5	3.0
Blackpool	Liverpool	−0 10	8.9	7.0
*Boulogne	London	−2 44	8.9	7.2
*Calais	London	−2 04	7.2	5.9
*Cherbourg	London	−6 00	6.4	5.0
Cobh	Liverpool	−5 55	4.2	3.2
Cowes	London	−2 38	4.2	3.5
Dartmouth	London	+4 25	4.9	3.8
*Dieppe	London	−3 03	9.3	7.3
Douglas, IoM	Liverpool	−0 04	6.9	5.4
Dover	London	−2 52	6.7	5.3
Dublin	London	−2 05	4.1	3.4
Dun Loaghaire	London	−2 10	4.1	3.4
*Dunkirk	London	−1 54	6.0	4.9
Fishguard	Liverpool	−4 01	4.8	3.4
Fleetwood	Liverpool	0 00	9.2	7.3
*Flushing	London	−0 15	4.7	3.9
Folkestone	London	−3 04	7.1	5.7
Galway	Liverpool	−6 08	5.1	3.9
Glasgow	Greenock	+0 26	4.7	4.0
Harwich	London	−2 06	4.0	3.4
*Le Havre	London	−3 55	7.9	6.6
Heysham	Liverpool	+0 05	9.4	7.4
Holyhead	Liverpool	−0 50	5.6	4.4
*Hook of Holland	London	−0 01	2.1	1.7
Hull (Albert Dock)	London	−7 40	7.5	5.8
Immingham	London	−8 00	7.3	5.8
Larne	London	−2 40	2.8	2.5
Lerwick	Leith	−3 48	2.2	1.6
Londonderry	London	−5 37	2.7	2.1
Lowestoft	London	−4 25	2.4	2.1
Margate	London	−1 53	4.8	3.9
Milford Haven	Liverpool	−5 08	7.0	5.2
Morecambe	Liverpool	+0 07	9.5	7.4
Newhaven	London	−2 46	6.7	5.1
Oban	Greenock	+5 43	4.0	2.9
*Ostend	London	−1 32	5.1	4.2
Plymouth	London	+4 05	5.5	4.4
Portland	London	+5 09	2.1	1.4
Portsmouth	London	−2 38	4.7	3.8
Ramsgate	London	−2 32	5.2	4.1
Richmond Lock	London	+1 00	4.9	3.7
Rosslare Harbour	Liverpool	−5 24	1.9	1.4
Rosyth	Leith	+0 09	5.8	4.7
*Rotterdam	London	+1 45	2.0	1.7
St Helier	London	+4 48	11.0	8.1
St Malo	London	+4 27	12.2	9.2
St Peter Port	London	+4 54	9.3	7.0
Scrabster	Leith	−6 06	5.0	4.0
Sheerness	London	−1 19	5.8	4.7
Shoreham	London	−2 44	6.3	4.9
Southampton (1st high water)	London	−2 54	4.5	3.7
Spurn Head	London	−8 25	6.9	5.5
Stornoway	Liverpool	−4 16	4.8	3.7
Stranraer	Greenock	−0 20	3.0	2.4
Stromness	Leith	−5 26	3.6	2.7
Swansea	London	−7 35	9.5	7.2
Tees (River Entrance)	Leith	+1 09	5.5	4.3
Tilbury	London	−0 49	6.4	5.4
Tobermory	Liverpool	−5 11	4.4	3.3
Tyne River (North Shields)	London	−10 30	5.0	3.9
Ullapool	Leith	−7 40	5.2	3.9
Walton-on-the-Naze	London	−2 10	4.2	3.4
Wick	Leith	−3 26	3.5	2.8
Zeebrugge	London	−0 55	4.8	3.9

PREDICTIONS

The data on pages 98–103 are daily predictions of the time and height of high water at London Bridge, Liverpool, Greenock and Leith. The time of the of the data is Greenwich Mean Time; this applies also to data for the months when British Summer Time is in operation and the hour's time difference should be allowed for. The datum of predictions for each port shows the difference of height, in metres from Ordnance data (Newlyn).

The tidal information for London Bridge, Liverpool, Greenock and Leith is reproduced with the permission of the UK Hydrographic Office and the Controller of HMSO. Crown copyright reserved.

JANUARY 2002   *High Water*   GMT

		LONDON BRIDGE				LIVERPOOL				GREENOCK				LEITH			
		*Datum of Predictions 3.20m below				*Datum of Predictions 4.93m below				*Datum of Predictions 1.62m below				*Datum of Predictions 2.90m below			
		hr	m	ht hr	m	hr	m	ht hr	m	hr	m	ht hr	m	hr	m	ht hr	m
1	Tuesday	02 48	6.9	15 14	7.1	00 05	9.4	12 26	9.5	01 34	3.3	13 41	3.7	03 35	5.6	15 54	5.6
2	Wednesday	03 32	6.9	16 01	7.2	00 53	9.4	13 13	9.6	02 22	3.3	14 23	3.8	04 20	5.7	16 37	5.6
3	Thursday	04 15	6.8	16 48	7.1	01 41	9.3	14 01	9.5	03 10	3.3	15 06	3.8	05 08	5.6	17 24	5.5
4	Friday	04 59	6.8	17 37	7.0	02 30	9.1	14 51	9.3	03 59	3.2	15 52	3.7	05 58	5.4	18 15	5.4
5	Saturday	05 46	6.6	18 28	6.7	03 22	8.8	15 44	9.0	04 51	3.2	16 41	3.6	06 51	5.2	19 11	5.2
6	Sunday	06 37	6.4	19 25	6.4	04 18	8.4	16 42	8.6	05 47	3.1	17 35	3.5	07 52	4.9	20 18	5.1
7	Monday	07 38	6.2	20 29	6.2	05 22	8.1	17 47	8.3	06 48	3.0	18 37	3.3	08 59	4.8	21 28	5.0
8	Tuesday	08 49	6.1	21 36	6.1	06 31	7.9	18 58	8.2	07 59	3.0	19 50	3.2	10 06	4.7	22 35	4.9
9	Wednesday	09 59	6.1	22 40	6.2	07 41	8.0	20 08	8.2	09 14	3.0	21 15	3.2	11 12	4.8	23 40	5.0
10	Thursday	11 04	6.3	23 38	6.4	08 43	8.3	21 09	8.4	10 15	3.2	22 23	3.2	12 13	4.9	—	—
11	Friday	12 02	6.5	—	—	09 36	8.6	22 02	8.7	11 06	3.3	23 19	3.2	00 40	5.1	13 07	5.0
12	Saturday	00 31	6.6	12 56	6.7	10 23	8.9	22 47	8.8	11 51	3.4	—	—	01 34	5.2	13 54	5.2
13	Sunday	01 20	6.7	13 46	6.8	11 04	9.1	23 28	8.9	00 08	3.2	12 33	3.5	02 22	5.2	14 35	5.3
14	Monday	02 04	6.7	14 31	6.8	11 43	9.2	—	—	00 53	3.2	13 11	3.6	03 04	5.2	15 14	5.3
15	Tuesday	02 43	6.7	15 12	6.8	00 05	8.9	12 20	9.2	01 34	3.2	13 48	3.6	03 44	5.2	15 50	5.3
16	Wednesday	03 17	6.6	15 48	6.6	00 41	8.8	12 56	9.1	02 11	3.2	14 23	3.6	04 21	5.1	16 25	5.3
17	Thursday	03 48	6.5	16 21	6.5	01 15	8.7	13 31	9.0	02 47	3.2	14 57	3.6	04 57	5.0	16 59	5.2
18	Friday	04 19	6.5	16 54	6.5	01 50	8.5	14 08	8.8	03 23	3.2	15 32	3.5	05 33	4.9	17 35	5.1
19	Saturday	04 53	6.4	17 30	6.4	02 26	8.3	14 45	8.6	04 00	3.2	16 07	3.4	06 11	4.8	18 15	4.9
20	Sunday	05 31	6.3	18 09	6.3	03 04	8.0	15 25	8.3	04 38	3.1	16 46	3.3	06 53	4.6	18 58	4.7
21	Monday	06 14	6.2	18 54	6.1	03 47	7.7	16 11	7.9	05 20	3.0	17 28	3.1	07 39	4.5	19 46	4.6
22	Tuesday	07 02	6.0	19 44	6.0	04 39	7.4	17 07	7.6	06 06	2.9	18 18	3.0	08 31	4.4	20 42	4.4
23	Wednesday	07 59	5.8	20 42	5.9	05 42	7.2	18 12	7.5	06 58	2.9	19 16	2.9	09 31	4.3	21 48	4.4
24	Thursday	09 03	5.8	21 48	5.8	06 54	7.3	19 21	7.7	08 00	2.8	20 30	2.8	10 35	4.4	22 57	4.5
25	Friday	10 13	5.9	22 58	6.0	08 02	7.7	20 27	8.0	09 15	2.9	21 49	2.9	11 39	4.6	—	—
26	Saturday	11 23	6.1	—	—	09 01	8.2	21 25	8.5	10 22	3.1	22 54	3.0	00 03	4.7	12 39	4.8
27	Sunday	00 01	6.3	12 26	6.5	09 52	8.8	22 17	8.9	11 14	3.3	23 47	3.1	01 02	5.0	13 30	5.1
28	Monday	00 57	6.6	13 22	6.8	10 40	9.2	23 07	9.3	12 00	3.4	—	—	01 53	5.3	14 15	5.4
29	Tuesday	01 47	6.8	14 13	7.1	11 27	9.6	23 54	9.6	00 38	3.2	12 45	3.6	02 38	5.6	14 57	5.6
30	Wednesday	02 35	7.0	15 02	7.3	12 14	9.9	—	—	01 28	3.3	13 30	3.7	03 22	5.8	15 39	5.7
31	Thursday	03 20	7.1	15 49	7.4	00 42	9.7	13 01	10.0	02 16	3.3	14 13	3.8	04 06	5.8	16 22	5.8

FEBRUARY 2002   *High Water*   GMT

		LONDON BRIDGE				LIVERPOOL				GREENOCK				LEITH			
1	Friday	04 03	7.1	16 35	7.4	01 29	9.7	13 48	10.0	03 01	3.3	14 57	3.9	04 52	5.8	17 08	5.8
2	Saturday	04 46	7.1	17 20	7.3	02 14	9.5	14 34	9.7	03 44	3.3	15 40	3.9	05 39	5.6	17 55	5.6
3	Sunday	05 29	7.0	18 06	7.0	03 00	9.2	15 21	9.3	04 27	3.3	16 24	3.7	06 28	5.3	18 47	5.4
4	Monday	06 13	6.7	18 55	6.6	03 49	8.7	16 12	8.7	05 11	3.2	17 10	3.6	07 22	5.0	19 48	5.1
5	Tuesday	07 03	6.4	19 51	6.1	04 44	8.1	17 11	8.1	05 58	3.0	18 00	3.3	08 24	4.7	20 58	4.8
6	Wednesday	08 08	6.1	20 58	5.8	05 51	7.7	18 25	7.7	06 54	2.9	18 59	3.1	09 32	4.5	22 10	4.7
7	Thursday	09 28	5.9	22 09	5.8	07 10	7.5	19 48	7.6	08 23	2.9	20 35	2.9	10 43	4.5	23 24	4.6
8	Friday	10 43	5.9	23 14	5.9	08 24	7.8	20 58	7.9	09 52	3.0	22 16	2.9	11 55	4.6	—	—
9	Saturday	11 47	6.2	—	—	09 22	8.2	21 52	8.2	10 49	3.1	23 16	3.0	00 34	4.7	12 58	4.8
10	Sunday	00 11	6.2	12 43	6.5	10 10	8.6	22 37	8.5	11 36	3.3	—	—	01 31	4.9	13 47	5.0
11	Monday	01 03	6.5	13 33	6.7	10 52	9.0	23 17	8.7	00 04	3.0	12 19	3.4	02 16	5.0	14 27	5.1
12	Tuesday	01 48	6.6	14 17	6.8	11 29	9.1	23 51	8.8	00 47	3.1	12 58	3.5	02 54	5.1	15 02	5.3
13	Wednesday	02 28	6.6	14 57	6.8	—	—	12 04	9.2	01 24	3.1	13 34	3.5	03 28	5.2	15 34	5.3
14	Thursday	03 02	6.6	15 30	6.6	00 23	8.8	12 38	9.2	01 57	3.1	14 07	3.5	03 59	5.1	16 04	5.3
15	Friday	03 32	6.5	15 59	6.6	00 55	8.8	13 10	9.1	02 27	3.1	14 37	3.4	04 30	5.1	16 35	5.3
16	Saturday	04 00	6.5	16 28	6.5	01 26	8.7	13 43	9.0	02 56	3.1	15 07	3.4	05 03	5.0	17 07	5.2
17	Sunday	04 30	6.5	17 00	6.6	01 58	8.6	14 15	8.8	03 27	3.2	15 39	3.4	05 37	4.9	17 42	5.0
18	Monday	05 04	6.5	17 36	6.5	02 30	8.4	14 50	8.5	04 00	3.1	16 13	3.4	06 14	4.8	18 19	4.9
19	Tuesday	05 42	6.4	18 17	6.4	03 05	8.1	15 29	8.2	04 36	3.1	16 51	3.1	06 55	4.6	19 01	4.7
20	Wednesday	06 26	6.3	19 03	6.1	03 49	7.7	16 19	7.9	05 17	3.0	17 34	2.9	07 41	4.4	19 50	4.5
21	Thursday	07 18	6.0	19 57	5.9	04 47	7.3	17 24	7.4	06 04	2.8	18 29	2.8	08 38	4.3	20 56	4.3
22	Friday	08 20	5.8	21 01	5.7	06 01	7.2	18 41	7.3	07 03	2.7	19 43	2.7	09 48	4.2	22 16	4.3
23	Saturday	09 31	5.8	22 18	5.7	07 23	7.4	20 00	7.7	08 25	2.7	21 21	2.7	11 03	4.3	23 36	4.5
24	Sunday	10 53	6.0	23 34	6.0	08 35	7.9	21 07	8.2	09 51	2.9	22 40	2.9	—	—	12 12	4.7
25	Monday	—	—	12 06	6.4	09 34	8.6	22 03	8.9	10 52	3.1	23 37	3.1	00 42	4.9	13 09	5.0
26	Tuesday	00 36	6.4	13 06	6.6	10 24	9.3	22 52	9.4	11 42	3.4	—	—	01 36	5.3	13 55	5.4
27	Wednesday	01 29	6.8	13 58	7.2	11 12	9.8	23 39	9.8	00 27	3.2	12 29	3.6	02 21	5.6	14 38	5.7
28	Thursday	02 17	7.1	14 46	7.4	11 58	10.1	—	—	01 16	3.3	13 14	3.7	03 04	5.9	15 19	5.9

MARCH 2002 *High Water* GMT

		LONDON BRIDGE				LIVERPOOL				GREENOCK				LEITH			
		*Datum of Predictions 3.20m below				*Datum of Predictions 4.93m below				*Datum of Predictions 1.62m below				*Datum of Predictions 2.90m below			
		hr	m	ht hr	m	hr	m	ht hr	m	hr	m	ht hr	m	hr	m	ht hr	m
1	Friday	03 02	7.2	15 32	7.6	00 24	10.0	12 43	10.3	02 00	3.3	13 58	3.8	03 47	5.9	1602	6.0
2	Saturday	03 44	7.3	16 15	7.5	01 09	9.9	13 28	10.2	02 41	3.4	14 41	3.9	04 31	5.8	1647	6.0
3	Sunday	04 25	7.4	16 58	7.3	01 52	9.7	14 11	9.9	03 19	3.4	15 22	3.9	05 16	5.6	1734	5.8
4	Monday	05 06	7.2	17 39	7.0	02 35	9.3	14 55	9.3	03 55	3.4	16 03	3.8	06 03	5.3	1825	5.4
5	Tuesday	05 47	6.9	18 21	6.6	03 18	8.8	15 42	8.6	04 33	3.3	16 45	3.5	06 52	4.9	1923	5.0
6	Wednesday	06 32	6.5	19 07	6.1	04 08	8.1	16 38	7.8	05 15	3.1	17 30	3.2	07 50	4.6	2032	4.7
7	Thursday	07 29	6.0	20 08	5.6	05 12	7.5	17 55	7.2	06 05	2.9	18 24	2.9	08 59	4.4	2147	4.4
8	Friday	08 58	5.6	21 37	5.4	06 39	7.2	19 29	7.1	07 11	2.8	19 38	2.7	10 14	4.3	2308	4.4
9	Saturday	10 23	5.7	22 49	5.6	08 02	7.4	20 42	7.5	09 28	2.8	22 12	2.7	11 35	4.4	—	—
10	Sunday	11 28	6.0	23 48	6.0	09 03	7.9	21 35	8.0	10 30	3.0	23 06	2.9	00 25	4.6	1243	4.6
11	Monday	12 24	6.4	—	—	09 51	8.4	22 19	8.4	11 18	3.2	23 50	3.0	01 20	4.8	1332	4.9
12	Tuesday	00 41	6.3	13 13	6.7	10 32	8.8	22 56	8.7	12 00	3.3	—	—	02 02	5.0	1411	5.1
13	Wednesday	01 27	6.6	13 57	6.8	11 09	9.1	23 29	8.8	00 28	3.0	12 39	3.4	02 36	5.1	1443	5.2
14	Thursday	02 07	6.7	14 34	6.8	11 42	9.1	—	—	01 03	3.0	13 14	3.3	03 06	5.1	1512	5.3
15	Friday	02 42	6.6	15 05	6.7	00 00	8.9	12 14	9.1	01 33	3.0	13 44	3.3	03 34	5.2	1540	5.3
16	Saturday	03 11	6.5	15 33	6.6	00 30	8.9	12 45	9.1	01 59	3.1	14 11	3.3	04 02	5.2	1609	5.3
17	Sunday	03 38	6.5	16 00	6.6	00 59	8.8	13 15	9.0	02 25	3.1	14 39	3.3	04 33	5.1	1640	5.2
18	Monday	04 06	6.6	16 31	6.6	01 28	8.8	13 46	8.8	02 53	3.2	15 11	3.3	05 06	5.0	1714	5.1
19	Tuesday	04 38	6.6	17 05	6.6	01 58	8.6	14 19	8.6	03 25	3.2	15 45	3.2	05 41	4.9	1750	4.9
20	Wednesday	05 15	6.6	17 44	6.5	02 31	8.3	14 56	8.2	03 58	3.1	16 21	3.1	06 19	4.7	1831	4.7
21	Thursday	05 59	6.4	18 29	6.2	03 11	7.9	15 45	7.8	04 34	3.0	17 02	2.9	07 02	4.5	1921	4.5
22	Friday	06 50	6.1	19 22	5.8	04 07	7.5	16 50	7.3	05 17	2.8	17 55	2.7	07 56	4.3	2025	4.3
23	Saturday	07 52	5.8	20 25	5.6	05 24	7.1	18 13	7.2	06 15	2.7	19 14	2.6	09 08	4.2	2148	4.3
24	Sunday	09 05	5.7	21 46	5.6	06 53	7.3	19 39	7.5	07 42	2.7	21 04	2.6	10 32	4.3	2312	4.6
25	Monday	10 32	5.9	23 10	6.0	08 12	7.9	20 49	8.2	09 22	2.8	22 27	2.8	11 46	4.6	—	—
26	Tuesday	11 48	6.4	—	—	09 13	8.6	21 44	8.9	10 29	3.1	23 22	3.0	00 21	5.0	1244	5.1
27	Wednesday	00 13	6.4	12 47	6.9	10 04	9.3	22 33	9.	11 20	3.4	—	—	01 14	5.4	1331	5.5
28	Thursday	01 06	6.8	13 38	7.3	10 51	9.9	23 18	9.9	00 10	3.2	12 08	3.6	01 59	5.7	1414	5.8
29	Friday	01 54	7.2	14 25	7.5	11 37	10.2	—	—	00 55	3.3	12 54	3.7	02 42	5.9	1457	6.0
30	Saturday	02 38	7.3	15 09	7.6	00 02	10.0	12 21	10.2	01 37	3.4	13 39	3.8	03 24	5.9	1541	6.1
31	Sunday	03 21	7.5	15 52	7.5	00 45	10.0	13 05	10.1	02 15	3.4	14 21	3.8	04 07	5.8	1626	6.0

APRIL 2002 *High Water* GMT

		LONDON BRIDGE				LIVERPOOL				GREENOCK				LEITH			
1	Monday	04 03	7.4	16 32	7.3	01 27	9.7	13 47	9.7	02 50	3.5	15 02	3.8	04 51	5.6	17 14	5.7
2	Tuesday	04 43	7.3	17 10	7.0	02 08	9.3	14 30	9.1	03 25	3.4	15 41	3.7	05 37	5.3	18 06	5.3
3	Wednesday	05 25	7.0	17 48	6.6	02 50	8.7	15 15	8.4	04 02	3.3	16 23	3.4	06 25	4.9	19 04	4.9
4	Thursday	06 08	6.5	18 27	6.1	03 36	8.1	16 10	7.6	04 43	3.2	17 08	3.1	07 21	4.6	20 10	4.5
5	Friday	07 02	6.0	19 17	5.6	04 38	7.4	17 28	7.0	05 32	3.0	18 02	2.8	08 28	4.3	21 22	4.3
6	Saturday	08 32	5.6	20 59	5.3	06 07	7.1	19 01	6.9	06 35	2.8	19 15	2.6	09 43	4.2	22 42	4.3
7	Sunday	09 59	5.6	22 19	5.5	07 30	7.3	20 13	7.2	08 48	2.7	21 50	2.6	11 04	4.3	—	—
8	Monday	11 02	6.0	23 19	5.9	08 32	7.7	21 06	7.8	10 02	2.9	22 41	2.8	00 00	4.5	12 14	4.5
9	Tuesday	11 57	6.4	—	—	09 22	8.2	21 49	8.2	10 50	3.1	23 22	2.9	00 55	4.7	13 04	4.8
10	Wednesday	00 11	6.3	12 45	6.7	10 03	8.6	22 26	8.5	11 32	3.2	23 59	3.0	01 35	4.9	13 43	5.0
11	Thursday	00 58	6.5	13 28	6.8	10 41	8.9	22 59	8.7	12 10	3.2	—	—	02 08	5.0	14 15	5.1
12	Friday	01 39	6.6	14 04	6.8	11 15	9.0	23 30	8.8	00 32	3.0	12 45	3.2	02 37	5.1	14 44	5.2
13	Saturday	02 14	6.6	14 35	6.7	11 46	9.0	—	—	01 02	3.0	13 14	3.2	03 04	5.2	15 12	5.3
14	Sunday	02 45	6.5	15 04	6.6	00 00	8.9	12 17	9.0	01 27	3.1	13 41	3.2	03 33	5.2	15 43	5.3
15	Monday	03 13	6.5	15 32	6.6	00 29	8.8	12 47	8.9	01 53	3.2	14 12	3.2	04 04	5.2	16 15	5.2
16	Tuesday	03 43	6.6	16 04	6.6	00 59	8.8	13 19	8.8	02 22	3.2	14 45	3.2	04 38	5.1	16 51	5.1
17	Wednesday	04 17	6.6	16 39	6.6	01 31	8.7	13 55	8.6	02 54	3.3	15 21	3.1	05 13	5.0	17 29	5.0
18	Thursday	04 56	6.6	17 18	6.4	02 06	8.4	14 35	8.2	03 28	3.2	15 59	3.0	05 51	4.8	18 13	4.8
19	Friday	05 41	6.4	18 03	6.2	02 49	8.1	15 25	7.8	04 03	3.1	16 43	2.8	06 35	4.6	19 05	4.6
20	Saturday	06 33	6.1	18 56	5.8	03 46	7.6	16 31	7.4	04 46	2.9	17 42	2.6	07 29	4.4	20 08	4.5
21	Sunday	07 36	5.9	20 01	5.6	05 02	7.3	17 54	7.3	05 46	2.8	19 08	2.6	08 42	4.3	21 29	4.5
22	Monday	08 51	5.8	21 24	5.7	06 29	7.5	19 18	7.6	07 14	2.7	20 50	2.6	10 06	4.4	22 49	4.7
23	Tuesday	10 17	6.1	22 44	6.0	07 47	8.0	20 26	8.3	08 54	2.9	22 06	2.8	11 18	4.7	23 55	5.0
24	Wednesday	11 27	6.6	23 46	6.5	08 48	8.7	21 20	8.9	10 02	3.1	23 00	3.0	12 16	5.1	—	—
25	Thursday	—	—	12 23	7.0	09 40	9.3	22 09	9.4	10 56	3.4	23 46	3.2	00 48	5.4	13 05	5.5
26	Friday	00 39	6.9	13 14	7.3	10 28	9.8	22 54	9.9	11 44	3.5	—	—	01 34	5.6	13 50	5.8
27	Saturday	01 28	7.2	14 01	7.5	11 14	10.0	23 37	9.9	00 30	3.3	12 31	3.6	02 17	5.8	14 34	6.0
28	Sunday	02 14	7.3	14 45	7.4	11 58	10.0	—	—	01 11	3.4	13 17	3.7	03 00	5.8	15 20	6.0
29	Monday	02 59	7.4	15 27	7.3	00 19	9.8	12 42	9.7	01 48	3.4	14 00	3.7	03 44	5.7	16 08	5.8
30	Tuesday	03 42	7.4	16 06	7.1	01 01	9.5	13 25	9.3	02 24	3.5	14 42	3.6	04 28	5.5	16 57	5.6

MAY 2002   *High Water*   GMT

		LONDON BRIDGE *Datum of Predictions 3.20m below*				LIVERPOOL *Datum of Predictions 4.93m below*				GREENOCK *Datum of Predictions 1.62m below*				LEITH *Datum of Predictions 2.90m below*			
		hr	ht m	hr	ht m	hr	ht m	hr	ht m	hr	ht m	hr	ht m	hr	ht m	hr	ht m
1	Wednesday	04 24	7.2	16 44	6.9	01 42	9.1	14 07	8.8	03 00	3.5	15 23	3.5	05 13	5.3	17 49	5.2
2	Thursday	05 07	6.9	17 20	6.5	02 24	8.7	14 52	8.2	03 38	3.4	16 06	3.3	06 01	5.0	18 45	4.8
3	Friday	05 52	6.5	17 58	6.1	03 10	8.1	15 44	7.5	04 19	3.2	16 53	3.0	06 55	4.7	19 45	4.5
4	Saturday	06 44	6.0	18 44	5.7	04 08	7.6	16 55	7.0	05 08	3.0	17 49	2.8	07 58	4.4	20 50	4.3
5	Sunday	08 02	5.6	20 05	5.4	05 29	7.2	18 19	6.9	06 08	2.8	18 57	2.6	09 07	4.3	22 00	4.2
6	Monday	09 24	5.6	21 38	5.5	06 47	7.3	19 29	7.1	07 34	2.7	20 49	2.6	10 18	4.3	23 13	4.3
7	Tuesday	10 27	5.9	22 41	5.8	07 51	7.6	20 25	7.5	09 16	2.8	21 56	2.7	11 27	4.4	—	—
8	Wednesday	11 21	6.2	23 34	6.1	08 43	8.0	21 10	8.0	10 12	3.0	22 42	2.9	00 12	4.6	12 22	4.7
9	Thursday	12 08	6.5	—	—	09 27	8.4	21 49	8.3	10 56	3.1	23 21	2.9	00 56	4.8	13 03	4.9
10	Friday	00 21	6.4	12 51	6.7	10 06	8.6	22 25	8.6	11 34	3.1	23 56	3.0	01 30	4.9	13 39	5.0
11	Saturday	01 03	6.5	13 28	6.7	10 42	8.8	22 57	8.7	12 08	3.1	—	—	02 12	5.1	14 11	5.1
12	Sunday	01 41	6.6	14 03	6.7	11 15	8.8	23 29	8.8	00 26	3.1	12 40	3.1	02 33	5.2	14 44	5.2
13	Monday	02 16	6.6	14 35	6.7	11 48	8.8	—	—	00 55	3.1	13 11	3.1	03 05	5.2	15 18	5.2
14	Tuesday	02 50	6.6	15 09	6.7	00 01	8.8	12 22	8.8	01 24	3.2	13 47	3.1	03 38	5.2	15 54	5.2
15	Wednesday	03 25	6.6	15 43	6.6	00 35	8.8	12 59	8.8	01 57	3.3	14 25	3.1	04 13	5.2	16 32	5.2
16	Thursday	04 03	6.7	16 20	6.6	01 12	8.7	13 39	8.6	02 32	3.3	15 05	3.0	04 50	5.1	17 14	5.1
17	Friday	04 44	6.6	17 01	6.4	01 53	8.6	14 24	8.4	03 07	3.3	15 48	2.9	05 31	4.9	18 00	4.9
18	Saturday	05 32	6.5	17 47	6.2	02 40	8.3	15 16	8.0	03 46	3.2	16 39	2.8	06 18	4.8	18 53	4.8
19	Sunday	06 25	6.3	18 40	6.0	03 38	8.0	16 20	7.7	04 32	3.1	17 45	2.7	07 13	4.6	19 56	4.7
20	Monday	07 28	6.1	19 46	5.8	04 48	7.8	17 36	7.6	05 34	2.9	19 04	2.6	08 23	4.6	21 09	4.7
21	Tuesday	08 42	6.1	21 05	5.9	06 05	7.9	18 51	7.8	06 56	2.9	20 25	2.7	09 40	4.7	22 22	4.8
22	Wednesday	09 57	6.3	22 16	6.2	07 17	8.2	19 57	8.3	08 24	3.0	21 36	2.9	10 49	4.9	23 27	5.0
23	Thursday	11 02	6.6	23 18	6.5	08 20	8.7	20 54	8.8	09 34	3.2	22 32	3.0	11 47	5.2	—	—
24	Friday	11 58	7.0	—	—	09 15	9.1	21 44	9.2	10 30	3.3	23 20	3.1	00 21	5.3	12 39	5.4
25	Saturday	00 13	6.9	12 50	7.2	10 05	9.4	22 30	9.5	11 20	3.4	—	—	01 10	5.4	13 28	5.6
26	Sunday	01 04	7.1	13 37	7.3	10 53	9.6	23 14	9.6	00 04	3.3	12 09	3.5	01 55	5.6	14 16	5.7
27	Monday	01 53	7.2	14 22	7.2	11 38	9.5	23 57	9.5	00 46	3.3	12 56	3.5	02 39	5.6	15 04	5.7
28	Tuesday	02 40	7.2	15 05	7.1	12 22	9.3	—	—	01 25	3.4	13 41	3.4	03 23	5.6	15 53	5.6
29	Wednesday	03 25	7.2	15 45	7.0	00 39	9.3	13 06	9.0	02 03	3.5	14 25	3.4	04 08	5.4	16 42	5.4
30	Thursday	04 09	7.0	16 22	6.7	01 21	9.0	13 48	8.6	02 41	3.5	15 08	3.3	04 53	5.2	17 32	5.1
31	Friday	04 52	6.8	16 58	6.5	02 03	8.7	14 31	8.2	03 20	3.4	15 53	3.1	05 39	5.0	18 22	4.8

JUNE 2002   *High Water*   GMT

		LONDON BRIDGE				LIVERPOOL				GREENOCK				LEITH			
1	Saturday	05 36	6.4	17 36	6.2	02 47	8.3	15 18	7.7	04 01	3.3	16 40	3.0	06 28	4.8	19 15	4.6
2	Sunday	06 24	6.1	18 20	5.9	03 37	7.9	16 13	7.3	04 47	3.1	17 33	2.8	07 23	4.6	20 09	4.4
3	Monday	07 21	5.8	19 18	5.7	04 39	7.5	17 22	7.0	05 41	3.0	18 29	2.7	08 22	4.4	21 06	4.3
4	Tuesday	08 29	5.7	20 35	5.6	05 52	7.4	18 33	7.1	06 44	2.8	19 29	2.7	09 23	4.4	22 06	4.3
5	Wednesday	09 35	5.8	21 46	5.7	06 57	7.5	19 33	7.3	07 58	2.8	20 36	2.7	10 24	4.4	23 05	4.4
6	Thursday	10 31	6.0	22 44	5.9	07 55	7.7	20 25	7.7	09 13	2.8	21 42	2.8	11 21	4.5	23 59	4.6
7	Friday	11 22	6.2	23 36	6.1	08 44	8.0	21 09	8.1	10 09	2.9	22 34	2.9	12 13	4.7	—	—
8	Saturday	12 08	6.4	—	—	09 27	8.3	21 48	8.4	10 52	2.9	23 15	3.0	00 44	4.8	12 58	4.8
9	Sunday	00 23	6.3	12 51	6.6	10 07	8.5	22 24	8.6	11 30	3.0	23 52	3.1	01 24	5.0	13 39	5.0
10	Monday	01 07	6.5	13 31	6.7	10 45	8.7	23 00	8.8	12 07	3.0	—	—	02 02	5.1	14 18	5.1
11	Tuesday	01 49	6.6	14 11	6.7	11 23	8.8	23 37	8.9	00 26	3.2	12 46	3.0	02 39	5.2	14 57	5.2
12	Wednesday	02 30	6.7	14 50	6.7	12 03	8.8	—	—	01 01	3.3	13 28	3.0	03 16	5.2	15 36	5.3
13	Thursday	03 11	6.8	15 29	6.7	00 17	9.0	12 45	8.8	01 38	3.3	14 12	3.0	03 54	5.3	16 17	5.3
14	Friday	03 54	6.8	16 10	6.6	01 00	8.9	13 30	8.8	02 16	3.4	14 57	3.0	04 34	5.2	17 01	5.3
15	Saturday	04 39	6.8	16 52	6.5	01 46	8.9	14 18	8.6	02 56	3.4	15 46	2.9	05 17	5.2	17 49	5.2
16	Sunday	05 27	6.7	17 38	6.4	02 35	8.7	15 09	8.4	03 38	3.4	16 40	2.9	06 04	5.1	18 41	5.0
17	Monday	06 19	6.5	18 29	6.2	03 30	8.5	16 07	8.2	04 26	3.3	17 41	2.8	06 58	4.9	19 39	4.9
18	Tuesday	07 18	6.4	19 31	6.1	04 31	8.4	17 12	8.0	05 24	3.1	18 45	2.8	08 01	4.9	20 45	4.8
19	Wednesday	08 24	6.3	20 40	6.1	05 38	8.3	18 21	8.0	06 32	3.1	19 52	2.8	09 12	4.9	21 53	4.8
20	Thursday	09 31	6.3	21 47	6.2	06 46	8.3	19 27	8.2	07 49	3.1	21 01	2.9	10 19	5.0	22 57	4.9
21	Friday	10 35	6.5	22 51	6.4	07 52	8.5	20 28	8.5	09 04	3.1	22 03	3.0	11 21	5.1	23 56	5.0
22	Saturday	11 33	6.7	23 50	6.7	08 52	8.7	21 22	8.8	10 07	3.2	22 56	3.1	12 19	5.2	—	—
23	Sunday	12 27	6.9	—	—	09 47	8.9	22 11	9.1	11 02	3.2	23 44	3.2	00 48	5.2	13 14	5.4
24	Monday	00 45	6.9	13 17	7.0	10 37	9.0	22 56	9.2	11 53	3.3	—	—	01 37	5.3	14 05	5.4
25	Tuesday	01 37	7.0	14 04	7.0	11 24	9.0	23 40	9.2	00 27	3.3	12 42	3.2	02 23	5.4	14 54	5.4
26	Wednesday	02 26	7.0	14 47	6.9	12 08	8.9	—	—	01 09	3.4	13 29	3.2	03 08	5.4	15 41	5.4
27	Thursday	03 13	7.0	15 28	6.8	00 22	9.2	12 50	8.8	01 48	3.5	14 14	3.1	03 52	5.4	16 27	5.2
28	Friday	03 56	6.9	16 04	6.7	01 03	9.0	13 30	8.5	02 26	3.5	14 57	3.1	04 34	5.2	17 11	5.1
29	Saturday	04 37	6.7	16 39	6.5	01 43	8.8	14 09	8.3	03 04	3.4	15 39	3.0	05 16	5.1	17 54	4.9
30	Sunday	05 17	6.5	17 15	6.4	02 23	8.5	14 49	8.0	03 43	3.3	16 22	3.0	05 58	4.9	18 38	4.7

JULY 2002 *High Water* GMT

		LONDON BRIDGE *Datum of Predictions 3.20m below				LIVERPOOL *Datum of Predictions 4.93m below				GREENOCK *Datum of Predictions 1.62m below				LEITH *Datum of Predictions 2.90m below			
		hr	m ht	hr	m ht	hr	ht	hr	ht	hr	ht	hr	ht	hr	ht	hr	ht
1	Monday	05 56	6.3	17 55	6.2	03 05	8.2	15 31	7.7	04 24	3.2	17 06	2.9	06 43	4.8	19 23	4.5
2	Tuesday	06 39	6.0	18 41	6.0	03 51	7.9	16 20	7.4	05 08	3.1	17 52	2.9	07 32	4.6	20 12	4.4
3	Wednesday	07 28	5.9	19 35	5.8	04 44	7.6	17 18	7.2	05 57	2.9	18 40	2.8	08 25	4.5	21 05	4.3
4	Thursday	08 23	5.8	20 37	5.7	05 45	7.5	18 25	7.2	06 51	2.8	19 30	2.8	09 22	4.4	22 00	4.3
5	Friday	09 24	5.8	21 41	5.8	06 50	7.5	19 28	7.4	07 53	2.7	20 28	2.8	10 20	4.4	22 58	4.4
6	Saturday	10 25	6.0	22 44	5.9	07 51	7.7	20 23	7.8	09 03	2.8	21 35	2.8	11 20	4.5	23 56	4.6
7	Sunday	11 22	6.2	23 42	6.1	08 45	7.9	21 11	8.2	10 06	2.8	22 34	2.9	12 18	4.6	—	—
8	Monday	12 15	6.4	—	—	09 33	8.3	21 55	8.5	10 57	2.9	23 20	3.0	00 49	4.8	13 10	4.8
9	Tuesday	00 35	6.4	13 04	6.6	10 19	8.5	22 37	8.8	11 43	3.0	—	—	01 36	5.0	13 56	5.0
10	Wednesday	01 25	6.6	13 50	6.7	11 03	8.8	23 20	9.1	00 02	3.2	12 29	3.0	02 18	5.2	14 39	5.3
11	Thursday	02 13	6.8	14 35	6.8	11 49	8.9	—	—	00 43	3.3	13 16	3.0	02 58	5.3	15 21	5.4
12	Friday	02 59	7.0	15 18	6.8	00 04	9.2	12 35	9.1	01 23	3.4	14 05	3.0	03 38	5.4	16 03	5.5
13	Saturday	03 45	7.0	16 01	6.8	00 50	9.3	13 21	9.1	02 05	3.5	14 53	3.0	04 19	5.5	16 47	5.5
14	Sunday	04 31	7.1	16 43	6.8	01 37	9.3	14 08	9.1	02 47	3.5	15 41	3.0	05 02	5.5	17 34	5.4
15	Monday	05 17	7.0	17 27	6.7	02 25	9.3	14 56	8.9	03 30	3.5	16 30	3.0	05 49	5.4	18 23	5.3
16	Tuesday	06 06	6.8	18 13	6.6	03 15	9.1	15 47	8.6	04 16	3.5	17 20	3.0	06 39	5.3	19 17	5.1
17	Wednesday	06 58	6.6	19 06	6.4	04 08	8.8	16 43	8.3	05 06	3.4	18 12	2.9	07 36	5.1	20 17	4.9
18	Thursday	07 57	6.3	20 08	6.2	05 08	8.4	17 47	8.0	06 03	3.2	19 09	2.9	08 43	5.0	21 23	4.7
19	Friday	09 02	6.2	21 17	6.1	06 15	8.1	18 57	7.9	07 08	3.1	20 20	2.8	09 53	4.9	22 29	4.7
20	Saturday	10 08	6.2	22 27	6.2	07 28	8.1	20 06	8.1	08 31	3.0	21 37	2.9	11 01	4.9	23 34	4.8
21	Sunday	11 10	6.3	23 33	6.4	08 37	8.2	21 06	8.4	09 51	3.0	22 38	3.0	12 08	5.0	—	—
22	Monday	12 07	6.5	—	—	09 37	8.4	21 59	8.7	10 54	3.0	23 29	3.2	00 35	4.9	13 08	5.1
23	Tuesday	00 32	6.6	13 00	6.7	10 28	8.6	22 45	9.0	11 48	3.1	—	—	01 29	5.1	14 01	5.2
24	Wednesday	01 26	6.8	13 49	6.8	11 14	8.7	23 27	9.1	00 14	3.3	12 38	3.1	02 15	5.2	14 47	5.3
25	Thursday	02 15	6.9	14 33	6.8	11 56	8.8	—	—	00 56	3.4	13 23	3.1	02 57	5.3	15 29	5.3
26	Friday	03 01	6.9	15 13	6.8	00 07	9.1	12 35	8.7	01 35	3.4	14 04	3.0	03 37	5.3	16 09	5.2
27	Saturday	03 42	6.8	15 47	6.7	00 44	9.1	13 10	8.6	02 12	3.4	14 41	3.0	04 14	5.3	16 46	5.1
28	Sunday	04 18	6.7	16 19	6.6	01 20	9.0	13 44	8.5	02 47	3.4	15 17	3.0	04 50	5.2	17 22	5.0
29	Monday	04 51	6.5	16 50	6.5	01 56	8.8	14 18	8.3	03 21	3.4	15 53	3.0	05 26	5.1	17 59	4.8
30	Tuesday	05 24	6.4	17 26	6.4	02 32	8.5	14 53	8.1	03 55	3.3	16 30	3.0	06 04	5.0	18 39	4.7
31	Wednesday	06 00	6.3	18 05	6.3	03 10	8.2	15 32	7.8	04 32	3.2	17 09	3.0	06 45	4.8	19 23	4.5

AUGUST 2002 *High Water* GMT

		LONDON BRIDGE				LIVERPOOL				GREENOCK				LEITH			
1	Thursday	06 41	6.1	18 50	6.1	03 53	7.9	16 17	7.5	05 12	3.0	17 51	2.9	07 31	4.6	20 12	4.4
2	Friday	07 28	6.0	19 42	5.9	04 44	7.6	17 14	7.3	05 59	2.9	18 38	2.8	08 25	4.4	21 08	4.3
3	Saturday	08 23	5.8	20 42	5.7	05 46	7.3	18 24	7.2	06 56	2.7	19 32	2.8	09 27	4.3	22 09	4.3
4	Sunday	09 28	5.8	21 51	5.7	06 56	7.3	19 36	7.5	08 07	2.7	20 40	2.8	10 34	4.3	23 14	4.4
5	Monday	10 38	5.9	23 03	5.9	08 06	7.6	20 39	7.9	09 27	2.7	21 54	2.9	11 43	4.5	—	—
6	Tuesday	11 43	6.2	—	—	09 06	8.0	21 31	8.4	10 36	2.9	22 53	3.0	00 17	4.7	12 45	4.8
7	Wednesday	00 08	6.3	12 41	6.5	09 59	8.5	22 19	8.9	11 30	3.0	23 41	3.2	01 12	4.9	13 37	5.1
8	Thursday	01 05	6.6	13 32	6.7	10 48	8.9	23 04	9.3	12 19	3.1	—	—	01 58	5.2	14 21	5.4
9	Friday	01 56	7.0	14 19	6.9	11 35	9.2	23 50	9.6	00 25	3.4	13 08	3.1	02 39	5.5	15 04	5.6
10	Saturday	02 44	7.2	15 03	7.0	12 21	9.4	—	—	01 08	3.5	13 56	3.2	03 19	5.7	15 45	5.8
11	Sunday	03 30	7.3	15 45	7.1	00 35	9.8	13 06	9.5	01 51	3.6	14 41	3.2	04 00	5.8	16 29	5.8
12	Monday	04 15	7.3	16 26	7.1	01 21	9.8	13 51	9.4	02 34	3.7	15 24	3.2	04 43	5.8	17 13	5.7
13	Tuesday	04 59	7.2	17 07	7.1	02 07	9.7	14 35	9.2	03 16	3.7	16 05	3.2	05 28	5.7	18 00	5.4
14	Wednesday	05 44	7.0	17 50	6.9	02 53	9.4	15 21	8.9	03 58	3.7	16 46	3.2	06 17	5.5	18 51	5.2
15	Thursday	06 30	6.6	18 36	6.6	03 42	8.9	16 12	8.4	04 43	3.5	17 30	3.1	07 12	5.3	19 48	4.9
16	Friday	07 22	6.2	19 32	6.2	04 38	8.3	17 13	7.9	05 31	3.3	18 20	2.9	08 18	5.0	20 54	4.6
17	Saturday	08 27	5.9	20 47	5.9	05 48	7.7	18 31	7.6	06 28	3.0	19 25	2.8	09 33	4.7	22 05	4.5
18	Sunday	09 41	5.7	22 10	5.8	07 12	7.5	19 51	7.7	07 52	2.8	21 05	2.8	10 49	4.7	23 19	4.6
19	Monday	10 49	5.9	23 20	6.1	08 30	7.7	20 56	8.1	09 52	2.8	22 24	3.0	12 04	4.8	—	—
20	Tuesday	11 50	6.2	—	—	09 30	8.1	21 48	8.6	10 56	3.0	23 16	3.2	00 27	4.8	13 08	4.9
21	Wednesday	00 20	6.5	12 44	6.5	10 19	8.4	22 33	8.9	11 47	3.0	—	—	01 23	5.0	13 57	5.1
22	Thursday	01 14	6.8	13 32	6.7	11 02	8.6	23 13	9.1	00 01	3.3	12 32	3.1	02 07	5.2	14 37	5.2
23	Friday	02 02	7.0	14 16	6.8	11 39	8.7	23 49	9.2	00 42	3.4	13 11	3.1	02 44	5.3	15 13	5.2
24	Saturday	02 44	7.0	14 54	6.8	12 13	8.8	—	—	01 20	3.4	13 47	3.1	03 19	5.4	15 46	5.2
25	Sunday	03 21	6.8	15 27	6.7	00 22	9.1	12 44	8.7	01 54	3.4	14 18	3.1	03 50	5.4	16 17	5.2
26	Monday	03 52	6.7	15 54	6.6	00 55	9.0	13 15	8.6	02 25	3.4	14 47	3.1	04 21	5.3	16 49	5.1
27	Tuesday	04 20	6.5	16 23	6.5	01 26	8.9	13 45	8.5	02 54	3.4	15 19	3.0	04 53	5.2	17 23	5.0
28	Wednesday	04 48	6.5	16 54	6.5	01 58	8.7	14 16	8.3	03 25	3.3	15 49	3.0	05 28	5.1	17 59	4.8
29	Thursday	05 21	6.4	17 29	6.4	02 32	8.4	14 50	8.1	03 57	3.2	16 24	3.1	06 06	4.9	18 39	4.7
30	Friday	05 59	6.3	18 10	6.3	03 10	8.1	15 30	7.7	04 34	3.1	17 03	3.0	06 48	4.7	19 25	4.5
31	Saturday	06 41	6.1	18 58	6.0	03 57	7.6	16 22	7.3	05 16	2.9	17 48	2.9	07 37	4.4	20 19	4.3

SEPTEMBER 2002 _High Water_ GMT

		LONDON BRIDGE *Datum of Predictions 3.20m below						LIVERPOOL *Datum of Predictions 4.93m below						GREENOCK *Datum of Predictions 1.62m below						LEITH *Datum of Predictions 2.90m below					
		hr	m	ht	hr	m	ht	hr	m	ht	hr	m	ht	hr	m	ht	hr	m	ht	hr	m	ht	hr	m	ht
1	Sunday	07 33	5.8	19 56	5.8	04 58	7.2	17 31	7.1	06 12	2.7	18 44	2.8	08 40	4.3	21 25	4.3
2	Monday	08 35	5.6	21 05	5.7	06 13	7.1	18 54	7.2	07 26	2.6	19 55	2.8	09 55	4.3	22 38	4.4
3	Tuesday	09 53	5.6	22 27	5.8	07 36	7.4	20 12	7.7	09 01	2.7	21 20	2.9	11 13	4.5	23 49	4.6
4	Wednesday	11 14	5.9	23 45	6.2	08 46	7.9	21 11	8.4	10 24	2.9	22 28	3.1	12 22	4.8	—	—
5	Thursday	12 17	6.4	—	—	09 42	8.5	22 00	9.1	11 19	3.1	23 19	3.3	00 47	5.0	13 16	5.2
6	Friday	00 45	6.7	13 10	6.7	10 30	9.1	22 46	9.6	12 07	3.2	—	—	01 34	5.3	14 00	5.6
7	Saturday	01 37	7.1	13 57	7.0	11 16	9.5	23 31	9.9	00 05	3.5	12 53	3.3	02 16	5.7	14 42	5.9
8	Sunday	02 24	7.4	14 40	7.2	12 00	9.7	—	—	00 50	3.7	13 37	3.3	02 56	5.9	15 23	6.0
9	Monday	03 09	7.5	15 22	7.3	00 15	10.1	12 44	9.8	01 33	3.8	14 18	3.4	03 37	6.1	16 05	6.0
10	Tuesday	03 52	7.5	16 03	7.3	00 59	10.1	13 27	9.7	02 16	3.9	14 56	3.4	04 20	6.1	16 49	5.8
11	Wednesday	04 34	7.3	16 43	7.3	01 43	9.8	14 10	9.4	02 57	3.9	15 33	3.4	05 06	5.9	17 35	5.5
12	Thursday	05 16	7.0	17 24	7.1	02 28	9.4	14 53	8.9	03 37	3.8	16 10	3.4	05 55	5.6	18 24	5.2
13	Friday	05 57	6.6	18 08	6.7	03 15	8.7	15 41	8.3	04 18	3.6	16 51	3.2	06 51	5.2	19 20	4.8
14	Saturday	06 42	6.1	19 00	6.2	04 10	8.0	16 42	7.7	05 04	3.3	17 39	3.1	07 59	4.8	20 28	4.6
15	Sunday	07 42	5.6	20 21	5.7	05 26	7.3	18 08	7.3	05 57	3.0	18 39	2.9	09 17	4.6	21 44	4.5
16	Monday	09 13	5.4	21 55	5.7	07 03	7.2	19 35	7.5	07 19	2.7	20 53	2.9	10 38	4.5	23 03	4.5
17	Tuesday	10 28	5.6	23 05	6.0	08 19	7.5	20 40	8.0	09 55	2.8	22 07	3.1	11 58	4.7	—	—
18	Wednesday	11 29	6.0	—	—	09 15	8.0	21 31	8.5	10 50	3.0	22 57	3.3	00 15	4.8	12 58	4.9
19	Thursday	00 03	6.5	12 23	6.4	10 01	8.4	22 13	8.9	11 34	3.1	23 40	3.4	01 08	5.0	13 43	5.1
20	Friday	00 55	6.8	13 10	6.7	10 40	8.7	22 51	9.1	12 13	3.2	—	—	01 50	5.2	14 19	5.2
21	Saturday	01 40	7.0	13 53	6.9	11 15	8.8	23 25	9.2	00 20	3.5	12 48	3.2	02 24	5.4	14 50	5.3
22	Sunday	02 20	7.0	14 30	6.8	11 46	8.8	23 56	9.1	00 57	3.5	13 19	3.2	02 54	5.4	15 18	5.3
23	Monday	02 54	6.8	15 01	6.7	12 14	8.8	—	—	01 29	3.4	13 47	3.2	03 23	5.4	15 47	5.3
24	Tuesday	03 21	6.7	15 27	6.6	00 26	9.0	12 43	8.8	01 58	3.4	14 13	3.3	03 52	5.4	16 17	5.2
25	Wednesday	03 46	6.6	15 53	6.5	00 56	8.9	13 12	8.7	02 25	3.4	14 41	3.3	04 23	5.3	16 49	5.1
26	Thursday	04 13	6.6	16 23	6.5	01 26	8.7	13 42	8.5	02 55	3.3	15 11	3.3	04 57	5.2	17 24	5.0
27	Friday	04 44	6.5	16 57	6.5	01 58	8.5	14 14	8.3	03 27	3.3	15 45	3.3	05 34	5.0	18 02	4.8
28	Saturday	05 20	6.4	17 38	6.4	02 35	8.1	14 52	7.9	04 02	3.1	16 21	3.2	06 16	4.7	18 45	4.6
29	Sunday	06 02	6.2	18 26	6.1	03 21	7.7	15 43	7.5	04 42	2.9	17 03	3.0	07 05	4.5	19 37	4.4
30	Monday	06 52	5.8	19 24	5.8	04 23	7.2	16 53	7.1	05 36	2.7	17 58	2.9	08 06	4.3	20 46	4.3

OCTOBER 2002 _High Water_ GMT

		LONDON BRIDGE				LIVERPOOL				GREENOCK				LEITH			
1	Tuesday	07 54	5.6	20 33	5.7	05 43	7.0	18 21	7.2	06 59	2.6	19 16	2.8	09 25	4.3	22 06	4.4
2	Wednesday	09 12	5.5	21 58	5.8	07 13	7.3	19 45	7.7	08 44	2.7	20 48	2.9	10 46	4.5	23 20	4.7
3	Thursday	10 43	5.8	23 21	6.3	08 25	8.0	20 47	8.5	10 10	2.9	22 01	3.2	11 56	4.9	—	—
4	Friday	11 49	6.3	—	—	09 20	8.7	21 37	9.2	11 02	3.2	22 54	3.4	00 19	5.1	12 50	5.4
5	Saturday	00 21	6.8	12 41	6.8	10 07	9.3	22 23	9.8	11 47	3.3	23 41	3.6	01 07	5.5	13 35	5.7
6	Sunday	01 13	7.2	13 28	7.1	10 52	9.7	23 08	10.1	12 30	3.4	—	—	01 49	5.8	14 17	6.0
7	Monday	01 59	7.5	14 13	7.3	11 35	9.9	23 51	10.2	00 27	3.8	13 11	3.5	02 30	6.1	14 58	6.1
8	Tuesday	02 44	7.5	14 56	7.4	12 18	9.9	—	—	01 12	3.9	13 50	3.6	03 13	6.2	15 40	6.0
9	Wednesday	03 26	7.5	15 38	7.5	00 35	10.1	13 01	9.8	01 55	3.9	14 27	3.6	03 58	6.2	16 24	5.8
10	Thursday	04 07	7.3	16 20	7.4	01 19	9.7	13 43	9.4	02 36	3.9	15 02	3.6	04 46	5.9	17 10	5.5
11	Friday	04 47	7.0	17 02	7.1	02 04	9.2	14 26	8.9	03 16	3.8	15 40	3.6	05 37	5.6	17 59	5.2
12	Saturday	05 26	6.6	17 47	6.7	02 51	8.5	15 14	8.3	03 57	3.6	16 21	3.4	06 35	5.1	18 55	4.9
13	Sunday	06 05	6.1	18 39	6.1	03 46	7.7	16 15	7.6	04 43	3.3	17 09	3.2	07 44	4.8	20 04	4.6
14	Monday	06 54	5.6	20 03	5.6	05 07	7.1	17 43	7.3	05 39	2.9	18 10	3.0	08 59	4.5	21 21	4.5
15	Tuesday	08 42	5.3	21 34	5.6	06 42	7.0	19 08	7.4	07 08	2.7	20 08	3.0	10 18	4.5	22 38	4.5
16	Wednesday	10 00	5.5	22 40	6.0	07 54	7.4	20 12	7.9	09 37	2.9	21 37	3.1	11 36	4.6	23 48	4.8
17	Thursday	11 00	5.9	23 37	6.4	08 48	7.9	21 02	8.4	10 27	3.0	22 29	3.3	12 34	4.9	—	—
18	Friday	11 53	6.4	—	—	09 32	8.3	21 45	8.8	11 07	3.2	23 13	3.4	00 41	5.0	13 17	5.1
19	Saturday	00 26	6.8	12 41	6.7	10 10	8.6	22 23	9.0	11 43	3.3	23 52	3.5	01 22	5.2	13 51	5.2
20	Sunday	01 11	7.0	13 23	6.8	10 44	8.8	22 57	9.1	12 16	3.3	—	—	01 56	5.3	14 21	5.3
21	Monday	01 49	6.9	14 00	6.8	11 15	8.9	23 27	9.1	00 28	3.4	12 47	3.3	02 26	5.4	14 48	5.3
22	Tuesday	02 21	6.8	14 31	6.6	11 43	8.9	23 56	9.0	01 00	3.4	13 14	3.4	02 54	5.4	15 16	5.3
23	Wednesday	02 48	6.7	14 59	6.6	12 12	8.9	—	—	01 28	3.3	13 40	3.4	03 24	5.4	15 47	5.3
24	Thursday	03 14	6.6	15 27	6.5	00 26	8.9	12 42	8.8	01 56	3.3	14 08	3.5	03 57	5.3	16 20	5.2
25	Friday	03 42	6.6	15 58	6.6	00 58	8.7	13 13	8.6	02 28	3.3	14 40	3.5	04 33	5.2	16 54	5.1
26	Saturday	04 14	6.6	16 34	6.6	01 32	8.5	13 47	8.4	03 03	3.3	15 14	3.5	05 11	5.0	17 32	4.9
27	Sunday	04 50	6.5	17 16	6.4	02 11	8.2	14 28	8.1	03 40	3.1	15 49	3.4	05 54	4.8	18 14	4.7
28	Monday	05 33	6.2	18 05	6.2	02 59	7.8	15 20	7.7	04 21	3.0	16 30	3.2	06 44	4.6	19 06	4.5
29	Tuesday	06 23	5.9	19 04	5.9	04 01	7.3	16 29	7.4	05 17	2.8	17 24	3.1	07 44	4.5	20 14	4.4
30	Wednesday	07 24	5.6	20 13	5.8	05 20	7.2	17 52	7.4	06 43	2.7	18 42	3.0	08 59	4.5	21 35	4.5
31	Thursday	08 41	5.6	21 36	5.9	06 46	7.4	19 13	7.9	08 22	2.8	20 14	3.1	10 18	4.7	22 48	4.8

NOVEMBER 2002 *High Water* GMT

		LONDON BRIDGE *Datum of Predictions 3.20m below				LIVERPOOL *Datum of Predictions 4.93m below				GREENOCK *Datum of Predictions 1.62m below				LEITH *Datum of Predictions 2.90m below			
		hr	ht m	hr	ht m	hr	ht m	hr	ht m	hr	ht m	hr	ht m	hr	ht m	hr	ht m
1	Friday	10 08	5.9	22 53	6.4	07 57	8.1	20 17	8.6	09 42	3.0	21 30	3.3	11 26	5.0	23 47	5.2
2	Saturday	11 15	6.4	23 53	6.8	08 53	8.8	21 10	9.3	10 35	3.2	22 27	3.5	12 21	5.4	—	—
3	Sunday	12 09	6.8	—	—	09 41	9.4	21 58	9.8	11 21	3.4	23 16	3.7	00 37	5.6	13 08	5.7
4	Monday	00 45	7.2	12 59	7.1	10 26	9.8	22 44	10.1	12 03	3.5	—	—	01 22	5.9	13 51	5.9
5	Tuesday	01 33	7.4	13 46	7.3	11 10	9.9	23 29	10.1	00 03	3.8	12 44	3.6	02 06	6.1	14 33	6.0
6	Wednesday	02 18	7.4	14 32	7.4	11 53	9.9	—	—	00 50	3.9	13 23	3.7	02 52	6.1	15 17	5.9
7	Thursday	03 01	7.4	15 17	7.4	00 13	9.9	12 37	9.7	01 34	3.9	14 01	3.7	03 40	6.0	16 01	5.8
8	Friday	03 42	7.2	16 01	7.3	00 58	9.5	13 20	9.4	02 17	3.8	14 39	3.8	04 30	5.8	16 48	5.5
9	Saturday	04 22	6.9	16 46	7.0	01 43	9.0	14 04	8.9	02 59	3.7	15 17	3.7	05 23	5.5	17 37	5.2
10	Sunday	05 00	6.6	17 32	6.6	02 30	8.4	14 51	8.4	03 43	3.5	16 00	3.6	06 20	5.1	18 32	4.9
11	Monday	05 38	6.2	18 25	6.1	03 24	7.7	15 49	7.8	04 31	3.2	16 48	3.4	07 24	4.7	19 38	4.7
12	Tuesday	06 22	5.8	19 37	5.7	04 36	7.2	17 05	7.5	05 29	3.0	17 47	3.2	08 31	4.5	20 49	4.5
13	Wednesday	07 51	5.4	21 00	5.7	06 01	7.0	18 25	7.4	06 44	2.8	19 07	3.1	09 41	4.4	22 00	4.5
14	Thursday	09 21	5.5	22 05	5.9	07 13	7.2	19 31	7.7	08 42	2.9	20 48	3.1	10 52	4.5	23 06	4.7
15	Friday	10 23	5.8	23 00	6.2	08 09	7.6	20 25	8.1	09 43	3.0	21 50	3.3	11 53	4.7	—	—
16	Saturday	11 16	6.1	23 50	6.5	08 56	8.1	21 10	8.5	10 27	3.2	22 38	3.3	00 01	4.8	12 39	4.9
17	Sunday	12 04	6.4	—	—	09 35	8.4	21 50	8.7	11 05	3.3	23 19	3.4	00 46	5.0	13 16	5.0
18	Monday	00 34	6.7	12 47	6.6	10 11	8.7	22 25	8.9	11 41	3.3	23 56	3.3	01 23	5.1	13 48	5.2
19	Tuesday	01 12	6.7	13 26	6.6	10 43	8.8	22 58	8.9	12 13	3.4	—	—	01 56	5.2	14 18	5.3
20	Wednesday	01 46	6.7	14 00	6.6	11 14	8.9	23 29	8.9	00 29	3.3	12 43	3.5	02 28	5.3	14 49	5.3
21	Thursday	02 17	6.7	14 33	6.6	11 45	8.9	—	—	01 00	3.3	13 11	3.5	03 02	5.3	15 22	5.3
22	Friday	02 48	6.6	15 06	6.6	00 02	8.9	12 18	8.9	01 32	3.3	13 43	3.6	03 37	5.3	15 56	5.3
23	Saturday	03 19	6.6	15 41	6.6	00 38	8.8	12 54	8.8	02 08	3.3	14 17	3.6	04 14	5.2	16 31	5.2
24	Sunday	03 53	6.6	16 20	6.6	01 16	8.6	13 33	8.6	02 46	3.2	14 52	3.6	04 54	5.1	17 10	5.0
25	Monday	04 31	6.5	17 04	6.5	01 59	8.4	14 17	8.4	03 27	3.1	15 30	3.5	05 38	5.0	17 53	4.9
26	Tuesday	05 14	6.3	17 54	6.3	02 48	8.1	15 09	8.1	04 13	3.0	16 13	3.4	06 28	4.8	18 44	4.8
27	Wednesday	06 03	6.1	18 51	6.1	03 46	7.7	16 12	7.9	05 12	2.9	17 06	3.2	07 25	4.7	19 46	4.7
28	Thursday	07 02	5.9	19 57	6.0	04 56	7.6	17 24	7.9	06 27	2.8	18 16	3.2	08 33	4.7	21 01	4.7
29	Friday	08 15	5.8	21 11	6.1	06 12	7.7	18 37	8.1	07 48	2.9	19 36	3.2	09 45	4.8	22 13	4.9
30	Saturday	09 34	6.0	22 22	6.4	07 23	8.1	19 43	8.6	09 04	3.0	20 54	3.3	10 52	5.0	23 14	5.2

DECEMBER 2002 *High Water* GMT

		LONDON BRIDGE				LIVERPOOL				GREENOCK				LEITH			
1	Sunday	10 41	6.4	23 24	6.7	08 23	8.7	20 42	9.1	10 03	3.2	21 58	3.5	11 50	5.2	—	—
2	Monday	11 40	6.7	—	—	09 15	9.1	21 35	9.5	10 53	3.4	22 52	3.6	00 08	5.5	12 41	5.5
3	Tuesday	00 18	7.0	12 34	7.0	10 03	9.5	22 24	9.7	11 38	3.5	23 42	3.7	00 59	5.7	13 28	5.6
4	Wednesday	01 08	7.2	13 25	7.2	10 49	9.7	23 11	9.7	12 21	3.6	—	—	01 48	5.8	14 12	5.7
5	Thursday	01 55	7.2	14 14	7.3	11 34	9.7	23 57	9.6	00 31	3.7	13 02	3.7	02 37	5.9	14 57	5.7
6	Friday	02 40	7.1	15 01	7.3	12 18	9.6	—	—	01 18	3.7	13 42	3.8	03 27	5.8	15 43	5.6
7	Saturday	03 22	7.0	15 48	7.1	00 42	9.3	13 02	9.4	02 04	3.6	14 22	3.8	04 17	5.6	16 30	5.5
8	Sunday	04 02	6.8	16 33	6.9	01 27	8.9	13 46	9.0	02 48	3.5	15 02	3.8	05 09	5.3	17 18	5.3
9	Monday	04 40	6.6	17 18	6.6	02 13	8.4	14 31	8.7	03 33	3.4	15 45	3.7	06 01	5.1	18 09	5.0
10	Tuesday	05 18	6.3	18 05	6.3	03 00	7.9	15 20	8.2	04 21	3.2	16 30	3.5	06 55	4.8	19 04	4.8
11	Wednesday	05 59	6.0	18 59	5.9	03 53	7.5	16 17	7.8	05 13	3.1	17 22	3.3	07 51	4.5	20 05	4.6
12	Thursday	06 53	5.7	20 02	5.7	04 58	7.2	17 24	7.6	06 10	3.0	18 21	3.2	08 49	4.4	21 06	4.5
13	Friday	08 11	5.6	21 09	5.7	06 10	7.1	18 32	7.6	07 10	2.9	19 28	3.1	09 48	4.4	22 06	4.5
14	Saturday	09 26	5.6	22 08	5.8	07 15	7.3	19 34	7.7	08 18	2.9	20 46	3.1	10 47	4.4	23 04	4.6
15	Sunday	10 26	5.8	23 01	6.0	08 10	7.7	20 27	8.0	09 27	3.0	21 52	3.1	11 43	4.6	23 57	4.7
16	Monday	11 19	6.0	23 49	6.2	08 56	8.0	21 13	8.3	10 20	3.1	22 42	3.1	12 31	4.8	—	—
17	Tuesday	12 07	6.3	—	—	09 36	8.4	21 53	8.5	11 04	3.3	23 24	3.2	00 44	4.9	13 13	5.0
18	Wednesday	00 32	6.4	12 51	6.4	10 13	8.7	22 30	8.7	11 41	3.4	—	—	01 27	5.0	13 50	5.1
19	Thursday	01 12	6.6	13 32	6.5	10 49	8.8	23 07	8.8	00 01	3.2	12 15	3.4	02 06	5.1	14 27	5.2
20	Friday	01 51	6.6	14 13	6.6	11 24	9.0	23 44	8.8	00 37	3.2	12 48	3.5	02 44	5.2	15 02	5.3
21	Saturday	02 28	6.7	14 51	6.7	12 02	9.0	—	—	01 15	3.2	13 23	3.6	03 21	5.3	15 38	5.3
22	Sunday	03 05	6.6	15 31	6.8	00 24	8.9	12 42	9.0	01 55	3.2	14 00	3.6	04 00	5.3	16 15	5.3
23	Monday	03 42	6.6	16 13	6.8	01 07	8.8	13 25	8.9	02 37	3.2	14 39	3.6	04 41	5.3	16 54	5.2
24	Tuesday	04 21	6.6	16 58	6.7	01 51	8.7	14 10	8.9	03 21	3.1	15 19	3.6	05 24	5.2	17 37	5.2
25	Wednesday	05 03	6.5	17 45	6.6	02 38	8.5	14 59	8.7	04 08	3.1	16 03	3.5	06 12	5.1	18 25	5.1
26	Thursday	05 50	6.3	18 38	6.3	03 31	8.3	15 53	8.6	05 00	3.0	16 52	3.4	07 04	5.0	19 20	5.0
27	Friday	06 43	6.2	19 36	6.3	04 29	8.1	16 54	8.4	05 59	2.9	17 49	3.3	08 03	4.8	20 24	4.9
28	Saturday	07 46	6.1	20 42	6.2	05 36	7.9	18 01	8.3	07 03	2.9	18 54	3.3	09 10	4.8	21 35	4.9
29	Sunday	08 58	6.1	21 51	6.2	06 45	8.0	19 10	8.4	08 16	3.0	20 11	3.2	10 17	4.8	22 43	5.0
30	Monday	10 09	6.2	22 56	6.4	07 53	8.3	20 17	8.6	09 28	3.1	21 28	3.3	11 20	5.0	23 46	5.2
31	Tuesday	11 15	6.4	23 54	6.6	08 53	8.7	21 17	8.9	10 28	3.2	22 33	3.4	12 18	5.1	—	—

World Geographical Statistics

THE EARTH

The shape of the Earth is that of an oblate spheroid or solid of revolution whose meridian sections are ellipses, whilst the sections at right angles are circles.

DIMENSIONS

Equatorial diameter = 12,756.27 km (7,926.38 miles)
Polar diameter = 12,713.50 km (7,899.80 miles)
Equatorial circumference = 40,075.01 km (24,901.46 miles)
Polar circumference = 40,007.86 km (24,859.73 miles)
Mass = 5,974,000,000,000,000,000,000 tonnes (5.879×10^{21} tons)

The equatorial circumference is divided into 360 degrees of longitude, which is measured in degrees, minutes and seconds east or west of the Greenwich meridian (0°) to 180°, the meridian 180° E. coinciding with 180° W. This dateline was internationally ratified on 13 October 1884.

Distance north and south of the Equator is measured in degrees, minutes and seconds of latitude. The Equator is 0°, the North Pole is 90° N. and the South Pole is 90° S. The Tropics lie at 23° 27' N. (Tropic of Cancer) and 23° 27' S. (Tropic of Capricorn). The Arctic Circle lies at 66° 33' N. and the Antarctic Circle at 66° 33' S. (NB The Tropics and the Arctic and Antarctic circles are affected by the slow decrease in obliquity of the ecliptic, of about 0.47 arcseconds per year. The effect of this is that the Arctic and Antarctic circles are currently moving towards their respective poles by about 14 metres per annum, while the Tropics move towards the Equator by the same amount.

AREA, ETC.

The surface area of the Earth is 510,069,120 km² (196,938,800 miles²), of which the water area is 70.92 per cent and the land area is 29.08 per cent.

The radial velocity on the Earth's surface at the Equator is 1,669.79 km per hour (1,037.56 m.p.h.). The Earth's mean velocity in its orbit around the Sun is 107,229 km per hour (66,629 m.p.h.). The Earth's mean distance from the Sun is 149,597,870 km (92,955,807 miles).

OCEANS

AREA

	km²	miles²
Pacific	166,240,000	64,186,300
Atlantic	86,550,000	33,420,000
Indian	73,427,000	28,350,500
Arctic	9,485,000	5,105,700

The division by the Equator of the Pacific into the North and South Pacific and the Atlantic into the North and South Atlantic makes a total of six oceans.

GREATEST DEPTHS

Greatest depth	location	metres	feet
Mariana Trench	Pacific	10,924	35,840
Puerto Rico Trench	Atlantic	8,605	28,232
Java (Sunda) Trench	Indian	7,125	23,376
Molloy Deep	Arctic	5,680	18,400

SEAS

AREA

	km²	miles²
South China	2,974,600	1,148,500
Caribbean	2,515,900	971,400
Mediterranean	2,509,900	969,100
Bering	2,261,000	873,000
Gulf of Mexico	1,507,600	582,100
Okhotsk	1,392,000	537,500
Japan	1,012,900	391,100
Hudson Bay	730,100	281,900
East China	664,600	256,600
Andaman	564,880	218,100
Black Sea	507,900	196,100
Red Sea	453,000	174,900
North Sea	427,100	164,900
Baltic Sea	382,000	147,500
Yellow Sea	294,000	113,500
Persian/Arabian Gulf	230,000	88,800

GREATEST DEPTHS

	Maximum depth	
	metres	feet
Caribbean	8,605	28,232
East China (Ryu Kyu Trench)	7,507	24,629
South China	7,258	23,812
Mediterranean (Ionian Basin)	5,150	16,896
Andaman	4,267	14,000
Bering	3,936	12,913
Gulf of Mexico	3,504	11,496
Okhotsk	3,365	11,040
Japan	3,053	10,016
Red Sea	2,266	7,434
Black Sea	2,212	7,257
North Sea	439	1,440
Hudson Bay	111	364
Baltic Sea	90	295
Persian Gulf	73	240
Yellow Sea	58	190

THE CONTINENTS

There are six geographic continents, although America is often divided politically into North and Central America, and South America.

AFRICA is surrounded by sea except for the narrow isthmus of Suez in the north-east, through which is cut the Suez Canal. Its extreme longitudes are 17° 20' W. at Cape Verde, Senegal, and 51° 24' E. at Ras Hafun, Somalia. The extreme latitudes are 37° 20' N. at Cape Blanc, Tunisia, and 34° 50' S. at Cape Agulhas, South Africa, about 4,400 miles apart. The Equator passes through the middle of the continent.

NORTH AMERICA, including Mexico, is surrounded by ocean except in the south, where the isthmian states of CENTRAL AMERICA link North America with South America. Its extreme longitudes are 168° 5' W. at Cape

Prince of Wales, Alaska, and 55° 40′ W. at Cape Charles, Newfoundland. The extreme continental latitudes are the tip of the Boothia peninsula, NW Territories, Canada (71° 51′ N.) and 14° 22′ N. at Ocós in the south of Mexico.

SOUTH AMERICA lies mostly in the southern hemisphere; the Equator passes through the north of the continent. It is surrounded by ocean except where it is joined to Central America in the north by the narrow isthmus through which is cut the Panama Canal. Its extreme longitudes are 34° 47′ W. at Cape Branco in Brazil and 81° 20′ W. at Punta Pariña, Peru. The extreme continental latitudes are 12° 25′ N. at Punta Gallinas, Colombia, and 53° 54′ S. at the southernmost tip of the Brunswick peninsula, Chile. Cape Horn, on Cape Island, Chile, lies at 55° 59′ S.

ANTARCTICA lies almost entirely within the Antarctic Circle (66° 34′ S.) and is the largest of the world's glaciated areas. The continent has an area of 5.1 million square miles, 99 per cent of which is permanently ice-covered. The ice amounts to some 7.2 million cubic miles and represents more than 90 per cent of the world's fresh water. The environment is too hostile for unsupported human habitation. *See also* pages 786–7

ASIA is the largest continent and occupies 29.6 per cent of the world's land surface. The extreme longitudes are 26° 05′ E. at Baba Buran, Turkey and 169° 40′ W. at Mys Dežneva (East Cape), Russia, a distance of about 6,000 miles. Its extreme northern latitude is 77° 45′ N. at Cape Celjuskin, Russia, and it extends over 5,000 miles south to about 1° 15′ N. of the Equator.

AUSTRALIA is the smallest of the continents and lies in the southern hemisphere. It is entirely surrounded by ocean. Its extreme longitudes are 113° 11′ E. at Steep Point and 153° 11′ E. at Cape Byron. The extreme latitudes are 10° 42′ S. at Cape York and 39° S. at South East Point, Tasmania.

EUROPE, including European Russia, is the smallest continent in the northern hemisphere. Its extreme latitudes are 71° 11′ N. at North Cape in Norway, and 36° 23′ N. at Cape Matapan in southern Greece, a distance of about 2,400 miles. Its breadth from Cabo Carvoeiro in Portugal (9° 34′ W.) in the west to the Kara River, north of the Urals (66° 30′ E.) in the east is about 3,300 miles. The division between Europe and Asia is generally regarded as the watershed of the Ural Mountains; down the Ural river to Gur'yev, Kazakhstan; across the Caspian Sea to Apsheronskiy Poluostrov, near Baku; along the watershed of the Caucasus Mountains to Anapa and thence across the Black Sea to the Bosporus in Turkey; across the Sea of Marmara to Çanakkale Boğazi (Dardanelles).

	Area	
	km²	miles²
Asia	43,998,000	16,988,000
*America	41,918,000	16,185,000
Africa	29,800,000	11,506,000
Antarctica	13,209,000	5,100,000
†Europe	9,699,000	3,745,000
Australia	7,618,493	2,941,526

*North and Central America has an area of 24,255,000 km{Sup}2 (9,365,000 miles²)
†Includes 5,571,000 km² (2,151,000 miles²) of former USSR territory, including the Baltic states, Belarus, Moldova, the Ukraine, that part of Russia west of the Ural Mountains and Kazakhstan west of the Ural river. European Turkey (24,378 km²/9,412 miles²) comprises territory to the west and north of the Bosporus and the Dardanelles

GLACIATED AREAS

It is estimated that 15,915,000 km² (6,145,000 miles²) or 10.73 per cent of the world's land surface is permanently covered with ice.

	Area	
	km²	miles²
South Polar regions	13,830,000	5,340,000
North Polar regions (incl. Greenland or Kalaallit Nunaat)	1,965,000	758,500
Alaska-Canada	58,800	22,700
Asia	37,800	14,600
South America	11,900	4,600
Europe	10,700	4,128
New Zealand	1,015	391
Africa	238	92

The largest glacier is the 515 km/320 mile-long Lambert-Fisher Ice Passage, Antarctica.

PENINSULAS

	Area	
	km²	miles²
Arabian	3,250,000	1,250,000
Southern Indian	2,072,000	800,000
Alaskan	1,500,000	580,000
Labradorian	1,300,000	500,000
Scandinavian	800,300	309,000
Iberian	584,000	225,500

LARGEST ISLANDS

Island, and Ocean	*Area*	
	km²	miles²
Greenland (Kalaallit Nunaat), Arctic	2,175,500	840,000
New Guinea, Pacific	792,500	306,000
Borneo, Pacific	725,450	280,100
Madagascar, Indian	587,040	226,658
Baffin Island, Arctic	507,451	195,928
Sumatra, Indian	427,350	165,000
Honshu, Pacific	227,413	87,805
*Great Britain, Atlantic	218,077	84,200
Victoria Island, Arctic	217,292	83,897
Ellesmere Island, Arctic	196,236	75,767
Sulawesi (Celebes), Indian	189,036	72,987
South Island, NZ, Pacific	151,213	58,384
Java, Indian	126,650	48,900
North Island, NZ, (Pacific)	114,487	44,204
Cuba, Atlantic	110,862	42,804
Newfoundland, Atlantic	108,855	42,030
Luzon, Pacific	105,360	40,680
Iceland, Atlantic	102,820	39,700
Mindanao, Pacific	95,247	36,775
Ireland, Atlantic	82,462	31,839

*Mainland only

LARGEST DESERTS

	Area (approx.) km²	miles²
The Sahara, N. Africa	9,000,000	3,500,000
Australian Desert (Great Sandy, Gibson and Great Victoria)	1,350,000	520,000
The Gobi, Mongolia/China	1,300,000	500,000
Arabian Desert	1,000,000	385,000
Kalahari Desert, Botswana/ Namibia/S. Africa	570,000	220,000
Taklimakan Shamo, Mongolia/China	320,000	125,000
*Kara Kum, Turkmenistan	310,000	120,000
Namib Desert, Namibia	285,000	110,000
Thar Desert, India/Pakistan	260,000	100,000
Somali Desert, Somalia	260,000	100,000
Atacama Desert, Chile	180,000	70,000
Sonoran Desert, USA/Mexico	180,000	70,000
Dasht-e Lut, Iran	52,000	20,000
Mojave Desert, USA	38,850	15,000

*Together with the Kyzyl Kum known as the Turkestan Desert

DEEPEST DEPRESSIONS

	Maximum depth below sea level metres	feet
Dead Sea, Jordan/Israel	408	1,338
Lake Assal, Djibouti	156	511
Turfan Depression, Sinkiang, China	153	505
Qattara Depression, Egypt	132	436
Mangyshlak peninsula, Kazakhstan	131	433
Danakil Depression, Ethiopia	116	383
Death Valley, California, USA	86	282
Salton Sink, California, USA	71	235
W. of Ustyurt plateau, Kazakhstan	70	230
Prikaspiyskaya Nizmennost', Russia/Kazakhstan	67	220
Lake Sarykamysh, Uzbekistan/ Turkmenistan	45	148
El Faiyûm, Egypt	44	147
Península Valdés, Chubut, Argentina	40	131
Lake Eyre, South Australia	16	52

The world's largest exposed depression is the Prikaspiyskaya Nizmennost' covering the hinterland of the northern third of the Caspian Sea, which is itself 28 m (92 ft) below sea level.

Western Antarctica and Central Greenland largely comprise crypto-depressions under ice burdens. The Antarctic Bentley subglacial trench has a bedrock 2,538 m (8,326 ft) below sea-level. In Greenland (lat. 73° N., long. 39° W.) the bedrock is 365 m (1,197 ft) below sea-level.

Nearly one quarter of the area of The Netherlands lies marginally below sea-level, an area of more than 10,000 km²/3,860 miles².

LONGEST MOUNTAIN RANGES

Range, and location	Length km	miles
Cordillera de Los Andes, W. South America	7,200	4,500
Rocky Mountains, W. North America	4,800	3,000
Himalaya-Karakoram-Hindu Kush, S. Central Asia	3,800	2,400
Great Dividing Range, E. Australia	3,600	2,250
Trans-Antarctic Mts, Antarctica	3,500	2,200
Atlantic Coast Range, E. Brazil	3,000	1,900
West Sumatran-Javan Range, Indonesia	2,900	1,800
Aleutian Range, Alaska and NW Pacific	2,650	1,650
Tien Shan, S. Central Asia	2,250	1,400
Central New Guinea Range, Irian Jaya/ Papua New Guinea	2,000	1,250

HIGHEST MOUNTAINS

The world's 8,000-metre mountains (with six subsidiary peaks) are all in the Himalaya-Karakoram-Hindu Kush ranges.

Mountain	Height metres	feet
Mt Everest*	8,850	29,035
K2 (Chogori)†	8,611	28,251
Kangchenjunga	8,586	28,169
Lhotse	8,501	27,890
Makalu I	8,462	27,762
Lhotse Shar (II)	8,383	27,504
Cho Oyu	8,201	26,906
Dhaulagiri I	8,167	26,794
Manaslu I (Kutang I)	8,156	26,760
Nanga Parbat (Diamir)	8,125	26,660
Annapurna I	8,091	26,546
Gasherbrum I (Hidden Peak)	8,068	26,470
Broad Peak I	8,046	26,400
Shisham Pangma (Gosainthan)	8,013	26,287
Gasherbrum II	8,034	26,360
Makalu South-East	8,010	26,280
Broad Peak Central	8,000	26,246

*Named after Sir George Everest (1790–1866), Surveyor-General of India 1830–43, in 1863. He pronounced his name Eve-rest
†Formerly Col. H. H. Godwin-Austen (1834–1923)

The culminating summits in the other major mountain ranges are:

Mountain, by range or country	Height metres	feet
Pik Pobedy, Tien Shan	7,439	24,406
Cerro Aconcagua, Cordillera de Los Andes	6,960	22,834
Mt McKinley (S. Peak), Alaska Range	6,194	20,320
Kilimanjaro (Kibo), Tanzania	5,894	19,340
Hkakabo Razi, Myanmar	5,881	19,296
El'brus, (W. Peak), Caucasus	5,642	18,510
Citlaltépetl (Orizaba), Sierra Madre Oriental, Mexico	5,610	18,405
Vinson Massif, E. Antarctica	4,897	16,066
Puncak Jaya, Central New Guinea Range	4,884	16,023
Mt Blanc, Alps	4,807	15,771

Mountain, by range or country	Height metres	feet
Klyuchevskaya Sopka, Kamchatka peninsula, Russia	4,750	15,584
Ras Dashan, Ethiopian Highlands	4,620	15,158
Zard Kuh, Zagros Mts, Iran	4,547	14,921
Mt Kirkpatrick, Trans Antarctic	4,529	14,860
Mt Belukha, Altai Mts, Russia/ Kazakhstan	4,505	14,783
Mt Elbert, Rocky Mountains	4,400	14,433
Mt Rainier, Cascade Range, N. America	4,392	14,410
Nevado de Colima, Sierra Madre Occidental, Mexico	4,268	14,003
Jebel Toubkal, Atlas Mts, N. Africa	4,165	13,665
Kinabalu, Crocker Range, Borneo	4,101	13,455
Kerinci, West Sumatran-Javan Range, Indonesia	3,800	12,467
Jabal an NabiShu'ayb, N. Tihamat, Yemen	3,760	12,336
Mt Cook (Aorangi), Southern Alps, New Zealand	3,754	12,315
Teotepec, Sierra Madre del Sur, Mexico	3,703	12,149
Thaban Ntlenyana, Drakensberg, South Africa	3,482	11,425
Pico de Bandeira, Atlantic Coast Range	2,890	9,482
Shishaldin, Aleutian Range	2,861	9,387
Kosciusko, Great Dividing Range	2,228	7,310

HIGHEST VOLCANOES

Volcano (last major eruption), and location	Height metres	feet
Ojos del Salado (1981), Andes, Argentina/Chile	6,880	22,572
Llullaillaco (1877), Andes, Argentina/Chile	6,723	22,057
San Pedro (1960), Andes, Chile	6,199	20,325
Guallatiri (1960, 1993), Andes, Chile	6,071	19,918
Cotopaxi (1940, 1975), Andes, Ecuador	5,897	19,347
Tupungatito (1986), Andes, Chile	5,640	18,504
Láscar (2000), Andes, Chile	5,591	18,346
Popocatépetl (1999-2001), Mexico	5,465	17,930
Nevado del Ruiz (1985, 1991), Colombia	5,321	17,457
Sangay (1998), Andes, Ecuador	5,188	17,021
Irruputancu (1995), Chile	5,163	16,939
Klyuchevskaya Sopka (1999), Kamchatka peninsula, Russia	4,835	15,863
Guagua Pichincha (1999), Andes, Ecuador	4,784	15,696
Purace (1977), Colombia	4,756	15,601
Wrangel (1907), Alaska, USA	4,316	14,028
Shasta (1786), California, USA	4,316	14,162
Galeras (1993), Colombia	4,275	14,028
Mauna Loa (1984, 1987), Hawaii Is.	4,170	13,680
Cameroon (2000), Cameroon	4,095	13,435

OTHER NOTABLE VOLCANOES

	Height metres	feet
Erebus (1998), Ross Island, Antarctica	3,794	12,450
Fuji (1708), Honshu, Japan	3,775	12,388
Santa Maria (1902, 1998), Guatemala	3,772	12,375
Semeru (since 1967), Java, Indonesia	3,675	12,060
Mt Etna (1169, 1669, 1993, 1996-9, 2000), Sicily, Italy	3,368	11,053
Raung (1993, 1997), Java, Indonesia	3,322	10,932
Sheveluch (1997, 1999, 2000), Kamchatka, Russia	3,283	10,771
Llaima (1995), Chile	3,125	10,253
Mt St Helens (1980, 1986, 1991, 1998), Washington State, USA	2,549	8,363
Beerenberg (1985), Jan Mayen Island	2,277	7,470
Pinatubo (1991, 1995), Luzon, Philippines	1,598	5,249
Hekla (1981, 1991, 2000), Iceland	1,491	4,892
Mt Unzen (1792, 1991, 1996, 2000), Kyushu, Japan	1,360	4,462
Vesuvius (AD 79, 1631, 1944), Italy	1,281	4,203
Kilauea (1996, 1997, 2000), Hawaii, USA	1,249	4,009
Soufrière (1979, 1997), St Vincent	1,178	3,865
Soufrière Hills (1997–2000), Montserrat	914	3,001
Stromboli (1996, 1997-9, 2000), Lipari Is., Italy	926	3,038
Krakatau (1883, 1995, 1999, 2001), Sunda Strait, Indonesia	813	2,667
Santoríni (Thíra) (1628 BC, 1950), Aegean Sea, Greece	564	1,850
Tristan da Cunha (1961), South Atlantic	243	800
Surtsey (1963–7), off Iceland	173	568

LARGEST LAKES

The areas of some of these lakes are subject to seasonal variation.

	Area km^2	miles^2	Length km	miles
Caspian Sea, Iran/ Azerbaijan/Russia/ Turkmenistan/ Kazakhstan	371,000	143,000	1,171	728
*Michigan–Huron, USA/Canada	117,610	45,300	1,010	627
Superior, Canada/ USA	82,100	31,700	563	350
Victoria, Uganda/ Tanzania/Kenya	69,500	26,828	362	225
Tanganyika, Dem. Rep. of Congo/ Tanzania/Zambia/ Burundi	32,900	12,665	725	450
Great Bear, Canada	31,328	12,096	309	192
‡Aral Sea, Kazakhstan/ Uzbekistan	30,700	11,850	320	200
†Baykal (Baikal), Russia	30,500	11,776	620	385
Malawi (Nyasa), Tanzania/Malawi/ Mozambique	28,900	11,150	580	360
Great Slave, Canada	28,570	11,031	480	298
Erie, Canada/USA	25,670	9,910	388	241
Winnipeg, Canada	24,390	9,417	428	266
Ontario, Canada/USA	19,010	7,340	310	193

	Area km²	miles²	Length km	miles
Balkhash, Kazakhstan	18,427	7,115	605	376
Ladozhskoye (*Ladoga*), Russia	17,700	6,835	193	120

*Lakes Michigan and Huron are regarded as lobes of the same lake. The Michigan lobe has an area of 57,750 km² (22,300 miles²) and the Huron lobe an area of 59,570 km² (23,000 miles²)
†World's deepest lake (1,940 m/6,365 ft)
‡ Northern part (Little Aral Sea) dammed off in 1997

UNITED KINGDOM, BY COUNTRY

	Area km²	miles²	Length km	miles
Lough Neagh, Northern Ireland	381.73	147.39	28.90	18.00
Loch Lomond, Scotland	71.12	27.46	36.44	22.64
Windermere, England	14.74	5.69	16.90	10.50
Lake Vyrnwy, Wales (artificial)	4.53	1.75	7.56	4.70
Llyn Tegid (*Bala*), Wales (natural)	4.38	1.69	5.80	3.65

LONGEST RIVERS

River, source and outflow	Length km	miles
Nile (*Bahr-el-Nil*), R. Luvironza, Burundi – E. Mediterranean Sea	6,725	4,180
Amazon (*Amazonas*), Lago Villafro, Peru – S. Atlantic Ocean	6,448	4,007
Yangtze-Kiang (*Chang Jiang*), Kunlun Mts, W. China – Yellow Sea	6,380	3,964
Mississippi-Missouri-Red Rock, Montana – Gulf of Mexico	5,970	3,710
Yenisey-Angara, W. Mongolia – Kara Sea	5,536	3,440
Huang He (*Yellow River*), Bayan Har Shan range, central China – Yellow Sea	5,463	3,395
Ob'-Irtysh, W. Mongolia – Kara Sea	5,410	3,362
Lena-Kirenga, R. Kirenga, W. of Lake Baykal – Laptev Sea, Arctic Ocean	4,400	2,734
Amur-Argun, R. Argun, Khingan Mts, N. China – Sea of Okhotsk	4,416	2,744
Zaïre (*Congo*), R. Lualaba, Dem. Rep. of Congo-Zambia – S. Atlantic Ocean	4,665	2,900
Mekong, Lants'ang, Tibet – South China Sea	4,345	2,700
Mackenzie-Peace, Tatlatui Lake, British Columbia – Beaufort Sea	4,240	2,635
Paraná-Río de la Plata, R. Paranáiba, central Brazil – S. Atlantic Ocean	4,240	2,635
Niger, Loma Mts, Guinea – Gulf of Guinea, E. Atlantic Ocean	4,170	2,590
Murray-Darling, SE Queensland – Lake Alexandrina, S. Australia	3,717	2,310
Volga, Valdai plateau – Caspian Sea	3,685	2,290

OTHER NOTABLE RIVERS

River	Length km	miles
Rio Grande, USA–Mexican border	3,057	1,900
Ganges-Brahmaputra, R. Matsang, SW Tibet – Bay of Bengal	2,900	1,800
Indus, R. Sengge, SW Tibet – N. Arabian Sea	2,897	1,800
Danube (*Donau*), Black Forest, SW Germany – Black Sea	2,856	1,775
Tigris-Euphrates, R. Murat, E. Turkey – Persian Gulf	2,800	1,740
Zambezi, NW Zambia – S. Indian Ocean	2,735	1,700
Irrawaddy, R. Mali Hka, Myanmar – Andaman Sea	2,151	1,337
Don, SE of Novomoskovsk – Sea of Azov	1,969	1,224

BRITISH ISLES

River	km	miles
Shannon, Co. Cavan, Rep. of Ireland – Atlantic Ocean	386	240
Severn, Powys, Wales – Bristol Channel	354	220
Thames, Gloucestershire, England – North Sea	346	215
Tay, Perthshire, Scotland – North Sea	188	117
Clyde, Lanarkshire, Scotland – Firth of Clyde	158	98½
Tweed, Peeblesshire, Scotland – North Sea	155	96½
Bann (Upper and Lower), Co. Down, N. Ireland – Atlantic Ocean	122	76

GREATEST WATERFALLS – BY HEIGHT

Waterfall, river and location	Total drop metres	feet	Greatest single leap metres	feet
Saltó Angel, Carrao Auyán Tepuí, Venezuela	979	3,212	807	2,648
Utigård, Jostedal Glacier, Norway	800	2,625	600	1,970
Mongefossen, Monge, Norway	774	2,540	—	—
Yosemite, Yosemite Creek, USA	739	2,425	435	1,430
*Østre Mardøla Foss, Mardals, Norway	655	2,149	296	974
*Tyssestrengene, Tysso, Norway	646	2,120	289	948
Cuquenán, Arabopó, Venezuela	610	2,000	—	—
Tugela, Tugela, Natal, S. Africa	580	1,904	410	1,350
Sutherland, Arthur, NZ	580	1,904	248	815

*Volume much affected by hydroelectric harnessing

BRITISH ISLES, BY COUNTRY

Waterfall	metres	feet	
Eas a' Chuàl Aluinn, Glas Bheinn, Sutherland, Scotland	200	658	
Powerscourt Falls, Dargle, Co. Wicklow, Rep. of Ireland	106	350	
Pistyll-y-Llyn, Powys/ Dyfed border, Wales	c.72	c.235	(cascades)
Pistyll Rhyadr, Clwyd/ Powys border, Wales	71.5	235	(single leap)
Caldron Snout, R. Tees, Cumbria/Durham, England	61	200	(cascades)

GREATEST WATERFALLS – BY VOLUME

Waterfall, river and location	Mean annual flow	
	m³/sec	galls/sec
Inga (Congo dam site), Dem. Rep. of Congo	43,000	9,460,000
Khône, Mekong, Laos	42,500	9,350,000
Boyoma (Stanley), R. Lualaba, Dem. Rep. of Congo	c.17,000	c.3,750,000
Guayra (Sete Quedas), Brazil	13,000	2,860,000
Rio Paraná, Argentina/ Paraguay	11,900	2,619,000
Niagara (Horseshoe), R. Niagara/Lake Erie–Lake Ontario	6,000	1,320,000
Paulo Afonso, R. São Francisco, Brazil	2,830	622,500
Urubupunga, Alto Paraná, Brazil	2,745	604,000
Cataratas del Iguazú, R. Iguaçu, Brazil/Argentina	1,743	380,000
Patos-Maribando, Rio Grande, Brazil	1,500	330,000
Churchill, R. Churchill, Canada	1,132	215,000
Victoria (Mosi-oa-tunya), R. Zambezi, Zambia/Zimbabwe	1,087	242,000

TALLEST DAMS

	metres	feet
*Rogun, R. Vakhsh, Tajikistan	335	1,098
Nurek, R. Vakhsh, Tajikistan	300	984
Grande Dixence, Switzerland	285	935
*Longtan, R. Hangshui, China	285	935
Inguri, Georgia	272	892
Borucu, Costa Rica	269	883
Vaiont, Italy	262	859
Manuel M. Torres, Chicoasén, Mexico	261	856
Tehri, R. Bhagivathi, India	261	856

*Under construction

The world's most massive dam is the Syncrude Tailings dam in Alberta, Canada, which will have a volume of 540 million cubic metres/706 million cubic yards.

The Three Gorges Chang Jiang (Yangtze) Dam, China, with a crest length of 1,983 m/6,505 ft, is due for completion in 2009 (stage 3).

The Yacyretá-Apipe dam across the River Paraná, Argentina-Paraguay, is being completed to a length of 69,600 m/43.24 miles.

TALLEST INHABITED BUILDINGS

Building and city	Height	
	metres	feet
Pearl of the Orient	468	1535
Shanghai World Financial Centre	460	1,509
Chongqing Tower, China	457	1,499
Petronas Towers I and II, Kuala Lumpur, Malaysia (1998)	451.9	1,482
Sears Tower, Chicago[1] (1974)	443	1,454
Jin Mao, Shanghai, China (1999)	420	1,378
Xianmen Fairwell International Centre, China (2002)	397	1,302
Plaza Rakyat, Kuala Lumpur, Malaysia (1999)	382	1,254
Empire State Building, New York[2] (1931)	381	1,250
Central Plaza, Hong Kong (1992)	373	1,227
Bank of China Tower, Hong Kong (1998)	368	1,209
Emirates Tower One (2000)	350	1,148
Amoco Building, Chicago (1973)	346	1,136
Central Station, Hong Kong	346	1,136
John Hancock Center, Chicago (1969	343	1,127
Shun Hing Square, Shenzhen, China (1996)	384	1,260
CITIC Plaza, Guangzhou, China (1996)	391	1,283
Chicago Beach Tower, Dubai (1999)	321	1,053
Sky Central Plaza, Guangzhou	322	1,056
Baiyoke Tower, Bangkok, Thailand (1998)	320	1,050

1. With TV antennae, 520 m/1,707 ft

Note: The two World Trade Center towers, One or North (1972) 110 stories, 415 m 1,368 ft or 521.2 m 1,716 ft with TV antennae; and Two or South (1973) 110 stories, 415 m, 1,362 ft, were destroyed by two terrorist hijacked aircraft on 11 September 2001.

2. With TV tower (added 1950–1), 430.9 m/1,414 ft

TALLEST STRUCTURES

Structure and location	Height	
	metres	feet
*Warszawa Radio Mast, Konstantynow, Poland (1974)	646	2,120
KVLY (formerly KTHI)-TV Mast, Blanchard, North Dakota (guyed) (1963)	629	2,063
CN Tower, Metro Centre, Toronto, Canada (1975)	555	1,822
Ostankino Tower, Moscow (1967)	540	1,772

*Collapsed during renovation, August 1991. New structure planned on a site at Solkajawski

LONGEST BRIDGES – BY SPAN

Bridge and location	Length	
	Metres	feet
SUSPENSION SPANS		
Akashi-Kaikyo, Shikoku, Japan (1998)	1,990	6,529
Storebaelt East Bridge, Denmark (1998)	1,624	5,328
Humber Estuary, Humberside, England (1981)	1,410	4,626
Jiangyin (Yangtze), China (1999)	1,385	4,544
Tsing Ma, Hong Kong, China (1997)	1,377	4,518
Verrazano Narrows, Brooklyn–Staten I, USA (1964)	1,298	4,260
Golden Gate, San Francisco Bay, USA (1937)	1,280	4,200
Hoga Kusten, Sweden (1997)	1,210	3,970
Mackinac Straits, Michigan, USA (1957)	1,158	3,800
Chesapeake Bay No.2, Viginia, USA (1999)	1,158	3,800
Minami Bisan-Seto, Japan (1988)	1,100	3,609
Bosporus II, Istanbul, Turkey (1988)	1,089	3,576
Bosporus I, Istanbul, Turkey (1973)	1,074	3,524
George Washington, Hudson River, New York City, USA (1931)	1,067	3,500
Kurishima III, Japan (1999)	1,030	3,379
Kurishima II, Japan (1999)	1,020	3,346
Ponte 25 de Abril (Tagus), Lisbon, Portugal (1966)	1,013	3,323
Firth of Forth (road), nr Edinburgh, Scotland	1,006	3,300
Kita Bisan-Seto, Japan	990	3,248
*Severn River, Severn Estuary, England	988	3,240

*The main span of the 5.15 km/3.2 mile long Second Severn bridging, opened in 1996, is 456 m/1,496 ft.

Bridge and location	Length	
	Metres	feet
CANTILEVER SPANS		
Pont de Québec (rail-road), St Lawrence,		
Canada (1997)	548.6	1,800
Ravenswood, W. Virginia, USA	525.1	1,723
Firth of Forth (rail), nr Edinburgh, Scotland		
(two spans of 1,170ft each) (1890)	521.2	1,710
Nanko, Osaka, Japan (1974)	510.0	1,673
Commodore Barry, Chester,		
Pennsylvania, USA	494.3	1,622
Greater New Orleans, Louisiana,		
USA (1988)	480.0	1,575
Howrah (rail-road), Calcutta,		
India (1936-43)	457.2	1,500

STEEL ARCH SPANS

New River Gorge, Fayetteville,		
W. Virginia, USA (1977)	518.0	1,700
Bayonne (Kill van Kull), Bayonne,		
NJ – Staten I., USA (1931)	503.5	1,652
Sydney Harbour, Sydney, Australia (1932)	502.9	1,650

The 'floating' bridging at Evergreen Point, Seattle, Washington State, USA (1963), is 3,839 m/12,596 ft long, of which 2,310 m/7,578 ft floats.

The longest stretch of bridgings of any kind is that carrying the Interstate 55 and Interstate 10 highways at Manchac, Louisiana (1979), on twin concrete trestles over 55.21 km/34.31 miles.

LONGEST VEHICULAR TUNNELS

Tunnel and location	Length	
	km	miles
*Seikan (rail), Tsugaru Channel, Japan		
(1988)	53.90	33.49
*Channel Tunnel, (rail) Cheriton, Kent –		
Sangatte, Calais (1994)	49.94	31.03
Moscow metro, Belyaevo - Bittsevsky,		
Moscow, Russia (1979)	37.90	23.50
Northern line tube, East Finchley –		
Morden, London (1939)	27.84	17.30
Laerdal-Aurland Road Link (2000)	24.51	15.22
*Oshimizu (rail), Honshu, Japan (1982)	22.17	13.78
Simplon II (rail), Brigue, Switzerland –		
Iselle, Italy (1922)	19.82	12.31
Simplon I (rail), Brigue, Switzerland –		
Iselle, Italy (1906)	19.80	12.30
Vereina, Switzerland (1999)	19.06	11.84
*Shin-Kanmon (rail), Kanmon Strait, Japan		
(1975)	18.68	11.61
Appennino (rail), Vernio, Italy (1934)	18.49	11.49
St Gotthard (road), Göschenen –		
Airolo, Switzerland (1981)	16.91	10.51

*Sub-aqueous

The longest non-vehicular tunnelling in the world is the Delaware Aqueduct in New York State, USA, constructed in 1937–44 to a length of 168.9 km/105 miles. St Gotthard (rail) tunnel (2010) will be 56.9 km/33.6 miles.

BRITAIN – RAIL TUNNELS

	miles	yards
Severn, Bristol - Newport (1873-86)	4	484
Totley, Manchester – Sheffield	3	950

	miles	yards
Standedge, Manchester - Huddersfield		
(1811)	3	66
Sodbury, Swindon – Bristol	2	924
Disley, Stockport – Sheffield	2	346
Ffestiniog, Llandudno – Blaenau		
Ffestiniog	2	338
Bramhope, Leeds – Harrogate	2	241
Cowburn, Manchester – Sheffield	2	182

The longest road tunnel in Britain is the Mersey Road Tunnel (1934), 3.42 km/2 miles 228 yards long. The longest canal tunnel, at Standedge, W. Yorks, is 5.13 km/3 miles 330 yards long; it was closed in 1944 but is currently being restored.

LONGEST SHIP CANALS

Canal (opening date)	Length		Min. depth	
	km	miles	metres	feet
White Sea-Baltic				
(formerly Stalin) (1933),				
of which Canalised river;				
51.5 km/32 miles	235	146.02	5.0	16.5
*Suez (1869)				
Links Red and				
Mediterranean Seas	162	100.60	12.9	42.3
V. I. Lenin Volga-Don				
(1952)				
Links Black and				
Caspian Seas	100	62.20	n/a	n/a
Kiel (or North Sea) (1895)				
Links North and				
Baltic Seas	98	60.90	13.7	45.0
*Houston (1940)				
Links inland city with sea	91	56.70	10.4	34.0
Alphonse XIII (1926)				
Gives Seville access to sea	85	53.00	7.6	25.0
Panama (1914)				
Links Pacific Ocean				
and Caribbean Sea;				
lake chain, 78.9 km/49				
miles dug	82	50.71	12.5	41.0
Manchester Ship (1894)				
Links city with				
Irish Channel	64	39.70	8.5	28.0
Welland (1932)				
Circumvents Niagara				
Falls and Rapids	43.5	27.00	8.8	29.0
Brussels (Rupel Sea)				
(1922) Renders Brussels				
an inland port	32	19.80	6.4	21.0

*Has no locks

The first section of China's Grand Canal, running 1,782 km/1,107 miles from Beijing to Hangzhou, was opened AD 610 and completed in 1283. Today it is limited to 2,000 tonne vessels.

The St Lawrence Seaway comprises the Beauharnois, Welland and Welland Bypass and Seaway 54–59 canals, and allows access to Duluth, Minnesota, USA via the Great Lakes from the Atlantic end of Canada's Gulf of St Lawrence, a distance of 3,769 km/2,342 miles. The St Lawrence Canal, completed in 1959, is 293 km/182 miles long.

Distances from London by Air

This list details the distances in miles from London, Heathrow, to various cities (airports) abroad.

To	Miles
Abidjan	3,197
Abu Dhabi (International)	3,425
Addis Ababa	3,675
Adelaide (International)	10,111
Aden	3,670
Algiers	1,035
'Ammān (Queen Alia)	2,287
Amsterdam	230
Ankara (Esenboga)	1,770
Athens	1,500
Atlanta	4,198
Auckland	11,404
Baghdād (Saddam)	2,551
Bahrain	3,163
Baku	2,485
Bangkok	5,928
Barbados	4,193
Barcelona (Muntadas)	712
Basel	447
Beijing (Capital)	5,063
Beirut	2,161
Belfast (Aldergrove)	325
Belgrade	1,056
Berlin (Tegel)	588
Bermuda	3,428
Bern	476
Bogotá	5,262
Bombay (Mumbai)	4,478
Boston	3,255
Brasília	5,452
Bratislava	817
Brisbane (Eagle Farm)	10,273
Brussels	217
Bucharest (Otopeni)	1,307
Budapest	923
Buenos Aires	6,915
Cairo (International)	2,194
Calcutta	4,958
Calgary	4,357
Canberra	10,563
Cape Town	6,011
Caracas	4,639
Casablanca (Mohamed V)	1,300
Chicago (O'Hare)	3,941
Cologne	331
Colombo (Katunayake)	5,411
Copenhagen	608
Dakar	2,706
Dallas (Fort Worth)	4,736
Dallas (Lovefield)	4,732
Damascus (International)	2,223
Dar-es-Salaam	4,662
Darwin	8,613
Delhi	4,180
Denver	4,655
Detroit (Metropolitan)	3,754
Dhahran	3,143
Dhaka	4,976
Doha	3,253
Dubai	3,414

	Miles
Dublin	279
Durban	5,937
Düsseldorf	310
Entebbe	4,033
Frankfurt (Main)	406
Freetown	3,046
Geneva	468
Gibraltar	1,084
Gothenburg (Landvetter)	664
Hamburg	463
Harare	5,156
Havana	4,647
Helsinki (Vantaa)	1,148
Hobart	10,826
Ho Chi Minh City	6,345
Hong Kong	5,990
Honolulu	7,220
Houston (Intercontinental)	4,821
Houston (William P. Hobby)	4,837
Islamabad	3,767
Istanbul	1,560
Jakarta (Halim Perdanakusuma)	7,295
Jeddah	2,947
Johannesburg	5,634
Kabul	3,558
Karachi	3,935
Kathmandu	4,570
Khartoum	3,071
Kiev (Borispol)	1,357
Kiev (Julyany)	1,337
Kingston, Jamaica	4,668
Kuala Lumpur (Subang)	6,557
Kuwait	2,903
Lagos	3,107
Larnaca	2,036
Lima	6,303
Lisbon	972
Lomé	3,129
Los Angeles (International)	5,439
Madras	5,113
Madrid	773
Malta	1,305
Manila	6,685
Marseille	614
Mauritius	6,075
Melbourne (Essendon)	10,504
Melbourne (Tullamarine)	10,499
Mexico City	5,529
Miami	4,414
Milan (Linate)	609
Minsk	1,176
Montego Bay	4,687
Montevideo	6,841
Montreal (Mirabel)	3,241
Moscow (Sheremetievo)	1,557
Munich (Franz Josef Strauss)	584
Muscat	3,621
Nairobi (Jomo Kenyatta)	4,248
Naples	1,011
Nassau	4,333
New York (J. F. Kennedy)	3,440
Nice	645

	Miles
Oporto	806
Oslo (Fornebu)	722
Ottawa	3,321
Palma, Majorca (Son San Juan)	836
Paris (Charles de Gaulle)	215
Paris (Le Bourget)	215
Paris (Orly)	227
Perth, Australia	9,008
Port of Spain	4,404
Prague	649
Pretoria	5,602
Reykjavík (Domestic)	1,167
Reykjavík (Keflavík)	1,177
Rhodes	1,743
Rio de Janeiro	5,745
Riyadh (King Khaled) International	3,067
Rome (Fiumicino)	895
St John's, Newfoundland	2,308
St Petersburg	1,314
Salzburg	651
San Francisco	5,351
São Paulo	5,892
Sarajevo	1,017
Seoul (Kimpo)	5,507
Shanghai	5,725
Shannon	369
Singapore (Changi)	6,756
Sofia	1,266
Stockholm (Arlanda)	908
Suva	10,119
Sydney (Kingsford Smith)	10,568
Tangier	1,120
Tehran	2,741
Tel Aviv	2,227
Tōkyō (Narita)	5,956
Toronto	3,544
Tripoli (International)	1,468
Tunis	1,137
Turin (Caselle)	570
Ulaanbaatar	4,340
Valencia	826
Vancouver	4,707
Venice (Tessera)	715
Vienna (Schwechat)	790
Vladivostok	5,298
Warsaw	912
Washington (Dulles)	3,665
Wellington	11,692
Yangon/Rangoon	5,582
Yokohama (Aomori)	5,647
Zagreb	848
Zürich	490

The United Kingdom

The United Kingdom comprises Great Britain (England, Wales and Scotland) and Northern Ireland. The Isle of Man and the Channel Islands are Crown dependencies with their own legislative systems, and not a part of the United Kingdom.

AREA AS AT 31 MARCH 1981

	Land miles²	km²	*Inland water miles²	km²	Total miles²	km²
United Kingdom	93,006	240,883	1,242	3,218	94,248	244,101
England	50,058	129,652	293	758	50,351	130,410
Wales	7,965	20,628	50	130	8,015	20,758
Scotland	29,767	77,097	653	1,692	30,420	78,789
†Northern Ireland	5,225	13,532	249	628	5,467	14,160
Isle of Man	221	572	—	—	221	572
Channel Islands	75	194	—	—	75	194

*Excluding tidal water
†Excluding certain tidal waters that are parts of statutory areas in Northern Ireland

POPULATION

The first official census of population in England, Wales and Scotland was taken in 1801 and a census has been taken every ten years since, except in 1941 when there was no census because of war. The last official census in the United Kingdom was taken in April 2001.

The first official census of population in Ireland was taken in 1841. However, all figures given below refer only to the area which is now Northern Ireland. Figures for Northern Ireland in 1921 and 1931 are estimates based on the censuses taken in 1926 and 1937 respectively.

Estimates of the population of England before 1801, calculated from the number of baptisms, burials and marriages, are:

1570 4,160,221   1670 5,773,646
1600 4,811,718   1700 6,045,008
1630 5,600,517   1750 6,517,035

Thousands	United Kingdom Total	Male	Female	England and Wales Total	Male	Female	Scotland Total	Male	Female	Northern Ireland Total	Male	Female
CENSUS RESULTS 1801–1991												
1801	—	—	—	8,893	4,255	4,638	1,608	739	869	—	—	—
1811	13,368	6,368	7,000	10,165	4,874	5,291	1,806	826	980	—	—	—
1821	15,472	7,498	7,974	12,000	5,850	6,150	2,092	983	1,109	—	—	—
1831	17,835	8,647	9,188	13,897	6,771	7,126	2,364	1,114	1,250	—	—	—
1841	20,183	9,819	10,364	15,914	7,778	8,137	2,620	1,242	1,378	1,649	800	849
1851	22,259	10,855	11,404	17,928	8,781	9,146	2,889	1,376	1,513	1,443	698	745
1861	24,525	11,894	12,631	20,066	9,776	10,290	3,062	1,450	1,612	1,396	668	728
1871	27,431	13,309	14,122	22,712	11,059	11,653	3,360	1,603	1,757	1,359	647	712
1881	31,015	15,060	15,955	25,974	12,640	13,335	3,736	1,799	1,936	1,305	621	684
1891	34,264	16,593	17,671	29,003	14,060	14,942	4,026	1,943	2,083	1,236	590	646
1901	38,237	18,492	19,745	32,528	15,729	16,799	4,472	2,174	2,298	1,237	590	647
1911	42,082	20,357	21,725	36,070	17,446	18,625	4,761	2,309	2,452	1,251	603	648
1921	44,027	21,033	22,994	37,887	18,075	19,811	4,882	2,348	2,535	1,258	610	648
1931	46,038	22,060	23,978	39,952	19,133	20,819	4,843	2,326	2,517	1,243	601	642
1951	50,225	24,118	26,107	43,758	21,016	22,742	5,096	2,434	2,662	1,371	668	703
1961	52,709	25,481	27,228	46,105	22,304	23,801	5,179	2,483	2,697	1,425	694	731
1971	55,515	26,952	28,562	48,750	23,683	25,067	5,229	2,515	2,714	1,536	755	781
1981	55,848	27,104	28,742	49,155	23,873	25,281	5,131	2,466	2,664	*1,533	750	783
1991	56,467	27,344	29,123	49,890	24,182	25,707	4,999	2,392	2,607	1,578	769	809
†RESIDENT POPULATION: PROJECTIONS (MID-YEAR)												
2001	59,954	29,581	30,372	53,137	26,258	26,879	5,109	2,485	2,624	1,708	839	869
2011	61,773	30,696	30,077	54,915	27,328	27,587	5,087	2,492	2,595	1,771	876	895
2021	63,642	31,717	31,925	56,763	28,325	28,437	5,058	2,487	2,570	1,821	904	917

*Figures include 44,500 non-enumerated persons
† Projections are 1996 based
Source: The Stationery Office – *Annual Abstract 2001*; ONS – Census reports (Crown copyright)

ISLANDS: Census Results 1901–91

	Isle of Man Total	Male	Female	Jersey Total	Male	Female	*Guernsey Total	Male	Female
1901	54,752	25,496	29,256	52,576	23,940	28,636	40,446	19,652	20,794
1911	52,016	23,937	28,079	51,898	24,014	27,884	41,858	20,661	21,197
1921	60,284	27,329	32,955	49,701	22,438	27,263	38,315	18,246	20,069
1931	49,308	22,443	26,865	50,462	23,424	27,038	40,643	19,659	20,984
1951	55,123	25,749	29,464	57,296	27,282	30,014	43,652	21,221	22,431
1961	48,151	22,060	26,091	57,200	27,200	30,000	45,068	21,671	23,397
1971	56,289	26,461	29,828	72,532	35,423	37,109	51,458	24,792	26,666
1981	64,679	30,901	33,778	77,000	37,000	40,000	53,313	25,701	27,612
1991	69,788	33,693	36,095	84,082	40,862	43,220	58,867	28,297	30,570

* Population of Guernsey, Herm, Jethou and Lithou. Figures for 1901–71 record all persons present on census night; census figures for 1981 and 1991 record all persons resident in the islands on census night
Source: 1991 Census

RESIDENT POPULATION

MID-YEAR ESTIMATE

	1989	1999
United Kingdom	57,365,000	59,501,000
England	47,809,000	49,753,000
Wales	2,869,000	2,937,000
Scotland	5,097,000	5,119,000
Northern Ireland	1,590,000	1,692,000

Source: The Stationery Office – *Annual Abstract of Statistics 2001* (Crown copyright)

BY AGE AND SEX 1999

Males	Under 18	65 and over
United Kingdom	6,963,000	3,845,000
England	5,801,000	3,231,000
Wales	344,000	210,000
Scotland	581,000	315,000
Northern Ireland	237,000	89,000

Females	Under 18	60 and over
United Kingdom	6,614,000	6,908,000
England	5,506,000	5,760,000
Wales†	291,000	376,000
Scotland	555,000	606,000
Northern Ireland	226,000	169,000

† 1998 figures
Source: The Stationery Office – *Annual Abstract of Statistics 2001* (Crown copyright)

BY ETHNIC GROUP (1991 CENSUS (GREAT BRITAIN))

Ethnic group	Estimated population	As % of ethnic minority population
Caribbean	500,000	16.6
African	212,000	7
Other black	178,000	5.9
Indian	840,000	27.9
Pakistani	477,000	15.8
Bangladeshi	163,000	5.4
Chinese	157,000	5.2
Other Asian	198,000	6.6
Other	290,000	9.6
Total ethnic minority groups	3,015,000	100
White	51,874,000	—
All ethnic groups	54,889,000	—

Source: The Stationery Office – *Population Trends 72* (Crown copyright)

AVERAGE DENSITY *Persons per hectare*

	1981	1991
England	3.55	3.61
Wales	1.34	1.36
Scotland	0.66	0.65
Northern Ireland	1.12	1.11

Sources: ONS – Census reports (Crown copyright)

IMMIGRATION 1999
Acceptances for settlement in the UK by nationality

Region	Number of persons
Europe: total	15,990
European Economic Area	10
Remainder of Europe	15,980
Americas: total	8,520
USA	3,760
Canada	1,010
Africa: total	27,020
Asia: total	40,090
Indian sub-continent	21,440
Middle East	5,590
Oceania: total	4,120
British Overseas Citizens	560
Stateless	820
Total	97,120

Source: The Stationery Office – *Annual Abstract of Statistics 2001* (Crown copyright)

LIVE BIRTHS AND BIRTH RATES 1998

	Live births	Birth rate*
United Kingdom	700,000	11.8
England and Wales	622,000	11.8
Scotland	55,000	10.8
Northern Ireland	23,000	13.6

*Live births per 1,000 population
Source: The Stationery Office – *Annual Abstract of Statistics 2001* (Crown copyright)

LEGAL ABORTIONS 1999

Age group	England and Wales	Scotland†
Under 16	3,603	251
16-19	32,807	2,630
20-34	112,635	7,704
35-44	24,096	1,536
45 and over	502	23
Total	173,643	12,144

† provisional
Source: The Stationery Office – Annual Abstract of Statistics 2001 (Crown copyright)

BIRTHS OUTSIDE MARRIAGE (UK)

Age group	1989	1999
Under 20	49,000	49,000
20-24	79,000	77,000
25-29	46,000	68,000
Over 30	32,000	77,000
Total	207,000	272,000

Source: The Stationery Office – Annual Abstract of Statistics 2001 (Crown copyright)

MARRIAGE AND DIVORCE 1999

	Marriages	Divorces
United Kingdom	301,083	158,746
England and Wales	263,515	144,556
Scotland	29,940	11,864
Northern Ireland	7,628	2,326

Source: The Stationery Office – Annual Abstract of Statistics 2001 (Crown copyright)

DEATHS AND DEATH RATES 1999

Males	Deaths	Death rate*
United Kingdom	300,368	10.3
England and Wales	264,299	10.2
Scotland	28,605	11.3
Northern Ireland	7,464	8.9
Females		
United Kingdom	331,694	11.0
England and Wales	291,819	10.9
Scotland	31,676	11.8
Northern Ireland	8,199	8.9

* Deaths per 1,000 population
Sources: The Stationery Office – Annual Abstract of Statistics 2001 (Crown copyright); ONS; General Register Office for Scotland; General Register Office (Northern Ireland)

INFANT MORTALITY 1999
deaths of infants under 1 year of age per 1,000 live births

	Number
United Kingdom	5.8
England and Wales	5.8
Scotland	5.0
Northern Ireland	6.4

Source: The Stationery Office – Annual Abstract of Statistics 2001 (Crown copyright)

LIFE EXPECTANCY LIFE TABLES 1997–99 (INTERIM FIGURES)

Age	England and Wales Male	Female	Scotland Male	Female	Northern Ireland Male	Female
0	75.1	80.0	72.6	78.1	74.3	79.5
5	70.7	75.5	68.1	73.5	69.8	75.0
10	65.7	70.5	63.2	68.5	64.9	70.1
15	60.8	65.5	58.3	63.6	59.9	65.1
20	55.9	60.6	53.5	58.7	55.1	60.2
25	51.2	55.7	48.8	53.8	50.4	55.3
30	46.4	50.8	44.1	48.9	45.6	50.4
35	41.4	45.9	39.4	44.0	40.9	45.5
40	36.8	41.1	34.7	39.2	36.1	40.6
45	32.2	36.3	30.1	34.5	31.4	35.9
50	27.6	31.7	25.7	29.9	26.9	31.3
55	23.2	27.2	21.5	25.5	22.6	26.7
60	19.1	22.8	17.7	21.3	18.5	22.4
65	15.3	18.7	14.2	17.4	14.8	18.3
70	12.0	14.9	11.1	13.8	11.6	14.5
75	9.2	11.5	8.5	10.6	8.9	11.1
80	6.9	8.6	6.4	7.9	6.6	8.3
85	5.1	6.3	4.7	5.6	4.9	6.0
90	3.9	4.6	3.5	3.8	4.1	4.3

Source: The Stationery Office – Annual Abstract of Statistics 2001 (Crown copyright)

DEATHS ANALYSED BY CAUSE 1999

	England and Wales	Scotland	N. Ireland
TOTAL DEATHS	556,118	60,281	15,663
Deaths from natural causes	537,166	57,649	14,942
Infectious and parasitic diseases	3,613	498	47
Neoplasms	136,181	14,966	3,654
Malignant neoplasm of stomach	6,139	650	187
Malignant neoplasm of trachea, bronchus and lung	29,493	3,961	781
Malignant neoplasm of breast	11,670	1,136	289
Malignant neoplasm of uterus	1,231	138	26
Malignant neoplasm of cervix	1,107	122	36
Benign and unspecified neoplasms	1,656	124	67
Leukaemia	3,680	313	104
Endocrine, nutritional and metabolic diseases and immunity disorders	7,560	870	118
Diabetes mellitus	5,963	670	93
Nutritional deficiencies	59	17	3
Other metabolic and immunity disorders	1,150	147	20
Diseases of blood and blood-forming organs	1,855	204	24
Anaemias	584	80	9
Mental disorders	11,173	1,901	190
Diseases of the nervous system and sense organs	10,192	971	284
Meningitis	182	19	3
Diseases of the circulatory system	219,087	24,787	6,423
Rheumatic heart disease	1,638	173	35
Hypertensive disease	3,324	353	68
Ischaemic heart disease	115,119	13,337	3,568
Diseases of pulmonary circulation and other forms of heart disease	26,462	2,638	768
Cerebrovascular disease	56,051	6,785	1,680
Diseases of the respiratory system	97,755	8,870	3,161
Influenza	585	62	5
Pneumonia	59,273	4,526	2,130
Bronchitis, emphysema	3,452	322	93
Asthma	1,364	119	38
Diseases of the digestive system	21,698	2,787	507
Ulcer of stomach and duodenum	4,011	337	80
Appendicitis	133	9	3
Hernia of the abdominal cavity and other intestinal obstruction	2,126	213	49
Chronic liver disease and cirrhosis	4,718	896	92
Diseases of the genitourinary system	7,299	936	242
Nephritis, nephrotic syndrome and nephrosis	2,952	540	155
Hyperplasia of prostate	200	16	4
Complications of pregnancy, childbirth and the puerperium	30	7	—
Abortion	5	—	—
Diseases of the skin and subcutaneous tissue	1,152	90	27
Diseases of the musculo-skeletal system	3,554	295	54
Congenital anomalies	1,194	157	93
Certain conditions originating in the perinatal period	116	137	69
Birth trauma, hypoxia, birth asphyxia and other respiratory conditions	72	54	21
Signs, symptoms and ill-defined conditions	14,707	355	161
Sudden infant death syndrome	222	41	3
Deaths from injury and poisoning	16,517	2,450	609
All accidents	10,625	1,428	430
Motor vehicle accidents	3,003	320	134
Suicide and self-inflicted injury	3,690	637	121
All other external causes	2,202	385	58

Source: The Stationery Office – Annual Abstract of Statistics 2001 (Crown copyright)

The National Flag

The national flag of the United Kingdom is the Union Flag, generally known as the Union Jack.

The Union Flag is a combination of the cross of St George, patron saint of England, the cross of St Andrew, patron saint of Scotland, and a cross similar to that of St Patrick, patron saint of Ireland.

Cross of St George: cross Gules in a field Argent (red cross on a white ground)

Cross of St Andrew: saltire Argent in a field Azure (white diagonal cross on a blue ground)

Cross of St Patrick: saltire Gules in a field Argent (red diagonal cross on a white ground)

The Union Flag was first introduced in 1606 after the union of the kingdoms of England and Scotland under one sovereign. The cross of St Patrick was added in 1801 after the union of Great Britain and Ireland.

FLYING THE UNION FLAG

The correct orientation of the Union Flag when flying is with the broader diagonal band of white uppermost in the hoist (i.e. near the pole) and the narrower diagonal band of white uppermost in the fly (i.e. furthest from the pole).

It is the practice to fly the Union Flag daily on some customs houses. In all other cases, flags are flown on government buildings by command of The Queen. It is now customary for the Union Flag to be flown at Buckingham Palace when The Queen is not present.

Days for hoisting the Union Flag are notified to the Department for Culture, Media and Sport by The Queen's command and communicated by the department to the other government departments. On the days appointed, the Union Flag is flown on government buildings in the United Kingdom from 8 a.m. to sunset.

DAYS FOR FLYING FLAGS

The Queen's Accession	6 February
Birthday of The Duke of York	19 February
*St David's Day (in Wales only)	1 March
Birthday of The Earl of Wessex	10 March
Commonwealth Day** (2002)	11 March
Birthday of The Queen	21 April
*St George's Day (in England only)	23 April
†Europe Day	9 May
Coronation Day	2 June
Birthday of The Duke of Edinburgh	10 June
The Queen's Official Birthday (2002)	15 June
Birthday of Queen Elizabeth the Queen Mother	4 August
Birthday of The Princess Royal	15 August
Birthday of The Princess Margaret	21 August
Remembrance Sunday (2002)	10 November
Birthday of The Prince of Wales	14 November
The Queen's Wedding Day	20 November
*St Andrew's Day (in Scotland only)	30 November

‡The opening of Parliament by The Queen
‡The prorogation of Parliament by The Queen

*Where a building has two or more flagstaffs, the appropriate national flag may be flown in addition to the Union Flag, but not in a superior position

**Commonwealth Day is always the second Monday in March

†The Union Flag should fly alongside the European flag. On government buildings that have only one flagpole, the Union Flag should take precedence

‡Flags are flown whether or not The Queen performs the ceremony in person. Flags are flown only in the Greater London area

FLAGS AT HALF-MAST

Flags are flown at half-mast (i.e. two-thirds up between the top and bottom of the flagstaff) on the following occasions:

(a) From the announcement of the death up to the funeral of the Sovereign, except on Proclamation Day, when flags are hoisted right up from 11 a.m. to sunset

(b) The funerals of members of the royal family, subject to special commands from The Queen in each case

(c) The funerals of foreign rulers, subject to special commands from The Queen in each case

(d) The funerals of prime ministers and ex-prime ministers of the UK, subject to special commands from The Queen in each case

(e) Other occasions by special command of The Queen

On occasions when days for flying flags coincide with days for flying flags at half-mast, the following rules are observed. Flags are flown:

(a) although a member of the royal family, or a near relative of the royal family, may be lying dead, unless special commands are received from The Queen to the contrary

(b) although it may be the day of the funeral of a foreign ruler

If the body of a very distinguished subject is lying at a government office, the flag may fly at half-mast on that office until the body has left (provided it is a day on which the flag would fly) and then the flag is to be hoisted right up. On all other government buildings the flag will fly as usual.

THE ROYAL STANDARD

The Royal Standard is hoisted only when The Queen is actually present in the building, and never when Her Majesty is passing in procession.

The Royal Family

THE SOVEREIGN

ELIZABETH II, by the Grace of God, of the United Kingdom of Great Britain and Northern Ireland and of her other Realms and Territories Queen, Head of the Commonwealth, Defender of the Faith

Her Majesty Elizabeth Alexandra Mary of Windsor, elder daughter of King George VI and of HM Queen Elizabeth the Queen Mother
Born 21 April 1926, at 17 Bruton Street, London W1
Ascended the throne 6 February 1952
Crowned 2 June 1953, at Westminster Abbey
Married 20 November 1947, in Westminster Abbey, HRH The Prince Philip, Duke of Edinburgh
Official residences: Buckingham Palace, London SW1A 1AA; Windsor Castle, Berks; Palace of Holyroodhouse, Edinburgh
Private residences: Sandringham, Norfolk; Balmoral Castle, Aberdeenshire

HUSBAND OF THE QUEEN

HRH THE PRINCE PHILIP, DUKE OF EDINBURGH, KG, KT, OM, GBE, AC, QSO, PC, Ranger of Windsor Park
Born 10 June 1921, son of Prince and Princess Andrew of Greece and Denmark, naturalised a British subject 1947, created Duke of Edinburgh, Earl of Merioneth and Baron Greenwich 1947

CHILDREN OF THE QUEEN

HRH THE PRINCE OF WALES (Prince Charles Philip Arthur George), KG, KT, GCB and Great Master of the Order of the Bath, AK, QSO, PC, ADC(p)
Born 14 November 1948, created Prince of Wales and Earl of Chester 1958, succeeded as Duke of Cornwall, Duke of Rothesay, Earl of Carrick and Baron Renfrew, Lord of the Isles and Prince and Great Steward of Scotland 1952
Married 29 July 1981 Lady Diana Frances Spencer (Diana, Princess of Wales (1961–97), youngest daughter of the 8th Earl Spencer and the Hon. Mrs Shand Kydd), marriage dissolved 1996
Issue:
(1) HRH Prince William of Wales (Prince William Arthur Philip Louis), *born* 21 June 1982
(2) HRH Prince Henry of Wales (Prince Henry Charles Albert David), *born* 15 September 1984
Residences of the Prince of Wales: St James's Palace, London SW1A 1BS; Highgrove, Doughton, Tetbury, Glos GL8 8TN

HRH THE PRINCESS ROYAL (Princess Anne Elizabeth Alice Louise), KG, GCVO
Born 15 August 1950, declared The Princess Royal 1987
Married (1) 14 November 1973 Captain Mark Anthony Peter Phillips, CVO (*born* 22 September 1948); marriage dissolved 1992; (2) 12 December 1992 Captain Timothy James Hamilton Laurence, MVO, RN (*born* 1 March 1955)
Issue:
(1) Peter Mark Andrew Phillips, *born* 15 November 1977

(2) Zara Anne Elizabeth Phillips, *born* 15 May 1981
Residence: Gatcombe Park, Minchinhampton, Glos

HRH THE DUKE OF YORK (Prince Andrew Albert Christian Edward), CVO, ADC(P)
Born 19 February 1960, created Duke of York, Earl of Inverness and Baron Killyleagh 1986
Married 23 July 1986 Sarah Margaret Ferguson, now Sarah, Duchess of York (*born* 15 October 1959, younger daughter of Major Ronald Ferguson and Mrs Hector Barrantes), marriage dissolved 1996
Issue:
(1) HRH Princess Beatrice of York (Princess Beatrice Elizabeth Mary), *born* 8 August 1988
(2) HRH Princess Eugenie of York (Princess Eugenie Victoria Helena), *born* 23 March 1990
Residences: Buckingham Palace, London SW1A 1AA; Sunninghill Park, Ascot, Berks

HRH THE EARL OF WESSEX (Prince Edward Antony Richard Louis), CVO
Born 10 March 1964, created Earl of Wessex, Viscount Severn 1999
Married 19 June 1999 Sophie Helen Rhys-Jones, now HRH The Countess of Wessex (*born* 20 January 1965, daughter of Mr and Mrs Christopher Rhys-Jones)
Residence: Bagshot Park, Bagshot, Surrey GU19 5HS

SISTER OF THE QUEEN

HRH THE PRINCESS MARGARET, COUNTESS OF SNOWDON, CI, GCVO, Royal Victorian Chain, Dame Grand Cross of the Order of St John of Jerusalem
Born 21 August 1930, younger daughter of King George VI and HM Queen Elizabeth the Queen Mother
Married 6 May 1960 Antony Charles Robert Armstrong-Jones, GCVO (*born* 7 March 1930, created Earl of Snowdon 1961); marriage dissolved 1978
Issue:
(1) David Albert Charles, Viscount Linley, *born* 3 November 1961, *married* 8 October 1993 the Hon. Serena Stanhope, and has issue, Hon. Charles Patrick Inigo Armstrong-Jones, *born* 1 July 1999
(2) Lady Sarah Chatto (Sarah Frances Elizabeth), *born* 1 May 1964, *married* 14 July 1994 Daniel Chatto, and has issue, Samuel David Benedict Chatto, *born* 28 July 1996; Arthur Robert Nathaniel Chatto, *born* 5 February 1999
Residence: Kensington Palace, London W8 4PU

MOTHER OF THE QUEEN

HM QUEEN ELIZABETH THE QUEEN MOTHER (Elizabeth Angela Marguerite), Lady of the Garter, Lady of the Thistle, CI, GCVO, GBE, Dame Grand Cross of the Order of St John of Jerusalem, Royal Victorian Chain, Lord Warden and Admiral of the Cinque Ports and Constable of Dover Castle
Born 4 August 1900, youngest daughter of the 14th Earl of Strathmore and Kinghorne
Married 26 April 1923 (as Lady Elizabeth Bowes-Lyon) Prince Albert, Duke of York, afterwards King George VI
(*see* page 126)

Residences: Clarence House, St James's Palace, London SW1A 1BA; Royal Lodge, Windsor Great Park, Berks; Castle of Mey, Caithness

AUNT OF THE QUEEN

HRH PRINCESS ALICE, DUCHESS OF GLOUCESTER (Alice Christabel), GCB, CI, GCVO, GBE, Grand Cordon of Al Kamal
Born 25 December 1901, third daughter of the 7th Duke of Buccleuch and Queensberry
Married 6 November 1935 (as Lady Alice Montagu-Douglas-Scott) Prince Henry, Duke of Gloucester, third son of King George V (*see* page 126)
Residence: Kensington Palace, London W8 4PU

COUSINS OF THE QUEEN

HRH THE DUKE OF GLOUCESTER (Prince Richard Alexander Walter George), KG, GCVO, Grand Prior of the Order of St John of Jerusalem
Born 26 August 1944
Married 8 July 1972 Birgitte Eva van Deurs, now HRH The Duchess of Gloucester, GCVO (*born* 20 June 1946, daughter of Asger Henriksen and Vivian van Deurs)
Issue:
(1)   Earl of Ulster (Alexander Patrick Gregers Richard), *born* 24 October 1974
(2)   Lady Davina Windsor (Davina Elizabeth Alice Benedikte), *born* 19 November 1977
(3)   Lady Rose Windsor (Rose Victoria Birgitte Louise), *born* 1 March 1980
Residence: Kensington Palace, London W8 4PU

HRH THE DUKE OF KENT (Prince Edward George Nicholas Paul Patrick), KG, GCMG, GCVO, ADC(P)
Born 9 October 1935
Married 8 June 1961 Katharine Lucy Mary Worsley, now HRH The Duchess of Kent, GCVO (*born* 22 February 1933, daughter of Sir William Worsley, Bt.)
Issue:
(1)   Earl of St Andrews (George Philip Nicholas), *born* 26 June 1962, *married* 9 January 1988 Sylvana Tomaselli, and has issue, Edward Edmund Maximilian George, Baron Downpatrick, *born* 2 December 1988; Lady Marina Charlotte Alexandra Katharine Windsor, *born* 30 September 1992; Lady Amelia Sophia Theodora Mary Margaret Windsor, *born* 24 August 1995
(2)   Lady Helen Taylor (Helen Marina Lucy), *born* 28 April 1964, *married* 18 July 1992 Timothy Taylor, and has issue, Columbus George Donald Taylor, *born* 6 August 1994; Cassius Edward Taylor, *born* 26 December 1996
(3)   Lord Nicholas Windsor (Nicholas Charles Edward Jonathan), *born* 25 July 1970
Residence: Wren House, Palace Green, London W8 4PY

HRH PRINCESS ALEXANDRA, THE HON. LADY OGILVY (Princess Alexandra Helen Elizabeth Olga Christabel), GCVO
Born 25 December 1936
Married 24 April 1963 The Rt. Hon. Sir Angus Ogilvy, KCVO (*born* 14 September 1928, second son of 12th Earl of Airlie)
Issue:
(1)   James Robert Bruce Ogilvy, *born* 29 February 1964, *married* 30 July 1988 Julia Rawlinson, and has issue,

Flora Alexandra Ogilvy, *born* 15 December 1994; Alexander Charles Ogilvy, *born* 12 November 1996
(2)   Marina Victoria Alexandra, Mrs Mowatt, *born* 31 July 1966, *married* 2 February 1990 Paul Mowatt (marriage dissolved 1997), and has issue, Zenouska May Mowatt, *born* 26 May 1990; Christian Alexander Mowatt, *born* 4 June 1993
Residence: Thatched House Lodge, Richmond Park, Surrey

HRH PRINCE MICHAEL OF KENT (Prince Michael George Charles Franklin), KCVO
Born 4 July 1942
Married 30 June 1978 Baroness Marie-Christine Agnes Hedwig Ida von Reibnitz, now HRH Princess Michael of Kent (*born* 15 January 1945, daughter of Baron Gunther von Reibnitz)
Issue:
(1)   Lord Frederick Windsor (Frederick Michael George David Louis), *born* 6 April 1979
(2)   Lady Gabriella Windsor (Gabriella Marina Alexandra Ophelia), *born* 23 April 1981
Residences: Kensington Palace, London W8 4PU; Nether Lypiatt Manor, Stroud, Glos GL6 7LS

ORDER OF SUCCESSION

1   HRH The Prince of Wales
2   HRH Prince William of Wales
3   HRH Prince Henry of Wales
4   HRH The Duke of York
5   HRH Princess Beatrice of York
6   HRH Princess Eugenie of York
7   HRH The Earl of Wessex
8   HRH The Princess Royal
9   Peter Phillips
10   Zara Phillips
11   HRH The Princess Margaret, Countess of Snowdon
12   Viscount Linley
13   Hon. Charles Armstrong-Jones
14   Lady Sarah Chatto
15   Samuel Chatto
16   Arthur Chatto
17   HRH The Duke of Gloucester
18   Earl of Ulster
19   Lady Davina Windsor
20   Lady Rose Windsor
21   HRH The Duke of Kent
22   Baron Downpatrick
23   Lady Marina Charlotte Windsor
24   Lady Amelia Windsor
25   Lord Nicholas Windsor
26   Lady Helen Taylor
27   Columbus Taylor
28   Cassius Taylor
29   Lord Frederick Windsor
30   Lady Gabriella Windsor
31   HRH Princess Alexandra, the Hon. Lady Ogilvy
32   James Ogilvy
33   Alexander Ogilvy
34   Flora Ogilvy
35   Marina, Mrs Paul Mowatt
36   Christian Mowatt
37   Zenouska Mowatt
38   The Earl of Harewood

The Earl of St Andrews and HRH Prince Michael of Kent both lost the right of succession to the throne through marriage to a Roman Catholic. Their children remain in succession provided that they are in communion with the Church of England.

Private Secretaries to the Royal Family

Note to readers: the complete listings of members of the Royal Households as published in previous editions of *Whitaker's Almanack* are no longer made available for publication by Buckingham Palace. We apologise for any inconvenience this may cause.

THE QUEEN

Office: Buckingham Palace, London SW1A 1AA
Tel: 020-7930 4832
Web: www.royal.gov.uk
Private Secretary to The Queen, Sir Robin Janvrin, KCVO, CB

PRINCE PHILIP, THE DUKE OF EDINBURGH

Office: Buckingham Palace, London SW1A 1AA
Tel: 020-7930 4832
Private Secretary, Brig. M. G. Hunt-Davis, CVO, CBE

QUEEN ELIZABETH THE QUEEN MOTHER

Office: Clarence House, St James's Palace, London SW1A 1BA Tel: 020-7930 3141
Private Secretary, Capt. Sir Alastair Aird, GCVO

THE PRINCE OF WALES

Office: St James's Palace, London SW1A 1BS
Tel: 020-7930 4832
Private Secretary, S. M. J. Lamport, CVO

THE DUKE OF YORK

Office: Buckingham Palace, London SW1A 1AA
Tel: 020-7930 4832
Private Secretary, Miss C. Manly, OBE

THE EARL AND COUNTESS OF WESSEX

Office: The Old Stables, Bagshot Park, Surrey GU19 5PJ
Tel: 01276-700 843/022
Private Secretary, Lt.-Col. S. G. O'Dwyer, LVO

THE PRINCESS ROYAL

Office: Buckingham Palace, London SW1A 1AA
Tel: 020-7930 4832
Private Secretary, Col. T. Earl, OBE

THE PRINCESS MARGARET, COUNTESS OF SNOWDON

Office: Kensington Palace, London W8 4PU
Tel: 020-7930 3141
Private Secretary, The Viscount Ullswater, PC

PRINCESS ALICE, DUCHESS OF GLOUCESTER AND THE DUKE AND DUCHESS OF GLOUCESTER

Office: Kensington Palace, London W8 4PU
Tel: 020-7937 6374
Private Secretary, Maj. N. M. L. Barne, LVO

THE DUKE OF KENT

Office: St James's Palace, London, SW1A 1BQ
Tel: 020-7930 4872
Private Secretary, N. C. Adamson, OBE

THE DUCHESS OF KENT

Office: Palace Green, London, W8 4PU
Tel: 020-7937 2928
Personal Secretary, Miss V. Uttley, OBE

PRINCE AND PRINCESS MICHAEL OF KENT

Office: Kensington Palace, London W8 4PU
Tel: 020-7938 3519
Private Secretary, N. Chance

PRINCESS ALEXANDRA, THE HON. LADY OGILVY

Office: Buckingham Palace, London SW1A 1AA
Tel: 020-7930 1860
Private Secretary, Lt.-Col. R. Macfarlane

Offices of the Royal Household

PRIVATE SECRETARY'S OFFICE
The Private Secretary, assisted by the three Assistant Private Secretaries, is responsible for:

– Informing and advising The Queen on constitutional, governmental and political matters in the UK, her other realms and the wider Commonwealth, including communications with the Prime Minister and Government Departments.

- Organising The Queen's domestic and overseas official programme, including the Presentation of Credentials by incoming foreign ambassadors from overseas countries.
- The Queen's speeches and messages, The Queen's patronage, The Queen's photographs and official presents, portraits of The Queen and dedications and congratulatory messages.
- Communications in connection with the role of the Royal Family and other members of the Royal Family and their households.
- Dealing with correspondence to The Queen from members of the public.
- Organising and co-ordinating Royal travel through the Royal Travel Office.
- Co-ordinating and initiating research to support engagements by members of the Royal Family through the Co-ordination and Research Unit.

The Private Secretary is also responsible for communications and media affairs. The Communications Secretary reports to the Private Secretary and is responsible for:

- Developing communications strategies to enhance the public understanding of the role of the royal family, including an education strategy, encompassing website development and other multi-media initiatives.
- Co-ordinating communications across the Households, including the publication of internal newsletters and related literature.
- The Buckingham Palace Press Office.

Within the Press Office, the Press Secretary, assisted by the Deputy Press Secretary and two Assistant Press Secretaries, is responsible for:

- Briefing the British and international media on the role and duties of The Queen and issues relating to the Royal Family.
- Responding to media enquiries.
- Arranging media facilities in the United Kingdom and overseas to support royal functions and engagements.
- The management of the Royal website.

The Private Secretary is Keeper of the Royal Archives and is responsible for the care of the records of the Sovereign and the Royal Household from previous reigns, which are preserved in the Royal Archives at Windsor, where they are managed by the Assistant Keeper (a post combined with that of the Librarian of the Royal Library, q.v.) and made available for historical research. As keeper, it is the Private Secretary's responsibility to ensure the proper management of the records of the present reign with a view to their transfer to the archives as and when appropriate. The Private Secretary is an *ex officio* trustee of the Royal Collection Trust.

PRIVY PURSE AND TREASURER'S OFFICE

The Keeper of the Privy Purse and Treasurer to the Queen, assisted by the Deputy Treasurer (who is also Deputy Keeper of the Privy Purse) and the Assistant Keeper of the Privy Purse, is responsible for:

- The Queen's Civil List, which is the money paid from the Government's Consolidated Fund to meet official expenditure relating to the Queen's duties as Head of State and Head of the Commonwealth.
- Through the Director of Personnel, the identification, planning and management of personnel policy across the Household, the administration of all pension schemes provided for the Household and

Private Estates employees, and the allocation of employee and pensioner housing.
- Information technology systems for the household.
- Internal audit services.
- All insurance matters.
- The Privy Purse, which is mainly financed by the net income of the Duchy of Lancaster, and which meets both official expenditure incurred by The Queen as Sovereign and private expenditure.
- Liaison with other members of the Royal Family and their Households on Financial matters.
- The Queen's private estates at Sandringham and Balmoral, The Queen's Racing Establishment and the Royal Studs and liaison with the Ascot Authority.
- The Home Park at Windsor and liaison with the Crown Estate Commissioners concerning the Home Park and the Great Park at Windsor.
- The Royal Philatelic Collection, which is managed by the Keeper of the Royal Philatelic Collection.
- Administrative aspects of the Military Knights of Windsor and the Royal Almonry.
- Administration of the Royal Victorian Order, of which the Keeper of the Privy Purse is Secretary, Long and Faithful Service Medals, and the Queen's Cups, Medals and Prizes, and Policy on Commemorative Medals.

The Keeper of the Privy Purse is one of three Royal Trustees (in respect of his responsibilities for the Civil List) and is Receiver General of the Duchy of Lancaster and a member of the Duchy's Council.

The Keeper of the Privy Purse is also responsible for property services for the Occupied Royal Palaces in England, which comprise Buckingham Palace, St James' Palace and Clarence House, Marlborough House Mews, the residential, office and general areas of Kensington Palace, Windsor Castle and related areas and buildings, Frogmore House, and Hampton Court Mews and Paddocks. The costs of property services for the Occupied Royal Palaces are met from a Grant-in-aid from the Department for Culture, Media and Sport.

The Director of Property Services, assisted by the Director of Finance, Property Services, has day to day responsibility for the Royal Household's Property Section, which is responsible for:

- Fire, health and safety issues.
- Repairs and refurbishment of buildings and new buildings work.
- Utilities and telephones.
- Putting up stages, flags and tents and other work in connection with ceremonial occasions and garden parties and other official functions.

The Property Section is also responsible, in effect on a sub-contract basis from the Department for Culture, Media and Sport, for the maintenance of Marlborough House (Which is occupied by the Commonwealth Secretariat).

The Keeper of the Privy Purse, assisted by the Director of Finance, Property Services, also oversees Royal Communications and Information expenditure, which is met from the Property Services Grant-in-aid.

The Keeper of the Privy Purse is responsible for the financial aspects of royal travel, which are overseen on a day to day basis by the Director of Finance, Royal Travel, who is also the Director of Finance, Property Services. The costs of official royal travel by aeroplane and train are met from a Grant-in-aid provided by the Department of Transport.

The Keeper of the Privy Purse is an *ex officio* trustee of the Royal Collection Trust and is also chairman of its trading subsidiary Royal Collection Enterprises Limited (see Royal Collection Department). He is also an *ex officio* trustee of the Historic Royal Palaces Trust.

The Queen's Civil List and the Grants-in-aid for property services and royal travel are provided by the Government in return for the surrender by the Sovereign of the net surplus from the Crown Estate and other hereditary revenues.

MASTER OF THE HOUSEHOLD'S DEPARTMENT

The Master of the Household, assisted by the Deputy Master of the Household (who is also Equerry to the Queen, q.v.), is responsible for the staff and domestic arrangements at Buckingham Palace, Windsor Castle and the Palace of Holyroodhouse and at Balmoral Castle and Sandringham House when The Queen is in residence. These arrangements include:

- The provision of meals for The Queen and other members of the Royal Family, their guests and Royal Household employees.
- Service by liveried staff at meals, receptions and other events.
- Travel arrangements for employees and the movement of baggage between the Royal residences.
- Cleaning and laundry
- Furnishings and the internal decorative appearance of the Occupied Royal Palaces in collaboration with the Director of the Royal Collection.
- Liaison with the Royalty and Diplomatic Protection Department of the Metropolitan Police concerning security procedures at the Occupied Royal Palaces.

The Master of the Household is responsible for The Queen's official entertaining, both at home and overseas, including preparation of guest lists, invitations and seating plans, and overseeing aspects of The Queen's private entertaining.

LORD CHAMBERLAIN'S OFFICE

The Comptroller, Lord Chamberlain's Office, assisted by the Assistant Comptroller, is responsible for:

- The organisation of all ceremonial engagements, including state visits to The Queen in the United Kingdom, royal weddings and royal funerals, the state opening of Parliament, Guards of Honour at Buckingham Palace, Investitures, and the Garter and Thistle ceremonies.
- Garden Parties at Buckingham Palace and Palace at Holyroodhouse (except for catering and tents).
- The Crown Jewels, which are part of the Royal Collection, when they are in use on state occasions.
- Co-ordination of the arrangements for The Queen to be represented at funerals and memorial services and at the arrival and departure of visiting Heads of State.
- Advising on matters of precedence, style and titles, dress, flying of flags, gun salutes, mourning and other ceremonial questions.
- Supervising the applications from tradesmen for Royal Warrants of Appointment.
- Advising on the commercial use of royal emblems and contemporary royal photographs.
- The Ecclesiastical Household, the Medical Household, the Body Guards and certain ceremonial appointments such as Gentlemen Ushers and Pages of Honour.
- The personal Lords in Waiting, who represent The Queen on various occasions and escort the visiting Head of State during incoming state visits.
- The Queen's Bargemaster and Watermen and The Queen's Swans.

The Comptroller, Lord Chamberlain's Office is also responsible for the Royal Mews, assisted by the Crown Equerry, who has day-to-day responsibility for:

- The provision of carriage processions for the State Opening of Parliament, State Visits, Trooping of the Colour, Royal Ascot, the Garter Ceremony, the Thistle Service, the Presentation of credentials to The Queen by incoming foreign Ambassadors and High Commissioners, and other state and ceremonial occasions.
- The provision of chauffeur-driven cars.
- Co-ordinating the travelling and transport arrangements by road in respect of The Queen's official engagements.
- Supervision and administration of the Royal Mews at Buckingham Palace, Windsor Castle, Hampton Court and the Palace of Holyroodhouse.

The Comptroller, Lord Chamberlain's Office also has overall responsibility for the Marshal of the Diplomatic Corps, who is responsible for the relationship between the Royal Household and the Diplomatic Heads of Mission in London; and the Secretary of the central chancery of the orders of Knighthood, who administers the Orders of Chivalry and their records, makes arrangements for the recipients at Investitures and the distribution of insignia, and ensures the proper public notification of awards through the London Gazette. The Secretary of the Central Chancery is also the Assistant Comptroller.

ROYAL COLLECTION DEPARTMENT

The Royal Collection, which contains a large number of works of art of all kinds, is held by The Queen as Sovereign in trust for her successors and the nation and is not owned by her as an individual. The administration, conservation and presentation of the Royal Collection are funded by the Royal Collection Trust solely from income from visitors to Windsor Castle, Buckingham Palace and the Palace of Holyroodhouse in Edinburgh. The Royal Collection Trust is chaired by the Prince of Wales. The Lord Chamberlain, the Private Secretary and the Keeper of the Privy Purse are *ex officio* trustees and there are three external trustees appointed by The Queen.

The Director of the Royal Collection is responsible for:

- The administration and custodial control of the Royal Collection in all royal residences.
- The care, display, conservation and restoration of items in the Collection.
- Initiating and assisting research into the Collection and publishing catalogues and books on the Collection.
- Making the Collection accessible to the public by display in places open to the public (including the unoccupied palaces), The Queen's Gallery at Buckingham Palace and the Queen's Gallery at the Palace of Holyroodhouse, by travelling exhibitions organised by museums and galleries in the United Kingdom and abroad.
- Educating and informing the public about the Collection.

The Surveyor of the Queen's Pictures is responsible for pictures and miniatures, the Royal Librarian is responsible for all the books, manuscripts, coins and medals, insignia and works of art on paper including the watercolours, prints and drawings in the Print Room at Windsor Castle, and the Surveyor of the Queen's Works of art is responsible for furniture, ceramics and the other decorative arts in the Collection.

The Director of the Royal Collection has overall responsibility for the trading activities that fund the Royal Collection Department. These are administered by Royal Collection Enterprises Limited, the trading subsidiary of The Royal Collection Trust, which is run by the Managing Director, Royal Collection Enterprises. The company, whose chairman is the Keeper of the Privy Purse, is responsible for:

– Managing access by the public to Windsor Castle (including Frogmore House), Buckingham Palace (including the Royal Mews and The Queen's Gallery) and the Palace of Holyroodhouse.
– Running shops at each location.
– Managing the images and intellectual property rights of the Royal Collection.

The Director of the Royal Collection is also an *ex officio* trustee of the Historic Royal Palaces Trust.

Royal Salutes

ENGLAND
A salute of 62 guns is fired on the wharf at the Tower of London on the following occasions:
(a) the anniversaries of the birth, accession and coronation of the Sovereign
(b) the anniversary of the birth of HM Queen Elizabeth the Queen Mother
(c) the anniversary of the birth of HRH Prince Philip, Duke of Edinburgh
A salute of 41 guns only is fired on extraordinary and triumphal occasions, e.g. on the occasion of the Sovereign opening, proroguing or dissolving Parliament in person, or when passing through London in procession, except when otherwise ordered.

A salute of 41 guns is fired from the two saluting stations in London (the Tower of London and Hyde Park) on the occasion of the birth of a royal infant.
Constable of the Royal Palace and Fortress of London, Gen. Sir Roger Wheeler, GCB, CBE
Lieutenant of the Tower of London, Lt.-Gen. Sir Roderick Cordy-Simpson, KBE, CB
Resident Governor and Keeper of the Jewel House, Maj.-Gen. Geoffrey Field, CB, OBE

Master Gunner of St James's Park, Gen. Sir Alex Harley, KBE, CB
Master Gunner within the Tower, Col. James Ferguson, TD

SCOTLAND
Royal salutes are authorised at Edinburgh Castle and Stirling Castle, although in practice Edinburgh Castle is the only operating saluting station in Scotland.
A salute of 21 guns is fired on the following occasions:
(a) the anniversaries of the birth, accession and coronation of the Sovereign
(b) the anniversary of the birth of HM Queen Elizabeth the Queen Mother
(c) the anniversary of the birth of HRH Prince Philip, Duke of Edinburgh
A salute of 21 guns is fired in Edinburgh on the occasion of the opening of the General Assembly of the Church of Scotland.
A salute of 21 guns may also be fired in Edinburgh on the arrival of HM The Queen, HM Queen Elizabeth the Queen Mother, or a member of the royal family who is a Royal Highness on an official visit.

Royal Finances

FUNDING

THE CIVIL LIST
The Civil List dates back to the late 17th century. It was originally used by the sovereign to supplement hereditary revenues for paying the salaries of judges, ambassadors and other government officers as well as the expenses of the royal household. In 1760 on the accession of George III it was decided that the Civil List would be provided by Parliament to cover all relevant expenditure in return for the King surrendering the hereditary revenues of the Crown. At that time Parliament undertook to pay the salaries of judges, ambassadors, etc. In 1831 Parliament agreed also to meet the costs of the royal palaces in return for a reduction in the Civil List. Each sovereign has agreed to continue this arrangement.

The Civil List paid to The Queen is charged on the Consolidated Fund. Until 1972, the amount of money allocated annually under the Civil List was set for the duration of a reign. The system was then altered to a fixed annual payment for ten years but from 1975 high inflation made an annual review necessary. The system of payments reverted to the practice of a fixed annual payment for ten years from 1 January 1991.

The Civil List Acts provide for other members of the royal family to receive parliamentary annuities from government funds to meet the expenses of carrying out their official duties. Since 1975 The Queen has reimbursed the Treasury for the annuities paid to the Duke of Gloucester, the Duke of Kent and Princess Alexandra. Since 1993 The Queen has reimbursed all the annuities except those paid to herself, Queen Elizabeth the Queen Mother and the Duke of Edinburgh.

The Prince of Wales does not receive a parliamentary annuity. He derives his income from the revenues of the Duchy of Cornwall and these monies meet the official and private expenses of the Prince of Wales and his family.

The annual payments for the years 1991–2001:

The Queen	£7,900,000
Queen Elizabeth the Queen Mother	643,000
The Duke of Edinburgh	359,000
*The Duke of York	249,000
*†The Earl of Wessex	141,000
*The Princess Royal	228,000
*The Princess Margaret, Countess of Snowdon	219,000
*Princess Alice, Duchess of Gloucester	87,000
*The Duke of Gloucester	175,000
*The Duke of Kent	236,000
*Princess Alexandra	225,000
	10,462,000
*Refunded to the Treasury	1,560,000
Total	8,902,000

†The Earl of Wessex's annuity was increased from £96,000 upon his marriage in June 1999

GRANTS-IN-AID

The royal household receives grants-in-aid from two government departments to meet various official expenses. The Department for Culture, Media and Sport provides grant-in-aid to pay for the upkeep of English occupied royal palaces, which are used as offices, for official and ceremonial purposes and to which there is public access, and to meet the cost of media and information services. The Royal Travel grant-in-aid is provided by the Department of the Environment, Transport and the Regions to meet the cost of official royal travel by air and rail, using mainly aircraft from 32 (The Royal) Squadron, chartered commercial aircraft for major overseas state visits and the Royal Train.

Grants-in-aid for 2000–2001 were:

Property Services and Communications and Information	£15,000,000
Royal Travel	5,400,000

THE PRIVY PURSE

The funds received by the Privy Purse pay for official expenses incurred by The Queen as head of state and for some of The Queen's private expenditure. The revenues of the Duchy of Lancaster are the principal source of income for the Privy Purse. The revenues of the Duchy were retained by George III in 1760 when the hereditary revenues were surrendered in exchange for the Civil List.

PERSONAL INCOME

The Queen's personal income derives mostly from investments, and is used to meet private expenditure.

DEPARTMENTAL VOTES

Items of expenditure connected with the official duties of the royal family which fall directly on votes of government departments include:

Ministry of Defence – equerries

Foreign and Commonwealth Office – Marshal of the Diplomatic Corps; costs (other than travel costs) associated with overseas visits at the request of government departments

HM Treasury – Central Chancery of the Orders of Knighthood

The Post Office – postal services

TAXATION

The sovereign is not legally liable to pay income tax, capital gains tax or inheritance tax. After income tax was reintroduced in 1842, some income tax was paid voluntarily by the sovereign but over a long period these payments were phased out. In 1992 The Queen offered to pay tax on a voluntary basis from 6 April 1993, and the Prince of Wales offered to pay tax on a voluntary basis on his income from the Duchy of Cornwall. (He was already taxed in all other respects.)

The main provisions for The Queen and the Prince of Wales to pay tax, set out in a Memorandum of Understanding on Royal Taxation presented to Parliament on 11 February 1993, are that The Queen will pay income tax and capital gains tax in respect of her private income and assets, and on the proportion of the income and capital gains of the Privy Purse used for private purposes. Inheritance tax will be paid on The Queen's assets, except for those which pass to the next sovereign, whether automatically or by gift or bequest. The Prince of Wales will pay income tax on income from the Duchy of Cornwall used for private purposes.

The Prince of Wales has confirmed that he intends to pay tax on the same basis following his accession to the throne.

Other members of the royal family are subject to tax as for any taxpayer.

Military Ranks and Titles

THE QUEEN

Lord High Admiral of the United Kingdom

Colonel-in-Chief

The Life Guards; The Blues and Royals (Royal Horse Guards and 1st Dragoons); The Royal Scots Dragoon Guards (Carabiniers and Greys); The Queen's Royal Lancers; Royal Tank Regiment; Corps of Royal Engineers; Grenadier Guards; Coldstream Guards; Scots Guards; Irish Guards; Welsh Guards; The Royal Welsh Fusiliers; The Queen's Lancashire Regiment; The Argyll and Sutherland Highlanders (Princess Louise's); The Royal Green Jackets; Adjutant General's Corps; The Royal Mercian and Lancastrian Yeomanry;

The Governor General's Horse Guards (of Canada); The King's Own Calgary Regiment; Canadian Forces Military Engineers Branch; Royal 22e Regiment (of Canada); Governor-General's Foot Guards (of Canada); The Canadian Grenadier Guards; Le Regiment de la Chaudiere (of Canada); 2nd Bn Royal New Brunswick Regiment (North Shore); The 48th Highlanders of Canada; The Argyll and Sutherland Highlanders of Canada (Princess Louise's); The Calgary Highlanders; Royal Australian Engineers; Royal Australian Infantry Corps; Royal Australian Army Ordnance Corps; Royal Australian Army Nursing Corps; The Corps of Royal New Zealand Engineers; Royal New Zealand Infantry Regiment; Royal Malta Artillery; The Malawi Rifles

Affiliated Colonel-in-Chief
The Queen's Gurkha Engineers

Captain-General
Royal Regiment of Artillery; The Honourable Artillery Company; Combined Cadet Force Association; Royal Regiment of Canadian Artillery; Royal Regiment of Australian Artillery; Royal Regiment of New Zealand Artillery; Royal New Zealand Armoured Corps

Patron
Royal Army Chaplains' Department

Air Commodore-in-Chief
Royal Auxiliary Air Force; Royal Air Force Regiment; Air Reserve (of Canada); Royal Australian Air Force Reserve; Territorial Air Force (of New Zealand)

Commandant-in-Chief
Royal Air Force College, Cranwell

Hon. Air Commodore
RAF Marham

HRH THE PRINCE PHILIP, DUKE OF EDINBURGH

Admiral of the Fleet
Field Marshal
Marshal of the Royal Air Force

Admiral of the Fleet, Royal Australian Navy
Field Marshal, Australian Military Forces
Marshal of the Royal Australian Air Force

Admiral of the Fleet, Royal New Zealand Navy
Field Marshal, New Zealand Army
Marshal of the Royal New Zealand Air Force
Captain-General, Royal Marines

Admiral
Royal Canadian Sea Cadets

Colonel-in-Chief
The Royal Gloucestershire, Berkshire and Wiltshire Regiment; The Highlanders (Seaforth, Gordons and Camerons); Corps of Royal Electrical and Mechanical Engineers; Intelligence Corps; Army Cadet Force Association; The Royal Canadian Regiment; The Royal Hamilton Light Infantry (Wentworth Regiment) (of Canada); The Cameron Highlanders of Ottawa; The Queen's Own Cameron Highlanders of Canada; The Seaforth Highlanders of Canada; The Royal Canadian Army Cadets; The Royal Corps of Australian Electrical and Mechanical Engineers; The Australian Cadet Corps

Deputy Colonel-in-Chief
The Queen's Royal Hussars (Queen's Own and Royal Irish)

Colonel
Grenadier Guards

Hon. Colonel
City of Edinburgh Universities Officers' Training Corps; The Trinidad and Tobago Regiment

Air Commodore-in-Chief
Air Training Corps; Royal Canadian Air Cadets

Hon. Air Commodore
RAF Kinloss

HM QUEEN ELIZABETH THE QUEEN MOTHER

Colonel-in-Chief
1st The Queen's Dragoon Guards; The Queen's Royal Hussars (Queen's Own and Royal Irish); 9th/12th Royal Lancers (Prince of Wales's); The King's Regiment; The Royal Anglian Regiment; The Light Infantry; The Black Watch (Royal Highland Regiment); Royal Army Medical Corps; The Black Watch (Royal Highland Regiment) of Canada; The Toronto Scottish Regiment; Canadian Forces Medical Services; Royal Australian Army Medical Corps; Royal New Zealand Army Medical Corps

Hon. Colonel
The Royal Yeomanry; The London Scottish; Inns of Court and City Yeomanry

Commandant-in-Chief
Women in the Royal Navy; Women, Royal Air Force; Royal Air Force Central Flying School

HRH THE PRINCE OF WALES

Rear Admiral, Royal Navy

Major-General, Army

Air Vice-Marshal, Royal Air Force

Colonel-in-Chief
The Royal Dragoon Guards; The 22nd (Cheshire) Regiment; The Royal Regiment of Wales (24th/41st Foot); The Parachute Regiment; The Royal Gurkha Rifles; Army Air Corps; The Royal Canadian Dragoons; Lord Strathcona's Horse (Royal Canadians); Royal Regiment of Canada; Royal Winnipeg Rifles; Air Reserve Group of Air Command (of Canada); Royal Australian Armoured Corps; The Royal Pacific Islands Regiment; Queen's Own Yeomanry

Deputy Colonel-in-Chief
The Highlanders (Seaforth, Gordons and Camerons)

Colonel
Welsh Guards

Air Commodore-in-Chief
Royal New Zealand Air Force

Hon. Air Commodore
RAF Valley

HRH THE DUKE OF YORK

Commander, Royal Navy

Admiral
Sea Cadet Corps

Colonel-in-Chief
The Staffordshire Regiment (The Prince of Wales's); The Royal Irish Regiment (27th (Inniskilling), 83rd, 87th and The Ulster Defence Regiment); Royal New Zealand Army Logistic Regiment; The Queen's York Rangers (First Americans)

Hon. Air Commodore
RAF Lossiemouth

HRH THE PRINCESS ROYAL

Rear Admiral
Chief Commandant for Women in the Royal Navy

Colonel-in-Chief
The King's Royal Hussars; Royal Corps of Signals; The Royal Scots (The Royal Regiment); The Worcestershire and Sherwood Foresters Regiment (29th/45th Foot); The Royal Logistic Corps; 8th Canadian Hussars (Princess Louise's); Canadian Forces Communications and Electronics Branch; The Grey and Simcoe Foresters; The Royal Regina Rifle Regiment; Royal Australian Corps of Signals; Royal New Zealand Corps of Signals; Royal New Zealand Nursing Corps

Colonel
Blues and Royals

Affiliated Colonel-in-Chief
The Queen's Gurkha Signals; The Queen's Own Gurkha Transport Regiment

Hon. Colonel
University of London Officers' Training Corps

Hon. Air Commodore
RAF Lyneham; University of London Air Squadron

HRH THE PRINCESS MARGARET, COUNTESS OF SNOWDON

Colonel-in-Chief
The Light Dragoons; The Royal Highland Fusiliers (Princess Margaret's Own Glasgow and Ayrshire Regiment); Queen Alexandra's Royal Army Nursing Corps; The Royal Highland Fusiliers of Canada; The Princess Louise Fusiliers (of Canada); The Bermuda Regiment

Deputy Colonel-in-Chief
The Royal Anglian Regiment

Hon. Air Commodore
RAF Coningsby

HRH PRINCESS ALICE, DUCHESS OF GLOUCESTER

Air Chief Marshal
Colonel-in-Chief
The King's Own Scottish Borderers; Royal Australian Corps of Transport

Deputy Colonel-in-Chief
The King's Royal Hussars; The Royal Anglian Regiment

Air Chief Commandant
Women, Royal Air Force

HRH THE DUKE OF GLOUCESTER

Hon. Air Marshal

Deputy Colonel-in-Chief
The Royal Gloucestershire, Berkshire and Wiltshire Regiment; The Royal Logistic Corps

Hon. Colonel
Royal Monmouthshire Royal Engineers (Militia)

Hon. Air Commodore
RAF Odiham

HRH THE DUCHESS OF GLOUCESTER

Colonel-in-Chief
Royal Australian Army Educational Corps; Royal New Zealand Army Educational Corps; Royal Army Dental Corps

Deputy Colonel-in-Chief
Adjutant-General's Corps

HRH THE DUKE OF KENT

Field Marshal
Hon. Air Chief Marshal
Colonel-in-Chief
The Royal Regiment of Fusiliers; The Devonshire and Dorset Regiment; The Lorne Scots (Peel, Dufferin and Hamilton Regiment)

Deputy Colonel-in-Chief
The Royal Scots Dragoon Guards (Carabiniers and Greys)

Colonel
Scots Guards

Hon. Air Commodore
RAF Leuchars

HRH THE DUCHESS OF KENT

Hon. Major-General
Colonel-in-Chief
The Prince of Wales's Own Regiment of Yorkshire

Deputy Colonel-in-Chief
The Royal Dragoon Guards; Adjutant-General's Corps; The Royal Logistic Corps

HRH PRINCE MICHAEL OF KENT

Major (retd), The Royal Hussars (Prince of Wales's Own)

Hon. Commodore
Royal Naval Reserve

HRH PRINCESS ALEXANDRA, THE HON. LADY OGILVY

Patron
Queen Alexandra's Royal Naval Nursing Service

Colonel-in-Chief
The King's Own Royal Border Regiment; The Queen's Own Rifles of Canada; The Canadian Scottish Regiment (Princess Mary's)

Deputy Colonel-in-Chief
The Queen's Royal Lancers; The Light Infantry

Deputy Hon. Colonel
The Royal Yeomanry

Patron and Air Chief Commandant
Princess Mary's Royal Air Force Nursing Service

The House of Windsor

King George V assumed by royal proclamation (17 July 1917) for his House and family, as well as for all descendants in the male line of Queen Victoria who are subjects of these realms, the name of Windsor.

KING GEORGE V (George Frederick Ernest Albert), second son of King Edward VII, *born* 3 June 1865; *married* 6 July 1893 HSH Princess Victoria Mary Augusta Louise Olga Pauline Claudine Agnes of Teck (Queen Mary, *born* 26 May 1867; *died* 24 March 1953); *succeeded* to the throne 6 May 1910; *died* 20 January 1936. *Issue:*

1. HRH PRINCE EDWARD Albert Christian George Andrew Patrick David, *born* 23 June 1894; *succeeded* to the throne as King Edward VIII, 20 January 1936; *abdicated* 11 December 1936; *created Duke of Windsor* 1937; *married* 3 June 1937, Mrs Wallis Simpson (Her Grace The Duchess of Windsor, *born* 19 June 1896; *died* 24 April 1986), *died* 28 May 1972

2. HRH PRINCE ALBERT Frederick Arthur George, *born* 14 December 1895, *created* Duke of York 1920; *married* 26 April 1923, Lady Elizabeth Bowes-Lyon, youngest daughter of the 14th Earl of Strathmore and Kinghorne (HM Queen Elizabeth the Queen Mother, *see* page 117), *succeeded* to the throne as King George VI, 11 December 1936; *died* 6 February 1952, having had issue (*see* page 117)

3. HRH PRINCESS (Victoria Alexandra Alice) MARY, *born* 25 April 1897, *created* Princess Royal 1932; *married* 28 February 1922, Viscount Lascelles, later the 6th Earl of Harewood (1882–1947), *died* 28 March 1965. *Issue:*

(1) George Henry Hubert Lascelles, 7th Earl of Harewood, KBE, *born* 7 February 1923; *married* (1) 1949, Maria (Marion) Stein (marriage dissolved 1967); *issue,* (*a*) David Henry George, Viscount Lascelles, *born* 1950; (*b*) James Edward, *born* 1953; (*c*)

(Robert) Jeremy Hugh, *born* 1955; (2) 1967, Mrs Patricia Tuckwell; *issue,* (*d*) Mark Hubert, *born* 1964
(2) Gerald David Lascelles (1924–98), *married* (1) 1952, Miss Angela Dowding (marriage dissolved 1978); *issue,* (*a*) Henry Ulick, *born* 1953; (2) 1978, Mrs Elizabeth Colvin; *issue,* (*b*) Martin David, *born* 1962

4. HRH PRINCE HENRY William Frederick Albert, *born* 31 March 1900, *created* Duke of Gloucester, Earl of Ulster and Baron Culloden 1928, *married* 6 November 1935, Lady Alice Christabel Montagu-Douglas-Scott, daughter of the 7th Duke of Buccleuch (HRH Princess Alice, Duchess of Gloucester, *see* page 118); *died* 10 June 1974. *Issue:*
(1) HRH Prince William Henry Andrew Frederick, *born* 18 December 1941; *accidentally killed* 28 August 1972
(2) HRH Prince Richard Alexander Walter George (HRH The Duke of Gloucester), *see* page 118

5. HRH PRINCE GEORGE Edward Alexander Edmund, *born* 20 December 1902, *created* Duke of Kent, Earl of St Andrews and Baron Downpatrick 1934, *married* 29 November 1934, HRH Princess Marina of Greece and Denmark (*born* 30 November OS, 1906; *died* 27 August 1968); *killed on active service,* 25 August 1942. *Issue:*
(1) HRH Prince Edward George Nicholas Paul Patrick (HRH The Duke of Kent), *see* page 118
(2) HRH Princess Alexandra Helen Elizabeth Olga Christabel (HRH Princess Alexandra, the Hon. Lady Ogilvy), *see* page 118
(3) HRH Prince Michael George Charles Franklin (HRH Prince Michael of Kent), *see* page 118

6. HRH PRINCE JOHN Charles Francis, *born* 12 July 1905; *died* 18 January 1919

Descendants of Queen Victoria

QUEEN VICTORIA (Alexandrina Victoria), *born* 24 May 1819; *succeeded* to the throne 20 June 1837; *married* 10 February 1840 (Francis) Albert Augustus Charles Emmanuel, Duke of Saxony, Prince of Saxe-Coburg and Gotha (HRH Albert, Prince Consort, *born* 26 August 1819, *died* 14 December 1861); *died* 22 January 1901. *Issue:*
1. HRH PRINCESS VICTORIA Adelaide Mary Louisa (Princess Royal) (1840–1901), *m.* 1858, Friedrich III (1831–88), German Emperor March–June 1888. *Issue:*
(1) HIM Wilhelm II (1859–1941), German Emperor 1888–1918, *m.* (1) 1881 Princess Augusta Victoria of Schleswig-Holstein-Sonderburg-Augustenburg (1858–1921); (2) 1922 Princess Hermine of Reuss (1887–1947). *Issue:*
(*a*) Prince Wilhelm (1882–1951), Crown Prince 1888–1918, *m.* 1905 Duchess Cecilie of Mecklenburg-Schwerin; *issue:* Prince Wilhelm (1906–40); Prince Louis Ferdinand (1907–94), *m.* 1938 Grand Duchess Kira (*see* page 128); Prince Hubertus (1909–50); Prince Friedrich Georg (1911–66); Princess Alexandrine Irene (1915–80); Princess Cecilie (1917–75)
(*b*) Prince Eitel-Friedrich (1883–1942), *m.* 1906 Duchess Sophie of Oldenburg (marriage dissolved 1926)
(*c*) Prince Adalbert (1884–1948), *m.* 1914 Duchess Adelheid of Saxe-Meiningen; *issue:* Princess Victoria Marina (1917–81); Prince Wilhelm Victor (1919–89)
(*d*) Prince August Wilhelm (1887–1949), *m.* 1908 Princess Alexandra of Schleswig-Holstein-Sonderburg-Glücksburg (marriage dissolved 1920); *issue:* Prince Alexander (1912–85)
(*e*) Prince Oskar (1888–1958), *m.* 1914 Countess von Ruppin; *issue:* Prince Oskar (1915–39); Prince Burchard (1917–88); Princess Herzeleide (1918–89); Prince Wilhelm-Karl (*b.* 1922)
(*f*) Prince Joachim (1890–1920), *m.* 1916 Princess Marie of Anhalt; *issue:* Prince (Karl) Franz Joseph (1916–75), and has issue

(*g*) Princess Viktoria Luise (1892–1980), *m.* 1913 Ernst, Duke of Brunswick 1913–18 (1887–1953); *issue:* Prince Ernst (1914–87); Prince Georg (*b.* 1915), *m.* 1946 Princess Sophie of Greece (*see* page 128) and has issue (two sons, one daughter); Princess Frederika (1917–81), *m.* 1938 Paul I, King of the Hellenes (*see* page 128; Prince Christian (1919–81); Prince Welf Heinrich (*b.* 1923)
(2) Princess Charlotte (1860–1919), *m.* 1878 Bernhard, Duke of Saxe-Meiningen 1914 (1851–1914). *Issue:*
Princess Feodora (1879–1945), *m.* 1898 Prince Heinrich XXX of Reuss
(3) Prince Heinrich (1862–1929), *m.* 1888 Princess Irene of Hesse (*see* page 128). *Issue:*
(*a*) Prince Waldemar (1889–1945), *m.* Princess Calixta Agnes of Lippe
(*b*) Prince Sigismund (1896–1978), *m.* 1919 Princess Charlotte of Saxe-Altenburg; *issue:* Princess Barbara (1920–94); Prince Alfred (*b.* 1924)
(*c*) Prince Heinrich (1900–4)
(4) Prince Sigismund (1864–6)
(5) Princess Victoria (1866–1929), *m.* (1) 1890, Prince Adolf of Schaumburg-Lippe (1859–1916); (2) 1927 Alexander Zubkov
(6) Prince Waldemar (1868–79)
(7) Princess Sophie (1870–1932), *m.* 1889 Constantine I (1868–1923), King of the Hellenes 1913–17, 1920–3. *Issue:*
(*a*) George II (1890–1947), King of the Hellenes 1923–4 and 1935–47, *m.* 1921 Princess Elisabeth of Roumania (marriage dissolved 1935) (*see* page 127)
(*b*) Alexander I (1893–1920), King of the Hellenes 1917–20, *m.* 1919 Aspasia Manos; *issue:* Princess Alexandra (1921–93), *m.* 1944 King Petar II of Yugoslavia (*see* below)
(*c*) Princess Helena (1896–1982), *m.* 1921 King Carol of Roumania (*see* below), (marriage dissolved 1928)

(d) Paul I (1901–64), King of the Hellenes 1947–64, *m.* 1938 Princess Frederika of Brunswick (*see* page 126); *issue:* King Constantine II (*b.* 1940), *m.* 1964 Princess Anne-Marie of Denmark (*see* page 128), and has issue (three sons, two daughters); Princess Sophie (*b.* 1938), *m.* 1962 Juan Carlos I of Spain (*see* page 128); Princess Irene (*b.* 1942)
(e) Princess Irene (1904–74), *m.* 1939 4th Duke of Aosta; *issue:* Prince Amedeo, 5th Duke of Aosta (*b.* 1943)
(f) Princess Katherine (Lady Katherine Brandram) (*b.* 1913), *m.* 1947 Major R. C. A. Brandram, MC, TD; *issue:* R. Paul G. A. Brandram (*b.* 1948)
(8) Princess Margarethe (1872–1954), *m.* 1893 Prince Friedrich Karl of Hesse (1868–1940). *Issue:*
(a) Prince Friedrich Wilhelm (1893–1916)
(b) Prince Maximilian (1894–1914)
(c) Prince Philipp (1896–1980), *m.* 1925 Princess Mafalda of Italy (1902–44); *issue:* Prince Moritz (*b.* 1926); Prince Heinrich (1927–2000); Prince Otto (*b.* 1937); Princess Elisabeth (*b.* 1940)
(d) Prince Wolfgang (1896–1989), *m.* (1) 1924 Princess Marie Alexandra of Baden; (2) 1948 Ottilie Möller
(e) Prince Richard (1901–69)
(f) Prince Christoph (1901–43), *m.* 1930 Princess Sophie of Greece (*see* below) and has issue (two sons, three daughters)

2. HRH PRINCE ALBERT EDWARD (HM KING EDWARD VII), *b.* 9 November 1841, *m.* 1863 HRH Princess Alexandra of Denmark (1844–1925), *succeeded* to the throne 22 January 1901, *d.* 6 May 1910. *Issue:*
(1) Albert Victor, Duke of Clarence and Avondale (1864–92)
(2) George (HM KING GEORGE V) (*see* page 126)
(3) Louise (1867–1931) Princess Royal 1905–31, *m.* 1889 1st Duke of Fife (1849–1912). *Issue:*
(a) Princess Alexandra, Duchess of Fife (1891–1959), *m.* 1913 Prince Arthur of Connaught (*see* page 128)
(b) Princess Maud (1893–1945), *m.* 1923 11th Earl of Southesk (1893–1992); *issue:* The Duke of Fife (*b.* 1929)
(4) Victoria (1868–1935)
(5) Maud (1869–1938), *m.* 1896 Prince Carl of Denmark (1872–1957), later King Haakon VII of Norway 1905–57. *Issue:*
(a) Olav V (1903–91), King of Norway 1957–91, *m.* 1929 Princess Märtha of Sweden (1901–54); *issue:* Princess Ragnhild (*b.* 1930); Princess Astrid (*b.* 1932); Harald V, King of Norway (*b.* 1937)
(6) Alexander (6–7 April 1871)

3. HRH PRINCESS ALICE Maud Mary (1843–78), *m.* 1862 Prince Ludwig (1837–92), Grand Duke of Hesse 1877–92. *Issue:*
(1) Victoria (1863–1950), *m.* 1884 *Admiral of the Fleet* Prince Louis of Battenberg (1854–1921), *cr.* 1st Marquess of Milford Haven 1917. *Issue:*
(a) Alice (1885–1969), *m.* 1903 Prince Andrew of Greece (1882–1944); *issue:* Princess Margarita (1905–81), *m.* 1931 Prince Gottfried of Hohenlohe-Langenburg (*see* below); Princess Theodora (1906–69), *m.* Prince Berthold of Baden (1906–63) and has issue (two sons, one daughter); Princess Cecilie (1911–37), *m.* George, Grand Duke of Hesse (*see* below); Princess Sophie (*b.* 1914), *m.* (1) 1930 Prince Christoph of Hesse (*see* above); (2) 1946 Prince Georg of Hanover (*see* page 127); Prince Philip, Duke of Edinburgh (*b.* 1921) (*see* page 117)
(b) Louise (1889–1965), *m.* 1923 Gustaf VI Adolf (1882–1973), King of Sweden 1950–73
(c) George, 2nd Marquess of Milford Haven (1892–1938), *m.* 1916 Countess Nadejda, daughter of Grand Duke Michael of Russia; *issue:* Lady Tatiana (1917–88); David Michael, 3rd Marquess (1919–70)
(d) Louis, 1st Earl Mountbatten of Burma (1900–79), *m.* 1922 Edwina Ashley, daughter of Lord Mount Temple; *issue:* Patricia, Countess Mountbatten of Burma (*b.* 1924), Pamela (*b.* 1929)
(2) Elizabeth (1864–1918), *m.* 1884 Grand Duke Sergius of Russia (1857–1905)
(3) Irene (1866–1953), *m.* 1888 Prince Heinrich of Prussia (*see* page 126)
(4) Ernst Ludwig (1868–1937), Grand Duke of Hesse 1892–1918, *m.* (1) 1894 Princess Victoria Melita of Saxe-Coburg (*see* below) (marriage dissolved 1901); (2) 1905 Princess Eleonore of Solms-Hohensolmslich. *Issue:*

(a) Princess Elizabeth (1895–1903)
(b) George, Hereditary Grand Duke of Hesse (1906–37), *m.* Princess Cecilie of Greece (*see* above), and had issue, two sons, accidentally killed with parents 1937
(c) Ludwig, Prince of Hesse (1908–68), *m.* 1937 Margaret, daughter of 1st Lord Geddes
(5) Frederick William (1870–3)
(6) Alix (Tsaritsa of Russia) (1872–1918), *m.* 1894 Nicholas II (1868–1918) Tsar of All the Russias 1894–1917, assassinated 16 July 1918. *Issue:*
(a) Grand Duchess Olga (1895–1918)
(b) Grand Duchess Tatiana (1897–1918)
(c) Grand Duchess Marie (1899–1918)
(d) Grand Duchess Anastasia (1901–18)
(e) Alexis, Tsarevich of Russia (1904–18)
(7) Marie (1874–8)

4. HRH PRINCE ALFRED Ernest Albert, Duke of Edinburgh, *Admiral of the Fleet* (1844–1900), *m.* 1874 Grand Duchess Marie Alexandrovna of Russia (1853–1920); succeeded as Duke of Saxe-Coburg and Gotha 22 August 1893. *Issue:*
(1) Alfred, Prince of Saxe-Coburg (1874–99)
(2) Marie (1875–938), *m.* 1893 Ferdinand (1865–1927), King of Roumania 1914–27. *Issue:*
(a) Carol II (1893–1953), King of Roumania 1930–40, *m.* (2) 1921 Princess Helena of Greece (*see* above) (marriage dissolved 1928); *issue:* Michael (*b.* 1921), King of Roumania 1927–30, 1940–7, *m.* 1948 Princess Anne of Bourbon-Parma, and has issue (five daughters)
(b) Elisabeth (1894–1956),' *m.* 1921 George II, King of the Hellenes (*see* page 126)
(c) Marie (1900–61), *m.* 1922 Alexander (1888–1934), King of Yugoslavia 1921–34; *issue:* Petar II (1923–70), King of Yugoslavia 1934–45, *m.* 1944 Princess Alexandra of Greece (*see* above) and has issue (Crown Prince Alexander, *b.* 1945); Prince Tomislav (*b.* 1928), *m.* (1) 1957 Princess Margarita of Baden (daughter of Princess Theodora of Greece and Prince Berthold of Baden, *see* above); (2) 1982 Linda Bonney; and has issue (three sons, one daughter); Prince Andrej (1929–90), *m.* (1) 1956 Princess Christina of Hesse (daughter of Prince Christoph of Hesse and Princess Sophie of Greece, *see* above); (2) 1963 Princess Kira-Melita of Leiningen (*see* below); and has issue (three sons, two daughters)
(d) Prince Nicolas (1903–78)
(e) Princess Ileana (1909–91), *m.* (1) 1931 Archduke Anton of Austria; (2) 1954 Dr Stefan Issarescu; *issue:* Archduke Stefan (*b.* 1932); Archduchess Maria Ileana (1933–59); Archduchess Alexandra (*b.* 1935); Archduke Dominic (*b.* 1937); Archduchess Maria Magdalena (*b.* 1939); Archduchess Elisabeth (*b.* 1942)
(f) Prince Mircea (1913–16)
(3) Victoria Melita (1876–1936), *m.* (1) 1894 Grand Duke Ernst Ludwig of Hesse (*see* above) (marriage dissolved 1901); (2) 1905 the Grand Duke Kirill of Russia (1876–1938). *Issue:*
(a) Marie Kirillovna (1907–51), *m.* 1925 Prince Friedrich Karl of Leiningen; *issue:* Prince Emich (1926–91); Prince Karl (1928–90); Princess Kira-Melita (*b.* 1930), *m.* Prince Andrej of Yugoslavia (*see* above); Princess Margarita (*b.* 1932); Princess Mechtilde (*b.* 1936); Prince Friedrich (*b.* 1938)
(b) Kira Kirillovna (1909–67), *m.* 1938 Prince Louis Ferdinand of Prussia (*see* page 127); *issue:* Prince Friedrich Wilhelm (*b.* 1939); Prince Michael (*b.* 1940); Princess Marie (*b.* 1942); Princess Kira (*b.* 1943); Prince Louis Ferdinand (1944–77); Prince Christian (*b.* 1946); Princess Xenia (1949–92)
(c) Vladimir Kirillovich (1917–92), *m.* 1948 Princess Leonida Bagration-Mukhransky; *issue:* Grand Duchess Maria (*b.* 1953), and has issue
(4) Alexandra (1878–1942), *m.* 1896 Ernst, Prince of Hohenlohe Langenburg. *Issue:*
(a) Gottfried (1897–1960), *m.* 1931 Princess Margarita of Greece (*see* above); *issue:* Prince Kraft (*b.* 1935), Princess Beatrice (1936–97); Prince Georg Andreas (*b.* 1938), Prince Ruprecht (1944–76); Prince Albrecht (1944–92)
(b) Maria (1899–1967), *m.* 1916 Prince Friedrich of Schleswig-Holstein-Sonderburg-Glücksburg; *issue:* Prince Peter (1922–80); Princess Marie (*b.* 1927)
(c) Princess Alexandra (1901–63)
(d) Princess Irma (1902–86)

(5) Princess Beatrice (1884–1966), *m.* 1909 Alfonso of Orleans, Infante of Spain. *Issue:*
(*a*) Prince Alvaro (*b.* 1910), *m.* 1937 Carla Parodi-Delfino; *issue:* Doña Gerarda (*b.* 1939); Don Alonso (1941–75); Doña Beatriz (*b.* 1943); Don Alvaro (*b.* 1947)
(*b*) Prince Alonso (1912–36)
(*c*) Prince Ataulfo (1913–74)

5. HRH PRINCESS HELENA Augusta Victoria (1846–1923), *m.* 1866 Prince Christian of Schleswig-Holstein-Sonderburg-Augustenburg (1831–1917). *Issue:*
(1) Prince Christian Victor (1867–1900)
(2) Prince Albert (1869–1931), Duke of Schleswig-Holstein 1921–31
(3) Princess Helena (1870–1948)
(4) Princess Marie Louise (1872–1956), *m.* 1891 Prince Aribert of Anhalt (marriage dissolved 1900)
(5) Prince Harold (12–20 May 1876)

6. HRH PRINCESS LOUISE Caroline Alberta (1848–1939), *m.* 1871 the Marquess of Lorne, afterwards 9th Duke of Argyll (1845–1914); without issue

7. HRH PRINCE ARTHUR William Patrick Albert, Duke of Connaught, *Field Marshal* (1850–1942), *m.* 1879 Princess Louisa of Prussia (1860–1917). *Issue:*
(1) Margaret (1882–1920), *m.* 1905 Crown Prince Gustaf Adolf (1882–1973), afterwards King of Sweden 1950–73. *Issue:*
(*a*) Gustaf Adolf, Duke of Västerbotten (1906–47), *m.* 1932 Princess Sibylla of Saxe-Coburg-Gotha (*see below*); *issue:* Princess Margaretha (*b.* 1934); Princess Birgitta (*b.* 1937); Princess Désirée (*b.* 1938); Princess Christina (*b.* 1943); Carl XVI Gustaf, King of Sweden (*b.* 1946)
(*b*) Count Sigvard Bernadotte (*b.* 1907), *m.*; *issue:* Count Michael (*b.* 1944)
(*c*) Princess Ingrid (Queen Mother of Denmark) (1910–2000), *m.* 1935 Frederick IX (1899–1972), King of Denmark 1947–72; *issue:* Margrethe II, Queen of Denmark (*b.* 1940); Princess Benedikte (*b.* 1944); Princess Anne-Marie (*b.* 1946), *m.* 1964 Constantine II of Greece (*see* page 127)
(*d*) Prince Bertil, Duke of Halland (1912–97), *m.* 1976 Mrs Lilian Craig
(*e*) Count Carl Bernadotte (*b.* 1916), *m.* (1) 1946 Mrs Kerstin Johnson; (2) 1988 Countess Gunnila Bussler
(2) Arthur (1883–1938), *m.* 1913 HH the Duchess of Fife (*see* page 127). *Issue:*

Alastair Arthur, 2nd Duke of Connaught (1914–43)
(3) (Victoria) Patricia (1886–1974), *m.* 1919 Adm. Hon. Sir Alexander Ramsay. *Issue:*
Alexander Ramsay of Mar (*b.* 1919), *m.* 1956 Hon. Flora Fraser (Lady Saltoun)

8. HRH PRINCE LEOPOLD George Duncan Albert, Duke of Albany (1853–84), *m.* 1882 Princess Helena of Waldeck (1861–1922). *Issue:*
(1) Alice (1883–1981), *m.* 1904 Prince Alexander of Teck (1874–1957), *cr.* 1st Earl of Athlone 1917. *Issue:*
(*a*) Lady May (1906–94), *m.* 1931 Sir Henry Abel-Smith, KCMG, KCVO, DSO; *issue:* Anne (*b.* 1932); Richard (*b.* 1933); Elizabeth (*b.* 1936)
(*b*) Rupert, Viscount Trematon (1907–28)
(*c*) Prince Maurice (March–September 1910)
(2) Charles Edward (1884–1954), Duke of Albany 1884 until title suspended 1917, Duke of Saxe-Coburg-Gotha 1900–18, *m.* 1905 Princess Victoria Adelheid of Schleswig-Holstein-Sonderburg-Glücksburg. *Issue:*
(*a*) Prince Johann Leopold (1906–72), and has issue
(*b*) Princess Sibylla (1908–72), *m.* 1932 Prince Gustav Adolf of Sweden (*see above*)
(*c*) Prince Dietmar Hubertus (1909–43)
(*d*) Princess Caroline (1912–83), and has issue
(*e*) Prince Friedrich Josias (*b.* 1918), and has issue

9. HRH PRINCESS BEATRICE Mary Victoria Feodore (1857–1944), *m.* 1885 Prince Henry of Battenberg (1858–96). *Issue:*
(1) Alexander, 1st Marquess of Carisbrooke (1886–1960), *m.* 1917 Lady Irene Denison. *Issue:*
Lady Iris Mountbatten (1920–82), *m.*; *issue:* Robin A. Bryan (*b.* 1957)
(2) Victoria Eugénie (1887–1969), *m.* 1906 Alfonso XIII (1886–1941) King of Spain 1886–1931. *Issue:*
(*a*) Prince Alfonso (1907–38)
(*b*) Prince Jaime (1908–75), and has issue
(*c*) Princess Beatrice (*b.* 1909), and has issue
(*d*) Princess Maria (1911–96), and has issue
(*e*) Prince Juan (1913–93), Count of Barcelona; *issue:* Princess Maria (*b.* 1936); Juan Carlos I, King of Spain (*b.* 1938), *m.* 1962 Princess Sophie of Greece (*see* page 127) and has issue (one son, two daughters); Princess Margarita (*b.* 1939)
(*f*) Prince Gonzalo (1914–34)
(3) Major Lord Leopold Mountbatten (1889–1922)
(4) Maurice (1891–1914), died of wounds received in action

Kings and Queens

ENGLISH KINGS AND QUEENS 927 TO 1603

HOUSES OF CERDIC AND DENMARK

Reign

927–939 ÆTHELSTAN
Son of Edward the Elder, by Ecgwynn, and grandson of Alfred
Acceded to Wessex and Mercia *c.*924, established direct rule over Northumbria 927, effectively creating the Kingdom of England
Reigned 15 years

939–946 EDMUND I
Born 921, son of Edward the Elder, by Eadgifu
Married (1) Ælfgifu (2) Æthelflæd
Killed aged 25, *reigned* 6 years

946–955 EADRED
Son of Edward the Elder, by Eadgifu
Reigned 9 years

955–959 EADWIG
Born before 943, son of Edmund and Ælfgifu
Married Ælfgifu
Reigned 3 years

959–975 EDGAR I
Born 943, son of Edmund and Ælfgifu
Married (1) Æthelflæd (2) Wulfthryth (3) Ælfthryth
Died aged 32, *reigned* 15 years

975–978 EDWARD I (the Martyr)
*Born c.*962, son of Edgar and Æthelflæd
Assassinated aged *c.*16, *reigned* 2 years

978–1016 ÆTHELRED (the Unready)
*Born c.*968/969, son of Edgar and Ælfthryth
Married (1) Ælfgifu (2) Emma, daughter of Richard I, count of Normandy
1013–14 dispossessed of kingdom by Swegn Forkbeard (king of Denmark 987–1014)
Died aged *c.*47, *reigned* 38 years

1016 EDMUND II (Ironside)
Born before 993, son of Æthelred and Ælfgifu
Married Ealdgyth
Died aged over 23, *reigned* 7 months (April–November)

1016–1035 CNUT (Canute)
*Born c.*995, son of Swegn Forkbeard, king of Denmark, and Gunhild
Married (1) Ælfgifu (2) Emma, widow of Æthelred the Unready

Gained submission of West Saxons 1015, Northumbrians 1016, Mercia 1016, king of all England after Edmund's death
King of Denmark 1019–35, king of Norway 1028–35
Died aged *c.*40, *reigned* 19 years

1035–1040   HAROLD I (Harefoot)
*Born c.*1016/17, son of Cnut and Ælfgifu
Married Ælfgifu
1035 recognized as regent for himself and his brother Harthacnut; 1037 recognized as king
Died aged *c.*23, *reigned* 4 years

1040–1042   HARTHACNUT
*Born c.*1018, son of Cnut and Emma
Titular king of Denmark from 1028
Acknowledged king of England 1035–7 with Harold I as regent; effective king after Harold's death
Died aged *c.*24, *reigned* 2 years

1042–1066   EDWARD II (the Confessor)
Born between 1002 and 1005, son of Æthelred the Unready and Emma
Married Eadgyth, daughter of Godwine, earl of Wessex
Died aged over 60, *reigned* 23 years

1066   HAROLD II (Godwinesson)
*Born c.*1020, son of Godwine, earl of Wessex, and Gytha
Married (1) Eadgyth (2) Ealdgyth
Killed in battle aged *c.*46, *reigned* 10 months (January–October)

THE HOUSE OF NORMANDY

1066–1087   WILLIAM I (the Conqueror)
Born 1027/8, son of Robert I, duke of Normandy; obtained the Crown by conquest
Married Matilda, daughter of Baldwin, count of Flanders
Died aged *c.*60, *reigned* 20 years

1087–1100   WILLIAM II (Rufus)
Born between 1056 and 1060, third son of William I; succeeded his father in England only
Killed aged *c.*40, *reigned* 12 years

1100–1135   HENRY I (Beauclerk)
Born 1068, fourth son of William I
Married (1) Edith or Matilda, daughter of Malcolm III of Scotland (2) Adela, daughter of Godfrey, count of Louvain
Died aged 67, *reigned* 35 years

1135–1154   STEPHEN
Born not later than 1100, third son of Adela, daughter of William I, and Stephen, count of Blois
Married Matilda, daughter of Eustace, count of Boulogne
1141 (February–November) held captive by adherents of Matilda, daughter of Henry I, who contested the crown until 1153
Died aged over 53, *reigned* 18 years

THE HOUSE OF ANJOU (PLANTAGENETS)

1154–1189   HENRY II (Curtmantle)
Born 1133, son of Matilda, daughter of Henry I, and Geoffrey, count of Anjou
Married Eleanor, daughter of William, duke of Aquitaine, and divorced queen of Louis VII of France
Died aged 56, *reigned* 34 years

1189–1199   RICHARD I (Coeur de Lion)
Born 1157, third son of Henry II
Married Berengaria, daughter of Sancho VI, king of Navarre
Died aged 42, *reigned* 9 years

1199–1216   JOHN (Lackland)
Born 1167, fifth son of Henry II
Married (1) Isabella or Avisa, daughter of William, earl of Gloucester (divorced) (2) Isabella, daughter of Aymer, count of Angoulême
Died aged 48, *reigned* 17 years

1216–1272   HENRY III
Born 1207, son of John and Isabella of Angoulême

Married Eleanor, daughter of Raymond, count of Provence
Died aged 65, *reigned* 56 years

1272–1307   EDWARD I (Longshanks)
Born 1239, eldest son of Henry III
Married (1) Eleanor, daughter of Ferdinand III, king of Castile (2) Margaret, daughter of Philip III of France
Died aged 68, *reigned* 34 years

1307–1327   EDWARD II
Born 1284, eldest surviving son of Edward I and Eleanor
Married Isabella, daughter of Philip IV of France
Deposed January 1327, *killed* September 1327 aged 43, *reigned* 19 years

1327–1377   EDWARD III
Born 1312, eldest son of Edward II
Married Philippa, daughter of William, count of Hainault
Died aged 64, *reigned* 50 years

1377–1399   RICHARD II
Born 1367, son of Edward (the Black Prince), eldest son of Edward III
Married (1) Anne, daughter of Emperor Charles IV (2) Isabelle, daughter of Charles VI of France
Deposed September 1399, *killed* February 1400 aged 33, *reigned* 22 years

THE HOUSE OF LANCASTER

1399–1413   HENRY IV
Born 1366, son of John of Gaunt, fourth son of Edward III, and Blanche, daughter of Henry, duke of Lancaster
Married (1) Mary, daughter of Humphrey, earl of Hereford (2) Joan, daughter of Charles, king of Navarre, and widow of John, duke of Brittany
Died aged *c.* 47, *reigned* 13 years

1413–1422   HENRY V
Born 1387, eldest surviving son of Henry IV and Mary
Married Catherine, daughter of Charles VI of France
Died aged 34, *reigned* 9 years

1422–1471   HENRY VI
Born 1421, son of Henry V
Married Margaret, daughter of René, duke of Anjou and count of Provence
Deposed March 1461, *restored* October 1470
Deposed April 1471, *killed* May 1471 aged 49, *reigned* 39 years

THE HOUSE OF YORK

1461–1483   EDWARD IV
Born 1442, eldest son of Richard of York (grandson of Edmund, fifth son of Edward III, and son of Anne, great-granddaughter of Lionel, third son of Edward III)
Married Elizabeth Woodville, daughter of Richard, Lord Rivers, and widow of Sir John Grey
Acceded March 1461, *deposed* October 1470, *restored* April 1471
Died aged 40, *reigned* 21 years

1483   EDWARD V
Born 1470, eldest son of Edward IV
Deposed June 1483, *died* probably July–September 1483, aged 12, *reigned* 2 months (April–June)

1483–1485   RICHARD III
Born 1452, fourth son of Richard of York
Married Anne Neville, daughter of Richard, earl of Warwick, and widow of Edward, Prince of Wales, son of Henry VI
Killed in battle aged 32, *reigned* 2 years

THE HOUSE OF TUDOR

1485–1509   HENRY VII
Born 1457, son of Margaret Beaufort (great-granddaughter of John of Gaunt, fourth son of

Edward III) and Edmund Tudor, earl of Richmond
Married Elizabeth, daughter of Edward IV
Died aged 52, *reigned* 23 years

1509–1547 HENRY VIII
Born 1491, second son of Henry VII
Married (1) Catherine, daughter of Ferdinand II,
king of Aragon, and widow of his elder brother
Arthur (divorced) (2) Anne, daughter of Sir Thomas
Boleyn (executed) (3) Jane, daughter of Sir John
Seymour (died in childbirth) (4) Anne, daughter of
John, duke of Cleves (divorced) (5) Catherine
Howard, niece of the Duke of Norfolk (executed)
(6) Catherine, daughter of Sir Thomas Parr and
widow of Lord Latimer
Died aged 55, *reigned* 37 years

1547–1553 EDWARD VI
Born 1537, son of Henry VIII and Jane Seymour
Died aged 15, *reigned* 6 years

1553 JANE
Born 1537, daughter of Frances (daughter of Mary
Tudor, the younger daughter of Henry VII) and
Henry Grey, duke of Suffolk
Married Lord Guildford Dudley, son of the Duke of
Northumberland
Deposed July 1553, *executed* February 1554 aged 16,
reigned 14 days

1553–1558 MARY I
Born 1516, daughter of Henry VIII and Catherine
of Aragon
Married Philip II of Spain
Died aged 42, *reigned* 5 years

1558–1603 ELIZABETH I
Born 1533, daughter of Henry VIII and Anne
Boleyn
Died aged 69, *reigned* 44 years

BRITISH KINGS AND QUEENS SINCE 1603

THE HOUSE OF STUART

Reign

1603–1625 JAMES I (VI OF SCOTLAND)
Born 1566, son of Mary, queen of Scots
(granddaughter of Margaret Tudor, elder daughter
of Henry VII), and Henry Stewart, Lord Darnley
Married Anne, daughter of Frederick II of Denmark
Died aged 58, *reigned* 22 years
(*see also* page 133)

1625–1649 CHARLES I
Born 1600, second son of James I
Married Henrietta Maria, daughter of Henry IV of
France
Executed 1649 aged 48, *reigned* 23 years
COMMONWEALTH DECLARED 19 May 1649
1649–53 Government by a council of state
1653–8 Oliver Cromwell, *Lord Protector*
1658–9 Richard Cromwell, *Lord Protector*

1660–1685 CHARLES II
Born 1630, eldest son of Charles I
Married Catherine, daughter of John IV of Portugal
Died aged 54, *reigned* 24 years

1685–1688 JAMES II (VII of Scotland)
Born 1633, second son of Charles I
Married (1) Lady Anne Hyde, daughter of Edward,
earl of Clarendon (2) Mary, daughter of Alphonso,
duke of Modena
Reign ended with flight from kingdom December
1688
Died 1701 aged 67, *reigned* 3 years
INTERREGNUM 11 December 1688 to 12 February
1689

1689–1702 WILLIAM III
Born 1650, son of William II, prince of Orange, and
Mary Stuart, daughter of Charles I
Married Mary, elder daughter of James II
Died aged 51, *reigned* 13 years

and

1689–1694 MARY II
Born 1662, elder daughter of James II and Anne
Died aged 32, *reigned* 5 years

1702–1714 ANNE
Born 1665, younger daughter of James II and Anne
Married Prince George of Denmark, son of
Frederick III of Denmark
Died aged 49, *reigned* 12 years

THE HOUSE OF HANOVER

1714–1727 GEORGE I (Elector of Hanover)
Born 1660, son of Sophia (daughter of Frederick,
elector palatine, and Elizabeth Stuart, daughter of
James I) and Ernest Augustus, elector of Hanover
Married Sophia Dorothea, daughter of George
William, duke of Lüneburg-Celle
Died aged 67, *reigned* 12 years

1727–1760 GEORGE II
Born 1683, son of George I
Married Caroline, daughter of John Frederick,
margrave of Brandenburg-Anspach
Died aged 76, *reigned* 33 years

1760–1820 GEORGE III
Born 1738, son of Frederick, eldest son of George II
Married Charlotte, daughter of Charles Louis, duke
of Mecklenburg-Strelitz
Died aged 81, *reigned* 59 years
REGENCY 1811–20
Prince of Wales regent owing to the insanity of
George III

1820–1830 GEORGE IV
Born 1762, eldest son of George III
Married Caroline, daughter of Charles, duke of
Brunswick-Wolfenbüttel
Died aged 67, *reigned* 10 years

1830–1837 WILLIAM IV
Born 1765, third son of George III
Married Adelaide, daughter of George, duke of
Saxe-Meiningen
Died aged 71, *reigned* 7 years

1837–1901 VICTORIA
Born 1819, daughter of Edward, fourth son of
George III
Married Prince Albert of Saxe-Coburg and Gotha
Died aged 81, *reigned* 63 years

THE HOUSE OF SAXE-COBURG AND GOTHA

1901–1910 EDWARD VII
Born 1841, eldest son of Victoria and Albert
Married Alexandra, daughter of Christian IX of
Denmark
Died aged 68, *reigned* 9 years

THE HOUSE OF WINDSOR

1910–1936 GEORGE V
Born 1865, second son of Edward VII
Married Victoria Mary, daughter of Francis, duke of
Teck
Died aged 70, *reigned* 25 years

1936 EDWARD VIII
Born 1894, eldest son of George V
Married (1937) Mrs Wallis Simpson
Abdicated 1936, *died* 1972 aged 77, *reigned* 10
months (20 January to 11 December)

1936–1952 GEORGE VI
Born 1895, second son of George V
Married Lady Elizabeth Bowes-Lyon, daughter of
14th Earl of Strathmore and Kinghorne (*see also*
page 117)
Died aged 56, *reigned* 15 years

1952– ELIZABETH II
Born 1926, elder daughter of George VI
Married Philip, son of Prince Andrew of Greece (see also page 117)

KINGS AND QUEENS OF SCOTS 1016 TO 1603

Reign

1016–1034 MALCOLM II
Born c.954, son of Kenneth II
Acceded to Alba 1005, secured Lothian c.1016, obtained Strathclyde for his grandson Duncan c.1016, thus reigning over an area approximately the same as that governed by later rulers of Scotland
Died aged c.80, reigned 18 years

THE HOUSE OF ATHOLL

1034–1040 DUNCAN I
Son of Bethoc, daughter of Malcolm II, and Crinan, mormaer of Atholl
Married a cousin of Siward, earl of Northumbria
Reigned 5 years
1040–1057 MACBETH
Born c.1005, son of a daughter of Malcolm II and Finlaec, mormaer of Moray
Married Gruoch, granddaughter of Kenneth III
Killed aged c.52, reigned 17 years
1057–1058 LULACH
Born c.1032, son of Gillacomgan, mormaer of Moray, and Gruoch (and stepson of Macbeth)
Died aged c.26, reigned 7 months (August–March)
1058–1093 MALCOLM III (Canmore)
Born c.1031, elder son of Duncan I
Married (1) Ingibiorg (2) Margaret (St Margaret), granddaughter of Edmund II of England
Killed in battle aged c.62, reigned 35 years
1093–1097 DONALD III BÁN
Born c.1033, second son of Duncan I
Deposed May 1094, restored November 1094, deposed October 1097, reigned 3 years
1094 DUNCAN II
Born c.1060, elder son of Malcolm III and Ingibiorg
Married Octreda of Dunbar
Killed aged c.34, reigned 6 months (May–November)
1097–1107 EDGAR
Born c.1074, second son of Malcolm III and Margaret
Died aged c.32, reigned 9 years
1107–1124 ALEXANDER I (The Fierce)
Born c.1077, fifth son of Malcolm III and Margaret
Married Sybilla, illegitimate daughter of Henry I of England
Died aged c.47, reigned 17 years
1124–1153 DAVID I (The Saint)
Born c.1085, sixth son of Malcolm III and Margaret
Married Matilda, daughter of Waltheof, earl of Huntingdon
Died aged c.68, reigned 29 years
1153–1165 MALCOLM IV (The Maiden)
Born c.1141, son of Henry, earl of Huntingdon, second son of David I
Died aged c.24, reigned 12 years
1165–1214 WILLIAM I (The Lion)
Born c.1142, brother of Malcolm IV
Married Ermengarde, daughter of Richard, viscount of Beaumont
Died aged c.72, reigned 49 years
1214–1249 ALEXANDER II
Born 1198, son of William I
Married (1) Joan, daughter of John, king of England (2) Marie, daughter of Ingelram de Coucy Died aged 50, reigned 34 years

1249–1286 ALEXANDER III
Born 1241, son of Alexander II and Marie
Married (1) Margaret, daughter of Henry III of England (2) Yolande, daughter of the Count of Dreux
Killed accidentally aged 44, reigned 36 years
1286–1290 MARGARET (The Maid of Norway)
Born 1283, daughter of Margaret (daughter of Alexander III) and Eric II of Norway
Died aged 7, reigned 4 years
FIRST INTERREGNUM 1290–2
Throne disputed by 13 competitors. Crown awarded to John Balliol by adjudication of Edward I of England

THE HOUSE OF BALLIOL

1292–1296 JOHN (Balliol)
Born c.1250, son of Dervorguilla, great-great-granddaughter of David I, and John de Balliol
Married Isabella, daughter of John, earl of Surrey
Abdicated 1296, died 1313 aged c.63, reigned 3 years
SECOND INTERREGNUM 1296–1306
Edward I of England declared John Balliol to have forfeited the throne for contumacy in 1296 and took the government of Scotland into his own hands

THE HOUSE OF BRUCE

1306–1329 ROBERT I (Bruce)
Born 1274, son of Robert Bruce and Marjorie, countess of Carrick, and great-grandson of the second daughter of David, earl of Huntingdon, brother of William I
Married (1) Isabella, daughter of Donald, earl of Mar (2) Elizabeth, daughter of Richard, earl of Ulster
Died aged 54, reigned 23 years
1329–1371 DAVID II
Born 1324, son of Robert I and Elizabeth
Married (1) Joanna, daughter of Edward II of England (2) Margaret Drummond, widow of Sir John Logie (divorced)
Died aged 46, reigned 41 years
1332 Edward Balliol, son of John Balliol, crowned King of Scots September, expelled December
1333–6 Edward Balliol restored as King of Scots

THE HOUSE OF STEWART

1371–1390 ROBERT II (Stewart)
Born 1316, son of Marjorie (daughter of Robert I) and Walter, High Steward of Scotland
Married (1) Elizabeth, daughter of Sir Robert Mure of Rowallan (2) Euphemia, daughter of Hugh, earl of Ross
Died aged 74, reigned 19 years
1390–1406 ROBERT III
Born c.1337, son of Robert II and Elizabeth
Married Annabella, daughter of Sir John Drummond of Stobhall
Died aged c.69, reigned 16 years
1406–1437 JAMES I
Born 1394, son of Robert III
Married Joan Beaufort, daughter of John, earl of Somerset
Assassinated aged 42, reigned 30 years
1437–1460 JAMES II
Born 1430, son of James I
Married Mary, daughter of Arnold, duke of Gueldres
Killed accidentally aged 29, reigned 23 years
1460–1488 JAMES III
Born 1452, son of James II
Married Margaret, daughter of Christian I of Denmark
Assassinated aged 36, reigned 27 years
1488–1513 JAMES IV
Born 1473, son of James III
Married Margaret Tudor, daughter of Henry VII of England
Killed in battle aged 40, reigned 25 years

1513–1542	JAMES V
	Born 1512, son of James IV
	Married (1) Madeleine, daughter of Francis I of France (2) Mary of Lorraine, daughter of the Duc de Guise
	Died aged 30, *reigned* 29 years
1542–1567	MARY
	Born 1542, daughter of James V and Mary
	Married (1) the Dauphin, afterwards Francis II of France (2) Henry Stewart, Lord Darnley (3) James Hepburn, earl of Bothwell
	Abdicated 1567, prisoner in England from 1568, executed 1587, *reigned* 24 years
1567–1625	JAMES VI (and I of England)
	Born 1566, son of Mary, queen of Scots, and Henry, Lord Darnley
	Acceded 1567 to the Scottish throne, *reigned* 58 years
	Succeeded 1603 to the English throne, so joining the English and Scottish crowns in one person. The two kingdoms remained distinct until 1707 when the parliaments of the kingdoms became conjoined For British Kings and Queens since 1603, *see* pages 130–1

WELSH SOVEREIGNS AND PRINCES

Wales was ruled by sovereign princes from the earliest times until the death of Llywelyn in 1282. The first English Prince of Wales was the son of Edward I, who was born in Caernarvon town on 25 April 1284. According to a discredited legend, he was presented to the Welsh chieftains as their prince, in fulfilment of a promise that they should have a prince who 'could not speak a word of English' and should be native born. This son, who afterwards became Edward II, was created 'Prince of Wales and Earl of Chester' at the Lincoln Parliament on 7 February 1301.

The title Prince of Wales is borne after individual conferment and is not inherited at birth, though some Princes have been declared and styled Prince of Wales but never formally so created (*s.*). The title was conferred on Prince Charles by The Queen on 26 July 1958. He was invested at Caernarvon on 1 July 1969.

INDEPENDENT PRINCES AD 844 TO 1282

844–878	Rhodri the Great
878–916	Anarawd, son of Rhodri
916–950	Hywel Dda, the Good
950–979	Iago ab Idwal (or Ieuaf)
979–985	Hywel ab Ieuaf, the Bad
985–986	Cadwallon, his brother
986–999	Maredudd ab Owain ap Hywel Dda
999–1008	Cynan ap Hywel ab Ieuaf
1018–1023	Llywelyn ap Seisyll
1023–1039	Iago ab Idwal ap Meurig
1039–1063	Gruffydd ap Llywelyn ap Seisyll
1063–1075	Bleddyn ap Cynfyn
1075–1081	Trahaern ap Caradog
1081–1137	Gruffydd ap Cynan ab Iago
1137–1170	Owain Gwynedd
1170–1194	Dafydd ab Owain Gwynedd
1194–1240	Llywelyn Fawr, the Great
1240–1246	Dafydd ap Llywelyn
1246–1282	Llywelyn ap Gruffydd ap Llywelyn

ENGLISH PRINCES SINCE 1301

1301	Edward (Edward II)
1343	Edward the Black Prince, son of Edward III
1376	Richard (Richard II), son of the Black Prince
1399	Henry of Monmouth (Henry V)
1454	Edward of Westminster, son of Henry VI
1471	Edward of Westminster (Edward V)
1483	Edward, son of Richard III (d. 1484)
1489	Arthur Tudor, son of Henry VII
1504	Henry Tudor (Henry VIII)
1610	Henry Stuart, son of James I (d. 1612)

1616	Charles Stuart (Charles I)
c.1638 (s.)	Charles Stuart (Charles II)
1688 (s.)	James Francis Edward Stuart (The Old Pretender), son of James II (d. 1766)
1714	George Augustus (George II)
1729	Frederick Lewis, son of George II (d. 1751)
1751	George William Frederick (George III)
1762	George Augustus Frederick (George IV)
1841	Albert Edward (Edward VII)
1901	George (George V)
1910	Edward (Edward VIII)
1958	Charles, son of Elizabeth II

PRINCESSES ROYAL

The style Princess Royal is conferred at the Sovereign's discretion on his or her eldest daughter. It is an honorary title, held for life, and cannot be inherited or passed on. It was first conferred on Princess Mary, daughter of Charles I, in approximately 1642.

c.1642	Princess Mary (1631–60), daughter of Charles I
1727	Princess Anne (1709–59), daughter of George II
1766	Princess Charlotte (1766–1828), daughter of George III
1840	Princess Victoria (1840–1901), daughter of Victoria
1905	Princess Louise (1867–1931), daughter of Edward VII
1932	Princess Mary (1897–1965), daughter of George V
1987	Princess Anne (b. 1950), daughter of Elizabeth II

Precedence

The Sovereign
The Prince Philip, Duke of Edinburgh
The Prince of Wales
The Sovereign's younger sons
The Sovereign's grandsons
The Sovereign's cousins
Archbishop of Canterbury
Lord High Chancellor
Archbishop of York
The Prime Minister
Lord President of the Council
Speaker of the House of Commons
Lord Privy Seal
Ambassadors and High Commissioners
Lord Great Chamberlain
Earl Marshal
Lord Steward of the Household
Lord Chamberlain of the Household
Master of the Horse
Dukes, according to their patent of creation:
(1) of England
(2) of Scotland
(3) of Great Britain
(4) of Ireland
(5) those created since the Union
Ministers and Envoys
Eldest sons of Dukes of Blood Royal
Marquesses, according to their patent of creation:
(1) of England
(2) of Scotland
(3) of Great Britain
(4) of Ireland
(5) those created since the Union
Dukes' eldest sons
Earls, according to their patent of creation:
(1) of England
(2) of Scotland
(3) of Great Britain
(4) of Ireland
(5) those created since the Union
Younger sons of Dukes of Blood Royal
Marquesses' eldest sons
Dukes' younger sons
Viscounts, according to their patent of creation:
(1) of England
(2) of Scotland
(3) of Great Britain
(4) of Ireland
(5) those created since the Union
Earls' eldest sons
Marquesses' younger sons
Bishops of London, Durham and Winchester
Other English Diocesan Bishops, according to seniority of consecration

Suffragan Bishops, according to seniority of consecration
Secretaries of State, if of the degree of a Baron
Barons, according to their patent of creation:
(1) of England
(2) of Scotland
(3) of Great Britain
(4) of Ireland
(5) those created since the Union
Treasurer of the Household
Comptroller of the Household
Vice-Chamberlain of the Household
Secretaries of State under the degree of Baron
Viscounts' eldest sons
Earls' younger sons
Barons' eldest sons
Knights of the Garter
Privy Counsellors
Chancellor of the Exchequer
Chancellor of the Duchy of Lancaster
Lord Chief Justice of England
Master of the Rolls
President of the Family Division
Vice-Chancellor
Lords Justices of Appeal
Judges of the High Court
Viscounts' younger sons
Barons' younger sons
Sons of Life Peers
Baronets, according to date of patent
Knights of the Thistle
Knights Grand Cross of the Bath
Members of the Order of Merit
Knights Grand Commanders of the Star of India
Knights Grand Cross of St Michael and St George
Knights Grand Commanders of the Indian Empire
Knights Grand Cross of the Royal Victorian Order
Knights Grand Cross of the British Empire
Companions of Honour
Knights Commanders of the Bath
Knights Commanders of the Star of India
Knights Commanders of St Michael and St George
Knights Commanders of the Indian Empire
Knights Commanders of the Royal Victorian Order
Knights Commanders of the British Empire
Knights Bachelor
Vice-Chancellor of the County Palatine of Lancaster
Judges of the Technology and Construction Court
Circuit judges and judges of the Mayor's and City of London Court
Companions of the Bath

Companions of the Star of India
Companions of St Michael and St George
Companions of the Indian Empire
Commanders of the Royal Victorian Order
Commanders of the British Empire
Companions of the Distinguished Service Order
Lieutenants of the Royal Victorian Order
Officers of the British Empire
Companions of the Imperial Service Order
Eldest sons of younger sons of Peers
Baronets' eldest sons
Eldest sons of Knights, in the same order as their fathers
Members of the Royal Victorian Order
Members of the British Empire
Younger sons of the younger sons of Peers
Baronets' younger sons
Younger sons of Knights, in the same order as their fathers
Naval, Military, Air, and other Esquires by office

The Sovereign
The Prince Philip, Duke of Edinburgh
The Lord High Commissioner to the General Assembly (while that Assembly is sitting)
The Duke of Rothesay (eldest son of the Sovereign)
The Sovereign's younger sons
The Sovereign's cousins
Lord-Lieutenants
Lord Provosts of those Cities
Sheriffs Principal, successively, within their own localities and during holding of office
Lord Chancellor of Great Britain
Moderator of the General Assembly of the Church of Scotland
Keepers of the Great Seal
The Presiding Officer
The Secretary of State for Scotland
Hereditary Lord High Constable of Scotland
Hereditary Master of the Household
Dukes, in same order as in England
Eldest sons of Dukes of the Blood Royal
Marquesses, as in England
Dukes' eldest sons
Earls, as in England
Younger sons of Dukes of Blood Royal

Marquesses' eldest sons
Dukes' younger sons
Lord Justice General
Lord Clerk Register
Lord Advocate
The Advocate-General
Lord Justice Clerk
Viscounts, as in England
Earls' eldest sons
Marquesses' younger sons
Lord-Barons, as in England
Viscounts' eldest sons
Earls' younger sons
Lord-Barons' eldest sons
Knights of the Garter
Knights of the Thistle
Privy Counsellors
Senators of College of Justice (Lords
    of Session)
Viscounts' younger sons
Lord-Barons' younger sons
Sons of Life Peers
Baronets
Knights Grand Cross, Grand
    Commander, and Knight
    Commanders, as in England
Solicitor-General for Scotland
Lord Lyon King of Arms
Sheriffs Principal, except as shown
    above
Knights Bachelor
Sheriffs
Commanders of the Royal Victorian
    Order
Companions of Orders, as in
  . England
Commanders of the British Empire
Lieutenants of the Royal Victorian
    Order
Companions of the Distinguished
    Service Order
Eldest sons of younger sons of Peers
Baronets' eldest sons
Knights' eldest sons, as in England
Members of the Royal Victorian
    Order
Baronets' younger sons
Knights' younger sons
Queen's Counsel
Esquires
Gentlemen

WOMEN

Women take the same rank as their husbands or as their brothers; but the daughter of a peer marrying a commoner retains her title as Lady or Honourable. Daughters of peers rank next immediately after the wives of their elder brothers, and before their younger brothers' wives. Daughters of peers marrying peers of lower degree take the same order of precedence as that of their husbands; thus the daughter of a Duke marrying a Baron becomes of the rank of Baroness only, while her sisters married to commoners retain their rank and take precedence of the

Baroness. Merely official rank on the husband's part does not give any similar precedence to the wife.

Peeresses in their own right take the same precedence as peers of the same rank, i.e. from their date of creation.

LOCAL PRECEDENCE
England and Wales
No written code of county or city order of precedence has been promulgated, but in counties the Lord Lieutenant stands first, and secondly (normally) the Sheriff, and therefore in cities and boroughs the Lord Lieutenant has social precedence over the Mayor; but at city or borough functions the Lord Mayor or Mayor will preside. At Oxford and Cambridge the High Sheriff takes precedence of the Vice-Chancellor.

Scotland
The Lord Provosts of the city districts of Aberdeen, Dundee, Edinburgh and Glasgow are Lord Lieutenants for those districts *ex officio* and take precedence as such.

Forms of address

It is only possible to cover here the forms of address for peers, baronets and knights, their wife and children, and Privy Counsellors. Greater detail should be sought in one of the publications devoted to the subject.

Both formal and social forms of address are given where usage differs; nowadays, the social form is generally preferred to the formal, which increasingly is used only for official documents and on very formal occasions.

F_ represents forename
S_ represents surname

BARON – *Envelope (formal)*, The Right Hon. Lord _; *(social)*, The Lord_. *Letter (formal)*, My Lord; *(social)*, Dear Lord_. *Spoken*, Lord_.

BARON'S WIFE–*Envelope (formal)*, The Right Hon. Lady_; *(social)*, The Lady_. *Letter (formal)*, My Lady; *(social)*, Dear Lady_. *Spoken*, Lady_.

BARON'S CHILDREN – *Envelope*, The Hon. F_S_. *Letter*, Dear Mr/Miss/Mrs S_. *Spoken*, Mr/Miss/Mrs S_.

BARONESS IN OWN RIGHT – *Envelope*, may be addressed in same way as a Baron's wife or, if she prefers *(formal)*, The Right Hon. the Baroness _; *(social)*, The Baroness_. Otherwise as for a Baron's wife.

BARONET – *Envelope*, Sir F_S_, Bt. *Letter (formal)*, Dear Sir; *(social)*, Dear Sir F_. *Spoken*, Sir F_.

BARONET'S WIFE – *Envelope*, Lady S_. *Letter (formal)*, Dear Madam; *(social)*, Dear Lady S_. *Spoken*, Lady S_.

COUNTESS IN OWN RIGHT – As for an Earl's wife.

COURTESY TITLES–The heir apparent to a Duke, Marquess or Earl uses the highest of his father's other titles as a courtesy title. (For list, *see* pages 165–6.) The holder of a courtesy title is not styled The Most Hon. or The Right Hon., and in correspondence 'The' is omitted before the title. The heir apparent to a Scottish title may use the title 'Master' (*see* below).

DAME – *Envelope*, Dame F_, followed by appropriate post-nominal letters. *Letter (formal)*, Dear Madam; *(social)*, Dear Dame F_. *Spoken*, Dame F_.

DUKE–*Envelope (formal)*, His Grace the Duke of_ ; *(social)*, The Duke of_. *Letter (formal)*, My Lord Duke; *(social)*, Dear Duke. *Spoken (formal)*, Your Grace; *(social)*, Duke.

DUKE'S WIFE–*Envelope (formal)*, Her Grace the Duchess of_; *(social)*, The Duchess of_. *Letter (formal)*, Dear Madam; *(social)*, Dear Duchess. *Spoken*, Duchess.

DUKE'S ELDEST SON – *see* Courtesy titles.

DUKE'S YOUNGER SONS – *Envelope*, Lord F_S_. *Letter (formal)*, My Lord; *(social)*, Dear Lord F_. *Spoken (formal)*, My Lord; *(social)*, Lord F_.

DUKE'S DAUGHTER–*Envelope*, Lady F_S_. *Letter (formal)*, Dear Madam; *(social)*, Dear Lady F_. *Spoken*, Lady F_.

EARL –*Envelope (formal)*, The Right Hon. the Earl (of)_; *(social)*, The Earl (of)_. *Letter (formal)*, My Lord; *(social)*, Dear Lord _. *Spoken (formal)*, My Lord; *(social)*, Lord _s WIFE – *Envelope (formal)*, The Right Hon. the Countess (of)_; *(social)*, The Countess (of)_. *Letter (formal)*, Madam; *(social)*, Lady_. *Spoken (formal)*, Madam; *(social)*, Lady_.

EARL'S CHILDREN – *Eldest son*, see Courtesy titles. *Younger sons*, The Hon. F_S_ (for forms of address, *see* Baron's children). *Daughters*, Lady F_S_ (for forms of address, *see* Duke's daughter).

KNIGHT (BACHELOR) – *Envelope*, Sir F_S_. *Letter (formal)*, Dear Sir; *(social)*, Dear Sir F_. *Spoken*, Sir F_.

KNIGHT (ORDERS OF CHIVALRY) – *Envelope*, Sir F_S_ , followed by appropriate post-nominal letters. Otherwise as for Knight Bachelor.

KNIGHT'S WIFE – As for Baronet's wife.

LIFE PEER – As for Baron/Baroness in own right.

LIFE PEER'S WIFE – As for Baron's wife.

LIFE PEER'S CHILDREN – As for Baron's children.

MARQUESS–*Envelope (formal)*, The Most Hon. the Marquess of _; *(social)*, The Marquess of_. *Letter (formal)*, My Lord; *(social)*, Dear Lord_. *Spoken (formal)*, My Lord; *(social)*, Lord_.

MARQUESS'S WIFE – *Envelope (formal)*, The Most Hon. the Marchioness of _; *(social)*, The Marchioness of_. *Letter (formal)*, Madam; *(social)*, Dear Lady_. *Spoken*, Lady_.

MARQUESS'S CHILDREN–*Eldest son*, see Courtesy titles. *Younger sons*, Lord F_S_ (for forms of address, *see* Duke's younger sons). *Daughters*, Lady F_S_ (for forms of address, *see* Duke's daughter).

MASTER–The title is used by the heir apparent to a Scottish peerage, though usually the heir apparent to a Duke, Marquess or Earl uses his courtesy title rather than 'Master'. *Envelope*, The Master of_. *Letter (formal)*, Dear Sir; *(social)*, Dear Master of _. *Spoken (formal)*, Master, or Sir; *(social)*, Master, or Mr S_.

MASTER'S WIFE–Addressed as for the wife of the appropriate peerage style, otherwise as Mrs S_.

PRIVY COUNSELLOR–*Envelope*, The Right (or Rt.) Hon. F_S_. *Letter*, Dear Mr/Miss/Mrs S_. *Spoken*, Mr/Miss/Mrs S_. It is incorrect to use the letters PC after the name in conjunction with the prefix The Right Hon., unless the Privy Counsellor is a peer below the rank of Marquess and so is styled The Right Hon. because of his rank. In this case only, the post-nominal letters may be used in conjunction with the prefix The Right Hon.

VISCOUNT–*Envelope (formal)*, The Right Hon. the Viscount_; *(social)*, The Viscount_. *Letter (formal)*, My Lord; *(social)*, Dear Lord_. *Spoken*, Lord_.

VISCOUNT'S WIFE – *Envelope (formal)*, The Right Hon. the Viscountess_; *(social)*, The Viscountess_. *Letter (formal)*, Madam; *(social)*, Dear Lady _. *Spoken*, Lady _.

VISCOUNT'S CHILDREN – As for Baron's children.

The Peerage
and Members of the House of Lords

The rules which govern the creation and succession of peerages are extremely complicated. There are, technically, five separate peerages, the Peerage of England, of Scotland, of Ireland, of Great Britain, and of the United Kingdom. The Peerage of Great Britain dates from 1707 when an Act of Union combined the two kingdoms of England and Scotland and separate peerages were discontinued. The Peerage of the United Kingdom dates from 1801 when Great Britain and Ireland were combined under an Act of Union. Some Scottish peers have received additional peerages of Great Britain or of the United Kingdom since 1707, and some Irish peers additional peerages of the United Kingdom since 1801.

The Peerage of Ireland was not entirely discontinued from 1801 but holders of Irish peerages, whether predating or created subsequent to the Union of 1801, were not entitled to sit in the House of Lords if they had no additional English, Scottish, Great Britain or United Kingdom peerage. However, they are eligible for election to the House of Commons and to vote in parliamentary elections. An Irish peer holding a peerage of a lower grade which enabled him to sit in the House of Lords was introduced there by the title which enabled him to sit, though for all other purposes he was known by his higher title.

In the Peerage of Scotland there is no rank of Baron; the equivalent rank is Lord of Parliament, abbreviated to 'Lord' (the female equivalent is 'Lady'). All peers of England, Scotland, Great Britain or the United Kingdom who are 21 years or over, and of British, Irish or Commonwealth nationality were entitled to sit in the House of Lords until the House of Lords Act 1999, when hereditary peers lost the right to sit. Ninety-two hereditaries are to remain in the House of Lords for a transitional period. In the list below, these peers are indicated by the **. Ten hereditary peers received Life Peerages in 1999 enabling them to remain in the reformed chamber, and two further hereditary peers reverted to sitting by virtue of the Life Peerages they already held.

HEREDITARY WOMEN PEERS

Most hereditary peerages pass on death to the nearest male heir, but there are exceptions, and several are held by women.

A woman peer in her own right retains her title after marriage, and if her husband's rank is the superior she is designated by the two titles jointly, the inferior one second. Her hereditary claim still holds good in spite of any marriage whether higher or lower. No rank held by a woman can confer any title or even precedence upon her husband but the rank of a hereditary woman peer in her own right is inherited by her eldest son (or in some cases daughter).

After the Peerage Act 1963, hereditary women peers in their own right were entitled to sit in the House of Lords, subject to the same qualifications as men, until the House of Lords Act 1999.

LIFE PEERS

Since 1876 non-hereditary or life peerages have been conferred on certain eminent judges to enable the judicial functions of the House of Lords to be carried out. These Lords are known as Lords of Appeal or law lords and, to date, such appointments have all been male.

Since 1958 life peerages have been conferred upon distinguished men and women from all walks of life, giving them seats in the House of Lords in the degree of Baron or Baroness. They are addressed in the same way as hereditary Lords and Barons, and their children have similar courtesy titles.

PEERAGES EXTINCT SINCE THE LAST EDITION

EARLDOMS: Munster (cr. 1831)

VISCOUNTCIES: Lambert (cr. 1945); Leverhulme (cr. 1922)

LIFE PEERAGES: Aldington (cr. 1999); Bellwin (cr. 1979); Brooke of Ystrafellte (cr. 1964); Cledwyn of Penrhos (cr. 1979); Cocks of Hartcliffe (cr. 1987); Cowdry of Tonbridge (cr. 1997); Denton of Wakefield (cr. 1991); Greenhill of Harrow (cr. 1974); Hamlyn (cr. 1998); Harmar-Nicholls (cr. 1974); Harris of Greenwich (cr. 1974); Hartwell (cr. 1968); Kelvedon (cr. 1997); Low (cr. 1999); Lovell-Davis (cr. 1974); McConnell (cr. 1995); MacKay of Ardbrecknish (cr. 1991); Molloy (cr. 1981); Morris of Castle Morris (cr. 1990); Onslow of Woking (cr. 1997); Packenham of Cowely (cr. 1999); Plowden (cr. 1959); Prentice (cr. 1992); Ryder of Warsaw (cr. 1979); Sefton of Garston (cr. 1978); Shepherd of Spalding (cr. 1999); Sieff of Brimpton (cr. 1980); Taylor of Gryfe (cr. 1968).

DISCLAIMER OF PEERAGES

The Peerage Act 1963 enables peers to disclaim their peerages for life. Peers alive in 1963 could disclaim within twelve months after the passing of the Act (31 July 1963); a person subsequently succeeding to a peerage may disclaim within 12 months (one month if an MP) after the date of succession, or of reaching 21, if later. The disclaimer is irrevocable but does not affect the descent of the peerage after the disclaimant's death, and children of a disclaimed peer may, if they wish, retain their precedence and any courtesy titles and styles borne as children of a peer. The disclaimer permitted the disclaimant to sit in the House of Commons if elected as an MP. As the House of Lords Act 1999 removed hereditary peers from the House of Lords, they are now entitled to sit in the House of Commons without having to disclaim their titles.

The following peerages are currently disclaimed:

EARLDOMS: Durham (1970); Selkirk (1994)

VISCOUNTCIES: Hailsham (1963); Stansgate (1963)

BARONIES: Altrincham (1963); Merthyr (1977); Reith (1972); Sanderson of Ayot (1971); Silkin (1972)

PEERS WHO ARE MINORS (i.e. under 21 years of age)

EARLS: Craven (b. 1989)

CONTRACTIONS AND SYMBOLS

s. Scottish title

I. Irish title

*   The peer holds also an Imperial title, specified after the name by Engl., Brit. or UK

** Hereditary peer remaining in the House of Lords for a transitional period

°   there is no 'of' in the title

b. born

s. succeeded

m. married

w. widower or widow

M.minor

†   heir not ascertained at time of going to press

Hereditary Peers

PEERS OF THE BLOOD ROYAL

Style, His Royal Highness The Duke of _/His Royal Highness the Earl of_
Style of address (formal) May it please your Royal Highness; *(informal)* Sir

Created	Title, order of succession, name, etc.	Heir
	Dukes	
1337	*Cornwall,* Charles, Prince of Wales, *s.* 1952 (*see* page 117)	‡
1398	*Rothesay,* Charles, Prince of Wales, *s.* 1952 (*see* page 117)	‡
1986	*York* (1st), The Prince Andrew, Duke of York (*see* page 117)	None
1928	*Gloucester* (2nd), Prince Richard, Duke of Gloucester, *s.* 1974 (*see* page 118)	Earl of Ulster (*see* page 118)
1934	*Kent* (2nd), Prince Edward, Duke of Kent, *s.* 1942 (*see* page 118)	Earl of St Andrews (*see* page 118)
	Earl	
1999	*Wessex* (1st), The Prince Edward, Earl of Wessex (*see* page 117)	None

‡ The title is not hereditary but is held by the Sovereign's eldest son from the moment of his birth or the Sovereign's accession

DUKES

Coronet, Eight strawberry leaves
Style, His Grace the Duke of _
Wife's style, Her Grace the Duchess of _
Eldest son's style, Takes his father's second title as a courtesy title
Younger sons' style, 'Lord' before forename and family name
Daughters' style, 'Lady' before forename and family name
For forms of address, *see* page 135

Created	Title, order of succession, name, etc.	Heir
1868 I.	*Abercorn* (*5th*), James Hamilton, KG, *b.* 1934, *s.* 1979, *m.*	Marquess of Hamilton, *b.* 1969
1701 S.*	*Argyll* (*13th*) and 6th UK Duke Argyll, *1892*, Torquhil Campbell, *b.* 1968, *s.* 2001	None
1703 S.	*Atholl* (*11th*), John Murray, *b.* 1929, *s.* 1996, *m.*	Marquess of Tullibardine, *b.* 1960
1682	*Beaufort* (*11th*), David Robert Somerset, *b.* 1928, *s.* 1984, *w.*	Marquess of Worcester, *b.* 1952
1694	*Bedford* (*13th*), John Robert Russell, *b.* 1917, *s.* 1953, *m.*	Marquess of Tavistock, *b.* 1940
1663 S.*	*Buccleuch* (*9th*) and Queensberry (*11th*) (S. *1684*) and 8th Eng. Earl, Doncaster, 1662, Walter Francis John Montagu Douglas Scott, KT, VRD, *b.* 1923, *s.* 1973, *m.*	Earl of Dalkeith, *b.* 1954
1694	*Devonshire* (*11th*), Andrew Robert Buxton Cavendish, KG, MC, PC, *b.* 1920, *s.* 1950, *m.*	Marquess of Hartington, CBE, *b.* 1944
1947	*Edinburgh* (*1st*), HRH The Prince Philip, Duke of Edinburgh, (*see* page 117)	The Prince of Wales §, (see *page 117*)
1900	*Fife* (*3rd*) and 12th Scott. Earl, Southesk, 1633, (S. *1992*), James George Alexander Bannerman Carnegie, *b.* 1929, *s.* 1959 (*see* page 128)	Earl of Southesk, *b.* 1961
1675	*Grafton* (*11th*), Hugh Denis Charles FitzRoy, KG, *b.* 1919, *s.* 1970, *m.*	Earl of Euston, *b.* 1947
1643 S.*	*Hamilton* (*15th*) and Brandon (*12th*) (Brit. *1711*), Angus Alan Douglas Douglas-Hamilton, *b.* 1938, *s.* 1973, *Premier Peer of Scotland*	Marquess of Douglas and Clydesdale, *b.* 1978
1766 I.*	*Leinster* (*8th*) and 8th Brit. Visct., Leinster, 1747, Gerald FitzGerald, *b.* 1914, *s.* 1976, *m.,* *Premier Duke and Marquess of Ireland*	Marquess of Kildare, *b.* 1948
1719	*Manchester* (*12th*), Angus Charles Drogo Montagu, *b.* 1938, *s.* 1985, *m.*	Viscount Mandeville, *b.* 1962
1702	*Marlborough* (*11th*), John George Vanderbilt Henry Spencer-Churchill, *b.* 1926, *s.* 1972, *m.*	Marquess of Blandford, *b.* 1955
1707 S.*	** *Montrose* (*8th*) and 6th Brit. Earl, Graham, 1722, James Graham, *b.* 1935, *s.* 1992, *m.*	Marquess of Graham, *b.* 1973
1483	** *Norfolk* (*17th*) and 12th Eng. Baron, Beaumont, 1309, *s.* 1971, and 4th UK Baron Howard of Glossop, 1869, S. 1972, Miles Francis Stapleton Fitzalan-Howard, KG, GCVO, CB, CBE, MC, *b.* 1915, *s.* 1975, *m.,* *Premier Duke and Earl Marshal*	Earl of Arundel and Surrey, *b.* 1956

§ In June 1999 Buckingham Palace revealed that the current Earl of Wessex would be given the Dukedom of Edinburgh when the present title returns to the Crown

Created	Title, order of succession, name, etc.	Heir
1766	Northumberland (12th), Ralph George Algernon Percy, b. 1956, s. 1995, m.	Earl Percy, b. 1984
1675	Richmond (10th) and Gordon (5th) (UK 1876) and Scott. Duke Lennox (10th), Charles Henry Gordon Lennox, b. 1929, s. 1989, m.	Earl of March and Kinrara, b. 1955
1707 S.*	Roxburghe (10th) and 5th UK Earl, Innes, 1837, Guy David Innes-Ker, b. 1954, s. 1974, m., Premier Baronet of Scotland	Marquess of Bowmont and Cessford, b. 1981
1703	Rutland (11th), David Charles Robert Manners, b. 1959, s. 1999, m.	Marquis of Granby, b. 1999
1684	St Albans (14th), Murray de Vere Beauclerk, b. 1939, s. 1988, m.	Earl of Burford, b. 1965
1547	Somerset (19th), John Michael Edward Seymour, b. 1952, s. 1984, m.	Lord Seymour, b. 1982
1833	Sutherland (7th) and 6th UK Earl, Ellesmere, 1846, Francis Ronald Egerton, b. 1940, s. 2000, m.	Marquess of Stafford, b. 1975
1814	Wellington (8th) and 9th Irish Earl, Mornington, 1760, Arthur Valerian Wellesley, KG, LVO, OBE, MC, b. 1915, s. 1972, m.	Marquess of Douro, b. 1945
1874	Westminster (6th), Gerald Cavendish Grosvenor, OBE, b. 1951, s. 1979, m.	Earl Grosvenor, b. 1991

MARQUESSES

Coronet, Four strawberry leaves alternating with four silver balls
Style, The Most Hon. the Marquess (of) _ . In Scotland the spelling 'Marquis' is preferred for pre-Union creations
Wife's style, The Most Hon. the Marchioness (of) _
Eldest son's style, Takes his father's second title as a courtesy title
Younger sons' style, 'Lord' before forename and family name
Daughters' style, 'Lady' before forename and family name
For forms of address, see page 135

Created	Title, order of succession, name, etc.	Heir
1916	Aberdeen and Temair (6th) and Scott. Earl, Aberdeen, 1682, Alastair Ninian John Gordon, b. 1920, s. 1984, m.	Earl Haddo, b. 1955
1876	Abergavenny (6th), Christopher George Charles Nevill, b. 1955, s. 2000, m.	David M. R. N., b. 1941
1821	Ailesbury (8th), Michael Sidney Cedric Brudenell-Bruce, b. 1926, s. 1974	Earl of Cardigan, b. 1952
1831	Ailsa (8th) and 20th Scott. Earl, Cassillis, 1509, Archibald Angus Charles Kennedy, b. 1956, s. 1994	Lord David Kennedy, b. 1958
1815	Anglesey (7th), George Charles Henry Victor Paget, b. 1922, s. 1947, m.	Earl of Uxbridge, b. 1950
1789	Bath (7th), Alexander George Thynn, b. 1932, s. 1992, m.	Viscount Weymouth, b. 1974
1826	Bristol (8th), Frederick William Augustus Hervey, b. 1979, s. 1999	Timothy H. H., b. 1960
1796	Bute (7th) and 12th Scott. Earl, Dumfries, 1633, John Colum Crichton-Stuart, b. 1958, s. 1993, m.	Earl of Dumfries, b. 1989
1812	°Camden (6th), David George Edward Henry Pratt, b. 1930, s. 1983	Earl of Brecknock, b. 1965
1815	** Cholmondeley (7th) and 11th Irish Visct., Cholmondeley, 1661, David George Philip Cholmondeley, b. 1960, s. 1990, Lord Great Chamberlain	Charles G. C., b. 1959
1816	°Conyngham (7th) and 7th UK Baron, Minster, 1821, Frederick William Henry Francis Conyngham, b. 1924, s. 1974, m.	Earl of Mount Charles, b. 1951
1791 I.*	Donegall (7th) and 7th Brit. Baron, Fisherwick, 1790 and 6th Brit. Baron Templemore, 1831, S. 1953, Dermot Richard Claud Chichester, LVO, b. 1916, s. 1975, w.	Earl of Belfast, b. 1952
1789 I.*	Downshire (8th) and 8th Brit. Earl, Hillsborough, 1772, (Arthur) Robin Ian Hill, b. 1929, s. 1989, m.	Earl of Hillsborough, b. 1959
1801 I.*	Ely (8th) and 8th UK Baron, Loftus, 1801, Charles John Tottenham, b. 1913, s. 1969, m.	Viscount Loftus, b. 1943
1801	Exeter (8th), (William) Michael Anthony Cecil, b. 1935, s. 1988, m.	Lord Burghley, b. 1970
1800 I.*	Headfort (6th) and 4th UK Baron, Kenlis, 1831, Thomas Geoffrey Charles Michael Taylour, b. 1932, s. 1960, m.	Earl of Bective, b. 1959
1793	Hertford (9th) and 10th Irish Baron, Conway, 1712, Henry Jocelyn Seymour, b. 1958, s. 1997, m.	Earl of Yarmouth, b. 1958
1599 S.*	Huntly (13th) and 5th UK Baron, Meldrum, 1815, Granville Charles Gomer Gordon, b. 1944, s. 1987, m., Premier Marquess of Scotland	Earl of Aboyne, b. 1973
1784	Lansdowne (9th) and 9th Irish Earl, Kerry, 1723, Charles Maurice Mercer NairnePetty-Fitzmaurice, b. 1941, s. 1999, m.	Earl of Shelbourne, b. 1941
1902	Linlithgow (4th) and 10th Scott. Earl, Hopetoun, 1703, Adrian John Charles Hope, b. 1946, s. 1987, m.	Earl of Hopetown, b. 1969
1816 I.*	Londonderry (9th) and 6th UK Earl, Vane, 1823, Alexander Charles Robert Vane-Tempest-Stewart, b. 1937, s. 1955, m.	Viscount Castlereagh, b. 1972

Created	Title, order of succession, name, etc.	Heir
1701 S.*	Lothian (12th) and 6th UK Baron, Kerr, 1821, Peter Francis Walter Kerr, KCVO, b. 1922, s. 1940, m.	Earl of Ancram, PC, MP, b. 1945
1917	Milford Haven (4th), George Ivar Louis Mountbatten, b. 1961, s. 1970, m.	Earl of Medina, b. 1991
1838	Normanby (5th) and 9th Irish Baron, Mulgrave, 1767, Constantine Edmund Walter Phipps, b. 1954, s. 1994, m.	Earl of Mulgrave, b. 1994
1812	Northampton (7th), Spencer Douglas David Compton, b. 1946, s. 1978, m.	Earl Compton, b. 1973
1682 S.	Queensberry (12th), David Harrington Angus Douglas, b. 1929, s. 1954	Viscount Drumlanrig, b. 1967
1926	Reading (4th), Simon Charles Henry Rufus Isaacs, b. 1942, s. 1980, m.	Viscount Erleigh, b. 1986
1789	Salisbury (6th), Robert Edward Peter Cecil, b. 1916, s. 1972, m.	Viscount Cranborne, PC, b. 1946 (see also Baron Cecil)
1800 I.*	Sligo (11th) and 11th UK Baron, Monteagle, 1806, Jeremy Ulick Browne, b. 1939, s. 1991, m.	Sebastian U. B., b. 1964
1787	° Townshend (7th), George John Patrick Dominic Townshend, b. 1916, s. 1921, w.	Viscount Raynham, b. 1945
1694	° Tweeddale (13th) and 4th UK Baron Tweeddale, 1881, Edward Douglas John Hay, b. 1947, s. 1979	Lord Charles D. M. H., b. 1947
1789 I.*	Waterford (8th) and 8th Brit. Baron Tyrone, 1786, John Hubert de la Poer Beresford, b. 1933, s. 1934, m.	Earl of Tyrone, b. 1958
1551	Winchester (18th), Nigel George Paulet, b. 1941, s. 1968, m., Premier Marquess of England	Earl of Wiltshire, b. 1969
1892	Zetland (4th) and 6th UK Earl, Zetland, 1838 and 7th Brit. Baron Dundas, 1794, Lawrence Mark Dundas, b. 1937, s. 1989, m.	Earl of Ronaldshay, b. 1965

EARLS

Coronet, Eight silver balls on stalks alternating with eight gold strawberry leaves
Style, The Right Hon. the Earl (of) _
Wife's style, The Right Hon. the Countess (of) _
Eldest son's style, Takes his father's second title as a courtesy title
Younger sons' style, 'The Hon.' before forename and family name
Daughters' style, 'Lady' before forename and family name
For forms of address, see page 135

Created	Title, order of succession, name, etc.	Heir
1639 S.	Airlie (13th), David George Coke Patrick Ogilvy, KT, GCVO, PC, b. 1926, s. 1968, m.	Lord Ogilvy, b. 1958
1696	Albemarle (10th), Rufus Arnold Alexis Keppel, b. 1965, s. 1979	Crispian W. J. K., b. 1948
1952	° Alexander of Tunis (2nd), Shane William Desmond Alexander, b. 1935, s. 1969, m.	Hon. Brian J. A., b. 1939
1662	Annandale and Hartfell (11th), Patrick Andrew Wentworth Hope Johnstone, b. 1941, m., claim established 1985	Lord Johnstone, b. 1971
1789	° Annesley (10th), Patrick Annesley, b. 1924, s. 1979, m.	Hon. Philip H. A., b. 1927
1785	Antrim (9th), Alexander Randal Mark McDonnell, b. 1935, s. 1977, m.	Viscount Dunluce, b. 1967
1762	** Arran (9th) and 5th UK Baron Sudley, 1884, Arthur Desmond Colquhoun Gore, b. 1938, s. 1983, m.	Paul A. G., CMG, CVO, b. 1921
1955	°** Attlee (3rd), John Richard Attlee, b. 1956, s. 1991, m.	None
1714	Aylesford (11th), Charles Ian Finch-Knightley, b. 1918, s. 1958, w.	Lord Guernsey, b. 1947
1937	°** Baldwin of Bewdley (4th), Edward Alfred Alexander Baldwin, b. 1938, s. 1976, m.	Viscount Corvedale, b. 1973
1922	Balfour (4th), Gerald Arthur James Balfour, b. 1925, s. 1968, m.	Roderick F. A. G., b. 1948
1772	° Bathurst (8th), Henry Allen John Bathurst, b. 1927, s. 1943, m.	Lord Apsley, b. 1961
1919	° Beatty (3rd), David Beatty, b. 1946, s. 1972, m.	Viscount Borodale, b. 1973
1797	Belmore (8th), John Armar Lowry-Corry, b. 1951, s. 1960, m.	Viscount Corry, b. 1985
1739	Bessborough (11th) and 8th UK Baron Duncannon, 1834, Arthur Mountifort Longfield Ponsonby, b. 1912, s. 1993, m.	Viscount Duncannon, b. 1941
1815	Bradford (7th), Richard Thomas Orlando Bridgeman, b. 1947, s. 1981, m.	Viscount Newport, b. 1980
1469	Buchan (17th) and 8th UK Baron Erskine, 1806, Malcolm Harry Erskine, b. 1930, s. 1984, m.	Lord Cardross, b. 1960
1746	Buckinghamshire (10th), (George) Miles Hobart-Hampden, b. 1944, s. 1983, m.	Sir John Hobart, Bt., b. 1945
1800	° Cadogan (8th), Charles Gerald John Cadogan, b. 1937, s. 1997, m.	Viscount Chelsea, b. 1966
1878	° Cairns (6th), Simon Dallas Cairns, CBE, b. 1939, s. 1989, m.	Viscount Garmoyle, b. 1965
1455	** Caithness (20th), Malcolm Ian Sinclair, PC, b. 1948, s. 1965, w.	Lord Berriedale, b. 1981

Created	Title, order of succession, name, etc.	Heir
1800	Caledon (7th), Nicholas James Alexander, b. 1955, s. 1980, m.	Viscount Alexander, b. 1990
1661	Carlisle (13th) and 13th Scott. Baron Ruthven of Freeland, 1651, George William Beaumont Howard, b. 1949, s. 1994	Hon. Philip C. W. H., b. 1963
1793	Carnarvon (8th), George Reginald Oliver Molyneux Herbert, b. 1956, s. 2001, m.	Hon. George K. O. M. H., b. 1992
1748 I.*	Carrick (10th) and 4th UK Baron Butler, 1912, David James Theobald Somerset Butler, b. 1953, s. 1992, m.	Viscount Ikerrin, b. 1975
1800 I.°	Castle Stewart (8th), Arthur Patrick Avondale Stuart, b. 1928, s. 1961, m.	Viscount Stuart, b. 1953
1814	° Cathcart (7th) and 16th Scott. Baron Cathcart, 1447, Charles Alan Andrew Cathcart, b. 1952, s. 1999, m.	Lord Greenock, b. 1952
1647	Cavan. The 12th Earl died in 1988. Heir had not established his claim to the title at the time of going to press	Roger C. Lambart, b. 1944
1827	° Cawdor (7th), Colin Robert Vaughan Campbell, b. 1962, s. 1993, m.	Hon. Frederick W. C., b. 1965
1801	Chichester (9th), John Nicholas Pelham, b. 1944, s. 1944, m.	Richard A. H. P., b. 1952
1803 I.	Clancarty (9th) and 8th UK Visct. Clancarty, 1823, Nicholas Power Richard Le Poer Trench, b. 1952, s. 1995	None
1776 I.	Clanwilliam (7th) and 5th UK Baron Clanwilliam, 1828, John Herbert Meade, b. 1919, s. 1989, m.	Lord Gillford, b. 1960
1776	Clarendon (7th), George Frederick Laurence Hyde Villiers, b. 1933, s. 1955, m.	Lord Hyde, b. 1976
1620 I.	Cork and Orrery (14th) (I. 1660) and 10th Brit. Baron Boyle of Marston, 1711, John William Boyle, DSC, b. 1916, s. 1995, m.	Viscount Dungarvan, b. 1945
1850	Cottenham (8th), Kenelm Charles Everard Digby Pepys, b. 1948, s. 1968, m.	Viscount Crowhurst, b. 1983
1762 I.	** Courtown (9th) and 8th Brit. Baron Saltersford, 1796, James Patrick Montagu Burgoyne Winthrop Stopford, b. 1954, s. 1975, m.	Viscount Stopford, b. 1988
1697	Coventry (11th), George William Coventry, b. 1934, s. 1940, m.	Francis H. C., b. 1912
1857	° Cowley (7th), Garret Graham Wellesley, b. 1934, s. 1975, m.	Viscount Dangan, b. 1965
1892	Cranbrook (5th), Gathorne Gathorne-Hardy, b. 1933, s. 1978, m.	Lord Medway, b. 1968
1801	Craven (9th), Benjamin Robert Joseph Craven, b. 1989, s. 1990	Rupert J. E. C., b. 1926
1398 S.*	Crawford (29th) and 12th UK Baron, Wigan, 1826 (s. 1651) and 5th UK Baron, Wigan, 1826 and Baron Balniel (life peerage, 1974), Robert Alexander Lindsay, KT, PC, b. 1927, s. 1975, m., Premier Earl on Union Roll	Lord Balniel, b. 1958
1861	Cromartie (5th), John Ruaridh Blunt Grant Mackenzie, b. 1948, s. 1989, m.	Viscount Tarbat, b. 1987
1901	Cromer (4th), Evelyn Rowland Esmond Baring, b. 1946, s. 1991, m.	Viscount Errington, b 1994
1633 S.*	Dalhousie (17th) and 5th UK Baron Ramsay, 1875, James Hubert Ramsay, b. 1948, s. 1999, m.	Lord Ramsay, b. 1948
1725 I.	Darnley (11th) and 20th Engl. Baron Clifton of Leighton Bromswold, 1608, Adam Ivo Stuart Bligh, b. 1941, s. 1980, m.	Lord Clifton, b. 1968
1711	Dartmouth (10th), William Legge, b. 1949, s. 1997	Hon. Rupert L., b. 1951
1761	° De La Warr (11th), William Herbrand Sackville, b. 1948, s. 1988, m.	Lord Buckhurst, b. 1979
1622	Denbigh (12th) and Desmond (11th) (I. 1622), Alexander Stephen Rudolph Feilding, b. 1970, s. 1995, m.	William D. F, b. 1939
1485	Derby (19th), Edward Richard William Stanley, b. 1962, s. 1994, m.	Lord Stanley, b. 1998
1553	Devon (18th), Hugh Rupert Courtenay, b. 1942, s. 1998, m.	Lord Courtenay, b. 1942
1800 I.*	Donoughmore (8th) and 8th UK Visct. Hutchinson, 1821, Richard Michael John Hely-Hutchinson, b. 1927, s. 1981, m.	Viscount Suirdale, b. 1952
1661 I.*	Drogheda (12th) and 3rd UK Baron Moore, 1954, Henry Dermot Ponsonby Moore, b. 1937, s. 1989, m.	Viscount Moore, b. 1983
1837	Ducie (7th), David Leslie Moreton, b. 1951, s. 1991, m.	Lord Moreton, b. 1981
1860	Dudley (4th), William Humble David Ward, b. 1920, s. 1969, m.	Viscount Ednam, b. 1947
1660 S.*	** Dundee (12th) and 2nd UK Baron Glassary, 1954, Alexander Henry Scrymgeour, b. 1949, s. 1983, m.	Lord Scrymgeour, b. 1982
1669 S.	Dundonald (15th), Iain Alexander Douglas Blair Cochrane, b. 1961, s. 1986, m.	Lord Cochrane, b. 1991
1686 S.	Dunmore (12th), Malcolm Kenneth Murray, b. 1946, s. 1995, m.	Hon. Geoffrey C. M., b.1949
1822 I.	Dunraven and Mount-Earl (7th), Thady Windham Thomas Wyndham-Quin, b. 1939, s. 1965, m.	None
1833	Durham, Antony Claud Frederick Lambton, b. 1922, s. 1970, m., Disclaimed for life 1970	Hon. Edward R. L. (Baron Durham), b. 1961
1837	Effingham (7th) and 17th Engl. Baron Howard of Effingham, 1554, David Mowbray Algernon Howard, b. 1939, s. 1996, m.	Lord Howard of Effingham, b. 1971
1507 S.*	Eglinton (18th) and Winton (9th) and 6th UK Earl Winton, 1859, Archibald George Montgomerie, b. 1939, s. 1966, m.	Lord Montgomerie, b. 1966
1733 I.*	Egmont (11th) and 9th Brit. Baron Lovel and Holland, 1762, Frederick George Moore Perceval, b. 1914, s. 1932, m.	Viscount Perceval, b. 1934
1821	Eldon (5th), John Joseph Nicholas Scott, b. 1937, s. 1976, m.	Viscount Encombe, b. 1962

Created	Title, order of succession, name, etc.	Heir
1633 S.*	Elgin (11th) and Kincardine (15th) (s. 1647) and 4th UK Baron, Elgin, 1849, Andrew Douglas Alexander Thomas Bruce, KT, b. 1924, s. 1968, m.	Lord Bruce, b. 1961
1789 I.*	Enniskillen (7th) and 5th UK Baron, Grinstead, 1815, Andrew John Galbraith Cole, b. 1942, s. 1989, m.	Arthur G. C., b. 1920
1876 I.*	Erne (3rd) and 3rd UK Baron Fermanagh, 1876, Henry George Victor John Crichton, b. 1937, m.	Viscount Crichton, b. 1971
1452 S.	** Erroll (24th), Merlin Sereld Victor Gilbert Hay, b. 1948, s. 1978, m., Hereditary Lord High Constable and Knight Marischal of Scotland	Lord Hay, b. 1984
1661	Essex (10th), Robert Edward de Vere Capell, b. 1920, s. 1981, m.	Viscount Malden, b. 1944
1711	°** Ferrers (13th), Robert Washington Shirley, PC, b. 1929, s. 1954, m.	Viscount Tamworth, b. 1952
1789	° Fortescue (8th), Charles Hugh Richard Fortescue, b. 1951, s. 1993, m.	Hon. Martin D. F., b. 1924
1841	Gainsborough (5th), Anthony Gerard Edward Noel, b. 1923, s. 1927, m.	Viscount Campden, b. 1950
1623 S.*	Galloway (13th) and 6th Brit. Baron of Garlies, 1796, Randolph Keith Reginald Stewart, b. 1928, s. 1978, w.	Andrew C. S., b. 1949
1703 S.*	Glasgow (10th) and 4th UK Baron, Farlie, 1897, Patrick Robin Archibald Boyle, b. 1939, s. 1984, m.	Viscount of Kelburn, b. 1978
1806 I.*	Gosford (7th) and 5th UK Baron, Worlingham, 1835, Charles David Nicholas Alexander John Sparrow Acheson, b. 1942, s. 1966, m.	Hon. Patrick B. V. M. A., b. 1915
1945	Gowrie (2nd) and 3rd UK Baron Ruthven of Gowrie, 1919, Alexander Patric Greysteil Hore-Ruthven, PC, b. 1939, s. 1955, m.	Viscount Ruthven of Canberra, b. 1964
1684 I.*	Granard (10th) and 5th UK Baron, Granard, 1806, Peter Arthur Edward Hastings Forbes, b. 1957, s. 1992, m.	Viscount Forbes, b. 1981
1833	° Granville (6th), Granville George Fergus Leveson-Gower, b. 1959, s. 1996, m.	Hon. Niall J. L.-G., b. 1963
1806	° Grey (6th), Richard Fleming George Charles Grey, b. 1939, s. 1963, m.	Philip K. G., b. 1940
1752	Guilford (10th), Piers Edward Brownlow North, b. 1971, s. 1999, m.	Hon. Charles E. N., b. 1918
1619	Haddington (13th), John George Baillie-Hamilton, b. 1941, s. 1986, m.	Lord Binning, b. 1985
1919	° Haig (2nd), George Alexander Eugene Douglas Haig, OBE, b. 1918, s. 1928, m.	Viscount Dawick, b. 1961
1944	Halifax (3rd) and 5th UK Visct., Halifax, 1866, Charles Edward Peter Neil Wood, b. 1944, s. 1980, m.	Lord Irwin, b. 1977
1898	Halsbury (4th), Adam Edward Giffard, b. 1934, s. 2000, m.	†
1754	Hardwicke (10th), Joseph Philip Sebastian Yorke, b. 1971, s. 1974	Charles E. Y., b. 1951
1812	Harewood (7th), George Henry Hubert Lascelles, KBE, b. 1923, s. 1947, m. (see also page 127)	Viscount Lascelles, b. 1950 (see also page 126)
1742	Harrington (11th) and 8th Brit. Visct. Stanhope of Mahon, 1717, William Henry Leicester Stanhope, b. 1922, s. 1929, m.	Viscount Petersham, b. 1945
1809	Harrowby (7th), Dudley Danvers Granville Coutts Ryder, TD, b. 1922, s. 1987, m.	Viscount Sandon, b. 1951
1605	** Home (15th), David Alexander Cospatrick Douglas-Home, CVO, b. 1943, s. 1995, m.	Lord Dunglass, b. 1987
1821	° ** Howe (7th), Frederick Richard Penn Curzon, b. 1951, s. 1984, m.	Viscount Curzon, b. 1994
1529	Huntingdon (16th), William Edward Robin Hood Hastings Bass, LVO, b. 1948, s. 1990, m.	Hon. Simon A. R. H. H. B., b. 1950
1885	Iddesleigh (4th), Stafford Henry Northcote, b. 1932, s. 1970, m.	Viscount St Cyres, b. 1957
1756	Ilchester (9th), Maurice Vivian de Touffreville Fox-Strangways, b. 1920, s. 1970, m.	Hon. Raymond G. F.-S., b. 1921
1929	Inchcape (4th), (Kenneth) Peter (Lyle) Mackay, b. 1943, s. 1994, m.	Viscount Glenapp, b. 1979
1919	Iveagh (4th), Arthur Edward Rory Guinness, b. 1969, s. 1992	Hon. Rory M. B. G., b. 1974
1925	° Jellicoe (2nd) and Baron Jellicoe of Southampton (life peerage, 1999), George Patrick John Rushworth Jellicoe, KBE, DSO, MC, PC, FRS, b. 1918, s. 1935, m.	Viscount Brocas, b. 1950
1697	Jersey (10th) and 13th Visct. Grandison, 1620, George Francis William Child Villiers, b. 1976, s. 1998	Hon. Jamie C. V., b. 1994
1822 I.	Kilmorey (6th), Richard Francis Needham, KT, PC, b. 1942, s. 1977, m. (does not use title)	Viscount Newry and Morne, b. 1966
1866	Kimberley (4th), John Wodehouse, b. 1924, s. 1941, m.	Lord Wodehouse, b. 1951
1768 I.	Kingston (11th), Barclay Robert Edwin King-Tenison, b. 1943, s. 1948, m.	Viscount Kingsborough, b. 1969
1633 S.*	Kinnoull (15th) and 9th Brit. Baron Hay of Pedwardine, 1711, Arthur William George Patrick Hay, b. 1935, s. 1938, m.	Viscount Dupplin, b. 1962
1677 S.*	Kintore (13th) and 3rd UK Visct. Stonehaven, 1938, Michael Canning William John Keith, b. 1939, s. 1989, m.	Lord Inverurie, b. 1976
1914	° Kitchener of Khartoum (3rd), Henry Herbert Kitchener, TD, b. 1919, s. 1937	None
1624	Lauderdale (17th), Patrick Francis Maitland, b. 1911, s. 1968, m.	Viscount Maitland, b. 1937
1837	Leicester (7th), Edward Douglas Coke, b. 1936, s. 1994, m.	Viscount Coke, b. 1965
1641 S.*	Leven (14th) and Melville (13th) (s. 1690), Alexander Robert Leslie Melville, b. 1924, s. 1947, m.	Lord Balgonie, b. 1954
1831	Lichfield (5th), Thomas Patrick John Anson, b. 1939, s. 1960	Viscount Anson, b. 1978

Created	Title, order of succession, name, etc.	Heir
1803 I.*	*Limerick (6th) and 6th UK Baron Foxford*, 1815, Patrick Edmund Pery, KBE, b. 1930, s. 1967, m.	Viscount Glentworth, b. 1963
1572	*Lincoln (18th)*, Robert Edward Fiennes-Clinton, s. 2001	†
1633 S.	** *Lindsay (16th)*, James Randolph Lindesay-Bethune, b. 1955, s. 1989, m.	Viscount Garnock, b. 1990
1626	*Lindsey (14th) and Abingdon (9th) (1682)*, Richard Henry Rupert Bertie, b. 1931, s. 1963, m.	Lord Norreys, b. 1958
1776 I.	*Lisburne (8th)*, John David Malet Vaughan, b. 1918, s. 1965, m.	Viscount Vaughan, b. 1945
1822 I.*	** *Listowel (6th) and 4th UK Baron Hare*, 1869, Francis Michael Hare, b. 1964, s. 1997, m.	Hon. Timothy P. H., b. 1966
1905	** *Liverpool (5th)*, Edward Peter Bertram Savile Foljambe, b. 1944, s. 1969, m.	Viscount Hawkesbury, b. 1972
1945	° *Lloyd George of Dwyfor (3rd)*, Owen Lloyd George, b. 1924, s. 1968, m.	Viscount Gwynedd, b. 1951
1785 I.*	*Longford (8th) and 2nd UK Baron Pakenham*, 1945, Thomas Frank Dermot Pakenham, s. 2001, m.	Hon. Edward M. P., b. 1970
1807	*Lonsdale (7th)*, James Hugh William Lowther, b. 1922, s. 1953, m.	Viscount Lowther, b. 1949
1838	*Lovelace (5th) and 12th Brit. Baron King*, 1725, Peter Axel William Locke King, b. 1951, s. 1964, m.	None
1795 I.*	*Lucan (7th) and 3rd UK Baron Bingham*, 1934, Richard John Bingham, b. 1934, s. 1964, m.	Lord Bingham, b. 1967
1880	*Lytton (5th) and 18th Engl. Baron, Wentworth*, 1529, John Peter Michael Scawen Lytton, b. 1950, s. 1985, m.	Viscount Knebworth, b. 1989
1721	*Macclesfield (9th)*, Richard Timothy George Mansfield Parker, b. 1943, s. 1992, m.	Hon. J. David G. P., b. 1945
1800	*Malmesbury (6th)*, William James Harris, TD, b. 1907, s. 1950, w.	Viscount FitzHarris, b. 1946
1776 & 1792	*Mansfield and Mansfield (8th) and 14th Scott. Visct. Stormont*, 1621, William David Mungo James Murray, b. 1930, s. 1971, m.	Viscount Stormont, b. 1956
1565 S.*	** *Mar (14th) and Kellie (16th) (S. 1616) and Baron Erkine of Alloa Tower (life peerage, 2000)*, James Thorne Erskine, b. 1949, s. 1994, m.	Hon. Alexander D. E., b. 1952
1785 I.	*Mayo (10th)*, Terence Patrick Bourke, b. 1929, s. 1962	Lord Naas, b. 1953
1627 I.*	*Meath (15th) and 6th UK Baron, Chaworth*, 1831, John Anthony Brabazon, b. 1941, s. 1998, m.	Lord Ardee, b. 1941
1766	*Mexborough (8th)*, John Christopher George Savile, b. 1931, s. 1980, m.	Viscount Pollington, b. 1959
1813	*Minto (6th)*, Gilbert Edward George Lariston Elliot-Murray-Kynynmound, OBE, b. 1928, s. 1975, m.	Viscount Melgund, b. 1953
1562 S.*	*Moray (20th) and 12th Brit. Baron Stuart of Castle Stuart*, 1796, Douglas John Moray Stuart, b. 1928, s. 1974, m.	Lord Doune, b. 1966
1815	*Morley (6th)*, John St Aubyn Parker, KCVO, b. 1923, s. 1962, m.	Viscount Boringdon, b. 1956
1458	*Morton (22nd)*, John Charles Sholto Douglas, b. 1927, s. 1976, m.	Lord Aberdour, b. 1952
1789	*Mount Edgcumbe (8th)*, Robert Charles Edgcumbe, b. 1939, s. 1982	Piers V. E., b. 1946
1805	° *Nelson (9th)*, Peter John Horatio Nelson, b. 1941, s. 1981, m.	Viscount Merton, b. 1971
1660 S.	*Newburgh (12th)*, Don Filippo Giambattista Camillo Francesco Aldo Ma Rospigliosi, b. 1942, s. 1986, m.	Princess Donna Benedetta F. M. R., b. 1974
1827 I.	*Norbury (6th)*, Noel Terence Graham-Toler, b. 1939, s. 1955, m.	Viscount Glandine, b. 1967
1806 I.*	*Normanton (6th) and 9th Brit. Baron Mendip, 1794, and 4th UK Baron, Somerton*, 1873, Shaun James Christian Welbore Ellis Agar, b. 1945, s. 1967, m.	Viscount Somerton, b. 1982
1647 S.**	*Northesk (14th)*, David John MacRae Carnegie, b. 1954, s. 1994, m.	Lord Rosehill, b. 1980
1801	** *Onslow (7th)*, Michael William Coplestone Dillon Onslow, b. 1938, s. 1971, m.	Viscount Cranley, b. 1967
1696 S.	*Orkney (9th)*, (Oliver) Peter St John, b. 1938, s. 1998, m.	Viscount Kirkwall, b. 1969
1328	*Ormonde and Ossory.* The 8th Marquess of Ormonde died in 1997, when the marquessate became extinct. The heir to his earldoms had not established his claim at the time of going to press.	Viscount Mountgarret, b. 1936 (see page 146)
1925	*Oxford and Asquith (2nd)*, Julian Edward George Asquith, KCMG, b. 1916, s. 1928, w.	Viscount Asquith, OBE, b. 1952
1929	°** *Peel (3rd) and 4th UK Viscount Peel*, 1895, William James Robert Peel, b. 1947, s. 1969, m.	Viscount Clanfield, b. 1976
1551	*Pembroke (17th) and Montgomery (14th) (1605)*, Henry George Charles Alexander Herbert, b. 1939, s. 1969	Lord Herbert, b. 1978
1605	*Perth (17th)*, John David Drummond, PC, b. 1907, s. 1951, w.	Viscount Strathallan, b. 1935
1905	*Plymouth (3rd) and 15th Engl. Baron, Windsor*, 1529, Other Robert Ivor Windsor-Clive, b. 1923, s. 1943, m.	Viscount Windsor, b. 1951
1785	*Portarlington (7th)*, George Lionel Yuill Seymour Dawson-Damer, b. 1938, s. 1959, m.	Viscount Carlow, b. 1965
1689	*Portland (12th)*, Count Timothy Charles Robert Noel Bentinck, b. 1953, s. 1997, m.	Viscount Woodstock, b. 1984
1743	*Portsmouth (10th)*, Quentin Gerard Carew Wallop, b. 1954, s. 1984, m.	Viscount Lymington, b. 1981

Created	Title, order of succession, name, etc.	Heir
1804	Powis (8th) and 9th Irish Baron, Clive, 1762, John George Herbert, b. 1952, s. 1993, m.	Viscount Clive, b. 1979
1765	Radnor (8th), Jacob Pleydell-Bouverie, BT, b. 1927, s. 1968, m.	Viscount Folkestone, b. 1955
1831 I.*	Ranfurly (7th) and 8th UK Baron, Ranfurly, 1826, Gerald Françoys Needham Knox, b. 1929, s. 1988, m.	Edward J. K., b. 1957
1771	Roden (10th), Robert John Jocelyn, b. 1938, s. 1993, m.	Viscount Jocelyn, b. 1989
1801	Romney (7th), Michael Henry Marsham, b. 1910, s. 1975, m.	Julian C. M., b. 1948
1703 S.*	Rosebery (7th) and 3rd UK Earl Midlothian, 1911, Neil Archibald Primrose, b. 1929, s. 1974, m.	Lord Dalmeny, b. 1967
1806 I.	Rosse (7th), William Brendan Parsons, b. 1936, s. 1979, m.	Lord Oxmantown, b. 1969.
1801	** Rosslyn (7th), Peter St Clair-Erskine, b. 1958, s. 1977, m.	Lord Loughborough, b. 1986
1457 S.	Rothes (21st), Ian Lionel Malcolm Leslie, b. 1932, s. 1975, m.	Lord Leslie, b. 1958
1861	°** Russell (5th), Conrad Sebastian Robert Russell, FBA, b. 1937, s. 1987, m.	Viscount Amberley, b. 1968
1915	° St Aldwyn (3rd), Michael Henry Hicks Beach, b. 1950, s. 1992, m.	Hon. David S. H. B., b. 1955
1815	St Germans (10th), Peregrine Nicholas Eliot, b. 1941, s. 1988	Lord Eliot, b. 1966
1660	** Sandwich (11th), John Edward Hollister Montagu, b. 1943, s. 1995, m.	Viscount Hinchingbrooke, b. 1969
1690	Scarbrough (12th) and 13th Irish Visct. Lumley, 1628, Richard Aldred Lumley, b. 1932, s. 1969, m.	Viscount Lumley, b. 1973
1701 S.	Seafield (13th), Ian Derek Francis Ogilvie-Grant, b. 1939, s. 1969, m.	Viscount Reidhaven, b. 1963
1882	** Selborne (4th), John Roundell Palmer, KBE, FRS, b. 1940, s. 1971, m.	Viscount Wolmer, b. 1971
1646 S.	Selkirk. Disclaimed for life 1994. (see Lord Selkirk of Douglas, page 161)	Hon. John A. D.-H., b. 1978
1672	Shaftesbury (10th), Anthony Ashley-Cooper, b. 1938, s. 1961, m.	Lord Ashley, b. 1977
1756 I.*	Shannon (9th) and 8th Brit. Baron Carleton, 1786, Richard Bentinck Boyle, b. 1924, s. 1963	Viscount Boyle, b. 1960
1442	** Shrewsbury and Waterford (22nd) and 7th Engl. Earl Talbot, 1784, Charles Henry John Benedict Crofton Chetwynd Chetwynd-Talbot, b. 1952, s. 1980, m., Premier Earl of England and Ireland	Viscount Ingestre, b. 1978
1961	Snowdon (1st) and Baron Armstrong-Jones (life peerage, 1999), Antony Charles Robert Armstrong-Jones, GCVO, b. 1930, m. Constable of Caernarfon Castle (see also page 117)	Viscount Linley, b. 1961
1765	° Spencer (9th), Charles Edward Maurice Spencer, b. 1964, s. 1992	Viscount Althorp, b. 1994
1703 S.*	Stair (14th) and 7th UK Baron, Oxenfoord, 1841, John David James Dalrymple, b. 1961, s. 1996	Hon. David H. D., b. 1963
1984	Stockton (2nd), Alexander Daniel Alan Macmillan, MEP, b. 1943, s. 1986, m.	Viscount Macmillan of Ovenden, b. 1974
1821	Stradbroke (6th), Robert Keith Rous, b. 1937, s. 1983, m.	Viscount Dunwich, b. 1961
1847	Strafford (8th), Thomas Edmund Byng, b. 1936, s. 1984, m.	Viscount Enfield, b. 1964
1606 S.*	Strathmore and Kinghorne (18th) and 16th Scott. Earl, Strathmore, 1677 and 18th Scott. Earl, Kinghorne, 1606 and 5th UK Earl, Strathmore and Kinghorne, 1937, Michael Fergus Bowes Lyon, b. 1957, s. 1987, m.	Lord Glamis, b. 1986
1603	Suffolk (21st) and Berkshire (14th) (1626), Michael John James George Robert Howard, b. 1935, s. 1941, m.	Viscount Andover, b. 1974
1955	Swinton (2nd), David Yarburgh Cunliffe-Lister, b. 1937, s. 1972, m.	Hon. Nicholas J. C.-L., b. 1939
1714	Tankerville (10th), Peter Grey Bennet, b. 1956, s. 1980	Revd the Hon. George A. G. B., b. 1925
1822	° Temple of Stowe (8th), (Walter) Grenville Algernon Temple-Gore-Langton, b. 1924, s. 1988, m.	Lord Langton, b. 1955
1815	Verulam (7th) and 11th Irish Visct. Grimston, 1719 and 16th Scott. Baron Forrester of Corstorphine, 1633, John Duncan Grimston, b. 1951, s. 1973, m.	Viscount Grimston, b. 1978
1729	° Waldegrave (13th), James Sherbrooke Waldegrave, b. 1940, s. 1995, m.	Viscount Chewton, b. 1986
1759	Warwick (9th) and Brooke (9th) (Brit. 1746), Guy David Greville, b. 1957, s. 1996, m.	Lord Brooke, b. 1982
1633 S.*	Wemyss (12th) and March (8th) and 5th UK Baron Wemyss, 1821, Francis David Charteris, KT, b. 1912, s. 1937, m.	Lord Neidpath, b. 1948
1621 I.	Westmeath (13th), William Anthony Nugent, b. 1928, s. 1971, m.	Hon. Sean C. W. N., b. 1965
1624	Westmorland (16th), Anthony David Francis Henry Fane, b. 1951, s. 1993, m.	Hon. Harry St C. F., b. 1953
1876	Wharncliffe (5th), Richard Alan Montagu Stuart Wortley, b. 1953, s. 1987, m.	Viscount Carlton, b. 1980
1801	Wilton (8th) and Ebury (1857), Francis Egerton Grosvenor, b. 1934, s. 1999, m.	Hon. Julian F. M. G., b. 1959
1628	Winchilsea (17th) and Nottingham (12th) (1681), Daniel James Hatfield Finch Hatton, b. 1967, s. 1999, m.	Hon. Robin H. F.-H., b. 1939
1766	° Winterton (8th), (Donald) David Turnour, b. 1943, s. 1991, m.	Robert C. T., b. 1950
1956	Woolton (3rd), Simon Frederick Marquis, b. 1958, s. 1969, m.	None
1837	Yarborough (8th), Charles John Pelham, b. 1963, s. 1991, m.	Lord Worsley, b. 1990

COUNTESSES IN THEIR OWN RIGHT

Style, The Right Hon. the Countess (of) _
Husband, Untitled
Children's style, As for children of an Earl
For forms of address, *see* page 135

Created	Title, order of succession, name, etc.	Heir
1643 S.	*Dysart (11th in line)*, Rosamund Agnes Greaves, *b.* 1914, *s.* 1975	Lady Katherine Grant of Rothiemurchus, *b.* 1918
1633 S.	*Loudoun (13th in line)*, Barbara Huddleston Abney-Hastings, *b.* 1919, *s.* 1960, *m.*	Lord Mauchline, *b.* 1942
c.1115 S.	** *Mar (31st in line)*, Margaret of Mar, *b.* 1940, *s.* 1975, *m.*, *Premier Earldom of Scotland*	Mistress of Mar, *b.* 1963
1947	° *Mountbatten of Burma (2nd in line)*, Patricia Edwina Victoria Knatchbull, CBE, *b.* 1924, *s.* 1979, *m.*	Lord Romsey, *b.* 1947
c.1235 S.	*Sutherland (24th in line)*, Elizabeth Millicent Sutherland, *b.* 1921, *s.* 1963, *m.*	Lord Strathnaver, *b.* 1947

VISCOUNTS

Coronet, Sixteen silver balls
Style, The Right Hon. the Viscount _
Wife's style, The Right Hon. the Viscountess _
Children's style, 'The Hon.' before forename and family name
In Scotland, the heir apparent to a Viscount may be styled 'The Master of _ (title of peer)'
For forms of address, *see* page 135

Created	Title, order of succession, name, etc.	Heir
1945	*Addison (4th)*, William Matthew Wand Addison, *b.* 1945, *s.* 1992, *m.*	Hon. Paul W. A., *b.* 1973
1946	*Alanbrooke (3rd)*, Alan Victor Harold Brooke, *b.* 1932, *s.* 1972	None
1919	** *Allenby (3rd)*, Lt.-Col. Michael Jaffray Hynman Allenby, *b.* 1931, *s.* 1984, *m.*	Hon. Henry J. H. A., *b.* 1968
1911	*Allendale (3rd)*, Wentworth Hubert Charles Beaumont, *b.* 1922, *s.* 1956	Hon. Wentworth P. I. B., *b.* 1948
1642 S.	*Arbuthnott (16th)*, John Campbell Arbuthnott, KT, CBE, DSC, FRSE, *b.* 1924, *s.* 1966, *m.*	Master of Arbuthnott, *b.* 1950
1751 I.	*Ashbrook (11th)*, Michael Llowarch Warburton Flower, *b.* 1935, *s.* 1995, *m.*	Hon. Rowland F. W. F., *b.* 1975
1917	** *Astor (4th)*, William Waldorf Astor, *b.* 1951, *s.* 1966, *m.*	Hon. William W. A., *b.* 1979
1781 I.	*Bangor (8th)*, William Maxwell David Ward, *b.* 1948, *s.* 1993, *m.*	Hon. E. Nicholas W., *b.* 1953
1925	*Bearsted (5th)*, Nicholas Alan Samuel, *b.* 1950, *s.* 1996, *m.*	Hon. Harry R. S., *b.* 1988
1963	*Blakenham (2nd)*, Michael John Hare, *b.* 1938, *s.* 1982, *m.*	Hon. Caspar J. H., *b.* 1972
1935	** *Bledisloe (3rd)*, Christopher Hiley Ludlow Bathurst, QC, *b.* 1934, *s.* 1979	Hon. Rupert E. L. B., *b.* 1964
1712	*Bolingbroke (7th) and St John (8th) (1716)*, Kenneth Oliver Musgrave St John, *b.* 1927, *s.* 1974	Hon. Henry F. St J., *b.* 1957
1960	*Boyd of Merton (2nd)*, Simon Donald Rupert Neville Lennox-Boyd, *b.* 1939, *s.* 1983, *m.*	Hon. Benjamin A. L.-B., *b.* 1964
1717 I.*	*Boyne (11th) and 5th UK Baron Brancepeth*, 1866, Gustavus Michael Stucley Hamilton-Russell, *b.* 1965, *s.* 1995, *m.*	Brian G. H.-R., *b.* 1940
1929	*Brentford (4th)*, Crispin William Joynson-Hicks, *b.* 1933, *s.* 1983, *m.*	Hon. Paul W. J.-H., *b.* 1971
1929	** *Bridgeman (3rd)*, Robin John Orlando Bridgeman, *b.* 1930, *s.* 1982, *m.*	Hon. William O. C. B., *b.* 1968
1868	*Bridport (4th) and 7th Duke, Bronte in Sicily, 1799 and 6th Irish Baron Bridport*, 1794, Alexander Nelson Hood, *b.* 1948, *s.* 1969, *m.*	Hon. Peregrine A. N. H., *b.* 1974
1952	** *Brookeborough (3rd)*, Alan Henry Brooke, *b.* 1952, *s.* 1987, *m.*	Hon. Christopher A. B., *b.* 1954
1933	*Buckmaster (3rd)*, Martin Stanley Buckmaster, OBE, *b.* 1921, *s.* 1974	Hon. Colin J. B., *b.* 1923
1939	*Caldecote (3rd)*, Piers James Hampden Inskip, *b.* 1947, *s.* 1999, *m.*	Hon. Thomas J. H. I., *b.* 1985
1941	*Camrose (4th)*, Adrian Michael Berry, *s.* 2001, *m.*	Hon. Jonathan W. B., *b.* 1970
1954	*Chandos (3rd) and Baron Lyttelton of Aldershot (life peerage, 2000)* Thomas Orlando Lyttelton, *b.* 1953, *s.* 1980, *m.*	Hon. Oliver A. L., *b.* 1986

Created	Title, order of succession, name, etc.	Heir
1665 I.*	*Charlemont (14th) and 18th Irish Baron Caulfield of Charlemont*, 1620, John Day Caulfeild, *b.* 1934, *s.* 1985, *m.*	Hon. John D. C., *b.* 1966
1921	*Chelmsford (4th) and UK Baron Chelmsford*, 1858, Frederic Corin Piers Thesiger, *b.* 1962, *s.* 1999	To Barony only, Sir Wilfred P. T., KBE, *b.* 1910
1717 I.	*Chetwynd (10th)*, Adam Richard John Casson Chetwynd, *b.* 1935, *s.* 1965, *m.*	Hon. Adam D. C., *b.* 1969
1911	*Chilston (4th)*, Alastair George Akers-Douglas, *b.* 1946, *s.* 1982, *m.*	Hon. Oliver I. A.-D., *b.* 1973
1902	*Churchill (3rd) and 5th UK Baron Churchill*, 1815, Victor George Spencer, *b.* 1934, *s.* 1973	To Barony only, Richard H. R. S., *b.* 1926
1718	*Cobham (11th) and 8th Irish Baron Westcote*, 1776, John William Leonard Lyttelton, *b.* 1943, *s.* 1977, *m.*	Hon. Christopher C. L., *b.* 1947
1902	** *Colville of Culross (4th) and 13th Scott. Baron Colville of Culcross*, 1604, John Mark Alexander Colville, QC, *b.* 1933, *s.* 1945, *m.*	Master of Colville, *b.* 1959
1826	*Combermere (6th)*, Thomas Robert Wellington Stapleton-Cotton, *s.* 2001	Hon. David P. D., *b.* 1932
1917	*Cowdray (4th) and 4th UK Baron Cowdray*, 1910, Michael Orlando Weetman Pearson, *b.* 1944, *s.* 1995, *m.*	Hon. Peregrine J. D. P., *b.* 1994
1927	** *Craigavon (3rd)*, Janric Fraser Craig, *b.* 1944, *s.* 1974	None
1886	*Cross (3rd)*, Assheton Henry Cross, *b.* 1920, *s.* 1932	None
1943	*Daventry (4th)*, James Edward FitzRoy Newdegate, *b.* 1960, *s.* 2000, *m.*	Hon. Humphrey J. F. N., *b.* 1995
1937	*Davidson (2nd)*, John Andrew Davidson, *b.* 1928, *s.* 1970, *m.*	Hon. Malcolm W. M. D., *b.* 1934
1956	*De L'Isle (2nd) and 7th UK Baron de L'Isle and Dudley*, 1835, Philip John Algernon Sidney, MBE, *b.* 1945, *s.* 1991, *m.*	Hon. Philip W. E. S., *b.* 1985
1776 I.*	*De Vesci (7th) and 8th Irish Baron Knapton*, 1750, Thomas Eustace Vesey, *b.* 1955, *s.* 1983, *m.*	Hon. Oliver I. V., *b.* 1991
1917	*Devonport (3rd)*, Terence Kearley, *b.* 1944, *s.* 1973	Chester D. H. K., *b.* 1932
1964	*Dilhorne (2nd)*, John Mervyn Manningham-Buller, *b.* 1932, *s.* 1980, *m.*	Hon. James E. M.-B., *b.* 1956
1622 I.	*Dillon (22nd)*, Henry Benedict Charles Dillon, *b.* 1973, *s.* 1982	Hon. Richard A. L. D., *b.* 1948
1785 I.	*Doneraile (10th)*, Richard Allen St Leger, *b.* 1946, *s.* 1983, *m.*	Hon. Nathaniel W. R. St J. St L., *b.* 1971
1680 I.*	*Downe (11th) and 4th UK Baron Dawnay*, 1897, John Christian George Dawnay, *b.* 1935, *s.* 1965, *m.*	Hon. Richard H. D., *b.* 1967
1959	*Dunrossil (3rd)*, Andrew William Reginald Morrison, *b.* 1953, *s.* 2000, *m.*	Hon. Callum A. B. M., *b.* 1994
1964	*Eccles (2nd)*, John Dawson Eccles, CBE, *b.* 1931, *s.* 1999, *m.*	Hon. William D. E., *b.* 1960
1897	*Esher (4th)*, Lionel Gordon Baliol Brett, CBE, *b.* 1913, *s.* 1963, *m.*	Hon. Christopher L. B. B., *b.* 1936
1816	*Exmouth (10th)*, Paul Edward Pellew, *b.* 1940, *s.* 1970, *m.*	Hon. Edward F. P., *b.* 1978
1620 S.	** *Falkland (15th)*, Lucius Edward William Plantagenet Cary, *b.* 1935, *s.* 1984, *m.*, *Premier Scottish Viscount on the Roll*	Master of Falkland, *b.* 1963
1720	*Falmouth (9th) and 26th Engl. Baron Le Despencer*, 1264, George Hugh Boscawen, *b.* 1919, *s.* 1962, *m.*	Hon. Evelyn A. H. B., *b.* 1955
1720 I.*	*Gage (8th) and 7th Brit. Baron Gage*, 1790, (Henry) Nicolas Gage, *b.* 1934, *s.* 1993, *m.*	Hon. Henry W. G., *b.* 1975
1727 I.	*Galway (12th)*, George Rupert Monckton-Arundell, *b.* 1922, *s.* 1980, *m.*	Hon. J. Philip M., *b.* 1952
1478 I.*	*Gormanston (17th) and 5th UK Baron Gormanston*, 1868, Jenico Nicholas Dudley Preston, *b.* 1939, *s.* 1940, *w.*, *Premier Viscount of Ireland*	Hon. Jenico F. T. P., *b.* 1974
1816 I.	*Gort (9th)*, Foley Robert Standish Prendergast Vereker, *b.* 1951, *s.* 1995, *m.*	Hon. Robert F. P. V., *b.* 1993
1900	** *Goschen (4th)*, Giles John Harry Goschen, *b.* 1965, *s.* 1977, *m.*	John A. G., *b.* 1992
1849	*Gough (5th)*, Shane Hugh Maryon Gough, *b.* 1941, *s.* 1951	None
1937	*Greenwood (3rd)*, Michael George Hamar Greenwood, *b.* 1923, *s.* 1998	None
1929	*Hailsham*. Disclaimed for life 1963 (*see* Lord Hailsham of St Marylebone, page 159)	Rt. Hon. Douglas M. Hogg, QC, MP, *b.* 1945
1891	*Hambleden (4th)*, William Herbert Smith, *b.* 1930, *s.* 1948, *m.*	Hon. William H. B. S., *b.* 1955
1884	*Hampden (6th)*, Anthony David Brand, *b.* 1937, *s.* 1975, *m.*	Hon. Francis A. B., *b.* 1970
1936	*Hanworth (3rd)*, David Stephen Geoffrey Pollock, *b.* 1946, *s.* 1996, *m.*	Hon. Richard C. S. P., *b.* 1951
1791 I.	*Harberton (10th)*, Thomas de Vautort Pomeroy, *b.* 1910, *s.* 1980, *w.*	Henry R. P., *b.* 1958
1846	*Hardinge (6th)*, Charles Henry Nicholas Hardinge, *b.* 1956, *s.* 1984, *m.*	Hon. Andrew H. H., *b.* 1960
1791 I.	*Hawarden (9th)*, (Robert) Connan Wyndham Leslie Maude, *b.* 1961, *s.* 1991, *m.*	Hon. Varian J. C. E. M., *b.* 1997
1960	*Head (2nd)*, Richard Antony Head, *b.* 1937, *s.* 1983, *m.*	Hon. Henry J. H., *b.* 1980
1550	*Hereford (18th)*, Robert Milo Leicester Devereux, *b.* 1932, *s.* 1952, *Premier Viscount of England*	Hon. Charles R. de B. D., *b.* 1975
1842	*Hill (8th)*, Antony Rowland Clegg-Hill, *b.* 1931, *s.* 1974, *m.*	Peter D. R. C. C.-H., *b.* 1945
1796	*Hood (8th) and 7th Irish Baron, Hood* 1782, Henry Lyttleton Alexander Hood, *b.* 1958, *s.* 1999, *m.*	Hon. Archibald L. S. H., *b.* 1993
1956	*Ingleby (2nd)*, Martin Raymond Peake, *b.* 1926, *s.* 1966, *w.*	None
1945	*Kemsley (3rd)*, Richard Gomer Berry, *b.* 1951, *s.* 1999, *m.*	Hon. Edward A. M., *b.* 1960
1911	*Knollys (3rd)*, David Francis Dudley Knollys, *b.* 1931, *s.* 1966, *m.*	Hon. Patrick N. M. K., *b.* 1962

Created	Title, order of succession, name, etc.	Heir
1895	*Knutsford (6th)*, Michael Holland-Hibbert, *b.* 1926, *s.* 1986, *m.*	Hon. Henry T. H.-H., *b.* 1959
1954	*Leathers (3rd)*, Christopher Graeme Leathers, *b.* 1941, *s.* 1996, *m.*	Hon. James F. L., *b.* 1969
1781 I.	*Lifford (9th)*, (Edward) James Wingfield Hewitt, *b.* 1949, *s.* 1987, *m.*	Hon. James T. W. H., *b.* 1979
1921	*Long (4th)*, Richard Gerard Long, CBE, *b.* 1929, *s.* 1967, *m.*	Hon. James R. L., *b.* 1960
1957	*Mackintosh of Halifax (3rd)*, (John) Clive Mackintosh, *b.* 1958, *s.* 1980, *m.*	Hon. Thomas H. G. M., *b.* 1985
1955	*Malvern (3rd)*, Ashley Kevin Godfrey Huggins, *b.* 1949, *s.* 1978	Hon. M. James H., *b.* 1928
1945	*Marchwood (3rd)*, David George Staveley Penny, *b.* 1936, *s.* 1979, *w.*	Hon. Peter G. W. P., *b.* 1965
1942	*Margesson (2nd)*, Francis Vere Hampden Margesson, *b.* 1922, *s.* 1965, *m.*	Capt. Hon. Richard F. D. M., *b.* 1960
1660 I.*	*Massereene (14th) and Ferrard (7th) (1797) and 7th UK Baron, Oriel*, 1821, John David Clotworthy Whyte-Melville Foster Skeffington, *b.* 1940, *s.* 1992, *m.*	Hon. Charles J. C. W.-M. F. S., *b.* 1973
1802	*Melville (9th)*, Robert David Ross Dundas, *b.* 1937, *s.* 1971, *m.*	Hon. Robert H. K. D., *b.* 1984
1916	*Mersey (4th) and 13th Scott. Lord Nairne, 1681 s.* 1995, Richard Maurice Clive Bigham, *b.* 1934, *s.* 1979, *m.*	Master of Nairne, *b.* 1966
1717 I.*	*Midleton (12th) and 9th Brit. Baron Brodrick of Peper Harow*, 1796, Alan Henry Brodrick, *b.* 1949, *s.* 1988, *m.*	Hon. Ashley R. B., *b.* 1980
1962	*Mills (3rd)*, Christopher Philip Roger Mills, *b.* 1956, *s.* 1988, *m.*	None
1716 I.	*Molesworth (12th)*, Robert Bysse Kelham Molesworth, *b.* 1959, *s.* 1997	Hon. William J. C. M., *b.* 1960
1801 I.*	*Monck (7th) and 4th UK Baron, Monck*, 1866, Charles Stanley Monck, *b.* 1953, *s.* 1982. Does not use title.	Hon. George S. M., *b.* 1957
1957	*Monckton of Brenchley (2nd)*, Maj.-Gen. Gilbert Walter Riversdale Monckton, CB, OBE, MC, *b.* 1915, *s.* 1965, *m.*	Hon. Christopher W. M., *b.* 1952
1946	*Montgomery of Alamein (2nd)*, David Bernard Montgomery, CBE, *b.* 1928, *s.* 1976, *m.*	Hon. Henry D. M., *b.* 1954
• 1550 I.*	*Mountgarret (17th) and 4th UK Baron Mountgarret*, 1911, Richard Henry Piers Butler, *b.* 1936, *s.* 1966, *m.*	Hon. Piers J. R. B., *b.* 1961
1952	*Norwich (2nd)*, John Julius Cooper, CVO, *b.* 1929, *s.* 1954, *m.*	Hon. Jason C. D. B. C., *b.* 1959
1651 S.**	*of Oxfuird (13th)*, George Hubbard Makgill, CBE, *b.* 1934, *s.* 1986, *m.*	Master of Oxfuird, *b.* 1969
1873	*Portman (10th)*, Christopher Edward Berkeley Portman, *b.* 1958, *s.* 1999, *m.*	Hon. Luke O. B. P., *b.* 1984
1743 I.*	*Powerscourt (10th) and 4th UK Baron Powerscourt*, 1885, Mervyn Niall Wingfield, *b.* 1935, *s.* 1973, *m.*	Hon. Mervyn A. W., *b.* 1963
1900	*Ridley (4th)*, Matthew White Ridley, KG, GCVO, TD, *b.* 1925, *s.* 1964, *m.*, Lord Steward	Hon. Matthew W. R., *b.* 1958
1960	*Rochdale (2nd)*, St John Durival Kemp, *b.* 1938, *s.* 1993, *m.*	Hon. Jonathan H. D. K., *b.* 1961
1919	*Rothermere (4th)*, (Harold) Jonathan Esmond Vere Harmsworth, *b.* 1967, *s.* 1998, *m.*	Hon. Esmond V. H., *b.* 1967
1937	*Runciman of Doxford (3rd) and 4th UK Baron, Runciman*, 1933, Walter Garrison Runciman (Garry), CBE, FBA, *b.* 1934, *s.* 1989, *m.*	Hon. David W. R., *b.* 1967
1918	** *St Davids (3rd) and 20th Engl. Baron Strange of Knokin, 1299 and 8th Engl. Baron, Hungerford, 1426 and Baron De Moleyns*, 1445, Colwyn Jestyn John Philipps, *b.* 1939, *s.* 1991, *m.*	Hon. Rhodri C. P., *b.* 1966
1801	*St Vincent (7th)*, Ronald George James Jervis, *b.* 1905, *s.* 1940, *m.*	Hon. Edward R. J. J., *b.* 1951
1937	*Samuel (3rd)*, David Herbert Samuel, OBE, PH.D., *b.* 1922, *s.* 1978, *m.*	Hon. Dan J. S., *b.* 1925
1911	*Scarsdale (3rd) and 7th Brit. Baron Scarsdale*, 1761, Francis John Nathaniel Curzon, *b.* 1924, *s.* 1977, *m.*	Hon. Peter G. N. C., *b.* 1949
1905	*Selby (5th)*, Edward Thomas William Gully, *b.* 1967, *s.* 1997, *m.*	Hon. Christopher R. T. G., *b.* 1993
1805	*Sidmouth (7th)*, John Tonge Anthony Pellew Addington, *b.* 1914, *s.* 1976, *m.*	Hon. Jeremy F. A., *b.* 1947
1940	** *Simon (3rd)*, Jan David Simon, *b.* 1940, *s.* 1993, *m.*	None
1960	** *Slim (2nd)*, John Douglas Slim, OBE, *b.* 1927, *s.* 1970, *m.*	Hon. Mark W. R. S., *b.* 1960
1954	*Soulbury (2nd)*, James Herwald Ramsbotham, *b.* 1915, *s.* 1971, *w.*	Hon. Sir Peter E. R., GCMG, GCVO, *b.* 1919
1776 I.	*Southwell (7th)*, Pyers Anthony Joseph Southwell, *b.* 1930, *s.* 1960, *m.*	Hon. Richard A. P. S., *b.* 1956
1942	*Stansgate*, Rt. Hon. Anthony Neil Wedgwood Benn, *b.* 1925, *s.* 1960, *m.* Disclaimed for life 1963.	Stephen M. W. B., *b.* 1951
1959	*Stuart of Findhorn (3rd)*, James Dominic Stuart, *b.* 1948, *s.* 1999, *m.*	Hon. Andrew M. S., *b.* 1957
1957	** *Tenby (3rd)*, William Lloyd George, *b.* 1927, *s.* 1983, *m.*	Hon. Timothy H. G. L. G., *b.* 1962
1952	*Thurso (3rd)*, John Archibald Sinclair, *b.* 1953, *s.* 1995, *m.*	Hon. James A. R. S., *b.* 1984
1721	*Torrington (11th)*, Timothy Howard St George Byng, *b.* 1943, *s.* 1961, *m.*	John L. B., MC, *b.* 1919
1936	*Trenchard (3rd)*, Hugh Trenchard, *b.* 1951, *s.* 1987, *m.*	Hon. Alexander T. T., *b.* 1978
1921	*Ullswater (2nd)*, Nicholas James Christopher Lowther, PC, *b.* 1942, *s.* 1949, *m.*	Hon. Benjamin J. L., *b.* 1975
1621 I.	*Valentia (15th)*, Richard John Dighton Annesley, *b.* 1929, *s.* 1983, *m.*	Hon. Francis W. D. A., *b.* 1959
1952	** *Waverley (3rd)*, John Desmond Forbes Anderson, *b.* 1949, *s.* 1990	Hon. Forbes A. R. A., *b.* 1996
1938	*Weir (3rd)*, William Kenneth James Weir, *b.* 1933, *s.* 1975, *m.*	Hon. James W. H. W., *b.* 1965

Created	Title, order of succession, name, etc.	Heir
1918	*Wimborne (4th) and 5th UK Baron Wimborne*, 1880, Ivor Mervyn Vigors Guest, *b.* 1968, *s.* 1993	Hon. Julien J. G., *b.* 1945
1923	*Younger of Leckie (4th) and Baron Younger of Prestwick (life peerage, 1992)*, George Kenneth Hotson Younger, KT, KCVO, TD, PC, *b.* 1931, *s.* 1997, *m.*	Hon. James E. G. Y., *b.* 1955

BARONS/LORDS

Coronet, Six silver balls
Style, The Right Hon. the Lord _ . In the Peerage of Scotland there is no rank of Baron; the equivalent rank is Lord of Parliament (*see* page 136) and Scottish peers should always be styled 'Lord', never 'Baron'
Wife's style, The Right Hon. the Lady _
Children's style, 'The Hon.' before forename and family name
In Scotland, the heir apparent to a Lord may be styled 'The Master of _ (title of peer)'
For forms of address, *see* page 135

Created	Title, order of succession, name, etc.	Heir
1911	*Aberconway (3rd)*, Charles Melville McLaren, *b.* 1913, *s.* 1953, *m.*	Hon. H. Charles M., *b.* 1948
1873	** *Aberdare (4th)*, Morys George Lyndhurst Bruce, KBE, PC, *b.* 1919, *s.* 1957, *m.*	Hon. Alastair J. L. B., *b.* 1947
1835	*Abinger (8th)*, James Richard Scarlett, *b.* 1914, *s.* 1943, *m.*	Hon. James H. S., *b.* 1959
1869	*Acton (4th) and Baron Acton of Bridgnorth (life peerage, 2000)*, Richard Gerald Lyon-Dalberg-Acton, *b.* 1941, *s.* 1989, *m.*	Hon. John C. F. H. L.-D.-A., *b.* 1966
1887	** *Addington (6th)*, Dominic Bryce Hubbard, *b.* 1963, *s.* 1982	Hon. Michael W. L. H., *b.* 1965
1896	*Aldenham (6th) and Hunsdon of Hunsdon (4th) (1923)*, Vicary Tyser Gibbs, *b.* 1948, *s.* 1986, *m.*	Hon. Humphrey W. F. G., *b.* 1989
1962	*Aldington (2nd)*, Charles Harold Stuart Low, *b.* 1948, *s.* 2001, *m.*	Hon. Philip T. A. L., *b.* 1990
1945	*Altrincham.* John Edward Poynder Grigg, *b.* 1924, *s.* 1955, *m.* Disclaimed for life 1963.	Hon. Anthony U. D. D. G.., *b.* 1934
1929	*Alvingham (2nd)*, Maj.-Gen. Robert Guy Eardley Yerburgh, CBE, *b.* 1926, *s.* 1955, *m.*	Capt. Hon. Robert R. G. Y., *b.* 1956
1892	*Amherst of Hackney (4th)*, William Hugh Amherst Cecil, *b.* 1940, *s.* 1980, *m.*	Hon. H. William A. C., *b.* 1968
1881	** *Ampthill (4th)*, Geoffrey Denis Erskine Russell, CBE, PC, *b.* 1921, *s.* 1973	Hon. David W. E. R., *b.* 1947
1947	*Amwell (3rd)*, Keith Norman Montague, *b.* 1943, *s.* 1990, *m.*	Hon. Ian K. M., *b.* 1973
1863	*Annaly (6th)*, Luke Richard White, *b.* 1954, *s.* 1990, *m.*	Hon. Luke H. W., *b.* 1990
1885	*Ashbourne (4th)*, Edward Barry Greynville Gibson, *b.* 1933, *s.* 1983, *m.*	Hon. Edward C. d'O. G., *b.* 1967
1835	*Ashburton (7th)*, John Francis Harcourt Baring, KG, KCVO, *b.* 1928, *s.* 1991, *m.*	Hon. Mark F. R. B., *b.* 1958
1892	*Ashcombe (4th)*, Henry Edward Cubitt, *b.* 1924, *s.* 1962, *m.*	Mark E. C., *b.* 1964
1911	*Ashton of Hyde (3rd)*, Thomas John Ashton, TD, *b.* 1926, *s.* 1983, *m.*	Hon. Thomas H. A., *b.* 1958
1800 I.	*Ashtown (7th)*, Nigel Clive Crosby Trench, KCMG, *b.* 1916, *s.* 1990, *m.*	Hon. Roderick N. G. T., *b.* 1944
1956	** *Astor of Hever (3rd)*, John Jacob Astor, *b.* 1946, *s.* 1984, *m.*	Hon. Charles G. J. A., *b.* 1990
1789 I.*	*Auckland (10th) and 10th Brit. Baron Auckland*, 1793, Robert Ian Burnard Eden, *b.* 1962, *s.* 1997, *m.*	Hon. Ronald J. E., *b.* 1931
1313	*Audley.* The 25th Lord Audley died in July 1997, leaving three co-heiresses.	
1900	** *Avebury (4th)*, Eric Reginald Lubbock, *b.* 1928, *s.* 1971, *m.*	Hon. Lyulph A. J. L., *b.* 1954
1718 I.	*Aylmer (13th)*, Michael Anthony Aylmer, *b.* 1923, *s.* 1982, *m.*	Hon. A. Julian A., *b.* 1951
1929	*Baden-Powell (3rd)*, Robert Crause Baden-Powell, *b.* 1936, *s.* 1962, *m.*	Hon. David M. B.-P., *b.* 1940
1780	*Bagot (9th)*, Heneage Charles Bagot, *b.* 1914, *s.* 1979, *m.*	Hon. C. H. Shaun B., *b.* 1944
1953	*Baillieu (3rd)*, James William Latham Baillieu, *b.* 1950, *s.* 1973, *m.*	Hon. Robert L. B., *b.* 1979
1607 S.	*Balfour of Burleigh (8th)*, Robert Bruce, FRSE, *b.* 1927, *s.* 1967, *m.*	Hon. Victoria B., *b.* 1973
1945	*Balfour of Inchrye (2nd)*, Ian Balfour, *b.* 1924, *s.* 1988, *m.*	None
1924	*Banbury of Southam (3rd)*, Charles William Banbury, *b.* 1953, *s.* 1981, *m.*	None
1698	*Barnard (11th)*, Harry John Neville Vane, TD, *b.* 1923, *s.* 1964	Hon. Henry F. C. V., *b.* 1959
1887	*Basing (5th)*, Neil Lutley Sclater-Booth, *b.* 1939, *s.* 1983, *m.*	Hon. Stuart W. S.-B., *b.* 1969
1917	*Beaverbrook (3rd)*, Maxwell William Humphrey Aitken, *b.* 1951, *s.* 1985, *m.*	Hon. Maxwell F. A., *b.* 1977
1647 S.	*Belhaven and Stenton (13th)*, Robert Anthony Carmichael Hamilton, *b.* 1927, *s.* 1961, *m.*	Master of Belhaven, *b.* 1953
1848 I.	*Bellew (7th)*, James Bryan Bellew, *b.* 1920, *s.* 1981, *m.*	Hon. Bryan E. B., *b.* 1943

Created	Title, order of succession, name, etc.	Heir
1856	Belper (5th), Richard Henry Strutt, b. 1941, s. 1999, m.	Michael H. Richard H. S., b. 1969
1938	Belstead (2nd) and Baron Ganzoni (life peerage, 1999), John Julian Ganzoni, PC, b. 1932, s. 1958	None
1421	Berkeley (18th) and Baron Gueterbock (life peerage, 2000), Anthony Fitzhardinge Gueterbock, OBE, b. 1939, s. 1992, m.	Hon. Thomas F. G., b. 1969
1922	Bethell (4th), Nicholas William Bethell, MEP, b. 1938, s. 1967, m.	Hon. James N. B., b. 1967
1938	Bicester (3rd), Angus Edward Vivian Smith, b. 1932, s. 1968	Hugh C. V. S., b. 1934
1903	Biddulph (5th), (Anthony) Nicholas Colin Maitland Biddulph, b. 1959, s. 1988, m.	Hon. Robert J. M. B., b. 1994
1938	Birdwood (3rd), Mark William Ogilvie Birdwood, b. 1938, s. 1962, m.	None
1958	Birkett (2nd), Michael Birkett, b. 1929, s. 1962, m.	Hon. Thomas B., b. 1982
1907	Blyth (4th), Anthony Audley Rupert Blyth, b. 1931, s. 1977, m.	Hon. Riley A. J. B., b. 1955
1797	Bolton (8th), Harry Algar Nigel Orde-Powlett, b. 1954, s. 2001, m.	Hon. Thomas O.-P., b. 1979
1452 S.	Borthwick (24th), John Hugh Borthwick, b. 1940, s. 1997, m.	Hon. James H. A. B. of Glengelt, b. 1940
1922	Borwick (4th), James Hugh Myles Borwick, MC, b. 1917, s. 1961, m.	Hon. Robin S. B., b. 1927
1761	Boston (10th), Timothy George Frank Boteler Irby, b. 1939, s. 1978, m.	Hon. George W. E. B. I., b. 1971
1942	** Brabazon of Tara (3rd), Ivon Anthony Moore-Brabazon, b. 1946, s. 1974, m.	Hon. Benjamin R. M.-B., b. 1983
1880	Brabourne (7th), John Ulick Knatchbull, CBE, b. 1924, s. 1943, m.	Lord Romsey, b. 1947
1925	Bradbury (3rd), John Bradbury, b. 1940, s. 1994, m.	Hon. John B., b. 1973
1962	Brain (2nd), Christopher Langdon Brain, b. 1926, s. 1966, m.	Hon. Michael C. B., b. 1928
1938	Brassey of Apethorpe (3rd), David Henry Brassey, OBE, b. 1932, s. 1967, m.	Hon. Edward B., b. 1964
1788	Braybrooke (10th), Robin Henry Charles Neville, b. 1932, s. 1990, m.	George N., b. 1943
1957	** Bridges (2nd), Thomas Edward Bridges, GCMG, b. 1927, s. 1969, m.	Hon. Mark T. B., b. 1954
1945	Broadbridge (4th), Martin Hugh Broadbridge, b. 1929, s. 2000, m.	Hon. Richard J. M. B., b. 1959
1933	Brocket (3rd), Charles Ronald George Nall-Cain, b. 1952, s. 1967, m.	Hon. Alexander C. C. N.-C., b. 1984
1860	** Brougham and Vaux (5th), Michael John Brougham, CBE, b. 1938, s. 1967	Hon. Charles W. B., b. 1971
1945	Broughshane (3rd), (William) Kensington Davison, DSO, DFC, b. 1914, s. 1995	None
1776	Brownlow (7th), Edward John Peregrine Cust, b. 1936, s. 1978, m.	Hon. Peregrine E. Q. C., b. 1974
1942	Bruntisfield (2nd), John Robert Warrender, OBE, MC, TD, b. 1921, s. 1993, m.	Hon. Michael J. V. W., b. 1949
1950	Burden (3rd), Andrew Philip Burden, b. 1959, s. 1995	Hon. Fraser W. E. B., b. 1964
1529	Burgh (7th), Alexander Peter Willoughby Leith, b. 1935, s. 1959, m.	Hon. A. Gregory D. L., b. 1958
1903	** Burnham (6th), Hugh John Frederick Lawson, b. 1931, s. 1993, m.	Hon. Harry F. A. L., b. 1968
1897	Burton (3rd), Michael Evan Victor Baillie, b. 1924, s. 1962, m.	Hon. Evan M. R. B., b. 1949
1643	Byron (13th), Robert James Byron, b. 1950, s. 1989, m.	Hon. Charles R. G. B., b. 1990
1937	Cadman (3rd), John Anthony Cadman, b. 1938, s. 1966, m.	Hon. Nicholas A. J. C., b. 1977
1945	Calverley (3rd), Charles Rodney Muff, b. 1946, s. 1971, m.	Hon. Jonathan E. M., b. 1975
1383	Camoys (7th), (Ralph) Thomas Campion George Sherman Stonor, GCVO, PC, b. 1940, s. 1976, m., Lord Chamberlain	Hon. R. William R. T. S., b. 1974
1715 I.	Carbery (11th), Peter Ralfe Harrington Evans-Freke, b. 1920, s. 1970, m.	Hon. Michael P. E.-F., b. 1942
1834 I.*	Carew (7th) and 7th UK Baron, Carew, 1838, Patrick Thomas Conolly-Carew, b. 1938, s. 1994, m.	Hon. William P. C.-C., b. 1973
1916	Carnock (4th), David Henry Arthur Nicolson, b. 1920, s. 1982	Nigel N., MBE, b. 1917
1796 I.*	Carrington (6th) and 6th Brit. Baron Carrington, 1797 and Baron Carington of Upton (life peerage, 1999), Peter Alexander Rupert Carington, KG, GCMG, CH, MC, PC, b. 1919, s. 1938, m.	Hon. Rupert F. J. C., b. 1948
1812	Castlemaine (8th), Roland Thomas John Handcock, MBE, b. 1943, s. 1973, m.	Hon. Ronan M. E. H., b. 1989
1936	Catto (3rd), Innes Gordon Catto, b. 1950, s. 2001, m.	†
1918	Cawley (4th), John Francis Cawley, b. 1946, s. 2001, m.	Hon. William R. H. C., b. 1981
1603	Cecil. A subsidiary title of the Marquess of Salisbury. His heir Viscount Cranborne, was given a Writ in Acceleration in this title to enable him to sit in the House of Lords whilst his father is still alive (see also page 139).	
1937	Chatfield (2nd), Ernle David Lewis Chatfield, b. 1917, s. 1967, m.	None
1858	Chesham (6th), Nicholas Charles Cavendish, b. 1941, s. 1989, m.	Hon. Charles G. C. C., b. 1974
1945	Chetwode (2nd), Philip Chetwode, b. 1937, s. 1950, m.	Hon. Roger C., b. 1968
1945	Chorley (2nd), Roger Richard Edward Chorley, b. 1930, s. 1978, m.	Hon. Nicholas R. D. C., b. 1966
1858	Churston (5th), John Francis Yarde-Buller, b. 1934, s. 1991, m.	Hon. Benjamin F. A. Y.-B., b. 1974
1946	Citrine (3rd), Ronald Eric Citrine, b. 1919, s. 1997, m. Does not use title.	None
1800	Clanmorris (8th), Simon John Ward Bingham, b. 1937, s. 1988, m.	Robert D. de B. B., b. 1942

Created	Title, order of succession, name, etc.	Heir
1672	*Clifford of Chudleigh (14th)*, Thomas Hugh Clifford, *b.* 1948, *s.* 1988, *m.*	Hon. Alexander T. H. C., *b.* 1985
1299	*Clinton (22nd)*, Gerard Nevile Mark Fane Trefusis, *b.* 1934, *m.* Title called out of abeyance 1965.	Hon. Charles P. R. F. T., *b.* 1962
1955	*Clitheroe (2nd)*, Ralph John Assheton, *b.* 1929, *s.* 1984, *m.*	Hon. Ralph C. A., *b.* 1962
1919	*Clwyd (3rd)*, (John) Anthony Roberts, *b.* 1935, *s.* 1987, *m.*	Hon. J. Murray R., *b.* 1971
1948	*Clydesmuir (3rd)*, David Ronald Colville, *b.* 1949, *s.* 1996, *m.*	Hon. Richard C., *b.* 1980
1960	** *Cobbold (2nd)*, David Antony Fromanteel Lytton Cobbold, *b.* 1937, *s.* 1987, *m.*	Hon. Henry F. L. C., *b.* 1962
1919	*Cochrane of Cults (4th)*, (Ralph Henry) Vere Cochrane, *b.* 1926, *s.* 1990, *m.*	Hon. Thomas H. V. C., *b.* 1957
1954	*Coleraine (2nd)*, (James) Martin (Bonar) Law, *b.* 1931, *s.* 1980, *m.*	Hon. James P. B. L., *b.* 1975
1873	*Coleridge (5th)*, William Duke Coleridge, *b.* 1937, *s.* 1984, *m.*	Hon. James D. C., *b.* 1967
1946	*Colgrain (3rd)*, David Colin Campbell, *b.* 1920, *s.* 1973, *m.*	Hon. Alastair C. L. C., *b.* 1951
1917	** *Colwyn (3rd)*, (Ian) Anthony Hamilton-Smith, CBE, *b.* 1942, *s.* 1966, *m.*	Hon. Craig P. H.-S., *b.* 1968
1956	*Colyton (2nd)*, Alisdair John Munro Hopkinson, *b.* 1958, *s.* 1996, *m.*	Hon. James P. M. H., *b.* 1983
1841	*Congleton (8th)*, Christopher Patrick Parnell, *b.* 1930, *s.* 1967, *m.*	Hon. John P. C. P., *b.* 1959
1927	*Cornwallis (3rd)*, Fiennes Neil Wykeham Cornwallis, OBE, *b.* 1921, *s.* 1982, *m.*	Hon. F. W. Jeremy C., *b.* 1946
1874	*Cottesloe (5th)*, Cdr. John Tapling Fremantle, *b.* 1927, *s.* 1994, *m.*	Hon. Thomas F. H. F., *b.* 1966
1929	*Craigmyle (4th)*, Thomas Columba Shaw, *b.* 1960, *s.* 1998, *m.*	Hon. Alexander F. S., *b.* 1988
1899	*Cranworth (3rd)*, Philip Bertram Gurdon, *b.* 1940, *s.* 1964, *m.*	Hon. Sacha W. R. G., *b.* 1970
1959	** *Crathorne (2nd)*, Charles James Dugdale, *b.* 1939, *s.* 1977, *m.*	Hon. Thomas A. J. D., *b.* 1977
1892	*Crawshaw (5th)*, David Gerald Brooks, *b.* 1934, *s.* 1997, *m.*	Hon. John P. B., *b.* 1938
1940	*Croft (3rd)*, Bernard William Henry Page Croft, *b.* 1949, *s.* 1997, *m.*	None
1797 I.	*Crofton (7th)*, Guy Patrick Gilbert Crofton, *b.* 1951, *s.* 1989, *m.*	Hon. E. Harry P. C., *b.* 1988
1375	*Cromwell (7th)*, Godfrey John Bewicke-Copley, *b.* 1960, *s.* 1982, *m.*	Hon. David G. B.-C., *b.* 1997
1947	*Crook (2nd)*, Douglas Edwin Crook, *b.* 1926, *s.* 1989, *m.*	Hon. Robert D. E. C., *b.* 1955
1914	*Cunliffe (3rd)*, Roger Cunliffe, *b.* 1932, *s.* 1963, *m.*	Hon. Henry C., *b.* 1962
1927	*Daresbury (4th)*, Peter Gilbert Greenall, *b.* 1953, *s.* 1996, *m.*	Hon. Thomas E. G., *b.* 1984
1924	*Darling (2nd)*, Robert Charles Henry Darling, *b.* 1919, *s.* 1936, *m.*	Hon. R. Julian H. D., *b.* 1944
1946	*Darwen (3rd)*, Roger Michael Davies, *b.* 1938, *s.* 1988, *m.*	Hon. Paul D., *b.* 1962
1932	*Davies (3rd)*, David Davies, *b.* 1940, *s.* 1944, *m.*	Hon. David D. D., *b.* 1975
1812 I.	*Decies (7th)*, Marcus Hugh Tristram de la Poer Beresford, *b.* 1948, *s.* 1992, *m.*	Hon. Robert M. D. de la P. B., *b.* 1988
1299	*de Clifford (27th)*, John Edward Southwell Russell, *b.* 1928, *s.* 1982, *m.*	Hon. William S. R., *b.* 1930
1851	*De Freyne (7th)*, Francis Arthur John French, *b.* 1927, *s.* 1935, *m.*	Hon. Fulke C. A. J. F., *b.* 1957
1821	*Delamere (5th)*, Hugh George Cholmondeley, *b.* 1934, *s.* 1979, *m.*	Hon. Thomas P. G. C., *b.* 1968
1838	*de Mauley (6th)*, Gerald John Ponsonby, *b.* 1921, *s.* 1962, *m.*	Hon. Col. Thomas M. P., *b.* 1930
1937	** *Denham (2nd)*, Bertram Stanley Mitford Bowyer, KBE, PC, *b.* 1927, *s.* 1948, *m.*	Hon. Richard G. G. B., *b.* 1959
1834	*Denman (5th)*, Charles Spencer Denman, CBE, MC, TD, *b.* 1916, *s.* 1971, *w.*	Hon. Richard T. S. D., *b.* 1946
1885	*Deramore (6th)*, Richard Arthur de Yarburgh-Bateson, *b.* 1911, *s.* 1964, *m.*	None
1887	*De Ramsey (4th)*, John Ailwyn Fellowes, *b.* 1942, *s.* 1993, *m.*	Hon. Freddie J. F., *b.* 1978
1264	*de Ros (28th)*, Peter Trevor Maxwell, *b.* 1958, *s.* 1983, *m.*, Premier Baron of England	Hon. Finbar J. M., *b.* 1988
1881	*Derwent (5th)*, Robin Evelyn Leo Vanden-Bempde-Johnstone, LVO, *b.* 1930, *s.* 1986, *m.*	Hon. Francis P. H. V.-B.-J., *b.* 1965
1831	*de Saumarez (7th)*, Eric Douglas Saumarez, *b.* 1956, *s.* 1991, *m.*	Hon. Victor T. S., *b.* 1956
1910	*de Villiers (3rd)*, Arthur Percy de Villiers, *b.* 1911, *s.* 1934	Hon. Alexander C. de V., *b.* 1940
1930	*Dickinson (2nd)*, Richard Clavering Hyett Dickinson, *b.* 1926, *s.* 1943, *m.*	Hon. Martin H. D., *b.* 1961
1620 I.*	*Digby (12th)*, Edward Henry Kenelm Digby, KCVO, *b.* 1924, *s.* 1964, *m.*	Hon. Henry N. K. D., *b.* 1954
1765	*Digby (6th)*, Edward Henry Kenelm Digby, KCVO, *b.* 1924, *m.*	Hon. Henry N. K. D., *b.* 1954
1615	*Dormer (17th)*, Geoffrey Henry Dormer, *b.* 1920, *s.* 1995, *m.*	Hon. William R. D., *b.* 1960
1943	*Dowding (3rd)*, Piers Hugh Tremenheere Dowding, *b.* 1948, *s.* 1992	Hon. Mark D. J. D., *b.* 1949
1800 I.	*Dufferin and Clandeboye.* The 10th Baron died in 1991. Heir had not established his claim to the title at the time of going to press.	Sir John Blackwood, Bt., *b.* 1944
1929	*Dulverton (3rd)*, (Gilbert) Michael Hamilton Wills, *b.* 1944, *s.* 1992	Hon. Robert A. H. W., *b.* 1983
1800 I.	*Dunalley (7th)*, Henry Francis Cornelius Prittie, *b.* 1948, *s.* 1992, *m.*	Hon. Joel H. P., *b.* 1981
1324 I.	*Dunboyne (28th)*, Patrick Theobald Tower Butler, VRD, *b.* 1917, *s.* 1945, *m.*	Hon. John F. B., *b.* 1951
1892	*Dunleath (6th)*, Brian Henry Mulholland, *b.* 1950, *s.* 1997, *m.*	Hon. Andrew H. M., *b.* 1981
1439 I.	*Dunsany (20th)*, Edward John Carlos Plunkett, *b.* 1939, *s.* 1999, *m.*	Hon. Randal P., *b.* 1983
1780	*Dynevor (9th)*, Richard Charles Uryan Rhys, *b.* 1935, *s.* 1962	Hon. Hugo G. U. R., *b.* 1966
1963	*Egremont (2nd)* and 7th UK Baron Leconfield, 1859, John Max Henry Scawen Wyndham, *b.* 1948, *s.* 1972, *m.*	Hon. George R. V. W., *b.* 1983
1643	*Elibank (14th)*, Alan D'Ardis Erskine-Murray, *b.* 1923, *s.* 1973, *w.*	Master of Elibank, *b.* 1964

Created	Title, order of succession, name, etc.	Heir
1802	*Ellenborough (8th)*, Richard Edward Cecil Law, *b.* 1926, *s.* 1945, *m.*	Maj. Hon. Rupert E. H. L., *b.* 1955
1509 S.*	*Elphinstone (19th)* and 5th UK Baron Elphinstone, 1885, Alexander Mountstuart Elphinstone, *b.* 1980, *s.* 1994	Hon. Angus J. E., *b.* 1982
1934	** *Elton (2nd)*, Rodney Elton, TD, *b.* 1930, *s.* 1973, *m.*	Hon. Edward P. E., *b.* 1966
1627 S.	*Fairfax of Cameron (14th)*, Nicholas John Albert Fairfax, *b.* 1956, *s.* 1964, *m.*	Hon. Edward N. T. F., *b.* 1984
1961	*Fairhaven (3rd)*, Ailwyn Henry George Broughton, *b.* 1936, *s.* 1973, *m.*	Maj. Hon. James H. A. B., *b.* 1963
1916	*Faringdon (3rd)*, Charles Michael Henderson, *b.* 1937, *s.* 1977, *m.*	Hon. James H. H., *b.* 1961
1756	*Farnham (12th)*, Barry Owen Somerset Maxwell, *b.* 1931, *s.* 1957, *m.*	Hon. Simon K. M., *b.* 1933
1856	*Fermoy (6th)*, Patrick Maurice Burke Roche, *b.* 1967, *s.* 1984, *m.*	Hon. E. Hugh B. R., *b.* 1972
1826	*Feversham (6th)*, Charles Antony Peter Duncombe, *b.* 1945, *s.* 1963, *m.*	Hon. Jasper O. S. D., *b.* 1968
1798 I.	*ffrench (8th)*, Robuck John Peter Charles Mario ffrench, *b.* 1956, *s.* 1986, *m.*	Hon. John C. M. J. F. ff., *b.* 1928
1909	*Fisher (3rd)*, John Vavasseur Fisher, DSC, *b.* 1921, *s.* 1955, *m.*	Hon. Patrick V. F., *b.* 1953
1295	*Fitzwalter (21st)* (Fitzwalter) Brook Plumptre, *b.* 1914, *m.* Title called out of abeyance 1953.	Hon. Julian B. P., *b.* 1952
1776	*Foley (8th)*, Adrian Gerald Foley, *b.* 1923, *s.* 1927, *m.*	Hon. Thomas H. F., *b.* 1961
1445	*Forbes (22nd)*, Nigel Ivan Forbes, KBE, *b.* 1918, *s.* 1953, *m.*, *Premier Lord of Scotland*	Master of Forbes, *b.* 1946
1821	*Forester (8th)* (George Cecil) Brooke Weld-Forester, *b.* 1938, *s.* 1977, *m.*	Hon. C. R. George W.-F., *b.* 1975
1922	*Forres (4th)*, Alastair Stephen Grant Williamson, *b.* 1946, *s.* 1978, *m.*	Hon. George A. M. W., *b.* 1972
1917	*Forteviot (4th)*, John James Evelyn Dewar, *b.* 1938, *s.* 1993, *m.*	Hon. Alexander J. E. D., *b.* 1971
1951	** *Freyberg (3rd)*, Valerian Bernard Freyberg, *b.* 1970, *s.* 1993	None
1917	*Gainford (3rd)*, Joseph Edward Pease, *b.* 1921, *s.* 1971, *m.*	Hon. George P., *b.* 1926
1818	*Garvagh (5th)*, (Alexander Leopold Ivor) George Canning, *b.* 1920, *s.* 1956, *m.*	Hon. Spencer G. S. de R. C., *b.* 1953
1942	** *Geddes (3rd)*, Euan Michael Ross Geddes, *b.* 1937, *s.* 1975, *m.*	Hon. James G. N. G., *b.* 1969
1876	*Gerard (5th)*, Anthony Robert Hugo Gerard, *b.* 1949, *s.* 1992, *m.*	Hon. Rupert B. C. G., *b.* 1981
1824	*Gifford (6th)*, Anthony Maurice Gifford, QC, *b.* 1940, *s.* 1961, *m.*	Hon. Thomas A. G., *b.* 1967
1917	*Gisborough (3rd)*, Thomas Richard John Long Chaloner, *b.* 1927, *s.* 1951, *m.*	Hon. T. Peregrine L. C., *b.* 1961
1960	*Gladwyn (2nd)*, Miles Alvery Gladwyn Jebb, *b.* 1930, *s.* 1996	None
1899	*Glanusk (5th)*, Christopher Russell Bailey, *b.* 1942, *s.* 1997, *m.*	Hon. Charles H. B., *b.* 1976
1918	** *Glenarthur (4th)*, Simon Mark Arthur, *b.* 1944, *s.* 1976, *m.*	Hon. Edward A. A., *b.* 1973
1911	*Glenconner (3rd)*, Colin Christopher Paget Tennant, *b.* 1926, *s.* 1983, *m.*	Hon. Cody T., *b.* 1994
1964	*Glendevon (2nd)*, Julian John Somerset Hope, *b.* 1950, *s.* 1996	Hon. Jonathan C. H., *b.* 1952
1922	*Glendyne (3rd)*, Robert Nivison, *b.* 1926, *s.* 1967, *m.*	Hon. John N., *b.* 1960
1939	** *Glentoran (3rd)* (Thomas) Robin (Valerian) Dixon, CBE, *b.* 1935, *s.* 1995, *m.*	Hon. Daniel G. D., *b.* 1959
1909	*Gorell (4th)*, Timothy John Radcliffe Barnes, *b.* 1927, *s.* 1963, *m.*	Hon. Ronald A. H. B., *b.* 1931
1953	*Grantchester (3rd)*, Christopher John Suenson-Taylor, *b.* 1951, *s.* 1995, *m.*	Hon. Jesse D. S.-T., *b.* 1977
1782	*Grantley (8th)*, Richard William Brinsley Norton, *b.* 1956, *s.* 1995	Hon. Francis J. H. N., *b.* 1960
1794 I.	*Graves (9th)*, Evelyn Paget Graves, *b.* 1926, *s.* 1994, *m.*	Hon. Timothy E. G., *b.* 1960
1445 S.	*Gray (22nd)*, Angus Diarmid Ian Campbell-Gray, *b.* 1931, *s.* 1946, *m.*	Master of Grey, *b.* 1964
1950	*Greenhill (3rd)*, Malcolm Greenhill, *b.* 1924, *s.* 1989	None
1927	** *Greenway (4th)*, Ambrose Charles Drexel Greenway, *b.* 1941, *s.* 1975, *m.*	Hon. Mervyn S. K. G., *b.* 1942
1902	*Grenfell (3rd) and Baron Grenfell of Kilvey (life peerage, 2000)*, Julian Pascoe Francis St Leger Grenfell, *b.* 1935, *s.* 1976, *m.*	Francis P. J. G., *b.* 1938
1944	*Gretton (4th)*, John Lysander Gretton, *b.* 1975, *s.* 1989	None
1397	*Grey of Codnor (6th)*, Richard Henry Cornwall-Legh, *b.* 1936, *s.* 1996, *m.*	Hon. Richard S. C. C.-L., *b.* 1976
1955	*Gridley (3rd)*, Richard David Arnold Gridley, *b.* 1956, *s.* 1996, *m.*	Hon. Carl R. G., *b.* 1981
1964	*Grimston of Westbury (2nd)*, Robert Walter Sigismund Grimston, *b.* 1925, *s.* 1979, *m.*	Hon. Robert J. S. G., *b.* 1951
1886	*Grimthorpe (4th)*, Christopher John Beckett, OBE, *b.* 1915, *s.* 1963, *m.*	Hon. Edward J. B., *b.* 1954
1945	*Hacking (3rd)*, Douglas David Hacking, *b.* 1938, *s.* 1971, *m.*	Hon. Douglas F. H., *b.* 1968
1950	*Haden-Guest (5th)*, Christopher Haden-Guest, *b.* 1948, *s.* 1996, *m.*	Hon. Nicholas H.-G., *b.* 1951
1886	*Hamilton of Dalzell (4th)*, James Leslie Hamilton, *b.* 1938, *s.* 1990, *m.*	Hon. Gavin G. H., *b.* 1968
1874	*Hampton (6th)*, Richard Humphrey Russell Pakington, *b.* 1925, *s.* 1974, *m.*	Hon. John H. A. P., *b.* 1964
1939	*Hankey (3rd)*, Donald Robin Alers Hankey, *b.* 1938, *s.* 1996, *m.*	Hon. Alexander M. A. H., *b.* 1947
1958	*Harding of Petherton (2nd)*, John Charles Harding, *b.* 1928, *s.* 1989, *m.*	Hon. William A. J. H., *b.* 1969
1910	*Hardinge of Penshurst (4th)*, Julian Alexander Hardinge, *b.* 1945, *s.* 1997	Hon. Hugh F. H., *b.* 1948
1876	*Harlech (6th)*, Francis David Ormsby-Gore, *b.* 1954, *s.* 1985, *m.*	Hon. Jasset D. C. O.-G., *b.* 1986

Created	Title, order of succession, name, etc.	Heir
1939	*Harmsworth (3rd)*, Thomas Harold Raymond Harmsworth, *b.* 1939, *s.* 1990, *m.*	Hon. Dominic M. E. H., *b.* 1973
1815	*Harris (8th)*, Anthony Harris, *b.* 1942, *s.* 1996, *m.*	Anthony J. T. H., *b.* 1915
1954	*Harvey of Tasburgh (2nd)*, Peter Charles Oliver Harvey, *b.* 1921, *s.* 1968, *w.*	Charles J. G. H., *b.* 1951
1295	*Hastings (22nd)*, Edward Delaval Henry Astley, *b.* 1912, *s.* 1956, *m.*	Hon. Delaval T. H. A., *b.* 1960
1835	*Hatherton (8th)*, Edward Charles Littleton, *b.* 1950, *s.* 1985, *m.*	Hon. Thomas E. L., *b.* 1977
1776	*Hawke (11th)*, Edward George Hawke, TD, *b.* 1950, *s.* 1992, *m.*	Hon. William M. T. H., *b.* 1995
1927	*Hayter (3rd)*, George Charles Hayter Chubb, KCVO, CBE, *b.* 1911, *s.* 1967, *m.*	Hon. G. William M. C., *b.* 1943
1945	*Hazlerigg (2nd)*, Arthur Grey Hazlerigg, MC, TD, *b.* 1910, *s.* 1949, *w.*	Hon. Arthur G. H., *b.* 1951
1943	*Hemingford (3rd)* (Dennis) Nicholas Herbert, *b.* 1934, *s.* 1982, *m.*	Hon. Christopher D. C. H., *b.* 1973
1906	*Hemphill (5th)*, Peter Patrick Fitzroy Martyn Martyn-Hemphill, *b.* 1928, *s.* 1957, *m.*	Hon. Charles A. M. M.-H., *b.* 1954
1799 I.*	** *Henley (8th) and 6th UK Baron Northington*, 1885, Oliver Michael Robert Eden, *b.* 1953, *s.* 1977, *m.*	Hon. John W. O. E., *b.* 1988
1800 I.*	*Henniker (8th)* and 4th UK Baron Hartismere, 1866, John Patrick Edward Chandos Henniker-Major, KCMG, CVO, MC, *b.* 1916, *s.* 1980, *m.*	Hon. Mark I. P. C. H.-M., *b.* 1947
1886	*Herschell (3rd)*, Rognvald Richard Farrer Herschell, *b.* 1923, *s.* 1929, *m.*	None
1935	*Hesketh (3rd)*, Thomas Alexander Fermor-Hesketh, KBE, PC, *b.* 1950, *s.* 1955, *m.*	Hon. Frederick H. F.-H., *b.* 1988
1828	*Heytesbury (6th)*, Francis William Holmes à Court, *b.* 1931, *s.* 1971, *m.*	Hon. James W. H. à. C., *b.* 1967
1886	*Hindlip (6th)*, Charles Henry Allsopp, *b.* 1940, *s.* 1993, *m.*	Hon. Henry W. A., *b.* 1973
1950	*Hives (3rd)*, Matthew Peter Hives, *b.* 1971, *s.* 1997	Hon. Michael B. H., *b.* 1926
1912	*Hollenden (4th)*, Ian Hampden Hope-Morley, *b.* 1946, *s.* 1999, *m.*	Hon. Edward H.-M., *b.* 1981
1897	*Holm Patrick (4th)*, Hans James David Hamilton, *b.* 1955, *s.* 1991, *m.*	Hon. Ion H. J. H., *b.* 1956
1797 I.	*Hotham (8th)*, Henry Durand Hotham, *b.* 1940, *s.* 1967, *m.*	Hon. William B. H., *b.* 1972
1881	*Hothfield (6th)*, Anthony Charles Sackville Tufton, *b.* 1939, *s.* 1991, *m.*	Hon. William S. T., *b.* 1977
1597	*Howard de Walden (9th)*. The 9th Baron Howard de Walden died in 1999, leaving four co-heiresses.	
1930	*Howard of Penrith (3rd)*, Philip Esme Howard, *b.* 1945, *s.* 1999, *m.*	Hon. Thomas Philip H., *b.* 1974
1960	*Howick of Glendale (2nd)*, Charles Evelyn Baring, *b.* 1937, *s.* 1973, *m.*	Hon. David E. C. B., *b.* 1975
1796 I.	*Huntingfield (7th)*, Joshua Charles Vanneck, *b.* 1954, *s.* 1994, *m.*	Hon. Gerard C. A. V., *b.* 1985
1866	** *Hylton (5th)*, Raymond Hervey Jolliffe, *b.* 1932, *s.* 1967, *m.*	Hon. William H. M. J., *b.* 1967
1933	*Iliffe (3rd)*, Robert Peter Richard Iliffe, *b.* 1944, *s.* 1996, *m.*	Hon. Edward R. I., *b.* 1968
1543 I.	*Inchiquin (18th)*, Conor Myles John O'Brien, *b.* 1943, *s.* 1982, *m.*	Murrough R. O., *b.* 1910
1962	*Inchyra (2nd)*, Robert Charles Reneke Hoyer Millar, *b.* 1935, *s.* 1989, *m.*	Hon. C. James C. H. M., *b.* 1962
1964	** *Inglewood (2nd)* (William) Richard Fletcher-Vane, MEP, *b.* 1951, *s.* 1989, *m.*	Hon. Henry W. F. F.-V., *b.* 1990
1919	*Inverforth (4th)*, Andrew Peter Weir, *b.* 1966, *s.* 1982	Hon. John V. W., *b.* 1935
1941	*Ironside (2nd)*, Edmund Oslac Ironside, *b.* 1924, *s.* 1959, *m.*	Hon. Charles E. G. I., *b.* 1956
1952	*Jeffreys (3rd)*, Christopher Henry Mark Jeffreys, *b.* 1957, *s.* 1986, *m.*	Hon. Arthur M. H. J., *b.* 1989
1906	*Joicey (5th)*, James Michael Joicey, *b.* 1953, *s.* 1993, *m.*	Hon. William J. J., *b.* 1990
1937	*Kenilworth (4th)*, (John) Randle Siddeley, *b.* 1954, *s.* 1981, *m.*	Hon. William R. J. S., *b.* 1992
1935	*Kennet (2nd)*, Wayland Hilton Young, *b.* 1923, *s.* 1960, *m.*	Hon. W. A. Thoby Y., *b.* 1957
1776 I.*	*Kensington (8th)*, Hugh Ivor Edwardes, *b.* 1933, *s.* 1981, *m.*	Hon. W. Owen A. E., *b.* 1964
1886	*Kensington (5th)*, Hugh Ivor Edwardes, *b.* 1933, *m.*	Hon. W. Owen A. E., *b.* 1964
1951	*Kenswood (2nd)*, John Michael Howard Whitfield, *b.* 1930, *s.* 1963, *m.*	Hon. Michael C. W., *b.* 1955
1788	*Kenyon (6th)*, Lloyd Tyrell-Kenyon, *b.* 1947, *s.* 1993, *m.*	Hon. Lloyd N. T.-K., *b.* 1972
1947	*Kershaw (4th)*, Edward John Kershaw, *b.* 1936, *s.* 1962, *m.*	Hon. John C. E. K., *b.* 1971
1943	*Keyes (2nd)*, Roger George Bowlby Keyes, *b.* 1919, *s.* 1945, *m.*	Hon. Charles W. P. K., *b.* 1951
1909	*Kilbracken (3rd)*, John Raymond Godley, DSC, *b.* 1920, *s.* 1950	Hon. Christopher J. G., *b.* 1945
1900	*Killanin (4th)* (George) Redmond Fitzpatrick Morris, *b.* 1947, *s.* 1999, *m.*	Luke M. G. M., *b.* 1975
1943	*Killearn (3rd)*, Victor Miles George Aldous Lampson, *b.* 1941, *s.* 1996, *m.*	Hon. Miles H. M. L., *b.* 1977
1789 I.	*Kilmaine (7th)*, John David Henry Browne, *b.* 1948, *s.* 1978, *m.*	Hon. John F. S. B., *b.* 1983
1831	*Kilmarnock (7th)*, Alastair Ivor Gilbert Boyd, *b.* 1927, *s.* 1975, *m.*	Hon. Robin J. B., *b.* 1941
1941	*Kindersley (3rd)*, Robert Hugh Molesworth Kindersley, *b.* 1929, *s.* 1976, *m.*	Hon. Rupert J. M. K., *b.* 1955
1223 I.	*Kingsale (35th)*, John de Courcy, *b.* 1941, *s.* 1969, *Premier Baron of Ireland*	Nevinson R. de C., *b.* 1920
1902	*Kinross (5th)*, Christopher Patrick Balfour, *b.* 1949, *s.* 1985, *m.*	Hon. Alan I. B., *b.* 1978
1951	*Kirkwood (3rd)*, David Harvie Kirkwood, PH.D., *b.* 1931, *s.* 1970, *m.*	Hon. James S. K., *b.* 1937
1800 I.	*Langford (9th)*, Col. Geoffrey Alexander Rowley-Conwy, OBE, *b.* 1912, *s.* 1953, *m.*	Hon. Owain G. R.-C., *b.* 1958
1942	*Latham (2nd)*, Dominic Charles Latham, *b.* 1954, *s.* 1970	Anthony M. L., *b.* 1954
1431	*Latymer (8th)*, Hugo Nevill Money-Coutts, *b.* 1926, *s.* 1987, *m.*	Hon. Crispin J. A. N. M.-C., *b.* 1955
1869	*Lawrence (5th)*, David John Downer Lawrence, *b.* 1937, *s.* 1968	None
1947	*Layton (3rd)*, Geoffrey Michael Layton, *b.* 1947, *s.* 1989, *m.*	Hon. David L., *b.* 1914

Created	Title, order of succession, name, etc.	Heir
1839	Leigh (5th), John Piers Leigh, b. 1935, s. 1979, m.	Hon. Christopher D. P. L., b. 1960
1962	Leighton of St Mellons (3rd), Robert William Henry Leighton Seager, b. 1955, s. 1998	Hon. Simon J. L. S., b. 1957
1797	Lilford (7th), George Vernon Powys, b. 1931, s. 1949, m.	Hon. Mark V. P., b. 1975
1945	Lindsay of Birker (3rd), James Francis Lindsay, b. 1945, s. 1994, m.	Alexander S. L., b. 1940
1758 I.	Lisle (8th), Patrick James Lysaght, b. 1931, s. 1998	Hon. John N. G. L., b. 1960
1850	Londesborough (9th), Richard John Denison, b. 1959, s. 1968, m.	Hon. James F. D., b. 1990
1541 I.	Louth (16th), Otway Michael James Oliver Plunkett, b. 1929, s. 1950, m.	Hon. Jonathan O. P., b. 1952
1458 S.*	Lovat (16th) and 5th UK Baron, Lovat, 1837, Simon Fraser, b. 1977, s. 1995	Hon. Jack F., b. 1984
1946	Lucas of Chilworth (2nd), Michael William George Lucas, b. 1926, s. 1967, m.	Hon. Simon W. L., b. 1957
1663	** Lucas (11th) and Dingwall (14th) (s. 1609), Ralph Matthew Palmer, b. 1951, s. 1991	Hon. Lewis E. P., b. 1987
1929	** Luke (3rd), Arthur Charles St John Lawson-Johnston, b. 1933, s. 1996, m.	Hon. Ian J. St J. L.-J., b. 1963
1914	** Lyell (3rd), Charles Lyell, b. 1939, s. 1943	None
1859	Lyveden (6th), Ronald Cecil Vernon, b. 1915, s. 1973, m.	Hon. Jack L. V., b. 1938
1959	MacAndrew (3rd), Christopher Anthony Colin MacAndrew, b. 1945, s. 1989, m.	Hon. Oliver C. J. M., b. 1983
1776 I.	Macdonald (8th), Godfrey James Macdonald of Macdonald, b. 1947, s. 1970, m.	Hon. Godfrey E. H. T. M., b. 1982
1949	Macdonald of Gwaenysgor (2nd), Gordon Ramsay Macdonald, b. 1915, s. 1966, m.	None
1937	McGowan (3rd), Harry Duncan Cory McGowan, b. 1938, s. 1966, m.	Hon. Harry J. C. M., b. 1971
1922	Maclay (3rd), Joseph Paton Maclay, b. 1942, s. 1969, m.	Hon. Joseph P. M., b. 1977
1955	McNair (3rd), Duncan James McNair, b. 1947, s. 1989, m.	Hon. William S. A. M., b. 1958
1951	Macpherson of Drumochter (2nd) (James) Gordon Macpherson, b. 1924, s. 1965, m.	Hon. James A. M., b. 1979
1937	** Mancroft (3rd), Benjamin Lloyd Stormont Mancroft, b. 1957, s. 1987, m.	Hon. Arthur L. S. M., b. 1995
1807	Manners (5th), John Robert Cecil Manners, b. 1923, s. 1972, m.	Hon. John H. R. M., b. 1956
1922	Manton (3rd), Joseph Rupert Eric Robert Watson, b. 1924, s. 1968, m.	Maj. Hon. Miles R. M. W., b. 1958
1908	Marchamley (4th), William Francis Whiteley, b. 1968, s. 1994	None
1964	Margadale (2nd), James Ian Morrison, TD, b. 1930, s. 1996, m.	Hon. Alastair J. M., b. 1958
1961	Marks of Broughton (3rd), Simon Richard Marks, b. 1950, s. 1998, m.	Hon. Michael M., b. 1989
1964	Martonmere (2nd), John Stephen Robinson, b. 1963, s. 1989	David A. R., b. 1965
1776 I.	Massy (9th), Hugh Hamon John Somerset Massy, b. 1921, s. 1958, m.	Hon. David H. S. M., b. 1947
1935	May (3rd), Michael St John May, b. 1931, s. 1950, m.	Hon. Jasper B. St J. M., b. 1965
1928	Melchett (4th), Peter Robert Henry Mond, b. 1948, s. 1973	None
1925	Merrivale (3rd), Jack Henry Edmond Duke, b. 1917, s. 1951, m.	Hon. Derek J. P. D., b. 1948
1911	Merthyr. Trevor Oswin Lewis, Bt, CBE, b. 1935, s. 1977, m. Disclaimed for life 1977.	David T. L., b. 1977
1919	Meston (3rd), James Meston, b. 1950, s. 1984, m.	Hon. Thomas J. D. M., b. 1977
1838	** Methuen (7th), Robert Alexander Holt Methuen, b. 1931, s. 1994, m.	James P. A. M.-C., b. 1952
1711	Middleton (12th) (Digby) Michael Godfrey John Willoughby, MC, b. 1921, s. 1970, m.	Hon. Michael C. J. W., b. 1948
1939	Milford (4th), Guy Wogan Philipps, b. 1961, s. 1999, m.	Hon. Roland A. P., b. 1962
1933	Milne (2nd), George Douglass Milne, TD, b. 1909, s. 1948, m.	Hon. George A. M., b. 1941
1951	** Milner of Leeds (2nd), Arthur James Michael Milner, AE, b. 1923, s. 1967, m.	Hon. Richard J. M., b. 1959
1947	Milverton (2nd), Revd Fraser Arthur Richard Richards, b. 1930, s. 1978, m.	Hon. Michael H. R., b. 1936
1873	Moncreiff (5th), Harry Robert Wellwood Moncreiff, b. 1915, s. 1942, w.	Hon. Rhoderick H. W. M., b. 1954
1884	Monk Bretton (3rd), John Charles Dodson, b. 1924, s. 1933, m.	Hon. Christopher M. D., b. 1958
1885	Monkswell (5th), Gerard Collier, b. 1947, s. 1984, m.	Hon. James A. C., b. 1977
1728	** Monson (11th), John Monson, b. 1932, s. 1958, m.	Hon. Nicholas J. M., b. 1955
1885	** Montagu of Beaulieu (3rd), Edward John Barrington Douglas-Scott-Montagu, b. 1926, s. 1929, m.	Hon. Ralph D.-S.-M., b. 1961
1839	Monteagle of Brandon (6th), Gerald Spring Rice, b. 1926, s. 1946, m.	Hon. Charles J. S. R., b. 1953
1943	** Moran (2nd) (Richard) John (McMoran) Wilson, KCMG, b. 1924, s. 1977, m.	Hon. James M. W., b. 1952
1918	Morris (3rd), Michael David Morris, b. 1937, s. 1975, m.	Hon. Thomas A. S. M., b. 1982
1950	Morris of Kenwood (2nd), Philip Geoffrey Morris, b. 1928, s. 1954, m.	Hon. Jonathan D. M., b. 1968
1831	Mostyn (5th), Roger Edward Lloyd Lloyd-Mostyn, MC, b. 1920, s. 1965, m.	Hon. Llewellyn R. L. L.-M., b. 1948
1933	Mottistone (4th), David Peter Seely, CBE, b. 1920, s. 1966, m.	Hon. Peter J. P. S., b. 1949
1945	Mountevans (3rd), Edward Patrick Broke Evans, b. 1943, s. 1974, m.	Hon. Jeffrey de C. R. E., b. 1948

Created	Title, order of succession, name, etc.	Heir
1283	** *Mowbray (26th), Segrave (27th) and Stourton (23rd) (1448)*, Charles Edward Stourton, CBE, *b.* 1923, *s.* 1965, *m.*	Hon. Edward W. S. S., *b.* 1953
1932	*Moyne (3rd)*, Jonathan Bryan Guinness, *b.* 1930, *s.* 1992, *m.*	Hon. Jasper J. R. G., *b.* 1954
1929	** *Moynihan (4th)* Colin Berkeley Moynihan, *b.* 1955, *s.* 1997, *m.*	Hon. Nicholas E. B. M., *b.* 1994
1781 I.	*Muskerry (9th)* Robert Fitzmaurice Deane, *b.* 1948, *s.* 1988, *m.*	Hon. Jonathan F. D., *b.* 1986
1627 S.*	*Napier (14th) and Ettrick (5th) (UK 1872)*, Francis Nigel Napier, KCVO, *b.* 1930, *s.* 1954, *m.*	Master of Napier, *b.* 1962
1868	*Napier of Magdala (6th)*, Robert Alan Napier, *b.* 1940, *s.* 1987, *m.*	Hon. James R. N., *b.* 1966
1940	*Nathan (2nd)*, Roger Carol Michael Nathan, *b.* 1922, *s.* 1963, *m.*	Hon. Rupert H. B. N., *b.* 1957
1960	*Nelson of Stafford (3rd)*, Henry Roy George Nelson, *b.* 1943, *s.* 1995, *m.*	Hon. Alistair W. H. N., *b.* 1973
1959	*Netherthorpe (3rd)*, James Frederick Turner, *b.* 1964, *s.* 1982, *m.*	Hon. Andrew J. E. T., *b.* 1993
1946	*Newall (2nd)*, Francis Storer Eaton Newall, *b.* 1930, *s.* 1963, *m.*	Hon. Richard H. E. N., *b.* 1961
1776 I.	*Newborough (8th)*, Robert Vaughan Wynn, *b.* 1949, *s.* 1998, *m.*	Hon. Charles H. R. W., *b.* 1923
1892	*Newton (5th)*, Richard Thomas Legh, *b.* 1950, *s.* 1992, *m.*	Hon. Piers R. L., *b.* 1979
1930	*Noel-Buxton (3rd)*, Martin Connal Noel-Buxton, *b.* 1940, *s.* 1980, *m.*	Hon. Charles C. N.-B., *b.* 1975
1957	*Norrie (2nd) (George)* Willoughby Moke Norrie, *b.* 1936, *s.* 1977, *m.*	Hon. Mark W. J. N., *b.* 1972
1884	** *Northbourne (5th)*, Christopher George Walter James, *b.* 1926, *s.* 1982, *m.*	Hon. Charles W. H. J., *b.* 1960
1866	** *Northbrook (6th)*, Francis Thomas Baring, *b.* 1954, *s.* 1990, *m.*	Peter B., *b.* 1939
1878	*Norton (8th)*, James Nigel Arden Adderley, *b.* 1947, *s.* 1993, *m.*	Hon. Edward J. A. A., *b.* 1982
1950	*Ogmore (2nd)*, Gwilym Rees Rees-Williams, *b.* 1931, *s.* 1976, *m.*	Hon. Morgan R.-W., *b.* 1937
1870	*O'Hagan (4th)*, Charles Towneley Strachey, *b.* 1945, *s.* 1961	Hon. Richard T. S., *b.* 1950
1868	*O'Neill (4th)*, Raymond Arthur Clanaboy O'Neill, *b.* 1933, *s.* 1944, *m.*	Hon. Shane S. C. O'N., *b.* 1965
1836 I.*	*Oranmore and Browne (4th) and 2nd UK Baron, Mereworth*, 1926, Dominick Geoffrey Edward Browne, *b.* 1901, *s.* 1927, *m.*	Hon. Dominick G. T. B., *b.* 1929
1933	** *Palmer (4th)*, Adrian Bailie Nottage Palmer, *b.* 1951, *s.* 1990, *m.*	Hon. Hugo B. R. P., *b.* 1980
1914	*Parmoor (4th)*, (Frederick Alfred) Milo Cripps, *b.* 1929, *s.* 1977	Michael L. S. C., *b.* 1942
1937	*Pender (3rd)*, John Willoughby Denison-Pender, *b.* 1933, *s.* 1965, *m.*	Hon. Henry J. R. D.-P., *b.* 1968
1866	*Penrhyn (6th)*, Malcolm Frank Douglas-Pennant, DSO, MBE, *b.* 1908, *s.* 1967, *m.*	Hon. Nigel D.-P., *b.* 1909
1603	*Petre (18th)*, John Patrick Lionel Petre, *b.* 1942, *s.* 1989, *m.*	Hon. Dominic W. P., *b.* 1966
1918	*Phillimore (5th)*, Francis Stephen Phillimore, *b.* 1944, *s.* 1994, *m.*	Hon. Tristan A. S. P., *b.* 1977
1945	*Piercy (3rd)*, James William Piercy, *b.* 1946, *s.* 1981	Hon. Mark E. P. P., *b.* 1953
1827	*Plunket (8th)*, Robin Rathmore Plunket, *b.* 1925, *s.* 1975, *m.*	Hon. Shaun A. F. S. P., *b.* 1931
1831	*Poltimore (7th)*, Mark Coplestone Bampfylde, *b.* 1957, *s.* 1978, *m.*	Hon. Henry A. W. B., *b.* 1985
1690 S.	*Polwarth (10th)*, Henry Alexander Hepburne-Scott, TD, *b.* 1916, *s.* 1944, *m.*	Master of Polwarth, *b.* 1947
1930	*Ponsonby of Shulbrede (4th) and Baron Ponsonby of Roehampton (life peerage, 2000)*, Frederick Matthew Thomas Ponsonby, *b.* 1958, *s.* 1990	None
1958	*Poole (2nd)*, David Charles Poole, *b.* 1945, *s.* 1993, *m.*	Hon. Oliver J. P., *b.* 1972
1852	*Raglan (5th)*, FitzRoy John Somerset, *b.* 1927, *s.* 1964	Hon. Geoffrey S., *b.* 1932
1932	*Rankeillour (4th)*, Peter St Thomas More Henry Hope, *b.* 1935, *s.* 1967	Michael R. H., *b.* 1940
1953	*Rathcavan (3rd)*, Hugh Detmar Torrens O'Neill, *b.* 1939, *s.* 1994, *m.*	Hon. François H. N. O'N., *b.* 1984
1916	*Rathcreedan (3rd)*, Christopher John Norton, *b.* 1949, *s.* 1990, *m.*	Hon. Adam G. N., *b.* 1952
1868	*Rathdonnell (5th)*, Thomas Benjamin McClintock-Bunbury, *b.* 1938, *s.* 1959, *m.*	Hon. William L. M.-B., *b.* 1966
1911	*Ravensdale (3rd)*, Nicholas Mosley, MC, *b.* 1923, *s.* 1966, *m.*	Hon. Shaun N. M., *b.* 1949
1821	*Ravensworth (8th)*, Arthur Waller Liddell, *b.* 1924, *s.* 1950, *m.*	Hon. Thomas A. H. L., *b.* 1954
1821	*Rayleigh (6th)*, John Gerald Strutt, *b.* 1960, *s.* 1988, *m.*	Hon. John F. S., *b.* 1993
1937	** *Rea (3rd)*, John Nicolas Rea, MD, *b.* 1928, *s.* 1981, *m.*	Hon. Matthew J. R., *b.* 1956
1628 S.	** *Reay (14th)*, Hugh William Mackay, *b.* 1937, *s.* 1963, *m.*	Master of Reay, *b.* 1965
1902	*Redesdale (6th) and Baron Mitford (life peerage 2000)*, Rupert Bertram Mitford, *b.* 1967, *s.* 1991, *m.*	Hon. Bertram D. M., *b.* 2000
1940	*Reith.* Christopher John Reith, *b.* 1928, *s.* 1971, *m.* Disclaimed for life 1972.	Hon. James H. J. R., *b.* 1971
1928	*Remnant (3rd)*, James Wogan Remnant, CVO, *b.* 1930, *s.* 1967, *m.*	Hon. Philip J. R., *b.* 1954
1806	*Rendlesham (8th)*, Charles Anthony Hugh Thellusson, *b.* 1915, *s.* 1943, *w.*	Hon. Charles W. B. T., *b.* 1954
1933	*Rennell (3rd)* (John Adrian) Tremayne Rodd, *b.* 1935, *s.* 1978, *m.*	Hon. James R. D. T. R., *b.* 1978
1964	*Renwick (2nd)*, Harry Andrew Renwick, *b.* 1935, *s.* 1973, *m.*	Hon. Robert J. R., *b.* 1966
1885	*Revelstoke (5th)*, John Baring, *b.* 1934, *s.* 1994	Hon. James C. B., *b.* 1938
1905	*Ritchie of Dundee (5th)* (Harold) Malcolm Ritchie, *b.* 1919, *s.* 1978, *m.*	Hon. C. Rupert R. R., *b.* 1958
1935	*Riverdale (3rd)*, Anthony Robert Balfour, *b.* 1960, *s.* 1998	Hon. David R. B., *b.* 1938
1961	*Robertson of Oakridge (2nd)*, William Ronald Robertson, *b.* 1930, *s.* 1974, *m.*	Hon. William B. E. R., *b.* 1975
1938	*Roborough (3rd)*, Henry Massey Lopes, *b.* 1940, *s.* 1992, *m.*	Hon. Massey J. H. L., *b.* 1969
1931	*Rochester (2nd)*, Foster Charles Lowry Lamb, *b.* 1916, *s.* 1955, *w.*	Hon. David C. L., *b.* 1944
1934	*Rockley (3rd)*, James Hugh Cecil, *b.* 1934, *s.* 1976, *m.*	Hon. Anthony R. C., *b.* 1961
1782	*Rodney (10th)*, George Brydges Rodney, *b.* 1953, *s.* 1992, *m.*	Nicholas S. H. R., *b.* 1947

Created	Title, order of succession, name, etc.	Heir
1651 S.*	Rollo (14th) and 5th UK Baron Dunning, 1869, David Eric Howard Rollo, b. 1943, s. 1997, m.	Master , b. 1972
1959	Rootes (3rd), Nicholas Geoffrey Rootes, b. 1951, s. 1992, m.	William B. R., b. 1944
1796 I.*	Rossmore (7th) and 6th UK Baron, Rossmore, 1838, William Warner Westenra, b. 1931, s. 1958, m.	Hon. Benedict W. W., b. 1983
1939	** Rotherwick (3rd) (Herbert) Robin Cayzer, b. 1954, s. 1996, m.	Hon. H. Robin C., b. 1989
1885	Rothschild (4th) (Nathaniel Charles) Jacob Rothschild, GBE, b. 1936, s. 1990, m.	Hon. Nathaniel P. V. J. R., b. 1971
1911	Rowallan (4th), John Polson Cameron Corbett, b. 1947, s. 1993	Hon. Jason W. P. C. C., b. 1972
1947	Rugby (3rd), Robert Charles Maffey, b. 1951, s. 1990, m.	Hon. Timothy J. H. M., b. 1975
1919	Russell of Liverpool (3rd), Simon Gordon Jared Russell, b. 1952, s. 1981, m.	Hon. Edward C. S. R., b. 1985
1876	Sackville (6th), Lionel Bertrand Sackville-West, b. 1913, s. 1965, m.	Hugh R. I. S.-W., b. 1919
1964	St Helens (2nd), Richard Francis Hughes-Young, b. 1945, s. 1980, m.	Hon. Henry T. H.-Y., b. 1986
1559	** St John of Bletso (21st), Anthony Tudor St John, b. 1957, s. 1978, m.	Hon. Oliver B. St J., b. 1995
1887	St Levan (4th), John Francis Arthur St Aubyn, DSC, b. 1919, s. 1978, m.	Hon. O. Piers St. A., b. 1920
1885	St Oswald (6th), Charles Rowland Andrew Winn, b. 1959, s. 1999, m.	Hon. Rowland C. S. H. W., b. 1986
1960	Sanderson of Ayot. Alan Lindsay Sanderson, b. 1931, s. 1971, m. Disclaimed for life 1971.	Hon. Michael S., b. 1959
1945	Sandford (2nd), Revd John Cyril Edmondson, DSC, b. 1920, s. 1959, m.	Hon. James J. M. E., b. 1949
1871	Sandhurst (5th) (John Edward) Terence Mansfield, DFC, b. 1920, s. 1964, m.	Hon. Guy R. J. M., b. 1949
1802	Sandys (7th), Richard Michael Oliver Hill, b. 1931, s. 1961, m.	The Marquess of Downshire, (see page 138)
1888	Savile (3rd), George Halifax Lumley-Savile, b. 1919, s. 1931	Hon. Henry L. T. L.-S., b. 1923
1447	Saye and Sele (21st), Nathaniel Thomas Allen Fiennes, b. 1920, s. 1968, m.	Hon. Richard I. F., b. 1959
1826	Seaford (6th), Colin Humphrey Felton Ellis, b. 1946, s. 1999, m.	Benjamin F. T. E., b. 1976
1932	** Selsdon (3rd), Malcolm McEacharn Mitchell-Thomson, b. 1937, s. 1963, m.	Hon. Callum M. M. M.-T., b. 1969
1489 S.	Sempill (21st), James William Stuart Whitemore Sempill, b. 1949, s. 1995, m.	Master of Semphill, b. 1979
1916	Shaughnessy (3rd), William Graham Shaughnessy, b. 1922, s. 1938, w.	Hon. Michael J. S., b. 1946
1946	Shepherd (2nd), Malcolm Newton Shepherd, PC, b. 1918, s. 1954, w.	Hon. Graeme G. S., b. 1949
1964	Sherfield (2nd), Christopher James Makins, b. 1942, s. 1996, m.	Hon. Dwight W. M., b. 1951
1902	Shuttleworth (5th), Charles Geoffrey Nicholas Kay-Shuttleworth, b. 1948, s. 1975, m.	Hon. Thomas E. K.-S., b. 1976
1950	Silkin. Arthur Silkin, b. 1916, s. 1972, m. Disclaimed for life 1972.	Hon. Christopher L. S., b. 1947
1963	Silsoe (2nd), David Malcolm Trustram Eve, QC, b. 1930, s. 1976, m.	Hon. Simon R. T. E., b. 1966
1947	Simon of Wythenshawe (2nd), Roger Simon, b. 1913, s. 1960, m.	Hon. Matthew S., b. 1955
1449 S.	Sinclair (17th), Charles Murray Kennedy St Clair, CVO, b. 1914, s. 1957, m.	Master of Sinclair, b. 1968
1957	Sinclair of Cleeve (3rd), John Lawrence Robert Sinclair, b. 1953, s. 1985	None
1919	Sinha (6th), Arup Kumar Sinha, b. 1966, s. 1999	Hon. Dilip K. S., b. 1967
1828	** Skelmersdale (7th), Roger Bootle-Wilbraham, b. 1945, s. 1973, m.	Hon. Andrew B.-W., b. 1977
1916	Somerleyton (3rd), Savile William Francis Crossley, GCVO, b. 1928, s. 1959, m.	Hon. Hugh F. S. C., b. 1971
1784	Somers (9th), Philip Sebastian Somers Cocks, b. 1948, s. 1995	Alan B. C., b. 1930
1780	Southampton (6th), Charles James FitzRoy, b. 1928, s. 1989, m.	Hon. Edward C. F., b. 1955
1640	Stafford (15th), Francis Melfort William Fitzherbert, b. 1954, s. 1986, m.	Hon. Benjamin J. B. F., b. 1983
1938	Stamp (4th), Trevor Charles Bosworth Stamp, MD, FRCP, b. 1935, s. 1987, m.	Hon. Nicholas C. T. S., b. 1978
1839	Stanley of Alderley (8th) and Sheffield (8th) (I. 1738) and 7th UK Baron, Eddisbury, 1848, Thomas Henry Oliver Stanley, b. 1927, s. 1971, m.	Hon. Richard O. S., b. 1956
1318	** Strabolgi (11th), David Montague de Burgh Kenworthy, b. 1914, s. 1953, m.	Andrew D. W. K., b. 1967
1954	Strang (2nd), Colin Strang, b. 1922, s. 1978, m.	None
1955	Strathalmond (3rd), William Roberton Fraser, b. 1947, s. 1976, m.	Hon. William G. F., b. 1976
1936	Strathcarron (2nd), David William Anthony Blyth Macpherson, b. 1924, s. 1937, m.	Hon. Ian D. P. M., b. 1949
1955	** Strathclyde (2nd), Thomas Galloway Dunlop du Roy de Blicquy Galbraith, PC, b. 1960, s. 1985, m.	Hon. Charles W. du R. de B. G., b. 1962
1900	Strathcona and Mount Royal (4th), Donald Euan Palmer Howard, b. 1923, s. 1959, m.	Hon. D. Alexander S. H., b. 1961
1836	Stratheden (6th) and Campbell (6th) (1841) Donald Campbell, b. 1934, s. 1987, m.	Hon. David A. C., b. 1963
1884	Strathspey (6th), James Patrick Trevor Grant of Grant, b. 1943, s. 1992, m.	Hon. Michael P. F. G., b. 1953
1838	Sudeley (7th), Merlin Charles Sainthill Hanbury-Tracy, b. 1939, s. 1941	D. Andrew J. H.-T., b. 1928

Created	Title, order of succession, name, etc.	Heir
1786	Suffield (11th), Anthony Philip Harbord-Hamond, MC, b. 1922, s. 1951, w.	Hon. Charles A. A. H.-H., b. 1953
1893	Swansea (4th), John Hussey Hamilton Vivian, b. 1925, s. 1934, m.	Hon. Richard A. H. V., b. 1957
1907	Swaythling (5th), Charles Edgar Samuel Montagu, b. 1954, s. 1998, m.	Hon. Anthony T. S. M., b. 1931
1919	** Swinfen (3rd), Roger Mynors Swinfen Eady, b. 1938, s. 1977, m.	Hon. Charles R. P. S. E., b. 1971
1935	Sysonby (3rd), John Frederick Ponsonby, b. 1945, s. 1956	None
1831 I.	Talbot of Malahide (10th), Reginald John Richard Arundell, b. 1931, s. 1987, m.	Hon. Richard J. T. A., b. 1957
1946	Tedder (3rd), Robin John Tedder, b. 1955, s. 1994, m.	Hon. Benjamin J. T., b. 1985
1884	Tennyson (5th), Cdr. Mark Aubrey Tennyson, DSC, b. 1920, s. 1991, m.	Lt.-Cdr. James A. T., b. 1913
1940	Teviot (2nd), Charles John Kerr, b. 1934, s. 1968, m.	Hon. Charles R. K., b. 1971
1616	Teynham (20th), John Christopher Ingham Roper-Curzon, b. 1928, s. 1972, m.	Hon. David J. H. I. R.-C., b. 1965
1964	Thomson of Fleet (2nd), Kenneth Roy Thomson, b. 1923, s. 1976, m.	Hon. David K. R. T., b. 1957
1792	Thurlow (8th), Francis Edward Hovell-Thurlow-Cumming-Bruce, KCMG, b. 1912, s. 1971, w.	Hon. Roualeyn R. H.-T.-C.-B., b. 1952
1876	Tollemache (5th), Timothy John Edward Tollemache, b. 1939, s. 1975, m.	Hon. Edward J. H. T., b. 1976
1564 S.	Torphichen (15th), James Andrew Douglas Sandilands, b. 1946, s. 1975, m.	Douglas R. A. S., b. 1926
1947	** Trefgarne (2nd), David Garro Trefgarne, PC, b. 1941, s. 1960, m.	Hon. George G. T., b. 1970
1921	Trevethin (4th) and Oaksey (2nd) (1947), John Geoffrey Tristram Lawrence, OBE, b. 1929, s. 1971, m.	Hon. Patrick J. T. L., b. 1960
1880	Trevor (5th), Marke Charles Hill-Trevor, b. 1970, s. 1997, m.	Hon. Iain R. H.-T., b. 1971
1461 I.	Trimlestown (21st), Raymond Charles Barnewall, b. 1930, s. 1997	None
1940	Tryon (3rd), Anthony George Merrik Tryon, b. 1940, s. 1976	Hon. Charles G. B. T., b. 1976
1935	Tweedsmuir (3rd), William de l'Aigle Buchan, b. 1916, s. 1996, m.	Hon. John W. H. de l'A. B., b. 1950
1523	Vaux of Harrowden (10th), John Hugh Philip Gilbey, b. 1915, s. 1977, m.	Hon. Anthony W. G., b. 1940
1800 I.	Ventry (8th), Andrew Wesley Daubeny de Moleyns, b. 1943, s. 1987, m.	Hon. Francis W. D. de M., b. 1965
1762	Vernon (10th), John Lawrance Vernon, b. 1923, s. 1963, m.	Anthony W. Vernon-Harcourt, b. 1939
1922	Vestey (3rd), Samuel George Armstrong Vestey, b. 1941, s. 1954, m.	Hon. William G. V., b. 1983
1841	** Vivian (6th), Nicholas Crespigny Laurence Vivian, b. 1935, s. 1991, m.	Hon. Charles H. C. V., b. 1966
1934	Wakehurst (3rd) (John) Christopher Loder, b. 1925, s. 1970, m.	Hon. Timothy W. L., b. 1958
1723	** Walpole (10th) and 8th Brit. Baron Walpole of Wolterton, 1756, Robert Horatio Walpole, b. 1938, s. 1989, m.	Hon. Jonathan R. H. W., b. 1967
1780	Walsingham (9th), John de Grey, MC, b. 1925, s. 1965, m.	Hon. Robert de. G., b. 1969
1936	Wardington (2nd), Christopher Henry Beaumont Pease, b. 1924, s. 1950, m.	Hon. William S. P., b. 1925
1792 I.	Waterpark (7th), Frederick Caryll Philip Cavendish, b. 1926, s. 1948, m.	Hon. Roderick A. C., b. 1959
1942	Wedgwood (4th), Piers Anthony Weymouth Wedgwood, b. 1954, s. 1970, m.	John W., b. 1919
1861	Westbury (5th), David Alan Bethell, CBE, MC, b. 1922, s. 1961, m.	Hon. Richard N. B., b. 1950
1944	Westwood (3rd), (William) Gavin Westwood, b. 1944, s. 1991, m.	Hon. W. Fergus W., b. 1972
1544/5	Wharton (12th), Myles Christopher David Robertson, b. 1964, s. 2000, m.	Hon. Christopher J. R., b. 1969
1935	Wigram (2nd) (George) Neville (Clive) Wigram, MC, b. 1915, s. 1960, w.	Maj. Hon. Andrew F. C. W., b. 1949
1491	** Willoughby de Broke (21st), Leopold David Verney, b. 1938, s. 1986, m.	Hon. Rupert G. V., b. 1966
1946	Wilson (2nd), Patrick Maitland Wilson, b. 1915, s. 1964, w.	None
1937	Windlesham (3rd) and Baron Hennesy (life peerage, 1999), David James George Hennessy, CVO, PC, b. 1932, s. 1962, w.	Hon. James R. H., b. 1968
1951	Wise (2nd), John Clayton Wise, b. 1923, s. 1968, m.	Hon. Christopher J. C. W., b. 1949
1869	Wolverton (7th), Christopher Richard Glyn, b. 1938, s. 1988	Hon. Andrew J. G., b. 1943
1928	Wraxall (2nd), George Richard Lawley Gibbs, b. 1928, s. 1931	Hon. Sir Eustace H. B. G., b. 1929
1915	Wrenbury (3rd), Revd John Burton Buckley, b. 1927, s. 1940, m.	Hon. William E. B., b. 1966
1838	Wrottesley (6th), Clifton Hugh Lancelot de Verdon Wrottesley, b. 1968, s. 1977	Hon. Stephen J. W., b. 1955
1829	Wynford (8th), Robert Samuel Best, MBE, b. 1917, s. 1943, m.	Hon. John P. R. B., b. 1950
1308	Zouche (18th), James Assheton Frankland, b. 1943, s. 1965, m.	Hon. William T. A. F., b. 1984

BARONESSES/LADIES IN THEIR OWN RIGHT

Style, The Right Hon. the Lady _ , *or* The Right Hon. the Baroness _ , according to her preference. Either style may be used, except in the case of Scottish titles (indicated by S.), which are not baronies (*see* page 136) and whose holders are always addressed as Lady
Husband, Untitled
Children's style, As for children of a Baron
For forms of address, *see* page 135

Created	Title, order of succession, name, etc.	Heir
1664	*Arlington*, Jennifer Jane Forwood, *b.* 1939, *m.* title called out of abeyance 1999	Patrick John Dudley Forwood, *b.* 1967
1455	*Berners (16th)*, Pamela Vivien Kirkham, *b.* 1929, *m.*	Hon. Rupert W. T. K., *b.* 1953
1529	*Braye (8th)*, Mary Penelope Aubrey-Fletcher, *b.* 1941, *s.* 1985, *m.*	
1321	*Dacre (27th)*, Rachel Leila Douglas-Home, *b.* 1929, *w.*	Hon. James T. A. D.-H., *b.* 1952
1332	** *Darcy de Knayth (18th)*, Davina Marcia Ingrams, DBE, *b.* 1938, *s.* 1943, *w.*	Hon. Caspar D. I., *b.* 1962
1439	*Dudley (14th)*, Barbara Amy Felicity Hamilton, *b.* 1907, *s.* 1972, *m.*	Hon. Jim A. H. Wallace, *b.* 1930
1490 S.	*Herries of Terregles (14th)*, Anne Elizabeth Fitzalan-Howard, *b.* 1938, *s.* 1975, *w.*	Lady Mary Mumford, *b.* 1940
1602 S.	*Kinloss (12th)*, Beatrice Mary Grenville Freeman-Grenville, *b.* 1922, *s.* 1944, *m.*	Master, *b.* 1953
1445 S.	** *Saltoun (20th)*, Flora Marjory Fraser, *b.* 1930, *s.* 1979, *m.*	Hon. Katharine I. M. I. F., *b.* 1957
1628	** *Strange (16th)* (Jean) Cherry Drummond of Megginch, *b.* 1928, *m.*	Hon. Adam H. D. of M., *b.* 1953
1313	*Willoughby de Eresby (27th)*, (Nancy) Jane Marie Heathcote-Drummond-Willoughby, *b.* 1934, *s.* 1983	

Life Peers

NEW LIFE PEERAGES *1 September 2000 to 31 August 2001:*
Victor Abedowale, CBE; Sir Jeremy (Paddy) Ashdown, KBE; Richard Best, OBE; Peter Brooke, CH; Edmund Browne; Dale Campbell-Savours; David Clarke; Paul Condon, QPM; Robin Corbett; Ronald Fearn, OBE; *Prof.* Ilora Finlay; Peter Fowler; Bruce Grocott; *Gen.* Sir Charles Guthrie, GCB, LVO, OBE; Michael Heseltine CH; Valerie Howarth, OBE; Elspeth Howe, CBE; Stephen Jones; Thomas King, CH, PC; Richard Livsey, CBE; John MacGregor, CBE; Robert MacLennon, PC; Ken Maginnis, Sir Robert May, Kt., Janet Michie; John Morris, QC; Sir Claus Moser, KCB, CBE; Sir Herman Ouseley, Kt.; Thomas Pendry; Giles Radice; Robert Sheldon; Sir Stewart Sutherland, Kt.; John Taylor; Peter Temple-Morris;

CREATED UNDER THE APPELLATE
JURISDICTION ACT 1876 (AS AMENDED)

BARONS
Created
1986 Ackner, Desmond James Conrad, Ackner, PC, *b. 1920, m.*
1980 *Bridge of Harwich,* Nigel Cyprian, Bridge, PC, *b. 1917, m.*
1982 *Brightman,* John Anson, Brightman, PC, *b. 1911, m.*
1991 *Browne-Wilkinson,* Nicolas Christopher Henry, Browne-Wilkinson, PC, *b. 1930, m.*
1996 *Clyde,* James John, Clyde, *b. 1932, m. Lord of Appeal in Ordinary*
1986 *Goff of Chieveley,* Robert Lionel Archibald, Goff, PC, *b. 1926, m.*
1985 *Griffiths,* (William) Hugh, Griffiths, MC, PC, *b. 1923, m.*
1998 *Hobhouse of Woodborough,* John Stewart, Hobhouse, PC, *b. 1932, Lord of Appeal in Ordinary*
1995 *Hoffmann,* Leonard Hubert, Hoffmann, PC, *b. 1934, m. Lord of Appeal in Ordinary*
1997 *Hutton,* (James) Brian (Edward), Hutton, PC, *b. 1931, m. Lord of Appeal in Ordinary*
1988 *Jauncey of Tullichettle,* Charles Eliot, Jauncey, PC, *b. 1925, m.*
1977 *Keith of Kinkel,* Henry Shanks, Keith, GBE, PC, *b. 1922, m.*
1979 *Lane,* Geoffrey Dawson, Lane, AFC, PC, *b. 1918, m.*
1993 *Lloyd of Berwick,* Anthony John Leslie, Lloyd, PC, *b. 1929, m.*
1998 *Millett,* Peter Julian, Millett, PC, *b. 1932, m. Lord of Appeal in Ordinary*
1992 *Mustill,* Michael John, Mustill, PC, *b. 1931, m.*
1994 *Nicholls of Birkenhead,* Donald James, Nicholls, PC, *b. 1933, m. Lord of Appeal in Ordinary*
1994 *Nolan,* Michael Patrick, Nolan, PC, *b. 1928, m.*
1986 *Oliver of Aylmerton,* Peter Raymond, Oliver, PC, *b. 1921, m.*
1999 *Phillips of Worth Matravers,* Nicholas Addison, Phillips, *b. 1938, m. Master of the Rolls*
1997 *Saville of Newdigate,* Mark Oliver, Saville, PC, *b. 1936, m. Lord of Appeal in Ordinary*
1977 *Scarman,* Leslie George, Scarman, OBE, PC, *b. 1911, m.*

1992 *Slynn of Hadley,* Gordon, Slynn, PC, *b. 1930, m. Lord of Appeal in Ordinary*
1995 *Steyn,* Johan van Zyl, Steyn, PC, *b. 1932, m. Lord of Appeal in Ordinary*
1982 *Templeman,* Sydney William, Templeman, MBE, PC, *b. 1920, m.*
1964 *Wilberforce,* Richard Orme, Wilberforce, CMG, OBE, PC, *b. 1907, m.*
1992 *Woolf,* Harry Kenneth, Woolf, PC, *b. 1933, m. Lord Chief Justice of England and Wales*

CREATED UNDER THE LIFE
PEERAGES ACT 1958

---

*Hereditary Peer who has been granted a life peerage

BARONS
2000 *Acton of Bridgnorth,* Lord Acton, *m.* (see page 147)
2001 *Adebowale of Thornes,* Victor Olufemi, Adebowale, CBE,
1998 *Ahmed,* Nazir, Ahmed, *b. 1957, m.*
1996 *Alderdice,* John Thomas, Alderdice, *b. 1955, m.*
1988 *Alexander of Weedon,* Robert Scott, Alexander, QC, *b. 1936, m.*
1976 *Allen of Abbeydale,* Philip, Allen, GCB, *b. 1912, m.*
1998 *Alli,* Waheed, Alli,
1997 *Alton of Liverpool,* David Patrick Paul, Alton, *b. 1951, m.*
1992 *Archer of Sandwell,* Peter Kingsley, Archer, PC, QC, *b. 1926, m.*
1992 *Archer of Weston-super-Mare,* Jeffrey Howard, Archer, *b. 1940, m.*
1988 *Armstrong of Ilminster,* Robert Temple, Armstrong, GCB, CVO, *b. 1927, m.*
1999 *Armstrong-Jones,* Earl of Snowdon, GCVO, *m.* (see page 143)
2000 *Ashcroft,* Michael Anthony, Ashcroft, KCMG,
2001 *Ashdown of Norton-sub-Hamdon,* Jeremy John Durham (Paddy), Ashdown, KBE, *m.*
1992 *Ashley of Stoke,* Jack, Ashley, CH, PC, *b. 1922, m.*
1993 *Attenborough,* Richard Samuel, Attenborough, CBE, *b. 1923, m.*
1998 *Bach,* William Stephen Goulden, Bach, *b. 1946, m. Minister of State for Defence Procurement*
1997 *Bagri,* Raj Kumar, Bagri, CBE, *b. 1930, m.*
1997 *Baker of Dorking,* Kenneth Wilfred, Baker, CH, PC, *b. 1934, m.*
1974 *Balniel,* The Earl of Crawford and Balcarres, *m.* (see page 140)
1974 *Barber,* Anthony Perrinott Lysberg, Barber, TD, PC, *b. 1920, m.*
1992 *Barber of Tewkesbury,* Derek Coates, Barber, *b. 1918, m.*
1983 *Barnett,* Joel, Barnett, PC, *b. 1923, m.*
1997 *Bassam of Brighton,* (John) Steven, Bassam, *b. 1953, Lord-in-Waiting*
1982 *Bauer,* Prof. Peter Thomas, Bauer, D.SC., FBA, *b. 1915*
1967 *Beaumont of Whitley,* Revd Timothy Wentworth, Beaumont, *b. 1928, m.*
1998 *Bell,* Timothy John Leigh, Bell, *b. 1941, m.*
2000 *Bernstein of Craigweil,* Alexander, Bernstein, *b. 1936, m.*
2001 *Best,* Richard Stuart, Best, OBE, *b. 1945, m.*
1997 *Biffen,* (William) John, Biffen, PC, *b. 1930, m.*
1996 *Bingham of Cornhill,* Thomas Henry, Bingham, PC, *b. 1933, m. Lord of Appeal in Ordinary*

2000   *Birt*, John Francis Hodgess, Birt, *b.* 1944, *m.*
1997   *Blackwell*, Norman Roy, Blackwell, *b.* 1952, *m.*
1971   *Blake*, Robert Norman William, Blake, FBA, *b.* 1916, *w.*
1994   *Blaker*, Peter Allan Renshaw, Blaker, KCMG, PC, *b.* 1922, *m.*
1978   *Blease*, William John, Blease, *b.* 1914, *m.*
1995   *Blyth of Rowington*, James, Blyth, *b.* 1940, *m.*
1980   *Boardman*, Thomas Gray, Boardman, MC, TD, *b.* 1919, *m.*
1996   *Borrie*, Gordon Johnson, Borrie, QC, *b.* 1931, *m.*
1976   *Boston of Faversham*, Terence George, Boston, QC, *b.* 1930, *m.*
1996   *Bowness*, Peter Spencer, Bowness, CBE, *b.* 1943, *m.*
1999   *Bradshaw*, William Peter, Bradshaw, *b.* 1936, *m.*
1998   *Bragg*, Melvyn, Bragg, *b.* 1939, *m.*
1987   *Bramall*, Edwin Noel Westby, Bramall, KG, GCB, OBE, MC, *b.* 1923, *m.*
2000   *Brennan*, Daniel Joseph, Brennan, QC, *b.* 1942, *m.*
1999   *Brett*, William Henry, Brett, *b.* 1942, *m.*
1976   *Briggs*, Asa, Briggs, FBA, *b.* 1921, *m.*
2000   *Brittan of Spennithorne*, Leon, Brittan, PC, QC, *b.* 1939, *m.*
1997   *Brooke of Alverthorpe*, Clive, Brooke, *b.* 1942, *m.*
2001   *Brooke of Sutton Mandeville*, Peter Leonard, Brooke, CH, *b.* 1934, *m.*
1975   *Brookes*, Raymond Percival, Brookes, *b.* 1909, *m.*
1998   *Brookman*, David Keith, Brookman, *b.* 1937, *m.*
1979   *Brooks of Tremorfa*, John Edward, Brooks, *b.* 1927, *m.*
2001   *Browne of Madingley*, Edmund John Phillip, Browne, *b.* 1948
1974   *Bruce of Donington*, Donald William Trevor, Bruce, *b.* 1912, *m.*
1976   *Bullock*, Alan Louis Charles, Bullock, FBA, *b.* 1914, *m.*
1997   *Burlison*, Thomas Henry, Burlison, *b.* 1936, *m.*
1998   *Burns*, Terence, Burns, GCB, *b.* 1944, *m.*
1998   *Butler of Brockwell*, (Frederick Edward) Robin, Butler, GCB, CVO, *b.* 1938, *m.*
1985   *Butterworth*, John Blackstock, Butterworth, CBE, *b.* 1918, *m.*
1978   *Buxton of Alsa*, Aubrey Leland Oakes, Buxton, KCVO, MC, *b.* 1918, *m.*
1987   *Callaghan of Cardiff*, (Leonard) James, Callaghan, KG, PC, *b.* 1912, *m.*
1984   *Cameron of Lochbroom*, Kenneth John, Cameron, PC, *b.* 1931, *m.*
1981   *Campbell of Alloway*, Alan Robertson, Campbell, QC, *b.* 1917, *m.*
1974   *Campbell of Croy*, Gordon Thomas Calthrop, Campbell, MC, PC, *b.* 1921, *m.*
2001   *Campbell-Savours of Allerdale*, Dale Norman, Cambell-Savours, *b.* 1943, *m.*
1999   **Carington of Upton*, Lord Carrington, GCMG, *b.* 1919, *m. (see page 148)*
1999   *Carlile of Berriew*, Alexander Charles, Carlile, QC, *b.* 1948, *m.*
1987   *Carlisle of Bucklow*, Mark, Carlisle, QC, PC, *b.* 1929, *m.*
1983   *Carmichael of Kelvingrove*, Neil George, Carmichael, *b.* 1921
1975   *Carr of Hadley*, (Leonard) Robert, Carr, PC, *b.* 1916, *m.*
1987   *Carter*, Denis Victor, Carter, PC, *b.* 1932, *m. Chief Whip*
1977   *Carver*, (Richard) Michael (Power), Carver, GCB, CBE, DSO, MC, *b.* 1915, *m.*
1990   *Cavendish of Furness*, (Richard) Hugh, Cavendish, *b.* 1941, *m.*
1996   *Chadlington*, Peter Selwyn, Gummer, *b.* 1942, *m.*
1964   *Chalfont*, (Alun) Arthur, Gwynne Jones, OBE, MC, PC, *b.* 1919, *m.*

1985   *Chapple*, Francis (Frank) Joseph, Chapple, *b.* 1921, *w.*
1987   *Chilver*, (Amos) Henry, Chilver, FRS, FENG., *b.* 1926, *m.*
1977   *Chitnis*, Pratap Chidamber, Chitnis, *b.* 1936, *m.*
1998   *Christopher*, Anthony Martin Grosvenor, Christopher, CBE, *b.* 1925, *m.*
1992   *Clark of Kempston*, William Gibson Haig, Clark, PC, *b.* 1917, *m.*
         Clarke, David George, Clarke, *m.*
1998   *Clarke of Hampstead*, Anthony James, Clarke, CBE, *b.* 1932, *m.*
1998   *Clement-Jones*, Timothy Francis, Clement-Jones, CBE, *b.* 1949, *m.*
1990   *Clinton-Davis*, Stanley Clinton, Clinton-Davis, PC, *b.* 1928, *m.*
1978   *Cockfield*, (Francis) Arthur, Cockfield, PC, *b.* 1916, *w.*
2000   *Coe*, Sebastian Newbold, Coe, OBE, *b.* 1956, *m.*
2001   *Condon of Langdon Green*, Paul Leslie, Condon, QPM, *m.*
1981   *Constantine of Stanmore*, Theodore, Constantine, CBE, AE, *b.* 1910, *w.*
1992   *Cooke of Islandreagh*, Victor Alexander, Cooke, OBE, *b.* 1920, *m.*
1996   *Cooke of Thorndon*, Robin Brunskill, Cooke, KBE, PC, PH.D., *b.* 1926, *m.*
1997   *Cope of Berkeley*, John Ambrose, Cope, PC, *b.* 1937, *m.*
2001   *Corbett of Castle Vale*, Robin, Corbett, *b.* 1933, *m.*
1991   *Craig of Radley*, David Brownrigg, Craig, GCB, OBE, *b.* 1929, *m.*
1987   *Crickhowell*, (Roger) Nicholas, Edwards, PC, *b.* 1934, *m.*
1978   *Croham*, Douglas Albert Vivian, Allen, GCB, *b.* 1917, *w.*
1995   *Cuckney*, John Graham, Cuckney, *b.* 1925, *m.*
1996   *Currie of Marylebone*, David Anthony, Currie, *b.* 1946, *m.*
1979   *Dacre of Glanton*, Hugh Redwald, Trevor-Roper, *b.* 1914, *w.*
1993   *Dahrendorf*, Ralf, Dahrendorf, KBE, PH.D., D.PHIL., FBA, *b.* 1929, *m.*
1997   *Davies of Coity*, (David) Garfield, Davies, CBE, *b.* 1935, *m.*
1997   *Davies of Oldham*, Bryan, Davies, *b.* 1939, *m. Lord-in-Waiting*
1993   *Dean of Harptree*, (Arthur) Paul, Dean, PC, *b.* 1924, *m.*
1998   *Dearing*, Ronald Ernest, Dearing, CB, *b.* 1930, *m.*
1986   *Deedes*, William Francis, Deedes, KBE MC, PC, *b.* 1913, *m.*
1991   *Desai*, Prof. Meghnad Jagdishchandra, Desai, PH.D., *b.* 1940, *m.*
1997   *Dholakia*, Navnit, Dholakia, OBE, *b.* 1937, *m.*
1970   *Diamond*, John, Diamond, PC, *b.* 1907, *m.*
1997   *Dixon*, Donald, Dixon, PC, *b.* 1929, *m.*
1993   *Dixon-Smith*, Robert William, Dixon-Smith, *b.* 1934, *m.*
1988   *Donaldson of Lymington*, John Francis, Donaldson, PC, *b.* 1920, *m.*
1985   *Donoughue*, Bernard, Donoughue, D.PHIL., *b.* 1934
1987   *Dormand of Easington*, John Donkin, Dormand, *b.* 1919, *m.*
1994   *Dubs*, Alfred, Dubs, *b.* 1932, *m.*
1995   *Eames*, Robert Henry Alexander, Eames, PH.D., *b.* 1937, *m.*
1992   *Eatwell*, John Leonard, Eatwell, PH.D., *b.* 1945, *m.*
1983   *Eden of Winton*, John Benedict, Eden, PC, *b.* 1925, *m.*
1999   *Elder*, Thomas Murray, Elder,
1992   *Elis-Thomas*, Dafydd Elis, Elis-Thomas, *b.* 1946, *m.*

Life Peers 159

1985 *Elliott of Morpeth*, Robert William, Elliott, *b.* 1920, *m.*

1981 *Elystan-Morgan*, Dafydd Elystan, Elystan-Morgan, *b.* 1932, *m.*

1980 *Emslie*, George Carlyle, Emslie, MBE, PC, FRSE, *b.* 1919, *m.*

2000 **Erskine of Alloa Tower*, Earl of Mar and Kellie, *m.* (*see page 142*)

1997 *Evans of Parkside*, John, Evans, *b.* 1930, *m.*

2000 *Evans of Temple Guiting*, Matthew, Evans, CBE, *b.* 1941, *m.*

1998 *Evans of Watford*, David Charles, Evans, *b.* 1942, *m.*

1992 *Ewing of Kirkford*, Harry, Ewing, *b.* 1931, *m.*

1983 *Ezra*, Derek, Ezra, MBE, *b.* 1919, *m.*

1997 *Falconer of Thornton*, Charles Leslie, Falconer, QC, *b.* 1951, *m. Minister of State for Housing and Planning*

1983 *Fanshawe of Richmond*, Anthony Henry Fanshawe, Royle, KCMG, *b.* 1927, *m.*

1999 *Faulkner of Worcester*, Richard Oliver, Faulkner, *b.* 1946, *m.*

2001 *Fearn of Southport*, Ronald Cyril, Fearn, OBE, *b.* 1931, *m.*

1996 *Feldman*, Basil, Feldman, *b.* 1926, *m.*

1999 *Fellowes*, Robert, Fellowes, PC, GCB, GCVO, *b.* 1941, *m.*

1999 *Filkin*, David Geoffrey Nigel, Filkin, CBE, *b.* 1944, *Lord-in-Waiting*

1983 *Fitt*, Gerard, Fitt, *b.* 1926, *w.*

1979 *Flowers*, Brian Hilton, Flowers, FRS, *b.* 1924, *m.*

1967 *Foot*, John Mackintosh, Foot, *b.* 1909, *m.*

1999 *Forsyth of Drumlean*, Michael Bruce, Forsyth, *b.* 1954, *m.*

1982 *Forte*, Charles, Forte, *b.* 1908, *m.*

1999 *Foster of Thames Bank*, Norman Robert, Foster, OM, *b.* 1935, *m.*

2001 *Fowler of Sutton Coldfield*, (Peter) Norman, Fowler, *b.* 1938, *m.*

1989 *Fraser of Carmyllie*, Peter Lovat, Fraser, PC, QC, *b.* 1945, *m.*

1997 *Freeman*, Roger Norman, Freeman, PC, *b.* 1942, *m.*

2000 *Fyfe of Fairfield*, George Lennox, Fyfe, *b.* 1941, *m.*

1982 *Gallacher*, John, Gallacher, *b.* 1920, *m.*

1999 **Ganzoni*, Lord Belstead, PC, (*see page 148*)

1997 *Garel-Jones*, (William Armand) Thomas Tristan, Garel-Jones, PC, *b.* 1941, *m.*

1999 **Gascoyne-Cecil*, The Viscount Cranborne, PC, *m.* (*see Baron Cecil page 148*)

1999 *Gavron*, Robert, Gavron, CBE, *b.* 1930, *m.*

1992 *Geraint*, Geraint Wyn, Howells, *b.* 1925, *m.*

1975 *Gibson*, (Richard) Patrick (Tallentyre), Gibson, *b.* 1916, *m.*

1979 *Gibson-Watt*, (James) David, Gibson-Watt, MC, PC, *b.* 1918, *m.*

1997 *Gilbert*, John William, Gilbert, PC, PH.D., *b.* 1927, *m.*

1992 *Gilmour of Craigmillar*, Ian Hedworth John Little, Gilmour, PC, *b.* 1926, *m.*

1994 *Gladwin of Clee*, Derek Oliver, Gladwin, CBE, *b.* 1930, *m.*

1977 *Glenamara*, Edward Watson, Short, CH, PC, *b.* 1912, *m.*

2001 *Golding of Newcastle-under-Lyme*, Llinos , Golding, *b.* 1933, *m.*

1999 *Goldsmith*, Peter Henry, Goldsmith, QC, *b.* 1950, *m. Attorney-General*

1997 *Goodhart*, William Howard, Goodhart, QC, *b.* 1933, *m.*

1997 *Gordon of Strathblane*, James Stuart, Gordon, CBE, *b.* 1936, *m.*

1999 *Grabiner*, Anthony Stephen, Grabiner, QC, *b.* 1945, *m.*

1983 *Graham of Edmonton*, (Thomas) Edward, Graham, *b.* 1925, *m.*

1983 *Gray of Contin*, James (Hamish) Hector Northey, Gray, PC, *b.* 1927, *m.*

1974 *Greene of Harrow Weald*, Sidney Francis, Greene, CBE, *b.* 1910, *m.*

1975 *Gregson*, John, Gregson, *b.* 1924

2000 **Grenfell of Kilvey*, Lord Grenfell, (*see page 150*)

1991 *Griffiths of Fforestfach*, Brian, Griffiths, *b.* 1941, *m.*

2001 *Grocott*, Bruce Joseph, Grocott, *b.* 1940, *m. Lord-in-Waiting*

2000 **Gueterbock*, Lord Berkeley, OBE, (*see page 148*)

2001 *Guthrie of Craigiebank*, Charles Ronald Llewelyn, Guthrie, GCB, LVO, OBE, *b.* 1938, *m.*

1995 *Habgood*, Rt. Revd John Stapylton, Habgood, PC, PH.D., *b.* 1927, *m.*

1970 *Hailsham of St Marylebone*, Quintin McGarel, Hogg, KG, CH, PC, FRS, *b.* 1907, *w.*

1994 *Hambro*, Charles Eric Alexander, Hambro, *b.* 1930, *m.*

1998 *Hanningfield*, Paul Edward Winston, White, *b.* 1940

1983 *Hanson*, James Edward, Hanson, *b.* 1922, *m.*

1997 *Hardie*, Andrew Rutherford, Hardie, QC, PC, *b.* 1946, *m.*

1997 *Hardy of Wath*, Peter, Hardy, *b.* 1931, *m.*

1998 *Harris of Haringey*, (Jonathan) Toby, Harris, *b.* 1953, *m.*

1979 *Harris of High Cross*, Ralph, Harris, *b.* 1924, *m.*

1996 *Harris of Peckham*, Philip Charles, Harris, *b.* 1942, *m.*

1999 *Harrison*, Lyndon Henry Arthur, Harrison, *b.* 1947, *m.*

1993 *Haskel*, Simon, Haskel, *b.* 1934, *m.*

1998 *Haskins*, Christopher Robin, Haskins, *b.* 1937, *m.*

1990 *Haslam*, Robert, Haslam, *b.* 1923, *m.*

1997 *Hattersley*, Roy Sidney George, Hattersley, PC, *b.* 1932, *m.*

1992 *Hayhoe*, Bernard John (Barney), Hayhoe, PC, *b.* 1925, *m.*

1992 *Healey*, Denis Winston, Healey, CH, MBE, PC, *b.* 1917, *m.*

1999 **Hennessey*, Lord Windlesham, CVO, *w.* (*see page 155*)

2001 *Heseltine of Thenford*, Michael Ray Dibdin, Heseltine, CH, *b.* 1933, *m.*

1997 *Higgins*, Terence Langley, Higgins, KBE, PC, *b.* 1928, *m.*

1979 *Hill-Norton*, Peter John, Hill-Norton, GCB, *b.* 1915, *m.*

2000 *Hodgson of Astley Abbotts*, Robin Granville, Hodgson, CBE, *b.* 1937, *m.*

1997 *Hogg of Cumbernauld*, Norman, Hogg, *b.* 1938, *m.*

1979 *Holderness*, Richard Frederick, Wood, PC, *b.* 1920, *m.*

1991 *Hollick*, Clive Richard, Hollick, *b.* 1945, *m.*

1990 *Holme of Cheltenham*, Richard Gordon, Holme, CBE, *b.* 1936, *m.*

1979 *Hooson*, (Hugh) Emlyn, Hooson, QC, *b.* 1925, *m.*

1995 *Hope of Craighead*, (James Arthur) David, Hope, PC, *b.* 1938, *m. Lord of Appeal in Ordinary*

1992 *Howe of Aberavon*, (Richard Edward) Geoffrey, Howe, CH, PC, QC, *b.* 1926, *m.*

1997 *Howell of Guildford*, David Arthur Russell, Howell, PC, *b.* 1936, *m.*

1978 *Howie of Troon*, William, Howie, *b.* 1924, *m.*

1997 *Hoyle*, (Eric) Douglas Harvey, Hoyle, *b.* 1930, *w.*

1997 *Hughes of Woodside*, Robert, Hughes, *b.* 1932, *m.*

2001 *Hunt of Chesterton*, Julian Charles Roland, Hunt, CBE, *b.* 1941, *m.*

1997   *Hunt of Kings Heath*, Philip Alexander, Hunt, OBE, b. 1949, m.
1980   *Hunt of Tanworth*, John Joseph Benedict, Hunt, GCB, b. 1919, m.
1997   *Hunt of Wirral*, David James Fletcher, Hunt, MBE, PC, b. 1942, m.
1997   *Hurd of Westwell*, Douglas Richard, Hurd, CH, CBE, PC, b. 1930, m.
1996   *Hussey of North Bradley*, Marmaduke James, Hussey, b. 1923, m.
1978   *Hutchinson of Lullington*, Jeremy Nicolas, Hutchinson, QC, b. 1915, m.
1999   *Imbert*, Peter Michael, Imbert, QPM, b. 1933, m.
1997   *Inge*, Peter Anthony, Inge, GCB, b. 1935, m.
1982   *Ingrow*, John Aked, Taylor, OBE, TD, b. 1917, m.
1987   *Irvine of Lairg*, Alexander Andrew Mackay, Irvine, PC, QC, b. 1940, m. *Lord Chancellor*
1997   *Islwyn*, Royston John (Roy), Hughes, b. 1925, m.
1997   *Jacobs*, (David) Anthony, Jacobs, b. 1931, m.
1997   *Janner of Braunstone*, Greville Ewan, Janner, QC, b. 1928, w.
1999   *'Jellicoe of Southampton*, Earl Jellicoe, KBE, w. (see page 141)
1987   *Jenkin of Roding*, (Charles) Patrick (Fleeming), Jenkin, PC, b. 1926, m.
1987   *Jenkins of Hillhead*, Roy Harris, Jenkins, OM, PC, b. 1920, m.
1981   *Jenkins of Putney*, Hugh Gater, Jenkins, b. 1908, w.
2000   *Joffe*, Joel Goodman, Joffe, CBE, b. 1932, m.
1987   *Johnston of Rockport*, Charles Collier, Johnston, TD, b. 1915, m.
2001   *Jones of Deeside*, Stephen Barry, Jones, b. 1937, m.
1997   *Jopling*, (Thomas) Michael, Jopling, PC, b. 1930, m.
2000   *Jordan*, William Brian, Jordan, CBE, b. 1936, m.
1991   *Judd*, Frank Ashcroft, Judd, b. 1935, m.
1980   *Keith of Castleacre*, Kenneth Alexander, Keith, b. 1916, m.
1996   *Kilpatrick of Kincraig*, Robert, Kilpatrick, CBE, b. 1926, m.
1985   *Kimball*, Marcus Richard, Kimball, b. 1928, m.
2001   *King*, Thomas Jeremy, King, CH, PC, b. 1933, m.
1983   *King of Wartnaby*, John Leonard, King, b. 1918, m.
1999   *King of West Bromwich*, Tarsem, King
1993   *Kingsdown*, Robert (Robin), Leigh-Pemberton, KG, PC, b. 1927, m.
1994   *Kingsland*, Christopher James, Prout, TD, PC, QC, b. 1942
1999   *Kirkham*, Graham, Kirkham, b. 1944, m.
1975   *Kirkhill*, John Farquharson, Smith, b. 1930, m.
1987   *Knights*, Philip Douglas, Knights, CBE, QPM, b. 1920, m.
1991   *Laing of Dunphail*, Hector, Laing, b. 1923, m.
1999   *Laird*, John Dunn, Laird, b. 1944, m.
1998   *Laming*, (William) Herbert, Laming, CBE, b. 1936, m.
1998   *Lamont of Lerwick*, Norman Stewart Hughson, Lamont, PC, b. 1942, m.
1990   *Lane of Horsell*, Peter Stewart, Lane, b. 1925, w.
1997   *Lang of Monkton*, Ian Bruce, Lang, PC, b. 1940, m.
1992   *Lawson of Blaby*, Nigel, Lawson, PC, b. 1932, m.
2000   *Layard*, Peter Richard Grenville, Layard, b. 1934, m.
1999   *Lea of Crondall*, David Edward, Lea, OBE, b. 1937
1993   *Lester of Herne Hill*, Anthony Paul, Lester, QC, b. 1936, m.
1997   *Levene of Portsoken*, Peter Keith, Levene, KBE, b. 1941, m.
1997   *Levy*, Michael Abraham, Levy, b. 1944, m.
1989   *Lewis of Newnham*, Jack, Lewis, FRS, b. 1928, m.
1999   *Lipsey*, David Lawrence, Lipsey, b. 1948, m.
1999   *Livsey*, Richard, Livsey, CBE, b. 1948, m.

1997   *Lloyd-Webber*, Andrew Lloyd, Webber, b. 1948, m.
1997   *Lofthouse of Pontefract*, Geoffrey, Lofthouse, b. 1925, w.
2000   **Lyttelton of Aldershot*, The Viscount Chandos, m. (see page 144)
1988   *Macaulay of Bragar*, Donald, Macaulay, QC, b. 1933, m.
1998   *Macdonald of Tradeston*, Angus John, Macdonald, CBE, b. 1940, m. *Minister for the Cabinet Office and Chancellor of the Duchy of Lancaster*
1991   *Macfarlane of Bearsden*, Norman Somerville, Macfarlane, KT, FRSE, b. 1926, m.
2001   *MacGregor of Pulham Market*, John Roddick Russell, MacGregor, CBE, b. 1937, m.
1979   *Mackay of Clashfern*, James Peter Hymers, Mackay, KT, PC, FRSE, b. 1927, m.
1995   *Mackay of Drumadoon*, Donald Sage, Mackay, PC, b. 1946, m.
1999   *Mackenzie of Culkein*, Hector Uisdean, MacKenzie, b. 1940
1998   *Mackenzie of Framwellgate*, Brian, Mackenzie, OBE, b. 1943, m.
1974   *Mackie of Benshie*, George Yull, Mackie, CBE, DSO, DFC, b. 1919, m.
1996   *MacLaurin of Knebworth*, Ian Charter, MacLaurin, b. 1937, w.
2001   *Maclennon of Rogart*, Robert Adam Ross, Maclennan, PC, b. 1936, m.
2001   *Maginnis of Drumglass*, Kenneth Wiggins, Maginnis, b. 1938, m.
1991   *Marlesford*, Mark Shuldham, Schreiber, b. 1931, m.
1981   *Marsh*, Richard William, Marsh, PC, b. 1928, m.
1998   *Marshall of Knightsbridge*, Colin Marsh, Marshall, b. 1933, m.
1987   *Mason of Barnsley*, Roy, Mason, PC, b. 1924, m.
2001   *May of Oxford*, Robert McCredie, May, b. 1936, m.
1997   *Mayhew of Twysden*, Patrick Barnabas Burke, Mayhew, QC, PC, b. 1929, m.
1984   *McAlpine of West Green*, (Robert) Alistair, McAlpine, b. 1942, m.
1975   *McCarthy*, William Edward John, McCarthy, D.PHIL., b. 1925, m.
1976   *McCluskey*, John Herbert, McCluskey, b. 1929, m.
1989   *McColl of Dulwich*, Ian, McColl, CBE, FRCS, FRCSE, b. 1933, m.
1982   *McIntosh of Haringey*, Andrew Robert, McIntosh, b. 1933, m. *Deputy Chief Whip*
1995   *McNally*, Tom, McNally, b. 1943, m.
1992   *Merlyn-Rees*, Merlyn, Merlyn-Rees, PC, b. 1920, m.
1978   *Mishcon*, Victor, Mishcon, QC, b. 1915, m.
2001   *Mitchell*, Parry Andrew, Mitchell
2000   **Mitford*, Lord Redesdale, m. (see page 153)
1997   *Molyneaux of Killead*, James Henry, Molyneaux, KBE, PC, b. 1920
1997   *Monro of Langholm*, Hector Seymour Peter, Monro, AE, PC, b. 1922, m.
1992   *Moore of Lower Marsh*, John Edward Michael, Moore, PC, b. 1937, m.
1986   *Moore of Wolvercote*, Philip Brian Cecil, Moore, GCB, GCVO, CMG, PC, b. 1921, m.
2000   *Morgan*, Kenneth Owen, Morgan, b. 1934, m.
2001   *Morris of Aberavon*, John, Morris, QC, b. 1931, m.
1997   *Morris of Manchester*, Alfred, Morris, PC, b. 1928, m.
2001   *Moser of Regents Park*, Claus Adolf, Moser, KCB, CBE, b. 1922, m.
1971   *Moyola*, James Dawson, Chichester-Clark, PC (NI), b. 1923, m.
1985   *Murray of Epping Forest*, Lionel, Murray, OBE, PC, b. 1922, m.

1979   *Murton of Lindisfarne*, (Henry) Oscar, Murton, OBE, TD, PC, *b.* 1914, *m.*
1997   *Naseby*, Michael Wolfgang Laurence, Morris, PC, *b.* 1936, *m.*
1997   *Neill of Bladen*, (Francis) Patrick, Neill, QC, *b.* 1926, *m.*
1997   *Newby*, Richard Mark, Newby, OBE, *b.* 1953, *m.*
1997   *Newton of Braintree*, Antony Harold, Newton, OBE, PC, *b.* 1937, *m.*
1994   *Nickson*, David Wigley, Nickson, KBE, FRSE, *b.* 1929, *m.*
1975   *Northfield*, (William) Donald, Chapman, *b.* 1923
1998   *Norton of Louth*, Philip, Norton, *b.* 1951
1997   *Orme*, Stanley, Orme, PC, *b.* 1923, *m.*
2001   *Ouseley of Peckham Rye*, Herman George, Ouseley, *m.*
1992   *Owen*, David Anthony Llewellyn, Owen, CH, PC, *b.* 1938, *m.*
1999   *Oxburgh*, Ernest Ronald, Oxburgh, KBE, FRS, PH.D., *b.* 1934, *m.*
1991   *Palumbo*, Peter Garth, Palumbo, *b.* 1935, *m.*
2000   *Parekh*, Bhikhu Chhotalal, Parekh, *b.* 1935, *m.*
1992   *Parkinson*, Cecil Edward, Parkinson, PC, *b.* 1931, *m.*
1975   *Parry*, Gordon Samuel David, Parry, *b.* 1925, *m.*
1999   *Patel*, Narendra Babubhai, Patel, *b.* 1938
2000   *Patel of Blackburn*, Adam Hafejee, Patel
1997   *Patten*, John Haggitt Charles, Patten, PC, *b.* 1945, *m.*
1996   *Paul*, Swraj, Paul, *b.* 1931, *m.*
1990   *Pearson of Rannoch*, Malcolm Everard MacLaren, Pearson, *b.* 1942, *m.*
2001   *Pendry of Stalybridge*, Thomas, Pendry, *b.* 1934, *m.*
1979   *Perry of Walton*, Walter Laing Macdonald, Perry, OBE, FRS, FRSE, *b.* 1921, *m.*
1987   *Peston*, Maurice Harry, Peston, *b.* 1931, *m.*
1983   *Peyton of Yeovil*, John Wynne William, Peyton, PC, *b.* 1919, *m.*
1998   *Phillips of Sudbury*, Andrew Wyndham, Phillips, OBE, *b.* 1939, *m.*
1996   *Pilkington of Oxenford*, Revd Canon Peter, Pilkington, *b.* 1933, *w.*
1992   *Plant of Highfield*, Prof. Raymond, Plant, PH.D., *b.* 1945, *m.*
1987   *Plumb*, (Charles) Henry, Plumb, *b.* 1925, *m.*
1981   *Plummer of St Marylebone*, (Arthur) Desmond (Herne), Plummer, TD, *b.* 1914, *w.*
2000   **Ponsonby of Roehampton*, Lord Ponsonby of Shulbrede, (*see page 153*)
1990   *Porter of Luddenham*, George, Porter, OM, FRS, *b.* 1920, *m.*
2000   *Powell of Bayswater*, Charles David, Powell, KCMG, *b.* 1941
1987   *Prior*, James Michael Leathes, Prior, PC, *b.* 1927, *m.*
1982   *Prys-Davies*, Gwilym Prys, Prys-Davies, *b.* 1923, *m.*
1997   *Puttnam*, David Terence, Puttnam, CBE, *b.* 1941, *m.*
1987   *Pym*, Francis Leslie, Pym, MC, PC, *b.* 1922, *m.*
1982   *Quinton*, Anthony Meredith, Quinton, FBA, *b.* 1925, *m.*
1994   *Quirk*, Prof. (Charles) Randolph, Quirk, CBE, FBA, *b.* 1920, *m.*
2001   *Radice*, Giles Heneage, Radice, *b.* 1936
1997   *Randall of St Budeaux*, Stuart Jeffrey, Randall, *b.* 1938, *m.*
1978   *Rawlinson of Ewell*, Peter Anthony Grayson, Rawlinson, PC, QC, *b.* 1919, *m.*
1976   *Rayne*, Max, Rayne, *b.* 1918, *m.*
1997   *Razzall*, (Edward) Timothy, Razzall, CBE, *b.* 1943, *m.*

1987   *Rees*, Peter Wynford Innes, Rees, PC, QC, *b.* 1926, *m.*
1988   *Rees-Mogg*, William, Rees-Mogg, *b.* 1928, *m.*
1991   *Renfrew of Kaimsthorn*, (Andrew) Colin, Renfrew, FBA, *b.* 1937, *m.*
1999   *Rennard*, Christopher John, Rennard, MBE, *b.* 1960
1979   *Renton*, David Lockhart-Mure, Renton, KBE, TD, PC, QC, *b.* 1908, *w.*
1997   *Renton of Mount Harry*, (Ronald) Timothy, Renton, PC, *b.* 1932, *m.*
1997   *Renwick of Clifton*, Robin William, Renwick, KCMG, *b.* 1937, *m.*
1990   *Richard*, Ivor Seward, Richard, PC, QC, *b.* 1932, *m.*
1979   *Richardson*, John Samuel, Richardson, LVO, MD, FRCP, *b.* 1910, *w.*
1983   *Richardson of Duntisbourne*, Gordon William Humphreys, Richardson, KG, MBE, TD, PC, *b.* 1915, *m.*
1992   *Rix*, Brian Norman Roger, Rix, CBE, *b.* 1924, *m.*
1997   *Roberts of Conwy*, (Ieuan) Wyn (Pritchard), Roberts, PC, *b.* 1930, *m.*
1999   *Robertson of Port Ellen*, George Islay MacNeill, Robertson, PC, *b.* 1946, *m.*
1992   *Rodger of Earlsferry*, Alan Ferguson, Rodger, PC, QC, FBA, *b.* 1944
1992   *Rodgers of Quarry Bank*, William Thomas, Rodgers, PC, *b.* 1928, *m.*
1999   *Rogan*, Dennis Robert David, Rogan, *b.* 1942, *m.*
1996   *Rogers of Riverside*, Richard George, Rogers, RA, RIBA, *b.* 1933, *m.*
1977   *Roll of Ipsden*, Eric, Roll, KCMG, CB, *b.* 1907, *w.*
2001   *Rooker*, Jeffrey William, Rooker, PC, *b.* 1941, *m.*
2000   *Roper*, John Francis Hodgess, Roper, *b.* 1935, *m.*
1997   *Russell-Johnston*, (David) Russell, Russell-Johnston, *b.* 1932, *m.*
1975   *Ryder of Eaton Hastings*, Sydney Thomas Franklin (Don), Ryder, *b.* 1916, *m.*
1997   *Ryder of Wensum*, Richard Andrew, Ryder, OBE, PC, *b.* 1949, *m.*
1996   *Saatchi*, Maurice, Saatchi, *b.* 1946, *m.*
1989   *Sainsbury of Preston Candover*, John Davan, Sainsbury, KG, *b.* 1927, *m.*
1997   *Sainsbury of Turville*, David John, Sainsbury, *b.* 1940, *m.*
1997   *Sandberg*, Michael Graham Ruddock, Sandberg, CBE, *b.* 1927, *m.*
1985   *Sanderson of Bowden*, Charles Russell, Sanderson, *b.* 1933, *m.*
1998   *Sawyer*, Lawrence (Tom), Sawyer,
2000   *Scott of Foscote*, Richard Rashleigh Folliott, Scott, PC, *b.* 1934, *m. Lord of Appeal in Ordinary*
1997   *Selkirk of Douglas*, James Alexander, Douglas-Hamilton, MSP, PC, QC, *b.* 1942, *m.*
1996   *Sewel*, John Buttifant, Sewel, CBE, *b.* 1946
1999   *Sharman*, Colin Morven, Sharman, OBE, *b.* 1943, *m.*
1994   *Shaw of Northstead*, Michael Norman, Shaw, *b.* 1920, *m.*
1959   *Shawcross*, Hartley William, Shawcross, GBE, PC, QC, *b.* 1923, *m.*
2001   *Sheldon of Ashton-under-Lyne*, Robert Edward, Sheldon, *b.* 1923, *m.*
1994   *Sheppard of Didgemere*, Allan John George, Sheppard, KCVO, *b.* 1932, *m.*
1998   *Sheppard of Liverpool*, David Stuart, Sheppard, *b.* 1929, *m.*
1997   *Shore of Stepney*, Peter David, Shore, PC, *b.* 1924, *m.*
2000   *Shutt of Greetland*, David Trevor , Shutt, OBE
1971   *Simon of Glaisdale*, Jocelyn Edward Salis, Simon, PC, *b.* 1911, *m.*
1997   *Simon of Highbury*, David Alec Gwyn, Simon, CBE, *b.* 1939, *m.*

1997 Simpson of Dunkeld, George, Simpson, b. 1942, m.
1991 Skidelsky, Robert Jacob Alexander, Skidelsky,
        D.PHIL., b. 1939, m.
1997 Smith of Clifton, Trevor Arthur, Smith, b. 1937, m.
1999 Smith of Leigh, Peter Richard Charles, Smith,
        b. 1945, m.
1990 Soulsby of Swaffham Prior, Ernest Jackson Lawson,
        Soulsby, PH.D., b. 1926, m.
1987 St John of Fawsley, Norman Antony Francis, St
        John-Stevas, PC, b. 1929
1983 Stallard, Albert William, Stallard, b. 1921, m.
1997 Steel of Aikwood, David Martin Scott, Steel, PC,
        KBE, MSP, b. 1938, m.
1991 Sterling of Plaistow, Jeffrey Maurice, Sterling, CBE,
        b. 1934, m.
1987 Stevens of Ludgate, David Robert, Stevens, b. 1936,
        m.
1999 Stevenson of Coddenham, Henry Dennistoun,
        Stevenson, CBE, b. 1945, m.
1992 Stewartby, (Bernard Harold) Ian (Halley),
        Stewart, RD, PC, FBA, FRSE, b. 1935, m.
1981 Stodart of Leaston, James Anthony, Stodart, PC,
        b. 1916, w.
1983 Stoddart of Swindon, David Leonard, Stoddart,
        b. 1926, m.
1969 Stokes, Donald Gresham, Stokes, TD, FENG.,
        b. 1914, w.
1997 Stone of Blackheath, Andrew Zelig, Stone, b. 1942,
        m.
2001 Sutherland of Houndwood, Stewart Ross,
        Sutherland, b. 1941, m.
1971 Tanlaw, Simon Brooke, Mackay, b. 1934, m.
1996 Taverne, Dick, Taverne, QC, b. 1928, m.
2001 Taylor, John David, Taylor, b. 1937, m.
1978 Taylor of Blackburn, Thomas, Taylor, CBE, b. 1929,
        m.
1996 Taylor of Warwick, John David Beckett, Taylor,
        b. 1952, m.
1992 Tebbit, Norman Beresford, Tebbit, CH, PC, b. 1931,
        m.
2001 Temple-Morris of Llandaff, Peter , Temple-Morris,
        b. 1938, m.
1996 Thomas of Gresford, Donald Martin, Thomas, OBE,
        QC, b. 1937, m.
1987 Thomas of Gwydir, Peter John Mitchell, Thomas,
        PC, QC, b. 1920, w.
1997 Thomas of Macclesfield, Terence James, Thomas,
        CBE, b. 1937, m.
1981 Thomas of Swynnerton, Hugh Swynnerton,
        Thomas, b. 1931, m.
1977 Thomson of Monifieth, George Morgan, Thomson,
        KT, PC, b. 1921, m.
1990 Tombs, Francis Leonard, Tombs, FENG., b. 1924,
        m.
1998 Tomlinson, John Edward, Tomlinson, MEP, b. 1939
1994 Tope, Graham Norman, Tope, CBE, b. 1943, m.
1981 Tordoff, Geoffrey Johnson, Tordoff, b. 1928, m.
1999 Trotman, Alexander, Trotman, b. 1933
1993 Tugendhat, Christopher Samuel, Tugendhat,
        b. 1937, m.
1990 Varley, Eric Graham, Varley, PC, b. 1932, m.
1996 Vincent of Coleshill, Richard Frederick, Vincent,
        GBE, KCB, DSO, b. 1931, m.
1985 Vinson, Nigel, Vinson, LVO, b. 1931, m.
1990 Waddington, David Charles, Waddington, GCVO,
        PC, QC, b. 1929, m.
1990 Wade of Chorlton, (William) Oulton, Wade,
        b. 1932, m.
1992 Wakeham, John, Wakeham, PC, b. 1932, m.
1999 Waldegrave of North Hill, William Arthur,
        Waldegrave, PC, b. 1946, m.
1997 Walker of Doncaster, Harold, Walker, PC, b. 1927,
        m.

1992 Walker of Worcester, Peter Edward, Walker, MBE,
        PC, b. 1932, m.
1974 Wallace of Coslany, George Douglas, Wallace,
        b. 1906, m.
1995 Wallace of Saltaire, William John Lawrence,
        Wallace, PH.D., b. 1941, m.
1989 Walton of Detchant, John Nicholas, Walton, TD,
        FRCP, b. 1922, m.
1998 Warner, Norman Reginald, Warner, b. 1940, m.
1997 Watson of Invergowrie, Michael Goodall, Watson,
        MSP, b. 1949, m.
1999 Watson of Richmond, Alan John, Watson, CBE,
        b. 1941, m.
1992 Weatherill, (Bruce) Bernard, Weatherill, PC,
        b. 1920, m.
1977 Wedderburn of Charlton, (Kenneth) William,
        Wedderburn, FBA, QC, b. 1927, m.
1976 Weidenfeld, (Arthur) George, Weidenfeld,
        b. 1919, m.
1980 Weinstock, Arnold, Weinstock, b. 1924, m.
1978 Whaddon, (John) Derek, Page, b. 1927, m.
1996 Whitty, John Lawrence (Larry), Whitty, b. 1943,
        m.
1974 Wigoder, Basil Thomas, Wigoder, QC, b. 1921, m.
1985 Williams of Elvel, Charles Cuthbert Powell,
        Williams, CBE, b. 1933, m.
1992 Williams of Mostyn, Gareth Wyn, Williams, QC,
        b. 1941, m. Lord Privy Seal, Leader of the House of
        Lords
1999 Williamson of Horton, David (Francis),
        Williamson, GCMG, CB, b. 1934, m.
1992 Wilson of Tillyorn, David Clive, Wilson, GCMG,
        PH.D., KT, b. 1935, m.
1995 Winston, Robert Maurice Lipson, Winston,
        FRCOG, b. 1940, m.
1985 Wolfson, Leonard Gordon, Wolfson, b. 1927, m.
1991 Wolfson of Sunningdale, David, Wolfson, b. 1935,
        m.
1999 Woolmer of Leeds, Kenneth John, Woolmer,
        b. 1940, m.
1994 Wright of Richmond, Patrick Richard Henry,
        Wright, GCMG, b. 1931, m.
1978 Young of Dartington, Michael, Young, PH.D.,
        b. 1915, m.
1984 Young of Graffham, David Ivor, Young, PC, b. 1932,
        m.
1992 *Younger of Prestwick, The Viscount Younger of,
        Leckie, m. (see page 146)

BARONESSES

Created
1997 Amos, Valerie Ann, Amos, b. 1954
2000 Andrews, Elizabeth Kay, Andrews, OBE
1996 Anelay of St Johns, Joyce Anne, Anelay, DBE,
        b. 1947, m.
1999 Ashton of Upholland, Catherine Margaret, Ashton,
        m.
1999 Barker, Elizabeth Jean, Barker, b. 1961
1987 Blackstone, Tessa Ann Vosper, Blackstone, PH.D.,
        b. 1942, Minister of State for the Arts
1987 Blatch, Emily May, Blatch, CBE, PC, b. 1937, m.
1999 Blood, May, Blood, MBE, b. 1938
1990 Brigstocke, Heather Renwick, Brigstocke, b. 1929,
        m.
1998 Buscombe, Peta Jane, Buscombe, b. 1954, m.
1996 Byford, Hazel, Byford, DBE, b. 1941, m.
1982 Carnegy of Lour, Elizabeth Patricia Carnegy of,
        Lour, b. 1925
1990 Castle of Blackburn, Barbara Anne, Castle, PC,
        b. 1910, w.
1992 Chalker of Wallasey, Lynda, Chalker, PC, b. 1942,
        m.
2000 Cohen of Pimlico, Janet, Cohen, b. 1940, m.

1982   *Cox*, Caroline Anne, Cox, *b.* 1937, *m.*
1998   *Crawley*, Christine Mary, Crawley, MEP, *b.* 1950, *m.*
1990   *Cumberlege*, Julia Frances, Cumberlege, CBE, *b.* 1943, *m.*
1978   *David*, Nora Ratcliff, David, *b.* 1913, *w.*
1993   *Dean of Thornton-le-Fylde*, Brenda, Dean, PC, *b.* 1943, *m.*
1974   *Delacourt-Smith of Alteryn*, Margaret Rosalind, Delacourt-Smith, *b.* 1916, *m.*
1990   *Dunn*, Lydia Selina, Dunn, DBE, *b.* 1940, *m.*
1990   *Eccles of Moulton*, Diana Catherine, Eccles, *b.* 1933, *m.*
1972   *Elles*, Diana Louie, Elles, *b.* 1921, *m.*
1997   *Emerton*, Audrey Caroline, Emerton, DBE, *b.* 1935
1974   *Falkender*, Marcia Matilda, Falkender, CBE, *b.* 1932
1994   *Farrington of Ribbleton*, Josephine, Farrington, *b.* 1940, *m. Baroness-in-Waiting*
2001   *Finlay of Llandaff*, Ilora Gillian, Finlay, *m.*
1974   *Fisher of Rednal*, Doris Mary Gertrude, Fisher, *b.* 1919, *w.*
1990   *Flather*, Shreela, Flather, *m.*
1997   *Fookes*, Janet Evelyn, Fookes, DBE, *b.* 1936
1999   *Gale*, Anita, Gale, *b.* 1940
1981   *Gardner of Parkes*, (Rachel) Trixie (Anne), Gardner, *b.* 1927, *m.*
2000   *Gibson of Market Rasen*, Anne, Gibson, OBE, *b.* 1940, *m.*
1998   *Goudie*, Mary Teresa, Goudie, *b.* 1946, *m.*
1993   *Gould of Potternewton*, Joyce Brenda, Gould, *b.* 1932, *m.*
2000   *Greengross*, Sally Ralea, Greengross, OBE, *b.* 1935, *m.*
1991   *Hamwee*, Sally Rachel, Hamwee, *b.* 1947
1999   *Hanham*, Joan Brownlow, Hanham, CBE, *b.* 1939, *m.*
1999   *Harris of Richmond*, Angela Felicity, Harris, *b.* 1944
1996   *Hayman*, Helene Valerie, Hayman, *b.* 1949, *m.*
1991   *Hilton of Eggardon*, Jennifer, Hilton, QPM, *b.* 1936
1995   *Hogg*, Sarah Elizabeth Mary, Hogg, *b.* 1946, *m.*
1990   *Hollis of Heigham*, Patricia Lesley, Hollis, D.PHIL., *b.* 1941, *m.*
1985   *Hooper*, Gloria Dorothy, Hooper, *b.* 1939
2001   *Howarth of Breckland*, Valerie Georgina, Howarth, OBE, *m.*
2001   *Howe of Idlicote*, Elspeth Rosamond Morton, Howe, CBE, *b.* 1932, *m.*
1999   *Howells of St Davids*, Rosalind Patricia-Anne, Howells
1965   *Hylton-Foster*, Audrey Pellew, Hylton-Foster, DBE, *b.* 1908, *w.*
1991   *James of Holland Park*, Phyllis Dorothy White (P. D., James), OBE, *b.* 1920, *w.*
1992   *Jay of Paddington*, Margaret Ann, Jay, PC, *b.* 1939, *m.*
1979   *Jeger*, Lena May, Jeger, *b.* 1915, *w.*
1997   *Kennedy of the Shaws*, Helena Ann, Kennedy, QC, *b.* 1950, *m.*
1997   *Knight of Collingtree*, (Joan Christabel) Jill, Knight, DBE, *b.* 1923, *w.*
1997   *Linklater of Butterstone*, Veronica, Linklater, *b.* 1943, *m.*
1996   *Lloyd of Highbury*, Prof. June Kathleen, Lloyd, DBE, FRCP, FRCPE, FRCGP, *b.* 1928
1978   *Lockwood*, Betty, Lockwood, *b.* 1924, *w.*
1997   *Ludford*, Sarah Ann, Ludford, MEP, *b.* 1951
1997   *Maddock*, Diana Margaret, Maddock, *b.* 1945, *m.*
1991   *Mallalieu*, Ann, Mallalieu, QC, *b.* 1945, *m.*
1970   *Masham of Ilton*, Susan Lilian Primrose, Cunliffe-Lister, *b.* 1935, *m.*

1999   *Massey of Darwen*, Doreen Elizabeth, Massey, *b.* 1938, *m.*
1979   *McFarlane of Llandaff*, Jean Kennedy, McFarlane, *b.* 1926
1999   *McIntosh of Hudnall*, Genista Mary, McIntosh, *b.* 1946
2001   *Michie*, Janet Ray, Michie, *b.* 1934, *m.*
1998   *Miller of Chilthorne Domer*, Susan Elizabeth, Miller, *b.* 1954
1993   *Miller of Hendon*, Doreen, Miller, MBE, *b.* 1933, *m.*
2001   *Morgan of Huyton*, Sally, Morgan, *b.* 1959, *m.*
1997   *Nicholson of Winterbourne*, Emma Harriet, Nicholson, MEP, *b.* 1941, *m.*
1982   *Nicol*, Olive Mary Wendy, Nicol, *b.* 1923, *m.*
2000   *Noakes*, Shiela Valerie, Masters, DBE,*m.*
2000   *Northover*, Lindsay Patricia, Granshaw
1991   *O'Cathain*, Detta, O'Cathain, OBE, *b.* 1938, *m.*
1999   *O'Neill of Bengarve*, Onora Sylvia, O'Neill, CBE, PH.D., *b.* 1941
1989   *Oppenheim-Barnes*, Sally, Oppenheim-Barnes, PC, *b.* 1930, *m.*
1990   *Park of Monmouth*, Daphne Margaret Sybil Désirée, Park, CMG, OBE, *b.* 1921
1991   *Perry of Southwark*, Pauline, Perry, *b.* 1931, *m.*
1974   *Pike*, (Irene) Mervyn (Parnicott), Pike, DBE, *b.* 1918
1997   *Pitkeathley*, Jill Elizabeth, Pitkeathley, OBE, *b.* 1940
1981   *Platt of Writtle*, Beryl Catherine, Platt, CBE, FENG., *b.* 1923, *m.*
1999   *Prashar*, Usha Kumari, Prashar, CBE, *b.* 1948, *m.*
1996   *Ramsay of Cartvale*, Margaret Mildred (Meta), Ramsay, *b.* 1936
1994   *Rawlings*, Patricia Elizabeth, Rawlings, *b.* 1939
1997   *Rendell of Babergh*, Ruth Barbara, Rendell, CBE, *b.* 1930, *m.*
1998   *Richardson of Calow*, Kathleen Margaret, Richardson, OBE, *b.* 1938, *m.*
1997   *Scotland of Asthal*, Patricia Janet, Scotland, QC, *m.*
2000   *Scott of Needham Market*, Rosalind Carol, Scott
1991   *Seccombe*, Joan Anna Dalziel, Seccombe, DBE, *b.* 1930, *m.*
1967   *Serota*, Beatrice, Serota, DBE, *b.* 1919, *m.*
1998   *Sharp of Guildford*, Margaret Lucy, Sharp, *m.*
1973   *Sharples*, Pamela, Sharples, *b.* 1923, *m.*
1995   *Smith of Gilmorehill*, Elizabeth Margaret, Smith, *b.* 1940, *w.*
1999   *Stern*, Vivien Helen, Stern, CBE, *b.* 1941
1996   *Symons of Vernham Dean*, Elizabeth Conway, Symons, *b.* 1951, *Minister of State for Trade and the Foreign and Commonwealth Office*
1992   *Thatcher*, Margaret Hilda, Thatcher, KG, OM, PC, FRS, *b.* 1925, *m.*
1994   *Thomas of Walliswood*, Susan Petronella, Thomas, OBE, *b.* 1935, *m.*
1998   *Thornton*, (Dorothea) Glenys, Thornton, *b.* 1952, *m.*
1980   *Trumpington*, Jean Alys, Barker, PC, *b.* 1922, *w.*
1985   *Turner of Camden*, Muriel Winifred, Turner, *b.* 1927, *m.*
1998   *Uddin*, Manzila Pola, Uddin, *b.* 1959, *m.*
2000   *Walmsley*, Joan Margaret, Walmsley
1985   *Warnock*, Helen Mary, Warnock, DBE, *b.* 1924, *w.*
1999   *Warwick of Undercliffe*, Diana Mary, Warwick, *b.* 1945, *m.*
1999   *Whitaker*, Janet Alison, Whitaker
1996   *Wilcox*, Judith Ann, Wilcox, *w.*
1999   *Wilkins*, Rosalie Catherine, Wilkins, *b.* 1946
1993   *Williams of Crosby*, Shirley Vivien Teresa Brittain, Williams, PC, *b.* 1930, *m.*
1971   *Young*, Janet Mary, Young, PC, *b.* 1926, *m.*
1997   *Young of Old Scone*, Barbara Scott, Young, *b.* 1948

Lords Spiritual

The Lords Spiritual are the Archbishops of Canterbury and York and 24 diocesan bishops of the Church of England. The Bishops of London, Durham and Winchester always have seats in the House of Lords; the other 21 seats are filled by the remaining diocesan bishops in order of seniority. The Bishop of Sodor and Man and the Bishop of Gibraltar are not eligible to sit in the House of Lords.

ARCHBISHOPS

Style, The Most Revd and Right Hon. the Lord Archbishop of _
Addressed as Archbishop, *or* Your Grace

Introduced to House of Lords

1991   *Canterbury* (103rd), George Leonard Carey, PC, Ph.D., *b.* 1935, *m., cons.* 1987, *trans.* 1991
1990   *York* (96th), David Michael Hope, KCVO, PC, D.Phil., *b.* 1940, *cons.* 1985, *elected* 1985, *trans.* 1991, 1995

BISHOPS

Style, The Right Revd the Lord Bishop of _
Addressed as My Lord
elected date of election as diocesan bishop

Introduced to House of Lords (as at mid-2001)

1989   *Lichfield* (97th), Keith Norman Sutton, *b.* 1934, *m., cons.* 1978, *elected* 1984
1990   *Bristol* (54th), Barry Rogerson, *b.* 1936, *m., cons.* 1979, *elected* 1985
1993   *Lincoln* (70th), Robert Maynard Hardy, *b.* 1936, *m., cons.* 1980, *elected* 1986
1993   *Oxford* (41st), Richard Douglas Harries, *b.* 1936, *m., cons.* 1987, *elected* 1987
1994   *Birmingham* (7th), Mark Santer, *b.* 1936, *m., cons.* 1981, *elected* 1987
1994   *Durham* (93rd), (Anthony) Michael (Arnold) Turnbull, *b.* 1935, *m., cons.* 1988, *elected* 1988, *trans.* 1994
1995   *Blackburn* (7th), Alan David Chesters, *b.* 1937, *m., cons.* 1989, *elected* 1989
1996   *London* (132nd), Richard John Carew Chartres, *b.* 1947, *m., cons.* 1992
1996   *Winchester* (96th), Michael Charles Scott-Joynt, *b.* 1943, *m., cons.* 1987
1997   *Hereford* (103rd), John Keith Oliver, *b.* 1935, *m., cons.* 1990, *elected* 1990
1997   *Southwark* (9th), Thomas Frederick Butler, *b.* 1940, *m., cons.* 1985, *elected* 1991
1997   *Bath and Wells* (77th), James Lawton Thompson, *b.* 1936, *m., cons.* 1978, *elected* 1991
1997   *Wakefield* (11th), Nigel Simeon McCulloch, *b.* 1942, *m., cons.* 1986, *elected* 1992
1997   *Bradford* (8th), David James Smith, *b.* 1935, *m., cons.* 1987, *elected* 1992
1998   *Manchester* (10th), Christopher John Mayfield, *b.* 1935, *m., cons.* 1985, *elected* 1993

1998   *Salisbury* (77th), David Staffurth Stancliffe, *b.* 1942, *m., cons.* 1993, *elected* 1993
1998   *Gloucester* (39th), David Edward Bentley, *b.* 1935, *m., cons.* 1986, *elected* 1993
1999   *Rochester* (106th), Michael James Nazir-Ali, Ph.D., *b.* 1949, *m., cons.* 1984, *elected* 1995
1999   *Guildford* (8th), John Warren Gladwin, *b.* 1942, *m., cons.* 1994, *elected* 1994
1999   *Portsmouth* (8th), Kenneth William Stevenson, *b.* 1949, *m., cons.* 1995, *elected* 1995
1999   *Derby* (6th), Jonathan Sansbury Bailey, *b.* 1940, *m., cons.* 1992, *elected* 1995
1999   *St Albans* (9th), Christopher William Herbert, *b.* 1944, *m., cons.* 1995, *elected* 1995
2000   *Chelmsford* (8th), John Freeman Perry, *b.* 1935, *m., cons.* 1989, *elected* 1996
2001   *Peterborough* (37th), Ian Cundy, *b.* 1945, *m., cons.* 1992, *elected* 1996

Bishops awaiting seats, in order of seniority (as at mid-2001)

Chester (40th), Peter Robert Forster, Ph.D., *b.* 1950, *cons.* 1996, *elected* 1996
St Edmundsbury and Ipswich (9th), (John Hubert) Richard Lewis, *b.* 1943, *m., cons.* 1992, *elected* 1997
Truro (14th), William Ind, *b.* 1942, *m., cons.* 1987, *elected* 1997
Worcester (112th), Peter Stephen Maurice Selby, *b.* 1941, *cons.* 1984, *elected* 1997
Newcastle (11th), (John) Martin Wharton, *b.* 1944, *m., cons.* 1992, *elected* 1997
Sheffield (6th), John Nicholls, *b.* 1943, *m., cons.* 1990, *elected* 1997
Coventry (8th), Colin J. Bennetts, *b.* 1940, *m., cons.* 1994, *elected* 1997
Liverpool (7th), James Jones, *b.* 1948, *m., cons.* 1994, *elected* 1998
Leicester (6th), Timothy John Stevens, *b.* 1946, *m., cons.* 1999, *elected* 1999
Southwell (10th), George Henry Cassidy, *b.* 1942, *m., cons.* 1999, *elected* 1999
Norwich (71st), Graham R. James, *b.* 1951, *m., cons.* 1993, *elected* 1999
Exeter (70th), Michael L. Langrish, *b.* 1946, *m., cons.* 1993, *elected* 2000
Ripon and Leeds (12th), John R. Packer, *b.* 1946, *m., cons.* 1996, *elected* 2000
Ely (68th), Dr. Anthony Russell, *b.* 1943, *m., cons.* 1988, *elected* 2000
Carlisle (65th) Graham Dow, *b.* 1942, *m., cons.* 1985, *elected* 2000

COURTESY TITLES

From this list it will be seen that, for example, the Marquess of Blandford is heir to the Dukedom of Marlborough, and Viscount Amberley to the Earldom of Russell. Titles of second heirs are also given, and the courtesy title of the father of a second heir is indicated by *; e.g. Earl of Burlington, eldest son of *Marquess of Hartington

For forms of address, *see* page 135

MARQUESSES

*Blandford – *Marlborough, D.*
Bowmont and Cessford – *Roxburghe, D.*
Douglas and Clydesdale – *Hamilton, D.*
*Douro – *Wellington, D.*
Graham – *Montrose, D.*
Granby – *Rutland, D.*
Hamilton – *Abercorn, D.*
*Hartington – *Devonshire, D.*
*Kildare – *Leinster, D.*
Lorne – *Argyll, D.*
*Tavistock – *Bedford, D.*
Tullibardine – *Atholl, D.*
*Worcester – *Beaufort, D.*

EARLS

Aboyne – *Huntly, M.*
Ancram – *Lothian, M.*
Arundel and Surrey – *Norfolk, D.*
*Bective – *Headfort, M.*
*Belfast – *Donegall, M.*
Brecknock – *Camden, M.*
Burford – *St Albans, D.*
Burlington – **Hartington, M.*
*Cardigan – *Ailesbury, M.*
Compton – *Northampton, M.*
*Dalkeith – *Buccleuch, D.*
Dumfries – *Bute, M.*
*Euston – *Grafton, D.*
Glamorgan – **Worcester, M.*
Grosvenor – *Westminster, D.*
*Haddo – *Aberdeen and Temair, M.*
Hillsborough – *Downshire, M.*
Hopetoun – *Linlithgow, M.*
March and Kinrara – *Richmond, D.*
Medina – *Milford Haven, M.*
*Mount Charles – *Conyngham, M.*
Mornington – **Douro, M.*
Mulgrave – *Normanby, M.*
Percy – *Northumberland, D.*
Ronaldshay – *Zetland, M.*
*St Andrews – *Kent, D.*
*Shelburne – *Lansdowne, M.*
*Southesk – *Fife, D.*

Sunderland – **Blandford, M.*
*Tyrone – *Waterford, M.*
Ulster – *Gloucester, D.*
*Uxbridge – *Anglesey, M.*
Wiltshire – *Winchester, M.*
Yarmouth – *Hertford, M.*

VISCOUNTS

Althorp – *Spencer, E.*
Amberley – *Russell, E.*
Andover – *Suffolk and Berkshire, E.*
Anson – *Lichfield, E.*
Asquith – *Oxford and Asquith, E.*
Boringdon – *Morley, E.*
Borodale – *Beatty, E.*
Boyle – *Shannon, E.*
Brocas – *Jellicoe, E.*
Campden – *Gainsborough, E.*
Carlow – *Portarlington, E.*
Carlton – *Wharncliffe, E.*
Castlereagh – *Londonderry, M.*
Chelsea – *Cadogan, E.*
Chewton – *Waldegrave, E.*
Chichester – **Belfast, E.*
Clanfield – *Peel, E.*
Clive – *Powis, E.*
Coke – *Leicester, E.*
Corry – *Belmore, E.*
Corvedale – *Baldwin of Bewdley, E.*
Cranborne – *Salisbury, M.*
Cranley – *Onslow, E.*
Crichton – *Erne, E.*
Crowhurst – *Cottenham, E.*
Curzon – *Howe, E.*
Dangan – *Cowley, E.*
Dawick – *Haig, E.*
Drumlanrig – *Queensberry, M.*
Duncannon – *Bessborough, E.*
Dungarvan – *Cork and Orrery, E.*
Dunluce – *Antrim, E.*
Dunwich – *Stradbroke, E.*
Dupplin – *Kinnoull, E.*
Ebrington – *Fortescue, E.*
Ednam – *Dudley, E.*
Encombe – *Eldon, E.*
Enfield – *Strafford, E.*
Erleigh – *Reading, M.*
Errington – *Cromer, E.*

FitzHarris – *Malmesbury, E.*
Folkestone – *Radnor, E.*
Forbes – *Granard, E.*
Garmoyle – *Cairns, E.*
Garnock – *Lindsay, E.*
Glandine – *Norbury, E.*
Glenapp – *Inchcape, E.*
Glentworth – *Limerick, E.*
Grimstone – *Verulam, E.*
Gwynedd – *Lloyd George of Dwyfor, E.*
Hawkesbury – *Liverpool, E.*
Hinchingbrooke – *Sandwich, E.*
Ikerrin – *Carrick, E.*
Ingestre – *Shrewsbury, E.*
Ipswich – **Euston, E.*
Jocelyn – *Roden, E.*
Kelburn – *Glasgow, E.*
Kilwarlin – *Hillsborough, E.*
Kingsborough – *Kingston, E.*
Kirkwall – *Orkney, E.*
Knebworth – *Lytton, E.*
Lascelles – *Harewood, E.*
Linley – *Snowdon, E.*
Loftus – *Ely, M.*
Lowther – *Lonsdale, E.*
Lumley – *Scarbrough, E.*
Lymington – *Portsmouth, E.*
Macmillan of Ovenden – *Stockton, E.*
Maitland – *Lauderdale, E.*
Malden – *Essex, E.*
Mandeville – *Manchester, D.*
Melgund – *Minto, E.*
Merton – *Nelson, E.*
Moore – *Drogheda, E.*
Newport – *Bradford, E.*
Newry and Mourne – *Kilmorey, E.*
Parker – *Macclesfield, E.*
Perceval – *Egmont, E.*
Petersham – *Harrington, E.*
Pollington – *Mexborough, E.*
Raynham – *Townshend, M.*
Reidhaven – *Seafield, E.*
Ruthven of Canberra – *Gowrie, E.*
St Cyres – *Iddesleigh, E.*
Sandon – *Harrowby, E.*
Savernake – **Cardigan, E.*
Slane – **Mount Charles, E.*
Somerton – *Normanton, E.*
Stopford – *Courtown, E.*
Stormont – *Mansfield, E.*
Strathallan – *Perth, E.*
Stuart – *Castle Stewart, E.*
Suirdale – *Donoughmore, E.*
Tamworth – *Ferrers, E.*
Tarbat – *Cromartie, E.*
Vaughan – *Lisburne, E.*

Weymouth – *Bath, M.*
Windsor – *Plymouth, E.*
Wolmer – *Selborne, E.*
Woodstock – *Portland, E.*

BARONS (LORD)

Aberdour – *Morton, E.*
Apsley – *Bathurst, E.*
Ardee – *Meath, E.*
Ashley – *Shaftesbury, E.*
Balgonie – *Leven and Melville, E.*
Balniel – *Crawford and Balcarres, E.*
Berriedale – *Caithness, E.*
Bingham – *Lucan, E.*
Binning – *Haddington, E.*
Brooke – *Warwick, E.*
Bruce – *Elgin, E.*
Buckhurst – *De La Warr, E.*
Burghley – *Exeter, M.*
Cardross – *Buchan, E.*
Carnegie – **Southesk, E.*
Clifton – *Darnley, E.*
Cochrane – *Dundonald, E.*
Courtenay – *Devon, E.*
Dalmeny – *Rosebery, E.*
Doune – *Moray, E.*
Downpatrick – **St Andrews, E.*
Dunglass – *Home, E.*
Eliot – *St Germans, E.*
Eskdail – **Dalkeith, E.*
Formartine – **Haddo, E.*
Gillford – *Clanwilliam, E.*
Glamis – *Strathmore, E.*
Greenock – *Cathcart, E.*
Guernsey – *Aylesford, E.*
Hay – *Erroll, E.*
Herbert – *Pembroke, E.*
Howard of Effingham – *Effingham, E.*
Howland – **Tavistock, M.*
Hyde – *Clarendon, E.*
Inverurie – *Kintore, E.*
Irwin – *Halifax, E.*
Johnstone – *Annandale and Hartfell, E.*
Kenlis – **Bective, E.*
Langton – *Temple of Stowe, E.*
La Poer – **Tyrone, E.*
Leslie – *Rothes, E.*
Loughborough – *Rosslyn, E.*
Maltravers – **Arundel and Surrey, E.*
Mauchline – *Loudoun, C.*
Medway – *Cranbrook, E.*
Montgomerie – *Eglinton and Winton, E.*
Moreton – *Ducie, E.*
Naas – *Mayo, E.*
Neidpath – *Wemyss and March, E.*

Norreys – *Lindsey and Abingdon*, E.
Ogilvy – *Airlie*, E.
Oxmantown – *Rosse*, E.

Paget de Beaudesert – **Uxbridge*, E.
Porchester – *Carnarvon*, E.
Ramsay – *Dalhousie*, E.

Romsey – *Mountbatten of Burma*, C.
Rosehill – *Northesk*, E.
Scrymgeour – *Dundee*, E.
Seymour – *Somerset*, D.

Stanley – *Derby*, E.
Strathnaver – *Sutherland*, C.
Wodehouse – *Kimberley*, E.
Worsley – *Yarborough*, E.

PEERS' SURNAMES WHICH DIFFER FROM THEIR TITLES

The following symbols indicate the rank of the peer holding each title:

C.   Countess
D.   Duke
E.   Earl
M.   Marquess
V.   Viscount
*   Life Peer

Where no designation is given, the title is that of an hereditary Baron or Baroness

Abney-Hastings – *Loudoun*, C.
Acheson – *Gosford*, E.
Adderley – *Norton*
Addington – *Sidmouth*, V.
Adebowale – *A. of Thornes**
Agar – *Normanton*, E.
Aitken – *Beaverbrook*
Akers-Douglas – *Chilston*, V.
Alexander – *A. of Tunis*, E.
Alexander – *A. of Weedon**
Alexander – *Caledon*, E.
Allen – *A. of Abbeydale**
Allen – *Croham**
Allsopp – *Hindlip*
Alton – *A. of Liverpool**
Anderson – *Waverley*, V.
Anelay – *A. of St Johns**
Annesley – *Valentia*, V.
Anson – *Lichfield*, E.
Archer – *A. of Sandwell**
Archer – *A. of Weston-super-Mare**
Armstrong – *A. of Ilminster**
Armstrong-Jones – *Snowdon*, E.
Arthur – *Glenarthur*
Arundell – *Talbot of Malahide*
Ashdown – *A. of Norton-sub-Hamdon**
Ashley – *A. of Stoke**
Ashley-Cooper – *Shaftesbury*, E.
Ashton – *A. of Hyde*
Ashton – *A. of Upholland**
Asquith – *Oxford and Asquith*, E.
Assheton – *Clitheroe*
Astley – *Hastings*
Astor – *A. of Hever*
Aubrey-Fletcher – *Braye*
Bailey – *Glanusk*
Baillie – *Burton*

Baillie Hamilton – *Haddington*, E.
Baker – *B. of Dorking**
Baldwin – *B. of Bewdley*, E.
Balfour – *B. of Inchrye*
Balfour – *Kinross*
Balfour – *Riverdale*
Bampfylde – *Poltimore*
Banbury – *B. of Southam*
Barber – *B. of Tewkesbury**
Baring – *Ashburton*
Baring – *Cromer*, E.
Baring – *Howick of Glendale*
Baring – *Northbrook*
Baring – *Revelstoke*
Barker – *Trumpington**
Barnes – *Gorell*
Barnewall – *Trimlestown*
Bassam – *B. of Brighton**
Bathurst – *Bledisloe*, V.
Beauclerk – *St Albans*, D.
Beaumont – *Allendale*, V.
Beaumont – *B. of Whitley**
Beckett – *Grimthorpe*
Benn – *Stansgate*, V.
Bennet – *Tankerville*, E.
Bentinck – *Portland*, E.-
Beresford – *Decies*
Beresford – *Waterford*, M.
Bernstein – *B. of Craigweil**
Berry – *Camrose*, V.
Berry – *Kemsley*, V.
Bertie – *Lindsey*, E.
Best – *Wynford*
Bethell – *Westbury*
Bewicke-Copley – *Cromwell*
Bigham – *Mersey*, V.
Bingham – *B. of Cornhill**
Bingham – *Clanmorris*
Bingham – *Lucan*, E.
Bligh – *Darnley*, E.
Blyth – *B. of Rowington**
Bootle-Wilbraham – *Skelmersdale*
Boscawen – *Falmouth*, V.
Boston – *B. of Faversham**
Bourke – *Mayo*, E.
Bowes Lyon – *Strathmore*, E.
Bowyer – *Denham*
Boyd – *Kilmarnock*
Boyle – *Cork and Orrery*, E.
Boyle – *Glasgow*, E.
Boyle – *Shannon*, E.
Brabazon – *Meath*, E.
Brand – *Hampden*, V.
Brassey – *B. of Apethorpe*
Brett – *Esher*, V.
Bridge – *B. of Harwich**

Bridgeman – *Bradford*, E.
Brittan – *B. of Spennithorne**
Brodrick – *Midleton*, V.
Brooke – *Alanbrooke*, V.
Brooke – *B. of Alverthorpe**
Brooke – *Brookeborough*, V.
Brooke – *B. of Sutton Mandeville**
Brooks – *B. of Tremorfa**
Brooks – *Crawshaw*
Brougham – *Brougham and Vaux*
Broughton – *Fairhaven*
Browne – *Kilmaine*
Browne – *B. of Madingley**
Browne – *Oranmore and Browne*
Browne – *Sligo*, M.
Bruce – *Aberdare*
Bruce – *Balfour of Burleigh*
Bruce – *B. of Donington**
Bruce – *Elgin and Kincardine*, E.
Brudenell-Bruce – *Ailesbury*, M.
Buchan – *Tweedsmuir*
Buckley – *Wrenbury*
Butler – *B. of Brockwell**
Butler – *Carrick*, E.
Butler – *Dunboyne*
Butler – *Mountgarret*, V.
Buxton – *B. of Alsa**
Byng – *Strafford*, E.
Byng – *Torrington*, V.
Callaghan – *C. of Cardiff**
Cambell-Savours – *C.-S. of Allerdale**
Cameron – *C. of Lochbroom**
Campbell – *Argyll*, D.
Campbell – *C. of Alloway**
Campbell – *C. of Croy**
Campbell – *Cawdor*, E.
Campbell – *Colgrain*
Campbell – *Stratheden and Campbell*
Campbell-Gray – *Gray*
Canning – *Garvagh*
Capell – *Essex*, E.
Carington – *Carrington*
Carlisle – *C. of Berriew**
Carlisle – *C. of Bucklow**
Carmichael – *C. of Kelvingrove**
Carnegie – *Fife*, D.
Carnegie – *Northesk*, E.
Carr – *C. of Hadley**
Cary – *Falkland*, V.
Castle – *C. of Blackburn**
Caulfeild – *Charlemont*, V.
Cavendish – *C. of Furness**

Cavendish – *Chesham*
Cavendish – *Devonshire*, D.
Cavendish – *Waterpark*
Cayzer – *Rotherwick*
Cecil – *Amherst of Hackney*
Cecil – *Exeter*, M.
Cecil – *Rockley*
Cecil – *Salisbury*, M.
Chalker – *C. of Wallasey**
Chaloner – *Gisborough*
Charteris – *Wemyss and March*, E.
Chetwynd-Talbot – *Shrewsbury*, E.
Chichester – *Donegall*, M.
Chichester-Clark – *Moyola**
Child Villiers – *Jersey*, E.
Cholmondeley – *Delamere*
Chubb – *Hayter*
Clark – *C. of Kempston**
Clarke – *C. of Hampstead**
Clegg-Hill – *Hill*, V.
Clifford – *C. of Chudleigh*
Cochrane – *C. of Cults*
Cochrane – *Dundonald*, E.
Cocks – *Somers*
Cohen – *C. of Pimlico**
Coke – *Leicester*, E.
Cole – *Enniskillen*, E.
Collier – *Monkswell*
Colville – *Clydesmuir*
Colville – *C. of Culross*, V.
Compton – *Northampton*, M.
Condon – *C. of Langdon Green**
Conolly-Carew – *Carew*
Constantine – *C. of Stanmore**
Cooke – *C. of Islandreagh**
Cooke – *C. of Thorndon**
Cooper – *Norwich*, V
Cope – *C. of Berkeley**
Corbett – *C. of Castle Vale**.
Corbett – *Rowallan*
Cornwall-Leigh – *Grey of Condor*
Courtenay – *Devon*, E.
Craig – *C. of Radley**
Craig – *Craigavon*, V.
Crichton – *Erne*, E.
Crichton-Stuart – *Bute*, M.
Cripps – *Parmoor*
Crossley – *Somerleyton*
Cubitt – *Ashcombe*
Cunliffe-Lister – *Masham of Ilton**
Cunliffe-Lister – *Swinton*, E.

Currie – *C. of Marylebone**
Curzon – *Howe, E.*
Curzon – *Scarsdale, V.*
Cust – *Brownlow*
Dalrymple – *Stair, E.*
Daubeny de Moleyns –
  Ventry
Davies – *D. of Coity**
Davies – *Darwen*
Davies – *D. of Oldham**
Davison – *Broughshane*
Dawnay – *Downe, V.*
Dawson-Damer –
  Portarlington, E.
Dean – *D. of Harptree**
Dean – *D. of Thornton-le-
  Fylde**
Deane – *Muskerry*
de Courcy – *Kingsale*
de Grey – *Walsingham*
Delacourt-Smith –
  *Delacourt Smith of
  Alteryn**
Denison – *Londesborough*
Denison-Pender – *Pender*
Devereux – *Hereford, V.*
Dewar – *Forteviot*
De Yarburgh-Bateson –
  Deramore
Dixon – *Glentoran*
Dodson – *Monk Bretton*
Donaldson – *D. of
  Lymington**
Dormand – *D. of Easington**
Douglas – *Morton, E.*
Douglas – *Queensberry, M.*
Douglas-Hamilton –
  Hamilton, D.
Douglas-Hamilton –
  Selkirk, E.
Douglas-Hamilton –
  *Selkirk of Douglas**
Douglas-Home – *Dacre*
Douglas-Home – *Home, E.*
Douglas-Pennant–*Penrhyn*
Douglas-Scott-Montagu –
  Montagu of Beaulieu
Drummond – *Perth, E.*
Drummond of Megginch –
  Strange
Dugdale – *Crathorne*
Duke – *Merrivale*
Duncombe – *Feversham*
Dundas – *Melville, V.*
Dundas – *Zetland, M.*
Eady – *Swinfen*
Eccles – *E. of Moulton**
Eden – *Auckland*
Eden – *E. of Winton**
Eden – *Henley*
Edgcumbe – *Mount
  Edgcumbe, E.*
Edmondson – *Sandford*
Edwardes – *Kensington*
Edwards – *Crickhowell**
Egerton – *Sutherland, D.*
Eliot – *St Germans, E.*
Elliot-Murray-
  Kynynmound – *Minto,
  E.*

Ellis – *Seaford*
Erskine – *Buchan, E.*
Erskine – *Mar and Kellie, E.*
Erskine-Murray – *Elibank*
Evans – *E. of Parkside**
Evans – *E. of Temple
  Guiting**
Evans – *E. of Watford**
Evans – *Mountevans*
Evans-Freke – *Carbery*
Eve – *Silsoe*
Ewing – *E. of Kirkford**
Fairfax – *F. of Cameron*
Falconer – *F. of Thoroton**
Fane – *Westmorland, E.*
Farrington – *F. of Ribbleton**
Faulkner – *F. of Worcester**
Fearn – *F. of Southport**
Feilding – *Denbigh, E.*
Felton – *Seaford*
Fellowes – *De Ramsey*
Fermor-Hesketh – *Hesketh*
Fiennes – *Saye and Sele*
Fiennes-Clinton – *Lincoln,
  E.*
Finch Hatton – *Winchilsea,
  E.*
Finch-Knightley –
  Aylesford, E.
Finlay – *F. of Llandaff**
Fisher – *F. of Rednal**
Fitzalan-Howard – *Herries
  of Terregles*
Fitzalan-Howard – *Norfolk,
  D.*
FitzGerald – *Leinster, D.*
Fitzherbert – *Stafford*
FitzRoy – *Grafton, D.*
FitzRoy – *Southampton*
FitzRoy Newdegate –
  Daventry, V.
Fletcher-Vane – *Inglewood*
Flower – *Ashbrook, V.*
Foljambe – *Liverpool, E.*
Forbes – *Granard, E.*
Forsyth – *F. of Drumlean**
Forwood – *Arlington*
Foster – *F. of Thames Bank**
Fowler – *F. of Sutton
  Caulfield**
Fox-Strangways – *Ilchester,
  E.*
Frankland – *Zouche*
Fraser – *F. of Carmyllie**
Fraser – *F. of Kilmorack**
Fraser – *Lovat*
Fraser – *Saltoun*
Fraser – *Strathalmond*
Freeman-Grenville –
  Kinloss
Fremantle – *Cottesloe*
French – *De Freyne*
Fyfe – *F. of Fairfield**
Galbraith – *Strathclyde*
Ganzoni – *Belstead*
Gardner – *G. of Parkes**
Gathorne-Hardy –
  Cranbrook, E.
Gibbs – *Aldenham*
Gibbs – *Wraxall*

Gibson – *Ashbourne*
Gibson – *G. of Market
  Ransen**
Giffard – *Halsbury, E.*
Gilbey – *Vaux of Harrowden*
Gilmour – *G. of
  Craigmillar**
Gladwin – *G. of Clee**
Glyn – *Wolverton*
Godley – *Kilbracken*
Goff – *G. of Chieveley**
Golding – *G. of Newcastle-
  under-Lyme**
Gordon – *Aberdeen, M.*
Gordon – *G. of Strathblane**
Gordon – *Huntly, M.*
Gordon Lennox –
  Richmond, D.
Gore – *Arran, E.*
Gould – *G. of Potternewton**
Graham – *G. of Edmonton**
Graham – *Montrose, D.*
Graham-Toler – *Norbury,
  E.*
Granshaw – *Northover**
Grant of Grant – *Strathspey*
Granville – *G. of Eye**
Gray – *G. of Contin**
Greaves – *Dysart, C.*
Greenall – *Daresbury*
Greene – *G. of Harrow
  Weald**
Greville – *Warwick, E.*
Griffiths – *G. of Fforestfach**
Grigg – *Altrincham*
Grimston – *G. of Westbury*
Grimston – *Verulam, E.*
Grosvenor – *Westminster,
  D.*
Grosvenor – *Wilton and
  Ebury, E*
Guest – *Wimborne, V*
Gueterbock – *Berkeley*
Guinness – *Iveagh, E.*
Guinness – *Moyne*
Gully – *Selby, V.*
Gummer – *Chadlington**
Gurdon – *Cranworth*
Guthrie – *G. of
  Craigiebank**
Gwynne Jones – *Chalfont**
Hamilton – *Abercorn, D.*
Hamilton – *Belhaven and
  Stenton*
Hamilton – *Dudley*
Hamilton – *H. of Dalzell*
Hamilton – *Holm Patrick*
Hamilton-Russell – *Boyne,
  V.*
Hamilton-Smith – *Colwyn*
Hanbury-Tracy – *Sudeley*
Handcock – *Castlemaine*
Harbord-Hamond –
  Suffield
Harding – *H. of Petherton*
Hardinge – *H. of Penshurst*
Hardy – *H. of Wath**
Hare – *Blakenham, V.*
Hare – *Listowel, E.*

Harmsworth – *Rothermere,
  V.*
Harris – *H. of Haringey**
Harris – *H. of High Cross**
Harris – *H. of Peckham**
Harris – *H. of Richmond**
Harris – *Malmesbury, E.*
Harvey – *H. of Tasburgh*
Hastings Bass –
  Huntingdon, E.
Hay – *Erroll, E.*
Hay – *Kinnoull, E.*
Hay – *Tweeddale, M.*
Heathcote-Drummond-
  Willoughby –
  Willoughby de Eresby
Hely-Hutchinson –
  Donoughmore, E.
Henderson – *Faringdon*
Hennessy – *Windlesham*
Henniker-Major –
  Henniker
Hepburne-Scott – *Polwarth*
Herbert – *Carnarvon, E.*
Herbert – *Hemingford*
Herbert – *Pembroke, E.*
Herbert – *Powis, E.*
Hervey – *Bristol, M.*
Heseltine – *H. of Thenford**
Hewitt – *Lifford, V.*
Hicks Beach – *St Aldwyn, E.*
Hill – *Downshire, M.*
Hill – *Sandys*
Hill-Trevor – *Trevor*
Hilton – *H. of Eggardon**
Hobart-Hampden –
  Buckinghamshire, E.
Hobhouse – *H. of
  Woodborough**
Hodgson – *H. of Astley
  Abbotts**
Hogg – *Hailsham of St
  Marylebone**
Hogg – *H. of Cumbernauld**
Holland-Hibbert –
  Knutsford, V.
Hollis – *H. of Heigham**
Holme – *H. of Cheltenham**
Holmes à Court –
  Heytesbury
Hood – *Bridport, V.*
Hope – *Glendevon*
Hope – *H. of Craighead**
Hope – *Linlithgow, M.*
Hope – *Rankeillour*
Hope Johnstone –
  *Annandale and Hartfell,
  E.*
Hope-Morley – *Hollenden*
Hopkinson – *Colyton*
Hore Ruthven – *Gowrie, E.*
Hovell-Thurlow-
  Cumming-Bruce –
  Thurlow
Howard – *Carlisle, E.*
Howard – *Effingham, E.*
Howard – *H. of Penrith*
Howard – *Strathcona*
Howard – *Suffolk and
  Berkshire, E.*

Northcote – *Iddesleigh, E.*
Norton – *Grantley*
Norton – *N. of Louth**
Norton – *Rathcreedan*
Nugent – *Westmeath, E.*
O'Brien – *Inchiquin*
Ogilvie-Grant – *Seafield, E.*
Ogilvy – *Airlie, E.*
Oliver – *O. of Aylmerton**
O'Neill – *O'N of Bengarve**
O'Neill – *Rathcavan*
Orde-Powlett – *Bolton*
Ormsby-Gore – *Harlech*
Ouseley – *O. of Peckham Rye**
Page – *Whaddon**
Paget – *Anglesey, M.*
Pakenham – *Longford, E.*
Pakington – *Hampton*
Palmer – *Lucas and Dingwall*
Palmer – *Selborne, E.*
Park – *P. of Monmouth**
Parker – *Macclesfield, E.*
Parker – *Morley, E.*
Parnell – *Congleton*
Parsons – *Rosse, E.*
Patel – *P. of Blackburn**
Paulet – *Winchester, M.*
Peake – *Ingleby, V.*
Pearson – *Cowdray, V.*
Pearson – *P. of Rannoch**
Pease – *Gainford*
Pease – *Wardington*
Pelham – *Chichester, E.*
Pelham – *Yarborough, E.*
Pellew – *Exmouth, V*
Pendry – *P. of Stalybridge**.*
Penny – *Marchwood, V.*
Pepys – *Cottenham, E.*
Perceval – *Egmont, E.*
Percy – *Northumberland, D.*
Perry – *P. of Southwark**
Perry – *P. of Walton**
Pery – *Limerick, E.*
Peyton – *P. of Yeovil**
Philipps – *Milford*
Philipps – *St Davids, V.*
Phillips – *P. of Sudbury**
Phillips – *P. of Worth Matravers**
Phipps – *Normanby, M.*
Pilkington – *P. of Oxenford**
Plant – *P. of Highfield**
Platt – *P. of Writtle**
Pleydell-Bouverie – *Radnor, E.*
Plummer – *P. of St Marylebone**
Plumptre – *Fitzwalter*
Plunkett – *Dunsany*
Plunkett – *Louth*
Pollock – *Hanworth, V.*
Pomeroy – *Harberton, V.*
Ponsonby – *Bessborough, E.*
Ponsonby – *de Mauley*
Ponsonby – *P. of Shulbrede*
Ponsonby – *Sysonby*
Porter – *P. of Luddenham**
Powell – *P. of Bayswater**

Powys – *Lilford*
Pratt – *Camden, M.*
Preston – *Gormanston, V.*
Primrose – *Rosebery, E.*
Prittie – *Dunalley*
Prout – *Kingsland**
Ramsay – *Dalhousie, E.*
Ramsay – *R. of Cartvale**
Ramsbotham – *Soulbury, V.*
Randall – *R. of St. Budeaux**
Rawlinson – *R. of Ewell**
Rees-Williams – *Ogmore*
Rendell – *R. of Babergh**
Renfrew – *R. of Kaimsthorn**
Renton – *R. of Mount Harry**
Renwick – *R. of Clifton**
Rhys – *Dynevor*
Richards – *Milverton*
Richardson – *R. of Calow**
Richardson – *R. of Duntisbourne**
Ritchie – *R. of Dundee*
Roberts – *Clwyd*
Roberts – *R. of Conway**
Robertson – *R. of Oakridge*
Robertson – *R. of Port Ellen**
Robertson – *Wharton*
Robinson – *Martonmere*
Roche – *Fermoy*
Rodd – *Rennell*
Rodger – *R. of Earlsferry**
Rodgers – *R. of Quarry Bank**
Rogers – *R. of Riverside**
Roll – *R. of Ipsden**
Roper-Curzon – *Teynham*
Rospigliosi – *Newburgh, E.*
Rous – *Stradbroke, E.*
Rowley-Conwy – *Langford*
Royle – *Fanshawe of Richmond**
Runciman – *R. of Doxford, V.*
Russell – *Ampthill*
Russell – *Bedford, D.*
Russell – *de Clifford*
Russell – *R. of Liverpool*
Ryder – *Harrowby, E.*
Ryder – *R. of Eaton Hastings**
Ryder – *R. of Wensum**
Sackville – *De La Warr, E.*
Sackville-West – *Sackville*
Sainsbury – *S. of Preston Candover**
Sainsbury – *S. of Turville**
St Aubyn – *St Levan*
St Clair – *Sinclair*
St Clair-Erskine – *Rosslyn, E.*
St John – *Bolingbroke and St John, V.*
St John – *St John of Blesto*
St John-Stevas – *St John of Fawsley**
St Leger – *Doneraile, V.*
Samuel – *Bearsted, V.*
Sanderson – *S. of Ayot*
Sanderson – *S. of Bowden**

Sandilands – *Torphichen*
Saumarez – *De Saumarez*
Savile – *Mexborough, E.*
Saville – *S. of Newdigate**
Scarlett – *Abinger*
Schreiber – *Marlesford**
Sclater-Booth – *Basing*
Scotland – *S. of Asthal**
Scott – *Eldon, E*
Scott – *S. of Foscote**
Scott – *S. of Needham Market**.*
Scrymgeour – *Dundee, E.*
Seager – *Leighton of St Mellons*
Seely – *Mottistone*
Seymour – *Hertford, M.*
Seymour – *Somerset, D.*
Sharp – *S. of Guildford**
Shaw – *Craigmyle*
Shaw – *S. of Northstead**
Sheldon – *S. of Ashdon-under-Lyne**
Sheppard – *S. of Didgemere**
Sheppard – *S. of Liverpool**
Shirley – *Ferrers, E.*
Shore – *S. of Stepney**
Short – *Glenamara**
Shutt – *S. of Greetland**
Siddeley – *Kenilworth*
Sidney – *De L'Isle, V.*
Simon – *S. of Glaisdale**
Simon – *S. of Highbury**
Simon – *S. of Wythenshawe*
Simpson – *S. of Dunkeld**
Sinclair – *Caithness, E.*
Sinclair – *S. of Cleeve*
Sinclair – *Thurso, V.*
Skeffington – *Massereene,V.*
Slynn – *S. of Hadley**
Smith – *Bicester*
Smith – *Hambleden, V.*
Smith – *Kirkhill**
Smith – *S. of Clifton**
Smith – *S. of Gilmorehill**
Smith – *S. of Leigh**
Somerset – *Beaufort, D.*
Somerset – *Raglan*
Soulsby – *S. of Swaffham Prior**
Spencer – *Churchill, V.*
Spencer-Churchill – *Marlborough, D.*
Spring Rice – *Monteagle of Brandon*
Stanhope – *Harrington, E.*
Stanley – *Derby, E.*
Stanley – *Stanley of Alderley and Sheffield*
Stapleton-Cotton – *Combermere, V.*
Steel – *S. of Aikwood**
Sterling – *S. of Plaistow**
Stevens – *S. of Ludgate**
Stevenson – *S. of Coddenham**
Stewart – *Galloway, E.*
Stewart – *Stewartby**
Stodart – *S. of Leaston**
Stoddart – *S. of Swindon**

Stone – *S. of Blackheath**
Stonor – *Camoys*
Stopford – *Courtown, E.*
Stourton – *Mowbray*
Strachey – *O'Hagan*
Strutt – *Belper*
Strutt – *Rayleigh*
Stuart – *Castle Stewart, E.*
Stuart – *Moray, E.*
Stuart – *S. of Findhorn, V.*
Suenson-Taylor – *Grantchester*
Sutherland – *S. of Houndwood**
Symons – *S. of Vernham Dean**
Taylor – *Ingrow**
Taylor – *T. of Blackburn**
Taylor – *T. of Warwick**
Taylour – *Headfort, M.*
Temple-Gore-Langton – *Temple of Stowe, E*
Temple-Morris – *Temple-Morris of Llandaff**
Tennant – *Glenconner*
Thellusson – *Rendlesham*
Thesiger – *Chelmsford, V.*
Thomas – *T. of Gresford**
Thomas – *T. of Gwydir**
Thomas – *T. of Macclesfield**
Thomas – *T. of Swynnerton**
Thomas – *T. of Walliswood**
Thomson – *T. of Fleet*
Thomson – *T. of Monifieth**
Thynn – *Bath, M.*
Tottenham – *Ely, M.*
Trefusis – *Clinton*
Trench – *Ashtown*
Trevor-Roper – *Dacre of Glanton**
Tufton – *Hothfield*
Turner – *Netherthorpe*
Turner – *T. of Camden**
Turnour – *Winterton, E.*
Tyrell-Kenyon – *Kenyon*
Vanden-Bempde-Johnstone – *Derwent*
Vane – *Barnard*
Vane-Tempest-Stewart – *Londonderry, M.*
Vanneck – *Huntingfield*
Vaughan – *Lisburne, E.*
Vereker – *Gort, V.*
Verney – *Willoughby de Broke*
Vernon – *Lyveden*
Vesey – *De Vesci, V.*
Villiers – *Clarendon, E.*
Vincent – *V. of Coleshill**
Vivian – *Swansea*
Wade – *W. of Chorlton**
Waldegrave – *W. of North Hill**
Walker – *W. of Doncaster**
Walker – *W. of Worcester**
Wallace – *W. of Coslany**
Wallace – *W. of Saltaire**
Wallop – *Portsmouth, E.*
Walton – *W. of Detchant**
Ward – *Bangor, V.*

Orders of Chivalry

THE MOST NOBLE ORDER
OF THE GARTER (1348)

KG
Ribbon, Blue
Motto, Honi soit qui mal y pense
(*Shame on him who thinks evil of it*)
The number of Knights Companions
is limited to 24

SOVEREIGN OF THE ORDER
The Queen

LADIES OF THE ORDER
HM Queen Elizabeth the Queen
Mother, 1936
HRH The Princess Royal, 1994

ROYAL KNIGHTS
HRH The Prince Philip, Duke of
Edinburgh, 1947
HRH The Prince of Wales, 1958
HRH The Duke of Kent, 1985
HRH The Duke of Gloucester, 1997

EXTRA KNIGHTS COMPANIONS
AND LADIES
HRH Princess Juliana of the
Netherlands, 1958
HRH The Grand Duke of
Luxembourg, 1972
HM The Queen of Denmark, 1979
HM The King of Sweden, 1983
HM The King of Spain, 1988
HM The Queen of the Netherlands,
1989
HIM The Emperor of Japan, 1998

KNIGHTS AND LADY
COMPANIONS
The Earl of Longford, 1971
The Duke of Grafton, 1976
The Duke of Norfolk, 1983
The Lord Richardson of
Duntisbourne, 1983
The Lord Carrington, 1985
The Lord Callaghan of Cardiff, 1987
The Lord Hailsham of St
Marylebone, 1988
The Duke of Wellington, 1990
Field Marshal the Lord Bramall, 1990
Sir Edward Heath, 1992
The Viscount Ridley, 1992
The Lord Sainsbury of Preston
Candover, 1992
The Lord Ashburton, 1994
The Lord Kingsdown, 1994

Sir Ninian Stephen, 1994
The Baroness Thatcher, 1995
Sir Edmund Hillary, 1995
The Duke of Devonshire, 1996
Sir Timothy Colman, 1996
The Duke of Abercorn, 1999
Sir William Gladstone, 1999
Field Marshal The Lord Inge, 2001
Sir Anthony Acland, 2001
Prelate, The Bishop of Winchester
Chancellor, The Lord Carrington, KG,
GCMG, CH, MC
Register, The Dean of Windsor
Garter King of Arms, P. Gwynn-Jones,
CVO
Gentleman Usher of the Black Rod, Lt.
Gen. Sir Michael Willcocks, KCB
Secretary, D. H. B. Chesshyre, LVO

THE MOST ANCIENT AND
MOST NOBLE ORDER OF
THE THISTLE (REVIVED 1687)

KT
Ribbon, Green
Motto, Nemo me impune lacessit (*No
one provokes me with impunity*)
The number of Knights is limited to
16

SOVEREIGN OF THE ORDER
The Queen

LADIES OF THE THISTLE
HM Queen Elizabeth the Queen
Mother, 1937
HRH The Princess Royal, 2000

ROYAL KNIGHTS
HRH The Prince Philip, Duke of
Edinburgh, 1952
HRH The Prince of Wales, Duke of
Rothesay, 1977

KNIGHTS AND LADIES
The Earl of Wemyss and March, 1966
Sir Donald Cameron of Lochiel, 1973
The Duke of Buccleuch and
Queensberry, 1978
The Earl of Elgin and Kincardine,
1981
The Lord Thomson of Monifieth,
1981
The Earl of Airlie, 1985
Capt. Sir Iain Tennant, 1986

The Viscount Younger of Leckie,
1995
The Viscount of Arbuthnott, 1996
The Earl of Crawford and Balcarres,
1996
Lady Marion Fraser, 1996
The Lord Macfarlane of Bearsden,
1996
The Lord Mackay of Clashfern, 1997
The Lord Wilson of Tillyorn, 2000
Chancellor, The Duke of Buccleuch
and Queensberry, KT, VRD
Dean, The Very Revd G. I. Macmillan,
CVO
Secretary and Lord Lyon King of Arms,
R. O. Blair, LVO, WS
Usher of the Green Rod, Rear-Adm. C.
H. Layman, CB, DSO, LVO

THE MOST HONOURABLE
ORDER OF THE BATH (1725)

GCB *Military*   GCB *Civil*

GCB Knight (or Dame) Grand Cross
KCB Knight Commander
DCB Dame Commander
CB Companion
Ribbon, Crimson
Motto, Tria juncta in uno (*Three joined
in one*)
Remodelled 1815, and enlarged many
times since. The Order is divided into
civil and military divisions. Women
became eligible for the Order from 1
January 1971

THE SOVEREIGN
GREAT MASTER AND FIRST OR
PRINCIPAL KNIGHT GRAND CROSS
HRH The Prince of Wales, KG, KT,
GCB
Dean of the Order, The Dean of
Westminster
Bath King of Arms, Gen. Sir Brian
Kenny, GCB, CBE
Registrar and Secretary, Rear-Adm. D.
E. Macey, CB
Genealogist, P. Gwynn-Jones, CVO
Gentleman Usher of the Scarlet Rod, Air
Vice-Marshal Sir Richard Peirse,
KCVO, CB
Deputy Secretary, The Secretary of the
Central Chancery of the Orders of
Knighthood

Chancery, Central Chancery of the Orders of Knighthood, St James's Palace, London SW1A 1BH

THE ORDER OF MERIT (1902)

OM *Military*   OM *Civil*

OM

Ribbon, Blue and crimson

This Order is designed as a special distinction for eminent men and women without conferring a knighthood upon them. The Order is limited in numbers to 24, with the addition of foreign honorary members. Membership is of two kinds, military and civil, the badge of the former having crossed swords, and the latter oak leaves

THE SOVEREIGN

HRH The Prince Philip, Duke of Edinburgh, 1968
Sir George Edwards, 1971
Revd Prof. Owen Chadwick, KBE, 1983
Sir Andrew Huxley, 1983
Dr Frederick Sanger, 1986
Prof. Sir Ernst Gombrich, 1988
Dr Max Perutz, 1988
Dame Cicely Saunders, 1989
Prof. The Lord Porter of Luddenham, 1989
The Baroness Thatcher, 1990
Dame Joan Sutherland, 1991
Prof. Francis Crick, 1991
Dame Ninette de Valois, 1992
Sir Michael Atiyah, 1992
Lucian Freud, 1993
The Lord Jenkins of Hillhead, 1993
Sir Aaron Klug, 1995
The Lord Foster of Thames Bank, 1997
Sir Denis Rooke, 1997
Sir James Black, 2000
Sir Anthony Caro, 2000
Prof. Sir Roger Penrose, 2000
Sir Tom Stoppard, 2000
Honorary Member, Nelson Mandela, 1995

Secretary and Registrar, Sir Edward Ford, GCVO, KCB, ERD
Chancery, Central Chancery of the Orders of Knighthood, St James's Palace, London SW1A 1BH

THE MOST DISTINGUISHED ORDER OF ST MICHAEL AND ST GEORGE (1818)

GCMG   KCMG

GCMG   Knight (or Dame) Grand Cross
KCMG   Knight Commander
DCMG   Dame Commander
CMG   Companion

Ribbon, Saxon blue, with scarlet centre
Motto, Auspicium melioris aevi (*Token of a better age*)

THE SOVEREIGN
GRAND MASTER
HRH The Duke of Kent, KG, GCMG, GCVO, ADC

Prelate, The Rt. Revd Simon Barrington-Ward, KCMG
Chancellor, Sir Antony Acland, kG, GCMG, GCVO
Secretary, The Permanent Under-Secretary of State at the Foreign and Commonwealth Office and Head of the Diplomatic Service
Registrar, Sir John Graham, Bt., GCMG
King of Arms, Sir Ewen Fergusson, GCMG, GCVO
Gentleman Usher of the Blue Rod, Sir John Margetson, KCMG
Dean, The Dean of St Paul's
Deputy Secretary, The Secretary of the Central Chancery of the Orders of Knighthood
Chancery, Central Chancery of the Orders of Knighthood, St James's Palace, London SW1A 1BH

THE MOST EMINENT ORDER OF THE INDIAN EMPIRE (1868)

GCIE   Knight Grand Commander
KCIE   Knight Commander
CIE   Companion

Ribbon, Imperial purple
Motto, Imperatricis auspiciis (*Under the auspices of the Empress*)

THE SOVEREIGN
Registrar, The Secretary of the Central Chancery of the Orders of Knighthood
No conferments have been made since 1947

THE IMPERIAL ORDER OF THE CROWN OF INDIA (1877) FOR LADIES

CI
Badge, the royal cipher in jewels within an oval, surmounted by an heraldic crown and attached to a bow of light blue watered ribbon, edged white
The honour does not confer any rank or title upon the recipient
No conferments have been made since 1947

HM The Queen, 1947
HM Queen Elizabeth the Queen Mother, 1931
HRH The Princess Margaret, Countess of Snowdon, 1947
HRH Princess Alice, Duchess of Gloucester, 1937

THE ROYAL VICTORIAN ORDER (1896)

GCVO   KCVO

GCVO   Knight or Dame Grand Cross
KCVO   Knight Commander
DCVO   Dame Commander
CVO   Commander
LVO   Lieutenant
MVO   Member

Ribbon, Blue, with red and white edges
Motto, Victoria

THE SOVEREIGN
GRAND MASTER
HM Queen Elizabeth the Queen Mother
Chancellor, The Lord Chamberlain
Secretary, The Keeper of the Privy Purse
Registrar, The Secretary of the Central Chancery of the Orders of Knighthood
Chaplain, The Chaplain of the Queen's Chapel of the Savoy
Hon. Genealogist, D. H. B. Chesshyre, LVO

THE MOST EXCELLENT ORDER OF THE BRITISH EMPIRE (1917)

GBE   KBE

The Order was divided into military and civil divisions in December 1918

GBE   Knight or Dame Grand Cross
KBE   Knight Commander
DBE   Dame Commander
CBE   Commander
OBE   Officer
MBE   Member

Ribbon, Rose pink edged with pearl grey with vertical pearl stripe in centre (military division); without vertical pearl stripe (civil division)
Motto, For God and the Empire

THE SOVEREIGN

GRAND MASTER
HRH The Prince Philip, Duke of Edinburgh, KG, KT, OM, GBE, PC

Prelate, The Bishop of London
King of Arms, Air Chief Marshal Sir Patrick Hine, GCB, GBE
Registrar, The Secretary of the Central Chancery of the Orders of Knighthood
Secretary, The Secretary of the Cabinet and Head of the Home Civil Service
Dean, The Dean of St Paul's
Gentleman Usher of the Purple Rod, Sir Alexander Michael Graham, GBE, DCL*Chancery*, Central Chancery of the Orders of Knighthood, St James's Palace, London SW1A 1BH

ORDER OF THE COMPANIONS OF HONOUR (1917)

CH

Ribbon, Carmine, with gold edges

This Order consists of one class only and carries with it no title. The number of awards is limited to 65 (excluding honorary members)

Anthony, Rt. Hon. John, 1981
Ashley of Stoke, The Lord, 1975
Astor, Hon. David, 1993
Attenborough, Sir David, 1995
Baker, Dame Janet, 1993

Baker of Dorking, The Lord, 1992
Birtwistle, Sir Harrison, 2001
Brenner, Sydney, 1986
Brook, Peter, 1998
Brooke, Rt. Hon. Peter, 1992
Carrington, The Lord, 1983
De Chastelain, Gen. John, 1999
Doll, Prof. Sir Richard, 1995
Fraser, Rt. Hon. Malcolm, 1977
Freud, Lucian, 1983
Glenamara, The Lord, 1976
Gorton, Rt. Hon. Sir John, 1971
Hailsham of St Marylebone, The Lord, 1974
Hamilton, Richard, 1999
Hawking, Prof. Stephen, 1989
Healey, The Lord, 1979
Heseltine, Rt. Hon. Michael, 1997
Hobsbawm, Prof. Eric, 1998
Hockney, David, 1997
Howe of Aberavon, The Lord, 1996
Hurd of Westwell, The Lord, 1995
Jones, James, 1977
King, Rt. Hon. Tom, 1992
Lange, Rt. Hon. David, 1989
Lessing, Doris, 1999
Major, Rt. Hon. John, 1999
Milstein, César, 1994
Owen, The Lord, 1994
Patten, Rt. Hon. Christopher, 1998
Perutz, Dr Max, 1975
Powell, Sir Philip, 1984
Riley, Bridget, 1999
Sanger, Frederick, 1981
Scofield, Paul, 2000
Sisson, Charles, 1993
Smith, Sir John, 1993
Somare, Rt. Hon. Sir Michael, 1978
Talboys, Rt. Hon. Sir Brian, 1981
Tebbit, The Lord, 1987
Varah, Rev. Dr. Chad, 1999
Honorary Members, Lee Kuan Yew, 1970; Dr Joseph Luns, 1971

Secretary and Registrar, The Secretary of the Central Chancery of the Orders of Knighthood

THE DISTINGUISHED SERVICE ORDER (1886)

DSO

Ribbon, Red, with blue edges

Bestowed in recognition of especial services in action of commissioned officers in the Navy, Army and Royal Air Force and (since 1942) Mercantile Marine. The members are Companions only. A Bar may be awarded for any additional act of service

THE IMPERIAL SERVICE ORDER (1902)

ISO

Ribbon, Crimson, with blue centre

Appointment as Companion of this Order is open to members of the Civil Services whose eligibility is determined by the grade they hold. The Order consists of The Sovereign and Companions to a number not exceeding 1,900, of whom 1,300 may belong to the Home Civil Services and 600 to Overseas Civil Services. The then Prime Minister announced in March 1993 that he would make no further recommendations for appointments to the Order.

Secretary, The Secretary of the Cabinet and Head of the Home Civil Service
Registrar, The Secretary of the Central Chancery of the Orders of Knighthood, St James's Palace, London SW1A 1BH

THE ROYAL VICTORIAN CHAIN (1902)

It confers no precedence on its holders

HM THE QUEEN

HM Queen Elizabeth the Queen Mother, 1937
HRH Princess Juliana of the Netherlands, 1950
HM The King of Thailand, 1960
HM King Zahir Shah of Afghanistan, 1971
HM The Queen of Denmark, 1974
HM The King of Nepal, 1975
HM The King of Sweden, 1975
HM The Queen of the Netherlands, 1982
Gen. Antonio Eanes, 1985
HM The King of Spain, 1986
HM The King of Saudi Arabia, 1987
HRH The Princess Margaret, Countess of Snowdon, 1990
HE Richard von Weizsäcker, 1992
HM The King of Norway, 1994
The Earl of Airlie, 1997
The Duke of Norfolk, 2000

Baronetage and Knightage

BARONETS

Style, 'Sir' before forename and surname, followed by 'Bt.'
Wife's style, 'Lady' followed by surname
For forms of address, *see* page 135

There are five different creations of baronetcies: Baronets of England (creations dating from 1611); Baronets of Ireland (creations dating from 1619); Baronets of Scotland or Nova Scotia (creations dating from 1625); Baronets of Great Britain (creations after the Act of Union 1707 which combined the kingdoms of England and Scotland); and Baronets of the United Kingdom (creations after the union of Great Britain and Ireland in 1801).

Badge of Baronets of the   *Badge of Baronets*
United Kingdom   *of Nova Scotia*

Badge of Ulster

The patent of creation limits the destination of a baronetcy, usually to male descendants of the first baronet, although special remainders allow the baronetcy to pass, if the male issue of sons fail, to the male issue of daughters of the first baronet. In the case of baronetcies of Scotland or Nova Scotia, a special remainder of 'heirs male and of tailzie' allows the baronetcy to descend to heirs general, including women. There are four existing Scottish baronets with such a remainder.

The Official Roll of Baronets is kept at the Home Office by the Registrar of the Baronetage. Anyone who considers that he is entitled to be entered on the Roll may petition the Crown through the Home Secretary. Every person succeeding to a baronetcy must exhibit proofs of succession to the Home Secretary. A person whose name is not entered on the Official Roll will not be addressed or mentioned by the title of baronet in any official document, nor will he be accorded precedence as a baronet.

BARONETCIES EXTINCT SINCE THE LAST EDITION
Corbet (*cr.* 1808); Cradock (*cr.* 1796); Nicholls (now Harmar-Nicholls) (*cr*, 1960); Readhead (*cr.* 1922); Richmond (*cr.*1920)

Registrar of the Baronetage, Miss C. E. C. Sinclair
Assistant Registrar, Mrs F. G. Bright
Office, Home Office, 50 Queen Anne's Gate, London SW1H 9AT. Tel: 020 7273 3498

KNIGHTS

Style, 'Sir' before forename and surname, followed by appropriate post-nominal initials if a Knight Grand Cross, Knight Grand Commander or Knight Commander

Wife's style, 'Lady' followed by surname
For forms of address, *see* page 135

The prefix 'Sir' is not used by knights who are clerics of the Church of England, who do not receive the accolade. Their wives are entitled to precedence as the wife of a knight but not to the style of 'Lady'.

ORDERS OF KNIGHTHOOD

Knight Grand Cross, Knight Grand Commander, and Knight Commander are the higher classes of the Orders of Chivalry (*see* pages 171–3). Honorary knighthoods of these Orders may be conferred on men who are citizens of countries of which The Queen is not head of state. As a rule, the prefix 'Sir' is not used by honorary knights.

KNIGHTS BACHELOR

The Knights Bachelor do not constitute a Royal Order, but comprise the surviving representation of the ancient State Orders of Knighthood. The Register of Knights Bachelor, instituted by James I in the 17th century, lapsed, and in 1908 a voluntary association under the title of The Society of Knights (now The Imperial Society of Knights Bachelor by Royal Command) was formed with the primary objects of continuing the various registers dating from 1257 and obtaining the uniform registration of every created Knight Bachelor. In 1926 a design for a badge to be worn by Knights Bachelor was approved and adopted; in 1974 a neck badge and miniature were added.

Knight Principal, Sir Richard Gaskell
Prelate, Rt. Revd and Rt. Hon. The Bishop of London
Registrar, Sir Robert Balchin, DL
Hon. Treasurer, Sir Paul Judge.
Clerk to the Council, R. L. Jenkins, LVO, TD.
Office, 21 Old Buildings, Lincoln's Inn, London WC2A 3UJ

LIST OF BARONETS AND KNIGHTS

Revised to 31 August 2001
Peers are not included in this list

†	Not registered on the Official Roll of the Baronetage at the time of going to press
( )	The date of creation of the baronetcy is given in parenthesis
I	Baronet of Ireland
NS	Baronet of Nova Scotia
S	Baronet of Scotland

If a baronet or knight has a double-barrelled or hyphenated surname, he is listed under the final element of the name
A full entry in italic type indicates that the recipient of a knighthood died during the year in which the honour was conferred. The name is included for purposes of record

Abal, Sir Tei, Kt., CBE
Abbott, Sir Albert Francis, Kt., CBE
Abbott, *Adm.* Sir Peter Charles, GBE, KCB
Abdy, Sir Valentine Robert Duff, Bt. (1850)
Abel, Sir Seselo (Cecil) Charles Geoffrey, Kt., OBE
Abercromby, Sir Ian George, Bt. (S. 1636)
Acheson, *Prof.* Sir (Ernest) Donald, KBE
Ackers, Sir James George, Kt.
Ackroyd, Sir Timothy Robert Whyte, Bt. (1956)
Acland, Sir Antony Arthur, GCMG, GCVO
Acland, *Lt.-Col.* Sir (Christopher) Guy (Dyke), Bt., MVO (1890)
Acland, Sir John Dyke, Bt. (1644)
Acland, *Maj.-Gen.* Sir John Hugh Bevil, KCB, CBE
Adam, Sir Christopher Eric Forbes, Bt. (1917)
Adams, Sir Philip George Doyne, KCMG
Adams, Sir William James, KCMG
Adrien, *Hon.* Sir Maurice Latour-, Kt.
Adsetts, Sir William Norman, Kt., OBE
Adye, Sir John Anthony, KCMG
Agnew, Sir Crispin Hamlyn, Bt. (S. 1629)
Agnew, Sir John Keith, Bt. (1895)
Aiken, *Air Chief Marshal* Sir John Alexander Carlisle, KCB
Aikens, Sir Richard John Pearson, Kt., QC
†Ainsworth, Sir Anthony Thomas Hugh, Bt. (1916)
Aird, *Capt.* Sir Alastair Sturgis, GCVO
Aird, Sir (George) John, Bt. (1901)
Airy, *Maj.-Gen.* Sir Christopher John, KCVO, CBE
Aitchison, Sir Charles Walter de Lancey, Bt. (1938)
Akehurst, *Gen.* Sir John Bryan, KCB, CBE
Alberti, *Prof.* Kurt George Matthew Mayer, Kt.
Albu, Sir George, Bt. (1912)
Alcock, *Air Chief Marshal* Sir (Robert James) Michael, GCB, KBE
Aldous, *Rt. Hon.* Sir William, Kt.
Alexander, Sir Charles Gundry, Bt. (1945)
Alexander, Sir Claud Hagart-, Bt. (1886)
Alexander, Sir Douglas, Bt. (1921)
Alexander, Sir Michael O'Donal Bjarne, GCMG
†Alexander, Sir Patrick Desmond William Cable-, Bt. (1809)
Allan, Sir Anthony James Allan Havelock-, Bt. (1858)
Allen, *Prof.* Sir Geoffrey, Kt., ph.D., FRS
Allen, Sir John Derek, Kt., CBE
Allen, *Hon.* Sir Peter Austin Philip Jermyn, Kt.

Allen, Sir Thomas Boaz, Kt., CBE
Allen, *Hon.* Sir William Clifford, KCMG, MP
Allen, Sir William Guilford, Kt.
Alleyne, Sir George Allanmoore Ogarren, Kt.
Alleyne, *Revd* Sir John Olpherts Campbell, Bt. (1769)
Alliance, Sir David, Kt., CBE
Allinson, Sir (Walter) Leonard, KCVO, CMG
Alliott, *Hon.* Sir John Downes, Kt.
Allison, *Air Chief Marshal* Sir John Shakespeare, KCB, CBE
Alment, Sir (Edward) Anthony John, Kt.
Althaus, Sir Nigel Frederick, Kt.
Ambo, *Rt. Revd* George, KBE
Amet, *Hon.* Sir Arnold Karibone, Kt.
Amies, Sir (Edwin) Hardy, KCVO
Amory, Sir Ian Heathcoat, Bt. (1874)
Anderson, Sir John Anthony, KBE
Anderson, *Maj.-Gen.* Sir John Evelyn, KBE
Anderson, Sir John Muir, Kt., CMG
Anderson, *Hon.* Sir Kevin Victor, Kt.
Anderson, Sir Leith Reinsford Steven, Kt., CBE
Anderson, *Vice-Adm.* Sir Neil Dudley, KBE, CB
Anderson, *Prof.* Sir (William) Ferguson, Kt., OBE
Anderton, Sir (Cyril) James, Kt., CBE, QPM
Andrew, Sir Robert John, KCB
Andrews, Sir Derek Henry, KCB, CBE
Andrews, *Hon.* Sir Dormer George, Kt.
Angus, Sir Michael Richardson, Kt.
Annesley, Sir Hugh Norman, Kt., QPM
Anson, *Vice-Adm.* Sir Edward Rosebery, KCB
Anson, Sir John, KCB
Anson, *Rear-Adm.* Sir Peter, Bt., CB (1831)
Anstruther, *Maj.* Sir Ralph Hugo, Bt., GCVO, MC (S. 1694)
Antico, Sir Tristan Venus, Kt.
Antrobus, Sir Charles James, GCMG, OBE
Antrobus, Sir Edward Philip, Bt. (1815)
Appleyard, Sir Leonard Vincent, KCMG
Appleyard, Sir Raymond Kenelm, KBE
Arbuthnot, Sir Keith Robert Charles, Bt. (1823)
Arbuthnot, Sir William Reierson, Bt. (1964)
Arbuthnott, *Prof.* Sir John Peebles, Kt., ph.D., FRSE
Archdale, *Capt.* Sir Edward Folmer, Bt., DSC, RN (1928)
Arculus, Sir Ronald, KCMG, KCVO
Armitage, *Air Chief Marshal* Sir Michael John, KCB, CBE
Armour, *Prof.* Sir James, Kt., CBE
†Armstrong, Sir Christopher John Edmund Stuart, Bt., MBE (1841)

Armytage, Sir John Martin, Bt. (1738)
Arnold, *Rt. Hon.* Sir John Lewis, Kt.
Arnold, Sir Malcolm Henry, Kt., CBE
Arnold, Sir Thomas Richard, Kt.
Arnott, Sir Alexander John Maxwell, Bt. (1896)
Arrindell, Sir Clement Athelston, GCMG, GCVO, QC
Arthur, *Lt.-Gen.* Sir (John) Norman Stewart, KCB
Arthur, Sir Stephen John, Bt. (1841)
Ash, *Prof.* Sir Eric Albert, Kt., CBE, FRS, FREng.
Ashburnham, Sir James Fleetwood, Bt. (1661)
Ashcroft, Sir Michael, KCMG
Ashdown, *Rt. Hon.* Sir Jeremy John Durham (Paddy), KBE
Ashley, Sir Bernard Albert, Kt.
Ashmore, *Admiral of the Fleet* Sir Edward Beckwith, GCB, DSC
Ashmore, *Vice-Adm.* Sir Peter William Beckwith, KCB, KCVO, DSC
Aske, *Revd* Sir Conan, Bt. (1922)
Askew, Sir Bryan, Kt.
Asscher, *Prof.* Sir (Adolf) William, Kt., MD, FRCP
Astill, *Hon.* Sir Michael John, Kt.
Aston, Sir Harold George, Kt., CBE
Astwood, *Hon.* Sir James Rufus, KBE
Atcherley, Sir Harold Winter, Kt.
Atiyah, Sir Michael Francis, Kt., OM, Ph.D., FRS
Atkins, *Rt. Hon.* Sir Robert James, Kt.
Atkinson, *Prof.* Sir Anthony Barnes, Kt.
Atkinson, *Air Marshal* Sir David William, KBE
Atkinson, Sir Frederick John, KCB
Atkinson, Sir John Alexander, KCB, DFC
Atkinson, Sir Robert, Kt., DSC, FREng.
Atopare, Sir Sailas, GCMG
Attenborough, Sir David Frederick, Kt., CH, CVO, CBE, FRS
Atwill, Sir (Milton) John (Napier), Kt.
Audland, Sir Christopher John, KCMG
Audley, Sir George Bernard, Kt.
Augier, *Prof.* Sir Fitz-Roy Richard, Kt.
Auld, *Rt. Hon.* Sir Robin Ernest, Kt.
Austin, Sir Anthony Leonard, Bt. (1894)
Austin, *Vice-Adm.* Sir Peter Murray, KCB
Austin, *Air Marshal* Sir Roger Mark, KCB, AFC
Axford, Sir William Ian, Kt.
Ayckbourn, Sir Alan, Kt., CBE
Aykroyd, Sir James Alexander Frederic, Bt. (1929)
Aykroyd, Sir William Miles, Bt., MC (1920)
Aylmer, Sir Richard John, Bt. (I. 1622)
Ayre, Sir Douglas, Kt., JP
Bacha, Sir Bhinod, Kt., CMG
Backhouse, Sir Jonathan Roger, Bt. (1901)
Bacon, Sir Nicholas Hickman Ponsonby, Bt. *Premier Baronet of England* (1611 and 1627)

Bacon, Sir Sidney Charles, Kt., CB, FREng.
Baddeley, Sir John Wolsey Beresford, Bt. (1922)
Baddiley, *Prof.* Sir James, Kt., Ph.D., D.SC., FRS, FRSE
Badge, Sir Peter Gilmour Noto, Kt.
Badger, Sir Geoffrey Malcolm, Kt.
Baer, Sir Jack Mervyn Frank, Kt.
Bagge, Sir (John) Jeremy Picton, Bt. (1867)
Bagnall, *Air Marshal* Sir Anthony John Crowther, KCB, OBE
Bagnall, *Field Marshal* Sir Nigel Thomas, GCB, CVO, MC
Bailey, Sir Alan Marshall, KCB
Bailey, Sir Brian Harry, Kt., OBE
Bailey, Sir Derrick Thomas Louis, Bt., DFC (1919)
Bailey, Sir John Bilsland, KCB
Bailey, Sir Richard John, Kt., CBE
Bailey, Sir Stanley Ernest, Kt., CBE, QPM
Bailhache, Sir Philip Martin, Kt.
Baillie, Sir Gawaine George Hope, Bt. (1823)
Bain, *Prof.* Sir George Sayers, Kt.
Baines, *Prof.* Sir George Grenfell-, Kt., OBE
†Baird, Sir Charles William Stuart, Bt. (1809)
†Baird, Sir James Andrew Gardiner, Bt. (S. 1695)
Baird, *Lt.-Gen.* Sir James Parlane, KBE, MD
Baird, *Air Marshal* Sir John Alexander, KBE
Baird, *Vice-Adm.* Sir Thomas Henry Eustace, KCB
Bairsto, *Air Marshal* Sir Peter Edward, KBE, CB
Baker, Sir Bryan William, Kt.
Baker, Sir Robert George Humphrey Sherston-, Bt. (1796)
Baker, *Hon.* Sir (Thomas) Scott (Gillespie), Kt.
Balchin, Sir Robert George Alexander, Kt.
Balderstone, Sir James Schofield, Kt.
Baldwin, *Prof.* Sir Jack Edward, Kt., FRS
Baldwin, Sir Peter Robert, KCB
Ball, *Air Marshal* Sir Alfred Henry Wynne, KCB, DSO, DFC
Ball, Sir Charles Irwin, Bt. (1911)
Ball, Sir Christopher John Elinger, Kt.
Ball, *Prof.* Sir Robert James, Kt., Ph.D.
Bamford, Sir Anthony Paul, Kt.
Banham, Sir John Michael Middlecott, Kt.
Bannerman, Sir David Gordon, Bt., OBE (S. 1682)
Bannister, Sir Roger Gilbert, Kt., CBE, DM, FRCP
Barber, Sir (Thomas) David, Bt. (1960)
Barbour, *Very Revd* Sir Robert Alexander Stewart, KCVO, MC

Barclay, Sir Colville Herbert Sanford, Bt. (S. 1668)
Barclay, Sir David Rowat, Kt.
Barclay, Sir Frederick Hugh, Kt.
Barclay, Sir Peter Maurice, Kt., CBE
Barder, Sir Brian Leon, KCMG
Baring, Sir John Francis, Bt. (1911)
Barker, Sir Alwyn Bowman, Kt., CMG
Barker, Sir Colin, Kt.
Barker, *Hon.* Sir (Richard) Ian, Kt.
Barlow, Sir Christopher Hilaro, Bt. (1803)
Barlow, Sir Frank, Kt., CBE
Barlow, Sir (George) William, Kt., FREng.
Barlow, Sir John Kemp, Bt. (1907)
Barlow, Sir Thomas Erasmus, Bt., DSC (1902)
Barnard, Sir Joseph Brian, Kt.
Barnes, Sir (James) David (Francis), Kt., CBE
Barnes, Sir Kenneth, KCB
Barnewall, Sir Reginald Robert, Bt. (I. 1623)
Baron, Sir Thomas, Kt., CBE
Barraclough, *Air Chief Marshal* Sir John, KCB, CBE, DFC, AFC
Barran, Sir David Haven, Kt.
Barran, Sir John Napoleon Ruthven, Bt. (1895)
Barratt, Sir Lawrence Arthur, Kt.
Barratt, Sir Richard Stanley, Kt., CBE, QPM
Barrett, *Lt.-Gen.* Sir David William Scott-, KBE, MC
Barrett, Sir Stephen Jeremy, KCMG
Barrington, Sir Alexander (Fitzwilliam Croker), Bt. (1831)
Barrington, Sir Nicholas John, KCMG, CVO
Barron, Sir Donald James, Kt.
Barrow, *Capt.* Sir Richard John Uniacke, Bt. (1835)
Barrowclough, Sir Anthony Richard, Kt., QC
Barry, Sir (Lawrence) Edward (Anthony Tress), Bt. (1899)
Barter, Sir Peter Leslie Charles, Kt., OBE
†Bartlett, Sir Andrew Alan, Bt. (1913)
Barttelot, *Col.* Sir Brian Walter de Stopham, Bt., OBE (1875)
Batchelor, Sir Ivor Ralph Campbell, Kt., CBE
Bate, Sir David Lindsay, KBE
Bate, Sir (Walter) Edwin, Kt., OBE
Bates, Sir Geoffrey Voltelin, Bt., MC (1880)
Bates, Sir Malcolm Rowland, Kt.
Bates, Sir Richard Dawson Hoult, Bt. (1937)
Batho, Sir Peter Ghislain, Bt. (1928)
Bathurst, *Admiral of the Fleet* Sir (David) Benjamin, GCB
Bathurst, Sir Frederick John Charles Gordon Hervey-, Bt. (1818)
Bathurst, Sir Maurice Edward, Kt., CMG, CBE, QC
Batten, Sir John Charles, KCVO

Battersby, *Prof.* Sir Alan Rushton, Kt., FRS
Battishill, Sir Anthony Michael William, GCB
Batty, Sir William Bradshaw, Kt., TD
Baxendell, Sir Peter Brian, Kt., CBE, FREng.
Bayliss, Sir Richard Ian Samuel, KCVO, MD, FRCP
Bayne, Sir Nicholas Peter, KCMG
Baynes, Sir John Christopher Malcolm, Bt. (1801)
Bazley, Sir Thomas John Sebastian, Bt. (1869)
Beach, *Gen.* Sir (William Gerald) Hugh, GBE, KCB, MC
Beale, *Lt.-Gen.* Sir Peter John, KBE, FRCP
Beament, Sir James William Longman, Kt., SC.D., FRS
Beamish, Sir Adrian John, KCMG
Beattie, *Hon.* Sir Alexander Craig, Kt.
Beattie, *Hon.* Sir David Stuart, GCMG, GCVO
Beauchamp, Sir Christopher Radstock Proctor-, Bt. (1745)
Beaumont, *Capt.* the Hon. Sir (Edward) Nicholas (Canning), KCVO
Beaumont, Sir George (Howland Francis), Bt. (1661)
Beaumont, Sir Richard Ashton, KCMG, OBE
Beavis, *Air Chief Marshal* Sir Michael Gordon, KCB, CBE, AFC
Becher, Sir John William Michael Wrixon-, Bt. (1831)
Beck, Sir Edgar Philip, Kt.
†Beckett, Sir Richard Gervase, Bt., QC (1921)
Beckett, Sir Terence Norman, KBE, FREng.
Bedingfeld, *Capt.* Sir Edmund George Felix Paston-, Bt. (1661)
Beddoe, Sir David Sydney Rowe-, Kt.
Bedser, Sir Alec Victor, Kt., CBE
Beecham, Sir Jeremy Hugh, Kt.
Beecham, Sir John Stratford Roland, Bt. (1914)
Beetham, *Marshal of the Royal Air Force* Sir Michael James, GCB, CBE, DFC, AFC
Beevor, Sir Thomas Agnew, Bt. (1784)
Beldam, *Rt. Hon.* Sir (Alexander) Roy (Asplan), Kt.
Belich, Sir James, Kt.
Bell, Sir Brian Ernest, KBE
Bell, Sir (George) Raymond, KCMG, CB
Bell, Sir John Lowthian, Bt. (1885)
Bell, *Hon.* Sir Rodger, Kt.
Bell, Sir (William) Ewart, KCB
Bell, Sir William Hollin Dayrell Morrison-, Bt. (1905)
Bellamy, *Hon.* Sir Christopher William, Kt.
Bellew, Sir Henry Charles Gratton-, Bt. (1838)
Bellinger, Sir Robert Ian, GBE

Bellingham, Sir Anthony Edward Norman, Bt. (1796)
Bengough, *Col.* Sir Piers, KCVO, OBE
Benn, Sir (James) Jonathan, Bt. (1914)
Bennett, *Air Vice-Marshal* Sir Erik Peter, KBE, CB
Bennett, *Rt. Hon.* Sir Frederic Mackarness, Kt.
Bennett, *Hon.* Sir Hugh Peter Derwyn, Kt.
Bennett, Sir John Mokonuiarangi, Kt.
Bennett, *Gen.* Sir Phillip Harvey, KBE, DSO
Bennett, Sir Richard Rodney, Kt., CBE
Bennett, Sir Ronald Wilfrid Murdoch, Bt. (1929)
Benson, Sir Christopher John, Kt.
Benyon, Sir William Richard, Kt.
Beresford, Sir (Alexander) Paul, Kt., MP
Berger, *Vice-Adm.* Sir Peter Egerton Capel, KCB, LVO, DSC
Berghuser, *Hon.* Sir Eric, Kt., MBE
Beringer, *Prof.* Sir John Evelyn, Kt., CBE
Berman, Sir Franklin Delow, KCMG
Bernard, Sir Dallas Edmund, Bt. (1954)
Berney, Sir Julian Reedham Stuart, Bt. (1620)
Berridge, *Prof.* Sir Michael John, Kt., FRS
Berrill, Sir Kenneth Ernest, GBE, KCB
Berriman, Sir David, Kt.
Berry, *Prof.* Sir Colin Leonard, Kt., FRCPath.
Berry, *Prof.* Sir Michael Victor, Kt., FRS
Berthon, *Vice-Adm.* Sir Stephen Ferrier, KCB
Berthoud, Sir Martin Seymour, KCVO, CMG
Best, Sir Richard Radford, KCVO, CBE
Bethune, *Hon.* Sir (Walter) Angus, Kt.
Bett, Sir Michael, Kt., CBE
Bevan, Sir Martyn Evan Evans, Bt. (1958)
Bevan, Sir Nicolas, Kt., CB
Bevan, Sir Timothy Hugh, Kt.
Beverley, *Lt.-Gen.* Sir Henry York La Roche, KCB, OBE, RM
Bibby, Sir Derek James, Bt., MC (1959)
Bichard, Sir Michael George, KCB
Bick, *Hon.* Sir Martin James Moore-, Kt.
Bickersteth, *Rt. Revd* Sir John Monier, KCVO
Biddulph, Sir Ian D'Olier, Bt. (1664)
Bide, Sir Austin Ernest, Kt.
Bidwell, Sir Hugh Charles Philip, GBE
Biggam, Sir Robin Adair, Kt.
Biggs, *Vice-Adm.* Sir Geoffrey William Roger, KCB
Biggs, Sir Norman Paris, Kt.
Bilas, Sir Angmai Simon, Kt., OBE
Billière, *Gen.* Sir Peter Edgar de la Cour de la, KCB, KBE, DSO, MC
Bingham, *Hon.* Sir Eardley Max, Kt., QC

Birch, Sir John Allan, KCVO, CMG
Birch, Sir Roger, Kt., CBE, QPM
Bird, Sir Richard Geoffrey Chapman, Bt. (1922)
Birkin, Sir John Christian William, Bt. (1905)
Birkin, Sir (John) Derek, Kt., TD
Birkmyre, Sir James, Bt. (1921)
Birley, Sir Derek Sydney, Kt.
Birrell, Sir James Drake, Kt.
Birtwistle, Sir Harrison, Kt.
Bischoff, Winfried Franz Wilhelm, Kt.
Bishop, Sir Frederick Arthur, Kt., CB, CVO
Bishop, Sir Michael David, Kt., CBE
Bisson, *Rt. Hon.* Sir Gordon Ellis, Kt.
Black, *Prof.* Sir Douglas Andrew Kilgour, Kt., MD, FRCP
Black, Sir James Whyte, Kt., FRCP, FRS, OM
Black, *Adm.* Sir (John) Jeremy, GBE, KCB, DSO
Black, Sir Robert David, Bt. (1922)
Blackburne, *Hon.* Sir William Anthony, Kt.
Blacker, *Gen.* Sir (Anthony Stephen) Jeremy, KCB, CBE
Blacker, *Gen.* Sir Cecil Hugh, GCB, OBE, MC
Blackett, Sir Hugh Francis, Bt. (1673)
Blackham, *Vice-Adm.* Sir Jeremy Joe, KCB
Blacklock, *Surgeon Capt. Prof.* Sir Norman James, KCVO, OBE
Blackman, Sir Frank Milton, KCVO, OBE
Blackwell, Sir Basil Davenport, Kt., FREng.
Blackwood, Sir John Francis, Bt. (1814) (see also page 149)
Blair, *Lt.-Gen.* Sir Chandos, KCVO, OBE, MC
Blair, Sir Edward Thomas Hunter, Bt. (1786)
Blake, Sir Alfred Lapthorn, KCVO, MC
Blake, Sir Francis Michael, Bt. (1907)
Blake, Sir Peter James, KBE
Blake, Sir (Thomas) Richard (Valentine), Bt. (I. 1622)
Blaker, Sir John, Bt. (1919)
Blakiston, Sir Ferguson Arthur James, Bt. (1763)
Blanch, Sir Malcolm, KCVO
Bland, Sir (Francis) Christopher (Buchan), Kt.
Bland, *Lt.-Col.* Sir Simon Claud Michael, KCVO
Blank, Sir Maurice Victor, Kt.
Blatherwick, Sir David Elliott Spiby, KCMG, OBE
Blelloch, Sir John Nial Henderson, KCB
Blennerhassett, Sir (Marmaduke) Adrian Francis William, Bt. (1809)
Blewitt, *Maj.* Sir Shane Gabriel Basil, GCVO
Blofeld, *Hon.* Sir John Christopher Calthorpe, Kt.

Blois, Sir Charles Nicholas Gervase, Bt. (1686)
Blomefield, Sir Thomas Charles Peregrine, Bt. (1807)
Bloomfield, Sir Kenneth Percy, KCB
Blosse, *Capt.* Sir Richard Hely Lynch-, Bt. (1622)
Blount, Sir Walter Edward Alpin, Bt., DSC (1642)
Blundell, Sir Thomas Leon, Kt., FRS
Blunden, Sir George, Kt.
†Blunden, Sir Philip Overington, Bt. (I. 1766)
Blunt, Sir David Richard Reginald Harvey, Bt. (1720)
Blyth, Sir Charles (Chay), Kt., CBE, BEM
Boardman, *Prof.* Sir John, Kt., FSA, FBA
Bodey, *Hon.* Sir David Roderick Lessiter, Kt., QC
Bodmer, Sir Walter Fred, Kt., ph.D., FRS
Body, Sir Richard Bernard Frank Stewart, Kt., MP
Boevey, Sir Thomas Michael Blake Crawley-, Bt. (1784)
Bogan, Sir Nagora, KBE
Boileau, Sir Guy (Francis), Bt. (1838)
Boles, Sir Jeremy John Fortescue, Bt. (1922)
Boles, Sir John Dennis, Kt., MBE
Bolland, Sir Edwin, KCMG
Bollers, *Hon.* Sir Harold Brodie Smith, Kt.
Bolt, *Air Marshal* Sir Richard Bruce, KBE, CB, DFC, AFC
Bolton, Sir Frederic Bernard, Kt., MC
Bona, Sir Kina, KBE
Bonallack, Sir Michael Francis, Kt., OBE
Bond, Sir John Reginald Hartnell, Kt.
Bond, Sir Kenneth Raymond Boyden, Kt.
Bond, *Prof.* Sir Michael Richard, Kt., FRCPsych., FRCPGlas., FRCSE
Bondi, *Prof.* Sir Hermann, KCB, FRS
Bonfield, Sir Peter Leahy, Kt., CBE, FREng.
Bonham, *Maj.* Sir Antony Lionel Thomas, Bt. (1852)
Bonington, Sir Christian John Storey, Kt., CBE
Bonsall, Sir Arthur Wilfred, KCMG, CBE
Bonsor, Sir Nicholas Cosmo, Bt. (1925)
Boolell, Sir Satcam, Kt.
Boord, Sir Nicolas John Charles, Bt. (1896)
Boorman, *Lt.-Gen.* Sir Derek, KCB
Booth, Sir Christopher Charles, Kt., MD, FRCP
Booth, *Hon.* Sir David Alwyn Gore-, KCMG, KCVO
Booth, Sir Douglas Allen, Bt. (1916)
Booth, Sir Gordon, KCMG, CVO
Booth, Sir Josslyn Henry Robert Gore-, Bt. (I. 1760)
Booth, Sir Michael Addison John Wheeler-, KCB

Boothby, Sir Brooke Charles, Bt. (1660)

Boreel, Sir Francis David, Bt. (1645)

Boreham, *Hon.* Sir Leslie Kenneth Edward, Kt.

Bornu, The Waziri of, KCMG, CBE

Borthwick, Sir John Thomas, Bt., MBE (1908)

Borysiewicz, *Prof.* Sir Leszek Krzysztof, Kt.

Bossom, *Hon.* Sir Clive, Bt. (1953)

Boswall, Sir (Thomas) Alford Houstoun-, Bt. (1836)

Boswell, *Lt.-Gen.* Sir Alexander Crawford Simpson, KCB, CBE

Bosworth, Sir Neville Bruce Alfred, Kt., CBE

Bottoms, *Prof.* Sir Anthony Edward, Kt.

Bottomley, Sir James Reginald Alfred, KCMG

Boughey, Sir John George Fletcher, Bt. (1798)

Boulton, Sir Clifford John, GCB

Boulton, Sir (Harold Hugh) Christian, Bt. (1905)

Boulton, Sir William Whytehead, Bt., CBE, TD (1944)

Bourn, Sir John Bryant, KCB

Bovell, *Hon.* Sir (William) Stewart, Kt.

Bowater, Sir Euan David Vansittart, Bt. (1939)

Bowater, Sir (John) Vansittart, Bt. (1914)

Bowden, Sir Andrew, Kt., MBE

Bowden, Sir Frank, Bt. (1915)

Bowen, Sir Geoffrey Fraser, Kt.

Bowen, Sir Mark Edward Mortimer, Bt. (1921)

Bowett, *Prof.* Sir Derek William, Kt., CBE, QC, FBA

†Bowlby, Sir Richard Peregrine Longstaff, Bt. (1923)

Bowman, Sir Jeffery Haverstock, Kt.

Bowman, Sir Paul Humphrey Armytage, Bt. (1884)

Bowness, Sir Alan, Kt., CBE

Boyce, Sir Graham Hugh, KCMG

Boyce, *Adm.* Sir Michael Cecil, GCB, OBE

Boyce, Sir Robert Charles Leslie, Bt. (1952)

Boyd, Sir Alexander Walter, Bt. (1916)

Boyd, Sir John Dixon Iklé, KCMG

Boyd, The Hon. Sir Mark Alexander Lennox-, Kt.

Boyd, *Prof.* Sir Robert Lewis Fullarton, Kt., CBE, D.SC., FRS

Boyes, Sir Brian Gerald Barratt-, KBE

Boyle, Sir Stephen Gurney, Bt. (1904)

Boynton, Sir John Keyworth, Kt., MC

Boys, *Rt. Hon.* Sir Michael Hardie, GCMG

Boyson, *Rt. Hon.* Sir Rhodes, Kt.

Brabham, Sir John Arthur, Kt., OBE

Bradbeer, Sir John Derek Richardson, Kt., OBE, TD

Bradbury, *Surgeon Vice-Adm.* Sir Eric Blackburn, KBE, CB

Bradford, Sir Edward Alexander Slade, Bt. (1902)

Bradshaw, Sir Kenneth Anthony, KCB

Bradshaw, *Lt.-Gen.* Sir Richard Phillip, KBE

Brain, Sir (Henry) Norman, KBE, CMG

Braithwaite, Sir (Joseph) Franklin Madders, Kt.

Braithwaite, *Rt. Hon.* Sir Nicholas Alexander, Kt., OBE

Braithwaite, Sir Rodric Quentin, GCMG

Bramley, *Prof.* Sir Paul Anthony, Kt.

Branson, Sir Richard Charles Nicholas, Kt.

Bratza, Sir Nicolas Dušan, Kt., QC

Bray, Sir Theodor Charles, Kt., CBE

Brennan, *Hon.* Sir (Francis) Gerard, KBE

Brett, Sir Charles Edward Bainbridge, Kt., CBE

Brickwood, Sir Basil Greame, Bt. (1927)

Bridges, *Hon.* Sir Phillip Rodney, Kt., CMG

Brierley, Sir Ronald Alfred, Kt.

Bright, Sir Graham Frank James, Kt.

Bright, Sir Keith, Kt.

Brigstocke, *Adm.* Sir John Richard, KCB

Brinckman, Sir Theodore George Roderick, Bt. (1831)

†Brisco, Sir Campbell Howard, Bt. (1782)

Briscoe, Sir John Geoffrey James, Bt. (1910)

Brise, Sir John Archibald Ruggles-, Bt., CB, OBE, TD (1935)

Bristow, *Hon.* Sir Peter Henry Rowley, Kt.

Brittan, Sir Samuel, Kt.

Britton, Sir Edward Louis, Kt., CBE

†Broadbent, Sir Andrew George, Bt. (1893)

Brocklebank, Sir Aubrey Thomas, Bt. (1885)

Brodie, Sir Benjamin David Ross, Bt. (1834)

Broers, *Prof.* Sir Alec Nigel, Kt., ph.D., FRS

Bromhead, Sir John Desmond Gonville, Bt. (1806)

Bromley, Sir Michael Roger, KBE

Bromley, Sir Rupert Charles, Bt. (1757)

†Brooke, Sir Alistair Weston, Bt. (1919)

Brooke, Sir Francis George Windham, Bt. (1903)

Brooke, *Rt. Hon.* Sir Henry, Kt.

Brooke, Sir (Richard) David Christopher, Bt. (1662)

Brooksbank, Sir (Edward) Nicholas, Bt. (1919)

Broom, *Air Marshal* Sir Ivor Gordon, KCB, CBE, DSO, DFC, AFC

Broomfield, Sir Nigel Hugh Robert Allen, KCMG

†Broughton, Sir David Delves, Bt. (1661)

Broun, Sir William Windsor, Bt. (s. 1686)

Brown, Sir Allen Stanley, Kt., CBE

Brown, Sir (Austen) Patrick, KCB

Brown, *Adm.* Sir Brian Thomas, KCB, CBE

Brown, Sir (Cyril) Maxwell Palmer, KCB, CMG

Brown, Sir David, Kt.

Brown, *Vice-Adm.* Sir David Worthington, KCB

Brown, Sir Derrick Holden-, Kt.

Brown, Sir Douglas Denison, Kt.

Brown, *Hon.* Sir Douglas Dunlop, Kt.

Brown, Sir George Francis Richmond, Bt. (1863)

Brown, Sir George Noel, Kt.

Brown, Sir John, Kt.

Brown, Sir John Gilbert Newton, Kt., CBE

Brown, Sir Martin, Kt.

Brown, Sir Mervyn, KCMG, OBE

Brown, Sir Peter Randolph, Kt.

Brown, *Hon.* Sir Ralph Kilner, Kt., OBE, TD

Brown, Sir Robert Crichton-, KCMG, CBE, TD

Brown, *Rt. Hon.* Sir Simon Denis, Kt.

Brown, *Rt. Hon.* Sir Stephen, GBE

Brown, Sir Stephen David Reid, KCVO

Brown, Sir Thomas, Kt.

Brown, Sir William Brian Piggott-, Bt. (1903)

Browne, Sir Anthony Arthur Duncan Montague-, KCMG, CBE, DFC

Browne, Sir (Edmund) John (Phillip), Kt., FREng.

Brownrigg, Sir Nicholas (Gawen), Bt. (1816)

Browse, *Prof.* Sir Norman Leslie, Kt., MD, FRCS

Bruce, Sir (Francis) Michael Ian, Bt. (s. 1628)

Bruce, Sir Hervey James Hugh, Bt. (1804)

Bruce, *Rt. Hon.* Sir (James) Roualeyn Hovell-Thurlow-Cumming-, Kt.

Brunner, Sir John Henry Kilian, Bt. (1895)

Brunton, Sir (Edward Francis) Lauder, Bt. (1908)

Brunton, Sir Gordon Charles, Kt.

Bryan, Sir Arthur, Kt.

Bryan, Sir Paul Elmore Oliver, Kt., DSO, MC

Bryce, *Hon.* Sir (William) Gordon, Kt., CBE

Bryson, *Adm.* Sir Lindsay Sutherland, KCB, FREng.

Buchan, Sir John, Kt., CMG

Buchanan, Sir Andrew George, Bt. (1878)

Buchanan, Sir Charles Alexander James Leith-, Bt. (1775)

Buchanan, *Prof.* Sir Colin Douglas, Kt., CBE

Buchanan, *Vice-Adm.* Sir Peter William, KBE

Buchanan, Sir (Ranald) Dennis, Kt., MBE
Buchanan, Sir Robert Wilson (Robin), Kt.
Buck, Sir (Philip) Antony (Fyson), Kt., QC
Buckland, Sir Ross, Kt.
Buckley, *Lt.-Cdr.* Sir (Peter) Richard, KCVO
Buckley, *Hon.* Sir Roger John, Kt.
Budd, Sir Alan Peter, Kt.
Bulkeley, Sir Richard Thomas Williams-, Bt. (1661)
Bull, Sir George Jeffrey, Kt.
Bull, Sir Simeon George, Bt. (1922)
Bullard, Sir Julian Leonard, GCMG
Bulmer, Sir William Peter, Kt.
Bultin, Sir Bato, Kt., MBE
Bunbury, Sir Michael William, Bt. (1681)
Bunbury, Sir (Richard David) Michael Richardson-, Bt. (I. 1787)
Bunch, Sir Austin Wyeth, Kt., CBE
Bunyard, Sir Robert Sidney, Kt., CBE, QPM
Burbidge, Sir Herbert Dudley, Bt. (1916)
Burdett, Sir Savile Aylmer, Bt. (1665)
Burgen, Sir Arnold Stanley Vincent, Kt., FRS
Burgess, *Gen.* Sir Edward Arthur, KCB, OBE
Burgess, Sir (Joseph) Stuart, Kt., CBE, Ph.D., FRSC
Burgh, Sir John Charles, KCMG, CB
Burke, Sir James Stanley Gilbert, Bt. (I. 1797)
Burke, Sir (Thomas) Kerry, Kt.
Burley, Sir Victor George, Kt., CBE
Burnet, Sir James William Alexander (Sir Alastair Burnet), Kt.
Burnett, *Air Chief Marshal* Sir Brian Kenyon, GCB, DFC, AFC
Burnett, Sir David Humphery, Bt., MBE, TD (1913)
Burnett, Sir John Harrison, Kt.
Burnett, Sir Walter John, Kt.
Burney, Sir Cecil Denniston, Bt. (1921)
Burns, Sir (Robert) Andrew, KCMG
Burnton, *Hon.* Sir Stanley Jeffrey, Kt
Burrell, Sir John Raymond, Bt. (1774)
Burrows, Sir Bernard Alexander Brocas, GCMG
Burston, Sir Samuel Gerald Wood, Kt., OBE
Burt, *Hon.* Sir Francis Theodore Page, KCMG
Burton, Sir Carlisle Archibald, Kt., OBE
Burton, Sir George Vernon Kennedy, Kt., CMG
Burton, *Lt.-Gen.* Sir Edmund Fortescue Gerard, KBE
Burton, Sir Graham Stuart, KCMG
Burton, Sir Michael John, Kt., QC
Burton, Sir Michael St Edmund, KCVO, CMG
Bush, *Adm.* Sir John Fitzroy Duyland, GCB, DSC

Butler, *Rt. Hon.* Sir Adam Courtauld, Kt.
Butler, *Hon.* Sir Arlington Griffith, KCMG
Butler, Sir Michael Dacres, GCMG
Butler, Sir (Reginald) Michael (Thomas), Bt. (1922)
Butler, Sir Percy James, Kt., CBE, DL
Butler, *Hon.* Sir Richard Clive, Kt.
†Butler, Sir Richard Pierce, Bt. (1628)
Butter, *Maj.* Sir David Henry, KCVO, MC
Butterfield, *Hon.* Sir Alexander Neil Logie, Kt.
Buxton, Sir Jocelyn Charles Roden, Bt. (1840)
Buxton, *Rt. Hon.* Sir Richard Joseph, Kt.
Buzzard, Sir Anthony Farquhar, Bt. (1929)
Byatt, Sir Hugh Campbell, KCVO, CMG
Byatt, Sir Ian Charles Rayner, Kt.
Byers, Sir Maurice Hearne, Kt., CBE, QC
Byford, Sir Lawrence, Kt., CBE, QPM
Byron, Sir Charles Michael Dennis, Kt.
Cable, Sir James Eric, KCVO, CMG
Cadbury, Sir (George) Adrian (Hayhurst), Kt.
Cadbury, Sir (Nicholas) Dominic, Kt.
Cadogan, *Prof.* Sir John Ivan George, Kt., CBE, FRS, FRSE
Cahn, Sir Albert Jonas, Bt. (1934)
Cain, Sir Henry Edney Conrad, Kt.
Caine, Sir Michael (Maurice Micklewhite), Kt., CBE
Caines, Sir John, KCB
Calcutt, Sir David Charles, Kt., QC
Calderwood, Sir Robert, Kt.
Caldwell, *Surgeon Vice-Adm.* Sir (Eric) Dick, KBE, CB
Callan, Sir Ivan Roy, KCVO, CMG
Callaway, *Prof.* Sir Frank Adams, Kt., CMG, OBE
Calman, *Prof.* Sir Kenneth Charles, KCB, MD, FRCP, FRCS, FRSE
Calne, *Prof.* Sir Roy Yorke, Kt., FRS
Calthorpe, Sir Euan Hamilton Anstruther-Gough-, Bt. (1929)
Cameron of Lochiel, Sir Donald Hamish, KT, CVO, TD
Cameron, Sir Hugh Roy Graham, Kt., QPM
Campbell, Sir Alan Hugh, GCMG
Campbell, *Prof.* Sir Colin Murray, Kt.
Campbell, *Prof.* Sir Donald, Kt., CBE, FRCS, FRCPGlas.
Campbell, Sir Ian Tofts, Kt., CBE, VRD
Campbell, Sir Ilay Mark, Bt. (1808)
Campbell, Sir James Alexander Moffat Bain, Bt. (s. 1668)
Campbell, Sir Lachlan Philip Kemeys, Bt. (1815)
Campbell, Sir Niall Alexander Hamilton, Bt. (1831)
Campbell, Sir Robin Auchinbreck, Bt. (s. 1628)

Campbell, Sir Alexander Thomas Cockburn-, Bt. (1821)
Campbell, *Hon.* Sir Walter Benjamin, Kt.
Campbell, *Rt. Hon.* Sir William Anthony, Kt.
†Carden, Sir Christopher Robert, Bt. (1887)
Carden, Sir John Craven, Bt. (I. 1787)
Carew, Sir Rivers Verain, Bt. (1661)
Carey, Sir Peter Willoughby, GCB
Carlisle, Sir James Beethoven, GCMG
Carlisle, Sir John Michael, Kt.
Carlisle, Sir Kenneth Melville, Kt.
Carmichael, Sir David Peter William Gibson-Craig-, Bt. (s. 1702 and 1831)
Carnac, *Revd Canon* Sir (Thomas) Nicholas Rivett-, Bt. (1836)
Carnegie, *Lt.-Gen.* Sir Robin Macdonald, KCB, OBE
Carnegie, Sir Roderick Howard, Kt.
Carnwath, Sir Robert John Anderson, Kt., CVO
Caro, Sir Anthony Alfred, Kt., CBE, OM
Carpenter, *Lt.-Gen.* the Hon. Sir Thomas Patrick John Boyd-, KBE
Carr, Sir (Albert) Raymond (Maillard), Kt.
Carrick, *Hon.* Sir John Leslie, KCMG
Carrick, Sir Roger John, KCMG, LVO
Carsberg, *Prof.* Sir Bryan Victor, Kt.
Carswell, *Rt. Hon.* Sir Robert Douglas, Kt.
Carter, Sir Charles Frederick, Kt., FBA
Carter, *Prof.* Sir David Craig, Kt., FRCSE, FRCSGlas., FRCPE
Carter, *Gen.* Sir Evelyn John Webb-, KCVO, OBE
Carter, Sir John, Kt., QC
Carter, Sir John Alexander, Kt.
Carter, Sir John Gordon Thomas, Kt.
Carter, Sir Philip David, Kt., CBE
Carter, Sir Richard Henry Alwyn, Kt.
Cartland, Sir George Barrington, Kt., CMG
Cartledge, Sir Bryan George, KCMG
Cary, Sir Roger Hugh, Bt. (1955)
Casey, *Rt. Hon.* Sir Maurice Eugene, Kt.
Cash, Sir Gerald Christopher, GCMG, GCVO, OBE
Cass, Sir Geoffrey Arthur, Kt.
†Cassel, Sir Timothy Felix Harold, Bt. (1920)
Cassels, Sir John Seton, Kt., CB
Cassels, *Adm.* Sir Simon Alastair Cassillis, KCB, CBE
Cassidi, *Adm.* Sir (Arthur) Desmond, GCB
Castell, Sir William Martin, Kt.
Cater, Sir Jack, KBE
Catford, Sir (John) Robin, KCVO, CBE
Catherwood, Sir (Henry) Frederick (Ross), Kt.
Catling, Sir Richard Charles, Kt., CMG, OBE
Cave, Sir John Charles, Bt. (1896)

Cave, Sir Robert Cave-Browne-, Bt. (1641)
Cayley, Sir Digby William David, Bt. (1661)
Cayzer, Sir James Arthur, Bt. (1904)
Cazalet, *Hon.* Sir Edward Stephen, Kt.
Cazalet, Sir Peter Grenville, Kt.
Cecil, *Rear-Adm.* Sir (Oswald) Nigel Amherst, KBE, CB
Chadwick, *Revd Prof.* Sir Henry, KBE
Chadwick, *Rt. Hon.* Sir John Murray, Kt., ED
Chadwick, Sir Joshua Kenneth Burton, Bt. (1935)
Chadwick, *Revd Prof.* Sir (William) Owen, OM, KBE, FBA
Chalmers, Sir Iain Geoffrey, Kt.
Chalmers, Sir Neil Robert, Kt.
Chalstrey, Sir (Leonard) John, Kt., MD, FRCS
Chan, *Rt. Hon.* Sir Julius, GCMG, KBE
Chance, Sir (George) Jeremy ffolliott, Bt. (1900)
Chandler, Sir Colin Michael, Kt.
Chandler, Sir Geoffrey, Kt., CBE
Chaney, *Hon.* Sir Frederick Charles, KBE, AFC
Chantler, *Prof.* Sir Cyril, Kt., MD, FRCP
Chaplin, Sir Malcolm Hilbery, Kt., CBE
Chapman, Sir David Robert Macgowan, Bt. (1958)
Chapman, Sir George Alan, Kt.
Chapman, Sir Sidney Brookes, Kt., MP
Chapman, *Lt-Gen.* Sir Timothy John Granville-, KCB, CBE
Chapple, *Field Marshal* Sir John Lyon, GCB, CBE
Charles, *Hon.* Sir Arthur William Hessin, Kt
Charles, Sir George Frederick Lawrence, KCMG, CBE
Charlton, Sir Robert (Bobby), Kt., CBE
Charnley, Sir (William) John, Kt., CB, FREng.
Chataway, *Rt. Hon.* Sir Christopher, Kt.
Chatfield, Sir John Freeman, Kt., CBE
Chaytor, Sir George Reginald, Bt. (1831)
Checketts, *Sqn. Ldr.* Sir David John, KCVO
Checkland, Sir Michael, Kt.
Cheetham, Sir Nicolas John Alexander, KCMG
Cheshire, *Air Chief Marshal* Sir John Anthony, KBE, CB
Chessells, Sir Arthur David (Tim), Kt.
Chesterton, Sir Oliver Sidney, Kt., MC
Chetwood, Sir Clifford Jack, Kt.
Chetwynd, Sir Arthur Ralph Talbot, Bt. (1795)
Cheung, Sir Oswald Victor, Kt., CBE
Cheyne, Sir Joseph Lister Watson, Bt., OBE (1908)
Chichester, Sir (Edward) John, Bt. (1641)

Chilcot, Sir John Anthony, GCB
Child, Sir (Coles John) Jeremy, Bt. (1919)
Chilton, *Brig.* Sir Frederick Oliver, Kt., CBE, DSO
Chilwell, *Hon.* Sir Muir Fitzherbert, Kt.
Chinn, Sir Trevor Edwin, Kt., CVO
Chipperfield, Sir Geoffrey Howes, KCB
Chisholm, Sir John Alexander Raymond, Kt., FREng.
Chitty, Sir Thomas Willes, Bt. (1924)
Cholmeley, Sir Hugh John Frederick Sebastian, Bt. (1806)
Chow, Sir Chung Kong, Kt.
Chow, Sir Henry Francis, Kt., OBE
Christie, Sir George William Langham, Kt.
Christie, Sir William, Kt., MBE
Chung, Sir Sze-yuen, GBE, FREng.
Clapham, Sir Michael John Sinclair, KBE
Clark, Sir Francis Drake, Bt. (1886)
Clark, Sir John Allen, Kt.
Clark, Sir John Stewart-, Bt., MEP (1918)
Clark, Sir Jonathan George, Bt. (1917)
Clark, Sir Robert Anthony, Kt., DSC
Clark, Sir Robin Chichester-, Kt.
Clark, Sir Terence Joseph, KBE, CMG, CVO
Clark, Sir Thomas Edwin, Kt.
Clarke, *Hon.* Sir Anthony Petr, Kt.
Clarke, Sir Arthur Charles, Kt., CBE
Clarke, Sir (Charles Mansfield) Tobias, Bt. (1831)
Clarke, Sir Ellis Emmanuel Innocent, GCMG
Clarke, Sir Jonathan Dennis, Kt.
Clarke, *Maj.* Sir Peter Cecil, KCVO
Clarke, Sir Robert Cyril, Kt.
Clarke, Sir Rupert William John, Bt., MBE (1882)
Clarke, Sir Stanley William, Kt., CBE
Clay, Sir Richard Henry, Bt. (1841)
Clayton, Sir David Robert, Bt. (1732)
Cleaver, Sir Anthony Brian, Kt.
Cleminson, Sir James Arnold Stacey, KBE, MC
Clerk, Sir John Dutton, Bt., CBE, VRD (s. 1679)
Clerke, Sir John Edward Longueville, Bt. (1660)
Clifford, Sir Roger Joseph, Bt. (1887)
Clothier, Sir Cecil Montacute, KCB, QC
Clucas, Sir Kenneth Henry, KCB
Clutterbuck, *Vice-Adm.* Sir David Granville, KBE, CB
Coates, Sir Anthony Robert Milnes, Bt. (1911)
Coates, Sir David Frederick Charlton, Bt. (1921)
Coats, Sir Alastair Francis Stuart, Bt. (1905)
Coats, Sir William David, Kt.
Cobham, Sir Michael John, Kt., CBE

Cochrane, Sir (Henry) Marc (Sursock), Bt. (1903)
Cockburn, Sir John Elliot, Bt. (s. 1671)
Cockshaw, Sir Alan, Kt., FREng.
Codrington, Sir Simon Francis Bethell, Bt. (1876)
Codrington, Sir William Alexander, Bt. (1721)
†Coghill, Sir Patrick Kendal Farley, Bt. (1778)
Coghlin, *Hon.* Sir Patrick, Kt.
Cohen, Sir Edward, Kt.
Cohen, Sir Ivor Harold, Kt., CBE, TD
Cohen, *Prof.* Sir Philip, Kt., Ph.D, FRS
Cohen, Sir Ronald, Kt.
Cohen, Sir Stephen Harry Waley-, Bt. (1961)
Coldstream, Sir George Phillips, KCB, KCVO, QC
Cole, Sir (Alexander) Colin, KCB, KCVO, TD
Cole, Sir (Robert) William, Kt.
Coleridge, *Hon.* Sir Justice Paul James Duke, Kt.
Coles, Sir (Arthur) John, GCMG
Colfox, Sir (William) John, Bt. (1939)
Collett, Sir Christopher, GBE
Collett, Sir Ian Seymour, Bt. (1934)
Collins, *Hon.* Sir Andrew David, Kt.
Collins, Sir Bryan Thomas Alfred, Kt., OBE, QFSM
Collins, Sir John Alexander, Kt.
Collins, *Hon.* Sir Lawrence Antony, Kt.
Collyear, Sir John Gowen, Kt., FREng.
Colman, *Hon.* Sir Anthony David, Kt.
Colman, Sir Michael Jeremiah, Bt. (1907)
Colman, Sir Timothy, KG
Colquhoun of Luss, Sir Ivar Iain, Bt. (1786)
Colt, Sir Edward William Dutton, Bt. (1694)
Colthurst, Sir Richard La Touche, Bt. (1744)
Coltman, Sir (Arthur) Leycester Scott, KBE, CMG
Colvin, Sir Howard Montagu, Kt., CVO, CBE, FBA
Compton, *Rt. Hon.* Sir John George Melvin, KCMG
Conant, Sir John Ernest Michael, Bt. (1954)
Condon, Sir Paul Leslie, Kt., QPM
Connell, *Hon.* Sir Michael Bryan, Kt.
Connery, Sir Sean, Kt.
Conran, Sir Terence Orby, Kt.
Cons, *Hon.* Sir Derek, Kt.
Constable, Sir Frederic Strickland-, Bt. (1641)
Constantinou, Sir Georkios, Kt., OBE
Cook, *Prof.* Sir Alan Hugh, Kt.
Cook, Sir Christopher Wymondham Rayner Herbert, Bt. (1886)
Cooke, Sir Charles Fletcher-, Kt., QC
Cooke, *Col.* Sir David William Perceval, Bt. (1661)
Cooke, Sir Howard Felix Hanlan, GCMG, GCVO

Cooksey, Sir David James Scott, Kt.
Cooper, *Rt. Hon.* Sir Frank, GCB, CMG
Cooper, Sir (Frederick Howard) Michael Craig-, Kt., CBE, TD
Cooper, *Gen.* Sir George Leslie Conroy, GCB, MC
Cooper, Sir Henry, Kt.
Cooper, Sir Louis Jacques Blom-, Kt., QC
Cooper, Sir Patrick Graham Astley, Bt. (1821)
Cooper, Sir Richard Powell, Bt. (1905)
Cooper, Sir Robert George, Kt., CBE
Cooper, *Maj.-Gen.* Sir Simon Christie, GCVO
Cooper, Sir William Daniel Charles, Bt. (1863)
Coote, Sir Christopher John, Bt., *Premier Baronet of Ireland* (I. 1621)
Copas, *Most Revd* Sir Virgil, KBE, DD
Copisarow, Sir Alcon Charles, Kt.
Corbett, *Maj.-Gen.* Sir Robert John Swan, KCVO, CB
Corby, Sir (Frederick) Brian, Kt.
Corfield, *Rt. Hon.* Sir Frederick Vernon, Kt., QC
Corfield, Sir Kenneth George, Kt., FREng.
Cork, Sir Roger William, Kt.
Corley, Sir Kenneth Sholl Ferrand, Kt.
Cormack, Sir Patrick Thomas, Kt., MP
Corness, Sir Colin Ross, Kt.
Cornforth, Sir John Warcup, Kt., CBE, D.Phil., FRS
Cortazzi, Sir (Henry Arthur) Hugh, GCMG
Cory, Sir (Clinton Charles) Donald, Bt. (1919)
Cossons, Sir Neil, Kt., OBE
Cotter, *Lt.-Col.* Sir Delaval James Alfred, Bt., DSO (I. 1763)
Cotterell, Sir John Henry Geers, Bt. (1805)
Cotton, Sir John Richard, KCMG, OBE
Cotton, *Hon.* Sir Robert Carrington, KCMG
Cotton, Sir William Frederick, Kt., CBE
Cottrell, Sir Alan Howard, Kt., Ph.D., FRS, FREng.
†Cotts, Sir Richard Crichton Mitchell, Bt. (1921)
Couper, Sir (Robert) Nicholas (Oliver), Bt. (1841)
Court, *Hon.* Sir Charles Walter Michael, KCMG, OBE
Courtenay, Sir Thomas Daniel, Kt.
Cousins, *Air Chief Marshal* Sir David, KCB, AFC
Coutts, Sir David Burdett Money-, KCVO
Couzens, Sir Kenneth Edward, KCB
Covacevich, Sir (Anthony) Thomas, Kt., DFC
Coville, *Air Marshal* Sir Christopher Charles Cotton, KCB
Cowan, *Gen.* Sir Samuel, KCB, CBE

Coward, *Vice-Adm.* Sir John Francis, KCB, DSO
Cowen, *Rt. Hon. Prof.* Sir Zelman, GCMG, GCVO, QC
Cowie, Sir Thomas (Tom), Kt., OBE
Cowperthwaite, Sir John James, KBE, CMG
Cox, Sir Alan George, Kt., CBE
Cox, *Prof.* Sir David Roxbee, Kt., FRS
Cox, Sir Geoffrey Sandford, Kt., CBE
Cox, *Vice-Adm.* Sir John Michael Holland, KCB
Cradock, *Rt. Hon.* Sir Percy, GCMG
Craig, Sir (Albert) James (Macqueen), GCMG
Crane, *Hon.* Sir Peter Francis, Kt.
Craufurd, Sir Robert James, Bt. (1781)
Craven, Sir John Anthony, Kt.
Craven, *Air Marshal* Sir Robert Edward, KBE, CB, DFC
Crawford, *Prof.* Sir Frederick William, Kt., FREng.
Crawford, Sir (Robert) Stewart, GCMG, CVO
Crawford, *Vice-Adm.* Sir William Godfrey, KBE, CB, DSC
Creagh, *Maj.-Gen.* Sir (Kilner) Rupert Brazier-, KBE, CB, DSO
Crew, Sir (Michael) Edward, Kt., QPM
Cresswell, *Hon.* Sir Peter John, Kt.
Crill, Sir Peter Leslie, KBE
Cripps, Sir Cyril Humphrey, Kt.
Crisp, Sir (John) Peter, Bt. (1913)
Critchett, Sir Ian (George Lorraine), Bt. (1908)
Crocker, Sir Walter Russell, KBE
Croft, Sir Owen Glendower, Bt. (1671)
Croft, Sir Thomas Stephen Hutton, Bt. (1818)
†Crofton, Sir Hugh Denis, Bt. (1801)
Crofton, *Prof.* Sir John Wenman, Kt.
Crofton, Sir Malby Sturges, Bt. (1838)
Crookenden, *Lt.-Gen.* Sir Napier, KCB, DSO, OBE
Cross, *Air Chief Marshal* Sir Kenneth Brian Boyd, KCB, CBE, DSO, DFC
Crossland, *Prof.* Sir Bernard, Kt., CBE, FREng.
Crossley, Sir Julian Charles, Bt. (1909)
Cruthers, Sir James Winter, Kt.
Cubbon, Sir Brian Crossland, GCB
Cubitt, Sir Hugh Guy, Kt., CBE
Cullen, Sir (Edward) John, Kt., FREng.
Culpin, Sir Robert Paul, Kt.
Cumming, Sir William Gordon Gordon-, Bt. (1804)
Cuninghame, Sir John Christopher Foggo Montgomery-, Bt. (NS 1672)
Cuninghame, Sir Robert Henry Fairlie-, Bt. (S. 1630)
Cunliffe, Sir David Ellis, Bt. (1759)
Cunningham, *Lt.-Gen.* Sir Hugh Patrick, KBE
Cunynghame, Sir Andrew David Francis, Bt. (S. 1702)
†Currie, Sir Donald Scott, Bt. (1847)

Currie, Sir Neil Smith, Kt., CBE
Curry, Sir Donald Thomas Younger, Kt., CBE
Curtis, Sir Barry John, Kt.
Curtis, Sir (Edward) Leo, Kt.
Curtis, *Hon.* Sir Richard Herbert, Kt.
Curtis, Sir William Peter, Bt. (1802)
Curtiss, *Air Marshal* Sir John Bagot, KCB, KBE
Curwen, Sir Christopher Keith, KCMG
Cuschieri, *Prof.* Sir Alfred, Kt.
Cutler, Sir (Arthur) Roden, VC, KCMG, KCVO, CBE
Cutler, Sir Charles Benjamin, KBE, ED
Dacie, *Prof.* Sir John Vivian, Kt., MD, FRS
Dain, Sir David John Michael, KCVO
Dalrymple, *Maj.* Sir Hew Fleetwood Hamilton-, Bt., GCVO, KCVO (S. 1697)
Dalton, Sir Alan Nugent Goring, Kt., CBE
Dalton, *Vice-Adm.* Sir Geoffrey Thomas James Oliver, KCB
Daly, *Lt.-Gen.* Sir Thomas Joseph, KBE, CB, DSO
Dalyell, Sir Tam (Thomas), Bt., MP (NS 1685)
Daniel, Sir Goronwy Hopkin, KCVO, CB, D.Phil.
Daniel, Sir John Sagar, Kt., D.Sc.
Daniel, Sir Wilred St Clair-, Kt., CBE, JP
Daniell, Sir Peter Averell, Kt., TD
Darby, Sir Peter Howard, Kt., CBE, QFSM
Darell, Sir Jeffrey Lionel, Bt., MC (1795)
Dargie, Sir William Alexander, Kt., CBE
Dark, Sir Anthony Michael Beaumont-, Kt.
Darling, Sir Clifford, GCVO
Darvall, Sir (Charles) Roger, Kt., CBE
†Dashwood, Sir Edward John Francis, Bt., *Premier Baronet of Great Britain* (1707)
Dashwood, Sir Richard James, Bt. (1684)
Daunt, Sir Timothy Lewis Achilles, KCMG
Davey, *Hon.* Sir David Herbert Penry-, Kt.
David, Sir Jean Marc, Kt., CBE, QC
David, *His Hon.* Sir Robin (Robert) Daniel George, Kt., QC
Davidge, Sir Leonard Edward, Kt.
Davidson, Sir Robert James, Kt., FREng.
†Davie, Sir Michael Ferguson-, Bt. (1847)
Davies, Sir Alan Seymour, Kt.
Davies, *Hon.* Sir (Alfred William) Michael, Kt.
Davies, Sir (Charles) Noel, Kt.
Davies, *Prof.* Sir David Evan Naughton, Kt., CBE, FRS, FREng.
Davies, *Hon.* Sir (David Herbert) Mervyn, Kt., MC, TD

Davies, Sir David John, Kt.
Davies, Sir Frank John, Kt., CBE
Davies, *Prof.* Sir Graeme John, Kt., FREng.
Davies, Sir John Howard, Kt.
Davies, *Vice-Adm.* Sir Lancelot Richard Bell, KBE
Davies, Sir Peter Maxwell, Kt., CBE
Davies, Sir Rhys Everson, Kt., QC
Davis, Sir Andrew Frank, Kt., CBE
Davis, Sir Colin Rex, Kt., CBE, CH
Davis, Sir (Ernest) Howard, Kt., CMG, OBE
Davis, Sir John Gilbert, Bt. (1946)
Davis, Sir Peter John, Kt.
Davis, *Hon.* Sir Thomas Robert Alexander Harries, KBE
Davison, *Rt. Hon.* Sir Ronald Keith, GBE, CMG
Davson, Sir Christopher Michael Edward, Bt. (1927)
Dawanincura, Sir John Norbert, Kt., OBE
Dawbarn, Sir Simon Yelverton, KCVO, CMG
Dawson, *Hon.* Sir Daryl Michael, KBE, CB
Dawson, Sir Hugh Michael Trevor, Bt. (1920)
Dawtry, Sir Alan (Graham), Kt., CBE, TD
Day, Sir Derek Malcolm, KCMG
Day, *Air Marshal* Sir John Romney, KCB, OBE
Day, Sir (Judson) Graham, Kt.
Day, Sir Michael John, Kt., OBE
Day, Sir Simon James, Kt.
Deakin, Sir (Frederick) William (Dampier), Kt., DSO
Deane, *Hon.* Sir William Patrick, KBE
Dear, Sir Geoffrey James, Kt., QPM
Dearlove, Sir Richard Billing, KCMG, OBE
de Bellaigue, Sir Geoffrey, GCVO
Debenham, Sir Gilbert Ridley, Bt. (1931)
de Deney, Sir Geoffrey Ivor, KCVO
de Hoghton, Sir (Richard) Bernard (Cuthbert), Bt. (1611)
De la Bère, Sir Cameron, Bt. (1953)
de la Rue, Sir Andrew George Ilay, Bt. (1898)
Dellow, Sir John Albert, Kt., CBE
de Montmorency, Sir Arnold Geoffroy, Bt. (I. 1631)
Denholm, Sir John Ferguson (Ian), Kt., CBE
Denman, Sir (George) Roy, KCB, CMG
Denny, Sir Anthony Coningham de Waltham, Bt. (I. 1782)
Denny, Sir Charles Alistair Maurice, Bt. (1913)
Dent, Sir John, Kt., CBE, FREng.
Denton, *Prof.* Sir Eric James, Kt., CBE, FRS
Derbyshire, Sir Andrew George, Kt.
Derham, Sir Peter John, Kt.
de Trafford, Sir Dermot Humphrey, Bt. (1841)

Deverell, *Lt.-Gen.* Sir John Freegard, KCB, OBE
Devesi, Sir Baddeley, GCMG, GCVO
De Ville, Sir Harold Godfrey Oscar, Kt., CBE
Devitt, Sir James Hugh Thomas, Bt. (1916)
de Waal, Sir (Constant Henrik) Henry, KCB, QC
Dewar, Sir John James Evelyn, Bt. (1907)
Dewey, Sir Anthony Hugh, Bt. (1917)
Dewhurst, *Prof.* Sir (Christopher) John, Kt.
d'Eyncourt, Sir Mark Gervais Tennyson-, Bt. (1930)
Dhenin, *Air Marshal* Sir Geoffrey Howard, KBE, AFC, GM, MD
Dhrangadhra, HH the Maharaja Raj Saheb of, KCIE
Dibela, *Hon.* Sir Kingsford, GCMG
Dick, *Maj.-Gen.* Sir Iain Charles Mackay-, KCVO, MBE
Dickenson, Sir Aubrey Fiennes Trotman-, Kt.
Dickinson, Sir Harold Herbert, Kt.
Dickinson, Sir Samuel Benson, Kt.
Dilke, Sir Charles John Wentworth, Bt. (1862)
Dillon, *Rt. Hon.* Sir (George) Brian (Hugh), Kt.
Dixon, Sir Jeremy, Kt.
Dixon, Sir Jonathan Mark, Bt. (1919)
Djanogly, Sir Harry Ari Simon, Kt., CBE
Dobbs, *Capt.* Sir Richard Arthur Frederick, KCVO
Dobson, *Vice-Adm.* Sir David Stuart, KBE
Dobson, *Gen.* Sir Patrick John Howard-, GCB
Dodds, Sir Ralph Jordan, Bt. (1964)
Dodson, Sir Derek Sherborne Lindsell, KCMG, MC
Dodsworth, Sir John Christopher Smith-, Bt. (1784)
Doll, *Prof.* Sir (William) Richard (Shaboe), Kt., CH, OBE, FRS, DM, MD, D.Sc.
Dollery, Sir Colin Terence, Kt.
Donald, Sir Alan Ewen, KCMG
Donald, *Air Marshal* Sir John George, KBE
Donne, *Hon.* Sir Gaven John, KBE
Donne, Sir John Christopher, Kt.
Dookun, Sir Dewoonarain, Kt.
Dorey, Sir Graham Martyn, Kt.
Dorman, Sir Philip Henry Keppel, Bt. (1923)
Dougherty, *Maj.-Gen.* Sir Ivan Noel, Kt., CBE, DSO, ED
Doughty, Sir Graham Martin, Kt.
Doughty, Sir William Roland, Kt.
Douglas, Sir (Edward) Sholto, Kt.
Douglas, *Hon.* Sir Roger Owen, Kt.
Douglas, *Rt. Hon.* Sir William Randolph, KCMG
Dover, *Prof.* Sir Kenneth James, Kt., D.Litt., FBA, FRSE
Dowell, Sir Anthony James, Kt., CBE

Down, Sir Alastair Frederick, Kt., OBE, MC, TD
Downes, Sir Edward Thomas, Kt., CBE
Downey, Sir Gordon Stanley, KCB
Downs, Sir Diarmuid, Kt., CBE, FREng.
Downward, *Maj.-Gen.* Sir Peter Aldcroft, KCVO, CB, DSO, DFC
Downward, Sir William Atkinson, Kt.
Dowson, Sir Philip Manning, Kt., CBE, PRA
Doyle, Sir Reginald Derek Henry, Kt., CBE
D'Oyly, Sir Nigel Hadley Miller, Bt. (1663)
Drake, *Hon.* Sir (Frederick) Maurice, Kt., DFC
Drewry, *Lt.-Gen.* Sir Christopher Francis, KCB, CBE
Dreyer, *Adm.* Sir Desmond Parry, GCB, CBE, DSC
Drinkwater, Sir John Muir, Kt., QC
Driver, Sir Antony Victor, Kt.
Driver, Sir Eric William, Kt.
Drummond, Sir John Richard Gray, Kt., CBE
Drury, Sir (Victor William) Michael, Kt., OBE
Dryden, Sir John Stephen Gyles, Bt. (1733 and 1795)
du Cann, *Rt. Hon.* Sir Edward Dillon Lott, KBE
†Duckworth, Sir Edward Richard Dyce, Bt. (1909)
du Cros, Sir Claude Philip Arthur Mallet, Bt. (1916)
Duffell, *Lt.-Gen.* Sir Peter Royson, KCB, CBE, MC
Duffus, *Hon.* Sir Herbert George Holwell, Kt.
Duffy, Sir (Albert) (Edward) Patrick, Kt., Ph.D.
Dugdale, Sir William Stratford, Bt., MC (1936)
Dummett, *Prof.* Sir Michael Anthony Eardley, Kt., FBA
Dunbar, Sir Archibald Ranulph, Bt. (S. 1700)
Dunbar, Sir David Hope-, Bt. (S. 1664)
Dunbar, Sir Robert Drummond Cospatrick, Bt. (S. 1698)
Dunbar, Sir James Michael, Bt. (S. 1694)
†Dunbar of Hempriggs, Sir Richard Francis, Bt. (S. 1706)
Duncan, Sir James Blair, Kt.
Duncombe, Sir Philip Digby Pauncefort-, Bt. (1859)
Dunham, Sir Kingsley Charles, Kt., Ph.D., FRS, FRSE, FREng.
Dunlop, Sir Thomas, Bt. (1916)
Dunn, *Air Marshal* Sir Eric Clive, KBE, CB, BEM
Dunn, *Air Marshal* Sir Patrick Hunter, KBE, CB, DFC
Dunn, *Rt. Hon.* Sir Robin Horace Walford, Kt., MC
Dunne, Sir Thomas Raymond, KCVO

Dunning, Sir Simon William Patrick, Bt. (1930)

Dunstan, *Lt.-Gen.* Sir Donald Beaumont, KBE, CB

Dunt, *Vice-Adm.* Sir John Hugh, KCB

†Duntze, Sir Daniel Evans, Bt. (1774)

Dupre, Sir Tumun, Kt., MBE

Dupree, Sir Peter, Bt. (1921)

Durand, Sir Edward Alan Christopher David Percy, Bt. (1892)

Durant, Sir (Robert) Anthony (Bevis), Kt.

Durham, Sir Kenneth, Kt.

Durkin, *Air Marshal* Sir Herbert, KBE, CB

Durrant, Sir William Alexander Estridge, Bt. (1784)

Duthie, *Prof.* Sir Herbert Livingston, Kt.

Duthie, Sir Robert Grieve (Robin), Kt., CBE

Dwyer, Sir Joseph Anthony, Kt.

Dyer, *Prof.* Sir (Henry) Peter (Francis) Swinnerton-, Bt., KBE, FRS (1678)

Dyke, Sir David William Hart, Bt. (1677)

Dyson, *Hon.* Sir John Anthony, Kt.

Eady, *Hon.* Sir David, Kt.

Earle, Sir (Hardman) George (Algernon), Bt. (1869)

Easton, Sir Robert William Simpson, Kt., CBE

Eaton, *Adm.* Sir Kenneth John, GBE, KCB

Eberle, *Adm.* Sir James Henry Fuller, GCB

Ebrahim, Sir (Mahomed) Currimbhoy, Bt. (1910)

Echlin, Sir Norman David Fenton, Bt. (I. 1721)

Eckersley, Sir Donald Payze, Kt., OBE

Edge, *Capt.* Sir (Philip) Malcolm, KCVO

†Edge, Sir William, Bt. (1937)

Edmonstone, Sir Archibald Bruce Charles, Bt. (1774)

Edwardes, Sir Michael Owen, Kt.

Edwards, Sir Christopher John Churchill, Bt. (1866)

Edwards, Sir George Robert, Kt., OM, CBE, FRS, FREng.

Edwards, Sir Llewellyn Roy, Kt.

Edwards, *Prof.* Sir Samuel Frederick, Kt., FRS

Egan, Sir John Leopold, Kt.

Egerton, Sir John Alfred Roy, Kt.

Egerton, Sir (Philip) John (Caledon) Grey-, Bt. (1617)

Egerton, Sir Stephen Loftus, KCMG

Eichelbaum, *Rt. Hon.* Sir Thomas, GBE

Elias, Sir Patrick, Kt., QC

Eliott of Stobs, Sir Charles Joseph Alexander, Bt. (S. 1666)

Ellerton, Sir Geoffrey James, Kt., CMG, MBE

Elliot, Sir Gerald Henry, Kt.

Elliott, Sir Clive Christopher Hugh, Bt. (1917)

Elliott, Sir David Murray, KCMG, CB

Elliott, *Prof.* Sir John Huxtable, Kt., FBA

Elliott, Sir Randal Forbes, KBE

Elliott, *Prof.* Sir Roger James, Kt., FRS

Elliott, Sir Ronald Stuart, Kt.

Ellis, Sir Ronald, Kt., FREng.

Ellison, *Col.* Sir Ralph Harry Carr-, KCVO, TD

Elphinstone, Sir John, Bt. (S. 1701)

Elphinstone, Sir John Howard Main, Bt. (1816)

Elton, Sir Arnold, Kt., CBE

Elton, Sir Charles Abraham Grierson, Bt. (1717)

Elwes, Sir Jeremy Vernon, Kt., CBE

Elwood, Sir Brian George Conway, Kt., CBE

Elworthy, Sir Peter Herbert, Kt.

Elyan, Sir (Isadore) Victor, Kt.

Emery, *Rt. Hon.* Sir Peter Frank Hannibal, Kt., MP

Empey, Sir Reginald Norman Morgan, Kt., OBE

Engle, Sir George Lawrence Jose, KCB, QC

English, Sir Terence Alexander Hawthorne, KBE, FRCS

Epstein, *Prof.* Sir (Michael) Anthony, Kt., CBE, FRS

Errington, *Col.* Sir Geoffrey Frederick, Bt., OBE (1963)

Errington, Sir Lancelot, KCB

Erskine, Sir (Thomas) David, Bt. (1821)

Esmonde, Sir Thomas Francis Grattan, Bt. (I. 1629)

Espie, Sir Frank Fletcher, Kt., OBE

Esplen, Sir John Graham, Bt. (1921)

Essenhigh, *Adm.* Sir Nigel Richard, Kt.

Etherton, *Hon.* Sir Terence Michael Elkan Barnet, KT.

Evans, Sir Anthony Adney, Bt. (1920)

Evans, *Rt. Hon.* Sir Anthony Howell Meurig, Kt., RD

Evans, *Prof.* Sir Christopher Thomas, Kt., OBE

Evans, *Air Chief Marshal* Sir David George, GCB, CBE

Evans, *Air Chief Marshal* Sir David Parry-, GCB, CBE

Evans, *Hon.* Sir David Roderick, Kt.

Evans, *Hon.* Sir Haydn Tudor, Kt.

Evans, *Prof.* Sir John Grimley, Kt., FRCP

Evans, Sir John Stanley, Kt., QPM

Evans, Sir Richard Harry, Kt., CBE

Evans, Sir Richard Mark, KCMG, KCVO

Evans, Sir Robert, Kt., CBE, FREng.

Evans, Sir (William) Vincent (John), GCMG, MBE, QC

Eveleigh, *Rt. Hon.* Sir Edward Walter, Kt., ERD

Everard, Sir Robin Charles, Bt. (1911)

Every, Sir Henry John Michael, Bt. (1641)

Ewans, Sir Martin Kenneth, KCMG

†Ewart, Sir William Michael, Bt. (1887)

Ewbank, *Hon.* Sir Anthony Bruce, Kt.

Ewin, Sir (David) Ernest Thomas Floyd, Kt., OBE, LVO

Ewing, Sir (Alistair) Simon Orr-, Bt. (1963)

Ewing, Sir Ronald Archibald Orr-, Bt. (1886)

Eyre, *Maj.-Gen.* Sir James Ainsworth Campden Gabriel, KCVO, CBE

Eyre, Sir Reginald Edwin, Kt.

Eyre, Sir Richard Charles Hastings, Kt., CBE

Faber, Sir Richard Stanley, KCVO, CMG

Fagge, Sir John William Frederick, Bt. (1660)

Fairbairn, Sir (James) Brooke, Bt. (1869)

Fairclough, Sir John Whitaker, Kt., FREng.

Fairhall, *Hon.* Sir Allen, KBE

Fairweather, Sir Patrick Stanislaus, KCMG

Falconer, *Hon.* Sir Douglas William, Kt., MBE

†Falkiner, Sir Benjamin Simon Patrick, Bt. (I. 1778)

Fall, Sir Brian James Proetel, GCVO, KCMG

Falle, Sir Samuel, KCMG, KCVO, DSC

Fang, *Prof.* Sir Harry, Kt., CBE

Fareed, Sir Djamil Sheik, Kt.

Farmer, Sir Thomas, Kt., CBE

Farquhar, Sir Michael Fitzroy Henry, Bt. (1796)

Farquharson, *Rt. Hon.* Sir Donald Henry, Kt.

Farquharson, Sir James Robbie, KBE

Farrell, Sir Terence, Kt., CBE

Farrer, Sir (Charles) Matthew, GCVO

Farrington, Sir Henry Francis Colden, Bt. (1818)

Fat, Sir (Maxime) Edouard (Lim Man) Lim, Kt.

Faulkner, Sir (James) Dennis (Compton), Kt., CBE, VRD

Fawcus, Sir (Robert) Peter, KBE, CMG

Fawkes, Sir Randol Francis, Kt.

Fay, Sir (Humphrey) Michael Gerard, Kt.

Fayrer, Sir John Lang Macpherson, Bt. (1896)

Fearn, Sir (Patrick) Robin, KCMG

Feilden, Sir Bernard Melchior, Kt., CBE

Feilden, Sir Henry Wemyss, Bt., (1846)

Fell, Sir David, KCB

Fender, Sir Brian Edward Frederick, Kt., CMG, Ph.D.

Fenn, Sir Nicholas Maxted, GCMG

Fennell, *Hon.* Sir (John) Desmond Augustine, Kt., OBE

Fennessy, Sir Edward, Kt., CBE

Fergus, Sir Howard Archibald, KBE, CBE

Ferguson, Sir Alexander Chapman, Kt., CBE

Ferguson, Sir Ian Edward Johnson-, Bt. (1906)
Fergusson of Kilkerran, Sir Charles, Bt. (s. 1703)
Fergusson, Sir Ewan Alastair John, GCMG, GCVO
Fergusson, Sir James Herbert Hamilton Colyer-, Bt. (1866)
Feroze, Sir Rustam Moolan, Kt., FRCS
Ferris, Hon. Sir Francis Mursell, Kt., TD
ffolkes, Sir Robert Francis Alexander, Bt, OBE (1774)
Field, Sir Malcolm David, Kt.
Fielding, Sir Colin Cunningham, Kt., CB
Fielding, Sir Leslie, KCMG
Fieldsend, Hon. Sir John Charles Rowell, KBE
Fiennes, Sir Ranulph Twisleton-Wykeham-, Bt., OBE (1916)
Figg, Sir Leonard Clifford William, KCMG
Figgis, Sir Anthony St John Howard, KCVO, CMG
Figures, Sir Colin Frederick, KCMG, OBE
Fingland, Sir Stanley James Gunn, KCMG
Finlay, Sir David Ronald James Bell, Bt. (1964)
Finney, Sir Thomas, Kt., OBE
Firth, Prof. Sir Raymond William, Kt., Ph.D., FBA
Fisher, Sir George Read, Kt., CMG
Fisher, Hon. Sir Henry Arthur Pears, Kt.
Fison, Sir (Richard) Guy, Bt., DSC (1905)
†Fitzgerald, Revd (Sir) Daniel Patrick, Bt. (1903)
†FitzGerald, Sir Adrian James Andrew, Bt. (1880)
FitzHerbert, Sir Richard Ranulph, Bt. (1784)
Fitzpatrick, Gen. Sir (Geoffrey Richard) Desmond, GCB, GCVO, DSO, MBE, MC
Fitzpatrick, Air Marshal Sir John Bernard, KBE, CB
Flanagan, Sir Ronald, Kt., OBE
Fletcher, Sir Henry Egerton Aubrey-, Bt. (1782)
Fletcher, Sir James Muir Cameron, Kt.
Fletcher, Sir Leslie, Kt., DSC
Floissac, Hon. Sir Vincent Frederick, Kt., CMG, OBE, QC
Floyd, Sir Giles Henry Charles, Bt. (1816)
Foley, Lt.-Gen. Sir John Paul, KCB, OBE, MC
Foley, Sir (Thomas John) Noel, Kt., CBE
Follett, Prof. Sir Brian Keith, Kt., FRS
Foot, Sir Geoffrey James, Kt.
Foots, Sir James William, Kt.
Forbes, Maj. Sir Hamish Stewart, Bt., MBE, MC (1823)

Forbes of Craigievar, Sir John Alexander Cumnock, Bt. (s. 1630)
Forbes, Vice-Adm. Sir John Morrison, KCB
Forbes, Hon. Sir Thayne John, Kt.
†Forbes, Sir William Daniel Stuart-, Bt. (s. 1626)
Ford, Sir Andrew Russell, Bt. (1929)
Ford, Sir David Robert, KBE, LVO, OBE
Ford, Maj. Sir Edward William Spencer, GCVO, KCB, ERD
Ford, Air Marshal Sir Geoffrey Harold, KBE, CB, FREng.
Ford, Prof. Sir Hugh, Kt., FRS, FREng.
Ford, Sir James Anson St Clair-, Bt. (1793)
Ford, Sir John Archibald, KCMG, MC
Ford, Gen. Sir Robert Cyril, GCB, CBE
Foreman, Sir Philip Frank, Kt., CBE, FREng.
Forman, Sir John Denis, Kt., OBE
Forrest, Prof. Sir (Andrew) Patrick (McEwen), Kt.
Forrest, Rear-Adm. Sir Ronald Stephen, KCVO
Forster, Sir Archibald William, Kt., FREng.
Forte, Hon. Sir Rocco John Vincent, Kt.
Forwood, Sir Dudley Richard, Bt. (1895)
Foster, Sir Andrew William, Kt.
Foster, Prof. Sir Christopher David, Kt.
Foster, Sir John Gregory, Bt. (1930)
Foster, Sir Robert Sidney, GCMG, KCVO
Foulis, Sir Ian Primrose Liston-, Bt. (s. 1634)
Foulkes, Sir Arther Alexander, KCMG
Foulkes, Sir Nigel Gordon, Kt.
Fountain, Hon. Sir Cyril Stanley Smith, Kt.
Fowden, Sir Leslie, Kt., FRS
Fowke, Sir David Frederick Gustavus, Bt. (1814)
Fowler, Sir (Edward) Michael Coulson, Kt.
Fowler, Rt. Hon. Sir (Peter) Norman, Kt., MP
Fox, Rt. Hon. Sir (John) Marcus, Kt., MBE
Fox, Rt. Hon. Sir Michael John, Kt.
Fox, Sir Paul Leonard, Kt., CBE
France, Sir Christopher Walter, GCB
Francis, Sir Horace William Alexander, Kt., CBE, FREng.
Frank, Sir Douglas George Horace, Kt., QC
Frank, Sir Robert Andrew, Bt. (1920)
Franklin, Sir Michael David Milroy, KCB, CMG
Franklin, Sir Michael George Charles, Kt
Franks, Sir Arthur Temple, KCMG
Fraser, Sir Alasdair MacLeod, Kt.
Fraser, Sir Charles Annand, KCVO
Fraser, Gen. Sir David William, GCB, OBE

Fraser, Sir Iain Michael Duncan, Bt. (1943)
Fraser, Sir Ian James, Kt., CBE, MC
Fraser, Sir (James) Campbell, Kt.
Fraser, Sir James Murdo, KBE
Fraser, Sir William Kerr, GCB
Frayling, Prof. Sir Christopher John, Kt.
Frederick, Sir Christopher St John, Bt. (1723)
Freeland, Sir John Redvers, KCMG
Freeman, Sir James Robin, Bt. (1945)
Freer, Air Chief Marshal Sir Robert William George, GBE, KCB
Freeth, Hon. Sir Gordon, KBE
French, Hon. Sir Christopher James Saunders, Kt.
Frere, Vice-Adm. Sir Richard Tobias, KCB
Fretwell, Sir (Major) John (Emsley), GCMG
Freud, Sir Clement Raphael, Kt.
Froggatt, Sir Leslie Trevor, Kt.
Froggatt, Sir Peter, Kt.
Frossard, Sir Charles Keith, KBE
Frost, Sir David Paradine, Kt., OBE
Frost, Sir Terence Ernest Manitou, Kt., RA
Fry, Sir Peter Derek, Kt.
Fry, Hon. Sir William Gordon, Kt.
Fuller, Sir James Henry Fleetwood, Bt. (1910)
Fuller, Hon. Sir John Bryan Munro, Kt.
Fung, Hon. Sir Kenneth Ping-Fan, Kt., CBE
Furness, Sir Stephen Roberts, Bt. (1913)
Gadsden, Sir Peter Drury Haggerston, GBE, FREng.
Gage, Hon. Sir William Marcus, Kt.
Gainsford, Sir Ian Derek, Kt., DDS
Gaius, Rt. Revd Saimon, KBE
Gallwey, Sir Philip Frankland Payne-, Bt. (1812)
Galsworthy, Sir Anthony Charles, KCMG
Galway, Sir James, Kt., OBE
Gam, Rt. Revd Sir Getake, KBE
Gamble, Sir David Hugh Norman, Bt. (1897)
Gambon, Sir Michael John, Kt., CBE
Garden, Air Marshal Sir Timothy, KCB
Gardiner, Sir George Arthur, Kt.
Gardiner, Sir John Eliot, Kt., CBE
Gardner, Sir Robert Henry Bruce-, Bt. (1945)
Garland, Hon. Sir Patrick Neville, Kt.
Garland, Hon. Sir Ransley Victor, KBE
Garlick, Sir John, KCB
Garner, Sir Anthony Stuart, Kt.
Garnett, Vice-Adm. Sir Ian David Graham, KCB
Garnier, Rear-Adm. Sir John, KCVO, CBE
Garrett, Sir Anthony Peter, Kt., CBE
Garrick, Sir Ronald, Kt., CBE, FREng.
Garrioch, Sir (William) Henry, Kt.

Garrod, *Lt.-Gen.* Sir (John) Martin Carruthers, KCB, OBE

Garthwaite, Sir (William) Mark (Charles), Bt. (1919)

Gaskell, Sir Richard Kennedy Harvey, Kt.

Gatehouse, *Hon.* Sir Robert Alexander, Kt.

Geno, Sir Makena Viora, KBE

Gent, Sir Christopher Charles, Kt.

George, Sir Arthur Thomas, Kt.

George, *Prof.* Sir Charles Frederick, MD, FRCP

George, Sir Edward, Kt.

George, *Rt. Hon.* Sir Edward Alan John, GBE

George, Sir Richard William, Kt., CVO

Gerken, *Vice-Adm.* Sir Robert William Frank, KCB, CBE

Gery, Sir Robert Lucian Wade-, KCMG, KCVO

Gethin, Sir Richard Joseph St Lawrence, Bt. (I. 1665)

Getty, Sir (John) Paul, KBE

Ghurburrun, Sir Rabindrah, Kt.

Gibb, Sir Francis Ross (Frank), Kt., CBE, FREng.

Gibbings, Sir Peter Walter, Kt.

Gibbons, Sir (John) David, KBE

Gibbons, Sir William Edward Doran, Bt. (1752)

Gibbs, *Hon.* Sir Eustace Hubert Beilby, KCVO, CMG

Gibbs, *Rt. Hon.* Sir Harry Talbot, GCMG, KBE

Gibbs, *Hon.* Sir Richard John Hedley, Kt.

Gibbs, Sir Roger Geoffrey, Kt.

Gibbs, *Field Marshal* Sir Roland Christopher, GCB, CBE, DSO, MC

†Gibson, *Revd* Sir Christopher Herbert, Bt. (1931)

Gibson, Sir Ian, Kt., CBE

Gibson, *Rt. Hon.* Sir Peter Leslie, Kt.

Gibson, *Rt. Hon.* Sir Ralph Brian, Kt.

Giddings, *Air Marshal* Sir (Kenneth Charles) Michael, KCB, OBE, DFC, AFC

Gielgud, Sir (Arthur) John, Kt., OM, CH

Giffard, Sir (Charles) Sydney (Rycroft), KCMG

Gilbert, *Air Chief Marshal* Sir Joseph Alfred, KCB, CBE

Gilbert, Sir Martin John, Kt., CBE

†Gilbey, Sir Walter Gavin, Bt. (1893)

Giles, *Rear-Adm.* Sir Morgan Charles Morgan-, Kt., DSO, OBE, GM

Gill, Sir Anthony Keith, Kt., FREng.

Gillam, Sir Patrick John, Kt.

Gillen, *Hon.* Sir John de Winter, Kt.

Gillett, Sir Robin Danvers Penrose, Bt., GBE, RD (1959)

Gilmour, *Col.* Sir Allan Macdonald, KCVO, OBE, MC

Gilmour, Sir John Edward, Bt., DSO, TD (1897)

Gina, Sir Lloyd Maepeza, KBE

Gingell, *Air Chief Marshal* Sir John, GBE, KCB, KCVO

Girolami, Sir Paul, Kt.

Girvan, *Hon.* Sir (Frederick) Paul, Kt.

Gladstone, Sir (Erskine) William, KG, Bt. (1846)

Glen, Sir Alexander Richard, KBE, DSC

Glenn, Sir (Joseph Robert) Archibald, Kt., OBE

Glidewell, *Rt. Hon.* Sir Iain Derek Laing, Kt.

Glover, *Gen.* Sir James Malcolm, KCB, MBE

Glover, Sir Victor Joseph Patrick, Kt.

Glyn, Sir Richard Lindsay, Bt. (1759 and 1800)

Goavea, Sir Sinaka Vakai, KBE

Gobbo, Sir James Augustine, Kt., AC

Godber, Sir George Edward, GCB, DM

Goff, Sir Robert (William) Davis-, Bt. (1905)

Gold, Sir Arthur Abraham, Kt., CBE

Gold, Sir Joseph, Kt.

Goldberg, *Prof.* Sir Abraham, Kt., MD, D.Sc., FRCP

Goldberg, *Prof.* Sir David Paul Brandes, Kt.

Goldman, Sir Samuel, KCB

Goldring, Sir John Bernard, Kt.

Gombrich, *Prof.* Sir Ernst Hans Josef, Kt., OM, CBE, Ph.D., FBA, FSA

Gomersall, Sir Stephen John, KCMG

Gooch, Sir Timothy Robert, Bt., MBE (1746)

Gooch, Sir Trevor Sherlock (Sir Peter), Bt. (1866)

Good, Sir John Kennedy-, KBE

Goodall, Sir (Arthur) David Saunders, GCMG

Goodall, *Air Marshal* Sir Roderick Harvey, KBE, CB, CBE, AFC RAF

Goode, *Prof.* Sir Royston Miles, Kt., CBE, QC

Goodenough, Sir Anthony Michael, KCMG

Goodenough, Sir William McLernon, Bt. (1943)

Goodhart, Sir Philip Carter, Kt.

Goodhart, Sir Robert Anthony Gordon, Bt. (1911)

Goodhew, Sir Victor Henry, Kt.

Gooding, Sir Alan, Kt.

Goodison, Sir Alan Clowes, KCMG

Goodison, Sir Nicholas Proctor, Kt.

Goodlad, *Rt. Hon.* Sir Alastair Robertson, KCMG

Goodman, Sir Patrick Ledger, Kt., CBE

Goodson, Sir Mark Weston Lassam, Bt. (1922)

Goodwin, Sir Matthew Dean, Kt., CBE

†Goold, Sir George William, Bt. (1801)

Gordon, Sir Andrew Cosmo Lewis Duff-, Bt. (1813)

Gordon, Sir Charles Addison Somerville Snowden, KCB

Gordon, Sir Gerald Henry, Kt., CBE, QC

Gordon, Sir Keith Lyndell, Kt., CMG

Gordon, Sir (Lionel) Eldred (Peter) Smith-, Bt. (1838)

Gordon, Sir Robert James, Bt. (S. 1706)

Gordon, Sir Sidney Samuel, Kt., CBE

Gordon Lennox, Lord Nicholas Charles, KCMG, KCVO

†Gore, Sir Nigel Hugh St George, Bt. (I. 1622)

Gorham, Sir Richard Masters, Kt., CBE, DFC

Goring, Sir William Burton Nigel, Bt. (1627)

Gorman, Sir John Reginald, Kt., CVO, CBE, MC

Gorst, Sir John Michael, Kt.

Gorton, *Rt. Hon.* Sir John Grey, GCMG, CH

Goschen, Sir Edward Christian, Bt., DSO (1916)

Gosling, Sir (Frederick) Donald, Kt.

Goswell, Sir Brian Lawrence, Kt.

Goulden, Sir (Peter) John, KCMG, GCMG

Goulding, Sir Marrack Irvine, KCMG

Goulding, Sir (William) Lingard Walter, Bt. (1904)

Gourlay, *Gen.* Sir (Basil) Ian (Spencer), KCB, OBE, MC, RM

Gourlay, Sir Simon Alexander, Kt.

Govan, Sir Lawrence Herbert, Kt.

Gow, *Gen.* Sir (James) Michael, GCB

Gowans, Sir James Learmonth, Kt., CBE, FRCP, FRS

†Graaff, Sir David de Villiers, Bt., MBE (1911)

Grabham, Sir Anthony Henry, Kt.

Graham, Sir Alexander Michael, GBE

Graham, Sir James Bellingham, Bt. (1662)

Graham, Sir James Fergus Surtees, Bt. (1783)

Graham, Sir James Thompson, Kt., CMG

Graham, Sir John Alexander Noble, Bt., GCMG (1906)

Graham, Sir John Alistair, Kt.

Graham, Sir John Moodie, Bt. (1964)

Graham, Sir Norman William, Kt., CB

Graham, Sir Peter, KCB, QC

Graham, Sir Peter Alfred, Kt., OBE

Graham, *Lt.-Gen.* Sir Peter Walter, KCB, CBE

†Graham, Sir Ralph Stuart, Bt. (1629)

Graham, *Hon.* Sir Samuel Horatio, Kt., CMG, OBE

Grandy, *Marshal of the Royal Air Force* Sir John, GCB, GCVO, KBE, DSO

Grant, Sir Archibald, Bt. (S. 1705)

Grant, Sir Clifford, Kt.

Grant, Sir (John) Anthony, Kt.

Grant, Sir Patrick Alexander Benedict, Bt. (S. 1688)

Grant, *Lt.-Gen.* Sir Scott Carnegie, KCB

Gray, *Hon.* Sir Charles Anthony St John, Kt., QC

Gray, *Prof.* Sir Denis John Pereira, Kt., OBE, FRCGP

Gray, Sir John Archibald Browne, Kt., SC.D., FRS

Gray, Sir John Walton David, KBE, CMG

Gray, *Lt.-Gen.* Sir Michael Stuart, KCB, OBE

Gray, Sir Robert McDowall (Robin), Kt.

Gray, Sir William Hume, Bt. (1917)

Graydon, *Air Chief Marshal* Sir Michael James, GCB, CBE

Grayson, Sir Jeremy Brian Vincent Harrington, Bt. (1922)

Green, Sir Allan David, KCB, QC

Green, Sir Andrew Fleming, KCMG

Green, *Hon.* Sir Guy Stephen Montague, KBE

Green, Sir Kenneth, Kt.

Green, Sir Owen Whitley, Kt.

†Green, Sir Simon Lycett, Bt., TD (1886)

Greenaway, Sir John Michael Burdick, Bt. (1933)

Greenbury, Sir Richard, Kt.

Greene, Sir (John) Brian Massy-, Kt.

Greener, Sir Anthony Armitage, Kt.

Greengross, Sir Alan David, Kt.

Greening, *Rear-Adm.* Sir Paul Woollven, GCVO

Greenstock, Sir Jeremy Quentin, KCMG

Greenwell, Sir Edward Bernard, Bt. (1906)

Gregson, Sir Peter Lewis, GCB

Greig, Sir (Henry Louis) Carron, KCVO, CBE

Grenside, Sir John Peter, Kt., CBE

Grey, Sir Anthony Dysart, Bt. (1814)

Grierson, Sir Michael John Bewes, Bt. (S. 1685)

Grierson, Sir Ronald Hugh, Kt.

Griffin, *Maj.* Sir (Arthur) John (Stewart), KCVO

Griffin, Sir (Charles) David, Kt., CBE

Griffiths, Sir Eldon Wylie, Kt.

Griffiths, Sir John Norton-, Bt. (1922)

Grigson, *Hon.* Sir Geoffrey Douglas, Kt.

Grimwade, Sir Andrew Sheppard, Kt., CBE

Grindrod, *Most Revd* Sir John Basil Rowland, KBE

Grinstead, Sir Stanley Gordon, Kt.

Grose, *Vice-Adm.* Sir Alan, KBE

Grossart, Sir Angus McFarlane McLeod, Kt., CBE

Grotrian, Sir Philip Christian Brent, Bt. (1934)

Grove, Sir Charles Gerald, Bt. (1874)

Grove, Sir Edmund Frank, KCVO

Grugeon, Sir John Drury, Kt.

Guinness, Sir Howard Christian Sheldon, Kt., VRD

Guinness, Sir John Ralph Sidney, Kt., CB

Guinness, Sir Kenelm Ernest Lee, Bt. (1867)

Guise, Sir John Grant, Bt. (1783)

Gull, Sir Rupert William Cameron, Bt. (1872)

Gumbs, Sir Emile Rudolph, Kt.

Gunn, *Prof.* Sir John Currie, Kt., CBE

Gunn, Sir Robert Norman, Kt.

Gunn, Sir William Archer, KBE, CMG

†Gunning, Sir Charles Theodore, Bt. (1778)

Gunston, Sir John Wellesley, Bt. (1938)

Gurdon, *Prof.* Sir John Bertrand, Kt., D.Phil., FRS

Guthrie, *Gen.* Sir Charles Ronald Llewelyn, GCB, LVO, OBE

Guthrie, Sir Malcolm Connop, Bt. (1936)

Guy, *Gen.* Sir Roland Kelvin, GCB, CBE, DSO

Habakkuk, Sir John Hrothgar, Kt., FBA

Haddacks, *Vice-Adm.* Sir Paul Kenneth, KCB

Hadfield, Sir Ronald, Kt., QPM

Hadlee, Sir Richard John, Kt., MBE

Hague, *Prof.* Sir Douglas Chalmers, Kt., CBE

Halberg, Sir Murray Gordon, Kt., MBE

Hall, Sir Basil Brodribb, KCB, MC, TD

Hall, Sir Douglas Basil, Bt., KCMG (S. 1687)

Hall, Sir Ernest, Kt., OBE

Hall, Sir (Frederick) John (Frank), Bt. (1923)

Hall, Sir John, Kt.

Hall, Sir John Bernard, Bt. (1919)

Hall, Sir Laurence Charles Brodie-, Kt., AO, CMG

Hall, Sir Percival Burton Curtis, Kt.

Hall, Sir Peter Edward, KBE, CMG

Hall, *Prof.* Sir Peter Geoffrey, Kt., FBA

Hall, Sir Peter Reginald Frederick, Kt., CBE

Hall, Sir Robert de Zouche, KCMG

Hall, *Brig.* Sir William Henry, KBE, DSO, ED

Halliday, *Vice-Adm.* Sir Roy William, KBE, DSC

Halpern, Sir Ralph Mark, Kt.

Halsey, *Revd* Sir John Walter Brooke, Bt. (1920)

Halstead, Sir Ronald, Kt., CBE

Ham, Sir David Kenneth Rowe-, GBE

Hambling, Sir (Herbert) Hugh, Bt. (1924)

Hamburger, Sir Sidney Cyril, Kt., CBE

Hamer, *Hon.* Sir Rupert James, KCMG, ED

Hamilton, *Rt. Hon.* Sir Archibald Gavin, Kt., MP

Hamilton, Sir Edward Sydney, Bt. (1776 and 1819)

Hamilton, Sir James Arnot, KCB, MBE, FREng.

Hamilton, Sir Malcolm William Bruce Stirling-, Bt. (S. 1673)

Hamilton, Sir (Robert Charles) Richard Caradoc, Bt. (S. 1646)

Hammick, Sir Stephen George, Bt. (1834)

Hammond, Sir Anthony Hilgrove, KCB, QC

Hampel, Sir Ronald Claus, Kt.

Hampshire, Sir Stuart Newton, Kt., FBA

Hampson, Sir Stuart, Kt.

Hampton, Sir (Leslie) Geoffrey, Kt.

Hancock, Sir David John Stowell, KCB

Hancock, *Air Marshal* Sir Valston Eldridge, KBE, CB, DFC

Hand, *Most Revd* Geoffrey David, KBE

Handley, Sir David John Davenport-, Kt., OBE

Hanham, Sir Michael William, Bt., DFC (1667)

Hanley, *Rt. Hon.* Sir Jeremy James, KCMG

Hanmer, Sir John Wyndham Edward, Bt. (1774)

Hann, Sir James, Kt., CBE

Hannam, Sir John Gordon, Kt.

Hannay, Sir David Hugh Alexander, GCMG

Hanson, Sir (Charles) Rupert (Patrick), Bt. (1918)

Hanson, Sir John Gilbert, KCMG, CBE

Hardcastle, Sir Alan John, Kt.

Hardie, Sir Douglas Fleming, Kt., CBE

Harding, Sir George William, KCMG, CVO

Harding, *Marshal of the Royal Air Force* Sir Peter Robin, GCB

Harding, Sir Roy Pollard, Kt., CBE

Hardy, Sir David William, Kt.

Hardy, Sir James Gilbert, Kt., OBE

Hardy, Sir Richard Charles Chandos, Bt. (1876)

Hare, Sir David, Kt., FRSL

Hare, Sir Nicholas Patrick, Bt. (1818)

Harford, Sir (John) Timothy, Bt. (1934)

Hargroves, *Brig.* Sir Robert Louis, Kt., CBE

Harington, *Gen.* Sir Charles Henry Pepys, GCB, CBE, DSO, MC

Harington, Sir Nicholas John, Bt. (1611)

Harland, *Air Marshal* Sir Reginald Edward Wynyard, KBE, CB

Harley, *Gen.* Sir Alexander George Hamilton, KBE, CB

Harman, *Gen.* Sir Jack Wentworth, GCB, OBE, MC

Harman, *Hon.* Sir Jeremiah LeRoy, Kt.

Harman, Sir John Andrew, Kt.

Harmsworth, Sir Hildebrand Harold, Bt. (1922)

Harris, *Prof.* Sir Henry, Kt., FRCP, FRCPath., FRS

Harris, Sir Jack Wolfred Ashford, Bt. (1932)

Harris, *Air Marshal* Sir John Hulme, KCB, CBE

Harris, *Prof.* Sir Martin Best, Kt., CBE

Harris, Sir William Gordon, KBE, CB, FREng.
Harrison, Sir David, Kt., CBE, FREng.
Harrison, *Prof.* Sir Donald Frederick Norris, Kt., FRCS
Harrison, Sir Ernest Thomas, Kt., OBE
Harrison, Sir Francis Alexander Lyle, Kt., MBE, QC
Harrison, *Surgeon Vice-Adm.* Sir John Albert Bews, KBE
Harrison, *Hon.* Sir (John) Richard, Kt., ED
Harrison, *Hon.* Sir Michael Guy Vicat, Kt.
Harrison, Sir Michael James Harwood, Bt. (1961)
Harrison, *Prof.* Sir Richard John, Kt., FRS
Harrison, Sir (Robert) Colin, Bt. (1922)
Harrison, Sir Terence, Kt., FREng
Harrop, Sir Peter John, KCB
Hart, Sir Graham Allan, KCB
Hart, *Hon.* Sir Michael Christopher Campbell, Kt.
Hartwell, Sir (Francis) Anthony Charles Peter, Bt. (1805)
Harvey, Sir Charles Richard Musgrave, Bt. (1933)
Harvie, Sir John Smith, Kt., CBE
Haselhurst, *Rt. Hon.* Sir Alan Gordon Barraclough, Kt., MP
Haskard, Sir Cosmo Dugal Patrick Thomas, KCMG, MBE
Haslam, *Rear-Adm.* Sir David William, KBE, CB
Hassett, *Gen.* Sir Francis George, KBE, CB, DSO, LVO
Hastings, Sir Stephen Lewis Edmonstone, Kt., MC
Hatter, Sir Maurice, Kt.
Havelock, Sir Wilfrid Bowen, Kt.
Hawkins, Sir Paul Lancelot, Kt., TD
Hawkins, Sir Richard Caesar, Bt. (1778)
Hawley, Sir Donald Frederick, KCMG, MBE
†Hawley, Sir Henry Nicholas, Bt. (1795)
Haworth, Sir Philip, Bt. (1911)
Hawthorne, Sir Nigel Barnard, Kt., CBE
Hawthorne, *Prof.* Sir William Rede, Kt., CBE, SC.D., FRS, FREng.
Hay, Sir David Osborne, Kt., CBE, DSO
Hay, Sir David Russell, Kt., CBE, FRCP, MD
Hay, Sir Hamish Grenfell, Kt.
Hay, Sir James Brian Dalrymple-, Bt. (1798)
Hay, Sir John Erroll Audley, Bt. (S. 1663)
†Hay, Sir Ronald Frederick Hamilton, Bt. (S. 1703)
Hayes, Sir Brian, Kt., CBE, QPM
Hayes, Sir Brian David, GCB
Hayward, Sir Anthony William Byrd, Kt.

Hayward, Sir Jack Arnold, Kt., OBE
Haywood, Sir Harold, KCVO, OBE
Head, Sir Francis David Somerville, Bt. (1838)
Healey, Sir Charles Edward Chadwyck-, Bt. (1919)
Heap, Sir Peter William, KCMG
Heap, *Prof.* Sir Robert Brian, Kt., CBE, FRS
Hearne, Sir Graham James, Kt., CBE
Heath, *Rt. Hon.* Sir Edward Richard George, KG, MBE, MP
Heath, Sir Mark Evelyn, KCVO, CMG
Heathcote, *Brig.* Sir Gilbert Simon, Bt., CBE (1733)
Heathcote, Sir Michael Perryman, Bt. (1733)
Heatley, Sir Peter, Kt., CBE
Heaton, Sir Yvo Robert Henniker-, Bt. (1912)
Heiser, Sir Terence Michael, GCB
Hellaby, Sir (Frederick Reed) Alan, Kt.
Henao, Revd Sir Ravu, Kt., OBE
Henderson, Sir Denys Hartley, Kt.
Henderson, Sir (John) Nicholas, GCMG, KCVO
Henley, Sir Douglas Owen, KCB
Hennessy, Sir James Patrick Ivan, KBE, CMG
†Henniker, Sir Adrian Chandos, Bt. (1813)
Henriques, *Hon.* Sir Richard Henry Quixano, Kt.
Henry, *Rt. Hon.* Sir Denis Robert Maurice, Kt.
Henry, *Hon.* Sir Geoffrey Arama, KBE
†Henry, Sir Patrick Denis, Bt. (1923)
Henry, *Hon.* Sir Trevor Ernest, Kt.
Hepburn, Sir John Alastair Trant Kidd Buchan-, Bt. (1815)
Herbecq, Sir John Edward, KCB
Herbert, *Adm.* Sir Peter Geoffrey Marshall, KCB, OBE
Herbert, Sir Walter William, Kt.
Hermon, Sir John Charles, Kt., OBE, QPM
Heron, Sir Conrad Frederick, KCB, OBE
Heron, Sir Michael Gilbert, Kt.
Hervey, Sir Roger Blaise Ramsay, KCVO, CMG
Heseltine, *Rt. Hon.* Sir William Frederick Payne, GCB, GCVO
Hetherington, Sir Arthur Ford, Kt., DSC, FREng.
Hetherington, Sir Thomas Chalmers, KCB, CBE, TD, QC
Hewetson, Sir Christopher Raynor, Kt., TD
Hewitt, Sir (Cyrus) Lenox (Simson), Kt., OBE
Hewitt, Sir Nicholas Charles Joseph, Bt. (1921)
Heygate, Sir Richard John Gage, Bt. (1831)
Heywood, Sir Peter, Bt. (1838)
Hezlet, *Vice-Adm.* Sir Arthur Richard, KBE, CB, DSO, DSC
Hibbert, Sir Jack, KCB

Hibbert, Sir Reginald Alfred, GCMG
Hickey, Sir Justin, Kt.
Hickman, Sir (Richard) Glenn, Bt. (1903)
Hicks, Sir Robert, Kt.
Hidden, *Hon.* Sir Anthony Brian, Kt.
Hielscher, Sir Leo Arthur, Kt.
Higgins, *Hon.* Sir Malachy Joseph, Kt.
Higginson, Sir Gordon Robert, Kt., Ph.D., FREng.
Hill, Sir Alexander Rodger Erskine-, Bt. (1945)
Hill, Sir Arthur Alfred, Kt., CBE
Hill, Sir Brian John, Kt.
Hill, Sir James Frederick, Bt. (1917)
Hill, Sir John McGregor, Kt., Ph.D., FREng.
Hill, Sir John Maxwell, Kt., CBE, DFC
†Hill, Sir John Rowley, Bt. (I. 1779)
Hill, *Vice-Adm.* Sir Robert Charles Finch, KBE, FREng.
Hillary, Sir Edmund, KG, KBE
Hillhouse, Sir (Robert) Russell, KCB
Hills, Sir Graham John, Kt.
Hine, *Air Chief Marshal* Sir Patrick Bardon, GCB, GBE
Hinston, Sir Harry Lee, Kt.
Hirsch, *Prof.* Sir Peter Bernhard, Kt., Ph.D., FRS
Hirst, *Rt. Hon.* Sir David Cozens-Hardy, Kt.
Hirst, Sir Michael William, Kt.
Hoare, *Prof.* Sir Charles Anthony Richard, Kt., FRS
Hoare, Sir Peter Richard David, Bt. (1786)
Hoare, Sir Timothy Edward Charles, Bt., OBE (I. 1784)
Hobart, Sir John Vere, Bt. (1914)
Hobbs, *Maj.-Gen.* Sir Michael Frederick, KCVO, CBE
Hobday, Sir Gordon Ivan, Kt.
Hobhouse, Sir Charles John Spinney, Bt. (1812)
Hockaday, Sir Arthur Patrick, KCB, CMG
Hockley, *Gen.* Sir Anthony Heritage Farrar-, GBE, KCB, DSO, MC
†Hodge, Sir Andrew Rowland, Bt. (1921)
Hodge, Sir James William, KCVO, CMG
Hodge, Sir Julian Stephen Alfred, Kt.
Hodges, *Air Chief Marshal* Sir Lewis MacDonald, KCB, CBE, DSO, DFC
Hodgkin, Sir Gordon Howard Eliot, Kt., CBE
Hodgkinson, *Air Chief Marshal* Sir (William) Derek, KCB, CBE, DFC, AFC
Hodgson, Sir Maurice Arthur Eric, Kt., FREng.
Hodgson, *Hon.* Sir (Walter) Derek (Thornley), Kt.
Hodson, Sir Michael Robin Adderley, Bt. (I. 1789)
Hoffenberg, *Prof.* Sir Raymond, KBE
Hogg, Sir Christopher Anthony, Kt.
Hogg, *Vice-Adm.* Sir Ian Leslie Trower, KCB, DSC

†Hogg, Sir Piers Michael James, Bt. (1846)

†Hogg, Sir Michael Edward Lindsay-, Bt. (1905)

Holcroft, Sir Peter George Culcheth, Bt. (1921)

Holderness, Sir Martin William, Bt. (1920)

Holden, Sir Edward, Bt. (1893)

Holden, Sir John David, Bt. (1919)

Holder, Sir John Henry, Bt. (1898)

Holdgate, Sir Martin Wyatt, Kt., CB, Ph.D.

Holdsworth, Sir (George) Trevor, Kt., CVO

Holland, *Hon.* Sir Alan Douglas, Kt.

Holland, *Hon.* Sir Christopher John, Kt.

Holland, Sir Clifton Vaughan, Kt.

Holland, Sir Geoffrey, KCB

Holland, Sir Kenneth Lawrence, Kt., CBE, QFSM

Holland, Sir Philip Welsby, Kt.

Holliday, *Prof.* Sir Frederick George Thomas, Kt., CBE, FRSE

Hollings, *Hon.* Sir (Alfred) Kenneth, Kt., MC

Hollis, *Hon.* Sir Anthony Barnard, Kt.

Hollom, Sir Jasper Quintus, KBE

Holloway, *Hon.* Sir Barry Blyth, KBE

Holm, Sir Carl Henry, Kt., OBE

Holm, Sir Ian (Ian Holm Cuthbert), Kt., CBE

Holman, *Hon.* Sir (Edward) James, Kt.

Holmes, *Prof.* Sir Frank Wakefield, Kt.

Holmes, Sir John Eaton, KBE, CMG, CVO

Holmes, Sir Peter Fenwick, Kt., MC

Holroyd, *Air Marshal* Sir Frank Martyn, KBE, CB, FREng.

Holt, *Prof.* Sir James Clarke, Kt.

Holt, Sir Michael, Kt., CBE

Home, Sir William Dundas, Bt. (S. 1671)

Hone, Sir Michael, Kt.

Honeycombe, *Prof.* Sir Robert William Kerr, Kt., FRS, FREng.

Honywood, Sir Filmer Courtenay William, Bt. (1660)

Hood, Sir Harold Joseph, Bt., TD (1922)

Hookway, Sir Harry Thurston, Kt.

Hooper, *Hon.* Sir Anthony, Kt.

Hope, Sir Colin Frederick Newton, Kt.

Hope, *Rt. Revd and Rt. Hon.* Sir David Michael, KCVO

Hope, Sir John Carl Alexander, Bt. (S. 1628)

Hopkin, Sir (William Aylsham) Bryan, Kt., CBE

Hopkins, Sir Anthony Philip, Kt., CBE

Hopkins, Sir Michael John, Kt., CBE, RA, RIBA

Hopwood, *Prof.* Sir David Alan, Kt., FRS

Hordern, *Rt. Hon.* Sir Peter Maudslay, Kt.

Horlick, *Vice-Adm.* Sir Edwin John, KBE, FREng.

Horlick, Sir James Cunliffe William, Bt. (1914)

Horlock, *Prof.* Sir John Harold, Kt., FRS, FREng.

Hornby, Sir Derek Peter, Kt.

Hornby, Sir Simon Michael, Kt.

Horne, Sir Alan Gray Antony, Bt. (1929)

Horsfall, Sir John Musgrave, Bt., MC, TD (1909)

Horsley, *Air Marshal* Sir (Beresford) Peter (Torrington), KCB, CBE, LVO, AFC

†Hort, Sir Andrew Edwin Fenton, Bt. (1767)

Horton, Sir Robert Baynes, Kt.

Hosker, Sir Gerald Albery, KCB, QC

Hoskyns, Sir Benedict Leigh, Bt. (1676)

Hoskyns, Sir John Austin Hungerford Leigh, Kt.

Hotung, Sir Joseph Edward, Kt.

Houghton, Sir John Theodore, Kt., CBE, FRS

Houldsworth, Sir Richard Thomas Reginald, Bt. (1887)

Hounsfield, Sir Godfrey Newbold, Kt., CBE

Hourston, Sir Gordon Minto, Kt.

House, *Lt.-Gen.* Sir David George, GCB, KCVO, CBE, MC

Houssemayne du Boulay, Sir Roger William, KCVO, CMG

Howard, Sir David Howarth Seymour, Bt. (1955)

Howard, Sir George Marshall, Kt.

Howard, *Prof.* Sir Michael Eliot, Kt., CBE, MC

Howard, *Maj.-Gen.* Lord Michael Fitzalan-, GCVO, CB, CBE, MC

Howell, Sir Ralph Frederic, Kt.

Howells, Sir Eric Waldo Benjamin, Kt., CBE

Howes, Sir Christopher Kingston, KCVO, CB

Howlett, *Gen.* Sir Geoffrey Hugh Whitby, KBE, MC

Hoyos, *Hon.* Sir Fabriciano Alexander, Kt.

Huggins, *Hon.* Sir Alan Armstrong, Kt.

Hughes, *Hon.* Sir Anthony Philip Gilson, Kt.

Hughes, Sir David Collingwood, Bt. (1773)

Hughes, Hon. Sir Davis, Kt.

Hughes, Sir Jack William, Kt.

Hughes, Sir Trevor Denby Lloyd-, Kt.

Hughes, Sir Trevor Poulton, KCB

Hull, *Prof.* Sir David, Kt.

Hulse, Sir Edward Jeremy Westrow, Bt. (1739)

Hume, Sir Alan Blyth, Kt., CB

Humphreys, Sir (Raymond Evelyn) Myles, Kt.

Hunt, Sir John Leonard, Kt.

Hunt, *Adm.* Sir Nicholas John Streynsham, GCB, LVO

Hunt, *Hon.* Sir Patrick James, Kt.

Hunt, Sir Rex Masterman, Kt., CMG

Hunt, Sir Robert Frederick, Kt., CBE, FREng.

Hunt, Sir Julian Charles Roland, CB, Bt.

Hunter, Sir Alistair John, KCMG

Hunter, Sir Ian Bruce Hope, Kt., MBE

Hunter, *Prof.* Sir Laurence Colvin, Kt., CBE, FRSE

Hurn, Sir (Francis) Roger, Kt.

Hurrell, Sir Anthony Gerald, KCVO, CMG

Hurst, Sir Geoffrey Charles, Kt., MBE

Husbands, Sir Clifford Straugh, GCMG

Hutchinson, *Hon.* Sir Ross, Kt., DFC

Hutchison, *Lt.-Cdr.* Sir (George) Ian Clark, Kt., RN

Hutchison, Sir James Colville, Bt. (1956)

Hutchison, *Rt. Hon.* Sir Michael, Kt.

Hutchison, Sir Robert, Bt. (1939)

Huxley, *Prof.* Sir Andrew Fielding, Kt., OM, FRS

Huxtable, *Gen.* Sir Charles Richard, KCB, CBE

Hyatali, *Hon.* Sir Isaac Emanuel, Kt.

Hyslop, Sir Robert John (Robin) Maxwell-, Kt.

Ibbs, Sir (John) Robin, KBE

Imray, Sir Colin Henry, KBE, CMG

Ingham, Sir Bernard, Kt.

Ingilby, Sir Thomas Colvin William, Bt. (1866)

Inglis, Sir Brian Scott, Kt.

Inglis of Glencorse, Sir Roderick John, Bt. (S. 1703)

Ingram, Sir James Herbert Charles, Bt. (1893)

Ingram, Sir John Henderson, Kt., CBE

Inkin, Sir Geoffrey David, Kt., OBE

†Innes, Sir David Charles Kenneth Gordon, Bt. (NS 1686)

Innes of Edingight, Sir Malcolm Rognvald, KCVO

Innes, Sir Peter Alexander Berowald, Bt. (S. 1628)

Irvine, Sir Donald Hamilton, Kt., CBE, MD, FRCGP

Irving, *Prof.* Sir Miles Horsfall, Kt., MD, FRCS, FRCSE

Isaacs, Sir Jeremy Israel, Kt.

Isham, Sir Ian Vere Gyles, Bt. (1627)

Jack, *Hon.* Sir Alieu Sulayman, Kt.

Jack, Sir David, Kt., CBE, FRS, FRSE

Jack, Sir David Emmanuel, GCMG, MBE

Jack, *Hon.* Sir Raymond Evan, Kt.

Jackling, Sir Roger Tustin, KCB. CBE

Jackson, Sir Barry Trevor, Kt.

Jackson, Sir (John) Edward, KCMG

Jackson, Sir Kenneth Joseph, Kt.

Jackson, *Lt.-Gen.* Sir Michael David, KCB, CBE

Jackson, Sir Michael Roland, Bt. (1902)

Jackson, Sir Nicholas Fane St George, Bt. (1913)
Jackson, Sir Robert, Bt. (1815)
Jackson, Hon. Sir Rupert Matthew, Kt., QC
Jackson, Sir William Thomas, Bt. (1869)
Jacob, Sir Isaac Hai, Kt., QC
Jacob, Hon. Sir Robert Raphael Hayim (Robin), Kt.
Jacobi, Sir Derek George, Kt., CBE
Jacobi, Dr Sir James Edward, Kt., OBE
Jacobs, Hon. Sir Kenneth Sydney, KBE
Jacobs, Sir Wilfred Ebenezer, GCMG, GCVO, OBE, QC
Jacomb, Sir Martin Wakefield, Kt.
Jaffray, Sir William Otho, Bt. (1892)
James, Sir Cynlais Morgan, KCMG
James, Sir Jeffrey Russell, KBE, CBE
James, Sir John Nigel Courtenay, KCVO, CBE
James, Sir Stanislaus Anthony, GCMG, OBE
Jamieson, Air Marshal Sir David Ewan, KBE, CB
Jansen, Sir Ross Malcolm, KBE
Jansen van Rensburg, Lt.-Gen. Sir Jurinus Lindo, Kt.
Janvrin, Sir Robin Berry, KCVO, CB
Jardine of Applegirth, Sir Alexander Maule, Bt. (S. 1672)
Jardine, Sir Andrew Colin Douglas, Bt. (1916)
Jardine, Maj. Sir (Andrew) Rupert (John) Buchanan-, Bt., MC (1885)
Jarman, Prof. Sir Brian, Kt., OBE
Jarratt, Sir Alexander Anthony, Kt., CB
Jarvis, Sir Gordon Ronald, Kt.
Jawara, Hon. Sir Dawda Kairaba, Kt.
Jay, Sir Antony Rupert, Kt., CVO
Jay, Sir Michael Hastings, KCMG
Jeewoolall, Sir Ramesh, Kt.
Jefferson, Sir George Rowland, Kt., CBE, FREng.
Jefferson, Sir Mervyn Stewart Dunnington-, Bt. (1958)
Jeffreys, Prof. Sir Alec John, Kt., FRS
Jeffries, Hon. Sir John Francis, Kt.
Jehangir, Sir Cowasji, Bt. (1908)
Jejeebhoy, Sir Jamsetjee, Bt. (1857)
Jenkins, Sir Brian Garton, GBE
Jenkins, Sir Elgar Spencer, Kt., OBE
Jenkins, Sir James Christopher, KCB, QC
Jenkins, Sir Michael Nicholas Howard, Kt., OBE
Jenkins, Sir Michael Romilly Heald, KCMG
Jenkinson, Sir John Banks, Bt. (1661)
Jenks, Sir Maurice Arthur Brian, Bt. (1932)
Jenner, Air Marshall Sir Timothy Ivo, KCB
Jennings, Sir John Southwood, Kt., CBE, FRSE
Jennings, Sir Peter Neville Wake, Kt., CVO
Jennings, Prof. Sir Robert Yewdall, Kt., QC

Jephcott, Sir (John) Anthony, Bt. (1962)
Jessel, Sir Charles John, Bt. (1883)
Jewkes, Sir Gordon Wesley, KCMG
Job, Sir Peter James Denton, Kt.
John, Sir David Glyndwr, KCMG
John, Sir Elton Hercules (Reginald Kenneth Dwight), Kt., CBE
Johns, Air Chief Marshal Sir Richard Edward, GCB, CBE, LVO
Johnson, Gen. Sir Garry Dene, KCB, OBE, MC
Johnson, Sir John Rodney, KCMG
†Johnson, Sir Patrick Eliot, Bt. (1818)
Johnson, Sir Peter Colpoys Paley, Bt. (1755)
Johnson, Hon. Sir Robert Lionel, Kt.
Johnson, Sir Vassel Godfrey, Kt., CBE
Johnston, Sir John Baines, GCMG, KCVO
Johnston, Lt.-Col. Sir John Frederick Dame, GCVO, MC
Johnston, Lt.-Gen. Sir Maurice Robert, KCB, OBE
Johnston, Sir Thomas Alexander, Bt. (S. 1626)
Johnston, Sir William Robert Patrick Knox- (John Robin), Kt., CBE, RD
Johnstone, Sir (George) Richard Douglas, Bt. (S. 1700)
Johnstone, Sir (John) Raymond, Kt., CBE
Jolliffe, Sir Anthony Stuart, GBE
Jolly, Sir Aurthur Richard, KCMG
Jonas, Sir John Peter Jens, Kt., CBE
Jones, Gen. Sir (Charles) Edward Webb, KCB, CBE
Jones, Sir Christopher Lawrence-, Bt. (1831)
Jones, Sir David Akers-, KBE, CMG
Jones, Air Marshal Sir Edward Gordon, KCB, CBE, DSO, DFC
Jones, Sir Ewart Ray Herbert, Kt., D.Sc., Ph.D., FRS
Jones, Sir Harry George, Kt., CBE
Jones, Sir (John) Derek Alun-, Kt.
Jones, Sir John Henry Harvey-, Kt., MBE
Jones, Sir John Prichard-, Bt. (1910)
Jones, Sir Keith Stephen, Kt.
Jones, Hon. Sir Kenneth George Illtyd, Kt.
Jones, Sir Lyndon, Kt.
Jones, Sir (Owen) Trevor, Kt.
Jones, Sir (Peter) Hugh (Jefferd) Lloyd-, Kt.
Jones, Sir Richard Anthony Lloyd, KCB
Jones, Sir Robert Edward, Kt.
Jones, Sir Simon Warley Frederick Benton, Bt. (1919)
Jones, Sir William Gwynoro, Kt.
Jones, Sir Wynn Normington Hugh-, Kt., LVO
†Joseph, Hon. Sir James Samuel, Bt. (1943)
Jowitt, Hon. Sir Edwin Frank, Kt.
Joyce, Lt.-Gen. Sir Robert John Hayman-, KCB, CBE
Judge, Rt. Hon. Sir Igor, Kt.

Judge, Sir Paul Rupert, Kt.
Jugnauth, Rt. Hon. Sir Anerood, KCMG, QC
Jungius, Vice-Adm. Sir James George, KBE
Jupp, Hon. Sir Kenneth Graham, Kt., MC
Kaberry, Hon. Sir Christopher Donald, Bt. (1960)
Kalms, Sir (Harold) Stanley, Kt.
Kalo, Sir Kwamala, Kt., MBE
Kan Yuet-Keung, Sir, GBE
Kapi, Hon. Sir Mari, Kt., CBE
Kaputin, Sir John Rumet, KBE, CMG
Katz, Sir Bernard, Kt., FRS
Kausimae, Sir David Nanau, KBE
Kavali, Sir Thomas, Kt., OBE
Kawashima, Sir Maurice Masaaki, Kt.
Kawharu, Prof. Sir Ian Hugh, Kt.
Kay, Prof. Sir Andrew Watt, Kt.
Kay, Hon. Sir John William, Kt.
Kay, Hon. Sir Maurice Ralph, Kt.
Kaye, Sir John Phillip Lister Lister-, Bt. (1812)
Kaye, Sir Paul Henry Gordon, Bt. (1923)
Keane, Sir Richard Michael, Bt. (1801)
Kearney, Hon. Sir William John Francis, Kt., CBE
Keeble, Sir (Herbert Ben) Curtis, GCMKeegan, Sir John Desmond Patrick, Kt., OBE
Keene, Hon. Sir David Wolfe, Kt.
Keirlie, Sir Dennis Robert, Kt
Keith, Prof. Sir James, KBE
Kellett, Sir Stanley Charles, Bt. (1801)
Kelly, Sir Christopher William, KCB
Kelly, Sir David Robert Corbett, Kt., CBE
Kelly, Rt. Hon. Sir (John William) Basil, Kt.
Kemakeza, Sir Allan, Kt.
Kemball, Air Marshal Sir (Richard) John, KCB, CBE
Kemp, Sir (Edward) Peter, KCB
Kenilorea, Rt. Hon. Sir Peter, KBE
Kennaway, Sir John Lawrence, Bt. (1791)
Kennedy, Sir Francis, KCMG, CBE
Kennedy, Hon. Sir Ian Alexander, Kt.
Kennedy, Sir Ludovic Henry Coverley, Kt.
†Kennedy, Sir Michael Edward, Bt. (1836)
Kennedy, Rt. Hon. Sir Paul Joseph Morrow, Kt.
Kennedy, Air Chief Marshal Sir Thomas Lawrie, GCB, AFC
Kenny, Sir Anthony John Patrick, Kt., D.Phil., D.Litt., FBA
Kenny, Gen. Sir Brian Leslie Graham, GCB, CBE
Kentridge, Sir Sydney Woolf, KCMG, QC
Kenyon, Sir George Henry, Kt.
Kermode, Sir (John) Frank, Kt., FBA
Kermode, Sir Ronald Graham Quale, KBE
Kerr, Hon. Sir Brian Francis, Kt.

Kerr, *Adm.* Sir John Beverley, GCB

Kerr, Sir John (Olav), GCMG, KCMG

Kerr, *Rt. Hon.* Sir Michael Robert Emanuel, Kt.

Kerruish, Sir (Henry) Charles, Kt., OBE

Kerry, Sir Michael James, KCB, QC

Kershaw, Sir (John) Anthony, Kt., MC

Keswick, Sir John Chippendale Lindley, Kt.

Keys, Sir (Alexander George) William, Kt., OBE, MC

Kidd, Sir Robert Hill, KBE, CB

Kikau, *Ratu* Sir Jone Latianara, KBE

Killen, *Hon.* Sir Denis James, KCMG

Killick, Sir John Edward, GCMG

Kimber, Sir Charles Dixon, Bt. (1904)

King, Sir John Christopher, Bt. (1888)

King, *Vice-Adm.* Sir Norman Ross Dutton, KBE

King, Sir Wayne Alexander, Bt. (1815)

Kingman, *Prof.* Sir John Frank Charles, Kt., FRS

Kingsland, Sir Richard, Kt., CBE, DFC

Kinloch, Sir David, Bt. (S. 1686)

Kinloch, Sir David Oliphant, Bt. (1873)

Kipalan, Sir Albert, Kt.

Kirby, *Hon.* Sir Richard Clarence, Kt.

Kirkpatrick, Sir Ivone Elliott, Bt. (S. 1685)

Kirkwood, *Hon.* Sir Andrew Tristram Hammett, Kt.

Kitcatt, Sir Peter Julian, Kt., CB

Kitson, *Gen.* Sir Frank Edward, GBE, KCB, MC

Kitson, Sir Timothy Peter Geoffrey, Kt.

Kleinwort, Sir Richard Drake, Bt. (1909)

Klevan, *Hon.* Sir Rodney (Conrad), Kt., QC

Klug, Sir Aaron, Kt., OM

Kneller, Sir Alister Arthur, Kt.

Knight, Sir Arthur William, Kt.

Knight, Sir Harold Murray, KBE, DSC

Knight, *Air Chief Marshal* Sir Michael William Patrick, KCB, AFC

Knill, *Prof.* Sir John Lawrence, Kt., FREng.

†Knill, Sir Thomas John Pugin Bartholomew, Bt. (1893)

Knowles, Sir Charles Francis, Bt. (1765)

Knowles, Sir Durward Randolph, Kt., OBE

Knowles, Sir Leonard Joseph, Kt., CBE

Knowles, Sir Richard Marchant, Kt.

Knox, Sir Bryce Muir, KCVO, MC, TD

Knox, Sir David Laidlaw, Kt.

Knox, *Hon.* Sir John Leonard, Kt.

Knox, *Hon.* Sir William Edward, Kt.

Koraea, Sir Thomas, Kt.

Kornberg, *Prof.* Sir Hans Leo, Kt., D.Sc., Sc.D., Ph.D., FRS

Korowi, Sir Wiwa, GCMG

Krebs, *Prof.* Sir John Richard, Kt., D.Phil., FRS

Kroto, *Prof.* Sir Harold Walter, Kt., FRS

Kulukundis, Sir Elias George (Eddie), Kt., OBE

Kurongku, *Most Revd* Peter, KBE

Lacon, Sir Edmund Vere, Bt. (1818)

Lacy, Sir Patrick Brian Finucane, Bt. (1921)

Lacy, Sir John Trend, Kt., CBE

Laddie, *Hon.* Sir Hugh Ian Lang, Kt.

Laidlaw, Sir Christophor Charles Fraser, Kt.

Laing, Sir (John) Martin (Kirby), Kt., CBE

Laing, Sir (John) Maurice, Kt.

Laing, Sir (William) Kirby, Kt., FREng.

Laird, Sir Gavin Harry, Kt., CBE

Lake, Sir (Atwell) Graham, Bt. (1711)

Laker, Sir Frederick Alfred, Kt.

Lakin, Sir Michael, Bt. (1909)

Laking, Sir George Robert, KCMG

Lamb, Sir Albert Thomas, KBE, CMG, DFC

Lambert, Sir Anthony Edward, KCMG

Lambert, Sir John Henry, KCVO, CMG

†Lambert, Sir Peter John Biddulph, Bt. (1711)

Lampl, Sir Frank William, Kt.

Landale, Sir David William Neil, KCVO

Landau, Sir Dennis Marcus, Kt.

Lander, Sir Stephen James, KCB

Lane, Prof. Sir David Philip, Kt., FRS, FRSE

Langham, Sir James Michael, Bt. (1660)

Langlands, Sir Robert Alan, Kt.

Langley, *Hon.* Sir Gordon Julian Hugh, Kt.

Langley, *Maj.-Gen.* Sir Henry Desmond Allen, KCVO, MBE

Langrishe, Sir James Hercules, Bt. (I. 1777)

Lankester, Sir Timothy Patrick, KCB

Lapun, *Hon.* Sir Paul, Kt.

Larcom, Sir (Charles) Christopher Royde, Bt. (1868)

Large, Sir Andrew McLeod Brooks, Kt.

Large, Sir Peter, Kt., CBE

Latham, *Hon.* Sir David Nicholas Ramsey, Kt.

Latham, Sir Martin Stuart, Kt., OBE

Latham, Sir Michael Anthony, Kt.

Latham, Sir Richard Thomas Paul, Bt. (1919)

Latimer, Sir (Courtenay) Robert, Kt., CBE

Latimer, Sir Graham Stanley, KBE

Lauder, Sir Piers Robert Dick-, Bt. (S. 1690)

Laughton, Sir Anthony Seymour, Kt.

Laurantus, Sir Nicholas, Kt., MBE

Laurence, Sir Peter Harold, KCMG, MC

Laurie, Sir Robert Bayley Emilius, Bt. (1834)

Lauterpacht, Sir Elihu, Kt., CBE, QC

Lauti, *Rt. Hon.* Sir Toaripi, GCMG

Lavan, *Hon.* Sir John Martin, Kt.

Law, *Adm.* Sir Horace Rochfort, GCB, OBE, DSC

Lawes, Sir (John) Michael Bennet, Bt. (1882)

Lawler, Sir Peter James, Kt., OBE

Lawrence, Sir David Roland Walter, Bt. (1906)

Lawrence, Sir George Alexander Waldemar, Bt. (1858)

Lawrence, Sir Ivan John, Kt., QC

Lawrence, Sir John Patrick Grosvenor, Kt., CBE

Lawrence, Sir William Fettiplace, Bt. (1867)

Laws, *Rt. Hon.* Sir John Grant McKenzie, Kt.

Lawson, Sir Christopher Donald, Kt.

Lawson, *Col.* Sir John Charles Arthur Digby, Bt., DSO, MC (1900)

Lawson, Sir John Philip Howard-, Bt. (1841)

Lawson, *Gen.* Sir Richard George, KCB, DSO, OBE

Layard, *Adm.* Sir Michael Henry Gordon, KCB, CBE

Lea, *Vice-Adm.* Sir John Stuart Crosbie, KBE

Lea, Sir Thomas William, Bt. (1892)

Leach, *Admiral of the Fleet* Sir Henry Conyers, GCB

Leahy, Sir Daniel Joseph, Kt.

Leahy, Sir John Henry Gladstone, KCMG

Learmont, *Gen.* Sir John Hartley, KCB, CBE

Leask, *Lt.-Gen.* Sir Henry Lowther Ewart Clark, KCB, DSO, OBE

Leather, Sir Edwin Hartley Cameron, KCMG, KCVO

Leaver, Sir Christopher, GBE

Le Bailly, *Vice-Adm.* Sir Louis Edward Stewart Holland, KBE, CB

Le Cheminant, *Air Chief Marshal* Sir Peter de Lacey, GBE, KCB, DFC

†Lechmere, Sir Reginald Anthony Hungerford, Bt. (1818)

Ledger, Sir Philip Stevens, Kt., CBE, FRSE

Lee, Sir Arthur James, KBE, MC

Lee, *Air Chief Marshal* Sir David John Pryer, GBE, CB

Lee, *Brig.* Sir Leonard Henry, Kt., CBE

Lee, Sir Quo-wei, Kt., CBE

Leeds, Sir Christopher Anthony, Bt. (1812)

Lees, Sir David Bryan, Kt.

Lees, Sir Thomas Edward, Bt. (1897)

Lees, Sir Thomas Harcourt Ivor, Bt. (1804)

Lees, Sir (William) Antony Clare, Bt. (1937)

Leese, Sir John Henry Vernon, Bt. (1908)

Le Fanu, *Maj.* Sir (George) Victor (Sheridan), KCVO

le Fleming, Sir David Kelland, Bt. (1705)

Legard, Sir Charles Thomas, Bt. (1660)

Legg, Sir Thomas Stuart, KCB, QC

Leggatt, Rt. Hon. Sir Andrew Peter, Kt.

Leggatt, Sir Hugh Frank John, Kt.

Leggett, Sir Clarence Arthur Campbell, Kt., MBE

Leigh, Sir Geoffrey Norman, Kt.

Leigh, Sir Richard Henry, Bt. (1918)

Leighton, Sir Michael John Bryan, Bt. (1693)

Leitch, Sir George, KCB, OBE

Leith, George Ian David Forbes-, Bt. (1923)

Le Marchant, Sir Francis Arthur, Bt. (1841)

Lemon, Sir (Richard) Dawnay, Kt., CBE

Leng, Gen. Sir Peter John Hall, KCB, MBE, MC

Lennard, Revd Sir Hugh Dacre Barrett-, Bt. (1801)

Leon, Sir John Ronald, Bt. (1911)

Leonard, Rt. Revd Monsignor and Rt. Hon. Graham Douglas, KCVO

Leonard, Hon. Sir (Hamilton) John, Kt.

Lepping, Sir George Geria Dennis, GCMG, MBE

Le Quesne, Sir (Charles) Martin, KCMG

Le Quesne, Sir (John) Godfray, Kt., QC

Leslie, Sir Colin Alan Bettridge, Kt.

Leslie, Sir John Norman Ide, Bt. (1876)

†Leslie, Sir (Percy) Theodore, Bt. (S. 1625)

Leslie, Sir Peter Evelyn, Kt.

Lester, Sir James Theodore, Kt.

Lethbridge, Sir Thomas Periam Hector Noel, Bt. (1804)

Lever, Sir Paul, KCMG

Lever, Sir (Tresham) Christopher Arthur Lindsay, Bt. (1911)

Leveson, Hon. Sir Brian Henry, Kt.

Levey, Sir Michael Vincent, Kt., LVO

Levine, Sir Montague Bernard, Kt.

Levinge, Sir Richard George Robin, Bt. (I. 1704)

Lewando, Sir Jan Alfred, Kt., CBE

Lewinton, Sir Christopher, Kt.

Lewis, Sir David Courtenay Mansel, KCVO

Lewis, Sir Terence Murray, Kt., OBE, GM, QPM

Lewthwaite, Brig. Sir Rainald Gilfrid, Bt., CVO, OBE, MC (1927)

Ley, Sir Ian Francis, Bt. (1905)

Leyland, Sir Philip Vyvyan Naylor-, Bt. (1895)

Lickiss, Sir Michael Gillam, Kt.

Liddington, Sir Bruce, Kt.

Liggins, Prof. Sir Graham Collingwood, Kt., CBE, FRS

Lightman, Hon. Sir Gavin Anthony, Kt.

Lighton, Sir Thomas Hamilton, Bt. (I. 1791)

Likierman, Prof. Sir John Andrew, Kt.

Limon, Sir Donald William, KCB

Linacre, Sir (John) Gordon (Seymour), Kt., CBE, AFC, DFM

Lindop, Sir Norman, Kt.

Lindsay, Sir James Harvey Kincaid Stewart, Kt.

Lindsay, Hon. Sir John Edmund Frederic, Kt.

Lindsay, Sir Ronald Alexander, Bt., (1962)

Lipton, Sir Stuart Anthony, Kt.

Lipworth, Sir (Maurice) Sydney, Kt.

Lithgow, Sir William James, Bt. (1925)

Little, Most Revd Sir Thomas Francis, KBE

Littler, Sir (James) Geoffrey, KCB

Livesay, Adm. Sir Michael Howard, KCB

Llewellyn, Sir David St Vincent, Bt. (1922)

Llewelyn, Sir John Michael Dillwyn-Venables-, Bt. (1890)

Lloyd, Prof. Sir Geoffrey Ernest Richard, Kt., FBA

Lloyd, Sir Ian Stewart, Kt.

Lloyd, Sir Nicholas Markley, Kt.

Lloyd, Rt. Hon. Sir Peter Robert Cable, Kt., MP

Lloyd, Sir Richard Ernest Butler, Bt. (1960)

Lloyd, Hon. Sir Timothy Andrew Wigram, Kt.

Loader, Sir Leslie Thomas, Kt., CBE

Loane, Most Revd Sir Marcus Lawrence, KBE

Lobo, Sir Rogerio Hyndman, Kt., CBE

Lockhart, Sir Simon John Edward Francis Sinclair-, Bt. (S. 1636)

†Loder, Sir Edmund Jeune, Bt. (1887)

Logan, Sir David Brian Carleton, KCMG

Logan, Sir Donald Arthur, KCMG

Logan, Sir Raymond Douglas, Kt.

Lokoloko, Sir Tore, GCMG, GCVO, OBE

Lombe, Hon. Sir Edward Christopher Evans-, Kt.

Longmore, Hon. Sir Andrew Centlivres, Kt.

Loram, Vice-Adm. Sir David Anning, KCB, CVO

Lord, Sir Michael Nicholson, Kt.

Lorimer, Sir (Thomas) Desmond, Kt.

Los, Hon. Sir Kubulan, Kt., CBE

Lovell, Sir (Alfred Charles) Bernard, Kt., OBE, FRS

Lovelock, Sir Douglas Arthur, KCB

Loveridge, Sir John Warren, Kt.

Lovill, Sir John Roger, Kt., CBE

Low, Sir Alan Roberts, Kt.

Low, Sir James Richard Morrison-, Bt. (1908)

Lowe, Air Chief Marshal Sir Douglas Charles, GCB, DFC, AFC

Lowe, Sir Frank Budge, Kt.

Lowe, Sir Thomas William Gordon, Bt. (1918)

Lowson, Sir Ian Patrick, Bt. (1951)

Lowther, Col. Sir Charles Douglas, Bt. (1824)

Lowther, Sir John Luke, KCVO, CBE

Loyd, Sir Francis Alfred, KCMG, OBE

Loyd, Sir Julian St John, KCVO

Lu, Sir Tseng Chi, Kt.

Lucas, Sir Cyril Edward, Kt., CMG, FRS

Lucas, Sir Thomas Edward, Bt. (1887)

Luce, Rt. Hon. Sir Richard Napier, Kt.

Lucy, Sir Edmund John William Hugh Cameron-Ramsay-Fairfax, Bt. (1836)

Luddington, Sir Donald Collin Cumyn, KBE, CMG, CVO

Lumsden, Sir David James, Kt.

Lus, Hon. Sir Pita, Kt., OBE

Lush, Hon. Sir George Hermann, Kt.

Lushington, Sir John Richard Castleman, Bt. (1791)

Luttrell, Col. Sir Geoffrey Walter Fownes, KCVO, MC

Lyell, Rt. Hon. Sir Nicholas Walter, Kt., QC, MP

Lygo, Adm. Sir Raymond Derek, KCB

Lyle, Sir Gavin Archibald, Bt. (1929)

Lyne, Sir Roderic Michael John, KBE, CMG

Lyons, Sir Edward Houghton, Kt.

Lyons, Sir James Reginald, Kt.

Lyons, Sir John, Kt.

Lyons, Sir Michael Thomas, Kt.

McAlpine, Sir William Hepburn, Bt. (1918)

Macara, Sir Alexander Wiseman, Kt., FRCP, FRCGP

†Macara, Sir Hugh Kenneth, Bt. (1911)

Macartney, Sir John Barrington, Bt. (I. 1799)

MacCormick, Prof. Sir Donald Neil, Kt., MEP, QC

Maclean, Sir Murdo, Kt.

MacSween, Prof. Sir Roderick Norman McIver, Kt.

McAvoy, Sir (Francis) Joseph, Kt., CBE

McCaffrey, Sir Thomas Daniel, Kt.

McCall, Sir (Charles) Patrick Home, Kt., MBE, TD

McCallum, Sir Donald Murdo, Kt., CBE, FREng.

McCamley, Sir Graham Edward, KBE

McCarthy, Rt. Hon. Sir Thaddeus Pearcey, KBE

McCartney, Sir (James) Paul, Kt., MBE

MacCormac, Sir Richard Cornelius, Kt., CBE

McClellan, Col. Sir Herbert Gerard Thomas, Kt., CBE, TD

McClintock, Sir Eric Paul, Kt.

McColl, Sir Colin Hugh Verel, KCMG

McCollum, Rt. Hon. Sir William, Kt.

McCombe, Hon. Sir Richard George Bramwell, Kt.

McConnell, Sir Robert Shean, Bt. (1900)

McCorkell, Col. Sir Michael William, KCVO, OBE, TD

McCowan, *Rt. Hon.* Sir Anthony James Denys, Kt.

†McCowan, Sir David William, Bt. (1934)

McCullough, *Hon.* Sir (Iain) Charles (Robert), Kt.

MacDermott, *Rt. Hon.* Sir John Clarke, Kt.

McDermott, Sir (Lawrence) Emmet, KBE

Macdonald of Sleat, Sir Ian Godfrey Bosville, Bt. (S. 1625)

Macdonald, Sir Kenneth Carmichael, KCB

McDonald, Sir Tom, Kt., OBE

McDonald, Sir Trevor, Kt., OBE

MacDougall, Sir (George) Donald (Alastair), Kt., CBE, FBA

McDowell, Sir Eric Wallace, Kt., CBE

McDowell, Sir Henry McLorinan, KBE

Mace, *Lt.-Gen.* Sir John Airth, KBE, CB

McEwen, Sir John Roderick Hugh, Bt. (1953)

McFarland, Sir John Talbot, Bt. (1914)

Macfarlane, Sir (David) Neil, Kt.

Macfarlane, Sir George Gray, Kt., CB, FREng.

McFarlane, Sir Ian, Kt.

McGeoch, *Vice-Adm.* Sir Ian Lachlan Mackay, KCB, DSO, DSC

McGrath, Sir Brian Henry, GCVO

Macgregor, Sir Edwin Robert, Bt. (1828)

MacGregor of MacGregor, Sir Gregor, Bt. (1795)

McGregor, Sir Ian Alexander, Kt., CBE, FRS

McGrigor, *Capt.* Sir Charles Edward, Bt. (1831)

McIntosh, *Vice-Adm.* Sir Ian Stewart, KBE, CB, DSO, DSC

McIntosh, Sir Neil William David, Kt., CBE

McIntosh, Sir Ronald Robert Duncan, KCB

McIntyre, Sir Donald Conroy, Kt., CBE

McIntyre, Sir Meredith Alister, Kt.

Mackay, *Hon.* Sir Colin Crichton, Kt.

MacKay, *Prof.* Sir Donald Iain, Kt., FRSE

McKay, Sir John Andrew, Kt., CBE

McKay, Sir William Robert, KCB, CB

Mackechnie, Sir Alistair John, Kt.

McKee, *Maj.* Sir (William) Cecil, Kt., ERD

McKellen, Sir Ian Murray, Kt., CBE

Mackenzie, Sir Alexander Alwyne Henry Charles Brinton Muir-, Bt. (1805)

†Mackenzie, Sir (James William) Guy, Bt. (1890)

Mackenzie, *Gen.* Sir Jeremy John George, GCB, OBE

†Mackenzie, Sir Peter Douglas, Bt. (S. 1673)

†Mackenzie, Sir Roderick McQuhae, Bt. (S. 1703)

McKenzie, Sir Roy Allan, KBE

Mackerras, Sir (Alan) Charles (MacLaurin), Kt., CBE

Mackeson, Sir Rupert Henry, Bt. (1954)

MacKinlay, Sir Bruce, Kt., CBE

McKinnon, Sir James, Kt.

McKinnon, *Hon.* Sir Stuart Neil, Kt.

Mackintosh, Sir Cameron Anthony, Kt.

Macklin, Sir Bruce Roy, Kt., OBE

Mackworth, Sir Digby (John), Bt. (1776)

McLaren, Sir Robin John Taylor, KCMG

McLaughlin, Sir Justice, Kt.

Maclean of Dunconnell, Sir Charles Edward, Bt. (1957)

Maclean, Sir Donald Og Grant, Kt.

MacLean, *Vice-Adm.* Sir Hector Charles Donald, KBE, CB, DSC

Maclean, Sir Lachlan Hector Charles, Bt. (NS 1631)

McLeod, Sir Charles Henry, Bt. (1925)

McLeod, Sir Ian George, Kt.

MacLeod, Sir (John) Maxwell Norman, Bt. (1924)

Macleod, Sir (Nathaniel William) Hamish, KBE

McLintock, Sir (Charles) Alan, Kt.

McLintock, Sir Michael William, Bt. (1934)

Maclure, Sir John Robert Spencer, Bt. (1898)

McMahon, Sir Brian Patrick, Bt. (1817)

McMahon, Sir Christopher William, Kt.

Macmillan, Sir (Alexander McGregor) Graham, Kt.

MacMillan, *Lt.-Gen.* Sir John Richard Alexander, KCB, CBE

McMullin, *Rt. Hon.* Sir Duncan Wallace, Kt.

McMurtry, Sir David, Kt., CBE

Macnaghten, Sir Patrick Alexander, Bt. (1836)

McNamara, *Air Chief Marshal* Sir Neville Patrick, KBE

Macnaughton, *Prof.* Sir Malcolm Campbell, Kt.

McNee, Sir David Blackstock, Kt., QPM

McNulty, Sir (Robert William) Roy, Kt., CBE

MacPhail, Sir Bruce Dugald, Kt.

Macpherson, Sir Ronald Thomas Steward (Tommy), CBE, MC, TD

Macpherson of Cluny, *Hon.* Sir William Alan, Kt., TD

McQuarrie, Sir Albert, Kt.

MacRae, Sir (Alastair) Christopher (Donald Summerhayes), KCMG

Macready, Sir Nevil John Wilfrid, Bt. (1923)

Mactaggart, Sir John Auld, Bt. (1938)

Macwhinnie, Sir Gordon Menzies, Kt., CBE

McWilliam, Sir Michael Douglas, KCMG

McWilliams, Sir Francis, GBE, FREng.

Madden, Sir Peter John, Bt. (1919)

Maddox, Sir John Royden, Kt.

Madel, Sir (William) David, Kt., MP

Madigan, Sir Russel Tullie, Kt., OBE

Magnus, Sir Laurence Henry Philip, Bt. (1917)

Mahon, Sir (John) Denis, Kt., CBE

Mahon, Sir William Walter, Bt. (1819)

Maiden, Sir Colin James, Kt., D.Phil.

Main, Sir Peter Tester, Kt., ERD

Maingard de la Ville ès Offrans, Sir Louis Pierre René, Kt., CBE

Maino, Sir Charles, KBE

†Maitland, Sir Charles Alexander, Bt. (1818)

Maitland, Sir Donald James Dundas, GCMG, OBE

Malbon, *Vice-Adm.* Sir Fabian Michael, KBE

Malcolm, Sir James William Thomas Alexander, Bt. (S. 1665)

Malet, Sir Harry Douglas St Lo, Bt. (1791)

Mallaby, Sir Christopher Leslie George, GCMG, GCVO

Mallick, *Prof.* Sir Netar Prakash, Kt., FRCP, FRCPEd.

Mallinson, Sir William James, Bt. (1935)

Malone, *Hon.* Sir Denis Eustace Gilbert, Kt.

Malpas, Sir Robert, Kt., CBE, FREng

Mamo, Sir Anthony Joseph, Kt., OBE

Mance, *Hon.* Sir Jonathan Hugh, Kt.

Manchester, Sir William Maxwell, KBE

Mander, Sir Charles Marcus, Bt. (1911)

Manduell, Sir John, Kt., CBE

Mann, *Rt. Revd* Sir Michael Ashley, KCVO

Mann, Sir Rupert Edward, Bt. (1905)

Manning, Sir David Geoffrey, KCMG, CMG

Mansel, Sir Philip, Bt. (1622)

Mansfield, *Vice-Adm.* Sir (Edward) Gerard (Napier), KBE, CVO

Mansfield, *Prof.* Sir Peter, Kt., FRS

Mansfield, Sir Philip (Robert Aked), KCMG

Mantell, *Rt. Hon.* Sir Charles Barrie Knight, Kt.

Manton, Sir Edwin Alfred Grenville, Kt.

Manuella, Sir Tulaga, GCMG, MBE

Manzie, Sir (Andrew) Gordon, KCB

Mara, *Rt. Hon. Ratu* Sir Kamisese Kapaiwai Tuimacilai, GCMG, KBE

Margetson, Sir John William Denys, KCMG

Marjoribanks, Sir James Alexander Milne, KCMG

Mark, Sir Robert, GBE

Markham, Sir Charles John, Bt. (1911)

Marking, Sir Henry Ernest, KCVO, CBE, MC

Marling, Sir Charles William Somerset, Bt. (1882)
Marmot, Prof. Sir Michael Gideon, Kt.
Marr, Sir Leslie Lynn, Bt. (1919)
Marriner, Sir Neville, Kt., CBE
Marriott, Sir Hugh Cavendish Smith-, Bt. (1774)
†Marsden, Sir Simon Neville Llewelyn, Bt. (1924)
Marsh, *Prof.* Sir John Stanley, Kt., CBE
Marshall, Sir Arthur Gregory George, Kt., OBE
Marshall, Sir Denis Alfred, Kt.
Marshall, *Prof.* Sir (Oshley) Roy, Kt., CBE
Marshall, Sir Peter Harold Reginald, KCMG
Marshall, Sir Robert Braithwaite, KCB, MBE
Marshall, Sir (Robert) Michael, Kt.
Martin, Sir Clive Haydon, Kt., OBE
Martin, Sir George Henry, Kt., CBE
Martin, *Vice-Adm.* Sir John Edward Ludgate, KCB, DSC
Martin, *Prof.* Sir Laurence Woodward, Kt.
Martin, Sir (Robert) Bruce, Kt., QC
Marychurch, Sir Peter Harvey, KCMG
Masefield, Sir Charles Beech Gordon, Kt.
Masefield, Sir Peter Gordon, Kt.
Masire, Sir Ketumile, GCMG
Mason, *Hon.* Sir Anthony Frank, KBE
Mason, Sir (Basil) John, Kt., CB, D.SC., FRS
Mason, *Prof.* Sir David Kean, Kt., CBE
Mason, Sir Frederick Cecil, KCVO, CMG
Mason, Sir Gordon Charles, Kt., OBE
Mason, Sir John Charles Moir, KCMG
Mason, Sir John Peter, Kt., CBE
Mason, *Prof.* Sir Ronald, KCB, FRS
Matane, Sir Paulias Nguna, Kt., CMG, OBE
Mather, Sir (David) Carol (Macdonell), Kt., MC
Mathers, Sir Robert William, Kt.
Matheson of Matheson, Sir Fergus John, Bt. (1882)
Matheson, Sir (James Adam) Louis, KBE, CMG, FREng.
Mathewson, Sir George Ross, Kt., CBE, Ph.D., FRSE
Matthews, Sir Peter Alec, Kt.
Matthews, Sir Peter Jack, Kt., CVO, OBE, QPM
Matthews, Sir Terence Hedley, Kt., OBE
Maud, The Hon. Sir Humphrey John Hamilton, KCMG
Mawhinney, *Rt. Hon.* Sir Brian Stanley, Kt., MP
Maxwell, Sir Michael Eustace George, Bt. (S. 1681)
Maxwell, Sir Nigel Mellor Heron-, Bt. (S. 1683)
May, *Rt. Hon.* Sir Anthony Tristram Kenneth, Kt.
May, Sir Kenneth Spencer, Kt., CBE

May, *Prof.* Sir Robert McCredie, Kt., FRS
Maynard, *Hon.* Sir Clement Travelyan, Kt.
Mayne, *Very Revd* Sir Michael Clement Otway, KCVO
Meadow, *Prof.* Sir (Samuel) Roy, Kt., FRCP, FRCPE
Medlycott, Sir Mervyn Tregonwell, Bt. (1808)
Megarry, *Rt. Hon.* Sir Robert Edgar, Kt., FBA
Meldrum, Sir George William, LVO
Melhuish, Sir Michael Ramsay, KBE, CMG
Mellon, Sir James, KCMG
Melville, Sir Leslie Galfreid, KBE
Melville, Sir Ronald Henry, KCB
Menter, Sir James Woodham, Kt., Ph.D., Sc.D., FRS
Menteth, Sir James Wallace Stuart-, Bt. (1838)
Merifield, Sir Anthony James, KCVO, CB
Meyer, Sir Anthony John Charles, Bt. (1910)
Meyer, Sir Christopher John Rome, KCMG
Meyjes, Sir Richard Anthony, Kt.
Meyrick, Sir David John Charlton, Bt. (1880)
Meyrick, Sir George Christopher Cadafael Tapps-Gervis-, Bt. (1791)
Miakwe, *Hon.* Sir Akepa, KBE
Michael, Sir Duncan, Kt.
Michael, Sir Peter Colin, Kt., CBE
Middleton, Sir Peter Edward, GCB
Miers, Sir (Henry) David Alastair Capel, KBE, CMG
Milbank, Sir Anthony Frederick, Bt. (1882)
Milburn, Sir Anthony Rupert, Bt. (1905)
Mildmay, Sir Walter John Hugh St John-, Bt. (1772)
Miles, Sir Peter Tremayne, KCVO
Miles, Sir William Napier Maurice, Bt. (1859)
Millais, Sir Geoffrey Richard Everett, Bt. (1885)
Millar, Sir Oliver Nicholas, GCVO, FBA
Millard, Sir Guy Elwin, KCMG, CVO
Miller, Sir Donald John, Kt., FRSE, FREng.
Miller, Sir Harry Holmes, Bt. (1705)
Miller, Sir Hilary Duppa (Hal), Kt.
Miller, *Lt.-Col.* Sir John Mansel, GCVO, DSO, MC
Miller, Sir (Oswald) Bernard, Kt.
Miller, Sir Peter North, Kt.
Miller, Sir Ronald Andrew Baird, Kt., CBE
Miller of Glenlee, Sir Stephen William Macdonald, Bt. (1788)
Miller, Sir William R., Kt.
Millichip, Sir Frederick Albert (Bert), Kt.
Mills, *Vice-Adm.* Sir Charles Piercy, KCB, CBE, DSC

Mills, Sir Ian, Kt.
Mills, Sir Frank, KCVO, CMG
Mills, Sir John Lewis Ernest Watts, Kt., CBE
Mills, Sir Peter Frederick Leighton, Bt. (1921)
Milman, Sir David Patrick, Bt. (1800)
Milne, Sir John Drummond, Kt.
Milner, Sir Timothy William Lycett, Bt. (1717)
Mirrlees, *Prof.* Sir James Alexander, Kt., FBA
Mitchell, *Air Cdre* Sir (Arthur) Dennis, KBE, CVO, DFC, AFC
Mitchell, Sir David Bower, Kt.
Mitchell, Sir Derek Jack, KCB, CVO
Mitchell, *Prof.* Sir (Edgar) William John, Kt., CBE, FRS
Mitchell, *Rt. Hon.* Sir James FitzAllen, KCMG
Mitchell, *Very Revd* Sir Patrick Reynolds, KCVO
Mitchell, *Hon.* Sir Stephen George, Kt.
Mitting, *Hon.* Sir John Edward, Kt.
Moate, Sir Roger Denis, Kt.
Mobbs, Sir (Gerald) Nigel, Kt.
Moberly, Sir John Campbell, KBE, CMG
Moberly, Sir Patrick Hamilton, KCMG
Moffat, Sir Brian Scott, Kt., OBE
Moffat, *Lt.-Gen.* Sir (William) Cameron, KBE
Mogg, *Gen.* Sir (Herbert) John, GCB, CBE, DSO
†Moir, Sir Christopher Ernest, Bt. (1916)
†Molony, Sir Thomas Desmond, Bt. (1925)
Monck, Sir Nicholas Jeremy, KCB
Montagu, Sir Nicholas Lionel John, KCB, CB
Montgomery, Sir (Basil Henry) David, Bt. (1801)
Montgomery, Sir (William) Fergus, Kt.
Mookerjee, Sir Birendra Nath, Kt.
Moollan, Sir Abdool Hamid Adam, Kt.
Moollan, *Hon.* Sir Cassam (Ismael), Kt.
Moon, Sir Peter Wilfred Giles Graham-, Bt. (1855)
†Moon, Sir Roger, Bt. (1887)
Moore, *Most Revd* Sir Desmond Charles, KBE
Moore, Sir Francis Thomas, Kt.
Moore, Sir Henry Roderick, Kt., CBE
Moore, *Maj.-Gen.* Sir (John) Jeremy, KCB, OBE, MC
Moore, Sir John Michael, KCVO, CB, DSC
Moore, Sir Lee Llewellyn, KCMG, QC
Moore, *Vice Adm.* Sir Michael Antony Claës, KBE, LVO
Moore, *Prof.* Sir Norman Winfrid, Bt. (1919)
Moore, Sir Patrick Alfred Caldwell, Kt., CBE

Moore, Sir Patrick William Eisdell, Kt., OBE

Moore, Sir William Roger Clotworthy, Bt., TD (1932)

Morauta, Sir Mekere, Kt.

Mordaunt, Sir Richard Nigel Charles, Bt. (1611)

Moreton, Sir John Oscar, KCMG, KCVO, MC

Morgan, Vice-Adm. Sir Charles Christopher, KBE

Morgan, His Hon. Maj.-Gen. Sir David John Hughes-, Bt., CB, CBE (1925)

Morgan, Sir Graham, Kt.

Morgan, Sir John Albert Leigh, KCMG

Morison, Hon. Sir Thomas Richard Atkin, Kt.

Morland, Hon. Sir Michael, Kt.

Morland, Sir Robert Kenelm, Kt.

Morpeth, Sir Douglas Spottiswoode, Kt., TD

†Morris, Sir Allan Lindsay, Bt. (1806)

Morris, Air Marshal Sir Arnold Alec, KBE, CB, FREng.

Morris, Sir (James) Richard (Samuel), Kt., CBE, FREng.

Morris, Rt. Hon. Sir John, Kt., QC

Morris, Sir Keith Elliot Hedley, KBE, CMG

Morris, Prof. Sir Peter John, Kt., FRS

Morris, Sir Trefor Alfred, Kt., CBE, QPM

Morris, Very Revd Sir William James, KCVO, Ph.D.

Morrison, Sir (Alexander) Fraser, Kt., CBE

Morrison, Hon. Sir Charles Andrew, Kt.

Morrison, Sir Howard Leslie, Kt., OBE

Morrison, Sir Kenneth Duncan, Kt., CBE

Morritt, Hon. Sir (Robert) Andrew, Kt., CVO

Morrow, Sir Ian Thomas, Kt.

Morse, Sir Christopher Jeremy, KCMG

Mortimer, Sir Laird, Kt.

Mortimer, Sir John Clifford, Kt., CBE, QC

Morton, Adm. Sir Anthony Storrs, GBE, KCB

Morton, Sir (Robert) Alastair (Newton), Kt.

Moseley, Sir George Walker, KCB

Moser, Prof. Sir Claus Adolf, KCB, CBE, FBA

Moses, Hon. Sir Alan George, Kt.

†Moss, Sir David John Edwards-, Bt. (1868)

Moss, Sir David Joseph, KCVO, CMG

Moss, Sir Stirling Craufurd, Kt., OBE

Mostyn, Gen. Sir (Joseph) David Frederick, KCB, CBE

†Mostyn, Sir William Basil John, Bt. (1670)

Mott, Sir John Harmer, Bt. (1930)

Mottram, Sir Richard Clive, KCB

†Mount, Sir (William Robert) Ferdinand, Bt. (1921)

Mountain, Sir Denis Mortimer, Bt. (1922)

Mountfield, Sir Robin, KCB

Mowbray, Sir John, Kt.

Mowbray, Sir John Robert, Bt. (1880)

Muir, Sir Laurence Macdonald, Kt.

†Muir, Sir Richard James Kay, Bt. (1892)

Mulcahy, Sir Geoffrey John, Kt.

Mullens, Lt.-Gen. Sir Anthony Richard Guy, KCB, OBE

Mummery, Hon. Sir John Frank, Kt.

Munby, Hon. Sir James Lawrence, Kt.

Munn, Sir James, Kt., OBE

Munro, Sir Alan Gordon, KCMG

†Munro, Sir Kenneth Arnold William, Bt. (S. 1634)

†Munro, Sir Keith Gordon, Bt. (1825)

Munro, Sir Sydney Douglas Gun-, GCMG, MBE

Muria, Hon. Sir Gilbert John Baptist, Kt.

Murphy, Sir Leslie Frederick, Kt.

Murray, Rt. Hon. Sir Donald Bruce, Kt.

Murray, Sir James, KCMG

Murray, Sir John Antony Jerningham, Kt., CBE

Murray, Prof. Sir Kenneth, Kt., FRCPath., FRS, FRSE

Murray, Sir Nigel Andrew Digby, Bt. (S. 1628)

Murray, Sir Patrick Ian Keith, Bt. (S. 1673)

†Murray, Sir Rowland William, Bt. (S. 1630)

Mursell, Sir Peter, Kt., MBE

Musgrave, Sir Christopher Patrick Charles, Bt. (1611)

Musson, Gen. Sir Geoffrey Randolph Dixon, GCB, CBE, DSO

Myers, Sir Philip Alan, Kt., OBE, QPM

Myers, Prof. Sir Rupert Horace, KBE

Mynors, Sir Richard Baskerville, Bt. (1964)

Naipaul, Sir Vidiadhar Surajprasad, Kt.

Nairn, Sir Michael, Bt. (1904)

Nairn, Sir Robert Arnold Spencer-, Bt. (1933)

Nairne, Rt. Hon. Sir Patrick Dalmahoy, GCB, MC

Naish, Sir (Charles) David, Kt.

Nall, Sir Michael Joseph, Bt., RN (1954)

Namaliu, Rt. Hon. Sir Rabbie Langanai, KCMG

†Napier, Sir Charles Joseph, Bt. (1867)

Napier, Sir John Archibald Lennox, Bt. (S. 1627)

Napier, Sir Oliver John, Kt.

Napier, Rt. Hon. Sir Richard, GCVO

Nasmith, Prof. Sir James Duncan Dunbar-, Kt., CBE, RIBA, FRSE

Neal, Sir Eric James, Kt., CVO

Neal, Sir Leonard Francis, Kt., CBE

Neale, Sir Gerrard Anthony, Kt.

Neave, Sir Paul Arundell, Bt. (1795)

Needham, Rt. Hon. Sir Richard (The Earl of Kilmorey, see page 141)

Neill, Rt. Hon. Sir Brian Thomas, Kt.

Neill, Rt. Hon. Sir Ivan, Kt., PC (NI)

Neill, Sir (James) Hugh, KCVO, CBE, TD

†Nelson, Sir Jamie Charles Vernon Hope, Bt. (1912)

Nelson, Hon. Sir Robert Franklyn, Kt.

Nelson, Air Marshal Sir (Sidney) Richard (Carlyle), KCB, OBE, MD

Nepean, Lt.-Col. Sir Evan Yorke, Bt. (1802)

Neuberger, Hon. Sir David Edmond, Kt.

Neubert, Sir Michael John, Kt.

Neville, Sir Roger Albert Gartside, Kt., VRD

New, Maj.-Gen. Sir Laurence Anthony Wallis, Kt., CB, CBE

Newall, Sir Paul Henry, Kt., TD

Newby, Prof. Sir Howard Joseph, Kt., CBE

Newington, Sir Michael John, KCMG

Newman, Sir Francis Hugh Cecil, Bt. (1912)

Newman, Sir Geoffrey Robert, Bt. (1836)

Newman, Hon. Sir George Michael, Kt.

Newman, Sir Kenneth Leslie, GBE, QPM

Newman, Vice-Adm. Sir Roy Thomas, KCB

Newman, Col. Sir Stuart Richard, Kt., CBE, TD

Newsam, Sir Peter Anthony, Kt.

Newton, Sir (Charles) Wilfred, Kt., CBE

Newton, Sir (Harry) Michael (Rex), Bt. (1900)

Newton, Sir Kenneth Garnar, Bt., OBE, TD (1924)

Ngata, Sir Henare Kohere, KBE

Nichol, Sir Duncan Kirkbride, Kt., CBE

Nicholas, Sir David, Kt., CBE

Nicholas, Sir John William, KCVO, CMG

Nicholls, Air Marshal Sir John Moreton, KCB, CBE, DFC, AFC

Nicholls, Sir Nigel Hamilton, KCVO, CBE

Nicholls, Sir Charles Harmar-, Bt. (1960)

Nichols, Sir Richard Everard, Kt.

Nicholson, Sir Bryan Hubert, Kt.

†Nicholson, Sir Charles Christian, Bt. (1912)

Nicholson, Rt. Hon. Sir Michael, Kt.

Nicholson, Sir Paul Douglas, Kt.

Nicholson, Sir Robin Buchanan, Kt., Ph.D., FRS, FREng.

Nicoll, Sir William, KCMG

Nightingale, Sir Charles Manners Gamaliel, Bt. (1628)

Nightingale, Sir John Cyprian, Kt., CBE, BEM, QPM

Nixon, Sir Simon Michael Christopher, Bt. (1906)

Nixon, Sir Edwin Ronald, Kt., CBE
Noble, Sir David Brunel, Bt. (1902)
Noble, Sir Iain Andrew, Bt., OBE (1923)
Noble, Sir (Thomas Alexander) Fraser, Kt., MBE
Nombri, Sir Joseph Karl, Kt., ISO, BEM
Norman, Sir Arthur Gordon, KBE, DFC
Norman, Sir Mark Annesley, Bt. (1915)
Norman, Sir Robert Henry, Kt., OBE
Norman, Sir Ronald, Kt., OBE
Norrington, Sir Roger Arthur Carver, Kt., CBE
Norris, *Air Chief Marshal* Sir Christopher Neil Foxley-, GCB, DSO, OBE
Norris, Sir Eric George, KCMG
Norriss, Air Marshal Sir Peter Coulson, KBE, CB, AFC
North, Sir Peter Machin, Kt., CBE, QC, DCL, FBA
North, Sir Thomas Lindsay, Kt.
North, Sir (William) Jonathan (Frederick), Bt. (1920)
Norton, *Vice-Adm. Hon.* Sir Nicholas John Hill-, KCB
Norwood, Sir Walter Neville, Kt.
Nossal, Sir Gustav Joseph Victor, Kt., CBE
Nott, *Rt. Hon.* Sir John William Frederic, KCB
Nourse, *Rt. Hon.* Sir Martin Charles, Kt.
Nugent, Sir John Edwin Lavallin, Bt. (I. 1795)
Nugent, *Maj.* Sir Peter Walter James, Bt. (1831)
Nugent, Sir Robin George Colborne, Bt. (1806)
Nursaw, Sir James, KCB, QC
Nurse, Sir Paul Maxime, Kt., Ph.D.
Nuttall, Sir Nicholas Keith Lillington, Bt. (1922)
Nutting, Sir John Grenfell, Bt., QC (1903)
Oakeley, Sir John Digby Atholl, Bt. (1790)
Oakes, Sir Christopher, Bt. (1939)
Oakshott, Hon. Sir Anthony Hendrie, Bt. (1959)
Oates, Sir Thomas, Kt., CMG, OBE
Obolensky, *Prof.* Sir Dimitri, Kt.
O'Brien, Sir Frederick William Fitzgerald, Kt.
O'Brien, Sir Richard, Kt., DSO, MC
O'Brien, Sir Timothy John, Bt. (1849)
O'Brien, *Adm.* Sir William Donough, KCB, DSC
O'Connell, Sir Maurice James Donagh MacCarthy, Bt. (1869)
O'Dea, Sir Patrick Jerad, KCVO
Odell, Sir Stanley John, Kt.
Odgers, Sir Graeme David William, Kt.
O'Dowd, Sir David Joseph, Kt., CBE, QPM
Ogden, Sir (Edward) Michael, Kt., QC

Ogden, Sir Robert, Kt., CBE
Ogilvy, *Rt. Hon.* Sir Angus James Bruce, KCVO
Ogilvy, Sir Francis Gilbert Arthur, Bt. (s. 1626)
Ognall, *Hon.* Sir Harry Henry, Kt.
Ohlson, Sir Brian Eric Christopher, Bt. (1920)
Okeover, *Capt.* Sir Peter Ralph Leopold Walker-, Bt. (1886)
Olewale, *Hon.* Sir Niwia Ebia, Kt.
Oliphant, Sir Mark (Marcus Laurence Elwin), KBE, FRS
O'Loghlen, Sir Colman Michael, Bt. (1838)
Olson, Sir Ralph, Kt.
Olver, Sir Stephen John Linley, KBE, CMG
Omand, Sir David Bruce, KCB
O'Neil, *Hon.* Sir Desmond Henry, Kt.
Ongley, *Hon.* Sir Joseph Augustine, Kt.
O'Nions, *Prof.* Sir Robert Keith, Kt., FRS, Ph.D.
Onslow, Sir John Roger Wilmot, Bt. (1797)
Oppenheim, Sir Duncan Morris, Kt.
Oppenheimer, Sir Michael Bernard Grenville, Bt. (1921)
Orde, Sir John Alexander Campbell-, Bt. (1790)
O'Regan, *Dr* Sir Stephen Gerard (Tipene), Kt.
O'Reilly, Anthony John Francis, Kt.
Orr, Sir David Alexander, Kt., MC
Orr, Sir John, Kt., OBE
Osborn, Sir John Holbrook, Kt.
Osborn, Sir Richard Henry Danvers, Bt. (1662)
Osborne, Sir Peter George, Bt. (I. 1629)
Osifelo, Sir Frederick Aubarua, Kt., MBE
Osmond, Sir Douglas, Kt., CBE
O'Sullevan, Sir Peter John, Kt., CBE
Oswald, *Admiral of the Fleet* Sir (John) Julian Robertson, GCB
Oswald, Sir (William Richard) Michael, KCVO
Otton, Sir Geoffrey John, KCB
Otton, *Rt. Hon.* Sir Philip Howard, Kt.
Oulton, Sir Antony Derek Maxwell, GCB, QC
Ouseley, *Hon.* Sir Brian Walter, Kt.
Ouseley, Sir Herman George, Kt.
Outram, Sir Alan James, Bt. (1858)
Overall, Sir John Wallace, Kt., CBE, MC
Owen, Sir Geoffrey, Kt.
Owen, Sir Hugh Bernard Pilkington, Bt. (1813)
Owen, Sir Hugo Dudley Cunliffe-, Bt. (1920)
Owen, *Hon.* Sir John Arthur Dalziel, Kt.
Owen, *Hon.* Sir Robert Michael, Kt.
Packer, Sir Richard John, KCB
Page, Sir (Arthur) John, Kt.

Page, Sir Frederick William, Kt., CBE, FREng.
Page, Sir John Joseph Joffre, Kt., OBE
Paget, Sir Julian Tolver, Bt., CVO (1871)
Paget, Sir Richard Herbert, Bt. (1886)
Pain, *Lt.-Gen.* Sir (Horace) Rollo (Squarey), KCB, MC
Pain, *Hon.* Sir Peter Richard, Kt.
Paine, Sir Christopher Hammon, Kt., FRCP, FRCR
Palin, *Air Chief Marshal* Sir Roger Hewlett, KCB, OBE
Palliser, *Rt. Hon.* Sir (Arthur) Michael, GCMG
Palmar, Sir Derek James, Kt.
Palmer, Sir (Charles) Mark, Bt. (1886)
Palmer, Sir Geoffrey Christopher John, Bt. (1660)
Palmer, *Rt. Hon.* Sir Geoffrey Winston Russell, KCMG
Palmer, Sir John Chance, Kt.
Palmer, Sir John Edward Somerset, Bt. (1791)
Palmer, *Maj.-Gen.* Sir (Joseph) Michael, KCVO
Palmer, Sir Reginald Oswald, GCMG, MBE
Pantlin, Sir Dick Hurst, Kt., CBE
Paolozzi, Sir Eduardo Luigi, Kt., CBE, RA
Parbo, Sir Arvi Hillar, Kt.
Park, *Hon.* Sir Andrew Edward Wilson, Kt.
Parker, Sir (Arthur) Douglas Dodds-, Kt.
Parker, Sir Eric Wilson, Kt.
Parker, Sir John, Kt.
Parker, *Hon.* Sir Jonathan Frederic, Kt.
Parker, *Maj.* Sir Michael John, KCVO, CBE
Parker, Sir Peter, KBE, LVO
Parker, Sir Richard (William) Hyde, Bt. (1681)
Parker, *Rt. Hon.* Sir Roger Jocelyn, Kt.
Parker, Sir Thomas John, Kt.
Parker, *Vice-Adm.* Sir (Wilfred) John, KBE, CB, DSC
Parker, Sir William Peter Brian, Bt. (1844)
Parkes, Sir Edward Walter, Kt., FREng.
Parkinson, Sir Nicholas Fancourt, Kt.
Parsons, Sir (John) Michael, Kt.
Parsons, Sir Richard Edmund (Clement Fownes), KCMG
Partridge, Sir Michael John Anthony, KCB
Pascoe, *Gen.* Sir Robert Alan, KCB, MBE
Pasley, Sir John Malcolm Sabine, Bt. (1794)
Paterson, Sir Dennis Craig, Kt.
Patnick, Sir (Cyril) Irvine, Kt., OBE
Patten, *Hon.* Sir Justice Nicholas John, Kt.
Pattie, *Rt. Hon.* Sir Geoffrey Edwin, Kt.
Pattinson, Sir (William) Derek, Kt.

Pattison, *Prof.* Sir John Ridley, Kt., DM, FRCPath.

Pattullo, Sir (David) Bruce, Kt., CBE

Paul, Sir John Warburton, GCMG, OBE, MC

Paul, *Air Marshal* Sir Ronald Ian Stuart-, KBE

Payne, Sir Norman John, Kt., CBE, FREng.

Peach, Sir Leonard Harry, Kt.

Peacock, *Prof.* Sir Alan Turner, Kt., DSC

Pearce, Sir Austin William, Kt., CBE, ph.D., FREng.

Pearce, Sir (Daniel Norton) Idris, Kt., CBE, TD

Pearse, Sir Brian Gerald, Kt.

Pearson, Sir Francis Nicholas Fraser, Bt. (1964)

Pearson, *Gen.* Sir Thomas Cecil Hook, KCB, CBE, DSO

Peart, *Prof.* Sir William Stanley, Kt., MD, FRS

Pease, Sir (Alfred) Vincent, Bt. (1882)

Pease, Sir Richard Thorn, Bt. (1920)

Peat, Sir Gerrard Charles, KCVO

Peat, Sir Michael Charles Gerrard, KCVO

Peck, Sir Edward Heywood, GCMG

Peckham, *Prof.* Sir Michael John, Kt., FRCP, FRCPGlas., FRCR, FRCPath.

Pedder, *Air Marshal* Sir Ian Maurice, KCB, OBE, DFC

Peek, *Vice-Adm.* Sir Richard Innes, KBE, CB, DSC

Peek, Sir William Grenville, Bt. (1874)

Peel, Sir John Harold, KCVO

Peel, Sir (William) John, Kt.

Peirse, Sir Henry Grant de la Poer Beresford-, Bt. (1814)

Peirse, *Air Vice-Marshal* Sir Richard Charles Fairfax, KCVO, CB

Pelgen, Sir Harry Friedrich, Kt., MBE

Peliza, Sir Robert John, KBE, ED

Pelly, Sir Richard John, Bt. (1840)

Pemberton, Sir Francis Wingate William, Kt., CBE

Penrose, *Prof.* Sir Roger, Kt., FRS, OM

Pereira, Sir (Herbert) Charles, Kt., D.SC., FRS

Perowne, *Vice-Adm.* Sir James Francis, KBE, OBE

Perring, Sir John Raymond, Bt. (1963)

Perris, Sir David (Arthur), Kt., MBE

Perry, Sir David Howard, KCB

Perry, Sir (David) Norman, Kt., MBE

Perry, Sir Michael Sydney, Kt., CBE

Pervez, Sir Mohammed Anwar, Kt., OBE

Pestell, Sir John Richard, KCVO

Peterkin, Sir Neville, Kt.

Peters, *Prof.* Sir David Keith, Kt., FRCP

Petersen, Sir Jeffrey Charles, KCMG

Petersen, Sir Johannes Bjelke-, KCMG

Peterson, Sir Christopher Matthew, Kt., CBE, TD

†Petit, Sir Jehangir, Bt. (1890)

Peto, Sir Henry George Morton, Bt. (1855)

Peto, Sir Michael Henry Basil, Bt. (1927)

Peto, *Prof.* Sir Richard, Kt., FRS

Petrie, Sir Peter Charles, Bt., CMG (1918)

Pettigrew, Sir Russell Hilton, Kt.

Pettit, Sir Daniel Eric Arthur, Kt.

Pettitt, Sir Dennis, Kt.

Philips, *Prof.* Sir Cyril Henry, Kt.

Phillips, Sir Fred Albert, Kt., CVO

Phillips, Sir (Gerald) Hayden, KCB

Phillips, Sir Henry Ellis Isidore, Kt., CMG, MBE

Phillips, Sir Horace, KCMG

Phillips, Sir John David, Kt., QPM

Phillips, Sir Peter John, Kt., OBE

Phillips, Sir Robin Francis, Bt. (1912)

Pickard, Sir (John) Michael, Kt.

Pickering, Sir Edward Davies, Kt.

Pickthorn, Sir James Francis Mann, Bt. (1959)

Pidgeon, Sir John Allan Stewart, Kt.

†Piers, Sir James Desmond, Bt. (I. 1661)

Pigot, Sir George Hugh, Bt. (1764)

Pigott, *Lt.-Gen.* Sir Anthony David, KCB, CBE

Pigott, Sir Berkeley Henry Sebastian, Bt. (1808)

Pike, *Lt.-Gen.* Sir Hew William Royston, KCB, DSO, MBE

Pike, Sir Michael Edmund, KCVO, CMG

Pike, Sir Philip Ernest Housden, Kt., QC

Pilditch, Sir Richard Edward, Bt. (1929)

Pile, Sir Frederick Devereux, Bt., MC (1900)

Pilkington, Sir Thomas Henry Milborne-Swinnerton-, Bt. (S. 1635)

Pill, *Rt. Hon.* Sir Malcolm Thomas, Kt.

Pilling, Sir Joseph Grant, KCB, CB

Pinker, Sir George Douglas, KCVO

Pinsent, Sir Christopher Roy, Bt. (1938)

Pippard, *Prof.* Sir (Alfred) Brian, Kt., FRS

Pirie, *Gp Capt* Sir Gordon Hamish, Kt., CVO, CBE

Pitakaka, Sir Moses Puibangara, GCMG

Pitcher, Sir Desmond Henry, Kt.

Pitchford, *Hon.* Sir Christopher John, Kt

Pitman, Sir Brian Ivor, Kt.

Pitoi, Sir Sere, Kt., CBE

Pitt, Sir Harry Raymond, Kt., ph.D., FRS

Pitts, Sir Cyril Alfred, Kt.

Plastow, Sir David Arnold Stuart, Kt.

Platt, Sir Harold Grant, Kt.

Pledger, *Air Marshal* Sir Malcolm David, KCB, OBE, AFC

Plowman, *Hon.* Sir John Robin, Kt., CBE

Plumb, *Prof.* Sir John Harold, Kt.

Plumbly, Sir Derek John, KCMG

Pogo, *Rev.* Sir Ellison Leslie, Kt.

Pohai, Sir Timothy, Kt., MBE

Pole, Sir (John) Richard (Walter Reginald) Carew, Bt. (1628)

Pole, Sir Peter Van Notten, Bt. (1791)

Polkinghorne, *Revd Canon* Sir John Charlton, KBE, FRS

Pollard, Sir Charles, Kt.

Pollen, Sir John Michael Hungerford, Bt. (1795)

Pollock, Sir George Frederick, Bt. (1866)

Pollock, Sir Giles Hampden Montagu-, Bt. (1872)

Pollock, *Admiral of the Fleet* Sir Michael Patrick, GCB, LVO, DSC

Ponsonby, Sir Ashley Charles Gibbs, Bt., KCVO, MC (1956)

Poole, *Hon.* Sir David Anthony, Kt.

Poore, Sir Herbert Edward, Bt. (1795)

Pope, Sir Joseph Albert, Kt., D.SC., Ph.D.

Popplewell, *Hon.* Sir Oliver Bury, Kt.

†Porritt, Sir Jonathon Espie, Bt. (1963)

Portal, Sir Jonathan Francis, Bt. (1901)

Porter, Sir John Simon Horsbrugh-, Bt. (1902)

Porter, Sir Leslie, Kt.

Porter, *Air Marshal* Sir (Melvin) Kenneth (Drowley), KCB, CBE

Porter, *Rt. Hon.* Sir Robert Wilson, Kt., PC (NI), QC

Posnett, Sir Richard Neil, KBE, CMG

Potter, *Rt. Hon.* Sir Mark Howard, Kt.

Potter, *Maj.-Gen.* Sir (Wilfrid) John, KBE, CB

Potts, *Hon.* Sir Francis Humphrey, Kt.

Pound, Sir John David, Bt. (1905)

Pountain, Sir Eric John, Kt.

Povey, Sir Keith, Kt., QPM

Powell, Sir (Arnold Joseph) Philip, Kt., CH, OBE, RA, FRIBA

Powell, Sir Nicholas Folliott Douglas, Bt. (1897)

Powell, Sir Raymond, Kt., MP

Powell, Sir Richard Royle, GCB, KBE, CMG

Power, Sir Alastair John Cecil, Bt. (1924)

Power, *Hon.* Sir Noel Plunkett, Kt.

Prance, *Prof.* Sir Ghillean Tolmie, Kt., FRS

Prendergast, Sir (Walter) Kieran, KCVO, CMG

Prentice, *Hon.* Sir William Thomas, Kt., MBE

Prescott, Sir Mark, Bt. (1938)

†Preston, Sir Philip Charles Henry Hulton, Bt. (1815)

Prevost, Sir Christopher Gerald, Bt. (1805)

Price, Sir Charles Keith Napier Rugge-, Bt. (1804)

Price, Sir David Ernest Campbell, Kt.

Price, Sir Francis Caradoc Rose, Bt. (1815)

Price, Sir Frank Leslie, Kt.
Price, Sir Norman Charles, KCB
Price, Sir Robert John Green-, Bt. (1874)
Prickett, *Air Chief Marshal* Sir Thomas Other, KCB, DSO, DFC
Prideaux, Sir Humphrey Povah Treverbian, Kt., OBE
†Primrose, Sir John Ure, Bt. (1903)
Pringle, *Air Marshal* Sir Charles Norman Seton, KBE, FREng.
Pringle, *Hon.* Sir John Kenneth, Kt.
Pringle, *Lt.-Gen.* Sir Steuart (Robert), Bt., KCB, RM (S. 1683)
Pritchard, Sir Neil, KCMG
Proby, Sir Peter, Bt. (1952)
Prosser, Sir Ian Maurice Gray, Kt.
Pryke, Sir Christopher Dudley, Bt. (1926)
Puapua, *Rt. Hon.* Sir Tomasi, KBE
Pugh, Sir Idwal Vaughan, KCB
Pullinger, Sir (Francis) Alan, Kt., CBE
Pumfrey, *Hon.* Sir Nicholas Richard, Kt.
Pumphrey, Sir (John) Laurence, KCMG
Purchas, *Rt. Hon.* Sir Francis Brooks, Kt.
Purves, Sir William, Kt., CBE, DSO
Purvis, *Vice-Adm.* Sir Neville, KCB
Quicke, Sir John Godolphin, Kt., CBE
Quigley, Sir (William) George (Henry), Kt., CB, Ph.D.
Quilliam, *Hon.* Sir (James) Peter, Kt.
Quilter, Sir Anthony Raymond Leopold Cuthbert, Bt. (1897)
Quinlan, Sir Michael Edward, GCB
Quinton, Sir James Grand, Kt.
Radcliffe, Sir Sebastian Everard, Bt. (1813)
Radda, *Prof.* Sir George Karoly, Kt., CBE, FRS
Rae, *Hon.* Sir Wallace Alexander Ramsay, Kt.
Raeburn, Sir Michael Edward Norman, Bt. (1923)
Raeburn, *Maj.-Gen.* Sir (William) Digby (Manifold), KCVO, CB, DSO, MBE
Raikes, *Vice-Adm.* Sir Iwan Geoffrey, KCB, CBE, DSC
Raison, *Rt. Hon.* Sir Timothy Hugh Francis, Kt.
Ralli, Sir Godfrey Victor, Bt., TD (1912)
Ramdanee, Sir Mookteswar Baboolall Kailash, Kt.
Ramphal, Sir Shridath Surendranath, GCMG
Ramphul, Sir Baalkhristna, Kt.
Ramphul, Sir Indurduth, Kt.
Ramsay, Sir Alexander William Burnett, Bt. (1806)
Ramsay, Sir Allan John (Hepple), KBE, CMG
Ramsbotham, *Gen.* Sir David John, GCB, CBE
Ramsbotham, *Hon.* Sir Peter Edward, GCMG, GCVO

Ramsden, Sir John Charles Josslyn, Bt. (1689)
Randle, *Prof.* Sir Philip John, Kt.
Rank, Sir Benjamin Keith, Kt., CMG
Rankin, Sir Ian Niall, Bt. (1898)
Rasch, Sir Simon Anthony Carne, Bt. (1903)
Rashleigh, Sir Richard Harry, Bt. (1831)
Ratford, Sir David John Edward, KCMG, CVO
Rattee, *Hon.* Sir Donald Keith, Kt.
Rattle, Sir Simon Dennis, Kt., CBE
Rault, Sir Louis Joseph Maurice, Kt.
Rawlins, *Surgeon Vice-Adm.* Sir John Stuart Pepys, KBE
Rawlins, *Prof.* Sir Michael David, Kt., FRCP, FRCPED.
Rawlinson, Sir Anthony Henry John, Bt. (1891)
Read, *Air Marshal* Sir Charles Frederick, KBE, CB, DFC, AFC
Read, Sir John Emms, Kt.
†Reade, Sir Kenneth Ray, Bt. (1661)
Reay, *Lt.-Gen.* Sir (Hubert) Alan John, KBE
Redgrave, *Maj.-Gen.* Sir Roy Michael Frederick, KBE, MC
Redgrave, Sir Steven Geoffrey, Kt., CBE
Redmayne, Sir Nicholas, Bt. (1964)
Redwood, Sir Peter Boverton, Bt. (1911)
Reece, Sir Charles Hugh, Kt.
Reece, Sir James Gordon, Kt.
Rees, Sir David Allan, Kt., Ph.D., D.Sc., FRS
Rees, *Prof.* Sir Martin John, Kt., FRS
Reeve, Sir Anthony, KCMG, KCVO
Reeves, *Most Revd* Paul Alfred, GCMG, GCVO
Reffell, *Adm.* Sir Derek Roy, KCB
Refshauge, *Maj.-Gen.* Sir William Dudley, Kt., CBE
Reid, Sir Alexander James, Bt. (1897)
Reid, Sir (Harold) Martin (Smith), KBE, CMG
Reid, Sir Hugh, Bt. (1922)
Reid, Sir Norman Robert, Kt.
Reid, Sir Robert Paul, Kt.
Reid, Sir William Kennedy, KCB
Reiher, Sir Frederick Bernard Carl, KBE, CMG
Reilly, *Lt.-Gen.* Sir Jeremy Calcott, KCB, DSO
Renals, Sir Stanley, Bt. (1895)
Rennie, Sir John Shaw, GCMG, OBE
Renouf, Sir Clement William Bailey, Kt.
Renshaw, Sir (Charles) Maurice Bine, Bt. (1903)
Renwick, Sir Richard Eustace, Bt. (1921)
Reporter, Sir Shapoor Ardeshirji, KBE
Reynolds, Sir David James, Bt. (1923)
Reynolds, Sir Peter William John, Kt., CBE
Rhodes, Sir Basil Edward, Kt., CBE, TD

Rhodes, Sir John Christopher Douglas, Bt. (1919)
Rhodes, Sir Peregrine Alexander, KCMG
Rice, *Maj.-Gen.* Sir Desmond Hind Garrett, KCVO, CBE
Rice, Sir Timothy Miles Bindon, Kt.
Richard, Sir Cliff, Kt., OBE
Richards, Sir Brian Mansel, Kt., CBE, Ph.D.
Richards, Sir (Francis) Brooks, KCMG, DSC
Richards, *Lt.-Gen.* Sir John Charles Chisholm, KCB, KCVO, RM
Richards, Sir Rex Edward, Kt., D.Sc., FRS
Richards, *Hon.* Sir Stephen Price, Kt.
Richardson, Sir Anthony Lewis, Bt. (1924)
Richardson, *Rt. Hon.* Sir Ivor Lloyd Morgan, Kt.
Richardson, Sir (John) Eric, Kt., CBE
Richardson, Sir Michael John de Rougemont, Kt.
Richardson, *Lt.-Gen.* Sir Robert Francis, KCB, CVO, CBE
Richardson, Sir Simon Alaisdair Stewart-, Bt. (S. 1630)
Richardson, Sir Thomas Legh, KCMG
Richmond, *Prof.* Sir Mark Henry, Kt., FRS
Ricketts, Sir Robert Cornwallis Gerald St Leger, Bt. (1828)
Riddell, Sir John Charles Buchanan, Bt., CVO (S. 1628)
Ridley, Sir Adam (Nicholas), Kt.
Ridley, Sir Michael Kershaw, KCVO
Ridsdale, Sir Julian Errington, Kt., CBE
Rifkind, *Rt. Hon.* Sir Malcolm Leslie, KCMG, QC
Rigby, Sir Anthony John, Bt. (1929)
Rimer, *Hon.* Sir Colin Percy Farquharson, Kt.
Ringadoo, *Hon.* Sir Veerasamy, GCMG
Ripley, Sir Hugh, Bt. (1880)
Risk, Sir Thomas Neilson, Kt.
Ritako, Sir Thomas Baha, Kt., MBE
Rix, *Hon.* Sir Bernard Anthony, Kt.
Rix, Sir John, Kt., MBE, FREng.
Robati, Sir Pupuke, KBE, OBE
Robb, Sir John Weddell, Kt.
Roberts, *Hon.* Sir Denys Tudor Emil, KBE, QC
Roberts, Sir Derek Harry, Kt., CBE, FRS, FREng.
Roberts, Sir (Edward Fergus) Sidney, Kt., CBE
Roberts, *Prof.* Sir Gareth Gwyn, Kt., FRS
Roberts, Sir Gilbert Howland Rookehurst, Bt. (1809)
Roberts, Sir Gordon James, Kt., CBE
Roberts, Sir Hugh Ashley, KCVO, CVO
Roberts, Sir Ivor Anthony, KCMG
Roberts, Sir Samuel, Bt. (1919)
Roberts, Sir Stephen James Leake, Kt.
Roberts, Sir William James Denby, Bt. (1909)

Robertson, Sir John Fraser, KCMG, CBE
Robertson, Sir Lewis, Kt., CBE, FRSE
Robertson, *Prof.* Sir Rutherford Ness, Kt., CMG
Robins, Sir Ralph Harry, Kt., FREng.
Robinson, Sir Albert Edward Phineas, Kt.
†Robinson, Sir Christopher Philipse, Bt. (1854)
Robinson, Sir Dominick Christopher Lynch-, Bt. (1920)
Robinson, Sir Ian, Kt.
Robinson, Sir John James Michael Laud, Bt. (1660)
Robinson, Sir Wilfred Henry Frederick, Bt. (1908)
Robson, *Prof.* Sir James Gordon, Kt., CBE
Robson, Sir John Adam, KCMG
Robson, Sir Stephen Arthur, Kt., CB
Roch, *Rt. Hon.* Sir John Ormond, Kt.
Roche, Sir David O'Grady, Bt. (1838)
Roche, Sir Henry John, Kt.
Rodgers, Sir (Andrew) Piers (Wingate Aikin-Sneath), Bt. (1964)
Rodley, *Prof.* Sir Nigel, KBE
Rodrigues, Sir Alberto Maria, Kt., CBE, ED
Roe, *Air Chief Marshal* Sir Rex David, GCB, AFC
Rogers, Sir Frank Jarvis, Kt.
Rogers, *Air Chief Marshal* Sir John Robson, KCB, CBE
Rooke, Sir Denis Eric, Kt., OM, CBE, FRS, FREng.
Ropner, Sir John Bruce Woollacott, Bt. (1952)
Ropner, Sir Robert Douglas, Bt. (1904)
Roscoe, Sir Robert Bell, KBE
Rose, *Rt. Hon.* Sir Christopher Dudley Roger, Kt.
Rose, Sir Clive Martin, GCMG
Rose, Sir David Lancaster, Bt. (1874)
Rose, *Gen.* Sir (Hugh) Michael, KCB, CBE, DSO, QGM
Rose, Sir Julian Day, Bt. (1872 and 1909)
Ross, Sir (James) Keith, Bt., RD, FRCS (1960)
Ross, *Lt.-Gen.* Sir Robert Jeremy, KCB, OBE
Ross, *Lt.-Col.* Sir Walter Hugh Malcolm, KCVO, OBE
Rosser, Sir Melvyn Wynne, Kt.
Rossi, Sir Hugh Alexis Louis, Kt.
Rotblat, *Prof.* Sir Joseph, KCMG, CBE, FRS
Roth, *Prof.* Sir Martin, Kt., MD, FRCP
Rothschild, Sir Evelyn Robert Adrian de, Kt.
Rougier, *Hon.* Sir Richard George, Kt.
Rowell, Sir John Joseph, Kt., CBE
Rowland, *Air Marshal* Sir James Anthony, KBE, DFC, AFC
Rowland, Sir (John) David, Kt.
Rowlands, *Air Marshal* Sir John Samuel, GC, KBE

Rowley, Sir Charles Robert, Bt. (1836) †(1786)
Rowlinson, *Prof.* Sir John Shipley, Kt., FRS
Roxburgh, *Vice-Adm.* Sir John Charles Young, KCB, CBE, DSO, DSC
Royden, Sir Christopher John, Bt. (1905)
Rudd, Sir (Anthony) Nigel (Russell), Kt.
Rudge, Sir Alan Walter, Kt., CBE, FRS
Rumbold, Sir Henry John Sebastian, Bt. (1779)
Rumbold, Sir Jack Seddon, Kt.
Runchorelal, Sir (Udayan) Chinubhai Madhowlal, Bt. (1913)
Rusby, *Vice-Adm.* Sir Cameron, KCB, LVO
†Russell, Sir (Arthur) Mervyn, Bt. (1812)
Russell, Sir Charles Dominic, Bt. (1916)
Russell, *Hon.* Sir David Sturrock West-, Kt.
Russell, Sir George, Kt., CBE
Russell, Sir Muir, KCB
Russell, *Prof.* Sir Peter Edward Lionel, Kt., D.Litt., FBA
Russell, Sir (Robert) Mark, KCMG
Russell, *Rt. Hon.* Sir (Thomas) Patrick, Kt.
Rutter, Sir Frank William Eden, KBE
Rutter, *Prof.* Sir Michael Llewellyn, Kt., CBE, MD, FRS
Ryan, Sir Derek Gerald, Bt. (1919)
Rycroft, Sir Richard John, Bt. (1784)
Ryrie, Sir William Sinclair, KCB
Sabola, *Hon.* Sir Joaquim Claudino Gonsalves-, Kt.
Sachs, *Hon.* Sir Michael Alexander Geddes, Kt.
Sainsbury, *Rt. Hon.* Sir Timothy Alan Davan, Kt.
†St Aubyn, Sir William Molesworth-, Bt. (1689)
†St George, Sir John Avenel Bligh, Bt. (I. 1766)
St Johnston, Sir Kerry, Kt.
Sainty, Sir John Christopher, KCB
Salisbury, Sir Robert William, Kt.
Salt, Sir Patrick MacDonnell, Bt. (1869)
Salt, Sir (Thomas) Michael John, Bt. (1899)
Sampson, Sir Colin, Kt., CBE, QPM
Samuel, Sir John Michael Glen, Bt. (1898)
Samuelson, Sir (Bernard) Michael (Francis), Bt. (1884)
Samuelson, Sir Sydney Wylie, Kt., CBE
Sanders, Sir John Reynolds Mayhew-, Kt.
Sanders, Sir Robert Tait, KBE, CMG
Sanderson, Sir Frank Linton, Bt. (1920)
Sarei, Sir Alexis Holyweek, Kt., CBE
Satchwell, Sir Kevin Joseph, Kt.
Saunders, *Hon.* Sir John Anthony Holt, Kt., CBE, DSO, MC

Saunders, Sir Peter, Kt.
Savage, Sir Ernest Walter, Kt.
Savile, Sir James Wilson Vincent, Kt., OBE
Say, *Rt. Revd* Richard David, KCVO
Scheele, Sir Nicholas Vernon, KCMG
Schiemann, *Rt. Hon.* Sir Konrad Hermann Theodor, Kt.
Scholar, Sir Michael Charles, KCB
Scholey, Sir David Gerald, Kt., CBE
Scholey, Sir Robert, Kt., CBE, FREng.
Scholtens, Sir James Henry, KCVO
Schreier, Sir Bernard, Kt.
Schubert, Sir Sydney, Kt.
Scipio, Sir Hudson Rupert, Kt.
Scoon, Sir Paul, GCMG, GCVO, OBE
Scott, Sir Anthony Percy, Bt. (1913)
Scott, Sir (Charles) Peter, KBE, CMG
Scott, Sir David Aubrey, GCMG
Scott, Sir Dominic James Maxwell-, Bt. (1642)
Scott, Sir Ian Dixon, KCMG, KCVO, CIE
Scott, Sir James Jervoise, Bt. (1962)
Scott, Sir Kenneth Bertram Adam, KCVO, CMG
Scott, Sir Michael, KCVO, CMG
Scott, *Rt. Hon.* Sir Nicholas Paul, KBE
Scott, Sir Oliver Christopher Anderson, Bt. (1909)
Scott, *Prof.* Sir Philip John, KBE
Scott, *Rt. Hon.* Sir Richard Rashleigh Folliott, Kt.
Scott, Sir Robert David Hillyer, Kt.
Scott, Sir Walter John, Bt. (1907)
Scott, *Rear-Adm.* Sir (William) David (Stewart), Kt.
Scowen, Sir Eric Frank, Kt., MD, D.Sc., LL D, FRCP, FRCS
Seale, Sir Clarence David, Kt.
Seale, Sir John Henry, Bt. (1838)
Seaman, Sir Keith Douglas, KCVO, OBE
Sebastian, Sir Cuthbert Montraville, GCMG, OBE
†Sebright, Sir Peter Giles Vivian, Bt. (1626)
Seccombe, Sir (William) Vernon Stephen, Kt.
Seconde, Sir Reginald Louis, KCMG, CVO
Sedley, *Rt. Hon.* Sir Stephen John, Kt.
Seely, Sir Nigel Edward, Bt. (1896)
Seeto, Sir Ling James, Kt., MBE
Seeyave, Sir Rene Sow Choung, Kt., CBE
Seligman, Sir Peter Wendel, Kt., CBE
Sellors, Sir Patrick John Holmes-, KCVO, FRCS
Semple, Sir John Laughlin, KCB
Sergeant, Sir Patrick, Kt.
Series, Sir (Joseph Michel) Emile, Kt., CBE
Serota, Sir Nicholas Andrew, Kt.
Serpell, Sir David Radford, KCB, CMG, OBE
†Seton, Sir Charles Wallace, Bt. (s. 1683)
Seton, Sir Iain Bruce, Bt. (s. 1663)
Severne, *Air Vice-Marshal* Sir John de Milt, KCVO, OBE, AFC

†Seymour, Sir Michael Patrick Culme-, Bt. (1809)

Shackleton, *Prof.* Sir Nicholas John, Kt., ph.D., FRS

Shaffer, Sir Peter Levin, Kt., CBE

Shakerley, Sir Geoffrey Adam, Bt. (1838)

Shakespeare, Sir Thomas William, Bt. (1942)

Shand, Sir James, Kt., MBE

Sharp, Sir Adrian, Bt. (1922)

Sharp, Sir George, Kt., OBE

Sharp, Sir Kenneth Johnston, Kt., TD

Sharp, Sir Leslie, Kt., QPM

Sharp, Sir Richard Lyall, KCVO, CB

Sharp, Sir Sheridan Christopher Robin, Bt. (1920)

Sharpe, *Hon.* Sir John Henry, Kt., CBE

Sharples, Sir James, Kt., QPM

Shattock, Sir Gordon, Kt.

Shaw, Sir Brian Piers, Kt.

Shaw, Sir (Charles) Barry, Kt., CB, QC

Shaw, Sir (George) Neville Bowman-, Kt.

Shaw, *Prof.* Sir John Calman, Kt., CBE, FRSE

Shaw, Sir (John) Giles (Dunkerley), Kt.

Shaw, Sir John Michael Robert Best-, Bt. (1665)

Shaw, Sir Neil McGowan, Kt.

Shaw, Sir Robert, Bt. (1821)

Shaw, Sir Roy, Kt.

Shaw, Sir Run Run, Kt., CBE

Sheehy, Sir Patrick, Kt.

Sheen, *Hon.* Sir Barry Cross, Kt.

Sheffield, Sir Reginald Adrian Berkeley, Bt. (1755)

Shehadie, Sir Nicholas Michael, Kt., OBE

Sheil, *Hon.* Sir John, Kt.

Sheinwald, Sir Nigel Elton, KCMG

Sheldon, *Hon.* Sir (John) Gervase (Kensington), Kt.

Shelley, Sir John Richard, Bt. (1611)

Shelton, Sir William Jeremy Masefield, Kt.

Shepheard, Sir Peter Faulkner, Kt., CBE

Shepherd, Sir Colin Ryley, Kt.

Shepherd, Sir John Alan, KCVO, CMG

Shepperd, Sir Alfred Joseph, Kt.

Sher, Sir Antony, KBE

Sherlock, Sir Philip Manderson, KBE

Sherman, Sir Alfred, Kt.

Sherman, Sir Louis, Kt., OBE

Shields, Sir Neil Stanley, Kt., MC

Shields, *Prof.* Sir Robert, Kt., MD

Shiffner, Sir Henry David, Bt. (1818)

Silber, *Rt. Hon.* Sir Stephen Robert, Kt.

Shinwell, Sir (Maurice) Adrian, Kt.

Shock, Sir Maurice, Kt.

Short, Sir Apenera Pera, KBE

Shuckburgh, Sir Rupert Charles Gerald, Bt. (1660)

Siaguru, Sir Anthony Michael, KBE

Siddall, Sir Norman, Kt., CBE, FREng.

Sidey, *Air Marshal* Sir Ernest Shaw, KBE, CB, MD

Sieff, *Hon.* Sir David, Kt.

Simeon, Sir John Edmund Barrington, Bt. (1815)

Simmons, *Air Marshal* Sir Michael George, KCB, AFC

Simmons, Sir Stanley Clifford, Kt., FRCS, FRCOG

Simms, Sir Neville Ian, Kt., FREng.

Simonet, Sir Louis Marcel Pierre, Kt., CBE

Simons, Sir Robert Stuart, Kt., QHP

Simpson, *Hon.* Sir Alfred Henry, Kt.

Simpson, *Lt.-Gen.* Sir Roderick Alexander Cordy-, KBE, CB

Simpson, Sir William James, Kt.

Sims, Sir Roger Edward, Kt.

Sinclair, Sir Clive Marles, Kt.

Sinclair, Sir George Evelyn, Kt., CMG, OBE

Sinclair, Sir Ian McTaggart, KCMG, QC

Sinclair, *Air Vice-Marshal* Sir Laurence Frank, GC, KCB, CBE, DSO

Sinclair, Sir Patrick Robert Richard, Bt. (s. 1704)

Sinclair, Sir Robert John, Kt.

Sinden, Sir Donald Alfred, Kt., CBE

Singer, *Prof.* Sir Hans Wolfgang, Kt.

Singer, *Hon.* Sir Jan Peter, Kt.

Singh, *Hon.* Sir Vijay Raghubir, Kt.

Sione, Sir Tomu Malaefone, GCMG, OBE

Sitwell, Sir (Sacheverell) Reresby, Bt. (1808)

Skeet, Sir Trevor Herbert Harry, Kt.

Skeggs, Sir Clifford George, Kt.

Skehel, Sir John James, Kt., FRSSkingsley, *Air Chief Marshal* Sir Anthony Gerald, GBE, KCB

Skinner, Sir (Thomas) Keith (Hewitt), Bt. (1912)

Skipwith, Sir Patrick Alexander d'Estoteville, Bt. (1622)

Skyrme, Sir (William) Thomas (Charles), KCVO, CB, CBE, TD

Slack, Sir William Willatt, KCVO, FRCS

Slade, Sir Benjamin Julian Alfred, Bt. (1831)

Slade, *Rt. Hon.* Sir Christopher John, Kt.

Slaney, *Prof.* Sir Geoffrey, KBE

Slater, *Adm.* Sir John (Jock) Cunningham Kirkwood, GCB, LVO

Sleight, Sir Richard, Bt. (1920)

Sloan, Sir Andrew Kirkpatrick, Kt., QPM

Sloman, Sir Albert Edward, Kt., CBE

Smart, *Prof.* Sir George Algernon, Kt., MD, FRCP

Smart, Sir Jack, Kt., CBE

Smedley, *Hon.* Sir (Frank) Brian, Kt.

Smedley, Sir Harold, KCMG, MBE

Smiley, *Lt.-Col.* Sir John Philip, Bt. (1903)

Smith, Sir Alan, Kt., CBE, DFC

Smith, Sir Alexander Mair, Kt., ph.D.

Smith, *Hon.* Sir Andrew Charles, Kt.

Smith, Sir Andrew Colin Hugh-, Kt.

Smith, *Lt.-Gen.* Sir Anthony Arthur Denison-, KBE

Smith, Sir Charles Bracewell-, Bt. (1947)

Smith, *Prof.* Sir Christopher Hubert Llewellyn-, Kt.

Smith, Sir Christopher Sydney Winwood, Bt. (1809)

Smith, *Prof.* Sir Colin Stansfield, Kt., CBE

Smith, Sir Cyril, Kt., MBE

Smith, *Prof.* Sir David Cecil, Kt., FRS

Smith, *Air Chief Marshal* Sir David Harcourt-, GBE, KCB, DFC

Smith, Sir David Iser, KCVO

Smith, Sir Douglas Boucher, KCB

Smith, Sir Dudley (Gordon), Kt.

Smith, *Prof.* Sir Eric Brian, Kt., ph.D.

Smith, *Maj.-Gen.* Sir (Francis) Brian Wyldbore-, Kt., CB, DSO, OBE

Smith, *Prof.* Sir Francis Graham-, Kt., FRS

Smith, Sir Geoffrey Johnson, Kt., MP

Smith, Sir Graham William, Kt., CBE

Smith, Sir John Alfred, Kt., QPM

Smith, *Prof.* Sir John Cyril, Kt., CBE, QC, FBA

Smith, Sir John Hamilton-Spencer-, Bt. (1804)

Smith, Sir John Jonah Walker-, Bt. (1960)

Smith, Sir John Lindsay Eric, Kt., CH, CBE

Smith, Sir John Rathbone Vassar-, Bt. (1917)

Smith, Sir Joseph William Grenville, Kt., MD, FRCP

Smith, Sir Leslie Edward George, Kt.

Smith, *Maj.-Gen.* Sir Michael Edward Carleton-, Kt., CBE

Smith, Sir Michael John Llewellyn, KCVO, CMG

Smith, *Rt. Hon.* Sir Murray Stuart-, Kt.

Smith, Sir (Norman) Brian, Kt., CBE, ph.D.

Smith, Sir Peter Brierley, Kt., CBE

†Smith, Sir Peter Frank Graham Newson-, Bt. (1944)

Smith, Sir Raymond Horace, KBE

Smith, Sir Robert Courtney, Kt., CBE

Smith, Sir Robert Haldane, Kt.

Smith, Sir Robert Hill, Bt., MP (1945)

Smith, *Prof.* Sir Roland, Kt.

Smith, *Air Marshal* Sir Roy David Austen-, KBE, CB, CVO, DFC

Smith, *Gen.* Sir Rupert Anthony, KCB, DSO, OBE, QGM

Smith, Sir (Thomas) Gilbert, Bt. (1897)

Smith, Sir (William) Antony (John) Reardon-, Bt. (1920)

Smith, Sir (William) Richard Prince-, Bt. (1911)

Smithers, Sir Peter Henry Berry Otway, Kt., VRD, D.Phil.

Smyth, Sir Thomas Weyland Bowyer-, Bt. (1661)

Smyth, Sir Timothy John, Bt. (1955)

Soakimori, Sir Frederick Pa-
Nukuanca, KBE, CPM
Soame, Sir Charles John Buckworth-
Herne-, Bt. (1697)
Sobers, Sir Garfield St Auburn, Kt.
Solomon, Sir Harry, Kt.
Somare, *Rt. Hon.* Sir Michael
Thomas, GCMG, CH
Somers, *Rt. Hon.* Sir Edward
Jonathan, Kt.
Somerville, *Brig.* Sir John Nicholas,
Kt., CBE
Somerville, Sir Quentin Charles
Somerville Agnew-, Bt. (1957)
Sorrell, Sir Martin Stuart, Kt.
Soulsby, Sir Peter Alfred, Kt.
Soutar, *Air Marshal* Sir Charles John
Williamson, KBE
South, Sir Arthur, Kt.
Southby, Sir John Richard Bilbe, Bt.
(1937)
Southgate, Sir Colin Grieve, Kt.
Southgate, Sir William David, Kt.
Southward, Sir Leonard Bingley, Kt.,
OBE
Southwood, *Prof.* Sir (Thomas)
Richard (Edmund), Kt., FRS
Souyave, *Hon.* Sir (Louis) Georges,
Kt.
Sowrey, *Air Marshal* Sir Frederick
Beresford, KCB, CBE, AFC
Sparkes, Sir Robert Lyndley, Kt.
Sparrow, Sir John, Kt.
Spearman, Sir Alexander Young
Richard Mainwaring, Bt. (1840)
Spedding, *Prof.* Sir Colin Raymond
William, Kt., CBE
Speed, Sir (Herbert) Keith, Kt., RD
Speelman, Sir Cornelis Jacob, Bt.
(1686)
Speight, *Hon.* Sir Graham Davies, Kt.
Spencer, Sir Derek Harold, Kt., QC
Spencer, *Vice-Adml.* Sir Peter, KCB
Spicer, Sir James Wilton, Kt.
Spicer, Sir Nicholas Adrian Albert,
Bt., MB (1906)
Spicer, Sir (William) Michael Hardy,
Kt., MP
Spiers, Sir Donald Maurice, Kt., CB,
TD
Spooner, Sir James Douglas, Kt.
Spotswood, *Marshal of the Royal Air
Force* Sir Denis Frank, GCB, CBE,
DSO, DFC
Spratt, *Col.* Sir Greville Douglas, GBE,
TD
Spring, Sir Dryden Thomas, Kt.
Squire, *Air Chief Marshal* Sir Peter
Ted, KCB, DFC, AFC, GCB
Stabb, *Hon.* Sir William Walter, Kt.,
QC
Stainton, Sir (John) Ross, Kt., CBE
Stamer, Sir (Lovelace) Anthony, Bt.
(1809)
Stanbridge, *Air Vice-Marshal* Sir Brian
Gerald Tivy, KCVO, CBE, AFC
Standard, Sir Kenneth Livingstone,
Kt., MD
Stanier, Sir Beville Douglas, Bt.
(1917)

Stanier, *Field Marshal* Sir John
Wilfred, GCB, MBE
Stanley, *Rt. Hon.* Sir John Paul, Kt.,
MP
Staples, Sir Richard Molesworth, Bt.
(I. 1628)
Stark, Sir Andrew Alexander Steel,
KCMG, CVO
Starkey, Sir John Philip, Bt. (1935)
Starrit, Sir James, KCVO
Statham, Sir Norman, KCMG, CVO
Staughton, *Rt. Hon.* Sir Christopher
Stephen Thomas Jonathan Thayer,
Kt.
Staveley, Sir John Malfroy, KBE, MC
Stear, *Air Chief Marshal* Sir Michael
James Douglas, KCB, CBE
Steel, Sir David Edward Charles, Kt.,
DSO, MC, TD
Steel, *Hon.* Sir David William, Kt.
Steele, Sir (Philip John) Rupert, Kt.
Steere, Sir Ernest Henry Lee-, KBE
Stephen, *Rt. Hon.* Sir Ninian Martin,
KG, GCMG, GCVO, KBE
Stephens, Sir (Edwin) Barrie, Kt.
Stephenson, Sir Henry Upton, Bt.
(1936)
Sternberg, Sir Sigmund, Kt.
Stevens, Sir Jocelyn Edward Greville,
Kt., CVO
Stevens, Sir John, Kt.
Stevens, Sir Laurence Houghton, Kt.,
CBE
Stevenson, *Vice-Adm.* Sir (Hugh)
David, KBE
Stevenson, Sir Simpson, Kt.
Stewart, Sir Alan, KBE
Stewart, Sir Alan d'Arcy, Bt. (I. 1623)
Stewart, Sir David James
Henderson-, Bt. (1957)
Stewart, Sir David John Christopher,
Bt. (1803)
Stewart, Sir Edward Jackson, Kt.
Stewart, *Prof.* Sir Frederick Henry,
Kt., Ph.D., FRS, FRSE
Stewart, Sir Houston Mark Shaw-,
Bt., MC, TD (S. 1667)
Stewart, Sir James Douglas, Kt.
Stewart, Sir James Moray, KCB
Stewart, Sir (John) Simon (Watson),
Bt. (1920)
Stewart, Sir John Young, Kt., OBE
Stewart, Sir Robertson Huntly, Kt.,
CBE
Stewart, Sir Robin Alastair, Bt. (1960)
Stewart, *Prof.* Sir William Duncan
Paterson, Kt., FRS, FRSE
Stibbon, *Gen.* Sir John James, KCB,
OBE
Stirling, Sir Alexander John Dickson,
KBE, CMG
Stirling, Sir Angus Duncan Aeneas,
Kt.
Stockdale, Sir Arthur Noel, Kt.
Stockdale, Sir Thomas Minshull, Bt.
(1960)
Stoddart, *Wg Cdr.* Sir Kenneth
Maxwell, KCVO, AE
Stoker, *Prof.* Sir Michael George
Parke, Kt., CBE, FRCP, FRS, FRSE

Stokes, Sir John Heydon Romaine,
Kt.
Stones, Sir William Frederick, Kt.,
OBE
Stonhouse, *Revd* Sir Michael Philip,
Bt. (1628)
Stonor, *Air Marshal* Sir Thomas
Henry, KCB
Stoppard, Sir Thomas, Kt., CBE, OB
Storey, *Hon.* Sir Richard, Bt., CBE
(1960)
Stott, Sir Adrian George Ellingham,
Bt. (1920)
Stoute, Sir Michael Ronald, Kt.
Stow, Sir Christopher Philipson-, Bt.,
DFC (1907)
Stowe, Sir Kenneth Ronald, GCB, CVO
Stracey, Sir John Simon, Bt. (1818)
Strachan, Sir Curtis Victor, Kt., CVO
Strachey, Sir Charles, Bt. (1801)
Strang Steel, Sir (Fiennes) Michael,
Bt. (1938)
Strawson, *Prof.* Sir Peter Frederick,
Kt., FBA
Street, *Hon.* Sir Laurence Whistler,
KCMG
Streeton, Sir Terence George, KBE,
CMG
Stringer, Sir Donald Edgar, Kt., CBE
Stringer, Sir Howard, Kt.
Strong, Sir Roy Colin, Kt., Ph.D., FSA
Stronge, Sir James Anselan Maxwell,
Bt. (1803)
Stroud, *Prof.* Sir (Charles) Eric, Kt.,
FRCP
Strutt, Sir Nigel Edward, Kt., TD
Stuart, Sir James Keith, Kt.
Stuart, Sir Kenneth Lamonte, Kt.
Stuart, Sir Mark Moody-, KCMG
†Stuart, Sir Phillip Luttrell, Bt. (1660)
Stubbs, Sir William Hamilton, Kt.,
Ph.D.
Stucley, *Lt.* Sir Hugh George
Coplestone Bampfylde, Bt. (1859)
Studd, Sir Edward Fairfax, Bt. (1929)
Studd, Sir Peter Malden, GBE, KCVO
Studholme, Sir Henry William, Bt.
(1956)
†Style, Sir William Frederick, Bt.
(1627)
Sugar, Sir Alan Michael, Kt.
Sugden, Sir Arthur, Kt.
Sullivan, *Hon.* Sir Jeremy Mirth, Kt.
Sullivan, Sir Richard Arthur, Bt.
(1804)
Sulston, Sir John Edward, Kt.
Sumner, *Hon.* Sir Christopher John,
Kt.
Sutherland, Sir John Brewer, Bt.
(1921)
Sutherland, Sir Maurice, Kt.
Sutherland, *Prof.* Sir Stewart Ross,
Kt., FBA
Sutherland, Sir William George
MacKenzie, Kt.
Suttie, Sir James Edward Grant-, Bt.
(S. 1702)
Sutton, Sir Frederick Walter, Kt., OBE
Sutton, *Air Marshal* Sir John Matthias
Dobson, KCB

Sutton, Sir Richard Lexington, Bt. (1772)
Swaffield, Sir James Chesebrough, Kt., CBE, RD
Swaine, Sir John Joseph, Kt., CBE
Swan, Sir Conrad Marshall John Fisher, KCVO, ph.D.
Swan, Sir John William David, KBE
Swann, Sir Michael Christopher, Bt., TD (1906)
Swanwick, Sir Graham Russell, Kt., MBE
Swartz, Hon. Sir Reginald William Colin, KBE, ED
Sweeney, Sir George, Kt.
Sweetnam, Sir (David) Rodney, KCVO, CBE, FRCS
Swinburn, Lt.-Gen. Sir Richard Hull, KCB
Swinson, Sir John Henry Alan, Kt., OBE
Swinton, Maj.-Gen. Sir John, KCVO, OBE
Swire, Sir Adrian Christopher, Kt.
Swire, Sir John Anthony, Kt., CBE
Swynnerton, Sir Roger John Massy, Kt., CMG, OBE, MC
Sykes, Sir Francis John Badcock, Bt. (1781)
Sykes, Sir Hugh Ridley, Kt.
Sykes, Sir John Charles Anthony le Gallais, Bt. (1921)
Sykes, Prof. Sir (Malcolm) Keith, Kt.
Sykes, Sir Richard, Kt.
Sykes, Sir Tatton Christopher Mark, Bt. (1783)
Symington, Prof. Sir Thomas, Kt., MD, FRSE
Symons, Vice-Adm. Sir Patrick Jeremy, KBE
Synge, Sir Robert Carson, Bt. (1801)
Tait, Adm. Sir (Allan) Gordon, KCB, DSC
Talbot, Hon. Sir Hilary Gwynne, Kt.
Talboys, Rt. Hon. Sir Brian Edward, CH, KCB
Tancred, Sir Henry Lawson-, Bt. (1662)
Tangaroa, Hon. Sir Tangoroa, Kt., MBE
Tange, Sir Arthur Harold, Kt., CBE
Tapsell, Sir Peter Hannay Bailey, Kt., MP
Tate, Sir (Henry) Saxon, Bt. (1898)
Tavaiqia, Ratu Sir Josaia, KBE
Tavare, Sir John, Kt., CBE
Tavener, Prof. Sir John Kenneth, Kt.
Taylor, Lt.-Gen. Sir Allan Macnab, KBE, MC
Taylor, Sir (Arthur) Godfrey, Kt.
Taylor, Sir Cyril Julian Hebden, Kt.
Taylor, Sir Edward Macmillan (Teddy), Kt., MP
Taylor, Rt. Revd John Bernard, KCVO
Taylor, Sir John Lang, KCMG
Taylor, Sir Nicholas Richard Stuart, Bt. (1917)
Taylor, Prof. Sir William, Kt., CBE
Teagle, Vice-Adm. Sir Somerford Francis, KBE

Tebbit, Sir Donald Claude, GCMG
Telford, Sir Robert, Kt., CBE, FREng.
Temple, Sir Rawden John Afamado, Kt., CBE, QC
Temple, Maj. Sir Richard Anthony Purbeck, Bt., MC (1876)
Templeton, Sir John Marks, Kt.
Tenison, Sir Richard Hanbury-, KCVO
Tennant, Sir Anthony John, Kt.
Tennant, Capt. Sir Iain Mark, KT
Teo, Sir Fiatau Penitala, GCMG, GCVO, ISO, MBE
Terry, Air Marshal Sir Colin George, KBE, CB
Terry, Sir Michael Edward Stanley Imbert-, Bt. (1917)
Terry, Air Chief Marshal Sir Peter David George, GCB, AFC
Thatcher, Sir Denis, Bt., MBE, TD (1990)
Thesiger, Sir Wilfred Patrick, KBE, DSO
Thomas, Sir Derek Morison David, KCMG
Thomas, Sir (Godfrey) Michael (David), Bt. (1694)
Thomas, Sir Jeremy Cashel, KCMG
Thomas, Sir (John) Alan, Kt.
Thomas, Sir John Maldwyn, Kt.
Thomas, Prof. Sir John Meurig, Kt., FRS
Thomas, Sir Keith Vivian, Kt.
Thomas, Sir Quentin Jeremy, Kt., CB
Thomas, Sir Robert Evan, Kt.
Thomas, Hon. Sir Roger John Laugharne, Kt.
Thomas, Hon. Sir Swinton Barclay, Kt.
Thomas, Sir William James Cooper, Bt., TD (1919)
Thomas, Sir (William) Michael (Marsh), Bt. (1918)
Thompson, Sir Christopher Peile, Bt. (1890)
Thompson, Sir Clive Malcolm, Kt.
Thompson, Sir Donald, Kt.
Thompson, Sir Gilbert Williamson, Kt., OBE
Thompson, Surgeon Vice-Adm. Sir Godfrey James Milton-, KBE
Thompson, Sir (Humphrey) Simon Meysey-, Bt. (1874)
Thompson, Prof. Sir Michael Warwick, Kt., D.Sc
Thompson, Sir Nicholas Annesley, Bt. (1963)
Thompson, Sir Paul Anthony, Bt. (1963)
Thompson, Sir Peter Anthony, Kt.
Thompson, Sir Thomas d'Eyncourt John, Bt. (1806)
Thomson, Sir (Frederick Douglas) David, Bt. (1929)
Thomson, Sir John Adam, GCMG
Thomson, Sir John (Ian) Sutherland, KBE, CMG
Thomson, Sir Mark Wilfrid Home, Bt. (1925)

Thomson, Sir Thomas James, Kt., CBE, FRCP
Thorn, Sir John Samuel, Kt., OBE
Thorne, Sir Neil Gordon, Kt., OBE, TD
Thorne, Sir Peter Francis, KCVO, CBE
Thornton, Sir (George) Malcolm, Kt.
Thornton, Sir Peter Eustace, KCB
Thornton, Sir Richard Eustace, KCVO, OBE
†Thorold, Sir (Anthony) Oliver, Bt. (1642)
Thorpe, Hon. Sir Mathew Alexander, Kt.
Thouron, Sir John Rupert Hunt, KBE
Thwaites, Sir Bryan, Kt., ph.D.
Tibbits, Capt. Sir David Stanley, Kt., DSC
Tickell, Sir Crispin Charles Cervantes, GCMG, KCVO
Tidbury, Sir Charles Henderson, Kt.
Tikaram, Sir Moti, KBE
Tilt, Sir Robin Richard, Kt.
Tims, Sir Michael David, KCVO
Tindle, Sir Ray Stanley, Kt., CBE
Tippet, Vice-Adm. Sir Anthony Sanders, KCB
†Tipping, Sir David Gwynne Evans-, Bt. (1913)
Tirvengadum, Sir Harry Krishnan, Kt.
Titman, Sir John Edward Powis, KCVO
Tod, Air Marshal Sir John Hunter Hunter-, KBE, CB
Tod, Vice-Adm. Sir Jonathan James Richard, KCB, CBE
Todd, Prof. Sir David, Kt., CBE
Todd, Sir Ian Pelham, KBE, FRCS
Todd, Hon. Sir (Reginald Stephen) Garfield, Kt.
Tollemache, Sir Lyonel Humphry John, Bt. (1793)
Tololo, Sir Alkan, KBE
Tomkins, Sir Edward Emile, GCMG, CVO
Tomkys, Sir (William) Roger, KCMG
Tomlinson, Prof. Sir Bernard Evans, Kt., CBE
Tomlinson, Hon. Sir Stephen Miles, Kt.
Tooley, Sir John, Kt.
Tooth, Sir (Hugh) John Lucas-, Bt. (1920)
ToRobert, Sir Henry Thomas, KBE
Tory, Sir Geofroy William, KCMG
Touche, Sir Anthony George, Bt. (1920)
Touche, Sir Rodney Gordon, Bt. (1962)
Toulson, Hon. Sir Roger Grenfell, Kt.
Tovey, Sir Brian John Maynard, KCMG
ToVue, Sir Ronald, Kt., OBE
Towneley, Sir Simon Peter Edmund Cosmo William, KCVO
Townsend, Sir Cyril David, Kt.
Traill, Sir Alan Towers, GBE
Trant, Gen. Sir Richard Brooking, KCB

Treacher, *Adm.* Sir John Devereux, KCB

Trehane, Sir (Walter) Richard, Kt.

Treitel, *Prof.* Sir Guenter Heinz, Kt., FBA, QC

Trelawny, Sir John Barry Salusbury-, Bt. (1628)

Trench, Sir Peter Edward, Kt., CBE, TD

Trescowthick, Sir Donald Henry, KBE

†Trevelyan, Sir Edward (Norman), Bt. (1662)

Trevelyan, Sir Geoffrey Washington, Bt. (1874)

Trezise, Sir Kenneth Bruce, Kt., OBE

Trippier, Sir David Austin, Kt., RD

Tritton, Sir Anthony John Ernest, Bt. (1905)

Trollope, Sir Anthony Simon, Bt. (1642)

Trotter, Sir Neville Guthrie, Kt.

Trotter, Sir Ronald Ramsay, Kt.

Troubridge, Sir Thomas Richard, Bt. (1799)

Troup, *Vice-Adm.* Sir (John) Anthony (Rose), KCB, DSC

Trowbridge, *Rear-Adm.* Sir Richard John, KCVO

Truscott, Sir George James Irving, Bt. (1909)

Tsang, Sir Donald Yam-keun, KBE

Tuck, Sir Bruce Adolph Reginald, Bt. (1910)

Tucker, *Hon.* Sir Richard Howard, Kt.

Tuckey, *Hon.* Sir Simon Lane, Kt.

Tuita, Sir Mariano Kelesimalefo, Kt., OBE

Tuite, Sir Christopher Hugh, Bt., Ph.D. (1622)

Tuivaga, Sir Timoci Uluiburotu, Kt.

Tumim, *His Hon.* Sir Stephen, Kt.

Tupper, Sir Charles Hibbert, Bt. (1888)

Turbott, Sir Ian Graham, Kt., CMG, CVO

Turing, Sir John Dermot, Bt. (s. 1638)

Turnbull, Sir Andrew, KCB, CVO

Turner, Sir Colin William Carstairs, Kt., CBE, DFC

Turner, *Hon.* Sir Michael John, Kt.

Turnquest, Sir Orville Alton, GCMG, QC

Tuti, *Revd* Dudley, KBE

Tweedie, *Prof.* Sir David Philip, Kt.

Tyree, Sir (Alfred) William, Kt., OBE

Tyrwhitt, Sir Reginald Thomas Newman, Bt. (1919)

Unsworth, *Hon.* Sir Edgar Ignatius Godfrey, Kt., CMG

Unwin, Sir (James) Brian, KCB

Ure, Sir John Burns, KCMG, LVO

Urquhart, Sir Brian Edward, KCMG, MBE

Urwick, Sir Alan Bedford, KCVO, CMG

Usher, *Sir Andrew John, Bt.* (1899)

Usher, Sir Leonard Gray, KBE

Ustinov, Sir Peter Alexander, Kt., CBE

Utting, Sir William Benjamin, Kt., CB

Vai, Sir Mea, Kt., CBE, ISO

Vallance, Sir Iain David Thomas, Kt.

Vallat, Sir Francis Aimé, GBE, KCMG, QC

Vallings, *Vice-Adm.* Sir George Montague Francis, KCB

Vanderfelt, Sir Robin Victor, KBE

Vane, Sir John Robert, Kt., D.Phil., D.Sc., FRS

Vardy, Sir Peter, Kt.

Vasquez, Sir Alfred Joseph, Kt., CBE, QC

Vaughan, Sir Gerard Folliott, Kt., FRCP

Vavasour, Sir Eric Michael Joseph Marmaduke, Bt. (1828)

Veale, Sir Alan John Ralph, Kt., FREng.

Venner, Sir Kenneth Dwight Vincent, KBE

Vereker, Sir John Michael Medlicott, KCB

†Verney, Sir John Sebastian, Bt. (1946)

Verney, *Hon.* Sir Lawrence John, Kt., TD

Verney, Sir Ralph Bruce, Bt., KBE (1818)

Vernon, Sir James, Kt., CBE

Vernon, Sir Nigel John Douglas, Bt. (1914)

Vernon, Sir (William) Michael, Kt.

Vestey, Sir (John) Derek, Bt. (1921)

Vial, Sir Kenneth Harold, Kt., CBE

Vickers, *Lt.-Gen.* Sir Richard Maurice Hilton, KCB, CVO, OBE

Vincent, Sir William Percy Maxwell, Bt. (1936)

Vinelott, *Hon.* Sir John Evelyn, Kt.

Vines, Sir William Joshua, Kt., CMG

von Schramek, Sir Eric Emil, Kt.

†Vyvyan, Sir Ralph Ferrers Alexander, Bt. (1645)

Waddell, Sir James Henderson, Kt., CB

Wade, *Prof.* Sir Henry William Rawson, Kt., QC, FBA

Wade, *Air Chief Marshal* Sir Ruthven Lowry, KCB, DFC

Waine, *Rt. Revd* John, KCVO

Waite, *Rt. Hon.* Sir John Douglas, Kt.

Wake, Sir Hereward, Bt., MC (1621)

Wakefield, Sir (Edward) Humphry (Tyrell), Bt. (1962)

Wakefield, Sir Norman Edward, Kt.

Wakefield, Sir Peter George Arthur, KBE, CMG

Wakeford, *Air Marshal* Sir Richard Gordon, KCB, OBE, LVO, AFC

Wakeley, Sir John Cecil Nicholson, Bt., FRCS (1952)

†Wakeman, Sir Edward Offley Bertram, Bt. (1828)

Wales, Sir Robert Andrew, Kt.

Walford, Sir Christopher Rupert, Kt.

Walker, *Revd* Alan Edgar, Kt., OBE

Walker, *Gen.* Sir Antony Kenneth Frederick, KCB

Walker, Sir Baldwin Patrick, Bt. (1856)

Walker, Sir (Charles) Michael, GCMG

Walker, Sir David Alan, Kt.

Walker, Sir Harold Berners, KCMG

Walker, *Maj.* Sir Hugh Ronald, Bt. (1906)

Walker, Sir James Graham, Kt., MBE

Walker, Sir James Heron, Bt. (1868)

Walker, Sir John Ernest, Kt., D.Phil., FRS

Walker, *Air Marshal* Sir John Robert, KCB, CBE, AFC

Walker, *Gen.* Sir Michael John Dawson, GCB, CMG, CBE

Walker, Sir Michael Leolin Forestier-, Bt. (1835)

Walker, Sir Miles Rawstron, Kt., CBE

Walker, Sir Patrick Jeremy, KCB

Walker, *Rt. Hon.* Sir Robert, Kt.

Walker, Sir Rodney Myerscough, Kt.

Walker, *Hon.* Sir Timothy Edward, Kt.

Wall, Sir John Anthony, Kt., CBE

Wall, Sir (John) Stephen, KCMG, LVO

Wall, *Hon.* Sir Nicholas Peter Rathbone, Kt.

Wall, Sir Robert William, Kt., OBE

Wallace, *Lt.-Gen.* Sir Christopher Brooke Quentin, KBE

Wallace, Sir Ian James, Kt., CBE

Waller, *Hon.* Sir (George) Mark, Kt.

Waller, Sir Robert William, Bt. (I. 1780)

Walley, Sir John, KBE, CB

Wallis, Sir Peter Gordon, KCVO

Wallis, Sir Timothy William, Kt.

Walmsley, *Vice-Adm.* Sir Robert, KCB

Walsh, *Prof.* Sir John Patrick, KBE

†Walsham, Sir Timothy John, Bt. (1831)

Walters, *Prof.* Sir Alan Arthur, Kt.

Walters, Sir Dennis Murray, Kt., MBE

Walters, Sir Frederick Donald, Kt.

Walters, Sir Peter Ingram, Kt.

Walters, Sir Roger Talbot, KBE, FRIBA

Wamiri, Sir Akapite, KBE

Wan, Sir Wamp, Kt., MBE

Wanstall, *Hon.* Sir Charles Gray, Kt.

Ward, *Rt. Hon.* Sir Alan Hylton, Kt.

Ward, Sir John Devereux, Kt., CBE

Ward, Sir Joseph James Laffey, Bt. (1911)

Ward, *Maj.-Gen.* Sir Philip John Newling, KCVO, CBE

Ward, *Rt. Rev.* Simon Barrington-, KCMG

Ward, Sir Timothy James, Kt.

Wardale, Sir Geoffrey Charles, KCB

Wardlaw, Sir Henry (John), Bt. (s. 1631)

Waring, Sir (Alfred) Holburt, Bt. (1935)

Warmington, Sir David Marshall, Bt. (1908)

Warner, Sir (Edward Courtenay) Henry, Bt. (1910)

Warner, Sir Edward Redston, KCMG, OBE

Warner, *Prof.* Sir Frederick Edward, Kt., FRS, FREng.

Warner, Sir Gerald Chierici, KCMG

Warner, *Hon.* Sir Jean-Pierre Frank Eugene, Kt.

Warren, Sir (Frederick) Miles, KBE

Warren, Sir Kenneth Robin, Kt.

†Warren, Sir Michael Blackley, Bt. (1784)

Wass, Sir Douglas William Gretton, GCB

Waterhouse, *Hon.* Sir Ronald Gough, Kt.

Waterlow, Sir Christopher Rupert, Bt. (1873)

Waterlow, Sir (James) Gerard, Bt. (1930)

Waters, *Gen.* Sir (Charles) John, GCB, CBE

Waters, Sir (Thomas) Neil (Morris), Kt.

Wates, Sir Christopher Stephen, Kt.

Watkins, *Rt. Hon.* Sir Tasker, VC, GBE

Watson, Sir Andrew Michael Milne-, Bt. (1937)

Watson, Sir Bruce Dunstan, Kt.

Watson, *Prof.* Sir David John, Kt., Ph.D.

Watson, Sir (James) Andrew, Bt. (1866)

Watson, Sir John Forbes Inglefield-, Bt. (1895)

Watson, *Vice-Adm.* Sir Philip Alexander, KBE, LVO

Watson, Sir Ronald Matthew, Kt., CBE

Watt, *Surgeon Vice-Adm.* Sir James, KBE, FRCS

Watt, Sir James Harvie-, Bt. (1945)

Watts, Sir John Augustus Fitzroy, KCMG, CBE

Watts, Sir Arthur Desmond, KCMG

Watts, *Lt.-Gen.* Sir John Peter Barry Condliffe, KBE, CB, MC

Wauchope, Sir Roger (Hamilton) Don-, Bt. (S. 1667)

Weatherall, *Prof.* Sir David John, Kt., FRS

Weatherall, *Vice-Adm.* Sir James Lamb, KCVO, KBE

Weatherstone, Sir Dennis, KBE

Webb, *Prof.* Sir Adrian Leonard, Kt.

Webb, Sir Thomas Langley, Kt.

Webster, *Very Revd* Alan Brunskill, KCVO

Webster, *Vice-Adm.* Sir John Morrison, KCB

Webster, *Hon.* Sir Peter Edlin, Kt.

Wedderburn, Sir Andrew John Alexander Ogilvy-, Bt. (1803)

Wedgwood, Sir (Hugo) Martin, Bt. (1942)

Weekes, Sir Everton DeCourcey, KCMG, OBE

Weinberg, Sir Mark Aubrey, Kt.

Weir, Sir Michael Scott, KCMG

Weir, Sir Roderick Bignell, Kt.

Welby, Sir (Richard) Bruno Gregory, Bt. (1801)

Welch, Sir John Kemp-, Kt.

Welch, Sir John Reader, Bt. (1957)

Weldon, Sir Anthony William, Bt. (I. 1723)

Weller, Sir Arthur Burton, Kt., CBE

Wellings, Sir Jack Alfred, Kt., CBE

†Wells, Sir Christopher Charles, Bt. (1944)

Wells, Sir John Julius, Kt.

Wells, Sir William Henry Weston, Kt., FRICS

West, *Vice-Adm.* Sir Alan William John, KCB

Westbrook, Sir Neil Gowanloch, Kt., CBE

Westerman, Sir (Wilfred) Alan, Kt., CBE

Weston, Sir Michael Charles Swift, KCMG, CVO

Weston, Sir (Philip) John, KCMG

Whalen, Sir Geoffrey Henry, Kt., CBE

Wheeler, Sir Harry Anthony, Kt., OBE

Wheeler, *Air Chief Marshal* Sir (Henry) Neil (George), GCB, CBE, DSO, DFC, AFC

Wheeler, *Rt. Hon.* Sir John Daniel, Kt.

Wheeler, Sir John Hieron, Bt. (1920)

Wheeler, *Gen.* Sir Roger Neil, GCB, CBE

Wheler, Sir Edward Woodford, Bt. (1660)

Whent, Sir Gerald Arthur, Kt., CBE

Whishaw, Sir Charles Percival Law, Kt.

Whitaker, Sir John James Ingham (Jack), Bt. (1936)

White, *Prof.* Sir Christopher John, Kt., CVO

White, Sir Christopher Robert Meadows, Bt. (1937)

White, *Hon.* Sir Christopher Stuart Stuart-, Kt.

White, Sir David Harry, Kt.

White, Sir Frank John, Kt.

White, Sir George Stanley James, Bt. (1904)

White, *Wg Cdr.* Sir Henry Arthur Dalrymple-, Bt., DFC (1926)

White, *Adm.* Sir Hugo Moresby, GCB, CBE

White, *Hon.* Sir John Charles, Kt., MBE

White, Sir John Albert

White, Sir John Woolmer, Bt. (1922)

White, Sir Lynton Stuart, Kt., MBE, TD

White, Sir Nicholas Peter Archibald, Bt. (1802)

White, *Adm.* Sir Peter, GBE

Whitehead, Sir John Stainton, GCMG, CVO

Whitehead, Sir Rowland John Rathbone, Bt. (1889)

Whiteley, Sir Hugo Baldwin Huntington-, Bt. (1918)

Whiteley, *Gen.* Sir Peter John Frederick, GCB, OBE, RM

Whitfield, Sir William, Kt., CBE

Whitford, *Hon.* Sir John Norman Keates, Kt.

Whitmore, Sir Clive Anthony, GCB, CVO

Whitmore, Sir John Henry Douglas, Bt. (1954)

Whitney, Sir Raymond William, Kt., OBE, MP

Wickerson, Sir John Michael, Kt.

Wicks, Sir Nigel Leonard, GCB, CVO, CBE

†Wigan, Sir Michael Iain, Bt. (1898)

Wiggin, Sir Alfred William (Jerry), Kt., TD

†Wiggin, Sir Charles Rupert John, Bt. (1892)

Wigram, *Maj.* Sir Edward Robert Woolmore, Bt. (1805)

Wignall, Sir Trevor Charles, Kt.

Wilbraham, Sir Richard Baker, Bt. (1776)

Wilford, Sir (Kenneth) Michael, GCMG

Wilkes, *Prof.* Sir Maurice Vincent, Kt.

Wilkes, *Gen.* Sir Michael John, KCB, CBE

Wilkins, Sir Graham John, Kt.

Wilkinson, Sir (David) Graham (Brook) Bt. (1941)

Wilkinson, *Prof.* Sir Denys Haigh, Kt., FRS

Wilkinson, Sir Philip William, Kt.

Willcocks, Sir David Valentine, Kt., CBE, MC

Willcocks, *Lt.-Gen.* Sir Michael Alan, Kt., CB

Williams, Sir Alastair Edgcumbe James Dudley-, Bt. (1964)

Williams, Sir Alwyn, Kt., Ph.D., FRS, FRSE

Williams, Sir Arthur Dennis Pitt, Kt.

Williams, Sir (Arthur) Gareth Ludovic Emrys Rhys, Bt. (1918)

Williams, *Prof.* Sir Bernard Arthur Owen, Kt., FBA

Williams, *Prof.* Sir Bruce Rodda, KBE

Williams, Sir Charles Othniel, Kt.

Williams, Sir Daniel Charles, GCMG, QC

Williams, *Prof.* Sir David Glyndwr Tudor, Kt.

Williams, Sir David Innes, Kt.

Williams, Sir David Reeve, Kt., CBE

Williams, *Hon.* Sir Denys Ambrose, KCMG

Williams, Sir Donald Mark, Bt. (1866)

Williams, *Prof.* Sir (Edward) Dillwyn, Kt., FRCP

Williams, *Hon.* Sir Edward Stratten, KCMG, KBE

Williams, Sir Francis Owen Garbett, Kt., CBE

Williams, *Prof.* Sir Glanmor, Kt., CBE, FBA

Williams, Sir Henry Sydney, Kt., OBE

Williams, Sir (John) Kyffin, Kt., OBE, DL, RA

Williams, Sir (Lawrence) Hugh, Bt. (1798)

Williams, Sir Leonard, KBE, CB

Williams, Sir Osmond, Bt., MC (1909)

Williams, Sir Peter Michael, Kt.

Williams, *Prof.* Sir Robert Evan Owen, Kt., MD, FRCP

Williams, Sir (Robert) Philip
Nathaniel, Bt. (1915)
Williams, Sir Robin Philip, Bt. (1953)
Williams, Sir (William) Maxwell
(Harries), Kt.
Williamson, *Marshal of the Royal Air
Force* Sir Keith Alec, GCB, AFC
Williamson, Sir Robert Brian, Kt.,
CBE
Willink, Sir Charles William, Bt.
(1957)
Willis, *Vice-Adm.* Sir (Guido) James,
KBE
Willis, *Air Chief Marshal* Sir John
Frederick, GBE, KCB
Willison, *Lt.-Gen.* Sir David John,
KCB, OBE, MC
Willison, Sir John Alexander, Kt., OBE
Wills, Sir David James Vernon, Bt.
(1923)
Wills, Sir David Seton, Bt. (1904)
Wilmot, Sir Henry Robert, Bt. (1759)
Wilmot, Sir Michael John Assheton
Eardley-, Bt. (1821)
Wilsey, *Gen.* Sir John Finlay Willasey,
GCB, CBE
Wilshaw, Sir Michael, Kt.
Wilson, *Prof.* Sir Alan Geoffrey, Kt.
Wilson, *Lt.-Gen.* Sir (Alexander)
James, KBE, MC
Wilson, Sir Anthony, Kt.
Wilson, *Vice-Adm.* Sir Barry Nigel,
KCB
Wilson, *Lt.-Col.* Sir Blair Aubyn
Stewart-, KCVO
Wilson, Sir Charles Haynes, Kt.
Wilson, *Prof.* Sir Colin Alexander St
John, Kt., RA, FRIBA
Wilson, Sir David, Bt. (1920)
Wilson, Sir David Mackenzie, Kt.
Wilson, Sir Geoffrey Masterman,
KCB, CMG
Wilson, Sir James William Douglas,
Bt. (1906)
Wilson, *Brig.* Sir Mathew John
Anthony, Bt., OBE, MC (1874)
Wilson, *Hon.* Sir Nicholas Allan Roy,
Kt.
Wilson, Sir Patrick Michael Ernest
David McNair-, Kt.
Wilson, Sir Richard Thomas James,
KCB, GCB
Wilson, Sir Robert, Kt., CBE
Wilson, *Rt. Revd* Roger Plumpton,
KCVO, DD
Wilson, Sir Robert Peter, KCMG
Wilson, *Air Chief Marshal* Sir
(Ronald) Andrew (Fellowes), KCB,
AFC
Wilson, *Hon.* Sir Ronald Darling,
KBE, CMG
Wilton, Sir (Arthur) John, KCMG,
KCVO, MC
Wingate, *Capt.* Sir Miles Buckley,
KCVO
Winkley, Sir David Ross, Kt.
Winnington, Sir Francis Salwey
William, Bt. (1755)

Winskill, *Air Cdre* Sir Archibald
Little, KCVO, CBE, DFC
Winterbottom, Sir Walter, Kt., CBE
Wisdom, Sir Norman, Kt., OBE
Wiseman, Sir John William, Bt.
(1628)
Wolfendale, *Prof.* Sir Arnold
Whittaker, Kt., FRS
Wolfson, Sir Brian Gordon, Kt.
Wolseley, Sir Charles Garnet Richard
Mark, Bt. (1628)
†Wolseley, Sir James Douglas, Bt.
(I. 1745)
Wolstenholme, Sir Gordon Ethelbert
Ward, Kt., OBE
Wombwell, Sir George Philip
Frederick, Bt. (1778)
Womersley, Sir Peter John Walter,
Bt. (1945)
Woo, Sir Leo Joseph, Kt.
Woo, Sir Po-Shing, Kt.
Wood, Sir Alan Marshall Muir, Kt.,
FRS, FREng.
Wood, Sir Andrew Marley, GCMG
Wood, Sir Anthony John Page, Bt.
(1837)
Wood, Sir David Basil Hill-, Bt.
(1921)
Wood, Sir Frederick Ambrose Stuart,
Kt.
Wood, Sir Ian Clark, Kt., CBE
Wood, *Prof.* Sir John Crossley, Kt.,
CBE
Wood, *Hon.* Sir John Kember, Kt., MC
Wood, Sir Martin Francis, Kt., OBE
Wood, Sir Russell Dillon, KCVO, VRD
Wood, Sir William Alan, KCVO, CB
Woodard, *Rear Adm.* Sir Robert
Nathaniel, KCVO
Woodcock, Sir John, Kt., CBE, QPM
Woodhead, *Vice-Adm.* Sir (Anthony)
Peter, KCB
Woodhouse, *Rt. Hon.* Sir (Arthur)
Owen, KBE, DSC
Wooding, Sir Norman Samuel, Kt.,
CBE
Woodroffe, *Most Revd* George
Cuthbert Manning, KBE
Woodroofe, Sir Ernest George, Kt.,
Ph.D.
Woods, Sir Colin Philip Joseph,
KCVO, CBE
Woods, Sir Robert Kynnersley, Kt.,
CBE
Woodward, *Hon.* Sir (Albert) Edward,
Kt., OBE
Woodward, *Adm.* Sir John Forster,
GBE, KCB
Worsley, *Gen.* Sir Richard Edward,
GCB, OBE
Worsley, Sir (William) Marcus
(John), Bt. (1838)
Worsthorne, Sir Peregrine Gerard,
Kt.
Wratten, *Air Chief Marshal* Sir
William John, GBE, CB, AFC
Wraxall, Sir Charles Frederick
Lascelles, Bt. (1813)

Wrey, Sir George Richard Bourchier,
Bt. (1628)
Wrigglesworth, Sir Ian William, Kt.
Wright, Sir Allan Frederick, KBE
Wright, Sir David John, KCMG, LVO
Wright, Sir Denis Arthur Hepworth,
GCMG
Wright, Sir Edward Maitland, Kt.,
D.Phil., LL D, D.Sc., FRSE
Wright, *Hon.* Sir (John) Michael, Kt.
Wright, Sir (John) Oliver, GCMG,
GCVO, DSC
Wright, Sir Paul Hervé Giraud,
KCMG, OBE
Wright, Sir Peter Robert, Kt., CBE
Wright, Sir Richard Michael Cory-,
Bt. (1903)
Wrightson, Sir Charles Mark
Garmondsway, Bt. (1900)
Wrigley, *Prof.* Sir Edward Anthony
(Sir Tony), Kt., Ph.D., PBA
Wu, Sir Gordon Ying Sheung, KCMG
Wynn, Sir David Watkin Williams-,
Bt. (1688)
Yacoub, *Prof.* Sir Magdi Habib, Kt.,
FRCS
Yaki, Sir Roy, KBE
Yang, *Hon.* Sir Ti Liang, Kt.
Yapp, Sir Stanley Graham, Kt.
Yardley, Sir David Charles Miller,
Kt., LL D
Yarranton, Sir Peter George, Kt.
Yarrow, Sir Eric Grant, Bt., MBE
(1916)
Yellowlees, Sir Henry, KCB
Yocklunn, Sir John (Soong Chung),
KCVO
Yoo Foo, Sir (François) Henri, Kt.
Young, Sir Brian Walter Mark, Kt.
Young, Sir Colville Norbert, GCMG,
MBE
Young, Sir Dennis Charles, KCMG
Young, *Rt. Hon.* Sir George Samuel
Knatchbull, Bt., MP (1813)
Young, *Hon.* Sir Harold William,
KCMG
Young, Sir John Kenyon Roe, Bt.
(1821)
Young, *Hon.* Sir John McIntosh,
KCMG
Young, Sir John Robertson, KCMG
Young, Sir Leslie Clarence, Kt., CBE
Young, Sir Nicholas Charles, Kt.
Young, Sir Richard Dilworth, Kt.
Young, Sir Roger William, Kt.
Young, Sir Stephen Stewart
Templeton, Bt. (1945)
Young, Sir William Neil, Bt. (1769)
Younger, *Maj.-Gen.* Sir John William,
Bt., CBE (1911)
Yuwi, Sir Matiabe, KBE
Zeeman, *Prof.* Sir (Erik) Christopher,
Kt., FRS
Zissman, Sir Bernard Philip, Kt.
Zochonis, Sir John Basil, Kt.
Zoleveke, Sir Gideon Pitabose, KBE
Zunz, Sir Gerhard Jacob (Jack), Kt.,
FREng.
Zurenuoc, Sir Zibang, KBE

Dames Grand Cross and Dames Commanders

Style, 'Dame' before forename and surname, followed by appropriate post-nominal initials. Where such an award is made to a lady already in enjoyment of a higher title, the appropriate initials follow her name
Husband, Untitled
For forms of address, *see* page 135

Dame Grand Cross and Dame Commander are the higher classes for women of the Order of the Bath, the Order of St Michael and St George, the Royal Victorian Order, and the Order of the British Empire. Dames Grand Cross rank after the wives of Baronets and before the wives of Knights Grand Cross. Dames Commanders rank after the wives of Knights Grand Cross and before the wives of Knights Commanders.

Honorary Dames Commanders may be conferred on women who are citizens of countries of which The Queen is not head of state.

LIST OF DAMES
Revised to 31 August 2001

Women peers in their own right and life peers are not included in this list. Female members of the royal family are not included in this list; details of the orders they hold are given on pages 117–8

If a dame has a double barrelled or hyphenated surname, she is listed under the final element of the name

A full entry in italic type indicates that the recipient of an honour died during the year in which the honour was conferred. The name is included for the purposes of record

Abaijah, Dame Josephine, DBE
Abel Smith, Lady, DCVO
Abergavenny, The Marchioness of, DCVO
Airlie, The Countess of, DCVO
Albemarle, The Countess of, DBE
Albon, Dame Yvonne Jeanne, DBE
Allen, *Prof.* Dame Ingrid Victoria, DBE, CBE, DL
Anderson, *Brig. Hon.* Dame Mary Mackenzie (Mrs Pihl), DBE
Andrews, Dame Julie, DBE
Anglesey, The Marchioness of, DBE
Anson, Lady (Elizabeth Audrey), DBE
Anstee, Dame Margaret Joan, DCMG
Arden, *Hon.* Dame Mary Howarth (Mrs Mance), DBE
Bainbridge, Dame Beryl, DBE
Baker, Dame Janet Abbott (Mrs Shelley), CH, DBE
Ballin, Dame Reubina Ann, DBE
Barletta, Dame Nelia, DBE
Barrow, Dame Jocelyn Anita (Mrs Downer), DBE
Barstow, Dame Josephine Clare (Mrs Anderson), DBE
Basset, Lady Elizabeth, DCVO
Bassey, Dame Shirley, DBE
Bean, Dame Majorie Louise, DBE
Beaurepaire, Dame Beryl Edith, DBE
Beer, *Prof.* Dame Gillian Patricia Kempster, DBE, FBA
Bergquist, *Prof.* Dame Patricia Rose, DBE
Berry, Dame Alice Miriam, DBE
Bewley, Dame Beulah Rosemary, DBE
Black, *Hon.* Dame Jill Margaret, DBE
Blaize, Dame Venetia Ursula, DBE
Blaxland, Dame Helen Frances, DBE
Booth, *Hon.* Dame Margaret Myfanwy Wood, DBE

Bowman, Dame (Mary) Elaine Kellett-, DBE
Bowtell, Dame Ann Elizabeth, DCB
Boyd, Dame Vivienne Myra, DBE
Bracewell, *Hon.* Dame Joyanne Winifred (Mrs Copeland), DBE
Brain, Dame Margaret Anne (Mrs Wheeler), DBE
Brazill, Dame Josephine (Sister Mary Philippa), DBE
Bridges, Dame Mary Patricia, DBE
Browne, Lady Moyra Blanche Madeleine, DBE
Bryans, Dame Anne Margaret, DBE
Buttfield, Dame Nancy Eileen, DBE
Byatt, Dame Antonia Susan, DBE, FRSL
Bynoe, Dame Hilda Louisa, DBE
Caldicott, Dame Fiona, DBE, FRCP, FRCPsych.
Cartwright, Dame Silvia Rose, DBE
Casey, Dame Stella Katherine, DBE
Charles, Dame (Mary) Eugenia, DBE
Chesterton, Dame Elizabeth Ursula, DBE
Clark, *Prof.* Dame Jill MacLeod, DBE
Clark, *Prof.* Dame (Margaret) June, DBE, Ph.D.
Collins, Dame Diana Clavering, DBE
Clay, Dame Marie Mildred, DBE
Clayton, Dame Barbara Evelyn (Mrs Klyne), DBE
Cleland, Dame Rachel, DBE
Coll, Dame Elizabeth Anne Loosemore Esteve-, DBE
Collarbone, Dame Patricia, DBE
Corsar, The Hon. Dame Mary Drummond, DBE
Davies, Dame Audrey Joan, DBE
Davies, Dame Wendy Patricia, DBE
Davis, Dame Karlene Cecile, DBE
Daws, Dame Joyce Margaretta, DBE
Cates, Dame Emma De-, DBE
Dell, Dame Miriam Patricia, DBE
Dench, Dame Judith Olivia (Mrs Williams), DBE
Descartes, Dame Marie Selipha Sesenne, BEM
Devonshire, The Duchess of, DCVO
Digby, Lady, DBE
Donaldson, Dame (Dorothy) Mary (Lady Donaldson of Lymington), GBE
Duffield, Dame Vivien Louise, DBE, CBE
Dugdale, Kathryn, Lady, DCVO
Dumont, Dame Ivy Leona, DCMG
Dyche, Dame Rachael Mary, DBE

Ebsworth, *Hon.* Dame Ann Marian, DBE
Ellison, Dame Jill, DBE
Else, Dame Jean, DBE
Engel, Dame Pauline Frances (Sister Pauline Engel), DBE
Evans, Dame Anne Elizabeth Jane, DBE
Evans, Dame Lois Marie Browne-, DBE
Evans, Dame Hilda Mary, DBE, BEM
Evison, Dame Helen June Patricia, DBE
Fenner, Dame Peggy Edith, DBE
Fielding, Dame Pauline, DBE
Fitton, Dame Doris Alice (Mrs Mason), DBE
Fort, Dame Maeve Geraldine, DCMG, DCVO
Fraser, Dame Dorothy Rita, DBE
Friend, Dame Phyllis Muriel, DBE
Fritchie, Dame Irene Tordoff (Dame Rennie Fritchie), DBE
Frost, Dame Phyllis Irene, DBE
Fry, Dame Margaret Louise, DBE
Gallagher, Dame Monica Josephine, DBE
Gardiner, Dame Helen Louisa, DBE, MVO
Giles, *Air Comdt.* Dame Pauline (Mrs Parsons), DBE, RRC
Goltra, Dame Seipp, DBE
Goodman, Dame Barbara, DBE
Gordon, Dame Minita Elmira, GCMG, GCVO
Gow, Dame Jane Elizabeth (Mrs Whiteley), DBE
Grafton, The Duchess of, GCVO
Grant, Dame Mavis, DBE
Green, Dame Mary Georgina, DBE
Grey, Dame Beryl Elizabeth (Mrs Svenson), DBE
Grimthorpe, The Lady, DCVO
Guilfoyle, Dame Margaret Georgina Constance, DBE
Guthardt, *Revd Dr* Dame Phyllis Myra, DBE
Haig, Dame Mary Alison Glen-, DBE
Hale, *Hon.* Dame Brenda Marjorie (Mrs Farrand), DBE
Hallett, Dame Heather Carol, DBE, QC
Harper, Dame Elizabeth Margaret Way, DBE
Dames Grand Cross and Dame Commanders
Heilbron, *Hon.* Dame Rose, DBE
Herbison, Dame Jean Marjory, DBE, CMG
Hercus, *Hon.* Dame (Margaret) Ann, DCMG

Higgins, *Prof.* Dame Julia Stretton, DBE, CBE, FRS
Higgins, *Prof.* Dame Rosalyn, DBE, QC
Hill, *Air Cdre* Dame Felicity Barbara, DBE
Hiller, Dame Wendy (Mrs Gow), DBE
Hine, Dame Deirdre Joan, DBE, FRCP
Hird, Dame Thora (Mrs Scott), DBE
Hogg, *Hon.* Dame Mary Claire (Mrs Koops), DBE
Hollows, Dame Sharon, DBE
Hurley, *Prof.* Dame Rosalinde (Mrs Gortvai), DBE
Hussey, Lady Susan Katharine (Lady Hussey of North Bradley), DCVO
Imison, Dame Tamsyn, DBE
Isaacs, Dame Albertha Madeline, DBE
James, Dame Naomi Christine (Mrs Haythorne), DBE
Jenkins, Dame (Mary) Jennifer (Lady Jenkins of Hillhead), DBE
Jones, Dame Gwyneth (Mrs Haberfeld-Jones), DBE
Jones, Dame (Lilian) Pauline Neville-, DCMG
Keegan, Dame Geraldine Mary Marcella, DBE, OBE
Kekedo, Dame Rosalina Violet, DBE
Kelleher, Dame Joan, DBE
Kelly, Dame Lorna May Boreland, DBE
Kershaw, Dame Janet Elizabeth Murray (Dame Betty), DBE
Kettlewell, *Comdt.* Dame Marion Mildred, DBE
Kilpatrick, Dame Judith Ann Gladys, DBE
King, Dame Thea, DBE, OBE
Kirby, Dame Georgina Kamiria, DBE
Kirk, Dame (Lucy) Ruth, DBE
Kramer, *Prof.* Dame Leonie Judith, DBE
Laine, Dame Cleo (Clementine) Dinah (Mrs Dankworth), DBE
Lamb, Dame Dawn Ruth, DBE
Lewis, Dame Edna Leofrida (Lady Lewis), DBE
Litchfield, Dame Ruby Beatrice, DBE
Lott, Dame Felicity Ann Emwhyla (Mrs Woolf), DBE
Louisy, Dame (Calliopa) Pearlette, DBE, GCSL, GCMG
Lowrey, *Air Comdt.* Dame Alice, DBE, RRC
Lympany, Dame Moura, DBE
Lynn, Dame Vera (Mrs Lewis), DBE
Mackinnon, Dame (Una) Patricia, DBE
McKechnie, Dame Sheila Marshall, DBE, OBE
McLaren, Dame Anne Laura, DBE, FRCOG, FRS
Macmillan of Ovenden, Katharine, Viscountess, DBE
Major, Dame Malvina Lorraine (Mrs Fleming), DBE
Major, Dame Norma Christina Elizabeth, DBE
Markova, Dame Alicia, DBE
Metcalf, Dame Helen, DBE
Metge, *Dr* Dame (Alice) Joan, DBE
Middleton, Dame Elaine Madoline, DCMG, MBE
Miller, Dame Mary Elizabeth Hedley-, DCVO, CB
Mills, Dame Barbara Jean Lyon, DBE, QC

Mitchell, Dame Mona, DCVO
Moores, Dame Yvonne, DBE
Morrison, *Hon.* Dame Mary Anne, DCVO
Mueller, Dame Anne Elisabeth, DCB
Muirhead, Dame Lorna Elizabeth Fox, DBE
Muldoon, Thea Dale, Lady, DBE, QSO
Mumford, Lady Mary Katharine, DCVO
Munro, Dame Alison, DBE
Murdoch, Dame Elisabeth Joy, DBE
Murray, Dame (Alice) Rosemary, DBE, D.Phil.
Ogilvie, Dame Bridget Margaret, DBE, Ph.D., D.Sc.
Oliver, Dame Gillian Frances, DBE
Ollerenshaw, Dame Kathleen Mary, DBE, D.Phil.
Oxenbury, Dame Shirley Anne, DBE
Park, Dame Merle Florence (Mrs Bloch), DBE
Paterson, Dame Betty Fraser Ross, DBE
Peake, *Air Cdre* Dame Felicity Hyde, DBE, AE
Penhaligon, Dame Annette (Mrs Egerton), DBE
Peters, Dame Mary Elizabeth, DBE, CBE
Poole, Dame Avril Anne Barker, DBE
Porter, Dame Shirley (Lady Porter), DBE
Powell, Dame Sally Ann Vickers, DBE
Prendergast, Dame Simone Ruth, DBE
Prentice, Dame Winifred Eva, DBE
Preston, Dame Frances Olivia Campbell-, DCVO
Price, Dame Margaret Berenice, DBE
Purves, Dame Daphne Helen, DBE
Pyke, Lady, DBE
Quinn, Dame Sheila Margaret Imelda, DBE
Rafferty, *Hon.* Anne Judith, DBE
Rankin, Lady Jean Margaret Florence, DCVO
Rees, *Prof.* Dame Lesley Howard, DBE
Reeves, Dame Helen May, DBE
Richardson, Dame Mary, DBE
Riddelsdell, Dame Mildred, DCB, CBE
Ridley, Dame (Mildred) Betty, DBE
Ridsdale, Dame Victoire Evelyn Patricia (Lady Ridsdale), DBE
Rigg, Dame Diana, DBE
Rimington, Dame Stella, DCB
Robertson, *Cmdt.* Dame Nancy Margaret, DBE
Robottom, Dame Marlene, DBE
Roe, Dame Raigh Edith, DBE
Rothschild, Hon. Dame Miriam Louisa, DBE, FRS
Rue, Dame (Elsie) Rosemary, DBE
Rumbold, *Rt. Hon.* Dame Angela Claire Rosemary, DBE
Runciman of Doxford, The Viscountess, DBE
Salas, Dame Margaret Laurence, DBE
Salmond, *Prof.* Dame Mary Anne, DBE
Saunders, Dame Cicely Mary Strode, OM, DBE, FRCP
Sawyer, *Hon.* Dame Joan Augusta, DBE
Schwarzkopf, Dame Elisabeth Friederike Marie Olga Legge-, DBE
Scott, Barbara, DBE
Scott, Dame Jean Mary Monica Maxwell-, DCVO

Seward, Dame Margaret Helen Elizabeth, DBE
Shenfield, Dame Barbara Estelle, DBE
Sherlock, *Prof.* Dame Sheila Patricia Violet, DBE, MD, FRCP
Shirley, Dame Stephanie, DBE
Shovelton, Dame Helena, DBE
Sibley, Dame Antoinette (Mrs Corbett), DBE
Sloss, *Rt. Hon.* Dame (Ann) Elizabeth (Oldfield) Butler-, DBE
Smieton, Dame Mary Guillan, DBE
Smith, Dame Dela, DBE
Smith, *Hon.* Dame Janet Hilary (Mrs Mathieson), DBE
Smith, Dame Margaret Natalie (Maggie) (Mrs Cross), DBE
Smith, Dame Margot, DBE
Smyth, Dame Frances Mary, DBE
Soames, Mary, Lady, DBE
Southgate, Prof. Dame Lesley Jill, DBE
Spark, Dame Muriel Sarah, DBE
Spencer, Dame Rosemary Jane, DCMG
Steel, *Hon.* Dame (Anne) Heather (Mrs Beattie), DBE
Stephens, *Air Cmdt.* Dame Anne, DBE
Stewart, Dame Muriel Acadia, DBE
Strachan, Dame Valerie Patricia Marie, DCB
Strathern, *Prof.* Dame Anne Marilyn, DBE
Sutherland, Dame Joan (Mrs Bonynge), OM, DBE
Sutherland, Dame Veronica Evelyn, DBE, CMG
Szaszy, Dame Miraka Petricevich, DBE
Taylor, Dame Elizabeth, DBE
Taylor, Dame Jean Elizabeth, DCVO
Te Atairangikaahu, Te Arikinui, Dame, DBE
Te Kanawa, Dame Kiri Janette, DBE
Thomas, Dame Maureen Elizabeth (Lady Thomas), DBE
Thorneycroft, Carla, Lady, DBE
Tinson, Dame Sue, DBE
Tizard, Dame Catherine Anne, GCMG, GCVO, DBE
Tokiel, Dame Rosa, DBE
Trotter, Dame Janet Olive, DBE
Uprichard, Dame Mary Elizabeth, DBE
Varley, Dame Joan Fleetwood, DBE
Wagner, Dame Gillian Mary Millicent (Lady Wagner), DBE
Wall, (Alice) Anne, (Mrs Michael Wall), DCVO
Warburton, Dame Anne Marion, DCVO, CMG
Warwick, Dame Margaret Elizabeth Harvey Turner-, DBE, FRCP, FRCPEd.
Waterhouse, Dame Rachel Elizabeth, DBE, Ph.D.
Webb, Prof. Dame Patricia, DBE
Weir, Dame Gillian Constance (Mrs Phelps), DBE
Weston, Dame Margaret Kate, DBE
Williamson, Dame (Elsie) Marjorie, DBE, Ph.D.
Winstone, Dame Dorothy Gertrude, DBE, CMG
Wong Yick-ming, Dame Rosanna, DBE
Wright, Dame Clarice Betty, DBE
Wright, Dame Gail, DBE

Decorations and Medals

PRINCIPAL DECORATIONS AND MEDALS
In order of precedence

VICTORIA CROSS (VC), 1856 (*see* page 208)
GEORGE CROSS (GC), 1940 (*see* pages 208–9)

BRITISH ORDERS OF KNIGHTHOOD AND DISTINGUISHED
SERVICE ORDER.
Baronet's Badge
Knight Bachelor's Badge

DECORATIONS

Conspicuous Gallantry Cross (CGC), 1995
Royal Red Cross Class I (RRC), 1883
Distinguished Service Cross (DSC), 1914. For all ranks for
   actions at sea
Military Cross (MC), December 1914. For all ranks for
   actions on land
Distinguished Flying Cross (DFC), 1918. For all ranks for
   acts of gallantry when flying in active operations against
   the enemy
Air Force Cross (AFC), 1918. For all ranks for acts of
   courage when flying, although not in active operations
   against the enemy
Royal Red Cross Class II (ARRC)
Order of British India
Kaisar-i-Hind Medal
Order of St John

MEDALS FOR GALLANTRY AND DISTINGUISHED
CONDUCT

Union of South Africa Queen's Medal for Bravery, in Gold
Distinguished Conduct Medal (DCM), 1854
Conspicuous Gallantry Medal (CGM), 1874
Conspicuous Gallantry Medal (Flying)
George Medal (GM), 1940
Queen's Police Medal for Gallantry
Queen's Fire Service Medal for Gallantry
*Royal West African Frontier Force Distinguished Conduct
   Medal*
King's African Rifles Distinguished Conduct Medal
Indian Distinguished Service Medal
Union of South Africa Queen's Medal for Bravery, in Silver
Distinguished Service Medal (DSM), 1914
Military Medal (MM), 1916
Distinguished Flying Medal (DFM), 1918
Air Force Medal (AFM)
Constabulary Medal (Ireland)
Medal for Saving Life at Sea
Sea Gallantry Medal
Indian Order of Merit (Civil)
Indian Police Medal for Gallantry
Ceylon Police Medal for Gallantry
Sierra Leone Police Medal for Gallantry
Sierra Leone Fire Brigades Medal for Gallantry
Colonial Police Medal for Gallantry (CPM)
Queen's Gallantry Medal (QGM), 1974
Royal Victorian Medal (RVM), Gold, Silver and Bronze
British Empire Medal (BEM), (formerly the Medal of the
   Order of the British Empire, for Meritorious Service;
   also includes the Medal of the Order awarded before 29
   December 1922)
Canada Medal
Queen's Police (QPM) *and Queen's Fire Service Medals*
   (QFSM) *for Distinguished Service*

Queen's Volunteer Reserves Medal
Queen's Medal for Chiefs

WAR MEDALS AND STARS (in order of date)
Polar Medals (in order of date)

POLICE MEDALS FOR VALUABLE SERVICE

JUBILEE, CORONATION AND DURBAR MEDALS

*King George V, King George VI and Queen Elizabeth II Long
   and Faithful Service Medals*

EFFICIENCY AND LONG SERVICE DECORATIONS AND
MEDALS

Medal for Meritorious Service
Accumulated Campaign Service Medal
The Medal for Long Service and Good Conduct (Military)
Naval Long Service and Good Conduct Medal
Royal Marines Meritorious Service Medal
Royal Air Force Meritorious Service Medal
Royal Air Force Long Service and Good Conduct Medal
Medal for Long Service and Good Conduct (Ulster Defence
   Regiment)
Police Long Service and Good Conduct Medal
Fire Brigade Long Service and Good Conduct Medal
Colonial Police and Fire Brigades Long Service Medals
Colonial Prison Service Medal
Hong Kong Disciplined Services Medal
Army Emergency Reserve Decoration (ERD), 1952
Volunteer Officers' Decoration (VD)
Volunteer Long Service Medal
Volunteer Officers' Decoration for India and the Colonies
Volunteer Long Service Medal for India and the Colonies
Colonial Auxiliary Forces Officers' Decoration
Colonial Auxiliary Forces Long Service Medal
Medal for Good Shooting (Naval)
Militia Long Service Medal
Imperial Yeomanry Long Service Medal
Territorial Decoration (TD), 1908
Efficiency Decoration (ED)
Territorial Efficiency Medal
Efficiency Medal
Special Reserve Long Service and Good Conduct Medal
Decoration for Officers, Royal Navy Reserve (RD), 1910
Decoration for Officers, RNVR (VRD)
Royal Naval Reserve Long Service and Good Conduct Medal
RNVR Long Service and Good Conduct Medal
*Royal Naval Auxiliary Sick Berth Reserve Long Service and
   Good Conduct Medal*
Royal Fleet Reserve Long Service and Good Conduct Medal
*Royal Naval Wireless Auxiliary Reserve Long Service and Good
   Conduct Medal*
Air Efficiency Award (AE), 1942
Volunteer Reserves Service Medal
Ulster Defence Regiment Medal
Northern Ireland Home Service Medal
The Queen's Medal. For champion shots in the RN, RM,
   RNZN, Army, RAF
Cadet Forces Medal, 1950
Coastguard Auxiliary Service Long Service Medal (formerly
   Coast Life Saving Corps Long Service Medal)
Special Constabulary Long Service Medal
Royal Observer Corps Medal
Civil Defence Long Service Medal

Ambulance Service (Emergency Duties) Long Service and Good
   Conduct Medal
Royal Fleet Auxiliary Service Medal
Rhodesia Medal
Royal Ulster Constabulary Service Medal
Northern Ireland Prison Service Medal
Service Medal of the Order of St John
Badge of the Order of the League of Mercy
Voluntary Medical Service Medal, 1932
Women's Voluntary Service Medal
Colonial Special Constabulary Medal

FOREIGN ORDERS, DECORATIONS AND MEDALS (IN
ORDER OF DATE)

THE VICTORIA CROSS (1856)
FOR CONSPICUOUS BRAVERY

VC
Ribbon, Crimson, for all Services (until 1918 it was blue for
the Royal Navy)

Instituted on 29 January 1856, the Victoria Cross was
awarded retrospectively to 1854, the first being held by Lt.
C. D. Lucas, RN, for bravery in the Baltic Sea on 21 June
1854 (gazetted 24 February 1857). The first 62 Crosses
were presented by Queen Victoria in Hyde Park, London,
on 26 June 1857.
   The Victoria Cross is worn before all other decorations,
on the left breast, and consists of a cross-pattée of bronze,
one and a half inches in diameter, with the Royal Crown
surmounted by a lion in the centre, and beneath there is the
inscription For Valour. Holders of the VC receive a tax-
free annuity of £1,300, irrespective of need or other
conditions. In 1911, the right to receive the Cross was
extended to Indian soldiers, and in 1920 to matrons, sisters
and nurses, and the staff of the Nursing Services and other
services pertaining to hospitals and nursing, and to
civilians of either sex regularly or temporarily under the
orders, direction or supervision of the naval, military, or
air forces of the Crown.

SURVIVING RECIPIENTS OF THE VICTORIA CROSS

as at 31 August 2001

Annand, Capt. R. W. (Durham Light Infantry)
1940 World War
Bhan Bhagta Gurung, Havildar (2nd Gurkha Rifles)
1945 World War
Bhandari Ram, Capt. (10th Baluch Regiment)
1944 World War
Chapman, Sgt. E. T., BEM (Monmouthshire Regiment)
1945 World War
Cruickshank, Flt. Lt. J. A. (RAFVR)
1944 World War
Cutler, Capt. Sir Roden, AK, KCMG, KCVO, CBE (Australian
Military Forces, 2/5th Field Artillery)
1941 World War
Fraser, Lt.-Cdr. I. E., DSC (RNR)
1945 World War
Gardner, Capt. P. J., MC (Royal Tank Regiment)
1941 World War

Gould, Lt. T. W. (RN)
1942 World War
Kenna, Pte. E. (Australian Military Forces, 2/4th (NSW))
1945 World War
Lachhiman Gurung, Havildar (8th Gurkha Rifles)
1945 World War
Norton, Capt. G. R., MM (South African Forces, Kaffrarian
Rifles)
1944 World War
Payne, WO K., DSC (USA) (Australian Army Training
Team)
1969 Vietnam
Rambahadur Limbu, Capt., MVO (10th Princess Mary's
Gurkha Rifles)
1965 Sarawak
Reid, Flt. Lt. W. (RAFVR)
1943 World War
Smith, Sgt. E. A., CD (Seaforth Highlanders of Canada)
1944 World War
Speakman-Pitts, Sgt. W. (Black Watch, attached KOSB)
1951 Korea
Tulbahadur Pun, Lt. (6th Gurkha Rifles)
1944 World War
Umrao Singh, Sub Major (Royal Indian Artillery)
1944 World War
Watkins, Maj. Rt. Hon. Sir Tasker, GBE (Welch Regiment)
1944 World War
Wilson, Lt.-Col. E. C. T. (East Surrey Regiment)
1940 World War

THE GEORGE CROSS (1940)
FOR GALLANTRY

GC
Ribbon, Dark blue, threaded through a bar adorned with
laurel leaves
Instituted 24 September 1940 (with amendments,
3 November 1942)

The George Cross is worn before all other decorations
(except the VC) on the left breast (when worn by a woman
it may be worn on the left shoulder from a ribbon of the
same width and colour fashioned into a bow). It consists of
a plain silver cross with four equal limbs, the cross having
in the centre a circular medallion bearing a design showing
St George and the Dragon. The inscription For Gallantry
appears round the medallion and in the angle of each limb
of the cross is the Royal cypher 'G VI' forming a circle
concentric with the medallion. The reverse is plain and
bears the name of the recipient and the date of the award.
The cross is suspended by a ring from a bar adorned with
laurel leaves on dark blue ribbon one and a half inches
wide.
   The cross is intended primarily for civilians; awards to
the fighting services are confined to actions for which
purely military honours are not normally granted. It is
awarded only for acts of the greatest heroism or of the most
conspicuous courage in circumstances of extreme danger.
From 1 April 1965, holders of the Cross have received a
tax-free annuity, which is now £1,300. The cross has twice
been awarded collectively rather than to an individual: to
Malta (1942) and the Royal Ulster Constabulary (1999).

The royal warrant which ordained that the grant of the Empire Gallantry Medal should cease authorised holders of that medal to return it to the Central Chancery of the Orders of Knighthood and to receive in exchange the George Cross. A similar provision applied to posthumous awards of the Empire Gallantry Medal made after the outbreak of war in 1939. In October 1971 all surviving holders of the Albert Medal and the Edward Medal exchanged those decorations for the George Cross.

SURVIVING RECIPIENTS OF THE GEORGE CROSS
as at 31 August 2001

If the recipient originally received the Empire Gallantry Medal (EGM), the Albert Medal (AM) or the Edward Medal (EM), this is indicated by the initials in parenthesis.

Archer, *Col.* B. S. T., GC, OBE, ERD, 1941
Bamford, J., GC, 1952
Beaton, J., GC, CVO, 1974
Bridge, *Lt.-Cdr.* J., GC, GM and Bar, 1944
Butson, *Lt.-Col.* A. R. C., GC, CD, MD (AM), 1948
Bywater, R. A. S., GC, GM, 1944
Errington, H., GC, 1941
Farrow, K., GC (AM), 1948
Flintoff, H. H., GC (EM), 1944
Gledhill, A. J., GC, 1967
Gregson, J. S., GC (AM), 1943
Hawkins, E., GC (AM), 1943
Johnson, *WO1 (SSM)* B., GC, 1990
Kinne, D. G., GC, 1954
Lowe, A. R., GC (AM), 1949
Lynch, J., GC, BEM (AM), 1948
Moore, R. V., GC, CBE, 1940
Naughton, F., GC (EGM), 1937
Pratt, M. K., GC, 1978
Purves, Mrs M., GC (AM), 1949
Raweng, Awang anak, GC, 1951
Riley, G., GC (AM), 1944
Rowlands, *Air Marshal* Sir John, GC, KBE, 1943
Sinclair, *Air Vice-Marshal* Sir Laurence, GC, KCB, CBE, DSO, 1941
Stevens, H. W., GC, 1958
Styles, *Lt.-Col.* S. G., GC, 1972
Walker, C., GC, 1972
Walker, C. H., GC (AM), 1942
Walton, E. W. K., GC (AM), DSO, 1948
Wilcox, C., GC (EM), 1949
Wiltshire, S. N., GC (EGM), 1930
Wooding, E. A., GC (AM), 1945

210

Chiefs of Clans and Names in Scotland

Only chiefs of whole Names or Clans are included, except certain special instances (marked *) who, though not chiefs of a whole name, were or are for some reason (e.g. the Macdonald forfeiture) independent. Under decision (*Campbell-Gray*, 1950) that a bearer of a 'double or triple-barrelled' surname cannot be held chief of a part of such, several others cannot be included in the list at present.

THE ROYAL HOUSE: HM The Queen

AGNEW: Sir Crispin Agnew of Lochnaw, Bt., QC, 6 Palmerston Road, Edinburgh EH9 1TN

ANSTRUTHER: Sir Ralph Anstruther of that Ilk, Bt., GCVO, MC, Balcaskie, Pittenweem, Fife KY10 2RD

ARBUTHNOTT: The Viscount of Arbuthnott, KT, CBE, DSC, Arbuthnott House, Laurencekirk, Kincardineshire AB30 1PA

BARCLAY: Peter C. Barclay of Towie Barclay and of that Ilk, 69 Oakwood Court, W14 8JF

BORTHWICK: The Lord Borthwick, Crookston, Heriot, Midlothian EH38 5YS

BOYD: The Lord Kilmarnock, 194 Regent's Park Road, London NW1 8XP

BOYLE: The Earl of Glasgow, Kelburn, Fairlie, Ayrshire KA29 0BE

BRODIE: Ninian Brodie of Brodie, Brodie Castle, Forres, Morayshire IV36 0TE

BRUCE: The Earl of Elgin and Kincardine, KT, Broomhall, Dunfermline, Fife KY11 3DU

BUCHAN: David S. Buchan of Auchmacoy, Auchmacoy House, Ellon, Aberdeenshire

BURNETT: J. C. A. Burnett of Leys, Crathes Castle, Banchory, Kincardineshire

CAMERON: Sir Donald Cameron of Lochiel, KT, CVO, TD, Achnacarry, Spean Bridge, Inverness-shire

CAMPBELL: The Duke of Argyll, Inveraray, Argyll PA32 8XF

CARMICHAEL: Richard J. Carmichael of Carmichael, Carmichael, Thankerton, Biggar, Lanarkshire

CARNEGIE: The Duke of Fife, Elsick House, Stonehaven, Kincardineshire AB3 2NT

CATHCART: The Earl Cathcart, 14 Smith Terrace, SW3 4DL

CHARTERIS: The Earl of Wemyss and March, KT, Gosford House, Longniddry, East Lothian EH32 0PX

CLAN CHATTAN: M. K. Mackintosh of Clan Chattan, Maxwell Park, Gwelo, Zimbabwe

CHISHOLM: Hamish Chisholm of Chisholm (*The Chisholm*), Elmpine, Beck Row, Bury St Edmunds, Suffolk

COCHRANE: The Earl of Dundonald, Lochnell Castle, Ledaig, Argyllshire

COLQUHOUN: Sir Ivar Colquhoun of Luss, Bt., Camstraddan, Luss, Dunbartonshire G83 8NX

CRANSTOUN: David A. S. Cranstoun of that Ilk, Corehouse, Lanark

CRICHTON: vacant

CUMMING: Sir William Cumming of Altyre, Bt., Altyre, Forres, Moray

DARROCH: Capt. Duncan Darroch of Gourock, The Red House, Branksome Park Road, Camberley, Surrey

DAVIDSON: Alister G. Davidson of Davidston, 21 Winscombe Street, Takapuna, Auckland, New Zealand

DEWAR: Michael Dewar of that Ilk and Vogrie, Rectory Farm House, Charleton Musgrove, Wincanton, Somerset BA9 8ET

DRUMMOND: The Earl of Perth, PC, Stobhall, Perth PH2 6DR

DUNBAR: Sir James Dunbar of Mochrum, Bt., 211 Gardenville Drive, Yorktown, Va 23693, USA

DUNDAS: David D. Dundas of Dundas, 8 Derna Road, Kenwyn 7700, South Africa

DURIE: Andrew Durie of Durie, CBE, Finnich Malise, Croftamie, Stirlingshire G63 0HA

ELIOTT: Mrs Margaret Eliott of Redheugh, Redheugh, Newcastleton, Roxburghshire

ERSKINE: The Earl of Mar and Kellie, Erskine House, Kirk Wynd, Alloa, Clackmannan FK10 4JF

FARQUHARSON: Capt. A. Farquharson of Invercauld, MC, Invercauld, Braemar, Aberdeenshire AB35 5TT

FERGUSSON: Sir Charles Fergusson of Kilkerran, Bt., Kilkerran, Maybole, Ayrshire

FORBES: The Lord Forbes, KBE, Balforbes, Alford, Aberdeenshire AB33 8DR

FORSYTH: Alistair Forsyth of that Ilk, Ethie Castle, by Arbroath, Angus DD11 5SP

FRASER: The Lady Saltoun, Inverey House, Braemar, Aberdeenshire AB35 5YB

* FRASER (OF LOVAT): The Lord Lovat, Beaufort Lodge, Beauly, Inverness-shire IV4 7AZ

GAYRE: R. Gayre of Gayre and Nigg, Minard Castle, Minard, Inverary, Argyll PA32 8YB

GORDON: The Marquess of Huntly, Aboyne Castle, Aberdeenshire AB34 5JP

GRAHAM: The Duke of Montrose, Buchanan Auld House, Drymen, Stirlingshire

GRANT: The Lord Strathspey, The School House, Lochbuie, Mull, Argyllshire PA62 6AA

GRIERSON: Sir Michael Grierson of Lag, Bt., 40C Palace Road, London SW2 3NJ

HAIG: The Earl Haig, OBE, Bemersyde, Melrose, Roxburghshire TD6 9DP

HALDANE: Martin Haldane of Gleneagles, Gleneagles, Auchterarder, Perthshire

HANNAY: Ramsey Hannay of Kirkdale and of that Ilk, Cardoness House, Gatehouse-of-Fleet, Kirkcudbrightshire

HAY: The Earl of Erroll, Woodbury Hall, Sandy, Beds

HENDERSON: John Henderson of Fordell, 7 Owen Street, Toowoomba, Queensland, Australia

HUNTER: Pauline Hunter of Hunterston, Plovers Ridge, Lon Cecrist, Treaddur Bay, Holyhead, Gwynedd

IRVINE OF DRUM: David C. Irvine of Drum, Holly Leaf Cottage, Inchmarlo, Banchory, Aberdeenshire AB31 4BR

JARDINE: Sir Alexander Jardine of Applegirth, Bt., Ash House, Thwaites, Millom, Cumbria LA18 5HY

JOHNSTONE: The Earl of Annandale and Hartfell, Raehills, Lockerbie, Dumfriesshire

KEITH: The Earl of Kintore, The Stables, Keith Hall, Inverurie, Aberdeenshire AB51 0LD

KENNEDY: The Marquess of Ailsa, Cassillis House, Maybole, Ayrshire

KERR: The Marquess of Lothian, KCVO, Ferniehurst Castle, Jedburgh, Roxburghshire TN8 6NX

KINCAID: Arabella Kincaid of Stoneyeld, Downton Kincaid, Ludlow, Shropshire

LAMONT: Peter N. Lamont of that Ilk, 209 Bungarribee Road, Blacktown, Australia

LEASK: Madam Leask of Leask, 1 Vincent Road, Sheringham, Norfolk

LENNOX: Edward J. H. Lennox of that Ilk, Tods Top Farm, Downton on the Rock, Ludlow, Shropshire

LESLIE: The Earl of Rothes, Tanglewood, West Tytherley, Salisbury, Wilts SP5 1LX

LINDSAY: The Earl of Crawford and Balcarres, KT, PC, Balcarres, Colinsburgh, Fife

LOCKHART: Angus H. Lockhart of the Lee, Newholme, Dunsyre, Lanark

LUMSDEN: Gillem Lumsden of that Ilk and Blanerne, Stapely Howe, Hoe Benham, Newbury, Berks

MACALESTER: William St J. S. McAlester of Loup and Kennox, Dun Skeig, 27 Durnham Road, Burton, Christchurch, Dorset BH23 7ND

McBAIN: J. H. McBain of McBain, 7025 North Finger Rock Place, Tucson, Arizona, USA

MACDONALD: The Lord Macdonald (*The Macdonald of Macdonald*), Kinloch Lodge, Sleat, Isle of Skye

*MACDONALD OF CLANRANALD: Ranald A. Macdonald of Clanranald, Mornish House, Killin, Perthshire FK21 8TX

*MACDONALD OF SLEAT (CLAN HUSTEAIN): Sir Ian Macdonald of Sleat, Bt., Thorpe Hall, Rudston, Driffield, N. Humberside YO25 0JE

*MACDONELL OF GLENGARRY: Ranald MacDonell of Glengarry, Elonbank, Castle Street, Fortrose, Ross-shire IV10 8TH

MACDOUGALL: vacant

MACDOWALL: Fergus D. H. Macdowall of Garthland, 16 Rowe Road, Ottawa, Ontario K29 2ZS

MACGREGOR: Brig. Sir Gregor MacGregor of MacGregor, Bt., Bannatyne, Newtyle, Blairgowrie, Perthshire PH12 8TR

MACINTYRE: James W. MacIntyre of Glenoe, 15301 Pine Orchard Drive, Apartment 3H, Silver Spring, Maryland, USA

MACKAY: The Lord Reay, 98 Oakley Street, London SW3

MACKENZIE: The Earl of Cromartie, Castle Leod, Strathpeffer, Ross-shire IV14 9AA

MACKINNON: Madam Anne Mackinnon of Mackinnon, 16 Purleigh Road, Bridgwater, Somerset

MACKINTOSH: *The Mackintosh of Mackintosh*, Moy Hall, Inverness IV13 7YQ

MACLAREN: Donald MacLaren of MacLaren and Achleskine, Achleskine, Kirkton, Balquhidder, Lochearnhead

MACLEAN: The Hon. Sir Lachlan Maclean of Duart, Bt., CVO, Arngask House, Glenfarg, Perthshire PH2 9QA

MACLENNAN: Ruaraidh MacLennan of MacLennan, Oldmill, Dores, Inverness-shire IV2 6R

MACLEOD: John MacLeod of MacLeod, Dunvegan Castle, Isle of Skye

MACMILLAN: George MacMillan of MacMillan, Finlaystone, Langbank, Renfrewshire

MACNAB: J. C. Macnab of Macnab (*The Macnab*), Leuchars Castle Farmhouse, Leuchars, Fife KY16 0EY

MACNAGHTEN: Sir Patrick Macnaghten of Macnaghten and Dundarave, Bt., Dundarave, Bushmills, Co. Antrim

MACNEACAIL: Iain Macneacail of Macneacail and Scorrybreac, 12 Fox Street, Ballina, NSW, Australia

MACNEIL OF BARRA: Ian R. Macneil of Barra (*The Macneil of Barra*), 95/6 Grange Loan, Edinburgh

MACPHERSON: The Hon. Sir William Macpherson of Cluny, TD, Newtown Castle, Blairgowrie, Perthshire

MACTAVISH: E. S. Dugald MacTavish of Dunardry, 2519 Vivaldi Lane, Four Seasons Estates, Gambrills, MD21 054, USA

MACTHOMAS: Andrew P. C. MacThomas of Finegand, c/o Roslin Cottage, Pitmedden, Aberdeenshire AB41 7NY

MAITLAND: The Earl of Lauderdale, 12 St Vincent Street, Edinburgh

MAKGILL: The Viscount of Oxfuird, Kenback, Stoke, Nr Andover, Hampshire SP11 0NP

MALCOLM (MACCALLUM): Robin N. L. Malcolm of Poltalloch, Duntrune Castle, Lochgilphead, Argyll

MAR: The Countess of Mar, St Michael's Farm, Great Witley, Worcs WR6 6JB

MARJORIBANKS: Andrew Marjoribanks of that Ilk, 10 Newark Street, Greenock

MATHESON: Maj. Sir Fergus Matheson of Matheson, Bt., Old Rectory, Hedenham, Bungay, Suffolk NR35 2LD

MENZIES: David R. Menzies of Menzies, Wester Auchnagallin Farmhouse, Braes of Castle Grant, Grantown on Spey PH26 3PL

MOFFAT: Madam Moffat of that Ilk, St Jasual, Bullocks Farm Lane, Wheeler End Common, High Wycombe

MONCREIFFE: Peregrine Moncreiffe of Moncreiffe, Easter Moncreiffe, Bride of Earn, Perthshire

MONTGOMERIE: The Earl of Eglinton and Winton, Balhomie, Cargill, Perth PH2 6DS

MORRISON: Dr Iain M. Morrison of Ruchdi, Magnolia Cottage, The Street, Walberton, Sussex

MUNRO: Hector W. Munro of Foulis, Foulis Castle, Evanton, Ross-shire IV16 9UX

MURRAY: The Duke of Atholl, Blair Castle, Blair Atholl, Perthshire

NESBITT (or NISBET): Mark Nesbitt of that Ilk, 1 Pier Head, Wapping High Street, London E12 1PN

NICOLSON: The Lord Carnock, 90 Whitehall Court, London SW1A 2EL

OGILVY: The Earl of Airlie, KT, GCVO, PC, Cortachy Castle, Kirriemuir, Angus

RAMSAY: The Earl of Dalhousie, Brechin Castle, Brechin, Angus DD7 6SH

RATTRAY: James S. Rattray of Rattray, Craighall, Rattray, Perthshire

RIDDELL; Sir John Riddell of Riddell, CB, CVO, Hepple, Morpeth, Northumberland

ROBERTSON: Alexander G. H. Robertson of Struan (*Struan-Robertson*), The Breach Farm, Goudhurst Road, Cranbrook, Kent

ROLLO: The Lord Rollo, Pitcairns, Dunning, Perthshire

ROSE: Miss Elizabeth Rose of Kilravock, Kilravock Castle, Croy, Inverness

ROSS: David C. Ross of that Ilk and Balnagowan, Shandwick, Perth Road, Stanley, Perthshire

RUTHVEN: The Earl of Gowrie, PC, 34 King Street, Covent Garden, London WC2

SCOTT: The Duke of Buccleuch and Queensberry, KT, VRD, Bowhill, Selkirk

SCRYMGEOUR: The Earl of Dundee, Birkhill, Cupar, Fife

SEMPILL: The Lord Sempill, 3 Vanburgh Place, Edinburgh, EH6 8AE

SHAW: John Shaw of Tordarroch, East Craig an Ron, 22 Academy Mead, Fortrose IV10 8TW

SINCLAIR: The Earl of Caithness, 137 Claxton Grove, London W6 8HB

SKENE: Danus Skene of Skene, Nether Pitlour, Strathmiglo, Fife

STIRLING: Fraser J. Stirling of Cader, 44A Oakley Street, London SW3 5HA

STRANGE: Maj. Timothy Strange of Balcaskie, Little Holme, Porton Road, Amesbury, Wilts

SUTHERLAND: The Countess of Sutherland, House of Tongue, Brora, Sutherland

SWINTON: John Swinton of that Ilk, 123 Superior Avenue SW, Calgary, Alberta, Canada

TROTTER: Alexander Trotter of Mortonhall, Charterhall, Duns, Berwickshire

URQUHART: Kenneth T. Urquhart of Urquhart, 507 Jefferson Park Avenue, Jefferson, New Orleans, La. 70121, USA

WALLACE: Ian F. Wallace of that Ilk, 5 Lennox Street, Edinburgh EH4 1QB

WEDDERBURN OF THAT ILK: The Master of Dundee, Birkhill, Cupar, Fife

WEMYSS: David Wemyss of that Ilk, Invermay, Forteviot, Perthshire

The Privy Council

The Sovereign in Council, or Privy Council, was the chief source of executive power until the system of Cabinet government developed in the 18th century. Now the Privy Council's main functions are to advise the Sovereign and to exercise its own statutory responsibilities independent of the Sovereign in Council (*see also* page 215).

Membership of the Privy Council is automatic upon appointment to certain government and judicial positions in the United Kingdom, e.g. Cabinet ministers must be Privy Counsellors and are sworn in on first assuming office. Membership is also accorded by The Queen to eminent people in the UK and independent countries of the Commonwealth of which Her Majesty is Queen, on the recommendation of the British Prime Minister. Membership of the Council is retained for life, except for very occasional removals.

The administrative functions of the Privy Council are carried out by the Privy Council Office (*see* page 354) under the direction of the President of the Council, who is always a member of the Cabinet.

President of the Council, The Rt. Hon. Robin Cook, MP
Clerk of the Council, A. Galloway

MEMBERS *as at 31 August 2001*

HRH The Duke of Edinburgh, 1951
HRH The Prince of Wales, 1977

Aberdare, Lord, 1974
Ackner, Lord, 1980
Airlie, Earl of, 1984
Aldington, Lord, 1954
Aldous, Sir William, 1995
Alebua, Ezekiel, 1988
Alison, Michael, 1981
Ampthill, Lord, 1995
Ancram, Michael, 1996
Anderson, Donald, 2000
Anthony, Douglas, 1971
Arbuthnot, James, 1998
Archer of Sandwell, Lord, 1977
Arden, Dame Mary, 2000
Armstrong, Hilary, 1999
Arnold, Sir John, 1979
Arthur, Hon. Owen, 1995
Ashdown of Norton-sub-Hamdon, Lord, 1989
Ashley of Stoke, Lord, 1979
Atkins, Sir Robert, 1995
Auld, Sir Robin, 1995

Baker of Dorking, Lord, 1984
Barber, Lord, 1963
Barnett, Lord, 1975
Beckett, Margaret, 1993
Beith, Alan, 1992
Beldam, Sir Roy, 1989
Belstead, Lord, 1983
Benn, Anthony, 1964
Bennett, Sir Frederic, 1985
Biffen, Lord, 1979
Bingham of Cornhill, Lord, 1986
Birch, William, 1992
Bisson, Sir Gordon, 1987
Blackstone, Baroness, 2001
Blair, Tony, 1994
Blaker, Lord, 1983
Blanchard, Peter, 1998
Blatch, Baroness, 1993
Blunkett, David, 1997
Boateng, Paul, 1999
Bolger, James, 1991
Booth, Albert, 1976
Boothroyd, Baroness, 1992
Boscawen, Hon. Robert, 1992
Bottomley, Virginia, 1992
Boyd, Colin, 2000
Boyson, Sir Rhodes, 1987
Bradley, Keith, 2001
Brathwaite, Sir Nicholas, 1991
Bridge of Harwich, Lord, 1975
Brightman, Lord, 1979
Brittan of Spennithorne, Lord, 1981
Brook, Sir Henry, 1996
Brooke of Sutton Mandeville, Lord, 1988
Brown, Gordon, 1996
Brown, Nicholas, 1997
Brown, Sir Simon, 1992
Brown, Sir Stephen, 1983
Browne-Wilkinson, Lord, 1983
Butler, Sir Adam, 1984
Butler-Sloss, Dame Elizabeth, 1988
Buxton, Sir Richard, 1997
Byers, Stephen, 1998
Caborn, Richard, 1999
Caithness, Earl of, 1990
Callaghan of Cardiff, Lord, 1964
Cameron of Lochbroom, Lord, 1984
Camoys, Lord, 1997
Campbell of Croy, Lord, 1970
Campbell, Walter Menzies, 1999
Campbell, Sir William, 1999
Canterbury, The Archbishop of, 1991
Carlisle of Bucklow, Lord, 1979
Carr of Hadley, Lord, 1963
Carrington of Upton, Lord, 1959
Carswell, Sir Robert, 1993
Carter, Lord, 1997
Casey, Sir Maurice, 1986
Castle of Blackburn, Baroness, 1964
Chadwick, Sir John, 1997
Chalfont, Lord, 1964
Chalker of Wallasey, Baroness, 1987
Chan, Sir Julius, 1981
Chataway, Sir Christopher, 1970
Clark of Windermere, Lord, 1997
Clark, Helen, 1990
Clark of Kempston, Lord, 1990

Clarke, Sir Anthony, 1998
Clarke, Charles, 2001
Clarke, Kenneth, 1984
Clarke, Thomas, 1997
Clinton-Davis, Lord, 1998
Clyde, Lord, 1996
Cockfield, Lord, 1982
Colman, Fraser, 1986
Compton, Sir John, 1983
Concannon, John, 1978
Cook, Robin, 1996
Cooke of Thorndon, Lord, 1977
Cooper, Sir Frank, 1983
Cope of Berkeley, Lord, 1988
Corfield, Sir Frederick, 1970
Coulsfield, Lord, 2000
Cowen, Sir Zelman, 1981
Cradock, Sir Percy, 1993
Cranborne, Viscount, 1994
Crawford and Balcarres, Earl of, 1972
Creech, *Hon.* Wyatt, 1999
Crickhowell, Lord, 1979
Croom-Johnson, Sir David, 1984
Cullen, *Hon.* Lord, 1997
Cunningham, Jack, 1993
Curry, David, 1996
Darling, Alistair, 1997
Davies, Denzil, 1978
Davies, Ronald, 1997
Davis, David, 1997
Davis, Terence, 1999
Davison, Sir Ronald, 1978
Dean of Harptree, Lord, 1991
Dean of Thornton-le-Fylde, Baroness, 1998
Deedes, Lord, 1962
Denham, John, 2000
Denham, Lord, 1981
Devonshire, Duke of, 1964
Diamond, Lord, 1965
Dillon, Sir Brian, 1982
Dixon, Lord, 1996
Dobson, Frank, 1997
Donaldson of Lymington, Lord, 1979
Dorrell, Stephen, 1994
Douglas, Sir William, 1977
du Cann, Sir Edward, 1964
Dunn, Sir Robin, 1980
Dyson, Sir John, 2001
East, Paul, 1998
Eden of Winton, Lord, 1972
Eggar, Timothy, 1995
Eichelaum, Sir Thomas, 1989
Elias, *Hon.* Dame, Sian, 1999
Emery, Sir Peter, 1993
Emslie, Lord, 1972
Erroll of Hale, Lord, 1960
Esquivel, Manuel, 1986
Evans, Sir Anthony, 1992
Eveleigh, Sir Edward, 1977
Farquharson, Sir Donald, 1989
Fellowes, Lord, 1990
Ferrers, Earl, 1982
Field, Frank, 1997
Floissac, Sir Vincent, 1992
Foot, Michael, 1994
Forsyth of Drumlean, The Lord, 1995
Forth, Eric, 1997

Foster, Derek, 1993
Fowler, Lord, 1979
Fox, Sir Marcus, 1995
Fox, Sir Michael, 1981
Fraser, Malcolm, 1976
Fraser of Carmyllie, Lord, 1989
Freeman, John, 1966
Freeman, Lord, 1993
Freeson, Reginald, 1976
Garel-Jones, Lord, 1992
Gault, Thomas, 1992
George, Bruce, 2000
George, Sir Edward, 1999
Georges, Telford, 1986
Gibbs, Sir Harry, 1972
Gibson, Sir Peter, 1993
Gibson, Sir Ralph, 1985
Gibson-Watt, Lord, 1974
Gilbert, Lord, 1978
Gilmour of Craigmillar, Lord, 1973
Glenamara, Lord, 1964
Glidewell, Sir Iain, 1985
Goff of Chieveley, Lord, 1982
Goodlad, Sir Alastair, 1992
Gorton, Sir John, 1968
Gowrie, Earl of, 1984
Graham, Sir Douglas, 1998
Graham of Edmonton, Lord, 1998
Gray of Contin, Lord, 1982
Griffiths, Lord, 1980
Gummer, John, 1985
Habgood, Rt. Revd Lord, 1983
Hague, William, 1995
Hailsham of St Marylebone, Lord, 1956
Hain, Peter, 2001
Hale, Dame Brenda, 1999
Hamilton, Sir Archie, 1991
Hanley, Sir Jeremy, 1994
Hardie, Lord, 1997
Hardie Boys, Sir Michael, 1989
Harman, Harriet, 1997
Harrison, Walter, 1977
Haselhurst, Sir Alan, 1999
Hattersley, Lord, 1975
Hayhoe, Lord, 1985
Hayman, Baroness, 2000
Healey, Lord, 1964
Heath, Sir Edward, 1955
Heathcoat-Amory, David, 1996
Henry, Sir Denis, 1993
Henry, John, 1996
Heseltine, Lord, 1979
Heseltine, Sir William, 1986
Hesketh, Lord, 1991
Hewitt, Patricia, 2001
Higgins, Lord, 1979
Hirst, Sir David, 1992
Hobhouse, Sir John, 1993
Hoffmann, Lord, 1992
Hogg, Hon. Douglas, 1992
Holderness, Lord, 1959
Hollis of Heigham, Baroness, 1999
Holme of Cheltenham, Lord, 2000
Hoon, Geoffrey, 1999
Hope of Craighead, Lord, 1989
Hordern, Sir Peter, 1993
Howard, Michael, 1990
Howe of Aberavon, Lord, 1972
Howell of Guildford, Lord, 1979
Hunt, Jonathan, 1989
Hunt of Wirral, Lord, 1990
Hurd of Westwell, Lord, 1982
Hutchison, Sir Michael, 1995
Hutton, Lord, 1988

Hutton, John, 2001
Ingraham, Hubert, 1993
Ingram, Adam, 1998
Irvine of Lairg, Lord, 1997
Jack, Michael, 1997
Janvrin, Sir Robin, 1998
Jauncey of Tullichettle, Lord, 1988
Jay of Paddington, Baroness, 1998
Jellicoe, Earl, 1963
Jenkin of Roding, Lord, 1973
Jenkins of Hillhead, Lord, 1964
Jones, Aubrey, 1955
Jones, Lord, 1999
Jopling, Lord, 1979
Jowell, Tessa, 1998
Judge, Sir Igor, 1996
Jugnauth, Sir Anerood, 1987
Kaufman, Gerald, 1978
Kay, Sir John, 2000
Keene, Sir David, 2000
Keith, Sir Kenneth, 1998
Keith of Kinkel, Lord, 1976
Kelly, Sir Basil, 1984
Kelvedon, Lord, 1980
Kenilorea, Sir Peter, 1979
Kennedy, Charles, 1999
Kennedy, Sir Paul, 1992
Kerr, Sir Michael, 1981
King of Bridgwater, Lord, 1979
Kingsdown, Lord, 1987
Kingsland, Lord, 1994
Kinnock, Neil, 1983
Kirkwood, Lord, 2000
Knight, Gregory, 1995
Lamont of Lerwick, Lord, 1986
Lane, Lord, 1975
Lang of Monkton, Lord, 1990
Lange, David, 1984
Latasi, Kamuta, 1996
Latham, Sir David, 2000
Lauti, Sir Toaripi, 1979
Laws, Sir John, 1999
Lawson of Blaby, Lord, 1981
Lawton, Sir Frederick, 1972
Leggatt, Sir Andrew, 1990
Leonard, Rt. Revd Graham, 1981
Liddell, Mrs Helen, 1998
Lilley, Peter, 1990
Lloyd of Berwick, Lord, 1984
Lloyd, Sir Peter, 1994
London, The Bishop of, 1995
Longmore, Sir Andrew, 2001
Louisy, Allan, 1981
Luce of Adur, Lord, 1986
Lyell, Sir Nicholas, 1990
Mabon, Dickson, 1977
McCartney, Ian, 1999
McCollum, Sir Liam, 1997
McCowan, Sir Anthony, 1989
MacDermott, Sir John, 1987
Macdonald of Tradeston, Lord, 1999
MacGregor of Pulham Market, Lord, 1985
MacIntyre, Duncan, 1980
Mackay, Andrew, 1998
McKay, Ian, 1992
Mackay of Clashfern, Lord, 1979
Mackay of Drumadoon, Lord, 1996
McKinnon, Donald, 1992
Maclean, David, 1995
Maclean, Lord, 2001
McLeish, Henry, 2000
Maclennan of Rogart, Lord, 1997
McMullin, Sir Duncan, 1980

Major, John, 1987
Mance, Sir Jonathan, 1999
Mandelson, Peter, 1998
Mantell, Sir Charles, 1997
Mara, Ratu Sir Kamisese, 1973
Marnoch, Lord, 2001
Marsh, Lord, 1966
Martin, Michael, 2000
Mason of Barnsley, Lord, 1968
Maude, Hon. Francis, 1992
Mawhinney, Sir Brian, 1994
May, Sir Anthony, 1998
Mayhew of Twysden, Lord, 1986
Meacher, Michael, 1997
Megarry, Sir Robert, 1978
Mellor, David, 1990
Merlyn-Rees, Lord, 1974
Michael, Alun, 1998
Milburn, Alan, 1998
Millan, Bruce, 1975
Millett, Lord, 1994
Milligan, Lord, 2000
Mitchell, Sir James, 1985
Molyneaux of Killead, Lord, 1983
Monro of Langholm, Lord, 1995
Moore, Michael, 1990
Moore of Lower Marsh, Lord, 1986
Moore of Wolvercote, Lord, 1977
Morgan, Rhodri, 2000
Morris, Charles, 1978
Morris, Estelle, 1999
Morris of Aberavon, Lord, 1970
Morris of Manchester, Lord, 1979
Morritt, Sir Robert, 1994
Mowlam, Marjorie, 1997
Moyle, Roland, 1978
Mummery, Sir John, 1996
Murphy, Paul, 1998
Murray, Hon. Lord, 1974
Murray, Sir Donald, 1989
Murray of Epping Forest, Lord, 1976
Murton of Lindisfarne, Lord, 1976
Mustill, Lord, 1985
Nairne, Sir Patrick, 1982
Namaliu, Sir Rabbie, 1989
Naseby, Lord, 1994
Needham, Sir Richard, 1994
Neill, Sir Brian, 1985
Newton of Braintree, Lord, 1988
Nicholls of Birkenhead, Lord, 1995
Nicholson, Sir Michael, 1995
Nolan, Lord, 1991
Nott, Sir John, 1979
Nourse, Sir Martin, 1985
Oakes, Gordon, 1979
O'Connor, Sir Patrick, 1980
O'Donnell, Turlough, 1979
O'Flynn, Francis, 1987
Ogilvy, Sir Angus, 1997
Oliver of Aylmerton, Lord, 1980
Onslow of Woking, Lord, 1988
Oppenheim-Barnes, Baroness, 1979
Orme, Lord, 1974
Osbourne, Lord, 2001
Otton, Sir Philip, 1995
Owen, Lord, 1976
Paeniu, Bikenibeu, 1991
Palliser, Sir Michael, 1983
Palmer, Sir Geoffrey, 1986
Parker, Sir Jonathan, 2000
Parker, Sir Roger, 1983
Parkinson, Lord, 1981
Patten, Christopher, 1989
Patten, Lord, 1990

Patterson, Percival, 1993
Pattie, Sir Geoffrey, 1987
Pendry, Lord, 2000
Penrose, Lord, 2000
Perth, Earl of, 1957
Peters, Winston, 1998
Peyton of Yeovil, Lord, 1970
Phillips of Worth Matravers, Lord, 1995
Pill, Sir Malcolm, 1995
Pindling, Sir Lynden, 1976
Portillo, Michael, 1992
Potter, Sir Mark, 1996
Prentice, Lord, 1966
Prescott, John, 1994
Price, George, 1982
Prior, Lord, 1970
Prosser, Lord, 2000
Puapua, Sir Tomasi, 1982
Purchas, Sir Francis, 1982
Pym, Lord, 1970
Quin, Ms Joyce, 1998
Radice, Lord, 1999
Raison, Sir Timothy, 1982
Ramsden, James, 1963
Rawlinson of Ewell, Lord, 1964
Raynsford, Nick, 2001
Redwood, John, 1993
Rees, Lord, 1983
Reid, John, 1998
Renton, Lord, 1962
Renton of Mount Harry, Lord, 1989
Richard, Lord, 1993
Richardson, Sir Ivor, 1978
Richardson of Duntisbourne, Lord, 1976
Rifkind, Sir Malcolm, 1986
Roberts of Conwy, Lord, 1991
Robertson of Port Ellen, Lord, 1997
Roch, Sir John, 1993
Rodger of Earlsferry, Lord, 1992
Rodgers of Quarry Bank, Lord, 1975
Rooker of Perry Barr, Lord, 1999
Rose, Sir Christopher, 1992
Ross, *Hon.* Lord, 1985
Rumbold, Dame Angela, 1991
Russell, Sir Patrick, 1987
Ryder of Wensum, Lord, 1990

Sainsbury, Sir Timothy, 1992
St John of Fawsley, Lord, 1979
Sandiford, Erskine, 1989
Saville of Newdigate, Lord, 1994
Scarman, Lord, 1973
Schiemann, Sir Konrad, 1995
Scott, Sir Nicholas, 1989
Scott, Sir Richard, 1991
Seaga, Edward, 1981
Sedley, Sir Stephen, 1999
Selkirk of Douglas, Lord, 1996
Shawcross, Lord, 1946
Shearer, Hugh, 1969
Sheldon, Lord, 1977
Shephard, Gillian, 1992
Shipley, Jennifer, 1998
Shore of Stepney, Lord, 1967
Short, Clare, 1997
Simmonds, Kennedy, 1984
Simon of Glaisdale, Lord, 1961
Sinclair, Ian, 1977
Slade, Sir Christopher, 1982
Slynn of Hadley, Lord, 1992
Smith, Andrew, 1997
Smith, Christopher, 1997
Smith, Sir Geoffrey Johnson, 1996
Somare, Sir Michael, 1977
Somers, Sir Edward, 1981
Spellar, John, 2001
Stanley, Sir John, 1984
Staughton, Sir Christopher, 1988
Steel of Aikwood, Lord, 1977
Stephen, Sir Ninian, 1979
Stewartby, Lord, 1989
Steyn, Lord, 1992
Stodart of Leaston, Lord, 1974
Strang, Gavin, 1997
Strathclyde, Lord, 1995
Straw, Jack, 1997
Stuart-Smith, Sir Murray, 1988
Sutherland, Lord, 2000
Symons of Vernham Dean, Baroness, 2001
Talboys, Sir Brian, 1977
Taylor, Ann, 1997
Tebbit, Lord, 1981
Templeman, Lord, 1978
Thatcher, Baroness, 1970

Thomas, Edmund, 1996
Thomas of Gwydir, Lord, 1964
Thomas, Sir Swinton, 1994
Thomson of Monifieth, Lord, 1966
Thorpe, Jeremy, 1967
Thorpe, Sir Matthew, 1995
Tipping, Andrew, 1998
Tizard, Robert, 1986
Trefgarne, Lord, 1989
Trimble, David, 1997
Trumpington, Baroness, 1992
Tuckey, Sir Simon, 1998
Ullswater, Viscount, 1994
Upton, Simon, 1999
Varley, Lord, 1974
Waddington, Lord, 1987
Waite, Sir John, 1993
Wakeham, Lord, 1983
Waldegrave of North Hill, Lord, 1990
Walker of Doncaster, Lord, 1979
Walker of Worcester, Lord, 1970
Walker, Sir Robert, 1997
Wallace, James, 2000
Waller, Sir Mark, 1996
Ward, Sir Alan, 1995
Watkins, Sir Tasker, 1980
Weatherill, Lord, 1980
Wheeler, Sir John, 1993
Widdecombe, Ann, 1997
Wigley, Dafydd, 1997
Wilberforce, Lord, 1964
Williams, Alan, 1977
Williams of Crosby, Baroness, 1974
Williams of Mostyn, Lord
Windlesham, Lord, 1973
Winti, Paias, 1987
Withers, Reginald, 1977
Woolfe, Sir David, 2000
Woodhouse, Sir Owen, 1974
Woolf, Lord, 1986
Wylie, *Hon.* Lord, 1970
York, The Archbishop of, 1991
Young, Baroness, 1981
Young, Sir George, 1993
Young of Graffham, Lord, 1984
Younger of Leckie, Viscount, 1979
Zacca, Edward, 1992

The Privy Council of Northern Ireland

The Privy Council of Northern Ireland had responsibilities in Northern Ireland similar to those of the Privy Council in Great Britain until the Northern Ireland Act 1974 instituted direct rule and a UK Cabinet minister became responsible for the functions previously exercised by the Northern Ireland government.

Membership of the Privy Council of Northern Ireland is retained for life. Since the Northern Ireland Constitution Act 1973 no further appointments

have been made. The postnominal initials PC (NI) are used to differentiate its members from those of the Privy Council.

MEMBERS *as at 31 August 2001*

Bailie, Robin, 1971
Bleakley, David, 1971

Craig, William, 1963
Dobson, John, 1969
Kelly, Sir Basil, 1969
Kirk, Herbert, 1962
Long, William, 1966
McConnell, The Lord, 1964
McIvor, Basil, 1971
Moyola, Lord, 1966
Neill, Sir Ivan, 1950
Porter, Sir Robert, 1969
Taylor, John, MP, 1970
West, Henry, 1960

Parliament

The United Kingdom constitution is not contained in any single document but has evolved in the course of time, formed partly by statute, partly by common law and partly by convention. A constitutional monarchy, the United Kingdom is governed by Ministers of the Crown in the name of the Sovereign, who is head both of the state and of the government.

The organs of government are the legislature (Parliament), the executive and the judiciary. The executive consists of HM Government (Cabinet and other Ministers), government departments, local authorities (*see* Local Government and Government Departments and Public Offices). The judiciary (*see* Law Courts and Offices) pronounces on the law, both written and unwritten, interprets statutes and is responsible for the enforcement of the law; the judiciary is independent of both the legislature and the executive.

THE MONARCHY

The Sovereign personifies the state and is, in law, an integral part of the legislature, head of the executive, head of the judiciary, commander-in-chief of all armed forces of the Crown and 'Supreme Governor' of the Church of England. The seat of the monarchy is in the United Kingdom. In the Channel Islands and the Isle of Man, which are Crown dependencies, the Sovereign is represented by a Lieutenant-Governor. In the member states of the Commonwealth of which the Sovereign is head of state, her representative is a Governor-General; in UK dependencies the Sovereign is usually represented by a Governor, who is responsible to the British Government.

Although in practice the powers of the monarchy are now very limited, restricted mainly to the advisory and ceremonial, there are important acts of government which require the participation of the Sovereign. These include summoning, proroguing and dissolving Parliament, giving royal assent to bills passed by Parliament, appointing important office-holders, e.g. government ministers, judges, bishops and governors, conferring peerages, knighthoods and other honours, and granting pardon to a person wrongly convicted of a crime. The Sovereign appoints the Prime Minister; by convention this office is held by the leader of the political party which enjoys, or can secure, a majority of votes in the House of Commons. In international affairs the Sovereign as head of state has the power to declare war and make peace, to recognise foreign states and governments, to conclude treaties and to annex or cede territory. However, as the Sovereign entrusts executive power to Ministers of the Crown and acts on the advice of her Ministers, which she cannot ignore, royal prerogative powers are in practice exercised by Ministers, who are responsible to Parliament.

Ministerial responsibility does not diminish the Sovereign's importance to the smooth working of government. She holds meetings of the Privy Council (*see* below), gives audiences to her Ministers and other officials at home and overseas, receives accounts of Cabinet decisions, reads dispatches and signs state papers; she must be informed and consulted on every aspect of national life; and she must show complete impartiality.

COUNSELLORS OF STATE

In the event of the Sovereign's absence abroad, it is necessary to appoint Counsellors of State under letters patent to carry out the chief functions of the Monarch, including the holding of Privy Councils and giving royal assent to acts passed by Parliament. The normal procedure is to appoint as Counsellors three or four members of the royal family among those remaining in the UK.

In the event of the Sovereign on accession being under the age of 18 years, or at any time unavailable or incapacitated by infirmity of mind or body for the performance of the royal functions, provision is made for a regency.

THE PRIVY COUNCIL

The Sovereign in Council, or Privy Council, was the chief source of executive power until the system of Cabinet government developed. Nowadays its main function is to advise the Sovereign to approve Orders in Council and to advise on the issue of royal proclamations. The Council's own statutory responsibilities (independent of the powers of the Sovereign in Council) include powers of supervision over the registering bodies for the medical and allied professions. A full Council is summoned only on the death of the Sovereign or when the Sovereign announces his or her intention to marry. (For full list of Counsellors, *see* The Privy Council section.)

There are a number of advisory Privy Council committees, whose meetings the Sovereign does not attend. Some are prerogative committees, such as those dealing with legislative matters submitted by the legislatures of the Channel Islands and the Isle of Man or with applications for charters of incorporation; and some are provided for by statute, e.g. those for the universities of Oxford and Cambridge and the Scottish universities.

The Judicial Committee of the Privy Council is the final court of appeal from courts of the UK dependencies, courts of independent Commonwealth countries which have retained the right of appeal, courts of the Channel Islands and the Isle of Man, some professional and disciplinary committees, and church sources. The Committee is composed of Privy Counsellors who hold, or have held, high judicial office, although usually only three or five hear each case.

Administrative work is carried out by the Privy Council Office under the direction of the President of the Council, a Cabinet Minister.

PARLIAMENT

Parliament is the supreme law-making authority and can legislate for the UK as a whole or for any parts of it separately (the Channel Islands and the Isle of Man are Crown dependencies and not part of the UK). The main functions of Parliament are to pass laws, to provide (by voting taxation) the means of carrying on the work of government and to scrutinise government policy and administration, particularly proposals for expenditure.

International treaties and agreements are by custom presented to Parliament before ratification.

Parliament emerged during the late 13th and early 14th centuries. The officers of the King's household and the King's judges were the nucleus of early Parliaments, joined by such ecclesiastical and lay magnates as the King might summon to form a prototype 'House of Lords', and occasionally by the knights of the shires, burgesses and proctors of the lower clergy. By the end of Edward III's reign a 'House of Commons' was beginning to appear; the first known Speaker was elected in 1377.

Parliamentary procedure is based on custom and precedent, partly formulated in the Standing Orders of both Houses of Parliament, and each House has the right to control its own internal proceedings and to commit for contempt. The system of debate in the two Houses is similar; when a motion has been moved, the Speaker proposes the question as the subject of a debate. Members speak from wherever they have been sitting. Questions are decided by a vote on a simple majority. Draft legislation is introduced, in either House, as a bill. Bills can be introduced by a Government Minister or a private Member, but in practice the majority of bills which become law are introduced by the Government. To become law, a bill must be passed by each House (for parliamentary stages, see Bill, page 220) and then sent to the Sovereign for the royal assent, after which it becomes an Act of Parliament.

Proceedings of both Houses are public, except on extremely rare occasions. The minutes (called Votes and Proceedings in the Commons, and Minutes of Proceedings in the Lords) and the speeches (*The Official Report of Parliamentary Debates*, Hansard) are published daily. Proceedings are also recorded for transmission on radio and television and stored in the Parliamentary Recording Unit before transfer to the National Sound Archive. Television cameras have been allowed into the House of Lords since 1985 and into the House of Commons since 1989; committee meetings may also be televised.

By the Parliament Act of 1911, the maximum duration of a Parliament is five years (if not previously dissolved), the term being reckoned from the date given on the writs for the new Parliament. The maximum life has been prolonged by legislation in such rare circumstances as the two world wars (31 January 1911 to 25 November 1918; 26 November 1935 to 15 June 1945). Dissolution and writs for a general election are ordered by the Sovereign on the advice of the Prime Minister. The life of a Parliament is divided into sessions, usually of one year in length, beginning and ending most often in October or November.

DEVOLUTION

The Scottish Parliament elected in 1999 has legislative power over all devolved matters, i.e. matters not reserved to Westminster or otherwise outside its powers. The National Assembly for Wales elected in May 1999 has power to make secondary legislation in the areas where executive functions have been transferred to it. The New Northern Ireland Assembly elected in June 1998 was due to be formally established by legislation in 1999. The Assembly started sitting in July 1998. Following suspension in February 2000, it resumed sitting on 5 June 2000. It will have legislative authority in the fields currently administered by the Northern Ireland departments.

THE HOUSE OF LORDS
London SW1A 0PW
Tel: 020-7219 3000
Information Office: 020-7219 3107
E-mail: hlinfo@parliament.uk
Web: www.parliament.uk

The members of the House of Lords consist of the Lords Spiritual and Temporal. The Lords Spiritual are the Archbishops of Canterbury and York, the Bishops of London, Durham and Winchester, and the 21 senior diocesan bishops of the Church of England. The Lords Temporal currently consist of, life peers created under the Life Peerages Act 1958, 92 hereditary peers elected under the House of Lords Act 1999, and those Lords of Appeal in Ordinary created life peers under the Appellate Jurisdiction Act 1876, as amended (i.e. Law Lords). The House of Lords Act provides for 92 hereditary peers (42 Conservative, 28 cross-bench, three Liberal Democrat, two Labour, the Earl Marshal, the Lord Great Chamberlain and 15 others) to remain in the House of Lords until longer-term reform of the House has been carried out; elections to select those who remain were held in October and November 1999.

Peers are disqualified from sitting in the House if they are:

– aliens, i.e. any peer who is not a British citizen, a Commonwealth citizen (under the British Nationality Act 1981) or a citizen of the Republic of Ireland
– under the age of 21
– undischarged bankrupts or, in Scotland, those whose estate is sequestered
– convicted of treason

Bishops retire from their sees on reaching the age of 70 and cease to be members of the house at that time.

Peers who do not wish to attend sittings of the House of Lords may apply for leave of absence for the duration of a Parliament.

Until the beginning of this century the House of Lords had considerable power, being able to veto any bill submitted to it by the House of Commons, but those powers were greatly reduced by the Parliament Acts of 1911 and 1949 (see page 221).

Combined with its legislative role, the House of Lords has judicial powers as the ultimate Court of Appeal for courts in Great Britain and Northern Ireland, except for criminal cases in Scotland. These powers are exercised by the Lord Chancellor and the Lords of Appeal in Ordinary (the Law Lords) (see Law Courts and Officers).

Members of the House of Lords are unpaid. However, they are entitled to reimbursement of travelling expenses on parliamentary business within the UK and certain other expenses incurred for the purpose of attendance at sittings of the House, within a maximum for each day of £84.00 for overnight subsistence, £37.00 for day subsistence and incidental travel, and £36.00 for secretarial costs, postage and certain additional expenses.

COMPOSITION *as at 25 July 2001*

Archbishops and Bishops, 26
Life peers under the Appellate Jurisdiction Act 1876, 28
Life peers under the Life Peerages Act 1958, 569 (113 women)
Peers under the House of Lords Act 1999, 92 (4 women)
Total 715
Of whom:
Peers on leave of absence from the House, 6

The Houses of Parliament: Lords, Commons 217

STATE OF PARTIES *as at 25 July 2001**
Conservative, 223
Labour, 195
Liberal Democrats, 61
Cross-bench, 173
Archbishops and Bishops, 26
Other, 31
Total: 709
* Excluding peers on leave of absence from the House

OFFICERS

The House is presided over by the Lord Chancellor, who is *ex officio* Speaker of the House. A panel of deputy Speakers is appointed by Royal Commission. The first deputy Speaker is the Chairman of Committees, appointed at the beginning of each session, a salaried officer of the House who takes the chair in committee of the whole House and in some select committees. He is assisted by a panel of deputy chairmen, headed by the salaried Principal Deputy Chairman of Committees, who is also chairman of the European Communities Committee of the House.

The permanent officers include the Clerk of the Parliaments, who is in charge of the administrative and procedural staff collectively known as the Parliament Office; the Gentleman Usher of the Black Rod, who is also Serjeant-at-Arms in attendance upon the Lord Chancellor and is responsible for security and for accommodation and services in the House of Lords; and the Yeoman Usher who is Deputy Serjeant-at-Arms and assists Black Rod in his duties.

Speaker (£173,875), The Lord Irvine of Lairg, PC, QC
Private Secretary, Ms E. Hutchinson
Chairman of Committees (£68,283), The Lord Tordoff
Principal Deputy Chairman of Committees (£63,626), The Lord Brabazon of Tara

DEPARTMENT OF THE CLERK OF THE PARLIAMENTS
Clerk of the Parliaments (£132,603), J. M. Davies
Clerk Assistant (£64,768– £100,292), P. D. G. Hayter
Reading Clerk and Principal Finance Officer (£64,768–£101,292), M. G. Pownall
Counsel to Chairman of Committees (£64,768–£104,292), Sir James Nursaw, KCB, QC: Dr C. S. Kerse; D. W. Saunders
Principal Clerks (£48,552–£77,869), J. A. Vallance White, CB (*Judicial Office and Fourth Clerk at the Table*); B. P. Keith (*Journals*); D. R. Beamish (*Committees and Overseas Office*); R. H. Walters, D.Phil. (*Clerk of Public Bills*)
Chief Clerks (£48,552–£77,869), E. C. Ollard, D.Phil. (*Establishment Officer*); T. V. Mohan (*Private Bills*); S. P. Burton (*Public Bills*); A. Makower; T. V. Mohan (*Select Committees*)
Senior Clerks (£32,931–£49,896), Miss M. B. Robertson (*seconded as Secretary to the Leader of the House and Chief Whip*); T. E. Radice; D. J. Batt; E. R. Morgan; J. A. Vaughan; Miss C. Salmon; Mr A. Rawsthorne; A. J. Mackersie; Miss K. Ball; P. F. Wogan
Clerks (£20,000–£27,500), R. A. McLean; C. S. Johnson; Miss C. K. S. K. Mawson; Mr T. Elias; Miss A. Murphy; R. R. Neal
Clerk of the Records (£48,552–£77,869), S. K. Ellison
Assistant Clerks of the Records (£32,931–£49,896), D. L. Prior; Dr C. Shenton; P. F. Grey
Librarian (£53,534–£87,598), D. L. Jones
Deputy Librarian (£37,293–£60,509), P. G. Davis, PH.D.
Senior Library Clerks (£32,931–£49,896), Miss I. L. Victory, Ph.D.; S. Kennedy; H. C. Deadman
Library Clerk (£20,000–£27,500), I. S. Cruse; A. J. C. Brocklehurst
Examiners of Petitions for Private Bills (£48,552–£77,869), T. V. Morgan; F. A. Cramer

Editor, Official Report (Hansard), (£48,552–£77,869), Mrs C. J. Bowden
Deputy Editor, Official Report (£37,293–£60,509), Miss J. A. Bradshaw

DEPARTMENT OF THE GENTLEMAN USHER OF THE BLACK ROD
Gentleman Usher of the Black Rod and Serjeant-at-Arms (£64,768–£104, 292), Lt.-Gen. Sir Michael Willcocks
Yeoman Usher of the Black Rod and Deputy Serjeant-at-Arms (£32,931–£49,896), Brig. H. D. C. Duncan, MBE

SELECT COMMITTEES

The main House of Lords select committees, as at June 2001, are as follows:
European Union – Chair, The Lord Brabazon of Tara; *Clerk*, T.V. Mohan
European Union – Sub-committees:
A (*Economic and Financial Affairs, Trade and External Relations*) – *Chair*, The Lord Grenfell; *Clerk*, Miss A. E. Murphy
B (*Energy, Industry and Transport*) – *Chair*, The Lord Brook of Alverthorpe; *Clerk*, P. F. M. Wogan
C (*Common Foreign and Security Policy*) – *Chair*, The Lord Jopling; *Clerk*, D. Batt
D (*Environment, Agriculture, Public Health and Consumer Protection*) – *Chair*, The Earl of Selborne; *Clerk*, T. E. Radice
E (*Law and Institutions*) – *Chair*, The Lord Scott of Foscote; *Clerk*, S. P. Burton
F (*Social Affairs, Education and Home Affairs*) – *Chair*, The Lord Harris of Richmond; *Clerk*, Dr C. S. Johnson
Science and Technology – Chair, Lord Oxburgh, FRCOG; *Clerk*, A. Makower
Delegated Powers and Deregulation – Chair, The Lord Alexander of Weedon, QC; *Clerk*, Dr F. P. Tudor
Constitution Committee – Chair, The Lord Norton of Louth; *Clerk*, S. P. Burton
Economic Affairs – Chair, The Lord Preston; *Clerk*, Ms C. Salmon
Animals in Scientific Procedures – Chair, The Lord Smith of Clifton; *Clerk*, Anon
Stem Cell Research – Chair, The Bishop of Oxford; *Clerk*, A. R. Rawsthorne

THE HOUSE OF COMMONS
London SW1A 0AA
Tel 020-7219 3000
Information Office: 020-7219 4272
Forthcoming business: 020-7219 5532
E-mail: hcinfo@parliament.uk
Web: www.parliament.uk

The members of the House of Commons are elected by universal adult suffrage. For electoral purposes, the United Kingdom is divided into constituencies, each of which returns one member to the House of Commons, the member being the candidate who obtains the largest number of votes cast in the constituency. To ensure equitable representation, the four Boundary Commissions keep constituency boundaries under review and recommend any redistribution of seats which may seem necessary because of population movements, etc. The number of seats was raised to 640 in 1945, reduced to 625 in 1948, and subsequently rose to 630 in 1955, 635 in 1970, 650 in 1983, 651 in 1992 and 659 in 1997. Of the present 659 seats, there are 529 for England, 40 for Wales, 72 for Scotland and 18 for Northern Ireland. The number of

Scottish MPs at Westminster is likely to be cut by about 12 by 2007.

An electoral reform commission headed by Lord Jenkins of Hillhead proposed in October 1998 that the 'first-past-the-post' system of electing members of the House of Commons should be replaced by an alternative vote top-up system, under which 80–85 per cent of MPs would be elected by an alternative vote method and the remaining 15–20 per cent by an open-list system of proportional representation. A referendum will be held on the proposals at an unspecified future date.

ELECTIONS

Elections are by secret ballot, each elector casting one vote; voting is not compulsory. For entitlement to vote in parliamentary elections, *see* Legal Notes section. When a seat becomes vacant between general elections, a by-election is held.

British subjects and citizens of the Irish Republic can stand for election as Members of Parliament (MPs) provided they are 21 or over and not subject to disqualification. Those disqualified from sitting in the House include:

- undischarged bankrupts
- people sentenced to more than one year's imprisonment
- members of the House of Lords (but hereditary peers not sitting in the Lords are eligible)
- holders of certain offices listed in the House of Commons Disqualification Act 1975, e.g. members of the judiciary, Civil Service, regular armed forces, police forces, some local government officers and some members of public corporations and government commissions

A candidate does not require any party backing but his or her nomination for election must be supported by the signatures of ten people registered in the constituency. A candidate must also deposit with the returning officer £500, which is forfeit if the candidate does not receive more than 5 per cent of the votes cast. All election expenses at a general election, except the candidate's personal expenses, are subject to a statutory limit of £5,483, plus 4.6 pence for each elector in a borough constituency or 6.2 pence for each elector in a county constituency.

See pages for an alphabetical list of MPs, pages for the results of the last general election, and page for the results of by-elections since the general election.

STATE OF PARTIES *as at 18 July 2001*

Conservative, 164 (14 women)
Labour, 411 (94 women)
Liberal Democrats, 52 (5 women)
Plaid Cymru, 4
Scottish Nationalist, 5 (1 woman)
Sinn Fein, 4 (1 woman)
Social Democratic Labour, 3
Ulster Democratic Unionist, 5 (1 woman)
Ulster Unionist, 6 (1 woman)
Independent (Dr Richard Taylor-Wyre Forest), 1
The Speaker and three Deputy Speakers, 4
Total, 659 (118 women)
Government majority, 167

BUSINESS

The week's business of the House is outlined each Thursday by the Leader of the House, after consultation between the Chief Government Whip and the Chief Opposition Whip. A quarter to a third of the time will be taken up by the Government's legislative programme and the rest by other business. As a rule, bills likely to raise political controversy are introduced in the Commons before going on to the Lords, and the Commons claims exclusive control in respect of national taxation and expenditure. Bills such as the Finance Bill, which imposes taxation, and the Consolidated Fund Bills, which authorise expenditure, must begin in the Commons. A bill of which the financial provisions are subsidiary may begin in the Lords; and the Commons may waive its rights in regard to Lords' amendments affecting finance.

The Commons has a public register of MPs' financial and certain other interests; this is published annually as a House of Commons paper. Members must also disclose any relevant financial interest or benefit in a matter before the House when taking part in a debate, in certain other proceedings of the House, or in consultations with other MPs, with Ministers or with civil servants.

MEMBERS' PAY AND ALLOWANCES

Since 1911 members of the House of Commons have received salary payments; facilities for free travel were introduced in 1924. Salary rates since 1911 are as follows:

1911	£400 p.a.	1984 Jan	£16,106 p.a.
1931	360	1985 Jan	16,904
1934	380	1986 Jan	17,702
1935	400	1987 Jan	18,500
1937	600	1988 Jan	22,548
1946	1,000	1989 Jan	24,107
1954	1,250	1990 Jan	26,701
1957	1,750	1991 Jan	28,970
1964	3,250	1992 Jan	30,854
1972 Jan	4,500	1994 Jan	31,687
1975 June	5,750	1995 Jan	33,189
1976 June	6,062	1996 Jan	34,085
1977 July	6,270	1996 July	43,000
1978 June	6,897	1997 April	43,860
1979 June	9,450	1998 April	45,066
1980 June	11,750	1999 April	47,008
1981 June	13,950	2000 April	48,371
1982 June	14,510	2001 April	49,822
1983 June	15,308		

In 1969 MPs were granted an allowance for secretarial and research expenses, now known as the Office Costs Allowance. From April 2001 the allowance is £52,760 a year.

Since 1972 MPs have been able to claim reimbursement for the additional cost of staying overnight away from their main residence while on parliamentary business; this is known as the Additional Costs Allowance and from April 2001 is £13,622 a year.

Since 1980 each MP in receipt of the Office Costs Allowance has been able to contribute sums to an approved pension scheme for the provision of a pension, or other benefits, for or in respect of persons whose salary is met by him/her from the Office Costs Allowance.

MEMBERS' PENSIONS

Pension arrangements for MPs were first introduced in 1964. The arrangements currently provide a pension of one-fiftieth of salary for each year of pensionable service with a maximum of two-thirds of salary at age 65. Pension is payable normally at age 65, for men and women, or on later retirement. Pensions may be paid earlier, e.g. on retirement due to ill health or at age 60 after 20 years' service. The widow/widower of a former MP receives a pension of five-eighths of the late MP's pension. Pensions are index-linked. Members currently contribute six per cent of salary to the pension fund; there is an Exchequer contribution, currently slightly more than the amount contributed by MPs.

The House of Commons Members' Fund provides for annual or lump sum grants to ex-MPs, their widows or widowers, and children whose incomes are below certain limits or who are experiencing severe hardship. Members contribute £24 a year and the Exchequer £215,000 a year to the fund.

OFFICERS AND OFFICIALS

The House of Commons is presided over by the Speaker, who has considerable powers to maintain order in the House. A deputy Speaker, called the Chairman of Ways and Means, and two Deputy Chairmen may preside over sittings of the House of Commons; they are elected by the House, and, like the Speaker, neither speak nor vote other than in their official capacity.

The staff of the House are employed by a Commission chaired by the Speaker. The heads of the six House of Commons departments are permanent officers of the House, not MPs. The Clerk of the House is the principal adviser to the Speaker on the privileges and procedures of the House, the conduct of the business of the House, and committees. The Serjeant-at-Arms is responsible for security, ceremonial, and for accommodation in the Commons part of the Palace of Westminster.

Speaker (£114,543), The Rt. Hon. Michael J. Martin, MP (Glasgow Springburn)
Chairman of Ways and Means (£82,697), Sir Alan Haselhurst, MP (Saffron Walden)
First Deputy Chairman of Ways and Means (£78,539), Sylvia Heal, MP
Second Deputy Chairman of Ways and Means (£78,539), Sir Michael Lord, MP (Suffolk Central and Ipswich North)

OFFICES OF THE SPEAKER AND CHAIRMAN OF WAYS AND MEANS

Speaker's Secretary (£45,810–£73,470), N. Bevan, CB
Chaplain to the Speaker, Revd Canon R. Wright
Secretary to the Chairman of Ways and Means (£30,967–£46,848 –£45,795), M. Hennessy

DEPARTMENT OF THE CLERK OF THE HOUSE

Clerk of the House of Commons (£123,787), W. R. McKay, CB
Clerk Assistant (£70,905–£110,428), R. B. Sands
   Clerk of Committees (£70,905–£11,428), G. Cubie
Clerk of Legislation (£70,905–£110,428), D. G. Millar
Principal Clerks (£64,768–£104,292)
   Journals, A. J. Hastings, CB
   Table Office, Ms H. E. Irwin
Principal Clerks (£53,534–£87,598)
   Overseas Office, R. W. G. Wilson
   Bills, Ms H. E. Irwin
   Select Committees, Mrs J. Sharpe; D. L. Natzler; R. J. Rogers
   Delegated Legislation, W. A. Proctor
Deputy Principal Clerks (£48,552–£77,869), Ms A. Barry; C. R. M. Ward, ph.D.; D. W. N. Doig; A. Sandall; A. R. Kennon; L. C. Laurence Smyth; S. J. Patrick; D. J. Gerhold; C. J. Poyser; D. F. Harrison; S. J. Priestley; A. H. Doherty; P. A. Evans; R. I. S. Phillips; R. G. James, ph.D.; Ms P. A. Helme; D. R. Lloyd; J. S. Benger, D.Phil.; N. P. Walker; M. D. Hamlyn; Mrs E. J. Flood; A. Y. A. Azad; C. G. Lee; C.D. Stanton
Senior Clerks (£31,710–£47,972), K. J. Brown, OBE, M. Clark; T. Goldsmith; D. H. Griffiths (*acting*) M. Hennessy; Mrs J. N. St J. Mulley; T. W. P. Healey; J. D. Whatley; Mrs C. Oxborough; S. T. Fiander (*acting*); Ms R. Melling, CBE (*acting*)

Examiners of Petitions for Private Bills, F. A. Cranmer; Dr F. P. Tudor
Registrar of Members' Interests (£53,534–£87,598), Ms A. Barry
Taxing Officer, F. A. Cranmer

VOTE OFFICE

Deliverer of the Vote (£48,552–£77,869), J. F. Collins
Deputy Deliverers of the Vote (£31,710–£58,164), O. B. T. Sweeney (*Parliamentary*); F. W. Hallett (*Production*); A. Powell (*Development*)

SPEAKER'S COUNSEL

Speaker's Counsel and Head of Legal Services Office (£64,768–£104,292), J. E. G. Vaux
Speaker's Counsel (European legislation) (£64,768–£104,292), M. Carpenter
Assistant Counsel (£48,552–£77,869), A. Akbar; P. Brooksbank

DEPARTMENT OF THE SERJEANT-AT-ARMS

Serjeant-at-Arms (£64,768–£104,292), M. J. A. Cummins
Deputy Serjeant-at-Arms (£48,552–£77,869), R. M. Morton
Assistant Serjeants-at-Arms (£35,914–£58,164), P. A. J. Wright; J. M. Robertson; M. Harvey

DEPARTMENT OF THE LIBRARY

Librarian (£64,768–£104,292), Miss P. Baines
Directors (£48,552–£77,869), K. G. Cuninghame; Mrs J. Wainwright; R. Clements; Mrs C. Gillie; R; Miss E. M. McInnes.
Heads of Sections (£35,914–£58,164), C. Pond, ph.D.; Mrs C. Andrews; Mrs J. Lourie; C. Barclay; Mrs C. Gillie; RG. Allen; R. Cracknell; E. Wood; P. Richards, ph.D.
Senior Library Clerks (£31,710–£47,972), Ms F. Poole; T. Edmonds; Ms O. Gay; Dr D. Gore; B. Winetrobe; Miss M. Baber; Ms A. Walker; Mrs H. Holden; Mrs P. Carling; S. Wise; Mrs J. Hough; Mrs K. Greener; Ms P. Strickland; Miss V. Miller; M. P. Hillyard; Ms J. Roll; Ms W. Wilson; S. Wise; E. Wood; P. Bowers, ph.D.; A. Seely; G. Danby, ph.D.; B. C. Morgan; Miss L. Conway; C. Blair, ph.D.; G. Vidler; C. Sear; Ms F. Whittle; M. Oakes (*period*); Ms G. Garton Grimwood; Ms S. Broadbridge (*period*)

DEPARTMENT OF FINANCE AND ADMINISTRATION

Director of Finance and Administration (£64,768–£104,292), A. J. Walker
Director of Operations (£48,552–£77,869), A. A. Cameron
Director of Personnel Policy (£48,552–£77,869) Ms S. Craig
Director of Finance Policy (£48,552–£77,869), M. Barram
Director of Internal Review Services (£35,914–£58,164), R. Russell

DEPARTMENT OF THE OFFICIAL REPORT

Editor (£53,534–£87,598), I. Church
Deputy Editors (£44,038–£69,178), W. G. Garland; Miss L. Sutherland; Ms C. Fogarty

REFRESHMENT DEPARTMENT

Director of Catering Services (£53,534–£87,598), Mrs S. Harrison
Catering Operations Manager (Outbuildings (£31,710–£47,972), Ms Della Herd
Executive Chef (£31,710–£47,972), D. Dorricott
Financial Controller (£31,710–£47,972), Mr Robert Gibbs

SELECT COMMITTEES

The more important committees, as at July 2001, are:

DEPARTMENTAL COMMITTEES

Accomodation and Works Chair, Derek Conway, MP
Administration Chair, Mrs Marion Roe
Culture, Media and Sport Chair, Rt. Hon. Gerald Kaufman, MP; *Clerks,* C. G. Lee; R. Cooke
Defence Chair, Rt. Hon. Bruce George, MP; *Clerks,* P. A. Evans; Mrs C. Oxborough
Education and Skills Chair, Barry Sheerman,MP; *Clerks,* L. C. Laurence-Smyth; T. P.W. Healey
Environment, Food and Rural Affairs Chair, Rt. Hon. David Curry, MP; *Clerks,* Dr. D. F. Harrison; H. Yardley; G. Devine
Foreign Affairs Chair, Rt. Hon. Donald Anderson, MP; *Clerks,* E. P. Silk; Ms T. Brufal
Health Chair, David Hinchliffe, MP; *Clerks,* J. S. Benger, D.Phil.; T. Goldsmith
Home Affairs Chair, Chris Mullin, MP; *Clerks,* A. R. Kennon; M. P. Atkins
International Development Chair, Tony Baldry, MP; *Clerks,* A. Y. A. Azad; Ms J. Hughes
Northern Ireland – Chair, Michael Mates, MP; *Clerk,* C. R. M. Ward
Scottish Affairs – Chair, to be announced; *Clerk,* J. D. Whatley
Trade and Industry – Chair, Martin O'Neill, MP; *Clerks,* D. L. Natzler; Ms C. Littleboy
Transport, Local Government and the Regions Chair, Hon. Mrs Gwyneth Dunwoody, MP
Treasury – Chair, Rt. Hon. John McFall, MP; *Clerks,* S. J. Patrick; M. Egan
Treasury sub-committee: Chair, Michael Fallon, MP; *Clerk,* M. Egan
Urban Affairs sub committee: Chair, Andrew Bennett, MP
Welsh Affairs – Chair, Martyn Jones, MP; *Clerk,* Ms P. A. Helme
Work and Pensions – Chair, Archy Kirkwood, MP

NON-DEPARTMENTAL COMMITTEES

Selection – Chair, John McWilliam, MP
Statutory Instruments – Chair, David Tredinnick, MP
Deregulation and Regulatory Reform – Chair, Peter Pike, MP; *Clerk,* Mrs S. Craig
Environmental Audit – Chair, John Horam, MP; *Clerk,* F. J. Reid
European Scrutiny – Chair, James Hood, MP; *Clerks,* Mrs E. J. Flood; Mrs S. Craig
Human Rights (Joint Committee) – Chair, Jean Carston
Modernisation of the House of Commons – Chair, Rt. Hon. Robin Cook, MP; *Clerks,* C. B. Winnifrith, CB; A. Sandall
Procedure – Chair, Nicholas Winterton, MP; *Clerks,* Dr R. G. James; Ms S. McGlashan
Public Accounts – Chair, Rt. Hon. David Davis, MP; *Clerk,* K. J. Brown, OBE
Public Administration – Chair, Tony Wright, MP; *Clerk,* Ms A. Barry

PARLIAMENTARY INFORMATION

The following is a short glossary of aspects of the work of Parliament. Unless otherwise stated, references are to House of Commons procedures.

BILL – Proposed legislation is termed a bill. The stages of a public bill (for private bills, *see* page 221) in the House of Commons are as follows:
First Reading: This stage nowadays merely constitutes an order to have the bill printed
Second Reading: The debate on the principles of the bill

Committee Stage: The detailed examination of a bill, clause by clause. In most cases this takes place in a standing committee, or the whole House may act as a committee. A special standing committee may take evidence before embarking on detailed scrutiny of the bill. Very rarely, a bill may be examined by a select committee (*see* page)
Report Stage: Detailed review of a bill as amended in committee
Third Reading: Final debate on a bill

Public bills go through the same stages in the House of Lords, except that in almost all cases the committee stage is taken in committee of the whole House.

A bill may start in either House, and has to pass through both Houses to become law. Both Houses have to agree the same text of a bill, so that the amendments made by the second House are then considered in the originating House, and if not agreed, sent back or themselves amended, until agreement is reached.

CHILTERN HUNDREDS – A nominal office of profit under the Crown, the acceptance of which requires an MP to vacate his/her seat. The Manor of Northstead is similar. These are the only means by which an MP may resign.

CONSOLIDATED FUND BILL – A bill to authorise issue of money to maintain Government services. The bill is dealt with without debate.

EARLY DAY MOTION – A motion put on the notice paper by an MP without in general the real prospect of its being debated. Such motions are expressions of back-bench opinion.

FATHER OF THE HOUSE – The Member whose continuous service in the House of Commons is the longest. The present Father of the House is the Rt. Hon. Tam Dalyell.

HOURS OF MEETING – The House of Commons normally meets Monday, Tuesday and Wednesday at 2.30 p.m., Thursdays at 11.30 a.m. and some Fridays at 9.30 a.m. There are ten Fridays without sittings in each session. (*See also* Westminster Hall Sittings, below.) The House of Lords normally meets at 2.30 p.m. Monday to Wednesday and at 3 p.m. on Thursday. In the latter part of the session, the House of Lords sometimes sits on Fridays at 11 a.m.

LEADER OF THE OPPOSITION – In 1937 the office of Leader of the Opposition was recognised and a salary was assigned to the post. Since April 2001 this has been £110,481 (including parliamentary salary of £49,822). The present Leader of the Opposition is Iain Duncan Smith.

THE LORD CHANCELLOR – The Lord High Chancellor of Great Britain is (*ex officio*) the Speaker of the House of Lords. Unlike the Speaker of the House of Commons, he is a member of the Government, takes part in debates and votes in divisions. He has none of the powers to maintain order that the Speaker in the Commons has, these powers being exercised in the Lords by the House as a whole. The Lord Chancellor sits in the Lords on one of the Woolsacks, couches covered with red cloth and stuffed with wool. If he wishes to address the House in any way except formally as Speaker, he leaves the Woolsack.

NORTHERN IRELAND GRAND COMMITTEE – The Northern Ireland Grand Committee consists of all MPs representing constituencies in Northern Ireland, together with not more than 25 other MPs nominated by the Committee of Selection. The business of the committee includes questions, short debates, ministerial statements, bills, legislative proposals and other matters relating exclusively to Northern Ireland, and delegated legislation. The Northern Ireland Affairs Committee is one of the departmental select committees, empowered to examine the expenditure, administration and policy of the Northern Ireland Office and the administration and expenditure of the Crown Solicitor's Office.

OPPOSITION DAY – A day on which the topic for debate is chosen by the Opposition. There are 20 such days in a normal session. On 17 days, subjects are chosen by the Leader of the Opposition; on the remaining three days by the leader of the next largest opposition party.

PARLIAMENT ACTS 1911 AND 1949 – Under these Acts, bills may become law without the consent of the Lords, though the House of Lords has the power to delay a public bill for 13 months from its first second reading in the House of Commons.

PRIME MINISTER'S QUESTIONS – The Prime Minister answers questions from 3.00 to 3.30 p.m. on Wednesdays.

PRIVATE BILL – A bill promoted by a body or an individual to give powers additional to, or in conflict with, the general law, and to which a special procedure applies to enable people affected to object.

PRIVATE MEMBER'S BILL – A public bill promoted by a Member who is not a member of the Government.

PRIVATE NOTICE QUESTION – A question adjudged of urgent importance on submission to the Speaker (in the Lords, the Leader of the House), answered at the end of oral questions, usually at 3.30 p.m.

PRIVILEGE – The following are covered by the privilege of Parliament:

(i) freedom from interference in going to, attending at, and going from, Parliament
(ii) freedom of speech in parliamentary proceedings
(iii) the printing and publishing of anything relating to the proceedings of the two Houses is subject to privilege
(iv) each House is the guardian of its dignity and may punish any insult to the House as a whole

QUESTION TIME – Oral questions are answered by Ministers in the Commons from 2.30 to 3.30 p.m. Monday to Wednesday and 11.30 a.m. to 12.30 p.m. on Thursdays. Questions are also taken at the start of the Lords sittings, with a daily limit of four oral questions.

ROYAL ASSENT – The royal assent is signified by letters patent to such bills and measures as have passed both Houses of Parliament (or bills which have been passed under the Parliament Acts 1911 and 1949). The Sovereign has not given royal assent in person since 1854. On occasion, for instance in the prorogation of Parliament, royal assent may be pronounced to the two Houses by Lords Commissioners. More usually royal assent is notified to each House sitting separately in accordance with the Royal Assent Act 1967. The old French formulae for royal assent are then endorsed on the acts by the Clerk of the Parliaments.

The power to withhold assent resides with the Sovereign but has not been exercised in the UK since 1707.

SELECT COMMITTEES – Consisting usually of ten to fifteen members of all parties, select committees are a means used by both Houses in order to investigate certain matters.

Most select committees in the House of Commons are tied to departments: each committee investigates subjects within a government department's remit. There are other select committees dealing with public accounts (i.e. the spending by the Government of money voted by Parliament) and European legislation, and also domestic committees dealing, for example, with privilege and procedure. Major select committees usually take evidence in public; their evidence and reports are published by The Stationery Office. House of Commons select committees are reconstituted after a general election. For main committees, see page 220.

The principal select committee in the House of Lords is that on the European Communities, which has, at present, six sub-committees dealing with all areas of Community policy. The House of Lords also has a select committee on science and technology, which appoints sub-committees to deal with specific subjects, and a select committee on delegated powers and deregulation. For committees, see page 217. In addition, ad hoc select committees have been set up from time to time to investigate specific subjects. There are also some joint committees of the two Houses, e.g. the committees on statutory instruments and on parliamentary privilege.

THE SPEAKER – The Speaker of the House of Commons is the spokesman and chairman of the Chamber. He or she is elected by the House at the beginning of each Parliament or when the previous Speaker retires or dies. The Speaker neither speaks in debates nor votes in divisions except when the voting is equal.

VACANT SEATS – When a vacancy occurs in the House of Commons during a session of Parliament, the writ for the by-election is moved by a Whip of the party to which the member whose seat has been vacated belonged. If the House is in recess, the Speaker can issue a warrant for a writ, should two members certify to him that a seat is vacant.

The Welsh Affairs Committee, one of the departmental select committees, was empowered to examine the expenditure, administration and policy of the Welsh Office. Following devolution, the role of the select committee has been questioned. If it continues, it will be concerned with the role and responsibilities of the relevant Secretary of State and on occasion the policy of the UK departments as it affects Wales.

WESTMINSTER HALL SITTINGS – Following a report by the Modernisation of the House of Commons Select Committee, the Commons decided in May 1999 to set up a second debating forum. It is known as 'Westminster Hall' and sittings are in the Grand Committee Room on Tuesdays and Wednesdays from 9.30 a.m. to 2 p.m. and Thursdays from 2.30 p.m. for up to three hours. Sittings will be open to the public at the times indicated.

WHIPS – In order to secure the attendance of Members of a particular party in Parliament, particularly on the occasion of an important vote, Whips (originally known as 'Whippers-in') are appointed. The written appeal or circular letter issued by them is also known as a 'whip', its urgency being denoted by the number of times it is underlined. Failure to respond to a three-line whip is tantamount in the Commons to secession (at any rate temporarily) from the party. Whips are provided with office accommodation in both Houses, and Government and some Opposition Whips receive salaries from public funds.

PARLIAMENTARY EDUCATION UNIT – Norman Shaw
Building (North), London SW1A 2TT.
Tel: 020-7219 2105
E-mail: edunit@parliament.uk
Web: www.explore-parliament.uk

GOVERNMENT OFFICE

The Government is the body of Ministers responsible for the administration of national affairs, determining policy and introducing into Parliament any legislation necessary to give effect to government policy. The majority of Ministers are members of the House of Commons but members of the House of Lords or of neither House may also hold ministerial responsibility. The Lord Chancellor is always a member of the House of Lords. The Prime Minister is, by current convention, always a member of the House of Commons.

THE PRIME MINISTER

The office of Prime Minister, which had been in existence for nearly 200 years, was officially recognised in 1905 and its holder was granted a place in the table of precedence. The Prime Minister, by tradition also First Lord of the Treasury and Minister for the Civil Service, is appointed by the Sovereign and is usually the leader of the party which enjoys, or can secure, a majority in the House of Commons. Other Ministers are appointed by the Sovereign on the recommendation of the Prime Minister, who also allocates functions amongst Ministers and has the power to obtain their resignation or dismissal individually.

The Prime Minister informs the Sovereign of state and political matters, advises on the dissolution of Parliament, and makes recommendations for important Crown appointments, the award of honours, etc.

As the chairman of Cabinet meetings and leader of a political party, the Prime Minister is responsible for translating party policy into government activity. As leader of the Government, the Prime Minister is responsible to Parliament and to the electorate for the policies and their implementation.

The Prime Minister also represents the nation in international affairs, e.g. summit conferences.

THE CABINET

The Cabinet developed during the 18th century as an inner committee of the Privy Council, which was the chief source of executive power until that time. The Cabinet is composed of about 20 Ministers chosen by the Prime Minister, usually the heads of government departments (generally known as Secretaries of State unless they have a special title, e.g. Chancellor of the Exchequer), the leaders of the two Houses of Parliament, and the holders of various traditional offices.

The Cabinet's functions are the final determination of policy, control of government and co-ordination of government departments. The exercise of its functions is dependent upon enjoying majority support in the House of Commons. Cabinet meetings are held in private, taking place once or twice a week during parliamentary sittings and less often during a recess. Proceedings are confidential, the members being bound by their oath as Privy Counsellors not to disclose information about the proceedings.

The convention of collective responsibility means that the Cabinet acts unanimously even when Cabinet Ministers do not all agree on a subject. The policies of departmental Ministers must be consistent with the policies of the Government as a whole, and once the Government's policy has been decided, each Minister is expected to support it or resign.

The convention of ministerial responsibility holds a Minister, as the political head of his or her department, accountable to Parliament for the department's work.

Departmental Ministers usually decide all matters within their responsibility, although on matters of political importance they normally consult their colleagues collectively. A decision by a departmental Minister is binding on the Government as a whole.

POLITICAL PARTIES

Before the reign of William and Mary the principal officers of state were chosen by and were responsible to the Sovereign alone and not to Parliament or the nation at large. Such officers acted sometimes in concert with one another but more often independently, and the fall of one did not, of necessity, involve that of others, although all were liable to be dismissed at any moment.

In 1693 the Earl of Sunderland recommended to William III the advisability of selecting a ministry from the political party which enjoyed a majority in the House of Commons and the first united ministry was drawn in 1696 from the Whigs, to which party the King owed his throne. This group became known as the Junto and was regarded with suspicion as a novelty in the political life of the nation, being a small section meeting in secret apart from the main body of Ministers. It may be regarded as the forerunner of the Cabinet and in course of time it led to the establishment of the principle of joint responsibility of Ministers, so that internal disagreement caused a change of personnel or resignation of the whole body of Ministers.

The accession of George I, who was unfamiliar with the English language, led to a disinclination on the part of the Sovereign to preside at meetings of his Ministers and caused the appearance of a Prime Minister, a position first acquired by Robert Walpole in 1721 and retained by him without interruption for 20 years and 326 days.

DEVELOPMENT OF PARTIES

In 1828 the Whigs became known as Liberals, a name originally given to it by its opponents to imply laxity of principles, but gradually accepted by the party to indicate its claim to be pioneers and champions of political reform and progressive legislation. In 1861 a Liberal Registration Association was founded and Liberal Associations became widespread. In 1877 a National Liberal Federation was formed, with headquarters in London. The Liberal Party was in power for long periods during the second half of the 19th-century and for several years during the first quarter of the 20th-century, but after a split in the party the numbers elected were small from 1931. In 1988, a majority of the Liberals agreed on a merger with the Social Democratic Party under the title Social and Liberal Democrats; since 1989 they have been known as Liberal Democrats. A minority continue separately as the Liberal Party.

Soon after the change from Whig to Liberal the Tory Party became known as Conservative, a name believed to have been invented by John Wilson Croker in 1830 and to have been generally adopted about the time of the passing of the Reform Act of 1832 to indicate that the preservation of national institutions was the leading principle of the party. After the Home Rule crisis of 1886 the dissentient Liberals entered into a compact with the Conservatives, under which the latter undertook not to contest their seats, but a separate Liberal Unionist organisation was maintained until 1912, when it was united with the Conservatives.

Labour candidates for Parliament made their first appearance at the general election of 1892, when there were 27 standing as Labour or Liberal-Labour. In 1900 the Labour Representation Committee was set up in order to establish a distinct Labour group in Parliament, with its own whips, its own policy, and a readiness to co-operate with any party which might be engaged in promoting legislation in the direct interest of labour. In 1906 the LRC became known as the Labour Party.

The Council for Social Democracy was announced by four former Labour Cabinet Ministers in January 1981 and in March 1981 the Social Democratic Party was launched. Later that year the SDP and the Liberal Party formed an electoral alliance. In 1988 a majority of the SDP agreed on a merger with the Liberal Party but a minority continued as a separate party under the SDP title. In 1990 it was decided to wind up the party organisation and its three sitting MPs were known as independent social democrats. None were returned at the 1992 general election.

Plaid Cymru was founded in 1926 to provide an independent political voice for Wales and to campaign for self-government in Wales.

The Scottish National Party was founded in 1934 to campaign for independence for Scotland.

The Social Democratic and Labour Party was founded in 1970, emerging from the civil rights movement of the 1960s, with the aim of promoting reform, reconciliation and partnership across the sectarian divide in Northern Ireland and of opposing violence from any quarter.

The Ulster Democratic Unionist Party was founded in 1971 to resist moves by the Ulster Unionist Party which were considered a threat to the Union. Its aim is to maintain Northern Ireland as an integral part of the UK.

The Ulster Unionist Council first met formally in 1905. Its objectives are to maintain Northern Ireland as an integral part of the UK and to promote the aims of the Ulster Unionist Party.

GOVERNMENT AND OPPOSITION

The government of the day is formed by the party which wins the largest number of seats in the House of Commons at a general election, or which has the support of a majority of members in the House of Commons. By tradition, the leader of the majority party is asked by the Sovereign to form a government, while the largest minority party becomes the official Opposition with its own leader and a 'Shadow Cabinet'. Leaders of the Government and Opposition sit on the front benches of the Commons with their supporters (the back-benchers) sitting behind them.

FINANCIAL SUPPORT

Financial support to Opposition parties in the House of Commons was introduced in 1975 and is commonly known as Short Money, after Edward Short, the Leader of the House at that time, who introduced the scheme. At 1 April 2001 the financial support was:

Conservative	£3,545,032
Liberal Democrats	1,138,615
Plaid Cymru	64,918
SNP	141,296
SDLP	56,787
Democratic Unionists	35,546
Ulster Unionists	145,612

A specific allocation for the Leader of the Opposition's office was introduced in April 1999 and has been set at £500,000 a year.

Financial support to the Opposition parties in the House of Lords was introduced in 1996 and is commonly known as Cranborne Money.

The parties included here are those with MPs sitting in the House of Commons in the present Parliament. Addresses of other political parties may be found in the Societies and Institutions section.

COMMONWEALTH PARLIAMENTARY
ASSOCIATION (1911)
Suite 700, Westminster House, 7 Millbank,
London SW1P 3JA.
Tel: 020-7799 1460; Fax: 020-7222 6073;
E.mail: hq.sec@cpahq.org; Web:www.cpahq.org;
The Commonwealth Parliamentary Association consists of 170 branches in the national, state, provincial or territorial parliaments in the countries of the Commonwealth. Conferences and general assemblies are held every year in different countries of the Commonwealth.
President (2001–2002), Rt. Hon. Kandi Nehova, MP

COMMONWEALTH PARLIAMENTARY
ASSOCIATION (UK BRANCH)
Westminster Hall, Houses of Parliament, London SW1A
0AA. Tel: 020-7219 5373; Fax: 020-7233 1202;
Email: cpa@parliament.uk
Hon. President, The Lord Chancellor, The Lord Irvine of Laird
Chairman of Branch, Rt. Hon. Tony Blair, MP
Chairman of the Executive Committee, Tom Cox, MP
Secretary, A. Pearson

CONSERVATIVE PARTY
Conservative Central Office, 32 Smith Square, London
SW1P 3HH
Tel: 020-7222 9000; Fax: 020-7222 1135
E-mail: ccoffice@conservative-party.org.uk
Web: www.conservatives.com
See Stop Press for details of the Opposition leader and Shadow Cabinet.

SCOTTISH CONSERVATIVE AND
UNIONIST CENTRAL OFFICE
83 Princes Street, Edinburgh EH2 2ER
Tel: 0131-247 6890; Fax: 0131-247 6891
Email: central.office@scottishtories.org.uk;
Web: www.scottishtories.org.uk
Chairman, D. Mitchell
Deputy Chairman, B. Walker
Hon. Treasurer, to be announced
Acting Director, M. McDonald

LABOUR PARTY
Millbank Tower, Millbank, London SW1P 4GT
Tel: 08705-900 200; Fax: 020-7802 1234
E-mail: join@labour.org.uk
Web: www.labour.org.uk
Parliamentary Party Leader, Rt. Hon. Tony Blair, MP
Deputy Party Leader, Rt. Hon. John Prescott, MP
Leader in the Lords, Lord Williams of Mostyn, QC
Chair, Clive Soley, MP
Vice-Chair, Tony Lloyd, MP
Treasurer, Ms M. Prosser
General Secretary, Ms M. McDonagh
General Secretary, Scottish Labour Party, L. Quinn

LIBERAL DEMOCRATS
4 Cowley Street, London SW1P 3NB
Tel: 020-7222 7999; Fax: 020-7799 2170
E-mail: libdems@cix.co.uk
Web: www.libdems.org.uk
President, Lord Dholakia
Hon. Treasurer, Reg Clark

Chief Executive, Hugh Rickard
Parliamentary Party Leader, Rt. Hon. Charles Kennedy, MP
Shadow Leader in the House of Commons, Paul Tyler, MP
Leader in the Lords, The Lord Rodgers of Quarry Bank, PC

LIBERAL DEMOCRAT SPOKESMEN *as at August 2001*

Deputy Leader, Rt. Hon. Alan Beith, MP
Culture, Media and Sport, Constitution, Rt. Hon. Nick Harvey, MP
Defence, Paul Keetch, MP
Education and Skills, Phil Willis, MP
Environment,Food and Rural Affairs, Malcolm Bruce, MP
Foreign Affairs, Defence and Europe, Rt. Hon. Menzies Campbell, MP
Home Affairs, Simon Hughes, MP
Health, Dr Evans Harry, MP
International Development, Dr Jenny Tonge, MP
Social Security and Welfare, Prof. Steve Webb, MP
Trade and Industry, Dr Vincent Cable, MP
Transport, Local Government and the Regions, Don Foster, MP
Treasury, Matthew Taylor, MP
Scotland, Rt. Hon. Michael Moore, MP
Wales and Northern Ireland, Lempit Opik, MP
Chair of the Parliamentary Party, Mark Oaten, MP

LIBERAL DEMOCRAT WHIPS

House of Lords, The Lord Roper of Thorney Island
House of Commons, Andrew Stunell, MP (*Chief Whip*)

WELSH LIBERAL DEMOCRATS

Bay View House, 102 Bute Street, Cardiff CF10 5AD
Tel: 029-2031 3400; Fax: 029-2031 3401
E-mail: ldwales@cix.co.uk

Party President, Clive Lindley
Party Leader, L. Opik, MP
Chairman, P. Lloyd
Treasurer, N. Burree
Secretary, J. Burree
Administrative Officer, Ms J. Batchelor
Chief Executive, C. Lines

SCOTTISH LIBERAL DEMOCRATS

4 Clifton Terrace, Edinburgh EH12 5DR
Tel: 0131-337 2314; Fax: 0131-337 3566
E-mail: scotlibdem@cix.co.uk
Web: www.scotlibdems.org.uk

Party President, Malcolm Bruce, MP
Party Leader, Jim Wallace, MSP
Convener, Cllr I. Yuill
Vice Convener, Neil Wallace; Moira Craig
Treasurer, D. R. Sullivan
Chief Executive, K. Croft

PLAID CYMRU – THE PARTY OF WALES

18 Park Grove, Cardiff CF10 3BN
Tel: 029-2064 6000; Fax: 029-2064 6001
E-mail: post@plaidcymru.org
Web: www.plaidcymru.org

Party President, Ieuan Wyn Jones, AM
Chairman, E. Jones, AM
Hon. Treasurer, Jeff Canning
Chief Executive/General Secretary, K. Davies

SCOTTISH NATIONAL PARTY

6 North Charlotte Street, Edinburgh EH2 4JH
Tel: 0131-226 3661; Fax: 0131-225 9597
Web: www.snp.org.uk

Parliamentary Party Leader, John Swinney, MSP
Chief Whip, K. Ullrich, MSP
National Convener, Alex Salmond, MP
Senior Vice-Convener, John Swinney, MSP
National Treasurer, Jim Mather
National Secretary, Stewart Hosie

NORTHERN IRELAND

SINN FEIN

147 Andersonstown Road, Belfast BT11 9BW
Tel: 028- 9030 1719; Web: www.sinnfein.ie
Party President, Gerry Adams, MP
Vice President, Pat Doherty, MP
Chief Negotiator, Martin McGuinness, MP

SOCIAL DEMOCRATIC AND LABOUR PARTY

Cranmore House, 121 Ormeau Road, Belfast BT7 1SH
Tel: 028-9024 7700; Fax: 028-9023 6699
E-mail: sdlp@indigo.ie
Web: www.sdlp.ie

Parliamentary Party Leader, vacant
Deputy Leader, Seamus Mallon, MP
Chief Whip, Eddie McGrady, MP
Chairman, A. Attwood, MLA
Hon. Treasurer, J. Stephenson
General Secretary, Mrs G. Cosgrove

ULSTER DEMOCRATIC UNIONIST PARTY

91 Dundela Avenue, Belfast BT4 3BU
Tel: 028-9047 1155; Fax: 028-9047 1797
E-mail: info@dup.org.uk
Web: www.dup.org.uk

Parliamentary Party Leader, Ian Paisley, MP, MEP, MLA
Deputy Leader, Peter Robinson, MP, MLA
Chairman, M. Morrow, MLA
Chief Executive, A. Ewart
Hon. Treasurer, G. Campbell, MP, MLA
Party Secretary, N. Dodds, MP, MLA

ULSTER UNIONIST PARTY

3 Glengall Street, Belfast BT12 5AE
Tel: 028-9032 4601; Fax: 028-9024 6738
E-mail: uup@uup.org
Web: www.uup.org

Party Leader, Rt. Hon. David Trimble, MP
Chief Whip, Cllr. Roy Beggs, MP

ULSTER UNIONIST COUNCIL

President, Revd Martin Smyth, MP
Leader, Rt. Hon. David Trimble, MP, MLA
Chairman of the Executive Committee, James Cooper
Hon. Treasurer, J. Allen, OBE
Vice Chairman, D. McConnell, OBE
Vice President, Jeffrey Donaldson, MP; Sir Reg Empey, OBE, MLA; Cllr K. Maginnis; Jim Nicholson, MEP

MEMBERS OF PARLIAMENT

*Abbott, Ms Diane (*b.* 1953) *Lab., Hackney North and Stoke Newington,* Maj. 13,651
*Adams, Gerard (Gerry) (*b.* 1948) *SF, Belfast West,* Maj. 19,342
*Adams, Mrs K. Irene JP (*b.* 1948) *Lab., Paisley North,* Maj. 9,321
*Ainger, Nicholas R. (*b.* 1949) *Lab., Carmarthen West and Pembrokeshire South,* Maj. 4,538
*Ainsworth, Peter M. (*b.* 1956) *C., Surrey East,* Maj. 13,203
*Ainsworth, Robert W. (*b.* 1952) *Lab., Coventry North East,* Maj. 15,751
*Alexander, Douglas G. (*b.* 1967) *Lab., Paisley South,* Maj. 11,910
Allan, Richard B. (*b.* 1966) *LD, Sheffield Hallam,* Maj. 9,347
*Allen, Graham W. (*b.* 1953) *Lab., Nottingham North,* Maj. 12,240
*Amess, David A. A. (*b.* 1952) *C., Southend West,* Maj. 7,941
*Ancram, Rt. Hon. Michael A.F.J.K. (Earl of Ancram) (*b.* 1945) *C., Devizes,* Maj. 11,896
*Anderson, Rt. Hon. Donald (*b.* 1939) *Lab., Swansea East,* Maj. 16,148
*Anderson, Mrs Janet (*b.* 1949) *Lab., Rossendale and Darwen,* Maj. 5,223
*Arbuthnot, Rt. Hon. James N. (*b.* 1952) *C., Hampshire North East,* Maj. 13,257
*Armstrong, Rt. Hon. Hilary J. (*b.* 1945) *Lab., Durham North West,* Maj. 16,333
Atherton, Ms Candy K. (*b.* 1955) *Lab., Falmouth and Camborne,* Maj. 4,527
Atkins, Ms Charlotte (*b.* 1950) *Lab., Staffordshire Moorlands,* Maj. 5,838
*Atkinson, David A. (*b.* 1940) *C., Bournemouth East,* Maj. 3,434
*Atkinson, Peter L. (*b.* 1943) *C., Hexham,* Maj. 2,529
*Austin, John E. (*b.* 1944) *Lab., Erith and Thamesmead,* Maj. 11,167
Bacon, Richard (*b.* 1962) *C., Norfolk South,* Maj. 6,893
*Bailey, Adrian (*b.* 1945) *Lab. Co-op, West Bromwich West,* Maj. 11,355
Baird, Vera (*b.* 1950) *Lab., Redcar,* Maj. 13,443
*Baker, Norman (*b.* 1957) *LD, Lewes,* Maj. 9,710
*Baldry, Anthony B. (*b.* 1950) *C., Banbury,* Maj. 5,219
*Banks, Anthony L. (*b.* 1943) *Lab., West Ham,* Maj. 15,645
Barker, Gregory (*b.* 1966) *C., Bexhill and Battle,* Maj. 10,503
*Barnes, Harold (*b.* 1936) *Lab., Derbyshire North East,* Maj. 12,258
Baron, John (*b.* 1959) *C., Billericay,* Maj. 5,013
Barrett, John (*b.* 1954) *LD, Edinburgh West,* Maj. 7,589
*Barron, Rt. Hon. Kevin J. (*b.* 1946) *Lab., Rother Valley,* Maj. 14,882
*Battle, John D. (*b.* 1951) *Lab., Leeds West,* Maj. 14,935
*Bayley, Hugh (*b.* 1952) *Lab., City of York,* Maj. 13,779
Beard, Nigel C. (*b.* 1936) *Lab., Bexleyheath and Crayford,* Maj. 1,472
*Beckett, Rt. Hon. Margaret (*b.* 1943) *Lab., Derby South,* Maj. 13,855
Begg, Ms Anne (*b.* 1955) *Lab., Aberdeen South,* Maj. 4,388
*Beggs, Roy (*b.* 1936) *UUP, Antrim East,* Maj. 128
*Beith, Rt. Hon. Alan J. (*b.* 1943) *LD, Berwick upon Tweed,* Maj. 8,458
*Bell, Stuart (*b.* 1938) *Lab., Middlesbrough,* Maj. 16,330
Bellingham, Henry (*b.* 1955) *Lab., Norfolk North West,* Maj. 3,485
*Benn, Hilary J. (*b.* 1953) *Lab., Leeds Central,* Maj. 14,381

*Bennett, Andrew F. (*b.* 1939) *Lab., Denton and Reddish,* Maj. 15,330
*Benton, Joseph E. (*b.* 1933) *Lab., Bootle,* Maj. 19,043
Bercow, John S. (*b.* 1963) *C., Buckingham,* Maj. 13,325
*Beresford, Sir Paul (*b.* 1946) *C., Mole Valley,* Maj. 10,153
*Berry, Dr Roger D.PHIL. (*b.* 1948) *Lab., Kingswood,* Maj. 13,962
*Best, Harold (*b.* 1939) *Lab., Leeds North West,* Maj. 5,236
*Betts, Clive J. C. (*b.* 1950) *Lab., Sheffield Attercliffe,* Maj. 18,844
Blackman, Ms Elizabeth M. (*b.* 1949) *Lab., Erewash,* Maj. 6,932
*Blair, Rt. Hon. Anthony C. L. (*b.* 1953) *Lab., Sedgefield,* Maj. 17,713
Blears, Hazel A. (*b.* 1956) *Lab., Salford,* Maj. 11,012
Blizzard, Robert J. (*b.* 1950) *Lab., Waveney,* Maj. 8,553
*Blunkett, Rt. Hon. David (*b.* 1947) *Lab., Sheffield Brightside,* Maj. 17,049
*Blunt, Crispin J. R. (*b.* 1960) *C., Reigate,* Maj. 8,025
*Boateng, Rt. Hon. Paul Y. (*b.* 1951) *Lab., Brent South,* Maj. 17,380
Borrow, David S. (*b.* 1952) *Lab., Ribble South,* Maj. 3,792
*Boswell, Timothy E. (*b.* 1942) *C., Daventry,* Maj. 9,649
*Bottomley, Peter J. (*b.* 1944) *C., Worthing West,* Maj. 9,037
*Bottomley, Rt. Hon. Virginia H. B. M. (*b.* 1948) *C., Surrey South West,* Maj. 861
*Bradley, Rt. Hon. Keith J. C. (*b.* 1950) *Lab., Manchester Withington,* Maj. 11,524
Bradley, Peter C. S. (*b.* 1953) *Lab., Wrekin, The,* Maj. 3,587
Bradshaw, Benjamin P. J. (*b.* 1960) *Lab., Exeter,* Maj. 11,759
*Brady, Graham (*b.* 1967) *C., Altrincham and Sale West,* Maj. 2,941
Brake, Thomas A. (*b.* 1962) *LD, Carshalton and Wallington,* Maj. 4,547
*Brazier, Julian W. H. TD (*b.* 1953) *C., Canterbury,* Maj. 2,069
Breed, Colin E. (*b.* 1947) *LD, Cornwall South East,* Maj. 5,375
Brennan, Kevin (*b.* 1959) *Lab., Cardiff West,* Maj. 11,321
Brooke, Annette (*b.* 1947) *LD, Dorset Mid and Poole North,* Maj. 384
*Brown, Rt. Hon. J. Gordon PH.D. (*b.* 1951) *Lab., Dunfermline East,* Maj. 15,063
*Brown, Rt. Hon. Nicholas H. (*b.* 1950) *Lab., Newcastle upon Tyne East and Wallsend,* Maj. 14,223
Brown, Russell L. (*b.* 1951) *Lab., Dumfries,* Maj. 8,834
Browne, Desmond (*b.* 1952) *Lab., Kilmarnock and Loudoun,* Maj. 10,334
*Browning, Mrs Angela F. (*b.* 1946) *C., Tiverton and Honiton,* Maj. 6,284
*Bruce, Malcolm G. (*b.* 1944) *LD, Gordon,* Maj. 7,879
Bryant, Chris (*b.* 1962) *Lab., Rhondda,* Maj. 16,047
Buck, Ms Karen P. (*b.* 1958) *Lab., Regent's Park and Kensington North,* Maj. 10,266
*Burden, Richard H. (*b.* 1954) *Lab., Birmingham Northfield,* Maj. 7,798
Burgon, Colin (*b.* 1948) *Lab., Elmet,* Maj. 4,171
Burnett, John P. A. (*b.* 1945) *LD, Devon West and Torridge,* Maj. 1,194
*Burnham, Andy (*b.* 1970) *Lab., Leigh,* Maj. 16,362
*Burns, Simon H. M. (*b.* 1952) *C., Chelmsford West,* Maj. 6,261
Burnside, David (*b.* 1952) *UUP, Antrim South,* Maj. 1,011

Burstow, Paul K. (*b.* 1962) *LD*, *Sutton and Cheam*, Maj. 4,304

Burt, Alastair (*b.* 1955) *C.*, *Bedfordshire North East*, Maj. 8,577

*Butterfill, John V. (*b.* 1941) *C.*, *Bournemouth West*, Maj. 4,718

*Byers, Rt. Hon. Stephen J. (*b.* 1953) *Lab.*, *Tyneside North*, Maj. 20,668

Cable, Dr J. Vincent (*b.* 1943) *LD*, *Twickenham*, Maj. 7,655

*Caborn, Rt. Hon. Richard G. (*b.* 1943) *Lab.*, *Sheffield Central*, Maj. 12,544

Cairns, David (*b.* 1966) *Lab.*, *Greenock and Inverclyde*, Maj. 9,890

Calton, Patsy (*b.* 1948) *LD*, *Cheadle*, Maj. 33

Cameron, David (*b.* 1966) *C.*, *Witney*, Maj. 7,973

Campbell, Alan (*b.* 1957) *Lab.*, *Tynemouth*, Maj. 8,678

*Campbell, Mrs Anne (*b.* 1940) *Lab.*, *Cambridge*, Maj. 8,579

Campbell, Gregory (*b.* 1953) *DUP*, *Londonderry East*, Maj. 1,901

*Campbell, Ronald (*b.* 1943) *Lab.*, *Blyth Valley*, Maj. 12,188

*Campbell, Rt. Hon. W. Menzies CBE, QC (*b.* 1941) *LD*, *Fife North East*, Maj. 9,736

*Cann, James C. (*b.* 1946) *Lab.*, *Ipswich*, Maj. 8,081

*Caplin, Ivor K. (*b.* 1958) *Lab.*, *Hove*, Maj. 3,171

Carmichael, Alistair (*b.* 1965) *LD*, *Orkney and Shetland*, Maj. 3,475

Casale, Roger M. (*b.* 1960) *Lab.*, *Wimbledon*, Maj. 3,744

*Cash, William N. P. (*b.* 1940) *C.*, *Stone*, Maj. 6,036

Caton, Martin P. (*b.* 1951) *Lab.*, *Gower*, Maj. 7,395

*Cawsey, Ian A. (*b.* 1960) *Lab.*, *Brigg and Goole*, Maj. 3,961

Challen, Colin (*b.* 1953) *Lab.*, *Morley and Rothwell*, Maj. 12,090

*Chapman, J. K. (Ben) (*b.* 1940) *Lab.*, *Wirral South*, Maj. 5,049

*Chapman, Sir Sydney (*b.* 1935) *C.*, *Chipping Barnet*, Maj. 2,701

*Chaytor, David M. (*b.* 1949) *Lab.*, *Bury North*, Maj. 6,532

*Chidgey, David W. G. (*b.* 1942) *LD*, *Eastleigh*, Maj. 3,058

*Chope, Christopher R. OBE (*b.* 1947) *C.*, *Christchurch*, Maj. 13,544

*Clapham, Michael (*b.* 1943) *Lab.*, *Barnsley West and Penistone*, Maj. 12,352

*Clappison, W. James (*b.* 1956) *C.*, *Hertsmere*, Maj. 4,902

Clark, Ms Helen R. (*b.* 1954) *Lab.*, *Peterborough*, Maj. 384

Clark, Dr Lynda M. QC (*b.* 1949) *Lab.*, *Edinburgh Pentlands*, Maj. 1,742

Clark, Paul G. (*b.* 1957) *Lab.*, *Gillingham*, Maj. 2,272

Clarke, Anthony R. (*b.* 1963) *Lab.*, *Northampton South*, Maj. 885

*Clarke, Rt. Hon. Charles R. (*b.* 1950) *Lab.*, *Norwich South*, Maj. 8,816

*Clarke, Rt. Hon. Kenneth H. QC (*b.* 1940) *C.*, *Rushcliffe*, Maj. 7,357

*Clarke, Rt. Hon. Thomas CBE (*b.* 1941) *Lab.*, *Coatbridge and Chryston*, Maj. 15,314

*Clelland, David G. (*b.* 1943) *Lab.*, *Tyne Bridge*, Maj. 14,889

*Clifton-Brown, Geoffrey R. (*b.* 1953) *C.*, *Cotswold*, Maj. 11,983

*Clwyd, Anne (*b.* 1937) *Lab.*, *Cynon Valley*, Maj. 12,998

*Coaker, Vernon R. (*b.* 1953) *Lab.*, *Gedling*, Maj. 5,598

*Coffey, Ms M. Ann (*b.* 1946) *Lab.*, *Stockport*, Maj. 11,569

*Cohen, Harry M. (*b.* 1949) *Lab.*, *Leyton and Wanstead*, Maj. 12,904

Coleman, Iain (*b.* 1958) *Lab.*, *Hammersmith and Fulham*, Maj. 2,015

Collins, Timothy W. G. CBE (*b.* 1964) *C.*, *Westmorland and Lonsdale*, Maj. 3,147

Colman, Anthony (*b.* 1943) *Lab.*, *Putney*, Maj. 2,771

*Connarty, Michael (*b.* 1947) *Lab.*, *Falkirk East*, Maj. 10,712

Conway, Derek (*b.* 1953) *C.*, *Old Bexley and Sidcup*, Maj. 3,345

*Cook, Frank (*b.* 1935) *Lab.*, *Stockton North*, Maj. 14,647

*Cook, Rt. Hon. R. F. (Robin) (*b.* 1946) *Lab.*, *Livingston*, Maj. 10,616

Cooper, Ms Yvette (*b.* 1969) *Lab.*, *Pontefract and Castleford*, Maj. 16,378

*Corbyn, Jeremy B. (*b.* 1949) *Lab.*, *Islington North*, Maj. 12,958

*Cormack, Sir Patrick FSA (*b.* 1939) *C.*, *Staffordshire South*, Maj. 6,881

*Corston, Ms Jean A. (*b.* 1942) *Lab.*, *Bristol East*, Maj. 13,392

Cotter, Brian J. (*b.* 1938) *LD*, *Weston-super-Mare*, Maj. 338

*Cousins, James M. (*b.* 1944) *Lab.*, *Newcastle upon Tyne Central*, Maj. 11,605

*Cox, Thomas M. (*b.* 1930) *Lab.*, *Tooting*, Maj. 10,400

*Cran, James D. (*b.* 1944) *C.*, *Beverley and Holderness*, Maj. 781

Cranston, Ross F. QC (*b.* 1948) *Lab.*, *Dudley North*, Maj. 6,800

*Crausby, David A. (*b.* 1946) *Lab.*, *Bolton North East*, Maj. 8,422

Cruddas, Jon (*b.* 1965) *Lab.*, *Dagenham*, Maj. 8,693

Cryer, Mrs C. Ann (*b.* 1939) *Lab.*, *Keighley*, Maj. 4,005

Cryer, John R. (*b.* 1964) *Lab.*, *Hornchurch*, Maj. 1,482

*Cummings, John S. (*b.* 1943) *Lab.*, *Easington*, Maj. 21,949

*Cunningham, Rt. Hon. Dr J. A. (Jack) PH.D. (*b.* 1939) *Lab.*, *Copeland*, Maj. 4,964

*Cunningham, James D. (*b.* 1941) *Lab.*, *Coventry South*, Maj. 8,279

Cunningham, Tony (*b.* 1952) *Lab.*, *Workington*, Maj. 10,850

*Curry, Rt. Hon. David M. (*b.* 1944) *C.*, *Skipton and Ripon*, Maj. 12,930

Curtis-Thomas, Ms Claire (*b.* 1958) *Lab.*, *Crosby*, Maj. 8,353

Daisley, Paul (*b.* 1957) *Lab.*, *Brent East*, Maj. 13,047

*Dalyell, Tam (*b.* 1932) *Lab.*, *Linlithgow*, Maj. 9,129

*Darling, Rt. Hon. Alistair M. (*b.* 1953) *Lab.*, *Edinburgh Central*, Maj. 8,142

Davey, Edward J. (*b.* 1965) *LD*, *Kingston and Surbiton*, Maj. 15,676

Davey, Ms Valerie (*b.* 1940) *Lab.*, *Bristol West*, Maj. 4,426

David, Wayne (*b.* 1957) *Lab.*, *Caerphilly*, Maj. 14,425

*Davidson, Ian G. (*b.* 1950) *Lab. Co-op.*, *Glasgow Pollok*, Maj. 11,268

*Davies, Rt. Hon. D. J. Denzil (*b.* 1938) *Lab.*, *Llanelli*, Maj. 6,403

Davies, Geraint R. (*b.* 1960) *Lab.*, *Croydon Central*, Maj. 3,984

*Davies, J. Quentin (*b.* 1944) *C.*, *Grantham and Stamford*, Maj. 4,518

*Davis, Rt. Hon. David M. (*b.* 1948) *C.*, *Haltemprice and Howden*, Maj. 1,903

*Davis, Rt. Hon. Terence A. G. (*b.* 1938) *Lab.*, *Birmingham Hodge Hill*, Maj. 11,618

Dawson, T. Hilton (*b.* 1953) *Lab.*, *Lancaster and Wyre*, Maj. 481

Dean, Ms Janet E. A. (*b.* 1949) *Lab.*, *Burton*, Maj. 4,849

*Denham, Rt. Hon. John Y. (*b.* 1953) *Lab.*, *Southampton Itchen*, Maj. 11,223

*Dhanda, Parmjit (*b.* 1971) *Lab.*, *Gloucester*, Maj. 3,880

*Dismore, Andrew H. (*b.* 1954) *Lab.*, *Hendon*, Maj. 7,417

Djanogly, Jonathan (*b.* 1965) *C.*, *Huntingdon*, Maj. 12,792

Dobbin, James (*b.* 1941) *Lab. Co-op., Heywood and Middleton*, Maj. 11,670

*Dobson, Rt. Hon. Frank G. (*b.* 1940) *Lab., Holborn and St Pancras*, Maj. 11,175

Dodds, Nigel MLA (*b.* 1958) *DUP, Belfast North*, Maj. 6,387

Doherty, Pat (*b.* 1945) *SF, Tyrone West*, Maj. 5,040

Donaldson, Jeffrey M. (*b.* 1962) *UUP, Lagan Valley*, Maj. 18,342

*Donohoe, Brian H. (*b.* 1948) *Lab., Cunninghame South*, Maj. 11,230

Doran, Frank (*b.* 1949) *Lab., Aberdeen Central*, Maj. 6,646

*Dorrell, Rt. Hon. Stephen J. (*b.* 1952) *C., Charnwood*, Maj. 7,739

Doughty, Sue (*b.* 1955) *LD, Guildford*, Maj. 538

*Dowd, James P. (*b.* 1951) *Lab., Lewisham West*, Maj. 11,920

Drew, David E. (*b.* 1952) *Lab. Co-op., Stroud*, Maj. 5,039

Drown, Ms Julia K. (*b.* 1962) *Lab., Swindon South*, Maj. 7,341

*Duncan, Alan J. C. (*b.* 1957) *C., Rutland and Melton*, Maj. 8,612

Duncan, Peter (*b.* 1965) *C., Galloway and Upper Nithsdale*, Maj. 74

*Duncan Smith, G. Iain (*b.* 1954) *C., Chingford and Woodford Green*, Maj. 5,487

*Dunwoody, Hon. Mrs Gwyneth P. (*b.* 1930) *Lab., Crewe and Nantwich*, Maj. 9,906

*Eagle, Ms Angela (*b.* 1961) *Lab., Wallasey*, Maj. 12,276

Eagle, Ms Maria (*b.* 1961) *Lab., Liverpool Garston*, Maj. 12,494

Edwards, Huw W. E. (*b.* 1953) *Lab., Monmouth*, Maj. 384

Efford, Clive S. (*b.* 1958) *Lab., Eltham*, Maj. 6,996

*Ellman, Ms Louise J. (*b.* 1945) *Lab. Co-op., Liverpool Riverside*, Maj. 13,950

*Ennis, Jeffrey (*b.* 1952) *Lab., Barnsley East and Mexborough*, Maj. 16,789

*Etherington, William (*b.* 1941) *Lab., Sunderland North*, Maj. 13,354

*Evans, Nigel M. (*b.* 1957) *C., Ribble Valley*, Maj. 11,238

Ewing, Annabelle (*b.* 1960) *SNP, Perth*, Maj. 48

*Fabricant, Michael (*b.* 1950) *C., Lichfield*, Maj. 4,426

*Fallon, Michael C. (*b.* 1952) *C., Sevenoaks*, Maj. 10,154

Farrelly, Paul (*b.* 1962) *Lab., Newcastle under Lyme*, Maj. 9,986

*Field, Rt. Hon. Frank (*b.* 1942) *Lab., Birkenhead*, Maj. 15,591

*Field, Mark (*b.* 1934) *C., Cities of London and Westminster*, Maj. 4,499

*Fisher, Mark (*b.* 1944) *Lab., Stoke-on-Trent Central*, Maj. 11,845

*Fitzpatrick, James (*b.* 1952) *Lab., Poplar and Canning Town*, Maj. 14,104

*Fitzsimons, Ms Lorna (*b.* 1967) *Lab., Rochdale*, Maj. 5,655

*Flight, Howard E. (*b.* 1948) *C., Arundel and South Downs*, Maj. 13,704

*Flint, Ms Caroline L. (*b.* 1961) *Lab., Don Valley*, Maj. 9,520

Flook, Adrian (*b.* 1963) *C., Taunton*, Maj. 235

*Flynn, Paul P. (*b.* 1935) *Lab., Newport West*, Maj. 9,304

Follett, Ms D. Barbara (*b.* 1942) *Lab., Stevenage*, Maj. 8,566

*Forth, Rt. Hon. Eric (*b.* 1944) *C., Bromley and Chislehurst*, Maj. 9,037

*Foster, Rt. Hon. Derek (*b.* 1937) *Lab., Bishop Auckland*, Maj. 13,926

*Foster, Donald M. E. (*b.* 1947) *LD, Bath*, Maj. 9,894

*Foster, Michael J. (*b.* 1946) *Lab., Hastings and Rye*, Maj. 4,308

Foster, Michael (*b.* 1963) *Lab., Worcester*, Maj. 5,766

*Foulkes, George (*b.* 1942) *Lab. Co-op., Carrick, Cumnock and Doon Valley*, Maj. 14,856

*Fox, Dr Liam (*b.* 1961) *C., Woodspring*, Maj. 8,798

Francis, David Hywel (*b.* 1946) *Lab., Aberavon*, Maj. 16,108

Francois, Mark PH.D. (*b.* 1965) *C., Rayleigh*, Maj. 8,290

*Gale, Roger J. (*b.* 1943) *C., Thanet North*, Maj. 6,650

*Galloway, George (*b.* 1954) *Lab., Glasgow Kelvin*, Maj. 7,260

*Gapes, Michael J. (*b.* 1952) *Lab. Co-op., Ilford South*, Maj. 13,997

Gardiner, Barry S. (*b.* 1957) *Lab., Brent North*, Maj. 10,205

*Garnier, Edward H. QC (*b.* 1952) *C., Harborough*, Maj. 5,252

George, Andrew H. (*b.* 1958) *LD, St Ives*, Maj. 10,053

*George, Rt. Hon. Bruce T. (*b.* 1942) *Lab., Walsall South*, Maj. 9,931

*Gerrard, Neil F. (*b.* 1942) *Lab., Walthamstow*, Maj. 15,181

*Gibb, Nicholas J. (*b.* 1960) *C., Bognor Regis and Littlehampton*, Maj. 5,643

*Gibson, Dr Ian (*b.* 1938) *Lab., Norwich North*, Maj. 5,863

*Gidley, Sandra (*b.* 1957) *LD, Romsey*, Maj. 2,370

Gildernew, Michelle (*b.* 1970) *SF, Fermanagh and South Tyrone*, Maj. 53

*Gillan, Mrs Cheryl E. K. (*b.* 1952) *C., Chesham and Amersham*, Maj. 11,882

Gilroy, Mrs Linda (*b.* 1949) *Lab. Co-op., Plymouth Sutton*, Maj. 7,517

*Godsiff, Roger D. (*b.* 1946) *Lab., Birmingham Sparkbrook and Small Heath*, Maj. 16,246

Goggins, Paul G. (*b.* 1953) *Lab., Wythenshawe and Sale East*, Maj. 12,608

Goodman, Paul (*b.* 1960) *C., Wycombe*, Maj. 3,168

Gray, James W. (*b.* 1954) *C., Wiltshire North*, Maj. 3,878

Grayling, Chris (*b.* 1962) *C., Epsom and Ewell*, Maj. 10,080

Green, Damian H. (*b.* 1956) *C., Ashford*, Maj. 7,359

Green, Mathew (*b.* 1970) *LD, Ludlow*, Maj. 1,630

*Greenway, John R. (*b.* 1946) *C., Ryedale*, Maj. 4,875

*Grieve, Dominic C. R. (*b.* 1956) *C., Beaconsfield*, Maj. 11,065

*Griffiths, Ms Jane P. (*b.* 1954) *Lab., Reading East*, Maj. 5,588

*Griffiths, Nigel (*b.* 1955) *Lab., Edinburgh South*, Maj. 5,499

*Griffiths, Winston J. (*b.* 1943) *Lab., Bridgend*, Maj. 10,045

*Grogan, John T. (*b.* 1961) *Lab., Selby*, Maj. 2,138

*Gummer, Rt. Hon. John S. (*b.* 1939) *C., Suffolk Coastal*, Maj. 4,326

*Hague, Rt. Hon. William J. (*b.* 1961) *C., Richmond*, Maj. 16,319

*Hain, Rt. Hon. Peter G. (*b.* 1950) *Lab., Neath*, Maj. 14,816

*Hall, Michael T. (*b.* 1952) *Lab., Weaver Vale*, Maj. 9,637

Hall, Patrick (*b.* 1951) *Lab., Bedford*, Maj. 6,157

*Hamilton, Fabian (*b.* 1955) *Lab., Leeds North East*, Maj. 7,089

Hamilton, David (*b.* 1950) *Lab., Midlothian*, Maj. 9,014

Hammond, Philip (*b.* 1955) *C., Runnymede and Weybridge*, Maj. 8,360

*Hancock, Michael T. CBE (*b.* 1946) *LD, Portsmouth South*, Maj. 6,094

*Hanson, David G. (*b.* 0) *Lab., Delyn*, Maj. 8,065

*Harman, Rt. Hon. Harriet QC (*b.* 1950) *Lab., Camberwell and Peckham*, Maj. 14,123

*Harris, Dr Evan (*b.* 1965) *LD, Oxford West and Abingdon*, Maj. 9,185

Harris, Tom (*b.* 1964) *Lab., Glasgow Cathcart*, Maj. 10,816

*Harvey, Nicholas B. (*b.* 1961) *LD, Devon North*, Maj. 2,984

*Haselhurst, Rt. Hon. Sir Alan (*b.* 1937) *C., Saffron Walden*, Maj. 12,004

Havard, Dai (*b.* 1949) *Lab.*, *Merthyr Tydfil and Rhymney*, Maj. 14,923

Hawkins, Nick (*b.* 0) *C.*, *Surrey Heath*, Maj. 10,819

Hayes, John H. (*b.* 1958) *C.*, *South Holland and the Deepings*, Maj. 11,099

*Heal, Mrs Sylvia L (*b.* 1942) *Lab.*, *Halesowen and Rowley Regis*, Maj. 7,359

*Heald, Oliver (*b.* 1954) *C.*, *Hertfordshire North East*, Maj. 3,444

Healey, John (*b.* 1960) *Lab.*, *Wentworth*, Maj. 16,449

Heath, David W. CBE (*b.* 1954) *LD*, *Somerton and Frome*, Maj. 668

*Heathcoat-Amory, Rt. Hon. David P. (*b.* 1949) *C.*, *Wells*, Maj. 2,796

*Henderson, Douglas J. (*b.* 1949) *Lab.*, *Newcastle upon Tyne North*, Maj. 14,450

Henderson, Ivan J. (*b.* 1958) *Lab.*, *Harwich*, Maj. 2,596

*Hendrick, Mark (*b.* 1958) *Lab.Co-op*, *Preston*, Maj. 12,268

Hendry, Charles (*b.* 1959) *C.*, *Wealden*, Maj. 13,772

Hepburn, Stephen (*b.* 1959) *Lab.*, *Jarrow*, Maj. 17,595

*Heppell, John (*b.* 1948) *Lab.*, *Nottingham East*, Maj. 10,320

Hermon, Lady Sylvia (*b.* 1956) *UUP*, *Down North*, Maj. 7,324

Hesford, Stephen (*b.* 1957) *Lab.*, *Wirral West*, Maj. 4,035

Hewitt, Rt. Hon. Patricia H. (*b.* 1948) *Lab.*, *Leicester West*, Maj. 9,639

Heyes, David (*b.* 1946) *Lab.*, *Ashton under Lyne*, Maj. 15,518

*Hill, T. Keith (*b.* 1943) *Lab.*, *Streatham*, Maj. 14,270

*Hinchliffe, David M. (*b.* 1948) *Lab.*, *Wakefield*, Maj. 7,954

Hoban, Mark (*b.* 1964) *C.*, *Fareham*, Maj. 7,009

*Hodge, Mrs Margaret E. MBE (*b.* 1944) *Lab.*, *Barking*, Maj. 9,534

*Hoey, Ms Catharine (Kate) L. (*b.* 1946) *Lab.*, *Vauxhall*, Maj. 13,018

*Hogg, Rt. Hon. Douglas M. QC (*b.* 1945) *C.*, *Sleaford and North Hykeham*, Maj. 8,622

Holmes, Paul (*b.* 1957) *LD*, *Chesterfield*, Maj. 2,586

*Hood, James (*b.* 1948) *Lab.*, *Clydesdale*, Maj. 7,794

*Hoon, Rt. Hon. Geoffrey W. (*b.* 1953) *Lab.*, *Ashfield*, Maj. 13,268

Hope, Philip I. (*b.* 1955) *Lab. Co-op.*, *Corby*, Maj. 5,700

Hopkins, Kelvin P. (*b.* 1941) *Lab.*, *Luton North*, Maj. 9,977

*Horam, John R. (*b.* 1939) *C.*, *Orpington*, Maj. 269

*Howard, Rt. Hon. Michael QC (*b.* 1941) *C.*, *Folkestone and Hythe*, Maj. 5,907

*Howarth, Rt. Hon. Alan CBE (*b.* 1967) *Lab.*, *Newport East*, Maj. 9,874

*Howarth, George E. (*b.* 1949) *Lab.*, *Knowsley North and Sefton East*, Maj. 18,927

Howarth, J. Gerald D. (*b.* 1947) *C.*, *Aldershot*, Maj. 6,564

*Howells, Dr Kim S. PH.D. (*b.* 1946) *Lab.*, *Pontypridd*, Maj. 17,684

Hoyle, Lindsay H. (*b.* 1957) *Lab.*, *Chorley*, Maj. 8,444

*Hughes, Ms Beverley J. (*b.* 1950) *Lab.*, *Stretford and Urmston*, Maj. 13,239

*Hughes, Kevin M. (*b.* 1952) *Lab.*, *Doncaster North*, Maj. 15,187

*Hughes, Simon H. W. (*b.* 1951) *LD*, *Southwark North and Bermondsey*, Maj. 9,632

Humble, Mrs Jovanka (Joan) (*b.* 1951) *Lab.*, *Blackpool North and Fleetwood*, Maj. 5,721

*Hume, John MEP (*b.* 1937) *SDLP*, *Foyle*, Maj. 11,550

*Hunter, Andrew R. F. (*b.* 1943) *C.*, *Basingstoke*, Maj. 880

Hurst, Alan A. (*b.* 1945) *Lab.*, *Braintree*, Maj. 358

*Hutton, Rt. Hon. John M. P. (*b.* 1955) *Lab.*, *Barrow and Furness*, Maj. 9,889

Iddon, Brian (*b.* 1940) *Lab.*, *Bolton South East*, Maj. 12,871

*Illsley, Eric E. (*b.* 1955) *Lab.*, *Barnsley Central*, Maj. 15,130

*Ingram, Rt. Hon. Adam P. (*b.* 1947) *Lab.*, *East Kilbride*, Maj. 12,755

*Jack, Rt. Hon. J. Michael (*b.* 1946) *C.*, *Fylde*, Maj. 9,610

*Jackson, Ms Glenda M. CBE (*b.* 1936) *Lab.*, *Hampstead and Highgate*, Maj. 7,876

*Jackson, Mrs Helen M. (*b.* 1939) *Lab.*, *Sheffield Hillsborough*, Maj. 14,569

*Jackson, Robert V. (*b.* 1946) *C.*, *Wantage*, Maj. 5,600

*Jamieson, David C. (*b.* 1947) *Lab.*, *Plymouth Devonport*, Maj. 13,033

*Jenkin, Hon. Bernard C. (*b.* 1959) *C.*, *Essex North*, Maj. 7,186

*Jenkins, Brian D. (*b.* 1942) *Lab.*, *Tamworth*, Maj. 4,598

*Johnson, Alan A. (*b.* 1950) *Lab.*, *Hull West and Hessle*, Maj. 10,951

Johnson, Boris (*b.* 1964) *C.*, *Henley*, Maj. 8,458

Johnson, Ms Melanie J. (*b.* 1955) *Lab.*, *Welwyn Hatfield*, Maj. 1,196

Jones, Ms Helen M. (*b.* 1954) *Lab.*, *Warrington North*, Maj. 15,156

*Jones, Jonathan O. (*b.* 1954) *Lab. Co-op.*, *Cardiff Central*, Maj. 659

Jones, Kevan (*b.* 1964) *Lab.*, *Durham North*, Maj. 18,683

*Jones, Ms Lynne M. PH.D. (*b.* 1951) *Lab.*, *Birmingham Selly Oak*, Maj. 10,339

*Jones, Martyn D. (*b.* 1947) *Lab.*, *Clwyd South*, Maj. 8,898

*Jones, Nigel D. (*b.* 1948) *LD*, *Cheltenham*, Maj. 5,255

*Jowell, Rt. Hon. Tessa J. H. D. (*b.* 1947) *Lab.*, *Dulwich and West Norwood*, Maj. 12,310

*Joyce, Eric (*b.* 1960) *Lab.*, *Falkirk West*, Maj. 8,532

*Kaufman, Rt. Hon. Gerald B. (*b.* 1930) *Lab.*, *Manchester Gorton*, Maj. 11,304

Keeble, Ms Sally C. (*b.* 1951) *Lab.*, *Northampton North*, Maj. 7,893

Keen, Mrs Ann L. (*b.* 1948) *Lab.Co-op*, *Brentford and Isleworth*, Maj. 10,318

*Keen, D. Alan (*b.* 1937) *Labour Co-op*, *Feltham and Heston*, Maj. 12,657

*Keetch, Paul S. (*b.* 1961) *LD*, *Hereford*, Maj. 968

*Kelly, Ms Ruth M. (*b.* 1968) *Lab.*, *Bolton West*, Maj. 5,518

*Kemp, Fraser (*b.* 1958) *Lab.*, *Houghton and Washington East*, Maj. 19,818

*Kennedy, Rt. Hon. Charles P. (*b.* 1959) *LD*, *Ross, Skye and Inverness West*, Maj. 12,952

*Kennedy, Mrs Jane E. (*b.* 1958) *Lab.*, *Liverpool Wavertree*, Maj. 12,319

*Key, S. Robert (*b.* 1945) *C.*, *Salisbury*, Maj. 8,703

*Khabra, Piara S. (*b.* 1922) *Lab.*, *Ealing Southall*, Maj. 13,683

*Kidney, David N. (*b.* 1955) *Lab.*, *Stafford*, Maj. 5,032

*Kilfoyle, Peter (*b.* 1946) *Lab.*, *Liverpool Walton*, Maj. 17,996

King, Andrew (*b.* 1948) *Lab.*, *Rugby and Kenilworth*, Maj. 2,877

*King, Ms Oona T. (*b.* 1967) *Lab.*, *Bethnal Green and Bow*, Maj. 10,057

*Kirkbride, Miss Julie (*b.* 1960) *C.*, *Bromsgrove*, Maj. 8,138

*Kirkwood, Archibald J. (*b.* 1946) *LD*, *Roxburgh and Berwickshire*, Maj. 7,511

Knight, Rt. Hon. Greg (*b.* 1949) *C.*, *Yorkshire East*, Maj. 4,682

Knight, Jim (*b.* 1965) *Lab.*, *Dorset South*, Maj. 153

*Kumar, Dr Ashok (*b.* 1956) *Lab.*, *Middlesbrough South and Cleveland East*, Maj. 9,351

*Ladyman, Dr Stephen J. (*b.* 1952) *Lab.*, *Thanet South*, Maj. 1,792

Laing, Mrs Eleanor F. (*b.* 1958) *C.*, *Epping Forest*, Maj. 8,426

*Lait, Ms Jacqueline A. H. (*b.* 1947) *C.*, *Beckenham*, Maj. 4,959

Lamb, Norman (*b.* 1957) *LD, Norfolk North*, Maj. 483
*Lammy, David (*b.* 1972) *Lab., Tottenham*, Maj. 16,916
*Lansley, Andrew D. CBE (*b.* 1956) *C., Cambridgeshire South*, Maj. 8,403
*Lawrence, Mrs Jacqueline R. (*b.* 1948) *Lab., Preseli Pembrokeshire*, Maj. 2,946
Laws, David (*b.* 1965) *LD, Yeovil*, Maj. 3,928
*Laxton, Robert (*b.* 1944) *Lab., Derby North*, Maj. 6,982
Lazarowicz, Mark (*b.* 1953) *Lab. Co-op., Edinburgh North and Leith*, Maj. 8,817
*Leigh, Edward J. E. (*b.* 1950) *C., Gainsborough*, Maj. 8,071
*Lepper, David (*b.* 1945) *Lab. Co-op., Brighton Pavilion*, Maj. 9,643
Leslie, Christopher M. (*b.* 1972) *Lab., Shipley*, Maj. 1,428
Letwin, Oliver (*b.* 1956) *C., Dorset West*, Maj. 1,414
*Levitt, Tom (*b.* 1954) *Lab., High Peak*, Maj. 4,489
*Lewis, Ivan (*b.* 1967) *Lab., Bury South*, Maj. 12,772
*Lewis, Dr Julian M. (*b.* 1951) *C., New Forest East*, Maj. 3,829
*Lewis, Terence (*b.* 1935) *Lab., Worsley*, Maj. 11,787
*Liddell, Rt. Hon. Helen (*b.* 1950) *Lab., Airdrie and Shotts*, Maj. 12,340
Liddell-Grainger, Ian (*b.* 1959) *C., Bridgwater*, Maj. 4,987
*Lidington, David R. PH.D. (*b.* 1956) *C., Aylesbury*, Maj. 10,009
*Lilley, Rt. Hon. Peter B. (*b.* 1943) *C., Hitchin and Harpenden*, Maj. 6,663
Linton, J. Martin (*b.* 1944) *Lab., Battersea*, Maj. 5,053
*Lloyd, Anthony J. (*b.* 1950) *Lab., Manchester Central*, Maj. 13,742
*Llwyd, Elfyn (*b.* 1951) *PC, Meirionnydd nant Conwy*, Maj. 5,684
*Lord, Sir Michael N. (*b.* 1938) *C., Suffolk Central and Ipswich North*, Maj. 3,469
*Loughton, Timothy P. (*b.* 1962) *C., Worthing East and Shoreham*, Maj. 6,139
*Love, Andrew (*b.* 1949) *Lab. Co-op., Edmonton*, Maj. 9,772
Lucas, Ian (*b.* 1960) *Lab., Wrexham*, Maj. 9,188
*Luff, Peter J. (*b.* 1955) *C., Worcestershire Mid*, Maj. 10,627
Luke, Ian (*b.* 1951) *Lab., Dundee East*, Maj. 4,475
Lyons, John (*b.* 1950) *Lab., Strathkelvin and Bearsden*, Maj. 11,717
*MacDonald, Calum A. PH.D. (*b.* 1956) *Lab., Western Isles*, Maj. 1,074
*MacDougall, John (*b.* 1947) *Lab., Fife Central*, Maj. 10,075
*Mackay, Rt. Hon. Andrew J. (*b.* 1949) *C., Bracknell*, Maj. 6,713
*Mackinlay, Andrew S. (*b.* 1949) *Lab., Thurrock*, Maj. 9,997
*Maclean, Rt. Hon. David J. (*b.* 1953) *C., Penrith and the Border*, Maj. 14,677
*MacShane, Denis PH.D. (*b.* 1948) *Lab., Rotherham*, Maj. 13,077
Mactaggart, Ms Fiona M. (*b.* 1953) *Lab., Slough*, Maj. 12,508
*McAvoy, Thomas M. (*b.* 1943) *Lab. Co-op., Glasgow Rutherglen*, Maj. 12,625
*McCabe, Stephen J. (*b.* 1955) *Lab., Birmingham Hall Green*, Maj. 6,648
*McCafferty, Ms Christine (*b.* 1945) *Lab., Calder Valley*, Maj. 3,094
*McCartney, Rt. Hon. Ian (*b.* 1951) *Lab., Makerfield*, Maj. 17,750
McDonagh, Ms Siobhain A. (*b.* 1960) *Lab., Mitcham and Morden*, Maj. 13,785
*McDonnell, John M. (*b.* 1951) *Lab., Hayes and Harlington*, Maj. 13,466
*McFall, John (*b.* 1944) *Lab. Co-op., Dumbarton*, Maj. 9,575
*McGrady, Edward K. (*b.* 1935) *SDLP, Down South*, Maj. 13,858
McGuinness, Martin (*b.* 1950) *SF, Ulster Mid*, Maj. 9,953

McGuire, Anne (*b.* 1949) *Lab., Stirling*, Maj. 6,274
*McIntosh, Miss Anne C. B. (*b.* 1954) *C., Vale of York*, Maj. 12,517
McIsaac, Ms Shona (*b.* 1960) *Lab., Cleethorpes*, Maj. 5,620
McKechin, Anne (*b.* 1961) *Lab., Glasgow Maryhill*, Maj. 9,888
McKenna, Ms Rosemary CBE (*b.* 1941) *Lab., Cumbernauld and Kilsyth*, Maj. 7,520
*McLoughlin, Patrick A. (*b.* 1957) *C., Derbyshire West*, Maj. 7,370
*McNamara, J. Kevin (*b.* 1934) *Lab., Hull North*, Maj. 10,721
*McNulty, Anthony J. (*b.* 1958) *Lab., Harrow East*, Maj. 11,124
*McWalter, Tony (*b.* 1945) *Lab. Co-op., Hemel Hempstead*, Maj. 3,742
*McWilliam, John D. (*b.* 1941) *Lab., Blaydon*, Maj. 7,809
Mahmood, Khalid (*b.* 1961) *Lab., Birmingham Perry Barr*, Maj. 8,753
*Mahon, Mrs Alice (*b.* 1937) *Lab., Halifax*, Maj. 6,129
Malins, Humfrey J. CBE (*b.* 1945) *C., Woking*, Maj. 6,759
*Mallaber, Ms C. Judith (*b.* 1951) *Lab., Amber Valley*, Maj. 7,227
*Mallon, Seamus (*b.* 1936) *SDLP, Newry and Armagh*, Maj. 3,575
*Mandelson, Rt. Hon. Peter B. (*b.* 1953) *Lab., Hartlepool*, Maj. 14,571
Mann, John (*b.* 1960) *Lab., Bassetlaw*, Maj. 9,748
*Maples, John C. (*b.* 1943) *C., Stratford-upon-Avon*, Maj. 11,802
Marris, Robert (*b.* 1955) *Lab., Wolverhampton South West*, Maj. 3,487
*Marsden, Gordon (*b.* 1953) *Lab., Blackpool South*, Maj. 8,262
*Marsden, Paul W. B. (*b.* 1968) *Lab., Shrewsbury and Atcham*, Maj. 3,579
*Marshall, David PH.D (*b.* 1941) *Lab., Glasgow Shettleston*, Maj. 9,818
*Marshall, James PH.D. (*b.* 1941) *Lab., Leicester South*, Maj. 13,243
*Marshall-Andrews, Robert G. QC (*b.* 1944) *Lab., Medway*, Maj. 3,780
*Martin, Rt. Hon. Michael J. (*b.* 1945) *The Speaker Lab., Glasgow Springburn*, Maj. 11,378
*Martlew, Eric A. (*b.* 1949) *Lab., Carlisle*, Maj. 5,702
*Mates, Michael J. (*b.* 1934) *C., Hampshire East*, Maj. 8,890
*Maude, Rt. Hon. Francis A. A. (*b.* 1953) *C., Horsham*, Maj. 13,666
*Mawhinney, Rt. Hon. Sir Brian PH.D. (*b.* 1940) *C., Cambridgeshire North West*, Maj. 8,101
*May, Mrs Theresa M. (*b.* 1956) *C., Maidenhead*, Maj. 3,284
*Meacher, Rt. Hon. Michael H. (*b.* 1939) *Lab., Oldham West and Royton*, Maj. 13,365
*Meale, J. Alan (*b.* 1949) *Lab., Mansfield*, Maj. 11,038
Mercer, Patrick OBE (*b.* 1956) *C., Newark*, Maj. 4,073
*Merron, Ms Gillian J. (*b.* 1959) *Lab., Lincoln*, Maj. 8,420
*Michael, Rt. Hon. Alun E. (*b.* 1943) *Lab. Co-op., Cardiff South and Penarth*, Maj. 12,287
*Milburn, Rt. Hon. Alan (*b.* 1958) *Lab., Darlington*, Maj. 9,529
Miliband, David (*b.* 1966) *Lab., South Shields*, Maj. 14,090
*Miller, Andrew P. (*b.* 1949) *Lab., Ellesmere Port and Neston*, Maj. 10,861
*Mitchell, Austin V. D.PHIL. (*b.* 1934) *Lab., Great Grimsby*, Maj. 11,484
Mitchell, Andrew (*b.* 1956) *C., Sutton Coldfield*, Maj. 10,104
*Moffatt, Mrs Laura J. (*b.* 1954) *Lab., Crawley*, Maj. 6,770

*Moonie, Dr Lewis G. (*b.* 1947) *Lab. Co-op., Kirkcaldy,* Maj. 8,963
*Moore, Michael (*b.* 1965) *LD, Tweeddale, Ettrick and Lauderdale,* Maj. 5,157
*Moran, Ms Margaret (*b.* 1955) *Lab., Luton South,* Maj. 10,133
Morgan, Ms Julie (*b.* 1944) *Lab., Cardiff North,* Maj. 6,165
*Morley, Elliot A. (*b.* 1952) *Lab., Scunthorpe,* Maj. 10,372
*Morris, Rt. Hon. Estelle (*b.* 1952) *Lab., Birmingham Yardley,* Maj. 2,578
*Moss, Malcolm D. (*b.* 1943) *C., Cambridgeshire North East,* Maj. 6,373
Mountford, Ms Kali C. J. (*b.* 1954) *Lab., Colne Valley,* Maj. 4,639
*Mudie, George E. (*b.* 1945) *Lab., Leeds East,* Maj. 12,643
*Mullin, Christopher J. (*b.* 1947) *Lab., Sunderland South,* Maj. 13,667
Munn, Meg (*b.* 1959) *Lab.Co-op, Sheffield Heeley,* Maj. 11,704
Murphy, Denis (*b.* 1948) *Lab., Wansbeck,* Maj. 13,101
Murphy, Jim (*b.* 1967) *Lab., Eastwood,* Maj. 9,141
*Murphy, Rt. Hon. Paul P. (*b.* 1948) *Lab., Torfaen,* Maj. 16,280
Murrison, Andrew (*b.* 1961) *C., Westbury,* Maj. 5,294
Naysmith, J. Douglas (*b.* 1941) *Lab. Co-op., Bristol North West,* Maj. 11,087
Norman, Archibald J. (*b.* 1954) *C., Tunbridge Wells,* Maj. 9,730
Norris, Dan (*b.* 1960) *Lab., Wansdyke,* Maj. 5,113
*Oaten, Mark (*b.* 1964) *LD, Winchester,* Maj. 9,634
*O'Brien, Michael (*b.* 1954) *Lab., Warwickshire North,* Maj. 9,639
*O'Brien, Stephen (*b.* 1957) *C., Eddisbury,* Maj. 4,568
*O'Brien, William (*b.* 1929) *Lab., Normanton,* Maj. 9,937
*O'Hara, Edward (*b.* 1937) *Lab., Knowsley South,* Maj. 21,316
*Olner, William J. (*b.* 1942) *Lab., Nuneaton,* Maj. 7,535
*O'Neill, Martin J. (*b.* 1945) *Lab., Ochil,* Maj. 5,349
Öpik, Lembit (*b.* 1965) *LD, Montgomeryshire,* Maj. 6,234
*Organ, Ms Diana M. (*b.* 1952) *Lab., Forest of Dean,* Maj. 2,049
Osborne, Mrs Sandra C. (*b.* 1956) *Lab., Ayr,* Maj. 2,545
Osborne, George (*b.* 1971) *C., Tatton,* Maj. 8,611
*Ottaway, Richard G. J. (*b.* 1945) *C., Croydon South,* Maj. 8,697
*Owen, Albert (*b.* 1960) *Lab., Ynys Môn,* Maj. 800
*Page, Richard L. (*b.* 1941) *C., Hertfordshire South West,* Maj. 8,181
*Paice, James E. T. (*b.* 1949) *C., Cambridgeshire South East,* Maj. 8,990
*Paisley, Revd Ian R. K. MEP (*b.* 1926) *DUP, Antrim North,* Maj. 14,224
Palmer, Nicholas D. (*b.* 1950) *Lab., Broxtowe,* Maj. 5,873
*Paterson, Owen W. (*b.* 1956) *C., Shropshire North,* Maj. 6,241
*Pearson, Ian P. PH.D. (*b.* 1959) *Lab., Dudley South,* Maj. 6,817
*Perham, Ms Linda (*b.* 1947) *Lab., Ilford North,* Maj. 2,115
Picking, Anne (*b.* 1958) *Lab., East Lothian,* Maj. 10,830
*Pickles, Eric J. (*b.* 1952) *C., Brentwood and Ongar,* Maj. 2,821
*Pickthall, Colin (*b.* 1944) *Lab., Lancashire West,* Maj. 9,643
*Pike, Peter L. (*b.* 1937) *Lab., Burnley,* Maj. 10,498
*Plaskitt, James A. (*b.* 1954) *Lab., Warwick and Leamington,* Maj. 5,953
Pollard, Kerry P. (*b.* 1944) *Lab., St Albans,* Maj. 4,466
*Pond, Christopher R. (*b.* 1952) *Lab., Gravesham,* Maj. 4,862
*Pope, Gregory J. (*b.* 1960) *Lab., Hyndburn,* Maj. 8,219

*Portillo, Rt. Hon. Michael (*b.* 1953) *C., Kensington and Chelsea,* Maj. 8,771
Pound, Stephen P. (*b.* 1948) *Lab., Ealing North,* Maj. 11,837
*Powell, Sir Raymond (*b.* 1928) *Lab., Ogmore,* Maj. 14,574
*Prentice, Ms Bridget T. (*b.* 1952) *Lab., Lewisham East,* Maj. 8,959
*Prentice, Gordon (*b.* 1951) *Lab., Pendle,* Maj. 4,275
*Prescott, Rt. Hon. John L. (*b.* 1938) *Lab., Hull East,* Maj. 15,325
Price, Adam (*b.* 1968) *PC, Carmarthen East and Dinefwr,* Maj. 2,590
*Primarolo, Ms Dawn (*b.* 1954) *Lab., Bristol South,* Maj. 14,181
*Prisk, Mark (*b.* 1962) *C., Hertford and Stortford,* Maj. 5,603
*Prosser, Gwynfor M. (*b.* 1943) *Lab., Dover,* Maj. 5,199
Pugh, John (*b.* 1949) *LD, Southport,* Maj. 3,007
*Purchase, Kenneth (*b.* 1939) *Lab. Co-op., Wolverhampton North East,* Maj. 9,965
Purnell, James (*b.* 1970) *Lab., Stalybridge and Hyde,* Maj. 8,859
*Quin, Rt. Hon. Joyce G. (*b.* 1944) *Lab., Gateshead East and Washington West,* Maj. 17,904
*Quinn, Lawrence W. (*b.* 1956) *Lab., Scarborough and Whitby,* Maj. 3,585
*Rammell, William E. (*b.* 1959) *Lab., Harlow,* Maj. 5,228
*Randall, A. John (*b.* 1955) *C., Uxbridge,* Maj. 2,098
Rapson, Sydney N. J. (*b.* 1942) *Lab., Portsmouth North,* Maj. 5,134
*Raynsford, Rt. Hon. W. R. N. (Nick) (*b.* 1945) *Lab., Greenwich and Woolwich,* Maj. 13,433
*Redwood, Rt. Hon. John A. D.PHIL. (*b.* 1951) *C., Wokingham,* Maj. 5,994
Reed, Andrew J. (*b.* 1964) *Lab., Loughborough,* Maj. 6,378
Reid, Alan (*b.* 1954) *LD, Argyll and Bute,* Maj. 1,653
*Reid, Rt. Hon. John PH.D. (*b.* 1947) *Lab., Hamilton North and Bellshill,* Maj. 13,561
*Rendel, David D. (*b.* 1949) *LD, Newbury,* Maj. 2,415
*Robathan, Andrew R. G. (*b.* 1951) *C., Blaby,* Maj. 6,209
*Robertson, John (*b.* 1952) *Lab., Glasgow Anniesland,* Maj. 11,054
Robertson, Angus (*b.* 1945) *SNP, Moray,* Maj. 11,054
Robertson, Hugh (*b.* 1962) *C., Faversham and Mid Kent,* Maj. 4,183
Robertson, Laurence A. (*b.* 1958) *C., Tewkesbury,* Maj. 8,663
*Robinson, Geoffrey (*b.* 1938) *Lab., Coventry North West,* Maj. 10,874
Robinson, Iris MLA (*b.* 1949) *DUP, Strangford,* Maj. 1,110
*Robinson, Peter D. (*b.* 1948) *DUP, Belfast East,* Maj. 7,117
*Roche, Mrs Barbara M. R. (*b.* 1954) *Lab., Hornsey and Wood Green,* Maj. 10,614
*Roe, Mrs Marion A. (*b.* 1936) *C., Broxbourne,* Maj. 8,993
*Rooney, Terence H. (*b.* 1950) *Lab., Bradford North,* Maj. 8,969
Rosindell, Andrew (*b.* 1966) *C., Romford,* Maj. 5,977
*Ross, Ernest (*b.* 1942) *Lab., Dundee West,* Maj. 6,800
*Roy, Frank (*b.* 1958) *Lab., Motherwell and Wishaw,* Maj. 10,956
*Ruane, Christopher S. (*b.* 1958) *Lab., Vale of Clwyd,* Maj. 5,761
*Ruddock, Mrs Joan M. (*b.* 1943) *Lab., Lewisham Deptford,* Maj. 15,293
Ruffley, David L. (*b.* 1962) *C., Bury St Edmunds,* Maj. 2,503
Russell, Ms Christine M. (*b.* 1945) *Lab., City of Chester,* Maj. 6,894
*Russell, Robert E. (*b.* 1946) *LD, Colchester,* Maj. 5,553
*Ryan, Ms Joan M. (*b.* 1955) *Lab., Enfield North,* Maj. 2,291

*Salmond, Alexander E. A. (*b.* 1954) *SNP, Banff and Buchan,* Maj. 10,503

Salter, Martin J. (*b.* 1954) *Lab., Reading West,* Maj. 8,849

*Sanders, Adrian M. (*b.* 1959) *LD, Torbay,* Maj. 6,708

*Sarwar, Mohammad (*b.* 1952) *Lab., Glasgow Govan,* Maj. 6,400

*Savidge, Malcolm K. (*b.* 1946) *Lab., Aberdeen North,* Maj. 4,449

*Sawford, Philip A. (*b.* 1950) *Lab., Kettering,* Maj. 665

*Sayeed, Jonathan (*b.* 1948) *C., Bedfordshire Mid,* Maj. 8,066

*Sedgemore, Brian C. J. (*b.* 1937) *Lab., Hackney South and Shoreditch,* Maj. 15,049

Selous, Andres (*b.* 1962) *C., Bedfordshire South West,* Maj. 776

*Shaw, Jonathan R. (*b.* 1966) *Lab., Chatham and Aylesford,* Maj. 4,340

*Sheerman, Barry J. (*b.* 1940) *Lab. Co-op., Huddersfield,* Maj. 10,046

*Shephard, Rt. Hon. Gillian P. (*b.* 1940) *C., Norfolk South West,* Maj. 9,366

*Shepherd, Richard C. S. (*b.* 1942) *C., Aldridge-Brownhills,* Maj. 3,768

Sheridan, Jim (*b.* 1952) *Lab., Renfrewshire West,* Maj. 8,575

*Shipley, Ms Debra A. (*b.* 1957) *Lab., Stourbridge,* Maj. 3,812

*Short, Rt. Hon. Clare (*b.* 1946) *Lab., Birmingham Ladywood,* Maj. 18,143

Simmonds, Mark (*b.* 1964) *C., Boston and Skegness,* Maj. 515

Simon, Sion (*b.* 1969) *Lab., Birmingham Erdington,* Maj. 9,962

*Simpson, Alan J. (*b.* 1948) *Lab., Nottingham South,* Maj. 9,989

*Simpson, Keith (*b.* 1949) *C., Norfolk Mid,* Maj. 4,562

Singh, Marsha (*b.* 1954) *Lab., Bradford West,* Maj. 4,165

*Skinner, Dennis E. (*b.* 1932) *Lab., Bolsover,* Maj. 18,777

*Smith, Rt. Hon. Andrew D. (*b.* 1951) *Lab., Oxford East,* Maj. 10,344

*Smith, Ms Angela E. (*b.* 1959) *Lab. Co-op., Basildon,* Maj. 7,738

*Smith, Rt. Hon. Christopher R. PH.D. (*b.* 1951) *Lab., Islington South and Finsbury,* Maj. 7,280

*Smith, Ms Geraldine (*b.* 1961) *Lab., Morecambe and Lunesdale,* Maj. 5,092

*Smith, Ms Jacqui (*b.* 1962) *Lab., Redditch,* Maj. 2,484

*Smith, John W. P. (*b.* 1951) *Lab., Vale of Glamorgan,* Maj. 4,700

*Smith, Llewellyn T. (*b.* 1944) *Lab., Blaenau Gwent,* Maj. 19,313

*Smith, Sir Robert BT. (*b.* 1958) *LD, Aberdeenshire West and Kincardine,* Maj. 4,821

*Smyth, Revd W. Martin (*b.* 1931) *UUP, Belfast South,* Maj. 5,399

*Soames, Hon. A. Nicholas W. (*b.* 1948) *C., Sussex Mid,* Maj. 6,898

*Soley, Clive S. (*b.* 1939) *Lab., Ealing Acton and Shepherd's Bush,* Maj. 10,789

Southworth, Ms Helen M. (*b.* 1956) *Lab., Warrington South,* Maj. 7,387

*Spellar, Rt. Hon. John F. (*b.* 1947) *Lab., Warley,* Maj. 11,850

Spelman, Mrs Caroline A. (*b.* 1958) *C., Meriden,* Maj. 3,784

*Spicer, Sir Michael (*b.* 1943) *C., Worcestershire West,* Maj. 5,374

Spink, Dr Robert (*b.* 1948) *C., Castle Point,* Maj. 985

*Spring, Richard J. G. (*b.* 1946) *C., Suffolk West,* Maj. 4,295

*Squire, Ms Rachel A. (*b.* 1954) *Lab., Dunfermline West,* Maj. 10,980

*Stanley, Rt. Hon. Sir John (*b.* 1942) *C., Tonbridge and Malling,* Maj. 8,250

Starkey, Dr Phyllis M. (*b.* 1947) *Lab., Milton Keynes South West,* Maj. 6,978

*Steen, Anthony (*b.* 1939) *C., Totnes,* Maj. 3,597

*Steinberg, Gerald N. (*b.* 1945) *Lab., City of Durham,* Maj. 13,441

*Stevenson, George W. (*b.* 1938) *Lab., Stoke-on-Trent South,* Maj. 10,489

*Stewart, David J. (*b.* 1956) *Lab., Inverness East, Nairn and Lochaber,* Maj. 4,716

*Stewart, Ian (*b.* 1950) *Lab., Eccles,* Maj. 14,528

*Stinchcombe, Paul D. (*b.* 1962) *Lab., Wellingborough,* Maj. 2,355

*Stoate, Dr Howard G. A. (*b.* 1954) *Lab., Dartford,* Maj. 3,306

*Strang, Rt. Hon Dr Gavin (*b.* 1943) *Lab., Edinburgh East and Musselburgh,* Maj. 12,168

*Straw, Rt. Hon. J. W. (Jack) (*b.* 1946) *Lab., Blackburn,* Maj. 9,249

*Streeter, Gary N. (*b.* 1955) *C., Devon South West,* Maj. 7,144

*Stringer, Graham E. (*b.* 1950) *Lab., Manchester Blackley,* Maj. 14,464

*Stuart, Mrs Gisela G. (*b.* 1955) *Lab., Birmingham Edgbaston,* Maj. 4,698

*Stunell, Andrew (*b.* 1942) *LD, Hazel Grove,* Maj. 8,435

*Sutcliffe, Gerard (*b.* 1953) *Lab., Bradford South,* Maj. 9,662

Swayne, Desmond A. (*b.* 1956) *C., New Forest West,* Maj. 13,191

Swire, Hugo (*b.* 1959) *C., Devon East,* Maj. 8,195

*Syms, Robert A. R. (*b.* 1956) *C., Poole,* Maj. 7,166

Tami, Mark (*b.* 1963) *Lab., Alyn and Deeside,* Maj. 9,222

*Tapsell, Sir Peter (*b.* 1930) *C., Louth and Horncastle,* Maj. 7,554

*Taylor, Rt. Hon. Ann (*b.* 1947) *Lab., Dewsbury,* Maj. 7,449

*Taylor, Ms Dari J. (*b.* 1944) *Lab., Stockton South,* Maj. 9,086

Taylor, David L. (*b.* 1946) *Lab., Leicestershire North West,* Maj. 8,157

*Taylor, Sir Edward (Teddy) (*b.* 1937) *C., Rochford and Southend East,* Maj. 7,034

*Taylor, Ian C. MBE (*b.* 1945) *C., Esher and Walton,* Maj. 11,538

*Taylor, John M. (*b.* 1941) *C., Solihull,* Maj. 9,407

*Taylor, Matthew O. J. (*b.* 1963) *LD, Truro and St Austell,* Maj. 8,065

Taylor, Dr Richard (*b.* 1935) *KHHC, Wyre Forest,* Maj. 17,630

Thomas, Gareth (*b.* 1954) *Lab., Clwyd West,* Maj. 1,115

*Thomas, Gareth R. (*b.* 1967) *Lab., Harrow West,* Maj. 6,156

*Thomas, Simon (*b.* 1963) *PC, Ceredigion,* Maj. 3,944

*Thurso, John (*b.* 1953) *LD, Caithness, Sutherland and Easter Ross,* Maj. 2,744

*Timms, Stephen C. (*b.* 1955) *Lab., East Ham,* Maj. 21,032

*Tipping, S. P. (Paddy) (*b.* 1949) *Lab., Sherwood,* Maj. 9,373

Todd, Mark W. (*b.* 1954) *Lab., Derbyshire South,* Maj. 7,851

Tonge, Dr Jennifer L. (*b.* 1941) *LD, Richmond Park,* Maj. 4,964

*Touhig, J. Donnelly (Don) (*b.* 1947) *Lab. Co-op., Islwyn,* Maj. 15,309

*Tredinnick, David A. S. (*b.* 1950) *C., Bosworth,* Maj. 2,280

*Trend, Hon. Michael St J. CBE (*b.* 1952) *C., Windsor,* Maj. 8,889

*Trickett, Jon H. (*b.* 1950) *Lab., Hemsworth,* Maj. 15,636

*Trimble, Rt. Hon. W. David (*b.* 1944) *UUP, Upper Bann,* Maj. 2,058

Truswell, Paul A. (*b.* 1955) *Lab., Pudsey,* Maj. 5,626

Turner, Andrew (*b.* 1953) *C.*, *Isle of Wight*, Maj. 2,826
*Turner, Dennis (*b.* 1942) *Lab.* *Co-op.*, *Wolverhampton South East*, Maj. 12,464
Turner, Desmond S. (*b.* 1939) *Lab.*, *Brighton Kemptown*, Maj. 4,922
*Turner, Neil (*b.* 1945) *Lab.*, *Wigan*, Maj. 13,743
*Twigg, J. Derek (*b.* 1959) *Lab.*, *Halton*, Maj. 17,428
*Twigg, Stephen (*b.* 1966) *Lab.*, *Enfield Southgate*, Maj. 5,546
*Tyler, Paul A. CBE (*b.* 1941) *LD*, *Cornwall North*, Maj. 9,832
*Tynan, Bill (*b.* 1940) *Lab.*, *Hamilton South*, Maj. 10,775
*Tyrie, Andrew G. (*b.* 1957) *C.*, *Chichester*, Maj. 11,355
*Vaz, N. Keith A. S. (*b.* 1956) *Lab.*, *Leicester East*, Maj. 13,422
*Viggers, Peter J. (*b.* 1938) *C.*, *Gosport*, Maj. 2,621
*Vis, R. J. (Rudi) (*b.* 1941) *Lab.*, *Finchley and Golders Green*, Maj. 3,716
*Walley, Ms Joan L. (*b.* 1949) *Lab.*, *Stoke-on-Trent North*, Maj. 11,784
*Walter, Robert J. (*b.* 1948) *C.*, *Dorset North*, Maj. 3,797
*Ward, Ms Claire M. (*b.* 1972) *Lab.*, *Watford*, Maj. 5,555
*Wareing, Robert N. (*b.* 1930) *Lab.*, *Liverpool West Derby*, Maj. 15,853
*Waterson, Nigel C. (*b.* 1950) *C.*, *Eastbourne*, Maj. 2,154
Watkinson, Angela (*b.* 1941) *C.*, *Upminster*, Maj. 1,241
*Watson, Tom (*b.* 1967) *Lab.*, *West Bromwich East*, Maj. 9,763
Watts, David L. (*b.* 1951) *Lab.*, *St Helens North*, Maj. 15,901
Webb, Prof. Steven J. (*b.* 1965) *LD*, *Northavon*, Maj. 9,877
Weir, Michael (*b.* 1957) *SNP*, *Angus*, Maj. 3,611
White, Brian A. R. (*b.* 1957) *Lab.*, *Milton Keynes North East*, Maj. 1,829
*Whitehead, Alan P. V. (*b.* 1950) *Lab.*, *Southampton Test*, Maj. 11,207
*Whittingdale, John F. L. OBE (*b.* 1959) *C.*, *Maldon and Chelmsford East*, Maj. 8,462
*Wicks, Malcolm H. (*b.* 1947) *Lab.*, *Croydon North*, Maj. 16,858
*Widdecombe, Rt. Hon. Ann N. (*b.* 1947) *C.*, *Maidstone and the Weald*, Maj. 10,318
Wiggin, Bill (*b.* 1966) *C.*, *Leominster*, Maj. 10,367
*Wilkinson, John A. D. (*b.* 1940) *C.*, *Ruislip-Northwood*, Maj. 7,537

*Willetts, David L. (*b.* 1956) *C.*, *Havant*, Maj. 4,207
*Williams, Rt. Hon. Alan J. (*b.* 1930) *Lab.*, *Swansea West*, Maj. 9,550
*Williams, Betty (*b.* 1944) *Lab.*, *Conwy*, Maj. 6,219
Williams, Hywel (*b.* 1953) *PC*, *Caernarfon*, Maj. 3,511
Williams, Roger (*b.* 1948) *LD*, *Brecon and Radnorshire*, Maj. 751
*Willis, G. Philip (*b.* 1941) *LD*, *Harrogate and Knaresborough*, Maj. 8,845
Wills, Michael D. (*b.* 1952) *Lab.*, *Swindon North*, Maj. 8,105
*Wilshire, David (*b.* 1943) *C.*, *Spelthorne*, Maj. 3,262
*Wilson, Brian D. H. (*b.* 1948) *Lab.*, *Cunninghame North*, Maj. 8,398
*Winnick, David J. (*b.* 1933) *Lab.*, *Walsall North*, Maj. 9,391
*Winterton, Mrs J. Ann (*b.* 1941) *C.*, *Congleton*, Maj. 7,134
*Winterton, Nicholas R. (*b.* 1938) *C.*, *Macclesfield*, Maj. 7,200
Winterton, Ms Rosalie (*b.* 1958) *Lab.*, *Doncaster Central*, Maj. 11,999
Wishart, Peter (*b.* 1962) *SNP*, *Tayside North*, Maj. 3,283
*Wood, Michael R. (*b.* 1946) *Lab.*, *Batley and Spen*, Maj. 5,064
Woodward, Shaun (*b.* 1958) *Lab.*, *St Helens South*, Maj. 8,985
*Woolas, Philip J. (*b.* 1959) *Lab.*, *Oldham East and Saddleworth*, Maj. 2,726
*Worthington, Anthony (*b.* 1941) *Lab.*, *Clydebank and Milngavie*, Maj. 10,724
*Wray, James (*b.* 1938) *Lab.*, *Glasgow Baillieston*, Maj. 9,839
Wright, Anthony D. (*b.* 1954) *Lab.*, *Great Yarmouth*, Maj. 4,564
*Wright, Anthony W. D.PHIL. (*b.* 1948) *Lab.*, *Cannock Chase*, Maj. 10,704
Wright, David (*b.* 1967) *Lab.*, *Telford*, Maj. 8,383
*Wyatt, Derek M. (*b.* 1949) *Lab.*, *Sittingbourne and Sheppey*, Maj. 3,509
*Yeo, Timothy S. K. (*b.* 1945) *C.*, *Suffolk South*, Maj. 5,081
*Young, Rt. Hon. Sir George BT. (*b.* 1941) *C.*, *Hampshire North West*, Maj. 12,009
Younger-Ross, Richard (*b.* 1953) *LD*, *Teignbridge*, Maj. 3,011

*Sitting MPs
For By-elections since 1997 *see* page 268
For MPs who stood down and defeated MPs *see* page 269.

GENERAL ELECTION STATISTICS

MAJORITIES IN THE COMMONS SINCE 1970

Year	Party	Maj.
1970	Conservative	31
1974 Feb.	No majority	
1974 Oct.	Labour	5
1979	Conservative	43
1983	Conservative	144
1987	Conservative	102
1992	Conservative	21
1997	Labour	178
2001	Labour	165

DISTRIBUTION OF SEATS BY COUNTRY 2001

	England	Wales	Scotland	N. Ireland
Conservative	165	—	1	—
Labour	323	34	55	—
Lib. Dem.	40	2	10	—
SNP	—	—	5	—
Plaid Cymru	—	4	—	—
Other	1	—	1*	18

* The Speaker

VOTES CAST 1997 AND 2001

	1997	2001
Conservative	9,600,940	8,357,622
Labour	13,517,911	10,724,895
Liberal Democrats	5,243,440	4,812,833
Scottish Nationalist	622,260	464,305
Plaid Cymru	161,030	195,892
N. Ireland parties	780,920	635,735
Others	1,361,701	1,177,516
Total	31,287,702	26,368,798

SIZE OF ELECTORATE 2001

England	37,101,328
Wales	2,238,211
Scotland	4,001,018
Northern Ireland	1,205,097
Total	44,545,654

PARLIAMENTARY CONSTITUENCIES AS AT 7 JUNE 2001

The results of voting in each parliamentary division at the general election of 7 June 2001 are given below. The majority in the 1997 general election, and any by-election between 1997 and 2001, is given below the 2001 result.

Symbols
* Sitting MP
† Previously MP in another seat

Abbreviations
AL	Asian League
Alliance	Alliance
Anti-Corrupt	Anti-Corruption Forum
BNP	British National Party
Bean	New Millennium Bean
CPA	Christian Peoples Alliance
Ch. D.	Christian Democrat
Choice	People's Choice
Comm.	Communist Party
Community	Independent Community Candidate Empowering Change
C.	Conservative
Country	Countryside Party
Customer	Direct Customer Service Party
DUP	Democratic Unionist Party
Def Welfare	Defend The Welfare State Against Blairism
Elvis	Church of the Militant Elvis Party
Ext. Club	Club Extinction Club
FDP	Fancy Dress Party

FP	Freedom Party
Green	Green Party
Grey	Grey Party
IOW	Isle of Wight Party
Ind.	Independent
Ind. UU	Independent United Unionist
Ind. Vote	Independent - Vote for Yourself Party
JLDP	John Lillburne Democratic Party
JP	Justice Party
KHHC	Kidderminster Hospital and Health Concern
LCA	Legalise Cannabis Alliance
LD	Liberal Democrat
LP	Liberated Party
Lab.	Labour
Lab. Co-op.	Labour and Co-operative
Left	All Left Alliance
Lib.	Liberal
Loony	Monster Raving Loony Party
Low Excise	Lower Excise Duty Party
Marxist	Marxist Party
Meb. Ker.	Mebyon Kernow
Muslim	Muslim Party
NBP	New Britain Party
NF	National Front
NI Unionist	Northern Ireland Unionist
PC	Plaid Cymru
PF	Pathfinders
PJP	People's Justice Party
PUP	Progressive Unionist Party
Pacifist	Pacifist for Peace, Justice, Cooperation, Environment
Pensioner	Pensioner Coalition
Pro Euro C	Pro Euro Conservative Party
ProLife	ProLife Alliance

Prog Dem	Progress Democratic Party Members Decide Policy
Qari	Qari
R & R Loony	Rock & Roll Loony Party
RP	Rate Payer
Ref. UK	Reform UK
Reform	Reform 2000
Res.	Motor Residents and Motorists of Great Britain
SDLP	Social Democratic and Labour Party
SF	Sinn Fein
SNP	Scottish National Party
SSP	Scottish Socialist Party
Scot. Ref.	Scottish Freedom Referendum Party
Scot. U.	Scottish Unionist
Soc.	Socialist Party
Soc. Alt.	Socialist Alternative Party
Soc. Lab.	Socialist Labour Party
Socialist	Socialist
Speaker	The Speaker
Stuck	Stuckist
Sunrise	Chairman of Sunrise Radio
Tatton	Tatton Group Independent
Third	Third Way
Truth	Truth Party
UK Ind.	UK Independence Party
UKU	United Kingdom Unionist
UUP	Ulster Unionist Party
Unrep.	Unrepresented People's Party
WFLOE	Women for Life on Earth
WP	Workers' Party
WRP	Workers' Revolutionary Party
Wessex Reg.	Wessex Regionalist
Women's Co.	Women's Coalition
Wrestling	Jam Wrestling Party

ENGLAND

ALDERSHOT
E.78,262 T. 45,315 (57.90%) C. hold
*Gerald Howarth, C.   19,106
Adrian Collett, LD   12,542
Luke Akehurst, Lab.   11,391
Derek Rumsey, UK Ind.   797
Adam Stacey, Green   630
Arthur Pendragon, Ind.   459
Alan Hope, Loony   390
C. majority 6,564 (14.49%)
1.13% swing LD to C.
(1997, C. maj. 6,621 (12.22%))

ALDRIDGE-BROWNHILLS
E.62,388 T. 37,810 (60.60%) C. hold
*Richard Shepherd, C.   18,974
Ian Geary, Lab.   15,206
Mrs Monica Howes, LD   3,251
John Rothery, Soc. All.   379
C. majority 3,768 (9.97%)
2.26% swing Lab. to C.
(1997, C. maj. 2,526 (5.44%))

ALTRINCHAM & SALE WEST
E.71,820 T. 43,568 (60.66%) C. hold
*Graham Brady, C.   20,113
Ms Janet Baugh, Lab.   17,172
Christopher Gaskell, LD   6,283
C. majority 2,941 (6.75%)
1.92% swing Lab. to C.
(1997, C. maj. 1,505 (2.91%))

AMBER VALLEY
E.73,798 T. 44,513 (60.32%) Lab. hold
*Ms Judy Mallaber, Lab.   23,101
Ms Gillian Shaw, C.   15,874
Ms Kate Smith, LD   5,538
Lab. majority 7,227 (16.24%)
2.49% swing Lab. to C.
(1997, Lab. maj. 11,613 (21.21%))

ARUNDEL & SOUTH DOWNS
E.70,956 T. 45,889 (64.67%) C. hold
*Howard Flight, C.   23,969
Derek Deedman, LD   10,265
Charles Taylor, Lab.   9,488
Robert Perrin, UK Ind.   2,167
C. majority 13,704 (29.86%)
1.26% swing LD to C.
(1997, C. maj. 14,035 (27.34%))

ASHFIELD
E.73,428 T. 39,350 (53.59%)Lab. hold
*Rt. Hon. G. Hoon, Lab.   22,875
Julian Leigh, C.   9,607
Bill Smith, LD   4,428
Melvin Harby, Ind.   1,471
George Watson, Soc. All.   589
Ms Katrina Howse, Soc. Lab.   380
Lab. majority 13,268 (33.72%)
5.60% swing Lab. to C.
(1997, Lab. maj. 22,728 (44.91%))

ASHFORD
E.76,699 T. 47,937 (62.50%) C. hold
*Damien Green, C.   22,739
John Adams, Lab.   15,380
Keith Fitchett, LD   7,236
Richard Boden, Green   1,353
David Waller, UK Ind.   1,229
C. majority 7,359 (15.35%)

2.84% swing Lab. to C.
(1997, C. maj. 5,355 (9.68%))

ASHTON UNDER LYNE
E.72,820 T. 35,764 (49.11%) Lab. hold
David Heyes, Lab.   22,340
Tim Charlesworth, C.   6,822
Mrs Kate Fletcher, LD   4,237
Roger Woods, BNP   1,617
Nigel Rolland, Green   748
Lab. majority 15,518 (43.39%)
2.59% swing Lab. to C.
(1997, Lab. maj. 22,965 (48.57%))

AYLESBURY
E.80,002 T. 49,087 (61.36%) C. hold
*David Lidington, C.   23,230
Peter Jones, LD   13,221
Keith White, Lab.   11,388
Justin Harper, UK Ind.   1,248
C. majority 10,009 (20.39%)
2.88% swing LD to C.
(1997, C. maj. 8,419 (14.63%))

BANBURY
E.83,392 T. 51,515 (61.77%) C. hold
*Tony Baldry, C.   23,271
Leslie Sibley, Lab.   18,052
Tony Worgan, LD   8,216
Bev Cotton, Green   1,281
Stephen Harris, UK Ind.   695
C. majority 5,219 (10.13%)
1.02% swing Lab. to C.
(1997, C. maj. 4,737 (8.10%))

BARKING
E.55,229 T. 25,126 (45.49%) Lab. hold
*Mrs Margaret Hodge, Lab.   15,302
Mike Weatherley, C.   5,768
Anura Keppetipola, LD   2,450
Mark Toleman, BNP   1,606
Lab. majority 9,534 (37.94%)
5.14% swing Lab. to C.
(1997, Lab. maj. 15,896 (48.22%))

BARNSLEY CENTRAL
E.60,086 T. 27,543 (45.84%) Lab. hold
*Eric Illsley, Lab.   19,181
Alan Hartley, LD   4,051
Ian McCord, C.   3,608
Henry Rajch, Soc. All.   703
Lab. majority 15,130 (54.93%)
6.26% swing Lab. to C.
(1997, Lab. maj. 24,501 (67.15%))

BARNSLEY EAST & MEXBOROUGH
E.65,655 T. 32,509 (49.51%) Lab. hold
*Jeff Ennis, Lab.   21,945
Mrs Sharron Brook, LD   5,156
Matthew Offord, C.   4,024
Terry Robinson, Soc. Lab.   722
George Savage, UK Ind.   662
Lab. majority 16,789 (51.64%)
5.57% swing Lab. to LD
(1997, Lab. maj. 26,763 (61.76%))

BARNSLEY WEST & PENISTONE
E.65,291 T. 34,564 (52.94%) Lab. hold
*Michael Clapham, Lab.   20,244
William Rowe, C.   7,892

Miles Crompton, LD   6,428
Lab. majority 12,352 (35.74%)
2.59% swing Lab. to C.
(1997, Lab. maj. 17,267 (40.91%))

BARROW & FURNESS
E.64,746 T. 39,020 (60.27%) Lab. hold
*Rt. Hon. J. Hutton, Lab.   21,724
James Airey, C.   11,835
Barry Rabone, LD   4,750
John Smith, UK Ind.   711
Lab. majority 9,889 (25.34%)
2.36% swing Lab. to C.
(1997, Lab. maj. 14,497 (30.06%))

BASILDON
E.74,121 T. 40,875 (55.15%) Lab. Co-op hold
*Ms Angela Smith, Lab. Co-op   21,551
Dominic Schofield, C.   13,813
Ms Jane Smithard, LD   3,691
Frank Mallon, UK Ind.   1,397
Dick Duane, Soc. All.   423
Lab. Co-op majority 7,738 (18.93%)
3.04% swing Lab. Co-op to C.
(1997, Lab. maj. 13,280 (25.02%))

BASINGSTOKE
E.79,110 T. 47,995 (60.67%) C. hold
*Andrew Hunter, C.   20,490
Jon Hartley, Lab.   19,610
Steve Sollitt, LD   6,693
Mrs Kim-Elisbeth Graham,
UK Ind.   1,202
C. majority 880 (1.83%)
1.18% swing C. to Lab.
(1997, C. maj. 2,397 (4.19%))

BASSETLAW
E.68,302 T. 38,895 (56.95%) Lab. hold
John Mann, Lab.   21,506
Mrs Alison Holley, C.   11,758
Neil Taylor, LD   4,942
Kevin Meloy, Soc. Lab.   689
Lab. majority 9,748 (25.06%)
5.68% swing Lab. to C.
(1997, Lab. maj. 17,460 (36.43%))

BATH
E.71,372 T. 46,296 (64.87%) LD hold
*Don Foster, LD   23,372
Ashley Fox, C.   13,478
Ms Marilyn Hawkings, Lab.   7,269
Mike Boulton, Green   1,469
Andrew Tettenborn, UK Ind.   708
LD majority 9,894 (21.37%)
2.06% swing C. to LD
(1997, LD maj. 9,319 (17.26%))

BATLEY & SPEN
E.63,665 T. 38,542 (60.54%) Lab. hold
*Mike Wood, Lab.   19,224
Mrs Elizabeth Peacock, C.   14,160
Ms Kath Pinnock, LD   3,989
Clive Lord, Green   595
Allen Burton, UK Ind.   574
Lab. majority 5,064 (13.14%)
0.03% swing C. to Lab.
(1997, Lab. maj. 6,141 (13.08%))

BATTERSEA
E.67,495 T. 36,804 (54.53%) Lab. hold

*Martin Linton, *Lab.*   18,498
Mrs Lucy Shersby, *C.*   13,445
Ms Siobhan Vitelli, *LD*   4,450
Thomas Barber, *Ind.*   411
Lab. majority 5,053 (13.73%)
1.21% swing C. to Lab.
(1997, Lab. maj. 5,360 (11.31%))

BEACONSFIELD
*E.*68,378   *T.* 42,044 (61.49%) C. hold
*Dominic Grieve, *C.*   22,233
Stephen Lathrope, *Lab.*   9,168
Stephen Lloyd, *LD*   9,017
Andrew Moffatt, *UK Ind.*   1,626
C. majority 13,065 (31.07%)
0.95% swing Lab. to C.
(1997, C. maj. 13,987 (27.86%))

BECKENHAM
*E.*72,241   *T.* 45,562 (63.07%) C. hold
*Mrs Jacqui Lait, *C.*   20,618
Richard Watts, *Lab.*   15,659
Alex Feakes, *LD*   7,308
Ms Karen Moran, *Green*   961
Christopher Pratt, *UK Ind.*   782
Rif Winfield, *Lib.*   234
C. majority 4,959 (10.88%)
0.89% swing Lab. to C.
(1997 Nov by-election, C. maj. 1,227
(3.85%); (1997, C. maj. 4,953 (9.11%))

BEDFORD
*E.*67,763   *T.* 40,579 (59.88%) Lab. hold
*Patrick Hall, *Lab.*   19,454
Mrs Nicky Attenborough, *C.*   13,297
Michael Headley, *LD*   6,425
Dr Richard Rawlins, *Ind.*   973
Mrs Jennifer Lo Bianco, *UK Ind.*   430
Lab. majority 6,157 (15.17%)
0.89% swing Lab. to C.
(1997, Lab. maj. 8,300 (16.96%))

BEDFORDSHIRE MID
*E.*70,594   *T.* 46,638 (66.07%) C. hold
*Jonathan Sayeed, *C.*   22,109
James Valentine, *Lab.*   14,043
Graham Mabbutt, *LD*   9,205
Christopher Laurence, *UK Ind.*   1,281
C. majority 8,066 (17.29%)
1.89% swing Lab. to C.
(1997, C. maj. 7,090 (13.51%))

BEDFORDSHIRE NORTH EAST
*E.*69,451   *T.* 45,246 (65.15%) C. hold
Alastair Burt, *C.*   22,586
Philip Ross, *Lab.*   14,009
Dan Rogerson, *LD*   7,409
Ms Ros Hill, *UK Ind.*   1,242
C. majority 8,577 (18.96%)
3.64% swing Lab. to C.
(1997, C. maj. 5,883 (11.68%))

BEDFORDSHIRE SOUTH WEST
*E.*72,126   *T.* 43,854 (60.80%) C. hold
Andrew Selous, *C.*   18,477
Andrew Date, *Lab.*   17,701
Martin Pantling, *LD*   6,473
Tom Wise, *UK Ind.*   1,203
C. majority 776 (1.77%)
0.76% swing Lab. to C.
(1997, C. maj. 132 (0.24%))

BERWICK-UPON-TWEED
*E.*56,918   *T.* 36,308 (63.79%)   LD hold
*Rt. Hon. A. Beith, *LD*   18,651
Glen Sanderson, *C.*   10,193
Martin Walker, *Lab.*   6,435
John Pearson, *UK Ind.*   1,029
LD majority 8,458 (23.30%)
0.94% swing C. to LD
(1997, LD maj. 8,042 (19.24%))

BETHNAL GREEN & BOW
*E.*79,192   *T.* 38,470 (48.58%) Lab. hold
*Ms Oona King, *Lab.*   19,380
Shahagir Faruk, *C.*   9,323
Ms Janet Ludlow, *LD*   5,946
Ms Anna Bragga, *Green*   1,666
Michael Davidson, *BNP*   1,267
Dennis Delderfield, *NBP*   888
Lab. majority 10,057 (26.14%)
0.44% swing C. to Lab.
(1997, Lab. maj. 11,285 (25.26%))

BEVERLEY & HOLDERNESS
*E.*75,146   *T.* 46,375 (61.71%) C. hold
*James Cran, *C.*   19,168
Stewart Willie, *LD*   7,356
Stephen Wallis, *UK Ind.*   1,464
C. majority 781 (1.68%)
0.08% swing Lab. to C.
(1997, C. maj. 811 (1.53%))

BEXHILL & BATTLE
*E.*69,010   *T.* 44,783 (64.89%) C. hold
Greg Barker, *C.*   21,555
Stephen Hardy, *LD*   11,052
Ms Anne Moore-Williams, *Lab.*   8,702
Nigel Farage, *UK Ind.*   3,474
C. majority 10,503 (23.45%)
0.40% swing LD to C.
(1997, C. maj. 11,100 (22.66%))

BEXLEYHEATH & CRAYFORD
*E.*63,580   *T.* 40,378 (63.51%) Lab. hold
*Nigel Beard, *Lab.*   17,593
David Evennett, *C.*   16,121
Nickolas O'Hare, *LD*   4,476
Colin Smith, *BNP*   1,408
John Dunford, *UK Ind.*   780
Lab. majority 1,472 (3.65%)
1.72% swing Lab. to C.
(1997, Lab. maj. 3,415 (7.08%))

BILLERICAY
*E.*78,528   *T.* 45,598 (58.07%) C. hold
John Baron, *C.*   21,608
Ms Amanda Campbell, *Lab.*   16,595
Frank Bellard, *LD*   6,323
Nick Yeomans, *UK Ind.*   1,072
C. majority 5,013 (10.99%)
4.27% swing Lab. to C.
(1997, Lab. maj. 1,356 (2.45%))

BIRKENHEAD
*E.*60,726   *T.* 28,967 (47.70%) Lab. hold
*Rt. Hon. F. Field, *Lab.*   20,418
Brian Stewart, *C.*   4,827
Roy Wood, *LD*   3,722
Lab. majority 15,591 (53.82%)
0.86% swing Lab. to C.
(1997, Lab. maj. 21,843 (55.55%))

BIRMINGHAM EDGBASTON
*E.*67,405   *T.* 37,749 (56.00%) Lab. hold
*Ms Gisela Stuart, *Lab.*   18,517
Nigel Hastilow, *C.*   13,819
Ms Nicola Davies, *LD*   4,528
John Gretton, *Pro Euro C*   454
Sam Brackenbury, *Soc. Lab.*   431
Lab. majority 4,698 (12.45%)
1.23% swing C. to Lab.
(1997, Lab. maj. 4,842 (9.99%))

BIRMINGHAM ERDINGTON
*E.*65,668   *T.* 30,604 (46.60%) Lab. hold
Sion Llewelyn Simon, *Lab.*   17,375
Oliver Lodge, *C.*   7,413
Ms Sandra Johnson, *LD*   3,602
Michael Shore, *NF*   681
Steve Goddard, *Soc. All.*   669
Mark Nattrass, *UK Ind.*   521
Ms Judith Sambrook-Marshall,
Soc. Lab.   343
Lab. majority 9,962 (32.55%)
0.62% swing to Lab.
(1997, Lab. maj. 12,657 (31.32%))

BIRMINGHAM HALL GREEN
*E.*57,563   *T.* 33,084 (57.47%) Lab. hold
*Stephen McCabe, *Lab.*   18,049
Chris White, *C.*   11,401
Punjab Singh, *LD*   2,926
Peter Johnson, *UK Ind.*   708
Lab. majority 6,648 (20.09%)
0.02% swing Lab. to C.
(1997, Lab. maj. 8,420 (20.14%))

BIRMINGHAM HODGE HILL
*E.*55,254   *T.* 26,465 (47.90%) Lab. hold
*Rt. Hon. T. Davis, *Lab.*   16,901
Mrs Debbie Lewis, *C.*   5,283
Alistair Dow, *LD*   2,147
Lee Windridge, *BNP*   889
Parwez Hussain, *PJP*   561
Dennis Cridge, *Soc. Lab.*   284
Harvey Vivian, *UK Ind.*   275
Ayub Khan, *Muslim*   125
Lab. majority 11,618 (43.90%)
1.16% swing C. to Lab.
(1997, Lab. maj. 14,200 (41.58%))

BIRMINGHAM LADYWOOD
*E.*71,113   *T.* 31,493 (44.29%) Lab. hold
*Rt. Hon. Ms C. Short, *Lab.*   21,694
Benjamin Prentice, *C.*   3,551
Mahmood Chaudhry, *LD*   2,586
Allah Ditta, *PJP*   2,112
Surinder Virdee, *Soc. Lab.*   443
Mahmood Hussain, *Muslim*   432
James Caffery, *ProLife*   392
Dr Anneliese Nattrass, *UK Ind.*   283
Lab. majority 18,143 (57.61%)
1.59% swing Lab. to C.
(1997, Lab. maj. 23,082 (60.78%))

BIRMINGHAM NORTHFIELD
*E.*55,922   *T.* 29,534 (52.81%) Lab. hold
*Richard Burden, *Lab.*   16,528
Nils Purser, *C.*   8,730
Trevor Sword, *LD*   3,322
Stephen Rogers, *UK Ind.*   550
Clive Walder, *Soc. All.*   193
Zane Carpenter, *Soc. Lab.*   151
Andrew Chaffer, *Comm.*   60

Lab. majority 7,798 (26.40%)
1.53% swing Lab. to C.
(1997, Lab. maj. 11,443 (29.46%))

BIRMINGHAM PERRY BARR
*E.*71,121 *T.* 37,417 (52.61%) Lab. hold
Khalid Mahmood, *Lab.* 17,415
David Binns, *C.* 8,662
Jon Hunt, *LD* 8,566
Avtar Singh Jouhl, *Soc. Lab.* 1,544
Ms Caroline Johnson, *Soc. All.* 465
Ms Natalya Nattrass, *UK Ind.* 352
Michael Roche, *Marxist* 221
Robert Davidson, *Muslim* 192
Lab. majority 8,753 (23.39%)
8.96% swing Lab. to C.
(1997, Lab. maj. 18,957 (41.32%))

BIRMINGHAM SELLY OAK
*E.*71,237 *T.* 40,100 (56.29%) Lab. hold
*Dr Lynne Jones, *Lab.* 21,015
Ken Hardeman, *C.* 10,676
David Osborne, *LD* 6,532
Barney Smith, *Green* 1,309
Mrs Beryl Williams, *UK Ind.* 568
Lab. majority 10,339 (25.78%)
1.04% swing Lab. to C.
(1997, Lab. maj. 14,088 (27.87%))

BIRMINGHAM SPARKBROOK &
SMALL HEATH
*E.*74,358 *T.* 36,647 (49.28%) Lab. hold
*Roger Godsiff, *Lab.* 21,087
Qassim Afzal, *LD* 4,841
Shafaq Hussain, *PJP* 4,770
Iftkhar Hussain, *C.* 3,948
Gul Mohammed, *Ind.* 662
Wayne Vincent, *UK Ind.* 634
Abdul Aziz, *Muslim* 401
Salman Mirza, *Soc. All.* 304
Lab. majority 16,246 (44.33%)
5.31% swing Lab. to LD
(1997, Lab. maj. 19,526 (46.76%))

BIRMINGHAM YARDLEY
*E.*52,444 *T.* 30,013 (57.23%) Lab. hold
*Rt. Hon. Ms E. Morris, *Lab.* 14,085
John Hemming, *LD* 11,507
Barrie Roberts, *C.* 3,941
Alan Ware, *UK Ind.* 329
Colin Wren, *Soc. Lab.* 151
Lab. majority 2,578 (8.59%)
2.74% swing Lab. to LD
(1997, Lab. maj. 5,315 (14.07%))

BISHOP AUCKLAND
*E.*67,377 *T.* 38,559 (57.23%) Lab. hold
*Rt. Hon. D. Foster, *Lab.* 22,680
Mrs Fiona McNish, *C.* 8,754
Chris Foote-Wood, *LD* 6,073
Carl Bennett, *Green* 1,052
Lab. majority 13,926 (36.12%)
4.85% swing Lab. to C.
(1997, Lab. maj. 21,064 (45.82%))

BLABY
*E.*73,907 *T.* 47,642 (64.46%) C. hold
*Andrew Robathan, *C.* 22,104
David Morgan, *Lab.* 15,895
Geoff Welsh, *LD* 8,286
Edward Scott, *BNP* 1,357
C. majority 6,209 (13.03%)
0.48% swing Lab. to C.

(1997, C. maj. 6,474 (12.08%))

BLACKBURN
*E.*72,621 *T.* 40,484 (55.75%) Lab. hold
*Rt. Hon. J. Straw, *Lab.* 21,808
John Cotton, *C.* 12,559
Imtiaz Patel, *LD* 3,264
Mrs Dorothy Baxter, *UK Ind.* 1,185
Paul Morris, *Ind.* 577
Terence Cullen, *Soc. Lab.* 559
Frederick Nichol, *Socialist* 532
Lab. majority 9,249 (22.85%)
3.79% swing Lab. to C.
(1997, Lab. maj. 14,451 (30.43%))

BLACKPOOL NORTH &
FLEETWOOD
*E.*74,456 *T.* 42,581 (57.19%) Lab. hold
*Ms Joan Humble, *Lab.* 21,610
Alan Vincent, *C.* 15,889
Steven Bate, *LD* 4,132
Colin Porter, *UK Ind.* 950
Lab. majority 5,721 (13.44%)
1.60% swing Lab. to C.
(1997, Lab. maj. 8,946 (16.64%))

BLACKPOOL SOUTH
*E.*74,311 *T.* 38,792 (52.20%) Lab. hold
*Gordon Marsden, *Lab.* 21,060
David Morris, *C.* 12,798
Ms Doreen Holt, *LD* 4,115
Mrs Val Cowell, *UK Ind.* 819
Lab. majority 8,262 (21.30%)
0.67% swing Lab. to C.
(1997, Lab. maj. 11,616 (22.63%))

BLAYDON
*E.*64,574 *T.* 37,086 (57.43%) Lab. hold
*John McWilliam, *Lab.* 20,340
Peter Maughan, *LD* 12,531
Mark Watson, *C.* 4,215
Lab. majority 7,809 (21.06%)
7.55% swing Lab. to LD
(1997, Lab. maj. 16,605 (36.16%))

BLYTH VALLEY
*E.*63,274 *T.* 34,550 (54.60%) Lab. hold
*Ronnie Campbell, *Lab.* 20,627
Jeff Reid, *LD* 8,439
Wayne Daley, *C.* 5,484
Lab. majority 12,188 (35.28%)
3.24% swing Lab. to LD
(1997, Lab. maj. 17,736 (41.75%))

BOGNOR REGIS &
LITTLEHAMPTON
*E.*66,903 *T.* 38,968 (58.25%) C. hold
*Nick Gibb, *C.* 17,602
George O'Neill, *Lab.* 11,959
Ms Pamela Peskett, *LD* 6,846
George Stride, *UK Ind.* 1,779
Ms Lilias Rider Haggard Cheyne,
Green 782
C. majority 5,643 (14.48%)
0.64% swing C. to Lab.
(1997, C. maj. 7,321 (15.76%))

BOLSOVER
*E.*67,537 *T.* 38,271 (56.67%) Lab. hold
*Dennis Skinner, *Lab.* 26,249
Simon Massey, *C.* 7,472
Ms Marie Bradley, *LD* 4,550
Lab. majority 18,777 (49.06%)

4.10% swing Lab. to C.
(1997, Lab. maj. 27,149 (57.26%))

BOLTON NORTH EAST
*E.*69,514 *T.* 38,950 (56.03%) Lab. hold
*David Crausby, *Lab.* 21,166
Michael Winstanley, *C.* 12,744
Tim Perkins, *LD* 4,004
Kenneth McIvor, *Green* 629
Ms Lynne Lowe, *Soc. Lab.* 407
Lab. majority 8,422 (21.62%)
2.06% swing Lab. to C.
(1997, Lab. maj. 12,669 (25.74%))

BOLTON SOUTH EAST
*E.*68,140 *T.* 34,154 (50.12%) Lab. hold
*Dr Brian Iddon, *Lab.* 21,129
Haroon Rashid, *C.* 8,258
Frank Harasiwka, *LD* 3,941
Dr William John Kelly, *Soc. Lab.* 826
Lab. majority 12,871 (37.69%)
5.74% swing Lab. to C.
(1997, Lab. maj. 21,311 (49.16%))

BOLTON WEST
*E.*66,033 *T.* 41,214 (62.41%) Lab. hold
*Ms Ruth Kelly, *Lab.* 19,381
James Stevens, *C.* 13,863
Ms Barbara Ronson, *LD* 7,573
David Toomer, *Soc. All.* 397
Lab. majority 5,518 (13.39%)
0.50% swing Lab. to C.
(1997, Lab. maj. 7,072 (14.39%))

BOOTLE
*E.*56,320 *T.* 27,594 (49.00%) Lab. hold
*Joe Benton, *Lab.* 21,400
Jim Murray, *LD* 2,357
Miss Judith Symes, *C.* 2,194
Dave Flynn, *Soc. Lab.* 971
Peter Glover, *Soc. All.* 672
Lab. majority 19,043 (69.01%)
4.05% swing Lab. to LD
(1997, Lab. maj. 28,421 (74.36%))

BOSTON & SKEGNESS
*E.*69,010 *T.* 40,313 (58.42%) C. hold
Mark Simmonds, *C.* 17,298
Ms Elaine Bird, *Lab.* 16,783
Duncan Moffatt, *LD* 4,994
Cyril Wakefield, *UK Ind.* 717
Martin Harrison, *Green* 521
C. majority 515 (1.28%)
0.06% swing C. to Lab.
(1997, C. maj. 647 (1.39%))

BOSWORTH
*E.*69,992 *T.* 45,106 (64.44%) C. hold
*David Tredinnick, *C.* 20,030
Andrew Furlong, *Lab.* 17,750
Jon Ellis, *LD* 7,326
C. majority 2,280 (5.05%)
1.54% swing Lab. to C.
(1997, C. maj. 1,027 (1.97%))

BOURNEMOUTH EAST
*E.*60,454 *T.* 35,799 (59.22%) C. hold
*David Atkinson, *C.* 15,501
Andrew Garratt, *LD* 12,067
Paul Nicholson, *Lab.* 7,107
George Chamberlaine, *UK Ind.* 1,124
C. majority 3,434 (9.59%)
0.21% swing C. to LD

(1997, C. maj. 4,346 (10.01%))

BOURNEMOUTH WEST
E.62,038   T. 33,648 (54.24%) C. hold
*John Butterfill, C.   14,417
David Stokes, Lab.   9,699
Ms Fiona Hornby, LD   8,468
Mrs Cynthia Blake, UK Ind.   1,064
C. majority 4,718 (14.02%)
1.54% swing C. to Lab.
(1997, C. maj. 5,710 (13.90%))

BRACKNELL
E.81,118   T. 49,225 (60.68%) C. hold
*Rt. Hon. A. Mackay, C.   22,962
Ms Janet Keene, Lab.   16,249
Ray Earwicker, LD   8,424
Lawrence Boxall, UK Ind.   1,266
Ms Dominica Roberts, ProLife   324
C. majority 6,713 (13.64%)
1.97% swing C. to Lab.
(1997, C. maj. 10,387 (17.58%))

BRADFORD NORTH
E.66,454   T. 35,017 (52.69%) Lab. hold
*Terry Rooney, Lab.   17,419
Zahid Iqbal, C.   8,450
David Ward, LD   6,924
John Brayshaw, BNP   1,613
Steven Schofield, Green   611
Lab. majority 8,969 (25.61%)
2.44% swing Lab. to C.
(1997, Lab. maj. 12,770 (30.49%))

BRADFORD SOUTH
E.68,450   T. 35,137 (51.33%) Lab. hold
*Gerry Sutcliffe, Lab.   19,603
Graham Tennyson, C.   9,941
Alexander Wilson-Fletcher, LD   3,717
Peter North, UK Ind.   783
Tony Kelly, Soc. Lab.   571
Ateeq Siddique, Soc. All.   302
George Riseborough, Def Welfare   220
Lab. majority 9,662 (27.50%)
0.61% swing Lab. to C.
(1997, Lab. maj. 12,936 (28.71%))

BRADFORD WEST
E.71,620   T. 38,370 (53.57%) Lab. hold
*Marsha Singh, Lab.   18,401
Mohammed Riaz, C.   14,236
John Robinson, Green   2,672
Abdul Rauf Khan, LD   2,437
Imran Hussain, UK Ind.   427
Farhan Khokhar, AL   197
Lab. majority 4,165 (10.85%)
1.17% swing C. to Lab.
(1997, Lab. maj. 3,877 (8.51%))

BRAINTREE
E.79,157   T. 50,315 (63.56%) Lab. hold
*Alan Hurst, Lab.   21,123
Brooks Newmark, C.   20,765
Peter Turner, LD   5,664
James Abbott, Green   1,241
Michael Nolan, LCA   774
Charles Cole, UK Ind.   748
Lab. majority 358 (0.71%)
0.95% swing Lab. to C.
(1997, Lab. maj. 1,451 (2.61%))

BRENT EAST
E.58,095   T. 28,992 (49.90%) Lab. gain

Paul Daisley, Lab.   18,325
David Gauke, C.   5,278
Ms Nowsheen Bhatti, LD   3,065
Ms Simone Aspis, Green   1,361
Ms Sarah Macken, ProLife   392
Ms Iris Cremer, Soc. Lab.   383
Ashwin Tanna, UK Ind.   188
Lab. majority 13,047 (45.00%)
0.01% swing Lab. to C.
(1997, Lab. maj. 15,882 (45.03%))

BRENT NORTH
E.58,789   T. 33,939 (57.73%) Lab. hold
*Barry Gardiner, Lab.   20,149
Philip Allott, C.   9,944
Paul Lorber, LD   3,846
Lab. majority 10,205 (30.07%)
9.77% swing C. to Lab.
(1997, Lab. maj. 4,019 (10.53%))

BRENT SOUTH
E.55,891   T. 28,637 (51.24%) Lab. hold
*Rt. Hon. P. Boateng, Lab.   20,984
Carupiah Selvarajah, C.   3,604
Havard Hughes, LD   3,098
Mick McDonnell, Soc. All.   491
Thomas Mac Stiofain (Res. Motor) 460
Lab. majority 17,380 (60.69%)
1.81% swing C. to Lab.
(1997, Lab. maj. 19,691 (57.08%))

BRENTFORD & ISLEWORTH
E.84,049   T. 44,514 (52.96%) Lab. hold
*Ms Ann Keen, Lab.   23,275
Tim Mack, C.   12,957
Gareth Hartwell, LD   5,994
Nic Ferriday, Green   1,324
Gerald Ingram, UK Ind.   412
Danny Faith, Soc. All.   408
Asa Khaira, Ind.   144
Lab. majority 10,318 (23.18%)
1.26% swing Lab. to C.
(1997, Lab. maj. 14,424 (25.70%))

BRENTWOOD & ONGAR
E.64,695   T. 43,542 (67.30%) C. hold
*Eric Pickles, C.   16,558
†Martin Bell (Ind Bell)   13,737
David Kendall, LD   6,772
Ms Diana Johnson, Lab.   5,505
Ken Gulleford, UK Ind.   611
Peter Pryke, Ind.   239
David Bishop, Elvis   68
Tony Appleton, Ind.   52
C. majority 2,821 (6.48%)
(1997, C. maj. 9,690 (19.10%))

BRIDGWATER
E.74,079   T. 47,847 (64.59%) C. hold
Ian Liddell-Grainger, C.   19,354
Ian Thorn, LD   14,367
William Monteith, Lab.   12,803
Ms Vicky Gardner, UK Ind.   1,323
C. majority 4,987 (10.42%)
3.57% swing LD to C.
(1997, C. maj. 1,796 (3.28%))

BRIGG & GOOLE
E.63,536   T. 41,054 (64.62%) Lab. hold
*Ian Cawsey, Lab.   20,066
Don Stewart, C.   16,105
David Nolan, LD   3,796
Godfrey Bloom, UK Ind.   688

Michael Kenny, Soc. Lab.   399
Lab. majority 3,961 (9.65%)
2.00% swing Lab. to C.
(1997, Lab. maj. 6,389 (13.65%))

BRIGHTON KEMPTOWN
E.67,621   T. 39,203 (57.97%) Lab. hold
*Dr Desmond Turner, Lab.   18,745
Geoffrey Theobald, C.   13,823
Ms Jan Marshall, LD   4,064
Hugh Miller, Green   1,290
Dr James Chamberlain-
Webber, UK Ind.   543
John McLeod, Soc. Lab.   364
Dave Dobbs, Free   227
Ms Elaine Cook, ProLife   147
Lab. majority 4,922 (12.56%)
2.45% swing C. to Lab.
(1997, Lab. maj. 3,534 (7.66%))

BRIGHTON PAVILION
E.69,200   T. 40,723 (58.85%) Lab. Co-
op hold
*David Lepper, Lab. Co-op   19,846
David Gold, C.   10,203
Ms Ruth Berry, LD   5,348
Keith Taylor, Green   3,806
Ian Fyvie, Soc. Lab.   573
Bob Dobbs, Free   409
Stuart Hutchin, UK Ind.   361
Ms Marie Paragallo, ProLife   177
Lab. Co-op majority 9,643 (23.68%)
1.63% swing Lab. Co-op to C.
(1997, Lab. maj. 13,181 (26.93%))

BRISTOL EAST
E.70,279   T. 40,334 (57.39%) Lab. hold
*Ms Jean Corston, Lab.   22,180
Jack Lo-Presti, C.   8,788
Brian Niblett, LD   6,915
Geoff Collard, Green   1,110
Roger Marsh, UK Ind.   572
Mike Langley, Soc. Lab.   438
Andy Pryor, Soc. All.   331
Lab. majority 13,392 (33.20%)
0.16% swing Lab. to C.
(1997, Lab. maj. 16,159 (33.52%))

BRISTOL NORTH WEST
E.76,756   T. 46,692 (60.83%) Lab. Co-
op hold
*Doug Naysmith, Lab. Co-op   24,436
Charles Hansard, C.   13,349
Peter Tyzack, LD   7,387
Miss Diane Carr, UK Ind.   1,149
Vince Horrigan, Soc. Lab.   371
Lab. Co-op majority 11,087 (23.74%)
1.57% swing C. to Lab. Co-op
(1997, Lab. maj. 11,382 (20.60%))

BRISTOL SOUTH
E.72,490   T. 40,970 (56.52%) Lab. hold
*Ms Dawn Primarolo, Lab.   23,299
Richard Eddy, C.   9,118
James Main, LD   6,078
Glenn Vowles, Green   1,233
Brian Drummond, Soc. All.   496
Chris Prasad, UK Ind.   496
Giles Shorter, Soc. Lab.   250
Lab. majority 14,181 (34.61%)
2.08% swing Lab. to C.
(1997, Lab. maj. 19,328 (38.77%))

BRISTOL WEST
E.84,821 T. 55,665 (65.63%) Lab. hold
*Ms Valerie Davey, *Lab.*   20,505
Stephen Williams, *LD*   16,079
Mrs Pamela Chesters, *C.*   16,040
John Devaney, *Green*   1,961
Bernard Kennedy, *Soc. Lab.*   590
Simon Muir, *UK Ind.*   490
Lab. majority 4,426 (7.95%)
0.37% swing LD to Lab.
(1997, Lab. maj. 1,493 (2.38%))

BROMLEY & CHISLEHURST
E.68,763 T. 43,231 (62.87%) C. hold
*Rt. Hon. E. Forth, *C.*   21,412
Ms Sue Polydorou, *Lab.*   12,375
Geoff Payne, *LD*   8,180
Rob Bryant, *UK Ind.*   1,264
C. majority 9,037 (20.90%)
0.09% swing C. to Lab.
(1997, C. maj. 11,118 (21.08%))

BROMSGROVE
E.68,115 T. 45,684 (67.07%) C. hold
*Miss Julie Kirkbride, *C.*   23,640
Peter McDonald, *Lab.*   15,502
Mrs Margaret Rowley, *LD*   5,430
Ian Gregory, *UK Ind.*   1,112
C. majority 8,138 (17.81%)
4.22% swing Lab. to C.
(1997, C. maj. 4,895 (9.38%))

BROXBOURNE
E.68,982 T. 37,845 (54.86%) C. hold
*Mrs Marion Roe, *C.*   20,487
David Prendergast, *Lab.*   11,494
Ms Julia Davies, *LD*   4,158
Martin Harvey, *UK Ind.*   858
John Cope, *BNP*   848
C. majority 8,993 (23.76%)
4.80% swing Lab. to C.
(1997, C. maj. 6,653 (14.16%))

BROXTOWE
E.73,675 T. 49,004 (66.51%) Lab. hold
*Nick Palmer, *Lab.*   23,836
Mrs Pauline Latham, *C.*   17,963
David Watts, *LD*   7,205
Lab. majority 5,873 (11.98%)
1.20% swing C. to Lab.
(1997, Lab. maj. 5,575 (9.59%))

BUCKINGHAM
E.65,270 T. 45,272 (69.36%) C. hold
*John Bercow, *C.*   24,296
Mark Seddon, *Lab.*   10,971
Ms Isobel Wilson, *LD*   9,037
Christopher Silcock, *UK Ind.*   968
C. majority 13,325 (29.43%)
2.18% swing Lab. to C.
(1997, C. maj. 12,386 (25.08%))

BURNLEY
E.66,393 T. 36,884 (55.55%) Lab. hold
*Peter Pike, *Lab.*   18,195
Robert Frost, *C.*   7,697
Paul Wright, *LD*   5,975
Steven Smith, *BNP*   4,151
Richard Buttrey, *UK Ind.*   866
Lab. majority 10,498 (28.46%)
4.62% swing Lab. to C.
(1997, Lab. maj. 17,062 (37.71%))

BURTON
E.75,194 T. 46,457 (61.78%) Lab. hold
*Ms Janet Dean, *Lab.*   22,783
Mrs Maggie Punyer, *C.*   17,934
David Fletcher, *LD*   4,468
Ian Crompton, *UK Ind.*   984
John Taylor, *ProLife*   288
Lab. majority 4,849 (10.44%)
0.59% swing Lab. to C.
(1997, Lab. maj. 6,330 (11.62%))

BURY NORTH
E.71,108 T. 44,788 (62.99%) Lab. hold
*David Chaytor, *Lab.*   22,945
John Walsh, *C.*   16,413
Bryn Hackley, *LD*   5,430
Lab. majority 6,532 (14.58%)
0.15% swing C. to Lab.
(1997, Lab. maj. 7,866 (14.29%))

BURY SOUTH
E.67,276 T. 39,539 (58.77%) Lab. hold
*Ivan Lewis, *Lab.*   23,406
Mrs Nicola Le Page, *C.*   10,634
Tim Pickstone, *LD*   5,499
Lab. majority 12,772 (32.30%)
3.80% swing C. to Lab.
(1997, Lab. maj. 12,433 (24.70%))

BURY ST EDMUNDS
E.76,146 T. 50,257 (66.00%) C. hold
*David Ruffley, *C.*   21,850
Mark Ereira, *Lab.*   19,347
Richard Williams, *LD*   6,998
John Howlett, *UK Ind.*   831
Mike Brundle, *Ind.*   651
Michael Benwell, *Soc. Lab.*   580
C. majority 2,503 (4.98%)
2.16% swing Lab. to C.
(1997, C. maj. 368 (0.66%))

CALDER VALLEY
E.75,298 T. 47,425 (62.98%) Lab. hold
*Mrs Christine McCafferty, *Lab.* 20,244
Mrs Sue Robson-Catling, *C.*   17,150
Michael Taylor, *LD*   7,596
Steve Hutton, *Green*   1,034
John Nunn, *UK Ind.*   729
Philip Lockwood, *LCA*   672
Lab. majority 3,094 (6.52%)
2.27% swing C. to Lab.
(1997, Lab. maj. 6,255 (11.07%))

CAMBERWELL & PECKHAM
E.53,694 T. 25,104 (46.75%) Lab. hold
*Rt. Hon. Ms H. Harman, *Lab.* 17,473
Donnachadh McCarthy, *LD*   3,350
Jonathan Morgan, *C.*   2,740
Storm Poorun, *Green*   805
John Mulrenan, *Soc. All.*   478
Robert Adams, *Soc. Lab.*   188
Frank Sweeney, *WRP*   70
Lab. majority 14,123 (56.26%)
0.91% swing Lab. to LD
(1997, Lab. maj. 16,351 (57.43%))

CAMBRIDGE
E.70,663 T. 42,836 (60.62%) Lab. hold
*Ms Anne Campbell, *Lab.*   19,316
David Howarth, *LD*   10,737
Graham Stuart, *C.*   9,829
Stephen Lawrence, *Green*   1,413
Howard Senter, *Soc. All.*   716

Len Baynes, *UK Ind.*   532
Ms Clare Underwood, *ProLife*   232
Ms Margaret Courtney, *WRP*   61
Lab. majority 8,579 (20.03%)
8.64% swing Lab. to LD
(1997, Lab. maj. 14,137 (27.54%))

CAMBRIDGESHIRE NORTH
EAST
E.79,891 T. 48,051 (60.15%) C. hold
*Malcolm Moss, *C.*   23,132
Dil Owen, *Lab.*   16,759
Richard Renaut, *LD*   6,733
John Stevens, *UK Ind.*   1,189
Tony Hoey, *ProLife*   238
C. majority 6,373 (13.26%)
2.03% swing Lab. to C.
(1997, C. maj. 5,101 (9.20%))

CAMBRIDGESHIRE NORTH
WEST
E.70,569 T. 43,956 (62.29%) C. hold
*Rt. Hon. Sir B. Mawhinney, *C.* 21,895
Ms Anthea Cox, *Lab.*   13,794
Alastair Taylor, *LD*   6,957
Barry Hudson, *UK Ind.*   881
David Hall, *Ind.*   429
C. majority 8,101 (18.43%)
1.27% swing Lab. to C.
(1997, C. maj. 7,754 (15.88%))

CAMBRIDGESHIRE SOUTH
E.72,095 T. 48,341 (67.05%) C. hold
*Andrew Lansley, *C.*   21,387
Ms Amanda Taylor, *LD*   12,984
Dr Joan Herbert, *Lab.*   11,737
Simon Saggers, *Green*   1,182
Mrs Helene Davies, *UK Ind.*   875
Ms Beata Klepacka, *ProLife*   176
C. majority 8,403 (17.38%)
0.58% swing LD to C.
(1997, C. maj. 8,712 (16.23%))

CAMBRIDGESHIRE SOUTH
EAST
E.81,663 T. 51,886 (63.54%) C. hold
*James Paice, *C.*   22,927
Ms Sal Brinton, *LD*   13,937
Andrew Inchley, *Lab.*   13,714
Neil Scarr, *UK Ind.*   1,308
C. majority 8,990 (17.33%)
0.27% swing C. to LD
(1997, C. maj. 9,349 (16.46%))

CANNOCK CHASE
E.73,423 T. 41,064 (55.93%) Lab. hold
*Dr Tony Wright, *Lab.*   23,049
Gavin Smithers, *C.*   12,345
Stewart Reynolds, *LD*   5,670
Lab. majority 10,704 (26.07%)
0.79% swing Lab. to C.
(1997, Lab. maj. 14,478 (27.65%))

CANTERBURY
E.74,159 T. 45,132 (60.86%) C. hold
*Julian Brazier, *C.*   18,711
Ms Emily Thornberry, *Lab.*   16,642
Peter Wales, *LD*   8,056
Ms Hazel Dawe, *Green*   920
Ms Lisa Moore, *UK Ind.*   803
C. majority 2,069 (4.58%)
1.37% swing C. to Lab.
(1997, C. maj. 3,964 (7.33%))

CARLISLE
E.58,811 T. 34,909 (59.36%) Lab. hold
*Eric Martlew, Lab.   17,856
Mike Mitchelson, C.   12,154
John Guest, LD   4,076
Colin Paisley, LCA   554
Paul Wilcox, Soc. All.   269
Lab. majority 5,702 (16.33%)
6.04% swing Lab. to C.
(1997, Lab. maj. 12,390 (28.41%))

CARSHALTON & WALLINGTON
E.67,337 T. 40,612 (60.31%) LD hold
*Tom Brake, LD   18,289
Ken Andrew, C.   13,742
Ms Margaret Cooper, Lab.   7,466
Simon Dixon, Green   614
Martin Haley, UK Ind.   501
LD majority 4,547 (11.20%)
3.26% swing C. to LD
(1997, LD maj. 2,267 (4.68%))

CASTLE POINT
E.68,108 T. 39,763 (58.38%) Con gain
Dr Robert Spink, C.   17,738
*Ms Christine Butler, Lab.   16,753
Billy Boulton, LD   3,116
Ron Hurrell, UK Ind.   1,273
Douglas Roberts, Ind.   663
Nik Searle, Truth   220
C. majority 985 (2.48%)
2.39% swing Lab. to C.
(1997, Lab. maj. 1,116 (2.30%))

CHARNWOOD
E.74,836 T. 48,265 (64.49%) C. hold
*Rt. Hon. S. Dorrell, C.   23,283
Sean Sheahan, Lab.   15,544
Ms Susan King, LD   7,835
Jamie Bye, UK Ind.   1,603
C. majority 7,739 (16.03%)
2.77% swing Lab. to C.
(1997, C. maj. 5,900 (10.50%))

CHATHAM & AYLESFORD
E.69,759 T. 39,735 (56.96%) Lab. hold
*Jonathan Shaw, Lab.   19,180
Sean Holden, C.   14,840
David Lettington, LD   4,705
Gregory Knopp, UK Ind.   1,010
Lab. majority 4,340 (10.92%)
2.62% swing C. to Lab.
(1997, Lab. maj. 2,790 (5.68%))

CHEADLE
E.69,002 T. 43,606 (63.20%) LD gain
Ms Patsy Calton, LD   18,477
*Stephen Day, C.   18,444
Howard Dawber, Lab.   6,086
Vincent Cavanagh, UK Ind.   599
LD majority 33 (0.08%)
3.07% swing C. to LD
(1997, C. maj. 3,189 (6.07%))

CHELMSFORD WEST
E.78,291   T. 48,143 (61.49%) C. hold
*Simon Burns, C.   20,446
Adrian Longden, Lab.   14,185
Stephen Robinson, LD   11,197
Mrs Eleanor Burgess, Green   837
Ken Wedon, UK Ind.   785
Christopher Philbin, LCA   693
C. majority 6,261 (13.01%)

0.62% swing C. to Lab.
(1997, C. maj. 6,691 (11.42%))

CHELTENHAM
E.67,563 T. 41,835 (61.92%) LD hold
*Nigel Jones, LD   19,970
Rob Garnham, C.   14,715
Andy Erlam, Lab.   5,041
Keith Bessant, Green   735
Dancing Ken Hanks, Loony   513
Jim Carver, UK Ind.   482
Anthony Gates, ProLife   272
Roger Everest, Ind.   107
LD majority 5,255 (12.56%)
0.32% swing LD to C.
(1997, LD maj. 6,645 (13.21%))

CHESHAM & AMERSHAM
E.70,021   T. 45,283 (64.67%) C. hold
*Mrs Cheryl Gillan, C.   22,867
John Ford, LD   10,985
Ken Hulme, Lab.   8,497
Ian Harvey, UK Ind.   1,367
Nick Wilkins, Green   1,114
Ms Gillian Duval, ProLife   453
C. majority 11,882 (26.24%)
0.16% swing C. to LD
(1997, C. maj. 13,859 (26.55%))

CHESTER, CITY OF
E.70,382 T. 44,877 (63.76%) Lab. hold
*Ms Christine Russell, Lab.   21,760
David Jones, C.   14,866
Tony Dawson, LD   6,589
Allan Weddell, UK Ind.   899
George Rogers, Ind.   763
Lab. majority 6,894 (15.36%)
1.70% swing Lab. to C.
(1997, Lab. maj. 10,553 (18.76%))

CHESTERFIELD
E.73,252 T. 44,441 (60.67%) LD gain
Paul Holmes, LD   21,249
Reg Race, Lab.   18,663
Simon Hitchcock, C.   3,613
Ms Jeannie Robinson, Soc. All.   437
Bill Harrison, Soc. Lab.   295
Christopher Rawson, Ind.   184
LD majority 2,586 (5.82%)
8.53% swing Lab. to LD
(1997, Lab. maj. 5,775 (11.24%))

CHICHESTER
E.77,703   T. 49,512 (63.72%) C. hold
*Andrew Tyrie, C.   23,320
Ms Lynne Ravenscroft, LD   11,965
Ms Celia Barlow, Lab.   10,627
Douglas Denny, UK Ind.   2,308
Gavin Graham, Green   1,292
C. majority 11,355 (22.93%)
2.74% swing LD to C.
(1997, C. maj. 9,734 (17.45%))

CHINGFORD & WOODFORD
GREEN
E.63,252   T. 36,982 (58.47%) C. hold
*Iain Duncan Smith, C.   17,834
Ms Jessica Webb, Lab.   12,347
John Beanse, LD   5,739
Ms Jean Griffin, BNP   1,062
C. majority 5,487 (14.84%)
0.99% swing Lab. to C.
(1997, C. maj. 5,714 (12.85%))

CHIPPING BARNET
E.70,217   T. 42,456 (60.46%) C. hold
*Sir Sydney Chapman, C.   19,702
Damien Welfare, Lab.   17,001
Sean Hooker, LD   5,753
C. majority 2,701 (6.36%)
2.14% swing Lab. to C.
(1997, C. maj. 1,035 (2.09%))

CHORLEY
E.77,036 T. 47,952 (62.25%) Lab. hold
*Lindsay Hoyle, Lab.   25,088
Peter Booth, C.   16,644
Stephen Fenn, LD   5,372
Graham Frost, UK Ind.   848
Lab. majority 8,444 (17.61%)
0.25% swing C. to Lab.
(1997, Lab. maj. 9,870 (17.10%))

CHRISTCHURCH
E.73,503   T. 49,567 (67.44%) C. hold
*Christopher Chope, C.   27,306
Ms Dorothy Webb, LD   13,762
Ms Judith Begg, Lab.   7,506
Ms Margaret Strange, UK Ind.   993
C. majority 13,544 (27.32%)
11.74% swing LD to C.
(1997, C. maj. 2,165 (3.85%))

CITIES OF LONDON &
WESTMINSTER
E.71,935   T. 33,975 (47.23%) C. hold
Mark Field, C.   15,737
Michael Katz, Lab.   11,238
Martin Horwood, LD   5,218
Hugo Charlton, Green   1,318
Colin Merton, UK Ind.   464
C. majority 4,499 (13.24%)
0.54% swing Lab. to C.
(1997, C. maj. 4,881 (12.16%))

CLEETHORPES
E.68,392 T. 42,418 (62.02%) Lab. hold
*Ms Shona McIsaac, Lab.   21,032
Stephen Howd, C.   15,412
Gordon Smith, LD   5,080
Ms Janet Hatton, UK Ind.   894
Lab. majority 5,620 (13.25%)
2.47% swing Lab. to C.
(1997, Lab. maj. 9,176 (18.18%))

COLCHESTER
E.78,955 T. 43,736 (55.39%) LD hold
*Bob Russell, LD   18,627
Kevin Bentley, C.   13,074
Chris Fegan, Lab.   10,925
Roger Lord, UK Ind.   631
Leonard Overy-Owen, Grey   479
LD majority 5,553 (12.70%)
4.83% swing C. to LD
(1997, LD maj. 1,581 (3.04%))

COLNE VALLEY
E.74,192 T. 46,987 (63.33%) Lab. hold
*Ms Kali Mountford, Lab.   18,967
Philip Davies, C.   14,328
Gordon Beever, LD   11,694
Richard Plunkett, Green   1,081
Dr Arthur Quarmby, UK Ind.   917
Lab. majority 4,639 (9.87%)
0.65% swing C. to Lab.
(1997, Lab. maj. 4,840 (8.58%))

CONGLETON
E.71,941 T. 45,083 (62.67%) C. hold
*Mrs Ann Winterton, C.   20,872
John Flanagan, Lab.   13,738
David Lloyd-Griffiths, LD   9,719
Bill Young, UK Ind.   754
C. majority 7,134 (15.82%)
1.08% swing Lab. to C.
(1997, C. maj. 6,130 (11.48%))

COPELAND
E.53,526 T. 34,750 (64.92%) Lab. hold
*Rt. Hon. Dr J. Cunningham, Lab.
                                     17,991
Mike Graham, C.   13,027
Mark Gayler, LD   3,732
Lab. majority 4,964 (14.28%)
7.30% swing Lab. to C.
(1997, Lab. maj. 11,944 (28.89%))

CORBY
E.72,304 T. 47,222 (65.31%) Lab. Co-
op hold
*Phil Hope, Lab. Co-op   23,283
Andrew Griffith, C.   17,583
Kevin Scudder, LD   4,751
Ian Gillman, UK Ind.   855
Andrew Dickson, Soc. Lab.   750
Lab. Co-op majority 5,700 (12.07%)
4.95% swing Lab. Co-op to C.
(1997, Lab. maj. 11,860 (21.98%))

CORNWALL NORTH
E.84,662 T. 53,983 (63.76%) LD hold
*Paul Tyler, LD   28,082
John Weller, C.   18,250
Mike Goodman, Lab.   5,257
Steve Protz, UK Ind.   2,394
LD majority 9,832 (18.21%)
2.79% swing LD to C.
(1997, LD maj. 13,933 (23.79%))

CORNWALL SOUTH EAST
E.79,090 T. 51,753 (65.44%) LD hold
*Colin Breed, LD   23,756
Ashley Gray, C.   18,381
Bill Stevens, Lab.   6,429
Graham Palmer, UK Ind.   1,978
Dr Ken George, Meb. Ker.   1,209
LD majority 5,375 (10.39%)
0.45% swing LD to C.
(1997, LD maj. 6,480 (11.28%))

COTSWOLD
E.68,154 T. 45,981 (67.47%) C. hold
*Geoffrey Clifton-Brown, C.   23,133
Ms Angela Lawrence, LD   11,150
Richard Wilkins, Lab.   10,383
Mrs Jill Stopps, UK Ind.   1,315
C. majority 11,983 (26.06%)
1.33% swing LD to C.
(1997, C. maj. 11,965 (23.41%))

COVENTRY NORTH EAST
E.73,998 T. 37,265 (50.36%) Lab. hold
*Bob Ainsworth, Lab.   22,739
Gordon Bell, C.   6,988
Geoffrey Sewards, LD   4,163
Dave Nellist, Soc. All.   2,638
Edward Sheppard, BNP   737
Lab. majority 15,751 (42.27%)
2.34% swing Lab. to C.
(1997, Lab. maj. 22,569 (46.94%))

COVENTRY NORTH WEST
E.76,652 T. 42,551 (55.51%) Lab. hold
*Geoffrey Robinson, Lab.   21,892
Andrew Fairburn, C.   11,018
Napier Penlington, LD   5,832
Ms Christine Oddy, Ind.   3,159
Mark Benson, UK Ind.   650
Lab. majority 10,874 (25.56%)
2.50% swing Lab. to C.
(1997, Lab. maj. 16,601 (30.56%))

COVENTRY SOUTH
E.72,527 T. 40,096 (55.28%) Lab. hold
*Jim Cunningham, Lab.   20,125
Ms Heather Wheeler, C.   11,846
Vincent McKee, LD   5,672
Rob Windsor, Soc. All.   1,475
Ms Irene Rogers, Ind.   564
Timothy Logan, Soc. Lab.   414
Lab. majority 8,279 (20.65%)
0.61% swing Lab. to C.
(1997, Lab. maj. 10,953 (21.86%))

CRAWLEY
E.71,626 T. 39,522 (55.18%) Lab. hold
*Ms Laura Moffatt, Lab.   19,488
Henry Smith, C.   12,718
Ms Linda Seekings, LD   5,009
Brian Galloway, UK Ind.   1,137
Ms Claire Staniford, Loony   388
Arshad Khan, JP   271
Karl Stewart, Soc. Lab.   260
Ms Muriel Hirsch, Soc. All.   251
Lab. majority 6,770 (17.13%)
3.05% swing Lab. to C.
(1997, Lab. maj. 11,707 (23.22%))

CREWE & NANTWICH
E.69,040 T. 41,547 (60.18%) Lab. hold
*Mrs Gwyneth Dunwoody, Lab. 22,556
Donald Potter, C.   12,650
David Cannon, LD   5,595
Roger Croston, UK Ind.   746
Lab. majority 9,906 (23.84%)
3.69% swing Lab. to C.
(1997, Lab. maj. 15,798 (31.22%))

CROSBY
E.57,375 T. 36,866 (64.25%) Lab. hold
*Ms Claire Curtis-Thomas, Lab. 20,327
Robert Collinson, C.   11,974
Tim Drake, LD   4,084
Mark Holt, Soc. Lab.   481
Lab. majority 8,353 (22.66%)
3.19% swing C. to Lab.
(1997, Lab. maj. 7,182 (16.27%))

CROYDON CENTRAL
E.77,567 T. 45,860 (59.12%) Lab. hold
*Geraint Davies, Lab.   21,643
David Congdon, C.   17,659
Paul Booth, LD   5,156
James Feisenberger, UK Ind.   545
Ms Lynda Miller, BNP   449
John Cartwright, Loony   408
Lab. majority 3,984 (8.69%)
0.85% swing C. to Lab.
(1997, Lab. maj. 3,897 (6.99%))

CROYDON NORTH
E.76,600 T. 41,882 (54.68%) Lab. hold
*Malcolm Wicks, Lab.   26,610
Simon Allison, C.   9,752

Ms Sandra Lawman, LD   4,375
Alan Smith, UK Ind.   606
Don Madgwick, Soc. All.   539
Lab. majority 16,858 (40.25%)
2.63% swing C. to Lab.
(1997, Lab. maj. 18,398 (35.00%))

CROYDON SOUTH
E.73,402   T. 45,060 (61.39%) C. hold
*Richard Ottaway, C.   22,169
Gerry Ryan, Lab.   13,472
Ms Anne Gallop, LD   8,226
Mrs Kathleen Garner, UK Ind.   998
Mark Samuel, Choice   195
C. majority 8,697 (19.30%)
1.35% swing C. to Lab.
(1997, C. maj. 11,930 (22.01%))

DAGENHAM
E.59,340 T. 27,580 (46.48%) Lab. hold
Jon Cruddas, Lab.   15,784
Michael White, C.   7,091
Adrian Gee-Turner, LD   2,820
David Hill, BNP   1,378
Berlyne Hamilton, Soc. All.   262
Robert Siggins, Soc. Lab.   245
Lab. majority 8,693 (31.52%)
7.82% swing Lab. to C.
(1997, Lab. maj. 17,054 (47.16%))

DARLINGTON
E.64,328 T. 40,754 (63.35%) Lab. hold
*Rt. Hon. A. Milburn, Lab.   22,479
Tony Richmond, C.   12,950
Robert Adamson, LD   4,358
Alan Docherty, Soc. All.   469
Craig Platt, Ind.   269
Ms Amanda Rose, Soc. Lab.   229
Lab. majority 9,529 (23.38%)
4.94% swing Lab. to C.
(1997, Lab. maj. 16,025 (33.27%))

DARTFORD
E.72,258 T. 44,740 (61.92%) Lab. hold
*Howard Stoate, Lab.   21,466
Bob Dunn, C.   18,160
Graham Morgan, LD   3,781
Mark Croucher, UK Ind.   989
Keith Davenport, FDP   344
Lab. majority 3,306 (7.39%)
0.47% swing Lab. to C.
(1997, Lab. maj. 4,328 (8.32%))

DAVENTRY
E.86,537   T. 56,684 (65.50%) C. hold
*Tim Boswell, C.   27,911
Kevin Quigley, Lab.   18,262
Jamie Calder, LD   9,130
Peter Baden, UK Ind.   1,381
C. majority 9,649 (17.02%)
2.54% swing Lab. to C.
(1997, C. maj. 7,378 (11.95%))

DENTON & REDDISH
E.69,236 T. 33,593 (48.52%) Lab. hold
*Andrew Bennett, Lab.   21,913
Paul Newman, C.   6,583
Roger Fletcher, LD   4,152
Alan Cadwallender, UK Ind.   945
Lab. majority 15,330 (45.63%)
0.78% swing C. to Lab.
(1997, Lab. maj. 20,311 (44.08%))

DERBY NORTH
E.76,489 T. 44,054 (57.60%) Lab. hold
*Bob Laxton, *Lab.*   22,415
Barrie Holden, *C.*   15,433
Robert Charlesworth, *LD*   6,206
Lab. majority 6,982 (15.85%)
1.53% swing Lab. to C.
(1997, Lab. maj. 10,615 (18.91%))

DERBY SOUTH
E.77,366 T. 43,075 (55.68%) Lab. hold
*Rt. Hon. Mrs M. Beckett, *Lab.*   24,310
Simon Spencer, *C.*   10,455
Anders Hanson, *LD*   8,310
Lab. majority 13,855 (32.16%)
0.54% swing C. to Lab.
(1997, Lab. maj. 16,106 (31.08%))

DERBYSHIRE NORTH EAST
E.71,527 T. 42,124 (58.89%) Lab. hold
*Harry Barnes, *Lab.*   23,437
James Hollingsworth, *C.*   11,179
Mark Higginbottom, *LD*   7,508
Lab. majority 12,258 (29.10%)
3.08% swing Lab. to C.
(1997, Lab. maj. 18,321 (35.25%))

DERBYSHIRE SOUTH
E.81,010 T. 51,945 (64.12%) Lab. hold
*Mark Todd, *Lab.*   26,338
James Hakewill, *C.*   18,487
Russell Eagling, *LD*   5,233
John Blunt, *UK Ind.*   1,074
Paul Liversuch, *Soc. Lab.*   564
James Taylor, *Ind.*   249
Lab. majority 7,851 (15.11%)
4.09% swing Lab. to C.
(1997, Lab. maj. 13,967 (23.29%))

DERBYSHIRE WEST
E.75,067 T. 50,589 (67.39%) C. hold
*Patrick McLoughlin, *C.*   24,280
Stephen Clamp, *Lab.*   16,910
Jeremy Beckett, *LD*   7,922
Stuart Bavester, *UK Ind.*   672
Nick Delves, *Loony*   472
Robert Goodall, *Ind.*   333
C. majority 7,370 (14.57%)
2.99% swing Lab. to C.
(1997, C. maj. 4,885 (8.59%))

DEVIZES
E.83,655 T. 53,249 (63.65%) C. hold
*Rt. Hon. M. Ancram, *C.*   25,159
Jim Thorpe, *Lab.*   13,263
Ms Helen Frances, *LD*   11,756
Alan Wood, *UK Ind.*   1,521
Ludovic Kennedy, *Ind.*   1,078
Ms Vanessa Potter, *Loony*   472
C. majority 11,896 (22.34%)
1.88% swing Lab. to C.
(1997, C. maj. 9,782 (16.29%))

DEVON EAST
E.70,278 T. 47,837 (68.07%) C. hold
Hugo Swire, *C.*   22,681
Tim Dumper, *LD*   14,486
Phil Starr, *Lab.*   7,974
David Wilson, *UK Ind.*   2,696
C. majority 8,195 (17.13%)
1.44% swing LD to C.
(1997, C. maj. 7,489 (14.25%))

DEVON NORTH
E.72,100 T. 49,254 (68.31%) LD hold
*Nick Harvey, *LD*   21,784
Clive Allen, *C.*   18,800
Ms Viv Gale, *Lab.*   4,995
Roger Knapman, *UK Ind.*   2,484
Tony Bown, *Green*   1,191
LD majority 2,984 (6.06%)
2.61% swing LD to C.
(1997, LD maj. 6,181 (11.27%))

DEVON SOUTH WEST
E.70,922 T. 46,904 (66.13%) C. hold
*Gary Streeter, *C.*   21,970
Christopher Mavin, *Lab.*   14,826
Phil Hutty, *LD*   8,616
Roger Bullock, *UK Ind.*   1,492
C. majority 7,144 (15.23%)
0.58% swing Lab. to C.
(1997, C. maj. 7,433 (14.07%))

DEVON WEST & TORRIDGE
E.78,976 T. 55,684 (70.51%) LD hold
*John Burnett, *LD*   23,474
Geoffrey Cox, *C.*   22,280
David Brenton, *Lab.*   5,959
Bob Edwards, *UK Ind.*   2,674
Martin Quinn, *Green*   1,297
LD majority 1,194 (2.14%)
0.58% swing LD to C.
(1997, LD maj. 1,957 (3.31%))

DEWSBURY
E.62,344 T. 36,651 (58.79%) Lab. hold
*Rt. Hon. Mrs A. Taylor, *Lab.*   18,524
Robert Cole, *C.*   11,075
Ian Cuthbertson, *LD*   4,382
Russell Smith, *BNP*   1,632
Ms Brenda Smithson, *Green*   560
David Peace, *UK Ind.*   478
Lab. majority 7,449 (20.32%)
0.50% swing C. to Lab.
(1997, Lab. maj. 8,323 (19.33%))

DON VALLEY
E.66,244 T. 36,630 (55.30%) Lab. hold
*Ms Caroline Flint, *Lab.*   20,009
James Browne, *C.*   10,489
Phillip Smith, *LD*   4,089
Tony Wilde, *Ind.*   800
David Cooper, *UK Ind.*   777
Nigel Ball, *Soc. Lab.*   466
Lab. majority 9,520 (25.99%)
3.84% swing Lab. to C.
(1997, Lab. maj. 14,659 (33.66%))

DONCASTER CENTRAL
E.65,087 T. 33,902 (52.09%) Lab. hold
*Ms Rosie Winterton, *Lab.*   20,034
Gary Meggitt, *C.*   8,035
Michael Southcombe, *LD*   4,390
David Gordon, *UK Ind.*   926
Ms Janet Terry, *Soc. All.*   517
Lab. majority 11,999 (35.39%)
2.85% swing Lab. to C.
(1997, Lab. maj. 17,856 (41.10%))

DONCASTER NORTH
E.62,124 T. 31,363 (50.48%) Lab. hold
*Kevin Hughes, *Lab.*   19,788
Mrs Anita Kapoor, *C.*   4,601
Colin Ross, *LD*   3,323
Martin Williams, *Ind.*   2,926

John Wallis, *UK Ind.*   725
Lab. majority 15,187 (48.42%)
3.28% swing Lab. to C.
(1997, Lab. maj. 21,937 (54.99%))

DORSET MID & POOLE NORTH
E.66,675 T. 43,718 (65.57%) LD gain
Ms Annette Brooke, *LD*   18,358
*Christopher Fraser, *C.*   17,974
James Selby-Bennett, *Lab.*   6,765
Jeff Mager, *UK Ind.*   621
LD majority 384 (0.88%)
1.11% swing C. to LD
(1997, C. maj. 681 (1.34%))

DORSET NORTH
E.72,140 T. 47,821 (66.29%) C. hold
*Robert Walter, *C.*   22,314
Miss Emily Gasson, *LD*   18,517
Mark Wareham, *Lab.*   5,334
Peter Jenkins, *UK Ind.*   1,019
Joseph Duthie, *Low Excise*   391
Mrs Cora Bone, *Ind.*   246
C. majority 3,797 (7.94%)
1.36% swing LD to C.
(1997, C. maj. 2,746 (5.23%))

DORSET SOUTH
E.69,233 T. 45,345 (65.50%) Lab. gain
Jim Knight, *Lab.*   19,027
*Ian Cameron Bruce, *C.*   18,874
Andrew Canning, *LD*   6,531
Laurence Moss, *UK Ind.*   913
Lab. majority 153 (0.34%)
0.25% swing C. to Lab.
(1997, C. maj. 77 (0.16%))

DORSET WEST
E.74,016 T. 49,571 (66.97%) C. hold
*Oliver Letwin, *C.*   22,126
Simon Green, *LD*   20,712
Richard Hyde, *Lab.*   6,733
C. majority 1,414 (2.85%)
0.29% swing C. to LD
(1997, C. maj. 1,840 (3.44%))

DOVER
E.69,025 T. 44,960 (65.14%) Lab. hold
*Gwyn Prosser, *Lab.*   21,943
Paul Watkins, *C.*   16,744
Antony Hook, *LD*   5,131
Lee Speakman, *UK Ind.*   1,142
Lab. majority 5,199 (11.56%)
5.05% swing Lab. to C.
(1997, Lab. maj. 11,739 (21.66%))

DUDLEY NORTH
E.68,964 T. 38,564 (55.92%) Lab. hold
*Ross Cranston, *Lab.*   20,095
Andrew Griffiths, *C.*   13,295
Richard Burt, *LD*   3,352
Simon Darby, *BNP*   1,822
Lab. majority 6,800 (17.63%)
1.08% swing Lab. to C.
(1997, Lab. maj. 9,457 (19.79%))

DUDLEY SOUTH
E.65,578 T. 36,344 (55.42%) Lab. hold
*Ian Pearson, *Lab.*   18,109
Jason Sugarman, *C.*   11,292
Ms Lorely Burt, *LD*   5,421
John Westwood, *UK Ind.*   859
Ms Angela Thompson, *Soc. All.*   663

Lab. majority 6,817 (18.76%)
4.22% swing Lab. to C.
(1997, Lab. maj. 13,027 (27.19%))

DULWICH & WEST NORWOOD
E.70,497 T. 38,247 (54.25%) Lab. hold
*Rt. Hon. Ms T. Jowell, Lab.   20,999
Nick Vineall, C.   8,689
Ms Caroline Pidgeon, LD   5,806
Ms Jenny Jones, Green   1,914
Brian Kelly, Soc. All.   839
Lab. majority 12,310 (32.19%)
2.29% swing Lab. to C.
(1997, Lab. maj. 16,769 (36.76%))

DURHAM NORTH
E.67,610 T. 38,568 (57.04%) Lab. hold
Kevan Jones, Lab.   25,920
Matthew Palmer, C.   7,237
Ms Carole Field, LD   5,411
Lab. majority 18,683 (48.44%)
3.65% swing Lab. to C.
(1997, Lab. maj. 26,299 (55.75%))

DURHAM NORTH WEST
E.67,062 T. 39,226 (58.49%) Lab. hold
*Rt. Hon. Ms H. Armstrong, Lab.   24,526
William Clouston, C.   8,193
Alan Ord, LD   5,846
Ms Joan Hartnell, Soc. Lab.   661
Lab. majority 16,333 (41.64%)
5.90% swing Lab. to C.
(1997, Lab. maj. 24,754 (53.44%))

DURHAM, CITY OF
E.69,633 T. 41,486 (59.58%) Lab. hold
*Gerry Steinberg, Lab.   23,254
Ms Carol Woods, LD   9,813
Nick Cartmell, C.   7,167
Mrs Chris Williamson, UK Ind.   1,252
Lab. majority 13,441 (32.40%)
7.82% swing Lab. to LD
(1997, Lab. maj. 22,504 (45.80%))

EALING ACTON & SHEPHERD'S
BUSH
E.70,697 T. 37,201 (52.62%) Lab. hold
*Clive Soley, Lab.   20,144
Miss Justine Greening, C.   9,355
Martin Tod, LD   6,171
Nick Grant, Soc. All.   529
Andrew Lawrie, UK Ind.   476
Carlos Rule, Soc. Lab.   301
Ms Rebecca Ng, ProLife   225
Lab. majority 10,789 (29.00%)
1.77% swing Lab. to C.
(1997, Lab. maj. 15,647 (32.55%))

EALING NORTH
E.77,524 T. 44,957 (57.99%) Lab. hold
*Stephen Pound, Lab.   25,022
Charles Walker, C.   13,185
Francesco Fruzza, LD   5,043
Ms Astra Seibe, Green   1,039
Daniel Moss, UK Ind.   668
Lab. majority 11,837 (26.33%)
4.94% swing C. to Lab.
(1997, Lab. maj. 9,160 (16.44%))

EALING SOUTHALL
E.82,373 T. 46,828 (56.85%) Lab. hold
*Piara Khabra, Lab.   22,239
Daniel Kawczynski, C.   8,556

Avtar Lit, Sunrise   5,764
Baldev Sharma, LD   4,680
Ms Jane Cook, Green   2,119
Salvinder Dhillon, Community   1,214
Mushtaq Choudhry, Ind.   1,166
Harpal Brar, Soc. Lab.   921
Mohammed Bhutta, Qari   169
Lab. majority 13,683 (29.22%)
5.00% swing Lab. to C.
(1997, Lab. maj. 21,423 (39.21%))

EASINGTON
E.61,532 T. 33,010 (53.65%) Lab. hold
*John Cummings, Lab.   25,360
Philip Lovel, C.   3,411
Christopher Ord, LD   3,408
Dave Robinson, Soc. Lab.   831
Lab. majority 21,949 (66.49%)
2.57% swing Lab. to C.
(1997, Lab. maj. 30,012 (71.64%))

EAST HAM
E.71,255 T. 37,277 (52.31%) Lab. hold
*Stephen Timms, Lab.   27,241
Peter Campbell, C.   6,209
Ms Bridget Fox, LD   2,600
Rod Finlayson, Soc. Lab.   783
Ms Johinda Pandhal, UK Ind.   444
Lab. majority 21,032 (56.42%)
3.95% swing C. to Lab.
(1997, Lab. maj. 19,358 (48.53%))

EASTBOURNE
E.73,784 T. 44,770 (60.68%) C. hold
*Nigel Waterson, C.   19,738
Chris Berry, LD   17,584
Ms Gillian Roles, Lab.   5,967
Barry Jones, UK Ind.   907
Ms Theresia Williamson, Lib.   574
C. majority 2,154 (4.81%)
0.51% swing LD to C.
(1997, C. maj. 1,994 (3.79%))

EASTLEIGH
E.74,603 T. 47,573 (63.77%) LD hold
*David Chidgey, LD   19,360
Conor Burns, C.   16,302
Sam Jaffa, Lab.   10,426
Stephen Challis, UK Ind.   849
Ms Martha Lyn, Green   636
LD majority 3,058 (6.43%)
2.54% swing C. to LD
(1997, LD maj. 754 (1.35%))

ECCLES
E.68,764 T. 33,182 (48.25%) Lab. hold
*Ian Stewart, Lab.   21,395
Peter Caillard, C.   6,867
Bob Boyd, LD   4,920
Lab. majority 14,528 (43.78%)
2.09% swing Lab. to C.
(1997, Lab. maj. 21,916 (47.96%))

EDDISBURY
E.69,181   T. 44,387 (64.16%) C. hold
*Stephen O'Brien, C.   20,556
Bill Eyres, Lab.   15,988
Paul Roberts, LD   6,975
David Carson, UK Ind.   868
C. majority 4,568 (10.29%)
3.95% swing Lab. to C.
(1999 Jul by-election, C. maj. 1,606)
(1997, C. maj. 1,185 (2.39%))

EDMONTON
E.62,294 T. 34,774 (55.82%) Lab. Co-
op hold
*Andy Love, Lab. Co-op   20,481
David Burrowes, C.   10,709
Douglas Taylor, LD   2,438
Miss Gwyneth Rolph, UK Ind.   406
Erol Basarik, Reform   344
Howard Medwell, Soc. All.   296
Dr Ram Saxena, Ind.   100
Lab. Co-op majority 9,772 (28.10%)
0.97% swing Lab. Co-op to C.
(1997, Lab. maj. 13,472 (30.04%))

ELLESMERE PORT & NESTON
E.68,147 T. 41,528 (60.94%) Lab. hold
*Andrew Miller, Lab.   22,964
Gareth Williams, C.   12,103
Stuart Kelly, LD   4,828
Henry Crocker, UK Ind.   824
Geoff Nicholls, Green   809
Lab. majority 10,861 (26.15%)
2.18% swing Lab. to C.
(1997, Lab. maj. 16,036 (30.51%))

ELMET
E.70,041 T. 45,937 (65.59%) Lab. hold
*Colin Burgon, Lab.   22,038
Andrew Millard, C.   17,867
Ms Madeleine Kirk, LD   5,001
Andrew Spence, UK Ind.   1,031
Lab. majority 4,171 (9.08%)
3.57% swing Lab. to C.
(1997, Lab. maj. 8,779 (16.22%))

ELTHAM
E.57,519 T. 33,792 (58.75%) Lab. hold
*Clive Efford, Lab.   17,855
Mrs Sharon Massey, C.   10,859
Martin Morris, LD   4,121
Terry Jones, UK Ind.   706
Andrew Graham, Ind.   251
Lab. majority 6,996 (20.70%)
1.37% swing Lab. to C.
(1997, Lab. maj. 10,182 (23.45%))

ENFIELD NORTH
E.67,756 T. 38,143 (56.29%) Lab. hold
*Ms Joan Ryan, Lab.   17,888
Nick De Bois, C.   15,597
Ms Hilary Leighter, LD   3,355
Ramon Johns, BNP   605
Brian Hall, UK Ind.   247
Michael Akerman, ProLife   241
Richard Course, Ind.   210
Lab. majority 2,291 (6.01%)
4.15% swing Lab. to C.
(1997, Lab. maj. 6,822 (14.31%))

ENFIELD SOUTHGATE
E.66,418 T. 41,908 (63.10%) Lab. hold
*Stephen Twigg, Lab.   21,727
John Flack, C.   16,181
Wayne Hoban, LD   2,935
Ms Elaine Graham-Leigh, Green   662
Roy Freshwater, UK Ind.   298
Andrew Malakouna, Ind.   105
Lab. majority 5,546 (13.23%)
5.08% swing C. to Lab.
(1997, Lab. maj. 1,433 (3.08%))

EPPING FOREST
E.72,645   T. 42,414 (58.39%) C. hold

*Mrs Eleanor Laing, C.   20,833
Christopher Naylor, Lab.   12,407
Michael Heavens, LD   7,884
Andrew Smith, UK Ind.   1,290
C. majority 8,426 (19.87%)
4.98% swing Lab. to C.
(1997, C. maj. 5,252 (9.91%))

EPSOM & EWELL
E.74,266   T. 46,643 (62.81%) C. hold
Chris Grayling, C.   22,430
Charles Mansell, Lab.   12,350
John Vincent, LD   10,316
G. Webster-Gardiner, UK Ind.   1,547
C. majority 10,080 (21.61%)
0.17% swing Lab. to C.
(1997, C. maj. 11,525 (21.27%))

EREWASH
E.78,484   T. 48,596 (61.92%) Lab. hold
*Ms Liz Blackman, Lab.   23,915
Gregor MacGregor, C.   16,983
Martin Garnett, LD   5,586
Ms Louise Smith, UK Ind.   692
Steven Belshaw, BNP   591
R U Seerius, Loony   428
Peter Waldock, Soc. Lab.   401
Lab. majority 6,932 (14.26%)
0.44% swing Lab. to C.
(1997, Lab. maj. 9,135 (15.14%))

ERITH & THAMESMEAD
E.66,371   T. 33,351 (50.25%) Lab. hold
*John Austin, Lab.   19,769
Mark Brooks, C.   8,602
James Kempton, LD   3,800
Hardev Dhillon, Soc. Lab.   1,180
Lab. majority 11,167 (33.48%)
4.21% swing Lab. to C.
(1997, Lab. maj. 17,424 (41.90%))

ESHER & WALTON
E.73,541   T. 45,531 (61.91%) C. hold
*Ian Taylor, C.   22,296
Joe McGowan, Lab.   10,758
Mark Marsh, LD   10,241
Bernard Collignon, UK Ind.   2,236
C. majority 11,538 (25.34%)
0.86% swing C. to Lab.
(1997, C. maj. 14,528 (27.07%))

ESSEX NORTH
E.71,680   T. 44,944 (62.70%) C. hold
*Bernard Jenkin, C.   21,325
Philip Hawkins, Lab.   14,139
Trevor Ellis, LD   7,867
George Curtis, UK Ind.   1,613
C. majority 7,186 (15.99%)
2.65% swing Lab. to C.
(1997, C. maj. 5,476 (10.69%))

EXETER
E.81,942   T. 52,616 (64.21%) Lab. hold
*Ben Bradshaw, Lab.   26,194
Mrs Anne Jobson, C.   14,435
Richard Copus, LD   6,512
David Morrish, Lib.   2,596
Paul Edwards, Green   1,240
John Stuart, UK Ind.   1,109
Francis Choules, Soc. All.   530
Lab. majority 11,759 (22.35%)
1.71% swing C. to Lab.
(1997, Lab. maj. 11,705 (18.92%))

FALMOUTH & CAMBORNE
E.72,833   T. 46,820 (64.28%) Lab. hold
*Ms Candy Atherton, Lab.   18,532
Nick Serpell, C.   14,005
Julian Brazil, LD   11,453
John Browne, UK Ind.   1,328
Ms Hilda Wasley, Meb. Ker.   853
Paul Holmes, Lib.   649
Lab. majority 4,527 (9.67%)
2.33% swing C. to Lab.
(1997, Lab. maj. 2,688 (5.01%))

FAREHAM
E.72,678   T. 45,447 (62.53%) C. hold
Mark Hoban, C.   21,389
James Carr, Lab.   14,380
Hugh Pritchard, LD   8,503
William O'Brien, UK Ind.   1,175
C. majority 7,009 (15.42%)
2.21% swing C. to Lab.
(1997, C. maj. 10,358 (19.85%))

FAVERSHAM & KENT MID
E.67,995   T. 41,051 (60.37%) C. hold
Hugh Robertson, C.   18,739
Grahame Birchall, Lab.   14,556
Mike Sole, LD   5,529
Jim Gascoyne, UK Ind.   828
Ms Penny Kemp, Green   799
Norman Davidson, R & R Loony   600
C. majority 4,183 (10.19%)
0.89% swing Lab. to C.
(1997, C. maj. 4,173 (8.41%))

FELTHAM & HESTON
E.73,229   T. 36,177 (49.40%) Lab. Co-op hold
*Alan Keen, Lab. Co-op   21,406
Mrs Liz Mammatt, C.   8,749
Andy Darley, LD   4,998
Surinder Cheema, Soc. Lab.   651
Warwick Prachar, Ind.   204
Asa Khaira, Ind.   169
Lab. Co-op majority 12,657 (34.99%)
1.11% swing C. to Lab. Co-op
(1997, Lab. maj. 15,273 (32.76%))

FINCHLEY & GOLDERS GREEN
E.76,175   T. 43,675 (57.34%) Lab. hold
*Rudi Vis, Lab.   20,205
John Marshall, C.   16,489
Ms Sarah Teather, LD   5,266
Ms Miranda Dunn, Green   1,385
John de Roeck, UK Ind.   330
Lab. majority 3,716 (8.51%)
1.08% swing C. to Lab.
(1997, Lab. maj. 3,189 (6.34%))

FOLKESTONE & HYTHE
E.71,503   T. 45,855 (64.13%) C. hold
*Rt. Hon. M. Howard, C.   20,645
Peter Carroll, LD   14,738
Albert Catterall, Lab.   9,260
John Baker, UK Ind.   1,212
C. majority 5,907 (12.88%)
0.36% swing LD to C.
(1997, C. maj. 6,332 (12.17%))

FOREST OF DEAN
E.66,240   T. 44,607 (67.34%) Lab. hold
*Ms Diana Organ, Lab.   19,350
Mark Harper, C.   17,301
David Gayler, LD   5,762

Simon Pickering, Green   1,254
Allen Prout, UK Ind.   661
Gerald Morgan, Ind.   279
Lab. majority 2,049 (4.59%)
4.02% swing Lab. to C.
(1997, Lab. maj. 6,343 (12.64%))

FYLDE
E.72,207   T. 44,737 (61.96%) C. hold
*Rt. Hon. M. Jack, C.   23,383
John Stockton, Lab.   13,773
John Begg, LD   6,599
Mrs Lesley Brown, UK Ind.   982
C. majority 9,610 (21.48%)
2.13% swing Lab. to C.
(1997, C. maj. 8,963 (17.22%))

GAINSBOROUGH
E.65,871   T. 42,319 (64.25%) C. hold
*Edward Leigh, C.   19,555
Alan Rhodes, Lab.   11,484
Steve Taylor, LD   11,280
C. majority 8,071 (19.07%)
2.39% swing Lab. to C.
(1997, C. maj. 6,826 (14.29%))

GATESHEAD EAST & WASHINGTON WEST
E.64,041   T. 33,615 (52.49%) Lab. hold
*Rt. Hon. Ms J. Quin, Lab.   22,903
Ron Beadle, LD   4,999
Ms Elizabeth Campbell, C.   4,970
Martin Rouse, UK Ind.   743
Lab. majority 17,904 (53.26%)
4.04% swing Lab. to LD
(1997, Lab. maj. 24,950 (57.92%))

GEDLING
E.68,540   T. 43,816 (63.93%) Lab. hold
*Vernon Coaker, Lab.   22,383
Jonathan Bullock, C.   16,785
Tony Gillam, LD   4,648
Lab. majority 5,598 (12.78%)
2.74% swing C. to Lab.
(1997, Lab. maj. 3,802 (7.29%))

GILLINGHAM
E.70,898   T. 42,212 (59.54%) Lab. hold
*Paul Clark, Lab.   18,782
Tim Butcher, C.   16,510
Jonathan Hunt, LD   5,755
Tony Scholefield, UK Ind.   933
Wynford Vaughan, Soc. All.   232
Lab. majority 2,272 (5.38%)
0.74% swing C. to Lab.
(1997, Lab. maj. 1,980 (3.91%))

GLOUCESTER
E.81,144   T. 48,223 (59.43%) Lab. hold
Parmjit Dhanda, Lab.   22,067
Paul James, C.   18,187
Tim Bullamore, LD   6,875
Terry Lines, UK Ind.   822
Stewart Smyth, Soc. All.   272
Lab. majority 3,880 (8.05%)
3.11% swing Lab. to C.
(1997, Lab. maj. 8,259 (14.26%))

GOSPORT
E.69,626   T. 39,789 (57.15%) C. hold
*Peter Viggers, C.   17,364
Richard Williams, Lab.   14,743
Roger Roberts, LD   6,011

John Bowles, *UK Ind.* 1,162
Kevin Chetwynd, *Soc. Lab.* 509
C. majority 2,621 (6.59%)
3.18% swing C. to Lab.
(1997, C. maj. 6,258 (12.94%))

GRANTHAM & STAMFORD
*E.*74,459 *T.* 46,289 (62.17%) C. hold
*Quentin Davies, *C.* 21,329
John Robinson, *Lab.* 16,811
Ms Jane Carr, *LD* 6,665
Miss Marilyn Swain, *UK Ind.* 1,484
C. majority 4,518 (9.76%)
2.34% swing Lab. to C.
(1997, C. maj. 2,692 (5.08%))

GRAVESHAM
*E.*69,590 *T.* 43,639 (62.71%) Lab. hold
*Chris Pond, *Lab.* 21,773
Jacques Arnold, *C.* 16,911
Bruce Parmenter, *LD* 4,031
William Jenner, *UK Ind.* 924
Lab. majority 4,862 (11.14%)
0.15% swing C. to Lab.
(1997, Lab. maj. 5,779 (10.85%))

GREAT GRIMSBY
*E.*63,157 *T.* 33,017 (52.28%) Lab. hold
*Austin Mitchell, *Lab.* 19,118
James Cousins, *C.* 7,634
Andrew de Freitas, *LD* 6,265
Lab. majority 11,484 (34.78%)
1.46% swing Lab. to C.
(1997, Lab. maj. 16,244 (37.70%))

GREAT YARMOUTH
*E.*69,131 *T.* 40,366 (58.39%) Lab. hold
*Tony Wright, *Lab.* 20,344
Charles Reynolds, *C.* 15,780
Maurice Leeke, *LD* 3,392
Bertie Poole, *UK Ind.* 850
Lab. majority 4,564 (11.31%)
3.21% swing Lab. to C.
(1997, Lab. maj. 8,668 (17.73%))

GREENWICH & WOOLWICH
*E.*62,530 *T.* 32,536 (52.03%) Lab. hold
*Rt. Hon. N. Raynsford, *Lab.* 19,691
Richard Forsdyke, *C.* 6,258
Russell Pyne, *LD* 5,082
Stan Gain, *UK Ind.* 672
Miss Kirstie Paton, *Soc. All.* 481
Ms Margaret Sharkey, *Soc. Lab.* 352
Lab. majority 13,433 (41.29%)
1.79% swing Lab. to C.
(1997, Lab. maj. 18,128 (44.87%))

GUILDFORD
*E.*76,046 *T.* 47,842 (62.91%) LD gain
Ms Sue Doughty, *LD* 20,358
*Nick St Aubyn, *C.* 19,820
Ms Joyce Still, *Lab.* 6,558
Ms Sonya Porter, *UK Ind.* 736
John Morris, *Pacifist* 370
LD majority 538 (1.12%)
4.77% swing C. to LD
(1997, C. maj. 4,791 (8.41%))

HACKNEY NORTH & STOKE
NEWINGTON
*E.*60,444 *T.* 29,621 (49.01%) Lab. hold
*Ms Diane Abbott, *Lab.* 18,081
Mrs Pauline Dye, *C.* 4,430

Ms Meral Ece, *LD* 4,170
Chit Yen Chong, *Green* 2,184
Sukant Chandan, *Soc. Lab.* 756
Lab. majority 13,651 (46.09%)
0.74% swing Lab. to C.
(1997, Lab. maj. 15,627 (47.57%))

HACKNEY SOUTH &
SHOREDITCH
*E.*63,990 *T.* 30,347 (47.42%) Lab. hold
*Brian Sedgemore, *Lab.* 19,471
Tony Vickers, *LD* 4,422
Paul White, *C.* 4,180
Ms Cecilia Prosper, *Soc. All.* 1,401
Saim Kokshal, *Reform* 471
Ivan Beavis, *Comm.* 259
William Rogers, *WRP* 143
Lab. majority 15,049 (49.59%)
2.60% swing LD to Lab.
(1997, Lab. maj. 14,980 (44.39%))

HALESOWEN & ROWLEY REGIS
*E.*65,683 *T.* 39,274 (59.79%) Lab. hold
*Ms Sylvia Heal, *Lab.* 20,804
Les Jones, *C.* 13,445
Patrick Harley, *LD* 4,089
Alan Sheath, *UK Ind.* 936
Lab. majority 7,359 (18.74%)
1.23% swing Lab. to C.
(1997, Lab. maj. 10,337 (21.20%))

HALIFAX
*E.*69,870 *T.* 40,390 (57.81%) Lab. hold
*Ms Alice Mahon, *Lab.* 19,800
James Walsh, *C.* 13,671
John Durkin, *LD* 5,878
Mrs Helen Martinek, *UK Ind.* 1,041
Lab. majority 6,129 (15.17%)
3.50% swing Lab. to C.
(1997, Lab. maj. 11,212 (22.18%))

HALTEMPRICE & HOWDEN
*E.*67,055 *T.* 43,928 (65.51%) C. hold
*Rt. Hon. D. Davis, *C.* 18,994
John Neal, *LD* 17,091
Leslie Howell, *Lab.* 6,898
Ms Joanne Robinson, *UK Ind.* 945
C. majority 1,903 (4.33%)
5.41% swing C. to LD
(1997, C. maj. 7,514 (15.16%))

HALTON
*E.*63,673 *T.* 34,470 (54.14%) Lab. hold
*Derek Twigg, *Lab.* 23,841
Chris Davenport, *C.* 6,413
Peter Walker, *LD* 4,216
Lab. majority 17,428 (50.56%)
1.33% swing Lab. to C.
(1997, Lab. maj. 23,650 (53.22%))

HAMMERSMITH & FULHAM
*E.*79,302 *T.* 44,700 (56.37%) Lab. hold
*Iain Coleman, *Lab.* 19,801
Matthew Carrington, *C.* 17,786
Jon Burden, *LD* 5,294
Daniel Lopez Dias, *Green* 1,444
Gerald Roberts, *UK Ind.* 375
Lab. majority 2,015 (4.51%)
1.30% swing Lab. to C.
(1997, Lab. maj. 3,842 (7.11%))

HAMPSHIRE EAST
*E.*78,802 *T.* 50,289 (63.82%) C. hold

*Michael Mates, *C.* 23,950
Robert Booker, *LD* 15,060
Ms Barbara Burfoot, *Lab.* 9,866
Stephen Coles, *UK Ind.* 1,413
C. majority 8,890 (17.68%)
1.13% swing C. to LD
(1997, C. maj. 11,590 (19.93%))

HAMPSHIRE NORTH EAST
*E.*71,323 *T.* 43,947 (61.62%) C. hold
*Rt. Hon. J. Arbuthnot, *C.* 23,379
Mike Plummer, *LD* 10,122
Barry Jones, *Lab.* 8,744
Graham Mellstrom, *UK Ind.* 1,702
C. majority 13,257 (30.17%)
1.00% swing LD to C.
(1997, C. maj. 14,398 (28.17%))

HAMPSHIRE NORTH WEST
*E.*76,359 *T.* 48,631 (63.69%) C. hold
*Rt. Hon. Sir G. Young, *C.* 24,374
Mick Mumford, *Lab.* 12,365
Alex Bentley, *LD* 10,329
Stanley Oram, *UK Ind.* 1,563
C. majority 12,009 (24.69%)
1.53% swing Lab. to C.
(1997, C. maj. 11,551 (21.13%))

HAMPSTEAD & HIGHGATE
*E.*65,309 *T.* 35,407 (54.21%) Lab. hold
*Ms Glenda Jackson, *Lab.* 16,601
Andrew Mennear, *C.* 8,725
Jonathan Simpson, *LD* 7,273
Andrew Cornwell, *Green* 1,654
Ms Helen Cooper, *Soc. All.* 559
Thomas McDermott, *UK Ind.* 316
Ms Sister XNunoftheabove, *Ind.* 144
Ms Mary Teale, *ProLife* 92
Amos Klein, *Ind.* 43
Lab. majority 7,876 (22.24%)
3.96% swing Lab. to C.
(1997, Lab. maj. 13,284 (30.17%))

HARBOROUGH
*E.*73,300 *T.* 46,427 (63.34%) C. hold
*Edward Garnier, *C.* 20,748
Ms Jill Hope, *LD* 15,496
Raj Jethwa, *Lab.* 9,271
David Knight, *UK Ind.* 912
C. majority 5,252 (11.31%)
0.49% swing C. to LD
(1997, C. maj. 6,524 (12.30%))

HARLOW
*E.*67,074 *T.* 40,115 (59.81%) Lab. hold
*Bill Rammell, *Lab.* 19,169
Robert Halfon, *C.* 13,941
Ms Lorna Spenceley, *LD* 5,381
Tony Bennett, *UK Ind.* 1,223
John Hobbs, *Soc. All.* 401
Lab. majority 5,228 (13.03%)
4.48% swing Lab. to C.
(1997, Lab. maj. 10,514 (21.99%))

HARROGATE &
KNARESBOROUGH
*E.*65,185 *T.* 42,179 (64.71%) LD hold
*Phil Willis, *LD* 23,445
Andrew Jones, *C.* 14,600
Alastair MacDonald, *Lab.* 3,101
Bill Brown, *UK Ind.* 761
John Cornforth, *ProLife* 272
LD majority 8,845 (20.97%)

3.94% swing C. to LD
(1997, LD maj. 6,236 (13.09%))

HARROW EAST
E.81,575 T. 48,077 (58.94%) Lab. hold
*Tony McNulty, Lab.   26,590
Peter Wilding, C.   15,466
George Kershaw, LD   6,021
Lab. majority 11,124 (23.14%)
3.02% swing C. to Lab.
(1997, Lab. maj. 9,738 (17.09%))

HARROW WEST
E.73,505 T. 46,648 (63.46%) Lab. hold
*Gareth Thomas, Lab.   23,142
Danny Finkelstein, C.   16,986
Christopher Noyce, LD   5,995
Peter Kefford, UK Ind.   525
Lab. majority 6,156 (13.20%)
5.42% swing C. to Lab.
(1997, Lab. maj. 1,240 (2.36%))

HARTLEPOOL
E.67,652 T. 38,051 (56.25%) Lab. hold
*Rt. Hon. P. Mandelson, Lab.   22,506
Gus Robinson, C.   7,935
Nigel Boddy, LD   5,717
Arthur Scargill, Soc. Lab.   912
Ian Cameron, Ind.   557
John Booth, Ind.   424
Lab. majority 14,571 (38.29%)
0.54% swing Lab. to C.
(1997, Lab. maj. 17,508 (39.38%))

HARWICH
E.77,539 T. 48,115 (62.05%) Lab. hold
*Ivan Henderson, Lab.   21,951
Ian Sproat, C.   19,355
Peter Wilcock, LD   4,099
Tony Finnegan-Butler, UK Ind.   2,463
Clive Lawrance, Ind.   247
Lab. majority 2,596 (5.40%)
1.56% swing C. to Lab.
(1997, Lab. maj. 1,216 (2.28%))

HASTINGS & RYE
E.70,632 T. 41,218 (58.36%) Lab. hold
*Michael Foster, Lab.   19,402
Mark Coote, C.   15,094
Graem Peters, LD   4,266
Alan Coomber, UK Ind.   911
Ms Sally Phillips, Green   721
Mrs Gillian Bargery, Ind.   486
John Ord-Clarke, Loony   198
Brett McLean, R & R Loony   140
Lab. majority 4,308 (10.45%)
2.62% swing C. to Lab.
(1997, Lab. maj. 2,560 (5.21%))

HAVANT
E.70,246 T. 40,437 (57.56%) C. hold
*David Willetts, C.   17,769
Peter Guthrie, Lab.   13,562
Ms Helena Cole, LD   7,508
Kevin Jacks, Green   793
Tim Cuell, UK Ind.   561
Roy Stanley, Ind.   244
C. majority 4,207 (10.40%)
1.34% swing Lab. to C.
(1997, C. maj. 3,729 (7.72%))

HAYES & HARLINGTON
E.57,561 T. 32,403 (56.29%) Lab. hold

*John McDonnell, Lab.   21,279
Robert McLean, C.   7,813
Ms Nahid Boethe, LD   1,958
Gary Burch, BNP   705
Wally Kennedy, Soc. Alt.   648
Lab. majority 13,466 (41.56%)
3.39% swing C. to Lab.
(1997, Lab. maj. 14,291 (34.78%))

HAZEL GROVE
E.65,107 T. 38,478 (59.10%) LD hold
*Andrew Stunell, LD   20,020
Ms Nadine Bargery, C.   11,585
Martin Miller, Lab.   6,230
Gerald Price, UK Ind.   643
LD majority 8,435 (21.92%)
1.01% swing LD to C.
(1997, LD maj. 11,814 (23.95%))

HEMEL HEMPSTEAD
E.72,086 T. 45,833 (63.58%) Lab. Co-op hold
*Tony McWalter, Lab. Co-op   21,389
Paul Ivey, C.   17,647
Neil Stuart, LD   5,877
Barry Newton, UK Ind.   920
Lab. Co-op majority 3,742 (8.16%)
0.78% swing C. to Lab. Co-op
(1997, Lab. maj. 3,636 (6.60%))

HEMSWORTH
E.67,948 T. 35,227 (51.84%) Lab. hold
*Jon Trickett, Lab.   23,036
Mrs Elizabeth Truss, C.   7,400
Ed Waller, LD   3,990
Paul Turek, Soc. Lab.   801
Lab. majority 15,636 (44.39%)
4.19% swing Lab. to C.
(1997, Lab. maj. 23,992 (52.76%))

HENDON
E.78,212 T. 40,851 (52.23%) Lab. hold
*Andrew Dismore, Lab.   21,432
Richard Evans, C.   14,015
Wayne Casey, LD   4,724
Craig Crosbie, UK Ind.   409
Ms Stella Taylor, WRP   164
Michael Stewart, Prog Dem   107
Lab. majority 7,417 (18.16%)
2.93% swing C. to Lab.
(1997, Lab. maj. 6,155 (12.30%))

HENLEY
E.69,081 T. 44,401 (64.27%) C. hold
Boris Johnson, C.   20,466
Ms Catherine Bearder, LD   12,008
Ms Janet Mathews, Lab.   9,367
Philip Collings, UK Ind.   1,413
Oliver Tickell, Green   1,147
C. majority 8,458 (19.05%)
1.31% swing C. to LD
(1997, C. maj. 11,167 (21.66%))

HEREFORD
E.70,305 T. 44,624 (63.47%) LD hold
*Paul Keetch, LD   18,244
Mrs Virginia Taylor, C.   17,276
David Hallam, Lab.   6,739
Clive Easton, UK Ind.   1,184
David Gillett, Green   1,181
LD majority 968 (2.17%)
5.24% swing LD to C.
(1997, LD maj. 6,648 (12.65%))

HERTFORD & STORTFORD
E.75,141 T. 47,176 (62.78%) C. hold
Mark Prisk, C.   21,074
Simon Speller, Lab.   15,471
Ms Mione Goldspink, LD   9,388
Stuart Rising, UK Ind.   1,243
C. majority 5,603 (11.88%)
0.37% swing C. to Lab.
(1997, C. maj. 6,885 (12.62%))

HERTFORDSHIRE NORTH EAST
E.68,790 T. 44,645 (64.90%) C. hold
*Oliver Heald, C.   19,695
Ivan Gibbons, Lab.   16,251
Ms Alison Kingman, LD   7,686
Michael Virgo, UK Ind.   1,013
C. majority 3,444 (7.71%)
0.89% swing Lab. to C.
(1997, Lab. maj. 3,088 (5.94%))

HERTFORDSHIRE SOUTH WEST
E.73,367 T. 47,269 (64.43%) C. hold
*Richard Page, C.   20,933
Graham Dale, Lab.   12,752
Ed Featherstone, LD   12,431
Colin Dale-Mills, UK Ind.   847
Ms Julia Goffin, ProLife   306
C. majority 8,181 (17.31%)
0.39% swing C. to Lab.
(1997, C. maj. 10,021 (18.08%))

HERTSMERE
E.68,780 T. 41,505 (60.34%) C. hold
*James Clappison, C.   19,855
Ms Hilary Broderick, Lab.   14,953
Paul Thompson, LD   6,300
James Dry, Soc. Lab.   397
C. majority 4,902 (11.81%)
2.85% swing C. to Lab.
(1997, C. maj. 3,075 (6.11%))

HEXHAM
E.59,807 T. 42,413 (70.92%) C. hold
*Peter Atkinson, C.   18,917
Paul Brannen, Lab.   16,388
Philip Latham, LD   6,380
Alan Patterson, UK Ind.   728
C. majority 2,529 (5.96%)
2.74% swing Lab. to C.
(1997, C. maj. 222 (0.49%))

HEYWOOD & MIDDLETON
E.73,005 T. 38,779 (53.12%) Lab. Co-op hold
*Jim Dobbin, Lab. Co-op   22,377
Mrs Marilyn Hopkins, C.   10,707
Ian Greenhalgh, LD   4,329
Philip Burke, Lib.   1,021
Ms Christine West, Ch. D.   345
Lab. Co-op majority 11,670 (30.09%)
2.30% swing Lab. Co-op to C.
(1997, Lab. maj. 17,542 (34.70%))

HIGH PEAK
E.73,774 T. 48,114 (65.22%) Lab. hold
*Tom Levitt, Lab.   22,430
Simon Chapman, C.   17,941
Peter Ashenden, LD   7,743
Lab. majority 4,489 (9.33%)
3.03% swing Lab. to C.
(1997, Lab. maj. 8,791 (15.38%))

HITCHIN & HARPENDEN
E.67,196   T. 44,924 (66.86%) C. hold
*Rt. Hon. P. Lilley, C.   21,271
Alan Amos, Lab.   14,608
John Murphy, LD   8,076
John Saunders, UK Ind.   606
Peter Rigby, Ind.   363
C. majority 6,663 (14.83%)
1.06% swing Lab. to C.
(1997, C. maj. 6,671 (12.72%))

HOLBORN & ST PANCRAS
E.62,813   T. 31,129 (49.56%) Lab. hold
*Rt. Hon. F. Dobson, Lab.   16,770
Nathaniel Green, LD   5,595
Mrs Roseanne Serelli, C.   5,258
Rob Whitley, Green   1,875
Ms Candy Udwin, Soc. All.   971
Joti Brar, Soc. Lab.   359
Magnus Nielsen, UK Ind.   301
Lab. majority 11,175 (35.90%)
8.31% swing Lab. to LD
(1997, Lab. maj. 17,903 (47.11%))

HORNCHURCH
E.61,008   T. 35,557 (58.28%) Lab. hold
*John Cryer, Lab.   16,514
Robin Squire, C.   15,032
Ms Sarah Lea, LD   2,928
Lawrence Webb, UK Ind.   893
Mr David Durant, Third   190
Lab. majority 1,482 (4.17%)
4.38% swing Lab. to C.
(1997, Lab. maj. 5,680 (12.93%))

HORNSEY & WOOD GREEN
E.75,967   T. 44,063 (58.00%) Lab. hold
*Ms Barbara Roche, Lab.   21,967
Ms Lynne Featherstone, LD   11,353
Jason Hollands, C.   6,921
Ms Jayne Forbes, Green   2,228
Ms Louise Christian, Soc. All.   1,106
Ms Ella Rule, Soc. Lab.   294
Erdil Ataman, Reform   194
Lab. majority 10,614 (24.09%)
13.21% swing Lab. to LD
(1997, Lab. maj. 20,499 (39.82%))

HORSHAM
E.79,604   T. 50,770 (63.78%) C. hold
*Rt. Hon. F. Maude, C.   26,134
Hubert Carr, LD   12,468
Ms Janet Sully, Lab.   10,267
Hugo Miller, UK Ind.   1,472
Jim Duggan, Ind.   429
C. majority 13,666 (26.92%)
0.46% swing LD to C.
(1997, C. maj. 14,862 (26.00%))

HOUGHTON & WASHINGTON EAST
E.67,946 T. 33,641 (49.51%) Lab. hold
*Fraser Kemp, Lab.   24,628
Tony Devenish, C.   4,810
Richard Ormerod, LD   4,203
Lab. majority 19,818 (58.91%)
2.29% swing Lab. to C.
(1997, Lab. maj. 26,555 (63.49%))

HOVE
E.70,889 T. 41,988 (59.23%) Lab. hold
*Ivor Caplin, Lab.   19,253
Mrs Jenny Langston, C.   16,082

Harold de Souza, LD   3,823
Ms Anthea Ballam, Green   1,369
Andy Richards, Soc. All.   531
Richard Franklin, UK Ind.   358
Nigel Donovan, Lib.   316
Simon Dobbshead, Free   196
Thomas Major, Ind.   60
Lab. majority 3,171 (7.55%)
0.34% swing Lab. to C.
(1997, Lab. maj. 3,959 (8.23%))

HUDDERSFIELD
E.64,349 T. 35,383 (54.99%) Lab. Co-op hold
*Barry Sheerman, Lab. Co-op   18,840
Paul Baverstock, C.   8,794
Neil Bentley, LD   5,300
John Phillips, Green   1,254
Mrs Judith Longman, UK Ind.   613
Graham Hellawell, Soc. All.   374
George Randall, Soc. Lab.   208
Lab. Co-op majority 10,046 (28.39%)
3.59% swing Lab. Co-op to C.
(1997, Lab. maj. 15,848 (35.57%))

HULL EAST
E.66,473 T. 30,875 (46.45%) Lab. hold
*Rt. Hon. J. Prescott, Lab.   19,938
Ms Jo Swinson, LD   4,613
Ms Sandip Verma, C.   4,276
Ms Jeanette Jenkinson, UK Ind.   1,218
Ms Linda Muir, Soc. Lab.   830
Lab. majority 15,325 (49.64%)
5.94% swing Lab. to LD
(1997, Lab. maj. 23,318 (57.60%))

HULL NORTH
E.63,022 T. 28,633 (45.43%) Lab. hold
*Kevin McNamara, Lab.   16,364
Ms Simone Butterworth, LD   5,643
Paul Charlson, C.   4,902
Ms Tineka Robinson, UK Ind.   655
Roger Smith, Soc. All.   490
Carl Wagner, LCA   478
Christopher Veasey, Ind.   101
Lab. majority 10,721 (37.44%)
6.89% swing Lab. to LD
(1997, Lab. maj. 19,705 (50.79%))

HULL WEST & HESSLE
E.63,077 T. 28,916 (45.84%) Lab. hold
*Alan Johnson, Lab.   16,880
John Sharp, C.   5,929
Ms Angela Wastling, LD   4,364
John Cornforth, UK Ind.   878
David Harris, Ind.   512
David Skinner, Soc. Lab.   353
Lab. majority 10,951 (37.87%)
1.38% swing Lab. to C.
(1997, Lab. maj. 15,525 (40.48%))

HUNTINGDON
E.78,604   T. 49,089 (62.45%) C. hold
Jonathan Djanogly, C.   24,507
Michael Pope, LD   11,715
Takki Sulaiman, Lab.   11,211
Derek Norman, UK Ind.   1,656
C. majority 12,792 (26.06%)
7.26% swing C. to LD
(1997, C. maj. 18,140 (31.84%))

HYNDBURN
E.66,445 T. 38,243 (57.56%) Lab. hold

*Greg Pope, Lab.   20,900
Peter Britcliffe, C.   12,681
Bill Greene, LD   3,680
John Tomlin, UK Ind.   982
Lab. majority 8,219 (21.49%)
1.11% swing Lab. to C.
(1997, Lab. maj. 11,448 (23.71%))

ILFORD NORTH
E.68,893 T. 40,234 (58.40%) Lab. hold
*Ms Linda Perham, Lab.   18,428
Vivian Bendall, C.   16,313
Gavin Stollar, LD   4,717
Martin Levin, UK Ind.   776
Lab. majority 2,115 (5.26%)
0.67% swing Lab. to C.
(1997, Lab. maj. 3,224 (6.60%))

ILFORD SOUTH
E.76,025 T. 41,295 (54.32%) Lab. Co-op hold
*Mike Gapes, Lab. Co-op   24,619
Suresh Kuma, C.   10,622
Ralph Scott, LD   4,647
Harun Khan, UK Ind.   1,407
Lab. Co-op majority 13,997 (33.90%)
2.75% swing C. to Lab. Co-op
(1997, Lab. maj. 14,200 (28.39%))

IPSWICH
E.68,198 T. 38,873 (57.00%) Lab. hold
*Jamie Cann, Lab.   19,952
Edward Wild, C.   11,871
Terry Gilbert, LD   5,904
William Vinyard, UK Ind.   624
Peter Leach, Soc. All.   305
Shaun Gratton, Soc. Lab.   217
Lab. majority 8,081 (20.79%)
0.40% swing Lab. to C.
(1997, Lab. maj. 10,439 (21.58%))

ISLE OF WIGHT
E.106,305 T. 63,482 (59.72%)   Con gain
Andrew Turner, C.   25,223
*Dr Peter Brand, LD   22,397
Ms Deborah Gardiner, Lab.   9,676
David Lott, UK Ind.   2,106
David Holmes, Ind.   1,423
Paul Scivier, Green   1,279
Philip Murray, IOW   1,164
James Spensley, Soc. Lab.   214
C. majority 2,826 (4.45%)
6.61% swing LD to C.
(1997, LD maj. 6,406 (8.76%))

ISLINGTON NORTH
E.61,970 T. 30,216 (48.76%) Lab. hold
*Jeremy Corbyn, Lab.   18,699
Ms Laura Willoughby, LD   5,741
Neil Rands, C.   3,249
Chris Ashby, Green   1,876
Steve Cook, Soc. Lab.   512
Emine Hassan, Reform   139
Lab. majority 12,958 (42.88%)
6.38% swing Lab. to LD
(1997, Lab. maj. 19,955 (55.64%))

ISLINGTON SOUTH & FINSBURY
E.59,515 T. 28,206 (47.39%) Lab. hold
*Rt. Hon. C. Smith, Lab.   15,217
Keith Sharp, LD   7,937

Mrs Nicky Morgan, *C.* 3,860
Ms Janine Booth, *Soc. All.* 817
Thomas McCarthy, *Ind.* 267
Charles Thomson, *Stuck* 108
Lab. majority 7,280 (25.81%)
7.71% swing Lab. to LD
(1997, Lab. maj. 14,563 (41.24%))

JARROW
*E.*63,172 *T.* 34,479 (54.58%) Lab. hold
*Stephen Hepburn, *Lab.* 22,777
James Selby, *LD* 5,182
Donald Wood, *C.* 5,056
Alan Badger, *UK Ind.* 716
Alan Le Blond, *Ind.* 391
John Bissett, *Soc.* 357
Lab. majority 17,595 (51.03%)
1.37% swing Lab. to LD
(1997, Lab. maj. 21,933 (49.91%))

KEIGHLEY
*E.*68,349 *T.* 43,333 (63.40%) Lab. hold
*Ms Ann Cryer, *Lab.* 20,888
Simon Cooke, *C.* 16,883
Mike Doyle, *LD* 4,722
Michael Cassidy, *UK Ind.* 840
Lab. majority 4,005 (9.24%)
2.30% swing Lab. to C.
(1997, Lab. maj. 7,132 (13.85%))

KENSINGTON & CHELSEA
*E.*62,007 *T.* 28,038 (45.22%) C. hold
*Rt. Hon. M. Portillo, *C.* 15,270
Simon Stanley, *Lab.* 6,499
Ms Kishwer Falkner, *LD* 4,416
Ms Julia Stephenson, *Green* 1,158
Nicholas Hockney, *UK Ind.* 416
Ms Josephine Quintavalle, *ProLife* 179
Ginger Crab, *Wrestling* 100
C. majority 8,771 (31.28%)
2.81% swing Lab. to C.
(1999 Nov by-election, C. maj. 6,706
(34.37%); 1997, C. maj. 9,519 (25.66%))

KETTERING
*E.*79,697 *T.* 53,752 (67.45%) Lab. hold
*Philip Sawford, *Lab.* 24,034
Philip Hollobone, *C.* 23,369
Roger Aron, *LD* 5,469
Barry Mahoney, *UK Ind.* 880
Lab. majority 665 (1.24%)
0.45% swing C. to Lab.
(1997, Lab. maj. 189 (0.33%))

KINGSTON & SURBITON
*E.*72,687 *T.* 49,093 (67.54%) LD hold
*Edward Davey, *LD* 29,542
David Shaw, *C.* 13,866
Phil Woodford, *Lab.* 4,302
Chris Spruce, *Green* 572
Miss Amy Burns, *UK Ind.* 438
John Hayball, *Soc. Lab.* 319
Jeremy Middleton, *Unrep.* 54
LD majority 15,676 (31.93%)
15.92% swing C. to LD
(1997, LD maj. 56 (0.10%))

KINGSWOOD
*E.*80,531 *T.* 52,676 (65.41%) Lab. hold
*Dr Roger Berry, *Lab.* 28,903
Robert Marven, *C.* 14,941
Christopher Greenfield, *LD* 7,747
David Smith, *UK Ind.* 1,085

Lab. majority 13,962 (26.51%)
1.35% swing C. to Lab.
(1997, Lab. maj. 14,253 (23.80%))

KNOWSLEY NORTH & SEFTON
EAST
*E.*70,781 *T.* 37,517 (53.00%) Lab. hold
*George Howarth, *Lab.* 25,035
Keith Chapman, *C.* 6,108
Richard Roberts, *LD* 5,173
Ron Waugh, *Soc. Lab.* 574
Thomas Rossiter, *Ind.* 356
David Jones, *Ind.* 271
Lab. majority 18,927 (50.45%)
1.08% swing Lab. to C.
(1997, Lab. maj. 26,147 (52.61%))

KNOWSLEY SOUTH
*E.*70,681 *T.* 36,590 (51.77%) Lab. hold
*Eddie O'Hara, *Lab.* 26,071
David Smithson, *LD* 4,755
Paul Jemetta, *C.* 4,250
Alan Fogg, *Soc. Lab.* 1,068
Ms Mona McNee, *Ind.* 446
Lab. majority 21,316 (58.26%)
5.27% swing Lab. to LD
(1997, Lab. maj. 30,708 (64.53%))

LANCASHIRE WEST
*E.*72,858 *T.* 42,971 (58.98%) Lab. hold
*Colin Pickthall, *Lab.* 23,404
Jeremy Myers, *C.* 13,761
John Thornton, *LD* 4,966
David Hill, *Ind.* 523
David Braid (Indep Braid) 317
Lab. majority 9,643 (22.44%)
4.42% swing Lab. to C.
(1997, Lab. maj. 17,119 (31.28%))

LANCASTER & WYRE
*E.*78,964 *T.* 52,350 (66.30%) Lab. hold
*Hilton Dawson, *Lab.* 22,556
Steve Barclay, *C.* 22,075
Ms Liz Scott, *LD* 5,383
Prof John Whitelegg, *Green* 1,595
Dr John Whittaker, *UK Ind.* 741
Lab. majority 481 (0.92%)
0.64% swing Lab. to C.
(1997, Lab. maj. 1,295 (2.20%))

LEEDS CENTRAL
*E.*65,497 *T.* 27,306 (41.69%) Lab. hold
*Hilary Benn, *Lab.* 18,277
Miss Victoria Richmond, *C.* 3,896
Stewart Arnold, *LD* 3,607
David Burgess, *UK Ind.* 775
Steve Johnson, *Soc. All.* 751
Lab. majority 14,381 (52.67%)
1.62% swing Lab. to C.
(1999 Jun by-election, Lab. maj. 2,293
(17.39%); 1997, Lab. maj. 20,689
(55.90%))

LEEDS EAST
*E.*56,400 *T.* 29,055 (51.52%) Lab. hold
*George Mudie, *Lab.* 18,290
Barry Anderson, *C.* 5,647
Brian Jennings, *LD* 3,923
Raymond Northgreaves, *UK Ind.* 634
Mark King, *Soc. Lab.* 419
Peter Socrates, *Ind.* 142
Lab. majority 12,643 (43.51%)
2.64% swing Lab. to C.

(1997, Lab. maj. 17,466 (48.80%))

LEEDS NORTH EAST
*E.*64,123 *T.* 39,773 (62.03%) Lab. hold
*Fabian Hamilton, *Lab.* 19,540
Owain Rhys, *C.* 12,451
Jonathan Brown, *LD* 6,325
Ms Celia Foote (Left All) 770
Jeffrey Miles, *UK Ind.* 382
Colin Muir, *Soc. Lab.* 173
Mohammed Zaman, *Ind.* 132
Lab. majority 7,089 (17.82%)
1.27% swing C. to Lab.
(1997, Lab. maj. 6,959 (15.29%))

LEEDS NORTH WEST
*E.*72,945 *T.* 42,451 (58.20%) Lab. hold
*Harold Best, *Lab.* 17,794
Adam Pritchard, *C.* 12,558
David Hall-Matthews, *LD* 11,431
Simon Jones, *UK Ind.* 668
Lab. majority 5,236 (12.33%)
2.27% swing C. to Lab.
(1997, Lab. maj. 3,844 (7.79%))

LEEDS WEST
*E.*64,218 *T.* 32,094 (49.98%) Lab. hold
*John Battle, *Lab.* 19,943
Kris Hopkins, *C.* 5,008
Darren Finlay, *LD* 3,350
David Blackburn, *Green* 2,573
William Finley, *UK Ind.* 758
Noel Nowosielski, *Lib.* 462
Lab. majority 14,935 (46.54%)
1.31% swing Lab. to C.
(1997, Lab. maj. 19,771 (49.16%))

LEICESTER EAST
*E.*65,527 *T.* 40,661 (62.05%) Lab. hold
*Keith Vaz, *Lab.* 23,402
John Mugglestone, *C.* 9,960
Ms Harpinder Athwal, *LD* 4,989
Dave Roberts, *Soc. Lab.* 837
Clive Potter, *BNP* 772
Shirley Bennett, *Ind.* 701
Lab. majority 13,442 (33.06%)
4.22% swing Lab. to C.
(1997, Lab. maj. 18,422 (41.49%))

LEICESTER SOUTH
*E.*72,671 *T.* 42,142 (57.99%) Lab. hold
*Jim Marshall, *Lab.* 22,958
Richard Hoile, *C.* 9,715
Parmjit Singh Gill, *LD* 7,243
Ms Margaret Layton, *Green* 1,217
Arnold Gardner, *Soc. Lab.* 676
Kirti Ladwa, *UK Ind.* 333
Lab. majority 13,243 (31.42%)
1.43% swing Lab. to C.
(1997, Lab. maj. 16,493 (34.28%))

LEICESTER WEST
*E.*65,267 *T.* 33,219 (50.90%) Lab. hold
*Rt. Hon. Ms P. Hewitt, *Lab.* 18,014
Chris Shaw, *C.* 8,375
Andrew Vincent, *LD* 5,085
Matthew Gough, *Green* 1,074
Sean Kirkpatrick, *Soc. Lab.* 350
Steve Score, *Soc. All.* 321
Lab. majority 9,639 (29.02%)
1.21% swing Lab. to C.
(1997, Lab. maj. 12,864 (31.44%))

248   Parliament

LEICESTERSHIRE NORTH
WEST
E.68,414 *T*. 45,009 (65.79%) Lab. Co-op hold
*David Taylor, *Lab. Co-op*   23,431
Nick Weston, *C*.   15,274
Charlie Fraser-Fleming, *LD*   4,651
William Nattrass, *UK Ind*.   1,021
Robert Nettleton, *Ind*.   632
Lab. Co-op majority 8,157 (18.12%)
3.64% swing Lab. Co-op to C.
(1997, Lab. maj. 13,219 (25.41%))

LEIGH
E.71,054 *T*. 35,298 (49.68%) Lab. hold
Andrew Burnham, *Lab*.   22,783
Andrew Oxley, *C*.   6,421
Ray Atkins, *LD*   4,524
William Kelly, *Soc. Lab*.   820
Chris Best, *UK Ind*.   750
Lab. majority 16,362 (46.35%)
3.50% swing Lab. to C.
(1997, Lab. maj. 24,496 (53.35%))

LEOMINSTER
E.68,695 *T*. 46,729 (68.02%) Con gain
Bill Wiggin, *C*.   22,879
Ms Celia Downie, *LD*   12,512
Stephen Hart, *Lab*.   7,872
Ms Pippa Bennett, *Green*   1,690
Christopher Kingsley, *UK Ind*. 1,590
John Haycock, *Ind*.   186
C. majority 10,367 (22.19%)
2.35% swing LD to C.
(1997, C. maj. 8,835 (17.48%))

LEWES
E.66,332 *T*. 45,433 (68.49%) LD hold
*Norman Baker, *LD*   25,588
Simon Sinnatt, *C*.   15,878
Paul Richards, *Lab*.   3,317
John Harvey, *UK Ind*.   650
LD majority 9,710 (21.37%)
9.36% swing C. to LD
(1997, LD maj. 1,300 (2.65%))

LEWISHAM DEPTFORD
E.62,869 *T*. 29,107 (46.30%) Lab. hold
*Joan Ruddock, *Lab*.   18,915
Ms Cordelia McCartney, *C*.   3,622
Andrew Wiseman, *LD*   3,409
Darren Johnson, *Green*   1,901
Ian Page, *Soc. All*.   1,260
Lab. majority 15,293 (52.54%)
1.78% swing Lab. to C.
(1997, Lab. maj. 18,878 (56.11%))

LEWISHAM EAST
E.58,302 *T*. 30,040 (51.52%) Lab. hold
*Ms Bridget Prentice, *Lab*.   16,116
David McInnes, *C*.   7,157
David Buxton, *LD*   4,937
Barry Roberts, *BNP*   1,005
Ms Jean Kysow, *Soc. All*.   464
Maurice Link, *UK Ind*.   361
Lab. majority 8,959 (29.82%)
1.30% swing Lab. to C.
(1997, Lab. maj. 12,127 (32.42%))

LEWISHAM WEST
E.60,947 *T*. 30,815 (50.56%) Lab. hold
*Jim Dowd, *Lab*.   18,816
Gary Johnson, *C*.   6,896

Richard Thomas, *LD*   4,146
Frederick Pearson, *UK Ind*.   485
Nick Long, *Ind*.   472
Lab. majority 11,920 (38.68%)
0.25% swing C. to Lab.
(1997, Lab. maj. 14,337 (38.19%))

LEYTON & WANSTEAD
E.61,549 *T*. 33,718 (54.78%) Lab. hold
*Harry Cohen, *Lab*.   19,558
Edward Heckels, *C*.   6,654
Alex Wilcock, *LD*   5,389
Ashley Gunstock, *Green*   1,030
Ms Sally Labern, *Soc. All*.   709
M. Skaife D'Ingerthorp, *UK Ind*. 378
Lab. majority 12,904 (38.27%)
0.17% swing Lab. to C.
(1997, Lab. maj. 15,186 (38.62%))

LICHFIELD
E.63,794 *T*. 41,680 (65.34%) C. hold
*Michael Fabricant, *C*.   20,480
Martin Machray, *Lab*.   16,054
Phillip Bennion, *LD*   4,462
John Phazey, *UK Ind*.   684
C. majority 4,426 (10.62%)
5.06% swing Lab. to C.
(1997, C. maj. 238 (0.49%))

LINCOLN
E.66,299 *T*. 37,125 (56.00%) Lab. hold
*Ms Gillian Merron, *Lab*.   20,003
Mrs Christine Talbot, *C*.   11,583
Ms Lisa Gabriel, *LD*   4,703
Roger Doughty, *UK Ind*.   836
Lab. majority 8,420 (22.68%)
0.61% swing Lab. to C.
(1997, Lab. maj. 11,130 (23.91%))

LIVERPOOL GARSTON
E.65,094 *T*. 32,651 (50.16%) Lab. hold
*Ms Maria Eagle, *Lab*.   20,043
Ms Paula Keaveney, *LD*   7,549
Miss Helen Sutton, *C*.   5,059
Lab. majority 12,494 (38.27%)
2.05% swing Lab. to LD
(1997, Lab. maj. 18,417 (42.36%))

LIVERPOOL RIVERSIDE
E.74,827 *T*. 25,503 (34.08%) Lab. Co-op hold
*Ms Louise Ellman, *Lab. Co-op* 18,201
Richard Marbrow, *LD*   4,251
Miss Judith Edwards, *C*.   2,142
Ms Cathy Wilson, *Soc. All*.   909
Lab. Co-op majority 13,950 (54.70%)
1.23% swing Lab. Co-op to LD
(1997, Lab. maj. 21,799 (57.16%))

LIVERPOOL WALTON
E.66,237 *T*. 28,458 (42.96%) Lab. hold
*Peter Kilfoyle, *Lab*.   22,143
Kiron Reid, *LD*   4,147
Stephen Horgan, *C*.   1,726
Paul Forrest, *UK Ind*.   442
Lab. majority 17,996 (63.24%)
2.00% swing Lab. to LD
(1997, Lab. maj. 27,038 (67.24%))

LIVERPOOL WAVERTREE
E.72,555 *T*. 32,138 (44.29%) Lab. hold
*Ms Jane Kennedy, *Lab*.   20,155
Christopher Newby, *LD*   7,836

Geoffrey Allen, *C*.   3,091
Michael Lane, *Soc. Lab*.   359
Mark O'Brien, *Soc. All*.   349
Neil Miney, *UK Ind*.   348
Lab. majority 12,319 (38.33%)
2.29% swing Lab. to LD
(1997, Lab. maj. 19,701 (42.91%))

LIVERPOOL WEST DERBY
E.67,921 *T*. 30,907 (45.50%) Lab. hold
*Robert Wareing, *Lab*.   20,454
Steve Radford, *Lib*.   4,601
Patrick Moloney, *LD*   3,366
Bill Clare, *C*.   2,486
Lab. majority 15,853 (51.29%)
5.15% swing Lab. to Lib.
(1997, Lab. maj. 25,965 (61.59%))

LOUGHBOROUGH
E.70,077 *T*. 44,254 (63.15%) Lab. Co-op hold
*Andy Reed, *Lab. Co-op*   22,016
Neil Lyon, *C*.   15,638
Ms Julie Simons, *LD*   5,667
John Bigger, *UK Ind*.   933
Lab. Co-op majority 6,378 (14.41%)
1.75% swing C. to Lab. Co-op
(1997, Lab. maj. 5,712 (10.91%))

LOUTH & HORNCASTLE
E.71,556 *T*. 44,460 (62.13%) C. hold
*Sir Peter Tapsell, *C*.   21,543
David Bolland, *Lab*.   13,989
Ms Fiona Martin, *LD*   8,928
C. majority 7,554 (16.99%)
1.59% swing Lab. to C.
(1997, C. maj. 6,900 (13.81%))

LUDLOW
E.63,053 *T*. 43,124 (68.39%) LD gain
Matthew Green, *LD*   18,620
Martin Taylor-Smith, *C*.   16,990
Nigel Knowles, *Lab*.   5,785
Jim Gaffney, *Green*   871
Phil Gutteridge, *UK Ind*.   858
LD majority 1,630 (3.78%)
8.27% swing C. to LD
(1997, C. maj. 5,909 (12.77%))

LUTON NORTH
E.65,998 *T*. 39,126 (59.28%) Lab. hold
*Kelvin Hopkins, *Lab*.   22,187
Mrs Amanda Sater, *C*.   12,210
Dr Bob Hoyle, *LD*   3,795
Colin Brown, *UK Ind*.   934
Lab. majority 9,977 (25.50%)
2.58% swing C. to Lab.
(1997, Lab. maj. 9,626 (20.34%))

LUTON SOUTH
E.68,985 *T*. 39,351 (57.04%) Lab. hold
*Ms Margaret Moran, *Lab*.   21,719
Gordon Henderson, *C*.   11,586
Rabi Martins, *LD*   4,292
Marc Scheimann, *Green*   798
Charles Lawman, *UK Ind*.   578
Joe Hearne, *Soc. All*.   271
Robert Bolton, *WRP*   107
Lab. majority 10,133 (25.75%)
1.13% swing C. to Lab.
(1997, Lab. maj. 11,319 (23.49%))

MACCLESFIELD
E.73,123   T. 45,585 (62.34%)   C. hold
*Nicholas Winterton, C.   22,284
Stephen Carter, Lab.   15,084
Mike Flynn, LD   8,217
C. majority 7,200 (15.79%)
0.09% swing C. to Lab.
(1997, C. maj. 8,654 (15.97%))

MAIDENHEAD
E.68,130   T. 43,318 (63.58%)   C. hold
*Mrs Theresa May, C.   19,506
Ms Kathryn Newbound, LD   16,222
John O'Farrell, Lab.   6,577
Dr Denis Cooper, UK Ind.   741
Lloyd Clarke, Loony   272
C. majority 3,284 (7.58%)
7.98% swing C. to LD
(1997, C. maj. 11,981 (23.54%))

MAIDSTONE & THE WEALD
E.74,002   T. 45,577 (61.59%)   C. hold
*Rt. Hon. Miss A. Widdecombe, C.
                                 22,621
Mark Davis, Lab.   12,303
Ms Allison Wainman, LD   9,064
John Botting, UK Ind.   978
Neil Hunt, Ind.   611
C. majority 10,318 (22.64%)
2.36% swing Lab. to C.
(1997, C. maj. 9,603 (17.91%))

MAKERFIELD
E.68,457   T. 34,856 (50.92%)   Lab. hold
*Rt. Hon. I. McCartney, Lab.   23,879
Mrs Jane Brooks, C.   6,129
David Crowther, LD   3,990
Malcolm Jones, Soc. All.   858
Lab. majority 17,750 (50.92%)
3.61% swing C. to Lab.
(1997, Lab. maj. 26,177 (58.15%))

MALDON & CHELMSFORD EAST
E.69,201   T. 44,100 (63.73%)   C. hold
*John Whittingdale, C.   21,719
Russell Kennedy, Lab.   13,257
Ms Jane Jackson, LD   7,002
Geoffrey Harris, UK Ind.   1,135
Walter Schwarz, Green   987
C. majority 8,462 (19.19%)
0.37% swing C. to Lab.
(1997, C. maj. 10,039 (19.92%))

MANCHESTER BLACKLEY
E.59,111   T. 26,523 (44.87%)   Lab. hold
*Graham Stringer, Lab.   18,285
Lance Stanbury, C.   3,821
Gary Riding, LD   3,015
Kevin Barr, Soc. Lab.   485
Ms Karen Reissmann, Soc. All.   461
Aziz Bhatti, Anti-Corrupt   456
Lab. majority 14,464 (54.53%
0.13% swing Lab. to C.
(1997, Lab. maj. 19,588 (54.79%))

MANCHESTER CENTRAL
E.66,268 T. 25,928 (39.13%) Lab. hold
*Tony Lloyd, Lab.   17,812
Philip Hobson, LD   4,070
Aaron Powell, C.   2,328
Ms Vanessa Hall, Green   1,018
Ron Sinclair, Soc. Lab.   484

Ms Terrenia Brosnan, ProLife   216
Lab. majority 13,742 (53.00%)
2.84% swing Lab. to LD
(1997, Lab. maj. 19,682 (58.69%))

MANCHESTER GORTON
E.63,834   T. 27,229 (42.66%)   Lab. hold
*Rt. Hon. G. Kaufman, Lab.   17,099
Ms Jackie Pearcey, LD   5,795
Christopher Causer, C.   2,705
Bruce Bingham, Green   835
Rashid Bhatti, UK Ind.   462
Ms Kirsty Muir, Soc. Lab.   333
Lab. majority 11,304 (41.51%)
3.12% swing Lab. to LD
(1997, Lab. maj. 17,342 (47.76%))

MANCHESTER WITHINGTON
E.67,480   T. 35,050 (51.94%)   Lab. hold
*Rt. Hon. K. Bradley, Lab.   19,239
Ms Yasmin Zalzala, LD   7,715
Julian Samways, C.   5,349
Ms Michelle Valentine, Green   1,539
John Clegg, Soc. All.   1,208
Lab. majority 11,524 (32.88%)
7.53% swing Lab. to LD
(1997, Lab. maj. 18,581 (42.20%))

MANSFIELD
E.66,748   T. 36,852 (55.21%)   Lab. hold
*Alan Meale, Lab.   21,050
William Wellesley, C.   10,012
Tim Hill, LD   5,790
Lab. majority 11,038 (29.95%)
6.65% swing Lab. to C.
(1997, Lab. maj. 20,518 (43.26%))

MEDWAY
E.64,930   T. 38,610 (59.46%)   Lab. hold
*Robert Marshall-Andrews, Lab.   18,914
Mark Reckless, C.   15,134
Geoffrey Juby, LD   3,604
Ms Nikki Sinclaire, UK Ind.   958
Lab. majority 3,780 (9.79%)
1.08% swing Lab. to C.
(1997, Lab. maj. 5,354 (11.96%))

MERIDEN
E.74,439   T. 44,559 (59.86%)   C. hold
*Mrs Caroline Spelman, C.   21,246
Ms Christine Shawcroft, Lab.   17,462
Nigel Hicks, LD   4,941
Richard Adams, UK Ind.   910
C. majority 3,784 (8.49%)
3.71% swing Lab. to C.
(1997, C. maj. 582 (1.07%))

MIDDLESBROUGH
E.67,659 T. 33,717 (49.83%) Lab. hold
*Stuart Bell, Lab.   22,783
Alex Finn, C.   6,453
Keith Miller, LD   3,512
Geoff Kerr-Morgan, Soc. All.   577
Kai Andersen, Soc. Lab.   392
Lab. majority 16,330 (48.43%)
2.92% swing Lab. to C.
(1997, Lab. maj. 25,018 (54.28%))

MIDDLESBROUGH SOUTH & CLEVELAND EAST
E.71,485 T. 43,991 (61.54%) Lab. hold
*Dr Ashok Kumar, Lab.   24,321
Mrs Barbara Harpham, C.   14,970

Ms Linda Parrish, LD   4,700
Lab. majority 9,351 (21.26%)
0.73% swing C. to Lab.
(1997, Lab. maj. 10,607 (19.79%))

MILTON KEYNES NORTH EAST
E.75,526 T. 47,094 (62.35%) Lab. hold
*Brian White, Lab.   19,761
Mrs Marion Rix, C.   17,932
David Yeoward, LD   8,375
Michael Phillips, UK Ind.   1,026
Lab. majority 1,829 (3.88%)
1.71% swing C. to Lab.
(1997, Lab. maj. 240 (0.47%))

MILTON KEYNES SOUTH WEST
E.76,607 T. 45,384 (59.24%) Lab. hold
*Dr Phyllis Starkey, Lab.   22,484
Iain Stewart, C.   15,506
Nazar Mohammad, LD   4,828
Alan Francis, Green   957
Clive Davies, UK Ind.   848
Patrick Denning, LCA   500
Dave Bradbury, Soc. All.   261
Lab. majority 6,978 (15.38%)
2.45% swing Lab. to C.
(1997, Lab. maj. 10,292 (20.28%))

MITCHAM & MORDEN
E.65,671 T. 37,961 (57.80%) Lab. hold
*Ms Siobhain McDonagh, Lab.   22,936
Harry Stokes, C.   9,151
Nicholas Harris, LD   3,820
Tom Walsh, Green   926
John Tyndall, BNP   642
Adrian Roberts, UK Ind.   486
Lab. majority 13,785 (36.31%)
3.83% swing C. to Lab.
(1997, Lab. maj. 13,741 (28.66%))

MOLE VALLEY
E.67,770   T. 47,072 (69.46%)   C. hold
*Sir Paul Beresford, C.   23,790
Ms Celia Savage, LD   13,637
Dan Redford, Lab.   7,837
Ron Walters, UK Ind.   1,333
William Newton, ProLife   475
C. majority 10,153 (21.57%)
1.41% swing LD to C.
(1997, C. maj. 10,221 (18.74%))

MORECAMBE & LUNESDALE
E.68,607 T. 41,655 (60.72%) Lab. hold
*Ms Geraldine Smith, Lab.   20,646
David Nuttall, C.   15,554
Chris Cotton, LD   3,817
Gregg Beaman, UK Ind.   935
Ms Cherith Adams, Green   703
Lab. majority 5,092 (12.22%)
0.05% swing C. to Lab.
(1997, Lab. maj. 5,965 (12.12%))

MORLEY & ROTHWELL
E.71,815 T. 38,442 (53.53%) Lab. hold
Colin Challen, Lab.   21,919
David Schofield, C.   9,829
Stewart Golton, LD   5,446
John Bardsley, UK Ind.   1,248
Lab. majority 12,090 (31.45%)
0.35% swing Lab. to C.
(1997, Lab. maj. 14,750 (32.14%))

NEW FOREST EAST
E.66,767 T. 42,178 (63.17%) C. hold
*Dr Julian Lewis, C. 17,902
Brian Dash, LD 14,073
Alan Goodfellow, Lab. 9,141
William Howe, UK Ind. 1,062
C. majority 3,829 (9.08%)
0.78% swing C. to LD
(1997, C. maj. 5,215 (10.63%))

NEW FOREST WEST
E.67,806 T. 44,087 (65.02%) C. hold
*Desmond Swayne, C. 24,575
Mike Bignell, LD 11,384
Ms Crada Onuegbu, Lab. 6,481
Michael Clark, UK Ind. 1,647
C. majority 13,191 (29.92%)
3.57% swing LD to C.
(1997, C. maj. 11,332 (22.78%))

NEWARK
E.71,089 T. 45,147 (63.51%) Con gain
Patrick Mercer, C. 20,983
*Ms Fiona Jones, Lab. 16,910
David Harding-Price, LD 5,970
Donald Haxby, Ind. 822
Ian Thomson, Soc. All. 462
C. majority 4,073 (9.02%)
7.41% swing Lab. to C.
(1997, Lab. maj. 3,016 (5.80%))

NEWBURY
E.75,490 T. 50,807 (67.30%) LD hold
*David Rendel, LD 24,507
Richard Benyon, C. 22,092
Steve Billcliffe, Lab. 3,523
Ms Delphine Gray-Fisk, UK Ind. 685
LD majority 2,415 (4.75%)
5.16% swing LD to C.
(1997, LD maj. 8,517 (15.08%))

NEWCASTLE UPON TYNE
CENTRAL
E.67,970 T. 34,870 (51.30%) Lab. hold
*Jim Cousins, Lab. 19,169
Stephen Psallidas, LD 7,564
Aidan Ruff, C. 7,414
Gordon Potts, Soc. Lab. 723
Lab. majority 11,605 (33.28%)
5.44% swing Lab. to LD
(1997, Lab. maj. 16,480 (35.75%))

NEWCASTLE UPON TYNE EAST
& WALLSEND
E.61,494 T. 32,694 (53.17%) Lab. hold
*Rt. Hon. N. Brown, Lab. 20,642
David Ord, LD 6,419
Tim Troman, C. 3,873
Andrew Gray, Green 651
Dr Harash Narang, Ind. 563
Ms Blanch Carpenter, Soc. Lab. 420
Martin Levy, Comm. 126
Lab. majority 14,223 (43.50%)
8.53% swing Lab. to LD
(1997, Lab. maj. 23,811 (57.25%))

NEWCASTLE UPON TYNE
NORTH
E.63,208 T. 36,368 (57.54%) Lab. hold
*Doug Henderson, Lab. 21,874
Phillip Smith, C. 7,424
Graham Soult, LD 7,070
Lab. majority 14,450 (39.73%)

1.50% swing Lab. to C.
(1997, Lab. maj. 19,332 (42.74%))

NEWCASTLE-UNDER-LYME
E.65,739 T. 38,674 (58.83%) Lab. hold
Paul Farrelly, Lab. 20,650
Mike Flynn, C. 10,664
Jerry Roodhouse, LD 5,993
Robert Fyson, Ind. 773
Paul Godfrey, UK Ind. 594
Lab. majority 9,986 (25.82%)
4.60% swing Lab. to C.
(1997, Lab. maj. 17,206 (35.02%))

NORFOLK MID
E.74,911 T. 52,548 (70.15%) C. hold
*Keith Simpson, C. 23,519
Daniel Zeichner, Lab. 18,957
Ms V. Clifford-Jackson, LD 7,621
John Agnew, UK Ind. 1,333
Peter Reeve, Green 1,118
C. majority 4,562 (8.68%)
3.18% swing Lab. to C.
(1997, C. maj. 1,336 (2.33%))

NORFOLK NORTH
E.80,061 T. 56,220 (70.22%) LD gain
Norman Lamb, LD 23,978
*David Prior, C. 23,495
Michael Gates, Lab. 7,490
Mike Sheridan, Green 649
Paul Simison, UK Ind. 608
LD majority 483 (0.86%)
1.53% swing C. to LD
(1997, C. maj. 1,293 (2.20%))

NORFOLK NORTH WEST
E.77,387 T. 51,203 (66.16%) Con gain
Henry Bellingham, C. 24,846
*Dr George Turner, Lab. 21,361
Dr Ian Mack, LD 4,292
Ian Durrant, UK Ind. 704
C. majority 3,485 (6.81%)
4.57% swing Lab. to C.
(1997, Lab. maj. 1,339 (2.33%))

NORFOLK SOUTH
E.82,710 T. 55,929 (67.62%) C. hold
Richard Bacon, C. 23,589
Dr Anne Lee, LD 16,696
Mark Wells, Lab. 13,719
Ms Stephanie Ross-Wagenknecht,
Green 1,069
Joseph Neal, UK Ind. 856
C. majority 6,893 (12.32%)
0.22% swing LD to C.
(1997, C. maj. 7,378 (11.88%))

NORFOLK SOUTH WEST
E.83,903 T. 52,949 (63.11%) C. hold
*Rt. Hon. Mrs G. Shephard, C. 27,633
Ms Anne Hanson, Lab. 18,267
Gordon Dean, LD 5,681
Ian Smith, UK Ind. 1,368
C. majority 9,366 (17.69%)
6.75% swing Lab. to C.
(1997, C. maj. 2,464 (4.19%))

NORMANTON
E.65,392 T. 34,155 (52.23%) Lab. hold
*William O'Brien, Lab. 19,152
Graham Smith, C. 9,215
Stephen Pearson, LD 4,990

Mick Appleyard, Soc. Lab. 798
Lab. majority 9,937 (29.09%)
3.93% swing Lab. to C.
(1997, Lab. maj. 15,893 (36.96%))

NORTHAMPTON NORTH
E.74,124 T. 41,494 (55.98%) Lab. hold
*Ms Sally Keeble, Lab. 20,507
John Whelan, C. 12,614
Richard Church, LD 7,363
Dusan Torbica, UK Ind. 596
Gordon White, Soc. All. 414
Lab. majority 7,893 (19.02%)
0.16% swing Lab. to C.
(1997, Lab. maj. 10,000 (19.34%))

NORTHAMPTON SOUTH
E.85,271 T. 51,029 (59.84%) Lab. hold
*Tony Clarke, Lab. 21,882
Shailesh Vara, C. 20,997
Andrew Simpson, LD 6,355
Derek Clark, UK Ind. 1,237
Miss Tina Harvey, LP 362
Ms Clare Johnson, ProLife 196
Lab. majority 885 (1.73%)
0.22% swing C. to Lab.
(1997, Lab. maj. 744 (1.30%))

NORTHAVON
E.78,841 T. 55,758 (70.72%) LD hold
*Steve Webb, LD 29,217
Dr Carrie Ruxton, C. 19,340
Robert Hall, Lab. 6,450
Mrs Carmen Carver, UK Ind. 751
LD majority 9,877 (17.71%)
7.15% swing C. to LD
(1997, LD maj. 2,137 (3.42%))

NORWICH NORTH
E.74,911 T. 45,614 (60.89%) Lab. hold
*Dr Ian Gibson, Lab. 21,624
Ms Kay Mason, C. 15,761
Ms Moira Toye, LD 6,750
Robert Tinch, Green 797
Guy Cheyney, UK Ind. 471
Michael Betts, Ind. 211
Lab. majority 5,863 (12.85%)
2.17% swing Lab. to C.
(1997, Lab. maj. 9,470 (17.20%))

NORWICH SOUTH
E.65,792 T. 42,592 (64.74%) Lab. hold
*Rt. Hon. C. Clarke, Lab. 19,367
Andrew French, C. 10,551
Andrew Aalders-Dunthorne, LD 9,640
Adrian Holmes, Green 1,434
Alun Buffrey, LCA 620
Edward Manningham, Soc. All. 507
Tarquin Mills, UK Ind. 473
Lab. majority 8,816 (20.70%)
3.67% swing Lab. to C.
(1997, Lab. maj. 14,239 (28.03%))

NOTTINGHAM EAST
E.65,339 T. 29,731 (45.50%) Lab. hold
*John Heppell, Lab. 17,530
Richard Allan, C. 7,210
Tim Ball, LD 3,874
Pete Radcliff, Soc. All. 1,117
Lab. majority 10,320 (34.71%)
2.04% swing Lab. to C.
(1997, Lab. maj. 15,419 (38.80%))

NOTTINGHAM NORTH
E.64,281 *T*. 30,042 (46.74%) Lab. hold
*Graham Allen, *Lab.*   19,392
Martin Wright, *C.*   7,152
Rob Lee, *LD*   3,177
Andrew Botham, *Soc. Lab.*   321
Lab. majority 12,240 (40.74%)
2.34% swing Lab. to C.
(1997, Lab. maj. 18,801 (45.42%))

NOTTINGHAM SOUTH
E.73,049 *T*. 36,605 (50.11%) Lab. hold
*Alan Simpson, *Lab.*   19,949
Mrs Wendy Manning, *C.*   9,960
Kevin Mulloy, *LD*   6,064
David Bartrop, *UK Ind.*   632
Lab. majority 9,989 (27.29%)
0.13% swing Lab. to C.
(1997, Lab. maj. 13,364 (27.55%))

NUNEATON
E.72,101 *T*. 43,312 (60.07%) Lab. hold
*Bill Olner, *Lab.*   22,577
Mark Lancaster, *C.*   15,042
Tony Ferguson, *LD*   4,820
Brian James, *UK Ind.*   873
Lab. majority 7,535 (17.40%)
3.95% swing Lab. to C.
(1997, Lab. maj. 13,540 (25.30%))

OLD BEXLEY & SIDCUP
E.67,841 *T*. 42,133 (62.11%) C. hold
Derek Conway, *C.*   19,130
Jim Dickson, *Lab.*   15,785
Ms Belinda Ford, *LD*   5,792
Mrs Janice Cronin, *UK Ind.*   1,426
C. majority 3,345 (7.94%)
0.49% swing Lab. to C.
(1997, C. maj. 3,569 (6.95%))

OLDHAM EAST &
SADDLEWORTH
E.74,511 *T*. 45,420 (60.96%) Lab. hold
*Phil Woolas, *Lab.*   17,537
Howard Sykes, *LD*   14,811
Craig Heeley, *C.*   7,304
Michael Treacy, *BNP*   5,091
Ms Barbara Little, *UK Ind.*   677
Lab. majority 2,726 (6.00%)
0.13% swing Lab. to C.
(1997, Lab. maj. 3,389 (6.26%))

OLDHAM WEST & ROYTON
E.69,409 *T*. 39,962 (57.57%) Lab. hold
*Rt. Hon. M. Meacher, *Lab.*   20,441
Duncan Reed, *C.*   7,076
Nick Griffin, *BNP*   6,552
Marc Ramsbottom, *LD*   4,975
David Roney, *Green*   918
Lab. majority 13,365 (33.44%)
0.99% swing Lab. to C.
(1997, Lab. maj. 16,201 (35.42%))

ORPINGTON
E.74,423 *T*. 50,912 (68.41%) C. hold
*John Horam, *C.*   22,334
Chris Maines, *LD*   22,065
Chris Purnell, *Lab.*   5,517
John Youles, *UK Ind.*   996
C. majority 269 (0.53%)
2.19% swing C. to LD
(1997, C. maj. 2,952 (4.91%))

OXFORD EAST
E.74,421 *T*. 39,848 (53.54%) Lab. hold
*Rt. Hon. A. Smith, *Lab.*   19,681
Steve Goddard, *LD*   9,337
Ms Cheryl Potter, *C.*   7,446
Pritam Singh, *Green*   1,501
John Lister, *Soc. All.*   708
Peter Gardner, *UK Ind.*   570
Fahim Ahmed, *Soc. Lab.*   274
Ms Linda Hodge, *ProLife*   254
Pathmanathan Mylvaganan, *Ind.*   77
Lab. majority 10,344 (25.96%)
8.08% swing Lab. to LD
(1997, Lab. maj. 16,665 (34.81%))

OXFORD WEST & ABINGDON
E.79,915 *T*. 51,568 (64.53%) LD hold
*Dr Evan Harris, *LD*   24,670
Ed Matts, *C.*   15,485
Ms Gillian Kirk, *Lab.*   9,114
Mike Woodin, *Green*   1,423
Marcus Watney, *UK Ind.*   451
Ms Sigrid Shreeve, *Ind.*   332
Robert Twigger, *Ext. Club*   93
LD majority 9,185 (17.81%)
3.77% swing C. to LD
(1997, LD maj. 6,285 (10.27%))

PENDLE
E.62,870 *T*. 39,732 (63.20%) Lab. hold
*Gordon Prentice, *Lab.*   17,729
Rasjid Skinner, *C.*   13,454
David Whipp, *LD*   5,479
Christian Jackson, *BNP*   1,976
Graham Cannon, *UK Ind.*   1,094
Lab. majority 4,275 (10.76%)
6.13% swing Lab. to C.
(1997, Lab. maj. 10,824 (23.02%))

PENRITH & THE BORDER
E.67,776 *T*. 44,249 (65.29%) C. hold
*Rt. Hon. D. Maclean, *C.*   24,302
Kenneth Geyve Walker, *LD*   9,625
Michael Boaden, *Lab.*   8,177
Thomas Lowther, *UK Ind.*   938
Mark Gibson, *LCA*   870
John Moffat, *Ind.*   337
C. majority 14,677 (33.17%)
6.13% swing LD to C.
(1997, C. maj. 10,233 (20.90%))

PETERBOROUGH
E.64,918 *T*. 39,812 (61.33%) Lab. hold
*Mrs Helen Brinton, *Lab.*   17,975
Stewart Jackson, *C.*   15,121
Nick Sandford, *LD*   5,761
Julian Fairweather, *UK Ind.*   955
Lab. majority 2,854 (7.17%)
3.98% swing Lab. to C.
(1997, Lab. maj. 7,323 (15.12%))

PLYMOUTH DEVONPORT
E.73,666 *T*. 41,719 (56.63%) Lab. hold
*David Jamieson, *Lab.*   24,322
John Glen, *C.*   11,289
Keith Baldry, *LD*   4,513
Michael Parker, *UK Ind.*   958
Tony Staunton, *Soc. All.*   334
Rob Hawkins, *Soc. Lab.*   303
Lab. majority 13,033 (31.24%)
2.73% swing Lab. to C.
(1997, Lab. maj. 19,067 (36.70%))

PLYMOUTH SUTTON
E.68,438 *T*. 39,073 (57.09%) Lab. Co-op hold
*Mrs Linda Gilroy, *Lab. Co-op*   19,827
Oliver Colvile, *C.*   12,310
Alan Connett, *LD*   5,605
Alan Whitton, *UK Ind.*   970
Henry Leary, *Soc. Lab.*   361
Lab. Co-op majority 7,517 (19.24%)
0.29% swing Lab. Co-op to C.
(1997, Lab. maj. 9,440 (19.81%))

PONTEFRACT & CASTLEFORD
E.63,181 *T*. 31,391 (49.68%) Lab. hold
*Ms Yvette Cooper, *Lab.*   21,890
Ms Pamela Singleton, *C.*   5,512
Wesley Paxton, *LD*   2,315
John Burdon, *UK Ind.*   739
Trevor Bolderson, *Soc. Lab.*   605
John Gill, *Soc. All.*   330
Lab. majority 16,378 (52.17%)
4.99% swing Lab. to C.
(1997, Lab. maj. 25,725 (62.15%))

POOLE
E.64,644 *T*. 39,233 (60.69%) C. hold
*Robert Syms, *C.*   17,710
David Watt, *Lab.*   10,544
Nick Westbrook, *LD*   10,011
John Bass, *UK Ind.*   968
C. majority 7,166 (18.27%)
1.15% swing C. to Lab.
(1997, C. maj. 5,298 (11.32%))

POPLAR & CANNING TOWN
E.75,173 *T*. 34,108 (45.37%) Lab. hold
*Jim Fitzpatrick, *Lab.*   20,862
Robert Marr, *C.*   6,758
Ms Alexi Sugden, *LD*   3,795
Paul Borg, *BNP*   1,743
Dr Kambiz Boomla, *Soc. All.*   950
Lab. majority 14,104 (41.35%)
3.41% swing Lab. to C.
(1997, Lab. maj. 18,915 (48.17%))

PORTSMOUTH NORTH
E.64,256 *T*. 36,866 (57.37%) Lab. hold
*Syd Rapson, *Lab.*   18,676
Chris Day, *C.*   13,542
Darren Sanders, *LD*   3,795
William McCabe, *UK Ind.*   559
Brian Bundy, *Ind.*   294
Lab. majority 5,134 (13.93%)
2.19% swing C. to Lab.
(1997, Lab. maj. 4,323 (9.55%))

PORTSMOUTH SOUTH
E.77,095 *T*. 39,215 (50.87%) LD hold
*Mike Hancock, *LD*   17,490
Philip Warr, *C.*   11,396
Graham Heaney, *Lab.*   9,361
John Molyneux, *Soc. All.*   647
Michael Tarrant, *UK Ind.*   321
LD majority 6,094 (15.54%)
3.58% swing C. to LD
(1997, LD maj. 4,327 (8.37%))

PRESTON
E.72,077 *T*. 36,041 (50.00%) Lab. Co-op hold
*Mark Hendrick, *Lab. Co-op*   20,540
Graham O'Hare, *C.*   8,272
Bill Chadwick, *LD*   4,746

Bilal Patel, *Ind.* 1,241
Richard Merrick, *Green* 1,019
The Rev David Braid, *Ind.* 223
Lab. Co-op majority 12,268 (34.04%)
2.41% swing Lab. Co-op to C.
(2000 Nov by-election, Lab. maj. 4,426)
(1997, Lab. maj. 18,680 (38.86%))

PUDSEY
*E.*71,405 *T.* 45,175 (63.27%) Lab. hold
*Paul Truswell, *Lab.* 21,717
John Procter, *C.* 16,091
Stephen Boddy, *LD* 6,423
David Sewards, *UK Ind.* 944
Lab. majority 5,626 (12.45%)
0.34% swing C. to Lab.
(1997, Lab. maj. 6,207 (11.77%))

PUTNEY
*E.*60,643 *T.* 34,254 (56.48%) Lab. hold
*Tony Colman, *Lab.* 15,911
Michael Simpson, *C.* 13,140
Tony Burrett, *LD* 4,671
Ms Pat Wild, *UK Ind.* 347
Ms Yvonne Windsor, *ProLife* 185
Lab. majority 2,771 (8.09%)
0.66% swing C. to Lab.
(1997, Lab. maj. 2,976 (6.76%))

RAYLEIGH
*E.*70,073 *T.* 42,773 (61.04%) C. hold
Mark Francois, *C.* 21,434
Paul Clark, *Lab.* 13,144
Geoff Williams, *LD* 6,614
Colin Morgan, *UK Ind.* 1,581
C. majority 8,290 (19.38%)
0.72% swing C. to Lab.
(1997, C. maj. 10,684 (20.83%))

READING EAST
*E.*74,637 *T.* 43,618 (58.44%) Lab. hold
*Ms Jane Griffiths, *Lab.* 19,531
Barry Tanswell, *C.* 13,943
Tom Dobrashian, *LD* 8,078
Ms Miriam Kennett, *Green* 1,053
Miss Amy Thornton, *UK Ind.* 525
Darren Williams, *Soc. All.* 394
Peter Hammerson, *Ind.* 94
Lab. majority 5,588 (12.81%)
2.63% swing C. to Lab.
(1997, Lab. maj. 3,795 (7.55%))

READING WEST
*E.*71,688 *T.* 41,986 (58.57%) Lab. hold
*Martin Salter, *Lab.* 22,300
Stephen Reid, *C.* 13,451
Ms Polly Martin, *LD* 5,387
David Black, *UK Ind.* 848
Lab. majority 8,849 (21.08%)
7.44% swing C. to Lab.
(1997, Lab. maj. 2,997 (6.20%))

REDCAR
*E.*66,179 *T.* 38,198 (57.72%) Lab. hold
Ms Vera Baird, *Lab.* 23,026
Chris Main, *C.* 9,583
Stan Wilson, *LD* 4,817
John Taylor, *Soc. Lab.* 772
Lab. majority 13,443 (35.19%)
4.53% swing C. to Lab.
(1997, Lab. maj. 21,664 (44.25%))

REDDITCH
*E.*62,543 *T.* 37,032 (59.21%) Lab. hold
*Ms Jacqui Smith, *Lab.* 16,899
Mrs Karen Lumley, *C.* 14,415
Michael Ashall, *LD* 3,808
George Flynn, *UK Ind.* 1,259
Richard Armstrong, *Green* 651
Lab. majority 2,484 (6.71%)
3.49% swing Lab. to C.
(1997, Lab. maj. 6,125 (13.69%))

REGENT'S PARK &
KENSINGTON NORTH
*E.*75,886 *T.* 37,052 (48.83%) Lab. hold
*Ms Karen Buck, *Lab.* 20,247
Peter Wilson, *C.* 9,981
David Boyle, *LD* 4,669
Dr Paul Miller, *Green* 1,268
China Mieville, *Soc. All.* 459
Alan Crisp, *UK Ind.* 354
Ms Charlotte Regan, *Ind.* 74
Lab. majority 10,266 (27.71%)
1.63% swing Lab. to C.
(1997, Lab. maj. 14,657 (30.96%))

REIGATE
*E.*65,023 *T.* 39,474 (60.71%) C. hold
*Crispin Blunt, *C.* 18,875
Simon Charleton, *Lab.* 10,850
Ms Jane Kulka, *LD* 8,330
Stephen Smith, *UK Ind.* 1,062
Harold Green, *Ref. UK* 357
C. majority 8,025 (20.33%)
2.13% swing Lab. to C.
(1997, C. maj. 7,741 (16.07%))

RIBBLE SOUTH (SOUTH
RIBBLE)
*E.*73,794 *T.* 46,130 (62.51%) Lab. hold
*David Borrow, *Lab.* 21,386
Adrian Owens, *C.* 17,594
Mark Alcock, *LD* 7,150
Lab. majority 3,792 (8.22%)
0.49% swing Lab. to C.
(1997, Lab. maj. 5,084 (9.20%))

RIBBLE VALLEY
*E.*74,319 *T.* 49,171 (66.16%) C. hold
*Nigel Evans, *C.* 25,308
Mike Carr, *LD* 14,070
Marcus Johnstone, *Lab.* 9,793
C. majority 11,238 (22.85%)
5.63% swing LD to C.
(1997, C. maj. 6,640 (11.60%))

RICHMOND (YORKS)
*E.*65,360 *T.* 44,034 (67.37%) C. hold
*Rt. Hon. W. Hague, *C.* 25,951
Ms Fay Tinnion, *Lab.* 9,632
Edward Forth, *LD* 7,890
Mrs Melodie Staniforth, *Loony* 561
C. majority 16,319 (37.06%)
8.00% swing Lab. to C.
(1997, C. maj. 10,051 (21.05%))

RICHMOND PARK
*E.*72,663 *T.* 49,151 (67.64%) LD hold
*Dr Jenny Tonge, *LD* 23,444
Tom Harris, *C.* 18,480
Barry Langford, *Lab.* 5,541
James Page, *Green* 1,223
Peter St John Howe, *UK Ind.* 348
Raymond Perrin, *Ind.* 115

LD majority 4,964 (10.10%)
2.45% swing C. to LD
(1997, LD maj. 2,951 (5.19%))

ROCHDALE
*E.*69,506 *T.* 39,412 (56.70%) Lab. hold
*Ms Lorna Fitzsimons, *Lab.* 19,406
Paul Rowen, *LD* 13,751
Ms Elaina Cohen, *C.* 5,274
Nick Harvey, *Green* 728
Mohammed Salim, *Ind.* 253
Lab. majority 5,655 (14.35%)
2.45% swing LD to Lab.
(1997, Lab. maj. 4,545 (9.45%))

ROCHFORD & SOUTHEND
EAST
*E.*69,991 *T.* 37,452 (53.51%) C. hold
*Sir Teddy Taylor, *C.* 20,058
Chris Dandridge, *Lab.* 13,024
Stephen Newton, *LD* 2,780
Adrian Hedges, *Green* 990
Brian Lynch, *Lib.* 600
C. majority 7,034 (18.78%)
4.86% swing Lab. to C.
(1997, C. maj. 4,225 (9.07%))

ROMFORD
*E.*59,893 *T.* 35,701 (59.61%) Con gain
Andrew Rosindell, *C.* 18,931
*Ms Eileen Gordon, *Lab.* 12,954
Nigel Meyer, *LD* 2,869
Stephen Ward, *UK Ind.* 533
Frank McAllister, *BNP* 414
C. majority 5,977 (16.74%)
9.14% swing Lab. to C.
(1997, Lab. maj. 649 (1.54%))

ROMSEY
*E.*70,584 *T.* 48,459 (68.65%) LD hold
*Mrs Sandra Gidley, *LD* 22,756
Paul Raynes, *C.* 20,386
Stephen Roberts, *Lab.* 3,986
Anthony McCabe, *UK Ind.* 730
Derrick Large, *LCA* 601
LD majority 2,370 (4.89%)
10.73% swing C. to LD
(2000 May by-election, LD maj. 3,311
(8.55%); 1997, C. maj. 8,585 (16.56%))

ROSSENDALE & DARWEN
*E.*70,280 *T.* 41,358 (58.85%) Lab. hold
*Ms Janet Anderson, *Lab.* 20,251
George Lee, *C.* 15,028
Brian Dunning, *LD* 6,079
Lab. majority 5,223 (12.63%)
4.38% swing Lab. to C.
(1997, Lab. maj. 10,949 (21.38%))

ROTHER VALLEY
*E.*69,174 *T.* 36,803 (53.20%) Lab. hold
*Rt. Hon. K. Barron, *Lab.* 22,851
James Duddridge, *C.* 7,969
Ms Win Knight, *LD* 4,603
David Cutts, *UK Ind.* 1,380
Lab. majority 14,882 (40.44%)
5.22% swing Lab. to C.
(1997, Lab. maj. 23,485 (50.88%))

ROTHERHAM
*E.*57,931 *T.* 29,354 (50.67%) Lab. hold
*Denis MacShane, *Lab.* 18,759
Richard Powell, *C.* 5,682

Charles Hall, *LD* 3,117
Peter Griffith, *UK Ind.* 730
Dick Penycate, *Green* 577
Ms Freda Smith, *Soc. All.* 352
Geoffrey Bartholomew, *JLDP* 137
Lab. majority 13,077 (44.55%)
6.24% swing Lab. to C.
(1997, Lab. maj. 21,469 (57.02%))

RUGBY & KENILWORTH
*E.*79,764 *T.* 53,796 (67.44%) Lab. hold
*Andy King, *Lab.* 24,221
David Martin, *C.* 21,344
Ms Gwen Fairweather, *LD* 7,444
Paul Garratt, *UK Ind.* 787
Lab. majority 2,877 (5.35%)
2.27% swing C. to Lab.
(1997, Lab. maj. 495 (0.81%))

RUISLIP-NORTHWOOD
*E.*60,788 *T.* 37,141 (61.10%) C. hold
*John Wilkinson, *C.* 18,115
Ms Gillian Travis, *Lab.* 10,578
Mike Cox, *LD* 7,177
Graham Lee, *Green* 724
Ian Edward, *BNP* 547
C. majority 7,537 (20.29%)
1.46% swing Lab. to C.
(1997, C. maj. 7,794 (17.38%))

RUNNYMEDE & WEYBRIDGE
*E.*75,569 *T.* 42,426 (56.14%) C. hold
*Philip Hammond, *C.* 20,646
Ms Jane Briginshaw, *Lab.* 12,286
Chris Bushill, *LD* 6,924
Christopher Browne, *UK Ind.* 1,332
Charles Gilman, *Green* 1,238
C. majority 8,360 (19.70%)
0.27% swing Lab. to C.
(1997, C. maj. 9,875 (19.16%))

RUSHCLIFFE
*E.*81,839 *T.* 54,446 (66.53%) C. hold
*Rt. Hon. K. Clarke, *C.* 25,869
Paul Fallon, *Lab.* 18,512
Jeremy Hargreaves, *LD* 7,395
Ken Browne, *UK Ind.* 1,434
Ashley Baxter, *Green* 1,236
C. majority 7,357 (13.51%)
2.69% swing Lab. to C.
(1997, C. maj. 5,055 (8.14%))

RUTLAND & MELTON
*E.*72,448 *T.* 47,056 (64.95%) C. hold
*Alan Duncan, *C.* 22,621
Matthew O'Callaghan, *Lab.* 14,009
Kim Lee, *LD* 8,386
Peter Baker, *UK Ind.* 1,223
Christopher Davies, *Green* 817
C. majority 8,612 (18.30%)
0.76% swing Lab. to C.
(1997, C. maj. 8,836 (16.78%))

RYEDALE
*E.*66,543 *T.* 43,899 (65.97%) C. hold
*John Greenway, *C.* 20,711
Keith Orrell, *LD* 15,836
David Ellis, *Lab.* 6,470
Stephen Feaster, *UK Ind.* 882
C. majority 4,875 (11.11%)
0.37% swing LD to C.
(1997, C. maj. 5,058 (10.37%))

SAFFRON WALDEN
*E.*76,724 *T.* 50,040 (65.22%) C. hold
*Rt. Hon. Sir A. Haselhurst, *C.* 24,485
Mrs E. Tealby-Watson, *LD* 12,481
Ms Tania Rogers, *Lab.* 11,305
Richard Glover, *UK Ind.* 1,769
C. majority 12,004 (23.99%)
2.73% swing LD to C.
(1997, C. maj. 10,573 (18.53%))

SALFORD
*E.*54,152 *T.* 22,514 (41.58%) Lab. hold
*Ms Hazel Blears, *Lab.* 14,649
Norman Owen, *LD* 3,637
Chris King, *C.* 3,446
Peter Grant, *Soc. All.* 414
Ms Hazel Wallace, *Ind.* 216
Roy Masterson, *Ind.* 152
Lab. majority 11,012 (48.91%)
4.89% swing Lab. to LD
(1997, Lab. maj. 17,069 (51.53%))

SALISBURY
*E.*80,538 *T.* 52,603 (65.31%) C. hold
*Robert Key, *C.* 24,527
Ms Y. Emmerson-Peirce, *LD* 15,824
Ms Sue Mallory, *Lab.* 9,199
Malcolm Wood, *UK Ind.* 1,958
Hamish Soutar, *Green* 1,095
C. majority 8,703 (16.54%)
2.88% swing LD to C.
(1997, C. maj. 6,276 (10.78%))

SCARBOROUGH & WHITBY
*E.*75,213 *T.* 47,523 (63.18%) Lab. hold
*Lawrie Quinn, *Lab.* 22,426
John Sykes, *C.* 18,841
Tom Pearce, *LD* 3,977
Jonathan Dixon, *Green* 1,049
John Jacob, *UK Ind.* 970
Ms Theresa Murray, *ProLife* 260
Lab. majority 3,585 (7.54%)
0.94% swing Lab. to C.
(1997, Lab. maj. 5,124 (9.43%))

SCUNTHORPE
*E.*59,689 *T.* 33,625 (56.33%) Lab. hold
*Elliot Morley, *Lab.* 20,096
Bernard Theobald, *C.* 9,724
Bob Tress, *LD* 3,156
John Cliff, *UK Ind.* 347
David Patterson, *Ind.* 302
Lab. majority 10,372 (30.85%)
1.62% swing Lab. to C.
(1997, Lab. maj. 14,173 (34.09%))

SEDGEFIELD
*E.*64,925 *T.* 40,258 (62.01%) Lab. hold
*Rt. Hon. A. Blair, *Lab.* 26,110
Douglas Carswell, *C.* 8,397
Andrew Duffield, *LD* 3,624
Andrew Spence, *UK Ind.* 974
Brian Gibson, *Soc. Lab.* 518
Christopher Driver, *R & R Loony* 375
Ms Helen John, *WFLOE* 260
Lab. majority 17,713 (44.00%)
4.69% swing Lab. to C.
(1997, Lab. maj. 25,143 (53.37%))

SELBY
*E.*77,924 *T.* 50,272 (64.51%) Lab. hold
*John Grogan, *Lab.* 22,652
Michael Mitchell, *C.* 20,514

Jeremy Wilcock, *LD* 5,569
Ms Helen Kenwright, *Green* 902
Bob Lewis, *UK Ind.* 635
Lab. majority 2,138 (4.25%)
1.28% swing Lab. to C.
(1997, Lab. maj. 3,836 (6.81%))

SEVENOAKS
*E.*66,648 *T.* 42,614 (63.94%) C. hold
*Michael Fallon, *C.* 21,052
Ms Caroline Humphreys, *Lab.* 10,898
Clive Gray, *LD* 9,214
Mrs Lisa Hawkins, *UK Ind.* 1,155
Mark Ellis, *PF* 295
C. majority 10,154 (23.83%)
1.48% swing Lab. to C.
(1997, C. maj. 10,461 (20.86%))

SHEFFIELD ATTERCLIFFE
*E.*68,386 *T.* 35,824 (52.38%) Lab. hold
*Clive Betts, *Lab.* 24,287
John Perry, *C.* 5,443
Ms Gail Smith, *LD* 5,092
Ms Pauline Arnott, *UK Ind.* 1,002
Lab. majority 18,844 (52.60%)
1.69% swing C. to Lab.
(1997, Lab. maj. 21,818 (49.23%))

SHEFFIELD BRIGHTSIDE
*E.*54,711 *T.* 25,552 (46.70%) Lab. hold
*Rt. Hon. D. Blunkett, *Lab.* 19,650
Matthew Wilson, *C.* 2,601
Ms Alison Firth, *LD* 2,238
Brian Wilson, *Soc. All.* 361
Robert Morris, *Soc. Lab.* 354
Mark Suter, *UK Ind.* 348
Lab. majority 17,049 (66.72%)
0.81% swing C. to Lab.
(1997, Lab. maj. 19,954 (58.92%))

SHEFFIELD CENTRAL
*E.*62,018 *T.* 30,069 (48.48%) Lab. hold
*Rt. Hon. R. Caborn, *Lab.* 18,477
Ali Qadar, *LD* 5,933
Miss Noelle Brelsford, *C.* 3,289
Bernard Little, *Green* 1,008
Nick Riley, *Soc. All.* 754
David Hadfield, *Soc. Lab.* 289
Ms Charlotte Schofield, *UK Ind.* 257
Michael Driver, *WRP* 62
Lab. majority 12,544 (41.72%)
2.36% swing Lab. to LD
(1997, Lab. maj. 16,906 (46.43%))

SHEFFIELD HALLAM
*E.*60,288 *T.* 38,246 (63.44%) LD hold
*Richard Allan, *LD* 21,203
John Harthman, *C.* 11,856
Ms Gillian Furniss, *Lab.* 4,758
Leslie Arnott, *UK Ind.* 429
LD majority 9,347 (24.44%)
3.12% swing C. to LD
(1997, LD maj. 8,271 (18.19%))

SHEFFIELD HEELEY
*E.*62,758 *T.* 34,139 (54.40%) Lab. hold
Ms Meg Munn, *Lab.* 19,452
David Willis, *LD* 7,748
Ms Carolyn Abbott, *C.* 4,864
Rob Unwin, *Green* 774
Brian Fischer, *Soc. Lab.* 667
David Dunn, *UK Ind.* 634
Lab. majority 11,704 (34.28%)

2.60% swing Lab. to LD
(1997, Lab. maj. 17,078 (39.48%))

SHEFFIELD HILLSBOROUGH
E.75,097 T. 42,536 (56.64%) Lab. hold
*Ms Helen Jackson, *Lab.*   24,170
John Commons, *LD*   9,601
Graham King, *C.*   7,801
Peter Webb, *UK Ind.*   964
Lab. majority 14,569 (34.25%)
1.62% swing LD to Lab.
(1997, Lab. maj. 16,451 (31.02%))

SHERWOOD
E.75,670 T. 45,900 (60.66%) Lab. hold
*Paddy Tipping, *Lab.*   24,900
Brandon Lewis, *C.*   15,527
Peter Harris, *LD*   5,473
Lab. majority 9,373 (20.42%)
4.66% swing Lab. to C.
(1997, Lab. maj. 16,812 (29.74%))

SHIPLEY
E.69,577 T. 46,020 (66.14%) Lab. hold
*Christopher Leslie, *Lab.*   20,243
David Senior, *C.*   18,815
Ms Helen Wright, *LD*   4,996
Martin Love, *Green*   1,386
Walter Whitacker, *UK Ind.*   580
Lab. majority 1,428 (3.10%)
1.28% swing Lab. to C.
(1997, Lab. maj. 2,996 (5.67%))

SHREWSBURY & ATCHAM
E.74,964 T. 49,909 (66.58%) Lab. hold
*Paul Marsden, *Lab.*   22,253
Miss Anthea McIntyre, *C.*   18,674
Jonathan Rule, *LD*   6,173
Henry Curteis, *UK Ind.*   1,620
Ms Emma Bullard, *Green*   931
James Gollins, *Ind.*   258
Lab. majority 3,579 (7.17%)
2.08% swing C. to Lab.
(1997, Lab. maj. 1,670 (3.02%))

SHROPSHIRE NORTH
E.73,716 T. 46,520 (63.11%) C. hold
*Owen Paterson, *C.*   22,631
Michael Ion, *Lab.*   16,390
Ben Jephcott, *LD*   5,945
David Trevanion, *UK Ind.*   1,165
Russell Maxfield, *Ind.*   389
C. majority 6,241 (13.42%)
4.58% swing Lab. to C.
(1997, C. maj. 2,195 (4.26%))

SITTINGBOURNE & SHEPPEY
E.65,825 T. 37,858 (57.51%) Lab. hold
*Derek Wyatt, *Lab.*   17,340
Adrian Lee, *C.*   13,831
Ms Elvie Lowe, *LD*   5,353
Michael Young, *R & R Loony*   673
Robert Oakley, *UK Ind.*   661
Lab. majority 3,509 (9.27%)
2.54% swing C. to Lab.
(1997, Lab. maj. 1,929 (4.18%))

SKIPTON & RIPON
E.75,201 T. 49,126 (65.33%) C. hold
*Rt. Hon. D. Curry, *C.*   25,736
Bernard Bateman, *LD*   12,806
Michael Dugher, *Lab.*   8,543
Mrs Nancy Holdsworth, *UK Ind.* 2,041

C. majority 12,930 (26.32%)
2.47% swing LD to C.
(1997, C. maj. 11,620 (21.38%))

SLEAFORD & NORTH
HYKEHAM
E.74,561 T. 48,719 (65.34%) C. hold
*Rt. Hon. D. Hogg, *C.*   24,190
Ms Elizabeth Donnelly, *Lab.*   15,568
Robert Arbon, *LD*   7,894
Michael Ward-Barrow, *UK Ind.*   1,067
C. majority 8,622 (17.70%)
4.03% swing Lab. to C.
(1997, C. maj. 5,123 (9.64%))

SLOUGH
E.72,429 T. 38,998 (53.84%) Lab. hold
*Ms Fiona MacTaggart, *Lab.*   22,718
Mrs Diana Coad, *C.*   10,210
Keith Kerr, *LD*   4,109
Michael Haines, *Ind.*   859
John Lane, *UK Ind.*   738
Choudry Nazir, *Ind.*   364
Lab. majority 12,508 (32.07%)
2.34% swing C. to Lab.
(1997, Lab. maj. 13,071 (27.39%))

SOLIHULL
E.77,094 T. 48,271 (62.61%) C. hold
*John Taylor, *C.*   21,935
Ms Jo Byron, *LD*   12,528
Brendan O'Brien, *Lab.*   12,373
Andy Moore, *UK Ind.*   1,061
Ms Stephanie Pyne, *ProLife*   374
C. majority 9,407 (19.49%)
0.07% swing LD to C.
(1997, C. maj. 11,397 (19.35%))

SOMERTON & FROME
E.74,991 T. 52,684 (70.25%) LD hold
*David Heath, *LD*   22,983
Jonathan Marland, *C.*   22,315
Andrew Perkins, *Lab.*   6,113
Peter Bridgwood, *UK Ind.*   919
Ms Jean Pollock, *Lib.*   354
LD majority 668 (1.27%)
0.52% swing C. to LD
(1997, LD maj. 130 (0.23%))

SOUTH HOLLAND & THE
DEEPINGS
E.73,880 T. 46,202 (62.54%) C. hold
*John Hayes, *C.*   25,611
Graham Walker, *Lab.*   14,512
Ms Grace Hill, *LD*   4,761
Malcolm Charlesworth, *UK Ind.* 1,318
C. majority 11,099 (24.02%)
4.04% swing Lab. to C.
(1997, C. maj. 7,991 (15.94%))

SOUTH SHIELDS
E.61,802 T. 30,448 (49.27%) Lab. hold
David Miliband, *Lab.*   19,230
Miss Joanna Gardner, *C.*   5,140
Marshall Grainger, *LD*   5,127
Alan Hardy, *UK Ind.*   689
Roger Nettleship, *Ind.*   262
Lab. majority 14,090 (46.28%)
5.28% swing Lab. to C.
(1997, Lab. maj. 22,153 (56.84%))

SOUTHAMPTON ITCHEN
E.76,603 T. 41,373 (54.01%) Lab. hold

*Rt. Hon. J. Denham, *Lab.*   22,553
Mrs Caroline Nokes, *C.*   11,330
Mark Cooper, *LD*   6,195
Kim Rose, *UK Ind.*   829
Gavin Marsh, *Soc. All.*   241
Michael Holmes, *Soc. Lab.*   225
Lab. majority 11,223 (27.13%)
0.37% swing C. to Lab.
(1997, Lab. maj. 14,209 (26.38%))

SOUTHAMPTON TEST
E.73,893 T. 41,575 (56.26%) Lab. hold
*Alan Whitehead, *Lab.*   21,824
Richard Gueterbock, *C.*   10,617
John Shaw, *LD*   7,522
Garry Rankin-Moore, *UK Ind.*   792
Mark Abel, *Soc. All.*   442
Paramjit Bahia, *Soc. Lab.*   378
Lab. majority 11,207 (26.96%)
0.43% swing C. to Lab.
(1997, Lab. maj. 13,684 (26.10%))

SOUTHEND WEST
E.64,116 T. 37,375 (58.29%) C. hold
*David Amess, *C.*   17,313
Paul Fisher, *Lab.*   9,372
Richard de Ste Croix, *LD*   9,319
Brian Lee, *UK Ind.*   1,371
C. majority 7,941 (21.25%)
2.64% swing Lab. to C.
(1997, C. maj. 2,615 (5.62%))

SOUTHPORT
E.70,785 T. 41,153 (58.14%) LD hold
John Pugh, *LD*   18,011
Laurence Jones, *C.*   15,004
Paul Brant, *Lab.*   6,816
David Green, *Lib.*   767
Gerry Kelley, *UK Ind.*   555
LD majority 3,007 (7.31%)
2.44% swing LD to C.
(1997, LD maj. 6,160 (12.18%))

SOUTHWARK NORTH &
BERMONDSEY
E.73,527 T. 36,862 (50.13%) LD hold
*Simon Hughes, *LD*   20,991
Kingsley Abrams, *Lab.*   11,359
Ewan Wallace, *C.*   2,800
Ms Ruth Jenkins, *Green*   752
Ms Lianne Shore, *NF*   612
Rob McWhirter, *UK Ind.*   271
John Davies, *Ind.*   77
LD majority 9,632 (26.13%)
8.91% swing Lab. to LD
(1997, LD maj. 3,387 (8.30%))

SPELTHORNE
E.68,731 T. 41,794 (60.81%) C. hold
*David Wilshire, *C.*   18,851
Andrew Shaw, *Lab.*   15,589
Martin Rimmer, *LD*   6,156
Richard Squire, *UK Ind.*   1,198
C. majority 3,262 (7.80%)
0.56% swing Lab. to C.
(1997, C. maj. 3,473 (6.69%))

ST ALBANS
E.66,040 T. 43,761 (66.26%) Lab. hold
*Kerry Pollard, *Lab.*   19,889
Charles Elphicke, *C.*   15,423
Nick Rijke, *LD*   7,847
Christopher Sherwin, *UK Ind.*   602

Lab. majority 4,466 (10.21%)
0.71% swing C. to Lab.
(1997, Lab. maj. 4,459 (8.78%))

ST HELENS NORTH
E.70,545 T. 37,601 (53.30%) Lab. hold
*Dave Watts, Lab.   22,977
Simon Pearce, C.   7,076
John Beirne, LD   6,609
Stephen Whatham, Soc. Lab.   939
Lab. majority 15,901 (42.29%)
2.64% swing Lab. to C.
(1997, Lab. maj. 23,417 (47.57%))

ST HELENS SOUTH
E.65,122 T. 33,804 (51.91%) Lab. hold
†Shaun Woodward, Lab.   16,799
Brian Spencer, LD   7,814
Dr Lee Rotherham, C.   4,675
Neil Thompson, Soc. All.   2,325
Mike Perry, Soc. Lab.   1,504
Bryan Slater, UK Ind.   336
Michael Murphy, Ind.   271
David Braid, Ind.   80
Lab. majority 8,985 (26.58%)
14.33% swing Lab. to LD
(1997, Lab. maj. 23,739 (53.63%))

ST IVES
E.74,256 T. 49,266 (66.35%) LD hold
*Andrew George, LD   25,413
Miss Joanna Richardson, C.   15,360
William Morris, Lab.   6,567
Mick Faulkner, UK Ind.   1,926
LD majority 10,053 (20.41%)
3.55% swing C. to LD
(1997, LD maj. 7,170 (13.30%))

STAFFORD
E.67,934 T. 44,366 (65.31%) Lab. hold
*David Kidney, Lab.   21,285
Philip Cochrane, C.   16,253
Ms Jeanne Pinkerton, LD   4,205
Earl of Bradford, UK Ind.   2,315
Michael Hames, R & R Loony   308
Lab. majority 5,032 (11.34%)
1.50% swing C. to Lab.
(1997, Lab. maj. 4,314 (8.34%))

STAFFORDSHIRE MOORLANDS
E.66,760 T. 42,658 (63.90%) Lab. hold
*Ms Charlotte Atkins, Lab.   20,904
Marcus Hayes, C.   15,066
John Redfern, LD   5,928
Paul Gilbert, UK Ind.   760
Lab. majority 5,838 (13.69%)
2.99% swing Lab. to C.
(1997, Lab. maj. 10,049 (19.66%))

STAFFORDSHIRE SOUTH
E.69,925 T. 42,180 (60.32%) C. hold
*Sir Patrick Cormack, C.   21,295
Paul Kalinauckas, Lab.   14,414
Ms Jo Harrison, LD   4,891
Mike Lynch, UK Ind.   1,580
C. majority 6,881 (16.31%)
0.51% swing Lab. to C.
(1997, C. maj. 7,821 (15.30%))

STALYBRIDGE & HYDE
E.66,265 T. 32,046 (48.36%) Lab. hold
James Purnell, Lab.   17,781
Andrew Reid, C.   8,922

Brendon Jones, LD   4,327
Frank Bennett, UK Ind.   1,016
Lab. majority 8,859 (27.64%)
3.36% swing Lab. to C.
(1997, Lab. maj. 14,806 (34.36%))

STEVENAGE
E.69,203 T. 42,453 (61.35%) Lab. hold
*Ms Barbara Follett, Lab.   22,025
Graeme Quar, C.   13,459
Harry Davies, LD   6,027
Steve Glennon, Soc. All.   449
Antal Losonczi, Ind.   320
Ms Sarah Bell, ProLife   173
Lab. majority 8,566 (20.18%)
1.18% swing Lab. to C.
(1997, Lab. maj. 11,582 (22.54%))

STOCKPORT
E.66,397 T. 35,383 (53.29%) Lab. hold
*Ms Ann Coffey, Lab.   20,731
John Allen, C.   9,162
Mark Hunter, LD   5,490
Lab. majority 11,569 (32.70%)
3.91% swing Lab. to C.
(1997, Lab. maj. 18,912 (40.52%))

STOCKTON NORTH
E.65,192 T. 35,427 (54.34%) Lab. hold
*Frank Cook, Lab.   22,470
Ms Amanda Vigar, C.   7,823
Ms Mary Wallace, LD   4,208
Bill Wennington, Green   926
Lab. majority 14,647 (41.34%)
3.34% swing Lab. to C.
(1997, Lab. maj. 21,357 (48.02%))

STOCKTON SOUTH
E.71,026 T. 44,209 (62.24%) Lab. hold
*Ms Dari Taylor, Lab.   23,414
Tim Devlin, C.   14,328
Mrs Suzanne Fletcher, LD   6,012
Lawrie Coombes, Soc. All.   455
Lab. majority 9,086 (20.55%)
0.84% swing Lab. to C.
(1997, Lab. maj. 11,585 (22.23%))

STOKE-ON-TRENT CENTRAL
E.59,750 T. 28,300 (47.36%) Lab. hold
*Mark Fisher, Lab.   17,170
Ms Jill Clark, C.   5,325
Gavin Webb, LD   4,148
Richard Wise, Ind.   1,657
Lab. majority 11,845 (41.86%)
3.83% swing Lab. to C.
(1997, Lab. maj. 19,924 (49.51%))

STOKE-ON-TRENT NORTH
E.57,998 T. 30,115 (51.92%) Lab. hold
*Ms Joan Walley, Lab.   17,460
Benjamin Browning, C.   5,676
Henry Jebb, LD   3,580
Lee Wanger, Ind.   3,399
Lab. majority 11,784 (39.13%)
2.92% swing Lab. to C.
(1997, Lab. maj. 17,392 (44.98%))

STOKE-ON-TRENT SOUTH
E.70,032 T. 36,028 (51.45%) Lab. hold
*George Stevenson, Lab.   19,366
Philip Bastiman, C.   8,877
Christopher Coleman, LD   4,724
Adrian Knapper, Ind.   1,703

Steven Batkin, BNP   1,358
Lab. majority 10,489 (29.11%)
5.23% swing Lab. to C.
(1997, Lab. maj. 18,303 (39.58%))

STONE
E.68,847 T. 45,642 (66.29%) C. hold
*William Cash, C.   22,395
John Palfreyman, Lab.   16,359
Brendan McKeown, LD   6,888
C. majority 6,036 (13.22%)
3.01% swing Lab. to C.
(1997, C. maj. 3,818 (7.20%))

STOURBRIDGE
E.64,610 T. 39,924 (61.79%) Lab. hold
*Ms Debra Shipley, Lab.   18,823
Stephen Eyre, C.   15,011
Chris Bramall, LD   4,833
John Knotts, UK Ind.   763
Mick Atherton, Soc. Lab.   494
Lab. majority 3,812 (9.55%)
0.91% swing Lab. to C.
(1997, Lab. maj. 5,645 (11.36%))

STRATFORD-ON-AVON
E.85,241 T. 54,914 (64.42%) C. hold
*John Maples, C.   27,606
Dr Susan Juned, LD   15,804
Mushtaq Hussain, Lab.   9,164
Ronald Mole, UK Ind.   1,184
Mick Davies, Green   1,156
C. majority 11,802 (21.49%)
0.61% swing C. to LD
(1997, C. maj. 14,106 (22.72%))

STREATHAM
E.76,021 T. 36,998 (48.67%) Lab. hold
*Keith Hill, Lab.   21,041
Roger O'Brien, LD   6,771
Stephen Hocking, C.   6,639
Mohammed Sajid, Green   1,641
Greg Tucker, Soc. All.   906
Lab. majority 14,270 (38.57%)
5.33% swing Lab. to LD
(1997, Lab. maj. 18,423 (41.04%))

STRETFORD & URMSTON
E.70,924 T. 38,973 (54.95%) Lab. hold
*Ms Beverley Hughes, Lab.   23,804
Jonathan Mackie, C.   10,565
John Bridges, LD   3,891
Ms Katie Price, Ind.   713
Lab. majority 13,239 (33.97%)
2.98% swing C. to Lab.
(1997, Lab. maj. 13,640 (28.01%))

STROUD
E.78,878 T. 55,175 (69.95%) Lab. Co-op hold
*David Drew, Lab. Co-op   25,685
Neil Carmichael, C.   20,646
Ms Janice Beasley, LD   6,036
Kevin Cranston, Green   1,913
Adrian Blake, UK Ind.   895
Lab. Co-op majority 5,039 (9.13%)
2.24% swing C. to Lab. Co-op
(1997, Lab. maj. 2,910 (4.66%))

SUFFOLK CENTRAL & IPSWICH NORTH
E.74,200 T. 47,104 (63.48%) C. hold
*Michael Lord, C.   20,924

Ms Carole Jones, *Lab.* — 17,455
Mrs Ann Elvin, *LD* — 7,593
Jonathan Wright, *UK Ind.* — 1,132
C. majority 3,469 (7.36%)
0.33% swing Lab. to C.
(1997, C. maj. 3,538 (6.70%))

SUFFOLK COASTAL
*E.*75,963   *T.* 50,407 (66.36%)   C. hold
*Rt. Hon. J. Gummer, *C.* — 21,847
Nigel Gardner, *Lab.* — 17,521
Tony Schur, *LD* — 9,192
Michael Burn, *UK Ind.* — 1,847
C. majority 4,326 (8.58%)
1.40% swing Lab. to C.
(1997, C. maj. 3,254 (5.79%))

SUFFOLK SOUTH
*E.*68,408   *T.* 45,293 (66.21%)   C. hold
*Tim Yeo, *C.* — 18,748
Marc Young, *Lab.* — 13,667
Mrs Tessa Munt, *LD* — 11,296
Derek Allen, *UK Ind.* — 1,582
C. majority 5,081 (11.22%)
1.59% swing Lab. to C.
(1997, C. maj. 4,175 (8.03%))

SUFFOLK WEST
*E.*71,220   *T.* 42,445 (59.60%)   C. hold
*Richard Spring, *C.* — 20,201
Michael Jeffreys, *Lab.* — 15,906
Robin Martlew, *LD* — 5,017
Will Burrows, *UK Ind.* — 1,321
C. majority 4,295 (10.12%)
3.16% swing Lab. to C.
(1997, C. maj. 1,867 (3.80%))

SUNDERLAND NORTH
*E.*60,846 *T.* 29,820 (49.01%) Lab. hold
*Bill Etherington, *Lab.* — 18,685
Michael Harris, *C.* — 5,331
John Lennox, *LD* — 3,599
Neil Herron, *Ind.* — 1,518
David Guynan, *BNP* — 687
Lab. majority 13,354 (44.78%)
3.38% swing Lab. to C.
(1997, Lab. maj. 19,697 (51.55%))

SUNDERLAND SOUTH
*E.*64,577 *T.* 31,187 (48.29%) Lab. hold
*Chris Mullin, *Lab.* — 19,921
Jim Boyd, *C.* — 6,254
Mark Greenfield, *LD* — 3,675
Joseph Dobbie, *BNP* — 576
Joseph Moore, *UK Ind.* — 470
Ms Rosalyn Warner, *Loony* — 291
Lab. majority 13,667 (43.82%)
2.68% swing Lab. to C.
(1997, Lab. maj. 19,638 (49.18%))

SURREY EAST
*E.*75,049   *T.* 47,049 (62.69%)   C. hold
*Peter Ainsworth, *C.* — 24,706
Jeremy Pursehouse, *LD* — 11,503
Ms Jo Tanner, *Lab.* — 8,994
Anthony Stone, *UK Ind.* — 1,846
C. majority 13,203 (28.06%)
0.23% swing LD to C.
(1997, C. maj. 15,093 (27.61%))

SURREY HEATH
*E.*75,858   *T.* 45,102 (59.46%)   C. hold
*Nicholas Hawkins, *C.* — 22,401

Mark Lelliott, *LD* — 11,582
James Norman, *Lab.* — 9,640
Nigel Hunt, *UK Ind.* — 1,479
C. majority 10,819 (23.99%)
2.89% swing C. to LD
(1997, C. maj. 16,287 (29.76%))

SURREY SOUTH WEST
*E.*74,127   *T.* 49,592 (66.90%)   C. hold
*Rt. Hon. Mrs V. Bottomley, *C.* 22,462
Simon Cordon, *LD* — 21,601
Martin Whelton, *Lab.* — 4,321
Timothy Clark, *UK Ind.* — 1,208
C. majority 861 (1.74%)
1.52% swing C. to LD
(1997, C. maj. 2,694 (4.77%))

SUSSEX MID
*E.*70,632   *T.* 45,822 (64.87%)   C. hold
*Nicholas Soames, *C.* — 21,150
Ms Lesley Wilkins, *LD* — 14,252
Paul Mitchell, *Lab.* — 8,693
Petrina Holdsworth, *UK Ind.* — 1,126
Peter Berry, *Loony* — 601
C. majority 6,898 (15.05%)
1.12% swing LD to C.
(1997, C. maj. 6,854 (12.82%))

SUTTON & CHEAM
*E.*63,648   *T.* 39,723 (62.41%)   LD hold
*Paul Burstow, *LD* — 19,382
Lady Olga Maitland, *C.* — 15,078
Ms Lisa Homan, *Lab.* — 5,263
LD majority 4,304 (10.84%)
3.19% swing C. to LD
(1997, LD maj. 2,097 (4.45%))

SUTTON COLDFIELD
*E.*71,856   *T.* 43,452 (60.47%)   C. hold
Andrew Mitchell, *C.* — 21,909
Robert Pocock, *Lab.* — 11,805
Martin Turner, *LD* — 8,268
Mike Nattrass, *UK Ind.* — 1,186
Ian Robinson, *Ind.* — 284
C. majority 10,104 (23.25%)
2.58% swing C. to Lab.
(1997, C. maj. 14,885 (28.41%))

SWINDON NORTH
*E.*69,335 *T.* 42,328 (61.05%) Lab. hold
*Michael Wills, *Lab.* — 22,371
Nick Martin, *C.* — 14,266
David Nation, *LD* — 4,891
Brian Lloyd, *UK Ind.* — 800
Lab. majority 8,105 (19.15%)
1.61% swing C. to Lab.
(1997, Lab. maj. 7,688 (15.93%))

SWINDON SOUTH
*E.*71,080 *T.* 43,384 (61.04%) Lab. hold
*Ms Julia Drown, *Lab.* — 22,260
Simon Coombs, *C.* — 14,919
Geoff Brewer, *LD* — 5,165
Mrs Vicki Sharp, *UK Ind.* — 713
Roly Gillard, *R & R Loony* — 327
Lab. majority 7,341 (16.92%)
2.94% swing C. to Lab.
(1997, Lab. maj. 5,645 (11.04%))

TAMWORTH
*E.*69,596 *T.* 40,250 (57.83%) Lab. hold
*Brian Jenkins, *Lab.* — 19,722
Ms Luise Gunter, *C.* — 15,124

Ms Jennifer Pinkett, *LD* — 4,721
Paul Sootheran, *UK Ind.* — 683
Lab. majority 4,598 (11.42%)
1.81% swing Lab. to C.
(1997, Lab. maj. 7,496 (15.04%))

TATTON
*E.*64,954   *T.* 41,278 (63.55%) Con gain
George Osborne, *C.* — 19,860
Steve Conquest, *Lab.* — 11,249
Mike Ash, *LD* — 7,685
Mark Sheppard, *UK Ind.* — 769
Peter Sharratt, *Ind.* — 734
Mrs Viviane Allinson, *Tatton* — 505
John Batchelor, *Ind.* — 322
Jonathan Boyd Hunt, *Ind.* — 154
C. majority 8,611 (20.86%)
(1997: Ind. maj 11,077 (22.70%))

TAUNTON
*E.*81,651   *T.* 55,225 (67.64%) Con gain
Adrian Flook, *C.* — 23,033
*Mrs Jackie Ballard, *LD* — 22,798
Andrew Govier, *Lab.* — 8,254
Michael Canton, *UK Ind.* — 1,140
C. majority 235 (0.43%)
2.21% swing LD to C.
(1997, LD maj. 2,443 (4.00%))

TEIGNBRIDGE
*E.*85,533 *T.* 59,310 (69.34%) LD gain
Richard Younger-Ross, *LD* — 26,343
*Patrick Nicholls, *C.* — 23,332
Christopher Bain, *Lab.* — 7,366
Paul Viscount Exmouth, *UK Ind.* 2,269
LD majority 3,011 (5.08%)
2.76% swing C. to LD
(1997, C. maj. 281 (0.45%))

TELFORD
*E.*59,486 *T.* 30,875 (51.90%) Lab. hold
David Wright, *Lab.* — 16,854
Andrew Henderson, *C.* — 8,471
Ms Sally Wiggin, *LD* — 3,983
Ms Nicola Brookes, *UK Ind.* — 1,098
Mike Jeffries, *Soc. All.* — 469
Lab. majority 8,383 (27.15%)
1.63% swing Lab. to C.
(1997, Lab. maj. 11,290 (30.42%))

TEWKESBURY
*E.*70,276   *T.* 45,195 (64.31%)   C. hold
*Laurence Robertson, *C.* — 20,830
Keir Dhillon, *Lab.* — 12,167
Stephen Martin, *LD* — 11,863
Charles Vernall, *Ind.* — 335
C. majority 8,663 (19.17%)
0.19% swing C. to Lab.
(1997, C. maj. 9,234 (17.71%))

THANET NORTH
*E.*70,581   *T.* 41,868 (59.32%)   C. hold
*Roger Gale, *C.* — 21,050
James Stewart Laing, *Lab.* — 14,400
Seth Proctor, *LD* — 4,603
John Moore, *UK Ind.* — 980
David Shortt, *Ind.* — 440
Thomas Holmes, *NF* — 395
C. majority 6,650 (15.88%)
5.12% swing Lab. to C.
(1997, C. maj. 2,766 (5.65%))

THANET SOUTH
*E.*61,462 *T.* 39,431 (64.16%) Lab. hold
*Dr Stephen Ladyman, *Lab.* 18,002
Mark Macgregor, *C.* 16,210
Guy Voizey, *LD* 3,706
William Baldwin, *Ind.* 770
Terry Eccott, *UK Ind.* 501
Bernard Franklin, *NF* 242
Lab. majority 1,792 (4.54%)
0.92% swing Lab. to C.
(1997, Lab. maj. 2,878 (6.39%))

THURROCK
*E.*76,524 *T.* 37,362 (48.82%) Lab. hold
*Andrew Mackinlay, *Lab.* 21,121
Mike Penning, *C.* 11,124
John Lathan, *LD* 3,846
Christopher Sheppard, *UK Ind.* 1,271
Lab. majority 9,997 (26.76%)
4.90% swing Lab. to C.
(1997, Lab. maj. 17,256 (36.55%))

TIVERTON & HONITON
*E.*80,646 *T.* 55,784 (69.17%) C. hold
*Mrs Angela Browning, *C.* 26,258
Jim Barnard, *LD* 19,974
Ms Isabel Owen, *Lab.* 6,647
Alan Langmaid, *UK Ind.* 1,281
Matthew Burgess, *Green* 1,030
Mrs Jennifer Roach, *Lib.* 594
C. majority 6,284 (11.26%)
4.23% swing LD to C.
(1997, C. maj. 1,653 (2.80%))

TONBRIDGE & MALLING
*E.*65,939 *T.* 42,436 (64.36%) C. hold
*Rt. Hon. Sir J. Stanley, *C.* 20,956
Ms Victoria Hayman, *Lab.* 12,706
Ms Merilyn Canet, *LD* 7,605
Ms Lynn Croucher, *UK Ind.* 1,169
C. majority 8,250 (19.44%)
0.67% swing C. to Lab.
(1997, C. maj. 10,230 (20.78%))

TOOTING
*E.*68,447 *T.* 37,591 (54.92%) Lab. hold
*Tom Cox, *Lab.* 20,332
Alexander Nicoll, *C.* 9,932
Simon James, *LD* 5,583
Matthew Ledbury, *Green* 1,744
Lab. majority 10,400 (27.67%)
2.45% swing Lab. to C.
(1997, Lab. maj. 15,011 (32.56%))

TORBAY
*E.*72,409 *T.* 47,569 (65.69%) LD hold
*Adrian Sanders, *LD* 24,015
Christian Sweeting, *C.* 17,307
John McKay, *Lab.* 4,484
Graham Booth, *UK Ind.* 1,512
Ms Pam Neale, *Ind.* 251
LD majority 6,708 (14.10%)
7.04% swing C. to LD
(1997, LD maj. 12 (0.02%))

TOTNES
*E.*72,548 *T.* 49,246 (67.88%) C. hold
*Anthony Steen, *C.* 21,914
Ms Rachel Oliver, *LD* 18,317
Thomas Wildy, *Lab.* 6,005
Craig Mackinlay, *UK Ind.* 3,010
C. majority 3,597 (7.30%)
2.84% swing LD to C.

(1997, C. maj. 877 (1.63%))

TOTTENHAM
*E.*65,567 *T.* 31,601 (48.20%) Lab. hold
*David Lammy, *Lab.* 21,317
Ms Uma Fernandes, *C.* 4,401
Ms Meher Khan, *LD* 3,008
Peter Budge, *Green* 1,443
Weyman Bennett, *Soc. All.* 1,162
Unver Shefki, *Reform* 270
Lab. majority 16,916 (53.53%)
0.03% swing Lab. to C.
(2000 Jun by-election, Lab. maj. 5,646
(34.39%); 1997, Lab. maj. 20,200
(53.58%))

TRURO & ST AUSTELL
*E.*79,219 *T.* 50,295 (63.49%) LD hold
*Matthew Taylor, *LD* 24,296
Tim Bonner, *C.* 16,231
David Phillips, *Lab.* 6,889
James Wonnacott, *UK Ind.* 1,664
Conan Jenkin, *Meb. Ker.* 1,137
John Lee, *Ind.* 78
LD majority 8,065 (16.04%)
3.00% swing LD to C.
(1997, LD maj. 12,501 (22.03%))

TUNBRIDGE WELLS
*E.*64,534 *T.* 40,201 (62.29%) C. hold
*Archie Norman, *C.* 19,643
Keith Brown, *LD* 9,913
Ian Carvell, *Lab.* 9,332
Victor Webb, *UK Ind.* 1,313
C. majority 9,730 (24.20%)
4.34% swing LD to C.
(1997, C. maj. 7,506 (15.52%))

TWICKENHAM
*E.*74,135 *T.* 49,938 (67.36%) LD hold
*Dr Vincent Cable, *LD* 24,344
Nick Longworth, *C.* 16,689
Dean Rogers, *Lab.* 6,903
Ms Judy Maciejowska, *Green* 1,423
Ray Hollebone, *UK Ind.* 579
LD majority 7,655 (15.33%)
3.98% swing C. to LD
(1997, LD maj. 4,281 (7.36%))

TYNE BRIDGE
*E.*58,900 *T.* 26,032 (44.20%) Lab. hold
*David Clelland, *Lab.* 18,345
James Cook, *C.* 3,456
Jonathan Wallace, *LD* 3,213
James Fitzpatrick, *Soc. Lab.* 533
Samuel Robson, *Soc. All.* 485
Lab. majority 14,889 (57.19%)
4.27% swing Lab. to C.
(1997, Lab. maj. 22,906 (65.73%))

TYNEMOUTH
*E.*65,184 *T.* 43,903 (67.35%) Lab. hold
*Alan Campbell, *Lab.* 23,364
Karl Poulsen, *C.* 14,686
Ms Penny Reid, *LD* 5,108
Michael Rollings, *UK Ind.* 745
Lab. majority 8,678 (19.77%)
1.14% swing Lab. to C.
(1997, Lab. maj. 11,273 (22.04%))

TYNESIDE NORTH
*E.*64,914 *T.* 37,569 (57.88%) Lab. hold
*Rt. Hon. S. Byers, *Lab.* 26,127

Mark Ruffell, *C.* 5,459
Simon Reed, *LD* 4,649
Alan Taylor, *UK Ind.* 770
Pete Burnett, *Soc. All.* 324
Ken Capstick, *Soc. Lab.* 240
Lab. majority 20,668 (55.01%)
2.02% swing Lab. to C.
(1997, Lab. maj. 26,643 (59.05%))

UPMINSTER
*E.*56,829 *T.* 33,851 (59.57%) C. gain
Mrs Angela Watkinson, *C.* 15,410
*Keith Darvill, *Lab.* 14,169
Peter Truesdale, *LD* 3,183
Terry Murray, *UK Ind.* 1,089
C. majority 1,241 (3.67%)
5.18% swing Lab. to C.
(1997, Lab. maj. 2,770 (6.70%))

UXBRIDGE
*E.*58,066 *T.* 33,418 (57.55%) C. hold
*John Randall, *C.* 15,751
David Salisbury-Jones, *Lab.* 13,653
Ms Catherine Royce, *LD* 3,426
Paul Cannons, *UK Ind.* 588
C. majority 2,098 (6.28%)
2.26% swing Lab. to C.
(1997 Jul by-election, C. maj. 3,766
(11.82%); 1997, C. maj. 724 (1.75%))

VALE OF YORK
*E.*73,335 *T.* 48,490 (66.12%) C. hold
*Miss Anne McIntosh, *C.* 25,033
Christopher Jukes, *Lab.* 12,516
Greg Stone, *LD* 9,799
Peter Thornber, *UK Ind.* 1,142
C. majority 12,517 (25.81%)
3.78% swing Lab. to C.
(1997, C. maj. 9,721 (18.25%))

VAUXHALL
*E.*74,474 *T.* 33,392 (44.84%) Lab. hold
*Ms Kate Hoey, *Lab.* 19,738
Anthony Bottrall, *LD* 6,720
Gareth Compton, *C.* 4,489
Shane Collins, *Green* 1,485
Ms Theresa Bennett, *Soc. All.* 853
Martin Boyd, *Ind.* 107
Lab. majority 13,018 (38.99%)
4.39% swing Lab. to LD
(1997, Lab. maj. 18,660 (47.77%))

WAKEFIELD
*E.*75,750 *T.* 41,254 (54.46%) Lab. hold
*David Hinchcliffe, *Lab.* 20,592
Mrs Thelma Karran, *C.* 12,638
Douglas Dale, *LD* 5,097
Ms Sarah Greenwood, *Green* 1,075
Ms Janice Cannon, *UK Ind.* 677
Abdul Aziz, *Soc. Lab.* 634
Mick Griffiths, *Soc. All.* 541
Lab. majority 7,954 (19.28%)
4.82% swing Lab. to C.
(1997, Lab. maj. 14,604 (28.93%))

WALLASEY
*E.*64,889 *T.* 37,346 (57.55%) Lab. hold
*Ms Angela Eagle, *Lab.* 22,718
Mrs Lesley Rennie, *C.* 10,442
Peter Reisdorf, *LD* 4,186
Lab. majority 12,276 (32.87%)
3.92% swing Lab. to C.
(1997, Lab. maj. 19,074 (40.72%))

WALSALL NORTH
E.66,020 T. 32,312 (48.94%) Lab. hold
*David Winnick, *Lab.*   18,779
Melvin Pitt, *C.*   9,388
Michael Heap, *LD*   2,923
Mrs Jenny Mayo, *UK Ind.*   812
Dave Church, *Soc. All.*   410
Lab. majority 9,391 (29.06%)
(1997, Lab. maj. 12,588 (29.07%))

WALSALL SOUTH
E.62,657 T. 34,899 (55.70%) Lab. hold
*Rt. Hon. B. George, *Lab.*   20,574
Mike Bird, *C.*   10,643
Bill Tomlinson, *LD*   2,365
Derek Bennett, *UK Ind.*   974
Peter Smith, *Soc. All.*   343
Lab. majority 9,931 (28.46%)
1.15% swing C. to Lab.
(1997, Lab. maj. 11,312 (26.16%))

WALTHAMSTOW
E.64,403 T. 34,429 (53.46%) Lab. hold
*Neil Gerrard, *Lab.*   21,402
Nick Boys Smith, *C.*   6,221
Peter Dunphy, *LD*   5,024
Simon Donovan, *Soc. Alt.*   806
William Phillips, *BNP*   389
Ms Gerda Mayer, *UK Ind.*   298
Ms Barbara Duffy, *ProLife*   289
Lab. majority 15,181 (44.09%)
0.64% swing C. to Lab.
(1997, Lab. maj. 17,149 (42.81%))

WANSBECK
E.62,989 T. 37,419 (59.41%) Lab. hold
*Denis Murphy, *Lab.*   21,617
Alan Thompson, *LD*   8,516
Mrs Rachael Lake, *C.*   4,774
Michael Kirkup, *Ind.*   1,076
Dr Nic Best, *Green*   954
Gavin Attwell, *UK Ind.*   482
Lab. majority 13,101 (35.01%)
7.25% swing Lab. to LD
(1997, Lab. maj. 22,367 (49.52%))

WANSDYKE
E.70,728 T. 49,047 (69.35%) Lab. hold
*Dan Norris, *Lab.*   22,706
Chris Watt, *C.*   17,593
Ms Gail Coleshill, *LD*   7,135
Francis Hayden, *Green*   958
Peter Sandell, *UK Ind.*   655
Lab. majority 5,113 (10.42%)
0.83% swing C. to Lab.
(1997, Lab. maj. 4,799 (8.77%))

WANTAGE
E.76,129   T. 49,129 (64.53%) C. hold
*Robert Jackson, *C.*   19,475
Stephen Beer, *Lab.*   13,875
Neil Fawcett, *LD*   13,776
David Brooks-Saxl, *Green*   1,062
Count Nicholas Tolstoy, *UK Ind.*   941
C. majority 5,600 (11.40%)
0.31% swing Lab. to C.
(1997, C. maj. 6,039 (10.77%))

WARLEY
E.58,071 T. 31,415 (54.10%) Lab. hold
*Rt. Hon. J. Spellar, *Lab.*   19,007
Mark Pritchard, *C.*   7,157
Ron Cockings, *LD*   3,315

Harbhajan Dardi, *Soc. Lab.*   1,936
Lab. majority 11,850 (37.72%)
1.00% swing Lab. to C.
(1997, Lab. maj. 15,451 (39.73%))

WARRINGTON NORTH
E.72,445 T. 38,910 (53.71%) Lab. hold
*Ms Helen Jones, *Lab.*   24,026
James Usher, *C.*   8,870
Roy Smith, *LD*   5,232
Jack Kirkham, *UK Ind.*   782
Lab. majority 15,156 (38.95%)
0.43% swing C. to Lab.
(1997, Lab. maj. 19,527 (38.10%))

WARRINGTON SOUTH
E.74,283 T. 45,487 (61.23%) Lab. hold
*Ms Helen Southworth, *Lab.*   22,409
Ms Caroline Mosley, *C.*   15,022
Roger Barlow, *LD*   7,419
Mrs Joan Kelley, *UK Ind.*   637
Lab. majority 7,387 (16.24%)
1.69% swing Lab. to C.
(1997, Lab. maj. 10,807 (19.62%))

WARWICK & LEAMINGTON
E.81,405 T. 53,539 (65.77%) Lab. hold
*James Plaskitt, *Lab.*   26,108
David Campbell Bannerman, *C.*   20,155
Ms Linda Forbes, *LD*   5,964
Ms Clare Kime, *Soc. All.*   664
Greville Warwick, *UK Ind.*   648
Lab. majority 5,953 (11.12%)
2.73% swing C. to Lab.
(1997, Lab. maj. 3,398 (5.65%))

WARWICKSHIRE NORTH
E.73,828 T. 44,409 (60.15%) Lab. hold
*Mike O'Brien, *Lab.*   24,023
Geoff Parsons, *C.*   14,384
William Powell, *LD*   5,052
John Flynn, *UK Ind.*   950
Lab. majority 9,639 (21.71%)
2.76% swing Lab. to C.
(1997, Lab. maj. 14,767 (27.23%))

WATFORD
E.75,724 T. 46,372 (61.24%) Lab. hold
*Ms Claire Ward, *Lab.*   20,992
Michael McManus, *C.*   15,437
Duncan Hames, *LD*   8,088
Ms Denise Kingsley, *Green*   900
Edmund Stewart-Mole, *UK Ind.*   535
Jon Berry, *Soc. All.*   420
Lab. majority 5,555 (11.98%)
0.75% swing C. to Lab.
(1997, Lab. maj. 5,792 (10.48%))

WAVENEY
E.76,585 T. 47,167 (61.59%) Lab. hold
*Bob Blizzard, *Lab.*   23,914
Lee Scott, *C.*   15,361
David Young, *LD*   5,370
Brian Aylett, *UK Ind.*   1,097
Graham Elliot, *Green*   983
Rupert Mallin, *Soc. All.*   442
Lab. majority 8,553 (18.13%)
1.93% swing Lab. to C.
(1997, Lab. maj. 12,453 (21.99%))

WEALDEN
E.83,066   T. 52,756 (63.51%) C. hold
Charles Hendry, *C.*   26,279

Steve Murphy, *LD*   12,507
Ms Kathy Fordham, *Lab.*   10,705
Keith Riddle, *UK Ind.*   1,539
Julian Salmon, *Green*   1,273
Cyril Thornton, *Pensioner*   453
C. majority 13,772 (26.11%)   1.03%
swing LD to C.
(1997, C. maj. 14,204 (24.04%))

WEAVER VALE
E.68,236 T. 39,271 (57.55%) Lab. hold
*Mike Hall, *Lab.*   20,611
Carl Cross, *C.*   10,974
Nigel Griffiths, *LD*   5,643
Michael Cooksley, *Ind.*   1,484
Jim Bradshaw, *UK Ind.*   559
Lab. majority 9,637 (24.54%)
1.65% swing Lab. to C.
(1997, Lab. maj. 13,448 (27.84%))

WELLINGBOROUGH
E.77,389 T. 51,006 (65.91%) Lab. hold
*Paul Stinchcombe, *Lab.*   23,867
Peter Bone, *C.*   21,512
Peter Gaskell, *LD*   4,763
Anthony Ellwood, *UK Ind.*   864
Lab. majority 2,355 (4.62%)
2.14% swing C. to Lab.
(1997, Lab. maj. 187 (0.33%))

WELLS
E.74,189   T. 51,314 (69.17%) C. hold
*Rt. Hon. D. Heathcoat-Amory, *C.*
                                      22,462
Graham Oakes, *LD*   19,666
Andy Merryfield, *Lab.*   7,915
Steve Reed, *UK Ind.*   1,104
Colin Bex, *Wessex Reg.*   167
C. majority 2,796 (5.45%)
2.25% swing LD to C.
(1997, C. maj. 528 (0.94%))

WELWYN HATFIELD
E.67,004 T. 42,821 (63.91%) Lab. hold
*Ms Melanie Johnson, *Lab.*   18,484
Grant Shapps, *C.*   17,288
Daniel Cooke, *LD*   6,021
Malcolm Biggs, *UK Ind.*   798
Ms Fiona Pinto, *ProLife*   230
Lab. majority 1,196 (2.79%)
3.89% swing Lab. to C.
(1997, Lab. maj. 5,595 (10.57%))

WENTWORTH
E.64,033 T. 33,778 (52.75%) Lab. hold
*John Healey, *Lab.*   22,798
Mike Roberts, *C.*   6,349
David Wildgoose, *LD*   3,652
John Wilkinson, *UK Ind.*   979
Lab. majority 16,449 (48.70%)
4.32% swing Lab. to C.
(1997, Lab. maj. 23,959 (57.34%))

WEST BROMWICH EAST
E.61,198 T. 32,664 (53.37%) Lab. hold
Tom Watson, *Lab.*   18,250
David MacFarlane, *C.*   8,487
Ian Garrett, *LD*   4,507
Steven Grey, *UK Ind.*   835
Sheera Johal, *Soc. Lab.*   585
Lab. majority 9,763 (29.89%)
1.43% swing Lab. to C.
(1997, Lab. maj. 13,584 (32.74%))

WEST BROMWICH WEST
E.66,777 T. 31,840 (47.68%) Lab. Co-op hold
*Adrian Bailey, Lab. Co-op   19,352
Mrs Karen Bissell, C.   7,997
Mrs Sadie Smith, LD   2,168
John Salvage, BNP   1,428
Kevin Walker, UK Ind.   499
Baghwant Singh, Soc. Lab.   396
Lab. Co-op majority 11,355 (35.66%)
(2000 Nov by-election, Lab. maj. 3,232
(17.12%); 1997: Speaker maj 15,423
(42.03%))

WEST HAM
E.59,828 T. 29,273 (48.93%) Lab. hold
*Tony Banks, Lab.   20,449
Syed Kamall, C.   4,804
Paul Fox, LD   2,166
Ms Jackie Chandler Oatts, Green   1,197
Gerard Batten, UK Ind.   657
Lab. majority 15,645 (53.45%)
2.24% swing Lab. to C.
(1997, Lab. maj. 19,494 (57.92%))

WESTBURY
E.75,911 T. 50,628 (66.69%) C. hold
Dr Andrew Murrison, C.   21,299
David Vigar, LD   16,005
Ms Sarah Cardy, Lab.   10,847
Charles Booth-Jones, UK Ind.   1,261
Bob Gledhill, Green   1,216
C. majority 5,294 (10.46%)
0.12% swing C. to LD
(1997, C. maj. 6,068 (10.69%))

WESTMORLAND & LONSDALE
E.70,637 T. 47,903 (67.82%) C. hold
*Tim Collins, C.   22,486
Tim Farron, LD   19,339
John Bateson, Lab.   5,234
Robert Gibson, UK Ind.   552
Tim Bell, Ind.   292
C. majority 3,147 (6.57%)
1.17% swing C. to LD
(1997, C. maj. 4,521 (8.90%))

WESTON-SUPER-MARE
E.74,343 T. 46,680 (62.79%) LD hold
*Brian Cotter, LD   18,424
John Penrose, C.   18,086
Derek Kraft, Lab.   9,235
Bill Lukins, UK Ind.   650
John Peverelle, Ind.   206
Richard Sibley, Ind.   79
LD majority 338 (0.72%)
0.83% swing LD to C.
(1997, LD maj. 1,274 (2.39%))

WIGAN
E.64,040 T. 33,591 (52.45%) Lab. hold
*Neil Turner, Lab.   20,739
Mark Page, C.   6,996
Trevor Beswick, LD   4,970
Dave Lowe, Soc. All.   886
Lab. majority 13,743 (40.91%)
5.38% swing Lab. to C.
(1999 Sept by-election, Lab. maj. 6,729)
(1997, Lab. maj. 22,643 (51.67%))

WILTSHIRE NORTH
E.79,524 T. 52,948 (66.58%) C. hold
*James Gray, C.   24,090

Hugh Pym, LD   20,212
Ms Jo Garton, Lab.   7,556
Neil Dowdney, UK Ind.   1,090
C. majority 3,878 (7.32%)
0.67% swing LD to C.
(1997, C. maj. 3,475 (5.99%))

WIMBLEDON
E.63,930 T. 41,109 (64.30%) Lab. hold
*Roger Casale, Lab.   18,806
Stephen Hammond, C.   15,062
Martin Pierce, LD   5,341
Rajeev Thacker, Green   1,007
Roger Glencross, Bean   479
Ms Mariana Bell, UK Ind.   414
Lab. majority 3,744 (9.11%)
1.47% swing C. to Lab.
(1997, Lab. maj. 2,980 (6.17%))

WINCHESTER
E.81,852 T. 59,158 (72.27%) LD hold
*Mark Oaten, LD   32,282
Andrew Hayes, C.   22,648
Stephen Wyeth, Lab.   3,498
Ms Joan Martin, UK Ind.   664
Ms Henrietta Rouse, Wessex Reg.   66
LD majority 9,634 (16.29%)
8.14% swing C. to LD
(1997 Nov by-election, LD maj. 21,556
(39.64%)
(1997, LD maj. 2 (0.00%))

WINDSOR
E.69,136 T. 42,110 (60.91%) C. hold
*Michael Trend, C.   19,900
Nick Pinfield, LD   11,011
Mark Muller, Lab.   10,137
John Fagan, UK Ind.   1,062
C. majority 8,889 (21.11%)
0.79% swing LD to C.
(1997, C. maj. 9,917 (19.53%))

WIRRAL SOUTH
E.60,653 T. 39,818 (65.65%) Lab. hold
*Ben Chapman, Lab.   18,890
Anthony Millard, C.   13,841
Phillip Gilchrist, LD   7,087
Lab. majority 5,049 (12.68%)
0.94% swing Lab. to C.
(1997, Lab. maj. 7,004 (14.56%))

WIRRAL WEST
E.62,294 T. 40,475 (64.97%) Lab. hold
*Stephen Hesford, Lab.   19,105
Chris Lynch, C.   15,070
Simon Holbrook, LD   6,300
Lab. majority 4,035 (9.97%)
2.06% swing C. to Lab.
(1997, Lab. maj. 2,738 (5.84%))

WITNEY
E.74,624 T. 49,203 (65.93%) C. gain
David Cameron, C.   22,153
Michael Bartlet, Lab.   14,180
Gareth Epps, LD   10,000
Mark Stevenson, Green   1,100
Barry Beadle, Ind.   1,003
Kenneth Dukes, UK Ind.   767
C. majority 7,973 (16.20%)
1.87% swing Lab. to C.
(1997, C. maj. 7,028 (12.46%))

WOKING
E.71,163 T. 42,910 (60.30%) C. hold
*Humfrey Malins, C.   19,747
Alan Hilliar, LD   12,988
Sabir Hussain, Lab.   8,714
Michael Harvey, UK Ind.   1,461
C. majority 6,759 (15.75%)
2.30% swing LD to C.
(1997, C. maj. 5,678 (11.15%))

WOKINGHAM
E.68,430 T. 43,848 (64.08%) C. hold
*Rt. Hon. J. Redwood, C.   20,216
Dr Royce Longton, LD   14,222
Matthew Syed, Lab.   7,633
Franklin Carstairs, UK Ind.   897
Peter "Top Cat" Owen, Loony   880
C. majority 5,994 (13.67%)
2.51% swing C. to LD
(1997, C. maj. 9,365 (18.69%))

WOLVERHAMPTON NORTH EAST
E.60,486 T. 31,494 (52.07%) Lab. Co-op hold
*Ken Purchase, Lab. Co-op   18,984
Ms Maria Miller, C.   9,019
Steven Bourne, LD   2,494
Thomas McCartney, UK Ind.   997
Lab. Co-op majority 9,965 (31.64%)
0.14% swing C. to Lab. Co-op
(1997, Lab. maj. 12,987 (31.37%))

WOLVERHAMPTON SOUTH EAST
E.53,931 T. 27,297 (50.61%) Lab. Co-op hold
*Dennis Turner (Lab. Co-op.)   18,409
Adrian Pepper, C.   5,945
Peter Wild, LD   2,389
James Barry, NF   554
Lab. Co-op majority 12,464 (45.66%)
1.04% swing C. to Lab. Co-op
(1997, Lab. maj. 15,182 (43.58%))

WOLVERHAMPTON SOUTH WEST
E.67,171 T. 40,897 (60.88%) Lab. hold
Robert Marris, Lab.   19,735
David Chambers, C.   16,248
Mike Dixon, LD   3,425
Ms Wendy Walker, Green   805
Doug Hope, UK Ind.   684
Lab. majority 3,487 (8.53%)
0.97% swing Lab. to C.
(1997, Lab. maj. 5,118 (10.46%))

WOODSPRING
E.71,023 T. 48,758 (68.65%) C. hold
*Dr Liam Fox, C.   21,297
Chanel Stevens, Lab.   12,499
Colin Eldridge, LD   11,816
David Shopland, Ind.   1,412
Dr Richard Lawson, Green   1,282
Fraser Crean, UK Ind.   452
C. majority 8,798 (18.04%)
2.86% swing C. to Lab.
(1997, C. maj. 7,734 (14.08%))

WORCESTER
E.71,255 T. 44,210 (62.04%) Lab. hold
*Michael Foster, Lab.   21,478
Richard Adams, C.   15,712

Paul Chandler, *LD*   5,578
Richard Chamings, *UK Ind.*   1,442
Lab. majority 5,766 (13.04%)
0.67% swing Lab. to C.
(1997, Lab. maj. 7,425 (14.38%))

WORCESTERSHIRE MID
*E.*71,985   *T.* 44,897 (62.37%) C. hold
*Peter Luff, *C.*   22,937
David Bannister, *Lab.*   12,310
R. Woodthorpe-Browne, *LD*   8,420
Tony Eaves, *UK Ind.*   1,230
C. majority 10,627 (23.67%)
2.57% swing Lab. to C.
(1997, C. maj. 9,412 (18.52%))

WORCESTERSHIRE WEST
*E.*66,769   *T.* 44,807 (67.11%) C. hold
*Sir Michael Spicer, *C.*   20,597
Mike Hadley, *LD*   15,223
Waquar Azmi, *Lab.*   6,275
Ian Morris, *UK Ind.*   1,574
Malcolm Victory, *Green*   1,138
C. majority 5,374 (11.99%)
2.10% swing LD to C.
(1997, C. maj. 3,846 (7.80%))

WORKINGTON
*E.*65,965   *T.* 41,822 (63.40%) Lab. hold
Tony Cunningham, *Lab.*   23,209
Tim Stoddart, *C.*   12,359
Ian Francis, *LD*   5,214
John Peacock, *LCA*   1,040
Lab. majority 10,850 (25.94%)
6.93% swing Lab. to C.
(1997, Lab. maj. 19,656 (39.81%))

WORSLEY
*E.*69,300   *T.* 35,363 (51.03%) Lab. hold
*Terry Lewis, *Lab.*   20,193
Tobias Ellwood, *C.*   8,406
Robert Bleakley, *LD*   6,188
Ms Dorothy Entwistle, *Soc. Lab.*   576
Lab. majority 11,787 (33.33%)
2.30% swing Lab. to C.
(1997, Lab. maj. 17,741 (37.93%))

WORTHING EAST &
SHOREHAM
*E.*71,890   *T.* 43,068 (59.91%) C. hold

*Tim Loughton, *C.*   18,608
Daniel Yates, *Lab.*   12,469
Paul Elgood, *LD*   9,876
Jim McCulloch, *UK Ind.*   1,195
Christopher Baldwin, *LCA*   920
C. majority 6,139 (14.25%)
1.14% swing C. to Lab.
(1997, C. maj. 5,098 (9.89%))

WORTHING WEST
*E.*72,419   *T.* 43,209 (59.67%) C. hold
*Peter Bottomley, *C.*   20,508
James Walsh, *LD*   11,471
Alan Butcher, *Lab.*   9,270
Tim Cross, *UK Ind.*   1,960
C. majority 9,037 (20.91%)
2.96% swing LD to C.
(1997, C. maj. 7,713 (15.00%))

WREKIN, THE
*E.*65,837   *T.* 41,490 (63.02%) Lab. hold
*Peter Bradley, *Lab.*   19,532
Jacob Rees-Mogg, *C.*   15,945
Ian Jenkins, *LD*   4,738
Denis Brookes, *UK Ind.*   1,275
Lab. majority 3,587 (8.65%)
0.98% swing C. to Lab.
(1997, Lab. maj. 3,025 (6.69%))

WYCOMBE
*E.*74,647   *T.* 44,974 (60.25%) C. hold
Paul Goodman, *C.*   19,064
Chauhdry Shafique, *Lab.*   15,896
Ms Dee Tomlin, *LD*   7,658
Christopher Cooke, *UK Ind.*   1,059
John Laker, *Green*   1,057
David Fitton, *Ind.*   240
C. majority 3,168 (7.04%)
1.26% swing Lab. to C.
(1997, C. maj. 2,370 (4.53%))

WYRE FOREST
*E.*72,152   *T.* 49,062 (68.00%) KHHC
gain
Dr Richard Taylor, *KHHC*   28,487
*David Lock, *Lab.*   10,857
Mark Simpson, *C.*   9,350
James Millington, *UK Ind.*   368
KHHC majority 17,630 (35.93%)

(1997, Lab. maj. 6,946 (12.62%))

WYTHENSHAWE & SALE EAST
*E.*72,127   *T.* 35,055 (48.60%) Lab. hold
*Paul Goggins, *Lab.*   21,032
Mrs Susan Fildes, *C.*   8,424
Ms Vanessa Tucker, *LD*   4,320
Lance Crookes, *Green*   869
Fred Shaw, *Soc. Lab.*   410
Lab. majority 12,608 (35.97%)
1.49% swing C. to Lab.
(1997, Lab. maj. 15,019 (32.99%))

YEOVIL
*E.*75,977   *T.* 48,132 (63.35%) LD hold
David Laws, *LD*   21,266
Marco Forgione, *C.*   17,338
Joe Conway, *Lab.*   7,077
Neil Boxall, *UK Ind.*   1,131
Alex Begg, *Green*   786
Tony Prior, *Lib.*   534
LD majority 3,928 (8.16%)
6.47% swing LD to C.
(1997, LD maj. 11,403 (21.10%))

YORK, CITY OF
*E.*80,431   *T.* 47,980 (59.65%) Lab. hold
*Hugh Bayley, *Lab.*   25,072
Michael McIntyre, *C.*   11,293
Andrew Waller, *LD*   8,519
Bill Shaw, *Green*   1,465
Frank Ormston, *Soc. All.*   674
Richard Bate, *UK Ind.*   576
Graham Cambridge, *Loony*   381
Lab. majority 13,779 (28.72%)
3.23% swing Lab. to C.
(1997, Lab. maj. 20,523 (35.17%))

YORKSHIRE EAST
*E.*72,342   *T.* 43,314 (59.87%) C. hold
Rt. Hon. G. Knight, *C.*   19,861
Ms Tracey Simpson-Laing, *Lab.* 15,179
Ms Mary-Rose Hardy, *LD*   6,300
Trevor Pearson, *UK Ind.*   1,661
Paul Dessoy, *Ind.*   313
C. majority 4,682 (10.81%)
1.99% swing Lab. to C.
(1997, C. maj. 3,337 (6.82%))

WALES

ABERAVON
*E.*49,660 *T.* 30,190 (60.79%) Lab. hold
Hywel Francis, *Lab.*   19,063
Ms Lisa Turnbull, *PC*   2,955
Chris Davies, *LD*   2,933
Ali Miraj, *C.*   2,296
Andrew Tutton, *RP*   1,960
Captain Beany, *Bean*   727
Mr Martin Chapman, *Soc. All.*   256
Lab. majority 16,108 (53.36%)
6.08% swing Lab. to PC
(1997, Lab. maj. 21,571 (59.98%))

ALYN & DEESIDE
*E.*60,478 *T.* 35,421 (58.57%) Lab. hold
Mark Tami, *Lab.*   18,525
Mark Isherwood, *C.*   9,303
Derek Burnham, *LD*   4,585
Richard Coombs, *PC*   1,182

Klaus Armstrong-Braun, *Green*   881
William Crawford, *UK Ind.*   481
Max Cooksey, *Ind.*   253
Glyn Davies, *Comm.*   211
Lab. majority 9,222 (26.04%)
6.53% swing Lab. to C.
(1997, Lab. maj. 16,403 (39.10%))

BLAENAU GWENT
*E.*53,353 *T.* 31,725 (59.46%) Lab. hold
*Llew Smith, *Lab.*   22,855
Adam Rykala, *PC*   3,542
Edward Townsend, *LD*   2,945
Huw Williams, *C.*   2,383
Lab. majority 19,313 (60.88%)
6.68% swing Lab. to PC
(1997, Lab. maj. 28,035 (70.74%))

BRECON & RADNORSHIRE
*E.*52,247 *T.* 37,516 (71.81%) LD hold
Roger Williams, *LD*   13,824
Dr Felix Aubel, *C.*   13,073
Huw Irranca-Davis, *Lab.*   8,024
Brynach Parri, *PC*   1,301
Ian Mitchell, *Ind.*   762
Mrs Elizabeth Phillips, *UK Ind.*   452
Robert Nicholson, *Ind.*   80
LD majority 751 (2.00%)
4.94% swing LD to C.
(1997, LD maj. 5,097 (11.89%))

BRIDGEND
*E.*61,496 *T.* 37,004 (60.17%) Lab. hold
*Win Griffiths, *Lab.*   19,422
Ms Tania Brisby, *C.*   9,377
Ms Jean Barraclough, *LD*   5,330
Ms Monica Mahoney, *PC*   2,652

Ms Sara Jeremy, *ProLife* 223
Lab. majority 10,045 (27.15%)
4.05% swing Lab. to C.
(1997, Lab. maj. 15,248 (35.24%))

CAERNARFON
*E.*47,354 *T.* 29,053 (61.35%) PC hold
Hywel Williams, *PC* 12,894
Martin Eaglestone, *Lab.* 9,383
Ms Bronwen Naish, *C.* 4,403
Mel ab Owain, *LD* 1,823
Ifor Lloyd, *UK Ind.* 550
PC majority 3,511 (12.08%)
4.75% swing PC to Lab
(1997, PC maj. 7,449 (21.59%))

CAERPHILLY
*E.*67,593 *T.* 38,831 (57.45%) Lab. hold
Wayne David, *Lab.* 22,597
Lindsay Whittle, *PC* 8,172
David Simmonds, *C.* 4,413
Rob Roffe, *LD* 3,649
Lab. majority 14,425 (37.15%)
10.49% swing Lab. to PC
(1997, Lab. maj. 25,839 (57.08%))

CARDIFF CENTRAL
*E.*59,785 *T.* 34,842 (58.28%) Lab. Co-op. hold
*Jon Owen Jones, *Lab. Co-op* 13,451
Ms Jenny Willott, *LD* 12,792
Gregory Walker, *C.* 5,537
Richard Grigg, *PC* 1,680
Stephen Bartley, *Green* 661
Julian Goss, *Soc. All.* 283
Frank Hughes, *UK Ind.* 221
Ms Madeleine Jeremy, *ProLife* 217
Lab. Co-op. maj 659 (1.89%) 8.43%
swing Lab. Co-op. to LD
(1997, Lab. maj. 7,923 (18.75%))

CARDIFF NORTH
*E.*62,634 *T.* 43,240 (69.04%) Lab. hold
*Ms Julie Morgan, *Lab.* 19,845
Alastair Watson, *C.* 13,680
John Dixon, *LD* 6,631
Sion Jobbins, *PC* 2,471
Don Hulston, *UK Ind.* 613
Lab. majority 6,165 (14.26%)
1.25% swing Lab. to C.
(1997, Lab. maj. 8,126 (16.76%))

CARDIFF SOUTH & PENARTH
*E.*62,125 *T.* 35,751 (57.55%) Lab. Co-op. hold
*Rt. Hon. A. Michael, *Lab. Co-op* 20,094
Ms Maureen Kelly Owen, *C.* 7,807
Dr Rodney Berman, *LD* 4,572
Ms Lila Haines, *PC* 1,983
Justin Callan, *UK Ind.* 501
Dave Bartlett, *Soc. All.* 427
Ms Anne Savoury, *ProLife* 367
Lab. Co-op. maj 12,287 (34.37%)
0.81% swing Con to Lab. Co-op.
(1997, Lab. maj. 13,881 (32.74%))

CARDIFF WEST
*E.*58,348 *T.* 34,083 (58.41%) Lab. hold
Kevin Brennan, *Lab.* 18,594
Andrew Davies, *C.* 7,273
Ms Jacqui Gasson, *LD* 4,458
Delme Bowen, *PC* 3,296
Ms Joyce Jenking, *UK Ind.* 462

Lab. majority 11,321 (33.22%)
2.79% swing Lab. to C.
(1997, Lab. maj. 15,628 (38.80%))

CARMARTHEN EAST &
DINEFWR
*E.*54,035 *T.* 38,053 (70.42%) PC gain
Adam Price, *PC* 16,130
*Alan Williams, *Lab.* 13,540
David N Thomas, *C.* 4,912
Doiran Evans, *LD* 2,815
Mike Squires, *UK Ind.* 656
PC majority 2,590 (6.81%)
7.54% swing Lab. to PC
(1997, Lab. maj. 3,450 (8.27%))

CARMARTHEN WEST &
PEMBROKESHIRE SOUTH
*E.*56,518 *T.* 36,916 (65.32%) Lab. hold
*Nick Ainger, *Lab.* 15,349
Robert Wilson, *C.* 10,811
Llyr Hughes Griffiths, *PC* 6,893
William Jeremy, *LD* 3,248
Ian Phillips, *UK Ind.* 537
Nick Turner, *Customer* 78
Lab. majority 4,538 (12.29%)
5.14% swing Lab. to C.
(1997, Lab. maj. 9,621 (22.57%))

CEREDIGION
*E.*56,118 *T.* 34,606 (61.67%) PC hold
*Simon Thomas, *PC* 13,241
Mark Williams, *LD* 9,297
Paul Davies, *C.* 6,730
David Grace, *Lab.* 5,338
PC majority 3,944 (11.40%)
6.89% swing PC to LD
(2000 Feb by-election: PC maj 4,948
(19.74%); 1997, PC maj. 6,961
(17.33%))

CLWYD SOUTH
*E.*53,680 *T.* 33,496 (62.40%) Lab. hold
*Martyn Jones, *Lab.* 17,217
Tom Biggins, *C.* 8,319
Dyfed Edwards, *PC* 3,982
David Griffiths, *LD* 3,426
Mrs Edwina Theunissen, *UK Ind.* 552
Lab. majority 8,898 (26.56%)
4.25% swing Lab. to C.
(1997, Lab. maj. 13,810 (35.07%))

CLWYD WEST
*E.*53,960 *T.* 34,600 (64.12%) Lab. hold
*Gareth Thomas, *Lab.* 13,426
Jimmy James, *C.* 12,311
Elfed Williams, *PC* 4,453
Ms Bobbie Feeley, *LD* 3,934
Matthew Guest, *UK Ind.* 476
Lab. majority 1,115 (3.22%)
0.68% swing Lab. to C.
(1997, Lab. maj. 1,848 (4.59%))

CONWY
*E.*54,751 *T.* 34,366 (62.77%) Lab. hold
*Mrs Betty Williams, *Lab.* 14,366
David Logan, *C.* 8,147
Ms Vicky Macdonald, *LD* 5,800
Ms Ann Owen, *PC* 5,665
Alan Barham, *UK Ind.* 388
Lab. majority 6,219 (18.10%)
3.66% swing Con to Lab
(1997, Lab. maj. 1,596 (3.84%))

CYNON VALLEY
*E.*48,591 *T.* 26,958 (55.48%) Lab. hold
*Ms Ann Clwyd, *Lab.* 17,685
Steven Cornelius, *PC* 4,687
Ian Parry, *LD* 2,541
Julian Waters, *C.* 2,045
Lab. majority 12,998 (48.22%)
5.44% swing Lab. to PC
(1997, Lab. maj. 19,755 (59.10%))

DELYN
*E.*54,732 *T.* 34,636 (63.28%) Lab. hold
*David Hanson, *Lab.* 17,825
Paul Brierley, *C.* 9,220
Tudor Jones, *LD* 5,329
Paul Rowlinson, *PC* 2,262
Lab. majority 8,605 (24.84%)
2.29% swing Lab. to C.
(1997, Lab. maj. 11,693 (29.42%))

GOWER
*E.*58,943 *T.* 37,353 (63.37%) Lab. hold
*Martin Caton, *Lab.* 17,676
John Bushell, *C.* 10,281
Ms Sheila Waye, *LD* 4,507
Ms Sian Caiach, *PC* 3,865
Ms Tina Shrewsbury, *Green* 607
Darran Hickery, *Soc. Lab.* 417
Lab. majority 7,395 (19.80%)
5.11% swing Lab. to C.
(1997, Lab. maj. 13,007 (30.02%))

ISLWYN
*E.*51,230 *T.* 31,691 (61.86%) Lab. Co-op. hold
*Don Touhig, *Lab. Co-op* 19,505
Kevin Etheridge, *LD* 4,196
Leigh Thomas, *PC* 3,767
Philip Howells, *C.* 2,543
Paul Taylor, *Ind.* 1,263
Ms Mary Millington, *Soc. Lab.* 417
Lab. Co-op. maj 15,309 (48.31%)
8.71% swing Lab. Co-op. to LD
(1997, Lab. maj. 23,931 (65.73%))

LLANELLI
*E.*58,148 *T.* 36,198 (62.25%) Lab. hold
*Rt. Hon. D. Davies, *Lab.* 17,586
Dyfan Jones, *PC* 11,183
Simon Hayes, *C.* 3,442
Ken Rees, *LD* 3,065
Ms Jan Cliff, *Green* 515
John Willock, *Soc. Lab.* 407
Lab. majority 6,403 (17.69%)
10.62% swing Lab. to PC
(1997, Lab. maj. 16,039 (38.92%))

MEIRIONNYDD NANT CONWY
*E.*33,175 *T.* 21,068 (63.51%) PC hold
*Elfyn Llwyd, *PC* 10,459
Ms Denise Idris Jones, *Lab.* 4,775
Ms Lisa Francis, *C.* 3,962
Dafydd Raw-Rees, *LD* 1,872
PC majority 5,684 (26.98%)
0.36% swing PC to Lab
(1997, PC maj. 6,805 (27.69%))

MERTHYR TYDFIL & RHYMNEY
*E.*55,368 *T.* 31,684 (57.22%) Lab. hold
Dai Havard, *Lab.* 19,574
Robert Hughes, *PC* 4,651
Keith Rogers, *LD* 2,385
Richard Cuming, *C.* 2,272

Jeff Edwards, *Ind.* 1,936
Ken Evans, *Soc. Lab.* 692
Anthony Lewis, *ProLife* 174
Lab. majority 14,923 (47.10%)
11.80% swing Lab. to PC
(1997, Lab. maj. 27,086 (69.20%))

MONMOUTH
*E.*62,202 *T.* 44,462 (71.48%) Lab. hold
*Huw Edwards, *Lab.* 19,021
Roger Evans, *C.* 18,637
Neil Parker, *LD* 5,080
Marc Hubbard, *PC* 1,068
David Rowlands, *UK Ind.* 656
Lab. majority 384 (0.86%)
3.83% swing Lab. to C.
(1997, Lab. maj. 4,178 (8.52%))

MONTGOMERYSHIRE
*E.*44,319 *T.* 28,983 (65.51%) LD hold
*Lembit Opik, *LD* 14,319
David Jones, *C.* 8,085
Paul Davies, *Lab.* 3,443
David Senior, *PC* 1,969
David William Rowlands, *UK Ind.* 786
Miss Ruth Davies, *ProLife* 210
Reg Taylor, *Ind.* 171
LD majority 6,234 (21.51%)
0.88% swing Con to LD
(1997, LD maj. 6,303 (19.74%))

NEATH
*E.*56,107 *T.* 35,020 (62.42%) Lab. hold
*Rt. Hon. P. Hain, *Lab.* 21,253
Alun Llywelyn, *PC* 6,437
David Davies, *LD* 3,335
David Devine, *C.* 3,310
Huw Pudner, *Soc. All.* 483
Gerardo Brienza, *ProLife* 202
Lab. majority 14,816 (42.31%)
11.56% swing Lab. to PC
(1997, Lab. maj. 26,741 (64.84%))

NEWPORT EAST
*E.*56,118 *T.* 31,282 (55.74%) Lab. hold
*Rt. Hon. A. Howarth, *Lab.* 17,120
Ian Oakley, *C.* 7,246
Alistair Cameron, *LD* 4,394
Madoc Batcup, *PC* 1,519
Ms Liz Screen, *Soc. Lab.* 420
Neal Reynolds, *UK Ind.* 410
Robert Griffiths, *Comm.* 173
Lab. majority 9,874 (31.56%)
2.36% swing Lab. to C.
(1997, Lab. maj. 13,523 (36.29%))

NEWPORT WEST
*E.*59,742 *T.* 35,063 (58.69%) Lab. hold
*Paul Flynn, *Lab.* 18,489
Dr William Morgan, *C.* 9,185
Ms Veronica Watkins, *LD* 4,095
Anthony Salkeld, *PC* 2,510
Hugh Moelwyn-Hughes, *UK Ind.* 506
Terry Cavill, *BNP* 278
Lab. majority 9,304 (26.54%)

4.81% swing Lab. to C.
(1997, Lab. maj. 14,537 (36.16%))

OGMORE
*E.*52,185 *T.* 30,353 (58.16%) Lab. hold
*Sir Ray Powell, *Lab.* 18,833
Ms Angela Pulman, *PC* 4,259
Ian Lewis, *LD* 3,878
Richard Hill, *C.* 3,383
Lab. majority 14,574 (48.02%)
9.46% swing Lab. to PC
(1997, Lab. maj. 24,447 (64.22%))

PONTYPRIDD
*E.*66,105 *T.* 38,309 (57.95%) Lab. hold
*Dr Kim Howells, *Lab.* 22,963
Bleddyn Hancock, *PC* 5,279
Ms Prudence Dailey, *C.* 5,096
Eric Brooke, *LD* 4,152
Ms Sue Warry, *UK Ind.* 603
Joseph Biddulph, *ProLife* 216
Lab. majority 17,684 (46.16%)
5.61% swing Lab. to PC
(1997, Lab. maj. 23,129 (50.44%))

PRESELI PEMBROKESHIRE
*E.*54,283 *T.* 36,777 (67.75%) Lab. hold
*Ms Jackie Lawrence, *Lab.* 15,206
Stephen Crabb, *C.* 12,260
Rhys Sinnet, *PC* 4,658
Alexander Dauncey, *LD* 3,882
Ms Trish Bowen, *Soc. Lab.* 452
Hugh Jones, *UK Ind.* 319
Lab. majority 2,946 (8.01%)
6.29% swing Lab. to C.
(1997, Lab. maj. 8,736 (20.60%))

RHONDDA
*E.*56,059 *T.* 34,002 (60.65%) Lab. hold
Chris Bryant, *Lab.* 23,230
Ms Leanne Wood, *PC* 7,183
Peter Hobbins, *C.* 1,557
Gavin Cox, *LD* 1,525
Glyndwr Summers, *Ind.* 507
Lab. majority 16,047 (47.19%)
6.95% swing Lab. to PC
(1997, Lab. maj. 24,931 (61.09%))

SWANSEA EAST
*E.*57,273 *T.* 30,072 (52.51%) Lab. hold
*Rt. Hon. D. Anderson, *Lab.* 19,612
John Ball, *PC* 3,464
Robert Speht, *LD* 3,064
Paul Morris, *C.* 3,026
Tony Young, *Green* 463
Tim Jenkins, *UK Ind.* 443
Lab. majority 16,148 (53.70%)
9.15% swing Lab. to PC
(1997, Lab. maj. 25,569 (66.12%))

SWANSEA WEST
*E.*57,074 *T.* 32,100 (56.24%) Lab. hold
*Rt. Hon. A. Williams, *Lab.* 15,644
Ms Margaret Harper, *C.* 6,094
Mike Day, *LD* 5,313

Ian Titherington, *PC* 3,404
Richard Lewis, *UK Ind.* 653
Martyn Shrewsbury, *Green* 626
Alec Thraves, *Soc. All.* 366
Lab. majority 9,550 (29.75%)
2.99% swing Lab. to C.
(1997, Lab. maj. 14,459 (35.73%))

TORFAEN
*E.*61,110 *T.* 35,242 (57.67%) Lab. hold
*Rt. Hon. P. Murphy, *Lab.* 21,883
Jason Evans, *C.* 5,603
Alan Masters, *LD* 3,936
Stephen Smith, *PC* 2,720
Mrs Brenda Vipass, *UK Ind.* 657
Steve Bell, *Soc. All.* 443
Lab. majority 16,280 (46.19%)
5.27% swing Lab. to C.
(1997, Lab. maj. 24,536 (56.74%))

VALE OF CLWYD
*E.*51,247 *T.* 32,346 (63.12%) Lab. hold
*Chris Ruane, *Lab.* 16,179
Brendan Murphy, *C.* 10,418
Graham Rees, *LD* 3,058
John Penri Williams, *PC* 2,300
William Campbell, *UK Ind.* 391
Lab. majority 5,761 (17.81%)
2.54% swing Lab. to C.
(1997, Lab. maj. 8,955 (22.89%))

VALE OF GLAMORGAN
*E.*67,071 *T.* 45,184 (67.37%) Lab. hold
*John Smith, *Lab.* 20,524
Lady Susan Inkin, *C.* 15,824
Dewi Smith, *LD* 5,521
Chris Franks, *PC* 2,867
Niall Warry, *UK Ind.* 448
Lab. majority 4,700 (10.40%)
4.57% swing Lab. to C.
(1997, Lab. maj. 10,532 (19.54%))

WREXHAM
*E.*50,465 *T.* 30,048 (59.54%) Lab. hold
Ian Lucas, *Lab.* 15,934
Ms Felicity Elphick, *C.* 6,746
Ron Davies, *LD* 5,153
Malcolm Evans, *PC* 1,783
Mrs Jane Brookes, *UK Ind.* 432
Lab. majority 9,188 (30.58%)
0.86% swing Lab. to C.
(1997, Lab. maj. 11,762 (32.30%))

YNYS MON
*E.*53,117 *T.* 34,018 (64.04%) Lab. gain
Albert Owen, *Lab.* 11,906
Eilian Williams, *PC* 11,106
Albie Fox, *C.* 7,653
Nick Bennett, *LD* 2,772
Francis Wykes, *UK Ind.* 359
Ms Nona Donald, *Ind.* 222
Lab. majority 800 (2.35%)
4.28% swing PC to Lab
(1997, PC maj. 2,481 (6.21%))

SCOTLAND

ABERDEEN CENTRAL
*E.*50,098 *T.* 26,429 (52.75%) Lab. hold
Frank Doran, Lab.	12,025
Wayne Gault, *SNP*	5,379
Ms Eleanor Anderson, *LD*	-4,547
Stewart Whyte, *C.*	3,761
Andy Cumbers, *SSP*	717

Lab. majority 6,646 (25.15%)
4.24% swing Lab. to SNP
(1997, Lab. maj. 10,801 (30.32%))

ABERDEEN NORTH
*E.*52,746 *T.* 30,357 (57.55%) Lab. hold
Malcolm Savidge, Lab.	13,157
Dr Alasdair Allan, *SNP*	8,708
Jim Donaldson, *LD*	4,991
Richard Cowling, *C.*	3,047
Ms Shona Forman, *SSP*	454

Lab. majority 4,449 (14.66%)
5.70% swing Lab. to SNP
(1997, Lab. maj. 10,010 (26.06%))

ABERDEEN SOUTH
*E.*58,907 *T.* 36,890 (62.62%) Lab. hold
Ms Anne Begg, Lab.	14,696
Ian Yuill, *LD*	10,308
Moray Macdonald, *C.*	7,098
Ian Angus, *SNP*	4,293
David Watt, *SSP*	495

Lab. majority 4,388 (11.89%)
2.13% swing LD to Lab.
(1997, Lab. maj. 3,365 (7.64%))

ABERDEENSHIRE WEST & KINCARDINE
*E.*61,180 *T.* 37,914 (61.97%) LD hold
Sir Robert Smith, LD	16,507
Tom Kerr, *C.*	11,686
Kevin Hutchens, *Lab.*	4,669
John Green, *SNP*	4,634
Alan Manley, *SSP*	418

LD majority 4,821 (12.72%)
3.28% swing C. to LD
(1997, LD maj. 2,662 (6.16%))

AIRDRIE & SHOTTS
*E.*58,349 *T.* 31,736 (54.39%) Lab. hold
Rt. Hon. Ms H. Liddell, Lab.	18,478
Ms Alison Lindsay, *SNP*	6,138
John Love, *LD*	2,376
Gordon McIntosh, *C.*	1,960
Ms Mary Dempsey, *Scot. U.*	1,439
Kenny McGuigan, *SSP*	1,171
Chris Herriot, *Lab.*	174

Lab. majority 12,340 (38.88%)
0.73% swing SNP to Lab.
(1997, Lab. maj. 15,412 (37.42%))

ANGUS
*E.*59,004 *T.* 35,013 (59.34%) SNP hold
Michael Weir, *SNP*	12,347
Marcus Booth, *C.*	8,736
Ian McFatridge, *Lab.*	8,183
Peter Nield, *LD*	5,015
Bruce Wallace, *SSP*	732

SNP majority 3,611 (10.31%)
6.67% swing SNP to C.
(1997, SNP maj. 10,189 (23.66%))

ARGYLL & BUTE
*E.*49,175 *T.* 30,957 (62.95%) LD hold

Alan Reid, *LD*	9,245
Hugh Raven, *Lab.*	7,592
David Petrie, *C.*	6,436
Ms Agnes Samuel, *SNP*	6,433
Des Divers, *SSP*	1,251

LD majority 1,653 (5.34%)
9.60% swing LD to Lab.
(1997, LD maj. 6,081 (17.03%))

AYR
*E.*55,630 *T.* 38,560 (69.32%) Lab. hold
Ms Sandra Osborne, Lab.	16,801
Phil Gallie, *C.*	14,256
Jim Mather, *SNP*	4,621
Stuart Ritchie, *LD*	2,089
James Stewart, *SSP*	692
Joseph Smith, *UK Ind.*	101

Lab. majority 2,545 (6.60%)
4.01% swing Lab. to C.
(1997, Lab. maj. 6,543 (14.62%))

BANFF & BUCHAN
*E.*56,496   *T.* 30,806 (54.53%)
		SNP hold
Alex Salmond, SNP		16,710
Alexander Wallace, *C.*		6,207
Edward Harris, *Lab.*		4,363
Douglas Herbison, *LD*		2,769
Ms Alice Rowan, *SSP*		447
Eric Davidson, *UK Ind.*		310

SNP majority 10,503 (34.09%)
1.06% swing C. to SNP
(1997, SNP maj. 12,845 (31.97%))

CAITHNESS, SUTHERLAND & EASTER ROSS
*E.*41,225 *T.* 24,867 (60.32%) LD hold
Viscount John Thurso, *LD*	9,041
Michael Meighan, *Lab.*	6,297
John Macadam, *SNP*	5,273
Robert Rowantree, *C.*	3,513
Ms Karn Mabon, *SSP*	544
Gordon Campbell, *Ind.*	199

LD majority 2,744 (11.03%)
1.64% swing Lab. to LD
(1997, LD maj. 2,259 (7.75%))

CARRICK, CUMNOCK & DOON VALLEY
*E.*64,919 *T.* 40,107 (61.78%) Lab. Co-op hold
George Foulkes, Lab. Co-op	22,174
Gordon Miller, *C.*	7,318
Tom Wilson, *SNP*	6,258
Ms Amy Rogers, *LD*	2,932
Ms Amanda McFarlane, *SSP*	1,058
James McDaid, *Soc. Lab.*	367

Lab. Co-op majority 14,856 (37.04%)
2.90% swing Lab. Co-op to C.
(1997, Lab. maj. 21,062 (42.84%))

CLYDEBANK & MILNGAVIE
*E.*52,534 *T.* 32,491 (61.85%) Lab. hold
Tony Worthington, Lab.	17,249
Jim Yuill, *SNP*	6,525
Rod Ackland, *LD*	3,909
Dr Catherine Pickering, *C.*	3,514
Ms Dawn Brennan, *SSP*	1,294

Lab. majority 10,724 (33.01%)
0.54% swing Lab. to SNP
(1997, Lab. maj. 13,320 (34.08%))

CLYDESDALE
*E.*64,423 *T.* 38,222 (59.33%) Lab. hold
Jimmy Hood, Lab.	17,822
Jim Wright, *SNP*	10,028
Kevin Newton, *C.*	5,034
Ms Moira Craig, *LD*	4,111
Paul Cockshott, *SSP*	974
Donald MacKay, *UK Ind.*	253

Lab. majority 7,794 (20.39%)
5.01% swing Lab. to SNP
(1997, Lab. maj. 13,809 (30.41%))

COATBRIDGE & CHRYSTON
*E.*52,178 *T.* 30,311 (58.09%) Lab. hold
Rt. Hon. T. Clarke, Lab.	19,807
Peter Kearney, *SNP*	4,493
Alistair Tough, *LD*	2,293
Patrick Ross-Taylor, *C.*	2,171
Ms Lynne Sheridan, *SSP*	1,547

Lab. majority 15,314 (50.52%)
0.39% swing Lab. to SNP
(1997, Lab. maj. 19,295 (51.30%))

CUMBERNAULD & KILSYTH
*E.*49,739 *T.* 29,699 (59.71%) Lab. hold
Ms Rosemary McKenna, Lab.	16,144
David McGlashan, *SNP*	8,624
John O'Donnell, *LD*	1,934
Ms Alison Ross, *C.*	1,460
Kenny McEwan, *SSP*	1,287
Thomas Taylor, *Scot. Ref.*	250

Lab. majority 7,520 (25.32%)
2.78% swing Lab. to SNP
(1997, Lab. maj. 11,128 (30.89%))

CUNNINGHAME NORTH
*E.*54,993 *T.* 33,816 (61.49%) Lab. hold
Brian Wilson, Lab.	15,571
Campbell Martin, *SNP*	7,173
Richard Wilkinson, *C.*	6,666
Ross Chmiel, *LD*	3,060
Sean Scott, *SSP*	964
Ms Louise McDaid, *Soc. Lab.*	382

Lab. majority 8,398 (24.83%)
3.51% swing Lab. to SNP
(1997, Lab. maj. 11,039 (26.84%))

CUNNINGHAME SOUTH
*E.*49,982 *T.* 28,009 (56.04%) Lab. hold
Brian Donohoe, Lab.	16,424
Bill Kidd, *SNP*	5,194
Mrs Pam Paterson, *C.*	2,682
John Boyd, *LD*	2,094
Ms Rosemary Byrne, *SSP*	1,233
Bobby Cochrane, *Soc. Lab.*	382

Lab. majority 11,230 (40.09%)
0.93% swing Lab. to SNP
(1997, Lab. maj. 14,869 (41.95%))

DUMBARTON
*E.*56,267 *T.* 33,994 (60.42%) Lab. Co-op hold
John McFall, Lab. Co-op	16,151
Iain Robertson, *SNP*	6,576
Eric Thompson, *LD*	5,265
Peter Ramsay, *C.*	4,648
Les Robertson, *SSP*	1,354

Lab. Co-op majority 9,575 (28.17%)
0.89% swing SNP to Lab. Co-op
(1997, Lab. maj. 10,883 (26.38%))

DUMFRIES
E.62,931 T. 42,586 (67.67%) Lab. hold
*Russell Brown, Lab.   20,830
John Charteris, C.   11,996
John Ross Scott, LD   4,955
Gerry Fisher, SNP   4,103
John Dennis, SSP   702
Lab. majority 8,834 (20.74%)
0.64% swing C. to Lab.
(1997, Lab. maj. 9,643 (19.47%))

DUNDEE EAST
E.56,535 T. 32,358 (57.24%) Lab. hold
Iain Luke, Lab.   14,635
Stewart Hosie, SNP   10,160
Alan Donnelly, C.   3,900
Raymond Lawrie, LD   2,784
Harvey Duke, SSP   879
Lab. majority 4,475 (13.83%)
5.38% swing Lab. to SNP
(1997, Lab. maj. 9,961 (24.58%))

DUNDEE WEST
E.53,760 T. 29,242 (54.39%) Lab. hold
*Ernie Ross, Lab.   14,787
Gordon Archer, SNP   7,987
Ian Hail, C.   2,656
Ms Elizabeth Dick, LD   2,620
Jim McFarlane, SSP   1,192
Lab. majority 6,800 (23.25%)
3.65% swing Lab. to SNP
(1997, Lab. maj. 11,859 (30.56%))

DUNFERMLINE EAST
E.52,811 T. 30,086 (56.97%) Lab. hold
*Rt. Hon. G. Brown, Lab.   19,487
John Mellon, SNP   4,424
Stuart Randall, C.   2,838
John Mainland, LD   2,281
Andy Jackson, SSP   770
Tom Dunsmore, UK Ind.   286
Lab. majority 15,063 (50.07%)
0.60% swing Lab. to SNP
(1997, Lab. maj. 18,751 (51.26%))

DUNFERMLINE WEST
E.54,293 T. 30,975 (57.05%) Lab. hold
*Ms Rachel Squire, Lab.   16,370
Brian Goodall, SNP   5,390
Russell McPhate, LD   4,832
James Mackie, C.   3,166
Ms Kate Stewart, SSP   746
Alastair Harper, UK Ind.   471
Lab. majority 10,980 (35.45%)
0.77% swing SNP to Lab.
(1997, Lab. maj. 12,354 (33.91%))

EAST KILBRIDE
E.66,572 T. 41,690 (62.62%) Lab. hold
*Rt. Hon. A. Ingram, Lab.   22,205
Archie Buchanan, SNP   9,450
Ewan Hawthorn, LD   4,278
Mrs Margaret McCulloch, C.   4,238
David Stevenson, SSP   1,519
Lab. majority 12,755 (30.59%)
2.52% swing Lab. to SNP
(1997, Lab. maj. 17,384 (35.63%))

EAST LOTHIAN
E.58,987 T. 36,871 (62.51%) Lab. hold
Mrs Anne Picking, Lab.   17,407
Hamish Mair, C.   6,577
Ms Judy Hayman, LD   6,506

Ms Hilary Brown, SNP   5,381
Derrick White, SSP   624
Jake Herriot, Soc. Lab.   376
Lab. majority 10,830 (29.37%)
1.68% swing Lab. to C.
(1997, Lab. maj. 14,221 (32.74%))

EASTWOOD
E.68,378 T. 48,368 (70.74%) Lab. hold
*Jim Murphy, Lab.   23,036
Raymond Robertson, C.   13,895
Allan Steele, LD   6,239
Stewart Maxwell, SNP   4,137
Peter Murray, SSP   814
Dr Manar Tayan, Ind.   247
Lab. majority 9,141 (18.90%)
6.35% swing C. to Lab.
(1997, Lab. maj. 3,236 (6.19%))

EDINBURGH CENTRAL
E.66,089 T. 34,390 (52.04%) Lab. hold
*Rt. Hon. A. Darling, Lab.   14,495
Andrew Myles, LD   6,353
Alastair Orr, C.   5,643
Dr Ian McKee, SNP   4,832
Graeme Farmer, Green   1,809
Kevin Williamson, SSP   1,258
Lab. majority 8,142 (23.68%)
5.15% swing Lab. to LD
(1997, Lab. maj. 11,070 (25.90%))

EDINBURGH EAST &
MUSSELBURGH
E.59,241 T. 34,454 (58.16%) Lab. hold
*Rt. Hon. Dr G. Strang, Lab.   18,124
Rob Munn, SNP   5,956
Gary Peacock, LD   4,981
Peter Finnie, C.   3,906
Derek Durkin, SSP   1,487
Lab. majority 12,168 (35.32%)
0.41% swing SNP to Lab.
(1997, Lab. maj. 14,530 (34.50%))

EDINBURGH NORTH & LEITH
E.62,475 T. 33,234 (53.20%) Lab. hold
Mark Lazarowicz, Lab.   15,271
Sebastian Tombs, LD   6,454
Ms Kaukab Stewart, SNP   5,290
Iain Mitchell, C.   4,626
Ms Catriona Grant, SSP   1,334
Don Jacobsen, Soc. Lab.   259
Lab. majority 8,817 (26.53%)
3.67% swing Lab. to LD
(1997, Lab. maj. 10,978 (26.81%))

EDINBURGH PENTLANDS
E.59,841 T. 38,932 (65.06%) Lab. hold
*Dr Lynda Clark, Lab.   15,797
Sir Malcolm Rifkind, C.   14,055
David Walker, LD   4,210
Stewart Gibb, SNP   4,210
James Mearns, SSP   555
William McMurdo, UK Ind.   105
Lab. majority 1,742 (4.47%)
3.08% swing Lab. to C.
(1997, Lab. maj. 4,862 (10.63%))

EDINBURGH SOUTH
E.64,012 T. 37,166 (58.06%) Lab. hold
*Nigel Griffiths, Lab.   15,671
Ms Marilyne MacLaren, LD   10,172
Geoffrey Buchan, C.   6,172
Ms Heather Williams, SNP   3,683

Colin Fox, SSP   933
Ms Linda Hendry, LCA   535
Lab. majority 5,499 (14.80%)
7.19% swing Lab. to LD
(1997, Lab. maj. 11,452 (25.54%))

EDINBURGH WEST
E.61,895 T. 39,478 (63.78%) LD hold
John Barrett, LD   16,719
Ms Elspeth Alexandra, Lab.   9,130
Iain Whyte, C.   8,894
Alyn Smith, SNP   4,047
Bill Scott, SSP   688
LD majority 7,589 (19.22%)
2.59% swing LD to Lab.
(1997, LD maj. 7,253 (15.22%))

FALKIRK EAST
E.57,633 T. 33,702 (58.48%) Lab. hold
*Michael Connarty, Lab.   18,536
Ms Isabel Hutton, SNP   7,824
Bill Stevenson, C.   3,252
Ms Karen Utting, LD   2,992
Tony Weir, SSP   725
Raymond Stead, Soc. Lab.   373
Lab. majority 10,712 (31.78%)
0.20% swing Lab. to SNP
(1997, Lab. maj. 13,385 (32.18%))

FALKIRK WEST
E.53,583 T. 30,891 (57.65%) Lab. hold
*Eric Joyce, Lab.   16,022
David Kerr, SNP   7,490
Simon Murray, C.   2,321
Hugh O'Donnell, LD   2,203
William Buchanan, Ind.   1,464
Ms Mhairi McAlpine, SSP   707
Hugh Lynch, Ind.   490
Ronnie Forbes, Soc. Lab.   194
Lab. majority 8,532 (27.62%)
4.15% swing Lab. to SNP
2000 Dec by-election, Lab. maj. 705
(3.61%) (1997, Lab. maj. 13,783
(35.92%))

FIFE CENTRAL
E.59,597 T. 32,512 (54.55%) Lab. hold
John MacDougall, Lab.   18,310
David Alexander, SNP   8,235
Ms Elizabeth Riches, LD   2,775
Jeremy Balfour, C.   2,351
Ms Morag Balfour, SSP   841
Lab. majority 10,075 (30.99%)
1.33% swing Lab. to SNP
(1997, Lab. maj. 13,713 (33.64%))

FIFE NORTH EAST
E.61,900 T. 34,692 (56.05%) LD hold
*Rt. Hon. M. Campbell, LD   17,926
Mike Scott-Hayward, C.   8,190
Ms Claire Brennan, Lab.   3,950
Ms Kris Murray-Browne, SNP   3,596
Keith White, SSP   610
Mrs Leslie Von Goetz, LCA   420
LD majority 9,736 (28.06%)
1.66% swing C. to LD
(1997, LD maj. 10,356 (24.75%))

GALLOWAY & UPPER
NITHSDALE
E.52,756 T. 35,914 (68.08%) C. gain
Peter Duncan, C.   12,222
Malcolm Fleming, SNP   12,148

Thomas Sloan, *Lab.*   7,258
Neil Wallace, *LD*   3,698
Andy Harvey, *SSP*   588
C. majority 74 (0.21%)
6.80% swing SNP to C.
(1997, SNP maj. 5,624 (13.39%))

GLASGOW ANNIESLAND
*E.*53,290 *T.* 26,722 (50.14%) Lab. hold
*John Robertson, *Lab.*   15,102
Grant Thoms, *SNP*   4,048
Christopher McGinty, *LD*   3,244
Stewart Connell, *C.*   2,651
Charlie McCarthy, *SSP*   1,486
Ms Katherine McGavigan, *Soc. Lab.* 191
Lab. majority 11,054 (41.37%)
1.68% swing Lab. to SNP
2000 Nov by-election, Lab. maj. 6,337
(31.35%) (1997, Lab. maj. 15,154
(44.73%))

GLASGOW BAILLIESTON
*E.*49,268 *T.* 23,261 (47.21%) Lab. hold
*Jimmy Wray, *Lab.*   14,200
Lachlan McNeill, *SNP*   4,361
David Comrie, *C.*   1,580
Jim McVicar, *SSP*   1,569
Charles Dundas, *LD*   1,551
Lab. majority 9,839 (42.30%)
2.15% swing Lab. to SNP
(1997, Lab. maj. 14,840 (46.59%))

GLASGOW CATHCART
*E.*52,094 *T.* 27,386 (52.57%) Lab. hold
Tom Harris, *Lab.*   14,902
Mrs Josephine Docherty, *SNP*   4,586
Richard Cook, *C.*   3,662
Tom Henery, *LD*   3,006
Ronnie Stevenson, *SSP*   1,730
Lab. majority 10,816 (39.49%)
1.80% swing SNP to Lab.
(1997, Lab. maj. 12,245 (35.90%))

GLASGOW GOVAN
*E.*54,068 *T.* 25,284 (46.76%) Lab. hold
*Mohammad Sarwar, *Lab.*   12,464
Ms Karen Neary, *SNP*   6,064
Bob Stewart, *LD*   2,815
Mark Menzies, *C.*   2,167
Willie McGartland, *SSP*   1,531
John Foster, *Comm.*   174
Badar Mirza, *Ind.*   69
Lab. majority 6,400 (25.31%)
8.14% swing SNP to Lab.
(1997, Lab. maj. 2,914 (9.04%))

GLASGOW KELVIN
*E.*61,534 *T.* 26,802 (43.56%) Lab. hold
*George Galloway, *Lab.*   12,014
Ms Tamsin Mayberry, *LD*   4,754
Frank Rankin, *SNP*   4,513
Miss Davina Rankin, *C.*   2,388
Ms Heather Ritchie, *SSP*   1,847
Tim Shand, *Green*   1,286
Lab. majority 7,260 (27.09%)
4.85% swing Lab. to LD
(1997, Lab. maj. 9,665 (29.60%))

GLASGOW MARYHILL
*E.*55,431 *T.* 22,231 (40.11%) Lab. hold
Ms Ann McKechin, *Lab.*   13,420
Alex Dingwall, *SNP*   3,532
Stuart Callison, *LD*   2,372

Gordon Scott, *SSP*   1,745
Gawain Towler, *C.*   1,162
Lab. majority 9,888 (44.48%)
1.76% swing Lab. to SNP
(1997, Lab. maj. 14,264 (47.99%))

GLASGOW POLLOK
*E.*49,201 *T.* 25,277 (51.37%) Lab. Co-
op hold
*Ian Davidson, *Lab. Co-op*   15,497
David Ritchie, *SNP*   4,229
Keith Baldassara, *SSP*   2,522
Ms Isabel Nelson, *LD*   1,612
Rory O'Brien, *C.*   1,417
Lab. Co-op majority 11,268 (44.58%)
1.27% swing SNP to Lab. Co-op
(1997, Lab. maj. 13,791 (42.04%))

GLASGOW RUTHERGLEN
*E.*51,855 *T.* 29,213 (56.34%) Lab. Co-
op hold
*Tommy McAvoy, *Lab. Co-op*   16,760
Ms Anne McLaughlin, *SNP*   4,135
David Jackson, *LD*   3,689
Malcolm Macaskill, *C.*   3,301
Bill Bonnar, *SSP*   1,328
Lab. Co-op majority 12,625 (43.22%)
0.48% swing SNP to Lab. Co-op
(1997, Lab. maj. 15,007 (42.25%))

GLASGOW SHETTLESTON
*E.*51,557 *T.* 20,465 (39.69%) Lab. hold
*David Marshall, *Lab.*   13,235
Jim Byrne, *SNP*   3,417
Ms Rosie Kane, *SSP*   1,396
Lewis Hutton, *LD*   1,105
Campbell Murdoch, *C.*   1,082
Murdo Ritchie, *Soc. Lab.*   230
Lab. majority 9,818 (47.97%)
5.60% swing Lab. to SNP
(1997, Lab. maj. 15,868 (59.18%))

GLASGOW SPRINGBURN
*E.*55,192 *T.* 24,104 (43.67%) Speaker
hold
*Rt. Hon. M. Martin, *Speaker*   16,053
Sandy Bain, *SNP*   4,675
Ms Carolyn Leckie, *SSP*   1,879
Daniel Houston, *Scot. U.*   1,289
Richard Silvester, *Ind.*   208
Speaker maj 11,378 (47.20%)
(1997, Lab. maj. 17,326 (54.87%))

GORDON
*E.*59,996 *T.* 35,001 (58.34%) LD hold
*Malcolm Bruce, *LD*   15,928
Mrs Nanette Milne, *C.*   8,049
Mrs Rhona Kemp, *SNP*   5,760
Ellis Thorpe, *Lab.*   4,730
John Sangster, *SSP*   534
LD majority 7,879 (22.51%)
2.97% swing C. to LD
(1997, LD maj. 6,997 (16.57%))

GREENOCK & INVERCLYDE
*E.*47,884 *T.* 28,419 (59.35%) Lab. hold
David Cairns, *Lab.*   14,929
Chic Brodie, *LD*   5,039
Andrew Murie, *SNP*   4,248
Alistair Haw, *C.*   3,000
Davey Landels, *SSP*   1,203
Lab. majority 9,890 (34.80%)
3.77% swing Lab. to LD

(1997, Lab. maj. 13,040 (37.59%))

HAMILTON NORTH &
BELLSHILL
*E.*53,539 *T.* 30,404 (56.79%) Lab. hold
*Rt. Hon. Dr J. Reid, *Lab.*   18,786
Chris Stephens, *SNP*   5,225
Bill Frain Bell, *C.*   2,649
Keith Legg, *LD*   2,360
Ms Shareen Blackall, *SSP*   1,189
Steve Mayes, *Soc. Lab.*   195
Lab. majority 13,561 (44.60%)
0.16% swing Lab. to SNP
(1997, Lab. maj. 17,067 (44.92%))

HAMILTON SOUTH
*E.*46,665 *T.* 26,750 (57.32%) Lab. hold
*Bill Tynan, *Lab.*   15,965
John Wilson, *SNP*   5,190
John Oswald, *LD*   2,381
Neil Richardson, *C.*   1,876
Ms Gena Mitchell, *SSP*   1,187
Ms Janice Murdoch, *UK Ind.*   151
Lab. majority 10,775 (40.28%)
3.85% swing Lab. to SNP
1999 Sep by-election, Lab. maj. 556
(2.86%) (1997, Lab. maj. 15,878
(47.98%)

INVERNESS EAST, NAIRN &
LOCHABER
*E.*67,139 *T.* 42,461 (63.24%) Lab. hold
*David Stewart, *Lab.*   15,605
Angus MacNeil, *SNP*   10,889
Ms Patsy Kenton, *LD*   9,420
Richard Jenkins, *C.*   5,653
Steve Arnott, *SSP*   894
Lab. majority 4,716 (11.11%)
3.10% swing Lab. to SNP
(1997, Lab. maj. 2,339 (4.90%))

KILMARNOCK & LOUDOUN
*E.*61,049 *T.* 37,665 (61.70%) Lab. hold
*Des Browne, *Lab.*   19,926
John Brady, *SNP*   9,592
Donald Reece, *C.*   3,943
John Stewart, *LD*   3,177
Jason Muir, *SSP*   1,027
Lab. majority 10,334 (27.44%)
6.07% swing Lab. to SNP
(1997, Lab. maj. 7,256 (15.30%))

KIRKCALDY
*E.*51,559 *T.* 28,157 (54.61%) Lab. Co-
op hold
*Dr Lewis Moonie, *Lab. Co-op*   15,227
Ms Shirley-Anne Somerville, *SNP*
                                   6,264
Scott Campbell, *C.*   3,013
Andrew Weston, *LD*   2,849
Dougie Kinnear, *SSP*   804
Lab. Co-op majority 8,963 (31.83%)
0.60% swing SNP to Lab. Co-op
(1997, Lab. maj. 10,710 (30.63%))

LINLITHGOW
*E.*54,599 *T.* 31,655 (57.98%) Lab. hold
*Tam Dalyell, *Lab.*   17,207
Jim Sibbald, *SNP*   8,078
Gordon Lindhurst, *C.*   2,836
Martin Oliver, *LD*   2,628
Eddie Cornoch, *SSP*   695
Ms Helen Cronin, *R & R Loony*   211

Lab. majority 9,129 (28.84%)
0.75% swing SNP to Lab.
(1997, Lab. maj. 10,838 (27.33%))

LIVINGSTON
*E.*64,850 *T.* 36,033 (55.56%) Lab. hold
*Rt. Hon. R. Cook, *Lab.*   19,108
Graham Sutherland, *SNP*   8,492
Gordon Mackenzie, *LD*   3,969
Ian Mowat, *C.*   2,995
Ms Wendy Milne, *SSP*   1,110
Robert Kingdon, *UK Ind.*   359
Lab. majority 10,616 (29.46%)
1.02% swing SNP to Lab.
(1997, Lab. maj. 11,747 (27.43%))

MIDLOTHIAN
*E.*48,625 *T.* 28,724 (59.07%) Lab. hold
David Hamilton, *Lab.*   15,145
Ian Goldie, *SNP*   6,131
Ms Jacqueline Bell, *LD*   3,686
Robin Traquair, *C.*   2,748
Bob Goupillot, *SSP*   837
Terence Holden, *ProLife*   177
Lab. majority 9,014 (31.38%)
1.69% swing SNP to Lab.
(1997, Lab. maj. 9,870 (28.00%))

MORAY
*E.*58,008 *T.* 33,223 (57.27%) SNP hold
Angus Robertson, *SNP*   10,076
Mrs Catriona Munro, *Lab.*   8,332
Frank Spencer-Nairn, *C.*   7,677
Ms Linda Gorn, *LD*   5,224
Ms Norma Anderson, *SSP*   821
Bill Jappy, *Ind.*   802
Nigel Kenyon, *UK Ind.*   291
SNP majority 1,744 (5.25%)
8.25% swing SNP to Lab.
(1997, SNP maj. 5,566 (14.00%))

MOTHERWELL & WISHAW
*E.*52,418 *T.* 29,673 (56.61%) Lab. hold
*Frank Roy, *Lab.*   16,681
Jim McGuigan, *SNP*   5,725
Mark Nolan, *C.*   3,155
Iain Brown, *LD*   2,791
Stephen Smellie, *SSP*   1,260
Ms Claire Watt, *Soc. Lab.*   61
Lab. majority 10,956 (36.92%)
1.00% swing SNP to Lab.
(1997, Lab. maj. 12,791 (34.93%))

OCHIL
*E.*57,554 *T.* 35,303 (61.34%) Lab. hold
*Martin O'Neill, *Lab.*   16,004
Keith Brown, *SNP*   10,655
Alasdair Campbell, *C.*   4,235
Paul Edie, *LD*   3,253
Ms Pauline Thompson, *SSP*   751
Flash Gordon Approaching, *Loony*   405
Lab. majority 5,349 (15.15%)
2.26% swing SNP to Lab.
(1997, Lab. maj. 4,652 (10.63%))

ORKNEY & SHETLAND
*E.*31,909 *T.* 16,733 (52.44%) LD hold
Alistair Carmichael, *LD*   6,919
Robert Mochrie, *Lab.*   3,444
John Firth, *C.*   3,121
John Mowat, *SNP*   2,473

Peter Andrews, *SSP*   776
LD majority 3,475 (20.77%)
6.48% swing LD to Lab.
(1997, LD maj. 6,968 (33.72%))

PAISLEY NORTH
*E.*47,994 *T.* 27,153 (56.58%) Lab. hold
*Ms Irene Adams, *Lab.*   15,058
George Adam, *SNP*   5,737
Ms Jane Hook, *LD*   2,709
Craig Stevenson, *C.*   2,404
Jim Halfpenny, *SSP*   982
Robert Graham, *ProLife*   263
Lab. majority 9,321 (34.33%)
1.61% swing Lab. to SNP
(1997, Lab. maj. 12,814 (37.54%))

PAISLEY SOUTH
*E.*53,351 *T.* 30,536 (57.24%) Lab. hold
*Douglas Alexander, *Lab.*   17,830
Brian Lawson, *SNP*   5,920
Brian O'Malley, *LD*   3,178
Andrew Cossar, *C.*   2,301
Ms Frances Curran, *SSP*   835
Ms Patricia Graham, *ProLife*   346
Terence O'Donnell, *Ind.*   126
Lab. majority 11,910 (39.00%)
2.44% swing SNP to Lab.
(1997 Nov by-election, Lab. maj. 2,731)
(1997, Lab. maj. 12,750 (34.13%))

PERTH
*E.*61,497 *T.* 37,816 (61.49%) SNP hold
Ms Annabelle Ewing, *SNP*   11,237
Miss Elizabeth Smith, *C.*   11,189
Ms Marion Dingwall, *Lab.*   9,638
Ms Vicki Harris, *LD*   4,853
Frank Byrne, *SSP*   899
SNP majority 48 (0.13%)
3.46% swing SNP to C.
(1997, SNP maj. 3,141 (7.05%))

RENFREWSHIRE WEST
*E.*52,889 *T.* 33,497 (63.33%) Lab. gain
James Sheridan, *Lab.*   15,720
Ms Carol Puthucheary, *SNP*   7,145
David Sharpe, *C.*   5,522
Ms Clare Hamblen, *LD*   4,185
Ms Arlene Nunnery, *SSP*   925
Lab. majority 8,575 (25.60%)
2.77% swing SNP to Lab.
(1997, Lab. maj. 7,979 (20.05%))

ROSS, SKYE & INVERNESS
WEST
*E.*56,522 *T.* 34,812 (61.59%) LD hold
*Rt. Hon. C. Kennedy, *LD*   18,832
Donald Crichton, *Lab.*   5,880
Ms Jean Urquhart, *SNP*   4,901
Angus Laing, *C.*   3,096
Dr Eleanor Scott, *Green*   699
Stuart Topp, *SSP*   683
Philip Anderson, *UK Ind.*   456
James Crawford, *Country*   265
LD majority 12,952 (37.21%)
13.57% swing Lab. to LD
(1997, LD maj. 4,019 (10.06%))

ROXBURGH & BERWICKSHIRE
*E.*47,059 *T.* 28,797 (61.19%) LD hold
*Archy Kirkwood, *LD*   14,044

George Turnbull, *C.*   6,533
Ms C. Maxwell-Stuart, *Lab.*   4,498
Roderick Campbell, *SNP*   2,806
Ms Amanda Millar, *SSP*   463
Peter Neilson, *UK Ind.*   453
LD majority 7,511 (26.08%)
1.73% swing C. to LD
(1997, LD maj. 7,906 (22.63%))

STIRLING
*E.*53,097 *T.* 35,930 (67.67%) Lab. hold
*Ms Anne McGuire, *Lab.*   15,175
Geoff Mawdsley, *C.*   8,901
Ms Fiona Macaulay, *SNP*   5,877
Clive Freeman, *LD*   4,208
Dr Clarke Mullen, *SSP*   1,012
Mark Ruskell, *Green*   757
Lab. majority 6,274 (17.46%)
1.27% swing C. to Lab.
(1997, Lab. maj. 6,411 (14.93%))

STRATHKELVIN & BEARSDEN
*E.*62,729 *T.* 41,486 (66.14%) Lab. hold
John Lyons, *Lab.*   19,250
Gordon Macdonald, *LD*   7,533
Calum Smith, *SNP*   6,675
Murray Roxburgh, *C.*   6,635
Willie Telfer, *SSP*   1,393
Lab. majority 11,717 (28.24%)
7.44% swing Lab. to LD
(1997, Lab. maj. 16,292 (32.77%))

TAYSIDE NORTH
*E.*61,645 *T.* 38,517 (62.48%) SNP hold
Peter Wishart, *SNP*   15,441
Murdo Fraser, *C.*   12,158
Thomas Docherty, *Lab.*   5,715
Ms Julia Robertson, *LD*   4,363
Ms Rosie Adams, *SSP*   620
Ms Tina MacDonald, *Ind.*   220
SNP majority 3,283 (8.52%)
0.30% swing SNP to C.
(1997, SNP maj. 4,160 (9.13%))

TWEEDDALE, ETTRICK &
LAUDERDALE
*E.*51,966 *T.* 33,217 (63.92%) LD hold
*Michael Moore, *LD*   14,035
Keith Geddes, *Lab.*   8,878
Andrew Brocklehurst, *C.*   5,118
Richard Thomson, *SNP*   4,108
Norman Lockhart, *SSP*   695
John Hein, *Lib.*   383
LD majority 5,157 (15.53%)
5.86% swing Lab. to LD
(1997, LD maj. 1,489 (3.81%))

WESTERN ISLES
*E.*21,807 *T.* 13,159 (60.34%) Lab. hold
*Calum MacDonald, *Lab.*   5,924
Alasdair Nicholson, *SNP*   4,850
Douglas Taylor, *C.*   1,250
John Horne, *LD*   849
Ms Joanne Telfer, *SSP*   286
Lab. majority 1,074 (8.16%)
7.02% swing Lab. to SNP
(1997, Lab. maj. 3,576 (22.20%))

NORTHERN IRELAND

ANTRIM EAST
E.60,897 T.36,000 (59.12%) UUP hold
*Roy Beggs, UUP   13,101
Sammy Wilson, DUP   12,973
John Mathews, Alliance   4,483
Danny O'Connor, SDLP   2,641
Robert Mason, Ind   1,092
Ms Jeanette Graffin, SF   903
Alan Greer, C.   807
UUP majority 128 (0.36%)
9.48% swing UUP to DUP
(1997, UUP maj. 6,389 (18.60%))

ANTRIM NORTH
E.74,451 T.49,217 (66.11%) DUP hold
*Revd Ian Paisley, DUP   24,539
Lexie Scott, UUP   10,315
Sean Farren, SDLP   8,283
John Kelly, SF   4,822
Miss Jayne Dunlop, Alliance   1,258
DUP majority 14,224 (28.90%)
3.01% swing UUP to DUP
(1997, DUP maj. 10,574 (22.89%))

ANTRIM SOUTH
E.70,651 T.44,158 (62.50%) UUP gain
David Burnside, UUP   16,366
*Revd Robert McCrea, DUP   15,355
Sean McKee, SDLP   5,336
Martin Meehan, SF   4,160
David Ford, Alliance   1,969
Norman Boyd, NI Unionist   972
UUP majority 1,011 (2.29%)
10.21% swing UUP to DUP
(2000 Sep by-election, DUP maj. 822)
(1997, UUP maj. 16,611 (41.33%))

BELFAST EAST
E.58,455 T.36,829 (63.00%) DUP hold
*Peter Robinson, DUP   15,667
Tim Lemon, UUP   8,550
Dr David Alderdice, Alliance   5,832
David Ervine, PUP   3,669
Joe O'Donnell, SF   1,237
Ms Ciara Farren, SDLP   880
Terry Dick, C.   800
Joe Bell, WP   123
Rainbow George Weiss, Ind. Vote   71
DUP majority 7,117 (19.32%)
1.01% swing UUP to DUP
(1997, DUP maj. 6,754 (17.30%))

BELFAST NORTH
E.60,941 T.40,932 (67.17%) DUP gain
Nigel Dodds, DUP   16,718
Gerry Kelly, SF   10,331
Alban Maginness, SDLP   8,592
*Cecil Walker, UUP   4,904
Ms Marcella Delaney, WP   253
Rainbow George Weiss, Ind. Vote   134
DUP majority 6,387 (15.60%)
(1997, UUP maj. 13,024 (31.42%))

BELFAST SOUTH
E.59,436 T.37,952 (63.85%) UUP hold
*Revd Martin Smyth, UUP   17,008
Dr Alasdair McDonnell, SDLP   11,609
Prof Monica McWilliams (Women's
Co.)   2,968

Alex Maskey, SF   2,894
Ms Geraldine Rice, Alliance   2,042
Ms Dawn Purvis, PUP   1,112
Paddy Lynn, WP   204
Rainbow George Weiss, Ind. Vote   115
UUP majority 5,399 (14.23%)
1.29% swing SDLP to UUP
(1997, UUP maj. 4,600 (11.65%))

BELFAST WEST
E.59,617 T. 40,982 (68.74%) SF hold
*Gerry Adams, SF   27,096
Alex Attwood, SDLP   7,754
The Rev Eric Smyth, DUP   2,641
Chris McGimpsey, UUP   2,541
John Lowry, WP   736
Mr David Kerr, Third   116
Rainbow George Weiss, Ind. Vote   98
SF majority 19,342 (47.20%)
14.98% swing SDLP to SF
(1997, SF maj. 7,909 (17.24%))

DOWN NORTH
E.63,212 T.37,189 (58.83%) UUP gain
Lady Sylvia Hermon, UUP   20,833
*Robert McCartney, UKU   13,509
Ms Marietta Farrell, SDLP   1,275
Julian Robertson, C.   815
Chris Carter, Ind   444
Eamon McConvey, SF   313
UUP majority 7,324 (19.69%)
11.83% swing UKU to UUP
(1997, UKU maj. 1,449 (3.96%))

DOWN SOUTH
E.73,519 T. 52,074 (70.83%) SDLP hold
*Eddie McGrady, SDLP   24,136
Mick Murphy, SF   10,278
Dermot Nesbitt, UUP   9,173
Jim Wells, DUP   7,802
Ms Betty Campbell, Alliance   685
SDLP majority 13,858 (26.61%)
7.97% swing SDLP to SF
(1997, SDLP maj. 9,933 (20.08%))

FERMANAGH & SOUTH TYRONE
E.66,640 T. 51,974 (77.99%) SF gain
Ms Michelle Gildernew, SF   17,739
James Cooper, UUP   17,686
Tommy Gallagher, SDLP   9,706
Jim Dixon, Ind. UU   6,843
SF majority 53 (0.10%)
14.22% swing UUP to SF
(1997, UUP maj. 13,688 (28.34%))

FOYLE
E.70,943 T. 48,879 (68.90%) SDLP hold
*John Hume, SDLP   24,538
Mitchel McLaughlin, SF   12,988
William Hay, DUP   7,414
Andrew Davidson, UUP   3,360
Colm Cavanagh, Alliance   579
SDLP majority 11,550 (23.63%)
2.47% swing SDLP to SF
(1997, SDLP maj. 13,664 (28.57%))

LAGAN VALLEY
E.72,671 T.45,941 (63.22%) UUP hold
*Jeffrey Donaldson, UUP   25,966
Seamus Close, Alliance   7,624

Edwin Poots, DUP   6,164
Ms Patricia Lewsley, SDLP   3,462
Paul Butler, SF   2,725
UUP majority 18,342 (39.93%)
0.86% swing Alliance to UUP
(1997, UUP maj. 16,925 (38.20%))

LONDONDERRY EAST
E.60,276 T.39,862 (66.14%) DUP gain
Gregory Campbell, DUP   12,813
*William Ross, UUP   10,912
John Dallat, SDLP   8,298
Francie Brolly, SF   6,221
Mrs Yvonne Boyle, Alliance   1,625
DUP majority 1,901 (4.77%)
7.36% swing UUP to DUP
(1997, UUP maj. 3,794 (9.95%))

NEWRY & ARMAGH
E.72,466 T. 55,621 (76.75%) SDLP hold
*Seamus Mallon, SDLP   20,784
Conor Murphy, SF   17,209
Paul Berry, DUP   10,795
Mrs Sylvia McRoberts, UUP   6,833
SDLP majority 3,575 (6.43%)
7.75% swing SDLP to SF
(1997, SDLP maj. 4,889 (9.17%))

STRANGFORD
E.72,192 T.43,254 (59.92%) DUP gain
Mrs Iris Robinson, DUP   18,532
*David McNarry, UUP   17,422
Kieran McCarthy, Alliance   2,902
Danny McCarthy, SDLP   2,646
Liam Johnstone, SF   930
Cedric Wilson, NI Unionist   822
DUP majority 1,110 (2.57%)
8.32% swing UUP to DUP
(1997, UUP maj. 5,852 (14.07%))

TYRONE WEST
E.60,739 T. 48,530 (79.90%) SF gain
Pat Doherty, SF   19,814
*William Thompson, UUP   14,774
Ms Brid Rodgers, SDLP   13,942
SF majority 5,040 (10.39%)
7.05% swing UUP to SF
(1997, UUP maj. 1,161 (2.51%))

ULSTER MID
E.61,390 T.49,936 (81.34%) SF hold
*Martin McGuinness, SF   25,502
Ian McCrea, DUP   15,549
Ms Eilis Haughey, SDLP   8,376
Francie Donnelly, WP   509
SF majority 9,953 (19.93%)
8.11% swing DUP to SF
(1997, SF maj. 1,883 (3.71%))

UPPER BANN
E.72,574 T.51,036 (70.32%) UUP hold
*Rt. Hon. D. Trimble, UUP   17,095
David Simpson, DUP   15,037
Dr Dara O'Hagan, SF   10,770
Ms Dolores Kelly, SDLP   7,607
Tom French, WP   527
UUP majority 2,058 (4.03%)
14.05% swing UUP to DUP
(1997, UUP maj. 9,252 (19.36%))

BY-ELECTIONS SINCE THE 1997 GENERAL ELECTION

UXBRIDGE
(31 July 1997)
E.57,446 T.55.5%

J. Randall, C.	16,288
A. Slaughter, Lab.	12,522
K. Kerr, LD	1,792
'Lord Sutch', Loony	396
Ms J. Leonard, Soc.	259
Ms F. Taylor, BNP	205
I. Anderson, Nat. Dem.	157
J. McCauley, NF	110
H. Middleton, Original Lib. Party	69
J. Feisenberger, UK Ind.	39
R. Carroll, Emerald Rainbow Islands Dream Ticket	30
C. majority	3,766

PAISLEY SOUTH
(6 November 1997)
E.54,386 T.43.1%

D. Alexander, Lab.	10,346
I. Blackford, SNP	7,615
Ms E. McCartin, LD	2,582
Ms S. Laidlaw, C.	1,643
J. Deighan, ProLife	578
F. Curran, Soc. All. Fighting Corruption	306
C. McLauchlan, Scottish Ind. Lab.	155
C. Herriot, Soc. Lab.	153
K. Blair, NLP	57
Lab. majority	2,731

BECKENHAM
(20 November 1997)
E.73,232 T.43.6%

Ms J. Lait, C.	13,162
R. Hughes, Lab.	11,935
Ms R. Vetterlein, LD	5,864
P. Rimmer, Lib.	330
J. McAuley, NF	267
L. Mead, New Britain Ref.	237
T. Campion, Social Foundation	69
J. Small, NLP	44
C. majority	1,227

WINCHESTER
(20 November 1997)
E.79,116 T.68.7%

M. Oaten, LD	37,006
G. Malone, C.	15,450
P. Davies, Lab.	944
R. Page, Ref./UK Ind.	521
Lord' Sutch, Loony	316
R. Huggett, Literal Dem.	59
Ms R. Barry, NLP	48
R. Everest, European C.	40
LD majority	21,556

LEEDS CENTRAL
(10 June 1999)
E.67,280 T.19.6%

H. Benn, Lab.	6,361
P. Wild, LD	4,068
E. Wild, C.	1,618
D. Blackburn, Green	478
R. Northgreaves, UK Ind.	353
C. Hill, C.	258
J. Fitzgerald, Equal Parenting Campaign	51
Lab. majority	2,293

EDDISBURY
(22 July 1999)
E.67,086 T.51.4 %

S. O'Brien, C.	15,465

Ms M. Hanson, Lab.	13,859
P. Roberts, LD	4,757
A. Hope, Loony	238
R. Everest, Ind. Euro C.	98
Ms D. Grice, NLP	80
C. majority	1,606

WIGAN
(23 September 1999)
E.64,775 T.25.0%

N. Turner, Lab.	9,641
T. Peet, C.	2,912
J. Rule, LD	2,148
J. Whittaker, UK Ind.	834
W. Kelly, Soc. Lab.	240
C. Maile, Green	190
S. Ebbs, Nat. Dem. Res.	100
P. Davis, NLP	64
D. Braid, Rev.	58
C. majority	6,729

HAMILTON SOUTH
(23 September 1999)
E.47,081 T.41.3%

B. Tynan, Lab.	7,172
A. Ewing, SNP	6,616
S. Blackall, SSP	1,847
C. Ferguson, C.	1,406
S. Mungall, Watson	1,075
M. MacLaren, LD	634
M. Burns, ProLife.	257
T. Dewar, Soc. Lab.	238
J. Reid, SU	113
A. McConnachie, UK Ind.	61
G. Stidolph, NLP	18
J. Moray, SQ	17
Lab. majority	556

KENSINGTON AND CHELSEA
(25 November 1999)
E.65,806 T.29.7%

Rt. Hon. M. Portillo, C.	11,004
R. Atkinson, Lab.	4,298
R. Woodthorpe Browne, LD	1,831
J. Stevens, ProECP	740
D. Hockney, UK Ind.	450
H. Charlton, Green	446
C. de Vere Beauclerk, Dem.	182
C. Paisley, LCA	141
M. Irwin, LWLC	97
G. Oliver, UKPP	75
S. Scott-Fawcett, Ref.	57
L. Hodges, DSSP	48
G. Valente, NLP	35
L. Lovebucket, PNDTP	26
J. Davies, Ind. ESCC	24
P. May, EPP	24
A. Hope, Loony	20
T. Samuelson, Stop	15
C. majority	6,706

CEREDIGION
(3 February 2000)
E.55,025 T. 45.6%

S. Thomas, PC	10,716
M. Williams, LD	5,768
P. Davies, C.	4,138
M. Battle, Lab.	3,612
J. Bufton, UK Ind.	487
J. Berkeley Davies, Ind. Green	289
M. Shipton, Match.	55
PC majority	4,948

ROMSEY
(4 May 2000)
E.69,701 T. 55.5%

S. Gidley, LD	19,571
T. Palmer, C	16,260

A. Howard, Lab	1,451
G. Rankin-Moore, UK Ind	901
D. Large, LCA	417
T. Lamont, Ind	109
LD majority	3,311

TOTTENHAM
(22 June 2000)
E.64,554 T.25.4%

D. Lammy, Lab.	8,785
D. Hames, LD	3,139
J. Ellison, C	2,634
W. Bennett, London Soc. All.	885
P. Budge, Green	606
E. Basarik, Reform 2000	177
A. Tanna, UK Ind	136
D. de Braam, Ind. C.	55
Lab. majority	5,646

SOUTH ANTRIM
(21 September 2000)
E.71,047 T.43.0%

W. McCrea, DUP	11,601
D. Burnside, UUP	10,779
D. McClelland, SDLP	3,496
M. Meehan, SF	2,611
D. Ford, Alliance	2,031
D. Collins, NLP	49
DUP majority	822

PRESTON
(23 November 2000)
E.72,229 T.29.6%

M. Hendrick, Lab	9,765
G. O'Hare, C.	5,339
W. Chadwick, LD	3,454
T. Cartwright, Lancashire Social Alliance	1,210
G. Beaman, UK Ind	458
R. Merrick, Green	441
P Garrett, Preston Alliance, Christian People's Alliance	416
C. Jackson, BNP	229
D. Franklin-Braid, Battle of Britain Christian Alliance	51
Lab. majority	4,426

WEST BROMWICH WEST
(23 November 2000)
E.68,408 T.27.6%

A. Bailey, Lab	9,640
K. Bissell, C.	6,408
S. Smith, LD	1,791
N. Griffin, BNP	794
J. Oakton, UK Ind	246
Lab. majority	3,232

GLASGOW, ANNIESLAND
(23 November 2000)
E.52,609 T.38.4%

J. Robertson, Lab	10,539
G. Thomas, SNP	4,202
D. Luckhurst, C.	2,188
C. McGinty, LD	1,630
C. McCarthy, Scottish Socialist	1,441
W. Lyden, Family	212
Lab. majority	6,337

FALKIRK WEST
(21 December 2000)
E.53,851 T.36.2%

E. Joyce, Lab	8,492
D. Kerr, SNP	7,787
C. Stevenson C.	1,621
I. Hunter, Scottish Socialist	989
H O'Donnell, LD	615
Lab. majority	705

RETIRING MPS

Ashdown, Rt. Hon. Sir Paddy; KBE, *LD*, *Yeovil*; Ashton, Joe, *Lab.*, *Bassetlaw*; Benn, Rt. Hon. Tony, *Lab.*, *Chesterfield*; Bermingham, Gerry, *Lab.*, *St Helens South*; Body, Sir Richard, *C.*, *Boston & Skegness*; Brooke, Rt. Hon. Peter; CH, *C.*, *Cities of London & Westminster*; Campbell-Savours, Dale, *Lab.*, *Workington*; Chisholm, Malcolm; MSP, *Lab.*, *Edinburgh North & Leith*; Church, Judith, *Lab.*, *Dagenham*; Clark, Rt. Hon. Dr David, *Lab.*, *South Shields*; Clark, Dr Michael, *C.*, *Rayleigh*; Clarke, Eric, *Lab.*, *Midlothian*; Corbett, Robin, *Lab.*, *Birmingham Erdington*; Cunliffe, Lawrence, *Lab.*, *Leigh*; Cunningham, Roseanna; MSP, *SNP*, *Perth*; Davies, Rt. Hon. Ron; AM, *Lab.*, *Caerphilly*; Emery, Rt. Hon. Sir Peter, *C.*, *Devon East*; Ewing, Margaret; MSP, *SNP*, *Moray*; Faber, David, *C.*, *Westbury*; Fearn, Ronnie; OBE, *LD*, *Southport*; Fowler, Rt. Hon. Sir Norman, *C.*, *Sutton Coldfield*; Fyfe, Maria, *Lab.*, *Glasgow Maryhill*; Galbraith, Sam; MSP, *Lab.*, *Strathkelvin & Bearsden*; Gill, Christopher; RD, *C.*, *Ludlow*; Godman, Dr Norman A, *Lab.*, *Greenock & Inverclyde*; Golding, Llin, *Lab.*, *Newcastle-under-Lyme*; Gorman, Teresa, *C.*, *Billericay*; Gorrie, Donald; MSP, *LD*, *Edinburgh West*; Graham, Thomas, *Scot Lab.*, *Renfrewshire West*; Grocott, Bruce, *Lab.*, *Telford*; Gunnell, John, *Lab.*, *Morley & Rothwell*; Hamilton, Rt. Hon. Sir Archibald, *C.*, *Epsom & Ewell*; Heath, Rt. Hon. Sir Edward; KG MBE, *C.*, *Old Bexley & Sidcup*; Heseltine, Rt. Hon. Michael; CH, *C.*, *Henley*; Home Robertson, John; MSP, *Lab.*, *East Lothian*; Johnson Smith, Rt. Hon. Sir Geoffrey, *C.*, *Wealden*; Jones, Ieuan Wyn, AM, *PC*, *Ynys Mon*; Jones, Jenny, *Lab.*, *Wolverhampton South West*; Jones, Rt. Hon. Barry, *Lab.*, *Alyn & Deeside*; King, Rt. Hon. Tom; CH, *C.*, *Bridgwater*; Kingham, Tess, *Lab.*, *Gloucester*; Livingstone, Ken, *Ind.*, *Brent East*; Livsey, Richard, *LD*, *Brecon & Radnorshire*; Lloyd, Rt. Hon. Sir Peter, *C.*, *Fareham*; Lyell, Rt. Hon. Sir Nicholas; QC, *C.*, *Bedfordshire North East*; MacGregor, Rt. Hon. John; OBE, *C.*, *Norfolk South*; Maclennan, Rt. Hon. Robert, *LD*, *Caithness, Sutherland & Easter Ross*; Madel, Sir David, *C.*, *Bedfordshire South West*; Maginnis, Ken, *UU*, *Fermanagh & South Tyrone*; Major, Rt. Hon. John; CH, *C.*, *Huntingdon*; Marek, Dr John; MP, *Lab.*, *Wrexham*; Maxton, John, *Lab.*, *Glasgow Cathcart*; McAllion, John; MSP, *Lab.*, *Dundee East*; McLeish, Rt. Hon. Henry; MSP, *Lab.*, *Fife Central*; Michie, Bill, *Lab.*, *Sheffield Heeley*; Michie, Hon Janet Ray, *LD*, *Argyll & Bute*; Morgan, Alasdair; MSP, *SNP*, *Galloway & Upper Nithsdale*; Morgan, Rt. Hon. Rhodri; AM, *Lab.*, *Cardiff West*; Morris, Rt. Hon. Sir John; QC, *Lab.*, *Aberavon*; Mowlam, Rt. Hon. Mo, *Lab.*, *Redcar*; Pendry, Rt. Hon. Tom, *Lab.*, *Stalybridge & Hyde*; Radice, Rt. Hon. Giles, *Lab.*, *Durham North*; Rogers, Allan R, *Lab.*, *Rhondda*; Rooker, Rt. Hon. Jeff, *Lab.*, *Birmingham Perry Barr*; Rowe, Andrew, *C.*, *Faversham & Mid Kent*; Rowlands, Ted, *Lab.*, *Merthyr Tydfil & Rhymney*; Sheldon, Rt. Hon. Robert, *Lab.*, *Ashton-under-Lyne*; Snape, Peter, *Lab.*, *West Bromwich East*; Swinney, John; MSP, *SNP*, *Tayside North*; Taylor, Rt. Hon. Dr John D, *UU*, *Strangford*; Temple-Morris, Peter, *Lab.*, *Leominster*; Townend, John, *C.*, *Yorkshire East*; Wallace, Rt. Hon. Jim; QC, MSP, *LD*, *Orkney & Shetland*; Wardle, Charles, *Ind.*, *Bexhill & Battle*; Wells, Bowen, *C.*, *Hertford & Stortford*; Welsh, Andrew; MSP. MP, *SNP*, *Angus*; Whitney, Sir Raymond; OBE, *C.*, *Wycombe*; Wigley, Rt. Hon. Dafydd; AM, *PC*, *Caernarfon*

DEFEATED MPS

Balard, Jackie, *LD*, *Taunton*; Bell, Martin, *Ind.*, *Tatton (contesting Brentwood and Ongar)*; Brand, Dr Peter, *LD*, *Isle of Wight*; Bruce, Ian, *C.*, *Dorset South*; Butler, Christine, *Lab.*, *Castle Point*; Darvill, Keith, *Lab.*, *Upminster*; Day, Stephen, *C.*, *Cheadle*; Fraser, Christopher, *C.*, *Dorset Mid and Poole North*; Gordon, Eileen, *Lab.*, *Romford*; Jones, Fiona, *Lab.*, *Newark*; Lock, David, *Lab.*, *Wyre Forest*; McCartney, Robert, *UK Unionist*, *Down North*; McCrea, Rev. Dr William, *DUP*, *Antrim South*; Nicholls, Patrick, *C.*, *Teignbridge*; Prior, David, *C.*, *Norfolk North*; Ross, William, *UU*, *Londonderry East*; St Aubyn, Nick, *C.*, *Guildford*; Thompson, William, *UU*, *Tyrone West*; Turner, Dr. George, *Lab.*, *Norfolk North West*; Walker, Cecil, *UU*, *Belfast North*; Wynne Williams, Alan, *Lab.*, *Carmarthen East and Dinefwr*

DEFEATED MPS BY PARTY

Labour,	7
Conservative,	6
Ulster Unionist,	3
Liberal Democrat,	2
Democratic Unionist Party,	1
Independent,	1
United Kingdom Unionist,	1
TOTAL	21

Regional Government

GREATER LONDON AUTHORITY (GLA)
Romney House, 43 Marsham Street, London SW21P 3PY
Tel: 020-7983 4000; Press Office: 020-7983 4071/4072/
4090/4067/4228; Email: mayor@london.gov.uk;
Web: www.london.gov.uk

On the 7 May 1998 London voted in favour of the formation of the Greater London Authority. The first elections
to the GLA were on Thursday, 4 May 2000 and the new
Authority took over its responsibilities on 3 July 2000.

The structure and objectives of the GLA stem from its
eight main areas of responsibility. These are transport,
planning, economic development and regeneration, the
environment, police, fire and emergency planning, culture
and health. The bodies that co-ordinate these functions
and report to the GLA are: Transport for London (TfL),
London Development Agency (LDA), Metropolitan
Police Authority (MPA), London Fire and Emergency
Planning Authority (LFEPA). The GLA also absorbs a
number of other London bodies, such as the London
Planning Advisory Committee, the London Ecology Unit
and the London Research Centre.

The GLA consists of a directly elected Mayor, The
Mayor of London and a separately elected assembly, The
London Assembly. The Mayor has the key role of decision
making with the Assembly performing the tasks of
regulating and scrutinising these decisions. In addition,
the GLA has around 400 permanent staff to support the
activities of the Mayor and the Assembly, which are
overseen by a Head of Paid Service. The Mayor may
appoint two political advisors but he/she may not appoint
the Chief Executive the Monitoring Officer or the Chief
Finance Officer. These must be appointed by the
Assembly.

The Mayor is also responsible for appointing a Cabinet.
The Cabinet functions as part of the Mayor's objective of
eliminating barriers to effective decision making and
enabling the GLA to speak with one voice on behalf of
London. The function of the Mayor's Cabinet is to
provide the Mayor with the most sound advice on policy
and strategy. Meetings of the Cabinet are designed to be a
powerful forum for discussing the issues affecting
Londoners. The Cabinet is not intended to fit the
Whitehall Cabinet model in that GLA members will not
be bound by the convention of collective responsibility,
the absence of which does not mean that the Mayor will
devolve or federalise his powers. All decisions are made by
the Mayor acting on the honest advice of his Cabinet.
Cabinet members can be broadly categorised into (a) those
with specific policy brief (e.g. in the areas of planning,
policing or fire and civil defence) and (b) those who have
been chosen to give advice and/or reflect political breadth.

The role of the Mayor can be broken down into a
number of key areas: to represent and promote London at
home and abroad and speak up for Londoners; to devise
strategies and plans to tackle London-wide issues, such as
transport, economic development and regeneration, air
quality, noise, waste, bio-diversity, planning and culture;
to set budgets for the Transport for London, the London
Development Agency, the Metropolitan Police Authority
and the London Fire and Emergency Planning Authority;
to control new transport and economic development
bodies and appoint their members; to make appointments
to the new police and fire authorities; to publish regular
reports on the state of the environment in London.

The role of the Assembly can be broken down into a
number of key areas:

- to provide a check and balance on the Mayor
- to scrutinise the Mayor
- to have the power to amend the Mayor's budget by a
  majority of 2/3
- to investigate issues of London wide significance and
  make proposals to the Mayor
- to provide the Deputy Mayor and the members serving
  on the police, fire and emergency planning authorities.

ELECTIONS AND THE VOTING SYSTEMS

The Assembly will be elected every four years at the same
time as the Mayor and consists of 25 members. There is
one member from each of the 14 GLA Constituencies
topped up with 11 London members who are representatives of political parties or individuals standing as
independent candidates.

The GLA constituencies are: Barnet and Camden;
Bexley and Bromley; Brent and Harrow; City and London
East, covering Barking and Dagenham and the City of
London; Newham and Tower Hamlets; Croydon and
Sutton; Ealing and Hillingdon; Enfield and Haringey;
Greenwich and Lewisham; Havering and Redbridge;
North East, covering Hackney, Islington and Waltham
Forest; Lambeth and Southwark; West Central, covering
Hammersmith and Fulham, Kensington and Chelsea and
Westminster; South West, covering Hounslow, Kingston
upon Thames and Richmond upon Thames; Merton and
Wandsworth.

FUNCTIONS AND STRUCTURE

Every aspect of the Assembly and its activities must be
open to the view of the public and therefore accountable.
Assembly meetings are open to the public and the reports
it produces are available to the public. Other measures
such as a twice yearly 'people's question time' also take
place. The meetings where the Assembly questions the
Mayor are also open to the public.

FUNDING

The GLA is responsible for funding Transport for
London, the London Development Agency, the Metro-
politan Police Authority and the London Fire and
Emergency Planning Authority. Budgets are set by the
Mayor, and scrutinised by the Assembly. Funds are
allocated subject to safeguards on service standards

TRANSPORT FOR LONDON (TfL)

The TfL is run by a board of 8-15 members appointed by
the Mayor. Its role is:

- to manage the buses, Croydon Tramlink and the
  Docklands Light Railway (DLR).
- to manage the underground once Public Private
  partnership contracts are in place
- to manage an important network of roads to be known as
  the GLA Road Network
- to regulate taxis and minicabs
- to run the London River services and promote the river
  for passenger and freight movement
- to help to co-ordinate the Dial-a-Ride and Taxicard
  schemes for door-to-door services for transport users
  with mobility problems
- to take responsibility for traffic lights

London Borough Councils maintain the role of highway and traffic authorities for 95 per cent of London's roads.

Transport Commissioner for London, Robert Kiley

SPATIAL DEVELOPMENT STRATEGY (SDS)

The Mayor of London is responsible for strategic planning in London in the form of a Spatial Planning Strategy. This sets priorities and provides direction for the future development of London. It replaces regional planning guidance provided by the Secretary of State. The SDS incorporates the key aspects of the many other areas of the Mayor's responsibility including sustainable development, transport, economic development, housing, the built environment, the natural and open environment, waste, town centres, cultural and community facilities, London's Capital and World City roles and the River Thames.

London Borough Councils continue to deal with all planning applications and produce development plans.

LONDON DEVELOPMENT AGENCY (LDA)

The LDA promotes economic development and regeneration. It is one of the eight regional development agencies set up around the country to perform this task. The key aspects of the LDA's role are:

- to promote business efficiency, investment and competitiveness
- to promote employment
- to enhance the skills of local people
- to create sustainable development

The London Boroughs retain powers to promote economic development in their local areas.

THE ENVIRONMENT

The Mayor is required to formulate strategies to tackle London's environmental issues including the quality of water, air and land; the use of energy and London's contribution to climate change targets; ground water levels and traffic emissions; municipal waste management.

METROPOLITAN POLICE AUTHORITY (MPA)

This body, which oversees the policing of London consists of 12 members of the assembly, including the deputy Mayor, 4 magistrates and 7 independents. One of the independents was appointed by the Home Secretary. The role of the MPA is:

- to maintain an efficient and effective police force
- to publish and annual policing plan
- to set police targets and monitor performance
- to be part of the appointment, discipline and removal of senior officers
- to be responsible for the performance budget

The boundaries of the metropolitan police districts have been changed to be in line with the 32 London boroughs. Areas beyond the GLA remit have been incorporated into the Surrey, Hertfordshire and Essex police areas. The City of London has its own police force.

LONDON FIRE AND EMERGENCY PLANNING AUTHORITY (LFEPA)

On 3 July 2000 the existing London Fire and Civil defence authority became the London Fire and Emergency Planning Authority. It consists of 17 members, 9 drawn from the assembly and 8 nominated by the London Boroughs. The role of LFEPA is:

- to set the strategy for the provision of fire services

- to ensure that the fire brigade can meet all the normal requirements efficiently
- to ensure that effective arrangements are made for the fire brigade to receive emergency calls and deal with them promptly
- to ensure that information useful to the development of the fire brigades is gathered
- to assist the boroughs with their emergency planning training and exercises.

HEALTH

Healthcare in London continues to be the remit of the NHS and the London Ambulance Service. The NHS London Regional Office are fully supported by the GLA in its development of strategies to improve the health of Londoners.

THE CULTURAL STRATEGY GROUP FOR LONDON (CSGL)

The GLA aims to provide a wide ranging culture strategy, encompassing the arts, sport and tourism. The CSGL provides advice and guidance to the GLA on this matter. Its role is:

- to produce a strategy for the cultural development of London
- to endorse and bid for major sporting events which London may host
- to develop the creative industries' contribution to the London economy
- to take over management of Trafalgar Square and Parliament Square
- to develop a policy for the development of tourism in London

The GLA will be housed at the temporary address shown above until its new premises are complete. The new GLA building is being built on a brown field site on the south bank of the river Thames, adjacent to Tower Bridge. The building is a distinctive glass globe with a purpose built assembly chamber and offices for 400 people. It will stand fifty metres high, with 21,700 square metres of floor space.

SALARIES *as at March 2001*

Mayor,	£86,832
Deputy Mayor,	£53,243
Assembly Member,	£35,436

MAYOR'S ADVISORY CABINET

Deputy Mayor and Spatial development and strategic planning, Nicky Gavron
Police, Toby Harris
Human rights and equalities, Graham Tope
Chair, London Fire and Emergency Planning Authority, Val Shawcross
Environment, Darren Johnson
City and business, Judith Mayhew
Homelessness, Glenda Jackson
Consultation and local government, John McDonnell
Chair of the London Development Agency, George Barlow
Regeneration, Kumar Murshid
Race relations, Lee Jasper
Women and equality, Diane Abbott
Community relations, Richard Stone
London Voluntary Services Council, Sean Baine
Disability rights, Caroline Gooding

GREATER LONDON ASSEMBLY MEMBERS
as at 31 July 2001

The Mayor, Ken Livingstone (*Ind.*)
Anderson, Victor (*Green*), *London List*
Arnold, Jeanette Arnold (*Lab.*) *London List*
Arbour, Anthony (*C.*), *South West,* maj. 7,059
Barnes, Richard (*C.*), *Ealing and Hillingdon,* maj. 6,812
Briggs, John (*Lab.*), *City and East,* maj. 26,121
Bloom, Louise (*LD*), *London List*
Bray, Angie (*C.*), *West Central,* maj. 18,279
Coleman, Brian (*C.*), *Barnet and Camden,* maj. 551
Duvall, Len (*Lab.*), *Greenwich and Lewisham,* maj. 17,985
Evans, Jeremy Roger (*C.*), *Havering and Redbridge,* maj. 8,269
Featherstone, Lynne (*LD*), *London List*

Gavron, Nicky (*Lab.*), *Enfield and Haringey,* maj. 3,302
Hamwee, Baroness (Sally) (*LD*), *London List*
Harris, Lord Toby (*Lab.*), *Brent and Harrow,* maj. 4,380
Heath, Samantha (*Lab.*), *London List*
Hillier, Meg (*Lab.*), *North East,* maj. 17,603
Howlett, Elizabeth (*C.*), *Merton and Wandsworth,* maj. 12,870
Johnson, Darren (*Green*), *London List*
Jones, Jennifer (*Green*), *London List*
Neill, Bob (*C.*), *Bexley and Bromley,* maj. 34,559
Ollerenshaw, Eric (*C.*), *London List*
Pelling, Andrew John (*C.*), *Croydon and Sutton,* maj. 17,087
Phillips, Trevor (*Lab.*), *London List*
Shawcross, Valerie (*Lab.*), *Lambeth and Southwark,* maj. 15,493
Tope, Graham (*LD*), *London List*

OVERALL RESULTS IN MAYORAL ELECTION AS AT MAY 2000

First Pref	*Party*	*Votes*	%
Ken Livingstone	Ind.	667,877	39.0
Steven Norris	C.	464,434	27.1
Frank Dobson	Lab.	223,884	13.1
Susan Kramer	LD	203,452	11.9
Ram Gidoomal	CPA	42,060	2.4
Darren Johnson	Green	38,121	2.2
Michael Newland	BNP	33,569	2.0
Damian Hockney	UK Ind	16,234	1.0
Geoffrey Ben-Nathan	PMSS	9,956	0.6
Ashwin Kumar Tanna	Ind.	9,015	0.5
Geoffrey Clements	Natural Law Party	5,470	0.3

Second Pref	*Party*	*Votes*	%
Susan Kramer	LD	404,815	28.5
Frank Dobson	Lab.	228,095	16.0
Darren Johnson	Green	192,764	13.6
Steven Norris	C.	188,041	13.2
Ken Livingstone	Ind.	178,809	12.6
Ram Gidoomal	CPA	56,489	4.0
Michael Newland	BNP	45,337	3.2
Damian Hockney	UK Ind.	43,672	3.1
Ashwin Kumar Tanna	Ind.	41,766	2.9
Geoffrey Ben-Nathan	PMSS	23,021	1.6
Geoffrey Clements	Natural Law Party	18,185	1.3

THE NATIONAL ASSEMBLY FOR WALES

Cathays Park, Cardiff CF1 3NQ
Tel: 029-2082 5111
National Assembly Information Line: 029-2089 8200
E-mail: webmaster@wales.gov.uk
Web: www.wales.gov.uk

In July 1997 the Government announced plans to establish a National Assembly for Wales. In a referendum on 18 September 1997 about 50 per cent of the electorate voted, of whom 50.3 per cent voted in favour of the Assembly. Elections are to be held every four years. The First elections were held on 6 May 1999 when about 46 per cent of the electorate voted. The first session was held on 10 May 1999 and the Assembly was officially opened on 26 May at Crickhowell House, Cardiff; a new building to house the Assembly is under construction in Cardiff.
    The Assembly has 60 members (including the Presiding Officer), comprising 40 constituency members and 20 additional regional members from party lists. It can introduce only secondary legislation and has no power to raise or lower income tax.
    The National Assembly for Wales has responsibility in Wales for ministerial functions relating to health and personal social services; education, except for terms and conditions of service and student awards; training; the Welsh language, arts and culture; the implementation of the Citizen's Charter in Wales; local government; housing; water and sewerage; environmental protection; sport; agriculture and fisheries; forestry; land use, including town and country planning and countryside and nature conservation; new towns; non-departmental public bodies and appointments in Wales; ancient monuments and historic buildings and the Welsh Arts Council; roads; tourism; financial assistance to industry; the Strategic Development Scheme in Wales and the Programme for the Valleys; and the operation of the European Regional Development Fund in Wales and other European Union matters.

SALARIES FROM 1 APRIL 2001:

First Secretary	£68,158
Assembly Secretary/Presiding Officer	£35,357
Assembly Members	£38,000*

*Reduced by two-thirds if the member is already an MP or an MEP
First Secretary, Assembly Member and Presiding Officer also receive the Assembly Member salary

THE WELSH CABINET
First Secretary of the Assembly and Acting Minister for Economic Development, Rhodri Morgan, AM
Principal Private Secretary, L. Conway
Special Advisers, P. Griffiths; M. Drakeford; Dr R. Jones; L. Punter; N. Bennett; M. Hines
Deputy First Minister (acting), Jenny Randerson, AM
Minister for Education and Lifelong Learning, Jane Davidson, AM
Minister for Health and Social Services, Jane Hutt, AM
Minister for Finance and Communities, Edwina Hunt, AM
Minister for Rural Affairs, Carwyn Jones, AM
Minister for Environment, Planning and Transport, Sue Essex, AM
Minister for Sport, Culture and the Welsh Language, Jenny Randerson, AM
Minister for Assembly Business, Andrew Davies, AM
Permanent Secretary (G1), J. D. Shortridge
Clerk to the Assembly, P. Silk , CB

OFFICE OF THE PRESIDING OFFICER
Deputy Clerk (G3), vacant

COMMITTEE SECRETARIAT
Grade 5, Ms M. Knox

CABINET EXECUTIVE
Head, B. Mitchell

CABINET SECRETARIAT
Grade 5, L. Conway

OFFICE OF THE COUNSEL GENERAL
Counsel General, W. Roddick, QC

COMMUNICATIONS DIRECTORATE
Head, M. Brooke

FINANCE GROUP
Principal Finance Officer (G3), D. T. Richards

ECONOMIC AFFAIRS, TRANSPORT, PLANNING AND ENVIRONMENT
Senior Director (G2), D. W. Jones

AGRICULTURE DEPARTMENT
Head of Department (G3), H. D. Brodie

ECONOMIC DEVELOPMENT DEPARTMENT
Head of Department (G3), D. Pritchard

SOCIAL POLICY AND LOCAL GOVERNMENT
Senior Director (G2), G. C. G. Craig

TRAINING AND EDUCATION DEPARTMENT
Head of Department (G3), R. J. Davies

OFFICE OF HM CHIEF INSPECTOR FOR SCHOOLS IN WALES – ESTYN
†*Chief Inspector (G4)*, Miss S. Lewis

SOCIAL SERVICES AND COMMUNITIES GROUP
Director, Ms H. Thomas

LOCAL GOVERNMENT GROUP
Head of Group (G3), A. Peat

NHS DIRECTORATE
Director (G3), vacant

HEALTH PROTECTION AND IMPROVEMENT DIRECTORATE
Chief Medical Officer (G3), Dr R. Hall
Chief Dental Officer (G5), P. Langmaid
Chief Scientific Adviser (G5), Dr J. A. V. Pritchard
Chief Pharmaceutical Adviser (G5), Miss C. W. Howells
Chief Environmental Health Adviser (G5), R. Alexander

NURSING DIVISION
Chief Nursing Officer, Miss R. Kennedy

TRANSPORT, PLANNING AND ENVIRONMENT GROUP
Head of Group (G3), M. L. Evans
Director of Transport (G4), R. Shaw

EXECUTIVE AGENCIES
CADW: WELSH HISTORIC MONUMENTS
Crown Building, Cathays Park, Cardiff CF1 3NQ
Tel: 029-2050 0200; Fax: 029-2082 6375

Cadw supports the preservation, conservation, appreciation and enjoyment of the built heritage in Wales.
Chief Executive, T. Cassidy

PLANNING INSPECTORATE
Crown Buildings, Cathays Park, Cardiff CF1 3NQ
Tel: 029-2082 5150 ; Fax: 029-2082 5111
Chief Executive and Chief Planning Inspector (G3), K. Powell

MEMBERS OF THE WELSH ASSEMBLY
AS AT MAY 2001

Barrett, Ms Lorraine, *Lab. Co-op., Cardiff South and Penarth*, maj. 6,803
Bates, Mick, *LD, Montgomeryshire*, maj. 5,504
Black, Peter, *LD, South Wales West region*
Bourne, Prof. Nicholas, *C., Wales Mid and West region*
Burham, Elenor, *LD, Wales North region*
Butler, Ms Rosemary, *Lab., Newport West*, maj. 4,710
Cairns, Alun, *C., South Wales West region*
Chapman, Ms Christine, *Lab. Co-op., Cynon Valley*, maj. 677
Dafis, Cynog G., *PC, Wales Mid and West region*
Davidson, Ms Jane, *Lab., Pontypridd*, maj. 1,575
Davies, Andrew, *Lab., Swansea West*, maj. 1,926
Davies, David, *C., Monmouth*, maj. 2,712
Davies, Geraint, *PC, Rhondda*, maj. 2,285
Davies, Glyn, *C., Wales Mid and West region*
Davies, Ms Janet, *PC, South Wales West region*
Davies, Ms Jocelyn, *PC, South Wales East region*
Davies, Rt. Hon. Ronald, *Lab., Caerphilly*, maj. 2,861
Edwards, Richard, *Lab., Preseli Pembrokeshire*, maj. 2,738
Elis Thomas, Dafydd, *PC, Meirionnydd Nant Conwy*, maj. 8,742
Essex, Ms Sue, *Lab., Cardiff North*, maj. 2,304
Evans, Delyth, *Lab., Wales Mid and West region*
Feld, Ms Val, *Lab., Swansea East*, maj. 3,781
German, Michael, *LD, South Wales East region*
Gibbons, Brian, *Lab., Aberavon*, maj. 6,743
Graham, William, *C., South Wales East region*
Gregory, Ms Janice, *Lab., Ogmore*, maj. 4,565
Griffiths, John, *Lab. Co-op., Newport East*, maj. 5,111

Gwyther, Ms Christine, *Lab.*, *Carmarthen West and Pembrokeshire South*, maj. 1,492
Halford, Ms Alison, *Lab.*, *Delyn*, maj. 5,417
Hancock, Brian, *PC*, *Islwyn*, maj. 604
Hart, Ms Edwina, *Lab.*, *Gower*, maj. 3,160
Hutt, Ms Jane, *Lab.*, *Vale of Glamorgan*, maj. 926
Jarman, Ms Pauline, *PC*, *South Wales Central region*
Jones, Ms Ann, *Lab.*, *Vale of Clwyd*, maj. 3,341
Jones, Carwyn, *Lab.*, *Bridgend*, maj. 4,258
Jones, Elin, *PC*, *Ceredigion*, maj. 10,249
Jones, Gareth, *PC*, *Conwy*, maj. 114
Jones, Ms Helen Mary, *PC*, *Llanelli*, maj. 688
Jones, Ieuan W., *PC*, *Ynys Môn*, maj. 9,288
Law, Peter, *Lab. Co-op.*, *Blaenau Gwent*, maj. 10,568
Lewis, Huw, *Lab. Co-op.*, *Merthyr Tydfil and Rhymney*, maj. 4,214
Lloyd, Dr David, *PC*, *South Wales West region*
Marek, John, Ph.D., *Lab.*, *Wrexham*, maj. 6,472
Melding, David, *C.*, *South Wales Central region*
Middlehurst, Tom, *Lab.*, *Alyn and Deeside*, maj. 6,359
Morgan, H. Rhodri, *Lab.*, *Cardiff West*, maj. 10,859
Morgan, Jonathan, *C.*, *South Wales Central region*
Neagle, Ms Lynne, *Lab.*, *Torfaen*, maj. 5,285
Pugh, Alun, *Lab.*, *Clwyd West*, maj. 760
Randerson, Ms Jenny, *LD*, *Cardiff Central*, maj. 3,168

Richards, Rod, *C.*, *Wales North region*
Rogers, Peter, *C.*, *Wales North region*
Ryder, Ms Janet, *PC*, *Wales North region*
Sinclair, Ms Karen, *Lab.*, *Clwyd South*, maj. 3,685
Thomas, Ms Gwenda, *Lab.*, *Neath*, maj. 2,618
Thomas, Owen John, *PC*, *South Wales Central region*
Thomas, Rhodri, *PC*, *Carmarthen East and Dinefwr*, maj. 6,980
Wigley, Rt. Hon. Dafydd, *PC*, *Caernarfon*, maj. 12,273
Williams, Ms Kirsty, *LD*, *Brecon and Radnorshire*, maj. 5,852
Williams, Dr Phil, *PC*, *South Wales East region*

STATE OF THE PARTIES *as at May 2001*

	Constituency AMs	Regional AMs	Total
Labour	27	1	28
Plaid Cymru	8†	8	16†
Conservative	1	8	9
Liberal Democrats	3	3	6
The Presiding Officer (The Lord Elis-Thomas)	1	0	1

† Excludes the Presiding Officer, who has no party allegiance while in post

Welsh Assembly AS AT JULY 2001

CONSTITUENCIES

ABERAVON (S. WALES WEST)
E. 49,786 T. 46.79%
B. Gibbons, *Lab.* 11,941
Ms J. Davies, *PC* 5,198
K. Davies, *LD* 3,165
Ms M. E. Davies, *C.* 1,624
Beany, *Bean* 849
D. Pudner, *United Soc.* 517
Lab. majority 6,743

ALYN AND DEESIDE (WALES N.)
E. 59,386 T. 32.04%
T. Middlehurst, *Lab.* 9,772
N. Formstone, *C.* 3,413
Ms A. Owen, *PC* 2,304
J. Clarke, *LD* 1,879
J. Cooksey, *Ind.* 1,333
G. Davies, *Comm.* 329
Lab. majority 6,359

BLAENAU GWENT (S. WALES EAST)
E. 53,919 T. 48.21%
P. Law, *Lab. Co-op.* 16,069
P. Williams, *PC* 5,501
K. Rogers, *LD* 2,980
D. Thomas, *C.* 1,444
Lab. Co-op. majority 10,568

BRECON AND RADNORSHIRE (WALES MID AND W.)
E. 51,166 T. 57.10%
Ms K. Williams, *LD* 13,022
N. Bourne, *C.* 7,170
I. Janes, *Lab. Co-op.* 5,165
D. Patterson, *PC* 2,356
M. Shaw, *Ind.* 1,502
LD majority 5,852

BRIDGEND (S. WALES WEST)
E. 60,234 T. 41.56%
C. Jones, *Lab.* 9,321
A. Cairns, *C.* 5,063
J. Canning, *PC* 4,919
R. Humphreys, *LD* 3,910
A. Jones, *Ind.* 1,819
Lab. majority 4,258

CAERNARFON (WALES N.)
E. 47,213 T. 60.32%
D. Wigley, *PC* 18,748
T. Jones, *Lab.* 6,475
Ms B. Naish, *C.* 2,464
D. Shankland, *LD* 791
PC majority 12,273

CAERPHILLY (S. WALES EAST)
E. 65,997 T. 43.20%
R. Davies, *Lab.* 12,602
R. Gough, *PC* 9,741
M. German, *LD* 3,543
Ms M. Taylor, *C.* 2,213
T. Richards, *United Soc.* 412
Lab. majority 2,861

CARDIFF CENTRAL (S. WALES CENTRAL)
E. 57,815 T. 44.75%
Ms J. Randerson, *LD* 10,937
M. Drakeford, *Lab.* 7,769
O. J. Thomas, *PC* 3,795
S. Jones, *C.* 3,034
J. Goss, *United Soc.* 338
LD majority 3,168

CARDIFF NORTH (S. WALES CENTRAL)
E. 61,398 T. 51.33%
Ms S. Essex, *Lab.* 12,198

J. Morgan, *C.* 9,894
A. Meikle, *LD* 5,088
C. Mann, *PC* 4,337
Lab. majority 2,304

CARDIFF SOUTH AND PENARTH (S. WALES CENTRAL)
E. 61,149 T. 37.67%
Ms L. Barrett, *Lab. Co-op.* 11,057
Ms M. Davies, *C.* 4,254
J. Rowlands, *PC* 3,931
Ms J. Maw-Cornish, *LD* 2,890
D. Bartlett, *United Soc.* 355
J. Foreman, *Ind. Lab.* 339
T. Davies, *Celtic All.* 210
Lab. Co-op. majority 6,803

CARDIFF WEST (S. WALES CENTRAL)
E. 57,717 T. 40.22%
R. Morgan, *Lab.* 14,305
Ms M. Boult, *C.* 3,446
Ms E. Bush, *PC* 3,402
D. Garrow-Smith, *LD* 2,063
Lab. majority 10,859

CARMARTHEN EAST AND DINEFWR (WALES MID AND W.)
E. 53,634 T. 60.88%
R. Thomas, *PC* 17,328
C. Llewellyn, *Lab.* 10,348
Ms H. Stoddart, *C.* 2,776
Ms J. Hughes, *LD* 2,202
PC majority 6,980

CARMARTHEN WEST AND PEMBROKESHIRE SOUTH (WALES MID AND W.)
E. 55,655 T. 50.58%
Ms C. Gwyther, *Lab.* 9,891

R. Llewellyn, *PC*	8,399
D. Edwards, *C.*	5,079
E. Davies, *Ind.*	2,090
R. Williams, *LD*	1,875
G. Fry, *TFPW*	815
Lab. majority 1,492	

CEREDIGION (WALES MID AND W.)
E. 55,311 *T.* 57.67%

E. Jones, *PC*	15,258
Ms M. Battle, *Lab.*	5,009
D. Lloyd Evans, *Ind.*	4,114
D. Evans, *LD*	3,571
H. Lloyd Davies, *C.*	2,944
D. Bradney, *Green*	1,002
PC majority 10,249	

CLWYD SOUTH (WALES N.)
E. 53,843 *T.* 40.51%

Ms K. Sinclair, *Lab.*	9,196
H. Williams, *PC*	5,511
D. R. Jones, *C.*	4,167
D. Burnham, *LD*	2,432
M. Jones, *United Soc.*	508
Lab. majority 3,685	

CLWYD WEST (WALES N.)
E. 53,952 *T.* 46.77%

A. Pugh, *Lab.*	7,824
R. Richards, *C.*	7,064
Ms E. Williams, *PC*	6,886
Ms R. Feeley, *LD*	3,462
Lab. majority 760	

CONWY (WALES N.)
E. 55,189 *T.* 49.11%

G. Jones, *PC*	8,285
Ms C. Sherrington, *Lab.*	8,171
D. I. Jones, *C.*	5,006
*Ms C. Humphreys, *LD*	4,480
G. Edwards, *Ind.*	1,160
PC majority 114	

**C. Humphreys resigned in April 2001.*
Replaced by Ms E. Burham.

CYNON VALLEY (S. WALES CENTRAL)
E. 47,619 *T.* 45.50%

Ms C. Chapman, *Lab. Co-op.*	9,883
P. Richards, *PC*	9,206
Ms A. Willott, *LD*	1,531
E. Hayward, *C.*	1,046
Lab. Co-op. majority 677	

DELYN (WALES N.)
E. 54,047 *T.* 44.13%

Ms A. Halford, *Lab.*	10,672
Ms K. Lumley, *C.*	5,255
Ms M. Ellis, *PC*	4,837
Ms E. Burnham, *LD*	3,089
Lab. majority 5,417	

GOWER (S. WALES WEST)
E. 58,523 *T.* 47.33%

Ms E. Hart, *Lab.*	9,813
D. Jones, *PC*	6,653
A. Jones, *C.*	3,912
H. Evans, *LD*	3,260
R. Lewis, *Ind.*	2,307
I. Richard, *PRP*	1,755

Lab. majority 3,160	

ISLWYN (S. WALES EAST)
E. 50,600 *T.* 47.29%

B. Hancock, *PC*	10,042
S. Williams, *Lab.*	9,438
Ms C. Bennett, *LD*	2,351
C. Stevens, *C.*	1,621
I. Thomas, *United Soc.*	475
PC majority 604	

LLANELLI (WALES MID AND W.)
E. 58,371 *T.* 48.63%

Ms H. M. Jones, *PC*	11,973
Ms A. Garrard, *Lab. Co-op.*	11,285
T. Dumper, *LD*	2,920
B. Harding, *C.*	1,864
A. Popham, *Ind.*	345
PC majority 688	

MEIRIONNYDD NANT CONWY (WALES MID AND W.)
E. 32,922 *T.* 57.33%

D. Elis Thomas, *PC*	12,034
Ms D. Jones, *Lab.*	3,292
O. J. Williams, *C.*	2,170
G. Worley, *LD*	1,378
PC majority 8,742	

MERTHYR TYDFIL AND RHYMNEY (S. WALES EAST)
E. 55,858 *T.* 44.91%

H. Lewis, *Lab. Co-op.*	11,024
A. Cox, *PC*	6,810
A. Rogers, *Ind.*	3,746
E. Jones, *LD*	1,682
Ms C. Hyde, *C.*	1,246
M. Jenkins, *United Soc.*	580
Lab. Co-op. majority 4,214	

MONMOUTH (S. WALES EAST)
E. 61,999 *T.* 51.13%

D. Davies, *C.*	12,950
Ms C. Short, *Lab.*	10,238
C. Lines, *LD*	4,639
M. Hubbard, *PC*	1,964
A. Carrington, *TFPW*	1,911
C. majority 2,712	

MONTGOMERYSHIRE (WALES MID AND W.)
E. 43,386 *T.* 49.41%

M. Bates, *LD*	10,374
G. Davies, *C.*	4,870
D. Senior, *PC*	3,554
C. Hewitt, *Lab.*	2,638
LD majority 5,504	

NEATH (S. WALES WEST)
E. 56,085 *T.* 47.95%

Ms G. Thomas, *Lab.*	12,234
T. Jones, *PC*	9,616
D. Davies, *LD*	2,631
Ms J. Chambers, *C.*	1,895
N. Duncan, *United Soc.*	519
Lab. majority 2,618	

NEWPORT EAST (S. WALES EAST)
E. 54,196 *T.* 35.45%

J. Griffiths, *Lab. Co-op.*	9,497
M. Major, *C.*	4,386
A. Cameron, *LD*	2,684

C. Holland, *PC*	2,647
Lab. Co-op. majority 5,111	

NEWPORT WEST (S. WALES EAST)
E. 57,243 *T.* 42.34%

Ms R. Butler, *Lab.*	11,538
W. Graham, *C.*	6,828
R. Vickery, *PC*	3,053
Ms V. Watkins, *LD*	2,820
Lab. majority 4,710	

OGMORE (S. WALES WEST)
E. 51,998 *T.* 41.54%

Ms J. Gregory, *Lab.*	10,407
J. Rogers, *PC*	5,842
R. Hughes, *Ind.*	2,439
Ms S. Waye, *LD*	1,496
C. Smart, *C.*	1,415
Lab. majority 4,565	

PONTYPRIDD (S. WALES CENTRAL)
E. 64,597 *T.* 45.71%

Ms J. Davidson, *Lab.*	11,330
B. Hancock, *PC*	9,755
G. Orsi, *LD*	5,240
Ms S. Ingerfield, *C.*	2,485
P. Phillips, *Ind.*	436
R. Griffiths, *Comm.*	280
Lab. majority 1,575	

PRESELI PEMBROKESHIRE (WALES MID AND W.)
E. 54,225 *T.* 53.63%

R. Edwards, *Lab.*	9,977
C. Bryant, *PC*	7,239
F. Aubel, *C.*	6,585
D. Lloyd, *LD*	3,338
A. Luke, *Ind.*	1,944
Lab. majority 2,738	

RHONDDA (S. WALES CENTRAL)
E. 55,398 *T.* 50.22%

G. Davies, *PC*	13,558
W. David, *Lab.*	11,273
M. Williams, *LD*	1,303
G. Summers, *Ind.*	913
P. Hobbins, *C.*	774
PC majority 2,285	

SWANSEA EAST (S. WALES WEST)
E. 57,766 *T.* 36.07%

*Ms V. Feld, *Lab.*	9,495
J. Ball, *PC*	5,714
P. Black, *LD*	3,963
W.Hughes, *C.*	1,663
Lab. majority 3,781	

**Awaiting by-election results following*
the death of Ms Feld, See Stop Press

SWANSEA WEST (S. WALES WEST)
E. 59,369 *T.* 39.97%

A. Davies, *Lab.*	8,217
D. Lloyd, *PC*	6,291
P. Valerio, *C.*	3,643
J. Newbury, *LD*	3,543
D. Evans, *Ind.*	996
J. Harris, *PRP*	774
A. Thraves, *United Soc.*	263
Lab. majority 1,926	

TORFAEN (S. WALES EAST)
E. 61,037 T. 39.19%
Ms L. Neagle, *Lab.* 9,080
M. Gough, *Ind. Lab.* 3,795
Ms I. Nutt, *Ind.* 2,828
N. Turner, *PC* 2,614
Ms J. Gray, *LD* 2,614
Ms K. Thomas, *C.* 2,152
S. Smith, *Local Soc.* 839
Lab. majority 5,285

VALE OF CLWYD (WALES N.)
E. 51,124 T. 43.43%
Ms A. Jones, *Lab.* 8,359
R. Salisbury, *C.* 5,018
Ms S. Brynach, *PC* 4,295
G. Clague, *Dem. All.* 1,908
P. Lloyd, *LD* 1,376
D. Roberts, *Ind.* 661
D. Pennant, *Ind.* 586
Lab. majority 3,341

VALE OF GLAMORGAN (S. WALES
CENTRAL)
E. 67,804 T. 48.31%
Ms J. Hutt, *Lab.* 11,448
D. Melding, *C.* 10,522
C. Franks, *PC* 7,848
F. Little, *LD* 2,938
Lab. majority 926

WREXHAM (WALES N.)
E. 50,932 T. 34.19%
J. Marek, *Lab.* 9,239
Ms C. O'Toole, *LD* 2,767
Ms F. Elphick, *C.* 2,747
Ms J. Ryder, *PC* 2,659
Lab. majority 6,472

YNYS MON (WALES N.)
E. 52,571 T. 59.56%
I. W. Jones, *PC* 16,469
A. Owen, *Lab.* 7,181
P. Rogers, *C.* 6,031
J. Clarke, *LD* 1,630
PC majority 9,288

REGIONS

SOUTH WALES CENTRAL
E. 473,494 T. 45.51%
Lab. 79,564 (36.92%)
PC 58,080 (26.95%)
C. 34,944 (16.22%)
LD 30,911 (14.35%)
Green 5,336 (2.48%)
Soc. Lab. 2,822 (1.31%)
Ind. Matt. 1,524 (0.71%)
NLP 665 (0.31%)
Comm. 652 (0.30%)
United Soc. 602 (0.28%)
Ind. Phill. 378 (0.18%)
Lab. majority 21,484
(May 1997, Lab. maj. 131,398)
Additional Members elected: J.
Morgan, *C.*; D. Melding, *C.*; Ms P.
Jarman, *PC*; O. J. Thomas, *PC*

SOUTH WALES EAST
E. 460,846 T. 43.95%
Lab. 83,953 (41.45%)
PC 49,139 (24.26%)
C. 33,947 (16.76%)
LD 24,757 (12.22%)
Soc. Lab. 4,879 (2.41%)
Green 4,055 (2.00%)
United Soc. 903 (0.45%)
NLP 898 (0.44%)
Lab. majority 34,814
(May 1997, Lab. maj. 163,134)
Additional Members elected: W.
Graham, *C.*; M. German, *LD*; Ms J.
Davies, *PC*; Dr P. Williams, *PC*

SOUTH WALES WEST
E. 393,758 T. 42.44%
Lab. 70,625 (42.26%)
PC 50,757 (30.37%)
C. 20,993 (12.56%)
LD 18,527 (11.09%)
Green 4,082 (2.44%)

United Soc. 1,257 (0.75%)
NLP 676 (0.40%)
PRP 204 (0.12%)
Lab. majority 19,868
(May 1997, Lab. maj. 142,286)
Additional Members elected: A.
Cairns, *C.*; P. Black, *LD*; Dr D.
Lloyd, *PC*; Ms J. Davies, *PC*

WALES MID AND WEST
E. 404,667 T. 54.21%
PC 84,554 (38.55%)
Lab. 53,842 (24.55%)
C. 36,622 (16.70%)
LD 31,683 (14.44%)
Green 7,718 (3.52%)
Soc. Lab. 3,019 (1.38%)
Ind. Turner 1,214 (0.55%)
NLP 705 (0.32%)
PC majority 30,712
(May 1997, Lab. maj. 52,382)
Additional Members elected: G.
Davies, *C.*; Prof. N. Bourne, *C.*; *A.
Michael, *Lab.*; C. Dafis, *PC*
*A. Michael resigned in March 2000.
Replaced by D. Evans.

WALES NORTH
E. 478,252 T. 45.06%
Lab. 73,673 (34.19%)
PC 69,518 (32.26%)
C. 41,700 (19.35%)
LD 22,130 (10.27%)
Green 4,667 (2.17%)
Rhuddlan 1,353 (0.63%)
NLP 917 (0.43%)
United Soc. 828 (0.38%)
Comm. 714 (0.33%)
Lab. majority 4,155
(May 1997, Lab. maj. 80,590)
Additional Members elected: P.
Rogers, *C.*; R. Richards, *C.*; Ms C.
Humphreys, *LD*; Ms J. Ryder, *PC*
*C. Humpreys resigned in April 2001.
Replaced by Ms E. Burham.

THE SCOTTISH PARLIAMENT
Edinburgh EH99 1SP. Tel: 0131-348 5000;
Web www.scotland.gov.uk

In July 1997 the Government announced plans to establish a Scottish Parliament. In a referendum on 11 September 1997 about 62 per cent of the electorate voted, of whom 74.3 per cent voted in favour of the Parliament and 63.5 in favour of its having tax-raising powers. Elections are to be held every four years. The first elections were held on 6 May 1999 when about 59 per cent of the electorate voted. The first session was held on 12 May 1999 and the Scottish Parliament was officially opened on 1 July 1999 at the Edinburgh Assembly Hall; a new building to house the Parliament is under construction in Edinburgh.

The Scottish Parliament has 129 members (including the Presiding Officer), comprising 73 constituency members and 56 additional regional members from party lists. It can introduce primary legislation and has the power to raise or lower the basic rate of income tax by up to three pence in the pound.

The Scottish Parliament is responsible for: education, health, law, environment, economic development, local government, housing, police, fire services, planning, financial assistance to industry, tourism, some transport, heritage and the arts, agriculture, forestry, food standards.

SALARIES FROM 1 APRIL 2001:
First Minister £68,159*
Ministers £35,358*
Lord Advocate £86,103
Solicitor-General for Scotland £73,684
Junior Ministers £18,342*
MSPs £42,493†
Presiding Officer £35,358
Deputy Presiding Officers £18,342
*In addition to the MSP salary
†Reduced by two-thirds if the member is already an MP or an MEP

THE SCOTTISH EXECUTIVE

St Andrew's House, Regent Road, Edinburgh EH1 3DG
Tel: 0131-556 8400; E-mail: ceu@scotland.gov.uk
Web: www.scotland.gov.uk

The Scottish Executive is responsible in Scotland for all matters not reserved to Westminster under devolution, including education, health, social work, law and order, agriculture and the environment. In addition there are a number of Scottish departments for which the Executive has some degree of responsibility; these include the Scottish Courts Administration, the General Register Office, the National Archives of Scotland (formerly the Scottish Record Office) and the Department of the Registers of Scotland.

First Minister, The Rt. Hon. Henry McLeish, MSP (*Lab.*)
Deputy First Minister and Minister for Justice, Jim Wallace, QC, MSP (*LD*)
Finance Minister, Jack McConnell, MSP (*Lab.*)
Minister for Health and Community Care, Susan Deacon, MSP (*Lab.*)
Minister for Transport and Planning, Sarah Boyack, MSP (*Lab.*)
Minister for Enterprise and Lifelong Learning, Wendy Alexander, MSP (*Lab.*)
Minister for Finance and Local Government, Angus MacKay, MSP (*Lab.*)
Minister for Environment and Rural Development, Ross Finnie, MSP (*LD*)
Minister for Education, Europe and External and External Affairs, Jack McConnell MSP (*Lab.*)
Minister for Parliament and Chief Whip, Tom McCabe, MSP (*Lab.*)
Lord Advocate, Colin Boyd, QC
Solicitor General, Neil Davidson, QC

JUNIOR MINISTERS (NOT MEMBERS OF THE SCOTTISH EXECUTIVE)
Deputy Minister for Social Justice, Margaret Curran, MSP (*Lab.*)
Deputy Minister for Community Care, Iain Gray, MSP
Deputy Minister for Finance and Local Government, Peter Peacock, MSP (*Lab.*)
Deputy Minister Health and Community Care, Malcolm Chisholm, MSP (*Lab.*)
Deputy Minister for Enterprise and Lifelong Learning, Alasdair Morrison, MSP
Deputy Minister for Education, Europe and External Affairs, Nicol Stephen, MSP (*Lab.*)
Deputy Minister for Sport, The Arts and Culture, Allan Wilson, MSP (*Lab.*)
Deputy Minister for Environment and Rural Development, Rhonda Brankin, MSP (*Lab.*)
Deputy Minister for Parliament and Whip, Euan Robertson, MSP (*LD*)

SCOTTISH EXECUTIVE CORPORATE SERVICES

16 Waterloo Place, Edinburgh EH1 3DN
Tel: 0131-556 8400

Principal Establishment Officer (*SCS*), Mrs A. Robson
Head of Personnel (*SCS*), Dr Ingrid Clayden

DIRECTORATE OF ADMINISTRATIVE SERVICES
Saughton House, Broomhouse Drive, Edinburgh EH11 3DX
Tel: 0131-556 8400

Director of Administrative Services (*SCS*), J. Meldrum
Director of Information Technology (*SCS*), P. Gray
Director of Procurement and Commercial Services, N. Bowd

Director of Corporate Development, I. Walford
Director of Accommodation, P. A. Rhodes
Chief Quantity Surveyor (*SCS*), A. J. Wyllie
Head of Procurement (*SCS*), N. Bowd

SCOTTISH EXECUTIVE FINANCE

Victoria Quay, Edinburgh EH6 6QQ
Tel: 0131-556 8400

Principal Finance Officer (*SCS*), Dr P. S. Collings
Head of Accountancy Services Unit, I. M. Smith

SCOTTISH EXECUTIVE SECRETARIAT

St Andrew's House, Regent Road, Edinburgh EH1 3DG
Tel: 0131-556 8400

Head of Secretariat, R. S. B. Gordon, CB
Constitutional Policy and Parliamentary Secretariat, C. M. A. Lugton
Head, Cabinet Secretariat, B. Campbell
Head, Audit Unit, W.T. Tait
Head of Accountancy Services Unit, I. M. Smith
Head, External Relations, B. Doig
Head, Brussels Office, G. Calder
Chief Economic Adviser, A. W. Goudie
Legal Secretary to the Lord Advocate, P. J. Layden
Head, Equality and Voluntary Issues, V. M. Macniven

SCOTTISH EXECUTIVE POLICY UNIT
Head of Unit (*SCS*), P. J. Rycroft

SCOTTISH EXECUTIVE INFORMATION DIRECTORATE
For the Scottish Executive and certain UK services in Scotland
Head of New Media Presentation (*SCS*), R. Williams
Head of News, O. D. Kelly

SOLICITOR'S OFFICE
Solicitor (*SCS*), R. M. Henderson
Deputy Solicitor (*SCS*), J. S. G. Maclean

SCOTTISH EXECUTIVE RURAL AFFAIRS DEPARTMENT

Pentland House, 47 Robb's Loan, Edinburgh EH14 1TY
Tel: 0131-556 8400

Head of Department (*SCS*), J. S. Graham
Group Heads (*SCS*), D. J. Crawley (*Food and Agriculture*); S. F. Hampson (*Environment*); A. J. Rushworth (*Agriculture and Biological Research*); A. J. Robertson (*Chief Agriculture Officer*)
Chief Agricultural Economist, A. Moxey
Chief Food and Dairy Officer, S. D. Rooke
Senior Principal Scientific Officers, Dr Linda Saunderson; Dr Maureen Bruce

EXECUTIVE AGENCIES

FISHERIES RESEARCH SERVICES
Marine Laboratory, PO Box 101, Victoria Road, Aberdeen AB11 9DB
Tel: 01224-876544; Fax: 01224-295511
Chief Executive, Dr A. D. Hawkins
Deputy Director, Dr R. Stagg

SCOTTISH AGRICULTURAL SCIENCE AGENCY
82 Craigs Road, East Craig, Edinburgh EH12 8NJ
Tel: 0131-244 8890; Fax: 0131-244 8988
Director, Dr R. K. M. Hay

SCOTTISH FISHERIES PROTECTION AGENCY
Pentland House, 47 Robb's Loan, Edinburgh EH14 1TY
Tel: 0131-556 8400; Fax: 0131-244 6086
Chief Executive, Capt. P. Du Vivier, RN

SCOTTISH EXECUTIVE DEVELOPMENT DEPARTMENT
Victoria Quay, Edinburgh EH6 6QQ
Tel: 0131-556 8400

Head of Department (SCS), K. MacKenzie, CB
Heads of Groups (SCS), D. J. Belfall; J. S. B. Martin
Senior Economic Adviser (SCS), N. Jackson

PROFESSIONAL STAFF
Chief Planner (SCS), J. MacKinnon

INQUIRY REPORTERS
2 Greenside Lane, Edinburgh EH1 3AG
Tel: 0131-244 5649; Fax: 0131-244 5680

Chief Reporter (SCS), R. M. Hickman

TRUNK ROADS DESIGN AND CONSTRUCTION DIVISION
Victoria Quay, Edinburgh EH6 6QQ
Tel: 0131-556 8400

Chief Engineers (SCS), J. A. Howison (*Roads*); N. B. MacKenzie (*Bridges*)

SCOTTISH EXECUTIVE EDUCATION DEPARTMENT
Victoria Quay, Edinburgh EH6 6QQ
Tel: 0131-556 8400

Secretary (SCS), J. Elvidge
Under-Secretaries (SCS), Mrs G. Stewart; Dr M. Ewart; Ms I. Low
Chief Statistician (SCS), R. C. Wishart
Chief Architect (SCS), J. E. Gibbons, PH.D., FSA Scot.
Chief Inspector of Social Work Services, A. Skinner
Assistant Chief Inspectors, V. A. Cox ; D. Perrott; I. C. Robertson

HM INSPECTORS OF SCHOOLS
Senior Chief Inspector (SCS), D. A. Osler
Depute Senior Chief Inspectors (SCS), G. H. C. Donaldson
Chief Inspectors (SCS), P. Banks; J. Boyes; W. C. Calder; F. Crawford; Miss K. M. Fairweather; A. S. McGlynn; H. M. Stalker

EXECUTIVE AGENCIES

HISTORIC SCOTLAND
Longmore House, Salisbury Place, Edinburgh EH9 1SH
Tel: 0131-668 8600; Fax: 0131-668 8699

Chief Executive (G3), G. N. Munro

SCOTTISH PUBLIC PENSIONS AGENCY
St Margaret's House, 151 London Road, Edinburgh EH8 7TG
Tel: 0131-556 8400; Fax: 0131-244 3334

Chief Executive, R. Garden

SCOTTISH EXECUTIVE ENTERPRISE AND LIFELONG LEARNING DEPARTMENT
Meridian Court, 5 Cadogan Street, Glasgow G2 6AT
Tel 0141-248 2855

Secretary (SCS), E. Frizzell
Under Secretary (SCS), vacant
Industrial Adviser, D. B. Blair
Scientific Adviser, Prof. D. J. Tedford

ECONOMIC DEVELOPMENT, ADVICE AND EMPLOYMENT ISSUES
Under-Secretaries (SCS), M. B. Foulis

ENTERPRISE AND INDUSTRIAL EXPANSION
Meridian Court, 5 Cadogan Street, Glasgow G2 6AT
Tel: 0141-248 2855

Under-Secretary (SCS), S. Hampson
Industrial Adviser, D. Blair

LIFELONG LEARNING GROUP
Europa House, 450 Argyle Street G2 8LG
Tel: 0141-248 2855

Under Secretary (SCS), E. J. Weeple

LOCATE IN SCOTLAND
120 Bothwell Street, Glasgow G2 7JP
Tel: 0141-248 2700

Director (SCS), M. Togneri

SCOTTISH TRADE INTERNATIONAL
120 Bothwell Street, Glasgow G2 7JP
Tel: 0141-248 2700

Director, D. Taylor

EXECUTIVE AGENCY

STUDENT AWARDS AGENCY FOR SCOTLAND
Gyleview House, 3 Redheughs Rigg, Edinburgh EH12 9HH
Tel: 0131-476 8212; Fax: 0131-244 5887

Chief Executive, K. MacRae

SCOTTISH EXECUTIVE HEALTH DEPARTMENT
St Andrew's House, Edinburgh EH1 3DG
Tel: 0131-244 2410

NATIONAL HEALTH SERVICE IN SCOTLAND MANAGEMENT EXECUTIVE
Chief Executive (SCS), T. Jones
Director of Nursing, Miss A. Jarvie
Chief Medical Officer, Dr M. Armstrong
Head of Community Care, T. Teale
Chief Pharmacist (SCS), W. Scott
Chief Scientist, Prof. Roland Young
Chief Dental Officer, T. R. Watkins

PUBLIC HEALTH POLICY UNIT
Director, Geofrey Robinson
Head of Policy and Chief Medical Officer (SCS), Dr Armstrong Keel

STATE HOSPITAL
Carstairs Junction, Lanark ML11 8RP
Tel: 01555-840293

Chairman, D. N. James
General Manager, R. Manson

COMMON SERVICES AGENCY
Trinity Park House, South Trinity Road, Edinburgh EH5 3SE
Tel: 0131-552 6255

Chairman, G. R. Scaife, CB
General Manager, Dr F. Gibb

SCOTTISH EXECUTIVE JUSTICE DEPARTMENT
Saughton House, Broomhouse Drive, Edinburgh EH11 3XD
Tel: 0131-556 8400

Secretary (SCS), J. Gallagher
Under-Secretaries (SCS), C. Baxter; N. G. Campbell; V. Macniven

SOCIAL WORK AND SERVICES GROUP AND
INSPECTORATE
James Craig Walk, Edinburgh EH1 3BA
Tel: 0131-556 8400

Under Secretary (SCS), Mrs G. M. Stewart
Chief Inspector of Social Work and Services for Scotland, A.
Skinner

OTHER APPOINTMENTS
HM Chief Inspector of Constabulary, W. Taylor, QPM
HM Chief Inspector of Prisons, C. Fairweather, OBE
Commandant, Scottish Police College, H. I. Watson, OBE,
QPM
HM Chief Inspector of Fire Services, D. Davis, CBE, QFSM
Head of Training, Scottish Fire Service Training School,
J. Robson

OFFICE OF THE SCOTTISH
PARLIAMENTARY COUNSEL
Victoria Quay, Edinburgh EH6 6QQ
Tel: 0131-556 8400
First Scottish Parliamentary Counsel, J. C. McCluskie, CB,
QC
Scottish Parliamentary Counsel, G. M. Clark;
C. A. M. Wilson

PRIVATE LEGISLATION OFFICE UNDER
THE PRIVATE LEGISLATION
PROCEDURE (SCOTLAND) ACT 1936
50 Frederick Street, Edinburgh EH2 1EN
Tel: 0131-226 6499
Senior Counsel, G. S. Douglas, QC
Junior Counsel, N. M. P. Morrison

EXECUTIVE AGENCIES

NATIONAL ARCHIVES OF SCOTLAND

REGISTERS OF SCOTLAND

SCOTTISH PRISON SERVICE

GENERAL REGISTER OFFICE FOR SCOTLAND
New Register House, Edinburgh EH1 3YT
Tel: 0131-334 0380; Fax: 0131-314 4400;
Web www.gro-scotland.gov.uk
Registrar-General (SCS), J. N. Randall

MENTAL WELFARE COMMISSION FOR
SCOTLAND
K Floor, Argyle House, 3 Lady Lawson Street, Edinburgh
EH3 9SH
Tel: 0131-222 6111
Chairman, I. J. Miller, OBE
Vice-Chairman, Mrs N. Bennie

MEMBERS OF THE SCOTTISH PARLIAMENT

Adam, Brian, *SNP, Scotland North East region*
Aitken, William, *C., Glasgow region*
Alexander, Ms Wendy, *Lab., Paisley North*, maj. 4,616
Baillie, Ms Jackie, *Lab., Dumbarton*, maj. 4,758
Barrie, Scott, *Lab., Dunfermline West*, maj. 5,021
Boyack, Ms Sarah, *Lab., Edinburgh Central*, maj. 4,626
Brankin, Ms Rhona, *Lab. Co-op., Midlothian*, maj. 5,525
Brown, Robert, *LD, Glasgow region*
Butler, Bill, *Lab., Glasgow Anniesland*, maj. 5,376

Campbell, Colin, *SNP, Scotland West region*
Canavan, Dennis A., *MP, Lab., Falkirk West*, maj. 12,192
Chisholm, Malcolm G. R., *MP, Lab., Edinburgh North and
Leith*, maj. 7,736
Craigie, Ms Cathy, *Lab., Cumbernauld and Kilsyth*, maj.
4,259
Crawford, Bruce, *SNP, Scotland Mid and Fife region*
Cunningham, Ms Roseanna, *MP, SNP, Perth*, maj. 2,027
Curran, Ms Margaret, *Lab., Glasgow Baillieston*, maj. 3,072
Davidson, David, *C., Scotland North East region*
Deacon, Ms Susan, *Lab., Edinburgh East and Musselburgh*,
maj. 6,714
Selkirk of Douglas, The Lord, *PC, QC, C., Lothians region*
Eadie, Ms Helen, *Lab. Co-op., Dunfermline East*, maj. 8,699
Elder, Ms Dorothy, *SNP, Glasgow region*
Ewing, Fergus, *SNP, Inverness East, Nairn and Lochaber*,
maj. 441
Ewing, Mrs Margaret A., *MP, SNP, Moray*, maj. 4,129
Ewing, Dr Winnifred, *SNP, Highlands and Islands region*
Fabiani, Ms Linda, *SNP, Scotland Central region*
Farquhar-Munro, John, *LD, Ross, Skye and Inverness West*,
maj. 1,539
Ferguson, Ms Patricia, *Lab., Glasgow Maryhill*, maj. 4,326
Fergusson, Alex, *C., Scotland South region*
Finnie, Ross, *LD, Scotland West region*
Fitzpatrick, Brian, *Lab., Strathkelvin and Bearsden*, maj.
7,829
Fraser, Murdo, *C., Scotland Mid and Fife region*
Gallie, Phil, *C., Scotland South region*
Gibson, Kenneth, *SNP, Glasgow region*
Gillon, Ms Karen, *Lab., Clydesdale*, maj. 3,880 *(elected as
Karen Turnbull)*
Godman, Ms Patricia, *Lab., Renfrewshire West*, maj. 2,893
Goldie, Miss Annabel, *C., Scotland West region*
Gorrie, Donald C. E., *MP, OBE, LD, Scotland Central region*
Grahame, Ms Christine, *SNP, Scotland South region (elected
as Christine Creech)*
Grant, Ms Rhoda, *Lab., Highlands and Islands region*
Gray, Iain, *Lab., Edinburgh Pentlands*, maj. 2,885
Hamilton, Duncan, *SNP, Highlands and Islands region*
Harding, Keith, *C., Scotland Mid and Fife region*
Harper, Robin, *Green, Lothians region*
Henry, Hugh, *Lab., Paisley South*, maj. 4,495
Home Robertson, John D., *MP, Lab., East Lothian*, maj.
10,946
Hughes, Ms Janice, *Lab., Glasgow Rutherglen*, maj. 7,287
Hyslop, Ms Fiona, *SNP, Lothians region*
Ingram, Adam, *SNP, Scotland South region*
Jackson, Gordon, *QC, Lab., Glasgow Govan*, maj. 1,756
Jackson, Dr Sylvia, *Lab., Stirling*, maj. 3,981
Jamieson, Ms Cathy, *Lab. Co-op., Carrick, Cumnock and
Doon Valley*, maj. 8,803
Jamieson, Ms Margaret, *Lab., Kilmarnock and Loudoun*,
maj. 2,760
Jenkins, Ian, *LD, Tweeddale, Ettrick and Lauderdale*, maj.
4,478
Johnstone, Alex, *C., Scotland North East region*
Kerr, Andy, *Lab., East Kilbride*, maj. 6,499
Lamont, Johann, *Lab. Co-op., Glasgow Pollock*, maj. 4,642
Livingstone, Ms Marilyn, *Lab. Co-op., Kirkcaldy*, maj. 4,475
Lochhead, Richard, *SNP, Scotland North East region*
Lyon, George, *LD, Argyll and Bute*, maj. 2,057
McAllion, John, *MP, Lab., Dundee East*, maj. 2,854
MacAskill, Kenny, *SNP, Lothians region*
McAveety, Frank, *Lab. Co-op., Glasgow Shettleston*, maj.
5,467
McCabe, Tom, *Lab., Hamilton South*, maj. 7,176
McConnell, Jack, *Lab., Motherwell and Wishaw*, maj. 5,076
Macdonald, Lewis, *Lab., Aberdeen Central*, maj. 2,696
MacDonald, Ms Margo, *SNP, Lothians region*

MacGrigor, Jamie, C., *Highlands and Islands region*
McGugan, Ms Irene, SNP, *Scotland North East region*
Macintosh, Ken, *Lab.*, *Eastwood*, maj. 2,125
McIntosh, Mrs Lindsay, C., *Scotland Central region*
MacKay, Angus, *Lab.*, *Edinburgh South*, maj. 5,424
MacLean, Ms Kate, *Lab.*, *Dundee West*, maj. 121
McLeish, Henry B., MP, *Lab.*, *Fife Central*, maj. 8,675
McLeod, Ms Fiona, SNP, *Scotland West region*
McLetchie, David, C., *Lothians region*
McMahon, Michael, *Lab.*, *Hamilton North and Bellshill*, maj. 5,606
Macmillan, Ms Maureen, *Lab.*, *Highlands and Islands region*
McNeil, Duncan, *Lab.*, *Greenock and Inverclyde*, maj. 4,313
McNeill, Ms Pauline, *Lab.*, *Glasgow Kelvin*, maj. 4,408
McNulty, Des, *Lab.*, *Clydebank and Milngavie*, maj. 4,710
Martin, Paul, *Lab.*, *Glasgow Springburn*, maj. 7,893
Marwick, Ms Tricia, SNP, *Scotland Mid and Fife region*
Matheson, Michael, SNP, *Scotland Central region*
Monteith, Brian, C., *Scotland Mid and Fife region*
Morgan, Alasdair N., MP, SNP, *Galloway and Upper Nithsdale*, maj. 3,201
Morrison, Alasdair, *Lab.*, *Western Isles*, maj. 2,093
Muldoon, Bristow, *Lab.*, *Livingston*, maj. 3,904
Mulligan, Ms Mary, *Lab.*, *Linlithgow*, maj. 2,928
Mundell, David, C., *Scotland South region*
Murray, Dr Elaine, *Lab.*, *Dumfries*, maj. 3,654
Neil, Alex, SNP, *Scotland Central region*
Oldfather, Ms Irene, *Lab.*, *Cunninghame South*, maj. 6,541
Paterson, Gil, SNP, *Scotland Central region*
Peacock, Peter, *Lab.*, *Highlands and Islands region*
Peattie, Ms Cathy, *Lab.*, *Falkirk East*, maj. 4,139
Quinan, Lloyd, SNP, *Scotland West region*
Radcliffe, Ms Nora, LD, *Gordon*, maj. 4,195
Raffan, Keith, LD, *Scotland Mid and Fife region*
Reid, George, SNP, *Scotland Mid and Fife region*
Robison, Ms Shona, SNP, *Scotland North East region*
Robson, Euan, LD, *Roxburgh and Berwickshire*, maj. 3,585
Rumbles, Mike, LD, *Aberdeenshire West and Kincardine*, maj. 2,289
Russell, Michael, SNP, *Scotland South region*
Scanlon, Mrs Mary, C., *Highlands and Islands region*
Scott, John, C., *Ayr*, maj. 3,344
Scott, Tavish, LD, *Shetland*, maj. 3,194
Sheridan, Tommy, SSP, *Glasgow region*

Simpson, Richard, *Lab.*, *Ochil*, maj. 1,303
Smith, Ms Elaine, *Lab.*, *Coatbridge and Chryston*, maj. 10,404
Smith, Iain, LD, *Fife North East*, maj. 5,064
Smith, Ms Margaret, LD, *Edinburgh West*, maj. 4,583
Steel, Rt. Hon. Sir David (The Lord Steel of Aikwood), KBE, PC, LD, *Lothians region*
Stephen, Nicol, LD, *Aberdeen South*, maj. 1,760
Stone, Jamie, LD, *Caithness, Sutherland and Easter Ross*, maj. 4,391
Sturgeon, Ms Nicola, SNP, *Glasgow region*
Swinney, John R., MP, SNP, *Tayside North*, maj. 4,192
Thomson, Ms Elaine, *Lab.*, *Aberdeen North*, maj. 398
Tosh, Murray, C., *Scotland South region*
Ullrich, Ms Kay, SNP, *Scotland West region*
Wallace, Ben, C., *Scotland North East region*
Wallace, James R., MP, QC, LD, *Orkney*, maj. 4,619
Watson, Mike (The Lord Watson of Invergowrie), *Lab.*, *Glasgow Cathcart*, maj. 5,374
Welsh, Andrew P., MP, SNP, *Angus*, maj. 8,901
White, Ms Sandra, SNP, *Glasgow region*
Whitefield, Ms Karen, *Lab.*, *Airdrie and Shotts*, maj. 8,985
Wilson, Allan, *Lab.*, *Cunninghame North*, maj. 4,796
Wilson, Andrew, SNP, *Scotland Central region*
Young, John, OBE, C., *Scotland West region*

STATE OF THE PARTIES *as at July 2001*

	Constituency MSPs	Regional MSPs	Total
Scottish Labour Party	52	3	55
Scottish National Party	7	28	35
Scottish Conservative and Unionist Party	1	18	19
Scottish Liberal Democrats	12	4†	16†
Scottish Green Party	0	1	1
Scottish Socialist Party	0	1	1
Independent (Dennis Canavan)	1	0	1
The Presiding Officer (Rt. Hon. Sir David Steel, KBE, MSP)	0	1	1

† *Excludes the Presiding Officer, who has no party allegiance while in post*

Deputy Presiding Officers, Patricia Ferguson, MSP (*Lab.*); George Reid, MSP (SNP)

Scottish Parliament

CONSTITUENCIES

ABERDEEN CENTRAL
(*Scotland North East region*)
E. 52,715 T. 50.26%
L. Macdonald, *Lab.*   10,305
R. Lochhead, SNP   7,609
Ms E. Anderson, LD   4,403
T. Mason, C.   3,655
A. Cumbers, SSP   523
Lab. majority 2,696

ABERDEEN NORTH
(*Scotland North East region*)
E. 54,553 T. 51.00%
Ms E. Thomson, *Lab.*   10,340
B. Adam, SNP   9,942
J. Donaldson, LD   4,767
I. Haughie, C.   2,772
Lab. majority 398

ABERDEEN SOUTH
(*Scotland North East region*)
E. 60,579 T. 57.26%
N. Stephen, LD   11,300
M. Elrick, *Lab.*   9,540
Ms N. Milne, C.   6,993
Ms I. McGugan, SNP   6,651
S. Sutherland, SWP   206
LD majority 1,760

ABERDEENSHIRE WEST AND KINCARDINE
(*Scotland North East region*)
E. 60,702 T. 58.87%
M. Rumbles, LD   12,838
B. Wallace, C.   10,549
Ms M. Watt, SNP   7,699
G. Guthrie, *Lab.*   4,650
LD majority 2,289

AIRDRIE AND SHOTTS
(*Scotland Central region*)

E. 58,481 T. 56.79%
Ms K. Whitefield, *Lab.*   18,338
G. Paterson, SNP   9,353
P. Ross-Taylor, C.   3,177
D. Miller, LD   2,345
Lab. majority 8,985

ANGUS
(*Scotland North East region*)
E. 59,891 T. 57.66%
A. Welsh, SNP   16,055
R. Harris, C.   7,154
I. McFatridge, *Lab.*   6,914
R. Speirs, LD   4,413
SNP majority 8,901

ARGYLL AND BUTE
(*Highlands and Islands region*)
E. 49,609 T. 64.86%
G. Lyon, LD   11,226
D. Hamilton, SNP   9,169
H. Raven, *Lab.*   6,470

D. Petrie, *C.*   5,312
LD majority 2,057

AYR
(Scotland South region)
E. 56,338 *T.* 66.48%
I. Welsh, *Lab.*   14,263
P. Gallie, *C.*   14,238
R. Mullin, *SNP*   7,291
Ms E. Morris, *LD*   1,662
Lab. majority 25
By-election held on 16 March 2000
see p 284

BANFF AND BUCHAN
(Scotland North East region)
E. 57,639 *T.* 55.06%
A. Salmond, *SNP*   16,695
D. Davidson, *C.*   5,403
M. Mackie, *LD*   5,315
Ms M. Harris, *Lab.*   4,321
SNP majority 11,292
By-election held on 7 June 2001 *see*
p 284

CAITHNESS, SUTHERLAND AND
EASTER ROSS
(Highlands and Islands region)
E. 41,581 *T.* 62.60%
J. Stone, *LD*   10,691
J. Hendry, *Lab.*   6,300
Ms J. Urquhart, *SNP*   6,035
R. Jenkins, *C.*   2,167
J. Campbell, *Ind.*   554
E. Stewart, *Ind.*   282
LD majority 4,391

CARRICK, CUMNOCK AND DOON
VALLEY
(Scotland South region)
E. 65,580 *T.* 62.66%
Ms C. Jamieson, *Lab. Co-op.*   19,667
A. Ingram, *SNP*   10,864
J. Scott, *C.*   8,123
D, Hannay, *LD*   2,441
Lab. Co-op. majority 8,803

CLYDEBANK AND MILNGAVIE
(Scotland West region)
E. 52,461 *T.* 63.55%
D. McNulty, *Lab.*   15,105
J. Yuill, *SNP*   10,395
R. Ackland, *LD*   4,149
Ms D. Luckhurst, *C.*   3,688
Lab. majority 4,710

CLYDESDALE
(Scotland South region)
E. 64,262 *T.* 60.61%
Ms K. Turnbull, *Lab.*   16,755
Ms A. Winning, *SNP*   12,875
C. Cormack, *C.*   5,814
Ms S. Grieve, *LD*   3,503
Lab. majority 3,880

COATBRIDGE AND CHRYSTON
(Scotland Central region)
E. 52,178 *T.* 57.87%
Ms E. Smith, *Lab.*   17,923
P. Kearney, *SNP*   7,519
G. Lind, *C.*   2,867
Ms J. Hook, *LD*   1,889
Lab. majority 10,404

CUMBERNAULD AND KILSYTH
(Scotland Central region)
E. 49,395 *T.* 61.97%
Ms C. Craigie, *Lab.*   15,182
A. Wilson, *SNP*   10,923
H. O'Donnell, *LD*   2,029
R. Slack, *C.*   1,362
K. McEwan, *SSP*   1,116
Lab. majority 4,259

CUNNINGHAME NORTH
(Scotland West region)
E. 55,867 *T.* 59.95%
A. Wilson, *Lab.*   14,369
Ms K. Ullrich, *SNP*   9,573
M. Johnston, *C.*   6,649
C. Irving, *LD*   2,900
Lab. majority 4,796

CUNNINGHAME SOUTH
(Scotland South region)
E. 50,443 *T.* 56.06%
Ms I. Oldfather, *Lab.*   14,936
M. Russell, *SNP*   8,395
M. Tosh, *C.*   3,229
S. Ritchie, *LD*   1,717
Lab. majority 6,541

DUMBARTON
(Scotland West region)
E. 56,090 *T.* 61.86%
Ms J. Baillie, *Lab.*   15,181
L. Quinan, *SNP*   10,423
D. Reece, *C.*   5,060
P. Coleshill, *LD*   4,035
Lab. majority 4,758

DUMFRIES
(Scotland South region)
E. 63,162 *T.* 60.93%
Ms E. Murray, *Lab.*   14,101
D. Mundell, *C.*   10,447
S.Norris, *SNP*   7,625
N. Wallace, *LD*   6,309
Lab. majority 3,654

DUNDEE EAST
(Scotland North East region)
E. 57,222 *T.* 55.33%
J. McAllion, *Lab.*   13,703
Ms S. Robison, *SNP*   10,849
I. Mitchell, *C.*   4,428
R. Lawrie, *LD*   2,153
H. Duke, *SSP*   530
Lab. majority 2,854

DUNDEE WEST
(Scotland North East region)
E. 55,725 *T.* 52.19%
Ms K. MacLean, *Lab.*   10,925
C. Cashley, *SNP*   10,804
G. Buchan, *C.*   3,345
Ms E. Dick, *LD*   2,998
J. McFarlane, *SSP*   1,010
Lab. majority 121

DUNFERMLINE EAST
(Scotland Mid and Fife region)
E. 52,087 *T.* 56.94%
Ms H. Eadie, *Lab. Co-op.*   16,576
D. McCarthy, *SNP*   7,877
Ms C. Ruxton, *C.*   2,931
F. Lawson, *LD*   2,275

Lab. Co-op. majority 8,699

DUNFERMLINE WEST
(Scotland Mid and Fife region)
E. 53,112 *T.* 57.75%
S. Barrie, *Lab.*   13,560
D. Chapman, *SNP*   8,539
Ms E. Harris, *LD*   5,591
J. Mackie, *C.*   2,981
Lab. majority 5,021

EAST KILBRIDE
(Scotland Central region)
E. 66,111 *T.* 62.49%
A. Kerr, *Lab.*   19,987
Ms L. Fabiani, *SNP*   13,488
C. Stevenson, *C.*   4,465
E. Hawthorn, *LD*   3,373
Lab. majority 6,499

EAST LOTHIAN
(Scotland South region)
E. 58,579 *T.* 64.16%
J. Home Robertson, *Lab.*   19,220
C. Miller, *SNP*   8,274
Ms C. Richard, *C.*   5,941
Ms J. Hayman, *LD*   4,147
Lab. majority 10,946

EASTWOOD
(Scotland West region)
E. 67,248 *T.* 67.51%
K. Macintosh, *Lab.*   16,970
J. Young, *C.*   14,845
Ms R. Findlay, *SNP*   8,760
Ms A. McCurley, *LD*   4,472
M. Tayan, *Ind.*   349
Lab. majority 2,125

EDINBURGH CENTRAL
(Lothians region)
E. 65,945 *T.* 56.73%
Ms S. Boyack, *Lab.*   14,224
I. McKee, *SNP*   9,598
A. Myles, *LD*   6,187
Ms J. Low, *C.*   6,018
K. Williamson, *SSP*   830
B. Allingham, *Ind. Dem.*   364
W. Wallace, *Braveheart*   191
Lab. majority 4,626

EDINBURGH EAST AND
MUSSELBURGH
(Lothians region)
E. 60,167 *T.* 61.48%
Ms S. Deacon, *Lab.*   17,086
K. MacAskill, *SNP*   10,372
J. Balfour, *C.*   4,600
Ms M. Thomas, *LD*   4,100
D. White, *SSP*   697
M. Heavey, *Ind. You*   134
Lab. majority 6,714

EDINBURGH NORTH AND LEITH
(Lothians region)
E. 62,976 *T.* 58.19%
M. Chisholm, *Lab.*   17,203
Ms A. Dana, *SNP*   9,467
J. Sempill, *C.*   5,030
S. Tombs, *LD*   4,039
R. Brown, *SSP*   907
Lab. majority 7,736

EDINBURGH PENTLANDS
(Lothians region)
E. 60,029 *T.* 65.97%
I. Gray, *Lab.*   14,343
D. McLetchie, *C.*   11,458
S. Gibb, *SNP*   8,770
I. Gibson, *LD*   5,029
Lab. majority 2,885

EDINBURGH SOUTH
(Lothians region)
E. 64,100 *T.* 62.61%
A. MacKay, *Lab.*   14,869
Ms M. MacDonald, *SNP*   9,445
M. Pringle, *LD*   8,961
I. Whyte, *C.*   6,378
W. Black, *SWP*   482
Lab. majority 5,424

EDINBURGH WEST
(Lothians region)
E. 61,747 *T.* 67.34%
Ms M. Smith, *LD*   15,161
Lord J. Douglas-
Hamilton, *C.*   10,578
Ms C. Fox, *Lab.*   8,860
G. Sutherland, *SNP*   6,984
LD majority 4,583

FALKIRK EAST
(Scotland Central region)
E. 57,345 *T.* 61.40%
Ms C. Peattie, *Lab.*   15,721
K. Brown, *SNP*   11,582
A. Orr, *C.*   3,399
G. McDonald, *LD*   2,509
R. Stead, *Soc. Lab.* 1,643
V. MacGrain, *SFPP* 358
Lab. majority 4,139

FALKIRK WEST
(Scotland Central region)
E. 53,404 *T.* 63.04%
D. Canavan, *Falkirk W.* 18,511
R. Martin, *Lab.*   6,319
M. Matheson, *SNP*   5,986
G. Miller, *C.*   1,897
A. Smith, *LD*   954
Falkirk W. majority 12,192

FIFE CENTRAL
(Scotland Mid and Fife region)
E. 58,850 *T.* 55.82%
H. McLeish, *Lab.*   18,828
Ms P. Marwick, *SNP*   10,153
Ms J. A. Liston, *LD*   1,953
K. Harding, *C.*   1,918
Lab. majority 8,675

FIFE NORTH EAST
(Scotland Mid and Fife region)
E. 60,886 *T.* 59.03%
I. Smith, *LD*   13,590
E. Brocklebank, *C.*   8,526
C. Welsh, *SNP*   6,373
C. Milne, *Lab.*   5,175
D. Macgregor, *Ind.*   1,540
R. Beveridge, *Ind.* 737
LD majority 5,064

GALLOWAY AND UPPER
NITHSDALE
(Scotland South region)

E. 53,057 *T.* 66.56%
A. Morgan, *SNP*   13,873
A. Fergusson, *C.*   10,672
J. Stevens, *Lab.*   7,209
Ms J. Mitchell, *LD*   3,562
SNP majority 3,201

GLASGOW ANNIESLAND
(Glasgow region)
E. 54,378 *T.* 52.37%
D. Dewar, *Lab.*   16,749
K. Stewart, *SNP*   5,756
W. Aitken, *C.*   3,032
I. Brown, *LD*   1,804
Ms A. Lynch, *SSP*   1,000
E. Boyd, *Soc. Lab.* 139
Lab. majority 10,993
By-election held on 23 November
2000 *see* p 284

GLASGOW BAILLIESTON
(Glasgow region)
E. 49,068 *T.* 48.32%
Ms M. Curran, *Lab.*   11,289
Ms D. Elder, *SNP*   8,217
J. McVicar, *SSP*   1,864
Ms K. Pickering, *C.*   1,526
Ms J. Fryer, *LD* 813
Lab. majority 3,072

GLASGOW CATHCART
(Glasgow region)
E. 51,338 *T.* 52.55%
M. Watson, *Lab.*   12,966
Ms M. Whitehead, *SNP*   7,592
Ms M. Leishman, *C.*   3,311
C. Dick, *LD*   2,187
R. Slorach, *SWP* 920
Lab. majority 5,374

GLASGOW GOVAN
(Glasgow region)
E. 53,257 *T.* 49.52%
G. Jackson, *Lab.*   11,421
Ms N. Sturgeon, *SNP*   9,665
Ms T. Ahmed-Sheikh, *C.*   2,343
M. Aslam Khan, *LD*   1,479
C. McCarthy, *SSP*   1,275
J. Foster, *Comm. Brit.* 190
Lab. majority 1,756

GLASGOW KELVIN
(Glasgow region)
E. 61,207 *T.* 46.34%
Ms P. McNeill, *Lab.*   12,711
Ms S. White, *SNP*   8,303
Ms M. Craig, *LD*   3,720
A. Rasul, *C.*   2,253
Ms H. Ritchie, *SSP*   1,375
Lab. majority 4,408

GLASGOW MARYHILL
(Glasgow region)
E. 56,469 *T.* 40.75%
Ms P. Ferguson, *Lab.*   11,455
W. Wilson, *SNP*   7,129
Ms C. Hamblen, *LD*   1,793
G. Scott, *SSP*   1,439
M. Fry, *C.*   1,194
Lab. majority 4,326

GLASGOW POLLOCK
(Glasgow region)

E. 47,970 *T.* 54.37%
J. Lamont, *Lab. Co-op.*   11,405
K. Gibson, *SNP*   6,763
T. Sheridan, *SSP*   5,611
R. O'Brien, *C.*   1,370
J. King, *LD* 931
Lab. Co-op. majority 4,642

GLASGOW RUTHERGLEN
(Glasgow region)
E. 51,012 *T.* 56.89%
Ms J. Hughes, *Lab.*   13,442
T. Chalmers, *SNP*   6,155
R. Brown, *LD*   5,798
I. Stewart, *C.*   2,315
W. Bonnar, *SSP* 832
J. Nisbet, *Soc. Lab.* 481
Lab. majority 7,287

GLASGOW SHETTLESTON
(Glasgow region)
E. 50,592 *T.* 40.58%
F. McAveety, *Lab. Co-op.*   11,078
J. Byrne, *SNP*   5,611
Ms R. Kane, *SSP*   1,640
C. Bain, *C.*   1,260
L. Clarke, *LD* 943
Lab. Co-op. majority 5,467

GLASGOW SPRINGBURN
(Glasgow region)
E. 55,670 *T.* 43.77%
P. Martin, *Lab.*   14,268
J. Brady, *SNP*   6,375
M. Roxburgh, *C.*   1,293
M. Dunnigan, *LD*   1,288
J. Friel, *SSP* 1,141
Lab. majority 7,893

GORDON
(Scotland North East region)
E. 59,497 *T.* 56.51%
Ms N. Radcliffe, *LD*   12,353
A. Stronach, *SNP*   8,158
A. Johnstone, *C.*   6,602
Ms G. Carlin-Kulwicki, *Lab.*   3,950
H. Watt, *Ind.*   2,559
LD majority 4,195

GREENOCK AND INVERCLYDE
(Scotland West region)
E. 48,584 *T.* 58.95%
D. McNeil, *Lab.*   11,817
R. Finnie, *LD*   7,504
I. Hamilton, *SNP*   6,762
R. Wilkinson, *C.*   1,699
D. Landels, *SSP* 857
Lab. majority 4,313

HAMILTON NORTH AND
BELLSHILL
(Scotland Central region)
E. 53,992 *T.* 57.82%
M. McMahon, *Lab.*   15,227
Ms K. McAlorum, *SNP*   9,621
S. Thomson, *C.*   3,199
Ms J. Struthers, *LD*   2,105
Ms K. McGavigan, *Soc. Lab.* 1,064
Lab. majority 5,606

HAMILTON SOUTH
(Scotland Central region)
E. 46,765 *T.* 55.43%

T. McCabe, *Lab.* 14,098
A. Ardrey, *SNP* 6,922
Ms M. Mitchell, *C.* 2,918
J. Oswald, *LD* 1,982
Lab. majority 7,176

INVERNESS EAST, NAIRN AND
LOCHABER
(Highlands and Islands region)
E. 66,285 T. 63.10%
F. Ewing, *SNP* 13,825
Ms J. Aitken, *Lab.* 13,384
D. Fraser, *LD* 8,508
Ms M. Scanlon, *C.* 6,107
SNP majority 441

KILMARNOCK AND LOUDOUN
(Scotland Central region)
E. 61,454 T. 64.03%
Ms M. Jamieson, *Lab.* 17,345
A. Neil, *SNP* 14,585
L. McIntosh, *C.* 4,589
J. Stewart, *LD* 2,830
Lab. majority 2,760

KIRKCALDY
(Scotland Mid and Fife region)
E. 51,640 T. 54.88%
M. Livingstone, *Lab. Co-op.* 13,645
S. Hosie, *SNP* 9,170
M. Scott-Hayward, *C.* 2,907
J. Mainland, *LD* 2,620
Lab. Co-op. majority 4,475

LINLITHGOW
(Lothians region)
E. 54,262 T. 62.26%
Ms M. Mulligan, *Lab.* 15,247
S. Stevenson, *SNP* 12,319
G. Lindhurst, *C.* 3,158
J. Barrett, *LD* 2,643
Ms I. Ovenstone, *Ind.* 415
Lab. majority 2,928

LIVINGSTON
(Lothians region)
E. 62,060 T. 58.93%
B. Muldoon, *Lab.* 17,313
G. McCarra, *SNP* 13,409
D. Younger, *C.* 3,014
M. Oliver, *LD* 2,834
Lab. majority 3,904

MIDLOTHIAN
(Lothians region)
E. 48,374 T. 61.51%
Ms R. Brankin, *Lab. Co-op.* 14,467
A. Robertson, *SNP* 8,942
J. Elder, *LD* 3,184
G. Turnbull, *C.* 2,544
D. Pryde, *Ind.* 618
Lab. Co-op. majority 5,525

MORAY
(Highlands and Islands region)
E. 58,388 T. 57.50%
Mrs M. Ewing, *SNP* 13,027
A. Farquharson, *Lab.* 8,898
A. Findlay, *C.* 8,595
Ms P. Kenton, *LD* 3,056
SNP majority 4,129

MOTHERWELL AND WISHAW
(Scotland Central region)
E. 52,613 T. 57.71%
J. McConnell, *Lab.* 13,955
J. McGuigan, *SNP* 8,879
W. Gibson, *C.* 3,694
J. Milligan, *Soc. Lab.* 1,941
R. Spillane, *LD* 1,895
Lab. majority 5,076

OCHIL
(Scotland Mid and Fife region)
E. 57,083 T. 64.58%
R. Simpson, *Lab.* 15,385
G. Reid, *SNP* 14,082
*N. Johnston, *C.* 4,151
Earl of Mar and Kellie, *LD* 3,249
Lab. majority 1,303
*N. Johnston resigned on 10 August
2001. He was replaced by
Murdo Fraser

ORKNEY
(Highlands and Islands region)
E. 15,658 T. 56.95%
J. Wallace, *LD* 6,010
C. Zawadzki, *C.* 1,391
J. Mowat, *SNP* 917
A. Macleod, *Lab.* 600
LD majority 4,619

PAISLEY NORTH
(Scotland West region)
E. 49,020 T. 56.61%
Ms W. Alexander, *Lab.* 13,492
I. Mackay, *SNP* 8,876
P. Ramsay, *C.* 2,242
Ms T. Mayberry, *LD* 2,133
Ms F. Macdonald, *SSP* 1,007
Lab. majority 4,616

PAISLEY SOUTH
(Scotland West region)
E. 53,637 T. 57.15%
H. Henry, *Lab.* 13,899
W. Martin, *SNP* 9,404
S. Callison, *LD* 2,974
Ms S. Laidlaw, *C.* 2,433
P. Mack, *Ind.* 1,273
Ms J. Forrest, *SWP* 673
Lab. majority 4,495

PERTH
(Scotland Mid and Fife region)
E. 61,034 T. 61.27%
Ms R. Cunningham, *SNP* 13,570
I. Stevenson, *C.* 11,543
Ms J. Richards, *Lab.* 8,725
C. Brodie, *LD* 3,558
SNP majority 2,027

RENFREWSHIRE WEST
(Scotland West region)
E. 52,452 T. 64.89%
Ms P. Godman, *Lab.* 12,708
C. Campbell, *SNP* 9,815
Ms A. Goldie, *C.* 7,243
N. Ascherson, *LD* 2,659
A. McGraw, *Ind.* 1,136
P. Clark, *SWP* 476
Lab. majority 2,893

ROSS, SKYE AND INVERNESS
WEST
(Highlands and Islands region)
E. 55,845 T. 63.42%
J. Farquhar-Munro, *LD* 11,652
D. Munro, *Lab.* 10,113
J. Mather, *SNP* 7,997
J. Scott, *C.* 3,351
D. Briggs, *Ind.* 2,302
LD majority 1,539

ROXBURGH AND BERWICKSHIRE
(Scotland South region)
E. 47,639 T. 58.52%
E. Robson, *LD* 11,320
A. Hutton, *C.* 7,735
S. Crawford, *SNP* 4,719
Ms S. McLeod, *Lab.* 4,102
LD majority 3,585

SHETLAND
(Highlands and Islands region)
E. 16,978 T. 58.77%
T. Scott, *LD* 5,435
J. Wills, *Lab.* 2,241
W. Ross, *SNP* 1,430
G. Robinson, *C.* 872
LD majority 3,194

STIRLING
(Scotland Mid and Fife region)
E. 52,904 T. 67.68%
Ms S. Jackson, *Lab.* 13,533
Ms A. Ewing, *SNP* 9,552
B. Monteith, *C.* 9,158
I. Macfarlane, *LD* 3,407
S. Kilgour, *Ind.* 155
Lab. majority 3,981

STRATHKELVIN AND BEARSDEN
(Scotland West region)
E. 63,111 T. 67.17%
S. Galbraith, *Lab.* 21,505
Ms F. McLeod, *SNP* 9,384
C. Ferguson, *C.* 6,934
Ms A. Howarth, *LD* 4,144
Ms M. Richards, *Anti-Drug* 423
Lab. majority 12,121
By-election held on 7 June 2001 *see
below*

TAYSIDE NORTH
(Scotland Mid and Fife region)
E. 61,795 T. 61.58%
J. Swinney, *SNP* 16,786
M. Fraser, *C.* 12,594
Ms M. Dingwall, *Lab.* 5,727
P. Regent, *LD* 2,948
SNP majority 4,192

TWEEDDALE, ETTRICK AND
LAUDERDALE
(Scotland South region)
E. 51,577 T. 65.37%
I. Jenkins, *LD* 12,078
Ms C. Creech, *SNP* 7,600
G. McGregor, *Lab.* 7,546
J. Campbell, *C.* 6,491
LD majority 4,478

WESTERN ISLES
(*Highlands and Islands region*)
E. 22,412 T. 62.26%

A. Morrison, *Lab.*	7,248
A. Nicholson, *SNP*	5,155
J. MacGrigor, *C.*	1,095
J. Horne, *LD*	456
Lab. majority 2,093	

BY-ELECTIONS

AYR (16 March 2000)
T. 57%

J. Scott, *C.*	12,580
J. Mather, *SNP*	9,236
R. Millar, *Lab.*	7,054
J. Stewart, *SSP*	1,345
S. Ritchie, *LD*	800
G. Corbett, *Green*	460
W. Botcherby, *Ind.*	186
A. McConnachie, *UK Ind*	113
R. Graham, *ProLife*	111
K. Dhillon, *Ind*	15
C. majority 3,344	

GLASGOW ANNIESLAND
(23 November 2000)
T. 20,221

Bill Butler, *Lab.*	9,838
Tom Chalmers, *SNP*	4,462
Kate Pickering, *C.*	2,148
R. Kane, *SSP*	1,429
Judith Fryer, *LD*	1,384
Alasdair Whitelaw, *Green*	662
Murdo Ritchie, *Lab.*	298
Lab. majority 5,376	

BANFF AND BUCHAN (7 June 2001)
T. 30,838

Stewart Stevenson, *SNP*	15,386
Ted Brocklebank, *C.*	6,819
Megan Harris, *Lab.*	4,597
Canon Kenyon Wright, *LD*	3,231
Peter Anderson, *SSP*	682
SNP majority 8,567	

STRATHKELVIN AND BEARSDEN
(7 June 2001)
T. 41,734

Brian Fitzpatrick, *Lab.*	15,401
Jean M. Turner, *Ind.*	7,275
John Morrison, *LD*	7,147
Janet E. Law, *SNP*	6,457
Charles Ferguson, *C.*	5,037
Lab. majority, 8,126	

REGIONS

GLASGOW
E. 531,956 T. 48.19%

Lab.	112,588 (43.92%)
SNP	65,360 (25.50%)
C.	20,239 (7.90%)
SSP	18,581 (7.25%)
LD	18,473 (7.21%)
Green	10,159 (3.96%)
Soc. Lab.	4,391 (1.71%)
ProLife	2,357 (0.92%)
SUP	2,283 (0.89%)
Comm. Brit.	521 (0.20%)
Humanist	447 (0.17%)
NLP	419 (0.16%)
SPGB	309 (0.12%)
Choice	221 (0.09%)
Lab. majority 47,228	

(May 1997, Lab. maj. 166,061)
Additional Members elected: W.
Aitken, *C.*; R. Brown, *LD*; Ms D.
Elder, *SNP*; Ms S. White, *SNP*; Ms
N. Sturgeon, *SNP*; K. Gibson,
SNP; T. Sheridan, *SSP*

HIGHLANDS AND ISLANDS
E. 326,553 T. 61.76%

SNP	55,933 (27.73%)
Lab.	51,371 (25.47%)
LD	43,226 (21.43%)
C.	30,122 (14.94%)
Green	7,560 (3.75%)
Ind. Noble	3,522 (1.75%)
Soc. Lab.	2,808 (1.39%)
Highlands	2,607 (1.29%)
SSP	1,770 (0.88%)
Mission	1,151 (0.57%)
Int. Ind.	712 (0.35%)
NLP	536 (0.27%)
Ind. R.	354 (0.18%)
SNP majority 4,562	

(May 1997, LD maj. 1,388)

Additional Members
J. MacGrigor, *C.*; Mrs M. Scanlon,
C.; Ms M. MacMillan, *Lab.*;
P. Peacock, *Lab.*; Ms R. Grant, *Lab.*;
Mrs W. Ewing, *SNP*; D. Hamilton,
SNP

LOTHIANS
E. 539,656 T. 61.25%

Lab.	99,908 (30.23%)
SNP	85,085 (25.74%)
C.	52,067 (15.75%)
LD	47,565 (14.39%)
Green	22,848 (6.91%)
Soc. Lab.	10,895 (3.30%)
SSP	5,237 (1.58%)
Lib.	2,056 (0.62%)
Witchery	1,184 (0.36%)
ProLife	898 (0.27%)
Rights	806 (0.24%)
NLP	564 (0.17%)
Braveheart	557 (0.17%)
SPGB	388 (0.12%)
Ind. Voice	256 (0.08%)
Ind. Ind.	145 (0.04%)
Anti-Corr.	54 (0.02%)
Lab. majority 14,823	

(May 1997, Lab. maj. 101,991)

Additional Members
Lord James Douglas Hamilton, *C.*;
D. McLetchie, *C.*; Rt. Hon. Sir David
Steel, *LD*; K. MacAskill, *SNP*; Ms M.
MacDonald, *SNP*; Ms F. Hyslop,
SNP; R. Harper, *Green*

SCOTLAND CENTRAL
E. 551,733 T. 59.90%

Lab.	129,822 (39.28%)
SNP	91,802 (27.78%)
C.	30,243 (9.15%)
Falkirk W.	27,700 (8.38%)
LD	20,505 (6.20%)
Soc. Lab.	10,956 (3.32%)
Green	5,926 (1.79%)
SSP	5,739 (1.74%)
SUP	2,886 (0.87%)
ProLife	2,567 (0.78%)
SFPP	1,373 (0.42%)
NLP	719 (0.22%)
Ind. Prog.	248 (0.08%)
Lab. majority 38,020	

(May 1997, Lab. maj. 143,376)

Additional Members
Mrs L. McIntosh, *C.*; D. Gorrie, *LD*;
A. Neil, *SNP*; M. Matheson, *SNP*; Ms
L. Fabiani, *SNP*; A. Wilson, *SNP*; G.
Paterson, *SNP*

SCOTLAND MID AND FIFE
E. 509,387 T. 60.01%

Lab.	101,964 (33.36%)
SNP	87,659 (28.68%)
C.	56,719 (18.56%)
LD	38,896 (12.73%)
Green	11,821 (3.87%)
Soc. Lab.	4,266 (1.40%)
SSP	3,044 (1.00%)
ProLife	735 (0.24%)
NLP	558 (0.18%)
Lab. majority 14,305	

(May 1997, Lab. maj. 54,087)

Additional Members
*N. Johnston, *C.*; B. Monteith, *C.*; K.
Harding, *C.*; K. Raffan, *LD*; B.
Crawford, *SNP*; G. Reid, *SNP*; Ms
P. Marwick, *SNP*; *N. Johnston
*resigned on 10 August 2001. He was
replaced by Murdo Fraser*

SCOTLAND NORTH EAST
E. 518,521 T. 55.05%

SNP	92,329 (32.35%)
Lab.	72,666 (25.46%)
C.	52,149 (18.27%)
LD	49,843 (17.46%)
Green	8,067 (2.83%)
Soc. Lab.	3,557 (1.25%)
SSP	3,016 (1.06%)
Ind. Watt.	2,303 (0.81%)
Ind. SB	770 (0.27%)
NLP	746 (0.26%)
SNP majority 19,663	

(May 1997, Lab. maj. 17,518)

Additional Members
D. Davidson, *C.*; A. Johnstone, *C.*; B.
Wallace, *C.*; R. Lochhead, *SNP*; Ms
S. Robison, *SNP*; B. Adam, *SNP*; Ms
I. McGugan, *SNP*

SCOTLAND SOUTH
E. 510,634 T. 62.35%

Lab.	98,836 (31.04%)
SNP	80,059 (25.15%)
C.	68,904 (21.64%)
LD	38,157 (11.99%)
Soc. Lab.	13,887 (4.36%)
Green	9,468 (2.97%)

Lib.	3,478 (1.09%)	SCOTLAND WEST		NLP	589 (0.19%)	
SSP	3,304 (1.04%)	E. 498,466 T. 62.27%		Ind. Water	565 (0.18%)	
UK Ind.	1,502 (0.47%)	Lab.	119,663 (38.55%)	Lab. majority 39,246		
NLP	775 (0.24%)	SNP	80,417 (25.91%)	(May 1997, Lab. maj. 115,995)		
Lab. majority 18,777		C.	48,666 (15.68%)			

Lib. 3,478 (1.09%)
SSP 3,304 (1.04%)
UK Ind. 1,502 (0.47%)
NLP 775 (0.24%)
Lab. majority 18,777
(May 1997, Lab. maj. 79,585)

Additional Members
P. Gallie, *C.*; D. Mundell, *C.*; M. Tosh, *C.*; A. Fergusson, *C.*; M. Russell, *SNP*; A. Ingram, *SNP*; Ms C. Creech, *SNP*

SCOTLAND WEST
E. 498,466 T. 62.27%
Lab. 119,663 (38.55%)
SNP 80,417 (25.91%)
C. 48,666 (15.68%)
LD 34,095 (10.98%)
Green 8,175 (2.63%)
SSP 5,944 (1.91%)
Soc. Lab. 4,472 (1.44%)
ProLife 3,227 (1.04%)
Individual 2,761 (0.89%)
SUP 1,840 (0.59%)

NLP 589 (0.19%)
Ind. Water 565 (0.18%)
Lab. majority 39,246
(May 1997, Lab. maj. 115,995)

Additional Members
Miss A. Goldie, *C.*; J. Young, *C.*; R. Finnie, *LD*; L. Quinan, *SNP*; Ms F. McLeod, *SNP*; Ms K. Ullrich, *SNP*; C. Campbell, *SNP*

NORTHERN IRELAND ASSEMBLY

Parliament Buildings, Stormont, Belfast BT4 3XX
Tel: 028-9052 1333; Fax: 028-9052 1961
Web: www.ni-assembly.gov.uk

The Assembly has 108 members elected by single transferable vote (six from each of the 18 Westminster constituencies). The first elections took place on 25 June 1998 and members met for the first time on 1 July. Safeguards ensure that key decisions have cross-community support. The executive powers of the Assembly are discharged by an Executive Committee comprising a First Minister and Deputy First Minister (jointly elected by the Assembly on a cross-community basis) and up to ten ministers with departmental responsibilities. Ministerial posts are allocated on the basis of the number of seats each party holds.

The Assembly met in shadow form, pending the establishment of an Executive and the transfer of powers from Parliament. Following devolution it has executive and legislative authority over those areas formerly the responsibility of the Northern Ireland government departments. Its powers might be extended further in future.

Power was initially due to be transferred to the new Executive on 10 March 1999, but disagreements emerged over whether Sinn Fein should be allowed to enter the Executive before IRA weapons had been decommissioned. Further deadlines of 2 April and 30 June were also missed. On 15 July the Assembly met to nominate ministers, with the transfer of power to follow on 18 July. However, as the decommissioning issue had still not been resolved, Unionists failed to nominate ministers (the UUP boycotting the meeting itself) and the process collapsed. On 20 July the two prime ministers announced a review of the implementation of the Agreement to be facilitated by Senator George Mitchell. The scope of the review was tightly drawn, focusing only on the practical implementation of the three principles set out above, effectively decommissioning the Executive. The timing of the review dove-tailed with the inevitably sensitive publication of the Patten Commission's report on policing.

Following a series of meetings involving the parties in London, Mitchell's interim report of 15 November stated that he was increasingly more confident that the parties could find a way through the impasse.

On 18 November, following statements from the UUP, Sinn Fein and one from the IRA, Senator Mitchell concluded the review indicating that he now believed there was a basis for devolution to occur, for the institutions to be established and for decommissioning to take place as soon as possible. He concluded that devolution should take effect, the Executive Committee should meet and paramilitary organisations should

appoint their authorised representatives to the IICD in that order and all in the same day. On 20 November the Secretary of State announced support for the Mitchell proposals and stated that the assembly should meet on 29 November for the purpose of running d'Hondt procedure for appointing shadow ministers and devolution should take effect after the necessary Parliamentary procedures had been completed by 2 December 1999.

Powers were devolved to Assembly and other institutions established on 2 December on a basis agreed by the parties during the Mitchell review. The Mitchell review created the expectation that the establishment of the institutions and the appointment of authorised representatives produced conditions in which Sinn Fein could influence bringing about the start of decommissioning. But it was a matter of political reality that if decommissioning did not occur by the end of January 2000 it would be very difficult for David Trimble to continue as leader of the Ulster Unionist Party beyond this. In Late November the Council of the UUP had endorsed the Mitchell outcome but, reflecting the political reality, also recommend that progress on the timing and modalities of decommissioning be reviewed at the end of January 2000 through reports presented to the two governments by the IICD.

Devolution and the institutions were able to flourish on the basis of sufficient cross community support. Unfortunately that support began to ebb when the anticipated progress on decommissioning failed to materialise at the end of January. The two Governments took receipt of General de Chastelain's 31 January report but held back publication in order to explore any hope of credible progress on decommissioning. Both governments tried further efforts to gain clarity on the decommissioning issue.

The Secretary of State announced the suspension legislation on 3 February and warned publicly that it would come into effect on Friday 11 February . On the morning of 11 February , there was some sign that a new IRA proposal was emerging. The Irish Government presented a new position from its leadership. There were still only words and no timescale, but it did include clearer and less equivocal words than before. Unfortunately this was not enough to avert the collapse of the institutions.

Suspension meant that the Assembly could not meet or conduct any business. Parliament Buildings remained open for use by Assembly Members for the purpose of carrying out constituency work and they continued to be paid salaries and allowances - set at the lower pre-devolution shadow rate to reflect the suspension of Assembly business.

Following a period of intensive discussions with pro-Agreement parties during 4 and 5 May at Hillsborough, the Prime Minister and Taoiseach issued a joint statement committing both Government's proposals. On May 6, the

IRA responded with a significant and forthcoming statement in which they recognised that:
- the implementation of what the Governments had agreed would provide a new context in which Republicans could pursue their political objectives peacefully.
- in that new context the IRA leadership would initiate a process that would completely and verifiably put arms beyond use.
- the IRA would renew contact with the Decommissioning Commission.
- agreed, as a confidence building measure, to open a number of arms dumps to independent inspectors reporting to the Decommissioning Commission on a regular basis to verify that arms remain secure.

The pro-Agreement parties welcomed these developments. The UUP leader, David Trimble said that the IRA statement 'appeared to break new ground'. The Prime Minister and the Taoiseach announced on 8 May that they were asking the former Finnish President Martti Ahtisaari and Cyril Ramaphosa, the ANC negotiator, to become the independent inspectors. On 9 May, the Chief Constable of the RUC recognised that the IRA statement marked a significant reduction in the overall threat and announced a number of measures, spread across Northern Ireland, designed as a return to more normal policing.

The Government published the Police Bill on 16 May and gave assurances to Unionists that the legal description of the new police service would incorporate the RUC, while the operational and working name would change to Police Service of Northern Ireland. The Government also took an enabling power to resolve the flying of flags over Government buildings if the devolved Executive could not.

A week later than originally envisaged the Ulster Unionist Council endorsed the Government's proposals on 27 May and devolved government was restored to Northern Ireland with effect from midnight on 29 May 2000.

Following considerable political unrest, David Trimble resigned as Northern Ireland First Minister on 30 June 2001. His resignation was an ultimatum to encourage the IRA to start decommissioning their weapons. The administrative elements of his post have been passed to Sir Reg Empey. The future of the Assembly remains uncertain at the time of going to press.

SALARIES *as at April 2001*

First Minister	£108,471*
Deputy First Minister	£108,471*
Assembly Member	£40,315

*Also receive the Assembly Member salary

NORTHERN IRELAND EXECUTIVE

CASTLE BUILDINGS, STORMONT, BELFAST BT4 3SG
Tel: 028-9052 0700; Fax: 028-9052 8195
Web: www.northernireland.gov.uk

First Minister, vacant
Deputy First Minister, Seamus Mallon, MLA
Minister of Agriculture and Rural Development, Brid Rodgers, MLA
Minister of Culture and Arts and Leisure, Michael McGimpsey, MLA
Minister of Education, Martin McGuiness, MLA
Minister for Enterprise, Trade and Investment, Sir Reg Empey, MLA
Minister for Environment, Sam Foster, MLA
Minister for Finance and Personnel, Mark Durkan, MLA

Minister of Health, Social Services and Public Safety, Bairbre de Brún, MLA
Minister of Higher and Further Education, Training and Employment, Sean Farren, MLA
Minister for Regional Development, Gregory Campbell, MLA
Minister for Social Development, Morris Morrow, MLA

OFFICE OF THE FIRST MINISTER AND DEPUTY MINISTER

Castle Buildings, Stormont Estate, Belfast BT4 3SR
Tel: 028-9052 8400
First Minister, vacant
Deputy First Minister, Seamus Mallon, MLA

DEPARTMENT OF AGRICULTURE AND RURAL DEVELOPMENT

Dundonald House, Upper Newtownards Road, Belfast BT4 3SB
Tel: 028-9052 0100; Fax: 028-9052 5015

Minister for Agriculture and Rural Development, Brid Rodgers, MLA
Permanent Secretary (SCS), Peter Small
Under-Secretaries (SCS), (Central Services and Rural Development); (Food, Farming and Environmental Policy); (Veterinary); (Science); (Agri-Food Development)

EXECUTIVE AGENCIES

RIVERS AGENCY, 4 Hospital Road, Belfast BT8 8JP.
Tel: 028-9025 3355
FOREST SERVICE, Dundonald House, Upper Newtownards Road, Belfast BT4 3SB.
Tel: 028-9052 4480

DEPARTMENT OF CULTURE, ARTS AND LEISURE

20-24 York Street, Belfast BT15 1AQ
Tel: 028-9025 8825

Minister for Culture, Arts and Leisure, Michael McGimpsey, MLA
Permanent Secretary (SCS), Dr Aideen Meginley

DEPARTMENT OF EDUCATION

Rathgael House, 43 Balloo Road, Bangor, Co. Down BT19 7PR
Tel: 028-9127 9279; Fax: 028-9127 9100

Minister of Education, Martin McGuinness, MLA
Permanent Secretary (SCS), Jerry McGinn

DEPARTMENT OF ENTERPRISE, TRADE AND INVESTMENT

Netherleigh, Massey Avenue, Belfast BT4 2JP
Tel: 028-9052 9900; Fax: 028 9052 9550

Minister for Enterprise, Trade and Investment, Sir Reg Empey, MLA
Permanent Secretary (SCS), Bruce Robinson
Under-Secretaries (SCS), Greg McConnell (Policy Group); R. Hamilton (Management Services Group)
INDUSTRIAL DEVELOPMENT BOARD, IDB House, 64 Chichester Street, Belfast BT1 4JX. Tel: 028-9023 3233

EXECUTIVE AGENCIES

INDUSTRIAL RESEARCH AND TECHNOLOGY UNIT, 17 Antrim Road, Lisburn BT28 3AL. Tel: 028-9262 3000

DEPARTMENT OF THE ENVIRONMENT FOR NORTHERN IRELAND

Clarence Court, 10–18 Adelaide Street, Belfast BT2 8GB
Tel: 028-90 540540

Minister for the Environment, Sam Foster, MLA
Permanent Secretary (SCS), Stephen Quinn
Under-Secretaries (SCS), C. Smith (Local Government and Planning); F. Dillon (Environment and Heritage, Road Safety, DVT (NI), DVL (NI) and Environmental Policy)

EXECUTIVE AGENCIES
DRIVER AND VEHICLE LICENSING AGENCY (NORTHERN IRELAND), County Hall, Castlerock Road, Coleraine, Co. Londonderry BT51 3HS. Tel: 028-703 41469
DRIVER AND VEHICLE TESTING AGENCY (NORTHERN IRELAND), Balmoral Road, Belfast BT12 6QL. Tel: 028-90681 831
ENVIRONMENT AND HERITAGE SERVICE, Commonwealth House, Castle Street, Belfast BT1 1GU. Tel: 028-90251477
PLANNING SERVICE, Clarence Court, 10–18 Adelaide Street, Belfast BT2 8GB. Tel: 028-9054 0540

ADVISORY BODIES
HISTORIC BUILDINGS COUNCIL FOR NORTHERN IRELAND, c/o Environment and Heritage Service, Historic Monuments and Buildings, Commonwealth House, Castle Street, Belfast BT1 1GU. Tel: 028-9025 1477
COUNCIL FOR NATURE CONSERVATION AND THE COUNTRYSIDE, c/o Environment and Heritage Service, Commonwealth House, Castle Street, Belfast BT1 1GU. Tel: 028-9025 1477

DEPARTMENT OF FINANCE AND PERSONNEL
Rathgael House, Balloo Road, Bangor BT19 7NA
Tel: 028-9127 9279
Minister of Finance and Personnel, Mark Durkan, MLA
Permanent Secretary (SCS), P. Carvill
Under-Secretaries (SCS), Dr A. MacCormick (Central Finances Group); Carol Muir (Central Personnel Group) J. Goldring (Law Reform)
GENERAL REGISTER OFFICE (NORTHERN IRELAND), Oxford House, 49–55 Chichester Street, Belfast BT1 4HH. Tel: 028-9025 2000. *Registrar-General (G5)*

EXECUTIVE AGENCIES
BUSINESS DEVELOPMENT SERVICE, Craigantlet Buildings, Stoney Road, Belfast BT4 3SX. Tel: 028-9052 0400
CONSTRUCTION SERVICE, Churchill House, Victoria Square, Belfast BT1 4QW. Tel: 028-9052 0250
GOVERNMENT PURCHASING AGENCY, Rosepark House, Upper Newtownards Road, Belfast BT4 3NR. Tel: 028-9052 0400
LAND REGISTERS OF NORTHERN IRELAND, Lincoln Building, 27–45 Great Victoria Street, Belfast BT2 7SL. Tel: 028-9025 1555
NORTHERN IRELAND STATISTICS AND RESEARCH AGENCY, McAuley House, 2-14 Castle Street, Belfast BT1 1SA. Tel: 028-9034 8100
RATE COLLECTION AGENCY, Oxford House, 49–55 Chichester Street, Belfast BT1 4HH Tel: 028-9025 2252
VALUATION AND LANDS AGENCY, Queen's Court, 56–66 Upper Queen Street, Belfast BT1 6FD. Tel: 028-9025 0700

DEPARTMENT OF HEALTH SOCIAL SERVICES AND PUBLIC SAFETY NORTHERN IRELAND
Castle Buildings, Stormont, Belfast BT4 3SJ
Tel: 028-9052 0000; Fax: 028-9052 0572

Minister for Health, Social Services and Public Safety: Bairbre de Brún, MLA
Permanent Secretary (SCS), Clive Gowdy
Chief Medical Officer (SCS), Dr H. Campbell
Under-Secretaries (SCS), D. Hill (Planning and Resources Group); P. Simpson (HPSS Management Group)

EXECUTIVE AGENCIES
NORTHERN IRELAND HEALTH AND SOCIAL SERVICES ESTATES AGENCY, Stoney Road, Dundonald, Belfast BT16 1US. Tel: 028-9052 0025

DEPARTMENT FOR EMPLOYMENT AND LEARNING
Adelaide House, Adelaide Street, Belfast BT2 8FD
Tel: 028-9025 7777; Fax: 028-9025 7783
Minister for Higher and Further Education, Training and Employment, Sean Farren, MLA
Permanent Secretary (SCS), Allan Shannon
Private Secretary (SCS), (Training and Employment Agency) Bernie Rooney

DEPARTMENT FOR REGIONAL DEVELOPMENT
Clarence Court, 10-18 Adelaide Street, Belfast BT2 8GB
Tel: 028-9054 0540; Fax: 028-9054 0064
Minister for Regional Development, Gregory Cambell, MLA
Permanent Secretary (SCS), N. Hamilton
Deputy Secretaries (SCS), Paul Swinney (Strategic Planning, Transport and Finance); Linda Brown (Roads, Water, Personnel and Management Services)

DEPARTMENT FOR SOCIAL DEVELOPMENT
Churchill House, Victoria Square, Belfast BT2 4BA
Tel: 028-9056 9100
Minister for Social Development, Morris Morrow
Permanent Secretary (SCS), John Hunter
Deputy Secretaries (SCS), Cliff Radcliffe (Urban Regeneration and Community Development); vacant (Resources, Housing and Social Group)

OTHER BODIES
BRITISH-IRISH COUNCIL
NORTH/SOUTH MINISTERIAL COUNCIL
CIVIC FORUM
BRITISH-IRISH INTERGOVERNMENTAL CONFERENCE

NORTHERN IRELAND ASSEMBLY MEMBERS AS AT 31 JULY 2001
Adams, Gerry, (*SF*), *West Belfast*
Adamson, Dr Ian, (*UUP*), *East Belfast*
*Agnew, Fraser, (*UUAP*), *North Belfast*
Alderdice, Lord, (*Speaker*), *East Belfast*
Armitage, Ms Pauline, (*UUP*) *East Londonderry*
Armstrong, Billy, (*UUP*), *Mid Ulster*
Attwood, Alex, (*SDLP*), *West Belfast*
Beggs, Roy, (*UUP*), *East Antrim*
Bell, Billy, (*UUP*) *Lagan Valley*
Bell, Eileen, (*All.*), *North Down*
Berry, Paul, (*DUP*), *Newry and Armagh*
Birnie, Esmond, (*UUP*), *South Belfast*
†Boyd, Norman, (*NIUP*), *South Antrim*
Bradley, P. J. (*SDLP*), *South Down*
Brun, Ms Bairbre de, (*SF*), *West Belfast*
Byrne, Joe, (*SDLP*), *West Tyrone*
Campbell, Gregory, (*DUP*), *East Londonderry*
Carrick, Mervyn, (*DUP*), *Upper Bann*
Carson, Ms Joan, (*UUP*), *Ferm and South Tyrone*
Close, Seamus, (*All.*), *Lagan Valley*

Clyde, Wilson, (DUP), South Antrim
Cobain, Fred, (UUP), North Belfast
Coulter, Robert, (UUP), North Antrim
**Courtney, Anne, (SDLP), Foyle
Dallat, John, (SDLP), East Londonderry
Davis, Ivan, (UUP), Lagan Valley
Dodds, Nigel, (DUP), North Belfast
Doherty, Arthur, (SDLP), East Londonderry
Doherty, Pat, (SF), West Tyrone
*Douglas, Boyd, (UUAP), East Londonderry
Durkan, Mark, (SDLP), Foyle
Empey, Reg, (UUP), East Belfast
Ervine, David, (PUP), East Belfast
Farren, Sean, (SDLP), North Antrim
Fee, John, (SDLP), Newry and Armagh
Ford, David, (All.), South Antrim
Foster, Sam, (UUP), Ferm and South Tyrone
Gallagher, Tommy, (SDLP), Ferm and South Tyrone
Gibson, Oliver, (DUP), West Tyrone
Gildernew, Michelle, (SF), Ferm and South Tyrone
‡Gorman, John, (UUP), North Down
***Hamilton, Tom, (UUP), Strangford
Hanna, Carmel, (SDLP), South Belfast
Haughey, Denis, (SDLP), Mid Ulster
Hay, William, (DUP), Foyle
Hendron, Joe, (SDLP), West Belfast
Hilditch, David, (DUP), East Antrim
Hussey, Derek, (UUP), West Tyrone
Hutchinson, Bill, (PUP), North Belfast
§Hutchinson, Roger, (Ind Unionist), East Antrim
Kane, Gardiner, (DUP), North Antrim
Kelly, Gerry (SF), North Belfast
Kelly, John, (SF), Mid Ulster
Kennedy, Danny, (UUP), Newry and Armagh
Leslie, James, (UUP), North Antrim
Lewsley, Patricia, (SDLP), Lagan Valley
Maginness, Alban, (SDLP), North Belfast
Mallon, Seamus, (SDLP), Newry and Armagh
Maskey, Alex, (SF), West Belfast
McCarthy, Keiran, (All.), Strangford
McCartney, Robert, (UKUP), North Down
McClarty, David, (UUP), East Londonderry
McCrea, William, (DUP), Mid Ulster
‡McClelland, Donovan, (SDLP), South Antrim
McDonnell, Alasdair, (SDLP), South Belfast
McElduff, Barry, (SF), West Tyrone
McFarland, Alan, (UUP), North Down
McGimpsey, Michael, (UUP), South Belfast
McGrady, Eddie, (SDLP), South Down
McGuiness, Martin, (SF), Mid Ulster
McHugh, Gerry, (SF), Ferm and South Tyrone
McLaughlin, Mitchel, (SF), Foyle
McMenamin, Eugene, (SDLP), West Tyrone
McNamee, Pat, (SF), Newry and Armagh
McWilliams, Prof. Monica, (NIWC), South Belfast
Molloy, Francie, (SF), Mid Ulster
Murphy, Connor, (SF), Newry and Armagh
Murphy, Mick, (SF), South Down
‡Morrice, Ms Jane, (NIWC), North Down
Morrow, Maurice, (DUP), Ferm and South Tyrone
Neeson, Sean, (All.), East Antrim
Nelis, Ms Mary, (SF), Foyle
Nesbitt, Dermot, (UUP), South Down
O'Connor, Danny, (SDLP), East Antrim
O'Hagan, Dara, (SF), Upper Bann
O'Neill, Eamon, (SDLP), South Down
Paisley, Rev Dr Ian, (DUP), North Antrim
Poots, Edwin, (DUP), Lagan Valley
Ramsey, Sue, (SF), West Belfast
Robinson, Iris, (DUP), Strangford

Robinson, Ken, (UUP), East Anrtim
Robinson, Mark, (DUP), South Belfast
Robinson, Peter, (DUP), East Belfast
†Roche, Patrick, (NIUP), Lagan Valley
Rodgers, Brid, (SDLP), Upper Bann
Savage, George, (UUP), Upper Bann
Shannon, Jim, (DUP), Strangford
Shipley-Dalton, Duncan, (UUP), South Antrim
Taylor, The Rt. Hon. John, (UUP), Strangford
Tierney, John, (SDLP), Foyle
Trimble, The Rt. Hon. David, (UUP), Upper Bann
Watson, Denis, (UUAP), Upper Bann
Weir, Peter, (UUP), North Down
Wells, Jim, (DUP), South Down
†Wilson, Cedric, (NIUP), Strangford
Wilson, Jim, (UUP) South Antrim
Wilson, Sammy, (DUP), East Belfast

* Elected as independent candidates, formed the United Unionist Assembly Party (UUAP) with effect from 21 September 1998
† Elected as UK Unionist Candidates, formed Northern Ireland Unionist Party (NIUP) with effect from 15 January 1999
‡ Elected as Deputy Speakers of the Northern Ireland Assembly 31 January 2000
§ Mr Hutchinson was expelled from the Northern Ireland Unionist Party (NIUP) with effect from 2 December 1999
** John Hume, MP, MEP, resigned from the Northern Ireland Assembly with effect from 1 December 2000. He was replaced by Anne Courtney
*** Tom Benson died on 24 December 2000. He was replaced by Tom Hamilton

POLITICAL COMPOSITION

UUP	Ulster Unionist Party	28
SDLP	Social Democratic and Labour Party	24
DUP	Democratic Unionist Party	20
SF	Sinn Fein	18
All.	All.	6
*NIUP	Northern Ireland Unionist Party	3
†UUAP	United Unionist Assembly Party	3
NIWC	Northern Ireland Women's Coalition	2
PUP	Progressive Unionist Party	2
UKUP	UK Unionist Party	1
‡Ind Unionist	Independent Unionist	1

The Government

Prime Minister, First Lord of the Treasury and Minister for the Civil Service
The Rt. Hon. Anthony (Tony) Blair, MP, since May 1997
Deputy Prime Minister and First Secretary of State
The Rt. Hon. John Prescott, MP, since May 1997
Chancellor of the Exchequer
The Rt. Hon. Gordon Brown, MP, since May 1997
Secretary of State for Foreign and Commonwealth Affairs
The Rt. Hon Jack Straw, MP, since June 2001
Lord Chancellor
The Lord Irvine of Lairg, PC, QC, since May 1997
Secretary of State for the Home Department
The Rt. Hon. David Blunkett, MP, since June 2001
Secretary of State for Education and Skills
The Rt. Hon. Estelle Morris, MP, since June 2001
President of the Council and Leader of the House of Commons
The Rt. Hon. Robin Cook, MP, since June 2001
Minister for the Cabinet Office and Chancellor of the Duchy of Lancaster
The Rt. Hon. Lord MacDonald of Tradeston, CBE
Secretary of State for Scotland
The Rt. Hon. Helen Liddell, MP, since June 2001
Secretary of State for Defence
The Rt. Hon. Geoff Hoon, MP, since October 1999
Secretary of State for Health
The Rt. Hon. Alan Milburn, MP, since October 1999
Parliamentary Secretary to the Treasury (Chief Whip)
The Rt. Hon. Hilary Armstrong, MP, since June 2001
Secretary of State for Culture, Media and Sport
The Rt. Hon. Tessa Jowell, MP, since June 2001
Secretary of State for Northern Ireland
The Rt. Hon. Dr John Reid, MP, since June 2001
Secretary of State for Wales
The Rt. Hon. Paul Murphy, MP, since July 1999
Secretary of State for International Development
The Rt. Hon. Clare Short, MP, since May 1997
Secretary of State for Work and Pensions
The Rt. Hon. Alistair Darling, MP, since July 1998
Secretary of State for Environment, Food and Rural Affairs
The Rt. Hon. Margaret Beckett, MP, since June 2001
Secretary of State for Transport, Local Government and The Regions
The Rt. Hon. Stephen Byers, MP, since June 2001
Lord Privy Seal, Leader of the House of Lords, The Lord Williams of Mostyn, QC, since June 2001
Secretary of State for Trade and Industry and Minister for Women
The Rt. Hon. Patricia Hewitt, MP, since June 2001
Chief Secretary to the Treasury
The Rt. Hon. Andrew Smith, MP, since October 1999
Minister without Portfolio and Party Chair
Charles Clarke, MP

The Government Chief Whip in the House of Lords will attend Cabinet meetings although they are not members of the Cabinet.
* Appointed as Lord Privy Seal

LAW OFFICERS

Attorney-General
Lord Goldsmith, QC, since June 2001
Lord Advocate
Colin Boyd, QC, since February 2000
Solicitor-General
The Rt. Hon. Harriet Harman, QC, MP, since June 2001
Solicitor-General for Scotland
Neil Davidson, QC, since February 2001
Advocate-General for Scotland
Dr Lynda Clark, QC, MP, since May 1999

MINISTERS OF STATE

Cabinet Office
Ms Barbara Roche, MP
Baroness Morgan of Huyton
Culture and Media
The Rt. Hon. Richard Caborn, MP (*Sport*)
The Rt. Hon. Baroness Blackstone (*Arts*)
Defence
The Rt. Hon. Adam Ingram, MP (*Armed Forces*)
Lord Bach (*Defence Procurement*)
Education and Skills
Stephen Timms, MP (*Schools*)
Mrs Margaret Hodge, MP, MBE (*Universities*)
Environment, Food and Rural Affairs
The Rt. Hon. Michael Meacher, MP (*Environment*)
The Rt. Hon. Alun Michael, MP (*Rural Affairs*)
Foreign and Commonwealth Office
Peter Hain, MP (*Minister for Europe*)
The Rt. Hon. Baroness Symons of Vernham Dean (*Trade and FCO*)
Health
John Hutton, MP (*NHS Structure and Resources*)
Ms Jacqui Smith, MP (*Social Care and Mental Health*)
Home Office
The Rt. Hon. John Denham, MP (*Crime Reduction Policing and Community Safety*)
The Rt. Hon. Keith Bradley, MP (*Criminal Justice Sentencing and Law Reform*)
The Lord Rooker of Perry Barr (*Citizenship and Immigration*)
Northern Ireland Office
Ms Jane Kennedy, MP
Scotland Office
George Foulkes, MP
Trade and Industry
Douglas Alexander, MP (*E-Commerce and Competitiveness*)
The Rt. Hon. Baroness Symons of Vernham Dean (*Trade and Investment*)
Brian Wilson, MP (*Industry and Energy*)
Alan Johnson, MP (*Employment Relations and the Regions*)
Transport, Local Government and the Regions
The Rt. Hon. John Spellar, MP (*Transport*)
The Rt. Hon. Nick Raynsford, MP (*Local Government and the Regions*)
Lord Falconer of Thoroton, QC (*Housing, Planning and Regeneration*)

Treasury
Dawn Primarolo, MP (*Paymaster-General*)
The Rt. Hon. Paul Boateng, MP (*Financial Secretary*)
Ms Ruth Kelly, MP (*Economic Secretary*)
Work and Pensions
The Rt. Hon. Nick Brown, MP (*Work*)
The Rt. Hon. Ian McCartney, MP (*Pensions*)

UNDER-SECRETARIES OF STATE

Cabinet
Christopher Leslie§, MP
Culture, Media and Sport
Dr Kim Howells, MP
Defence
Dr Lewis Moonie, MP (*Veterans*)
Lord Bach of Lutterworth (*Defence Procurement*)
Education and Skills
Baroness Ashton of Upholland (*Early Years and Skill Standards*)
Ivan Lewis, MP (*Young People and Learning*)
John Healey, MP (*Adult Skills*)
Environment, Food and Rural Affairs
Elliot Morley, MP (*Animal Health and Welfare and Fisheries*)
The Lord Whitty (*Food and Farming*)
Foreign and Commonwealth Office
Ben Bradshaw, MP
Baroness Amos
Dr Denis MacShane, MP
Health
Ms Hazel Blears, MP
The Lord Hunt of King's Heath, OBE
Yvette Cooper, MP
Home Office
Ms Beverley Hughes, MP (*Community and Custodial Sentences*)
Robert Ainsworth, MP (*Anti-Drugs Co-ordination and Organised Crime*)
Ms Angela Eagle, MP (*Europe, Community and Race*)
International Development
Hilary Benn, MP
Lord Chancellor's Department
Baroness Scotland of Asthal, QC
Michael Wills, MP
Ms Rosie Winterton, MP
Northern Ireland Office
Des Browne, MP
Trade and Industry
Lord Sainsbury of Turville (*Science and Innovation*)
Ms Melanie Johnson§, MP (*Competition, Consumers and Markets*)
Nigel Griffiths§, MP (*Small Business*)
Transport, Local Government and the Regions
David Jamieson, MP (*Transport*)
Ms Sally Keeble, MP (*Housing, Planning and Regeneration*)
Dr Alan Whitehead, MP (*Local Government and the Regions*)
Wales Office
Don Touhig, MP
Work and Pensions
The Rt. Hon. Baroness Hollis of Heigham
Malcolm Wicks, MP
Marcia Eagle, MP
§ Unpaid

GOVERNMENT WHIPS

HOUSE OF LORDS
Captain of the Honourable Corps of Gentlemen-at-Arms (Chief Whip)
The Rt. Hon. The Lord Carter, PC
Captain of The Queen's Bodyguard of the Yeoman of the Guard (Deputy Chief Whip)
The Lord McIntosh of Haringey
Lords-in-Waiting
The Lord Davies of Oldham
The Lord Grocott
The Lord Filkin, CBE
The Lord Bassam of Brighton
Baronesses-in-Waiting
The Baroness Farrington of Ribbleton

HOUSE OF COMMONS
Parliamentary Secretary to the Treasury (Chief Whip)
The Rt. Hon. Hilary Armstrong, MP
Treasurer of HM Household (Deputy Chief Whip)
Keith Hill, MP
Comptroller of HM Household
Thomas McAvoy, MP
Vice-Chamberlain of HM Household
Gerry Sutcliffe, MP
Lords Commissioners
Mrs Anne McGuire, MP; John Heppell, MP; Tony McNulty, MP; Nick Ainger, MP; Graham Stringer, MP
Assistant Whips
Ian Pearson, MP; Ms Angela Smith, MP; Ivor Caplin, MP; Jim Fitzpatrick, MP; Fraser Kemp, MP; Philip Woolas, MP; Dan Norris, MP

Government Departments and Public Offices

This section covers central Government departments, executive agencies, regulatory bodies, other statutory independent organisations, and bodies which are government-financed or whose head is appointed by a Government Minister.

THE CIVIL SERVICE

Under the Next Steps programme, launched in 1988, many semi-autonomous executive agencies have been established to carry out much of the work of the Civil Service. Executive agencies operate within a framework set by the responsible minister which specifies policies, objectives and available resources. All executive agencies are set annual performance targets by their minister. Each agency has a chief executive, who is responsible for the day-to-day operations of the agency and who is accountable to the minister for the use of resources and for meeting the agency's targets. The minister accounts to Parliament for the work of the agency. Nearly 80 per cent of civil servants now work in executive agencies. In October 1999 there were about 466,500 permanent civil servants.

The Senior Civil Service was created in 1996 and on 1 April 2000 comprised 3,180 staff from Permanent Secretary to the former Grade 5 level, including all agency chief executives. All Government departments and executive agencies are now responsible for their own pay and grading systems for civil servants outside the Senior Civil Service. In practice the grades of the former Open structure are still in use in some organisations. The Open structure represented the following:

Grade	Title
1	Permanent Secretary
1A	Second Permanent Secretary
2	Deputy Secretary
3	Under-Secretary
4	Chief Scientific Officer B, Professional and Technology Directing A
5	Assistant Secretary, Deputy Chief Scientific Officer, Professional and Technology Directing B
6	Senior Principal, Senior Principal Scientific Officer, Professional and Technology Superintending Grade
7	Principal, Principal Scientific Officer, Principal Professional and Technology Officer

SALARIES 2001–2

MINISTERIAL SALARIES *from 1 April 2001*

Ministers who are Members of the House of Commons receive a parliamentary salary (£49,822) in addition to their ministerial salary.

*Prime Minister	£113,596
*Cabinet minister (Commons)	£68,157
*†Cabinet minister (Lords)	£88,562
Minister of State (Commons)	£35,356
Minister of State (Lords)	£68,283
Parliamentary Under-Secretary (Commons)	£26,835
Parliamentary Under-Secretary (Lords)	£58,941

† Except the Lord Chancellor, who receives a salary of £173,875

SPECIAL ADVISERS' SALARIES *from 1 April 2001*

Special advisers to Government Ministers are paid out of public funds; their salaries are negotiated individually, but are usually in the range £28,328 to £82,867.

CIVIL SERVICE SALARIES *from 1 April 2001*

Senior Civil Service (SCS)

Secretary of the Cabinet and Head of the Home Civil Service	£98,400–£168,910
Permanent Secretary	£104,292 –£179,022
Band 9	£92,696 –£131,276
Band 8	£84,811 –£123,856
Band 7	£77,635 –£116,904
Band 6	£70,905 –£110,428
Band 5	£64,768 –£104,292
Band 4	£59,088 –£98,494
Band 3	£53,534 –£87,598
Band 2	£48,552 –£77,869
Band 1	£44,038 –£69,178

Staff are placed in pay bands according to their level of responsibility and taking account of other factors such as experience and marketability. Movement within and between bands is based on performance.

Other Civil Servants

Following the delegation of responsibility for pay and grading to Government departments and agencies from 1 April 1996, it is no longer possible to show service-wide pay rates for staff outside the Senior Civil Service. The following table will however give an indication of the percentage of civil servants at a given salary level.

Non-Industrial Staff by Gross Salary Band
as at 1 April 2000

Salary Band	Per Cent
£5,001–£10,000	6.1
£10,001–£15,000	36.8
£15,001–£20,000	23.2
£20,001–£25,000	16.8
£25,001–£30,000	6.9
£30,001–£35,000	3.4
£35,001–£40,000	1.9
£40,001–£45,000	1.4
£45,001–£50,000	0.8
£50,001–£55,000	0.4
£55,001–£60,000	0.3
£60,001–£65,000	0.2
£65,001–£70,000	0.1
£70,001–£75,000	0.1
£75,001 +	0.1

Source: Government Statistical Service – *Civil Service Statistics 2000*

GOVERNMENT DEPARTMENTS

THE CABINET OFFICE
70 Whitehall, London SW1A 2AS
Tel: 020-7270 3000
Web: www.cabinet-office.gov.uk

The Cabinet Office has responsibility for a wide range of work. This includes a secretariat role for the Cabinet and Civil Contingencies work, devolution and regional work, a central role for civil service strategy and management, public service reform, government policy delivery, social exclusion and work for women and equality. The department also takes the lead on issues such as e-government and regulatory impact.
Prime Minister and Minister for the Civil Service, The Rt. Hon. Antony (Tony) Blair, MP
Deputy Prime Minister and First Secretary of State, The Rt. Hon. John Prescott, MP
Minister for the Cabinet Office and Chancellor of the Duchy of Lancaster, The Rt. Hon. The Lord MacDonald of Tradeston, CBE
Principal Private Secretary (SCS), Dr J. Fuller
Parliamentary Private Secretary, Alan Campbell, MP
Private Secretary, Fiona Butler
Minister of State, Barbara Roche, MP
Private Secretary, Mark Langdale
Parliamentary Secretary, Tom Levitt, MP
Minister of State, Baroness Morgan of Huyton
Private Secretary, N. Pitts
Parliamentary Private Secretary, Magaret Moran, MP
Parliamentary Under-Secretary of State, Christopher Leslie, MP
Secretary of the Cabinet and Head of the Home Civil Service, Sir Richard Wilson, KCB
Private Secretary (SCS), A. Allbellry
Permanent Secretary, Ms M. MacDonald
Private Secretary, Julie Eason

PRIME MINISTER'S OFFICE
10 Downing Street, London SW1A 2AA
Tel: 020-7270 3000; Fax: 020-7925 0918
Web: www.number-10.gov.uk

Prime Minister, The Rt. Hon. Antony (Tony) Blair, MP
Principal Private Secretary, Jeremy Heywood
Chief of Staff, Jonathan Powell
Deputy Chief of Staff, P. McFadden
Private Secretaries, Claire Sumner (*Parliamentary Affairs*); David North (*Home Affairs*); Simon Virley (*Economic Affairs*); Anna Wechsberg, Michael Tatham (*Assistants on Foreign Affairs*)
Personal Assistant to PM (Diary), Katie Kay
Political Secretary, Robert Hill
Head of Policy Unit, Andrew Adonis
Policy Directorate: Carey Oppenheim; Ed Richards, Brian Hackland; Simon Virley; Geoffrey Norris; Mike Emmerich; Sarah Hunter; Simon Stevens; Justin Russell; David North; Clare Sumner; Alasdair McGowan
Parliamentary Private Secretary, David Hanson, MP
Research and Information Unit, Phil Bassett
Corporate Communications, James Humphreys
Director of Communications and Strategy, Alastair Campbell
Strategic Communications Unit, Peter Hyman
Executive Secretary, Pat Dixon
Director of Events and Visits, Fiona Millar
Director of Government Relations, Anji Hunter
Secretary for Appointments, and Ecclesiastical Secretary to the Lord Chancellor, William Chapman

Head of Secretariat and Advisor on Foreign Policy and Head of Overseas Defence Secretariat, Sir David Manning
Parliamentary Clerk, Clive Barbour

SECRETARIATS

ECONOMIC AND DOMESTIC SECRETARIAT
Head (SCS), S. Chakrabarti
Deputy Heads (SCS), Ms. L. Bell; P. Britton

DEFENCE AND OVERSEAS AFFAIRS SECRETARIAT
Foreign Policy, M. Tatham; A. Wechberg; I. Lloyd; R. Liddle
Delivery Unit Head, M. Barber
Office of Public Service Reform Head; W. Thomson
Forward Strategy Unit Head; G. Mulgan

EUROPEAN AFFAIRS SECRETARIAT
Head (SCS), S. Wall
Deputy Heads (SCS), M. Donnelly

CONSTITUTION SECRETARIAT
Director (SCS), J. Tross
Head of Other Constitutional Reform Team (SCS), Ms J. Simpson
Head of Legal Advisers, Ms R. Jeffreys

CENTRAL SECRETARIAT
Director (SCS), Ms S. Phippard
Deputy Director (SCS), P. Calcutt, OBE

CEREMONIAL BRANCH
Ashley House, 2 Monck Street, London SW1P 2BQ
Tel: 020-7270 1234
Honours Nomination Unit: Tel: 020-7276 2775
Ceremonial Officer (SCS), Mrs G. Catto

PUBLIC SERVICE DELIVERY

MODERNISING PUBLIC SERVICES GROUP
Director (SCS), J. Stephens
Deputy Directors (SCS), S. O'Leary, OBE; M. Sweetman; A. Whysall; J. Cowper

CENTRAL IT UNIT
Tel: 020-7270 1234
Director (SCS), D. Cooke
Deputy Directors (SCS), J. Crump; M. Gladwyn; Mrs A. Steward; I. White; P. Waller

REGULATORY IMPACT UNIT
Director (SCS), P. Wynn Owen
Deputy Directors (SCS), D. Hayler; C. Hayes; Ms A. French
Legal Adviser, P. Bovey

MODERNISING GOVERNMENT
Director, A. Wells
Deputy Director (SCS), J. Cowper

CIVIL SERVICE MANAGEMENT
CENTRAL GOVERNMENT NATIONAL TRAINING ORGANISATION (CGNTO)
Room 69/1 GOOGS, Horse Guards Road, London SW1P 3AL Tel: 020-7270 1597; Fax: 020-7270 6640; Email: secretariat@cgnto.org.uk

Council Members, B. Fox; J. Barker; R. Green; Ms A. Perkins; R. Dudding; C. Macdonald; B. Mitchell; B. Richardson; M. Grannatt; P. Joyce; J. Sheldon; Cllr J. Stocks; N. Starritt; D. Laughrin; I. Magee
Head of Secretariat, John Barker

CENTRE FOR MANAGEMENT AND POLICY STUDIES (CMPS)

Director-General, Prof. R. Amman
Directors (SCS), R. Green; S. Duncan

CIVIL SERVICE COLLEGE DIRECTORATE

Sunningdale Park, Larch Avenue, Ascot, Berks SL5 0QE
Tel: 01344-634000; Fax: 01344-634233
11 Belgrave Road, London SW1 4RB
Tel: 020-7834 6644; Fax: 01344-634451
1 St Colme Street, Edinburgh EH3 6AA
Tel: 0131-220 8267; Fax: 0131-220 8367
The Civil Service College Directorate of CMPS which is part of the Cabinet Office provides training in management and professional skills for the public and private sectors.
Director, E. Wooldridge
Deputy Directors M. Barnes; R. Behrens; E. Goodison; G. Llewellyn; M. Timmis

CIVIL SERVICE CORPORATE MANAGEMENT COMMAND

Senior Director (SCS), B. M. Fox, CB
Directors (SCS), J. Barker; Ms S. Hinkley, CBE
Deputy Directors (SCS), Ms A. Schofield; Ms J. Lemprière; C. J. Parry; Ms E. Goodison; D. G. Pain; S. Mitha

GOVERNMENT INFORMATION AND COMMUNICATION SERVICES

Head of Government Information and Communication Services (SCS), M. Granatt
Director, Development Centre (SCS), C. Skinner
Deputy Director, Ms S. Jenkins

OFFICE OF THE COMMISSIONER FOR PUBLIC APPOINTMENTS (OCPA)

Tel: 020-7270 6472
The role of the Commissioner for Public Appointments is to monitor, regulate, report and advise on 12,500 ministerial public appointments to executive non-departmental public bodies, public corporations, nationalised industries, utility regulators and NHS bodies. The Commissioner is appointed by an Order-in-Council.
Commissioner, Dame Rennie Fritchie
Head of Office (SCS), J. Barron

OFFICE OF THE CIVIL SERVICE COMMISSIONERS (OCSC)

3rd Floor, 35 Great Smith Street, London, SW1P 3BQ
Tel: 020-7276 2615; Fax: 020-7276 2606
The Civil Service Commissioners are responsible for upholding the principle of selection on merit on the basis of fair and open competition in recruitment to the Civil Service. They also hear and determine appeals in cases of concerns about propriety and conscience raised by civil servants under the Civil Service Code which cannot be resolved through internal procedures. The Commissioners are appointed by an Order-in-Council.
First Commissioner, The Baroness Usha Prashar, CBE
Commissioners (part-time), D. Bell; P. Bounds; J.Boyle; Ms B. Curtis; Ms S. Forbes; Dame Rennie Fritchie; Prof. E.

Gallagher, CBE; J. Hamill, CB; G. Lemos; A. Macdonald, CB; G. Maddrell; Rabbi Julia Neuberger; G. Peacock, CBE; Dr M. Semple, OBE; J. Shrigley; C. Stevens, CB
Secretary to the Commissioners and Head of the Office (SCS), J. K. Barron

CROSS-CUTTING ISSUES

SOCIAL EXCLUSION UNIT

Tel: 020-7270 5211
Director of Unit (SCS), Ms M. Wallace, OBE
Deputy Directors, Ms Z. Peatfield; A. Patel

UK ANTI DRUGS CO-ORDINATION UNIT

Tel: 020-7270 5399
UK Anti-Drugs Co-ordinator (£106,057), K. Hellawell
Deputy Co-ordinator, M. Trace
Private Secretary, V. Baggarley
Director, J. Critchley

WOMEN'S UNIT

10 Great George Street, London SW1P 3AE
Tel: 020-7273 8808
Head of Unit (SCS), Ms F. Reynolds, CBE
Deputy Director, G. Kidd

PERFORMANCE AND INNOVATION UNIT

Tel: 020-7270 1512
Director (SCS), vacant
Deputy Director (SCS), J. Rentoul

INFORMATION, ESTABLISHMENT AND ORGANISATION

Queen Anne's Chambers, 28 Broadway, London SW1H 9JS
Director of Information (SCS), P. Martin
Principal Establishment and Finance Officer (SCS), P. Wardle
Deputy Directors (SCS), Miss E. Chennells; D. Brennan; R. Harris; K. Tolladay
Ministers' Adviser on Agencies, C. Brendish, CBE

HER MAJESTY'S STATIONERY OFFICE

St Clements House, 2–16 Colegate, Norwich NR3 1BQ
Tel: 01603-621000
Controller (SCS), Mrs C. Tullo

EXECUTIVE AGENCY

GOVERNMENT CAR AND DESPATCH AGENCY

46 Ponton Road, London SW8 5AX
Tel: 020-7217 3839; Fax: 020-7217 3840;
Email: info@gcda.gsi.gov.uk The Agency provides secure transport and document transfers between Government departments.
Chief Executive, N. Matheson

CENTRAL OFFICE OF INFORMATION
Hercules Road, London SE1 7DU
Tel: 020-7928 2345; Fax: 020-7928 5037

The Central Office of Information (COI) is a Government department which offers consultancy, procurement and project management services to central Government for publicity. Administrative responsibility for the COI rests with the Minister for the Cabinet Office.
Chief Executive (G3), Miss Carol Fisher
Senior Personal Secretary, Mrs Ira MacMull

MANAGEMENT BOARD

Members, K. Williamson; P. Buchanan; I. Hamilton; R. Haslam; Mrs S. Whetton; M. Reid
Secretary, Mrs I. MacMull

DIRECTORS

Director, Client Services, I. Hamilton
Director, Marketing Communications, P. Buchanan
Director, Films, Radio and Events, S. Whetton
Director, Publications, M. Reid
Director, Central Services, K. Williamson
Director, Regional Network, R. Haslam

NETWORK OFFICES

EASTERN, 2nd Floor, Block A1, Westbrook Centre, Milton Road, Cambridge CB4 1YG. *Network Director*, Ms. M. Basham
MIDLANDS EAST, Belgrave Centre, Talbot Street, Nottingham NG1 5GG. *Network Director*, P. Smith
MIDLANDS WEST, Five Ways House, Islington Row, Middleway, Edgbaston, Birmingham B15 1SH. *Network Director* , B. Garner
NORTH-EAST, Wellbar House, Gallowgate, Newcastle upon Tyne NE1 4TB. *Network Director*, Ms L. Taylor
NORTH-WEST, Sunley Tower, Piccadilly Plaza, Manchester M1 4BD. *Network Director*, Mrs E. Jones
SOUTH-EAST, Hercules Road, London SE1 7DU. *Network Director*, Ms V. Burdon
SOUTH-WEST, The Pithay, Bristol BS1 2NF. *Network Director*, P. Whitbread
YORKSHIRE AND HUMBERSIDE, City House, New Station Street, Leeds LS1 4JG. *Network Director*, Ms W. Miller

---

DEPARTMENT FOR CULTURE, MEDIA AND SPORT
2–4 Cockspur Street, London SW1Y 5DH
Tel: 020-7211 6200; Fax: 020-7211 6032
Email: enquiries@culture.gov.uk
Web: www.culture.gov.uk

The Department for Culture, Media and Sport was established in July 1997 and is responsible for Government policy relating to the arts, broadcasting, the press, museums and galleries, libraries, sport and recreation, historic buildings and ancient monuments, tourism, and the music industry.
Secretary of State for Culture, Media and Sport, The Rt. Hon. Tessa Jowell, MP
  Principal Private Secretary, Simon Cooper
  Special Advisers, Bill Bush; Ms Ruth Mackenzie, OBE
  Parliamentary Private Secretary, Bill Rammell, MP;
Minister of State, Baroness Tessa Blackstone (*Arts, Museums and Galleries*)
  Private Secretary, David McLaren
Minister of State, Richard Caborn, MP (*Sport*)
  Parliamentary Private Secretary, Ben Chapman, MP
  Private Secretary, Graeme Cornell
Parliamentary Under-Secretary, Kim Howells, MP
  Private Secretary, Tim Owen Edmunds
Permanent Secretary (SCS), Nicholas Kroll

MUSEUMS, GALLERIES, LIBRARIES AND HERITAGE GROUP

Head of Group (SCS), Ms A. Stewart
Head, Museums, Libraries and Archives (SCS), J. Evans
Head, Architecture and Historic Environment (SCS), C. Pullman

Head, Museums, and Libraries Sponsorship Unit (*AU*), H. Bauer
Director, Government Art Collection (SCS), P. Johnson

STRATEGY AND COMMUNICATION GROUP

Head of Group (SCS), vacant
Head of News, P. Fearney
Head of Communications, G. Newsom
Head of Strategy, vacant

CORPORATE SERVICES GROUP

Head of Group (SCS), vacant
Head, Finance and Planning Division (SCS), A. McLellan
Head, National Lottery Division (SCS), J. Zest
Head, Personnel and Central Services Division (SCS), P. Heron
Head, Public Appointments and Honours Unit, S. Roberts
Head, Internal Audit, D. Rix

CREATIVE INDUSTRIES AND BROADCASTING GROUP

Head of Group (SCS), A. Ramsay
Head, Broadcasting Division (SCS), D. Kahn
Head, Creative Industries Division (SCS), M. Seeney

REGIONS, TOURISM, MILLENNIUM AND INTERNATIONAL GROUP

Head of Group, B. Leonard
Head, Tourism Division (SCS), S. Broadley
Head, Millennium Unit, H. Ind
Head, Local, Regional and International Division (SCS), P. Douglas

EDUCATION, TRAINING, ARTS AND SPORT

Head of Group, Ms P. Drew
Head, Arts Division (SCS), A. Davey
Head, Sports Division (SCS), H. Reeves
Head, Education (SCS), vacant
QUEST Chief Executive, (SCS), T. Suter

EXECUTIVE AGENCY

ROYAL PARKS AGENCY

The Old Police House, Hyde Park, London W2 2UH
Tel: 020-7298 2000; Fax: 020-7298 2005

The Agency is responsible for maintaining and developing the royal parks.
Chief Executive (G5), W. Weston

DEPARTMENT FOR EDUCATION AND SKILLS
Sanctuary Buildings, Great Smith Street, London SW1P 3BT Tel: 0870-001 2345; Fax: 020-7925 6000
Email: info@dfes.gov.uk Web: www.dfes.gov.uk
Caxton House, Tothill Street, London SW1H 9NF
Tel: 020-7273 3000; Fax: 020-7273 5124
Castle View House, East Lane, Runcorn,WA7 2GJ.
Tel: 0114-275 3275; Fax: 0114-259 4724
Mowden Hall, Staindrop Road, Darlington DL3 9BG.
Tel: 01325-460155

The Department for Education and Employment was formed in July 1995, bringing together the functions of the former Department for Education with the training and labour market functions of the former Employment Department. It includes an executive agency, the Employment Service. The Department aims to support economic growth and improve the nation's competitiveness and quality of life by raising standards of education and training and by promoting an efficient and flexible labour market. The department was renamed following the 2001 general election.

Secretary of State for Education and Skills, The Rt. Hon.
  Estelle Morris, MP
  Principal Private Secretary, Mike Wardle
  Special Advisers, vacant
  Parliamentary Private Secretary, David Lammy, MP
  Private Secretary, D. Jefferson
Minister of State (Schools), Stephen Timms, MP
  Parliamentary Private Secretary, Vernon Coaker, MP
  Private Secretary, Nick Carson
Minister in the Lords, Baroness Catherine Blackstone
  Private Secretary, M. Hopkinson
Minister of State (Universities), Margaret Hodge, MBE, MP
Parliamentary Under-Secretaries of State, John Healey, MP
  (Adult Skills); Ivan Lewis, MP (Young People and
  Learning); Baroness Catherine Ashton of Upholland,
  (Early Years and School Standards)
  Parliamentary Private Secretary, Mike Foster, MP
  Private Secretaries, Margaret Doherty; Steve Bartlett; J.
  Grundy; Karen Lumley
Permanent Secretary, David Normington, CB

EMPLOYMENT, EQUALITY AND INTERNATIONAL RELATIONS DIRECTORATE
Director-General, P. Shaw

INTERNATIONAL

Director, C. Tucker, CB
Heads of Divisions, Ms W. Harris (European Union); J. Evans
  (European Social Fund); M. Evans (International Relations)

EMPLOYMENT POLICY

Director, M. J. Richardson
Heads of Divisions, J. Moore (Structural Unemployment
  Policy); J. Fuller (Adults Disadvantage Policy Division); C.
  Hunter (Welfare to Work); B. Wells (Economy and Labour
  Market); N. Atkinson (Learning and Workbank Project);
  M. Daly (DfEE/ES New Agency Division)

OPPORTUNITY AND DIVERSITY GROUP

Director, Ms S. Trundle, OBE
Heads of Divisions, Ms J. Eastabrook, (Equality and Diversity
  Division); Ms E. Tillett (Disability Policy Division); M.
  Craske (Work Permits UK)

EARLY YEARS AND CHILDCARE UNIT

Heads of Divisions, A. Cranston (Quality Standards);
  C. Slowcock (Affordability and Accessibility Division)

FINANCE AND ANALYTICAL SERVICES DIRECTORATE
Director-General, P. Makeham

FINANCE

Director, Ms R. Thompson
Heads of Divisions, Mrs S. Todd (Expenditure); vacant
  (Capital Investment); Dr J. Pugh (Programmes); R. Wye
  (Efficiency); M. Maddox; P. Connor (Financial
  Accounting); N. Thirtle (Internal Audit)

ANALYTICAL SERVICES

Director General, P. Makeham
Director, P. Johnson

Heads of Divisions, M. Britton (Qualifications, Pupil
  Assessment and IT); J. Elliott (Youth and Further
  Education); A. Ray (Higher Education, Evaluation Strategy
  and International); Dr B. Butcher (Employability and
  Adult Learning); R. Bartholomew (Equal Opportunities
  and Research Programmes); Ms A. Brown (Schools,
  Teachers and Resources)

LIFELONG LEARNING DIRECTORATE
Director-General, N. Stuart
Heads of Division below the Director General, A. Clarke;
  (Prisoners Learning and Skills Unit); J. Temple (Strategy and
  Funding); M. Boo (Adult Basic Skills)

DIRECTORATES UNDER THE DIRECTOR GENERAL
ADULT BASIC SKILLS STRATEGY UNIT

Director, S. Pember

ADULT LEARNING GROUP

Director, D. Grover
Heads of Divisions, T. Down (Access to Learning for Adults
  Division); O. Crouch (Lifelong Learning and Technologies
  Division); E. Galvin (Skills for Employment); H.
  Tollyfield (Workplace Learning Division); P. Thorpe
  (Review of Basic Skills Agency)

CONNEXIONS SERVICE UNIT

Director, A. Weinstock
Heads of Divisions, J. Haywood (Activities for Young People
  and Volunteering Division); P. Bailey (Communications
  Division); S. Geary (Partnership Formation & Delivery
  Division); C. Tyler (Policy and Strategy Division);
  J. Mackey (Quality Unit); Jane Benham (Standards and
  Effectiveness Unit)

HIGHER EDUCATION GROUP

Director, N. Sanders
Heads of Division, M. Hipkins (Higher Education Funding
  and Organisation Division); N. Flint (Student Support
  Division 1); N. Graham (Student Support Division 2); P.
  Cohen (Quality and Employability Division)

LEARNING DELIVERY AND STANDARDS GROUP

Director, P. Lauener
Heads of Divisions, S. Hillier (FE Funding Division); P.
  Mucklow (Learning and Skills Council and Partnership
  Division); S. Orr (Raising Standards Division); J. Reid
  (Learning Skills Council); R. Hinchcliffe and M. Stock
  (LSC/ALI Information and Business Systems Division); P.
  Houten (Transition Division); M. Stark (LSC Corporate
  Planning Division)

QUALIFICATIONS AND YOUNG PEOPLE GROUP

Director, R. Hull
Heads of Divisions, S. Marshall (Qualifications for Work
  Division); C. Johnson (School and College Qualifications
  Division); T. Fellowes (Young People Learner Support
  Division); A. Davies (Young People's Policy Division)

LEGAL ADVISER'S OFFICE
Director, D. Macrae
Heads of Divisions, S. Harker (Legal Advisers Division 1,
  School); F. Clarke (Legal Advisers Division 2, Post 16); D.
  Aries (Legal Advisers Division 3, HE and Teachers and
  Support Directorates); D. Collins (Legal Advisers Division
  4, Equality and External); P. Kilgarriff (Legal Advisers
  Division 5, Standards)

CORPORATE SERVICES AND DEVELOPMENT DIRECTORATE

Director-General, S. Thomas
Heads of Divisions, T. Eves (*Personnel Division*); J. McIntyre (*Learning Academy*) C. Moore (*Information Service Division*); P. Neill; G. Archer (*Leadership and Change Division*); D. Jarvis (*Equal Opportunities Unit*)

SCHOOLS DIRECTORATE

Director-General, H. Williams

CURRICULUM AND COMMUNICATIONS GROUP

Director, I. Wilde
Heads of Divisions, G. McKenzie (*Curriculum Division*); S. Edwards (*School Communications Division*); D. Brown (*NGFL-National Grid for Learning Division*); N. Baxter (*Parents and Performance Division*); D. Palmer (*ICT Strategy Unit*); vacant (*Future Development of the NGFL*)

PUPIL SUPPORT AND INCLUSION GROUP

Director, T. Jeffrey
Heads of Divisions, B. Shaw (*School Inclusion Division*); Ms S. Johnson and Ms. R. Pratt (*Schools Plus*); M. Phipps; (*Pupil Support and Independent Schools Division*); C. Wells

SURE START UNIT

Director, N. Eisenstadt
Head of Division, A. Esunshile
Divisional Managers, J. Doughty; T. A. McCully (*Children and Young People's Unit*); T. Finkelstein (*Policy*)

TEACHERS GROUP

Director, S. Kershaw
Heads of Divisions, G. Holley (*Teachers' Supply and Training Division*); A. Jackson (*Teacher's Pay and Policy Division*); P. Swift (*School Leadership Division*); P. Jones (*Teacher's Standards and Pensions Division*); R. Harrison (*Teacher's Professional Development Division*); M. Williams (*Teacher Rapid Response Unit*)

SCHOOL ORGANISATION AND FUNDING GROUP

Director, H. Williams
Heads of Divisions, K. Beeton (*Schools Capital and Buildings Division*); M. Patel (*Architects and Building*); A. Wye (*School and LEA Funding Division*); C. Macready (*School Admissions Organisation and Governance Division*)

STANDARDS AND EFFECTIVENESS UNIT

Acting Director, S. Crowne
Heads of Divisions, R. Wood (*Diversity and Best Practice Division*); vacant (*LEA Improvement Division*); S. Adamson (*Pupil Standards Division*); C. Wormald (*School Improvements and Excellence*); S. Imbriano (*Local Implementation Unit*)
Divisional Managers, C. Bienkowska (*Diversity in Secondary Education*); J. Benham (*14 to 19 year-olds*); S. Crowne (*City Academies Unit*)
Heads of Division, R. Graham (*Schools Communications Unit*); J. Coles (*Green Paper Implementation Division*)

STRATEGY AND COMMUNICATIONS DIRECTORATE

Director, P. Wanless
Heads of Divisions, J. Simpson (*Media Relations Division*); T. Cook (*Deputy Head of Media Relations*); C. Bicknell (*Communications and Knowledge Management Division*); M. Lord (*Strategy Division*); N. Houston (*Team Leader*) (*Speeches, Presentations and General Briefing Unit*);

Y. Diamond (*Welfare to Work Communication Division*); J. Ross (*Publicity Division*); G. McKenzies (*Regional Policy Division*); B. Glickman (*Employer Relations*)
Private Office Head of Division, N. Roache

EXECUTIVE AGENCY

THE EMPLOYMENT SERVICE

Caxton House, Tothill Street, London SW1H 9NA
Tel: 020-7273 6060; Fax: 020-7273 6099

The aims of the Employment Service are to contribute to high levels of employment and growth by helping all people without a job to find work and by helping employers to fill their vacancies, and to help individuals lead rewarding working lives.

From 1 October 2001 The Employment Service, and some parts of the Benefits Agency will merge into a new organisation called 'Jobcentre Plus.'

Chief Executive, L. Lewis, CB
Director of Jobcentre Services, Ms C. Dodgson,
Director of Human Resources, K. White
Director of Welfare to Work Delivery, R. Foster
Director for Finance, Commercial and Corporate Services, M. Neale
Non-Executive Directors, R. Dykes; Ms L. de Groot; C. Cox
Regional Directors, M. Groves (*East Midlands and Eastern*); S. Holt, OBE (*London and South-East*); V. Robinson; OBE (*Northern*); L. Brown; (*North-West*); Ms D. Ross; (*South-West*); Ms R. Thew (*West Midlands*); R. Lasko (*Yorkshire and Humberside*)
Director for Scotland, A. R. Brown
Director for Wales, Mrs S. Keyse

DEPARTMENT FOR ENVIRONMENT, FOOD AND RURAL AFFAIRS

Nobel House, 17 Smith Square, London SW1P 3JR
Tel: 020-7238 3000; Fax: 020-7238 6591
Email: helpline@infdefra.gov.uk
Web: www.defra.gov.uk

The Department for Environment, Food, and Rural Affairs is responsible for Government policies on agriculture, horticulture and fisheries in England and for policies relating to the safety and quality of food in the UK as a whole, including composition, labelling, additives, contaminants and new production processes. In association with the agriculture departments of the Scottish Executive, the National Assembly for Wales and Northern Ireland Office and with the Intervention Board, the Ministry is responsible for negotiations in the EU on the common agricultural and fisheries policies, and on single European market questions relating to its responsibilities. Its remit also includes international agricultural and food trade policy.

The department exercises responsibilities for the protection and enhancement of the countryside and the marine environment, for flood defence and for other rural issues. It is the licensing authority for veterinary medicines and the registration authority for pesticides. It administers policies relating to the control of animal, plant and fish diseases. It provides scientific, technical and professional services and advice to farmers, growers and ancillary industries, and it commissions research to assist in the formulation and assessment of policy and to underpin applied research and development work done by industry. Responsibility for food safety and standards was transferred to the new Food Standards Agency in April 2000.

Ssecretary of State for Environment, Food and Rural Affairs,
The Rt. Hon. Margaret Beckett, MP
Principal Private Secretary (G7), Andrew Slade
Private Secretary, Alexia Flowerday
Parliamentary Private Secretary, Andrew Reed, MP
Special Advisers, Sheila Watson; Nicci Collins
Minister of State (Environment), The Rt. Hon. Michael
Meacher, MP
Parliamentary Private Secretary, Terry Rooney, MP
Private Secretary, Gabriel Edwards
Minister of State (Rural Affairs), The Rt. Hon. A. Michael,
MP
Parliamentary Private Secretary, Peter Bradley, MP
Private Secretary, Becky Taylor
Parliamentary Under-Secretary, Elliot Morley, MP
Private Secretary, Robert Hitchen
Parliamentary Under Secretary, The Lord Whitty
Permanent Secretary (SCS), Brian Bender, CB

ESTABLISHMENTS GROUP
Director of Establishments (SCS), R. A. Saunderson

CORPORATE SERVICES DIVISION
Head of Division (SCS), B. Jones

PERSONNEL DIVISION
Head of Division (SCS), Ms T. Newell

BUILDING AND ESTATE MANAGEMENT
Eastbury House, 30–34 Albert Embankment,
London SE1 7TL
Tel: 020-7238 6000
Head of Division (SCS), J. A. S. Nickson

INFORMATION TECHNOLOGY DIRECTORATE
Government Buildings, Epsom Road, Guildford, Surrey
GU1 2LD Tel: 01483-403757

E-BUSINESS
E-Business Director, D. Rossington
IT Director, S. Soper
Assistant Director (Applications), P. Barber
Assistant Director (Infrastructure), D. Brown
Assistant Director (E-Business), A. Hill

COMMUNICATIONS DIRECTORATE
Nobel House, 17 Smith Square, London SW1P 3JR
Tel: 020-7238 6000; Helpline 0645-335577
Director of Communications (SCS), R. Lowson
Head of News, M. Smith
Chief Publicity Officer (G7), N. Wagstaffe
Principal Librarian (G7), P. McShane

AGENCY OWNERSHIP UNIT
3-8 Whitehall House (West Block), London SW1A 2HH
Head of Unit (SCS), Dr M. Tas

FINANCE DEPARTMENT
3–8 Whitehall Place (West Block), London SW1A 2HH
Tel: 020-7238 6000
Finance Director, (SCS), P. Elliott

FINANCIAL POLICY DIVISION
Head of Division (SCS), F. Marlow

PROCUREMENT AND CONTRACTS DIVISION
19–29 Woburn Place, London WC1H 0LU
Tel: 020-7273 3000
Head of Division (SCS), D. Rabey

AUDIT, CONSULTANCY AND MANAGEMENT SERVICES
19–29 Woburn Place, London WC1H 0LU
Tel: 020-7273 3000
Director of Audit (SCS), D. V. Fisher

RESOURCE MANAGEMENT STRATEGY UNIT
19–29 Woburn Place, London WC1H 0LU
Tel: 020-7273 3000
Head of Unit (SCS), D. V. Fisher

RESOURCE MANAGEMENT DIVISION
Foss House, Kings Pool, 1–2 Peasholme Green, York YO1
7PX Tel: 01904-455328
Head of Division (G6), R. Atkinson

BUSINESS IMPROVEMENT DIVISION
Head of Unit (G7), Ms. J. Flint and G. Holt

LEGAL DEPARTMENT
55 Whitehall, London SW1A 2EY
Tel: 020-7238 6000
Legal Adviser and Solicitor (SCS), Miss K. M. S. Morton
Principal Assistant Solicitors (SCS), S. Parker; Ms C. A.
Crisham

LEGAL DIVISIONS
Assistant Solicitor, Division A1, P. Davis
Assistant Solicitor, Division A2, Ms A. Werbicki
Assistant Solicitor, Division A3, C. Gregory
Assistant Solicitor, Division A4 , C. Allen
Assistant Solicitor, Division A5 , N. Lambert
Assistant Solicitor, Division A6, B. Dickinson
Assistant Solicitor, Division B1, Ms S. Spence
Assistant Solicitor, Division B2, M. Patel
Assistant Solicitor, Division B3, I. Corbett

INVESTIGATION UNIT
Chief Investigation Officer (G7), Miss J. Panting

ECONOMICS AND STATISTICS
3–8 Whitehall Place (West Block), London SW1A 2HH
Tel: 020-7238 6000
Director of Economics and Statistics Group (SCS),
D. Thompson

DIVISIONS
*Senior Economic Adviser, Economics and Statistics (Farm
Business) (G6),* J. Watson
Senior Economic Adviser, Economics (International) (SCS),
N. Atkinson
Senior Economic Adviser, Economics (Resource Use) (SCS),
J. P. Muriel

STATISTICS DIVISION
Foss House, Kings Pool, 1–2 Peasholme Green, York YO1
7PX Tel: 01904-455332
Chief Statistician (Commodities and Food) (SCS), S. Platt
Chief Statistician (Census and Surveys) (SCS), P. F. Helm

CHIEF SCIENTIST'S GROUP

Cromwell House, Dean Stanley Street, Westminster, London, SW1P 3JH.
Tel: 020-7238 6000
Chief Scientist (SCS), Dr D. W. F. Shannon

DIVISIONS

Head, Agriculture, Environment and Food Technology (SCS), Dr J. C. Sherlock
Head, Veterinary, Food and Aquatic Science (SCS), vacant
Head, Research Policy and International (SCS), A. R. Burne

FISHERIES DEPARTMENT

Nobel House, 17 Smith Square, London SW1P 3JR
Fisheries Director (SCS), S. Wentworth

DIVISIONS

Head, Fisheries I (SCS), P. M. Boyling
Head, Fisheries II (SCS), R. Cowan
Head, Fisheries III (SCS), C. Ryder
Head, Fisheries IV (SCS), B. S. Edwards
Chief Inspector, Sea Fisheries Inspectorate (G6), S. G. Ellson

AGRICULTURAL CROPS AND COMMODITIES DIRECTORATE

3–8 Whitehall Place (West Block), London SW1A 2HH
Tel: 020-7238 6000
Director General (SCS), vacant

EUROPEAN UNION AND INTERNATIONAL POLICY

Director (SCS), A. J. Lebrecht

DIVISIONS

Head, European Union and Agriculture Strategy (SCS), T. Eddy
Head, European Union and International Division (SCS), D. Dawson
Head, Cap Schemes Policy, Ms J. Purnell

AGRICULTURE GROUP

Head of Group (SCS), D. Hunter

DIVISIONS

Head, Horticulture, Potatoes and HMI (SCS), D. Jones
Head Genetic Modification and Industrial Crops, Ms S. Henry
Head, Arable Crops (SCS), A. Kuyk
Head, Beef and Sheep (SCS), I. Llewelyn
Head, Livestock Schemes (SCS), A. Taylor
Head, Milk, Pigs, Eggs and Poultry (SCS), G. Ross
Head Plant Health and PHSI, S. Hunter

FOOD INDUSTRY, COMPETITIVENESS AND CONSUMERS

Director, (SCS), J. Robbs

DIVISIONS

Head, Food and Drinks Industry (SCS), C. Young
Head, International Relations and Export Promotion (SCS), N. Denton
Head, Agricultural Resources and Better Regulations (SCS), L. Harris
Head, Marketing, Competition and Consumers (SCS), Ms J. Allfrey
Head, Flood and Coastal Defence (SCS), J. Park

PLANT VARIETY RIGHTS OFFICE AND SEED DIVISION

White House Lane, Huntingdon road, Cambridge CB3 0LF
Head of Office (SCS), H. Hamilton

POLICY AND CORPORATE STRATEGY

3–8 Whitehall Place (West Block), London SW1A 2HH
Tel: 020-7238 6000
Director, B. Harding
EAST OF ENGLAND, Building A, Westbrook Centre, Milton Road, Cambridge, CB4 1YG. Tel: 01223-346700.
Rural Director, J. Rabagliati
EAST MIDLANDS, The Belgrave Centre, The Stanley Place, Talbot Street, Nottingham, NG1 5GG.
Rural Director, Graham Norbury
NORTH-EAST, Welbar House, Gallowgate, Newcastle-upon-Tyne, NE1 4TD. Tel: 0191-201 3300.
Rural Director, John Bainton
NORTH WEST, Sunley Tower, Picadilly Plaza, Manchester, M1 4BE. Tel: 0161-952 4000.
Regional Director, Neil Cumberlidge
SOUTH-EAST, Bridge House, 1 Walnut Tree Close, Guildford, Surrey, GU1 4GA. Tel: 01483-882255.
Regional Director, Alison Parker
SOUTH-WEST, 4th and 5th Floors, The Pithay, Bristol, BS1 2PB. Tel: 0117-900 1700.
Regional Director, Tim Render
WEST MIDLANDS, 77 Paradise Circus, Queensway, Birmingham, B1 2DT. Tel: 0121-212 5000.
Regional Director, Brin Davies
YORKSHIRE AND THE HUMBERSIDE, PO Box 213, City House, New Station Street, Leeds, LS1 4US. Tel: 0113-280 0600. *Regional Director*, *(Acting)*, Ms C. Deakins

ANIMAL HEALTH AND ENVIRONMENT GROUP

Deputy Secretary (SCS), Ms J. Bacon

ENVIRONMENT AND RURAL DEVELOPMENT GROUP

Head of Group (SCS), Mrs K. A. J. Brown

DIVISIONS

Head, Conservation Management, J. Osmond
Head, Rural Division, Ms. L. Cornish
Head, Land Use, A. Perrins
Head, Rural Marine and Environment, P. Cleasby
Head, Corporate Strategy Unit, Ms A. Tarran

RURAL DEVELOPMENT SERVICE

Head of Group, S. Nason
Technical Advice, A. Hooper
Business Process Director, J. Robinson

RURAL DEVELOPMENT CENTRES

EAST, Government Buildings, Brooklands Avenue Cambridge, CB2 2DR , Tel: 01223-462727.
Regional Manager, M. Edwards
EAST-MIDLANDS , Block 7, Government Buildings, Chalfont Drive, Nottingham, NG8 3SN. Tel: 0115-929 1191. *Regional Manager*, S. Buckenham
NORTH-EAST , Government Buildings Kenton Bar, Newcastle-upon-Tyne, NE5 3EW. Tel: 0191-286 3377.
Regional Manager, F. Gough
NORTH-WEST , Electra Way, Crewe Business Park, Crewe, Cheshire, CW1 6GJ. Tel: 01270-754000.
Regional Manager, Tony Percival

SOUTH-EAST , Government Buildings, Coley Park, Reading, Berkshire, RG1 6DT. Tel: 01189-581 222, *Regional Manager*, Nick Beard
SOUTH-WEST , Block 3, Government Buildings, Burghill Road, Westbury-on-Trym, Bristol, BS10 6NJ. Tel: 0117-959 1000. *Regional Manager*, David Sisson
WEST MIDLANDS , Block C, Government Buildings, Whittington Road, Worcester, WR5 2LQ. Tel: 01905-763355. *Regional Manager*, C. Deakin
YORKSHIRE AND THE HUMBERSIDE , Government Buildings, Otley Road, Lawnswood, Leeds, LS16 5QT. Tel: 0113 261 3333. *Regional Manager*, M. Silverwood

ANIMAL HEALTH GROUP
1A Page Street, London SW1P 4PQ. Tel: 020-7904 6000
Head of Group (SCS), N. Thornton

DIVISIONS
Head of Animal Indentification and Animal International Trade, Mrs V. Smith
Animal Disease Control, R. Hathaway
Head Animal Health Services, Ms C. Harold
Animal Welfare, G. Noble
TSE Group Director, P. Nash
Head, BSE and Scrapie, J. A. Bailey
Head Sheep TSE, N. Cleary

ANIMAL HEALTH AND ENVIRONMENT DIRECTORATE
Nobel House, 17 Smith Square, London, SW1P 3JR
Director General, Ms J. Bacon

WILDLIFE AND COUNTRYSIDE GROUP
Eland House, Bressenden Place, London, SW1E 5DU
Tel: 020-7944 3000.
Director, Ms S. Lamberet

DIVISIONS
Countryside, S. Carter
European Wildlife, H. Neal
Global Wildlife, M. Brasher
Rural Development, H. Cleary
Rural Task Force Secretariat, C. Dunabin

CHIEF VETERINARY OFFICER'S GROUP
1A Page Street, London SW1P 4PQ. Tel: 020-7904 6000
Chief Veterinary Officer (SCS), J. M. Scudamore
Deputy Chief Veterinary Officer (Services) (SCS), M. Atkinson

DIVISIONS
Head of Veterinary Services East (SCS), G. Jones
Head of Veterinary Services West (SCS), J. Cross
Head of Veterinary Services North (SCS), R. Drummond
Head of Veterinary Services Resources (SCS), Ms B. Phillip
Assistant Chief Veterinary Officer (Scotland), L. Gardner
Head of Veterinary Services (Scotland) (SCS), D. McIntosh
Assistant Chief Veterinary Officer (Wales), A. Edwards
Deputy Chief Veterinary Officer (Policy) (SCS), R. Cawthorne
Head, Veterinary International Trade Team (SCS), R. A. Bell
Head, Veterinary Notifiable Disease Team (Exotic Diseases) (SCS), Dr D. Matthews
Head, Veterinary Notifiable Disease Team (Endemic Animal Diseases and Zoonosis) (SCS), vacant
Head, Welfare Team (SCS), D. Pritchard

EXECUTIVE AGENCIES

CENTRAL SCIENCE LABORATORY

Sand Hutton, York YO41 1LZ
Tel: 01904-462000; Fax: 01904-462111
The agency provides advice, technical and enforcement support, underpinned by appropriate research, to meet both the statutory and policy objectives of DEFRA; and it provides research and development and advice on a commercial basis to other government departments and to public and private sector organisations both overseas and UK-based.
The main areas are: safeguarding food supplies through the identification and control of invertebrate pests, plant pests and diseases; the management of vertebrate wildlife; food and consumer safety with the emphasis on the microbiological and chemical safety, and the quality and nutritional value of food. The agency is also concerned with environmental protection through the investigation of the impact of agriculture on the environment, and the promotion of biodiversity in agricultural habitats.
Chief Executive (G3), Prof. M. Roberts
Research Directors (G5), Prof. Tony Hardy (*Agriculture and Environment*); Prof. John Gilbert (*Food*)
Commercial Director, Dr Robert Bolton
Corporate Services Director, Dr Helen Crews
Finance and Procurement Director, Richard Shaw

CENTRE FOR ENVIRONMENT, FISHERIES AND AQUACULTURE SCIENCE

Pakefield Road, Lowestoft, Suffolk NR33 0HT
Tel: 01502-562244; Fax: 01502-513865
The Agency, established in April 1997, provides research and consultancy services in fisheries science and management, aquaculture, fish health and hygiene, environmental impact assessment, and environmental quality assessment.
Chief Executive, Dr P. Greig-Smith

PESTICIDES SAFETY DIRECTORATE

Mallard House, Kings Pool, 3 Peasholme Green, York YO1 7PX. Tel: 01904-640500; Fax: 01904-455733
The Pesticides Safety Directorate is responsible for the evaluation and approval of agricultural pesticides and the development of policies relating to them, in order to protect consumers, users and the environment.
Chief Executive (G4), Dr H. K. Wilson
Director (Policy) (G5), Dr S. Popple
Director (Approvals) (G5), R. Davis

VETERINARY LABORATORIES AGENCY

Woodham Lane, New Haw, Addlestone, Surrey KT15 3NB
Tel: 01932-341111; Fax: 01932-347046
The Veterinary Laboratories Agency provides scientific and technical expertise in animal and public health.
Chief Executive, Dr S. Edwards
Director of Research, Dr J. A. Morris
Director of Surveillance and Laboratory Services, R. Hancock
Director of Finance, C. Morrey
Laboratory Secretary, C. Edwards

VETERINARY MEDICINES DIRECTORATE

Woodham Lane, New Haw, Addlestone, Surrey KT15 3LS
Tel: 01932-336911; Fax: 01932-336618

The Veterinary Medicines Directorate is responsible for all aspects of the authorisation and control of veterinary medicines, including post-authorisation surveillance of residues in animals and animal products, and the provision of policy advice to Ministers.

Chief Executive (G4), Dr J. M. Rutter
Director (Policy) (G5), R. Anderson
Director (Licensing) (G5), S. Dean
Secretary and Head of Business Unit (G6), J. FitzGerald
Licensing Manager, Pharmaceuticals and Feed Additives (G6), J. P. O'Brien
Licensing Manager, Immunologicals (G6), Dr D. J. K. Mackay

FOREIGN AND COMMONWEALTH OFFICE
King Charles Street, London SW1A 2AH
Tel: 020-7270 1500
Web: www.fco.gov.uk

The Foreign and Commonwealth Office provides, through its staff in the UK and through its diplomatic missions abroad, the means of communication between the British Government and other governments and international governmental organisations on all matters falling within the field of international relations. It is responsible for alerting the British Government to the implications of developments overseas; for promoting British interests overseas; for protecting British citizens abroad; for explaining British policies to, and cultivating relationships with, governments overseas; for the discharge of British responsibilities to the overseas territories; for entry clearance (through the Joint Entry Clearance Unit, with the Home Office) and for promoting British business overseas (jointly with the Department of Trade and Industry through British Trade International).

Secretary of State for Foreign and Commonwealth Affairs, The Rt. Hon. Jack Straw, MP
Principal Private Secretary, Simon McDonald
Special Advisers, Michael Williams; Ed Owen
Parliamentary Private Secretary, Colin Pickthall, MP
Minister for Europe, The Rt. Hon. Peter Hain, MP
Private Secretary, James Morrison
Minister of State for Trade, The Rt. Hon. Baroness Symons of Vernham Dean,
Private Secretary, Robin Gwynn
Parliamentary Under-Secretary of State, Ben Bradshaw, MP
Private Secretary, Hugo Shorter
Parliamentary Under-Secretary of State, Dr. Denis MacShane, MP
Private Secretary, Fiona Gibb
Parliamentary Under-Secretary of State, Baroness Amos
Private Secretary, David Cairns
Parliamentary Private Secretaries, Charlotte Atkins, MP; Caroline Flint, MP
Permanent Under-Secretary of State and Head of HM Diplomatic Service, Sir John Kerr, KCMG
Private Secretary, Susan Hyland
Chief Executive, †*British Trade International*, Sir David Wright, KCMG, LVO
Deputy Under-Secretaries, Peter Collecott (*Chief Clerk*); Michael. Arthur, CMG (*Economic Director*); M. Wood, CMG (*Legal Adviser*); Peter Westmacott, CMG, LVO; Emyr Jones Parry, CMG (*Political Director*); Stephen Wright, CMG

DIRECTORS
Africa, M. Lyall Grant
Americas/Overseas Territories, R. Wilkinson, CVO
International Security, W. Ehrman
Wider Europe, J. Macgregor, CVO
European Union, K. Darroch, CMG
Chief Executive FCO Services, S. Sage
Global Issues, N. Brewer
South East Europe, A. Charlton CMG
Middle East and North Africa, A. Goulty CMG
Asia Pacific, R. Marsden
British Trade International, D. Hall CMG
Personnel, D. Holt
Public Services, D. Reddaway
Resources, S. Gass

HEADS OF DEPARTMENTS
African Department (Equatorial), F. Baker
African Department (Southern), A. Pocock
Aviation and Maritime Department, C. Segar
Central and North-West European Department, Sir John Ramsden, Bt.
Change Management Unit, Ms S. Matthews
China/Hong Kong Department, A. Seaton
Common Foreign and Security Policy Department, T. Barrow
Commonwealth Co-ordination, C. Bright
Consular Division, J. Watt
Counter-Terrorism Policy Department, K. Bloomfield
Cultural Relations Department, Dr M. Reilly
Diplomatic Service Families Association; E. Salvesen
Diplomatic Service Trade Union Side (DSTUS), S. Watson
Drugs and International Crime Department, M. Ryder
Eastern Department, S. Butt
Eastern Adriatic Department, S. Wordsworth
Economic Policy, C. Butler
Environment Policy, J. Ashton
Estate Strategy, J. Metcalfe
European Unit (Bi-lateral), K. Pierce
European Union Department (External), S. Featherstone
European Union Department (Internal), J. Bevan
Financial Compliance Unit, D. Major
FCO Association, D. Burns (*Chairman*)
FCO Services, J. Clark (*Head, Conference and Visits Group*); J. Elgie (*Head, Estates Group*); J. Thompson, MBE (*Head, Information Management Group*); V. Life (*Head Management Consultancy Services*); V. Davies (*Head Language Group*); Ms J. Link (*Head, Resource Management Group*); M. Carr (*Head, Support Group*); N. Stickells (*Head, Technical Group*)
Human Rights Policy; Dr C. Browne
Internal Audit (FCO/DFID), R. Elias
IT Strategy Unit, M. Kirk
Joint Entry Clearance Unit (Joint FCO/Home Office Unit), R. Brinkley
Latin America and Caribbean Department, J. Dew
Legal Advisers, M. Wood, CMG
Middle East Department, W. Patey
National Audit Office, J. Pearce
Near East and North Africa Department, C. Prentice
News, J. Williams
Non-Proliferation Department, T. Dowse
North America Department, N. Armour
North-East Asia and Pacific Department, N. Archer
Organisation for Security Co-operation in Europe, P. January
Overseas Territories Department, A. Huckle
Parliamentary Relations and Devolution, M. Hutton
Personnel Command, T. Simmons (*Performance and Development*); Ms E. Kennedy (*Asst. Director*, *Medical and Welfare*); P. Jones (*Personnel Management*); S.

Wightman (*Personnel Policy*); R. White (*Personnel Services*); C. Edgerton and T. Malcomson (*Prosper*); A. Cookson-Hall (*Recruitment*); G. Deacon (*Interchange*); C. Dharwarker (*Training*); R. Clarke (*Policy Planning Staff*)
Protocol Department, Mrs K. F. Colvin
Public Diplomacy, J. Buck
Purchasing Directorate, M. Gower
Quality and Efficiency, K. Jackson
Records and Historical, H. Yasamee
Research Analysis, R. D. Lavers
Resource Accounting, M. Brown
Resource Budgeting, M. Williamson
Science and Technology, R. Barnett
Security Strategy Unit, J. Macgregor
Security Policy, A. M. Thomson
South Asia, S. N. Evans, OBE
South-East Asian Department, R. Gordon
Southern European, G. Gillham
United Nations, S. Pattison
Whitehall Liaison Department, M. Kidd

BRITISH TRADE INTERNATIONAL

Central Services Group
Group Director, D. Hall

REGIONAL GROUP

Group Director, I. Jones

INTERNATIONAL GROUP

Group Director, Q. Quayle

BUSINESS GROUP

Group Director, D. Warren
Strategy and Communications Group
Group Director, S. Lyle Smythe

INVEST UK

Chief Executive, W. Pedder
*Joint Foreign and Commonwealth Office/Department for International Development department
† Joint Foreign and Commonwealth Office/Department of Trade and Industry directorate

EXECUTIVE AGENCY

WILTON PARK CONFERENCE CENTRE

Wiston House, Steyning, W. Sussex BN44 3DZ
Tel: 01903-815020; Fax: 01903-879647

Wilton Park organises international affairs conferences and is hired out to Government departments and commercial users.
Chief Executive, C. B. Jennings

CORPS OF QUEEN'S MESSENGERS

Support Group, Foreign and Commonwealth Office, London SW1A 2AH Tel: 020-7270 2779

Superintendent of the Corps of Queen's Messengers, A. C. Brown
Queen's Messengers, P. Allen; R. Allen; Maj. A. N. D. Bols; Maj. P. C. H. Dening-Smitherman; Sqn. Ldr. J. S. Frizzell; Capt. N. C. E. Gardner; Maj. D. A. Griffiths; A. Hill; R. Long; Maj. K. J. Rowbottom; Maj. M. R. Senior; Maj. J. E. A. Andre; W. Lisle; Maj. J. H. Steele; J. A. Hatfield; P. J. Hearn; D. J. Bufton

DEPARTMENT OF HEALTH
Richmond House, 79 Whitehall, London SW1A 2NL
Tel: 020-7210 3000
Web: www.open.gov.uk/doh/dhhome.htm

The Department of Health is responsible for the provision of the National Health Service in England and for social care, including oversight of personal social services run by local authorities in England for children (except day care, which is now the responsibility of the DfES), the elderly, the infirm, the handicapped and other persons in need. It is responsible for health promotion and has functions relating to public and environmental health, food safety and nutrition. The Department is also responsible for the ambulance and emergency first aid services, under the Civil Defence Act 1948. The Department represents the UK at the European Union and other international organisations including the World Health Organisation. It also supports UK-based healthcare and pharmaceutical industries. Responsibility for food safety was transferred to the Food Standards Agency in April 2000.
Secretary of State for Health, The Rt. Hon. Alan Milburn, MP
    Principal Private Secretary, H. Rodgers
    Private Secretaries, S. Sinclair; S. Waring
    Special Advisers, P. Corrigan; D. Murphy
    Parliamentary Private Secretary, M. Hall , MP
Minister of State, The Rt. Hon. John Hutton, MP (*Structure and Resources*)
    Private Secretary, T. Fretten
    Parliamentary Private Secretary, Claire Ward, MP
Minister of State, Jacqui Smith, MP (*Social Care and Mental Health*)
    Private Secretary, J. Adedeji
Parliamentary Under-Secretaries of State, Yvette Cooper, MP; The Lord Hunt of Kings Heath, OBE; Hazel Blears, MP
    Parliamentary Private Secretary, Andy Love, MP
    Private Secretaries, P. Mcnaught; Ms H. McLain; K. Holton
    Parliamentary Clerk, J. Mean
Permanent Secretary (SCS), N. Crisp
    Private Secretary, R. Wetterstand
Chief Medical Officer (SCS), Prof. L. Donaldson, FRCSEd, FRCP
Chief Executive, Operations Officer (SCS), Neil McKay

STATISTICS DIVISION

Director of Statistics (SCS), J. Fox
Chief Statisticians (SCS), R. K. Willmer; A. Roberts; J. Stokoe; A. Sutherland

INTERNATIONAL AND CONSTITUTIONAL BRANCH (ICB)
Branch Head (SCS), N. Boyd

PERSONNEL SERVICES

Director of Personnel (SCS), F. Goldhill
Heads of Branches (SCS), C. Muir; Mrs W. Honeyghan-Williams; J. Sinclair

INFORMATION SERVICES DIVISION

Head of Division (SCS), Dr A. A. Holt
Heads of Branches, Mrs L. Wishart; C. Horsey; M. Rainsford; Mrs J. Dainty; R. Long; P. G. Cobb; Mrs D. McDonagh
Joint Service Managers, P. Dowler and T. Shaw

RESOURCE MANAGEMENT
Head of Division (SCS), D. Clark
Head of Branch, S. Mitchell,

FINANCE DIRECTORATE
Director of Finance, (SCS), R. Douglas
Deputy Directors of Finance, C. Daws; vacant
Head of Branches, L. Eccles; I. Ellul; M. Sturges,
J. Stopes-Roe; J. Tomlinson; P. Coates; P. Taylor;
A. MacLellan; P. Kendall

MEDICINES, PHARMACY AND INDUSTRY
DIVISION (MPI)
Head of Division, A. McKeon
Heads of Branches, M. Brownlee; K. Guiness; J. Middleton;
Dr J. Smith

ECONOMICS AND OPERATIONAL RESEARCH DIVISION
(HEALTH)
Chief Economic Adviser (SCS), C. H. Smee, CBE
Heads of Branches, Dr S. Harding; Dr G. Royston; A. Hare;
N. York;

COMMUNICATIONS DIRECTORATE
Director of Communications (SCS), vacant
Deputy Directors, S. Jarvis (*Media*); W. Roberts
(*Campaigns*); P. Addison-Child (*Corporate
Communications*)

SOLICITOR'S OFFICE
Solicitor (SCS), M. Morgan, CB
Director of Legal Services (SCS), Mrs G. S. Kerrigan

PUBLIC HEALTH POLICY GROUP

PUBLIC HEALTH DIVISION
Head of Division, Prof. D. Nutbeam
Heads of Branches, M. Fry; Ms I. Sharp; M. Haroon;
R. Carter; D. Harper; Ms C. Hamlyn; E. Waterhouse,
Dr Pui-Ling; Dr D. Macpherson; Mrs E. Johnson;
Dr M. O'Mahony

WINTER AND EMERGENCY SERVICES CAPACITY
PLANNING TEAM (WEST)
Division Head, Ms A. Sergeant
Head of Branch, C. Hetherington

SOCIAL CARE GROUP
Chief Social Services Inspector, Ms D. Platt, CBE
Head of Social Care Policy, D. Walden
Deputy Chief Inspectors, D. Gilroy; Ms A. Nottage
Heads of Branches (SCS), Miss A. Stephenson; R. Wilson
(*Section Head*); Ms. C. Brock; B. Clark; Ms A. Gross;
R. Campbell; C. Hume
Assistant Chief Inspector (HQ), J. Cleary
Assistant Chief Inspectors (Regions), J. Cypher; B. Riddell; A.
Jones; C. P. Brearley; J. Fraser; Mrs L. Hoare; Ms J.
Owen; Miss F. McCabe; R. Balfe; J. Bolton

NURSING GROUP
Chief Nursing Officer/Director of Nursing (SCS), Ms S.
Mullally
Assistant Chief Nursing Officers (SCS), Mrs G. Stephens;
D. Moore; K. Billingham

QUALITY MANAGEMENT BRANCH
Branch Head, Julian Brookes

RESEARCH AND DEVELOPMENT
DIVISION
Director of Research and Development, Prof. Sir John
Pattison
Heads of Branches (SCS), Dr P. Greenaway; Mrs J. Griffin;
Ms A. Kauder; M. Taylor

NHS EXECUTIVE
Quarry House, Quarry Hill, Leeds LS2 7UE
Tel: 0113-254 5000
Chief Executive, N. Crisp
Director of Human Resources, A. Foster
Director of Finance, R. Douglas
Health Services Director, Dr S. Adam
Director of Research and Development, Prof. Sir John
Pattison
Head of Planning, M. P. Dash
Director of National Cancer Services, Prof. M. Richards, CBE
Director of Counter Fraud Services, J. Gee
Director of Operation, R. Kerr, CBE

HUMAN RESOURCES
Director of Human Resources, A. Foster
Deputy Director of Human Resources (SCS), S. Barnett
Heads of Branches, B. Dyson; R. Mailly; Ms J. Hargadon; S.
Barnett; R. Cairncross; T. Sands; H. Fields; D. Amos;
Dr R. J. Moore

INFORMATION POLICY UNIT
Head of Unit (SCS), Dr P. Drury

PLANNING DIVISION
Director (SCS), vacant
Chief Economic Adviser, C. Smee, CBE
Head of Planning, Ms P. Dash
Head of Information Policy Unit, P. Drury
Director of Statistics, J. Fox

HEALTH SERVICES DIRECTORATE
Director (SCS), Dr Sheila Adam
Heads of Branches, Ms J. McKessack; L. Percival; Ms K.
Tyson; H. Shirely-Quirk; A. Sheehan; J. Mahoney; A.
Humphrey; A. Mithani; Dr G. Chapman; Dr J.
Carpenter; J. Boyington; Dr F. Harvey; Ms H.
Robinson; A. Berland; Ms K. Tyson; A. Sheehan; Ms S.
White; Ms K. Doran; R. Webster; L. Smith, R.
Armstrong; Prof. Ian Phillip; Ms H. Gwynn

PRIMARY CARE DIVISION
Head of Division, Ms K. Dovan
Chief Dental Officer, Dame Margaret Seward
Chief Pharmaceutical Officer, Dr J. Smith
Heads of Branches, Miss H. Robinson (*Dental and Optical
Services*); K. Guinness (*Pharmacy and Prescribing*); vacant
(*White Paper Implementation Team*); R. Webster
(*General Medical Services*); H. Gwynn (*Cardiac Services*)

FINANCE DIRECTORATE
Director (SCS), R. Douglas
Deputy Directors, Ms C. Daws; vacant
Heads of Branches, M. Sturges; P. Coates; P. Taylor; A.
MacLellan; I. Ellul; J. Stopes-Roe; L. Eccles; J.
Tomlinson

PERFORMANCE DIRECTORATE
Heads of Branches, S. Peck; Dr J. Bibby, Ms J. Copeland

DIRECTORATE OF COUNTER FRAUD SERVICES
Director, J. Gee

REGIONAL OFFICES
– *see* Social Welfare section

ADVISORY COMMITTEES

ADVISORY COMMITTEE ON THE MICROBIOLOGICAL SAFETY OF FOOD Room 808C, Aviation House, 125 Kingsway, London, WC2B 6NH. Tel: 020-7276 8946.
Chairman, Prof. D. Georgarla, CBE, Ph.D.
COMMITTEE ON THE SAFETY OF MEDICINES, Market Towers, 1 Nine Elms Lane, London SW8 5NQ. Tel: 020-7273 0000. *Director,* I. Hudson Breckenridge, CBE, FRCP, FRCPEd., FRSE
MEDICINES COMMISSION, Market Towers, 1 Nine Elms Lane, London SW8 5NQ. Tel: 020-7273 0652. *Chairman,* Prof. D. H. Lawson, CBE, FRCPed, FRCP(Glas)

SPECIAL HEALTH AUTHORITIES

DENTAL VOCATIONAL TRAINING AUTHORITY, Master's House, Temple Grove, Compton Place Road, Eastbourne, E. Sussex BN20 8AD. Tel: 01323-431189. *Chairman,* R. Davies; *Secretary,* Ms J. Verity
FAMILY HEALTH SERVICES APPEAL AUTHORITY, 30 Victoria Avenue, Harrogate HG1 5PR. Tel: 01423-535415. *Chief Executive,* D. J. Laverick
HEALTH DEVELOPMENT AGENCY, Trevelyan House, 30 Great Peter Street, London SW1P 2HW. Tel: 0171-222 5300. *Chair,* Ms Y. Buckland; *Chief Executive,* Prof R. Parish
MENTAL HEALTH ACT COMMISSION – *see* page 343
MICROBIOLOGICAL RESEARCH AUTHORITY, Porton Down, Salisbury, Wilts SP4 0JG. Tel: 01980-612100. *Chairman,* Sir William Stewart, FRS; *Director,* Dr R. H. Gilmour
NATIONAL BLOOD SERVICE , Oak House, Reeds Crescent, Watford, Herts WD24 4QN. Tel: 01923-486800. *Chairman,* M. Fogden, CB; *Chief Executive,* M. Gorham
NATIONAL INSTITUTE OF CLINICAL EXCELLENCE, 90 Long Acre, London WC2E 9RZ. Tel: 020-7849 3444. *Chairman,* Sir Michael Rawlins; *Chief Executive,* A. Dillon
NHS INFORMATION AUTHORITY, 15 Frederick Road, Edgbaston, Birmingham B15 1JD. Tel: 0121-625 1992. *Chairman,* Prof. A. Bellingham, CBE; *Chief Executive,* N. Bell
NHS LITIGATION AUTHORITY, Mapier Health, 24-28 High Holburn, London WC13 6AZ. Tel: 020-7430 8700. *Chief Executive,* S. Walker
NHS PURCHASING AND SUPPLY AGENCY, Premier House, 60 Caversham Road, Reading, Berks RG1 7EB. Tel 0118-980 8600. *Chairman,* D. Hall, CBE, TD; *Chief Executive,* D. Eaton
PRESCRIPTION PRICING AUTHORITY, Bridge House, 152 Pilgrim Street, Newcastle upon Tyne NE1 6SN. Tel: 0191-232 5371. *Chairman,* Prof. D. J. Johns; *Chief Executive,* N. Scholte
UK TRANSPLANT SUPPORT SERVICE AUTHORITY, Fox Den Road, Stoke Gifford, Bristol BS34 8RR. Tel: 0117-975 7575. *Chairman,* J. F. Shaw; *Chief Executive,* Mrs R. Balderson

SPECIAL HOSPITALS

ASHWORTH HOSPITAL, Parkbourn, Maghull, Merseyside L31 1HW. Tel: 0151-473 0303. *Chief Executive,* L. Boswell

BROADMOOR HOSPITAL, Crowthorne, Berks RG45 7EG. Tel: 01344-773111. *Chief Executive,* Dr J. Hollyman
RAMPTON HOSPITAL, Retford, Notts DN22 0PD. Tel: 01777-248321. *Chief Executive,* J. Taylor

EXECUTIVE AGENCIES

MEDICINES CONTROL AGENCY (MCA)

Market Towers, 1 Nine Elms Lane, London SW8 5NQ
Tel: 020-7273 0000; Fax: 020-7273 0353
The MCA is responsible for safeguarding public health by ensuring all medicines on the UK market meet appropriate standards of safety, quality and efficacy. This is achieved by a system of licensing, inspection, enforcement and monitoring of medicines after they have been licensed.
Chief Executive, Dr K. H. Jones, CB

MEDICAL DEVICES AGENCY

Hannibal House, Elephant and Castle, London SE1 6TQ
Tel: 020-7972 8000; Fax: 020-7972 8108;
Email mail@medical-devices.gov.uk;
Web www.medical-devices.gov.uk
The Agency safeguards the performance, quality and safety of medical devices and ensures that they comply with relevant EU directives.
Chief Executive, Dr D. Jefferys

NHS ESTATES

1 Trevelyan Square, Boar Lane, Leeds LS1 6AE
Tel: 0113-254 7000; Fax: 0113-254 7299;
Email: nhs.estates@doh.gov.uk
NHS Estates provides advice and guidance in the area of healthcare estate and facilities management to the NHS and the healthcare industry.
Acting Chief Executive, Peter Wearmouth

NHS PENSIONS

Hesketh House, 200–220 Broadway, Fleetwood, Lancs FY7 8LG. Tel: 01253-774774; Fax: 01253-774860
NHS Pensions administers the NHS occupational pension scheme.
Chief Executive, A. F. Cowan

HOME OFFICE
Home Office, Room 1024, 50 Queen Anne's Gate, London SW1H 9AT
Tel: 020-7273 4000; Fax: 020-7273 2190
Email: gen.ho@gtnet.gov.uk
Web: www.homeoffice.gov.uk

The Home Office deals with those internal affairs in England and Wales which have not been assigned to other Government departments. The Home Secretary personally is the link between The Queen and the public, and exercises certain powers on her behalf, including that of the royal pardon.
   The Home Office's statement of purpose is to build a safe, just and tolerant society, enhancing opportunities for all and in which rights and responsibilities go hand in hand, and the protection and security of the public are maintained and enhanced; to support and mobilise communities so that, through active citizenship, they are able to shape policy and improvement for their locality, overcome nuisance, anti-social behaviour, maintain and enhance social cohesion and enjoy their homes and public spaces peacefully; to deliver the Departments policies and

responsibilities fairly, effectively and efficiently, through the most up to date project and day to day management; and to make the best use of resources and the development of partnership working. These are also supported by the Department's aims, which reflect the priorities of the Government and the Home Secretary in areas of crime, citizenship and communities. They are to reduce crime and the fear of crime; to reduce organised and international crime; to combat terrorism and other threats to national security; to ensure the effective delivery of justice; to deliver effective custodial and community sentences; to reduce re-offending and protect the public; to reduce the availability and abuse of dangerous drugs; to regulate entry to and settlement in the United Kingdom effectively in the interests of sustainable growth and social inclusion; and to support strong active communities in which people of all races and backgrounds are valued and participate on equal terms.

The Home Office delivers these aims by working through the prison, probation and immigration services; its agencies and non-departmental public bodies, including Forensic Science Service, Police Information Technology Organisation, UK Passport Agency; and by working with partners in private, public and voluntary sectors, individuals and communities.

The Home Secretary is also the link between the UK Government and the governments of the Channel Islands and the Isle of Man.

Secretary of State for the Home Department, The Rt. Hon. David Blunkett, MP
Principal Private Secretary (SCS), Ms H. Jackson
Private Secretaries, G. Hills; S. Harrison; Ms M. Goldstein, Judith Simpson
Special Advisers, Nick Pearce; Katherine Raymond; Sophie Linden; Huw Evans
Minister of State, The Rt. Hon. John Denham, MP
Private Secretary, Richard Riley
Minister of State, The Rt. Hon. Keith Bradley, MP
Private Secretary, J. Laurie
Minister of State, Lord Rooker of Perry Barr
Private Secretary, C. Cumming
Parliamentary Under-Secretaries of State, Bob Ainsworth, MP; Beverley Hughes, MP
Private Secretaries, Peter Grime
Parliamentary Clerk, Ms D. Caddle
Permanent Under-Secretary of State (SCS), J. Grieve
Private Secretary, Phillip. Colligan
Chief Medical Officer (at Department of Health), Prof. L. Donaldson, QHP, FRCSEd, FRCP

COMMUNICATION DIRECTORATE

Director (SCS), B. Butler
Deputy Director of Communication (Head of News), Julia Simpson, *Deputy Director of Communication (Head of Corporate Communication Strategy) (SCS)*, A. Nash; *(Head of Strategic Communications) (SCS)*, P. Teare; *Head of Internal Communications) (SCS)*, P. Samuels
Assistant Director and Head of Information Services Group (G6), P. Griffiths
Head of Business Support Group (G6), G. Samples

CONSTITUTIONAL AND COMMUNITY POLICY DIRECTORATE

Director (SCS), Miss C. Sinclair
Heads of Units (SCS), E. L. Avery; Dr R. Richmond; T. Cobley; J. Lane; M. Boyle

ANIMALS (SCIENTIFIC PROCEDURES) INSPECTORATE

Chief Inspector (SCS), Dr J. Richmond
Superintendent Inspector (SCS), Dr J. Anderson
Inspectors (G6), Dr R. Curtis; Dr V. Navaratnam; Dr C. Wilkins; P. Buckley; Dr M. Hinton; Dr A. M. Farmer; Mrs S. Houlton; D. Buist

GAMING BOARD FOR GREAT BRITAIN

— *see* page 334

CORPORATE DEVELOPMENT AND SERVICES GROUP

Grenadier House, 99–105 Horseferry Road, London SW1P 2DD
Tel: 020-7273 4000
Queen Anne's Gate, London SW1H 9AT
Tel: 020-7273 4000

Director (SCS), Ms L. Lockyer
Heads of Units (SCS), Ms D. Loudon; Ms E. Moody; B. Gudgin; J. Potts; N. Benger; G. Jones; T. Edwards; D. McDonaugh; F. Spencer; S. Whaston
Senior Principals (G6), P. Roascorla, P. Vagg, J. Lawler; M. Fitzpatrick; V. Clayton; C. McCombie; D. G. Jones

CRIMINAL POLICY GROUP

Directors (SCS), Mrs S. Street; D. Cooke; Dr E. Wallis
Heads of Units (SCS), S. Atkins; Bob Eagle; M. Lewer; Dr D. Jones; I. Chisholm; S. Hickson; A. M. Field; T. Williams; M. Gladwyn; J. Sedgwick; Lord Warner; Miss C. Stewart; H. Webber; T. Woolfenden
Senior Principals (G6), S. Bryans; D. Grice; J. Furniss; Mrs A. Johnstone; S. Limpkin (G5); R. Ritchie; S. Trimmins; D. Perry; M. Wilkinson; S. Hart; D. Rigby

HOME OFFICE CRIME PREVENTION COLLEGE

The Hawkhills, Easingwold, York YO6 3EG
Tel: 01347-825060
Director, S. Trimmins

HM INSPECTORATE OF PROBATION

Chief Inspector (SCS), Sir. G. Smith, CBE
Deputy Chief Inspector (G5), J. Furnis
Assistant Chief Inspector (G6), J. Kuipers

IMMIGRATION AND NATIONALITY DIRECTORATE, AND EUROPEAN AND INTERNATIONAL UNIT

Advance House, 15 Wellesley Road, Croydon, Surrey CR9 3LY Tel: 020-8760 3023
Apollo House, 36 Wellesley Road, Croydon, Surrey CR9 3RR Tel: 020-8760 0333
50 Queen Anne's Gate, London SW1H 9AT
Tel: 020-7273 4000
India Buildings, 3rd Floor, Water Street, Liverpool L2 0QN
Tel: 0151-237 5200

Director-General (SCS), S. Boys Smith
Deputy Directors-General (SCS), P. Welch, *(Policy)*; Dr C. Mace *(Operations)*
Heads of Directorates (SCS), J. Actan; U. Wiffen; M. Craske; R. Reynolds

WORK PERMITS UK

Moorfort, Sheffield, S1 4PQ.
Director, M. Caske

IMMIGRATION SERVICE

Director (Ports) (SCS), P. Higgins
Deputy Director (G6), D. Roberts; D. Ingham
Director (Enforcement) (SCS), I. Boon
Deputy Director (G6), C. Harbin, A. Ramlagan-Singh

EUROPEAN INTERNATIONAL UNIT

Head of Unit (SCS), L. Pallett

LEGAL ADVISERS' BRANCH

Legal Adviser (SCS), D. Seymour
Deputy Legal Advisers (SCS), D. Noble; T. Middleton
Assistant Legal Advisers (SCS), R. J. Clayton; J. R. O'Meara;
S. Bramley; C. Price; H. Carter; S. Weston; R. Collins-
Rice; R. Davies; C. Osborn

ORGANISED AND INTERNATIONAL
CRIME DIRECTORATE

Director (SCS), J. Warne
Deputy Director, Dr K. Collins

PLANNING, FINANCE AND
PERFOMANCE GROUP

50 Queen Anne's Gate, London SW1H 9AT
Tel: 020-7273 4000
Horseferry House, Dean Ryle Street, London SW1P 2AW
Tel: 020-7273 4000

Directors (SCS), R. Fulton; L. Haugh
Heads of Units (G7), A. Potter; A. Corry; *Senior Principals
(G6)*, K. Venosi; B. Sanders; C. Jones

POLICING AND CRIME REDUCTION
GROUP

Director (SCS), J. Lyon
Director of Police Services and Volume Crime (SCS), J. Daniell
Senior Principals (G6), S. Pike; C. Lee; B. Lane; A.
McFarlane; R. Henderson; S. King; S. Trimmins; Dr S.
Martin; P. McFarlane; D. Buge; J. Cooke; P. Duffin; C.
Passey; T. Hepple
Heads of Units (SCS), J. Duke-Evans; V. Hogg; J.
Nicholson; B. Moxam; P. Pugh; C. Byrne; M. Du
Pulford; R. Karnicki; C. Everett

NATIONAL POLICE TRAINING

National Director of Police Training, C. Mould
Corporate Services; Senior Principal (G6), S. Wells

NATIONAL POLICE TRAINING

Bramshill House, Bramshill, Hook, Hants RG27 0JW
Tel: 01256-602100
Head of Higher Training, I. McDonald

HENDON DATA CENTRE

Aerodrome Road, Colindale, London NW9 5LN
Tel: 020-8200 2424
Head of Unit (G6), J. Ladley

POLICE SCIENTIFIC DEVELOPMENT BRANCH

Sandridge, St Albans, Herts AL4 9HQ
Tel: 01727-865051

Director (SCS), B. R. Coleman, OBE
Chief Scientist/Deputy Director (G6), Dr P. Young

Langhurst House, Langhurstwood Road, Nr Horsham,
W. Sussex RH12 4WX
Tel: 01403-255451
Head of Langhurst Facility (G6), M. Thompson

UK ANTI DRUGS CO-ORDINATION
UNIT

4 Central Buildings, Matthew Parker Street, London,
SW1H 9NL. Tel: 020 -7270 1234
Director, S. Killen
Deputy Director (SCS), J. Lempriese
Senior Principals (G6), T. Campbell; K. Lidbetter

HM INSPECTORATE OF
CONSTABULARY

HM Chief Inspector of Constabulary (SCS), Sir David
O'Dowd, CBE, QPM
HM Inspectors (SCS), D. Crompton, CBE, QPM; K. Povey,
QPM; C. Smith, CBE, CVO, QPM; P. J. Winship, CBE, QPM;
D. Blakey, CBE, QPM
Senior Principal (G6), L. Robinson

METROPOLITAN POLICE COMMITTEE AND
SECRETARIAT

Clive House, Petty France, London SW1H 9HD
Tel: 020-7273 4000

Head of Secretariat (SCS), P. Honour

RESEARCH, DEVELOPMENT AND
STATISTICS DIRECTORATE

Director (SCS), Dr P. Wiles
Heads of Units (SCS), Prof. D. Pyle; Mrs C. Lehman; D.
Moxam; Dr J. Yovell; C. Lewis; P. Ward C. Willis;
Senior Principals (G6), P. Ibrahim M. Koudra; L. Singer;
Mrs P. Mayhew, OBE; B. Webb; J. Simmons; P.
Dowdeswell; P. Collier; M. Collidge

HM INSPECTORATE OF PRISONS

HM Chief Inspector, Sir David Ramsbotham, GCB, CBE
HM Deputy Chief Inspector, C. Allen
HM Inspectors (Governor 1), R. Jacques; G. Hughes; J.
Podmore

PRISONS OMBUDSMAN

— see page 354

PAROLE BOARD FOR ENGLAND AND
WALES

— see page 353

HM PRISON SERVICE

— see Prison Service Section pages 391–5

UK PASSPORT SERVICE

Globe House, 89 Ecclestone Square, London SW1V 1PN
Tel: 020-7901 2000

Chief Executive (SCS), B. L. Herdan
Deputy Chief Executive and Director of Operations (G6), K. J.
Sheehan
Director of Systems (G6), J. Davies
Director Finance; A. Cook
Director of Human Resources, R. Mycroft
CRIMINAL RECORDS BUREAU, Horton House, Exchange
Flags, Liverpool L2 3YL. Tel: 0151-236 8068.
Director of Operation, K. Broadbent
Programme Manager (G7), G. Ryan

DEPARTMENT FOR INTERNATIONAL DEVELOPMENT
94 Victoria Street, London SW1E 5JL
Tel: 020-7917 7000; Fax: 020-7917 0019
Web: www.dfid.gov.uk
Abercrombie House, Eaglesham Road, East Kilbride, Glasgow G75 8EA
Tel: 01355-844000; Fax: 01355-844099

The Department for International Development (DFID) is the UK Government department responsible for promoting development and the reduction of poverty. The governments aim is to strengthening the department and increase its budget. The central focus of the Government's policy, set out in the 1997 White Paper on International Development, is a commitment to internationally agreed target to halve the proportion of people living in extreme poverty by 2015, together with associated targets, including basic health care provision and universal access to primary education, by the same date. A second White Paper on International Development, published in December 2000, reaffirmed this commitment, while focusing specifically on how to manage the process of globalisation to benefit poor people. DFID seeks to work in partnership with governments committed to these targets, and with business, civil society and the research community.

DFID also works with multilateral institutions including the World Bank, United Nations agencies and the European Community. The bulk of assistance is concentrated on the poorest countries in Asia and sub-Saharan Africa. DFID also contributes to poverty elimination and sustainable development in middle-income countries in Latin America, the Caribbean and elsewhere. In the transition countries of central and Eastern Europe, DFID is working to ensure the process of change brings benefits to all people, and particularly to the poorest.

Secretary of State for International Development,
The Rt. Hon. Clare Short, MP
Private Secretary, Anna Bewes
Special Advisers, Susan Cox; David Mepham
Parliamentary Private Secretary, Dennis Turner, MP
Parliamentary Under-Secretary, Hilary Benn, MP
Private Secretary, James Price
Permanent Secretary (SCS), Sir John Vereker, KCB
Private Secretary, Joanne Graham

PROGRAMMES
Director-General (SCS), B. R. Ireton

AFRICA DIVISION

Head (SCS), G. Stegmann
Heads of Departments, T. Craddock *(SCS, Africa Great Lakes and Horn)*; O. Barder *(Africa Policy and Economics)*; B. Thomson *(SCS, West and North Africa)*; J. Winter *(DFID Central Africa)*; M. Wood *(SCS, DFIDCA Malawi)*; E. Cassidy *(DFIDCA Mozambique)*; Ms H. Mealins *(DFIDCA Zambia)*; M. Wyatt *(DFID Eastern Africa)*; D. Bell *(DFID Eastern Africa Kenya)*; Ms C. Sergeant *(DFID Eastern Africa Tanzania)*; M. Hammond *(DFID Eastern Africa Uganda)*; P. Spray *(DFID Nigeria)*; S. Sharpe *(SCS, DFID Southern Africa)*

ASIA AND PACIFIC

Head (SCS), M. Dinham
Heads of Departments (SCS), P. Grant *(Asia Regional Economics and Policy)*; Ms M. H. Vowles *(SCS, Eastern Asia and Pacific)*; C. Austin *(Western Asia)*; P. Ackroyd

(SCS, DFID Bangladesh); R. Graham-Harrison *(SCS, DFID India)*; D. Wod *(DFID Nepal)*; J. Medhurst *(DFID Pacific)*; M. Mallalieu *(SCS, DFID South East Asia)*

EASTERN EUROPE AND WESTERN HEMISPHERE DIVISION

Head (SCS), Ms C. Miller
Heads of Departments (SCS), Ms B. Killen *(Americas and Transition Economies Policy)*; S. Ray *(SCS, Central and South Eastern Europe)*; D. Batt *(SCS, Eastern Europe and Central Asia)*; vacant *(Latin America)*; Ms R. Eyben *(SCS, DFID Bolivia)*; D. Curran *(DFID Caribbean)*; Ms G. Taylor *(DFID Central America)*; C. Warren *(Overseas Territories Unit)*; J. Kerby *(SCS UK Delegation to the EBRD)*

INTERNATIONAL DIVISION

Director (SCS), J. A. L. Faint
Heads of Departments (SCS), Dr M. Kapila *(Conflict and Humanitarian Affairs)* A. Smith *(European Affairs)*; Ms C. Cund *(International Financial Institutions)*; M. Mosselmans *(United Nations Commonwealth)*; A. Beattie *(UK Permanent Representation to the UN Food and Agriculture Agencies)*; D. L. Stanton *(UK Permanent Delegation to UNESCO)*

CIVIL SOCIETY DEPARTMENT

Head, R. Calvert

RURAL LIVELIHOODS AND ENVIRONMENT

Chief Natural Resources Adviser (SCS), A. J. Bennett, CMG
Head, Environment Policy Department (SCS), A. Davis
Head, Rural Livelihoods, J. M. Scott

RESOURCES
Director-General (SCS), R. G. Manning, CB

ECONOMICS, BUSINESS AND STATISTICS DIVISION

Chief Economist (SCS) A. Wood
Heads of Departments (SCS) P. Landymore *(Economic Policy and Research)*; D. L. Stanton *(Chief Enterprise Development Adviser)*; Ms C. Seymour-Smith *(International Trade)*; Ms V. Harris *(Private Sector Policy)*; A. Williams *(Chief Statistician)*

FINANCE AND DEVELOPMENT POLICY DIVISION

Principal Finance Officer (SCS), M. Lowcock
Heads of Department, R. Teuten *(Acting, Development Policy)*; C. Kirk; *(SCS, Evaluation)*; K. Sparkhall *(SCS, Finance)*; M. Smithson *(Accounts)*; R. A. Elias *(SCS, Internal Audit)*; S. Chard *(SCS, Procurement)*

HUMAN RESOURCES DIVISION

Head (SCS), D. Fish
Heads of Departments, J. Anning *(Human Resources Operations)*; D. Richards; *(Human Resources Policy)*; P. Brough *(Overseas Pensions)*

ADVISORY GROUPS

Heads of Departments (SCS), Prof. Stephen Matlin *(Chief Education Adviser)*; R. Wilson *(Chief Governance Adviser)*; Dr J. Lob-Levyt *(Chief Health and Population Adviser)*; J.W. Hodges *(Chief Engineering Adviser)*; Dr M. Schultz *(Chief Social Development Adviser)*; Prof. Stephen Matlin *(Chief Education Adviser)*; R. Wilson *(Chief Governance Adviser)*; Dr J. Lob-Levyt *(Chief Health and Population Adviser)*; J.W. Hodges *(Chief Engineering Adviser)*; Dr M. Schultz *(Chief Social Development Adviser)*

INFORMATION SYSTEMS AND SERVICES
DEPARTMENT
Head (SCS), D. Gillett

INFORMATION DEPARTMENT
Head (SCS), R. Calvert

OTHER RELATED ORGANISATIONS

CDC CAPITAL PARTNERS
One Bessborough Gardens, London SW1V 2JQ
Tel: 020-7828 4488; Fax: 020-7282 6505
The Commonwealth Development Corporation has now
become CDC Capital Partners, a public limited company
with the Department of International Development as its
100% shareholder. At a later date CDC plans to become a
public-private partnership with the Government main-
taining the majority of the shareholding.
Chairman, The Lord Cairns, CBE
Deputy Chairman, Ms J. Almond
Chief Executive, Dr A. Gillespie

LORD CHANCELLOR'S DEPARTMENT
Selborne House, 54–60 Victoria Street, London
SW1E 6QW
Tel: 020-7210 8500
Email: enquiries.lcdhq@gtnet.gov.uk
Web: www.open.gov.uk/lcd

The Lord Chancellor appoints Justices of the Peace
(except in the Duchy of Lancaster) and advises the Crown
on the appointment of most members of the higher
judiciary. He is responsible for promoting general reforms
in the civil law, for the procedure of the civil courts and for
the Community Legal Service. He is a member of the
Cabinet. He also has ministerial responsibility for
magistrates' courts, which are administered locally.
Administration of the Supreme Court and county courts
in England and Wales was taken over by the Court Service,
an executive agency of the department, in 1995.
The Lord Chancellor is also responsible for ensuring
that letters patent and other formal documents are passed
in the proper form under the Great Seal of the Realm, of
which he is the custodian. The work in connection with
this is carried out under his direction in the Office of the
Clerk of the Crown in Chancery.
The Lord Chancellor is also the senior Lord of Appeal
in Ordinary and speaker of the House of Lords.
Lord Chancellor (£173,875), The Lord Irvine of Lairg,
  PC, QC
Principal Private Secretary, Ms Debra Matthews
Special Adviser, Gary Hart
Parliamentary Under-Secretary, Baroness Scotland of
  Asthal, QC; Michael Wills, MP; Rosie Winterton, MP
Private Secretaries, David Liddemore; Mel Charles
Parliamentary Private Secretaries, Laura Moffatt, MP;
  Gordon Marsden, MP
Permanent Secretary, Sir Hayden Phillips, KCB
Private Secretary, Bridgete Lee

CROWN OFFICE
House of Lords, London SW1A 0PW
Tel: 020-7219 4713
Clerk of the Crown in Chancery, Sir Hayden Phillips, KCB
Deputy Clerk of the Crown in Chancery, M. Huebner, CB
Clerk of the Chamber, C. I. P. Denyer

JUDICIAL GROUP
Tel: 020-7210 8500
Director General, Mrs J. Williams
Director (SCS), Mrs E. J. Grimsey
Heads of Divisions (SCS), D. E. Staff *(Policy and Conditions of
  Service)*; D. Gladwell *(Senior Appointment and Silk)*; Mrs
  C. Pulford *(District Bench and Tribunals)*; S. Humphries
  (Magistrates' Appointments)

JUDICIAL STUDIES BOARD
9th Floor, Millbank Tower, London SW1P 4QW
Tel: 020-7925 4762
Secretary (SCS), E. S. Adams

POLICY GROUP
Tel: 020-7210 8719
Director-General (SCS), Ms J. MacNaughton
Heads of Divisions (SCS), A. Cogbill *(Civil Justice and Legal
  Services Directorate)*; J. Tanner *(Civil Justice)*; H. Burns
  (Civil Law Development); D. A. Hill *(Public Legal
  Services)*; C. Myerscough *(Community Legal Services)*; P.
  Harris *(Legal Services)*; Ms A. Finlay *(Public and Private
  Rights Directorate)*; Ms M. Pigott, Ms J. Killick *(Family
  Policy)*; B. Wells *(Administrative Justice)*; D. Lye
  (Children and Advisory Service); Ms C. Colins, Ms K.
  Di Lorenzo *(Human Rights and Constitution Division)*;
  Mrs K. Allen *(Policy Group Secretariat)*; M. Ormerod
  (Criminal Justice Group); M. Kron *(Criminal Courts
  Review)*; P. Stockton *(Criminal Justice)*; Ms. S. Field
  (Magistrates' Court); P. White *(Magistrates' Courts IT)*

LEGAL ADVISER'S GROUP
Tel: 020-7210 0711
Modernising Government, D. Nooney
Legal Adviser (SCS), P. Jenkins
Heads of Divisions (SCS), P. Fish *(Legal Advice and
  Litigation)*; A. Wallace *(International and Common Law
  Services)*; M. Collon *(Drafting Services)*

COMMUNICATIONS GROUP
Tel: 020-7210 8672
Director of Communications (SCS), A. Percival, LVO

CORPORATE SERVICES GROUP
Tel: 020-7210 8503
Director of Corporate Services (SCS), Ms. J. Rowe
Heads of Divisions (SCS), R. Sams *(Personnel)*; S. Smith
  (Finance) A. Pay *(Accountancy)*; A. Rummins *(Internal
  Assurance)*; A. Maultby *(Information Management Unit)*;
  R. Atkinson *(Facilities and Support Services)*; K. Garrett
  (Statutory Publications); vacant *(Information Technology)*;
  B. Eadie *(Corporate Services Secretariat)*

ECCLESIASTICAL PATRONAGE
10 Downing Street, London SW1A 2AA
Tel: 020-7930 4433
Secretary for Ecclesiastical Patronage, J. H. Holroyd, CB
Assistant Secretary for Ecclesiastical Patronage, N. C.
  Wheeler

HM MAGISTRATES' COURTS' SERVICE
INSPECTORATE
Southside, 105 Victoria Street, London SW1E 6QJ
Tel: 020-7210 1655
Chief Inspector (SCS), C. J. A. Chivers

Senior Inspectors (SCS), D. Gear; C. Monson; Ms S. Steel; Dr S. Dixon

LORD CHANCELLOR'S ADVISORY COMMITTEE ON STATUTE LAW

Room 6.06, Selborne House, 54–60 Victoria Street, London SW1E 6QW
Tel: 020-7210 2615; Fax: 020-7210 2678

The Advisory Committee advises the Lord Chancellor on all matters relating to the revision, modernisation and publication of the statute book.
Chairman, The Lord Chancellor, The Rt. Hon. the Lord Irvine of Lairg
Deputy Chairman, Sir Hayden Phillips, KCB
Members, The Hon. Mr Justice Carnwath, CVO; The Hon. Lord Gill; J. M. Davies; J. C. McCluskie, CB, QC; R. Henderson; P. Jenkins; Mrs C. Tullo; W. R. McKay, CB; K. Garrett; E. G. Cauldwell, CB; P. J. Layden, TD; G. Gray; Miss J. Wheldon, CB, QC; Ms J. Rowe; A. Pawsey
Secretary, N. Hodgett

EXECUTIVE AGENCY

THE COURT SERVICE

Southside, 105 Victoria Street, London SW1E 6QT
Tel: 020-7210 1646; Fax: 020-7210 2059;
E mail cust.ser.cs@gtnet.gov.uk;
Web www.courtservice.gov.uk

The Court Service provides administrative support to the Supreme Court, the Crown Court, county courts and a number of tribunals in England and Wales.
Chief Executive (SCS), I. Magee
Director of Field Services, P. Handcock
Director of Operational Policy (SCS), Miss B. Kenny
Director of Finance (SCS), P. Commins
Change Director (SCS), vacant
Director of Purchasing and Contract Management (SCS), C. Lyne
Director of Information Services Division (SCS), Ms A. Vernon
Director of Personnel and Training (SCS), Ms H. Dudley
Director of Civil and Family Business (SCS), J. Sills; *Director of Crown Court Operations (SCS)*, M. Camley; *Director of Tribunals (SCS)*, S. Smith

SUPREME COURT GROUP

Strand, London WC2A 2LL
Tel: 020-7936 6000
Director (SCS), I. Hyams

NORTHERN IRELAND OFFICE

11 Millbank, London SW1P 4PN
Tel: 020-7210 3000
Castle Buildings, Stormont, Belfast BT4 3SG
Tel: 01232-520700; Fax: 01232-528195
Web: www.nio.gov.uk

The Northern Ireland Office was established in 1972, when the Northern Ireland (Temporary Provisions) Act transferred the legislative and executive powers of the Northern Ireland Parliament and Government to the UK Parliament and a Secretary of State.

The Northern Ireland Office is responsible primarily for security issues, law and order and prisons, and for matters relating to the political and constitutional future of the province. It also deals with international issues as they affect Northern Ireland. Following an earlier suspension of the Assembly, devolution took place on 29 May 2000.

Under the terms of the 1998 Belfast Agreement, power was due to be devolved to the New Northern Ireland Assembly in 1999; the Assembly would then have taken on responsibility for the relevant areas of work currently undertaken by the departments of the Northern Ireland Office. In December 1998 the creation of ten new departments was agreed: agriculture and rural development; the environment; regional development; social development; education; higher education, training and employment; enterprise, trade and investment, culture, arts and leisure; health, social services and public safety; and finance and personnel. Each department is headed by a member of the power-sharing executive which is headed by the First Minister and Deputy First Minister. Six cross-border implementation bodies have also been established, dealing with inland waterways, food safety, trade and business development, EU programmes, language, and aquaculture.
Secretary of State for Northern Ireland, The Rt. Hon. Dr John Reid, MP
Parliamentary Private Secretary, Gillian Merron, MP
Minister of State, Jane Kennedy, MP
Parliamentary Private Secretary, Shona McIsaac, MP
Parliamentary Under-Secretary of State, Des Browne, MP
Permanent Under-Secretary of State (SCS), Sir Joseph Pilling, CB
Second Permanent Under-Secretary of State, Head of the Northern Ireland Civil Service, Gerry Loughran

NORTHERN IRELAND INFORMATION SERVICE

Castle Buildings, Stormont, Belfast BT4 3SG
Tel: 01232-520700

EXECUTIVE AGENCIES

COMPENSATION AGENCY, Royston House, Upper Queen Street, Belfast BT1 6FD. Tel: 01232-2499444
FORENSIC SCIENCE AGENCY, Seapark, 151 Belfast Road, Carrickfergus, Co. Antrim BT38 8PL. Tel: 01232-365744
NORTHERN IRELAND PRISON SERVICE, *see* Prison Service section

SCOTLAND OFFICE

Dover House, Whitehall, London SW1A 2AU
Tel: 020-7270 6754; Fax: 020-7270 6812;
Web: www.scottishsecretary.gov.uk

The Scotland Office is the department of the Secretary of State for Scotland, who represents Scottish interests in the Cabinet on matters reserved to the UK Parliament, i.e. constitutional matters, financial and economic matters, defence and international relations, immigration, social security, various matters relating to the single market with the UK (energy, transport, consumer protection) and employment. It also supports the Advocate General, the legal adviser to the UK Government on Scottish law. *See also* Scottish Executive, Regional Government section
Secretary of State for Scotland, The Rt. Hon. Helen Liddell, MP
Private Secretary, Ms J. Colquhoun
Minister of State, George Foulkes, MP
Private Secretary, Greig Chalmers
Parliamentary Private Secretary, Jim Murphy, MP; Sandra Osborne, MP
Advocate-General for Scotland, Dr Lynda Clark, QC, MP
Private Secretary, Gary Whyte

DEPARTMENT OF TRADE AND INDUSTRY
1 Victoria Street, London SW1H 0ET
Tel: 020-7215 5000; Fax: 020-7222 2629
Web: www.dti.gov.uk

The Department is responsible for international trade policy, including the development of UK trade interests in the European Union, GATT, OECD, UNCTAD and other international organisations; policy in relation to industry and commerce, including industrial relations policy; policy towards small firms; regional industrial assistance; legislation and policy in relation to the Post Office; competition policy and consumer protection; the development of national policies in relation to all forms of energy and the development of new sources of energy, including international aspects of energy policy; policy on science and technology research and development; space policy; standards, quality and design; and company legislation.

Secretary of State for Trade and Industry, Minister for Women, and E-Minister in Cabinet, The Rt. Hon. Patricia Hewitt, MP
Principal Private Secretary, Ms Bernadette Kelly
Private Secretaries, Elleanor Brooks; Damien Nussbourn
Minister of State, Douglas Alexander, MP (*E-Commerce and Competitiveness*)
Minister of State, The Rt. Hon. Baroness Symons of Vernham Dean (*Trade and Investment and Deputy Leader of the House of Lords*)
Minister of State for Industry and Energy, Brian Wilson, MP
Minister of State, for the Regions and Employment Relations, Alan Johnson, MP
Parliamentary Under-Secretaries of State, Melanie Johnson, MP (*Competition, Consumers and Markets*); The Lord Sainsbury of Turville, MP (*Science and Innovation*); Nigel Griffiths, MP (*Small Business*)
Private Secretaries, Gareth Maybury; Ms Gaynor-. Jeffrey; Ms Becky Eggleton
Parliamentary Clerk, Tim Williams
Permanent Secretary, Robin Young, CB
Private Secretary, Fergus Harradence
Chief Scientific Adviser and Head of Office of Science and Technology, Prof. David King
Private Secretary, Anne Harris
British Trade International Chief Executive, Sir David Wright, KCMG, LVO
Directors-General, Dr J. Taylor, OBE, FEng, FRS (*Director-General of the Research Councils*); R. Carden (*Trade Policy*); M. Gibson (*Enterprise and Innovation*); Dr C. Bell (*Competition and Markets Group*); D. Nissen, CB (*The Solicitor*); Ms A. Walker (*Energy*); J. Phillips (*Resources and Services*); J. Spencer (*Business Competitiveness*)

DIVISIONAL ORGANISATION

†BRITISH NATIONAL SPACE CENTRE
Director-General (SCS), Dr C. Hicks
Deputy Director-General (SCS), D. Leadbeater
Directors (SCS), A. Cooper; Dr P. Murdin; Miss P. Freedman

BPT DIRECTORATE - BNFL PUBLIC PRIVATE PARTNERSHIP
Directors, J. Rhodes; Dr. D. Walker
Deputy Directors, Ms R. Loebl; Ms P. Ciniewicz; N. Woodage

CENTRAL DIRECTORATE
Director of Competitiveness Unit (SCS), S. Lyle Smythe
Directors (SCS), S. Chambers; E. Zimmon

†CHEMICALS AND BIOTECHNOLOGY DIRECTORATE
Director of Chemicals and Biotechnology (SCS), D. Davis
Directors (SCS), Ms M. Darnbrough; Dr D. Jennings
Directorate/Newsroom
Deputy Director of News (SCS), I. Heppleshile
Director of Public Information (SCS), P. Burke
†COMMUNICATIONS AND INFORMATION INDUSTRIES DIRECTORATE
Director of Communications and Information Industries (SCS), W. MacIntyre
Directors (SCS), N. Worman; D. Lumley; D. Love; C. Holmes; Mrs G. Alliston

COAL DIRECTORATE
Director of Coal Directorate (SCS) R. Wright
Directors (SCS) G. Rigs; A. Taylor; S. Pride

COMPANY LAW AND INVESTIGATIONS DIRECTORATE
Director of Company Law and Investigations (SCS), R. Rogers
Directors (SCS), J. Grewe; G. Harp; J. Gardner; J. Sibley; R. Burns; Ms B. Chase; A. Robertshaw; K. Harre; P. Masson

COMPETITION POLICY AND UTILITIES REVIEW DIRECTORATE
Director of Team (SCS), Ms R. Anderson
Directors (SCS), P. Sellers; J. Swift; D. Miner; J. May; R. Bent

CONSUMER AFFAIRS DIRECTORATE
Director of Consumer Affairs (SCS), J. Rees
Directors (SCS), P. Wilson; C. Durkin; B. Habbajam; A. Willcocks

CONSUMER GOODS, BUSINESS AND POSTAL SERVICES DIRECTORATE
Director of Consumer Goods, Business and Postal Services (SCS), D. Davis
Directors (SCS), B. Hopson; Ms J. Britton; M. Higsen

ECONOMICS AND STATISTICS DIRECTORATE
Chief Economic Adviser (SCS), D. R. Coates
Directors (SCS), K. Warwick; G. Everitt; A. Rees

EMPLOYMENT RELATIONS DIRECTORATE
Director of Industrial Relations (SCS), M. Beatson; J. Munday; S. Rhodes: J. Startup

ENERGY POLICY, ANALYSIS, TECHNOLOGY COUNCIL
Director of Energy Policy, Analysis, Technology and Coal (SCS), N. Hirst
Directors (SCS), G. C. White; N. Peace; J. Doddrell; Dr A. Heyes; G. White

ENERGY UTILITIES DIRECTORATE (ENU)
Deputy Director General, N. Hirst
Director, I. Fletcher
Deputy Director, Dr G. Bryce

†ENGINEERING INDUSTRIES DIRECTORATE
Director of Engineering Industries (SCS), M. O'Shea
Directors (SCS), J. Hunt; N. Carter ; R. Kingcombe; H. Brown; I. Cameron; J. Dennis; S. Bishop

ENGINEERING INSPECTORATE

Director of Engineering Inspectorate (SCS), Dr P. Fenwick

ENVIRONMENT DIRECTORATE

Director of Environment (SCS), Dr J. Dennis
Director (SCS), D. Prior

ESTATES AND FACILITIES MANAGEMENT DIRECTORATE

Director (SCS), M. Coolican

EUROPEAN POLICY DIRECTORATE

Kingsgate House, 66–74 Victoria Street, London SW1E 6SW

Directors (SCS), J. Alty; H. Savill

EXPORT CONTROL AND NON-PROLIFERATION DIRECTORATE
Kingsgate House, 66–74 Victoria Street, London SW1E 6SW

Director of Export Control and Non-Proliferation (SCS), Ms S. Haird
Director (SCS), J. Neve

FINANCE AND RESOURCE MANAGEMENT DIRECTORATE

Director of Finance and Resource Management (SCS), E. Hosker
Directors (SCS), P. Lloyd; R. Niblett

‡INDUSTRY ECONOMICS AND STATISTICS DIRECTORATE

Director (SCS), Dr N. Owen

†INFORMATION MANAGEMENT AND PROCESS ENGINEERING DIRECTORATE

Director (SCS), R. Wheeler

INNOVATION SERVICES

Director of Innovation Policy and Standards (SCS), Dr A. Kaddie
Directors (SCS), J. Barber; D. Reed; S. I. Chanik

†INTERNAL AUDIT DIRECTORATE

Director of Internal Audit (SCS), C. Juman

INTERNATIONAL ECONOMICS DIRECTORATE

Kingsgate House, 66–74 Victoria Street, London SW1E 6SW

Director (SCS), C. Moir

INVEST UK

Chief Executive (SCS), W. Pedder
Director, Operations, A. Morgan
Director, International, D. Cockerham

LEGAL RESOURCE MANAGEMENT AND BUSINESS LAW UNIT

10 Victoria Street, London SW1H 0NN

The Solicitor and Director-General (SCS), D. Nissen, CB
Director (SCS), C. Warren

LEGAL SERVICES DIRECTORATE A

10 Victoria Street, London SW1H 0NN

Director of Legal A (SCS), J. Stanley

Legal Directors (SCS), J. Roberts; S. Hyett; Miss G. Richmond

LEGAL SERVICES DIRECTORATE B

10 Victoria Street, London SW1H 0NN

Director of Legal B (SCS), A. Brett-Holt
Legal Directors (SCS), R. Baker; B. Welch; R. Perkins; Ms S. Hardy; C. Raikes; Ms N. Arora

LEGAL SERVICES DIRECTORATE C

10 Victoria Street, London SW1H 0NN

Director of Legal C (SCS), P. Beug
Legal Directors (SCS), M. Bucknill; A. Woods; M. Smith; T. Susman; B. Welch

LEGAL SERVICES DIRECTORATE D

10 Victoria Street, London SW1H 0NN

Director of Legal D (SCS), S. Milligan; L. Nawbatt

TRADE POLICY

Kingsgate House, 66–74 Victoria Street, London SW1E 6SW

Director (SCS), Dr E. Draige

NUCLEAR INDUSTRIES DIRECTORATE

Director of Nuclear Industries (SCS), H. Leiser
Directors (SCS), I. Downing; S. Bowen; P. Robinson; Dr P. Heyes

OFFICE OF SCIENCE AND TECHNOLOGY: SCIENCE AND ENGINEERING BASE DIRECTORATE

Albany House, 84–86 Petty France, London SW1H 9ST

Director, Science and Engineering Base (SCS), C. Henshall
Directors (SCS), Dr F. Saunders; R. King; Dr K. Root

OFFICE OF SCIENCE AND TECHNOLOGY: TRANSDEPARTMENTAL SCIENCE AND TECHNOLOGY DIRECTORATE

Albany House, 84–86 Petty France, London SW1H 9ST

Director, Transdepartmental Science and Technology (SCS), Ms J. Durning
Directors (SCS), S. Spivey; M. Parker; Ms J. Darrell

OIL AND GAS DIRECTORATE

1 Victoria Street, London SW1H 0ET

Director of Oil and Gas (SCS), G. Dart
Directors (SCS), J. R. V. Brooks, CBE; Dr A. Eggington; S. Toole; M. Graham

Atholl House, 86–88 Guild Street, Aberdeen AB11 6AR
Tel: 01224-254059

Director of Reform and Energy Regulation, K. Long
Directors of Oil and Gas (SCS), S. Toole; J. Campbell

REGIONAL ASSISTANCE DIRECTORATE

Director of Regional Assistance (SCS), A. Steele

REGIONAL EUROPEAN FUNDS DIRECTORATE

Director (SCS), J. Neve

REGIONAL POLICY DIRECTORATE

Director (SCS), P. Bunn

SENIOR STAFF MANAGEMENT DIRECTORATE
Director (SCS), Ms K. Elliott

SMALL BUSINESS SERVICE
Chief Executive, D. Irwin
Deputy Chief Executive, Dr D. Evans
Directors, H. Merrifield; P. Jackson; J. Hobday; M. Cocks; R. Allpress

STAFF PERSONNEL OPERATIONS DIRECTORATE
Director (SCS), R. Heyhoe

STAFF POLICY AND PAY DIRECTORATE
Director (SCS), F. Sonne

TRADE POLICY DIRECTORATE
Kingsgate House, 66–74 Victoria Street, London SW1E 6SW
Director (SCS), C. Bridge

TRADE FACILITATION AND IMPORT POLICY DIRECTORATE
Kingsgate House, 66–74 Victoria Street, London SW1E 6SW
Director (SCS), A. Berry

BRITISH TRADE INTERNATIONAL
Kingsgate House, 66–74 Victoria Street, London SW1E 6SW
Tel: 020-7215 5000

British Trade International brings together the Department of Trade and Industry and the Foreign and Commonwealth Office export and investment operations.
Chairmen, The Rt. Hon. Baroness Symons of Vernham Dean (*Minister for Trade, DTI*)
Vice-Chairmen, HRH The Duke of York GCMG, GCVO; Sir David John, KCMG
Chief Executive, Sir David Wright, KCMG, LVO
Group Members, R. Turner, OBE; V. Brown; A. Summers; Ms G. Goucher, MBE; R. Orgill; K. Pathak; P. Westmacott; W. Thomson; G. Robson; D. Jones; J. Spencer; P. Mason; A. Hingston

TRADE PARTNERS UK
The Trade Partners UK network provides services to British exporters and investors at home and overseas.
Deputy Chief Executive and Group Director, Central Services Group (SCS), D. Hall
Group Director, Regional Group, I. Jones
Group Director, International Group (SCS), Q. Quayle
Group Director, Business Group (SCS), D. Warren
Group Director, Strategy and Communications Group (SCS), J. Reynolds

EXECUTIVE AGENCIES
COMPANIES HOUSE
Companies House, Crown Way, Cardiff CF14 3UZ
Tel: 0870-333 3636; Fax: 029-2038 0900
London Information Centre, 21 Bloomsbury Street, London WC1B 3XD
Edinburgh, 37 Castle Terrace, Edinburgh EH1 2EB
Tel: 0131-535 5800; Fax: 0131-535 5820;
Web: www.companies.gov.uk
Birmingham, Central Library, Chamberlain Square,
Leeds, 25 Queen Street, Leeds, LS1 2TW; 9am to 4pm
Manchester, 75 Mosley Street, Manchester, M2 2HR; 9am to 4pm
Glasgow, Small Business Gateway, 7 West George Street, Glasgow, G2 1BQ; 9am to 5pm

Companies House incorporates companies, registers company documents and provides company information.
Registrar of Companies for England and Wales, J. Holden
Registrar for Scotland, J. Henderson

EMPLOYMENT TRIBUNALS SERVICE
19–29 Woburn Place, London WC1H 0LU
Tel: 020-7273 8666; Fax: 020-7273 8670
The Service became an executive agency in 1997 and brought together the administrative support for the employment tribunals and the Employment Appeal Tribunal.
Chief Executive, R. Heathcote

THE INSOLVENCY SERVICE
PO Box 203, 21 Bloomsbury Street, London WC1B 3QW
Tel: 020-7637 1110; Fax: 020-7636 4709
The Service administers and investigates the affairs of bankrupts and companies in compulsory liquidation; deals with the disqualification of directors in all corporate failures; regulates insolvency practitioners and their professional bodies; provides banking and investment services for bankruptcy and liquidation estates; and advises Ministers on insolvency policy issues.
Inspector-General and Chief Executive, D. J. Flynn
Deputy Inspectors-Generals, D. J. Flynn; L. T. Cramp

NATIONAL WEIGHTS AND MEASURES LABORATORY (NWML)
Stanton Avenue, Teddington, Middx TW11 0JZ
Tel: 020-8943 7272; Fax: 020-8943 7270;
Web: www.nwml.gov.uk
The Laboratory administers weights and measures legislation, carries out type examination, calibration and testing, and runs courses on legal meteorological topics.
Chief Executive, Dr S. Bennett

PATENT OFFICE
— *see* page 353

RADIOCOMMUNICATIONS AGENCY
Wyndham House, 189 Marsh Wall, London E14 9SX
Tel: 020-7211 0211; Fax: 020-7211 0507;
Email: library@ra.gsi.gov.uk; Web www.radio.gov.uk
The Agency is responsible for the management of the radio spectrum used for civilian purposes within the UK. It also represents UK radio interests internationally.
Chief Executive, D. Hendon

DEPARTMENT OF TRANSPORT, LOCAL GOVERNMENT AND THE REGIONS
Eland House, Bressenden Place, London SW1E 5DU
Great Minster House, 76 Marsham Street, London SW1P 4DR
Ashdown House, 123 Victoria Street, London SW1E 6DE Tel: 020-7944 3000 Web: www.dtlr.gov.uk

Due to major changes at Whitehall following the 2001 General Election, the DETR has been re-organised to create the Department for Transport, Local Government and the Regions (DTLR).
Environment Protection and Wildlife & Countryside policy have moved to the former MAFF to create the Department for Environment, Food and Rural Affairs (DEFRA).

Construction has moved to the DTI although DTLR retain Building Regulations, which have been merged with Fire Policy from the Home Office to create a new Directorate.

Responsibility for Local and Parliamentary bylaws has also moved from the Home Office to DTLR.

Sponsorship of the RDAs has moved to the DTI and the Regional Co-ordination Unit and Government Offices now report to the Cabinet Office.

The Department's Ministers are based at Eland House.

Secretary of State for Transport, Local Government and the Regions, The Rt. Hon. Stephen Byers, MP

Private Secretary, Peter Unwin

Special Advisers, Jo Moore; Dan Corrie

Parliamentary Private Secretary, David Watts, MP

Minister of State for Transport, The Rt. Hon. John Spellar, MP

Private Secretary, *Phil West*

Special Adviser, A. Long

Parliamentary Private Secretary, D. Watts, MP

Minister of State, Local Government and The Regions, The Rt. Hon. Nick Raynsford, MP

Private Secretary, Matt Leach

Parliamentary Private Secretary, Linda Gilray, MP

Minister of State for Housing, Planning and Regeneration, The Rt. Hon. Lord Falconer of Thoroton, QC, MP

Parliamentary Private Secretary, Paul Clark, MP

Parliamentary Under-Secretaries of State, David Jamieson, MP (*Transport*); Sally Keeble, MP (*Housing, Planning and Regeneration*); Dr Alan Whitehead, MP (*Local Government and the Regions*)

Private Secretaries, Rory O'Donnell; Kirsty Gibson; Shane Snow; Tom Wechsler; P. West

* Based at Eland House

† Based at Ashdown House

‡ Based at Great Minster House

*DIRECTORATE OF COMMUNICATION

Director of Communication (SCS), A. Evans

DIRECTORATE OF FINANCE

Director of Finance, P. Ward

DIRECTORATE OF LAW

Legal Director, D. Hogg

*HOUSING, URBAN POLICY AND PLANNING (HUPP)

Director-General (SCS), G. Turton, CB

HOUSING

Director (SCS), M. Gahagan, CB

Heads of Divisons (SCS), B. Provan (*Housing Care and Support*); B. Oelman (*Housing Data and Statistics*) A.Waquar (*Research, Analysis and Evaluation*); P. Cox (*Housing and Urban Economics*); M. Jones (*Housing Policy, Renewal and Ownership*); M. Faulkner (*Housing Private Rented Sector*); N. McDonald (*Local Authority Housing*); R. Horsman (*Housing Associations and Private Finance*); B. Hill (*Homelessness and Housing Management*)

URBAN POLICY UNIT

Director, Dr P. Evans

Heads of Divisions, S. Bonfanti (*Urban White Paper*); J. Bridges (*Strategic Development*); J. Sienkiewicz (*Thames Gateway*); M. Leigh-Pollitt (*LPD–Land and Property*); P. Houston (*Physical Regeneration and English Partnerships*); vacant (*Regional Funding*)

PLANNING

Director, P. Britton

Divisional Managers, J. Channing (*Planning Policies*); L. Hicks (*Minerals and Waste Policy*); C. Bowden (*Development Control Policy*); M. Ash (*Plans, Compensation and International*); A. Gray (*Environmental Assessment, Transport and Works, Management and Finance*); P. Capell (*Planning and Land Use Statistics*)

ROUGH SLEEPERS UNIT

Divisional Director, L. Casey

INTEGRATED TRANSPORT TASKFORCE TEAM

Director-General (SCS), W. Rickett

Deputy Director (SCS), Ms M. Phillips, CB

Heads of Divisons (SCS), Ms L. Robinson (*Transport, Delivery and Presentation*); I. Todd (*Transport, Environment and Taxation*); D. Hulls (*Transport Finance*); Ms B. Hills (*Transport Strategy*)

COMMERCIAL, HOUSING AND LOCAL GOVERNMENT

Director (SCS), C. Muttukamaru

Heads of Divisions (SCS), J. Comber (*Environment (National)*); D. Jordan (*Local Government (Finance)*); Ms P. Conlon (*Local Government (General)*); J. Wright (*Housing and Land*); N. Thomas (*Greater London Authority Implementation*); D. Aries (*Commercial and Establishments*); Ms D. Phillips (*Devolution and Regional Government*)

*LOCAL AND REGIONAL GOVERNMENT GROUP

Director-General (SCS), P. Wood

LOCAL GOVERNMENT DIRECTORATE

Director (SCS), A. Whetnall

Heads of Divisions (SCS), P. Rowsell (*Local Government Sponsorship*); J. R. Footitt (*Local Government Competition and Quality*); T. Redpath (*Local Government Legislation*); T. Crossley (*Local Government Pensions*); vacant (*Electoral Reform*); J. Haunton (*G7*) (*Local Government Modernisation*); V. Sherwood (*SEO*) (*Honours Secretariat*)

LOCAL GOVERNMENT FINANCE POLICY DIRECTORATE

Director (SCS), M. Lambirth

Heads of Divisions (SCS), R. Davies (*Modernisation and Grant Distribution*); S. Claughton (*Taxation, Valuation and General Policy*); M. Green (*Statistics, Payments and IT Division*); P. Williams (*Capital Finance and Accountancy Advice*)

REGIONAL POLICY UNIT

Director (SCS), R. Allan

Heads of Divisions (SCS), A. Murray (*Devolution and Regional Governance*)

FIRE AND BUILDING REGULATIONS

Director, vacant

Divisional Managers, P. Everall (*Building Regulations*); E. Guy (*Fire Policy Unit*); D. Peace (*Fire Research and Development*); G. Meldrum (*HM Fire Service Inspectorate*)

‡ TRANSPORT STRATEGY, ROADS AND
LOCAL TRANSPORT (TSRLT)
Director-General (SCS), W. Pickett
Director DVO Group, J. Plowman

INTEGRATED AND LOCAL TRANSPORT

Director, A. Davis
Divisional Managers, R. Verge (*DVO Secretariat*); M.
Walsh (*Economics, Local Transport and General*);
K. Lloyd (*Local Transport Policy*); M. Talbot (*Traffic
Management*); H. Hillier (*Transport Statistics: Personal
Travel*); J. Rogers and A. Rutherford (*Buses and Taxis*)

MOBILITY UNIT

Head of Unit, A. Frye, OBE,
Director Roads and Traffic, D. Roberts
Divisional Managers, A. Oliver (*Transport Statistics: Roads*);
R. Jones (*Licensing, Road Worthiness and Insurance*);
R. Peel (*Road Safety*); T. Carter (*Road Safety:
Chief Medical Advisor*); H. Chipping (*Roads Policy*);
M. Fendick (*Vehicle Standards and Engineering*)

TRANSPORT STRATEGY

Director, D. Phillips, CB
Divisional Managers, T. Worsley (*Integrated Transport
Economics and Appraisal*); P. Collins (*Multi-Modal Studies
Division*); G. Smith (*Transport Research Unit*); E.
Robinson (*Transport Strategy and Finance*) E. Sampson
(*Transport Technology and Telematics*); L. Packer
(*Transport, Environment and Taxation*)

‡ RAILWAYS, AVIATION LOGISTICS AND
MARITIME (RALM)
Director-General (SCS), D. Rowlands

RAILWAYS

Director (SCS), R. Linnard
Heads of Divisions (SCS), Ms A. Munro (*Railways Major
Project*); S. Connolly (*Railways Economics and Finance*); P.
Thomas (*Railways International and General*); M.
Coulshed (*Railways Sponsorship*)

AVIATION

Director (SCS), R. Griffins
Heads of Divisions (SCS), M. Fawcett (*Airports Policy*); M.
Mann (*Economics, Aviation, Maritime and International*);
Ms E. Duthie (*Aviation Environmental*); M. Smethers
(*Multilateral*); A. T. Baker (*International Aviation
Negotiation*); D. McMillan (*Air Traffic*); I. McBrayne
(*Civil Aviation*)

TRANSPORT SECURITY

Director (SCS), I. Devlin
Deputy Director of Transport Security, W. Gillan

LONDON UNDERGROUND TASK GROUP

Director (SCS), M. Fuhr
Heads of Divisions (SCS), I. Jordan (*London Underground
Task Group 1*); R. Bennett (*London Underground Task
Group 2*); E. West (*London Underground Task Group 3*) P.
Sanders (*London Underground Task Group 4*)

LOGISTICS AND MARITIME TRANSPORT

Director (SCS), B. Wadsworth
Divisional Managers, J. Lang (*Marine Accident Investigation
Branch*); S. Reeves (*Ports Policy*); Ms B. A. Bostock (*Road
Haulage Regulation*); T. Wellburn (*Road Haulage
Sponsorship and Logistics*); T. Allan (*Logistics and Maritime
Transport*); M. Hughes (*Transport Statistics Freight*); D.
Liston-Jones (*Traffic Area Network Unit*); D. Cooke
(*Shipping Policy 1*); G. D. Rowe (*Shipping Policy 2*); J. F.
Wall, CMG (*Shipping Policy 3*)

*STRATEGY AND CORPORATE
SERVICES GROUP
Director (SCS), R. S. Dudding

EXECUTIVE AGENCIES

DRIVER AND VEHICLE LICENSING AGENCY
Longview Road, Morriston, Swansea SA6 7JL
Tel: 01792-782 341; Fax: 01792-782 793
Web www.dvla.gov.uk
The Agency is responsible for registering and licensing
drivers and vehicles, and the collection and enforcement of
vehicle excise duty.
Chief Executive, C. Bennett

DRIVING STANDARDS AGENCY
Stanley House, Talbot Street, Nottingham NG1 5GU
Tel: 0115-901 2500; Fax: 0115-901 2940
Web www.dsa.gov.uk
The Agency is responsible for carrying out theory and
practical driving tests for car drivers, motorcyclists, bus
and lorry drivers and for maintaining the registers of
Approved Driving Instructors and Large Goods Vehicle
Instructors, as well as supervising Compulsory Basic
Training (CBT) for learner motorcyclists. There are five
area offices, which manage over 430 practical test centres
across Britain.
Chief Executive, G. Austin

FIRE SERVICE COLLEGE
Moreton-in-Marsh, Gloucestershire, GL56 ORH
Tel: 01608-650 831; Fax: 01608-651 788;
Web: www.fireservicecollege.ac.uk
The Fire Service College provides unique facilities for
both practical and theoretical fire fighting, fire safety and
accident and emergency training.
Chief Executive, T. Glossop

HIGHWAYS AGENCY
St Christopher House, Southwark Street, London SE1 0TE
Tel: 020-7921 4574; Fax:020-7921 4592
Web: www.highways.gov.uk
The Agency is responsible for delivering the DTLR's
road programme and for maintaining the national road
network in England.
Chief Executive, T. Matthews

MARITIME AND COASTGUARD AGENCY
Spring Place, 105 Commercial Road, Southampton
SO15 1EG
Tel: 023-8032 9100; Fax: 023-8032 9477
Web: www.mcga.gov.uk
The Agency aims to develop, promote and enforce high
standards of marine safety and pollution prevention; to
minimise the loss of life among seafarers and coastal users;
and to minimise pollution from ships to sea and coastline.
Chief Executive, M. Storey
Chief Coastguard, J. Astbury

ORDNANCE SURVEY
Romsey Road, Maybush, Southampton, SO16 4GU.
Tel: 023-8079 2000; Fax: 023-8079 2660;
Web: www.ordsvy.gov.uk

The Ordnance Survey department carries out official surveying and definitive mapping of Great Britain.
Chief Executive, V. Lawrence

PLANNING INSPECTORATE

Crown Buildings, Cathays Park, Cardiff CF10 3NQ.
Tel: 029-2082 3866; Fax; 029- 2082 5150;
Web: www.planning-inspectorate.gov.uk
The Inspectorate appeals against the decisions of local authorities on planning applications and appeals against local authority enforcement notices. Also provides inspectors to hold enquiries into objections to local authority planning.
Chief Executive and Chief Planning Inspector, C. Shepley

QUEEN ELIZABETH II CONFERENCE CENTRE

Broad Sanctuary, London SW1P 3EE
Tel: 020-7222 5000; Fax: 020-7798 4200
Web: www.qeiicc.co.uk
The Centre provides secure conference facilities for national and international government and private sector use.
Chief Executive, M. C. Buck, CBE

THE RENT SERVICE

Clifton House, 1st Floor, 87-113 Euston Road, London NW1 2RA Tel: 020-7554 2450 Fax: 020-7554 2490
Web: www.vca.gov.uk
The Agency combines 77 independent units previously administered by local authorities.
Chief Executive, D. Harvey

VEHICLE CERTIFICATION AGENCY

1 Eastgate Office Centre, Eastgate Road, Bristol BS5 6XX
Tel: 0117-951 5151; Fax: 0117-952 4103;
Web: www.vca.gov.uk
The Agency brings together 77 independent units previously administered by local authorities. It tests and certificates vehicles to UK and international Standards.
Chief Executive, D. W. Harvey

VEHICLE INSPECTORATE (VI)

Berkeley House, Croydon Street, Bristol BS5 0DA
Tel: 0117-954 3200; Fax: 0117-954 3212
Web www.via.gov.uk
The Agency tests and certifies the roadworthiness of heavy goods and public service vehicles and supervises MOT testing.
Chief Executive, M. Newey

TRAFFIC AREA OFFICES AND COMMISSIONERS

Senior Traffic Commissioner, M. W. Betts, CBE
Eastern, G. Simms
North-Eastern, T. Macartney
North-Western, B. Bell
Scottish, M. W. Betts, CBE
South-Eastern and Metropolitan, C. Heaps
Western, P. Brown
Wales and West Midlands, D. Dixon

HM TREASURY
Parliament Street, London SW1P 3AG
Tel: 020-7270 5000
Email: public.enquiries@hm-treasury.gov.uk
Web: www.hm-treasury.gov.uk

The Office of the Lord High Treasurer has been continuously in commission for well over 200 years. The Lord High Commissioners of HM Treasury are the First Lord of the Treasury (who is also the Prime Minister), the Chancellor of the Exchequer and five junior Lords. This Board of Commissioners is assisted at present by the Chief Secretary, the Parliamentary Secretary (who is also the Government Chief Whip in the House of Commons), the Paymaster-General, the Financial Secretary, and the Economic Secretary. The Prime Minister as First Lord is not primarily concerned in the day-to-day aspects of Treasury business; neither are the Parliamentary Secretary and the Junior Lords as Government Whips. Treasury business is managed by the Chancellor of the Exchequer and the other Treasury Ministers, assisted by the Permanent Secretary.

The Chief Secretary is responsible for public expenditure planning and control; public sector pay; value for money in the public services; public service agreements public/private partnerships and procurement policy; strategic oversight of banking, financial services and insurance; departmental investment strategies; including the Capital Modernisation Fund and Invest to Save Budget; welfare reform; devolution; and resource accounting and budgeting.

The Paymaster-General is responsible for the Inland Revenue and the Valuation Office, with overall responsibility for the Finance Bill. She leads on personal taxation, business taxation, European and international tax issues.

The Financial Secretary is responsible for Customs and Excise; growth and productivity; science, research and development; competition and deregulation policy; export credit; VAT and road and fuel duties; and parliamentary financial business (Public Accounts Committee, National Audit Office).

The Economic Secretary is responsible for National Savings, the Debt Management Office, the National Investment and Loans Office, the Office of National Statistics, the Royal Mint, and the Government Actuary's Department; banking, financial services and insurance; foreign exchange reserves; debt management policy; financial services tax issues and charity taxation. She provides support to the Chancellor on EU issues.

Prime Minister and First Lord of the Treasury, The Rt. Hon. Anthony (Tony) Blair, MP
Chancellor of the Exchequer, The Rt. Hon. Gordon Brown, MP
Principal Private Secretary, Tom Scholar
Private Secretaries, Beth Russell ; Mark Bowman
Special Advisers, Ed Miliband; Ian Austin; Paul Andrew; Spencer Livermore
Council of Economic Advisers, Chris Wales; Paul Gregg; Ms Shriti Vadera; Paul Gregg; Maeve Sherlock, Stewart Wood
Parliamentary Private Secretaries, Mrs Ann Keen, MP, Joan Ryan, MP; Chris Pond, MP; Helen Southworth, MP
Chief Secretary to the Treasury, The Rt. Hon. Andrew Smith, MP
Chief Economic Adviser to the Treasury, Ed Balls
Private Secretary, Lucy Makinson
Paymaster-General, Dawn Primarolo, MP

Private Secretary, Heidi Popperwell
Financial Secretary to the Treasury, The Rt. Hon. Paul Boateng , MP
Private Secretary, Helen Watson
Economic Secretary to the Treasury, Ruth Kelly, MP
Private Secretary, Niki Cleal
Parliamentary Clerk, David Martin
Parliamentary Secretary to the Treasury and Government Chief Whip, The Rt. Hon. Hilary Armstrong, MP
Private Secretary, Roy Stone
Treasurer of HM Household and Deputy Chief Whip, Keith Hill , MP
Comptroller of HM Household, Thomas McAvoy, MP
Vice-Chamberlain of HM Household, Gerry Sutcliffe, MP
Lord Commissioners of the Treasury (Whips), Anne McGuire, MP; John Heppel, MP; Nick Ainger, MP; Tony McNulty, MP; Graham Stringer, MP; *Assistant Whips*, Ian Pearson, MP; Fraser Kemp, MP; Angela Smith , MP; Ivor Caplin, MP; Phil Woolas, MP; Dan Norris, MP; Jim Fitzpatrick, MP
Permanent Secretary to the Treasury, Sir Andrew Turnbull, KCB

DIRECTORATES

Head of Ministerial Support Team (SCS), T. Scholar
Head of Communications and Strategy Team (SCS), M. Elham
Head of Strategy Finance and Purchasing Team (SCS), R. Brightwell

MACROECONOMIC POLICY AND INTERNATIONAL FINANCE

Managing Director, G. O'Donnell
Directors (SCS), S. Brooks; S. Pickford; J. Cunliffe; J. Taylor; I. Rogers
Heads of Teams (SCS), C. M. Kelly; A. Kilpatrick; D. Ramsden; M. Glycopantis; P. Mills; J. de Berkker; G. Lloyd; R. Lawrence K. Peters; A. Lewis; M. Richardson; D. Lawton; M. Manuel

BUDGET AND PUBLIC FINANCES

Managing Director (SCS), R. Culpin
Directors (SCS), N. Holgate ; C. J. Mowl
Heads of Teams (SCS), P. Curwen; P. Betts; S. Pickford; I. Taylor; M. P. Williams; G. Parker; A. Gibbs; D. Deaton; C. Maxwell; P. Rankin; M. Swan; M. Dawes; A. Sharples; A. Ritche; P. Williams; W. Nye

PUBLIC SERVICES

Managing Director, N. Macpherson
Directors, M. Aldred; L. de Groot; A. Sharples; J. Grice
Heads of Teams, R. Brown; A. Bridges; R. Dunn; H. John; J. Richardson; P. Kane; M. Wheatley; D. Franklin; P. Brook; A. Charlesworth

CORPORATE SERVICES AND DEVELOPMENT (CSD)

Managing Director (SCS), H. Douglas
Heads of Teams (SCS), C. Pearson; J. Dodds; P. Pelger; R. Brightwell

FINANCIAL MANAGEMENT, REPORTING AND AUDIT

Managing Director (SCS), A. Likierman
Director and Head of Treasury Office of Accounts Team (SCS), B. Glicksman
Heads of Teams (SCS), D. Loweth; K. Ross; I. Carruthers; R. Brightwell
Heads of Teams, K. Ross; C. Butler; Miss A. M. Jones; I. Carruthers; D. Loweth

FINANCE, REGULATION AND INDUSTRY

Managing Director (SCS), J. Cunliffe
Directors (SCS), H. J. Bush, CB; R. Fellgett
Heads of Teams (SCS), S. Mullen; S. Meek; D. Griffiths; J. Halligan; P. Rutnan; P. Schofield; J. Kingman; R. Bent; S. Beckett; D. Storey

EXECUTIVE AGENCIES

NATIONAL SAVINGS

— *see* pages 625–6

OFFICE FOR NATIONAL STATISTICS

— *see* page 349

ROYAL MINT

— *see* page 357

UNITED KINGDOM DEBT MANAGEMENT OFFICE

Eastcheap Court, 11 Philpot Lane, London, EC3M 8UD
Tel: 020-7862 6500; Fax: 020- 7862 6509

The UK Debt Management Office was launched as an executive agency of the Treasury in April 1998 after the transfer from the Bank of England to the Treasury of responsibility for debt management, the sale of gilts and oversight of the gilts market. It took over responsibility for the management of the Exchequer's daily cash flows in April 2000.
Chief Executive, M. L. Williams

OTHER BODIES

OFFICE OF GOVERNMENT COMMERCE (OGC)

Fleetbank House, 2-6 Salisbury Square, London EC4Y 8JX
Tel: 020-7211 1300; Web: www.ogc.gov.uk
The Office of Government Commerce was set up on the 1 April 2000. It is a unique body within government, overseen by a supervisory board of Ministers and officials from across the departments of government. Its aim is to achieve the best value for money for the Government's commercial relationships and coherence of purchasing activity across 200 Government departments, non-governmental bodies and agencies. The OGC is an office of HM Treasury.
Chief Executive, P. Gershon
Deputy Chief Executive, B. Rigby

OGC.BUYING.SOLUTIONS

Royal Liver Building, Pier Head, Liverpool L3 1PE
Tel: 0151-227 4262; Fax: 0151-258 1249
Web: www. ogcbuyingsolutions.gov.uk
The Agency provides a professional purchasing service to Government departments and other public bodies. From April 2000 it became part of the Office of Government Commerce reporting to the Chief Secretary to the Treasury.
Chief Executive (SCS), D. J. Court

THE TREASURY SOLICITOR

DEPARTMENT OF HM PROCURATOR-GENERAL AND TREASURY SOLICITOR
Queen Anne's Chambers, 28 Broadway, London SW1H 9JS Tel: 020-7210 3000; Fax: 020-7210 3004

The Treasury Solicitor's Department provides legal services for many Government departments. Those without their own lawyers are provided with legal advice, and both they and other departments are provided with litigation services. The Treasury Solicitor is also the Queen's Proctor, and is responsible for collecting Bona Vacantia on behalf of the Crown. The Department became an executive agency in 1996.

HM Procurator-General and Treasury Solicitor (SCS), Juliet Wheldon
Deputy Treasury Solicitor (SCS), Anthony M. Inglese

LITIGATION DIVISION

SCS, R. Aitken; Mrs D. Babar; Peter Bennett; David Brummell; Lee John-Charles; Anthony D. Lawton; A. Leithead; B. McHenry; Barrie McKay; Peter R. Messer; Ms Lyndsey Nicoll; Mrs J. B. C. Oliver; David Palmer; Stephen Parkinson; Roland Phillips; A. J. Sandal

QUEEN'S PROCTOR DIVISION

Queen's Proctor (SCS), Juliet Wheldon
Assistant Queen's Proctor (SCS), Sue Cochrane

RESOURCES AND SERVICES DIVISION

Principal Establishment and Finance Officer and Security Officer (SCS), J. P. Burnett
Assistant Director Establishments (G7), Ms H. Donnelly
Assistant Director Finance (G7), C. A. Woolley
Assistant Director Information Systems (G7), M. Gabbidon
Business Support Manager (SEO), E. Blishen
Assistant Director Personnel and Training, Ms M Esplin

BONA VACANTIA DIVISION

SCS, Ms L. Addison

EUROPEAN DIVISION

SCS, J. E. Collins; A. Ridout; M. C. P. Thomas

CULTURE, MEDIA AND SPORT DIVISION

SCS, Ms I. Letwin

CABINET OFFICE AND CENTRAL ADVISORY DIVISION

SCS, M. C. L. Carpenter; C. House

MINISTRY OF DEFENCE ADVISORY DIVISION

Metropole Building, Northumberland Avenue, London WC2N 5BL Tel: 020-7218 4691
SCS, N. Beach; Mrs V. Collett; M. Hemming; Ms F. Nash

DEPARTMENT FOR EDUCATION AND EMPLOYMENT ADVISORY DIVISION

Caxton House, Tothill Street, London SW1H 9NF
Tel: 020-7273 3000

SCS, F. D. W. Clarke; Ms D. Collins; S. T. Harker; P. Kilgarriff; N. A. D. Lambert; D. Macrae; A. Preston

HM TREASURY ADVISORY DIVISION

Allington Towers, 19 Allington Street, London SW1E 5EB
Tel: 020-7270 3000

SCS, M. A. Blythe; J. R. J. Braggins; Ms R. Ford; J. Jones; R. Ricks; Miss J. V. Stokes

CONSTITUTIONAL REFORM DIVISION

70 Whitehall, London SW1A 2AS
Tel: 020-7270 6093

SCS, Miss R. A. Jeffreys

WALES OFFICE
Gwydyr House, Whitehall, London SW1A 2ER
Tel: 020-7270 0549;
Email: wales@planning-inspectorate.gov.uk

The Wales Office is the Office of the Secretary of State for Wales, who represents Welsh interests in the Cabinet.
Secretary of State for Wales, The Rt. Hon. Paul Murphy, MP
Parliamentary Under-Secretary, Don Touhig, MP
Head of Department, Ms Alison. Jackson

DEPARTMENT FOR WORK AND PENSIONS
Richmond House, 79 Whitehall, London SW1A 2NS
Tel: 020-7238 0800; Web: dwp.gov.uk

The Department for Work and Pensions was formed on 8 June 2001 from parts of the former Department of Social Security and Department for Education and Employment and the Employment Service. The Department provides people of working age, pensioners and children with the advice and help they need to achieve financial independence and to make the most of life. Its stated aims are to create a single point of delivery for jobs, benefits advice and support through a modern nationwide service called Jobcentre Plus; to provide employers with a professional service for filling job vacancies; to provide a new Pension Service; to provide information and support to today's and tomorrow's pensioners; to ensure delivery of a simplified and efficient Child Support system and quality of opportunity and social inclusion for all.
Secretary of State for Work and Pensions, The Rt. Hon. Alistair Darling, MP
Principal Private Secretary, Neil Couling
Special Advisers, Andrew Maugham
Ministers of State, The Rt. Hon. Nick Brown, MP(*Work*); The Rt. Hon. Ian McCartney, MP (*Pensions*)
Privaties Secretary for Work , D. Jefferson; A. Holt; S. Jones
Private Secretary for Pensions, D. Whitehead
Private Secretary for Work, D. Jefferson; A. Holt; S. Jones
Private Secretary for Disabled People, E. Davies
Parliamentary Under-Secretaries of State, The Baroness Hollis of Heigham, D.Phil. (*Children and the Family*); Malcolm Wicks, MP (*Work*); Marion Eagle, MP (*Pensions*)
Private Secretaries, C. Jennings; Ms M. Curran
Parliamentary Private Secretaries, Anne Coffey, MP; Bob Blizzard, MP
Permanent Secretary (SCS), Ms R. Lomax
Private Secretary, J. Tunstall

CORPORATE SERVICES DEPARTMENT
Director (SCS), S. Hickey

HUMAN RESOURCES DIRECTORATE
Director, K. White

ANALYTICAL SERVICES DIVISION

The Adelphi, 1–11 John Adam Street, London WC2N 6HT
Tel: 020-7962 8000

Director (SCS), D. Stanton
Chief Statistician (SCS), F. Johnson
Director Information Centre (SCS), N. Dyson
Senior Economic Advisers (SCS), J. Ball; G. Harris; R. Enden; T. Huddleston

Operational Research Service (SCS), D. Barnbrook
Chief Research Officers (SCS), G. Clark; S. Rice

FINANCE DIRECTORATE

Director, J. Codling

COMMUNICATIONS DIRECTORATE

Director (SCS), S. MacDowall
Deputy Directors (SCS), J. Bretherton; A. Hall
Head of Media Relations, (SCS), K. Young
Head of Marketing (SCS), S. O'Neil

PENSIONS, CHILDREN AND DISABLED CLIENT GROUPS DIRECTORATE

Director (SCS), P. R. C. Gray
Director, Children (SCS), H. Ghosh
Director, Disability and Carer Benefits (SCS), D. Burton
Director, Pensions Credit Programme (SCS), G. McCorkell
Director, Pensions Change and Specification, H. Reynolds

WORKING AGE GROUP

Director (SCS), U. Brennan
Director, Change, S. Hewitt
Director, Strategy, R. Devereux
Director, Employment, M. Richardson

SOLICITOR'S OFFICE

Solicitor and Head of Law and Special Policy Group (SCS), Mrs
M. A. Morgan, CB

SOLICITOR'S DIVISION A

New Court, 48 Carey Street, London WC2A 2LS
Tel: 020-7412 1326
Legal Director (SCS), J. A. Catlin
Assistant Legal Director (SCS), Ms F. A. Logan; S. Cooper;
Ms C. Cooper; P. Milledge; Ms A. McGaughrin

SOLICITOR'S DIVISION B

New Court, 48 Carey Street, London WC2A 2LS
Tel: 020-7412 1528
Solicitor and Head of Law and Special Policy Group (SCS), Mrs
M. A. Morgan, CB
Assistant Solicitors (SCS), Ms S. Edwards; R. S. Powell; Mrs
A. James

SOLICITOR'S DIVISION C

New Court, 48 Carey Street, London WC2A 2LS
Tel: 020-7412 1342
Legal Director (SCS), Mrs G. S. Kerrigan
Assistant Solicitors (SCS), Miss M. E. Trefgarne; Mrs S.
Walker; K. Baulblys; D. Dunleavy; Ms R. Sandby-
Thomas

BENEFIT FRAUD INSPECTORATE

Berkeley House, 12A North Park Road, Harrogate HG1
5QA Tel: 01423-832922
Director-General (SCS), C. Bull

EXECUTIVE AGENCIES

APPEALS SERVICE AGENCY

— *see* Tribunals Section

DWP BENEFITS AGENCY

Quarry House, Quarry Hill, Leeds LS2 7UA
Tel: 0113-232 4000

The Agency administers claims for and payments of social
security benefits.
Chief Executive, A. Cleveland
Private Secretary, R. Baldwin
Directors, J. Codling *(Finance)*; M. Fisher *(Personnel and
Communications)*; S. Heminsley *(Strategic and Planning)*;
A. Cleveland *(Operations Support)*; N. Haighton
(Projects)
Medical Policy
Principal Medical Officers, Dr M. Aylward; Dr P. Dewis; Dr
P. Sawney; Dr A. Braidwood; Dr P. Stidolph

CHILD SUPPORT AGENCY

DSS and Inland Revenue, CSA, Long Benton, Benton
Park Road, Newcastle upon Tyne NE98 1YX
Tel: 0191-213 5000

The Agency was set up in April 1993. It is responsible for
the administration of the Child Support Act and for the
assessment, collection and enforcement of maintenance
payments for all new cases.
Chief Executive, Ms F. Boardman
Directors, M. Davison; C. Peters; M. Isaacs; T. Read

WAR PENSIONS AGENCY

Norcross, Blackpool, Lancs FY5 3WP
Tel: 01253-338816
Email: warpensions@gtnet.gov.uk

The Agency administers the payment of war disablement
and war widows' pensions and provides welfare services
and support to war disablement pensioners, war widows
and their dependants and carers.
Acting Chief Executive, A. Burnham
Secretary, C. Pike

ADVISORY BODIES

SOCIAL SECURITY ADVISORY COMMITTEE
New Court, 48 Carey Street, London WC2A 2LS.
Tel: 020-7412 1508; Fax: 020-7412 1570;
Email: ssac@ms42.dwp.gov.uk; Web www.ssac.org.uk
Chairman, Sir Thomas Boyd-Carpenter, KBE; *Secretary*,
Ms G. Saunders

PUBLIC OFFICES

ADJUDICATOR'S OFFICE

Haymarket House, 28 Haymarket, London SW1Y 4SP
Tel: 020-7930 2292; Fax: 020-7930 2298;
Web: www.adjucatorsoffice.gov.uk

The Adjudicator's Office opened in 1993 and investigates complaints about the way the Inland Revenue (including the Valuation Office Agency) and Customs and Excise have handled a person's affairs.
The Adjudicator, Dame Barbara Mills, DBE, QC
Head of Office, C. Gordon

ADVISORY, CONCILIATION AND ARBITRATION SERVICE

Brandon House, 180 Borough High Street, London
SE1 1LW Tel: 020-7210 3613; Fax: 020-7210 3708

The Advisory, Conciliation and Arbitration Service (ACAS) was set up under the Employment Protection Act 1975 (the provisions now being found in the Trade Union and Labour Relations (Consolidation) Act 1992). ACAS is directed by a Council consisting of a full-time chairman and part-time employer, trade union and independent members, all appointed by the Secretary of State for Trade and Industry. The functions of the Service are to promote the improvement of industrial relations in general, to provide facilities for conciliation, mediation and arbitration as means of avoiding and resolving industrial disputes, and to provide advisory and information services on industrial relations matters to employers, employees and their representatives.

ACAS has regional offices in Birmingham, Bristol, Cardiff, Fleet, Glasgow, Leeds, Liverpool, London, Manchester, Newcastle upon Tyne and Nottingham.
Chairman, R. Donaghy, OBE
Chief Conciliator (G4), D. Evans

ANCIENT MONUMENTS BOARD FOR SCOTLAND

Longmore House, Salisbury Place, Edinburgh
EH9 1SH Tel: 0131-668 8764; Fax: 0131-668 8765;
Email: ancient.monuments@scotland.gov.uk

The Ancient Monuments Board for Scotland advises the Scottish Ministers on the exercise of their functions, under the Ancient Monuments and Archaeological Areas Act 1979, of providing protection for monuments of national importance.
Chairman, Prof. Michael Lynch, Ph.D., FRSE, FSA Scot.
Members, AR. J. Mercer, FRSE, FSA, FSA Scot.; Miss Lisbeth. M. Thoms, FSA Scot.; J. Higgitt, FSA, FSA Scot.; Dr C. Swanson, Ph.D., FSA Scot.; M. Baughan; Dr J. Cannizzo, Ph.D., FSA Scot.; Dr S. Peake, Ph.D.; M. J. Taylor; Ms Jill. Harden, FSA Scot.; A. Saville, FSA Scot; Cllr J. A. McFadden, CBE; Cllr E. F. Scott, FSA Scot; Prof C. D. Morris, FRSE, FSA, FSA Scot; A.P.K. Wright, OBE
Secretary, R. A. J. Dalziel
Assessor, Dr D. J. Breeze, Ph.D., FRSE, FSA, FSA Scot.

ANCIENT MONUMENTS BOARD FOR WALES

Crown Buildings, Cathays Park, Cardiff CF10 3NQ
Tel: 029-2050 0200; Fax: 029-2082 6375;
Email: cadw@wales.gsi.gov.uk;
Web: www.cadw.wales.gov.uk

The Ancient Monuments Board for Wales advises the National Assembly for Wales on its statutory functions in respect of ancient monuments.
Chairman, Prof. R. R. Davies, CBE, D.Phil. FBA
Members, R. G. Keen; Prof. W. Davies, Ph.D. FBA, FSA; M. J. Garner; Prof. R. A. Griffiths, Ph.D., D.Litt.; R. Brewer, FSA; Prof. A. Whittle, D.Phil, FBA; C. Musson, MBE, FSA; Prof. M. Adhoose-Green, Ph.D., FSA
Secretary, Mrs J. Booker

ARTS COUNCILS

The Arts Council of Great Britain was established as an independent body in 1946 to be the principal channel for the Government's support of the arts. In 1994 the Scottish and Welsh Arts Councils became autonomous and the Arts Council of Great Britain became the Arts Council of England.

The Arts Councils are responsible for the distribution of the proceeds of the National Lottery allocated to the arts. (*see* Lotteries and Gaming Section).

ARTS COUNCIL OF ENGLAND

14 Great Peter Street, London SW1P 3NQ
Tel: 020-7333 0100; Fax: 020-7973 6590;
Web: www.artscouncil.org.uk

The Arts Council is the national, strategic policy body for the arts. It works in partnership with the Regional Arts Boards, which are responsible for funding and development of the arts in their areas. The Arts Council and the Regional Arts Boards commission new work, conduct research, provide advice and information, promote the case for publicly funded arts and work together to create partnerships and access new money for artistic activity. It receives funding from Government, but is an independent non-political body working at arm's length from the Government.

There are currently proposals to combine the Arts Council and the 10 Regional Arts Boards to create a new national arts funding and development organisation.

The Government grant for 2001–2002 is £252 million.
Chairman, G. Robinson
Members, D. Brierley, CBE, D. Bull , CBE; E. Cooper; A. Kapoor; Prof. J. MacGregor; B. McMaster, CBE; Dr J. Ritterman; W. Sieghart H. Strong
Chief Executive, P. Hewitt

REGIONAL ARTS BOARDS

Web: www.arts.org.uk

EAST ENGLAND ARTS, Cherry Hinton Hall, Cherry Hinton Road, Cambridge CB1 8DW. Tel: 01223-215355.
Chair, Prof. S. Timperley
EAST MIDLANDS ARTS BOARD, Mountfields House, Epinal Way, Loughborough, Leics LE11 0QE.
Tel: 01509-218292. *Acting Chair*, S. Lowe
LONDON ARTS , 2 Pear Tree Court, London, EC1R 0DS
Tel: 020-7608 6100. *Chair*, Lady Hollick

NORTHERN ARTS BOARD, Central Square, Forth Street, Newcastle upon Tyne NE7 3PJ. Tel: 0191-255 8500. *Chair*, G. Loggie

NORTH-WEST ARTS BOARD, Manchester House, 22 Bridge Street, Manchester M3 3AB. Tel: 0161-834 6644. *Chair*, T. Bloxham, MBE

SOUTH-EAST ARTS BOARD, Union House, Eridge Road, Tunbridge Wells, Kent TN4 8HF. Tel: 01892-507200. *Joint Chair*, J. White; N. Chapman

SOUTHERN ARTS , 13 St Clement Street, Winchester SO23 9DQ. Tel: 01962-855099. *Chair*, D. Astor

SOUTH WEST ARTS, Bradninch Place, Gandy Street, Exeter EX4 3LS. Tel: 01392-218188. *Chair*, Prof. A. Livingston

WEST MIDLANDS ARTS BOARD, 82 Granville Street, Birmingham B1 2LH. Tel: 0121-631 3121. *Chair*, R. Natkiel

YORKSHIRE ARTS BOARD, 21 Bond Street, Dewsbury, W. Yorks WF13 1AX. Tel: 01924-455555. *Chair*, R. Guthrie

SCOTTISH ARTS COUNCIL

12 Manor Place, Edinburgh EH3 7DD
Tel: 0131-226 6051; Fax: 0131-225 9833;
Email: administrator@scottisharts.org.uk;
Web: www.sac.org.uk

The Scottish Arts Council funds arts organisations in Scotland with the concept of providing leadership and developing new ideas and initiatives. It has two main sources of funding: the Scottish Executive (2001–2002: £34.9m) and Lottery funding through the Department of Culture, Media and Sport (2001–2002: £207m).

Chairman, J. Boyle
Members, Ms S. Ainsley; Cllr E. Cameron; R. Chester; W. English; J. Faulds; Ms D. Idiens; Ms M. Marshall; Dr Ann Matheson, OBE; J. Scott Moncrieff; R. Presswood; W. Speirs; J. Baker; L. Mitchell
Director, Ms T. Jackson

ARTS COUNCIL OF WALES

9 Museum Place, Cardiff CF10 3NX
Tel: 029-2037 6500; Fax: 029-2022 1447

The Arts Council of Wales funds arts organisations in Wales and is funded by the National Assembly for Wales. The grant for 2000–2001 was £15.4 million.

Chairman, Ms S. Crouch
Members, D. Davies; Dr H. Walford Davies; E. Fivet; S. Garrett; E. ap Gwyn; H. James; D. Jones; P. Ryan, OBE; R. Davies; G. Lewis; A. Lloyd; C. Thomas
Acting Chief Executive, F. Medley

ARTS COUNCIL OF NORTHERN IRELAND

MacNeice House, 77 Malone Road, Belfast BT9 6AQ
Tel: 028-90-38 5210; Fax: 028-9066 1715;
Email: publicaffairs@artscouncil-ni.org;
Web: www.artscouncil-ni.org

The Arts Council of Northern Ireland is the prime distributor of Government funds in support of the arts in Northern Ireland. It is funded by the Department of Culture, Arts and Leisure, and the grant for 2001–2002 is £7.881 million including £250,000 for 'cultural traditional funding.'

Chairman, Prof. B. Walker
Vice-Chairman, Ms E. O'Baoill
Members, Ms M. Armstrong; D. Boyd; Dr M. Crozier; R. Dunn; Dr T. Maginess; D. Hyndman; Ms J. Jordan; J. Kerr; Prof. B. McClelland; Ms G. Moriarty; A. Shortt; Mrs. M. Yeomans
Chief Executive, Ms R. McDonough

ART GALLERIES AND ASSOCIATED BODIES

NATIONAL GALLERIES OF SCOTLAND

The Mound, Edinburgh EH2 2EL
Tel: 0131-624 6200; Fax: 0131-343 3250

The National Galleries of Scotland comprise the National Gallery of Scotland, the Scottish National Portrait Gallery, the Scottish National Gallery of Modern Art and the Dean Gallery. There are also outstations at Paxton House, Berwickshire, and Duff House, Banffshire. Total Government grant-in-aid for 2001–2002 is £7.7 million.

TRUSTEES

Chairman of the Trustees, Mr B.Ivory, CBE
Trustees, Ms V. Atkinson; J. Hunter Blair; DL; G. J. N. Gemmell, CBE; Lord Gordon of Strathblane, CBE; A. P. Leitch; Prof. Christina Lodder; Dr I. McKenzie Smith, OBE; G. Weaver; Prof. I. Whyte

OFFICERS

Director-General (G4), T. Clifford
Keeper of Conservation (G6), M. Gallagher
Head of Press and Information (G7), C. Black
Head of Education (G7), M. Finn *Registrar (G7)*, Miss A. Buddle
Buildings (G7), R. Galbraith
Director, National Gallery of Scotland (G6), M. Clarke
Director, Scottish National Portrait Gallery (G6), J. Holloway
Curator of Photography, Miss S. F. Stevenson
Director, Scottish National Gallery of Modern Art and Dean Gallery (G6), R. Calvocoressi

NATIONAL GALLERY

Trafalgar Square, London WC2N 5DN
Tel: 020-7839 3321; Fax: 020-7747 2403

The National Gallery, which houses a permanent collection of western painting from the 13th to the 20th century, was founded in 1824, following a parliamentary grant of £60,000 for the purchase and exhibition of the Angerstein collection of pictures. The present site was first occupied in 1838; an extension to the north of the building with a public entrance in Orange Street was opened in 1975, and the Sainsbury wing was opened in 1991. Total Government grant-in-aid for 2000–2001 was £19.215 million.

BOARD OF TRUSTEES

Chairman, P. Scott, QC
Trustees, Sir Mark Richmond, SC.D., FRS; Sir Ewen Fergusson, GCMG, CGVO; Lord R. Gavron, CBE; P. Hughes, CBE C.Le Brun; Dr D. Landau; Sir Colin Southgate; J. Snow; Prof. Dawn Ades; Lady Hopkins; M. Getty; R. Sondhi; Prof. J. Higgins

OFFICERS

Director, R. N. MacGregor
Keeper, Dr N. Penny
Head of Curational Department, Dr S. Foister
Senior Curator, D. Jaffé
Chief Restorer, M. H. Wyld, CBE
Head of Exhibitions, M. J. Wilson
Scientific Adviser, Dr A. Roy
Director of Administration, J. MacAuslan
Director of Communications, D. Savelkoul
Head of Education, K. Adler

NATIONAL PORTRAIT GALLERY

St Martin's Place, London WC2H 0HE
Tel: 020-7306 0055; Fax: 020-7306 0056

A grant was made in 1856 to form a gallery of the portraits of the most eminent persons in British history. The present building was opened in 1896 and the Ondaatje wing; including a new Balcony Gallery, Tudor Gallery, IT Gallery, State-of-the-art Lecture Theatre, and roof-top restaurant opened in May 2001. There are four regional partnerships displaying portraits in appropriate settings: Montacute House, Beningbrough Hall and Bodelwyddan Castle. Total Government grant-in-aid for 2001–2002 is £5.460 million.

BOARD OF TRUSTEES
Chairman, Sir D. Scholey, CBE
Trustees, The Rt. Hon. Margaret Beckett, MP; Prof. Phillip King; Ms F. Fraser; Ms T. Green; M. Hastings; T. Phillips, RA; Prof. The Earl Russell, FBA; Ms C. Tomalin; D. Scholey, CBE; Ms A. Shulman; Sir John Weston; Baroness Willoughby de Eresby; Prof. D. Cannadine; Prof. L. Jordanova
Director (G3), C. Saumarez Smith, PH.D.

ROYAL FINE ART COMMISSION FOR SCOTLAND

Bakehouse Close, 146 Canongate, Edinburgh EH8 8DD
Tel: 0131-556 6699; Fax: 0131-556 6633;
Web: www.royfinartcomforsco.gov.uk

The Commission was established in 1927 and advises Ministers and local authorities on the visual impact and quality of design of construction projects. It is an independent body and gives its opinions impartially.
Chairman, The Rt. Hon. The Lord Cameron of Lochbroom, PC, FRSE
Commissioners, Ms J. Malvenan; R. G. Maund; M. Murray; D. Page; B. Rae; Prof. R. Russell; M. Turnbull; A. Wright
Secretary, C. Prosser

TATE BRITAIN

Millbank, London SW1P 4RG
Tel: 020-7887 8000; Fax: 020-7887 8007
Web: www.tate.org.uk

Tate Britain displays the national collection of British art. The gallery opened in 1897, the cost of erection (£80,000) being defrayed by Sir Henry Tate, who also contributed the nucleus of the present collection. The Turner wing was opened in 1910, and further galleries and a new sculpture hall followed in 1937. In 1979 a further extension was built, and the Clore Gallery, for the Turner collection, was opened in 1987. Tate consists of four galleries: Tate Britain and Tate Modern in London, Tate Liverpool and Tate St Ives.

BOARD OF TRUSTEES
Chairman, D. Verey
Trustees, Prof. Dawn Ades; Ms V. Barnsley; The Hon. P. Doig; Prof. J. Latto; Sir Christopher Mallaby, GCMG, GCVO; J. Snow; J. Studzinski; Ms G. Wearing; C. Ofili

OFFICERS
Director, Sir Nicholas Serota
Director of National Programmes, S. Nairne
Director of Collections, J. Lewison
Director, Tate Modern, vacant
Director, Tate Britain, S. Deuchar
Curator, Tate Liverpool, C. Gruneberg
Curator, Tate St Ives, S. Daniel-McElvoy

TATE MODERN

Bankside, London SE1 9TG
Tel: 020-7887 8000

Opened on 11 May 2000, Tate Modern displays the Tate collection of international modern art dating from 1900 to the present day. It includes works by Dalí, Picasso, Matisse, and Warhol as well as many contemporary works. It is housed in the former Bankside Power Station in London, redesigned by the Swiss architects Herzog & de Meuron.

WALLACE COLLECTION

Hertford House, Manchester Square, London W1M 6BN
Tel: 020-7563 9516; Fax: 020-7224 2155

The Wallace Collection was bequeathed to the nation by the widow of Sir Richard Wallace, Bt. in 1897, and Hertford House was subsequently acquired by the Government. Total Government grant-in-aid for 1999–2000 was £2.453 million.
Director, vacant
Head of Administration, N. Paladina

ASSEMBLY OMBUDSMAN FOR NORTHERN IRELAND AND NORTHERN IRELAND COMMISSIONER FOR COMPLAINTS

Progressive House, 33 Wellington Place, Belfast BT1 6HN Tel: 028-9023 3821; Fax: 028-9023 4912;
Email: ombudsman@ni-ombudsman.org.uk;
Web: www.ni-ombudsman.org.uk

The Ombudsman is appointed under legislation with powers to investigate complaints by people claiming to have sustained injustice in consequence of maladministration arising from action taken by a Northern Ireland Government department, or any other public body within his remit. Staff are presently seconded from the Northern Ireland Civil Service.
Ombudsman, T. Frawley
Deputy Ombudsman, J. MacQuarrie
Directors, C. O'Hare; R. Doherty; H. Mallon

AUDIT COMMISSIONS

ACCOUNTS COMMISSION FOR SCOTLAND

see Audit Scotland

AUDIT COMMISSION FOR LOCAL AUTHORITIES AND THE NATIONAL HEALTH SERVICE IN ENGLAND AND WALES

1 Vincent Square, London SW1P 2PN
Tel: 020-7828 1212; Fax: 020-7976 6187

The Audit Commission was set up in 1983 and is responsible for appointing external auditors to local authorities, including the Greater London Authority, and local National Health Service bodies in England and Wales. It is also responsible for promoting the proper stewardship of public finances and value for money in the services provided by local authorities and health bodies.

The Commission has a chairman, a deputy chairman and up to 18 members who are appointed by the Secretary of State for the Transport, Local Government and the Regions in consultation with the Secretary of State for Wales and the Health Secretaries in England and Wales.
Chair, Dame Helena Shovelton, DBE
Deputy Chairman, A. Fresko
Members, J. R. Foster; Sir Ronald Watson, CBE; Dr P. Lane; G. Lemos; N. Skellett; C. Swinson; D. Moss; Ms R. Lowe; Cllr R. Arthur; Sir David Williams; Prof. S. Richards; Dr J. Curson; Sir G. Hart; Ms E. Filkin; B. Wolfe; Ms J. Baddeley
Controller of Audit, A. Foster
Commission Secretary, C. Morales-Oyarce
Chief Executive of District Audit Service, A. Meekings

AUDIT SCOTLAND
110 George Street, Edinburgh EH2 4LH
Tel: 0131-477 1234; Fax: 0131-477 4567;
Web: www.audit-scotland.gov.uk
Audit Scotland was set up on 1 April 2000 to provide services to the Accounts Commission and the Auditor General for Scotland. Together they help to ensure that the Scottish Executive and public sector bodies in Scotland are held accountable for the proper, efficient and effective use of around £17 billion of public funds.
Audit Scotland's work covers around 250 bodies including local authorities, police and fire boards; NHS boards and trusts; further education colleges; water authorities; departments of the Scottish Executive; executive agencies such as the Prison Service and non-departmental public bodies such as Scottish Enterprise.
Audit Scotland carries out financial and regularity audits to ensure that the public sector bodies adhere to the highest standards of financial management and governance. It also performs audits to ensure that these bodies achieve the best value for money. All of Audit Scotland's work in connection with local authorities, fire and police boards is carries out for the Accounts Commission while its other work is undertaken for the Auditor General.
Auditor General, R. W. Black
Controller of Audit, R. Hinds
Secretary, W. F. Magee

BANK OF ENGLAND
Threadneedle Street, London EC2R 8AH
Tel: 020-7601 4444; Fax: 020-7601 4771;
Email: enquiries@bankofengland.co.uk;
Web: www.bankofengland

The Bank of England was incorporated in 1694 under royal charter. It is the banker of the Government and manages the note issue. Since May 1997 it has been operationally independent and its Monetary Policy Committee has had responsibility for setting short-term interest rates to meet the Government's inflation target. As the central reserve bank of the country, the Bank keeps the accounts of British banks, who maintain with it a proportion of their cash resources, and of most overseas central banks. The Bank has three main areas of activity: Monetary Stability, Market Operations and Financial Stability. Its responsibility for banking supervision has been transferred to the Financial Services Authority. (*See also* Financial Services Regulation section).
Governor, The Rt. Hon. E. A. J. George
Deputy Governors, D. Clementi; M. A. King

Non-Executive Directors, R. Bailie, OBE; Sir David Cooksey; H. J. Davies; Sir Ian Gibson; Ms S. McKechnie, OBE; W. Morris; J. Neill, CBE, Ph.D.; N. I. Simms; J. Stretton; Ms K. A. O'Donovan; G. Hall; Dr D. Julius; Sir J. Bond; Ms M Francis; Ms B Blow; Sir B. S. Moffat
Monetary Policy Committee, The Governor; the Deputy Governors; I. Plenderleith; J. Vickers; Dr S. Wadhwani; Prof. S. Nickell, C. J. Allsopp; C, Bean; Ms K. Barker
Advisers to the Governor, Sir Peter Petrie; M. Glover
Chief Cashier and Deputy Director, Banking and Market Services, Ms M. V. Lowther
Chief Registrar, G. P. Sparkes
General Manager, Printing Works, M. Thompson
Secretary, P. D. Rodgers
The Auditor, K. Butler

BOARD OF CUSTOMS AND EXCISE
*New King's Beam House, 22 Upper Ground, London SE1 9PJ; Tel: 020-7620 1313;
National Advice Line: 0845 010 900;
Web: www.open.gov.uk/customs/c&ehome.htm

Commissioners of Customs were first appointed in 1671 and housed by the King in London. The Excise Department was formerly under the Inland Revenue Department and was amalgamated with the Customs Department in 1909.
HM Customs and Excise is responsible for collecting and administering customs and excise duties and VAT, and advises the Chancellor of the Exchequer on any matters connected with them. The Department is also responsible for preventing and detecting the evasion of revenue laws and for enforcing a range of prohibitions and restrictions on the importation of certain classes of goods. In addition, the Department undertakes certain agency work on behalf of other departments, including the compilation of UK overseas trade statistics from customs import and export documents.

THE BOARD
Chairman (G1), R. Broadbent
Private Secretaries, Ms D. Morris, Ms A. Lakemen
Commissioners (G3), P. R. H. Allen; M. R. Brown; R. N. McAfee; M. W. Norgrove; T. Byrne; M. Eland; M. Hansons (*Non Executive*) Ms R. Pickauence; D. Spencer
Solicitor, D. Pickup
* Unless otherwise stated, this is the address and telephone number of directorates of the Board

COMMUNICATIONS DIVISION
Tel: 020-7865 5335
Head of Communications Division, P. Rose

LOGISTICS GROUP
Alexander House, 21 Victoria Avenue, Southend-on-Sea SS99 1AA Tel: 01702-348944
Director, A. Fazer

ENFORCEMENT GROUP
Director, T. Byrne

POLICY GROUP
Director, M. Eland

HUMAN RESOURCE GROUP
Director, M. Rickwood

TARIFF AND STATISTICAL OFFICE

Portcullis House, 27 Victoria Avenue, Southend-on-Sea
SS2 6AL Tel: 01702-348944
Controller, M. McDowall

ACCOUNTING SERVICES DIVISION

Alexander House, 21 Victoria Avenue, Southend-on-Sea
SS99 1AA Tel: 01702-348944
Accountant and Comptroller-General, D. Robinson

NATIONAL INVESTIGATION SERVICE

Custom House, Lower Thames Street, London EC3R 6EE
Tel: 020-7283 5353
Chief Investigation Officer, P. Evans

SOLICITOR'S OFFICE
Solicitor, D. Pickup
Deputy Solicitor, G. Fotherby

BOARD OF INLAND REVENUE
Somerset House, Strand, London WC2R 1LB
Tel: 020-7438 6622

The Board of Inland Revenue was constituted under the Inland Revenue Board Act 1849. The Board administers and collects direct taxes – income tax, corporation tax, capital gains tax, inheritance tax, stamp duty, and petroleum revenue tax – and advises the Chancellor of the Exchequer on policy questions involving them. The Department's Valuation Office is an executive agency responsible for valuing property for tax purposes. The Contributions Agency of the Department for Work and Pensions which is responsible for the collection of contributions under the National Insurance scheme, became part of the Inland Revenue in April 1999 and is now an executive office called the National Insurance Contributions Office. The Contributions Unit of the Social Security Agency in Northern Ireland also transferred to the Inland Revenue in April 1999.

THE BOARD

Chairman (G1), N. Montagu, CB
  Private Secretary, S. Hardy
Deputy Chairmen (G2), T. J. Flesher; A. Chaut

DIVISIONS

Director, Human Resources Division (G3), A. Walker
Director of Business (G3), J. Yard
Head, Strategy and Planning, S. Norris
Principal of Financial Institutions (G3), R. R. Martin
Director, Business Operations (G3), S. Banyard
Director of Analysis Research (G3), R. G. Ward
Director Business Tax (G3), Mary Hay
Director International (G3), G. Makhlouf
Director of Special Compliance, J. Middleton
Director, Personal Tax (G3), T. Orhinal
Director, Capital and Savings (G3), M. Williams
Head, Revenue Policy (G3), D. Hartnett

EXECUTIVE OFFICES

ACCOUNTS OFFICE (CUMBERNAULD), St Mungo's Road, Cumbernauld, Glasgow G70 5TR. *Director*, A. Geddes, OBE
ACCOUNTS OFFICE (SHIPLEY), Shipley, Bradford, W. Yorks BD98 8AA. *Director*, vacant

INLAND REVENUE CAPITAL TAXES, Ferrers House, PO Box 38, Castle Meadow Road, Nottingham NG2 1BB. *Director*, J. Lee Pemberton
CAPITAL TAXES OFFICE (SCOTLAND), Meldrum House, 15 Drumshugh Gardens, Edinburgh, EH3 7UG. *Registrar*, Mrs J. Templeton
MARKETING AND COMMUNICATIONS, Ground Floor, New Wing Somerset House, Strand, London WC2R 1LB. *Director of Communications*, Ms N. Walters
ENFORCEMENT OFFICE, Durrington Bridge House, Barrington Road, Worthing, W. Sussex BN12 4SE. *Director*, D. Ellis
FINANCIAL ACCOUNTING OFFICE, South Block, Barrington Road, Worthing, W. Sussex BN12 4XH. *Director*, Ms M. McLeish
CENTRE FOR NON-RESIDENTS , St John's House, Merton Road, Bootle L26 9BB; Fitz Roy House, PO Box 46, Castle Meadow, Nottingham NG2 1BD. *Director*, J. Johnson
INTERNAL AUDIT OFFICE, 2nd Floor (North), 22 Kingsway, London WC2B 6NR. *Director*, N. R. Buckley
NATIONAL INSURANCE CONTRIBUTIONS OFFICE, DSS Longbenton, Benton Park Road, Newcastle upon Tyne NE98 1ZZ. *Chief Executive (G3)*, B. Woodley
OIL TAXATION OFFICE, Melbourne House, Aldwych, London WC2B 4LL. *Director*, R. Dyall
SAVINGS PENSIONS AND SHARES, Yorke House, PO Box 62, Castle Meadow Road, Nottingham NG2 1BG. *Director*, R. Hurcombe
SOLICITOR'S OFFICE, East Wing, Somerset House, London WC2R 1LB. *Solicitor (G2)*, P. Ridd
SOLICITOR'S OFFICE (SCOTLAND), Clarendon House, 114–116 George Street, Edinburgh EH2 4LH. *Solicitor*, I. K. Laing
SPECIAL COMPLIANCE OFFICE, Angel Court, 199 Borough High Street, London SE1 1HZ. *Director*, J. Middleton
STAMP OFFICE, Ground Floor, PO Box 38, Ferrers House, Castle Meadow, Nottingham NG2 1BB. *Director*, vacant
TRAINING OFFICE, Lawress Hall, Riseholme Park, Lincoln LN2 2BJ. *Director*, Ms L. Hinnigan

REGIONAL EXECUTIVE OFFICES

INLAND REVENUE CENTRAL ENGLAND, Churchgate, New Road, Peterborough PE1 1TD. *Director*, E. McKeegan
INLAND REVENUE LARGE BUSINESS OFFICE, 1st Floor North, 22 Kingsway, London WC2B 6NR. *Director*, S. Jones
INLAND REVENUE LONDON, New Court, Carey Street, London WC2A 2JE. *Director*, C. R. Massingale
INLAND REVENUE NORTHERN ENGLAND, The Triad, Stanley Road, Bootle, Merseyside L75 2DD. *Director*, G. W. Lunn
INLAND REVENUE SOUTHERN ENGLAND 4th Floor, Dukes Court, Dukes Street, Woking GU21 5XR. *Director*, T. Sleeman
INLAND REVENUE WALES, 1st Floor, Phase II Building, Ty Glas Avenue, Llanishen, Cardiff CF14 5TS. *Director*, J. Harra
INLAND REVENUE SCOTLAND, Clarendon House, 114–116 George Street, Edinburgh EH2 4LH. *Director*, I. S. Gerrie
INLAND REVENUE NORTHERN IRELAND, Dorchester House, 52–58 Great Victoria Street, Belfast BT2 7QE. *Director*, D. Hinstridge

VALUATION OFFICE AGENCY
New Court, 48 Carey Street, London WC2A 2JE
Tel: 020-7506 1700; Fax: 020-7506 1998;
Web: www.voa.gov.uk
50 Frederick Street, Edinburgh EH2 1NG

Tel: 0131-465 0701; Fax 0131-465 0799
Chief Executive, M. A. Johns
Chief Valuer, Scotland, A. Ainslie
Chief Valuer, Wales, P. Clement

ADJUDICATOR'S OFFICE
— *see* page 318

BOUNDARY COMMISSIONS

The Commissions are constituted under the Parliamentary Constituencies Act 1986. The Speaker of the House of Commons is *ex officio* chairman of all four commissions in the UK. Each of the four commissions is required by law to keep the parliamentary constituencies in their part of the UK under review. The latest Boundary Commission report for England was completed in April 1995, and its proposals took effect at the 1997 general election. The next report must be submitted before April 2006. The latest Scottish report was completed in December 1994, with the European constituencies completed in April 1996.

ENGLAND

1 Drummond Gate, London SW1V 2QQ
Tel: 020-7533 5177; Fax: 020-7533 5176
Deputy Chairman, The Hon. Mr Justice Harrison
Joint Secretaries, R. Farrance; M. Rawlings

WALES

1 Drummond Gate, London SW1V 2QQ
Tel: 020-7533 5172; Fax: 020-7533 5176
Deputy Chairman, The Hon. Mr Justice Kay
Joint Secretaries, R. Farrance; M. Rawlings

SCOTLAND

3 Drumsheugh Gardens, Edinburgh EH3 7QJ
Tel: 0131-538 7510; Fax: 0131-538 7240
Deputy Chairman, The Hon. Lady Cosgrove
Secretary, R. Smith

NORTHERN IRELAND

REL Division, 11 Millbank, London SW1P 4QE
Tel: 020-7210 6569
Deputy Chairman, The Hon. Mr Justice Coghlin
Secretary, Mrs L. Rogers

BRITISH BROADCASTING CORPORATION
Broadcasting House, Portland Place, London
W1A 1AA Tel: 020-7580 4468;
BBC Information Line: 0870 010 0222;
Web: www.bbc.co.uk
Television Centre, Wood Lane, London W12 7RJ

The BBC was incorporated under royal charter in 1926 as successor to the British Broadcasting Company Ltd. The BBC's current charter came into force on 1 May 1996 and extends to 31 December 2006. The chairman, vice-chairman and other governors are appointed by The Queen-in-Council. The BBC is financed by revenue from receiving licences for the home services and by grant-in-aid from Parliament for the World Service (radio).
For services, *see* Broadcasting section.

BOARD OF GOVERNORS
Chairman, Sir Christopher Bland
Vice-Chairman, G. Davies
National Governors, Prof. F. Monds (*N. Ireland*); R. S. Jones, OBE (*Wales*); Sir Robert Smith (*Scotland*)
Governors, Sir Richard Eyre, CBE; D. Glecson; Dame Pauline Neville-Jones, DCMG; A. Young; Ms H. Rabbatts; Baroness Hogg; R. Sondhi

BOARD OF MANAGEMENT
EXECUTIVE COMMITTEE

Director-General and Editor-in-Chief G. Dyke (from April 2000)
Directors, M. Thompson (*Television*); Ms J. Abramsky (*Radio*); M. Byford (*BBC World Service*); R. Sambrook (*News*); G. Benson (*Joint Director, Factual and Learning*) A. Yentob (*Drama, Entertainment and Children*); R. Flynn (*Business Commercial*); P. Loughrey (*National and Regions*); J. Smith (*Finance, and Business Affairs*); G. Jones (*Human Resources and Internal Communications*); A. Duncan (*Marketing and Communications*); M. Stevenson (*Joint Director, Factual and Learning*); P. Salmon (*Sport*); Ms C. Thomson (*Public Policy*); Ms C. Fairbairn (*Strategy and Distribution*); A. Highfield (*New Media and Distribution*);
Chief Executives, D. Green (*Acting*), BBC Resources and Technology Ltd); P. Langsdale (*BBC Technology*); R. Gavin (*BBC Worldwide*)

OTHER SENIOR STAFF

Controller, BBC1, L. Heggessey
Controller, BBC2, Ms J. Root
Controller, Radio 1, A. Parfitt
Controller, Radio 2, J. Moir
Controller, Radio 3, R. Wright
Controller, Radio 4, H. Boaden
Controller, Radio 5 Live, B. Shennan
Controller, BBC Scotland, J. McCormick
Controller, BBC Wales, M. Richards
Controller, BBC N. Ireland, A. Carragher
Controller, English Regions, A. Griffee
Secretary, G. Milner

THE BRITISH COUNCIL
10 Spring Gardens, London SW1A 2BN
Tel: 020-7930 8466; Fax: 020-7839 6347
Bridgewater House, 58 Whitworth Street, Manchester M1 6BB Tel: 0161-957 7000;
Fax: 0161-957 7111; 11 Portland Place, London W1B 1EJ Tel: 020-7930 3194; Fax: 020-7389 3199

The British Council was established in 1934, incorporated by Royal Charter in 1940 and granted a supplemental charter in 1993. It is an independent, non-political organisation which promotes Britain abroad. It is the UK's international organisation for educational and cultural relations. The British Council is represented in 229 towns and cities in 111 countries. Total income in 2000–2001, including Foreign and Commonwealth Office grants and contracted money, was £451.560 million.
Chairman, The Baroness Kennedy of The Shaws, QC
Deputy Chairman, Sir Tim Lankester, KCB
Director-General, D. Green, CMG

BRITISH FILM COMMISSION
10 Little Portland Street, London W1N 5DF
Tel: 020-7224 5000; Fax: 020-7224 1013

The British Film Commission was set up in 1991 and is funded by the Department for Culture, Media and Sport. The Commission promotes the UK as an international production centre, encourages the use of locations, facilities, services and personnel, and provides, at no charge to the film makers, comprehensive advice and information relating to the practical aspects of filming in the UK.

In April 2000, the Government. launched the Film Council to take a leading role in the development of the British film industry.

Commissioner and Chief Executive, S. Norris

BRITISH FILM INSTITUTE
21 Stephen Street, London W1T 1LN
Tel: 020-7255 1444; Fax: 020-7436 0439;
Web: www.bfi.org.uk

The British Film Institute was established in in 1933. It consists of three main departments: bfi Education, which comprises the bfi National Library, bfi publishing and bfi education projects, which encourages life-long learning about the moving image; bfi Exhibition, which runs the National Film Theatre, the London Film Festival and supports local cinemas and festivals UK wide; and bfi Collections, which preserves and promotes the UK's moving image heritage. The bfi also runs the London Imax Cinema, featuring the UK's largest screen. In April 2000, the Government launched the Film Council to take a leading role in the development of the British film industry.

Chairman, Ms J. Bakewell, CBE
Deputy Chairman, E. Senat
Director, J. Teckman
Deputy Director, R. Collins

BRITISH PHARMACOPOEIA COMMISSION
Market Towers, 1 Nine Elms Lane, London
SW8 5NQ Tel: 020-7273 0561; Fax: 020-7273 0566

The British Pharmacopoeia Commission sets standards for medicinal products used in human and veterinary medicines and is responsible for publication of the British Pharmacopoeia (a publicly available statement of the standard that a product must meet throughout its shelf-life), the British Pharmacopoeia (Veterinary) and the selection of British Approved Names. It has 13 members who are appointed by the Secretary of State for Health, the Minister for Environment, Food and Rural Affairs, the Scottish Ministers, the National Assembly for Wales, and the relevant Northern Ireland departments.

Chairman, Prof. D. Calam, OBE, D.Phil.
Vice-Chairman, Prof. J. A. Goldsmith
Secretary and Scientific Director, Dr R. C. Hutton

BRITISH STANDARDS INSTITUTION (BSI)
389 Chiswick High Road, London W4 4AL
Tel: 020-8996 9000; Fax: 020-8996 7344

The British Standards Institution is the recognised authority in the UK for the preparation and publication of national standards for industrial and consumer products. About 90 per cent of its standards work is now internationally linked. British Standards are issued for voluntary adoption, though in a number of cases compliance with a British Standard is required by legislation. Industrial and consumer products certified as complying with the relevant British Standard may carry the Institution's certification trade mark, known as the 'Kitemark'.

Chairman, V. E. Thomas, CBE

BRITISH TOURIST AUTHORITY
Thames Tower, Black's Road, London W6 9EL
Tel: 020-8846 9000; Fax: 020-8563 0302

Established under the Development of Tourism Act 1969, the British Tourist Authority is responsible for promoting tourism to Britain from overseas. It also has a general responsibility for the promotion and development of tourism and tourist facilities within Britain as a whole, and for advising the Secretary of State for Culture, Media and Sport on tourism matters.

Chairman, D. Quarmby
Chief Executive, J. Hamblin

BRITISH WATERWAYS
Willow Grange, Church Road, Watford, Herts
WD17 4QA Tel: 01923-226422; Fax: 01923-201400;
Email: enquirieshq@britishwaterways.co.uk
Web: www.britishwaterways.co.uk

British Waterways conserves and manages over 2,000 miles of canals and rivers in England, Scotland and Transport, Local Government and the Regions. Its responsibilities include maintaining the waterways and structures on and around them; looking after wildlife and the waterway environment; and ensuring that canals and rivers are safe and enjoyable places to visit.

Chairman (part-time), Dr G. Greener
Members (part-time),D. Langslow; I. Darling; H. Gorden; Ms C. Dobson; P. King; P. Soulsby; C. Christie
Chief Executive, D. Fletcher

BROADCASTING STANDARDS COMMISSION
7 The Sanctuary, London SW1P 3JS
Tel: 020-7808 1000; Fax: 020-7233 0397

The Commission was established in April 1997 under the Broadcasting Act 1996. It is an independent organisation representing the interests of the consumer, and its remit covers all television and radio broadcasting. The Commission considers the portrayal of violence and sexual conduct and matters of taste and decency. It also provides redress for people who believe they have been unfairly treated or subjected to unwarranted infringement of privacy. The Commission conducts research into stan-

dards and fairness in broadcasting and produces codes of practice, and it considers and adjudicates on complaints. Members of the Commission are appointed by the Secretary of State for Culture, Media and Sport. The appointments are part-time.
Chair, Lord Dobs of Battersea
Deputy Chairmen (£34,000–£36,000), Ms J. Leighton; Lady S. Warner
Commissioners, D. Boulton; U. Dholakia; G. Elliott; S. Heppel, CB; Revd Rose Hudson Wilkin; The Rt. Revd R. Holloway; Ms M. Redfern; Ms S. O'Sullivan;
Director, P. Bolt

THE BROADS AUTHORITY
Thomas Harvey House, 18 Colegate, Norwich NR3 1BQ Tel: 01603-610734; Fax: 01603-765710; Web: www.broads-authority.gov.uk

The Broads Authority is a special statutory authority set up under the Norfolk and Suffolk Broads Act 1988. The functions of the Authority are to conserve and enhance the natural beauty of the Broads; to provide integrated management of the land and water space of the area; to promote the enjoyment of the Broads by the public; and to protect the interests of navigation. The Authority comprises 35 members, appointed by the local authorities in the area covered, environmental conservation bodies, the Environment Agency, and the Great Yarmouth Port Authority.
Chairman, The Viscountess Knollys
Chief Executive, Dr J. Packman

CENTRAL ARBITRATION COMMITTEE
Third Floor, Discovery House, 28–42 Banner Street, London EC1Y 8QE Tel: 020-7251 9747; Fax: 020 7251 3114; Web: www.cac.gov.uk

The Central Arbitration Committee determines claims for statutory recognition and de-recognition of trade unions under the Employment Relations Act 1999, it also adjudicates on disclosure of information cases, issues relating to the European Works Council Directive and arbitrates on trade disputes.
Chairman, Sir Michael Burton
Secretary, C. Johnston

CERTIFICATION OFFICE FOR TRADE UNIONS AND EMPLOYERS' ASSOCIATIONS
180 Borough High Street, London SE1 1LW Tel: 020-7210 3734/5; Fax: 020-7210 3612

The Certification Office is an independent statutory authority. The Certification Officer is appointed by the Secretary of State for Trade and Industry and is responsible for receiving and scrutinising annual returns from trade unions and employers' associations; for determining complaints concerning trade union elections, certain ballots and certain breaches of trade union rules; for ensuring observance of statutory requirements governing mergers between trade unions and employers' associations; for overseeing the political funds and finances of trade unions and employers' associations; and for certifying the independence of trade unions.
Certification Officer, Mr Cockburn
Assistant Certification Officer, G. S. Osborne

SCOTLAND
58 Frederick Street, Edinburgh EH2 1NB Tel: 0131-226 3224; Fax: 0131-200 1300
Assistant Certification Officer for Scotland, J. L. J. Craig

CHARITY COMMISSION
Harmsworth House, 13–15 Bouverie Street, London EC4Y 8DP Tel: 0870 333 0123; Fax: 020-7674 2310
Web: www.charity-commission.gov.uk
2nd Floor, 20 King's Parade, Queen's Dock, Liverpool L3 4DQ Tel: 0870 333 0123; Fax: 0151-703 1555
Woodfield House, Tangier, Taunton, Somerset TA1 4BL Tel: 0870 333 0123; Fax: 01823-345003

The Charity Commission for England and Wales is the Government Department whose aim is to give the public confidence in the integrity of charity. It also carries out the functions of the registration, monitoring and support of charities and the investigation of alleged wrong-doing. The Commission maintains a computerised register of some 187,000 charities. It is accountable to the courts and for its efficiency to the Home Secretary. There are five Commissioners appointed by the Home Office for a fixed term and the Commission has Offices in London, Liverpool and Taunton.
Chief Commissioner (G3), J. Stoker
Legal Commissioner (G3), M. Carpenter
Commissioners (part-time) (G4), D. Taylor; Ms J. Warburton; Ms J. Unwin
Heads of Legal Sections (G5), J. A. Dutton; G. S. Goodchild; K. M. Dibble; S. Slack
Director of Operations (G4), S. Gillespie
Head of Policy Division (G5), Ms R. Chapman
Establishment Officer (G5), Ms C. Stewart
Information Systems Controller (G5), K. Chaun

The offices responsible for charities in Scotland and Northern Ireland are:
SCOTLAND – Scottish Charities Office, Crown Office, 25 Chambers Street, Edinburgh EH1 1LA. Tel: 0131-226 2626
NORTHERN IRELAND – Department for Social Development, Charities Branch, 5th Floor, Churchill House, Victoria Square, Belfast BT1 4SD

CHURCH COMMISSIONERS
1 Millbank, London SW1P 3JZ Tel: 020-7898 1000; Fax: 020-7898 1131
Email: commissioners.enquiry@c-of-e.org
Web: www.churchcommissioners

The Church Commissioners were established in 1948 by the amalgamation of Queen Anne's Bounty (established 1704) and the Ecclesiastical Commissioners (established 1836). They are responsible for the management of most of the Church of England's assets, the income from which is predominantly used to pay, house and pension the clergy. The Commissioners own 128,000 acres of agricultural land, a number of residential estates in central London, and commercial property in Great Britain. They also carry out administrative duties in connection with pastoral reorganisation and redundant churches.

The Commissioners are: the Archbishops of Canterbury and of York; four bishops, three clergy and four lay persons elected by the respective houses of the General Synod; two deans or provosts elected by all the deans and provosts; three persons nominated by The Queen; three persons nominated by the Archbishops of Canterbury and York; three persons nominated by the Archbishops after consultation with others including the lord mayors of London and York and the vice-chancellors of the universities of Oxford and Cambridge; the First Lord of the Treasury; the Lord President of the Council; the Home Secretary; the Lord Chancellor; the Secretary of State for Culture, Media and Sport; and the Speaker of the House of Commons.

INCOME AND EXPENDITURE

for year ended 31 December 2000
£160m

	£ *million*
Net income	125.3
Investments	76.8
Property	41.4
Interest from loans, etc.	16.1
Total expenditure	160.0
Parish ministry support	22.4
Bishop and cathedral clergy stipends	6.7
Bishops' housing	3.0
Grants to cathedrals	2.5
Financial provision for resigning clergy	1.2
Clergy pensions and CHARM subsidy	92.4
Transitional support for pension contributions	11.3
Church buildings	1.2
Bishops' working cost	9.3
Commissioners' administration of national church functions	5.0
Administration costs of other church bodies	2.0

CHURCH ESTATES COMMISSIONERS

First, vacant
Second, S. Bell, MP
Third, The Viscountess Brentford

OFFICERS

Secretary, H. H. Hughes
Deputy Secretary (Finance and Investment), C. W. Daws
Official Solicitor, S. Jones
Assistant Secretaries:
  The Accountant, M. Adams
  Management Accountant, B. J. Hardy
  Chief Surveyor and Deputy Secretary, A. C. Brown
  Computer Manager, J. W. Ferguson
  Bishoprics Secretary, R. Badger
  Investments Manager, M. Chaloner
  Pastoral, Houses and Redundant Churches, M. D. Elengorn
  Senior Architect, J. A. Taylor

CIVIL AVIATION AUTHORITY
CAA House, 45–59 Kingsway, London WC2B 6TE
Tel: 020-7379 7311; Fax: 020-7240 1153;
Web: www.caa.co.uk

The CAA is responsible for the economic regulation of UK airlines and for the safety regulation of UK civil aviation by the certification of airlines and aircraft and by licensing aerodromes, flight crew and aircraft engineers.
  The CAA advises the Government on aviation issues, represents consumer interests, conducts economic and scientific research, produces statistical data, and provides specialist services and other training and consultancy services to clients world-wide. It also regulates UK airspace and runs the ATOL flight and air holiday protection scheme.

Chairman, Sir Malcolm Field
Secretary, R. J. Britton

THE COAL AUTHORITY
200 Lichfield Lane, Mansfield, Notts NG18 4RG
Tel: 01623-427162; Fax: 01623-622072;
Email: coalauthority@coal.gov.uk;
Web: www.coal.gov.uk

The Coal Authority was established under the Coal Industry Act 1994 to manage certain functions previously undertaken by British Coal, including ownership of unworked coal. It is responsible for licensing coal mining operations and for providing information on coal reserves and past and future coal mining. It settles subsidence claims not falling on coal mining operators. It deals with the management and disposal of property, and with surface hazards such as abandoned coal mine shafts.

Chairman, J. Harris, DL
Chief Executive, Dr I. Roxburgh

COLLEGE OF ARMS (OR HERALDS COLLEGE)
Queen Victoria Street, London EC4V 4BT
Tel: 020-7248 2762; Fax: 020-7248 6448
Email: enquiries@college-of-arms.gov.uk;
Web: www.college-of-arms.gov.uk

The Sovereign's Officers of Arms (Kings, Heralds and Pursuivants of Arms) were first incorporated by Richard III. The powers vested by the Crown in the Earl Marshal (the Duke of Norfolk) with regard to state ceremonial are largely exercised through the College. The College is also the official repository of the arms and pedigrees of English, Welsh, Northern Irish and Commonwealth (except Canadian) families and their descendants, and its records include official copies of the records of Ulster King of Arms, the originals of which remain in Dublin. The 13 officers of the College specialise in genealogical and heraldic work for their respective clients.
  Arms have been and still are granted by letters patent from the Kings of Arms. A right to arms can only be established by the registration in the official records of the College of Arms of a pedigree showing direct male line descent from an ancestor already appearing therein as being entitled to arms, or by making application through the College of Arms for a grant of arms. Grants are made to corporations as well as to individuals.
  The College of Arms is open Monday–Friday 10–4.
Earl Marshal, The Duke of Norfolk, KG, GCVO, CB, CBE, MC

KINGS OF ARMS

Garter, P. L. Gwynn-Jones, CVO, FSA
Clarenceux, D. H. B. Chesshyre, LVO, FSA
Norroy and Ulster, T. Woodcock, LVO, FSA

HERALDS

Richmond (and Earl Marshal's Secretary), P. L. Dickinson
York, H. E. Paston-Bedingfeld
Chester (and Registrar), T. H. S. Duke

Lancaster, R. J. B. Noel
Windsor, W. G. Hunt, TD
PURSUIVANTS
Rouge Croix, D. V. White
Rouge Dragon, C. E. A. Cheesman

Deputy Chairmen, Ms B. Bernard; Dr M. Jogee
Commissioners, M. Amran; Dr R. Chandran; M. Hastings; S. Malik; Ms J. Mellor; P. Passley; Ms S. Patel; B. Purkiss; Ms C. Short; Dr J. Singh; R. Singh; Ms G. Sootarsing; K. Jandu
Acting Chief Executive, A. Housley

COMMISSION FOR ARCHITECTURE AND THE BUILT ENVIRONMENT
The Tower Building, 11 York Road, London SE1 7NX Tel: 020-7960 2400; Fax: 020-7960 2444; Email: enquiries@cabe.org.uk; Web: www.cabe.org.uk

---

The Commission for Architecture and the Built Environment (CABE) is responsible for promoting the importance of high quality architecture and urban design and encouraging the understanding of architecture through educational and regional initiatives CABE offers free advice to Local Authorities, public sector clients and others embarking on building projects of any size or purpose.
Chairman, Sir Stuart Lipton
Chief Executive, J. Rouse

COMMISSION FOR INTEGRATED TRANSPORT
Romney House, 5th Floor, Tufton Street, London SW1P 3RA Tel: 020-7944 4101; Fax: 020-7944 2919; Email: cfit@dtlr.gsi.gov.uk; Web: www.cfit.gov.uk

The Commission for Integrated Transport was proposed in the 1998 Transport White Paper and was set up in June 1999. Its role is to provide independent expert advice to the Government in order to achieve a transport system that supports sustainable development. Members of the Commission are appointed by the Secretary of State for Transport, Local Government and the Regions.
Chairman (£25,000), Prof. D. Begg
Vice-Chairman (£17,500), Sir Trevor Chinn
Members (£5,000 each), Lord Bradshaw; L. Christensen, CBE; N. Gavron; S. Joseph; D. Leeder; Ms L. Matson; W. Morris; J. O'Brien; Ms V. Palmer; M. Parker; N. Reilly
Ex-Officio Members, Sir Malcolm Field (*Chairman, Civil Aviation Authority*); T. Matthews (*Chief Executive, Highways Agency*); Sir Alastair Morton (*Chairman, British Railways Board and Head, Strategic Rail Authority*); Ms J. Wilmot (*Chair, Disabled Persons Transport Advisory Committee*)
Secretary (G7), A. Braithwaite

COMMISSION FOR RACIAL EQUALITY
Elliot House, 10–12 Allington Street, London SW1E 5EH Tel: 020-7828 7022; Fax: 020-7630 7605

The Commission was established in 1977 under the Race Relations Act 1976. Its duties are to work towards the elimination of discrimination and promote equality of opportunity, to encourage good relations between different racial groups and to monitor the working of the Race Relations Act. It is funded by the Home Office.
Chairman, Gurbux Singh (£81,000)

COMMITTEE ON STANDARDS IN PUBLIC LIFE
35 Great Smith Street, London SW1P 3BQ Tel: 020-7276 2595; Fax: 020-7276 2585; Email: nigel.wicks@gtnet.gov.uk; Web: www.public-standards.gov.uk

---

The Committee on Standards in Public Life was set up in October 1994. It is a standing body whose chairman and members are appointed by the Prime Minister; three members are nominated by the leaders of the three main political parties. The committee's remit is to examine concerns about standards of conduct of all holders of public office, including arrangements relating to financial and commercial activities, and to make recommendations as to any changes in present arrangements which might be required to ensure the highest standards of propriety in public life. It is also charged with reviewing issues in relation to the funding of political parties. The committee does not investigate individual allegations of misconduct.
Chair, Sir Nigel Wicks
Members, Ms A.Abraham; Prof. Alice Brown; Sir Anthony Cleaver; The Lord Goodhart, QC; F. Heaton The Rt. Hon. J. MacGregor, OBE, R. Donaghy, OBE; Rabbi Julia Neuberger; The Lord Shore of Stepney,
Secretary (SCS), Mrs S. Tyerman

COMMONWEALTH INSTITUTE
230 Kensington High Street, London W8 6NQ Tel: 020-7603 4535; Fax: 020-7602 7374; Email: info@commonwealth.org.uk; Web: www.commonwealth.org.uk

---

The Commonwealth Institute is an independent agency working with young people across the Commonwealth. Central to the Institute's mission is running schools education programmes, supplying learning resources and support to schools, teachers and young people, on citizenship, development and issues dealing with managing and celebrating cultural diversity.
The Institute was established in 1958 as an independent statutory body funded by the British Government. In January 2000, the Institute became an Independent Commonwealth agency after forty years as an agency of the Foreign and Commonwealth Office. It is a registered charity and a company limited by guarantee. It is controlled by a Board of Trustees elected by a Board of Governors. All the Commonwealth High Commissioners in London are *ex-officio* governors of the Institute in addition to other governors appointed by the Board of Trustees.
Chairman, D. A. Thompson
Vice-Chairman, Lord Fellowes
Chief Executive, D. French
Commercial Director, P. Kennedy
Director of Education, S. Brace
Finance Director, Ms J. Curry
Director of Public Affairs, G. Carter

COMMUNITIES FUND
St Vincent House, 16 Suffolk Street, London
SW1Y 4NL Tel: 020-7747 5299; Fax: 020-7747 5220;
Web: www.nlcb.org.uk

The Fund was set up under the National Lottery Act 1993
to distribute funds from the Lottery to support charitable,
benevolent and philanthropic organisations. The chair
and members are appointed by the Secretary of State for
Culture, Media and Sport. The Fund's main aim is to help
meet the needs of those at greatest disadvantage in society
and to improve the quality of life in the community
through grants programmes in the UK and an international grants programme for UK-based agencies working
abroad.
Chair, Lady Brittan, CBE
Deputy Chairman, Dame Valerie Stracham
Members, T. Baring, CBE; R. Bevan; S. Burkeman; J.
    Carroll; A. Clark; D. Graham; K. Hampton; Prof. J.
    Kearney; M. Lee; B. Lowndes, MBE; S. Malley; R.
    Martineau; Dr N. Stewart, OBE; E. Watkins; B.
    Whitaker, CBE *Chief Executive*, N. Pittman

COMMONWEALTH WAR GRAVES
COMMISSION
2 Marlow Road, Maidenhead, Berks SL6 7DX
Tel: 01628-634221; Fax: 01628-771208;
Email: generalenq@cwgc.org; Web: www.cwgc.org

The Commonwealth War Graves Commission (formerly
Imperial War Graves Commission) was founded by royal
charter in 1917. It is responsible for the commemoration
of 1,693,786 members of the forces of the Commonwealth
who fell in the two world wars. More than one million
graves are maintained in 23,247 burial grounds throughout the world. Over three-quarters of a million men and
women who have no known grave or who were cremated
are commemorated by name on memorials built by the
Commission.
    The funds of the Commission are derived from the six
participating governments, i.e. the UK, Canada, Australia,
India, New Zealand and South Africa.
President, HRH The Duke of Kent, KG, GCMG, GCVO, ADC
Chairman, The Secretary of State for Defence in the UK
Vice-Chairman, Gen. Sir John Wilsey, GCB, CBE, DC
Members, The High Commissioners in London for New
    Zealand, South Africa, India, Australian and Canada;
    Mrs L. Golding, MP; J. Wilkinson, MP; Sir John Gray,
    KBE, CMG; P. D. Orchard-Lisle, CBE, TD; Air Chief
    Marshal Sir Michael Stear, KCB, CBE, DL,; Dame Susan
    Tinson, DBE; Gen. Sir John Keegan, OBE; Adm. Sir
    Peter Abbott, GBE
Director-General and Secretary to the Commission, R. E.
    Kellaway
Deputy Director-General, R. J. Dalley
Legal Adviser and Solicitor, G. C. Reddie
Directors, D. R. Parker (*Information and Secretariat*); A.
    Coombe (*Works*); R. D. Wilson (*Administration*); D. C.
    Parker (*Horticulture*); D. G. Stacey (*Personnel*)

IMPERIAL WAR GRAVES ENDOWMENT FUND

Trustees, A. C. Barker (*Chairman*); C. G. Clarke; Gen. Sir
    John Wilsey, DC, CBE
Secretary to the Trustees, R. D. Wilson

COMMUNITIES FUND
St Vincent House, 16 Suffolk Street, London
SW1Y 4NL Tel: 020-7747 5299; Fax: 020-7747 5220;
Web: www.nlcb.org.uk

The Fund was set up under the National Lottery Act 1993
to distribute funds from the Lottery to support charitable,
benevolent and philanthropic organisations. The chair
and members are appointed by the Secretary of State for
Culture, Media and Sport. The Fund's main aim is to help
meet the needs of those at greatest disadvantage in society
and to improve the quality of life in the community
through grants programmes in the UK and an international grants programme for UK-based agencies working
abroad.
Chair, Lady Brittan, CBE
Deputy Chairman, Dame Valerie Stracham
Members, T. Baring, CBE; R. Bevan; S. Burkeman; J.
    Carroll; A. Clark; D. Graham; K. Hampton; Prof. J.
    Kearney; M. Lee; B. Lowndes, MBE; S. Malley; R.
    Martineau; Dr N. Stewart, OBE; E. Watkins; B.
    Whitaker, CBE
Chief Executive, N. Pittman

COMPETITION COMMISSION
New Court, 48 Carey Street, London WC2A 2JT
Tel: 020-7271 0100; Fax: 020-7271 0367

The Commission was established in 1948 as the Monopolies and Restrictive Practices Commission (later the
Monopolies and Mergers Commission); it became
the Competition Commission in April 1999 under the
Competition Act 1998. Its role is to investigate and report
on matters which are referred to it by the Secretary of State
for Trade and Industry or the Director-General of Fair
Trading or, in the case of regulated utilities, by the
appropriate regulator. It has no power to initiate its own
investigations.
    The Appeals Tribunal of the Competition Commission
hears appeals against decisions by the Director-General of
Fair Trading and the utility regulators in respect of the
prohibitions on anti-competitive agreements and abuse of
a dominant position.
    The Commission has a full-time chairman, two part-
time deputy chairmen and about 36 reporting panel
members and 25 specialist panel members to carry out
investigations. All are appointed by the Secretary of State
for Trade and Industry.
Chairman, Dr D. Morris, Ph.D.
Deputy Chairmen, Prof. P. Geroski; Mrs D. P. B.
    Kingsmill, CBE
President, Appeal Tribunals, His Hon. Sir Christopher
    Bellamy, QC
Members Prof. J. Beatson, QC; R. Bertram; Mrs S. Brown;
    Prof. M. Cave; A. T. Clothier; R. H. F. Croft, CB; C.
    Darke; N. Garthwaite; Prof. C. Graham; G. H. Hadley;
    D. B. Hammond; Ms J. C. Hanratty; C. Henderson, CB;
    D. J. Jenkins, MBE; P. MacKay, CB; Dr E. M. Monck; Ms
    K. M. H. Mortimer; R. J. Munson; Prof. D. M. G.
    Newbery, FBA; Dr Gill Owen; Prof. D. Parker; A. Pryor,
    CB; R. A. Rawlinson; Prof. Judith Rees; T. S. Richmond,
    MBE; J. Rickford; E. J. Seddon; Dame Helena Shovelton,
    DBE; G. H. Stacy, CBE; J. D. Stark; Prof. A. Steele; M. R.
    Webster; A. M. Young
Appeal Panel Members, Prof. A. Bain, OBE, M. Blair, QC; Sir
    Christopher Bellamy, QC; P. Clayton; B. D. Colgate; M.

Davey; P. Grant-Hutchinson; Prof. P. Grinyer; Mrs S. Hewitt; Ms A. M. Kelly; The Rt. Hon. A. Lewis; G. Mather; P. Quigley; Prof. J. Pickering; M. R. Prosser, OBE; Dr A. J. Pryor, CB; A. Scott, TD; Mrs V. Smith-Hillman; Prof P. Stoneman; D. L. Summers; Prof. G. Zellick
Appeal Panel Registrar, C. Dhanowa
Secretary, R. Foster

COUNCIL ON TRIBUNALS
7th Floor, 22 Kingsway, London WC2B 6LE
Tel: 020-7947 7045; Fax: 020-7947 7044;
Web: www.council-on-tribunals.gov.uk

The Council on Tribunals is an independent body that operates under the Tribunals and Inquiries Act 1992. It consists of 16 members appointed by the Lord Chancellor and the Scottish Ministers; one member is appointed to represent the interests of people in Wales. The Scottish Committee of the Council generally considers Scottish tribunals and matters relating only to Scotland.
The Council advises on and keeps under review the constitution and working of administrative tribunals, and considers and reports on administrative procedures relating to statutory inquiries. Some 80 tribunals are currently under the Council's supervision. It is consulted by and advises Government departments on a wide range of subjects relating to adjudicative procedures.
Chairman, The Rt. Hon. The Lord Newton of Braintree
Members, The Parliamentary Commissioner for Administration (*ex officio*); R. J. Elliot, WS (*Chairman of the Scottish Committee*); Mrs C. Berkeley; S. M. D. Brown; S. R. Davie, CB; J. H. Eames; Mrs A. Galbraith; Mrs S. R. Howdle; I. J. Irvine; S. Jones, CBE; Prof.G. Richardson; I. D. Penman, CB; D. G. Readings; E. P. Roberts; P. A. A. Waring
Secretary, Mrs P. J. Fairbairn

SCOTTISH COMMITTEE OF THE COUNCIL ON TRIBUNALS

44 Palmerston Place, Edinburgh EH12 5BJ
Tel: 0131-220 1236; Fax: 0131-225 4271;
Email: sccot@gtnet.gov.uk
Chairman, R. J. Elliot
Members, The Parliamentary Commissioner for Administration (*ex officio*); Mrs M. Wood
Secretary, Mrs E. M. MacRae

CONSIGNIA
148 Old Street, London EC1V 9HQ
Tel: 020-7250 2888

Crown services for the carriage of Government dispatches were set up in about 1516. The conveyance of public correspondence began in 1635 and the mail service was made a parliamentary responsibility with the setting up of a Post Office in 1657. Telegraphs came under Post Office control in 1870 and the Post Office Telephone Service began in 1880. The National Girobank service of the Post Office began in 1968. The Post Office ceased to be a Government department in 1969 when responsibility for the running of the postal, telecommunications, giro and remittance services was transferred to a public authority called The Post Office. The 1981 British Telecommunications Act separated the functions of the Post Office,

making it solely responsible for postal services and Girobank. Girobank was privatised in 1990. The Postal Services Act 2000 turned The Post Office into a wholly owned public limited company establishing a regulatory regime under the Postal Service Commission. The Post Office Group changed its name to Consignia plc on 26 March 2001 when its new corporate structure took effect.
The chairman, chief executive and members of the Consignia Board are appointed by the Secretary of State for Trade and Industry but responsibility for the running of Consignia as a whole rests with the Board in its corporate capacity.

CONSIGNIA BOARD
Chairman, Dr N. Bain
Chief Executive, J. Roberts, CBE
Members, M. Cassoni (*Managing Director, Finance*); J. Cope (*Managing Director, Strategy and Personnel*)
Secretary, J. Evans

COUNTRYSIDE AGENCY
John Dower House, Crescent Place, Cheltenham, Glos GL50 3RA Tel: 01242-521381;
Fax: 01242-584270

The Countryside Agency was set up in April 1999 by the merger of the Countryside Commission with parts of the Rural Development Commission. It is a Government agency which promotes the conservation and enhancement of the countryside in England and undertakes activities aimed at stimulating job creation and the provision of essential services in the countryside. The Agency is funded by an annual grant from the Department Transport, Local Government and the Regions, and board members are appointed by the Secretary of State.
Chairman, E. Cameron
Deputy Chair, Ms P. Warhurst
Members, Ms K. Ashbrook; Ms J. Bradbury; the Rt. Revd Bishop of Norwich; M. Doughty; Dr Victoria Edwards, FRICS; P. Fane; A. Hams, OBE; Prof. P. Lowe; Ms C. Mack; FCA; L. Frank-Riley; Ms F. Rowe; Ms S. Stapley
Chief Executive, R. G. Wakeford
Directors, Miss M. A. Clark, OBE; D. Coleman; J. Tomlinson; S. Sleet

COUNTRYSIDE COUNCIL FOR WALES/ CYNGOR CEFN GWLAD CYMRU
Plas Penrhos, Ffordd Penrhos, Bangor LL57 2LQ
Tel: 01248-385500; Fax: 01248-385505

The Countryside Council for Wales is the Government's statutory adviser on sustaining natural beauty, wildlife and the opportunity for outdoor enjoyment in Wales and its inshore waters. It is funded by the National Assembly for Wales and accountable to the First Secretary, who appoints its members.
Chairman, J. Lloyd Jones, OBE
Chief Executive, P. E. Loveluck, CBE
Senior Director and Chief Scientist, Dr M. E. Smith
Director, Countryside Policy, Dr J. Taylor
Director, Conservation, Dr D. Parker

COURT OF THE LORD LYON
HM New Register House, Edinburgh EH1 3YT
Tel: 0131-556 7255; Fax: 0131-557 2148

The Court of the Lord Lyon is the Scottish Court of Chivalry (including the genealogical jurisdiction of the *Ri-Sennachie* of Scotland's Celtic Kings). The Lord Lyon King of Arms has jurisdiction, subject to appeal to the Court of Session and the House of Lords, in questions of heraldry and the right to bear arms. The Court also administers the Scottish Public Register of All Arms and Bearings and the Public Register of All Genealogies. Pedigrees are established by decrees of Lyon Court and by letters patent. As Royal Commissioner in Armory, the Lord Lyon grants patents of arms (which constitute the grantee and heirs noble in the Noblesse of Scotland) to 'virtuous and well-deserving' Scotsmen and to petitioners (personal or corporate) in The Queen's overseas realms of Scottish connection, and issues birthbrieves.
Lord Lyon King of Arms, R. O. Blair, LVO, WS

HERALDS

Albany, J. A. Spens, MVO, RD, WS
Rothesay, Sir Crispin Agnew of Lochnaw, Bt., QC
Ross, C. J. Burnett, FSA Scot.

PURSUIVANTS

Unicorn, Alastair Campbell of Airds, FSA Scot.
Carrick, Mrs C. G. W. Roads, MVO, FSA Scot.

EXTRAORDINARY OFFICERS

Orknell Herald Extrordinary, Sir Malcolm Innes of Edingight, KCVO, WS
Linlithgow Pursuant Extraordinary, J. C. G. George
Lyon Clerk and Keeper of Records, Mrs C. G. W. Roads, MVO, FSA Scot.
Procurator-Fiscal, D. I. K. MacLeod, WS
Herald Painter, Mrs J. Phillips
Macer, A. M. Clark

COVENT GARDEN MARKET AUTHORITY
Covent House, New Covent Garden Market,
London SW8 5NX
Tel: 020-7720 2211; Fax: 020-7622 5307;
Email: info@cgma.gov.uk; Web: www.cgma.gov.uk

The Covent Garden Market Authority is constituted under the Covent Garden Market Acts 1961 to 1977, the members being appointed by the Minister of Environment, Food and Rural Affairs. The Authority owns and operates the 56-acre New Covent Garden Markets (fruit, vegetables, flowers) which have been trading since 1974.
Chairman (part-time), L. Mills, CBE
General Manager, Dr P. M. Liggins
Secretary, C. Farey

CRIMINAL CASES REVIEW COMMISSION
Alpha Tower, Suffolk Street Queensway,
Birmingham B1 1TT
Tel: 0121-633 1800; Fax: 0121-633 1823/1804

The Criminal Cases Review Commission is an independent body set up under the Criminal Appeal Act 1995. It is a non-departmental public body reporting to Parliament

via the Home Secretary. It is responsible for investigating suspected miscarriages of justice in England, Wales and Northern Ireland, and deciding whether or not to refer cases back to an appeal court. Membership of the Commission is by royal appointment; the senior executive staff are appointed by the Commission.
Chairman, Sir Frederick Crawford, FREng.
Members, B. Capon; L. Elks; A. Foster; Ms F. King; J. Knox; D. Kyle; Prof. L. Leigh; J. MacKeith; K. Singh; B. Skitt; E. Weiss
Chief Executive, vacant
Director of Finance and Personnel, D. Robson
Legal Advisers, J. Wagstaff; M. Aspinall
Police Adviser, R. Barrington

CRIMINAL INJURIES COMPENSATION AUTHORITY (CICA)
Morley House, Holborn Viaduct, London EC1A 2JQ
Tel: 020-7842 6800; Fax: 020-7436 0804;
Web: www.cica.gov.uk
Tay House, 300 Bath Street, Glasgow G2 4JR
Tel: 0141-331 2726; Fax: 0141-331 2287

All applications for compensation for personal injury arising from crimes of violence in England, Scotland and Wales are dealt with at the above locations. (Separate arrangements apply in Northern Ireland.) Applications received up to 31 March 1996 are assessed on the basis of common law damages under the 1990 compensation scheme. Applications received later than 1 April 1996 are assessed under a tariff-based scheme, made under the Criminal Injuries Compensation Act 1995, by the Criminal Injuries Compensation Authority (CICA). There is a separate avenue of appeal to the Criminal Injuries Compensation Appeals Panel (CICAP). In 1999-2000 total compensation paid was £194.34 million.
Chief Executive, Howard Webber
Deputy Chief Executive, E. McKeown
Head of Legal Services, Ms A. M. Johnstone
Press enquiries, Ms J Hay

CRIMINAL INJURIES COMPENSATION APPEALS PANEL (CICAP)
11th Floor, Cardinal Tower, 12 Farringdon Road,
London EC1M 3HS
Tel: 020-7549 4600; Fax: 020-7549 4643;
Email: info@cicap.gov.uk; Web: www.cicap.gov.uk
Chairman, Michael Lewer, QC
Secretary, Ms V. Jenson

CROFTERS COMMISSION
4–6 Castle Wynd, Inverness IV2 3EQ
Tel: 01463-663450; Fax: 01463-711820

The Crofters Commission was established in 1955 under the Crofters (Scotland) Act. It advises the Scottish Ministers on all matters relating to crofting. It seeks to develop and promote thriving crofting communities and to simplify relevant legislation. It administers the Crofting Counties Agricultural Grants Scheme, Livestock Improvement Schemes and the Croft Entrant Scheme. It also provides a free enquiry service.
Chairman, I. MacAskill
Chief Executive, S. Rankin

CROWN ESTATE
16 Carlton House Terrace, London SW1Y 5AH
Tel: 020-7210 4377; Fax: 020-7930 8187

The Crown Estate includes substantial blocks of urban property, primarily in London, almost 120,000 hectares of agricultural land and extensive marine holdings throughout the United Kingdom. Its origins go back to the reign of King Edward the Confessor and, until the accession of King George III, the Sovereign received its rents and profits. However, since 1760 the annual surplus, after deducting management expenses, has been surrendered by the Sovereign to Parliament to help meet the cost of civil government. In return, the Sovereign receives the Civil List and the Government meets other official expenditure incurred in support of the Sovereign.

In the year ended 31 March 2001, the gross revenue from the Crown Estate totalled £204.9 million and £147.7 million was paid to the Exchequer as surplus revenue.

First Commissioner and Chairman (part-time), Sir Denys Henderson
Second Commissioner and Chief Executive, R, Bright
Commissioners (part-time), The Lord De Ramsey; I. D. Grant, CBE; Mrs H. M. R. Chapman, CBE, FRICS; R. R. Spinney, FRICS; D. T. Y. Curry, CBE
Director of Urban Estates, D. A. Bickmore
Rural Estate, C. Bourchier
Urban, Central London Estate, Ms E. Miller
Urban, Regent Street Estate, M. W. Dillon
Urban, Regional Estate, A. Meakin
Urban, Residential Estate, R, Wyatt
Urban, Special Projects, L. Colgan
Marine Estate, F. G. Parrish
Finance and Information Systems, J. G. Lelliott
Internal Audit, J. Ford
Corporate Policy and Personnel, M. J. Gravestock
Commuinications Manager, I. Belcher

SCOTLAND

10 Charlotte Square, Edinburgh EH2 4BR
Tel: 0131-226 7241; Fax: 0131-220 1366
Head of Scottish Estate, M. Cunliffe

WINDSOR ESTATE

The Great Park, Windsor, Berks SL4 2HT
Tel: 01753-860222; Fax: 01753-859617
Deputy Ranger, P. Everrett

DEER COMMISSION FOR SCOTLAND
Knowsley, 82 Fairfield Road, Inverness IV3 5LH
Tel: 01463-231751; Fax: 01463-712931;
Email: deercom@aol.com; Web: www.dcs.gov.uk

The Deer Commission for Scotland has the general functions of furthering the conservation and control of deer in Scotland. It has the statutory duty, with powers, to prevent damage to agriculture, forestry and the habitat by deer. It is funded by the Scottish Executive.
Chairman (part-time), A. Raven
Director, N. Reiter
Technical Director, D. Balharry

DESIGN COUNCIL
34 Bow Street, London WC2E 7DL
Tel: 020-7420 5200; Fax: 020-7420 5300

The Design Council is a campaigning and lobbying organisation which works with partners in business, education and Government to promote the effective use of good design. It is a registered charity with a Royal Charter and is funded by grant-in-aid from the Department of Trade and Industry.
Chairman, C. Frayling
Chief Executive, A. Summers

DISABILITY RIGHTS COMMISSION (DRC)
DRC, Stratford upon Avon CV37 9BR
Helpline: 08457-622633; Web: www.drc-gb.org

The Commission is an executive non-departmental public body established in April 2000. Its role is to advise Government on issues of discrimination against disabled people and the operation of the Disability Discrimination Act 1995. It promotes good practice to employers and service providers and provides advice, information and sometimes legal support to disabled people.
Chair, B. Massie
Chief Executive, R. Niven
Commissioners, Saghir Alam; Ms K. Allen; Ms J. Campbell; M. Deveney; R. Exell; Dr K. Fitzpatrick; J. Hougham; P. Humphrey; C. Low; Mrs E. Noad; Ms E. Rank-Petruzzietto; Ms P. Russell; J. Strachan; Ms J. White

THE DUCHY OF CORNWALL
10 Buckingham Gate, London SW1E 6LA
Tel: 020-7834 7346; Fax: 020-7931 9541

The Duchy of Cornwall was created by Edward III in 1337 for the support of his eldest son Edward, later known as the Black Prince. It is the oldest of the English duchies. The duchy is acquired by inheritance by the sovereign's eldest son either at birth or on the accession of his parent to the throne, whichever is the later. The primary purpose of the estate remains to provide an income for the Prince of Wales. The estate is mainly agricultural and based in the south-west of England. A recent purchase has increased the landholding to approximately 150,000 acres in 26 counties. The duchy also has some residential property, a number of shops and offices, and a Stock Exchange portfolio. Prince Charles is the 24th Duke of Cornwall.

THE PRINCE'S COUNCIL

Chairman, HRH The Prince of Wales, KG, KT, GCB
Lord Warden of the Stannaries, The Earl Peel
Receiver-General, The Rt. Hon. J. H. Leigh-Pemberton
Attorney-General to the Prince of Wales, N. Underhill, QC
Secretary and Keeper of the Records, W. R. A. Ross
Other members, R. Broadhurst; A. M. J. Galsworthy; W. N. Hood, CBE; Sir Christopher Howes, CB; S. Lamport; The Marquess of Lansdowne; J. E. Pugsley

OTHER OFFICERS

Auditors, I. Brindle; R. Hughes
Sheriff (2001–2002), J. M. Williams

THE DUCHY OF LANCASTER
Lancaster Place, Strand, London WC2E 7ED
Tel: 020-7836 8277; Fax: 020-7836 3098

The estates and jurisdiction known as the Duchy of Lancaster have belonged to the reigning monarch since 1399 when John of Gaunt's son came to the throne as Henry IV. As the Lancaster Inheritance it goes back as far as 1265 when Henry III granted his youngest son Edmund lands and possessions following the Baron's war. In 1267 Henry gave Edmund the County, Honor and Castle of Lancaster and created him the first Earl of Lancaster. In 1351 Edward III created Lancaster a County Palatine.

The Chancellor of the Duchy of Lancaster is responsible for the administration of the Duchy, the appointment of justices of the peace in Lancashire, Greater Manchester and Merseyside and ecclesiastical patronage in the Duchy gift.

Chancellor of the Duchy of Lancaster (and Minister for the Cabinet Office), The Rt. Hon.The Lord Macdonald of Tradeston, CBE
Chairman of the Duchy Council, Sir Michael Bunbury, Bt
Attorney-General, M. T. F. Briggs, QC
Receiver-General, Sir Michael Peat, KCVO
Clerk of the Council and Chief Executive, P. R. Clarke
Secretary for Appointments, Col. F. N. J. Davies

ECGD (EXPORT CREDITS GUARANTEE DEPARTMENT)
PO Box 2200, 2 Exchange Tower, Harbour Exchange Square, London E14 9GS
Tel: 020-7512 7000; Fax: 020-7512 7649

ECGD (Export Credits Guarantee Department), the UK's official export credit insurer, is a Government department responsible for the Secretary of State for Trade and Industry and functions under the Export and Investment Guarantees Act 1991. This enables ECGD to facilitate UK exports by making available export credit insurance to firms engaged in selling overseas and to guarantee repayment to banks providing finance for capital goods. The Act also empowers ECGD to insure UK companies investing overseas against political risks such as war, expropriation and restrictions on remittances.
Chief Executive, H. V. B. Brown
Group Directors (G3), V. P. Lunn-Rockliffe (*Portfolio Asset Management*); J. R. Weiss (*Business*); T. M. Jaffray (*Risk Management*)

DIVISIONS

Director, Finance (G5), R. J. Healey
Director, Central Services (G5), S. R. Dodgson
*Directors, Business Divisions (G5),*G. G. Welsh *(Division A);* R. Gotts *(Division B);* M. D. Pentecost *(Division C)*; J.C.W. Croall *(Capital Management)*
Director, Office of the General Counsel (G5), N. Ridley
Director, International Debt (G5), Ms L. Woods
Director, Claims (G5), R. F. Lethbridge
Director, Active Portfolio Management), J. S. Snowdon
Director, Strategy and Communications, J. Ormerod
Director, Risk Management, P. J. Radford
Director, IT Services (G6), E. J. Walsby
Director, Internal Audit (G6), G. Cassell
Director, Operational Research (G6), Ms R. Kaufman

EXPORT GUARANTEES ADVISORY COUNCIL
Chairman, D. H. A. Harrison, CBE
Other Members, E. L. Airey; J. Armitt; A. Brown, J. Elkington; Prof. J. Kydd; D. MacLachlan; Prof. K. Phylaktis; A. Shepherd; Dr R. Thamotheram; Sir David Wright

ENGLISH HERITAGE (HISTORIC BUILDINGS AND MONUMENTS COMMISSION FOR ENGLAND)
23 Savile Row, London W1S 2ET Tel: 020-7973 3000; Fax: 020-7973 3001

English Heritage was established under the National Heritage Act 1983. On 1 April 1999 it merged with the Royal Commission on the Historical Monuments of England to become the new lead body for England's historic environment. Its duties are to carry out and sponsor archaeological, architectural and scientific survey and research designed to increase the understanding of England's past and its changing condition; to offer expert advice and skills and give grants to secure the preservation of listed buildings, cathedrals, churches, archaeological sites, ancient monuments and historic houses of England; to encourage the imaginative re-use of historic buildings to aid regeneration of the centres of cities, towns and villages; to manage the historic monuments and historic buildings in England; and to curate and make publicly accessible the National Monuments Record, whose records of over one million historic sites and buildings, and collections of more that 12 million photographs, maps, drawings and reports constitute the central database and archive to England's historic environment.
Chairman, Sir Neil Cossons
Commissioners, Miss A. Arrowsmith; M. Cairns; Ms B. Cherry; HRH The Duke of Gloucester, KG, GCVO; P. Gough, CBE; J. Grenville; L. Grossman; Ms K. McLeod; Prof. R. Morris, FSA; L. Sparks; Miss S. Underwood
Chief Executive, Ms P. Alexander

NATIONAL MONUMENTS RECORD, National Monuments Record Centre, Kemble Drive, Swindon SN2 2GZ. Tel: 01793-414600; Fax: 01793-414606. *London Search Room:* 55 Blandford Street, London SW1H 3AF. Tel: 020-7208 8200; Fax: 020-7224 5333

ENGLISH NATURE
Northminster House, Peterborough PE1 1UA
Tel: 01733-455000; Fax: 01733-568834

English Nature (the Nature Conservancy Council for England) was established in 1991 and is responsible for advising the Secretary of State for the Transport, Local Government and the Regions on nature conservation in England. It promotes, directly and through others, the conservation of England's wildlife and natural features. It selects, establishes and manages National Nature Reserves and identifies and notifies Sites of Special Scientific Interest. It provides advice and information about nature conservation, and supports and conducts research relevant to these functions. Through the Joint Nature Conservation Committee, it works with its sister organisations in Scotland and Wales on UK and international nature conservation issues.

Chairman, M. Doughty
Chief Executive, D. Arnold-Forster
Directors, Dr K. L. Duff; Miss C. E. M. Wood; Ms S.
  Collins; A. E. Brown

THE ENVIRONMENT AGENCY
Rio House, Waterside Drive, Aztec West,
Almondsbury, Bristol BS32 4UD
Tel: 01454-624400; Fax: 01454-624409;
Email: enquiries@environment-agency.gov.uk

The Environment Agency was established in 1996 under
the Environment Act 1995 and is a non-departmental
public body sponsored by the Department of the
Environment, Food and Rural Affairs and the National
Assembly for Wales. The Agency is responsible for
pollution prevention and control in England and Wales,
and for the management and use of water resources,
including flood defences, fisheries and navigation. It has
head offices in London and Bristol and eight regional
offices.

THE BOARD

Chairman, Sir John Harman
Members, C. Beardwood; A. J. P. Dalton; A. Dare, CBE; E.
  Gallagher; N. Haigh, OBE; C. Hampson, CBE; Prof. R.
  Macrory; Prof. Jacqueline McGlade; G. Manning, OBE;
  Dr A. Powell; Prof. D. Ritchie; A. Rogers; G. Wardell

THE EXECUTIVE

Chief Executive, B. Young
Director of Finance, N. Reader
Director of Personnel, G. Duncan
Director of Environmental Protection, Dr P. Leinster
Director of Water Management, G. Mance
Director of Operations, A. Robertson
Director of Corporate Affairs, H. McCallum
Director of Legal Services, R. Navarro
Chief Scientist, Dr John Murlis

EQUAL OPPORTUNITIES COMMISSION
Arndale House, Arndale Centre, Manchester M4 3EQ
Tel: 0161-833 9244; Fax: 0161-838 8312

Press Office, 36 Broadway, London SW1H 0XH. Tel: 020-
7222 1110
Other Offices, St Stephens House, 279 Bath Street,
Glasgow G2 4JL Tel: 0141-248 5833; Windsor House,
Windsor Place, Cardiff CF10 3GE Tel: 029-2034 3552

The Commission was set up in 1975 as a result of the
passing of the Sex Discrimination Act. It works towards
the elimination of discrimination on the grounds of sex or
marital status and to promote equality of opportunity
between men and women generally. It is responsible to
The Cabinet Office.
Chair, Ms J. Mellor
Deputy Chair, Ms J. Watson
Members, T. Akpeki; S. Ashtiany; R. Arashad, OBE; K.
  Carberry; Ms F. Cannon; J. Drake;. Hodder; S. Pearce;
  R. Penn; S. Pierce; Prof. T. Rees; S. Sharma; Dr J.
  Stringer; T. Woodcraft
Chief Executive, L. Berry
Acting Chief Executive, G. Ashmore

EQUALITY COMMISSION FOR NORTHERN
IRELAND
Equality House, 7–9 Shaftesbury Square, Belfast,
BT2 7DP Tel: 028-9050 0600; Fax: 028-9033 1544;
Email: information@equalityni.org;
Web: www.equallityni.org

The Equality Commission was set up in 1999 and is
responsible for promoting equality and eliminating
discrimination on the grounds of race, disability, gender,
religion and political opinion.
Chief Commissioner, Ms J. Harbison
Chief Executive, E. Collins

FILM COUNCIL
10 Little Portland Street, London W1W 7JG
Tel: 020-7861 7861; Fax: 020-7861 7862

The Council was created in April 2000 by the Department
for Culture, Media and Sport to develop a coherent
strategy for the development and leadership of film culture
and the film industry. It is responsible for the majority of
the Department for Culture, Media and Sport funding for
film as well as lottery and grant-in-aid (with the exception
of the National Film and Television School).
Chairman, A. Parker
Deputy Chairman, S. Till
Chief Executive, J. Woodward

FOOD STANDARDS AGENCY (UK)
Aviation House, 125 Kingsway, London, WC2 BNH
Tel: 020-7276 8100; Fax: 020-7276 84104;
Web: www.foodstandards.gov.uk

The Food Standards Agency was established by Act of
Parliament (the Food Standards Act 1999) in April 2000 to
protect public health from risks arising in connection with
the consumption of food, and otherwise to protect the
interests of consumers in relation to food. The Agency has
the general function of developing policy in these areas
and provides information and advice to the Government,
other public bodies and consumers. It also sets standards
for and monitors food law enforcement by local authorities. The Agency is a UK body and has executive offices
in Scotland, Wales and Northern Ireland. It is advised by
advisory committees on food safety matters of special
interest to each of these areas.
Chairman, Prof. Sir John Krebs
Deputy Chairman, Ms S. Leather
Chief Executive, G. J. F. Podger

EXECUTIVE AGENCY
MEAT HYGIENE SERVICE

Foss House, Kings Pool, 1–2 Peasholme Green, York YO1
7PX Tel: 01904-455501; Fax: 01904-455502
The Agency was launched in April 1995 and from the 1
April became an executive agency of the Food Standards
Agency. It protects public health and promotes animal
welfare through veterinary supervision and meat inspec-
tion in licensed fresh meat establishments.
Chief Executive (G4), C. S. Lawson

FOOD STANDARDS AGENCY SCOTLAND
St Magnus House, 25 Guild Street, Aberdeen, AB11 6NJ
Tel: 01224 285100; Fax: 01224 285167;
Email: scotland@foodstandards.gsi.gov.uk;
Web: www.foodstandards.gov.uk

FOOD STANDARDS AGENCY WALES
1st Floor, Southgate House, Wood Street, Cardiff
CF10 1EW Tel: 029-2067 8999;
Email: foodstandards@Wales.gsi.gov.uk
Web: www.foodstandards.gov.uk/wales
Advisory Committee for Wales
Chair, Ms A. Hemingway

FOOD STANDARDS AGENCY NORTHERN IRELAND
10b and 10c Clarendon Road, Belfast, BT1 3BG
Tel: 028-9041 7700; Fax: 028-9041 7726;
Email: gerry.rickard@dhsspsni.gov.uk;
Web: www.foodstandards.gov.uk/n_ireland
Advisory Committee for Northern Ireland
Chairman, M. Walker

FOREIGN COMPENSATION COMMISSION
Room SG/III, Old Admiralty Building, Whitehall,
London SW1A 2PA
Tel: 020-7008 1321; Fax: 020-7008 0160

The Commission was set up by the Foreign Compensation Act 1950 primarily to distribute, under Orders in Council, funds received from other governments in accordance with agreements to pay compensation for expropriated British property and other losses sustained by British nationals.
Chairman, A. W. E. Wheeler, CBE
Secretary, A. N. Grant

FORESTRY COMMISSION
231 Corstorphine Road, Edinburgh EH12 7AT
Tel: 0131-334 0303; Fax: 0131-334 3047

The Forestry Commission is the Government department responsible for forestry policy in Great Britain. It reports directly to forestry Ministers (i.e. the Minister of Environment, Food and Rural Affairs., the Scottish Ministers and the National Assembly for Wales), to whom it is responsible for advice on forestry policy and for the implementation of that policy.

The Commission's principal objectives are to protect Britain's forests and woodlands; expand Britain's forest area; enhance the economic value of the forest resources; conserve and improve the biodiversity, landscape and cultural heritage of forests and woodlands; develop opportunities for woodland recreation; and increase public understanding of and community participation in forestry. Forest Enterprise, a trading body operating as an executive agency of the Commission, manages its forestry estate on a multi-use basis.
Chairman (part-time), Sir Peter Hutchison, Bt., CBE
Director-General and Deputy Chairman (G2), D. J. Bills
Secretary to the Commissioners (G5), F. Strang

FOREST ENTERPRISE HEADQUARTERS, 231 Corstorphine
Road, Edinburgh EH12 7AT. Tel: 0131-334 0303.
Chief Executive, Dr B. McIntosh

FOREST RESEARCH, Alice Holt Lodge, Wrecclesham,
Farnham, Surrey GU10 4LU. Tel: 01420-222555;
Northern Research Station, Roslin, Midlothian
EH25 9SY. Tel: 0131-445 2176. *Chief Executive*, J. Dewar

FRIENDLY SOCIETIES COMMISSION
15th Floor, 25 The North Colonnade, Canary
Wharf, London E14 5HS
Tel: 020-7676 1000; Fax: 020-7676 9700;
Web: www.fsa.gov.uk

The Friendly Societies Commission was established by the Friendly Societies Act 1992. It is responsible for the supervision of friendly societies and administers the system of prudential regulation. It also advises the Treasury and other Government departments on matters relating to friendly societies.

The Government has decided that the functions of the Commission should pass to the Financial Services Authority on implementation of the Financial Services and Markets Act.

FRIENDLY SOCIETIES COMMISSION

Chairman, M. Roberts
Commissioners, F. da Rocha; *B. Richardson; *J. A. Geddes;
*Ms S. Brown; *Ms P. Triggs
* non executive

SECRETARIAT
Miss J. Erskine; Miss L. Gammans

GAMING BOARD FOR GREAT BRITAIN
Berkshire House, 168–173 High Holborn, London
WC1V 7AA Tel: 020-7306 6200; Fax: 020-7306 6266;
Web: www.gbgb.org.uk

The Board was established in 1968 and is responsible to the Home Secretary. It is the regulatory body for casinos, bingo clubs, gaming machines and the larger society and all local authority lotteries in Great Britain. Its functions are to ensure that those involved in organising gaming and lotteries are fit and proper to do so and to keep gaming free from criminal infiltration; to ensure that gaming and lotteries are run fairly and in accordance with the law; and to advise the Home Secretary on developments in gaming and lotteries.
Chairman (part-time) (£39,826), P. Dean, CBE
Secretary, T. Kavanagh

GOVERNMENT ACTUARY'S DEPARTMENT
New King's Beam House, 22 Upper Ground,
London SE1 9RJ
Tel: 020-7211 2601; Fax: 020-7211 2640/2650;
Email: enquiries@gad.gov.uk; Web: www.gad.gov.uk

The Government Actuary provides a consulting service to Government departments, the public sector, and overseas governments. The actuaries advise on social security schemes and superannuation arrangements in the public sector at home and abroad, on population and other statistical studies, and on supervision of insurance companies and pension funds.
Government Actuary, C. D. Daykin, CB

Directing Actuaries, D. G. Ballantine; A. G. Young
Chief Actuaries, E. I. Battersby; I. A. Boonin; A. I. Johnston;
D. Lewis; G. T. Russell

GOVERNMENT HOSPITALITY
Lancaster House, Stable Yard, St Jame's, London
SW1A 1BB Tel: 020-7008 8196; Fax: 020-7210 4301

The Government Hospitality Fund was instituted in 1908
for the purpose of organising official hospitality on a
regular basis with a view to the promotion of international
goodwill. It is responsible to the Foreign and Commonwealth Office.

Government Hospitality is now incorporated as part of
the Foreign and Commonwealth Office's Conference and
Visitors Group.

Minister in Charge, Dr Dennis MacShane
Head of Government Hospitality, R. Alexander

GOVERNMENT OFFICES FOR THE REGIONS

The Government Offices for the Regions manage
expenditure programmes amounting to over £7 billion
per year for various Government Departments. The
programmes cover areas such as sustainable development,
Neighbourhood Renewal, Social Inclusion, regeneration,
competitiveness and rural affairs.

Government Offices handle land use planning, housing
and countryside work, road schemes decisions, local
transport priorities, transport interaction with land uses
planning and statutory casework. Government Offices
have a sponsorship role for the eight Regional Development Agencies and the London Development Agency and
are also involved in training and education and business
support issues.

REGIONAL CO-ORDINATION UNIT, Riverwalk House,
157–161 Millbank, London SW1P 4RR Tel: 020-7217
3595; Fax: 020-7217 3590
Email: username.rcu@go-regions.gsi.gov.uk
Director General, R. Smith
Director (G3), A. Wells
Directors, A. Modu *(Corporate Relations)*; A. Sargeant
(Strategy); T. Vokes *(Business Development)*

EAST MIDLANDS
Secretariat: The Belgrave Centre, Stanley Place, Talbot
Street, Nottingham NG1 5GG
Tel: 0115-971 9971; Fax: 0115-971 2404;
Email: enquiries.goem@go-regions.gsi.gov.uk;
Web: www.go-em.gov.uk
Regional Director (G3), D. Morrison
Directors (G5), Dr S. Kennett *(Infrastructure and
Community Affairs)*; S. Brookes *(Regional Crime
Reduction)*; G. Norbury *(European and Rural Affairs
Policy)*, R. Poole *(Industry, Education and Skills,
Leicestershire and Derby)*; R. Smith *(Corporate Affairs)*

EAST OF ENGLAND
Secretariat: Building A, Westbrook Centre, Milton Road,
Cambridge CB4 1YG
Tel: 01223 346719; Fax: 01223-346705
Email: username.go-east@go-regions.gsi.gov.uk
Regional Director (G3), A. Riddell

Directors (G5), Ms C. Bowdler *(Planning and Transport)*; M.
Oldham *(Business and Europe)*; J. Street *(Learning and
Local Government)*; *(G6)*, J. Rabagliati *(DEFRA,
Agriculture, Countryside and Sustainability)*; H. Cooper
(Temporary Strategy and Services); H. Tam *(HO
Community Safety and Regeneration)*

GOVERNMENT OFFICE LONDON
Secretariat: Riverwalk House, 157–161 Millbank, London
SW1P 4RR
Tel: 020-7217 3456; Fax: 020-7217 3450
Email: username.gol@go-regions.gsi.gov.uk
Regional Director (G3), L. Meek
Directors (G3), J. Anderson and S. Webber *(Job Share
Government/FGLA Liaison Unit)*; S. Ebanja *(Local
Government and Europe)*; C. Lyons *(Corporate and Change
Management)*; A. Melville *(London Co-Ordination and
Environment Division)*; E. Roy *(Crime Reduction)*; K.
Timmins *(Trade and Industry)*; R. Wragg *(Skills and
Education)*

NORTH-EAST
Secretariat: Wellbar House, Gallow Gate, Newcastle upon
Tyne NE1 4TD Tel: 0191-201 3300; Fax: 0191-201 3300;
Web: www.go-ne.gov.uk
Email: general.enquiries.gone@go-regions.gsi.gov.uk
Regional Director (G3), Dr R. Dobbie, CB
Directors (G5), J. Darlington *(Planning, Environment and
Transport)*; D. Caudle *(Education, Skills, Enterprise and
Regeneration)*; J. Bainton *(DEFRA)*; A. Brown *(Crime
Reduction)*; D. Pearce *(Strategy and Resources)*; D. Slater
(Competitiveness in Europe)

NORTH-WEST
Secretariat: 12th Floor, Sunley Tower, Piccadilly Plaza,
Manchester M1 4BE
Tel: 0161-952 4000; Fax: 0161-952 4099
Regional Director (G3), K. Barnes
Directors (G5), P. Styche *(Communities)*; Dr D. Highham
(Business and Europe); *(G6)*, I. Jamieson *(Business and
Europe)*; Ms S. Yates *(Europe, Liverpool)*; E. Hughes
*(Planning and Environment/Regional Policy and Co-
ordination)*; D. Duff, OBE *(Tec Transition)*; D. Hopewell
(Corporate Services); N. Burke *(Education and Social
Exclusion)*; M. Hill *(Commonwealth Games)*; J. Flannon
(Objective 1); Dr D. Higham *(Business Connexions)*; T.
Walker *(Small Business Team)*

SOUTH-EAST
Secretariat: 2nd Floor, Bridge House, 1 Walnut Tree
Close, Guildford, Surrey GU1 4GA
Tel: 01483-882481; Fax: 01483-882250
Regional Director (G3), D. Saunders
Directors (G5), C. Byrne *(Hants/IOW)*; S. Burt *(Skills and
Enterprise Berks/Oxon/Bucks)*; A. Campbell *(A.
Campbell (Regeneration, Housing and Environment,
Kent)*; A. Parker *(DEFRA and Europe, Surrey and Sussex)*;
C. Dixon *(Transport and Strategy)*; P. Craggs *(Finance
and Corporate Management)*; H. Marriage *(Crime
Reduction)*

SOUTH-WEST
Secretariat: 4th and 5th Floor, The Pithay, Bristol BS1 2PB
Tel: 0117-900 1700; Fax: 0117-900 1900;
Email: receptionist.gosw@go-regions.gsi.gov.uk;
Web: www.gosw.gov.uk
Regional Director (G3), Ms J. Henderson

Directors (G5), R. Bayly (*Transport, Devon and Cornwall*); C. Carrington (*Local Government and Neighbourhood Renewal-Former West/West of England*); T. Shearer (*Enterprise Intelligence and Young People-Gloucestershire/ Wiltshire*); (*G6*) M. Davey (*Corporate Services*); P. Rowlandson (*Crime Reduction*); T. Render (*Food Farming and Rural Development, Somerset and Dorset*)

WEST MIDLANDS

Secretariat: 6th Floor, 77 Paradise Circus, Queensway, Birmingham B1 2DT
Tel: 0121-212 5050; Fax: 0121-212 1010;
Email: enquiries.gowm@go-regions.gsi.gov.uk
Regional Director (G3), G. Garbutt
Directors (G5), C. Marsh (*Corporate Affairs and Europe*); P. Holland (*Local Government*); (*G6*) C. Beesley (*Business and Learning Division*); B. Davies (*DEFRA*); M. Greary (*Crime Reduction*)

YORKSHIRE AND THE HUMBER

Secretariat: PO Box 213, City House, New Station Street, Leeds LS1 4US
Tel: 0113-280 0600; Fax: 0113-283 6394
Email: enquiries.goyh@go-regions.gsi.gov.uk
Regional Director (G3), F. Everiss
Directors (G5), G. Dyche (*HO Crime Reduction and Voluntary Sector*); S. Perryman (*People and Communities*); (*G6*), J. Jarvis (*Regional Affairs*); N. Best (*Corporate Services*); G. Kingston (*DEFRA-Rural*); I. Mills (*Europe*); S. Yates (*Objective 1*); M. Jackson (*Competitiveness and Sensibilities*)

HEALTH AND SAFETY COMMISSION
Rose Court, 2 Southwark Bridge, London SE1 9HS
Tel: 020-7717 6000; Fax: 020-7717 6644

The Health and Safety Commission was created under the Health and Safety at Work etc. Act 1974, with duties to reform health and safety law, to propose new regulations, and generally to promote the protection of people at work and of the public from hazards arising from industrial and commercial activity, including major industrial accidents and the transportation of hazardous materials.
Chairman, W. Callaghan
Members, J. Donovan; M. Rooney; Ms J. Edmond-Smith; G. Brumwell; Ms M. Burns; S. Hamid; A. Chowdry; O. Tudor; R. Symons, CBE
Secretary, A. Adams

HEALTH AND SAFETY EXECUTIVE
Rose Court, 2 Southwark Bridge, London SE1 9HS
Tel: 020-7717 6000; Fax: 020-7717 6717

The Health and Safety Executive is the Health and Safety Commission's major instrument. Through its inspectorates it enforces health and safety law in the majority of industrial premises. The Executive advises the Commission in its major task of laying down safety standards through regulations and practical guidance for many industrial processes. The Executive is also the licensing authority for nuclear installations and the reporting officer on the severity of nuclear incidents in Britain, and it is responsible for the Channel Tunnel Safety Authority.
Director-General, T. Walker
Deputy Director-General, D. C. T. Eves, CB

Director, Field Operations Unit, Dr A. Ellis
Director, Safety Policy, N. Starling
Director, Health Directorate, S. Caldwell
Director/Chief Inspector of the Nuclear Safety Directorate, L. Williams
Director, Strategy and Analytical Support Directorate, Dr P. Graham
Director, Hazardous Installations Directorate and Chief Scientist, Dr P. Davies
Director, Resource and Planning Directorate, R. Hiller
Director Railways Directorate, C. Norris

HIGHLANDS AND ISLANDS ENTERPRISE
Bridge House, 20 Bridge Street, Inverness IV1 1QR
Tel: 01463-234171; Fax: 01463-244469
Email: hie.general@hient.co.uk;
Web: www.hie.co.uk

Highlands and Islands Enterprise (HIE) was set up under the Enterprise and New Towns (Scotland) Act 1991. Its role is to design, direct and deliver enterprise development, training, environmental and social projects and services. HIE is made up of a strategic core body and ten Local Enterprise Companies (LECs) to which many of its individual functions are delegated.
Chairman, Dr J. Hunter
Chief Executive, J. R. S Cumming

HISTORIC BUILDINGS COUNCIL FOR SCOTLAND
Longmore House, Salisbury Place, Edinburgh EH9 1SH Tel: 0131-668 8799; Fax: 0131-668 8788

The Historic Buildings Council for Scotland is the advisory body to the Scottish Ministers on matters related to buildings of special architectural or historical interest and in particular to proposals for awards by them of grants for the repair of buildings of outstanding architectural or historical interest or lying within outstanding conservation areas.
Chairman, Sir Raymond Johnstone, CBE
Members, R. Cairns; Mrs P. Chalmers; Bishop M. Conti; Ms L. Davidson; Mrs A. Dundas-Bekker; Revd G. Forbes; Dr J. Frew; D. Gauci; M. Hopton; E. Jamieson; Mrs P. Robertson; Ms F. Sinclair
Secretary, Mrs S. Williamson

HISTORIC BUILDINGS COUNCIL FOR WALES
Cathays Park, Cardiff CF1 3NQ
Tel: 029-2050 0200; Fax: 029-20-82 6375

The Council's function is to advise the National Assembly for Wales on the historic buildings through Cadw: Welsh Historic Monuments, which is an executive agency of the Assembly.
Chairman, T. Lloyd, FSA
Members, Dr P. Morgan; Mrs S. Furse; Dr S. Unwin; Dr E. William; Miss E. Evans; Dr R. Wools
Secretary, Mrs J. Booker

HISTORIC ROYAL PALACES
Hampton Court Palace, East Molesey, Surrey
KT8 9AU Tel: 020-8781 9500; Fax: 020-8781 9754

Historic Royal Palaces is a non-departmental public body with charitable status. The Secretary of State for Culture, Media and Sport is still accountable to Parliament for the care, conservation and presentation of the palaces, which are owned by the Sovereign in right of the Crown. The chairman of the trustees is appointed by The Queen on the advice of the Secretary of State.

Historic Royal Palaces is responsible for the Tower of London, Hampton Court Palace, Kensington Palace State Apartments and the Royal Ceremonial Dress Collection, Kew Palace with Queen Charlotte's Cottage, and the Banqueting House, Whitehall.

TRUSTEES

Chairman, The Earl of Airlie, KT, GCVO, PC
Appointed by The Queen, The Lord Luce, GCVO, DL; Sir Michael Peat, KCVO; H. Roberts, CVO, FSA
Appointed by the Secretary of State, M. Herbert, CBE; Ms A. Heylin, OBE; S. Jones, LVO; Ms J. Sharman, CBE
Ex officio, Field Marshal the Lord Inge, GCB (*Constable of the Tower of London*)

OFFICERS

Chief Executive, A. Coppin
Director of Finance, Ms A. McLeish
Director of Human Resources, G. Josephs
Director, Palaces Group, H. Player
Resident Governor, HM Tower of London, Maj.-Gen. G. Field, CB, OBE
Retail Director, Ms A. Boyes
Marketing Director, D. Homan
Director of Conservation, Vacant

HOME-GROWN CEREALS AUTHORITY
Caledonia House, 223 Pentonville Road, London
N1 9HY Tel: 020-7520 3926; Fax: 020-7520 3954

Set up under the Cereals Marketing Act 1965, the HGCA Board consists of seven members representing UK cereal growers, seven representing dealers in, or processors of, grain and two independent members. HGCA's functions are to improve the production and marketing of UK-grown cereals and oilseeds through a research and development programme, to provide a market information service, and to promote UK cereals in export markets.
Chairman (part-time) (£23,576), A. Pike
Chief Executive, P. V. Biscoe

HONOURS SCRUTINY COMMITTEE
Ashley House, 2 Monck Street, London SW1P 2BQ
Tel: 020-7276 2770; Fax: 020-7276 2766

The functions of the Honours Scrutiny Committee (a committee of Privy Councillors) are set out in full in an Order of Council. The Prime Minister submits certain particulars to the Committee about persons proposed to be recommended for honour at any level other than a peerage for their political services, or for an honour at the level of Knight or Dame for non-political services. The Committee, after such enquiry as it thinks fit, reports to

the Prime Minister whether, so far as it believes, the political candidates are fit and proper persons to be recommended and for any non-political candidate, who may have made a political donation, whether this was a factor in the recommendation for an honour.
Chairman, The Lord Thomson of Monifieth, KT, PC
Members, The Baroness Dean of Thornton-le-Fylde, PC; The Lord Hurd of Westwell, CH, CBE
Secretary, Mrs P. G. W. Catto

HORSERACE TOTALISATOR BOARD
Tote House, 74 Upper Richmond Road, London
SW15 2SU Tel: 020-8874 6411; Fax: 020-8874 6107;
Web: www.tote.co.uk

The Horserace Totalisator Board (the Tote) was established by the Betting, Gaming and Lotteries Act 1963. Its function is to operate totalisators on approved racecourses in Great Britain, and it also provides on- and off-course cash and credit offices. Under the Horserace Totalisator and Betting Levy Board Act 1972, it is further empowered to offer bets at starting price (or other bets at fixed odds) on any sporting event, and under the Horserace Totalisator Board Act 1997 to take bets on any event, except the National Lottery. The chairman and members of the Board are appointed by the Secretary of State, Department of Culture, Media and Sport.

The Government announced in March 2000 that the Tote would be sold to a racing trust, subject to the necessary legislation going through Parliament.
Chairman, P. I. Jones
Chief Executive, W. J. Heaton

HOUSING CORPORATION
149 Tottenham Court Road, London W1T 7BN
Tel: 020-7393 2000; Fax: 020-7393 2111;
Email: enquiries@housingcorp.gsx.gov.uk;
Web: www.housingcorp.gov.uk

Established by Parliament in 1964, the Housing Corporation regulates, funds and promotes the proper performance of registered social landlords, which are non-profit making bodies run by voluntary committees. There are over 2,200 registered social landlords, most of which are housing associations, and they now provide homes for more than 1.5 million people. Under the Housing Act 1996, the Corporation's regulatory role was widened to embrace new types of landlords, in particular local housing companies. The Corporation is funded by the Department of Transport, Local Government and the Regions.
Chairman, The Rt. Hon. the Baroness Dean of Thornton-le-Fylde, PC
Deputy Chairman, E. Armitage
Chief Executive, Dr N. Perry

HUMAN FERTILISATION AND EMBRYOLOGY AUTHORITY
Paxton House, 30 Artillery Lane, London E1 7LS
Tel: 020-7377 5077; Fax: 020-7377 1871

The Human Fertilization and Embryology Authority (HFEA) was established under the Human Fertilisation and Embryology Act 1990. Its function is to license the following activities: the creation or use of embryos outside

338 **Government Departments and Public Offices**

the body in the provision of infertility treatment services; the use of donated gametes in infertility treatment; the storage of gametes or embryos; and research on human embryos. It maintains a confidential database of all such treatments and of egg and sperm donors, and provides information to patients, clinics and the public. The HFEA also keeps under review information about embryos and, when requested to do so, gives advice to the Secretary of State for Health.
Chairman, Lady Julia Tugendhat
Deputy Chairman, Mrs J. Denton
Members, Prof. Brenda Almond; Dr S. Avery; Prof T. Baldwin; Prof. D. Barlow; Prof. P. Brande; Prof. I. Cameron; J. Denton; Prof. Christine Gosden; Prof. A. Grubb; Prof. H. Leese; Prof. S. Lewis; Dr Anne McLaren; Dr S. Muhammed; Ms S. Nathan; Ms S. Nebhrajani; The Rt. Revd the Lord Bishop of Rochester; Dr F. Shenfield; Mrs L. Woods
Chief Executive, Dr M. Dalziel

HUMAN GENETICS COMMISSION
Area 652C, Skipton House, 80 London Road, London, SE1 6LH
Tel: 020-7972 1578; Fax: 020-7972 1717;
Email: hgc@doh.gov.uk; Web: www.hgc.gov.uk

The Human Genetics Commission was established in 1999, subsuming three previous advisory committees. Its remit is to give Ministers strategic advice on how developments in human genetics will impact on people and on health care, focusing in particular on the special and ethical implications.
Chairman, Baroness H. Kennedy of the Shaws, QC
Vice Chair, Prof. A. McCall Smith
Members Dr W. Albert, Prof. E. Anionwu; Prof. J. Burn; Ms R. Evans; Prof. P. Goodfellow; Dr H. Harris; Prof. J. Harris; Ms H. Newiss; Revd Dr J. Polkinghorne; Prof. M. Richards; Dr G. Samuels; Mr G. Watts; Mr P. Webb; Prof. V. von Heyningen; Ms R. Deech; Mrs J. Axelby; Dr Patrick Morrison; Dr R. Skinner
Head of Secretariat, Mark Bale

INDEPENDENT HOUSING OMBUDSMAN
Norman House, 105–109 Strand, London WC2R 0AA
Tel: 020-7836 3630; 0345-125973; Fax: 020-7836 3900; Email: ombudsman@ihos.org.uk;
Web: www.ihos.org.uk

The Independent Housing Ombudsman (IHO) was established in 1997 under the Housing Act 1996. The Ombudsman deals with complaints against registered social landlords (not including local authorities) and some private landlords. IHO is also managing the pilot Tenancy Deposit Scheme aimed at protecting the deposits of private tenants and resolving any disputes over their return quickly, cheaply and fairly.
Ombudsman, M. Biles
Chair of Board, K. Lampard
General Manager, L. Greenberg

INDEPENDENT INTERNATIONAL COMMISSION ON DECOMMISSIONING
Dublin Castle, Block M, Ship Street, Dublin 2
Tel: 00 353 1-478 0111; Fax: 00 353 1-478 0600
Rosepark House, Upper Newtownards Road, Belfast BT4 3NX
Tel: 028-90-48 8600; Fax: 028-9048 8601

The Commission was established by agreement between the British and Irish Governments in August 1997. Its objective is to facilitate the decommissioning of illegally-held firearms and explosives in accordance with the relevant legislation in both jurisdictions. Its members are appointed jointly by the two Governments; staff are appointed by the Commission. All are drawn from countries other than the UK and the Republic of Ireland.
Chairman, Gen. J. de Chastelain (Canada)
Commissioners, Brig. T. Nieminen (Finland); A. Sens (USA)
Chief of Staff, C. E. Garrard (Canada)

INDEPENDENT REVIEW SERVICE FOR THE SOCIAL FUND
4th Floor, Centre City Podium, 5 Hill Street, Birmingham B5 4UB
Tel: 0121-606 2100; Fax: 0121-606 2180

The Social Fund Commissioner is appointed by the Secretary of State for Work and Pensions. The Commissioner appoints Social Fund Inspectors, who provide an independent review of decisions made by Social Fund Officers in the Benefits Agency of the Department of Work and Pensions.
Social Fund Commissioner, Sir R. Tilt

INDEPENDENT TELEVISION COMMISSION
33 Foley Street, London W1P 7LB
Tel: 0845-601 3608; Fax: 020-7306 7800

The Independent Television Commission replaced the Independent Broadcasting Authority in 1991. The Commission is responsible for licensing and regulating all commercially funded television services broadcast from the UK. Members are appointed by the Secretary of State for Culture, Media and Sport.
Chairman, Sir Robin Biggam
Members, A. Balls, CB; C. Brendish; Ms B. Donoghue; Sir Michael Checkland; Ms J. Goffe; J. Kelly; C. Bharucha (*Member for Northern Ireland*); Prof. D. L. Morgan, D.Phil. (*Member for Wales*); Dr M. Shea, CVO (*Member for Scotland*)
Chief Executive, P. Hodgson
Secretary and Director of Administration, M. Redley

INDUSTRIAL INJURIES ADVISORY COUNCIL
6th Floor, The Adelphi, 1–11 John Adam Street, London WC2N 6HT
Tel: 020-7962 8066; Fax: 020-7712 2255;
Email: iiac@dial.pipex.com; Web: www.iiac.org.uk

The Industrial Injuries Advisory Council is a statutory body under the Social Security Administration Act 1992 which considers and advises the Secretary of State for

Social Security on regulations and other questions relating to industrial injuries benefits or their administration.
Chairman, Prof. A. J. Newman Taylor, OBE, FRCP
Secretary, H. Leigh

INFORMATION COMMISSIONER'S OFFICE
Wycliffe House, Water Lane, Wilmslow, Cheshire SK9 5AF Tel: 01625-545745; Fax: 01625-524510;
Email: data@dataprotection.gov.uk;
Web: www.dataprotection.gov.uk

The Data Protection Act 1998 sets rules for processing personal information and applies to some paper records as well as those held on computers.

The Data Protection Act works in two ways. It says those who record and use personal information (data controllers) must be open about how the information is used and must follow the eight principles of 'good information handling'. It also gives data subjects (individuals who are the subject of personal data) certain rights.

The Commissioner has a number of specific duties under the Act. She is given discretion in the manner in which she fulfils those duties and much of her work, and that of her staff involves informal advice and consultation with data controllers, and data subjects and the various bodies that represent them.

It is the Commissioner's duty to compile and maintain the register of data controllers, and provide facilities for members of the public to examine the register; promote observance of the data protection principles; and disseminate information to the public about the Act and her function under the Act. The Commissioner also has the power to produce codes of practice.

The Commissioner reports annually to parliament on the performance of her functions under the Act and has obligations to assess breaches of the Act.

The Information Commissioner is also responsible for Freedom of Information.
Commissioner, Mrs E. France

JOINT NATURE CONSERVATION COMMITTEE
Monkstone House, City Road, Peterborough PE1 1JY
Tel: 01733-562626; Fax: 01733-555948

The Committee was established under the Environmental Protection Act 1990. It advises the Government and others on UK and international nature conservation issues and disseminates knowledge on these subjects. It establishes common standards for the monitoring of nature conservation and research, and provides guidance to English Nature, Scottish Natural Heritage, the Countryside Council for Wales and the Department of the Environment for Northern Ireland.
Chairman, Sir Angus Stirling
Managing Director, D. Steer
Director, Dr M. A. Vincent

LAND REGISTRIES

HM LAND REGISTRY
Lincoln's Inn Fields, London WC2A 3PH
Tel: 020-7917 8888; Fax: 020-7955 0110

The registration of title to land was first introduced in England and Wales by the Land Registry Act 1862; HM Land Registry operates today under the Land Registration Acts 1925 to 1997. The object of registering title to land is to create and maintain a register of landowners whose title is guaranteed by the state and so to simplify the transfer, mortgage and other dealings with real property. Registration on sale is now compulsory throughout England and Wales. The register has been open to inspection by the public since 1990.

HM Land Registry is an executive agency and Trading Fund administered under the Lord Chancellor by the Chief Land Registrar.

HEADQUARTERS OFFICE

Chief Land Registrar and Chief Executive, P. Collis
Solicitor to Land Registry, C. J. West
Director of Corporate Services, E. G. Beardsall
Director of Operations, A. Howarth
Director of Practice and Legal Services, J. V. Timothy
Director of Information Systems, P. J. Smith, OBE
Director of Facilities, P. R. Laker
Director of Personnel, J. Hodder
Director of Finance, Ms H. Jackson
Director of Communication, A. Pemberton
Director of Service Development, P. Norman

COMPUTER SERVICES DIVISION

Burrington Way, Plymouth PL5 3LP
Tel: 01752-635600
Head of IT Services Division, P. A. Maycock
Head of IT Development Division, J. Formby
Head of IT Management Services, K. Deards

LAND CHARGES AND AGRICULTURAL CREDITS DEPARTMENT
Burrington Way, Plymouth PL5 3LP
Tel: 01752-635600
Superintendent of Land Charges, J. Hughes

DISTRICT LAND REGISTRIES

BIRKENHEAD (OLD MARKET) – Old Market House, Hamilton Street, Birkenhead CH41 5FL. Tel: 0151-473 1110. *District Land Registrar*, P. J. Brough
BIRKENHEAD (ROSEBRAE) – Rosebrae Court, Woodside Ferry Approach, Birkenhead CH41 6DU. Tel: 0151-472 6666. *District Land Registrar*, M. G. Garwood
COVENTRY – Leigh Court, Torrington Avenue, Newline Coventry CV4 9XZ. Tel: 024-7686 0860. *District Land Registrar*, T. H. O. Lewis
CROYDON – Sunley House, Bedford Park, Croydon CR9 3LE. Tel: 020-8781 9100. *District Land Registrar*, F. M. Twambley
DURHAM (BOLDON HOUSE) – Boldon House, Wheatlands Way, Pity Me, Durham DH1 5GJ. Tel: 0191-301 2345. *District Land Registrar*, R. B. Fearnley
DURHAM (SOUTHFIELD HOUSE) – Southfield House, Southfield Way, Durham DH1 5TR. Tel: 0191-301 3500. *District Land Registrar*, P. J. Timothy
GLOUCESTER – Twyver House, Bruton Way, Gloucester GL1 1DQ. Tel: 01452-511111. *District Land Registrar*, W. W. Budden
HARROW – Lyon House, Lyon Road, Harrow, Middx HA1 2EU. Tel: 020-8235 1181. *District Land Registrar*, C. Tate
KINGSTON UPON HULL – Earle House, Portland Street, Hull HU2 8JN. Tel: 01482-223244. *District Land Registrar*, S. R. Coveney

LANCASHIRE – Wrea Brook Court, Lytham Road, Warton, Preston PR4 1TE. Tel: 01772 836 700 *District Land Registrar*, Mrs L. Wallwork
LEICESTER – Westbridge Place, Leicester LE3 5DR. Tel: 0116-265 4000. *District Land Registrar*, Mrs J. A. Goodfellow
LYTHAM – Birkenhead House, East Beach, Lytham, Lancs FY8 5AB. Tel: 01253-849849. *District Land Registrar*, J. G. Cooper
NOTTINGHAM (EAST) – Robins Wood Road, Nottingham NG8 3RQ. Tel: 0115-906 5353. *District Land Registrar*, P. A. Brown
NOTTINGHAM (WEST) – Chalfont Drive, Nottingham NG8 3RN. Tel: 0115-935 1166. *District Land Registrar*, Ms A. M. Goss
PETERBOROUGH – Touthill Close, City Road, Peterborough PE1 1XN. Tel: 01733-288288. *District Land Registrar*, C. W. Martin
PLYMOUTH – Plumer House, Tailyour Road, Crownhill, Plymouth PL6 5HY. Tel: 01752-636000. *District Land Registrar*, A. J. Pain
PORTSMOUTH – St Andrew's Court, St Michael's Road, Portsmouth PO1 2JH. Tel: 023-9276 8888. *District Land Registrar*, S. R. Sehrawat
STEVENAGE – Brickdale House, Swingate, Stevenage, Herts SG1 1XG. Tel: 01438-788888. *District Land Registrar*, M. Croker
SWANSEA – Ty Bryn Glas, High Street, Swansea SA1 1PW. Tel: 01792-458877. *District Land Registrar*, G. A. Hughes
TELFORD – Parkside Court, Hall Park Way, Telford TF3 4LR. Tel: 01952-290355. *District Land Registrar*, A. M. Lewis
TUNBRIDGE WELLS – Forest Court, Forest Road, Tunbridge Wells, Kent TN2 5AQ. Tel: 01892-510015. *District Land Registrar*, G. R. Tooke
WALES – Ty Cwm Tawe, Phoenix Way, Llansamlet, Swansea SA7 9FQ. Tel: 01792-355000. *District Land Registrar*, T. M. Lewis
WEYMOUTH – Melcombe Court, 1 Cumberland Drive, Weymouth, Dorset DT4 9TT. Tel: 01305-363636. *District Land Registrar*, Mrs P. M. Reeson
YORK – James House, James Street, York YO10 3YZ. Tel: 01904-450000. *District Land Registrar*, Mrs R. F. Lovel

REGISTERS OF SCOTLAND
Meadowbank House, 153 London Road, Edinburgh EH8 7AU
Tel: 0131-659 6111; Fax: 0131-479 3688
Customer Service Centre: 0845-6070161
Registers of Scotland is the executive agency responsible for framing and maintaining records relating to property and other legal documents in Scotland. The agency holds 15 registers: two property registers (General Register of Sasines and Land Register of Scotland) and 13 chancery and judicial registers (Register of Deeds in the Books of Council and Session; Register of Protests; Register of Judgments; Register of Service of Heirs; Register of the Great Seal; Register of the Quarter Seal; Register of the Prince's Seal; Register of Crown Grants; Register of Sheriffs' Commissions; Register of the Cachet Seal; Register of Inhibitions and Adjudications; Register of Entails; and Register of Hornings).
Chief Executive and Keeper of the Registers of Scotland, A. W. Ramage
Deputy Keeper, A. G. Rennie
Managing Director, F. Manson

LAW COMMISSION
Conquest House, 37–38 John Street, London WC1N 2BQ Tel: 020-7453 1220; Fax: 020-7453 1297; Web: www.lawcom.gov.uk

The Law Commission was set up in 1965, under the Law Commissions Act 1965, to make proposals to the Government for the examination of the law in England and Wales and for its revision where it is unsuited to modern requirements, obscure, or otherwise unsatisfactory. It recommends to the Lord Chancellor programmes for the examination of different branches of the law and suggests whether the examination should be carried out by the Commission itself or by some other body. The Commission is also responsible for the preparation of Consolidation and Statute Law (Repeals) Bills.
Chairman, The Hon. Mr Justice Carnwath, CVO
Commissioners, C. Harpum; Miss D. Faber; Judge A. Wilkie, QC; Prof H. Beale
Secretary, M. W. Sayers

LAW OFFICERS' DEPARTMENTS
Legal Secretariat to the Law Officers, Attorney-General's Chambers, 9 Buckingham Gate, London SW1E 6JP Tel: 020-7271 2400; Fax: 020-7271 2430; Email: lslo@gtnet.gov.uk; Web: www.lslo.gov.uk
Attorney-General's Chambers, Royal Courts of Justice, Belfast BT1 3JY
Tel: 02890 546082; Fax: 02890-546049

The Law Officers of the Crown for England and Wales are the Attorney-General and the Solicitor-General. The Attorney-General, assisted by the Solicitor-General, is the chief legal adviser to the Government and is also ultimately responsible for all Crown litigation. He has overall responsibility for the work of the Law Officers' Departments (the Treasury Solicitor's Department, the Crown Prosecution Service, the Serious Fraud Office and the Legal Secretariat to the Law Officers). He has a specific statutory duty to superintend the discharge of their duties by the Director of Public Prosecutions (who heads the Crown Prosecution Service) and the Director of the Serious Fraud Office. The Director of Public Prosecutions for Northern Ireland is also responsible to the Attorney-General for the performance of his functions. The Attorney-General has additional responsibilities in relation to aspects of the civil and criminal law.
Attorney-General (*£90,125), The Lord Goldsmith, QC
Private Secretary, R. Cazalet
Parliamentary Private Secretary, M. Foster, DL, MP
Solicitor-General, Rt. Hon. Harriet Harman, QC
Legal Secretary (G2), D. Brammell
*Deputy Legal Secretary (G3), S. Parkinson
In addition to a parliamentary salary of £48,371

LEARNING AND SKILLS COUNCIL
Cheylesmore House, Quinton Road, Coventry, West Midlands, CV1 2WT

The Learning and Skills Council was established in April 2001 to replace the Further Education Funding and the Training and Enterprise Councils. It is a non-departmental public body that advises the government on future National Learning Targets and is responsible for the

allocation of £6 billion of public money. Its objective is to ensure that high quality post-16 provision is available to meet the needs of employers, individuals and communities. The LSC operates through 47 local departments, which work to promote the equality of opportunity in the workplace, aiming to ensure that the needs of the most disadvantaged in the labour market are met. These local departments in most cases have coterminous boundaries with Small business service franchises.
Chairman, B. Sanderson
Chief Executive, J. Harwood

LEGAL SERVICES COMMISSION
85 Gray's Inn Road, London WC1X 8TX
Tel: 020-7759 0000; Web: www.legalservices.gov.uk

On 1 April 2000, the Legal Aid Board was replaced by the Legal Services Commission (LSC), which runs two schemes - the civil scheme for funding civil cases as part of the Community Legal Service, and the Criminal Defence Service. The LSC has an important role in co-ordinating and working in a partnership with other funders of legal services, such as local authorities. The LSC also directly funds legal services for eligible clients.
The Criminal Defence Services provides access to advice, assistance and representation to people accused of a crime, as the interests of justice require.
Chairman, P. G. Birch, CBE
Members, S. Orchard, CBE (*Chief Executive*); M. Barnes, CBE; R. Buxton (*Director of Operations*); A. Edwards; P. Ely; B. Harvey (*Director of Resources and Supplier Development*); Ms J. Herzog; Mrs S. Hewitt; Ms Y. Mosquito; R. Penn; J. Shearer

LIBRARIES

THE BRITISH LIBRARY
96 Euston Road, London NW1 2DB
Tel: 020-7412 7000
The British Library was established in 1973. It is the UK's national library and occupies a key position in the library and information network. The Library aims to serve scholarship, research, industry, commerce and all other major users of information. Its services are based on collections which include over 18 million volumes, 1 million discs, and 55,000 hours of tape recordings. The Library is now based at two sites: London (St Pancras and Colindale) and Boston Spa, W. Yorks. Government grant-in-aid to the British Library in 2001-2002 is £86.2 million. The Library's sponsoring department is the Department for Culture, Media and Sport.
Access to the reading rooms at St Pancras is limited to holders of a British Library Reader's Pass; information about eligibility is available from the Reader Admissions Office. The exhibition galleries and public areas are open to all, free of charge.
Opening hours of services vary; some services may close for one week each year. Specific information should be checked by telephone.

BRITISH LIBRARY BOARD

Chairman, Dr J. M. Ashworth
Chief Executive and Deputy Chairman, L. Brindley
Part-time Members, H. Boyd-Carpenter, CVO; Prof. M. Anderson, OBE, FBA, FRSE; C. G. R. Leach, ph.D.; B.

Naylor; Prof. Jessica Rawson, CBE, FBA; J. Ritblat, FRICS; The Viscount Runciman of Doxford, CBE, FBA; P. Scherer; Prof. L. Colley, FRHist; S. Olswang

BRITISH LIBRARY, BOSTON SPA
Boston Spa, Wetherby, W. Yorks LS23 7BQ
Tel: 01937-546000

BRITISH LIBRARY, ST PANCRAS
96 Euston Road, London NW1 2DB
Tel: 020-7412 7000

PRESS AND PUBLIC RELATIONS. Tel: 020-7412 7111
EXHIBITIONS SERVICE AND VISITOR SERVICES. Tel: 020-7412 7332
EDUCATION SERVICE. Tel: 020-7412 7797
READER SERVICES AND COLLECTION DEVELOPMENT.
Reader Admissions. Tel: 020-7412 7677
Reader Services. Tel: 020-7412 7676
West European Collections, Slavonic and East European Collections, English Language Collections. Tel: 020-7412 7676
Newspaper Library, Colindale Avenue, London NW9 5HE. Tel: 020-7412 7353
NATIONAL PRESERVATION OFFICE. Tel: 020-7412 7612
SPECIAL COLLECTIONS. Tel: 020-7412 7513
Oriental and India Office Collections. Tel: 020-7412 7873
Western Manuscripts. Tel: 020-7412 7513
Map Library. Tel: 020-7412 7700
Music Library. Tel: 020-7412 7772
Philatelic Collections. Tel: 020-7412 7635
National Sound Archive. Tel: 020-7412 7440

SCIENCE, TECHNOLOGY AND BUSINESS
Science and Technology. Tel: 020-7412 7494/7496
British and EPO Patents. Tel: 020-7412 7919
Foreign Patents. Tel: 020-7412 7902
Business. Tel: 020-7412 7454
Social Policy Information Service. Tel: 020-7412 7536
LIBRARIES AND INFORMATION COMMISSION (former) – *see* Resource: The Council for Museums, Libraries and Archives

NATIONAL LIBRARY OF SCOTLAND
George IV Bridge, Edinburgh EH1 1EW
Tel: 0131-226 4531; Fax: 0131-622 4803

The Library, which was founded as the Advocates' Library in 1682, became the National Library of Scotland in 1925. It is funded by the Scottish Executive. It contains about seven million books and pamphlets, 20,000 current periodicals, 350 newspaper titles and 120,000 manuscripts. It has an unrivalled Scottish collection.
The Reading Room is for reference and research which cannot conveniently be pursued elsewhere. Admission is by ticket issued to an approved applicant. Opening hours: Reading Room, weekdays, 9.30–8.30 (Wednesday, 10–8.30); Saturday 9.30–1. Map Library, weekdays, 9.30–5 (Wednesday, 10–5); Saturday 9.30–1. Exhibition, weekdays, 10–5; Saturday 10–5; Sunday 2–5. Scottish Science Library, weekdays, 9.30–5 (Wednesday, 10–8.30).
Chairman of the Trustees, Prof. Michael Anderson, OBE, Ph.D., FBA, FRSE
Librarian and Secretary to the Trustees (G4), I. D. McGowan
Secretary of the Library (G6), M. C. Graham
Director of General Collections, C. Newton
Director of Special Collections, M. C. T. Simpson
Director of Public Services, A. M. Marchbank

NATIONAL LIBRARY OF WALES/ LLYFRGELL GENEDLAETHOL CYMRU

Aberystwyth SY23 3BU
Tel: 01970-632800; Fax: 01970-615709

The National Library of Wales was founded by royal charter in 1907, and is funded by the National Assembly for Wales. It contains about four million printed books, 40,000 manuscripts, four million deeds and documents, numerous maps, prints and drawings, and a sound and moving image collection. It specialises in manuscripts and books relating to Wales and the Celtic peoples. It is the repository for pre-1858 Welsh probate records, manorial records and tithe documents, and certain legal records. Readers' room open weekdays, 9.30–6 (Saturday 9.30–5); closed first week of October. Admission by reader's ticket to the Reading Rooms but free entry to the exhibition programme.

President, Dr R. Brinley Jones
Librarian (G4), A. M. W. Green
Heads of Departments (G6), M. W. Mainwaring (*Corporate Services*); G. Jenkins (*Collection Services*); Dr W. R. M. Griffiths (*Public Services*)

LIGHTHOUSE AUTHORITIES

CORPORATION OF TRINITY HOUSE

Trinity House, Tower Hill, London EC3N 4DH
Tel: 020-7481 6900; Fax: 020-7480 7662

Trinity House, the first general lighthouse and pilotage authority in the kingdom, was granted its first charter by Henry VIII in 1514. The Corporation is the general lighthouse authority for England, Wales and the Channel Islands and maintains 72 lighthouses, 13 major floating aids to navigation (e.g. light vessels) and more than 420 buoys. The Corporation also has certain statutory jurisdiction over aids to navigation maintained by local harbour authorities and is responsible for dealing with wrecks dangerous to navigation, except those occurring within port limits or wrecks of HM ships.

The Trinity House Lighthouse Service is maintained out of the General Lighthouse Fund which is provided from light dues levied on ships calling at ports of the UK and the Republic of Ireland. The Corporation is also a deep-sea pilotage authority and a charitable organisation.

The affairs of the Corporation are controlled by a board of Elder Brethren and the Secretary. A separate board, which comprises Elder Brethren, senior staff and outside representatives, currently controls the Lighthouse Service. The Elder Brethren also act as nautical assessors in marine cases in the Admiralty Division of the High Court of Justice.

ELDER BRETHREN

Master, HRH The Prince Philip, Duke of Edinburgh, KG KT
Deputy Master, Rear-Adm. P. B. Rowe, CBE, LVO
Wardens, Capt. C. M. C. Stewart; Sir Brian Shaw
Elder Brethren, HRH The Prince of Wales, KG, KT; HRH The Duke of York, CVO, ADC; Capt. Sir David Tibbits, DSC, RN; Capt. D. A. G. Dickins; Capt. J. E. Bury; Capt. J. A. N. Bezant, DSC, RD, RNR (retd.); Capt. D. J. Cloke; Capt. Sir Miles Wingate, KCVO; The Rt. Hon. Sir Edward Heath, KG, MBE, Capt. I. R. C. Saunders; Capt. P. F. Mason, CBE; Capt.T. Woodfield, OBE; The Lord Simon of Glaisdale; Capt. D. T. Smith, RN; Cdr. Sir Robin Gillett, Bt., GBE, RD, RNR; Capt. Sir Malcolm

Edge, KCVO; The Lord Cuckney; Capt. D. J. Orr; The Lord Carrington, KG, GCMG, CH, MC, PC; The Lord Mackay of Clashfern, KT, PC; Sir Adrian Swire; The Lord Sterling of Plaistow, CBE, RNR; Cdr. M. J. Rivett-Carnac, RN; Adm. Sir Jock Slater, GCB, LVO, ADC; Capt. J. R. Burton-Hall, RD; Capt. I. Gibb, FRSA; Cdre P. J. Melson, CBE, RN; Capt. D. C. Glass

OFFICERS

Secretary, R. F. Dobb
Director of Finance, K. W. Clark
Director of Engineering, D. Golden
Director of Administration, D. I. Brewer
Head of Human Resources, P. F. Morgan
Legal and Insurance Manager, J. D. Price
Navigation Manager, Mrs K. Hossain
Head of Management Services, S. J. W. Dunning
Deputy Director of Engineering, P. N. Hyde
Senior Inspector of Shipping, J. R. Dunnett
Media and Communication Officer, H. L. Cooper

NORTHERN LIGHTHOUSE BOARD

84 George Street, Edinburgh EH2 3DA
Tel: 0131-473 3100; Fax: 0131-220 2093;
Email: enquiries@nlb.org.uk; Web: www.nlb.org.uk

The Lighthouse Board is the general lighthouse authority for Scotland and the Isle of Man. The board owes its origin to an Act of Parliament passed in 1786. At present the Commissioners operate under the Merchant Shipping Act 1995 and are 19 in number.

The Commissioners control 83 major automatic lighthouses, 117 minor lights and many lighted and unlighted buoys. They have a fleet of two motor vessels.

COMMISSIONERS

The Lord Advocate; the Solicitor-General for Scotland; the Lord Provosts of Edinburgh, Glasgow and Aberdeen; the Provost of Inverness; the Convener of Argyll and Bute Council; the Sheriffs-Principal of North Strathclyde, Tayside, Central and Fife, Grampian, Highlands and Islands, South Strathclyde, Dumfries and Galloway, Lothians and Borders, and Glasgow and Strathkelvin; Capt. D. M. Cowell; Adm. Sir Michael Livesay, KCB; The Lord Maclay; P. MacKay, CB; Capt. K. MacLeod

OFFICERS

Chief Executive, Capt. J. B. Taylor, RN
Director of Finance, D. Gorman
Director of Engineering, M. Waddell
Director of Operations and Navigational Requirements, P. J. Christmas

---

LOCAL COMMISSIONERS

COMMISSION FOR LOCAL ADMINISTRATION IN ENGLAND

21 Queen Anne's Gate, London SW1H 9BU
Tel: 020-7915 3210; Fax: 020-7233 0396

Local Commissioners (local government ombudsmen) are responsible for investigating complaints from members of the public against local authorities (but not town and parish councils); English Partnerships (planning matters only); Housing Action Trusts; education appeal committees; police authorities and certain other authorities. The Commissioners are appointed by the Crown on the

Mental Health Act Commission 343

recommendation of the Secretary of State for Transport, Local Government, and the Regions.

Certain types of action are excluded from investigation, including personnel matters and commercial transactions unless they relate to the purchase or sale of land. Complaints can be sent direct to the Local Government Ombudsman or through a councillor, although the Local Government Ombudsman will not consider a complaint unless the council has had an opportunity to investigate and reply to a complainant.

A free leaflet 'Complaint about the council? How to complain to the Local Government Ombudsman' is available from the Commission's office.

Chairman and Chief Executive of the Commission and Local Commissioner (£132,603), E. B. C. Osmotherly, CB
Vice-Chairman and Local Commissioner (£100,420), Mrs P. A. Thomas
Local Commissioner (£99,420), J. R. White
Member (ex officio), The Parliamentary Commissioner for Administration
Deputy Chief Executive and Secretary (£62,658), N. J. Karney

COMMISSION FOR LOCAL ADMINISTRATION IN WALES

Derwen House, Court Road, Bridgend CF31 1BN
Tel: 01656-661325; Fax: 01656-658317;
Email: enquiries@ombudsman-wales.org;
Web: www.ombudsman-wales.org

The Local Commissioner for Wales has similar powers to the Local Commissioners in England, but by the end of 2001 he will also have additional powers (similar to the Standards Board for England) to investigate allegations made against local authority members of misconduct. The Commissioner is appointed by the Crown on the recommendation of the Secretary of State for Wales. A free leaflet 'Your Local Government Ombudsman in Wales' is available from the Commissioners office.

Local Commissioner, E. R. Moseley
Secretary, D. Bowen
Member (ex officio), The Parliamentary Commissioner for Administration

COMMISSIONER FOR LOCAL ADMINISTRATION IN SCOTLAND

23 Walker Street, Edinburgh EH3 7HX
Tel: 0131-225 5300; Fax: 0131-225 9495;
Email: commissioner@ombudslgscot.org.uk;
Web: www.ombudslgscot.org.uk

The Local Commissioner for Scotland has similar powers to the Local Commissioners in England, and is appointed by the Crown on the recommendation of the First Minister.

Local Commissioner, I. F. Smith
Deputy Commissioner and Secretary, Ms J. H. Renton

LONDON REGIONAL TRANSPORT

55 Broadway, London SW1H 0BD
Tel: 020-7222 5600

Subject to the financial objectives and principles approved by the Secretary of State for Transport, Local Government and the Regions, London Regional Transport has a general duty to provide or secure the provision of public transport services for Greater London.

Chairman (non-executive), B. Kiley

Member, and Managing Director of London Underground Ltd, D. Smith

LORD GREAT CHAMBERLAIN'S OFFICE

House of Lords, London SW1A 0PW
Tel: 020-7219 3100; Fax: 020-7219 2500

The Lord Great Chamberlain is a Great Officer of State, the office being hereditary since the grant of Henry I to the family of De Vere, Earls of Oxford. It is now a joint hereditary office between the Cholmondeley and Carington families. The Lord Great Chamberlain is responsible for the royal apartments of the Palace of Westminster, i.e. The Queen's Robing Room, the Royal Gallery and, in conjunction with the Lord Chancellor and the Speaker, Westminster Hall. The Lord Great Chamberlain has particular responsibility for the internal administrative arrangements within the House of Lords for State Openings of Parliament.

Lord Great Chamberlain, The Marquess of Cholmondeley
Secretary to the Lord Great Chamberlain, Lt.-Gen. Sir Michael Willcocks, KCB
Clerks to the Lord Great Chamberlain, Ms J. Perodeau; Ms A. Feuz

LORD PRIVY SEAL'S OFFICE

Privy Council Office, 68 Whitehall, London SW1A 2AT Tel: 020-7270 3000;
Web: www.cabinetoffice.gov.uk

The Lord Privy Seal is a member of the Cabinet and Leader of the House of Lords. He has no departmental portfolio, but is a member of a number of Cabinet committees. He is responsible to the Prime Minister for the organisation of Government business in the House and has a responsibility to the House itself to advise it on procedural matters and other difficulties which arise.

Lord Privy Seal, Leader of the House of Lords, The Lord Williams of Mostyn, QC, PC
Principal Private Secretary, P. Richardson
Private Secretary (House of Lords), Miss M. Robertson

MENTAL HEALTH ACT COMMISSION

Maid Marian House, 56 Hounds Gate, Nottingham NG1 6BG Tel: 0115-943 7100; Fax: 0115-943 7101

The Mental Health Act Commission was established in 1983. Its functions are to keep under review the operation of the Mental Health Act 1983; to visit and meet patients detained under the Act; to investigate complaints falling within the Commission's remit; to operate the consent to treatment safeguards in the Mental Health Act; to publish a biennial report on its activities; to monitor the implementation of the Code of Practice; and to advise Ministers. Commissioners are appointed by the Secretary of State for Health.

Chairman, Miss M. Clayton
Vice-Chairman, Prof. R. Williams
Chief Executive, P. Hampshire

MILLENNIUM COMMISSION
Portland House, Stag Place, London SW1E 5EZ
Tel: 020-7880 2001; Fax: 020-7880 2000;
Email: info@millennium.gov.uk

The Millennium Commission was established in February 1994 and is accountable to the Department for Culture, Media and Sport. It is an independent body which distributes money from National Lottery proceeds to projects to mark the millennium.
Chairman, The Rt. Hon. T. Jowell, MP
Members, Dr H. Couper; The Earl of Dalkeith; Ms F. Benjamin; The Rt. Hon. M. Heseltine, MP; Ms J. Donovan, CBE; M. D' Ancona. Lord Gletoran
Director, M. O'Connor

MUSEUMS

THE BRITISH MUSEUM
Great Russell Street, London WC1B 3DG
Tel: 020-7323 8000; Fax: 020-7323 8616

The British Museum houses the national collection of antiquities, ethnography, coins and paper money, medals, and prints and drawings. The British Museum may be said to date from 1753, when Parliament approved the holding of a public lottery to raise funds for the purchase of the collections of Sir Hans Sloane and the Harleian manuscripts, and for their proper housing and maintenance. The building (Montagu House) was opened in 1759. The present buildings were erected between 1823 and the present day, and the original collection has increased to its present dimensions by gifts and purchases. Total government grant-in-aid for 2000–2001 was £34.8 million.

BOARD OF TRUSTEES

Appointed by the Sovereign, HRH The Duke of Gloucester, KG, GCVO
Appointed by the Prime Minister, C. Allen-Jones; H. Askari; N. Barber; Dame Gillian Beer, FBA; Sir John Boyd, KCMG; Sir John Browne, FREng.; The Rt. Hon. Countess of Dalkeith; Sir Michael Hopkins, CBE, RA, RIBA; Dr J. Montagu, FBA; Sir Claus Moser, KCB, CBE, FBA; Sir Joseph Hotung; Prof. M. Kemp, FBA; Prof. Barry Cunliffe, CBE; D. Lindsell; C. McCall, QC; Sir Martin Rees, FRS, Dr Anna Ritchie; E. Salama
Nominated by the Learned Societies, Prof. Jean Thomas, CBE (*Royal Society*); T. Phillips, RA (*Royal Academy*); Sir Keith Thomas, FBA (*British Academy*)
Appointed by the Trustees of the British Museum, G. C. Greene, CBE (*Chairman*); Sir David Attenborough, CH, CVO, CBE, FRS; Dr Jennifer Montagu, FBA; Sir Claus Moser, KCB, CBE, FBA; J. Tusa

OFFICERS

Director, Dr R. G. W. Anderson, FRSC, FSA
Managing Director, Ms S. Taverne
Director of Marketing and Public Affairs, Dr C. Homden
Director of Finance and Resources, C. Herring
Secretary, T. Doubleday
Head of Exhibitions, G. A. L. House
Head of Media Relations, A. E. Hamilton
Head of Design, Miss M. Hall, OBE
Head of Education, J. F. Reeve
Director of Operations, C. E. I. Jones

Head of Building Development and Planning, K. T. Stannard
Head of Building Management, T. R. A. Giles
Head of Finance, D. Allcorn
Director of Human Resources, I. Black ,
Head of Visitor Services, Ms L. Lee
Head of Membership Development, Ms S. Carthew
Head of Marketing Communications, M. Ladds

KEEPERS

Senior Keeper, Dr B. J. Mack
Keeper of Prints and Drawings, A. V. Griffiths
Keeper of Coins and Medals, Dr A. M. Burnett
Keeper of Egyptian Antiquities, W. V. Davies
Keeper of Ancient Near East Antiquities, Dr J. E. Curtis
Keeper of Greek and Roman Antiquities, Dr D. J. R. Williams
Keeper of Medieval and Modern Europe, J. Cherry
Keeper of Prehistory and Early Europe, Dr C. Malone
Keeper of Japanese Antiquities, V. T. Harris
Keeper of Oriental Antiquities, R. J. Knox
Keeper of Ethnography, Dr B. Durrans
Keeper of Scientific Research, Dr S. G. E. Bowman
Keeper of Conservation, W. A. Oddy

IMPERIAL WAR MUSEUM
Lambeth Road, London SE1 6HZ
Tel: 020-7416 5320; Fax: 020-7416 5374

The Museum, founded in 1917, illustrates and records all aspects of the two world wars and other military operations involving Britain and the Commonwealth since 1914. It was opened in its present home, formerly Bethlem Hospital or Bedlam, in 1936. The Museum also administers *HMS Belfast* in the Pool of London, Duxford Airfield near Cambridge and the Cabinet War Rooms in Westminster.
Government grant-in-aid for 2001-2002 is £11.347 million.

OFFICERS

Director-General, R. W. K. Crawford
Secretary and Director of Finance, J. Card
Assistant Directors, D. A. Needham (*Administration*); Miss K. J. Carmichael (*Collections*); G. Marsh (*Planning and Development*)
Director of Duxford Airfield, E. O. Inman, OBE
Director of HMS Belfast, E. J. Wenzel

KEEPERS

Public Services Division, C. Dowling, D.Phil.
Department of Documents, R. W. A. Suddaby
Department of Exhibits and Firearms, D. J. Penn
Department of Printed Books, R. Golland
Department of Art, Miss A. H. Weight
Department of Film, R. B. N. Smither
Department of Sound Records, Mrs M. A. Brooks
Department of Marketing and Trading, Miss A. Godwin
Curator of the Cabinet War Rooms, P. Reed

MUSEUM OF LONDON
London Wall, London EC2Y 5HN
Tel: 020-7600 3699; Fax: 020-7600 1058;
Email: info@museumoflondon.org.uk;
Web: www.museumoflondon.org.uk

The Museum of London illustrates the history of London from prehistoric times to the present day. It opened in 1976 and is based on the amalgamation of the former Guildhall Museum and London Museum. The Museum is controlled by a Board of Governors, appointed (nine each) by the Government and the Corporation of London. The

Museums 345

Museum is currently funded jointly by the Department for Culture, Media and Sport and the Corporation of London, each contributing £4.519 million in 2000–2001.
Chairman of Board of Governors, R. Hambro
Director, Dr S. Thurley

NATIONAL ARMY MUSEUM

Royal Hospital Road, London SW3 4HT
Tel: 020-7730 0717; Fax: 020-7823 6573;
Web: www.national-army-museum.ac.uk;
Email: info@national-army-museum.ac.uk

The National Army Museum covers the history of five centuries of the British Army. It was established by royal charter in 1960. Total Government grant-in-aid for 1999–2000 was £4.5 million.
Director, I. G. Robertson
Assistant Directors, D. K. Smurthwaite; A. J. Guy; P. B. Boyden

NATURAL HISTORY MUSEUM

Cromwell Road, London SW7 5BD
Tel: 020-7942 5000

The Natural History Museum originates from the natural history departments of the British Museum, which grew extensively during the 19th century; in 1860 the natural history collection was moved from Bloomsbury to a new location. Part of the site of the 1862 International Exhibition in South Kensington was acquired for the new museum, and the Museum opened to the public in 1881. In 1963 the Natural History Museum became completely independent with its own board of trustees. The Walter Rothschild Zoological Museum, Tring, bequeathed by the second Lord Rothschild, has formed part of the Museum since 1938. The Geological Museum merged with the Natural History Museum in 1985. Total Government grant-in-aid for 2001-2002 is £32.377 million.

BOARD OF TRUSTEES

Appointed by the Prime Minister, The Lord Oxburgh, KBE, Ph.D., FRS (*Chairman*); Sir Crispin Tickell, GCMG, KCVO; Dame Anne McLaren, DBE, FRS, FRCOG; Sir Richard Sykes, FRS; Miss J. Mayhew; Ms J. Bennett; Prof. M. Hassell, FRS; O. Stocken
Appointed by the Secretary of State for Culture, Media and Sport, Prof. C. Leaver, CBE, FRS,
Appointed by the Trustees of the Natural History Museum, The Lord Palumbo; Prof. Sir K. O'Nions, FRS; Prof. Linda Partridge, FRS, FRSE

SENIOR STAFF

Director, Dr N. R. Chalmers
Director of Science, Prof. P. Henderson, D.Phil
Head of Audit and Review, D. Thorpe
Keeper of Botany, Dr R. Bateman
Director of Development and Marketing, Ms S. Ament
Keeper of Entomology, Dr R. Vane-Wright
Director of Estates, K. Rellis
Head of Education and Exhibitions, Dr G. Clarke
Director of Finance, N. Greenwood
Head of Library and Information Services, Dr R. G. Lester
Keeper of Mineralogy, Prof. A. Fleet
Keeper of Palaeontology, Prof. S. K. Donovan
Director of Human Resources, D. Hill
Head of Visitor Services, D. Candlin
Keeper of Zoology, Prof. P. Rainbow
Policy and Planning Co-ordinator, vacant
Director, Tring Zoological Museum, Mrs T. Wild

NATIONAL MARITIME MUSEUM

Greenwich, London SE10 9NF
Tel: 020-8858 4422; Fax: 020-8312 6632

Established by Act of Parliament in 1934, the National Maritime Museum illustrates the maritime history of Great Britain in the widest sense, underlining the importance of the sea and its influence on the nation's power, wealth, culture, technology and institutions. The Museum is in three groups of buildings in Greenwich Park – the main building, the Queen's House (built by Inigo Jones, 1616–35) and the Royal Observatory (including Wren's Flamsteed House). In May 1999, a £20 million Heritage Lottery supported project opened 16 new galleries in a glazed courtyard in the Museum's west wing. Total Government grant-in-aid for 1999–2000 was £10.425 million.
Director, R. Clare

NATIONAL MUSEUMS AND GALLERIES ON MERSEYSIDE

PO Box 33, 127 Dale Street, Liverpool L69 3LA
Tel: 0151-207 0001; Fax: 0151-478 4790

The Board of Trustees of the National Museums and Galleries on Merseyside is responsible for the Liverpool Museum, the Merseyside Maritime Museum (incorporating HM Customs and Excise National Museum), the Museum of Liverpool Life, the Lady Lever Art Gallery, the Walker Art Gallery and Sudley House, and the Conservation Centre. Total Government grant-in-aid for 2001–2002 is £13.6 million.
Chairman of the Board of Trustees, D. McDonnell
Director, Dr David Fleming
Keeper of Art Galleries, J. Treuherz
Keeper of Conservation, A. Durham
Keeper, Liverpool Museum, Ms L. Knowles
Keeper, Merseyside Maritime Museum and Museum of Liverpool Life, M. Stammers

NATIONAL MUSEUMS AND GALLERIES OF WALES/AMGUEDDFEYDD AC ORIELAU CENEDLAETHOL CYMRU

Cathays Park, Cardiff CF10 3NP
Tel: 029-2039 7951; Fax: 029-2037 3219;
Email: post@nmgw.ac.uk; Web: www//nmgw.ac.uk

The National Museums and Galleries of Wales comprise the National Museum and Gallery Cardiff, the Museum of Welsh Life St Fagans, Big Pit National Museum of Wales, Blaenafon, the Roman Legionary Museum Caerleon, Turner House Gallery Penarth, the Welsh Slate Museum Llanberis, the Segontium Roman Museum Caernarfon and the Museum of the Welsh Woollen Industry Drefach, Felindre. Total funding from the National Assembly for Wales for 2000–2001 is £16 million.
President, M. C. T. Prichard, CBE
Vice-President, R. G. Thomas, OBE

OFFICERS

Director, A. Southall
Directors, Dr E. William (*Collections and Education and Deputy Director*); J. Williams-Davies (*Museum of Welsh Life*); M. Tooby (*National Museum and Gallery*); R. Gwyn (*Strategic Communications*); M. Richards (*Resource Planning*)
Keeper of Geology, M. G. Bassett, Ph.D.
Keeper of Bio-diversity and Systematic Biology, Dr P. G. Oliver
Keeper of Art, O. Fairclough
Keeper of Archaeology, R. Brewer

Manager, Roman Legionary Museum, B. Lewis
Keeper in Charge, Turner House Gallery, O. Fairclough
Keeper, Welsh Slate Museum and Segontium Roman Museum, D. Roberts, Ph.D.
Manager, Museum of the Welsh Woollen Industry, S. Moss
Manager, Big Pit National Museum of Wales, P. Walker

NATIONAL MUSEUMS OF SCOTLAND

Chambers Street, Edinburgh EH1 1JF
Tel: 0131-225 7534; Fax: 0131-220 4819

The National Museums of Scotland comprise the Royal Museum of Scotland, the Scottish United Services Museum, the Museum of Scottish County Life, the Museum of Flight, Shambellie House Museum of Costume and the Museum of Scotland. Total funding from the Scottish Executive for 2001–2002 is £17.0 million.

BOARD OF TRUSTEES

Chairman, Sir Robert Smith, FSA Scot.
Members, Prof. T. Devine; Dr L. Glasser, MBE, FRSE; G. Johnston, OBE, TD; Ms C. Macaulay; N. McIntosh, CBE; Mrs N. Mahal; Prof. A. Manning, OBE; Prof. J. Murray; Sir William Purves, CBE, DSO; Dr A. Ritchie, OBE; I. Smith; The Lord Wilson of Tillyorn, GCMG

OFFICERS

Director, vacant
Acting Director, Miss D. Idiens, FRSA, FSA Scot.
Development Director, C. McCallum
Keeper of Archaeology, D. V. Clarke, Ph.D., FSA, FSA Scot.
Keeper of Geology and Zoology, M. Shaw, D.Phil.
Keeper of Social and Technological History, G. Sprott
Head of Public Affairs, Ms M. Bryden
Head of Museum Services, S. R. Elson, FSA Scot.
Acting Keeper of History and Applied Art, Dr D. Caldwell, FSA

RESOURCE: THE COUNCIL FOR MUSEUMS, ARCHIVES AND LIBRARIES

16 Queen Anne's Gate, London SW1H 9AA
Tel: 020-72733 1444; Fax: 020-72733 1404;
Web: www.resource.gov.uk

On 1 April 2000, the Museums and Galleries Commission and the Library and Information Commission merged to form Resource: The Council for Museums, Archives and Libraries. This new strategic agency will work with museums, libraries and archives across the UK.
Chairman, Lord Evans
Chief Executive, N. Mackay
Board Members, L. Grossman; V. Gray; M. Wood; A. Chowdhury; Dr M. Crozier; V. Griffiths; N. Hodgson; M. Jones; N. MacGregor; E. J. Ryder; M. Stevenson; Prof. L. Young; A. Watkin; D. Barrie

ROYAL AIR FORCE MUSEUM

Grahame Park Way, London NW9 5LL
Tel: 020-8205 2266; Fax: 020-8200 1751

Situated on the former airfield at RAF Hendon, the Museum illustrates the development of aviation from before the Wright brothers to the present-day RAF. Total Government grant-in-aid for 2001–2002, including funding for the aerospace museum at Cosford, is £5.245 million.
Director, Dr M. A. Fopp
Assistant Directors, H. Hall; A. Wright
Senior Keeper, P. Elliott

THE SCIENCE MUSEUM

Exhibition Road, London SW7 2DD
Tel: 0870 870 4868; Fax: 020-7942 4447

The Science Museum, part of the National Museum of Science and Industry, houses the national collections of science, technology, industry and medicine. The Museum began as the science collection of the South Kensington Museum and first opened in 1857. In 1883 it acquired the collections of the Patent Museum and in 1909 the science collections were transferred to the new Science Museum, leaving the art collections with the Victoria and Albert Museum. The Wellcome Wing was opened in July 2000.

Some of the Museum's commercial aircraft, agricultural machinery, and road and rail transport collections are at Wroughton, Wilts. The National Museum of Science and Industry also incorporates the National Railway Museum, York and the National Museum of Photography, Film and Television, Bradford.

Total Government grant-in-aid for 2000–1 was £24,329 million.

BOARD OF TRUSTEES

Chairman, Sir Peter Williams, CBE, Ph.D., FREng.
Members, HRH The Duke of Kent, KG, GCMG, GCVO, ADC; Dr M. Archer; Prof. Anne Dowling; G. Dyke; Prof. Susan Greenfield; Dr Ann Grocock; Mrs A. Higham, OBE; Mrs J. Kennedy, OBE; Dr N. Myhrvold; Dame Bridget Ogilvie, DBE; The Lord Puttnam, CBE; Sir Michael Quinlan, GCB; D. E. Rayner, CBE; Prof. M. Richards; M. G. Smith; Sir Christopher Wates

OFFICERS

Director, Dr. L. Sharp
Head of Personnel and Legal Services, A. Mather
Head of Finance, Ms A. Caine
Head of Information Systems, S. Gordon
Head of Estates, J. Bevin
Assistant Director and Head of Collections Division, D. Swade
Head of Physical Sciences and Engineering Group (acting), Dr A. Q. Morton
Head of Life and Communications Technologies Group, Dr R. F. Bud
Head of Collections Management Group, Dr S. Keene
Assistant Director and Head of Public Affairs Division, C. M. Pemberton
Head of Corporate Relations, F. Kirk
Head of Commercial Development, M. Sullivan
Head of Marketing and Communications, R. Hopson
Head of Wellcome Wing Commercial and Access, B. Jones
Assistant Director, Wellcome Wing Project Director and Head of Science Communication Division, Prof. J. R. Durant
Head of Education and Programmes, Dr R. Jackson
Head of Exhibition and Wellcome Wing Content, Dr G. Farmelo
Head of Design, T. Molloy
Head of National Railway Museum, A. Scott
Head of National Museum of Photography, Film and Television, Ms A. Nevill

VICTORIA AND ALBERT MUSEUM

Cromwell Road, London SW7 2RL
Tel: 020-7942 2000

The Victoria and Albert Museum is the national museum of fine and applied art and design. It descends directly from the Museum of Manufactures, which opened in Marlborough House in 1852 after the Great Exhibition of 1851. The Museum was moved in 1857 to become part of the South Kensington Museum. It was renamed the Victoria and Albert Museum in 1899. It also houses the National Art Library and Print Room.

The Museum administers three branch museums: the National Museum of Childhood in Bethnal Green, the Theatre Museum in Covent Garden, and the Wellington Museum at Apsley House. The museum in Bethnal Green was opened in 1872 and the building is the most important surviving example of the type of glass and iron construction used by Paxton for the Great Exhibition. Total Government grant-in-aid for 2001–2002 is £32.387 million.

BOARD OF TRUSTEES

Chairman, Paula Ridley
Deputy Chairman, J. Scott, CBE, FSA
Members, Prof M. Buck; Penelope, Viscountess Cobham; R. Dickins CBE; Sir Christopher Frayling, Ph.D.; Sir Terence Heiser, GCB; Mrs J. Gordon Clark; Mrs A. Heseltine; R. Mather; P. Rogers; A. Snow; Sir Christopher White, CVO, FBA
Acting Secretary to the Board of Trustees, J.F.Rider

OFFICERS

Director, M. Jones, MA
Assistant Director, J. W. Close
Senior Chief Curator, Dr D. Swallow
Chief Curator, Ceramics and Glass, Dr O. Watson
Director of Collections, vacant
Director of Collections Services, vacant
Head of Conservation, Dr J. Ashley-Smith
Director of Corporate Communications, vacant
Director of Development, Mrs L. Blythe
Director of Facilities Management, vacant
Chief Curator, Far Eastern, Miss R. Kerr
Director of Finance and Central Services, Miss R. M. Sykes
Chief Curator, Furniture and Woodwork, C. Wilk
Chief Curator, Indian and South-East Asian, R. Crill
Head of Information Systems Services, I. Croxford
Director of Learning and Visitor Services, D. Anderson, OBE
Director of Major Projects, Mrs G. F. Miles
Chief Curator, Metalwork, Silver and Jewellery, vacant
Chief Librarian, National Art Library, vacant
Director of Personnel, Mrs G. Henchley
Chief Curator, Prints, Drawings and Paintings, Miss S. B. Lambert
Head of Records and Collections Services, A. Seal
Acting Head of Research, C. Sargentson
Chief Curator, Sculpture, Dr P. E. D. Williamson
Acting Chief Curator, Textiles and Dress, L. Parry
Managing Director, V. and A. Enterprises Ltd, M. Cass
Director of the National Museum of Childhood, Ms D. Lees
Director of the Theatre Museum, Miss M. Benton
Director of the Wellington Museum, Miss A. Robinson

NATIONAL AUDIT OFFICE
157–197 Buckingham Palace Road, London
SW1W 9SP
Tel: 020-7798 7000; Fax: 020-7828 3774
Audit House, 23–24 Park Place, Cardiff CF1 3BA
Tel: 02920-378661; Fax: 02920 678501;
Email: enqiries@nao.gsi.gov.uk
Web: www.nao.gov.uk

The National Audit Office came into existence under the National Audit Act 1983 to replace and continue the work of the former Exchequer and Audit Department. The Act reinforced the Office's total financial and operational

independence from the Government and brought its head, the Comptroller and Auditor-General, into a closer relationship with Parliament as an officer of the House of Commons.

The National Audit Office provides independent information, advice and assurance to Parliament and the public about all aspects of the financial operations of Government departments and many other bodies receiving public funds. It does this by examining and certifying the accounts of these organisations and by regularly publishing reports to Parliament on the results of its value for money investigations of the economy, efficiency and effectiveness with which public resources have been used. The National Audit Office is also the auditor by agreement of the accounts of certain international and other organisations. In addition, the Office authorises the issue of public funds to Government departments.

Comptroller and Auditor-General, Sir John Bourn, KCB
Private Secretary, M. Davies
Deputy Comptroller and Auditor-General, T. Burr
Deputy Auditor-General, M. C. Pfleger
Assistant Auditors-General, J. Colman; J. Marshall; Miss C. Mawhood; M. Sinclair; Ms W. Kenway-Smith

NATIONAL CONSUMER COUNCIL
20 Grosvenor Gardens, London SW1W 0DH
Tel: 020-7730 3469; Fax: 020-7730 0191;
Web: www.ncc.org.uk

The National Consumer Council (NCC) was set up by the Government in 1975 to give an independent voice to consumers in the UK. Its role is to advocate the consumer interest to decision-makers in national and local government, industry and regulatory bodies, business and the professions. It does this through a combination of research and campaigning. NCC is a non-profit making company limited by guarantee and is largely funded by grant-in-aid from the Department of Trade and Industry.

Chairman, D. Hutton, CBE
Director, Ms A. Bradley

NATIONAL ENDOWMENT FOR SCIENCE, TECHNOLOGY AND THE ARTS (NESTA)
Fishmongers' Chambers, 110 Upper Thames Street, London EC4R 3TW Tel: 020-7645 9500; Fax: 020-7645 9501

The National Endowment for Science, Technology and the Arts (NESTA) was established under the National Lottery Act 1998 with a £200 million endowment from the proceeds of the National Lottery. Its aims are to help talented individuals; to enable innovative ideas to be successfully commercially exploited; and to promote public knowledge of science, technology and the arts.

Chairman, The Lord Puttnam, CBE
Trustees, Dame Bridget Ogilvie, DBE; Prof. Sir Martin Rees, FRS; Dr C. Evans, OBE; Ms C. Vorderman; D. Wardell; F. Matarasso; The Baroness McIntosh of Hudnall; Ms C. McKeever; Ms J. Kirkpatrick; Ms S. Hunter; D. Alexander; D. Wanless
Chief Executive, J. Newton

348   Government Departments and Public Offices

NATIONAL HERITAGE MEMORIAL FUND
7 Holbein Place, London SW1W 8NR
Tel: 020-7591 6000; Fax: 020-7591 6001

The National Heritage Memorial Fund is an independent body established in 1980 as a memorial to those who have died for the UK. The Fund is empowered by the National Heritage Act 1980 to give financial assistance towards the cost of acquiring, maintaining or preserving land, buildings, works of art and other objects of outstanding interest which are also of importance to the national heritage. The Fund is administered by 13 trustees who are appointed by the Prime Minister.

The National Lottery Act 1993 designated the Fund as distributor of the heritage share of proceeds from the National Lottery. As a result, the Fund now operates two funds: the Heritage Memorial Fund and the Heritage Lottery Fund. The Heritage Memorial Fund receives an annual grant from the Department for Culture, Media and Sport; the grant for 2000 - 2001 is £5 million.
Chairman, L. Forgan
Trustees, Prof. C. Baines; R. Boas; N. Dodd; Sir Angus Grossart; G. Waterfield; Mrs P. Lankester; P. Wilson; S. Palmer; Earl of Dalkeith; Prof. T. Pritchard; Ms M. A. Sieghart; J. Wright
Director, Ms A. Case

NATIONAL INVESTMENT AND LOANS OFFICE
1 King Charles Street, London SW1A 2AP
Tel: 020-7270 3861; Fax: 020-7270 3860

The National Investment and Loans Office is a non-ministerial Government department which was set up in 1980 by the merger of the National Debt Office and the Public Works Loan Board. The Office provides the staff and administrative support for the National Debt Commissioners, the Public Works Loan Commissioners and the Office of HM Paymaster-General. The National Debt Office is responsible for managing the investment portfolios of certain public funds and the management of some residual operations relating to the national debt. The function of the Public Works Loan Board is to make loans from the National Loans Fund to local authorities and certain other statutory bodies, primarily for capital purposes.

The Office of HM Paymaster-General has continuously existed in its present form since 1836; the Paymaster-General has responsibilities assigned from time to time by the Prime Minister and is currently a Treasury minister. The Assistant Paymaster-General is responsible for the banking and financial information services provided to the Government and public sector bodies by the Office of HM Paymaster-General.
Director, I. Peattie
Establishment Officer, D. Hockey

NATIONAL DEBT OFFICE
020-7270 3868
Comptroller-General, Ian Peattie

PUBLIC WORKS LOAN BOARD
020-7270 3874
Chairman, A. D. Loehnis, CMG
Deputy Chairman, Miss V. J. Di Palma, OBE

Other Commissioners, Mrs R. V. Hale; J. A. Parkes, CBE; B. Tanner, CBE; Mrs R. Terry; D. W. Midgley; L. M. Nippers; Mrs S. Wood
Secretary, Ian Peattie
Assistant Secretary, M. Frankel

OFFICE OF HM PAYMASTER-GENERAL
020-7270 6074
Paymaster-General, Dawn Primarolo, MP
Assistant Paymaster-General, I. Peattie
Head of Banking, L. Palmer
Banking Manager, P. Harris

NATIONAL LOTTERY COMMISSION
2 Monck Street, London SW1P 2BQ
Tel: 020-7227 2000; Fax: 020-7227 2005;
Web: www.natlotcomm.gov.uk

The National Lottery Commission replaced the Office of the National Lottery (OFLOT) in April 1999 under the National Lottery Act 1998. The Commission is responsible for the granting, varying and enforcing of licences to run the National Lottery. Its duties are to ensure that the National Lottery is run with all due propriety, that the interests of players are protected, and, subject to these two objectives, that returns to the 'good causes' are maximised.
Chairman, Lord Terry Burns
Commissioners, Ms H. Spicer; B. Pomeroy; R. Gilmore; T. Horwsby
Chief Executive, M. Harris
Director of Licensing, K. Jones
Director of Compliance and Resources, Ms M. Phillips

See also Lotteries and Gaming section

NATIONAL PHYSICAL LABORATORY
Queens Road, Teddington, Middx TW11 0LW
Tel: 020-8977 3222; Fax: 020-8943 6458

The Laboratory is the UK's national standards laboratory. It develops, maintains and disseminates national measurement standards for physical quantities such as mass, length, time, temperature, voltage, force and pressure. It also conducts underpinning research on engineering materials and information technology and disseminates good measurement practice. It is Government-owned but contractor-operated.
Managing Director, Dr R. McGuiness
Director of Marketing and Knowledge Transfer, D. C. Richardson

NATIONAL RADIOLOGICAL PROTECTION BOARD
Chilton, Didcot, Oxon OX11 0RQ
Tel: 01235-831600; Fax: 01235-833891;
Web: www.nrpb.org.uk

The National Radiological Protection Board is an independent statutory body created by the Radiological Protection Act 1970. It is the national point of authoritative reference on radiological protection for both ionising and non-ionising radiations, and has issued recommendations on limiting human exposure to electromagnetic fields and radiation from a range of sources,

including X-rays, the Sun, base stations and mobile phones. Its sponsoring department is the Department of Health.
Chairman, Sir Walter Bodmer, ph.D., FRCPath., FRS
Director, Prof. R. H. Clarke

NATIONAL SAVINGS
375 Kensington High Street, London W14 8SD
Tel: 020-7348 9200; Fax: 020-7048 9755;
Web: www.nationalsavings.co.uk

National Savings was established as a Government department in 1969. It became an executive agency of the Treasury in 1996 and is responsible for the design, marketing and administration of savings and investment products for personal savers and investors. In April 1999 Siemens Business Services took over all the back office functions at National Savings.
Chief Executive, P. Bareau
Personnel Director, D. S. Speedie
Finance Director, T. Bayley
Commercial Director, W. Cattanach
Sourcing Director, Ms J. Bevan

For details of schemes, *see* National Savings section

NEW OPPORTUNITIES FUND
Heron House, 322 High Holborn, London WC1V 7PW Tel: 020-7211 1800; Fax: 020-7211 1750; Email: enquiries@nof.org.uk; Web: www.nof.org.uk

The New Opportunities Fund is a Lottery Distributor created to distribute grants to health, education and environment projects across the UK. The New Opportunities Fund intends to fund projects that will improve people's quality of life, address the needs of those people who are most disadvantaged in society, encourage community participation and complement relevent local and national strategies and programmes.
Chair of the Board, The Baroness Pitkeathley
Members of the Board, Ms J. Barrow; Prof. E. Bolton, CB; Ms N. Clarke; Prof. A. Patmore, CBE; D. Mackie; D. Campbell; Prof. S. Griffiths; Prof. B. Gaad
Chief Executive, S. Dunmore

NORTHERN IRELAND AUDIT OFFICE
106 University Street, Belfast BT7 1EU
Tel: 02890-251000; Fax: 02890-251106

The primary aim of the Northern Ireland Audit Office is to provide independent assurance, information and advice to the Northern Ireland Assembly on the proper accounting for Northern Ireland departmental and certain other public expenditure, revenue, assets and liabilities; on regularity and propriety; and on the economy, efficiency and effectiveness of the use of resources.
Comptroller and Auditor-General for Northern Ireland, J. M. Dowdall

NORTHERN IRELAND HUMAN RIGHTS COMMISSION
Temple Court, 39–41 North Street, Belfast BT1 1NA
Tel: 028-9024 3987; Fax: 028-9024 7844;
Email: nihrc@belfast.org.uk; Web: www.nihrc.org

The Northern Ireland Human Rights Commission was set up in March 1999. Its main functions are to keep under review the law and practice relating to human rights in Northern Ireland, to advise the Government and to promote an awareness of human rights in Northern Ireland. It can also take cases to court. The Commission currently consists of one full-time commissioner and eight part-time commissioners, all appointed by the Secretary of State for Northern Ireland.
Chief Commissioner (£57,500), Prof. B. Dickson
Commissioners (£8,000 each), Prof. C. Bell; Ms M-A. Dinsmore, QC; T. Donnelly, MBE; The Revd H. Good, OBE; Prof. T. Hadden; Ms P. Kelly; Ms I. McCormack; F. McGuinness

OCCUPATIONAL PENSIONS REGULATORY AUTHORITY
Invicta House, Trafalgar Place, Brighton BN1 4DW
Tel: 01273-627600; Fax: 01273-627760;
Email: helpdesk@opra.gov.uk

The Occupational Pensions Regulatory Authority (OPRA) was set up under the Pensions Act 1995 and became fully operational on 6 April 1997. It is the independent, statutory regulator of occupational and stakeholder pension schemes in the UK.
Chairman, H. Maunsell, OBE
Chief Executive, Mrs C. Instance

OFFICE FOR NATIONAL STATISTICS
1 Drummond Gate, London SW1V 2QQ
Tel: 020-7533 5888; Email: info@statistics.gov.uk;
Web: www.statistics.gov.uk

The Office for National Statistics was created in 1996 by the merger of the Central Statistical Office and the Office of Population Censuses and Surveys. It is both a government department and an executive agency of the Treasury and is responsible for preparing and interpreting key economic statistics for Government policy; collecting and publishing business statistics; publishing annual and monthly statistical digests; providing researchers, analysts and other customers with a statistical service; administration of the marriage laws and local registration of births, marriages and deaths in England and Wales; provision of population estimates and projections and statistics on health and other demographic matters in England and Wales; population censuses in England and Wales; surveys for Government departments and public bodies; and promoting these functions within the UK, the European Union and internationally to provide a statistical service to meet European Union and international requirements.

Following the publication of the White Paper, 'Building Trust in Statistics', National Statistics was launched in June 2000. Headed by the National Statistician, with an independent Statistics Commission, providing assurance to Parliament about the integrity of official statistics and statistical practice. The National Statistics brand encompasses the output of the ONS, plus many of the key public interest statistics produced by other Government departments.

National Statistician, Registrar General for England and Wales and the Head of the Government Statistical Service, L. Cook
Directors, Ms S. Linacre (*Method and Quality*); J. Kidgell (*Economic Statistics*); K. Drunnell (*Social Statistics*); J. Pullinger (*Information Age Access Project*); P. Walton (*Business Change*)
Principal Establishment Officer, E. Williams
Head of Communication, Ms H. Rafalowska
Parliamentary Clerk, J. Bailey

FAMILY RECORDS CENTRE, 1 Myddelton Street, London EC1R 1UW. Tel: 020-8392 5300

OFFICE FOR STANDARDS IN EDUCATION (OFSTED)
Alexandra House, 33 Kingsway, London WC2B 6SE
Tel: 020-7421 6800; Fax: 020-7421 6707

OFSTED is a non-ministerial Government department established under the Education (Schools Act) 1992 to keep the Secretary of State and the public informed about the standards and management of schools in England, and to establish and monitor an independent inspection system for maintained schools in England. Its inspection role also includes the inspection of local education authorities, teacher training institutions, youth work and funded education. Its staff include HMI, who draw on inspection evidence to report on good practice in schools and on a wide range of educational issues.
See also Education section.
HM Chief Inspector, M. J. Tomlinson, CBE
Directors of Inspection, D. Taylor; E. Passmore
Director of Policy, Planning and Resources, J. M. Phillips, CBE
Director of Early Years, M. Smith
Director of Finance, P. Jolly
Director of Corporate Services, R. Knight

DIVISION MANAGERS

Personnel Management, A. White
Contracts, C. Bramley
Communications, Media and Public Relations, J. Lawson
Information Systems, M. Worthy
Administrative Support and Estate Management, K. Francis
Early Years Inspection Quality, D. Bradley
Inspection Quality, P. Matthews
LEA Inspections, D. Singleton
School Improvement, K. Cross
Primary, K. Lloyd
Secondary, M. Raleigh
Curriculum Advice and Inspection, B. McCafferty
Post-Compulsory, S. Grix
Special Educational Needs, C. Marshall
Research, Analysis and International, G. Goodwin
Teacher Education, C. Gould
Nursery Education Scheme, D. Bradley
There are about 200 HM Inspectors

OFFICE FOR THE REGULATION OF ELECTRICITY AND GAS
Brookmount Buildings, 42 Fountain Street, Belfast BT1 5EE Tel: 028-9031 1575 (*Electricity*); 028-9031 4212 (*Gas*); Fax: 028-9031 1740;
Email: ofreg@nics.gov.uk;
Web: www.ofreg.nics.gov.uk

The Office for the Regulation of Electricity and Gas (OFREG) is the combined regulatory body for the electricity and gas supply industries in Northern Ireland.
Director-General of Electricity Supply and Director-General of Gas for Northern Ireland, D. B. McIldoon

OFFICE OF GAS AND ELECTRICITY MARKETS
9 Millbank, London, SW1P 3GE.
Tel: 020-7901 7000; Fax: 020-7901 7066
SCOTLAND: Regent Court, 70 West Regent Street, Glasgow G2 2QZ
Tel: 0141-331 2678; Fax: 0141-331 2777

The Office of Gas and Electricity Markets (Ofgem) regulates the gas and electricity industries in England, Scotland and Wales. Ofgem's aim is to bring choice and value to all gas and electricity customers by prompting competition and regulating monopolies. Ofgem is governed by an authority and its powers are provided for under the Gas Act 1986, the Electricity Act 1989 and the Utilities Act 2000.
Chief Executive, C. McCarthy
Managing Directors, J. Neilson (*Customers and Supply*); Dr Marshall, CBE (*Competition and Trading Arrangements*); R. Ramsay (*Regulation and Financial Affairs*); C. Coulthard (*Scotland*)
Chief Operating Officer, Ms G. Whittington

OFFICE OF FAIR TRADING
Fleetbank House, 2–6 Salisbury Square, London EC4Y 8JX Tel: 020-7211 8000; Fax: 020-7211 8800

The Office of Fair Trading is a non-ministerial Government department headed by the Director-General of Fair Trading. It keeps commercial activities in the UK under review and seeks to protect consumers against unfair trading practices. The Director-General's consumer protection duties under the Fair Trading Act 1973, together with his responsibilities under the Consumer Credit Act 1974, the Estate Agents Act 1979, the Control of Misleading Advertisements Regulations 1988, and the Unfair Terms in Consumer Contracts Regulations 1999, are administered by the Office's Consumer Affairs Division. The Competition Policy Division is concerned with monopolies and mergers (under the Fair Trading Act 1973) and the Director-General's other responsibilities for competition matters, including those under the Competition Act 1998, the Financial Services Act 1986 and the Broadcasting Act 1990. The Office is the UK competent authority on the application of the European Commission's competition rules, and also liaises with the Commission on consumer protection initiatives.
Director-General, J. Vickers

CONSUMER AFFAIRS DIVISION
Director (G3), Miss C. Banks
Branch Directors (G5), R. Watson; M. Graham; D. Wray

Office of the Parliamentary Commissioner for Administration 351

COMPETITION POLICY DIVISION
Divisional Director (G3), Mrs M. J. Bloom
Branch Directors (G5), A. J. White; A. Walker-Smith; E. L. Whitehorn; S. Wood; Dr D. Mason; Dr G. Davis; A. Williams
Chief Economist, vacant

LEGAL DIVISION
Divisional Director (G3), Miss P. Edwards
Branch Directors (G5), M. A. Khan; S. Brindley
Establishment and Finance Officer (G5), Mrs R. Heyhoe
Chief Information Officer (G6), M. Ricketts

COMMUNICATIONS DIVISION
Director of Communications (Chief Information Officer) (G5), M. Ricketts

RESOURCES AND SERVICES
Director of Resources and Services (Chief Establishment and Finance Officer) (G5), D. Fisher

OFFICE OF MANPOWER ECONOMICS
Oxford House, 76 Oxford Street, London W1N 9FD
Tel: 020-7467 7244; Fax: 020-7467 7248

The Office of Manpower Economics was set up in 1971. It is an independent non-statutory organisation which is responsible for servicing independent review bodies which advise on the pay of various public service groups, the Pharmacists Review Panel and the Police Negotiating Board. The Office is also responsible for servicing *ad hoc* bodies of inquiry and for undertaking research into pay and associated matters as requested by the Government.
OME Director, M. J. Horsman
Director, Health Secretariat, and OME Deputy Director, G. S. Charles
Director, Armed Forces' Secretariat, C. Haworth
Director, Senior Salaries and Police Negotiating Board Secretariat, Ms R. McCarthy-Ward
Director, School Teachers' Secretariat, Mrs E. M. Melling
Director, Prison Service Secretariat, M. C. Cahill
Press Liaison Officer, C. P. Jordan

OFFICE OF TELECOMMUNICATIONS
(OFTEL)
50 Ludgate Hill, London EC4M 7JJ
Tel: 020-7634 8700; Fax: 020-7 634 8943;
Web: www.oftel.gov.uk

The Office of Telecommunications (Oftel) is the regulator, or 'watchdog', for the UK telecommunications industry. Oftel is a Government department but is independent of ministerial control. Oftel's aim is for customers to get the best deal in terms of quality, choice and value for money. Its strategy to achieve this goal is through four objectives: effective competition benefiting consumers; well informed consumers; adequately protected consumers; and prevention of significant anti-competitive practice. Oftel is responsible for ensuring that holders of telecommunications licences comply with their licence conditions, and has powers under the Competition Act 1999 to deal with anti-competitive practices and cartels. The Director-General has a duty to consider all reasonable complaints about telecommunications services.
Oftel, is one of the first regulators, along with the Independent Television Commission, the Broadcast

Standards Council, the Radio Authority and the Radio Communications Agency that under Government plans will merge to become the Office of Communication, the new regulator for the communications sector.
Director-General, D. Edmonds
Director of Operations, Miss A. Lambert
Director of Regulatory Policy, C. Kenny
Director of Compliance, K. Long
Director of Technology, P. Walker
Director of Strategy and Forecasting, A. Bell
Director of Business Support, D. Smith
Director of Communications, D. Stroud

OFFICE OF THE LEGAL SERVICES OMBUDSMAN
22 Oxford Court, Oxford Street, Manchester M2 3WQ Tel: 0845 601 0794; Fax: 0161-236 2651; Email: enquiries.olso@gtnet.gov.uk

The Legal Services Ombudsman is appointed by the Lord Chancellor under the Courts and Legal Services Act 1990 to oversee the handling of complaints against solicitors, barristers, licensed conveyancers, legal executives and patent agents by their professional bodies. A complainant must first complain to the relevant professional body before raising the matter with the Ombudsman. The Ombudsman is independent of the legal profession and her services are free of charge.
Legal Services Ombudsman, Ms A. Abraham
Secretary Manager, S. D. Entwistle

OFFICE OF THE SCOTTISH LEGAL SERVICES OMBUDSMAN
17 Waterloo Place, Edinburgh, EH1 3DL
Tel: 0131-244 3055; Fax: 0131-244 3065;
Email: Ombudsman@slso.org.uk; Web: www.slso.org.uk
The Ombudsman is appointed by Scottish Ministers, and cannot be a lawyer.
Scottish Legal Services Ombudsman, Ms L. Costelloe Baker

OFFICE OF THE LORD ADVOCATE
Crown Office, 25 Chambers Street, Edinburgh EH1 1LA Tel: 0131-226 2626; Fax: 0131-226 6910

The Law Officers for Scotland are the Lord Advocate and the Solicitor-General for Scotland.
Lord Advocate, The Rt. Hon. Colin Boyd, QC
Solicitor-General for Scotland, Neil F. Davidson, QC
Private Secretary to the Law Officers, J. Gibbons

OFFICE OF THE PARLIAMENTARY COMMISSIONER FOR ADMINISTRATION AND HEALTH SERVICE COMMISSIONER
Millbank Tower, Millbank, London SW1P 4QP
Tel: 0845-015 4033; Fax: 020-7217 4000
Web: www.ombudsman.org.uk

The Parliamentary Commissioner for Administration (the Parliamentary Ombudsman) is independent of Government and is an officer of Parliament. He is responsible for investigating complaints referred to him by MPs from members of the public who claim to have sustained injustice in consequence of maladministration by or on behalf of Government departments and certain non-departmental public bodies. In March 1999 an additional 158 public bodies were brought within the jurisdiction of the Parliamentary Commissioner. Certain types of action by Government departments or bodies are excluded from investigation. The Parliamentary Commissioner is also responsible for investigating complaints, referred by MPs, alleging that access to official information has been wrongly refused under the Code of Practice on Access to Government Information 1994.

The Health Service Commissioners (the Health Service Ombudsmen) for England, for Scotland and for Wales are responsible for investigating complaints against National Health Service authorities and trusts that are not dealt with by those authorities to the satisfaction of the complainant. Complaints can be referred direct by the member of the public who claims to have sustained injustice or hardship in consequence of the failure in a service provided by a relevant body, failure of that body to provide a service or in consequence of any other action by that body. The Ombudsmens' jurisdiction now covers complaints about family doctors, dentists, pharmacists and opticians, and complaints about actions resulting from clinical judgement.

The Health Service Ombudsmen are also responsible for investigating complaints that information has been wrongly refused under the Code of Practice on Openness in the National Health Service 1995. The three offices are presently held by the Parliamentary Commissioner.

Parliamentary Commissioner and Health Service Commissioner (G1), M. S. Buckley
Deputy Parliamentary Commissioner (G3), A. Watson
Deputy Health Service Commissioner (G3), Ms H. Scott
Directors, Parliamentary Commissioner (G5), G. Monk; D. Reynolds; Ms C. Corrigan;
Directors, Health Service Commissioners (G5), Ms H. Bainbridge; N. J. Jordan; D. R. G. Pinchin; L. Charlton
Finance and Establishment Officer (G5), J. Stevens

For Scotland, *see* Scottish Parliamentary Commissioner for Administration
For Wales, *see* Welsh Administration Ombudsman

OFFICE OF THE PENSIONS OMBUDSMAN
6th Floor, 11 Belgrave Road, London sw1v 1RB
Tel: 020-7834 9144; Fax: 020-7821 0065

The Pensions Ombudsman is appointed under the Pension Schemes Act 1993 as amended by the Pensions Act 1995. He investigates and decides complaints and disputes concerning occupational pension schemes. Complaints concerning personal pensions would normally be dealt with only if outside the jurisdiction of the Personal Investment Authority. The Ombudsman is completely independent and there is no charge for bringing a complaint or dispute to him.
Pensions Ombudsman, Dr J. T. Farrand, QC

OFFICE OF THE RAIL REGULATOR
1 Waterhouse Square, 138–142 Holborn, London
EC1N 2TQ Tel: 020-7282 2000; Fax: 020-7282 2047;
Email: orr@dial.pipex.com;
Web: www.rail-reg.gov.uk

The Office of the Rail Regulator was set up under the Railways Act 1993. The Regulator's main functions are

the licensing of operators of railway assets; the approval of agreements for access by those operators to track, stations and light maintenance depots; the enforcement of domestic competition law; and consumer protection. The Rail Regulator will become subject to strategic guidance from the Secretary of State.
Rail Regulator, T. Winsor
Director of Strategy Planning and Communications, K. Webb
Director of Network Regulation, M. Beswick
Director of Access, Competition and Licensing, S. Gooding
Chief Economist and Director of Economics and Finance, T. Martin
Chief Legal Adviser and Director of Legal Services, S. Barrett-Williams

---

OFFICE OF WATER SERVICES
Centre City Tower, 7 Hill Street, Birmingham
B5 4UA Tel: 0121-625 1300; Fax: 0121-625 1400;
Email: enquiries@ofwat.gsi.gov.uk;
Web: www.ofwat.gov.uk

The Office of Water Services (Ofwat) was set up under the Water Act 1989 and is a non-ministerial Government department headed by the Director-General of Water Services. It is the independent economic regulator of the water and sewerage companies in England and Wales. Ofwat's main duties are to ensure that the companies can finance and carry out the functions specified in the Water Industry Act 1991 and to protect the interests of water customers. There are ten regional customer service committees which are concerned solely with the interests of water customers. Representation of customer interests at national level is the responsibility of the Ofwat National Customer Council (ONCC).
Director-General of Water Services, P. Fletcher
Chairman, Ofwat National Customer Council, M. Terry

OMBUDSMEN
— *see* Local Commissioners *and* Parliamentary Commissioner. For non-statutory Ombudsmen, *see* Index

---

ORDNANCE SURVEY
Romsey Road, Maybush, Southampton so16 4GU
Tel: 023-8079 2000; Fax: 023-8079 2615

Ordnance Survey is the national mapping agency for Britain. It is a Government department and executive agency operating as a Trading Fund and reporting to the Secretary of State for Transport, Local Government and the Regions.
Director-General and Chief Executive, Ms V. Lawrence

PARADES COMMISSION
12th Floor, Windsor House, 6–12 Bedford Street,
Belfast BT2 7EL
Tel: 029-9054 8900; Fax: 029-9032 2988

The Parades Commission was set up under the Public Processions (Northern Ireland) Act 1998. Its function is to encourage and facilitate local accommodation on contentious parades; where this is not possible, the Commission is empowered to make legal determinations about such parades, which may include imposing conditions on aspects of the notified parade.

The chairman and members are appointed by the Secretary of State for Northern Ireland; the membership must, as far as is practicable, be representative of the community in Northern Ireland.
Chairman, A. J. Holland
Members, J. Cousins; Revd R. Magee; W. Martin; P. Osborne; Sir J. Pringle; P. Quinn
Secretary (G5), A. Elliott

PARLIAMENTARY COMMISSIONER FOR STANDARDS
House of Commons, London SW1A 0AA
Tel: 020-7219 0320

Following recommendations of the Committee on Standards in Public Life, the House of Commons agreed to the appointment of an independent Parliamentary Commissioner for Standards with effect from November 1995. The Commissioner has responsibility for maintaining and monitoring the operation of the Register of Members' Interests; advising Members of Parliament and the Select Committee on Sandards and Privileges, on the interpretation of the rules on disclosure and advocacy, and on other questions of propriety; and receiving and, if she thinks fit, investigating complaints about the conduct of MPs.
Parliamentary Commissioner for Standards, Ms E. Filkin

PARLIAMENTARY COUNSEL
36 Whitehall, London SW1A 2AY
Tel: 020-7210 6611; Fax: 020-7210 6632

Parliamentary Counsel draft all Government bills (i.e. primary legislation) except those relating exclusively to Scotland. They also advise on all aspects of parliamentary procedure in connection with such bills and draft Government amendments to them as well as any motions (including financial resolutions) necessary to secure their introduction into, and passage through, Parliament.
First Counsel (SCS), E. G. Caldwell, CB
Counsel (SCS), E. G. Bowman, CB; G. B. Sellers, CB; E. R. Sutherland, CB; P. F. A. Knowles, CB; S. C. Laws, CB; R. S. Parker, CB; Miss C. E. Johnston, CB; P. J. Davies, CB; J. M. Sellers

PAROLE BOARD FOR ENGLAND AND WALES
Abell House, John Islip Street, London SW1P 4LH
Tel: 020-7217 5314; Fax: 020-7217 5793;
Email: info@paroleboard.gov.uk
Web: www.paroleboard.gov.uk

The Board was constituted under the Criminal Justice Act 1967 and continued under the Criminal Justice Act 1991. It is an executive non-departmental public body and its duty is to advise the Home Secretary with respect to matters referred to it by him which are connected with the early release or recall of prisoners. Its functions include giving directions concerning the release on licence of prisoners serving discretionary life sentences and of certain prisoners serving long-term determinate sentences.
Chairman, D. Hatch, CBE
Vice-Chairman, The Hon. Mr Justice Scott Baker
Chief Executive, J. Casey

PAROLE BOARD FOR SCOTLAND
Saughton House, Broomhouse Drive, Edinburgh EH11 3XD Tel: 0131-244 8755; Fax: 0131-244 69740

The Board directs and advises the Scottish Minister on the release of prisoners on licence, and related matters.
Chairman, Dr J. J. McManus
Vice-Chairman, H. Hyslop
Secretary, H. P. Boyle

PATENT OFFICE
Concept House, Cardiff Road, Newport NP10 8QQ
Tel: 0845-9500505; Fax: 01633-814444;
Email: enquiries@patent.gov.uk
Web: www.patent.gov.uk

The Patent Office is an executive agency of the Department of Trade and Industry. The duties of the Patent Office are to administer the Patent Acts, the Registered Designs Act and the Trade Marks Act, and to deal with questions relating to the Copyright, Designs and Patents Act 1988. The Search and Advisory Service carries out commercial searches through patent information.
Comptroller-General, Ms A. Brimelow
Director, Intellectual Property Policy Directorate, G. Jenkins
Director, Patents and Designs, R. J. Marchant
Director and Assistant Registrar of Trade Marks, P. Lawrence
Director, Administration and Resources and Secretary to the Patent Office, C. Clancy
Director, Copyright, A. Murphy
Director, Finance, J. Thompson

HM PAYMASTER-GENERAL, OFFICE
— *see* National Investment and Loans Office

PENSIONS COMPENSATION BOARD
11 Belgrave Road, London SW1V 1RB
Tel: 020-7828 9794; Fax: 020-7931 7239

The Pensions Compensation Board was established under the Pensions Act 1995 and is funded by a levy paid by all eligible occupational pension schemes. Its function is to compensate occupational pension schemes for losses due to dishonesty where the employer is insolvent.
Chairman, Dr J. T. Farrand, QC
Secretary, M. Lydon

POLICE COMPLAINTS AUTHORITY
10 Great George Street, London SW1P 3AE
Tel: 020-7273 6450; Fax: 020-7273 6401;
Web: www.pca.gov.uk

The Police Complaints Authority was established under the Police and Criminal Evidence Act 1984 to provide an independent system for dealing with complaints by members of the public against police officers in England and Wales. It is funded by the Home Office. The authority has powers to supervise the investigation of certain categories of serious complaints and examines all completed investigations to decide whether officers should face misconduct proceedings. It does not deal with police operational matters; these are usually dealt with by the Chief Constable of the relevant force.

Chairman, Sir Alistair Graham
Deputy Chair, M. Meacher
2nd Deputy Chair, I. Bynoe
Members, Mrs A. Boustred; Ms J. Dobry; J. Elliott;
D. Gear; Miss M. Mian; Mrs C. Mitchell; D. Petch;
Mrs W. Towers; S. Swindell; D. Hughes; D. Glass;
L. Pilkington; A. Macdougall

POLICE OMBUDSMAN FOR NORTHERN IRELAND
New Cathedral Buildings, St Anne's Square,
11 Church Street, Belfast BT 1PG
Tel: 028-9082 8600; Fax: 028-9082 8659;
Web: www.policeombudsman.org;
Email: info@policeombudsman.org

Founded in November 2000 under the Police (Northern Ireland) Act 1998, the function of the Police Ombudsman for Northern Ireland is to investigate complaints against the police in an impartial, efficient, effective and (as far as possible) transparent way, to win the confidence of the public and the police. It must report on trends in complaints and react to incidents involving the police, where it is in the public interest, even if no individual complaint has been made.
Ombudsman, N. O'Loan

PORT OF LONDON AUTHORITY
Bakers' Hall, 7 Harp Lane, London EC3R 6LB
Tel: 020-7743 7900; Fax: 020-7743 7999;
Web: www.portoflondon.co.uk

The Port of London Authority is a public trust constituted under the Port of London Act 1908 and subsequent legislation. It is the governing body for the Port of London, covering the tidal portion of the River Thames from Teddington to the seaward limit. The Board comprises a chairman and up to seven but not less than four non-executive members appointed by the Secretary of State for Transport, Local Government and the Regions, and up to four but not less than one executive members appointed by the Board.
Chairman, S. Sherrard
Vice-Chairman, The Baroness Wilcox
Chief Executive, S. Cuthbert
Secretary, G. E. Ennals

PRIME MINISTER'S OFFICE
— *see* page 292

PRISONS OMBUDSMAN FOR ENGLAND AND WALES
Ashley House, 2 Monck Street, London SW1P 2BQ
Tel: 020-7276 2876; Fax: 020-7276 2860
Email: prisonsombudsman@homeoffice.gsi.gov.uk

The post of Prisons Ombudsman was instituted in 1994. The Ombudsman is appointed by the Home Secretary and is an independent point of appeal for prisoners' grievances about their lives in prison, including disciplinary issues. The Ombudsman can investigate complaints about almost any aspect of prison life, assuming prisoners have completed the Prison Service's internal complaints procedure.
Prisons Ombudsman, S. Shaw

For Scotland, *see* Scottish Prisons Complaints Commission

PRIVY COUNCIL OFFICE
2 Carlton Gardens, London SW1Y 5AA
Tel: 020-7210 1033; Fax: 020-7210 1071

The Office is responsible for the arrangements leading to the making of all royal proclamations and Orders in Council; for certain formalities connected with ministerial changes; for considering applications for the granting (or amendment) of royal charters; for the scrutiny and approval of by-laws and statutes of chartered bodies; and for the appointment of high sheriffs and many Crown and Privy Council appointments to governing bodies.
President of the Council (and Leader of the House of Commons), The Rt. Hon. Margaret Beckett, MP
Private Secretary, R. Holderness
Parliamentary Secretary, Paddy Tipping, MP
Clerk of the Council, A. Galloway
Deputy Clerk of the Council, G. Donald
Senior Clerk, M. McCullagh
Registrar, J. Watherston

PUBLIC HEALTH LABORATORY SERVICE
61 Colindale Avenue, London NW9 5DF
Tel: 020-8200 1295; Fax: 020-8358 3130/3131;
Email: phls@phls.nhs.uk

The Public Health Laboratory Service comprises eight groups of laboratories, the Central Public Health Laboratory, the Communicable Disease Surveillance Centre, a Regional Epidemiology service and the Headquarters. The PHLS seeks to protect the population from infection through detection, diagnosis, surveillance, prevention and control of infections and communicable diseases. It keeps track of what infections are appearing where, advises on remedial or preventive action and provides clinical diagnostic services.
Chairman, Lord Leslie Turnberg, MD
Deputy Chairman, R. Tabor
Director, Dr D. Walford, FRCP, FRCPath.
Deputy Directors, Prof. B. I. Duerden, MD, FRCPath. *(Medical Director)*; K. M. Saunders *(Corporate Planning and Resources)*

CENTRAL PUBLIC HEALTH LABORATORY
Colindale Avenue, London NW9 5HT
Director, Prof. S. P. Borriello

COMMUNICABLE DISEASES SURVEILLANCE CENTRE
Colindale Avenue NW9 5EQ
Director, Dr A. Nicoll

PHLS GROUPS OF LABORATORIES AND GROUP DIRECTORS
East, Dr P. M. B. White
Midlands, Dr R. E. Warren
North, Dr N. F. Lightfoot
North-West, Dr I. Farrell
South-West, Prof. K. A. V. Cartwright
London and South-East, Dr R. Gross
Trent, Dr P. J. Wilkinson
Wales, Dr A. J. Howard

OTHER SPECIAL LABORATORIES AND UNITS

ANAEROBE REFERENCE UNIT, Public Health Laboratory, Cardiff. *Head*, Prof. B. I. Duerden
ANTIVIRAL SUSCEPTIBILITY REFERENCE UNIT, Public Health Laboratory, Birmingham. *Head*, Dr D. P. Pillay
CRYPTOSPRORIDIUM REFERENCE UNIT, Public Health Laboratory, Rhyl. *Head*, Dr Rachel Chalmers
FOOD MICROBIOLOGY RESEARCH UNIT, Public Health Laboratory, Exeter. *Head*, Prof. T. J. Humphrey
GENITO-URINARY INFECTIONS REFERENCE LABORATORY, Public Health Laboratory, Bristol. *Head*, Dr A. J. Herring
LEPTOSPIRA REFERENCE LABORATORY, Public Health Laboratory, Hereford. *Director*, Dr T. J. Coleman
LYME DISEASE REFERENCE UNIT, Public Health Laboratory, Southampton. *Head*, Dr S. O'Connell
MALARIA REFERENCE LABORATORY, London School of Hygiene and Tropical Medicine, London WC1E 7HT. *Directors*, Prof. D. J. Bradley; Dr D. C. Warhurst
MENINGOCOCCAL REFERENCE LABORATORY, Public Health Laboratory, Manchester. *Director*, Dr E. Kaczmarski
MYCOBACTERIUM REFERENCE UNIT, Public Health Laboratory, Dulwich, London. *Director*, Dr F. Drobniewski
MYCOLOGY REFERENCE LABORATORY, Public Health Laboratory, Bristol. *Head*, University of Leeds. *Head*, Prof. E. G. V. Evans
PARASITOLOGY REFERENCE LABORATORY, Hospital for Tropical Diseases, London. *Director*, Dr P. L. Chiodini
TOXOPLASMA REFERENCE LABORATORY, Public Health Laboratory, Swansea. *Head*, D. H. M. Joynson
WATER AND ENVIRONMENTAL MICROBIOLOGY RESEARCH UNIT, Public Health Laboratory, Nottingham. *Head*, Dr J. V. Lee

PUBLIC GUARDIANSHIP OFFICE

Stewart House, 24 Kingsway, London WC2B 6JX
Tel 020-7664 7000; Fax 020-7664 7702
COURT FUNDS OFFICE, 22 Kingsway, London WC2B 6LE Tel 020-7936 6000; Fax 020-7936 6882;
Email: custerv@guardianship.gov.uk
Web: www.gurdianship.gov.uk

The Public Guardianship Office (PGO) is the administrative office of the Court of Protection, based within the Lord Chancellor's Department.
Established on the 1st of April 2001, it has taken over the mental health functions previously undertaken by the Public Trust Office (PTO), which also provides services that promote the financial and social well being of people with mental incapacity.
Chief Executive (Accountant-General), D. Lye
Director of Finance, I. Rees
Director of Client Services, K. Launchbury
Director of Mental Health, F. Eddy
Interim Director of Human Resource, H. Daley
Director of Communication, L. Joy

PUBLIC WORKS LOAN BOARD

— *see* National Investment and Loans Office TY

QUEST (THE QUALITY, EFFICIENCY AND STANDARDS TEAM)

c/o Department for Culture, Media and Sport,
2–4 Cockspur Street, London SW1Y 5DH
Tel: 020-7211 2206; Fax: 020-7211 2220

Quest was established in 1999. Its role is to monitor the quality of performance in organisations sponsored by the Department for Culture, Media and Sport and to provide independent advice to the Secretary of State.
Chief Executive, T. Suter

THE RADIO AUTHORITY

Holbrook House, 14 Great Queen Street, London WC2B 5DG Tel: 020-7430 2724; Fax: 020-7405 7062; Web: www.radioauthority.org.uk

The Radio Authority was established in 1991 under the Broadcasting Act 1990. It is the regulator and licensing authority for all independent radio services. Members of the Authority are appointed by the Secretary of State for Culture, Media and Sport; senior executive staff are appointed by the Authority.
Chairman, Richard Hooper
Deputy Chairman, David Witherow
Members, M. Adair; T. Prag; G. Talfan Davies; F. Sharkey; Ms S. Hewitt; Ms S. Nathan; Ms K. O'Rourke
Chief Executive, T. Stoller
Deputy Chief Executive, D. Vick
Secretary to the Authority and Director of Legal Affairs, Ms E. Salomon

RECORD OFFICES

ADVISORY COUNCIL ON PUBLIC RECORDS

Secretariat: Public Record Office, Kew, Richmond, Surrey TW9 4DU
Tel: 020-8876 3444 ext. 2351; Fax: 020-8392 5295
Web: www.pro.gov.uk/advisorycouncil/default.htm

Council members are appointed by the Lord Chancellor, under the Public Records Act 1958, to advise him on matters concerning public records in general and, in particular, on those aspects of the work of the Public Record Office which affect members of the public who make use of it.
Chairman, The Master of the Rolls
Secretary, T. R. Padfield

CORPORATION OF LONDON RECORDS OFFICE

Guildhall, London EC2P 2EJ
Tel: 020-7332 1251; Fax: 020-7710 8682
Email: clro@corpoflondon.gov.uk
Web: www.cityoflondon.gov.uk/archives/clro

The Corporation of London Records Office contains the municipal archives of the City of London which are regarded as the most complete collection of ancient municipal records in existence. The collection includes charters of William the Conqueror, Henry II, and later kings and queens to 1957; ancient custumals: Liber Horn, Dunthorne, Custumarum, Ordinacionum, Memorandorum and Albus, Liber de Antiquis Legibus, and collections

of statutes; continuous series of judicial rolls and books from 1252 and Council minutes from 1275; records of the Old Bailey and Guildhall sessions from 1603; financial records from the 16th century; the records of London Bridge from the 12th century; and numerous subsidiary series and miscellanea of historical interest.
Keeper of the City Records, The Town Clerk
City Archivist, J. R. Sewell, OBE
Deputy City Archivist, J. M. Bankes

HISTORICAL MANUSCRIPTS COMMISSION

Quality House, Quality Court, Chancery Lane, London WC2A 1HP Tel: 020-7242 1198; Fax: 020-7831 3550; Email: nra@hmc.gov.uk; Web: www.hmc.gov.uk

The Commission was set up by royal warrant in 1869 to enquire and report on collections of papers of value for the study of history which were in private hands. In 1959 a new warrant enlarged these terms of reference to include all historical records, wherever situated, outside the Public Records and gave it added responsibilities as a central co-ordinating body to promote, assist and advise on their proper preservation and storage. The Commission is sponsored by the Department for Culture, Media and Sport.

The Commission also maintains the National Register of Archives (NRA), which contains over 43,000 unpublished lists and catalogues of manuscript collections describing the holdings of local record offices, national and university libraries, specialist repositories and others in the UK and overseas. The NRA can be searched using computerised indices which are available in the Commission's search room.

The Commission also administers the Manorial and Tithe Documents Rules on behalf of the Master of the Rolls.
Chairman, The Lord Bingham of Cornhill, PC
Commissioners, Sir Patrick Cormack, FSA, MP; The Lord Egremont and Leconfield; Sir Matthew Farrer, GCVO; Sir John Sainty, KCB, FSA; Very Revd H. E. C. Stapleton, FSA; Sir Keith Thomas, FBA; The Earl of Scarbrough; A. Dundas-Bekker; Mrs S. J. Davies, Ph.D.; Prof. Peter Clarke; Mr Victor Gray; A. Prochaska, Ph.D.; Miss R. Dunhill, FSA; Dr Caroline Barron, FSA; Prof. T. C. Smout, CBE, Ph.D., FBA, FRSE, FSAScot.; Prof. Lola Young
Secretary, C. J. Kitching, Ph.D., FSA

HOUSE OF LORDS RECORD OFFICE (THE PARLIAMENTARY ARCHIVES)

House of Lords, London SW1A 0PW
Tel: 020-7219 3074; Fax: 020-7219 2570
Web: www.parliament.uk; Email: hlro@parliament.uk

Since 1497, the records of Parliament have been kept within the Palace of Westminster. They are in the custody of the Clerk of the Parliaments. In 1946 a record department was established to supervise their preservation and their availability to the public. The search room of the office is open to the public by appointment.

Some three million documents are preserved, including Acts of Parliament from 1497, journals of the House of Lords from 1510, minutes and committee proceedings from 1610, and papers laid before Parliament from 1531. Amongst the records are the Petition of Right, the Death Warrant of Charles I, the Declaration of Breda, and the Bill of Rights. The House of Lords Record Office also has charge of the journals of the House of Commons (from 1547), and other surviving records of the Commons (from 1572), including documents relating to private bill

legislation from 1818. Among other documents are the records of the Lord Great Chamberlain, the political papers of certain members of the two Houses, and documents relating to Parliament acquired on behalf of the nation. A permanent exhibition was established in the Royal Gallery in 1979.
Clerk of the Records, S. K. Ellison
Assistant Clerks of the Records, D. L. Prior; Dr C. Shenton

NATIONAL ARCHIVES OF SCOTLAND

HM General Register House, Edinburgh EH1 3YY
Tel: 0131-535 1314; Fax: 0131-535 1360
Web: www.nas.gov.uk; Email: enquiries@nas.gov.uk

The history of the national archives of Scotland can be traced back to the 13th century. The National Archives of Scotland (formerly the Scottish Record Office) is an executive agency of the Scottish Executive and keeps the administrative records of pre-Union Scotland, the registers of central and local courts of law, the public registers of property rights and legal documents, and many collections of local and church records and private archives. Certain groups of records, mainly the modern records of Government departments in Scotland, the Scottish railway records, the plans collection, and private archives of an industrial or commercial nature, are preserved in the branch repository at the West Register House in Charlotte Square. The National Register of Archives (Scotland) is based in the West Register House.
Keeper of the Records of Scotland, G. P. MacKenzie
Deputy Keeper, Dr P. D. Anderson

THE PUBLIC RECORD OFFICE

Kew, Richmond, Surrey TW9 4DU
Tel: 020-8876 3444; Fax: 020-8878 8905

The Public Record Office, originally established in 1838 under the Master of the Rolls, was placed under the direction of the Lord Chancellor in 1958; it became an executive agency in 1992. The Lord Chancellor appoints a Keeper of Public Records, whose duties are to co-ordinate and supervise the selection of records of Government departments and the law courts for permanent preservation, to safeguard the records and to make them available to the public. There is a separate record office for Scotland, now called the National Archives of Scotland.

The Office holds records of central Government dating from the Domesday Book (1086) to the present. Under the Public Records Act 1967 they are normally open to inspection when 30 years old, and are then available, without charge, in the reading rooms.
Keeper of Public Records (G3), Mrs S. Tyacke, CB
Director, Public Services Division (G5), Dr E. Hallam Smith
Director, Government, Corporate and Information Services Division (G5), Dr D. Simpson

PUBLIC RECORD OFFICE OF NORTHERN IRELAND

66 Balmoral Avenue, Belfast BT9 6NY
Tel: 02890-251318; Fax: 02890-255999

The Public Record Office of Northern Ireland is responsible for identifying and preserving Northern Ireland's archival heritage and making it available to the public. It is an executive agency of the Department of Culture, Arts and Leisure.
Chief Executive, Dr G. Slater

Royal Botanic Garden Edinburgh 357

SCOTTISH RECORDS ADVISORY COUNCIL
HM General Register House, Edinburgh EH1 3YY
Tel: 0131-535 1314; Fax: 0131-535 1360;
Web: www.nas.gov.uk

The Council was established under the Public Records (Scotland) Act 1937. Its members are appointed by the First Minister and it may submit proposals or make representations to the First Minister, the Lord Justice General or the Lord President of the Court of Session on questions relating to the public records of Scotland.
Chairman, Prof. H. MacQueen
Secretary, Dr A. Rosie

REGISTRAR OF PUBLIC LENDING RIGHT
Richard House, Sorbonne Close, Stockton on Tees
TS17 6DA Tel: 01642-604699; Fax: 01642-615641

Under the Public Lending Right system, in operation since 1983, payment is made from public funds to authors whose books are lent out from public libraries. Payment is made once a year and the amount each author receives is proportionate to the number of times (established from a sample) that each registered book has been lent out during the previous year. The Registrar of PLR, who is appointed by the Secretary of State for Culture, Media and Sport, compiles the register of authors and books. From 1 July 2000 authors resident in all EC countries are eligible to apply. (The term 'author' covers writers, illustrators, translators, and some editors/compilers.)

A payment of 2.49 pence was made in 2000–2001 for each estimated loan of a registered book, up to a top limit of £6,000 for the books of any one registered author; the money for loans above this level is used to augment the remaining PLR payments. In February 2001, the sum of £4,477 million was made available for distribution to 30,127 registered authors and assignees as the annual payment of PLR.
Registrar, Dr J. G. Parker
Chairman of Advisory Committee, C. Francis

REVIEW BODIES

The secretariat for these bodies is provided by the Office of Manpower Economics (*see* page 351)

ARMED FORCES PAY
The Review Body on Armed Forces Pay was appointed in 1971. It advises the Prime Minister and Government on the pay and allowances of members of naval, military and air forces of the Crown.
Chairman, The Baroness Dean of Thornton-le-Fylde, PC
Members, Mrs K. Coleman, OBE; J. Davies; Vice-Adm. Sir Toby Frere, KCB; The Lord Gladwin of Clee, CBE; Prof. D. Greenaway; Prof. The Lord Patel of Dunkeld; M. Ward

DOCTORS' AND DENTISTS'
The Review Body on Doctors' and Dentists' Remuneration was set up in 1971. It advises the Prime Minister and Government on the remuneration of doctors and dentists taking any part in the National Health Service.
Chairman, M. Blair, QC
Members, Prof. F. Burchill; Prof. A. Dow; A. Hawksworth; Miss C. Hui; Dr G. Jones; R. Malone

NURSING STAFF, MIDWIVES, HEALTH VISITORS AND PROFESSIONS ALLIED TO MEDICINE
The Review Body for nursing staff, midwives, health visitors and professions allied to medicine was set up in 1983. It advises the Prime Minister and Government on the remuneration of nursing staff, midwives and health visitors employed in the National Health Service; and also of physiotherapists, radiographers, occupational therapists, orthoptists, chiropodists, dietitians and related grades employed in the National Health Service.
Chairman, Prof. C. Booth
Members, M. Banerjee; J. Bartlett; Mrs M. Davies; C. Monks, OBE; Prof P. Weetman; D. Evans; Sir Patrick Symons

SCHOOL TEACHERS
The School Teachers' Review Body (STRB) was set up under the School Teachers' Pay and Conditions Act 1991. It is required to examine and report on such matters relating to statutory conditions of employment of school teachers in England and Wales as may be referred to it by the Secretary of State for Education and Skills.
Chairman, A. Vineall
Members, C. Ferguson; R. Gardner; P. Gedling; Miss J. Langdon; R. Pearson; J. Singh; Mrs P. Sloane

SENIOR SALARIES
The Senior Salaries Review Body (formerly the Top Salaries Review Body) was set up in 1971 to advise the Prime Minister on the remuneration of the judiciary, senior civil servants and senior officers of the armed forces. In 1993 its remit was extended to cover the pay, pensions and allowances of MPs, Ministers and others whose pay is determined by a Ministerial and Other Salaries Order, and the allowances of peers. It also advises on the pay of officers and members of the devolved Parliament and Assemblies.
Chairman, Sir Michael Perry, CBE

PRISON SERVICE

The Prison Service Pay Review Body (PSPRB) was set up in 2001. It makes independent recommendations on the pay of prison governors, prison officers and related grades for the Prison Service in England and Wales and for the Northern Ireland Prison.
Chairman, Sir Toby Frere, KCB
Members, D. Bourn; B. Brewer; A. Faulder; A. Gallico; P. Heard; F. Horisk; Prof. A. Smith

ROYAL BOTANIC GARDEN EDINBURGH
20A Inverleith Row, Edinburgh EH3 5LR
Tel: 0131-552 7171; Fax: 0131-248 2901;
Email: press@rbge.org.uk; Web: www.rbge.org.uk

The Royal Botanic Garden Edinburgh (RBGE) originated as the Physic Garden, established in 1670 beside the Palace of Holyroodhouse. The Garden moved to its present 28-hectare site at Inverleith, Edinburgh, in 1821. There are also three Regional Gardens: Benmore Botanic Garden, near Dunoon, Argyll; Logan Botanic Garden, near Stranraer, Wigtownshire; and Dawyck Botanic Garden, near Stobo, Peeblesshire. Since 1986 RBGE has been administered by a board of trustees established under the National Heritage (Scotland) Act 1985. It receives an annual grant from the Rural Affairs Department of the Scottish Executive.

RBGE is an international centre for scientific research on plant diversity and for horticulture education and conservation. It has an extensive library, a herbarium with over two million preserved plant specimens, and over 20,00 species in the living collections. Public opening hours: Edinburgh site, daily (except Christmas Day and New Year's Day) November–January 9.30–4; February and October 9.30–5; March and September 9.30–6; April–August 9.30–7; Regional Gardens, 1 March–31 October 9.30–6. Admission free to Edinburgh site; admission charge to Regional Gardens.

Chairman of the Board of Trustees, Dr P. Nicholson
Regius Keeper, Prof. S. Blackmore, FRSE

ROYAL BOTANIC GARDENS KEW
Richmond, Surrey TW9 3AB
Tel: 020-8332 5000; Fax: 020-8332 5197
Wakehurst Place, Ardingly, nr Haywards Heath,
W. Sussex RH17 6TN
Tel: 01444-894066; Fax: 01444-894069

The Royal Botanic Gardens (RBG) Kew were originally laid out as a private garden for Kew House for George III's mother, Princess Augusta, in 1759. They were much enlarged in the 19th century, notably by the inclusion of the grounds of the former Richmond Lodge. In 1965 the garden at Wakehurst Place was acquired; it is owned by the National Trust and managed by RBG Kew. Under the National Heritage Act 1983 a board of trustees was set up to administer the gardens, which in 1984 became an independent body supported by grant-in-aid from the Department of Environment, Food and Rural Affairs.

The functions of RBG Kew are to carry out research into plant sciences, to disseminate knowledge about plants and to provide the public with the opportunity to gain knowledge and enjoyment from the gardens' collections. There are extensive national reference collections of living and preserved plants and a comprehensive library and archive. The main emphasis is on plant conservation and bio-diversity.

The gardens are open daily (except Christmas Day and New Year's Day) from 9.30 a.m. (Wakehurst, 10 a.m.). The closing hour varies from 4 p.m. in mid-winter to 6 p.m. on weekdays and 7.30 p.m. on Sundays and Bank Holidays in mid-summer. Admission, 2001, £6.50 (free for children under 16); concessionary schemes available. Glasshouses (Kew only), 9.30–4.30 (winter); 9.30–5.30 (summer). No dogs except guide-dogs for the blind.

BOARD OF TRUSTEES

Chairman, The Viscount Blakenham
Members, Sir Jeffery Bowman (*Queen's Trustee*); Miss M. Black, CBE; Prof. M. Crawley; Prof. H. Dickinson; Miss A. Ford; Mrs R. Franklin; S. de Grey, CBE; R. Lapthorne, CBE; I. Oag; Prof. J. S. Parker; Prof. C. Payne, OBE
Director, Prof. P. Crane, FRS

ROYAL COMMISSION FOR THE EXHIBITION OF 1851
Sherfield Building, Imperial College of Science, Technology and Medicine, London SW7 2AZ
Tel: 020-7594 8790; Fax: 020-7594 8794;
Email: royalcom1851@ic.ac.uk;
Web: www.royalcommission1851.org.uk

The Royal Commission was incorporated by supplemental charter as a permanent commission after winding up the affairs of the Great Exhibition of 1851. Its object is to promote scientific and artistic education by means of funds derived from its Kensington estate, purchased with the surplus left over from the Great Exhibition. Annual charitable expenditure on educational grants is about £1 million.

President, HRH The Prince Philip, Duke of Edinburgh, KG, KT, PC
Chairman, Board of Management, Sir Alan Rudge, CBE, FRS, FREng.
Secretary to Commissioners, J. P. W. Middleton, CB

ROYAL COMMISSION ON ENVIRONMENTAL POLLUTION
1st Floor, Steel House, 11 Tothill Street, London SW1H 9RE Tel: 020-7273 6635;
Email: enquiries@rcep.org.uk;
Web: www.rcep.org.uk

The Commission was set up in 1970 to advise on national and international matters concerning the pollution of the environment.

Chairman, Prof. Sir Thomas Blundell
Members, Revd Prof. M. C. Banner; Dr I. Graham-Bryce; CBE; Prof. R. Clift, OBE, FREng.; J. Flemming; Sir Brian Folett, FRS; Sir Martin Holdgate, CB; Prof. B. Hoskins, CBE, FRS; Prof. R. Macrory; Sir Michael Marmot, PH.D.; Mrs C. Miller, FRSA; Dr Susan Owens, OBE; Prof. Jane Plant, CBE, FRSA; J. Roberts
Secretary, D. R. Lewis

ROYAL COMMISSION ON THE ANCIENT AND HISTORICAL MONUMENTS OF SCOTLAND
John Sinclair House, 16 Bernard Terrace, Edinburgh EH8 9NX
Tel: 0131-662 1456; Fax: 0131-662 1477

The Royal Commission was established in 1908 and is appointed to provide for the survey and recording of ancient and historical monuments connected with the culture, civilisation and conditions of life of the people in Scotland from the earliest times. It is funded by the Scottish Executive. The Commission compiles and maintains the National Monuments Record of Scotland as the national record of the archaeological and historical environment. The National Monuments Record is open for reference Monday–Friday 9.30–4.30.

Chairman, Mrs Kathleen Dalyell,
Commissioners, Prof. J. M. Coles, PH.D., FBA, FSA; Prof. R. A. Paxton, MBE, FRSE; Dr Barbara E. Crawford, FSA, FSAScot.; Miss A. C. Riches, OBE, FSA; J. W. T. Simpson, FSAScot.; Dr M. A. Mackay, PH.D.; Dr J. Murray, PH.D.;

Dr A. Macdonald Ph.D., FSAScot; Prof. C. D. Morris, FSA, FRSE, FSAScot; Dr Stana Nenadic, Ph.D.
Secretary, R. J. Mercer, FSA, FRSE

ROYAL COMMISSION ON THE ANCIENT AND HISTORICAL MONUMENTS OF WALES
Crown Building, Plas Crug, Aberystwyth SY23 1NJ
Tel: 01970-621200; Fax: 01970-627701

The Royal Commission was established in 1908 and is currently empowered by a Royal Warrant of 2001 to survey, record, publish and maintain a database of ancient and historical and maritime sites and structures, and landscapes in Wales. The Commission is funded by the National Assembly for Wales and is also responsible for the National Monuments Record of Wales, which is open daily for public reference, for the supply of archaeological information to the Ordnance Survey, for the co-ordination of archaeological aerial photography in Wales, and for sponsorship of the regional Sites and Monuments Records.
Chairman, Prof. R. A. Griffiths, Ph.D., D.Litt.
Commissioners, D. W. Crossley, FSA; J. Newman, FSA; U. B. Smith, Ph.D.; Prof. P. Sims-Williams, FBA; Prof. G. J. Wainwright, MBE, Ph.D., FSA; E. Wiliam, Ph.D., FSA
Secretary, P. R. White, FSA

THE ROYAL MINT
Llantrisant, Pontyclun CF72 8YT
Tel: 01443-623060; Fax: 01443-623185;
Web: www.royalmint.com

The prime responsibility of the Royal Mint is the provision of United Kingdom coinage, but it actively competes in world markets for a share of the available circulating coin business and about half of the 25,000 tonnes of coins and blanks it produces annually are exported. The Mint also manufactures special proof and uncirculated quality coins in gold, silver and other metals; military and civil decorations and medals; commemorative and prize medals; and royal and official seals.
The Royal Mint became an executive agency of the Treasury in 1990. The Government announced in July 1999 that the Royal Mint would be given greater commercial freedom to expand its business into new areas and develop partnerships with the private sector.
Master of the Mint, The Chancellor of the Exchequer (*ex officio*)
Deputy Master and Comptroller, R. de L. Holmes

THE ROYAL NATIONAL THEATRE
South Bank, London, SE1 9PX
Tel: 020-7452 3333; Fax: 020-7452 3344;
Email: secretariat@royalmint.gov.uk

Chairman, Sir Christopher Hogg
Members, Ms J. Bakewell, CBE; The Hon. P. Benson; Sir David Hancock, KCB; G. Hutchings; Ms K. Jones; Ms S. MacGregor, OBE; B. Okri; M. Oliver; Sir Tom Stoppard, OM, CBE; E. Walker-Arnott; P. Wiegand; Prof. Lola Young; A. Ptaszynski
Company Secretary, Mrs M. McGregor
Director, T. Nunn, CBE
Executive Director, The Baroness McIntosh of Hudnall

RURAL PAYMENTS AGENCY
PO Box 69, Reading RG1 3YD
Tel: 0118-958 3626; Fax: 0118-953 1370

The Rural Payments Agency (previously the Intervention Board) was established as a Government department in 1972 and became an executive agency in 1990. It is responsible for the implementation of European Union regulations covering the market support arrangements of the Common Agricultural Policy. Members are appointed by and are responsible to the agriculture Ministers in the UK.
Chief Executive (G3), J. Mcneill
Directors (G5), H. MacKinnon (*Operations*); A. Kerr, (*Finance*); vacant (*Corporate Services*); P. Kent (*Legal*); R. Gregg (*Acting Human Resources Director*); J. Welch (*Acting I.S.S*)

SCOTTISH CRIMINAL CASES REVIEW COMMISSION
5th Floor, Portland House, 17 Renfield Street, Glasgow G2 5AH
Tel: 0141-270 7030; Fax: 0141-270 7040

The Commission is a non-departmental public body which started operating on 1 April 1999. It took over from the Secretary of State for Scotland powers to consider alleged miscarriages of justice in Scotland and refer cases meeting the relevant criteria to the High Court for review. Members are appointed by Her Majesty The Queen on the recommendation of the First Minister; senior executive staff are appointed by the Commission.
Chairperson (£372 per day), Prof. Sheila McLean
Members (£217 per day), A. Bonnington; Prof. P. Duff; The Very Revd G. Forbes; A. Gallen; Sir G. Gordon, CBE, QC; W. Taylor, QC
Chief Executive, Ms C. A. Kelly

SCOTTISH ENTERPRISE
120 Bothwell Street, Glasgow G2 7JP
Tel: 0141-248 2700; Fax: 0141-221 3217

Scottish Enterprise was established in 1991 and its purpose is to create jobs and prosperity for the people of Scotland. It is funded largely by the Scottish Executive and is responsible to the Scottish Ministers. Working in partnership with the private and public sectors, Scottish Enterprise aims to further the development of Scotland's economy, to enhance the skills of the Scottish workforce and to promote Scotland's international competitiveness. Scottish Enterprise has a network of 12 Local Enterprise Companies that deliver economic development services at local level.
Chairman (£33,883), Sir Ian Robinson, CBE
Chief Executive, Dr R. Crawford

SCOTTISH ENVIRONMENT PROTECTION AGENCY

Erskine Court, The Castle Business Park, Stirling FK9 4TR Tel: 01786-457700; Hotline: 0800-60 70 60 Fax: 01786-446885

The Scottish Environment Protection Agency (SEPA) is the public body responsible for environmental protection in Scotland. It regulates potential pollution to land, air and water, the storage, transport and disposal of controlled waste and the safe keeping and disposal of radioactive materials. It does this witin a complex legislative framework of Acts of Parliament, EC Directives and Regulations, granting licenses to operations of industrial processes and waste disposal.
Chairman, K. Collins
Chief Executive, M. P. Henton

SCOTTISH EXECUTIVE

— *see* Regional Government Section

SCOTTISH HOMES

Thistle House, 91 Haymarket Terrace, Edinburgh EH12 5HE Tel: 0131-313 0044; Fax: 0131-313 2680

Scottish Homes, aims to improve the quality and variety of housing available in Scotland by working in partnership with the public and private sectors. The agency is a major funder of new and improved housing provided by housing associations and private developers. It is also involved in housing research. Board members are appointed by the First Minister.

On 1 November 2001 Scottish Homes became a new executive agency directly accountable to ministers and the Scottish Parliament.
Chairman, J. Ward, CBE
Chief Executive, B. Millar

SCOTTISH LAW COMMISSION

140 Causewayside, Edinburgh EH9 1PR
Tel: 0131-668 2131; Fax: 0131-662 4900

The Commission keeps the law in Scotland under review and makes proposals for its development and reform. It is responsible to the Scottish Ministers through the Scottish Executive Justice Department.
Chairman (*part-time*), The Hon. Lord Gill
Commissioners (*full-time*), Prof. G. Maher; Prof. K. G. C. Reid; Prof. J. M. Thomson; (*part-time*) P. S. Hodge, QC

SCOTTISH LEGAL AID BOARD

44 Drumsheugh Gardens, Edinburgh EH3 7SW
Tel: 0131-226 7061; Fax: 0131-220 4878

The Scottish Legal Aid Board was set up under the Legal Aid (Scotland) Act 1986. It is responsible for ensuring that advice, assistance and representation are available in accordance with the Act. Members are appointed by Scottish Ministers.
Chairman, Mrs J. Couper

SCOTTISH NATURAL HERITAGE

12 Hope Terrace, Edinburgh EH9 2AS
Tel: 0131-447 4784; Fax: 0131-446 2277;
Web: www.snh.org.uk

Scottish Natural Heritage was established in 1992 under the Natural Heritage (Scotland) Act 1991. It provides advice on nature conservation to all those whose activities affect wildlife, landforms and features of geological interest in Scotland, and seeks to develop and improve facilities for the enjoyment and understanding of the Scottish countryside. It is funded by the Scottish Executive.
Chairman, Dr J. Markland, CBE
Chief Executive, R. Crofts, CBE

SCOTTISH PARLIAMENTARY COMMISSIONER FOR ADMINISTRATION

28 Thistle Street, Edinburgh EH2 1EN
Tel: 0845-601 0456; Fax: 0131-226 4447
Web: www.ombudsman.org.uk

The Scottish Parliamentary Commissioner for Administration was appointed in July 1999 to investigate complaints made to him by Members of the Scottish Parliament on behalf of members of the public who have suffered an injustice through maladministration by the Scottish Executive and a wide range of public bodies involved in devolved Scottish affairs.
Scottish Parliamentary Commissioner for Administration, M. S. Buckley

SCOTTISH PRISONS COMPLAINTS COMMISSION

Government Buildings, Broomhouse Drive, Edinburgh EH11 3XD
Tel: 0131-244 8423; Fax: 0131-244 8430;
Email: joan.aitken@scotland.gsi.gov.uk

The Commission was established in 1994. It is an independent body to which prisoners in Scottish prisons can make application in relation to any matter where they have failed to obtain satisfaction from the Scottish Prison Service's internal grievance procedures. Clinical judgments made by medical officers, matters which are the subject of legal proceedings and matters relating to sentence, conviction and parole decision-making are excluded from the Commission's jurisdiction. The Commissioner is appointed by the First Minister.
Commissioner, Miss J. N. Aitken

SEA FISH INDUSTRY AUTHORITY

18 Logie Mill, Logie Green Road, Edinburgh EH7 4HG
Tel: 0131-558 3331; Fax: 0131-558 1442

Established under the Fisheries Act 1981, the Authority is required to promote the efficiency of the sea fish industry. It carries out research relating to the industry and gives advice on related matters. It provides training, promotes the marketing, consumption and export of sea fish and sea fish products, and may provide financial assistance for the

improvement of fishing vessels in respect of essential safety equipment. It is responsible to the Department of the Environment, Food and Rural Affairs.
Chairman, E. Davey
Chief Executive, A. C. Fairbairn

THE SECURITY AND INTELLIGENCE SERVICES

Under the Intelligence Services Act 1994, the Intelligence and Security Committee of Parliamentarians was established to oversee the work of GCHQ, MI5 and MI6; in 1999 an Investigator was appointed to the committee in order to reinforce the authority of its findings and establish public confidence in the oversight system. The Act also established the Intelligence Services Tribunal, which hears complaints made against GCHQ and MI6. The Security Service Tribunal and Commissioner (*see* below) investigate complaints about MI5.

DEFENCE INTELLIGENCE STAFF
— *see* Defence section

GOVERNMENT COMMUNICATIONS HEADQUARTERS (GCHQ)
Priors Road, Cheltenham, Glos GL52 5AJ
Tel: 01242-221491; Fax: 01242-574349
GCHQ produces signals intelligence in support of national security and the UK's economic wellbeing, and in the prevention or detection of serious crime. Additionally, GCHQ Communications-Electronics Security Group (CESG) provides advice and assistance to Government departments, the armed forces and other national infrastructure bodies on the security of their communications and information systems. GCHQ was placed on a statutory footing by the Intelligence Services Act 1994 and is headed by a director who is directly accountable to the Foreign Secretary. A new building to house GCHQ is being constructed in Cheltenham, with the anticipated completion date of early 2003.
Director, F. N. Richards, CVO, CMG

INVESTIGATORY POWERS TRIBUNAL
PO Box 33220, London, SW1H 9ZQ Tel: 020-7273 4095
The Investigatory Powers Tribunal replaces the Interception of Communications Tribunal, the Intelligence Services Tribunal, the Security Services Tribunal and the complaints function of the Commissioner appointed under the Police Act 1997.
The Regulation of Investigatory Powers Act 2000 provides for a Tribunal made up of senior members of the legal profession, independent of the Government and appointed by The Queen, to investigate complaints from any person about anything which they believe the Intelligence Services or various public authorities has carried out in relation to them, their property or their communications.
President, The Rt. Hon. Lord Justice John Mummery

NATIONAL CRIMINAL INTELLIGENCE SERVICE
PO Box 8000, London SE11 5EN
Tel: 020-7238 8000; Web: www.ncis.gov.uk
The National Criminal Intelligence Service (NCIS) provides intelligence about serious and organised crime to law enforcement, government and other relevant national and international agencies. On 1 April 1998 NCIS was placed on a statutory footing. It is accountable to the NCIS Service Authority.
Director-General, J. Abbott, QPM, CBE

SERVICE AUTHORITY
PO Box 2600, London SW1V 2WG
Tel: 020-7238 2600
The Service Authority for NCIS is responsible for ensuring its effective operation. It operates with the Service Authority for the National Crime Squad. There are 26 members of the authorities, of whom the chairman and nine others serve as 'core members' on both authorities.
Chairman, Rt. Hon. Sir John Wheeler

THE SECRET INTELLIGENCE SERVICE (MI6)
PO Box 1300, London SE1 1BD
The Secret Intelligence Service produces secret intelligence in support of the Government's security, defence, foreign and economic policies. It was placed on a statutory footing by the Intelligence Services Act 1994 and is headed by a chief, known as 'C', who is directly accountable to the Foreign Secretary.
Chief, Sir R. B. Dearlove, OBE, KCMG

THE SECURITY SERVICE (MI5)
PO Box 3255, London SW1P 1AE
Tel: 020-7930 9000
The function of the Security Service is the protection of national security, in particular against threats from espionage, terrorism, sabotage and the proliferation of weapons of mass destruction, from the activities of agents of foreign powers, and from actions intended to overthrow or undermine parliamentary democracy by political, industrial or violent means. It is also the Service's function to safeguard the economic well-being of the UK against threats posed by the actions or intentions of persons outside the British Islands. Under the Security Service Act 1996, the Service's role was extended to support the police and customs in the prevention and detection of serious crime.
Director-General, Sir Stephen Lander, KCB

INTELLIGENCE COMMISSIONER
c/o PO Box 33220, London SW1H 1ZQ
Tel: 020-7273 4514

The Commissioner is appointed by the Prime Minister. He keeps under review the issue of warrants by the Home Secretary under the Regulation of Investigatory Powers Act (RIPA) 2000. The Commisioner is also required to submit an annual report on the discharge of his functions to the Prime Minister.
Commissioner, The Rt. Hon. Lord Justice Simon Brown

SENTENCE REVIEW COMMISSIONERS
PO Box 1011, Belfast BT2 7SR
Tel: 01232-549412; Fax: 01232-549427;
Email: sentrev@belfast.org.uk;
Web: www.sentencereview.org.uk

The Sentence Review Commissioners are appointed by the Secretary of State for Northern Ireland to consider applications from prisoners serving sentences in Northern Ireland for declarations that they are entitled to early release in accordance with the provisions of the Northern Ireland (Sentences) Act 1998. The commissioners have been appointed until 31 July 2005 and are served by staff seconded from the Northern Ireland Office.

Joint Chairmen, Sir John Belloch, KCB; B. Currin

SERIOUS FRAUD OFFICE

Elm House, 10–16 Elm Street, London WC1X 0BJ
Tel: 020-7239 7272; Fax: 020-7837 1689;
Email: public.enquiries@sfo.gsigov.uk

The Serious Fraud Office works under the superintendence of the Attorney-General. Its remit is to investigate and prosecute serious and complex fraud. (Other fraud cases are handled by the fraud divisions of the Crown Prosecution Service.) The scope of its powers covers England, Wales and Northern Ireland. The staff includes lawyers, accountants and other support staff, investigating teams work closely with the police.

Director, Mrs R. Wright

SMALL BUSINESS COUNCIL

1 Victoria Street, London SW1H 0ET Tel: 020-7215 5399; Email: sbcsecretariat@sbs.gsi.gov.uk;
Web: www.businessadviceonline.org

The Small Business Council was set up in March 2000. It is a Non-Departmental Public Body independent of Government acting in an advisory capacity to the Small Business Service. The Council also reports to the Secretary for Trade and Industry on the needs of small businesses.

Chairman, W. Sargent

SMALL BUSINESS SERVICE

1 Victoria Street, London SW1H 0ET
Tel: 020-7215 5365;
Email: enquiries@sbs.gsi.gov.uk;
Web: www.businessadviceonline.org

The Small Business Service was set up by the government in April 2000. The role of the Service will be to provide a voice for small businesses in Government, to improve the coherence and quality of Government support for the small business, and to help small businesses on issues of regulation. There are 45 local Business Link franchises throughout England largely coterminous in their boundaries with the new Learning and Skills Councils.

Chief Executive, D. Irwin

STATISTICS COMMISSION

10 Great George Street, London SW1P 3AE
Tel: 020-7273 8000;
Email: statscom@statscom.org.uk
Web: www.statscom.org.uk

The statistics Commission has been set up to advise on the quality, quality assurance and priority-setting for National Statistics, and on the procedures designed to deliver statistical integrity, to help ensure National Statistics are trustworthy and responsive to public needs. It is independent of both Ministers and the procedures of National Statistics. It operates in a transparent way with the minutes of its meetings, correspondence and evidence it receives, and advice it gives, all normally publicly available for scrutiny.

Chairman, Sir John Kingman, FRS

STRATEGIC RAIL AUTHORITY

55 Victoria Street, London SW1H 0EU
Tel: 020-7654 6000; Fax: 020-7654 6010

The Strategic Rail Authority formally came into being on 1 February 2001 following the passage of the Transport Act 2000.

The SRA's key role is to promote and develop the rail network and encourage integration. As well as providing overall strategic direction for Britain's railways, SRA has responsibility for consumer protection, administering freight grants and steering forward the investment projects. It is responsible for letting and managing passenger rail franchises. The SRA operates under Directions and Guidance Issued by the Secretary of State for Transport, Local Government and the Regions. Where Scotland is concerned it is also subject to Directions from the Scottish Minister for Transport. The SRA has subsumed the powers of the Office of Passenger Rail Franchising (OPRAF) and the British Railways Board (BRB).

Chairman, Sir Alastair Morton
Chief Executive, Mike Grant

TOURISM BODIES

The English Tourism Council, the Scottish Tourist Board, the Wales Tourist Board and the Northern Ireland Tourist Board are responsible for developing and marketing the tourist industry in their respective countries.

ENGLISH TOURISM COUNCIL, Thames Tower, Black's Road, London W6 9EL. Tel: 020-8563 3000;
Web: www.englishtourism.org.uk.
VISIT SCOTLAND, 23 Ravelston Terrace, Edinburgh EH4 3TP. Tel: 0131-332 2433; Thistle House, Beechwood Park North, Inverness IV2 3ED. Tel: 01463-716996. Web: www.visitscotland.com.
WALES TOURIST BOARD, Brunel House, 2 Fitzalan Road, Cardiff CF24 0UY. Tel: 02920-499909 Fax: 02920-485031 Web: www.visitwales.com
NORTHERN IRELAND TOURIST BOARD, St Anne's Court, 59 North Street, Belfast BT1 1NB. Tel: 028- 9023 1221

UNITED KINGDOM SPORTS COUNCIL (UK SPORT)

40 Bernard Street, London WC1N 1ST
Tel: 020-7841 9500; Fax: 020-7841 8850;
Web: www.uksport.gov.uk

The UK Sports Council (UK Sport) was established by Royal Charter in January 1997. Its role is to focus on high performance sport at UK level, with the aim of achieving sporting excellence in world competition. It works to combat drug misuse, deals with international relations and supports major events. It also distributes the funds

allocated to sport from the proceeds of the National Lottery.
Chairman, Sir Rodney Walker
Chief Executive, R. Callicott

UNRELATED LIVE TRANSPLANT REGULATORY AUTHORITY
Department of Health, c/o Room 420, Wellington House, 133–155 Waterloo Road, London SE1 8UG
Tel: 020-7972 4812; Fax: 020-7972 4852

The Unrelated Live Transplant Regulatory Authority (ULTRA) is a statutory body established in 1990. In every case where the transplant of an organ within the definition of the Human Organ Transplants Act 1989 is proposed between a living donor and a recipient who are not genetically related, the proposal must be referred to ULTRA. Applications must be made by registered medical practitioners.

The Authority comprises a chairman and ten members appointed by the Secretary of State for Health. The secretariat is provided by Department of Health officials.
Chairman, Prof. Sir Roddy MacSween

UK ATOMIC ENERGY AUTHORITY
Harwell, Didcot, Oxon OX11 0RA
Tel: 01235-820220; Fax: 01235-436401

The UKAEA was established by the Atomic Energy Authority Act 1954 and took over responsibility for the research and development of the civil nuclear power programme. The Authority's commercial arm, AEA Technology PLC, was privatised in 1996. UKAEA is now responsible for the safe management and decommissioning of its radioactive plant and for maximising the income from the buildings and land on its sites. UKAEA also undertakes special nuclear tasks for the Government, including the UK's contribution to the international fusion programme.
Chairman, Adm. Sir Kenneth Eaton
Chief Executive, Dr J. McKeown

WALES YOUTH AGENCY
Leslie Court, Lon-y-Llyn, Caerphilly CF83 1BQ
Tel: 029-2085 5700; Fax: 029-2085 5701;
Email: wya@wya.org.uk; Web: www.wya.org.uk

The Wales Youth Agency is an independent organisation funded by the National Assembly for Wales to support the youth service in Wales. Its functions include the encouragement and development of the partnership between statutory and voluntary agencies relating to young people; the promotion of staff development and training; and the extension of marketing and information services in the relevant fields. The board of directors do not receive a salary.
Chairman of the Board of Directors, R. Noble
Vice-Chairman of the Board of Directors, Dr H. Williamson
Chief Executive, B. Williams

WELSH ADMINISTRATION OMBUDSMAN
5th Floor, Capital Tower, Greyfriars Road, Cardiff CF10 3AG Tel: 0845-601 0987; Fax: 029-2022 6909;
Email: wao.enquiries@ombudsman.gsi.gov.uk
Web: www.ombudsman.org.uk

The Welsh Administration Ombudsman was appointed in July 1999 to investigate complaints by members of the public who have suffered an injustice through maladministration by the National Assembly for Wales and certain public bodies involved in devolved Welsh affairs.
Welsh Administration Ombudsman, M. S. Buckley

WELSH DEVELOPMENT AGENCY
Principality House, The Friary, Cardiff CF10 3FE
Tel: 0845-777 5577; Fax: 01443-845589

The Agency was established under the Welsh Development Agency Act 1975. Its remit is to help further the regeneration of the economy and improve the environment in Wales. Under the Government of Wales Act 1998, the Land Authority for Wales and the Development Board for Rural Wales merged with the Welsh Development Agency. The Agency is sponsored by the National Assembly for Wales.

The Agency's priorities are to create new businesses and to encourage existing small firms to grow. Its main activities include promoting Wales as a location for inward investment, helping to boost the growth, profitability and competitiveness of indigenous Welsh companies, providing investment capital for industry, encouraging investment by the private sector in property development, grant-aiding land reclamation, and stimulating quality urban and rural development.
Chairman, Sir David Rowe-Beddoe
Deputy Chairman, T. G. Jones, CBE
Chief Executive, G. Hawker, CBE

WOMEN'S NATIONAL COMMISSION
Room 56/4, Cabinet Office, Horse Guards Road, London SW1P 3AL
Tel: 020-7238 0386; Fax: 020-7238 0387

The Women's National Commission is an independent advisory committee to the Government. Its remit is to ensure that the informed opinions of women are given their due weight in the deliberations of the Government and in public debate on matters of public interest including those of special interest to women. The Commission's sponsoring department is the Cabinet Office.
Chair, Baroness Christine Crawley of Edgbaston
Director, Ms J. Veitch

European Parliament

European Parliament elections take place at five-yearly intervals; the first direct elections to the Parliament were held in 1979. In mainland Britain MEPs were elected in all constituencies on a first-past-the-post basis until the elections of June 1999; in Northern Ireland three MEPs have been elected by the single transferable vote system of proportional representation since 1979. From 1979 to 1994 the number of seats held by the UK in the European Parliament was 81. At the June 1994 election the number of seats increased to 87 (England 71, Wales 5, Scotland 8, Northern Ireland 3).

At the European Parliament elections held on 10 June 1999, all British MEPs were elected under a 'closed-list' regional system of proportional representation, with England being divided into nine regions and Scotland and Wales each constituting a region. Parties submitted a list of candidates for each region in their own order of preference. Voters voted for a party or an independent candidate, and the first seat in each region was allocated to the party or candidate with the highest number of votes. The rest of the seats in each region were then allocated broadly in proportion to each party's share of the vote. Each region returned the following number of members: East Midlands, 6; Eastern, 8; London, 10; North East, 4; North West, 10; South East, 11; South West, 7; West Midlands, 8; Yorkshire and the Humber, 7; Wales, 5; Scotland, 8.

If a vacancy occurs due to the resignation or death of an MEP, the vacancy is filled by the next available person on that party's list. If an independent MEP resigns or dies, a by-election is held. Where an MEP leaves the party on whose list he/she was elected, there is no requirement to resign and he/she can remain in office until the next election.

British subjects and citizens of the Irish Republic are eligible for election to the European Parliament provided they are 21 or over and not subject to disqualification. Since 1994, nationals of member states of the European Union have had the right to vote in elections to the European Parliament in the UK as long as they are entered on the electoral register.

MEPs currently receive a salary from the parliaments or governments of their respective member states, set at the level of the national parliamentary salary and subject to national taxation rules (for salary of British MPs, *see* Parliament section). A proposal that all MEPs should be paid the same rate of salary out of the EU budget, and subject to the EC tax rate, was under negotiation between the European Parliament and the Council of Ministers at the time of going to press.

UK MEMBERS AS AT 28 JULY 2001

*Denotes membership of the last European Parliament
†*See* Replacements since the last election
‡Subsequently left UK Independence Party and now sits as an independent
**Subsequently left the Conservative Party and sits with the Liberal Democrats

Atkins, Rt. Hon. Sir Robert (*b.* 1946), *C., North West*
Attwooll, Ms Elspeth M.-A. (*b.* 1943), *LD, Scotland*
*Balfe, Richard A. (*b.* 1944), *Lab., London*
Beazley, Christopher J. P. (*b.* 1952), *C., Eastern*
Bethell, The Lord (*b.* 1938), *C., London*

*Bowe, David R. (*b.* 1955), *Lab., Yorkshire and the Humber*
Bowis, John C., OBE (*b.* 1945), *C., London*
Bradbourn, Philip, OBE (*b.* 1951), *C., West Midlands*
Bushill-Matthews, Philip (*b.* 1943), *C., West Midlands*
Callanan, Martin (*b.* 1961), *C., North East*
Cashman, Michael (*b.* 1950), *Lab., West Midlands*
*Chichester, Giles B. (*b.* 1946), *C., South West*
Clegg, Nicholas W. P. (*b.* 1967), *LD, East Midlands*
*Corbett, Richard (*b.* 1955), *Lab., Yorkshire and the Humber*
*Corrie, John A. (*b.* 1935), *C., West Midlands*
Davies, Christopher G. (*b.* 1954), *LD, North West*
Deva, Niranjan J. A. (Nirj), FRSA (*b.* 1948), *C., South East*
†*Donnelly, Alan J. (*b.* 1957), *Lab., North East*
Dover, Den (*b.* 1938), *C., North West*
Duff, Andrew N. (*b.* 1950), *LD, Eastern*
*Elles, James E. M. (*b.* 1949), *C., South East*
Evans, Ms Jillian R. (*b.* 1959), *PC, Wales*
Evans, Jonathan P., FRSA (*b.* 1950), *C., Wales*
*Evans, Robert J. E. (*b.* 1956), *Lab., London*
Farage, Nigel (*b. 1964*), *UK Ind., South East*
*Ford, J. Glyn (*b.* 1950), *Lab., South West*
Foster, Mrs Jacqui (*b.* 1947), *C., North West*
Gill, Ms Neena (*b.* 1956), *Lab., West Midlands*
Goodwill, Robert (*b.* 1956), *C., Yorkshire and the Humber*
†*Green, Mrs Pauline (*b.* 1948), *Lab., London*
Hannan, Daniel (*b.* 1971), *C., South East*
Harbour, Malcolm (*b.* 1947), *C., West Midlands*
Heaton-Harris, Christopher (*b.* 1967), *C., East Midlands*
Helmer, Roger (*b.* 1944), *C., East Midlands*
‡Holmes, Michael (*b. 1938*), *UK Ind., South West*
*Howitt, Richard (*b.* 1961), *Lab., Eastern*
Hudghton, Ian (*b.* 1951), *SNP, Scotland*
*Hughes, Stephen S. (*b.* 1952), *Lab., North East*
Huhne, Christopher M. P., OBE (*b.* 1954), *LD, South East*
*Hume, John, MP (*b.* 1937), *SDLP, Northern Ireland*
Inglewood, The Lord (*b.* 1951), *C., North West*
*Jackson, Mrs Caroline F., D.Phil. (*b.* 1946), *C., South West*
Khanbhai, Bashir (*b.* 1945), *C., Eastern*
*Kinnock, Mrs Glenys E. (*b.* 1944), *Lab., Wales*
Kirkhope, Timothy J. R. (*b.* 1945), *C., Yorkshire and the Humber*
Lambert, Ms Jean D. (*b.* 1950), *Green, London*
Lucas, Ms Caroline, PH.D. (*b.* 1960), *Green, South East*
Ludford, The Baroness (*b.* 1951), *LD, London*
Lynne, Ms Elizabeth (*b.* 1948), *LD, West Midlands*
*McAvan, Ms Linda (*b.* 1962), *Lab., Yorkshire and the Humber*
*McCarthy, Ms Arlene (*b.* 1960), *Lab., North West*
MacCormick, Prof. D. Neil, FBA (*b.* 1941), *SNP, Scotland*
*McMillan-Scott, Edward H. C. (*b.* 1949), *C., Yorkshire and the Humber*
*McNally, Mrs Eryl M. (*b.* 1942), *Lab., Eastern*
*Martin, David W. (*b.* 1954), *Lab., Scotland*
*Miller, William (*b.* 1954), *Lab., Scotland*
Moraes, Claude (*b. 1965*), *Lab., London*
*Morgan, Ms Eluned (*b.* 1967), *Lab., Wales*
*Murphy, Simon F., PH.D. (*b.* 1962), *Lab., West Midlands*
**Newton Dunn, William F. (Bill) (*b.* 1941), *LD, East Midlands*
Nicholson of Winterbourne, The Baroness (*b.* 1941), *LD, South East*
*Nicholson, James F. (*b.* 1945), *UUP, Northern Ireland*
O'Toole, Ms Barbara M. (Mo) (*b.* 1960), *Lab., North East*

*Paisley, Revd Ian R. K., MP (b. 1926), DUP, Northern Ireland
Parish, Neil (b. 1956), C., South West
*Perry, Roy J. (b. 1943), C., South East
*Provan, James L. C. (b. 1936), C., South East
Purvis, John R., CBE (b. 1938), C., Scotland
*Read, Ms I. M. (Mel) (b. 1939), Lab., East Midlands
*Simpson, Brian (b. 1953), Lab., North West
*Skinner, Peter W. (b. 1959), Lab., South East
Stevenson, Struan (b. 1948), C., Scotland
Stihler, Catherine D. (elected Catherine Taylor) (b. 1973), Lab., Scotland
Stockton, The Earl of (b. 1943), C., South West
*Sturdy, Robert W. (b. 1944), C., Eastern

Sumberg, David A. G. (b. 1941), C., North West
Tannock, Dr Charles (b. 1957), C., London
Titford, Jeffrey (b. 1933), UK Ind., Eastern
*Titley, Gary (b. 1950), Lab., North West
Van Orden, Geoffrey (b. 1945), C., Eastern
Villiers, Ms Theresa (b. 1968), C., London
Wallis, Ms Diana P. (b. 1954), LD, Yorkshire and the Humber
*Watson, Graham R. (b. 1956), LD, South West
*Watts, Mark F. (b. 1964), Lab., South East
*Whitehead, Philip (b. 1937), Lab., East Midlands
Wyn, Eurig (b. 1944), PC, Wales
*Wynn, Terence (b. 1946), Lab., North West

UK REGIONS AS AT 10 JUNE 1999

Abbreviations		
ACPFCA	Anti-Corruption Pro Family Christian Alliance	
AHRPE	Architect Human Rights Peace in Europe	
Anti VAT	Independent Anti Value Added Tax	
EFP	English Freedom Party	
Ind. Profit	Independent Making a Profit in Europe	
Ind. Stable	Independent Open Democracy for Stability	
Lower Tax	Account for Lower Scottish Taxes	
MEP Ind.	MEP Independent Labour	
Soc. All.	Socialist Alliance	
SSP	Scottish Socialist Party	
WW	Weekly Worker	

For other abbreviations, 233

EASTERN

(Bedfordshire; Cambridgeshire; Essex; Hertfordshire; Luton; Norfolk; Peterborough; Southend-on-Sea; Suffolk; Thurrock)

E.4,019,916	T.24.74%	
C.	425,091	(42.75%)
Lab.	250,132	(25.15%)
LD	118,822	(11.95%)
UK Ind.	88,452	(8.89%)
Green	61,334	(6.17%)
Lib.	16,861	(1.70%)
Pro Euro C.	16,340	(1.64%)
BNP	9,356	(0.94%)
Soc. Lab.	6,143	(0.62%)
NLP	1,907	(0.19%)

C. majority 174,959
(June 1994, Lab. maj. 90,087)

MEMBERS ELECTED
*R. Sturdy, C.
C. Beazley, C.
B. Khanbhai, C.
G. Van Orden, C.
*Ms E. McNally, Lab.
*R. Howitt, Lab.
A. Duff, LD
J. Titford, UK Ind.

EAST MIDLANDS

(Derby; Derbyshire; Leicester; Leicestershire; Lincolnshire; Northamptonshire; Nottingham; Nottinghamshire; Rutland)

E.3,170,517	T.22.83%	
C.	285,662	(39.47%)

Lab.	206,756	(28.57%)
LD	92,398	(12.77%)
UK Ind.	54,800	(7.57%)
Green	38,954	(5.38%)
Alt. Lab.	17,409	(2.41%)
Pro Euro C.	11,359	(1.57%)
BNP	9,342	(1.29%)
Soc. Lab.	5,528	(0.76%)
NLP	1,525	(0.21%)

C. majority 78,906
(June 1994, Lab. maj. 229,680)

MEMBERS ELECTED
R. Helmer, C.
**W. Newton Dunn, LD.
C. Heaton-Harris, C.
*Ms M. Read, Lab.
*P. Whitehead, Lab.
N. Clegg, LD

LONDON

E.4,940,493	T.23.10%	
Lab.	399,466	(35.00%)
C.	372,989	(32.68%)
LD	133,058	(11.66%)
Green	87,545	(7.67%)
UK Ind.	61,741	(5.41%)
Soc. Lab.	19,632	(1.72%)
BNP	17,960	(1.57%)
Lib.	16,951	(1.49%)
Pro Euro C.	16,383	(1.44%)
AHRPE	4,851	(0.43%)
Anti VAT	2,596	(0.23%)
Hum.	2,586	(0.23%)
Hemp	2,358	(0.21%)
NLP	2,263	(0.20%)
WW	846	(0.07%)

Lab. majority 26,477
(June 1994, Lab. maj. 346,850)

MEMBERS ELECTED
Miss T. Villiers, C.
Dr C. Tannock, C.
The Lord Bethell, C.
J. Bowis, C.
*Ms P. Green, Lab.
C. Moraes, Lab.
*R. Evans, Lab.
*R. Balfe, Lab.
Ms S. Ludford, LD
Ms J. Lambert, Green

NORTH EAST

(Co. Durham; Darlington;

Hartlepool; Middlesbrough; Northumberland; Redcar and Cleveland; Stockton-on-Tees; Tyne and Wear)

E.1,954,076	T.19.74%	
Lab.	162,573	(42.15%)
C.	105,573	(27.37%)
LD	52,070	(13.50%)
UK Ind.	34,063	(8.83%)
Green	18,184	(4.71%)
Soc. Lab.	4,511	(1.17%)
BNP	3,505	(0.91%)
Pro Euro C.	2,926	(0.76%)
SPGB	1,510	(0.39%)
NLP	826	(0.21%)

Lab. majority 57,000
(June 1994, Lab. maj. 330,689)

MEMBERS ELECTED
M. Callanan, C.
*A. Donnelly, Lab.
*S. Hughes, Lab.
Ms M. O'Toole, Lab.

NORTHERN IRELAND

Northern Ireland forms a three-member seat with a single transferable vote system

E.1,190,160	T.57.77%

First Count
*Revd I. Paisley, DUP	192,762
*J. Hume, SDLP	190,731
*J. Nicholson, UUP	119,507
M. McLaughlin, SF	117,643
D. Ervine, PUP	22,494
R. McCartney, UKU	20,283
S. Neeson, All.	14,391
J. Anderson, NLP	998

MEMBERS ELECTED
*Revd I. Paisley, DUP
*J. Hume, SDLP
*J. Nicholson, UUP (elected on third count)

NORTH WEST

(Blackburn-with-Darwen; Blackpool; Cheshire; Cumbria; Greater Manchester; Halton; Lancashire; Merseyside; Warrington)

E.5,170,524	T.19.67%	
C.	360,027	(35.39%)
Lab.	350,511	(34.46%)
LD	119,376	(11.74%)

UK Ind.   66,779 (6.57%)
Green   56,828 (5.59%)
Lib.   22,640 (2.23%)
BNP   13,587 (1.34%)
Soc. Lab.   11,338 (1.11%)
Pro Euro C.   9,816 (0.97%)
ACPFCA   2,251 (0.22%)
NLP   2,114 (0.21%)
Ind. Hum.   1,049 (0.10%)
WW   878 (0.09%)
C. majority   9,516
(June 1994, Lab. maj. 444,569)

MEMBERS ELECTED
The Lord Inglewood, C.
Sir Robert Atkins, C.
D. Sumberg, C.
D. Dover, C.
Mrs J. Foster, C.
*Ms A. McCarthy, Lab.
*G. Titley, Lab.
*T. Wynn, Lab.
*B. Simpson, Lab.
C. Davies, LD

SCOTLAND
E.3,979,845   T.24.83%
Lab.   283,490 (28.68%)
SNP   268,528 (27.17%)
C.   195,296 (19.76%)
LD   96,971 (9.81%)
Green   57,142 (5.78%)
SSP   39,720 (4.02%)
Pro Euro C.   17,781 (1.80%)
UK Ind.   12,549 (1.27%)
Soc. Lab.   9,385 (0.95%)
BNP   3,729 (0.38%)
NLP   2,087 (0.21%)
Lower Tax   1,632 (0.17%)
Lab. majority   14,962
(June 1994, Lab. maj. 148,718)

MEMBERS ELECTED
S. Stevenson, C.
J. Purvis, C.
*D. Martin, Lab.
*W. Miller, Lab.
Ms C. Taylor, Lab.
Ms E. Attwooll, LD
*I. Hudghton, SNP
Prof. N. MacCormick, SNP

SOUTH EAST
(Bracknell Forest; Brighton and Hove;
Buckinghamshire; East Sussex;
Hampshire; Isle of Wight; Kent;
Medway; Milton Keynes; Oxfordshire;
Portsmouth; Reading; Slough;
Southampton; Surrey; West
Berkshire; West Sussex; Windsor and
Maidenhead; Wokingham)
E.5,972,945   T.24.95%
C.   661,931 (44.42%)
Lab.   292,146 (19.61%)
LD   228,136 (15.31%)
UK Ind.   144,514 (9.70%)
Green   110,571 (7.42%)
Pro Euro C.   27,305 (1.83%)
BNP   12,161 (0.82%)
Soc. Lab.   7,281 (0.49%)

NLP   2,767 (0.19%)
Ind. Stable   1,857 (0.12%)
Ind. Profit   1,400 (0.09%)
C. majority   369,785
(June 1994, C. maj. 230,122)

MEMBERS ELECTED
*J. Provan, C.
*R. Perry, C.
D. Hannan, C.
*J. Elles, C.
N. Deva, C.
*P. Skinner, Lab.
*M. Watts, Lab.
The Baroness Nicholson of Winter-
bourne, LD
C. Huhne, LD
Dr Caroline Lucas, Green
N. Farage, UK Ind.

SOUTH WEST
(Bath and North-East Somerset;
Bournemouth; Bristol; Cornwall;
Devon; Dorset; Gloucestershire;
North Somerset; Plymouth; Poole;
Scilly Isles; Somerset; South
Gloucestershire; Swindon; Torbay;
Wiltshire)
E.3,747,620   T.27.81%
C.   434,645 (41.70%)
Lab.   188,362 (18.07%)
LD   171,498 (16.45%)
UK Ind.   111,012 (10.65%)
Green   86,630 (8.31%)
Lib.   21,645 (2.08%)
Pro Euro C.   11,134 (1.07%)
BNP   9,752 (0.94%)
Soc. Lab.   5,741 (0.55%)
NLP   1,968 (0.19%)
C. majority   246,283
(June 1994, LD maj. 3,796)

MEMBERS ELECTED
*Dr Caroline Jackson, C.
*G. Chichester, C.
The Earl of Stockton, C.
N. Parish, C.
*G. Ford, Lab.
*G. Watson, LD
M. Holmes, UK Ind.

WALES
E.2,211,162   T.28.33%
Lab.   199,690 (31.88%)
PC   185,235 (29.57%)
C.   142,631 (22.77%)
LD   51,283 (8.19%)
UK Ind.   19,702 (3.15%)
Green   16,146 (2.58%)
Pro Euro C.   5,834 (0.93%)
Soc. Lab.   4,283 (0.68%)
NLP   1,621 (0.26%)
Lab. majority   14,455
(June 1994, Lab. maj. 368,271)

MEMBERS ELECTED
J. Evans, C.
*Ms G. Kinnock, Lab.
*Ms E. Morgan, Lab.
Ms J. Evans, PC
E. Wyn, PC

WEST MIDLANDS
(Herefordshire; Shropshire;
Staffordshire; Stoke-on-Trent;
Telford and Wrekin; Warwickshire;
West Midlands Metropolitan County;
Worcestershire)
E.4,001,942   T.21.21%
C.   321,719 (37.91%)
Lab.   237,671 (28.00%)
LD   95,769 (11.28%)
UK Ind.   49,621 (5.85%)
Green   49,440 (5.83%)
MEP Ind.   36,849 (4.34%)
Lib.   14,954 (1.76%)
BNP   14,344 (1.69%)
Pro Euro C.   11,144 (1.31%)
Soc. All.   7,203 (0.85%)
Soc. Lab.   5,257 (0.62%)
EFP   3,066 (0.36%)
NLP   1,647 (0.19%)
C. majority   84,048
(June 1994, Lab. maj. 268,888)

MEMBERS ELECTED
*J. Corrie, C.
P. Bushill-Matthews, C.
M. Harbour, C.
P. Bradbourn, C.
*S. Murphy, Lab.
M. Cashman, Lab.
Ms N. Gill, Lab.
Ms E. Lynne, LD

YORKSHIRE AND THE
HUMBER
(East Riding of Yorkshire; Kingston-
upon-Hull; North East Lincolnshire;
North Lincolnshire; North Yorkshire;
South Yorkshire; West Yorkshire;
York)
E.3,767,227   T.19.75%
C.   272,653 (36.64%)
Lab.   233,024 (31.32%)
LD   107,168 (14.40%)
UK Ind.   52,824 (7.10%)
Green   42,604 (5.73%)
Alt. Lab.   9,554 (1.28%)
BNP   8,911 (1.20%)
Pro Euro C.   8,075 (1.09%)
Soc. Lab.   7,650 (1.03%)
NLP   1,604 (0.22%)
C. majority   39,629
(June 1994, Lab. maj. 344,310)

MEMBERS ELECTED
*E. McMillan-Scott, C.
T. Kirkhope, C.
R. Goodwill, C.
*Ms L. McAvan, Lab.
*D. Bowe, Lab.
*R. Corbett, Lab.
Ms D. Wallis, LD

REPLACEMENTS SINCE
THE LAST ELECTION
London 2000; Pauline Green replaced
by Mary Honeyball, Lab
North East 2000; Alan Donnelly
replaced by Gordon Adam, Lab

Law Courts and Offices

THE JUDICIAL COMMITTEE OF THE PRIVY COUNCIL

The Judicial Committee of the Privy Council is primarily the final court of appeal for the United Kingdom overseas and those independent Commonwealth countries which have retained this avenue of appeal (Antigua and Barbuda, The Bahamas, Barbados, Belize, Brunei, Dominica, Grenada, Jamaica, Kiribati, Mauritius, New Zealand, St Christopher and Nevis, St Lucia, St Vincent and the Grenadines, Trinidad and Tobago, and Tuvalu). The Committee also hears appeals from the Channel Islands and the Isle of Man and the disciplinary and health committees of the medical and allied professions. It has a limited jurisdiction to hear appeals under the Pastoral Measure 1983. In 2000 the Judicial Committee heard 76 appeals and 64 petitions for special leave to appeal.

Under the devolution legislation enacted in 1998, the Judicial Committee of the Privy Council is the final arbiter in disputes as to the legal competence of things done or proposed by the devolved legislative and Executive authorities in Scotland, Wales and Northern Ireland.

The members of the Judicial Committee include the Lord Chancellor, the Lords of Appeal in Ordinary (see page 368), other Privy Counsellors who hold or have held high judicial office and certain judges from the Commonwealth countries.

PRIVY COUNCIL OFFICE (JUDICIAL COMMITTEE), Downing Street, London SW1A 2AJ. Tel: 020-7270 0483. *Registrar of the Privy Council*, J. A. C. Watherston; *Chief Clerk*, F. G. Hart

The Judicature of England and Wales

The legal system of England and Wales is separate from those of Scotland and Northern Ireland and differs from them in law, judicial procedure and court structure, although there is a common distinction between civil law (disputes between individuals) and criminal law (acts harmful to the community).

The supreme judicial authority for England and Wales is the House of Lords, which is the ultimate Court of Appeal from all courts in Great Britain and Northern Ireland (except criminal courts in Scotland) for all cases except those concerning the interpretation and application of European Community law, including preliminary rulings requested by British courts and tribunals, which are decided by the European Court of Justice (see pages 773–81). Under the Human Rights Act 1998, which came into force on 2 October 2000, the European Convention on Human Rights is incorporated into British law; unresolved cases are still referred to the European Court of Human Rights. As a Court of Appeal the House of Lords consists of the Lord Chancellor and the Lords of Appeal in Ordinary (law lords).

SUPREME COURT OF JUDICATURE

The Supreme Court of Judicature comprises the Court of Appeal, the High Court of Justice and the Crown Court. The High Court of Justice is the superior civil court and is divided into three divisions. The Chancery Division is concerned mainly with equity, bankruptcy and contentious probate business. The Queen's Bench Division deals with commercial and maritime law, serious personal injury and medical negligence cases, cases involving a breach of contract and professional negligence actions. The Family Division deals with matters relating to family law. Sittings are held at the Royal Courts of Justice in London or at 126 District Registries outside the capital. High Court judges sit alone to hear cases at first instance. The Restrictive Practices Court, set up under the Restrictive Trade Practices Act 1956, and the Technology and Construction Court, which deals with cases which require expert evidence on technical and other issues concerning mainly the construction industry, defective products, property valuations, and landlord and tenant disputes, are also currently part of the High Court, although the Restrictive Practices Court is due to be abolished following the establishment of the Competition Commission. Appeals from the High Court are heard in the Court of Appeal (Civil Division), presided over by the Master of the Rolls, and may go on to the House of Lords.

In December 1999 the Lord Chancellor began a wide ranging, independent review of the criminal courts in England and Wales. Lord Justice Auld lead the review into how the criminal courts work at every level.

CRIMINAL CASES

In criminal matters the decision to prosecute in the majority of cases rests with the Crown Prosecution Service, the independent prosecuting body in England and Wales (see page 376). The Service is headed by the Director of Public Prosecutions, who works under the superintendence of the Attorney-General. Certain categories of offence continue to require the Attorney-General's consent for prosecution.

The Crown Court sits in about 90 centres, divided into six circuits, and is presided over by High Court judges, full-time circuit judges, and (part-time recorders and assistant recorders), sitting with a jury in all trials which are contested. Since the 12 April 2000, the Lord Chancellor changed the distinction between assistant recorders and recorders. Consequently, there are now only full recorders. The post of Assistant Recorder remains on the statute book but the Lord Chancellor no longer appoints any. There were 1400 full recorders at 30 June 2000. The Crown Court deals with trials of the more serious criminal offences, the sentencing of offenders committed for sentence by magistrates' courts (when the magistrates consider their own power of sentence inadequate), and appeals from magistrates' courts. Magistrates usually sit with a circuit judge or recorder to deal with appeals and committals for sentence. Appeals from the Crown Court, either against sentence or conviction, are made to the Court of Appeal (Criminal Division), presided over by the Lord Chief Justice. A further appeal from the Court of Appeal to the House of Lords can be brought if a point of law of general public importance is considered to be involved.

Minor criminal offences (summary offences) are dealt with in magistrates' courts, which usually consist of three unpaid lay magistrates (justices of the peace) sitting without a jury, who are advised on points of law and procedure by a legally-qualified clerk to the justices. There were 28,735 justices of the peace at 1 April 2001. In busier courts a full-time, salaried and legally-qualified stipendiary magistrate presides alone. Cases involving people under 18 are heard in youth courts, specially constituted magistrates' courts which sit apart from other courts. Preliminary proceedings in a serious case to decide whether there is evidence to justify committal for trial in the Crown Court are also dealt with in the magistrates' courts. Appeals from magistrates' courts against sentence or conviction are made to the Crown Court. Appeals upon a point of law are made to the High Court, and may go on to the House of Lords.

CIVIL CASES

Most minor civil cases are dealt with by the county courts, of which there are about 222 (details may be found in the local telephone directory). Cases are heard by circuit judges, courts or district judges (magistrates courts). There were 399 district judges, and 97 District Judges (magistrates courts), formerly stipendiary magistrates at 1 May 2001. For cases involving small claims there are special simplified procedures. Where there are financial limits on county court jurisdiction, claims which exceed those limits may be tried in the county courts with the consent of the parties, subject to the Court's agreement, or in certain circumstances on transfer from the High Court. Outside London, bankruptcy proceedings can be heard in designated county courts. Magistrates' courts can deal with certain classes of civil case and committees of magistrates license public houses, clubs and betting shops. For the implementation of the Children Act 1989, a new structure of hearing centres was set up in 1991 for family proceedings cases, involving magistrates' courts (family proceedings courts), divorce county courts, family hearing centres and care centres. Appeals in family matters heard in the family proceedings courts go to the Family Division of the High Court; affiliation appeals and appeals from decisions of the licensing committees of magistrates go to the Crown Court. Appeals from county courts may be heard in the High Court of Appeal (civil division) and may go on to the House of Lords.

CORONERS' COURTS

Coroners' courts investigate violent and unnatural deaths or sudden deaths where the cause is unknown. Cases may be brought before a local coroner (a senior lawyer or doctor) by doctors, the police, various public authorities or members of the public. Where a death is sudden and the cause is unknown, the coroner may order a post-mortem examination to determine the cause of death rather than hold an inquest in court.

Judicial appointments are made by The Queen; the most senior appointments are made on the advice of the Prime Minister and other appointments on the advice of the Lord Chancellor.

Under the provisions of the Criminal Appeal Act 1995, a Commission was set up to direct and supervise investigations into possible miscarriages of justice and to refer cases to the courts on the grounds of conviction and sentence these functions were formerly the responsibility of the Home Secretary.

THE HOUSE OF LORDS
AS FINAL COURT OF APPEAL

The Lord High Chancellor (£167,760)
The Rt. Hon. the Lord Irvine of Lairg, *born* 1940, *apptd* 1997
LORDS OF APPEAL IN ORDINARY (each £152,072)

Style, The Rt. Hon. Lord—
Rt. Hon. Lord Bingham of Cornhill, *born* 1933, *apptd* 2000
Rt. Hon. Lord Slynn of Hadley, *born* 1930, *apptd* 1992
Rt. Hon. Lord Nicholls of Birkenhead, *born* 1933, *apptd* 1994
Rt. Hon. Lord Steyn, *born* 1932, *apptd* 1995
Rt. Hon. Lord Hoffman, *born* 1934, *apptd* 1995
Rt. Hon. Lord Hope of Craighead, *born* 1938, *apptd* 1996
Rt. Hon. Lord Clyde, *born* 1932, *apptd* 1996
Rt. Hon. Lord Hutton, *born* 1931, *apptd* 1997
Rt. Hon. Lord Saville of Newdigate, *born* 1936, *apptd* 1997
Rt. Hon. Lord Hobhouse of Woodborough, *born* 1932, *apptd* 1998
Rt. Hon. Lord Millett, *born* 1932, *apptd* 1998
Rt. Hon. Lord Scott Foscote , *born* 1934, *apptd* 2000
Judicial Office of the House of Lords, House of Lords, London SW1A 0PW. Tel: 020-7219 3111
Registrar, The Clerk of the Parliaments (*see* page 217)

SUPREME COURT OF JUDICATURE

COURT OF APPEAL

The Master of the Rolls (£163,213), The Rt. Hon. Lord Phillips of Worth Matravers, *born* 1938, *apptd* 2000, *Secretary*, Mrs L. Grace
Clerk, Ms J. Jones

LORDS JUSTICES OF APPEAL (each £149,897)
Style, The Rt. Hon. Lord/Lady Justice [surname]

Rt. Hon. Sir Paul Kennedy, *born* 1935, *apptd* 1992
Rt. Hon. Sir Simon Brown, *born* 1937, *apptd* 1992
Rt. Hon. Sir Christopher Rose, *born* 1937, *apptd* 1992
Rt. Hon. Sir John Roch, *born* 1934, *apptd* 1993
Rt. Hon. Sir Peter Gibson, *born* 1934, *apptd* 1993
Rt. Hon. Sir Denis Henry, *born* 1931, *apptd* 1993
Rt. Hon. Sir Swinton Thomas, *born* 1931, *apptd* 1994
Rt. Hon. Sir Philip Otton, *born* 1933, *apptd* 1995
Rt. Hon. Sir Robin Auld, *born* 1937, *apptd* 1995
Rt. Hon. Sir Malcolm Pill, *born* 1938, *apptd* 1995
Rt. Hon. Sir William Aldous, *born* 1936, *apptd* 1995
Rt. Hon. Sir Alan Ward, *born* 1938, *apptd* 1995
Rt. Hon. Sir Konrad Schiemann, *born* 1937, *apptd* 1995
Rt. Hon. Sir Mathew Thorpe, *born* 1938, *apptd* 1995
Rt. Hon. Sir Mark Potter, *born* 1937, *apptd* 1996
Rt. Hon. Sir Henry Brooke, *born* 1936, *apptd* 1996
Rt. Hon. Sir Igor Judge, *born* 1941, *apptd* 1996
Rt. Hon. Sir Mark Waller, *born* 1940, *apptd* 1996
Rt. Hon. Sir John Mummery, *born* 1938, *apptd* 1996
Rt. Hon. Sir Charles Mantell, *born* 1937, *apptd* 1997
Rt. Hon. Sir John Chadwick, ED, *born* 1941, *apptd* 1997
Rt. Hon. Sir Robert Walker, *born* 1938, *apptd* 1997
Rt. Hon. Sir Richard Buxton, *born* 1938, *apptd* 1997
Rt. Hon. Sir Anthony May, *born* 1940, *apptd* 1997
Rt. Hon. Sir Simon Tuckey, *born* 1941, *apptd* 1998
Rt. Hon. Sir Anthony Clarke, *born* 1943, *apptd* 1998
Rt. Hon. Sir John Laws, *born* 1945, *apptd* 1999
Rt. Hon. Sir Stephen Sedley, *born* 1939, *apptd* 1999
Rt. Hon. Sir Jonathan Mance, *born* 1943, *apptd* 1999
Rt. Hon. Dame Brenda Hale, *born* 1945, *apptd* 1999
Rt Hon. Sir David Latham, *born* 1942, *apptd* 2000
Rt. Hon Sir John William Kay, *born* 1943, *apptd.* 2000
Rt. Hon. Sir Bernard Anthony Rix, *born* 1944, *apptd.*
Rt. Hon. Sir Jonathan Parker, *born* 1937, *apptd* 2000
Rt. Hon. Dame Mary Howarth Alden, DBE, *born* 1947, *apptd* 2000
Rt. Hon. Sir David Wolfe Keene, *born* 1941, *apptd* 2000

Rt. Hon. Sir John Anthony Dyson, *born* 1943, *apptd* 2001
Rt. Hon. Sir Andrew Centlivres Longmore, *born* 1944, *apptd* 2001
Ex officio Judges, The Lord High Chancellor; the Lord Chief Justice of England; the Master of the Rolls; the President of the Family Division; and the Vice-Chancellor

COURT OF APPEAL (CIVIL DIVISION)
Vice-President, The Rt. Hon. Lord Justice Nourse

COURT OF APPEAL (CRIMINAL DIVISION)
Vice-President, The Rt. Hon. Lord Justice Rose
Judges, The Lord Chief Justice of England; the Master of the Rolls; Lords Justices of Appeal; and Judges of the High Court of Justice

COURTS-MARTIAL APPEAL COURT
Judges, The Lord Chief Justice of England; the Master of the Rolls; Lords Justices of Appeal; and Judges of the High Court of Justice

HIGH COURT OF JUSTICE

CHANCERY DIVISION
President, The Lord High Chancellor
The Vice-Chancellor (£157,699), The Rt. Hon. Sir Andrew Moritt, CVO, *born*, 1938 *apptd* 1994
Clerk, W. Northfield, BEM

JUDGES (each £132,603)
Style, The Hon. Mr/Mrs Justice [surname]

Hon. Sir Francis Ferris, TD, *born* 1932, *apptd* 1990
Hon. Sir John Lindsay, *born* 1935, *apptd* 1992
Hon. Sir Edward Evans-Lombe, *born* 1937, *apptd* 1993
Hon. Sir Robin Jacob, *born* 1941, *apptd* 1993
Hon. Sir William Blackburne, *born* 1944, *apptd* 1993
Hon. Sir Gavin Lightman, *born* 1939, *apptd* 1994
Hon. Sir Robert Carnwath, *born* 1945, *apptd* 1994
Hon. Sir Colin Rimer, *born* 1944, *apptd* 1994
Hon. Sir Hugh Laddie, *born* 1946, *apptd* 1995
Hon. Sir Timothy Lloyd, *born* 1946, *apptd* 1996
Hon. Sir David Neuberger, *born* 1948, *apptd* 1996
Hon. Sir Andrew Park, *born* 1939, *apptd* 1997
Hon. Sir Nicholas Pumfrey, *born* 1951, *apptd* 1997
Hon. Sir Michael Hart, *born* 1948, *apptd* 1998
Hon. Sir Lawrence Collins, *born* 1941, *apptd* 2000
Hon. Sir Nicholas John Pattern, *born* 1950, apptd 2000
Hon Sir Terence Michael Barnet Etherton, *born* 1951, *apptd* 2001
Rt. Hon. Sir Andrew Morritt, CVO, *born* 1938, *apptd* 2000

HIGH COURT OF JUSTICE IN BANKRUPTCY
Judges, The Vice-Chancellor and judges of the Chancery Division of the High Court

COMPANIES COURT
Judges, The Vice Chancellor and judges of the Chancery Division of the High Court

PATENT COURT (APPELLATE SECTION)
Judge, The Hon. Mr Justice Jacob

QUEEN'S BENCH DIVISION
The Lord Chief Justice of England and Wales (£171,375) The Rt. Hon. the Lord Woolf, *born* 1933, *apptd* 2000
Private Secretary, E. Adams
Clerk, J. Bond

Vice-President, The Rt. Hon. Lord Justice Kennedy until 1 February 2002 when The Rt. Hon. Lord Justice May will take office.

JUDGES (each £132,603)

Style, The Hon. Mr/Mrs Justice [surname]

Hon. Sir Patrick Garland, *born* 1929, *apptd* 1985
Hon. Sir Michael Turner, *born* 1931, *apptd* 1985
Hon. Sir Humphrey Potts, *born* 1931, *apptd* 1986
Hon. Sir Richard Rougier, *born* 1932, *apptd* 1986
Hon. Sir Stuart McKinnon, *born* 1938, *apptd* 1988
Hon. Sir Scott Baker, *born* 1937, *apptd* 1988
Hon. Sir Michael Morland, *born* 1929, *apptd* 1989
Hon. Sir Roger Buckley, *born* 1939, *apptd* 1989
Hon. Sir Anthony Hidden, *born* 1936, *apptd* 1989
Hon. Sir Michael Wright, *born* 1932, *apptd* 1990
Hon. Sir John Blofeld, *born* 1932, *apptd* 1990
Hon. Sir Peter Cresswell, *born* 1944, *apptd* 1991
Hon. Dame Ann Ebsworth, DBE, *born* 1937, *apptd* 1992
Hon. Sir Christopher Holland, *born* 1937, *apptd* 1992
Hon. Sir Richard Curtis, *born* 1933, *apptd* 1992
Hon. Dame Janet Smith, DBE, *born* 1940, *apptd* 1992
Hon. Sir Anthony Colman, *born* 1938, *apptd* 1992
Hon. Sir Thayne Forbes, *born* 1938, *apptd* 1993
Hon. Sir Michael Sachs, *born* 1932, *apptd* 1993
Hon. Sir Stephen Mitchell, *born* 1941, *apptd* 1993
Hon. Sir Rodger Bell, *born* 1939, *apptd* 1993
Hon. Sir Michael Harrison, *born* 1939, *apptd* 1993
Hon. Dame Heather Steel, DBE, *born* 1940, *apptd* 1993
Hon. Sir William Gage, *born* 1938, *apptd* 1993
Hon. Sir Thomas Morison, *born* 1939, *apptd* 1993
Hon. Sir Andrew Collins, *born* 1942, *apptd* 1994
Hon. Sir Maurice Kay, *born* 1942, *apptd* 1995
Hon. Sir Anthony Hooper, *born* 1937, *apptd* 1995
Hon. Sir Alexander Butterfield, *born* 1942, *apptd* 1995
Hon. Sir George Newman, *born* 1941, *apptd* 1995
Hon. Sir David Poole, *born* 1938, *apptd* 1995
Hon. Sir Martin Moore-Bick, *born* 1946, *apptd* 1995
Hon. Sir Gordon Langley, *born* 1943, *apptd* 1995
Hon. Sir Roger Thomas, *born* 1947, *apptd* 1996
Hon. Sir Robert Nelson, *born* 1942, *apptd* 1996
Hon. Sir Roger Toulson, *born* 1946, *apptd* 1996
Hon. Sir Michael Astill, *born* 1938, *apptd* 1996
Hon. Sir Alan Moses, *born* 1945, *apptd* 1996
Hon. Sir Timothy Walker, *born* 1946, *apptd* 1996
Hon. Sir David Eady, *born* 1943, *apptd* 1997
Hon. Sir Jeremy Sullivan, *born* 1945, *apptd* 1997
Hon. Sir David Penry-Davey, *born* 1942, *apptd* 1997
Hon. Sir Stephen Richards, *born* 1950, *apptd* 1997
Hon. Sir David Steel, *born* 1943, *apptd* 1998
Hon. Sir Rodney Klevan, *born* 1940, *apptd* 1998
Hon. Sir Charles Gray, *born* 1942, *apptd* 1998
Hon. Sir Nicolas Bratza, *born* 1945, *apptd* 1998
Hon. Sir Michael Burton, *born* 1946, *apptd* 1998
Hon. Sir Rupert Jackson, *born* 1948, *apptd* 1998
Hon. Dame Heather Hallett, *born* 1949, *apptd* 1999
Hon. Sir Patrick Elias, *born* 1947, *apptd* 1999
Hon. Sir Richard Aikens, *born* 1948, *apptd* 1999
Hon. Sir Stephen Silber, *born* 1944, apptd 1999
Hon. Sir Peter Crane, *born* 1940, *apptd* 2000
Hon. Dame Anne Rafferty, *born* 1951, *apptd* 2000
Hon. Sir Geoffrey Grigson, *born* 1944, *apptd* 2000
Hon. Sir Richard Gibbs, *born* 1941, *apptd* 2000
Hon. Sir Richard Henriques, *born* 1943, *apptd* 2000
Hon. Sir Stephen Tomlinson, *born* 1952, *apptd* 2000
Hon. Sir Andrew Smith, *born* 1947, *apptd* 2000
Hon. Sir Stanley Burnton, *born* 1942, *apptd* 2000
Hon. Sir Patrick Hunt, *born* 1943, *apptd* 2000
Hon. Sir Brian Leveson, *born* 1949, *apptd* 2000

Hon. Sir Raymond Jack, *born* 1942, *apptd* 2000
Hon. Sir Duncan Ouseley, *born* 1950, *apptd* 2000
Hon. Sir Colin Mackay, *born* 1943, *apptd* 2001
Hon. Sir John Edward Mitting, *born* 1947, *apptd* 2001
Hon. Sir David Roderick Evans, *born* 1946, *apptd* 2001
Hon. Sir Brian Richard Keith, *born* 1944, *apptd* 2001
Hon. Sir Richard George Bramwell McCombe, *born* 1952 *appt* 2001
Hon. Sir Raymond Evan Jack, *born* 1942, *apptd* 2001
Hon. Sir Robert Michael Owen, *born* 1944, *apptd* 2001

FAMILY DIVISION

President (£157,699), The Rt. Hon. Dame Elizabeth Butler-Sloss, DBE, *born* 1933, *apptd* 1999
Secretary, Mrs S. Leung
Clerk, Mrs S. Bell

JUDGES (each £132,603)

Hon. Sir Robert Johnson, *born* 1933, *apptd* 1989
Hon. Dame Joyanne Bracewell, DBE, *born* 1934, *apptd* 1990
Hon. Sir Michael Connell, *born* 1939, *apptd* 1991
Hon. Sir Peter Singer, *born* 1944, *apptd* 1993
Hon. Sir Nicholas Wilson, *born* 1945, *apptd* 1993
Hon. Sir Nicholas Wall, *born* 1945, *apptd* 1993
Hon. Sir Andrew Kirkwood, *born* 1944, *apptd* 1993
Hon. Sir Hugh Bennett, *born* 1943, *apptd* 1995
Hon. Sir Edward Holman, *born* 1947, *apptd* 1995
Hon. Dame Mary Hogg, DBE, *born* 1947, *apptd* 1995
Hon. Sir Christopher Sumner, *born* 1939, *apptd* 1996
Hon. Sir Anthony Hughes, *born* 1948, *apptd* 1997
Hon. Sir Arthur Charles, *born* 1948, *apptd* 1998
Hon. Sir David Bodey, *born* 1947, *apptd* 1998
Hon. Dame Jill Black, *born* 1954, *apptd* 1999
Hon. Sir James Munby, *born* 1949, *apptd* 2000
Hon. Sir Paul Coleridge, *born* 1949, *apptd* 2000

RESTRICTIVE PRACTICES COURT

Room 410, Thomas More Building, Royal Courts of Justice, Strand, London WC2A 2LL
Tel: 020-7947 6727

President, The Hon. Mr Justice Buckley
Judges, The Hon. Mr Justice Ferris; The Hon. Mr Justice Lightman
Lay Members, B. M. Currie; Sir Lewis Robertson, CBE; R. Garrick, CBE; S. J. Ahearne; J. A. Graham; Mrs D. H. Hatfield; J. A. Scott; B. D. Colgate; J. A. C. King
Clerk of the Court, M. Buckley

TECHNOLOGY AND CONSTRUCTION COURT

St Dunstan's House, 133–137 Fetter Lane, London EC4A 1HD. Tel: 020-7947 7427

JUDGES (each £107,346)

The Hon. Mr Justice Forbes (*Presiding Judge*)
His Hon. Judge Bowsher, QC
His Hon. Judge Havery, QC
His Hon. Judge Seymour, QC
His Hon. Judge Thornton, QC
His Hon. Judge Wilcox
His Hon. Judge Toulmin, CMG, QC
Her Hon. Judge Kirkham

Court Manager, Mrs S. Morson

LORD CHANCELLOR'S DEPARTMENT
— *see* Government Departments and Public Offices

SUPREME COURT DEPARTMENTS AND OFFICES
Royal Courts of Justice, London WC2A 2LL
Tel: 020-7947 6000

DIRECTOR'S OFFICE
Director, I. Hyams
Group Manager and Deputy Director, J. Selch
Group Manager, Family Proceedings and Probate Service, R. P. Knight
Finance and Performance Officer, vacant

ADMIRALTY AND COMMERCIAL REGISTRY AND MARSHAL'S OFFICE
Registrar (£79,767), P. Miller
Admiralty Marshal and Court Manager, K. Houghton

BANKRUPTCY DEPARTMENT
Chief Registrar (£99,420), M. C. B. Buckley
Bankruptcy Registrars (£79,767), W. S. James; J. A. Simmonds; P. J. S. Rawson; S. Baister; G. W. Jaques
Court Manager, Mrs J. O'Connor

CENTRAL OFFICE OF THE SUPREME COURT
Senior Master of the Supreme Court (QBD), and Queen's Remembrancer (£99,420), R. L. Turner
Masters of the Supreme Court (QBD) (£79,767), D. L. Prebble; G. H. Hodgson; J. Trench; M. Tennant; P. Miller; N. O. G. Murray; I. H. Foster; G. H. Rose; P. G. A. Eyre; H. J. Leslie; J. G. G. Ungley
Court Manager, M. A. Brown

CHANCERY CHAMBERS
Chief Master of the Supreme Court (£99,420), J. I. Winegarten
Masters of the Supreme Court (£79,767), J. A. Moncaster; R. A. Bowman; N. W. Bragge; T. J. Bowles
Court Manager, G. Robinson
Conveyancing Counsel of the Supreme Court, W. D. Ainger; H. M. Harrod; A. C. Taussig

COMPANIES COURT
Registrar (£79,767), M. Buckley
Court Manager, Mrs O'Connel

COURT OF APPEAL CIVIL DIVISION
Head of the Civil Appeals Office R. A. Venne
Court Manager, Miss H. M. Goddard

COURT OF APPEAL CRIMINAL DIVISION
Registrar (£99,420), M. McKenzie, CB, QC
Deputy Registrar, Mrs L. G. Knapman
Chief Clerk, M. Bishop

COURTS-MARTIAL APPEALS OFFICE
Registrar (£99,420), M. McKenzie, CB, QC
Chief Clerk, M. Bishop

CROWN OFFICE OF THE SUPREME COURT
Master of the Crown Office, and Queen's Coroner and Attorney (£99,420), M. McKenzie, CB, QC
Head of Crown Office, Mrs L. G. Knapman
Chief Clerk, M. Bishop

EXAMINERS OF THE COURT
Empowered to take examination of witnesses in all Divisions of the High Court

A. G. Dyer; A. W. Hughes; Mrs G. M. Kenne; R. M. Planterose; Miss V. E. I. Selvaratnam

SUPREME COURT COSTS OFFICE

Senior Cost Judge (£99,420), P. T. Hurst
Masters of the Supreme Court (£79,767), M. Ellis; T. H. Seager Berry; C. C. Wright; P. R. Rogers; G. N. Pollard; J. E. O'Hare; C. D. N. Campbell
Court Manager, D. O'Riordan

COURT OF PROTECTION

Stewart House, 24 Kingsway, London WC2B 6HD
Tel: 020-7664 7000
Master (£99,420), D. A. Lush

ELECTION PETITIONS OFFICE

Room E218, Royal Courts of Justice, Strand, London WC2A 2LL. Tel: 020-7947 6131

The office accepts petitions and deals with all matters relating to the questioning of parliamentary, European Parliament and local government elections, and with applications for relief under the Representation of the People legislation.
Prescribed Officer, R. L. Turner
Chief Clerk, Miss J. L. Waine

OFFICE OF THE LORD CHANCELLOR'S VISITORS

Stewart House, 24 Kingsway, London WC2B 6HD
Tel: 020-7664 7317
Legal Visitor, A. R. Tyrrell
Medical Visitors, K. Khan; W. B. Sprey; E. Mateu; S. E. Mahapatra; A. Bailey; A. Kaeser

OFFICIAL RECEIVERS' DEPARTMENT

21 Bloomsbury Street, London WC1B 3SS
Tel: 020-7323 3090
Senior Official Receiver, M. C. A. Osborne
Official Receivers, M. J. Pugh; L. T. Cramp; J. Norris

OFFICIAL SOLICITOR'S DEPARTMENT

81 Chancery Lane, London WC2B 6HD
Tel: 020-7911 7105
Official Solicitor to the Supreme Court, P. M. Harris
Deputy Official Solicitor, H. J. Baker
Chief Clerk, R. Lancaster

PRINCIPAL REGISTRY (FAMILY DIVISION)

First Avenue House, 42–49 High Holborn, London WC1V 6NP. Tel: 020-7947 6000
Senior District Judge (£99,420), G. B. N. A. Angel
District Judges (£80,921), B. P. F. Kenworthy-Browne; Mrs K. T. Moorhouse; M. J. Segal; R. Conn; Miss I. M. Plumstead; G. J. Maple; Miss H. C. Bradley; K. J. White; A. R. S. Bassett-Cross; N. A. Grove; M. C. Berry; Miss S. M. Bowman; C. Million; P. Waller; Miss P. Cushing; R. Harper; G. C. Brasse; Miss D. C. Redgrave
Family and Probate Service Group Manager, R. P. Knight

District Probate Registrars
Birmingham and Stoke-on-Trent, C. Marsh
Brighton and Maidstone, P. Ellwood
Bristol, Exeter and Bodmin, R. H. P. Joyce
Cardiff, Bangor and Carmarthen, R. F. Yeldam
Ipswich, Norwich and Peterborough, D. N. Mee
Leeds, Lincoln and Sheffield, A. P. Dawson
Liverpool, Lancaster and Chester, C. Fox
Manchester and Nottingham, M. A. Moran
Newcastle, Carlisle, York and Middlesbrough, P. Sanderson

Oxford, Gloucester and Leicester, R. R. Da Costa
Winchester, A. K. Biggs

JUDGE ADVOCATES

OFFICE OF THE JUDGE ADVOCATE OF THE FLEET

c/o The Crown Court at Chichester, Southgate, Chichester PO19 1SX. Tel: 01243 520741
Judge Advocate of the Fleet (£99,420), His Hon. Judge Sessions

OFFICE OF THE JUDGE ADVOCATE-GENERAL OF THE FORCES

(*Joint Service for the Army and the Royal Air Force*)
22 Kingsway, London WC2B 6LE. Tel: 020-7218 8089
Judge Advocate-General (£99,420), His Hon. Judge J. W. Rant, CB, QC
Vice-Judge Advocate-General (£95,666), E. G. Moelwyn-Hughes
Judge Advocates (£79,767), M. A. Hunter; J. P. Camp; C. R. Burn; R. C. C. Seymour; I. H. Pearson; R. G. Chapple; J. F. T. Bayliss
Style for Judge Advocates, Judge Advocate [surname]

HIGH COURT AND CROWN COURT CENTRES

First-tier centres deal with both civil and criminal cases and are served by High Court and circuit judges. Second-tier centres deal with criminal cases only and are served by High Court and circuit judges. Third-tier centres deal with criminal cases only and are served only by circuit judges.

MIDLAND CIRCUIT

First-tier – Birmingham, Lincoln, Nottingham, Oxford, Stafford, Warwick
Second-tier – Leicester, Northampton, Shrewsbury, Worcester
Third-tier – Coventry, Derby, Hereford, Stoke-on-Trent, Wolverhampton
Circuit Administrator, P. Risk , The Priory Courts, 6th Floor, 33 Bull Street, Birmingham B4 6DS. Tel: 0121-681 3201
Group Managers: Birmingham Group, Mrs D. Ponsonby; *West Midlands/Warwickshire Group*; D. Bennett, *Staffordshire/West Mercia*; A. Phillips, *East Midlands*

NORTH-EASTERN CIRCUIT

First-tier – Leeds, Newcastle upon Tyne, Sheffield, Teesside
Second-tier – Bradford, York
Third-tier – Doncaster, Durham, Kingston-upon-Hull
Circuit Administrator, P. J. Farmer, 18th Floor, West Riding House, Albion Street, Leeds LS1 5AA. Tel: 0113-251 1200
Group Managers: P. M. Norris *North and West Yorkshire Group*, Newcastle upon Tyne Group, Miss S. Proudlock; *Sheffield Group* D.Keane; *Teesside Group*, Miss E. Yates

NORTHERN CIRCUIT

First-tier – Carlisle, Liverpool, Manchester (Crown Square), Preston

Third-tier – Barrow-in-Furness, Bolton, Burnley, Lancaster; Manchester (Minshull Street)
Circuit Administrator, R. A. Vincent, 15 Quay Street, Manchester M60 9FD. Tel: 0161-833 1005
Group Managers:Greater Manchester Group, Miss G. Hague; *Merseyside Group*, R. Knott; *Lancashire and Cumbria Group*; S. McNally

SOUTH-EASTERN CIRCUIT

First-tier – Chelmsford, Lewes, Norwich
Second-tier – Ipswich, London (Central Criminal Court), Luton, Maidstone, Reading, St Albans
Third-tier – Aylesbury, Basildon, Bury St Edmunds, Cambridge, Canterbury, Chichester, Croydon, Guildford, King's Lynn, London (Blackfriars, Harrow, Inner London Sessions House, Isleworth, Kingston, Middlesex Guildhall, Snaresbrook, Southwark, Wood Green, Woolwich), Southend
Circuit Administrator, K. Pogson, New Cavendish House, 18 Maltravers Street, London WC2R 3EU. Tel: 020-7947 7235
Group Managers: K. Budgen (*London Crime*); D. Thompson (*London City*); L. Lennon (*Kent and Sussex*); M. Littlewood (*East Anglia, Bedfordshire and Hertfordshire*), S. Townley (*Thames Valley, Surrey and Oxford*).
The High Court in Greater London sits at the Royal Courts of Justice.

WALES AND CHESTER CIRCUIT

First-tier – Caernarfon, Cardiff, Chester, Mold, Swansea
Second-tier – Carmarthen, Merthyr Tydfil, Newport, Welshpool
Third-tier – Dolgellau, Haverfordwest, Knutsford, Warrington
Circuit Administrator, N. Chipnall, Churchill House, Churchill Way, Cardiff CF10 4HH. Tel: 029-2041 5500
Group Managers:South Wales Group, G. Pickett; *North Wales and Cheshire Group*, G. Kenney; *Swansea Group*, Mrs D. Thomas

WESTERN CIRCUIT

First-tier – Bristol, Exeter, Truro, Winchester
Second-tier – Dorchester, Gloucester, Plymouth, Weymouth
Third-tier – Barnstaple, Bournemouth, Newport (IOW), Portsmouth, Salisbury, Southampton, Swindon, Taunton
Circuit Administrator, D. Ryan, Bridge House, Sion Place, Clifton, Bristol BS8 4BN. Tel: 0117-974 3763
Group Managers: East Group, N. Jeffery; *Exeter Group*, D. Gentry; *West Group*, D. Gentry

CIRCUIT JUDGES

Senior Circuit Judges, each £107,346
Circuit Judges at the Central Criminal Court, London (Old Bailey Judges), each £107,346
Circuit Judges, each £99,420
Style, His/Her Hon. Judge [surname]
Senior Presiding Judge, The Rt. Hon. Lord Justice Judge

MIDLAND CIRCUIT

Presiding Judges, The Hon. Mr Justice Astill (until 1 January 2002 when The Hon. Mr Justice Goldring will take office).

Miss C. Alton; B. J. Appleby, QC; D. P. Bennett; R. S. A. Benson; R. W. A. Bray; D. W. Brunning; N. B. Cameron Coles, QC; J. R. Case; J. J. Cavell; F. A. Chapman; P. N. R. Clark (Shared with South-East Circuit); M. F. Coates; R.

R. B. Cole; I. Collis; T. G. E. Corrie; *Mrs P. A. Deeley; P. N. de Mille (Shared with South-East Circuit); C. H. Durman; R. M. Eades; H. W. P. Eccles, QC; T. M. Faber; Miss E. N. Fisher; J. E. Fletcher; A. C. Geddes; R.H. Griffith-Jones; J. Hall; V. E. Hall; A. N. Hamilton; D. R. D. Hamilton; S. T. Hammond; G. C. W. Harris, QC; M. J. Heath; Miss E. J. Hindley, QC; C. R. Hodson; J. R. Hopkin; Mrs H. M. Hughes; R. A. G. Inglis; A. W. P. King; Ms F. M. Kirkham; P. G. McCahill, QC; D. L. McCarthy; A. W. McCreath; M. N. McKenna; A. G. MacDuff, QC; D. D. McEvoy, QC; J. V. Machin; M. H. Mander; L. Marshall; W. D. Matthews; H. R. Mayor, QC; C. Metcalf; A. P. Mitchell; P. R. Morrell; J. I. Morris; M. D. Mott; A. J. D. Nicholl; S. Oliver-Jones, QC; R. Onions; R. T. N. Orme; R. C. C. O'Rorke; J. F. F. Orrell; D. S. Perrett, QC; C. J. Pitchers; D. P. Pugsley; J. R. Pyke; R. J. Rubery; R. Rundell; J. A. O. Shand; D. P. Stanley; M. G. T. Stokes, QC; P. J. Stretton; G. C. Styler; A. B. Taylor; J. J. Teare; R. S. W. F. Tonking; S. Waine; *R.M.Wakerley, QC (Recorder of Birmingham) J. J. Wait; J. C. Warner; C.T. Wide QC

Following a boundary review in April 2001 the Oxford Circuit has now become part of the South-East Circuit.

NORTH-EASTERN CIRCUIT

Presiding Judges, The Hon. Mr Justice Henriques; The Hon. Mr Justice Bennett

NORTH AND WEST YORKSHIRE GROUP

R. Adams; G. N. Barr Young; J. E. Barry; C. O. J. Behrens; C. Benson; B. Bush; P. J. Charlesworth; G. Cliffe; P. J. Cockroft; G. J. K. Coles; J. Dobkin; J. Dowse; A. C. Finnerty; M. S. Garner; R. A. Grant; S. P. Grenfell; S. J. Gullick; T. S. A. Hawkesworth, QC; P. M. L. Hoffman; R. Ibbotson; N. H. Jones, QC; G. H. Kamil; R. Keen, QC; T. D. Kent-Jones, TD; P. Langan, QC; K. M. P. Macgill; A. G. McCallum; C. I. McGonigal; J. Prophet; R. M. Scott; J. Spencer, QC; T. Walsh; J. S. Wolstenholme

NEWCASTLE GROUP

P. J. B. Armstrong; B. Bolton; P. H. Bowers; A. N. J. Briggs; D. M. A. Bryant; M. C. Carr; M. L. Cartlidge; W. H. R. Crawford, QC; E. J. Faulks; P. J. Fox, QC; G. F. R. Harkins; T. D. T. Hodson; A. T. Lancaster; P. Lowden; J. P. Moir; M.G.C. Moorhouse; D. A. Orde; L. Spittle; M. Taylor; C. T. Walton; G. Walford; G. Whitburn, QC; D. R. Wood

SHEFFIELD GROUP

T. W. Barber; R. Bartfield; D. R. Bentley, QC; J. W. Bullimore; A. C. Carr; J. Crabtree; J. Cracknell; J. Davies; A. R. Goldsack, QC; P. J. M. Heppel, QC; T. Hewitt; L. Hull; P. Jones; M. K. Mettyear; R. J. Moore; M. J. A. Murphy, QC; J. H. Reddihough; P. E. Robertshaw; J. Shipley; L. Sutcliffe; J. A. Swanson; M. Walker

NORTHERN CIRCUIT

Presiding Judge, The Hon. Mr Justice Perry-Davey; The Hon. Mr Justice Douglas Brown (until 1 January 2001 when The Hon. Mr Justice Leveson will take office).

M. P. Allweis; J. F. Appleton; E. K. Armitage, QC; R. K. Atherton; Miss H. P. Badley; S. W. Baker; R. C. W. Bennett;A. N. H. Blake; C. Bloom, QC; D. J. Boulton; L. F. M. Brown; R. Brown; J. K. Burke, QC; I. B. Campbell; B. I. Caulfield; D. Clark; *D. C. Clarke, QC (Recorder of Liverpool); G. M. Clifton; I. W. Crompton; Miss J. M. P. Daley;*R. E. Davies, QC (Recorder of Manchester); Miss A. E. Downey; B. R. Duckworth; S. B. Duncan; Miss D. B. Eaglestone; T. K. Earnshaw; G. A. Ensor; D. M. Evans,

QC; S. J. D. Fawcus; P. S. Fish; J. R. B. Geake; D. S. Gee; W. George; J. A. D. Gilliland, QC; N.B.D. Gilmour, QC; I. M. Hamilton; J. A. Hammond; D. Harris, QC; M. Hedley; T. B. Hegarty, QC; M. J. Henshell; F. R. B. Holloway; R. C. Holman; N. J. G. Howarth; G. W. Humphries; C. E. F. James; P. M. Kershaw, QC (*Commercial Circuit Judge*); Miss L. J. Kushner, QC; P. M. Lakin; B. L. Lever; B. W. Lewis; R. J. D. Livesey, QC; A. C. Lowcock; A. P. Lyon; D. Lynch; D. I. Mackay; J. B. Macmillan; D. G. Maddison; B. C. Maddocks; C. J. Mahon; J. A. Morgan; W. P. Morris; T. J. Mort; L. Newton; *C. P. L. Openshaw, QC; F. D. Owen, TD; J. A. Phillips; J. C. Phipps; P. R. Raynor, QC; J. H. Roberts; Miss M. Roddy; Miss G. D. Ruaux; H. S. Singer; E. Slinger; A. C. Smith; W. P. Smith; Miss E. M. Steel; M. Steiger, QC; D. R. Swift; P. Sycamore; C. B. Tetlow; I. J. C. Trigger; Miss B. J. Watson; K. H. P. Wilkinson; B. Woodward

SOUTH-EASTERN CIRCUIT

Presiding Judges, The Hon. Mr Justice Aikens; The Hon. Mr Justice Moses

J. D. R. Adams; M. F. Addison; P. C. Ader; J. Altman; Mrs S. C. Andrew; A. R. L. Ansell; M. G. Anthony; S. A. Anwyl, QC; E. H. Bailey; M. F. Baker, QC; C. G. Ball, QC; A. F. Balston; G. S. Barham; B. J. Barker; C. J. A. Barnett, QC; W. E. Barnett, QC; R. A. Barratt, QC; K. Bassingthwaighte; *G. A. Bathurst Norman; P. J. L. Beaumont, QC (*Common Serjeant*); N. E. Beddard; R. V. M. E. Behar; Mrs C. V. Bevington; N.C. van der Bijl; I. G. Bing; M. G. Binning; J. E. Bishop; B. M. Black; H. O. Blacksell, QC; J. G. Boal, QC; A. V. Bradbury; P. N. Brandt; G. B. Breen; R. G. Brown; J. M. Bull, QC; The Hon. C. W. Byers; H. J. Byrt, QC; J. Q. Campbell; M. J. Carroll; M.T. Caterson; B. E. F. Catlin; *B. L. Charles, QC; P. C. L. Clark; P. C. Clegg; Miss S. Coates; N. J. Coleman; S. H. Colgan; *P. H. Collins, CBE; C. C. Colston, QC; S. S. Coltart; ; C. D. Compston; T. A. C. Coningsby, QC; J. G. Connor; R. D. Connor; M. J. Cook; R. A. Cooke; M. R. Coombe; P. E. Copley; T. G. E. Corrie; P. Crawford, QC; Dr E. Cotran; P. R. Cowell; R. C. Cox; M. L. S. Cripps; C. A. Critchlow; J. F. Crocker; D. L. Croft, QC; D. M. Cryan; P. Curl; Mrs P. M. T. Dangor; A. M. Darroch; M. Dean, QC; P. G. Dedman; J. E. Devaux; M. N. Devonshire, TD; P. Dodgson; P. H. Downes; W. H. Dunn, QC; C. M. Edwards; D. R. Ellis; R. C. Elly; C. Elwen; F. P. L. Evans; Miss D. Faber; J. D. Farnworth; P. Fingret; P. E. J. Focke, QC; P. Ford; G. C. F. Forrester; Ms D. A. Freedman; L. Gerber; C. A. H. Gibson; Miss A. F. Goddard, QC; S. A. Goldstein; C. G. M. Gordon; J. B. Gosschalk; A. A. Goymer; B. S. Green, QC; A. E. Greenwood; P.Grobel; TD, VRD D. A. B. R. Hallgarten, QC; Miss G. Hallon; J. Hamilton; Miss S. Hamilton; C. R. H. Hardy; B. Hargrove, OBE, QC; C. Harris; M. F. Harris; A. M. Harvey; W. G. Hawkesworth; R. G. Hawkins, QC; J. M. Haworth; R. J. Haworth; R. M. Hayward; A. N. Hitching; H. E. G. Hodge, OBE; K. M. J. Hollis; J. F. Holt; A. C. W. Hordern, QC; K. A. D. Hornby; M. Hucker; J.C.A. Hughes; M. J. Hyam (*Recorder of London*); D. A. Inman; A. B. Issard-Davies; D. G. A. Jackson; Dr P. J. E. Jackson; T. J. C. Joseph; I. G. F. Karsten, QC; S. S. Katkhuda; C. J. B. Kemp; M. Kennedy, QC; W. A. Kennedy; A. M. Kenny; A.W.P. King; T. R. King; B. J. Knight, QC; P.E. Knowles; L. G. Krikler; L. H. C. Lait; P. QC; Capt. J. B. R. Langdon, RN; P. H. Latham; R. Laurie; T. Lawrence; D. M. Levy, QC; C. C. D. Lindsay, QC; S. H. Lloyd; F. R. Lockhart; J. A. M. Lowen; Mrs C. M. Ludlow; Capt. S. Lyons; A. G. McDowall; R. J. McGregor-Johnson; B. M. McIntyre; K. A. Machin; R. G. McKinnon; W. N. McKinnon; N. A. McKittrick; K. C. Macrae; T. Maher; F. J. M. Marr-

Johnson; D. N. N. Martineau; D. Matheson, QC; N. A. Medawar, QC; D. B. Meier; D. J. Mellor; G. D. Mercer; P.N. De Mille; D. Q. Miller; Miss A. E. Mitchell; D.C. Mitchell; F. I. Mitchell; H. M. Morgan; D. Morton Jack; R. T. Moss; Miss M. J. S. Mowat; T. M. E. Nash; M. H. D. Neligan; Mrs M. F. Norrie; Brig. A. P. Norris, OBE; P. W. O'Brien; M. A. Oppenheimer; D. C. J. Paget, QC; J. Parry; A. Patience, QC; Mrs N. Pearce; Prof. D. S. Pearl; Miss V. A. Pearlman; B. P. Pearson; N. A. J. Philpot; T. D. Pillay; D. C. Pitman; J. R. Platt; J. R. Playford, QC; Miss I. M. Plumstead; P. B. Pollock; T. G. Pontius; W. D. C. Poulton; S. Pratt; R. J. C. V. Prendergast; B. H. Pryor, QC; D. W. Radford; J. W. Rant, CB, QC; E. V. P. Reece; D. J. Rennie; J. R. Reid, QC; M. P. Reynolds; M. S. Rich, QC; D. J. Richardson; N. P. Riddell; G. Rivlin, QC; S. D. Robbins; W. M. Rose; T. R. G. Ryland; J. E. A. Samuels, QC; R. B. Sanders; A. R. G. Scott-Gall; J. S. Sennitt; D. Serota, QC; J. L. Sessions; D. R. A. Sich; A. G. Simmons; K. T. Simpson; P. R. Simpson; M. Singh, QC; S. P. Sleeman; C. M. Smith, QC; S. A. R. Smith; Miss Z. P. Smith; E. Southwell; S. B. Spence; S. M. Stephens, QC; N. A. Stewart; D. M. A. Stokes, QC; G. Stone, QC; T. M. F. Stow, QC; J. B. C. Tanzer, QC; A. M. Tapping; C. Thomas; P. J. Thompson; A. G. Y. Thorpe; C. H. Tilling; C. J. M. Tyrer; Mrs A. P. Uziell-Hamilton; J. E. van der Werff; T. L. Viljoen; J. P. Wadsworth, QC; Miss A. P. Wakefield; R. Wakefield; R. Walker; S. P. Waller; A. R. Webb; C. S. Welchman; R. J. Wilkie, QC; S. R. Wilkinson; Miss J. A. Williams; R. J. Winstanley; S.E. Woollam; D. Worsley; M. P. Yelton; M. K. Zeidman, QC; K. H. Zucker, QC

WALES AND CHESTER CIRCUIT

Presiding Judges, The Hon. Mr Justice Richard; The Hon. Mr Justice Connell; The Hon. Mr Justice Thomas (until 1 January 2001 when The Hon. Mr Justice Pitchford will take office).

K. E. Barnett; M. R. Burr; G. H. F. Carson; J. R. Case; N. M. Chambers, QC; S. P. Clarke; J. T. Curran; Miss J. M. P. Daley; G. H. M. Daniel; D. T. A. Davies; J. B. S. Diehl, QC; R. T. Dutton; D. E. H. Edwards; G. O. Edwards, QC; The Lord Elystan-Morgan; P. M. Farmer; M. R. Furness; J. W. Gaskell; D. R. Halbert; D. J. Hale; Miss J. E. Hayward; G. R. Hickinbottom; R. P. Hughes; T. M. Hughes, QC; P. J. Jacobs; G. J. Jones; H. D. H. Jones; G. E. Kilfoil; C. G. Masterman; D. G. Morris; D. C. Morton; T. H. Moseley, QC; G. A. L. Price, QC; P. J. Price, QC; D. W. Richards; P. B. Richards; J. M. T. Rogers, QC; A. A. Wallace; *J. G. Williams, QC; N. F. Woodward

WESTERN CIRCUIT

Presiding Judges, The Hon. Mrs Justice Hallett, DBE; The Hon. Mr Justice Toulson

P. R. Barclay; J. F. Beashel; R. H. Bond; Miss J. A. M. Bonvin; C. L. Boothman; M. J. L. Brodrick; J. M. J. Burford, QC; R. D. H. Bursell, QC; M. G. Cotterill; *T. Crowther, QC; G. W. A. Cottle; K. C. Cutler; P. M. Darlow; S. C. Darwall Smith; Mrs L. H. Davies; J. D. Foley; F. H. S. Gilbert, QC; D. L. Griffiths; J. D. Griggs; Mrs C. M. A. Hagen; J. A. Havelock-Allan, QC; P. J. C. R. Hooton; M. K. Harrington; G. B. Hutton; J. R. Jarvis; A. G. H. Jones; C. H. de V. Leigh, QC; T. Longbotham; T. K. Mackean; Miss S. M. D. McKinney; I. S. McKintosh; J. G. McNaught; The Lord Meston, QC; T. J. Milligan; J. O. Neligan; S. K. O'Malley; S. W. Overend; R. Price; R. C. Pryor, QC; M. W. Roach; R. Rucker; J. N. P. Rudd; A. Rutherford; Miss A. O. H. Sander; D. H. D. Selwood; R. M. Shawcross; D. A. Smith, QC; W. E. M. Taylor; P. M. Thomas; A. A. R. Thompson, QC; D. K. Ticehurst, QC; D.

I. H. Tyzack, QC; R. C. B. Wade; D. MacLaren Webster, QC; J. H. Weeks, QC; J. S. Wiggs;

RECORDERS (each £422 per day)

F. A. Abbott; R. D. I. Adam; J. F. Akast; D. J. Ake; R. Akenhead, QC; I. D. G. Alexander, QC; C. D. Allan, QC; C. J. Alldis; J. H. Allen, QC; D. M. Altaras; A. J. Anderson, QC; W. P. Andreae-Jones, QC; Mrs E. H. Andrew; P. J. Andrews, QC; R. A. Anelay, QC; J. M. Appleby; Miss L. E. Appleby, QC; B. J. Argyle; G. K. Arran; S. J. Ashurst; E. G. Aspley; P. Atherton; N. J. Atkinson, QC; D. J. M. Aubrey, QC; D. S. Aubrey; M. G. Austin-Smith, QC; M. J. S. Axtell; W. S. Aylen, QC; P. D. Babb; J. F. Badenoch, QC; P. G. N. Badge; A. B. Baillie; N. R. J. Baker, QC; Miss A. Ball, QC; A. Barker, QC; G. E. Barling, QC; D. N. Barnard; H. J. Barnes; T. P. Barnes, QC; A. J. Barnett; Miss F. J. Baron, QC; D. A. Bartlett; G. R. Bartlett, QC; J. C. T. Barton, QC; D. C. Bate, QC; S. D. Batten, QC; P. D. Batty, QC; J. J. Baughan, QC; J. F. T. Bayliss; R. A. Bayliss; D. M. Bean; C. M. Beale; J. Beatson; S. J. Bedford; R. W. Belben; J. K. Benson; P. C. Benson; R. A. Benson, QC; H. L. Bentham, QC; D. M. Berkson; C. R. Berry; M. Bethel, QC; J. P. V. Bevan; Mrs M. O. Bickford-Smith; N. Bidder; P. V. Birkett, QC; M. I. Birnbaum; W. J. Birtles; P. W. Birts, QC; M. J. Black, QC; B. G. D. Blair, QC; W. J. L. Blair, QC; P. E. Bleasdale; R. H. L. Blomfield, TD; D. J. Blunt, QC; O. S. P. Blunt, QC; G. T. K. Boney, QC; Ms C. Booth, QC; J. J. Boothby; S. N. Bourne-Arton, QC; M. J. Bowerman; Ms M. R. Bowron; W. Boyce; S. C. Boyd, QC; J. J. Boyle; D. L. Bradshaw; W. T. S. Braithwaite, QC; D. J. Brennan, QC; M. L. Brent, QC; G. J. B. G. Brice, QC; A. J. Brigden; D. R. Bright; R. P. Brittain; R. A. Britton; J. Bromley-Davenport; S. C. Brown, QC; D. J. M. Browne, QC; J. N. Browne; A. J. N. Brunner, QC; R. V. Bryan; Miss B. M. Bucknall, QC; J. E. Bullen; J. P. Burke, QC; L. S. Burn; H. W. Burnett, QC; R. H. Burns; F. G. Burrell, QC; K. Bush; A. J. Butcher, QC; C. M. Butler; Miss J. Butler; M. D. Byrne; D. W. Caddick; D. Calvert-Smith, QC; R. Camden Pratt, QC; Miss S. M. C. Cameron, QC; A. N. Campbell, QC; Ms A. R. Campbell; J. M. Caplan, QC; G. M. C. Carey, QC; A. C. Carlile, QC, MP; H. B. H. Carlisle, QC; J. J. Carter-Manning, QC; R. Carus, QC; Mrs J. R. Case; P. D. Cattan; R. M. Challinor; Miss D. C. Champion; C. B. Chandler; V. R. Chapman; J. M. Cherry, QC; A. C. Chippindall; C. F. Chruszcz, QC; C. H. Clark, QC; C. S. C. S. Clarke, QC; T. N. Clark; P. W. Clarke; P. R. J. Clarkson, QC; T. Clayson; A. S. L. Cleary; W. Clegg, QC; P. Clements; T. A. Clover; W. P. Coates; D. J. Cocks, QC; J. J. Coffey, QC; T. A. Coghlan, QC; J. L. Cohen; L. F. R. Cohen, QC; W. J. Coker, QC; A. J. S. Coleman; A. R. Collender, QC; P. N. Collier, QC; M. G. Collins, QC; Mrs J. R. Comyns; D. G. Conlin; A. D. Conrad; C. S. Cook; J. L. Cooke, QC; N. O. Cooke; K. B. Coonan, QC; A. E. M. Cooper; P. J. Cooper, QC; C. J. Cornwall; P. J. Cosgrove, QC; Miss D. R. Cotton; J. S. Coward, QC; T. G. Cowling; Mrs L. M. Cox, QC; P. Crampin, QC; L. S. Crawford; N. Crichton; D. I. Crigman, QC; D. R. Crome; S. R. Crookenden, QC; Mrs J. E. Crowley; J. D. Crowley, QC; T. S. Culver; Miss E. A. M. Curnow, QC; P. D. Curran; J. W. O. Curtis; M. J. Curwen; A. J. G. Dalziel; C. P. M. Davidson; A. M. Davies; A. R. M. Davies; H. Davies; J. T. L. Davies; Miss N. V. Davies, QC; R. L. Davies, QC; N. A. L. Davis, QC; W. E. Davis; A. W. Dawson; D. H. Day, QC; Ms M. R. de Haas, QC; P. A. de la Piquerie; M. A. de Navarro, QC; R. L. Denyer, QC; H. A. D. de Silva; P. N. Digney; C. E. Dines; A. D. Dinkin, QC; D. R. Dobbin; R. S. Dodds; R. A. M. Doggett; Ms B. Dohmann, QC; D. T. Donaldson, QC; A. M. Donne, QC; A. F. S. Donovan; A. K. Dooley; Ms J. M. R. Dowell; M. J. Dudley; J. R. Duggan; P. R. Dunkels, QC; J. D. Durham Hall, QC; R. M. C. N. Edelman, QC; A. J. C.

Edis, QC; A. H. Edwards; Miss S. M. Edwards, QC; A. J. C. Edwards-Stuart, QC; A. J. Elleray, QC; G. Elias, QC; E. A. Elliott; J. A. Elvidge; R. M. Englehart, QC; D. A. Evans, QC; D. H. Evans, QC; F. W. H. Evans, QC; G. J. Evans; G. W. R. Evans, QC; I. Evans; M. Evans, QC; M. J. Evans; M. A. Everall, QC; R. B. Farley, QC; D. J. Farrer, QC; P. E. Feinberg, QC; J. F. Q. Fenwick, QC; R. Fernyhough, QC; M. C. Field; R. A. Field, QC; J. E. Finestein; D. T. Fish; D. P. Fisher, QC; G. D. Flather, CBE, QC; R. A. Flowerdew; N. M. Ford, QC; R. A. Fordham, QC; B. C. Forster; M. D. P. Fortune; D. R. Foskett, QC; I. H. Foster; J. R. Foster, QC; D. P. Friedman; S. A. Furst, QC; C. J. E. Gardner, QC; P. R. Garlick, QC; C. R. Garside, QC; R. C. Gaskell; J. B. Gateshill; S. A. G. L. Gault; A. H. Gee, QC; I. W. Geering, QC; D. S. Geey; C. R. George, QC; S. M. Gerlis; D. C. Gerrey; J. S. Gibbons, QC; A. J. Gilbart, QC; N. J. Gilchrist; K. Gillance; N. B. D. Gilmour, QC; L. Giovenne; R. P. Glancy, QC; A. T. Glass, QC; M. G. J. Gledhill; H. B. Globe, QC; Miss E. Gloster, QC; H. K. Goddard, QC; H. A. Godfrey, QC; Ms L. S. Godfrey, QC; J. J. Goldberg, QC; I. S. Goldrein, QC; P. H. Goldsmith, QC; A. J. Goldstaub, QC; L. C. Goldstone, QC; A. J. J. Gompertz, QC; Miss R. M. Goode; J. R. W. Goss; T. J. C. Goudie, QC; G. Gozem; The Lord Grabiner, QC; H. Green, QC; Miss J. E. G. Greenberg, QC; J. C. Greenwood; J. G. Grenfell, QC; D. E. Griffith-Jones; J. P. G. Griffiths, QC; M. G. Grills; M. S. E. Grime, QC; P. H. Gross, QC; B. P. Gulbenkian; J. D. Guthrie, QC; A. S. Hacking, QC; J. W. Haines; N. J. Hall; S. J. Hall; P. N. Hallam; G. M. Hamilton, TD, QC; P. L. Hamlin; J. L. Hand, QC; G. T. Harrap; P. J. Harrington, QC; R. D. Harrison; R. M. Harrison, QC; H. M. Harrod; J. M. Harrow; C. A. Hart-Leverton, QC; B. Harvey; J. G. Harvey; M. L. T. Harvey, QC; D. W. Hatton, QC; A. M. D. Havelock-Allan, QC; The Hon. P. N. Havers, QC; R. W. P. H. Hay; Prof. D. J. Hayton; R. Hayward-Smith, QC; R. Hedgeland; A. T. Hedworth, QC; R. A. Henderson, QC; B. C. Herman; M. S. Heslop, QC; J. W. Hillyer; A. J. H. Hilton, QC; J. W. Hirst; W. T. J. Hirst; J. D. Hitchen; S. A. Hockman, QC; A. J. C. Hoggett, QC; T. V. Holroyde, QC; R. M. Hone; G. A. J. Hooper; A. D. Hope; S. J. Hopkins; M. A. P. Hopmeier; M. Horowitz, QC; Miss R. Horwood-Smart; C. P. Hotten, QC; B. F. Houlder, QC; M. N. Howard, QC; C. I. Howells; M. J. Hubbard, QC; D. L. Hughes; Miss K. L. Hughes; P. T. Hughes, QC; L. D. Hull; Capt. D. R. Humphrey, RN; W. G. B. Hungerford; D. R. N. Hunt, QC; I. G. A. Hunter, QC; M. A. Hunter; G. N. N. Huskinson; M. Hussain, QC; J. G. K. Hyland; M. D. Inman, QC; P. R. Isaacs; S. L. Isaacs, QC; S. M. Jack; M. R. Jackson; I. E. Jacob; N. F. B. Jarman, QC; J. M. Jarvis, QC; A. H. Jeffreys; D. A. Jeffreys, QC; J. D. Jenkins, QC; J. J. Jenkins; Miss A. M. Jolles; D. A. F. Jones; D. L. Jones; S. E. Jones, QC; W. J. Jones; R. C. Jose; Ms W. R. Joseph, QC; H. M. Joy; P. S. L. Joyce, QC; R. W. S. Juckes; M. L. Kallipetis, QC; Miss L. N. R. Kamill; R. G. Kaye, QC; C. B. Kealy; K. R. Keen, QC; Mrs S. M. Keen; D. Kennett Brown; D. M. Kerr; L. D. Kershen, QC; M. I. Khan; G. M. P. F. Khayat, QC; C. A. Kinch; T. R. A. King, QC; M. S. Knott; C. J. Knox; Miss J. C. M. Korner, QC; S. E. Kramer, QC; P. E. Kyte, QC; N. R. W. Lambert; D. C. Lamdin; D. A. Landau; D. G. Lane, QC; B. F. J. Langstaff, QC; R. B. Latham, QC; S. W. Lawler, QC; Sir Ivan Lawrence, QC; Miss E. A. Lawson, QC; M. H. Lawson, QC; G. S. Lawson-Rogers, QC; P. L. O. Leaver, QC; D. Lederman, QC; B. W. T. Leech; I. Leeming, QC; H. B. G. Lett; A. E. Levy, QC; M. E. Lewer, QC; J. A. Lewis; K. M. J. Lewison, QC; S. J. Linehan, QC; R. A. Lissack, QC; G. W. Little; B. J. E. Livesey, QC; C. G. Llewellyn-Jones, QC; L. J. R. Lobo; C. J. Lockhart-Mummery, QC; A. J. C. Lodge, QC; D. C. Lovell-Pank, QC; G. W. Lowe; Rt. Hon. Sir Nicholas Lyell, QC, MP; R. G. B. McCombe, QC; G. F. McDermott; A. E. McFarlane, QC;

R. D. Machell, QC; D. L. Mackie; I. A. B. McLaren, QC; I. McLeod; N. R. B. Macleod; QC; Ms J. Macur, QC; A. G. Mainds; A. H. R. Maitland; A. R. Malcolm; H. J. Malins; M. E. Mann, QC; The Hon. G. R. J. Mansfield; R. L. Marks; J. W. Marrin, QC; A. L. Marriott, QC; G. M. Marriott; A. S. Marron, QC; P. Marsh; R. G. Marshall-Andrews, QC; G. C. Marson; H. R. A. Martineau; S. A. Maskrey, QC; C. P. Mather; P. R. Matthews; Mrs S. P. Matthews, QC; P. B. Mauleverer, QC; R. B. Mawrey, QC; J. F. M. Maxwell; R. Maxwell, QC; Mrs P. R. May; R. M. J. Meeke; G. M. Mercer; N. F. Merriman, QC; C. S. J. Metcalf; J. T. Milford, QC; K. S. H. Miller; P. W. Miller; R. A. Miller; S. M. Miller, QC; C. J. Millington; C. E. Million; J. B. M. Milmo, QC; D. C. Milne, QC; C. J. M. Miskin, QC; Miss C. M. Miskin; A. R. Mitchell, QC; C. R. Mitchell; D. C. Mitchell; J. R. Mitchell; F. R. Moat; E. G. Moelwyn-Hughes; C. R. D. Moger, QC; D. R. P. Mole, QC; M. G. C. Moorhouse; A. G. Moran, QC; P. B. Morgan; A. P. Morris, QC; C. Morris-Coole; H. A. C. Morrison, OBE; R. F. Morrison; G. E. Morrow, QC; M. G. M. Morse; C. J. Moss, QC; P. C. Mott, QC; R. W. Moxon-Brown, QC; J. H. Muir; F. J. Muller, QC; A. H. Munday, QC; G. S. Murdoch, QC; I. P. Murphy, QC; A. C. Murray; C. M. Murray; N. O. G. Murray; N. J. Mylne, QC; H. G. Narayan; A. R. H. Newman, QC; A. I. Niblett; G. Nice, QC; A. E. R. Noble; B. Nolan, QC; M. C. Norman; J. M. Norris; P. H. Norris; G. Nuttall; J. G. Nutting, QC; D. P. O'Brien, QC; Mrs F. M. T. Oldham, QC; M. D. Oldham; R. W. Onions; M. N. O'Sullivan; N. D. Padfield, QC; Miss A. M. Page, QC; S. R. Page; A. O. Palmer; A. W. Palmer, QC; D. P. Pannick, QC; A. D. W. Pardoe, QC; S. A. B. Parish; P. L. Parker; G. C. Parkins, QC; G. E. Parkinson; M. P. Parroy, QC; D. J. T. Parry; E. O. Parry; N. S. K. Pascoe, QC; Miss A. E. H. Pauffley, QC; J. G. Pauslusz; W. E. Pawlak; F. M. Pearce; D. J. Pearce-Higgins, QC; R. J. Pearse Wheatley; The Hon. I. J. C. Peddie, QC; J. V. Pegden; J. Perry, QC; M. Pert, QC; N. M. Peters, QC; J. R. D. Philips; D. J. Phillips, QC; W. B. Phillips; M. A. Pickering, QC; J. K. Pickup; The Hon. B. M. D. Pitt; Miss E. F. Platt, QC; R. Platts; R. O. Plender, QC; Miss J. C. Plumptre; S. D. Popat; A. R. Porten, QC; L. R. Portnoy; J. R. L. Posnansky, QC; Mrs R. M. Poulet, QC; S. R. Powles, QC; D. Price; J. A. Price, QC; J. C. Price; N. P. L. Price, QC; R. Price Lewis; R. B. L. Prior; F. S. K. Privett; H. W. Prosser; A. C. Pugh, QC; G. V. Pugh, QC; G. F. Pulman, QC; C. P. B. Purchas, QC; R. M. Purchas, QC; N. R. Purnell, QC; P. O. Purnell, QC; Q. C. W. Querelle; N. P. Quinn; D. A. Radcliffe; Mrs N. P. Radford, QC; T. W. H. Raggatt, QC; Miss E. A. Ralphs; J. Y. Randall, QC; A. D. Rawley, QC; J. E. Rayner James, QC; J. H. Reddihough; M. H. Redfern, QC; A. R. F. Redgrave; D. W. Rees; G. W. Rees; P. Rees; C. E. Reese, QC; P. C. Reid; R. E. Rhodes, QC; T. Rigby; S. V. Riordan, QC; G. Risius; Miss J. H. Ritchie, QC; T. D. Roberts; A. J. Robertson; G. R. Robertson; V. Robinson; D. E. H. Robson, QC; G. W. Roddick, QC; Miss D. J. Rodgers; P. F. G. Rook, QC; J. G. Ross; J. G. Ross Martyn; P. C. Rouch; J. J. Rowe, QC; R. J. Royce, QC; M. W. Rudland; P. E. B. M. Rueff; A. A. Rumbelow, QC; N. J. Rumfitt, QC; R. J. Rundell; J. R. T. Rylance; C. R. A. Sallon, QC; C. N. Salmon; D. A. Salter; G. R. Sankey, QC; N. L. Sarony; J. H. B. Saunders, QC; M. P. Sayers, QC; R. J. Scholes, QC; T. J. W. Scott; Miss P. Scriven, QC; R. J. Seabrook, QC; C. Seagroatt, QC; W. P. L. Sellick; O. M. Sells, QC; A. J. Seys-Llewellyn; A. R. F. Sharp; P. P. Shears; S. J. Sher, QC; Miss D. A. Sherwin; P. C. H. Simon, QC; Miss E. A. Slade, QC; A. T. Smith, QC; D. Smith; P. W. Smith, QC; R. D. H. Smith, QC; C. J. Smyth; R. C. Southwell, QC; M. H. Spence, QC; Sir Derek Spencer, QC; J. Spencer, QC; M. G. Spencer, QC; R. G. Spencer; S. M. Spencer, QC; R. V. Spencer Bernard; D. P. Spens, QC; R. W. Spon-Smith; D. Steer, QC; Mrs L. J.

Stern, QC; A. W. Stevenson, TD; J. S. H. Stewart, QC; S. P. McLeod; N. R. B. Macleod; QC; Ms J. Macur, QC; A. G. Stewart, QC; W. R. Stewart Smith; A. C. Steynor; G. J. C. Still; D. A. Stockdale, QC; Mrs D. M. Stocken; J. B. Storey, QC; D. M. A. Strachan, QC; M. Stuart-Moore, QC; J. H. Stuart-Smith, QC; F. R. C. Such; A. B. Suckling, QC; Ms L. E. Sullivan, QC; D. M. Sumner; J. P. C. Sumption, QC; M. A. Supperstone, QC; P. J. Susman; R. P. Sutton, QC; N. H. Sweeney; Miss C. J. Swift, QC; M. R. Swift, QC; Miss H. H. Swindells, QC; C. J. M. Symons, QC; J. P. Tabor, QC; J. A. Tackaberry, QC; P. J. Talbot, QC; R. K. K. Talbot; R. B. Tansey, QC; G. F. Tattersall, QC; E. T. H. Teague; N. J. M. Teare, QC; R. H. Tedd, QC; A. D. Temple, QC; V. B. A. Temple, QC; M. H. Tennant; The Lord Thomas of Gresford, OBE, QC; P. A. Thomas; R. L. Thomas, QC; R. M. Thomas; R. U. Thomas, QC; Miss S. M. Thomas; C. F. J. Thompson; R. E. T. Thorn, QC; A. R. Thornhill, QC; P. R. Thornton, QC; A. C. Tickle; M. B. Tillett, QC; J. W. Tinnion; R. N. Titheridge, QC; P. J. H. Towler; J. B. S. Townend, QC; C. M. Treacy, QC; H. B. Trethowan; A. D. H. Trollope, QC; D. W. Tucker; M. G. Tugendhat, QC; H. W. Turcan; D. A. Turner, QC; J. Turner; P. A. Twigg, QC; J. F. Uff, QC; R. P. A. Ullstein, QC; N. E. Underhill, QC; J. G. G. Ungley; P. C. Upward, QC; H. V. C. Vagg; N. P. Valios, QC; D. A. J. Vaughan, QC; M. J. D. Vere-Hodge, QC; C. J. Vosper; S. P. Waine; R. A. Walker, QC; R. J. Walker, QC; Sir Jonah Walker-Smith, Bt.; J. J. Wardlow; B. B. Warner; J. Warren, QC; N. J. Warren; N. R. Warren, QC; D. E. B. Waters; Miss B. J. Watson; Sir James Watson, Bt.; B. J. Waylen; A. S. Webster, QC; M. R. West; L. J. West-Knights; G. B. N. White; W. J. M. White; D. R. B. Whitehouse, QC; R. P. Whitehurst; P. G. Whiteman, QC; P. J. M. Whitman, TD; A. Whitfield, QC; S. J. P. Widdup; R. Wigglesworth; Mrs M. Wilby; N. V. M. Wilkinson, QC; Miss E. Willers; G. H. G. Williams, QC; J. L. Williams, QC; M. J. Williams; W. L. Williams, QC; Miss H. E. Williamson; C. S. W. Williamson, QC; A. J. D. Wilson, QC; A. M. Wilson, QC; I. K. R. Wilson; C. Wilson-Smith, QC; G. W. Wingate-Saul, QC; Miss S. E. Wollam; H. Wolton, QC; M. M. Wood, QC; N. A. Wood; R. L. J. Wood, QC; W. R. Wood; Miss S. Woodley, QC; J. T. Woods; W. C. Woodward, QC; A. P. L. Woolman; T. H. Workman; Miss A. M. Worrall, QC; P. F. Worsley, QC; J. J. Wright; N. A. Wright; D. E. M. Young, QC

DISTRICT JUDGES (MAGISTRATES' COURTS)

The Provincial and Metropolitan Divisions have now been changed, all former Provincial and Metropolitan Stipendiary Magistrates can serve nationally within any district and are now called District Judges (Magistrates' Courts).

District Judges (each £80,921)
Former Provincial Magistrates (each £79,767 and £4,000 additional London allowance)

M. A. Abelson, *apptd* 1998; Mrs J. H. Alderson, *apptd* 1997; R. W. Anderson, *apptd* 1999; Mrs A. M. Arnold, *apptd* 1999; J. A. Browne, *apptd* 1992; P. H. R. Browning, *apptd* 1994; N. R. Cadbury, *apptd* 1997; G. E. Cawdron, *apptd* 1993; D. J. Chinery, *apptd* 1998; T. G. Cowling, *apptd* 1989; C. R. Darnton, *apptd* 1994; S. N. Day, *apptd* 1991; Mrs S. E. Driver, *apptd* 1995; P. K. Dodd, OBE, *apptd* 1991; P. R. Farmer, *apptd* 1998; J. Finestein, *apptd* 1992; P. J. Firth, *apptd* 1994; M. J. Friel, *apptd* 1997; I. Gillespie, *apptd* 1991; K. A. Gray, *apptd* 1995; M. L. R. Harris, *apptd* 1991; N. P. Heley, *apptd* 1994; Mrs P. A. Hewitt, *apptd* 1990; G.

A. K. Hodgson, *apptd* 1993; R. Holland, *apptd* 1999; M. F. James, *apptd* 1991; J. A. Jellema, *apptd* 1998; P. H. F. Jones, *apptd* 1995; C. M. McColl, *apptd* 1994; D. V. Manning-Davies, *apptd* 1996; D. M. Meredith, *apptd* 1995; B. Morgan, *apptd* 1989; P. F. Nuttall, *apptd* 1991; W. M. Probert, *apptd* 1983; M. A. Rosenberg, *apptd* 1993; Mrs M. Shelvey, *apptd* 1999; P. C. Tain, *apptd* 1992; D. R. G. Tapp, *apptd* 1992; D. L. Thomas, *apptd* 1999; W. D. Thomas, *apptd* 1989; P. S. Ward, *apptd* 1994; P. H. Wassall, *apptd* 1994; G. R. Watkins, *apptd* 1993; Miss P. J. Watkins, *apptd* 1995; N. H. White, *apptd* 1985; C. S. Wiles, *apptd* 1996; J. I. Woollard, *apptd* 1998

METROPOLITAN DISTRICTS

Bow Street, The Chief Magistrate; H. N. Evans, *apptd* 1994; C. L. Pratt, *apptd* 1990; T. Workman, *apptd* 1986
Camberwell Green, C. P. M. Davidson, *apptd* 1984; K. Grant, *appt* 1999; R. House, *apptd* 1995; Mrs L. Morgan, *appt* 1995; Miss C. S. R. Tubbs, *apptd* 1996
Greenwich, D. A. Cooper, *apptd* 1991; M. Kelly, *apptd* 1992; H. C. F. Riddle, *apptd* 1995; P. S. Wallis, *apptd* 1993
Highbury Corner, I. M. Baker, *apptd* 1990; P. A. M. Clark, *apptd* 1996; A. T. Evans, *apptd* 1990; M. A. Johnstone, *apptd* 1980; Mrs L. Morgan, *apptd* 1995; J. Perkins, *apptd* 1999; Miss D. Quick, *apptd* 1984
Horseferry Road, G. Breen, *apptd* 1986; A. R. Davies, *apptd* 1985; Mrs K. R. Keating, *apptd* 1987; Mrs E. Rees, *apptd* 1994; G. Wicks, *apptd* 1987
Inner London and City Family Proceedings Court, N. Crichton, *apptd* 1987
Marylebone, Ms G. Babington-Browne, *apptd* 1991; D. Kennett Brown, *apptd* 1982; Miss E. Roscoe, *apptd* 1994
South-Western, A. W. Ormerod, *apptd* 1988; C. D. Voelcker, *apptd* 1982; Miss D. Wickham, *apptd* 1989
Thames, A. Baldwin, *apptd* 1990; I. G. Bing, *apptd* 1989; Mrs J. Comyns, *apptd* 1982; S. E. Dawson, *apptd* 1984
Tower Bridge, C. S. F. Black, *apptd* 1993; M. Read, *apptd* 1993; S. Somjee, *apptd* 1995
West London Magistrates' Court, J. Coleman, *apptd* 1995; T. English, *apptd* 1986; Miss D. Lachhar, apptd 1996; B. Loosley, *apptd* 1989; K. L. Maitland-Davies, *apptd* 1984; J. Philips, *apptd* 1989; D. Simpson, *apptd* 1993; D. L. Thomas, *apptd* 1990

GREATER LONDON MAGISTRATES' COURTS

185 Marylebone Road, London, NW1 5QL. Tel: 0845 601-3600

Justices' Chief Executive and Clerk to the Committee (£93,203), Maj.-Gen. A. Truluck
Training Manager (£27,600–£37,500), Miss J. Whitby

CROWN PROSECUTION SERVICE
50 Ludgate Hill, London EC4M 7EX
Tel: 020-7796 8000
E-mail enquiries@cps.gov.uk
Web www.cps.gov.uk

The Crown Prosecution Service (CPS) is responsible for the independent review and conduct of criminal proceedings instituted by police forces in England and Wales, with the exception of cases conducted by the Serious Fraud Office and certain minor offences.

The Service is headed by the Director of Public Prosecutions (DPP), who works under the superintendence of the Attorney-General, and a chief executive. The Service comprises a headquarters and 42 Areas, each Area corresponding to a police area in England and Wales.

Each Area is headed by a Chief Crown Prosecutor, supported by an Area Business Manager.

Director of Public Prosecutions (SCS), D. Calvert-Smith, QC
Chief Executive (SCS), M. E. Addison
Directors (SCS), C. Newell (*Casework*); G. Patten (*Policy*); J. Graham (*Finance*); L. Carey (*Business Information Systems*); I. Seehra (Human Resources
Head of Communications (SCS), Mrs L. Salisbury
Head of Management Audit Services (SCS), Ms. R. Read

CPS AREAS

ENGLAND

CPS AVON AND SOMERSET, 2nd Floor, Froomsgate House, Rupert Street, Bristol BS1 2QJ. Tel: 0117-930 2800. *Chief Crown Prosecutor (SCS)*, D. Archer; *Area Business Manager*, Mrs L. Burton
CPS BEDFORDSHIRE, Sceptre House, 7–9 Castle Street, Luton LU1 3AJ. Tel: 01582-816600. *Acting Chief Crown Prosecutor (SCS)*, Mrs S. Brown; *Area Business Manager*, Ms J. Altham
CPS CAMBRIDGESHIRE, Justinian House, Spitfire Close, Ermine Business Park, Huntingdon, Cambs PE28 6XY. Tel: 01480-825200. *Chief Crown Prosecutor (SCS)*, R. Crowley; *Area Business Manager*, A. Mardell
CPS CHESHIRE, 2nd Floor, Windsor House, Pepper Street, Chester CH1 1TD. Tel: 01244-408600. *Chief Crown Prosecutor (SCS)*, B. Hughes; *Area Business Manager*, Mrs E. Sherwood
CPS CLEVELAND, 5 Linthorpe Road, Middlesbrough, Cleveland TS1 1TX. Tel: 01642-204500. *Chief Crown Prosecutor (SCS)*, D. Magson; *Area Business Manager*, Mrs M. Phillips
CPS CUMBRIA, 1st Floor, Stocklund House, Castle Street, Carlisle CA3 8SY. Tel: 01228-882900. *Chief Crown Prosecutor (SCS)*, D. Farmer; *Area Business Manager*, J. Pears
CPS DERBYSHIRE, 7th Floor, St Peter's House, Gower Street, Derby DE1 1SB. Tel: 01332-614000. *Chief Crown Prosecutor (SCS)*, D. Adams; *Area Business Manager*, Mrs A. Clarke
CPS DEVON AND CORNWALL, Hawkins House, Pynes Hill, Rydon Lane, Exeter EX2 5SS. Tel: 01392-288000. *Chief Crown Prosecutor (SCS)*, A. Cresswell; *Area Business Manager*, J. Nettleton
CPS DORSET, 1st Floor, Oxford House, Oxford Road, Bournemouth BH8 8HA. Tel: 01202-498700. *Chief Crown Prosecutor (SCS)*, J. Revell; *Area Business Manager*, J. Putman
CPS DURHAM, Elvet House, Hallgarth Street, Durham DH1 3AT. Tel: 0191-383 5800. *Chief Crown Prosecutor (SCS)*, J. Corringhan; *Area Business Manager*, to be announced
CPS ESSEX County House, 100 New London Road, Chelmsford CM2 0RG. Tel: 01245-455800. *Chief Crown Prosecutor (SCS)*, J. Bell; *Area Business Manager*, P. Overett
CPS GLOUCESTERSHIRE, 2 Kimbrose Way, Gloucester GL1 2DB. Tel: 01452-872400. *Chief Crown Prosecutor (SCS)*, W. Cole; *Area Business Manager*, W. Hollins
CPS GREATER MANCHESTER, PO Box 237, 8th Floor, Sunlight House, Quay Street, Manchester M60 3PS. Tel: 0161-827 4700. *Chief Crown Prosecutor (SCS)*, T. Taylor; *Area Business Manager*, K. Fox
CPS HAMPSHIRE, 3rd Floor, Black Horse House, 810 Leigh Road, Eastleigh, Hants SO50 9FH. Tel: 02380-673800. *Chief Crown Prosecutor (SCS)*, R. Daw; *Area Business Manager*, M. Sunderland

CPS HERTFORDSHIRE, Queen's House, 58 Victoria Street, St Albans, Herts AL1 3HZ. Tel: 01727-798700. *Chief Crown Prosecutor (SCS)*, C. Ingham; *Area Business Manager*, L. Carroll

CPS HUMBERSIDE, 2nd Floor, King William House, Lowgate, Hull HU1 1RS. Tel: 01482-621000. *Chief Crown Prosecutor (SCS)*, B. Marshall; *Area Business Manager*, Ms C. Skidmore

CPS KENT, Priory Gate, 29 Union Street, Maidstone, Kent ME14 1PT. Tel: 01622-356300. *Chief Crown Prosecutor (SCS)*, Ms E. Howe; *Area Business Manager*, K. Mitchell

CPS LANCASHIRE, 3rd Floor, Unicentre, Lord's Walk, Preston PR1 1DH. Tel: 01772-208100. *Chief Crown Prosecutor (SCS)*, D. Dickenson; *Area Business Manager*, G. Rankin

CPS LEICESTERSHIRE, Princes Court, 34 York Road, Leicester LE1 5TU. Tel: 0116-204 6700. *Chief Crown Prosecutor (SCS)*, M. Howard; *Area Business Manager*, Ms L. Jones

CPS LINCOLNSHIRE, Crosstrend House, 10A Newport, Lincoln LN1 3DF. Tel: 01522-585900. *Chief Crown Prosecutor (SCS)*, Ms A. Kerr; *Area Business Manager*, Ms A. Garbett

CPS LONDON (METROPOLITAN), 4th Floor, 50 Ludgate Hill, London EC4M 8000. *Chief Crown Prosecutor (SCS)*, P. Boeuf; *Assistant Chief Crown Prosecutors (SCS)*: R. Barcaly; Ms M. Werrett; H. Cohen; M. Townsend; *Area Business Manager*, A. Machray

CPS MERSEYSIDE, 7th Floor (South), Royal Liver Building, Pier Head, Liverpool L3 1HN. Tel: 0151-239 6400. *Chief Crown Prosecutor (SCS)*, J. Holt; *Area Business Manager*, Ms D. King

CPS NORFOLK, Haldin House, Old Bank of England Court, Queen Street, Norwich NR2 4SX. Tel: 01603-693000. *Chief Crown Prosecutor (SCS)*, P. Tidey; *Area Business Manager*, Ms F. CampbellCPS NORTH YORKSHIRE 6th Floor, Ryedale Building, 60 Piccadilly, York YO1 1NS. Tel: 01904-731700. *Chief Crown Prosecutor (SCS)*, R. Turnbull; *Area Business Manager*, R. Cragg

CPS NORTHAMPTONSHIRE Beaumont House, Cliftonville, Northampton NN1 5BE. Tel: 01604-823600. *Chief Crown Prosecutor (SCS)*, C. Chapman; *Area Business Manager*, J. Stephenson

CPS NORTHUMBRIA 1st Floor, Benton House, 136 Sandyford Road, Newcastle upon Tyne NE2 1QE. Tel: 0191-260 4200. *Chief Crown Prosecutor (SCS)*, Ms N. Reasbeck; *Area Business Manager*, I. Groundwell

CPS NOTTINGHAMSHIRE, 2 King Edward Court, King Edward Street, Nottingham NG1 1EL. Tel: 0115-852 3300. *Chief Crown Prosecutor (SCS)*, P. Lewis; *Area Business Manager*, Mrs G. Pessol

CPS SOUTH YORKSHIRE, Greenfield House, 32 Scotland Street, Sheffield S3 7DQ. Tel: 0114-229 8600. *Chief Crown Prosecutor (SCS)*, Mrs J. Walker; *Area Business Manager*, C. Day

CPS STAFFORDSHIRE, 11A Princes Street, Stafford ST16 2EU. Tel: 01785-272200. *Chief Crown Prosecutor (SCS)*, H. Ireland; *Area Business Manager*, B. Laybourne

CPS SUFFOLK, Saxon House, 1 Cromwell Square, Ipswich IP1 1TS. Tel: 01473-282100. *Chief Crown Prosecutor (SCS)*, C. Yule; *Area Business Manager*, Mrs A. Saunders

CPS SURREY, One Onslow Street, Guildford, Surrey GU1 4YA. Tel: 01483-468200. *Chief Crown Prosecutor (SCS)*, Ms S. Hebblethwaite; *Area Business Manager*, M. Wray

CPS SUSSEX Unit 3, Clifton Mews, Clifton Hill, Brighton BN1 3HR. Tel: 01273-765600. *Chief Crown Prosecutor (SCS)*, Mrs A. Saunders; *Area Business Manager*, B. Shepherd

CPS THAMES VALLEY, The Courtyard, Lombard Street, Abingdon, Oxon OX14 5SE. Tel: 01235-551900. *Chief Crown Prosecutor (SCS)*, S. Clements; *Area Business Manager*, G. Choldcroft

CPS WARWICKSHIRE, Rossmore House, 10 Newbold Terrace, Leamington Spa, Warks CV32 4EA. Tel: 01926-455000. *Chief Crown Prosecutor (SCS)*, M. Lynn; *Area Business Manager*, Mrs S. Petyt

CPS WEST MERCIA, Artillery House, Heritage Way, Droitwich, Worcester WR9 8YB. Tel: 01905-825000. *Chief Crown Prosecutor (SCS)*, J. England; *Area Business Manager*, L. Sutton

CPS WEST MIDLANDS, 14th Floor, Colmore Gate, 2 Colmore Row, Birmingham B3 2QA. Tel: 0121-262 1300. *Chief Crown Prosecutor (SCS)*, D. Blundell; *Area Business Manager*, M. Grist

CPS WEST YORKSHIRE, Oxford House, Oxford Row, Leeds LS1 3BE Tel: 0113-290 2700. *Chief Crown Prosecutor (SCS)*, N. Franklin; *Area Business Manager*, R. Stevenson

CPS WILTSHIRE 2nd Floor, Fox Talbot House, Bellinger Close, Malmesbury Road, Chippenham, Wilts SN15 1BN. Tel: 01249-766100. *Chief Crown Prosecutor (SCS)*, N. Hawkins; *Area Business Manager*, N. Nabi

WALES

CPS DYFED-POWYS, Heol Penlanffos, Tanerdy, Carmarthen, Dyfed SA31 2EZ. Tel: 01267-242100. *Chief Crown Prosecutor (SCS)*, S. Rowlands; *Area Business Manager*, Mrs C. Jones

CPS GWENT 6th Floor, Chartist Tower, Upper Dock Street, Newport, Gwent NP9 1DW. Tel: 01633-261100. *Chief Crown Prosecutor (SCS)*, C. Woolley; *Area Business Manager*, Ms H. Phillips

CPS NORTH WALES Bromfield House, Ellice Way, Wrexham LL13 7YW. Tel: 01978 346000. *Chief Crown Prosecutor (SCS)*, P. Whittaker; *Area Business Manager*, Mrs A. Walsh

CPS SOUTH WALES 20th Floor, Capital Tower, Greyfriars Road, Cardiff CF1 3PL. Tel: 029-2080 3900. *Chief Crown Prosecutor (SCS)*, H. Heycock; *Area Business Manager*, I. Edmondson

The Scottish Judicature

Scotland has a legal system separate from and differing greatly from the English legal system in enacted law, judicial procedure and the structure of courts.

In Scotland the system of public prosecution is headed by the Lord Advocate and is independent of the police, who have no say in the decision to prosecute. The Lord Advocate, discharging his functions through the Crown Office in Edinburgh, is responsible for prosecutions in the High Court, sheriff courts and district courts. Prosecutions in the High Court are prepared by the Crown Office and conducted in court by one of the law officers, by an advocate-depute, or by a solicitor advocate. In the inferior courts the decision to prosecute is made and prosecution is preferred by procurators fiscal, who are lawyers and full-time civil servants subject to the directions of the Crown Office. A permanent legally-qualified civil servant known as the Crown Agent is responsible for the running of the Crown Office and the organisation of the Procurator Fiscal Service, of which he is the head.

Scotland is divided into six sheriffdoms, each with a full-time sheriff principal. The sheriffdoms are further divided into sheriff court districts, each of which has a legally-qualified resident sheriff or sheriffs, who are the judges of the court.

In criminal cases sheriffs principal and sheriffs have the same powers; sitting with a jury of 15 members, they may try more serious cases on indictment, or, sitting alone, may try lesser cases under summary procedure. Minor summary offences are dealt with in district courts which are administered by the district and the islands local government authorities and presided over by lay justices of the peace (of whom there are about 4,000) and, in Glasgow only, by district judges (magistrates courts). Juvenile offenders (children under 16) may be brought before an informal children's hearing comprising three local lay people. The superior criminal court is the High Court of Justiciary which is both a trial and an appeal court. Cases on indictment are tried by a High Court judge, sitting with a jury of 15, in Edinburgh and on circuit in other towns. Appeals from the lower courts against conviction or sentence are heard also by the High Court, which sits as an appeal court only in Edinburgh. There is no further appeal to the House of Lords in criminal cases.

In civil cases the jurisdiction of the sheriff court extends to most kinds of action. Appeal against decisions of the sheriff may be made to the sheriff principal and thence to the Court of Session, or direct to the Court of Session, which sits only in Edinburgh. The Court of Session is divided into the Inner and the Outer House. The Outer House is a court of first instance in which cases are heard by judges sitting singly, sometimes with a jury of 12. The Inner House, itself subdivided into two divisions of equal status, is mainly an appeal court. Appeals may be made to the Inner House from the Outer House as well as from the sheriff court. An appeal may be made from the Inner House to the House of Lords.

The judges of the Court of Session are the same as those of the High Court of Justiciary, the Lord President of the Court of Session also holding the office of Lord Justice General in the High Court. Senators of the College of Justice are Lords Commissioners of Justiciary as well as judges of the Court of Session. On appointment, a Senator takes a judicial title, which is retained for life. Although styled 'The Hon./Rt. Hon. Lord —', the Senator is not a peer.

The office of coroner does not exist in Scotland. The local procurator fiscal inquires privately into sudden or suspicious deaths and may report findings to the Crown Agent. In some cases a fatal accident inquiry may be held before the sheriff.

COURT OF SESSION AND HIGH COURT OF JUSTICIARY

The Lord President and Lord Justice General (£163,213)
The Rt. Hon. the Lord Rodger of Earlsferry, *born* 1944, *apptd* 1996
Secretary, A. Maxwell

INNER HOUSE
Lords of Session (each £149,897)

FIRST DIVISION
The Lord President
Rt. Hon. Lord Prosser (William Prosser), *born* 1934, *apptd* 1986

Rt. Hon. Lord Cameron of Lochbroom, *born* 1931, *apptd* 1989
Hon. Lord Marnoch (Michael Bruce), *born* 1938, *apptd* 1990

SECOND DIVISION
Lord Justice Clerk (£157,699), The Rt. Hon. Lord Cullen (William Cullen), *born* 1935, *apptd* 1997
Rt. Hon. Lord Kirkwood (Ian Kirkwood), *born* 1932, *apptd* 1987
Rt. Hon. Lord Coulsfield (John Cameron), *born* 1934, *apptd* 1987
Hon. Lord MacLean (Ranald MacLean), *born* 1938, *apptd* 1990.
Hon. Lord Osborne (Kenneth Osborne), *born* 1937, *apptd* 1990
Lord Penrose (George Penrose), *born* 1938, *apptd* 1990

OUTER HOUSE
Lords of Session (each £132,603)

Hon. Lord Abernethy (Alistair Cameron), *born* 1938, *apptd* 1992
Hon. Lord Johnston (Alan Johnston), *born* 1942, *apptd* 1994
Hon. Lord Gill (Brian Gill), *born* 1942, *apptd* 1994
Hon. Lord Hamilton (Arthur Hamilton), *born* 1942, *apptd* 1995
Hon. Lord Dawson (Thomas Dawson), *born* 1948, *apptd* 1995
Hon. Lord Macfadyen (Donald Macfadyen), *born* 1945, *apptd* 1995
Hon. Lady Cosgrove (Hazel Aronson), *born* 1946, *;apptd* 1996
Hon. Lord Nimmo Smith (William Nimmo Smith), *born* 1942, *apptd* 1996
Hon. Lord Philip (Alexander Philip), *born* 1942, *apptd* 1996
Hon. Lord Kingarth (Derek Emslie), *born* 1949, *apptd* 1997
Hon. Lord Bonomy (Iain Bonomy), *born* 1946, *apptd* 1997
Hon. Lord Eassie (Ronald Mackay), *born* 1945, *apptd* 1997
Hon. Lord Reed (Robert Reed), *born* 1956, *apptd* 1998
Hon. Lord Wheatley (John Wheatley), *born* 1941, *apptd* 2000
Hon. Lady Paton (Ann Paton), *born* 1952, *apptd* 2000
Hon. Lord Carloway (Colin Sutherland), *born* 1954, *apptd* 2000
Hon. Lord Clarke (Matthew Clarke), *born* 1947, *apptd* 2000
Rt. Hon. Lord Hardie (Andrew Hardie), *born* 1946, *apptd* 2000
Rt. Hon. Lord Mackay of Drumadoon (Donald Mackay), *born* 1946, *apptd* 2000
Hon. Lord McEwan (Robin McEwan), *born* 1943, *apptd* 2000
Hon. Lord Menzies (Duncan Menzies), *born* 1953, *apptd* 2001
Hon. Lord Drummond Young (James Drummond Young), *born* 1950, *apptd* 2001

COURT OF SESSION AND HIGH COURT OF JUSTICIARY

Parliament House, Parliament Square, Edinburgh EH1 1HQ Tel: 0131-225 2595

Principal Clerk of Session and Justiciary (£33,391–£55,711), J. L. Anderson
Deputy Principal Clerk of Justiciary (£29,277–£45,365), T. Higgins

Deputy Principal Clerk of Session and Principal Extractor (£29,277–£45,365), D. Shand
Deputy in Charge of Offices of Court, Mrs P. McFarlane
Deputy Principal Clerk (Keeper of the Rolls) (£29,277–£5,365), D. Shand
Depute Clerks of Session and Justiciary (£22,348–£29,381), N. J. Dowie; I. F. Smith; T. Higgins; T. B. Cruickshank; Q. A. Oliver; F. Shannly; A. S. Moffat; G. G. Ellis; W. Dunn; A. M. Finlayson; C. C. Armstrong; R. Jenkins; J. O. McLean; M. Weir; R. M. Sinclair; E. G. Appelbe; B. Watson; D. W. Cullen; I. D. Martin; N. McGinley; J. Lynn; E. Dickson; K. D. Carter; F. Petrie; D. Fraser; S. M. Fowler; W. G. Combe; R. T. MacPherson; P. A. Johnston; D. Bruton

SCOTTISH EXECUTIVE JUSTICE DEPARTMENT
Hayweight House, 23 Lauriston Street, Edinburgh EH3 9DQ
Tel: 0131-229 9200

Courts Group is responsible for the provision of sufficient Judges and Sheriffs for the needs of the programme of the supreme and Sheriffs Court in Scotland. It is also responsible for the promotion, through the reform of law of Scotland, of the independence, integrity and quality of the judicial process in civil proceedings (and in relation to evidence, in criminal proceedings). It also has a role in the development of the private international law of Scotland and the relationship between the Scottish Legal System and other legal systems including those in Europe and the United Kingdom; and provides resources for the efficient administration of a number of tribunals and small departments.
Head of Judicial Appointments and Finance Division (SCS), D. Stewart
Head of Civil Law and International Division (SCS), P. M. Beaton

SCOTTISH COURT SERVICE
Hayweight House, 23 Lauriston Street, Edinburgh EH3 9DQ Tel: 0131-229 9200

The Scottish Court Service is an executive agency within the Scottish Executive Justice Department. It is responsible to the Scottish Ministers for the provision of staff, court houses and associated services for the Supreme and Sheriff Courts.
Chief Executive, J. Ewing

SHERIFF COURT OF CHANCERY
27 Chambers Street, Edinburgh EH1 1LB
Tel: 0131-225 2525

The Court deals with service of heirs and completion of title in relation to heritable property.
Sheriff of Chancery, C. G. B. Nicholson, QC

HM COMMISSARY OFFICE
27 Chambers Street, Edinburgh EH1 1LB
Tel: 0131-225 2525

The Office is responsible for issuing confirmation, a legal document entitling a person to execute a deceased person's will, and other related matters.
Commissary Clerk, J. M. Ross

SCOTTISH LAND COURT
1 Grosvenor Crescent, Edinburgh EH12 5ER
Tel: 0131-225 3595

The court deals with disputes relating to agricultural and crofting land in Scotland.
Chairman (£107,346), The Hon. Lord McGhie (James McGhie), QC
Members, D. J. Houston; D. M. Macdonald; J. Kinloch *(part-time)*
Principal Clerk, K. H. R. Graham, WS

SHERIFFDOMS

SALARIES

Sheriff Principal	£107,346
Sheriff	£99,420
Area Director	£32,293–£63,490
Sheriff Clerk	£12,719–£43,873

*Floating Sheriff

GRAMPIAN, HIGHLANDS AND ISLANDS
Sheriff Principal, Sir Stephen John, Bt
Area Director North, J. Robertson

SHERIFFS AND SHERIFF CLERKS
Aberdeen and Stonehaven, L. A. S. Jessop; A. Pollock; Mrs A. M. Cowan; C. J. Harris, QC; P. M. Bowman; *G. K. Buchanan; *Sheriff Clerks*, Mrs E. Laing *(Aberdeen)*; A. Hempseed *(Stonehaven)*
Peterhead and Banff, K. A. McLernan; *D. J. Cusine; *Sheriff Clerk*, *(Peterhead)*; *Sheriff Clerk Depute*, Mrs F. L. MacPherson *(Banff)*
Elgin, I. A. Cameron; *Sheriff Clerk*, M. McBey
Inverness, Lochmaddy, Portree, Stornoway, Dingwall, Tain, Wick and Dornoch, W. J. Fulton; D. Booker-Milburn; J. O. A. Fraser; D. O. Sutherland; *Sheriff Clerk*, M. McBey *(Dingwall)*; *Sheriff Clerks Depute*, Miss M. Campbell *(Lochmaddy and Portree)*; Miss A. B. Armstrong *(Stornoway)*; L. MacLachlan *(Tain)*; Mrs J. McEwan *(Wick)*; K. Kerr *(Dornoch)*
Kirkwall and Lerwick, C. S. Mackenzie; *Sheriff Clerks Depute*, A. Moore *(Kirkwall)*; M. Flanagan *(Lerwick)*
Fort William, W. D. Small (also *Oban*); *Sheriff Clerk Depute*, S. McKenna

TAYSIDE, CENTRAL AND FIFE
Sheriff Principal, R. A. Dunlop, QC
Area Director East, M. Bonar

SHERIFFS AND SHERIFF CLERKS
Arbroath and Forfar, K. A. Veal; *C. N. R. Stein; *Sheriff Clerks*, M. Herbertson *(Arbroath)*; S. Munro *(Forfar)*
Dundee, R. A. Davidson; A. L. Stewart, QC; J. P. Scott; G. J. Evans (also *Cupar*); P. P. Davies; F. R. Crowe; *Sheriff Clerk*, D. Nicoll
Perth, M. J. Fletcher; J. K, Tierney; D. Pyle; *L. D. R. Foulis *Sheriff Clerk*, J. Murphy
Falkirk, A. V. Sheehan; A. J. Murphy; *C. Caldwell; *Sheriff Clerk*, R. McMillan
Stirling, The Hon. R. E. G. Younger; W. Robertson; W. M. Reid; *Sheriff Clerk*, R. G. McKeand
Cupar, G. J. Evans (also *Dundee*); *Sheriff Clerk*, A. Nicol
Dunfermline, J. S. Forbes; *G. W. M. Liddle; Mrs I. G. McColl; *R. J. Macleod; N. C. Stewart; *Sheriff Clerk*, W. McCulloch
Kirkcaldy, F. J. Keane; Mrs L. G. Patrick; *B. G. Donald; *Sheriff Clerk*, W. Jones

LOTHIAN AND BORDERS

Sheriff Principal, C. G. B. Nicholson, QC
Area Director East, M. Bonar

SHERIFFS AND SHERIFF CLERKS

Edinburgh, R. G. Craik, QC (also *Peebles*); R. J. D. Scott
(also *Peebles*); Miss I. A. Poole; A. M. Bell; J. M. S.
Horsburgh, QC; G. W. S. Presslie (also *Haddington*); J.
A. Farrell; A. Lothian; I. D. Macphail, QC; C. N.
Stoddart; M. McPartlin; J.D.Allan; N. M. P. Morrison,
QC; Miss M. M. Stephen; Mrs M. L. E. Jarvie, QC; *Mrs
K. E. C. Mackie; *N. J. MacKinnon; D.W.M. McIntyre;
Sheriff Clerk, J. Ross
Peebles, R. G. Craik, QC (also *Edinburgh*); R. J. D. Scott
(also *Edinburgh*); *Sheriff Clerk Depute*, M. L. Kubeczka
Linlithgow, H. R. MacLean; G. R. Fleming; *P. Gillam; W.
D. Muirhead; *Sheriff Clerk*, R. D. Sinclair
Haddington, G. W. S. Presslie (also *Edinburgh*); *Sheriff
Clerk*, J. O'Donnell
Jedburgh and Duns, T. A. K. Drummond, QC; *Sheriff Clerk*,
I. W. Williamson
Selkirk, T. A. K. Drummond, QC; *Sheriff Clerk Depute*,
L. McFarlane

NORTH STRATHCLYDE

Sheriff Principal, B. A. Kerr, QC
Area Director West, I. Scott

SHERIFFS AND SHERIFF CLERKS

Oban, W. D. Small (also *Fort William*); *Sheriff Clerk
Depute*, D. Irwin
Dumbarton, J. T. Fitzsimons; T. Scott; S. W. H. Fraser;
Sheriff Clerk, S. Bain
Paisley, J. Spy; C. K. Higgins; N. Douglas; D. J. Pender;
*W. Dunlop; G. C. Kavanagh (also *Campbeltown*); Mrs I.
S. McDonald; *Sheriff Clerk*, Miss S. Hindes
Greenock, J. Herald (also *Rothesay*); Sir Stephen Young;
*Mrs R. Swanney; *Sheriff Clerk*, J. Tannahill
Kilmarnock, T. M. Croan; D. B. Smith; T. F. Russell; *Mrs
I. S. Donald; *Sheriff Clerk*, G. Waddell
Dunoon, Mrs C. M. A. F. Gimblett; *Sheriff Clerk Depute*,
J. McGraw
Campbeltown, *W. Dunlop (also *Paisley*); *Sheriff Clerk
Depute*, Miss E. Napier
Rothesay, J. Herald (also *Greenock*); *Sheriff Clerk Depute*,
Mrs C. K. McCormick

GLASGOW AND STRATHKELVIN

Sheriff Principal, E. F. Bowen, QC
Area Director West, I. Scott

SHERIFFS AND SHERIFF CLERKS

Glasgow, B. Kearney; B. A. Lockhart; Mrs A. L. A. Duncan;
A. C. Henry; J. K. Mitchell; A. G. Johnston; Miss S. A.
O. Raeburn, QC; D. Convery; I. A. S. Peebles, QC; C. W.
McFarlane, QC; K. M. Maciver; H. Matthews, QC; J. A.
Baird; Miss R. E. A. Rae, QC; A. W. Noble; J. D. Friel;
Mrs D. M. MacNeill, QC; J. A. Taylor; C. A. L. Scott; * S.
Cathcart; *Ms L. M. Ruxton; I. H. L. Miller; Mrs F. L.
Reith; W. J. Totten; M. G. O'Grady; *Sheriff Clerk*, C.
Binning

SOUTH STRATHCLYDE, DUMFRIES AND GALLOWAY

Sheriff Principal, J. C. McInnes, QC
Area Director West, I. Scott

SHERIFFS AND SHERIFF CLERKS

Hamilton, L. Cameron; D. C. Russell; V. J. Canavan (also
Airdrie); W. E. Gibson; J. H. Stewart; Miss J. Powie H.
S. Neilson; S. C. Pender; *Sheriff Clerk*, P. Feeney; T.
Welsh, QC; D.M.Bicker; *Mrs M. Smart; *H. K. Small
Lanark, Ms N.C. Stewart; *A. D. Vannett; *Sheriff Clerk*,
Mrs M. McLean, N. Gow, QC; C. B. Miller; J.
McGowan; *Sheriff Clerk*, Miss C. D. Cockburn
Stranraer and Kirkcudbright, J. R. Smith (also *Dumfries*);
Sheriff Clerks, W. McIntosh (*Stranraer*); B. Lindsay
(*Kirkcudbright*)
Dumfries, K. G. Barr; J. R. Smith (also *Stranraer and
Kirkcudbright*); K. A. Ross; *Sheriff Clerk*, P. McGonigle
Airdrie, V. J. Canavan (also *Hamilton*); R. H. Dickson; I. C.
Simpson; J. C. Morris, QC; A. D. Vannet (also *Lanark*)
Sheriff Clerk, D. Forrester

STIPENDIARY MAGISTRATES

GLASGOW
R. Hamilton, *apptd* 1984; J. B. C. Nisbet, *apptd* 1984; R. B.
Christie, *apptd* 1985; Mrs J. A. M. MacLean, *apptd* 1990

CROWN OFFICE AND PROCURATOR FISCAL SERVICE

CROWN OFFICE

25 Chambers Street, Edinburgh EH1 1LA
Tel: 0131-226 2626; Web www.crownoffice.gov.uk
Crown Agent (£80,020–£116,860), A. C. Normand
Deputy Crown Agent (£57,367–£95,625), W. A. Gilchrist

PROCURATORS FISCAL

SALARIES

Regional Procurator Fiscal –	
(*SCS Band 5*)	£62,882–£101,254
Regional Procurator Fiscal –	£57,367–£95,6256
(*SCS Band 4*)	£55,750–£92,930
Procurator Fiscal – upper level	£42,755–£67,163
Procurator Fiscal – lower level	£38,00–£46,200

GRAMPIAN, HIGHLAND AND ISLANDS REGION
Regional Procurator Fiscal, Mrs E. Angiolini (*Aberdeen*)
Procurators Fiscal, E. K. Barbour (*Stonehaven*); A. J. M.
Colley (*Banff*); A. B. Hutchinson (*Peterhead*); D. J.
Dickson (*Elgin*); G. Aitken (*Wick*); J. F. Bamber (*Portree,
Lochmaddy*); D. S. Teale (*Stornoway*); G. Napier
(*Inverness*); Miss Susenn (*Kirkwall, Lerwick*); A. Wylie
(*Fort William*); R. Urquhart (*Dingwall, Dornoch, Tain*)

TAYSIDE, CENTRAL AND FIFE REGION
Regional Procurator Fiscal, B. K. Heywood (*Dundee*)
Procurators Fiscal, J. I. Craigen (*Forfar*); I. A. McLeod
(*Perth*); W. J. Gallacher (*Falkirk*); C. Ritchie (*Stirling
and Alloa*); E. B. Russell (*Cupar*); R. G. Stott
(*Dunfermline*); Miss H. M. Clark (*Kirkcaldy*); A. J.
Wheelan (*Arbroath*)

LOTHIAN AND BORDERS REGION
Regional Procurator Fiscal, N. McFadyen (*Edinburgh*)
Procurators Fiscal, Mrs C. P. Dyer (*Linlithgow*); A. J. P.
Reith (*Haddington*); A. R. G. Fraser (*Duns, Jedburgh*);
Mrs L. E. Thomson (*Selkirk, Peebles*)

NORTH STRATHCLYDE REGION

Regional Procurator Fiscal, W. A. Gilchrist (*Paisley*)
Procurators Fiscal, F. Redman (*Campbeltown*); C. C.
Donnelly (*Dumbarton*); W. S. Carnegie (*Greenock, Rothesay*); D. L. Webster (*Dunoon*); J. Watt (*Kilmarnock*); B. R. Maguire (*Oban*)

GLASGOW AND STRATHKELVIN REGION

Regional Procurator Fiscal, L. A. Higson (*Glasgow*)

SOUTH STRATHCLYDE, DUMFRIES AND GALLOWAY REGION

Regional Procurator Fiscal, D. A. Brown (*Hamilton*)
Procurators Fiscal, S. R. Houston (*Lanark*); J. T. O'Donnell (*Ayr*); A. S. Kennedy (*Stranraer*); D. J. Howdle (*Dumfries, Kirkcudbright*); D. Spiers (*Airdrie*)

Northern Ireland Judicature

In Northern Ireland the legal system and the structure of courts closely resemble those of England and Wales; there are, however, often differences in enacted law.

The Supreme Court of Judicature of Northern Ireland comprises the Court of Appeal, the High Court of Justice and the Crown Court. The practice and procedure of these courts is similar to that in England. The superior civil court is the High Court of Justice, from which an appeal lies to the Northern Ireland Court of Appeal; the House of Lords is the final civil appeal court.

The Crown Court, served by High Court and county court judges, deals with criminal trials on indictment. Cases are heard before a judge and, except those involving offences specified under emergency legislation, a jury. Appeals from the Crown Court against conviction or sentence are heard by the Northern Ireland Court of Appeal; the House of Lords is the final court of appeal.

The decision to prosecute in cases tried on indictment and in summary cases of a serious nature rests in Northern Ireland with the Director of Public Prosecutions, who is responsible to the Attorney-General. Minor summary offences are prosecuted by the police.

Minor criminal offences are dealt with in magistrates' courts by a legally qualified resident magistrate and, where an offender is under 17, by juvenile courts each consisting of a resident magistrate and two lay members specially qualified to deal with juveniles (at least one of whom must be a woman). On 26 July 2001 there were 901 justices of the peace in Northern Ireland. Appeals from magistrates' courts are heard by the county court, or by the Court of Appeal on a point of law or an issue as to jurisdiction. Magistrates' courts in Northern Ireland can deal with certain classes of civil case but most minor civil cases are dealt with in county courts. Judgments of all civil courts are enforceable through a centralised procedure administered by the Enforcement of Judgments Office.

SUPREME COURT OF JUDICATURE

The Royal Courts of Justice, Belfast BT1 3JF
Tel: 028-9023 5111
Lord Chief Justice of Northern Ireland (£163,213)
The Rt. Hon. Sir Robert Carswell, *born* 1934, *apptd* 1997
Principal Secretary, G. W. Johnston

LORDS JUSTICES OF APPEAL (each £149,897)

Style, The Rt. Hon. Lord Justice [surname]

Rt. Hon. Sir Michael Nicholson, *born* 1933, *apptd* 1995
Rt. Hon. Sir William McCollum, *born* 1933, *apptd* 1997
Rt. Hon. Sir Anthony Campbell, *born* 1936, *apptd* 1998

PUISNE JUDGES (each £132,603)

Style, The Hon. Mr Justice [surname]

Hon. Sir John Sheil, *born* 1938, *apptd* 1989
Hon. Sir Brian Kerr, *born* 1948, *apptd* 1993
Hon. Sir Malachy Higgins, *born* 1944, *apptd* 1993
Hon. Sir Paul Girvan, *born* 1948, *apptd* 1995
Hon. Sir Patrick Coghlin, *born* 1945, *apptd* 1997
Hon. Sir John Gillen, *born* 1947, *apptd* 1998
Hon. Sir Richard McLaughlin, *born* 1947, *apptd* 1999

MASTERS OF THE SUPREME COURT (each £79,767)

Master, Queen's Bench and Appeals and Clerk of the Crown, J. W. Wilson, QC
Master, High Court, C.J. McCorry
Master, Office of Care and Protection, F. B. Hall
Master, Chancery Office, R. A. Ellison
Master, Bankruptcy and Companies Office, C. W. G. Redpath
Master, Probate and Matrimonial Office, Miss M. McReynolds
Master, Taxing Office, J. C. Napier

OFFICIAL SOLICITOR

Official Solicitor to the Supreme Court of Northern Ireland, Miss B. M. Donnelly

COUNTY COURTS

JUDGES (each £107,346)

Style, His/Her Hon. Judge [surname]

Judge Curran, QC; Judge Gibson, QC; Judge Markey, QC; Judge McKay, QC; Judge Smyth, QC; Judge Martin (*Chief Social Security and Child Support Commissioner*); Judge Brady, QC; Judge Foote, QC; Her Hon. Judge Philpott, QC; Judge McFarland; Judge Lockie; Her Hon. Judge Kennedy; Judge Finnegan

RECORDERS (each £107,346)

Belfast, Judge Hart, QC
Londonderry, Judge Burgess

MAGISTRATES' COURTS

RESIDENT MAGISTRATES (EACH £79,767)

There are 19 resident magistrates in Northern Ireland.

CROWN SOLICITOR'S OFFICE

PO Box 410, Royal Courts of Justice, Belfast BT1 3JY
Tel: 028-9054 2555

Crown Solicitor, W. A. Palmer

DEPARTMENT OF THE DIRECTOR OF PUBLIC PROSECUTIONS

Royal Courts of Justice, Belfast BT1 3NX
Tel: 028-9054 2444

Director of Public Prosecutions, A. Fraser, CB, QC
Deputy Director of Public Prosecutions, W. R. Junkin

NORTHERN IRELAND COURT SERVICE

Windsor House, Bedford Street, Belfast BT2 7LT
Tel: 028-9032 8594

Director (G3)

Tribunals

AGRICULTURAL LAND TRIBUNALS
c/o Rural and Marine Environment Division, Ministry of Agriculture, Fisheries and Food, Nobel House, 17 Smith Square, London SW1P 3JR
Tel: 020-7238 6991

Agricultural Land Tribunals settle disputes and other issues between agricultural landlords and tenants, and drainage disputes between neighbours.
There are seven tribunals covering England and one covering Wales. For each tribunal the Lord Chancellor appoints a chairman and one or more deputies (barristers or solicitors of at least seven years standing). The Lord Chancellor also appoints lay members to three statutory panels: the 'landowners' panel, the 'farmers' panel and the 'drainage' panel.
Each tribunal is an independent statutory body with jurisdiction only within its own area. A separate tribunal is constituted for each case, and consists of a chairman (who may be the chairman or one of the deputy chairmen) and two lay members nominated by the chairman.
Chairmen (England) (£280 a day), W. D. M. Wood; P. A. de la Piquerie; A. G. Donn; His Hon. Judge J. V. Machin; N. Thomas G. L. Newsom; His Hon. Judge Robert Taylor
Chairman (Wales) (£280 a day), W. J. Owen

THE APPEALS SERVICE
Whittington House, 19–30 Alfred Place, London WC1E 7LW
Tel: 020-7712 2600

The Service (formerly the Independent Tribunal Service) is responsible for the functioning of tribunals hearing appeals concerning child support assessments, social security benefits and vaccine damage payments. Judicial authority for the Service rests with the President, while administrative responsibility is exercised by the Appeals Service Agency, which is an executive agency of the Department of Work and Pensions.
President, His Hon. Judge Michael Harris
Chief Executive, Appeals Service Agency, N. Ward

COMMONS COMMISSIONERS
Room Zone 1/05b, Temple Quay House, 2 The Square, Temple Quay, Bristol BS1 6EB
Tel: 0117-372 8928

The Commons Commissioners are responsible for deciding disputes arising under the Commons Registration Act 1965. They also enquire into the ownership of unclaimed common land and village greens. Commissioners are appointed by the Lord Chancellor.
Chief Commons Commissioner (part-time), I. L. R. Romer
Clerk, P. Lawrence

COPYRIGHT TRIBUNAL
Harmsworth House, 13–15 Bouverie Street, London EC4Y 8DP
Tel: 020-7596 6510; Fax; Minicom: 0845-9222250 020-7596-6526;
Email: copyright.tribunal@patent.gov.uk;
Web: www.patent.gov.uk

The Copyright Tribunal resolves disputes over copyright licences, principally where there is collective licensing.
The chairman and two deputy chairmen are appointed by the Lord Chancellor. Up to eight ordinary members are appointed by the Secretary of State for Trade and Industry.
Chairman (£316 a day), C. P. Tootal
Secretary, Miss J. E. M. Durdin

GENERAL COMMISSIONERS OF INCOME TAX
Lord Chancellor's Department, Selborne House, 54–60 Victoria Street, London SW1E 6QW
Tel: 020-7210 0680

General Commissioners of Income Tax operate under the Taxes Management Act 1970. They are unpaid judicial officers who sit in some 460 Divisions throughout the United Kingdom to hear appeals against decisions by the Inland Revenue on a variety of taxation matters. The Commissioners' jurisdiction was extended in 1999 to hear National Insurance appeals. The Lord Chancellor appoints General Commissioners (except in Scotland, where they are appointed by the Scottish Executive). There are approximately 3,000 General Commissioners appointed throughout the United Kingdom. In each Division, Commissioners appoint a Clerk, who is normally legally qualified, who makes the administrative arrangements for appeal hearings and advises Commissioners on points of law and procedure. The Lord Chancellor's Department pays the Clerks' remuneration.
Appeals from the General Commissioners are by way of case stated, on a point of law, to the High Court (the Court of Session in Scotland or the Court of Appeal in Northern Ireland).
In 2000, approximately 80,000 cases were listed before the General Commissioners.

INFORMATION TRIBUNAL
c/o The Home Office, Queen Anne's Gate, London SW1H 9AT
Tel 020-7273 3755

The Information Tribunal determines appeals against decisions of the Information Commissioner. The chairman and deputy chairman are appointed by the Lord Chancellor and must be legally qualified. Lay members are appointed by the Lord Chancellor to represent the interests of data users or data subjects. A tribunal consists of a legally-qualified chairman sitting with equal numbers of the lay members appointed to represent the interests of data users and data subjects. There is a separate panel of the tribunal which hears national security appeals, the president of this panel is the Rt. Hon. Sir Anthony Evans, RD.

Chairman, J. A. C. Spokes, QC
Secretary, R. Hartley
Information Commissoner, Elizabeth France

EMPLOYMENT TRIBUNALS

CENTRAL OFFICE (ENGLAND AND WALES)
19–29 Woburn Place, London WC1H 0LU
Tel: 020-7273 8666
Employment Tribunals for England and Wales sit in 12 regions. The tribunals deal with matters of employment law, redundancy, dismissal, contract disputes, sexual, racial and disability discrimination, and related areas of dispute which may arise in the workplace. A central registration unit records all applications and maintains a public register at Southgate Street, Bury St Edmunds, Suffolk IP33 2AQ. The tribunals are funded by the Department of Trade and Industry; administrative support is provided by the Employment Tribunals Service.
Chairmen, who may be full-time or part-time, are legally qualified. They are appointed by the Lord Chancellor. Tribunal members are appointed by the Secretary of State for Trade and Industry.
President (£103,516), His Hon. Judge Prophet

CENTRAL OFFICE (SCOTLAND)
Eagle Building, 215 Bothwell Street, Glasgow G2 7TS
Tel: 0141-204 0730
Tribunals in Scotland have the same remit as those in England and Wales. Chairmen are appointed by the Lord President of the Court of Session and lay members by the Secretary of State for Trade and Industry.
President (£99,420), C. M. Milne

EMPLOYMENT APPEAL TRIBUNAL
Central Office: Audit House, 58 Victoria Embankment, London EC4Y 0DS
Tel: 020-7273 1041; Fax: 020-7273 1045
Divisional Office: 52 Melville Street, Edinburgh EH3 7HF
Tel: 0131-225 3963;
Web: www.employmentappeals.gov.uk

The Employment Appeal Tribunal hears appeals on a question of law arising from any decision of an employment tribunal. A tribunal consists of a high court judge and two lay members, one from each side of industry. They are appointed by The Queen on the recommendation of the Lord Chancellor and the Secretary of State for Trade and Industry. Administrative support is provided by the Employment Tribunals Service.
President, The Hon. Mr Justice Lindsay
Scottish Chairman, The Hon. Lord Johnston
Registrar, P. Donleavy
Deputy Registrar, Ms J. Johnson

IMMIGRATION APPELLATE AUTHORITIES
Taylor House, 88 Rosebery Avenue, London EC1R 4QU
Tel: 020-7862 4200

The Immigration Appellate Authorities' powers are now derived from the immigration and Assylum Act 1999. Immigration Adjudicators hear appeals from immigration decisions concerning the need for, and the refusal of, leave to enter or remain in the UK, refusals to grant asylum, decisions to make deportation orders and directions to remove persons subject to immigration control from the UK.
The Immigration Appeal Tribunal provides a second appellate level for those dissatisfied with an Adjudicator's decision. Leave to appeal needs to be obtained. From the Tribunal there is an appeal to the Court of Appeal on a point of law only.
An adjudicator sits alone. The Tribunal sits in divisions of three, normally a legally qualified member and two lay members.

IMMIGRATION APPEAL TRIBUNAL
Field House, 15–25 Bream's Buildings, Chancery Lane, London, EC4A 1DZ
Tel: 020-7073 4200

President, The Hon. Mr Justice Collins
Deputy President, C. M. G. Ockelton
Vice-Presidents, J. Barnes; K. Eshun; J. R. A. Fox; M. W. Rapinet; G. Warr; M. Rapinet; A. O'Brien-Quinn; Dr H. H. W. Storey; J. G. Freeman; D. K. Allen; K. Drabu; J. Fox; P. Moulden; C. Ockelton; A. Mackey; H. J. E. Latter

IMMIGRATION APPEAL ADJUDICATORS

Chief Adjudicator, His Hon. Judge Dunn, QC
Deputy Chief Adjudicator, E. Arfon-Jones

IMMIGRATION SERVICES TRIBUNAL
48/49 Chancery Lane, London WC2A 1JR
Tel: 020-7947 7200; Fax; 020-7947 7215

The Immigration Services Tribunal is an independent Judicial body set up to provide a forum in which appeals against decisions of the Immigration Services Commissioner and complaints made by the Immigration Services Commissioner can be heard and determined. The cases exclusively concern people providing advice and representation services in connection with immigration matters.
The Tribunal forms part of the Court Service. It is the responsibility of the Lord Chancellor. There is a President, who is the judicial head; other judicial members, who must be legally qualified; lay members who must have substantial experience in immigration services or in the law and procedure relating to immigration; and a secretary who is responsible for administration. The tribunal can sit anywhere in the UK.
President, Hon. Judge Seddon Crisp
Members, D. Bean, QC; G. Marriott; P. Barnett; O. Conway; M. Hoare; S. Maguire; A. Montgomery; I. Newton; M. Quayum; S. Rowland; P. Fisher
Immigration Services Tribunal Staff, D. Duncan

384   Tribunals

INDUSTRIAL TRIBUNALS AND THE FAIR EMPLOYMENT TRIBUNAL (NORTHERN IRELAND)
Long Bridge House, 20–24 Waring Street, Belfast BT1 2EB
Tel: 028-9032 7666

The industrial tribunal system in Northern Ireland was set up in 1965 and has a similar remit to the employment tribunals in the rest of the UK. There is also in Northern Ireland a Fair Employment Tribunal, which hears and determines individual cases of alleged religious or political discrimination in employment. Employers can appeal to the Fair Employment Tribunal if they consider the directions of the Equality Commission to be unreasonable, inappropriate or unnecessary, and the Equality Commission can make application to the Tribunal for the enforcement of undertakings or directions with which an employer has not complied.

The president, vice-president and part-time chairmen of the Fair Employment Tribunal are appointed by the Lord Chancellor. The full-time chairman and the part-time chairmen of the industrial tribunals and the panel members to both the industrial tribunals and the Fair Employment Tribunal are appointed by the Department of Higher and Further Education Training and Employment.

President of the Industrial Tribunals and the Fair Employment Tribunal (£103,516), J. Maguire, CBE
Vice-President of the Industrial Tribunals and the Fair Employment Tribunal, Mrs M. P. Price
Secretary, Mrs P. McVeigh

LANDS TRIBUNAL
48–49 Chancery Lane, London WC2A 1JR
Tel: 020-7947 7200

The Lands Tribunal is an independent judicial body which determines questions relating to the valuation of land, rating appeals from valuation tribunals, the discharge or modification of restrictive covenants, and compulsory purchase compensation. The tribunal may also arbitrate under references by consent. The president and members are appointed by the Lord Chancellor.
President (£103,516), G. R. Bartlett, QC
Members (£95,873), P. H. Clarke, FRICS; N. J. Rose, FRICS; P. R. Francis
Member (part-time), His Hon. Judge Rich, QC
Registrar, D. Scannell

LANDS TRIBUNAL FOR SCOTLAND
1 Grosvenor Crescent, Edinburgh EH12 5ER
Tel: 0131-225 7996

The Lands Tribunal for Scotland has the same remit as the tribunal for England and Wales but also covers questions relating to tenants' rights to buy their homes under the Housing (Scotland) Act 1987. The president is appointed by the Lord President of the Court of Session.
President (£103,516), The Hon. Lord McGhie, QC
Members (£95,873), J. Devine, FRICS; A. R. MacLeary, FRICS
Member (part-time) (£33,409), J. N. Wright, QC
Clerk, N. M. Tainsh

MENTAL HEALTH REVIEW TRIBUNALS
Secretariat: Health Service Directorate, Room 326 Wellington House, 133–155 Waterloo Road, London SE1 8UG
Tel: 020-7972 4503/4577; Fax: 020-7972 4884

The Mental Health Review Tribunals are independent judicial bodies which review the cases of patients compulsorily detained under the provisions of the Mental Health Act 1983. They have the power to discharge the patient, to recommend leave of absence, delayed discharge, transfer to another hospital or that a guardianship order be made, to reclassify both restricted and unrestricted patients, and to recommend consideration of a supervision application. There are four tribunals in England, each headed by a regional chairman who is appointed by the Lord Chancellor on a part-time basis. Each tribunal is made up of at least three members, and must include a lawyer, who acts as president, a medical member and a lay member.
There are five regional offices:

LIVERPOOL, 3rd Floor, Cressington House, 249 St Mary's Road, Garston, Liverpool L19 0NF. Tel: 0151-728 5400
LONDON (NORTH), Spur 3, Block 1, Government Buildings, Honeypot Lane, Stanmore, Middx HA7 1AY. Tel: 020-7972 3754
LONDON (SOUTH), Block 3, Crown Offices, Kingston Bypass Road, Surbiton, Surrey KT6 5QN. Tel: 020-8268 4549
NOTTINGHAM, Spur A, Block 5, Government Buildings, Chalfont Drive, Western Boulevard, Nottingham NG8 3RZ. Tel: 0115-942 8308
WALES, 4th Floor, Crown Buildings, Cathays Park, Cardiff CF1 3NQ. Tel: 029-2082 5328

NATIONAL HEALTH SERVICE TRIBUNAL
380 Rayleigh Rod, Thundersley, Essex, SS7 3TA
Tel: 01268-774481; Fax: 01268-71565

The NHS Tribunal considers representations that the continued inclusion of a doctor, dentist, optician or pharmacist on a health authority's list would be prejudicial to the efficiency of the service concerned. The tribunal sits when required, usually in London. The chairman is appointed by the Lord Chancellor and members by the Secretary of State for Health.
Chairman, A. Whitfield, QC
Deputy Chairmen, Miss E. Platt, QC; Dr R. N. Ough; S. Rodway; W. Edis; T. Thorne
Clerk, T. L. Rayson, OBE, 380 Rayleigh Road, Thundersley, Essex SS7 3TA. Tel 01268 774481

NATIONAL HEALTH SERVICE TRIBUNAL (SCOTLAND)
Clerk: 40 Craiglockhart Road, North, Edinburgh EH14 1BT
Tel: 0131-443 2575

The tribunal considers representations that the continued inclusion of a doctor, dentist, optometrist or pharmacist on a health board's list would be prejudicial to the efficiency of the service concerned. The tribunal sits when required and is composed of a chairman, one lay member, and one practitioner member drawn from a representative

professional panel. The chairman is appointed by the Lord President of the Court of Session, and the lay member and the members of the professional panel are appointed by the First Minister.
Chairman, M. G. Thomson, QC
Lay member, J. D. M. Robertson
Clerk to the Tribunal, W. Bryden

PENSIONS APPEAL TRIBUNALS
CENTRAL OFFICE (ENGLAND AND WALES)
48–49 Chancery Lane, London WC2A 1JF
Tel: 020-7947 7034; Fax: 020-7947 7492

The Pensions Appeal Tribunals are responsible for hearing appeals from ex-servicemen or women and widows who have had their claims for a war pension rejected by the Secretary of State for Social Security. The Entitlement Appeal Tribunals hear appeals in cases where the Secretary of State has refused to grant a war pension. The Assessment Appeal Tribunals hear appeals against the Secretary of State's assessment of the degree of disablement caused by an accepted condition. The tribunal members are appointed by the Lord Chancellor.
President (£76,921), Dr H. M. G. Concannon
Tribunal Manager, Miss L. Nay

PENSIONS APPEAL TRIBUNALS FOR SCOTLAND
20 Walker Street, Edinburgh EH3 7HS
Tel: 0131-220 1404
President (£307 a day), C. N. McEachran, QC

OFFICE OF THE SOCIAL SECURITY AND CHILD SUPPORT COMMISSIONERS
5th Floor, Newspaper House, 8–16 Great New Street, London EC4A 3BN
Tel: 020-7353 5145
23 Melville Street, Edinburgh EH3 7PW
Tel: 0131-225 2201

The Social Security Commissioners are the final statutory authority to decide appeals relating to entitlement to social security benefits. The Child Support Commissioners are the final statutory authority to decide appeals relating to child support. Appeals may be made in relation to both matters only on a point of law. The Commissioners' jurisdiction covers England, Wales and Scotland. There are 17 commissioners; they are all qualified lawyers.
Chief Social Security Commissioner and Chief Child Support Commissioner (£103,516), His Hon. Judge Machin, QC
Secretary, L. Salder (*London*); S. Niven (*Edinburgh*)

OFFICE OF THE SOCIAL SECURITY COMMISSIONERS AND CHILD SUPPORT COMMISSIONERS FOR NORTHERN IRELAND
Lancashire House, 5 Linenhall Street, Belfast BT2 8AA
Tel: 028-9033 2344; Fax: 028-9031 3510
Email: socialsecuritycommissioners@courtsni.gov.uk

The role of Northern Ireland Social Security Commissioners and Child Support Commissioners is similar to that of the Commissioners in Great Britain. There are two commissioners for Northern Ireland.

Chief Commissioner (£103,516), His Hon. Judge Martin, QC
Deputy Commissioner, Mrs M. S. Brown
Registrar of Appeals, W. R. Brown

THE SOLICITORS' DISCIPLINARY TRIBUNAL
3rd Floor, Gate House, 1 Farringdon Street, London EC4M 7NS
Tel: 020-7329 4808; Fax: 020-7329 4833

The Solicitors' Disciplinary Tribunal is an independent statutory body whose members are appointed by the Master of the Rolls. The tribunal considers applications made to it alleging either professional misconduct and/or a breach of the statutory rules by which solicitors are bound against an individually named solicitor, former solicitor, registered foreign lawyer, or solicitor's clerk. The president and solicitor members do not receive remuneration.
President, A. Issacs
Clerk, Mrs S. C. Elson

THE SCOTTISH SOLICITORS' DISCIPLINE TRIBUNAL
22 Rutland Square, Edinburgh EH1 2BB
Tel: 0131-229 5860

The Scottish Solicitors' Discipline Tribunal is an independent statutory body with a panel of 18 members, ten of whom are solicitors; members are appointed by the Lord President of the Court of Session. Its principal function is to consider complaints of misconduct against solicitors in Scotland.
Chairman, J. W. Laughland
Clerk, J. M. Barton, WS

SPECIAL COMMISSIONERS OF INCOME TAX
15–19 Bedford Avenue, London WC1B 3AS
Tel: 020-7631 4242

The Special Commissioners are an independent body appointed by the Lord Chancellor to hear complex appeals against decisions of the Board of Inland Revenue and its officials.
Presiding Special Commissioner, His Hon. Stephen Oliver, QC
Clerk, R. P. Lester

SPECIAL IMMIGRATION APPEALS COMMISSION
Taylor House, 88 Rosebery Avenue, London EC1R 4QU
Tel: 020-7862 4200

The Commission was set up under the Special Immigration Appeals Commission Act 1998. Its main function is to consider appeals against orders for deportations in cases which involve, in the main, considerations of national security. Members are appointed by the Lord Chancellor.
Chairman, The Hon. Mr Justice Potts
Secretary, S. Hill

TRAFFIC COMMISSIONERS
c/o Scottish Traffic Area, Argyle House, 3 Lady Lawson Street, Edinburgh EH3 9SE
Tel: 0131-529 8500

The Traffic Commissioners are responsible for licensing operators of heavy goods and public service vehicles. They also have responsibility for licensing operators of heavy goods and public service vehicles. They also have responsibility for disciplinary cases involving the conduct of drivers of these vehicles. There are Seven Commissioners in the eight traffic areas covering Britain. Each Traffic Commissioner constitutes a tribunal for the purposes of the Tribunals and Inquiries Act 1992.
Senior Traffic Commissioner M. W. Betts, CBE

TRANSPORT TRIBUNAL
48-49 Chancery Lane, London WC2A 1JR
Tel: 020-7947 7493

The Transport Tribunal hears appeals against decisions made by Traffic Commissioners at public inquiries. The tribunal consists of a legally-qualified president, two legal members who may sit as chairmen, and five lay members. The president and legal members are appointed by the Lord Chancellor and the lay members by the Secretary of State for Transport, Local Government and the Regions.
President (part-time), H. B. H. Carlisle, QC
Legal member (part-time) (£258 a day), His Hon. Judge Brodrick; J. Beech
Lay members (£258 a day), D. Yeomans; J. W. Whitworth; P. Steel; P. Rogers; L. Milliken
Secretary, E. Miles

VALUATION TRIBUNALS
Valuation Tribunal Management Board 2nd Floor, Walton House, 11 Parade, Leamington Spa, Warks CV32 4DG
Tel: 01926-421875

The Valuation Tribunals hear appeals concerning the council tax, non-domestic rating and land drainage rates in England and Wales. There are 56 tribunals in England and four in Wales; those in England are funded by the Department of Transport Local G'ment and the Regions (DTLR) and those in Wales by the National Assembly for Wales. A separate tribunal is constituted for each hearing, and normally consists of a chairman and two other members. Members are appointed by the local authorities and serve on a voluntary basis. The Valuation Tribunal Management Board considers all matters affecting valuation tribunals in England, and the Council of Wales Valuation Tribunals performs the same function in Wales.
Chairman, Valuation Tribunal Management Board, P. Wood, OBE
Valuation Tribunals National Officer, B. P. Massen, MBE
President, Council of Wales Valuation Tribunals, J. H. Owens

VAT AND DUTIES TRIBUNALS
15-19 Bedford Avenue, London WC1B 3AS
Tel: 020-7631 4242

VAT and Duties Tribunals are administered by the Lord Chancellor in England and Wales, and by the First Minister in Scotland. They are independent, and decide disputes between taxpayers and Customs and Excise. In England and Wales, the president and chairmen are appointed by the Lord Chancellor and members by the Treasury. Chairmen in Scotland are appointed by the Lord President of the Court of Session.
President, His Hon. Stephen Oliver, QC
Vice-President, England and Wales, J. D. Demack
Vice-President, Scotland, T. G. Coutts, QC
Vice-President, Northern Ireland, His Hon. J. McKee, QC
Registrar, R. P. Lester

TRIBUNAL CENTRES

EDINBURGH, 44 Palmerston Place, Edinburgh EH12 5BJ. Tel: 0131-226 3551
LONDON (including Belfast), 15-19 Bedford Avenue, London WC1B 3AS. Tel: 020-7631 4242
MANCHESTER, 9th Floor, Westpoint, 501 Chester Road, Manchester M16 5HU. Tel: 0161-868 6600

The Police Service

There are 52 police forces in the United Kingdom, each responsible for policing in its area. Most forces' area is coterminous with one or more local authority areas. Policing in London is carried out by the Metropolitan Police and the City of London Police; in Northern Ireland by the Royal Ulster Constabulary (RUC); and by the Isle of Man, States of Jersey, and Guernsey forces in their respective islands and bailiwicks. National services include the National Missing Persons Bureau and the National Crime Squad.

The police authorities of English and Welsh forces comprise local councillors, magistrates and independent members. In Scotland, there are six joint police boards made up of local councillors; the other two police authorities are councils. In London the newly established Metropolitan Police Authority oversees police operations; for the City of London Police, a committee of the Corporation of London exists including councillors and magistrates. In Northern Ireland the Secretary of State appoints the police authority.

Police authorities are financed by central and local government grants and a precept on the council tax. Subject to the approval of the Home Secretary (in England and Wales) and to regulations, they appoint the chief constable. In England and Wales they are responsible for publishing annual policing plans and annual reports, setting local objectives and a budget, and levying the precept. The police authorities in Scotland are responsible for setting a budget, providing the resources necessary to police the area adequately, appointing officers of the rank of Assistant Chief Constable and above, and determining the number of officers and civilian staff in the force. The structure and responsibilities of the police authority in Northern Ireland are under review.

The Home Secretary, the Secretary of State for Northern Ireland and the Scottish Executive are responsible for the organisation, administration and operation of the police service. They make regulations covering matters such as police ranks, discipline, hours of duty, and pay and allowances. All police forces are subject to inspection by HM Inspectors of Constabulary, who report to the Home Secretary, Scottish Executive or Secretary of State for Northern Ireland. In Northern Ireland a commission on policing was established by the Belfast Agreement in April 1998. The Police Act, based on the commission's report and passed in November 2000, provided for the creation of a Policing Board to oversee the RUC.

In April 1999 the Home Secretary set targets for recruitment of officers from ethnic minorities for each force in England and Wales to achieve within ten years. In July 1999 targets for promotion and retention of these officers were also set.

COMPLAINTS

The investigation and resolution of a serious complaint against a police officer in England and Wales is subject to the scrutiny of the Police Complaints Authority. An officer who is dismissed, required to resign or reduced in rank, whether as a result of a complaint or not, may appeal to a police appeals tribunal established by the relevant police authority. In Scotland, chief constables are obliged to investigate a complaint against one of their officers; if there is a suggestion of criminal activity, the complaint is investigated by an independent public prosecutor. In Northern Ireland complaints are investigated by the Police Ombudsman.

BASIC RATES OF PAY
since 1 September 2000

Chief Constable	
No fixed term	£75,825–£112,353
Fixed term appointment	£79,620–£117,837
Assistant Chief Constable – designated Deputy	
No fixed term	80% of their Chief Constable's pay or £72,630, whichever is higher
Fixed term appointment	80% of their Chief Constable's pay or £76,260, whichever is higher
Assistant Chief Constable	
No fixed term	£63,270–£72,630
Fixed term appointment	£66,435–£76,260
Superintendent	£46,038–£57,150
Chief Inspector	£37,830–£42,426
Inspector	£33,849–£38,385
Sergeant	£26,169–£30,522
Constable	£17,133–£27,114

Metropolitan Police

Metropolitan Commissioner	£130,469–£143,527
Deputy Commissioner	£106,251–£120,057
Assistant Commissioner	£96,075–£105,780
Commander	£63,270–£76,260

The rank of Chief Superintendent was abolished in April 1995. Existing appointments continue and receive the higher ranges of the pay scale for Superintendents

THE SPECIAL CONSTABULARY

Each police force has its own special constabulary, made up of volunteers who work in their spare time. Special Constables have full police powers within their force and adjoining force areas, and assist regular officers.

NATIONAL CRIME SQUAD

The National Crime Squad (NCS) was established on 1 April 1998, replacing the six regional crime squads in England and Wales. It investigates national and international organised and serious crime. It also supports police forces investigating serious crime. The squad is accountable to the National Crime Squad Service Authority.

Headquarters: PO Box 2500, London SW1V 2WF.
Tel: 020-7238 2500
Director General, W. Hughes, QPM

NCS SERVICE AUTHORITY

The Service Authority is responsible for ensuring the effective operation of the National Crime Squad. It fulfils a similar role to a police authority. It works alongside the National Criminal Intelligence Service Service Authority. There are 17 members, of whom the chairman and nine others serve as 'core members' on both authorities.

Headquarters: PO Box 2600, London SW1V 2WG.
Tel: 020-7238 2600
Chairman, Rt. Hon. Sir John Wheeler, JP, DL
Clerk, T. Simmons
Treasurer, S. Atkins

POLICE NATIONAL MISSING PERSONS BUREAU
The Police National Missing Persons Bureau (PNMPB)
acts as a central clearing house of information, receiving
reports about vulnerable missing persons that are still
outstanding after 14 days and details of unidentified
persons or remains within 48 hours of being found from
all forces in England and Wales. Reports are also
received from Scottish police forces, the RUC, and
foreign police forces via Interpol.
Headquarters: New Scotland Yard, Broadway, London
SW1H 0BG. Tel: 020-7230 1212
Director, C. J. Coombes

POLICE INFORMATION TECHNOLOGY
ORGANISATION
The Police Information Technology Organisation
(PITO) develops and manages the delivery of national
police information technology services, such as the
Police National Computer, co-ordinates the
development of local information technology systems
where common standards and systems are needed, and
provides a procurement service.
Headquarters: New Kings Beam House, 22 Upper
Ground, London SE1 9QY. Tel: 020-8358 5678
Chairman, Sir Edmund Burton
Chief Executive, V. Dews

FORENSIC SCIENCE SERVICE
The Forensic Science Service (FSS) provides forensic
science support to the police forces in England and
Wales for the investigation of scenes of crime, scientific
analysis of material, and interpretation of scientific
results. The FSS is organised into serious crime, volume
crime, drugs and specialist services, supported by
intelligence and consultancy services.
Headquarters: Priory House, Gooch Street North,
Birmingham B5 6QQ. Tel: 0121-607 6800
Chief Executive, Dr J. Thompson

POLICE FORCES AND AUTHORITIES

Strength: actual strength of force as at mid 2000
Chair: chairman/convener of the police authority/police
committee/joint police board

ENGLAND
AVON AND SOMERSET CONSTABULARY, PO Box 37, Valley
Road, Portishead, North Somerset BS20 8QJ.
Tel: 01275-818181; Fax: 01275-816112; *Strength*,
2,978; *Chief Constable*, S. Pilkington, QPM
BEDFORDSHIRE POLICE, Police Headquarters, Woburn
Road, Kempston, Bedford MK43 9AX.
Tel: 01234-841212; Fax: 01234-842006; *Strength*,
1,065; *Chief Constable*, P. Hancock, QPM
CAMBRIDGESHIRE CONSTABULARY, Hinchingbrooke
Park, Huntingdon, Cambs PE29 6NP. Tel: 01480-
456111; Fax: 01480-422447; *Strength*, 1,288; *Chief
Constable*, D. G. Gunn
CHESHIRE CONSTABULARY, Police Headquarters, Nuns
Road, Chester CH1 2PP. Tel: 01244-350000; Fax: 01244-
612269; *Strength*, 2,029; *Chief Constable*, N. K. Burgess,
QPM

CLEVELAND POLICE, PO Box 70, Ladgate Lane,
Middlesbrough TS8 9EH. Tel: 01642-326326;
Fax: 01642-301200; *Strength*, 1,426; *Chief Constable*, B.
Shaw
CUMBRIA CONSTABULARY, Carleton Hall, Penrith,
Cumbria CA10 2AU. Tel: 01768-891999; Fax: 01768-
217099; *Strength*, 1,029; *Chief Constable*, C. Phillips
DERBYSHIRE CONSTABULARY, Butterley Hall, Ripley,
Derbys DE5 3RS. Tel: 01773-570100; Fax: 01773-
572225; *Strength*, 1,836; *Chief Constable*, D. F. Coleman
DEVON AND CORNWALL CONSTABULARY, Middlemoor,
Exeter EX2 7HQ. Tel: 08705-777444; Fax: 08705-
452346; *Strength*, 3,058; *Chief Constable*, Sir John Evans,
QPM
DORSET POLICE HEADQUARTERS, Winfrith, Dorchester,
Dorset DT2 8DZ. Tel: 01929-462727; Fax: 01202-
223987; *Strength*, 1,355; *Chief Constable*, Mrs J.
Stichbury
DURHAM CONSTABULARY HEADQUARTERS, Aykley
Heads, Durham City DH1 5TT. Tel: 0191-386 4929;
Fax: 0191-375 2160; *Strength*, 1,602; *Chief Constable*, G.
Hedges, QPM
ESSEX POLICE, PO Box 2, Springfield, Chelmsford, Essex
CM2 6DA. Tel: 01245-491491; Fax: 01245-452259;
Strength, 2,906; *Chief Constable*, D. F. Stevens, QPM, LLB
GLOUCESTERSHIRE CONSTABULARY, Holland House,
Lansdown Road, Cheltenham, Glos GL51 6QH.
Tel: 01242-521321; Fax: 01242-221362; *Strength*,
1,179; *Chief Constable*, T. Brain
GREATER MANCHESTER POLICE, PO Box 22, Chester
House, Boyer Street, Manchester M16 0RE. Tel: 0161-
872 5050; Fax: 0161-856 2666; *Strength*, 7,000; *Chief
Constable*, D. Wilmot
HAMPSHIRE CONSTABULARY, Police Headquarters, West
Hill, Winchester, Hampshire SO22 5DB. Tel: 0845-045
4545; Fax: 01962-871204; *Strength*, 3,465; *Chief
Constable*, P. R. Kernaghan, QPM, LLB
HERTFORDSHIRE CONSTABULARY, Stanborough Road,
Welwyn Garden City, Herts AL8 6XF. Tel: 01707-
354200; Fax: 01707-354409; *Strength*, 1,886; *Chief
Constable*, P. Acres
HUMBERSIDE POLICE, Queens Gardens, Kingston upon
Hull HU1 3DJ. Tel: 01482-326111; Fax: 01482-220037;
Strength, 2,000; *Chief Constable*, D. Westwood, QPM
KENT CONSTABULARY, Sutton Road, Maidstone, Kent
ME15 9BZ. Tel: 01622-690690; Fax: 01622-690511;
Strength, 3,325; *Chief Constable*, Sir David Phillips, QPM
LANCASHIRE CONSTABULARY, PO Box 77, Hutton,
Preston, Lancashire PR4 5SB. Tel: 01772-614444;
Fax: 01772-618843; *Strength*, 3,313; *Chief Contstable*,
Ms P. Clare
LEICESTERSHIRE CONSTABULARY, St John's, Narborough,
Leicester LE9 5BX. Tel: 0116-222 2222; Fax: 0116-248
2227; *Strength*, 2,017; *Chief Constable*, D. J. Wyrko, QPM
LINCOLNSHIRE POLICE, PO Box 999, Lincoln LN5 7PH.
Tel: 01522-532222; Fax: 01522-558229; *Strength*,
1,231; *Chief Constable*, R. J. N. Childs
MERSEYSIDE POLICE, PO Box 59, Canning Place,
Liverpool L69 1JD. Tel: 0151-709 6010; Fax: 0151-777
8999; *Strength*, 4,190; *Chief Constable*, N. Bettison, QPM
NORFOLK CONSTABULARY, Police Headquarters,
Martineau Lane, Norwich NR1 2DJ. Tel: 01603-768769;
Fax: 01603-276215; *Strength*, 1,390; *Chief Constable*, K.
Williams
NORTHAMPTONSHIRE POLICE, Wootton Hall,
Northampton NN4 0JQ. Tel: 01604-700700; Fax: 01604-
703028; *Strength*, 1,171; *Chief Executive*, C. Fox

NORTHUMBRIA POLICE, Force Headquarters, North Road, Ponteland, Newcastle upon Tyne NE20 0BL. Tel: 01661-872555; Fax: 01661-868928; *Strength*, 3,294; *Chief Constable*, C. Strachan

NORTH YORKSHIRE POLICE, Newby Wiske Hall, Newby Wiske, Northallerton, N. Yorks DL7 9HA. Tel: 01609-783131; Fax: 01609-789213; *Strength*, 1,337; *Chief Constable*, D. R. Kenworthy

NOTTINGHAMSHIRE POLICE, Sherwood Lodge, Arnold, Nottingham NG5 8PP. Tel: 0115-967 0999; Fax: 0115-967 0900; *Strength*, 2,258; *Chief Constable*, S. M. Green

SOUTH YORKSHIRE POLICE, Snig Hill, Sheffield S3 8LY. Tel: 0114-220 2020; Fax: 0114-252 3154; *Strength*, 3,202; *Chief Constable*, M. Hedges

STAFFORDSHIRE POLICE, Cannock Road, Stafford ST17 0QG. Tel: 01785-257717; Fax: 01785-232313; *Strength*, 2,211; *Chief Constable*, J. Giffard

SUFFOLK CONSTABULARY HEADQUARTERS, Force Headquarters, Portal Avenue, Martlesham Heath, Ipswich IP5 3QS. Tel: 01473-613500; Fax: 01473-610876; *Strength*, 1,136; *Chief Constable*, P. J. Scott-Lee, QPM

SURREY POLICE, Mount Browne, Sandy Lane, Guildford, Surrey GU3 1HG. Tel: 01483-571212; Fax: 01483-300279; *Strength*, 2,088; *Chief Constable*, D. O'Connor

SUSSEX POLICE, Malling House, Church Lane, Lewes, E. Sussex BN7 2DZ. Tel: 0845-6070 999; Fax: 01273-404274; *Strength*, 2,812; *Chief Constable*, P. C. Whitehouse, QPM

THAMES VALLEY POLICE, Oxford Road, Kidlington, Oxon OX5 2NX. Tel: 01865-846000; Fax: 01865-846160; *Strength*, 3,971; *Chief Constable*, C. Pollard, QPM

WARWICKSHIRE CONSTABULARY, PO Box 4, Leek Wootton, Warwick CV35 7QB. Tel: 01926-415000; Fax: 01926-850362; *Strength*, 920; *Chief Constable*, A. C. Timpson

WEST MERCIA CONSTABULARY, Hindlip Hall, PO Box 55, Worcester WR3 8SP. Tel: 01905-723000; Fax: 01905-454226; *Strength*, 1,936; *Chief Constable*, P. Hampson, QPM

WEST MIDLANDS POLICE, PO Box 52, Lloyd House, Colmore Circus, Queensway, Birmingham B4 6NQ. Tel: 0121-626 5000; Fax: 0121-626 5695; *Strength*, 7,322; *Chief Constable*, Sir Edward Crew, QPM

WEST YORKSHIRE POLICE, PO Box 9, Laburnum Road, Wakefield, W. Yorks WF1 3QP. Tel: 01924-375222; Fax: 01924-292182; *Strength*, 4,839; *Chief Constable*, G. Moore

WILTSHIRE CONSTABULARY, Police Headquarters, London Road, Devizes, Wilts SN10 2DN. Tel: 01380-722341; Fax: 01380-734176; *Strength*, 1,074; *Chief Constable*, Miss E. Neville

WALES

DYFED-POWYS POLICE, PO Box 99, Llangunnor, Carmarthen, Carmarthenshire SA31 2PF. Tel: 01267-222020; Fax: 01267-222185; *Strength*, 1,064; *Chief Constable*, T. Grange

GWENT POLICE, Police Headquarters, Turnpike Road, Croesyceiliog, Cwmbran, Gwent NP44 2XJ. Tel: 01633-838111; Fax: 01633-865211; *Strength*, 1,260; *Chief Constable*, K. Turner

NORTH WALES POLICE, Glan-y-don, Colwyn Bay, Conwy LL29 8AW. Tel: 01492-517171; Fax: 01492-511232; *Strength*, 1,426; *Chief Constable*, R. Brunstrom

SOUTH WALES POLICE, Police Headquarters, Cowbridge Road, Bridgend CF31 3SU. Tel: 01656-655555; Fax: 01656-869399; *Strength*, 3,105; *Chief Constable*, A. T. Burden

SCOTLAND

CENTRAL SCOTLAND POLICE, Randolphfield, Stirling FK8 2HD. Tel: 01786-456000; Fax: 01786-451177; *Strength*, 733; *Chief Constable*, A. Cameron *Convenor, Joint Police Board*, I. Miller

DUMFRIES AND GALLOWAY CONSTABULARY, Police Headquarters, Cornwall Mount, Dumfries DG1 1PZ. Tel: 01387-252112; Fax: 01387-260501; *Strength*, 483; *Chief Constable*, D. Strang

FIFE CONSTABULARY, Police Headquarters, Detroit Road, Glenrothes, Fife KY6 2RJ. Tel: 01592-418888; Fax: 01592-418444; *Strength*, 855; *Chief Constable*, P. M. Wilson, QPM, LLB

GRAMPIAN POLICE, Force Headquarters, Queen Street, Aberdeen AB10 1ZA. Tel: 01224-386000; Fax: 01224-643366; *Strength*, 1,221; *Chief Constable*, A. G. Brown *Convenor of Police Authority Committee*, Ms M. Stewart

LOTHIAN AND BORDERS POLICE, Fettes Avenue, Edinburgh EH4 1RB. Tel: 0131-311 3131; Fax: 0131-311 3580; *Strength*, 2,602; *Chief Constable*, Sir Roy Cameron, Kt., QPM *Convenor of Police Authority*, Ms L. Hinds

NORTHERN CONSTABULARY, Police Headquarters, Old Perth Road, Inverness IV2 3SY. Tel: 01463-715555; Fax: 01463-720373; *Strength*, 667; *Chief Constable*, W. Robertson

STRATHCLYDE POLICE, HQ, 173 Pitt Street, Glasgow G2 4JS. Tel: 0141-532 2000; Fax: 0141-532 2475; *Strength*, 7,078; *Chief Constable*, W. Rae, QPM *Convenor of Strathyclyde Joint Police Board*, B. A. Mann, CBE, JP

TAYSIDE POLICE, PO Box 59, 4 West Bell Street, Dundee DD1 9JU. Tel: 01382-223200; Fax: 01382-200449; *Strength*, 1,160; *Chief Constable*, J. Vine

NORTHERN IRELAND

ROYAL ULSTER CONSTABULARY, G. C.

Royal Ulster Constabulary, G. C., RUC Headquarters, Brooklyn, 65 Knock Road, Belfast BT5 6LD. Tel: 028-9065 0222; Fax: 028-9070 0124; *Strength*, 7935; *Chief Constable*, Sir Ronnie Flanagan, KT., OBE

ISLANDS

ISLAND POLICE FORCE

Island Police Force, Hospital Lane, St Peter Port, Guernsey GY1 2QN. Tel: 01481-725111; Fax: 01481-45136; *Strength*, 137; *Chief Constable*, M. H. Wyeth *President, Committee of Home Affairs*, M. Torode

STATES OF JERSEY POLICE

States of Jersey Police, Rouge Bouillon, PO Box 789, St Helier, Jersey JE2 3ZA. Tel: 01534-612612; Fax: 01534-612116; *Strength*, 240; *Chief Officer*, G. Power *Committee President*, A. Layzell

ISLE OF MAN CONSTABULARY

Isle of Man Constabulary, Police Headquarters, Glencrutchery Road, Douglas, Isle of Man IM2 4RG. Tel: 01624-631212; Fax: 01624-628113; *Strength*, 240; *Chief Constable*, M. Culverhouse *Chairman, Minister for Home Affairs*, A. Bell

METROPOLITAN POLICE SERVICE
New Scotland Yard, Broadway, London SW1H 0BG
Tel 020-7230 1212

Strength (July 2001), 25,485
Commissioner, Sir John Stevens, QPM
Deputy Commissioner, Ian Blair, QPM

OPERATIONAL AREAS
Assistant Commissioners, T. Ghaffur *(Policy, Review and Standards)*; M. Todd *(Territorial Policing)*

SPECIALIST OPERATIONS DEPARTMENT
Assistant Commissioner, A. C. Veness, QPM

COMPLAINTS INVESTIGATION BUREAU
Deputy Assistant Commissioner, A. C. Hayman

PAN LONDON UNITS
Assistant Commissioner, B. Hogan-Howe

OTHER DEPARTMENTS
Director, Public Affairs, R. Fedorcio
Solicitor, D. Hamilton
Director, Information, Miss A. Beaton
Director, Property Services, T. G. Lawrence

CITY OF LONDON POLICE
26 Old Jewry, London EC2R 8DJ
Tel: 020-7601 2222

Strength (July 2001), 707
The City of London Police is responsible for policing the City of London. Though small, the area includes one of the most important financial centres in the world and the force has particular expertise in areas such as fraud investigation as well as the areas required of any police force.
  The force has a wholly elected police authority, the police committee of the Corporation of London, which appoints the Commissioner.
Commissioner, P. Nove, QPM
Assistant Commissioner, J. Hart, QPM

BRITISH TRANSPORT POLICE
15 Tavistock Place, London WC1H 9SJ
Tel: 020-7388 7541

Strength (March 2001), 2,109
British Transport Police is the national police force for the railways in England, Wales and Scotland, including the London Underground system, the Docklands Light Railway, the Midland Metro Tram system and Croydon Tramlink. The Chief Constable reports to the British Transport Police Committee.
Chief Constable, I. Johnston, QPM

MINISTRY OF DEFENCE POLICE
MDP Wethersfield, Braintree, Essex CM7 4AZ
Tel: 01371-854000

Strength (March 2001), 3,526 operational staff and 266 civilian support staff
The Ministry of Defence Police is a civilian police force geared to meeting the requirements of the MOD and other customers including visiting forces, the Royal Mint and the Royal Ordnance. The Policing Team initiative has recently been expanded to meet policing demands across a wider area than previously. Other specialist services include marine policing, dogs, firearms and Police Search Teams.
Chief Constable, L. Clarke, OBE

ROYAL PARKS CONSTABULARY
The Old Police House, Hyde Park, London W2 2UH
Tel: 020-7298 2000

Strength (August 2001), 140
The Royal Parks Constabulary is maintained by the Royal Parks Agency, an executive agency of the Department for Culture, Media and Sport, and is responsible for the policing of eight royal parks in and around London.
Chief Officer (Acting), D. Pollack

UK ATOMIC ENERGY AUTHORITY CONSTABULARY
Building E6, Culham Science Centre, Abingdon, Oxon OX14 3DB
Tel: 01235-463760

Strength (June 2001), 539
The Constabulary is responsible for policing UK Atomic Energy Authority and British Nuclear Fuels PLC establishments and for escorting nuclear material between establishments.
Chief Constable, W. F. Pryke

STAFF ASSOCIATIONS

Police officers are not permitted to join a trade union or to take strike action. All ranks have their own staff associations.
ASSOCIATION OF CHIEF POLICE OFFICERS OF ENGLAND, WALES AND NORTHERN IRELAND, 7th Floor, 25 Victoria Street, London SW1H 0EX. Tel: 020-7227 3434. Represents Chief Constables, Deputy and Assistant Chief Constables in England, Wales and Northern Ireland; officers of the rank of Commander and above in the Metropolitan and City of London Police and senior civilian members of these forces.
THE POLICE SUPERINTENDENTS' ASSOCIATION OF ENGLAND AND WALES, 67A Reading Road, Pangbourne, Reading RG8 7JD. Tel: 0118-984 4005. Represents officers of the rank of Superintendent.
THE POLICE FEDERATION OF ENGLAND AND WALES, 15–17 Langley Road, Surbiton, Surrey KT6 6LP. Tel: 020-8399 2224. Represents officers up to and including the rank of Chief Inspector.
ASSOCIATION OF CHIEF POLICE OFFICERS IN SCOTLAND, Police Headquarters, Fettes Avenue, Edinburgh EH4 1RB. Tel: 0131-311 3051. Represents Chief Constables, Deputy and Assistant Chief Constables of the Scottish police forces.
THE ASSOCIATION OF SCOTTISH POLICE SUPERINTENDENTS, Secretariat, 173 Pitt Street, Glasgow G2 4JS. Tel: 0141-221 5796. Represents officers of the rank of Superintendent.
THE SCOTTISH POLICE FEDERATION, 5 Woodside Place, Glasgow G3 7QF. Tel: 0141-332 5234. Represents officers up to and including the rank of Chief Inspector.
THE SUPERINTENDENTS' ASSOCIATION OF NORTHERN IRELAND, RUC Training Centre, Garnerville Road, Belfast BT4 2NX. Tel: 028-9070 0660. Represents Superintendents and Chief Superintendents in the RUC.
THE POLICE FEDERATION FOR NORTHERN IRELAND, Royal Ulster Constabulary, Garnerville, Garnerville Road, Belfast BT4 2NX. Tel: 028-9076 0831. Represents officers up to and including the rank of Chief Inspector.

The Prison Service

The prison services in the United Kingdom are the responsibility of the Home Secretary, the Scottish Executive Justice Department and the Secretary of State for Northern Ireland. The chief director generals (Chief Executive in Scotland) officers of the Prison Service, the Scottish Prison Service and the Northern Ireland Prison Service are responsible for the day-to-day running of the system.

There are 137 prison establishments in England and Wales, 20 in Scotland and four in Northern Ireland. Convicted prisoners are classified according to their assessed security risk and are housed in establishments appropriate to that level of security. There are no open prisons in Northern Ireland. Female prisoners are housed in women's establishments or in separate wings of mixed prisons. Remand prisoners are, where possible, housed separately from convicted prisoners. Offenders under the age of 21 are usually detained in a young offenders' institution, which may be a separate establishment or part of a prison.

Nine prisons are now run by the private sector, and in England and Wales all escort services have been contracted out to private companies. Two prisons are being built and financed under the Private Finance Initiative and will also be run by private contractors. In Scotland, one prison (Kilmarnock) was built and financed by the private sector and is being operated by private contractors.

There are independent prison inspectorates in England and Wales and Scotland which report annually on conditions and the treatment of prisoners. HM Chief Inspector of Prisons for England and Wales also performs an inspectorate role for prisons in Northern Ireland. Every prison establishment also has an independent board of visitors or visiting committee made up of local volunteers. Any prisoner whose complaint is not satisfied by the internal complaints procedures may complain to the Prisons Ombudsman for England and Wales or the Scottish Prisons Complaints Commission. There is no Prisons Ombudsman for Northern Ireland, but complaints by prisoners regarding maladministration may be made to the Parliamentary Commissioner for Administration.

AVERAGE PRISON POPULATION 2000–2001 (UK)

	Remand	Sentenced	Other
ENGLAND AND WALES			
Male	10,296	50,480	641
Female	700	2,684	22
Total	10,996	53,164	663
SCOTLAND			
Male	n/a	n/a	—
Female	n/a	n/a	—
Total	975	4,999	—
N. IRELAND			
Male	284	699	5
Female	9	13	0
Total	293	712	5
UK TOTAL	12,264	58,875	673

The projected prison population for 2007 in England and Wales is 69,500 if custody rates and sentence lengths remain at 2000 levels

Sources: Home Office – *Research Development Statistics*; Scottish Prison Service – *Annual Report and Accounts 1999–2000*; Northern Ireland Prison Service – *Annual Report 2000–2001*

SENTENCED PRISON POPULATION BY SEX AND OFFENCE (ENGLAND AND WALES) *as at 30 June 2000.*

	Male	Female
Violence against the person	10,807	410
Sexual offences	5,070	20
Burglary	8,824	158
Robbery	6,158	195
Theft, handling	4,537	507
Fraud and forgery	885	131
Drugs offences	7,526	947
Other offences	5,829	222
Offence not known	797	69
In default of payment of a fine	80	7
Total	50,514	2,666

Source: Home Office – *Research Development Statistics*

AVERAGE SENTENCED POPULATION BY LENGTH OF SENTENCE 2000 (ENGLAND AND WALES)

	Adults	Young Offenders
Less than 12 months	6,053	2,414
12 months to less than 4 years	15,161	4,517
4 years to less than 10 years	16,181	1,338
10 years less than life	2,384	19
Life	4,406	147
Total	44,185	8,435

Source: Home Office – *Research Development Statistics*

AVERAGE DAILY SENTENCED POPULATION BY LENGTH OF SENTENCE 1999–2000 (SCOTLAND)

	Adults	Young Offenders
Less than 4 years	1,987	502
4 years or over (including life)	2,333	176
Total	4,320	678

Source: Scottish Prison Service – *Annual Report and Accounts 1999–2000*

PRISON SUICIDES 2001 (ENGLAND AND WALES)

Males	73
Females	8
Total	81
Rate per 1,000 prisoners in custody	1.25

Source: Home Office – *Research Development Statistics*

AVERAGE NUMBER OF PRISON SERVICE STAFF 2000–2001 (GREAT BRITAIN)

	England and Wales	Scotland
No. of prison service staff	43,845	4,870

Sources: HM Prison Service – *Annual Report and Accounts 2000–2001*; Scottish Prison Service – *Annual Report and Accounts 1999–2000*

392   The Prison Service

OPERATING COSTS OF PRISON SERVICE IN
ENGLAND AND WALES 2000–2001

	£ million
Staff costs	1,094.5
Other operating costs	925.1
Operating income	(144.8)
Net operating costs before notional charge on capital employed	1,874.8
Charge on capital employed	259.9
Net operating costs	2,134.7
Average cost per prisoner place (reflecting establishment costs only)	£22,890

Source: HM Prison Service – Annual Report and Accounts 2000–2001

OPERATING COSTS OF SCOTTISH PRISON SERVICE
1999–2000

	£
Total income	1,734,000
Total expenditure	219,975,000
Staff costs	127,724,000
Running costs	73,489,000
Other current expenditure	18,762,000
Operating cost	(218,241,000)
Cost of capital charges	(23,349,000)
Interest payable and similar charges	(15,000)
Interest receivable	93,000
Lockerbie Trial Costs	3,387
Deficit for financial year	(244,899,000)
Average annual cost per prisoner per place	£28,375

Source: Scottish Prison Service – Annual Report and Accounts 1999–2000

OPERATING COSTS OF NORTHERN IRELAND PRISON
SERVICE 2000–2001

	£'000
Income	105
Expenditure	
Staff Costs	82,256
Depreciation and other charges,	5,417
Other Operating Costs,	21,719
Total,	109,392
Net cost of Operations,	107,657
Average annual cost per prisoner place	74,580

Source: Northern Ireland Prison Service – Annual Report and Accounts 2000–2001

THE PRISON SERVICES

HM PRISON SERVICE

Cleland House, Page Street, London SW1P 4LN
Tel: 020-7217 6000; Fax: 020-7217 6403

SALARIES 2000–2001

Grade1A1	£42,500–£61,376
Grade 1B	£41,000–£58,573
Grade 1C	£36,500–£52,738
Grade 1D/2A	£32,500–£48,293
Grade 2B/3A	£23,000–£36,346
Grade 2C/3B	£19,000–£37,090
Grade 3C	£18,000–£25,233

THE PRISON SERVICE MANAGEMENT BOARD

Director-General (SCS), M. Narey
  Private Secretary, Ms R. Goodwin
  Staff Officer, C. Stuart
*Prisons and Probation Minister, Chairman of the Strategy
  Board for Correctional Services*, Beverley J. Huges, MP
Director, Criminal Policy Group, Home Office, Ms S. Street
Deputy Director-General (SCS), P. Wheatley
Director of High Security Prisons (SCS), P. Atherton
Director of Security (SCS), B. Clark
Director of Personnel (SCS), G. Hadley
Director of Finance Procurement (SCS), J. Le Vay
Director of Corporate Affairs (SCS), Ms C. Pelham
Director of Resettlement (SCS), K. D. Sutton
Head of the Prison Health Policy Unit (SCS), Dr F. Harvey
Non-Executive Members, Sir Duncan Nichol, CBE; Mrs R.
  Thomson, CBE; P. Carter; R. Rosser; Lord Laming
Board Secretary and Head of Secretariat, Ms C. Checksfield
Chaplain-General and Archdeacon of the Prison Service,
  W. Noblett
Muslim Advisor, M. Ahmed
Race Equality Advisor, Ms J. Clements
Legal Adviser, S. Bramley

AREA MANAGERS (SCS)

Eastern, M. Spurr; *East Midlands (North)*, D. Shaw; *East
Midlands (South)*, M. Egan; *London*, A. Smith; *North East*,
R. Mitchell; *North West (Lancashire and Cumbria)*,
T. Fitzpatrick; *North West (Manchester, Mersey and
Cheshire)*, I. Lockwood; *South East (Thames Valley
and Hampshire)*, Mrs S. Payne; *South East (Kent Surrey
and Sussex)*, T. Murtagh; *South West*, J. Petherick;
Wales, J. May; *West Midlands*, B. Payling; *Yorkshire and
Humberside*, P. Earnshaw
Operational Manager for Women's Prisons, N. Clifford
Operational Manager for Juvenile Estate, D. Walplington
Operational Manager for High Security Prisons, P. Atherton

PRISON ESTABLISHMENTS – ENGLAND AND WALES

CNA – Average number of in use certified normal
  accommodation places without overcrowding 2000-
  2001 *Prisoners*, 63,462
Prisoners/Young Offenders Average number of prisoners/
  young offenders 2000-2001, *Prisoners*, 64,520, *Young
  Offenders 10,980*
ACKLINGTON, Morpeth, Northumberland NE65 9XH.
  CNA, 782. *Prisoners*, 727. *Governor*, P. Atkinson
ALBANY, Newport, Isle of Wight PO30 5RS. *CNA*, 446.
  Prisoners, 438. *Governor*, K. Munns
ALTCOURSE (private prison), Higher Lane, Fazakerley,
  Liverpool L9 7AG. *CNA*, 614. *Prisoners*,768. *Director*,
  W. MacGowan
††ASHFIELD (from December 1999), Shortwood Road,
  Pucklechurch, Bristol BS16 9QT. *CNA*, 407. *Prisoners*,
  356. *Director*, D. Bramley
ASHWELL, Oakham, Leics LE15 7LF. *CNA*, 407. *Prisoners*,
  384. *Governor*, D. Walmsley
*††ASKHAM GRANGE, Askham Richard, York YO23PT. *CNA*,
  132. *Prisoners and Young Offenders*, 120. *Governor*,
  I. Simmonds
‡AYLESBURY, Bierton Road, Aylesbury, Bucks HP20 1EH.
  CNA, 418. *Young Offenders*, 355. *Governor*, S. Bryans
BEDFORD, St Loyes Street, Bedford MK40 1HG. *CNA*, 352.
  Prisoners, 413. *Governor*, A. Cross
†BELMARSH, Western Way, Thamesmead, London
  SE28 0EB. *CNA*, 843. *Prisoners*, 817. *Governor*, H. Banks
BIRMINGHAM, Winson Green Road, Birmingham B18 4AS.
  CNA, 722. *Prisoners*, 817. *Governor*, M. Shann

BLAKENHURST (private prison), Hewell Lane, Redditch, Worcs B97 6QS. *CNA,* 647. *Prisoners,* 833. *Director,* P. Siddons

BLANTYRE HOUSE, Goudhurst, Cranbrook, Kent TN17 2NH. *CNA,* 120. *Prisoners,* 109. *Governor,* C. Bartlett

BLUNDESTON, Lowestoft, Suffolk NR32 5BG. *CNA,* 424. *Prisoners,* 412. *Governor,* J. Knight

†‡BRINSFORD, New Road, Featherstone, Wolverhampton WV10 7PY. *CNA,* 477. *Young Offenders,* 473. *Governor,* D. McAllister

BRISTOL, Cambridge Road, Bristol BS7 8PS. *CNA,* 489. *Prisoners,* 537. *Governor,* N. Wall

BRIXTON, PO Box 369, Jebb Avenue, London SW2 5XF. *CNA,* 651. *Prisoners,* 766. *Governor,* S. Twinn

*†‡BROCKHILL, Redditch, Worcs B97 6RD. *CNA,* 166. *Prisoners and Young Offenders,* 151. *Governor,* M. Sheppard

BUCKLEY HALL (private prison), Buckley Farm Lane, Rochdale, Lancs OL12 9DP. *CNA,* 350. *Prisoners,* 367. *Director,* P. Norbury

BULLINGDON, PO Box 50, Bicester, Oxon OX6 0PR. *CNA,* 773. *Prisoners,* 864. *Acting Governor,* L. Serjeant

*†‡BULLWOOD HALL, High Road, Hockley, Essex SS5 4TE. *CNA,* 180. *Prisoners and Young Offenders,* 167. *Governor,* Mrs V. Hart

CAMP HILL, Newport, Isle of Wight PO30 5PB. *CNA,* 481 *Prisoners,* 525. *Governor,* S. Metcalf

CANTERBURY, 46 Longport, Canterbury CT1 1PJ. *CNA,* 198. *Prisoners,* 273. *Governor,* Ms J. Galbally

†‡CARDIFF, Knox Road, Cardiff CF2 1UG. *CNA,* 525. *Prisoners and Young Offenders,* 619. *Governor,* J. Thomas-Ferrand

‡CASTINGTON, Morpeth, Northumberland NE65 9XG. *CNA,* 460. *Young Offenders,* 271. *Governor,* M. Lees

CHANNINGS WOOD, Denbury, Newton Abbott, Devon TQ12 6DW. *CNA,* 594. *Prisoners,* 587. *Governor,* N. Evans

†‡CHELMSFORD, 200 Springfield Road, Chelmsford, Essex CM2 6LQ. *CNA,* 50. *Prisoners and Young Offenders,* 459. *Governor,* P. Haley

COLDINGLEY, Bisley, Woking, Surrey GU24 9EX. *CNA,* 370. *Prisoners,* 356 *Governor,* J. Dixon

*COOKHAM WOOD, Rochester, Kent ME1 3LU. *CNA,* 120. *Prisoners,* 146. *Governor,* S. West

DARTMOOR, Princetown, Yelverton, Devon PL20 6RR. *CNA,* 691. *Prisoners,* 636. *Governor,* J. Lawrence

‡DEERBOLT, Bowes Road, Barnard Castle, Co. Durham DL12 9BG. *CNA,* 474. *Young Offenders,* 389. *Governor,* P. Copple

†‡DONCASTER (private prison), Off North Bridge, Marshgate, Doncaster DN5 8UX. *CNA,* 771. *Prisoners and Young Offenders,* 1,048. *Director,* K. Rogers

†‡DORCHESTER, North Square, Dorchester DT1 1JD. *CNA,* 172. *Prisoners and Young Offenders,* 225. *Governor,* R. Bateman

‡DOVER, The Citadel, Western Heights, Dover CT17 9DR. *CNA,* 316. *Young Offenders,* 288. *Governor,* C. Kershaw

DOWNVIEW, Sutton Lane, Sutton, Surrey SM2 5PD. *CNA,* 327. *Prisoners,* 328. *Governor,* B. Chapman

*‡DRAKE HALL, Eccleshall, Staffs ST21 6LQ. *CNA,* 311. *Prisoners and Young Offenders,* 199. *Governor,* P. Tidball

DOVEGATE (Private prison), UTTOXETER, ST14 8XR. *CNA,* 200, *Prisoners and Young Offenders,* 199. *Director,* P. Wright.

*†DURHAM, Old Elvet, Durham DH1 3HU. *CNA,* 670. *Prisoners,* 696. *Governor,* M. Newell

*‡EAST SUTTON PARK, Sutton Valence, Maidstone, Kent ME17 3DF. *CNA,* 94. *Prisoners and Young Offenders,* 85. *Governor,* Revd R. Carter

*†‡EASTWOOD PARK, Falfield, Wotton-under-Edge, Glos GL12 8DB. *CNA,* 295. *Prisoners and Young Offenders,* 303. *Governor,* P. Winkley.

ELMLEY, Church Road, Eastchurch, Sheerness, Kent ME12 4AY. *CNA,* 763. *Prisoners,* 894. *Governor,* B. Pollett

ERLESTOKE HOUSE, Devizes, Wilts SN10 5TU. *CNA,* 326. *Prisoners,* 315. *Governor,* Mrs J. Blake

EVERTHORPE, Brough, E. Yorks HU15 1RB. *CNA,* 438. *Prisoners,* 460. *Governor,* P. Midgley

†‡EXETER, New North Road, Exeter EX4 4EX. *CNA,* 321. *Prisoners and Young Offenders,* 469. *Governor,* G. Deighton

FEATHERSTONE, New Road, Wolverhampton WV10 7PU. *CNA,* 599. *Prisoners,* 592. *Governor,* M. Pascoe

†‡FELTHAM, Bedfont Road, Feltham, Middx TW13 4ND. *CNA,* 860. *Prisoners and Young Offenders,* 660. *Governor,* N. Pascoe

FORD, Arundel, W. Sussex BN18 0BX. *CNA,* 501. *Prisoners,* 319. *Governor,* K. Kan

FOREST BANK, Agecroft Road, Pendlebury, Manchester M27 8UE. *CNA,* 800. *Prisoners,* 726. *Director,* M. Goodwin

*‡FOSTON HALL, Foston, Derbys DE65 5DN. *CNA,* 174. *Prisoners and Young Offenders,* 154. *Governor,* Ms P. Scriven

FRANKLAND, Brasside, Durham DH1 5YD. *CNA,* 653. *Prisoners,* 622. *Governor,* I. Woods

FULL SUTTON, Full Sutton, York YO41 1PS. *CNA,* 603. *Prisoners,* 584. *Governor,* D. Roberts

GARTH, Ulnes Walton Lane, Leyland, Preston PR5 3NE. *CNA,* 633. *Prisoners,* 618. *Governor,* J. Illingsworth

GARTREE, Gallow Field Road, Market Harborough, Leics LE16 7RP. *CNA,* 366. *Prisoners,* 286. *Governor,* S. McAllister

†‡GLEN PARVA, Tigers Road, Wigston, Leicester LE8 4TN. *CNA,* 460. *Young Offenders,* 763. *Governor,* C. Bushell

†‡GLOUCESTER, Barrack Square, Gloucester GL1 2JN. *CNA,* 236. *Prisoners and Young Offenders,* 260. *Governor,* R. Booty

GRENDON/SPRING HILL, Grendon Underwood, Aylesbury, Bucks HP18 0TL. *CNA,* 509. *Prisoners,* 434. *Governor,* T. C. Newell

‡GUYS MARSH, Shaftesbury, Dorset SP7 0AH. *CNA,* 487. *Prisoners and Young Offenders,* 507. *Governor,* Mrs D. Calvert

§HASLAR, 2 Dolphin Way, Gosport, Hants PO12 2AW. *CNA,* 160. *Prisoners,* 147. *Governor,* B. Bennett

‡HATFIELD, Thorne Road, Hatfield, Doncaster DN7 6EL. *CNA,* 180. *Young Offenders,* 169. *Governor,* T. Watson

HAVERIGG, Millom, Cumbria LA18 4NA. *CNA,* 554. *Prisoners,* 518. *Governor,* G. Brunskill

HEWELL GRANGE, Redditch, Worcs B97 6QQ. *CNA,* 193. *Prisoners,* 142. *Governor,* N. Croft

HIGH DOWN, Sutton Lane, Sutton, Surrey SM2 5PJ. *CNA,* 649. *Prisoners,* 700. *Governor,* T. Butt

*HIGHPOINT, Stradishall, Newmarket, Suffolk CB8 9YG. *CNA,* 850. *Prisoners,* 794. *Governor,* R. Haley

†‡HINDLEY, Gibson Street, Bickershaw, Wigan, Lancs WN2 5TH. *CNA,* 538. *Prisoners and Young Offenders,* 510. *Governor,* J. Heavens

‡HOLLESLEY BAY COLONY, Woodbridge, Suffolk IP12 3JW. *CNA,* 463. *Prisoners and Young Offenders,* 311. *Governor,* S. Robinson

*†‡HOLLOWAY, Parkhurst Road, London N7 0NU. *CNA,* 517. *Prisoners and Young Offenders,* 470. *Governor,* D. Lancaster

HOLME HOUSE, Holme House Road, Stockton-on-Tees TS18 2QU. *CNA,* 971. *Prisoners,* 918. *Governor,* R. Crouch

†‡HULL, Hedon Road, Hull HU9 5LS. *CNA,* 615. *Prisoners and Young Offenders,* 554. *Governor,* S. Wagstaffe

394   The Prison Service

‡HUNTERCOMBE, Huntercombe Place, Nuffield, Henley-on-Thames RG9 5SB. *CNA*, 360. *Young Offenders*, 325. *Governor*, P. Manwaring

KINGSTON, 122 Milton Road, Portsmouth PO3 6AS. *CNA*, 193. *Prisoners*, 181. *Governor*, A. Munro

KIRKHAM, Freckleton Road, Preston PR4 2RN. *CNA*, 577. *Prisoners*, 479. *Governor*, A. F. Jennings, OBE

KIRKLEVINGTON GRANGE, Yarm, Cleveland TS15 9PA. *CNA*, 183. *Prisoners*, 179. *Governor*, Ms S. Anthony

LANCASTER, The Castle, Lancaster LA1 1YL. *CNA*, 240. *Prisoners*, 229. *Governor*, T. Williams

†‡LANCASTER FARMS, Far Moor Lane, Stone Row Head, off Quernmore Road, Lancaster LA1 3QZ. *CNA*, 496. *Prisoners and Young Offenders*, 457. *Governor*, D. Thomas

LATCHMERE HOUSE, Church Road, Ham Common, Richmond, Surrey TW10 5HH. *CNA*, 193. *Prisoners*, 169. *Governor*, T. Hinchliffe

LEEDS, Armley, Leeds LS12 2TJ. *CNA*, 770. *Prisoners*, 1,256. *Governor*, S. Tasker

LEICESTER, Welford Road, Leicester LE2 7AJ. *CNA*, 219. *Prisoners*, 334. *Governor*, D. Bamber

†‡LEWES, Brighton Road, Lewes, E. Sussex BN7 1EA. *CNA*, 485. *Prisoners and Young Offenders*, 445. *Governor*, P. Carroll

LEYHILL, Wotton-under-Edge, Glos GL12 8BT. *CNA*, 410. *Prisoners*, 319. *Governor*, R. Booty

LINCOLN, Greetwell Road, Lincoln LN2 4BD. *CNA*, 436. *Prisoners*, 486. *Governor*, R. Peacock

§LINDHOLME, Bawtry Road, Hatfield Woodhouse, Doncaster DN7 6EE. *CNA*, 641 *Prisoners*, 590. *Governor*, M. Read

LITTLEHEY, Perry, Huntingdon, Cambs PE18 0SR. *CNA*, 624. *Prisoners*, 627. *Governor*, J. Morgan

LIVERPOOL, 68 Hornby Road, Liverpool L9 3DF. *CNA*, 1,216. *Prisoners*, 1,257. *Governor*, C. Sheffield

LONG LARTIN, South Littleton, Evesham, Worcs WR11 5TZ. *CNA*, 599. *Prisoners*, 448. *Governor*, J. Mullen

LOWDHAM GRANGE (private prison), Lowdham, Notts NG14 7TA. *CNA*, 504. *Prisoners*, 489. *Director*, A. Bramley

*†‡LOW NEWTON, Brasside, Durham DH1 5SD. *CNA*, 215. *Prisoners and Young Offenders*, 237. *Governor*, M. Kirby

MAIDSTONE, 36 County Road, Maidstone ME14 1UZ. *CNA*, 549. *Prisoners*, 371. *Governor*, M. Conway

MANCHESTER, Southall Street, Manchester M60 9AH. *CNA*, 953. *Prisoners*, 1,105. *Acting Governor*, J. Smith

‡MOORLAND, Bawtry Road, Hatfield Woodhouse, Doncaster DN7 6BW. *CNA*, 753. *Prisoners and Young Offenders*, 760. *Governor*, B. McCourt

MORTON HALL, Swinderby, Lincoln LN6 9PS. *CNA*, 192. *Prisoners*, 119. *Governor*, M. Murphy

THE MOUNT, Molyneaux Avenue, Bovingdon, Hemel Hempstead HP3 0NZ. *CNA*, 705. *Prisoners*, 717. *Governor*, P. Wailen

*†‡NEW HALL, Dial Wood, Flockton, Wakefield WF4 4AX. *CNA*, 327. *Prisoners and Young Offenders*, 334. *Governor*, V. Bird

†‡NORTHALLERTON, 15A East Road, Northallerton, N. Yorks DL6 1NW. *CNA*, 152. *Prisoners and Young Offenders*, 198. *Governor*, D. P. G. Appleton

NORTH SEA CAMP, Freiston, Boston, Lincs PE22 0QX. *CNA*, 226. *Prisoners*, 182. *Governor*, M. A. Lewis

†‡NORWICH, Mousehold, Norwich NR1 4LU. *CNA*, 561. *Prisoners and Young Offenders*, 652. *Governor*, M. Knight

NOTTINGHAM, Perry Road, Sherwood, Nottingham NG5 3AG. *CNA*, 519. *Prisoners*, 484. *Governor*, K. Beaumont

‡ONLEY, Willoughby, Rugby, Warks CV23 8AP. *CNA*, 640. *Young Offenders*, 576. *Governor*, R. Fielder

†‡PARC (private prison), Heol Hopcyn John, Bridgend CF35 6AR. *CNA*, 844. *Prisoners and Young Offenders*, 869. *Director*, R. Woolford

PARKHURST, Newport, Isle of Wight PO30 5NX. *CNA*, 482. *Prisoners*, 427. *Governor*, D. Kennedy

PENTONVILLE, Caledonian Road, London N7 8TT. *CNA*, 897. *Prisoners*, 1,122. *Governor*, G. Davies

‡PORTLAND, Easton, Portland, Dorset DT5 1DL. *CNA*, 512. *Young Offenders*, 480. *Governor*, K. Lockyer

‡PRESCOED, 47 Maryport Street, Usk, Gwent NP5 1XP. *CNA*, 120. *Prisoners and Young Offenders*, 111. *Governor*, R. J. Comber

PRESTON, 2 Ribbleton Lane, Preston PR1 5AB. *CNA*, 425. *Prisoners*, 542. *Governor*, A. Scott

RANBY, Ranby, Retford, Notts DN22 8EV. *CNA*, 725. *Prisoners*, 738. *Governor*, J. Slater

†‡READING, Forbury Road, Reading RG1 3HY. *CNA*, 204. *Prisoners and Young Offenders*, 229. *Governor*, C. Norman

*RISLEY, Risley, Warrington WA3 6BP. *CNA*, 818. *Prisoners*, 790. *Governor*, C. McConnell

†‡ROCHESTER, 1 Fort Road, Rochester, Kent ME1 3QS. *CNA*, 433. *Prisoners and Young Offenders*, 367. *Governor*, T. Robson

RYE HILL (Private Prison), ONLEY, RUGBY CV23 8A9. *CNA*, 600. *Prisoners and Young Offenders*, 458, *Director*, A. Rose-Quirie

*SEND, Ripley Road, Send, Woking, Surrey GU23 7LJ. *CNA*, 220. *Prisoners*, 216. *Governor*, T. Beeston

SHEPTON MALLET, Cornhill, Shepton Mallet, Somerset BA4 5LU. *CNA*, 195. *Prisoners*, 150. *Governor*, B. McAlley

SHREWSBURY, The Dana, Shrewsbury SY1 2HR. *CNA*, 185. *Prisoners*, 325. *Governor*, A. Bramley

STAFFORD, 54 Gaol Road, Stafford ST16 3AW. *CNA*, 627. *Prisoners*, 619. *Governor*, L. Taylor

STANDFORD HILL, Church Road, Eastchurch, Isle of Sheppey, Kent ME12 4AA. *CNA*, 384. *Prisoners*, 332. *Governor*, J. Robinson

STOCKEN, Stocken Hall Road, Stretton, nr Oakham, Leics LE15 7RD. *CNA*, 556. *Prisoners*, 578. *Governor*, R. Curtis

‡STOKE HEATH, Stoke Heath, Market Drayton, Shropshire TF9 2JL. *CNA*, 634. *Young Offenders*, 509. *Governor*, C. James

*‡STYAL, Wilmslow, Cheshire SK9 4HR. *CNA*, 412. *Prisoners and Young Offenders*, 421. *Governor*, Ms M. Moulden

SUDBURY, Ashbourne, Derbys DE6 5HW. *CNA*, 519. *Prisoners*, 498. *Governor*, P. Salter

SWALESIDE, Brabazon Road, Eastchurch, Isle of Sheppey, Kent ME12 4AX. *CNA*, 752. *Prisoners*, 746. *Governor*, E. Willett

†SWANSEA, 200 Oystermouth Road, Swansea SA1 3SR. *CNA*, 249. *Prisoners*, 346. *Governor*, Miss V. O'Dea

‡SWINFEN HALL, Lichfield, Staffs WS14 9QS. *CNA*, 320. *Young Offenders*, 308 *Governor*, Ms J. Mosley

‡THORN CROSS, Arley Road, Appleton Thorn, Warrington WA4 4RL. *CNA*, 316. *Young Offenders*, 212. *Governor*, C. Davies

USK, 47 Maryport Street, Usk, Gwent NP5 1XP. *CNA*, 131. *Prisoners*, 216. *Governor*, R. J. Comber

THE VERNE, Portland, Dorset DT5 1EQ. *CNA*, 552. *Prisoners*, 562. *Governor*, M. Cook

WAKEFIELD, 5 Love Lane, Wakefield WF2 9AG. *CNA*, 746. *Prisoners*, 558. *Governor*, D. Shaw

WANDSWORTH, Heathfield Road, London SW18 3HS. *CNA*, 1,162. *Prisoners*, 1,301. *Governor*, S. Rimmer

WAYLAND, Griston, Thetford, Norfolk IP25 6RL. *CNA*, 620. *Prisoners*, 623. *Governor*, Mrs K. Crawley

WEALSTUN, Wetherby, W. Yorks LS23 7AZ. *CNA*, 616. *Prisoners*, 603. *Governor*, S. Tilley

WEARE, Portland Dock, Castletown, Portland, Dorset DT5 1PZ. *CNA*, 400. *Prisoners*, 374. *Governor*, Ms S. F. McCormick

WELLINGBOROUGH, Millers Park, Doddington Road, Wellingborough, Northants NN8 2NH. *CNA*, 518. *Prisoners*, 449. *Governor*, Dr P. Bennett

‡WERRINGTON, Werrington, Stoke-on-Trent ST9 0DX. *CNA*, 106. *Young Offenders*, 105. *Governor*, S. Habgood

‡WETHERBY, York Road, Wetherby, W. Yorks LS22 5ED. *CNA*, 309. *Young Offenders*, 347. *Governor*, S. McEwan

WHATTON, 14 Cromwell Road, Nottingham NG13 9FQ. *CNA*, 275. *Prisoners*, 272. *Governor*, B. Greenberry

WHITEMOOR, Longhill Road, March, Cambs PE15 0PR. *CNA*, 532. *Prisoners*, 381. *Governor*, B. Perry

*WINCHESTER, Romsey Road, Winchester SO22 5DF. *CNA*,439. *Prisoners*, 590. *Governor*, J. Gomersall

THE WOLDS (private prison), Everthorpe, Brough, E. Yorks HU15 2JZ. *CNA*, 360. *Prisoners*, 397. *Director*, D. McDonnell

††§WOODHILL, Tattenhoe Street, Milton Keynes MK4 4DA. *CNA*, 677. *Prisoners and Young Offenders*, 660. *Governor*, B. Mullen

WORMWOOD SCRUBS, PO Box 757, Du Cane Road, London W12 0AE. *CNA*, 1,212. *Prisoners*, 947. *Governor*, K. Munns

WYMOTT, Ulnes Walton Lane, Leyland, Preston PR5 3LW. *CNA*, 809. *Prisoners*, 793. *Governor*, R. Doughty

SCOTTISH PRISON SERVICE

Calton House, 5 Redheughs Rigg, Edinburgh EH12 9HW
Tel: 0131-556 8400

SALARIES 2000–2001

Senior managers in the Scottish Prison Service, including governors and deputy governors of prisons, are paid across three pay bands:

Band I	£37,375–£37,700
Band H	£31,150 –£48,100
Band G	£26,050–£39,600

Chief Executive of Scottish Prison Service, A. Cameron
Director, Human Resources, P. Russell
Director, Finance and Information Systems, W. Pretswell
Director, Strategy and Business Performance, B. Allison
Deputy Director, Rehabilitation and Care, A. Spencer
Deputy Director, Estates and Buildings, D. Bentley
Operations Director, South and West, M. Duffy
Operations Director, North and East, P. Withers
Head of Training, Scottish Prison Service College, J. Matthews
Head of Communications, T. Fox

PRISON ESTABLISHMENTS

Prisoners/Young Offenders Average number of prisoners/ young offenders 2000–2001

*ABERDEEN, Craiginches, Aberdeen AB9 2HN. *Prisoners*, 181. *Governor*, I. Gunn

BARLINNIE, Barlinnie, Glasgow G33 2QX. *Prisoners*, 1,124. *Governor*, R. L. Houchin

CASTLE HUNTLY, Castle Huntly, Longforgan, nr Dundee DD2 5HL. *Prisoners*, 106. *Governor*, M. McAlpine

*‡CORNTON VALE, Cornton Road, Stirling FK9 5NY. *Prisoners and Young Offenders*, 180. *Governor*, S. Swan

*‡DUMFRIES, Terregles Street, Dumfries DG2 9AX. *Young Offenders*, 137. *Governor*, C. McGeever

EDINBURGH, 33 Stenhouse Road, Edinburgh EH1 3LN. *Prisoners*, 731. *Governor*, R. MacCowan

‡GLENOCHIL, King O'Muir Road, Tullibody, Clackmannanshire FK10 3AD. *Prisoners and Young Offenders*, 573. *Governor*, K. Donegan

GREENOCK, Gateside, Greenock PA16 9AH. *Prisoners*, 236. *Governor*, A. Park

*INVERNESS, Porterfield, Inverness IV2 3HH. *Prisoners*, 122. *Governor*, A. MacDonald

KILMARNOCK (private prison), Bowhouse, Mauchline Road, Kilmarnock KA1 5JH. *Prisoners*, 500. *Director*, J. Bywalec

LOW MOSS, Low Moss, Bishopbriggs, Glasgow G64 2QB. *Prisoners*, 362. *Governor*, E. Murch

NORANSIDE, Noranside, Fern, by Forfar, Angus DD8 3QY. *Prisoners*, 102. *Governor*, K. Rennie

PERTH, 3 Edinburgh Road, Perth PH2 8AT. *Prisoners*, 477. *Governor*, W. Millar

PETERHEAD, Salthouse Head, Peterhead, Aberdeenshire AB4 6YY. *Prisoners*, 297. *Governor*, W. Rattray

‡POLMONT, Brightons, Falkirk, Stirlingshire FK2 0AB. *Young Offenders*, 443. *Governor*, D. Gunn

SHOTTS, Shotts ML7 4LF. *Prisoners*, 467. *Governor*, W. McKinlay

NORTHERN IRELAND PRISON SERVICE

Dundonald House, Upper Newtownards Road, Belfast BT4 3SU. Tel: 028-9052 2922; Fax 028-9052 5100; Web: www.niprisonservice.gov.uk

Salaries 1999–2000

Governor 1	£55,536–£57,453
Governor 2	£50,148–£51,687
Governor 3	£43,309–£44,532
Governor 4	£36,317–£38,249
Governor 5	£25,461–£34,261

A Northern Ireland allowance is also payable

PRISON ESTABLISHMENTS

Prisoners/Young Offenders Average number of prisoners/ young offenders 2000–2001

†HYDEBANK WOOD, Hospital Road, Belfast BT8 8NA. *Young Offenders*, 136

*‡MAGHABERRY, Old Road, Ballinderry Upper, Lisburn, Co. Antrim BT28 2PT. *Prisoners and Young Offenders*, 481

§MAGILLIGAN, Point Road, Magilligan, Co. Londonderry BT49 0LR. *Prisoners*, 364

*Women's establishment or establishment with units for women
†Remand Centre or establishment with units for remand prisoners
‡Young Offender Institution or establishment with units for young offenders
§Immigration Holding Centre

Defence

The armed forces of the United Kingdom comprise the Royal Navy, the Army and the Royal Air Force. The Queen is commander-in-chief of all the armed forces. The Ministry of Defence, headed by a Secretary of State, provides the support structure for the armed forces. Within the Ministry of Defence, the Defence Council has overall responsibility for running the armed forces. The Chief of Staff of each service reports through the Chief of the Defence Staff to the Secretary of State on matters relating to the running of his service. The Chief of Staff also chairs the executive committee of the appropriate service board, which manages the service in accordance with centrally determined objectives and budgets. The military-civilian Central Staffs, headed by the Vice-Chief of the Defence Staff and the Second Permanent Under-Secretary of State, are responsible for policy, operational requirements, commitments, financial management, resource planning and civilian personnel management. The Defence Procurement Agency is responsible for purchasing equipment. The Defence Scientific Staff and the Defence Intelligence Staff also form part of the Ministry of Defence.

A permanent Joint Headquarters for the conduct of joint operations was set up at Northwood in 1996. The Joint Headquarters connects the policy and strategic functions of the MoD Head Office with the conduct of operations and is intended to strengthen the policy/executive division. A Joint Rapid Deployment Force was established in August 1996 and a Joint Rapid Reaction Force was set up in April 1999.

Britain pursues its defence and security policies through its membership of NATO (to which most of its armed forces are committed), the Western European Union, the European Union, the Organisation for Security and Co-operation in Europe and the UN (*see* International Organisations section).

ARMED FORCES STRENGTHS *as at 1 July 2001*

All Services	203,730
Men	187,054
Women	16,676
Royal Naval Services	41,864
Army	108,475
Royal Air Force	53,391

Source: Ministry of Defence: Defence Analytical Service Agency

SERVICE PERSONNEL

1 August 2001

	Royal Navy	Army	RAF	All Services
1975 strength	76,200	167,100	95,000	338,300
1990 strength	63,200	152,800	89,700	305,700
1999 strength	43,700	113,500	55,200	212,400
2001 strength	41,864	108,475	53,391	203,730

Source: Ministry of Defence: *The Military Balance 2000–2001 (OUP)*

CIVILIAN PERSONNEL

1975 level	316,700
1990 level	172,300
1999 level	117,700
2000 level	99,142
2001 level	98,384

Source: The Ministry of Defence: *The Military Balance 1999–2000 (OUP) and UK Defence Statistics 2001*

DEPLOYMENT OF UK PERSONNEL

SERVICE PERSONNEL IN UK *as at July 2000*

	England	Wales	Scotland	N. Ireland	Unknown	Total
All Services	143,039	3,223	15,080	8,387	566	170,295
Officers	25,039	402	1,759	889	147	28,236
Other Ranks	118,000	2,821	13,321	7,498	419	142,059
Army [2]	68,040	864	4,165	7,110	343	80,522
Officers	9,745	106	422	729	36	11,038
Ranks	58,295	758	3,743	6,381	307	69,484
Navy [1,2]	34,858	29	4,962	189	13	40,051
Officers	6,496	12	590	15	5	7,118
Ranks	28,362	17	4,372	174	8	32,933
RAF [2]	40,141	2,330	5,953	1,088	210	49,722
Officers	8,798	284	747	145	106	10,080
Ranks	31,343	2,046	5,206	943	104	39,642

1. Naval Service personnel on sea service in home waters are included against the local authority containing the home port of their ship.
2. The titles Naval Service, Army and Royal Air Force include Nursing services.
3. The Home battalions of the Royal Irish Regiment are excluded from the UK Northern Ireland figures.

Source: Ministry of Defence: Defence Analytical Service Agency

SERVICE PERSONNEL OVERSEAS

as at 1 January 2001

All Services	37,657
Officers	5,480
Other Ranks	32,177
Army	29,372
Officers	3,668
Ranks	25,704
Navy	1,924
Officers	559
Ranks	1,365
RAF	6,361
Officers	1,253
Ranks	5,108

Source: Ministry of Defence: Defence Analytical Service Agency

NUCLEAR FORCES

Britain's nuclear forces comprise four ballistic missile submarines carrying Trident missiles and equipped with nuclear warheads. All nuclear free-fall bombs have been taken out of service.

ARMS CONTROL

The 1990 Conventional Armed Forces in Europe Treaty (the CFE Treaty), which is currently being revised, commits all NATO and former Warsaw Pact members to limiting five major classes of conventional weapons. In 1968 Britain signed the Nuclear Non-Proliferation Treaty, which was indefinitely and unconditionally extended in 1995 and in 1996 signed a Comprehensive Nuclear Test Ban Treaty. Britain was a party to the 1972 Biological and Toxin Weapons Convention, which provides for a world-wide ban on biological weapons, and the 1993 Chemical Weapons Convention, which came into force in 1997 and provides for a world-wide ban on chemical weapons. In 1997 Britain signed the Ottawa

Ministry of Defence 397

Convention, which provides for an immediate ban on the use, production and transfer of anti-personnel land-mines; Britain ratified the Convention on 31 July 1998 and it came into force on 1 March 1999.

DEFENCE BUDGET

Estimated Outturn | £ billion
2000–2001 | 22.820
2001–2002 | 23.408
2002–2003 | 24.036
2003–2004 | 24.816

Source: Ministry of Defence: Defence Analytical Service Agency

The defence settlement under the 2000 Comprehensive Spending Review estimates that defence expenditure will rise from approximately £23 billion this year to almost £25 billion by 2004–05.

Over the period of the Spending Review, defence as a percentage of GDP will fall from 2.4 per cent this year to 2.3 per cent by 2003–04, reflecting the fact that GDP is forecast to grow strongly. As a share of total Government expenditure, defence spending will remain at around 6 per cent.

MINISTRY OF DEFENCE
Main Building, Whitehall, London SW1A 2HB
Tel 020-7218 9000
Public Enquiry Office: Tel 020-7218 6645
Web: www.mod.uk

For ministerial and civil service salaries, *see* page 291
For Services salaries, *see* pages 406–8
Officers promoted in an acting capacity to a more senior rank are listed under the more senior rank. Promotion to five-star rank is no longer usual in peacetime.

Secretary of State for Defence, Rt. Hon. Geoffrey Hoon, MP
  Private Secretary (SCS), P. Watkins
  Special Adviser, R. Taylor
  Parliamentary Private Secretary, Mrs L. Blackman
Minister of State for the Armed Forces, Adam Ingram, MP
  Private Secretary (SCS), D. Applegate
Parliamentary Under Secretary and Minister of State for Defence Procurement, Lord Bach
  Private Secretary (SCS), D. E. A. Hatcher
  Parliamentary Private Secretary, Gillian Merron, MP
Parliamentary Under-Secretary of State (Veterans), Dr Lewis Moonie, MP
  Private Secretary (SCS), K. Alford
Permanent Under-Secretary of State (SCS), K. R. Tebbit, CMG
Chief of the Defence Staff, Admiral Sir Michael Boyce GCB, OBE

THE DEFENCE COUNCIL

The Defence Council is responsible for running the Armed Forces. The Crown Office announced that as of the 5th November 1999, the constitution of the defence council would be arranged in the following way. It is chaired by the Principal Secretary of State for Defence and consists of: the Ministers of State for the Armed Forces; the Minister of State for Defence Procurement; the Parliamentary Under-Secretary of State for Defence; the Chief of the Defence Staff; the Permanent Under-Secretary of State of the Ministry of Defence; the Chief of the Naval Staff and First Sea Lord; the Chief of the General Staff; the Chief of the Air Staff; the Vice-Chief of

the Defence Staff; the Chief of Defence Procurement for the Ministry of Defence; the Chief Scientific Adviser of the Ministry of Defence; the Chief of Defence Logistics and the Second Permanent Under-Secretary of State of the Ministry of Defence.

CHIEFS OF STAFF

CHIEF OF THE NAVAL STAFF
Chief of the Naval Staff and First Sea Lord, Adm. Sir Nigel Essenhigh, KCB
Asst Chief of the Naval Staff, Rear-Adm. T. P. McClement OBE
Secretariat (Naval Staff) (SCS), C. Verey

CHIEF OF THE GENERAL STAFF
Chief of the General Staff, Gen. Sir Michael Walker, GCB, CMG, CBE, ADC
Asst Chief of the General Staff, Maj.-Gen. F. R. Dannatt CBE MC; Lt-Gen. K. O'Donoghue, CBE MCBE, MC
Director-General, Development and Doctrine, Maj.-Gen. C. L. Elliott, CB, MBE

CHIEF OF THE AIR STAFF
Chief of the Air Staff, Air Chief Marshal Sir Peter Squire AFC, ADC, KCB, DFC, GCB
Asst Chief of the Air Staff, Air Vice-Marshal P. O. Sturley
British-American Community Relations Co-ordinator, Air Marshal Sir John Kemball, KCB, CBE, RAF (retd)
Chief Executive, National Air Traffic Services (SCS), D. J. McLauchlan
Director, Airspace Policy, Air Vice-Marshal J. R. D. Arscott

CENTRAL STAFFS

Vice-Chief of the Defence Staff, Adm. Sir Anthony Bagnall, KCB, OBE
Second Permanent Under-Secretary of State (SCS), R. T. Jackling, CB, CBE
Deputy CDS (Equipment Capability), Vice-Adm. Sir Jeremy Blackham, KCB
Asst CDS, Operational Requirements (Sea Systems), Rear-Adm. R. J. G. Ward
Asst CDS, Operational Requirements (Land Systems), to be announced
Asst CDS, Operational Requirements (Air Systems), Air Vice-Marshal S. M. Nicholl, CBE, AFC
Deputy CDS (Personnel), Air Marshal M. D. Pledger, KCB, OBE, AFC
Asst CDS (Programmes), Maj.-Gen. J. P. Kiszely, MC
Asst Under-Secretary of State (Service Personnel Policy) (SCS), D. Bowen
Defence Housing Executive (SCS), C. J. I. James
Surgeon-General, Lt.-Gen. R. C. Menzies, OBE, QHS
Chief Executive, Defence Medical Training Organisation, Brig. J. R. Brown
Chief Executive, Defence Secondary Care Organisation, C. Callow
Deputy Under-Secretary of State (Resources, Programmes and Finance) (SCS), C. V. Balmer
Asst Under-Secretary of State (Programmes) (SCS), T. A. Woolley
Asst Under-Secretary of State (Systems) (SCS), N. K. J. Witney
Asst Under-Secretary of State (Financial Management) (SCS), D. G. Jones
Asst Under-Secretary of State (General Finance) (SCS), C. Sanders
Defence Services Secretary, Maj.-Gen. C. H. Elliott
Deputy CDS (Commitments), Lt.-Gen. A. D. Pigott, CBE

Asst CDS (Operations) and Air Officer Commanding No 1 Group, Air Vice-Marshal G. L. Torpy, CBE, DSO
Chief of Defence Logistics, Gen. Sir Samuel Cowan, KCB, CBE
Chief of Staff to the Chief of Defence Logistics, (Operations and Business Development) and Chief Naval Engineer Officer Rear-Adm. M. G. Wood, CBE
Deputy to the Chief of Defence Logistics, J. R. C. Oughton
Asst CDS (Logistics), Air Vice-Marshal D. C. Couzens
Director of Policy (SCS), R. P. Hatfield, CBE
Asst CDS (Policy), Lt. Gen. J. G. Reith, CBE
Deputy Under-Secretary of State (Civilian Management) (SCS), J. Howe
Asst Under-Secretary of State, Civilian Management (Personnel) (SCS), B. A. E. Taylor
Chief Constable, MOD Police, W. E. E. Boreham, OBE
Asst Under-Secretary of State (Security and Support) (SCS), A. G. Rucker
Legal Adviser (SCS), M. J. Hemming
Director-General, Information and Communications Services (SCS), A. C. Sleigh
Defence Estates (SCS), B. L. Hirst
Commandant, Joint Services Command and Staff College, Air Vice-Marshal B. K. Burridge, CBE

DEFENCE INFORMATION STAFF
Director-General of Corporate Communications (SCS), J. Pitt-Brooke
Director, News, M. Howard
Director, Internal Communications and Media Training (SCS), A. Boardman
Director, Corporate Communications (Navy), Cdre H. Edelston
Director, Corporate Communications (Army), Brig. S. Roberts
Director, Corporate Communications (RAF), Air Cdre D. Walker

DEFENCE INTELLIGENCE STAFF
Old War Office Building, Whitehall, London SW1A 2EU
Tel 020-7218 6645; fax 020-7218 1562
Chief of Defence Intelligence, Air Marshal Joseph French, CBE
Deputy Chief of Defence Intelligence and Head of Defence Intelligence Analysis Staff (SCS), Anthony Cragg, CMG
Director, Intelligence Programmes and Resources (SCS), P. I. Bailey
Director, Defence Intelligence Secretariat and Communications Information Systems (SCS), C. A. Younger
Director, Regional Assessments, Brig. N. J. COTTAM
Director, Intelligence Global Issues (SCS), J. M. Cunningham
Director-General, Intelligence and Geographic Resources, Maj.-Gen. M. Laurie

DEFENCE SCIENTIFIC STAFF
Chief Scientific Adviser (SCS), Prof. Sir Keith O'Nions, FRS
Chief Scientist, H. B. Jordan
Director General (Scrutiny and Analysis) (SCS), M. J. Earwicker; P. M. Sutcliffe
Asst Chief Scientific Adviser (Nuclear) (SCS), P. W. Roper
Nuclear Weapon Safety Adviser (SCS), Rear-Adm. Fred Scourse

SECOND SEA LORD/COMMANDER-IN-CHIEF NAVAL HOME COMMAND
Second Sea Lord and C.-in-C. Naval Home Command, Vice-Adm. Sir P. Spencer, ADC
Director-General, Naval Personnel (Strategy and Plans) and Chief of Staff to Second Sea Lord and C.-in-C. Naval Home Command, Rear-Adm. R. G. Lockwood

Asst Under-Secretary of State (Naval Personnel) (SCS), E. Cassidy
Flag Officer Training and Recruiting and Chief Executive, Naval Recruiting and Training Agency, Rear-Adm. J. Chadwick
Naval Secretary and Chief Executive, Naval Manning Agency, Rear-Adm. J. M. de Halpert
Medical Director, General Navy Surgeon, Rear-Adm. I. L. Jenkins *Director-General, Naval Chaplaincy Services*, Revd Dr C. Stewart

NAVAL SUPPORT COMMAND
Chief of Fleet Support, Rear-Adm. B. B. Perowne
Asst Under-Secretary of State (Fleet Support) (SCS), D. J. Gould
Chief Executive, Warships Support Agency (SCS), J. Coles
Chief Naval Engineer Officer, Rear-Adm. M. G. Wood, CBE
Flag Officer Scotland, N. England and N. Ireland, and Naval Base Commander Clyde, Rear-Adm. D. J. Anthony, CBE

COMMANDER-IN-CHIEF FLEET
C.-in-C. Fleet, Adm. Sir Alan West KCB, DSC
Deputy Commander Fleet, Vice-Adm. J. Band
Chief of Staff (Operations) and Flag Officer Submarines, Rear-Adm. R. P. Stevens, OBE
Chief of Staff (Corporate Development), Rear-Adm. P. D. Greenish
Flag Officer Surface Flotilla, Rear-Adm. A. K. Backus, OBE, *Flag Officer Sea Training and Flag Officer Surface Flotilla*, Rear-Adm A. K. Backus, OBE.
Commander, UK Task Group/Commander, Anti-Submarine Warfare Strike Force, Rear-Adm. J. M. Burnell-Nugent
Flag Officer Maritime Aviation, Rear-Adm. I. R. Henderson, CBE
Commandant-General, Royal Marines, Maj.-Gen. R. A. Fry, MBE

ADJUTANT-GENERAL'S DEPARTMENT
Adjutant-General, Lt.-Gen. T. J. Granville-Chapman, KCB, CBE
Chief of Staff, Brig. K. H. Cima
Head, Command Secretariat (SCS), M. E. McLoughlin
Director-General, Army Training and Recruiting and Chief Executive, Army Training and Recruiting Agency, Maj.-Gen. A. M. D. Palmer, CBE
Chaplain-General, Revd Ven. J Blackburn
Director-General, Army Medical Services, Maj.-Gen. D. S. Jolliffe, QHP
Director, Army Legal Services, Maj.-Gen. G. Risius
Military Secretary and Chief Executive, Army Personnel Centre, Maj.-Gen. A. P. Grant Peterkin
Commandant, Royal Military Academy, Sandhurst, Maj.-Gen. P. C. C. Trousdell, CB

COMMANDER-IN-CHIEF LAND COMMAND
C.-in-C., Land Command, Gen. Sir Michael Jackson, KCB, CBE, DSO (*Commander-in-Chief Headquarters Land Command*)
Deputy C.-in-C., Land Command, and Inspector-General, Territorial Army and C-in-C Allied Forces Northern Europe, Lt.-Gen. C. N. G. Delves, CBE, DSO
Chief of Staff, HQ Land Command, Maj.-Gen. F. R. Viggers, MBE
Deputy Chief of Staff, HQ Land Command, Maj.-Gen. P. A. Chambers, MBE

HQ STRIKE COMMAND
Air Officer Commanding-in-Chief, Air Chief Marshal Sir John Day, KCB, ADC,

Chief of Air Staff, Air Chief marshallSir Peter Squire .
Deputy Chief of Staff Operations, Air Vice-Marshal N. J.
Sudborough OBE
*Air Officer Logistics and Communications Information
Systems,* Air Vice-Marshal P. J. Scott
Air Officer Administration, Air Vice-Marshal A. J. Burton
Head, Command Secretariat (SCS), C. J. Wright
Air Officer Commanding, No. 1 Group, Air Vice-Marshal G.
L. Torpy
Air Officer Commanding No 3 Group, Rear Adm. S.
Lidbetter
Air Officer Commanding, No. 38 Group, Air Vice-Marshal
K. D. Filbey, CBE
Deputy Commander-in-Chief Strike Command, Air Marshal
G. E. Stirrup, KCB

HQ LOGISTICS COMMAND
Air Officer Commanding-in-Chief, Air Vice-Marshal G.
Skinner, CBE
Command Secretary (SCS), H. Griffiths
*Air Officer Communications Information Systems and Support
Services,* Air Vice-Marshal P. Liddell
Director-General, Support Management (RAF),
Air Vice-Marshal P. W. Henderson, CB, MBE

HQ PERSONNEL AND TRAINING
COMMAND
*Air Member for Personnel and Commander-in-Chief
Personnel and Training Command and Commander-in-
Chief Strike Command,* Air Chief Marshal Sir John Day
Chief of Staff, Air Vice-Marshal R. A. Wright, AFC
Chief Executive, Training Group Defence Agency,
Air Vice-Marshal I. S. Corbitt
*Air Officer Administration and Air Officer Commanding
Directly Administered Units,* Air Vice-Marshal C.
Davison, MBE
Commandant, RAF College, Cranwell, Air Vice-Marshall
H. G. Mackay, OBE, AFC
*Air Secretary and Chief Executive, RAF Personnel
Management Agency,* Air Vice-Marshal I. M. Stewart,
AFC
Director-General, Medical Services (RAF), Air Vice-Marshal
C. J. Sharples, QHP
Director, Legal Services (RAF), Air Vice-Marshal J. Weeden
Chaplain-in-Chief (RAF), Revd A. P. Bishop, QHC
Command Secretary (SCS), R. Rooks

DEFENCE PROCUREMENT AGENCY
(DPA)
215 MOD Abbey Wood, Bristol BS34 8JH
Tel: 0117-913 0249; Fax: 0117-913 0902
*Chief of Defence Procurement and Chief Executive, Defence
Procurement Agency,* Sir Robert Walmsley, KCB
Deputy Chief Executive (SCS), David Gould
Executive Director 1 (SCS), I. Fauset
Executive Director 2, Maj.-Gen P. Gilchrist
Executive Director 3 (SCS), B. M. Thornton
Executive Director 4, and Controller of the Navy,
Rear-Adm. N. C. F. Guild
Executive Director 5 (SCS), S. Porter
Executive Director 6 (SCS), N. Evans

OTHER DEFENCE AGENCIES
ARMED FORCES PERSONNEL ADMINSTRATION AGENCY,
Building 182, RAF Innsworth, Gloucester GL3 1HW.
Tel: 01452-712612 ext. 6250. *Chief Executive,* T. S.
Lord

ABRO, Building 200, Monxton Road, Andover, Hants
SP11 8HT. Tel: 01264-383295. Acting *Chief Executive,*
Dr L. Sammon
ARMY PERSONNEL CENTRE, Kentigern House, 65 Brown
Street, Glasgow G2 8EX. Tel: 0141-224 3010. *Chief
Executive,* Lt-Gen. A. S. H. Irwin, CBE
ARMY TRAINING AND RECRUITING AGENCY, Trenchard
Lines, Upavon, Pewsey, Wilts SN9 6BE. Tel: 01980-
615033. *Chief Executive,* Maj.-Gen. A. M. D. Palmer,
CBE
BRITISH FORCES POST OFFICE, Inglis Barracks, Mill Hill,
London NW7 1PX. Tel: 020-8818 6310.
Email: bfpo@compuserve.com; Web: bfpo.org.uk
Director and Chief Executive, Brig. B. J. Cash
CHILDREN'S EDUCATION, HQ SCE, Building 5, Wegberg
Military Complex, BFPO 40. Tel: 00-49 2161-908
2372. *Chief Executive,* D. G. Wadsworth
DEFENCE ANALYTICAL SERVICES AGENCY, St. Giles
Court, 1–13 St Giles High Street, London WC2H 8LD.
Tel: 020-7218 0729; Fax; 020-7218 5203.
Chief Executive, C. Youngson
DEFENCE AVIATION REPAIR AGENCY, DARA Head Office,
Building 145, St Athan, Barry, Vale of Glamorgan CF62
4WA. Tel: 01446-798893. *Chief Executive,* S. R. Hill, OBE
DEFENCE BILLS AGENCY, Room 410, Mersey House,
Drury Lane, Liverpool L2 7PX. Tel: 0151-242 2234.
Chief Executive, I. S. Elrick
DEFENCE COMMUNICATION SERVICES AGENCY (DCSA),
Building 111 Basil Hill Site, Park Lane, Wilts SN13 9NR.
Tel: 01225-814785 *Chief Executive,* Maj.-Gen. A. J.
Raper, CBE
DEFENCE COMMUNICATION SERVICES AGENCY/
DIRECTORATE ENGINEERING AND INTEROPERABILITY
(DSCA/DEI), RAF Henlow, Beds, SG16 6DN.
Tel: 01462-8515 ext 7625/7250
Chief Executive, Brig. J. E.Thomas
DEFENCE DENTAL AGENCY, RAF Halton, Aylesbury,
Bucks HP22 5PG. Tel: 01296-623535, ext. 6851. *Chief
Executive,* Maj.-Gen. J. A. Gamon , QHDS
DEFENCE ESTATES, St George's House, Blakemore Drive,
Sutton Coldfield, W. Midlands B75 7RL. Tel: 0121-311
2140. *Chief Executive,* I. Andrews, CBE
DEFENCE GEOGRAPHIC AND IMAGERY INTELLIGENCE
AGENCY (DGIA), Watson Building, Elmwood Avenue,
Feltham, Middx TW13 7AH. Tel: 020-8818 2133; Fax:
020-8818 2426 *Chief Executive,* Brig. A. P. Walker, OBE
The former Military Survey and the Joint Air
Reconnaissance Intelligence Centre (JARIC)
converged in April 2000 to form one agency, the DGIA.
DEFENCE HOUSING EXECUTIVE, 8th Floor, St
Christopher House, Southwark Street, London SE1
0TD. Tel: 020-7305-2035 *Chief Executive,* J. Wilson
DEFENCE INTELLIGENCE AND SECURITY CENTRE,
Chicksands, Shefford, Beds SG17 5PR. Tel: 01462-
752125. *Chief Executive,* Brig. C. G. Holtom
DEFENCE MEDICAL TRAINING ORGANISATION, Building
87, Fort Blockhouse, Gosport, Hants PO12 2AB.
Tel: 023-9276 5284/5438
Chief Executive, Brig. J. R. Brown
DEFENCE SECONDARY CARE AGENCY, Room 4/168, St
Christopher House, Southwark Street, London, SE1
0TD. Tel: 020-7305 6190 . *Chief Executive,* Mr J.
Tuckett
DEFENCE STORAGE AND DISTRIBUTION AGENCY,
Ploughley Road, Lower Arncott, Bicester, Oxon OX25
2LD. Tel: 01869-256840. *Chief Executive,* Brig. P. D.
Foxton, CBE,
DEFENCE TRANSPORT AND MOVEMENTS AGENCY,
Monxton Road, Andover, Hants SP11 8HT. Tel: 01264-
382537. *Chief Executive,* Air Cdre Whalley

DEFENCE VETTING AGENCY, Room Building 107 , Imphal Barracks, Fulford Road, York YO10 4AS . Tel: 01904 662444 . *Chief Executive*, M. P. B. G. Wilson

DISPOSAL SERVICES AGENCY, 7th Floor, 6 Hercules Road, London SE1 7DJ. Tel: 020-7261 8879; Fax: 020-7261 8696; Email: disposalservices.agency.mod.uk *Chief Executive*, S. Taylor, CBE

LOGISTIC APPLICATIONS IPT, Monxton Road, Andover, Hants SP11 8HT. Tel: 01264-382025; Email: hq.laipt@gtnet.gov.uk *Team Leader*, Brig. P. A. Flenagan

MEDICAL SUPPLIES AGENCY, Drummond Barracks, Ludgershall, Andover, Hants SP11 9RU. Tel: 01264-798622. *Acting Chief Executive*, J. Baines

MET OFFICE, London Road, Bracknell, Berks RG12 2SZ. Tel: 01344-420242; Email:enquiries@metoffice.com; Web:www.metoffice.com *Chief Executive*, P. D. Ewins

MINISTRY OF DEFENCE POLICE, Wethersfield, Braintree, Essex CM7 4AZ. Tel: 01371-854000. *Chief Executive*, Chief Constable D. L. Clarke

NAVAL MANNING AGENCY, Victory Building, HM Naval Base, Portsmouth PO1 3LS. Tel: 023-9272 7408. *Chief Executive*, Rear-Adm. J. M. de Halpert

NAVAL RECRUITING AND TRAINING AGENCY, Victory Building, HM Naval Base, Portsmouth PO1 3LS. Tel: 023-9272 7600; Fax: 023-9272 7613 *Chief Executive*, Rear-Adm. P.R. Davies, CBE

PAY AND PERSONNEL AGENCY, Warminster Road, Bath BA1 5AA. Tel: 01225-828533. *Chief Executive*, D.C.J. Ball

QINETIQ PLC, Ively Road, Farnborough, Hants GU14 0LX. Tel: 01252-394500; Web: www.qiuetiq.com. *Chief Executive*, Sir John Chisholm

RAF PERSONNEL MANAGEMENT AGENCY, RAF Innsworth, Gloucester GL3 1EZ. Tel: 01452-712612, ext. 7849. *Chief Executive*, Air Vice-Marshal I. M. Stewart, AFC

RAF SIGNALS ENGINEERING ESTABLISHMENT RAF Henlow, Beds SG16 6DN. Tel: 01452-712612 ext. 7849. *Chief Executive*, Air Vice-Marshal I. M. Stewart, AFC

WARSHIP SUPPORT AGENCY, B Block, Management Suite, Foxhill, Bath BA1 5AB. Tel: 01225-882348; Fax: 01225-884313; Email: cessa@navynet.gtnet.gov.uk *Chief Executive*, J. D. Coles

TRAINING GROUP DEFENCE AGENCY, RAF Innsworth, Gloucester GL3 1EZ. Tel: 01452-712612, ext. 5344. *Chief Executive*, Air Vice-Marshal I. S. Corbitt

UNITED KINGDOM HYDROGRAPHIC OFFICE, Admiralty Way, Taunton, Somerset TA1 2DN. Tel: 01823-337900. E-mail: name.surname@ukho.gov.uk Web: www.ukho.gov.uk *Chief Executive, and National Hydrographer*, Dr David Winford Williams

The Royal Navy

LORD HIGH ADMIRAL OF THE UNITED KINGDOM
HM The Queen

ADMIRALS OF THE FLEET
HRH The Prince Philip, Duke of Edinburgh, KG, KT, OM, GBE, AC, QSO, PC, *apptd* 1953
The Lord Hill-Norton, GCB, *apptd* 1971
Sir Michael Pollock, GCB, LVO, DSC, *apptd* 1974
Sir Edward Ashmore, GCB, DSC, *apptd* 1977
Sir Henry Leach, GCB, *apptd* 1982

Sir Julian Oswald, GCB, *apptd* 1993
Sir Benjamin Bathurst, GCB, *apptd* 1995

ADMIRALS
Boyce, Sir Michael, GCB, OBE, ADC (*Chief of Defence Staff and Aide-de-Camp to Her Majesty The Queen*)
Abbott, Sir Peter, GBE, KCB (*Vice Chief of the Defence Staff*)
Essenhigh, Sir Nigel, KCB (*Chief of Naval Staff and First Sea Lord*)
Perowne, Sir James, KBE (*Deputy Saclant*)
West, Sir Alan, KCB (*Commander-in-Chief Fleet, Cinceastlant and Commander Allied Naval Forces North Europe*)
Forbes, I. A., CBE (*Deputy Supreme Allied Commander Atlantic*)
Garnett, Sir Ian, KCB (*Chief of Joint Operations Chief of Staff Supreme Headquarters Allied Powers Europe*)

VICE-ADMIRALS
Haddacks, Sir Paul, KCB (*Director of International Military Staff*)
Blackham, Sir Jeremy, KCB (*Deputy CDS (Equipment Capability)*)
Malbon, F. M. (*Director TOPMAST*)
Band, J. (*Deputy Commander-in-Chief Fleet*)
Spencer, Sir P., KCB, ADC (*C.-in-C. Naval Home Command and Second Sea Lord*)

REAR-ADMIRALS
Lippiett, R. J., MBE (*Chief of Staff to Commander, Allied Naval Forces Southern Europe*)
Dunt, P. A. (*Senior Directing Staff (Navy)*)
Stevens, R. P., OBE (*Chief of Staff (Operations), Flag Officer Submarines, COMSUBEASTLANT and COMSUBNORTHWEST*)
Chadwick, J. (*Flag Officer Training and Recruiting and Chief Executive, Naval Recruiting and Training Agency*)
de Halpert, J. M. (*Naval Secretary/Chief Executive, Naval Manning Agency*)
Wood, M. G., CBE (*Director General Defence Logistics (Operations and Business Development)*)
Stanford, C. D. (*Chief of Staff to the Surgeon-General*)
Burnell-Nugent, J. M., CBE (*Commander UK Maritime Forces and Commander Anti Submarine Warfare Striking Force*)
Meyer, S. R. (*Chief of Staff, Permanent Joint Headquarters*)
Backus, A. K., OBE (*Flag officer Sea Training and Flag Officer Surface Flotilla*)
Guild, N. C. F. (*Executive Director 4, Defence Procurement Agency, Controller of the Navy*)
Ward, R. J. G. (*Capability Manager (Strategic Deployment)*)
Dymock, A. K. (*Deputy COMSTRIKFORTHS*)
Anthony, D. J., MBE (*Flag Officer Scotland, N. England and N. Ireland, and Naval Base Commander Clyde*)
Reeve, J. (*Deputy Chief Executive of the Warship Support Agency*)
Lockwood, R. G. (*Director-General, Naval Personnel (Strategy and Plans) and Chief of Staff to Second Sea Lord and C.-in-C. Naval Home Command*)
Greenish, P. D. (*Chief of Staff (Corporate Development)*)
Stanhope, M., OBE (*Director of Operational Management, NATO Regional Command North*)
McLean, R. A. I., OBE (*Asst Chief of Defence Staff (Resource and Planning)*)
McClement, T. P., OBE (*Asst Chief of Naval Staff*)
S. Lidbetter (*Air Officer Commanding 3 Group/Flag Officer Maritime Aviation, Commander Air East Atlantic and Commander Maritime Air North*)

HM FLEET *as at autumn 2001*

SUBMARINES

Trident	Vanguard, Vengeance, Victorious, Vigilant
Fleet	Sceptre, Sovereign, Spartan, Splendid, Superb, Talent, Tireless, Torbay, Trafalgar, Trenchant, Triumph, Turbulent
ANTI-SUBMARINE WARFARE CARRIERS	Ark Royal, Illustrious, Invincible
ASSAULT SHIPS	Fearless, Intrepid
LANDING PLATFORM HELICOPTER	Ocean
DESTROYERS	
Type 42	Cardiff, Edinburgh, Exeter, Glasgow, Gloucester, Liverpool, Manchester, Newcastle, Nottingham, Southampton, York
FRIGATES	
Type 23	Argyll, Grafton, Iron Duke, Kent, Lancaster, Marlborough, Monmouth, Montrose, Norfolk, Northumberland, Portland, Richmond, Somerset, St Albans, Sutherland, Westminster
Type 22	Campbeltown, Chatham, Cornwall, Coventry, Cumberland, Sheffield
OFFSHORE PATROL	
Castle Class	Dumbarton Castle, Leeds Castle
Island Class	Alderney, Anglesey, Guernsey, Lindisfarne, Shetland
MINEHUNTERS	
Hunt Class	Atherstone, Brecon, Brocklesby, Cattistock, Chiddingfold, Cottesmore, Dulverton, Hurworth, Ledbury, Middleton, Quorn
Sandown Class	Bangor, Blyth, Bridport, Cromer, Grimsby, Inverness, Pembroke, Penzance, Ramsay, Sandown, Shoreham, Walney
PATROL CRAFT	
River Class	Orwell
Coastal Training Craft	Archer, Biter, Blazer, Charger, Dasher, Example, Exploit, Explorer, Express, Puncher, Pursuer, Raider, Smiter, Tracker
Gibraltar Search and Rescue Craft	Ranger, Trumpeter
ICE PATROL SHIP	Endurance
SURVEY SHIPS	Beagle, Gleaner, Roebuck, Scott

OTHER PARTS OF THE NAVAL SERVICE

ROYAL MARINES

The Royal Marines were formed in 1664 and are part of the Naval Service. Their primary purpose is to conduct amphibious and land warfare. The principal operational units are 3 Commando Brigade Royal Marines, an amphibious all-arms brigade trained to operate in arduous environments, which is a core element of the UK's Joint Rapid Reaction Force; Comacchio Group Royal Marines, which is responsible for the security of nuclear weapon facilities; and Special Boat Service Royal Marines, the maritime special forces. The Royal Marines also provide detachments for warships and land-based naval parties as required. The Royal Marines Band Service provides military musical support for the Naval Service. The headquarters of the Royal Marines is at Portsmouth, along with the Royal Marines School of Music, and principal bases are at Plymouth, Arbroath, Poole, Taunton and Chivenor. The Corps of Royal Marines is about 6,500 strong.

Capability Manager (Information Superiority), Maj.-Gen. R. H. G. Fulton
Chief of Staff, NATO Joint Headquarters North, Maj.-Gen. D. Wilson, OBE
Director-General, Joint Doctrine and Concepts Centre, Maj.-Gen. A. A. Milton, OBE, ADC

ROYAL MARINES RESERVE (RMR)

The Royal Marines Reserve is a commando-trained volunteer force with the principal role, when mobilised, of supporting the Royal Marines. There are RMR centres in London, Glasgow, Bristol, Liverpool and Newcastle. The current strength of the RMR is about 1,000.
Director, RMR, Col. A. W. MacCormick

ROYAL FLEET AUXILIARY service (RFA)

The Royal Fleet Auxiliary Service is a civilian-manned flotilla of 22 ships. Its primary role is to supply the Royal Navy at sea with food, fuel, ammunition and spares, enabling it to maintain operations away from its home ports. In addition the RFA provides the Royal Navy with sea-borne aviation training facilities as well as secure logistic support and amphibious operations capability for the Army and Royal Marines.

FLEET AIR ARM

The Fleet Air Arm was founded in 1914 as the Royal Naval Air Service and operates some 240 fixed wing aircraft and helicopters for the Royal Navy. Sea Harrier fighters provide air defence/strike capability for the fleet, and Sea King, Merlin and Lynx helicopters provide commando support, anti-submarine, anti-surface, airborne early warning and search and rescue capability. In 2001 the strength of the FAA was 5,500.

ROYAL NAVAL RESERVE (RNR)

The Royal Naval Reserve is an integral part of the Naval Service. It comprises up to 3,850 men and women nationwide who volunteer to train in their spare time to enable the Royal Navy to meet its operational commitments, at sea and ashore, in crisis or war.

The standard annual training commitment is 24 days, including 12 days' continuous training. Daily pay scales range from £47 to £154 for officers and from £27 to £67 for ratings. A tax-free bounty is also payable, the amount depending on the length of service.
Director, Naval Reserves, Capt C. G. Massie-Taylor, OBE, RN

QUEEN ALEXANDRA'S ROYAL NAVAL NURSING SERVICE

The first nursing sisters were appointed to naval hospitals in 1884 and the Queen Alexandra's Royal Naval Nursing Service (QARNNS) gained its current title in 1902.

Nursing ratings were introduced in 1960 and men were integrated into the Service in 1982; QARNNS recruits qualified nurses as both officers and ratings and student nurse training can be undertaken in the Service. Female medical assistants were introduced between 1987-1998, although no longer recruited some continue to serve in QARNNS.

Patron, HRH Princess Alexandra, the Hon. Lady Ogilvy, GCVO

Matron-in-Chief and Director of Naval Nursing Services, Capt. M. Bowen

The Army

THE QUEEN

FIELD MARSHALS

HRH The Prince Philip, Duke of Edinburgh, KG, KT, OM, GBE, AC, QSO, PC, *apptd* 1953

The Lord Carver, GCB, CBE, DSO, MC, *apptd* 1973

Sir Roland Gibbs, GCB, CBE, DSO, MC, *apptd* 1979

The Lord Bramall, KG, GCB, OBE, MC, *apptd* 1982

The Lord Vincent GBE, KCB, DSO

Sir John Stanier, GCB, MBE, *apptd* 1985

Sir Nigel Bagnall, GCB, CVO, MC, *apptd* 1988

Sir John Chapple, GCB, CBE, *apptd* 1992

HRH The Duke of Kent, KG, GCMG, GCVO, ADC, *apptd* 1993

The Lord Inge, GCB (Col. Green Howards, Col. Cmdt. APTC), *apptd* 1994

GENERALS

Sir Michael Boyce, GCB, OBE, ADC (*Chief of the Defence Staff*)

Walker, Sir Michael, GCB, CMG, CBE, ADC (*Chief of the General Staff*)

Harley, Sir Alexander, KBE, CB, ADC (*Gen.*), Col. Cmdt. RHA

Cowan, Sir Samuel, KCB, CBE, Col. Cmdt. Bde of Gurkhas (*Chief of Defence Logistics*)

Smith, Sir Rupert, KCB, DSO, OBE, QGM, Col. Cmdt. REME (*D.SACEUR*)

Jackson, Sir Michael, KCB, CBE, DSO, Col. Cmdt. Parachute Regiment, Col. Cmdt. AG Corps, Hon. Col. The Rifle Volunteers (*C.-in-C., Land*)

Deverell, Sir John, KCB, OBE, Col. Cmdt. LI, Col. Cmdt. SASC (*Deputy C.-in-C., Land Command, and Inspector-General, Territorial Army and C-in-C Allied Forces Northern Europe*)

LIEUTENANT-GENERALS

Willcocks, Sir Michael, KCB, Col. Cmdt. RA (*UK Military Rep. at NATO HQ*)

Drewry, C. F., CBE (*Commander, ACE Rapid Reaction Corps*)

Pigott, A. D., CBE, Col. The Queen's Gurkha Engineers, Col. Cmdt. RE (*Deputy CDS (Commitments)*)

Menzies, R. C., OBE, QHS (*Surgeon-General*)

Irwin, A. S. H., CBE, General Officer Commanding Northern Ireland; Col. Cmdt. The Scottish Division (*Military Secretary and Chief Executive, Army Personnel Centre*)

Delves, C. N. G. (*Chief of Joint Forces Operational Readiness and Training*)

O'Donoghue, K., CBE (*Asst Chief of the General Staff*)

Reith, J. G., CB, CBE (*Asst CDS (Policy)*)

MAJOR-GENERALS

Sullivan, T. J. CBE (*GOC HQ 4 Div*)

Elliott, C. L., CB, MBE (*Director-General, Development and Doctrine*)

Kiszely, J. P., MC (*Asst CDS (Programmes)*)

Moore-Bick, J. D., CBE, (*Military Assistant to the High Representative in Bosnia-Hercegovina*)

Trousdell, P. C. C., Col. The Queen's Own Gurkha Transport Regiment (*Deputy Commander (Operations) Stabilisation Force Bosnia Hercegovina*)

Chambers, P. A., MBE (*Deputy Chief of Staff, HQ Land Command*)

Besgrove, P. V. R., CBE, Col. Cmdt. REME (*Asst. Chief of Staff (Resources) HQ Allied Forces Southern Europe*)

Searby, R. V. (*Senior British Loan Service Officer, Oman*)

Risius, G. (*Director, Army Legal Services*)

Ramsay, A. I., CBE, DSO, Col. Cmdt. (*Commander British Forces Cyprus*)

Elliott, C. H., CBE (*Defence Services Secretary*)

Pringle, A. R. D., CB, CBE, Col. Cmdt. RGJ (*Chief of Staff to Chief of Joint Operations*)

Raper, A. J., CBE (*Chief Executive, Defence Communications Services Agency*)

Ridgway, A. P., CBE (*Chief of Staff HQ ACE Rapid Reaction Corps*)

Currie, A. P. N. (*Chief of Staff to Adjutant-General*)

Watt, C. R., CBE, (*GOG 1 (UK) Armed Division*)

HRH The Prince of Wales, KG, KT, GCB and Great Master of the Order of the Bath, AK, QSO, PC, ADC(P)

Dannatt, F. R., CBE, MC (*GOC 3 (UK) Divn, Asst Chief of the General Staff*)

Grant Peterkin, A. P., OBE (*General Officer, Commanding 5th Division*)

Palmer, A. M. D., CBE (*Director-General, Army Training and Recruiting and Chief Executive, Army Training and Recruiting Agency*)

Sutherell, J. C. B., CBE, Col. Cmdt. The Queens Division (*Commandant, RMCS*)

Viggers, F. R., MBE (*Chief of Staff, HQ Land Command*)

Gordon, R. D. S., CBE (*GOC HQ 2 Divn*)

Plummer, B. P.

Judd, D. L. (*Quartermaster General*)

Brims, R. V., CBE (*Commander Multinational Divn. (South West) Bosnia Hercegovina*)

Gilchrist, P. (*Master General of the Ordnance, Col. Cmdt. RAC Executive Director 2, Defence Procurement Agency*)

Jolliffe, D. S., QHP (*Director-General, Army Medical Services*)

Cross, T. CBE

Messervy-Whiting, G. G. (*Head Interim Military Staff EU Brussels*)

Figgures, A. C., CBE (*Asst CDS, Operational Requirements (Land Systems)*)

Laurie, M. I., CBE,

McColl, J. C., CBE (*Director-General Intelligence and Geographic Resources*)

Charlton-Weedy, M. A. CBE,

Gamon, J. A. (*Chief Executive of the Defence Dental Agency*)

Holmes, J. T., OBE,

Denaro, A. G. (*Commandant of Sandurst and Middle Eastern Adviser to the Secretary of State for Defence, General Officer Commanding 5th Division*)

CONSTITUTION OF THE ARMY

The regular forces include the following arms, branches and corps. They are listed in accordance with the order of precedence within the British Army. All enquiries with regard to records of serving personnel (Regular and Territorial Army) should be directed to Relations with the Public, Army Personnel Office, Kentigern House, 65 Brown Street, Glasgow G2 8EX. Tel: 0141-224 2023/3303. DASD, Rm 643, Metroploe Building, Northumberland Avenue, London WC2N 5BP. Contact , RO2 Pubs IM, Tel: 020-7218 2922 or Chief Clerk, Tel: 020-7218 2619

THE ARMS

HOUSEHOLD CAVALRY – The Household Cavalry Regiment (The Life Guards and The Blues and Royals)
ROYAL ARMOURED CORPS – Cavalry Regiments: 1st The Queen's Dragoon Guards; The Royal Scots Dragoon Guards (Carabiniers and Greys); The Royal Dragoon Guards; The Queen's Royal Hussars (The Queen's Own and Royal Irish); 9th/12th Royal Lancers (Prince of Wales's); The King's Royal Hussars; The Light Dragoons; The Queen's Royal Lancers; Royal Tank Regiment, comprising two regular regiments
ARTILLERY – Royal Regiment of Artillery
ENGINEERS – Corps of Royal Engineers
SIGNALS – Royal Corps of Signals

THE INFANTRY

The Foot Guards and regiments of Infantry of the Line are grouped in divisions as follows:
GUARDS DIVISION – Grenadier, Coldstream, Scots, Irish and Welsh Guards. *Divisional Office*, HQ Infantry, Warminster Training Centre, Warminster, Wilts. *Training Centre*, Infantry Training Centre, Vimy Barracks, Catterick, N. Yorks
SCOTTISH DIVISION – The Royal Scots (The Royal Regiment); The Royal Highland Fusiliers (Princess Margaret's Own Glasgow and Ayrshire Regiment); The King's Own Scottish Borderers; The Black Watch (Royal Highland Regiment); The Highlanders (Seaforth, Gordons and Camerons); The Argyll and Sutherland Highlanders (Princess Louise's). *Divisional Office*, HQ Infantry, Warminster Training Centre, Warminster, Wilts. *Training Centre*, Infantry Training Centre, Vimy Barracks, Catterick, N. Yorks
QUEEN'S DIVISION – The Princess of Wales's Royal Regiment (Queen's and Royal Hampshire's); The Royal Regiment of Fusiliers; The Royal Anglian Regiment. *Divisional Office*, HQ Infantry, Warminster Training Centre, Warminster, Wilts. *Training Centre*, Infantry Training Centre, Vimy Barracks, Catterick, N. Yorks
KING'S DIVISION – The King's Own Royal Border Regiment; The King's Regiment; The Prince of Wales's Own Regiment of Yorkshire; The Green Howards (Alexandra, Princess of Wales's Own Yorkshire Regiment); The Queen's Lancashire Regiment; The Duke of Wellington's Regiment (West Riding). *Divisional Office*, HQ Infantry, Warminster Training Centre, Warminster, Wilts. *Training Centre*, Infantry Training Centre, Vimy Barracks, Catterick, N. Yorks
PRINCE OF WALES'S DIVISION – The Devonshire and Dorset Regiment; The Cheshire Regiment; The Royal Welch Fusiliers; The Royal Regiment of Wales (24th/41st Foot); The Royal Gloucestershire, Berkshire and Wiltshire Regiment; The Worcestershire and Sherwood Foresters Regiment (29th/45th Foot); The Staffordshire Regiment (The Prince of Wales's). *Divisional Office*, HQ Infantry, Warminster Training Centre, Warminster, Wilts. *Training Centre*, Infantry Training Centre, Vimy Barracks, Catterick, N. Yorks
LIGHT DIVISION – The Light Infantry; The Royal Green Jackets. *Divisional Office*, HQ Infantry, Warminster

Training Centre, Warminster, Wilts. *Training Centre*, Infantry Training Centre, Vimy Barracks, Catterick, N. Yorks
THE ROYAL IRISH REGIMENT (one general service and six home service battalions) – 27th (Inniskilling), 83rd, 87th and the Ulster Defence Regiment. *Regimental HQ* and *Training Centre*, St Patrick's Barracks, BFPO 808
BRIGADE OF GURKHAS – The Royal Gurkha Rifles; The Queen's Gurkha Engineers; Queen's Gurkha Signals; The Queen's Own Gurkha Transport Regiment. *Regimental HQ*, Airfield Camp, Netheravon, Wilts. *Gurkha Company*, Infantry Training Centre, Vimy Barracks, Catterick, N. Yorks
THE PARACHUTE REGIMENT (three regular battalions) – *Regimental HQ*, Browning Barracks, Aldershot, Hants. *Training Centre*, Infantry Training Centre, Vimy Barracks, Catterick, N. Yorks
SPECIAL AIR SERVICE REGIMENT – *Regimental HQ* and *Training Centre*, Stirling Lines, Hereford
ARMY AIR CORPS – *Regimental HQ* and *Training Centre*, Middle Wallop, Stockbridge, Hants

SERVICES/ARMS*

Royal Army Chaplains' Department – *Regimental HQ*, HQ AG, Upavon, Pewsey, Wilts. *Training Centre*, Armed Forces Chaplaincy Centre, Amport House, Amport, Andover, Hants
The Royal Logistic Corps – *Regimental HQ*, Blackdown Barracks, Deepcut, Camberley, Surrey. *Training Centre*, Princess Royal Barracks, Deepcut, Camberley, Surrey
Royal Army Medical Corps – *Regimental HQ, Training Centre*, Defence Medical Services Training Centre, former Army Staff Collge, Slim Road, Cambereley, Surrey.
Corps of Royal Electrical and Mechanical Engineers – *Regimental HQ* and *Training Centre*, Hazebrouck Barracks, Isaac Newton Road, Arborfield, Reading, Berks
Adjutant-General's Corps – *Directorate HQ* and *Training Centre*, Worthy Down, Winchester, Hants
Royal Army Veterinary Corps – *Regimental HQ*, Small Arms School Corps - *Regimental HQ*, Warminster Training Centre, Warminster, Wilts
Royal Army Dental Corps – *Regimental HQ*, Keogh Barracks, Ash Vale, Aldershot, Hants. *Training Centre*, Defence Dental Agency Trainingformer Army Staff Collge, Slim Road, Cambereley, Surrey *Intelligence Corps – *Directorate HQ* and *Training Centre*, Chicksands, Shefford, Beds
Army Physical Training Corps – *Regimental HQ*, Army School of Physical Training, Fox Lines, Queen's Avenue, Aldershot, Hants General Service Corps
Queen Alexandra's Royal Army Nursing Corps – *Regimental HQ*, Former Army Staff Collge, Slim Road, Cambereley, Surrey Corps of Army Music - *Directorate HQ* and *Training Centre*, Army School of Music, Kneller Hall, Kneller Road, Twickenham, Middx

ARMY EQUIPMENT HOLDINGS *as at August 2000*

Tanks	373
Armoured combat vehicles	2,920
Artillery pieces	406
Large landing craft	2
Helicopters	232

THE TERRITORIAL ARMY (TA)

The Territorial Army provides formed units and individuals as an essential part of the Army's order of battle for operations across all military tasks in order to ensure that the Army is capable of mounting and sustaining operations at nominated states of readiness. It also provides a basis for regeneration, while at the same time maintaining links with the local community and society at large. From 1 July 1999 its established strength is 41,204.

Members of the TA receive pay at the rate appropriate to their rank. From 1 April 2000, the minimum daily pay for an officer is £47.85 and for a soldier is £27.29. Pay rises with rank and length of service. Members who complete their annual training requirements (27 and 19 days respectively for members of the Independent and Specialist TA) and are certified as efficient receive a single bounty ranging from £110 to £1,290.

Inspector-General, Lt.-Gen. C.N.G. Delves, CBE, DSO

QUEEN ALEXANDRA'S ROYAL ARMY NURSING CORPS

The Queen Alexandra's Royal Army Nursing Corps (QARANC) was founded in 1902 as Queen Alexandra's Imperial Military Nursing Service (QAIMNS) and gained its present title in 1949. The QARANC has trained nurses for the register since 1950 and also trains and employs Health Care Assistants to Level 3 NVQ. The Corps also recruits qualified nurses as Officers and other ranks and in 1992 male nurses already serving in the Army were transferred to the QARANC. QARANC personnel serve in all four corners of the world in both peacetime and operational environments.

Colonel-in-Chief, HRH The Princess Margaret, Countess of Snowdon, CI, GCVO

Director of Army Nursing Services (DANS) and Matron in Chief Army, Col. B. C. McEvilly

---

The Royal Air Force

THE QUEEN

MARSHALS OF THE ROYAL AIR FORCE

HRH The Prince Philip, Duke of Edinburgh, KG, KT, OM, GBE, AC, QSO, PC, *apptd* 1953
Sir John Grandy, GCB, GCVO, KBE, DSO, *apptd* 1971
Sir Denis Spotswood, GCB, CBE, DSO, DFC, *apptd* 1974
Sir Michael Beetham, GCB, CBE, DFC, AFC, *apptd* 1982
Sir Keith Williamson, GCB, AFC, *apptd* 1985
The Lord Craig of Radley, GCB, OBE, *apptd* 1988

AIR CHIEF MARSHALS

Johns, Sir Richard, GCB, CBE, LVO, ADC (*Chief of the Air Staff*)
Cheshire, Sir John, KBE, CB Squire, Sir Peter, KCB, DFC, AFC, ADC, GCB (*Chief of the Air Staff*) *Air Officer Commanding-in-Chief, HQ Strike Command, and Commander Allied Air Forces NW Europe*)
Bagnall, Sir Anthony, KCB, OBE (*Vice Chief of Defence Staff and Commander-in-Chief Strike Command*)
Day, Sir John, KCB, OBE (*Air Member for Personnel/C-in-C Personnel and Training Command and Commander-in-Chief Strike Command*)

AIR MARSHALS

Coville, Sir Christopher, KCB (*Deputy C.-in-C. Allied Forces Central Europe*)
Jenner, T. I., CB (*Chief of Staff*)

Norriss, Sir Peter, KBE, CB, AFC (*Deputy Chief of Defence Procurement (Operations) and Controller of the Navy*)
Pledger, M. D., KCB, OBE, AFC (*Deputy CDS (Personnel*))
Goodall, R. H., CB, CBE, AFC (*Chief of Staff, Component Command Air North*)
Spink, C. R., CBE (*Director General, Saudi Arabia Armed Forces Project*)

AIR VICE-MARSHALS

French, J. C., CBE (*Director-General, Intelligence and Geographic Resources*)
Thompson, J. H., CB (*Defence Attaché and Head of British Defence Staff Washington*)
Stewart, I. M., AFC (*Air Secretary and Chief Executive, RAF Personnel Management Agency*)
Weeden, J. (*Director, Legal Services (RAF)*)
Wright, R. A., AFC (*Chief of Staff, HQ Personnel and Training Command and Asst Chief of Staff Policy and Requirements SHAPE*)
McIntyre, I. G., QHDS (*Chief Executive, Defence Dental Agency*)
Sharples, C. J., QHP (*Director-General, Medical Services (RAF)*)
Burridge, B. K., CBE (*Commandant, Joint Services Command and Staff College*)
Filbey, K. D., CBE (*AOC No. 38 Group*)
Sturley, P. O., CB, MBE (*Asst. Chief of the Air Staff)*)
Henderson, P. W., CB, MBE (*Director-General, Support Management, HQ Logistics Command*)
Day, N. J., CBE (*Capability Manager (Strike) (Air Systems*))
Niven, D. M., CBE (*Commander, Joint Helicopter Command*)
Scott, P. J. (*Air Officer Logistics and Communications Information Systems, HQ Strike Command*)
Burton, A. J., OBE (*Air Officer Administration, HQ Strike Command*)
Rimmer, T. W., OBE (*Commander British Forces Cyprus and Administrator of the Sovereign Base Areas of Akrotiri and Dhekelia*)
Nicholson, A. A., CBE, LVO (*Integration and Aerospace Adviser, Defence Procurement Agency*)
HRH The Prince of Wales, KG, KT, GCB and Great Master of the Order of the Bath, AK, QSO, PC, ADC(P)
Gardiner, M. J., OBE (*Deputy Commander, Interim Combined Air Operations Centre No. 4 and Military Assistant to the High Representative Sarajevo*)
Couzens, D. C. (*Asst CDS (Logistics*))
Liddell, P. (*Air Officer Communications Information Systems and Support Services*)
Arscott, J. R. D. (*Director, Airspace Policy*)
Skinner, G., CBE (*Air Officer C.-in-C., HQ Logistics Command*)
Corbitt, I. S. (*Air Officer Training and Chief Executive, Training Group Defence Agency*)
Roser, P. W., MBE (*Senior Directing Staff (Air), Royal College of Defence Studies*)
Davison, C., MBE (*Air Officer Administration and Air Officer Commanding Directly Administered Units, HQ Personnel and Training Command*)
Sudborough, N.J, OBE (*Deputy Chief of Staff Operations Strike Command*)
Torpy, G. L., CBE, DSO (*Asst CDS (Operations) and Air Officer Commanding No 1 Group*)
Mackay, H. G, OBE, AFC (*Commandant, RAF College, Cranwell*)
Davidson, C. M. (*Air Officer Administration and Air Officer Commanding Directly Administered Units Headquarters Personnel and Training Command*)
Stirrup, G. E., CB (*Deputy C-in-C*)
Walker P. B. (*Asst Chief of Defence Staff (Operations*))
Hobart D. A. (*Asst Chief of Defence Staff (Policy and Nuclear*))

CONSTITUTION OF THE ROYAL AIR FORCE

The RAF consists of three commands: Strike Command, Personnel and Training Command and Logistics Command. Strike Command is responsible for all the RAF's front-line forces. The restructured Strike Command, implemented on 1 April 2000, was split into three organisational groups, each responsible for specific operational duties. No 1 Group now contains the tactical fast jet forces, with No 2 Group providing the overarching enabling forces - Air Transport, Air Refuelling and Strategic Reconnaissance. No 3 Group is comprised of the Nimrod MPA force, Search and Rescue helicopters and the newly created Joint Force 2000 - a combination of the RAF Harrier GR7 and RN Harrier FA2 squadrons. Personnel and Training Command is responsible for personnel administration and training in the RAF. Logistics Command is responsible for all logistics, engineering and material support.

Enquiries regarding records of serving officers should be directed to the RAF Personnel Management Agency (*see* Defence Agencies, above).

PRINCESS MARY'S ROYAL AIR FORCE NURSING SERVICE

The Princess Mary's Royal Air Force Nursing Service (PMRAFNS) was formed on 1 June 1918 as the Royal Air Force Nursing Service. In June 1923, His Majesty King George V gave his Royal Assent for the Royal Air Force Nursing Service to be known as the Princess Mary's Royal Air Force Nursing Service. Men were integrated into the PMRAFNS in 1980 and now serve as officers and other ranks. Student nurse training is undertaken and qualified RN's, RM's and RMN's are recruited to the commissioned branches of the PMRAFNS.

Patron and Air Chief Commandant, HRH Princess Alexandra, the Hon. Lady Ogilvy, GCVO
Matron-in-Chief and Director RAF Nursing Service, Air Cdre R. H. Williams

RAF EQUIPMENT *as at 1 July 2001*

AIRCRAFT
Tornado	195
Harrier	48
Jaguar	43
Canberra	4
Nimrod	24
VC10	10
Tristar	8
Hercules	50
BAe 125	5
BAe 146	2
Sentry	6
Hawk	98
Domenie	8
Islander	1
Jetstream	10
Tucano	74

HELICOPTERS
Chinook	31
Puma	28
Sea King	19
Wessex	11
Gazelle	1

ROYAL AUXILIARY AIR FORCE (RAUXAF)

Formed in 1924, the Auxiliary Air Force received the prefix 'Royal' in 1947 in recognition of its war record. The RAuxAF amalgamated with the Royal Air Force Volunteer Reserve in 1997. The RAuxAF supports the RAF in many roles, including maritime air operations, air and ground defence of airfields, air movements, aero-medical evacuation, intelligence and public relations.   The minimum annual commitment for reservists is 27 days, including 15 days' continuous training. Pay scales are equivalent to regular rates less a percentage, made on a pro-rata daily basis. An annual bounty is also payable, the amount depending on the length of service.
Air Commodore-in-Chief, HM The Queen
Inspector Royal Auxiliary Air Force, Gp. Capt. R. G. Kemp

SERVICE SALARIES

The following rates of pay apply from 1 April 2001. Annual salaries are derived from daily rates in whole pence and rounded to the nearest £.

The pay rates shown are for Army personnel. The rates apply also to personnel of equivalent rank and pay band in the other services (*see* page 407 for table of relative ranks).

Rank	Daily	Annual
Second Lieutenant	£51.50	£18,797.50
Lieutenant		
On appointment	£61.91	£22,597.15
After 1 year in rank	£63.54	£23,192.10
After 2 years in rank	£65.17	£23,787.05
After 3 years in rank	£66.79	£24,378.35
After 4 years in rank	£68.42	£24,973.30
Captain		
On appointment	£78.94	£28,813.10
After 1 year in rank	£81.07	£29,590.55
After 2 years in rank	£83.21	£30,371.65
After 3 years in rank	£85.35	£31,152.75
After 4 years in rank	£87.48	£31,930.20
After 5 years in rank	£89.62	£32,711.30
After 6 years in rank	£91.75	£33,488.75
After 7 years in rank	£92.82	£33,879.30
After 8 years in rank	£93.89	£34,269.85
Major		
On appointment	£99.44	£36,295.60
After 1 year in rank	£101.90	£37,193.50
After 2 years in rank	£104.35	£38,087.75
After 3 years in rank	£106.81	£38,985.65
After 4 years in rank	£109.27	£39,883.55
After 5 years in rank	£111.73	£40,781.45
After 6 years in rank	£114.18	£41,675.70
After 7 years in rank	£116.64	£42,573.60
After 8 years in rank	£119.10	£43,471.50

Rank	Daily	Annual
Lieutenant Colonel		
On appointment	£140.25	£51,191.25
After 1 year in rank	£142.10	£51.866.50
After 2 years in rank	£143.95	£52.541.75
After 3 years in rank	£145.79	£53,213.35
After 4 years in rank	£147.64	£53,888.60
After 5 years in rank	£149.48	£54,560.20
After 6 years in rank	£151.33	£55,235.45
After 7 years in rank	£153.17	£55,907.05
After 8 years in rank	£155.03	£56,585.95
On appointment	£162.41	£59,279.65
After 1 year in the rank	£164.55	£60,060.75
After 2 years in the rank	£166.69	£60.841.85
After 3 years in the rank	£168.82	£61,619.30
After 4 years in the rank	£170.96	£62,400.40
After 5 years in the rank	£173.10	£63,181.50
After 6 years in the rank	£175.23	£63,958.95
After 7 years in the rank	£177.37	£64,740.05
After 8 years in the rank	£179.51	£65,521.15
Brigadier		
On appointment	£194.81	£71,107.65
After 1 year in the rank	£169.89	£71,864.85
After 2 years in the rank	£198.96	£72,620.40
After 3 years in the rank	£201.03	£73,375.95
After 4 years in the rank	£203.11	£74,135.15

Field Marshal – appointments to this rank will not usually be made in peacetime. The salary for existing holders of the rank is equivalent to the salary of a range 8 General

SALARIES OF OFFICERS COMMISSIONED FROM THE RANKS (LIEUTENANTS AND CAPTAINS ONLY)

YEARS OF COMMISSIONED SERVICE	YEARS OF NON-COMMISSIONED SERVICE FROM AGE 18					
	Less than 12 years		12 years but less than 15 years		15 years or more	
	Daily	Annual	Daily	Annual	Daily	Annual
On commissioning	£87.19	£31,824.35	£91.25	£33,306.25	£95.32	£34,791.80
After 1 year's service	£89.22	£32,565.30	£93.29	£34,050.85	£97.39	£35,547.80
After 2 years' service	£91.25	£33,306.25	£95.32	£34,791.80	£98.75	£36,043.75
After 3 years' service	£93.29	£34,050.85	£97.39	£35,547.35	£100.10	£36,536.50
After 4 years' service	£95.32	£34,791.80	£98.75	£36,043.75	£101.46	£37,032.90
After 5 years' service	£97.39	£35,547.35	£100.10	£36,536.50	£102.81	£37,525.65
After 6 years' service	£98.75	£36,043.75	£101.46	£37,032.90	£104.17	£38,022.05
After 8 years' service	£100.10	£36,536.50	£102.81	£37,525.65	£105.53	£38,518.45
After 10 years' service	£101.46	£37,032.90	£104.17	£38,022.05	£105.53	£38,518.45
After 12 years' service	£102.81	£37,525.65	£105.53	£38,518.45	£105.53	£38,518.45
After 14 years' service	£104.17	£38,022.05	£105.53	£38,518.45	£105.53	£38,518.45
After 16 years' service	£105.53	£38,518.45	£105.53	£38,518.45	£105.53	£38,518.45

SOLDIERS' SALARIES

The pay structure below officer level is divided into pay bands. Jobs at each rank are allocated to bands according to their score in the job evaluation system. Length of service is from age 18.

Scale A: committed to serve for less than 6 years, or those with less than 9 years' service who are serving on Open Engagement

Scale B: committed to serve for 6 years but less than 9 years

Scale C: committed to serve for 9 years or more, or those with more than 9 years' service who are serving on Open Engagement

Daily rates of pay effective from 1 April 2001 are:

SCALE A

RANK	Lower Band Daily	Annual	Higher Band Daily	Annual
Private				
Level 1	£33.07	£12,070.55	£33.07	£12,070.55
Level 2	£35.02	£12,782.30	£38.38	£14,008.70
Level 3	£36.96	£13.490.40	£42.36	£15,461.40
Level 4	£40.20	£14,673.00	£45.55	£16,625.75
Lance Corporal				
Level 5	£42.36	£15,461.40	£50.38	£18,388.70
Level 6	£44.13	£16,107.45	£52.83	£19,282.95
Level 7	£46.03	£16,800.95	£55.25	£20,166.25
Level 8	£48.13	£17,567.45	£57.75	£21,067.80
Level 9	£49.88	£18,206.20	£60.55	£22,100.75

SCALE B

	Lower Band Daily	Annual	Higher Band Daily	Annual
Corporal				
Level 1	£54.28	£19,812.20	£56.37	£20,575.05
Level 2	£56.81	£20,735.65	£59.95	£21,881.75
Level 3	£57.80	£21,097.00	£63.51	£23,181.15
Level 4	£59.56	£21,739.40	£64.99	£23,721.35
Level 5	£60.46	£22,067.90	£66.57	£24,298.05
Level 6	£61.19	£22,067.90	£67.95	£24,801.75
Level 7	£62.02	£22,637.30	£69.43	£25,341.95

SCALE C

	Lower Band Daily	Annual	Higher Band Daily	Annual
Sergeant				
Level 1	£62.81	£22,925.65	£68.54	£25,017.10
Level 2	£64.44	£23,520.60	£70.31	£25,663.15
Level 3	£66.06	£24,111.90	£72.09	£26,312.85
Level 4	£66.73	£24,356.45	£73.00	£26,645.00
Level 5	£67.93	£24,794.45	£74.42	£27,163.30
Level 6	£69.31	£25,298.15	£75.84	£27,681.60
Level 7	£70.93	£25,889.45	£77.26	£28,199.90

	Lower Band Daily	Annual	Higher Band Daily	Annual
Staff Sergeant				
Level 1	£69.31	£25,298.15	£77.31	£28,218.15
Level 2	£70.42	£25,703.15	£79.19	£28,904.35
Level 3	£72.71	£26,539.15	£81.07	£29,590.55
Level 4	£74.41	£27,159.65	£82.95	£30,276.75
Warrant Officer II				
Level 5	£75.43	£27,531.95	£84.84	£30,966.60
Level 6	£77.31	£28,218.15	£86.71	£31,649.15
Level 7	£79.19	£28,904.35	£87.97	£32,109.05
Level 8	£81.07	£29,590.55	£89.23	£32,568.95
Level 9	£82.91	£30,262.15	£90.49	£33,028.85

	Lower Band Daily	Annual	Higher Band Daily	Annual
Warrant Officer I				
Level 1	£79.95	£29,181.75	£87.69	£32,006.85
Level 2	£81.51	£29,751.15	£89.33	£32,605.45
Level 3	£83.07	£30,320.55	£90.78	£33,134.70
Level 4	£84.64	£30,893.60	£92.35	£33,707.75
Level 5	£86.20	£31,463.00	£93.91	£34,277.15
Level 6	£87.69	£32,006.85	£95.48	£34,850.20
Level 7	£89.33	£32,605.45	£97.04	£35,419.60

RELATIVE RANK – ARMED FORCES

	Royal Navy		*Army*		*Royal Air Force*
1	Admiral of the Fleet	1	Field Marshal	1	Marshal of the RAF
2	Admiral (Adm.)	2	General (Gen.)	2	Air Chief Marshal
3	Vice-Admiral (Vice-Adm.)	3	Lieutenant-General (Lt.-Gen.)	3	Air Marshal
4	Rear-Admiral (Rear-Adm.)	4	Major-General (Maj.-Gen.)	4	Air Vice-Marshal
5	Commodore (Cdre)	5	Brigadier (Brig.)	5	Air Commodore (Air Cdre)
6	Captain (Capt.)	6	Colonel (Col.)	6	Group Captain (Gp Capt.)
7	Commander (Cdr.)	7	Lieutenant-Colonel (Lt.-Col.)	7	Wing Commander (Wg Cdr.)
8	Lieutenant-Commander (Lt.-Cdr.)	8	Major (Maj.)	8	Squadron Leader (Sqn Ldr)
9	Lieutenant (Lt.)	9	Captain (Capt.)	9	Flight Lieutenant (Flt. Lt.)
10	Sub-Lieutenant (Sub-Lt.)	10	Lieutenant (Lt.)	10	Flying Officer (FO)
11	Acting Sub-Lieutenant (Acting Sub-Lt.)	11	Second Lieutenant (2nd Lt.)	11	Pilot Officer (PO)

SERVICE RETIRED PAY ON COMPULSORY RETIREMENT

Those who leave the services having served at least five years, but not long enough to qualify for the appropriate immediate pension, now qualify for a preserved pension and terminal grant, both of which are payable at age 60. The tax-free resettlement grants shown below are payable on release to those who qualify for a preserved pension and who have completed nine years service from age 21 (officers) or 12 years from age 18 (other ranks).

The annual rates for army personnel are given. The rates apply also to personnel of equivalent rank in the other services, including the nursing services.

OFFICERS

Applicable to officers who give full pay service on the active list on or after 31 March 2001. Senior officers (*) can elect to receive a pension calculated as a percentage of their pensionable earnings.

No. of years reckonable service over age 21	Capt. and below	Major	Lt.-Col.	Colonel	Brigadier	Major-General*	Lieutenant-General*	General*
16	£9,544	£11,367	£14,974	—	—	—	—	—
17	£9,984	£11,907	£15,667	—	—	—	—	—
18	£10,424	£12,447	£16,360	£18,944	—	—	—	—
19	£10,864	£12, 986	£17,052	£19,746	—	—	—	—
20	£ 11,304	£13,526	£17,745	£20,548	—	—	—	—
21	£11,743	£14,066	£18,438	£21,351	—	—	—	—
22	£12,183	£14,606	£19,131	£22,153	£26,345	—	—	—
23	£12,623	£15,146	£19,823	£22,955	£26,345	—	—	—
24	£13,063	£15,686	£20,516	£23,757	£27,152	£29,496	—	—
25	£13,503	£16,225	£21,209	£24,559	£27,959	£30,372	—	—
26	£13,943	£16,765	£21,902	£25,361	£28,766	£31,249	—	—
27	£14,383	£17,305	£22,595	£26,163	£29,573	£32,125	£37,176	—
28	£14,823	£17,845	£23,287	£26,965	£30,380	£33,002	£38,190	—
29	£15,263	£18,385	£23,980	£27, 767	£31,187	£33,878	£39,204	—
30	£15,702	£18,925	£24,673	£28,570	£31,993	£34,755	£40,219	£52, 809
31	£16,142	£19,464	£25,366	£29,372	£32,800	£35,632	£41,233	£54,141
32	£16,582	£20,004	£26,058	£30,174	£32,800	£36,508	£42,247	£55,472
33	£17,022	£20,544	£26,751	£30,976	£34,414	£37,385	£43,262	£56,804
34	£17,462	£21,084	£27,444	£31,778	£35,221	£38,261	£44,276	£58,136

WARRANT OFFICERS, NCOS AND PRIVATES

Applicable to soldiers who give full pay service on or after 31 March 2001.

No. of years reckonable service	Below Corporal	Corporal	Sergeant	Staff Sergeant	Warrant Officer Level II	Warrant Officer Level I
22	£5,633	£7,236	£8,026	£9,142	£9,312	£10,283
23	£5,830	£7,489	£8,306	£9,461	£9,637	£10,642
24	£6,026	£7,741	£8,586	£9,780	£9,962	£11,001
25	£6,223	£7,994	£8,867	£10,099	£10,287	£11,360
26	£6,419	£8,246	£9,147	£10,418	£10,612	£11,719
27	£6,616	£8,499	£9,427	£10,737	£10,937	£12,078
28	£6,813	£8,752	£9,707	£11,056	£11,262	£12,437
29	£7,009	£9,004	£9,987	£11,375	£11,587	£12,796
30	£7,206	£9,257	£10,268	£11,695	£11,912	£13,154
31	£7,402	£9,509	£10,548	£12,014	£12,237	£13,513
32	£7,599	£9,762	£10,828	£12,333	£12,562	£13,872
33	£7,796	£10,015	£11,108	£12,652	£12,887	£14,231
34	£7,992	£10,267	£11,388	£12,971	£13,212	£14,590
35	£8,189	£10,520	£11,669	£13,290	£13,537	£14,949
36	£8,385	£10,772	£11,949	£13,609	£13,862	£15,308
37	£8,582	£11,025	£12,229	£13,928	£14,187	£15,667

RESETTLEMENT GRANTS

Terminal grants are in each case three times the rate of retired pay or pension. There are special rates of retired pay for certain other ranks not shown above. Lower rates are payable in cases of voluntary retirement.

A gratuity of £3,130 is payable for officers with short service commissions for each year completed. Resettlement grants are: officers £10,765; non-commissioned ranks £7,034.

Religion in the UK

There are two established, i.e. state, churches in the United Kingdom: the Church of England and the Church of Scotland. There are no established churches in Wales or Northern Ireland, though the Church in Wales, the Scottish Episcopal Church and the Church of Ireland are members of the Anglican Communion.

About 65 per cent of the population of the UK (38.1 million people) would call itself broadly Christian (in the Trinitarian sense), with 45 per cent (26.1 million) identifying with Anglican churches, 10 per cent (5.7 million) with the Roman Catholic Church, 4 per cent (2.6 million) with Presbyterian Churches, 2 per cent (1.3 million) with the Methodist Churches and 4 per cent (2.6 million) with other Christian churches; but only about 8.7 per cent of the population of Great Britain (3.98 million people) regularly attends a Christian church. Church attendance in Northern Ireland is estimated at 30–35 per cent of the population.

About 2 per cent of the population (1.3 million people) is affiliated to non-Trinitarian churches, e.g. Jehovah's Witnesses, the Church of Jesus Christ of Latter-Day Saints (Mormons), the Church of Christ, Scientist and the Unitarian churches.

A further 5 per cent of the population (3.25 million people) are adherents of other faiths, including Hinduism, Islam, Judaism and Sikhism.

About 28 per cent of the population is non-religious.

ADHERENTS TO RELIGIONS IN UK *(millions)*

	1975	1985	1995
Christian (Trinitarian)	40.2	39.1	38.1
Non-Trinitarian	0.7	1.0	1.3
Hindu	0.3	0.4	0.4
Jew	0.4	0.3	0.3
Muslim	0.4	0.9	1.2
Sikh	0.2	0.3	0.6
Other	0.1	0.3	0.3
Total	42.3	42.3	42.2

PERCENTAGE OF UK POPULATION ADHERING TO RELIGIONS

	1975	1985	1995
Christian (Trinitarian)	72	69	65
Non-Trinitarian	1	2	2
Non-Christian religions	3	3	5
All religions	76	74	72

Source: Christian Research/Paternoster Publishing – *UK Christian Handbook Religious Trends No. 1 1998–9;* figures in text are for 1995

INTER-CHURCH AND INTER-FAITH CO-OPERATION

The main umbrella body for the Christian churches in the UK is the Churches Together in Britain and Ireland (formerly the Council of Churches for Britain and Ireland). There are also ecumenical bodies in each of the constituent countries of the UK: Churches Together in England, Action of Churches Together in Scotland, CYTUN (Churches Together in Wales), and the Irish Council of Churches. The Free Churches' Council comprises most of the Free Churches in England and Wales, and the Evangelical Alliance represents evangelical Christians.

The Inter Faith Network for the United Kingdom promotes co-operation between faiths, and the Council of Christians and Jews works to improve relations between the two religions. Churches Together in Britain and Ireland also has a Commission on Inter-Faith Relations.

ACTION OF CHURCHES TOGETHER IN SCOTLAND, Scottish Churches House, Kirk Street, Dunblane, Perthshire FK15 0AJ. Tel: 01786-823588; Fax: 01786-825844; E-mail: acts.ecum@dial.pipex.com; Web: www.acts-scotland.org. *General Secretary,* Revd Dr K. Franz

CHURCHES TOGETHER IN BRITAIN AND IRELAND, Inter-Church House, 35–41 Lower Marsh, London SE1 7SA. Tel: 020-7523 2121; Fax: 020-7928 0010; Email: gensec@ctbi.org.uk; Web: www.ctbi.org.uk. *General Secretary,* Dr D. Goodbourn

CHURCHES TOGETHER IN ENGLAND, 27 Tavistock Square, London WC1H 9HH. Tel: 020-7529 8141; Fax: 020-7529 8134; Web: www.churches-together.org.uk. *General Secretary:* The Revd Bill Snelson

COUNCIL OF CHRISTIANS AND JEWS, Camelford House, 87-89 Albert Embankment, London, SE1 7TP. Tel: 020-7820 0090; Fax: 020-7820 0504; Email: cjrelalations@ccj.org.uk; Web: www.ccj.org.uk. *Director,* Sr M. Shepherd, NDS

CYTUN (CHURCHES TOGETHER IN WALES) - Ty John Penri, 11 St Helen's Road, Swansea SA1 4AL. Tel: 01792-460876. *General Secretary,* Revd G. Abraham-Williams

EVANGELICAL ALLIANCE, Whitefield House, 186 Kennington Park Road, London SE11 4BT. Tel: 020-7207 2100; Fax: 020-7207 2150; Email: london@eauk.org; Web: www.eauk.org. *General Director,* Revd J. Edwards

INTER FAITH NETWORK FOR THE UNITED KINGDOM, 5–7 Tavistock Place, London WC1H 9SN. Tel: 020-7388 0008; Fax: 020-7387 7968; Email: ifnet.uk@interfaith.org.uk; Web: www.interfaith.org.uk. *Director,* B. Pearce, OBE

IRISH COUNCIL OF CHURCHES, Inter-Church Centre, 48 Elmwood Avenue, Belfast BT9 6AZ. Tel: 028-9066 3145. *General Secretary,* Dr R. D. Stevens

Christianity

Christianity is a monotheistic faith based on the person and teachings of Jesus Christ and all Christian denominations claim his authority. Central to its teaching is the concept of God and his son Jesus Christ, who was crucified and resurrected in order to enable mankind to attain salvation.

The Jewish scriptures predicted the coming of a *Messiah,* an 'anointed one', who would bring salvation. To Christians, Jesus of Nazareth, a Jewish rabbi (teacher), who was born in Palestine, was the promised Messiah. Jesus' birth, teachings, crucifixion and subsequent resurrection are recorded in the *Gospels,* which, together with other scriptures that summarise Christian belief, form the *New Testament.* This, together with the Hebrew scriptures, entitled the *Old Testament* by Christians, makes up the *Bible,* the sacred texts of Christianity.

BELIEFS

Christians believe that sin distanced mankind from God, and that Jesus was the Son of God, sent to redeem mankind from that sin by his death. In addition, many believe that Jesus will return again at some future date, triumph over evil and establish a kingdom on earth, thus inaugurating a new age. The Gospel assures Christians that those who believe in Jesus and obey his teachings will be forgiven their sins and will be resurrected from the dead.

PRACTICES

Christian practices vary widely between different Christian churches, but prayer is universal to all, as is charity, giving for the maintenance of the church buildings, for the work of the church, and to the poor and needy. In addition, certain days of observance, i.e. the *Sabbath, Easter*, and *Christmas* are celebrated by most Christians. The Orthodox, Roman Catholic and Anglican churches celebrate many more days of observance, based on saints and significant events in the life of Jesus. The belief in sacraments, physical signs believed to have been ordained by Jesus Christ to symbolise and convey spiritual gifts, varies greatly between Christian denominations; *Baptism* and the *Eucharist* are practised by most Christians. Baptism, symbolising repentance and faith in Jesus is an act marking entry into the Christian community; the Eucharist, the ritual re-enactment of the Last Supper, Jesus' final meal with his disciples, is also practised by most denominations. Other sacraments, such as anointing the sick, the laying on of hands to symbolise the passing on of the office of priesthood or to heal the sick and speaking in tongues, where it is believed that the person is possessed by the Holy Spirit, the Spirit of God, are less common. In denominations where infant baptism is practised, confirmation is common, where the person now repeats the commitments made for him or her at infancy. Matrimony and the ordination of priests are also widely believed to be sacraments. Many Protestants only view baptism and the Eucharist as sacraments; the Quakers and the Salvation Army reject the use of sacraments.

Most Christians believe that God actively guides the Church.

THE EARLY CHURCH

The apostles were Jesus' first converts and are recognised by Christians as the founders of the Christian community. The new faith spread rapidly throughout the eastern provinces of the Roman Empire. Early Christianity was subject to great persecution until 313 AD, when Emperor Constantine's Edict of Toleration confirmed its right to exist and it became established as the religion of the Roman Empire in 381AD.

The Christian faith was slowly formulated in the first millennium of the Christian era. Between AD 325 and 787 there were seven Oecumenical Councils at which bishops from the entire Christian world assembled to resolve various doctrinal disputes. The estrangement between East and West began after Constantine moved the centre of the Roman Empire from Rome to Constantinople, and it grew after the division of the Roman Empire into eastern and western halves. Linguistic and cultural differences between Greek East and Latin West served to encourage separate ecclesiastical developments which became pronounced in the tenth and early 11th centuries.

Administration of the church was divided between five ancient patriarchates: Rome and all the West, Constantinople (the imperial city – the 'New Rome'), Jerusalem and all Palestine, Antioch and all the East, and Alexandria and all Africa. Of these, only Rome was in the Latin West

and after the schism in 1054, Rome developed a structure of authority centralised on the Papacy, while the Orthodox East maintained the style of localised administration.

Papal authority over the doctrine and jurisdiction of the Church in western Europe was unrivalled after the split with the Eastern Orthodox Church until the Protestant Reformation in the 16th century.

CHRISTIANITY IN BRITAIN

An English Church already existed when Pope Gregory sent Augustine to evangelise the English in AD 596. Conflicts between Church and State during the Middle Ages culminated in the Act of Supremacy in 1534, which repudiated papal supremacy and declared King Henry VIII to be the supreme head of the Church in England. Since 1559 the English monarch has been termed the Supreme Governor of the Church of England.

In 1560 the jurisdiction of the Roman Catholic Church in Scotland was abolished and the first assembly of the Church of Scotland ratified the Confession of Faith, drawn up by a committee including John Knox. In 1592 Parliament passed an Act guaranteeing the liberties of the Church and its presbyterian government. King James VI (James I of England) and later Stuart monarchs attempted to reintroduce episcopacy, but a presbyterian church was finally restored in 1690 and secured by the Act of Settlement (1690) and the Act of Union (1707).

PORVOO DECLARATION

The Porvoo Declaration was drawn up by representatives of the British and Irish Anglican churches and the Nordic and Baltic Lutheran churches and was approved by the General Synod of the Church of England in July 1995. Churches that approve the Declaration regard baptised members of each other's churches as members of their own, and allow free interchange of episcopally ordained ministers within the rules of each church.

Non-Christian Religions

BAHÁ'Í FAITH

Mirza Husayn-'Ali, known as *Bahá'u'lláh* (Glory of God) was born in Iran in 1817 and became a follower of the *Báb*, a religious reformer and prophet who was imprisoned for his beliefs and executed on the grounds of heresy in 1850. *Bahá'u'lláh* was himself imprisoned in 1852, and in 1853 he had a vision that he was the Promised One foretold by the *Báb*. He was exiled after his release from prison and eventually was exiled to Acre, now in Israel, where he continued to compose the Bahá'í sacred scriptures. He died in 1892 and was succeeded by his son, Abdu'l-Bahá, as spiritual leader, under whose guidance the faith spread to Europe and North America. He was followed by Shoghi Effendi, his grandson, who translated many of *Bahá'u'l-láh*'s works into English. Upon his death in 1957, a democratic system of leadership was brought into operation.

The Bahá'í faith recognises the unity and relativity of religious truth and teaches that there is only one God, whose will has been revealed to mankind by a series of messengers, such as Zoroaster, Abraham, Moses, Buddha, Krishna, Christ, Muhammad, the Báb and Bahá'u'lláh, who were seen as the founders of separate religions, but whose common purpose was to bring God's message to mankind. It teaches that all races and both sexes are equal and deserving of equal opportunities and treatment, that education is a fundamental right and encourages a fair distribution of wealth. In addition, mankind is exhorted to establish a world federal system to promote peace, tolerance and the free movement of people, goods and ideas.

A Feast is held every 19 days, which consists of prayer and readings of Bahá'í scriptures, consultation on community business, and social activities. Music, food and beverages usually accompany the proceedings. There is no clergy; each local community elects a local assembly, which co-ordinates community activities, enrols new members, counsels and assists members in need, and conducts Bahá'í marriages and funerals. A national assembly is elected annually by locally elected delegates, and every five years the national spiritual assemblies meet together to elect the Universal House of Justice, the supreme international governing body of the Bahá'í Faith. World-wide there are about 12,535 local spiritual assemblies; there are around five million members residing in about 235 countries, of which 181 have national organisations.

THE BAHÁ'Í INFORMATION OFFICE, 27 Rutland Gate, London SW7 1PD. Tel: 020-7584 2566; Fax: 020-7584 9402; Email: nsa@bahai.org.uk; Web: www.bahai.org.uk; *Secretary General*: The Hon. Barnabas Leith

BUDDHISM

Buddhism originated in northern India, in the teachings of Siddharta Gautama, who was born near Kapilavastu about 560 BC and became the *Buddha* (Enlightened One).

Fundamental to Buddhism is the concept of rebirth. Each life carries with it the consequences of the conduct of earlier lives (known as the law of *karma*). This cycle of death and rebirth is broken only when the state of *nirvana* has been reached. Buddhism steers a middle path between belief in personal immortality and belief in death as the final end.

The Four Noble Truths of Buddhism (*dukkha*, suffering; *tanha*, a thirst or desire for continued existence which causes dukkha; *nirvana*, the final liberation from desire and ignorance; and *ariya*, the path to nirvana) are all held to be universal and to sum up the *dhamma* or true nature of life. Necessary qualities to promote spiritual development are *sila* (morality), *samadhi* (meditation) and *panna* (wisdom).

There are two main schools of Buddhism: *Theravada* Buddhism, the earliest extant school, which is more traditional, and *Mahayana* Buddhism, which began to develop about 100 years after the Buddha's death and is more liberal; it teaches that all people may attain Buddhahood. Important schools that have developed within Mahayana Buddhism are *Zen* Buddhism, *Nichiren* Buddhism and Pure Land Buddhism or *Amidism*. There are also distinctive Tibetan forms of Buddhism. Buddhism began to establish itself in the West in the early 20th century.

The scripture of Theravada Buddhism is the *Pali Canon*, which dates from the first century BC. Mahayana Buddhism uses a Sanskrit version of the Pali Canon but also has many other works of scripture.

There is no set time for Buddhist worship, which may take place in a temple or in the home. Worship centres around meditation, acts of devotion centring on the image of the Buddha, and, where possible, offerings to a relic of the Buddha. Buddhist festivals vary according to local traditions and within Theravada and Mahayana Buddhism. For religious purposes Buddhists use solar and lunar calendars, the New Year being celebrated in April. Other festivals mark events in the life of the Buddha.

There is no supreme governing authority in Buddhism. In the United Kingdom communities representing all schools of Buddhism have developed and operate independently. The Buddhist Society was established in 1924; it runs courses and lectures, and publishes books about Buddhism. It represents no one school of Buddhism.

There are estimated to be at least 300 million Buddhists world-wide, and more than 500 groups and centres, an estimated 25,000 adherents and up to 20 temples or monasteries in the UK.

THE BUDDHIST SOCIETY, 58 Eccleston Square, London SW1V 1PH. Tel: 020-7834 5858; Fax: 020-7976 5238; Email: info@thebuddhistsociety.org.uk; Web: www.thebuddhistsociety.org.uk. *General Secretary*, R. C. Maddox
FRIENDS OF THE WESTERN BUDDHIST ORDER, London Buddhist Centre, 51 Roman Road, E2 0HU. Tel: 020-8901 1225
THE NETWORK OF BUDDHIST ORGANISATIONS, The Old Courthouse, 43 Renfrew Road, London SE11 4NB. Tel: 020-8682 3442; fax: 020-8767 3210; Email: secretary@nbo.org.uk; Web: www.nbo.org.uk
OFFICE OF TIBET (The Official UK Agency for HH the Dalai Lama) Tibet House, 1 Culworth Street, London NW8 7AF. TEL: 020-7722 5378
SOKA GAKKAI UK, Taplow Court, Taplow, Maidenhead, Berkshire SL6 0ER. Tel: 01628-773 163

HINDUISM

Hinduism has no historical founder but had become highly developed in India by about 1200 BC. Its adherents originally called themselves Aryans; Muslim invaders first called the Aryans 'Hindus' (derived from 'Sindhu', the name of the river Indus) in the eighth century.

Most Hindus hold that *satya* (truthfulness), *ahimsa* (non-violence), honesty, sincerity and devotion to God are essential for good living. They believe in one supreme spirit (*Brahman*), and in the transmigration of *atman* (the soul). Most Hindus accept the doctrine of *karma* (consequences of actions), the concept of *samsara* (successive lives) and the possibility of all atmans achieving *moksha* (liberation from samsara) through *jnana* (knowledge), *yoga* (meditation), *karma* (work or action) and *bhakti* (devotion).

Most Hindus offer worship to *murtis* (images of deities) representing different incarnations or aspects of Brahman, and follow their *dharma* (religious and social duty) according to the traditions of their *varna* (social class), *ashrama* (stage in life), *jati* (caste) and *kula* (family).

Hinduism's sacred texts are divided into *shruti* ('that which is heard'), including the *Vedas*; or *smriti* ('that which is remembered'), including the *Ramayana*, the *Mahabharata*, the *Puranas* (ancient myths), and the sacred law books. Most Hindus recognise the authority of the *Vedas*, the oldest holy books, and accept the philosophical teachings of the *Upanishads*, the *Vedanta Sutras* and the *Bhagavad-Gita*.

Brahman is omniscient, omnipotent, limitless and all-pervading, and is usually worshipped in His deity form. Brahma, Vishnu and Shiva are the most important gods worshipped by Hindus; their respective consorts are Saraswati, Lakshmi and Durga or Parvati, also known as Shakti. There are believed to have been ten *avatars* (incarnations) of Vishnu, of whom the most important are Rama and Krishna. Other popular gods are Ganesha,

Hanuman and Subrahmanyam. All gods are seen as aspects of the supreme God, not as competing deities.

Orthodox Hindus revere all gods and goddesses equally, but there are many denominations, including the Hare-Krishna movement (ISKCon), the Arya Samaj, the Swami Narayan Hindu mission and the Satya Sai-Baba movement, in which worship is concentrated on one deity. The *guru* (spiritual teacher) is seen as the source of spiritual guidance.

Hinduism does not have a centrally-trained and ordained priesthood. The pronouncements of the *shankaracharyas* (heads of monasteries) of Shringeri, Puri, Dwarka and Badrinath are heeded by the orthodox but may be ignored by the various sects.

The commonest form of worship is a *puja*, in which offerings of water, flowers, food, fruit, incense and light are made to a deity. Puja may be done either in a home shrine or a *mandir* (temple). Many British Hindus celebrate *samskars* (purification rights) to name a baby, the sacred thread (an initiation ceremony), marriage and cremation.

The largest communities of Hindus in Britain are in Leicester, London, Birmingham and Bradford, and developed as a result of immigration from India, eastern Africa and Sri Lanka.

There are an estimated 800 million Hindus world-wide; there are about 380,000 adherents and over 150 temples in the UK.

ARYA PRATINIDHI SABHA (UK) AND ARYA SAMAJ LONDON, 69A Argyle Road, London W13 0LY. Tel: 020-8991 1732. *President*, Prof. S. N. Bharadwaj

BHARATIYA VIDYA BHAVAN, Institute of Indian Art and Culture, 4A Castletown Road, London W14 9HQ. Tel: 020-7381 4608. *Executive Director*, Dr M. N. Nandakumara

INTERNATIONAL SOCIETY FOR KRISHNA CONSCIOUSNESS (ISKCon), Bhaktivedanta Manor, Dharam Marg, Hilfield Lane, Aldenham, Watford, Herts WD2 8EZ. Tel: 01923-857244; Email: bhaktivedanta.manor@pamho.net; Web: www.iskcon.org. *Governing Body Commissioner*, H. H. Sivarama Swami

NATIONAL COUNCIL OF HINDU TEMPLES (UK), Bhakrivedanta Manor, Dharam Marg, Hilfield Lane, Aldenham, Watford WD2 8EZ. Tel: 01923-856269/ 857244; Email: bimal.krsna.bcs@pamho.net. *Secretary*, V. A. Aery

SWAMINARAYAN HINDU MISSION (SHREE SWAMINARAYAN MANDIR), 105–119 Brentfield Road, London NW10 8JP. Tel: 020-8965 2651; Fax: 020-8965 6313; Email: shm@swaminarayan-baps.org.uk; Web: www.swaminarayan-baps.org.uk. *Secretary*, A. Patel

VISHWA HINDU PARISHAD (UK), 48 Wharfedale Gardens, Thornton Heath, Surrey CR7 6LB. Tel: 020-8684 9716. *General Secretary*, K. Ruparelia

ISLAM

Islam (which means 'peace arising from submission to the will of Allah' in Arabic) is a monotheistic religion which was taught in Arabia by the Prophet Muhammad, who was born in Mecca (Al-Makkah) in 570 CE. Islam spread to Egypt, North Africa, Spain and the borders of China in the century following the Prophet's death, and is now the predominant religion in Indonesia, the Near and Middle East, northern and parts of western Africa, Pakistan,

Bangladesh, Malaysia and some of the former Soviet republics. There are also large Muslim communities in other countries.

For Muslims (adherents of Islam), there is one God (*Allah*), who holds absolute power. His commands were revealed to mankind through the prophets, who include Abraham, Moses and Jesus, but His message was gradually corrupted until revealed finally and in perfect form to Muhammad through the angel *Jibril* (Gabriel) over a period of 23 years. This last, incorruptible message has been recorded in the *Qur'an* (Koran), which contains 114 divisions called *surahs*, each made up of *ayahs*, and is held to be the essence of all previous scriptures. The *Ahadith* are the records of the Prophet Muhammad's deeds and sayings (the *Sunnah*) as recounted by his immediate followers. A culture and a system of law and theology gradually developed to form a distinctive Islamic civilisation. Islam makes no distinction between sacred and worldly affairs and provides rules for every aspect of human life. The *Shari'ah* is the sacred law of Islam based upon prescriptions derived from the Qur'an and the *Sunnah* of the Prophet.

The 'five pillars of Islam' are *shahadah* (a declaration of faith in the oneness and supremacy of Allah and the messengership of Muhammad); *salat* (formal prayer, to be performed five times a day facing the Ka'bah (sacred house in the holy city of Makkah); *zakat* (welfare due); *sawm* (fasting during the month of Ramadan); and *hajj* (pilgrimage to Makkah); some Muslims would add *jihad* (striving for the cause of good and resistance to evil).

Two main groups developed among Muslims. *Sunni* Muslims accept the legitimacy of Muhammad's first four *caliphs* (successors as head of the Muslim community) and of the authority of the Muslim community as a whole. About 90 per cent of Muslims are Sunni Muslims. *Shi'ites* recognise only Muhammad's son-in-law Ali as his rightful successor and the *Imams* (descendants of Ali, not to be confused with *imams* (prayer leaders or religious teachers)) as the principal legitimate religious authority. The largest group within Shi'ism is *Twelver Shi'ism*, which has been the official school of law and theology in Iran since the 16th century; other subsects include the *Ismailis* and the *Druze*, the latter being an offshoot of the Ismailis and differing considerably from the main body of Muslims.

There is no organised priesthood, but learned men such as *ulama*, *imams* and *ayatollahs* are accorded great respect. The *Sufis* are the mystics of Islam. Mosques are centres for worship and teaching and also for social and welfare activities.

Islam was first known in western Europe in the eighth century AD when 800 years of Muslim rule began in Spain. Later, Islam spread to eastern Europe. More recently, Muslims came to Europe from Africa, the Middle East and Asia in the late 19th century. Both the Sunni and Shi'ah traditions are represented in Britain, but the majority of Muslims in Britain adhere to Sunni Islam.

Efforts to establish a representative central organisation recognised by all Muslims in Britain are beginning to yield good results. Meanwhile, the Islamic Cultural Centre, which is the London Central Mosque, and the Imams and Mosques Council are influential bodies; there are many other Muslim organisations in Britain.

There are about 1,000 million Muslims world-wide, with nearly two million adherents and about 1,200 mosques in Britain.

IMAMS AND MOSQUES COUNCIL, 20–22 Creffield Road, London W5 3RP. Tel: 020-8992 6636. *Director of the Council and Principal of the Muslim College*, Dr M. A. Z. Badawi

ISLAMIC CULTURAL CENTRE, 146 Park Road, London
NW8 7RG. Tel: 020-7724 3363. *Director*, Dr A. Al-
Dubayan
MUSLIM COUNCIL OF BRITAIN, P.O. Box 52, Wembley,
Middx HA9 0XW. Tel: 020-8903 9024; Fax: 020-8903
9026; Email: admin@mcb.org.uk;
Web: www.mcb.org.uk. *Secretary-General*, Yousuf
Bhailok
MUSLIM WORLD LEAGUE, 46 Goodge Street, London
W1P 1FJ. Tel: 020-7636 7568. *Deputy Director*, G.
Rahman
UNION OF MUSLIM ORGANISATIONS OF THE UK AND
ÉIRE, 109 Campden Hill Road, London W8 7TL.
Tel: 020-7229 0538/7221 6608. *General Secretary*, Dr S.
A. Pasha

JAINISM

Jainism traces its history to Vardhamana Jnatiputra,
known as *Tirthankara Mahavira* (The Great Hero)
whose traditional dates were 599-527 BC. He was the last
of a series of 24 *Jinas* (those who overcome all passions and
desires) or *Tirthankaras* (those who show a way across the
ocean of life) stretching back to remote antiquity. Born to a
noble family in north-eastern Indian, he renounced the
world for the life of a wandering ascetic and after 12 years
of austerity and meditation he attained enlightenment. He
then preached his message until, at the age of 72, he passed
away and reached *moksha*, total liberation from the cycle of
death and rebirth.

Jains deny the authority of the *Vedas*, the Hindu sacred
scriptures. They recognise some of the minor deities of the
Hindu pantheon, but the supreme objects of worship are
the *Tirthankaras*. The pious Jain does not ask favours from
the *Tirthankaras*, but seeks to emulate their example in his
or her own life.

Jains believe that the universe is eternal and self-
subsisting: there is no omnipotent creator God ruling it
and the destiny of the individual is in his or her own hands.
Karma, the fruit of past actions, determines the place of
every living being and rebirth may be in the heavens, on
earth as a human, an animal or other lower being, or in the
hells. The ultimate goal of existence is *moksha* or *nirvana*, a
state of perfect knowledge and tranquility for each
individual soul, which can be achieved only by gaining
enlightenment.

The path to liberation is defined by the Three Jewels,
samyak darsana (right thought), *samyak jnana* (right
knowledge) and *samyak charitra* (right conduct).

There are about 25,000 Jains in Britain, sizeable
communities in North America and East Africa and
smaller groups in many other countries.

INSTITUTE OF JAINOLOGY, Unit 18, Silicon Business
Centre, 26/28 Wadsworth Road, Greenford, Middx,
UB6 7JZ Tel: 020-8997 2300; Fax: 020-8997 4964
JAIN CENTRE, Oxford Street, Leicester, LE1 5XU Tel: 0116-
254 3091

JUDAISM

Judaism is the oldest monotheistic faith. The primary
authority of Judaism is the Hebrew Bible or *Tanakh*, which
records how the descendants of Abraham were led by
Moses out of their slavery in Egypt to Mount Sinai where
God's law (*Torah*) was revealed to them as the chosen
people. The *Talmud*, which consists of commentaries on

the *Mishnah* (the first text of rabbinical Judaism), is also
held to be authoritative, and may be divided into two main
categories: the *halakah* (dealing with legal and ritual
matters) and the *Aggadah* (dealing with theological and
ethical matters not directly concerned with the regulation
of conduct). The *Midrash* comprises rabbinic writings
containing biblical interpretations in the spirit of the
Aggadah. The *halakah* has become a source of division;
Orthodox Jews regard Jewish law as derived from God and
therefore unalterable; Reform and Liberal Jews seek to
interpret it in the light of contemporary considerations;
and Conservative Jews aim to maintain most of the
traditional rituals but to allow changes in accordance with
tradition. Reconstructionist Judaism, a 20th-century
movement, regards Judaism as a culture rather than a
theological system and accepts all forms of Jewish practice.

The family is the basic unit of Jewish ritual, with the
synagogue playing an important role as the centre for
public worship and religious study. A synagogue is led by a
group of laymen who are elected to office. The Rabbi is
primarily a teacher and spiritual guide. The Sabbath is the
central religious observance. Most British Jews are
descendants of either the *Ashkenazim* of central and
eastern Europe or the *Sephardim* of Spain, Portugal and
the Middle East.

The Chief Rabbi of the United Hebrew Congregations
of the Commonwealth is appointed by a Chief Rabbinate
Conference, and is the rabbinical authority of the mainstream Orthodox sector of the Ashkenazi Jewish community, the largest body of which is the United Synagogue.
His authority is not recognised by the Reform Synagogues
of Great Britain (the largest progressive group), the Union
of Liberal and Progressive Synagogues, the Union of
Orthodox Hebrew Congregations, the Federation of
Synagogues, the Sephardi community, or the Assembly
of Masorti Synagogues. He is, however, generally
recognised both outside the Jewish community and within
it as the public religious representative of the totality of
British Jewry. The Chief Rabbi is President of the *Beth Din*
of the United Synagogue.

A *Beth Din* (Court of Judgement) is a rabbinic court.
The *Dayanim* (Assessors) adjudicate in disputes or on
matters of Jewish law and tradition; they also oversee
dietary law administration.

The Board of Deputies of British Jews, established in
1760, is the representative body of British Jewry. The basis
of representation is mainly synagogal, but communal
organisations are also represented. It watches over the
interests of British Jewry, acts as the central voice of the
community and seeks to counter anti-Jewish discrimination and antisemitic activities.

In November 1998 a Consultative Committee was
established comprising representatives of the Assembly of
Masorti Synagogues, Reform Synagogues of Great
Britain, Union of Liberal and Progressive Synagogues
and the United Synagogue. The Committee holds
discussions to further communal harmony and development.

There are over 12.5 million Jews world-wide; in Great
Britain and Ireland there are an estimated 285,000
adherents and about 365 synagogues. Of these, 191
congregations and about 150 rabbis and ministers are
under the jurisdiction of the Chief Rabbi; 99 orthodox
congregations have a more independent status; and 79
congregations are outside the jurisdiction of the Chief
Rabbi.

CHIEF RABBINATE, Adler House, 735 High Road, London
N12 0US. Tel: 020-8343 6301. *Chief Rabbi*, Prof. Jonathan
Sacks; *Executive Director*, Mrs S. Weinberg

BETH DIN (COURT OF THE CHIEF RABBI), 735 High Road, London N12 0US. Tel: 020-8343 6280; Fax: 020-8343 6257; Email: info@londonbethdin.fsnet.co.uk. *Registrar*, D. Frei; *Dayanim*, Dayan C. Ehrentreu; Dayan I. Binstock; Rabbi C. D. Kaplin; Dayan M. Gelley

BOARD OF DEPUTIES OF BRITISH JEWS, Commonwealth House, 1–19 New Oxford Street, London WC1A 1NU. Tel: 020-7543 5400; Email: info@bod.org.uk; Web: www.bod.org.uk. *President*, Jo Wagerman, OBE; *Director-General*, N. A. Nagler

ASSEMBLY OF MASORTI SYNAGOGUES, 1097 Finchley Road, London NW11 0PU. Tel: 020-8201 8772; Fax: 020-8201 8917; Email: office@masorti.org.uk; Web: www.masorti.org.uk. *Director*, M. Gluckman

FEDERATION OF SYNAGOGUES, 65 Watford Way, London NW4 3AQ. Tel: 020-8202 2263. *Chief Executive*, G. D. Coleman

BETH DIN OF THE FEDERATION OF SYNAGOGUES, 65 Watford Way, London NW4 3AQ. Tel: 020-8202 2263. *Registrar*, Rabbi S. Zaiden; *Dayanim*, Dayan Y. Y. Lichtenstein, Dayan B. Berkovits, Dayan M. D. Elzas

REFORM SYNAGOGUES OF GREAT BRITAIN, The Sternberg Centre for Judaism, 80 East End Road, London N3 2SY. Tel: 020-8349 5640; Fax: 020-8349 5699; Email: admin@reformjudaism.org.uk; Web: www.reformjudaism.org.uk. *Chief Executive*, Rabbi T. Bayfield

SPANISH AND PORTUGUESE JEWS' CONGREGATION, 2 Ashworth Road, London W9 1JY. Tel: 020-7289 2573. *Chief Executive*, H. Miller

UNION OF LIBERAL AND PROGRESSIVE SYNAGOGUES, The Montagu Centre, 21 Maple Street, London W1T 4BE. Tel: 020-7580 1663; Fax: 020-7436 4184; Email: montagu@ulps.org; Web: www.ulps.org. *Executive Director*, Rabbi Dr C. H. Middleburgh

UNION OF ORTHODOX HEBREW CONGREGATIONS, 140 Stamford Hill, London N16 6QT. Tel: 020-8802 6226. *Principal Rabbinical Authority*, M. C. E. Padwa

UNITED SYNAGOGUE HEAD OFFICE, Adler House, 735 High Road, London N12 0US. Tel: 020-8343 8989. *Chief Executive*, J. Wayne

SIKHISM

The Sikh religion dates from the birth of Guru Nanak in the Punjab in 1469. 'Guru' means teacher but in Sikh tradition has come to represent the divine presence of God giving inner spiritual guidance. Nanak's role as the human vessel of the divine guru was passed on to nine successors, the last of whom (Guru Gobind Singh) died in 1708. The immortal guru is now held to reside in the sacred scripture, *Guru Granth Sahib*, and so to be present in all Sikh gatherings.

Guru Nanak taught that there is one God and that different religions are like different roads leading to the same destination. He condemned religious conflict, ritualism and caste prejudices. The fifth Guru, Guru Arjan Dev, largely compiled the Sikh Holy Book, a collection of hymns (*gurbani*) known as the *Adi Granth*. It includes the writings of the first five Gurus and the ninth Guru, and selected writings of Hindu and Muslim saints whose views are in accord with the Gurus' teachings. Guru Arjan Dev also built the Golden Temple at Amritsar, the centre of Sikhism. The tenth Guru, Guru Gobind Singh, passed on the guruship to the sacred scripture, Guru Granth Sahib. He also founded the *Khalsa*, an order intended to fight against tyranny and injustice. Male

initiates to the order added 'Singh' to their given names and women added 'Kaur'. Guru Gobind Singh also made five symbols obligatory: *kaccha* (a special undergarment), *kara* (a steel bangle), *kirpan* (a small sword), *kesh* (long unshorn hair, and consequently the wearing of a turban), and *kangha* (a comb). These practices are still compulsory for those Sikhs who are initiated into the Khalsa (the *Amritdharis*). Those who do not seek initiation are known as *Sehajdharis*.

There are no professional priests in Sikhism; anyone with a reasonable proficiency in the Punjabi language can conduct a service. Worship can be offered individually or communally, and in a private house or a *gurdwara* (temple). Sikhs are forbidden to eat meat prepared by ritual slaughter; they are also asked to abstain from smoking, alcohol and other intoxicants. Such abstention is compulsory for the *Amritdharis*.

There are about 20 million Sikhs world-wide and about 500,000 adherents and 250 gurdwaras in Great Britain. Every gurdwara manages its own affairs and there is no central body in the UK. The Sikh Missionary Society provides an information service.

SIKH MISSIONARY SOCIETY UK, 10 Featherstone Road, Southall, Middx UB2 5AA. Tel: 020-8574 1902. *Hon. General Secretary*, K. S. Rai

WORLD SIKH FOUNDATION (THE SIKH COURIER INTERNATIONAL), 33 Wargrave Road, South Harrow, Middx HA2 8LL. Tel: 020-8864 9228. *Secretary*, Mrs H. B. Bharara

ZOROASTRIANISM

Zoroastrianism was founded by Zarathushtra (or Zoroaster in its hellenised form) in Persia. Linguistic analysis of the earliest extant Zoroastrian texts suggests that he lived around 1500 BC. Zarathushtra's words are recorded in five poems called the *Gathas*, which, together with other scriptures, forms the *Avestan*.

Zoroastrianism teaches that there is one God, *Ahura Mazda* (the Wise Lord), and that all creation stems ultimately from God; the Gathas teach that human beings have free will, are responsible for their own actions and can choose between good and evil: Choosing *Asha* (truth or righteousness) leads to happiness for the individual and society, whereas choosing evil leads to unhappiness and conflict. The *Gathas* also encourage hard work, good deeds and charitable acts. Zoroastrians believe that after death, the immortal soul is judged by God, and is then sent to paradise or hell.

In Zoroastrian places of worship, an urn containing fire is the central feature; the fire symbolises purity, light, and truth and is a visible symbol of the *Fravashi* or *Farohar*, the presence of *Ahura Mazda* in every human being.

Zoroastrians respect nature and much importance is attached to cultivating land and protecting the air, the earth and water. The practice of leaving corpses on mountain tops or towers developed to avoid pollution.

Zoroastrians were persecuted in Iran following the Arab invasion of Persia in the seventh century AD, which also brought Islam and a group migrated to India in the tenth century AD to avoid harassment and persecution; there are fewer than 150,000 Zoroastrians worldwide.

ZOROASTRIAN ASSOCIATION OF EUROPE, 88 Compayne Gardens, London NW6. Tel: 020-7328 6018

The Churches

For changes notified after 31 August, *see* Stop-press

The Church of England

The Church of England is the established (i.e. national) church in England and seeks to serve the nation through its dioceses and parishes. It traces its life back to the first coming of Christianity to England. Its position is defined by the ancient creeds of the Church and by the Thirty-nine articles of Religion (1571), the Book of Common Prayer (1662) and the Ordinal. The Church of England is thus both catholic and reformed. It is the mother church of the Anglican Communion.

THE ANGLICAN COMMUNION

The Anglican Communion consists of 40 independent provincial or national Christian churches throughout the world, many of which are in Commonwealth countries and originated from missionary activity by the Church of England. Every ten years all the bishops in the Communion meet at the Lambeth Conference, convened by the Archbishop of Canterbury. The Conference has no policy-making authority but is an important forum for discussing and forming consensus around issues common concern. The Anglican Consultative Council was set up in 1968 to liaise between the member churches and provinces of the Anglican Communion. It meets every three years. Meetings of the Anglican primates have taken place every two years since 1979.

There are about 70 million Anglicans and 800 archbishops and bishops world-wide.

STRUCTURE

The Church of England is divided into the two provinces of Canterbury and York, each under an archbishop. The two provinces are subdivided into 44 dioceses.

Decisions on matters concerning the Church of England are made by the General Synod, established in 1970. It also discusses and expresses opinion on any other matter of religious or public interest. The General Synod has 580 members in total, divided between three houses: the House of Bishops, the House of Clergy and the House of Laity. It is presided over jointly by the Archbishops of Canterbury and York and normally meets twice a year. The Synod has the power, delegated by Parliament, to frame statute law (known as a Measure) on any matter concerning the Church of England. A Measure must be laid before both Houses of Parliament, who may accept or reject it but cannot amend it. Once accepted the Measure is submitted for royal assent and then has the full force of law. In addition to the General Synod, there are Synods at diocesan level

The Archbishops' Council was established in January 1999. Its creation was the result of changes to the Church of England's national structure proposed in 1995 and subsequently approved by the Synod and Parliament. The Council's purpose, set out in the National Institutions Measure 1998, is 'to co-ordinate, promote and further the work and mission of the Church of England. It reports frequently to the General Synod. The Archbishops' Council comprises three *ex-officio* members: the Archbishops of Canterbury and York (joint presidents) and a Church Estates Commissioners, ten elected members: the two persons elected by the Convocations of Prolocutors; the Chairman and Vice-Chairman of the House of Laity,

elected by that House; two bishops, two clergy and two lay members each elected by their respective Houses of the General Synod; and up to six members appointed by the two archbishops with the approval of the General Synod.

There are also a number of national Boards, Councils and other bodies working on matters such as social responsibility, mission, Christian unity and education which report to the General Synod through the Archbishops' Council.

GENERAL SYNOD OF THE CHURCH OF ENGLAND, Church House, Great Smith Street, London SW1P 3NZ. Tel: 020-7898 1000. *Joint Presidents*, The Archbishops of Canterbury and York. *Secretary-General*, P. Mawer
HOUSE OF BISHOPS: *Chairman*, The Archbishop of Canterbury; *Vice-Chairman*, The Archbishop of York
HOUSE OF CLERGY: *Chairmen (alternating)*, Canon Bob Baker; Canon Glyn Webster
HOUSE OF LAITY: *Chairman*, Dr Christina Baxter; *Vice-Chairman*, Brian McHenry
ARCHBISHOPS' COUNCIL, Church House, Great Smith Street, London SW1P 3NZ. Tel: 020-7898 1000. *Joint Presidents*, The Archbishops of Canterbury and York. *Secretary-General*, P. Mawer.

THE ORDINATION OF WOMEN

The canon making it possible for women to be ordained to the priesthood was promulgated in the General Synod in February 1994 and the first 32 women priests were ordained on 12 March 1994.

MEMBERSHIP

In 1999, 179,000 people were baptised. In 1998 the Church of England had an electoral roll membership of 1.4 million, and each week about 1 million people attended Sunday services. At December 2000 there were two archbishops and 108 diocesan, suffragan and (stipendiary) assistant bishops. In 2000 there were 8,398 other male and 1,140 female full-time stipendiary clergy, and over 16,000 churches and places of worship.

FULL-TIME DIOCESAN CLERGY 1999 AND CHURCH ELECTORAL ROLLS 1997

| | Clergy | | Membership |
	Male	Female	
Bath and Wells	210	29	43,000
Birmingham	177	26	19,300
Blackburn	226	13	38,600
Bradford	106	10	13,100
Bristol	122	20	20,400
Canterbury	159	19	22,300
Carlisle	139	14	25,000
Chelmsford	367	48	54,200
Chester	250	25	52,100
Chichester	329	9	61,300
Coventry	130	17	18,200
Derby	168	17	21,900
Durham	211	28	27,700

| | Clergy | | Membership |
	Male	Female	
Ely	130	24	21,500
Europe	113	13	9,100
Exeter	232	19	34,600
Gloucester	141	18	26,900
Guildford	170	31	31,900
Hereford	96	19	20,100

Leicester	143	23	16,700
Lichfield	304	46	54,800
Lincoln	187	39	30,700
Liverpool	215	37	33,300
London	497	60	59,900
Manchester	256	40	39,800
Newcastle	130	16	18,300
Norwich	183	18	26,800
Oxford	369	71	63,200
Peterborough	151	17	19,600
Portsmouth	107	10	19,300
Ripon and Leeds	123	22	20,000
Rochester	194	25	32,800
St Albans	228	48	46,100
St Edmundsbury and Ipswich	139	15	26,500
Salisbury	199	30	47,500
Sheffield	156	31	21,800
Sodor and Man	20	0	2,900
Southwark	304	66	47,200
Southwell	144	26	18,600
Truro	124	6	18,100
Wakefield	155	24	24,700
Winchester	220	19	43,500
Worcester	129	22	23,400
York	245	30	39,800
TOTAL	8,398	1,140	1,347,400

STIPENDS 2001–2002

Archbishop of Canterbury	£57,320
Archbishop of York	£50,220
Bishop of London	£46,840
Other diocesan bishops	£31,110
Suffragan bishops	£25,530
Assistant Bishops (full-time)	£25,520
Deans and provosts	£25,530
Residentiary canons	£20,800
Incumbents and clergy of similar status	£16,910*

*National Stipends Benchmark

CANTERBURY

103RD ARCHBISHOP AND PRIMATE OF ALL ENGLAND
Most Revd and Rt. Hon. George L. Carey, Ph.D., cons. 1987, trans. 1991, apptd 1991; Lambeth Palace, London SE1 7JU. Signs George Cantuar

BISHOPS SUFFRAGAN
Dover, Rt. Revd Stephen S. Venner, cons 1994, apptd 1999; Upway, St Martin's Hill, Canterbury, Kent CT1 1PR
Maidstone, Rt. Revd Graham Cray Bishop's House, Pett Lane, Charing, Ashford, Kent TN27 0DL
Ebbsfleet, Rt. Revd Andrew Burnham, cons. 2001, apptd 2001 (provincial episcopal visitor); Bishop's House, Dry Sandsford, Oxon OX13 6JP
Richborough, Rt. Revd Edwin Barnes, cons. 1995, apptd 1995 (provincial episcopal visitor); 14 Hall Place Gardens, St Albans, Herts AL1 3SP

DEAN
Very Revd Robert Andrew Willis, apptd 2001

CANONS RESIDENTIARY
P. Brett, apptd 1983; R. H. C. Symon, apptd 1994; Dr M. Chandler, apptd 1995; Ven. J. Pritchard, apptd 1996
Organist, D. Flood, FRCO, apptd 1988

ARCHDEACONS
Canterbury, Ven. J. Pritchard, apptd 1996

Maidstone, Ven. P. Evans, apptd 1989
Vicar-General of Province and Diocese, Chancellor S. Cameron, QC
Commissary-General, His Hon. Judge Richard Walker
Joint Registrars of the Province, F. E. Robson, OBE; B. J. T. Hanson, CBE
Diocesan Registrar and Legal Adviser, R. H. B. Sturt
Diocesan Secretary, D. Kemp, Diocesan House, Lady Wootton's Green, Canterbury CT1 1NQ. Tel: 01227-459401

YORK

96TH ARCHBISHOP AND PRIMATE OF ENGLAND
Most Revd and Rt. Hon. David M. Hope, KCVO, D.Phil., LL D, cons. 1985, trans. 1995, apptd 1995; Bishopthorpe, York YO23 2GE. Signs David Ebor

BISHOPS SUFFRAGAN
Hull, Rt. Revd Richard M. C. Frith, cons. 1998, apptd 1998; Hullen House, Woodfield Lane, Hessle, Hull HU13 0ES
Selby, Rt. Revd Humphrey V. Taylor, cons. 1991, apptd 1991; 10 Precentor's Court, York YO1 2EJ
Whitby, Rt. Revd Robert S. Ladds, cons. 1999, apptd 1999; 60 West Green, Stokesley, Middlesbrough TS9 5BD
Beverley, Rt. Revd M. Jarrett, apptd 2000 (provincial episcopal visitor); 3 North Lane, Roundhay, Leeds LS8 2QJ

DEAN
Very Revd Raymond Furnell, apptd 1994

CANONS RESIDENTIARY
G. Webster, apptd 1999; E. R. Norman, Ph.D., DD, apptd 1999; J. L. Draper, apptd 2000

CANONS LAY
J. L. Mackinlay, apptd 2000; Mrs E. C. Rymer, apptd 2000; Dr A. J. Warren, apptd 2000; Brig. P. J. Lyddon (as Chapter Steward), apptd 2000
Organist, P. Moore, FRCO, apptd 1983

ARCHDEACONS
Cleveland, Ven. P. J. Ferguson, apptd 2001
East Riding, Ven. P. R. W. Harrison, apptd 1998
York, Ven. R. Seed, apptd 1999

Official Principal and Auditor of the Chancery Court, Sir John Owen, QC
Chancellor of the Diocese, His Hon. Judge Coningsby, QC, apptd 1977
Vicar-General of the Province and Official Principal of the Consistory Court, His Hon. Judge Coningsby, QC
Registrar and Legal Secretary, L. P. M. Lennox
Diocesan Secretary, C. Sheppard, Diocesan House, Aviator Court, Clifton Moor, York YO30 4WJ. Tel: 01904-699500

LONDON (Province of Canterbury)

132ND BISHOP
Rt. Revd and Rt. Hon Richard J. C. Chartres, cons. 1992, apptd. 1995; The Old Deanery, Dean's Court, London EC4V 5AA. Signs Richard Londin

AREA BISHOPS
Edmonton, Rt. Revd Peter W. Wheatley, cons. 1999, apptd 1999; 27 Thurlow Road, London NW3 5PP

Kensington, Rt. Revd Michael Colclough, *cons.* 1996, *apptd* 1996; 19 Campden Hill Square, London W8 7JY
Stepney, Rt. Revd Dr John M. Sentamu, *cons.* 1996, *apptd* 1996; 63 Coborn Road, London E3 2DB
Willesden, Rt. Revd Peter Broadbent, *cons.*, *apptd* 2000; 173 Willesden Lane, London NW6 7YN

BISHOP SUFFRAGAN
Fulham, Rt. Revd John Broadhurst, *cons.* 1996, *apptd* 1996; 26 Canonbury Park South, London N1 2FN

DEAN OF ST PAUL'S
Very Revd John H. Moses, PH.D., *apptd* 1996

CANONS RESIDENTIARY
R. J. Halliburton, *apptd* 1990; S. J. Oliver, *apptd* 1997; P. Buckler, *apptd* 1999; Edmund Newall, *apptd* 2001
Registrar and Receiver of St Paul's, vacant
Organist, J. Scott, FRCO, *apptd* 1990

ARCHDEACONS
Charing Cross, Ven. Dr W. Jacob, *apptd* 1996
Hackney, Ven. L. Dennen, *apptd* 1999
Hampstead, Ven. M. Lawson, *apptd* 1999
London, Ven. P. Delaney, *apptd* 1999
Middlesex, Ven. M. Colmer, *apptd* 1996
Northolt, Ven. Christopher Chessum, *apptd* 2001

Chancellor, Nigel Seed, QC, *apptd* 2001
Registrar and Legal Secretary, P. C. E. Morris
Diocesan Secretary, K. Robinson, London Diocesan House, 36 Causton Street, London SW1P 4AU.
Tel: 020-7932 1100

DURHAM (Province of York)

70TH BISHOP
Rt. Revd A. Michael A. Turnbull, *cons.* 1988, *apptd* 1994; Auckland Castle, Bishop Auckland DL14 7NR.
Signs Michael Dunelm

BISHOP SUFFRAGAN
Jarrow, Rt. Revd Alan Smithson, *cons.* 1990, *apptd* 1990; The Old Vicarage, Hallgarth, Pittington, Durham DH6 1AB

DEAN
Very Revd John R. Arnold, *apptd* 1989

CANONS RESIDENTIARY
D. W. Brown, *apptd* 1990; T. Willmott, *apptd* 1997; M. Kitchen, *apptd* 1997; D. J. Whittington, *apptd* 1998; D. J. Kennedy, *apptd* 2001
Organist, J. B. Lancelot, FRCO, *apptd* 1985

ARCHDEACONS
Auckland, Ven. I. Jagger, *apptd* 2001
Durham, Ven. T. Willmott, *apptd* 1997
Sunderland, Ven. F. White, *apptd* 1997

Chancellor, His Hon. Judge Bursell, QC, *apptd* 1989
Registrar and Legal Secretary, A. N. Fairclough
Diocesan Secretary, J. P. Cryer, Auckland Castle, Bishop Auckland, Co. Durham DL14 7QJ. Tel: 01388-604515

WINCHESTER (Canterbury)

96TH BISHOP
Rt. Revd Michael C. Scott-Joynt, *cons.* 1987, *trans.* 1995, *apptd* 1995; Wolvesey, Winchester SO23 9ND. *Signs* Michael Winton

BISHOPS SUFFRAGAN
Basingstoke, vacant
Southampton, Rt. Revd Jonathan M. Gledhill, *cons.* 1996, *apptd* 1996; Ham House, The Crescent, Romsey SO51 7NG

DEAN
Very Revd Michael Till, *apptd* 1996
Dean of Jersey (*A Peculiar*), Very Revd John Seaford, *apptd* 1993
Dean of Guernsey (*A Peculiar*), Very Revd Marc Trickey, *apptd* 1995

CANONS RESIDENTIARY
A. K. Walker, *apptd* 1987; C. Stewart, *apptd* 1997; Ven. J. A. Guille, *apptd* 1998
Organist, D. Hill, FRCO, *apptd* 1988

ARCHDEACONS
Bournemouth, Ven. A. G. Harbidge, *apptd* 1998
Winchester, Ven. J. A. Guille, *apptd* 1998

Chancellor, C. Clark, *apptd* 1993
Registrar and Legal Secretary, P. M. White
Diocesan Secretary, R. Anderton, Church House, 9 The Close, Winchester, Hants SO23 9LS. Tel: 01962-844644

BATH AND WELLS (Canterbury)

76TH BISHOP
Rt. Revd James L. Thompson, *cons.* 1978, *apptd* 1991; The Palace, Wells BA5 2PD. *Signs* James Bath & Wells

BISHOP SUFFRAGAN
Taunton, Rt. Revd Andrew John Radford, *cons.* Dec. 1998, *apptd* 1998; The Bishop's Lodge, Monkton Heights, West Monkton, Taunton, Somerset TA2 8LU

DEAN
Very Revd Richard Lewis, *apptd* 1990

CANONS RESIDENTIARY
R. Acworth, *apptd* 1993; P. G. Walker, *apptd* 1994; M. W. Matthews, *apptd* 1997; P. H. F. Woodhouse, *apptd* 2000
Organist, M. Archer, *apptd* 1996

ARCHDEACONS
Bath, Ven. R. J. S. Evens, *apptd* 1996
Taunton, Ven. J. P. C. Reed, *apptd* 1999
Wells, Ven. R. Acworth, *apptd* 1993

Chancellor, T. Briden, *apptd* 1993
Registrar and Legal Secretary, T. Berry
Diocesan Secretary, N. Denison, The Old Deanery, Wells, Somerset BA5 2UG. Tel: 01749-670777

BIRMINGHAM (Canterbury)

7TH BISHOP
Rt. Revd Mark Santer, *cons.* 1981, *apptd* 1987; Bishop's Croft, Harborne, Birmingham B17 0BG. *Signs* Mark Birmingham

BISHOP SUFFRAGAN
Aston, Rt. Revd John Austin, *cons.* 1992, *apptd* 1992; Strensham House, 8 Strensham Hill, Moseley, Birmingham B13 8AG

PROVOST
The Very Revd Gordon Mursell, *apptd* 2000

CANONS RESIDENTIARY
Ven. C. J. G. Barton, *apptd* 1990; Revd D. Lee, *apptd* 1996; Revd G. O'Neill, *apptd* 1997
Organist, M. Huxley, FRCO, *apptd* 1986

ARCHDEACONS
Aston, Ven. C. J. G. Barton, *apptd* 1990
Birmingham, Ven. H. J. Osborne, *apptd* 2001
Chancellor, His Hon. Judge Aglionby, *apptd* 1970
Registrar and Legal Secretary, H. Carslake
Diocesan Secretary, J. Drennan, 175 Harborne Park Road, Harborne, Birmingham B17 0BH. Tel: 0121-426 0400

BLACKBURN (York)

7TH BISHOP
Rt. Revd Alan D. Chesters, *cons.* 1989, *apptd* 1989; Bishop's House, Ribchester Road, Blackburn BB1 9EF. *Signs* Alan Blackburn

BISHOPS SUFFRAGAN
Burnley, Rt. Revd John W. Goddard, *cons.* 2000, *apptd* 2000; Dean House, 449 Padiham Road, Burnley BB12 6TE
Lancaster, Rt. Revd Stephen Pedley, *cons.* 1998, *apptd* 1997; The Vicarage, Shireshead, Forton, Preston PR3 0AE

PROVOST
Very Revd David Frayne, *apptd* 1992

CANONS RESIDENTIARY
D. M. Galilee, *apptd* 1995; A. D. Hindley, *apptd* 1996; P. J. Ballard, *apptd* 1998; A. Clitherow, *apptd* 2000
Organist, R. Tanner, *apptd* 1998

ARCHDEACONS
Blackburn, Ven. F. J. Marsh, *apptd* 1996
Lancaster, Ven. C. H. Williams, *apptd* 1999
Chancellor, J. W. M. Bullimore, *apptd* 1990
Registrar and Legal Secretary, T. A. Hoyle
Diocesan Secretary, Revd M. J. Wedgeworth, Diocesan Office, Cathedral Close, Blackburn BB1 5AA. Tel: 01254-54421

BRADFORD (York)

8TH BISHOP
Rt. Revd David J. Smith, *cons.* 1987, *apptd* 1992; Bishopscroft, Ashwell Road, Heaton, Bradford BD9 4AU. *Signs* David Bradford

DEAN
Very Revd John S. Richardson, *apptd* 1990

CANONS RESIDENTIARY
C. G. Lewis, *apptd* 1993; D. Jackson, *apptd* 2000
Organist, A. Horsey, FRCO, *apptd* 1986

ARCHDEACONS
Bradford, Ven. G. A. Wilkinson, *apptd* 1999
Craven, Ven. M. L. Grundy, *apptd* 1994
Chancellor, J. de G. Walford, *apptd* 1999
Registrar and Legal Secretary, J. G. H. Mackrell
Diocesan Secretary, M. Halliday, Cathedral Hall, Stott Hill, Bradford BD1 4ET. Tel: 01274-725958

BRISTOL (Canterbury)

54TH BISHOP
Rt. Revd Barry Rogerson, *cons.* 1979, *apptd* 1985; Bishop's House, Clifton Hill, Bristol BS8 1BW. *Signs* Barry Bristol:

BISHOP SUFFRAGAN
Swindon, Rt. Revd Michael Doe, *cons.* 1994, *apptd* 1994; Mark House, Field Rise, Old Town, Swindon SN1 4HP

DEAN
Very Revd Robert W. Grimley, *apptd* 1997

CANONS RESIDENTIARY
P. F. Johnson, *apptd* 1990; D. R. Holt, *apptd* 1998; B. D. Clover, *apptd* 1999
Organist, M. Lee, *apptd* 1998

ARCHDEACONS
Bristol, Ven. T. E. McClure, apptd 1999
Swindon, Ven. A. F. Hawker, *apptd* 1998
Chancellor, Sir David Calcutt, QC, *apptd* 1971
Registrar and Legal Secretary, T. Berry
Diocesan Secretary, Mrs L. Farrall, Diocesan Church House, 23 Great George Street, Bristol, Avon BS1 5QZ. Tel: 0117-921 4411

CARLISLE (York)

65TH BISHOP
Rt. Revd Graham Dow, *cons.* 1985, *apptd* 2000; Rose Castle, Dalston, Carlisle CA5 7BZ. *Signs* Graham Carlisle

BISHOP SUFFRAGAN
Penrith, Rt. Revd Richard Garrard, *cons.* 1994, *apptd* 1994; Holm Croft, Castle Road, Kendal, Cumbria LA9 7AU

DEAN
Very Revd Graeme P. Knowles, *apptd* 1998

CANONS RESIDENTIARY
R. A. Chapman, *apptd* 1978; D. W. V. Weston, *apptd* 1994; C. Hill, *apptd* 1996
Organist, J. Suter, FRCO, *apptd* 1991

ARCHDEACONS
Carlisle, vacant
West Cumberland, Ven. A. N. Davis, *apptd* 1996
Westmorland and Furness, Ven. G. A. Howe, *apptd* 2000
Chancellor, His Hon. Judge Aglionby, *apptd* 1991
Registrar and Legal Secretary, Mrs S. Holmes

Diocesan Secretary, Canon C. Hill, Church House, West Walls, Carlisle CA3 8UE. Tel: 01228-522573

CHELMSFORD (Canterbury)

8TH BISHOP
Rt. Revd John F. Perry, *cons.* 1989, *apptd* 1996; Bishopscourt, Margaretting, Ingatestone CM4 0HD. *Signs* John Chelmsford

BISHOPS SUFFRAGAN
Barking, Rt. Revd Roger F. Sainsbury, *cons.* 1991, *apptd* 1991; 110 Capel Road, Forest Gate, London E7 0JS
Bradwell, Rt. Revd Laurence Green, *cons.* 1993, *apptd* 1993; The Vicarage, Orsett Road, Horndon-on-the-Hill, Stanford-le-Hope, Essex SS17 8NS
Colchester, vacant

PROVOST
Very Revd Peter S. M. Judd, *apptd* 1997

CANONS RESIDENTIARY
A. Knowles, *apptd* 1998; W. King, *apptd* 2001
Master of Music, P. Nardone, *apptd* 2000

ARCHDEACONS
Colchester, Ven. M. W. Wallace, *apptd* 1997
Harlow, Ven. P. F. Taylor, *apptd* 1996
Southend, Ven. David Lowman, *apptd* 2001
West Ham, Ven. M. J. Fox, *apptd* 1996

Chancellor, George Pulman, *apptd* 2001
Registrar and Legal Secretary, B. Hood
Diocesan Secretary, D. Phillips, 53 New Street, Chelmsford, Essex CM1 1AT. Tel: 01245-294400

CHESTER (York)

40TH BISHOP
Rt. Revd Peter R. Forster, ph.D., *cons.* 1996, *apptd* 1996; Bishop's House, Chester CH1 2JD. *Signs* Peter Cestr

BISHOPS SUFFRAGAN
Birkenhead, Rt. Revd David A. Urquhart, *cons.* 2000, *apptd* 2000; Bishop's Lodge, 67 Bidston Road, Oxton, Birkenhead CH43 6TR
Stockport, Rt. Revd Nigel Stock, *cons.* 2000, *apptd* 2000; Bishop's Lodge, Back Lane, Dunham Town, Altrincham, Cheshire WA14 4SG

DEAN
vacant

CANONS RESIDENTIARY
J. M. Roff, *apptd* 2000; Dr T. J. Dennis, *apptd* 1994; J. W. S. Newcome, *apptd* 1994; C. P. Burkett, *apptd* 2000
Organist and Director of Music, D. G. Poulter, FRCO, *apptd* 1997

ARCHDEACONS
Chester, Ven. C. Hewetson, *apptd* 1994
Macclesfield, Ven. R. J. Gillings, *apptd* 1994

Chancellor, D. G. P. Turner, QC, *apptd* 1998
Registrar and Legal Secretary, A. K. McAllester
Diocesan Secretary, S. P. A. Marriott, Church House, Lower Lane, Aldford, Chester CH3 6HP. Tel: 01244-620444

CHICHESTER (Canterbury)

102ND BISHOP
Rt. Revd John Hind, *cons.* 1991, *apptd* 2001; The Palace, Chichester PO19 1PY. *Signs* John Cicestr

BISHOPS SUFFRAGAN
Horsham, Rt. Revd Lindsay G. Urwin, *cons.* 1993, *apptd* 1993; Bishop's House, 21 Guildford Road, Horsham, W. Sussex RH12 1LU
Lewes, Rt. Revd Wallace P. Benn, *cons.* 1997, *apptd* 1997; 16A Prideaux Road, Eastbourne, E. Sussex BN21 2NB

DEAN
Very Revd John D. Treadgold, LVO, *apptd* 1989

CANONS RESIDENTIARY
J. M. Brotherton, *apptd* 1991; P. G. Atkinson, *apptd* 1997; M. R. J. Manktelow, *apptd* 1997; P. C. Kefford, *apptd* 2001
Organist, A. J. Thurlow, FRCO, *apptd* 1980

ARCHDEACONS
Chichester, Ven. M. Brotherton, *apptd* 1991
Horsham, Ven. W. C. L. Filby, *apptd* 1983
Lewes and Hastings, Ven. N. S. Reade, *apptd* 1997

Chancellor, M. Hill
Registrar and Legal Secretary, C. Butcher
Diocesan Secretary, J. Prichard, Diocesan Church House, 211 New Church Road, Hove, E. Sussex BN3 4ED. Tel: 01273-421021

COVENTRY (Canterbury)

8TH BISHOP
Rt. Revd Colin J. Bennetts; *cons.* 1994, *apptd* 1997; The Bishop's House, 23 Davenport Road, Coventry CV5 6PW. *Signs* Colin Coventry

BISHOP SUFFRAGAN
Warwick, Rt. Revd Anthony M. Priddis, *cons.* 1996, *apptd* 1996; 139 Kenilworth Road, Coventry CV4 7AF

DEAN
Very Revd John Irvine, *apptd* 2001

CANONS RESIDENTIARY
J. C. Burch, *apptd* 1995; A. White, *apptd* 1998; S. A. Beake, *apptd* 2000
Director of Music, R. Jeffcoat, *apptd* 1997

ARCHDEACONS
Coventry, Ven. M. W. Bryant, *apptd* 2001
Warwick, Ven. M. J. J. Paget-Wilkes, *apptd* 1990

Chancellor, Sir William Gage, *apptd* 1980
Registrar and Legal Secretary, D. J. Dumbleton
Diocesan Secretary, Mrs I. Chapman, Church House, Palmerston Road, Coventry CV5 6FJ. Tel: 024-7667 4328

DERBY (Canterbury)

6TH BISHOP
Rt. Revd Jonathan S. Bailey, *cons.* 1992, *apptd* 1995; Derby Church House, Full Street, Derby DE1 3DR. *Signs* Jonathan Derby

BISHOP SUFFRAGAN
Repton, Rt. Revd David C. Hawtin, *cons.*1999, *apptd* 1999;
Repton House, Lea, Matlock, Derbys DE4 5JP

PROVOST
Very Revd Michael F. Perham, *apptd* 1998

CANONS RESIDENTIARY
G. A. Chesterman, *apptd* 1989; B. V. Gauge, *apptd* 1999; G.
O. Marshall, *apptd* 1992; D. C. Truby, *apptd* 1998
Organist, P. Gould, *apptd* 1982

ARCHDEACONS
Chesterfield, Ven. D. C. Garnett, *apptd* 1996
Derby, Ven. I. Gatford, *apptd* 1992

Chancellor, J. W. M. Bullimore, *apptd* 1981
Registrar and Legal Secretary, J. S. Battie
Diocesan Secretary, R. J. Carey, Derby Church House, Full
Street, Derby DE1 3DR. Tel: 01332-382233

ELY (Canterbury)

BISHOP
Rt. Revd Dr Anthony Russell, *cons.* 1988, *apptd* 2000; The
Bishop's House, Ely, Cambs CB7 4DW *Signs* Anthony Ely

BISHOP SUFFRAGAN
Huntingdon, Rt. Revd John R. Flack, *cons.* 1997, *apptd* 1996;
14 Lynn Road, Ely, Cambs CB6 1DA

DEAN
Very Revd Michael Higgins, *apptd* 1991

CANONS RESIDENTIARY
J. Inge, *apptd* 1996; P. M. Sills, *apptd* 2000
Organist, P. Trepte, FRCO, *apptd* 1991

ARCHDEACONS
Ely, Ven. J. Watson, *apptd* 1993
Huntingdon, Ven. J. Beer, *apptd* 1997
Wisbech, Ven. J. Rone, *apptd* 1995

Chancellor, W. Gage, QC
Joint Registrars, W. H. Godfrey; P. F. B. Beesley (*Legal
Secretary*)
Diocesan Secretary, Dr M. Lavis, Bishop Woodford House,
Barton Road, Ely, Cambs CB7 4DX. Tel: 01353-652701

EXETER (CANTERBURY)

70TH BISHOP
Rt. Revd Michael L. Langrish, *cons.* 1993, *apptd* 2000; The
Palace, Exeter, EX1 1HY. *Signs* Michael Exon

BISHOPS SUFFRAGAN
Crediton, Rt. Revd Richard S. Hawkins, *cons.* 1988, *apptd*
1996; 10 The Close, Exeter EX1 1EZ
Plymouth, Rt. Revd John H. Garton, *cons.* 1996, *apptd*
1996; 31 Riverside Walk, Tamerton Foliot, Plymouth
PL5 4AQ

DEAN
Very Revd Keith B. Jones, *apptd* 1996

CANONS RESIDENTIARY
N. Collings, *apptd* 1999; D. J. Ison, *apptd* 1997; C. Turner,
apptd 2001

Director of Music, A. T. S. Millington, *apptd* 1999

ARCHDEACONS
Barnstaple, Ven. T. Lloyd, *apptd* 1989
Exeter, Ven. A. F. Tremlett, *apptd* 1994
Plymouth, Ven. T. Wilds, *apptd* 2001
Totnes, Preb. R. T. Gilpin, *apptd* 1996

Chancellor, Sir David Calcutt, QC, *apptd* 1971
Registrar and Legal Secretary, R. K. Wheeler
Diocesan Secretary, M. Beedell, Diocesan House, Palace
Gate, Exeter, Devon EX1 1HX. Tel: 01392-272686

GIBRALTAR IN EUROPE (Canterbury)

BISHOP
Rt. Revd Geoffrey Rowell, *cons.* 1994, *apptd* 2001; 14
Tufton Street, London SW1P 3QZ

BISHOP SUFFRAGAN
In Europe Rt. Revd Henry Scriven, *cons.* 1995, *apptd* 1994;
14 Tufton Street, London SW1P 3QZ

Dean, Cathedral Church of the Holy Trinity, Gibraltar, Very
Revd J. K. Robinson
Chancellor, Pro-Cathedral of St Paul, Valletta, Malta, Canon
A. Woods
*Chancellor, Pro-Cathedral of the Holy Trinity, Brussels,
Belgium*, Canon N. Walker

ARCHDEACONS
Eastern, Rt. Revd H. Scriven (acting)
North-West Europe, Ven. G. G. Allen
France, Ven. M. Draper, OBE
Gibraltar, Very Revd K. Robinson
Italy, Ven. W. G. Reid
Scandinavia and Germany, Ven. D. Ratcliff
Switzerland, Ven. P. J. Hawker, OBE

Chancellor, Sir David Calcutt, QC
Registrar and Legal Secretary, J. G. Underwood
Diocesan Secretary, A. C. Mumford, 14 Tufton Street,
London SW1P 3QZ. Tel: 020-7898 1155

GLOUCESTER (Canterbury)

39TH BISHOP
Rt. Revd David Bentley, *cons.* 1986, *apptd* 1993;
Bishopscourt, Pitt Street, Gloucester GL1 2BQ. *Signs*
David Gloucestr

BISHOP SUFFRAGAN
Tewkesbury, Rt. Revd John S. Went, *cons.* 1995, *apptd* 1995;
Green Acre, 166 Hempsted Lane, Hempsted,
Gloucester GL2 5LG

DEAN
Very Revd Nicholas A. S. Bury, *apptd* 1997

CANONS RESIDENTIARY
R. D. M. Grey, *apptd* 1982; N. Chatfield, *apptd* 1992; N.
Heavisides, *apptd* 1993; C. H. Morgan, *apptd* 1996
Organist, D. Briggs, FRCO, *apptd* 1994

ARCHDEACONS
Cheltenham, Ven. H. S. Ringrose, *apptd* 1998
Gloucester, Ven. G. H. Sidaway, *apptd* 2000

Chancellor and Vicar-General, Ms D. J. Rodgers, *apptd* 1990
Registrar and Legal Secretary, C. G. Peak

Diocesan Secretary, M. Williams, Church House, College Green, Gloucester GL1 2LY. Tel: 01452-410022

GUILDFORD (Canterbury)

8TH BISHOP
Rt. Revd John W. Gladwin, *cons.* 1994, *apptd* 1994; Willow Grange, Woking Road, Guildford GU4 7QS. Tel: 01483-590500; Fax: 01483-590501 *Signs* John Guildford

BISHOP SUFFRAGAN
Dorking, Rt. Revd Ian Brackley, *cons.* 1996, *apptd* 1995; Dayspring, 13 Pilgrims Way, Guildford GU4 8AD

DEAN
vacant

CANONS RESIDENTIARY
Dr Maureen Palmer, *apptd* 1996; Dr Nicholas Thistlethwaite, *apptd* 1999; Julian Hubbard, *apptd* 1999
Organist, S. Farr, FRCO, *apptd* 1999

ARCHDEACONS
Dorking, Ven. M. Wilson, *apptd* 1996
Surrey, Ven. R. Reiss, *apptd* 1996

Chancellor, His Hon. Judge Goodman
Registrar and Legal Secretary, P. Beesley
Diocesan Secretary, S. Marriott

HEREFORD (Canterbury)

103RD BISHOP
Rt. Revd John Oliver, *cons.* 1990, *apptd* 1990; The Palace, Hereford HR4 9BN. *Signs* John Hereford

BISHOP SUFFRAGAN
Ludlow, Rt. Revd Dr John Saxbee, *cons.* 1994, *apptd* 1994; Bishop's House, Halford, Craven Arms, Shropshire SY7 9BT

DEAN
Vacant

CANONS RESIDENTIARY
P. Iles, *apptd* 1983; J. Tiller, *apptd* 1984; M. W. Hooper, *apptd* 1997
Organist, Geraint Bowen, FRCO, *apptd* 2001

ARCHDEACONS
Hereford, Ven. M. W. Hooper, *apptd* 1997
Ludlow, Rt. Revd J. C. Saxbee, *apptd* 1992

Chancellor, Roger Kaye QC
Joint Registrars and Legal Secretaries, V. T. Jordan; P. F. B. Beesley
Diocesan Secretary, Miss S. Green, The Palace, Hereford HR4 9BL. Tel: 01432-353863

LEICESTER (CANTERBURY)

6TH BISHOP
Rt. Revd Timothy J. Stevens, *cons.* 1995, *apptd* 1999; Bishop's Lodge, 10 Springfield Road, Leicester LE2 3BD. *Signs* Timothy Leicester

STIPENDIARY ASSISTANT BISHOP
Vacant

PROVOST
Very Revd Vivienne F. Faull, *apptd* 2000

CANONS RESIDENTIARY
M. T. H. Banks, *apptd* 1988; M. Wilson, *apptd* 1988
Organist, J. T. Gregory, *apptd* 1994

ARCHDEACONS
Leicester, Ven. M. Edson, *apptd* 1994
Loughborough, Ven. I. Stanes, *apptd* 1992

Chancellor, vacant
Registrars and Legal Secretaries, P. C. E. Morris; R. H. Bloor
Diocesan Secretary, A. Howard; Church House, 3–5 St Martin's East, Leicester LE1 5FX. Tel: 0116-262 7445

LICHFIELD (Canterbury)

97TH BISHOP
Rt. Revd Keith N. Sutton, *cons.* 1978, *apptd* 1984; Bishop's House, The Close, Lichfield WS13 7LG. *Signs* Keith Lichfield

BISHOPS SUFFRAGAN
Shrewsbury, vacant
Stafford, Rt. Revd Christopher J. Hill, *cons.* 1996, *apptd* 1996; Ash Garth, Broughton Crescent, Barlaston, Staffs ST12 9DD
Wolverhampton, Rt. Revd Michael G. Bourke, *cons.* 1993, *apptd* 1993; 61 Richmond Road, Wolverhampton WV3 9JH

DEAN
Very Revd Michael Yorke, *apptd* 1999

CANONS RESIDENTIARY
A. N. Barnard, *apptd* 1977; C. W. Taylor, *apptd* 1995; Ven. C. F. Liley, *apptd* 2001
Organist, A. Lumsden, *apptd* 1992

ARCHDEACONS
Lichfield, Ven. C. F. Liley, *apptd* 2001
Salop, Ven . J. B. Hall, *apptd* 1998
Stoke-on-Trent, Ven. A. G. C. Smith, *apptd* 1997
Walsall, Ven. A. G. Sadler, *apptd* 1997

Chancellor, His Hon. Judge Shand
Registrar and Legal Secretary, J. P. Thorneycroft
Diocesan Secretary, D. R. Taylor, St Mary's House, The Close, Lichfield, Staffs WS13 7LD. Tel: 01543-306030

LINCOLN (Canterbury)

70TH BISHOP
Rt. Revd Robert M. Hardy, *cons.* 1980, *apptd* 1987; Bishop's House, Eastgate, Lincoln LN2 1QQ. *Signs* Robert Lincoln

BISHOPS SUFFRAGAN
Grantham, Rt. Revd Alastair L. J. Redfern, *cons.* 1997, *apptd* 1997; Fairacre, 234 Barrowby Road, Grantham, Lincs NG31 8NP
Grimsby, Rt. Revd David D. J. Rossdale, *cons.* 2000, *apptd* 2000; Bishop's House, Church Lane, Irby-upon-Humber, Grimsby DN37 7JR

DEAN
Very Revd Alexander F. Knight, *apptd* 1998

CANONS RESIDENTIARY
B. R. Davis, *apptd* 1977; A. J. Stokes, *apptd* 1992; V. White, *apptd* 1994
Organist, C. S. Walsh, FRCO, *apptd* 1988

ARCHDEACONS
Lincoln, Ven. A. Hawes, *apptd* 1995
Lindsey, Ven. Dr T. W. Ellis, *apptd* 2001
Stow, Ven. Dr T. W. Ellis, *apptd* 2001

Chancellor, Peter N. Collier, QC, *apptd* 1999
Registrar and Legal Secretary, D. M. Wellman
Diocesan Secretary, P. Hamlyn Williams, The Old Palace, Lincoln LN2 1PU. Tel: 01522-529241

LIVERPOOL (York)

7TH BISHOP
Rt. Revd James Jones, *cons.* 1994, *apptd* 1998; Bishop's Lodge, Woolton Park, Liverpool L25 6DT. *Signs* James Liverpool

BISHOP SUFFRAGAN
Warrington, Rt. Revd David Jennings; 34 Central Avenue, Eccleston Park, Prescot, Merseyside L34 2QP

DEAN
Rt. Revd Dean Dr Rupert W. N. Hoare

CANONS RESIDENTIARY
D. J. Hutton, *apptd* 1983; M. C. Boyling, *apptd* 1994; N. T. Vincent, *apptd* 1995
Organist, Prof. I. Tracey, *apptd* 1980

ARCHDEACONS
Liverpool, Ven. R. L. Metcalf, *apptd* 1994
Warrington, Ven. C. D. S. Woodhouse, *apptd* 1981

Chancellor, R. G. Hamilton
Registrar and Legal Secretary, R. H. Arden
Diocesan Secretary, Mike Eastwood, Church House, 1 Hanover Street, Liverpool L1 3DW. Tel: 0151-709 9722

MANCHESTER (York)

10TH BISHOP
Rt. Revd Christopher J. Mayfield, *cons.* 1985, *apptd* 1993; Bishopscourt, Bury New Road, Manchester M7 4LE. *Signs* Christopher Manchester

BISHOPS SUFFRAGAN
Bolton, Rt. Revd David K. Gillett, *cons.* 1999, *apptd* 1999; 4 Bishop's Lodge, Bolton Road, Hawkshaw, Bury BL8 4JN
Hulme, Rt. Revd Stephen R. Lowe, *cons.* 1999, *apptd.* 1999; 14 Moorgate Avenue, Withington, Manchester M20 1HE
Middleton, Rt. Revd Michael A. O. Lewis, *cons.* 1999, *apptd* 1999; The Hollies, Manchester Road, Rochdale OL11 3QY

DEAN
Very Revd Kenneth Riley, *apptd* 1993

CANONS RESIDENTIARY
J. R. Atherton, PH.D., *apptd* 1984; P. Denby, *apptd* 1995
Organist, C. Stokes, *apptd* 1992

ARCHDEACONS
Bolton, Ven. L. M. Davies, *apptd* 1992

Manchester, Ven A. Wolstencroft, *apptd* 1998
Rochdale, Ven. A. Ballard, *apptd* 2000

NEWCASTLE (York)

11TH BISHOP
Rt. Revd J. Martin Wharton, *cons.* 1992, *apptd* 1997; Bishop's House, 29 Moor Road South, Gosforth, Newcastle upon Tyne NE3 1PA. *Signs* Martin Newcastle

STIPENDIARY ASSISTANT BISHOP
Rt. Revd Paul Richardson, *cons.* 1987, *apptd* 1999

HON. ASSISTANT BISHOP
Rt. Revd K. E. Gill, *cons.* 1972, *apptd* 1998

PROVOST
Very Revd Nicholas G. Coulton, *apptd* 1990

CANONS RESIDENTIARY
P. R. Strange, *apptd* 1986; Ven. P. Elliott, *apptd* 1993; G. V. Miller, *apptd* 1999
Organist, T. G. Hone, FRCO, *apptd* 1987

ARCHDEACONS
Lindisfarne, Ven. R. Langley, *apptd* 2001
Northumberland, Ven. P. Elliott, *apptd* 1993

Chancellor, Prof. D. McClean, *apptd* 1998
Registrar and Legal Secretary, Mrs B. J. Lowdon
Diocesan Secretary, P. Davies, Church House, Grainger Park Road, Newcastle upon Tyne NE4 8SX. Tel: 0191-273 0120

NORWICH (Canterbury)

71ST BISHOP
Rt. Revd Graham R. James, *cons.* 1993, *apptd* 2000; Bishop's House, Norwich NR3 1SB. *Signs* Graham Norvic

BISHOPS SUFFRAGAN
Lynn, Rt. Revd A. C. Foottit, *cons.* 1999, *apptd* 1999; The Old Vicarage, Castle Acre, King's Lynn, Norfolk PE32 2AA.
Thetford, Rt. Revd David J. Atkinson, *cons.* 2001, *apptd* 2001; Rectory Meadow, Bramerton, Norwich NR14 7DW

DEAN
Very Revd Stephen Platten, *apptd* 1995

CANONS RESIDENTIARY
J. M. Haselock, *apptd* 1998; Ven. C. J. Offer, *apptd* 1994; R. J. Hanmer, *apptd* 1994; M. Kitchener, *apptd* 1999
Organist, D. Dunnett, *apptd* 1996

ARCHDEACONS
Lynn, Ven. M. C. Gray, *apptd* 1999
Norfolk, Ven. A. M. Handley, *apptd* 1993
Norwich, Ven. C. J. Offer, *apptd* 1994

Chancellor, The Hon. Mr Justice Blofeld, *apptd* 1998
Registrar and Legal Secretary, J. W. F. Herring
Diocesan Secretary, D. Adeney, Diocese House, 109 Dereham Road, Easton, Norwich, Norfolk NR9 5ES. Tel: 01603-880853

OXFORD (Canterbury)

41ST BISHOP
Rt. Revd Richard D. Harries, *cons.* 1987, *apptd* 1987;
Diocesan Church House, North Hinksey, Oxford OX2
0NB. *Signs* Richard Oxon

AREA BISHOPS
Buckingham, Rt. Revd Michael A. Hill *cons.* 1998, *apptd*
1998; 28 Church Street, Great Missenden, Bucks HP16
0AZ
Dorchester, Rt. Revd Colin Fletcher, *cons.* 2000, *apptd* 2000;
12 Sandy Lane, Yarnton, Oxon OX5 1PB
Reading, Rt. Revd Dominic Walker, *cons.* 1997, *apptd* 1997;
Bishop's House, Tidmarsh Lane, Tidmarsh, Reading
RG8 8HA

DEAN OF CHRIST CHURCH
Very Revd John H. Drury, *apptd* 1991

CANONS RESIDENTIARY
O. M. T. O'Donovan, D.Phil., *apptd* 1982; M. Parry, *apptd*
2001; J. S. K. Ward, *apptd* 1991; R. Jeffery, *apptd* 1996;
Prof. J. Webster, *apptd* 1996; Prof. H. M. R. E. Mayr-
Harting, *apptd* 1997; Ven. J. A. Morrison, *apptd* 1998; M.
Parry, *apptd* 2001
Organist, S. Darlington, FRCO, *apptd* 1985

ARCHDEACONS
Berkshire, Ven. N. A. Russell, *apptd* 1998
Buckingham, Ven. D. Goldie, *apptd* 1998
Oxford, Ven. J. A. Morrison, *apptd* 1998

Acting Chancellor, Dr Frank Robson, *apptd* 2001
Joint Registrars and Legal Secretaries, Dr F. E. Robson and
Revd. J. Rees
Diocesan Secretary, R. Pearce, Diocesan Church House,
North Hinksey, Oxford OX2 0NB. Tel: 01865-208202

PETERBOROUGH (Canterbury)

37TH BISHOP
Rt. Revd Ian P. M. Cundy, *cons.* 1992, *apptd* 1996; The
Palace, Peterborough PE1 1YA. *Signs* Ian Petriburg

BISHOP SUFFRAGAN
Brixworth, Rt. Revd Paul E. Barber, *cons.* 1989, *apptd* 1989;
4 The Avenue, Dallington, Northampton NN1 4RZ

DEAN
Very Revd Michael Bunker, *apptd* 1992

CANONS RESIDENTIARY
T. R. Christie, *apptd* 1980; J. Higham, *apptd* 1983; D.
Painter, *apptd* 2000; W. S. Croft, *apptd* 2001
Organist, C. S. Gower, FRCO, *apptd* 1977

ARCHDEACONS
Northampton, Ven. M. R. Chapman, *apptd* 1991
Oakham, Ven. D. Painter, *apptd* 2000

Chancellor, T. A. C. Coningsby, QC, *apptd* 1989
Registrar and Legal Secretary, R. Hemingray
Diocesan Secretary, R. L. Pestell, The Palace,
Peterborough, Cambs PE1 1YB. Tel: 01733-887000

PORTSMOUTH (Canterbury)

8TH BISHOP
Rt. Revd Dr Kenneth W. Stevenson, *cons.* 1995, *apptd*
1995; Bishopsgrove, 26 Osborn Road, Fareham, Hants
PO16 7DQ. *Signs* Kenneth Portsmouth

DEAN
The Very Revd Dr William H. Taylor, *apptd* 2000; The
Deanery, 13 Pembroke Road, Portsmouth PO1 2NS.

CANONS RESIDENTIARY
D. T. Isaac, *apptd* 1990; G. Kirk, *apptd* 1998
Organist, D. J. C. Price, *apptd* 1996

ARCHDEACONS
Isle of Wight, Ven. K. M. L. H. Banting, *apptd* 1996
Portsdown, Ven. C. Lowson, *apptd* 1999
The Meon, Ven. P. Hancock, *apptd* 1999

Chancellor, His Hon. Judge Aglionby, *apptd* 1978
Registrar and Legal Secretary, Miss H. A. G. Tyler
Diocesan Secretary, M. F. Jordan, Cathedral House, St
Thomas's Street, Portsmouth, Hants PO1 2HA. Tel: 023-
9282 5731

RIPON AND LEEDS (York)

12TH BISHOP
Rt. Revd John R. Packer, *apptd* 2000; Bishop Mount,
Ripon HG4 5DP. *Signs* John Ripon and Leeds

BISHOP SUFFRAGAN
Knaresborough, Rt. Revd Frank V. Weston, *cons.* 1997,
apptd 1997; 16 Shaftesbury Avenue, Roundhay, Leeds
LS8 1DT

DEAN
Very Revd John Methuen, *apptd* 1995

CANONS RESIDENTIARY
M. R. Glanville-Smith, *apptd* 1990; K. Punshon, *apptd*
1996
Organist, K. Beaumont, FRCO, *apptd* 1994

ARCHDEACONS
Leeds, Ven. J. M. Oliver, *apptd* 1992
Richmond, Ven. K. Good, *apptd* 1993
Chancellor, His Hon. Judge Grenfell, *apptd* 1992
Registrars and Legal Secretaries, C. T. Tunnard, Mrs N.
Harding
Diocesan Secretary, P. M. Arundel, Diocesan Office, St
Mary's Street, Leeds LS9 7DP. Tel: 0113-248 7487

ROCHESTER (Canterbury)

106TH BISHOP
Rt. Revd Dr Michael Nazir-Ali, *cons.* 1984, *apptd* 1994;
Bishopscourt, Rochester ME1 1TS. *Signs* Michael Roffen

BISHOP SUFFRAGAN
Tonbridge, Rt. Revd Brian A. Smith, *cons.* 1993, *apptd* 1993;
Bishop's Lodge, 48 St Botolph's Road, Sevenoaks TN13
3AG

DEAN
Very Revd Edward F. Shotter, *apptd* 1990

CANONS RESIDENTIARY
C. J. Meyrick, *apptd* 1998; Ven. P. Lock, *apptd* 2000
Organist, R. Sayer, FRCO, *apptd* 1995

ARCHDEACONS
Bromley, Ven. G. Norman, *apptd* 1994
Rochester, Ven. P. Lock, *apptd* 2000
Tonbridge, Ven. Judith Rose, *apptd* 1996

Chancellor, His Hon. Judge Goodman, *apptd* 1971
Registrar and Legal Secretary, M. Thatcher
Diocesan Secretary, Mrs L. Gilbert, St Nicholas Church, Boley Hill, Rochester ME1 1SL. Tel: 01634-830333

ST ALBANS (Canterbury)

9TH BISHOP
Rt. Revd Christopher W. Herbert, *cons.* 1995, *apptd* 1995; Abbey Gate House, St Albans AL3 4HD. *Signs* Christopher St Albans

BISHOPS SUFFRAGAN
Bedford, Rt. Revd John H. Richardson, *cons.* 1994, *apptd* 1994; 168 Kimbolton Road, Bedford MK41 8DN
Hertford, Rt. Revd Christopher R. J. Foster, *cons.* 2001, *apptd* 2001; Hertford House, Abbey Mill Lane, St Albans AL3 4HE

DEAN
Very Revd Christopher Lewis, *apptd* 1993

CANONS RESIDENTIARY
M. Sansom, *apptd* 1988; A. K. Bergquist, *apptd* 1997; I. R. Lane, *apptd* 2000
Organist, A. Lucas, *apptd* 1998

ARCHDEACONS
Bedford, Ven. M. L. Lesiter, *apptd* 1993
Hertford, Ven. T. P. Jones, *apptd* 1997
St Albans, Ven. R. I. Cheetham, *apptd* 1999

Chancellor, His Hon. Judge Bursell, QC, *apptd* 1992
Registrar and Legal Secretary, D. N. Cheetham
Diocesan Secretary, S. Pope, Holywell Lodge, 41 Holywell Hill, St Albans AL1 1HE. Tel: 01727-854532

ST EDMUNDSBURY AND IPSWICH (Canterbury)

9TH BISHOP
Rt. Revd J. H. Richard Lewis, *cons.* 1992, *apptd* 1997; Bishop's House, 4 Park Road, Ipswich IP1 3ST. *Signs* Richard St Edmundsbury and Ipswich

BISHOP SUFFRAGAN
Dunwich, Rt. Revd Clive Young, *cons.* 1999, *apptd* 1999; 28 Westerfield Road, Ipswich IP4 2UJ

DEAN
Very Revd J. Atwell, *apptd* 1995

CANONS RESIDENTIARY
A. M. Shaw, *apptd* 1989; M. E. Mingins, *apptd* 1993
Organist, J. Thomas, *apptd* 1997

ARCHDEACONS
Ipswich, Ven. T. A. Gibson, *apptd* 1987
Sudbury, Ven. J. Cox, *apptd* 1995

Suffolk, Ven. G. Arrand, *apptd* 1994

Chancellor, The Hon. Mr Justice Blofeld, *apptd* 1974
Registrar and Legal Secretary, J. Hall
Diocesan Secretary, N. Edgell, Churchgates House, Cutler Street, Ipswich IP1 1QU. Tel: 01473-298500

SALISBURY (Canterbury)

77TH BISHOP
Rt. Revd David S. Stancliffe, *cons.* 1993, *apptd* 1993; South Canonry, The Close, Salisbury SP1 2ER. *Signs* David Sarum

BISHOPS SUFFRAGAN
Ramsbury, Rt. Revd Peter F. Hullah, *cons.* 1999, *apptd* 1999
Sherborne, vacant

DEAN
Very Revd Derek Watson, *apptd* 1996

CANONS RESIDENTIARY
D. J. C. Davies, *apptd* 1985; D. M. K. Durston, *apptd* 1992; June Osborne, *apptd* 1995
Organist, S. R. A. Lole, *apptd* 1997

ARCHDEACONS
Dorset, Ven. A. J. Magowan, *apptd* 2000
Sherborne, Ven. P. C. Wheatley, *apptd* 1991
Wilts, Ven. B. J. Hopkinson, *apptd* 1986 (Sarum), 1998 (Wilts)

Chancellor, His Hon. Judge Wiggs, *apptd* 1997
Registrar and Legal Secretary, A. Johnson
Diocesan Secretary, Revd Karen Curnock, Church House, Crane Street, Salisbury SP1 2QB. Tel: 01722-411922

SHEFFIELD (York)

6TH BISHOP
Rt. Revd John (Jack) Nicholls, *cons.* 1990, *apptd* 1997; Bishopscroft, Snaithing Lane, Sheffield S10 3LG. *Signs* Jack Sheffield

BISHOP SUFFRAGAN
Doncaster, Rt. Revd Cyril Guy Ashton, *cons.* 2000, *apptd* 2000; Bishop's House, 3 Farrington Court, Wickersley, Rotherham S66 1JQ

DEAN
Very Revd Michael Sadgrove, *apptd* 1995

CANONS RESIDENTIARY
C. M. Smith, *apptd* 1991; Jane E. M. Sinclair, *apptd* 1993; Ven. R. F. Blackburn, *apptd* 1999
Master of Music, N. Taylor, *apptd* 1997

ARCHDEACONS
Doncaster, Ven. R. A. Fitzharris, *apptd* 2001
Sheffield, Ven. R. F. Blackburn, *apptd* 1999

Chancellor, Prof. J. D. McClean, *apptd* 1992
Registrar and Legal Secretary, Mrs M. Myers
Diocesan Secretary, C. A. Beck, FCIS, Diocesan Church House, 95–99 Effingham Street, Rotherham S65 1BL. Tel: 01709-511116

SODOR AND MAN (York)

79TH BISHOP
Rt. Revd Noel D. Jones, CB, *cons.* 1989, *apptd* 1989; The Bishop's House, Quarterbridge Road, Douglas, Isle of Man IM2 3RF. *Signs* Noel Sodor and Man

CANONS
B. H. Kelly, *apptd* 1980; F. H. Bird, *apptd* 1993; D. Whitworth, *apptd* 1996; M. Convery, *apptd* 1999

ARCHDEACON
Isle of Man, Ven. B. H. Partington, *apptd* 1996

Vicar-General and Chancellor, Ms C. Faulds
Registrar and Legal Secretary, C. J. Callow
Diocesan Secretary, Mrs C. Roberts, Holly Cottage, Ballaughton Meadows, Douglas, Isle of Man IM2 1JG. Tel: 01624-626994

SOUTHWARK (Canterbury)

9TH BISHOP
Rt. Revd Thomas F. Butler, *cons.* 1985, *apptd* 1998; Bishop's House, 38 Tooting Bec Gardens, London SW16 1QZ. *Signs* Thomas Southwark

AREA BISHOPS
Croydon, Rt. Revd Dr Wilfred D. Wood, DD, *cons.* 1985, *apptd* 1985; St Matthew's House, George Street, Croydon CR0 1PE
Kingston upon Thames, Rt. Revd Peter B. Price, *cons.* 1997, *apptd* 1998; *Kingston Episcopal Area Office*, Whitelands College, West Hill, London SW15 3SN
Woolwich, Rt. Revd Colin O. Buchanan, *cons.* 1985, *apptd* 1996; 37 South Road, Forest Hill, London SE23 2UJ

DEAN
Very Revd Colin B. Slee, *apptd* 1994

CANONS RESIDENTIARY
Helen Cunliffe, *apptd* 1995; J. John, *apptd* 1997; B. Saunders, *apptd* 1997; A. P. Nunn, *apptd* 1999; S. Roberts, *apptd* 2000
Organist, P. Wright, FRCO, *apptd* 1989

ARCHDEACONS
Croydon, Ven. V. A. Davies, *apptd* 1994
Lambeth, Ven. N. Baines, *apptd* 2000
Lewisham, Ven. Christine H. Ardman, *apptd* 2001
Reigate, Ven. Daniel Kajumba, *apptd* 2001
Southwark, Ven. D. L. Bartles-Smith, *apptd* 1985
Wandsworth, Ven. D. Gerrard, *apptd* 1989

Chancellor, C. George, QC
Registrar and Legal Secretary, P. Morris
Diocesan Secretary, S. Parton, Trinity House, 4 Chapel Court, Borough High Street, London SE1 1HW. Tel: 020-7403 8686

SOUTHWELL (York)

10TH BISHOP
Rt. Revd George H. Cassidy, *cons.* 1999, *apptd* 1999; Bishop's Manor, Southwell NG25 0JR. *Signs* George Southwell

BISHOP SUFFRAGAN
Sherwood, Rt. Revd Alan W. Morgan, *cons.* 1989, *apptd* 1989; Dunham House, Westgate, Southwell, Notts NG25 0JL

DEAN
Very Revd David Leaning, *apptd* 1991

CANONS RESIDENTIARY
I. G. Collins, *apptd* 1985; G. A. Hendy *apptd* 1997; R. H. Davey, *apptd* 1999
Organist, P. Hale, *apptd* 1989

ARCHDEACONS
Newark, Ven. N. Peyton, *apptd* 1999
Nottingham, Ven. G. Ogilvie, *apptd* 1996

Chancellor, J. Shand, *apptd* 1981
Registrar and Legal Secretary, C. C. Hodson
Diocesan Secretary, P. Prentis, Dunham House, Westgate, Southwell, Notts NG25 0JL. Tel: 01636-814331

TRURO (Canterbury)

14TH BISHOP
Rt. Revd William Ind, *cons.* 1987, *apptd* 1997; Lis Escop, Truro TR3 6QQ. *Signs* William Truro

BISHOP SUFFRAGAN
St Germans, Revd Royden Screech, *cons.* 2000, *apptd* 2000

DEAN
Very Revd Michael A. Moxon, LVO, *apptd* 1998

CANONS RESIDENTIARY
P. R. Gay, *apptd* 1994; K. P. Mellor, *apptd* 1994; P. A. A. Walker, *apptd* 2001
Organist, A. Nethsingha, FRCO, *apptd* 1994

ARCHDEACONS
Cornwall, Ven. R. D. C. Whiteman, *apptd* 2000
Bodmin, Ven. C. Cohen, *apptd* 2000

Chancellor, T. Briden, *apptd* 1998
Registrar and Legal Secretary, M. J. Follett
Diocesan Secretary, B. C. Laite, Diocesan House, Kenwyn, Truro TR1 1UQ. Tel: 01872-274351

WAKEFIELD (York)

11TH BISHOP
Rt. Revd Nigel S. McCulloch, *cons.* 1986, *apptd* 1992; Bishop's Lodge, Woodthorpe Lane, Wakefield WF2 6JL. *Signs* Nigel Wakefield

BISHOP SUFFRAGAN
Pontefract, Rt. Revd David C. James, *cons.* 1998, *apptd* 1998; Pontefract House, 181A Manygates Lane, Wakefield WF2 7DR

DEAN
Very Revd George P. Nairn-Briggs, *apptd* 1997

CANONS RESIDENTIARY
R. Capper, *apptd* 1997; R. Gage, *apptd* 1997; I. Gaskell, *apptd* 1998; J. Holmes, *apptd* 1998
Organist, J. Bielby, FRCO, *apptd* 1972

ARCHDEACONS
Halifax, Ven. R. Inwood, *apptd* 1995
Pontefract, Ven. A. Robinson, *apptd* 1997

Chancellor, P. Collier, QC, *apptd* 1992
Registrar and Legal Secretary, L. Box
Diocesan Secretary, A. W. Ellis, Church House, 1 South
Parade, Wakefield WF1 1LP. Tel: 01924-371802

WORCESTER (Canterbury)

112TH BISHOP
Rt. Revd Dr Peter S. M. Selby, *cons.* 1984, *apptd* 1997; The
Bishop's House, Hartlebury Castle, Kidderminster
DY11 7XX. *Signs* Peter Wigorn

AREA BISHOP
Dudley, Rt. Revd David S. Waker, *cons.* 2000, *apptd* 2000;
The Bishop's House, Bishop's Walk, Cradley Heath
B64 7JF

DEAN
Very Revd Peter J. Marshall, *apptd* 1997

CANONS RESIDENTIARY
B. B. Ruddock, *apptd.* 1999; J. D. Tetley, *apptd* 1999
Organist, A. Lucas, *apptd* 1996

ARCHDEACONS
Dudley, Ven. F. M. Trethewey, *apptd* 2001
Worcester, Ven. Dr J. D. Tetley

Chancellor, C. Mynors, *apptd* 1999
Registrar and Legal Secretary, M. Huskinson
Diocesan Secretary, R. Higham, The Old Palace,
Deansway, Worcester WR1 2JE. Tel: 01905-20537

ROYAL PECULIARS

WESTMINSTER
The Collegiate Church of St Peter
Dean, Very Revd Dr A. W. Carr, *apptd* 1997
Sub Dean and Archdeacon, D. H. Hutt, *apptd* 1995
Canons of Westminster, D. H. Hutt, *apptd* 1995; M. J.
Middleton, *apptd* 1997; R. Wright, *apptd* 1998; Dr N. T.
Wright, *apptd* 1999
Chapter Clerk and Receiver-General, Maj.-Gen. D. Burden,
CB, CBE, *apptd* 199, Chapter Office, 20 Dean's Yard,
London SW1P 3PA
Organist, J. O'Donnell, *apptd* 1999
Registrar, S. J. Holmes, MVO
Legal Secretary, C. Vyse, *apptd* 2000

WINDSOR
*The Queen's Free Chapel of St George within Her Castle of
Windsor*

Dean, Rt. Revd D. J. Conner, *apptd* 1998
Canons Residentiary, J. A. White, *apptd* 1982; L. F. P.
Gunner, *apptd* 1996; B. P. Thompson, PH.D., *apptd* 1998;
J. A. Ovenden, *apptd* 1998
Chapter Clerk, Lt.-Col. N. J. Newman, *apptd* 1990,
Chapter Office, The Cloisters, Windsor Castle,
Windsor, Berks SL4 1NJ
Organist, J. Rees-Williams, FRCO, *apptd* 1991

Other Anglican Churches

THE CHURCH IN WALES

The Anglican Church was the established church in Wales
from the 16th century until 1920, when the estrangement
of the majority of Welsh people from Anglicanism
resulted in disestablishment. Since then the Church in
Wales has been an autonomous province consisting of six
sees. The bishops are elected by an electoral college
comprising elected lay and clerical members, who also
elect one of the diocesan bishops as Archbishop of Wales.
The legislative body of the Church in Wales is the
Governing Body, which has 365 members divided
between the three orders of bishops, clergy and laity. Its
President is the Archbishop of Wales and it meets twice
annually. Its decisions are binding upon all members of the
Church. The Church's property and finances are the
responsibility of the Representative Body. There are about
96,000 members of the Church in Wales, with about 700
stipendiary clergy and 1,142 parishes.

THE GOVERNING BODY OF THE CHURCH IN WALES, 39
Cathedral Road, Cardiff CF1 9XF. Tel: 029-2023 1638.
Secretary-General, J. W. D. McIntyre

10TH ARCHBISHOP OF WALES, Most Revd Dr Rowan D.
Williams, *elected* 1999, installed 2000

BISHOPS
Bangor (79th), Rt. Revd F. J. Saunders Davies, *b.* 1937, *cons.*
2000, *elected* 1999; Ty'r Esgob, Bangor, Gwynedd LL57
2SS. *Signs* Saunders Bangor, *Stipendiary clergy*, 60
Llandaff (102nd), Rt. Revd Dr Barry C. Morgan, *b.* 1947,
cons. 1993, *elected* 1999; Llys Esgob, The Cathedral
Green, Llandaff, Cardiff CF5 2YE. *Signs* Barry Landav.
Stipendiary clergy, 164
Monmouth (8th), Most Revd Dr Rowan D. Williams, *b.*
1950, *cons.* 1992, *elected* 1992; Bishopstow, Stow Hill,
Newport NP20 4EA. *Signs* Rowan Cambrensis.
Stipendiary clergy, 106
St Asaph (74th), Rt. Revd John S. Davies, *b.* 1943, *cons.*
1999, *elected* 1999; Esgobty, St Asaph, Denbighshire
LL17 0TW. *Signs* John St Asaph. *Stipendiary clergy*, 112
St David's (126th), Rt. Revd D. Huw Jones, *b.* 1934, *cons.*
1993, *elected* 1995; Llys Esgob, Abergwili, Carmarthen
SA31 2JG. *Signs* Huw St Davids. *Stipendiary clergy*, 124
Swansea and Brecon (8th), Rt. Revd Anthony E. Pierce, *b.*
1941, *cons.* 1999, *elected* 1999; Ely Tower, Brecon,
Powys LD3 9DE. *Signs* Anthony Swansea *Stipendiary
clergy*, 86

The stipend of a diocesan bishop of the Church in Wales is
£26,674 a year from 1998

THE SCOTTISH EPISCOPAL CHURCH

The Scottish Episcopal Church was founded after the Act
of Settlement (1690) established the presbyterian nature of
the Church of Scotland. The Scottish Episcopal Church is
in full communion with the Church of England but is
autonomous. The governing authority is the General
Synod, an elected body of approximately 170 members
which meets once a year. The diocesan bishop who
convenes and presides at meetings of the General Synod is
called the Primus and is elected by his fellow bishops.
There are 48,385 members of the Scottish Episcopal

Church, of whom 30,988 are communicants. There are seven bishops, 457 serving clergy, and 327 churches and places of worship.

THE GENERAL SYNOD OF THE SCOTTISH EPISCOPAL CHURCH, 21 Grosvenor Crescent, Edinburgh EH12 5EE. Tel: 0131-225 6357. *Secretary-General*, J. F. Stuart

PRIMUS OF THE SCOTTISH EPISCOPAL CHURCH, Most Revd A. Bruce Cameron (Bishop of Aberdeen and Orkney), *elected* 2000

BISHOPS

Aberdeen and Orkney, A. Bruce Cameron, *b*. 1941, *cons*. 1992, *elected* 1992. *Clergy*, 53
Argyll and the Isles, Douglas M. Cameron, *b*. 1935, *cons*. 1993, *elected* 1992. *Clergy*, 24
Brechin, Neville Chamberlain, *b*. 1939, *cons*. 1997, *elected* 1997. *Clergy*, 30
Edinburgh, Brian Smith, *b*. 1943, *cons*. 1993, *elected* 2001. *Clergy*, 143
Glasgow and Galloway, Idris Jones, *b*. 1943, *cons*. 1998, *elected* 1998. *Clergy*, 105
Moray, Ross and Caithness, John Crook, *b*. 1940, *cons*. 1999, *elected* 1999. *Clergy*, 32
St Andrews, Dunkeld and Dunblane, Michael H. G. Henley, *b*. 1938, *cons*. 1995, *elected* 1995. *Clergy*, 70

The minimum stipend of a diocesan bishop of the Scottish Episcopal Church was £24,354 in 2001 (i.e. 1.5 × the minimum clergy stipend of £16,236)

THE CHURCH OF IRELAND

The Anglican Church was the established church in Ireland from the 16th century but never secured the allegiance of a majority of the Irish and was disestablished in 1871. The Church of Ireland is divided into the provinces of Armagh and Dublin, each under an archbishop. The provinces are subdivided into 12 dioceses. The legislative body is the General Synod, which has 660 members in total, divided between the House of Bishops and the House of Representatives. The Archbishop of Armagh is elected by the House of Bishops; other episcopal elections are made by an electoral college.
There are about 375,000 members of the Church of Ireland, with two archbishops, ten bishops, about 550 clergy and about 1,000 churches and places of worship.

CENTRAL OFFICE, Church of Ireland House, Church Avenue, Rathmines, Dublin 6. Tel: 00-353-1-4978422. *Chief Officer and Secretary of the Representative Church Body*, R. H. Sherwood; *Assistant Secretary of the General Synod*, V. F. Beatty

PROVINCE OF ARMAGH

ARCHBISHOP OF ARMAGH AND PRIMATE OF ALL IRELAND, Most Revd Robert H. A. Eames, PH.D., *b*. 1937, *cons*. 1975, *trans*. 1986. *Clergy*, 51

BISHOPS

Clogher, Brian D. A. Hannon, *b*. 1936, *cons*. 1986, *apptd* 1986. *Clergy*, 32
Connor, James E. Moore, *b*. 1933, *cons*. 1995, *apptd* 1995. *Clergy*, 106
Derry and Raphoe, James Mehaffey, PH.D., *b*. 1931, *cons*. 1980, *apptd* 1980. *Clergy*, 50
Down and Dromore, Harold C. Miller, *b*. 1950, *cons*. 1997, *apptd* 1997. *Clergy*, 109
Kilmore, Elphin and Ardagh, Kenneth H. Clarke, *b*. 1949, *cons* 2001, *apptd* 2001. *Clergy*, 24

Tuam, Killala and Achonry, Richard C. A. Henderson, *b*. 1957, *cons*. 1998, *apptd* 1998. *Clergy*, 12

PROVINCE OF DUBLIN

ARCHBISHOP OF DUBLIN, BISHOP OF GLENDALOUGH, AND PRIMATE OF IRELAND, Most Revd Walton N. F. Empey, *b*. 1934, *cons*. 1981, *trans*. 1985, 1996. *Clergy*, 90

BISHOPS

Cashel and Ossory, John R. W. Neill, *b*. 1945, *cons*. 1986, *trans*. 1997. *Clergy*, 37
Cork, Cloyne and Ross, W. Paul Colton, *b*. 1960, *cons*. 1999, *apptd* 1999. *Clergy*, 28
Limerick and Killaloe, Michael H. G. Mayes, *b*. 1941, *cons*. 1993, *apptd* 2000
Meath and Kildare, (Most Revd) Richard L. Clarke, PH.D., *b*. 1949, *cons*. 1996, *apptd* 1996. *Clergy*, 23

OVERSEAS

PRIMATES

PRIMATE AND PRESIDING BISHOP OF AOTEAROA, NEW ZEALAND AND POLYNESIA, Rt. Revd John Paterson (Bishop of Auckland), *cons*. 1995, *apptd* 1998
PRIMATE OF AUSTRALIA, Most Revd Peter Carnley (Archbishop of Perth), *cons*. 1981, *apptd* 2000
PRIMATE OF BRAZIL, Most Revd Glauco Soares de Lima (Bishop of São Paulo), *cons*. 1989, *apptd* 1994
ARCHBISHOP OF THE PROVINCE OF BURUNDI, Most Revd Samuel Ndayisenga (Bishop of Buye), *apptd* 1998
ARCHBISHOP AND PRIMATE OF CANADA, Most Revd Michael G. Peers, *cons*. 1977, *elected* 1986
ARCHBISHOP OF THE PROVINCE OF CENTRAL AFRICA, Most Revd Bernard A. Malango, *elected* 2000
PRIMATE OF THE CENTRAL REGION OF AMERICA, Most Revd Cornelius J. Wilson (Bishop of Costa Rica), *cons*. 1978, *apptd* 1998
ARCHBISHOP OF THE PROVINCE OF CONGO, Most Revd Patrice Byankya Njojo (Bishop of Boga), *cons*. 1980, *apptd* 1992
PRIMATE OF THE PROVINCE OF HONG KONG SHENG KUNG HUI, Most Revd Peter Kwong (Bishop of Hong Kong Island), *cons*.1981, *apptd* 1998
ARCHBISHOP OF THE PROVINCE OF THE INDIAN OCEAN, Most Revd Remi Rabenirina (Bishop of Antananarivo), *cons*. 1984, *apptd* 1995
PRESIDENT-BISHOP OF JERUSALEM AND THE MIDDLE EAST, Most Revd Iraj Mottahedeh, *apptd* 2000A
ARCHBISHOP OF THE PROVINCE OF KENYA, Most Revd Dr David M. Gitari (Bishop of Nairobi), *cons*. 1975, *apptd* 1996
ARCHBISHOP OF THE PROVINCE OF KOREA, Most Revd Paul Hwan Yoon (Bishop of Taejon), *cons*. 1987, *apptd* 2000
ARCHBISHOP OF THE PROVINCE OF MELANESIA, Most Revd Ellison L. Pogo (Bishop of Central Melanesia), *cons*. 1981, *apptd* 1994
ARCHBISHOP OF MEXICO, Most Revd Samuel Espinoza (Bishop of Western Mexico), *cons*. 1981, *elected* 1995
ARCHBISHOP OF THE PROVINCE OF MYANMAR, Most Revd Samuel San Si Htay (Bishop of Yangon), *cons*. *apptd* 2001
ARCHBISHOP OF THE PROVINCE OF NIGERIA, Most Revd Peter Akinola (Bishop of Abuja), *cons*. 1989, *apptd* 2000
PRIMATE OF NIPPON SEI KO KAI, Rt. Revd John Jun'Ichiro Furumoto (Bishop of Kobe), *elected* 2000
ARCHBISHOP OF PAPUA NEW GUINEA, Most Revd James Ayong (Bishop of Aipo Rongo), *cons*. 1995, *elected* 1996

PRIME BISHOP OF THE PHILIPPINES, Most Revd Ignacio C. Soliba, *cons.* 1991, *apptd* 1997

ARCHBISHOP OF THE PROVINCE OF RWANDA, Most Revd Emmanuel Kolini Mboni (Bishop of Kigali), *cons.* 1980, *apptd* 1997

PRIMATE OF THE PROVINCE OF SOUTH EAST ASIA, Most Revd Ping Chung Yong (Bishop of Sabah), *cons.* 1990 *apptd* 1999

METROPOLITAN OF THE PROVINCE OF SOUTHERN AFRICA, Most Revd Winston H. N. Ndungane (Archbishop of Cape Town), *cons.* 1991, *trans.* 1996

PRESIDING BISHOP OF THE SOUTHERN CONE OF AMERICA, Rt. Revd Maurice Sinclair (Bishop of Northern Argentina), *cons.* 1990

ARCHBISHOP OF THE PROVINCE OF THE SUDAN, Most Revd Joseph Marona (Bishop of Juba) *cons.*1984, *apptd* 2000

ARCHBISHOP OF THE PROVINCE OF TANZANIA, Most Revd Donald L. Mtetemela (Bishop of Ruaha), *cons.* 1982, *apptd* 1998

ARCHBISHOP OF THE PROVINCE OF UGANDA, Most Revd Livingstone Mpalanyi-Nkoyoyo. *cons.* 1980

PRESIDING BISHOP AND PRIMATE OF THE USA, Most Revd Frank T. Griswold III, *cons.* 1985, *apptd* 1997

ARCHBISHOP OF THE PROVINCE OF WEST AFRICA, Most Revd Robert Okine (Bishop of Koforidua), *cons.* 1981, *apptd* 1993

ARCHBISHOP OF THE PROVINCE OF THE WEST INDIES, Most Revd Drexel Gomez (Bishop of Nassau and the Bahamas), *cons.* 1972, *apptd* 1998

OTHER CHURCHES AND EXTRA-PROVINCIAL DIOCESES

ANGLICAN CHURCH OF BERMUDA, Rt. Revd Ewen Ratteray, *apptd* 1996

CHURCH OF CEYLON: This Church comes under the Metropolitical authority of the Archbishop of Canterbury.
Bishop of Colombo, Rt. Revd. Kenneth Michael James Fernando, *cons.* 1992
Bishop of Kurunagala, Rt. Revd Andrew O. Kumarage, *cons.* 1984

EPISCOPAL CHURCH OF CUBA, Rt. Revd Jorge Perera Hurtado, *apptd* 1995

LUSITANIAN CHURCH (*Portuguese Episcopal Church*), Rt. Revd Fernando da Luz Soares, *apptd* 1971

SPANISH REFORMED EPISCOPAL CHURCH, Rt. Revd Carlos Lozano Lopez, *apptd* 1995

EXTRA-PROVINCIAL TO PROVINCE IX OF THE EPISCOPAL CHURCH IN THE USA:
PUERTO RICO, Rt. Revd David Andres Alvarez-Velazquez, *cons.* 1987
VENEZUELA, Rt. Revd Orlando Guerrero, *cons.* 1995

MODERATORS OF CHURCHES IN FULL COMMUNION WITH THE ANGLICAN COMMUNION

CHURCH OF NORTH INDIA, Most Revd Zechariah J. Terom (Bishop of Chotanagpur), *apptd*

CHURCH OF SOUTH INDIA, Most Revd Joseph Samuel (Bishop of East Kerala), *cons.* 1990, *apptd* 2000

CHURCH OF PAKISTAN, Rt. Revd Samuel Azariah, Bishop of Raiwind

CHURCH OF BANGLADESH, Rt. Revd Barnabas Mondal, *cons.* 1975, *apptd* 1975

The Church of Scotland

The Church of Scotland is the established (i.e. national) church of Scotland. The Church is Reformed and evangelical in doctrine, and presbyterian in constitution, i.e. based on a hierarchy of councils of ministers and elders and, since 1990, of members of a diaconate. At local level the kirk session consists of the parish minister and ruling elders. At district level the presbyteries, of which there are 47, consist of all the ministers in the district, one ruling elder from each congregation, and those members of the diaconate who qualify for membership. The General Assembly is the supreme authority, and is presided over by a Moderator chosen annually by the Assembly. The Sovereign, if not present in person, is represented by a Lord High Commissioner who is appointed each year by the Crown.

The Church of Scotland has about 600,000 members, 1,200 ministers and 1,600 churches. There are about 100 ministers and other personnel working overseas.

Lord High Commissioner (2000), HRH The Prince of Wales
Moderator of the General Assembly (2001), The Rt. Revd John Miller
Principal Clerk, Revd F. A. J. Macdonald
Depute Clerk, Revd M. A. MacLean
Procurator, P. S. Hodge
Law Agent and Solicitor of the Church, Mrs J. S. Wilson
Parliamentary Agent, I. McCulloch (*London*)
General Treasurer, D. F. Ross
Secretary, Church and Nation Committee, Revd Dr D. Sinclair
CHURCH OFFICE, 121 George Street, Edinburgh EH2 4YN. Tel: 0131-225 5722

PRESBYTERIES AND CLERKS

Edinburgh, Revd W. P. Graham
West Lothian, Revd D. Shaw
Lothian, J. D. McCulloch

Melrose and Peebles, Revd J. H. Brown
Duns, Revd J. S. H. Cutler
Jedburgh, Revd A. D. Reid

Annandale and Eskdale, Revd C. B. Haston
Dumfries and Kirkcudbright, Revd G. M. A. Savage
Wigtown and Stranraer, Revd D. W. Dutton

Ayr, Revd J. Crichton
Irvine and Kilmarnock, Revd R. Travers (acting)
Ardrossan, Revd D. Broster

Lanark, Revd G. J. Elliott
Paisley, Revd D. Kay
Greenock, Revd D. Mill
Glasgow, Revd A. Cunningham
Hamilton, Revd J. H. Wilson
Dumbarton, Revd D. P. Munro
South Argyll, Revd M. A. J. Gossip
Dunoon, Revd R. Samuel
Lorn and Mull, Revd J. A. McCormick

Falkirk, Revd I. W. Black
Stirling, Revd G. G. Gringles

Dunfermline, Revd W. E. Farquhar
Kirkcaldy, Revd B. L. Tomlinson
St Andrews, Revd P. Meager

Dunkeld and Meigle, Revd B. Dempsey
Perth, Revd D. G. Lawson
Dundee, Revd J. A. Roy
Angus, Revd M. I. G. Rooney

Aberdeen, Revd A. M. Douglas

Kincardine and Deeside, Revd J. W. S. Brown
Gordon, Revd E. Glen
Buchan, Revd R. Neilson
Moray, Revd G. Melvyn Wood
Abernethy, Revd J. A. I. MacEwan
Inverness, Revd A. S. Younger
Lochaber, Revd A. Ramsay
Ross, Revd T. M. McWilliam
Sutherland, Revd J. L. Goskirk
Caithness, Mrs M. Gillies, MBE
Lochcarron/Skye, Revd A. I. Macarthur
Uist, Revd M. Smith
Lewis, Revd T. S. Sinclair
Orkney (Finstown), Revd T. Hunt
Shetland (Lerwick), Revd C. H. M.Greig
England (London), Revd W. A. Cairns
Europe (Geneva), Revd J. A. Cowie

The minimum stipend of a minister in the Church of Scotland in 2001 was £18,016

The Roman Catholic Church

The Roman Catholic Church is one world-wide Christian Church acknowledging as its head the Bishop of Rome, known as the Pope (Father). The Pope is held to be the successor of St Peter and thus invested with the power which was entrusted to St Peter by Jesus Christ. A direct line of succession is therefore claimed from the earliest Christian communities. With the fall of the Roman Empire the Pope also became an important political leader. His temporal power is now limited to the 107 acres of the Vatican City State.

The Pope exercises spiritual authority over the Church with the advice and assistance of the Sacred College of Cardinals, the supreme council of the Church. He is also advised about the concerns of the Church locally by his ambassadors, who liaise with the Bishops' Conference in each country.

In addition to advising the Pope, those members of the Sacred College of Cardinals who are under the age of 80 also elect a successor following the death of a Pope. The assembly of the Cardinals at the Vatican for the election of a new Pope is known as the Conclave in which, in complete seclusion, the Cardinals elect by a secret ballot; a two-thirds majority is necessary before the vote can be accepted as final. When a Cardinal receives the necessary votes, the Dean of the Sacred College formally asks him if he will accept election and the name by which he wishes to be known. On his acceptance of the office the Conclave is dissolved and the First Cardinal Deacon announces the election to the assembled crowd in St Peter's Square. On the first Sunday or Holyday following the election, the new Pope assumes the pontificate at High Mass in St Peter's Square. A new pontificate is dated from the assumption of the pontificate.

The number of cardinals was fixed at 70 by Pope Sixtus V in 1586, but has been steadily increased since the pontificate of John XXIII and at the end of July 2001 stood at 189, plus two cardinals created 'in pectore' (their names being kept secret by the Pope for fear of persecution; they are thought to be Chinese).

The Roman Catholic Church universally and the Vatican City State are run by the Curia, which is made up of the Secretariat of State, the Sacred Council for the Public Affairs of the Church, and various congregations, secretariats and tribunals assisted by commissions and

offices. The congregations are permanent commissions for conducting the affairs of the Church and are made up of cardinals, one of whom occupies the office of prefect. Below the Secretariat of State and the congregations are the secretariats and tribunals, all of which are headed by cardinals. (The Curial cardinals are analagous to ministers in charge of government departments.)

The Vatican State has its own diplomatic service, with representatives known as nuncios. Papal nuncios with full diplomatic recognition are given precedence over all other ambassadors to the country to which they are appointed; where precedence is not recognised the Papal representative is known as a pro-nuncio. Where the representation is only to the local churches and not to the government of a country, the Papal representative is known as an apostolic delegate. The Roman Catholic Church has an estimated 890.9 million adherents world-wide.

SOVEREIGN PONTIFF

His Holiness Pope John Paul II (Karol Wojtyla), *born* Wadowice, Poland, 18 May 1920; *ordained priest* 1946; *appointed Archbishop* of Kraków 1964; *created Cardinal* 1967; *assumed pontificate* 16 October 1978

SECRETARIAT OF STATE

Secretary of State, HE Cardinal Angelo Sodano
First Section (General Affairs), HE Cardinal G. Re (Archbishop of Vescovio)
Second Section (Relations with other states), Mgr J. L. Tauran (Archbishop of Telepte)

BISHOPS' CONFERENCE

The Roman Catholic Church in England and Wales is governed by the Bishops' Conference, membership of which includes the Diocesan Bishops, the Apostolic Exarch of the Ukrainians, the Bishop of the Forces and the Auxiliary Bishops. The Conference is headed by the President (*HE Cardinal Cormac M. O'Connor*) and Vice-President (*Archbishop Kelly*). There are five departments, each with an episcopal chairman: the Department for Christian Life and Worship (the Bishop of Menevia), the Department for Mission and Unity (the Bishop of Portsmouth), the Department for Catholic Education and Formation (the Bishop of Leeds), the Department for Christian Responsibility and Citizenship (the Bishop of East Anglia), and the Department for International Affairs (the Bishop of Leeds).

The Bishops' Standing Committee, made up of all the Archbishops and the chairman of each of the above departments, has general responsibility for continuity and policy between the plenary sessions of the Conference. It prepares the Conference agenda and implements its decisions. It is serviced by a General Secretariat. There are also agencies and consultative bodies affiliated to the Conference.

The Bishops' Conference of Scotland had until recently as its president the late Cardinal Winning of Glasgow and is the permanently constituted assembly of the Bishops of Scotland. To promote its work, the Conference establishes various agencies which have an advisory function in relation to the Conference. The more important of these agencies are called Commissions and each one has a Bishop President who, with the other members of the Commissions, are appointed by the Conference.

The Irish Episcopal Conference has as its president Archbishop Brady of Armagh. Its membership comprises all the Archbishops and Bishops of Ireland and it appoints various Commissions to assist it in its work. There are three types of Commissions: (a) those made up of lay and clerical members chosen for their skills and experience, and staffed by full-time expert secretariats; (b) Commissions whose members are selected from existing institutions and whose services are supplied on a part-time basis; and (c) Commissions of Bishops only.

The Roman Catholic Church in Britain and Ireland has an estimated 8,992,000 members, 11 archbishops, 67 bishops, 11,260 priests, and 8,588 churches and chapels open to the public.

Bishops' Conferences secretariats:

ENGLAND AND WALES, 39 Eccleston Square, London SW1V 1PD. Tel: 020-7630 8220; Fax: 020-7630 5166; Email: secretariat@cbcew.org.uk; Web: www.catholic-ew.org.uk. *General Secretary*, The Revd Andrew Summersgill

SCOTLAND, 64 Aitken Street, Airdrie, Lanarkshire ML6 6LT. *General Secretary*, Mgr Henry Docherty

IRELAND, Iona, 65 Newry Road, Dundalk, Co. Louth. *Executive Secretaries*, Revd Aidan O'Boyle; The Rt. Revd William Lee (Bishop of Waterford and Lismore)

GREAT BRITAIN

APOSTOLIC NUNCIO TO GREAT BRITAIN
The Most Revd Pablo Puente, 54 Parkside, London SW19 5NE. Tel: 020-8946 1410

ENGLAND AND WALES

THE MOST REVD ARCHBISHOPS
Westminster, H. E. Cardinal Cormac Murphy-O'Connor, *cons.* 1977, *apptd* 2000
Auxiliaries, James J. O'Brien, *cons.* 1977; Patrick O'Donoghue, *cons.* 1993; Arthur Roche, *cons* 2001; George Stack, *cons* 2001
Clergy, 762
Archbishop's Residence, Archbishop's House, Ambrosden Avenue, London SW1P 1QJ. Tel: 020-7798 9033
Birmingham, Vincent Nichols, *cons.* 1992, *apptd* 2000
Auxiliaries, Philip Pargeter, *cons.* 1990
Clergy, 511
Diocesan Curia, Cathedral House, St Chad's Queensway, Birmingham B4 6EX. Tel: 0121-236 5535
Cardiff, John A. Ward, *cons.* 1980, *apptd* 1983 (*The Rt Revd Edwin Regan has been appointed at present as apostolic administrator whilst the Archbishop recovers from illness*)
Clergy, 126
Diocesan Curia, Archbishop's House, 41–43 Cathedral Road, Cardiff CF1 9HD. Tel: 029-2022 0411
Liverpool, Patrick Kelly, *cons.* 1984, *apptd* 1996
Auxiliary, Vincent Malone, *cons.* 1989
Clergy, 522
Diocesan Curia, Archdiocese of Liverpool, Centre for Evengelisation, Croxteth Drive, Sefton Park, Liverpool L17 1AA. Tel: 0151-522 1000
Southwark, Michael Bowen, *cons.* 1970, *apptd* 1977
Auxiliaries, John Hine, *cons.* 2001; Howard Tripp, *cons.* 1980; John Jukes, *cons.* 1980
Clergy, 518
Diocesan Curia, Archbishop's House, 150 St George's Road, London SE1 6HX. Tel: 020-7928 5592

THE RT. REVD BISHOPS
Arundel and Brighton, Kieran Conry, *cons.* 2001
Clergy, 274. *Diocesan Curia*, Bishop's House, The Upper Drive, Hove, E. Sussex BN3 6NE. Tel: 01273-506387
Brentwood, Thomas McMahon, *cons.* 1980, *apptd* 1980. *Clergy*, 175. *Bishop's Office*, Cathedral House, Ingrave Road, Brentwood, Essex CM15 8AT. Tel: 01277-232266

Clifton, Declan Lang, *cons.* 2001. *Clergy*, 254. *Diocesan Curia*, Egerton Road, Bishopston, Bristol BS7 8HU. Tel: 0117-983 3907
East Anglia, Peter Smith, *cons.* 1995, *apptd* 1995. *Clergy*, 164. *Diocesan Curia*, The White House, 21 Upgate, Poringland, Norwich NR14 7SH. Tel: 01508-492202
Hallam, John Rawsthorne, *cons.* 1981, *apptd* 1997. *Clergy*, 91. *Bishop's Residence*, 'Quarters', Carsick Hill Way, Sheffield S10 3LY. Tel: 0114-230 9101
Hexham and Newcastle, Michael Ambrose Griffiths, *cons.* 1992. *Clergy*, 261. *Diocesan Curia*, Bishop's House, East Denton Hall, 800 West Road, Newcastle upon Tyne NE5 2BJ. Tel: 0191-228 0003
Lancaster, Patrick O'Donoghue, *cons.* 2001
Clergy, 248. *Bishop's Residence*, Bishop's House, Cannon Hill, Lancaster LA1 5NG. Tel: 01524-32231
Leeds, David Konstant, *cons.* 1977, *apptd* 1985. *Clergy*, 254. *Diocesan Curia*, Hinsley Hall, 62 Headingley Lane, Leeds LS6 2BU. Tel: 0113-261 8000
Menevia (*Wales*), Mark Jabalé, *cons.* 2001. *Clergy*, 60. *Diocesan Curia*, 27 Convent Street, Greenhill, Swansea SA1 2BX. Tel: 01792-644017
Middlesbrough, John Crowley, *cons.* 1986, *apptd* 1992. *Clergy*, 182. *Diocesan Curia*, 50A The Avenue, Linthorpe, Middlesbrough, Cleveland TS5 6QT. Tel: 01642-850505
Northampton, Kevin McDonald, *cons.* 2001. *Clergy*, 159. *Diocesan Curia*, Bishop's House, Marriott Street, Northampton NN2 6AW. Tel: 01604-715635
Nottingham, Malcolm McMahon, *cons.* 2000. *Clergy*, 214. *Diocesan Curia*, Willson House, Derby Road, Nottingham NG1 5AW. Tel: 0115-953 9800
Plymouth, Christopher Budd, *cons.* 1986. *Clergy*, 170. *Diocesan Curia*, Bishop's House, 31 Wyndham Street West, Plymouth PL1 5RZ. Tel: 01752-224414
Portsmouth, F. Crispian Hollis, *cons.* 1987, *apptd* 1989. *Clergy*, 282. *Bishop's Residence*, Bishop's House, Edinburgh Road, Portsmouth, Hants PO1 3HG. Tel: 023-9282 0894
Salford, Terence J. Brain, *cons.* 1991, *apptd* 1997. *Clergy*, 380. *Diocesan Curia*, Cathedral House, 250 Chapel Street, Salford M3 5LL. Tel: 0161-834 9052
Shrewsbury, Brian Noble, *cons.* 1995, *apptd* 1995. *Clergy* 202. *Diocesan Curia*, 2 Park Road South, Prenton, Wirral CH43 4UX. Tel: 0151-652 9855
Wrexham (*Wales*), Edwin Regan, *apptd* 1994. *Clergy*, 83. *Diocesan Curia*, Bishop's House, Sontley Road, Wrexham, Clwyd LL13 7EW. Tel: 01978-262726

SCOTLAND
THE MOST REVD ARCHBISHOPS
St Andrews and Edinburgh, Keith Patrick O'Brien, *cons.* 1985
Clergy, 188
Diocesan Curia, 113 Whitehouse Loan, Edinburgh EH9 1BD. Tel: 0131-452 8244
Glasgow, awaiting appointment
Clergy, 257
Diocesan Curia, 196 Clyde Street, Glasgow G1 4JY. Tel: 0141-226 5898

THE RT. REVD BISHOPS
Aberdeen, Mario Conti, *cons.* 1977. *Clergy*, 54. *Bishop's Residence*, 3 Queen's Cross, Aberdeen AB2 6BR. Tel: 01224-319154
Argyll and the Isles, Ian Murray, *cons.* 1999. *Clergy*, 33. *Diocesan Curia*, St Columba's Cathedral, Esplanade, Oban, Argyll PA34 5AB. Tel: 01631-571003
Dunkeld, Vincent Logan, *cons.* 1981. *Clergy*, 52. *Diocesan Curia*, 29 Roseangle, Dundee DD1 4LR. Tel: 01382-25453

Galloway, Maurice Taylor, *cons.* 1981. *Clergy*, 59. *Diocesan Curia*, 8 Corsehill Road, Ayr KA7 2ST. Tel: 01292-266750

Motherwell, Joseph Devine, *cons.* 1977, *apptd* 1983. *Clergy*, 163. *Diocesan Curia*, Coursington Road, Motherwell ML1 1PW. Tel: 01698-269114

Paisley, John A. Mone, *cons.* 1984, *apptd* 1988. *Clergy*, 87. *Diocesan Curia*, Cathedral House, 8 East Buchanan Street, Paisley, Renfrewshire PA1 1HS. Tel: 0141-889 3601

BISHOPRIC OF THE FORCES

Francis Walmsley, *cons.* 1979. Administration: AGPDO, Middle Hill, Aldershot, Hants GU11 1PP. Tel: 01252-349004

IRELAND

There is one hierarchy for the whole of Ireland. Several of the dioceses have territory partly in the Republic of Ireland and partly in Northern Ireland.

APOSTOLIC NUNCIO TO IRELAND

Most Revd Giovanni Ceirano (titular Archbishop of Tigimma), 183 Navan Road, Dublin 7. Tel: (00 353) (1) 380577

THE MOST REVD ARCHBISHOPS

Armagh, Sean Brady, *cons.* 1995, *apptd* 1996
Auxiliary, Gerard Clifford, *cons.* 1991
Clergy, 183
Diocesan Curia, Ara Coeli, Armagh BT61 7QY. Tel: 028-3752 2045

Cashel, Dermot Clifford, *cons.* 1986, *apptd* 1988
Clergy, 136
Archbishop's Residence, Archbishop's House, Thurles, Co. Tipperary. Tel: (00 353) (504) 21512

Dublin, H. E. Cardinal Desmond Connell, *cons.* 1988, *apptd* 1988
Auxiliaries, James Moriarty, *cons.* 1991; Eamonn Walsh, *cons.* 1990; Fiachra O'Ceallaigh, *cons* 1994; Martin Drennan, *cons.* 1997; Raymond Field, *cons.* 1997
Clergy, 994
Archbishop's Residence, Archbishop's House, Drumcondra, Dublin 9. Tel: (00 353) (1) 8373732

Tuam, Michael Neary, *cons.* 1992, *apptd* 1995
Clergy, 180
Archbishop's Residence, Archbishop's House, Tuam, Co. Galway. Tel: (00 353) (93) 24166

THE MOST REVD BISHOPS

Achonry, Thomas Flynn, *cons.* 1975. *Clergy*, 62. *Bishop's Residence*, Bishop's House, Ballaghadaderreen, Co. Roscommon. Tel: (00 353) (907) 60021

Ardagh and Clonmacnois, Colm O'Reilly, *cons.* 1983. *Clergy*, 100. *Diocesan Office*, Bishop's House, St Michael's, Longford, Co. Longford. Tel: (00 353) (43) 46432

Clogher, Joseph Duffy, *cons.* 1979. *Clergy*, 108. *Bishop's Residence*, Bishop's House, Monaghan. Tel: (00 353) (47) 81019

Clonfert, John Kirby, *cons.* 1988. *Clergy*, 71. *Bishop's Residence*, St Brendan's, Coorheen, Loughrea, Co. Galway. Tel: (00 353) (91) 41560

Cloyne, John Magee, *cons.* 1987. *Clergy*, 158. *Diocesan Centre*, Cobh, Co. Cork. Tel: (00 353) (21) 811430

Cork and Ross, John Buckley, *cons.* 1984, *apptd* 1998. *Clergy*, 338. *Diocesan Office*, Bishop's House, Redemption Road, Cork. Tel: (00 353) (21) 301717

Derry, Seamus Hegarty, *cons.* 1984, *apptd* 1994. *Clergy*, 157. *Bishop's Residence*, Bishop's House, St Eugene's Cathedral, Derry BT48 9AP. Tel: 028-7126 2302
Auxiliary, Francis Lagan, *cons.* 1988

Down and Connor, Patrick J. Walsh, *cons.* 1983, *apptd* 1991. *Clergy*, 248. *Bishop's Residence*, Lisbreen, 73 Somerton Road, Belfast, Co. Antrim BT15 4DE. Tel: 028-9077 6185
Auxiliaries, *Anthony Farquhar*, cons. *1983; Michael Dallat*, cons. *1994*

Dromore, John McAreavey, *cons.* 1999. *Clergy*, 78. *Bishop's Residence*, Bishop's House, Violet Hill, Newry, Co. Down BT35 6PN. Tel: 028-3026 2444

Elphin, Christopher Jones, *cons.* 1994. *Clergy*, 101. *Bishop's Residence*, St Mary's, Sligo. Tel: (00 353) (71) 62670

Ferns, Brendon Comiskey, *cons.* 1980. *Clergy*, 161. *Bishop's Office*, Bishop's House, Summerhill, Wexford. Tel: (00 353) (53) 22177

Galway and Kilmacduagh, James McLoughlin, *cons.* 1993. *Clergy*, 90. *Diocesan Office*, The Cathedral, Galway. Tel: (00 353) (91) 63566

Kerry, William Murphy, *cons.* 1995. *Clergy*, 149. *Bishop's Residence*, Bishop's House, Killarney, Co. Kerry. Tel: (00 353) (64) 31168

Kildare and Leighlin, Laurence Ryan, *cons.* 1984. *Clergy*, 136. *Bishop's Residence*, Bishop's House, Carlow. Tel: (00 353) (503) 31102

Killala, Thomas Finnegan, *cons.* 1970. *Clergy*, 62. *Bishop's Residence*, Bishop's House, Ballina, Co. Mayo. Tel: (00 353) (96) 21518

Killaloe, William Walsh, *cons.* 1994. *Clergy*, 149. *Bishop's Residence*, Westbourne, Ennis, Co. Clare. Tel: (00 353) (65) 28638

Kilmore, Leo O'Reilly, *cons.* 1972, *apptd* 2000. *Clergy*, 115. *Bishop's Residence*, Bishop's House, Cullies, Co. Cavan. Tel: (00 353) (49) 31496

Limerick, Donal Murray, *cons.* 1996. *Clergy*, 152. *Diocesan Offices*, 66 O'Connell Street, Limerick. Tel: (00 353) (61) 315856

Meath, Michael Smith, *cons.* 1984, *apptd* 1990. *Clergy*, 141. *Bishop's Residence*, Bishop's House, Dublin Road, Mullingar, Co. Westmeath. Tel: (00 353) (44) 48841

Ossory, Laurence Forristal, *cons.* 1980. *Clergy*, 111. *Bishop's Residence*, Sion House, Kilkenny. Tel: (00 353) (56) 62448

Raphoe, Philip Boyce, *cons.* 1995. *Clergy*, 96. *Bishop's Residence*, Ard Adhamhnáin, Letterkenny, Co. Donegal. Tel: (00 353) (74) 21208

Waterford and Lismore, William Lee, *cons.* 1993. *Clergy*, 130. *Bishop's Residence*, Woodleigh, Summerville Avenue, Waterford. Tel: (00 353) (51) 71432

PATRIARCHS IN COMMUNION WITH THE ROMAN CATHOLIC CHURCH

Alexandria, HB Cardinal Stephanos II Ghattas (Patriarch for Catholic Copts)

Antioch, HB Ignace Antoine II Hayek (Patriarch for Syrian rite Catholics); HB Maximos V. Hakim (Patriarch for Greek Melekite rite Catholics); HE Cardinal Nasrallah Pierre Sfeir (Patriarch for Maronite rite Catholics)

Jerusalem, HB Michel Sabbah (Patriarch for Latin rite Catholics); HB Maximos V. Hakim (Patriarch for Greek Melekite rite Catholics)

Babilonia of the Chaldeans, HB Raphael I Bidawid

Cilicia of the Armenians, HB Jean Pierre XVIII Kasparian (Patriarch for Armenian rite Catholics)

Oriental India, Archbishop Raul Nicolau Gonsalves

Lisbon, vacant

Venice, HE Cardinal Marco Ce

Other Churches in the UK

AFRICAN AND AFRO-CARIBBEAN CHURCHES

There are more than 160 Christian churches or groups of African or Afro-Caribbean origin in the UK. These include the Apostolic Faith Church, the Cherubim and Seraphim Church, the New Testament Church Assembly, the New Testament Church of God, the Wesleyan Holiness Church and the Aladura Churches.

The Afro-West Indian United Council of Churches and the Council of African and Afro-Caribbean Churches UK (which was initiated as the Council of African and Allied Churches in 1979 to give one voice to the various Christian churches of African origin in the UK) are the media through which the member churches can work jointly to provide services they cannot easily provide individually.

There are about 70,000 adherents of African and Afro-Caribbean churches in the UK, and over 1,000 congregations. The Afro-West Indian United Council of Churches has about 30,000 individual members, 135 ministers and own over 100 places of worship. The Council of African and Afro-Caribbean Churches UK has about 17,000 members, 250 ministers and 125 congregations.

AFRO-WEST INDIAN UNITED COUNCIL OF CHURCHES, c/o New Testament Church of God, Arcadian Gardens, High Road, London N22 5AA. Tel: 020-8888 9427. *Secretary*, Bishop E. Brown

COUNCIL OF AFRICAN AND AFRO-CARIBBEAN CHURCHES UK, 31 Norton House, Sidney Road, London SW9 0UJ. Tel: 020-7274 5589; Fax: 020-7274 4726. *Chairman*, His Grace The Most Revd Father Olu A. Abiola

ASSOCIATED PRESBYTERIAN CHURCHES OF SCOTLAND

The Associated Presbyterian Churches came into being in 1989 as a result of a division within the Free Presbyterian Church of Scotland. Following two controversial disciplinary cases, the culmination of deepening differences within the Church, a presbytery was formed calling itself the Associated Presbyterian Churches (APC). The Associated Presbyterian Churches has about 1,000 members, 15 ministers and 20 churches.

Clerk of the Scottish Presbytery, Revd A. N. McPhail, Fernhill, Polvinster Road, Oban PA34 5TN. Tel: 01631-567076

THE BAPTIST CHURCH

Baptists trace their origins to John Smyth, who in 1609 in Amsterdam reinstituted the baptism of conscious believers as the basis of the fellowship of a gathered church. Members of Smyth's church established the first Baptist church in England in 1612. They came to be known as 'General' Baptists and their theology was Arminian, whereas a later group of Calvinists who adopted the baptism of believers came to be known as 'Particular' Baptists. The two sections of the Baptists were united into one body, the Baptist Union of Great Britain and Ireland, in 1891. In 1988 the title was changed to the Baptist Union of Great Britain.

Baptists emphasise the complete autonomy of the local church, although individual churches are linked in various kinds of associations. There are international bodies (such as the Baptist World Alliance) and national bodies, but some Baptist churches belong to neither. However, in Great Britain the majority of churches and associations belong to the Baptist Union of Great Britain. There are also Baptist Unions in Wales, Scotland and Ireland which are much smaller than the Baptist Union of Great Britain, and there is some overlap of membership.

There are over 40 million Baptist church members world-wide; in the Baptist Union of Great Britain there are 144,056 members, 1,756 pastors and 2,125 churches. In the Baptist Union of Scotland there are 14,463 members, 156 pastors and 171 churches. In the Baptist Union of Wales (Undeb Bedyddwyr Cymru) there are 19,850 members, 106 pastors and 498 churches. In the Association of Baptist Churches (formerly the Baptist Union of Ireland) there are 8,436 members, 94 pastors and 111 churches.

President of the Baptist Union of Great Britain (2001–2), Revd Peter Worley

General Secretary, Revd D. R. Coffey, Baptist House, PO Box 44, 129 Broadway, Didcot, Oxon OX11 8RT. Tel: 01235-517700; Email: baptistuniongb@baptist.org.uk; Web: www.baptist.org.uk

President of the Baptist Union of Scotland (2001–2) Revd John Greenshields

General Secretary, Revd William Slack, 14 Aytoun Road, Glasgow G41 5RT. Tel: 0141-423 6169; fax: 0141-424 1422; Email; admin@scottishbaptist.org.uk

General Secretary of the Baptist Union of Wales, Revd P. D. Richards, 94 Stryd Mansel, Swansea SA1 5TZ. Tel: 01792-655468

General Secretary of the Association of Baptist Churches in Ireland, Revd W. Colville, 117 Lisburn Road, Belfast BT9 7AF. Tel: 028-9066 3108

THE CONGREGATIONAL FEDERATION

The Congregational Federation was founded by members of Congregational churches in England and Wales who did not join the United Reformed Church in 1972. There are also churches in Scotland, France and Australia affiliated to the Federation. The Federation exists to encourage congregations of believers to worship in free assembly, but it has no authority over them and emphasises their right to independence and self-government.

The Federation has 11,104 members, 71 recognised ministers and 313 churches in England, Wales and Scotland.

President of the Federation (2001–2), Revd Barry Osborne

General Secretary, Revd. M. Heaney, The Congregational Centre, 4–8 Castle Gate, Nottingham NG1 7AS. Tel: 0115-911 1460

THE FREE CHURCH OF ENGLAND

The Free Church of England is a union of two bodies in the Anglican tradition, the Free Church of England, founded in 1844 as a protest against the Oxford Movement in the established Church, and the Reformed Episcopal Church, founded in America in 1873 but which also had congregations in England. As both Churches sought to maintain the historic faith, tradition and practice of the Anglican Church since the Reformation, they decided to unite as one body in England in 1927. The historic episcopate was conferred on the English Church in 1876 through the line of the American bishops, who had pioneered an open table Communion policy towards members of other denominations.

The Free Church of England has 1,400 members, 41 ministers and 25 churches in England. It also has three house churches and three ministers in New Zealand and one church and one minister in St Petersburg, Russia.

General Secretary, Revd R. E. Talbot, 32 Bonnywood Road, Hassocks, W. Sussex BN6 8HR. Tel: 01273-845092

THE FREE CHURCH OF SCOTLAND

The Free Church of Scotland was formed in 1843 when over 400 ministers withdrew from the Church of Scotland as a result of interference in the internal affairs of the church by the civil authorities. In 1900, all but 26 ministers joined with others to form the United Free Church (most of which rejoined the Church of Scotland in 1929). In 1904 the remaining 26 ministers were recognised by the House of Lords as continuing the Free Church of Scotland.

The Church maintains strict adherence to the Westminster Confession of Faith (1648) and accepts the Bible as the sole rule of faith and conduct. Its General Assembly meets annually. It also has links with Reformed Churches overseas. The Free Church of Scotland has 4,600 communicating members, 90 ministers and 110 churches.

General Treasurer, I. D. Gill, The Mound, Edinburgh EH1 2LS. Tel: 0131-226 5286

THE FREE PRESBYTERIAN CHURCH OF SCOTLAND

The Free Presbyterian Church of Scotland was formed in 1893 by two ministers of the Free Church of Scotland who refused to accept a Declaratory Act passed by the Free Church General Assembly in 1892. The Free Presbyterian Church of Scotland is Calvinistic in doctrine and emphasises observance of the Sabbath. It adheres strictly to the Westminster Confession of Faith of 1648.

The Church has about 3,000 members in Scotland and about 4,000 in overseas congregations. It has 19 ministers and 50 churches in the UK.

Moderator, Revd D. J. MacDonald, Free Presbyterian Manse, Evelix, Dornoch, Sutherland IV25 3RD. Tel: 01862-811 138

Clerk of Synod, Revd J. MacLeod, 16 Matheson Road, Stornoway, Isle of Lewis HS1 2LA. Tel: 01851-702755

THE HOLY APOSTOLIC CATHOLIC ASSYRIAN CHURCH OF THE EAST

The Holy Apostolic Catholic Assyrian Church of the East traces its beginnings to the middle of the first century. It spread from Upper Mesopotamia throughout the territories of the Persian Empire. The Church is headed by the Catholicos Patriarch and is episcopal in government. The liturgical language is Syriac (Aramaic).

The Church numbers about 400,000 members in the Middle East, India, Europe, North America and Australasia. There are around 1,000 members in the UK

The Church in Great Britain forms part of the diocese of Europe under Mar Odisho Oraham.

Representative in Great Britain, Very Revd Younan Y. Younan, 66 Montague Road, London W7 3PQ. Tel: 020-8579 7259.

THE INDEPENDENT METHODIST CHURCHES

The Independent Methodist Churches seceded from the Wesleyan Methodist Church in 1805 and remained independent when the Methodist Church in Great Britain was formed in 1932. They are mainly concentrated in the industrial areas of the north of England.

The churches are Methodist in doctrine but their organisation is congregational. All the churches are members of the Independent Methodist Connexion of Churches. The controlling body of the Connexion is the Annual Meeting, to which churches send delegates. The Connexional President is elected annually. Between annual meetings the affairs of the Connexion are handled by departmental committees. Ministers are appointed by the churches and trained through the Connexion. The ministry is open to both men and women and is unpaid.

There are 2,552 members, 108 ministers and 96 churches in Great Britain.

Connexional President (2001–2), C. Scholes

General Secretary, W. C. Gabb, 66 Kirkstone Drive, Loughborough LE11 3RW. Tel: 01942-223526

THE LUTHERAN CHURCH

Lutheranism is based on the teachings of Martin Luther, the German leader of the Protestant Reformation. The authority of the scriptures is held to be supreme over Church tradition and creeds, and the key doctrine is that of justification by faith alone.

Lutheranism is one of the largest Protestant denominations and it is particularly strong in northern Europe and the USA. Some Lutheran churches are episcopal, while others have a synodal form of organisation; unity is based on doctrine rather than structure. Most Lutheran churches are members of the Lutheran World Federation, based in Geneva.

Lutheran services in Great Britain are held in seventeen languages to serve members of different nationalities. Services usually follow ancient liturgies. English-language congregations are members either of the Lutheran Church in Great Britain, or of the Evangelical Lutheran Church of England. The Lutheran Church in Great Britain and other Lutheran churches in Britain are members of the Lutheran Council of Great Britain, which represents them and co-ordinates their common work.

There are over 70 million Lutherans world-wide; in Great Britain there are about 100,000 members, 50 clergy and 100 congregations.

General Secretary of the Lutheran Council of Great Britain, Revd T. Bruch, 30 Thanet Street, London WC1H 9QH. Tel: 020-7554 2900; Fax 020-7383 3081; Email: enquiries@lutheran.org.uk Web: www.lutheran.org.uk

THE METHODIST CHURCH

The Methodist movement started in England in 1729 when the Revd John Wesley, an Anglican priest, and his brother Charles met with others in Oxford and resolved to conduct their lives and study by 'rule and method'. In 1739 the Wesleys began evangelistic preaching and the first Methodist chapel was founded in Bristol in the same year. In 1744 the first annual conference was held, at which the Articles of Religion were drawn up. Doctrinal emphases included repentance, faith, the assurance of salvation, social concern and the priesthood of all believers. After John Wesley's death in 1791 the Methodists withdrew from the established Church to form the Methodist Church. Methodists gradually drifted into many groups, but in 1932 the Wesleyan Methodist Church, the United Methodist Church and the Primitive Methodist Church united to form the Methodist Church in Great Britain as it now exists.

The governing body and supreme authority of the Methodist Church is the Conference, but there are also 33 district synods, consisting of all the ministers and selected lay people in each district, and circuit meetings of the ministers and lay people of each circuit.

There are over 60 million Methodists world-wide; in Great Britain (1998 figures) there are 353,330 members, 3,727 ministers, 10,746 lay preachers and 6,452 churches.
President of the Conference in Great Britain (2001–2), Revd C. Le Moignan
Vice-President of the Conference (2001–2), A. Leck
Secretary of the Conference, Revd Dr N. T. Collinson, Methodist Church, Conference Office, 25 Marylebone Road, London NW1 5JR. Tel: 020-7486 5502; Fax: 020-7467 5226;
Email: conferenceoffice@methodistchurch.org.uk;
Web: www.methodist.org.uk

THE METHODIST CHURCH IN IRELAND

The Methodist Church in Ireland is closely linked to British Methodism but is autonomous. It has a community roll of 55,701, 16,191 members, 200 ministers, 293 lay preachers and 222 churches.
President of the Methodist Church in Ireland (2001–2), Revd G. Harold Good, OBE, 49 Old Forge Manor, Belfast BT10 0HY. Tel: 028-9060 4200
Secretary of the Methodist Church in Ireland, Revd E. T. I. Mawhinney, 1 Fountainville Avenue, Belfast BT9 6AN. Tel: 028-9032 4554

THE (EASTERN) ORTHODOX CHURCH

The Eastern (or Byzantine) Orthodox Church is a communion of self-governing Christian churches recognising the honorary primacy of the Oecumenical Patriarch of Constantinople.

The position of Orthodox Christians is that the faith was fully defined during the period of the Oecumenical Councils. In doctrine it is strongly trinitarian, and stresses the mystery and importance of the sacraments. It is episcopal in government. The structure of the Orthodox Christian year differs from that of western Churches. Orthodox Christians throughout the world are estimated to number about 300 million.

PATRIARCHS OF THE EASTERN ORTHODOX CHURCH
Archbishop of Constantinople, New Rome and Oecumenical Patriarch, Vartholomaeos, *elected* 1991
Pope and Patriarch of Alexandria and All Africa, Petros VII, *elected* 1997
Patriarch of Antioch and All the East, Ignatios IV, *elected* 1979
Patriarch of Jerusalem and All Palestine, vacant
Patriarch of Moscow and All Russia, Alexei II, *elected* 1990
Archbishop of Pec, Metropolitan of Belgrade and Karlovci, Patriarch of Serbia, Pavle, *elected* 1990
Archbishop of Bucharest and Patriarch of Romania, Teoctist, *elected* 1986

Metropolitan of Sofia and Patriarch of Bulgaria, Maxim, *elected* 1971
Archbishop of Tbilisi and Mtskheta, Catholicos-Patriarch of All Georgia, Ilia II, *elected* 1977

HEADS OF AUTOCEPHALOUS ORTHODOX CHURCHES

Archbishop of Cyprus, Chrysostomos, *elected* 1977
Archbishop of Athens and All Greece, Christodoulos, *elected* 1998
Metropolitan of Warsaw and All Poland, Sawa, *elected* 1998
Archbishop of Tirana and All Albania, Anastas, *elected* 1992
Archbishop of Prague and All the Czech Lands and Slovakia, Nikolaj, *elected* 2000

EASTERN ORTHODOX CHURCHES IN THE UK

THE PATRIARCHATE OF ANTIOCH
There are ten parishes served by 14 clergy. In Great Britain the Patriarchate is represented by the Revd Fr Samir Gholam, St George's Cathedral, 1A Redhill Street, London NW1 4BG. Tel: 020-7383 0403.

THE GREEK ORTHODOX CHURCH (PATRIARCHATE OF CONSTANTINOPLE)
The presence of Greek Orthodox Christians in Britain dates back at least to 1677 when Archbishop Joseph Geogirenes of Samos fled from Turkish persecution and came to London. The present Greek cathedral in Moscow Road, Bayswater, was opened for public worship in 1879 and the Diocese of Thyateira and Great Britain was established in 1922. There are now 120 parishes and other communities (including monasteries) in the UK, served by seven bishops, 106 clergy, nine cathedrals and about 93 churches.

In Great Britain the Patriarchate of Constantinople is represented by Archbishop Gregorios of Thyateira and Great Britain, Thyateira House, 5 Craven Hill, London W2 3EN. Tel: 020-7723 4787; fax: 020-7224 9301.

THE RUSSIAN ORTHODOX CHURCH (PATRIARCHATE OF MOSCOW) AND THE RUSSIAN ORTHODOX CHURCH OUTSIDE RUSSIA
The records of Russian Orthodox Church activities in Britain date from the visit to England of Tsar Peter I in the early 18th century. Clergy were sent from Russia to serve the chapel established to minister to the staff of the Imperial Russian Embassy in London.

In Great Britain the Patriarchate of Moscow is represented by Metropolitan Anthony of Sourozh, 67 Ennismore Gardens, London SW7 1NH. Fax only: 020-7584 9864. He is assisted by one archbishop, one vicar bishop and 28 clergy. There are 27 parishes and smaller communities.

The Russian Orthodox Church Outside Russia is represented by Archbishop Mark of Berlin, Germany and Great Britain, c/o 57 Harvard Road, London W4 4ED. Tel: 020-8742 3493. There are eight communities, including two monasteries, served by nine clergy.

THE SERBIAN ORTHODOX CHURCH (PATRIARCHATE OF SERBIA)
There are 33 parishes and smaller communities in Great Britain served by 11 clergy. The Patriarchate of Serbia is represented by the Episcopal Vicar, the Very Revd Milenko Zebic, 131 Cob Lane, Bournville, Birmingham B30 1QE. Tel: 0121-486 1220.

OTHER NATIONALITIES

Most of the Ukrainian parishes in Britain have joined the Patriarchate of Constantinople, leaving a small number of Ukrainian parishes in Britain under the care of other patriarchates (not all of which are recognised by the other Orthodox Churches). The Latvian, Polish and some Belorussian parishes are also under the care of the Patriarchate of Constantinople. The Patriarchate of Romania has one parish served by two clergy. The Patriarchate of Bulgaria has one parish served by one priest. The Belorussian Autocephalous Orthodox Church has five parishes served by two priests.

THE ORIENTAL ORTHODOX CHURCHES

The term 'Oriental Orthodox Churches' is now generally used to describe a group of six ancient eastern churches which reject the Christological definition of the Council of Chalcedon (AD 451) and use Christological terms in different ways from the Eastern Orthodox Church. There are about 34 million members of the Oriental Orthodox Churches.

PATRIARCHS OF THE ORIENTAL ORTHODOX CHURCHES

ARMENIAN ORTHODOX CHURCH – *Supreme Patriarch Catholicos of All Armenians (Etchmiadzin)*, Karekin II, *elected* 1999; *Catholicos of Cilicia*, Aram I, *elected* 1995; *Patriarch of Jerusalem*, Torkom II, *elected* 1994; *Patriarch of Constantinople*, Mesrob II, *elected* 1998
COPTIC ORTHODOX CHURCH – *Pope of Alexandria and Patriarch of the See of St Mark*, Shenouda III, *elected* 1971
ERITREAN ORTHODOX CHURCH – *Patriarch of Eritrea*, Philipos I, *elected* 1998
ETHIOPIAN ORTHODOX CHURCH – *Patriarch of Ethiopia*, Paulos, *elected* 1992
MALANKARA ORTHODOX SYRIAN CHURCH – *Catholicos of the East*, Basilios Mar Thoma Mathews II, *elected* 1991
SYRIAN ORTHODOX CHURCH – *Patriarch of Antioch and All the East*, Ignatius Zakka I, *elected* 1980

ORIENTAL ORTHODOX CHURCHES IN THE UK

THE ARMENIAN ORTHODOX CHURCH
(PATRIARCHATE OF ETCHMIADZIN)
The Armenian Orthodox Church is the longest-established Oriental Orthodox community in Great Britain. It is represented by the Rt. Revd Bishop Nathan Hovhannisian, Armenian Primate of Great Britain, Armenian Vicarage, Iverna Gardens, London W8 6TP. Tel: 020-7937 0152.

THE COPTIC ORTHODOX CHURCH
The Coptic Orthodox Church is the largest Oriental Orthodox community in Great Britain. It has five dioceses (London; Birmingham; Scotland, Ireland and North-East England; the British Orthodox Church; and churches directly under Pope Shenouda III). The senior bishop in Great Britain is Metropolitan Seraphim, 10 Heathwood Gardens, London SE7 8EP. Tel: 020-8854 3090.

THE ERITREAN ORTHODOX CHURCH
In Great Britain the Eritrean Orthodox Church is represented by Bishop Markos, 11 Anfield Close, Weir Road, London SW12 0NT. Tel: 020-8675 5115.

THE ETHIOPIAN ORTHODOX CHURCH
The Ethiopian Orthodox Church in Great Britain is represented by Like Teguhan Tekle Mariam Edwards, PO Box 14738, London N15 3NJ. Tel: 020-8889 9355.

THE MALANKARA ORTHODOX SYRIAN CHURCH
The Malankara Orthodox Syrian Church is part of the Diocese of Europe under Metropolitan Thomas Mar Makarios. His representative in Great Britain is Fr M. S. Skariah, Paramula House, 44 Newbury Road, Newbury Park, Ilford, Essex IG2 7HD. Tel: 020-8599 3836.

THE SYRIAN ORTHODOX CHURCH
The Syrian Orthodox Church in Great Britain comes under the Patriarchal Vicar, whose representative is Fr Touma Hazim Dakkama, Antiochian, 5 Canning Road, Croydon CR0 6QA. Tel: 020-8654 7531. The Indian congregation under the Syrian Patriarch of Antioch is represented by Fr Eldhose Koungampillil, 1 Roslyn Court, Roslyn Avenue, East Barnet, Herts EN4 8DJ. Tel: 020-8368 2794.
THE COUNCIL OF ORIENTAL ORTHODOX CHURCHES, 34 Chertsey Road, Church Square, Shepperton, Middx TW17 9LF. Tel: 020-8368 8447; *Secretary*, Deacon Aziz M. A. Nour

PENTECOSTAL CHURCHES

Pentecostalism is inspired by the descent of the Holy Spirit upon the apostles at Pentecost. The movement began in Los Angeles, USA, in 1906 and is characterised by baptism with the Holy Spirit, divine healing, speaking in tongues (glossolalia), and a literal interpretation of the scriptures. The Pentecostal movement in Britain dates from 1907. Initially, groups of Pentecostalists were led by laymen and did not organise formally. However, in 1915 the Elim Foursquare Gospel Alliance (more usually called the Elim Pentecostal Church) was founded in Ireland by George Jeffreys and in 1924 about 70 independent assemblies formed a fellowship, the Assemblies of God in Great Britain and Ireland. The Apostolic Church grew out of the 1904–5 revivals in South Wales and was established in 1916, and the New Testament Church of God was established in England in 1953. In recent years many aspects of Pentecostalism have been adopted by the growing charismatic movement within the Roman Catholic, Protestant and Eastern Orthodox churches.
There are about 105 million Pentecostalists worldwide, with about 200,000 adult adherents in Great Britain and Ireland.

THE APOSTOLIC CHURCH, International Administration Offices, PO Box 389, 24–27 St Helens Road, Swansea SA1 1ZH. Tel: 01792-473992. *President*, Pastor R. W. Jones; *Administrator*, Pastor A. Saunders. The Apostolic Church has about 110 churches, 5,500 adherents and 91 ministers
THE ASSEMBLIES OF GOD IN GREAT BRITAIN AND IRELAND, General Offices, 16 Bridgford Road, West Bridgford, Nottingham NG2 6AF. Tel: 0115-981 1188. *General Superintendent*, P.C. Weaver; *General Administrator*, D. H. Gill. The Assemblies of God has 630 churches, about 75,000 adherents (including children) and 890 accredited ministers
THE ELIM PENTECOSTAL CHURCH, PO Box 38, Cheltenham, Glos GL50 3HN. Tel: 01242-519904. *General Superintendent*, Revd J. J. Glass; *Administrator*, Pastor B. Hunter. The Elim Pentecostal Church has 600 churches, 68,500 adherents and 650 accredited ministers

436   The Churches

THE NEW TESTAMENT CHURCH OF GOD, Main House, Overstone Park, Overstone, Northampton NN6 0AD. Tel: 01604-643311. *National Overseer*, Revd Dr R. O. Brown. The New Testament Church of God has 104 organised congregations, about 8,500 baptised members, about 10,000 adherents and 256 accredited ministers

THE PRESBYTERIAN CHURCH IN IRELAND

The Presbyterian Church in Ireland is Calvinistic in doctrine and presbyterian in constitution. Presbyterianism was established in Ireland as a result of the Ulster plantation in the early 17th century, when English and Scottish Protestants settled in the north of Ireland.

There are 21 presbyteries and five regional synods under the chief court known as the General Assembly. The General Assembly meets annually and is presided over by a Moderator who is elected for one year. The ongoing work of the Church is undertaken by 18 boards under which there are a number of specialist committees.

There are about 285,000 Presbyterians in Ireland, mainly in the north, in 557 congregations and with 400 ministers.

Moderator (2001–2), Rt. Revd Dr H. A Dunlop
Clerk of Assembly and General Secretary, Very Revd Dr S. Hutchinson, Church House, Belfast BT1 6DW. Tel: 028-9032 2284

THE PRESBYTERIAN CHURCH OF WALES

The Presbyterian Church of Wales or Calvinistic Methodist Church of Wales is Calvinistic in doctrine and presbyterian in constitution. It was formed in 1811 when Welsh Calvinists severed the relationship with the established church by ordaining their own ministers. It secured its own confession of faith in 1823 and a Constitutional Deed in 1826, and since 1864 the General Assembly has met annually, presided over by a Moderator elected for a year. The doctrine and constitutional structure of the Presbyterian Church of Wales was confirmed by Act of Parliament in 1931–2.

The Church has 43,606 members, 119 ministers and 869 churches.

Moderator (2001–2), Dr B. F. Roberts
General Secretary, Revd W. G. Edwards, 53 Richmond Road, Cardiff CF24 3WJ. Tel: 029-2049 4913

THE RELIGIOUS SOCIETY OF FRIENDS (QUAKERS)

Quakerism is a movement, not a church, which was founded in the 17th century by George Fox and others in an attempt to revive what they saw as 'primitive Christianity'. The movement was based originally in the Midlands, Yorkshire and north-west England, but there are now Quakers in 36 countries around the world. The colony of Pennsylvania, founded by William Penn, was originally Quaker.

Emphasis is placed on the experience of God in daily life rather than on sacraments or religious occasions. There is no church calendar. Worship is largely silent and there are no appointed ministers; the responsibility for conducting a meeting is shared equally among those present. Social reform and religious tolerance have always been important to Quakers, together with a commitment to non-violence in resolving disputes.

There are 213,800 Quakers world-wide, with over 19,000 in Great Britain and Ireland. There are about 490 meeting houses in Great Britain.

CENTRAL OFFICES: (GREAT BRITAIN) Friends House, 173 Euston Road, London NW1 2BJ. Tel: 020-7663 1000; Fax: 020-7663 1001; Email: qhs@quaker.org.uk; Web: www.quaker.org.uk;(IRELAND) Swanbrook House, Morehampton Road, Dublin 4. Tel: (00 353) (1) 668 3684

THE SALVATION ARMY

The Salvation Army was founded by a Methodist minister, William Booth, in the east end of London in 1865, and has since become established in 108 countries world-wide. In 1878 it adopted a quasi-military command structure intended to inspire and regulate its endeavours and to reflect its view that the Church was engaged in spiritual warfare. Salvationists emphasise evangelism and the provision of social welfare.

There are over 1.5 million members worldwide, 17,201 active officers (full-time ordained ministers) and 15,670 worship centres and outposts world-wide. In Great Britain and Ireland there are 62,836 members, 1,638 active officers and 810 worship centres.

International Leader, Gen. John Gowans
UK Leader, Commissioner Alex Hughes
TERRITORIAL HEADQUARTERS, 101 Newington Causeway, London SE1 6BN. Tel: 020-7367 4500

THE SEVENTH-DAY ADVENTIST CHURCH

The Seventh-day Adventist Church was founded in 1863 in the USA. Its members look forward to the second coming of Christ and observe the Sabbath (the seventh day) as a day of rest, worship and ministry. The Church bases its faith and practice wholly on the Bible and has developed 27 fundamental beliefs.

The World Church is divided into 13 divisions, each made up of unions of churches. The Seventh-day Adventist Church in the British Isles is known as the British Union Conference of Seventh-day Adventists and is a member of the Trans-European Division. In the British Isles the administrative organisation of the church is arranged in three tiers: the local churches; the regional conferences for south England, north England, Wales, Scotland and Ireland; and the national headquarters.

There are over 11 Adventists and 45,715 churches in 205 countries world-wide. In the UK and Ireland there are 20,651 members, 153 ministers and 243 churches.

President of the British Union Conference, Pastor C. R. Perry
BRITISH ISLES HEADQUARTERS, Stanborough Park, Watford WD25 6JZ. Tel: 01923-672251

THE (SWEDENBORGIAN) NEW CHURCH

The New Church is based on the teachings of the 18th century Swedish scientist and theologian Emanuel Swedenborg (1688-1772), who believed that Jesus Christ appeared to him and instructed him to reveal the spiritual meaning of the Bible. He claimed to have visions of the spiritual world, including heaven and hell, and conversations with angels and spirits. He published several theological works, including descriptions of the spiritual world and a Bible commentary.

The Second Coming of Jesus Christ is believed to have already taken place and is still taking place, being not an actual physical reappearance of Christ, but rather His return in spirit. It is also believed that concurrent with our life on earth is life in a parallel spiritual world, of which we are usually unconscious until death, when our final judgement is our realisation of our individual essential nature.

There are around 30,000 Swedenborgians world-wide, with about 1,300 members, 30 Churches and 11 ministers in the UK.

THE GENERAL CONFERENCE OF THE NEW CHURCH, Swedenborg House, 20 Bloomsbury Way, London WC1A 2TH. Tel: 020-7229 9340

THE SWEDENBORG MOVEMENT, 98 Abbotts Drive, Wembley, Middx, HA0 3SQ. Tel: 020-8904 3433

UNDEB YR ANNIBYNWYR CYMRAEG
The Union of Welsh Independents

The Union of Welsh Independents was formed in 1872 and is a voluntary association of Welsh Congregational Churches and personal members. It is mainly Welsh-speaking. Congregationalism in Wales dates back to 1639 when the first Welsh Congregational Church was opened in Gwent. Member churches are Calvinistic in doctrine, although a wide range of interpretations is permitted, and congregationalist in organisation. Each church has complete independence in the government and administration of its affairs.

The Union has 34,885 members, 204 ministers and 514 member churches.
President of the Union (2001–2002), Revd I. W. Gryffydd
General Secretary, Revd D. Myrddin Hughes, Tyy John Penry, 11 Heol Sant Helen, Swansea SA1 4AL. Tel: 01792-652542

THE UNITED REFORMED CHURCH

The United Reformed Church was first formed by the union of most of the Congregational churches in England and Wales with the Presbyterian Church of England in 1972.

Congregationalism dates from the mid 16th century. It is Calvinistic in doctrine, and its followers form independent self-governing congregations bound under God by covenant, a principle laid down in the writings of Robert Browne (1550–1633). From the late 16th century the movement was driven underground by persecution, but the cause was defended at the Westminster Assembly in 1643 and the Savoy Declaration of 1658 laid down its principles. Congregational churches formed county associations for mutual support and in 1832 these associations merged to form the Congregational Union of England and Wales.

Presbyterianism in England also dates from the mid 16th century, and was Calvinistic and evangelical in its doctrine. It was governed by a hierarchy of courts.

In the 1960s there was close co-operation locally and nationally between Congregational and Presbyterian Churches. This led to union negotiations and a Scheme of Union, supported by Act of Parliament in 1972. In 1981 a further unification took place, with the Reformed Association of Churches of Christ becoming part of the URC. In 2000 a third union took place, with the Congregational Union of Scotland. In its basis the United Reformed Church reflects local church initiative and responsibility with a conciliar pattern of oversight. The General Assembly is the central body, and is made up of equal numbers of ministers and lay members.

The United Reformed Church is divided into 13 Synods, each with a Synod Moderator, and 78 Districts. There are 96,500 members, 657 full-time stipendiary ministers, 77 part-time stipendiary ministers, 190 non-stipendiary ministers, 10 active church related community workers, and 1,765 local churches.
General Secretary, Revd Dr David C. Cornick, 86 Tavistock Place, London WC1H 9RT. Tel: 020-7916 2020; Fax: 7916 2021; Email: david.cornick@urc.org.uk

THE WESLEYAN REFORM UNION

The Wesleyan Reform Union was founded by Methodists who left or were expelled from Wesleyan Methodism in 1849 following a period of internal conflict. Its doctrine is conservative evangelical and its organisation is congregational, each church having complete independence in the government and administration of its affairs. The main concentration of churches is in Yorkshire.

The Union has 2,072 members, 17 ministers, 127 lay preachers and 110 churches.
President (2001–2), B. J. Armitt
General Secretary, Revd A. J. Williams, Wesleyan Reform Church House, 123 Queen Street, Sheffield S1 2DU. Tel: 0114-272 1938

Non-Trinitarian Churches

CHRISTADELPHIANISM

Christadelphians believe in the Bible as the literal truth and that the Second Coming of Jesus Christ to establish God's kingdom is imminent. Mankind is mortal by nature and only those who have been baptised and saved by their faith in Jesus will be resurrected to eternal life on earth.

Christadelphianism was founded by Dr John Thomas, an Englishman who emigrated to the USA, where he joined a religious group which he left after disagreements on doctrine, taking many of the group with him, who were later to be called Christadelphians. He founded several magazines and returned to England several times, where several congregations had formed on the basis of his teachings.

There are around 18,700 Christadelphians in the UK and some 282 ecclesias (churches).
THE CHRISTADELPHIAN MAGAZINE AND PUBLISHING ASSOCIATION, 404 Shaftmoor Lane, Birmingham B28 8SZ. Tel: 0121-777 6324; fax: 0121-778 5024

THE CHURCH OF CHRIST, SCIENTIST

The Church of Christ, Scientist was founded by Mary Baker Eddy in the USA in 1879 to 'reinstate primitive Christianity and its lost element of healing'. Christian Science teaches the need for spiritual regeneration and salvation from sin, but is best known for its reliance on prayer alone in the healing of sickness. Adherents believe that such healing is a law, or science, and is in direct line with that practised by Jesus Christ (revered, not as God, but as the Son of God) and by the early Christian Church.

The denomination consists of The First Church of Christ, Scientist, in Boston, Massachusetts, USA (the Mother Church) and its branch churches in over 60 countries world-wide. Branch churches are democratically governed by their members, while a five-member Board of Directors, based in Boston, is authorised to transact the business of the Mother Church. The Bible and Mary Baker Eddy's book, *Science and Health with Key to the Scriptures*, are used at services; there are no clergy. Those engaged in full-time healing are called practitioners, of whom there are 3,500 world-wide.

No membership figures are available, since Mary Baker Eddy felt that numbers are no measure of spiritual vitality and ruled that such statistics should not be published. There are over 2,400 branch churches world-wide, including nearly 200 in the UK.

CHRISTIAN SCIENCE COMMITTEE ON PUBLICATION, 9 Elysium Gate, 126 New Kings Road, London SW6 4LZ. Tel: 020-7384 8600; Fax: 020-7371 9204; Email: joynesh@compub.org; *District Manager for Great Britain and Ireland*, H. Joynes

THE CHURCH OF JESUS CHRIST OF LATTER-DAY SAINTS

The Church (often referred to as 'the Mormons') was founded in New York State, USA, in 1830, and came to Britain in 1837. The oldest continuous branch in the world is to be found in Preston, Lancs. Mormons are Christians who claim to belong to the 'Restored Church' of Jesus Christ. They believe that true Christianity died when the last original apostle died, but that it was given back to the world by God and Christ through Joseph Smith, the Church's founder and first president. They accept and use the Bible as scripture, but believe in continuing revelation from God and use additional scriptures, including *The Book of Mormon: Another Testament of Jesus Christ*. The importance of the family is central to the Church's beliefs and practices. Church members set aside Monday evenings as Family Home Evenings when Christian family values are taught. Polygamy was formally discontinued in 1890.

The Church has no paid ministry; local congregations are headed by a leader chosen from amongst their number. The world governing body, based in Utah, USA, is the three-man First Presidency, assisted by the Quorum of the Twelve Apostles.

There are more than 11 million members world-wide, with about 180,000 adherents in Britain in over 350 congregations.

President of the Europe North Area (including Britain), Elder W. Rolfe Kerr

BRITISH HEADQUARTERS, Church Offices, 751 Warwick Road, Solihull, W. Midlands B91 3DQ. Tel: 0121-712 1202

JEHOVAH'S WITNESSES

The movement now known as Jehovah's Witnesses grew from a Bible study group formed by Charles Taze Russell in 1872 in Pennsylvania, USA. In 1896 it adopted the name of the Watch Tower Bible and Tract Society, and in 1931

its members became known as Jehovah's Witnesses. Jehovah's (God's) Witnesses believe in the Bible as the word of God, and consider it to be inspired and historically accurate. They take the scriptures literally, except where there are obvious indications that they are figurative or symbolic, and reject the doctrine of the Trinity. Witnesses also believe that the earth will remain for ever and that all those approved of by Jehovah will have eternal life on a cleansed and beautified earth; only 144,000 will go to heaven to rule with Christ. They believe that the second coming of Christ began in 1914 and his thousand-year reign on earth is imminent, and that Armageddon (a final battle in which evil will be defeated) will precede Christ's rule of peace. They refuse to take part in military service, and do not accept blood transfusions. They publish two magazines, *The Watchtower* and *Awake!*

The 11-member world governing body is based in New York, USA. Witnesses world-wide are divided into branches, countries or areas, districts, circuits and congregations. There are overseers at each level, and two assemblies are held annually for each circuit. There is no paid ministry, but each congregation has elders assigned to look after various duties and every Witness is assigned homes to visit in their congregation.

There are over 6 million Jehovah's Witnesses world-wide, with 130,000 Witnesses in the UK organised into over 1,400 congregations.

BRITISH ISLES HEADQUARTERS, Watch Tower House, The Ridgeway, London NW7 1RN. Tel: 020-8906 2211 Fax: 020-8371 0051; Email: pr@wtbts.org.uk; Web: www.watchtower.org

UNITARIAN AND FREE CHRISTIAN CHURCHES

Unitarianism has its historical roots in the Judaeo-Christian tradition but rejects the deity of Christ and the doctrine of the trinity. It allows the individual to embrace insights from all the world's faiths and philosophies, as there is no fixed creed. It is accepted that beliefs may evolve in the light of personal experience.

Unitarian communities first became established in Poland and Transylvania in the 16th century. The first avowedly Unitarian place of worship in the British Isles opened in London in 1774. The General Assembly of Unitarian and Free Christian Churches came into existence in 1928 as the result of the amalgamation of two earlier organisations. There are about 7,000 Unitarians in Great Britain and Ireland, and 150 Unitarian ministers. Nearly 200 self-governing congregations and fellowship groups, including a small number overseas, are members of the General Assembly.

GENERAL ASSEMBLY OF UNITARIAN AND FREE CHRISTIAN CHURCHES, Essex Hall, 1–6 Essex Street, London WC2R 3HY. Tel: 020-7240 2384; Fax: 020-7240 3089; Email: ga@unitarian.org.uk; Web: www.unitarian.org.uk. *General Secretary*, Jeffrey J. Teagl

Education

Responsibility for education in England lies with the Secretary of State for Education and Skills (formerly of Education and Employment); in Wales, with the First Secretary of the National Assembly for Wales; in Scotland, with Scottish Ministers; and with Education Ministers in Northern Ireland.

The main concerns of the education departments (the Department for Education and Skills (DfES) in England; the National Assembly for Wales Education Department; the Scottish Executive Department of Education and Department of Enterprise and Lifelong Learning; the Department of Education (DED) and Department for Employment and Learning (DEL) (formerly Department of Higher and Further Education, Training and Employment) in the Northern Ireland Executive) are the formulation of national policies for education and the maintenance of consistency in educational standards. They are responsible for the broad allocation of resources for education, for the rate and distribution of educational building and for the supply, training and superannuation of teachers (in England through the Teacher Training Agency).

EXPENDITURE

In the UK in 1998–9, expenditure on education was (£ million):

Schools	22,482.5
Further and higher education	12,284.3
Other education and related expenditure	1,886.3

Most of this expenditure, except that for higher and further education, is incurred by local authorities, which make their own expenditure decisions according to their local situations and needs. Expenditure on education by central government departments, in real terms, was (£ million):

	2000–1 estimated outturn	2001–2 planned
DfES	18,549	21,583
National Assembly for Wales	877.4	932.4
Scottish Executive	1,469.6	1,672.0
Northern Ireland Assembly	1,645.0	1,660.0

The bulk of direct expenditure by the DfES, the National Assembly for Wales and the Scottish Executive is directed towards supporting higher education in universities and colleges through the Higher Education Funding Councils (HEFCs) and further education and, in England and Wales, sixth form colleges, through the funding councils for the sector. In addition, the DfES funds student support in England and Wales, the City Technology Colleges, the City College for the Technology of the Arts, and pays grants under the specialist schools programme.

In Wales the National Assembly also funds curriculum development, educational services and research and supports bilingual education. In Scotland the main elements of central government expenditure, in addition to those outlined above, are grant-aided special schools, student awards and bursaries (through the Student Awards Agency for Scotland), teachers, curriculum development, special educational needs, community education and further and higher education through the Funding

Councils. In Northern Ireland the DED also administers the teachers' superannuation scheme, pays teachers' salaries and funds grant-maintained integrated schools, and voluntary grammar schools. The DEL directly funds higher education, student awards and further education.

Current net expenditure on education by local education authorities in England, Wales, and Scotland, and education and library boards in Northern Ireland is (£ million):

	2000–1 estimated outturn	2001–2 planned
England	20,577	22,573
Wales	1,476	1,586
Scotland	2,752.4	2,952.8
Northern Ireland	940*	912

*provisional

LOCAL EDUCATION ADMINISTRATION

In England and Wales the education service is administered by local education authorities (LEAs), which carry the day-to-day responsibility for providing most state primary and secondary education in their areas. They share with the funding bodies the duty to provide adult education to meet local needs.

The LEAs own and maintain most schools and some colleges, build new ones and provide equipment. LEAs are financed largely from the council tax and aggregate external finance from the Department for Transport, Local Government and the Regions in England and the National Assembly for Wales.

All LEA-maintained schools manage their own budgets. The LEA allocates funds to the school, largely on the basis of pupil numbers, and the school governing body is responsible for overseeing spending and for most aspects of staffing, including appointments and dismissals. LEAs have powers to monitor, maintain and improve standards. An Education Association can be set up to take over the management of failing schools where both the LEA and the governing body have not brought about improvements identified as necessary by inspection.

The duty of providing education locally in Scotland rests with the education authorities. They are responsible for the construction of buildings, the employment of teachers and other staff and the provision of equipment and materials. Devolved School Management is in place for all primary, secondary and special schools. Education authorities are required to establish school boards consisting of parents and teachers as well as co-opted members, responsible, among other things, for the appointment of staff.

Education is administered locally in Northern Ireland by five education and library boards, whose costs are met in full by central government. All grant-aided schools include elected parents and teachers on their boards of governors. Provision has been made for schools wishing to provide integrated education to have grant-maintained integrated status from the outset. All schools and colleges of further education have full responsibility for their own budgets, including staffing costs. The Council for Catholic Maintained Schools forms an upper tier of management for Catholic schools and provides advice on matters relating to management and administration.

THE INSPECTORATE

The Office for Standards in Education (OFSTED) is a non-ministerial government department in England headed by HM Chief Inspector of Schools (HMCI). OFSTED's remit is regularly to inspect and report on all maintained schools in England; local education authorities (supported by the Audit Commission); initial teacher training; youth work; all 16–19 education including sixth form and further education colleges; and funded education for three- and four-year-olds. OFSTED also has responsibility for the regulation of day care services for all children under eight.

Teams of OFSTED-trained accredited inspectors, including educationalists and lay people, carry out inspections in schools according to the Framework for Inspection of Schools to ensure consistency in the process of inspection and the criteria used. HM Inspectors (HMI) within OFSTED report on good practice in schools and on other educational issues based on inspection evidence. From 1997 for secondary and from 1998 for primary, schools are inspected once every six years or more frequently if there is cause. A summary of the inspection report must be sent to the parents of each pupil by the school, followed by a copy of the governors' action plan thereon.

There are about 200 HMIs on OFSTED's permanent staff, about 1,500 registered inspectors, about 7,500 team inspectors, and about 700 lay inspectors, who work on contract to OFSTED.

Estyn: Arolygiaeth Ei Mawrhydi dros Addysg a Hyfforddiant yng Nghymru (Her Majesty's Inspectorate for Education and Training in Wales) inspects funded nursery provision, maintained schools, local education authorities, teacher education and training, work-based training, careers companies, adult and youth education, and colleges of further education in Wales. Its remit also includes advice to the National Assembly for Wales on a wide range of education and training matters.

There are 54 HMIs, 149 registered inspectors and 562 team members in Wales.

HM Inspectorate of Education (HMIE) is an executive agency of the Scottish Executive. HM Inspectors (HMI) inspect or review and report on education in pre-school centres, nursery, primary and special schools, further education institutions (under contract to the Scottish Further Education Funding Council), initial teacher education, community learning; care and welfare of pupils; the education functions of local authorities; and in other contexts as necessary. HMIs work in teams alongside lay members and associate assessors, who are practising teachers seconded for the inspection. The inspection of higher education is the responsibility of inspectors appointed to the Higher Education Funding Council for Scotland.

In 2000–1 there were 87 HMIs and five Chief Inspectors in Scotland.

Inspection is carried out in Northern Ireland by the Education and Training Inspectorate which provides services for the Department of Education and the Department for Employment and Learning, among others. Schools are inspected once every five to seven years. In further education and training, extended inspections are carried out once every four years and focused inspections at least every eight years. In addition to its monitoring and evaluating activity, the Inspectorate also provides advice to Ministers and Departments.

The Inspectorate comprises a Chief Inspector, four assistant inspectors and 56 inspectors. Inspectorate teams also include on occasion lay persons and associate assessors.

SCHOOLS AND PUPILS

Schooling is compulsory in Great Britain for all children between five and 16 years and between four and 16 years in Northern Ireland. Provision is being increased for pre-school children and many pupils remain at school after the minimum leaving age. No fees are charged in any publicly maintained school in England, Wales and Scotland. In Northern Ireland, fees may be charged in voluntary schools and are paid by pupils in preparatory departments of grammar schools, but pupils admitted to the secondary departments of grammar schools, unless they come from outside the province, do not pay fees.

The 'Parents' Charter', available free from education departments, is a booklet telling parents about the education system. Schools are now required to make available information about themselves, their truancy rates, destinations of leavers, public examination and national test results. Parents in England and Wales must receive a written yearly progress report on all aspects of their child's achievements. There is a similar commitment for Northern Ireland. In Scotland the school report card gives parents information on their child's progress.

FALL AND RISE IN NUMBERS

In primary education, and increasingly in secondary education, pupil numbers in the UK increased through the 1990s. In maintained primary schools they stood at 4.9 million in 1991, had risen to 5.5 million by 2000 but are expected to decline to 4.9 million by 2006. In secondary schools pupil numbers stood at 3.4 million in 1991 and had risen to 3.9 million by 2000, where they are projected to remain until 2010.

ENGLAND AND WALES

There are two main types of school in England and Wales: publicly maintained schools, which charge no fees; and independent schools, which charge fees. Publicly maintained schools, with the exception in England of City Technology Colleges, are maintained by local education authorities (LEAs).

Publicly funded schools are classified as community, voluntary or foundation schools. Community (formerly county) schools are owned by LEAs and wholly funded by them. They are non-denominational and provide primary and secondary education. Schools in the voluntary category provide primary and secondary education and many have a particular religious ethos. Although the buildings are in many cases provided by the voluntary bodies, they are financially maintained by an LEA. The category comprises two subdivisions, voluntary controlled and voluntary aided. In the case of voluntary controlled schools the LEA bears all costs. In voluntary aided schools, although the managers or governors are responsible for repairs, improvements and alterations to the building, central government may reimburse up to 85 per cent of approved capital expenditure, while the LEA pays for internal maintenance and other running costs. That subdivision also includes schools formerly classed as special agreement and those former grant-maintained schools which were originally voluntary aided or special agreement schools or were founded by promoters. In the case of former special agreement schools, the LEA may, at special agreement, pay between one-half and three-quarters of the cost of building a new or extending an existing school, usually a secondary school. Foundation schools are former grant-maintained schools which were originally county or voluntary controlled schools or were established by the Funding Agency for Schools. Under the previous administration all secondary and primary schools, whether maintained or independent, were eligible to apply for grant-maintained status subject to a ballot of parents. Grant-maintained schools were maintained directly by the Secretary of State (through the Funding Agency for Schools) and the former Welsh Office, not the LEA; those arrangements no longer apply and they are now included in LEA funding arrangements. They are wholly run by their own governing body. About 60 per cent of schools established were secondary schools.

The number of schools by category in 2000 was:

	England	Wales
Maintained schools	24,288	1,872
Community	16,094	1,584
Voluntary	7,314	276
controlled	2,889	116
aided	4,425	160
Foundation	880	12
CTCs and CCTAs*	15	–
Independent schools	3,050	55
TOTAL	27,353	1,927

* In England only

Under the Local Management of Schools initiative, LEAs are required to delegate the entire school budget, including staffing costs, directly to those schools that wish it. LEAs continue to retain responsibility for various common services, including transport and special educational needs units. The LEA acts as admission authority for most community and some voluntary schools.

Governing bodies – All publicly maintained schools have a governing body, usually made up of a number of parent and local community representatives, governors appointed by the LEA if the school is LEA maintained, the headteacher (unless he or she chooses otherwise), and serving teachers. Schools can appoint up to four sponsor governors from business who will be expected to provide financial and managerial assistance. Governing bodies are responsible for the overall policies of schools and their academic aims and objectives. They also control matters of school discipline, the appointment and dismissal of staff and act as the admission authority for voluntary aided and all foundation schools.

City Technology Colleges (CTCs) and City Colleges for the Technology of the Arts (CCTAs) are state-aided but independent of LEAs. Their aim is to widen the choice of secondary education in disadvantaged urban areas and to teach a broad curriculum with an emphasis on science, technology, business understanding and arts technologies. Capital costs are shared by government and business sponsors, and running costs are covered by a per capita grant from the DfES in line with comparable costs in an LEA maintained school. The first city technology college opened in 1988 in Solihull. The first CCTA, known as Britschool, opened in Croydon in 1991.

The Specialist Schools Programme – The programme is open to all state secondary schools in England, which wish to specialise in the teaching of a particular subject area (technology, mathematics and science, modern foreign languages, sports and the arts). The schools must raise £50,000 sponsorship, prepare four-year development plans with measurable targets in the specialist subject area and make provision to involve other schools and the wider community. In return, in addition to the normal funding arrangements, the schools receive business sponsorship (up to four sponsor governors may sit on governing bodies) and a capital grant of up to £100,000 from central government, together with extra annual funding of £123 per pupil (for four years initially) to assist the delivery of an enhanced curriculum. By September 2001, there were 367 technology colleges, 126 language colleges, 101 sports colleges and 91 arts colleges.

City Academies – The first City Academies, publicly funded independent secondary schools involving sponsors from the private and voluntary sectors, opened in September 2001. They are usually in deprived communities and replace either seriously failing schools with poor examination results or are established to meet a demand for places.

SCOTLAND

Education authority schools (known as public schools) are financed by local government, partly through revenue support grants from central government, and partly from local taxation. Devolved management from the local authority to the school is in place for more than 88 per cent of all school level expenditure. A small number of grant-aided schools, mainly in the special sector, are conducted by boards of managers and receive grants direct from the Scottish Executive Education Department. Under the previous administration a category of self-governing schools was created. Such schools opted to be managed entirely by a board of management but remained in the public sector and were funded by direct government grant. Two were established but one has since been returned to the education authority framework.

Independent schools charge fees and receive no direct grant, but are subject to inspection and registration.

The number of schools by category in 2000 was:

Publicly maintained schools:	
Education authority	4,850
Self-governing	1
Independent schools	209
TOTAL	5,060

NORTHERN IRELAND

Controlled schools are maintained by the education and library boards with all costs paid from public funds. Voluntary maintained schools, mainly under Roman Catholic management, receive grants towards capital costs and running costs in whole or in part. Voluntary grammar schools may be under denominational or non-denominational management and receive grants from the Department for Education (DED). Voluntary maintained and voluntary grammar schools can apply for designation as a new category of voluntary school, which is eligible for a 100 per cent as opposed to 85 per cent grant. Such schools are managed by a board of governors on which no single interest group has a majority of nominees. All grant-aided schools include elected parents and teachers on their boards of governors, whose responsibilities also include financial management under the Local Management of Schools initiative. All schools now have fully delegated budgets. The majority of children in Northern Ireland are educated in schools which have a religious affiliation. Integrated schools exist to educate Protestant and Roman Catholic children together. There are two types: grant-maintained integrated schools which are funded by DED; and controlled integrated schools funded by the education and library boards. Procedures are in place for balloting parents in existing religiously affiliated schools to determine whether they want their school to become integrated, subject to the satisfaction of certain criteria. By September 2001, 45 integrated schools had been established, 17 of them secondary.

The number of schools by category in 2000–2001 was:

Grant-aided schools:

Controlled	646
Maintained	542
Voluntary grammar	54
Integrated schools	45
Independent schools	27
TOTAL	1,314

THE STATE SYSTEM

PRE-SCHOOL EDUCATION – Pre-school education is for children from two to five years and is not compulsory, although a free place is available for each four-year-old who requires it and provision for three-year-olds in the public sector is being increased. Northern Ireland has a compulsory school starting age of four as of September each year but there too pre-school provision is being increased. Pre-school education takes place variously in nursery schools (2,826 in the public sector in 2000), nursery classes in primary schools, or pre-school education centres. The number of children receiving pre-school education in the UK in 1999–2000 was (thousands):

In maintained nursery schools	143.8
In primary schools	963.0
In non-maintained nursery schools	71.0
In special schools	7.0
TOTAL	1,184.8

Education authorities are responsible for planning, co-ordinating and delivering nursery education in their areas using a range of providers on the basis of an Early Years Development Plan, in partnership with parents and the private and voluntary sectors. All providers of pre-school education are subject to inspection.

PRIMARY EDUCATION – Primary education begins at five years in Great Britain and four years in Northern Ireland. In England, Wales and Northern Ireland the transfer to secondary school is generally made at 11 years. In Scotland, the primary school course lasts for seven years and pupils transfer to secondary courses at about the age of 12.

Primary schools consist mainly of infant schools for children aged five to seven, junior schools for those aged seven to 11, and combined junior and infant schools for both age groups. First schools in some parts of England cater for ages five to ten as the first stage of a three-tier system: first, middle and secondary.

Primary schools (UK) 1999–2000

No. of primary schools	23,052
No. of pupils (thousands)	5,338.3
Pupils aged 2–4 years (thousands)	992.3

Pupil–teacher ratios in maintained primary schools were:

	1998–9	1999–2000
England	23.5	23.3
Wales	23.0	22.3
Scotland	19.4	19.1
Northern Ireland	19.9	20.2
UK	23.0	22.7

The average size of classes 'as taught' was 25.3 in 1999–2000.

MIDDLE SCHOOLS – Middle schools (which take children from first schools), mostly in England, cover varying age ranges between eight and 14 and usually lead on to comprehensive upper schools.

SECONDARY EDUCATION – Secondary schools are for children aged 11 to 16 and for those who choose to stay on

to 18. At 16, many students prefer to move on to tertiary or sixth form colleges. Most secondary schools in England, Wales and Scotland are co-educational. The largest secondary schools have over 1,500 pupils; thirty-five per cent of schools take over 1,000 pupils.

Secondary schools 1999–2000

	England	Wales	Scotland	Northern Ireland
No. of pupils (000s)	3,181.8	204.2	316.6	155.0
% 16 to 17 years old	31.2	34.1	29.2	43.1
Average class size	22.2	20.6	19.2	n/a
Pupil–teacher ratio	17.2	16.5	13.0	14.7

In England and Wales the main types of maintained secondary schools (January 2000) were: comprehensive schools (86.2 per cent of pupils in England, 100 per cent in Wales), whose admission arrangements are without reference to ability or aptitude; deemed middle schools for children aged between eight and 14 years who then move on to senior comprehensive schools at 12, 13 or 14 (4.8 per cent of pupils in England); secondary modern schools (3.4 per cent of pupils in England) providing a general education with a practical bias; secondary grammar schools (4.4 per cent of pupils in England) with selective intake providing an academic course from 11 to 16–18 years; and technical schools (0.009 per cent of pupils in England), providing an integrated academic and technical education.

In Scotland all pupils in education authority secondary schools attend schools with a comprehensive intake. Most of these schools provide a full range of courses appropriate to all levels of ability from first to sixth year.

In most areas of Northern Ireland there is a selective system of secondary education with pupils transferring either to grammar schools (34.8 per cent of pupils in 2000) or secondary schools (65.2 per cent of pupils in 2000) at 10–11 years of age. Parents can choose the school they would like their children to attend and all those who apply must be admitted if they meet the criteria. If a school is over-subscribed beyond its statutory admissions number, selection is on the basis of published criteria, which, for most grammar schools, place emphasis on performance in the transfer procedure tests which are set and administered by the Northern Ireland Council for the Curriculum, Examinations and Assessment. When parents consider that a school has not applied its criteria fairly they have access to independent appeals tribunals. Grammar schools provide an academic type of secondary education with A-levels at the end of the seventh year, while secondary non-grammar schools follow a curriculum suited to a wider range of aptitudes and abilities.

SPECIAL EDUCATION – Wherever possible, taking the parents' wishes into account, children with special needs are educated in ordinary schools, which are required to publish their policy for pupils with special educational needs. Local education authorities in England and Wales and education and library boards in Northern Ireland are required to identify and secure provision for the needs of children with learning difficulties, to involve the parents in any decision and draw up a formal statement of the child's special educational needs and how they intend to meet them, all within statutory time limits.

In Scotland, school placing is a matter of agreement between education authorities and parents. Parents have the right to say which school they want their child to attend, and a right of appeal where their wishes are not being met. Whenever possible, children with special needs are integrated into ordinary schools.

Maintained special schools are run by education

authorities which pay all the costs of maintenance, but under the terms of Local Management of Schools, those able and wishing to manage their own budgets may choose to do so. Non-maintained special schools are run by voluntary bodies; they may receive some grant from central government for capital expenditure and for equipment but their current expenditure is met primarily from the fees charged to education authorities for pupils placed in the schools. Some independent schools provide education wholly or mainly for children with special educational needs and are required to meet similar standards to those for maintained and non-maintained special schools.

The number of pupils with statements of special needs in January 2000 was (thousands):

In special schools:

Total	101.0
England	86.9
Wales	3.7
Scotland	6.5
N. Ireland	3.9

In public sector primary and secondary schools:

Total	93.7
England	79.8
Wales	6.8
Scotland	4.8
N. Ireland	2.3

ALTERNATIVE PROVISION

There is no legal obligation on parents in the UK to educate their children at school provided that the local education authority is satisfied that the child is receiving full-time education suited to its age, abilities and aptitudes. The education authority need not be informed that a child is being educated at home unless the child is already registered at a state school. In that case the parents must arrange for the child's name to be removed from the school's register (by writing to the headteacher) before education at home can begin. Failure to do so leaves the parents liable to prosecution for condoning non-attendance.

INDEPENDENT SCHOOLS

Independent schools charge fees and are owned and managed under special trusts, with profits being used for the benefit of the schools concerned. There is a wide variety of provision, from kindergartens to large day and boarding schools, and from experimental schools to traditional institutions. A number of independent schools have been instituted by religious and ethnic minorities.

The term public schools is applied to those independent schools in membership of the Headmasters' and Headmistresses' Conference, the Governing Bodies Association or the Governing Bodies of Girls' Schools Association.

Most independent schools in Scotland follow the same examination system as England, Wales and Northern Ireland, i.e. GCSE followed by A-levels.

Preparatory schools are so-called because they prepare pupils for the common entrance examination to senior independent schools. Most cater for pupils from about seven to 13 years. The common entrance examination is set by the Common Entrance Examination Board, but marked by the independent school to which the pupil intends to go. It is taken at 13 by boys, and between 11 and 13 by girls.

The Assisted Places Scheme was funded by central government in England, Wales and Scotland and enabled children to attend independent secondary schools which

their parents could not otherwise afford. It ceased to operate after the September 1997 intake but pupils holding their places at the beginning of the 1997–8 school year will keep them until they have completed their education at their current school.

The number of schools and pupils in 1999–2000 was:

	No. of Schools	No. of pupils (000s)	% of school population	Pupil-teacher ratio
England	2,204	577.3	7.4	9.9
Wales	54	9.7	1.9	9.8
Scotland	176	30.2	3.6	10.3
N. Ireland	22	1.2	0.3	8.8

THE CURRICULUM

ENGLAND

The national curriculum was introduced in primary and secondary schools between autumn 1989 and autumn 1996, for the period of compulsory schooling from five to 16. It is mandatory in all maintained schools. As originally proposed, it was widely criticised for being too prescriptive and time-consuming. Following revision in 1994 its requirements were substantially reduced; the revisions were implemented from September 1995 for key stages one to three and from September 1996 for key stage four. A second review was completed in August 1999 and a revised curriculum was introduced in schools from September 2000.

The statutory subjects at key stages one and two (five–11-year olds) are:

Core subjects	Foundation subjects
English	Design and technology
Mathematics	Information and communication technology
Science	History
	Geography
	Music
	Art and design
	Physical education

At key stage three (11- to 14-year-olds) a modern foreign language is introduced. At key stage four (14- to 16-year-olds) pupils are required to continue to study the core subjects, physical education, design and technology and information and communication technology. Citizenship will become a compulsory subject for secondary pupils from September 2002. Other foundation subjects are optional and others, such as drama, dance and classical languages are taught when the resources of individual schools permit. Religious education must be taught across all key stages, following a locally agreed syllabus; parents have the right to remove their children if they wish.

Statutory assessment takes place on entry to primary school and national tests and tasks in English and mathematics at key stage one, with the addition of science at key stages two and three, are in place. Teachers make their own assessments of their pupils' progress to set alongside the test results. At key stage four the GCSE and vocational equivalents are the main form of assessment.

The DfES publishes tables showing pupils' performance in A-level, AS-level, GCSE, GNVQ and Vocational A-level examinations school by school. Local education authorities are required to publish similar information in November each year showing the results of national curriculum tests and teacher assessments for seven, 11- and 14-year-olds. Approximately 600,000 pupils in each of the age groups take the tests each year.

NATIONAL TESTING (TEACHERS' ASSESSMENT RESULTS IN PARENTHESIS) IN CORE SUBJECTS 2000
Percentage of pupils reaching or exceeding the expected level of performance at that age:

	Key stage 1 7-year olds (level 2)	Key stage 2 11-year-olds (level 4)	Key stage 3 14-year-olds (level 5)
English	84 (83)	74.5 (70.5)	63.5 (64.5)
Mathematics	90 (88)	71.5 (72.5)	64.5 (66.5)
Science	– (88)	84.5 (79)	59.5 (61.5)

National targets for 2004 proposed for 11-year-olds are: 85 per cent to reach level four in English and mathematics and 35 per cent to reach level five. Targets for 14-year-olds are: 75 per cent to reach level five in English, mathematics and information and communication technology and 70 per cent in science by 2004; by 2007, 85 and 80 per cent respectively.

The Qualifications and Curriculum Authority (QCA) is an independent government agency funded by the DfES. It is responsible for ensuring that the curriculum and qualifications available to young people and adults are of high quality, coherent and flexible and its remit ranges from the under-fives to higher level vocational qualifications.

WALES

The national curriculum was introduced simultaneously in Wales and, although it is broadly similar, has separate and distinctive characteristics which are reflected, where appropriate, in the programmes of study. A review of the curriculum in Wales has been completed and changes were introduced from September 2000. Welsh is compulsory for pupils at all key stages, either as a teaching medium or as a second language. In 1999–2000 some 27 per cent of primary schools used Welsh as the sole or main medium of instruction and over five per cent used it for part of the curriculum. More than 23.7 per cent of secondary schools taught Welsh both as a first and second language, while 67.5 per cent taught it as a second language only. Schools perform tests and tasks in Welsh in addition to those in the other subjects of the national curriculum. Approximately 38,000 pupils in each of the age groups take the tests each year.

Information about pupils' performance in examinations and national curriculum tests is made available by schools to parents but will no longer be published.

NATIONAL TESTING (TEACHERS' ASSESSMENT RESULTS IN PARENTHESIS) IN CORE SUBJECTS 2000
Percentage of pupils reaching or exceeding the expected level of performance at that age:

	Key stage 1 7-year-olds (level 2)	Key stage 2 11-year-olds (level 4)	Key stage 3 14-year-olds (level 5)
English	82.5 (81.5)	73.5 (69)	59.5 (62.5)
Welsh (first language)	83.0 (82.7)	73.0 (70)	62.0 (65)
Mathematics	90.0 (87.5)	69.0 (70)	60.5 (64.5)
Science	– (88)	80.5 (78)	59.0 (60.5)

National targets have been set as follows: by 2004 80-85 per cent of 11-year-olds to reach level four or better and 80-85 per cent of 14-year-olds to reach level five or better in English, Welsh (first language), mathematics and science.

Awdurdod Cymwysterau, Cwricwlwm ac Asesu Cymru (ACCAC)/the Qualifications, Curriculum and Assessment Authority for Wales advises government on the matters within its remit. ACCAC is funded by the National Assembly for Wales.

SCOTLAND

The content and management of the curriculum in Scotland are not prescribed by statute but are the responsibility of education authorities and individual headteachers. Advice and guidance are provided by the Scottish Executive Education Department and Learning and Teaching Scotland, which also has a developmental role. Those bodies have produced guidelines on the structure and balance of the curriculum as well as for each of the curriculum areas for the five to 14 age group. There are also guidelines on assessment across the whole curriculum, on reporting to parents, and on standardised national tests for English language and mathematics at five levels. Testing is carried out on a voluntary basis when the teacher deems it appropriate; most pupils are expected to move from one level to the next at roughly two-year intervals. National testing is largely in place in most primary schools but secondary school participation rates are lower.

The curriculum for 14- to 16-year-olds includes study within each of eight modes: language and communication; mathematical studies; science; technology; social studies; creative activities; physical education; and religious and moral education. There is a recommended percentage of time to be devoted to each area over the two years. Provision is made for teaching in Gaelic in Gaelic-speaking areas.

For 16- to 18-year-olds National Qualifications, a unified framework of courses and awards, which brings together both academic and vocational courses, was introduced in 1999. The Scottish Qualifications Authority awards the certificates.

NORTHERN IRELAND

A curriculum common to all grant-aided schools exists. Pupils are required to study religious education and, depending on which key stage they have reached, certain subjects from six broad areas of study: English, mathematics, science and technology; the environment and society; creative and expressive studies and, in key stages three and four, language studies. The statutory curriculum requirements at key stages one to three have been revised and new programmes of study were introduced in September 1996. Six cross-curricular educational themes, which include information technology and education for mutual understanding, are woven through the main subjects of the curriculum. Irish is a foundation subject in schools that use it as a medium of instruction.

The assessment of pupils is broadly in line with practice in England and Wales and takes place at the ages of eight, 11 and 14. The GCSE is used to assess 16-year-olds. From 2001 the Department of Education ceased to publish the national testing results, as a consultation exercise showed that parents and others preferred the option of individual schools providing information to parents.

National targets have been set as follows for achievement by 2002: for key stage 2 (11-year-olds), 77 per cent to reach level four in English and mathematics; and for key stage 3 (14-year-olds), 75 per cent in English and mathematics and 70 per cent in science to reach level five and above.

The Northern Ireland Council for the Curriculum, Examinations and Assessment (NICCEA) monitors and advises the Department of Education and teachers on all matters relating to the curriculum, assessment arrangements and examinations in grant-aided schools. It conducts GCSE, A- and AS-level examinations, pupil assessment at key stages one, two and three and administers the transfer procedure tests.

PUBLIC EXAMINATIONS AND QUALIFICATIONS

ENGLAND, WALES AND NORTHERN IRELAND

Until the end of 1987, secondary school pupils at the end of compulsory schooling around the age of 16, and others, took the General Certificate of Education (GCE) Ordinary-level or the Certificate of Secondary Education (CSE). From 1988 these were replaced by a single system of examinations, the General Certificate of Secondary Education (GCSE), which is usually taken after five years of secondary education. The GCSE is the main method of assessing the performance of pupils at age 16 in all national curriculum subjects required to be assessed at the end of compulsory schooling. The structure of the examination is being adapted in accordance with national curriculum requirements; new subject criteria were published in 1995 to govern GCSE syllabuses introduced in 1996 for first examination in 1998. GCSE short-course qualifications are available in some subjects. As a rule the syllabus takes half the time of a full GCSE course.

The GCSE differs from its predecessors in that there are syllabuses based on national criteria covering course objectives, content and assessment methods; differentiated assessment (i.e. different papers or questions for different ranges of ability) and grade-related criteria (i.e. grades awarded on absolute rather than relative performance). The GCSE certificates are awarded on an eight-point scale, A* to G. Grades A to C are the equivalent of the corresponding O-level grades A to C or CSE grade 1. Grades D, E, F and G record achievement at least as high as that represented by CSE grades 2 to 5. All GCSE syllabuses, assessments and grading procedures are monitored by the Qualifications and Curriculum Authority to ensure that they conform to the national criteria

In the UK in 1998–9, 73.9 per cent of all 15 to 16-year-old entrants achieved one or more graded GCSE, SCE Standard Grade, or equivalent result, while 49.1 per cent achieved five or more results at grade C or better.

Students are increasingly encouraged to continue their education post-16. For those who do so, in addition to the vocational qualifications outlined below, there are General Certificate of Education (GCE) Advanced (A-level) examinations. A-level courses usually last two years and have traditionally provided the foundation for entry to higher education. A-level reforms have introduced revised syllabuses from Summer 2000 for examination in summer 2002. Advanced Subsidiary (AS) level examinations replaced Advanced Supplementary level examinations (introduced in 1987 and requiring not less than half the teaching time and content of the corresponding A-level course) for examination in summer 2001. The government is considering changes in response to the criticism that the introduction of AS-level examinations has imposed too heavy a burden in the first year of the A-level course on students and teachers. The new A-level qualification is normally composed of six units (three A2 units and three AS units), the latter being less demanding and constituting the new AS-level qualification, which represents the first half of a full A-level. Students who go on to complete the full A-level will be assessed on their attainment in all six units, which may be taken either in stages or all at the end

of the course. Candidates have the choice between end-of-course or staged assessment, with limits on coursework. A-levels and AS-levels are marked on a six-point scale: from A to E (pass) and U (unclassified), which is not certificated.

Many maintained schools offer BTEC Firsts and an increasing number offer BTEC Nationals. National Vocational Qualifications (NVQs) in the form of General NVQs (GNVQs) are also available to students in schools. The Vocational Certificates of Education (VCE) exist at Advanced and AS levels.

In the UK in 1998–9, 33.7 per cent of young students in schools and colleges achieved two or more passes at A-level or SCE H-grade (an increase of 0.2 per cent on the previous year). Of those in Great Britain who entered for A-level or SCE H-grade examinations, the greatest number of entries were in the following subjects: English (13 per cent of students, 9 per cent boys, 16.3 per cent girls); general studies (9.7 per cent of students, 10.0 boys, 9.5 girls); mathematics (9.6 per cent of students, 12.8 per cent boys, 7.0 per cent of girls); and biological sciences (6.9 per cent of students, 5.7 per cent boys, 8.0 per cent girls).

There is also the opportunity for A-level candidates to take additional papers of greater difficulty, known as Advanced Extension Awards (formerly Special-level or Scholarship-level). Papers are available in most of the traditional academic subjects and are marked on a two-point scale (Merit and Distinction).

The City & Guilds Diploma of Vocational Education is intended for a wide ability range. Within guidelines and to meet specified criteria, schools and colleges design their own courses, which stress activity-based learning, core skills which include application of number, communication and information technology, and work experience. The Diploma is of value to those who want to find out what aptitudes they may have and to prepare themselves for work, but who may not yet be committed to a particular occupation. It can be taken alongside GCSEs and can provide a context for the introduction of GNVQ units into the key stage four curriculum.

The various examining boards in England have combined into three Unitary Awarding Bodies (UABs), which offer both academic and vocational qualifications: GNVQs, GCSEs, AS and A-levels. The new bodies are the Assessment and Qualifications Alliance (AQA), Edexcel and Oxford, Cambridge and RSA Examinations (OCR). The UABs are separate bodies, although they work together in many ways to meet the needs of schools and colleges. The Joint Council for General Qualifications (JCGQ) comprises the three English UABs, the Welsh Joint Education Committee and the Northern Ireland Council for the Curriculum, Examinations and Assessment.

SCOTLAND

Scotland has its own system of public examinations. At the end of the fourth year of secondary education, at about the age of 16, pupils take the Standard Grade of the Scottish Certificate of Education. Standard Grade courses and examinations have been designed to suit every level of ability, with assessment against nationally determined standards of performance.

For most courses there are three separate examination papers at the end of the two-year Standard Grade course. They are set at three levels: Credit (leading to awards at grade 1 or 2); General (leading to awards at grade 3 or 4); and Foundation (leading to awards at grade 5 or 6). Grade 7 is available to those who, although they have completed the course, have not attained any of these levels. Normally pupils will take examinations covering two pairs of grades, either grades 1–4 or grades 3–6. Most candidates take seven or eight Standard Grade examinations.

Post-16 a new system of courses and qualifications is being phased in under the 'Higher Still' reforms, bringing together academic and vocational qualifications. National Qualifications will replace the Certificate of Sixth Year Studies (from 2001–2) and Highers, National Certificate modules, and General Scottish Vocational Qualifications (from 2004) for everyone studying beyond Standard Grade in Scottish schools and further education colleges. Standard Grade and Scottish Vocational Qualifications will remain. National Qualifications are available at five levels: Access, Intermediate 1, Intermediate 2, Higher and Advanced Higher. Courses are made up of internally assessed units with external assessment of the full course determining the grade (A to C). The core skills of communication, numeracy, problem-solving, information technology and working with others are embedded in the Higher Still qualifications, although the skills and levels covered vary between subjects; there are also separate core skills units.

All these qualifications are awarded by the Scottish Qualifications Authority (SQA).

THE INTERNATIONAL BACCALAUREATE

The International Baccalaureate is an internationally recognised two-year pre-university course and examination designed to facilitate the mobility of students and to promote international understanding. There are 43 schools and colleges in the UK which offer the International Baccalaureate diploma.

RECORDS OF ACHIEVEMENT

The National Record of Achievement is under review. Subject to evaluation, it will be replaced in England, Wales and Northern Ireland by the 'Progress file' after a three year trial period from July 1999. In Scotland the Scottish Qualifications Authority issues a Scottish Qualifications Certificate recording all qualifications achieved at all levels which it has either awarded or accredited.

TEACHERS

ENGLAND AND WALES

New entrants to the teaching profession in state primary and secondary schools are required to be graduates and to have Qualified Teacher Status (QTS). QTS is achieved by successfully completing a course of initial teacher training, traditionally either a Bachelor of Education (B Ed) degree or the Postgraduate Certificate of Education (PGCE) at an accredited institution. New entrants are statutorily required to serve a one-year induction period during which they will have a structured programme of support. In recent years various employment-based routes to QTS have been developed. The Graduate Teacher Programme allows graduates of at least 24 years of age with teaching experience to undergo between one term's and one year's school-based training. The schools involved receive up to £13,000 to cover the trainee's salary in addition to a grant of up to £4,000 for undertaking training. The Registered Teacher Scheme is designed to attract into the teaching profession entrants over 24 years of age without a degree or formal teaching qualification but with at least two years higher education and with relevant experience; entrants are paid a salary and complete a degree while undergoing training. Teachers in further education are not required to have QTS, though roughly half have a teaching qualification and most have industrial, commercial or professional experience. A qualification for aspiring head-teachers, the National Professional Qualification for Headship, was

introduced in September 1997 and will be mandatory by 2002. The National College for School Leadership administers this qualification and others and acts as a focus for development and support.

Teacher training is now largely school-based, with student teachers on secondary PGCE courses spending two-thirds of their training in the classroom. Changes have also been made to primary phase teacher training to make it more school-based and to give schools a role in course design and delivery. Individual schools or consortia of schools and CTCs can bid for funds from the DfES to carry out their own teacher training, including recruitment of students, subject to approval of their proposed training programme by the Teacher Training Agency (TTA) and monitoring and evaluation by OFSTED and Estyn. Funds are given to schools to meet the costs of designing and delivering the courses.

The TTA funds all types of teacher training in England, whether run by universities, colleges or schools, and some educational research. In Wales funding is undertaken by the Higher Education Funding Council for Wales (HEFCW). On an integrated England and Wales basis the TTA also acts as a central source of information and advice about entry to teaching, and has responsibilities relating to the continuing professional development of teachers. An independent professional council, the General Teaching Council, has been established to advise the Secretary of State and the TTA, with a separate council for Wales.

The Specialist Teacher Assistant (STA) scheme provides trained support to qualified teachers in the teaching of reading, writing and arithmetic to young pupils.

SHORTAGE SUBJECTS

The government has introduced various schemes in an attempt to address the shortage of teachers in England and Wales. Graduates training for a PGCE in certain secondary subjects (English, modern foreign languages, mathematics, science, technology, and Welsh (in Wales)), who then take up a teaching post, receive a training salary of £6,000 (£150 per week) and a further £4,000 lump sum after completing their first year of work. In Wales the scheme applies to all postgraduate trainee teachers, although only those teaching shortage subjects receive the lump sum. The latter will moreover be assisted to pay off their student loans over 10 years. Furthermore, providers of initial teacher training in England and Wales may receive funds from the TTA to help promote courses in certain subjects and to offer students on courses in those subjects financial support. The subjects are: design and technology; geography; information technology; mathematics; modern languages; music; religious education; science; and Welsh in Wales. A training salary for postgraduates training as primary teachers was trialled during 2000–1 and for trainee teachers in post-16 non-degree craft subjects from September 2001.

The TTA administers a returners' programme for qualified teachers who wish to refresh their skills before returning to the profession. They benefit from the waiving of course fees, a grant of up to £150 per week while studying and supplementary grants for childcare.

SCOTLAND

The General Teaching Council (GTC) for Scotland advises central government on matters relating to teacher supply and the professional suitability of all teacher training courses. The GTC is also the body responsible for disciplinary procedures in cases of professional misconduct. All teachers in maintained schools must be registered with the GTC, initially for a two-year probationary period which can be extended if necessary. Only graduates are accepted as entrants to the profession; primary school teachers undertake either a four-year vocational degree course or a one-year postgraduate course, while teachers of academic subjects in secondary schools undertake the latter. Most initial teacher training is classroom-based. The Scottish Qualification for Headship has been introduced for aspiring head teachers. The colleges of education provide both in-service and pre-service training for teachers which is subject to inspection by HM Inspectorate of Education. The colleges are funded by the Scottish Higher Education Funding Council, which also sets intake levels for teacher education courses.

NORTHERN IRELAND

All new entrants to teaching in grant-aided schools are graduates and hold an approved teaching qualification. Initial teacher training is provided by the two universities and two colleges of education, but is integrated with induction and early in-service training, the latter over a period of three years. The colleges are concerned with teacher education mainly for the primary school sector. They also provide B Ed courses for intending secondary school teachers of religious education, commercial studies, and craft, design and technology. With these exceptions, the professional training of teachers for secondary schools is provided in the education departments of the universities. A review of primary and secondary teacher training has taken place as a result of which all student teachers spend more time in the classroom. The General Teaching Council for Northern Ireland is to be established in 2002 to advise government on professional issues, to maintain a register of teachers and to act as a disciplinary body.

ACCREDITATION OF TRAINING INSTITUTIONS

Advice to central government on the accreditation, content and quality of initial teacher training courses is given in England by the TTA, in Wales by the HEFCW and in Northern Ireland by validating bodies (by the General Teaching Council for Northern Ireland when established). These bodies also monitor and disseminate good practice, assisted in Northern Ireland by the Teacher Education Committee. The GTC performs those functions in Scotland.

SERVING TEACHERS 1998–9 (*full-time and part-time*)(thousands):

Public sector schools	
Nursery and primary	230.2
Secondary	239.8
Special (public sector and non-maintained)	18.2
Independent schools	60.4
TOTAL	548.6

SALARIES

Qualified teachers in England, Wales and Northern Ireland, other than heads and deputy heads, are paid on an 18-point scale. Entry points and placement depend on qualifications and experience. There are additional cash allowances for management responsibilities, special needs work and recruitment and retention factors as calculated by the relevant body, i.e. the governing body or the LEA. The grade of 'Advanced Skills Teacher' was introduced to enhance prospects in the classroom for the most able teachers. High-performing teachers as assessed against national standards receive a performance-related pay increase of an extra £3,000 a year. There is a statutory superannuation scheme in maintained schools.

Salary scales for teachers in England Wales and Northern Ireland from 1 April 2001 are as follows:

Head	£33,375–£78,783
Deputy head	from £29,499
Advanced skills teacher	£27,973–£44,571
Teacher	£16,038–£31,128

Teachers in Scotland are paid on a nine-point scale. The entry point depends on type of qualification and additional allowances are payable under a range of circumstances.

Salary scales for teachers in Scotland are:

	from 1 April 2001	from 1 April 2002
Head	£32,526–£60,252	£33,826–£62,661
Depute Head	£32,526–£45,084	£33,826–£46,887
Principal teacher	£28,932–£33,750	£30,090–£35,100
Senior teacher	£26,424–£27,954	£27,480–£29,073
Teacher	£16,005–£25,644	£16,644–£25,670

FURTHER EDUCATION

Further education is defined as provision outside schools to people aged over 16 of education up to and including A-level and its equivalent.

ENGLAND AND WALES

Further education and sixth form colleges are funded directly by central government through the Learning and Skills Council in England (which assumed the role of the former Further Education Funding Council for England and the Training and Enterprise Councils and operates through 47 regional centres) and the National Council for Education and Training in Wales (formerly the Further Education Funding Council for Wales). The Councils have a duty to secure provision of adequate facilities in their areas and are also responsible for the assessment of quality, in which their inspectors play a key role. The colleges are controlled by autonomous further education corporations, which include substantial representation from industry and commerce, and which own their own assets and employ their own staff. Their funding is determined in part by the number of students enrolled and their level of achievement.

Teaching staff in further education establishments are not necessarily required to have teaching qualifications although many do so, but they are subject to regular appraisal of teaching performance. It is planned to introduce a mandatory professional qualification for college principals.

Much further education tends to be broadly vocational in purpose and employers are often involved in designing courses. It ranges from lower-level technical and commercial courses and government-sponsored training, through courses for those aiming at higher-level posts in industry, commerce and administration, to professional courses. Facilities exist for GCE A- and AS-levels, GCSEs, GNVQs and a full range of vocational qualifications. These courses can form the foundation for progress to higher education qualifications. Many students attend part-time, either through day or block release from employment, or in the evenings.

The main courses and examinations in the vocational field, all of which link in with the National Vocational

Qualification (NVQ) framework, are offered by the following bodies, but there are also many others.

The Edexcel Foundation was formed by the merger of the Business and Technology Education Council (BTEC) and London Examinations. It provides programmes of study across a wide range of subject areas. Qualifications offered include GNVQs, NVQs, GCSEs, AS and A-levels, National and Higher National diplomas and certificates and other BTEC qualifications.

City & Guilds specialise in developing qualifications and assessments for work-related and leisure qualifications. They offer nationally and internationally recognised certificates in over 500 vocational qualifications. The progressive structure of awards spans seven levels, from foundation to the highest level of professional competence.

Oxford, Cambridge and RSA Examinations cover the full range of academic and vocational qualifications. The latter include accounting, business administration, customer service, management, language schemes, information technology and teaching qualifications. A wide range of NVQs and GNVQs are offered and a policy operates of credit accumulation, so that candidates can take a single unit or complete qualifications.

There are 428 further education establishments (of which 105 are sixth form colleges) in England and 24 in Wales. In England (1998–9) there were 963.5 thousand full-time and sandwich-course students and 2,506.1 thousand part-time students. In Wales (1998–9) there were 43.9 thousand full-time and sandwich students and 162.4 thousand part-time students.

SCOTLAND

Responsibility for further education lies with the Scottish Executive under the Minister for Enterprise and Lifelong Learning. The Executive liaises with the Scottish Further Education Funding Council to administer further education funding. There are 47 further education colleges of which 43 are self-governing incorporated colleges run by their own boards of management. The boards include the principal, staff and student representatives among their ten to 16 members; at least half of whom must have experience of commerce, industry or professional practice. Two colleges, on Orkney and Shetland, are under Islands Council control and two others, Sabhal Mor Ostaig (the Gaelic college on Skye) and Newbattle Abbey are run by trustees.

The Scottish Qualifications Authority (SQA) is the statutory awarding body for qualifications in the national education and training system in Scotland. It is both the main awarding body for qualifications for work including Scottish Vocational Qualifications (SVQs) and is also their accrediting body. The SQA is by statute required clearly to separate its awarding and accrediting functions.

There are three main qualification families in Scottish further education: National Qualifications; Higher National Qualifications (HNC and HND); and SVQs. In addition to Standard Grade qualifications, National Qualifications are available at five levels: Access, Intermediate 1, Intermediate 2, Higher and Advanced Higher. Another feature of the qualifications system is the Scottish Group Award (SGA). SGAs are built up unit by unit and allow opportunity for credit transfer from other qualifications (such as Standard Grade or SVQ) providing a further option for learners, especially adult returners.

Advanced-level HNC/HND qualifications are available in further education colleges and higher education institutions. SQA accredits and awards SVQs which have mutual recognition with the NVQs available in the rest of the UK. SVQs are competence-based qualifications

suitable for work-place delivery but they can also be taken in further education colleges and other centres where work-place conditions can be simulated.

In the academic year 1999–2000 there were 38,176 full-time and sandwich-course students and 273,360 part-time students on non-advanced vocational courses of further education in further education colleges (excluding Newbattle Abbey College).

NORTHERN IRELAND

All further education colleges are free-standing corporate bodies like their counterparts in the rest of the UK. Planning is the responsibility of the Department for Employment and Learning, which funds the colleges directly. The colleges own their own property, are responsible for their own services and employ their own staff.

The governing bodies of the colleges must include at least 50 per cent membership from the professions, local business or industry, or other fields of employment relevant to the activities of the college.

In 2000–1 Northern Ireland had 17 institutions of further education, and there were 20,966 full-time and 58,323 part-time enrolments on vocational further education courses.

STUDENT SUPPORT

At present 16- to 19-year-olds may receive means-tested discretionary payments from LEAs, while adults may apply for funds including financial help with childcare allocated by central government through the funding bodies. The means-tested Education Maintenance Allowance (EMA) for 16- to 19-year-old students continuing their education beyond school leaving age in both schools and colleges is a weekly allowance worth up to £30 which is being piloted in certain areas in England and Scotland where there are problems of poverty and low staying-on rates. EMAs are payable subject to conditions laid out under a learning agreement. The access fund scheme is also being extended. Various similar options are under consideration in Northern Ireland.

NATIONAL VOCATIONAL QUALIFICATIONS

National Vocational Qualifications (NVQs) are workplace based occupational qualifications. General National Vocational Qualifications (GNVQs) provide a vocational alternative to academic qualifications in colleges and schools. GNVQs cover six broad categories in the NVQ framework and are aimed at those wishing to familiarise themselves with a range of opportunities. The Vocational A-level, introduced in September 2000, operates at three levels: the three unit vocational A-level (known as Vocational AS), equivalent to one GCE AS-level; the 6 unit Vocational A-level, equivalent to one GCE A-level; and the 12 unit Vocational A-level (double award) equivalent to two A-levels (formerly Advanced GNVQ). Part one GNVQ comprises Intermediate GNVQ, equivalent to two GCSEs at A* to C grade and Foundation GNVQ, equivalent to two GCSEs at D to G grade. The full GNVQ, also at Intermediate and Foundation level, is similarly equivalent to four GCSEs.

HIGHER EDUCATION

The term higher education is used to describe education above A-level, Higher and Advanced Higher Grade and their equivalent, which is provided in universities, colleges of higher education and in some further education colleges.

The Further and Higher Education Act 1992 and parallel legislation in Scotland removed the distinction between higher education provided by the universities and that provided in England and Wales by the former polytechnics and colleges of higher education and in Scotland by the former central institutions and others. It allowed all polytechnics, and other higher education institutions which satisfy the necessary criteria, to award their own taught course and research degrees and to adopt the title of university. All the polytechnics, art colleges and some colleges of higher education have since done so. The change of name does not affect the legal constitution of the institutions. Funding is by the Higher Education Funding Councils for England, Wales and Scotland and directly by the Department for Employment and Learning in Northern Ireland.

The number of students in higher education in the UK in 1999–2000 was (thousands):

Full-time, sandwich	1,259.7
% female	53.0%
Part-time	764.4
% female	55.4%
TOTAL	2,024.1
of which overseas	11.0%

The proportion of the 18- to 21-year-old population undertaking full-time and part-time courses in higher education was about 33 per cent in England and Wales, about 40 per cent in Scotland and about 45 per cent in Northern Ireland in 1999–2000. In the same year about twenty-five per cent of undergraduates in the first year of a first degree course were aged 21 years or over, while over 70 per cent of first year postgraduate students were aged 25 years or over. During that period 54.6 per cent of the student population were female (56.5 per cent of UK domiciled undergraduates). Women formed the majority of students in subjects allied to medicine (82.9 per cent), education (72 per cent), languages (69.3 per cent), veterinary science (68.1 per cent), information science (62.3 per cent), biological sciences (60.8 per cent) and social, economic and political studies (60.6 per cent). Men formed the majority of those studying engineering and technology (85.2 per cent), computer science (76.9 per cent), architecture, building and planning (72.2 per cent), physical sciences (62.8 per cent) and mathematics (63.1 per cent).

Responsibility for universities rests in England with the Secretary of State for Education and Skills and with Education Ministers in Scotland, Northern Ireland and Wales. Advice to government on matters relating to the universities is provided by the Higher Education Funding Councils for England, Wales and Scotland, and by the Higher Education Council in Northern Ireland. The Councils receive a block grant from central government which they allocate to the universities and colleges. The grant is allocated directly to institutions by the Department for Employment and Learning in Northern Ireland on the advice of the Northern Ireland Higher Education Council.

There are now 88 universities in the UK, where only 47 existed prior to the Further and Higher Education Acts 1992. Of the 88, 71 are in England (including one federal university), two (one a federal institution) in Wales, 13 in Scotland and two in Northern Ireland.

The pre-1992 universities each have their own system of internal government but broad similarities exist. Most are run by two main bodies: the senate, which deals primarily with academic issues and consists of members elected from within the university; and the council, which is the supreme body and is responsible for all appointments and promotions, and bidding for and allocation of financial resources. At least half the members of the council are drawn from outside the university. Joint committees of senate and council are common.

Those universities which were formerly polytechnics (38) or other higher education institutions (three) and the colleges of higher education (61) are run by higher education corporations, which are controlled by boards of governors. At least half the members of each board must be drawn from industry, business, commerce and the professions.

The non-residential Open University provides courses nationally leading to degrees. Teaching is through a combination of television and radio programmes, correspondence, tutorials, short residential courses and local audio-visual centres. No qualifications are needed for entry. The Open University offers a modular programme of undergraduate courses by credit accumulation and post-experience and postgraduate courses, including a programme of higher degrees which comprises BPhil, MPhil and PhD through research, and MA, MBA and MSc through taught courses. The Open University in England, Wales and Northern Ireland is funded by the Higher Education Funding Council for England (HEFCE) and in Scotland by the Scottish Higher Education Funding Council (SHEFC). The Open University's recurrent grant for 1999–2000 was £133.0 million from the HEFCE and £2.3 million from the Teacher Training Agency. In 2001 about 134,000 undergraduates were registered of whom about 54 per cent were women. Estimated cost (2001) of a six-credit degree was around £4,500 including course fees of about £3,300.

The University for Industry (UfI) was launched in autumn 2000 to promote learning ranging from basic skills to specialised technological and management skills. UfI operates through learning centres. The Scottish UfI operates within the distinctive Scottish system.

The independent University of Buckingham receives no public funding and provides a two-year course (four terms per year) leading to a bachelor's degree. Its tuition fees from October 2001 are £2,625 per term.

ENGLAND AND WALES

In 1999–2000 full-time and part-time student enrolments were (thousands):

England	
Undergraduates	1,091.1
% overseas	9.8%
Postgraduates	262.4
% overseas	30.4%
Wales	
Undergraduates	74.3
% overseas	8.6%
Postgraduates	14.1
% overseas	30.0%

Higher education courses funded by the funding bodies are also taught in some further education colleges. In England in 1999–2000 there were about 73.1 thousand full-time and part-time students (4.7 per cent of total higher education student numbers) on such courses and 716 enrolments (0.8 per cent of higher education student numbers) in Wales.

SCOTLAND

SHEFC funds 22 institutions of higher education, including 13 universities. The universities are broadly managed as described above and the remaining colleges are managed by independent governing bodies which include representatives of industrial, commercial, professional and educational interests. Most of the courses outside the universities have a vocational orientation and a substantial number are sandwich courses.

Student enrolments in 1999–2000 in universities and other higher education institutions were (thousands):

Undergraduates	133.7
% overseas	7.4%
Postgraduates	48.6
% overseas	27.3%

There were about 72 thousand students on higher education courses in further education colleges, amounting to about 27.8 per cent of the total number.

NORTHERN IRELAND

In Northern Ireland higher education is provided in the 17 colleges of further education, the two universities and two university colleges. These institutions offer a range of courses, which may include first and postgraduate degrees, PGCEs, undergraduate diplomas and certificates, and professional qualifications. Enrolments in higher education institutions in 2000–1 were:

Undergraduates	33,879
% overseas* students	2.4%
Postgraduates	8,113
% overseas* students	8.1%

*classified as non-UK or Republic of Ireland domiciled

In addition to the above, in 2000–1 there were 12,021 enrolments on higher education courses in Northern Ireland institutions of further education, which equates to 22.3 per cent of all higher education enrolments in Northern Ireland.

ACADEMIC STAFF

Each university and college appoints its own academic staff on its own conditions. However, there is a common salary structure and, except for Oxford and Cambridge, a common career structure in the pre-1992 universities and a common salary structure for the post-1992 universities. The Universities and Colleges Employers Association acts as a pay agency for universities and colleges.

Teaching staff in higher education require no formal teaching qualification, but the Institute of Teaching and Learning in Higher Education, funded by the funding Councils, has been established to set up an accreditation scheme for higher education teachers and to encourage innovation in teaching and learning. Teacher trainers are required to spend a certain amount of time in schools to ensure that they have sufficient recent practical experience.

In 1999–2000, there were 106,410 full-time and part-time teaching and research staff (UK nationals) in institutions of higher education in the UK.

Salary scales for staff in the pre-1992 universities differ from those in the former polytechnics and colleges; it is planned eventually to amalgamate them. The salary scales for non-clinical academic staff in the pre-1992 universities are (2000–1):

Professor	from £37,493
Senior lecturer	£32,510–£39,718
Lecturer grade B	£25,213–£30,967
Lecturer grade A	£18,731–£24,227

The salaries of clinical academic staff are kept broadly comparable to those of doctors and dentists in the National Health Service.

Salary scales for lecturers in the former polytechnics, now universities, and colleges of higher education in England, Wales and Northern Ireland are:

	1 September 2001	1 February 2002
Head of Department	from £26,304	from £26,304
Principal lecturer	£30,519–£38,373	£31,129–£39,141
Senior lecturer	£24,417–£32,265	£24,906–£32,910
Lecturer	£19,191–£26,163	£19,575–£26,686

and in Scotland:

	1 September 2001	1 March 2002
Head of Department	£45,697–£51,578	£46,154–£52,094
Senior Lecturer	£28,999–£42,143	£29,289–£42,605
Lecturer	£17,616–£35,109	£17,792–35,460

FINANCE

Although universities and colleges are expected to look to a wider range of funding sources than before, and to generate additional revenue in collaboration with industry, they are still largely financed, directly or indirectly, from government resources.

In 1999–2000 the total income of institutions of higher education in the UK was £12,779.7 million (£12,087.4 million in 1998–9) comprising (*percentage of income in parenthesis*):

	1999–2000 £ million	1998–9 £ million
Funding Council grants	£5,147.1 (40.3%)	£4,992.1 (40.7%)
Tuition fees and education contracts	£2,872.4 (22.5%)	£2,722.6 (22.5%)
Research grants and contracts	£1,973.4 (15.4%)	£1,831.4 (15.2%)
Other income*	£2,786.9 (21.8%)	£2,611.2 (21.6%)

*includes fees, services, endowments and investments

In the academic year 1999–2000 the HEFCE's and HEFCW's recurrent grant to institutions outside their sector for the provision of higher education courses was £143.5 million.

COURSES

In the UK all universities and some colleges award their own degrees and other qualifications and may act as awarding and validating bodies for neighbouring colleges which are not yet accredited. The Quality Assurance Agency for Higher Education, funded by institutional contributions, advises government on applications for degree-awarding powers.

Higher education courses last full-time for at least four weeks or, if part-time, involve more than 60 hours of instruction. Facilities exist for full-time and part-time study, day release, sandwich or block release. Credit accumulation and transfer (CATS) is a system of study which allows a student to achieve a final qualification by accumulating credits for courses of study successfully achieved, or even professional experience, over a period. Credit transfer information and values are carried on an electronic database called ECCTIS 2000, which is available in most careers offices and many schools and colleges.

Higher education courses comprise: first degree and postgraduate (including research); Diploma in Higher Education (DipHE); Higher National Diploma (HND) and Higher National Certificate (HNC); and preparation for professional examinations. The in-service training of teachers is also included, but is funded in England by the Teacher Training Agency, not the HEFCE.

The Diploma of Higher Education (DipHE) is a two-year diploma usually intended to serve as a stepping-stone to a degree course or other further study. The DipHE is awarded by the institution itself if it is accredited; by an accredited institution of its choice if not. The BTEC Higher National Certificate (HNC) is awarded after two years part-time study. The BTEC Higher National Diploma (HND) is awarded after two years full-time, or three years sandwich-course or part-time study.

With the exception of certain Scottish universities where master is sometimes used for a first degree in arts subjects, undergraduate courses lead to the title of Bachelor, Bachelor of Arts (BA) and Bachelor of Science (BSc) being the most common. For a higher degree the titles are: Master of Arts (MA), Master of Science (MSc) and the research degrees of Master of Philosophy (MPhil) and Doctor of Philosophy (PhD or, at a few universities, DPhil).

Most undergraduate courses at universities and colleges of higher education run for three years, but some take up to four years. They include modern language courses and honours courses at Scottish universities and the University of Keele. Professional courses in subjects such as medicine, veterinary science and architecture take longer.

Postgraduate studies vary in length. Certificates, diplomas or masters degrees usually take one year full-time or two years part-time. Research degrees take from two to three years full-time.

Post-experience short courses are forming an increasing part of higher education provision, reflecting the need to update professional and technical training. Most of these courses fund themselves.

ADMISSIONS

The target proportion of the 18- to 19-year-old age group entering full-time higher education for 2001–2 was set at 33 to 35 per cent. Institutions suffer financial penalties if the number of students laid down for them by the funding Councils is exceeded, but the individual university or college decides which students to accept. The formal entry requirements to most degree courses are two A-levels at grade E or above (or equivalent), and to HND courses one A-level (or equivalent). In practice, most offers of places require qualifications in excess of this, higher requirements usually reflecting the popularity of a course or institution. These requirements do not, however, exclude applications from students with a variety of non-GCSE qualifications or unquantified experience and skills.

For admission to a degree, DipHE or HND, potential students apply through a central clearing house, the Universities and Colleges Admission Service (UCAS). Applicants are supplied with an application form and the UCAS Handbook, available from schools, colleges and careers offices or direct from UCAS, and may apply to a maximum of six institutions/courses. The only exception among universities is the Open University, which conducts its own admissions.

Applications for undergraduate teacher training courses are made through UCAS. Details of initial teacher training courses in Scotland can be obtained from colleges of education and those universities offering such courses, and from the Committee of Scottish Higher Education Principals (COSHEP).

For admission as a postgraduate student, universities and colleges normally require a good first degree in a subject related to the proposed course of study or research,

but other experience and qualifications will be considered on merit. Most applications are made to individual institutions but there are two clearing houses of relevance. All postgraduate teacher training courses in England and Wales and most of those in Scotland utilise the Graduate Teacher Training Registry. Applications for post graduate certificate of education (PGCE) courses at institutions in Northern Ireland are made directly to the institutions. For social work the Social Work Admissions System operates.

FEES

From September 1998 entrants to undergraduate courses have paid, directly to the institution, an annual contribution to their fees (up to £1,075 in 2001–2) depending on their own level of income and that of their spouse or parents. The average cost of a higher education course in the UK is £4,000 and the balance is paid by the education authority or, in Northern Ireland, by the Education and Libraries Board. Students from EU member countries pay fees at home student rates and, if studying at institutions in England, Wales and Northern Ireland, are liable to make an annual contribution to fees assessed against family income. Among the classes of students exempt from payment are: Scottish domiciled and EU students at Scottish institutions; students from England, Wales and Northern Ireland in the fourth year of a four-year degree course at a Scottish institution; existing students with mandatory awards (see below), for whom the grant-awarding body pays; PGCE students; medical students in the fifth year of their course; health professionals on National Health Service bursaries; and full-time or part-time students on benefit or low incomes.

Universities and colleges are free to set their own charges for students from non-EU countries, whose fees are meant to cover the cost of their education. Financial help is available under a number of schemes.

For postgraduate students, the maximum tuition fee that will be reimbursed through the awards system is £2,805 (full-time) or £1,402.50 (part-time) in 2001–2.

STUDENT SUPPORT

LOANS

The means-tested interest-free loan is the main form of support for most undergraduate students in the UK who started full-time or sandwich undergraduate courses of higher education from the academic year commencing in September 1998. Students apply through LEAs in England and Wales, education and library boards in Northern Ireland and the Students Awards Agency in Scotland. The maximum loan available to full-time students in 2001–2 is £4,700, of which £3,525 (75%) is not subject to means testing.

Loan rates for 2001–2 (final year rates in parenthesis):

Living in college/ lodgings in London area	£4,700 (£4,075)
Living in college/ lodgings elsewhere	£3,815 (£3,310)
Living in parental home	£2,635 (£1,975)

Extra income assessed loans are available to students whose courses last over 30 term-time weeks or who need to study abroad in certain high-cost countries. Loans of up to £500 are available to part-time students on low incomes or with dependent children.

Loans are available to students on designated courses, which comprise those full-time or sandwich courses leading to: a degree; the Diploma of Higher Education;

the Higher National Diploma; initial teacher-training courses (not in Scotland), including those for the PGCE and the art teachers' certificate or diploma; a university certificate or diploma course lasting at least three years; and other qualifications which are specifically designated as being comparable to first degree courses. Certain residency conditions also apply. In 1999–2000, 723.6 thousand loans were taken up, to the value of £1,823.0 million.

Repayment arrangements differ for students who embarked upon higher education courses before the 1998–9 academic year and those starting thereafter. The former normally repay on a mortgage-style basis over five to seven years, although repayment can be deferred if annual income is at or below 85 per cent of national average earnings. The latter are not required to make repayments until their annual income is above £10,000 when nine per cent of the income above that amount is taken to repay the loan. Interest on the loan is linked to inflation in line with the Retail Prices Index. Providing repayments have been kept up, the loan is automatically cancelled on death; if the recipient becomes permanently disabled; or at age 65.

NON-REPAYABLE GRANTS AND ALLOWANCES

Eligible students, such as single parents and others with dependants, are entitled to apply for various additional means-tested supplementary grants for help in meeting certain living costs, for childcare and for each child at school. Disabled students are eligible for non means-tested Disabled Students Allowances.

MANDATORY GRANTS

Students who started their courses before September 1998 and certain others continue, for the duration of their course, to be eligible for means-tested maintenance grants from which a parental contribution is deductible on a sliding scale dependent on income or, for married students, from their spouse's income. However, a parental contribution is not deducted from the grant to students over 25 years of age who have been self-supporting for any three years before the beginning of their course.

Grants are paid by the local education authority for the area in which the student lives in England, Wales and Northern Ireland. The cost is reimbursed by central government. For students resident in Scotland grants are made by central government through the Student Awards Agency.

The means-tested maintenance grant, usually paid once a term, covers periods of attendance during term as well as the Christmas and Easter vacations, but not the summer vacation.

The basic grant rates for 2000–1 (rates for Scottish students in parentheses) are:

Living in College/lodgings in London area £2,335 (£2,255)
College/lodgings outside London area £1,900 (£1,825)
Parental home £1,555 (£1,345)

Additional allowances are available if, for example, the course requires a period of study abroad. Expenditure on mandatory awards in 1999–2000 was £470.9 million.

ACCESS FUNDS

Access funds are allocated by central government to the appropriate funding Councils in England and Wales and to the Student Awards Agency in Scotland and administered by further and higher education institutions. In Northern Ireland they are allocated by central govern-

ment directly to the institution. All students, whether full-or part-time, undergraduate or postgraduate, may apply but those whose courses attract a student loan must already have applied for their full entitlement before applying to the access funds. Access funds may be paid as a short-term loan but are usually paid as a grant. The amount payable depends on individual circumstances and on the amount the institution has available. Some colleges offer non-repayable bursaries from access funds, i.e. a payment for each year of the course, to students who might be prevented from completing their studies due to financial problems.

POSTGRADUATE AWARDS

Grants for postgraduate study are discretionary and competition for them is fierce. They comprise: maintenance grants for studentships, which cover students undertaking research degrees or taught masters degrees, are not means-tested and are dependent on the class of first degree (especially for research degrees); and flat-rate maintenance grants which replaced the former 30-week bursaries for new entrants from the academic year 2000–1. There are additional allowances for disabled students, those with dependants and for fieldwork expenses. Postgraduate students, with the exception of students in England, Wales and Northern Ireland on loan-bearing diploma courses such as teacher training, are not eligible to apply for student loans.

Awards are funded by The British Academy, the Higher Education Funding Councils for England and Wales, the Department for Employment and Learning (DEL) for Northern Ireland, and the Scottish Higher Education Funding Council.

Prospective students should apply for awards (depending on the subject domain) to the following bodies: the Arts and Humanities Research Board or to one of the six Research Council in England, Wales and Northern Ireland (where application may also be made to DEL) and to the Student Awards Agency in Scotland.

The rates of awards in 2001–2 are:

	London	Elsewhere
Studentships	£9,250	£7,500
Professional and vocational	£5,100	£4,300

ADULT AND CONTINUING EDUCATION

In the UK, the duty of securing adult and continuing education leading to academic or vocational qualifications is statutory. The Learning and Skills Council in England, the National Council for Education and Training in Wales and the Further Education Funding Council in Scotland are responsible for and fund those courses which take place in their sector and lead to academic and vocational qualifications, prepare students to undertake further or higher education courses, or confer basic skills; the Higher Education Funding Councils fund advanced courses of continuing education. The LEAs have the power, although not the duty, to provide those courses which do not fall within the remit of the funding bodies. Funding in Northern Ireland is through the education and library boards.

Adult education is provided in adult education centres and colleges run by LEAs (England and Wales), further education colleges and evening centres (Scotland), community schools (Northern Ireland), and the adult studies departments of higher education institutions.

The involvement of universities in adult education and continuing education has diversified considerably. Birkbeck College in the University of London caters solely for part-time students. The post-1992 universities and the colleges of higher education, because of their range of courses and flexible patterns of student attendance, provide opportunities in the field of adult and continuing education. The Forum for the Advancement of Continuing Education promotes collaboration between institutions of higher education active in this area. The Open University, in partnership with the BBC, provides distance teaching leading to first degrees, and also offers post-experience and higher degree courses.

Of the voluntary bodies, the biggest is the Workers' Educational Association (WEA) which operates throughout the UK, reaching about 150,000 adult students annually. The further education funding bodies and LEAs make grants towards provision.

NIACE, the National Organisation for Adult Learning, has a broad remit to promote lifelong learning opportunities for adults. NIACE works to develop increased participation in education and training. It does this through research and project work, conferences, publications and the provision of an information service to educational providers. NIACE Cymru, the Welsh committee, receives financial support from the National Assembly for Wales, support in kind from local authorities, and advises government, voluntary bodies and education providers on adult continuing education and training matters in Wales. In Scotland advice on adult and community education, and promotion thereof, is provided by Community Learning Scotland. In Northern Ireland those functions are undertaken by the Department for Employment and Learning.

The Universities' Association for Continuing Education (UACE) represents the continuing education community within higher education and is open to universities and higher education institutions in the UK with additional provision for international, associate and individual members.

GRANTS

Adult education bursaries for students at the long-term residential colleges of adult education are the responsibility of the colleges themselves. The awards are administered for the colleges by the Awards Officer of the Residential Colleges Committee for students resident in England. They are funded for colleges in England and Wales by the respective Councils; for colleges in Scotland by the Department for Lifelong Learning and administered by the Scottish Further Education Funding Council; and for colleges in Northern Ireland by the Department for Employment and Learning and administered by the education and library boards.

Education Directory

LOCAL EDUCATION AUTHORITY

ENGLAND

COUNTY COUNCILS

BEDFORDSHIRE, County Hall, Cauldwell Street, Bedford MK42 9AP. Tel: 01234-363222. *Director*, David Doran

BUCKINGHAMSHIRE, County Hall, Walton Street, Aylesbury HP20 1UA. Tel: 01296-382603. *Chief Education Officer*, P. J. Mooney

CAMBRIDGESHIRE, Education Information Office, Box ELH 1500, Shire Hall, Castle Hill, Cambridge CB3 0AP. Tel: 01223-717667. *Director*, A. Baxter

CHESHIRE, County Hall, Chester CH1 1SQ. Tel: 01244-602424. *Director of Education*, D. Cracknell

CORNWALL, County Hall, Truro TR1 3AY. Tel: 01872-322000. *Director of Education, Arts and Libraries*, J. Harris

CUMBRIA, 5 Portland Square, Carlisle CA1 1PU. Tel: 01228-606877. *Director of Education*, J. Nellist

DERBYSHIRE, County Hall, Matlock DE4 3AG. Tel: 01629-585641. *Chief Education Officer*, R. V. Taylor

DEVON, County Hall, Topsham Road, Exeter EX2 4QG. Tel: 01392-382059. *Director of Education, Arts and Libraries*, A. G. Smith

DORSET, County Hall, Colliton Park, Dorchester DT1 1XJ. Tel: 01305-224164. *Director*, D. Goddard

DURHAM, County Hall, Durham DH1 5UJ. Tel: 0191-383 3319. *Director*, K. Mitchell

EAST SUSSEX, County Hall, St Anne's Crescent, Lewes BN7 1SG. Tel: 01273-481000. *Director of Education*, Ms D. Stokoe

ESSEX, PO Box 47, Chelmsford CM2 6WN. Tel: 01245-492211. *Director of Learning Services*, P. A. Lincoln

GLOUCESTERSHIRE, Shire Hall, Westgate Street, Gloucester GL1 2TG. Tel: 01452-425300. *Acting Director*, S. King

HAMPSHIRE, The Castle, Winchester SO23 8UG. Tel: 01962-841841. *County Education Officer*, A. J. Seber

HERTFORDSHIRE, County Hall, Pegs Lane, Hertford SG13 8DE. Tel: 01992-555555. *Director*, R. Shostak

ISLE OF WIGHT, County Hall, High Street, Newport PO30 1UD. Tel: 01983-823400. *Director*, A. Kaye

KENT, Sessions House, County Hall, Maidstone ME14 1XQ. Tel: 01622-671411. *Strategic Director Education and Libraries*, N. Henwood

LANCASHIRE, PO Box 61, County Hall, Preston PR1 8RJ. Tel: 01772-254868. *Director of Education and Cultural Services*, C. J. Trinick

LEICESTERSHIRE, County Hall, Glenfield, Leicester LE3 8RF. Tel: 0116-265 6301. *Director*, Mrs J. A. M. Strong

LINCOLNSHIRE, County Offices, Newland, Lincoln LN1 1YQ. Tel: 01522-552222. *Director*, Dr C. Berry

NORFOLK, County Hall, Martineau Lane, Norwich NR1 2DH. Tel: 01603-222146. *Director*, Dr B. C. Slater

NORTHAMPTONSHIRE, Education and Community Learning, PO Box 233, County Hall, Northampton NN1 1AZ. Tel: 01604-236252. *Corporate Director*, Mrs B. Bignold

NORTHUMBERLAND, County Hall, Morpeth NE61 2EF. Tel: 01670-533601. *Director*, Dr L. Davis

NORTH YORKSHIRE, County Hall, Northallerton, N. Yorks DL7 8AE. Tel: 01609-780780. *Director*, Miss C. Welbourn

NOTTINGHAMSHIRE, County Hall, West Bridgford, Nottingham NG2 7QP. Tel: 0115-982 3823. *Director*, P. Tulley

OXFORDSHIRE, Education Department, Macclesfield House, New Road, Oxford OX1 1NA. Tel: 01865-815449. *Chief Education Officer*, G. Badman

SHROPSHIRE, The Shirehall, Abbey Foregate, Shrewsbury SY2 6ND. Tel: 01743-254307. *Corporate Director - Education Services*, Mrs E. Nicholson

SOMERSET, County Hall, Taunton TA1 4DY. Tel: 01823-355790. *Corporate Director - Education*, M. Jennings

STAFFORDSHIRE, Education Offices, Tipping Street, Stafford ST16 2DH. Tel: 01785-223121. *Director*, Mrs J. S. Hawkins

SUFFOLK, St Andrew House, County Hall, Ipswich IP4 1LJ. Tel: 01473-584631. *Director*, D. J. Peachey

SURREY, County Hall, Penrhyn Road, Kingston upon Thames KT1 2DJ. Tel: 0845-600 9009. *Director*, Dr P. Gray

WARWICKSHIRE, PO Box 24, 22 Northgate Street, Warwick CV34 4SP. Tel: 01926-410410. *County Education Officer*, E. Wood

WEST SUSSEX, County Hall, Chichester PO19 1RF. Tel: 01243-777129. *Director of Education and the Arts*, R. D. C. Bunker

WILTSHIRE, County Hall, Bythesea Road, Trowbridge BA14 8JB. Tel: 01225-713000. *Chief Education Officer*, R. W. Wolfson

WORCESTERSHIRE, County Hall, Spetchley Road, Worcester WR5 2NP. Tel: 01905-766895. *Director of Educational Services*, J. Kramer

UNITARY COUNCILS

BARNSLEY, Berneslai Close, Barnsley S70 2HS. Tel: 01226-773500. *Executive Director, Education*, Ms J. Potter

BATH AND NORTH-EAST SOMERSET, PO Box 25, Riverside, Temple Street, Keynsham, Bristol BS31 1DN. Tel: 01225-394200. *Director*, D. Williams

BIRMINGHAM, Education Offices, Margaret Street, Birmingham B3 3BU. Tel: 0121-303 2590. *Chief Education Officer*, Prof. T. Brighouse

BLACKBURN WITH DARWEN, Town Hall, Blackburn BB1 7DY. Tel: 01254-585541. *Director of Education and Training*, M. Pattison

BLACKPOOL, Progress House, Clifton Road, Blackpool FY4 4US. Tel: 01253-476555. *Director of Education and Cultural Services*, Dr D. Sanders

BOLTON, Paderborn House, Civic Centre, Bolton BL1 1JW. Tel: 01204-333333. *Director*, Mrs M. Blenkinsop

BOURNEMOUTH, Dorset House, 20–22 Christchurch Road, Bournemouth BH1 3NL. Tel: 01202-456219. *Director*, K. Shaikh

BRACKNELL FOREST, Edward Elgar House, Skimped Hill Lane, Bracknell, Berks RG12 1LY. Tel: 01344-424642. *Director of Education*, T. Eccleston

EDUCATION BRADFORD, Support Office, Flockton Road, Bradford BD4 7RY. Tel: 01274-751840. *Director of Educational Services*, Mr Paul Brett

BRIGHTON AND HOVE, PO Box 2503, Kings House, Grand Avenue, Hove BN3 2SU. Tel: 01273-290000. *Strategic Director of Education and Lifelong Learning*, D. Hawker

BRISTOL, The Council House, College Green, Bristol BS99 7EB. Tel: 0117-903 7961. *Director of Education and Lifelong Learning*, R. Riddell

BURY, Athenaeum House, Market Street, Bury BL9 0SW. Tel: 0161-253 5652. *Chief Education Officer*, H. Williams

CALDERDALE, Northgate House, Northgate, Halifax HX1 1UN. Tel: 01422-357257. *Director*, Ms C. White

COVENTRY, Council Offices, Earl Street, Coventry CV1 5RS. Tel: 024-7683 1511. *Director*, Ms C. Goodwin

DARLINGTON, Town Hall, Darlington DL1 5QT. Tel: 01325-380651. *Director*, G. Pennington

DERBY, Middleton House, 27 St Mary's Gate, Derby DE1 3NN. Tel: 01332-716924. *Director*, A. Flack

DONCASTER, Directorate of Education and Culture, The Council House, College Road, Doncaster DN1 3AD. Tel: 01302-737103. *Executive Director*, M. Simpson

DUDLEY, Westox House, 1 Trinity Road, Dudley DY1 1JQ. Tel: 01384-814225. *Interim Director of Education*, J. Freeman

EAST RIDING OF YORKSHIRE, County Hall, Beverley HU17 9BA. Tel: 01482-392000. *Director of Education, Leisure and Libraries*, J. Ginnever

GATESHEAD, Civic Centre, Regent Street, Gateshead NE8 1HH. Tel: 0191-433 3000. *Director*, B. H. Edwards

HALTON, Halton Borough Council, Grosvenor House, Halton Lea, Runcorn WA7 2WD. Tel: 0151-424 2061. *Director*, G. Talbot

HARTLEPOOL, Civic Centre, Victoria Road, Hartlepool TS24 8AY. Tel: 01429-266522. *Director*, J. J. Fitt

HEREFORDSHIRE, Education and Conference Centre, 4 Blackfriars Street, Hereford HR4 9ZR. Tel: 01432-260000. *Director*, Dr E. Oram

KINGSTON UPON HULL, Essex House, Manor Street, Kingston upon Hull HU1 1YD. Tel: 01482-613161. *Acting Group Director Learning Services*, Mr S. Jenkins

KIRKLEES, Oldgate House, 2 Oldgate, Huddersfield HD1 6QW. Tel: 01484-225242. *Director of Lifelong Learning*, G. Tonkin

KNOWSLEY, Education Offices, Huyton Hey Road, Huyton, Knowsley L36 9YH. Tel: 0151-443 3220. *Director of Education and Lifelong Learning*, S. Munby

EDUCATION LEEDS, Merrion House, Merrion Way, 110 Merrion Centre, Leeds LS2 8DT. Tel: 0113-247 5590. *Chief Executive*, C. Edwards

LEICESTER, Marlborough House, 38 Welford Road, Leicester LE2 7AA. Tel: 0116-252 7807. *Director*, S. Andrews

LIVERPOOL, 4th Floor, Lewis Buildings, 4 Renshaw Street, Liverpool L1 4AD. Tel: 0151-233 3000. *Executive Director*, C. Hilton

LUTON, Unity House, 111 Stuart Street, Luton LU1 5NP. Tel: 01582-546000. *Corporate Director, Lifelong Learning*, T. Dessent

MANCHESTER, Overseas House, Quay Street, Manchester M3 3BB. Tel: 0161-234 7125. *Chief Education Officer*, D. Johnston

MEDWAY, Compass Centre, Chatham Maritime, Chatham, Kent ME4 4YN. Tel: 01634-331011. *Director*, R. Bolsin

MIDDLESBROUGH, PO Box 69, Vancouver House, Gurney Street, Middlesbrough TS1 1EL. Tel: 01642-262001. *Corporate Director of Education*, Dr B. Comiskey

MILTON KEYNES, Learning and Development Directory, Saxon Court, 502 Avebury Boulevard, Milton Keynes MK9 3HS. Tel: 01908-253325. *Head of School Effectiveness and Early Years Services*, J. McElligott

NEWCASTLE UPON TYNE, Civic Centre, Newcastle upon Tyne NE1 8PU. Tel: 0191-232 8520 ext. 5301. *Director of Education and Libraries*, P. Turner

NORTH EAST LINCOLNSHIRE, Education Department, 7 Eleanor Street, Grimsby DN32 9DU. Tel: 01472-323025. *Director of Learning and Child Care*, G. Hill

NORTH LINCOLNSHIRE, PO Box 35, Hewson House, Station Road, Brigg DN20 8XJ. Tel: 01724-297240. *Director of Education and Personal Development*, Dr T. W. Thomas

NORTH SOMERSET, PO Box 51, Town Hall, Weston-super-Mare BS23 1ZZ. Tel: 01934-888888. *Director*, J. Simpson

NORTH TYNESIDE, Town Hall, High Street East, Wallsend, Tyne & Wear NE28 7RR. Tel: 0191-200 6565. *Chief Education Officer*, Anne Marie Carrie

NOTTINGHAM CITY, Sandfield Centre, Sandfield Road, Lenton, Nottingham NG7 1QH. Tel: 0115-915 0706. *Director*, Heather Tomlinson

OLDHAM, PO Box 40, Civic Centre, West Street, Oldham OL1 1XJ. Tel: 0161-911 4200. *Executive Director*, Ms C. Berry

PETERBOROUGH, Bayard Place, Broadway, Peterborough PE1 1FB. Tel: 01733-748000. *Director*, R. Clayton

DEPARTMENT FOR LIFELONG LEARNING, PLYMOUTH, Plymouth PL1 2AA. Tel: 01752-307400. *Director for Lifelong Learning*, S. Faruqi

POOLE, Civic Centre, Poole, Dorset BH15 2RU. Tel: 01202-633202. *Policy Director – Education*, Dr S. Goodwin

PORTSMOUTH, Civic Offices, Guildhall Square, Portsmouth PO1 2AL. Tel: 023-9284 1209. *City Education Officer*, J. Gaskin

READING, Civic Centre, PO Box 2623, Reading RG1 7WA. Tel: 0118-939 0900. *Director*, A. J. Daykin

REDCAR AND CLEVELAND, Council Offices, Kirkleatham Street, Redcar TS10 1YA. Tel: 01642-444342. *Director*, P. Scott

ROCHDALE, PO Box 70, Municipal Offices, Smith Street, Rochdale OL16 1YD. Tel: 01706-647474. *Director of Education*, T. Piggott

ROTHERHAM, Education Office, Norfolk House, Walker Place, Rotherham S65 1AS. Tel: 01709-382121. *Acting Executive Director for Education, Culture and Leisure Services*, Ms D. Billups

RUTLAND, Catmose, Oakham, Rutland LE15 6HP. Tel: 01572-722577. *Director of Education and Youth*, Ms C. Chambers

ST HELENS, Rivington Centre, Rivington Road, St Helens WA10 4ND. Tel: 01744-455321. *Director of Community Education and Leisure Services*, Ms S. Richardson

SALFORD, Pendlebury Road, Swinton, Manchester *Director of Education and Leisure*, M. Carriline

SANDWELL, PO Box 41, Shaftesbury House, 402 High Street, West Bromwich B70 9LT. Tel: 0121-525 7366. *Executive Director, Education and Lifelong Learning*, E. Griffiths

SEFTON, Town Hall, Trinity Road, Bootle, Merseyside L20 7AE. Tel: 0151-922 4040. *Director*, Ms E. Simpson

SHEFFIELD, Education Directorate, Leopold Street, Sheffield S1 2HH. Tel: 0114-273 5722. *Executive Director of Education*, J. Crossley-Holland

SLOUGH, Town Hall, Bath Road, Slough SL1 3UQ. Tel: 01753-875712. *Chief Education Officer*, J. Christie

SOLIHULL, PO Box 20, Council House, Solihull B91 3QU. Tel: 0121-704 6656. *Director of Education, Libraries and Arts*, D. Nixon

SOUTHAMPTON, Education Services, Southampton City Council, 5th Floor, Frobisher House, Nelson Gate, Southampton SO15 1S2. Tel: 023-8083 2771. *Director*, R. Hogg

456   Education

SOUTH GLOUCESTERSHIRE EDUCATION, Bowling Hill, Chipping Sodbury, S. Glos BS37 6JX. Tel: 01454-868686. *Director of Education*, Ms T. Gillespie

SOUTHEND, Civic Centre, Victoria Avenue, Southend-on-Sea SS2 6ER. Tel: 01702-215890. *Education and Library Services Director*, S. Hay

SOUTH TYNESIDE, Town Hall and Civic Offices, Westoe Road, South Shields NE33 2RL. Tel: 0191-427 1717. *Director*, Ms B. Hughes

STOCKPORT, Town Hall, Stockport SK1 3XE. Tel: 0161-474 3808. *Chief Education Officer*, M. K. J. Hunt

STOCKTON-ON-TEES, Municipal Buildings, PO Box 228, Church Road, Stockton-on-Tees TS18 1XE. Tel: 01642-393441. *Director*, S. T. Bradford

STOKE-ON-TRENT, Floor 2, Civic Centre, Glebe Street, Stoke-on-Trent ST4 1HH. Tel: 01782-232014. *Director*, N. Rigby

SUNDERLAND, PO Box 101, Civic Centre, Sunderland SR2 7DN. Tel: 0191-553 1000. *Director of Education and Community Services*, Dr J. A. Williams

SWINDON, Sandord House, Sanford Street, Swindon SN1 1QN. Tel: 01793-463069. *Director, Education and Community*, M. Lusty

TAMESIDE, Council Offices, Wellington Road, Ashton under Lyne, Lancs OL6 6DL. Tel: 0161-342 2201. *Director of Education and Cultural Services*, P. Lawday

TELFORD AND WREKIN, Civic Offices, Telford, Shropshire TF3 4WF. Tel: 01952-202402. *Corporate Director: Education*, Mrs C. Davies

THURROCK, PO Box 118, Grays, Essex RM17 6GF. Tel: 01375-652652. *Interim Director of Education*, Jenny Cairns

TORBAY, Oldway Mansion, Paignton, Devon TQ3 2TE. Tel: 01803-208208. *Director*, G. Cane

TRAFFORD, PO Box 40, Trafford Town Hall, Talbot Road, Stretford, Trafford, Greater Manchester M32 0EL. Tel: 0161-912 1212. *Executive Director, Lifelong Learning*, C. Pratt

WAKEFIELD, County Hall, Bond Street, Wakefield WF1 2QW. Tel: 01924-305500. *Chief Education Officer*, J. McLeod

WALSALL, Civic Centre, Darwall Street, Walsall WS1 1TP. Tel: 01922-652301. *Director*, C. Green

WARRINGTON, New Town House, Buttermarket Street, Warrington, Cheshire WA1 2NJ. Tel: 01925-442901. *Director*, M. L. Roxburgh

WEST BERKSHIRE, Avonbank House, West Street, Newbury, Berks RG14 1BZ. Tel: 01635-519722. *Corporate Director for Children and Young People*, R. Hubbard

WIGAN, Gateway House, Standishgate, Wigan, Lancs WN1 1AE. Tel: 01942-828891. *Director*, R. J. Clark

WINDSOR AND MAIDENHEAD, Town Hall, St Ives Road, Maidenhead, Berks SL6 1RF. Tel: 01628-796367. *Director*, M. Peckham

WIRRAL, Hamilton Building, Conway Street, Birkenhead CH41 4FD. Tel: 0151-666 2121. *Director*, C. Rice

WOKINGHAM, Education and Cultural Services, Shute End, Wokingham, Berks RG40 1WN. Tel: 0118-974 6100. *Director*, A. Roberts

WOLVERHAMPTON, Civic Centre, St Peter's Square, Wolverhampton WV1 1RR. Tel: 01902-554100. *Co-ordinating Director for Lifelong Learning*, R. Lockwood

YORK, 10–12 George Hudson Street, York YO1 6ZG. Tel: 01904-613161. *Director of Education and Leisure*, Patrick Scott

LONDON

*Inner London borough

BARKING AND DAGENHAM, Town Hall, Barking, Essex IG11 7LU. Tel: 020-8227 3181/3662. *Director of Education, Arts and Libraries*, A. Larbalestier

BARNET, The Old Town Hall, Friern Barnet Lane, London N11 3DL. Tel: 020-8359 3048. *Chief Education Officer*, Ms L. Stone

BEXLEY, Hill View, Hill View Drive, Welling, Kent DA16 3RY. Tel: 020-8303 7777. *Director*, P. McGee

BRENT, Chesterfield House, 9 Park Lane, Wembley, Middx HA9 7RW. Tel: 020-8937 3190. *Director of Education, Arts and Libraries*, Ms Jackie Griffin

BROMLEY, Civic Centre, Stockwell Close, Bromley BR1 3UH. Tel: 020-8313 4066. *Director*, K. Davis

*CAMDEN, Crowndale Centre, 218–220 Eversholt Street, London NW1 1BD. Tel: 020-7974 1505. *Director*, R. Litchfield

*CITY OF WESTMINSTER, City Hall, 64 Victoria Street, London SW1E 6QP. Tel: 020-7641 1947. *Director*, J. Harris

*CORPORATION OF LONDON, Education Service, Corporation of London, PO Box 270, Guildhall, London EC2P 2EJ. Tel: 020-7332 1750. *City Education Officer*, D. Smith

CROYDON, Taberner House, Park Lane, Croydon CR9 3JS. Tel: 020-8760 5452. *Director*, D. Sands

EALING, Perceval House, 14–16 Uxbridge Road, London W5 2HL. Tel: 020-8758 5410. *Director*, A. Parker

ENFIELD, PO Box 56, Civic Centre, Silver Street, Enfield, Middx EN1 3XQ. Tel: 020-8379 3201. *Director*, Ms E. Graham

*GREENWICH, Riverside House, Woolwich High Street, London SE18 6DN. Tel: 020-8921 8238. *Director*, G. Gyte

*HACKNEY, Edith Cavell Building, Enfield Road, London N1 5BA. Tel: 020-8356 8436. *Director*, Mr A. Wood

*HAMMERSMITH AND FULHAM, Cambridge House, Cambridge Grove, London W6 0LE. Tel: 020-8748 3020. *Director*, Ms C. Whatford

HARINGEY, 48 Station Road, Wood Green, London N22 7TY. Tel: 020-8489 0000. *Director*, S. Jenkin

HARROW, PO Box 22, Civic Centre, Station Road, Harrow HA1 2UW. Tel: 020-8863 5611. *Director*, P. A. Osburn

HAVERING, The Broxhill Centre, Broxhill Road, Harold Hill, Romford RM4 1XN. Tel: 01708-432488. *Executive Director*, S. Evans

HILLINGDON, Civic Centre, High Street, Uxbridge UB8 1UW. Tel: 01895-250528. *Corporate Director*, P. O'Hear

HOUNSLOW, Civic Centre, Lampton Road, Hounslow, Middx TW3 4DN. Tel: 020-8583 2000. *Director*, J. D. Tricket

*ISLINGTON EDUCATION DEPARTMENT, Laycock Street, Islington, London N1 1TH. Tel: 020-7527 5566. *Director of Education*, J. Slater

*KENSINGTON AND CHELSEA, Town Hall, Hornton Street, London W8 7NX. Tel: 020-7361 3303. *Executive Director*, R. Wood

KINGSTON UPON THAMES, Guildhall 2, Kingston upon Thames KT1 1EU. Tel: 020-8547 5220. *Director*, Mr J. Braithwaite

*LAMBETH LOCAL EDUCATION SERVICES, International House, Canterbury Crescent, London SW9 7QE. Tel: 020-7926 1000. *Acting Director*, A. Wood

*LEWISHAM, 3rd Floor, Laurence House, 1 Catford Road, London SE6 4RU. Tel: 020-8314 8527. *Executive Director – Education and Culture*, Ms F. Sulke

MERTON, Civic Centre, London Road, Morden, Surrey SM4 5DX. Tel: 020-8545 3251. *Acting Director of Education, Leisure and Libraries*, Mr Tony Lenney

NEWHAM, Broadway House, 322 High Street, Stratford, London E15 1AJ. Tel: 020-8430 2000. *Director*, Ms P. Maddison

REDBRIDGE, Lynton House, 255–259 High Road, Ilford, Essex IG1 1NN. Tel: 020-8478 3020. *Director*, E. Grant

RICHMOND UPON THAMES, 1st Floor, Regal House, London Road, Twickenham TW1 3QS. Tel: 020-8891 7500. *Chief Education Officer*, Anji Phillips

*SOUTHWARK, John Smith House, 144–152 Walworth Road, London SE17 1JL. Tel: 020-7525 5050/5001. *Strategic Director of Education and Lifelong Learning*, Dr Roger Smith

SUTTON, The Grove, Carshalton, Surrey SM5 3AL. Tel: 020-8770 5000. *Strategic Director of Learning for Life*, Dr I. Birnbaum

*TOWER HAMLETS, Town Hall, Mulberry Place, 5 Clove Crescent, London E14 2BG. Tel: 020-7364 5000. *Corporate Director – Education*, Ms C. Gilbert

WALTHAM FOREST, Leyton Municipal Offices, High Road, Leyton, London E10 5QJ. Tel: 020-8527 5544 ext. 5015

*WANDSWORTH, Town Hall, Wandsworth High Street, London SW18 2PU. Tel: 020-8871 8013. *Director*, P. Robinson

WALES

ANGLESEY, Swyddfa'r Sir, Llangefni, Anglesey LL77 7EY. Tel: 01248-752921. *Director of Lifelong Learning and Leisure*, R. P. Jones

BLAENAU GWENT, Victoria House, Victoria Business Park, Ebbw Vale, Blaenau Gwent NP23 8ER. Tel: 01495-355434. *Director*, B. Mawby

BRIDGEND, Sunnyside, Bridgend CF31 4AR. Tel: 01656-642600. *Director of Education, Leisure and Community Services*, D. Matthews

CAERPHILLY, Council Offices, Caerphilly Road, Ystrad Mynach, Hengoed CF82 7EP. Tel: 01443-815588. *Director*, D. Hopkins

CARDIFF, County Hall, Atlantic Wharf, Cardiff CF10 4UW. Tel: 029-2087 2700. *Head of Service – Schools Services*, H. Knight

CARMARTHENSHIRE, Pibwrlwyd, Carmarthen SA31 2NH. Tel: 01267-224501. *Director of Education and Community Services*, A. Davies

CEREDIGION, Swyddfa'r Sir, Marine Terrace, Aberystwyth SY23 2DE. Tel: 01970-633600. *Director*, R. J. Williams

CONWY, Government Buildings, Dinerth Road, Colwyn Bay LL28 4UL. Tel: 01492-575031/032. *Director*, R. E. Williams

DENBIGHSHIRE, Caledfryn, Smithfireld Road, Dengbigh, Denbighshire LL16 3RJ. Tel: 01824-706777. *Director*, S. Bowen

FLINTSHIRE, County Hall, Mold CH7 6ND. Tel: 01352-704010. *Director*, K. McDonogh

GWYNEDD, Shirehall Street, Caernarfon LL55 1SH. Tel: 01286-679162. *Director, Education, Culture and Leisure*, D. Whittall

MERTHYR TYDFIL EDUCATION DEPARTMENT, Ty Keir Hardie, Riverside Court, Avenue De Clichy, Merthyr Tydfil CF47 8XD. Tel: 01685-724600. *Corporate Chief Officer (Education)*, Mr W. V. Morgan

MONMOUTHSHIRE, County Hall, Cwmbran NP44 2XH. Tel: 01633-644487. *Director of Lifelong Learning and Leisure*, P. Cookoe

NEATH PORT TALBOT, Civic Centre, Port Talbot SA13 1PJ. Tel: 01639-763298. *Director*, K. Napieralla

NEWPORT, Civic Centre, Newport NP20 4UR. Tel: 01633-232257. *Chief Education Officer*, D. Griffiths

PEMBROKESHIRE, County Hall, Haverfordwest SA61 1TP. Tel: 01437-764551. *Director of Education and Community Services*, G. Davies

POWYS, County Hall, Llandrindod Wells LD1 5LG. Tel: 01597-826000. *Director*, M. Barker

RHONDDA, CYNO, TAFF, Education Centre, Grawen Street, Porth CF39 0BU. Tel: 01443-687666. *Group Director, Education and Children's Services*, D. Jones

SWANSEA, County Hall, Oystermouth Road, Swansea SA1 3SN. Tel: 01792-636351. *Director*, R. Parry

TORFAEN, County Hall, Croesyceiliog, Cwmbran, Torfaen NP44 2WN. Tel: 01633-648610. *Director*, M. de Val

VALE OF GLAMORGAN, Civic Offices, Holton Road, Barry CF63 4RU. Tel: 01446-709138. *Director of Learning and Development*, B. Jeffreys

WREXHAM, Ty Henblas, Queen's Square, Wrexham LL13 8AZ. Tel: 01978-297421. *Director*, T. Garner

SCOTLAND

ABERDEEN CITY, Summerhill Education Centre, Stronsay Drive, Aberdeen AB15 6JA. Tel: 01224-346060. *Director*, J. Stodter

ABERDEENSHIRE, Woodhill House, Westburn Road, Aberdeen AB16 5GJ. Tel: 01224-665420. *Director*, H. Vernal

ANGUS COUNCIL EDUCATION AUTHORITY, County Buildings, Market Street, Forfar DD8 3WE. Tel: 01307-461460. *Director of Education*, J. Anderson

ARGYLL AND BUTE COUNCIL, EDUCATION, Argyll House, Alexandra Parade, Dunoon PA23 8AJ. Tel: 01369-704000. *Director of Education*, A. C. Morton

CITY OF EDINBURGH, Wellington Court, 10 Waterloo Place, Edinburgh EH1 3EG. Tel: 0131-469 3000. *Director, Education*, Mr R. Jobson

CLACKMANNANSHIRE, Lime Tree House, Alloa FK10 1EX. Tel: 01259-452431. *Acting Executive Director Education and Community Services*, Mr J. Goodall

DUMFRIES AND GALLOWAY, Education Department, 30 Edinburgh Road, Dumfries DG1 1JG. Tel: 01387-260419. *Director for Education*, F. Sanderson

DUNDEE CITY COUNCIL EDUCATION DEPARTMENT, Floor 8, Tayside House, Crichton Street, Dundee DD1 3RJ. Tel: 01382-433088. *Director of Education*, Mrs A. Wilson

EAST AYRSHIRE, Council Headquarters, London Road, Kilmarnock KA3 7BU. Tel: 01563-576017. *Director*, J. Mulgrew

EAST DUNBARTONSHIRE, Boclair House, 100 Milngavie Road, Bearsden, Glasgow G61 2TQ. Tel: 0141-578 8000. *Strategic Director – Community*, Ms S. Bruce

EAST LOTHIAN, John Muir House, Haddington EH41 3HA. Tel: 01620-827562. *Director of Education and Community Services*, A. Blackie

EAST RENFREWSHIRE, Council Offices, Eastwood Park, Rouken Glen Road, Giffnock G46 6UG. Tel: 0141-577 3431. *Director*, Mrs E. J. Currie

FALKIRK, McLaren House, Marchmont Avenue, Polmont, Falkirk FK2 0NZ. Tel: 01324-506600. *Director*, Dr G. Young

FIFE, Fife House, North Street, Glenrothes KY7 5PN. Tel: 01592-413667. *Head of Education*, A. McKay

GLASGOW CITY, Nye Bevan House, 20 India Street, Glasgow G2 4PF. Tel: 0141-287 6898. *Director*, K. Corsar

HIGHLAND, Council Buildings, Glenurquhart Road, Inverness IV3 5NX. Tel: 01463-702802. *Director*, B. Robertson

INVERCLYDE, 105 Dalrymple Street, Greenock PA15 1HT. Tel: 01475-712824. *Director*, B. McLeary

MIDLOTHIAN, Fairfield House, 8 Lothian Road, Dalkeith EH22 3ZG. Tel: 0131-270 7500. *Director*, D. MacKay

MORAY, Council Offices, High Street, Elgin IV30 1BX. Tel: 01343-563171. *Director of Educational Services*, D. M. Duncan

NORTH AYRSHIRE, Cunninghame House, Irvine KA12 8EE. Tel: 01294-324400. *Corporate Director – Educational Services*, J. Travers

NORTH LANARKSHIRE, Municipal Buildings, Kildonan Street, Coatbridge ML5 3BT. Tel: 01236-812222. *Director*, M. O'Neill

ORKNEY ISLANDS, Council Offices, School Place, Kirkwall, Orkney KW15 1NY. Tel: 01856-873535. *Director of Education and Recreation*, L. Manson

PERTH AND KINROSS EDUCATION AND CHILDREN'S SERVICES, Pullar House, 35 Kinnoull Street, Perth PH1 5GD. Tel: 01738-476200. *Education Director and Children's Services*, W. Frew

RENFREWSHIRE COUNCIL EDUCATION AND LEISURE DEPT, Council Headquarters, South Building, Cotton Street, Paisley PA1 1LE. Tel: 0141-842 5601. *Director of Education and Leisure*, Ms S. Rae

SCOTTISH BORDERS, Council Headquarters, Newtown St Boswells, Melrose, Roxburghshire TD6 0SA. Tel: 01835-824000. *Director*, J. Christie

SHETLAND ISLANDS, Hayfield House, Hayfield Lane, Lerwick, Shetland ZE1 0QD. Tel: 01595-744000. *Head of Education Service*, M. Payton

SOUTH AYRSHIRE, County Buildings, Wellington Square, Ayr KA7 1DR. Tel: 01292-612201. *Director of Education, Culture and Lifelong Learning*, M. McCabe

SOUTH LANARKSHIRE, Council Headquarters, Almada Street, Hamilton ML3 0AE. Tel: 01698-454545. *Executive Director*, Ms M. Allan

STIRLING, Viewforth, Stirling FK8 2ET. Tel: 01786-442678. *Director of Children's Services*, G. Jeyes

WEST DUNBARTONSHIRE, Garshake Road, Dumbarton G82 3PU. Tel: 01389-737301. *Director of Education and Cultural Services*, I. McMurdo

EILEAN SIAR/WESTERN ISLES, Council Offices, Sandwick Road, Stornoway, Isle of Lewis HS1 2BW. Tel: 01851-703773. *Director of Education*, M. Macleod

WEST LOTHIAN COUNCIL EDUCATION SERVICES, Lindsay House, South Bridge Street, Bathgate EH48 1TS. Tel: 01506-776000. *Corporate Manager*, R. Stewart

NORTHERN IRELAND

BELFAST EDUCATION AND LIBRARY BOARD, 40 Academy Street, Belfast BT1 2NQ. Tel: 028-9056 4000. *Chief Executive*, D. Cargo

NORTH EASTERN EDUCATION AND LIBRARY BOARD, County Hall, 182 Galgorm Road, Ballymena, Co. Antrim BT42 1HN. Tel: 028-2565 3333. *Chief Executive*, G. Topping

SOUTH EASTERN EDUCATION AND LIBRARY BOARD, Grahamsbridge Road, Dundonald BT16 2HS. Tel: 028-9056 6200. *Chief Executive*, J. B. Fitzsimons

SOUTHERN EDUCATION AND LIBRARY BOARD, 3 Charlemont Place, The Mall, Armagh BT61 9AX. Tel: 028-3751 2200. *Chief Executive*, Mrs H. McClenaghan

WESTERN EDUCATION AND LIBRARY BOARD, 1 Hospital Road, Omagh, Co. Tyrone BT79 0AW. Tel: 028-8241 1411. *Chief Executive*, P. J. Martin

ISLANDS

GUERNSEY, The Grange, St Peter Port, Guernsey GY1 1RQ. Tel: 01481-710821. *Director*, D. T. Neale

JERSEY, PO Box 142, Jersey JE4 8QJ. Tel: 01534-509500. *Director*, T. W. McKeon

ISLE OF MAN, Murray House, 5–11 Mount Havelock, Douglas, Isle of Man IM1 2SG. Tel: 01624-685820. *Director*, R. B. Cowin

ISLES OF SCILLY, Town Hall, St Mary's, Isles of Scilly TR21 0LW. Tel: 01720-422537 ext. 145. *Secretary for Education*, P. S. Hygate

ADVISORY BODIES

SCHOOLS

BRITISH EDUCATIONAL COMMUNICATIONS AND TECHNOLOGY AGENCY, Milburn Hill Road, Science Park, Coventry CV4 7JJ. Tel: 024-7641 6994; Fax: 024-7641 1418. *Chief Executive*, O. Lynch

EDUCATION OTHERWISE, PO Box 7420, London N9 9SG. Tel: Helpline: 0870-730 0074

INTERNATIONAL BACCALAUREATE ORGANIZATION, Peterson House, Malthouse Avenue, Cardiff Gate, Cardiff CF23 8GL. Tel: 029-2054 7777; Fax: 029-2054 7778. *Director of Academic Affairs*, Dr H. Drennen

LEARNING AND SKILLS COUNCIL, 101 Lockhurst Lane, Coventry CV6 5SF. Tel: 024-7670 3241; Fax: 024-7670 3334

LEARNING AND SKILLS COUNCIL, Cheylesmore House, Quinton Road, Coventry CV1 2WT. Tel: 0845-019 4170; Fax: 024-7686 3100

SPECIAL EDUCATIONAL NEEDS TRIBUNAL, 7th Floor, Windsor House, 50 Victoria Street, London SW1H 0NW. Tel: 020-7925 6925; Fax: 020-7925 6926. *President*, T. Aldridge

INDEPENDANT SCHOOLS

GOVERNING BODIES ASSOCIATION, The Ancient Foresters, Bush End, Takeley, Bishop's Stortford, Herts CM22 6NN. Tel: 01279-871865; Fax: 01279-871865. *Secretary*, F. V. Morgan

GOVERNING BODIES OF GIRLS' SCHOOLS ASSOCIATION, The Ancient Foresters, Bush End, Takeley, Bishop's Stortford, Herts CM22 6NN. Tel: 01279-871865; Fax: 01279-871865. *Secretary*, F. V. Morgan

INDEPENDENT SCHOOLS COUNCIL, Grosvenor Gardens House, 35–37 Grosvenor Gardens, London SW1W 0BS. Tel: 020-7 798 1590; Fax: 020-7 798 1591. *General Secretary*, Dr A. B. Cooke

INDEPENDENT SCHOOLS EXAMINATIONS BOARD, Jordan House, Christchurch Road, New Milton, Hants BH25 6QJ. Tel: 01425-621111; Fax: 01425-620044. *Administrator*, Mrs J. Williams

FURTHER EDUCATION

AOSEC, Building 33, The University of Reading, London Road, Reading RG1 5AQ. Tel: 0118-931 6320; Fax: 0118-931 6324. *Chief Executive*, B. J. Knowles

Regional Advisory Councils

ASSOCIATION OF COLLEGES IN THE EASTERN REGION, Suite 1, Lancaster House, Meadow Lane, St Ives, Huntingdon, Cambs PE27 4LG. Tel: 01480-468198; Fax: 01480-468601. *Chief Executive*, N. Brenton

CENTRA (EDUCATION AND TRAINING SERVICES) LTD, Duxbury Park, Duxbury Hall Road, Chorley, Lancs PR7 4AT. Tel: 01257-241428; Fax: 01257-260357. *Chief Executive*, P. Wren

EMFEC (EAST MIDLAND FURTHER EDUCATION COUNCIL), Robins Wood House, Robins Wood Road, Aspley, Nottingham NG8 3NH. Tel: 0115-854 1616; Fax: 0115-854 1617. *Chief Executive*, Ms J. Gardiner
LEARNING AND SKILLS DEVELOPMENT AGENCY, Citadel Place, Tinworth Street, London SE11 5EH. Tel: 020-7 840 5400; Fax: 020-7 840 5401. *Chief Executive*, C. Hughes
NCFE, Portland House, New Bridge Street, Newcastle upon Tyne NE1 8AN. Tel: 0191-201 3100; Fax: 0191-2013101. *Chief Executive*, I. M. Sutcliffe
SOUTH WEST ASSOCIATION FOR EDUCATION AND TRAINING, Bishops Hull House, Bishops Hull, Taunton, Somerset TA1 5EP. Tel: 01823-335491; Fax: 01823-323388. *Chief Executive*, Ms L. McGrath
WELSH JOINT EDUCATION COMMITTEE, 245 Western Avenue, Cardiff CF5 2YX. Tel: 029-2026 5000; Fax: 029-2057 5894

HIGHER EDUCATION

ASSOCIATION OF COMMONWEALTH UNIVERSITIES, John Foster House, 36 Gordon Square, London WC1H 0PF. Tel: 020-7380 6700; Fax: 020-7387 2655.. *Secretary-General*, Prof. M. G. Gibbons
NORTHERN IRELAND HIGHER EDUCATION COUNCIL, 4th Floor, Room 407, Adelaide House, 39–49 Adelaide Street, Belfast BT2 8FD. Tel: 028-9025 7702; Fax: 028-9025 7701. *Chairman*, Sir Kenneth Bloomfield
QUALITY ASSURANCE AGENCY FOR HIGHER EDUCATION, Southgate House, Southgate Street, Gloucester GL1 1UB. Tel: 01452-557000; Fax: 01452-557070. *Chief Executive*, J. Randall
UNIVERSITIES SCOTLAND, 53 Hanover Street, Edinburgh EH2 2PJ. Tel: 0131-226 1111; Fax: 0131-226 1100. *Director*, D. Caldwell
UNIVERSITIES UK, Woburn House, 20 Tavistock Square, London WC1H 9HQ. Tel: 020-7 419 4111; Fax: 020-7388 8649. *President*, Prof. R. Floud

CURRICULUM COUNCILS

AWDURDOD CYMWYSTERAU, CWRICWLWM AC ASESU CYMRU/QUALIFICATIONS, CURRICULUM AND ASSESSMENT AUTHORITY FOR WALES, Castle Buildings, Womanby Street, Cardiff CF10 1SX. Tel: 029-20 375400; Fax: 029-20 343612. *Chief Executive*, J. V. Williams
LEARNING AND TEACHING SCOTLAND, Gardyne Road, Dundee DD5 1NY. Tel: 01382-443600; Fax: 01382-443645. *Chief Executive*, M. Baughan
NORTHERN IRELAND COUNCIL FOR THE CURRICULUM, EXAMINATIONS AND ASSESSMENT, Clarendon Dock, 29 Clarendon Road, Belfast BT1 3BG. Tel: 028-9026 1200; Fax: 028-9026 1234. *Chief Executive*, G. Boyd
QUALIFICATIONS AND CURRICULUM AUTHORITY, 83 Piccadilly, London W1Y 8QA. Tel: 020-7509 5555; Fax: 020-7 509 6666. *Chairman*, Sir William Stubbs, PH.D.

EXAMINING BODIES

ASSESSMENT AND QUALIFICATIONS ALLIANCE (AQA), Devas Street, Manchester M15 6EX. Tel: 0161-953 1180; Fax: 0161-273 7572. *Director General*, Ms K. Tattersall

ASSESSMENT AND QUALIFICATIONS ALLIANCE (AQA), Stag Hill House, Guildford, Surrey GU2 7XJ. Tel: 01483-506506; Fax: 01483-300152. *Director General*, Ms K. Tattersall
EDEXCEL, Stewart House, 32 Russell Square, London WC1B 5DN. Tel: 0870-240 9800; Fax: 020-7758 6960. *Chief Executive*, Dr C. Townsend
OCR (OXFORD CAMBRIDGE AND RSA EXAMINATIONS), Head Office, 1 Regent Street, Cambridge CB2 1GG. Tel: 01223-552552; Fax: 01223-552553. *Chief Executive*, Dr R. McLone
NORTHERN IRELAND COUNCIL FOR THE CURRICULUM, EXAMINATIONS AND ASSESSMENT, 29 Clarendon Road, Belfast, County Antrim BT1 3BG. Tel: 01232-261200; Fax: 01232-261234. *Chief Executive*, G. Boyd
WELSH JOINT EDUCATION COMMITTEE, 245 Western Avenue, Cardiff CF5 2YX. Tel: 029-2026 5000; Fax: 029-2057 5894. *Chief Executive*, W. G. Roberts

GCSE – *see* above

EDEXCEL
NORTHERN IRELAND COUNCIL FOR THE CURRICULUM, EXAMINATIONS AND ASSESSMENT
WELSH JOINT EDUCATION COMMITTEE

A-LEVEL – *see* above

ASSESSMENT AND QUALIFICATIONS ALLIANCE (AQA)
EDEXCEL
NORTHERN IRELAND COUNCIL FOR THE CURRICULUM, EXAMINATIONS AND ASSESSMENT EXAMINATIONS AND ASSESSMENT
OCR (OXFORD, CAMBRIDGE AND RSA EXAMINATIONS)

SCOTLAND

SCOTTISH QUALIFICATIONS AUTHORITY, Hanover House, 24 Douglas Street, Glasgow G2 7NQ. Tel: 0141-248 7900; Fax: 0141-242 2244. *Chief Executive*, B. Morton

FURTHER EDUCATION – *see* above

CITY GUILDS, 1 Giltspur Street, London EC1A 9DD. Tel: 020-7 294 2468; Fax: 020-7294 2400. *Director-General*, C. Humphries, CBE
EDEXCEL
OCR (OXFORD, CAMBRIDGE AND RSA EXAMINATIONS)

FUNDING COUNCILS

FURTHER EDUCATION

LEARNING AND SKILLS COUNCIL, Cheylesmore House, Quinton Road, Coventry CV1 2WT. Tel: 0845-019 4170; Fax: 024-7686 3100. *Chief Executive*, J. Harwood
NATIONAL COUNCIL – ELWA, Linden Court, The Orchards, Ilex Close, Cardiff CF14 5DZ. Tel: 029-2076 1861; Fax: 029-2076 3163. *Director of Operations*, L. Bloomfield
SCOTTISH FURTHER EDUCATION FUNDING COUNCIL, Donaldson House, 97 Haymarket Terrace, Edinburgh EH12 5HD. Tel: 0131-313 6500; Fax: 0131-313 6501. *Chief Executive*, Prof. J. Sizer, CBE

HIGHER EDUCATION

HIGHER EDUCATION COUNCIL-ELWA, Linden Court, The Orchards, Ilex Close, Cardiff CF14 5DZ. Tel: 029-2076 1861; Fax: 029-2076 3163. *Chief Executive*, S. Martin

HIGHER EDUCATION FUNDING COUNCIL FOR ENGLAND, Northavon House, Coldharbour Lane, Bristol BS16 1QD. Tel: 0117-931 7317; Fax: 0117-931 7203. *Chief Executive*, Sir Brian Fender, KT.

SCOTTISH HIGHER EDUCATION FUNDING COUNCIL, Donaldson House, 97 Haymarket Terrace, Edinburgh EH12 5HD. Tel: 0131-313 6500; Fax: 0131-313 6501. *Chief Executive*, Prof. J. Sizer, CBE

STUDENT AWARDS AGENCY FOR SCOTLAND, Gyleview House, 3 Redheughs Rigg, Edinburgh EH12 9HH. Tel: 0131-476 8212; Fax: 0131-244 5717. *Chief Executive*, D. Stephen

STUDENT LOANS COMPANY LTD, 100 Bothwell Street, Glasgow G2 7JD. Tel: 0141-306 2000. *Chief Executive*, C. Ward

TEACHER TRAINING AGENCY, Portland House, Stag Place, London SW1E 5TT. Tel: 020-7925 3700; Fax: 020-7925 3790. *Chairman*, Prof. C. Booth

---

ADMISSIONS AND COURSE INFORMATION

CAREERS RESEARCH AND ADVISORY CENTRE, Sheraton House, Castle Park, Cambridge CB3 0AX. Tel: 01223-460277; Fax: 01223-311708. *Chief Executive*, D. Thomas

GRADUATE TEACHER TRAINING REGISTRY, Rosehill, New Barn Lane, Cheltenham, Glos GL52 3LZ. Tel: 01242-544600; Fax: 01242-544962. *Small Systems Unit Manager*, Mrs J. Pearce

SOCIAL WORK ADMISSIONS SYSTEM, Rosehill, New Barn Lane, Cheltenham, Glos GL52 3LZ. Tel: 01242-544600; Fax: 01242-544962. *Small Systems Unit Manager*, Mrs J. Pearce

UNIVERSITIES AND COLLEGES ADMISSIONS SERVICE, Rosehill, New Barn Lane, Cheltenham, Glos GL52 3LZ. Tel: 01242-222444; Fax: 01242-544963. *Chief Executive*, M. A. Higgins

UNIVERSITIES SCOTLAND, 53 Hanover Street, Edingburgh EH2 2PJ. Tel: 0141-353 1880; Fax: 0141-353 1881. *Director*, D. Caldwell

---

UNIVERSITIES

UNIVERSITY OF ABERDEEN (1495)
Aberdeen AB24 3FX. Scotland
Tel: 01224-272000
Chancellor, The Lord Wilson of Tillyorn, GCMG (1997)
Rector, Miss C. Dickson Wright
Vice-Chancellor and Principal, Prof. C. D. Rice

UNIVERSITY OF ABERTAY DUNDEE (1994)
Bell Street, Dundee DD1 1HG. Scotland
Tel: 01382-308000
Chancellor, The Rt. Hon. Earl of Airlie, KT, GCVO, PC (1994)
Registrar, Dr D. Button
Vice-Chancellor, Prof. B. King

ANGLIA POLYTECHNIC UNIVERSITY (1992)
Bishop Hall Lane, Chelmsford, Essex CM1 1SQ.
Tel: 01245-493131
Chancellor, vacant
Vice-Chancellor, M. Malone-Lee, CB

ANGLIA POLYTECHNIC UNIVERSITY (1992)
East Road, Cambridge CB1 1PT.

Tel: 01223-363271
Chancellor, vacant
Vice-Chancellor, M. Malone-Lee, CB

ASTON UNIVERSITY (1895)
Aston Triangle, Birmingham B4 7ET.
Tel: 0121-359 3611
Chancellor, Sir Adrian Cadbury, (1979)
Registrar and Secretary, R. D. A. Packham
Vice-Chancellor, Prof. M. Wright

UNIVERSITY OF BATH (1966)
Claverton Down, Bath BA2 7AY.
Tel: 01225-826826
Chancellor, The Lord Tugendhat, (1998)
Registrar, J. A. Bursey
Vice-Chancellor, Prof. G. Breakwell

UNIVERSITY OF BIRMINGHAM (1900)
Edgbaston, Birmingham BH15 2TT.
Tel: 0121-414 3344
Chancellor, Sir Alexander Jarratt, CB (1983)
Registrar and Secretary, D. E. Hall
Vice-Chancellor, Prof. M. Sterling, DENG, FRENG

BOURNEMOUTH UNIVERSITY (1992)
Christchurch Road, Bournemouth BH1 3LT.
Tel: 01202-524111
Chancellor, The Baroness Cox of Queensbury, (1992)
Registrar, N. O. G. Richardson
Vice-Chancellor, Prof. G. Slater

BOURNEMOUTH UNIVERSITY (1992)
Fern Barrow, Poole, Dorset BH12 5BB.
Tel: 01202-524111
Chancellor, The Baroness Cox of Queensbury, (1992)
Registrar, N. O. G. Richardson
Vice-Chancellor, Prof. G. Slater

UNIVERSITY OF BRADFORD (1966)
Richmond Road, Bradford, W. Yorks BD7 1DP.
Tel: 01274-232323
Chancellor, The Baroness Lockwood of Dewsbury, (1997)
Registrar and Secretary, N. J. Andrew
Vice-Chancellor, Prof. C. Bell

UNIVERSITY OF BRIGHTON (1992)
Lewes Road, Brighton BN2 4AT.
Tel: 01273-600900
Chairman of the Board, C. Hume
Director, Prof. Sir David Watson
Deputy Director, D. E. House
Secretary, Ms C. E. Moon

UNIVERSITY OF BRISTOL (1909)
Tyndall Avenue, Bristol BS8 1TH.
Tel: 0117-928 9000
Chancellor, Sir Jeremy Morse, KCMG (1989)
Registrar, D. Pretty
Vice-Chancellor, Prof. Eric Thomas

BRUNEL UNIVERSITY (1966)
Uxbridge, Middx UB8 3PH.
Tel: 01895-274000
Academic and Principal Registrar, J. B. Alexander
Chancellor, The Rt. Hon Lord Wakeham, PC, JP, DL, FCA, HON AND UNIV, HON PHD (1998)
Vice-Chancellor and Principal, Prof. M. J. H. Sterling, PH.D, FRENG.

UNIVERSITY OF BUCKINGHAM (1983)
Buckingham MK18 1EG.
Tel: 01280-814080

Chancellor, Sir Martin Jacomb, (1998)
Registrar and Secretary, S. Cooksey
Vice-Chancellor, Dr Terence Kealey

UNIVERSITY OF CAMBRIDGE
Trinity Lane, Cambridge CB2 1TN.
Tel: 01223-337733

UNIVERSITY OFFICERS, ETC.
Chancellor, HRH The Prince Philip, Duke of Edinburgh, KG, KT, OM, GBE, PC (1977)
Commissary, The Lord Oliver of Aylmerton (*Trinity Hall*), PC (1989)
Deputy High Steward, The Lord Richardson of Duntisbourne, MBE, TD, PC (1983)
Director of the Fitzwilliam Museum, D. D. Robinson (*Clare*), (1995)
Librarian, P. K. Fox (*Selwyn*), (1994)
Orator, A. J. Bowen (*Jesus*), (1993)
Proctors, Dr D. J. Chivers (Selwyn); V. E. Izzet (Christ's), (2001)
Registrary, T. J. Mead (*Wolfson*), PH.D. (1997)
Secretary-General of the Faculties, D. A. Livesey (*Emmanuel*), PH.D. (1992)
Treasurer, Mrs J. Womack (*Trinity Hall*), (1993)
Vice-Chancellor, Prof. Sir Alec Broers, FRS (1996)

COLLEGES AND HALLS *with dates of foundation*
CHRIST'S, (1505), *Master*, A. J. Munro, PH.D. (1995)
CHURCHILL, (1960), *Master*, Sir John Boyd, KCMG (1996)
CLARE, (1326), *Master*, Prof. B. A. Hepple, LLD (1993)
CLARE HALL, (1966), *President*, Prof. Dame Gillian Beer, DBE, LITTD., FBA (1994)
CORPUS CHRISTI, (1352), *Master*, Prof. H. Ahmed, PH.D. (2000)
DARWIN, (1964), *Master*, Prof. W. Brown (2000)
DOWNING, (1800), *Master*, Dr S. G. Fleet, PHD (2001)
EMMANUEL, (1584), *Master*, Prof. J. E. Ffowcs-Williams, SC.D. (1996)
FITZWILLIAM, (1966), *Master*, Prof. B. F. G. Johnson (1999)
GIRTON, (1869), *Mistress*, Prof. A. M. Strathern, PH.D. (1998)
GONVILLE AND CAIUS, (1348), *Master*, N. McKendrick (1996)
HOMERTON, (1824) (for B.Ed. Students), *Principal*, Dr K. B. Pretty (1991)
HUGHES HALL, (1885) (for post-graduate students), *President*, Prof. P. Richards, PHD (1998)
JESUS, (1496), *Master*, Prof. R. Mair, SRENG
KING'S, (1441), *Provost*, Prof. P. P. G. B. Bateson, SC.D., FRS (1987)
*LUCY CAVENDISH COLLEGE, (1965) (for women research students and mature and affiliated undergraduates), *President*, Dame Veronica Sutherland (2001)
MAGDALENE, (1542), *Master*, Prof. Sir John Gurdon, D.PHIL., FRS (1995)
*NEW HALL, (1954), *President*, Mrs A. Lonsdale (1996)
*NEWNHAM, (1871), *Principal*, Baroness O'Neill, CBE (1992)
PEMBROKE, (1347), *Master*, Sir Roger Tomkys, KCMG (1992)
PETERHOUSE, (1284), *Master*, Prof. Sir John Meuric Thomas, FRS (1993)
QUEENS', (1448), *President*, The Lord Eatwell (1997)
ROBINSON, (1977), *Warden*, Prof. the Lord Lewis of Newnham, SC.D., FRS (1977)
SELWYN, (1882), *Master*, Prof. R. J. Bowring, LITT.D. (2000)

SIDNEY SUSSEX, (1596), *Master*, Prof. S. J. N. Dawson (1999)
ST CATHARINE'S, (1473), *Master*, Prof. D. S. Ingram, SC.D. (2000)
ST EDMUND'S, (1896), *Master*, Prof. R. B. Heap, SC.D. (1996)
ST JOHN'S, (1511), *Master*, Prof. P. Goddard, PH.D., FRS (1994)
TRINITY, (1546), *Master*, Prof. A. K. Sen , PHD (1998)
TRINITY HALL, (1350), *Master*, Prof. P. Clarke (1984)
WOLFSON, (1965), *President*, G. Johnson, PH.D. (1994)
*College for women only

UNIVERSITY OF CENTRAL ENGLAND IN BIRMINGHAM (1992)
Perry Barr, Birmingham B42 2SU.
Tel: 0121-331 5000
Chancellor, I. McArdle
Registrar and Secretary, Ms M. Penlington
Vice-Chancellor, Dr P. C. Knight, CBE

UNIVERSITY OF CENTRAL LANCASHIRE (1992)
Preston PR1 2HE.
Tel: 01772-201201
Chancellor, Richard Evans, (1995)
Registrar, Ms L. Munro
Vice-Chancellor, Dr M. McVicar

CITY UNIVERSITY (1966)
Northampton Square, London EC1V 0HB.
Tel: 020-7040 5060
Academic Registrar, A. H. Sevilleb (until Dec 2001), PH.D.
Chancellor, The Rt. Hon. the Lord Mayor of London
Vice-Chancellor, Prof. D. W. Rhind

COVENTRY UNIVERSITY (1992)
Priory Street, Coventry CV1 5FB.
Tel: 024-7688 7688
Academic Registrar, Dr J. Gledhill, PH.D.
Chancellor, The Lord Plumb, DL (1995)
Secretary, Mrs L. Arlidge
Vice-Chancellor, Dr M. Goldstein, CBE, PH.D.

CRANFIELD UNIVERSITY (1969)
Cranfield, Beds MK43 0AL.
Tel: 01234-750111
Academic Registrar and Secretary, D. J. Buck
Chancellor, The Lord Vincent of Coleshill, GBE, KCB, DSO (1998)
Vice-Chancellor, Prof. F. R. Hartley, D.SC.

DE MONTFORT UNIVERSITY (1992)
The Gateway, Leicester LE1 9BH.
Tel: 0116-255 1551
Academic Registrar, V. E. Critchlow
Chancellor, Baroness Prashar of Runnymede, CBE (1998)
Vice-Chancellor, Prof. P. Tasker

UNIVERSITY OF DERBY (1992)
Kedleston Road, Derby DE22 1GB.
Tel: 01332-590500
Chancellor, Sir Christopher Ball, FRSA
Registrar, Mrs J. M. Fry, BSC
Vice-Chancellor, Prof. R. Waterhouse

UNIVERSITY OF DUNDEE (1967)
Dundee DD1 4HN. Scotland
Tel: 01382-344000
Academic Secretary, Dr I. K. Francis
Chancellor, Sir James Black, FRCP, FRS (1992)
Rector, F. MacAualy, 1998–2001
Vice-Chancellor, Sir Alan Langlands

UNIVERSITY OF DURHAM Durham DH1 3HP.
Tel: 0191-374 2000
Chancellor, Sir Peter Ustinov, CBE, FRSL, KT, HON DLITT, FRSA, FRSL
Registrar and Secretary, J. V. Hogan, PH.D.
Vice-Chancellor, Prof. Sir Kenneth Calman, KCB, MD, FRCP, FRCGP, FRCR, FRSE, PH.D.

COLLEGES

COLLINGWOOD, *Principal*, Prof. G. H. Blake, PH.D. (1987)
GRADUATE SOCIETY, *Principal*, M. J. Rowell, PH.D. (2000)
GREY, *Master*, V. E. Watts (1989)
HATFIELD, *Master*, Prof. T. P. Burt, PH.D. (1996)
ST AIDAN'S, *Principal*, J. S. Ashworth (1998)
ST CHAD'S, *Principal*, Revd J. P. M. Cassidy, PH.D. (1997)
ST CUTHBERT'S SOCIETY, *Principal*, B. Robertson (1999)
ST HILD AND ST BEDE, *Principal*, J. A. Pearson, PH.D. (2000)
ST JOHN'S, *Principal*, Rt. Revd. Prof. S. W. Sykes (1999)
ST MARY'S, *Principal*, Miss J. L. Hobbs (1999)
STOCKTON CAMPUS, *Provost*, Prof. Sir Kenneth Calman
TREVELYAN, *Principal*, N. Martin, PH.D (2000)
UNIVERSITY, *Master*, Prof. M. E. Tucker, PH.D. (1998)
USHAW, *President*, Revd J. O'Keefe (1996)
VAN MILDERT, *Principal*, G. Patterson (2000)

UNIVERSITY OF EAST ANGLIA (1963)
Norwich NR4 7TJ.
Tel: 01603-456161
Chancellor, Sir Geoffrey Allen, FRS, FRENG. (1994)
Registrar and Secretary, B. Summers
Vice-Chancellor, V. Watts

UNIVERSITY OF EAST LONDON (1898)
Longbridge Road, Dagenham, Essex RM8 2AS.
Tel: 020-8223 3000
Chancellor, The Lord Rix, CBE, DL, KT. (1997)
Registrar and Secretary, A. Ingle
Vice-Chancellor, Prof. F. W. Gould

UNIVERSITY OF EDINBURGH (1583)
South Bridge, Edinburgh EH8 9YL. Scotland
Tel: 0131-650 1000
Chancellor, HRH The Prince Philip, Duke of Edinburgh, KG, KT, OM, GBE, PC, FRS (1952)
Rector, R. Harper, MSP
Vice-Chancellor, Prof. Sir Stewart Sutherland, FBA, FRSE

UNIVERSITY OF ESSEX (1964)
Wivenhoe Park, Colchester CO4 3SQ.
Tel: 01206-873333
Chancellor, The Lord Nolan, PC (1997)
Registrar and Secretary, T. Rich, PH.D.
Vice-Chancellor, Prof. I. Crewe

UNIVERSITY OF EXETER (1955)
The Queen's Drive, Exeter EX4 4QJ.
Tel: 01392-263263
Chancellor, The Lord Alexander of Weedon (1998), QC
Registrar and Secretary, I. H. C. Powell
Vice-Chancellor, Sir Geoffrey Holland, KCB

UNIVERSITY OF GLAMORGAN (1992)
Pontypridd CF37 1DL. Wales
Tel: 01443-480480; Freephone: 0800-716925
Chancellor, The Rt. Hon. Lord Merlyn-Rees, PC, QC (1994)
Registrar, J. O'Shea
Secretary, J. L. Bracegirdle,
Vice-Chancellor, Prof. Sir Adrian Webb

UNIVERSITY OF GLASGOW (1451)
University Avenue, Glasgow G12 8QQ. Scotland

Tel: 0141-339 8855
Chancellor, Sir William Kerr Fraser, GCB, FRSE
Vice-Chancellor, Prof. Sir Graeme Davies, FRENG, FRSE

GLASGOW CALEDONIAN UNIVERSITY (1993)
Cowcaddens Road, Glasgow G4 0BA. Scotland
Tel: 0141-331 3000
Principal and Vice-Chancellor, Dr I. A. Johnston, PH.D., CB, FIPO, FRSA
Pro Vice Chancellor Learning, Prof. P. Abbott, KBE (1993)
Secretary to University Court, B. M. Murphy

UNIVERSITY OF GREENWICH (1992)
Park Row, Greenwich, London SE10 9LS.
Tel: 020-8331 8000
Academic Registrar, Miss C. Rose
Chancellor, Lord Holme of Cheltenham, CBE
Vice-Chancellor, Prof. R. Trainor

HERIOT-WATT UNIVERSITY (1966)
Edinburgh EH14 4AS. Scotland
Tel: 0131-449 5111
Chancellor, The Lord Mackay of Clashfern, KT, PC (1979)
Vice-Chancellor, Prof. J. S. Archer, FRENG.

UNIVERSITY OF HERTFORDSHIRE (1992)
College Lane, Hatfield, Herts AL10 9AB.
Tel: 01707-284000
Chancellor, The Lord MacLaurin of Knebworth, (1996)
Registrar and Secretary, P. G. Jeffreys,
Vice-Chancellor, Prof. N. K. Buxton,

UNIVERSITY OF HUDDERSFIELD (1992)
Queensgate, Huddersfield HD1 3DH.
Tel: 01484-422288
Chancellor, Sir Ernest Hall, OBE (1996)
Vice-Chancellor, Prof. J. R. Tarrant

UNIVERSITY OF HULL (1954)
Cottingham Road, Hull HU6 7RX.
Tel: 01482-346311
Chancellor, The Lord Armstrong of Ilminster, GCB, CVO (1994)
Registrar, D. J. Lock
Vice-Chancellor, Dr D. J. Drewry

KEELE UNIVERSITY (1962)
Keele, Staffs ST5 5BG.
Tel: 01782-621111
Chancellor, Sir Claus Moser, KCB, CBE, FBA (1986)
Registrar and Secretary, S. J. Morris
Vice-Chancellor, Prof. J. V. Finch, CBE, DL, PH.D.

UNIVERSITY OF KENT AT CANTERBURY (1965)
Canterbury, Kent CT2 7NZ.
Tel: 01227-764000
Chancellor, Sir Crispin Tickell, GCMG, KCVO
Registrar and Secretary, N. A. McHard,
Vice-Chancellor, Prof. D. Melville, PH.D.

KINGSTON UNIVERSITY (1992)
Kingston upon Thames, Surrey KT1 1LQ.
Tel: 020-8547 2000
Academic Registrar, Mrs A. Stokes
Chancellor, Sir Peter Hall
Secretary, R. S. Abdula, MBE
Vice-Chancellor, Prof. P. Scott

UNIVERSITY OF LANCASTER (1964)
Bailrigg, Lancaster LA1 4YW.
Tel: 01524-65201
Chancellor, HRH Princess Alexandra, the Hon. Lady Ogilvy, GCVO (1994)
Secretary, Miss F. Aiken
Vice-Chancellor, Prof. W. Ritchie, OBE

UNIVERSITY OF LEEDS (1904)
Leeds LS2 9JT.
Tel: 0113-243 1751
Academic Registrar, A. Parkinson
Chancellor, Lord Bragg of Wigton
Vice-Chancellor, Prof. A. G. Wilson

LEEDS METROPOLITAN UNIVERSITY (1992)
Calverley Street, Leeds LS1 3HE.
Tel: 0113-283 2600
Chancellor, L. Silver, OBE (1989)
Vice-Chancellor, Prof. L. Wagner, CBE

UNIVERSITY OF LEICESTER (1957)
University Road, Leicester LE1 7RH.
Tel: 0116-252 2522
Chancellor, Sir Michael Atiyah, OM, FRS, PH.D., D.SC. (1995)
Registrar and Secretary, K. J. Julian,
Vice-Chancellor, Prof. R. Burgess, PH.D.

UNIVERSITY OF LINCOLN (1992)
Brayford Pool, Lincoln, LN7 6TS.
Tel: 01522-882000
Chancellor, Dame Elizabeth Esteve
Registrar, Dr Kevin Pardoe
Vice-Chancellor, Prof. David Chiddick

UNIVERSITY OF LIVERPOOL (1903)
Abercromby Square, Liverpool L69 3BX.
Tel: 0151-794 2000
Chancellor, The Lord Owen, CH, PC (1996)
Registrar and Secretary, M. D. Carr
Vice-Chancellor, Prof. P. N. Love, CBE

LIVERPOOL JOHN MOORES UNIVERSITY (1992)
2 Rodaney Street, Liverpool L3 5UX.
Tel: 0151-231 2121
Chancellor, Ms C. Booth, QC
Registrar and Secretary, Ms A. Wild
Vice-Chancellor, Prof. M. Brown

UNIVERSITY OF LONDON (1836)
Malet Street, London WC1E 7HU.
Tel: 020-7862 8000
Visitor, HM The Queen in Council
Academic Registrar, Mrs G. F. Roberts
Chairman of Convocation, D. D. A. Leslie
Chairman of the Council, The Lord Woolf, PC
Chancellor, HRH The Princess Royal, KG, GCVO, FRS (1981)
Director of Administration, J. R. Davidson
Vice-Chancellor, Prof. G. Zellick, PH.D.

COLLEGES

BIRKBECK, Malet Street, London WC1E7HX. *Master,* Prof. T. O'Shea, PH.D. (1998)
GOLDSMITHS COLLEGE, Lewisham Way, New Cross, London SE146NW *Warden,* Prof. B. Pimlott, FBA (1998)
HEYTHROP COLLEGE, Kensington Square, London W85HQ. *Principal,* Revd Dr J. McDade, SJ, BD (1999)
IMPERIAL COLLEGE OF SCIENCE, TECHNOLOGY AND MEDICINE (includes Imperial College Schools of Medicine at Charing Cross, Hammersmith and St Mary's hospitals and at the National Heart and Lung Institute), South Kensington, London SW72AZ. *Rector,* Sir Richard Sykes, FRS (2001)
INSTITUTE OF EDUCATION, 20 Bedford Way, London WC1H0AL. *Director,* Prof. G. Whitty (2000)
KING'S COLLEGE LONDON, (includes King's College School of Medicine and Dentistry, United Medical and Dental Schools of Guy's and St Thomas' Hospitals), Strand, London WC2R2LS. *Principal,* Prof. A. Lucas, PH.D. (1993)

LONDON BUSINESS SCHOOL, Sussex Place, Regent's Park, London NW14SA. *Dean,* Prof. L. D'Andrea Tyson (2002)
LONDON SCHOOL OF ECONOMICS AND POLITICAL SCIENCE, Houghton Street, London WC2A2AE. *Director,* Prof. A. Giddens (1997)
LONDON SCHOOL OF HYGIENE AND TROPICAL MEDICINE, Keppel Street, London WC1E7HT. *Dean,* Prof. A. Hairies (2001)
QUEEN MARY (incorporating St Bartholomew's and the Royal London School of Medicine and Dentistry and the London Hospital Medical College), Mile End Road, London E14NS. *Principal,* Prof. A. Smith, FRS, PH. D. (1998)
ROYAL ACADEMY OF MUSIC, Marylebone Road, London NW12BS. *Principal,* Prof. Curtis Price, PH.D., HON. RAM, FKC (1995)
ROYAL HOLLOWAY, Egham Hill, Egham, Surrey TW20 0EX. *Principal,* Prof. D. Bone, FRSA (2000)
ROYAL VETERINARY COLLEGE, Royal College Street, London NW10TU. *Principal and Dean,* Prof. L. E. Lanyon, CBE (1989)
SCHOOL OF ORIENTAL AND AFRICAN STUDIES, Thornhaugh Street, Russell Square, London WC1H0XG. *Director,* Prof. C. Bundy (2001)
SCHOOL OF PHARMACY, 29–39 Brunswick Square, London WC1N1AX. *Dean,* Prof. A. T. Florence, CBE, PH.D. (1989)
ST GEORGE'S HOSPITAL MEDICAL SCHOOL, Cranmer Terrace, London SW170RE. *Principal,* Prof. R. Boyd (1996)
UNIVERSITY COLLEGE LONDON (including UCL Medical School), Gower Street, London WC1E6BT. *Provost and President,* Prof. Sir C. Llewellyn-Smith, FRS (1998)

INSTITUTES

BRITISH INSTITUTE IN PARIS, 9–11 rue de Constantine, 75340 Paris, Cedex 07, France. *Director,* Prof. C. L. Campos, *London office:* Senate House, Malet Street, London WC1E7HU, OBE, PH.D.
CENTRE FOR DEFENCE STUDIES, King's College London, Strand, London WC2R2LS. *Honorary Director,* Prof. L. Freedman, CBE, FBA
COURTAULD INSTITUTE OF ART, North Block, Somerset House, Strand, London WC2R0RN. *Director,* Prof. E. C. Fernie, CBE, FSA, FRSE

ASSOCIATE INSTITUTES

INSTITUTE OF CANCER RESEARCH, Royal Cancer Hospital, Chester Beatty Laboratories, 17A Onslow Gardens, London SW73AL. *Chief Executive,* Dr P. Rigby

LONDON GUILDHALL UNIVERSITY (1992)
31 Jewry Street, London EC3N 2EY.
Tel: 020-7 320 1000
Chancellor, Lord Limerick,
Patron, HRH The Prince Philip, Duke of Edinburgh, KG, KT, OM, GBE, PC (1952)
Secretary and Registrar, Ms J. Grinstead,
Vice Chancellor, Prof. R. Floud, D.PHIL.

SCHOOL OF ADVANCED STUDIES

INSTITUTE OF ADVANCED LEGAL STUDIES, Charles Clore House, 17 Russell Square, London WC1B5DR. *Director,* Prof. B. A. K. Rider
INSTITUTE OF CLASSICAL STUDIES, Senate House, Malet Street, London WC1E 7HU. *Director,* Prof. G. B. Waywell, FSA
INSTITUTE OF COMMONWEALTH STUDIES, 27–28 Russell Square, London WC1B5DS. *Director,* Prof. T. Shaw
INSTITUTE OF ENGLISH STUDIES, Senate House, Malet Street, London WC1E 7HU *Director,* Prof. W. Gould

INSTITUTE OF GERMANIC STUDIES, 29 Russell Square, London WC1B5DP. *Director*, Prof. R. Görner, PH. D.
INSTITUTE OF HISTORICAL RESEARCH, Senate House, Malet Street, London WC1E7HU. *Director*, Prof. D. Cannadine
INSTITUTE OF LATIN AMERICAN STUDIES, 31 Tavistock Square, London WC1H9HA. *Director*, Prof. J. Dunkerley
INSTITUTE OF ROMANCE STUDIES, Senate House, Malet Street, London WC1E7HU. *Director*, Prof. J. Labanyi
INSTITUTE OF UNITED STATES STUDIES, Senate House, Malet Street, London WC1E7HU *Director*, Prof. G. L. McDowell, PH.D.
WARBURG INSTITUTE, Woburn Square, London WC1H0AB. *Director*, Prof. C. N. J. Mann, PH.D., CBE

LOUGHBOROUGH UNIVERSITY (1966)
Loughborough, Leics LE11 3TU.
Tel: 01509-263171
Chancellor, Sir Denis Rooke, CBE, FRS, FRENG. (1989)
Registrar and Secretary, J. Town
Vice-Chancellor, Prof. D.Wallace, FRS, FRSE

UNIVERSITY OF LUTON (1993)
Park Square, Luton LU1 3JU.
Tel: 01582-734111
Chancellor, Sir Robin Biggam
Vice-Chancellor, Dr D. John

UNIVERSITY OF MANCHESTER (1851)
Oxford Road, Manchester M13 9PL.
Tel: 0161-275 2000
Chancellor, The Lord Flowers, FRS (1994)
Registrar and Secretary, E. Newcomb, FRSA
Vice-Chancellor, Prof. M. B. Harris, CBE, DL, PH.D.

UNIVERSITY OF MANCHESTER INSTITUTE OF SCIENCE AND TECHNOLOGY (UMIST) (1824)
Manchester M60 1QD.
Tel: 0161-236 3311
Chancellor, Prof. Sir Roland Smith, PH.D. (1995)
Registrar and Secretary, J. Baldwin
Vice-Chancellor, Prof. J. Garside, PH.D.

MANCHESTER METROPOLITAN UNIVERSITY (1992)
All Saints, Manchester M15 6BH.
Tel: 0161-247 2000
Academic Registrar, J. D. M. Karczewski-Slowikowski
Chancellor, The Duke of Westminster, OBE, TD (1993)
Vice-Chancellor, Mrs A. V. Burslem, OBE

MIDDLESEX UNIVERSITY (1992)
White Hart Lane, London N17 8HR.
Tel: 020-8 411 5000
Chancellor, The Rt. Hon. Lord Sheppard of Didgemere, KT., KGVC
Registrar, G. Jones
Vice-Chancellor, Prof. M. Driscoll, FRSA

NAPIER UNIVERSITY (1992)
219 Colinton Road, Edinburgh EH14 1DJ. Scotland
Tel: 0131-444 2266
Academic Registrar, Mrs L. Fraser
Chancellor, The Viscount Younger of Leckie, KT, KCVO, TD, PC, FRSE (1993)
Vice-Chancellor, Prof. J. Mavor

UNIVERSITY OF NEWCASTLE UPON TYNE (1834)
6 Kensington Terrace, Newcastle upon Tyne NE1 7RU.
Tel: 0191-222 6000
Chancellor, Rt. Hon. C. Patten, CH
Registrar, D. E. T. Nicholson
Vice-Chancellor, Prof. C. R. W. Edwards

UNIVERSITY OF NORTH LONDON (1992)
166–220 Holloway Road, London N7 8DB.
Tel: 020-7 607 2789
Secretary, J. McParland
Vice-Chancellor, B. A. Roper

UNIVERSITY OF NORTHUMBRIA AT NEWCASTLE (1992)
Ellison Place, Newcastle upon Tyne NE1 8ST.
Tel: 0191-232 6002
Chancellor, The Lord Glenamara, CH, PC (1984)
Registrar, Mrs C. Penna
Vice-Chancellor, Kel Fidler

UNIVERSITY OF NOTTINGHAM (1948)
University Park, Nottingham NG7 2RD.
Tel: 0115-951 5151
Chancellor, Prof. F. Yang (1993)
Registrar, K. H. Jones
Vice-Chancellor, Prof. Sir Colin Campbell, DL, LLB, FRSA

NOTTINGHAM TRENT UNIVERSITY (1992)
Burton Street, Nottingham NG1 4BU.
Tel: 0115-941 8418
Chairman of the Board of Governors, John Peace
Registrar, D. W. Samson
Vice-Chancellor, Prof. R. Cowell, PH.D.

OPEN UNIVERSITY (1969)
Milton Keynes MK7 6AA.
Tel: 01908-274066
Chancellor, Baroness Betty Boothroyd
Head of Student Services Registry, Ms H. Niven
Vice-Chancellor, Prof. Brenda Gourley

UNIVERSITY OF OXFORD
Wellington Square, Oxford OX1 2JD.
Tel: 01865-270000
Assessor, Dr B Ward-Perkins (*Trinity*), *elected* 2001
Bodley's Librarian, R. P. Carr (*Balliol*), *elected* 1997
Chancellor, The Lord Jenkins of Hillhead (*Balliol*), *elected* 1987, OM, PC
Director of the Ashmolean Museum, Dr C. Brown (*Worcester*), *elected* 1998
High Steward, The Lord Goff of Chieveley (*Lincoln* and *New College*), *elected* 1990, PC
Keeper of Archives, S. Bayiley, *elected* 2000
Proctors, Dr D Womersley (*Jesus*); Prof. G, Walford (*Green*), *elected* 2001
Public Orator, Prof. J. Griffin (*Balliol*), *elected* 1992
Registrar of the University, D. R. Holmes (*St John's*), *elected* 1998
Secretary of Faculties, A. P. Weale (*Worcester*), *elected* 1984
Secretary of the Chest, J. R. Clements (*Merton*), *elected* 1995
Surveyor to the University, P. M. R. Hill (*St Cross*),*elected* 1993
Vice-Chancellor, Dr C. R. Lucas (*Balliol*), *elected* 1997

OXFORD COLLEGES AND HALLS
with dates of foundation

ALL SOULS (1438), *Warden*, Prof. J. Davis, FBA, PH.D. (1995)
BALLIOL (1263), *Master*, A. Graham (1998)
BLACKFRIARS (1221), *Regent*, Revd F. G. Kerr (1998)
BRASENOSE (1509), *Principal*, The Lord Windlesham, BT, CVO, PC, D.LITT (1989)
CAMPION HALL (1896), *Master*, Revd Dr G. J. Hughes (1998)
CHRIST CHURCH (1546), *Dean*, Very Revd J. H. Drury (1991)
CORPUS CHRISTI (1517), *President*, Sir Timothy Lankester, KCB (1986)

EXETER (1314), *Rector*, Dr M. Butler (1993)
GREEN (1979), *Warden*, Sir John Hanson, KCMG, CBE (1997)
GREYFRIARS (1910), *Warden*, Revd Dr T. G. Weinandy (1996)
HARRIS MANCHESTER (1786), *Principal*, Revd R. Waller, PH.D. (1988)
HERTFORD (1874), *Principal*, Sir Walter Bodmer, FRS, FRCPATH. (1996)
JESUS (1571), *Principal*, Sir Peter North, CBE, QC, FBA (1984)
KEBLE (1868), *Warden*, Dr A. Cameron, CBE, PHD, FBA, FSA (1994)
KELLOGG (1990), *President*, Dr G. P. Thomas (1990)
LADY MARGARET HALL (1878), *Principal*, Sir Brian Fall, GVCO, KCMG (1995)
LINACRE (1962), *Principal*, Dr P. A. Slack, FBA (1996)
LINCOLN (1427), *Rector*, Prof. P. Langford (2000)
MAGDALEN (1458), *President*, A. D. Smith, CBE (1988)
MANSFIELD (1886), *Principal*, Prof. D. I. Marquand, FRSA, FBA, FRHISTS (1996)
MERTON (1264), *Warden*, Dr J. Rawson, CBE, FBA (1994)
NEW COLLEGE (1379), *Warden*, Dr. A. J. Ryan, FBA (1996)
NUFFIELD (1958), *Warden*, Sir Tony Atkinson, FBA (1994)
ORIEL (1326), *Provost*, Dr E. W. Nicholson, DD, FBA (1990)
PEMBROKE (1624), *Master*, Giles Henderson, CBE (2001)
QUEEN'S (1340), *Provost*, Sir Alan Budd, D.PHIL. (1999)
REGENT'S PARK (1810), *Principal*, Revd Dr P. S. Fiddes (1989)
SOMERVILLE (1879), *Principal*, Dame Fiona Caldicott, DBE, FRCP, FRCPSYCH., FRCPI (1996)
ST ANNE'S (1952 (Society of Oxford Home-Students (1879)), *Principal*, Mrs R. L. Deech (1991)
ST ANTONY'S (1953), *Warden*, Sir Marrack Goulding, KCMG (1997)
ST BENET'S HALL (1897), *Master*, Revd H. Wansbrough, OSB (1991)
ST CATHERINE'S (1963), *Master*, Sir Peter Williams, CBE, FRENG., FRS (2000)
ST CROSS (1965), *Master*, Dr R. C. Repp (1987)
ST EDMUND HALL (*c*.1278), *Principal*, Prof. D. M. P. Mingos, FRS, FRSC (1999)
*ST HILDA'S (1893), *Principal*, Judith Milne (2001)
ST HUGH'S (1886), *Principal*, D. Wood, CBE, QC (1991)
ST JOHN'S (1555), *President*, Sir Michael Scholar, KCB (2001)
ST PETER'S (1929), *Master*, Dr J. P. Barron, FSA (1991)
TEMPLETON (1965), *President*, Sir David Rowland (1998)
TRINITY (1554), *President*, The Hon. Michael J. Beloff, QC, FRSA (1996)
UNIVERSITY (1249), *Master*, Baron Butler of Brockwell, GCB, CVO (1998)
WADHAM (1610), *Warden*, J. S. Flemming, FBA (1993)
WOLFSON (1966), *President*, Prof. Sir Gareth Roberts, FRS, PHD (2000)
WORCESTER (1714), *Provost*, R. G. Smethurst (1991)
*WYCLIFFE HALL (1877), *Principal*, Revd Dr A. E. McGrath (1995)

OXFORD BROOKES UNIVERSITY (1992)
Gipsy Lane, Oxford OX3 0BP.
Tel: 01865-484848
Chancellor, John Snow
Deputy Vice-Chancellor (Academic Affairs), Linda Challis
Vice-Chancellor, Prof. G. Upton

UNIVERSITY OF PAISLEY (1992)
Paisley PA1 2BE. Scotland
Tel: 0141-848 3000

Chancellor, Sir Robert Easton, CBE (1993)
Registrar, D. Rigg
Vice-Chancellor and Principal, Prof. R. W. Shaw, CBE

UNIVERSITY OF PLYMOUTH (1992)
Drake Circus, Plymouth PL4 8AA.
Tel: 01752-600600
Academic Registrar and University Secretary, Miss J. Hopkinson
Vice-Chancellor, Prof. J. Bull

UNIVERSITY OF PORTSMOUTH (1992)
Winston Churchill Avenue, Portsmouth PO1 2UP.
Tel: 023-9284 8484
Chancellor, The Lord Palumbo (1992)
Pro Vice-Chancellor (Academic), A. Glasner
Pro Vice-Chancellor (Resources), Dr M. Bateman
Vice-Chancellor, Prof. J. Craven

QUEEN'S UNIVERSITY OF BELFAST (1908)
Belfast BT7 1NN. Northern Ireland
Tel: 028-9024 5133
Chancellor, Sen. G. Mitchell
Registrar, J. O'Kane
Vice-Chancellor, Prof. G. Bain

UNIVERSITY OF READING (1926)
PO Box 217, Reading RG6 6AH.
Tel: 0118-987 5123
Chancellor, The Rt. Hon. The Lord Carrington, KG, GCMG, CH, MC, PC (1992)
Registrar, D. C. R. Frampton
Vice-Chancellor, Prof. R. Williams

ROBERT GORDON UNIVERSITY (1992)
Schoolhill, Aberdeen AB10 1FR. Scotland
Tel: 01224-262000
Chancellor, Sir Bob Reid (1993)
Vice-Chancellor and Principal, Prof. W. Stevely, B.SC., D.PHIL.

ROYAL COLLEGE OF ART (1837)
Kensington Gore, London SW7 2EU.
Tel: 020-7590 4444
Provost, The Earl of Snowdon, GCVO (1995)
Rector, Prof. C. Frayling, PH.D.
Registrar, A. Selby, B.SC.

ROYAL COLLEGE OF MUSIC
Prince Consort Road, London SW7 2BS.
Tel: 020-7 589 3643
Dean and Deputy Director, Dr J. Cox
Director, Dr J. Ritterman
Registrar and Secretary, K. A. Porter

UNIVERSITY OF SURREY ROEHAMPTON
Roehampton Lane, London SW15 5PU.
Tel: 020-8392 3000/3232
Chancellor, HRH The Duke of Kent, KG
Rector & Chief Executive, Dr Bernadette Porter
Secretary, A. Skinner

UNIVERSITY OF ST ANDREWS (1411)
College Gate, St Andrews, Fife KY16 9AJ. Scotland
Tel: 01334-476161
Chancellor, Sir Kenneth Dover, DLITT., FRSE, FBA (1981)
Rector, A. Neil (2000–2003)
Secretary and Registrar, D. J. Corner
Vice-Chancellor, Dr B. Lang

UNIVERSITY OF SALFORD (1967)
Salford, Greater Manchester M5 4WT.
Tel: 0161-295 5000

Chancellor, Sir Walter Bodmer, PH.D., FRS
Registrar, Dr M. D. Winton, PH.D.
Vice-Chancellor, Prof. M. Harloe

UNIVERSITY OF SHEFFIELD (1905)
Western Bank, Sheffield S10 2TN.
Tel: 0114-222 2000
Chancellor, Sir Peter Middleton, GCB
Registrar and Secretary, Dr D. E. Fletcher, PH.D.
Vice-Chancellor, Prof. R. F. Boucher, CBE, PH.D.

SHEFFIELD HALLAM UNIVERSITY (1992)
Howard Street, Sheffield S1 1WB.
Tel: 0114-225 5555
Chancellor, Sir Bryan Nicholson (1992)
Registrar, Ms J. Tory
Vice-Chancellor, Prof. D. Green

UNIVERSITY OF SOUTHAMPTON (1952)
Highfield, Southampton SO17 1BJ.
Tel: 023-8059 5000
Chancellor, The Rt Hon. The Earl of Selbourne, KBE, FRS
(1996)
Registrar and Secretary, J. F. D. Lauwerys
Vice-Chancellor, Prof. Sir H. Newby, CBE, PH.D.

SOUTH BANK UNIVERSITY (1992)
103 Borough Road, London SE1 0AA.
Tel: 020-7928 8989
Chancellor, Sir Trevor McDonald
Registrar, R. Phillips
Vice-Chancellor, Prof. D. Hopkin

STAFFORDSHIRE UNIVERSITY (1992)
College Road, Stoke-on-Trent ST4 2DE.
Tel: 01782-294000
Chancellor, The Lord Ashley of Stoke, CH, PC (1993)
Dean of Students and Academic Registrar, Ms F. Francis
Vice-Chancellor, Prof. C. E. King, PH.D., DL, D.LITT, FRSA

UNIVERSITY OF STIRLING (1967)
Stirling FK9 4LA. Scotland
Tel: 01786-473171
Chancellor, Dame Diana Rigg, DBE
Principal and Academic Registrar, D. G. Wood
Vice-Chancellor, Prof.Colin Bell, FRSE

UNIVERSITY OF STRATHCLYDE (1796)
John Anderson Campus, Glasgow G1 1XQ. Scotland
Tel: 0141-552 4400
Chairman of Court, Dr R. A. Johnson
Chancellor, The Rt. Hon. Lord Hope of Craighead, PC
(1998)
Vice-Chancellor, Prof. A. Hamnett

UNIVERSITY OF SUNDERLAND (1992)
Ryhope Road, Sunderland SR2 7EE.
Tel: 0191-515 2000
Chancellor, The Lord Puttnam of Queensgate, CBE (1998)
Rector, Revd P. Hutchinson
Registrar, S. Porteous
Vice-Chancellor, Prof. P. Fidler, MBE

UNIVERSITY OF SURREY (1966)
Guildford, Surrey GU2 7XH.
Tel: 01483-300800
Chancellor, HRH The Duke of Kent, KG, GCMG, GCVO
(1977)
Secretary and Registrar, H. W. B. Davies
Vice-Chancellor, Prof. P. J. Dowling, CBE, FRS, FRENG.

UNIVERSITY OF SUSSEX (1961)
Falmer, Brighton BN1 9RH.
Tel: 01273-606755

Chancellor, The Lord Attenborough, KT, CBE (1998)
Registrar, N. Gershon
Vice-Chancellor, Prof. M. A. M. Smith

UNIVERSITY OF TEESSIDE (1992)
Middlesbrough TS1 3BA.
Tel: 01642-218121
Chancellor, The Rt. Hon. Sir Leon Brittan, QC (1993)
Registrar, Ms J. Walters
Vice-Chancellor, Prof. D. Fraser

THAMES VALLEY UNIVERSITY (1992)
St Mary's Road, Ealing, London W5 5RF.
Tel: 020-8579 5000
Pro-Chancellor, The Lord Paul of Marylebone, CBE
Vice-Chancellor, Prof. K. Barker, CBE

UNIVERSITY OF ULSTER (1984)
Cromore Road, Coleraine, Co. Londonderry BT52 1SA.
Northern Ireland
Tel: 028-7034 4141
Chancellor, vacant
Registrar, Dr A. Scott
Vice-Chancellor, Prof. P. G. McKenna, PH.D.

UNIVERSITY OF WALES (1893)
King Edward VII Avenue, Cathays Park, Cardiff CF10 3NS.
Wales
Tel: 029-2038 2656
Chancellor, HRH The Prince of Wales, KG, KT, GCB, PC
(1976)
Secretary to the Council, L. E. Williams, PH.D.
Secretary-General, Lynne E. Williams, PH. D.
Senior Vice-Chancellor, Prof. D. Llwyd Morgan, D.PHIL.,
DLITT.
UNIVERSITY OF WALES, ABERYSTWYTH, Old College,
King Street, Aberystwyth SY23 2AX. Tel: 01970-623111.
Vice-Chancellor, Prof. D. Llwyd Morgan, D.PHIL, D.LITT
UNIVERSITY OF WALES BANGOR, Bangor, LL57 2DG. Tel:
01248-351151 *Vice-Chancellor*, Prof. H. R. Evans, PH.D.,
FRENG

MEMBER INSTITUTES

UNIVERSITY OF WALES, CARDIFF, PO Box 920, Cardiff
CF10 3XP. Tel: 01222-874000. *Vice-Chancellor*, Dr D.
Grant, CBE, FENG
UNIVERSITY OF WALES, INSTITUTE, CARDIFF, Llandaff
Centre, Western Avenue, Cardiff CF5 2SG. Tel:
01222-506070. *Principal*, A. J. Chapman, PH.D.
UNIVERSITY OF WALES, LAMPETER, Lampeter SA48 7ED.
Tel: 01570-422351. *Vice-Chancellor*, Prof. K. G.
Robbins, D.LITT, D.PHIL., FRSED
UNIVERSITY OF WALES COLLEGE OF MEDICINE, Heath
Park, Cardiff CF14 4XN. Tel: 01222-747747.
Vice-Chancellor, Prof. S. Tomlinson, MD, FRCP
UNIVERSITY OF WALES COLLEGE, NEWPORT, Caerleon
Campus, PO Box 179, Newport NP6 1YG. Tel:
01633-430088. *Principal*, Prof. K. J. Overshott, PH.D.
UNIVERSITY OF WALES, SWANSEA, Singleton Park,
Swansea SA28PP. Tel: 01792-205678. *Vice-Chancellor*,
Prof. R. H. Williams, PH.D., D.SC., FRS

UNIVERSITY OF WARWICK (1965)
Coventry CV4 7AL.
Tel: 024-7652 3523
Chancellor, Sir Shridath Surendranath Ramphal, GCMG,
QC (1989)
Registrar, Dr J. W. Nicholls
Vice-Chancellor, Prof. V. D. Vondelinde, FRS

UNIVERSITY OF WESTMINSTER (1992)
309 Regent Street, London W1B 2UW.

Tel: 020-7911 5000
Academic Registrar, Ms E. Green
Vice-Chancellor and Rector, Dr G. M. Copland (1996)

UNIVERSITY OF THE WEST OF ENGLAND (1992) Coldharbour Lane, Bristol BS16 1QY.
Tel: 0117-965 6261
Chancellor, The Rt. Hon. Dame Elizabeth Butler-Sloss, DBE (1993)
Vice-Chancellor, A. C. Morris
Academic Secretary, Ms C. Webb

UNIVERSITY OF WOLVERHAMPTON (1992) Wulfruna Street, Wolverhampton WV1 1SB.
Tel: 01902-321000
Chancellor, Lord Paul of Marylebone
Clerk to the Board of Governors, A. W. Lee
Vice-Chancellor, Prof. J. S. Brooks, PH.D.

UNIVERSITY OF YORK (1963)
Heslington, York YO10 5DD.
Tel: 01904-430000
Chancellor, Dame Janet Baker, CH, DBE (1991)
Registrar and Secretary, D. J. Foster
Vice-Chancellor, Prof. R. U. Cooke, PH.D.

COLLEGES

It is not possible to name here all the colleges offering courses of higher or further education. The list does not include colleges forming part of a polytechnic or a university. The English colleges that follow are confined to those in the Higher Education Funding Council for England sector; there are many more colleges in England providing higher education courses, some with HEFCFE funding.

The list of colleges in Wales, Scotland and Northern Ireland include institutions providing at least one full-time course leading to a first degree granted by an accredited validating body.

ENGLAND

BATH SPA UNIVERSITY COLLEGE, Newton Park, Newton St Loe, Bath BA2 9BN. Tel: 01225-875875. *Director*, F. Morgan

BISHOP GROSSETESTE COLLEGE, Lincoln LN1 3DY. Tel: 01522-527347. *Principal*, Prof. E. Baker

BOLTON INSTITUTE OF HIGHER EDUCATION, Deane Road, Bolton BL3 5AB. Tel: 01204-528851. *Principal*, Ms M. Temple

BUCKINGHAMSHIRE CHILTERNS UNIVERSITY COLLEGE, Queen Alexandra Road, High Wycombe, Bucks HP11 2JZ. Tel: 01494-603015. *Director*, Prof. P. B. Mogford

CANTERBURY CHRIST CHURCH UNIVERSITY COLLEGE, North Holmes Road, Canterbury, Kent CT1 1QU. Tel: 01227-767700. *Principal*, Prof. M. Wright

THE CENTRAL SCHOOL OF SPEECH AND DRAMA SPEECH AND DRAMA, Embassy Theatre, 64 Eton Avenue, London NW3 3HY. Tel: 020-7 722 8183. *Principal*, Prof. G. Crossley

CHELTENHAM AND GLOUCESTER COLLEGE OF HIGHER EDUCATION COLLEGE OF HIGHER EDUCATION, PO Box 220, The Park, Cheltenham, Glos GL50 2QF. Tel: 01242-532700. *Director*, Miss J. O. Trotter, OBE

CHESTER COLLEGE OF HIGHER EDUCATION, Parkgate Road, Chester CH1 4BJ. Tel: 01244-375444. *Principal*, Prof. T. J. Wheeler

DARTINGTON COLLEGE OF ARTS, Totnes, Devon TQ9 6EJ. Tel: 01803-862224. *Principal*, Prof. K. Thompson

EDGE HILL COLLEGE OF HIGHER EDUCATION, St Helens Road, Ormskirk, Lancs L39 4QP. Tel: 01695-575171. *Chief Executive*, Dr J. Cater

FALMOUTH COLLEGE OF ARTS, Woodlane, Falmouth, Cornwall TR11 4RH. Tel: 01326-211077. *Principal*, Prof. A. G. Livingston

HARPER ADAMS UNIVERSITY COLLEGE, Newport, Shropshire TF10 8NB. Tel: 01952-815000. *Principal*, Prof. E. W. Jones

HOMERTON COLLEGE, Cambridge CB2 2PH. Tel: 01223-507111. *Principal*, Dr K. Pretty, Ph.D.

KENT INSTITUTE OF ART AND DESIGN, Oakwood Park, Maidstone, Kent ME16 8AG. Tel: 01622-757286. *Director*, Prof. V. Grylls

KING ALFRED'S COLLEGE, Sparkford Road, Winchester, Hants SO22 4NR. Tel: 01962-841515. *Principal*, Prof. P. Light

LIVERPOOL HOPE, Hope Park, Liverpool L16 9JD. Tel: 0151-291 3000. *Rector and Chief Executive*, Prof. S. Lee

THE LONDON INSTITUTE, 65 Davies Street, London W1Y 2AA. Tel: 020-7 514 6000. *Rector*, Sir William Stubbs

NEWMAN COLLEGE OF HIGHER EDUCATION, Genners Lane, Bartley Green, Birmingham B32 3NT. Tel: 0121-476 1181. *Principal and Chief Executive*, Mrs P. Taylor

THE COLLEGE OF RIPON AND YORK ST JOHN, Lord Mayor's Walk, York YO31 7EX. Tel: 01904-656771. *Principal*, Prof. D. Willcocks

RCN INSTITUTE, The Royal College of Nursing, 20 Cavendish Square, London W1G 0RN. Tel: 020-7647 3700. *Director*, Prof. A. L. Kitson

ROSE BRUFORD COLLEGE, Lamorbey Park, Sidcup, Kent DA15 9DF. Tel: 020-8 300 3024. *Principal*, Prof. A. Pearce

ROYAL AGRICULTURAL COLLEGE, Cirencester, Glos GL7 6JS. Tel: 01285-652531. *Principal*, Prof. J. B. Dent

ROYAL NORTHERN COLLEGE OF MUSIC, 124 Oxford Road, Manchester M13 9RD. Tel: 0161-907 5200. *Principal*, Prof. E. Gregson

ST MARTIN'S COLLEGE, Lancaster LA1 3JD. Tel: 01524-384384. *Principal and Chief Executive*, Prof. C. J. Carr

SOUTHAMPTON INSTITUTE, East Park Terrace, Southampton SO14 0YN. Tel: 023-80 319000. *Principal*, Dr R. Brown

SURREY INSTITUTE OF ART AND DESIGN, UNIVERSITY COLLEGE, Falkner Road, Farnham, Surrey GU9 7DS. Tel: 01252-722441. *Director*, Prof. E. Thomas

TRINITY AND ALL SAINTS' COLLEGE, Brownberrie Lane, Horsforth, Leeds LS18 5HD. Tel: 0113-283 7100. *Principal*, Dr M. J. Coughlan

UNIVERSITY COLLEGE CHICHESTER, College Lane, Chichester, W. Sussex PO19 4PE. Tel: 01243-816000. *Director*, P. E. D. Robinson

UNIVERSITY COLLEGE NORTHAMPTON, Park Campus, Boughton Green Road, Northampton NN2 7AL. Tel: 01604-735500. *Rector*, Dr S. M. Gaskell

THE COLLEGE OF ST MARK AND ST JOHN, Derriford Road, Plymouth PL6 8BH. Tel: 01752-636700. *Principal*, Dr W. J. Rea

WINCHESTER SCHOOL OF ART, Park Avenue, Winchester, Hants SO23 8DL. Tel: 023-8059 6900. *Principal*, Prof. P. Pilgrim

UNIVERSITY COLLEGE WORCESTER, Henwick Grove, Worcester WR2 6AJ. Tel: 01905-855000. *Principal*, Ms D. Urwin

WALES

CARMARTHENSHIRE COLLEGE, Graig Campus, Sandy Road, Llanelli SA15 4DN. Tel: 01554-748000. *Principal*, B. Robinson
COLEG LLANDRILLO, Llandudno Road, Rhos-on-Sea, Colwyn Bay, Conwy LL28 4HZ. Tel: 01492-546666. *Principal*, W. S. H. Evans
NORTH EAST WALES INSTITUTE OF HIGHER EDUCATION, Plas Coch, Mold Road, Wrexham LL11 2AW. Tel: 01978-290666. *Principal and Chief Executive*, Prof. M. Scott
SWANSEA INSTITUTE OF HIGHER EDUCATION, Mount Pleasant, Swansea SA1 6ED. Tel: 01792-481000. *Principal*, Prof. D. Warner
TRINITY COLLEGE, College Road, Carmarthen SA31 3EP. Tel: 01267-676767. *Principal*, Dr M. Hughes
UNIVERSITY OF WALES INSTITUTE CARDIFF, Llandaff Campus, Western Avenue, Cardiff CF5 2YB. Tel: 029-20 416070. *Principal*, Prof A. J. Chapman
WELSH COLLEGE OF MUSIC AND DRAMA, Castle Grounds, Cathays Park, Cardiff CF10 3ER. Tel: 029-2034 2854. *Principal*, E. Fivet

SCOTLAND

BELL COLLEGE OF TECHNOLOGY, Almada Street, Hamilton, Lanarkshire ML3 0JB. Tel: 01698-283100. *Principal*, Dr K. J. MacCallum
DUMFRIES AND GALLOWAY COLLEGE, Heathhall, Dumfries DG1 3QZ. Tel: 01387-261261. *Principal*, T. Jakimciw
FIFE COLLEGE OF FURTHER AND HIGHER EDUCATION, St Brycedale Avenue, Kirkcaldy, Fife KY1 1EX. Tel: 01592-268591. *Principal*, Mrs J. S. R. Johnston
GLASGOW SCHOOL OF ART, 167 Renfrew Street, Glasgow G3 6RQ. Tel: 0141-353 4500. *Director*, Ms S. Reid
INVERNESS COLLEGE, 3 Longman Road, Inverness IV1 1SA. Tel: 01463-273000. *Principal*, Dr G. Clark
LEWS CASTLE COLLEGE, Stornoway, Isle of Lewis HS2 0XR. Tel: 01851-770000. *Principal*, D. Green
MORAY COLLEGE, Moray Street, Elgin, Moray IV30 1JJ. Tel: 01343-576000. *Acting Principal*, Dr Logan
NORTHERN COLLEGE, Hilton Place, Aberdeen AB24 4FA. Tel: 01224-283500. *Principal*, D. Adams
NORTH ISLAND COLLEGE, Ormlie Road, Thurso, Caithness KW14 7EE. Tel: 01847-896161. *Principal*, H. Logan
ORKNEY COLLEGE, Kirkwall, Orkney KW15 1LX. Tel: 01856-569000. *Principal*, P. Scott
QUEEN MARGARET UNIVERSITY COLLEGE, Clerwood Terrace, Edinburgh EH12 8TS. Tel: 0131-317 3000. *Principal*, Prof. J. Stringer
ROYAL SCOTTISH ACADEMY OF MUSIC AND DRAMA, 100 Renfrew Street, Glasgow G2 3DB. Tel: 0141-332 4101. *Principal*, Sir Philip Ledger, Kt., CBE, FRSE
SÀBHAL MÒR OSTAIG, Sleat, Isle of Skye IV44 8RQ. Tel: 01471-888000
SAC (SCOTTISH AGRICULTURAL COLLEGE), Central Office, West Mains Road, Edinburgh EH9 3JG. Tel: 0131-535 4000. *Principal*, K. A. Linklater

NORTHERN IRELAND

ST MARY'S UNIVERSITY COLLEGE, 191 Falls Road, Belfast BT12 6FE. Tel: 028-9032 7678. *Principal*, Very Revd Prof. M. O'Callaghan

ADULT CONTINUING EDUCATION

COMMUNITY LEARNING SCOTLAND, Rosebery House, 9 Haymarket Terrace, Edinburgh EH12 5EZ. Tel: 0131-313 2488. *Chief Executive*, C. McConnell
NATIONAL INSTITUTE OF ADULT CONTINUING EDUCATION, 21 De Montfort Street, Leicester LE1 7GE. Tel: 0116-204 4200. *Director*, A. Tuckett
NIACE DYSGU CYMRU, Ground Floor, 35 Cathedral Road, Cardiff CF11 9HB. Tel: 029-2037 0900. *Acting Director*, R. Griffiths
THE RESIDENTIAL COLLEGES COMMITTEE, c/o Ruskin College, Oxford OX1 2HE. Tel: 01865-556360. *Awards Officer*, Mrs C. Gregory
THE UNIVERSITIES ASSOCIATION FOR CONTINUING EDUCATION, University of Cambridge Board of Continuing Education, Madingley Hall, Madingley, Cambridge CB3 8AQ. Tel: 01954-280280. *Administrator*, Ms S. Irwin
THE WIDENING PARTICIPATION UNIT, Regional Office, Widening Participation Unit, University of East London, Romford Road, London E15 4LZ. Tel: 020-8223 4936
WORKERS' EDUCATIONAL ASSOCIATION, Temple House, 17 Victoria Park Square, London E2 9PB. Tel: 020-8983 1515. *General Secretary*, R. Lochrie

LONG-TERM RESIDENTIAL COLLEGES FOR ADULT EDUCATION

COLEG HARLECH/WEA(N), Harlech, Gwynedd LL46 2PU. Tel: 01766-780363. *Principal*, A. Williams
CO-OPERATIVE COLLEGE, Holyoake House, Hanover Street, Manchester M60 0AS. Tel: 0161-246 2909. *Chief Executive and Principal*, M. Wilson
FIRCROFT COLLEGE, 1018 Bristol Road, Selly Oak, Birmingham B29 6LH. Tel: 0121-472 0116. *Principal*, Ms F. Larden
HILLCROFT COLLEGE, South Bank, Surbiton, Surrey KT6 6DF. Tel: 020-8 399 2688. *Principal*, Mrs J. Ireton
NEWBATTLE ABBEY COLLEGE, Newbattle Road, Dalkeith, Midlothian EH22 3LL. Tel: 0131-663 1921. *Principal*, Ms A. Southwood
NORTHERN COLLEGE, Wentworth Castle, Stainborough, Barnsley, S. Yorks S75 3ET. Tel: 01226-776000. *Principal and Chief Executive*, Prof. J. A. Jowitt
PLATER COLLEGE, Pullens Lane, Oxford OX3 0DT. Tel: 01865-740500. *Principal*, M. Blades
RUSKIN COLLEGE, Walton Street, Oxford OX1 2HE. Tel: 01865-554331. *Principal*, J. Durcan

PROFESSIONAL EDUCATION
Excluding postgraduate study

The organisations listed below are those which, by providing specialist training or conducting examinations, control entry into a profession, or are responsible for maintaining a register of those with professional qualifications in their sector.

EU RECOGNITION

It is now possible for those with professional qualifications obtained in the UK to have these recognised in other European Union countries. A booklet, *Europe Open for Professions*, and further information can be obtained from: DEPARTMENT OF TRADE AND INDUSTRY, Bay 212, Kingsgate House, 66–74 Victoria Street, London SW1E 6SW. Tel: 020-7215 4648. *Contact*, Mrs P. Campbell

ACCOUNTANCY

The main bodies granting membership on examination after a period of practical work are:
ASSOCIATION OF CHARTERED CERTIFIED ACCOUNTANTS (ACCA), 29 Lincoln's Inn Fields, London WC2A 3EE. Tel: 020-7396 7000; Email: info@accaglobal.com; Web: www.accaglobal.com. *Chief Executive*, Ms A. Rose
CIMA (THE CHARTERED INSTITUTE OF MANAGEMENT ACCOUNTANTS), 26 Chapter Street, London SW1P 4NP. Web: www.cimaglobal.com. *Chief Executive*, C. Tilley
INSTITUTE OF CHARTERED ACCOUNTANTS IN ENGLAND AND WALES, Chartered Accountants' Hall, PO Box 433, Moorgate Place, London EC2P 2BJ. Tel: 020-7920 8100; Email: comms@icaew.co.uk; Web: www.icaew.co.uk. *Secretary General*, J. Collier
INSTITUTE OF CHARTERED ACCOUNTANTS OF SCOTLAND, CA House, 21 Haymarket Yards, Edinburgh EH12 5BG. Tel: 0131-347 0100; Email: enquiries@icas.org.uk; Web: www.icas.org.uk. *Chief Executive*, D. A. Brew

ACTUARIAL SCIENCE

Two professional organisations grant qualifications after examination:
THE FACULTY OF ACTUARIES IN SCOTLAND, Maclaurin House, 18 Dublin Street, Edinburgh EH2 3PP. Tel: 0131-240 1300; Email: faculty@actuaries.org.uk; Web: www.actuaries.org.uk.
INSTITUTE OF ACTUARIES, Staple Inn Hall, High Holborn, London WC1V 7QJ. Tel: 020-7632 2100; Email: institute@actuaries.org.uk; Web: www.actuaries.org.uk.

ARCHITECTURE

The Education Committee of the Royal Institute of British Architects sets standards and guides the whole system of architectural education throughout the UK. RIBA recognises courses at 36 schools of architecture in the UK for exemption from their own examinations as well as 57 courses overseas.
ARCHITECTS REGISTRATION BOARD, 8 Weymouth Street, London W1W 5BU. Tel: 020-7580 5861; Email: info@arb.org.uk; Web: www.arb.org.uk. *Chief Executive and Registrar*, R. Vaughan
ROYAL INSTITUTE OF BRITISH ARCHITECTS, 66 Portland Place, London W1N 4AD. Tel: 020-7580 5533; Email: admin@inst.riba.org; Web: www.architecture.com.
THE ARCHITECTURAL ASSOCIATION (INC.), 34–36 Bedford Square, London WC1B 3ES. Tel: 020-7887 4018; Email: arch-assoc@arch-assoc.org.uk; Web: www.aaschool.ac.uk.

THE PRINCE'S FOUNDATION, 19–22 Charlotte Road, London EC2A 3SG. Tel: 020-7613 8500; Email: info@princes-foundation.org; Web: www.princes-foundation.org/school.

BANKING

Professional organisations granting qualifications after examination are:
THE CHARTERED INSTITUTE OF BANKERS, 90 Bishopsgate, London EC2N 4DQ. Tel: 020-7444 7111; Email: institute@ifslearning.com; Web: www.ifslearning.com. *Chief Executive Officer*, G. Shreeve
THE CHARTERED INSTITUTE OF BANKERS IN SCOTLAND, Drumsheugh House, 38b Drumsheugh Gardens, Edinburgh EH3 7SW. Tel: 0131-473 7777; Email: info@ciobs.org.uk; Web: www.ciobs.org.uk. *Chief Executive*, C. W. Munn

BUILDING

Examinations are conducted by:
THE CHARTERED INSTITUTE OF BUILDING, Englemere, King's Ride, Ascot, Berks SL5 7TB. Tel: 01344-630700; Email: reception@ciob.org.uk; Web: www.ciob.org.uk. *Chief Executive*, C. Blythe
RICS (ROYAL INSTITUTE OF CHARTERED SURVEYORS), 12 Great George Street, Parliament Square, London SW1P 3AD. Tel: 020-7222 7000; Web: www.rics.org.uk. *Chief Executive*, J. Parrott
THE INSTITUTE OF CLERKS OF WORKS OF GREAT BRITAIN, 41 The Mall, London W5 3TJ. Tel: 020-8579 2917/8. *General Secretary*, D. McGeorge

BUSINESS, MANAGEMENT AND ADMINISTRATION

Professional bodies conducting training and/or examinations include:
THE ASSOCIATION OF MBAS, 15 Duncan Terrace, London N1 8BZ. Tel: 020-7837 3375; Email: info@mba.org.uk; Web: www.mba.org.uk. *Director General*, M. A. Jones
THE CAM FOUNDATION, Moore Hall, Cookham, Maidenhead, Berks SL6 9QH. Tel: 01628-427180; Web: www.camfoundation.com. *Chief Executive*, D. Royston-Lee
THE CHARTERED INSTITUTE OF HOUSING, Octavia House, Westwood Business Park, Westwood Way, Coventry CV4 8JP. Tel: 024-7685 1700; Email: customer.services@cih.org; Web: www.cih.org. *Chief Executive*, D. Butler
THE CHARTERED INSTITUTE OF PURCHASING AND SUPPLY, Easton House, Easton on the Hill, Stamford, Lincs PE9 3NZ. Tel: 01780-756777; Email: info@cips.org; Web: www.cips.org. *Chief Executive*, K. James
HENLEY MANAGEMENT COLLEGE, Greenlands, Henley on Thames, Oxon RG9 3AU. Tel: 01491-571454; Web: www.henleymc.ac.uk. *Principal*, S. Watson
THE INSTITUTE OF ADMINISTRATIVE MANAGEMENT, 40 Chatsworth Parade, Petts Wood, Orpington, Kent BR5 1RW. Tel: 01689-875555; Email: enquiries@instam.org; Web: www.instam.org.
INSTITUTE OF CHARTERED SECRETARIES AND ADMINISTRATORS, 16 Park Crescent, London W1B 1AH. Tel: 020-7580 4741; Email: icsa@dial.pipex.com; Web: www.icsa.org.uk. *Chief Executive*, M. J. Ainsworth
INSTITUTE OF CHARTERED SHIPBROKERS, 3 St Helen's Place, London EC3A 6EJ. Tel: 020-7628 5559; Email: info@ics.org.uk; Web: www.ics.org.uk. *Director*, Mrs B. Fletcher
THE INSTITUTE OF EXPORT, Export House, Minerva Business Park, Lynch Wood, Peterborough PE2 6FT. Tel: 01733-404400; Email: institute@export.org.uk; Web: www.export.org.uk. *Director-General*, I. J. Campbell

THE INSTITUTE OF HEALTHCARE MANAGEMENT, 46–48 Grosvenor Gardens, London SW1W 0WN. Tel: 020-7881 9235; Email: enquiries@ihm.org.uk; Web: www.ihm.org.uk. *Chief Executive*, S. Marples
INSTITUTE OF MANAGEMENT, 3rd Floor, 2 Savoy Court, The Strand, London WC2R 0EZ. Tel: 01536-204222; Email: marketing@imgt.org.uk; Web: www.inst-mgt.org.uk. *Director-General*, Ms M. Chapman
CHARTERED INSTITUTE OF PERSONNEL AND DEVELOPMENT, CIPD House, Camp Road, London SW19 4UX. Tel: 020-8971 9000; Email: cipd@cipd.co.uk; Web: www.cipd.co.uk. *Director General*, G. Armstrong
INSTITUTE OF QUALITY ASSURANCE, 12 Grosvenor Crescent, London SW1X 7EE. Tel: 020-7245 6722; Email: iqa@iqa.org; Web: www.iqa.org. *Chief Executive*, Frank Steer

CHIROPRACTIC

The General Chiropractic Council (GCC) is the statutory regulatory body for chiropractors and its role and remit is defined in the Chiropractors Act 1994. The GCC's register of chiropractors opened in June 1999; nearly 1800 chiropractors are expected to be registered with the GCC by the end of 2001.
BRITISH CHIROPRACTIC ASSOCIATION, Blagrave House, Blagrave Street, Reading, Berks RG1 1QB. Tel: 0118-950 5950; Email: enquiries@chiropractic-uk.co.uk; Web: www.chiropractic-uk.co.uk.
COLLEGE OF CHIROPRACTORS, PO Box 2739, 106 London Street, Reading RG1 4BF. Tel: 0118-950 2070.
GENERAL CHIROPRACTIC COUNCIL, 344-354 Gray's Inn Road, London WC1X 8BP. Tel: 020-7713 5155; Email: enquiries@gcc-uk.org; Web: www.gcc-uk.org.
MCTIMONEY CHIROPRACTIC ASSOCIATION, 21 High Street, Eynsham, OX8 1HE. Tel: 01865-880974; Web: www.mctimoney-chiropractic.org.uk.
SCOTTISH CHIROPRACTIC ASSOCIATION, St Boswells Chiropractic Clinic, 16 Jenny Moores Road, St Boswells, Roxburghshire TD6 0AL. Tel: 01835-824026; Email: sca@scottishborders.co.uk. Web: www.sca-chiropractic.org.uk.
UNITED CHIROPRACTIC ASSOCIATION, 145A London Road, Kingston upon Thames, Surrey KT2 6SR. Tel: 020-8549 0020.

DANCE

The Council for Dance Education and Training (CDET) has accredited courses at the following: Arts Education Schools, Tring Park and London; Central School of Ballet; Doreen Bird College of Performing Arts; Elmhurst–The School for Dance and Performing Arts; English National Ballet School; The Hammond School; The Italia Conti Academy of Theatre Arts Ltd; Laban Centre, London; Laine Theatre Arts Ltd; London Contemporary Dance School; London Studio Centre; Midlands Academy of Dance and Drama; Merseyside Dance and Drama Centre; Northern Ballet School; Performers College; Stella Mann College; Studios La Pointe; Royal Academy of Dancing; The Urdang Academy.
  The accreditation of a course in a school does not necessarily imply that other courses of a different type or duration in the same school are also accredited.
  CDET has approved the teacher registration systems of the following: Association of American Dancing; British Ballet Organisation; British Theatre Dance Association; Cecchetti Society; Imperial Society of Teachers of Dancing; Royal Academy of Dancing.
IMPERIAL SOCIETY OF TEACHERS OF DANCING, Imperial House, 22-26 Paul Street, London EC2A 4QE. Tel: 020-7377 1577; Email: admin@istd.org; Web: www.istd.org. *Chief Executive*, M. J. Browne

INTERNATIONAL DANCE TEACHERS' ASSOCIATION, International House, 76 Bennett Road, Brighton BN2 5JL. Tel: 01273-685652; Email: info@idta.co.uk; Web: www.idta.co.uk.
ROYAL ACADEMY OF DANCE, 36 Battersea Square, London SW11 3RA. Tel: 020-7326 8000; Email: info@rad.org.uk. *Chief Executive*, L. Rittner
ROYAL BALLET SCHOOL, 155 Talgarth Road, London W14 9DE. Tel: 020-8748 6335; Web: www.royalballetschool.co.uk. *Director*, Ms G. Stock

DEFENCE

ROYAL COLLEGE OF DEFENCE STUDIES, Seaford House, 37 Belgrave Square, London SW1X 8NS. Tel: 020-7915 4800; Email: des@rcds.ac.uk; Web: www.rcds.ac.uk. *Commandant*, Lt Gen (Retd) Sir Christopher Wallace
JOINT SERVICES COMMAND AND STAFF COLLEGE, Faringdon Road, Watchfield, Swindon, Wilts SN6 8TS. Tel: 01793-788555; Email: registry@jscsc.org.uk; Web: www.jscsc.org.uk. *Commandant*, Air Vice-Marshal B. K. Burridge

ROYAL NAVAL COLLEGE

BRITANNIA ROYAL NAVAL COLLEGE, Dartmouth, Devon TQ6 0HJ. Tel: 01803-677108. *Commodore*, Cdre M. W. G. Kerr

MILITARY COLLEGES

DIRECTORATE OF EDUCATIONAL AND TRAINING SERVICES (ARMY), Trenchard Lines, Upavon, Pewsey, Wilts SN9 6BE. Tel: 01980-618719/618701; Email: dets_a@gtnet.gov.uk. *Director*, Brig. P. S. Purves
ROYAL MILITARY ACADEMY SANDHURST, Camberley, Surrey GU15 4PQ. Tel: 01276-63344. *Commandant*, Maj. Gen. PCC Trousdell
ROYAL MILITARY COLLEGE OF SCIENCE, Cranfield University, RMCS Shrivenham, Swindon SN6 8LA. Tel: 01793-785435; Web: www.rmcs.cranfield.ac.uk.

ROYAL AIR FORCE COLLEGES

ROYAL AIR FORCE COLLEGE, Cranwell, Sleaford, Lincs NG34 8HB. Tel: 01400-261201; Web: www.cranwell.raf.mod.uk.
ROYAL AIR FORCE TRAINING, DEVELOPMENT AND SUPPORT UNIT, RAF Halton, Aylesbury, Bucks HP22 5PG. Tel: 01296-623535 ext. 6210; Email: octdsu@raf-tdsu.demon.co.uk. *Commanding Officer*, PO J. Turner
ROYAL AIR FORCE COLLEGE, Provides initial training for all officer entrants to the RAF. Also provides initial specialist and postgraduate training for engineering and supply officers. The RAF College is the site of the Joint Elementary Flying School for pilots of all three services, Number 3 Flying Training School and the RAF Central Flying School. It is also the headquarters for the RAF University Air Squadrons, and is responsible for super-vision of the Air Cadet Organisation. *Air Officer Commanding and Commandant*, Air Vice-Marshal H. G. Mackay, OBE, AFC, BSC, FRAES, RAF

DENTISTRY

In order to practise in the UK, a dentist must be registered with the General Dental Council. To be registered a person must be qualified in one of the following ways: hold the degree or diploma in dental surgery of a university in the UK or hold the licentiate in dental surgery awarded by one of the Royal Surgical Colleges in the UK; completed the Council's statutory examination (soon to be replaced by the International Qualifying Examination (IQE)); be an European Community or European Economic Area national holding an appropriate European diploma; hold a registered overseas diploma or be an EEA national holding a primary dental qualification from outside the EEA but has acquired a right to practise in the EEA. The holder of a dental degree or diploma other than those

referred to above may be eligible for temporary registration to enable him or her to practise dentistry in the United Kingdom for a limited period and in specified posts without the need to take further examinations. The Dentists Register and Rolls of Dental Auxiliaries are maintained by:
GENERAL DENTAL COUNCIL, 37 Wimpole Street, London W1G 8DQ. Tel: 020-7887 3800; Email: information@gdc-uk.org Web: www.gdc-uk.org.

DIETETICS

See also FOOD AND NUTRITION SCIENCE

The professional association is the British Dietetic Association. Full membership is open to dieticians holding a recognised qualification, who may also become State Registered Dieticians through the Council for Professions Supplementary to Medicine (*see* Medicine).
THE BRITISH DIETETIC ASSOCIATION, 5th Floor, Charles House, 148-149 Craig Charles Street Queensway, Birmingham B3 3HT. Tel: 0121-200 8080.

DRAMA

The national validating body for courses providing training in drama for the professional theatre is the National Council for Drama Training. It currently has accredited courses at the following: Academy of Live and Recorded Arts; Arts Educational Schools; Birmingham School of Speech Training and Dramatic Art; Bristol Old Vic Theatre School; Central School of Speech and Drama; Drama Centre, London; Drama Studio, London; Guildford School of Acting; Guildhall School of Music and Drama, London; London Academy of Music and Dramatic Art; Manchester Metropolitan University School of Theatre; Mountview Theatre School; Oxford School of Drama, Woodstock; Queen Margaret University College, Edinburgh; Rose Bruford College, Sidcup; Royal Academy of Dramatic Art, London; Royal Scottish Academy of Music and Drama; Webber Douglas Academy of Dramatic Art, London; Welsh College of Music and Drama.
The accreditation of a course in a school does not necessarily imply that other courses of a different type or duration in the same school are also accredited.
NATIONAL COUNCIL FOR DRAMA TRAINING, 5 Tavistock Place, London WC1H 9SS. Tel: 020-7387 3650; Email: ncdt@lineone.net; Web: www.ncdt.co.uk.

ENGINEERING

The Engineering Council provides a central resource for supporting and promoting the engineering profession through the nominated engineering institutions represented on its Board for Engineers' Regulation. The Council's register of over 250,000 professionals, qualified to internationally recognised standards, reflects engineers and technicians across the broad spectrum of the industry. Working with and through the institutions, the Council sets the standards for the registration of individuals, and also the accreditation for academic courses in universities and colleges and the practical training in industry.
The principal qualifying bodies are:
THE ENGINEERING COUNCIL, 10 Maltravers Street, London WC2R 3ER. Tel: 020-7240 7891; Email: publicaffairs@engc.org.uk; Web: www.engc.org.uk.
BRITISH COMPUTER SOCIETY, 1 Sanford Street, Swindon SN1 1HJ. Tel: 01793-417417; Email: bcshq@hq.bcs.org.uk; Web: www.bcs.org. *Chief Executive*, Ms J. Scott
CHARTERED INSTITUTE OF BUILDING SERVICES ENGINEERS, 222 Balham High Road, London SW12 9BS. Tel: 020-8675 5211; Email: enquiries@cibse.org.uk; Web: www.cibse.org.uk. *Deputy Secretary*, S. Brown

INSTITUTION OF CHEMICAL ENGINEERS, Davis Building, 165–189 Railway Terrace, Rugby, Warks CV21 3HQ. Tel: 01788-578214; Web: www.icheme.org.
INSTITUTION OF CIVIL ENGINEERS, 1 Great George Street, London SW1P 3AA. Tel: 020-7222 7722; Email: library@ice.org.uk; Web: www.ice.org.uk. *Chief Executive and Secretary*, M. Casebourne
INSTITUTION OF ELECTRICAL ENGINEERS, Savoy Place, London WC2R 0BL. Tel: 020-7344 5445; Email: postmaster@iee.org.uk; Web: www.iee.org.uk. *Chief Executive*, Dr A. Roberts
INSTITUTION OF GAS ENGINEERS, 21 Portland Place, London W1B 1PY. Tel: 020-7636 6603; Email: general@igaseng.demon.co.uk; Web: www.igaseng.com.
THE INSTITUTE OF MARINE ENGINEERS, 80 Coleman Street, London EC2R 5BJ. Tel: 020-7382 2600; Email: imare@imare.org.uk; Web: www.imare.org.uk. *Director-General*, K. F. Read
THE INSTITUTE OF MATERIALS, 1 Carlton House Terrace, London SW1Y 5DB. Tel: 020-7451 7300; Email: admin@materials.org.uk; Web: www.materials.org.uk. *Chief Executive*, Dr B. Rickinson
THE INSTITUTE OF MEASUREMENT AND CONTROL, 87 Gower Street, London WC1E 6AF. Tel: 020-7387 4949; Email: education@instmc.org.uk; Web: www.instmc.org.uk. *Secretary*, M. Yates
INSTITUTION OF MECHANICAL ENGINEERS, 1 Birdcage Walk, London SW1H 9JJ. Tel: 020-7222 7899; Email: enquiries@imeche.org.uk; Web: www.imeche.org.uk. *Director-General*, Sir Michael Moore
INSTITUTION OF MINING AND METALLURGY, Danum House, South Parade, Doncaster, S. Yorks DN1 2DY. Tel: 01302-320486; Email: hq@imm.org.uk; Web: www.imm.org.uk. *Secretary*, Dr G. J. M. Woodrow
THE INSTITUTE OF PHYSICS, 76 Portland Place, London W1B 1NT. Tel: 020-7470 4800; Email: physics@iop.org; Web: www.iop.org. *Chief Executive*, Dr A. Jones
INSTITUTION OF STRUCTURAL ENGINEERS, 11 Upper Belgrave Street, London SW1X 8BH. Tel: 020-7235 4535; Email: mail@istructe.org.uk; Web: www.istructe.org.uk. *Chief Executive and Secretary*, Dr K. J. Eaton
INSTITUTION OF STRUCTURAL ENGINEERS, (Scottish Branch), 15 Beresford Place, East Trinity Road, Edinburgh EH5 3SL. Tel: 0131-552 8852.
ROYAL AERONAUTICAL SOCIETY, 4 Hamilton Place, London W1J 7BQ. Tel: 020-7670 4300; Email: raes@raes.org.uk; Web: www.raes.org.uk.
ROYAL INSTITUTION OF NAVAL ARCHITECTS, 10 Upper Belgrave Street, London SW1X 8BQ. Tel: 020-7235 4622; Email: hq@rina.org.uk; Web: www.rina.org.uk. *Chief Executive*, T. Blakeley

FILM AND TELEVISION

Postgraduate training for those intending to make a career in film, television and media production is provided by the National Film and Television School, which provides courses in animation direction, documentary direction, fiction direction, producing, screenwriting, screen design, editing, cinematography, screen sound, screen music and television producing/direction. Short courses, enabling professionals to update or expand their skills are run by the National Short Course Training Programme. There is also the Finishing School, a new industry-accredited, Digital Post-Production training workshop and creative laboratory.
NATIONAL FILM AND TELEVISION SCHOOL, Station Road, Beaconsfield, Bucks HP9 1LJ. Tel: 01494-671234; Email: admin@nftsfilm-tv.ac.uk Web: www.nftsfilm-tv.ac.uk. *Director*, S. Bayly

FOOD AND NUTRITION SCIENCE
See also DIETETICS
Scientific and professional bodies include:
THE BRITISH DIETETIC ASSOCIATION, 5th Floor, Charles House, 148-149 Craig Charles Street Queensway, Birmingham B3 3HT. Tel: 0121-200 8080.

FORESTRY AND TIMBER STUDIES
Professional organisations include:
COMMONWEALTH FORESTRY ASSOCIATION, c/o Oxford Forestry Institute, South Parks Road, Oxford OX1 3RB. Tel: 01865-271037; Email: cfa_oxford@hotmail.com. *Chairman*, Dr J. S. Maini
INSTITUTE OF CHARTERED FORESTERS, 7a St Colme Street, Edinburgh EH3 6AA. Tel: 0131-225 2705; Email: icf@charteredforesters.org; Web: www.charteredforesters.org.
ROYAL FORESTRY SOCIETY OF ENGLAND, WALES AND NORTHERN IRELAND, 102 High Street, Tring, Herts HP23 4AF. Tel: 01442-822028; Email: rfshq@rfs.org.uk; Web: www.rfs.org.uk. *Director*, Dr J. E. Jackson
ROYAL SCOTTISH FORESTRY SOCIETY, Hagg-on-Esk, Canonbie, Dumfriesshire DG14 0BE. Tel: 01387-371518. *President*, P. J. Fothergill

FUEL AND ENERGY SCIENCE
The principal professional bodies are:
THE INSTITUTE OF PETROLEUM, 61 New Cavendish Street, London W1G 7AR. Tel: 020-7467 7100; Email: ip@petroleum.co.uk; Web: www.petroleum.co.uk. *Director-General*, J. Pym

HOTELKEEPING, CATERING AND INSTITUTIONAL MANAGEMENT
See also DIETETICS, AND FOOD AND NUTRITION SCIENCE
The qualifying professional body in these areas is:
HOTEL AND CATERING INTERNATIONAL MANAGEMENT ASSOCIATION, 191 Trinity Road, London SW17 7HN. Tel: 020-8772 7400; Email: general@hcima.co.uk; Web: www.hcima.org.uk. *Chief Executive*, D. Wood

INDUSTRIAL AND VOCATIONAL TRAINING
The NTO National Council represents the network of employer-led national training organisations (NTOs). NTOs represent the education and training interests of their respective sectors to government and ensure the development and adoption of occupational standards, particularly through National and Scottish Vocational Qualifications and learning initiatives including Modern Apprenticeship and National Traineeship.
NTO NATIONAL COUNCIL, 10 Meadowcourt, Amos Road, Sheffield S9 1BX. Tel: 0114-261 9926; Email: info@nto-nc.org; Web: www.nto-nc.org.

INSURANCE
Organisations conducting examinations and awarding diplomas are:
ASSOCIATION OF AVERAGE ADJUSTERS, The Baltic Exchange, St Mary Axe, London EC3A 8BH. Tel: 020-7623 5501; Email: aaa@balticexchange.com; Web: www.average-adjusters.co.uk. *Chairman*, M. Duncan
THE CHARTERED INSTITUTE OF LOSS ADJUSTERS, Peninsular House, 36 Monument Street, London EC3R 8LJ. Tel: 020-7337 9960; Email: info@cila.co.uk; Web: www.cila.co.uk. *Executive Director*, G. L. Cave
THE CHARTERED INSURANCE INSTITUTE, 20 Aldermanbury, London EC2V 7HY. Tel: 020-8989 8464; Email: customer.serv@cii.co.uk; Web: www.cii.co.uk. *Director-General*, A. W. M. Scott

JOURNALISM
Courses for trainee newspaper journalists are available at 30 centres. One-year full-time courses are available for selected students and 18-week courses for graduates. Particulars of all these courses are available from the National Council for the Training of Journalists. Short courses for mid-career development can be arranged, as can various distance learning courses. The NCTJ also offers Assessor, Internal Verifier (IV) and Accreditation of Prior Achievement (APA) training, and NVQs.
For periodical journalists, there are nine centres running courses approved by the Periodicals Training Council (PTC). The PTC also provides career information for people wishing to join the industry.
NATIONAL COUNCIL FOR THE TRAINING OF JOURNALISTS, Latton Bush Centre, Southern Way, Harlow, Essex CM18 7BL. Tel: 01279-430009; Email: info@nctj.com; Web: www.nctj.com.
THE PERIODICALS TRAINING COUNCIL, Queens House, 55–56 Lincoln Inn Field, London WC2A 3LJ. Tel: 020-7404 4168; Email: training@ppa.co.uk; Web: www.ppa.co.uk/ptc.

LAW
THE BAR
Admission to the Bar of England and Wales is controlled by the Inns of Court, admission to the Bar of Northern Ireland by the Honorable Society of the Inn of Court of Northern Ireland and admission as an Advocate of the Scottish Bar is controlled by the Faculty of Advocates. The governing body of the barristers' branch of the legal profession in England and Wales is the General Council of the Bar (the Bar Council). The governing body in Northern Ireland is the Honorable Society of the Inn of Court of Northern Ireland, and the Faculty of Advocates is the governing body of the Scottish Bar. The education and examination of students training for the Bar of England and Wales is regulated by the General Council of the Bar. Those who intend to practise at the Bar of England and Wales must pass the Bar's vocational course. The Inns of Court School of Law is the largest provider of initial training (both full and part time) for those wishing to practise at the Bar, but seven other institutions have been validated to provide the course. Applications are handled by the Bar Council's Centralised Applications Clearing House (CACH).
CACH, The General Council of the Bar, 2–3 Curistor Street, London EC4A 1NE. Tel: 020-7440 4000; Email: CACH@barcouncil.org.uk; Web: www.barcouncil.org.uk. *Chief Executive*, N. Morison
FACULTY OF ADVOCATES, Advocates Library, Parliament House, Edinburgh EH1 1RF. Tel: 0131-226 5071. *Dean*, G. N. H. Emslie
THE GENERAL COUNCIL OF THE BAR, 3 Bedford Row, London WC1R 4DB. Tel: 020-7242 0082; Email: chiefexec@barcouncil.org.uk; Web: www.barcouncil.org.uk.
THE HONORABLE SOCIETY OF THE INN OF COURT OF NORTHERN IRELAND, Royal Courts of Justice, Belfast BT1 3JF. Tel: 028-9056 2349.
INNS OF COURT SCHOOL OF LAW, 4 Gray's Inn Place, Gray's Inn, London WC1R 5DX. Tel: 020-7404 5787; Email: icslcourses@icsl.ac.uk; Web: www.icsl.ac.uk.

The Inns of Court
GRAY'S INN, 8 South Square, London WC1R 5ET. Tel: 020-7458 7800; Web: www.graysinn.org.uk. *Treasurer*, The Rt. Hon. Sir Paul Kennedy
INNER TEMPLE, London EC4Y 7HL. Tel: 020-7797 8250; Web: www.innertemple.org.uk. *Treasurer*, The Rt. Hon. Sir Swinton Thomas
MIDDLE TEMPLE, London EC4Y 9AT. Tel: 020-7427 4800; Email: studentenquiries@middletemple.org.uk. *Treasurer*, Rt Hon. Lord Alexander of Weedon
HONORABLE SOCIETY OF LINCOLN'S INN, Treasury Office, Lincoln's Inn, London WC2A 3TL. Tel: 020-7405

1393; Email: mail@lincolnsinn.org.uk;
Web: www.lincolnsinn.org.uk.
Under-Treasurer, Col. D. Hills

SOLICITORS

Qualifications for solicitors are obtainable only from one of the Law Societies, which control the education and examination of trainee solicitors and the admission of solicitors.
THE COLLEGE OF LAW, Braboeuf Manor, Portsmouth Road, St Catherine's, Guildford, Surrey GU3 1HA. Tel: 01483-460200; Web: www.lawcol.org.uk.
THE LAW SOCIETY OF ENGLAND AND WALES, 113 Chancery Lane, London WC2A 1PL. Tel: 020-7320 5902; Web: www.lawsociety.org.uk.
LAW SOCIETY OF NORTHERN IRELAND, Law Society House, 98 Victoria Street, Belfast BT1 3JZ. Tel: 028-9023 1614; Email: info@lawsoc-ni.org; Web: www.lawsoc-ni.org.
LAW SOCIETY OF SCOTLAND, 26 Drumsheugh Gardens, Edinburgh EH3 7YR. Tel: 0131-226 7411; Email: lawscot@lawscot.org.uk; Web: www.lawscot.org.uk.
OFFICE FOR THE SUPERVISION OF SOLICITORS, Victoria Court, 8 Dormer Place, Leamington Spa, Warks CV32 5AE. Tel: 01926-820082; Email: enquiries@lawsociety.org.uk; Web: www.oss.lawsociety.org.uk.
Director, J. Plane

LIBRARIANSHIP AND INFORMATION SCIENCE/MANAGEMENT

The Library Association accredits degree and postgraduate courses in library and information science which are offered by 17 universities in the UK. A full list of accredited degree and postgraduate courses is available from its International Relations and Information Services Department and on its web site (*see* below) The Association also maintains a professional register of Chartered Members.
THE LIBRARY ASSOCIATION, 7 Ridgmount Street, London WC1E 7AE. Tel: 020-7636 7543 Web: www.la-hq.uk.

MEDICINE

All doctors must be registered with the General Medical Council (GMC), which is responsible for protecting the public by setting standards for professional practice, overseeing medical education, keeping a register of qualified doctors and taking action where a doctor's fitness to practise is in doubt. A doctor not registered with the GMC is not a "legally qualified" medical practitioner for the purposes of the Medical Act 1983. In order to be eligible for registration, doctors must obtain a primary medical qualification recognised by the GMC and have satisfactorily completed a year of general clinical training. Special arrangements apply to doctors qualified outside the UK. Once registered, doctors undertake general professional and basic specialist training as senior house officers. Further specialist training is provided by the royal colleges, faculties and societies listed below.
    The United Examining Board holds qualifying examinations for candidates who have trained overseas. These candidates must also have spent a period at a UK medical school.
GENERAL MEDICAL COUNCIL, 178 Great Portland Street, London W1N 6JE. Tel: 020-7580 7642; Web: www.gmc-uk.org.
UNITED EXAMINING BOARD, Apothecaries Hall, Black Friars Lane, London EC4V 6EJ. Tel: 020-7236 1180; Email: examoffice@apothecaries.org.

COLLEGES/SOCIETIES HOLDING POSTGRADUATE MEMBERSHIP AND DIPLOMA EXAMINATIONS

FACULTY OF ACCIDENT AND EMERGENCY MEDICINE, 35–43 Lincoln's Inn Fields, London WC2A 3PE. Tel: 020-7405 7071; Email: faem@compuserve.com; Web: www.faem.org.uk. *President*, I. W. R. Anderson
FACULTY OF PUBLIC HEALTH MEDICINE, 4 St Andrews Place, London NW1 4LB. Tel: 020-7935 0243; Email: enquiries@fphm.org.uk; Web: www.fphm.org.uk.
ROYAL COLLEGE OF ANAESTHETISTS, 48–49 Russell Square, London WC1B 4JY. Tel: 020-7813 1900; Email: info@rcoa.ac.uk; Web: www.rcoa.ac.uk. *President*, Prof. P. Hatton
ROYAL COLLEGE OF OBSTETRICIANS AND GYNAECOLOGISTS, 27 Sussex Place, Regent's Park, London NW1 4RG. Tel: 020-7772 6200; Email: coll.sec@rcog.org.uk; Web: www.rcog.org.uk. *College Secretary*, P. A. Barnett
ROYAL COLLEGE OF PAEDIATRICS AND CHILD HEALTH, 50 Hallam Street, London W1W 6DE. Tel: 020-7307 5600; Email: enquiries@rcpch.ac.uk. *Secretary*, L. Tyler
ROYAL COLLEGE OF PATHOLOGISTS, 2 Carlton House Terrace, London SW1Y 5AF. Tel: 020-7451 6700; Email: info@rcpath.org; Web: www.rcpath.org. *Chief Executive*, D. Ross
ROYAL COLLEGE OF PHYSICIANS, 11 St Andrews Place, Regent's Park, London NW1 4LE. Tel: 020-7935 1174; Web: www.rcplondon.ac.uk. *President*, Prof. Sir George Alberti
ROYAL COLLEGE OF PHYSICIANS AND SURGEONS OF GLASGOW, 232–242 St Vincent Street, Glasgow G2 5RJ. Tel: 0141-221 6072; Email: registrar@rcpsglasg.ac.uk; Web: www.rcpsglasg.ac.uk. *President*, Prof. A. R. Lorimer
ROYAL COLLEGE OF PHYSICIANS OF EDINBURGH, 9 Queen Street, Edinburgh EH2 1JQ. Tel: 0131-225 7324; Web: www.rcpe.ac.uk. *President*, Dr N. D. C. Finlayson
ROYAL COLLEGE OF PSYCHIATRISTS, 17 Belgrave Square, London SW1X 8PG. Tel: 020-7235 2351; Email: rcpsych@rcpsych.ac.uk; Web: www.rcpsych.ac.uk. *President*, Prof J. L. Cox
ROYAL COLLEGE OF RADIOLOGISTS, 38 Portland Place, London W1N 4JQ. Tel: 020-7636 4432; Email: enquiries@rcr.ac.uk; Web: www.rcr.ac.uk. *President*, Dr D. V. Ash
ROYAL COLLEGE OF SURGEONS OF EDINBURGH, Nicolson Street, Edinburgh EH8 9DW. Tel: 0131-527 1600; Email: information@rcsed.ac.uk. Web: www.rcsed.ac.uk. *President*, Prof. J. G. Temple
THE ROYAL COLLEGE OF SURGEONS OF ENGLAND, 35–43 Lincoln's Inn Fields, London WC2A 3PE. Tel: 020-7405 3474; Web: www.rcseng.ac.uk. *President*, Prof. Sir Peter Morris
SOCIETY OF APOTHECARIES OF LONDON, 14 Black Friars Lane, London EC4V 6EJ. Tel: 020-7236 1189; Email: clerk@apothecaries.org; Web: www.apothecaries.org. *The Clerk*, R. J. Stringer

PROFESSIONS SUPPLEMENTARY TO MEDICINE

The standard of professional education in art, drama and music therapies, biomedical sciences, chiropody, dietetics, occupational therapy, orthoptics, prosthetics and orthotics, physiotherapy and radiography is the responsibility of nine professional boards, which also publish an annual register of qualified practitioners. The work of the boards is co-ordinated by the Council for Professions Supplementary to Medicine.
    In January 2000 three new boards were established, covering speech and language therapists, clinical scientists and paramedics.

474   Education

COUNCIL FOR PROFESSIONS SUPPLEMENTARY TO MEDICINE, Park House, 184 Kennington Park Road, London SE11 4BU. Tel: 020-7582 0866; Web: www.cpsm.org.uk.

ART, DRAMA AND MUSIC THERAPIES

A postgraduate qualification in the relevant therapy is required. There are five institutions in the UK offering courses in art therapy and six offering courses in music therapy.

ASSOCIATION OF PROFESSIONAL MUSIC THERAPISTS, 26 Hamlyn Road, Glastonbury, Somerset BA6 8HT. Tel: 01458-834919; Email: apmtoffice@aol.com; Web: www.apmt.org.uk.

BRITISH ASSOCIATION OF ART THERAPISTS, Mary Ward House, 5 Tavistock Place, London WC1H 9SN. Tel: 020-7383 3774; Web: www.baat.co.uk.

BRITISH ASSOCIATION OF DRAMA THERAPISTS, 41 Broomhouse Lane, London SW6 3DP. Tel: 020-7731 0160; Email: gillian@badth.demon.co.uk.

BIOMEDICAL SCIENCES

Qualifications from higher education establishments and training in medical laboratories are required for membership of the Institute of Biomedical Science.

INSTITUTE OF BIOMEDICAL SCIENCES, 12 Coldbath Square, London EC1R 5HL. Tel: 020-7713 0214; Email: mail@ibms.org; Web: www.ibms.org.

CHIROPODY

Professional recognition is granted by the Society of Chiropodists and Podiatrists to students who are awarded BSc. degrees in Podiatry or Podiatric Medicine after attending a course of full-time training for three or four years at one of the 13 recognised schools in the UK (ten in England and Wales, two in Scotland and one in Northern Ireland). Qualifications granted and degrees recognised by the Society are approved for the purpose of State Registration, which is a condition of employment within the National Health Service.

SOCIETY OF CHIROPODISTS AND PODIATRISTS, 1 Fellmongers Path, Tower Bridge Road, London SE1 3LY. Tel: 020-7234 8620; Email: eng@scpod.org; Web: www.feetforlife.org.

OCCUPATIONAL THERAPY

The professional qualification may be obtained upon successful completion of a validated course in any of the 28 institutions approved by the College of Occupational Therapists. The courses are normally degree-level courses based in higher education institutions.

COLLEGE OF OCCUPATIONAL THERAPISTS, 106–114 Borough High Street, London SE1 1LB. Tel: 020-7357 6480; Email: cot@cot.co.uk; Web: www.cot.co.uk.

FACULTY OF OCCUPATIONAL THERAPY, 6 St Andrew's Place, London NW1 4LB. Tel: 020-7317 5890; Email: fom@facoccmed.ac.uk; Web: www.facoccmed.ac.uk. *Secretary*, Ms F. Quinn

ORTHOPTICS

Orthoptists undertake the diagnosis and treatment of all types of squint and other anomalies of binocular vision, working in close collaboration with ophthalmologists. The training and maintenance of professional standards are the responsibility of the Orthoptists Board of the Council for the Professions Supplementary to Medicine. The professional body is the British Orthoptic Society. Training is at degree level.

THE BRITISH ORTHOPTIC SOCIETY, Tavistock House North, Tavistock Square, London WC1H 9HX. Tel: 020-7387 7992; Email: bos@orthoptics.org.uk.

PHYSIOTHERAPY

Full-time three- or four-year degree courses are available at 30 higher education institutions in the UK. Information about courses leading to eligibility for Membership of the Chartered Society of Physiotherapy and to State Registration is available from the Chartered Society of Physiotherapy.

THE CHARTERED SOCIETY OF PHYSIOTHERAPY, 14 Bedford Row, London WC1R 4ED. Tel: 020-7306 6666; Email: careersadviser@csphysio.org.uk; Web: www.csphysio.org.uk.

PROSTHETICS AND ORTHOTICS

Prosthetists provide artificial limbs, while orthotists provide devices to support or control a part of the body. It is necessary to obtain an honours degree to become a prosthetist/orthotist. Courses are available at two institutions in the UK.

BRITISH ASSOCIATION OF PROSTHETISTS AND ORTHOTISTS, Sir James Clark Building, Abbey Mill Business Centre, Paisley PA1 1TJ. Tel: 0141-561 7217; Email: admin@bapo.com; Web: www.bapo.com.

RADIOGRAPHY AND RADIOTHERAPY

In order to practise both diagnostic and therapeutic radiography in the UK, it is necessary to have successfully completed a course of education and training recognised by the Privy Council. Such courses are offered by universities throughout the UK and lead to the award of a degree in radiography. Further information is available from the college.

COLLEGE OF RADIOGRAPHERS, 27 Providence Square, Mill Street, London SE1 2EW. Tel: 020-7740 7200; Email: info@sor.org; Web: www.sor.org.

COMPLEMENTARY MEDICINE

Professional courses are validated by:

INSTITUTE FOR COMPLEMENTARY MEDICINE, PO Box 194, London SE16 7QZ. Tel: 020-7237 5165; Email: icm@icmedicine.co.uk; Web: www.icmedicine.co.uk. *Director*, A. Baird

MERCHANT NAVY TRAINING SCHOOLS

OFFICERS

WARSASH MARITIME CENTRE, Southampton Institute, Newtown Road, Warsash, Southampton SO31 9ZL. Tel: 01489-576161; Email: wmc@solent.ac.uk; Web: www.solent.ac.uk/wmc/. *Head*, J. Milligan

SEAFARERS

NATIONAL SEA TRAINING CENTRE, North West Kent College, Dering Way, Gravesend, Kent DA12 2JJ. Tel: 01322-629600; Email: rodgermacdonald@nwkent.ac.uk; Web: www.nwkent.ac.uk/nstc. *Director of Faculty – NSTC*, R. MacDonald

MUSIC

Associated Board of the Royal Schools of Music, conducts graded music examinations in over 80 countries and provides other services to music education through its professional development department and publishing company.

ASSOCIATED BOARD OF THE ROYAL SCHOOLS OF MUSIC, 24 Portland Place, London W1B 1LU. Tel: 020-7636 5400; Email: abrsm@abrsm.ac.uk; Web: www.abrsm.ac.uk.

GUILDHALL SCHOOL OF MUSIC DRAMA, Silk Street, Barbican, London EC2Y 8DT. Tel: 020-7628 2571; Web: www.gsmd.ac.uk. *Principal*, Dr I. Horsbrugh

LONDON COLLEGE OF MUSIC AND MEDIA, Thames Valley University, St Mary's Road, London W5 5RF. Tel: 020-8231 2304; Web: www.elgar.tvu.ac.uk. *Acting Dean*, H. Swain

ROYAL ACADEMY OF MUSIC, Marylebone Road, London NW1 5HT. Tel: 020-7873 7373; Email: registry@ram.ac.uk; Web: www.ram.ac.uk. *Principal*, C. Price

ROYAL COLLEGE OF ORGANISTS, 7 St Andrew Street, London EC4A 3LQ. Tel: 020-7936 3606; Email: admin@rco.org.uk; Web: www.rco.org.uk. *Senior Executive*, A. Dear

ROYAL NORTHERN COLLEGE OF MUSIC, 124 Oxford Road, Manchester M13 9RD. Tel: 0161-907 5200; Email: info@rncm.ac.uk; Web: www.rncm.ac.uk. *Principal*, Prof. E. Gregson

ROYAL SCOTTISH ACADEMY OF MUSIC AND DRAMA, 100 Renfrew Street, Glasgow G2 3DB. Tel: 0141-332 4101; Email: registry@rsamd.ac.uk; Web: www.rsamd.ac.uk. *Principal*, Sir Philip Ledger

TRINITY COLLEGE OF MUSIC, 11-13 Mandeville Place, London W1M 6AQ. Tel: 020-7487 9647; Web: www.tcm.ac.uk. *Principal*, G. Henderson

NURSING

All nurses must be registered with the UK Central Council for Nursing, Midwifery and Health Visiting. Please note that it will cease to exist in March 2002 and a new regulating body – the Nursing and Midwifery Council – will be set up; its functions were not yet known at the time of going to press. Courses leading to registration as a nurse are at least three years in length. There are also some programmes which are combined with degrees. Students study in colleges of nursing or in institutions of higher education. Courses offer a combination of theoretical and practical experience in a variety of settings. Different courses lead to different types of registration, including Registered Nurse (RN), Registered Mental Nurse (RMN), Registered Mental Handicap Nurse (RMHN), Registered Sick Children's Nurse (RSCN), Registered Midwife (RM) and Registered Health Visitor (RHV). The various national boards, listed below, are responsible for validating courses in nursing. In February 1999 the Government announced plans to replace these boards and the UK Central Council with a single UK-wide body. Health visitors will continue to have separate registration and representation on the new body.

The Royal College of Nursing is the largest professional union representing nurses and provides higher education through its Institute.

ENGLISH NATIONAL BOARD FOR NURSING, MIDWIFERY AND HEALTH VISITING, Victory House, 170 Tottenham Court Road, London W1T 7HA. Tel: 020-7391 6229; Email: ceo@enb.org.uk; Web: www.enb.org.uk.

NATIONAL BOARD FOR NURSING, MIDWIFERY AND HEALTH VISITING FOR NORTHERN IRELAND, Centre House, 79 Chichester Street, Belfast BT1 4JE. Tel: 028-9023 8152; Email: enquiries@nbni.n-i.nhs.uk; Web: www.n-i.nhs.uk/NBNI/index.htm.

NATIONAL BOARD FOR NURSING, MIDWIFERY AND HEALTH VISITING FOR SCOTLAND, 22 Queen Street, Edinburgh EH2 1NT. Tel: 0131-226 7371; Email: david.ferguson@nbs.org.uk; Web: www.nbs.org.uk.

UK CENTRAL COUNCIL FOR NURSING, MIDWIFERY AND HEALTH VISITING, 23 Portland Place, London W1N 4JT. Tel: 020-7637 7181; Email: communication@ukcc.org.uk; Web: www.ukcc.org.uk.

WELSH NATIONAL BOARD FOR NURSING, MIDWIFERY AND HEALTH VISITING, 2nd Floor, Golate House, 101 St Mary Street, Cardiff CF10 1DX. Tel: 029-2026 1400; Email: info@wnb.org.uk; Web: www.wnb.org.uk.

OPHTHALMIC AND DISPENSING OPTICS

Professional bodies are:

THE ASSOCIATION OF BRITISH DISPENSING OPTICIANS, 6 Hurlingham Business Park, Sulivan Road, London SW6 3DU. Tel: 020-7736 0088; Email: general@abdo.org.uk. *General-Secretary*, Sir Anthony Garrett

THE COLLEGE OF OPTOMETRISTS, 42 Craven Street, London WC2N 5NG. Tel: 020-7839 6000; Email: optometry@college-optometrists.org; Web: www.optometrists.org. *Secretary*, P. D. Leigh

OSTEOPATHY

Osteopathy is the first of the professions previously outside conventional medical services to achieve statutory recognition under a new body the General Osteopathic Council. Since May 2000 all practising osteopaths have had to be registered with the General Osteopathic Council and the title 'osteopath' is protected by law. To gain entry to the register all newly qualified osteopaths have to be in possession of a recognised qualification from a course of training accredited by the General Osteopathic Council. The General Osteopathic Council is responsible for regulating, developing, and promoting the profession.

GENERAL OSTEOPATHIC COUNCIL, Osteopathy House, 176 Tower Bridge Road, London SE1 3LU. Tel: 020-7357 6655; Email: info@osteopathy.org.uk; Web: www.osteopathy.org.uk.

PHARMACY

The Royal Pharmaceutical Society of Great Britain is the professional statutory body for practising pharmacists in Great Britain. It maintains the Register of Pharmaceutical Chemists where all pharmacists must be registered before being able to practice.

FACULTY OF PHARMACEUTICAL MEDICINE, 1 St Andrew's Place, London NW1 4LB. Tel: 020-7224 0343; Email: fpm@f-pharm-med.org.uk; Web: www.fpm.org.uk. *Faculty Administrator*, Mrs K. Swanston

PHOTOGRAPHY

The professional body is:

BRITISH INSTITUTE OF PROFESSIONAL PHOTOGRAPHY, Fox Talbot House, Amwell End, Ware, Herts SG12 9HN. Tel: 01920-464011; Email: bipp@compuserve.com; Web: www.bipp.com. *Chief Executive*, A. Mair

PRINTING

Details of training courses in printing can be obtained from the Institute of Printing and the British Printing Industries Federation. In addition to these examining and organising bodies, examinations are held by various independent regional examining boards in further education.

BRITISH PRINTING INDUSTRIES FEDERATION, Farringdon Point, 29-35 Farringdon Rd, London EC1M 3JF. Tel: 020-7915 8300; Email: info@bpif.org.uk; Web: www.bpif.org.uk.

INSTITUTE OF PRINTING, The Mews, Hill House, Clanricarde Road, Tunbridge Wells, Kent TN1 1PJ. Tel: 01892-538118; Email: david@iop.ftech.co.uk; Web: www.instituteofprinting.org.

SCIENCE

Professional qualifications are awarded by:

THE INSTITUTE OF BIOLOGY, 20-22 Queensberry Place, London SW7 2DZ. Tel: 020-7581 8333; Email: info@iob.org; Web: www.iob.org. *Chief Executive*, Prof. A. D. B. Malcolm

THE ROYAL SOCIETY OF CHEMISTRY, Burlington House, Piccadilly, London W1J 0BA. Tel: 020-7437 8656; Email: rsc@rsc.org; Web: www.rsc.org. *Secretary-General and Chief Executive*, Dr D. Giachardi

SPEECH AND LANGUAGE THERAPY

The Royal College of Speech and Language Therapists accredits education and training courses leading to qualification as a speech and language therapist.

ROYAL COLLEGE OF SPEECH AND LANGUAGE THERAPISTS,
2 White Hart Yard, London SE1 1NX. Tel: 020-7378
1200; Email: info@rcslt.org.uk;
Web: www.rcslt.org.uk.

SURVEYING

The qualifying professional bodies include:
ARCHITECTURE AND SURVEYING INSTITUTE, St Mary
House, 15 St Mary Street, Chippenham, Wilts
SN15 3WD. Tel: 01249-444505; Email: mail@asi.org.uk;
Web: www.asi.org.uk. *Chief Executive*, I. N. Norris
ASSOCIATION OF BUILDING ENGINEERS, Lutyens House,
Billing Brook Road, Weston Favell, Northampton
NN3 8NW. Tel: 01604-404121;
Email: building.engineers@abe.org.uk;
Web: www.abe.org.uk. *Chief Executive*, D. R. Gibson
INSTITUTE OF REVENUES, RATING AND VALUATION, 41
Doughty Street, London WC1N 2LF. Tel: 020-7831 3505;
Email: enquiries@irrv.org.uk; Web: www.irrv.org.uk.
Director, Ms K. Aldred
THE ROYAL INSTITUTION OF CHARTERED SURVEYORS, 12
Great George Street, London SW1P 3AD. Tel: 020-7222
7000; Email: info@rics.org.uk; Web: www.rics.org.
Chief Executive, J. H. A. J. Armstrong

TEACHING

Teachers in maintained schools must acquire Qualified
Teacher Status (QTS) by completing a programme of
Initial Teacher Training. Those without a first degree may
take a Bachelor of Education (BEd) or a Bachelor of Arts/
Science (BA/BSc) with QTS, full-time for three or four
years, depending on the programme followed. These
degrees combine subject and professional studies with
teaching practice. Shortened courses of these degrees are
available for those who have successfully completed one or
two years of higher education. Flexible routes into
teaching are increasing, including part-time, distance
learning and modular courses. Alternatively, teachers can
gain QTS through employment-based training, following
individual training plans while in post.

For those who already have a first degree, the most
common route is through a one-year Postgraduate
Certificate of Education (PGCE). This may be taken
full-time or part-time, or as a distance-learning programme. Postgraduates may also gain QTS through
training in a school (School-Centred Initial Teacher
Training). Since January 1998, graduates have been able to
join the Graduate Teacher Programme which provides
teaching and training for one year.

Details of courses in England and Wales are contained
in the *NATFHE Handbook of Initial Teacher Training in
England and Wales 2000*, in *University and College Entrance:
2000 (The Big Book)* published by UCAS and on the UCAS
website. Further information about teaching in England
and Wales is available from the Teaching Information
Line, 0845 600 0991. Details of courses in Scotland can be
obtained from universities and the Graduate Teacher
Training Registry (GTTR). Details of courses in Northern Ireland can be obtained from the Department of
Education for Northern Ireland. Applications for teacher
training courses in Northern Ireland are made to the
institutions direct.
TEACHER TRAINING AGENCY, Portland House, Stag
Place, London SW1E 5TT. Tel: 020-7925 3700;
Web: www.canteach.gov.uk.

TEXTILES

THE TEXTILE INSTITUTE, 4th Floor, St James's
Buildings, Oxford Street, Manchester M1 6FQ.
Tel: 0161-237 1188; Email: tiihq@textileinst.org.uk;
Web: www.texi.org.uk.
Director-General, T. D. Hennessey

THEOLOGICAL COLLEGES

ANGLICAN
COLLEGE OF THE RESURRECTION, Mirfield, W. Yorks
WF14 0BW. Tel: 01924-490441;
Email: registrar@mirfield.org.uk;
Web: www.mirfield.org.uk. *Principal*, Revd C. Irvine
CRANMER HALL, St John's College, Durham DH1 3RJ.
Tel: 0191-374 3579; Web: www.dur.ac.uk/cranmer.
Principal, The Rt. Revd S. W. Sykes
OAK HILL COLLEGE, Chase Side, Southgate, London
N14 4PS. Tel: 020-8449 0467;
Email: mailbox@oakhill.ac.uk;
Web: www.oakhill.ac.uk.
Principal, Revd Dr D. Peterson
RIDLEY HALL, Cambridge CB3 9HG. Tel: 01223-741080;
Email: ridley-pa@lists.cam.ac.uk;
Web: www.ridley.cam.ac.uk. *Principal*, The Revd
Canon Dr Christopher Cocksworth
RIPON COLLEGE, Cuddesdon, Oxford OX44 9EX.
Tel: 01865-874427; Email: admin@ripon-
cuddesdon.ac.uk; Web: www.ripon-cuddesdon.ac.uk.
Principal, Canon J. Clarke
ST JOHN'S COLLEGE, Chilwell Lane, Bramcote,
Nottingham NG9 3DS. Tel: 0115-925 1114;
Email: principal@stjohns-nottm.ac.uk;
Web: www.stjohns-nottm.ac.uk.
Principal, Canon Dr C. Baxter
ST MICHAEL'S THEOLOGICAL COLLEGE, Llandaff,
Cardiff CF5 2YJ. Tel: 029-2056 3379;
Email: stmichael@nildram.co.uk.
Principal, Revd Dr J. Holdsworth
ST STEPHEN'S HOUSE, 16 Marston Street, Oxford
OX4 1JX. Tel: 01865-247874;
Email: jeremy.sheehy@theology.oxford.ac.uk.
Principal, Revd Dr J. P. Sheehy
THEOLOGICAL INSTITUTE OF THE SCOTTISH EPISCOPAL
CHURCH, Old Coates House, 32 Manor Place,
Edinburgh EH3 7EB. Tel: 0131-220 2272;
Email: office@stisec.scotland.anglican.org.
Principal, Revd Canon Dr M. Fuller
TRINITY COLLEGE, Stoke Hill, Bristol BS9 1JP.
Tel: 0117-968 2803; Email: principal@trinity-
bris.ac.uk; Web: www.trinity-bris.ac.uk.
Principal, Revd Dr F. Bridger
WESTCOTT HOUSE, Jesus Lane, Cambridge CB5 8BP.
Tel: 01223-741000;
Email: westcott.house@lists.cam.ac.uk;
Web: www.ely.anglican.org/westcott.
Principal, Revd M. Roberts
WYCLIFFE HALL THEOLOGICAL COLLEGE, 54 Banbury
Road, Oxford OX2 6PW. Tel: 01865-274200;
Email: enquiries@wycliffe.ox.ac.uk;
Web: www.wycliffe.ox.ac.uk.
Principal, Revd Prof. A. E. McGrath

BAPTIST
BRISTOL BAPTIST COLLEGE, The Promenade, Clifton,
Bristol BS8 3NF. Tel: 0117-946 7050;
Email: admin@bristol-baptist.ac.uk
Web: www.bristol-baptist.ac.uk.
Principal, Revd C. Ellis
NORTHERN BAPTIST COLLEGE, Luther King House,
Brighton Grove, Rusholme, Manchester M14 5JP.
Tel: 0161-224 6404;
Email: richard.kidd@appleonline.net.
Principal, Revd Dr R. Kidd
NORTH WALES BAPTIST COLLEGE, Ffordd Ffriddoedd,
Bangor LL57 2EH. Tel: 01248-362608;
Web: www.bangor.ac.uk/rs/gttest.html.
Warden, Revd Dr D. D. Morgan
REGENT'S PARK COLLEGE, Oxford OX1 2LB.
Tel: 01865-288120;
Email: postmaster@regents.ox.ac.uk;
Web: www.rpc.ox.ac.uk/rpc.
Principal, Revd Dr P. S. Fiddes

THE SCOTTISH BAPTIST COLLEGE, 12 Aytoun Road, Glasgow G41 5RN. Tel: 0141-424 0747; Web: www.scottishbaptistcollege.org.uk. *Principal*, Dr K. B. E. Roxburgh
SOUTH WALES BAPTIST COLLEGE, 54 Richmond Road, Cardiff CF24 3UR. Tel: 029-2025 6066; Email: swbc@cardiff.ac.uk; Web: www.welshbaptists.com. *Principal*, Revd Dr J. Weaver

CHURCH OF SCOTLAND
NEW COLLEGE, Mound Place, Edinburgh EH1 2LX. Tel: 0131-650 8916/8900; Email: lyalld@div.ed.ac.uk; Web: www.divinity.ed.ac.uk. *Principal*, Revd Dr D. Lyall
TRINITY COLLEGE, Faculty of Divinity, University of Glasgow, Glasgow G12 8QQ. Tel: 0141-330 6840; Email: d.murray@arts.gla.ac.uk. *Principal*, Revd Dr D. M. Murray

CONGREGATIONAL
THE QUEEN'S FOUNDATION FOR ECUMENICAL THEOLOGICAL INFORMATION, Somerset Road, Edgbaston, Birmingham B15 2QH. Tel: 0121-454 1527; Email: enquire@queens.ac.uk; Web: www.queens.ac.uk. *Principal*, Revd Canon P. Fisher

METHODIST
EDGHILL THEOLOGICAL COLLEGE, 9 Lennoxvale, Belfast BT9 5BY. Tel: 028-9066 5870. *Principal*, Revd Dr D. Cooke
HARTLEY VICTORIA COLLEGE, Luther King House, Brighton Grove, Rusholme, Manchester M14 5JP. Tel: 0161-249 2516. *Principal*, Revd Dr J. A. Harrod
WESLEY COLLEGE, College Park Drive, Henbury Road, Bristol BS10 7QD. Tel: 0117-959 1200; Email: admin@wescoll.demon.co.uk; Web: www.wescoll.demon.co.uk. *Principal*, Revd Dr N. Richardson
WESLEY THEOLOGICAL COLLEGE, Wesley House, Jesus Lane, Cambridge CB5 8BJ. Tel: 01223-741033; Email: bursar@wesley.org.uk; Web: www.wesley.org.uk. *Principal*, Revd Dr P. Luscombe
WESLEY STUDY CENTRE, 55 The Avenue, Durham DH1 4EB. Tel: 0191-374 3580. *Director*, Revd R. Walton

NON-DENOMINATIONAL
CHRIST'S College, 25 High Street, Old Aberdeen, Aberdeen AB24 3EE. Tel: 01224-272138. *Master*, Revd Prof. Iain R. Torrance
ST MARY'S COLLEGE, The University, St Andrews, Fife KY16 9JU. Tel: 01334-462850; Email: divinity@st-andrews.ac.uk; Web: www.st-andrews.ac.uk. *Principal*, Prof. R. A. Piper
SPURGEON'S COLLEGE, South Norwood Hill, London SE6 6DJ. Tel: 020-8653 0850; Email: enquiries@spurgeons.ac.uk; Web: www.spurgeons.ac.uk. *Principal*, Revd Dr N. Wright

PRESBYTERIAN
UNION THEOLOGICAL COLLEGE, 108 Botanic Avenue, Belfast BT7 1JT. Tel: 028-9020 5080; Email: admin@union.ac.uk; Web: www.union.ac.uk. *Principal*, Revd J. C. McCullough

PRESBYTERIAN CHURCH OF WALES
UNITED THEOLOGICAL COLLEGE, Aberystwyth, Ceredigion SY23 2LT. Tel: 01970-624574; Web: www.ebcpcw.org.uk.

ROMAN CATHOLIC
ALLEN HALL, 28 Beaufort Street, London SW3 5AA. Tel: 020-7351 1296; Email: secretary@allenhall.co.uk. *Rector*, Revd P. McGinn
CAMPION HOUSE COLLEGE, 112 Thornbury Road, Isleworth, Middx TW7 4NN. Tel: 020-8560 1924; Email: campionhouseosterley@compuserve.com; Web: www.campionhouse.org.uk. *Principal*, Revd M. Barrow
OSCOTT COLLEGE, Chester Road, Sutton Coldfield, West Midlands B73 5AA. Tel: 0121-321 5000; Email: oscott@dial.pipex.com. *Rector*, Monsignor K. McDonald
ST JOHN'S SEMINARY, Wonersh, Guildford, Surrey GU5 0QX. Tel: 01483-892217. *Rector*, Revd K. Haggerty
SCOTUS COLLEGE, 2 Chesters Road, Bearsden, Glasgow G61 4AG. Tel: 0141-942 8384. *Rector*, Revd N. Donnachie
USHAW COLLEGE, Durham DH7 9RH. Tel: 0191-373 8501; Email: j.p.o'keefe@dur.ac.uk; Web: www.dur.ac.uk/ushaw. *President*, Revd J. O'Keefe

UNITARIAN
Unitarian College, Luther King House, Brighton Grove, Rusholme, Manchester M14 5JP. Tel: 0161-224 2849; Email: ucm@ptem.freeserve.co.uk. *Principal*, Revd Dr L. Smith

UNITED REFORMED
NORTHERN COLLEGE, Luther King House, Brighton Grove, Rusholme, Manchester M14 5JP. Tel: 0161-249 2506; Email: reception@lkh.co.uk. *Principal*, Revd Dr D. R. Peel
WESTMINSTER COLLEGE, Madingley Road, Cambridge CB3 0AA. Tel: 01223-741084; Email: mr258@cam.ac.uk; Web: www.westminster.cam.ac.uk. *Principal*, Revd Dr S. Orchard

JEWISH
LEO BAECK COLLEGE, Sternberg Centre for Judaism, 80 East End Road, London N3 2SY. Tel: 020-8349 5600; Email: info@lbc.ac.uk; Web: www.lbc.ac.uk. *Principal*, Rabbi Prof. J. Magonet
LONDON SCHOOL OF JEWISH STUDIES, Schaller House, 44a Albert Road, London NW4 2SJ. Tel: 020-8203 6427; Email: enquiries@lsjs.ac.uk; Web: www.lsjs.ac.uk. *Principal*, Dr A. Weiss

VETERINARY MEDICINE

The regulatory body for veterinary medicine is the Royal College of Veterinary Surgeons, which keeps the register of those entitled to practise veterinary medicine. In order to be registered, a person must complete a five-year undergraduate degree (BVetMed, BVSc., BVMS, BVM and S) at one of the six authorised institutions in the UK.
The British Veterinary Association is the professional body representing veterinary surgeons. The British Veterinary Nursing Association is the professional body representing veterinary nurses who are also registered with the Royal College of Veterinary Surgeons.
BRITISH VETERINARY NURSING ASSOCIATION, Level 15, Terminus House, Terminus Street, Harlow, Essex CM20 1XA. Tel: 01279-450567; Email: bvna@bvna.co.uk; Web: www.bvna.org.uk.
ROYAL COLLEGE OF VETERINARY SURGEONS, Belgravia House, 62-64 Horseferry Road, London SW1P 2AF. Tel: 020-7222 2001; Email: admin@rcvs.org.uk; Web: www.rcvs.org.uk.

Health

SELECTED CAUSES OF DEATH, BY GENDER AND
AGE 1999 (UNITED KINGDOM)

	Under 1*	1–14	15–24	25–34	35–54	55–64	65–74	75 and over	All ages
Males									
Circulatory diseases	28	64	90	368	6,969	13,097	31,293	67,821	119,730
Cancer	6	195	207	426	6,109	12,320	24,727	34,820	78,810
Respiratory diseases	94	93	76	143	1,245	2,944	9,675	34,640	48,910
Injury and poisoning	39	280	1,613	2,387	3,666	1,156	1,056	2,175	12,372
Infectious diseases	77	64	54	100	386	222	395	805	2,103
Other causes	2074	336	598	1,092	4,420	3,599	6,590	19,734	38,443
All males (number)	2,318	1,032	2638	4516	22,795	33,338	73,763	159,995	300,368
Females									
Circulatory diseases	23	44	90	214	2,629	5,365	18,852	103,349	130,566
Cancer	8	137	132	509	7,285	10,304	18,887	36,404	73,666
Respiratory diseases	51	70	62	97	929	2118	7,525	50,024	60,876
Injury and poisoning	30	153	414	543	1,134	499	719	3,712	7,204
Infectious diseases	69	50	51	42	168	165	327	1,183	2,055
Other causes*	1,546	319	277	519	2,654	2,594	5,930	43,485	57,327
All females (number)	1,727	773	1,026	1,924	14,802	21,045	52,240	238,157	331,694

* Deaths at under 28 days are not assigned a specific cause and are entered under 'other'.
Source: Office for National Statistics, Mortality Statistics Section, GRO Scotland and NISRA

NOTIFICATIONS OF INFECTIOUS DISEASES
(UK) 1999

Measles	2,953
Mumps	2,005
Rubella	2,581
Whooping cough	1,461
Scarlet fever	2,951
Dysentery	1,627
Food poisoning	96,944
Typhoid and paratyphoid fevers	278
Hepatitis	4,346
Tuberculosis	6,703
Malaria	1,039

Source: The Stationery Office – Annual Abstract of Statistics 2001
(Crown copyright)

HIV/AIDS AND SEXUALLY TRANSMITTED
DISEASES (ENGLAND)

	1987	2000
HIV cases diagnosed	1,917	3,551
Exposure category		
Homosexual intercourse	73%	39%
Heterosexual intercourse	9%	49%
Injecting drug use	12%	2.6%
Blood products	2%	0.6%
Mother to infant	—	2.4%
Other/undetermined	4%	6.4%
Aids cases diagnosed	640	718

Source: Public Health Laboratory Service

CURRENT SMOKERS (UNITED KINGDOM)
By gender and socio-economic group
Percentage

	1982	1998-99
Males		
Professional	20	13
Employers and managers	29	20
Intermediate and junior non-manual	30	23
Skilled manual	42	34
Semi-skilled manual	47	39
Unskilled manual	49	44
Females		
Professional	21	14
Employers and managers	29	24
Intermediate and junior non-manual	30	23
Skilled manual	39	28
Semi-skilled manual	36	34
Unskilled manual	41	33

Source: The Stationery Office - Social Trends 31 (Crown
copyright)

ADULTS CONSUMING OVER SELECTED WEEKLY
LIMITS OF ALCOHOL, BY GENDER AND AGE
Percentage

	1998	1998-99
Men		
16-24	31	37
25-44	34	28
45-64	24	17
65 and over	13	4
All aged 16 and over	26	21
Women		
16-24	15	23
25-44	14	11
45-64	9	4
65 and over	4	1
All aged 16 and over	10	8

Source: The Stationery Office - Social Trends 31 (Crown
copyright)

Social Welfare

National Health Service

The National Health Service (NHS) came into being on 5 July 1948 under the National Health Service Act 1946, covering England and Wales, and under separate legislation for Scotland and Northern Ireland. The NHS is now administered by the Secretary of State for Health (in England), the National Assembly for Wales, the Scottish Executive and the Secretary of State for Northern Ireland.

The function of the NHS is to provide a comprehensive health service designed to secure improvement in the physical and mental health of the people and to prevent, diagnose and treat illness. It was founded on the principle that treatment should be provided according to clinical need rather than ability to pay, and should be free at the point of delivery. However, prescription charges were provided for by legislation in 1949 and implemented in 1952, and charges for some dental and ophthalmic treatment have also been introduced.

The NHS covers a comprehensive range of hospital, specialist, family practitioner (medical, dental, ophthalmic and pharmaceutical), artificial limb and appliance, ambulance, and community health services. Everyone normally resident in the UK is entitled to use any of these services.

STRUCTURE

The structure of the NHS remained relatively stable for the first 30 years of its existence. In 1974, a three-tier management structure comprising Regional Health Authorities, Area Health Authorities and District Management Teams was introduced in England, and the NHS became responsible for community health services. In 1979 Area Health Authorities were abolished and District Management Teams were replaced by District Health Authorities.

The National Health Service and Community Care Act 1990 provided for more streamlined Regional Health Authorities and District Health Authorities, and for the establishment of Family Health Services Authorities (FHSAs) and NHS Trusts. The concept of the 'internal market' was introduced into health care, whereby care was provided through NHS contracts where health authorities or boards and GP fundholders (the purchasers) were responsible for buying health care from hospitals, non-fundholding GPs, community services and ambulance services (the providers).

NHS Trusts operate as self-governing health care providers independent of health authority control and responsible to the Secretary of State. Until 1999 they derived their income principally from contracts to provide services to health authorities and fund-holding GPs. In Northern Ireland, 20 health and social services trusts are responsible for providing health and social services in an organisational model unique to Northern Ireland.

The Act also paved the way for the Community Care reforms, which were introduced in April 1993 and changed the way care is administered for elderly people, the mentally ill, the physically handicapped and people with learning disabilities.

The eight Regional Health Authorities in England were abolished in April 1996 and replaced by eight regional offices which, together with the headquarters in Leeds, form the NHS Executive. The regional offices are part of the Department of Health, and their functions include financial and performance monitoring of local purchasers and providers, public health, regional research and development, and education programmes.

In April 1996 the District Health Authorities and Family Health Service Authorities were merged to form 100 unified Health Authorities (HAs) in England. The HAs are responsible for health and health services in their areas. They are also responsible for assessing the health care needs of the local population and developing integrated strategies for meeting these needs in partnership with GPs and in consultation with the public, hospitals and others. HAs' resources are allocated by the NHS Executive headquarters, to which they are also accountable for their performance. HA chairmen are appointed by the Health Secretary and non-executive members by the regional offices of the NHS Executive.

In Wales the chairman and non-executive members of the five HAs which replaced the former 17 HAs and FHSAs in April 1996 are appointed by the First Secretary. Health Solutions Wales provides a range of specialist services to the NHS in Wales. In Scotland there are 15 Health Boards with similar responsibilities to those of HAs. In Northern Ireland there are four Health and Social Services Boards.

There are also Community Health Councils (called Local Health Councils in Scotland and Health and Social Services Councils in Northern Ireland) throughout the UK; their role is to represent the interests of the public to health authorities and boards. The Government announced in March 1998 that public consultation and patient representation in the NHS would be increased.

Under the Health Act 1999 the NHS internal market in England was replaced by teams of GPs and community nurses working together in primary care groups (*see* pages 481–2) from 1 April 1999. Long-term service agreements are beginning to replace annual contracts between primary care groups, health authorities, and NHS Trusts. A National Institute for Clinical Excellence has been established to produce new national guidelines and National Service Frameworks are being prepared to guarantee consistency in access to services. The first of these, published in late 1999, addressed mental health and coronary heart disease services. A Commission for Health Improvement was established in autumn 1999 to promote best practice. In Scotland, the Act replaced the internal market with Local Health Care Co-operatives (see page 482) from 1 April 1999. The NHS Trusts were reorganised into 13 primary care trusts and 15 acute care trusts, responsible to the Health Boards. In Wales the internal market was replaced by a system of Local Health Groups (see page 482). In Scotland the Scottish Health Technology Assessment Centre provide guidelines to promote best practice.

In March 2000 the government launched The NHS Plan, an extensive programme of reforms intended to modernise the NHS. Under a system of 'earned autonomy' power over spending will be devolved to local health organisations that achieve the government's targets for providing healthcare and they will have access to a £500 million performance fund. Increased overlap between the social services and the NHS will be co-ordinated by the care trusts, with a focus on providing care for the elderly in their own homes. The Plan also outlines a concordat with

480   Social Welfare

private healthcare providers whereby the NHS will pay for the use of facilities in private hospitals. In 2000 the NHS spent £1.25 billion on healthcare from the private sector.

The implementation of The Plan is to be overseen by The Modernisation Board which meets on a quarterly basis and is chaired by the Secretary of State.

FINANCE

UNITED KINGDOM

The NHS is still funded mainly through general taxation, although in recent years more reliance has been placed on the NHS element of National Insurance contributions, patient charges and other sources of income. In 2000–01 80.4 per cent of NHS expenditure was financed from general taxation and 12.1 per cent from National Insurance Contributions. Forecast UK Gross Expenditure on the NHS in 2000–01 is 6.2 per cent of GDP and is set to rise to 6.3 per cent in 2001–02. The Government announced in July 1998 that an additional £21,000 million would be spent on the NHS between 1999 and 2002. In the March 2000 Budget the Government unveiled its plans to put extra funding into the NHS in order for it to grow by one half in cash terms and by one third in real terms by 2005. Their objectives include 7,000 extra beds in hospitals and intermediate care; over 100 new hospitals by 2010 and 500 new one-stop primary care centres; over 3,000 GP premises modernised and 250 new scanners; cleaner wards and better hospital food; more IT systems in every hospital and GP surgery; 7,500 more consultants and 2,000 more GPs; 20,000 extra nurses and 6,500 extra therapists; 1,000 more medical school places and childcare support for NHS staff with 100 on-site nurseries.

NATIONAL HEALTH CURRENT EXPENDITURE 1999–2000

	£ million
National Health Service:	
Hospitals, Community Health Services and Family Health Services	48,279
Departmental administration	231
Other central services	1,601
Less payments by patients	–1,089
TOTAL	49,022

PERSONAL SOCIAL SERVICES CURRENT EXPENDITURE 1999–2000

	£ million
Central government	50
Local authorities running expenses	11,563
Capital expenditure	145
TOTAL	11,758

Source: The Stationery Office – *Annual Abstract of Statistics 2001* (Crown copyright)

TOTAL NHS EXPENDITURE PER HEAD OF POPULATION 2000–1

	NET £	GROSS £
UK	967	906
England	949	885
Scotland	1,094	1,026
Wales	976	958
Northern Ireland	912	898

Source: Department of Health

ORGANISATIONS

HEALTH AUTHORITIES (ENGLAND)

There are 100 health authorities in England. For details, contact the relevant NHS Executive regional office (*see* below).

NHS EXECUTIVE REGIONAL OFFICES
EASTERN, Capital Park, Fulbourn, Cambridge CB1 5XB. Tel: 01223 597500. *Regional Director*, P. Houghton
LONDON, 40 Eastbourne Terrace, London W2 3QR. Tel: 020-7725 5300. *Regional Director*, J. Bacon
NORTHERN AND YORKSHIRE, John Snow House, Durham University Science Park, Durham DH1 3YG. Tel: 0191-301 1325. *Regional Director*, P. Garland
NORTH WEST, 930–932 Birchwood Boulevard, Millennium Park, Birchwood, Warrington WA3 7QN. Tel: 01925-704000. *Regional Director*, Prof. R. Tinston
SOUTH EAST, 40 Eastbourne Terrace, London W2 3QR. Tel: 020-7725 2500. *Regional Director*, R. Cavnall
SOUTH WEST, Westward House, Lime Kiln Close, Stoke Gifford, Bristol BS34 8SR. Tel: 0117-984 1750. *Regional Director*, T. Laurance
TRENT, Fulwood House, Old Fulwood Road, Sheffield S10 3TH. Tel: 0114-263 0300. *Regional Director*, D. Nicholson
WEST MIDLANDS, Bartholomew House, 142 Hagley Road, Birmingham B16 9PA. Tel: 0121-224 4600. *Regional Director*, S. Day

HEALTH BOARDS (SCOTLAND)

ARGYLL AND CLYDE, Ross House, Hawkhead Road, Paisley PA2 7BN. Tel: 0141-842 7200. *Chairman*, J. Mullin; *Chief Executive*, N. McConachie
AYRSHIRE AND ARRAN, Boswell House, 10 Arthur Street, Ayr KA7 1QJ. Tel: 01292-611040. *Chairman*, Dr J. Morrow; *Chief Executive*, Mrs W. Hatton
BORDERS, Newstead, Melrose, Roxburghshire TD6 9TD. Tel: 01896-825500. *Chairman*, T. Keeler, OBE; *Chief Executive*, Dr L. Burley
DUMFRIES AND GALLOWAY, Grierson House, The Crichton Royal, Bankend Road, Dumfries DG1 4ZG. Tel: 01387-272700. *Chairman*, J. Ross, CBE; *Chief Executive*, M. Wright
FIFE, Springfield House, Cupar KY15 5UP. Tel: 01334-656200. *Chairman*, Ms E. Roberton; *Chief Executive*, T. Ranzetta
FORTH VALLEY, 33 Spittal Street, Stirling FK8 1DX. Tel: 01786-463031. *Chairman*, F. Clark; *General Manager*, D. Hird
GRAMPIAN, Summerfield House, 2 Eday Road, Aberdeen AB15 6RE. Tel: 01224-663456. *Chairman*, Dr C. E. MacLeod, CBE; *General Manager*, F. E. L. Hartnell, OBE
GREATER GLASGOW, Dalian House, 350 St Vincent Street, Glasgow G3 8YZ. Tel: 0141-201 4444. *Chairman*, Prof. D. Hamblen; *Chief Executive*, C. J. Spry
HIGHLAND, Assynt House, Beechwood Park, Inverness IV2 3HG. Tel: 01463-717123. *Chairman*, Mrs C. Thomson; *General Manager*, R. Gibbins
LANARKSHIRE, 14 Beckford Street, Hamilton, Lanarkshire ML3 0TA. Tel: 01698-281313. *Chairman*, I. Livingstone, CBE; *General Manager*, Prof. T. A. Divers
LOTHIAN, Deaconess House, 148 Pleasance, Edinburgh EH8 9RS. Tel: 0131-536 9000. *Chairman*, R. Findlay; *Chief Executive*, J. Barbour
ORKNEY, Garden House, New Scapa Road, Kirkwall, Orkney KW15 1BQ. Tel: 01856-885400. *Chairman*, I. Leslie; *General Manager*, J. Wellden

SHETLAND, Brevik House, South Road, Lerwick ZE1 0TG. Tel: 01595-696767. *Chairman*, J. Telford; *Chief Executive*, Miss S. Laurenson

TAYSIDE, Gateway House, Luna Place, Dundee Technology Park, Dundee DD2 1TP. Tel: 01382-561818. *Chairman*, P. Bates; *General Manager*, T. Brett

WESTERN ISLES, 37 South Beach Street, Stornoway, Isle of Lewis HS1 2BN. Tel: 01851-702997. *Chairman*, A. Matheson; *General Manager*, M. Maclennan

HEALTH AUTHORITIES (WALES)

BRO TAF, 17 Churchill House, Churchill Way, Cardiff CF102TW. Tel: 029-2040 2402. *Chairman*, S. Jones; *Chief Executive*, Mrs J. Williams

DYFED POWYS, PO Box 13, St David's Hospital, Carmarthen SA31 3YH. Tel: 01267-225225. *Chairman*, Ms M. Price; *Chief Executive*, S. Gray

GWENT, Mamhilad House, Mamhilad Park Estate, Pontypool NP4 0YP. Tel: 01495-765065. *Chairman*, Mrs F. Peel; *Chief Executive*, B. Hudson

IECHYD MORGANNWG, 41 High Street, Swansea SA1 1LT. Tel: 01792-458066. *Chairman*, D. H. Thomas; *Chief Executive*, Ms J. Perrin

NORTH WALES, Preswylfa, Hendy Road, Mold CH7 1PZ. Tel: 01352-700227. *Chairman*, Mrs P. Wood; *Chief Executive*, D. Hands

HEALTH SOLUTIONS WALES, Brunnell House, 2 Fitzellen Road, Cardiff CF24 0HA. Tel: 029-2050 0500.

NORTHERN IRELAND HEALTH AND SOCIAL SERVICES BOARDS

EASTERN, Champion House, 12–22 Linenhall Street, Belfast BT2 8BS. Tel: 028-9032 1313. *Chairman*, D. Russell; *Chief Executive*, Dr M. P. J. Kilbane, FRCP

NORTHERN, County Hall, 182 Galgorm Road, Ballymena BT42 1QB. Tel: 028-2565 3333. *Chairman*, M. A. Wood; *Chief Executive*, J. S. MacDonell

SOUTHERN, Tower Hill, Armagh BT61 7DR. Tel: 028-3741 0041. *Chairman*, W. Gillespie; *Chief Executive*, B. P. Cunningham

WESTERN, 15 Gransha Park, Clooney Road, Londonderry BT47 6FN. Tel: 028-7186 0086. *Chairman*, J. Bradley; *Chief Executive*, S. Lindsay

HEALTH PROMOTION AUTHORITIES

HEALTH PROMOTION ENGLAND, 40 Eastbourne Terrace, London W2 3QR. Tel: 020-7725 9030. *General Manager*, Mrs D. Ashdon

HEALTH EDUCATION BOARD FOR SCOTLAND, Woodburn House, Canaan Lane, Edinburgh EH10 4SG. Tel: 0131-536 5500. *Chairman*, D. R. Campbell; *Chief Executive*, Prof. A. Tannahill

HEALTH PROMOTION AGENCY FOR NORTHERN IRELAND, 18 Ormeau Avenue, Belfast BT2 8HS. Tel: 028-9031 1611; *Chief Executive*, Dr B. Gaffney

EMPLOYEES AND SALARIES

EMPLOYEES

NHS HOSPITAL AND COMMUNITY HEALTH SERVICES – ALL NON-MEDICAL STAFF (*England*) *as at September 1999**

Ambulance service	15,910
Administration and estates	204,617
Healthcare assistants and other support staff	115,024
Nursing, midwifery and health visiting	431,103
Nursing, midwifery and health visiting learners	1,945
Scientific, therapeutic and technical	128,293
Other non-medical staff	675
All non-medical staff	897,567

* Figures exclude agency staff
Source: The Department of Health – *1999 Non-medical Workforce Census*

SALARIES *as at 1 April 2001*

General Practitioners (GPs), dentists, optometrists and pharmacists are self-employed, and are employed by the NHS under contract. GPs are paid for their NHS work in accordance with a scheme of remuneration which includes a basic practice allowance, capitation fees, reimbursement of certain practice expenses and payments for out-of-hours work. Dentists receive payment for items of treatment for individual adult patients and, in addition, a continuing care payment for those registered with them. Optometrists receive approved fees for each sight test they carry out. Pharmacists receive professional fees from the NHS and are refunded the cost of prescriptions supplied.

Consultant	£50,810–£66,120
Specialist Registrar	£25,015–£36,460
Registrar	£25,015–£30,340
Senior House Officer	£22,380–£29,880
House Officer	£17,935–£20,245
GP	*£54,220
Nursing Grades G–I (Senior Ward Sister)	£21,605–£30,720
Nursing Grade F (Ward Sister)	£18,310–£22,865
Nursing Grade E (Senior Staff Nurse)	£16,510–£19,935
Nursing Grade D (Staff Nurse)	£15,445–£17,055
Nursing Grade C (Enrolled Nurse)	£12,585–£15,445
Nursing Grades A–B (Nursing Auxiliary)	£9,335–£12,585

*average intended net remuneration

HEALTH SERVICES

PRIMARY AND COMMUNITY HEALTH CARE

Primary and community health care services comprise the family health services (i.e. the general medical, personal medical, pharmaceutical, dental, and ophthalmic services) and community services (including preventive activities such as vaccination, immunisation and fluoridation) commissioned by HAs and provided by NHS Trusts, health centres and clinics. Nursing services including practice nurses, district nurses and health visitors, community psychiatric nurses, school nurse and ante- and post-natal care are also an integral part of primary and community health care.

FAMILY DOCTOR SERVICE

In England and Wales the Family Doctor Service (or General Medical Service) is now the responsibility of the HAs. In late 1999 a pilot scheme of 19 walk-in centres, where people may consult a doctor without an appointment between the hours of 7 a.m. and 10 p.m., was introduced. The scheme has since been expanded to cover 43 walk-in centres around the country. They are responsible to HAs and work closely with primary care groups.

Any doctor may take part in the Family Doctor Service (provided the area in which he/she wishes to practise has not already an adequate number of doctors) and 27,700 GPs in England do so. The distribution of GPs is controlled by the Medical Practices Committee, a statutory body. The average number of patients on a doctor's list in the UK as at August 2001 was 1,853.GPs may also have private fee-paying patients.

The Government has replaced the fundholding system by allowing the new primary care groups and trusts to assume one of four levels of responsibility. In April 1999 481 primary care groups became operational in England, covering populations of between 46,000 and 257,000. They operate as a committee of a Health Authority and are responsible for health improvement, primary and community health service development and commissioning secondary care services where appropriate. Primary care groups operate at one of two levels of responsibility. At level one, the group advises the Health Authority and is responsible for less than 40 per cent of the group's unified budget. Level two primary care groups are responsible for 40 per cent of the group's unified budget, rising to 60 per cent in their second year of operation. A board consisting of GPs, nurses, a social services officer, a health authority representative and a local member of the public administers each group.

From 1 April 2000, Primary Care Trusts became operational in England. They are free-standing statutory bodies undertaking many of the functions previously exercised by Health Authorities. They operate at one of two levels. Level three Trusts are able to commission services with greater scope than a level two primary care group, but not directly provide them. Those at level four are able to commission and directly provide services and run community hospitals and health services.

In Scotland, fundholding was replaced by over 70 Local Health Care Co-operatives on 1 April 1999. These, consisting of GPs and others involved in primary care, are responsible for developing health care in their area.

In Wales 22 Local Health Groups were set up by the Health Authorities and began work in April 1999. They are coterminous with local authority areas. At present, they advise Health Authorities but in the future they will assume responsibility for commissioning services and devising strategies for improved health. They will also integrate the delivery of primary and community care. A governing body including GPs and other health professionals, social services and community representatives administers each group.

Everyone aged 16 or over can choose their doctor (parents or guardians choose for children under 16); the doctor is free to accept or refuse an individual. Should a patient have difficulty in registering with a doctor, HAs have powers to assign the patient to a GP. A person may change their doctor if they wish, by going to the surgery of a GP of their choice who is willing to accept them, and either handing in their medical card to register or filling in a form. When people are away from home they can still use the Family Doctor Service if they ask to be treated as temporary residents, and in an emergency, any doctor in the service will give treatment and advice. A number of drop-in medical centres are being set up where anyone can consult a doctor.

PHARMACEUTICAL SERVICE

Patients may obtain medicines, appliances and oral contraceptives prescribed under the NHS from any pharmacy whose owner has entered into arrangements with the HA to provide this service; the number of these pharmacies in England and Wales in December 2000 was 12,257. There are also some appliance suppliers who only provide special appliances. In rural areas, where access to a pharmacy may be difficult, patients may be able to obtain medicines, etc., from their doctor.

Except for contraceptives (for which there is no charge), a charge of £6.10 is payable for each item supplied unless the patient is exempt and the declaration on the back of the prescription form is completed. Prepayment certificates (£31.90 valid for four months, £87.60 valid for a year) may be purchased by those patients not entitled to exemption who require frequent prescriptions.

The following people are exempt from prescription charges:
– children under 16
– full-time students under 19
– men and women aged 60 and over
– pregnant women who hold an exemption certificate
– women who have had a baby in the last 12 months and who hold an exemption certificate
– people suffering from certain medical conditions who hold an exemption certificate
– people who receive income support, full working families' tax credit or credit reduced by up to £70, full disabled person's tax credit or credit reduced by up to £70 or income-based jobseeker's allowance, and their partners
– people who are named on an HC2 certificate issued by the Health Benefits Division
– war pensioners (for their accepted disablements)

Booklet HC11, available from main post offices and local social security offices, gives further details.

The number of prescriptions dispensed in the community in 2000 was:

England and Wales	551,800,000
Scotland	60,900,000
Northern Ireland	22,171,000*

*1998 figure

DENTAL SERVICE

Dentists, like doctors, may take part in the NHS and also have private patients. About 17,000 dentists in England provide NHS general dental services. They are responsible to the HAs in whose areas they provide services.

Patients may go to any dentist who is taking part in the NHS and is willing to accept them. Patients are required to pay 80 per cent of the cost of NHS dental treatment. Since 1 April 1999 the maximum charge for a course of treatment has been £348. There is no charge for arrest of bleeding or repairs to dentures; home visits by the dentist or reopening a surgery in an emergency are charged for as treatment given in the normal way. The following people are exempt from dental charges or have charges remitted:
– people under 18
– full-time students under 19
– women who were pregnant when accepted for treatment
– women who have had a child in the previous 12 months
– people who receive income support, full working families' tax credit or credit reduced by up to £70, full disabled person's tax credit or credit reduced by up to £70, or income-based jobseeker's allowance, and their partners
– people who are named on an HC2 certificate issued by the Health Benefits Division

Booklet HC11, available from main post offices and local social security offices, gives further details.

GENERAL DENTAL SERVICE 2000–1 (ENGLAND)

Number of dentists	18,107
Number of patients registered	
Adults	16,900,000
Children	6,800,000

Number of courses of treatment
Adults   26,400,000
Expenditure (£ million)
Gross expenditure   1,550
Paid by patients   450
Paid out of public funds   1,100

Source: Department of Health

GENERAL OPHTHALMIC SERVICES
General Ophthalmic Services are administered by HAs. Testing of sight may be carried out by any ophthalmic medical practitioner or ophthalmic optician (optometrist). The optician must give the prescription to the patient, who can take this to any supplier of glasses to have them dispensed. Only registered opticians can supply glasses to children and to people registered as blind or partially sighted. At the end of March 2001 there were 7,548 practising Optometrists in Great Britain. 16.5 million sight tests were carried out in 2000–1.

The NHS sight test costs £15.01. Those on a low income may qualify for help with the cost. The test is available free to:

- people aged 60 or over
- children under 16*
- full-time students under 19*
- people who receive income support, income-based jobseeker's allowance, full working families' tax credit or credit reduced by up to £70, full disabled person's tax credit or credit reduced by up to £70, and their partners*
- people who are named on an HC2 certificate issued by the Health Benefits Division*
- people prescribed complex lenses*
- people registered as blind or partially sighted
- diagnosed diabetic and glaucoma patients
- people advised by an ophthalmologist that they are at risk of glaucoma

The categories indicated by * above are automatically entitled to help with the purchase of glasses under an NHS voucher scheme, as are people whose spectacles are lost or damaged as a result of illness. Booklet HC11, available from main post offices and local social security offices, gives further details.

COMMUNITY CHILD HEALTH SERVICES
Pre-school services at GP surgeries or child health clinics provide regular monitoring of children's physical, mental and emotional health and development, and advice to parents on their children's health and welfare.

The School Health Service provides for the medical and dental examination of schoolchildren, and advises the local education authority, the school, the parents and the pupil of any health factors which may require special consideration during the pupil's school life. GPs are increasingly undertaking child health monitoring in order to improve the preventive health care of children.

HEALTH ACTION ZONES
Health Action Zones aim to improve health services and tackle health inequalities in certain areas, working with the primary care groups in their area. The first 11 zones were set up in April 1998 and there are currently a total of 26 in existence. Each zone receives funding for seven years.

HOSPITALS AND OTHER SERVICES
Hospital, medical, dental, nursing, ophthalmic and ambulance services are provided by the NHS to meet all reasonable requirements. Facilities for the care of expectant and nursing mothers and young children, and

other services required for the diagnosis and treatment of illness, are also provided. Rehabilitation services (occupational therapy, physiotherapy and speech therapy) may also be provided, and surgical and medical appliances are supplied where appropriate. Specialists and consultants who work in NHS hospitals can also engage in private practice, including the treatment of their private patients in NHS hospitals although, under the terms of the NHS plan, newly qualified consultants are unable to do private work for up to seven years.

PRIVATE FINANCE INITIATIVE
The Private Finance Initiative (PFI) was launched in 1992, and involves the private sector in designing, building, financing and operating new hospitals, which are then leased to the NHS. In July 1997 a new programme of hospital building under the PFI was announced by the Government.

CHARGES
Certain hospitals have accommodation in single rooms or small wards which, if not required for patients who need privacy for medical reasons, may be made available to patients who desire it as an amenity for a small charge. These patients are still NHS patients and are treated as such.

In a number of hospitals, accommodation is available for the treatment of private in-patients who undertake to pay the full costs of hospital accommodation and services and (usually) separate medical fees to a specialist as well. The amount of the medical fees is a matter for agreement between doctor and patient. Hospital charges for private in-patients are set locally at a commercial rate.

There is no charge for drugs supplied to NHS hospital in-patients, but out-patients pay £6.10 an item unless they are exempt. With certain exceptions, hospital out-patients have to pay fixed charges for dentures, contact lenses and certain appliances. Glasses may be obtained either from the hospital or an optician, and the charge will be related to the type of lens prescribed and the choice of frame.

AMBULANCE SERVICE
The NHS provides emergency ambulance services free of charge via the 999 emergency telephone service. There are 35 ambulance services in the UK. Helicopter ambulances are used in some areas where access may be difficult or heavy traffic could hinder road progress, and an air ambulance service is available throughout Scotland. Non-emergency ambulance services are provided free of charge to patients who are deemed to require them on medical grounds.

In 2000–01 in England approximately 4,140,000 emergency calls were made to the ambulance service, an increase of 6 per cent on the previous year. There were about 2,900,000 emergency patient journeys. The Patients' Charter requires emergency ambulances to respond to 95 per cent of calls within 14 minutes in urban areas and 19 minutes in rural areas, and to reach 50 per cent of cases within eight minutes. In 2000–01, of the 31 ambulance services that had introduced call prioritisation by 1 January 2001, 26 ambulance services met the Charter standard for responding to life-threatening emergencies and 13 met the standard for non-life threatening emergencies.

NHS DIRECT
NHS Direct is a telephone service staffed by nurses which gives patients advice on how to look after themselves as well as directing them to the appropriate part of the NHS for treatment if necessary. Tel: 0845-4647.

BLOOD SERVICES

There are four national bodies which co-ordinate the blood donor programme in each constituent country of the UK. About two million donations of blood are given each year; donors give blood at local centres on a voluntary basis.

NATIONAL BLOOD AUTHORITY, Oak House, Reeds Crescent, Watford, Herts WD24 4GN. Tel: 01923-486800. *Chairman*, M. Fogden, CB; *Chief Executive*, M. Gorham

SCOTTISH NATIONAL BLOOD TRANSFUSION SERVICE, 21 Ellens Glen Road, Edinburgh EH17 7QT. Tel: 0131-536 5700. *National Director*, Dr D. Perry

WELSH BLOOD SERVICE, Ely Valley Road, Talbot Green, Pontyclun CF72 9WB. Tel: 01443-622000. *Director*, Dr F. G. Williams

NORTHERN IRELAND BLOOD TRANSFUSION SERVICE, Belfast City Hospital Complex, Lisburn Road, Belfast BT9 7TS. Tel: 028-9032 1414

HOSPICES

Hospice or palliative care may be available for patients with life-threatening illnesses. It may be provided at the patient's home or in a voluntary or NHS hospice or in hospital, and is intended to ensure the best possible quality of life for the patient during their illness, and to provide help and support to both the patient and the patient's family. The National Council for Hospices and Specialist Palliative Care Services co-ordinates NHS and voluntary services in England, Wales and Northern Ireland; the Scottish Partnership Agency for Palliative and Cancer Care performs the same function in Scotland.

NATIONAL COUNCIL FOR HOSPICE AND SPECIALIST PALLIATIVE CARE SERVICES, 1st Floor, 34–44 Britannia Street, London WC1X 9JG. Tel: 020-7520 8299. *Executive Director*, Ms E. S. Richardson

SCOTTISH PARTNERSHIP AGENCY FOR PALLIATIVE AND CANCER CARE, 1A Cambridge Street, Edinburgh EH1 2DY. Tel: 0131-229 0538. *Director*, Mrs M. Stevenson

NUMBER OF BEDS AND PATIENT ACTIVITY 1999

	England*	Wales
In-patients:		
Average daily available beds	190,000	14,700
Average daily occupation of beds	157,000	11,800
Persons waiting for admission at 31 March	1,298,000	75,400
Day-case admissions	3,421,000	342,200
Ordinary admissions	8,563,000	516,300
Out-patient attendances:		
New patients	11,778,000	694,100
Total attendances	42,154,000	2,706,200
Accident and emergency:		
New patients	12,811,000	868,000
Total attendances	14,280,000	026,400
Ward attendances	1,068,000	n/a

* 1998 figures
n/a not available

SCOTLAND

In-patients:	
Average available staffed beds	35,200
Average occupied beds	28,200
Out-patient attendances:	
New patients	2,734,000
Total attendances	6,424,000

Source: The Stationery Office – *Annual Abstract of Statistics 2001* (Crown copyright)

WAITING LISTS

At the end of June 2001 the total number of patients waiting to be admitted to NHS hospitals in England was 1,037,900, a decrease of 1.0 per cent on the previous year. The number of patients who had been waiting more than one year was 46,000, an increase of 9.2 per cent on the previous year. Under the Patient's Charter, patients are guaranteed admission within 18 months of being placed on a waiting list however, 356 patients had been waiting longer than 18 months at the end of June 2001.

COMPLAINTS

The Patient's Charter includes the right to have any complaint about the service provided by the NHS dealt with quickly, with a full written reply being provided by a relevant chief executive. There are two levels to the NHS complaints procedure: the first level involves resolution of a complaint locally, following a direct approach to the relevant service provider; the second level involves an independent review procedure if the complaint is not resolved locally. As a final resort, patients may approach the Health Service Commissioner or Ombudsman (*see* page 350) (in Northern Ireland, the Commissioner for Complaints if they are dissatisfied with the response of the NHS to a complaint).

In 1999–2000 there were 86,536 written complaints about hospital and community health services, of which 60 per cent were resolved locally within the target period of four weeks; just over two per cent of complainants requested an independent review. Hospital and Community Trusts received 93 per cent of the total number of complaints with Ambulance Trusts receiving four per cent and Health Authorities three per cent.

RECIPROCAL ARRANGEMENTS

Citizens of countries in the European Economic Area (EEA *see* European Union) are entitled to receive emergency health care either free of charge or for a reduced charge when they are temporarily visiting other member states of the EEA. Form E111, available at post offices, should be obtained before travelling. Non-EEA nationals, or visitors receiving routine, non-emergency care, are normally required to pay for treatment in Britain. There are bilateral agreements with several other countries, including Australia and New Zealand, for provision of urgent medical treatment either free of charge or for a reduced charge.

Personal Social Services

The Secretary of State for Health is responsible, under the Local Authority Social Services Act 1970, for the provision of social services for elderly people, disabled people, families and children, and those with mental disorders. Personal Social Services are administered by local authorities according to policies and standards set by central government. Each authority has a Director of Social Services and a Social Services Committee responsible for the social services functions placed upon them. Local authorities provide, enable and commission care after assessing the needs of their population.

The Community Care reforms introduced in 1993 were intended to enable vulnerable groups to live in the community rather than in residential homes wherever possible, and to offer them as independent a lifestyle as possible.

At 31 March 2000, there were 345,600 residential places in 24,800 residential and nursing care homes in England. About 267,500 residents were supported by local authorities (compared to 216,000 in 1996).

FINANCE

The Personal Social Services programme is financed partly by central government, with decisions on expenditure allocations being made at local authority level.

STAFF

STAFF OF LOCAL AUTHORITY SOCIAL SERVICES
DEPARTMENTS 2000 (ENGLAND)

Full-time equivalents

Area office/field work staff	108,800
Residential care staff	56,600
Day care staff	30,800
Central/strategic HQ staff	19,400
Other staff	1,500
Total staff	217,200

Source: Department of Health

ELDERLY PEOPLE

Services for elderly people are designed to enable them to remain living in their own homes for as long as possible. Local authority services include advice, domestic help, meals in the home, alterations to the home to aid mobility, emergency alarm systems, day and/or night attendants, laundry services and the provision of day centres and recreational facilities. Charges may be made for these services. Respite care may also be provided in order to allow carers temporary relief from their responsibilities.

Local authorities and the private sector also provide 'sheltered housing' for elderly people, sometimes with resident wardens.

If an elderly person is admitted to a residential home, charges are made according to a means test; if the person cannot afford to pay, the costs are met by the local authority.

In line with the recommendations made by The Royal Commission on Long-Term Care the government has created a National Care Standards Commission to oversee the registration, regulation and enforcement of care standards. It is due to assume its powers in April 2002.

DISABLED PEOPLE

Services for disabled people are designed to enable them to remain living in their own homes wherever possible. Local authority services include advice, adaptations to the home, meals in the home, help with personal care, occupational therapy, educational facilities and recreational facilities. Respite care may also be provided in order to allow carers temporary relief from their responsibilities.

Special housing may be available for disabled people who can live independently, and residential accommodation for those who cannot.

FAMILIES AND CHILDREN

Local authorities are required to provide services aimed at safeguarding the welfare of children in need and, wherever possible, allowing them to be brought up by their families. Services include advice, counselling, help in the home and the provision of family centres. Many authorities also provide short-term refuge accommodation for women and children.

DAY CARE

In allocating day-care places to children, local authorities give priority to children with special needs, whether in terms of their health, learning abilities or social needs.

They also provide a registration and inspection service in relation to childminders, play groups and private day nurseries in the local authority area. In England in August 2000 there were approximately 7,000 day nurseries providing 170,000 places, 98,500 registered child-minders providing 365,000 places, and 14,500 play groups providing 362,000 places.

A national child care strategy is being developed by the Government, under which day care and out-of-school child care facilities will be extended to match more closely the needs of working parents.

CHILD PROTECTION

Children considered to be at risk of physical injury, neglect or sexual abuse are placed on the local authority's child protection register. Local authority social services staff, school nurses, health visitors and other agencies work together to prevent and detect cases of abuse. In England at 31 March 2000 there were 30,300 children on child protection registers, a five per cent decrease from March 1999. This figure represents 28 children per 10,000 of population aged under 18. Of these, 46 per cent were at risk of neglect, 29 per cent of physical injury, 18 per cent of sexual abuse and 18 per cent of emotional abuse.

LOCAL AUTHORITY CARE

Local authorities are required to provide accommodation for children who have no parent or guardian or whose parents or guardians are unable or unwilling to care for them. A family proceedings court may also issue a care order in cases where a child is being neglected or abused, or is not attending school; the court must be satisfied that this would positively contribute to the well-being of the child.

The welfare of children in local authority care must be properly safeguarded. Children may be placed with foster families, who receive payments to cover the expenses of caring for the child or children, or in residential care. Children's homes may be run by the local authority or by the private or voluntary sectors; all homes are subject to inspection procedures. In England at 31 June 2000, 58,100 children were in the care of local authorities. Of these, 65 per cent were placed with foster parents and four per cent were placed for adoption.

ADOPTION

Local authorities are required to provide an adoption service, either directly or via approved voluntary societies. In England and Wales in 1998, 4,387 children (2,214 boys and 2,173 girls) were adopted.

PEOPLE WITH LEARNING DISABILITIES

Services for people with learning disabilities (i.e. mental handicap) are designed to enable them to remain living in the community wherever possible. Local authority services include short-term care, support in the home, the provision of day care centres, and help with other activities outside the home. Residential care is provided for the severely or profoundly disabled.

MENTALLY ILL PEOPLE

Under the Care Programme Approach, mentally ill people should be assessed by specialist services and receive a care plan, and a key worker should be appointed for each patient. Regular reviews of the patient's progress should be conducted. Local authorities provide help and advice to mentally ill people and their families, and places in day centres and social centres. Social workers can apply for a mentally disturbed person to be compulsorily detained in hospital. Where appropriate, mentally ill people are

LOCAL AUTHORITY PERSONAL SOCIAL SERVICES GROSS EXPENDITURE BY CLIENT GROUP 1998–9
(ENGLAND)

£ million	Elderly	Children	Learningdisability	Adults	Mental health	Other	Total
HQ costs	—	—	—	—	—	149	149
Area officers/senior managers	103	161	26	29	28	—	348
Care management/care assessment	329	505	76	101	126	—	1,136
Residential care	3,180	724	838	218	224	—	5184
Non-residential care	1,605	1,074	555	402	186	—	3,822
Other	—	—	—	—	—	208	208
TOTAL	5,216	2,465	1,495	750	564	357	10,847

Source: *The Department of Health* – Health and Personal Social Services Statistics for England 2000 *(Crown copyright)*

provided with accommodation in special hospitals, local authority accommodation, or homes run by private or voluntary organisations. Patients who have been discharged from hospitals may be placed on a supervision register. In July 1998 the Government announced that the system of care for mentally ill people would be replaced. A Mental Health National Service Framework was published in September 1999 setting the first ever national standards on how to prevent and treat mental illness. The government has pledged £700 million in the next two years in a drive to build modern and dependable mental health services.

LOCAL AUTHORITY-SUPPORTED RESIDENTS IN STAFFED RESIDENTIAL AND NURSING CARE (ENGLAND)
as at 31 March 2000

All staffed homes	261,139
Local authority staffed	47,611
Independent residential care	139,150
Independent nursing care	74,378
People aged 65 and over	210,638
People aged under 65	
Physically/sensorily disabled adults	9,876
People with mental health problems	10,969
People with learning disabilities	30,931
Other people	2,111

Source: Department of Health

National Insurance and Related Cash Benefits

The state insurance and assistance schemes, comprising schemes of national insurance and industrial injuries insurance, national assistance, and non-contributory old age pensions, came into force from 5 July 1948. The Ministry of Social Security Act 1966 replaced national assistance and non-contributory old age pensions with a scheme of non-contributory benefits. These and subsequent measures relating to social security provision in Great Britain were consolidated by the Social Security Act 1975, the Social Security (Consequential Provisions) Act 1975, and the Industrial Injuries and Diseases (Old Cases) Act 1975. Corresponding measures were passed for Northern Ireland. The Social Security Pensions Act 1975 introduced a new state pensions scheme in 1978, and the graduated pension scheme 1961 to 1975 has been wound up, existing rights being preserved. Under the Pensions Act 1995 the age of retirement is to be 65 for both men and women, this being phased in between 2010 and 6

April 2020. The Pensioners' Payments and Social Security Act 1979 provided for a Christmas bonus for pensioners in 1979 and in succeeding years. The Child Benefit Act 1975 replaced family allowances (introduced 1946) with child benefit and one-parent benefit. Some of this legislation has been superseded by the provisions of the Social Security Acts 1969 to 1992. The Government is reforming the social security system. The Welfare Reform and Pensions Act became law on 11 November 1999. Changes in benefits came into effect from April 2001.

NATIONAL INSURANCE SCHEME

The National Insurance (NI) scheme operates under the Social Security Contributions and Benefits Act 1992 and the Social Security Administration Act 1992, and orders and regulations made thereunder. The scheme is financed by contributions payable by earners, employers and others (*see* below) and by a Treasury grant. Money collected under the scheme is used to finance the National Insurance Fund (from which contributory benefits are paid) and to contribute to the cost of the National Health Service.

National Insurance Fund
Receipts and payments of the National Insurance Fund for the year ended 31 March 2000 were:

Receipts	£'000
National Insurance contributions	50,592,578
Grant from Inland Revenue	2,200
Compensation from Consolidated Fund for Statutory Sick Pay and Statutory Maternity Pay recoveries	607,000
Income from investments	714,737
State scheme premiums	126,294
Other receipts	123,211
Redundancy receipts	20,685
	52,186,705

Payments	£'000
Benefits	46,215,093
Personal pensions	2,573,715
Transfers to Northern Ireland	230,000
Administration	816,694
Redundancy payments (net)	170,895
Other payments	19,159
	50,025,556

Balances	£'000
Opening balance	12,277,381
Excess of receipts over payments	2,161,149
Closing balance, 31 March 2000	14,438,530

CONTRIBUTIONS

There are six classes of NI contributions:

Class 1   paid by employees and their employers
Class 1A   paid by employers who provide employees
           with cars/fuel for private use
Class 1B   paid by employers in value of any items
           included on a PAYE settlement with the
           Inland Revenue
Class 2   paid by self-employed people
Class 3   voluntary contributions paid to protect
           entitlement to certain benefits
Class 4   paid by the self-employed on their taxable
           profits over a set limit

The lower and upper earnings limits and the percentage rates referred to below apply from 3 April 2001 to 2 April 2002 unless otherwise stated.

CLASS 1

Class 1 contributions are paid where a person:

- is an employed earner (employee) or office holder (e.g. company director)
- is 16 or over and under state pension age
- earns at or above £76.00 per week (including overtime pay, bonus, commission, etc., without deduction of superannuation contributions)

Class 1 contributions are made up of primary and secondary contributions. Primary contributions are those paid by the employee and these are deducted from earnings by the employer. From 6 April 2001 the employee's earnings threshold has been raised to the same level as the employer's earnings threshold, they will now be referred to as the earnings threshold. Primary contributions are not paid on earnings below the earnings threshold of £87.00. Contributions are payable at the rate of ten per cent on earnings between the earnings threshold and the upper earnings limit of £575.00 per week (8.4 per cent for contracted-out employment, *see* page 496).

Some married women or widows pay a reduced rate of 3.85 per cent on earnings between the lower and upper earnings limits. It is no longer possible to elect to pay the reduced rate but those who had reduced liability before 12 May 1977 may retain it so long as certain conditions are met. *See* leaflet CA09 (widows) or leaflet CA13 (married women).

Secondary contributions are paid by employers of employed earners at the rate of 11.9 per cent on all earnings at or above the earnings threshold of £87.00 per week. Employers operating contracted-out salary related schemes (*see* page 489) pay reduced contributions of 8.9 per cent; those with contracted-out money-purchase schemes (*see* page 489) pay 11.3 per cent. There is no upper earnings limit for employers' contributions. The contracted-out rate applies only to that portion of earnings between the earnings threshold and the upper earnings limits. Employers' contributions below and above those respective limits are assessed at the appropriate not contracted-out rate.

CLASS 2

Class 2 contributions are paid where a person is self-employed and is 16 or over and under state pension age. Contributions are paid at a flat rate of £2.00 per week regardless of the amount earned. However, those with earnings of less than £3,955 a year can apply for Small Earnings Exception, e.g. exemption from liability to pay Class 2 contributions. Those granted exemption from Class 2 contributions may pay Class 2 or Class 3 contributions voluntarily. Self-employed earners

(whether or not they pay Class 2 contributions) may also be liable to pay Class 4 contributions based on profits. There are special rules for those who are concurrently employed and self-employed.

Married women and widows can no longer choose not to pay Class 2 contributions but those who elected not to pay Class 2 contributions before 12 May 1977 may retain the right so long as certain conditions are met.

Class 2 contributions are collected by the National Insurance Contributions Office (NICO), an executive agency of the Inland Revenue, by direct debit or quarterly bills. *See* leaflets CA03 and CA02.

CLASS 3

Class 3 contributions are voluntary flat-rate contributions of £6.75 per week payable by persons over the age of 16 who would otherwise be unable to qualify for retirement pension and certain other benefits because they have an insufficient record of Class 1 or Class 2 contributions. This may include those who are not working, those not liable for Class 1 or Class 2 contributions or those excepted from Class 2 contributions. Married women and widows who on or before 11 May 1977 elected not to pay Class 1 (full rate) or Class 2 contributions cannot pay Class 3 contributions while they retain this right.

Class 3 contributions are collected by the NICO by quarterly bills or direct debit. *See* leaflet CA08.

CLASS 4

Self-employed people whose profits and gains are over £4,535 a year pay Class 4 contributions in addition to Class 2 contributions. This applies to self-employed earners over 16 and under the state pension age. Class 4 contributions are calculated at seven per cent of annual profits or gains between £4,535 and £29,900. The maximum Class 4 contribution payable on £29,900 or more is £2,093.00.

Class 4 contributions are assessed and collected by the Inland Revenue together with Schedule D tax. It is possible, in some circumstances, to apply for exceptions from liability to pay Class 4 contributions or to have the amount of contribution reduced (where Class 1 contributions are payable on earnings assessed for Class 4 contributions). *See* leaflet CA03.

PENSIONS

The Social Security Pensions Act came into force in 1978. It aimed to:

- reduce reliance on means-tested benefit in old age, widowhood and chronic ill-health
- ensure that occupational pension schemes which are contracted out of the state scheme fulfil the conditions of a good scheme
- ensure that pensions are adequately protected against inflation
- ensure that men and women are treated equally in state and occupational schemes

Legislation and regulations introduced since 1978 go further towards fulfilling these aims and more changes came into effect in April 1997 (*see* below). One of the changes is to equalise the state pension age for men (currently 65 years) and women (currently 60 years) from 6 April 2020. The change will be phased in over the ten years leading up to 6 April 2020. As a result the state pension age is as follows:

- the pension age for men remains at 65
- the pension age for women born on or before 5 April 1950 remains at 60

- the pension age for women born on or after 6 April 1955 is now 65
- for women born after 5 April 1950 and before 6 April 1955, the pension age is 60 plus one month for every month, or part of a month, that their date of birth fell after 5 April 1950.

The Welfare Reform and Pensions Bill provides for the sharing of pensions between divorcing couples.

STATE PENSION SCHEME

The state pension scheme consists of the basic flat-rate pension and the state earnings-related pension scheme (SERPS), also known as additional pension.

The amount of basic pension paid is dependent on the number of 'qualifying years' a person has in their 'working life'. A 'qualifying year' is a tax year in which a person pays Class 1 (at the standard rate), 2 or 3 NI contributions for the whole year (see above). Those in receipt of invalid care allowance, disabled person's tax credit, jobseeker's allowance, incapacity benefit, severe disablement allowance or approved training have contributions credited to them for each week they receive benefit or fulfil certain other conditions. For those reaching pensionable age on or after 6 April 1999, a Class 3 credit of earnings will be awarded for each week from 6 April 1995 that family credit or, subsequently, working families tax credit, has been received. 'Working life' is counted from the start of the tax year in which a person reaches 16 to the end of the tax year before the one in which they reach pensionable age: for men this is normally 49 years and for women this varies between 44 and 49 years because the pension ages vary (see above). To get the full rate (100 per cent) basic pension a person must have qualifying years for about 90 per cent of their working life. To get the minimum basic pension (25 per cent) a person will need ten or eleven qualifying years. Married women who are not entitled to a pension on their own contributions may get a pension on their husband's contributions. It is possible for people who are unable to work because they care for children or a sick or disabled person at home to reduce the number of qualifying years required. This is called home responsibilities protection (HRP) and can be given for any tax year since April 1978; the number of years for which HRP is given is deducted from the number of qualifying years needed.

The amount of SERPS or additional pension paid depends on the amount of earnings a person has between the lower and upper earnings limits (see page 487) for each complete tax year between 6 April 1978 (when the scheme started) and the tax year before they reach state pension age. The right to additional pension does not depend on the person's right to basic pension. The amount of additional pension paid also depends on when a person reaches retirement; changes phased in from 6 April 1999 mean that pensions are calculated differently from that date. Men or Women widowed before 5 October 2002 inherit all their late spouse's additional pension. Those widowed on or after this date will inherit a proportion of their spouse's additional pension, up to weekly maximum of £131.35, in line with the table below:

Maximum % SERPS entitlement for surviving spouse	Date when contributor reaches state pension age
100%	5/10/2002 or earlier
90%	6/10/2002–5/10/04
80%	6/10/2004–5/10/06
70%	6/10/2006–5/10/08
60%	6/10/2008–5/10/10
50%	6/10/2010 or later

There are four categories of state pension provided under the Social Security Contributions and Benefits Act 1992:
- Category A, a contributory pension made up of basic and additional elements, payable to those of pensionable age who satisfy the entitlement conditions described above (see pages 491–2)
- Category B, a contributory pension made up of basic and additional elements, payable to married women and widows and based on their husband's contributions. This category of pension is to be extended to men whose wives were born after 5 April 1950 from 6 April 2010 (see pages 491–2)
- Category C, a non-contributory pension payable to those who reached pensionable age before 5 July 1948 (see page 493)
- Category D, a non-contributory pension for those over 80 (see page 493)

Graduated retirement benefit is also available to those who paid graduated NI contributions into the scheme when it existed between April 1961 and April 1975.

It is possible to find out how much basic and additional pension a person might receive by filling in form BR19, available from local social security offices or by telephoning the Retirement Pensions Forecasting and Advice Unit on 0191-218 7585.

The Welfare Reform and Pensions Bill will make changes to pensions. SERPS will be replaced by a second state pension from 2002. This will initially be earnings-related, but will subsequently be paid at a flat rate, targeted towards low earners. It will provide a guaranteed minimum income. Under certain circumstances, people not working (such as disabled people and those caring for children or sick relatives) will receive credits into the scheme as though they had earned £9,000 per year. As with SERPS, a person will be entitled to contract out into an occupational, personal or new stakeholder pension scheme.

CONTRACTED-OUT OCCUPATIONAL AND PERSONAL PENSION SCHEMES

Under the Pensions Schemes Act 1993, an employer can contract out of SERPS those employees who are members of an occupational scheme, so long as the occupational pension scheme satisfies certain conditions. The occupational pension took the place of the additional pension from April 1997 (previously it took the place of part of the additional pension); the state remains responsible for the flat rate state basic pension. Until April 1997 members of contracted-out occupational and personal pension schemes accrued additional pension in the same way as someone who is not contracted-out but the rate payable was reduced by contracted-out deductions. Since 5 April 1997, it has not been possible to accrue any SERPS while being a member of a contracted-out occupational or personal pension scheme. Members are still entitled to those rights earned before April 1997. Since April 1997 there have been age-related NI contribution rebates for people who leave SERPS and become members of either a COMP (see below), a stakeholder or an appropriate personal pension scheme; these will be lower for younger people and higher for older people.

There are three types of contracted-out occupational schemes.

Contracted-Out Salary-Related Scheme (COSR)
- this scheme must provide a pension related to earnings
- the pension provided must not be less than a person's guaranteed minimum pension (GMP), i.e. worth

about the same as the additional pension provided by the state scheme had the member remained in the State scheme

- any notional additional pension earned from 6 April 1978 to 5 April 1997 will be reduced by the amount of GMP earned during that period (the contracted-out deduction)
- from 6 April 1997 these schemes no longer provide a GMP but do have to satisfy a new scheme-based test, certified by an actuary, before a contracting-out certificate can be issued

Contracted-Out Money Purchase Scheme (COMP)
- this scheme must provide a pension based on the value of the fund built up, i.e. the money paid in, along with returns from investment
- part of the pension, known as protected rights, takes the place of the additional pension. A contracted-out deduction, which may be more or less than the pension provided by the scheme, will be made from any additional pension earned from 6 April 1987 to 5 April 1997

In contracted-out occupational pension schemes, both the employee and employer pay lower NI contribution rates in recognition that SERPS will not be paid.

Contracted-Out Mixed Benefit Scheme (COMBS)
A mixed benefit scheme has two active sections, one salary-related and the other money purchase. Scheme rules set out which section individual employees may join and the circumstances (if any) in which members may move between sections. Each section must satisfy the respective contracting-out conditions for COSRs and COMPs.

Appropriate Personal Pension Schemes
The option of a personal pension scheme is open to all employees, even if their employer has an occupational pension scheme. A personal pension scheme must provide a pension based on the value of the fund built up, i.e. the money paid in, along with returns from investment. Part of the pension, known as protected rights, takes the place of the additional pension. A contracted-out deduction, which may be more or less than the pension provided by the scheme, will be made from any additional pension earned from 6 April 1987 to 5 April 1997.

Employees who are members of a personal pension plan and their employers pay NI contributions at the full rate and the Inland Revenue pays the difference between the full rate and the contracted-out rate into the personal pension scheme.

A Pensions Ombudsman deals with complaints about maladministration of pensions schemes. The Occupational Pensions Board, which supervised contracting-out and approved personal pension schemes, was abolished in April 1997 and replaced by the Occupational Pensions Regulatory Authority (OPRA). *See* leaflet NP46.

Stakeholder Pensions
Stakeholder pensions became available in April 2001. They are targeted at those earning between £9,000 and £20,000 who have no occupational or appropriate personal scheme to join although higher earners are able to join a stakeholder scheme if they wish. It is possible to invest up to £3,600 (including tax relief) annually in a stakeholder pension scheme without evidence of earnings. The minimum contribution cannot be set higher than £20 and providers are prohibited from levying a charge of more than 1%. People who are already members of occupational pension schemes may also contribute to a stakeholder pension scheme and it is possible to contribute to a scheme that is not your own, for example that of a non-working partner.

Normally there will be tax relief on any payments made into a stakeholder pension. If an individual contracts out of SERPS using a stakeholder pension plan, a rebate of National Insurance contributions is paid into their stakeholder plan. *See* leaflet PSO2.

For further information contact the Office of the Pensions Advisory Service on 020-7233 8080.

BENEFITS

Leaflets relating to the various benefits and contribution conditions for different benefits are available from local social security offices; leaflets NI196 *Social Security Benefit Rates*, FB2 *Which Benefit?* and MG1 *A Guide to Benefits* are general guides to benefits, benefit rates and contributions.

The benefits payable under the Social Security Acts are:

CONTRIBUTORY BENEFITS
Jobseeker's allowance (contribution-based)
Incapacity benefit
Maternity allowance
Widow's benefit (comprising widow's payment, widowed mother's allowance and widow's pension)
Retirement pensions, categories A and B

NON-CONTRIBUTORY BENEFITS AND TAX CREDITS
Child benefit
Guardian's allowance
Jobseeker's allowance (income-based)
Invalid care allowance
Severe disablement allowance
Attendance allowance
Disability living allowance
Disabled person's tax credit
Retirement pensions, categories C and D
Income support
Working families tax credit
Housing benefit
Council tax benefit
Social fund

BENEFITS FOR INDUSTRIAL INJURIES AND DISABLEMENT
Other
Statutory sick pay
Statutory maternity pay

TAX CREDITS
Under the Tax Credits Act 1999, Family Credit and Disability Working Allowance (both non-contributory benefits) were replaced by Working Families Tax Credit and Disabled Person's Tax Credit from 5 October 1999. Both of these are administered by the Inland Revenue. The first payments were made from April 2000. People receiving Family Credit or Disability Working Allowance on 5 October 1999 continue to receive their benefits until the award expires, when they will be able to change to the new tax credits. From April 2000 employees will receive the credits from their employer along with their wages or salary. Self-employed applicants will be paid direct by the Inland Revenue. Further information and application forms are available from Inland Revenue Tax Enquiry Centres, Benefits Agency offices, Jobcentres, post offices and Citizens' Advice Bureaux.

WORKING FAMILIES TAX CREDIT
Working Families Tax Credit is a system of tax credits paid to couples (married or unmarried) or lone parents who

have at least one child living with them and where at least one partner works at least 16 hours per week. The credit is not payable if any savings exceed £8,000.

Working Families Tax Credit will usually be paid at the same rate for 26 weeks. There are four elements:
- a basic credit of £59.00 per family per week
- a credit of £11.45 per week where one earner works at least 30 hours per week
- a credit for each child at the rate of £26.00 per week from birth and £26.75 from the September following their 16th birthday up to the day before their 19th birthday
- a childcare credit (in certain circumstances) of up to 70 per cent of eligible childcare costs up to a maximum of £135 per week for one child and £200 per week for two or more children.

If net income is below £92.90 per week, the maximum tax credit is payable. If net income exceeds £92.90 per week, the total tax credit is reduced by 55p for each £1.00 above £92.90.

DISABLED PERSON'S TAX CREDIT

Disabled Person's Tax Credit is a system of tax credits for people who are working at least 16 hours per week but have an illness or disability which puts them at a disadvantage in getting a job. To qualify, a person must have one of the 'qualifying benefits' or have had them up to 182 days before applying. The credit is not payable if any savings exceed £16,000.

Disabled Person's Tax Credit will usually be paid at the same rate for 26 weeks. There are six elements:
- a basic credit of £61.05 per week for a single person or £91.25 for a couple or lone parent
- enhanced disability tax credit (where applicant or partner is entitled to the highest rate care component of Disability Living Allowance) £11.05 or £16.00 for a couple or lone parent
- a credit of £11.45 per week where one applicant works at least 30 hours per week
- a credit for each child at the rate of £26.00 from birth and £26.75 from the September following their 16th birthday up to the day before their 19th birthday
- a disabled child's tax credit of £30.00 per week or an enhanced disabled child's credit of £41.05 for each severely disabled child
- a childcare credit (in certain circumstances) of up to 70 per cent of eligible childcare costs up to a maximum of £135 per week for one child and £200 per week for two or more children.

If net income is below £70 per week for a single person or £90 per week for a couple or lone parent, the maximum tax credit is payable. If net income exceeds these thresholds, the total tax credit is reduced by 55p for each £1.00 above the threshold.

CONTRIBUTORY BENEFITS

Entitlement to contributory benefits depends on contribution conditions being satisfied either by the claimant or by some other person (depending on the kind of benefit). The class or classes of contribution which for this purpose are relevant to each benefit are:

Jobseeker's allowance (contribution-based)	Class 1
Incapacity benefit	Class 1 or 2
Maternity allowance	Class 1 or 2
Widow's benefits	Class 1, 2 or 3
Retirement pensions, categories A and B	Class 1, 2 or 3

The system of contribution conditions relates to yearly levels of earnings on which contributions have been paid.

JOBSEEKER'S ALLOWANCE

Jobseeker's allowance (JSA) replaced unemployment benefit and income support for unemployed people under pension age from 7 October 1996. There are two routes of entitlement. Contribution-based JSA is paid as a personal rate (i.e. additional benefit for dependants is not paid) to those who have made sufficient NI contributions in two particular tax years. Savings and partner's earnings are not taken into account and payment can be made for up to six months. Those who do not qualify for contribution-based JSA, those who have exhausted their entitlement to contribution-based JSA or those for whom contribution-based JSA provides insufficient income may qualify for income-based JSA. The amount paid depends on age and number of dependants and income and savings are taken into account. Income-based JSA may comprise three parts: a personal allowance for the jobseeker and his/her partner and one for each child or young person for whom they are responsible; premiums for groups of people with special needs; and housing costs. This is payable for the claimant and their dependants for as long as they satisfy the rules. Rates of jobseeker's allowance correspond to income support rates.

Claims for this benefit are made through Employment Service Jobcentres. A person wishing to claim jobseeker's allowance must be unemployed, capable of work and available for any work which they can reasonably be expected to do, usually for at least 40 hours per week. They must agree and sign a 'jobseeker's agreement', which will set out each claimant's plans to find work, and must actively seek work. If they refuse work or training their benefit may be suspended for between two and six weeks.

A person will be disqualified from jobseeker's allowance if they have left a job voluntarily or through misconduct, if they refuse to take up an offer of employment or if they fail to attend a training scheme or employment programme. In these circumstances, it may be possible to receive hardship payments, particularly where the claimant or their family is vulnerable, e.g. if sick or pregnant, or for those with children or caring responsibilities. See leaflet JSAL5.

INCAPACITY BENEFIT

Incapacity benefit is available to those who are incapable of work but cannot get statutory sick pay from their employer. It is not payable to those over state pension age. However, people who are already in receipt of short-term incapacity benefit when they reach state pension age may continue to receive this benefit for up to 52 weeks. The Welfare Reform and Pensions Bill 1999 restricts eligibility for incapacity benefit to people who have paid National Insurance contributions for one of the previous three years. The Bill also provides for the reduction of the amount of incapacity benefit payable where a claimant receives more than a specified amount of occupational or personal pension. Severely disabled people aged between 16 and 19 should receive incapacity benefit without meeting the national insurance contribution conditions under the Government's proposals. There are three rates of incapacity benefit:
- short-term lower rate for the first 28 weeks of sickness
- short-term higher rate from weeks 29 to 52
- long-term rate after week 52

The terminally ill and those entitled to the highest rate care component of disability living allowance are paid the long-term rate after 28 weeks. Incapacity benefit is taxable after 28 weeks.

Two rates of age addition are paid with long-term benefit based on the claimant's age when incapacity started. The higher rate is payable where incapacity for

work commenced before the age of 35; and the lower rate where incapacity commenced before the age of 45. Increases for dependants are also payable with short and long-term incapacity benefit.
There are two medical tests of incapacity: the 'own occupation' test and the 'all work' test. Those who worked before becoming incapable of working will be assessed, for the first 28 weeks of incapacity, on their ability to do their own job. After 28 weeks (or from the start of incapacity for those who were not working) claimants are assessed on their ability to carry out a range of work-related activities. The 'all work' test applies to most former sickness and invalidity benefit claimants. The Government plans to replace the 'all work' test with a new 'personal capability assessment.' *See* leaflets IB202 and SD1.

MATERNITY ALLOWANCE
The maternity allowance (MA) scheme covers women who are self-employed or otherwise do not qualify for statutory maternity pay (*see* page 496). In order to qualify, the woman must have been working and paying standard rate NI contributions for at least 26 weeks in the 66-week period which ends with the week before the week in which the baby is due. A woman can choose to start receiving MA between the beginning of the 11th week before the week in which the baby is due and the Sunday after the baby is born, depending on when she stops working. MA is paid for a period of up to 18 weeks. MA is only paid while the woman is not working. *See* leaflet NI17A.

BEREAVEMENT BENEFITS
Bereavement benefits replaced widows' benefits on 9 April 2001. Those claiming widows' benefits before this date will continue to receive them under the old scheme for as long as they qualify. The new system provides bereavement benefits for widows and widowers providing that their deceased spouse paid National Insurance contributions. The new system offers benefits in three forms:
Bereavement payment – may be received by a man or woman who is under the state pension age at the time of their spouse's death, or whose husband or wife was not entitled to a Category A retirement pension when he or she died. It is a single tax-free lump sum of £2,000 payable immediately on becoming a widow or widower.
Widowed parent's allowance – a taxable benefit payable to the surviving partner if he or she is entitled or treated as entitled to child benefit, or to a widow if she is expecting her husband's baby
Bereavement allowance – a taxable weekly benefit paid for 52 weeks after the spouse's death. A widow or widower may receive this pension if aged 45 or over at the time of his or her spouse's death (40 or over if widowed before 11 April 1988) or when his or her widowed parent's allowance ends. If aged 55 or over he or she will receive the full bereavement allowance
It is not possible to receive widowed parent's allowance and bereavement allowance at the same time, and bereavement benefit in any form ceases upon remarriage or during a period of cohabitation as man and wife without being legally married. *See* leaflet NP45.

RETIREMENT PENSION: CATEGORIES A AND B
A Category A pension is payable for life to men and women who reach state pension age and who satisfy the contributions conditions (*see* page 488). A Category B pension is payable for life to a spouse and is based on their wife or husband's contributions. It becomes payable only when the wife or husband has claimed their pension and the spouse has reached state pension age. It is also payable on widowhood after the state retirement age regardless of

whether the wife or husband had qualified for their pension. There are special rules for those who are widowed before reaching pensionable age.
A person may defer claiming their pension for five years after state pension age. In doing so they may earn increments which will increase the weekly amount paid when they claim their pension. If a married man defers his Category A pension, his wife cannot claim a Category B pension on his contributions but she may earn increments on her pension during this time. A woman can defer her Category A and B pension, and earn increments, even if her husband is claiming his Category A pension.
The basic state pension is £72.50 per week plus any additional (earnings-related) pension the person may be entitled to (*see* page 488). An increase of £43.40 is paid for an adult dependant, providing the dependant's earnings do not exceed the rate of jobseeker's allowance for a single person (*see* below). It is also possible to get an increase of Category A and B pensions for a child or children. An age addition of 25p per week is payable if a retirement pensioner is aged 80 or over.
Since 1989 pensioners have been allowed to have unlimited earnings without affecting their retirement pension. Income support is payable on top of a pension where a pension does not give the person enough to live on and to those who are entitled to retirement pension but who have not claimed it. Pensioners may also be entitled to housing and council tax benefits.

GRADUATED RETIREMENT BENEFIT
Graduated NI contributions were first payable from 1961 and were calculated as a percentage of earnings between certain bands. They were discontinued in 1975. Any graduated pension which an employed person over 18 and under 70 (65 for a woman) had earned by paying graduated contributions will be paid when the contributor claims retirement pension or at 70 (65 for a woman), in addition to any retirement pension for which he or she qualifies. A wife can get a graduated pension in return for her own graduated contributions, but not for her husband's.
Graduated retirement benefit is at a weekly rate for each 'unit' of graduated contributions paid by the employee (half a unit or more counts as a whole unit); the rate varies from person to person. A unit of graduated pension can be calculated by adding together all graduated contributions and dividing by 7.5 (men) or 9.0 (women). If a person defers making a claim beyond 65 (60 for a woman), entitlement may be increased by one seventh of a penny per £1 of its weekly rate for each complete week of deferred retirement, as long as the retirement is deferred for a minimum of seven weeks.

WEEKLY RATES OF BENEFIT
from April 2001

Jobseeker's allowance (contribution-based)

Person under 18	£31.95
Person aged 18–24	42.00
Person over 25	53.05

Short-term incapacity benefit

Person under pension age – lower rate	52.60
*Person under pension age – higher rate	62.20
Increase for adult dependant	32.55
*Person over pension age	66.90
Increase for adult dependant	32.55

Long-term incapacity benefit

Person (under or over pension age)	69.75
Increase for adult dependant	41.75
Age addition – lower rate	7.35
Age addition – higher rate	14.65

Invalidity allowance: maximum amount payable
Higher rate	14.65
Middle rate	9.30
Lower rate	4.65

Maternity allowance
Employed	62.20
Maternity rate threshold	30.00

Widow's benefits (before 9 April 2001)
Widow's payment (lump sum)	1,000.00
Widowed mother's allowance	72.50
Widow's pension	72.50

Bereavement benefit (from 9 April 2001)
Bereavement payment (lump sum)		2,000.00
*Widowed parents allowance		72.50
*Bereavement allowance		72.50
*Age related	54	67.43
	53	62.35
	52	57.28
	51	52.20
	50	47.13
	49	42.05
	48	36.98
	47	31.90
	46	26.83
	45	21.75

Retirement pension: categories A and B
Single person	72.50
Increase for wife/other adult dependant	43.40

*These benefits attract an increase for each dependent child (in addition to child benefit) of £9.70 for the first or only child and £11.35 for each subsequent child

NON-CONTRIBUTORY BENEFITS

These benefits are paid from general taxation and are not dependent on NI contributions. Unless otherwise stated, a benefit is tax-free and is not means tested.

CHILD BENEFIT

Child benefit is payable for virtually all children aged under 16, and for those aged 16 to 18 who are studying full-time up to and including A-level or equivalent standard. It is also payable for a short period if the child has left school recently and is registered for work or work-based training for young people at a careers office.

A higher rate of benefit (child benefit (lone parent)) may be paid to a person who is responsible for bringing up one or more children on his/her own. It is a flat rate benefit payable for the eldest child only. Since 6 July 1998 child benefit (lone parent) has not been available to new lone parents but it may still be payable in certain circumstances. *See* leaflets CH1 and CH11.

GUARDIAN'S ALLOWANCE

Where the parents of a child are dead, the person who has the child in his/her family may claim a guardian's allowance in addition to child benefit. In exceptional circumstances the allowance is payable on the death of only one parent. *See* leaflet NI14.

INVALID CARE ALLOWANCE

Invalid care allowance (ICA) is a taxable benefit payable to people of working age who give up the opportunity of full-time paid employment because they are regularly and substantially engaged (spending at least 35 hours per week) in caring for a severely disabled person. To qualify for ICA a person must be caring for someone in receipt of one of the following benefits:
- the middle or highest rate of disability living allowance care component

- either rate of attendance allowance
- constant attendance allowance, paid at not less than the normal maximum rate, under the industrial injuries or war pension schemes

See leaflets FB31 and SD1.

SEVERE DISABLEMENT ALLOWANCE

From April 2001 Severe Disablement Allowance (SDA) has not been available to new claimants. Those claiming SDA before that date will continue to receive it for as long as they qualify. *See* leaflet NI252.

ATTENDANCE ALLOWANCE

This is payable to disabled people who claim after the age of 65 and who need a lot of care or supervision because of physical or mental disability for a period of at least six months. People not expected to live for six months because of an illness do not have to wait six months. The allowance has two rates: the lower rate is for day or night care, and the higher rate is for day and night care. *See* leaflets DS702 and SD1.

DISABILITY LIVING ALLOWANCE

This is payable to disabled people who claim before the age of 65 who have personal care and mobility needs because of an illness or disability for a period of at least three months and are likely to have those needs for a further six months or more. People not expected to live for six months because of an illness do not have to wait three months. The allowance has two components: the care component, which has three rates, and the mobility component, which has two rates. The rates depend on the care and mobility needs of the claimant. *See* leaflets DS704 and SD1.

RETIREMENT PENSION: CATEGORIES C AND D

A Category C pension is provided, subject to a residence test, for persons who were over pensionable age on 5 July 1948, and for the wives and widows of men who qualified if they are over pension age. A Category D pension is provided for people aged 80 and over if they are not entitled to another category of pension or are entitled to less than the Category D rate.

WEEKLY RATES OF BENEFIT
from April 2001

Child benefit
Eldest child	£15.50
Eldest child of certain lone parents	17.35
Each subsequent child	10.35

Guardian's allowance
Eldest child	9.85
Each subsequent child	11.35

Invalid care allowance
Increase for wife/other adult dependant	41.75
	24.95

Severe disablement allowance
†Basic rate	42.15
Under 40	14.65
40–49	9.30
50–59	4.65
Increase for wife/other adult dependant	25.00

Attendance allowance
Higher rate	55.30
Lower rate	37.00

Disability living allowance
Care component
Higher rate	55.30
Middle rate	37.00
Lowest rate	14.65

Mobility component
Higher rate 38.65
Lower rate 14.65
Retirement pension: categories *C and D
Single person 43.40
Increase for wife/other adult dependant 24.95
(not payable with Category D pension)

*These benefits attract an increase for each dependent child (in addition to child benefit) of £9.85 for the first or only child and £11.35 for each subsequent child
†The age addition applies to the age when incapacity began

INCOME SUPPORT

Income support is a benefit for those aged 16 and over whose income is below a certain level. It can be paid to people who are not expected to sign on as unemployed (income support for unemployed people was replaced by jobseeker's allowance in October 1996) and who are:
– incapable of work due to sickness or disability
– bringing up children alone
– 60 or over
– looking after a person who has a disability
– registered blind
Some people who are not in these categories may also be able to claim income support.

Income support is also payable to people who work for less than 16 hours a week on average (or 24 hours for a partner). Some people can claim income support if they work longer hours.

Income support is not payable if the claimant, or claimant and partner, have capital or savings in excess of £8,000. For capital and savings in excess of £3,000, a deduction of £1 is made for every £250 or part of £250 held. Different limits apply to people permanently in residential care and nursing homes: the upper limit is £16,000 and deductions apply for capital in excess of £10,000.

Sums payable depend on fixed allowances laid down by law for people in different circumstances. If both partners are entitled to income support, either may claim it for the couple. People receiving income support may be able to receive housing benefit, help with mortgage or home loan interest and help with health care. They may also be eligible for help with exceptional expenses from the Social Fund. Special rates may apply to some people living in residential care or nursing homes. Leaflet IS20 gives a detailed explanation of income support.

In October 1998 the Government's voluntary New Deal for Lone Parents programme became available throughout the UK. All lone parents receiving income support are assigned a personal adviser at a jobcentre who will provide guidance and support with a view to enabling the claimant to find work.

INCOME SUPPORT PREMIUMS

Income support premiums are additional weekly payments for those with special needs. People qualifying for more than one premium will normally only receive the highest single premium for which they qualify. However, family premium, disabled child premium, severe disability premium and carer premium are payable in addition to other premiums.

People with children may qualify for:
– the family premium if they have at least one child (a higher rate is paid to lone parents, although from 6 April 1998 it has not generally been available to new claimants)

– the disabled child premium if they have a child who receives disability living allowance or is registered blind

Carers may qualify for:
– the carer premium if they or their partner are in receipt of invalid care allowance

Long-term sick or disabled people may qualify for:
– the disability premium if they or their partner are receiving certain benefits because they are disabled or cannot work; are registered blind; or if the claimant has been incapable of work or receiving statutory sick pay for at least 364 days (196 days if the person is terminally ill), including periods of incapacity separated by eight weeks or less

– the severe disability premium if the person lives alone and receives attendance allowance or the middle or higher rate of disability living allowance care component and no one receives invalid care allowance for caring for that person. This premium is also available to couples where both partners meet the above conditions

People aged 60 and over may qualify for:
– the pensioner premium if they or their partner are aged 60 to 74.
– the enhanced pensioner premium if they or their partner are aged 75 to 79
– the higher pensioner premium if they or their partner are aged 80 or over. This is also available to people over 60 who receive attendance allowance, disability living allowance, long-term incapacity benefit or severe disablement allowance, or who are registered blind

WEEKLY RATES OF BENEFIT

from April 2001
Income support
Single person
under 18	£31.95
under 18 (higher)	42.00
aged 18–24	42.00
aged 25 and over	53.05
aged under 18 and a single parent (lower)	31.95
aged under 18 and a single parent (higher)	42.00
aged 18 and over and a single parent	53.05
Couples*	
Both under 18	63.35
one or both aged 18 or over	83.25
For each child in a family from birth	
until September following 16th birthday	31.45
†from September following 16th birthday to day before 19th birthday	32.25
Premiums	
Family premium	14.50
Family (lone parent) premium	15.90
Disabled child premium	30.00
Carer premium	24.40
Disability premium	
Single	22.60
Couple	32.25
Enhanced disability premium	
Single	11.05
Disabled child rate	11.05
Couple	32.25
Severe disability premium	
Single	41.55
Couple (one person qualified)	41.55
Couple (both qualified)	83.10
Pensioner premium	
Single	39.10
Couple	57.30

Higher pensioner premium	
Single	39.10
Couple	57.30
Enhanced pensioner premium	
Single	39.10
Couple	57.30
Bereavement premium	19.45

*Where one or both partners are aged under 18, their personal allowance will depend on their situation
†If in full-time education up to A-level or equivalent standard

HOUSING BENEFIT

Housing benefit is designed to help people with rent (including rent for accommodation in guest houses, lodgings or hostels). It does not cover mortgage payments. The amount of benefit paid depends on:
- the income of the claimant, and partner if there is one, including earned income, unearned income (any other income including some other benefits) and savings
- number of dependants
- certain extra needs of the claimant, partner or any dependants
- number and gross income of people sharing the home who are not dependent on the claimant
- how much rent is paid

Housing benefit is not payable if the claimant, or claimant and partner, have savings of over £16,000. The amount of benefit is affected if savings held exceed £3,000. Housing benefit is not paid for meals, fuel or certain service charges that may be included in the rent. Deductions are also made for most non-dependants who live in the same accommodation as the claimant (and their partner).

The maximum amount of benefit (which is not necessarily the same as the amount of rent paid) may be paid where the claimant is in receipt of income support or income-based jobseeker's allowance or where the claimant's income is less than the amount allowed for their needs. Any income over that allowed for their needs will mean that their benefit is reduced.

Claims for housing benefit are made to the local council. Those who are also claiming income support or income-based jobseeker's allowance may claim housing benefit at the local benefits or employment services office. See leaflets RR1 and RR2.

COUNCIL TAX BENEFIT

Nearly all the rules which apply to housing benefit apply to council tax benefit, which helps people on low incomes to pay council tax bills. The amount payable depends on how much council tax is paid and who lives with the claimant. The benefit may be available to those receiving income support or income-based jobseeker's allowance or to those whose income is less than that allowed for their needs. Any income over that allowed for their needs will mean that their council tax benefit is reduced. Deductions are made for non-dependants.

The maximum amount that is payable for those living in properties in council tax bands A to E is 100 per cent of the claimant's council tax liability. This also applies to those living in properties in bands F to H who were in receipt of the benefit at 31 March 1998 if they have remained in the same property. From 1 April 1998 council tax benefit for new claimants living in property bands F to H (or existing claimants moving into these bands) was restricted to the level payable for band E.

If a person shares a home with one or more adults (not their partner) who are on a low income, it may be possible to claim a second adult rebate. Those who are entitled to both council tax benefit and second adult rebate will be awarded whichever is the greater. Second adult rebate may be claimed by those not in receipt of council tax benefit.

THE SOCIAL FUND

The Social Fund helps people with expenses which are difficult to meet from regular income. Regulated maternity and funeral payments are decided by Decision Makers; cold weather payments and winter fuel payments are made automatically. These payments are not limited by the district's Social Fund budget. Discretionary community care grants, and budgeting and crisis loans are decided by Social Fund Officers and come out of a yearly budget which is allocated to each district (1999–2000, grants £98 million; loans £436.7 million; £0.5 million set aside as a contingency reserve). See leaflet SB16.

REGULATED PAYMENTS

Maternity Payments
From April 2000 the Maternity Payment Scheme was replaced by the State Maternity Grant Scheme. A payment of up to £200 for each baby expected, born, adopted or the subject of a parental order (in the case of surrogacy), will be linked to the claimant seeking advice on the welfare of the baby. It is payable to people on income support, income-based jobseeker's allowance, disabled person's tax credit and working families tax credit and does not have to be repaid.

Funeral Payments
Payable for the necessary cost of burial or cremation, plus other funeral expenses reasonably incurred up to £600, to people receiving income support, income-based jobseeker's allowance, disabled person's tax credit, working families' tax credit, council tax benefit or housing benefit who have good reason for taking responsibility for the funeral expenses. These payments are recoverable from any estate of the deceased.

Cold Weather Payments
A payment of £8.50 when the average temperature over seven consecutive days is recorded as or forecast to be 0°C or below in their area. Payments are made to people on income support or income-based jobseeker's allowance and who have a child under five or whose benefit includes a pensioner or disability premium. They do not have to be repaid.

Winter Fuel Payments
An annual payment of £100 per household paid automatically to eligible pensioners. Payments are made before Christmas and do not have to be repaid.

DISCRETIONARY PAYMENTS

Community Care Grants
These are intended to help people on income support or income-based jobseeker's allowance (or those likely to receive these benefits on leaving residential or institutional accommodation) to live as independently as possible in the community; ease exceptional pressures on families; care for a prisoner or young offender released on temporary licence; help people set up home as part of a resettlement programme and/or assist with certain travelling expenses. They do not have to be repaid.

Budgeting Loans
These are interest-free loans to people who have been receiving income support or income-based jobseeker's allowance for at least 26 weeks, for intermittent expenses that may be difficult to budget for.

Crisis Loans
These are interest-free loans to anyone, whether receiving benefit or not, who is without resources in an emergency, where there is no other means of preventing serious damage or serious risk to their health or safety.

SAVINGS
Savings over £500 (£1,000 for people aged 60 or over) are taken into account for maternity and funeral payments, community care grants and budgeting loans. All savings are taken into account for crisis loans. Savings are not taken into account for cold weather or winter fuel payments.

INDUSTRIAL INJURIES AND DISABLEMENT BENEFITS

The industrial injuries scheme, administered under the Social Security Contributions and Benefits Act 1992, provides a range of benefits designed to compensate for disablement resulting from an industrial accident (i.e. an accident arising out of and in the course of an employed earner's employment) or from a prescribed disease due to the nature of a person's employment. Those who are self-employed are not covered by this scheme.

INDUSTRIAL INJURIES DISABLEMENT BENEFIT
A person must be at least 14 per cent disabled (except for certain respiratory diseases) in order to qualify for this benefit. The amount paid depends on the degree of disablement:
– those assessed as 14–19 per cent disabled are paid at the 20 per cent rate
– those with disablement of over 20 per cent will have the percentage rounded up or down to the nearest ten per cent, e.g. a disablement of 44 per cent will be paid at the 40 per cent rate while a disablement of 45 per cent will be paid at the 50 per cent rate
Benefit is payable 15 weeks (90 days) after the date of the accident or onset of the disease and may be payable for a limited period or for life. The benefit is payable whether the person works or not and those who are incapable of work are entitled to draw statutory sick pay or incapacity benefit in addition to industrial injuries disablement benefit. It may also be possible to claim the following allowances:
– reduced earnings allowance for those who are unable to return to their regular work or work of the same standard and who had their accident (or whose disease started) before 1 October 1990
– retirement allowance for those who were entitled to reduced earnings allowance who have reached state pension age
– constant attendance allowance for those with a disablement of 100 per cent who need constant care. There are four rates of allowance depending on how much care the person needs
– exceptionally severe disablement allowance for those who are entitled to constant care attendance allowance at one of the higher rates and who need constant care permanently
See leaflets NI6 and N12.

OTHER BENEFITS
People who are disabled because of an accident or disease that was the result of work that they did before 5 July 1948 are not entitled to industrial injuries disablement benefit. They may, however, be entitled to payment under the workmen's compensation scheme or the pneumoconiosis, byssinosis and miscellaneous diseases benefit scheme. *See* leaflets WS1 and PN1.

WEEKLY RATES OF BENEFIT
from April 2001
*Disablement benefit/pension

Degree of disablement	
100 per cent	£112.90
90	101.61
80	90.32
70	79.03
60	67.74
50	56.45
40	45.16
30	33.87
20	22.58
†Unemployability supplement	69.75
Addition for adult dependant (subject to earnings rule)	40.40
Reduced earnings allowance (maximum)	45.16
Retirement allowance (maximum)	11.29
Constant attendance allowance (normal maximum rate)	45.20
Exceptionally severe disablement allowance	45.20

*There is a weekly benefit for those under 18 with no dependants which is set at a lower rate
†This benefit attracts an increase for each dependent child (in addition to child benefit) of £9.85 for the first child and £11.35 for each subsequent child

CLAIMS AND QUESTIONS

With a few exceptions, claims and questions relating to social security benefits are decided in agencies. The decision makers act impartially. *See* leaflets GL24 and NI260(DMA).
Entitlement to benefit (including disablement questions) and regulated Social Fund payments is determined by decision makers. A claimant who is dissatisfied with that decision can ask for an explanation and review of the decision. If they are still dissatisfied they can go to the Appeals Service, an independent tribunal. There is a further right of appeal to a Social Security Commissioner against the tribunal's decision but leave to appeal must first be obtained. Appeals to the Commissioner must be on a point of law. Provision is also made for the determination of certain questions by the Secretary of State for Social Security.
Decisions on applications to the discretionary Social Fund are made by Social Fund Officers. Applicants can ask for a review within 28 days of the date on the decision letter. The Social Fund Review Officer will review the case and there is a further right of review to an independent Social Fund Inspector.
Reviews of housing and council tax benefit decisions are dealt with initially by the council. The claimant must ask for a review within six weeks of being told how much benefit they will receive. Further reviews are dealt with by an independent review board.

OTHER BENEFITS

STATUTORY SICK PAY
Employers usually pay statutory sick pay (SSP) to their employees for up to 28 weeks of sickness in any period of incapacity for work that lasts longer than four days. SSP is

paid at £62.20 per week and is subject to PAYE tax and NI deductions. Employees who cannot obtain SSP may be able to claim incapacity benefit. Employers may be able to recover some SSP costs. *See* leaflets NI244 and NI245.

STATUTORY MATERNITY PAY

In general, employers pay statutory maternity pay (SMP) to pregnant women who have been employed by them full or part-time for at least 26 weeks before the end of the 'qualifying week', which is 15 weeks before the week the baby is due, and whose earnings on average at least equal the lower earnings limit applied to NI contributions. All women who meet these conditions receive payment of 90 per cent of their average earnings for six weeks, followed by a maximum of 12 weeks at £62.20. SMP can be paid from the beginning of the 11th week before the week in which the baby is due but women can decide to begin maternity leave later than this. SMP is not payable for any week in which the woman works. Employers are reimbursed for 92 per cent of the SMP they pay (105 per cent for those whose annual NI liability (excluding Class 1A) is £20,000 or less). *See* Leaflet NI17A.

War Pensions

The War Pensions Agency, which became an executive agency of the Ministry of Defence in June 2001, awards war pensions under The Naval, Military and Air Forces, Etc. (Disablement and Death) Service Pensions Order 1983 to members of the armed forces in respect of service after 4 August 1914. There is also a scheme for civilians and civil defence workers in respect of the 1939–45 war, and other schemes for groups such as merchant seamen and Polish armed forces who served under British command.

PENSIONS

War disablement pension is awarded for the disabling effects of any injury, wound or disease which is the result of, or has been aggravated by, conditions of service in the armed forces. It can only be paid once the person has left the armed forces. The amount of pension paid depends on the severity of disablement, which is assessed by comparing the health of the claimant with that of a healthy person of the same age and sex. The person's earning capacity or occupation are not taken into account in this assessment. A pension is awarded if the person has a disablement of 20 per cent or more and a lump sum is usually payable to those with a disablement of less than 20 per cent. No award is made for noise-induced sensorineural hearing loss where the assessment of disablement is less than 20 per cent.

War widow's pension is payable where the husband's death was due to, or hastened by, his service in the armed forces or where the husband was in receipt of a war disablement pension constant attendance allowance (or would have been had he not been in hospital). A war widow's pension is also payable if the husband was getting unemployability supplement at the time of his death and his pensionable disablement was at least 80 per cent. Most war widows receive a standard rank-related rate but a lower weekly rate is payable to war widows of men below the rank of Lieutenant-Colonel who are under the age of

40, without children and capable of maintaining themselves. This is increased to the standard rate at age 40. Allowances are paid for children (in addition to child benefit) and adult dependants. An age allowance may also be given when the woman reaches 65 and increased at age 70 and age 80.

A war widower's pension may be payable to a man whose wife died because of service in the armed forces, if he was dependent on his wife before her death and cannot support himself.

All war pensions and war widow's pensions are tax-free and pensioners living overseas receive the same amount as those resident in the UK.

SUPPLEMENTARY ALLOWANCES

A number of supplementary allowances may be awarded to a war pensioner which are intended to meet various needs which may result from disablement or death and take account of its particular effect on the pensioner or spouse. The principal supplementary allowances are unemployability supplement, allowance for lowered standard of occupation and constant attendance allowance. Others include exceptionally severe disablement allowance, severe disablement occupational allowance, treatment allowance, mobility supplement, comforts allowance, clothing allowance, age allowance and widow's age allowance. There is a rent allowance available on a war widow's pension.

DEPARTMENT FOR WORK AND PENSIONS BENEFITS

Benefits formerly administered by the Department of Social Services are now overseen by the Department of Work and Pensions. Most benefits are paid in addition to the basic war disablement pension or war widow's pension. Any retirement pension for which a war widow qualifies on her own NI contribution record can be paid in addition to her war widow's pension.

A war pensioner or war widow who claims income support, working families tax credit or disabled person's tax credit has the first £10 a week of pension disregarded. A similar provision operates for housing benefit and council tax benefit; but the local authority may, at its discretion, disregard any or all of the balance.

CLAIMS AND QUESTIONS

To claim a war pension it is necessary to contact the nearest war pensioners' welfare service office, the address of which is available from local social security offices, or to write to the War Pensions Agency, Norcross, Blackpool FY5 3WP. Claims can also be made through authorised agents, usually ex-service organisations such as the RBL, BLESMA etc. Claim forms are also available from the WPA website listed below.

The war pensioners' welfare service advises and assists war pensioners and widows on any matters affecting their welfare. General advice on any war pensions matter can be obtained by ringing the War pensions Freeline (UK only) on 0800-169 2277. If living overseas ring 00 44 1253 866043; E-mail warpensions@gtnet.gov.uk; Web: www.dss.gov.uk/wpa

The Water Industry

ENGLAND AND WALES

The water industry supplies 58 million people 18,000 million litres of water every day. Around 2.8 million tests are carried out to check water quality every year and 99.82 per cent of samples meet all British/European standards. In England and Wales the Secretary of State for Environment, Food and Rural Affairs and the National Assembly for Wales have overall responsibility for water policy and set the environmental and health and safety standards for the water industry. The Drinking Water Inspectorate acts on their behalf as the regulator of drinking water quality.

The Director-General of Water Services, as the independent economic regulator, is responsible for ensuring that the private water companies are able to fulfil their statutory obligation to provide water supply and sewerage services, and for protecting the interests of consumers.

The Secretary of State for Environment, Food and Rural Affairs and the National Assembly for Wales are responsible for policy relating to land drainage, flood protection, sea defences and the protection and development of fisheries.

The Environment Agency is responsible for water quality and the control of pollution, the management of water resources and nature conservation.

THE WATER COMPANIES

Until 1989, nine regional water authorities in England and the Welsh Water Authority in Wales were responsible for water supply and the development of water resources, sewerage and sewage disposal, pollution control, freshwater fisheries, flood protection, water recreation, and environmental conservation. The Water Act 1989 provided for the creation of a privatised water industry under public regulation, and the functions of the regional water authorities were taken over by ten holding companies and the regulatory bodies and has since been consolidated into the Water Industry Act 1991.

Of the 99 per cent of the population of England and Wales who are connected to a public water supply, 78 per cent are supplied by the water companies (through their principal operating subsidiaries, the water service companies). The remaining 22 per cent are supplied by statutory water companies which were already in the private sector. Most of these have public limited company (PLC) status and many are now in foreign ownership or are part of larger multi-utility companies. They are represented by Water UK, which also represents the ten water service companies responsible for sewerage and sewage disposal in England and Wales, and the state-owned water authorities of Scotland and Northern Ireland. Water UK is the trade association for all the water service companies except Mid Kent Water.

Limited competition exists in the water industry, with large industrial customers being able to negotiate separate supply arrangements. Discussions are underway to determine the feasibility and future extent of competition.

WATER UK, 1 Queen Anne's Gate, London, SW1H 9BT. Tel: 020-7344 1844 Web: www.water.org.uk. *Chief Executive*, Ms P. Taylor

Water Service Companies

ANGLIAN WATER SERVICES LTD, Anglian House, Ambury Road, Huntingdon, Cambs PE18 6NZ
DWR CYMRU (WELSH WATER), Pentwyn Road, Nelson, Treharris, Mid Glamorgan CF46 6LY
NORTHUMBRIAN WATER LTD, Abbey Road, Pity Me, Durham DH1 5FJ
SEVERN TRENT WATER LTD, 2297 Coventry Road, Sheldon, Birmingham B26 3PU

WATER SUPPLY AND CONSUMPTION 1999–2000

	Supply		Consumption			
	Supply from treatment works (Ml/day)	Total leakage (Ml/day)	Household (l/head/day) Unmetered	Non-household (l/prop/day) Metered	Unmetered	Metered
WATER SERVICE COMPANIES						
Anglian	1,140.3	189.9	165.8	143.4	542.3	3,282.4
Dwr Cymru (Welsh)	929.8	228.4	158.8	149.4	744.7	2,627.1
North West	1,947.2	487.1	152.1	137.4	698.9	2,690.2
Northumbrian	757.6	167.8	167.0	148.7	922.4	4,935.8
Severn Trent	1,878.0	340.1	155.8	142.6	600.0	2,352.9
South West	431.4	83.7	175.2	127.3	859.9	1,659.1
Southern	584.8	92.7	171.8	150.7	816.3	2,597.6
Thames	2,553.3	661.9	189.4	164.1	976.6	3,640.8
Wessex	376.2	88.3	161.0	137.6	2,266.1	2,579.4
Yorkshire	1,283.3	316.5	154.9	138.4	147.1	2,726.3
Total	11,881.9	2,716.3	—	—	—	—
Average	—	—	164.8	145.5	783.0	2,844.0
WATER COMPANIES						
Total	3,175.9	589.9	—	—	—	—
Average	—	—	177.6	151.7	852.2	2,962.6

Source: Office of Water Services

SOUTHERN WATER SERVICES LTD, Southern House, Yeoman Road, Worthing, W. Sussex BN13 3NX
SOUTH WEST WATER SERVICES LTD, Peninsula House, Rydon Lane, Exeter EX2 7HR
THAMES WATER UTILITIES LTD, Reading Bridge House, c/o Blake House, Manor Farm Road, Reading RG2 0JN
UNITED UTILITIES WATER LTD (formerly NORTH WEST WATER), Dawson House, Liverpool Road, Great Sankey, Warrington WA5 3LW
WESSEX WATER SERVICES LTD, Claverton Down Road, Claverton Down, Bath BA2 7WW
YORKSHIRE WATER SERVICES LTD, Western House, Western Way, Halifax Road, Bradford BD6 2LZ

REGULATORY BODIES

The Office of Water Services (Ofwat) was set up under the Water Act 1989 and is the independent economic regulator of the water and sewerage companies in England and Wales. Ofwat's main duty is to ensure that the companies can finance and carry out their statutory functions and to protect the interests of water customers. Ofwat is a non-ministerial government department headed by the Director-General of Water Services, who is appointed by the Secretary of State for Environment, Food and Rural Affairs and the Secretary of State for Wales. Under the Competition Act 1998, from 1 March 2000 the Competition Commission has heard appeals against the regulator's decisions regarding anti-competitive agreements and abuse of a dominant position in the marketplace. The Environment Agency has statutory duties and powers in relation to water resources, pollution control, flood defence, fisheries, recreation, conservation and navigation in England and Wales.

The Drinking Water Inspectorate is responsible for assessing the quality of the drinking water supplied by the water companies, inspecting the companies themselves and investigating any accidents affecting drinking water quality. The Chief Inspector presents an annual report to the Secretary of State for the Environment, Food and Rural Affairs and to the National Assembly for Wales.

METHODS OF CHARGING

In England and Wales, most domestic customers still pay for domestic water supply and sewerage services through charges based on the old rateable value of their property, although about 20 per cent of householders are now charged according to consumption, which is recorded by meter. Industrial and most commercial customers are charged according to consumption.

Under the Water Industry Act 1999, water companies can continue basing their charges on the old rateable value of property. Domestic customers can continue paying on an unmeasured basis unless they choose to pay according to consumption. After having a meter installed (which is free of charge), a customer can revert to unmeasured charging within 12 months. Domestic, school and hospital customers cannot be disconnected for non-payment.

In November 1999 Ofwat decided to set new price limits for the period 2000-5. The average reduction in prices for the first year, 2000-1, was 12.3 per cent.

SCOTLAND

Overall responsibility for national water policy in Scotland rested with the Secretary of State for Scotland until July 1999 when it was devolved to the Scottish Ministers.

Until The Local Government etc. (Scotland) Act 1994, water supply and sewerage services were local authority responsibilities. The Central Scotland Water Development Board had the function of developing new sources of water supply for the purpose of providing water in bulk to

water authorities whose limits of supply were within the board's area. Under the Act, three new public water authorities, covering the north, east and west of Scotland respectively, took over the provision of water and sewerage services from April 1996. The Central Scotland Water Development Board was then abolished. The new authorities were accountable to the Secretary of State for Scotland, and since July 1999 have been accountable to the Scottish Ministers. The Act also established the Scottish Water and Sewerage Customers Council representing consumer interests. It monitored the performance of the authorities; approved charges schemes; investigated complaints; and advised the Secretary of State. The Water Industry Act 1999, whose Scottish provisions were accepted by the Scottish Executive, abolished the Scottish Water and Sewerage Customers Council and replaced it in November 1999 by a Water Industry Commissioner who promotes the interests of customers. The Commissioner makes long-term recommendations about charging and efficiency to the Scottish Ministers and is advised by three water industry consultative committees (one for each water authority).

The Scottish Environment Protection Agency (SEPA) is responsible for promoting the cleanliness of Scotland's rivers, lochs and coastal waters. SEPA is also responsible for controlling pollution.

WATER RESOURCES 1999

	No.	Yield (Ml/day)
Reservoirs and lochs	322	3,099
Feeder intakes	23	—
River intakes	249	452
Bore-holes	45	100
Underground springs	84	27
TOTAL	*723	3,678

* Including compensation reservoirs

WATER CONSUMPTION 1999

TOTAL (Ml/day)	2,363
Potable	2,352.3
Unmetered	1,912.3
Metered	520.2
Non-potable†	10.7
TOTAL (l/head/day)	474.4
Unmetered	383.9
Metered and non-potable†	106.3

† 'Non-potable' supplied for industrial purposes. Metered supplies in general relate to commercial and industrial use and unmetered to domestic use
Source: The Scottish Office; *Public Water Supplies in Scotland 1999-2000*

EAST OF SCOTLAND WATER AUTHORITY, 55 Buckstone Terrace, Edinburgh EH10 6XH. Tel: 0131-453 7500. *Chief Executive*, J. Hargreaves
NORTH OF SCOTLAND WATER AUTHORITY, Cairngorm House, Beechwood Business Park, Inverness IV2 3ED. Tel: 01463-245400. *Chief Executive*, K. Bryan
WATER INDUSTRY COMMISSIONER FOR SCOTLAND, Ochil House, Springkerse Business Park, Stirling FK7 7XE. Tel: 01786-430200. *Commissioner*, A. D. A. Sutherland
WEST OF SCOTLAND WATER AUTHORITY, 419 Balmore Road, Glasgow G22 6NU. Tel: 0141-355 5333. *Chief Executive*, C. Cornish

METHODS OF CHARGING

The water authorities set charges for domestic and non-domestic water and sewerage provision through charges schemes which have to be approved by the Water

Industries Commissioner. The authorities must publish a summary of their charges schemes.

NORTHERN IRELAND

In Northern Ireland ministerial responsibility for water services lies with The Minister of the Department for Regional Development. The Water Service, which is an executive agency of the Department for Regional Development, is responsible for policy and co-ordination with regard to supply, distribution and cleanliness of water, and the provision and maintenance of sewerage services.

The Water Service is divided into four regions, the Eastern, Northern, Western and Southern Divisions. These are based in Belfast, Ballymena, Londonderry and Craigavon respectively.

Methods of Charging

Until last year Water Service was funded mainly through the regional rate (part of which was appropriated in-aid of the Department) and direct charges principally for metered water. However, the regional rate is no longer appropriated-in-aid and following Devolution the Water service is now funded by Parliamentary Vote and direct charges.

All properties, which are not exclusively domestic, are metered. The are, however, granted an allowance of 200 cubic metres per annum to reflect domestic usage - this is known as the domestic usage allowance. Customers are charged only for water used in excess of the domestic usage allowance together with a standing charge, which is intended to cover the costs of meter provision, maintenance, reading and billing. This allowance is not granted if rates are not paid on the property. Traders operating from rated premises are required to pay for the treatment and disposal of trade effluent which they discharge into the public sewer.

Energy

The main primary sources of energy in Britain are oil, natural gas, coal, nuclear power and water power. The main secondary sources (e.g. sources derived from the primary sources) are electricity, coke and smokeless fuels, and petroleum products. The Department for the Environment, Food and Rural Affairs (DEFRA) is responsible for promoting energy efficiency.

INDIGENOUS PRODUCTION OF PRIMARY FUELS

Million tonnes of oil equivalent

	1999	2000p
Coal	25.2	21.9
Petroleum	150.3	138.4
Natural gas	99.3	108.5
Primary electricity		
Nuclear	22.68	20.26
Natural flow hydro	0.54	0.52
Total	298.0	289.6

p provisional

INLAND ENERGY CONSUMPTION BY PRIMARY FUEL

Million tonnes of oil equivalent, seasonally adjusted

	1999	2000p
Coal	38.3	40.6
Petroleum	7.4	73.1
Natural gas	92.6	96.2
Primary electricity	24.45	22.0
Nuclear	22.68	20.26
Natural flow hydro	0.54	0.52
Net imports	1.23	1.22
Total	229.9	231.9

p provisional

TRADE IN FUELS AND RELATED MATERIALS 2000

	Quantity*	Value†
IMPORTS		
Coal and other solid fuel	16.5	696
Crude petroleum	40.5	5,026
Petroleum products	20.7	3,424
Natural gas	1.2	91
Electricity	1.2	373
Total	78.8	9,610
Total (fob)‡	—	8,886
EXPORTS		
Coal and other solid fuel	0.2	73
Crude petroleum	83.4	10,287
Petroleum products	32.4	4,842
Natural gas	6.9	507
Electricity	—	5
Total	122.9	15,714
Total (fob)‡	—	15,714

* Million tonnes of oil equivalent
† *£ million*
‡ Adjusted to exclude estimated costs of insurance, freight, etc.
Source: *Department of Trade and Industry*

OIL

Until the 1960s Britain imported almost all its oil supplies. In 1969 oil was discovered in the UK Continental Shelf (UKCS). The first oilfield to be brought into production was the Argyll field in 1975, and since the mid-1970s Britain has been a major producer of crude oil.

Licences for exploration and production are granted to companies by the Department of Trade and Industry; the leading British oil companies are British Petroleum (BP) and Shell Transport and Trading. At the end of 1998, 1,021 offshore licences and 150 onshore licences had been awarded, and there were 121 offshore oilfields in production. In 1998 there were 10 oil refineries and four smaller refining units processing crude and process oils. There are estimated to be reserves of 1,800 million tonnes of oil in the UKCS. Royalties are payable on fields approved before April 1982 and petroleum revenue tax is levied on fields approved between 1975 and March 1993.

DRILLING ACTIVITY 2000

Number of wells started	Offshore	Onshore
Exploration and appraisal	59	14
Exploration	26	—
Appraisal	33	—
Development	216	11

VALUE OF UKCS OIL AND GAS PRODUCTION AND INVESTMENT

£ million

	1999	2000
Total income	19,427	27,009
Operating costs	4,249	4,288
Exploration expenditure	457	377
Gross trading profits*	13,493	21,196
Percentage contribution to GVA	1.9	2.7
Capital investment	3,116	2,848
Percentage contribution to industrial investment	13	12

* Net of stock appreciation

INDIGENOUS PRODUCTION AND REFINERY RECEIPTS

	1999	2000
Indigenous production (thousand tonnes)	137,125	126,245
Crude oil	128,286	128,262
NGLs*	8,839	8,363
Refinery receipts (thousand tonnes)		
Indigenous	50,886	34,519
Other†	2,113	3,493
Net foreign imports	36,346	45,771

* Natural gas liquids: condensates and petroleum gases derived at onshore treatment plants
† Mainly recycled products

DELIVERIES OF PETROLEUM PRODUCTS FOR INLAND
CONSUMPTION BY ENERGY USE

Thousand tonnes

	1999	2000
Electricity generators	1,018	798
Gas works	47	40
Iron and steel industry	485	429
Other industries	5,638	5,690
Transport	48,486	49,203
Domestic	2,874	2,279
Other	3,060	2,866
Total	61,608	61,305

Source: Department of Trade and Industry

GAS

From the late 18th-century gas in Britain was produced from coal. In the 1960s town gas began to be produced from oil-based feedstocks using imported oil. In 1965 gas was discovered in the North Sea in the West Sole field, which became the first gasfield in production in 1967, and from the late 1960s natural gas began to replace town gas. Britain is now the world's fourth largest producer of gas and in 1998 only 1.5 per cent of gas available for consumption in the UK was imported. From October 1998 Britain was connected to the continental European gas system via a pipeline from Bacton, Norfolk to Zeebrugge, Belgium.

By the end of 1998 there were 80 offshore gasfields producing natural gas and associated gas (mainly methane). There is estimated to be 1,795,000 million cubic metres of recoverable gas reserves. There are about 9,419km of major submarine pipelines for transporting hydrocarbons, and onshore pipelines for carrying refined products and chemicals. Natural gas is transported around Britain by about 273,000km of pipelines supplied by seven coastal terminals. This pipeline system is owned by Transco and licensed gas shippers are allowed access under a network code. New arrangements for trading within the pipeline system were introduced on 1 October 1999. Greater efficiency in balancing supply and demand is expected to achieve savings which will be reflected in lower prices.

The Office of Gas and Electricity Markets is the regulator for the gas industry. It was formed in 1999 by the merger of the Office of Gas Supply and the Office of Electricity Regulation. Under the Competition Act 1998, from 1 March 2000 the Competition Commission has heard appeals against the regulator's decisions regarding anti-competitive agreements and abuse of a dominant position in the marketplace.

The gas industry in Britain was nationalised in 1949 and operated as the Gas Council. The Gas Council was replaced by the British Gas Corporation in 1972 and the industry became more centralised. The British Gas Corporation was privatised in 1986 as British Gas PLC.

In 1993 the Monopolies and Mergers Commission found that British Gas's integrated business in Great Britain as a gas trader and the owner of the gas transportation system could be expected to operate against the public interest. In February 1997, British Gas demerged its trading arm and became two separate companies: BG PLC, which was responsible for the Transco pipeline business in Britain and oil and gas exploration and production in the UK and abroad; and Centrica PLC, which runs the trading and services operations under the British Gas brand name in Great

Britain. In October 2000 Transco demerged from BG PLC and became part of Lattice Group PLC.

Competition was gradually introduced into the industrial gas market from 1986. Supply of gas to the domestic market was opened to companies other than British Gas, starting in April 1996 with a pilot project in the West Country and Wales. From spring 1997 competition was progressively introduced throughout the rest of Britain in stages which were completed in May 1998. With the electricity market also open, many suppliers now offer their customers both gas and electricity. Some gas companies have become part of larger multi-utility companies, often operating internationally.

BG PLC, 100 Thames Valley Park Drive, Reading RG6 1PT. Tel: 0118-935 3222. *Chairman*, R. V. Giordano; *Chief Executive*, F. Chapman
CENTRICA PLC, Charter Court, 50 Windsor Road, Slough, Berks SL1 2HA. Tel: 01753-758000. *Chief Executive*, R. Gardner
LATTICE GROUP PLC, 130 Jermyn Street, London SW14 4UR. Tel: 020 7389 3200. *Chairman*, J. Parker

NATURAL GAS PRODUCTION AND SUPPLY

GWh

	1999	2000
Gross gas production	1,152,154	1,258,549
Exports	84,433	146,342
Imports	12,862	26,032
Gas available	1,011,157	1,062,187
Gas transmitted‡	1,011,284	1,061,953

‡ Figures differ from gas available mainly because of stock changes

NATURAL GAS CONSUMPTION

GWh

	1999	2000
Electricity generators	313,319	323,371
Iron and steel industry	22,664	22,383
Other industries	180,950	193,244
Domestic	356,067	373,400
Public administration, commerce and agriculture	121,560	122,277
Total	994,560	1,034,675

Source: Department of Trade and Industry

COAL

Coal has been mined in Britain for centuries and the availability of coal was crucial to the industrial revolution of the 18th- and 19th-centuries. Mines were in private ownership until 1947 when they were nationalised and came under the management of the National Coal Board, later the British Coal Corporation. In addition to producing coal at its own deep-mine and opencast sites, of which there were 850 in 1955, British Coal was responsible for licensing private operators.

Under the Coal Industry Act 1994, the Coal Authority was established to take over ownership of coal reserves and to issue licences to private mining companies as part of the privatisation of British Coal. The Coal Authority also deals with the physical legacy of mining, e.g. subsidence damage claims, and is responsible for holding and making available all existing records. The mines were sold as five separate businesses in 1994 and coal production in the UK is now undertaken entirely in the private sector. At the end of 2000 there were 17 large deep mines in operation.

502 Energy

The main UK customer for coal is the electricity supply industry. A review of energy policy was undertaken during 1998 and the Government announced measures in its October 1998 Energy White Paper which included a freeze on new applications to build gas-fired power stations in order to increase opportunities for coal-fired power stations. The moratorium on new gas-fired power stations was lifted in 2000 in the light of two measures to improve the competitiveness of coal fired generation. Firstly the government reached agreement with the European Commission to make available temporary state aid for the coal industry; such aid to end with the termination of the European Coal and Steel Community Treaty in 2002. Secondly there was the reform of the electricity wholesale market and the replacement of The Pool with the New Electricity Trading Arrangement (NETA) which took effect from 27 March 2001.

COAL PRODUCTION AND FOREIGN TRADE

Thousand tonnes

	1999	2000p
Total production	37,077	31,972
Deep-mined	20,888	17,611
Opencast	15,275	13,564
Imports	20,758	23,446
Exports	762	660

p provisional

INLAND COAL USE

Thousand tonnes

	1999	2000
Fuel producers		
Collieries	10	12
Electricity generators	40,471	46,052
Coke ovens	8,558	8,697
Other conversion industries	643	540
Final users		
Industry	2,836	1,449
Domestic	2,693	1,919
Public administration, commerce and agriculture	318	355
Total	55,529	59,024

p provisional
Source: Department of Trade and Industry

ELECTRICITY

The first power station in Britain generating electricity for public supply began operating in 1882. In the 1930s a national transmission grid was developed, and it was reconstructed and extended in the 1950s and 1960s. Power stations were operated by the Central Electricity Generating Board.

Under the Electricity Act 1989, 12 regional electricity companies (RECs), which are responsible for the distribution of electricity from the national grid to consumers, were formed from the former area electricity boards in England and Wales. Four companies were formed from the Central Electricity Generating Board: three generating companies (National Power PLC, Nuclear Electric PLC and PowerGen PLC) and the National Grid Company PLC, which owns and operates the transmission system. National Power and PowerGen were floated on the stock market in 1991. National Power was demerged in October 2000 to form two separate companies:

International Power PLC and Innogy PLC, which manages the bulk of National Power's UK assets. Nuclear Electric was split into two parts in 1995; the part comprising the more modern nuclear stations was incorporated into a new company, British Energy, which was floated on the stock market in 1996. Magnox Electric, which owns the magnox nuclear reactors, remained in the public sector and was integrated into British Nuclear Fuels (BNFL) in 1999. Ownership of the National Grid Company was transferred to the RECs and it was subsequently floated in 1995.

Generators and suppliers participate in a competitive wholesale trading market known as NETA (New Electricity Trading Arrangements) which began in March 2001, replacing the Electricity Pool. The introduction of competition into the domestic electricity market was completed in May 1999. With the gas market also open, many suppliers now offer their customers both gas and electricity.

Electricity companies can now also sell gas to their customers. Similarly, gas companies can also offer electricity. Some electricity companies have bought others, and there is a trend towards larger multi-utility companies, often operating internationally.

In Scotland, three new companies were formed under the Electricity Act 1989: Scottish Power PLC and Scottish Hydro-Electric PLC, which are responsible for generation, transmission, distribution and supply; and Scottish Nuclear Ltd. Scottish Power and Scottish Hydro-Electric were floated on the stock market in 1991 (the latter merged with Southern Electric in 1998 to become Scottish and Southern Energy PLC); Scottish Nuclear was incorporated into British Energy in 1995.

In Northern Ireland, Northern Ireland Electricity PLC was set up in 1993 under a 1991 Order in Council. It is responsible for transmission, distribution and supply and has been floated on the stock market. There is no Pool in Northern Ireland; three private companies are responsible for electricity generation and the electricity is sold to Northern Ireland Electricity under a series of power purchase agreements.

The Office of Gas and Electricity Markets is the regulator for the electricity industry. It was formed in 1999 by the merger of the Office of Electricity Regulation and the Office of Gas Supply. Under the Competition Act 1998, the Competition Commission hears appeals against the regulator's decisions regarding anti-competitive agreements and abuse of a dominant position in the marketplace.

The Electricity Association is the electricity industry's main trade association, providing representational and professional services for the electricity companies. EA Technology Ltd provides distribution and utilisation research, development and technology transfer.

NUCLEAR POWER

Nuclear reactors began to supply electricity to the national grid in 1956. It is generated at six magnox reactors, seven advanced gas-cooled reactors (AGRs) and one pressurised water reactor (PWR), Sizewell 'B' in Suffolk. Nuclear stations now generate about 29 per cent of the UK's electricity.

In preparation for privatisation, the nuclear industry was restructured in December 1995. A holding company, British Energy PLC, was formed with two operational subsidiaries, Nuclear Electric Ltd and Scottish Nuclear Ltd. Nuclear Electric operates the five AGRs and the PWR in England and Wales; Scottish Nuclear operates the two AGRs in Scotland. British Energy was floated on the stock market in 1996. The Magnox reactors were transferred to Magnox Electric PLC, and later to British

Nuclear Fuels Ltd (BNFL). BNFL is in public ownership, providing reprocessing, waste management and effluent treatment services. The UK Atomic Energy Authority is responsible for the decommissioning of nuclear reactors and other nuclear facilities used in research and development. UK Nirex, which is owned by the nuclear generating companies and the Government, is responsible for the disposal of intermediate and some low-level nuclear waste. The Nuclear Installations Inspectorate of the Health and Safety Executive is the nuclear industry's regulator.

ELECTRICITY UTILITIES

BRITISH ENERGY PLC, 10 Lochside Place, Edinburgh EH12 9DF. Tel: 0131-527 2000
BNFL MAGNOX GENERATION PLC, Berkeley Centre, Berkeley, Glos GL13 9PB. Tel: 01453-810451
EAST MIDLANDS ELECTRICITY PLC, PO Box 44, Wollaton, Nottingham NG8 1EZ. Tel: 0115-929 1151
EASTERN ENERGY PLC, PO Box 40, Wherstead Park, Wherstead, Ipswich IP9 2AQ. Tel: 01473-688688
FIRST HYDRO COMPANY, Bala House, Lakeside Business Village, St David's Park, Ewloe CH5 3XJ. Tel: 01244-520234
GENERAL PUBLIC UTILITIES, Whittington Hall, Whittington WR5 2RB. Tel: 0845-735 3637.
GUERNSEY ELECTRICITY, PO Box 4, Electricity House, North Side, Vale, Guernsey GY1 3AD. Tel: 01481-46931
HYDER PLC, Newport Road, St Mellons, Cardiff CF3 9XW. Tel: 029-2079 2111
INNOGY PLC (formerly NATIONAL POWER), Windmill Hill Business Park, Whitehill Way, Swindon, Wilts SN5 9FH. Tel: 01793-877777
JERSEY ELECTRICITY, PO Box 45, Queens Road, St Helier, Jersey JE4 8NY. Tel: 01534-505000
LONDON ELECTRICITY PLC, Templar House, 81–87 High Holborn, London WC1V 6NU. Tel: 020-7242 9050
MANWEB PLC, Manweb House, Kingsfield Court, Chester Business Park, Chester CH4 9RF. Tel: 0845-272 3636
MANX ELECTRICITY AUTHORITY, PO Box 177, Douglas, Isle of Man IM99 1PS. Tel: 01624-687687
NATIONAL GRID COMPANY PLC, National Grid House, Kirby Corner Road, Coventry CV4 8JY. Tel: 024-7642 3000
NIGEN Ltd., AES Kilroot Power Station, Larne Road, Carrickfergus, Co. Antrim BT38 7LX. Tel: 028-9335 1644
NORTHERN ELECTRIC PLC, Carliol House, Market Street, Newcastle upon Tyne NE1 6NE. Tel: 0191-210 2000
NORTHERN IRELAND ELECTRICITY PLC, 120 Malone Road, Belfast BT9 5HT. Tel: 028-9066 1100
NORWEB ENERGI PLC, Oakland House, Talbot Road, Old Trafford, Manchester M16 0HQ. Tel: 0161-873 8000
POWERGEN PLC, Westwood Way, Westwood Business Park, Coventry CV4 8LG. Tel: 024-7642 4000
PREMIER POWER LTD, Ballylumford, Islandmagee, Larne, Co. Antrim BT40 3RS. Tel: 028-9335 1644
SCOTTISH AND SOUTHERN ENERGY PLC, 10 Dunkeld Road, Perth PH1 5WA. Tel: 01738-452100
SCOTTISHPOWER PLC, 1 Atlantic Quay, Glasgow G2 8SP. Tel: 0141-248 8200
SEEBOARD PLC, Forest Gate, Brighton Road, Crawley, W. Sussex RH11 9BH. Tel: 01293-565888
SWEB PLC, 300 Park Avenue, Aztec West, Almondsbury, Bristol BS32 4SE. Tel: 01454-201101
YORKSHIRE ELECTRICITY GROUP PLC, Wetherby Road, Scarcroft, Leeds LS15 3HS. Tel: 0113-289 2123
ELECTRICITY ASSOCIATION LTD, 30 Millbank, London SW1P 4RD. Tel: 020-7963 5700

EA TECHNOLOGY LTD, Capenhurst, Chester CH1 6ES. Tel: 0151-339 4181

ELECTRICITY GENERATION, SUPPLY AND CONSUMPTION

GWh

	1998	1999
Electricity generated: total	362,014	366,798
Major power producers: total	335,145	337,142
Conventional steam stations	134,317	118,453
Nuclear stations	100,140	96,281
Gas turbines and oil engines	229	196
Combined cycle gas turbine stations	93,832	114,242
Hydro-electric stations:		
Natural flow	4,357	4,422
Pumped storage	1,624	2,902
Renewables other than hydro	646	646
Other generators	26,870	29,656
Electricity used on works: total	17,686	17,456
Major generating companies	16,471	16,182
Other generators	1,215	1,215
Electricity supplied (gross): total	344,328	349,342
Major power producers: total	318,674	320,960
Conventional steam stations	127,581	112,552
Nuclear stations	91,186	87,672
Gas turbines and oil engines	210	186
Combined cycle gas turbine stations	93,005	112,763
Hydro-electric stations:		
Natural flow	4,344	4,409
Pumped storage	1,569	2,804
Renewables other than hydro	572	574
Other generators	25,655	28,302
Electricity used in pumping		
Major power producers	2,594	3,774
Electricity supplied (net): total	341,734	345,568
Major power producers	316,080	317,186
Other generators	25,655	28,382
Net imports	12,468	14,244
Electricity available	354,202	359,812
Losses in transmission, etc.	29,161	29,842
Electricity consumption: total	325,040	329,940
Fuel industries	8,130	8,315
Final users: total	316,910	321,625
Industrial sector	106,810	109,710
Domestic sector	109,610	110,408
Other sectors	100,490	101,430

Source: The Stationery Office – Annual Abstract of Statistics 2001

RENEWABLE SOURCES

Renewable sources of energy principally include biofuels, hydro, wind and solar. Renewable sources accounted for 3.0 million tonnes of oil equivalent of primary energy use in 2000; of this, about 2.2 million tonnes was used to generate electricity and about 0.8 million tonnes to generate heat.

The Non-Fossil Fuel Obligation (NFFO) Renewables Orders have, to date, been the Government's principal mechanism for developing renewable energy sources. NFFO Renewables Orders require the regional electricity companies to buy specified amounts of electricity from specified non-fossil fuel sources. The technologies covered by NFFO Orders have included landfill gas, municipal and industrial waste, small-scale hydro, onshore wind and energy crops. The fifth NFFO Renewables Order was made in September 1998. In Scotland a similar system of Scottish Renewables Orders exists. The third Order was made in February 1999 and covers wave energy, the first time that this technology has been supported by a Renewables Order.

Since February 2000 the United Kingdom's renewables policy has consisted of four key strands:
– a new obligation for all electricity suppliers to supply a specific proportion of electricity from renewables
– the exemption of renewable electricity sources from the Climate Change Levy
– an expanded support programme for new and renewble energy, including capital grants and an expanded research and development programme
– development of a regional strategic approach to planning and targets for renewables

The Government intends to achieve 10 per cent of the UK's electricity needs from renewables by 2010.

RENEWABLE ENERGY SOURCES 2000

	Percentages
Biofuels	82.3
Landfill gas	24.4
Sewage gas	5.4
Wood combustion	16.8
Straw combustion	2.4
Refuse combustion	21.2
Other biofuels	12.1
Hydro	14.6
Large-scale	14.02
Small-scale	0.6
Wind	2.7
Active solar heating	0.4
Total	100

Source: Department of Trade and Industry

Transport

CIVIL AVIATION

Since the privatisation of British Airways in 1987, UK airlines have been operated entirely by the private sector. In 2000, total capacity on British airlines amounted to 43 billion tonne-km, of which 33 billion tonne-km was on scheduled services. British airlines carried 103.7 million passengers, 70.3 million on scheduled services and 33.4 million on charter flights.

Leading British airlines include British Airways, Britannia Airways, British Midland, Air 2000, Airtours, JMC and Virgin Atlantic.

There are 142 licensed civil aerodromes in Britain, with Heathrow and Gatwick handling the highest volume of passengers. BAA PLC owns and operates the seven major airports: Heathrow, Gatwick, Stansted, Southampton, Glasgow, Edinburgh and Aberdeen, which between them handle about 70 per cent of air passengers and 81 per cent of air cargo traffic in Britain. Many other airports, including Manchester, are controlled by local authorities or private companies.

The Civil Aviation Authority (CAA), an independent statutory body, is responsible for the economic regulation of UK airlines and for the safety regulation of the UK civil aviation industry.

The CAA is responsible for ensuring that UK airlines meet stringent safety standards. It is also responsible for the economic regulation of the larger airports.

All commercial airline companies must be granted an Air Operator's Certificate, which is issued by the CAA to operators meeting the required safety standards. The CAA also issues airport safety licences, which must be obtained by any airport used for public transport and training flights. All British-registered aircraft must be granted an airworthiness certificate, and the CAA also issues professional licences to pilots, flight crew, ground engineers and air traffic controllers.

The Transport Act, passed by parliament on 29 November 2000, separated the CAA from its subsidiary, National Air Traffic Services (NATS), which plans and provides air traffic control services throughout the United Kingdom and over the North Atlantic - more than a million square miles - and at most of Britain's major airports. In March 2001, the Airline Group, comprising 7 of Britain's major airlines, was selected by the government as its strategic partner for NATS. The Airline Group plans to invest 1 billion of private capital in NATS over 10 years. Under the terms of a Public Private Partnership 46 per cent of shares in NATS were sold to The Airline Group, 5 per cent to staff and 49 per cent were retained by the government.

AIR PASSENGERS 2000*

ALL UK AIRPORTS: TOTAL	181,178,687
LONDON AREA AIRPORTS: TOTAL	116,528,429
Battersea Heliport	6,452
Gatwick (BAA)	32,068,540
Heathrow (BAA)	64,620,286
London City	1,583,843
Luton	6,190,499
Southend	3,568
Stansted (BAA)	11,879,693

OTHER UK AIRPORTS: TOTAL	64,805,826
Aberdeen (BAA)	2,488,597
Barra	7,796
Barrow-in-Furness	77
Belfast City	1,290,566
Belfast International	3,148,577
Benbecula (HIAL)	35,805
Biggin Hill	6,168
Birmingham	7,596,893
Blackpool	108,806
Bournemouth	275,198
Bristol	2,142,626
Cambridge	20,094
Campbeltown (HIAL)	8,369
Cardiff	1,519,920
Carlisle	456
Coventry	3,993
Dundee	49,682
East Midlands	2,234,494
Edinburgh (BAA)	5,523,559
Exeter	328,450
Glasgow (BAA)	6,965,500
Gloucestershire	2,038
Hawarden	2,490
Humberside	447,738
Inverness (HIAL)	360,698
Islay (HIAL)	20,813
Isle of Man	728,846
Kent International	7,594
Kirkwall (HIAL)	94,093
Leeds/Bradford	1,585,039
Lerwick (Tingwall)	4,650
Liverpool	1,982,714
Londonderry	162,704
Lydd	1,522
Manchester	18,568,709
Newcastle upon Tyne	3,208,734
Norwich	367,457
Penzance Heliport	126,409
Plymouth	151,874
Prestwick	910,023
St Mary's, Isles of Scilly	128,269
Scatsta	240,489
Sheffield City	60,636
Shoreham	1,379
Southampton (BAA)	856,957
Stornoway (BAA)	90,490
Sumburgh (HIAL)	129,918
Teesside	751,839
Tiree (HIAL)	5,011
Tresco, Isles of Scilly (H)	39,789
Unst	1,429
Wick (HIAL)	29,832
CHANNEL IS. AIRPORTS: TOTAL	2,681,695
Alderney	75,199
Guernsey	931,894
Jersey	1,674,602

*Total terminal, transit, scheduled and charter passengers

Source: Civil Aviation Authority

RAILWAYS

Britain pioneered railways and a railway network was developed across Britain by private companies in the course of the 19th century. In 1948 the main railway companies were nationalised and were run by a public authority, the British Transport Commission. The Commission was replaced by the British Railways Board in 1963, operating as British Rail. On 1 April 1994, responsibility for managing the railway infrastructure passed to a newly-formed company, Railtrack; the British Railways Board continued as operator of all train services until they were sold or franchised to the private sector. All passenger activities have now been franchised and all British Rail's freight, technical support and specialist function businesses have been sold. The Board still has certain functions, including overall responsibility for the British Transport Police.

PRIVATISATION

Since 1 April 1994, ownership of operational track and land has been vested in Railtrack, which was floated on the Stock Exchange in 1996. Railtrack manages the track and charges for access to it and is responsible for signalling and timetables. It does not operate train services. It owns the stations, and leases most of them out to the train operating companies. Infrastructure support functions are now provided by private sector companies. Railtrack invests in infrastructure principally using finance raised by track charges, and takes investment decisions in consultation with rail operators. Railtrack is also responsible for overall safety on the railways.

OTHER RAIL SYSTEMS

The government announced plans for a public-private partnership for London Underground on 20 March 1998. London underground will remain responsible for all aspects of operations and safety, in the public sector. Three long-term contracts for maintainance and renewal of infrastructure will be awarded to private sector companies. There are two groupings of 'deep tube' lines and one group for the sub-surface lines. London Underground announced preferred bidders for the two deep tube contracts on 2 May 2001. A preferred bidder for the sub-surface lines is expected to be announced in summer 2001. In 2000-1 there were 972 million passenger journeys on the London Underground, up 5 per cent on the previous year.

Light rail and metro systems in Great Britain contributed to the growth in public transport, with 109 million passenger journeys in 1999-2000, up 9 per cent on the previous year. The Government's 10-year Transport Plan announced up to 25 new rapid transit lines and set a target to double light rail use in England over the next decade.

RAIL REGULATOR

The independent Rail Regulator is responsible for the licensing of new railway operators, approving access agreements, promoting the use and development of the network, preventing anti-competitive practices (in conjunction with the Director-General of The Office of Fair Trading) and protecting the interests of rail users.

Regulations, which took effect on 28 June 1998, established licensing and access arrangements for certain international train services in Great Britain. These are overseen by the International Rail Regulator.

The White Paper *New Deal for Transport*, published in

July 1998, announced plans to establish a Strategic Rail Authority (SRA) to manage passenger railway franchising, take responsibility for increasing the use of the railways for freight transport, and lead strategic planning of passenger and freight rail services. The SRA began work in shadow form in July 1999, using the existing powers of the Franchising Director and British Rail, and became a fully operational authority in February 2001 when its shadow status was dropped.

SERVICES

For privatisation, domestic passenger services were divided into 25 train-operating units, which have been franchised to private sector operators via a competitive tendering process overseen by the Strategic Rail Authority (SRA). The franchise agreements were for between five and 15 years. The Government continues to subsidise loss-making but socially necessary rail services. The SRA is responsible for monitoring the performance of the franchisees, allocating and administering government subsidy payments, proposing closures to the Rail Regulator and designating experimental services.

There are currently 25 train operating companies (TOCs): Anglia Railways; Arriva Trains Merseyside; Arriva Trains Northern; C2C; Cardiff Railway; Central Trains; Chiltern Railways; Connex South Eastern; Gatwick Express; GO-Via; Great Eastern Railway; Great North Eastern Railway; Great Western Trains; Island Line (Isle of Wight); Midland Mainline; North Western Trains; Scotrail Railways; Silverlink Train Services (North London); South West Trains; Thameslink Rail; Thames Trains; Virgin Crosscountry; Virgin West Coast; Wales and West Passenger Trains; and West Anglia Great Northern Railway (WAGN).

In addition to these 25 franchised TOCs, Eurostar and Eurotunnel provide services through the channel tunnel, but are not subject to the franchise process. The first phase of the Channel Tunnel high speed link through Kent is due open in 2003. The Heathrow Express service is a subsidiary of the airports group BAA and is also exempt from the franchise process.

The SRA is currently replacing the short term franchises that are due to expire on or before 2004 with the aim of completing the process by the end of 2001. New, long term franchises lasting 15-20 years will take their place.

Railtrack publishes a national timetable which contains details of rail services operated over the Railtrack network, coastal shipping information and connections with Ireland, the Isle of Man, the Isle of Wight, the Channel Islands and some European destinations.

The national rail enquiries service offers information about train times and fares for any part of the country:

National Rail Enquiries   08457-484950;
                        Web: www.nationalrail.co.uk
Transport for London   020-7941 4500
Eurostar   0345-303030;
                        Web: www.eurostar.com

Rail Users' Consultative Committees monitor the policies and performance of train and station operators in their area (there are nine, covering Britain). They are statutory bodies and have a legal right to make recommendations for changes. The London Regional Passengers Committee represents users of buses, the Underground and the Docklands Light Railway as well as the users of rail services in the London area. In summer 2000 the Greater London Assembly and Mayor established Transport for London with a view to developing a strategy for transport in the capital.

British Rail's passenger rolling stock was divided between three subsidiary companies, which were privatised in 1996. The companies lease rolling stock to passenger service operators. On privatisation, British Rail's bulk freight haulage companies and Rail Express Systems, which carries Royal Mail traffic, were sold to English, Welsh and Scottish Railways, which also purchased Railfreight Distribution (international freight) in 1997. In 1999–2000 102.9 million tonnes of freight was transported by an average of 1,600 trains a day.

RAILTRACK, Railtrack House, Euston Square, London NW1 2EE. Tel: 020-7557 8000.
Web: www.railtrack.co.uk *Chairman*, J. Robinson. *Chief Executive*, S. Marshall
ASSOCIATION OF TRAIN OPERATING COMPANIES, 40 Bernard Street, London WC1N 1BY. Tel: 020-7904 3010. *Chairman*, R. Brown
OFFICE OF THE RAIL REGULATOR (ORR) 1 Waterhouse Square, 138–142 Holborn, London EC1N 2TQ. Tel: 020-7282 2000. Web: www.rail-reg.gov.uk
Rail Regulator, T. Winsor
STRATEGIC RAIL AUTHORITY, 55 Victoria Street, London, SW1H 0EU. Tel: 020-7654 6000 Web: www.sra.gov.uk
Chairman, Sir Alastair Morton

RAILTRACK

At 31 March 2001, Railtrack had about 20,000 miles of standard gauge lines and sidings in use, representing 10,343 miles of route of which 3,208 miles were electrified. Standard rail on main line has a weight of 110 lb per yard. Railtrack owns 2,495 stations, 90 light maintenance depots, about 40,000 bridges, viaducts and tunnels, and over 9,000 level crossings.

Passenger journeys made in 1999–2000 totalled 947 million, including 404 million made by holders of season tickets. This national total was the largest since the early 1960s. Passenger kilometres in the year totalled 38.3 billion, earning a total revenue of £3,368 million.

In 1999–2000 Railtrack showed an operating profit of £471 million and a pre-tax profit of £428 million. In 1999-2000 Railtrack employed over 10,000 people.

RAIL SAFETY

The Railways (Safety Case) Regulations 1994 require infrastructure controllers (e.g. Railtrack, London Underground) to have systems in place to manage safety on the railway networks for which they are responsible.

Each infrastructure controller is required to present a Railway Safety Case (RSC) to the Railway Inspectorate (part of the Health and Safety Executive). The RSC must be accepted by the Inspectorate, and is subject to regular compliance audits.

The infrastructure controllers require companies wishing to operate services to present an RSC. The RSC must be accepted by the infrastructure controller before a train or station operator can receive a licence and begin to provide services. If any revision is required, the RSC must be re-presented. RSCs must be thoroughly reviewed at least every three years. The Inspectorate may examine the RSC of train and service operators as part of its general inspection activities.

Following consultation the Railways (Safety Case) Regulations were amended to transfer the responsibility for acceptance of RSCs of train and station operators from the infrastructure controllers to the Health and Safety Executive. The new regulations and guidance came into force on 31 December 2000.

ACCIDENTS ON RAILWAYS

	1998-9	1999-2000
Train accidents: total	1,835	1,895
Persons killed: total	3	33
Passengers	0	29
Railway staff	0	2
Others	3	2
Persons injured: total	84	332
Passengers	40	290
Railway staff	31	23
Others	13	19
Other accidents through movement of railway vehicles		
Persons killed	27	27
Persons injured	962	906
Other accidents on railway premises		
Persons killed	7	5
Passengers	3	4
Railway staff	3	1
Others	1	0
Persons injured	4,172	3,992
Trespassers and suicides		
Persons killed	249	274
Persons injured	149	144

THE CHANNEL TUNNEL

The earliest recorded scheme for a submarine transport connection between Britain and France was in 1802. Tunnelling has begun simultaneously on both sides of the Channel three times: in 1881, in the early 1970s, and on 1 December 1987, when construction workers began to bore the first of the three tunnels which form the Channel Tunnel. They 'holed through' the first tunnel (the service tunnel) on 1 December 1990 and tunnelling was completed in June 1991. The tunnel was officially inaugurated by The Queen and President Mitterrand of France on 6 May 1994.

The submarine link comprises three tunnels. There are two rail tunnels, each carrying trains in one direction, which measure 24.93 ft (7.6 m) in diameter. Between them lies a smaller service tunnel, measuring 15.75 ft (4.8 m) in diameter. The service tunnel is linked to the rail tunnels by 130 cross-passages for maintenance and safety purposes. The tunnels are 31 miles (50 km) long, 24 miles (38 km) of which is under the sea-bed at an average depth of 132 ft (40 m). The rail terminals are situated at Folkestone and Calais, and the tunnels go underground at Shakespeare Cliff, Dover, and Sangatte, west of Calais.

Eurostar is the high speed passenger train connecting London with Paris in three hours and Brussels in two hours 40 minutes, via the Channel Tunnel. There are up to 24 trains each way per day on the Paris route and ten each way per day on the Brussels route. Some trains stop en route at Ashford (Kent), Calais and Lille. Connecting services from Edinburgh and Manchester via London began in 1997. Vehicle shuttle services operate between Folkestone and Calais.

RAIL LINKS

The route for the British Channel Tunnel Rail Link will run from Folkestone to a new terminal at St Pancras station, London, with new intermediate stations at Ebbsfleet, Kent, and Stratford, east London; at present services run into a terminal at Waterloo station, London.

Construction of the rail link is being financed by the private sector with a substantial government contribution. A private sector consortium, London and Continental Railways Ltd (LCR), is responsible for the design, construction and ownership of the rail link, and comprises Union Railways and the UK operator of Eurostar. Construction was expected to be completed in 2003, but on 28 January 1998 LCR informed the Government that it was unable to fulfil its obligations. On 3 June 1998 the Government announced a new funding agreement with LCR. The rail link will be constructed in two phases: phase one, from the Channel Tunnel to Fawkham Junction (where an existing connection allows trains to continue to Waterloo), began in October 1998 and will be completed in 2003; phase two, from Fawkham Junction to St Pancras, will be built between 2001 and 2007. Railtrack will buy phase one when it is completed and has an option to buy phase two by 2003.

Infrastructure developments in France have been completed and high-speed trains run from Calais to Paris, linking the Channel Tunnel with the high-speed European network.

ROADS

HIGHWAY AUTHORITIES

The powers and responsibilities of highway authorities in England and Wales are set out in the Highways Acts 1980; for Scotland there is separate legislation.

Responsibility for trunk road motorways and other trunk roads in Great Britain rests in England with the Secretary of State for Transport, Local Government and the Regions, in Scotland with the Scottish Parliament, and in Wales with the National Assembly for Wales. The costs of construction, improvement and maintenance are paid for by central government. The White Paper *New Deal for Transport*, published in July 1998, restated and revised the Highways Agency's responsibility for operating, maintaining and improving the trunk road network.

The highway authority for non-trunk roads in England, Wales and Scotland is, in general, the unitary authority, county council or London borough council in whose area the roads lie.

In Northern Ireland the Department of Regional Development is the statutory road authority responsible for public roads and their maintenance and construction; the Roads Service executive agency carries out these functions on behalf of the Department.

FINANCE

The Government contributes towards capital expenditure through grants and credit approvals in England and Transport Grant (TG) in Wales. Grant rates are determined by the Secretary of State for Transport, Local Government and the Regions in England, the Scottish Ministers and the National Assembly for Wales in each country respectively. Grant is paid at 50 per cent of expenditure accepted for grant in England and Wales.

In England Transport Supplementary Grant (TSG) is paid towards capital spending on highways and the regulation of traffic; other capital spending is financed by credit approvals and specific grants. Current expenditure is funded by revenue support grant (i.e. central government grants to local authorities for non-specific services). From 2000 all bridge assessment and strengthening, and structural maintenance of principal road carriageways has been funded entirely through credit approvals. In Wales TG is paid towards capital expenditure only; current expenditure is funded by revenue support grant.

For the financial year 2000–1 local authorities in England received £22 million in TSG and £720 million in credit approvals. Total estimated expenditure on building and maintaining motorways and trunk roads in England in 1999–2000 was £1,389 million; estimated outturn for 2000–1 was £1,430 million.

In Wales total expenditure on trunk roads, motorways, and transport services in 2000–01 was £117.9 million and estimated expenditure in 2001–02 is £131.2 million.

Until 1999, the Scottish Office received a block vote from Parliament, and the Secretary of State for Scotland determined how much was spent on roads. Since 1 July 1999 all decisions on transport expenditure have been devolved to the Scottish Ministers. Total expenditure on building and maintaining trunk roads in Scotland was estimated at £17 million in 1998–9.

In Northern Ireland estimated expenditure on roads for 2000–1 was £176.0 million and £190.5 million has been allocated for expenditure in 2001–2.

The Government is considering the possibility of introducing tolls on certain roads. The Transport Bill currently before Parliament contains proposals to enable local authorities to levy charges for driving cars in congested areas or for workplace charging. In 2000–1, £18 million was allocated to a number of pilot authorities to develop charging schemes.

PRIVATE FINANCE

Private finance is being increasingly used to help finance road schemes. The current targeted programme of road improvements contains two design, build, finance and operate road contracts with a capital value of £360 million which will deliver five of the road schemes in the Government's targeted programme of improvements.

TARGETED PROGRAMME OF IMPROVEMENTS (TPI)

The 1998 Roads Review increased the emphasis given to making better use of the existing road network and improving road maintenance. It resulted in a carefully targeted £1,400 million programme of 37 trunk road improvements to be started by 2005. In February 2000, the Government announced the acceleration of the TPI with the result that 13 rather than seven schemes were started in 2000–1. A series of studies are also underway looking at traffic problems not addressed by the TPI. Road schemes that emerge from these studies will be progressed through the regional planning guidance (RPG) system. This is now the method by which truck road schemes will enter the TPI. Four additional schemes with a value of £100 million were added to the TPI in March 2000.

ROAD LENGTHS
(in miles) *2000*

	Total roads	Trunk roads (including Motorways)	Motorways*
England	230,958	6,290	1,705
Wales	20,917	1,062	82
Scotland	33,115	2,154	229
N. Ireland	15,374	765†	83

*There were in addition 26.1 miles of local authority motorway in England
† Including motorways and slip roads

MOTORWAYS

England and Wales:

M1	London to Yorkshire
M2	London to Faversham
M3	London to Southampton
M4	London to South Wales
M5	Birmingham to Exeter
M6	Catthorpe to Carlisle
M10	St Albans spur
M11	London to Cambridge
M18	Rotherham to Goole
M20	London to Folkestone
M23	London to Gatwick
M25	London orbital
M26	M20 to M25 spur
M27	Southampton bypass
M32	M4 to Bristol spur
M40	London to Birmingham
M41	London to West Cross
M42	South-west of Birmingham to Measham
M45	Dunchurch spur
M50	Ross spur
M53	Chester to Birkenhead
M54	M6 to Telford
M55	Preston to Blackpool
M56	Manchester to Chester
M57	Liverpool outer ring
M58	Liverpool to Wigan
M60	Manchester ring road
M61	Manchester to Preston
M62	Liverpool to Hull
M65	Calder Valley
M67	Manchester Hyde to Denton
M69	Coventry to Leicester
M180	South Humberside

Scotland:

M8	Edinburgh-Newhouse, Baillieston-West Ferry Interchange
M9	Edinburgh to Dunblane
M73	Maryville to Mollinsburn
M74	Glasgow-Gretna,
M77	Ayr Road Route
M80	Stirling to Haggs/Glasgow (M8) to Stepps
M90	Inverkeithing to Perth
M876	Dennyloanhead (M80) to Kincardine Bridge

Northern Ireland:

M1	Belfast to Dungannon
M2	Belfast to Antrim
M2	Ballymena bypass
M3	Belfast Cross Harbour Bridge
M5	M2 to Greencastle
M12	M1 to Craigavon
M22	Antrim to Randalstown

ROAD USE

ESTIMATED TRAFFIC ON ALL ROADS (GREAT BRITAIN) 1999

Million vehicle kilometres

All motor vehicles	467,100
Cars and taxis	380,300
Two-wheeled motor vehicles	4,000
Buses and coaches	5,000
Light vans	44,400
Other goods vehicles	32,800
Total goods vehicles	77,200
Pedal cycles	4,200

ROAD GOODS TRANSPORT (GREAT BRITAIN) 1999

Analysis by mode of working and by gross weight of vehicle

Estimated tonne kilometres (thousand million)	149.2
Own account	38.3
Public haulage	110.9
By gross weight of vehicle (billion tonne kilometres)	
Estimated tonnes carried (millions)	1,567.0
Own account	576.0
Public haulage	991.0
By gross weight of vehicle (million tonnes)	
Not over 25 tonnes	346.0
Over 25 tonnes	1,221.0

ROAD PASSENGER SERVICES

Until 1988 most road passenger transport services in Great Britain were provided by the public sector; the National Bus Company was the largest bus and coach operator in England and Wales and the Scottish Bus Group the largest operator in Scotland. The privatisation of the National Bus Company was completed in 1988 and that of the Scottish Bus Group in 1991. London Transport's bus operating subsidiaries were privatised by the end of 1994. Almost all bus and coach services in Great Britain are now provided by private sector companies.

Bus services outside London were deregulated in 1986, although local authorities can subsidise the provision of socially necessary services after competitive tendering. In London, Transport for London retains overall responsibility for the running of the bus network.

The largest bus operators in Great Britain are Stagecoach Holdings, FirstGroup (formerly FirstBus) and Arriva (formerly Cowie British Bus), which between them account for over 50 per cent of all bus services (by turnover). There are also 17 municipal bus companies in England and Wales, and thousands of smaller private sector operators. National Express runs a national network of coach routes, operating through a number of contractors.

In Northern Ireland, almost all passenger transport services are provided by Ulsterbus Limited and Citybus Limited, two wholly owned subsidiaries of the Northern Ireland Transport Holding Company. Along with Northern Ireland Railways, Ulsterbus and Citybus operate under the brand name of Translink and are publicly owned. Ulsterbus operates long distance, rural, town and Londonderry City bus services while Citybus provide the bulk of internal bus services in Greater Belfast. There are also 136 small private sector operators.

The transport White Paper and the subsequent 10-year transport plan intend to promote bus use, primarily through agreements between local authorities and bus operators to improve the standard and efficiency of services. The 10-year plan sets targets for bus patronage and reliability of services in England.

There are about 70,000 licensed taxis in Great Britain, of which about 20,000 are in London. There are also around 76,000 licensed private hire vehicles in England and Wales outside London, and an estimated 60,000 in London (where there has been no licensing system). The Greater London Assembly and Mayor control the licensing of taxis and private hire vehicles, through the Public Carriage Office. Licensing of private hire vehicle operators in London is in progress.

BUSES AND COACHES (GREAT BRITAIN) 1999–2000

Number of vehicles (31 March 2000)	80,000
Vehicle kilometres (millions)	4,016
Local bus passenger journeys (millions)	4,279
Passenger receipts (£ million)	4,043

510   Transport

ROAD SAFETY

The Government in 1987 set a target of reducing road traffic casualties by a third by the year 2000 compared to the average for 1981–5. Measures to achieve this were successful in reducing the number of deaths on the road by 39 per cent by 1998, and the number of serious casualties by 45 per cent. Over the same period the number of slight casualties increased by 16 per cent, but as road traffic increased by 55 per cent, the number of casualties per 100 km travelled has increased by only 1 per cent. In 1998, fatalities were reduced by 5 per cent from 1997, and all casualties decreased by 1 per cent.

In March 2000, the Government published a new road safety strategy, Tomorrow's Roads - Safer for Everyone which set new casualty reduction targets for 2010. The new targets include a 40 per cent reduction in the overall number of people killed or seriously injured in road accidents, a 50 per cent reduction in the number of children killed or seriously injured and a 10 per cent reduction in the slight casualty rate, all compared with the average for 1994-8.

The previous target was to reduce casualties by a third by 2000 compared to the average for 1981-5. Measures to achieve this were successful in reducing the number of deaths on the road by 39 per cent by 1998 and the number of seriously injured by 45 per cent. Both figures represent a 5 per cent reduction compared to 1997. The total number of casualties rose by 1 per cent taking into account a 16 per cent rise in slight casualties although this is considerably less than the 55 per cent rise in traffic between the average for 1981-9 and 1998.

ROAD ACCIDENT CASUALTIES 2000

	Fatal	Serious	Slight	All Severities
England	2,915	32,951	249,855	285,721
Wales	169	1,652	12,266	13,918
Scotland	325	3,552	16,598	20,150
Great Britain	3,409	38,155	278,719	320,283

	Killed	Injured
1965	7,952	389,985
1970	7,499	355,869
1975	6,366	318,584
1980	6,010	323,000
1985	5,165	312,359
1990	5,217	335,924
1995	3,621	306,885
1996	3,598	316,704
1997	3,599	323,945
1998	3,421	321,791
1999	3,429	316,887

Source: Department of Transport, Local Government and the Regions

DRIVING LICENCES

It is necessary to hold a valid full licence in order to drive unaccompanied on public roads in the UK. Learner drivers must obtain a provisional driving licence before starting to learn to drive and must then pass theory and practical tests to obtain a full driving licence.

There are separate tests for driving motor cycles, cars, passenger-carrying vehicles (PCVs) and large goods vehicles (LGVs). Drivers must hold full car entitlement before they can apply for PCV or LGV entitlements.

The Driver and Vehicle Licensing Agency (DVLA) no longer issues paper licenses, however, those currently in circulation will remain valid until they expire or the details on them change. The photocard driving license was introduced to comply with the second EC directive on driving licenses. This requires a photograph of the driver to be included on all UK licenses issued from July 2001. In March 2000 the DVLA ceased issuing paper licenses and over 10 million photocards have since been issued. Some 39 million people in the UK (21 million male, 18 million female) hold either a valid provisional or full driving license.

To apply for a first photocard driving license, individuals are required to complete the forms Application for a Driving License (D1) and Application for a Photocard Driving License (D 750). Application forms are available from post offices.

The minimum age for driving motor cars, light goods vehicles up to 3.5 tonnes and motor cycles is 17 (moped, 16). Since June 1997, drivers who collect six or more penalty points within two years of qualifying lose their licence and are required to take another test. A leaflet, What You Need to Know About Driving Licences (form D100), is available from post offices.

The DVLA is responsible for issuing driving licences, registering and licensing vehicles, and collecting excise duty in Great Britain. In Northern Ireland the Driver and Vehicle Licensing Agency (Northern Ireland) has similar responsibilities.

DRIVING LICENCE FEES as at 1 April 2001

First provisional licence	£27.50
Changing a provisional to a full licence after passing a driving test	£12.50
Renewal of licence	£6.00
Renewal of licence including PCV or LGV entitlements	£32.50
Renewal after disqualification	£27.50
Renewal after drinking and driving disqualification	£37.50
Medical renewal	Free
Medical renewal (over 70)	Free
Duplicate Licence	£17.50
Exchange licence	£17.50
Removing endorsements	£17.50
Replacement (change of name or address)	Free

DRIVING TESTS

The Driving Standards Agency is responsible for carrying out driving tests and approving driving instructors in Great Britain. In Northern Ireland the Driver and Vehicle Testing Agency (Northern Ireland) is responsible for testing drivers and vehicles.

In 1999-2000, almost 1.2 million driving tests, nearly 55,500 vocational tests (lorries and buses) and over 96,500 motorcycle tests were conducted in Great Britain. In the same period, 1.1 million theory tests were conducted. In 1998–9, almost 1.2 million car driving tests were conducted in Great Britain of which 45.9 per cent resulted in a pass. In addition over 49,000 lorry tests were undertaken, of which 51.9 per cent were successful. 83,000 motorcycle tests were undertaken, of which 67.9 per cent were successful. There were more than 7,600 bus tests, with a pass rate of 47.8 per cent. In the same period, 1.2 million theory tests were conducted. A new, longer driving test was introduced on 4 May 1999.

Since 1 March 1997 driving test candidates have been required to produce photographic confirmation of their identity.

*DRIVING TEST FEES (weekday rate/evening and Saturday rate) as at 1 July 2001

For cars	£36.75/£46
†For motor cycles	£45/£55
For lorries, buses	£73.50/£92

*Since 1 July 1996 most candidates for car and motor cycle tests have also been required to take a written driving theory test, for which there is a separate fee of £15.50. Theory tests for lorry and bus drivers were introduced on 1 January 1997

†Before riding on public roads, learner motor cyclists and learner moped riders are required to have completed Compulsory Basic Training, provided by DSA-approved training bodies. The Compulsory Basic Training certificate costs £8.00. All exemptions from CBT were removed on 1 January 1997

An extended driving test was introduced in 1992 for those convicted of dangerous driving. The fee is £73.50/£92 (car) or £90/£110 (motorcycle).

MOTOR VEHICLES

Vehicles must be licensed by the DVLA or the DVLNI before they can be driven on public roads. They must also be approved as roadworthy by the Vehicle Certification Agency. The Vehicle Inspectorate carries out annual testing and inspection of goods vehicles, buses and coaches.

There were approximately 27 million vehicles registered at the DVLA at March 2001: (approximate figures)

Private and light goods	23,900,000
Motor cycles, scooters, mopeds	800,000
Coaches and buses	83,500
Large goods vehicles	450,000
Electric vehicles	10,200
Others	1,750,000
TOTAL:	27,000,000

Source: DVLA

VEHICLE LICENCES

Registration and first licensing of vehicles is through local offices of the Driver and Vehicle Licensing Agency in Swansea. Local facilities for relicensing are available at any post office which deals with vehicle licensing. Applicants will need to take their vehicle registration document; if this is not available the applicant must complete form V62 which is held at post offices. Postal applications can be made to the post offices shown on form V100, available at any post office. This form also provides guidance on registering and licensing vehicles.

Details of the present duties chargeable on motor vehicles are available at post offices and Vehicle Registration Offices. The Vehicle Excise and Registration Act 1994 provides *inter alia* that any vehicle kept on a public road but not used on roads is chargeable to excise duty as if it were in use. All non-commercial vehicles constructed before 1 January 1973 are exempt from vehicle excise duty.

VEHICLE EXCISE DUTY RATES *from 1 July 2001*
REGISTERED BEFORE 1 MARCH 2001

	Twelve months £	Six Months £
Motor Cars		
Light vans, cars, taxis, etc.		
Under 1549cc	105.00	57.75
Over 1549cc	160.00	88.00
Motor Cycles		
With or without sidecar, not over 150 cc	15.00	—
With or without sidecar, 150–250 cc	40.00	—
Others	65.00	35.75
Electric motorcycles (including tricycles)	15.00	—
Tricycles (not over 450 kg)		
Not over 150 cc	15.00	—
Others	65.00	35.75

*Buses**

Seating 9–16 persons	165.00	90.75
	(160.00)	(88.00)
Seating 17–35 persons	220.00	121.00
	(160.00)	(88.00)
Seating 36–60 persons	330.00	181.00
	(160.00)	(88.00)
Seating over 60 persons	500.00	275.00
	(160.00)	(88.00)

* Figures in parentheses refer to reduced pollution vehicles.

REGISTERED ON OR AFTER 1 MARCH 2001

Band	CO_2 Emissions (g/km)	Diesel Car 12 month rate £	6 month rate £
A	Up to 150	110.00	60.50
B	151-165	130.00	71.50
C	166-185	150.00	82.50
D	Over 185	160.00	88.00

Petrol Car 12 month rate £	6 month rate £	Alternative Fuel Car 12 month rate £	6 month rate £
100.00	55.00	90.00	49.50
120.00	66.00	110.00	60.50
140.00	77.00	130.00	71.50
155.00	85.25	150.00	82.50

MoT TESTING

Cars, motor cycles, motor caravans, light goods and dual-purpose vehicles more than three years old must be covered by a current MoT test certificate. However, some vehicles i.e. minibuses may require a certificate at one year old. All certificates must be renewed annually. The MoT testing scheme is administered by the Vehicle Inspectorate on behalf of the Secretary of State for Transport.

A fee is payable to MoT testing stations, which must be authorised to carry out tests. The maximum fees, which are prescribed by regulations, are:

For cars and light vans	£34.00
For solo motor cycles	£13.70
For motor cycle combinations	£22.70
For three-wheeled vehicles	£24.60
Private passenger vehicles and ambulance Including seat-belt installation check	
With 9-12 passenger seats	£36.90 £40.75*
13-16 passenger seats	£41.70 £50.60*
Over 16 passenger seats	£54.15 £80.80*
For light goods vehicles between 3,000 and 3,500 kg	£35.75

* including seatbelt installation check

METHOD OF TRAVEL TO WORK, *Great Britain* (*percentage**)

	1993	1997
Car, van, minibus, works van	68	71
Bus, coach, private bus	9	8
Train (incl. Underground and light rail)	5	6
Walk	12	11
Other	5	5
All	100	100

* All figures are rounded

Source: DETR/The Stationery Office – *Focus on Personal Travel 1998* (Crown copyright)

SHIPPING AND PORTS

Since earliest times sea trade has played a central role in Britain's economy. By the 17th century Britain had built up a substantial merchant fleet and by the early 20th century it dominated the world shipping industry. In recent years the size and tonnage of the UK-registered trading fleet have declined; the UK-flagged merchant fleet now constitutes about 1 per cent of the world fleet. In December 1998 the Government published a document, *British Shipping: Charting a New Course*, which outlined strategies to promote the long-term interests of British shipping.

Freight is carried by liner and bulk services, almost all scheduled liner services being containerised. About 95 per cent by weight of Britain's overseas trade is carried by sea; this amounts to 75 per cent of its total value. Passengers and vehicles are carried by roll-on, roll-off ferries, hovercraft, hydrofoils and high-speed catamarans. There are about 53 million ferry passengers a year, of whom 32 million travel internationally. The leading British operators of passenger services are P&O Stena, Stena Line (which has a Swedish parent company) and P&O European Ferries.

Lloyd's of London provides the most comprehensive shipping intelligence service in the world. *Lloyd's Shipping Index*, published daily, lists some 25,000 ocean-going vessels and gives the latest known report of each.

PORTS

There are about 70 commercially significant ports in Great Britain, including such ports as London, Dover, Forth, Tees and Hartlepool, Grimsby and Immingham, Sullom Voe, Milford Haven, Southampton, Felixstowe and Liverpool. Belfast is the principal freight port in Northern Ireland.

Broadly speaking, ports are owned and operated by private companies, local authorities or trusts. The largest operator is Associated British Ports (formerly the British Transport Docks Board, privatised in 1981), which owns 23 ports. Total traffic through UK ports in 2000 amounted to 577 million tonnes, an increase of 2 per cent on the previous year's figure of 566 million tonnes.

MARINE SAFETY

By 1 October 2002 all roll-on, roll-off ferries operating to and from the UK will be required to meet the new international safety standards on stability established by the Stockholm Agreement.

The Maritime and Coastguard Agency (MCA) was established on 1 April 1998 by the merger of the Coastguard Agency and the Marine Safety Agency. It is an executive agency of the Department for Transport, Local Government and the Regions. The Agency's aims are to minimise loss of life amongst seafarers and coastal users, respond to maritime emergencies 24 hours a day, develop, promote and enforce high standards of marine safety and to minimise the risk of pollution of the marine environment from ships and where pollution occurs, minimise the impact on UK interests. Each year HM Coastguard co-ordinate Search and Rescue for around 11,000 incidents saving around 250 lives.   Locations hazardous to shipping in coastal waters are marked by lighthouses and other lights and buoys. The lighthouse authorities are the Corporation of Trinity House (for England, Wales and the Channel Islands), the Northern Lighthouse Board (for Scotland and the Isle of Man), and the Commissioners of Irish Lights (for Northern Ireland

and the Republic of Ireland). Trinity House maintains 72 lighthouses, 13 major floating aids to navigation and more than 429 buoys; and the Northern Lighthouse Board 84 lighthouses, 116 minor lights and many buoys.

Harbour authorities are responsible for pilotage within their harbour areas; and the Ports Act 1991 provides for the transfer of lights and buoys to harbour authorities where these are used for mainly local navigation.

UK-REGISTERED TRADING VESSELS OF 500 GROSS TONS AND OVER *as at end 1999*

Type of vessel	No.	Gross tonnage
Tankers[1]	67	552,000
Bulk carriers[2]	3	29,000
Specialised carriers[3]	10	54,000
Container (fully cellular)[4]	32	1,151,000
Ro-Ro[5]	78	937,000
Other general cargo[6]	63	85,000
Passenger[7]	11	363,000
TOTAL	264	3,171,000

[1] Includes oil, gas, chemical and other specialised tankers
[2] Includes combination bulk carriers: ore/oil and ore/bulk/oil carriers
[3] Includes livestock, car and chemical carriers
[4] Fully cellular container ships only.
[5] Ro-Ro passenger and cargo vessels
[6] Reefer vessels, general cargo/passenger vessels, and single and multi-deck general cargo vessels.
[7] Cruise liner and other passenger

Source: The Department of Transport, Local Government and the Regions

PASSENGER MOVEMENT BY SEA 1999

Arrivals plus departures at UK seaports by place of embarkation or landing*

All passenger movements	31,382,000
Irish Republic	4,343,000
Belgium	1,592,000
France†	22,454,000
Netherlands	1,939,000
Other EU countries	843,000
Other European and Mediterranean countries‡	211,000

* Passengers are included at both departure and arrival if their journeys begin and end at a UK seaport
† Includes hovercraft passengers
‡ Includes North Africa and Middle East Mediterranean countries

Source: The The Department of Transport, Local Government and the Regions

Communications

Postal Services

On the 26 March 2001 the Post Office became a public limited company and adopted a new name, Consignia plc. Responsibility for running postal services in the UK remains with Consignia. While the company has signalled its eagerness to expand into the global market, domestic services including Royal Mail, Parcelforce and the local branches of the Post Office remain unchanged. An independent postal services regulator, The Postal Services Commission (Postcomm), has been appointed by the Government to oversee Consignia's operation. The Secretary of State for Trade and Industry has powers to suspend Consignia's letter monopoly in certain areas and to issue licences to other bodies to provide an alternative service.

For further details please contact the relevant service provider, i.e Royal Mail or Parcelforce. For a quick reference guide to the price of postal services consult the Royal Mail's postal calculator at www.royalmail.com.

INLAND POSTAL SERVICES AND REGULATIONS

INLAND LETTER POST RATES*

Not over	1st class†	2nd class†
60 g	27p	19p
100 g	41p	33p
150 g	57p	44p
200 g	72p	54p
250 g	84p	66p
300 g	96p	76p
350 g	£1.09	87p
400 g	£1.24	£1.00
450 g	£1.41	£1.14
500 g	£1.58	£1.30
600 g	£1.90	£1.52
700 g	£2.39	£1.74
750 g	£2.56	£1.85 (not
800 g	£2.77	Admissible
900 g	£3.05	over 750 g)
1,000 g	£3.32	
Each extra 250 g or part thereof	81p	

UK PARCEL RATES

Parcel Force Standard Tariff

Not over	
1 kg	£3.10
2 kg	£4.30
4 kg	£6.50
6 kg	£7.05
8 kg	£8.05
10 kg	£8.65

*Postcards travel at the same rates as letter post
† First class letters are normally delivered the following day and second class post within three days

OVERSEAS SURFACE MAIL RATES

Letters

Not over		Not over	
20 g	36p	450 g	£3.14
60 g	58p	500 g	£3.47
100 g	83p	750 g	£5.12
150 g	£1.16	1,000 g	£6.77
200 g	£1.49	1,250 g	£8.42
250 g	£1.82	1,500 g	£10.07
300 g	£2.15	1,750 g	£11.72
350 g	£2.48	2,000 g	£13.77
400 g	£2.81		

Postcards travel at 20 g letter rate

AIRMAIL LETTER RATES

Europe: Letters

Not over		Not over	
20 g	36p	280 g	£2.30
40 g	50p	300 g	£2.45
60 g	65p	320 g	£2.60
80 g	80p	340 g	£2.75
100 g	95p	360 g	£2.90
120 g	£1.10	380 g	£3.05
140 g	£1.25	400 g	£3.20
160 g	£1.40	420 g	£3.35
180 g	£1.55	440 g	£3.50
200 g	£1.70	460 g	£3.65
220 g	£1.85	480 g	£3.80
240 g	£2.00	500 g	£3.95
260 g	£2.15	1,000 g	£7.70
		*2,000 g	£15.20

* Max. 2 kg
Postcards to Europe travel at 20 g letter rate

Outside Europe: Letters

	Not over 10 g	Not over 20 g	Over 20 g
Zones 1 & 2	45p	65p	Varies

For airmail letter zones outside Europe, see pages 515-7

STAMPS

Postage stamps are sold in values of 1p, 2p, 4p, 5p, 8p, 10p, 19p, 20p, 27p, 33p, 41p, 45p, 50p, 65p, £1, £2.00, £3.00 and £5.00.

PREPAID STATIONERY

Airletters to all destinations are 40p, with a packet of six costing £2.20. Pictorial aerogrammes are 49p; a packet of six, £2.70. Forces aerogrammes are free to certain destinations.

Special Delivery prepaid envelopes:

Not over	
500 g (C4 and C5 size)	£3.80
1 kg	£4.95

Printed postage stamps cut from envelopes, postcards, newspaper wrappers, etc., may be used as stamps in payment of postage, provided that they are not imperfect or defaced.

RESTRICTIONS

Advice at to what articles may not be sent through the post is available from Royal Mail (Tel: 08457-950950) for letters and small packets; Parcelforce (Tel: 0800-224466) for parcels; or local post office counter staff.

The exportation of some goods by post is prohibited except under Department of Trade licence. Enquiries should be addressed to the Export Data Branch, Overseas Trade Divisions, Department of Trade and Industry, 1 Victoria Street, London SW1H 0ET Tel: 020-7215 5000.

SPECIAL DELIVERY SERVICES

DATAPOST

A guaranteed service for the delivery of documents and packages: (i) Datapost Sameday offers same working day collection and delivery in many areas; (ii) Datapost 10 (for delivery before 10 a.m.) and Datapost 12 (for delivery before noon) offer next working day delivery nationwide and are available only to certain destinations.

ROYAL MAIL SPECIAL DELIVERY

A guaranteed next working day delivery service by 12.00 p.m. to most UK destinations for first class letters and packets. The fee is £3.50. Compensation of up to £250 can be awarded for an item if next working day delivery is not achieved, provided that items are posted before latest recommended posting times. Details of other compensation levels can be obtained by telephoning 08457-950950.

SWIFTAIR

An express airmail service. Items are placed on the first available flight to the destination country. Although Swiftair mail receives priority treatment, delivery times are not guaranteed.

OTHER SERVICES

CERTIFICATE OF POSTING

Issued free on request at time of posting.

COMPENSATION (INLAND AND INTERNATIONAL)

Inland: compensation up to a maximum of £27 may be paid where it can be shown that a letter was damaged or lost in the post due to the fault of the Post Office, its employees or agents. The Post Office does not accept responsibility for loss or damage arising from faulty packing.

International: if a certificate of posting is produced, compensation up to a maximum of £27 may be given for loss or damage in the UK to uninsured parcels to or from most overseas countries. No compensation will be paid for any loss or damage due to the action of the Queen's Enemies.

NEWSPAPER POST

Copies of newspapers registered at the Post Office may be posted only by the publisher or their agents in open-ended wrappers or unsealed envelopes approved by the Post Office, or tied with string removable without cutting. Wrappers and envelopes must be prominently marked 'newspaper post' in the top left-hand corner.

POSTE RESTANTE

Poste Restante is solely for travellers and is for three months in any one town. A packet may be addressed to any post office, except town sub-offices, and should state 'Poste Restante' or 'to be called for' in the address. Redirection from a Poste Restante is undertaken for up to three months. Letters for an expected ship at a port are kept for two months, otherwise letters are kept for two weeks, or one month if from abroad.

PRIVATE BOX

Provides an alternative address (e.g. PO Box 123) and mail is held at the local delivery office for collection.

RECORDED MAIL

Provides a record of posting and delivery of letters and ensures a signature on delivery. This service is recommended for items of little or no monetary value. All packets must be handed to the post office and a certificate of posting issued. Charges: 63p plus postage (inland); £2.60 plus postage (international).

REDIRECTION

By agent of addressee: mail other than parcels, business reply and freepost items may be reposted free not later than the day after delivery (not counting Sundays and public holidays) if unopened and if original addressee's name is unobscured. Parcels may be redirected free within the same time limits only if the original and substituted address are in the same local parcel delivery area (or the London postal area). Registered packets must be taken to a post office and re-registered free up to the day after delivery.

By the Post Office: a printed form obtainable from the Post Office must be signed by the person to whom the letters are to be addressed. A fee is payable for each different surname on the application form. Charges: up to 1 calendar month, £6.30 (abroad via airmail, £12.60); up to 3 calendar months, £13.65 (£27.30); up to 12 calendar months, £31.50 (£63.00).

REGISTERED MAIL (INTERNATIONAL)

All packets must be handed to the post office and a certificate of posting obtained. Charges (plus postage):

Compensation up to	*Registered fee plus postage*
£500	£3.15

Compensation in respect of currency or other forms of monetary worth is given only if money is sent by registered letter post. Compensation is only paid for well-packed fragile articles and not for exceptionally fragile or perishable articles.

SMALL PACKETS POST AND PRINTED PAPERS (INTERNATIONAL)

Permits the transmission of goods up to 2 kg to all countries, in the same mails as printed papers. Packets can be sealed and can contain personal correspondence relating to the contents. Registration is allowed as insurance as long as the item is packed in a way complying with any insurance regulations. A customs declaration is required and the packet must be marked with 'small packet' and a return address. Instructions for the disposal of undelivered packets must be given at the time of posting. An undeliverable packet will be returned to the sender at his/her expense.

Surface mail: worldwide

Not over		Not over	
100 g	57p	450 g	£1.90
150 g	76p	500 g	£2.09
200 g	95p	750 g	£3.04
250 g	£1.14	1,000 g	£3.99
300 g	£1.33	1,500 g	£5.89
350 g	£1.52	2,000 g	£7.79
400 g	£1.71		

UNDELIVERED AND UNPAID MAIL

Undelivered mail is returned to the sender provided the return address is indicated either on the outside of the envelope or inside. If the sender's address is not available items not containing property are destroyed.

If the packet contains something of value it is retained for up to three months. Undeliverable second class mail containing newspapers, magazines or commercial advertising is destroyed.

Airmail and IDD Codes

AIRMAIL ZONES (AZ)

The table includes airmail letter zones for countries outside Europe, and destinations to which European and European Union airmail letter rates apply (*see also* page 513).
(*Source:* Post Office)
1   airmail zone 1
2   airmail zone 2
e   Europe

INTERNATIONAL DIRECT DIALLING (IDD)

International dialling codes are composed of four elements which are dialled in sequence:
(i)   the international code
(ii)   the country code (*see* below)
(iii)   the area code
(iv)   the customer's telephone number

Calls to some countries must be made via the international operator. (*Source:* BT)
p   A pause in dialling is necessary whilst waiting for a second tone
*   Varies in some areas
**   Varies depending on carrier

Country	AZ	IDD from UK	IDD to UK
Afghanistan	1	00 93	00 44
Albania	e	00 355	00 44
Algeria	1	00 213	00p44
Andorra	e	00 376	00 44
Angola	1	00 244	00 44
Anguilla	1	00 1 264	011 44
Antigua and Barbuda	1	00 1 268	011 44
Argentina	1	00 54	00 44
Armenia	e	00 374	810 44
Aruba	1	00 297	00 44
Ascension Island	1	00 247	00 44
Australia	2	00 61	00 11 44
Austria	e	00 43	00 44
Azerbaijan	e	00 994	810 44
Azores	e	00 351	00 44
Bahamas	1	00 1 242	011 44
Bahrain	1	00 973	0 44
Bangladesh	1	00 880	00 44
Barbados	1	00 1 246	011 44
Belarus	e	00 375	810 44
Belgium	e	00 32	00 44
Belize	1	00 501	00 44
Benin	1	00 229	00p44
Bermuda	1	00 1 441	011 44
Bhutan	1	00 975	00 44
Bolivia	1	00 591	00 44
Bosnia-Hercegovina	e		
Muslim-Croat Federation		00 387	00 44
Republika Srpska		00 381	00 44
Botswana	1	00 267	00 44
Brazil	1	00 55	00 44
British Virgin Islands	1	00 1 284	011 44

Country	AZ	IDD from UK	IDD to UK
Brunei	1	00 673	00 44
Bulgaria	e	00 359	00 44
Burkina Faso	1	00 226	00 44
Burundi	1	00 257	90 44
Cambodia	1	00 855	00 44
Cameroon	1	00 237	00 44
Canada	1	00 1	011 44
Canary Islands	e	00 34	00 44
Cape Verde	1	00 238	0 44
Cayman Islands	1	00 1 345	011 44
Central African Republic	1	00 236	19 44
Chad	1	00 235	15 44
Chile	1	00 56	00 44
China	2	00 86	00 44
Hong Kong	1	00 852	001 44
Macao	1	00 853	00 44
Colombia	1	00 57	009 44
Comoros	1	00 269	00 44
Congo, Dem. Rep. of	1	00 243	00 44
Congo, Republic of	1	00 242	00 44
Cook Islands	2	00 682	00 44
Costa Rica	1	00 506	00 44
Côte d'Ivoire	1	00 225	00 44
Croatia	e	00 385	00 44
Cuba	1	00 53	119 44
Cyprus	e	00 357	00 44
Czech Republic	e	00 420	00 44
Denmark	e	00 45	00 44
Djibouti	1	00 253	00 44
Dominica	1	00 1 767	011 44
Dominican Republic	1	00 1 809	011 44
Ecuador	1	00 593	00 44
Egypt	1	00 20	00 44
Equatorial Guinea	1	00 240	00 44
Eritrea	1	00 291	00 44
Estonia	e	00 372	800 44
Ethiopia	1	00 251	00 44
Falkland Islands	1	00 500	0 44
Faroe Islands	e	00 298	009 44
Fiji	2	00 679	05 44
Finland	e	00 358	00 44**
France	e	00 33	00 44
French Guiana	1	00 594	00 44
French Polynesia	2	00 689	00 44
Gabon	1	00 241	00 44
The Gambia	1	00 220	00 44
Georgia	e	00 995	810 44
Germany	e	00 49	00 44
Ghana	1	00 233	00 44
Gibraltar	e	00 350	00 44
Greece	e	00 30	00 44
Greenland	e	00 299	009 44
Grenada	1	00 1 473	011 44
Guadeloupe	1	00 590	00 44
Guam	2	00 1 671	001 44
Guatemala	1	00 502	00 44
Guinea	1	00 224	00 44
Guinea-Bissau	1	00 245	099 44
Guyana	1	00 592	001 44
Haiti	1	00 509	00 44

Country	AZ	IDD from UK	IDD to UK
Honduras	1	00 504	00 44
Hungary	e	00 36	00 44
Iceland	e	00 354	00 44
India	1	00 91	00 44
Indonesia	1	00 62	001 44** / 00844**
Iran	1	00 98	00 44
Iraq	1	00 964	00 44
Ireland, Republic of	e	00 353	00 44
Israel	1	00 972	00 44**
Italy	e	00 39	00 44
Jamaica	1	00 1 876	011 44
Japan	2	00 81	001 44** / 004144** / 006144**
Jordan	1	00 962	00 44*
Kazakhstan	e	00 7	810 44
Kenya	1	00 254	00 44
Kiribati	2	00 686	00 44
Korea, North	2	00 850	00 44
Korea, South	2	00 82	001 44** / 00244**
Kuwait	1	00 965	00 44
Kyrgystan	e	00 996	00 44
Laos	1	00 856	00 44
Latvia	e	00 371	00 44
Lebanon	1	00 961	00 44
Lesotho	1	00 266	00 44
Liberia	1	00 231	00 44
Libya	1	00 218	00 44
Liechtenstein	e	00 423	00 44
Lithuania	e	00 370	810 44
Luxembourg	e	00 352	00 44
Macedonia	e	00 389	99 44
Madagascar	1	00 261	00 44
Madeira	e	00 351 91	00 44*
Malawi	1	00 265	101 44
Malaysia	1	00 60	00 44
Maldives	1	00 960	00 44
Mali	1	00 223	00 44
Malta	e	00 356	00 44
Mariana Islands, Northern	2	00 1 670	011 44
Marshall Islands	2	00 692	011 44
Martinique	1	00 596	00 44
Mauritania	1	00 222	00 44
Mauritius	1	00 230	00 44
Mayotte	1	00 269	10 44
Mexico	1	00 52	98 44
Micronesia, Federated States of	2	00 691	011 44
Moldova	e	00 373	810 44
Monaco	e	00 377	00 44
Mongolia	2	00 976	00 44
Montenegro	e	00 381	99 44
Montserrat	1	00 1 664	011 44
Morocco	1	00 212	00p44
Mozambique	1	00 258	00 44
Myanmar	1	00 95	00 44
Namibia	1	00 264	00 44
Nauru	2	00 674	00 44
Nepal	1	00 977	00 44
Netherlands	e	00 31	00 44
Netherlands Antilles	1	00 599	00 44
New Caledonia	2	00 687	00 44
New Zealand	2	00 64	00 44
Nicaragua	1	00 505	00 44
Niger	1	00 227	00 44

Country	AZ	IDD from UK	IDD to UK
Nigeria	1	00 234	009 44
Niue	2	00 683	00 44
Norfolk Island	2	00 672	0101 44
Norway	e	00 47	00 44
Oman	1	00 968	00 44
Pakistan	1	00 92	00 44
Palau	2	00 680	011 44
Panama	1	00 507	00 44
Papua New Guinea	2	00 675	05 44
Paraguay	1	00 595	00 44** / 003 44**
Peru	1	00 51	00 44
Philippines	2	00 63	00 44
Poland	e	00 48	00 44
Portugal	e	00 351	00 44
Puerto Rico	1	00 1 787	011 44
Qatar	1	00 974	00 44
Réunion	1	00 262	00 44
Romania	e	00 40	00 44
Russia	e	00 7	810 44
Rwanda	1	00 250	00 44
St Christopher and Nevis	1	00 1 869	011 44
St Helena	1	00 290	0 44
St Lucia	1	00 1 758	011 44
St Pierre and Miquelon	1	00 508	00 44
St Vincent and the Grenadines	1	00 1 784	001 44
El Salvador	1	00 503	0 44
Samoa	2	00 685	0 44
Samoa, American	2	00 684	00 44
San Marino	e	00 378	00 44
São Tomé and Príncipe	1	00 239	00 44
Saudi Arabia	1	00 966	00 44
Senegal	1	00 221	00p44
Serbia	e	00 381	99 44
Seychelles	1	00 248	00 44
Sierra Leone	1	00 232	00 44
Singapore	1	00 65	001 44
Slovak Republic	e	00 421	00 44
Slovenia	e	00 386	00 44
Solomon Islands	2	00 677	00 44
Somalia	1	00 252	16 44
South Africa	1	00 27	09 44
Spain	e	00 34	00 44
Sri Lanka	1	00 94	00 44
Sudan	1	00 249	00 44
Suriname	1	00 597	00 44
Swaziland	1	00 268	00 44
Sweden	e	00 46	007 44** / 00944** / 008744**
Switzerland	e	00 41	00 44
Syria	1	00 963	00 44
Taiwan	2	00 886	002 44
Tajikistan	e	00 7	810 44
Tanzania	1	00 255	00 44
Thailand	1	00 66	001 44
Tibet	1	00 86	00 44
Togo	1	00 228	00 44
Tonga	2	00 676	00 44
Trinidad and Tobago	1	00 1 868	011 44
Tristan da Cunha	1	00 2 897	‡
Tunisia	1	00 216	00 44
Turkey	e	00 90	00 44
Turkmenistan	e	00 993	810 44
Turks and Caicos Islands	1	00 1 649	0 44

Country	AZ	IDD from UK	IDD to UK
Tuvalu	2	00 688	00 44
Uganda	1	00 256	00 44
Ukraine	e	00 380	810 44
United Arab Emirates	1	00 971	00 44
Uruguay	1	00 598	00 44
USA	1	00 1	011 44
Alaska		00 1 907	011 44
Hawaii		00 1 808	011 44
Uzbekistan	e	00 998	810 44

Country	AZ	IDD from UK	IDD to UK
Vanuatu	2	00 678	00 44
Vatican City State	e	00 390 66982	00 44
Venezuela	1	00 58	00 44
Vietnam	1	00 84	00 44
Virgin Islands (US)	1	00 1 340	011 44
Yemen	1	00 967	00 44
Yugoslav Fed. Rep.	e	00 381	99 44
Zambia	1	00 260	00 44
Zimbabwe	1	00 263	00 44

The UK Mobile Communications Industry

General Introduction

The UK's mobile market has historically been among the most mature of the world's mobile markets. Liberalisation was introduced early and competition has been actively encouraged by a progressive regulator. The UK now boasts one of the world's most competitive markets with a range of services offered through a number of forward-thinking suppliers.

REGULATION

The Regulator is responsible for setting the controls for the UK mobile market and ensuring that none of the industry players indulge in anti-competitive behaviour.

The two government bodies covering the regulation of the mobile industry in the UK are the Radiocommunications Agency and Oftel. The Radiocommunications Agency is part of the Department of Trade and Industry (DTI) and is responsible for radio frequency allocation. The greater part of regulation falls under the jurisdiction of Oftel. Oftel was created by the 1984 Telecommunications Act and empowered to ensure competition in the UK market. It was therefore given authority over licensing procedures, tariffing, interconnection (where one operator has access to another's infrastructure) as well as acting as an arbitrator between operators in disputes. Oftel has authority over the UK's other communications sectors as well.

The policies adopted and enforced by Oftel are largely driven by the European Commission (with the support of the Parliament and Council of Ministers). This follows the European Court of Justice's ruling allowing the European Commission to apply the competition rules of the Treaty of Rome to telecommunications (in 1985). This ruling also prompted the formation of DGXIII (Telecommunications, Information Industries and Innovation) in 1986.

In general policy has been aimed at providing access to networks and public services and guarantee harmonised, objective, transparent and non-discriminatory conditions based on the so called 'Open Network Provision' (ONP) principles which endeavour to ensure fair competition and access for new entrants. Among other things that have impacted on the mobile industry, the Commission has addressed:

- *Universal Service*
  This is the stipulation by which services must be provided to all customers irrespective of their location. New entrants often have to contribute to the cost of universal service provision. In the UK in 1996, the government and the EU agreed to offer grants to Vodafone and BT Cellnet to extend their mobile telephony coverage to sparsely populated areas of Scotland.

- *Number Portability*
  This allows the customer to keep his or her telephone number even if they change service provider so the telephone number is seen to belong to the customer not the service provider. Number portability was introduced to the UK's fixed line communications industry in June 1997 and to the mobile industry in January 1999.

- *Licensing*
  The provision of and requirements of the licensing process.

- *Incumbent's Tariffs*
  This provision is to stop incumbent operators abusing their positions as providers of both local, national and long distance services by cross-subsidising one with another.

In the UK the two major pieces of legislation that have shaped the communications industry are the 1981 and the 1984 Telecommunications Acts. The former divided the General Post Office (which prior to this had provided both telecommunications and postal services) into British Telecommunications and the Post Office and made provision for the introduction of competition. The latter established BT as a public limited company and created Oftel as the industry watchdog.

Since its creation, Oftel has licensed hundreds of companies to compete in the various sectors of the UK communications industry. These licenses are divided into the following four categories:

- PTO or Public Telecommunications Operator (a total of 39 licensed to date)
- IFS or International Facilities Based Service Provider (110 licensed to date)
- ISVR or International Simple Voice Reseller (179 licensed to date)
- Satellite Services Provider (36 licensed to date)

It must be noted that not all these licenses are current, some operators may have ceased to exist or may never have begun operations.

PTOs can provide either fixed or mobile services and will own their network (the physical infrastructure over which the call is routed). IFS providers also own infrastructure although this is limited by the nature of the services they offer i.e. international calls only. ISR providers do not own any infrastructure but buy capacity from other operators. Finally, as the name suggests, Satellite Services Providers offer satellite-based services.

Much of the early regulation of the UK telecommunications industry was concerned with the promotion of competition and since this has by and large been achieved in most of the sectors covered by Oftel, the regulator has announced that it intends to take a much 'softer' approach in the future. In light of this, Oftel's activities can now broadly be described as:

- Continuing to review its current customer protection policies to promote the interests of consumers
- Policing the regulation of licenses
- Conducting separate twice yearly reviews of each sector – fixed, mobile, Internet access and interactive broadcasting – to monitor for anti-competitive behaviour, excessive profits and market share

Oftel's three directorates – Regulatory Policy, Compliance and Business Support – conduct these activities. The Regulatory Policy Directorate is responsible for developing telecommunications policies. The Compliance Directorate makes sure phone companies meet the obligations of their licenses and existing telecoms regulations. Finally, the Business Support Directorate supports the entire organisation.

One aspect of the mobile sector which is currently not covered by Oftel regulation is mobile Internet access.

INDUSTRY PLAYERS

The provision of mobile services in the UK is offered through Network Operators, Service Providers and MVNOs.

The Network Operator owns the license to provide cellular services as well as the physical network. Network operators are responsible for billing and maintaining the networks, can set tariffs and have a direct billing relationship with the end users. There are currently four Network Operators in the UK (*see table below*).

The Service Providers were introduced into the UK market at the very beginning when their role was to increase competition within the market. They buy airtime wholesale from the network operators and sell it onto the end users. This agreement means that they can set their own tariff structures and they have a billing relationship with the end users.

The incumbent operators (those who have been operating since the start) BT Cellnet and Vodafone, have an obligation under the terms of their licenses to offer wholesale minutes of airtime to Service Providers. The next two entrants Orange and One2One were never obliged to offer this and although this came up for review in April 1998, both these operators were considered at this time to have insignificant market share. There are around 50 Service Providers still operating in the market including One.Tel, Sainsbury's, Sony Cellular Services and Martin Dawes. In order to maintain a viable business operation, many of these Service Providers have diversified their product offer away from pure mobile service offering to other telecom or Internet-based services.

Finally, the newest entrants to the market are MVNOs, Mobile Virtual Network Operators. Unlike the Service Providers there is no obligation for the Network operators to open their networks to MVNOs rather it is an entirely commercial agreement where the Network Operator allows the MVNO access to their network. This differs from the Service Provider in that a true MVNO that has its own mobile network code, issues its own SIM cards (Subscriber Identity Module card – the 'brain' of the handset), operates its own mobile switching centre and has a pricing structure fully independent from the network operator. As these are commercial agreements there are as yet no regulations covering MVNOs, but, as with mobile Internet access, the regulator is currently observing development closely and may step in as MVNOs become

a more important force. To date, the most successful MVNO is Virgin which operates on the One2One network although others are emerging including Energis (operating on the Orange network) and Carphone Warehouse which claims to operate on all four networks.

CURRENT MOBILE MARKET

Operator	Ownership	Technology	Launch Date
BT Cellnet	100% BT	Tacs-900	January 1985
		GSM	January 1994
Vodafone	100% Vodafone AirTouch	Tacs-900	January 1985
		GSM	July 1992
One2One	100% Deutsche Telekom	GSM 1800	September 1993
Orange	100% France Telecom	GSM 1800	April 1994
Hutchison 3G	65% Hutchison Whampoa, 20% DoCoMo & 15% KPN	UMTS	To begin operations 2002

MARKET SHARE

	BT Cellnet	Vodafone	One2One	Orange
Current Subscriber Base	11,158,000	12,279,000	8,981,000	11,030,000
Total Market Share	25.7%	28.3%	20.7%	25.3%

SUBSCRIBER GROWTH

Date	Jan 1997	Jan 1998	Jan 1999	Jan 2000	Mar 2001
Subscriber Base	6,810,000	8,344,000	13,001,000	23,944,000	43,448,000
Penetration Rate	11.7%	14.3%	22.3%	41%	73.8%

Subscriber growth in the UK has been driven by a number of factors. The most important of these are

- Promotion of prepaid services
- Subsidised handsets
- Number portability

PREPAID SERVICES

There are two methods of paying for mobile services in the UK, monthly contracts or pre-paid cards. With monthly contracts, the end user pays a fixed subscription fee each month which entitles them to a number of basic services (for example voicemail) and gives them a certain amount of 'airtime' each month. Prepaid subscribers have access to the same services but pay in advance. Initially this allowed industry players to target additional consumer groups in particular the youth market and those people who would normally not pass the credit checks necessary for a contract. It has proved to be a very popular option as it allows people to control their spend and is a low entry cost method to mobile services.

NUMBER PORTABILITY

All UK operators have been obliged to provide number portability since the beginning of 1999. This means that any end user who wishes to change Network Operator (or service provider) must be given the option of retaining their existing number i.e. taking their mobile number with them to the new service provider. This was considered to be a barrier to competition. The regulator is currently looking at how the administrative system for number portability can be improved in order to enforce this obligation.

TECHNOLOGY

Services were introduced to the UK in 1985 using an analogue technology called TACS. In 1992 Vodafone launched a new digital 'GSM' network. The introduction of GSM was therefore referred to as 2G or second-generation services. BT Cellnet and two more entrants launched GSM services in the following two years making the UK one of Europe's most competitive markets.

The UK was the third European country to license 3G operators after Finland and Spain but was the first to auction its licenses. Auctions are not new to the European communications industry. Many of the second and third entrants had to bid for their license, what is spectacular about the UK's 3G auction is the height of the bids. While industry observers has speculated that the auction might reach £4 billion, in the event a total of £22 billion was raised from the sale of spectrum.

There is continued speculation about the impact of the UK's 3G spectrum auction. Since operators must recoup the investment in the license it is expected that this will result in higher costs for the consumer thus hindering the UK's migration to 3G services.

UK 3G License Winners and Total Cost

Hutchison 3G UK	License A	2 x 15MHz paired 5MHz unpaired	7 billion
Vodafone	License B	2 x 15MHz paired	9.6 billion
BT Cellnet	License C	2 x 10 MHz paired 5MHz unpaired	6.5 billion
One2One	License D	2 x 10 MHz paired 5MHz unpaired	6.4 billion
Orange	License E	2 x 10 MHz paired 5MHz unpaired	6.6 billion
TOTAL			36.1 billion

DATA SERVICES

As in the fixed line communications, mobile operators are no longer content to offer connection, voice telephony and standard applications i.e. voicemail, bundled airtime and so on. Competition has driven down price and therefore revenue from the basic services and operators are now seeking to differentiate themselves by offering innovative value added services. The most important of these to date is the development of SMS and WAP applications.

SMS (Short Messaging Services) or 'text messaging' as it is more commonly referred to allows consumers to send and receive text messages up to 160 characters long on their mobile phones. These messages can be personal messages sent from one user to another or can be information based services specified by the end user and sent by the network operator. Most popular SMS information services are sports results and news headlines. Due to its simplicity and popularity among young users, the number of SMS messages being sent each day has increased dramatically (see table below).

TOTAL NUMBER OF SMS SENT IN THE UK

Date	December '98	December '99	December '00	March '01
Number of Messages	170 million	271 million	756 million	864 million

SMS is a relatively simple technology but the more complicated offering is WAP, or Wireless Application Protocol. WAP is a language that allows Internet-style

data to be viewed from a mobile phone. To date, applications have be uninspiring, news and weather reports, sports information, horoscopes etc and uptake much slower than anticipated. However, it is key to Operators' future business plans that users accept and use more sophisticated services to prepare them for the changes that 3G services are expected to herald. 3G will offer much faster data transfer rates (up to 2Mbps is commonly quoted) which will expand the facility of the network to include full Internet browsing and streamed video content. The question remains as to whether ordinary consumers will want or use these enhanced services.

PMR

There is a fifth operational national mobile network which must be mentioned in a discussion of the communications industry in the UK. Dolphin Telecom operates a national mobile network based on the TETRA standard. PMR (Public Mobile Radio) or PAMR (Public Access Mobile Radio) as it is also referred to differs from other mobile networks in its ability to allow group communication, a single user has the ability to push a button which allows him to broadcast to members of a pre-selected group. Most often PMR is used by the emergency services but the Dolphin network interconnects with the fixed network and is offered primarily to business users as the UK's fifth mobile network. However, the take up of services has been much slower than anticipated.

OFTEL
50 Ludgate Hill, London EC4M 7JJ
Tel: 020-7634 8700; Fax: 020-7634 8943
Web: www.oftel.co.uk

DEPARTMENT OF TRADE AND INDUSTRY (DTI)
Telecommunications Division, 151 Buckingham Palace Road, London SW1W 9SS
Tel: 020-7215 5000; Fax: 020-7215 2909

BT CELLNET
260 Bath Road Slough, Berkshire SL1 4DX
Tel: 01753 565000; Fax: 01753 565010
Web: www.cellnet.co.uk

DOLPHIN TELECOM
The Crescent, Jays Close, That Viables, Basingstoke Hampshire RG22 4BS
Tel: 01256 811822; Fax: 01256 474537
Web: www.dolphin-telecom.co.uk

HUTCHISON 3G UK
43 New Bond Street, London W1Y 9HB
Tel: 020-7499 1886; Fax: 020-7491 7266

ORANGE PLC
The Economist Building, 25 St James Street, London SW1A 1HA
Tel: 020-7766 1766; Fax: 020-7766 1767
Web: www.orange.co.uk

ONE2ONE
Imperial Place, Maxwell Road, Borehamwood WD6 1EA
Tel: 020-8214 2121; Fax: 020-8214 3601
Web: www.one2one.co.uk

VODAFONE GROUP
The Courtyard, 2–4 London Road, Newbury, Berkshire RG14 1JX
Tel: 01635 33251; Fax: 01635 45713
Web: www.vodafone.co.uk

Information Technology and Computer Science

It can be asserted that there have been three marvels of the twentieth century: modern medicine, nuclear fusion and the computer. It can be further asserted that modern medicine and nuclear fusion might not have so advanced were it not for the invention of the computer. This article provides an overview of the rapid and broad development of computers and computer science.

ANCESTRY

The ancestors of the modern century computer are the Difference Engine and Analytical Engine devised by mathematician Charles Babbage. Designed in 1820 to automatically compute mathematical tables, construction of his mechanical, clockwork-like Difference Engine was abandoned by Babbage in the 1840s due to financial problems, personal tragedy and a disagreement with head engineer Joseph Clement.

In 1834 Babbage began work on his Analytical Engine. Unlike the Difference Engine, the Analytical Engine was designed as a general purpose tool with a store to hold information and a mill to take information input on punched cards and translate it into results, or output, on similar punched cards.

Following the financial problems with the incomplete Difference Engine project, Babbage was unable to secure further government funding for his Analytical Engine and it was not until 1991 that an actual engine was built by a group of historical enthusiasts.

FIRST GENERATION

Babbage's work relied heavily on mechanics and physical machinery. It was not until the twentieth century invention of the electrical vacuum tube and then the transistor that computers became a feasible means to solving problems.

War has been a significant factor in the development of the computer. In 1943, during World War II, the British and Americans developed electronic computers. Colossus, a British effort, was specifically developed to crack the German coding cipher Lorenz whilst an American effort, Harvard Mark I, was developed as a more general purpose electromechanical programmable computer.

Regarded as early 'first generation' computers, these machines primarily comprised wired circuits and vacuum valves. Punched cards were employed as the input, output and main storage systems.

Following on from initial developments, ENIAC (Electronic Numerical Integrator and Computer) was completed in 1946 by the Americans. Capable of carrying out 100,000 calculations a second, it was remarkable for its day. Like all first generation machines, ENIAC was huge and power hungry (weighing 30 tonnes and consuming 25 kilowatts of electricity).

SECOND GENERATION

Similar to light bulbs, valves were prone to failure, requiring tedious checks to resolve problems (ENIAC alone contained 18,000 vacuum valves). In 1947, the transistor was invented. Performing the same role as a vacuum valve but less prone to failure, smaller and more efficient, the transistor allowed smaller 'second generation' computers to be developed throughout the 1950s and early 1960s.

Computers remained the province of government and universities due to their scale of cost and size. Their use

was significant in nuclear weapon and power generation research and development.

THIRD GENERATION

In 1958 Jack St Claire Kilby produced the first integrated circuit, or 'micro-chip'. A micro-chip is comprised of a large number of transistors and other components bonded to a single substrate – typically a wafer of silicon, interconnected by a surface film of conductive material rather than by wires. By reducing distance between components, savings are made in both size and electricity. In 1963 the first 'third generation' computers based on 'micro-chip' technology appeared.

FOURTH GENERATION

In 1971 Intel produced the first 'microprocessor' heralding a 'fourth generation' of computers. The Intel 4004 (capable of 60,000 instructions per second) grouped much of the processing functions onto a single micro-chip. Around the same time, Intel invented the RAM (random access memory) chip which grouped significant amounts of memory onto a single chip. Intel remains today a leading chip manufacturer. Successive microprocessors had ever-increasing calculating ability while the capacity of RAM also increased. Supercomputers and mainframes utilising scores of microprocessors had terrific power in the order of 150 million instructions per second.

The power of the computer has exponentially increased as science has scaled down the size and electrical consumption of the core component (the transistor) from thumb size to far smaller than the thickness of a human hair, allowing a greater density and thus increasing the total power of the computer. Developments such as multiple-layer circuits and the use of copper instead of gold continue to yield gains in size and performance through miniaturisation.

The microprocessor facilitated the advent of immensely powerful supercomputers and also allowed small and affordable micro or personal computers. Early micro computers included the Altair 8800 in 1974, the Apple I & II, Commodore PET through to the IBM PC based on Intel's 8086 in 1981. The 8086 chip began a dynasty of hugely successful microprocessors for Intel that continues today with the Pentium III range.

IBM's original PC set a standard which was effectively wrestled from IBM by companies making clones or copies of the IBM design. IBM designed the initial PC only to see other companies take the lion's share of the market. The operating system supplier Microsoft made thousands of times more money out of the IBM PC than IBM ever did.

In the mid 1980s Apple Computer abandoned its highly successful Apple II computer range to produce the Apple Lisa and Apple Macintosh computers utilising the Motorola 68000 processor. Being the first widely available commercial computers with a graphical mouse/pointer driven interface they were relatively expensive compared to the command line (text only) operated IBM PC clones.

The Lisa was abandoned but the Apple Macintosh today ranks as the second largest personal computer system.

In the early 1990s RISC (reduced instruction set computing) became common. Compared with conventional CISC (complex instruction set computing) chips, a RISC processor uses a small set of highly efficient instruction types in combinations to achieve the same result as one CISC instruction. Because of performance optimisation the RISC chip can often perform some tasks more quickly than a CISC chip.

The first RISC chips were installed in UNIX servers and workstations. In the mid-1990s Apple Computer teamed up with IBM and Motorola to produce the PowerPC chip. Apple stopped shipping personal computers with the ageing 68040 CISC chip and instead utilised the PowerPC chip. Around that time Intel began shipping the Pentium CISC chip. Successive releases have produced ever faster versions of the PowerPC and Intel chip sets. For example: from an initial speed of 66 MHz in the mid-1990s, the PowerPC chip was released at 1,000 MHz in 2000.

NEXT GENERATION

Most modern computers are still regarded as 'fourth generation' as they use essentially the same technology, albeit highly miniaturised. The future of computer technology is widely thought to be dependent on the physics of light. Already used extensively in the computer industry for high speed communications, laser light offers possibilities for both calculation and storage.

As has been seen, there is huge diversity in the field of computer science and processor types are no exception – there have been literally hundreds of design families and thousands of processor models.

PROGRAMMING LANGUAGES

A multitude of programming languages have been devised with the common purpose of devising a program of instructions for computers to follow to achieve a task. Programming languages are categorised by generation:

1GL or first-generation language is the machine language that the processor chips execute. Instructions and arguments are in binary form (strings of zeros and ones). For the very early computers, machine language was the only choice as there was often insufficient resources to support assembly language or even an operating system. Machine language tends to be highly specific to a particular processor or processor family.

2GL or second-generation language. Assembly language is a human-understandable language insofar as it uses names instead of numbers. An assembler program takes assembly language and turns it into a machine code program. Very common on early systems where resources (speed, storage) were at a premium, it is typically only used today as an output from 3GL and higher systems. It is rare for the assembly language of two different processor families to be identical but they all share similar syntax. Assembly language programs do not lend themselves to being used on different hardware platforms.

3GL or third-generation language is a 'high-level' programming language. Typically more readable and concise than assembly language, 3GL programs are converted by a compiler program into either machine or assembly language for later execution. 3GL languages allow programs to be converted or ported from one operating system or hardware platform to another (with varying degrees of effort) and allow more complex data structures and program flows than 2GLs. 4GL or fourth generation language is designed to be closer to natural language than a 3GL language. Languages for accessing databases are often described as 4GLs.

5GL or fifth-generation language programming uses graphical development environments to create source language to be compiled with a 3GL or 4GL language compiler. Often 5GLs are used to develop prototype applications which have the look and feel of a final application but often without the underlying power provided by a 3GL or 4GL. Often a mix of generations is used, with a high level language (4 or 5GL) used to produce interface elements and a lower level language used to provide the processing power.

OPERATING SYSTEMS

An operating system (OS) is a set of utility programs that acts as the liaison between the computer user, the computer hardware (processor unit, memory) and its peripherals (hard disk, mouse, display, printer, network etc) and the program that a user is running (e.g. a spreadsheet).

The first computers had no operating system, and each program had to directly control the hardware on its own adding greatly to the burden of programming a computer. Initial input was by setting dials and switches (or even plugging cables), with calculation results shown on dials. The input was in the form of elementary machine language encoded in binary.

The early code-breaking systems utilised teletype paper tape. Then came punched cards – where instructions were laboriously encoded onto cardboard cards that were fed through the machine telling it both what to do and giving it the information or data to compute. The result was either produced onto further punched cards or output on to rudimentary display panels.

The use of punched cards allowed some routine components or programs to be re-used (by re-using routines on sets of cards). Later, the development of memory chips, magnetic tape and hard disks has allowed more extensive programs and information to be stored, executed and re-executed.

Early OS were hardware and vendor-specific with assembly language or machine code as the programming language. Each computer model or series tended to have its own specific operating system.

In 1969 a major mainstream operating systems, UNIX, was first released. Originated at Bell Labs in the USA, it was based on 'Multics', an earlier time-sharing system. UNIX was one of the first operating systems that could be ported (converted) to a variety of system hardware. UNIX's ability was made largely through the use of the 'C' programming language which was first defined and developed around the same time.

UNIX has evolved into many different versions or 'strains' due in part to the fact that the source code is largely free and written in C. UNIX systems were keystones in the development of the Internet and a large proportion of Internet servers today are UNIX-driven. UNIX is available on more hardware platforms than any other OS, although there is no dominant version of UNIX with a dozen or so major versions.

In 1979 Digital Equipment Corporation (DEC) released VMS (Virtual Memory System) as the operating system for the DEC VAX mini-computer. The main features of VMS was the adoption of a 32-bit virtual memory system that allowed use of hard disk as virtual memory in place of actual RAM chips. There have been many operating systems devised and abandoned over the years.

PERSONAL COMPUTER OPERATING SYSTEMS

Throughout the 1990s the personal computer world has been dominated by two main players: Microsoft and Apple Computer. Although not a significant manufacturer of computer equipment itself, Microsoft Corporation has built on its market share secured in the 1980s with MSDOS to become the market leading operating system provider. Microsoft's MS Windows range of personal computer operating systems are installed on more computers than any other commercial operating system.

Concern over the market dominance of Microsoft has led to legislatures in the US and European Union bringing anti-trust (anti-monopoly) lawsuits against the company. Success or failure for Microsoft in such litigation is likely to significantly shape the future of computing over the first decade of the new millennium.

Microsoft's main rival is Apple Computer. Established in the 1970s, Apple became highly successful with its Apple I, II and III range of personal computers and is one of the few of a flock of personal computer companies from that time that has continued to manufacture both its own operating system and hardware to run upon it.

Unlike Microsoft, Apple's strategy has been to control both the hardware and software of its systems. The Apple Macintosh operating system (MacOS) can only be run on Apple Macintosh hardware. This has resulted in a benefit that is also a curse: the Macintosh is a quality product but quality tends to cost. Microsoft benefited from the production of a huge volume of less expensive PCs, while Apple sells on quality and features. Both have significant benefits and downfalls. Many other operating systems exist but tend to be brand or hardware-specific.

'THE NET'

Prior to the Internet or 'the Net' as it is known colloquially, computers tended to be connected together by hardware and protocols that were peculiar to each particular connection. Typically, links were point-to-point (a link had to be directly and physically established between the two computers).

As in other areas of computing, the military had an important influence on the development of what was to become 'the Net'. In 1969 ARPANET was formed by the US Department of Defence. A main concern was to establish a way for the computer capability of the military to be dispersed so that no one centre was critical to the operation of the network as a whole. This was achieved by interconnecting computers both directly and by way of other intermediary computers; thus if one link or 'node' computer was hit by a nuclear bomb, other pathways of communication could be established. The interconnections, when drawn, appeared as a mesh or net or web.

ARPANET was extended to non-military users such as universities early in the 1970s, with initial international links appearing in 1972. Early network research lead to the protocol of request for comments (RFC) whereby ideas in development can be adopted and studied by other computer users, who will comment on it, expand it and improve on it allowing a de facto standard to quickly evolve. The collaboration ethos instilled in the RFC protocol has fuelled development of the Internet and related computer fields. RFC number 1 was written in 1969 and there are well over 2,000 today.

Early Internet was merely a means for computers rather than people to communicate and was a side-effect of research into networking. It was not 'the Web', and web pages and email as we know it did not exist – these were the days of command line, text-only green screens (if not Teletype printer/keyboards).

The introduction of domain names (e.g. ditdit.co.uk) in 1984 offered an easier means of using the Web. Prior to domain names one had to remember IP numbers (e.g.192.168.1.100) for accessing destination computers. The use of email increased and implementations improved as various RFCs were adopted as standards; however, the Internet was primarily limited to government agencies, the military, academic and research organisations and some big businesses.

In 1989 what most people perceive as 'the Net' was born. It was effectively invented at CERN (the European Particle Physics Laboratory) by Tim Berners-Lee as a way for scientists to share information by placing it in a prescribed format (defined in an RFC) on a server. Initially text only, development of computer capability allowed inclusion of images through use of a program called NCSA Mosaic – the first graphical 'browser' (*see glossary*).

By 1993 a whole new industry of ISPs (Internet Service Providers) had begun, allowing computer users to dial up via a modem and access the Internet and to view the Web through their browser of choice. The leading two browsers today, Netscape and Microsoft Explorer, were both based on the open source code of NCSA Mosaic.

In the mid 1990s the term 'information superhighway' was coined to refer to the Internet. Sadly, the Internet is not a superhighway – it suffers from rush hours, traffic jams and link closures despite the fact that new connections are added at a frantic pace.

Developments of the late 1990s have allowed music, video, games, text, graphics and even telephone conversations to co-exist on the same Internet. The core technologies underpinning the Internet are TCP/IP, routers and domain names (*see glossary*).

The future of the Internet is likely to see the majority of telephone calls and probably video being transmitted over the Internet for at least part of its journey. Expansion of fibre-optic cable networks to homes and businesses will underpin this. The advent of high-capacity mobile phones will also facilitate and demand expansion of the Internet.

Simple but successful virus attacks like the 'love bug' computer virus of early 2000 show how much the world depends on and is affected by Internet technology. With no central governing body or legal jurisdiction, the legal implications of the Internet will continue to puzzle for years to come.

GLOSSARY OF IT TERMS

The following is a selected list of modern computing terms. It is by no means exhaustive but is intended to cover those that the average computer user might encounter.

Kbps: kilo bits per second – measure of transmission speed, denoting 1,000 bits transmitted per second.

Mbps: mega bits per second – denoting 1 million bits transmitted per second.

Gbps: giga bits per second – denoting 1,000 million bits transmitted per second.

10-BaseT: 10 Mbps Ethernet. *See also* Ethernet.

100-BaseT: 100 Mbps Ethernet. *See also* Ethernet.

1000-BaseT: 1000 Mbps or 1 Gbps Ethernet also known as Gigabit Ethernet. *See also* Ethernet.

10-Base2: 2 Mbps Ethernet over co-axial cable. (*See* Ethernet).

ADB: a defunct proprietary standard formerly built into Apple Macintosh computers to connect keyboard and mice and other input peripherals, ADB has now been supplanted by USB. *See also* USB.

ADSL: Asymmetric Digital Subscriber Line – a high speed digital protocol that allows continuous connection over standard copper wire to the Internet at over 265 kbps for sending and at least twice as fast for receiving. First available in the United Kingdom in 2000, ADSL is ideal for receiving streamed video and audio and is seen as the replacement for modems and ISDN. *See also* DSL, SDSL and ISDN.

Animated Gif: a multi-layered Gif file that allows simple animations to be created by transitions between the layers. Banner advertising on the Internet tends to utilise animated Gifs. *See also* Gif.

Applet: a very small application that is run in a special environment to provide a specialised function. For example Java applets provide special functions to web pages and are run in the Java virtual machine environment from which they derive their functionality.

ATA: Advanced Technology Attachment – ANSI name for IDE. *See also* IDE.

Browser: typically referring to a 'web browser' that allows a computer user to view web page content on their computer. Browsers can be designed for different specialist functions such as presenting image libraries, databases or computer code to users in a friendly format.

BASIC: Beginners All Purpose Symbolic Instruction Code – was designed for mainframe computers in 1963. Included on many personal computers in the 1970s (due to its minimal memory requirements) it became popular for beginners and non-professional programmers. Available on most operating systems, BASIC has been further popularised by Microsoft Visual Basic (an object-oriented graphical language).

Bluetooth: a de facto standard for wireless connectivity between devices. Bluetooth is based on short-range (10 metre) radio link and allows devices such as laptops, cellphones and printers to interact without wires. Developed primarily by joint initiatives between several of the large telecommunication and computer companies as a way for applicances of any type (including household appliances) to interact.

Burn: to 'Burn' or 'toast' a file or files to a CD-ROM or similar media means to copy the files to the media from hard disk (or other source). Derived from the fact that CD-ROMs are burnt by a laser during the process of writing to the disk.

Bytecode: file format which is the product of a compiler. Bytecode allows programs written in Java or PERL to be executed on virtual machines on any supporting platform.

Cat-5: an electrical performance and cable quality standard prescribed to support high-speed Ethernet networks. There are higher category specifications denoted by higher numbers but Cat-5 is the most commonly installed today.

C: a 3GL programming language developed in the late 1960s in parallel with the UNIX operating systems. Primarily limited to UNIX until the mid 1980s when standards emerged (the POSIX standard among others) allowing C to be widely adopted on many operating systems. UNIX used C as its core programming language.

C++: 3GL programming language invented by Bell Labs in 1985 with a final standard ratified in the late 1990s. Hugely popular, it has overthrown C as the language of choice for professional operating system and application developers. Based on C, it uses the object-oriented programming model.

CD: Compact Disc – a digital disk format capable of storing 650 megabytes of information on each of its two sides. Information is read by a laser head that detects pits etched into the substrate of the spinning disk and interprets them as information. Widely used in an audio format for storing recorded music. The computer format CD-ROM is likely to be superseded by the higher capacity DVD in the next few years. CD-RAM/CD-RW is a modifiable version and CD-R is a write once, read many format – both use lasers to alter the disk substrate to make the pits interpreted later as information. (CD-ROM is pressed by machine and die). *See also* DVD.

CGI: Common Gateway Interface – specification for how a web server and web page interact with applications on the server to accept, process and return web content dynamically. Typically, CGI handles form submission and searches, converting user input into database entries etc.

COBOL: Common Business Oriented Language – was released in 1960. Its authors aimed to produce a programming language that was easy to understand and use, more like English and less like code. COBOL in all its versions has been widely adopted for the development of business and financial systems. Millennium preparation for many organisations involved replacing legacy COBOL systems with more modern solutions using standard relational database and Internet tools. COBOL is still commercially available today.

DNS: Domain Name Server – a server that translates domain names into the IP numbers used by programs to directly access computers on the Internet. Each server has a telephone number and a name and DNS is analogous to the directory enquiries service, providing a means of locating a computer connected to the Internet.

Domain: a set of words, numbers and letters separated by dots used to identify an Internet server or group of servers, e.g. www.whitakers-almanack.co.uk, where 'www' denotes a web (http) server, 'whitakers-almanack' denotes the organisation name, 'co' denotes that the organisation is a company and 'uk' denotes United Kingdom (there are alternates for every country but 'us' is seldom used for United States). Alternatives include: org - organisation; net - network; gov - government; co/com - company (and many more).

DVD: Digital Versatile Disc – DVD-ROM is a high capacity (read only) disk format that has the same form factor as CD-ROM. Unlike the CD-ROM, however, DVD-ROM can store several Gigabytes of information on each surface and can have four readable surfaces (through laser focusing technology) compared with CD-ROM's two surfaces of 650 Megabytes. DVD-RAM is a modifiable version of DVD. Various formats of DVD are available, the most common being that used to store high-quality digital video, an alternative to the laser disk or video tape. *See also* CD.

DSL: Digital Subscriber Line – A family of high speed digital technologies for connection to the Internet over ordinary copper telephone cable. *See also* ADSL and SDSL.

Email: Electronic mail – An email message is a document that is addressed to one or more persons from an individual. Usually containing a message, it can also include other documents and email is the modern version of the telex, telegram, postcard and letter for exchanging information electronically. The advent of the Internet has seen an explosion in the use of email in modern life. Without encryption or digital signature, an Internet email is not secure.

Ethernet: a local area network type that typically utilises twisted pair cables directly between a central switch or hub. Utilising simple, standard and relatively cheap cable and connectors (RJ-45) Ethernet has become the standard for local area networks. Speeds of 10 Mbps (10-BaseT) and 100 Mbps (100-BaseT) are common with 1000 Mbps (1000-BaseT) also available. Ethernet employs a system whereby each computer listens for information addressed to its own unique address. Before transmitting, each computer waits for silence on the line; if multiple computers start transmitting simultaneously, they each detect the 'collision' and wait a random period of time before listening for silence and retransmitting, thus allowing communications to resume much like polite society. Ethernet reliability depends on the hub or switch rather than on one individual computer. Ethernet is also available over co-axial (television style) cable typically at 2 Mbps (10-Base2); although higher speeds are available, they are less common as co-axial cable is less resilient than twisted pair. 10-Base2 does not typically employ hubs or switches and comprises an open ended 'daisy-chain' of computers connected to the network. A break in the chain will divide the network into two or ever cause it to fail.

Extranet: secure subset of the Internet, using Internet protocols. Common today for exchanging information and services between a specific group or organisation. Security prevents outsiders from accessing the Extranet.

File Server: a computer on a network that stores computer files that users can access from other computers on the network. Popular modern systems include Windows NT, UNIX, Novell NetWare and AppleShare IP.

Fire Wall: computer or device to protect a network from security risks posed by the Internet, just as a firewall or fire-door protects parts of a building from a fire raging on the other side.

Firewire: Apple Computer trade mark for their implementation of the IEEE 1394 standard. *See also* SCSI, IEEE 1394, iLink.

Flash: a de facto standard for providing online animated web content from something as simple as an animated logo or button to an online video game. Flash is primarily produced by Macromedia Director and can be programmed with the logo language.

FORTRAN: FORmula TRANslation is a 3GL programming language designed for users and creators of scientific algorithms rather than business solutions. Today it has been succeeded by C for most applications but many legacy FORTRAN applications still exist and many developers still use it.

FTP: File Transfer Protocol – an Internet protocol whereby an FTP client program can request listings of files on a remote server and exchange files with that server. Publicly accessible FTP servers allow Anonymous FTP which does not require a password or user name, whereas private ones do.

GIF: Graphics Interchange Format – compressed graphic format most suitable for logos and non-photographic images. Invented by Unisys to allow images to be electronically sent in an efficient manner. Royalties due to Unisys for any implementation of GIF have lead to the development of a replacement format, PNG.

Hot-plugable: adjective to describe the ability of a protocol or device to be connected and disconnected as required without restarting the computer or device.

HTML: HyperText Mark-up Language – A small programming language used to denote or mark-up how an Internet page should be presented to a user from a HTTP server via a web browser. HTTP is an evolving standard that has grown greatly from its first version in order to accommodate new types of web content and features provided by the different web browsers (e.g. Netscape and Internet Explorer).

HTTP: Hypertext Transfer Protocol – an Internet protocol whereby a web server sends web pages, images and files to a web browser. HTTP is a perpetually evolving application protocol.

HUB: An Ethernet HUB connects a 10/100-BaseT network together with each machine or network device connected to the hub by a cable, with the hub linking them all together. Any traffic on any HUB 'Port' (connection) is echoed to all Ports. A USB hub performs a similar function allowing multiple USB devices to be connected to a single Computer via the HUB. *See also* Ethernet, 10/100-BaseT, USB. *See also* Switch.

IDE: Integrated Drive Electronics – a standard electronic interface used between computer disk storage devices. The IDE interface is based on the IBM PC ISA 16-bit bus standard. *See also* ATA.

IEEE 1394: developed primarily by Apple Computer (as FireWire) and Sony (as iLink), IEEE 1394 is a high-performance hot-plugable replacement for SCSI for connection of hard disks, scanners and digital video and still cameras. *See also* SCSI, FireWire, iLink.

iLink: Sony Corporation trade mark for their implementation of the IEEE 1394 standard. *See also* SCSI, IEEE 1394, iLink.

IMAP: Internet Mail Access Protocol – an Internet protocol offered as a replacement for POP3. IMAP allows a user to review, manipulate and store email on a central server from one or more workstations without necessitating message removal from the server. Advanced versions such as IMAP4 allow multiple users to have shared mailboxes or folders on the email server.

Internet: an abstract concept applied to describe the global network of INTER-connected computer NET-works of computers. *See body of article.*

Intranet: subset of the Internet, using Internet protocols but on a local area network. Common today for publishing information and services within a company or office.

IP Address/IP Number: typically in number form e.g. 192.168.1.100, an IP Address is unique to the computer that possesses it. Its purpose is similar to that of a telephone number, each digit allowing an Internet or network connection to be made between computers. When transmitting, a computer quotes the destination address and its own address and the information is routed accordingly using those numbers. *See also* Router. The widely used IP Address scheme is running out of unique numbers and an extended scheme is being phased in to replace it, although this is likely to take many years.

IRC: Internet Relay Chat – protocol that allows users to 'chat' online with other users using their keyboards. Under IRC a user can log into various chat rooms under their own name or an alias and have a text 'conversation' in real time with other users. IRC spans the globe and allows a person to build a persona based entirely on what they type.

ISDN: Integrated Services Digital Network – widely adopted in the United Kingdom and Europe but not North America, ISDN allows both digital computer data and voice telephony to coexist simultaneously on the same cable circuits. Data can be digitally exchanged at 64 kbps on one pair of copper wires, and at 128 kbps for a typical installation of two pairs. Typically used for point-to-point file transfer of large documents when first introduced, more recently it has been used for 'dialup' Internet for small to medium-sized business. In the UK, widespread adoption has been hampered by pricing structures (a 128 kbps connection incurs call charges for two lines per minute). Introduction of ADSL is likely to limit or reduce market penetration of ISDN.

Java: a development environment that allows development of cross-platform applications or applets typically utilised by web sites or Intranets. Java applications are compiled into Java Virtual Machine code in the same way as normal programs and thus cannot be modified by end users and is relatively efficient when compared to Java Script. Java is related to C++, an object-oriented development language used to develop many modern operating systems and as such can be used to develop sophisticated web-based programs.

Java Script: Netscape version of Java code that is executed or interpreted on the web user's machine each time it is run and is thus less efficient than compiled Java applets. Unlike Java, Java Script is typically provided in source form and is modifiable by the end user.

Java Virtual Machine (JVM): Java applets are required by Java standard to be able to run on any operating system that has a Java Virtual Machine which must provide a standard suite of facilities to the Java program. Microsoft, among others, has produced its own extensions to Java that are outside the standard, causing problems to MacOS users and others who do not have access to the Microsoft extensions.

JPEG: Joint Photographic Experts Group – compressed graphic format most suitable for compression of photographic images. Image data is compressed in manner that simplifies the image, losing definition in the process. As the level of compression increases so too does the image degradation.

MacOS: operating system developed by Apple Computer for use on their own Macintosh personal and server computers. A co-operative multi-tasking system up to version 9.1, it has become a more powerful operating system with MacOS X (10) which is a preemptive multi-tasking operating system based on UNIX.

Novell NetWare: introduced in the late 1980s, NetWare was one of the first network server operating systems and until MS Windows NT4 overtook it in the mid-to late1990s it was the market leader.

Modem: modulator/demodulator – a device that modulates digital signals from a computer into analogue signals for transmission over a standard telephone line and demodulates an incoming analogue signal and converts it to a digital signal for the computer.

MP3: motion picture group 1 layer 3 – popular format for compressing audio information for transmission over the Internet for later playback on personal computers and hand-held music players and other devices.

MPEG: Motion Picture Encoding Group – popular format standards for compressing video and audio information for transmission over the Internet for later playback on personal computers and on some hand-held devices.

MS-DOS: Microsoft Corporation's Disk Operating System – an early OS developed but not invented by Microsoft for use on early Intel-based personal computers. MS-DOS is believed by many to still be a core for Microsoft's more modern operating systems. *See also* PC-DOS; Operating System.

Name Server: see DNS Network Server: both Print Servers and File Servers are types of network server. Other types of network service include provision of configuration or security controls.

News: see NNTP.

News Group: see NNTP.

NNTP: Network News Transfer Protocol – an Internet protocol that implements a bulletin board, but on a global scale. Using a NNTP browser one can subscribe to one or more news groups of a huge diversity of topics from Archaeology to Zebras. Messages are posted to a virtual notice board by users through their news browser software to a news group on their local server which in turn passes it to other servers higher up in the hierarchy. To simplify, the hierarchy ends at a server for each country which passes the messages back down the chain in its own country and to its peers abroad (in actuality countries are irrelevant and network boundaries are important). Network News generates huge volumes each day and messages are discarded off servers after an amount of time specified by the individual server manager for each specific group. This period could be minutes, hours or days. Moderated news requires a news group administrator to approve each message before it is posted to a moderated news group. News groups can be specific to a particular organisation, country or network. There is no central store for news and no central control of content.

Operating System (OS): computer software developed to provide computer programs with standard facilities to interact with users and with computer hardware (via drivers). *See also* MS-DOS, PC-DOS, UNIX, MacOS, MS Windows.

PERL: Practical Extraction and Reporting Language – powerfull text processing language typically used to develop CGI's for web servers. Compiled into Byte-code, a PERL program can be run on any computer supporting the PERL virtual machine.

Parallel: adjective to describe a communications type to denote that bits of information are sent in groups simultaneously side by side over multiple pairs within a single cable. Commonly used to connect PCs and printers.

PC-DOS: very closely related to MS-DOS and providing the same functionality. Initially adopted by IBM as the operating system for their personal computers but was effectively abandoned as MS-DOS became ubiquitous. *See also* PC-DOS; Operating System.

PGP: Pretty Good Privacy – an implementation of the Public Key System of data encryption. Available on many different platforms PGP is a widely used program. Developed by Philip R Zimmermann in 1991 it is typically used for email security and digital signatures. There are two versions Rivest-Shamire-Adleman (RSA) and Diffie-Hellman. The RSA version incurs a licence fee to RSA. PGP is available in restricted shareware and commercial versions. Availability of PGP has until recently been heavily restricted by the US government (via classification as a war munition). *See also* Public Key System.

PNG: an improved royalty-free graphics file replacement for GIF.

POP3: Post Office Protocol 3 – an Internet protocol whereby a workstation can collect email from a personal mailbox on an email server and move it to a mailbox typically on a user's own machine. Mail collection typically copies the messages from the server to the local machine before deleting them from the server.

Public Key: a virtual key generated and publicly available from a destination (e.g. email or web site) for use in encryption of information sent to that destination. Akin to a recipient providing unlocked padlocks for which only the recipient has the key. The sender uses the key (padlock) to encrypt (secure) the contents of the message or web submission (cargo) for the recipient to receive and unlock.

Print Server: a computer or device on a network that manages the sharing of one or more printers between multiple computers over a network. Many modern printers have a print server built in, although early printers almost always needed a print server to be actively shared.

RJ-45: a standard for cable connectors in Ethernet networks.

RIP: Raster Image Processor – Hardware and/or Software product that generates a raster graphic (or bitmap) from images in vector graphic format.

Router: where multiple networks are joined together, a router acts like a very fast sorting office, examining the destination address of each information packet and passing or routing it to the appropriate network.

Routers select the most efficient general route for packets of information based on current system demands.

SCSI: Small Computer System Interface – available in a variety of performance specifications. Typically used for connection of high speed hard disks, scanners, specialist printers and removable drives, SCSI was until recently shipped as standard on all Apple Macintosh computers and is common on UNIX servers and workstations. SCSI has been replaced by Firewire on Apple Macintosh and is becoming more common on other platforms.

SDSL: Symetric Digital Subscriber Line – Form of DSL providing high speed connection to the Internet over ordinary copper telephone cables. Unlike ADSL, SDSL offers the same transfers in each direction. Common in North America and Europe but not in the United Kingdom. *See also* DSL, ADSL.

Serial: adjective to describe a communication type to denote that bits of information are sent one after another down a single wire pair as opposed to being sent in parallel. Commonly used for mice and keyboards, and on Macintosh computers for printers (*see* Parallel).

SMTP: Simple Mail Transfer Protocol – an Internet protocol whereby a workstation can send email to a server or whereby two servers can exchange email.

SNMP: Simple Network Management Protocol – Widely used protocol for remotely monitoring and managing network device status and function.

Stuffit: popular Apple Macintosh mechanism to compress information for transmission and later expansion without loss of information. Stuffit is a proprietary brand name of Aladdin Systems. *See also* Zip.

Switch: Unlike an Ethernet HUB the Ethernet switch only passes network traffic between the parties to a connection. For example when printing from Workstation A to Printer B, the switch only passes information to the switch ports (connections) for the workstation and the printer, not all ports. Typically a good switch is more expensive and provides better performance on average than a HUB. *See also* HUB.

TCP/IP: Transmission Control Protocol/Internet Protocol – a protocol which is the lifeblood of the Internet, TCP/IP defines how information and requests generated by all other protocols are transmitted and received over the Internet. The majority of information on the Internet is chopped up into small chunks or packets of information which are addressed with a destination and origination address. It sometimes happens that a packet gets lost and TCP/IP dictates how such a loss is handled.

Token ring: historically popular but less so today, a token ring is a form of network that takes the form of a ring connecting each computer. An electronic token (or tokens) is passed around the ring to each computer in turn. Possession of the token allows a computer to transmit for a limited period of time. Token ring is less resilient than Ethernet as any break or flaw in the ring can seriously degrade performance or cause it to fail completely.

USB: Universal Serial Bus – new standard for connecting serial devices such as scanners, mice, keyboards, modems and printers to computers. With USB, speeds of 10 Mbps and higher are possible. Has replaced standard serial ports and ADB connections on Apple Macintosh computers. USB devices can be hot-plugged as required. *See also* ADB.

URL: Uniform Resource Locator – address of an Internet file accessible on the Internet. Typically the server and path to an image, HTML page, CGI, Java applet or other Internet content available to web browsers.

Virus: a computer program or script written for the express purpose of replicating itself onto as many machines as possible (much like its biological namesake) often with negative side effects to the host computer and computer network. Such effects vary from harmless screen messages to deletion or corruption of document integrity, network overload or compromising of security or privacy. A typical motive is notoriety for the author. Most viruses are not particularly sophisticated and tend to capitalise on specific flaws or features of a particular operating system or program. Very few viruses are truly self-modifying and simply robotically clone themselves. Historically transmitted by floppy disk between offices and over networks within offices, the prevalence of email means viruses can spread globally within hours.

WAP: Wireless Application Protocol – a set of standards to defined how portable devices connected via radio waves (such as cell phones) can access Internet services. Launched in 2000 into the United Kingdom, WAP has not been as widely used as expected.

Windows ME: Windows Millennium Edition – operating system successor to Windows 98 for Pentium compatible personal computers. *See also* Windows 98.

Windows 3.1.1: Microsoft's first credible implementation of an graphical user interface operating system (GUI OS) implementation. Still used by many companies but superseded by successive MS Windows releases.

Windows 2000 Professional: Replacement for Windows NT Workstation. *See also* Windows NT.

Windows 2000 Server: Replacement for Windows NT Server. Available in various optimised and targeted versions. *See also* Windows NT.

Windows 95: Microsoft's highly successful upgrade to 3.1.1 providing more features but consuming more resources.

Windows 98: essentially a bug-fix, correcting problems with Windows 95.

Windows NT 3: appearing to the user as a 32 bit implementation of Windows 3.1.1, Windows NT was marketed as a stable and powerful business operating system. NT was mainly adopted by organisations as a server operating system and thus competing with Novell NetWare. Subsequently has been superseded by Windows NT 4.

Windows NT 4: this evolution of Windows NT 3 was marketed as Windows NT 4 Workstation for business machines and as NT4 Workstation for network servers. Significant in-built network administration and work group features coupled with the highly successful graphical interface of Windows 95 led to Windows NT being a leading operating system.

XML: Extensible Mark-up Language; similar to HTML but more powerful, XML allows pages of information to be encoded for publishing on the web and for traditional paper publishing. It is extensible insomuch as XML primaries can be combined to extend the language providing greater functionality.

Zip: compression – a popular mechanism on PCs to compress information for transmission and later expansion without loss of information. *See also* Stuffit.

Zip DRIVE: a popular 3.5" inexpensive removable disk format capable of storing either 100 or 250 Megabytes of information depending on format. Zip is a proprietary brand name of Iomega.

Local Government

Major changes in local government were introduced in England and Wales in 1974 and in Scotland in 1975 by the Local Government Act 1972 and the Local Government (Scotland) Act 1973. Further significant alterations were made in England by the Local Government Acts of 1985, 1992 and 2000.

The structure in England was based on two tiers of local authorities (county councils and district councils) in the non-metropolitan areas; and a single tier of metropolitan councils in the six metropolitan areas of England and London borough councils in London.

Following reviews of the structure of local government in England by the Local Government Commission, 46 unitary (all-purpose) authorities were created between April 1995 and April 1998 to cover certain areas in the non-metropolitan counties. The remaining county areas continue to have two tiers of local authorities. The county and district councils in the Isle of Wight were replaced by a single unitary authority on 1 April 1995; the former counties of Avon, Cleveland, Humberside and Berkshire have been replaced by unitary authorities; and Hereford and Worcester was replaced by a new county council for Worcestershire (with district councils) and a unitary authority for Herefordshire.

The Local Government (Wales) Act 1994 and the Local Government etc. (Scotland) Act 1994 abolished the two-tier structure in Wales and Scotland with effect from 1 April 1996, replacing it with a single tier of unitary authorities.

Local authorities are empowered or required by various Acts of Parliament to carry out functions in their areas. The legislation concerned comprises public general Acts and 'local' Acts which local authorities have promoted as private bills.

ELECTIONS

Local elections are normally held on the first Thursday in May. Generally, all British subjects, citizens of the Republic of Ireland, Commonwealth and other European Union citizens who are 18 years or over and resident on the qualifying date in the area for which the election is being held, are entitled to vote at local government elections. A register of electors is prepared and published annually by local electoral registration officers.

A returning officer has the overall responsibility for an election. Voting takes place at polling stations, arranged by the local authority and under the supervision of a presiding officer specially appointed for the purpose. Candidates, who are subject to various statutory qualifications and disqualifications designed to ensure that they are suitable persons to hold office, must be nominated by electors for the electoral area concerned.

In England, the Local Government Commission is responsible for carrying out periodic reviews of electoral arrangements and making recommendations to the Secretary of State for changes found necessary. In Wales and Scotland these matters are the responsibility of the Local Government Boundary Commission for Wales and the Local Boundary Commission for Scotland respectively. The Local Government Act 2000 provided for the Secretary of State to change the frequency and phasing of elections.

LOCAL GOVERNMENT COMMISSION FOR ENGLAND, Dolphyn Court, 10–11 Great Turnstile, Lincoln's Inn Fields, London WC1V 7JU. Tel: 020-7430 8400
LOCAL GOVERNMENT BOUNDARY COMMISSION FOR WALES, Caradog House, 1–6 St Andrew's Place, Cardiff CF1 3BE. Tel: 029-2039 5031
LOCAL GOVERNMENT BOUNDARY COMMISSION FOR SCOTLAND, 3 Drumsheugh Gardens, Edinburgh EH3 7QJ. Tel: 0131-538 7510

INTERNAL ORGANISATION

The council as a whole is the final decision-making body within any authority. Councils are free to a great extent to make their own internal organisational arrangements. The Local Government Act, given Royal assent on 28 July 2000, allows councils to adopt one of three broad categories of a new constitution which include a separate executive. These three categories are:

- A directly elected mayor with a cabinet selected by that mayor.
- A cabinet, either elected by the council or appointed by its leader.
- A directly elected mayor and council manager.

Normally, questions of policy are settled by the full council, while the administration of the various services is the responsibility of committees of councillors. Day-to-day decisions are delegated to the council's officers, who act within the policies laid down by the councillors.

FINANCE

Local government in England, Wales and Scotland is financed from four sources: the council tax, non-domestic rates, government grants, and income from fees and charges for services.

COUNCIL TAX

Under the Local Government Finance Act 1992, from 1 April 1993 the council tax replaced the community charge (which had been introduced in April 1989 in Scotland and April 1990 in England and Wales in place of domestic rates).

The council tax is a local tax levied by each local council. Liability for the council tax bill usually falls on the owner-occupier or tenant of a dwelling which is their sole or main residence. Council tax bills may be reduced because of the personal circumstances of people resident in a property, and there are discounts in the case of dwellings occupied by fewer than two adults.

In England, each county council, each district council and each police authority sets its own council tax rate. The district councils collect the combined council tax, and the county councils and police authorities claim their share from the district councils' collection funds. In Wales, each unitary authority and each police authority sets its own council tax rate. The unitary authorities collect the combined council tax and the police authorities claim their share from the funds. In Scotland, each island council and unitary authority sets its own rate of council tax.

The tax relates to the value of the dwelling. Each dwelling is placed in one of eight valuation bands, ranging from A to H, based on the property's estimated market value as at 1 April 1991.

The valuation bands and ranges of values in England, Wales and Scotland are:

England

A	Up to £40,000	E	£88,001–£120,000
B	£40,001–£52,000	F	£120,001–£160,000
C	£52,001–£68,000	G	£160,001–£320,000
D	£68,001–£88,000	H	Over £320,000

Wales

A	Up to £30,000	E	£66,001–£90,000
B	£30,001–£39,000	F	£90,001–£120,000
C	£39,001–£51,000	G	£120,001–£240,000
D	£51,001–£66,000	H	Over £240,000

Scotland

A	Up to £27,000	E	£58,001–£80,000
B	£27,001–£35,000	F	£80,001–£106,000
C	£35,001–£45,000	G	£106,001–£212,000
D	£45,001–£58,000	H	Over £212,000

The council tax within a local area varies between the different bands according to proportions laid down by law. The charge attributable to each band as a proportion of the Band D charge set by the council is approximately:

A	67%	E	122%
B	78%	F	144%
C	89%	G	167%
D	100%	H	200%

The band D rate is given in the tables on the following pages. There may be variations from the given figure within each district council area because of different parish or community precepts being levied.

NON-DOMESTIC RATES

Non-domestic (business) rates are collected by billing authorities; these are the district councils in those areas of England with two tiers of local government and unitary authorities in other parts of England, in Wales and in Scotland. In respect of England and Wales, the Local Government Finance Act 1988 provides for liability for rates to be assessed on the basis of a poundage (multiplier) tax on the rateable value of property (hereditaments). Separate multipliers are set by the Secretary of State for Transport, Local Government and the Regions in England, the National Assembly for Wales and the Scottish Executive, and rates are collected by the billing authority for the area where a property is located. Rate income collected by billing authorities is paid into a national non-domestic rating (NNDR) pool and redistributed to individual authorities on the basis of the adult population figure as prescribed by the Secretary of State for Transport, Local Government and the Regions, the National Assembly for Wales or the Scottish Executive. The rates pools are maintained separately in England, Wales and Scotland. Actual payment of rates in certain cases is subject to transitional arrangements, to phase in the larger increases and reductions in rates resulting from the effects of the 2000 revaluation.

Rates are levied in Scotland in accordance with the Local Government (Scotland) Act 1975. For 1995–6, the Secretary of State for Scotland prescribed a single non-domestic rates poundage to apply throughout the country at the same level as the uniform business rate (UBR) in England. Rate income is pooled and redistributed to local authorities on a per capita basis. For the year 1995–6 payment of rates was subject to transitional arrangements to phase in the effect of the 1995 revaluation.

Rateable values for the 2000 rating lists came into force on 1 April 2000. They are derived from the rental value of property as at 1 April 1993 and determined on certain statutory assumptions by the Valuation Office Agency in England and Wales, and by Regional Assessors in Scotland. New property which is added to the list, and significant changes to existing property, necessitate amendments to the rateable value on the same basis. Rating lists (valuation rolls in Scotland) remain in force until the next general revaluation. Such revaluations take place every five years, the next being in 2005.

Certain types of property are exempt from rates, e.g. agricultural land and buildings, certain businesses and places of public religious worship. Charities and other non-profit-making organisations may receive full or partial relief. Empty property is liable to pay rates at 50 per cent, except for certain specified classes which are exempt entirely.

GOVERNMENT GRANTS

In addition to specific grants in support of revenue expenditure on particular services, central government pays revenue support grant to local authorities. This grant is paid to each local authority so that if each authority spends at the level of its standard spending assessment, all authorities in the same class can set broadly the same council tax.

COMPLAINTS

Commissioners for Local Administration in England, Wales and Scotland are responsible for investigating complaints from members of the public who claim to have suffered injustice as a consequence of maladministration in local government or in certain local bodies.

The Northern Ireland Commissioner for Complaints fulfils a similar function in Northern Ireland, investigating complaints about local authorities and certain public bodies.

Complaints are made to the relevant local authority in the first instance and complainants may approach the Commissioners if not satisfied. Complaints may also be made directly to the Commissioners.

The Local Government Act 2000 established a Standards Board and Adjudication Panel in England. The Standards Board investigates any allegations that councillors have breached the council's Code of Conduct and if there is evidence of wrongdoing the Adjudication Panel will consider the report of investigations and if it is upheld, impose a penalty. In Wales the Commission for Local Administration in Wales undertakes the role of the Standards Board.

THE QUEEN'S REPRESENTATIVES

The Lord-Lieutenant of a county is the permanent local representative of the Crown in that county. The appointment of Lord-Lieutenants is now regulated by the Lieutenancies Act 1997. They are appointed by the Sovereign on the recommendation of the Prime Minister. The retirement age is 75. The office of Lord-Lieutenant dates from 1551, and its holder was originally responsible for the maintenance of order and for local defence in the county. The duties of the post include attending on royalty during official visits to the county, performing certain duties in connection with armed forces of the Crown (and in particular the reserve forces), and making presentations of honours and awards on behalf of the Crown. In England, Wales and Northern Ireland, the Lord-Lieutenant usually also holds the office of *Custos Rotulorum*. As such, he or she acts as head of the county's commission of the peace (which recommends the appointment of magistrates).

The office of Sheriff (from the Old English shire-reeve) of a county was created in the tenth century. The Sheriff was the special nominee of the Sovereign, and the office reached the peak of its influence under the Norman kings. The Provisions of Oxford (1258) laid down a yearly tenure of office. Since the mid-16th century the office has been purely civil, with military duties taken over by the Lord-Lieutenant of the county. The Sheriff (commonly known as 'High Sheriff') attends on royalty during official visits to the county, acts as the returning officer during parliamentary elections in county constituencies, attends the opening ceremony when a High Court judge goes on circuit, executes High Court writs, and appoints under-sheriffs to act as deputies. The appointments and duties of the High Sheriffs in England and Wales are laid down by the Sheriffs Act 1887.

The serving High Sheriff submits a list of names of possible future sheriffs to a tribunal which chooses three names to put to the Sovereign. The tribunal nominates the High Sheriff annually on 12 November and the Sovereign picks the name of the Sheriff to succeed in the following year. The term of office runs from 25 March to the following 24 March (the civil and legal year before 1752). No person may be chosen twice in three years if there is any other suitable person in the county.

CIVIC DIGNITIES

District councils in England may petition for a royal charter granting borough or 'city' status to the district. Local councils in Wales may petition for a royal charter granting county borough or 'city' status to the council.

In England and Wales the chairman of a borough or county borough council may be called a mayor, and the chairman of a city council a Lord Mayor. Parish councils in England and community councils in Wales may call themselves 'town councils', in which case their chairman is the town mayor.

In Scotland the chairman of a local council may be known as a convenor; a provost is the equivalent of a mayor. The chairmen of the councils for the cities of Aberdeen, Dundee, Edinburgh and Glasgow are Lord Provosts.

ENGLAND

There are currently 34 non-metropolitan counties; all are divided into non-metropolitan districts. In addition, there are 45 unitary authorities (13 created in April 1996, 13 in April 1997 and 19 in April 1998). At present there are 238 non-metropolitan districts. The populations of most of the new unitary authorities are in the range of 100,000 to 300,000. The non-metropolitan districts have populations broadly in the range of 60,000 to 100,000; some, however, have larger populations, because of the need to avoid dividing large towns, and some in mainly rural areas have smaller populations.

The main conurbations outside Greater London – Tyne and Wear, West Midlands, Merseyside, Greater Manchester, West Yorkshire and South Yorkshire – are divided into 36 metropolitan districts, most of which have a population of over 200,000.

There are also about 10,000 parishes, in 219 of the non-metropolitan and 18 of the metropolitan districts.

ELECTIONS

For districts, non-metropolitan counties and for about 8,000 parishes, there are elected councils, consisting of directly elected councillors. The councillors elect annually one of their number as chairman.

Generally, councillors serve four years and there are no elections of district and parish councillors in county election years. In metropolitan districts, one-third of the councillors for each ward are elected each year except in the year when county elections take place elsewhere. Non-metropolitan districts can choose whether to have elections by thirds or whole council elections. In the former case, one-third of the council, as nearly as may be, is elected in each year of metropolitan district elections. If whole council elections are chosen, these are held in the year midway between county elections.

FUNCTIONS

In non-metropolitan areas, functions are divided between the districts and counties, those requiring the larger area or population for their efficient performance going to the county. The metropolitan district councils, with the larger population in their areas, already had wider functions than non-metropolitan councils, and following abolition of the metropolitan county councils were given most of their functions also. A few functions continue to be exercised over the larger area by joint bodies, made up of councillors from each district.

The allocation of functions is as follows:

County councils: education; strategic planning; traffic, transport and highways; fire service; consumer protection; refuse disposal; smallholdings; social services; libraries

Non-metropolitan district councils: local planning; housing; highways (maintenance of certain urban roads and off-street car parks); building regulations; environmental health; refuse collection; cemeteries and crematoria

Unitary councils: their functions are all those listed above, except that the fire service is exercised by a joint body

Concurrently by county and district councils: recreation (parks, playing fields, swimming pools); museums; encouragement of the arts, tourism and industry

The Police and Magistrates Court Act 1994 set up police authorities in England and Wales separate from the local authorities.

PARISH COUNCILS

Parishes with 200 or more electors must generally have parish councils, which means that over three-quarters of the parishes have councils. A parish council comprises at least five members, the number being fixed by the district council. Elections are held every four years, at the time of the election of the district councillor for the ward including the parish. All parishes have parish meetings, comprising the electors of the parish. Where there is no council, the meeting must be held at least twice a year.

Parish council functions include: allotments; encouragement of arts and crafts; community halls, recreational facilities (e.g. open spaces, swimming pools), cemeteries and crematoria; and many minor functions. They must also be given an opportunity to comment on planning applications. They may, like county and district councils, spend limited sums for the general benefit of the parish. They levy a precept on the district councils for their funds.

The Local Government and Rating Act 1997 gave additional powers to parish councils to spend money on community transport initiatives and crime prevention equipment.

FINANCE

Aggregate external finance for 2001-2002 was originally determined at £44,520 million. Of this, specific and special grants were estimated at £9,229 million; £21,122 million was in respect of revenue support grant and £15,137 million was support from the national non-domestic rate pool. Total standard spending by local authorities considered for grant purposes was £57,133 million.

In England, the average council tax per dwelling in 2000-2001 was £697, an increase of 6.2 per cent from the 1999-2000 level. The average council tax was £710 in shire areas, £713 in London and £650 in metropolitan areas. In England, the average council tax bill for a band D dwelling (occupied by two adults) for 2000-2001 was £847, an increase of 6.1 per cent from the 1999-2000 level. The average band D council tax was £843 in shire areas, £778 in London and £919 in metropolitan areas.

The provisional amount estimated to be raised from national non-domestic rates from central and local lists is £15,068 million. Total rateable value held on draft local authority lists at 30 December 2000 was £41,351 million. The amount of national non-domestic rates to be redistributed to authorities from the pool in 2001-2002 was £15,137 million. The national non-domestic rate multiplier, or poundage, for 2001-2002 is 43.0p. Under the Local Government and Housing Act 1989, local authorities have four main ways of paying for capital expenditure: borrowing and other forms of extended credit; capital grants from central government towards some types of capital expenditure; 'usable' capital receipts from the sale of land, houses and other assets; and revenue.

The amount of capital expenditure which a local authority can finance by borrowing (or other forms of credit) is effectively limited by the credit approvals issued to it by central government. Most credit approvals can be used for any kind of local authority capital expenditure; these are known as basic credit approvals. Others (supplementary credit approvals) can be used only for the kind of expenditure specified in the approval, and so are often given to fund particular projects or services.

Local authorities can use all capital receipts from the sale of property or assets for capital spending, except in the case of sales of council houses. Generally, the 'usable' part of a local authority's capital receipts consists of 25 per cent of receipts from the sale of council houses and 50 per cent of other housing assets such as shops or vacant land. The balance has to be set aside as provision for repaying debt and meeting other credit liabilities.

EXPENDITURE

Local authority budgeted net revenue expenditure for 2001–2002 was (2001–2002 cash prices):

Service	£m
Education	25,813
Personal social services	11,076
Police	7,861
Highway maintenance	1,615
Fire	1,842
Emergency Planning and other Home Office services	105
Magistrates courts	324
Public transport and parking	972
Housing benefit administration	6,167
Non-housing revenue account housing	434
Libraries, culture and heritage	1,201
Sport	557
Local environmental services	4,696
Other services	2,427
Net current expenditure	65,073
Capital charges	2,050
Capital charged to revenue	699
Other non-current expenditure	2,378
Interest receipts	–809

Gross revenue expenditure	69,390
Specific and special grants outside AEF	–8,119
Revenue expenditure	61,270
Specific and special grants inside AEF	–5,431
Net revenue expenditure	55,839

AEF = aggregate external finance

LONDON

Since the abolition of the Greater London Council in 1986, the Greater London area has not had a single local government body. The area is divided into 32 borough councils, which have a status similar to the metropolitan district councils in the rest of England, and the Corporation of the City of London.

In March 1998 the Government announced proposals for a Greater London Authority (GLA) covering the area of the 32 London boroughs and the City of London, which would comprise a directly elected mayor and a 25-member assembly. A referendum was held in London on 7 May 1998; the turnout was approximately 34 per cent, of whom 72 per cent voted in favour of the GLA. The independent candidate for London Mayor, Ken Livingstone, was elected on 4 May 2000 and the Authority assumed its responsibilities on 3 July 2000. The GLA is responsible for transport, economic development, strategic planning, culture, health, the environment, the police and fire and emergency planning. The separately elected assembly scrutinise the mayor's activities and approve plans and budgets. There are 14 Constituency Assembly members, each representing a separate area of London (each constituency is made up of two or three complete London boroughs). Eleven additional members, making up the total Assembly complement of 25 members, are elected on a Londonwide basis, either as independents or from party political lists on the basis of proportional representation. Parties or independent candidates must secure at least five per cent of the vote to be entitled to additional seats.

LONDON BOROUGH COUNCILS

The London boroughs have whole council elections every four years, in the year immediately following the county council election year. The next elections will be in 2002.

The borough councils have responsibility for the following functions: building regulations; cemeteries and crematoria; consumer protection; education; youth employment; environmental health; electoral registration; food; drugs; housing; leisure services; libraries; local planning; local roads; museums; parking; recreation (parks, playing fields, swimming pools); refuse collection and street cleansing; social services; town planning; and traffic management.

THE CORPORATION OF LONDON

The Corporation of London is the local authority for the City of London. Its legal definition is 'The Mayor and Commonalty and Citizens of the City of London'. It is governed by the Court of Common Council, which consists of the Lord Mayor, 24 other aldermen, and 130 common councilmen. The Lord Mayor and two sheriffs are nominated annually by the City guilds (the livery companies) and elected by the Court of Aldermen. Aldermen and councilmen are elected from the 25 wards into which the City is divided; councilmen must stand for re-election annually. The Council is a legislative assembly, and there are no political parties.

The Corporation has the same functions as the London borough councils. In addition, it runs the City of London Police; is the health authority for the Port of London; has health control of animal imports throughout Greater London, including at Heathrow airport; owns and manages public open spaces throughout Greater London; runs the Central Criminal Court; and runs Billingsgate, Smithfield and Spitalfields markets.

THE CITY GUILDS (LIVERY COMPANIES)

The livery companies of the City of London grew out of early medieval religious fraternities and began to emerge as trade and craft guilds, retaining their religious aspect, in the 12th century. From the early 14th century, only members of the trade and craft guilds could call themselves citizens of the City of London. The guilds began to be called livery companies, because of the distinctive livery worn by the most prosperous guild members on ceremonial occasions, in the late 15th century.

By the early 19th century the power of the companies within their trades had begun to wane, but those wearing the livery of a company continued to play an important role in the government of the City of London. Liverymen still have the right to nominate the Lord Mayor and sheriffs, and most members of the Court of Common Council are liverymen.

GREATER LONDON SERVICES

After the abolition of the Greater London Council (GLC) in 1986, the London boroughs took over most of its functions. Successor bodies have also been set up for certain functions. The London Residuary Body (LRB) was set up in 1986 to deal with residual matters of the GLC. It completed its work and was wound up in 1995.

WALES

The Local Government (Wales) Act 1994 abolished the two-tier structure of eight county and 37 district councils which had existed since 1974, and replaced it, from 1 April 1996, with 22 unitary authorities. The new authorities were elected in May 1995. Each unitary authority has inherited all the functions of the previous county and district councils, except fire services (which are provided by three combined fire authorities, composed of representatives of the unitary authorities) and National Parks (which are the responsibility of three independent National Park authorities).

The Police and Magistrates Courts Act 1994 set up four police authorities with effect from 1 April 1995: Dyfed-Powys, Gwent, North Wales, and South Wales.

COMMUNITY COUNCILS

In Wales community councils are the equivalent of parishes in England. Unlike England, where many areas are not in any parish, communities have been established for the whole of Wales, approximately 865 communities in all. Community meetings may be convened as and when desired.

Community councils exist in 735 communities and further councils may be established at the request of a community meeting. Community councils have broadly the same range of powers as English parish councils. Community councillors are elected for a term of four years.

FINANCE

Aggregate external finance for 2001-2002 (excluding specific grants) is £2,848 million. This comprises revenue

support grant of £2,147 million, support from the national non-domestic rate pool of £697 million, and £4 million in council tax reduction grants. Total standard spending by local authorities considered for grant purposes is £3,495 million.

The average Band D council tax levied in Wales for 2001-02 is £710, comprising unitary authorities £606, police authorities £86, community councils £18 and an average grant reduction of £4.

EXPENDITURE

Local authority budgeted net revenue expenditure for 2001–2 was:

Service	£m
Education	1,585.0
Personal social services	716.5
Police	426.2
Fire	102.9
Other law, order and protective services	34.8
Roads and Transport	192.3
Council tax benefit and administration	124.4
Non-housing revenue account housing, including housing benefit	280.0
Libraries, culture, heritage, sport and recreation	122.8
Local environmental services	293.7
National Parks	9.6
Debt financing costs	256.8
Other services	196.7
Gross Revenue Expenditure	4,342.2
Less specific government grants	–578.0
Net revenue expenditure	3,763.7

SCOTLAND

The Local Government etc. (Scotland) Act 1994 abolished the two-tier structure of nine regional and 53 district councils which had existed since 1975 and replaced it, from 1 April 1996, with 29 unitary authorities on the mainland; the three islands councils remained. The new authorities were elected in April 1995. Each unitary authority has inherited all the functions of the regional and district councils, except water and sewerage (now provided by three public bodies whose members were appointed by the Secretary of State for Scotland; this power has now been devolved to the Scottish Executive) and reporters panels (now a national agency).

In July 1999 the Scottish Parliament assumed responsibility for legislation on local government. The Government had established a Commission on Local Government and the Scottish Parliament (the McIntosh Commission) to make recommendations on the relationship between local authorities and the new Parliament and on increasing local authorities' accountability. The Commission reported to the First Minister of the Scottish Parliament in June 1999. Following this, the Scottish Executive established the 'Renewing Local Democracy' working group to consider ways in which council membership could be made more attractive and councils could become more representative of the make-up of the community and advise on the appropriate numbers of members for each council, taking account of new management arrangements and characteristics. They also investigated which method of election would be most appropriate, taking account of the following criteria; proportionality and the councillor-ward link, fair provision for independents, allowance for geographical diversity and a close fit between council wards and natural communities, and advise on an appropriate system of remuneration for councillors, taking account of available resources.

The Scottish Executive also set up the Leadership Advisory Panel in October 1999 following the recommendations of the McIntosh Report. The panel is working closely with all Scottish local authorities conducting reviews of their policy development and decision-making structures.

ELECTIONS

The unitary authorities consist of directly elected councillors. Elections take place every three years; the next elections are in 2002. In 2001 the register showed 3,984,306 electors in Scotland.

FUNCTIONS

The functions of the councils and islands councils are: education; social work; strategic planning; the provision of infrastructure such as roads; consumer protection; flood prevention; coast protection; valuation and rating; the police and fire services; civil defence; electoral registration; public transport; registration of births, deaths and marriages; housing; leisure and recreation; development control and building control; environmental health; licensing; allotments; public conveniences; and the administration of district courts.

COMMUNITY COUNCILS

Unlike the parish councils and community councils in England and Wales, Scottish community councils are not local authorities. Their purpose as defined in statute is to ascertain and express the views of the communities they represent, and to take in the interests of their communities such action as appears to be expedient or practicable. Over 1,000 community councils have been established under schemes drawn up by district and islands councils in Scotland.

Since April 1996 community councils have had an enhanced role, becoming statutory consultees on local planning issues and on the decentralisation schemes which the new councils have to draw up for delivery of services.

FINANCE

Figures for 2000–01 show total receipts from non-domestic rates of £1,535,173,000 (provisional). The unified business rate for 2001–2 was 45p for property with a rateable value of less than £10,000 and 47p otherwise. The average Band D council tax payable in 2001–2 was £929.

EXPENDITURE

The 2001–2 budget estimates for local authorities in Scotland were:

Service	£m
Education	3,245.9
Arts and Libraries	126.5
Social Work Services	1,334.0
Law, order and protective services	1,011.8
Roads and transport	365.3
Other environmental services	758.2
Tourism	9.1
Housing	3.3
Sub-total	6,854.6

Sheltered employment	9.6
Housing benefit administration	42.7
Consumer protection	70.8
Total	6,925.3

NORTHERN IRELAND

For the purpose of local government Northern Ireland has a system of 26 single-tier district councils.

ELECTIONS

There are 582 members of the councils, elected for periods of four years at a time on the principle of proportional representation.

FUNCTIONS

The district councils have three main roles. These are:

Executive: responsibility for a wide range of local services including building regulations; community services; consumer protection; cultural facilities; environmental health; miscellaneous licensing and registration provisions, including dog control; litter prevention; recreational and social facilities; refuse collection and disposal; street cleansing; and tourist development

Representative: nominating representatives to sit as members of the various statutory bodies responsible for the administration of regional services such as drainage, education, fire, health and personal social services, housing, and libraries

Consultative: acting as the medium through which the views of local people are expressed on the operation in their area of other regional services, notably conservation (including water supply and sewerage services), planning and roads, provided by those departments of central government which have an obligation, statutory or otherwise, to consult the district councils about proposals affecting their areas

FINANCE

Local government in Northern Ireland is funded by a system of rates (a local property tax calculated by using the rateable value of a property multiplied by an amount per pound of rateable value). Rates are collected by the Rate Collection Agency, an executive agency within the Department of the Environment for Northern Ireland. A general revaluation of non-domestic properties became effective on 1 April 1997. As a result of this, separate regional rates are now made at standard uniform amounts by the Department of Finance and Personnel for both domestic and non-domestic sectors. District councils now make their individual district rates on the same basis.

In 2000–01 approximately £607.9 million was raised in rates. The average domestic poundage levied was 227.83p and the average non-domestic rate poundage was 47.13p.

Political Composition of Local Councils

AS AT END JUNE 2001

Abbreviations:

C.	Conservative
Com.	Communist
Dem.	Democrat
Green	Green
Ind.	Independent
Lab.	Labour
Lib.	Liberal
LD	Liberal Democrat
MK	Mebyon Kernow
NP	Non-political/Non-party
PC	Plaid Cymru
RA	Ratepayers'/Resident's Associations
SD	Social Democrat
SNP	Scottish National Party

ENGLAND

COUNTY COUNCILS

Bedfordshire	*C.* 25, *Lab.* 14, *LD* 10
Buckinghamshire	*C.* 40, *Lab.* 5, *LD* 9
Cambridgeshire	*C.* 34, *Lab.* 9, *LD* 16
Cheshire	*C.* 28, *Ind.* 1, *Lab.* 17, *LD* 5
Cornwall	*C.* 9, *Ind.* 25, *Lab.* 9, *LD* 35, *Lib.* 1
Cumbria	*C.* 33, *Ind.* 1, *Lab.* 40, *LD* 10
Derbyshire	*C.* 13, *Ind.* 1, *Lab.* 43, *LD* 7
Devon	*C.* 22, *Ind.* 3, *Lab.* 5, *LD* 21, *Lib.* 2, *Other* 1
Dorset	*C.* 23, *Ind.* 1, *Lab.* 4, *LD* 14
Durham	*C.* 2, *Ind.* 2, *Lab.* 53, *LD* 4
East Sussex	*C.* 20, *Lab.* 7, *LD* 17
Essex	*C.* 40, *Ind.* 1, *Lab.* 24, *LD* 14
Gloucestershire	*C.* 24, *Ind.* 3, *Lab.* 15, *LD* 20, *Others* 1
Hampshire	*C.* 46, *Lab.* 9, *LD* 19
Hertfordshire	*C.* 40, *Lab.* 27, *LD* 10
Kent	*C.* 52, *Lab.* 22, *LD* 10
Lancashire	*C.* 26, *Green* 1, *Lab.* 44, *LD* 6, *Other* 1
Leicestershire	*C.* 25, *Lab.* 17, *LD* 11, *Other* 1
Lincolnshire	*C.* 49, *Ind.* 3, *Lab.* 21, *LD* 4
Norfolk	*C.* 37, *Ind.* 1, *Lab.* 33, *LD* 13
Northamptonshire	*C.* 33, *Lab.* 39, *LD* 1
Northumberland	*C.* 17, *Ind.* 3, *Lab.* 38, *LD* 9
North Yorkshire	*C.* 37, *Ind.* 5, *Lab.* 11, *LD* 21
Nottinghamshire	*C.* 20, *Lab.* 40, *LD* 3
Oxfordshire	*C.* 26, *Green* 2, *Lab.* 24, *LD* 18
Shropshire	*C.* 18, *Lab.* 11, *LD* 9, *Others* 6
Somerset	*C.* 24, *Lab.* 5, *LD* 29
Staffordshire	*C.* 24, *Lab.* 36, *LD* 2
Suffolk	*C.* 31, *Ind.* 1, *Lab.* 36, *LD* 12
Surrey	*C.* 51, *Lab.* 6, *LD* 13, *Others* 6
Warwickshire	*C.* 20, *Ind.* 1, *Lab.* 28, *LD* 13
West Sussex	*C.* 42, *Lab.* 11, *LD* 18
Wiltshire	*C.* 28, *Ind.* 3, *Lab.* 3, *LD* 13
Worcestershire	*C.* 26, *Ind.* 6, *Ind. Lib.* 3, *Lab* 14, *LD* 8

UNITARY COUNCIL

Barnsley	*C.* 3, *Ind.* 7, *Lab.* 52, *LD* 3 *Others* 1
Bath and North-East Somerset	*C.* 16, *Ind.Lab.* 2, *Lab.* 17, *LD* 30,
Birmingham	*C.* 28, *Lab.* 66, *LD* 18, *Others* 5
Blackburn with Darwen	*C.* 19, *Lab.* 37, *LD* 6
Blackpool	*C.* 15, *Lab.* 25, *LD* 4
Bolton	*C.* 15, *Lab.* 34, *LD* 11
Bournemouth	*C.* 27, *Ind.* 6, *Lab.* 6, *LD* 18
Bracknell Forest	*C.* 30, *Lab.* 9, *Lab.* 1
Bradford	*C.* 37, *Green* 1, *Lab.* 40, *LD* 11, *vacant* 1
Brighton and Hove	*C.* 26, *Green* 3, *Lab.* 45, *LD* 3, *vacant* 1
Bristol	*C.* 10, *Lab.* 35, *LD* 24, *Other* 1
Bury	*C.* 13, *Lab.* 31, *LD* 3, *vacant* 1
Calderdale	*C.* 28, *Ind.* 1, *Lab.* 8, *LD* 17
Coventry	*C.* 15, *Lab.* 35, *SD* 1, *Others* 3
Darlington	*C.* 15, *Lab.* 35 *LD* 2
Derby	*C.* 9, *Lab.* 29, *LD* 6
Doncaster	*C.* 6, *Ind.* 4, *Lab.* 40, *LD* 7, *Others* 6
Dudley	*C.* 18, *Lab.* 43, *LD* 11
East Riding of Yorkshire	*C.* 27, *Ind.* 6, *Lab.* 12, *LD* 22
Gateshead	*Lab.* 47, *LD* 18, *Lib.* 1
Halton	*C.* 2, *Lab.* 43, *LD* 7, *Others* 4
Hartlepool	*C.* 9, *Ind.* 3, *Lab.* 21, *LD* 14
Herefordshire	*C.* 22, *Ind.* 13, *Lab.* 5, *LD* 20
Isle of Wight	*C.* 15, *Ind.* 8, *Lab.* 4, *LD* 17, *Lib.* 2, *Others* 1
Kingston upon Hull	*C.* 2, *Ind. Lab.* 2, *Lab.* 44, *LD* 10, *Others* 2
Kirklees	*C.* 15, *Green* 3, *Lab.* 25, *LD* 29
Knowsley	*Lab.* 60, *LD* 4, *Others* 2
Leeds	*C.* 16, *Green* 2, *Ind.* 1, *Lab.* 61, *LD* 19
Leicester	*C.* 10, *Lab.* 30, *LD* 16
Liverpool	*Ind.* 1, *Lab.* 20, *Ind. Lab.* 3, *LD* 70, *Lib.* 3, *Others* 2
Luton	*C.* 3, *Lab.* 36, *LD* 9
Manchester	*Lab.* 77, *LD* 21, *Other* 1
Medway	*C.* 38, *Lab.* 25, *LD* 15, *Others* 2
Middlesbrough	*C.* 4, *Ind.* 1, *Lab.* 42, *LD* 6
Milton Keynes	*C.* 8, *Ind.* 1, *Lab.* 22, *LD* 20
Newcastle upon Tyne	*Lab.* 62, *LD* 16
North East Lincolnshire	*C.* 11, *Ind.* 4, *Lab.* 23, *LD* 5
North Lincolnshire	*C.* 19, *Lab.* 23
North Somerset	*C.* 32, *Green* 1, *Ind.* 3, *Lab.* 13, *LD* 11, *Others* 1
North Tyneside	*C.* 17, *Lab.* 35, *LD* 8
Nottingham City	*C.* 11, *Lab.* 40, *LD* 4
Oldham	*C.* 2, *Green* 2, *Ind.* 2, *Lab.* 24, *LD* 30
Peterborough	*C.* 27, *Lab.* 22, *LD* 3, *Lib.* 3, *Other* 2
Plymouth	*C.* 39, *Lab.* 21
Poole	*C.* 17, *Lab.* 3, *LD* 19
Portsmouth	*C.* 16, *Lab.* 15, *LD* 8
Reading	*C.* 3, *Lab.* 36, *LD* 5
Redcar and Cleveland	*C.* 14, *Lab.* 31, *LD* 10, *Others* 4
Rochdale	*C.* 8, *Lab.* 31, *LD* 21
Rotherham	*C.* 4, *Ind.* 4, *Lab.* 57, *LD* 1
Rutland	*C.* 1, *Green* 1, *Ind.* 10, *Lab.* 2, *LD* 4, *Others* 2
St Helens	*C.* 4, *Lab.* 35, *LD* 15
Salford	*C.* 3, *Lab.* 52, *LD* 5
Sandwell	*C.* 6, *Ind.* 1, *Lab.* 55, *Lib.* 10
Sefton	*C.* 19, *Lab.* 22, *LD* 25
Sheffield	*Ind.* 1, *Lab.* 37, *LD* 48, *Lib.* 1
Slough	*C.* 8, *Ind.* 1, *Lab.* 26, *LD* 1, *Lib.* 4, *Other* 1
Solihull	*C.* 29, *Lab.* 11, *LD* 8, *Others* 3
Southampton	*C.* 7, *Lab.* 22, *LD* 16

South Gloucestershire   *C.* 10, *Lab.* 23, *LD* 37
Southend   *C.* 32, *Lab.* 11, *LD* 7
South Tyneside   *Lab.* 50, *LD* 6, *Others* 4
Stockport   *C.* 6, *Ind.* 3, *Lab.* 22, *LD* 32
Stockton-on-Tees   *C.* 12, *Lab.* 38, *LD* 5
Stoke-on-Trent   *C.* 6, *Ind.* 15, *Lab.* 32, *LD* 7
Sunderland   *C.* 10, *Lab.* 61, *LD* 3
Swindon   *C.* 23, *Lab.* 28, *LD* 8
Tameside   *C.* 6, *Lab.* 47, *LD* 2, *Others* 2
Telford and Wrekin   *C.* 15, *Ind.* 4, *Lab.* 30, *LD* 4, *RA* 1
Thurrock   *C.* 10, *Ind.* 3, *Lab.* 36
Torbay   *C.* 31, *LD* 5
Trafford   *C.* 27, *Lab.* 33, *LD* 3
Wakefield   *C.* 6, *Ind. Lab.* 1, *Lab.* 55, *Lib. Dem.* 1
Walsall   *C.* 26, *Lab.* 27, *Lib.* 7
Warrington   *C.* 4, *Lab.* 43, *LD* 13
West Berkshire   *C.* 25, *Ind.* 1, *LD* 28
Wigan   *C.* 1, *Lab.* 69, *LD* 2
Windsor and Maidenhead *C.* 29, *Lab.* 1, *LD* 21, *Others* 7
Wirral   *C.* 20, *Lab.* 34, *LD* 12
Wokingham   *C.* 27, *LD* 27
Wolverhampton   *C.* 24, *Lab.* 33, *LD* 3
York   *C.* 3, *Ind.* 1, *Lab.* 25, *LD* 24

DISTRICT COUNCILS

*Denotes councils where one-third of Councillors retire each year except in the year of county council elections

*Adur, W. Sussex   *C.* 18, *Ind.* 2, *Lab.* 12, *LD* 7
Allerdale, Cumbria   *C.* 10, *Ind.* 2, *Lab.* 36, *LD* 7, *vacant* 1
Alnwick,   *C.* 2, *Ind.* 13, *Lab.* 2, *LD* 12,
Northumberland   *Others* 1
Amber Valley, Derbys   *C.* 32, *Ind.* 1, *Lab.* 12
Arun, W. Sussex   *C.* 36, *Ind.* 3, *Lab.* 8, *LD* 9
Ashfield, Notts   *C.* 1, *Ind.* 2, *Lab.* 30
Ashford, Kent   *C.* 24, *Ind.* 2, *Ind. C.* 1, *Lab.* 10, *LD* 9, *Others* 3
Aylesbury Vale, Bucks   *C.* 25, *Ind.* 7, *Lab.* 1, *LD* 25
Babergh, Suffolk   *C.* 10, *Ind.* 13, *Lab.* 5, *LD* 13, *Others* 1
*Barrow-in-Furness,   *C.* 16, *Lab.* 18, *Others* 4
Cumbria
*Basildon, Essex   *C.* 18, *Lab.* 19, *LD* 4, *vacant* 1
*Basingstoke and Deane,   *C.* 25, *Ind.* 2, *Lab.* 15, *LD* 15
Hants
*Bassetlaw, Notts   *C.* 14 *Ind.* 2, *Lab.* 31 *LD* 3
*Bedford, Beds   *C.* 7, *Ind.* C. 6,*Ind.*6, *Lab.* 18, *LD* 16
Berwick-upon-Tweed,   *C.* 3, *Ind.* 5, *Lab.* 1, *LD* 16, *Others* 4
Northumberland
Blaby, Leics   *C.* 25, *Lab.* 6, *LD* 8
Blyth Valley,   *C.* 2, *Ind.* 3, *Lab.* 35, *LD* 9, *vacant* 1
Northumberland
Bolsover, Derbys   *Ind.* 4, *Lab.* 32, *RA* 1
Boston, Lincs   *C.* 14, *Ind.* 5, *Lab.* 10, *LD* 3
Braintree, Essex   *Lab.* 31, *LD* 3, *Others* 3
Breckland, Norfolk   *C.* 34, *Ind.* 3, *Lab.* 14, *LD* 2
*Brentwood, Essex   *C.* 11, *Ind.C.* 1, *Lab.* 2, *LD* 24, *Lib.* 1
Bridgnorth, Shrops   *C.* 8, *Ind.* 10, *Ind. Al.* 9, *LD* 4, *Others* 2
Broadland, Norfolk   *C.* 25, Ind. *8*, Lab. 7, *LD* 9
Bromsgrove, Worcs   *C.* 30, *Ind.* C. 1, *Lab.* 6, *RA* 2
*Broxbourne, Herts   *C.* 35, *Lab.* 3
Broxtowe, Notts   *C.* 12, *Ind.* 1, *Lab.* 25, *LD* 11
*Burnley, Lancs   *C.* 3, *Ind.* 11, *Lab.* 24, *LD* 9, *Others* 1
*Cambridge, Cambs   *C.* 3, *Ind.* 1, *Lab.* 15, *LD* 23
*Cannock Chase, Staffs   *C.* 8, *Lab.* 27, *LD* 7
Canterbury, Kent   *C.* 18, *Lab.* 13, *LD* 17, *Other* 1
Caradon, Cornwall   *C.* 1, *Ind.* 20, *Lab.* 2, *LD* 18
*Carlisle, Cumbria   *C.* 29, *Ind.* 2, *Lab.* 16, *LD* 5
Carrick, Cornwall   *C.* 15, *Ind.* 6, *Lab.* 2, *LD* 18 *Ind. LD* 1

Castle Morpeth,   *C.* 4, *Green* 1, *Ind.* 10, *Lab.* 9, *LD* 8
Northumberland
Castle Point, Essex   *C.* 15, *Lab.* 22, *Others* 2
Charnwood, Leics   *C.* 20, *Ind.* C 1, *Lab.* 24, *LD* 6, *Other* 1
Chelmsford, Essex   *C.* 23, *Ind.* 2, *Lab.* 5, *LD* 26
*Cheltenham, Glos   *C.* 23, *Lab.* 2, *LD* 11, *Others* 5
*Cherwell, Oxon   *C.* 33, *Ind.* 3, *Lab.* 12, *LD* 4
Chesterfield, Derbys   *Lab.* 28, *LD* 19
Chester-le-Street, Co.   *C.* 1, *Ind.* 1, *Lab.* 30, *LD* 1
Durham
*Chester, Cheshire   *C.* 18, *Ind.* 2, *Lab.* 22, *LD* 18
Chichester, W. Sussex   *C.* 30, *Ind.* 2 *LD* 18
Chiltern, Bucks   *C.* 29, *LD* 19, *RA* 2
*Chorley, Lancs   *C.* 15, *Ind.* 2, *Lab.* 24, *LD* 7
Christchurch, Dorset   *C.* 17, *Ind.* 3, *LD* 5
*Colchester, Essex   *C.* 22, *Lab.* 14, *LD* 23, *RA* 1
*Congleton, Cheshire   *C.* 14, *Lab.* 2, *LD* 32
Copeland, Cumbria   *C.* 17, *Ind.* 3, *Lab.* 30, *LD* 1
Corby, Northants   *C.* 2, *Ind.* 1, *Lab.* 26
Cotswold, Glos   *C.* 11, *Ind.* 25, *Lab.* 2, *LD* 7
*Craven, N. Yorks   *C.* 18, *Ind.* 12, *LD* 4
*Crawley, W. Sussex   *C.* 6, *Lab.* 24, *LD* 2
*Crewe and Nantwich,   *C.* 21, *Ind.* 1, *Lab.* 26, *LD* 5,
Cheshire   *Others* 3
Dacorum, Herts   *C.* 27, *Ind.* 1, *Lab.* 20, *LD* 4
Dartford, Kent   *C.* 13, *Ind.* 5, *Lab.* 29
*Daventry, Northants   *C.* 20, *Ind.* 2, *Lab.* 13, *LD* 3
Derbyshire Dales, Derbys *C.* 21, *Ind.* 3, *Lab.* 6, *LD* 9
Derwentside, Co.   *Ind.* 7, *Lab.* 47, *Others* 1
Durham
Dover, Kent   *C.* 26, *Ind.* 1, *Lab.* 28, *LD* 1
Durham, Co. Durham   *Ind.* 3, *Lab.* 32, *Ind. Lab.* 1, *LD* 13
Easington, Co. Durham   *Ind.* 5, *Lab.* 45, *LD* 1
*Eastbourne, E. Sussex   *C.* 17, *LD* 13
East Cambridgeshire,   *Ind.* 13, *Lab.* 4, *LD* 20
Cambs
East Devon, Devon   *C.* 37, *Ind.* 6, *Lab.* 1, *LD* 15, *Lib.* 1
East Dorset, Dorset   *C.* 26, *Ind.* 1, *LD* 9
East Hampshire, Hants   *C.* 22, *Ind.* 3, *LD* 17
East Hertfordshire, Herts *C.* 32, *Ind.* 2, *Lab.* 7, *LD* 9
*Eastleigh, Hants   *C.* 9, *Lab.* 7, *LD* 28
East Lindsey, Lincs   *C.* 7, *Lab.* 9, *LD* 8, *Others* 36
East Northamptonshire,   *C.* 21, *Lab.* 15
Northants
East Staffordshire, Staffs *C.* 15, *Lab.* 28, *LD* 3
Eden, Cumbria   *C.* 4, *Ind.* 30, *Lab.* 1, *LD* 3
*Ellesmere Port and   *C.* 6, *Lab.* 36, *LD* 1
Neston, Cheshire
*Elmbridge, Surrey   *C.* 22, *Lab.* 1, *LD* 9, *RA* 28
*Epping Forest, Essex   *C.* 20, *Ind.* C. 3, *Lab.* 12, *LD* 16, *Others* 8
Epsom and Ewell, Surrey *Lab.* 3, *LD* 9, *RA* 27
Erewash, Derbys   *C.* 16, *Ind.* 3, *Lab.* 29, *LD* 3, *vacant* 1
*Exeter, Devon   *C.* 6, *Lab.* 22, *LD* 8, *Lib.* 4
*Fareham, Hants   *C.* 29, *Lab.* 2, *LD* 11
Fenland, Cambs   *C.* 27, *Ind.* 3, *Lab.* 7, *LD* 1, *vacant* 2
Forest Heath, Suffolk   *C.* 21, *Ind.* 1, *Lab.* 1, *LD* 2
Forest of Dean, Glos   *Con.* 2, *Ind.* 14, *Lab.* 28, *LD* 6
Fylde, Lancs   *C.* 20, *Ind.* 13, *Lab.* 2, *LD* 3, *Others* 11
Gedling, Notts   *C.* 29, *Ind.* 2, *Lab.* 19, *LD* 7
*Gloucester, Glos   *C.* 11, *Ind.* 1, *Lab.* 19, *LD* 8
*Gosport, Hants   *C.* 13, *Lab.* 12, *LD*5
Gravesham, Kent   *C.* 15, *Lab.* 29
*Great Yarmouth, Norfolk *C.* 26, *Lab.* 22
Guildford, Surrey   *C.* 17, *Ind.* 3, *Lab.* 6, *LD* 19
Hambleton, N. Yorks   *C.* 35, *Ind.* 6, *Lab.* 2, *LD* 4
Harborough, Leics   *C.* 17, *Ind.* 3, *Lab.* 3, *LD* 14
*Harlow, Essex   *C.* 8, *Ind.* 1, *Lab.* 25, *LD* 8
*Harrogate, N. Yorks   *C.* 18, *Lab.* 1, *LD* 40
*Hart, Hants   *Ind.* 17, *Con.* 18

*Hastings, E. Sussex — C. 6, Lab. 18, LD 8
*Havant, Hants — C. 19, Ind. 3, Lab. 11, LD 8
*Hertsmere, Herts — C. 22, Lab. 12, LD 5
High Peak, Derbys — C. 10, Ind. 2, Lab. 27, LD 5
Hinckley and Bosworth, Leics — C. 11, Lab. 9, LD 14
Horsham, W. Sussex — C. 24, Ind. 3, LD 16
*Huntingdonshire, Cambs — C. 37, Ind. 3, LD 13
*Hyndburn, Lancs — C. 31, Lab. 16
*Ipswich, Suffolk — C. 15, Lab. 31, LD 2
Kennet, Wilts — C. 23, Ind. 11, Lab. 4, LD 2
Kerrier, Cornwall — C. 4, Ind. 21, Lab. 9, LD 10
Kettering, Northants — C. 18, Ind. 4, Lab. 22, LD 1
King's Lynn and West Norfolk, Norfolk — C. 27, Lab. 27, LD 5, Others 1
Lancaster, Lancs — C. 9, Green 6, Ind. 23, Lab. 15, LD 7
Lewes, E. Sussex — C. 16, Ind. 1, LD 30, RA 1
Lichfield, Staffs — C. 29, Lab. 25, LD 2
*Lincoln, Lincs — C. 4, Lab. 29
*Macclesfield, Cheshire — C. 36, Lab. 6, LD 15, Others 3
*Maidstone, Kent — C. 16, Ind. 5, Lab. 12, LD 22
Maldon, Essex — C. 18, Ind. 6, Lab. 6
Malvern Hills, Worcs — C. 24, LD 13, Others 5
Mansfield, Notts — S. 5, Lab. 39, LD 2
Melton, Leics — C. 9, Ind. 6, Lab. 11
Mendip, Somerset — C. 18, Ind. 2, Lab. 10, LD 16
Mid Bedfordshire, Beds — C. 35, Ind. 5, Lab. 7, LD 6
Mid Devon, Devon — C. 2, Ind. 18, Lab. 1, LD 18, Lib. 1
Mid Suffolk, Suffolk — C. 18, Ind. Lab. 2, Lab. 6, LD 13, Ind. Lib. 1
*Mid Sussex, W. Sussex — C. 29, Ind. 2, Lab. 2, LD 21
*Mole Valley, Surrey — C. 19, Ind. 7, Lab. 1, LD 14
Newark and Sherwood, Notts — C. 21, Ind. 2, Lab. 26, LD 5
*Newcastle under Lyme, Staffs — C. 9, Ind. 1, Lab. 30, Lib. 16
New Forest, Hants — C. 33, Ind. 3, LD 22
Northampton, Northants — C. 8, Lab. 28, LD 11
North Cornwall, Cornwall — C. 3, Ind. 27, LD 11
North Devon, Devon — C. 5, Ind. 10, LD 27, Others 2
North Dorset, Dorset — C. 15, Ind. 8, LD 10
North East Derbyshire, Derbys — C. 9, Ind. 2, Lab. 39, LD 3
*North Hertfordshire, Herts — C. 27, Lab. 19, LD 3
North Kesteven, Lincs — C. 17, Ind. 4, Lab. 6, LD 6, Others 7
North Norfolk, Norfolk — Ind. 7, Lab. 7, Ind. Lab. 3, LD 12, Others 13
North Shropshire, Shrops — C. 12, Ind. 9, Lab. 5, LD 1, Others 13
North Warwickshire, Warks — C. 9, Ind. 1, Lab. 22, LD 2
North West Leicestershire, Leics — C. 8, Ind. C. 1, Lab. 31
North Wiltshire, Wilts — C. 20, Ind. 2, Lab. 4, LD 26
*Norwich, Norfolk — C. 1, Lab. 26, LD 21
*Nuneaton and Bedworth, Warks — C. 10, Lab. 35
*Oadby and Wigston, Leics — C. 5, LD 21
Oswestry, Shrops — C. 4, Ind. 13, Lab. 5, LD 6, vacant 1
*Oxford, Oxon — C. 1, Green 8, Lab. 22, LD 20
*Pendle, Lancs — C. 9, Lab. 23, LD 19
*Penwith, Cornwall — C. 11, Ind. 9, Lab. 3, LD 7, Others 5
*Preston, Lancs — C. 17, Ind. 1, Ind. Lab. 4, Lab. 25, LD 10
*Purbeck, Dorset — C. 16, Ind. C. 4, Ind. 4
*Redditch, Worcs — C. 10, Lab. 17, LD 2
*Reigate and Banstead, Surrey — C. 33, Lab. 8, LD 4, RA 6

Restormel, Cornwall — C. 13, Ind. 11, Lab. 1, LD 17, Others 1, vacant 1
Ribble Valley, Lancs — C. 19, Ind. 2, Lab. 1, LD 17
Richmondshire, N. Yorks — C. 6, Ind. 17, LD 9
*Rochford, Essex — C. 19, Lab. 9, LD 9, Others 3
*Rossendale, Lancs — C. 24, Lab. 12
Rother, E. Sussex — C. 29, Ind. 4, Lab. 4, LD 8
*Rugby, Warks — C. 14, Ind. 6, Lab. 17, LD 10, vacant 1
*Runnymede, Surrey — C. 33, Ind. 6, Lab. 3
Rushcliffe, Notts — C. 30, Ind. 1, Lab. 11, LD 12
*Rushmoor, Hants — C. 24, Ind. 1, Lab. 10, LD 10
Ryedale, N. Yorks — C. 11, Ind. 6, Lab. 1, LD 5
*St Albans, Herts — C. 19, Ind. 1, Lab. 15, LD 23
St Edmundsbury, Suffolk — C. 22, Ind. 4, Lab. 15, LD 2, vacant 1
Salisbury, Wilts — C. 29, Ind. 3, Lab. 11, LD 15
Scarborough, N. Yorks — C. 19, Ind. 14, Lab. 11, LD 5
Sedgefield, Co. Durham — Ind. 3, Lab. 44, LD 2
Sedgemoor, Somerset — C. 31, Lab. 16, LD 3
Selby, N. Yorks — C. 15, Ind. 6, Lab. 20
Sevenoaks, Kent — C. 33, Ind. 2, Lab. 9, LD 9
Shepway, Kent — C. 29, Lab. 11, LD 16
*Shrewsbury and Atcham, Shrops — C. 16, Ind. 4, Lab. 18, LD 10
*South Bedfordshire, Beds — C. 26, Ind. 3, Lab. 7, LD 17
South Bucks, Berks — C. 28, Ind. 10, LD 2
*South Cambridgeshire, Cambs — C. 20, Ind. 5, Lab. 13, LD 15, Other 1
South Derbyshire, Derbys — C. 10, Lab. 24
South Hams, Devon — C. 29, Ind. 4, Lab. 3, LD 4
South Holland, Lincs — C. 19, Ind. 10, Lab. 3, LD 1, Others 7
South Kesteven, Lincs — C. 30, Ind. 12, Lab. 12, LD 3, Other 1
*South Lakeland, Cumbria — C. 16, Ind. 4, Lab. 9, LD 22, vacant 1
South Norfolk, Norfolk — C. 16, Ind. 2, Lab. 2, LD 27
South Northamptonshire, Northants — C. 29, Ind. 4, Lab. 6, LD 3
South Oxfordshire, Oxon — C. 20, Ind. 3, Lab. 7, LD 20
South Ribble, Lancs — C. 18, Lab. 21, LD 12, Others 3
South Shropshire, Shrops — Green 2, Ind. 16, LD 16, Others 6
South Somerset, Somerset — C. 13, Ind. 6, LD 41
South Staffordshire, Staffs — C. 37, Ind. 2, Lab. 10, LD 1
Spelthorne, Surrey — C. 27, Lab. 9, LD 4
*Stafford Moorlands, Staffs — C. 17, Ind. 3, Lab. 14, LD 10, Others 10
Staffordshire, Staffs — C. 23, Ind. 1, Lab. 28, LD 8
*Stevenage, Herts — C. 3, Lab. 33, LD 3
*Stratford, Warks — C. 28, Ind. 5, Lab. 2, LD 18, Others 2
Stroud, Glos — C. 24, Green 4, Ind. 4, Lab. 18, LD 5
Suffolk Coastal, Suffolk — C. 35, Ind. 2, Lab. 7, LD 10
Surrey Heath, Surrey — C. 22 Lab. 6, LD 7
*Swale, Kent — C. 15, Lab. 12, LD 22
*Tamworth, Staffs — C. 13, Ind. 1, Lab. 16
*Tandridge, Surrey — C. 29, Lab. 3, LD 10
Taunton Deane, Somerset — C. 21, Green 1, Ind. 4, Lab. 5, LD 23
Teesdale, Co. Durham — C. 2, Ind. 12, Lab. 8, Others 9
Teignbridge, Devon — C. 20, Ind. 20, Lab. 1, LD 17
Tendring, Essex — C. 16, Ind. 8, Lab. 23, LD 9, RA 4
Test Valley, Hants — C. 28, Ind. 2, LD 14
Tewkesbury, Glos — C. 16, Ind. 5, Lab. 8, LD 4, Others 3
Thanet, Kent — C. 18, Ind. 3, Lab. 33
*Three Rivers, Herts — C. 15, Lab. 7, LD 26
*Tonbridge and Malling, Kent — C. 27, Lab. 7, LD 21
Torridge, Devon — C. 1, Green 1, Ind. 13, Lab. 2, LD 12, Others 6, vacant 1
*Tunbridge Wells, Kent — C. 31, Ind. 1, Lab. 5, LD 11
Tynedale, Northumberland — C. 23, Ind. 6, Lab. 12, LD 11

Uttlesford, Essex — *C.* 6, *Ind.* 8, *Lab.* 2, *LD* 29
Vale of White Horse, — *C.* 15, *Ind.* 1, *Lab.* 2, *LD* 33
  Oxon
Vale Royal, Cheshire — *C.* 16, *Lab.* 32, *LD* 8
Wansbeck, — *Lab.* 25, *LD* 20
  Northumberland
Warwick, Warks — *C.* 10, *Ind.* 6, *Lab.* 16, *LD* 13
*Watford, Herts — *C.* 8, *Lab.* 18, *LD* 10
*Waveney, Suffolk — *C.* 13, *Ind.* 3, *Lab.* 27, *LD* 4,
  Others 1
Waverley, Surrey — *C.* 31, *Lab.* 2, *LD* 24
Wealden, E. Sussex — *C.* 34, *Ind.* 2, *LD* 22
Wear Valley, Co. — *Ind.* 6, *Lab.* 30, *LD* 4
  Durham
Wellingborough, — *C.* 14, *Ind. C.* 1, *Ind.* 1, *Lab.* 20
  Northants
*Welwyn Hatfield, Herts — *C.* 23, *Lab.* 25
West Devon, Devon — *C.* 10, *Ind.* 12, *LD* 8
West Dorset, Dorset — *C.* 22, *Lab.* 4, *LD* 15, *Others* 14
*West Lancashire, Lancs — *C.* 23, *Ind.* 1, *Lab.* 24, *Others* 7
*West Lindsey, Lincs — *C.* 9, *Ind.* 9, *Lab.* 3, *LD* 16
*West Oxfordshire, Oxon — *C.* 26, *Ind.* 8, *Lab.* 2, *LD* 13
West Somerset, Somerset — *C.* 19, *Ind.* 7, *Lab.* 4, *LD* 1
West Wiltshire, Wilts — *C.* 11, *Ind.* 2, *Lab.* 2, *LD* 25, *Others* 3
*Weymouth and Portland, — *C.* 5, *Lab.* 13, *LD* 12, *Others* 5
  Dorset
*Winchester, Hants — *C.* 11, *Ind.* 5, *Lab.* 4, *LD* 35
*Woking, Surrey — *C.* 14, *Ind.* 1, *Lab.* 5, *LD* 16
*Worcester, Worcs — *C.* 15, *Ind. C.* 1, *Ind.* 4, *Lab.* 15, *LD* 1
*Worthing, W. Sussex — *C.* 20, *LD* 16
Wychavon, Worcs — *C.* 32, *Ind.* 2, *Lab.* 4, *LD* 11
Wycombe, Bucks — *C.* 42, *Ind.* 2, *Lab.* 9, *LD* 7
Wyre, Lancs — *C.* 35, *Lab.* 19, *LD* 2
*Wyre Forest, Worcs — *C.* 5, *Lab.* 11, *LD* 4, *Others* 22

GREATER LONDON COUNCILS

Barking and Dagenham — *Lab.* 47, *LD* 1, *RA* 3
Barnet — *C.* 28, *Lab.* 26, *LD* 6
Bexley — *C.* 32, *Lab.* 24, *LD* 6
Brent — *C.* 19, *Lab.* 43, *LD* 4
Bromley — *C.* 30, *Lab.* 7, *LD* 23
Camden — *C.* 11, *Lab.* 42, *LD* 6
City of Westminster — *C.* 47, *Lab.* 13
Croydon — *C.* 31, *Lab.* 38, *LD* 1
Ealing — *C.* 16, *Lab.* 52, *LD* 3
Enfield — *C.* 22, *Ind.* 1, *Lab.* 42
Greenwich — *C.* 8, *Lab.* 52, *LD* 2
Hackney — *C.* 10, *Green* 2, *Ind.* 1, *Lab.* 30, *LD* 15
Hammersmith and — *C.* 14, *Ind.* 1, *Lab.* 35
  Fulham
Haringey — *C.* 2, *Lab.* 52, *LD* 3
Harrow — *C.* 20, *Ind.* 2, *Lab.* 32, *Lib.* 9
Havering — *C.* 13, *Lab.* 31, *LD* 3, *RA* 16
Hillingdon — *C.* 33, *Lab.* 32, *LD* 4
Hounslow — *C.* 11, *Lab.* 43, *LD* 5, *Others* 1
Islington — *Lab.* 25, *LD* 27
Kensington and Chelsea — *C.* 39, *Lab.* 15
Kingston upon Thames — *C.* 20, *Ind. C.* 1, *Lab.* 10, *LD* 19
Lambeth — *C.* 5, *Lab.* 41, *LD* 18
Lewisham — *C.* 2, *Ind. Lab.* 1, *Lab.* 58, *LD* 4, *Other* 2
Merton — *C.* 13, *Ind. Lab.* 3, *Lab.* 35, *LD* 2,
  Other 1
Newham — *Lab.* 59, *Other* 1
Redbridge — *C.* 25, *Lab.* 28, *LD* 9
Richmond upon Thames — *C.* 14, *Lab.* 4, *LD* 34
Southwark — *C.* 4, *Ind.* 1, *Lab.* 31, *LD* 27
Sutton — *C.* 5, *Lab.* 5, *LD* 46
Tower Hamlets — *Ind.* 1, *Lab.* 41, *LD* 8
Waltham Forest — *C.* 14, *Ind.* 1, *Lab.* 30, *LD* 12
Wandsworth — *C.* 50, *Lab.* 11

WALES

Anglesey — *Ind.* 27, *Lab.* 4, *PC* 7
Blaenau Gwent — *Ind.* 2, *Ind. Lab.* 1, *Lab.* 34, *LD* 1,
  Others 4
Bridgend — *C.* 1, *Ind.* 4, *Ind. Lab.* 1, *Lab.* 40,
  LD 6, *PC* 2
Caerphilly — *Ind.* 3, *Lab.* 28, *LD* 4, *PC* 38
Cardiff — *C.* 5, *Ind.* 1, *Lab.* 50, *LD* 18, *PC* 1
Carmarthenshire — *Ind.* 28, *Ind. Lab* 2, *Lab.* 27, *LD* 1,
  PC 15, *RA* 1
Ceredigion — *Ind.* 22, *Lab.* 1, *LD* 7, *PC* 13, *Others* 1
Conwy — *C.* 5, *Ind.* 14, *Lab.* 19, *LD* 13, *PC* 8
Denbighshire — *C.* 2, *Ind.* 17, *Lab.* 14, *LD* 1, *NP* 1,
  PC 8, *Others* 4
Flintshire — *Lab.* 42, *LD* 7, *PC* 2, *Others* 19
Gwynedd — *Ind.* 21, *Lab.* 13, *LD* 6, *Others* 2, *PC*
  41
Merthyr Tydfil — *Ind.* 13, *Lab.* 16, *PC* 4
Monmouthshire — *C.* 19, *Ind.* 3, *Lab.* 18, *LD* 1, *Others* 1
Neath Port Talbot — *Ind.* 3, *Ind. Lab.* 1, *Lab.* 40, *LD* 2,
  PC 10, *RA* 5, *Others* 3
Newport — *C.* 5, *Ind.* 2, *Lab.* 39, *LD* 1
Pembrokeshire — *C.* 4, *Ind.* 38, *Lab.* 13, *LD* 3, *PC* 2
Powys — *C.* 1, *Ind.* 59, *Lab.* 6, *LD* 7
Rhondda, Cynon, Taff — *Ind.* 5, *Lab.* 26, *LD* 2, *PC* 42
Swansea — *C.* 5, *Ind.* 7, *Lab.* 46, *LD* 11, *PC* 2,
  Others 1
Torfaen — *C.* 1, *Ind.* 3, *Lab.* 39, *LD* 1
Vale of Glamorgan — *C.* 22, *Lab.* 18, *LD* 1, *PC* 6
Wrexham — *C.* 4, *Ind.* 11, *Lab.* 24, *Others* 13

SCOTLAND

Aberdeen City — *C.* 6, *Lab.* 22, *LD* 12, *SNP* 3
Aberdeenshire — *Com.* 7, *Ind.* 10, *LD* 28, *SNP* 23
Angus — *C.* 2, *Ind.* 3, *Lab.*1, *LD* 2, *SNP* 21
Argyll and Bute — *C.* 4, *Ind.* 3, *LD* 6, *NP* 19, *SNP* 4
City of Edinburgh — *C.* 13, *Lab.* 31, *LD* 13, *SNP* 1
Clackmannanshire — *C.*1 *Lab.* 7, *SNP* 10
Dumfries and Galloway — *C.* 8, *Ind.* 15, *Lab.* 13, *LD* 6, *SNP* 5
Dundee City — *C.* 4, *Ind.* 1, *Ind. Lab.* 1, *Lab.* 13,
  SNP 11
East Ayrshire — *C.* 1, *Lab.* 17, *SNP* 14
East Dunbartonshire — *C.* 3, *Lab.* 11, *LD* 10
East Lothian — *C.* 5, *Lab.* 16, *SNP* 2
East Renfrewshire — *C.* 8, *Lab.* 9, *LD* 2, *RA* 1
Eilean Siar/Western Isles — *Ind.* 23, *Lab.* 5, *SNP* 3
Falkirk — *C.* 2, *Ind.* 2, *Lab.* 14, *SNP* 10, *Others* 4
Fife — *C.* 2, *Lab.* 42, *LD* 21, *SNP* 10,
  Others 3
Glasgow City — *C.* 1, *Lab.* 74, *LD* 1, *SNP* 2, *SSP* 1
Highland — *Ind.* 50, *Lab.* 11, *LD* 10, *SNP* 9
Inverclyde — *C.* 1, *Lab.* 10, *LD* 9
Midlothian — *Lab.* 17, *LD* 1
Moray — *C.* 1, *Ind.* 13, *Lab.* 6, *LD* 2, *SNP* 2,
  Others 2
North Ayrshire — *C.* 2, *Ind.* 1, *Lab.* 25, *SNP* 2
North Lanarkshire — *Ind.* 2, *Lab.* 56, *SNP* 12
Orkney Islands — *Ind.* 21
Perth and Kinross — *C.* 11, *Ind.* 2, *Lab.* 6, *LD* 6, *SNP* 16
Renfrewshire — *C.* 1, *Lab.* 21, *LD* 3, *SNP* 15
Scottish Borders — *C.* 1, *Ind.* 15, *Lab.* 1, *LD* 14, *SNP* 3
Shetland Islands — *Ind.* 13, *LD* 9
South Ayrshire — *C.* 13, *Lab.* 15, *NP* 2
South Lanarkshire — *C.* 2, *Lab.* 53, *LD* 1, *SNP* 11
Stirling — *C.* 10, *Lab.* 11, *SNP* 1
West Dunbartonshire — *Lab.* 13, *SNP* 7, *Others* 2
West Lothian — *C.* 1, *Ind.* 1, *Lab.* 20, *SNP* 10

England

The Kingdom of England lies between 55° 46' and 49° 57' 30'' N. latitude (from a few miles north of the mouth of the Tweed to the Lizard), and between 1° 46' E. and 5° 43' W. (from Lowestoft to Land's End). England is bounded on the north by the Cheviot Hills; on the south by the English Channel; on the east by the Straits of Dover (Pas de Calais) and the North Sea; and on the west by the Atlantic Ocean, Wales and the Irish Sea. It has a total area of 50,351 sq. miles (130,410 sq. km): land 50,058 sq. miles (129,652 sq. km); inland water 293 sq. miles (758 sq. km).

POPULATION

The population at the 1991 census was 47,055,204. The average density of the population in 1991 was 3.6 persons per hectare.

FLAG

The flag of England is the cross of St George, a red cross on a white field (cross gules in a field argent). The cross of St George, the patron saint of England, has been used since the 13th century.

RELIEF

There is a marked division between the upland and lowland areas of England. In the extreme north the Cheviot Hills (highest point, The Cheviot, 2,674 ft) form a natural boundary with Scotland. Running south from the Cheviots, though divided from them by the Tyne Gap, is the Pennine range (highest point, Cross Fell, 2,930 ft), the main orological feature of the country. The Pennines culminate in the Peak District of Derbyshire (Kinder Scout, 2,088 ft). West of the Pennines are the Cumbrian mountains, which include Scafell Pike (3,210 ft), the highest peak in England, and to the east are the Yorkshire Moors, their highest point being Urra Moor (1,490 ft).

In the west, the foothills of the Welsh mountains extend into the bordering English counties of Shropshire (the Wrekin, 1,334 ft; Long Mynd, 1,694 ft) and Hereford and Worcester (the Malvern Hills –Worcestershire Beacon, 1,394 ft). Extensive areas of highland and moorland are also to be found in the south-western peninsula formed by Somerset, Devon and Cornwall: principally Exmoor (Dunkery Beacon, 1,704 ft), Dartmoor (High Willhays, 2,038 ft) and Bodmin Moor (Brown Willy, 1,377 ft). Ranges of low, undulating hills run across the south of the country, including the Cotswolds in the Midlands and south-west, the Chilterns to the north of London, and the North (Kent) and South (Sussex) Downs of the south-east coastal areas.

The lowlands of England lie in the Vale of York, East Anglia and the area around the Wash. The lowest-lying are the Cambridgeshire Fens in the valleys of the Great Ouse and the River Nene, which are below sea-level in places. Since the 17th century extensive drainage has brought much of the Fens under cultivation. The North Sea coast between the Thames and the Humber, low-lying and formed of sand and shingle for the most part, is subject to erosion and defences against further incursion have been built along many stretches.

HYDROGRAPHY

The Severn is the longest river in Great Britain, rising in the north-eastern slopes of Plynlimon (Wales) and entering England in Shropshire with a total length of 220 miles (354 km) from its source to its outflow into the Bristol Channel, where it receives on the east the Bristol Avon, and on the west the Wye, its other tributaries being the Vyrnwy, Tern, Stour, Teme and Upper (or Warwickshire) Avon. The Severn is tidal below Gloucester, and a high bore or tidal wave sometimes reverses the flow as high as Tewkesbury ($13\frac{1}{2}$ miles above Gloucester). The scenery of the greater part of the river is very picturesque and beautiful, and the Severn is a noted salmon river, some of its tributaries being famous for trout. Navigation is assisted by the Gloucester and Berkeley Ship Canal ($16\frac{1}{4}$ miles), which admits vessels of 350 tons to Gloucester. The Severn Tunnel was begun in 1873 and completed in 1886 at a cost of £2 million and after many difficulties from flooding. It is 4 miles 628 yards in length (of which $2\frac{1}{4}$ miles are under the river). The Severn road bridge between Haysgate, Gwent, and Almondsbury, Glos, with a centre span of 3,240 ft, was opened in 1966.

The longest river wholly in England is the Thames, with a total length of 215 miles (346 km) from its source in the Cotswold hills to the Nore, and is navigable by ocean-going ships to London Bridge. The Thames is tidal to Teddington (69 miles from its mouth) and forms county boundaries almost throughout its course; on its banks are situated London, Windsor Castle, the oldest royal residence still in regular use, Eton College and Oxford, the oldest university in the kingdom.

Of the remaining English rivers, those flowing into the North Sea are the Tyne, Wear, Tees, Ouse and Trent from the Pennine Range, the Great Ouse (160 miles), which rises in Northamptonshire, and the Orwell and Stour from the hills of East Anglia. Flowing into the English Channel are the Sussex Ouse from the Weald, the Itchen from the Hampshire Hills, and the Axe, Teign, Dart, Tamar and Exe from the Devonian hills. Flowing into the Irish Sea are the Mersey, Ribble and Eden from the western slopes of the Pennines and the Derwent from the Cumbrian mountains.

The English Lakes, noteworthy for their picturesque scenery and poetic associations, lie in Cumbria, the largest being Windermere (10 miles long), Ullswater and Derwent Water.

ISLANDS

The Isle of Wight is separated from Hampshire by the Solent. The capital, Newport, stands at the head of the estuary of the Medina, Cowes (at the mouth) being the chief port. Other centres are Ryde, Sandown, Shanklin, Ventnor, Freshwater, Yarmouth, Totland Bay, Seaview and Bembridge.

Lundy (the name means Puffin Island), 11 miles northwest of Hartland Point, Devon, is about two miles long and about half a mile wide on average, with a total area of about 1,116 acres, and a population of about 20. It became the property of the National Trust in 1969 and is now principally a bird sanctuary.

The Isles of Scilly consist of about 140 islands and skerries (total area, 6 sq. miles/10 sq. km) situated 28 miles south-west of Land's End. Only five are inhabited: St Mary's, St Agnes, Bryher, Tresco and St Martin's. The population is 1,978. The entire group has been designated a Conservation Area, a Heritage Coast, and an Area of Outstanding Natural Beauty, and has been given National Nature Reserve status by the Nature Conservancy Council because of its unique flora and fauna. Tourism and the winter/spring flower trade for the home market form the basis of the economy of the Isles. The island group is a recognised rural development area.

EARLY HISTORY

Archaeological evidence suggests that England has been inhabited since at least the Palaeolithic period, though the extent of the various Palaeolithic cultures was dependent upon the degree of glaciation. The succeeding Neolithic and Bronze Age cultures have left abundant remains throughout the country, the best-known of these being the henges and stone circles of Stonehenge (ten miles north of Salisbury, Wilts) and Avebury (Wilts), both of which are believed to have been of religious significance. In the latter part of the Bronze Age the Goidels, a people of Celtic race, and in the Iron Age other Celtic races of Brythons and Belgae, invaded the country and brought with them Celtic civilisation and dialects, place names in England bearing witness to the spread of the invasion over the whole kingdom.

THE ROMAN CONQUEST

The Roman conquest of Gaul (57–50 BC) brought Britain into close contact with Roman civilisation, but although Julius Caesar raided the south of Britain in 55 BC and 54 BC, conquest was not undertaken until nearly 100 years later. In AD 43 the Emperor Claudius dispatched Aulus Plautius, with a well-equipped force of 40,000, and himself followed with reinforcements in the same year. Success was delayed by the resistance of Caratacus (Caractacus), the British leader from AD 48–51, who was finally captured and sent to Rome, and by a great revolt in AD 61 led by Boudicca (Boadicea), Queen of the Iceni; but the south of Britain was secured by AD 70, and Wales and the area north to the Tyne by about AD 80.

In AD 122, the Emperor Hadrian visited Britain and built a continuous rampart, since known as Hadrian's Wall, from Wallsend to Bowness (Tyne to Solway). The work was entrusted by the Emperor Hadrian to Aulus Platorius Nepos, legate of Britain from AD 122 to 126, and it was intended to form the northern frontier of the Roman Empire.

The Romans administered Britain as a province under a Governor, with a well-defined system of local government, each Roman municipality ruling itself and its surrounding territory, while London was the centre of the road system and the seat of the financial officials of the Province of Britain. Colchester, Lincoln, York, Gloucester and St Albans stand on the sites of five Roman municipalities, and Wroxeter, Caerleon, Chester, Lincoln and York were at various times the sites of legionary fortresses. Well-preserved Roman towns have been uncovered at or near Silchester (*Calleva Atrebatum*), ten miles south of Reading, Wroxeter (*Viroconium Cornoviorum*), near Shrewsbury, and St Albans (*Verulamium*) in Hertfordshire.

Four main groups of roads radiated from London, and a fifth (the Fosse) ran obliquely from Lincoln through Leicester, Cirencester and Bath to Exeter. Of the four groups radiating from London, one ran south-east to Canterbury and the coast of Kent, a second to Silchester and thence to parts of western Britain and south Wales, a third (later known as Watling Street) ran through Verulamium to Chester, with various branches, and the fourth reached Colchester, Lincoln, York and the eastern counties.

In the fourth century Britain was subject to raids along the east coast by Saxon pirates, which led to the establishment of a system of coastal defences from the Wash to Southampton Water, with forts at Brancaster, Burgh Castle (Yarmouth), Walton (Felixstowe), Bradwell, Reculver, Richborough, Dover, Lympne, Pevensey and Porchester (Portsmouth). The Irish (Scoti) and Picts in the north were also becoming more aggressive; from about AD 350 incursions became more frequent and more formidable. As the Roman Empire came under attack increasingly towards the end of the fourth century, many troops were removed from Britain for service in other parts of the empire. The island was eventually cut off from Rome by the Teutonic conquest of Gaul, and with the withdrawal of the last Roman garrison early in the fifth century, the Romano-British were left to themselves.

SAXON SETTLEMENT

According to legend, the British King Vortigern called in the Saxons to defend him against the Picts, the Saxon chieftains being Hengist and Horsa, who landed at Ebbsfleet, Kent, and established themselves in the Isle of Thanet; but the events during the one and a half centuries between the final break with Rome and the re-establishment of Christianity are unclear. However, it would appear that in the course of this period the raids turned into large-scale settlement by invaders traditionally known as Angles (England north of the Wash and East Anglia), Saxons (Essex and southern England) and Jutes (Kent and the Weald), which pushed the Romano-British into the mountainous areas of the north and west, Celtic culture outside Wales and Cornwall surviving only in topographical names. Various kingdoms were established at this time which attempted to claim overlordship of the whole country, hegemony finally being achieved by Wessex (capital, Winchester) in the ninth century. This century also saw the beginning of raids by the Vikings (Danes), which were resisted by Alfred the Great (871–899), who fixed a limit to the advance of Danish settlement by the Treaty of Wedmore (878), giving them the area north and east of Watling Street, on condition that they adopt Christianity.

In the tenth century the kings of Wessex recovered the whole of England from the Danes, but subsequent rulers were unable to resist a second wave of invaders. England paid tribute (*Danegeld*) for many years, and was invaded in 1013 by the Danes and ruled by Danish kings from 1016 until 1042, when Edward the Confessor was recalled from exile in Normandy. On Edward's death in 1066, Harold Godwinson (brother-in-law of Edward and son of Earl Godwin of Wessex) was chosen King of England. After defeating (at Stamford Bridge, Yorkshire, 25 September) an invading army under Harald Hadraada, King of Norway (aided by the outlawed Earl Tostig of Northumbria, Harold's brother), Harold was himself defeated at the Battle of Hastings on 14 October 1066, and the Norman conquest secured the throne of England for Duke William of Normandy, a cousin of Edward the Confessor.

CHRISTIANITY

Christianity reached the Roman province of Britain from Gaul in the third century (or possibly earlier); Alban, traditionally Britain's first martyr, was put to death as a Christian during the persecution of Diocletian (22 June 303), at his native town Verulamium; and the Bishops of Londinium, Eboracum (York), and Lindum (Lincoln) attended the Council of Arles in 314. However, the Anglo-Saxon invasions submerged the Christian religion in England until the sixth century when conversion was undertaken in the north from 563 by Celtic missionaries from Ireland led by St Columba, and in the south by a mission sent from Rome in 597 which was led by St Augustine, who became the first archbishop of Canterbury. England appears to have been converted again by the end of the seventh century and followed, after the Council of Whitby in 663, the practices of the Roman Church, which brought the kingdom into the mainstream of European thought and culture.

PRINCIPAL CITIES

BIRMINGHAM

Birmingham is Britain's second city. It is a focal point in national communications networks with a rapidly expanding international airport. The generally accepted derivation of 'Birmingham' is the *ham* (dwelling-place) of the *ing* (family) of *Beorma*, presumed to have been Saxon. During the Industrial Revolution the town grew into a major manufacturing centre and in 1889 was granted city status.

Despite the decline in manufacturing, Birmingham is still a major hardware trade and motor component industry centre. As well as the National Exhibition Centre and the Aston Science Park, recent developments include the International Convention Centre, the National Indoor Arena and Brindleyplace.

The principal buildings are the Town Hall (1834–50); the Council House (1879); Victoria Law Courts (1891); Birmingham University (1906–9); the 13th-century Church of St Martin-in-the-Bull-Ring (rebuilt 1873); Our Lady, Help of Christians Church; the Cathedral (formerly St Philip's Church) (1711) and the Roman Catholic Cathedral of St Chad (1839–41).

BRADFORD

Bradford lies on the southern edge of the Yorkshire Dales National Park, including within its boundaries the village of Haworth, home of the Brontë sisters, and Ilkley Moor.

Originally a Saxon township, Bradford received a market charter in 1251 but developed only slowly until the industrialisation of the textile industry brought rapid growth during the 19th century; it was granted its city charter in 1897. The prosperity of that period is reflected in much of the city's architecture, particularly the public buildings: City Hall (1873), Wool Exchange (1867), St George's Hall (Concert Hall, 1853), Cartwright Hall (Art Gallery, 1904) and the Technical College (1882). Other chief buildings are the Cathedral (15th century) and Bolling Hall (14th century).

Textiles still play an important part in the city's economy but industry is now more broadly based, including engineering, micro-electronics, printing and chemicals. The city has a strong financial services sector, and a growing tourism industry.

BRIGHTON AND HOVE

Brighton and Hove was granted city status in December 2000. Originally a small fishing village, the city was transformed into a fashionable seaside retreat in the mid 18th century when Dr Richard Russell popularised the area with his 'sea-water' cure. The Prince Regent (later King George IV) visited Brighton in 1783 and the city's most prominent architectural feature, the Royal Pavilion, is the legacy of his love of the city.

The Pavilion, built on the site of a farmhouse rented for the Prince's initial visit, is the result of a succession of projects carried out between 1787 and 1823. The architect William Porden initiated the buildings' famous Indo-Saracenic style when he designed the royal stables. The Indian conceit was extended by John Nash in 1813 when he added the large central dome and the tent-like roofs over the banqueting hall and music room.

The city has numerous other examples of Regency architecture including Adelaide Crescent and Brunswick and Palmeira Squares in Hove, as well as hundreds of townhouses designed by Amon Wilds and Augustin Busby. There are also striking examples of Victorian design including Brighton's two piers.

BRISTOL

Bristol was a Royal Borough before the Norman Conquest. The earliest form of the name is *Bricgstow*. In 1373 Edward III granted Bristol county status.

The chief buildings include the 12th-century Cathedral (with later additions), with Norman chapter house and gateway, the 14th-century Church of St Mary Redcliffe, Wesley's Chapel, Broadmead, the Merchant Venturers' Almshouses, the Council House (1956), Guildhall, Exchange (erected from the designs of John Wood in 1743), Cabot Tower, the University and Clifton College. The Roman Catholic Cathedral at Clifton was opened in 1973.

The Clifton Suspension Bridge, with a span of 702 feet over the Avon, was projected by Brunel in 1836 but was not completed until 1864. Brunel's SS *Great Britain*, the first ocean-going propeller-driven ship, is now being restored in the City Docks from where she was launched in 1843. The docks themselves have been extensively restored and redeveloped and are becoming a focus for the arts and recreation.

CAMBRIDGE

Cambridge, a settlement far older than its ancient University, lies on the River Cam or Granta. The city is a county town and regional headquarters. Its industries include electronics, high technology research and development, and biotechnology. Among its open spaces are Jesus Green, Sheep's Green, Coe Fen, Parker's Piece, Christ's Pieces, the University Botanic Garden, and the Backs, or lawns and gardens through which the Cam winds behind the principal line of college buildings. East of the Cam, King's Parade, upon which stand Great St Mary's Church, Gibbs' Senate House and King's College Chapel with Wilkins' screen, joins Trumpington Street to form one of the most beautiful thoroughfares in Europe.

University and college buildings provide the outstanding features of Cambridge architecture but several churches (especially St Benet's, the oldest building in the city, and St Sepulchre's, the Round Church) are also notable. The Guildhall (1939) stands on a site of which at least part has held municipal buildings since 1224.

CANTERBURY

Canterbury, the Metropolitan City of the Anglican Communion, dates back to prehistoric times. It was the Roman *Durovernum Cantiacorum* and the Saxon *Cant-wara-byrig* (stronghold of the men of Kent). Here in 597 St Augustine began the conversion of the English to Christianity, when Ethelbert, King of Kent, was baptised. Of the Benedictine St Augustine's Abbey, burial place of the Jutish Kings of Kent (whose capital Canterbury was), only ruins remain. St Martin's Church, on the eastern outskirts of the city, is stated by Bede to have been the place of worship of Queen Bertha, the Christian wife of King Ethelbert, before the advent of St Augustine.

In 1170 the rivalry of Church and State culminated in the murder in Canterbury Cathedral, by Henry II's knights, of Archbishop Thomas Becket. His shrine became a great centre of pilgrimage, as described in Chaucer's *Canterbury Tales*. After the Reformation pilgrimages ceased, but the prosperity of the city was strengthened by an influx of Huguenot refugees, who introduced weaving. The poet and playwright Christopher Marlowe was born and reared in Canterbury, and there are also literary associations with Defoe, Dickens, Joseph Conrad and Somerset Maugham.

The Cathedral, with architecture ranging from the 11th to the 15th centuries, is world famous. Modern pilgrims are attracted particularly to the Martyrdom, the Black Prince's Tomb, the Warriors' Chapel and the many examples of medieval stained glass.

The medieval city walls are built on Roman foundations and the 14th-century West Gate is one of the finest buildings of its kind in the country.

The 1,000-seat Marlowe Theatre is a centre for the Canterbury Arts Festival each autumn.

CARLISLE

Carlisle is situated at the confluence of the River Eden and River Caldew, 309 miles north-west of London and about ten miles from the Scottish border. It was granted a charter in 1158.

The city stands at the western end of Hadrian's Wall and dates from the original Roman settlement of *Luguvalium*. Granted to Scotland in the tenth century, Carlisle is not included in the Domesday Book. William Rufus reclaimed the area in 1092 and the castle and city walls were built to guard Carlisle and the western border; the citadel is a Tudor addition to protect the south of the city. Border disputes were common until the problem of the Debateable Lands was settled in 1552. During the Civil War the city remained Royalist; in 1745 Carlisle was besieged for the last time by the Young Pretender.

The Cathedral, originally a 12th-century Augustinian priory, was enlarged in the 13th and 14th centuries after the diocese was created in 1133. To the south is a restored Tithe Barn and nearby the 18th-century church of St Cuthbert, the third to stand on a site dating from the seventh century.

Carlisle is the major shopping, commercial and agricultural centre for the area, and industries include the manufacture of metal goods, biscuits and textiles. However, the largest employer is the services sector, notably in central and local government, retailing and transport. The city has an important communications position at the centre of a network of major roads, as a stage on the main west coast rail services, and with its own airport at Crosby-on-Eden.

CHESTER

Chester is situated on the River Dee, and was granted borough and city status in 1974. Its recorded history dates from the first century when the Romans founded the fortress of *Deva*. The city's name is derived from the Latin *castra* (a camp or encampment). During the Middle Ages, Chester was the principal port of north-west England but declined with the silting of the Dee estuary and competition from Liverpool. The city was also an important military centre, notably during Edward I's Welsh campaigns and the Elizabethan Irish campaigns. During the Civil War, Chester supported the King and was besieged from 1643 to 1646. Chester's first charter was granted *c.* 1175 and the city was incorporated in 1506. The office of Sheriff is the earliest created in the country (*c.* 1120s), and in 1992 the Mayor was granted the title of Lord Mayor. He/she also enjoys the title 'Admiral of the Dee'.

The city's architectural features include the city walls (an almost complete two-mile circuit), the unique 13th-century Rows (covered galleries above the street-level shops), the Victorian Gothic Town Hall (1869), the Castle (rebuilt 1788 and 1822) and numerous half-timbered buildings. The Cathedral was a Benedictine abbey until the Dissolution. Remaining monastic buildings include the chapter house, refectory and cloisters and there is a modern free-standing bell tower. The Norman church of St John the Baptist was a cathedral church in the early Middle Ages.

Chester is a thriving retail, business and tourist centre.

COVENTRY

Coventry is an important industrial centre, producing vehicles, machine tools, agricultural machinery, man-made fibres, aerospace components and telecommunications equipment. New investment has come from financial services, power transmission, professional services, leisure and education.

The city owes its beginning to Leofric, Earl of Mercia, and his wife Godiva who, in 1043, founded a Benedictine monastery. The guildhall of St Mary dates from the 14th century, three of the city's churches date from the 14th and 15th centuries, and 16th-century almshouses may still be seen. Coventry's first cathedral was destroyed at the Reformation, its second in the 1940 blitz (the walls and spire remain) and the new cathedral designed by Sir Basil Spence, consecrated in 1962, now draws numerous visitors.

Coventry is the home of the University of Warwick and its Science Park, Coventry University, the Westwood Business Park, the Cable and Wireless College, the Museum of British Road Transport and the Coventry Arena.

DERBY

Derby stands on the banks of the River Derwent, and its name dates back to 880 when the Danes settled in the locality and changed the original Saxon name of *Northworthy* to *Deoraby*.

Derby has a wide range of industries including aero engines, cars, pipework, specialised mechanical engineering equipment, textiles, chemicals, plastics and the Royal Crown Derby porcelain. The city is an established railway centre with rail research, engineering, safety testing, infrastructure and train-operating companies.

Buildings of interest include St Peter's Church and the Old Abbey Building (14th century), the Cathedral (1525), St Mary's Roman Catholic Church (1839) and the Industrial Museum, formerly the Old Silk Mill (1721). The traditional city centre is complemented by the Eagle Centre and 'out-of-centre' retail developments. In addition to the Derby Playhouse, the Assembly Rooms are a multi-purpose venue.

The first charter granting a Mayor and Aldermen was that of Charles I in 1637. Previous charters date back to 1154. It was granted city status in 1977.

DURHAM

The city of Durham is a district in the county of Durham and a major tourist attraction because of its prominent Norman Cathedral and Castle set high on a wooded peninsula overlooking the River Wear. The Cathedral was founded as a shrine for the body of St Cuthbert in 995. The present building dates from 1093 and among its many treasures is the tomb of the Venerable Bede (673–735). Durham's Prince Bishops had unique powers up to 1836, being lay rulers as well as religious leaders. As a palatinate Durham could have its own army, nobility, coinage and courts. The Castle was the main seat of the Prince Bishops for nearly 800 years; it is now used as a college by the University. The University, founded on the initiative of Bishop William Van Mildert, is England's third oldest.

Among other buildings of interest is the Guildhall in the Market Place which dates originally from the 14th century. Work has been carried out to conserve this area as part of the city's contribution to the Council of Europe's Urban Renaissance Campaign. Annual events include Durham's Regatta in June (claimed to be the oldest rowing event in Britain) and the Annual Gala (formerly Durham Miners' Gala) in July.

The economy has undergone a significant change with the replacement of mining as the dominant industry by 'white collar' employment. Although still a predominantly rural area, the industrial and commercial sector is growing and a wide range of manufacturing and service industries are based on industrial estates in and around the city. A research and development centre, linked to the University, also plays an important role in the local economy.

EXETER

Exeter lies on the River Exe ten miles from the sea. It was granted a charter by Henry II. The Romans founded *Isca Dumnoniorum* in the first century AD, and in the third century a stone wall (much of which remains) was built, providing protection against Saxon, and then Danish invasions. After the Conquest, the city led resistance to William in the west until reduced by siege. The Normans built the ringwork castle of Rougemont, the gatehouse and one tower of which remain, although the rest was pulled down in 1784. The first bridge across the Exe was built in the early 13th century. The city's main port was situated downstream at Topsham until the construction in the 1560s of the first true canal in England, the redevelopment of which in 1700 brought seaborne trade direct to the city. Exeter was the Royalist headquarters in the west during the Civil War.

The diocese of Exeter was established by Edward the Confessor in 1050, although a minster existed near the Cathedral site from the late seventh century. A new cathedral was built in the 12th century but the present building, which incorporates the Norman Towers, was begun *c.* 1275 and completed about a century later. The Guildhall dates from the 12th century and there are many other medieval buildings in the city, as well as architecture in the Georgian and Regency styles, and the Custom House (1680). Damage suffered by bombing in 1942 led to the redevelopment of the city centre.

Exeter's prosperity from medieval times was based on trade in wool and woollen cloth (commemorated by Tuckers Hall), which flourished until the late 18th century when export trade was hit by the French wars. Subsequently Exeter has developed as an administrative and commercial centre, notably in the distributive trades, light manufacturing industries and tourism.

KINGSTON UPON HULL

Hull (officially Kingston upon Hull) lies at the junction of the River Hull with the Humber, 22 miles from the North Sea. It is one of the major seaports of the United Kingdom, comprising 2,000 acres in four main dock installations. The port provides a wide range of cargo services, including ro-ro and container traffic, and handles a million passengers annually on daily sailings to Rotterdam and Zeebrugge. There is a variety of manufacturing and service industries, as well as increasing tourism and conference business.

The city, restored after heavy air raid damage during the Second World War, has good office and administrative buildings, its municipal centre being the Guildhall, its educational centres the University of Hull and the University of Lincolnshire and Humberside and its religious centre the Parish Church of the Holy Trinity.

The old town area has been renovated and includes a marina and shopping complex. Just west of the city is the Humber Bridge, the world's longest single-span suspension bridge.

Kingston upon Hull was so named by Edward I. City status was accorded in 1897 and the office of Mayor raised to the dignity of Lord Mayor in 1914.

LEEDS

Leeds, situated in the lower Aire Valley, is a junction for road, rail, canal and air services and an important manufacturing and commercial centre. Seventy-three per cent of employment is in services, notably the distributive trades, public administration, medical services and business services. The main manufacturing industries are mechanical engineering, printing and publishing, metal goods and furniture.

The principal buildings are the Civic Hall (1933), the Town Hall (1858), the Municipal Buildings and Art Gallery (1884) with the Henry Moore Gallery (1982), the Corn Exchange (1863) and the University. The Parish Church (St Peter's) was rebuilt in 1841; the 17th-century St John's Church has a fine interior with a famous English Renaissance screen; the last remaining 18th-century church in the city is Holy Trinity in Boar Lane (1727). Kirkstall Abbey (about three miles from the centre of the city), founded by Henry de Lacy in 1152, is one of the most complete examples of Cistercian houses now remaining. Temple Newsam, birthplace of Lord Darnley, was acquired by the Council in 1922. The present house was largely rebuilt by Sir Arthur Ingram in about 1620. Adel Church, about five miles from the centre of the city, is a fine Norman structure. The new Royal Armouries Museum houses the collection of antique arms and armour formerly held at the Tower of London.

Leeds was first incorporated by Charles I in 1626. The earliest forms of the name are *Loidis* or *Ledes*, the origins of which are obscure.

LEICESTER

Leicester is situated geographically in the centre of England. It dates back to pre-Roman times and was one of the Five Danish Boroughs of the Danelaw. In 1589 Queen Elizabeth I granted a charter to the city and the ancient title was confirmed by letters patent in 1919.

The principal industries are hosiery, knitwear, footwear manufacturing and engineering. The growth of Leicester as a hosiery centre increased rapidly from the introduction there of the first stocking frame in 1670 and today it has some of the largest hosiery factories in the world.

The principal buildings are the Town Hall, the New Walk Centre, the University of Leicester, De Montfort University, De Montfort Hall, one of the finest concert halls in the provinces seating over 2,750 people, and the Granby Halls, an indoor sports facility. The ancient churches of St Martin (now Leicester Cathedral), St Nicholas, St Margaret, All Saints, St Mary de Castro, and buildings such as the Guildhall, the 14th-century Newarke Gate, the Castle and the Jewry Wall Roman site still exist. The Haymarket Theatre was opened in 1973 and The Shires shopping centre in 1992.

LINCOLN

Situated 40 miles inland on the River Witham, Lincoln derives its name from a contraction of *Lindum Colonia*, the settlement founded in AD 48 by the Romans to command the crossing of Ermine Street and Fosse Way. Sections of the third-century Roman city wall can be seen, including an extant gateway (Newport Arch), and excavations have discovered traces of a sewerage system unique in Britain.

The Romans also drained the surrounding fenland and created a canal system, laying the foundations of Lincoln's agricultural prosperity and also of the city's importance in the medieval wool trade as a port and Staple town.

As one of the Five Boroughs of the Danelaw, Lincoln was an important trading centre in the ninth and tenth centuries and medieval prosperity from the wool trade lasted until the 14th century, enabling local merchants to build parish churches (of which three survive), and attracting in the 12th century a Jewish community (Jew's House and Court, Aaron's House). However, the removal of the Staple to Boston in 1369 heralded a decline from which the city only recovered fully in the 19th century when improved fen drainage made Lincoln agriculturally important and improved canal and rail links led to industrial development, mainly in the manufacture of machinery, components and engineering products.

The castle was built shortly after the Conquest and is unusual in having two mounds; on one motte stands a Keep (Lucy's Tower) added in the 12th century. It currently houses one of the four surviving copies of the Magna Carta. The Cathedral was begun c. 1073 when the first Norman bishop moved the See of Lindsey to Lincoln, but was mostly destroyed by fire and earthquake in the 12th century. Rebuilding was begun by St Hugh and completed over a century later. Other notable architectural features are the 12th-century High Bridge, the oldest in Britain still to carry buildings, and the Guildhall situated above the 15th–16th-century Stonebow gateway.

LIVERPOOL

Liverpool, on the right bank of the River Mersey, three miles from the Irish Sea, is the United Kingdom's foremost port for the Atlantic trade. Tunnels link Liverpool with Birkenhead and Wallasey.

There are 2,100 acres of dockland on both sides of the river and the Gladstone and Royal Seaforth Docks can accommodate Panamax-sized vessels. Approximately 31 million tonnes of cargo is handled annually. The main cargoes are crude oil, grain, fossil fuels, edible oils, timber, scrap metal, containers and break-bulk cargo. Liverpool Free Port, Britain's largest, was opened in 1984.

Liverpool was created a free borough in 1207 and a city in 1880. From the early 18th century it expanded rapidly with the growth of industrialisation and the Atlantic trade. Surviving buildings from this period include the Bluecoat Chambers (1717, formerly the Bluecoat School), the Town Hall (1754, rebuilt to the original design 1795), and buildings in Rodney Street, Canning Street and the suburbs. Notable from the 19th and 20th centuries are the Anglican Cathedral, built from the designs of Sir Giles Gilbert Scott (the foundation stone was laid in 1904, and the building was completed only in 1980), the Catholic Metropolitan Cathedral (designed by Sir Frederick Gibberd, consecrated 1967) and St George's Hall (1838–54), regarded as one of the finest modern examples of classical architecture. The refurbished Albert Dock (designed by Jesse Hartley) contains the Merseyside Maritime Museum and Tate Gallery, Liverpool.

In 1852 an Act was obtained for establishing a public library, museum and art gallery; as a result Liverpool had one of the first public libraries in the country. The Brown, Picton and Hornby libraries now form one of the country's major libraries. The Victoria Building of Liverpool University, the Royal Liver, Cunard and Mersey Docks & Harbour Company buildings at the Pier Head, the Municipal Buildings and the Philharmonic Hall are other examples of the city's fine buildings.

MANCHESTER

Manchester (the *Mamucium* of the Romans, who occupied it in AD 79) is a commercial and industrial centre with a population engaged in the engineering, chemical, clothing, food processing and textile industries and in education. Banking, insurance and a growing leisure industry are among the prime commercial activities. The city is connected with the sea by the Manchester Ship Canal, opened in 1894, $35\frac{1}{2}$ miles long, and accommodating ships up to 15,000 tons. Manchester Airport handles 15 million passengers yearly.

The principal buildings are the Town Hall, erected in 1877 from the designs of Alfred Waterhouse, with a large extension of 1938; the Royal Exchange (1869, enlarged 1921); the Central Library (1934); Heaton Hall; the 17th-century Chetham Library; the Rylands Library (1900), which includes the Althorp collection; the University precinct; the 15th-century Cathedral (formerly the parish church) and G-MEX exhibition centre. Recent developments include the Manchester Arena, the largest indoor arena in Europe, and the Bridgewater Hall. Manchester is the home of the Hallé Orchestra, the Royal Northern College of Music, the Royal Exchange Theatre and seven public art galleries. Metrolink, the light rail system, opened in 1992.

The Commonwealth Games are to be held in Manchester in 2002 and new sports facilities include a stadium, a swimming pool complex and the National Cycling Centre.

The town received its first charter of incorporation in 1838 and was created a city in 1853.

NEWCASTLE UPON TYNE

Newcastle upon Tyne, on the north bank of the River Tyne, is eight miles from the North Sea. A cathedral and university city, it is the administrative, commercial and cultural centre for north-east England and the principal port. It is an important manufacturing centre with a wide variety of industries.

The principal buildings include the Castle Keep (12th century), Black Gate (13th century), Blackfriars (13th century), West Walls (13th century), St Nicholas's Cathedral (15th century, fine lantern tower), St Andrew's Church (12th–14th century), St John's (14th–15th century), All Saints (1786 by Stephenson), St Mary's Roman Catholic Cathedral (1844), Trinity House (17th century), Sandhill (16th-century houses), Guildhall (Georgian), Grey Street (1834–9), Central Station (1846–50), Laing Art Gallery (1904), University of Newcastle Physics Building (1962) and Medical Building (1985), Civic Centre (1963), Central Library (1969) and Eldon Square Shopping Development (1976). Open spaces include the Town Moor (927 acres) and Jesmond Dene. Nine bridges span the Tyne at Newcastle.

The city's name is derived from the 'new castle' (1080) erected as a defence against the Scots. In 1400 it was made a county, and in 1882 a city.

NORWICH

Norwich grew from an early Anglo-Saxon settlement near the confluence of the Rivers Yare and Wensum, and now serves as provincial capital for the predominantly agricultural region of East Anglia. The name is thought to relate to the most northerly of a group of Anglo-Saxon villages or *wics*. The city's first known charter was granted in 1158 by Henry II.

Norwich serves its surrounding area as a market town and commercial centre, banking and insurance being prominent among the city's businesses. From the 14th century until the Industrial Revolution, Norwich was the regional centre of the woollen industry, but now the biggest single industry is financial services and principal trades are engineering, printing, shoemaking, double glazing, the production of chemicals and clothing, food processing and technology. Norwich is accessible to seagoing vessels by means of the River Yare, entered at Great Yarmouth, 20 miles to the east.

Among many historic buildings are the Cathedral (completed in the 12th century and surmounted by a 15th-century spire 315 feet in height), the keep of the Norman castle (now a museum and art gallery), the 15th-century flint-walled Guildhall (now a tourist information centre), some thirty medieval parish churches, St Andrew's and Blackfriars' Halls, the Tudor houses preserved in Elm Hill and the Georgian Assembly House. The University of East Anglia is on the city's western boundary.

NOTTINGHAM

Nottingham stands on the River Trent and is connected by canal with the Atlantic Ocean and the North Sea. *Snotingaham* or *Notingeham*, literally the homestead of the people of Snot, is the Anglo-Saxon name for the Celtic settlement of *Tigguocobauc*, or the house of caves. In 878, Nottingham became one of the Five Boroughs of the Danelaw. William the Conqueror ordered the construction of Nottingham Castle, while the town itself developed rapidly under Norman rule. Its laws and rights were later formally recognised by Henry II's charter in 1155. The Castle became a favoured residence of King John. In 1642 King Charles I raised his personal standard at Nottingham Castle at the start of the Civil War.

Nottingham is home to Notts County FC (the world's oldest football league side), Nottingham Racecourse and the National Watersports Centre. The principal industries include textiles, pharmaceuticals, food manufacturing, engineering and telecommunications. There are two universities within the city boundaries.

Architecturally, Nottingham has a wealth of notable buildings, particularly those designed in the Victorian era by T. C. Hine and Watson Fothergill. The City Council owns the Castle, of Norman origin but restored in 1878, Wollaton Hall (1580–8), Newstead Abbey (home of Lord Byron), the Guildhall (1888) and Council House (1929). St Mary's, St Peter's and St Nicholas's Churches are of interest, as is the Roman Catholic Cathedral (Pugin, 1842–4).

Nottingham was granted city status in 1897.

OXFORD

Oxford is a university city, an important industrial centre, and a market town. Industry played a minor part in Oxford until the motor industry was established in 1912.

It is for its architecture that Oxford is of most interest to the visitor, its oldest specimens being the reputedly Saxon tower of St Michael's church, the remains of the Norman castle and city walls, and the Norman church at Iffley. It is chiefly famous, however, for its Gothic buildings, such as the Divinity Schools, the Old Library at Merton College, William of Wykeham's New College, Magdalen College and Christ Church and many other college buildings. Later centuries are represented by the Laudian quadrangle at St John's College, the Renaissance Sheldonian Theatre by Wren, Trinity College Chapel, and All Saints Church; Hawksmoor's mock-Gothic at All Souls College, and the 18th-century Queen's College. In addition to individual buildings, High Street and Radcliffe Square, just off it, both form architectural compositions of great beauty. Most of the Colleges have gardens, those of Magdalen, New College, St John's and Worcester being the largest.

PLYMOUTH

Plymouth is situated on the borders of Devon and Cornwall at the confluence of the Rivers Tamar and Plym. The city has a long maritime history; it was the home port of Sir Francis Drake and the starting point for his circumnavigation of the world, as well as the last port of call for the *Mayflower* when the Pilgrim Fathers sailed for the New World in 1620. Today Plymouth is host to many international yacht races. The Barbican harbour area has many Elizabethan buildings and on Plymouth Hoe stands Smeaton's lighthouse, the third to be built on the Eddystone Rocks 13 miles offshore.

The city centre was rebuilt following extensive war damage, and comprises a large shopping centre, municipal offices, law courts and public buildings. The main employment is provided at the naval base, though many industrial firms and service industries have become established in the post-war period and the city is a growing tourism centre. In 1982 the Theatre Royal was opened. In conjunction with the Cornwall County Council, the Tamar Bridge was constructed linking the city by road with Cornwall.

PORTSMOUTH

Portsmouth occupies Portsea Island, Hampshire, with boundaries extending to the mainland. It is a centre of industry and commerce, including many high technology and manufacturing industries. It is the British headquarters of several major international companies. The Royal Navy base still has a substantial work-force, although this has decreased in recent years. The commercial port and continental ferry port is owned and run by the City Council, and carries passengers and vehicles to France and northern Spain.

A major port since the 16th century, Portsmouth is also a thriving seaside resort catering for thousands of visitors annually. Among many historic attractions are Lord Nelson's flagship, HMS *Victory*, the Tudor warship *Mary Rose*, Britain's first 'ironclad' warship, HMS *Warrior*, the D-Day Museum, Charles Dickens' birthplace at 393 Old Commercial Road, the Royal Naval and Royal Marine museums, Southsea Castle (built by Henry VIII), Fort Nelson on Portsdown Hill, the Sealife Centre and the Round Tower and Point Battery, which for hundreds of years have guarded the entrance to Portsmouth Harbour.

ST ALBANS

The origins of St Albans, situated on the River Ver, stem from the Roman town of *Verulamium*. Named after the first Christian martyr in Britain, who was executed here, St Albans has developed around the Norman Abbey and Cathedral Church (consecrated 1115), built partly of materials from the old Roman city. The museums house Iron Age and Roman artefacts and the Roman Theatre, unique in Britain, has a stage as opposed to an amphitheatre. Archaeological excavations in the city centre have revealed evidence of pre-Roman, Saxon and medieval occupation.

The town's significance grew to the extent that it was a signatory and venue for the drafting of the Magna Carta. It was also the scene of riots during the Peasants' Revolt, the French King John was imprisoned there after the Battle of Poitiers, and heavy fighting took place there during the Wars of the Roses.

Previously controlled by the Abbot, the town achieved a charter in 1553 and city status in 1877. The street market, first established in 1553, is still an important feature of the city, as are many hotels and inns which survive from the days when St Albans was an important coach stop. Tourist attractions include historic churches and houses, and a 15th-century clock tower.

The city now contains a wide range of firms, with special emphasis on information and legal services. In addition, it is the home of the Royal National Rose Society, and of Rothamsted Park, the agricultural research centre.

SHEFFIELD

Sheffield, the centre of the special steel and cutlery trades, is situated at the junction of the Sheaf, Porter, Rivelin and Loxley valleys with the River Don. Though its cutlery, silverware and plate have long been famous, Sheffield has other and now more important industries: special and alloy steels, engineering, tool-making, medical equipment and media-related industries (in its new Cultural Industries Quarter). Sheffield has two universities and is an important research centre.

The parish church of St Peter and St Paul, founded in the 12th century, became the Cathedral Church of the Diocese of Sheffield in 1914. The Roman Catholic Cathedral Church of St Marie (founded 1847) was created Cathedral for the new diocese of Hallam in 1980. Parts of the present building date from c.1435. The principal buildings are the Town Hall (1897), the Cutlers' Hall (1832), City Hall (1932), Graves Art Gallery (1934), Mappin Art Gallery, the Crucible Theatre and the restored 19th-century Lyceum theatre, which dates from 1897 and was reopened in 1990. Three major sports venues were opened in 1990 to 1991. The National Centre for Popular Music was opened in 1999. Sheffield was created a city in 1893.

SOUTHAMPTON

Southampton is the leading British deep-sea port on the Channel and is situated on one of the finest natural harbours in the world. The first charter was granted by Henry II and Southampton was created a county of itself in 1447. In 1964 it was granted city status.

There were Roman and Saxon settlements on the site of the city, which has been an important port since Anglo-Saxon times due to its natural deep-water harbour. The oldest church is St Michael's (1070) which has an unusually tall spire built in the 18th century as a landmark for navigators of Southampton Water. Other buildings and monuments within the city walls are the Bargate, the Tudor House Museum, God's House Tower, the Tudor Merchants Hall, the Weigh-house, West Gate, King John's House, Long House, Wool House, the ruins of Holy Rood Church, St Julien's Church and the Mayflower Memorial. The medieval town walls, built for artillery, are among the most complete in the UK. Public open spaces total over 1,000 acres and comprise 9 per cent of the city's area.

STOKE-ON-TRENT

Stoke-on-Trent, standing on the River Trent and familiarly known as The Potteries, is the main centre of employment for the population of North Staffordshire. The city is the largest clayware producer in the world (china, earthenware, sanitary goods, refractories, bricks and tiles) and also has a wide range of other manufacturing industry, including steel, chemicals, engineering and tyres. Extensive reconstruction has been carried out in recent years.

The city was formed by the federation of the separate municipal authorities of Tunstall, Burslem, Hanley, Stoke, Fenton, and Longton in 1910 and received its city status in 1925.

WINCHESTER

Winchester, the ancient capital of England, is situated on the River Itchen. The city is rich in architecture of all types

but the Cathedral takes pride of place. The longest Gothic cathedral in the world, it was built in 1079–93 and exhibits examples of Norman, Early English and Perpendicular styles. The author Jane Austen is buried in the Cathedral. Winchester College, founded in 1382, is one of the most famous public schools, the original building (1393) remaining largely unaltered. St Cross Hospital, another great medieval foundation, lies one mile south of the city. The almshouses were founded in 1136 by Bishop Henry de Blois, and Cardinal Henry Beaufort added a new almshouse of 'Noble Poverty' in 1446. The chapel and dwellings are of great architectural interest, and visitors may still receive the 'Wayfarer's Dole' of bread and ale.

Excavations have done much to clarify the origins and development of Winchester. Part of the forum and several of the streets of the Roman town have been discovered; excavations in the Cathedral Close have uncovered the entire site of the Anglo-Saxon cathedral (known as the Old Minster) and parts of the New Minster which was built by Alfred's son Edward the Elder and is the burial place of the Alfredian dynasty. The original burial place of St Swithun, before his remains were translated to a site in the present cathedral, was also uncovered.

Excavations in other parts of the city have thrown much light on Norman Winchester, notably on the site of the Royal Castle (adjacent to which the new Law Courts have been built) and in the grounds of Wolvesey Castle, where the great house built by Bishops Giffard and Henry de Blois in the 12th century has been uncovered. The Great Hall, built by Henry III between 1222 and 1236 survives and houses the Arthurian Round Table.

WOLVERHAMPTON

Wolverhampton was awarded 'Millennium City' status by the Queen in December 2000. The city's first known charter was awarded in AD 985 by the Saxon King Aethelred to the Lady Wulfruna, grandmother of King Harold. The charter referred to the area as Heantun, or High Town, and it is from Wulfrun Heantun that city's current name is derived.

Wolverhampton has long been an industrial centre. Initially a focus for the medieval wool trade, from the 17th century the city has been famous for the quality of its metalwork.

The city's notable features include the municipal gardens and conservatory at West Park and St Peter's Collegiate Church.

YORK

The city of York is an archiepiscopal seat. Its recorded history dates from AD 71, when the Roman Ninth Legion established a base under Petilius Cerealis which later became the fortress of Eburacum. In Anglo-Saxon times the city was the royal and ecclesiastical centre of Northumbria, and after capture by a Viking army in AD 866 it became the capital of the Viking kingdom of Jorvik. By the 14th century the city had become a great mercantile centre, mainly because of its control of the wool trade, and was used as the chief base against the Scots. Under the Tudors its fortunes declined, though Henry VIII made it the headquarters of the Council of the North. Excavations on many sites, including Coppergate, have greatly expanded knowledge of Roman, Viking and medieval urban life.

The city is rich in examples of architecture of all periods. The earliest church was built in AD 627 and, in the 12th to 15th centuries, the present Minster was built in a succession of styles. Other examples within the city are the medieval city walls and gateways, churches and guildhalls. Domestic architecture includes the Georgian mansions of The Mount, Micklegate and Bootham.

English Counties and Shires

LORD-LIEUTENANTS AND HIGH SHERIFFS

County/Shire	Lord-Lieutenant	High Sheriff, 2001–2
Bedfordshire	S. C. Whitbread	Hon. Mrs Fiona Chapman
Berkshire	P. L. Wroughton	D. J. M. Roberts, MC
Bristol	J. Tidmarsh, MBE	Dr M. Campbell
Buckinghamshire	Sir Nigel Mobbs	M. H. T. Jourdan
Cambridgeshire	J. G. P. Crowden	W. H. Proby
Cheshire	W. A. Bromley-Davenport	A. W. A. Spiegelberg
Cornwall	Lady Mary Holborow	Lady Frances Banham
Cumbria	J. A. Cropper	R. B. Hassell-McCosh
Derbyshire	J. K. Bather	Miss J. K. Walker-Okeover, LVO
Devon	E. Dancer, CBE	Lt.-Col. A. Drake
Dorset	Capt. M. Fulford-Dobson, RN	C. A. G. Perry
Durham	Sir Paul Nicholson	T. M. Swan
East Riding of Yorkshire	R. Marriott, TD	Hon. Elizabeth Susan Cunliffe-Lister
East Sussex	P. Stewart-Roberts.	A. R. P. Carden
Essex	The Lord Braybrooke	G. Courtauld
Gloucestershire	H. W. G. Elwes	Mrs Jane Jenner-Fust
Greater London	The Lord Imbert, QPM	A. H. Scott
Greater Manchester	Col. J. B. Timmins, OBE, TD	Major J. N. Abbott, TD, DL
Hampshire	Mrs F. M. Fagan	A. R. C. B. Cooke
Herefordshire	Sir Thomas Dunne, KCVO	A. W. D. Perrins
Hertfordshire	S. A. Bowes Lyon	C. M. Laing
Isle of Wight	C. D. J. Bland	Capt. H. Wrigley
Kent	The Lord Kingsdown, KG, PC	R. H. B. Neame, CBE
Lancashire	The Lord Shuttleworth	R. N. Swarbrick, CBE, DL
Leicestershire	T. G. M. Brooks	M. C. C. Sandell
Lincolnshire	Mrs B. K. Cracroft-Eley	C. G. Rowles Nicholson
Merseyside	A. W. Waterworth	W. D. Fulton, JP, DL
Norfolk	Sir Timothy Colman, KG	Mrs Theresa Caroline Courtauld
Northamptonshire	Lady Juliet Townsend, LVO	Lady Robinson
Northumberland	Sir John Riddel, CVO	J. P. P. Anderson
North Yorkshire	The Lord Crathorne	D. G. H. Nelson, OBE
Nottinghamshire	Sir Andrew Buchanan, Bt.	Sir John Whitaker, Bt.
Oxfordshire	H. L. J. Brunner	Lady McLintock
Rutland	Air Chief Marshal Sir Thomas Kennedy, GCB, AFC	M. M. Allen
Shropshire	A. E. H. Heber-Percy	J. R. Ravenscroft
Somerset	Lady Gass	T. H. R. Poole, TD
South Yorkshire	The Earl of Scarbrough	A. M. C. Staniforth
Staffordshire	J. A. Hawley, TD	The Countess of Shrewsbury and Waterford
Suffolk	The Lord Belstead, PC	D. W. Barclay
Surrey	Mrs S. J. F. Goad	C. W. Biddell
Tyne and Wear	N. Sherlock	Mrs Anne Darling
Warwickshire	M. Dunne	Miss Sarah Holman
West Midlands	R. R. Taylor, OBE	Mrs Tessa King-Farlow
West Sussex	H. Wyatt	G. G. Ferguson
West Yorkshire	J. Lyles, CBE	J. D. N. Stoddart-Scott
Wiltshire	Lt.-Gen. Sir Maurice Johnston, KCB, OBE	R. D. Stratton, OBE
Worcestershire	Sir Thomas Dunne, KCVO	A. W. D. Perrins

COUNTY COUNCILS: AREA, POPULATION, FINANCE

Council	Administrative Headquarters	Area (Hectares)	Population	Net current expenditure 2000-1
Bedfordshire	County Hall, Bedford	119,220	380,500	£307,412,000.00
Buckinghamshire	County Hall, Aylesbury	156,538	476,200	£346,501,000.00
Cambridgeshire	Shire Hall, Cambridge	305,399	573,500	£397,377,000.00
Cheshire	County Hall, Chester	208,344	677,300	£523,362,000.00
Cornwall	County Hall, Truro	354,810	493,900	£367,006,000.00
Cumbria	The Courts, Carlisle	681,000	492,900	£398,563,000.00
Derbyshire	County Hall, Matlock	262,858	740,200	£546,862,000.00
Devon	County Hall, Exeter	670,343	692,400	£512,509,000.00
Dorset	County Hall, Dorchester	254,375	392,800	£279,328,000.00
Durham	County Hall, Durham	223,180	490,100	£407,210,000.00
East Sussex	Pelham House, St Andrew's Lane, Lewes	172,500	497,500	£373,393,000.00
Essex	County Hall, Chelmsford	344,781	1,295,000	£1,008,446,000.00
Gloucestershire	Shire Hall, Gloucester	265,535	565,200	£405,063,000.00
Hampshire	The Castle, Winchester	367,915	1,255,900	£485,995,000.00
Hertfordshire	County Hall, Hertford	164,306	1,051,300	£813,694,000.00
Kent	County Hall, Maidstone	354,296	1,332,000	£1,082,458,000.00
Lancashire	County Hall, Preston	289,780	1,147,300	£929,012,000.00
Leicestershire	County Hall, Glenfield, Leicester	208,380	602,000	£430,852,000.00
Lincolnshire	County Offices, Newland, Lincoln	588,000	635,300	£461,788,000.00
Norfolk	County Hall, Norwich	537,234	801,000	£578,212,000.00
Northamptonshire	County Hall, Northampton	236,737	622,800	£478,753,000.00
Northumberland	County Hall, Morpeth	502,594	312,000	£261,318,000.00
North Yorkshire	County Hall, Northallerton	830,399	572,200	£412,921,000.00
Nottinghamshire	County Hall, Nottingham	208,510	744,400	£593,807,000.00
Oxfordshire	County Hall, Oxford	260,595	625,400	£423,595,000.00
Shropshire	The Shirehall, Shrewsbury	319,736	283,000	£193,867,000.00
Somerset	County Hall, Taunton	345,233	494,600	£349,079,000.00
Staffordshire	County Buildings, Stafford	262,355	807,000	£589,598,000.00
Suffolk	County Hall, Ipswich	380,207	670,000	£475,480,000.00
Surrey	County Hall, Kingston upon Thames	167,011	1,055,400	£717,320,000.00
Warwickshire	Shire Hall, Warwick	198,054	510,000	£362,587,000.00
West Sussex	County Hall, Chichester	199,025	759,600	£535,143,000.00
Wiltshire	County Hall, Trowbridge	348,070	431,000	£306,454,000.00
Worcestershire	County Hall, Worcester	173,529	545,000	£374,950,000.00

Source of population statistics and net expenditure figures,
CIPFA

COUNTY COUNCILS: Officers and Chairmen

Council	Chief Executive	County Treasurer	Chairman of County Council
Bedfordshire	D. Bell	B. Dodds	A. P. Hendry
Buckinghamshire	C. Williams	S. Nolan	D. Shakespeare
Cambridgeshire	A. Barnish	M. Parsons	J. Eddy
Cheshire	C. Cheesman	A. Cope	B. Grange
Cornwall	P. Davies	F. P. Twyning	J. M. Philp
Cumbria	L. Victory	R. F. Mather	R. S. J. Edgar
Derbyshire	A. R. N. Hodgson	P. Swaby	Mrs K. M. Trueman
Devon	P. Jenkinson	Mrs J. Stanhope	S. Day
Dorset	D. H. Jenkins	A. P. Peel	J. C. Peake, MBE
Durham	K. W. Smith	J. Kirkby	C. Megee
East Sussex	Mrs C. Miller	J. Howes	M. Tunwell
Essex	S. Ashurst	K. D. Neale	J. Pike
Gloucestershire	J. Redfearn	R. Potter	Dr J. Cardwell
Hampshire	P. C. B. Robertson	J. C. Pittam	A. W. Rice
Hertfordshire	W. D. Ogley	Chris Sweeney	K. Gray
Kent	M. Pitt	D. Lewis	C. Thorton
Lancashire	M. B. Winterbottom	B. Aldred	D. Westell
Leicestershire	J. B. Sinnott	A. Youd	J. F. Howard
Lincolnshire	D. Bowles	P. Moore	Mrs H. D. Judge
Norfolk	T. J. Byles	R. D. Summers	Dr J. Norris
Northamptonshire	P. Gould	S. Wood	J. Gardner
Northumberland	A. Clarke	C. Burns	Dr G. H. Fisher
North Yorkshire	J. Walker	J. S. Moore	G. Rennie
Nottinghamshire	P. J. Housden	R. Latham	J. T. Napier
Oxfordshire	R. Shaw	C. Gray	C. Scholar
Shropshire	N. T. Pursey	L. Rowly	Maj. A. Coles, MBE, TD
Somerset	Dr D. Radford	C. N. Bilsland	R. J. E. Bush
Staffordshire	B. A. Price, CBE	R. G. Tettenborn, OBE	Dr. D. Mole
Suffolk	Mrs L. Homer	W. Banks	R. Sudds
Surrey	P. Coen	N. W. Skelett	Dr B. J. Coffin
Warwickshire	I. G. Caulfield	D. Clarke	M. Singh
West Sussex	D. P. Rigg	Mrs H. Kilpatrick	Mrs M. Johnson
Wiltshire	Dr K. Robinson	D. Chalker	J. P. Johnson
Worcestershire	R. Sykes	M. Weaver	P. Fallows

Unitary Councils

SMALL CAPITALS denote CITY status
§ Denotes Borough status

Council	Population	Band D charge 2001	Chief Eecutive	Mayor (a) Lord Mayor (b) Chairman 2001–2
§Barnsley	227,213	899.31	P. J. Coppard	C. Evans
Bath and North-East Somerset	158,692	923.00	J. Everitt	M. McVeir
§BIRMINGHAM	961,041	978.94	Sir Michael Lyons	(a) J. Wormwood
§Blackburn with Darwen	139,490	1,010.52	P. S. Watson	J. Williams
§Blackpool	154,000	810.47	G. E. Essex-Crosby	Mrs S. E. Wright
§Bolton	226,100	978.15	B. Knight	K. Helsby
§Bournemouth	162,000	839.93	D. Newell	D. Eyre
§Bracknell Forest	110,000	799.00	G. S. Mitchell	Mrs D. Hayes
BRADFORD	457,344	882.25	I. Stewart	(a) G. Khaliq
§Brighton and Hove	258,100	828.11	G. Jones	H. Steer
BRISTOL	399,600	1,004.00	R. Weston	(a) Mrs B. Hughill
§Bury	182,400	910.89	D. Taylor	P. Nesbit
§Calderdale	193,000	959.00	P. Sheehan	C. O'Connor
§COVENTRY	305,000	1,065.00	Mrs S. Manzie	(a) D. Chater
§Darlington	100,500	829.77	B. Keel	Mrs I. Harley
DERBY	235,000	873.16	R. H. Cowlishaw	J. Till
§Doncaster	288,854	842.18	D. Marlow	Mrs B. Roberts
§Dudley	311,468	896.00	A. Sparke	J. Walters
East Riding of Yorkshire	315,717	992.00	D. Stephenson	(b) Ms M. Kingston
§Gateshead	199,600	1,056.91	L. N. Elton	J. Hatton
§Halton	123,038	801.14	M. Cuff	Ms J. Devaney
Hartlepool	90,000	1,068.21	B. J. Dinsdale	D. Ferriday
Herefordshire	167,000	852.29	N. Pringle	R. Thomas
Isle of Wight	126,000	859.00	B. Quoroll	(b) V. J. Morey
KINGSTON UPON HULL	257,873	892.32	I. Crookham	(a) F. Beedle
§Kirklees	392,300	948.00	A. Elson	T. Elson
§Knowsley	153,252	1,027.17	S. Gallagher	T. Russell
§LEEDS	727,000	845.00	P. Rogerson	(a) D. Hudson
LEICESTER	290,900	920.68	R. Green	(a) J. Allen
§LIVERPOOL	468,000	1,171.54	D. Henshaw	(a) G. Scott
§Luton	180,600	805.14	D. Singh	B. Devenish
§MANCHESTER	431,052	1,027.42	H. Bernstein	(a) H. Barrett
Medway	250,000	745.02	Ms J. Armitt	T. Goulden
Middlesbrough	145,000	880.00	N. Sayer	P. Walker
§Milton Keynes	210,000	853.46	H. Miller	Mrs Pat Seymour
§NEWCASTLE UPON TYNE	273,000	1,049.43	K. G. Lavery	(a) Mrs M. J. Carr
North East Lincolnshire	156,243	984.53	J. Leivers	N. Lincoln
North Lincolnshire	152,287	1,051.00	M. Garnett	Mrs M. Simpson
North Somerset	189,776	818.00	G. Turner	(b) P. Bryant
§North Tyneside	198,000	1,009.57	vacant	C. Gambling
NOTTINGHAM CITY	284,000	983.00	E. F. Cantle	(a) R. Greensmith
§Oldham	220,000	1,069.97	A. W. Kilburn	C. Wheeler
PETERBOROUGH	159,900	858.30	P. Martin	R. Pobgee, MBE
PLYMOUTH	250,000	789.60	Mrs A. Stone	(a) D. Viney
§Poole	139,000	837.00	J. Brooks	R. Parker
PORTSMOUTH	188,800	744.00	N. Gurney	(a) Mrs E. Baker
§Reading	143,520	962.00	Ms J. Markham	T. Jones
Redcar and Cleveland	138,200	1,080.99	C. Moore	V. Collins
§Rochdale	202,000	972.00	R. Ellis	Ms I. Davidson
§Rotherham	251,637	940.22	G. B. Fitzgerald	R. Littleboy
Rutland	35,000	1,299.00	K. Franklin	(b) Mrs J. Bews
§St Helens	180,000	1,063.00	Mrs C. Hudson	K. Roberts
§SALFORD	229,300	1,084.00	J. C. Willis	J. King
§Sandwell	290,500	964.00	F. N. Summers	Lord Tarsem King
§Sefton	289,542	950.15	G. J. Haywood	A. Hill
§SHEFFIELD	529,000	999.78	R. W. Kerslake	(a) D. Baker
§Slough	108,000	760.12	Ms C. Coppell	J. Jones
§Solihull	205,600	852.00	Ms K. Kerswell	Mrs L. Kellie
SOUTHAMPTON	210,352	831.90	B. Roynton	Mrs C. Kelly
South Gloucestershire	252,000	906.00	M. Robinson	(b) A. Bracey

Council	Population	Band D charge 2001	Chief Ececutive	Mayor (a) Lord Mayor (b) Chairman 2001-2
§Southend	176,000	770.36	J. K. M. Krawiec	H. Briggs
§South Tyneside	154,057	972.36	P. J. Haigh	A. Kerr
§Stockport	292,000	1,018.74	J. R. Schultz	E. Pyle
§Stockton-on-Tees	178,300	952.90	G. Garlick	W. T. Bean
STOKE-ON-TRENT	254,400	853.05	B. Smith	(a) W. F. Austin
§SUNDERLAND	290,700	911.16	C. W. Sinclair	J. K. Murray
Swindon	177,500	793.00	P. Doherty	D. Cox
§Tameside	219,400	987.84	M. J. Greenwood	S. Poole
Telford and Wrekin	153,000	899.89	M. Frater	(b) A. Mackenzie
§Thurrock	150,000	769.00	E. Nath	B. Lawrence
§Torbay	124,100	848.84	A. J. Hodgkiss	B. Pudner
§Trafford	230,000	771.28	Ms C. Hassan	H. Faulkner
WAKEFIELD	319,600	819.46	M. Pullan	D. Kitchen
§Walsall	261,600	923.55	H. Bhogal	C. Belby
§Warrington	188,000	823.00	S. Broomhead	J. Richards
West Berkshire	145,000	940.00	Ms S. Manzie	(b) Mrs M. Lock
§Wigan	310,000	960.52	S. M. Jones	J. E. Hilton
§Windsor and Maidenhead	140,500	794.41	D. C. Lunn	J. Tryon
§Wirral	326,000	1,077.00	S. Maddox	J. Cocker
Wokingham	146,252	948.00	Ms J. Earl	(b) D. Swindells
§WOLVERHAMPTON	240,900	1,043.00	D. B. Anderson	Mrs J. Hill
YORK	178,000	790.65	D. Atkinson	(a) I. Waubby

District Councils

SMALL CAPITALS denote CITY status
§ Denotes Borough status

Council	Population	Band D charge 2001	Chief Ececutive	Chairman (a) Mayor (b) Lord Mayor 2001-2
Adur, W. Sussex	58,400	897.00	I. Lowrie	D. Philips
§Allerdale, Cumbria	96,000	952.71	P. J. Leonard	(a) A. Barry
Alnwick, Northumberland	31,400	956.25	L. A. B. St Ruth	V. Vaggs
Amber Valley, Derbys	115,000	990.00	P. M. Carney	(a) J. Nelson
Arun, W. Sussex	143,800	775.94	I. Sumnall	Mrs J. Maconachie
Ashfield, Notts	107,000	1,042.00	E. N. Bernasconi	Mrs Y. White
§Ashford, Kent	102,177	842.67	A. Baker	(a) L. G. Lawrie
Aylesbury Vale, Bucks	156,597	853.12	R. Carr	Mrs C. Lambert
Babergh, Suffolk	80,790	872.00	M. Hammond	Mrs S. Carpendale
§Barrow-in-Furness, Cumbria	71,000	987.00	T. O. Campbell	(a) Mrs P. J. M. Smith
Basildon, Essex	162,800	933.75	J. Robb	Mrs L. Gordon
§Basingstoke and Deane, Hants	156,700	843.52	Mrs K. E. P. Sporle	(a) Mrs R. Wellman
Bassetlaw, Notts	106,600	1,026.87	J. Molloy	Avril Borsley
§Bedford, Beds	140,700	959.98	S. Field	(a) P. Olney
§Berwick-upon-Tweed, Northumberland	26,731	1,002.55	P. Rutherford (Acting)	(a) W. R. Huntly
Blaby, Leics	86,400	920.00	E. Hemsley	R. Berrington
§Blyth Valley, Northumberland	79,900	995.61	G. Paul	(a) J. Newman
Bolsover, Derbys	71,000	1,020.02	J. R. Fotherby	B. W. Hendry
§Boston, Lincs	54,140	879.00	M. James	(a) S. Bakewell
Braintree, Essex	132,300	879.20	Ms A. F. Ralph	K. Boylan
Breckland, Norfolk	120,000	837.78	R. N. Garnett	Mrs S. Matthews
§Brentwood, Essex	71,400	886.00	B. McLintock	(a) A. Davies
Bridgnorth, Shrops	52,300	871.00	R. Heath	L. Jones
Broadland, Norfolk	116,000	882.00	C. Bland	D. Thompson
Bromsgrove, Worcs	85,210	873.00	R. F. Lewis	M. H. Gill
§Broxbourne, Herts	81,500	804.22	M. J. Walker	(a) D. C. Smith
§Broxtowe, Notts	110,319	1,007.14	M. Brown	(a) T. Syson
§Burnley, Lancs	89,900	1,043.42	Dr G. Taylor	(a) J. Alston
CAMBRIDGE, CAMBS	122,900	850.00	R. Hammond	(a) C. Lakin

Council	Population	Band D charge 2001	Chief Eecutive	Chairman (a) Mayor (b) Lord Mayor 2001-2
Cannock Chase, Staffs	91,000	908.00	M. G. Kemp	M. Holder
CANTERBURY, KENT	123,900	867.71	C. Carmichael	(b) F. Whitemore
Caradon, Cornwall	81,280	861.00	Dr J. Neal	E. J. Lewis
CARLISLE, CUMBRIA	102,317	975.00	P. Stybelski	(a) Mrs D. H. Parsons
Carrick, Cornwall	85,300	872.35	J. P. Winskill	L. Brokenshire
§Castle Morpeth, Northumberland	50,000	1,021.00	P. Wilson	(a) C. Cuthbertson
§Castle Point, Essex	84,800	935.00	B. Rollinson	(a) E. Brett
§Charnwood, Leics	155,400	910.67	S. M. Peatfield	(a) A. W. Stott
§Chelmsford, Essex	156,000	898.27	M. Easteal	(a) C. Rycroft
§Cheltenham, Glos	103,115	888.68	L. Davison	(a) Ms D. Pennell
Cherwell, Oxon	132,578	836.38	G. J. Handley	Mrs C. A. Fulljames
§Chesterfield, Derbys	101,000	960.02	D. R. Shaw	(a) J. McManus
Chester-le-Street, Co. Durham	53,000	907.20	M. W. Waterson	J. Tinnion
CHESTER, CHESHIRE	118,700	986.47	P. F. Durham	(b) G. Proctor
Chichester, W. Sussex	110,110	815.80	J. S. Marsland	B. B. Trinkwoh
Chiltern, Bucks	91,682	878.17	A. Goodrum	Ian Gomm
§Chorley, Lancs	98,075	987.10	J. W. Davies	(a) D. Edgerley
§Christchurch, Dorset	44,327	904.10	M. A. Turvey	(a) Mrs J. Spencer
§Colchester, Essex	159,000	882.99	J. Cobley	(a) M. Hogg
§Congleton, Cheshire	88,400	972.55	P. Cooper	(a) R.Giltrap
§Copeland, Cumbria	69,800	985.00	Dr J. Stanforth	(a) N. Williams
§Corby, Northants	53,000	856.00	N. Rudd	(a) Mrs B. Wade
Cotswold, Glos	83,000	893.00	N. C. Abbott	B. I. Evans
Craven, N. Yorks	52,100	838.01	Miss R. Mann	S. Butcher
§Crawley, W. Sussex	97,000	796.59	M. D. Sander	(a) C. Mullins
§Crewe and Nantwich, Cheshire	116,800	922.19	A. Wenham	(a) W. T. Beard
§Dacorum, Herts	130,000	839.00	P. Walker	(a) D. Pownsend
§Dartford, Kent	86,000	809.00	G. Harris	(a) T. A. Maddison
Daventry, Northants	69,000	820.08	S. Atkinson	A. Compling
Derbyshire Dales, Derbys	71,300	989.17	D. Wheatcroft	T. Boam
Derwentside, Co. Durham	87,300	981.20	L. Vaux	A. Watson
Dover, Kent	109,400	853.20	J. P. Moir, TD	W. Hansell
DURHAM, CO. DURHAM	80,669	931.44	C. Shearsmith	(a) J. G. Cowper
Easington, Co. Durham	97,824	1,041.00	P. Wilding	Mrs A. E. Laing
§Eastbourne, E. Sussex	90,000	926.00	vacant	(a) D. Stevens
East Cambridgeshire, Cambs	66,200	828.08	J. Hill	V. Leake
East Devon, Devon	130,600	861.00	F. J. Vallender	Dr W. H. Waterworth
East Dorset, Dorset	82,400	944.00	A. Breakwell	R. Daw
East Hampshire, Hants	112,432	883.14	P. Burton	P. Rodgers
East Hertfordshire, Herts	124,000	852.60	R. J. Bailey	R. Gilbert
§Eastleigh, Hants	113,500	882.00	C. Tapp	(a) Mrs M. A. Sollitt
East Lindsey, Lincs	124,160	843.12	P. Haigh	G. Allan
East Northamptonshire, Northants	76,750	864.00	G. Wise	A. Campbell
§East Staffordshire, Staffs	103,400	908.60	F. W. Saunders	(a) P. Davies
Eden, Cumbria	45,581	957.56	I. W. Bruce	J. Banks
§Ellesmere Port and Neston, Cheshire	81,200	980.00	S. Ewbank	(a) Mrs M. Andrews
§Elmbridge, Surrey	114,479	856.00	M. Lockwood	(a) Mrs M. Sheldrick
Epping Forest, Essex	118,000	904.00	J. Burgess	J. Gilliham
§Epsom and Ewell, Surrey	67,007	841.16	D. J. Smith	(a) A. C. Carlson
§Erewash, Derbys	108,160	974.00	Tony Harris	(a) P. Trueman
EXETER, DEVON	111,264	849.96	P. Bostock	(a) M. G. Baldwin
Fareham, Hants	107,000	845.00	A. A. Davies	(a) A. Mandry
Fenland, Cambs	81,900	854.00	N. R. Topliss	A. Carlisle
Forest Heath, Suffolk	69,200	827.70	D. W. Burnip	W. E. Sadler
Forest of Dean, Glos	75,351	911.11	Ms M. Holborow	D. Clarke
§Fylde, Lancs	74,900	967.00	K. Lee	(a) P. Fieldhouse
§Gedling, Notts	110,133	953.20	vacant	(a) M. Roach
GLOUCESTER, GLOS	101,608	889.00	P. Smith	(a) T. L. Haines
§Gosport, Hants	78,040	880.34	M. C. Crocker	(a) D. F. Wright
§Gravesham, Kent	92,454	846.00	E. C. Anderson	(a) V. Ashenden
§Great Yarmouth, Norfolk	89,900	880.73	R. W. Packham	D. W. Thompson
§Guildford, Surrey	129,200	850.00	D. T. Watts, FRSA	(a) Mrs J. E. Powell
Hambleton, N. Yorks	86,500	797.53	P. Simpson	M. J. Prest
Harborough, Leics	75,300	916.00	M. C. Wilson	P. Callis
Harlow, Essex	74,629	986.00	D. Patterson	R. Long

Council	Population	Band D charge 2001	Chief Eecutive	Chairman (a) Mayor (b) Lord Mayor 2001–2
§Harrogate, N. Yorks	143,000	879.00	P. M. Walsh	(a) P. Nash
Hart, Hants	80,921	869.00	G. R. Jelbart	S. Band
§Hastings, E. Sussex	84,500	953.63	R. Mawford	(a) J. Dowling
§Havant, Hants	120,113	862.82	R. D. Smith	(a) R. V. Bellinger
§Hertsmere, Herts	97,314	851.00	R. Higgins	(a) W. Hogan
§High Peak, Derbys	87,900	987.16	P. Sloman	(a) R. Priestly
§Hinckley and Bosworth, Leics	97,699	882.24	J. Corry	(a) W. G. Joy
Horsham, W. Sussex	122,405	837.35	M. J. Pearson	Mrs C. Vickers
Huntingdonshire, Cambs	153,000	860.00	D. Monks	K. Reynolds
§Hyndburn, Lancs	78,390	1,026.48	M. J. Chambers	(a) D. Parkins
§Ipswich, Suffolk	116,956	946.70	J. D. Hehir	(a) Mrs M. Corrington-Brown
Kennet, Wilts	79,500	894.00	M. J. Boden	K. R. F. Beard
Kerrier, Cornwall	87,566	879.75	G. G. Cox	Mrs B. Godolphin
§Kettering, Northants	81,320	860.30	D. Cook	(a) R. Civil
§King's Lynn and West Norfolk, Norfolk	133,420	886.16	G. Chilton	(a) G. Pratt
LANCASTER, LANCS	137,000	978.86	M. Cullinan	(a) Mrs P. Quinton
Lewes, E. Sussex	85,859	956.00	J. N. Crawford	P. R. Harper
Lichfield, Staffs	92,699	881.00	J. T. Thompson	J. R. T. Mercer
LINCOLN, LINCS	170,000	851.85	A. Taylor	(a) P. McGinley
§Macclesfield, Cheshire	151,590	959.71	D. W. Parr	(a) Mrs M. Clampett
§Maidstone, Kent	137,000	910.74	D. Petford	(a) Mrs P. Stockell
Maldon, Essex	57,300	885.64	S. W. Packham	Mrs P. A. Channer
Malvern Hills, Worcs	74,011	844.86	C. J. Bocock	Mrs B. Williams
Mansfield, Notts	100,300	1,055.00	R. P. Goad	M. Sage
§Melton, Leics	46,861	907.00	P. M. Murphy	(a) T. P. Cullen
Mendip, Somerset	100,000	887.00	G. Jeffs	T. O'Connel
Mid Bedfordshire, Beds	109,800	969.00	J. Salsbury	R. A. Holden
Mid Devon, Devon	68,600	880.96	P. Edwards	Mrs J. Campbell
Mid Suffolk, Suffolk	77,100	833.61	A. Good	T. Fowler
Mid Sussex, W. Sussex	126,000	854.00	W. J. H. Hatton	C. A. C. Hersey
Mole Valley, Surrey	79,220	826.97	Mrs H. Kerswell	M. Homewood
Newark and Sherwood, Notts	104,010	1,080.00	R. G. Dix	Ms. J. Dawn
§Newcastle under Lyme, Staffs	123,300	883.63	F. Harley	(a) Mrs G. Williams
New Forest, Hants	170,610	889.00	D. Yates	Ms. A. Drake
§Northampton, Northants	198,300	881.77	R. J. B. Morris	(a) T. Hadland
North Cornwall, Cornwall	81,000	873.56	D. Brown	E. T. Denholm
North Devon, Devon	87,740	894.00	D. T. Cunliffe	D. Paul
North Dorset, Dorset	62,000	910.40	A. Greaves	Mrs D. L. Jones
North East Derbyshire, Derbys	99,000	1,024.00	Ms C. A. Gilby	Mrs M. Treweek
North Hertfordshire, Herts	113,500	843.15	S. Philp	P. Burt
North Kesteven, Lincs	78,400	893.00	Mrs R. Marlow	B. Drain
North Norfolk, Norfolk	100,900	887.00	B. A. Barrell	V. Woodcock
North Shropshire, Shrops	54,100	905.71	R. J. Hughes	F. J. Udale
§North Warwickshire, Warks	60,747	977.00	J. Hutchinson	(a) M. E. Stanley
North West Leicestershire, Leics	86,000	921.71	M. J. Diaper	Mrs A. Harrop
North Wiltshire, Wilts	126,829	924.26	R. Marshall	B. Atfield
NORWICH, NORFOLK	123,500	934.00	Ms A. Seex	(b) K. Ratcliffe
§Nuneaton and Bedworth, Warks	117,052	951.00	Ms C. Kerr	(a) W. Hancox
§Oadby and Wigston, Leics	53,570	924.88	Mrs R. E. Hyde	(a) G. A. Boulter
§Oswestry, Shrops	33,508	907.00	P. Shevlin	(a) L. Dennis
OXFORD, OXON	146,100	955.25	M. Headicar	(b) P. Moss
§Pendle, Lancs	83,000	1,034.47	S. Barnes	(a) F. M. Hartley
Penwith, Cornwall	60,107	848.00	J. A. R. McKenna	R. A. Mann
§Preston, Lancs	135,000	1,050.00	J. E. Carr	(a) A. Hackett
Purbeck, Dorset	46,140	934.24	P. B. Croft	R. Anderson
§Redditch, Worcs	77,000	906.00	C. Smith	(a) D. Dudley
§Reigate and Banstead, Surrey	119,000	863.80	N. Clifford	(a) S. A. Gates
§Restormel, Cornwall	91,000	847.51	Mrs P. Crowson	(a) Mrs E. J. Vincent
§Ribble Valley, Lancs	52,444	978.31	D. G. Morris	(a) Mrs G. Pye
Richmondshire, N. Yorks	49,300	864.68	H. Tabiner	Mrs J. Metcalfe
Rochford, Essex	78,273	911.62	P. Warren	Mrs S. J. Lemmon
§Rossendale, Lancs	65,681	1,027.57	J. S. Hartley	(a) J. Grogan
Rother, E. Sussex	90,100	906.65	D. Stevens	W. H. Clements
§Rugby, Warks	87,000	938.00	Mrs D. M. Colley	(a) R. Kirby

Council	Population	Band D charge 2001	Chief Eecutive	Chairman (a) Mayor (b) Lord Mayor 2001–2
§Runnymede, Surrey	76,629	781.00	T. N. Williams	(a) J. R. Ashmore
§Rushcliffe, Notts	105,000	1,008.00	K. Beaumont	(a) T. D. Barlow
§Rushmoor, Hants	86,000	863.49	J. A. Lloyd	(a) C. S. Choudhary
Ryedale, N. Yorks	49,000	883.98	H. W. Mosley	C. R. Wainwright
ST ALBANS, HERTS	128,700	858.06	P. Learner	(a) J. Peters
§St Edmundsbury, Suffolk	97,000	850.00	G. R. N. Toft	(a) B. Bagnall
Salisbury, Wilts	115,000	891.06	R. Sheard	I. Tomes
§Scarborough, N. Yorks	106,067	796.54	J. M. Trebble	(a) Mrs L. Haycock
§Sedgefield, Co. Durham	89,500	1,055.49	N. Vaulks	(a) A. Gray
Sedgemoor, Somerset	104,000	865.00	K. Rickards	(a) K. Richards
Selby, N. Yorks	89,428	844.47	M. Connor	W. Norton
Sevenoaks, Kent	111,000	887.25	N. Howells	P. Deans
Shepway, Kent	96,460	899.00	R. J. Thompson	(a) D. Dickinson
§Shrewsbury and Atcham, Shrops	97,400	877.00	R. Hooper	(a) C. Forshaw
South Bedfordshire, Beds	111,250	1,019.53	J. Ruddick	Mrs Staples
South Bucks, Berks	62,482	858.79	C. R. Furness	J. R. A. Kennedy
South Cambridgeshire, Cambs	126,500	819.00	J. S. Ballantyne	G. Elsbury
South Derbyshire, Derbys	81,200	972.00	F. McArdle	C. H. Rose
South Hams, Devon	82,600	875.60	Miss R. E. Bagley	I. Longrigg
South Holland, Lincs	74,095	833.22	C. J. Simpkins	E. J. Poll
South Kesteven, Lincs	120,000	855.05	C. Farmer	A. Parkin
South Lakeland, Cumbria	103,240	956.00	P. J. Cunliffe	R. Bingham
South Norfolk, Norfolk	104,334	900.00	G. Rivers	Mrs P. Dore
South Northamptonshire, Northants	78,800	883.38	R. Tinlin	L. Richards
South Oxfordshire, Oxon	125,000	904.26	D. Buckle	Mrs E. Haros
§South Ribble, Lancs	104,300	974.82	Ms J. Hunter	(a) N. Crossley
South Shropshire, Shrops	282,500	908.00	G. C. Biggs, MBE	M. R. Williams
South Somerset, Somerset	155,000	891.47	Ms E. Peters	Mrs H. Merrifield
South Staffordshire, Staffs	105,487	823.60	L. T. Barnfield	R. Williams
§Spelthorne, Surrey	89,748	836.65	M. B. Taylor	(a) Ms J. Wood-Dow
Stafford Moorlands, Staffs	95,000	903.00	B. J. Preedy	R. Plant
§Staffordshire, Staffs	127,000	808.70	D. Rawlings	(a) P. Bruce
§Stevenage, Herts	77,000	856.26	I. Paske	(a) H. C. L. Tessier
Stratford, Warks	109,400	891.70	I. B. Prosser	L. Topham
Stroud, Glos	108,000	944.26	D. Hagg	Mrs S. M. Bruce
Suffolk Coastal, Suffolk	121,000	858.65	T. K. Griffin	Mrs D. Savage
§Surrey Heath, Surrey	85,000	846.00	B. R. Catchpole	(a) R. Christie
§Swale, Kent	120,000	874.00	C. Edwards	(a) Mrs B. Simpson
§Tamworth, Staffs	77,000	853.00	D. Weatherley	(a) M. Cooper
Tandridge, Surrey	76,316	846.76	J. D. Thomas	E. Morgan
§Taunton Deane, Somerset	100,000	857.00	S. Fletcher	(a) Mrs M. Whitmarsh
Teesdale, Co. Durham	24,992	913.89	C. M. Anderson	N. Wood
Teignbridge, Devon	116,500	886.00	H. Davies	D. Tracy
Tendring, Essex	130,328	885.00	J. Hawkins	Miss C. Jessop
§Test Valley, Hants	111,000	837.00	A. Jones	(a) J. E. Taylor
§Tewkesbury, Glos	74,478	851.79	T. Turner	(a) Mrs F. M. Ogden
Thanet, Kent	127,000	898.52	D. Ralls, CBE	W. E. Palmer
Three Rivers, Herts	84,000	865.00	A. Robertson	G. Emery
§Tonbridge and Malling, Kent	106,300	880.03	T. Thompson	(a) Mrs J. Oxely
Torridge, Devon	55,440	893.00	R. K. Brasington	P. Waters
§Tunbridge Wells, Kent	102,738	816.22	R. J. Stone	(a) M. Howell
Tynedale, Northumberland	58,181	987.14	P. A. Kemp	Mrs A. Hutchinson
Uttlesford, Essex	69,796	901.00	Mrs E. Forbes	D. Gregory
Vale of White Horse, Oxon	113,940	870.00	T. A. Stock	V. Butt
§Vale Royal, Cheshire	118,300	984.88	A. Bingham-Holmes	(a) S. Gough
Wansbeck, Northumberland	63,171	1,016.25	R. A. Stephenson	D. Armstrong
Warwick, Warks	124,500	900.07	Miss J. M. Barrett	H. Thomas
§Watford, Herts	81,000	926.49	A. Clarke	(a) Mrs S. Tuckwood
Waveney, Suffolk	108,163	839.00	Mrs M. McLean	Ms M. Rodgers
§Waverley, Surrey	113,212	865.77	Ms C. L. Pointer	(a) M. R. Goodridge
Wealden, E. Sussex	130,214	963.79	Ms S. Douglas	N. Buck
Wear Valley, Co. Durham	62,746	943.36	I. Phillips	W. Dobinson
§Wellingborough, Northants	70,400	805.66	A. D. W. McArdle	(a) Mrs P. Beirne
Welwyn Hatfield, Herts	92,366	863.06	M. Saminaden	T. Wilder
§West Devon, Devon	47,716	906.54	D. J. Incoll	(a) R. Pike

Council	Population	Band D charge 2001	Chief Ececutive	Chairman (a) Mayor (b) Lord Mayor 2001–2
West Dorset, Dorset	91,100	934.00	R. C. Rennison	Mrs N. M. Penfold
West Lancashire, Lancs	110,200	1,010.00	W. J. Taylor	R. Hodge
West Lindsey, Lincs	77,560	879.75	R. W. Nelsey	R. Rainforth
West Oxfordshire, Oxon	99,000	840.90	G. Bonner	A. Walker
West Somerset, Somerset	32,700	851.00	T. Howes	E. S. Taylor
West Wiltshire, Wilts	108,000	830.50	J. Ligo	Mrs A. Irving
§Weymouth and Portland, Dorset	63,000	936.90	T. Grainger	(a) Mrs J. Stanley
WINCHESTER, HANTS	110,000	863.00	D. H. Cowan	(a) Ms T. Evans
§Woking, Surrey	86,765	877.05	P. Russell	(a) B. J. Pope
WORCESTER, WORCS	95,500	864.91	D. Wareing	(a) D. Clark
§Worthing, W. Sussex	100,000	849.51	Miss S. Grady	(a) Mrs V. Sutton
Wychavon, Worcs	101,716	864.00	S. Pritchard	A. Hotham
Wycombe, Bucks	162,000	870.00	R. J. Cummins	R. W. Jennings
§Wyre, Lancs	105,010	974.60	M. Brown	(a) F. Baillie
Wyre Forest, Worcs	94,814	904.00	W. Delin	F. Bailly

1 Stockton-on-Tees
2 Middlesbrough
3 Blackpool
4 Blackburn
  with Darwen
5 Bolton
6 Bury
7 Rochdale
8 Salford
9 Oldham
10 Liverpool
11 Knowsley
12 St Helens
13 Halton
14 Warrington
15 Trafford
16 Manchester
17 Tameside
18 Stockport
19 Nottingham
20 Telford and
   Wrekin
21 Wolverhampton

22 Walsall
23 Sandwell
24 Dudley
25 Birmingham
26 Solihull
27 Coventry
28 Peterborough
29 South Glos
30 Bristol
31 Bath and
   NE Somerset
32 Windsor and
   Maidenhead
33 Slough
34 Reading
35 Wokingham
36 Bracknell Forest
37 Thurrock
38 Southend
39 Medway
40 Plymouth
41 Torbay

LONDON

1 Hillingdon
2 Harrow
3 Barnet
4 Enfield
5 Waltham Forest
6 Redbridge
7 Barking and Dagenham
8 Havering
9 Ealing
10 Brent
11 Camden
12 Haringey
13 Islington
14 Hackney
15 Newham
16 Hounslow
17 Hammersmith and Fulham

18 Kensington and Chelsea
19 City of Westminster
20 City of London
21 Tower Hamlets
22 Richmond upon Thames
23 Wandsworth
24 Lambeth
25 Southwark
26 Lewisham
27 Greenwich
28 Bexley
29 Kingston upon Thames
30 Merton
31 Sutton
32 Croydon
33 Bromley

London

THE CORPORATION OF LONDON

The City of London is the historic centre at the heart of London known as 'the square mile' around which the vast metropolis has grown over the centuries. The City's residential population is 5,500. The civic government is carried on by the Corporation of London through the Court of Common Council.

The City is an international financial centre, generating over £20 billion a year for the British economy. It includes the head offices of the principal banks, insurance companies and mercantile houses, in addition to buildings ranging from the historic Roman Wall and the 15th-century Guildhall, to the massive splendour of St Paul's Cathedral and the architectural beauty of Wren's spires.

The City of London was described by Tacitus in AD 62 as 'a busy emporium for trade and traders'. Under the Romans it became an important administration centre and hub of the road system. Little is known of London in Saxon times, when it formed part of the kingdom of the East Saxons. In 886 Alfred recovered London from the Danes and reconstituted it a burgh under his son-in-law. In 1066 the citizens submitted to William the Conqueror who in 1067 granted them a charter, which is still preserved, establishing them in the rights and privileges they had hitherto enjoyed.

THE MAYORALTY

The Mayoralty was probably established about 1189, the first Mayor being Henry Fitz Ailwyn who filled the office for 23 years and was succeeded by Fitz Alan (1212–14). A new charter was granted by King John in 1215, directing the Mayor to be chosen annually, which has ever since been done, though in early times the same individual often held the office more than once. A familiar instance is that of 'Whittington, thrice Lord Mayor of London' (in reality four times, 1397, 1398, 1406, 1419); and many modern cases have occurred. The earliest instance of the phrase 'Lord Mayor' in English is in 1414. It was used more generally in the latter part of the 15th century and became invariable from 1535 onwards. At Michaelmas the liverymen in Common Hall choose two Aldermen who have served the office of Sheriff for presentation to the Court of Aldermen, and one is chosen to be Lord Mayor for the following mayoral year.

LORD MAYOR'S DAY

The Lord Mayor of London was previously elected on the feast of St Simon and St Jude (28 October), and from the time of Edward I, at least, was presented to the King or to the Barons of the Exchequer on the following day, unless that day was a Sunday. The day of election was altered to 16 October in 1346, and after some further changes was fixed for Michaelmas Day in 1546, but the ceremonies of admittance and swearing-in of the Lord Mayor continued to take place on 28 and 29 October respectively until 1751. In 1752, at the reform of the calendar, the Lord Mayor was continued in office until 8 November, the 'New Style' equivalent of 28 October. The Lord Mayor is now presented to the Lord Chief Justice at the Royal Courts of Justice on the second Saturday in November to make the final declaration of office, having been sworn in at Guildhall on the preceding day. The procession to the Royal Courts of Justice is popularly known as the Lord Mayor's Show.

REPRESENTATIVES

Aldermen are mentioned in the 11th century and their office is of Saxon origin. They were elected annually between 1377 and 1394, when an Act of Parliament of Richard II directed them to be chosen for life.

The Common Council, elected annually on the first Friday in December, was, at an early date, substituted for a popular assembly called the *Folkmote*. At first only two representatives were sent from each ward, but the number has since been greatly increased. The Corporation is reducing the number of Common Councilmen from 130 to 100 through natural wastage. The Government has introduced legislation to remove anomalies from the election system and to extend the non-resident franchise.

OFFICERS

Sheriffs were Saxon officers; their predecessors were the *wic-reeves* and *portreeves* of London and Middlesex. At first they were officers of the Crown, and were named by the Barons of the Exchequer; but Henry I (in 1132) gave the citizens permission to choose their own Sheriffs, and the annual election of Sheriffs became fully operative under King John's charter of 1199. The citizens lost this privilege, as far as the election of the Sheriff of Middlesex was concerned, by the Local Government Act 1888; but the liverymen continue to choose two Sheriffs of the City of London, who are appointed on Midsummer Day and take office at Michaelmas.

The office of Chamberlain is an ancient one, the first contemporary record of which is 1237. The Town Clerk (or Common Clerk) is mentioned in 1274.

ACTIVITIES

The work of the Corporation is assigned to a number of committees which present reports to the Court of Common Council. These Committees are: City Lands and Bridge House Grants Estates, Policy and Resources, Finance, Planning and Transportation, Central Markets, Billingsgate and Leadenhall Markets, Spitalfields Market, Police, Port and City of London Health and Social Services, Libraries, Art Galleries and Records, Board of Governors of City of London Freemen's School, Music and Drama (Guildhall School of Music and Drama), Establishment, Housing and Sports Development, Gresham (City side), Hampstead Heath Management, Epping Forest and Open Spaces, West Ham Park, Privileges, Barbican Residential and Barbican Centre (Barbican Arts and Conference Centre).

The City's estate, in the possession of which the Corporation of London differs from other municipalities, is managed by the City Lands and Bridge House Grants Estates Committee, the chairmanship of which carries with it the title of Chief Commoner.

The Honourable the Irish Society, which manages the Corporation's estates in Ulster, consists of a Governor and five other Aldermen, the Recorder, and 19 Common Councilmen, of whom one is elected Deputy Governor.

THE LORD MAYOR 2000–2001*

The Rt. Hon. the Lord Mayor, Alderman Sir David Howard, TD *Private Secretary*, P. Tribe

* The Lord Mayor for 2001–2002 was elected on Michaelmas Day. *See* Stop-press

THE SHERIFFS 2001-2
Michael Savory (*Alderman Bread Street*) and David Mauleverer

OFFICERS, ETC
Town Clerk, T. Simmons
Chamberlain, P. Derrick
Chief Commoner (2001), A. Eskenzi
Clerk, The Honourable the Irish Society, S. Waley, The Irish Chamber, 1st Floor, 75 Watling Street, London EC4M 9BJ

THE ALDERMEN

Name and Ward	CC	Ald.	Shff.	Lord Mayor
Sir Christopher Leaver, GBE, *Dowgate*	1973	1974	1979	1981
Sir Alan Traill, GBE, *Langbourn*	1970	1975	1982	1984
Sir David Rowe-Ham, GBE, *Bridge* and *Bridge Wt.*	—	1976	1984	1986
Sir Christopher Collett, GBE, *Broad Street*	1973	1979	1985	1988
Sir Alexander Graham, GBE, *Queenhithe*	1978	1979	1986	1990
Sir Brian Jenkins, GBE, *Cordwainer*	—	1980	1987	1991
Sir Paul Newall, TD, *Walbrook*	1980	1981	1989	1993
Sir Christopher Walford, *Farringdon Wn.*	—	1982	1990	1994
Sir John Chalstrey, *Vintry*	1981	1984	1993	1995
Sir Roger Cork, *Tower*	1978	1983	1992	1996
Richard Nichols, *Candlewick*	1983	1984	1994	1997
Lord Levene of Portsoken, KBE, *Portsoken*	1983	1984	1995	1998
Clive Martin, Aldgate	—	1985	1996	1999

All the above have passed the Civic Chair

Michael Oliver, *Bishopsgate*	1980	1987	1997
Anthony Bull, *Cheap*	1968	1984	
Gavyn Arthur, *Cripplegate*	1988	1991	1998
Robert Finch, *Coleman Street*	—	1992	1999
Richard Agutter, *Castle Baynard*	—	1995	1999
Michael Savory, *Bread Street*	1980	1996	
David Brewer, *Bassishaw*	1992	1996	
Nicholas Anstee, *Aldersgate*	1987	1996	
Michael Everard, CBE, *Lime Street*	—	1996	
John Hughesdon, *Billingsgate*	1991	1997	
Simon Walsh, *Farringdon Wt.*	1989	2000	

THE COMMON COUNCIL

Deputy: Each Common Councilman so described serves as deputy to the Alderman of her/his ward.

Abrahams, G. (2000) — *Farringdon Wt*
Absalom, J. D. (1994) — *Farringdon Wt.*
Altman, L. P., CBE (1996) — *Cripplegate Wn.*
Angell, E. H. (1991) — *Cripplegate Wt.*
Archibald, *Deputy* W. W. (1986) — *Cornhill*
Ayers, K. E. (1996) — *Bassishaw*
Balls, H. D. (1970) — *Castle Baynard*
Barker, *Deputy* J. A. (1981) — *Cripplegate Wn.*
Barter, S. (1999) — *Langbourn*

Beale, *Deputy* M. J. (1979) — *Lime Street*
Bird, J. L., OBE (1977) — *Bridge*
Bradshaw, D. J. (1991) — *Cripplegate Wn.*
Bramwell, F. M. (1983) — *Langbourn*
Brewster, J. W., OBE (1994) — *Bassishaw*
Brighton, R. L. (1984) — *Portsoken*
Brooks, W. I. B. (1988) — *Billingsgate*
Byllam-Barnes, J. C. F. B. (1997) — *Cheap*
Caspi, D. R. (1994) — *Bridge*
Cassidy, *Deputy* M. J. (1989) — *Coleman Street*
Catt, B. F. (1982) — *Farringdon Wn.*
Chadwick, R. A. H. (1994) — *Tower*
Charkham, J. P. (1996) — *Farringdon Wt.*
Cohen, Mrs C. M. (1986) — *Lime Street*
Cotgrove, D. (1991) — *Lime Street*
Currie, *Deputy* Miss S. E. M. (1985) — *Cripplegate Wt.*
Daily-Hunt, R. B. (1989) — *Cripplegate Wt.*
Darwin, G. E. (1995) — *Farringdon Wn.*
Davis, C. B. (1991) — *Bread Street*
Dove, W. H., MBE (1993) — *Bishopsgate*
Duckworth, S. (2000) — *Bishopsgate*
Dunitz, A. A. (1984) — *Portsoken*
Eskenzi, *Deputy* A. N. (1970) — *Farringdon Wn.*
Eve, R. A. (1980) — *Cheap*
Everett, K. M. (1984) — *Candlewick*
Falk, F. A., TD (1997) — *Broad Street*
Farr, M. C. (1998) — *Walbrook*
Farrow, M. W. W. (1996) — *Farringdon Wt.*
Farthing, R. B. C. (1981) — *Aldgate*
FitzGerald, *Deputy* R. C. A. (1981) — *Bread Street*
Forbes, G. B. (1993) — *Bishopsgate*
Fraser, S. J. (1993) — *Coleman Street*
Fraser, W. B. (1981) — *Vintry*
Galloway, A. D. (1981) — *Broad Street*
Gillon, G. M. F. (1995) — *Cordwainer*
Ginsburg, S. (1990) — *Bishopsgate*
Gowman, *Deputy* Miss A. J. (1991) — *Dowgate*
Graves, A. C. (1985) — *Bishopsgate*
Green, C. (1994) — *Aldersgate*
Hall, B. R. H. (1995) — *Farringdon Wn.*
Halliday, Mrs P. (1992) — *Walbrook*
Hardwick, Dr P. B. (1987) — *Aldgate*
Harris, B. N. (1996) — *Broad Street*
Hart, *Deputy* M. G. (1970) — *Bridge*
Haynes, J. E. H. (1986) — *Cornhill*
Henderson-Begg, M. (1977) — *Coleman Street*
Holland, *Deputy* J., CBE (1972) — *Aldgate*
Holliday, Mrs E. H. L. (1987) — *Vintry*
Hook, J. W. (2000) — *Walbrook*
Jackson, L. St J. T. (1978) — *Bread Street*
Kellett, Mrs M. W. F. (1986) — *Tower*
Kemp, D. L. (1984) — *Coleman Street*
King, A. (1999) — *Queenhithe*
Knowles, S. K. (1984) — *Candlewick*
Lawrence, G. A. (1994) — *Farringdon Wt.*
Lawson, G. C. H. (1971) — *Portsoken*
Leck, P. (1998) — *Aldersgate*
Littlechild, Mrs V. (1998) — *Cripplegate Wt.*
Lord, C. E. (2000) — *Coleman Street*
Luder, I. D. (1998) — *Farringdon Wt.*
McGuinness, C. (1997) — *Castle Baynard*
McNeil, I. D. (1977) — *Lime Street*
Malins, *Deputy* J. H., QC (1981) — *Farringdon Wt.*
Martinelli, *Deputy* P. J. (1994) — *Bassishaw*
Mayhew, Miss J. (1986) — *Queenhithe*
Mayhew, J. P. (1996) — *Aldersgate*
Mead, Mrs W. (1997) — *Farringdon Wt.*
Mitchell, *Deputy* C. R. (1971) — *Castle Baynard*
Mobsby, *Deputy* D. J. L. (1985) — *Billingsgate*

Montgomery, B. (1999)	*Dowgate*
Mooney, B. D. F. (1998)	*Queenhithe*
Moss, A. D. (1989)	*Tower*
Moys, Mrs S. (2000)	*Aldgate*
Nash, *Deputy* Mrs J. C. (1983)	*Aldersgate*
Newman, Mrs P. B. (1989)	*Aldersgate*
Owen, Mrs J. (1975)	*Langbourn*
Owen-Ward, J. R. (1983)	*Bridge*
Parmley, A. C., Ph.D. (1992)	*Vintry*
Pembroke, *Deputy* Mrs A. M. F. (1978)	*Cheap*
Platts-Mills, J. F. F., QC	*Farringdon Wt.*
Price, E. E. (1996)	*Farringdon Wt.*
Pulman, *Deputy* G. A. G. (1983)	*Tower*
Punter, C. (1993)	*Cripplegate Wn.*
Quilter, S. D. (1998)	*Cripplegate Wt.*
Regan, R. D. (1998)	*Farringdon Wn.*
Rigby, P. P., CBE (1972)	*Farringdon Wn.*
Robinson, Mrs D. C. (1989)	*Bishopsgate*
Roney, E. P. T., CBE (1974)	*Bishopsgate*
Samuel, *Deputy* Mrs I., MBE (1971)	*Portsoken*
Sargant, K. A. (1991)	*Cornhill*
Scott, J. (1999)	*Broad Street*
Scriven, R. G., CBE (1984)	*Candlewick*
Shalit, D. M. (1972)	*Farringdon Wn.*
Sherlock, M. R. C. (1992)	*Dowgate*
Snyder, *Deputy* M. J. (1986)	*Cordwainer*
Stevenson, F. P. (1994)	*Cripplegate Wn.*
Taylor, J. A. F., TD (1991)	*Bread Street*
Thorp, C. R. (1996)	*Billingsgate*
Thorp, D. (2000)	*Farringdon Wt.*
Trotter, J. (1993)	*Billingsgate*
Warner, D. W. (1994)	*Cripplegate Wn.*
Willoughby, P. J. (1985)	*Bishopsgate*
Wilmot, R. T. D. (1973)	*Cordwainer*

The City Guilds (Livery Companies)

The constitution of the livery companies has been unchanged for centuries. There are three ranks of membership: freemen, liverymen and assistants. A person can become a freeman by patrimony (through a parent having been a freeman); by servitude (through having served an apprenticeship to a freeman); or by redemption (by purchase).

Election to the livery is the prerogative of the company, who can elect any of its freemen as liverymen. Assistants are usually elected from the livery and form a Court of Assistants which is the governing body of the company. The Master (in some companies called the Prime Warden) is elected annually from the assistants.

As at June 1998, 22,923 liverymen of the guilds were entitled to vote at elections at Common Hall.

The order of precedence, omitting extinct companies, is given in parenthesis after the name of each company in the list below. In certain companies the election of Master or Prime Warden for the year does not take place until the autumn. In such cases the Master or Prime Warden for 2000–1 is given.

THE TWELVE GREAT COMPANIES
In order of civic precedence

MERCERS *(1)*. Hall, Ironmonger Lane, London EC2V 8HE. *Livery*, 229. *Clerk*, C. H. Parker. *Master*, A. E. Hodson

GROCERS *(2)*. Hall, Princes Street, London EC2R 8AD. *Livery*, 319. *Clerk*, Brig. P. P. Rawlins. *Master*, J. G. Tregoning

DRAPERS *(3)*. Drapers' Hall, Throgmorton Avenue, London EC2N 2DQ. *Livery*, 262. *Clerk*, Rear-Admiral A. B. Ross. *Master*, Lord Luke, DL

FISHMONGERS *(4)*. Hall, London Bridge, London EC4R 9EL. *Livery*, 355. *Clerk*, K. S. Waters. *Prime Warden*, Sir Thomas Stockdale, BT

GOLDSMITHS *(5)*. Hall, Foster Lane, London EC2V 6BN. *Livery*, 293. *Clerk*, R. D. Buchanan-Dunlop. *Prime Warden*, B. L. Schroder

MERCHANT TAYLORS *(6/7)*. 30 Threadneedle Street, London EC2R 8JB. *Livery*, 323. *Clerk*, D. A. Peck. *Master*, David Brewer, CMG

SKINNERS *(6/7)*. Hall, 8 Dowgate Hill, London EC4R 2SP. *Livery*, 390. *Clerk*, Capt. D. Hart Dyke. *Master*, G. B. Thompson

HABERDASHERS *(8)*. 39–40 Bartholomew Close, London EC1A 7JN. *Livery*, 320. *Clerk*, Capt. R. J. Fisher. *Master*, (from 23 November 2001) H. N. Lund

SALTERS *(9)*. Salters Hall, 4 Fore Street, London EC2Y 5DE. *Livery*, 170. *Clerk*, Col. M. P. Barneby. *Master*, J. C. Russell

IRONMONGERS *(10)*. Hall, Shaftesbury Place, Barbican, London EC2Y 8AA. *Livery*, 129. *Clerk*, J. A. Oliver. *Master*, W. L. Weller, DL

VINTNERS *(11)*. Hall, Upper Thames Street, London EC4V 3BG. *Livery*, 290. *Clerk*, Brig. M. Smythe. *Master*, H. J. Newton

CLOTHWORKERS *(12)*. Hall, Dunster Court, Mincing Lane, London EC3R 7AH. *Livery*, 210. *Clerk*, A. C. Blessly. *Master*, R. Saunders

OTHER CITY GUILDS
In alphabetical order

ACTUARIES *(91)*. 81 Worrin Road, Shenfield, Brentwood, Essex CM15 8JN. *Livery*, 198. *Clerk*, Mrs J. V. Evans. *Master*, P. J. Derby

AIR PILOTS AND AIR NAVIGATORS, GUILD OF *(81)*. Cobham House, 9 Warwick Court, Gray's Inn, London WC1R 5DJ. *Livery*, 500. *Clerk*, Capt. J. G. F. Stoy. *Master*, H. Greyburn. *Grand Master*, HRH The Prince Philip, Duke of Edinburgh, KG, KT, OM, GBE, PC

APOTHECARIES, SOCIETY OF *(58)*. Hall, 14 Black Friars Lane, London EC4V 6EJ. *Livery*, 1700. *Clerk*, Lt.-Col. R. J. Stringer. *Master*, J. H. D. Briscoe

ARBITRATORS *(93)*. 13 Hall Gardens, Colney Heath, St Albans, Herts AL4 0QF. *Livery*, 220. *Clerk*, Mrs G. Duffy. *Master*, Miss Victoria Russell

ARMOURERS AND BRASIERS *(22)*. Hall, 81 Coleman Street, London EC2R 5BJ. *Livery*, 120. *Clerk*, Cdr. T. J. K. Sloane. *Master*, Rear-Admiral J. P. W. Middleton, CB

BAKERS *(19)*. Hall, Harp Lane, London EC3R 6DP. *Livery*, 380. *Clerk*, R. E. B. Sawyer. *Master*, A. G. Cavan

BARBERS *(17)*. Barber-Surgeons' Hall, Monkwell Square, Wood Street, London EC2Y 5BL. *Livery*, 225. *Clerk*, Brig. A. F. Eastburn. *Master*, W. S. Shand, MA, MD, FRCS, FRCS (ED)

BASKETMAKERS *(52)*. 48 Seymour Walk, London SW10 9NF. *Livery*, 308. *Clerk*, Maj. G. J. Flint-Shipman. *Prime Warden*, N. E. Woolley

558   Local Government

BLACKSMITHS *(40)*. 48 Upwood Road, London SE12 8AN. *Livery*, 224. *Clerk*, C. Jeal. *Prime Warden*, P. R. Allcard
BOWYERS *(38)*. 11 Aldermans Hill, London N13 4YD. *Livery*, 103. *Clerk*, J. R. Owen-Ward. *Master*, E. J. Burnett
BREWERS *(14)*. Hall, Aldermanbury Square, London EC2V7HR. *Livery*, 133. *Clerk*, Brig. D. J. Ross. *Master*, W. R. Lees-Jones, TD, DL
BRODERERS *(48)*. Ember House, 35–37 Creek Road, East Molesey, Surrey KT8 9BE. *Livery*, 175. *Clerk*, P. J. C. Crouch. *Master*, I. M. Brackenbury
BUILDERS MERCHANTS *(88)*. 4 College Hill, London EC4R 2RB. *Livery*, 200. *Clerk*, Miss S. M. Robinson. *Master*, C. G. Bence
BUTCHERS *(24)*. Hall, 87 Bartholomew Close, London EC1A 7EB. *Livery*, 582. *Clerk*, G. J. Sharp. *Master*, D. J. Noakes, MBE
CARMEN *(77)*. 8 Little Trinity Lane, London EC4V 2AN. *Livery*, 453. *Clerk*, Cdr. R. M. H. Bawtree. *Master*, B. H. Owen
CARPENTERS *(26)*. Hall, 1 Throgmorton Avenue, London EC2N 2JJ. *Livery*, 150. *Clerk*, Maj.-Gen. P. T. Stevenson. *Master*, R. S. Miller
CHARTERED ACCOUNTANTS *(86)*. The Rustlings, Valley Close, Studham, Dunstable LU6 2QN. *Livery*, 340. *Clerk*, C. Bygrave. *Master*, P. Brennan, OBE
CHARTERED ARCHITECTS *(98)*. 82A Muswell Hill Road, London N10 3JR. *Livery*, 161. *Clerk*, D. Cole-Adams. *Master*, M. P. West
CHARTERED SECRETARIES AND ADMINISTRATORS *(87)*. Sadler's Hall, 3rd Floor, 40 Gutter Lane, London EC2V6BR. *Livery*, 240. *Clerk*, G. E. L. Lintott. *Master*, P. M. Marcell, FCIS, FFA
CHARTERED SURVEYORS *(85)*. 16 St Mary-at-Hill, London EC3R 8EF. *Livery*, 350. *Clerk*, Mrs A. L. Jackson. *Master*, M. P. L. Baker
CLOCKMAKERS *(61)*. Room 66-67 Albert Buildings, 49 Queen Victoria Street, London EC4N 4SE. *Livery*, 230. *Clerk*, Gp Capt. P. H. Gibson. *Master*, M. M. Smith
COACHMAKERS AND COACH-HARNESS MAKERS *(72)*. 8 Chandlers Court, Burwell, Cambridge CB5 0AZ. *Livery*, 400. *Clerk*, Gp Capt. G. Bunn. *Master*, Hon. Roy Constantine
CONSTRUCTORS *(99)*. 181 Fentiman Road, London SW8 1JY. *Livery*, 136. *Clerk*, L. L. Brace. *Master*, J. M. Burrell
COOKS *(35)*. Registry Chambers, The Old Deanery, Deans Court, London EC4V5AA. *Livery*, 75. *Clerk*, M. C. Thatcher. *Master*, P. A. P. Wright
COOPERS *(36)*. Hall, 13 Devonshire Square, London EC2M 4TH. *Livery*, 260. *Clerk*, J. A. Newton. *Master*, J. W. S. Clarke, RD
CORDWAINERS *(27)*. 8 Warwick Court, Gray's Inn, London WC1R 5DJ. *Livery*, 161. *Clerk*, Lt.-Col. J. R. Blundell. *Master*, D. M. B. Skinner
CURRIERS *(29)*. Kestrel Cottage, East Knoyle, Salisbury SP3 6AD. *Livery*, 95. *Clerk*, Gp Capt. F. J. Hamilton. *Master*, P. D. MacCorkindale
CUTLERS *(18)*. Hall, Warwick Lane, London EC4M 7BR. *Livery*, 100. *Clerk*, J. P. Allen. *Master*, D. Barnes
DISTILLERS *(69)*. 71 Lincoln's Inn Fields, London WC2A3JF. *Livery*, 270. *Clerk*, C. V. Hughes. *Master*, R. R. Howell
DYERS *(13)*. Hall, 10 Dowgate Hill, London EC4R 2ST. *Livery*, 121. *Clerk*, J. R. Chambers. *Prime Warden*, E. R. Verney, BA, FRICS
ENGINEERS *(94)*. Kiln Bank, Bodle Street Green, Hailsham, E. Sussex BN27 4UA. *Livery*, 290. *Clerk*, Cdr. B. D. Gibson. *Master*, A. G. Jackson

ENVIRONMENTAL CLEANERS *(97)*. Woodside Cottage, 44 New Road, Bengeo, Herts SG14 3JL. *Livery*, 245. *Clerk*, J. C. M. Chapman. *Master*, M. G. O'Connor
FAN MAKERS *(76)*. 2 Bolts Hill, Castle Camps, Cambridge CB1 6TL. *Livery*, 210. *Clerk*, Lt.-Col. I. R. P. Green. *Master*, R. I. Simpson
FARMERS *(80)*. Farmers' and Fletchers' Hall, 3 Cloth Street, London EC1A 7LD. *Livery*, 300. *Clerk*, Miss M. L. Winter. *Master*, H. R. H. The Princess Royal
FARRIERS *(55)*. 19 Queen Street, Chipperfield, Kings Langley, Herts WD4 9BT. *Livery*, 345. *Clerk*, Mrs C. C. Clifford. *Master*, S. J. Curtis, FWCF
FELTMAKERS *(63)*. Providence Cottage, Chute Cadley, Andover, Hants SP11 9EB. *Livery*, 170. *Clerk*, Lt.-Col. C. J. Holroyd. *Master*, W. Horsham
FIREFIGHTERS *(No livery)*. The Insurance Hall, 20 Aldermanbury, London EC2V 7GF. *Freemen*, 130. *Clerk*, Mrs M. Holland-Prior. *Master*, W. W. A. Redford, QFSM
FLETCHERS *(39)*. Farmers' and Fletchers' Hall, 3 Cloth Street, London EC1A7LD. *Livery*, 130. *Clerk*, J. R. Owen-Ward. *Master*, C. J. Brown
FOUNDERS *(33)*. Founders' Hall, Number One, Cloth Fair, London EC1A 7JQ. *Livery*, 175. *Clerk*, A. J. Gillett. *Master*, A. C. Newman
FRAMEWORK KNITTERS *(64)*. Whitegarth Chambers, 37 The Uplands, Loughton, Essex IG10 1NQ. *Livery*, 211. *Clerk*, H. W. H. Ellis. *Master*, B. A. F. Smith
FRUITERERS *(45)*. Chapelstones, 84 High Street, Codford St Mary, Warminster BA12 0ND. *Livery*, 262. *Clerk*, Lt.-Col. L. G. French. *Master*, H. E. B. Kelsey
FUELLERS *(95)*. 22 Broadfields, Headstone Lane, Hatch End, Middx HA2 6NH. *Livery*, 85. *Clerk*, R. A. Riley. *Master*, R. J. Budge
FURNITURE MAKERS *(83)*. Painters' Hall, 9 Little Trinity Lane, London EC4V 2AD. *Livery*, 296. *Clerk*, Mrs J. A. Wright. *Master*, P. G. Keen
GARDENERS *(66)*. 25 Luke Street, London EC2A 4AR. *Livery*, 249. *Clerk*, Col. N. G. S. Gray. *Master*, A. H. K. Edwards
GIRDLERS *(23)*. Hall, Basinghall Avenue, London EC2V5DD. *Livery*, 80. *Clerk*, Lt.-Col. R. Sullivan. *Master*, F. M. French
GLASS-SELLERS *(71)*. 43 Aragon Avenue, Thames Ditton, Surrey KT7 0PY. *Livery*, 180. *Hon. Clerk*, B. J. Rawles. *Master*, R. Long FCA, ATII
GLAZIERS AND PAINTERS OF GLASS *(53)*. Glaziers' Hall, 9 Montague Close, London SE1 9DD. *Livery*, 248. *Clerk*, Col. D. W. Eking. *Master*, R. A. Stone
GLOVERS *(62)*. 71 Ifield Road, London SW10 9AU. *Livery*, 275. *Clerk*, Mrs M. Hood. *Master*, J. D. H. Clarke, BEM
GOLD AND SILVER WYRE DRAWERS *(74)*. 'Twizzletwig', The Ballands South, Fetcham, Leatherhead, Surrey KT22 9EP. *Livery*, 310. *Clerk*, T. J. Waller. *Master*, Sir Peter G. Yarranton
GUNMAKERS *(73)*. The Proof House, 48-50 Commercial Road, London E1 1LP. *Livery*, 238. *Clerk*, J. M. Riches. *Master*, S. Duckworth
HORNERS *(54)*. c/o St. Saviours Church, Warwick Avenue, London W9 2QB. *Livery*, 238. *Clerk*, A. R. Layard. *Master*, Miles St. C. Baird
INFORMATION TECHNOLOGISTS *(100)*. 39A Bartholomew Close, London EC1A 7JN. *Livery*, 265. *Clerk*, Mrs G. Davies. *Master*, J. C. Carrington
INNHOLDERS *(32)*. Innholders' Hall, 30 College Street, London EC4R 2RH. *Livery*, 139. *Clerk*, D. E. Bulger. *Master*, A. G. Fisher
INSURERS *(92)*. The Hall, 20 Aldermanbury, London EC2V7HY. *Livery*, 375. *Clerk*, L. J. Walters. *Master*, M. J. Bright

JOINERS AND CEILERS *(41)*. 75 Meadway Drive, Horsell, Woking, Surrey GU21 4TF. *Livery*, 124. *Clerk*, Mrs A. L. Jackson. *Master*, J. P. T. Brown

LAUNDERERS *(89)*. Hall, 9 Montague Close, London Bridge, London SE1 9DD. *Livery*, 250. *Clerk*, Mrs J. Polek. *Master*, D. A. Hargreaves

LEATHERSELLERS *(15)*. The Hall, 15 St Helen's Place, London EC3A 6DQ. *Livery*, 150. *Clerk*, Capt. J. G. F. Cooke. *Master*, D. R. Curtis

LIGHTMONGERS *(96)*. Crown Wharf, 11a Coldharbour, Blackwall Reach, London E14 9NS. *Livery*, 145. *Clerk*, D. B. Wheatley. *Master*, B. Hurst

LORINERS *(57)*. 8 Portland Square, London E1W 2QR. *Livery*, 355. *Clerk*, G. B. Forbes. *Master*, R. H. Walker-Arnott

MAKERS OF PLAYING CARDS *(75)*. 6 The Priory, Godstone, Surrey RH9 8NL. *Livery*, 140. *Clerk*, M. J. Smyth. *Master*, Y. Beresiner

MARKETORS *(90)*. 13 Hall Gardens, Colney Heath, St Albans, Herts AL4 0PF. *Livery*, 220. *Clerk*, Mrs G. Duffy. *Master*, W. S. C. Kennett

MASONS *(30)*. 22 Cannon Hill, Southgate, London N14 6LG. *Livery*, 122. *Clerk*, P. F. Clark. *Master*, T. F. Ackland

MASTER MARINERS, HONOURABLE COMPANY OF *(78)*. HQS Wellington, Temple Stairs, Victoria Embankment, London WC2R 2PN. *Livery*, 210. *Clerk*, J. A. V. Maddock. *Master*, Commodore A. D. Barrett, CBE, RD, DL, RNR. *Admiral*, HRH The Prince Philip, Duke of Edinburgh, KG, KT, OM, GBE, PC

MUSICIANS *(50)*. 75 Watling Street, London EC4M 9BJ. *Livery*, 365. *Clerk*, Mrs M. Alford. *Master*, D. R. Hill

NEEDLEMAKERS *(65)*. 5 Staple Inn, London WC1V 7QH. *Livery*, 230. *Clerk*, M. G. Cook. *Master*, M. Copsey

PAINTER-STAINERS *(28)*. Painters' Hall, 9 Little Trinity Lane, London EC4V 2AD. *Livery*, 320. *Clerk*, Col. W. J. Chesshyre. *Master*, Rev. G. Blacktop

PARISH CLERKS *(No livery)*. c/o 1 Dean Trench Street, London SW1P 3HB. *Members*, 95. *Clerk*, Lt. Col. B. J. N. Coombes. *Master*, S. J. Murray

PATTENMAKERS *(70)*. Vanguard House, Sutton Valence, Kent ME17 3JA. *Livery*, 200. *Clerk*, Lt. Col. R. W. Murfin. *Master*, M. P. Fincham

PAVIORS *(56)*. 3 Ridgemount Gardens, Enfield, Middx EN2 8QL. *Livery*, 230. *Clerk*, J. L. White. *Master*, K. C. White

PEWTERERS *(16)*. Hall, Oat Lane, London EC2V 7DE. *Livery*, 120. *Clerk*, Cdr. A. St J. Steiner. *Master*, M. M. Sutcliffe FRCS

PLAISTERERS *(46)*. 6th Floor, 19 Great Winchester Street, London EC2N 2BH. *Livery*, 213. *Clerk*, R. Vickers. *Master*, A. J. Turner

PLUMBERS *(31)*. Room 28, 49 Queen Victoria Street, London EC4N 4SA. *Livery*, 339. *Clerk*, Lt.-Col. R. J. A. Paterson-Fox. *Master*, A. K. Woollaston

POULTERS *(34)*. 53 Sandersfield Road, Banstead, Surrey 8M7 2DH. *Livery*, 178. *Clerk*, Mrs G. W. Butcher. *Master*, D. M. Jackson

SADDLERS *(25)*. Hall, 40 Gutter Lane, London EC2V 6BR. *Livery*, 75. *Clerk*, Gp Capt. W. S. Brereton Martin. *Master*, M. A. C. Lawrie

SCIENTIFIC INSTRUMENT MAKERS *(84)*. 9 Montague Close, London SE1 9DD. *Livery*, 240. *Clerk*, N. J. Watson. *Master*, Dr D. Cornish

SCRIVENERS *(44)*. HQS Wellington, Temple Stairs, Victoria Embankment, London WC2R 2PN. *Livery*, 228. *Clerk*, G. A. Hill. *Master*, D. M. F. Scott

SHIPWRIGHTS *(59)*. Ironmongers Hall, Barbican, London EC2Y 8AA. *Livery*, 400. *Clerk*, Capt. R. F. Channon. *Prime Warden*, Vice-Adm. Sir James Weatherall KCVO, KBE

Permanent Master, HRH The Prince Philip, Duke of Edinburgh, KG, KT, OM, GBE, PC

SOLICITORS *(79)*. 4 College Hill, London EC2R 2RB. *Livery*, 260. *Clerk*, N. Cameron. *Master*, M. J. Cassidy

SPECTACLE MAKERS *(60)*. Apothecaries' Hall, Black Friars Lane, London EC4V 6EL. *Livery*, 325. *Clerk*, Lt.-Col. J. A. B. Salmon. *Master*, G. W. D, McLaren FBDO, FLUSTD, MIMGT

STATIONERS AND NEWSPAPER MAKERS *(47)*. Stationers' Hall, Ave Maria Lane, London EC4M 7DD. *Livery*, 452. *Clerk*, Brig. D. G. Sharp. *Master*, R. J. Russell

TALLOW CHANDLERS *(21)*. Tallow Chandlers' Hall, 4 Dowgate Hill, London EC4R 2SH. *Livery*, 180. *Clerk*, Brig. W. K. L. Prosser. *Master*, C. P. Tootal

TAX ADVISERS *(No Livery)*. 504 Bryer Court, Barbican, London EC2Y 8DE. *Freemen*, 120. *Clerk*, E. Lord. *Master*, M. B. Squires

TIN PLATE WORKERS (ALIAS WIRE WORKERS) *(67)*. Bartholomew House, 66 Westbury Road, New Malden, Surrey KT3 5AS. *Livery*, 190. *Clerk*, M. Henderson-Begg. *Master*, J. H. Perry

TOBACCO PIPE MAKERS AND TOBACCO BLENDERS *(82)*. Hackhurst Farm, Lower Dicker, Hailsham, E. Sussex BN27 4BP. *Livery*, 156. *Clerk*, N. J. Hallings-Pott. *Master*, J. A. G. Murray

TURNERS *(51)*. 182 Temple Chambers, Temple Avenue, London EC4Y 0HP. *Livery*, 160. *Clerk*, E. A. Windsor Clive. *Master*, A. M. Sherred

TYLERS AND BRICKLAYERS *(37)*. Hawthorns, Claygate Lane, Thames Ditton, Surrey KT7 0DT. *Livery*, 128. *Clerk*, J. A. Norris. *Master*, A. P. Wallace

UPHOLDERS *(49)*. Hall in the Wood, 46 Quail Gardens, Selsdon Vale, Croydon CR2 8TF. *Livery*, 225. *Clerk*, J. P. Cody. *Master*, R. C. Olney

WATER CONSERVATORS *(102)*. Watermen's Hall, 16 St Mary-at-Hill, London EC2R 8EF. *Livery*, 148. *Hon. Clerk*, R. A. Riley. *Master*, P. N. Paul

WATERMEN AND LIGHTERMEN *(No livery)*. Watermen's Hall, 16 St Mary-at-Hill, London EC3R 8EF. *Craft Owning Freemen*, 362. *Clerk*, C. Middlemiss. *Master*, C. G. Newens

WAX CHANDLERS *(20)*. Hall, Gresham Street, London EC2V 7AD. *Livery*, 125. *Clerk*, J. R. Williamson. *Master*, His Hon. W. N. Denison QC

WEAVERS *(42)*. Saddlers' House, Gutter Lane, London EC2V 6BR. *Livery*, 125. *Clerk*, Mrs F. Newcombe. *Upper Bailiff*, P. Littlewood

WHEELWRIGHTS *(68)*. Ember House, 35–37 Creek Road, East Molesey, Surrey KT8 9BE. *Livery*, 212. *Clerk*, P. J. C. Crouch. *Master*, N. A. Joseph

WOOLMEN *(43)*. Hollands, Hedsor Road, Bourne End, Bucks SL8 5EE. *Livery*, 138. *Clerk*, F. Allen. *Master*, J. W. Bishop

WORLD TRADERS *(101)*. 36 Ladbroke Grove, London W11 2PA. *Livery*, 143. *Clerk*, N. R. Pullman. *Master*, B. K. Whalley TD

LONDON BOROUGH COUNCILS

Council	Municipal offices	Population	Band D charge 2001	Chief Executive	Mayor (a) Lord Mayor 2001–2
Barking and Dagenham	°Dagenham, RM10 7BN	156,000	£848.43	G. Farrant	P. Twomey
Barnet	†The Burroughs, Hendon, NW4 4BG	293,500	£874.29	L. Boland	Mrs A. Campbell
Bexley	‡Bexleyheath, Kent DA6 7LB	219,000	£882.00	C. Duffield	Mrs A. Beckwith
Brent	†Forty Lane, Wembley, HA9 9EZ	243,025	£779.00	G. Daniel	R. Patel
Bromley	°Bromley, BR1 3UH	297,600	£826.00	Dr M. Blanch	J. Holbrook
§Camden	†Judd Street, WC1H 9JE	192,000	£950.00	S. Bundred	R. Robinson
§City of Westminster	City Hall, Victoria Street, SW1E 6QP	175,000	£410.00	P. Rogers	(a) H. Marshall
Croydon	Taberner House, Park Lane, Croydon, CR9 3JS	337,500	£824.00	D. Wechsler	P. Hopson
Ealing	†Uxbridge Road, W5 2HL	298,000	£823.00	Ms G. Guy	R. Dheer
Enfield	°Enfield, EN1 3XA	257,417	£884.73	D. Plank	Y. Brett
§Greenwich	†Wellington Street, SE18 6PW	207,700	£911.00	Ms M. Ney	T. Malone
§Hackney	†Mare Street, E8 1EA	195,000	£923.00	M. Caller	S. Siddiqui
§Hammersmith and Fulham	†King Street, W6 9JU	157,000	£923.00	R. Harbord	A. Slaughter
Haringey	°Wood Green, N22 4LE	223,700	£960.00	D. Warwick	H. Brown
Harrow	°Harrow, HA1 2UJ	220,000	£938.95	T. Redmond	B. Currie
Havering	†Romford, RM1 3BD	229,800	£959.00	H. W. Tinworth	D. O'Flynn
Hillingdon	°Uxbridge, UB8 1UW	231,600	£911.71	D. Leatham	C. Dann
Hounslow	°Lampton Road, Hounslow, TW3 4DN	205,000	£955.00	M. Gilks	M. Gill
§Islington	†Upper Street, N1 2UD	176,393	£877.00	Ms L. Fullick	J. Trotter
§Kensington and Chelsea (RB)	†Hornton Street, W8 7NX	140,000	£688.86	D. Myers	T. Holt
Kingston upon Thames (RB)	Guildhall, Kingston upon Thames, KT1 1EU	144,000	£946.60	B. McDonald	J. Thorn
§Lambeth	†Brixton Hill, SW2 1RW	272,500	£741.00	L. Casey	Ms C. Hewitt
§Lewisham	†Catford, SE6 4RU	241,500	£876.77	Dr B. Quirk, CBE	D. Sullivan
Merton	°London Road, Morden, SM4 5DX	182,000	£952.00	R. Paine	S. Pickover
§Newham	†East Ham, E6 2RP	230,000	£827.66	D. Burbage	S. Marway
Redbridge	†Ilford, IG1 1DD	232,500	£870.00	M. Frater	L. Weinberg
Richmond upon Thames	°Richmond Road, Twickenham, TW1 3AA	182,700	£999.00	Mrs G. Norton	Ms E. Stanier
§Southwark	†Peckham Road, SE5 8UB	237,300	£845.00	R. A. Coomber	Ms H. Wines
Sutton	‡St Nicholas Way, Sutton, SM1 1EA	180,000	£872.64	Mrs J. Simons	J. Leach
§Tower Hamlets	107A Commercial Street, E1 6BG	176,000	£781.00	Ms E. Kelly	Ms L. Melvin
Waltham Forest	†Forest Road, Walthamstow, E17 4JF	219,000	£928.00	S. White	Mrs M. Broadley
§Wandsworth	†Wandsworth, SW18 2PU	266,300	£451.71	G. K. Jones	R. Smith

§ Inner London Borough
RB Royal Borough
° Civic Centre
† Town Hall
‡ Civic Offices

Wales

The Principality of Wales (Cymru) occupies the extreme west of the central southern portion of the island of Great Britain, with a total area of 8,015 sq. miles (20,758 sq. km): land 7,965 sq. miles (20,628 sq. km); inland water 50 sq. miles (130 sq. km). It is bounded on the north by the Irish Sea, on the south by the Bristol Channel, on the east by the English counties of Cheshire, Shropshire, Worcestershire and Gloucestershire, and on the west by St George's Channel.

Across the Menai Straits is the island of Anglesey (Ynys Môn) (276 sq. miles), communication with which is facilitated by the Menai Suspension Bridge (1,000 ft long) built by Telford in 1826, and by the tubular railway bridge (1,100 ft long) built by Stephenson in 1850. Holyhead harbour, on Holy Isle (north-west of Anglesey), provides accommodation for ferry services to Dublin (70 miles).

POPULATION

The population at the 1991 census was 2,835,073 (males 1,370,104; females 1,464,969). The average density of population in 1991 was 1.36 persons per hectare.

RELIEF

Wales is a country of extensive tracts of high plateau and shorter stretches of mountain ranges deeply dissected by river valleys. Lower-lying ground is largely confined to the coastal belt and the lower parts of the valleys. The highest mountains are those of Snowdonia in the north-west (Snowdon, 3,559 ft), Berwyn (Aran Fawddwy, 2,971 ft), Cader Idris (Pen y Gadair, 2,928 ft), Dyfed (Plynlimon, 2,467 ft), and the Black Mountain, Brecon Beacons and Black Forest ranges in the south-east (Carmarthen Van, 2,630 ft, Pen y Fan, 2,906 ft, Waun Fâch, 2,660 ft).

HYDROGRAPHY

The principal river rising in Wales is the Severn, which flows from the slopes of Plynlimon to the English border. The Wye (130 miles) also rises in the slopes of Plynlimon. The Usk (56 miles) flows into the Bristol Channel, through Gwent. The Dee (70 miles) rises in Bala Lake and flows through the Vale of Llangollen, where an aqueduct (built by Telford in 1805) carries the Pontcy-syllte branch of the Shropshire Union Canal across the valley. The estuary of the Dee is the navigable portion, 14 miles in length and about five miles in breadth, and the tide rushes in with dangerous speed over the 'Sands of Dee'. The Towy (68 miles), Teifi (50 miles), Taff (40 miles), Dovey (30 miles), Taf (25 miles) and Conway (24 miles), the last named broad and navigable, are wholly Welsh rivers.

The largest natural lake is Bala (Llyn Tegid) in Gwynedd, nearly four miles long and about one mile wide. Lake Vyrnwy is an artificial reservoir, about the size of Bala, and forms the water supply of Liverpool; Birmingham is supplied from reservoirs in the Elan and Claerwen valleys.

WELSH LANGUAGE

According to the 1991 census results, the percentage of persons of three years and over able to speak Welsh was:

Clwyd	18.2	Powys	20.2
Dyfed	43.7	S. Glamorgan	6.5
Gwent	2.4	W. Glamorgan	15.0
Gwynedd	61.0		
Mid Glamorgan	8.5	Wales	18.7

The 1991 figure represents a slight decline from 18.9 per cent in 1981 (1971, 20.8 per cent; 1961, 26 per cent).

FLAG

The flag of Wales, the Red Dragon (Y Ddraig Goch), is a red dragon on a field divided white over green (per fess argent and vert a dragon passant gules). The flag was augmented in 1953 by a royal badge on a shield encircled with a riband bearing the words *Ddraig Goch Ddyry Cychwyn* and imperially crowned, but this augmented flag is rarely used.

EARLY HISTORY

The earliest inhabitants of whom there is any record appear to have been subdued or exterminated by the Goidels (a people of Celtic race) in the Bronze Age. A further invasion of Celtic Brythons and Belgae followed in the ensuing Iron Age. The Roman conquest of southern Britain and Wales was for some time successfully opposed by Caratacus (Caractacus or Caradog), chieftain of the Catuvellauni and son of Cunobelinus (Cymbeline). South-east Wales was subjugated and the legionary fortress at Caerleon-on-Usk established by about AD 75–77; the conquest of Wales was completed by Agricola about AD 78. Communications were opened up by the construction of military roads from Chester to Caerleon-on-Usk and Caerwent, and from Chester to Conwy (and thence to Carmarthen and Neath). Christianity was introduced during the Roman occupation, in the fourth century.

ANGLO-SAXON ATTACKS

The Anglo-Saxon invaders of southern Britain drove the Celts into the mountain stronghold of Wales, and into Strathclyde (Cumberland and south-west Scotland) and Cornwall, giving them the name of *Waelisc* (Welsh), meaning 'foreign'. The West Saxons' victory of Deorham (AD 577) isolated Wales from Cornwall and the battle of Chester (AD 613) cut off communication with Strathclyde and northern Britain. In the eighth century the boundaries of the Welsh were further restricted by the annexations of Offa, King of Mercia, and counter-attacks were largely prevented by the construction of an artificial boundary from the Dee to the Wye (Offa's Dyke).

In the ninth century Rhodri Mawr (844–878) united the country and successfully resisted further incursions of the Saxons by land and raids of Norse and Danish pirates by sea, but at his death his three provinces of Gwynedd (north), Powys (mid) and Deheubarth (south) were divided among his three sons, Anarawd, Mervyn and Cadell. Cadell's son Hywel Dda ruled a large part of Wales and codified its laws but the provinces were not united again until the rule of Llewelyn ap Seisyllt (husband of the heiress of Gwynedd) from 1018 to 1023.

THE NORMAN CONQUEST

After the Norman conquest of England, William I created palatine counties along the Welsh frontier, and the Norman barons began to make encroachments into Welsh territory. The Welsh princes recovered many of their losses during the civil wars of Stephen's reign and in the early 13th century Owen Gruffydd, prince of Gwynedd, was the dominant figure in Wales. Under Llewelyn ap Iorwerth (1194–1240) the Welsh united in powerful resistance to English incursions and Llewelyn's privileges and *de facto* independence were recognised in

Magna Carta. His grandson, Llywelyn ap Gruffydd, was the last native prince; he was killed in 1282 during hostilities between the Welsh and English, allowing Edward I of England to establish his authority over the country. On 7 February 1301, Edward of Caernarvon, son of Edward I, was created Prince of Wales, a title which has subsequently been borne by the eldest son of the sovereign.

Strong Welsh national feeling continued, expressed in the early 15th century in the rising led by Owain Glyndŵr, but the situation was altered by the accession to the English throne in 1485 of Henry VII of the Welsh House of Tudor. Wales was politically assimilated to England under the Act of Union of 1535, which extended English laws to the Principality and gave it parliamentary representation for the first time.

EISTEDDFOD

The Welsh are a distinct nation, with a language and literature of their own, and the national bardic festival (Eisteddfod), instituted by Prince Rhys ap Griffith in 1176, is still held annually. These *Eisteddfodau* (sessions) form part of the *Gorsedd* (assembly), which is believed to date from the time of Prydian, a ruling prince in an age many centuries before the Christian era.

PRINCIPAL CITIES

CARDIFF

Cardiff, at the mouth of the Rivers Taff, Rhymney and Ely, is the capital city of Wales and a major administrative, commercial and business centre. The National Assembly for Wales was opened in Cardiff in 1999. It has many industries, including steel, and its flourishing port is within the Cardiff Bay area, subject of a major redevelopment continuing until the year 2000.

The many fine buildings include the City Hall, the National Museum of Wales, University Buildings, Law Courts, Welsh Office, County Hall, Police Headquarters, the Temple of Peace and Health, Llandaff Cathedral, the Welsh National Folk Museum at St Fagans, Cardiff Castle, the New Theatre, the Sherman Theatre and the Welsh College of Music and Drama. More recent buildings include St David's Hall, Cardiff International Arena and World Trade Centre, and the Welsh National Ice Rink. The Millennium Stadium is under construction for the 1999 rugby World Cup and the Centre for Visual Arts opened in 1999.

SWANSEA

Swansea (*Abertawe*) is a city and a seaport. The Gower peninsula was brought within the city boundary under local government reform in 1974. The trade of the port includes coal, steel products, containerised goods, petroleum products and petrochemicals.

The principal buildings are the Norman Castle (rebuilt *c*.1330), the Royal Institution of South Wales, founded in 1835 (including Library), the University of Wales Swansea at Singleton, and the Guildhall, containing Frank Brangwyn's British Empire panels. The Dylan Thomas Centre, formerly the old Guildhall, was restored in 1995. More recent buildings include the County Hall, the new Maritime Quarter and Marina and the leisure centre.

Swansea was chartered by the Earl of Warwick, *c*. 1158–84, and further charters were granted by King John, Henry III, Edward II, Edward III and James II, Cromwell (two) and the Marcher Lord William de Breos.

LOCAL COUNCILS

Key	County
1	Anglesey
2	Blaenau Gwent
3	Bridgend
4	Caerphilly
5	Cardiff
6	Carmarthenshire
7	Ceredigion
8	Conwy
9	Denbighshire
10	Flintshire
11	Gwynedd
12	Merthyr Tydfil
13	Monmouthshire
14	Neath Port Talbot
15	Newport
16	Pembrokeshire
17	Powys
18	Rhondda, Cynon, Taff
19	Swansea
20	Torfaen
21	Vale of Glamorgan
22	Wrexham

LORD-LIEUTENANTS AND HIGH SHERIFFS

County/Shire	Lord-Lieutenant	High Sheriff, 2001–2
Clwyd	T. Jones, CBE	R. J. Best
Dyfed	Sir David Mansel Lewis, KCVO	R. H. James
Gwent	Vacant	J. W. H. Tenison
Gwynedd	Prof. E. Sunderland, OBE	Mrs Bettina Harden
Mid Glamorgan	M. A. McLaggan	M. E. McGrane
Powys	The Hon. Mrs E. S. Legge-Bourke, LVO	D. P. Trant
S. Glamorgan	Capt. N. Lloyd-Edwards	Lt.-Col. Rhodri Llewellyn Traherne
W. Glamorgan	R. C. Hastie, CBE	D. P. Ll. Davies

LOCAL COUNCILS

SMALL CAPITALS denote CITY status
§ Denotes Borough status

Council	Administrative headquaters	Population	Band D charge 2000	Chief Executive	Chairman 2001–2 (a) Mayor (b) Lord Mayor
Anglesey	Llangefni	68,500	£647.10	G. F. Edwards	J. Williams
Blaenau Gwent	Ebbw Vale	73,000	£796.40	R. Leadbeter, OBE	(a) B. Clements
Bridgend	Bridgend	131,000	£768.40	I. K. Lewis	(a) D. Buttle
§Caerphilly	Hengoed	69,100	£696.60	M. Davies	A. Donaldson
CARDIFF	Cardiff	324,500	£691.40	B. Davies	(b) R. Goodway
Carmarthenshire	Carmarthen	170,000	£607.00	A. Howells	E. Williams
Ceredigion	Aberaeron	71,700	£760.60	O. Watkin	G. Edwards
§Conwy	Conwy	111,000	£599.73	C. D. Barker	A. Barrett
Denbighshire	Ruthin	90,000	£666.50	M. Hughes (Acting)	D. Jones
Flintshire	Mold	147,000	£702.39	P. McGreevy	Mrs A. Slowick
Gwynedd	Caernarfon	116,000	£694.70	G. R. Jones	I. L. Jones
§Merthyr Tydfil	Merthyr Tydfil	58,100	£869.30	G. W. Meredith	(a) R. Thomas
Monmouthshire	Cwmbran	86,000	£679.54	Mrs E. Raikes	D. Spencer
§Neath Port Talbot	Port Talbot	139,500	£884.19	K. R. Sawyers	(a) D. Davies
§Newport	Newport	139,000	£582.18	C. Freegard	(a) R. J. Morris
Pembrokeshire	Haverfordwest	114,000	£499.00	B. Parry-Jones	Mrs R. Hayes
Powys	Llandrindod Wells	126,000	£673.40	Miss J. Tonge	E. Jones
§Rhondda, Cynon, Taff	Tonypandy	240,000	£809.60	K. Ryley	Mrs L. Jones
SWANSEA	Swansea	231,000	£674.61	Ms V. Sugar	(b) R. Francis-Davies
§Torfaen	Pontypool	90,000	£646.09	Dr C. Grace	(a) Mrs C. Thomas
Vale of Glamorgan	Barry	121,300	£654.80	J. Maitland-Evans	M. Nugent
§Wrexham	Wrexham	125,000	£728.64	D. Griffin	(a) Mrs S. Mewies

Scotland

The Kingdom of Scotland occupies the northern portion of the main island of Great Britain and includes the Inner and Outer Hebrides, and the Orkney, Shetland, and many other islands. It lies between 60° 51′ 30″ and 54° 38′ N. latitude and between 1° 45′ 32″ and 6° 14′ W. longitude, with England to the south, the Atlantic Ocean on the north and west, and the North Sea on the east.

The greatest length of the mainland (Cape Wrath to the Mull of Galloway) is 274 miles, and the greatest breadth (Buchan Ness to Applecross) is 154 miles. The customary measurement of the island of Great Britain is from the site of John o' Groats house, near Duncansby Head, Caithness, to Land's End, Cornwall, a total distance of 603 miles in a straight line and approximately 900 miles by road.

The total area of Scotland is 30,420 sq. miles (78,789 sq. km); land 29,767 sq. miles (77,097 sq. km), inland water 653 sq. miles (1,692 sq. km).

POPULATION

The population at the 1991 census was 4,998,567 (males 2,391,961; females 2,606,606). The average density of the population in 1991 was 0.65 persons per hectare.

RELIEF

There are three natural orographic divisions of Scotland. The southern uplands have their highest points in Merrick (2,766 ft), Rhinns of Kells (2,669 ft), and Cairnsmuir of Carsphairn (2,614 ft), in the west; and the Tweedsmuir Hills in the east (Hartfell 2,651 ft, Dollar Law 2,682 ft, Broad Law 2,756 ft).

The central lowlands, formed by the valleys of the Clyde, Forth and Tay, divide the southern uplands from the northern Highlands, which extend almost from the extreme north of the mainland to the central lowlands, and are divided into a northern and a southern system by the Great Glen.

The Grampian Mountains, which entirely cover the southern Highland area, include in the west Ben Nevis (4,406 ft), the highest point in the British Isles, and in the east the Cairngorm Mountains (Cairn Gorm 4,084 ft, Braeriach 4,248 ft, Ben Macdui 4,296 ft). The north-western Highland area contains the mountains of Wester and Easter Ross (Carn Eige 3,880 ft, Sgurr na Lapaich 3,775 ft).

Created, like the central lowlands, by a major geological fault, the Great Glen (60 miles long) runs between Inverness and Fort William, and contains Loch Ness, Loch Oich and Loch Lochy. These are linked to each other and to the north-east and south-west coasts of Scotland by the Caledonian Canal, providing a navigable passage between the Moray Firth and the Inner Hebrides.

HYDROGRAPHY

The western coast is fragmented by peninsulas and islands, and indented by fjords (sea-lochs), the longest of which is Loch Fyne (42 miles long) in Argyll. Although the east coast tends to be less fractured and lower, there are several great drowned inlets (firths), e.g. Firth of Forth, Firth of Tay, Moray Firth, as well as the Firth of Clyde in the west.

The lochs are the principal hydrographic feature. The largest in Scotland and in Britain is Loch Lomond (27 sq. miles), in the Grampian valleys; the longest and deepest is Loch Ness (24 miles long and 800 feet deep), in the Great Glen; and Loch Shin (20 miles long) and Loch Maree in the Highlands.

The longest river is the Tay (117 miles), noted for its salmon. It flows into the North Sea, with Dundee on the

estuary, which is spanned by the Tay Bridge (10,289 ft) opened in 1887 and the Tay Road Bridge (7,365 ft) opened in 1966. Other noted salmon rivers are the Dee (90 miles) which flows into the North Sea at Aberdeen, and the Spey (110 miles), the swiftest flowing river in the British Isles, which flows into Moray Firth. The Tweed, which gave its name to the woollen cloth produced along its banks, marks in the lower stretches of its 96-mile course the border between Scotland and England.

The most important river commercially is the Clyde (106 miles), formed by the junction of the Daer and Portrail water, which flows through the city of Glasgow to the Firth of Clyde. During its course it passes over the picturesque Falls of Clyde, Bonnington Linn (30 ft), Corra Linn (84 ft), Dundaff Linn (10 ft) and Stonebyres Linn (80 ft), above and below Lanark. The Forth (66 miles), upon which stands Edinburgh, the capital, is spanned by the Forth (Railway) Bridge (1890), which is 5,330 feet long, and the Forth (Road) Bridge (1964), which has a total length of 6,156 feet (over water) and a single span of 3,000 feet.

The highest waterfall in Scotland, and the British Isles, is Eas a'Chùal Aluinn with a total height of 658 feet (200 m), which falls from Glas Bheinn in Sutherland. The Falls of Glomach, on a head-stream of the Elchaig in Wester Ross, have a drop of 370 feet.

GAELIC LANGUAGE

According to the 1991 census, 1.4 per cent of the population of Scotland, mainly in the Highlands and western coastal regions, were able to speak the Scottish form of Gaelic.

LOWLAND SCOTTISH LANGUAGE

Several regional Lowland Scottish dialects, known variously as Scots, Scotch, Lallans or Doric, are widely spoken. The General Register Office (Scotland) has estimated that 1.5 million people, or 30 per cent of the population, are Scots speakers.

FLAG

The flag of Scotland is known as the Saltire. It is a white diagonal cross on a blue field (saltire argent in a field azure) and represents St Andrew, the patron saint of Scotland.

THE SCOTTISH ISLANDS

ORKNEY

The Orkney Islands (total area 375½ sq. miles) lie about six miles north of the mainland, separated from it by the Pentland Firth. Of the 90 islands and islets (holms and skerries) in the group, about one-third are inhabited.

The total population at the 1991 census was 19,612; the 1991 populations of the islands shown here include those of smaller islands forming part of the same civil parish.

Mainland, 15,128	Rousay, 291
Burray, 363	Sanday, 533
Eday, 166	Shapinsay, 322
Flotta and Fara, 126	South Ronaldsay, 943
Graemsay and Hoy, 477	Stronsay, 382
North Ronaldsay, 92	Westray, 704
Papa Westray, 85	

The islands are rich in prehistoric and Scandinavian remains, the most notable being the Stone Age village of Skara Brae, the burial chamber of Maeshowe, the many brochs (towers) and the 12th-century St Magnus Cathedral. Scapa Flow, between the Mainland and Hoy, was the war station of the British Grand Fleet from 1914 to 1919 and the scene of the scuttling of the surrendered German High Seas Fleet (21 June 1919).

Most of the islands are low-lying and fertile, and farming (principally beef cattle) is the main industry. Flotta, to the south of Scapa Flow, is the site of the oil terminal for the Piper, Claymore and Tartan fields in the North Sea.

The capital is Kirkwall (population 6,881) on Mainland.

SHETLAND

The Shetland Islands have a total area of 551 sq. miles and a population at the 1991 census of 22,522. They lie about 50 miles north of the Orkneys, with Fair Isle about half-way between the two groups. Out Stack, off Muckle Flugga, one mile north of Unst, is the most northerly part of the British Isles (60° 51′ 30″ N. lat.).

There are over 100 islands, of which 16 are inhabited. Populations at the 1991 census were:

Mainland, 17,596	Muckle Roe, 115
Bressay, 352	Trondra, 117
East Burra, 72	Unst, 1,055
Fair Isle, 67	West Burra, 857
Fetlar, 90	Whalsay, 1,041
Housay, 85	Yell, 1,075

Shetland's many archaeological sites include Jarlshof, Mousa and Clickhimin, and its long connection with Scandinavia has resulted in a strong Norse influence on its place-names and dialect.

Industries include fishing, knitwear and farming. In addition to the fishing fleet there are fish processing factories, while the traditional handknitting of Fair Isle and Unst is supplemented now with machine-knitted garments. Farming is mainly crofting, with sheep being raised on the moorland and hills of the islands. Latterly the islands have become a centre of the North Sea oil industry, with pipelines from the Brent and Ninian fields running to the terminal at Sullom Voe, the largest of its kind in Europe. Lerwick is the main centre for supply services for offshore oil exploration and development.

The capital is Lerwick (population 7,901) on Mainland.

THE HEBRIDES

Until the late 13th century the Hebrides included other Scottish islands in the Firth of Clyde, the peninsula of Kintyre (Argyll), the Isle of Man, and the (Irish) Isle of Rathlin. The origin of the name is stated to be the Greek Eboudai, latinised as Hebudes by Pliny, and corrupted to its present form. The Norwegian name Sudreyjar (Southern Islands) was latinised as Sodorenses, a name that survives in the Anglican bishopric of Sodor and Man.

There are over 500 islands and islets, of which about 100 are inhabited, though mountainous terrain and extensive peat bogs mean that only a fraction of the total area is under cultivation. Stone, Bronze and Iron Age settlement has left many remains, including those at Callanish on Lewis, and Norse colonisation influenced language, customs and place-names. Occupations include farming (mostly crofting and stock-raising), fishing and the manufacture of tweeds and other woollens. Tourism is also an important factor in the economy.

The Inner Hebrides lie off the west coast of Scotland and relatively close to the mainland. The largest and best-known is Skye (area 643 sq. miles; pop. 8,868; chief town, Portree), which contains the Cuillin Hills (Sgurr Alasdair 3,257 ft), the Red Hills (Beinn na Caillich 2,403 ft), Bla Bheinn (3,046 ft) and The Storr (2,358 ft). Skye is also famous as the refuge of the Young Pretender in 1746. Other islands in the Highland council area include Raasay (pop. 163), Rum, Eigg and Muck.

Further south the Inner Hebridean islands include Arran (pop. 4,474) containing Goat Fell (2,868 ft); Coll and Tiree (pop. 940); Colonsay and Oronsay (pop. 106); Islay (area 235 sq. miles; pop. 3,538); Jura (area 160 sq. miles; pop. 196) with a range of hills culminating in the Paps of Jura (Beinn-an-Oir, 2,576 ft, and Beinn Chaolais, 2,477 ft); and Mull (area 367 sq. miles; pop. 2,708; chief town Tobermory) containing Ben More (3,171 ft).

The Outer Hebrides, separated from the mainland by the Minch, now form the Eilean Siar Western Isles Islands Council area (area 1,119 sq. miles; population at the 1991 census 29,600). The main islands are Lewis with Harris (area 770 sq. miles, pop. 21,737), whose chief town, Stornoway, is the administrative headquarters; North Uist (pop. 1,404); South Uist (pop. 2,106); Baleshare (55); Benbecula (pop. 1,803) and Barra (pop. 1,244). Other inhabited islands include Bernera (262), Berneray (141), Eriskay (179), Grimsay (215), Scalpay (382) and Vatersay (72).

EARLY HISTORY

There is evidence of human settlement in Scotland dating from the third millennium BC, the earliest settlers being Middle Stone Age hunters and fishermen. Early in the second millennium BC, New Stone Age farmers began to cultivate crops and rear livestock; their settlements were on the west coast and in the north, and included Skara Brae and Maeshowe (Orkney). Settlement by the Early Bronze Age 'Beaker folk', so-called from the shape of their drinking vessels, in eastern Scotland dates from about 1800 BC. Further settlement is believed to have occurred from 700 BC onwards, as tribes were displaced from further south by new incursions from the Continent and the Roman invasions from AD 43.

Julius Agricola, the Roman governor of Britain AD 77–84, extended the Roman conquests in Britain by advancing into Caledonia, culminating with a victory at Mons Graupius, probably in AD 84; he was recalled to Rome shortly afterwards and his forward policy was not pursued. Hadrian's Wall, mostly completed by AD 30, marked the northern frontier of the Roman empire except for the period between about AD 144 and 190 when the frontier moved north to the Forth–Clyde isthmus and a turf wall, the Antonine Wall, was manned.

After the Roman withdrawal from Britain, there were centuries of warfare between the Picts, Scots, Britons, Angles and Vikings. The Picts, believed to be a non-Indo-European race, occupied the area north of the Forth. The Scots, a Gaelic-speaking people of northern Ireland, colonised the area of Argyll and Bute (the kingdom of Dalriada) in the fifth century AD and then expanded eastwards and northwards. The Britons, speaking a Brythonic Celtic language, colonised Scotland from the south from the first century BC; they lost control of south-eastern Scotland (incorporated into the kingdom of Northumbria) to the Angles in the early seventh century but retained Strathclyde (south-western Scotland and Cumbria). Viking raids from the late eighth century were followed by Norse settlement in the western and northern isles, Argyll, Caithness and Sutherland from the mid-ninth century onwards.

UNIFICATION

The union of the areas which now comprise Scotland began in AD 843 when Kenneth mac Alpin, king of the Scots from c.834, became also king of the Picts, joining the two lands to form the kingdom of Alba (comprising Scotland north of a line between the Forth and Clyde rivers). Lothian, the eastern part of the area between the Forth and the Tweed, seems to have been leased to Kenneth II of Alba (reigned 971–995) by Edgar of England c.973/4, and Scottish possession was confirmed by Malcolm II's victory over a Northumbrian army at Carham c.1016. At about this time Malcolm II (reigned 1005–34) placed his grandson Duncan on the throne of the British kingdom of Strathclyde, bringing under Scots rule virtually all of what is now Scotland.

The Norse possessions were incorporated into the kingdom of Scotland from the 12th century onwards. An uprising in the mid-12th century drove the Norse from most of mainland Argyll. The Hebrides were ceded to Scotland by the Treaty of Perth in 1266 after a Norwegian expedition in 1263 failed to maintain Norse authority over the islands. Orkney and Shetland fell to Scotland in 1468–9 as a pledge for the unpaid dowry of Margaret of Denmark, wife of James III, though Danish claims of suzerainty were relinquished only with the marriage of Anne of Denmark to James VI in 1590.

From the 11th century, there were frequent wars between Scotland and England over territory and the extent of England's political influence. The failure of the Scottish royal line with the death of Margaret of Norway in 1290 led to disputes over the throne which were resolved by the adjudication of Edward I of England. He awarded the throne to John Balliol in 1292 but Balliol's refusal to be a puppet king led to war. Balliol surrendered to Edward I in 1296 and Edward attempted to rule Scotland himself. Resistance to Scotland's loss of independence was led by William Wallace, who defeated the English at Stirling Bridge (1297), and Robert Bruce, crowned in 1306, who held most of Scotland by 1311 and routed Edward II's army at Bannockburn (1314). England recognised the independence of Scotland in the Treaty of Northampton in 1328. Subsequent clashes include the disastrous battle of Flodden (1513) in which James IV and many of his nobles fell.

THE UNION

In 1603 James VI of Scotland succeeded Elizabeth I on the throne of England (his mother, Mary Queen of Scots, was the great-granddaughter of Henry VII), his successors reigning as sovereigns of Great Britain. Political union of the two countries did not occur until 1707.

THE JACOBITE REVOLTS

After the abdication (by flight) in 1688 of James VII and II, the crown devolved upon William III (grandson of Charles I) and Mary II (elder daughter of James VII and II). In 1689 Graham of Claverhouse roused the Highlands on behalf of James VII and II, but died after a military success at Killiecrankie.

After the death of Anne (younger daughter of James VII and II), the throne devolved upon George I (great-grandson of James VI and I). In 1715, armed risings on behalf of James Stuart (the Old Pretender, son of James VII and II) led to the indecisive battle of Sheriffmuir, and the Jacobite movement died down until 1745, when Charles Stuart (the Young Pretender) defeated the Royalist troops at Prestonpans and advanced to Derby (1746). From Derby, the adherents of 'James VIII and III' (the title claimed for his father by Charles Stuart) fell back on the defensive and were finally crushed at Culloden (16 April 1746).

PRINCIPAL CITIES

ABERDEEN

Aberdeen, 130 miles north-east of Edinburgh, received its charter as a Royal Burgh in 1179. Scotland's third largest city, Aberdeen is the second largest Scottish fishing port and the main centre for offshore oil exploration and production. It is also an ancient university town and distinguished research centre. Other industries include engineering, food processing, textiles, paper manufacturing and chemicals.

Places of interest include King's College, St Machar's Cathedral, Brig o' Balgownie, Duthie Park and Winter Gardens, Hazlehead Park, the Kirk of St Nicholas, Mercat Cross, Marischal College and Marischal Museum, Provost Skene's House, Art Gallery, Gordon Highlanders Museum, Satrosphere Hands-On Discovery Centre, and Aberdeen Maritime Museum in Provost Ross's House.

DUNDEE

Dundee, a Royal Burgh, is situated on the north bank of the Tay estuary. The city's port and dock installations are important to the offshore oil industry and the airport also provides servicing facilities. Principal industries include textiles, computers and other electronic industries, lasers, printing, tyre manufacture, food processing, carpets, engineering, clothing manufacture and tourism.

The unique City Churches – three churches under one roof, together with the 15th-century St Mary's Tower – are the most prominent architectural feature. Dundee has two historic ships: the Dundee-built RRS *Discovery* which took Capt. Scott to the Antarctic lies alongside Discovery Quay, and the frigate *Unicorn*, the only British-built wooden warship still afloat, is moored in Victoria Dock. Places of interest include Mills Public Observatory, the Tay road and rail bridges, McManus Galleries, Barrack Street Museum, Claypotts Castle, Broughty Castle and Verdant Works (Textile Heritage Centre).

EDINBURGH

Edinburgh is the capital of and seat of government in Scotland. The city is built on a group of hills and contains in Princes Street one of the most beautiful thoroughfares in the world.

The principal buildings are the Castle, which now houses the Stone of Scone and also includes St Margaret's Chapel, the oldest building in Edinburgh, and near it, the Scottish National War Memorial; the Palace of Holyroodhouse; Parliament House, the present seat of the judicature; three universities (Edinburgh, Heriot-Watt, Napier); St Giles' Cathedral; St Mary's (Scottish Episcopal) Cathedral (Sir George Gilbert Scott); the General Register House (Robert Adam); the National and the Signet Libraries; the National Gallery; the Royal Scottish Academy; the National Portrait Gallery; and the Edinburgh International Conference Centre, opened in 1995. A new Scottish Parliament building is under construction at Holyrood.

GLASGOW

Glasgow, a Royal Burgh, is the principal commercial and industrial centre in Scotland. The city occupies the north and south banks of the Clyde, formerly one of the chief commercial estuaries in the world. The principal industries include engineering, electronics, finance, chemicals and printing. The city has also developed recently as a tourism and conference centre.

The chief buildings are the 13th-century Gothic Cathedral, the University (Sir George Gilbert Scott), the City Chambers, the Royal Concert Hall, St Mungo Museum of Religious Life and Art, Pollok House, the School of Art (Mackintosh), Kelvingrove Art Galleries, the Gallery of Modern Art, the Burrell Collection museum and the Mitchell Library. The city is home to the Scottish National Orchestra, Scottish Opera and Scottish Ballet.

INVERNESS

Inverness was granted city status in January 2001. The city's name is derived from the Gaelic for 'the mouth of the Ness', referring to the river on which it lies. Inverness is recorded as being at the junction of the old trade routes since 565AD. Today the city is the main administrative centre for the north of Scotland and is the capital of the Highlands. Tourism is one of the city's main industries

Among the city's most notable buildings is Abertarff House, built in 1593 and the oldest secular building remaining in Inverness. Balnain House, built as a town house in 1726 is a fine example of early Georgian architecture. Once a hospital for Hanoverian soldiers after the battle of Culloden and as billets for the Royal Engineers when completing the 1st Ordnance Survey, today Balnain House is the National Trust of Scotland's regional HQ. The Old High Church, on St Michael's Mount, is the original Parish Church of Inverness and is built on the sight of the earliest Christian church in the city. Parts of the church date back to the 14th century.

LORD-LIEUTENANTS

Title	Name	Title	Name
Aberdeenshire	A. D. M. Farquharson, OBE	Moray	Air Vice-Marshal G. A. Chesworth, CB, OBE, DFC
Angus	Mrs G. L. Osborne		
Argyll and Bute	Vacant	Nairn	E. J. Brodie
Ayrshire and Arran	Maj. R. Y. Henderson, TD	Orkney	G. R. Marwick
Banffshire	J. A. S. McPherson, CBE	Perth and Kinross	Sir David Montgomery, Bt.
Berwickshire	Maj. A. Trotter	Renfrewshire	C. H. Parker, OBE
		Ross and Cromarty	Capt. R. W. K. Stirling of Fairburn, TD
Caithness	Maj. G. T. Dunnett, TD		
Clackmannan	Mrs S. G. Cruickshank	Roxburgh, Ettrick and Lauderdale	Dr June Paterson-Brown, CBE
Dumfries	Capt. R. C. Cunningham-Jardine		
		Shetland	J. H. Scott
Dunbartonshire	Brig. D. D. G. Hardie, TD	Stirling and Falkirk	Lt.-Col. J. Stirling of Garden, CBE, TD
East Lothian	W. Garth Morrison, CBE		
Eilean Siar/ Western Isles	A. Matheson, OBE	Sutherland	Maj.-Gen. D. Houston, CBE
		The Stewartry of Kirkcudbright	Lt.-Gen. Sir Norman Arthur, KCB
Fife	Mrs C. M. Dean		
Inverness	Rt. Hon. The Lord Gray of Contin, PC	Tweeddale	Capt. D. Younger
		West Lothian	*vacant*
Kincardineshire	J. D. B. Smart	Wigtown	Maj. E. S. Orr-Ewing
Lanarkshire	G. Cox, MBE		
Midlothian	Capt. G. W. Burnet, LVO		

The Lord Provosts of the four city districts of Aberdeen, Dundee, Edinburgh and Glasgow are Lord-Lieutenants for those districts *ex officio*.

LOCAL COUNCILS

Council	Administrative headquaters	Population (latest estimate)	Band D charge 2001	Chief Executive	Chairman (a) Convenor (b) Provost (c) Lord Provost
Aberdeen City	Aberdeen	217,200	£934.00	D. Paterson	(c) Ms M. Smith
Aberdeenshire	Aberdeen	228,000	£855.00	A. G. Campbell	(a) R. Bisset, OBE
Angus	Forfar	110,200	£821.00	A. B. Watson	(b) Mrs F. M. Duncan, OBE
Argyll and Bute	Lochgilphead	88,790	£984.00	J. A. McLellan	(a) W. Petrie
City of Edinburgh	Edinburgh	449,000	£960.00	T. N. Aitchison	(c) Rt. Hon. E. Milligan
Clackmannanshire	Alloa	48,500	£951.00	K. Bloom	(b) W. McAdam
Dumfries and Galloway	Dumfries	148,000	£857.00	P. N. Jones	(a) A. Campbell, OBE
Dundee City	Dundee	146,690	£1,046.00	A. Stephen	(c) Rt. Hon. H. W. Wright
East Ayrshire	Kilmarnock	124,000	£828.00	D. Montgomery	(b) J. Boyd
East Dunbartonshire	Glasgow	110,000	£872.00	Dr V. Nash	(b) R. McSkimming
East Lothian	Haddington	85,600	£909.00	J. Lindsay	(b) P. O'Brien
East Renfrewshire	Giffnock	89,280	£859.00	P. Daniels	(b) A. Steele
Eilean Siar/Western Isles	Stornoway	27,560	£765.00	W. Howat	(a) A. A. Macdonald

Council	Administrative headquaters	Population (latest estimate)	Band D charge 2001	Chief Executive	Chairman (a) Convenor (b) Provost (c) Lord Provost
Falkirk	Falkirk	144,688	£813.00	Mrs M. Pitcaithly	(b) J. Johnson
Fife	Glenrothes	352,000	£891.00	D. Sinclair	(a) J. MacDougall
Glasgow City	Glasgow	611,500	£1,120.00	J. Andrews	(c) A. Mosson
Highland	Inverness	208,700	£889.00	A. D. McCourt	(a) D. Green
Inverclyde	Greenock	85,000	£894.00	R. Cleary	(b) R. Jackson
Midlothian	Dalkeith	81,680	£1,001.00	T. Muir	(b) S. Campbell
Moray	Elgin	86,000	£825.00	A. Keddie	(a) E. Aldridge
North Ayrshire	Irvine	140,000	£877.00	B. Devine	(a) S. Taylor
North Lanarkshire	Motherwell	327,000	£844.00	G. Whitefield	(b) B. McCulloch
Orkney Islands	Kirkwall	19,817	£754.00	A. Buchan	(a) H. Halcro-Johnston
Perth and Kinross	Perth	134,000	£875.00	H. Robertson	(b) M. O'Malley
Renfrewshire	Paisley	177,000	£896.40	T. Scholes	(b) J. McDowell
Scottish Borders	Newtown St Boswells	106,400	£785.00	A. M. Croall	(a) A. L. Tulley
Shetland Islands	Lerwick	23,000	£747.00	M. Goodlad	(a) T. Stove
South Ayrshire	Ayr	114,000	£1,140.00	G. W. F. Thorley	(b) Ms E. Foulkes
South Lanarkshire	Hamilton	301,000	£924.00	M. Docherty	(b) A. Dick
Stirling	Stirling	85,200	£954.00	K. Yates	(b) T. Brookes
West Dunbartonshire	Dumbarton	93,977	£1,024.00	T. Huntingford	(b) A. Macdonald
West Lothian	Livingston	152,000	£919.00	A. M. Linkston	(b) J. Thomas

LOCAL COUNCILS

Key	Council
1	Aberdeen City
2	Aberdeenshire
3	Angus
4	Argyll and Bute
5	City of Edinburgh
6	Clackmannanshire
7	Dumfries and Galloway
8	Dundee City
9	East Ayrshire
10	East Dunbartonshire
11	East Lothian
12	East Renfrewshire
13	Falkirk
14	Fife
15	Glasgow City
16	Highland
17	Inverclyde
18	Midlothian
19	Moray
20	North Ayrshire
21	North Lanarkshire
22	Orkney
23	Perth and Kinross
24	Renfrewshire
25	Scottish Borders
26	Shetland
27	South Ayrshire
28	South Lanarkshire
29	Stirling
30	West Dunbartonshire
31	Western Isles (Eilean Siar)
32	West Lothian

Northern Ireland

Northern Ireland has a total area of 5,467 sq. miles (14,144 sq. km): land, 5,225 sq. miles (13,532 sq. km); inland water and tideways, 249 sq. miles (628 sq. km).

The population of Northern Ireland at the 1991 census was 1,577,836 (males, 769,071; females, 808,765). The average density of population in 1991 was 1.11 persons per hectare.

In 1991 the number of persons in the various religious denominations (expressed as percentages of the total population) were: Roman Catholic, 38.4; Presbyterian, 21.4; Church of Ireland, 17.7; Methodist, 3.8; others 7.7; none, 3.7; not stated, 7.3.

FLAG

The official national flag of Northern Ireland is now the Union Flag. The flag formerly in use (a white, six-pointed star in the centre of a red cross on a white field, enclosing a red hand and surmounted by a crown) has not been used since the imposition of direct rule.

PRINCIPAL CITIES

BELFAST

Belfast, the administrative centre of Northern Ireland, is situated at the mouth of the River Lagan at its entrance to Belfast Lough. The city grew, owing to its easy access by sea to Scottish coal and iron, to be a great industrial centre.

The principal buildings are of a relatively recent date and include the Parliament Buildings at Stormont, the City Hall, Waterfront Hall, the Law Courts, the Public Library and the Museum and Art Gallery.

Belfast received its first charter of incorporation in 1613 and was created a city in 1888; the title of Lord Mayor was conferred in 1892.

LONDONDERRY

Londonderry (originally Derry) is situated on the River Foyle, and has important associations with the City of London. The Irish Society was created by the City of London in 1610, and under its royal charter of 1613 it fortified the city and was for long closely associated with its administration. Because of this connection the city was incorporated in 1613 under the new name of Londonderry.

The city is famous for the great siege of 1688–9, when for 105 days the town held out against the forces of James II until relieved by sea. The city walls are still intact and form a circuit of almost a mile around the old city.

Interesting buildings are the Protestant Cathedral of St Columb's (1633) and the Guildhall, reconstructed in 1912 and containing a number of beautiful stained glass windows, many of which were presented by the livery companies of London.

CONSTITUTIONAL DEVELOPMENTS

Northern Ireland is subject to the same fundamental constitutional provisions which apply to the rest of the United Kingdom. It had its own parliament and government from 1921 to 1972, but after increasing civil unrest the Northern Ireland (Temporary Provisions) Act 1972 transferred the legislative and executive powers of the Northern Ireland parliament and government to the UK Parliament and a Secretary of State. The Northern Ireland Constitution Act 1973 provided for devolution in North-

ern Ireland through an assembly and executive, but a power-sharing executive formed by the Northern Ireland political parties in January 1974 collapsed in May 1974; since then Northern Ireland has been governed by direct rule under the provisions of the Northern Ireland Act 1974. This allows Parliament to approve all laws for Northern Ireland and places the Northern Ireland department under the direction and control of the Secretary of State for Northern Ireland.

Attempts were made by successive governments to find a means of restoring a widely acceptable form of devolved government to Northern Ireland. In 1985 the governments of the United Kingdom and the Republic of Ireland signed the Anglo-Irish Agreement, establishing an inter-governmental conference in which the Irish government may put forward views and proposals on certain aspects of Northern Ireland affairs.

Discussions between the British and Irish governments and the main Northern Ireland parties began in 1991. It was agreed that any political settlement would need to address relationships within Northern Ireland, within the island of Ireland (north/south) and between the British and Irish governments (east/west). Although round table talks ended in 1992 the process continued from September 1993 as separate bilateral discussions with three of the Northern Ireland parties (the DUP declined to participate).

In December 1993 the British and Irish governments published the Joint Declaration complementing the political talks, and making clear that any settlement would need to be founded on principles of democracy and consent. The declaration also stated that all democratically mandated parties could be involved in political talks as long as they permanently renounced paramilitary violence.

The provisional IRA and loyalist paramilitary groups announced cease-fires on 31 August and 13 October 1994 respectively. The Government initiated exploratory meetings with Sinn Fein and loyalist representatives in December 1994.

In February 1995 the then Prime Minister (John Major) launched *A Framework for Accountable Government in Northern Ireland* and, with the Irish Prime Minister, *A New Framework for Agreement*. These outlined what a comprehensive political settlement might look like. The ideas were intended to facilitate multilateral dialogue involving the Northern Ireland parties and the British government.

In autumn 1995 the Prime Minister said that Sinn Fein would not be invited to all-party talks until the IRA had decommissioned its arms; the IRA ruled out any decommissioning of weapons in advance of a political settlement. An international body chaired by a former US senator, George Mitchell, reported in January 1996 that no weapons would be decommissioned before the start of all-party talks and that a compromise agreement was necessary under which weapons would be decommissioned during negotiations. The Prime Minister accepted the report and proposed the election of representatives to conduct all-party talks. On 9 February 1996 the IRA called off its cease-fire.

PEACE TALKS

Following elections on 30 May 1996, all-party talks opened at Stormont Castle on 10 June 1996 which included nine of the ten parties returned at the election;

Sinn Fein representatives were turned away because the IRA had failed to reinstate its cease-fire. On 29 July 1996 the all-party talks were suspended after disagreements over the issue of decommissioning arms. An opening agenda for the talks was agreed in October 1996.

On 25 June 1997 the newly-elected Labour Government said that substantive negotiations should begin in September 1997 with a view to reaching conclusions by May 1998. The British and Irish governments issued a joint paper outlining their proposals for resolving the decommissioning issue. The Government also indicated that if the IRA were to call a cease-fire, it would assess whether it was genuine over a period of six weeks, and if satisfied that it was so, would then invite Sinn Fein to the talks. An IRA cease-fire was declared on 20 July 1997.

When the UK Government announced in August 1997 that Sinn Fein would be present when the substantive talks opened on 15 September, the Unionist and loyalist parties, unhappy at the terms on which Sinn Fein had been admitted, boycotted the opening session. The Ulster Unionist Party, the Progressive Unionist Party and the Ulster Democratic Party re-entered the negotiations on 17 September. Full-scale peace talks began on 7 October. The parties had agreed to concentrate on constitutional issues, with the issue of decommissioning terrorist weapons to be handled by a new independent commission.

On 12 January 1998 the British and Irish governments issued a joint document, *Propositions on Heads of Agreement*, proposing the establishment of various new cross-border bodies; further proposals were presented on 27 January. A draft peace settlement was issued by the talks' chairman, Sen. George Mitchell, on 6 April 1998 but was rejected by the Unionists the following day. On 10 April agreement was reached between the British and Irish governments and the eight Northern Ireland political parties still involved in the talks (the Good Friday/Belfast Agreement). The agreement provided for an elected New Northern Ireland Assembly; a North/South Ministerial Council, and a British-Irish Council comprising representatives of the British, Irish, Channel Islands and Isle of Man governments and members of the new assemblies for Scotland, Wales and Northern Ireland. Further points included the abandonment of the Republic of Ireland's constitutional claim to Northern Ireland; the decommissioning of weapons; the release of paramilitary prisoners; and changes in policing.   Referendums on the agreement were held in Northern Ireland and the Republic of Ireland on 22 May 1998. In Northern Ireland the turnout was 81 per cent, of which 71.12 per cent voted in favour of the agreement. In the Republic of Ireland, the turnout was about 55 per cent, of which 94.4 per cent voted in favour of both the agreement and the necessary constitutional change. In the UK, the Northern Ireland Act 1998, enshrining the provisions of the Agreement, received Royal Assent in November 1998.

For details of the *Northern Ireland Assembly and the further political developments in Northern Ireland, see* Regional Government section.

OTHER BODIES

Consultations between the First Minister and Deputy First Minister, the British and Irish Governments and the political parties concluded in early 1999 with an agreement to establish six areas for cross-border bodies and a further six areas for co-operation. Treaties between the British and Irish governments establishing the bodies and parallel domestic legislation to underpin them are now in place.

The intergovernmental conference established by the 1985 Anglo-Irish Agreement was replaced by a new British-Irish Intergovernmental Conference which will discuss all areas of mutual bilateral interest.

The British-Irish Council will operate on the basis of consensus and may reach agreements and pursue common policies in areas of mutual interest.

ECONOMY

FINANCE

Northern Ireland's expenditure is funded by the Northern Ireland Consolidated Fund (NICF). Up to date of devolution on 2 December 1999, the NICF was largely financed by Northern Ireland's attributed share of UK taxation and supplemented by a grant-in-aid. From devolution, these separate elements have been subsumed into a single Block Grant. In 2000–1 the provisional outturn for public expenditure falling within the Northern Ireland Departmental Expenditure Limit was £5,245 million. For 2001–2 the provisional estimate of required funds was £5,758 million.

PRODUCTION

The products of the engineering and allied industries, which employed 28,800 persons in 1997, were valued at £2,093 million. The textiles industry (manufacture of textiles and textile products), employing about 22,500 persons, produced goods valued at approximately £936 million. The food products, beverages and tobacco industry, employing about 20,700 persons, produced goods valued at £3,836 million.

In 1999, 1,724 persons were employed in mining and quarrying operations in Northern Ireland and the minerals raised (28,555,000 tonnes) were valued at £58,433,000.

COMMUNICATIONS

The total tonnage handled by Northern Ireland ports in 2000 was 22.8 million. Regular ferry, freight and container services operate to ports in Great Britain and Europe from a number of ports, with most trade passing through Belfast (58 per cent of the total), Larne and Warrenpoint.

The Northern Ireland Transport Holding Company is largely responsible for the supervision of the subsidiary companies, Ulsterbus and Citybus (which operate the public road passenger services) and Northern Ireland Railways (collectively known as Translink). Road freight services are also provided by a large number of hauliers operating competitively under licence.

Belfast International Airport, owned by TBI International, provides scheduled and chartered services on domestic and international routes. In 2000–1 the airport handled approximately 3 million passengers and 26,000 tonnes of freight. Scheduled services also operate from Belfast City Airport (BCA, owned by Shorts Bombardier Aerospace) to 16 UK destinations. In 2000–1 the airport handled approximately 1.2 million passengers. City of Derry Airport (Londonderry), owned and operated by Derry City Council) provides services to 3 UK and European destinations and to Belfast, providing links to many of the locations serviced by BCA. In 2000–1 City of Derry Airport served approximately 103,000 passengers.

NORTHERN IRELAND COUNTIES

County	Area* (sq. miles)	Lord-Lieutenant	High Sheriff, 2001
Antrim	1,093	The Lord O'Neill, TD	J. W. Wallace
Armagh	484	The Earl of Caledon	P. S. Kellet
‡Belfast City	25	Lady Carswell, OBE	A. R. Crow
Down	945	W. J. Hall	R. J. Gordon
Fermanagh	647	The Earl of Erne	Mrs E. G. Thompson
†Londonderry	798	J. Thompson Eaton, CBE, TD	Mrs F. M. Sloan, MBE
‡Londonderry City	3.4	D. F. Desmond, CBE	Mrs F. M. O'Kane
Tyrone	1,211	The Duke of Abercorn, KG	Mr J. G. Ferguson, OBE

* Excluding inland waters and tideways
‡ Denotes County Borough
† Excluding the City of Londonderry

DISTRICT COUNCILS

SMALL CAPITALS denotes CITY status
§ Denotes Borough Council

Council	Population (May 2000)	Net Annual Value £	Council Clerk	Chairman † Mayor 2000
§Antrim, Co. Antrim	49,100	32,562,784	S. J. Magee	† M. Rea
§Ards, Co. Down	72,300	29,416,655	D. J. Fallows	† Mrs M. Craig
§ARMAGH, Co. Armagh	54,200	21,485,083	V. Brownlees	† Mrs S. McRoberts
§Ballymena, Co. Antrim	59,500	34,649,252	M. G. Rankin	† T. Nicholl
§Ballymoney, Co. Antrim	26,200	8,977,431	J. Dempsey	† B. Kennedy
Banbridge, Co. Down	40,500	15,706,117	R. Gilmore	W. J. Martin
BELFAST, Co. Antrim and Co. Down	281,700	297,090,024	B. Hanna	† J. Rodgers
§Carrickfergus, Co. Antrim	38,400	16,236,190	A. Cardwell	† W. Ash
§Castlereagh, Co. Down	67,000	35,575,626	A. Donaldson	† K. Morton
§Coleraine, Co. Londonderry	55,900	30,201,937	W. Moore	† J. Dallot
Cookstown, Co. Tyrone	31,600	15,744,017	M. J. McGuckin	P. McAleer
§Craigavon, Co. Armagh	80,300	45,917,344	T. Reaney	† S. Gardner
DERRY, Co. Londonderry	106,100	60,041,828	C. Logue (acting)	† Mrs M. Garfield
Down, Co. Down	64,000	24,106,390	J. McGrillen	Mrs A. Aleenan
Dungannon, Co. Tyrone	48,500	25,842,535	W. J. Beattie	W. Beattie
Fermanagh, Co. Fermanagh	57,600	28,899,077	R. Connor	R. Martin
§Larne, Co. Antrim	31,000	17,539,967	C. McGarry	† D. Fleck
§Limavady, Co. Londonderry	31,300	12,369,586	J. K. Stevenson	† L. Lowry
§Lisburn, Co. Antrim and Co. Down	109,700	58,400,242	N. Davidson	† J. Dillon
Magherafelt, Co. Londonderry	39,200	15,485,660	J. A. McLaughlin	A. Hughes
Moyle, Co. Antrim	15,400	4,964,065	R. G. Lewis	R. McDonald
Newry and Mourne, Co. Down and Co. Armagh	87,800	39,082,703	T. McCall	D. Hyland
§Newtownabbey, Co. Antrim	81,800	44,591,040	N. Dunn	† Mrs V. McWilliams
§North Down, Co. Down	75,300	39,774,190	T. Polley	† I. Henry
Omagh, Co. Tyrone	47,200	23,326,205	D. McSorley	B. McElduss
Strabane, Co. Tyrone	37,800	13,591,913	J. Stewart (Acting)	I. Barr

The Isle of Man

Ellan Vannin

The Isle of Man is an island situated in the Irish Sea, in latitude 54° 3'–54° 25' N. and longitude 4° 18'–4° 47' W., nearly equidistant from England, Scotland and Ireland. Although the early inhabitants were of Celtic origin, the Isle of Man was part of the Norwegian Kingdom of the Hebrides until 1266, when this was ceded to Scotland. Subsequently granted to the Stanleys (Earls of Derby) in the 15th century and later to the Dukes of Atholl, it was brought under the administration of the Crown in 1765. The island forms the bishopric of Sodor and Man.

The total land area is 221 sq. miles (572 sq. km). The report on the 1991 census showed a resident population of 69,788 (males, 33,693; females, 36,095). The main language in use is English. There are no remaining native speakers of Manx Gaelic but 643 people are able to speak the language.

CAPITAL – ΨDouglas; population (1991), 22,214.

ΨCastletown (3,152) is the ancient capital; the other towns are ΨPeel (3,829) and ΨRamsey (6,496)

FLAG – A red flag charged with three conjoined armoured legs in white and gold

TYNWALD DAY – 5 July

GOVERNMENT

The Isle of Man is a self-governing Crown dependency, having its own parliamentary, legal and administrative system. The British Government is responsible for international relations and defence. Under the UK Act of Accession, Protocol 3, the island's relationship with the European Union is limited to trade alone and does not extend to financial aid. The Lieutenant-Governor is The Queen's personal representative in the island.

The legislature, Tynwald, is the oldest parliament in the world in continuous existence. It has two branches: the Legislative Council and the House of Keys. The Council consists of the President of Tynwald, the Bishop of Sodor and Man, the Attorney-General (who does not have a vote) and eight members elected by the House of Keys. The House of Keys has 24 members, elected by universal adult suffrage. The branches sit separately to consider legislation and sit together, as Tynwald Court, for most other parliamentary purposes.

The presiding officer of Tynwald Court is the President of Tynwald, elected by the members, who also presides over sittings of the Legislative Council. The presiding officer of the House of Keys is Mr Speaker, who is elected by members of the House.

The principal members of the Manx Government are the Chief Minister and nine departmental ministers, who comprise the Council of Ministers.

Lieutenant-Governor, HE Air-Marshal I. MacFadyen, CB, OBE
ADC to the Lieutenant-Governor, C. J. Tummon
President of Tynwald, The Hon. N. Q. Cringle
Speaker, House of Keys, The Hon. J. D. Q. Cannan
The First Deemster and Clerk of the Rolls, His Honour T. W. Cain, QC
Clerk of Tynwald, Secretary to the House of Keys and Counsel to the Speaker, Mr Malachy Cornwell-Kelly
Clerk of the Legislative Council and Deputy Clerk of Tynwald, Mrs M. Cullen
Attorney-General, W. J. H. Corlett, QC
Chief Minister, The Hon. D. J. Gelling
Chief Secretary, J. F. Kissack
Chief Financial Officer, Mrs M. Williams

ECONOMY

Most of the income generated in the island is earned in the services sector with financial and professional services accounting for just over half of the national income. Tourism and manufacturing are also major generators of income whilst the island's other traditional industries of agriculture and fishing now play a smaller role in the economy.

Under the terms of Protocol 3, the island has tariff-free access to EU markets for its goods.

The island's unemployment rate is approximately 0.5 per cent and price inflation is around 2.5 per cent per annum.

FINANCE

The budget for 2000–2001 provided for net revenue expenditure of £317 million. The principal sources of government revenue are taxes on income and expenditure. Income tax is payable at a rate of 14 per cent on the first £10,000 of taxable income for single resident individuals and 20 per cent on the balance, after personal allowances of £7,535. These bands are doubled for married couples. The rate of income tax is 14 per cent on the first £125,000 of taxable income of companies, rising to 20 per cent on the balance. Non-residents are charged tax at the rate of 20 per cent. By agreement with the British Government, the island keeps most of its rates of indirect taxation (VAT and duties) the same as those in the United Kingdom, but this agreement may be terminated by either party. However, VAT on tourist accommodation, property, repairs and renovations is charged at 5 per cent. A reciprocal agreement on national insurance benefits and pensions exists between the governments of the Isle of Man and the United Kingdom. Taxes are also charged on property (rates), but these are comparatively low.

The major government expenditure items are health, social security and education, which account for 60 per cent of the government budget. The island makes a voluntary annual contribution to the United Kingdom for defence and other external services.

The island has a special relationship with the European Union and neither contributes money to nor receives funds from the EU budget.

The Channel Islands

The Channel Islands, situated off the north-west coast of France (at distances of from ten to 30 miles), are the only portions of the Dukedom of Normandy still belonging to the Crown, to which they have been attached since the Norman Conquest of 1066. They were the only British territory to come under German occupation during the Second World War, following invasion on 30 June to 1 July 1940. The islands were relieved by British forces on 9 May 1945, and 9 May (Liberation Day) is now observed as a bank and public holiday.

The islands consist of Jersey (28,717 acres/11,630 ha), Guernsey (15,654 acres/6,340 ha), and the dependencies of Guernsey: Alderney (1,962 acres/795 ha), Brechou (74/30), Great Sark (1,035/419), Little Sark (239/97), Herm (320/130), Jethou (44/18) and Lihou (38/15) – a total of 48,083 acres/19,474 ha, or 75 sq. miles/194 sq. km. In 1996 the population of Jersey was 85,150; and of Guernsey, 58,681; Alderney, 2,147 and Sark, 575. The official languages are English and French but French is being supplanted by English, which is the language in daily use. In country districts of Jersey and Guernsey and throughout Sark a Norman-French *patois* is also in use, though to a declining extent.

GOVERNMENT

The islands are Crown dependencies with their own legislative assemblies (the States in Jersey, Guernsey and Alderney, and the Court of Chief Pleas in Sark), and systems of local administration and law, and their own courts. Acts passed by the States require the sanction of The Queen-in-Council. The British Government is responsible for defence and international relations. The Channel Islands have trading rights alone within the European Union; these rights do not include financial aid.

In both Bailiwicks the Lieutenant-Governor and Commander-in-Chief, who is appointed by the Crown, is the personal representative of The Queen and the channel of communication between the Crown (via the Privy Council) and the island's government.

The government of each Bailiwick is conducted by committees appointed by the States. Justice is administered by the Royal Courts of Jersey and Guernsey, each consisting of the Bailiff and 12 elected Jurats. The Bailiffs of Jersey and Guernsey, appointed by the Crown, are President of the States and of the Royal Courts of their respective islands.

Each Bailiwick constitutes a deanery under the jurisdiction of the Bishop of Winchester (*see* Index).

ECONOMY

A mild climate and good soil have led to the development of intensive systems of agriculture and horticulture, which form a significant part of the economy. Equally important are invisible earnings, principally from tourism and banking and finance, the low rate of income tax (20p in the £ in Jersey and Guernsey; no tax of any kind in Sark) and the absence of super-tax and death duties making the islands a popular tax-haven.

Principal exports are agricultural produce and flowers; imports are chiefly machinery, manufactured goods, food, fuel and chemicals. Trade with the UK is regarded as internal.

British currency is legal tender in the Channel Islands but each Bailiwick issues its own coins and notes (*see* page 617). They also issue their own postage stamps; UK stamps are not valid.

JERSEY

Lieutenant-Governor and Commander-in-Chief of Jersey, Chief Marshall Sir John Cheshire, KBE, CB, *apptd* 2001
Secretary and ADC, Lt.-Col. A. J. C. Woodrow, OBE, MC
Bailiff of Jersey, Sir Philip Bailhache, Kt.
Deputy Bailiff, M. C. St J. Birt, Esq
Attorney-General, W. J. Bailhache, QC, Esq
Receiver-General, Gp Capt. R. Green, OBE
Solicitor-General, Miss S. C. Nicolle, QC
Greffier of the States, Miss C. M. Newcombe
States Treasurer, Mr I. Black

FINANCE

Year to 31 Dec.	1999	2000
Revenue income	£478,161,000	£518,177,000
Revenue expenditure	405,162,000	446,605,000
Capital expenditure	79,687,000	51,861,000
Public debt	0	0

CHIEF TOWN – ΨSt Helier, on the south coast of Jersey
FLAG – A white field charged with a red saltire cross, and the arms of Jersey in the upper centre

GUERNSEY AND DEPENDENCIES

Lieutenant-Governor and Commander-in-Chief of the Bailiwick of Guernsey and its Dependencies, HE Lieutenant-General. Sir John Foley, KCB, OBE, MC, *apptd* 2000
Secretary and ADC, Colonel R. H. Graham, MBE
Bailiff of Guernsey, de V. G. Carey
Deputy Bailiff, A. C. K. Day, QC
HM Procureur and Receiver-General, G. R. Rowland, QC
HM Comptroller, H. E. Roberts, QC
States Supervisor, M. J. Brown

FINANCE

Year to 31 Dec.	1999	2000
Revenue	£238,216,000	£257,600,000
Expenditure	190,846,000	204,400,000

CHIEF TOWNS – ΨSt Peter Port, on the east coast of Guernsey; St Anne on Alderney
FLAG – White, bearing a red cross of St George, with a gold cross overall in the centre

ALDERNEY

President of the States, J. Kay-Mouat, OBE
Clerk of the States, D. V. Jenkins
Clerk of the Court, Mrs S. Kelly

SARK

Seigneur of Sark, J. M. Beaumont, OBE
The Seneschal, Lieutenant-Colonel R. J. Guille, MBE
The Greffier, J. P. Hamon

OTHER DEPENDENCIES

Herm and Lihou are owned by the States of Guernsey; Herm is leased. Jethou is leased by the Crown to the States of Guernsey and is sub-let by the States. Brecqhou is within the legislative and judicial territory of Sark.

The Environment

INTERNATIONAL CONVENTIONS

Legislation and strategies to protect the environment in the UK are driven by the requirements of international conventions and protocols (of which there are over 50) and European Directives (of which there are over 300), as well as the desires of the UK government. The Environment Agency, the Scottish Environment Protection Agency and the Environment and Heritage Service for Northern Ireland are responsible for regulation.

EUROPEAN UNION MEASURES

The European Union's (EU) work is developed based on its Environmental Action Programme. The Sixth Environmental Action Programme, *Environment 2010: Our Future, Our Choice*, sets the programme to 2010. It proposes five priority areas: improving the implementation of existing legislation; integration of environmental concerns into other policies; working more closely with the market; empowering private citizens and helping them to change behaviour; and taking account of the environment in land-use planning and management decisions.

SUSTAINABLE DEVELOPMENT AND LOCAL AGENDA 21

The environmental agenda in the UK, both at a business and government level is moving forward to address sustainability which incorporates social, environmental and economic development. The most commonly used definition is 'development that meets the needs of the present without compromising the ability of future generations to meet their own needs'.

The UK published its first national sustainable development strategy in 1994 and its first set of sustainable development indicators in 1996. The latest strategy *A Better Quality of Life* was published in May 1999. It establishes a framework for integrating social, environmental and economic policies to meet four objectives: social progress, to protect the environment, prudent use of natural resources, and to maintain high and stable levels of economic growth and employment. The strategy contains 14 headline indicators, which are backed by a further 150, against which progress in the UK is measured. Leading businesses are beginning to use the indicators in assessing and reporting their own progress towards achieving sustainability. Sustainable development indicators are also being developed for Scotland.

Local authorities also have a role to play in sustainable development. Under Local Agenda 21, which came out of the UN Conference on Environment and Development in Rio, Brazil in 1992, local authorities are to draw up sustainable development strategies for their areas. Although not a statutory obligation, the government wants all councils to have adopted Local Agenda 21 by the end of 2000. Currently some 93% have adopted it. Partnership between regional and local councils is needed. Regional Development Agencies will take Local Agenda 21 strategies into account in sustainable development frameworks for each English region. The EU is also developing a sustainable development strategy.

WASTE

Waste policy in the UK follows a number of principles: the waste hierarchy of reduce, reuse, recycle, dispose; the proximity principle of disposing of waste close to its generation; and national self sufficiency.

Directives from Europe are playing an increasingly important role in driving UK policy particularly regarding commercial and industrial waste: the recent Landfill Directive sets stringent targets for reducing the amount of waste sent to landfill and the planned integrated products policy aims to internalise the environmental costs of products throughout their life-cycle through market forces, by focusing on eco-design and incentives to ensure increased demand for greener products. Greater responsibility for end-of-life products is already being addressed with the producer responsibility directives for packaging waste, which came into force in the UK in 1997, and the end-of-life-vehicle directive, which entered into force in December last year.

In May 2000, the Waste Strategy for England and Wales was published. It aims to tackle the amount of waste produced; increase recycling rates through statutory targets for local authorities; reduce the amount of waste sent to landfill; and develop markets and end-uses for secondary materials. To meet the targets the public and local authorities will have to vastly increase their current recycling rates.

Scotland also has a national waste strategy which aims to encourage more effective use of natural resources through greater efficiency, waste minimisation, recycling and increased value recovery from waste. The Northern Ireland waste strategy is a framework to help achieve the goal of sustainable waste management and meet targets for the diversion of waste from landfill.

CLIMATE CHANGE AND AIR POLLUTION

The UK's response to climate change is driven by the Framework Convention on Climate Change. This is a binding agreement that has been signed and ratified by 184 countries. It was ratified in the UK in December 1993 and came into force in March 1994. It is intended to reduce risks of global warming by limiting 'greenhouse' gas emissions.

Progress towards the convention's targets are assessed at regular conferences. At Kyoto in 1997, a protocol (the Kyoto Protocol) to the convention was adopted. It covers the six main greenhouse gases - carbon dioxide, methane, nitrous oxide, hydrofluorocarbons (HFCs), perfluorocarbons (PFCs), and sulphur hexafloride. Under the protocol industrialised countries agreed to legally binding targets for cutting emissions of greenhouse gases by 5.2% below 1990 levels by 2008-2012. EU members agreed to an 8% reduction and the UK's target is a 12.5% cut.

The protocol set three ways (Kyoto mechanisms) for countries to increase the flexibility and reduce the cost of making emission cuts: the clean development mechanism, emissions trading and joint implementation. The sixth Conference of the Parties in The Hague, Netherlands in November 2000 was suspended. It had been hoped that the methodology of using sinks (such as offsetting emissions by growing forests) and a compliance regime to ensure countries meet their targets would be clarified. The talks are to resume in Bonn, Germany in July. Informal talks have been held since the failure of the November meeting, including a meeting in April that focused on the US statement that the Bush administration opposed the Kyoto Protocol.

In November 2000, a climate change programme was published which sets out how the UK intends to meet its Kyoto target and progress towards its domestic goal of a 20% cut in carbon dioxide emissions by 2010, some of the policies mentioned are already in place. The proposed measures include: a climate change levy which came into effect in April applied to sales of electricity, coal, natural gas, and liquified petroleum gas to the business and public sectors; agreements with energy intensive sectors to meet targets; integrated pollution prevention and control (see below); cutting transport congestion and pollution; energy efficiency standards of performance requiring electricity and gas suppliers to help domestic consumers save energy; better countryside management; cuts in fertiliser use; new targets for improving energy management of public buildings; and emissions trading.

The voluntary greenhouse gas emissions trading scheme is expected to start this year. Participants will agree to cap on emissions and can meet that cap, or reduce emission to below the cap and sell the excess allowance, or let emissions remain over the cap and buy allowances.

The government has also committed £50m to support offshore wind and biomass, while the EU is proposing a directive on renewable energy sources. This would expect the UK to increase its share of renewable energy sources from 1.7% to 10%. The Scottish climate change programme was published in November.

Other conventions covering air pollution include the Convention on Long Range Transboundary Air Pollution which was adopted in 1979 and came into force in 1993. Protocols to this convention cover various pollutants, such as sulphur and nitrogen oxides.

The UK has also developed its own policy on air pollution. The Environmental Protection Act 1990 established two regimes: integrated pollution control (IPC) to regulate emissions to any environmental medium from certain industrial processes and local air pollution control to regulate emissions to air from smaller processes. The recent European Integrated Pollution Prevention and Control (IPPC) Directive was largely based on the UK's IPC regime. This new regime came into force in the UK in August 2000 (and Scotland in September) after much deliberation and wrangling over details. Although IPPC is very similar to the UK's IPC it will cover many more installations and will include returning sites to a satisfactory state on closure, using energy efficiently and noise and vibration regulation.

The first National Air Quality Strategy was published in 1997 and was revised in January 2000. The strategy sets air quality objectives for the main pollutants (benzene, 1-3, butadiene, carbon monoxide, lead, nitrogen dioxide, sulphur dioxide, ozone, and particulates) to be met by 2003-2008.

Under the strategy, all district and unitary authorities have a duty to review air quality, including likely future air quality, in their areas. This is accompanied by an assessment of whether air quality objectives (set in the strategy) are being, or are likely to be, met. If authorities find that any part of their area breaches the objectives, an air quality management area must be declared and an action plan drawn up for improvements.

WATER

Water quality targets are set at both EU and UK levels for drinking water sources, wastewater discharges, rivers, coastal water and bathing water.

The EU's water framework directive, which entered into force in December, has an objective to achieve 'good water status' throughout the EU by 2015. Consultations later this year and next year will focus on how the directive will be implemented in the UK and on some initial draft regulations.

The EC Bathing Water Directive sets standards for bathing waters. This applies to 391 coastal and nine inland bathing waters in the UK. This directive is over 25 years old and a new version is being drafted.

The Environment Agency sets river quality objectives for each stretch of river. A survey, published last year, shows that 92% of rivers and canals are classified as of 'good' or 'fair' quality.

Water quality is currently protected through licensing abstraction and regulating discharges. Consents to discharge sewage and industrial effluent are regulated under the Water Resources Act 1991 and the Environmental Protection Act 1990 through its IPC regime and the IPPC regime. Discharge consents are based on the river quality objectives and relevant EU directives and specify the concentration and quantity permitted.

The European Urban Waste Water Treatment Directive sets minimum standards for sewage treatment before discharge into coastal waters with the levels of treatment needed depending on the sensitivity of the receiving water. In 1999 the government set more stringent UK targets for all significant coastal discharges to have a minimum of secondary treatment by 2005.

SELECTED UK TARGETS

Global atmosphere

- Reduce greenhouse gas emissions to 12.5% below 1990 levels by 2010
- Reduce carbon dioxide emissions to 20% below 1990 levels by 2010

Air quality

- Reduce sulphur dioxide emissions by 63% based on 1990 levels by 2010
- Reduce emissions of nitrogen oxides by 41% based on 1990 levels by 2010
- Reduce emissions of volatile organic compounds by 40% based on 1990 levels by 2010
- Reduce ammonia emissions by 17% based on 1990 levels by 2010

Fresh water and sea

- 97% of bathing waters to meet European directive standards consistently by 2005
- Provide secondary treatment for discharges above 15,000 population equivalent by 31 March 2002
- Provide secondary treatment for all significant coastal discharges (over 2,000 population equivalent) by 2005

Waste

- Reduce industrial and commercial waste going to landfill by 85% of 1998 levels by 2005
- Recover 40% of municipal waste by 2005, 45% by 2010 and 67% by 2015
- Recycle or compost 25% of household waste by 2005, 30% by 2010 and 33% by 2015
- Reduce biodegradable waste sent to landfill to 75% of 1995 levels by 2010, 50% by 2013 and 35% by 2020

- Ensure 60% of UK newspaper feedstock content is waste paper by end of 2001, 65% by end of 2003 and 70% by end of 2006
- The 2001 recovery and recycling target for packaging waste set at 56%, up from the 2000 target of 45%
- Proposed re-use and recovery of 85% of the mass of end-of-life vehicles with a minimum of 80% recycling by 2006, 95% and 85% by 2015
- EU target to reduce the amount of waste going to final disposal by 20% by 2010 and 50% by 2050

Land

- Ensure 60% of all new housing is built on re-used sites

CONTACTS

ADVISORY COMMITTEE ON BUSINESS AND THE ENVIRON-MENT, Zone 6/D12, Ashdown House, 123 Victoria Street, London SW1E 6DE. Tel: 020-7890 6278 Web: www.environment.detr.gov.uk/acbe/index.htm
DEPARTMENT FOR ENVIRONMENT, FOOD AND RURAL AFFAIRS, Nobel House, 17 Smith Square, London SW1P 3JR. Tel: 020-7238 3000
Web: www.defra.gov.uk
ENVIRONMENT AGENCY, Rivers House, Waterside Drive, Aztec West, Almondsbury, Bristol BS12 4UD
Tel: 01454-624400
Web: www.environment-agency.gov.uk
ENVIROWISE, THE ENVIRONMENT AND ENERGY HELP-LINE. Tel: 0800 585794
Web: www.environwise.gov.uk

EUROPEAN ENVIRONMENT AGENCY, Kongens Nytorv 6, DK-1050 Copenhagen K, Denmark
Tel: Copenhagen 3336 7100
Web: www.eea.eu.int
LOCAL AGENDA 21, Improvement and Development Agency, Layden House, 76-78 Turnmill Street, London EC1M 5QU
Tel: 020-7296 6599
Web: www.la21-uk.org.uk
ROYAL COMMISSION ON ENVIRONMENTAL POLLUTION, Steel House, 11 Tothill Street, London SW1H 9RE
Tel: 020-7273 6635
Web: www.rcep.org.uk
SCOTTISH ENVIRONMENTAL PROTECTION AGENCY, Erskine Court, Castle Business Park, Stirling FK9 4TR
Tel: 01786-457700
Web: www.sepa.org.uk
SUSTAINABLE DEVELOPMENT COMMISSION, 5th Floor, Romney House, Tufton Street, London SW1P 3RA
Tel: 020-7944 4964
Web: www.sd-commission.gov.uk
SUSTAINABLE DEVELOPMENT UNIT, 5/B2 Ashdown House, 123 Victoria Street, London SW1E 6DE
Tel: 020-7944 6485
Web: www.sustainable-development .gov.uk
UN COMMISSION ON SUSTAINABLE DEVELOPMENT, Division for Sustainable Development, 2 UN Plaza, Room DC2-2220, New York, NY 10017, USA.
Tel: New York 963 3170
Web: www.un.org/esa/sustdev

Conservation and Heritage

Conservation of the Countryside

NATIONAL PARKS

ENGLAND AND WALES

The ten National Parks of England and Wales were set up under the provisions of the National Parks and Access to the Countryside Act 1949 to conserve and protect scenic landscapes from inappropriate development and to provide access to the land for public enjoyment.

The Countryside Agency (established on 1 April 1999 from the merger of the Countryside Commission and the Rural Development Commission) is the statutory body which has the power to designate National Parks in England, and the Countryside Council for Wales is responsible for National Parks in Wales. Designations in England are confirmed by the Secretary of State for Environment, Food and Rural Affairs and those in Wales by the National Assembly for Wales. The designation of a National Park does not affect the ownership of the land or remove the rights of the local community. The majority of the land in the National Parks is owned by private landowners (74 per cent) or by bodies such as the National Trust (7 per cent) and the Forestry Commission (7 per cent). The National Park Authorities own only 2.3 per cent of the land.

The Environment Act 1995 replaced the existing National Park boards and committees with free-standing National Park Authorities (NPAs). NPAs are the sole local planning authorities for their areas and as such influence land use and development, and deal with planning applications. Their duties include conserving and enhancing the natural beauty, wildlife and cultural heritage of the National Parks; promoting opportunities for public understanding and enjoyment of the National Parks; and fostering the economic and social well-being of the communities within National Parks. The NPAs publish management plans as statements of their policies and appoint their own officers and staff.

Membership of the NPAs differs slightly between England and Wales. In England membership is split between representatives of the constituent local authorities and members appointed by the Secretary of State (of whom one half, minus one, are nominated by the parish councils in the park), with the local authority representatives in a majority of one. The Countryside Agency advises the Secretary of State on appointments not nominated by the parish councils. In Wales two-thirds of NPA members are appointed by the constituent local authorities and one-third by the National Assembly for Wales, advised by the Countryside Council for Wales.

Central government provides 75 per cent of the funding for the parks through the National Park Grant. The remaining 25 per cent is supplied by the local authorities concerned. Approved net expenditure for all National Parks in 2000–1 was £27,920,800 for England and £8,712,000 for Wales.

The National Parks (with date designation confirmed) are:

BRECON BEACONS (1957), Powys (66 per cent)/ Carmarthenshire/Rhondda, Cynon and Taff/Merthyr Tydfil/Blaenau Gwent/Monmouthshire, 1,351 sq. km/ 522 sq. miles – The park is centred on the Beacons, Pen y Fan, Corn Du and Cribyn, but also includes the valley of the Usk, the Black Mountains to the east and the Black Mountain to the west. There are information centres at Brecon, Craig-y-nos Country Park, Abergavenny and Llandovery, a study centre at Danywenallt and a day visitor centre near Libanus.
Information Office, 7 Glamorgan Street, Brecon, Powys LD3 7DP. Tel: 01874-624437. *National Park Officer*, C. Gledhill

DARTMOOR (1951 and 1994), Devon, 954 sq. km/368 sq. miles – The park consists of moorland and rocky granite tors, and is rich in prehistoric remains. There are information centres at Newbridge, Tavistock, Bovey Tracey, Steps Bridge, Princetown and Postbridge.
Information Office, Parke, Haytor Road, Bovey Tracey, Devon TQ13 9JQ. Tel: 01626-832093. *National Park Officer*, N. Atkinson

EXMOOR (1954), Somerset (71 per cent)/Devon, 693 sq. km/268 sq. miles – Exmoor is a moorland plateau inhabited by wild ponies and red deer. There are many ancient remains and burial mounds. There are information centres at Lynmouth, County Gate, Dulverton and Combe Martin.
Information Office, Exmoor House, Dulverton, Somerset TA22 9HL. Tel: 01398-322322. *National Park Officer*, N. Stone

LAKE DISTRICT (1951), Cumbria, 2,292 sq. km/885 sq. miles – The Lake District includes England's highest mountains (Scafell Pike, Helvellyn and Skiddaw) but it is most famous for its glaciated lakes. There are information centres at Keswick, Waterhead, Hawkshead, Seatoller, Bowness, Grasmere, Coniston, Glenridding and Pooley Bridge, an information van at Gosforth and a park centre at Brockhole, Windermere.
Information Office, Murley Moss, Oxenholme Road, Kendal, Cumbria, LA9 7RL. Tel: 01539-724555. *National Park Officer*, P. Tiplady

NORTHUMBERLAND (1956), Northumberland, 1,049 sq. km/405 sq. miles – The park is an area of hill country stretching from Hadrian's Wall to the Scottish Border. There are information centres at Ingram, Once Brewed, Rothbury, Housesteads, Harbottle and Kielder, and an information caravan at Cawfields.
Information Office, Eastburn, South Park, Hexham, Northumberland NE46 1BS. Tel: 01434-605555. *National Park Officer*, G. Taylor

NORTH YORK MOORS (1952), North Yorkshire (96 per cent)/Redcar and Cleveland, 1,436 sq. km/554 sq. miles – The park consists of woodland and moorland, and includes the Hambleton Hills and the Cleveland Way. There are information centres at Danby, Pickering, Sutton Bank, Ravenscar, Helmsley and Hutton-le-Hole, and a day study centre at Danby.
Information Office, The Old Vicarage, Bondgate, Helmsley, York YO6 5BP. Tel: 01439-770657. *National Park Officer*, D. Arnold-Forster

PEAK DISTRICT (1951), Derbyshire (64 per cent)/ Staffordshire/South Yorkshire/Cheshire/West Yorkshire/Greater Manchester, 1,438 sq. km/555 sq. miles – The Peak District includes the gritstone moors of the 'Dark Peak' and the limestone dales of the 'White Peak'. There are information centres at Bakewell, Edale, Fairholmes and Castleton, and information points at Torside (in the Longdendale Valley) and at Hartington (former station).
Information Office, Aldern House, Baslow Road, Bakewell, Derbyshire DE45 1AE. Tel: 01629-816200. *National Park Officer*, C. Harrison
PEMBROKESHIRE COAST (1952 and 1995), Pembrokeshire, 584 sq. km/225 sq. miles – The park includes cliffs, moorland and a number of islands, including Skomer. There are information centres at Tenby, St David's, Pembroke, Kilgetty and Haverfordwest.
Information Office, Winch Lane, Haverfordwest, Pembrokeshire SA61 1PY. Tel: 01437-764636. *National Park Officer*, N. Wheeler
SNOWDONIA (1951), Gwynedd/Conwy, 2,142 sq. km/827 sq. miles – Snowdonia is an area of deep valleys and rugged mountains. There are information centres at Aberdyfi, Bala, Betws y Coed, Blaenau Ffestiniog, Conwy, Harlech, Dolgellau and Llanberis.
Information Office, Penrhyndeudraeth, Gwynedd LL48 6LF. Tel: 01766-770274. *National Park Officer*, I. Huws
YORKSHIRE DALES (1954), North Yorkshire (88 per cent)/ Cumbria, 1,769 sq. km/683 sq. miles – The Yorkshire Dales are composed primarily of limestone overlaid in places by millstone grit. The three peaks of Ingleborough, Whernside and Pen-y-Ghent are within the park. There are information centres at Clapham, Grassington, Hawes, Aysgarth Falls, Malham and Sedbergh.
Information Office, Yorebridge House, Bainbridge, Leyburn, N. Yorks DL8 3EE. Tel: 01969-650456. *National Park Officer*, H. Hancock

Two other areas considered to have equivalent status to national parks are the Broads and the New Forest. The Broads Authority, a special statutory authority, was established in 1989 to develop, conserve and manage the Norfolk and Suffolk Broads. The Government declared in 1992 its intention of giving the New Forest a status equivalent to that of a National Park by declaring it an 'area of national significance'.

THE BROADS (1989), Norfolk, 303 sq. km/117 sq. miles – The Broads are located between Norwich and Great Yarmouth on the flood plains of the five rivers flowing through the area to the sea. The area is one of fens, winding waterways, woodland and marsh. The 40 or so broads are man-made, and are connected to the rivers by dykes, providing over 200 km of navigable waterways. There are information centres at Beccles, Hoveton, North-west Tower (Yarmouth), Ranworth and Toad Hole.
Broads Authority, Thomas Harvey House, 18 Colegate, Norwich NR3 1BQ. Tel: 01603-610734. *Chief Executive*, J. Packman
THE NEW FOREST, Hampshire, 376 sq. km/145 sq. miles – The forest has been protected since 1079 when it was declared a royal hunting forest. The area consists of forest, ancient woodland and heathland. Much of the Forest is managed by the Forestry Commission, which provides several camp-sites. The main villages are Brockenhurst, Burley and Lyndhurst, which has a visitor centre.

The New Forest Committee, 4 High Street, Lyndhurst, Hants SO43 7BD. Tel: 023-8028 2249. *Chief Executive*, Ted Johnson

SCOTLAND AND NORTHERN IRELAND

The National Parks and Access to the Countryside Act 1949 dealt only with England and Wales and made no provision for Scotland or Northern Ireland.

On 9 August 2000, The National Parks (Scotland) Bill received Royal Assent, providing the Parliament with the ability to create National Parks in Scotland in any area deemed to be appropriate. The first Scottish National Park, Loch Lomond and the Trossachs, is expected to be operational by May 2002, with the Cairngorms following a year later.

There is power to designate National Parks in Northern Ireland under the Amenity Lands Act 1965 and the Nature Conservation and Amenity Lands Order (Northern Ireland) 1985.

AREAS OF OUTSTANDING NATURAL BEAUTY

ENGLAND AND WALES

Under the National Parks and Access to the Countryside Act 1949, provision was made for the designation of Areas of Outstanding Natural Beauty (AONBs) by the Countryside Commission. The Countryside Agency is now responsible for AONBs in England and since April 1991 the Countryside Council for Wales has been responsible for the Welsh AONBs. Designations in England are confirmed by the Secretary of State for Environment, Food and Rural Affairs and those in Wales by the National Assembly for Wales. The Countryside and Rights of Way Act 2000 provided for the creation of conservation boards for individual AONBs and placed greater responsibility on local authorities to protect them.

Although less emphasis is placed upon the provision of open-air enjoyment for the public than in the national parks, AONBs are areas which are no less beautiful and require the same degree of protection to conserve and enhance the natural beauty of the countryside. This includes protecting flora and fauna, geological and other landscape features. In AONBs planning and management responsibilities are split between county and district councils and the newly established conservation boards (where they exist); where unitary authorities exist in Wales, they have sole responsibility for planning and management. Several AONBs cross local authority boundaries. Finance for the AONBs is provided by grant-aid.

The 41 Areas of Outstanding Natural Beauty (with date of designation confirmed) are:

ANGLESEY (1967), Anglesey, 221 sq. km/85 sq. miles
ARNSIDE AND SILVERDALE (1972), Cumbria/Lancashire, 75 sq. km/29 sq. miles
BLACKDOWN HILLS (1991), Devon/Somerset, 370 sq. km/ 143 sq. miles
CANNOCK CHASE (1958), Staffordshire, 68 sq. km/26 sq. miles
CHICHESTER HARBOUR (1964), Hampshire/West Sussex, 74 sq. km/29 sq. miles
CHILTERNS (1965; extended 1990), Bedfordshire/ Hertfordshire/Buckinghamshire/Oxfordshire, 833 sq. km/322 sq. miles

CLWYDIAN RANGE (1985), Denbighshire/Flintshire, 157 sq. km/60 sq. miles

CORNWALL (1959; Camel estuary 1983), 958 sq. km/370 sq. miles

COTSWOLDS (1966; extended 1990), Gloucestershire/ Wiltshire/Warwickshire/ Worcestershire/Somerset, 2,038 sq. km/787 sq. miles

CRANBORNE CHASE AND WEST WILTSHIRE DOWNS (1983), Dorset/Hampshire/Somerset/Wiltshire, 983 sq. km/379 sq. miles

DEDHAM VALE (1970; extended 1978, 1991), Essex/ Suffolk, 90 sq. km/35 sq. miles

DORSET (1959), 1,129 sq. km/436 sq. miles

EAST DEVON (1963), 268 sq. km/103 sq. miles

EAST HAMPSHIRE (1962), 383 sq. km/148 sq. miles

FOREST OF BOWLAND (1964), Lancashire/North Yorkshire, 802 sq. km/310 sq. miles

GOWER (1956), Swansea, 188 sq. km/73 sq. miles

HIGH WEALD (1983), Kent/Surrey/East Sussex/West Sussex, 1,460 sq. km/564 sq. miles

HOWARDIAN HILLS (1987), North Yorkshire, 204 sq. km/ 79 sq. miles

ISLE OF WIGHT (1963), 189 sq. km/73 sq. miles

ISLES OF SCILLY (1976), 16 sq. km/6 sq. miles

KENT DOWNS (1968), 878 sq. km/339 sq. miles

LINCOLNSHIRE WOLDS (1973), 558 sq. km/215 sq. miles

LLEYNN (1957), Gwynedd, 161 sq. km/62 sq. miles

MALVERN HILLS (1959), Herefordshire/Worcestershire/ Gloucestershire, 105 sq. km/40 sq. miles

MENDIP HILLS (1972; extended 1989), Somerset, 198 sq. km/76 sq. miles

NIDDERDALE (1994), North Yorkshire, 603 sq. km/233 sq. miles

NORFOLK COAST (1968), 451 sq. km/174 sq. miles

NORTH DEVON (1960), 171 sq. km/66 sq. miles

NORTH PENNINES (1988), Cumbria/Durham/ Northumberland, 1,983 sq. km/766 sq. miles

NORTHUMBERLAND COAST (1958), 135 sq. km/52 sq. miles

QUANTOCK HILLS (1957), Somerset, 99 sq. km/38 sq. miles

SHROPSHIRE HILLS (1959), 804 sq. km/310 sq. miles

SOLWAY COAST (1964), Cumbria, 115 sq. km/44 sq. miles

SOUTH DEVON (1960), 337 sq. km/130 sq. miles

SOUTH HAMPSHIRE COAST (1967), 77 sq. km/30 sq. miles

SUFFOLK COAST AND HEATHS (1970), 403 sq. km/156 sq. miles

SURREY HILLS (1958), 419 sq. km/162 sq. miles

SUSSEX DOWNS (1966), 983 sq. km/379 sq. miles

TAMAR VALLEY (1995), Cornwall/Devon, 195 sq. km/115 sq. miles

NORTH WESSEX DOWNS (1972), Berkshire/Hampshire/ Oxfordshire/Wiltshire, 1,730 sq. km/668 sq. miles

WYE VALLEY (1971), Monmouthshire/Gloucestershire/ Herefordshire, 326 sq. km/126 sq. miles

NORTHERN IRELAND

The Department of the Environment for Northern Ireland, with advice from the Council for Nature Conservation and the Countryside, designates Areas of Outstanding Natural Beauty in Northern Ireland. At present there are nine and these cover a total area of approximately 284,948 hectares (704,121 acres).

ANTRIM COAST AND GLENS, Co. Antrim, 70,600 ha/ 174,452 acres

CAUSEWAY COAST, Co. Antrim, 4,200 ha/10,378 acres

LAGAN VALLEY, Co. Down, 2,072 ha/5,119 acres

LECALE COAST, Co. Down, 3,108 ha/7,679 acres

MOURNE, Co. Down, 57,012 ha/140,876 acres

NORTH DERRY, Co. Londonderry, 12,950 ha/31,999 acres

RING OF GULLION, Co. Armagh, 15,353 ha/37,938 acres

SPERRIN, Co. Tyrone/Co. Londonderry, 101,006 ha/ 249,585 acres

STRANGFORD LOUGH, Co. Down, 18,647 ha/46,077 acres

NATIONAL SCENIC AREAS

In Scotland, National Scenic Areas have a broadly equivalent status to AONBs. Scottish Natural Heritage recognises areas of national scenic significance. At mid 1999 there were 40, covering a total area of 1,001,800 hectares (2,475,448 acres).

Development within National Scenic Areas is dealt with by local authorities, who are required to consult Scottish Natural Heritage concerning certain categories of development. Disagreements between Scottish Natural Heritage and local authorities are referred to the Scottish Executive. Land management uses can also be modified in the interest of scenic conservation.

ASSYNT-COIGACH, Highland, 90,200 ha/222,884 acres

BEN NEVIS AND GLEN COE, Highland/Argyll and Bute/ Perth and Kinross, 101,600 ha/251,053 acres

CAIRNGORM MOUNTAINS, Highland/Aberdeenshire/ Moray, 67,200 ha/166,051 acres

CUILLIN HILLS, Highland, 21,900 ha/54,115 acres

DEESIDE AND LOCHNAGAR, Aberdeenshire/Angus, 40,000 ha/98,840 acres

DORNOCH FIRTH, Highland, 7,500 ha/18,532 acres

EAST STEWARTRY COAST, Dumfries and Galloway, 4,500 ha/11,119 acres

EILDON AND LEADERFOOT, Scottish Borders, 3,600 ha/ 8,896 acres

FLEET VALLEY, Dumfries and Galloway, 5,300 ha/13,096 acres

GLEN AFFRIC, Highland, 19,300 ha/47,690 acres

GLEN STRATHFARRAR, Highland, 3,800 ha/9,390 acres

HOY AND WEST MAINLAND, Orkney Islands, 14,800 ha/ 36,571 acres

JURA, Argyll and Bute, 21,800 ha/53,868 acres

KINTAIL, Highland, 15,500 ha/38,300 acres

KNAPDALE, Argyll and Bute, 19,800 ha/48,926 acres

KNOYDART, Highland, 39,500 ha/97,604 acres

KYLE OF TONGUE, Highland, 18,500 ha/45,713 acres

KYLES OF BUTE, Argyll and Bute, 4,400 ha/10,872 acres

LOCH NA KEAL, MULL, Argyll and Bute, 12,700 ha/31,382 acres

LOCH LOMOND, Argyll and Bute/Stirling/West Dunbartonshire, 27,400 ha/67,705 acres

LOCH RANNOCH AND GLEN LYON, Perth and Kinross/ Stirling, 48,400 ha/119,596 acres

LOCH SHIEL, Highland, 13,400 ha/33,111 acres

LOCH TUMMEL, Perth and Kinross, 9,200 ha/22,733 acres

LYNN OF LORN, Argyll and Bute, 4,800 ha/11,861 acres

MORAR, MOIDART AND ARDNAMURCHAN, Highland, 13,500 ha/33,358 acres

NORTH-WEST SUTHERLAND, Highland, 20,500 ha/ 50,655 acres

NITH ESTUARY, Dumfries and Galloway, 9,300 ha/22,980 acres

NORTH ARRAN, North Ayrshire, 23,800 ha/58,810 acres

RIVER EARN, Perth and Kinross, 3,000 ha/7,413 acres

RIVER TAY, Perth and Kinross, 5,600 ha/13,838 acres

ST KILDA, Western Isles, 900 ha/2,224 acres

SCARBA, LUNGA AND THE GARVELLACHS, Argyll and Bute, 1,900 ha/4,695 acres

SHETLAND, Shetland Islands, 11,600 ha/28,664 acres
SMALL ISLES, Highland, 15,500 ha/38,300 acres
SOUTH LEWIS, HARRIS AND NORTH UIST, Western Isles, 109,600 ha/270,822 acres
SOUTH UIST MACHAIR, Western Isles, 6,100 ha/15,073 acres
THE TROSSACHS, Stirling, 4,600 ha/11,367 acres
TROTTERNISH, Highland, 5,000 ha/12,355 acres
UPPER TWEEDDALE, Scottish Borders, 10,500 ha/25,945 acres
WESTER ROSS, Highland, 145,300 ha/359,036 acres

THE NATIONAL FOREST

The National Forest is being planted across 200 square miles of Derbyshire, Leicestershire and Staffordshire. About 30 million trees, of mixed species but mainly broadleaved, will be planted, and will eventually cover about one-third of the designated area. The project is funded by the Department for Environment, Food and Rural Affairs. It was developed in 1992–5 by the Countryside Commission and is now run by the National Forest Company, which was established in April 1995. Since then 4 million trees have been planted on 2,500 hectares of land across 480 sites. Under the National Forest Tender Scheme, anybody wishing to undertake a project can submit a competitive bid to the National Forest Company.
NATIONAL FOREST COMPANY, Enterprise Glade, Bath Lane, Moira, Swadlincote, Derbys DE12 6BD. Tel: 01283-551211. *Chief Executive*, Miss S. Bell, OBE

Nature Conservation Areas

SITES OF SPECIAL SCIENTIFIC INTEREST

Site of Special Scientific Interest (SSSI) is a legal notification applied to land in England, Scotland or Wales which English Nature (EN), Scottish Natural Heritage (SNH), or the Countryside Council for Wales (CCW) identifies as being of special interest because of its flora, fauna, geological or physiographical features. In some cases, SSSIs are managed as nature reserves.

EN, SNH and CCW must notify the designation of a SSSI to the local planning authority, every owner/occupier of the land, and the Secretary of State for Environment, Food and Rural Affairs, the First Minister in Scotland or the National Assembly for Wales. Forestry and agricultural departments and a number of other bodies are also informed of this notification.

Objections to the notification of a SSSI can be made and ultimately considered at a full meeting of the Council of EN or CCW. In Scotland an objection will be dealt with by the appropriate area board or the main board of SNH, depending on the nature of the objection. Unresolved objections on scientific grounds must be referred to the Advisory Committee on SSSI.

The protection of these sites depends on the co-operation of individual landowners and occupiers. Owner/occupiers must consult EN, SNH or CCW and gain written consent before they can undertake certain listed activities on the site. Funds are available through management agreements and grants to assist owners and

occupiers in conserving sites' interests. As a last resort a site can be purchased.

The number and area of SSSIs in Britain as at 1 March 2001 was:

	no.	Hectares	Acres
England	4,115	1,089,260	2,690,472
Scotland	1,449	957,710	2,366,469
Wales	1,008	224,733	555,090

NORTHERN IRELAND
In Northern Ireland 161 Areas of Special Scientific Interest (ASSIs) have been established by the Department of the Environment for Northern Ireland. These cover a total area of 83,465.476 hectares (206,243.19 acres).

NATIONAL NATURE RESERVES

National Nature Reserves are defined in the National Parks and Access to the Countryside Act 1949 as land designated for the study and preservation of flora and fauna, or of geological or physiographical features.

English Nature (EN), Scottish Natural Heritage (SNH) or the Countryside Council for Wales (CCW) can designate as a National Nature Reserve land which is being managed as a nature reserve under an agreement with one of the statutory nature conservation agencies; land held and managed by EN, SNH or CCW; or land held and managed as a nature reserve by another approved body. EN, SNH or CCW can make by-laws to protect reserves from undesirable activities; these are subject to confirmation by the Secretary of State for Environment, Food and Rural Affairs, the National Assembly for Wales or the Scottish Ministers in Scotland.

The number and area of National Nature Reserves in Britain as at 1 March 2001 was:

	no.	Hectares	Acres
England	208	83,560	206,393
Scotland	72	114,327	282,498
Wales	65	19,269	47,594

NORTHERN IRELAND
National Nature Reserves are established and managed by the Department of the Environment for Northern Ireland, with advice from the Council for Nature Conservation and the Countryside. There are 46 National Nature Reserves covering 4,322.1 hectares (10,676 acres).

LOCAL NATURE RESERVES

Local Nature Reserves are defined in the National Parks and Access to the Countryside Act 1949 as land designated for the study and preservation of flora and fauna, or of geological or physiographical features. The Act gives local authorities in England, Scotland and Wales the power to acquire, declare and manage local nature reserves in consultation with English Nature, Scottish Natural Heritage and the Countryside Council for Wales. Conservation trusts can also own and manage non-statutory local nature reserves.

The number and area of designated Local Nature Reserves in Britain as at 1 March 2001 was:

	no.	hectares	Acres
England	665	30,702	75,834
Scotland	34	9,382	23,183
Wales	51	4,701	11,611

An additional 38 km of linear trails are designated as Local Nature Reserves.

FOREST NATURE RESERVES

Forest Enterprise (an executive agency of the Forestry Commission) is responsible for the management of the Commission's forests. It has created 46 Forest Nature Reserves with the aim of protecting and conserving special forms of natural habitat, flora and fauna. There are about 300 SSSIs on the estates, some of which are also Nature Reserves.

Forest Nature Reserves extend in size from under 50 hectares (124 acres) to over 500 hectares (1,236 acres). The largest include the Black Wood of Rannoch, by Loch Rannoch; Cannop Valley Oakwoods, Forest of Dean; Culbin Forest, near Forres; Glen Affric, near Fort Augustus; Kylerhea, Skye; Pembrey, Carmarthen Bay; Starr Forest, in Galloway Forest Park; and Wyre Forest, near Kidderminster.

Forest Enterprise also manages 18 Caledonian Forest Reserves in Scotland. These reserves are intended to protect and expand 16,000 hectares of native oak and pine woods in the Scottish highlands.

NORTHERN IRELAND

There are 35 Forest Nature Reserves in Northern Ireland, covering 1,637 hectares (4,043 acres). They are designated and administered by the Forest Service, an agency of the Department of Agriculture and Rural Development for Northern Ireland. There are also 16 National Nature Reserves on Forest Service-owned property.

MARINE NATURE RESERVES

The Secretary of State for Environment, Food and Rural Affairs, the National Assembly for Wales and the Scottish Executive have the power to designate Marine Nature Reserves. English Nature, Scottish Natural Heritage and the Countryside Council for Wales select and manage these reserves. Marine Nature Reserves may be established in Northern Ireland under a 1985 Order.

Marine Nature Reserves provide protection for marine flora and fauna, and geological and physiographical features on land covered by tidal waters or parts of the sea in or adjacent to the UK. Reserves also provide opportunities for study and research.

The three statutory Marine Nature Reserves are:

LUNDY (1986), Bristol Channel
SKOMER (1990), Dyfed
STRANGFORD LOUGH (1995), Northern Ireland

Two other areas proposed for designation as reserves are: the Menai Strait, and Bardsey Island and part of the Llŷn peninsula, both in Wales.

A number of non-statutory marine reserves have been set up by conservation groups.

EUROPEAN MARINE SITES

The 1992 EC Habitats Directive and the 1979 Birds Directive allow the UK government to establish Special Areas of Conservation (SACs) on Special Protection Areas (SPA) for birds on land and at sea. Where the designated area includes sea or seashore it is described as a European marine site. The UK Marine SACs project is a demonstration initiative, funded partly by the EU, to establish management schemes for twelve of the marine SACs in the UK.

582

World Heritage Sites

The Convention Concerning the Protection of the World Cultural and Natural Heritage was adopted by UNESCO in 1972 and ratified by the UK in 1984. By May 2000 the convention had been ratified by 156 states. The convention provides for the identification, protection and conservation of cultural and natural sites of outstanding universal value.

Cultural sites may be:
– monuments
– groups of buildings
– sites of historic, aesthetic, archaeological, scientific, ethnologic or anthropologic value
– historic areas of towns
– 'cultural landscapes', i.e. sites whose characteristics are marked by significant interactions between human populations and their natural environment

Natural sites may be:
– those with remarkable physical, biological or geological formations
– those with outstanding universal value from the point of view of science, conservation or natural beauty
– the habitat of threatened species and plants

Governments which are party to the convention nominate sites in their country for inclusion in the World Cultural and Natural Heritage List. Nominations are considered by the World Heritage Committee, an inter-governmental committee composed of 21 representatives of the parties to the convention. The committee is advised by the International Council on Monuments and Sites (ICOMOS) and the International Union for the Conservation of Nature (IUCN). ICOMOS evaluates and reports on proposed cultural sites and IUCN on proposed natural sites. The International Centre for the Study of the Preservation and Restoration of Cultural Property (ICCROM) provides the committee with expert advice on monument restoration. The Department for Culture, Media and Sport represents the UK government in matters relating to the convention.

A prerequisite for inclusion in the World Cultural and Natural Heritage List is the existence of an effective legal protection system in the country in which the site is situated (e.g. listing, conservation areas and planning controls in the United Kingdom) and a detailed management plan to ensure the conservation of the site. Inclusion in the list does not confer any greater degree of protection on the site than that offered by the national protection framework.

If a site is considered to be in serious danger of decay or damage the committee may add it to a complementary list, the World Heritage in Danger List. Sites on this list may benefit from particular attention or emergency measures.

Financial support for the conservation of sites on the World Cultural and Natural Heritage List is provided by the World Heritage Fund. This is administered by the World Heritage Committee, which determines the financial and technical aid to be allocated. The fund's income is derived from the obligatory contributions of the parties to the convention, amounting to 1 per cent of their contribution to UNESCO. The fund may also receive voluntary contributions from the parties to the convention, donations from institutions or individuals, and income from national and international promotional activities.

DESIGNATED SITES

As at December 2000 there were 690 sites in 122 countries on the World Cultural and Natural Heritage List. Of these, 17 were in the United Kingdom and three in British overseas territories; 15 were listed for their cultural significance (†) and five for their natural significance (*).

United Kingdom
†Bath – the city
†Blaenarvon, Wales
†Blenheim Palace and park, Oxfordshire
†Canterbury Cathedral, St Augustine's Abbey, St Martin's Church, Kent
†Castle and town walls of King Edward I, north Wales – Beaumaris, Anglesey, Caernarfon Castle, Conwy Castle, Harlech Castle
†Durham Cathedral and Castle
†Edinburgh Old and New Towns
*Giant's Causeway and Causeway coast, Co. Antrim
†Greenwich, London – maritime Greenwich, including the Royal Naval College, Old Royal Observatory, Queen's House, town centre
†Hadrian's Wall, northern England
†Heart of Neolithic Orkney
†Ironbridge Gorge, Shropshire – the world's first iron bridge and other early industrial sites
*St Kilda, Western Isles
†Stonehenge, Avebury and related megalithic sites, Wiltshire
†Studley Royal Park, Fountains Abbey, St Mary's Church, N. Yorkshire
†Tower of London
†Westminster Abbey, Palace of Westminster, St Margaret's Church, London

British Overseas Territories
*Henderson Island, Pitcairn Islands, South Pacific Ocean
*Gough Island wildlife reserve (part of Tristan da Cunha), South Atlantic Ocean
*St George town and related fortifications, Bermuda

BUILDINGS, MONUMENTS AND SITES DIVISION, Department for Culture, Media and Sport, 2-4 Cockspur Street, London SW1Y 5DH. Tel: 020-7211 6909
WORLD HERITAGE CENTRE, UNESCO, 7 place de Fontenoy, 75352 Paris, France. Tel: Paris 4568 1876; Email wh-info@unesco.org
INTERNATIONAL CENTRE FOR THE STUDY OF THE PRESERVATION AND RESTORATION OF CULTURAL PROPERTY (ICCROM), Via di San Michele 13, I-00153 Rome, Italy. Tel: Rome 585531
INTERNATIONAL COUNCIL ON MONUMENTS AND SITES (ICOMOS), 10 Barley Mow Passage, London W4 4PH. Tel. 020-8994 6477
INTERNATIONAL UNION FOR THE CONSERVATION OF NATURE (IUCN), UK Committee, c/o 36 Kingfisher Court, Hambridge Road, Newbury, Berks RG14 5SJ. Telephone: 01635-522925

Conservation of wildlife and habitats

The UK is party to a number of international conventions.

RAMSAR CONVENTION

The 1971 Ramsar Convention on Wetlands of International Importance especially as Waterfowl Habitat, entered into force in the UK in May 1976. By May 2001 124 countries were party to the convention.

The aim of the convention is the conservation and wise use of wetlands and their flora and fauna, especially waterfowl. Governments that are party to the convention must designate wetlands and include wetland conservation considerations in their land-use planning. A total of 1,069 wetland sites, totalling 81.2 million hectares have been designated for inclusion in the List of Wetlands of International Importance. The UK currently has 161 designated sites covering 805,669 hectares. The member countries meet every three years to assess the progress of the convention. The next meeting will be held in Spain next November.

The UK has set targets under its Ramsar Strategic Plan, 1997-2002. Progress towards these is monitored by the UK Ramsar Committee, known as the Joint Working Party. The UK and the Republic of Ireland have established a formal protocol to ensure common monitoring standards for waterbirds in the two countries.
RAMSAR CONVENTION BUREAU, Rue Mauverney 28,
    CH-1196 Gland, Switzerland. Tel: Gland 9990170.
    Web: www.ramsar.org

BIODIVERSITY

There is much synergy between the Ramsar Convention and the 1992 Convention on Biological Diversity. In 1996 the Ramsar Secretariat became a lead partner in implementing activities under the Convention on Biological Diversity with joint work plans. The UK ratified the Convention on Biological Diversity in June 1994. There are 180 parties to the convention.

The objectives are the conservation of biological diversity, the sustainable use of its components and the fair and equitable sharing of the benefits arising out of the use of genetic resources. There are thematic work programmes addressing marine and coastal, forest, inland waters, dry land, and sub-humid land.

The UK published its own Biodiversity Action Plan in 1994. A report from the UK Biodiversity Steering Group, published in 1995, identified some 400 priority species and 38 priority habitats, requiring urgent action.

A report on the plan's first five years, published in March, made a number of recommendations including to support actions for conservation of species and habitats at UK, county and local levels, and to enhance access to biological information. Individual action plans have been published for most areas of the UK.
THE BIODIVERSITY ACTION PLAN SECRETARIAT,
    European Wildlife Division, Department of the
    Environment Transport and the Regions, Room 902D,
    Tollgate House, Houlton Street, Bristol, BS2 9DJ.
    Tel: Bristol 987 8974. Web: www.ukbap.org.uk

CITIES

The 1973 Convention on International Trade in Endangered Species of Wild Fauna and Flora (CITES) came into force in the UK in July 1975. Currently 152 countries are members. The countries party to the convention ban commercial international trade in an agreed list of endangered species and regulate and monitor trade in others species that might become endangered. The convention covers around 30,000 species.

The Conference of the Parties to CITES meets every two to three years to review the convention's implementation

The Global Wildlife Division at the Department of the Environment, Transport and the Regions carries out the government's responsibilities under CITES and the Bonn Convention on the Conservation of Migratory Species of Wild Animals
CITES SECRETARIAT, 15 Chemin des Anemones,
    CH-1219 Châtelaine, Geneva, Switzerland.
    Tel: Geneva 917 8139/8140.
    Web: www:international.fws.gov/cites/cites.html

BONN CONVENTION

The 1979 Convention on Conservation of Migratory Species of Wild Animals came into force in the UK in October 1979. By May 2001 70 parties were party to the convention.

It requires the protection of listed endangered migratory species and encourages international agreements covering these and other threatened species. International agreements can range from legally-binding treaties to less formal memoranda of understanding.

Nine agreements have been concluded to date under the convention. They aim to conserve: bats in Europe; cetaceans of the Mediterranean and Black Seas; small cetaceans of the Baltic and North Seas; seals in the Wadden Sea; African-Eurasian migratory waterbirds; the Siberian Crane; the Slender-billed Curlew; marine turtles; and middle-European great bustards.

Further agreements are being developed for a wide range of migratory species, including Sahelo-Saharan ungulates and albatrosses of the southern hemisphere.
UNEP/CMS SECRETARIAT, United Nations Premises in
    Bonn, Martin-Luther-King Strasse 8, D-53175.
    Tel: Bonn 815 2401/2. Web: www.wcmc.org.uk/cms

BERN CONVENTION

The 1979 Bern Convention on the Conservation of European Wildlife and Natural Habitats came into force in the UK in June 1982. Over 40 countries are party to the convention and a number of other states attend meetings as observers.

The aims are to conserve wild flora and fauna and their natural habitats, especially where this requires the co-operation of several countries, and to promote such co-operation. The convention gives particular emphasis to endangered and vulnerable species.

All parties to the convention must promote national conservation policies and take account of the conservation of wild flora and fauna when setting planning and development policies.
SECRETARIAT OF THE BERN CONVENTION STANDING
    COMMITTEE, Council of Europe, F-67075 Strasbourg
    Cedex, France. Tel: Strasbourg 8841 3476.
    Web: www.nature.coe.int

EUROPEAN WILDLIFE TRADE REGULATION

The Council (EC) Regulation on the Protection of Species of Wild Fauna and Flora by Regulating Trade Therein came into force in the UK on 1 June 1997. It is

584 Conservation and Heritage

intended to standardise wildlife trade regulations across Europe and to improve the application of CITES. Approximately 30,000 plant and animal species are protected under the regulation.

UK LEGISLATION

The Wildlife and Countryside Act 1981 gives legal protection to a wide range of wild animals and plants. Subject to parliamentary approval, the Secretary of State for the Environment, Food and Rural Affairs may vary the animals and plants given legal protection. The most recent variation of Schedules 5 and 8 came into effect in March and April 1998.

Under Section 9 and Schedule 5 of the Act it is illegal without a licence to kill, injure, take, possess or sell any of the listed animals (whether alive or dead) and to disturb its place of shelter and protection or to destroy that place.

Under Section 13 and Schedule 8 of the Act it is illegal without a licence to pick, uproot, sell or destroy any of the listed plants and, unless authorised, to uproot any wild plant.

The Act lays down a close season for wild birds (other than game birds) from 1 February to 31 August inclusive, each year. Exceptions to these dates are made for:

Capercaillie and (except Scotland) *Woodcock* – 1 February to 30 September

Snipe – 1 February to 11 August

Wild Duck and *Wild Goose* (below high water mark) – 21 February to 31 August

Birds which may be killed or taken outside the close season (except on Sundays and on Christmas Day in Scotland, and on Sundays in prescribed areas of England and Wales) are the above-named, plus coot, certain wild duck (gadwall, goldeneye, mallard, pintail, pochard, shoveler, teal, tufted duck, wigeon), certain wild geese (Canada, greylag, pink-footed, white-fronted (in England and Wales only)), moorhen, golden plover and woodcock.

Certain wild birds may be killed or taken subject to the conditions of a general licence at any time by authorised persons: crow, collared dove, gull (great and lesser black-backed or herring), jackdaw, jay, magpie, pigeon (feral or wood), rook, sparrow (house), and starling. Conditions usually apply where the birds pose a threat to agriculture, public health, air safety, other bird species, and to prevent the spread of disease.

All other British birds are fully protected by law throughout the year.

Animals

‡Adder (*Vipera berus*)
Anemone, Ivell's Sea (*Edwardsia ivelli*)
Anemone, Starlet Sea (*Nematosella vectensis*)
Apus, Tadpole shrimp (*Triops cancriformis*)
Bat, Horseshoe (*Rhinolophidae*, all species)
Bat, Typical (*Vespertilionidae*, all species)
Beetle (*Graphoderus zonatus*)
Beetle (*Hypebaeus flavipes*)
Beetle, Lesser Silver Water (*Hydrochara caraboides*)
§§Beetle, Mire Pill (*Curimopsis nigrita*)
Beetle, Rainbow Leaf (*Chrysolina cerealis*)
*Beetle, Stag (*Lucanus cervus*)
Beetle, Violet Click (*Limoniscus violaceus*)
Beetle, Water (*Graphoderus zonatus*)
Beetle, Water (*Paracymus aeneus*)
Burbot (*Lota lota*)
*Butterfly, Adonis Blue (*Lysandra bellargus*)
*Butterfly, Black Hairstreak (*Strymonidia pruni*)

*Butterfly, Brown Hairstreak (*Thecla betulae*)
*Butterfly, Chalkhill Blue (*Lysandra coridon*)
*Butterfly, Chequered Skipper (*Carterocephalus palaemon*)
*Butterfly, Duke of Burgundy Fritillary (*Hamearis lucina*)
*Butterfly, Glanville Fritillary (*Melitaea cinxia*)
Butterfly, Heath Fritillary (*Mellicta athalia* (or *Melitaea athalia*))
Butterfly, High Brown Fritillary (*Argynnis adippe*)
Butterfly, Large Blue (*Maculinea arion*)
Butterfly, Large Copper (*Lycaena dispar*)
*Butterfly, Large Heath (*Coenonympha tullia*)
*Butterfly, Large Tortoiseshell (*Nymphalis polychloros*)
*Butterfly, Lulworth Skipper (*Thymelicus acteon*)
Butterfly, Marsh Fritillary (*Eurodryas aurinia*)
*Butterfly, Mountain Ringlet (*Erebia epiphron*)
*Butterfly, Northern Brown Argus (*Aricia artaxerxes*)
*Butterfly, Pearl-bordered Fritillary (*Boloria euphrosyne*)
*Butterfly, Purple Emperor (*Apatura iris*)
*Butterfly, Silver Spotted Skipper (*Hesperia comma*)
*Butterfly, Silver-studded Blue (*Plebejus argus*)
*Butterfly, Small Blue (*Cupido minimus*)
Butterfly, Swallowtail (*Papilio machaon*)
*Butterfly, White Letter Hairstreak (*Stymonida w-album*)
*Butterfly, Wood White (*Leptidea sinapis*)
Cat, Wild (*Felis silvestris*)
Cicada, New Forest (*Cicadetta montana*)
**Crayfish, Atlantic stream (*Austropotamobius pallipes*)
Cricket, Field (*Gryllus campestris*)
Cricket, Mole (*Gryllotalpa gryllotalpa*)
Damselfly, Southern (*Coenagrion mercuriale*)
Dolphin (*Cetacea*)
Dormouse (*Muscardinus avellanarius*)
Dragonfly, Norfolk Aeshna (*Aeshna isosceles*)
*Frog, Common (*Rana temporaria*)
Goby, Couch's (*Gobius couchii*)
Goby, Giant (*Gobius cobitis*)
Grasshopper, Wart-biter (*Decticus verrucivorus*)
Hatchet Shell, Northern (*Thyasira gouldi*)
Hydroid, Marine (*Clavopsella navis*)
Lagoon Snail (*Paludinella littorina*)
Lagoon Snail, De Folin's (*Caecum armoricum*)
Lagoon Worm, Tentacled (*Alkmaria romijni*)
Leech, Medicinal (*Hirudo medicinalis*)
Lizard, Sand (*Lacerta agilis*)
‡Lizard, Viviparous (*Lacerta vivipara*)
Marten, Pine (*Martes martes*)
Moth, Barberry Carpet (*Pareulype berberata*)
Moth, Black-veined (*Siona lineata* (or *Idaea lineata*))
Moth, Essex Emerald (*Thetidia smaragdaria*)
Moth, Fiery clearwing (*Bembecia chrysidiformis*)
Moth, Fisher's estuarine (*Gortyna borelii*)
Moth, New Forest Burnet (*Zygaena viciae*)
Moth, Reddish Buff (*Acosmetia caliginosa*)
Moth, Sussex Emerald (*Thalera fimbrialis*)
††Mussel, Fan (*Atrina fragilis*)
†Mussel, Freshwater Pearl (*Margaritifera margaritifera*)
Newt, Great Crested (or Warty) (*Triturus cristatus*)
*Newt, Palmate (*Triturus helveticus*)
*Newt, Smooth (*Triturus vulgaris*)
Otter, Common (*Lutra lutra*)
Porpoise (*Cetacea*)
Sandworm, Lagoon (*Armandia cirrhosa*)
††Sea Fan, Pink (*Eunicella verrucosa*)
Sea-Mat, Trembling (*Victorella pavida*)
Sea Slug, Lagoon (*Tenellia adspersa*)
‡‡Shad, Allis (*alosa alosa*)
§§Shad, Twaite (*alosa fallax*)
Shark, Basking (*Cetorhinus maximus*)
Shrimp, Fairy (*Chirocephalus diaphanus*)
Shrimp, Lagoon Sand (*Gammarus insensibilis*)

‡Slow-worm (*Anguis fragilis*)
Snail, Glutinous (*Myxas glutinosa*)
Snail, Sandbowl (*Catinella arenaria*)
‡Snake, Grass (*Natrix natrix* (*Natrix helvetica*))
Snake, Smooth (*Coronella austriaca*)
Spider, Fen Raft (*Dolomedes plantarius*)
Spider, Ladybird (*Eresus niger*)
Squirrel, Red (*Sciurus vulgaris*)
Sturgeon (*Acipenser sturio*)
*Toad, Common (*Bufo bufo*)
Toad, Natterjack (*Bufo calamita*)
Turtle, Marine (*Dermochelyidae* and *Cheloniidae*, all species)
Vendace (*Coregonus albula*)
§§Vole, Water (*Arvicola terrestris*)
Walrus (*Odobenus rosmarus*)
Whale (*Cetacea*)
Whitefish (*Coregonus lavaretus*)

* The offence relates to 'sale' only
** The offence relates to 'taking' and 'sale' only
† The offence relates to 'killing and injuring' only
‡ The offence relates to 'killing, injuring and sale'
§ The offence relates to 'killing, injuring and taking'
§§ The offence relates only to damaging, destroying or obstructing access to a shelter or protection
†† The offence relates to killing, injuring, taking, possession and sale
‡‡ The offence relates to killing, injuring, taking and damaging, etc., a shelter

Plants

Adder's tongue, Least (*Ophioglossum lusitanicum*)
Alison, Small (*Alyssum alyssoides*)
Blackwort (*Southbya nigrella*)
°Bluebell (*Hyacinthoides non-scripta*)
Broomrape, Bedstraw (*Orobanche caryophyllacea*)
Broomrape, Oxtongue (*Orobanche loricata*)
Broomrape, Thistle (*Orobanche reticulata*)
Cabbage, Lundy (*Rhynchosinapis wrightii*)
Calamint, Wood (*Calamintha sylvatica*)
Caloplaca, Snow (*Caloplaca nivalis*)
Catapyrenium, Tree (*Catapyrenium psoromoides*)
Catchfly, Alpine (*Lychnis alpina*)
Catillaria, Laurer's (*Catellaria laureri*)
Centaury, Slender (*Centaurium tenuiflorum*)
Cinquefoil, Rock (*Potentilla rupestris*)
Cladonia, Upright Mountain (*Cladonia stricta*)
Clary, Meadow (*Salvia pratensis*)
Club-rush, Triangular (*Scirpus triquetrus*)
Colt's-foot, Purple (*Homogyne alpina*)
Cotoneaster, Wild (*Cotoneaster integerrimus*)
Cottongrass, Slender (*Eriophorum gracile*)
Cow-wheat, Field (*Melampyrum arvense*)
Crocus, Sand (*Romulea columnae*)
Crystalwort, Lizard (*Riccia bifurca*)
Cudweed, Broad-leaved (*Filago pyramidata*)
Cudweed, Jersey (*Gnaphalium luteoalbum*)
Cudweed, Red-tipped (*Filago lutescens*)
Cut-grass (*Leersia oryzoides*)
Diapensia (*Diapensia lapponica*)
Dock, Shore (*Rumex rupestris*)
Earwort, Marsh (*Jamesoniella undulifolia*)
Eryngo, Field (*Eryngium campestre*)
Fern, Dickie's bladder (*Cystopteris dickieana*)
Fern, Killarney (*Trichomanes speciosum*)
Flapwort, Norfolk (*Leiocolea rutheana*)
Fleabane, Alpine (*Erigeron borealis*)
Fleabane, Small (*Pulicaria vulgaris*)
Fleawort, South stack (*Tephroseris integrifolia* (ssp maritima))

Frostwort, Pointed (*Gymnomitrion apiculatum*)
Fungus, Hedgehog (*Hericium erinaceum*)
Fungus, Oak polypore (*Buglossoporus pulvinus*)
Fungus, Royal bolete (*Boletus regius*)
Fungus, Sandy stilt puffball (*Battarraea phalloides*)
Galingale, Brown (*Cyperus fuscus*)
Gentian, Alpine (*Gentiana nivalis*)
Gentian, Dune (*Gentianella uliginosa*)
Gentian, Early (*Gentianella anglica*)
Gentian, Fringed (*Gentianella ciliata*)
Gentian, Spring (*Gentiana verna*)
Germander, Cut-leaved (*Teucrium botrys*)
Germander, Water (*Teucrium scordium*)
Gladiolus, Wild (*Gladiolus illyricus*)
Goosefoot, Stinking (*Chenopodium vulvaria*)
Grass-poly (*Lythrum hyssopifolia*)
Grimmia, Blunt-leaved (*Grimmia unicolor*)
Gyalecta, Elm (*Gyalecta ulmi*)
Hare's-ear, Sickle-leaved (*Bupleurum falcatum*)
Hare's-ear, Small (*Bupleurum baldense*)
Hawk's-beard, Stinking (*Crepis foetida*)
Hawkweed, Northroe (*Hieracium northroense*)
Hawkweed, Shetland (*Hieracium zetlandicum*)
Hawkweed, Weak-leaved (*Hieracium attenuatifolium*)
Heath, Blue (*Phyllodoce caerulea*)
Helleborine, Red (*Cephalanthera rubra*)
Helleborine, Young's (*Epipactis youngiana*)
Horsetail, Branched (*Equisetum ramosissimum*)
Hound's-tongue, Green (*Cynoglossum germanicum*)
Knawel, Perennial (*Scleranthus perennis*)
Knotgrass, Sea (*Polygonum maritimum*)
Lady's-slipper (*Cypripedium calceolus*)
Lecanactis, Churchyard (*Lecanactis hemisphaerica*)
Lecanora, Tarn (*Lecanora archariana*)
Lecidea, Copper (*Lecidea inops*)
Leek, Round-headed (*Allium sphaerocephalon*)
Lettuce, Least (*Lactuca saligna*)
Lichen, Alpine sulphur-tresses (*Alectoria ochroleuca*)
Lichen, Arctic kidney (*Nephroma arcticum*)
Lichen, Ciliate strap (*Heterodermia leucomelos*)
Lichen, Convoluted cladonia (*Cladonia convoluta*)
Lichen, Coralloid rosette (*Heterodermia propagulifera*)
Lichen, Ear-lobed dog (*Peltigera lepidophora*)
Lichen, Forked hair (*Bryoria furcellata*)
Lichen, Goblin lights (*Catolechia wahlenbergii*)
Lichen, Golden hair (*Teloschistes flavicans*)
Lichen, New Forest beech-lichen (*Enterographa elaborata*)
Lichen, Orange fruited Elm (*Caloplaca luteoalba*)
Lichen, River jelly (*Collema dichotomum*)
Lichen, Scaly breck (*Squamarina lentigera*)
Lichen, Stary breck (*Buellia asterella*)
Lily, Snowdon (*Lloydia serotina*)
Liverwort, Leafy (*Petallophyllum ralfsi*)
Liverwort, Lindenberg's (*Adelanthus lindenbergianus*)
Marsh-mallow, Rough (*Althaea hirsuta*)
Marshwort, Creeping (*Apium repens*)
Milk-parsley, Cambridge (*Selinum carvifolia*)
Moss (*Drepanocladius vernicosus*)
Moss, Alpine copper (*Mielichoferia mielichoferi*)
Moss, Anomodon, long-leaved (*Anomodon longifolius*)
Moss, Baltic bog (*Sphagnum balticum*)
Moss, Blue dew (*Saelania glaucescens*)
Moss, Blunt-leaved bristle (*Orthotrichum obtusifolium*)
Moss, Bright green cave (*Cyclodictyon laetevirens*)
Moss, Cordate beard (*Barbula cordata*)
Moss, Cornish path (*Ditrichum cornubicum*)
Moss, Derbyshire feather (*Thamnobryum angustifolium*)
Moss, Dune thread (*Bryum mamillatum*)
Moss, Flamingo (*Desmatodon cernuus*)
Moss, Glaucous beard (*Barbula glauca*)

Moss, Green shield (*Buxbaumia viridis*)
Moss, Hair silk (*Plagiothecium piliferum*)
Moss, Knothole (*Zygodon forsteri*)
Moss, Large yellow feather (*Scorpidium turgescens*)
Moss, Millimetre (*Micromitrium tenerum*)
Moss, Multifruited river (*Cryphaea lamyana*)
Moss, Nowell's limestone (*Zygodon gracilis*)
Moss, Polar feather-moss (*Hygrohypnum polare*)
Moss, Rigid apple (*Bartramia stricta*)
Moss, Round-leaved feather (*Rhyncostegium rotundifolium*)
Moss, Schleicher's thread (*Bryum schleicheri*)
Moss, Threadmoss, long-leaved (*Bryum neodamense*)
Moss, Triangular pygmy (*Acaulon triquetrum*)
Moss, Vaucher's feather (*Hypnum vaucheri*)
Mudwort, Welsh (*Limosella austeralis*)
Naiad, Holly-leaved (*Najas marina*)
Naiad, Slender (*Najas flexilis*)
Orache, Stalked (*Halimione pedunculata*)
Orchid, Early spider (*Ophrys sphegodes*)
Orchid, Fen (*Liparis loeselii*)
Orchid, Ghost (*Epipogium aphyllum*)
Orchid, Lapland marsh (*Dactylorhiza lapponica*)
Orchid, Late spider (*Ophrys fuciflora*)
Orchid, Lizard (*Himantoglossum hircinum*)
Orchid, Military (*Orchis militaris*)
Orchid, Monkey (*Orchis simia*)
Panneria, Caledonia (*Panneria ignobilis*)
Parmelia, New Forest (*Parmelia minarum*)
Parmentaria, Oil stain (*Parmentaria chilensis*)
Pear, Plymouth (*Pyrus cordata*)
Penny-cress, Perfoliate (*Thlaspi perfoliatum*)
Pennyroyal (*Mentha pulegium*)
Pertusaria, Alpine moss (*Pertusaria bryontha*)
Physcia, Southern grey (*Physcia tribacioides*)
Pigmyweed (*Crassula aquatica*)
Pine, Ground (*Ajuga chamaepitys*)
Pink, Cheddar (*Dianthus gratianopolitanus*)
Pink, Childing (*Petroraghia nanteuilii*)
Pink, Deptford (*Dianthus armeria*) (England and Wales only)
Plantain, Floating water (*Luronium natans*)
Pseudocyphellaria, Ragged (*Pseudocyphellaria lacerata*)
Psora, Rusty Alpine (*Psora rubiformis*)
Ragwort, Fen (*Senecio paludosus*)

Ramping-fumitory, Martin's (*Fumaria martinii*)
Rampion, Spiked (*Phyteuma spicatum*)
Restharrow, Small (*Ononis reclinata*)
Rock-cress, Alpine (*Arabis alpina*)
Rock-cress, Bristol (*Arabis stricta*)
Rustwort, Western (*Marsupella profunda*)
Sandwort, Norwegian (*Arenaria norvegica*)
Sandwort, Teesdale (*Minuartia stricta*)
Saxifrage, Drooping (*Saxifraga cernua*)
Saxifrage, Marsh (*Saxifrage hirulus*)
Saxifrage, Tufted (*Saxifraga cespitosa*)
Solenopsora, Serpentine (*Solenopsora liparina*)
Solomon's-seal, Whorled (*Polygonatum verticillatum*)
Sow-thistle, Alpine (*Cicerbita alpina*)
Spearwort, Adder's-tongue (*Ranunculus ophioglossifolius*)
Speedwell, Fingered (*Veronica triphyllos*)
Speedwell, Spiked (*Veronica spicata*)
Spike rush, Dwarf (*Eleocharis parvula*)
Star-of-Bethlehem, Early (*Gagea bohemica*)
Starfruit (*Damasonium alisma*)
Stonewort, Bearded (*Chara canescens*)
Stonewort, Foxtail (*Lamprothamnium papulosum*)
Strapwort (*Corrigiola litoralis*)
Turpswort (*Geocalyx graveolens*)
Violet, Fen (*Viola persicifolia*)
Viper's-grass (*Scorzonera humilis*)
Water-plantain, Ribbon-leaved (*Alisma gramineum*)
Wood-sedge, Starved (*Carex depauperata*)
Woodsia, Alpine (*Woodsia alpina*)
Woodsia, Oblong (*Woodsia ilvenis*)
Wormwood, Field (*Artemisia campestris*)
Woundwort, Downy (*Stachys germanica*)
Woundwort, Limestone (*Stachys alpina*)
Yellow-rattle, Greater (*Rhinanthus serotinus*)

° The sale of plants taken from the wild is prohibited; the sale of cultivated plants is still permitted

MOST UNDER THREAT

The animals and birds considered to be most under threat in Great Britain by the Joint Nature Conservation Committee are the high brown fritillary butterfly; violet click beetle; new forest burnet moth; corncrake; aquatic warbler; tree sparrow; wryneck; water vole; red squirrel; allis shad; and twaite shad.

Historic Buildings and Monuments

LISTING

Under the Planning (Listed Buildings and Conservation Areas) Act 1990, the Secretary of State for Culture, Media and Sport has a statutory duty to compile lists of buildings or groups of buildings in England which are of special architectural or historic interest. Under the Ancient Monuments and Archaeological Areas Act 1979 as amended by the National Heritage Act 1983, the Secretary of State is also responsible for compiling a schedule of ancient monuments. Decisions are taken on the advice of English Heritage (see page 332).

Listed buildings are classified into Grade I, Grade II* and Grade II. There are currently about 500,000 individual listed buildings in England, of which about 95 per cent are Grade II listed. Almost all pre-1700 buildings are listed, and most buildings of 1700 to 1840. English Heritage is carrying out thematic surveys of particular types of buildings with a view to making recommendations for listing, and members of the public may propose a building for consideration. The main purpose of listing is to ensure that care is taken in deciding the future of a building. No changes which affect the architectural or historic character of a listed building can be made without listed building consent (in addition to planning permission where relevant). Applications for listed building consent are normally dealt with by the local planning authority, although English Heritage is always consulted about proposals affecting Grade I and Grade II* properties. It is a criminal offence to demolish a listed building, or alter it in such a way as to affect its character, without consent.

There are currently about 22,500 scheduled monuments in England. English Heritage is carrying out a Monuments Protection Programme assessing archaeological sites with a view to making recommendations for scheduling, and members of the public may propose a monument for consideration. All monuments proposed for scheduling are considered to be of national importance. Where buildings are both scheduled and listed, ancient monuments legislation takes precedence. The main purpose of scheduling a monument is to preserve it for the future and to protect it from damage, destruction or any unnecessary interference. Once a monument has been scheduled, scheduled monument consent is required before any works are carried out. The scope of the control is more extensive and more detailed than that applied to listed buildings, but certain minor works, as detailed in the Ancient Monuments (Class Consents) Order 1994, may be carried out without consent. It is a criminal offence to carry out unauthorised work to scheduled monuments.

Under the Planning (Listed Buildings and Conservation Areas) Act 1990 and the Ancient Monuments and Archaeological Areas Act 1979, the Secretary of State for Wales is responsible for listing buildings and scheduling monuments in Wales on the advice of Cadw (see Regional Government section), the Historic Buildings Council for Wales (see page 336) and the Royal Commission on the Ancient and Historical Monuments of Wales (see page 359). The criteria for evaluating buildings are similar to those in England and the same listing system is used. There are approximately 19,200 listed buildings and approximately 3,000 scheduled monuments in Wales.

Under the Planning (Listed Buildings and Conservation Areas) (Scotland) Act 1997 and the Ancient Monuments and Archaeological Areas Act 1979, Scottish Ministers are responsible for listing buildings and scheduling monuments in Scotland on the advice of

Historic Scotland (see Regional Government section), the Historic Buildings Council for Scotland (see page 336) and the Royal Commission on the Ancient and Historical Monuments of Scotland (see page 358). The criteria for evaluating buildings are similar to those in England but an A, B, C categorisation is used. There are 45,498 listed buildings and 7,439 scheduled monuments in Scotland.

Under the Planning (Northern Ireland) Order 1991 and the Historic Monuments and Archaeological Objects (Northern Ireland) Order 1995, the Department of the Environment of the Northern Ireland Executive (see Regional Government section) is responsible for listing buildings and scheduling monuments in Northern Ireland on the advice of the Historic Buildings Council for Northern Ireland and the Historic Monuments Council for Northern Ireland. The criteria for evaluating buildings are similar to those in England but no statutory grading system is used. In March 1999 there were 8,563 listed buildings and 1,365 scheduled monuments in Northern Ireland.

OPENING TO THE PUBLIC

The following is a selection of the many historic buildings and monuments open to the public. Admission charges and opening hours vary. Many properties are closed in winter and some are also closed in the mornings. Most properties are closed on Christmas Eve, Christmas Day, Boxing Day and New Year's Day, and many are closed on Good Friday. During the winter season, most English Heritage monuments are closed on Mondays and Tuesdays and monuments in the care of Cadw are closed on Sunday mornings. In Northern Ireland most monuments are closed on Mondays except on bank holidays. Information about a specific property should be checked by telephone.

*Closed in winter (usually November-March)
†Closed in winter, and in mornings in summer

ENGLAND

For more information on any of the English Heritage properties listed below, the official website is: www.english-heritage.org.uk. For more information on any of the National Heritage properties lited below, the official website is: www.nationaltrust.org.uk

EH English Heritage property
NT National Trust property

*A LA RONDE (NT), Summer Lane, Exmouth, Devon. Tel: 01395-265514.
Unique 16-sided house completed c.1796

†ALNWICK CASTLE, Northumberland. Tel: 01665-510777. Seat of the Dukes of Northumberland since 1309; Italian Renaissance-style interior

ALTHORP, Northants. Tel: 01604-770107, ticket reservations 01604-592020.
Spencer family seat. Diana, Princess of Wales memorabilia

†ANGLESEY ABBEY (NT), Cambs. Tel: 01223-811200. House built c.1600. Outstanding grounds with unique statuary

APSLEY HOUSE, London W1. Tel: 020-7499 5676. Built by Robert Adam 1771-8, home of the Dukes of Wellington since 1817 and known as 'No. 1 London'. Collection of fine and decorative arts

†ARUNDEL CASTLE, W. Sussex. Tel: 01903-883136. Castle dating from the Norman Conquest. Seat of the Dukes of Norfolk

AVEBURY (NT), Wilts. Tel: 01672-539250. Remains of stone circles constructed 4,000 years ago surrounding the later village of Avebury. Also *Alexander Keiller Museum.*

BANQUETING HOUSE, Whitehall, London SW1. Tel: 020-7930 4179. Designed by Inigo Jones; ceiling paintings by Rubens. Site of the execution of Charles I

†BASILDON PARK (NT), Berks. Tel: 0118-984 3040. Palladian house built in 1776–83

BATTLE ABBEY (EH), E. Sussex. Tel: 01424-773792. Remains of the abbey founded by William the Conqueror on the site of the Battle of Hastings

BEAULIEU, Hants. Tel: 01590-612345. House and gardens, Beaulieu Abbey and exhibition of monastic life, National Motor Museum

BEESTON CASTLE (EH), Cheshire. Tel: 01829-260464. Thirteenth-century inner ward with gatehouse and towers, and remains of outer ward

†BELTON HOUSE (NT), Grantham, Lincs. Tel: 01476-566116. Fine 17th-century house in landscaped park

*BELVOIR CASTLE, nr Grantham, Lincs. Tel: 01476-870262. Seat of the Dukes of Rutland; 19th-century Gothic-style castle

*BERKELEY CASTLE, Glos. Tel: 01453-810332. Completed 1153; site of the murder of Edward II (1327)

*BLENHEIM PALACE, Woodstock, Oxon. Tel: 01993-811325. Seat of the Dukes of Marlborough and Winston Churchill's birthplace; designed by Vanbrugh

†BLICKLING HALL (NT), Norfolk. Tel: 01263-738030. Jacobean house with state rooms, temple and 18th-century orangery

BODIAM CASTLE (NT), E. Sussex. Tel: 01580-830436. Well-preserved medieval moated castle

BOLSOVER CASTLE (EH), Derbys. Tel: 01246-823349. Notable 17th-century buildings

BOSCOBEL HOUSE (EH), Shropshire. Tel: 01902-850244. Timber-framed 17th-century hunting lodge, refuge of fugitive Charles II

†BOUGHTON HOUSE, Northants. Tel: 01536-515731. A 17th-century house with French-style additions

*BOWOOD HOUSE, Wilts. Tel: 01249-812102. An 18th-century house in Capability Brown park, with lake, temple and arboretum

†BROADLANDS, Hants. Tel: 01794-505010. Palladian mansion in Capability Brown parkland. Mountbatten exhibition

BRONTË PARSONAGE, Haworth, W. Yorks. Tel: 01535-642323. Home of the Brontë sisters; museum and memorabilia

BUCKFAST ABBEY, Devon. Tel: 01364-642519. Benedictine monastery on medieval foundations

*BUCKINGHAM PALACE, London SW1. Tel: 020-7839 1377. Purchased by George III in 1762, and the Sovereign's official London residence since 1837. Eighteen state rooms, including the Throne Room, and Picture Gallery

BUCKLAND ABBEY (NT), Devon. Tel: 01822-853607. A 13th-century Cistercian monastery. Home of Sir Francis Drake

BURGHLEY HOUSE, Stamford, Lincs. Tel: 01780-752451. Late Elizabethan house; vast state apartments

†CALKE ABBEY (NT), Derbys. Tel: 01332-863822. Baroque 18th-century mansion

CARISBROOKE CASTLE (EH), Isle of Wight. Tel: 01983-522107. Norman castle; prison of Charles I 1647-8

CARLISLE CASTLE (EH), Cumbria. Tel: 01228-606000. Medieval castle, prison of Mary Queen of Scots

*CARLYLE'S HOUSE (NT), Cheyne Row, London SW3. Tel: 020-7352 7087. Home of Thomas Carlyle

CASTLE ACRE PRIORY (EH), Norfolk. Tel: 01760-755394. Remains include 12th-century church and prior's lodgings

*CASTLE DROGO (NT), Devon. Tel: 01647-433306. Granite castle designed by Lutyens

*CASTLE HOWARD, N. Yorks. Tel: 01653-648444. Designed by Vanbrugh 1699–1726; mausoleum designed by Hawksmoor

CASTLE RISING CASTLE (EH), Norfolk. Tel: 01553-631330. A 12th-century keep in a massive earthwork with gatehouse and bridge

*CHARTWELL (NT), Kent. Tel: 01732-866368. Home of Sir Winston Churchill

*CHATSWORTH, Derbys. Tel: 01246-582204. Tudor mansion in magnificent parkland

CHESTERS ROMAN FORT (EH), Northumberland. Tel: 01434-681379. Roman cavalry fort

*CHYSAUSTER ANCIENT VILLAGE (EH), Cornwall. Tel: 0831-757934. Romano-Cornish village, 2nd and 3rd century AD, on a probably late Iron Age site

CLIFFORD'S TOWER (EH), York. Tel: 01904-646940. A 13th-century tower built on a mound

†CLIVEDEN (NT), Berks. Tel: 01628-605069. House open Thurs. and Sun. only, gardens daily. Former home of the Astors, now an hotel in garden and woodland

CORBRIDGE ROMAN SITE (EH), Northumberland. Tel: 01434-632349. Excavated central area of a Roman town and successive military bases

CORFE CASTLE (NT), Dorset. Tel: 01929-481294. Ruined former royal castle dating from 11th-century

†CROFT CASTLE (NT), Herefordshire. Tel: 01568-780246. Pre-Conquest border castle with Georgian-Gothic interior

DEAL CASTLE (EH), Kent. Tel: 01304-372762. Largest of the coastal defence forts built by Henry VIII

DICKENS HOUSE, Doughty Street, London WC1. Tel: 020-7405 2127. House occupied by Dickens 1837–9; manuscripts, furniture and portraits

DR JOHNSON'S HOUSE, 17 Gough Square, London EC4. Tel: 020-7353 3745. Web: www.drjh.dircon.co.uk. Home of Samuel Johnson

DOVE COTTAGE, Grasmere, Cumbria. Tel: 01539-435544. Wordsworth's home 1799-1808; museum

DOVER CASTLE (EH), Kent. Tel: 01304-201628. Castle with Roman, Saxon and Norman features; wartime operations rooms

DUNSTANBURGH CASTLE (EH), Northumberland. Tel: 01665-576231. A 14th-century castle on a cliff, with a substantial gatehouse-keep

ELTHAM PALACE (EH), Court Yard, Eltham, London SE9 . Tel: 020-8294 2548. Combines a 1930s country house and remains of medieval palace set in moated gardens.

FARLEIGH HUNGERFORD CASTLE (EH), Somerset. Tel: 01225-754026. Late 14th-century castle with two courts; chapel with tomb of Sir Thomas Hungerford

*FARNHAM CASTLE KEEP (EH), Surrey. Tel: 01252-713393. Large 12th-century shell-keep

FOUNTAINS ABBEY (NT), nr Ripon, N. Yorks. Tel: 01765-608888. Deer park visitor centre, deer park and St Mary's Church. Ruined Cistercian monastery; 18th-century landscaped gardens of Studley Royal estate

FRAMLINGHAM CASTLE (EH), Suffolk. Tel: 01728-724189. Castle (c.1200) with high curtain walls enclosing an almshouse (1639)

FURNESS ABBEY (EH), Cumbria. Tel: 01229-823420. Remains of church and conventual buildings founded in 1123

GLASTONBURY ABBEY, Somerset. Tel: 01458-832267. Ruins of a 12th-century abbey rebuilt after fire. Site of an early Christian settlement

GOODRICH CASTLE (EH), Herefordshire. Tel: 01600-890538. Remains of 13th- and 14th-century castle with 12th-century keep

GREENWICH, London SE10. *Royal Observatory.* Tel: 020-8858 6575. Web: www.rof.nmm.ac.uk. Former Royal Observatory (founded 1675) housing the time ball and zero meridian of longitude. *The Queen's House.* Tel: 020-8858 4422. Designed for Queen Anne, wife of James I, by Inigo Jones. *Painted Hall and Chapel* (Royal Naval College). Visitors admitted to Sunday service (11 a.m.) in the chapel during college term

GRIME'S GRAVES (EH), Norfolk. Tel: 01842-810656. Neolithic flint mines. One shaft can be descended

GUILDHALL, London EC2. Tel: 020-7332 1460. Centre of civic government of the City. Built c.1441; facade built 1788-9

*HADDON HALL, Derbys. Tel: 01629-812855. Well-preserved 12th-century manor house

HAILES ABBEY (EH), Glos. Tel: 01242-602398. Ruins of a 13th-century Cistercian monastery

†HAM HOUSE (NT), Richmond, Surrey. Tel: 020-8940 1950. Garden open all year except Thurs. and Fri. Stuart house with fine interiors

HAMPTON COURT PALACE, East Molesey, Surrey. Tel: 020-8781 9500. A 16th-century palace with additions by Wren. Gardens with maze; Tudor tennis court (summer only)

†HARDWICK HALL (NT), Derbys. Tel: 01246-850430. Built 1591-7 for Bess of Hardwick; notable furnishings

*HARDY'S COTTAGE (NT), Dorset. Tel: 01305-262366. Higher Bockhampton, Dorset. Birthplace of Thomas Hardy

*HAREWOOD HOUSE, W. Yorks. Tel: 0113-288 6331. An 18th-century house designed by John Carr and Robert Adam; park by Capability Brown

†HATFIELD HOUSE, Herts. Tel: 01707-262823. Jacobean house built by Robert Cecil; surviving wing of Royal Palace of Hatfield (1497)

HELMSLEY CASTLE (EH), N. Yorks. Tel: 01439-770442. A 12th-century keep and curtain wall with 16th-century buildings. Spectacular earthwork defences

†HEVER CASTLE (NT), Kent. Tel: 01732-865224. A 13th-century double-moated castle, childhood home of Anne Boleyn

*HOLKER HALL, Cumbria. Tel: 015395-58328. Former home of the Dukes of Devonshire; award-winning gardens

†HOLKHAM HALL, Norfolk. Tel: 01328-710227. Fine Palladian mansion

HOUSESTEADS ROMAN FORT (EH), Northumberland. Tel: 01434-344363. Excavated infantry fort on Hadrian's Wall with extra-mural civilian settlement

†HUGHENDEN MANOR (NT), High Wycombe. Tel: 01494-755565. Home of Disraeli; small formal garden

JANE AUSTEN'S HOUSE, Chawton, Hants. Tel: 01420-83162. Jane Austen's home 1809-17

KEDLESTON HOUSE (NT), Derby. Tel: 01332-842191. A classical Palladian mansion built 1759-65; complete Robert Adam interiors.

*KELMSCOTT MANOR, nr Lechlade, Oxon. Tel: 01367-252486. Summer home of William Morris, with products of Morris and Co.

KENILWORTH CASTLE (EH), Warks. Tel: 01926-852078. Castle with building styles from 1155 to 1649

KENSINGTON PALACE, London W8. Tel: 020-7937 7079. Built in 1605 and enlarged by Wren; bought by William and Mary in 1689. Birthplace of Queen Victoria. Royal Ceremonial Dress Collection

KENWOOD (EH), Hampstead Lane, London NW3. Tel: 020-8348 1286. Adam villa housing the Iveagh bequest of paintings and furniture. Open-air concerts in summer

*KEW, Surrey. Tel: 020-8332 5189. *Queen Charlotte's Cottage*

†KINGSTON LACY HOUSE (NT), Dorset. Tel: 01202-883402. A 17th-century house with 19th-century alterations; important art collection

†KNEBWORTH HOUSE, Herts. Tel: 01438-812661. Tudor manor house concealed by 19th-century Gothic decoration; Lutyens gardens

*KNOLE (NT), Kent. Tel: 01732-450608. House dating from 1456 set in parkland; fine art treasures

LAMBETH PALACE, London SE1. Tel: 020-7898 1200. Web: www.archbishopofcanterbury.org. Official residence of the Archbishop of Canterbury. A 19th-century house with parts dating from the 12th century

*LANERCOST PRIORY (EH), Cumbria. Tel: 01697-73030. The nave of the Augustinian priory church, c.1166, is still used; remains of other claustral buildings

*LANHYDROCK (NT), Cornwall. Tel: 01208-73320. House dating from the 17th century; 45 rooms, including kitchen and nursery

LEEDS CASTLE, Kent. Tel: 01622-765400. Castle dating from 9th century, on two islands in lake

†LEVENS HALL, Cumbria. Tel: 01539-560321. Elizabethan house with unique topiary garden (1694). Steam engine collection

LINCOLN CASTLE. Tel: 01522-511068. Built by William the Conqueror in 1068

LINDISFARNE PRIORY (EH), Northumberland. Tel: 01289-389200. Bishopric of the Northumbrian kingdom destroyed by the Danes; re-established in the 11th-century as a Benedictine priory, now ruined

LITTLE MORETON HALL (NT), Cheshire. Tel: 01260-272018. Timber-framed moated manor house with knot garden

LONGLEAT HOUSE, Warminster, Wilts. Tel: 01985-844400. Elizabethan house in Italian Renaissance style

LULLINGSTONE ROMAN VILLA (EH), Kent. Tel: 01322-863467. Large villa occupied for much of the Roman period; fine mosaics

MANSION HOUSE, London EC4. Tel: 020-7626 2500. The official residence of the Lord Mayor of London

MARBLE HILL HOUSE (EH), Twickenham, Middx. Tel: 020-8892 5115. English Palladian villa with Georgian paintings and furniture

*MICHELHAM PRIORY, E. Sussex. Tel: 01323-844224. Tudor house built onto an Augustinian priory

MIDDLEHAM CASTLE (EH), N. Yorks. Tel: 01969-623899. A 12th-century keep within later fortifications. Childhood home of Richard III

†MONTACUTE HOUSE (NT), Somerset. Tel: 01935-823289. Elizabethan house with National Portrait Gallery portraits from period

MOUNT GRACE PRIORY (EH), N. Yorks. Tel: 01609-883494. Carthusian monastery, with remains of monastic buildings

NETLEY ABBEY (EH), Hants. Tel: 023-8045 3076. Remains of Cistercian abbey, used as house in Tudor period

OLD SARUM (EH), Wilts. Tel: 01722-335398. Earthworks enclosing remains of the castle and the 11th-century cathedral

ORFORD CASTLE (EH), Suffolk. Tel: 01394-450472. Circular keep of c.1170 and remains of coastal defence castle built by Henry II

*OSBORNE HOUSE (EH), Isle of Wight. Tel: 01983-200022. Queen Victoria's seaside residence

†OSTERLEY PARK HOUSE (NT), Isleworth, Middx. Tel: 020-8568 7714. Elizabethan mansion set in parkland

PENDENNIS CASTLE (EH), Cornwall. Tel: 01326-316594. Well-preserved coastal defence castle built by Henry VIII

†PENSHURST PLACE, Kent. Tel: 01892-870307. House with medieval Baron's Hall and 14th-century gardens

†PETWORTH (NT), W. Sussex. Tel: 01798-343929. Late 17th-century house set in deer park

PEVENSEY CASTLE (EH), E. Sussex. Tel: 01323-762604. Walls of a 4th-century Roman fort; remains of an 11th-century castle

PEVERIL CASTLE (EH), Derbys. Tel: 01433-620613. A 12th-century castle defended on two sides by precipitous rocks

†POLESDEN LACEY (NT), Surrey. Tel: 01372-458203. Regency villa remodelled in the Edwardian era. Fine paintings and furnishings

PORTCHESTER CASTLE (EH), Hants. Tel: 023-9237 8291. Walls of a late Roman fort enclosing a Norman keep and an Augustinian priory church

*POWDERHAM CASTLE, Devon. Tel: 01626-890243. Medieval castle with 18th- and 19th-century alterations

†RABY CASTLE, Co. Durham. Tel: 01833-660202. A 14th-century castle with walled gardens

*RAGLEY HALL, Warks. Tel: 01789-762090. A 17th-century house with gardens, park and lake

RICHBOROUGH ROMAN FORT (EH), Kent. Tel: 01304-612013. Landing-site of the Claudian invasion in AD 43, with 3rd-century stone walls

RICHMOND CASTLE (EH), N. Yorks. Tel: 01748-822493. A 12th-century keep with 11th-century curtain wall and domestic buildings

RIEVAULX ABBEY (EH), N. Yorks. Tel: 01439-798228. Remains of a Cistercian abbey founded c.1131

ROCHESTER CASTLE (EH), Kent. Tel: 01634-402276. An 11th-century castle partly on the Roman city wall, with a square keep of c.1130

†ROCKINGHAM CASTLE, Northants. Tel: 01536-770240. Built by William the Conqueror

ROYAL PAVILION, Brighton. Tel: 01273-290900. Palace of George IV, in Chinese style with Indian exterior and Regency gardens

†RUFFORD OLD HALL (NT), Lancs. Tel: 01704-821254. A 16th-century hall with unique screen

ST AUGUSTINE'S ABBEY (EH), Canterbury, Kent. Tel: 01227-767345. Remains of Benedictine monastery, with Norman church, on site of abbey founded AD 598 by St Augustine

ST MAWES CASTLE (EH), Cornwall. Tel: 01326-270526. Coastal defence castle built by Henry VIII

ST MICHAEL'S MOUNT (NT), Cornwall. Tel: 01736-710507. A 12th-century castle with later additions, off the coast at Marazion

*SANDRINGHAM, Norfolk. Tel: 01553-772675. The Queen's private residence; a neo-Jacobean house built in 1870

SCARBOROUGH CASTLE (EH), N. Yorks. Tel: 01723-372451. Remains of 12th-century keep and curtain walls

†SHERBORNE CASTLE, Dorset. Tel: 01935-813182. Web: www.sherbornecastle.com. Sixteenth-century castle built by Sir Walter Raleigh

*SHUGBOROUGH (NT), Staffs. Tel: 01889-881388. House set in 18th-century park with monuments, temples and pavilions in the Greek Revival style

SKIPTON CASTLE, N. Yorks. Tel: 01756-792442. D-shaped castle with six round towers and beautiful inner courtyard

†SMALLHYTHE PLACE (NT), Kent. Tel: 01580-762334. Half-timbered 16th-century house; home of Ellen Terry 1899-1928

†STANFORD HALL, Leics. Tel: 01788-860250. William and Mary house with Stuart portraits. Motorcycle museum

STONEHENGE (EH), Wilts. Tel: 01980-624715. Prehistoric monument consisting of concentric stone circles surrounded by a ditch and bank

†STONOR PARK, Oxon. Tel: 01491-638587. Medieval house with Georgian facade. Centre of Roman Catholicism after the Reformation

†STOURHEAD (NT), Wilts. Tel: 09001-335205. English Palladian mansion with famous gardens

*STRATFIELD SAYE HOUSE, Hants. Tel: 01256-882882. Web: www.stratfield-saye.co.uk. House built 1630-40; home of the Dukes of Wellington since 1817

STRATFORD-UPON-AVON, Warks. Shakespeare's Birthplace with Shakespeare Centre; Anne Hathaway's Cottage, home of Shakespeare's wife; Mary Arden's House, home of Shakespeare's mother; Nash's House and New Place, where Shakespeare died; and Hall's Croft, home of Shakespeare's daughter. Tel: 01789-204016. Web: www.shakespeare.org.uk. Also Grammar School attended by Shakespeare, Holy Trinity Church, where Shakespeare is buried, Royal Shakespeare Theatre (burnt down 1926, rebuilt 1932) and Swan Theatre (opened 1986)

*SUDELEY CASTLE, Glos. Tel: 01242-602308. Castle built in 1442; restored in the 19th century

SYON HOUSE, Brentford, Middx. Tel: 020-8560 0883. Built on the site of a former monastery; Adam interior

TILBURY FORT (EH), Essex. Tel: 01375-858489. A 17th-century coastal fort

TINTAGEL CASTLE (EH), Cornwall. Tel: 01840-770328. A 12th-century cliff-top castle and Dark Age settlement site

TOWER OF LONDON, London EC3N 4AB. Tel: 020-7709 0765. Web: www.hrp.org.uk. Royal palace and fortress begun by William the Conqueror in 1078. Houses the Crown Jewels

*TRERICE (NT), Cornwall. Tel: 01637-875404. Elizabethan manor house

TYNEMOUTH PRIORY AND CASTLE (EH), Tyne and Wear. Tel: 0191-257 1090. Remains of a Benedictine priory, founded c.1090, on Saxon monastic site

†UPPARK (NT), W. Sussex. Tel: 01730-825857. Late 17th-century house, completely restored after fire. Fetherstonhaugh art collection

WALMER CASTLE (EH), Kent. Tel: 01304-364288. One of Henry VIII's coastal defence castles, now the residence of the Lord Warden of the Cinque Ports

WALTHAM ABBEY (EH), Essex. Tel: 01992-702200. Ruined abbey including the nave of the abbey church, 'Harold's Bridge' and late 14th-century gatehouse. Traditionally the burial place of Harold II (1066)

WARKWORTH CASTLE (EH), Northumberland. Tel: 01665-711423. A 15th-century keep amidst earlier ruins, with 14th-century hermitage upstream

WARWICK CASTLE. Tel: 01926-406600. Medieval castle with Madame Tussaud's waxworks, in Capability Brown parkland

WHITBY ABBEY (EH), N. Yorks. Tel: 01947-603568. Remains of Norman church on the site of a monastery founded in AD 657

*WILTON HOUSE, Wilts. Tel: 01722-746720. A 17th-century house on the site of a Tudor house and Saxon abbey

WINDSOR CASTLE, Berks. Tel: 01753-831118. Official residence of The Queen; oldest royal residence still in regular use. Also *St George's Chapel*

*WOBURN ABBEY, Beds. Tel: 01525-290666. Built on the site of a Cistercian abbey; seat of the Dukes of Bedford. Important art collection; antiques centre

WROXETER ROMAN CITY (EH), Shropshire. Tel: 01743-761330. Second-century public baths and part of the forum of the Roman town of Viroconium

WALES

For more information on any of the National Trust properties listed below, the official website is: www.nationaltrust.org.uk. For more information on any of the Cadw properties listed below, the official website is: www.cadw.wales.gov.uk

(C) Property of Cadw: Welsh Historic Monuments
(NT) National Trust property

BEAUMARIS CASTLE (C), Anglesey. Tel: 01248-810361. Concentrically-planned castle, still almost intact

CAERLEON ROMAN BATHS AND AMPHITHEATRE (C), nr Newport. Tel: 01633-890104. Rare example of a legionary bath-house and late 1st-century arena surrounded by bank for spectators

CAERNARFON CASTLE (C). Tel: 01286-677617. Important Edwardian castle built, with the town wall, between 1283 and 1330

CAERPHILLY CASTLE (C). Tel: 029 2088 3143. Concentrically-planned castle (*c.*1270) notable for its scale and use of water defences

CARDIFF CASTLE. Tel: 029-2087 8100. Castle built on the site of a Roman fort; spectacular towers and rich interior

CASTELL COCH (C), nr Cardiff. Tel: 029-2081 0101. Rebuilt 1875-90 on medieval foundations

CHEPSTOW CASTLE (C). Tel: 01291-624065. Rectangular keep amid extensive fortifications

CONWY CASTLE (C). Tel: 01492-592358. Built by Edward I, 1283-7

*CRICCIETH CASTLE (C). Tel: 01766-522227. Native Welsh 13th-century castle, altered by Edward I

DENBIGH CASTLE (C). Tel: 01745-813385. Remains of the castle (begun 1282), including triple-towered gatehouse

HARLECH CASTLE (C). Tel: 01766-780552. Well-preserved Edwardian castle, constructed 1283-90, on an outcrop above the former shoreline

PEMBROKE CASTLE. Tel: 01646-681510. Web: www.pembrokecastle.co.uk. Castle founded in 1093; Great Tower built 1200; birthplace of King Henry VII

*PENRHYN CASTLE (NT), Bangor. Tel: 01248-353084. Neo-Norman castle built in the 19th-century. Industrial railway museum

PORTMEIRION, Penrhyndeudraeth. Tel: 01766-770228. Village in Italianate style

†POWIS CASTLE (NT), nr Welshpool. Tel: 01938-557018. Medieval castle with interior in variety of styles; 17th-century gardens and Clive of India museum

RAGLAN CASTLE (C). Tel: 01291-690228. Remains of 15th-century castle with moated hexagonal keep

ST DAVIDS BISHOP'S PALACE (C), St Davids. Tel: 01437-720517. Remains of residence of Bishops of St Davids built 1328-47

TINTERN ABBEY (C), nr Chepstow. Tel: 01291-689251. Remains of 13th-century church and conventual buildings of a Cistercian monastery

*TRETOWER COURT AND CASTLE (C), nr Crickhowell. Tel: 01874-730279. Medieval house with remains of 12th-century castle nearby

SCOTLAND

For more information on any of the Historic Scotland properties listed below, the official website is: www.historic-scotland.gov.uk
For more information on any of the National Trust For Scotland properties listed below, the official website is: www.nts.org.uk

(HS) Historic Scotland property
(NTS) National Trust for Scotland property

ANTONINE WALL, between the Clyde and the Forth. Built about AD 142, consists of ditch, turf rampart and road, with forts every two miles

BALMORAL CASTLE, nr Braemar. Tel: 013397-42334. Web: www.balmoralcastle.com. Baronial-style castle built for Victoria and Albert. The Queen's private residence

BLACK HOUSE, ARNOL (HS), Lewis, Western Isles. Tel: 01851-710395. Traditional Lewis thatched house

*BLAIR CASTLE, Blair Atholl. Tel: 01796-481207. Mid 18th-century mansion with 13th-century tower; seat of the Dukes of Atholl

*BONAWE IRON FURNACE (HS), Argyll and Bute. Tel: 01866-822432. Charcoal-fuelled ironworks founded in 1753

†BOWHILL, Selkirk. Tel: 01750-22204. Seat of the Dukes of Buccleuch and Queensberry; fine collection of paintings, including portrait miniatures

BROUGH OF BIRSAY (HS), Orkney. Remains of Norse church and village on the tidal island of Birsay

CAERLAVEROCK CASTLE (HS), nr Dumfries. Tel: 01387-770244. Fine early classical Renaissance building

CALANAIS STANDING STONES (HS), Lewis, Western Isles. Tel: 01851-621422. Standing stones in a cross-shaped setting, dating from 3000 BC

CATHERTUNS (BROWN AND WHITE) (HS), nr Brechin. Two large Iron Age hill forts

*CAWDOR CASTLE, Inverness. Tel: 01667-404615. A 14th-century keep with 15th- and 17th-century additions

CLAVA CAIRNS (HS), Highland. Late Neolithic or early Bronze Age cairns

*CRATHES CASTLE (NTS), nr Banchory. Tel: 01330-844525. A 16th-century baronial castle in woodland, fields and gardens

*CULZEAN CASTLE (NTS), S. Ayrshire. Tel: 01655-760274. An 18th-century Adam castle with oval staircase and circular saloon

DRYBURGH ABBEY (HS), Scottish Borders. Tel: 01835-822381. A 12th-century abbey containing tomb of Sir Walter Scott

*DUNVEGAN CASTLE, Skye. Tel: 01470-521206. A 13th-century castle with later additions; home of the chiefs of the Clan MacLeod; trips to seal colony

EDINBURGH CASTLE (HS). Tel: 0131-225 9846. Includes the Scottish National War Memorial, Scottish United Services Museum and historic apartments

EDZELL CASTLE (HS), nr Brechin. Tel: 01356-648631.
Medieval tower house; unique walled garden
*EILEAN DONAN CASTLE, Wester Ross. Tel: 01599-555202. A 13th-century castle with Jacobite relics
ELGIN CATHEDRAL (HS), Moray. Tel: 01343-547171.
A 13th-century cathedral with fine chapterhouse
*FLOORS CASTLE, Kelso. Tel: 01573-223333.
Largest inhabited castle in Scotland; seat of the Dukes of Roxburghe
FORT GEORGE (HS), Highland. Tel: 01667-462777.
An 18th-century fort
*GLAMIS CASTLE, Angus. Tel: 01307-840393. Seat of the Lyon family (later Earls of Strathmore and Kinghorne) since 1372
GLASGOW CATHEDRAL (HS). Tel: 0141-552 6891.
Medieval cathedral with elaborately vaulted crypt
GLENELG BROCH (HS), Highlands. Two broch towers with well-preserved structural features
*HOPETOUN HOUSE, nr Edinburgh. Tel: 0131-331 2451.
House designed by Sir William Bruce, enlarged by William Adam
HUNTLY CASTLE (HS). Tel: 01466-793191.
Ruin of a 16th- and 17th-century house
*INVERARAY CASTLE, Argyll. Tel: 01499-302203. Gothic-style 18th-century castle; seat of the Dukes of Argyll
IONA ABBEY, Inner Hebrides. Tel: 01681-700 793.
Monastery founded by St Columba in AD 563
*JARLSHOF (HS), Shetland. Tel: 01950-460112.
Remains from Stone Age
JEDBURGH ABBEY (HS), Scottish Borders. Tel: 01835-863925. Romanesque and early Gothic church founded c.1138
KELSO ABBEY (HS), Scottish Borders. Remains of great abbey church founded 1128
LINLITHGOW PALACE (HS). Tel: 01506-842896.
Ruin of royal palace in park setting. Birthplace of Mary, Queen of Scots
MAES HOWE (HS), Orkney. Tel: 01856-761606.
Neolithic tomb
*MEIGLE SCULPTURED STONES (HS), Angus. Tel: 01828-640612. Celtic Christian stones
MELROSE ABBEY (HS), Scottish Borders. Tel: 01896-822562. Ruin of Cistercian abbey founded c.1136
MOUSA BROCH (HS), Shetland. Finest surviving Iron Age broch tower
NETHER LARGIE CAIRNS (HS), Argyll and Bute. Bronze Age and Neolithic cairns
NEW ABBEY CORN MILL (HS), nr Dumfries. Tel: 01387-850260. Water-powered mill
PALACE OF HOLYROODHOUSE, Edinburgh.
Tel: 0131-556 7371. The Queen's official Scottish residence. Main part of the palace built 1671-9
RING OF BROGAR (HS), Orkney. Neolithic circle of upright stones with an enclosing ditch
RUTHWELL CROSS (HS), Dumfries and Galloway.
Seventh-century Anglian cross
ST ANDREWS CASTLE AND CATHEDRAL (HS), Fife.
Tel: 01334-477196 (castle); 01334-472563 (cathedral).
Ruins of 13th-century castle and remains of the largest cathedral in Scotland
*SCONE PALACE, Perth. Tel: 01738-552300.
House built 1802-13 on the site of a medieval palace
SKARA BRAE (HS), Orkney. Tel: 01856-841815.
Stone-Age village with adjacent 17th-century house
*SMAILHOLM TOWER (HS), Scottish Borders.
Tel: 01573-460365. Well-preserved tower-house
STIRLING CASTLE (HS). Tel: 01786-450000.
Great Hall and gatehouse of James IV, palace of James V, Chapel Royal remodelled by James VI

TANTALLON CASTLE (HS), E. Lothian.
Tel: 01620-892727. Fortification with earthwork defences and a 14th-century curtain wall with towers
*THREAVE CASTLE (HS), Dumfries and Galloway.
Tel: 0831-168512. Late 14th-century tower on an island; reached by boat, long walk to castle
URQUHART CASTLE (HS), Loch Ness. Tel: 01456-450551.
Castle remains with well-preserved tower

NORTHERN IRELAND

For more information on any of the National Trust properties listed below, the official website is: www.nationaltrust.org.uk
DE Property in the care of the Northern Ireland Department of the Environment
NT National Trust property
CARRICKFERGUS CASTLE (DE), Co. Antrim. Tel: 01960-351273. Castle begun in 1180 and garrisoned until 1928
†CASTLE COOLE (NT), Enniskillen. Tel: 01365-322690.
An 18th-century mansion by James Wyatt in parkland
†CASTLE WARD (NT), Co. Down. Tel: 01396-881204. An 18th-century house with Classical and Gothic facades
*DEVENISH ISLAND (DE), Co. Fermanagh.
Island monastery founded in the 6th century by St Molaise
DOWNHILL CASTLE (NT), Co. Londonderry.
Tel: 01265-848728. Ruins of palatial house in land-scaped estate including Mussenden Temple.
DUNLUCE CASTLE (DE), Co. Antrim. Tel: 012657-31938.
Ruins of 16th-century stronghold of the MacDonnells
†FLORENCE COURT (NT), Co. Fermanagh.
Tel: 01365-348249. Mid–18th-century house with rococo plasterwork
*GREY ABBEY (DE), Co. Down. Tel: 01247-788585.
Substantial remains of a Cistercian abbey founded in 1193
HILLSBOROUGH FORT (DE), Co. Down. Built in 1650
†MOUNT STEWART (NT), Co. Down. Tel: 012477-88387.
An 18th-century house, childhood home of Lord Castlereagh
NENDRUM MONASTERY (DE), Mahee Island, Co. Down.
Founded in the 5th century by St Machaoi
*TULLY CASTLE (DE), Co. Fermanagh.
Fortified house and bawn built in 1613
*WHITE ISLAND (DE), Co. Fermanagh. Tenth-century monastery and 12th-century church. Access by ferry

Presidents of the Royal Academy

The President is elected by members of the Royal Academy from among their number and is subject only to the authority of the Sovereign. The post was usually held for life until the early 20th century. The President now retires at his own discretion.

Sir Joshua Reynolds (1723–92), appointed 1768
Benjamin West (1738–1820), appointed 1792
James Wyatt (1746–1813), appointed 1805
Benjamin West (1738–1820), appointed 1806
Sir Thomas Lawrence (1769–1830), appointed 1820
Sir Martin Shee (1770–1850), appointed 1830
Sir Charles Eastlake (1793–1865), appointed 1850
Sir Francis Grant (1803–78), appointed 1866
Lord Leighton (1830–96), appointed 1878
Sir John Millais (1829–96), appointed 1896
Sir Edward Poynter (1836–1919), appointed 1896
Sir Aston Webb (1849–1930), appointed 1919
Sir Francis Dicksee (1853–1928), appointed 1924
Sir William Llewellyn (1863–1941), appointed 1928
Sir Edwin Lutyens (1869–1944), appointed 1938
Sir Alfred Munnings (1878–1959), appointed 1944
Sir Gerald Kelly (1879–1972), appointed 1949
Sir Albert Richardson (1880–1964), appointed 1954
Sir Charles Wheeler (1892–1974), appointed 1956
Sir Thomas Monnington (1902–76), appointed 1966
Sir Hugh Casson (1910–), appointed 1976
Sir Roger de Grey (1918–95), appointed 1984
Sir Philip Dowson (1924–), appointed 1993
Prof. Philip King (1934–), appointed 1999

Museums and Galleries

There are more than 2,500 museums and galleries in the United Kingdom. Over 1,800 are registered with Resource: The Council for Museums, Archives and Libraries, formerly the Museums and Galleries Commission, which indicates that they have an appropriate constitution, are soundly financed, have adequate collection management standards and public services, and have access to professional curatorial advice. Museums must achieve full or provisional registration status in order to be eligible for grants from Resource and from Area Museums Councils. Over 700 of the registered museums are run by a local authority.

The national museums and galleries receive direct government grant-in-aid. These are: British Museum; Imperial War Museum; National Army Museum; National Galleries of Scotland; National Gallery; National Maritime Museum; National Museums and Galleries on Merseyside; National Museum of Wales; National Museums of Scotland; National Portrait Gallery; Natural History Museum; RAF Museum; Royal Armouries; Science Museum; Tate Gallery; Ulster Folk and Transport Museum; Ulster Museum; Victoria and Albert Museum; Wallace Collection. An online art museum (Web: www.24hourmuseum.org.uk) has also been awarded national collection status.

Local authority museums are funded by the local authority and may also receive grants from Resource. Independent museums and galleries mainly rely on their own resources but are also eligible for grants from the Museums and Galleries Commission.

The former Museums and Galleries Commission identified 26 non-national museum bodies which have pre-eminent collections of more than local or regional importance. Some of those designated are museum services with a wide variety of collections; others are small and more focused in a particular field. Ten Area Museum Councils in the UK, which are independent charities, give advice and support to the museums in their area and may offer improvement grants. They also circulate exhibitions and assist with training and marketing.

Opening to the Public

The following is a selection of the museums and art galleries in the United Kingdom. Opening hours and admission charges vary. Most museums are closed on Christmas Eve, Christmas Day, Boxing Day and New Year's Day; many are closed on Good Friday, and some are closed on May Day Bank Holiday. Some smaller museums close at lunchtimes. Information about a specific museum or gallery should be checked by telephone.

ENGLAND

---

* Local authority museum/gallery
† Museum/gallery contains a collection designated pre-eminent

BARNARD CASTLE, Co. Durham – *†*The Bowes Museum*, Westwick Road DR12 8NP. Tel: 01833-690606; Web: www.barnard-castle.co.uk
European art from the late medieval period to the 19th century; music and costume galleries; English period rooms from Elizabeth I to Victoria; local archaeology

BATH – *American Museum in Britain*, Claverton Manor BA2 7BD. Tel: 01225-460503;
Web: www.americanmuseum.org
American decorative arts from the 17th to 19th century
*Museum of Costume, Bennett Street BA1 2EW. Tel: 01225-477752;
Web: www.museumofcostume.co.uk
Fashion from the 16th century to the present day
*Roman Baths Museum, Abbey Church Yard BA1 1LZ. Tel: 01225-477774; Web: www.romanbaths.co.uk
Museum adjoins the remains of a Roman baths and temple complex
*Victoria Art Gallery, Bridge Street BA2 4AT. Tel: 01225-477772; Web: www.victoria.gal.org.uk
European Old Masters and British art since the 18th century

BEAMISH, Co. Durham – *†*Beamish, The North of England Open Air Museum*, DH9 0RG Tel: 0191-370 4000; Web: www.countydurham.com/beamish.
Recreated northern town c.1900, with rebuilt and furnished local buildings, colliery village, farm, railway station, tramway, Pockerley Manor and horse-yard (set c.1800)

BEAULIEU, Hants – †*National Motor Museum*. SO42 7ZN. Tel: 01590-612345; Web: www.beaulieu.co.uk
Displays of over 250 vehicles dating from 1895 to the present day

BIRMINGHAM – *†*Aston Hall*, Trinity Road, B6 6JD. Tel: 0121-327 0062.
Jacobean House containing paintings, furniture and tapestries from 17th to 19th century
*†*Barber Institute of Fine Arts*, off Edgbaston Park Road, B15 2TS. Tel: 0121-472 0962; Web: www.barber.org.uk
Fine arts, including Old Masters
*Birmingham Nature Centre, Edgbaston, B5 7RL. Tel: 0121-472 7775.
Indoor and outdoor enclosures displaying wildlife, especially British and European
*†City Museum and Art Gallery, Chamberlain Square. Tel: 0121-303 2834;
Web: www.bmag.org.uk/museum_and_art_gallery
Includes notable collection of Pre-Raphaelites
*†Museum of the Jewellery Quarter, Vyse Street, Hockley. Tel: 0121-554 3598;
Web: www.bmag.org.uk/jewellery_quarter
Built around a real jewellery workshop
*†Soho House, Soho Avenue. Tel: 0121-554 9122;
Web: www.bmag.org.uk/soho_house
Eighteenth-century home of industrialist Matthew Boulton

BOVINGTON CAMP, Dorset – †*Tank Museum* BH20 6JD. Tel: 01929-405096; Web: www.tankmuseum.org.uk
Collection of 300 tanks from the earliest days of tank warfare to the present

BRADFORD – *Cartwright Hall Art Gallery, Lister Park BD9 4NS. Tel: 01274-493313.
British 19th- and 20th-century fine art
*Industrial Museum and Horses at Work, Moorside Road BD2 3HP. Tel: 01274-631756;
Web: www.bradford.gov.uk
Engineering, textiles, transport and social history exhibits, including recreated back-to-back cottages, shire horses and horse tram-rides
National Museum of Photography, Film and Television BD1 1NQ. Tel: 01274-202030; Web: www.nmpft.org.uk

Photography, film and television interactive exhibits. Features the UK's first IMAX cinema and the only public Cinerama screen in the world

BRIGHTON – *†*Booth Museum of Natural History*, Dyke Road. Tel: 01273-292777.
Zoology, botany and geology collections; British birds in recreated habitats

*†*Brighton Museum and Art Gallery*, Church Street, BN1 1UE. Tel: 01273-290900;
Web: www.royalpavilion.brighton.co.uk
Includes fine art and design, fashion, non-Western art, Brighton history

BRISTOL – *Arnolfini Gallery*, Narrow Quay BS1 4QA. Tel: 0117-929 9191; Web: www.arnolfini.demon.co.uk
Contemporary visual arts, dance, performance, music, talks and workshops

*†*Blaise Castle House Museum*, Henbury BS10 7QS. Tel: 0117-950 6789; Web: www.bristol-city.gov.uk
Agricultural and social history collections in an 18th-century mansion

*†*Bristol Industrial Museum*, Prince Street BS1 4RN. Tel: 0117-925 1470; Web: www.bristol-city.gov.uk
Industrial, maritime and transport collections

*†*City Museum and Art Gallery*, Queen's Road B58 1RL Tel: 0117-922 3571;
Web: www.bristol-city.gov.uk/museums
Includes fine and decorative art, oriental art, Egyptology and Bristol ceramics and paintings

CAMBRIDGE – *Duxford Airfield*, Duxford CB2 4QR Tel: 01223-835000; Web: www.iwm.org.uk
Displays of military and civil aircraft, tanks, guns and naval exhibits

†*Fitzwilliam Museum*, Trumpington Street CB2 1RB. Tel: 01223-332900; Web: www.fitzmuseum.cam.ac.uk
Antiquities, fine and applied arts, clocks, ceramics, manuscripts, furniture, sculpture, coins and medals, temporary exhibitions

†*Sedgwick Museum of Geology*, Downing Street, CB2 3EQ. Tel: 01223-333456;
Extensive geological collection

†*University Museum of Archaeology and Anthropology*, Downing Street CB2 3EJ. Tel: 01223-333516; Web: www.cumaa.archanth.cam/museum.htm
Archaeology and anthropology from all parts of the world

†*University Museum of Zoology*, Downing Street CB2 3EJ. Tel: 01223-336650; Web: www.zoo.cam.ac.uk
Extensive zoological collection

†*Whipple Museum of the History of Science*, Free School Lane CB2 3RH. Tel: 01223-330906
Scientific instruments from the 14th century to the present

CARLISLE – *Tullie House Museum and Art Gallery*, Castle Street CA3 8TP. Tel: 01228-534781.
Prehistoric archaeology, Hadrian's Wall, Viking and medieval Cumbria, and the social history of Carlisle; also British 19th- and 20th-century art and English porcelain

CHATHAM – *World Naval Base* ME44TZ Tel: 01634-823800; Web: www.worldnavalbase.org.uk
Maritime attractions including HMS *Cavalier*, the UK's last World War II destroyer

†*Royal Engineers Museum*, Brompton Barracks ME4 4U9. Tel: 01634-406397; Web: www.royalengineers.org.uk
Regimental history, ethnography, decorative art and photography

CHELTENHAM – *Art Gallery and Museum*, Clarence Street GL50 3JT. Tel: 01242-237431;
Web: www.cheltenhammuseum.org.uk
Paintings, arts and crafts

CHESTER – *Grosvenor Museum*, Grosvenor Street CH1 2DD. Tel: 01244-321616;
Web: www.chestercc.gov.uk
Roman collections, natural history, art, Chester silver, local history and costume

CHICHESTER – †*Weald and Downland Open Air Museum*, Singleton PO18 0EU. Tel: 01243-811348;
Web: www.wealddown.co.uk
Rebuilt vernacular buildings from south-east England; includes medieval houses, agricultural and rural craft buildings and a working watermill

COLCHESTER – *†*Colchester Castle Museum*, Castle Park CO1 1YG. Tel: 01206-282931;
Web: www.colchestercastle.co.uk
Largest Norman keep in Europe standing on foundations of roman Temple of Claudius; tours of the Roman vaults, castle walls and chapel with medieval and prison displays

COVENTRY – *Herbert Art Gallery and Museum*, Jordan Well CV1 5QP. Tel: 024-7683 2565;
Web: www.coventrymuseum.org.uk
Local history, archaeology and industry, and fine and decorative art

*†*Museum of British Road Transport*, Hales Street CV1 1PN. Tel: 024-7683 2425; Web: www.mbrt.co.uk
Hundreds of motor vehicles and bicycles

CRICH, nr Matlock, Derbys – †*National Tramway Museum* BE45DP. Tel: 01773-852565; Web: www.tramway.co.uk
Open-air working museum with tram rides

DERBY – *Derby Museum and Art Gallery*, The Strand DE1 1BS. Tel: 01332-716659;
Web: www.derby.gov.uk/museums
Includes paintings by Joseph Wright of Derby and Derby porcelain

Industrial Museum, off Full Street DE1 3AR. Tel: 01332-255308;
Web: www.derby.gov.uk/museums
Rolls-Royce aero engine collection and a railway engineering gallery

DEVIZES – †*Wiltshire Heritage Museum*, Long Street SN10 1NS. Tel: 01380-727369;
Web: www.devizes-dc.gov.uk/museums
Natural and local history, art gallery, archaeological finds from Bronze Age, Iron Age, Roman and Saxon sites

DORCHESTER – *Dorset County Museum*, High West Street, DT1 1XA. Tel: 01305-262735
Includes a collection of Thomas Hardy's manuscripts, books, notebooks and drawings

DOVER – *Dover Museum*, Market Square CT16 1PB. Tel: 01304-201066; Web: www.dovermuseum.co.uk
Contains Dover Bronze Age Boat Gallery and archaeological finds from the Bronze Age, Roman and Saxon sites.

ELLESMERE PORT – *Boat Museum*, South Pier Road CH65 4FW. Tel: 0151-355 5017;
Web: www.boatmuseum.co.uk
Craft and boating history

EXETER – *†*Royal Albert Memorial Museum*, Queen Street EX4 3RX. Tel: 01392-265858; Web: www.exeter.gov.uk
Natural history, archaeology, worldwide fine and decorative art including Exeter silver

GATESHEAD – *Shipley Art Gallery*, Prince Consort Road NE8 4JB. Tel: 0191-477 1495.
Contemporary crafts

GAYDON, Warwick – *British Motor Industry Heritage Trust*, Heritage Motor Centre, Banbury Road CB35 0BJ. Tel: 01926-641188; Web; www.heritage.org.uk

History of British motor industry from 1895 to present; classic vehicles; engineering gallery; Corgi and Lucas collections

GLOUCESTER, – †*National Waterways Museum*, Llanthony Warehouse, Gloucester Docks GL1 2EH. Tel: 01452-318054; Web: www.nwm.org.uk Two-hundred-year history of Britain's canals and inland waterways

GOSPORT, Hants – *Royal Navy Submarine Museum*, Haslar Jetty Road PO12 2AS. Tel: 023-9252 9217; Web: www.rnsbmus.co.uk Underwater warfare, including the submarine *Alliance*; historical and nuclear galleries; and first Royal Navy submarine

GRASMERE, Cumbria – †*Dove Cottage* and the *Wordsworth Museum* LA22 9SH. Web: www.wordsworth.org.uk

HALIFAX – *Eureka! The Museum for Children*, Discovery Road HX1 2NE. Tel: 01426-983191; Web: www.eureka.org.uk Hands-on museum designed for children up to age 12

HULL – *Ferens Art Gallery*, Queen Victoria Square HU1 3RA. Tel: 01482-613902; Web: www.hullcc.gov.uk/museums/index.htm European art, especially Dutch 17th-century paintings, British portraits from 17th- to 20th-century, and marine paintings

Town Docks Museum, Queen Victoria Square HU1 3DX. Tel: 01482-613902; Web: www.hullcc.gov.uk/museums Whaling, fishing and navigation exhibits

HUNTINGDON – *Cromwell Museum*, Grammar School Walk P29 3LS. Tel: 01480-375830; Web:www.cromwell.argonet.co.uk. Portraits and memorabilia relating to Oliver Cromwell

IPSWICH – *Christchurch Mansion and Wolsey Art Gallery*, Christchurch Park IP4 2BE. Tel: 01473-253246. Tudor house with paintings by Gainsborough, Constable and other Suffolk artists; furniture and 18th-century ceramics. Art gallery for temporary exhibitions

LEEDS – *†City Art Gallery*, The Headrow LS1 3AA. Tel: 0113-247 8248. British and European paintings including English watercolours, modern sculpture, Henry Moore gallery, print room

Leeds Industrial Museum at Armley Mills, Canal Road, Armley LS12 2QF. Tel: 0113-263 7861; Web: www.leeds.gov.uk. Largest woollen mill in world

†Lotherton Hall, Aberford. Tel: 0113-281 3259. Costume and oriental collections in furnished Edwardian house; deer park and bird garden

Royal Armouries Museum, Armouries Drive. Tel: 0113-220-1940. National collection of arms and armour from BC to present; demonstrations of foot combat in museum's five galleries; falconry and mounted combat in the tiltyard

†Temple Newsam House LS15 7SE. Tel: 0113-264 7321. Old Masters and 17th- and 18th-century decorative art in furnished Jacobean/Tudor house

LEICESTER – *Jewry Wall Museum*, St Nicholas Circle. Tel: 0116-247 3021 Archaeology, Roman Jewry Wall and baths, and mosaics

New Walk Museum and Art Gallery, New Walk LE1 7EA. Tel: 0116-255 4100; Web: www.leicestermuseums.ac.uk Natural history, geology, ancient Egypt gallery, European art and decorative arts

Snibston Discovery Park, Coalville LE67 3LN. Tel: 01530-510851. Open-air science and industry museum on site of a coal mine; country park with nature trail

LINCOLN – *Museum of Lincolnshire Life*, Burton Road LN1 3LY. Tel: 01522-528448. Social history and agricultural collection

Usher Gallery, Lindum Road LN2 1NN. Tel: 01522-527980. Watches, miniatures, porcelain, silver; collection of Peter de Wint works; Lincolnshire topography and Royal Lincs Regiment memorabilia

LIVERPOOL – *Lady Lever Art Gallery*, Wirral CH62 4EQ. Tel: 0151-478 4136; Web: www.portsunlight.org.uk Paintings, furniture and porcelain

Liverpool Museum, William Brown Street L3 8EN. Tel: 0151-478 4399; Web: www.nmgm.org.uk. Includes Egyptian mummies, weapons and classical sculpture; planetarium, aquarium, vivarium and natural history centre

Merseyside Maritime Museum, Albert Dock L3 4AQ. Tel: 0151-478 4499; Web: www.nmgm.org.uk. Floating exhibits, working displays and craft demonstrations; incorporates *HM Customs and Excise National Museum*

Museum of Liverpool Life, Mann Island L3 4AA. Tel: 0151-478 4080; Web: www.nmgm.org.uk. The history of Liverpool

Sudley House, Mossley Hill Road. Tel: 0151-724 3245. Late 18th- and 19th-century British paintings in former shipowner's home

Tate Gallery Liverpool, Albert Dock L3 4BB. Tel: 0151-709 3223; Web: www.tate.org.uk. Twentieth-century painting and sculpture

Walker Art Gallery, William Brown Street. Tel: 0151-478 4199. Paintings from the 14th to 20th century

LONDON: GALLERIES – *Barbican Art Gallery*, Barbican Centre EC2Y 8DS. Tel: 020-7382 7105; Web: www.barbican.org.uk. Temporary exhibitions

†*Courtauld Gallery*, Somerset House, Strand, WC2. Tel: 020-7848 2526. The University of London galleries

†*Dulwich Picture Gallery*, College Road, SE21 7AD. Tel: 020-8693 5254; Web: www.dulwichpicturegalleryorg.uk. Built by Sir John Soane to house 17th- and 18th-century paintings

Hayward Gallery, Belvedere Road, SE18 XE2. Tel: 020-7928 3144; Web: www.haywardgallery.org.uk Temporary exhibitions

National Gallery, Trafalgar Square, WC2N 5DN. Tel: 020-7839 3321; Web: www.nationalgallery.org.uk. Western painting from the 13th to 20th century; early Renaissance collection in the Sainsbury wing

National Portrait Gallery, St Martin's Place, WC2H 0HE. Tel: 020-7306 0055; Web: www.npg.org.uk. Portraits of eminent people in British history

Percival David Foundation of Chinese Art, Gordon Square, WC1H 0PD. Tel: 020-7387 3909. Chinese ceramics from tenth to 18th-century

Photographers Gallery, Great Newport Street, WC2. Tel: 020-7831 1772; Web: www.photonet.org.uk Temporary exhibitions

The Queen's Gallery, Buckingham Palace, SW1A 1AA. Tel: 020-7839 1377; Web: www.royal.org.uk Art from the Royal Collection

Royal Academy of Arts, Piccadilly, W1V 0DS.
Tel: 020-7300 8000; Web: www.royalacademy.org.uk.
British art since 1750 and temporary exhibitions; annual Summer Exhibition
Saatchi Gallery, Boundary Road, NW8 0RH.
Tel: 020-7624 8299; Web: www.saatchigallery.org.uk
Contemporary art including paintings, photographs, sculpture and installations
Serpentine Gallery, Kensington Gardens, W2 3XA.
Tel: 020-7298 1515;
Web: www.serpentinegallery.org.uk.
Temporary exhibitions of British and international contemporary art
Tate Britain, Millbank, SW1P 4RG. Tel: 020-7887 8000;
Web: www.tate.org.uk.
British painting and 20th-century painting and sculpture. In 2000 the Millbank site became the Tate Gallery of British Art, and the Tate Gallery of Modern Art opened on the South Bank, London SE1
Wallace Collection, Manchester Square, W1 U3BN.
Tel: 020-7935 0687;
Web: www.the-wallace-collection.org.uk.
Paintings and drawings, French 18th-century furniture, armour, porcelain, clocks and sculpture
Whitechapel Art Gallery, Whitechapel High Street, E1 7QZ. Tel: 020-7522 7878;
Web: www.whitechapel.org.uk
Temporary exhibitions of modern art
LONDON: MUSEUMS – *Bank of England Museum*, Threadneedle Street, EC2 (entrance from Bartholomew Lane). Tel: 020-7601 5545.
History of the Bank since 1694
Bethnal Green Museum of Childhood, Cambridge Heath Road, E2 1PA. Tel: 020-8983 5200;
Web: www.museumofchildhood.org.uk.
Toys, games and exhibits relating to the social history of childhood
British Museum, Great Russell Street, WC1 B3DG.
Tel: 020-7636 1555;
Web: www.thebritishmuseum.ac.uk
Antiquities, coins, medals, prints and drawings
Cabinet War Rooms, King Charles Street, SW1A 7AQ.
Tel: 020-7930 6961; Web: www.iwm.org.uk.
Underground rooms used by Churchill and the Government during the Second World War
Commonwealth Experience, Kensington High Street W8 6NQ. Tel: 020-7603 4535;
Web: www.commonwealth.org.uk
Exhibitions on Commonwealth nations, visual arts and crafts; Interactive World
Cutty Sark, Greenwich, SE10 9HT. Tel: 020-8858 3445;
Web: www.cuttysark.org.uk
Restored and re-rigged tea clipper with exhibits on board.
Design Museum, Shad Thames, SE1.
Tel: 020-7378 6055; Web: www.designmuseum.org.uk
The development of design and the mass-production of consumer objects
Estorick Collection, Canonbury Square, N1 2AN
Tel: 020-7704 9522;
Web: www.estorickcollection.com.
Stages the main Estorick Collection of modern Italian art together with temporary loan exhibitions.
Geffrye Museum, Kingsland Road, E2 8EA.
Tel: 020-7739 9893;
Web: www.geffrye-museum.org.uk.
English urban domestic interiors from 1600 to present day; also paintings, furniture, decorative arts, walled herb garden and period garden rooms

Firepower! The Royal Artillery Museum, Royal Arsenal, Woolwich, SE18 6ST. Tel: 020-8855 7755;
Web: www.firepower.org.uk
The history and development of artillery over the last 700 years including the collections of the Royal Regiment of Artillery
Gilbert Collection, The Strand WC2R 1LN.
Tel: 020-7240 4080;
Web: www.gilbert-collection.org.uk
The collection comprises some 800 works of art including European silver, gold snuff boxes and Italian mosaics.
HMS Belfast, Morgans Lane, Tooley Street, SE1 2TH.
Tel: 020-7940 6300; Web: www.hmsbelfast.org.uk
Life on a warship, illustrated on World War II warship
†*Horniman Museum and Gardens*, London Road SE23 3PQ.
Tel: 020-8699 1872;
Web: www.horniman.demon.co.uk
Museum of ethnography, musical instruments, natural history and aquarium; reference library; sunken, water and flower gardens
Imperial War Museum, Lambeth Road SE1 6HZ.
Tel: 020-7416 5000; Web: www.iwm.org.uk.
All aspects of the two world wars and other military operations involving Britain and the Commonwealth since 1914
†*Jewish Museum, Camden Town*, Albert Street NW1 7NB.
Tel: 020-7284 1997.
Jewish life, history and religion
†*Jewish Museum, Finchley*, East End Road N3 2SY.
Tel: 020-8349 1143; Web: www.jewmusm.ort.org.
Jewish life in London and Holocaust education
†*London Transport Museum*, Covent Garden WC2E 7BB.
Tel: 020-7379 6344;
Web: www.londontransport.co.uk/ltmuseum.
Vehicles, photographs and graphic art relating to the history of transport in London
MCC Museum, Lord's NW8 8QN. Tel: 020-7289 1611;
Web: www.lords.org
Cricket museum. Conducted tours by appointment with Tours Manager.
Museum of Garden History, Lambeth Palace Road SE1 7LB. Tel: 020-7401 8865;
Web: www.museumgardenhistory.org
Exhibition of aspects of garden history and re-created 17th-century garden
†*Museum of London*, London Wall, EC2Y 5HN
Tel: 020-7600 3699;
Web: www.museumoflondon.org.uk
History of London from prehistoric times to present day
National Army Museum, Royal Hospital Road SW3 4HT.
Tel: 020-7730 0717; Web: www.faille.com/nam
Five-hundred-year history of the British soldier; exhibits include model of the Battle of Waterloo and *Army for Today* gallery
National Maritime Museum, Greenwich SE10 9NF.
Tel: 020-8858 4422; Web: www.port.nmm.ac.uk
Comprises the main building, the Royal Observatory and the Queen's House. Maritime history of Britain; collections include globes, clocks, telescopes and paintings
Natural History Museum, Cromwell Road SW7 5BD.
Tel: 020-7938 9123; Web: www.nhm.ac.uk
Natural history collections
†*Petrie Museum of Egyptian Archaeology*, University College London. Tel: 020-7504 2884.
Egyptian archaeology collection
Royal Air Force Museum, Colindale, NW9 5LL.
Tel: 020-8205 2266; Web: www.rafmuseum.org.uk

National museum of aviation with over 70 full-size aircraft; aviation from before the Wright brothers to the present-day RAF; flight simulator
Royal Mews, Buckingham Palace SW1A 1AA.
Tel: 020-7839 1377.
Carriages, coaches, stables and horses
Science Museum, Exhibition Road, SW7 2DD.
Tel: 020-7942 4454;
Web: www.science museum.org.uk
Science, technology, industry and medicine collections
Shakespeare Globe Exhibition, Bankside SE1 9DT.
Tel: 020-7902 1500;
Web: www.shakespeares-globe.org
Recreation of Elizabethan theatre using 16th-century techniques
Sherlock Holmes Museum, Baker Street NW1 6XE.
Tel: 020-7935 8866;
Web: www.sherlock-holmes.co.uk
Recreated rooms of the fictional detective
Sir John Soane's Museum, Lincoln's Inn Fields WC2A 3BP.
Tel: 020-7430 0175; Web: www.soane.org
Art and antiques
Theatre Museum, Russell Street WC2.
Tel: 020-7836 2330.
History of the performing arts
*Tower Bridge Experience, SE1. Tel: 020-7940 3985.
History of the bridge and display of Victorian steam machinery; panoramic views from walkways
Victoria and Albert Museum, Cromwell Road SW7 2RL.
Tel: 020-7938 8500; Web: www.varn.ac.uk
Includes National Art Library and Print Room. Fine and applied art and design, including furniture, glass, textiles, dress collections (British Galleries closed for refurbishment)
Wellington Museum, Apsley House, W1
Wimbledon Lawn Tennis Museum, Church Road SW19.
Tel: 020-8946 6131.
Tennis trophies, fashion and memorabilia; view of Centre Court
MANCHESTER – **Gallery of Costume*, Rusholme M14 5LL
Tel: 0161-224 5217.
Exhibits from the 16th- to 20th-century
†*Manchester Museum*, Oxford Road M13 9PL
Tel: 0161-275 2634; Web: www.museum.man.ac.uk.
Archaeology, archery, botany, Egyptology, entomology, ethnography, geology, natural history, numismatics, oriental and zoology collections
†*Museum of Science and Industry*, Castlefield M3 4SP.
Tel: 0161-832 2244; Web: www.msim.org.uk
On site of world's oldest passenger railway station; galleries relating to space, energy, power, transport, aviation, textiles and social history; interactive science centre
†*Pump House People's History Museum*, for *National Museum of Labour History*, Left Bank M3 3ER.
Tel: 0161-228 7212; Web: www.nmlhweb.org
Political and and working life history
†*Whitworth Art Gallery*, Oxford Road M15 6ER.
Tel: 0161-275 7450; Web: www.whitworth.ac.uk
Watercolours, drawings, prints, textiles, wallpapers and 20th-century British art
MONKWEARMOUTH – **†Monkwearmouth Station Museum*, North Bridge Street SR5 1AP. Tel: 0191-567 7075.
Victorian train station
NEWCASTLE UPON TYNE – **†Hancock Museum*, Barras Bridge. Tel: 0191-222 7418.
Natural history
*†Laing Art Gallery, New Bridge Street.
Tel: 0191-232 7734.

British and European art, ceramics, glass, silver, textiles and costume; *Art on Tyneside* display
*†Newcastle Discovery Museum, Blandford Square NE1 4JA.
Tel: 0191-232 6789;
Web: www.thenortheast.com/museums/news.htm
Science and industry, local history, fashion and Tyneside's maritime history; *Turbinia* (first steam-driven vessel) gallery
NEWMARKET – *National Horseracing Museum*, High Street CB8 8JL. Tel: 01638-667333; Web: www.nhrm.co.uk
The Essential Horse Millennium Exhibition, horseracing exhibits and tours of local trainers' yards and studs
NORTHAMPTON – **†Central Museum and Art Gallery*, Guildhall Road NN1 1DP. Tel: 01604-238548;
Web: www.northampton.gov.uk/museums
Boot and shoe collection
NORTH SHIELDS – †*Stephenson Railway Museum*, Middle Engine Lane. Tel: 0191-200 7144.
Locomotive engines and rolling stock
NOTTINGHAM – **Brewhouse Yard Museum*,
Castle Boulevard NG7 1FB. Tel: 0115-915 3600.
Daily life from the 17th to 20th century
*Castle Museum and Art Gallery NG1 6EL.
Tel: 0115-915 3700.
Paintings, ceramics, silver and glass; history of Nottingham
*Industrial Museum, Wollaton Park. Tel: 0115-915 3910.
Lacemaking machinery, steam engines and transport exhibits
*Museum of Costume and Textiles, Castle Gate NG1 6AF.
Tel: 0115-915 3500.
Costume displays from 1790 to the mid-20th century in period rooms
*Natural History Museum, Wollaton Park.
Tel: 0115-915 3900.
Local natural history and wildlife dioramas
OXFORD – †*Ashmolean Museum*, Beaumont Street OX1 2PH.
Tel: 01865-278000; Web: www.ashmol.ox.ac.uk
European and Oriental fine and applied arts, archaeology, Egyptology and numismatics
Museum of Modern Art, Pembroke Street OX1 1BP.
Tel: 01865-722733; Web: www.moma.org.uk
Temporary exhibitions
†*Museum of the History of Science*, Broad Street OX1 3AZ.
Tel: 01865-277280; Web: www.mhs.ox.ac.uk
Displays include early scientific instruments, chemical apparatus, clocks and watches
†*Oxford University Museum of Natural History*, Parks Road. Tel: 01865-272950.
Entomology, geology, mineralogy and zoology
†*Pitt Rivers Museum*, South Parks Road OX1 3PP.
Tel: 01865-270927; Web: www.prm.ox.ac.uk
Ethnographic and archaeological artefacts.
PLYMOUTH – **†City Museum and Art Gallery*, Drake Circus PL4 8AJ. Tel: 01752-304774;
Web: www.plymouth.gov.co.uk
Local and natural history, ceramics, silver, Old Masters, temporary exhibitions
*The Dome, The Hoe. Tel: 01752-603300.
Maritime history museum
PORTSMOUTH – **Charles Dickens Birthplace Museum*, Old Commercial Road PO1 4QL. Tel: 023-9282 7261.
Dickens memorabilia
*D-Day Museum, Clarence Esplanade PO1 2LJ.
Tel: 023-9282 7261;
Web: www.portsmouthmuseums.co.uk
Includes the Overlord Embroidery

Flagship Portsmouth, HM Naval Base. Incorporates the *Royal Naval Museum* (Tel: 023-9272 7562), HMS *Victory* (Tel: 023-9282 2034), HMS *Warrior* (Tel: 023-9229 1379), the †*Mary Rose* (Tel: 023-9275 0521) and the *Dockyard Museum*. History of the Royal Navy and of the dockyard and the trades in it

PRESTON – **Harris Museum and Art Gallery*, Market Square PR1 2PP. Tel: 01772-258248;
Web: www.preston.gov.uk/harris
British art since the 18th century, ceramics, glass, costume and local history; also contemporary exhibitions

READING – †*Rural History Museum*, University of Reading. Tel: 0118-931 8660.
History of farming and the countryside over the last 200 years

ST ALBANS – **Verulamium Museum*, St Michael's AL3 4SW. Tel: 01727-866100;
Web: www.stalbansmuseums.org.uk.
Iron Age and Roman Verulamium, including wall plasters, jewellery, mosaics and room reconstructions

ST IVES, Cornwall – *Tate Gallery St Ives*, Porthmeor Beach TR26 1TG. Tel: 01736-796226; Web: www.tate.org.uk
Painting and sculpture by artists associated with St Ives

SALISBURY – *Salisbury and South Wiltshire Museum*, The Close SP1 2EN Tel: 01722-332151.
Archaeology collection

SHEFFIELD – **City Museum and Mappin Art Gallery*, Weston Park. Tel: 0114-276 8588.
Includes applied arts, natural history, Bronze Age archaeology and ethnography, 19th- and 20th-century art
**Graves Art Gallery*, Surrey Street. Tel: 0114-273 5158.
Twentieth-century British art, Grice Collection of Chinese ivories
**Kelham Island Industrial Museum*, off Alma Street. Tel: 0114-272 2106.
Local industrial and social history
**Ruskin Gallery and Ruskin Craft Gallery*, Norfolk Street LA21 8DU. Tel: 0114-273 5299/203 9416;
Web: www.coniston.org.uk.

SOUTHAMPTON – City Art Gallery, Civic Centre SO14 7LP. Tel: 023-8083 2277;
Web: www.southampton.gov.uk/leisure/arts
Fine art, especially 20th-century British
*†*Maritime Museum*, Town Quay SO14 2NY.
Tel: 023-8022 3941. Southampton maritime history
*†*Museum of Archaeology*, Town Quay SO14 2NY.
Tel: 023-8063 5904.
Roman, Saxon and medieval archaeology
*†*Tudor House Museum and Garden*, Bugle Street SO142AD. Tel: 023-8033 2513.
Restored 16th century garden; social history exhibitions

SOUTH SHIELDS – *Arbeia Roman Fort*, Baring Street. Tel: 0191-456 6612.
Excavated ruins
South Shields Museum and Art Gallery, Ocean Road NE33 2JA. Tel: 0191-456 8740.
South Tyneside history, including reconstructed street

STOKE-ON-TRENT – **Etruria Industrial Museum*, Etruria ST4 7AS. Tel: 01782-233144.
Britain's sole surviving steam-powered potter's mill
**Gladstone Pottery Museum*, Longton ST3 1PQ.
Tel: 01782-319232;
Web: www.stoke.gov.uk/gladstone
A working Victorian pottery
*†*Potteries Museum and Art Gallery*, Hanley ST1 3DE.
Tel: 01782-232323;
Web: www.stoke.gov.uk/citymuseum

Pottery, china and porcelain collections and a Mark XVI Spitfire. Pottery factory tours are available by arrangement, at the following: *Royal Doulton*, Burslem; *Spode*, Stoke; *Wedgwood*, Barlaston; *W. Moorcroft*, Cobridge; *Staffordshire Enamels*, Longton; *Royale Stratford China*, Fenton

STYAL, Cheshire – *Quarry Bank Mill* FK9 4LA.
Tel: 01625-527468; Web: www.quarrybankmill.org.uk
Working mill illustrating history of cotton industry; costumed guides at restored Apprentice House

SUNDERLAND – †*Sunderland Art Gallery*, Borough Road SO1 1PP. Tel: 0191-553 2323.
Fine and decorative art

WASHINGTON – †*Washington 'F' Pit Museum*, Albany Way
Colliery-related collection

TELFORD – *†*Ironbridge Gorge Museums* TF8 7AW.
Tel: 01952-432166; Web: www.ironbridge.org.uk
Includes first iron bridge; Blists Hill (late Victorian working town); Museum of Iron; Jackfield Tile Museum; Coalport China Museum; Tar Tunnel; Broseley Pipeworks

TRING, Herts – *Tring Zoological Museum*, Akeman Street HP23 6AT. Tel: 01442-824181.
Display of more than 4,000 animal species

WAKEFIELD – *Yorkshire Sculpture Park*, West Bretton WS4 4LG. Tel: 01924-830302.
Open-air sculpture gallery including works by Moore, Hepworth, Frink and others in 300 acres of parkland

WORCESTER – **City Museum and Art Gallery*, Foregate Street WR1 1DT. Tel: 01905-25371.
Includes a military museum, River Severn Gallery and changing art exhibitions
Museum of Worcester Porcelain and Royal Worcester Visitor Centre, Severn Street WR1 2NE. Tel: 01905-23221.
Factory tours

WROUGHTON, nr Swindon, Wilts – *Science Museum*, Wroughton Airfield. Tel: 01793-814466.
Aircraft displays and some of the Science Museum's transport and agricultural collection

YEOVIL, Somerset – *Fleet Air Arm Museum*, Royal Naval Air Station, Yeovilton BA22 8HT. Tel: 01935-840565;
Web: www.fleetairarm.com
History of naval aviation; historic aircraft, including Concorde 002
Montacute House, Montacute. Elizabethan and Jacobean portraits from the National Portrait Gallery

YORK – *Beningbrough Hall*, Shipton-by-Beningbrough YO6 1DD. Tel: 01904-470666.
Portraits from the National Portrait Gallery
*†*Castle Museum*. Tel: 01904-653611.
Reconstructed streets; costume and military collections
*†*City Art Gallery*, Exhibition Square YO1 7EW.
Tel: 01904-551861; Web: www.york.gov.uk.
European and British painting spanning seven centuries; modern pottery
Jorvik Viking Centre, Coppergate YO1 9WT.
Tel: 01904-643211; Web: www.vikingyorvik.com
Reconstruction of Viking York
National Railway Museum, Leeman Road YO2 4XJ.
Tel: 01904-621261; Web: www.nmsi.ac.uk/nrm
Includes locomotives, rolling stock and carriages
*†*Yorkshire Museum*, Museum Gardens WO1 7FR.
Tel: 01904-551800;
Web: www.theyorkshiremuseum.com.
Yorkshire life from Roman to medieval times; geology gallery

600   Conservation and Heritage

WALES

BODELWYDDAN, Denbighshire – *Bodelwyddan Castle* LL18 5YA. Tel: 01745-584060.
Portraits from the National Portrait Gallery, furniture from the Victoria and Albert Museum and sculptures from the Royal Academy
CAERLEON – *Roman Legionary Museum*. Tel: 01633-423134.
Material from the site of the Roman fortress of Isca and its suburbs
CARDIFF – *National Museum and Gallery Cardiff*, Cathays Park CF1 3NP. Tel: 029-2039 7951; Web: www.nmgw.ac.uk/index.htm
Includes natural sciences, archaeology and Impressionist paintings
Museum of Welsh Life, St Fagans CF5 6XB. Tel: 029-2057 3500; Web: www.nmgw.ac.uk
Open-air museum with re-erected buildings, agricultural equipment and costume
DRE-FACH FELINDRE, nr Llandysul – *Museum of the Welsh Woollen Industry* SA44 5UP. Tel: 01559-370929; Web: www.nmgw.ac.uk
Exhibitions, a working woollen mill and craft workshops
LLANBERIS, nr Caernarfon –*Welsh Slate Museum* WL55 4TY. Tel: 01286-870630; Web: www.nmgw.ac.uk.
Former slate quarry with original machinery and plant slate crafts demonstrations
LLANDRINDOD WELLS – *National Cycle Exhibition*, Automobile Palace, Temple Street. Tel: 01597-825531.
Over 200 bicycles on display, from 1818 to the present day
SWANSEA – *Glynn Vivian Art Gallery and Museum*, Alexandra Road. Tel: 01792-655006.
Paintings, ceramics, Swansea pottery and porcelain, clocks, glass and Welsh art
Swansea Maritime and Industrial Museum, Museum Square SA1 1SN. Tel: 01792-650351.
Includes a working woollen mill and historic boats afloat
Swansea Museum, Victoria Road SA1 1SN. Tel: 01792-653763; Web: www.swansea.gov.uk.
Archaeology, social history, Swansea pottery

SCOTLAND

ABERDEEN – *Aberdeen Art Gallery*, Schoolhill AB10 1FQ. Tel: 01224-523700.
Art from the 18th to 20th century
Aberdeen Maritime Museum, Shiprow AB11 5BY. Tel: 01224-337700; Web: www.aagm.co.uk
Maritime history, incl. shipbuilding and North Sea oil
EDINBURGH –*Britannia*, Leith docks. Tel: 0131-555 5566; Web: www.royal.gov.uk/faq/hmy.htm
Former royal yacht with royal barge and royal family picture gallery. Tickets must be pre-booked
City Art Centre, Market Street. Tel: 0131-529 3993.
Late 19th- and 20th-century art and temporary exhibitions
Huntly House Museum, Canongate EH8 8DD. Tel: 0131-529 4143; Web: www.cac.org.uk
Local history, silver, glass and Scottish pottery
Museum of Childhood, High Street EH1 1TG. Tel: 0131-529 4142; Web: www.cac.org.uk
Toys, games, clothes and exhibits relating to the social history of childhood

Museum of Flight, East Fortune Airfield, nr North Berwick. Tel: 01620-880308.
Display of aircraft
Museum of Scotland, Chambers Street EH1 1JF. Tel: 0131-247 4422; Web: www.nms.ac.uk
Scottish history from prehistoric times to the present
National Gallery of Scotland, The Mound EH2 2EL. Tel: 0131-624 6200; Web: www.natgalscot.ac.uk
Paintings, drawings and prints from the 16th- to 20th-century, and the national collection of Scottish art
The People's Story, Canongate EH8 8BN. Tel: 0131-529 4057.
Edinburgh life since the 18th–century
Royal Museum of Scotland, Chambers Street EH1 1JF. Tel: 0131-225 7534; Web: www.nms.ac.uk
Scottish and international collections from prehistoric times to the present
Scottish Agricultural Museum, Ingliston. Tel: 0131-333 2674.
History of agriculture in Scotland
Scottish National Gallery of Modern Art, Belford Road EH4 3DR.
Tel: 0131-624 6200; Web: www.natgalscot.ac.uk
Twentieth-century painting, sculpture and graphic art
Scottish National Portrait Gallery, Queen Street EH2 1JD. Tel: 0131-624 6200; Web; www.natgalscot.ac.uk
Portraits of eminent people in Scottish history, and the national collection of photography
The Writers' Museum, Lawnmarket EH1 2PA. Tel: 0131-529 4901; Web: www.edinburgh.gov.uk
Robert Louis Stevenson, Walter Scott and Robert Burns exhibits
FORT WILLIAM – *West Highland Museum*, Cameron Square PH33 6AJ. Tel: 01397-702169.
Includes tartan collections and exhibits relating to 1745 uprising
GLASGOW – *Burrell Collection*, Pollokshaws Road G43 1AT. Tel: 0141-287 2550.
Paintings, textiles, furniture, ceramics, stained glass and silver from classical times to the 19th century
Gallery of Modern Art, Queen Street G1 3AZ. Tel: 0141-229 1996.
Collection of contemporary Scottish and world art
Glasgow Art Gallery and Museum, Kelvingrove Tel: 0141-287 2699.
Includes Old Masters, 19th-century French paintings and armour collection
Hunterian Art Gallery, Hillhead Street G12 8QQ. Tel: 0141-330 5431; Web: www.hunterian.ac.uk
Rennie Mackintosh and Whistler collections; Old Masters, Scottish paintings and modern paintings, sculpture and prints
McLellan Galleries, Sauchiehall Street Tel: 0141-331 1854.
Temporary exhibitions
Museum of Transport, Bunhouse Road G3 8DP. Tel: 0141-287 2720;
Web: www.clyde-valley.com/glasgow/transmus.htm
Includes a reproduction of a 1938 Glasgow street, cars since the 1930s, trams and a Glasgow subway station
People's Palace Museum, Glasgow Green G3 8AG. Tel: 0141-554 0223; Web: www.glasgow.gov.uk
History of Glasgow since 1175
St Mungo Museum of Religious Life and Art, Castle Street G4 0RH. Tel: 0141-553 2557.
Explores universal themes through objects of all the main world religions

NORTHERN IRELAND

BELFAST – *Ulster Museum*, Botanic Gardens BT9 5AB. Tel: 028-9038 3000; Web: www.ulstermuseum.org.uk Irish antiquities, natural and local history, fine and applied arts
HOLYWOOD, Co. Down – *Ulster Folk and Transport Museum*, Cultra. Tel: 028-9042 8428.
Open-air museum with original buildings from Ulster town and rural life *c*.1900; indoor galleries including Irish rail and road transport and *Titanic* exhibitions

LONDONDERRY – *The Tower Museum*, Union Hall Place P248 6LU. Tel: 028-7137 2411.
Tells the story of Ireland through the history of Londonderry
OMAGH, Co. Tyrone – *Ulster American Folk Park*, Castletown BT78 5QY. Tel: 028-8224 3292.
Open-air museum telling the story of Ulster's emigrants to America; restored or recreated dwellings and workshops; ship and dockside gallery

Royal Academicians (as at August 2001)

Date of appointment in parentheses

PAINTERS

Senior Academicians
Diana Armfield (1989)
Jeffery Camp (1974)
John Craxton (1993)
Bernard Dunstan (1959)
Anthony Eyton (1976)
Mary Fedden (1992)
Sir Terry Frost (1992)
Frederick Gore, CBE (1964)
Colin Hayes (1963)
Albert Irvin (1998)
Flavia Irwin (1996)
Leonard Rosoman (1960)
Sir Kyffin Williams, OBE (1970)

Academicians
Norman Adams (1967)
Craigie Aitchison, CBE (1978)
Gillian Ayres (1991) (re-elected following resignation in 2000)
John Bellany, CBE (1986)
Adrian Berg, (1992)
Elizabeth Blackadder, OBE (1971)
Peter Blake, CBE (1974)
Sandra Blow (1971)
Olwyn Bowey (1970)
William Bowyer (1974)
Patrick Caulfield (1993)
Maurice Cockrill (1999)
Peter Coker (1965)
Jean Cooke (1965)
Frederick Cuming (1969)
Gus Cummins (1992)
Jennifer Durrant (1994)
Stephen Farthing (1998)
Donald Hamilton Fraser (1975)
Anthony Green (1971)
David Hockney, CH (1985)
Ken Howard (1983)
John Hoyland (1983)
Paul Huxley (1987)
William Jacklin (1989)
R. B. Kitaj (1984)
Sonia Lawson (1982)
Ben Levene (1975)
Patrick Procktor (1996)
Barbara Rae, CBE (1996)

Michael Rooney (1990)
Philip Sutton (1977)
David Tindle (1973)
Anthony Whishaw (1980)

SCULPTORS

Senior Academicians
Kenneth Armitage (1994)
Prof. Sir Eduardo Paolozzi, CBE (1979)

Academicians
Ivor Abrahams (1989)
Ralph Brown (1968)
James Butler (1964)
Ann Christopher (1980)
Geoffrey Clarke (1970)
Robert Clatworthy (1968)
Prof. Tony Cragg (1994)
Richard Deacon (1998)
Ken Draper (1990)
Barry Flanagan, OBE (1987)
Anish Kapoor, (1990)
Prof. Phillip King, CBE (1977)
Prof. Bryan Kneale (1970)
David Mach (1998)
John Maine (1995)
Dhruva Mistry (1991)
David Nash (1999)
William Tucker (1992)
Alison Wilding (1999)
John Wragg (1983)

ARCHITECTS

Senior Academicians
Prof. H.T. Cadbury-Brown, OBE (1971)
Prof. Trevor Dannatt (1977)
Sir Philip Dowson, CBE (1979)
Leonard Manasseh, OBE (1976)
John Partridge, CBE (1980)
Sir Philip Powell, CH, OBE (1972)
Prof. Sir Colin St John Wilson (1990)

Academicians
Will Alsop (2000)
Gordon Benson (2000)
Edward Cullinan, CBE (1989)

Lord Foster of Thames Bank, OM (1983)
Nicholas Grimshaw, CBE (1994)
Sir Michael Hopkins, CBE (1992)
Eva Jiricna, CBE (1997)
Paul Koralek, CBE (1986)
Richard MacCormac, CBE (1993)
Michael Manser, CBE (1994)
Ian Ritchie (1998)
Lord Rogers of Riverside (1978)

ENGRAVERS, PRINTMAKERS, AND DRAFTSMEN

Senior Academicians
Paul Hogarth, OBE (1974)

Academicians
Prof. Norman Ackroyd (1988)
Jennifer Dickson (1970)
Peter Freeth (1990)
Allen Jones (1981)
Christopher Le Brun (1996)
Leonard McComb (1987)
Mick Moon (1994)
Prof. Brendan Neiland (1992)
Prof. Chris Orr (1995)
Tom Phillips (1984)
Joe Tilson (1985)

Honorary Academicians
Georg Baselitz (1999)
Eduardo Chillida (1983)
Ralph Erskine (1984)
Frank O. Gehry (1998)
Arata Isozaki (1994)
Jasper Johns (1989)
Elsworth Kelly (2001)
Anselm Kiefer (1996)
Matta (1997)
Mimmo Paladino (1999)
Ieoh Ming Pei (1993)
Robert Rauschenberg (2000)
Richard Serra (1995)
Frank Stella (1993)
Antoni Tàpies (1992)
Cy Twombly (1998)
Jørn Utzon (1985)
Andrew Wyeth (1996)

Hallmarks

Hallmarks are the symbols stamped on gold, silver or platinum articles to indicate that they have been tested at an official Assay Office and that they conform to one of the legal standards. With certain exceptions, all gold, silver or platinum articles are required by law to be hallmarked before they are offered for sale. Hallmarking was instituted in England in 1300 under a statute of Edward I.

MODERN HALLMARKS

Since 1 January 1999, UK hallmarks have consisted of three compulsory symbols – the sponsor's mark, the fineness (standard) mark and the assay office mark. Traditional marks such as the year date letter, the Britannia for 958 silver, the lion passant for 925 silver (lion rampant in Scotland) and the orb for 950 platinum may be added voluntarily. The distinction between UK and foreign articles has been removed, and more finenesses are now legal, reflecting the more common finenesses elsewhere in Europe.

SPONSOR'S MARK

Instituted in England in 1363, the sponsor's mark was originally a device such as a bird or fleur-de-lis. Now it consists of the initial letters of the name or names of the manufacturer or firm. Where two or more sponsors have the same initials, there is a variation in the surrounding shield or style of letters.

FINENESS (STANDARD) MARK

The fineness (standard) mark indicates that the content of the precious metal in the alloy from which the article is made, is not less than the legal standard. The legal standard is the minimum content of precious metal by weight in parts per thousand, and the standards are:

Gold	999	
	990	
	916.6	(22 carat)
	750	(18 carat)
	585	(14 carat)
	375	(9 carat)
Silver	999	
	958.4	(Britannia)
	925	(sterling)
	800	
Platinum	999	
	950	
	900	
	850	

ASSAY OFFICE MARK

This mark identifies the particular assay office at which the article was tested and marked. The British assay offices are:

LONDON, Goldsmith's Hall, London EC2V 8AQ.
  Tel: 020-7606 8975

BIRMINGHAM, Newhall Street, Birmingham B3 1SB.
  Tel: 0121-236 6951

SHEFFIELD, 137 Portobello Street, Sheffield S1 4DS.
  Tel: 0114-275 5111

EDINBURGH, 24 Broughton Street, Edinburgh EH1 3RH.
  Tel: 0131-556 1144

Assay offices formerly existed in other towns, e.g. Chester, Exeter, Glasgow, Newcastle, Norwich and York, each having its own distinguishing mark.

DATE LETTER

The date letter shows the year in which an article was assayed and hallmarked. Each alphabetical cycle has a distinctive style of lettering or shape of shield. The date letters were different at the various assay offices and the particular office must be established from the assay office mark before reference is made to tables of date letters. Date letter marks became voluntary from 1 January 1999.

The table on page 608 shows specimen shields and letters used by the London Assay Office on silver articles in each period from 1498. The same letters are found on gold articles but the surrounding shield may differ. Since 1 January 1975, each office has used the same style of date letter and shield for all articles.

OTHER MARKS

FOREIGN GOODS

Foreign goods imported into the UK are required to be hallmarked before sale, unless they already bear a convention mark (see below) or a hallmark struck by an independent assay office in the European Economic Area which is deemed to be equivalent to a UK hallmark.

The following are the assay office marks used for gold until the end of 1998. For silver and platinum the symbols remain the same but the shields differ in shape.

  London

  Birmingham

  Sheffield

  Edinburgh

CONVENTION HALLMARKS

Special marks at authorised assay offices of the signatory countries of the International Convention on Hallmarking (Austria, the Czech Republic, Denmark, Finland, Ireland, the Netherlands, Norway, Portugal, Sweden, Switzerland and the UK) are legally recognised in the United Kingdom as approved hallmarks. These consist of a sponsor's mark, a common control mark, a fineness mark (arabic numerals showing the standard in parts per thousand), and an assay office mark. There is no date letter.

The fineness marks are:

Gold	750	(18 carat)
	585	(14 carat)
	375	(9 carat)
Silver	925	(sterling)
Platinum	950	

The common control marks are:

Gold (18 carat)

Silver

Platinum

DUTY MARKS

In 1784 an additional mark of the reigning sovereign's head was introduced to signify that the excise duty had been paid. The mark became obsolete on the abolition of the duty in 1890.

COMMEMORATIVE MARKS

There are three other marks to commemorate special events: the silver jubilee of King George V and Queen Mary in 1935, the coronation of Queen Elizabeth II in 1953, and her silver jubilee in 1977. During 1999 and 2000 there is a voluntary additional Millennium Mark.

LONDON (GOLDSMITHS' HALL) DATE LETTERS FROM 1498

	Black letter, small	1498–9 1517–8
	Lombardic	1518–9 1537–8
	Roman and other capitals	1538–9 1557–8
	Black letter, small	1558–9 1577–8
	Roman letter, capitals	1578–9 1597–8
	Lombardic, external cusps	1598–9 1617–8
	Italic letter, small	1618–9 1637–8
	Court hand	1638–9 1657–8
	Black letter, capitals	1658–9 1677–8
	Black letter, small	1678–9 1696–7
	Court hand	1697 1715–6
	Roman letter, capitals	1716–7 1735–6
	Roman letter, small	1736–7 1738–9
	Roman letter, small	1739–40 1755–6
	Old English, capitals	1756–7 1775–6
	Roman letter, small	1776–7 1795–6
	Roman letter, capitals	1796–7 1815–6
	Roman letter, small	1816–7 1835–6
	Old English, capitals	1836–7 1855–6
	Old English, small	1856–7 1875–6
	Roman letter, capitals [A to M square shield N to Z as shown]	1876–7 1895–6
	Roman letter, small	1896–7 1915–6
	Black letter, small	1916–7 1935–6
	Roman letter, capitals	1936–7 1955–6
	Italic letter, small	1956–7 1974
	Italic letter, capitals	1975

Countries of the World

WORLD AREA AND POPULATION

The total population of the world in mid-1990 was estimated at 5,292 million, compared with 3.019 million in 1960 and 2.070 million in 1930.

Continent, etc.	Area sq. miles '000	sq. km '000	Estimated population mid-1990
Africa	11,704	30,313	642,000,000
North America[1]	8,311	21,525	276,000,000
Latin America[2]	7,933	20,547	448,000,000
Asia[3]	10,637	27,549	3,113,000,000
Europe[4]	1,915	4,961	498,000,000
Former USSR	8,649	22,402	289,000,000
Oceania[5]	3,286	8,510	26,500,000
TOTAL	52,435	135,807	5,292,000,000

[1]Includes Greenland and Hawaii
[2]Mexico and the remainder of the Americas south of the USA
[3]Includes European Turkey, excludes former USSR
[4]Excludes European Turkey and former USSR
[5]Includes Australia, New Zealand and the islands inhabited by Micronesian, Melanesian and Polynesian peoples.
Source: UN Demographic Yearbook 1990 (pub. 1992)

A United Nations report The Sex and Age Distribution of the World Populations (revised 1994) puts the world's population in the late 20th and the 21st centuries at the following levels (medium variant data):

1995	5,176.4m	2030	8,670.6m
2000	6,158.0m	2040	9,318.2m
2010	7,032.3m	2050	9,833.2m
2020	7,887.8m		

The population forecast for the years 2000 and 2050 is:

Continent, etc.	Estimated population (million) 2000	2050
Africa	831.596	2,140.844
North America[1]	306.280	388.997
Latin America[2]	523.875	838.527
Asia	3,753.846	5,741.005
Europe	729.803	677.764
Oceania	30,651	46,070
TOTAL	6,158.051	9,833.207

[1]Includes Bermuda, Greenland, and St Pierre and Miquelon
[2]Mexico and the remainder of the Americas south of the USA

AREA AND POPULATION BY CONTINENT

No complete survey of many countries has yet been achieved and consequently accurate area figures are not always available. Similarly, may countries have not recently, or have never, taken a census. The areas of countries given below are derived from estimate figures published by the United Nations. The conversion factors used are:
(i) to convert square miles to square km, multiply by 2.589988
(ii) to convert square km to square miles, multiply by 0.3861022
Population figures for countries are derived from the most recent estimates available. Accurate and up-to-date data for the populations of capital cities are scarce, and definitions of cities' extent differ. The figures given below are the latest estimates available.

Ψ seaport

AFRICA

COUNTRY/TERRITORY	AREA Sq. miles	Sq. Km	POPULATION	CAPITAL	POPULATION OF CAPITAL
Algeria	919,595	2,381,741	29,050,000	Ψ Algiers (El Djazaïr)	1,507,241
Angola	481,354	1,246,700	11,569,000	Ψ Luanda	475,328
Benin	43,484	112,622	5,828,000	Ψ Porto Novo	179,138
Botswana	224,607	581,730	1,533,000	Gaborone	286,779
Burkina Faso	105,792	274,000	11,087,000	Ouagadougou	634,479
Burundi	10,747	27,834	6,194,000	Bujumbura	235,440
Cameroon	183,569	475,442	13,937,000	Yaoundé	653,670
Cape Verde	1,557	4,033	406,000	Ψ Praia	61,644
Central African Republic	240,535	622,984	3,245,000	Bangui	473,817
Chad	495,755	1,284,000	6,702,000	N'Djaména	179,000
Comoros	863	2,235	651,000	Moroni	17,267
Congo, Democratic Republic of	905,355	2,344,858	48,040,000	Kinshasa	2,664,309
Congo-Brazzaville, Rep. of	132,047	342,000	2,745,000	Brazzaville	596,200
Côte d'Ivoire	124,504	322,463	14,300,000	Yamoussoukro	126,191
Djibouti	8,958	23,200	634,000	Ψ Djibouti	62,000
Egypt	386,662	1,001,449	67,974,000	Cairo	6,800,000
Equatorial Guinea	10,831	28,051	420,000	Ψ Malabo	30,418
Eritrea	45,406	117,600	3,409,000	Asmara	358,100
Ethiopia	426,373	1,104,300	63,495,000	Addis Ababa	2,495,000
Gabon	103,347	267,668	1,138,000	Ψ Libreville	251,000
Gambia	4,361	11,295	1,169,000	Ψ Banjul	109,986

Country/Territory	Area Sq. miles	Sq. Km	Population	Capital	Population of Capital
Ghana	92,098	238,533	18,885,616	Ψ Accra	1,445,515
Guinea	94,926	245,857	7,614,000	Ψ Conakry	763,000
Guinea–Bissau	13,948	36,125	1,112,000	Ψ Bissau	109,214
Kenya	224,081	580,367	33,144,000	Nairobi	1,400,000
Lesotho	11,720	30,355	2,131,000	Maseru	367,000
Liberia	43,000	111,369	2,879,000	Ψ Monrovia	421,053
Libya	679,362	1,759,540	4,389,739	Ψ Tripoli (Tarābulus)	1,000,000
Madagascar	226,658	587,041	15,845,000	Antananarivo	1,052,835
Malawi	45,747	118,484	10,441,000	Lilongwe	233,973
Mali	478,841	1,240,192	11,480,000	Bamako	809,552
Mauritania	395,956	1,025,520	2,392,000	Nouakchott	850,000
Mauritius	788	2,040	1,160,000	Ψ Port Louis	146,499
Mayotte (Fr.)	144	372	94,410	Mamoudzou	12,000
Morocco	172,414	446,550	27,310,000	Ψ Rabat	1,220,000
Western Sahara	102,703	266,000	265,000	El-Aaiūn	20,010
Mozambique	309,494	801,590	16,916,600	Ψ Maputo	1,039,700
Namibia	318,261	824,292	1,613,000	Windhoek	147,056
Niger	489,191	1,267,000	9,788,000	Niamey	392,169
Nigeria	356,669	923,768	118,369,000	Abuja	378,671
Réunion (Fr.)	969	2,510	673,000	St Denis	121,999
Rwanda	10,169	26,338	5,883,000	Kigali	116,227
Saint Helena (UK)	47	122	6,000	Ψ Jamestown	884
Ascension (UK)	34	88	1,051	Ψ Georgetown	—
Tristan Da Cunha (UK)	38	98	288	Ψ Edinburgh of the Seven Seas	—
São Tomé And Príncipe	372	964	138,000	Ψ São Tomé	43,420
Senegal	75,955	196,722	8,802,000	Ψ Dakar	1,641,358
Seychelles	176	455	78,846	Ψ Victoria	24,324
Sierra Leone	27,699	71,740	4,428,000	Ψ Freetown	469,776
Somalia	246,201	637,657	10,217,000	Ψ Mogadishu	230,000
South Africa	471,445	1,221,037	43,336,000	{ Pretoria	822,925;
				Ψ Cape Town;	1,911,521;
				Bloemfontein	300,150
Sudan	967,500	2,505,813	27,889,000	Khartoum (Al-Khartūm)	947,483
Swaziland	6,704	17,364	906,000	Mbabane	38,290
Tanzania	341,216	883,749	31,507,000	Dodoma	85,000
Togo	21,925	56,785	4,317,000	Ψ Lomé	366,476
Tunisia	63,170	163,610	9,215,000	Ψ Tunis	1,830,634
Uganda	93,065	241,038	20,438,000	Kampala	750,000
Zambia	290,587	752,618	8,478,000	Lusaka	982,362
Zimbabwe	150,872	390,757	12,294,000	Harare	1,189,103

AMERICA

North America

Country/Territory	Area Sq. miles	Sq. Km	Population	Capital	Population of Capital
Canada	3,849,674	9,970,610	30,491,294	Ottawa	1,010,498
Greenland (Den.)	840,004	2,175,600	56,000	Ψ Godthåb (Nuuk)	12,483
Mexico	756,066	1,958,201	96,400,000	Mexico City	15,047,685
Saint Pierre and Miquelon (Fr.)	93	242	6,316	Ψ St Pierre	5,416
United States Of America	3,536,382	9,156,119	274,520,000	Washington DC	7,285,206

Central America and the West Indies

Country/Territory	Area Sq. miles	Sq. Km	Population	Capital	Population of Capital
Anguilla (UK)	37	96	12,394	The Valley	2,400
Antigua And Barbuda	171	442	67,000	Ψ St John's	22,342
Aruba (Neth)	75	193	87,000	Ψ Oranjestad	25,000
Bahamas	5,358	13,878	289,000	Ψ Nassau	172,196
Barbados	166	430	262,000	Ψ Bridgetown	108,000
Belize	8,763	22,696	230,000	Belmopan	44,087
Bermuda (UK)	20	53	60,000	Ψ Hamilton	2,277
Cayman Islands (UK)	102	264	38,000	Ψ George Town	20,000
Costa Rica	19,730	51,100	3,464,000	San José	1,220,412
Cuba	42,804	110,861	11,059,000	Ψ Havana	2,184,990
Dominica	290	751	71,000	Ψ Roseau	16,243
Dominican Republic	18,730	48,511	8,097,000	Ψ Santo Domingo	2,134,779

Country/Territory	Area Sq. miles	Sq. Km	Population	Capital	Population of Capital
El Salvador	8,124	21,041	5,928,000	San Salvador	1,200,000
Grenada	133	344	93,000	Ψ St George's	4,788
Guadeloupe *(Fr.)*	658	1,705	437,000	Ψ Basse Terre	29,522
Guatemala	42,042	08,889	10,517,000	Guatemala City	1,675,589
Haïti	10,714	27,750	7,492,000	Ψ Port-au-Prince	884,472
Honduras	43,277	112,088	6,338,000	Tegucigalpa	670,100
Jamaica	4,243	10,990	2,590,400	Ψ Kingston	524,638
Martinique *(Fr.)*	425	1,102	388,000	Ψ Fort de France	133,920
Montserrat *(UK)*	39	102	4,500	Ψ Plymouth	1,478
Netherlands Antilles (Neth)	309	800	207,333	Ψ Willemstad	50,000
Nicaragua	50,193	(130,000)	4,351,000	Managua	608,020
Panama	29,157	75,517	2,719,000	Ψ Panama City	464,928
Puerto Rico *(USA)*	3,427	8,875	3,771,000	Ψ San Juan	1,222,316
Saint Kitts – Nevis	101	261	41,000	Ψ Basseterre	12,200
Saint Lucia	240	622	146,000	Ψ Castries	51,994
Saint Vincent And The Grenadines	150	388	112,000	Ψ Kingstown	15,466
Trinidad And Tobago	1,981	5,130	1,307,000	Ψ Port of Spain	43,396
Turks And Caicos Islands *(UK)*	166	430	23,000	Ψ Grand Turk	3,691
Virgin Islands, British *(UK)*	58	151	20,000	Ψ Road Town	3,983
Virgin Islands, US *(USA)*	134	347	114,483	Ψ Charlotte Amalie	11,842

South America

Country/Territory	Area Sq. miles	Sq. Km	Population	Capital	Population of Capital
Argentina	1,073,518	2,780,400	35,672,000	Ψ Buenos Aires	11,298,030
Bolivia	424,165	1,098,581	8,140,000	La Paz	739,453
Brazil	3,300,171	8,547,403	159,884,000	Brasília	1,737,813
Chile	292,135	756,626	14,622,000	Santiago	4,640,635
Colombia	439,737	1,138,914	36,162,000	Bogotá	5,398,998
Ecuador	109,484	283,561	11,937,000	Quito	1,444,363
Falkland Islands *(UK)*	4,700	12,173	2,221	Ψ Stanley	1,636
French Guiana *(Fr.)*	34,749	90,000	159,000	Ψ Cayenne	41,164
Guyana	83,000	214,969	847,000	Ψ Georgetown	250,000
Paraguay	157,048	406,752	5,085,000	Asunción	718,690
Peru	496,225	1,285,216	25,015,000	Lima	6,321,173
South Georgia *(UK)*	1,580	4,092	—	—	—
Suriname	63,037	163,265	437,000	Ψ Paramaribo	265,000
Uruguay	67,574	175,016	3,221,000	Ψ Montevideo	1,303,182
Venezuela	352,145	912,050	22,777,000	Caracas	3,672,779

ASIA

Country/Territory	Area Sq. miles	Sq. Km	Population	Capital	Population of Capital
Afghanistan	251,773	652,090	22,132,000	Kābol (Kabul)	1,424,400
Bahrain	268	694	620,000	Ψ Manama (Al-Manāmah)	140,401
Bangladesh	55,598	143,998	122,013,000	Dhaka	3,397,187
Bhutan	18,147	47,000	1,862,000	Thimphu	15,000
Brunei Darussalam	2,226	5,765	307,000	Bandar Seri Begawan	49,902
Cambodia	69,898	181,035	10,516,000	Ψ Phnom Penh	832,000
China[1]	3,705,408	9,596,961	1,248,100,000	Beijing	7,362,426
Hong Kong *(China)*	415	1,075	6,687,200	—	—
Macao *(China)*	7	18	440,000	Ψ Macao	241,413
East Timor	5,743	14,874	839,719	Ψ Dili	62,000
India	1,269,213	3,287,263	970,930,000	New Delhi	301,297
Indonesia	735,358	1,904,569	199,867,000	Ψ Jakarta	9,160,500
Iran	630,574	1,633,188	60,694,000	Tehran	6,750,043
Iraq	169,235	438,317	21,177,000	Baghdād	3,841,268
Israel[2]	8,130	21,056	6,100,000	Tel Aviv	1,919,700
West Bank And Gaza Strip	2,406	6,231	1,635,000	Gaza City	120,000
Japan	145,880	377,829	125,638,000	Tokyo	11,680,296
Jordan	37,738	97,740	5,774,000	Ammān	1,270,000
Kazakhstan	1,052,085	2,724,900	15,671,000	Astana	275,100
Korea, Democratic People's Republic	46,540	120,538	22,082,000	Pyongyang	2,741,260
Korea, Republic of	38,327	99,268	46,858,460	Seoul	10,321,000

Country/Territory	Area Sq. miles	Sq. Km	Population	Capital	Population of Capital
Kuwait	6,880	17,818	1,866,104	Ψ Kuwait City (Al-Kuwayt)	388,663
Kyrgyzstan	77,181	199,900	4,856,000	Bishkek	589,400
Laos	91,429	236,800	5,035,000	Vientiane	132,253
Lebanon	4,015	10,400	3,144,000	Ψ Beirut	1,500,000
Malaysia	127,320	329,758	21,667,000	Kuala Lumpur; Putrajaya	1,145,342
Maldives	115	298	273,000	Ψ Malé	62,973
Mongolia	604,829	1,566,500	2,313,000	Ulaanbaatar	515,100
Myanmar	261,228	676,578	46,402,000	Ψ Yangon (Rangoon)	2,513,023
Nepal	56,827	147,181	22,591,000	Kathmandu	421,258
Oman	82,030	212,457	2,302,000	Ψ Muscat (Masqat)	400,000
Pakistan	307,374	796,095	138,150,000	Islamabad	350,000
Philippines	115,831	300,000	73,527,000	Ψ Manila	8,594,150
Qatar	4,247	11,000	569,000	Ψ Doha (Ad-Dawhah)	217,294
Saudi Arabia	830,000	2,149,690	19,494,000	Riyadh (Ar-Riyād)	3,100,000
Singapore	239	618	3,737,000	—	—
Sri Lanka	25,332	65,610	18,552,000	Ψ Colombo	615,000
Syria	71,498	185,180	14,951,000	Damascus	1,549,000
Taiwan	13,800	35,742	21,854,273	Taipei	2,638,565
Tajikistan	55,251	143,100	5,513,400	Dushanbe	528,600
Thailand	198,115	513,115	60,206,000	Ψ Bangkok	5,882,000
Turkey[3]	314,508	814,578	63,745,000	Ankara	3,258,026
Turkmenistan	188,456	488,100	3,808,900	Ashgabat	407,000
United Arab Emirates	32,278	83,600	2,940,000	Abu Dhabi (Abu Żaby)	450,000
Uzbekistan	172,742	447,400	21,206,800	Tashkent	2,200,000
Vietnam	128,066	331,689	76,548,000	Hanoi	1,073,760
Yemen	203,850	527,968	15,919,000	Sana'ā'	926,595

[1] Including Tibet
[2] Including East Jerusalem, the Golan Heights and Israeli citizens on the West Bank
[3] Including Turkey in Europe

EUROPE

Albania	11,099	28,748	3,731,000	Tirana	244,153
Andorra	181	468	65,877	Andorra la Vella	21,721
Armenia	11,506	29,800	3,798,400	Yerevan	1,254,400
Austria	32,378	83,859	8,086,000	Vienna	1,806,737
Azerbaijan	33,436	86,600	7,625,000	Ψ Baku	1,149,000
Belarus	80,155	207,600	10,179,000	Minsk	1,708,308
Belgium	11,787	30,528	10,188,000	Brussels	953,175
Bosnia-Hercegovina	19,767	51,197	3,784,000	Sarajevo	529,021
Bulgaria	42,823	110,912	8,306,000	Sofia	1,192,735
Croatia	21,824	56,538	4,498,000	Zagreb	867,717
Cyprus	3,572	9,251	766,000	Nicosia	193,000
Czech Republic	30,450	78,866	10,304,000	Prague	1,200,458
Denmark	16,639	43,094	5,284,000	Ψ Copenhagen	1,362,264
Færøe Islands	540	1,399	48,000	Ψ Tórshavn	16,218
Estonia	17,413	45,100	1,453,844	Tallinn	415,299
Finland	130,559	338,145	5,140,000	Ψ Helsinki	905,555
France	212,935	551,500	58,607,000	Paris	9,319,367
Georgia	26,911	69,700	5,434,000	Tbilisi	1,268,000
Germany	137,846	357,022	82,071,000	Berlin	3,472,009
Gibraltar (UK)	2.3	6.0	28,000	Ψ Gibraltar	—
Greece	50,949	131,957	10,522,000	Athens	3,072,922
Hungary	35,920	93,032	10,153,000	Budapest	1,896,507
Iceland	39,769	103,000	275,277	Ψ Reykjavík	107,764
Ireland, Republic of	27,132	70,273	3,626,087	Ψ Dublin	952,692
Italy	116,339	301,318	57,523,000	Rome	2,648,843
Latvia	24,942	64,600	2,474,000	Riga	805,997
Liechtenstein	62	160	32,015	Vaduz	5,106
Lithuania	25,174	65,200	3,701,300	Vilnius	580,099
Luxembourg	998	2,586	417,000	Luxembourg	77,400
Macedonia	9,928	25,713	2,190,000	Skopje	429,964
Malta	122	316	378,518	Ψ Valletta	7,100

Country/Territory	Area Sq. miles	Sq. Km	Population	Capital	Population of Capital
Moldova	13,012	33,700	4,335,000	Chişinău	655,940
Monaco	0.4	1	32,000	Monaco	27,063
Netherlands	16,033	41,526	15,604,000	Ψ Amsterdam	1,102,323
Norway[1]	125,050	323,877	4,445,460	Ψ Oslo	499,693
Poland	124,808	323,250	38,650,000	Warsaw	1,632,534
Portugal[2]	35,514	91,982	9,920,760	Ψ Lisbon	2,561,225
Romania	92,043	238,391	22,520,000	Bucharest	2,027,500
Russia[3]	6,592,850	17,075,400	146,100,000	Moscow	8,598,896
San Marino	24	61	26,000	San Marino	4,357
Slovakia	18,923	49,012	5,383,000	Bratislava	452,278
Slovenia	7,821	20,256	1,987,000	Ljubljana	273,000
Spain[4]	195,365	505,992	39,270,000	Madrid	3,084,673
Sweden	173,732	449,964	8,846,000	Ψ Stockholm	1,148,953
Switzerland	15,940	41,284	7,114,600	Bern	321,932
Ukraine	233,090	603,700	50,500,000	Kiev (Kyiv)	2,630,000
United Kingdom[5]	93,784	242,900	58,784,000	Ψ London	7,074,265
England	50,351	130,410	48,903,000	—	—
Northern Ireland	5,467	14,160	1,649,000	Ψ Belfast	297,300
Scotland	30,420	78,789	5,137,000	Ψ Edinburgh	448,850
Wales	8,015	20,758	2,917,000	Ψ Cardiff (Caerdydd)	315,040
Vatican City State	0.2	0.44	1,000	Vatican City	766
Yugoslavia	39,449	102,173	10,597,000	Belgrade	1,338,856

[1] Excludes Svalbard and Jan Mayen Islands (approx. 24,101 sq. miles (62,422 sq. km) and 3,000 population)
[2] Includes Madeira (314 sq. miles) and the Azores (922 sq. miles)
[3] Includes Russia in Asia
[4] Includes Balearic Islands, Canary Islands, Ceuta and Melilla
[5] Excludes Isle of Man (221 sq. miles (572 sq. km), 69,788 population), and Channel Islands (75 sq. miles (194 sq. km), 142,949 population)

OCEANIA

Country/Territory	Area Sq. miles	Sq. Km	Population	Capital	Population of Capital
American Samoa (USA)	77	199	58,000	Ψ Pago Pago	3,519
Australia	2,988,902	7,741,220	19,104,600	Canberra	309,500
Norfolk Island	14	36	1,772	Ψ Kingston	—
Fiji	7,056	18,274	809,000	Ψ Suva	141,273
French Polynesia (Fr.)	1,544	4,000	227,000	Ψ Papeete	36,784
Guam (USA)	212	549	145,780	Agana	1,139
Kiribati	280	726	81,000	Tarawa	17,921
Marshall Islands	70	181	61,000	Dalap-Uliga-Darrit	20,000
Micronesia, Federated States Of	271	702	130,000	Palikir	—
Nauru	8	21	11,000	Ψ Nauru	—
New Caledonia (Fr.)	7,172	18,575	193,000	Ψ Noumea	97,581
New Zealand	104,454	270,534	3,811,000	Ψ Wellington	346,700
Cook Islands	91	236	20,000	Rarotonga	9,281
Niue	100	260	2,000	Alofi	—
Ross Dependency[1]	175,000	453,248	—	—	—
Tokelau	5	12	2,000	—	—
Northern Mariana Islands (USA)	179	464	49,000	Saipan	52,706
Palau (USA)	177	459	17,000	Koror	10,493
Papua New Guinea	178,704	462,840	4,500,000	Ψ Port Moresby	173,500
Pitcairn Islands (UK)	2	5	54	—	—
Samoa	1,093	2,831	168,000	Ψ Apia	36,000
Solomon Islands	11,157	28,896	404,000	Ψ Honiara	40,000
Tonga	288	747	99,000	Ψ Nuku'alofa	29,018
Tuvalu	10	26	10,000	Ψ Fongafale	2,856
Vanuatu	4,706	12,189	178,000	Ψ Port Vila	26,100
Wallis And Futuna Islands (Fr.)	77	200	15,000	Ψ Mata–Utu	—

[1] Includes permanent ice shelf

Currencies of the World

AND EXCHANGE RATES AGAINST £ STERLING

COUNTRY/TERRITORY	MONETARY UNIT	AVERAGE RATE TO £ 14 September 2000	AVERAGE RATE TO £ 19 September 2001
Afghanistan	Afghani (Af) of 100 puls	Af 6936.19	Af 6945.45
Albania	Lek (Lk) of 100 qindraka	Lk 215.387	Lk 207.486
Algeria	Algerian dinar (DA) of 100 centimes	DA 112.936	DA 109.808
American Samoa	Currency is that of the USA	US$ 1.4603	US$
Andorra*	French and Spanish currencies in use	–	Francs – 10.6435
		–	Peseta – 269.976
Angola	Readjusted kwanza (Krzl) of 100 lwei	Krzl 10.7745	Kzrl 34.3712
Anguilla	East Caribbean dollar (EC$) of 100 cents	EC$ 3.9427	EC$
Antigua and Barbuda	East Caribbean dollar (EC$) of 100 cents	EC$ 3.9427	EC$ 3.9480
Argentina	Peso of 10,000 australes	Pesos 1.4593	Pesos 1.4617
Armenia	Dram of 100 louma	Dram 775.539	Dram 809.898
Aruba	Aruban florin	Florins 2.6139	Florins 2.6174
Ascension Island	Currency is that of St Helena	at parity with £ sterling	
Australia	Australian dollar ($A) of 100 cents	$A 2.5365	$A 2.9507
Norfolk Island	Currency is that of Australia	$A 2.5365	$A 2.9507
Austria*	Euro (€) of 100 cents/ Schilling of 100 Groschen	Schilling 22.3274	€ 1.5864/Schilling 21.8284
Azerbaijan	Manat of 100 gopik	Manat 6391.52	Manat 6862.10
The Bahamas	Bahamian dollar (B$) of 100 cents	B$ 1.4603	B$ 1.4622
Bahrain	Bahraini dinar (BD) of 1,000 fils	BD 0.5505	BD 0.5513
Bangladesh	Taka (Tk) of 100 poisha	Tk 78.9266	Tk 83.2724
Barbados	Barbados dollar (BD$) of 100 cents	BDS 2.9205	BDS 2.9098
Belarus	Belarusian rouble of 100 kopeks	BYR 1486.54 (market rate)	BYR 2152.36 (market rate)
Belgium*	Euro (€) of 100 cents/ Belgian franc (or frank) of 100 centimes (centiemen)	Francs 65.4551	€ 1.5864/Francs 63.9924
Belize	Belize dollar (BZ$) of 100 cents	BZ$ 2.9205	BZ$ 2.8952
Benin	Franc FCA	Francs 1064.35	Francs 1040.57
Bermuda	Bermuda dollar of 100 cents	$ 1.4603	$ 1.4622
Bhutan	Ngultrum of 100 chetrum (Indian currency is also legal tender)	Ngultrum 66.8065	Ngultrum 70.1417
Bolivia	Boliviano ($b) of 100 centavos	$b 9.0244	$b 9.8260
Bosnia-Hercegovina	Convertible marka	Marka 3.1735	Marka 3.1026
Botswana	Pula (P) of 100 thebe	P 7.5290	P 8.5609
Brazil	Real of 100 centavos	Real 2.6628 (floating rate)	Real 3.9136 (floating rate)
Brunei	Brunei dollar (B$) of 100 sen (fully interchangeable with Singapore currency)	B$ 2.5123	$ 2.5386
Bulgaria	Lev of 100 stotinki	Leva 3.1583	Leva 3.0878
Burkina Faso	Franc CFA	Francs 1064.35	Francs 1040.57
Burundi	Burundi franc of 100 centimes	Francs 1133.37	Francs 1230.44
Cambodia	Riel of 100 sen	Riel 5621.96	Riel 5607.54
Cameroon	Franc CFA	Francs 1064.35	Francs 1040.57
Canada	Canadian dollar (C$) 100 cents	C$ 2.1517	C$ 2.2974
Cape Verde	Escudo Caboverdiano of 100 centavos	Esc 181.384	Esc 175.099
Cayman Islands	Cayman Islands dollar (CI$) of 100 cents	CI$ 1.2168	CI$ 1.1990
Central African Republic	Franc CFA	Francs 1064.35	Francs 1040.57
Chad	Franc CFA	Francs 1064.35	Francs 1040.57
Chile	Chilean peso of 100 centavos	Pesos 822.632	Pesos 1009.65
China	Renminbi Yuan of 10 jiao or 100 fen	Yuan 12.0890	Yuan 12.1024
Hong Kong	Hong Kong (HK$) of 100 cents	HK$ 11.3886	HK$ 11.4051
Macao	Pataca of 100 avos	Pataca 11.7346	Pataca 11.7459
Colombia	Colombian peso of 100 centavos	Pesos 3234.45	Pesos 3419.65
The Comoros	Comorian franc (KMF) of 100 centimes	Francs 796.139	Francs 804.423
Congo, Dem. Rep. of	Congolese franc	CFr 6.5711	Francs 1040.57
Congo, Rep. of	Franc CFA	Francs 1064.35	CFr 6.57980
Costa Rica	Costa Rican colón (₡) of 100 céntimos	₡ 447.275	₡ 485.845
Côte d'Ivoire	Franc CFA	Francs 1064.35	Francs 1040.57
Croatia	Kuna of 100 lipa	Kuna 12.2506	Kuna 11.9834
Cuba	Cuban peso of 100 centavos	Pesos 30.6653	Pesos 30.7062
Cyprus	Cyprus pound (C£) of 100 cents	C£ 0.9289	C£ 0.9085
Czech Republic	Koruna (Kčs) of 100 haléřu	Kčs 57.3711	Kčs 54.3953

Country	Currency		
Denmark	Danish krone of 100 øre	Kroner 12.1033	Kroner 11.8059
Færøe Islands	Currency is that of Denmark	Kroner 12.1033	Kroner 11.8059
Dijbouti	Dijbouti franc of 100 centimes	Francs 253.646	Francs 250.767
Dominica	East Caribbean dollar (EC$) of 100 cents	EC$ 3.9427	EC$ 3.9480
Dominican Republic	Dominican Republic peso (RD$) of 100 centavos	RD$ 26.6350	RD$ 23.8339
East Timor	Currency is that of the USA	–	US$ 1.4622
Ecuador	Currency is that of the USA (formerly sucre of 100 centavos)	Sucres 36506.3 (official rate)	US$ 1.4622
Egypt	Egyptian pound (£E) of 100 piastres or 1,000 millièmes	£E 5.1365	£E 6.2144
El Salvador	El Salvador colón (₡) of 100 centavos	₡ 12.7334	₡ 12.7972
Equatorial Guinea	Franc CFA	Francs 1064.35	Francs 1040.57
Eritrea	Nakfa	–	–
Estonia	Kroon of 100 sents	Kroons 25.3740	Kroons 24.8343
Ethiopia	Ethiopian birr (EB) of 100 cents	EB 11.8894	EB 12.2869
Falkland Islands	Falkland pound of 100 pence	at parity with £ sterling	
Fiji	Fiji dollar (F$) of 100 cents	F$ 3.1608	F$ 33.3461
Finland*	Euro (€) of 100 cents/ Markka (Mk) of 100 penniä	Mk 9.6475	€ 1.5864/Mk 9.4319
France*	Euro (€) of 100 cents/ Franc of 100 centimes	Francs 10.6435	€ 1.5864/Francs 10.4057
French Guiana*	Currency is that of France	Francs 10.6435	€ 1.5864/Francs 10.4057
French Polynesia	Franc CFP	Francs 195.498	Francs 191.038
Gabon	Franc CFA	Francs 1064.35	Francs 1040.57
The Gambia	Dalasi (D) of 100 butut	D 19.1294	D 24.8940
Georgia	Laria of 100 tetri	Laria 2.8986	Laria 3.0412
Germany*	Euro (€) of 100 cents/ Deutsche Mark (DM) of 100 Pfennige	DM 3.1735	€ 1.5864/DM 3.1026
Ghana	Cedi of 100 pesewas	Cedi 10294.8	Cedi 10367.0
Gibraltar	Gibraltar pound of 100 pence	at parity with £ sterling	
Greece*	Euro (€) of 100 cents/ Drachma of 100 leptae	Drachmae 547.754	€ 1.5864/Drachmae 540.542
Greenland	Currency is that of Denmark	Kroner 12.1033	Kroner 11.8059
Grenada	East Caribbean dollar (EC$) of 100 cents	EC$ 3.9427	EC$ 3.9480
Guadeloupe*	Currency is that of France	Francs 10.6435	€ 1.5864/Francs 10.4057
Guam	Currency is that of the USA	US$ 1.4603	US$ 1.4622
Guatemala	Quetzal (Q) of 100 centavos	Q 11.4170	Q 11.5390
Guinea	Guinea franc of 100 centimes	Francs 2381.67	Francs 2865.92
Guinea-Bissau	Franc CFA	Francs 1064.35	Francs 1040.57
Guyana	Guyana dollar (G$) of 100 cents	G$ 266.204	G$ 263.196
Haiti	Gourde of 100 centimes	Gourdes 32.1255	Gourdes 34.7273
Honduras	Lempira of 100 centavos	Lempiras 21.7870	Lempiras 22.7665
Hungary	Forint of 100 fillér	Forints 424.071	Forints 408.005
Iceland	Icelandic króna (Kr) of 100 aurar	Kr 117.930	Kr 146.220
India	Indian rupee (Rs) of 100 paisa	Rs 66.8065	Rs 70.1417
Indonesia	Rupiah (Rp) of 100 sen	Rp 12083.6	Rp 14000.6
Iran	Rial	Rials 2551.79 (official rate)	Rials 2558.85 (official rate)
Iraq	Iraqi dinar (ID) of 1,000 fils	ID 0.4540	ID 0.4548
Ireland, Republic of*	Euro (€) of 100 cents/ Punt (IR£) of 100 pence	IR£ 1.2779	€ 1.5864/IR£ 1.2494
Israel	Shekel of 100 agora	Shekels 5.8629	Shekels 6.3767
Italy*	Euro (€) of 100 cents/ Lira of 100 centesimi	Lire 3141.77	€ 1.5864/Lire 3071.56
Jamaica	Jamaican dollar (J$) of 100 cents	J$ 61.3305	J$ 66.6032
Japan	Yen	Yen 154.422	Yen 171.699
Jordan	Jordanian dinar (JD) of 1,000 fils	JD 1.0382	JD 1.0393
Kazakhstan	Tenge	Tenge 208.356	Tenge 215.989
Kenya	Kenya shilling (Ksh) of 100 cents	Ksh 112.804	Ksh 115.368
Kiribati	Australian dollar ($A) of 100 cents	$A 2.5365	$A 2.9507
Korea, Dem. People's Rep. of	Won of 100 chon	Won 3.2126	Won 3.2169
Korea, Republic of	Won	Won 1614.53	Won 1896.47
Kuwait	Kuwaiti dinar (KD) of 1,000 fils	KD 0.4493	KD 0.4458
Kyrgyzstan	Som	Som 70.1436	Som 69.7818
Laos	Kip (K) of 100 at	K 11046.8	K 11112.7
Latvia	Lats of 100 santims	Lats 0.8872	Lats 0.9031
Lebanon	Lebanese pound (L£) of of 100 piastres	L£ 2210.82	L£ 2214.14
Lesotho	Loti (M) of 100 lisente	M 10.1670	M 12.6772
Liberia	Liberian dollar (L$) of 100 cents	L$ 1.4603	L$ 1.4622

Libya	Libyan dinar (LD) of 1,000 dirhams	LD 0.737	LD 0.9411
Liechtenstein	Swiss franc of 100 rappen (or centimes)	Francs 2.5143	Francs 2.3486
Lithuania	Litas of 100 centas	Litas 5.8425	Litas 5.8474
Luxembourg*	Euro (€) of 100 cents/ Luxembourg franc (LF) of 100 centimes (Belgian currency is also legal tender)	LF 65.4551	€ 1.5864/LF 63.9924
Macedonia	Denar of 100 deni	Den 95.4931	Den 96.2675
Madagascar	Franc malgache(FMG) of 100 centimes	FMG 9588.00	FMG 9011.54
Malawi	Kwacha (K) of 100 tambala	MK 89.1265	MK 90.0204
Malaysia	Malaysian dollar (ringgit) (M$) of 100 sen	M$ 5.5490 (official rate)	M$ 5.5564 (official rate)
Maldives	Rufiyaa of 100 laaris	Rufiyaa 17.1872	Rufiyaa 17.2101
Mali	Franc CFA	Francs 1064.35	Francs 1040.57
Malta	Maltese lira (LM) of 100 cents of 1,000 mils	LM 0.6534	LM 0.6461
Marshall Islands	Currency is that of the USA	US$ 1.4603	US$ 1.4622
Martinique*	Currency is that of France	Francs 10.6435	€ 1.5864/Francs 10.4057
Mauritania	Ouguiya (UM) of 5 khoums	UM 352.490	UM 374.353
Mauritius	Mauritius rupee of 100 cents	Rs 38.1856	Rs 43.2446
Mayotte*	Currency is that of France	Francs 10.6435	€ 1.5864/Francs 10.4057
Mexico	Peso of 100 centavos	Pesos 13.4343	Pesos 13.8105
Micronesia, Federated States of	Currency is that of the USA	US$ 1.4603	US$ 1.4622
Moldova	Moldovan leu of 100 bani	MDL 18.0706	MDL 18.8258
Monaco*	Currency is that of France	Francs 10.6435	€ 1.5864/Francs 10.4057
Mongolia	Tugrik of 100 möngö	Tugriks 1565.87	Tugriks 1608.42
Montserrat	East Caribbean dollar (EC$) of 100 cents	EC$ 3.9427	EC$ 3.9480
Morocco	Dirham (DH) of 100 centimes	DH 15.7328	DH 16.3950
Mozambique	Metical (MT) of 100 centavos	MT 23510.1	MT 31645.7
Myanmar	Kyat (K) of 100 pyas	K 9.1290	K 9.66380
Namibia	Namibian dollar of 100 cents	at parity with SA Rand	
Nauru	Australian dollar ($A) of 100 cents	$A 2.5365	$A 2.9507
Nepal	Nepalese rupee of 100 paisa	Rs 106.774	Rs 111.595
The Netherlands*	Euro (€) of 100 cents/ Gulden (guilder) of florin of 100 cents	Guilders 3.5757	€ 1.5864/Guilders 3.4959
Netherlands Antilles	Netherlands Antilles guilder of 100 cents	Guilders 2.5847	Guilders 2.6027
New Caledonia	Franc CFP	Francs 195.498	Francs 191.038
New Zealand	New Zealand dollar (NZ$) of 100 cents	NZ$ 3.4130	NZ$ 3.5703
Cook Islands	Currency is that of New Zealand	NZ$ 3.4130	NZ$ 3.5703
Niue	Currency is that of New Zealand	NZ$ 3.4130	NZ$ 3.5703
Tokelau	Currency is that of New Zealand	NZ$ 3.4130	NZ$ 3.5703
Nicaragua	Córdoba (C$) of 100 centavos	C$ 17.0192	C$ 19.9152
Niger	Franc CFA	Francs 1064.35	Francs 1040.57
Nigeria	Naira (N) of 100 kobo	N 151.355	N 164.732
Northern Mariana Islands	Currency is that of the USA	US$ 1.4603	US$ 1.4622
Norway	Krone of 100 øre	Kroner 13.1471	Kroner 12.6693
Oman	Rial Omani (OR) of 1,000 baisas	OR 0.5622	OR 0.5630
Pakistan	Pakistan rupee of 100 paisa	Rs 79.9560	Rs 93.9829
Palau	Currency is that of the USA	US$ 1.4603	US$ 1.4622
Panama	Balboa of 100 centésimos (US notes are also in circulation)	Balboa 1.4603	Balboa 1.4622
Papua New Guinea	Kina (K) of 100 toea	K 3.8916	K 5.0640
Paraguay	Guarani (Gs) of 100 céntimos	Gs 5117.45	Gs 6465.12
Peru	New Sol of 100 cénts	New Sol 5.0693	New Sol 5.1155
The Philippines	Philippine peso (P) of 100 centavos	P 65.9303	P 75.2302
Pitcairn Islands	Currency is that of New Zealand	NZ$ 3.4130	NZ$ 3.5703
Poland	Złoty of 100 groszy	Złotych 6.3915	Złotych 6.1832
Portugal*	Euro (€) of 100 cents/ Escudo (Esc) of 100 centavos	Esc 325.300	€ 1.5864/Esc 318.031
Puerto Rico	Currency is that of the USA	US$ 1.4603	US$ 1.4622
Qatar	Qatar riyal of 100 dirhams	Riyals 5.3157	Riyals 5.3234
Réunion*	Currency is that of France	Francs 10.6435	€ 1.5864/Francs 10.4057
Romania	Leu of 100 bani	Lei 33666.1	Lei 44238.9
Russia	Rouble of 100 kopeks	Rbl 40.5468	Rbl 43.0764
Rwanda	Rwanda franc of 100 centimes	Francs 524.271	Francs 638.981
St Christopher and Nevis	East Caribbean dollar (EC$) of 100 cents	EC$ 3.9427	EC$ 3.9480
St Helena	St Helena pound (£) of 100 pence	at parity with £ sterling	

St Lucia	East Caribbean dollar (EC$) of 100 cents	EC$ 3.9427	EC$ 3.9480
St Pierre and Miquelon*	Currency is that of France	Francs 10.6435	€ 1.5864/Francs 10.4057
St Vincent and the Grenadines	East Caribbean dollar (EC$) of 100 cents	EC$ 3.9427	EC$ 3.9480
Samoa	Tala (S$) of 100 sene	S$ 45.112	S$ 5.0507
San Marino*	San Marino and Italian currencies are in circulation	Lire 3141.77	€ 1.5864/Lire 3071.56
São Tomé and Príncipe	Dobra of 100 centavos	Dobra 3490.00	Dobra 13068.0
Saudi Arabia	Saudi riyal (SR) of 20 qursh or 100 halala	SR 5.4769	SR 5.4842
Senegal	Franc CFA	Francs 1064.35	Francs 1040.57
Seychelles	Seychelles rupee of 100 cents	Rs 8.3660	Rs 8.0531
Sierra Leone	Leone (Le) of 100 cents	Le 2976.21	Le 2846.90
Singapore	Singapore dollar (S$) of 100 cents	S$ 2.5123	S$ 2.5386
Slovakia	Koruna (Sk) of 100 halierov	Kčs 69.3437	Kčs 69.3560
Slovenia	Tolar (SIT) of 100 stotin	Tolars 339.107	Tolars 348.749
Solomon Islands	Solomon Islands dollar (SI$) of 100 cents	SI$ 7.3836	SI$ 7.8402
Somalia	Somali shilling of 100 cents	Shillings 3825.86	Shillings 3830.96
South Africa	Rand (R) of 100 cents	R 10.1670	R 12.6772
Spain*	Euro (€) of 100 cents/ Peseta of 100 céntimos	Pesetas 269.976	€ 1.5864/Pesetas 263.943
Sri Lanka	Sri Lankan rupee of 100 cents	Rs 114.119	Rs 131.795
Sudan	Sudanese dinar (SD) of 100 piastres	SD 377.913	SD 378.271
Suriname	Surinamese guilder of 100 cents	Guilders 1182.07	Guilders 1434.42
Swaziland	Lilangeni (E) of 100 cents (South African currency is also in circulation)	at parity with SA Rand	
Sweden	Swedish krona of 100 öre	Kronor 13.6183	Kronor 15.4366
Switzerland	Swiss franc of 100 rappen (or centimes)	Francs 2.5143	Francs 2.3486
Syria	Syrian pound (S£) of 100 piastres	S£ 76.6632	S£ 75.8151
Taiwan	New Taiwan dollar NT$) of 100 cents	NT$ 45.3846	NT$ 50.5483
Tajikistan	Somoni of 100 dirams	–	TJS 3.5341
Tanzania	Tanzanian shilling of 100 cents	Shillings 1166.74	Shillings 1302.82
Thailand	Baht of 100 satang	Baht 59.6878	Baht 64.5854
Togo	Franc CFA	Francs 10.6435	Francs 1040.57
Tonga	Pa'anga (T$) of 100 seniti	T$ 2.5365	T$ 2.9507
Trinidad and Tobago	Trinidad and Tobago dollar (TT$) of 100 cents	TT$ 9.0828	TT$ 8.8463
Tristan da Cunha	Currency is that of the UK		
Tunisia	Tunsian dinar of 1,000 millimes	Dinars 2.0456	Dinars 2.0712
Turkey	Turkish lira (TL) of 100 kurus	TL 952995.7	TL 2186722
Turkmenistan	Manat of 100 tenge	–	–
Turks and Caicos Islands	US dollar (US$)	US$ 1.4603	US$ 1.4622
Tuvalu	Australian dollar ($A) of 100 cents	$A 2.5365	$A 2.9507
Uganda	Uganda shilling of 100 cents	Shilling 2507.98	Shillings 2554.46
Ukraine	Hryvna of 100 kopiykas	UAH 7.9620	UAH 7.8115
United Arab Emirates	UAE dirham (Dh) of 100 fils	Dirham 5.3635	Dirham 5.3705
United Kingdom	Pound sterling (£) of 100 pence		
United States of America	US dollar (US$) of 100 cents	US$ 1.4603	US$ 1.4622
Uruguay	Uruguayan peso of 100 centésimos	Pesos 18.0487	Pesos 20.0066
Uzbekistan	Sum of 100 tiyin	Sum 1131.69	Sum 617.341
Vanatu	Vatu of 100 centimes	Vatu 204.654	Vatu 213.335
Vatican City State*	Italian currency is legal tender	Lire 3141.77	€ 1.5864/Lire 3071.56
Venezuela	Bolívar (Bs) of 100 céntimos	Bs 1005.46	Bs 1088.61
Vietnam	Dông of 10 hào or 100 xu	Dông 20618.7	Dông 21928.6
Virgin Islands, British	US dollar (US$) (£ sterling and ECS also circulate)	US$ 1.4603	US$ 1.4622
Virgin Islands, US	Currency is that of the USA	US$ 1.4603	US$ 1.4622
Wallis and Futuna Islands	Franc CFP	Francs 195.498	Francs 191.038
Yemen	Riyal of 100 fils	Riyals 237.145	Riyals 247.594
Yugoslavia	New dinar of 100 paras	New Dinars 17.7813	New Dinars 98.4090
Zambia	Kwacha (K) of 100 ngwee	K 4840.74	K 5468.64
Zimbabwe	Zimbabwe dollar (Z$) of 100 cents	Z$ 60.8129	Z$ 80.8963

* The euro is now the legal currency in these countries. Euro notes and coins will be introduced from 1 January 2002 and will circulate alongside national currencies for between four weeks and two months, after which time national notes and coins will cease to be legal tender.

Cost of Living and Inflation Rates

The first cost of living index to be calculated took July 1914 as 100 and was based on the pattern of expenditure of working-class families in 1914. The cost of living index was superseded in 1947 by the general index of retail prices (RPI), although the older term is still popularly applied to it.

GENERAL INDEX OF RETAIL PRICES

The general index of retail prices measures the changes month by month in the average level of prices of goods and services purchased by most households in the United Kingdom. The spending pattern on which the index is based is revised each year, mainly using information from the Family Expenditure Survey. The expenditure of certain higher income households and of households mainly dependent on state pensions is excluded.

The index is compiled using a selection of over 600 goods and services, and the prices charged for these items are collected at regular intervals in about 146 locations throughout the country. For the index, the price changes are weighted in accordance with the pattern of consumption of the average family.

INFLATION RATE

The twelve-monthly percentage change in the 'all items' index of the RPI is usually referred to as the rate of inflation. The percentage change in prices between any two months/years can be obtained using the following formula:

$$\frac{\text{Later date RPI} - \text{Earlier date RPI}}{\text{Earlier date RPI}} \times 100$$

e.g. to find the rate of inflation for 1988, using the annual averages for 1987 and 1988:

$$\frac{106.9 - 101.9}{101.9} \times 100 = 4.9\%$$

PURCHASING POWER OF THE POUND

Changes in the internal purchasing power of the pound may be defined as the 'inverse' of changes in the level of prices; when prices go up, the amount which can be purchased with a given sum of money goes down. To find the purchasing power of the pound in one month or year, given that it was 100p in a previous month or year, the calculation would be:

$$100p \times \frac{\text{Earlier month/year RPI}}{\text{Later month/year RPI}}$$

Thus, if the purchasing power of the pound is taken to be 100p in 1975, the comparable purchasing power in 1997 would be:

$$100p \times \frac{34.2}{157.5} = 21.71p$$

For longer term comparisons, it has been the practice to use an index which has been constructed by linking together the RPI for the period 1962 to date; an index derived from the consumers expenditure deflator for the period from 1938 to 1962; and the prewar 'cost of living' index for the period 1914 to 1938. This long-term index enables the internal purchasing power of the pound to be calculated for any year from 1914 onwards. It should be noted that these figures can only be approximate.

	Long-term index of consumer goods and services (Jan. 1987 = 100)	Comparable purchasing power of £1 in 1998	Rate of inflation (annual average)
1914	2.8	58.18	
1915	3.5	46.54	
1920	7.0	23.27	
1925	5.0	32.58	
1930	4.5	36.20	
1935	4.0	40.72	
1938	4.4	37.02	
There are no official figures for 1939–45			
1946	7.4	22.01	
1950	9.0	18.10	
1955	11.2	14.54	
1960	12.6	12.93	
1965	14.8	11.00	
1970	18.5	8.80	
1975	34.2	4.76	
1980	66.8	2.44	18.0
1981	74.8	2.18	11.9
1982	81.2	2.01	8.6
1983	84.9	1.92	4.6
1984	89.2	1.83	5.0
1985	94.6	1.72	6.1
1986	97.8	1.67	3.4
1987	101.9	1.60	4.2
1988	106.9	1.52	4.9
1989	115.2	1.41	7.8
1990	126.1	1.29	9.5
1991	133.5	1.22	5.9
1992	138.5	1.18	3.7
1993	140.7	1.16	1.6
1994	144.1	1.13	2.4
1995	149.1	1.09	3.5
1996	152.7	1.07	2.4
1997	157.5	1.03	3.1
1998	162.9	1.00	3.4
1999	165.4	0.98	1.5
2000	170.3	0.96	3.0

The RPI figures are published around the middle of each month. They are available as a recorded message which can be heard by telephoning 020-7533 5866. Each month an updated Consumer Price Indices bulletin is published by the Office of National Statistics.

OFFICE OF NATIONAL STATISTICS, 1 Drummond Gate, London SW1V 2QQ.
PUBLIC ENQUIRIES LINE: 020-7533 5874
WEB: www.statistics.gov.uk

Time Zones

Standard time differences from the Greenwich meridian

+ hours ahead of GMT
− hours behind GMT
* may vary from standard time at some part of the year (Summer Time or Daylight Saving Time)
‡ some areas may keep another time zone
h hours
m minutes

	h	m
Afghanistan	+ 4	30
*Albania	+ 1	
Algeria	+ 1	
*Andorra	+ 1	
Angola	+ 1	
Anguilla	− 4	
Antigua and Barbuda	− 4	
Argentina	− 3	
*Armenia	+ 4	
Aruba	− 4	
Ascension Island	0	
*Australia	+10	
ACT, NSW (except Broken Hill area) Qld, Tas., Vic, Whitsunday Islands		
*Broken Hill area (NSW)	+ 9	30
*Lord Howe Island	+10	30
Northern Territory	+ 9	30
*South Australia	+ 9	30
Western Australia	+ 8	
*Austria	+ 1	
*Azerbaijan	+ 4	
*Bahamas	− 5	
Bahrain	+ 3	
Bangladesh	+ 6	
Barbados	− 4	
*Belarus	+ 2	
*Belgium	+ 1	
Belize	− 6	
Benin	+ 1	
*Bermuda	− 4	
Bhutan	+ 6	
Bolivia	− 4	
*Bosnia-Hercegovina	+ 1	
Botswana	+ 2	
Brazil		
western states	− 5	
central states	− 4	
N. and NE coastal states	− 3	
*S. and E. coastal states, including Brasilia	− 3	
Fernando de Noronha Island	− 2	
British Antarctic Territory	− 3	
British Indian Ocean Territory	+ 5	
Diego Garcia	+ 6	
British Virgin Islands	− 4	
Brunei	+ 8	
*Bulgaria	+ 2	
Burkina Faso	0	
Burundi	+ 2	

	h	m
Cambodia	+ 7	
Cameroon	+ 1	
Canada		
*Alberta	− 7	
*‡British Columbia	− 8	
*‡Labrador	− 4	
*Manitoba	− 6	
*New Brunswick	− 4	
*Newfoundland	− 3	30
*Northwest Territories		
east of 85° W.	− 5	
85° W.–102° W.	− 6	
*Nunavut	− 7	
*Nova Scotia	− 4	
Ontario		
*east of 90° W.	− 5	
west of 90° W.	− 5	
*Prince Edward Island	− 4	
Québec		
east of 63° W.	− 4	
*west of 63° W.	− 5	
‡Saskatchewan	− 6	
*Yukon	− 8	
Cape Verde	− 1	
Cayman Islands	− 5	
Central African Republic	+ 1	
Chad	+ 1	
*Chatham Islands	+12	45
*Chile	− 4	
China (inc. Hong Kong and Macao)	+ 8	
Christmas Island (Indian Ocean)	+ 7	
Cocos (Keeling) Islands	+ 6	30
Colombia	− 5	
Comoros	+ 3	
Congo (Dem. Rep.)		
Haut-Zaïre, Kasai, Kivu, Shaba	+ 2	
Kinshasa, Mbandaka	+ 1	
Congo-Brazzaville	+ 1	
Costa Rica	− 6	
Côte d'Ivoire	0	
*Croatia	+ 1	
*Cuba	− 5	
*Cyprus	+ 2	
*Czech Republic	+ 1	
*Denmark	+ 1	
*Færøe Islands	0	
*Greenland	− 3	
Danmarkshavn, Mesters Vig	0	
*Scoresby Sound	− 1	
*Thule area	− 4	
Djibouti	+ 3	
Dominica	− 4	
Dominican Republic	− 5	
East Timor	+ 9	
Ecuador	− 5	
Galápagos Islands	− 6	
*Egypt	+ 2	
El Salvador	−6	
Equatorial Guinea	+ 1	
Eritrea	+ 3	
Estonia	+ 2	

	h	m
Ethiopia	+ 3	
*Falkland Islands	− 4	
Fiji	+12	
*Finland	+ 2	
*France	+ 1	
French Guiana	− 3	
French Polynesia	−10	
Guadeloupe	− 4	
Martinique	− 4	
Réunion	+ 4	
Marquesas Islands	− 9	30
Gabon	+ 1	
The Gambia	0	
*Georgia	+ 3	
*Germany	+ 1	
Ghana	0	
*Gibraltar	+ 1	
*Greece	+ 2	
Grenada	− 4	
Guam	+10	
Guatemala	− 6	
Guinea	0	
Guinea-Bissau	0	
Guyana	− 4	
Haïti	− 5	
Honduras	− 6	
*Hungary	+ 1	
Iceland	0	
India	+ 5	30
Indonesia		
Java, Kalimantan (west and central), Madura, Sumatra	+ 7	
Bali, Flores, Kalimantan (south and east), Lombok, Sulawesi, Sumbawa, West Timor	+ 8	
Irian Jaya, Maluku,	+ 9	
*Iran	+ 3	30
*Iraq	+ 3	
*Ireland, Republic of	0	
*Israel	+ 2	
*Italy	+ 1	
Jamaica	− 5	
Japan	+ 9	
*Jordan	+ 2	
*Kazakhstan		
western	+ 4	
central	+ 5	
eastern	+ 6	
Kenya	+ 3	
Kiribati	+12	
Line Islands	+14	
Phoenix Islands	+13	
Korea, North	+ 9	
Korea, South	+ 9	
Kuwait	+ 3	
*Kyrgyzstan	+ 5	
Laos	+ 7	
Latvia	+ 2	
*Lebanon	+ 2	
Lesotho	+ 2	
Liberia	0	
Libya	+ 2	
*Liechtenstein	+ 1	

	h	m
Line Islands not part of Kiribati	−10	
Lithuania	+ 1	
*Luxembourg	+ 1	
*Macedonia	+ 1	
Madagascar	+ 3	
Malaŵi	+ 2	
Malaysia	+ 8	
Maldives	+ 5	
Mali	0	
*Malta	+ 1	
Marshall Islands	+12	
Ebon Atoll	−12	
Mauritania	0	
Mauritius	+ 4	
*Mexico	− 6	
*Nayarit, Sinaloa, S. Baja California	− 7	
Sonora	− 7	
N. Baja California	− 8	
Micronesia		
Caroline Islands	+10	
Kosrae, Pingelap, Pohnpei	+11	
*Moldova	+ 2	
*Monaco	+ 1	
Mongolia	+ 8	
Montserrat	− 4	
Morocco	0	
Mozambique	+ 2	
Myanmar	+ 6	30
*Namibia	+ 1	
Nauru	+12	
Nepal	+ 5	45
*Netherlands	+ 1	
Netherlands Antilles	− 4	
New Caledonia	+11	
*New Zealand	+12	
*Cook Islands	−10	
Nicaragua	− 6	
Niger	+ 1	
Nigeria	+ 1	
Niue	−11	
Norfolk Island	+11	30
Northern Mariana Islands	+10	
*Norway	+ 1	
Oman	+ 4	
Pakistan	+ 5	
Palau	+ 9	
Panama	− 5	
Papua New Guinea	+10	
*Paraguay	− 4	
Peru	− 5	
Philippines	+ 8	
*Poland	+ 1	
*Portugal	0	
*Azores	− 1	
kern;*Madeira	0	
Puerto Rico	− 4	
Qatar	+ 3	
Réunion	+ 4	
*Romania	+ 2	
*Russia		
Zone 1	+ 2	
Zone 2	+ 3	
Zone 3	+ 4	
Zone 4	+ 5	
Zone 5	+ 6	
Zone 6	+ 7	

	h	m
Zone 7	+ 8	
Zone 8	+ 9	
Zone 9	+10	
Zone 10	+11	
Zone 11	+12	
Rwanda	+ 2	
St Helena	0	
St Christopher and Nevis	− 4	
St Lucia	− 4	
*St Pierre and Miquelon	− 3	
St Vincent and the Grenadines	− 4	
Samoa	−11	
Samoa, American	−11	
*San Marino	+ 1	
São Tomé and Princípe	0	
Saudi Arabia	+ 3	
Senegal	0	
Seychelles	+ 4	
Sierra Leone	0	
Singapore	+ 8	
*Slovakia	+ 1	
*Slovenia	+ 1	
Solomon Islands	+11	
Somalia	+ 3	
South Africa	+ 2	
South Georgia	− 2	
*Spain	+ 1	
*Canary Islands	0	
Sri Lanka	+ 6	
Sudan	+ 3	
Suriname	− 3	
Swaziland	+ 2	
*Sweden	+ 1	
*Switzerland	+ 1	
*Syria	+ 2	
Taiwan	+ 8	
Tajikistan	+ 5	
Tanzania	+ 3	
Thailand	+ 7	
Togo	0	
*Tonga	+13	
Trinidad and Tobago	− 4	
Tristan da Cunha	0	
Tunisia	+ 1	
*Turkey	+ 2	
Turkmenistan	+ 5	
*Turks and Caicos Islands	− 5	
Tuvalu	+12	
Uganda	+ 3	
*Ukraine	+ 2	
United Arab Emirates	+ 4	
*United Kingdom	0	
*United States of America		
Alaska	− 9	
Aleutian Islands, east of 169° 30′ W.	− 9	
Aleutian Islands, west of 169° 30′ W.	−10	
eastern time	− 5	
central time	− 6	
Hawaii	−10	
mountain time	− 7	
Pacific time	− 8	
Uruguay	− 3	
Uzbekistan	+ 5	
Vanuatu	+11	
*Vatican City State	+ 1	
Venezuela	− 4	

	h	m
Vietnam	+ 7	
Virgin Islands (US)	− 4	
Yemen	+ 3	
*Yugoslavia (Fed. Rep. of)	+ 1	
Zambia	+ 2	
Zimbabwe	+ 2	

Source: reproduced with permission from data produced by HM Nautical Almanac Office

Events of the Year

1 September 2000 to 31 August 2001

SEPTEMBER 2000

4. Cabinet Office Minister (Mo Mowlam) announced that she would be standing down as an MP at the next general election. **5.** 150 British paratroopers were flown into Sierra Leone, on standby to rescue the six British soldiers being held hostage by a rebel faction. **6.** The Government came under increasing pressure to reduce the VAT on fuel as petrol prices were expected to reach almost 87 pence a litre, due to the rising price of crude oil. **8.** Protesters in France set up road blocks at refineries and fuel depots to highlight the high cost of fuel. **9.** The fuel shortages continued as people began panic buying after Shell warned that the majority of their pumps would be dry by the end of the week. **10.** A British paratrooper was killed when airborne forces freed six captured soldiers in a raid deep in the Sierra Leone jungle. **11.** Following reports showing that over a quarter of all British petrol stations were dry, the Prime Minister (Tony Blair) declared that he would not cave in to the protestors. **12.** A limited number of tankers were released from blockades around the country in order to meet the needs of the emergency services and other essential industries. 90% of petrol stations remained closed. **13.** Troops were put on standby to intervene in the fuel crisis as the health service went on emergency alert. Schools and businesses closed and supermarkets introduced rationing. **14.** Protesters lifted the blockades at oil refineries around the country but threatened that the blockades would return if taxes on fuel were not cut within 60 days. **19.** The Tories called for the resignation of the Chancellor of the Exchequer (Gordon Brown) over allegations that he lied about a £1 million donation to the Labour Party by the head of Formula One motor racing Bernie Ecclestone.

OCTOBER 2000

4. The Conservative spokesperson for Home Affairs (Anne Widdecombe) was criticised by her own party for proposing that individuals caught in possession of cannabis should receive an automatic minimum fine of £100 and a criminal record. **11.** Scotland's First Minister (Donald Dewar) died of a brain haemorrhage following a fall outside his Edinburgh residence. Thousands attended the funeral of former East End gangster Reggie Kray. **14.** Former Paymaster General, Geoffrey Robinson, accused Peter Mandelson of initiating discussions about a home loan in the scandal that forced them both to resign. Figures showed that the size of secondary school classes had grown to a ten year high due to a shortage of teachers. **19.** Hundreds of thousands of doses of a polio vaccine were recalled by the Department of Health after it was discovered that it had been produced with material from British cows, in breach of European guidelines in force since 1999. **23.** It was announced that Railtrack was to receive a five-year grant of £4.7 billion from the rail industry regulator to 'deliver a modern safe railway with greater public accountability'. The Labour MP for Glasgow Springburn (Michael Martin) was elected Speaker of the House of Commons. **24.** Sir Edward Heath announced he was to retire from Parliament at the next election. French-owned rail company Connex became the first train operating company to lose its franchise since privatisation. Railtrack announced the immediate closure of the Scottish west coast mainline for urgent maintenance, causing major disruptions in Scotland. **26.** The official BSE inquiry found that Ministers and Whitehall were guilty of repeatedly misleading the public about the threat to human health posed by mad cow disease, but did not deliberately lie or protect farming interests at the cost of consumers. The House of Lords voted to delay part-privatisation of air traffic control until after the general election.

NOVEMBER 2000

4. Samples collected by researchers from the *Sunday Times* found traces of cocaine on surfaces in lavatories in the House of Commons. John Prescott, announced that an extra £51 million would be spent on improving flood defences around the British Isles over the next four years in response to the extreme flooding taking place around the country. **6.** Surgeons at St Mary's Hospital, Manchester, undertook the operation to separate Siamese twins Jodie and Mary following a ruling by the Court of Appeal. As surgeons suspected, the weaker twin Mary later died. Alan Milburn signed an agreement to recruit up to 5,000 nurses from Spain in order to address the shortfall within the NHS. **8.** In response to growing fears of public protest the Chancellor (Gordon Brown) in his pre-budget speech announced that duty on fuel would be frozen at current levels until April 2002. **10.** Fuel protesters began their convoy from Newcastle to London. **13.** For the third time in two years, the House of Lords rejected Government proposals to lower the age of consent from 18 to 16 for homosexuals. **15.** A report compiled by the Better Regulation Taskforce claimed that farmers in Britain were being driven to bankruptcy due to EU 'red tape'. A rebellion by 37 Labour MPs over plans to privatise the national air traffic control service was beaten by a Government majority of 93. **20.** The Agriculture Minister (Nick Brown) warned Tony Blair that BSE infected beef of French origin could be entering the UK due to legal loopholes in the importing mechanism and insufficient checking. Members of the European Union including the United Kingdom declared their commitment to a military European Rapid Reaction Force in a meeting in Brussels. **23.** By-elections took place for the seats of West Bromwich West (winner John Robertson (Lab) with a majority of 6,337), Preston (winner Mark Hendrick (Lab/Co-op) with a majority of 4,426) and Glasgow Anniesland (winner Adrian Bailey (Lab/Co-op) with a majority of 3,232). **27.** The Prime Minister met with the head of Railtrack and other train operating companies, emphasising that the rail network should be restored to its normal timetable by Christmas.

DECEMBER 2000

3. The Metropolitan Police Commissioner said that inner-city policing was in crisis due to difficulties in recruiting and retaining sufficient police officers and called on Government to provide resources to make up the shortfall of 3,000. **6.** The Queen's speech marked the official re-opening of Parliament. **18.** Brighton and Hove, Wolverhampton and Inverness were awarded city status. In an attempt to alleviate pressure on the National Health Service, the Government announced that the majority of nurses would receive a 3.7% pay increase and GPs a 3.9% increase. Senior nurses and nurses working in Inner London would get a larger increase of up to 9%. **19.** Camelot won the right to continue to run the National Lottery for another seven years, beating the rival bid from Richard Branson's People's Lottery. **20.** Following the second reading of the Hunting Bill, the Home Secretary (Jack Straw) stated in the House of Commons that he was in favour of the regulation of hunting with dogs rather than its abolition. **27.** John Prescott ordered an inquiry into why 1,000 Christmas travellers were stranded at Stansted airport after all train links to London were cancelled.

JANUARY 2001

2. Speculation about the identity of a £2 million donor to the Labour Party's election fund ended when the publisher Lord Hamlyn announced that it came from him. Following calls for an inquiry by war veterans, the Ministry of Defence admitted that it was aware of the health risks of using depleted uranium ammunition during the Gulf War and the Balkan conflicts. In a reversal of Government policy, the Defence Minister (John Spellar) announced that a voluntary screening programme would be introduced for all personnel and civilians deployed to the Balkans with concerns about their health. **3.** A series of checks undertaken by inspection teams revealed that more than one in three hospitals did not meet basic hygiene standards. **10.** Head Teachers of Schools, Chief Examiners and Trade Unions warned the Government that the examining boards were facing a serious shortage of qualified A-level markers which could lead to the collapse of the delivery of exam results in the summer. **15.** Railtrack announced that it needed an advance of £1 billion from the Government in funding if it was to avoid scrapping new schemes such as the Channel tunnel Rail Link. **16.** Figures released by the Metropolitan Police in September 2000 which showed that 281 officers from ethnic minorities had joined the service, were reported to be inaccurate: 214 of the officers came from Irish and other Caucasian backgrounds. A British couple was widely criticised for paying £8,200 to adopt twin baby girls over the Internet. **17.** MPs voted by a majority of more than 200 for an outright ban on hunting with dogs. **23.** The Northern Ireland Secretary (Peter Mandelson) admitted that he had personally intervened in the passport application of the wealthy Indian businessmen Srichand Hinduja, who later contributed £1 million to the Millennium Dome project. Mr Mandelson denied that he had given any preferential treatment to Mr Hinduja's family but resigned the following day. The Rt. Hon. John Reid was immediately appointed to be the new Northern Ireland Secretary, and in turn, Helen Liddell was appointed Secretary of State for Scotland to replace him. **25.** Figures released by the Home Office showed that Britain had become the most popular destination for asylum-seekers, with over 10,000 arriving in the year 2000. **26.** The Alder Hey Hospital in Liverpool and the Birmingham Children's Hospital admitted they had routinely removed the thymus glands from children undergoing heart surgery and sold them to a French drug company, without prior knowledge or consent of the children's parents. **29.** Peers voted 177 to 95 against a motion in the House of Lords, proposed by Baroness Young, to prevent the sale of the morning-after pill over the counter in pharmacies.

FEBRUARY 2001

7. Tony Blair stated during Prime Minister's questions that a re-elected Labour Government would set a two-year deadline for deciding whether the conditions for entry into the single European currency have been met. **15.** The Strategic Rail Authority announced that it was to strip Railtrack of its responsibility for expanding the rail network after deciding that the company could not stop costs spiralling out of control. **18.** John Prescott ordered a complete reorganisation of the rules governing the sale of the Millennium Dome. **21.** The first case of foot-and-mouth disease for 20 years was discovered at an abattoir in Essex. The European Commission immediately imposed a world-wide ban on shipments of all cattle and meat until March 1. The Pope appointed the Archbishop of Westminster, The Most Reverend Cormack Murphy-O'Connor, as a Cardinal. **22.** The third case of foot-and-mouth disease was confirmed and 600 farms around Britain were under emergency restrictions. **23.** The Government banned livestock movements throughout the country for seven days as the number of confirmed outbreaks of foot-and-mouth-disease rose to six. **24.** Mass culls of pigs and cattle got underway in an attempt to prevent further spread of foot-and-mouth-disease. **25.** Fears were raised that Britain might have exported the disease to France through exports from a farm in Devon, which was later found to be infected. The number of British outbreaks grew to 8. **27.** As a result of the outbreak horse racing was suspended for a week, a £5,000 fine was introduced for walking on closed footpaths, and the ban on movement of animals was extended by a further two weeks. Tony Blair and Gordon Brown approved £167 million in compensation for beef, sheep and dairy farmers.

MARCH 2001

1. Cases of foot-and-mouth were confirmed in Scotland and Northern Ireland for the first time since the start of the outbreak. **2.** The House of Commons passed a Bill to allow priests and clergymen to sit as MPs. **6.** The European Commission suspended all livestock markets in the EU for two weeks in an unprecedented emergency measure aimed at preventing the spread of foot-and-mouth. **7.** The Chancellor (Gordon Brown) presented the Budget to the House of Commons. **8.** Bluebird, the jet-powered boat in which Donald Campbell died while attempting to break the world water speed record in 1967, was recovered from the waters of Coniston. **14.** The Prince of Wales donated £500,000 to farmers who were dealing with the outbreak of the disease. **27.** Control of Britain's air traffic control was awarded to the Airline Group – including British Airways, Virgin Atlantic and British Midland, who had promised to spend £1 billion on improving the system. **29.** Princess Margaret suffered a third stroke. **31.** Tony Blair confirmed that the General Election and all English local elections would be postponed due to the foot-and-mouth crisis.

APRIL 2001

7. The Countess of Wessex was forced to resign from her PR company R-JH, after a reporter, claiming to be a potential client, recorded her making unsuitable remarks about the Government, the monarchy and British affairs. **8.** The Scottish Executive announced that it was to post a senior civil servant in the USA in a bid to boost tourism and inward investment links. **11.** Scotland's premier farming event, The Royal Highland Show, was cancelled due to the foot-and-mouth outbreak. **22.** The Department of Health launched an investigation into the effects of the inhalation of smoke and pollution from pyres used to burn foot-and-mouth diseased animals. The Queen appointed the Most Reverend Peter Hollingworth, Archbishop of Brisbane, as

Australia's new Governor-General. **23.** David Hart, The General Secretary of the National Association of Head Teachers, asked for a Government enquiry into pay and conditions in schools. **26.** The Government created the first of 15 'people's peers'. The Master of Dominicans, Fr. Timothy Radcliffe stated that the Roman Catholic Church was in a state of institutional crisis and needed reform. **27.** British Roman Catholic bishops agreed to create a national child protection unit to vet potential child abuse by clergy, lay staff or volunteers. **28.** A Californian businessman, Dennis Tito, paid £14 million to the Russian space agency to go on an eight-day excursion orbiting the earth on the Soyuz spacecraft. **29.** The Army admitted to supplying untreated waste food to the pig farm where the foot-and-mouth broke out.

MAY 2001

1. May Day demonstrators held anti-capitalist protests in London, 6,000 police officers were drafted in to keep the peace. Stephen Byers announced that new mothers would have the right to 52 weeks unpaid maternity leave, but would have to give employers additional notice. The Association of British Insurers agreed to reduce the use of genetic test results for insurance policies worth £300,000 or more following recommendations by the Human Genetics Commission. **2.** The NHS admitted that one in three women with cervical cancer had been wrongly given the all-clear. Statistics from the United Kingdom Central Council showed a 70% rise in the number of foreign nurses registering to work in the UK. **3.** Mike Tomlinson, the Chief Inspector of OFSTED, said that basic school inspections would continue every six years, but the amount of information that schools had to provide would be 'streamlined'. **4.** Oxford University announced the creation of a £15 million institute to study the Internet. **6.** A survey by The Institute of Education in London found that more than 5,000 maths teachers were needed in Britain to reduce the chronic shortfall of qualified teachers. **7.** It was announced that schools in Southwark, where Damilola Taylor was stabbed to death in a gang attack, were to be given their own full-time police officers to tackle crime. **8.** An official industrial investigation found that Railtrack was aware that the line at Hatfield was cracked two years before the derailment, which caused four deaths. **11.** Fuel protesters demonstrated at refineries and petrol stations prior to the general election in a bid to force the Prime Minister to cut fuel tax. **12.** A study commissioned by the Police Federation found that Britain had the lowest number of officers per capita among comparable countries. **18.** It was announced that train companies had recovered all their lost passenger business resulting from the Hatfield train disaster. Figures released from the Child Support Agency showed that the number of absent mothers targeted by the CSA had increased from 23,300 in 1996 to 61,000. **20.** Doug McAvoy, General Secretary of the National Union of Teachers, said that regulation should be introduced to protect children from advertisers marketing products by sending text messages to their mobile phones. **21.** The European Commission labelled Windermere unfit for bathing in an annual survey of seaside and freshwater holiday resorts. A report showed that women smokers were twice as likely to suffer from chest cancer as men who smoke the same number of cigarettes. **25.** Cancer-causing chemicals from foot-and-mouth funeral pyres may have contaminated milk on nearby farms, said the Food Standard Agency. The Ministry of Agriculture Fisheries and Food (MAFF) said the total number of foot-and-mouth cases was likely to be 3,000 – almost double the official total of 1,640.

26. Rioting occurred in Oldham, as fighting broke out between whites and Asians.

JUNE 2001

4. A report by the National Audit Office found that some hospital trusts 'massaged' waiting lists to reduce the numbers. British Airways agreed to compensate more than 500 stewardesses who were transferred to lower paid ground duties after they became pregnant. **6.** A report by the Royal Society for The Prevention of Accidents found that nearly three million people were injured at home every year, of whom 4,000 died. Timothy McVeigh, in prison for the Oklahoma City bombing, which killed 168 people, withdrew his appeal against receiving the death sentence. **7.** Tony Blair became the first Labour leader to secure a second full term in office after another landslide general election victory. The election had the lowest turnout since 1918. For full details of the new cabinet *see* p. 289. **8.** William Hague resigned as Leader of the Conservative Party following his party's defeat at the General Election. **10.** Around a million people in Britain could be suffering from undiagnosed diabetes, which could result in life-threatening complications according to a report issued by Diabetes UK. **11.** Following a ruling by the European Commission, employers must consult their employees before taking any decisions on redundancies and closures. The new legislation will take effect in three years time. **11.** Janardan Dhasmana, a surgeon involved in the Bristol heart babies scandal, operated on 38 children of whom 20 died according to the General Medical Council. **12.** Philanthropist Sir Paul Getty made a £5 million donation to the Conservative Party to boost the party leadership contest. The Education and Skills Secretary (Estelle Morris) ordered an emergency review of the new sixth-form curriculum. **13.** The Family Planning Association won the right to a judicial review over abortion rights in Northern Ireland. **15.** The surviving Siamese twin Gracie Attard (alias Jodie) went home to Gozo after being released from St Mary's Hospital, Manchester. **17.** The first of two parole hearings took place to decide whether the two boys convicted of the murder of Jamie Bulger would be released from detention. **18.** Liberal Democrat Leader (Charles Kennedy) completed a reshuffle of his front bench team: Norman Baker became the junior spokesperson on Home Affairs; Colin Breed became junior agricultural spokesman; David Heath became spokesman on work, family and pensions; and Sarah Gidley – deputy spokeswoman on health and women's issues. The Serious Fraud Office began an investigation into the collapse of Independent Insurance, whose liquidation affected more than 40,000 British firms. **20.** Cancer-causing chemical 3-MCPD was found in a number of imported soy sauces. **26.** Shahid Malik, a member of the Government's National Executive Committee and the Commission for Racial Equality, was hit by a police riot shield and beaten by officers whilst intervening during disturbances in Burnley. **29.** British tourists were stranded at airports in the Balearic Islands, after bus drivers went on strike over pay. **30.** The Prince of Wales told an inquiry into the future of the monarchy, that the Earl and Countess of Wessex must give up their business careers entirely if they were to continue to receive royal privileges and participate in official duties. British Members of the European Parliament (MEPs) were given a 36% pay rise to £61,488 per year.

JULY 2001

2. The Government set new academic targets for 14-year-olds to increase literacy and numeracy levels by 2004, 75% of 14-year-olds will be expected to achieve level 5 in national curriculum tests in English, maths and information technology. Liverpool Airport was renamed Liverpool John Lennon Airport. **3.** Bumi Shagaya, an eleven-year old schoolgirl from Brixton, London, went missing whilst on a school trip in Dieppe, France. *The Sun* newspaper was cleared by the Press Complaints Committee for breaking its code of conduct after paying for Ronnie Biggs, his son and Bruce Reynolds, a fellow Great Train Robber, to fly back to Britain. Under new Government welfare reform plans individuals claiming invalidity benefit will have to have to prove every three years that they are still unwell. **5.** Bumi Shagaya's, dead body was found floating in the Lac de Caniel near Dieppe. MPs voted in favour of an increase to their pay, pensions, expenses and allowances worth £24,000 per year. Kenneth Clarke, Michael Portillo, David Davis, Iain Duncan Smith and Michael Ancram were nominated for leadership of the Conservative Party. **7.** Lord Jenkins and Lord Baker, both former Home Secretaries, called for the possession of cannabis to be decriminalised. Around 120 police officers were injured and two people were stabbed during a riot in Bradford, following disturbances between far right gangs and Asian youths. **8.** The Church of England's General Synod announced that it would end its secret selection of bishops. Members of the Royal family would maintain the right to pursue business careers in new guidelines drawn up by senior officials and approved by the Queen. **10.** London Mayor (Ken Livingstone) announced plans to cut traffic congestion in the capital by introducing a £5 charge for traffic entering central London, the scheme is likely to be implemented in 2003. Jean Corston, MP for Bristol East, became the first woman to be elected chairman of the Parliamentary Labour Party. The Royal Navy announced plans to replace warships designed in the 1960s with six new generation Type 45 destroyers costing £4.5 billion which would create 3,000 new jobs. John Prescott was appointed head of a new Cabinet committee responsible for drawing up policy and reform. Labour MPs called for the banning of far right organisations following the race riots in Bradford. **11.** The Government abandoned most of its A-level education reforms by scrapping its key skills tests for A/S-level exams. **14.** SMA Nutrition baby milk was withdrawn from sale amid fears that it might have been responsible for a recent case of infant botulism. **17.** The Government fired Bob Kiley as the Chairman of London Transport, two months after his appointment to oversee reforms of the Government's Public Private Partnership. **19.** US President George Bush began a state visit to Britain and met the Queen at Buckingham Palace. **20.** Three police officers were injured when 120 youths rioted following a peaceful protest over the death of Derek Bennett, who was shot dead by a police marksman. **25.** The Home Office announced that the backlog for asylum applications had risen to 47,000. The Food Standards Agency announced fines up to £500 on restaurants, pubs, food manufacturers or supermarkets that mislead the members of the public about food descriptions. Forty-seven British tourists returned to Heathrow airport after fleeing a Tamil Tiger attack at Colombo airport in Sri Lanka. **26.** James Archer, 27, the son of Lord Jeffrey Archer of Western-Super-Mare, was banned from working in the city by the Securities and Futures Authority over a 'blatant attempt to swindle the stock market'. **29.** Ministers ordered an investigation into allegations that farmers were deliberately spreading foot-and-mouth to gain compensation. Channel 4 apologised to victims of sex abuse following the screening of a spoof about media treatment of paedophilia; the programme *Brass Eye* was condemned by Government ministers and some 500 complaints were received from the general public. MPs

called for an investigation into allegations of teachers' cheating following the results of national tests. **30.** Ken Livingstone lost his High Court attempt to block the Government's part-privatisation plans for the London Underground. A report by the Day Care Trust, entitled The Price Parents Pay, found that one in eight parents could not afford to send their children to nursery or a childminder. **31.** Louis Farrakhan, the leader of the Nation of Islam, was given leave to enter Britain after a High Court Judge overruled a ban by the Home Office. The Prime Minister (Tony Blair) made a historic visit to Argentina to meet both President de la Rua of Argentina and President Cardoso of Brazil.

AUGUST 2001

2. A car bomb exploded at Ealing tube station; several people were injured and a nearby pub was damaged in the explosion. 2,000 teachers were to be given Government help to buy their homes. Queen Elizabeth the Queen Mother received a blood transfusion for anaemia at King Edward VII Hospital in London. British tourists on a cruise of the Spice Islands were attacked by machete-wielding robbers on the island of Shungu Mbili. **4.** The Queen Mother celebrated her 101st birthday. The Church of England's General Synod appointed a review group to look at ways of modernising the practice of reading marriage banns. The European Commission announced that the Department of Health could face legal action if it refused to allow British NHS patients to obtain surgical treatment abroad. The Government launched a national register to match children with families wishing to adopt, in an attempt to reduce the numbers of young people in care. It was announced by the Roman Catholic and Church of England that clergymen previously jailed for paedophile offences were to be treated in safe houses financed by church parishes. **5.** Leader of the Liberal Democrats (Charles Kennedy) announced that he was likely to end his party's links with Labour by ending the Joint Cabinet Committee (JCC) established four years ago by Tony Blair and Paddy Ashdown. Hundreds of asylum-seekers marched in Glasgow in protest over the death of a 22-year-old Turkish man who police believe was killed in a racist attack. **7.** Three Welsh teenagers in Pill, Newport South Wales, contracted typhoid fever, the first outbreak in Britain for nine years. **9.** A report by The Howard League for Penal Reform stated that conditions in young offenders institutes failed to meet standards set by the United Nations. **20.** The British Medical Association issued a warning to general practitioners to combat female genital mutilation, a cultural practice carried out amongst some refugee communities in the UK. Baroness Thatcher, the former Conservative Prime Minister, gave her support to Ian Duncan Smith's candidacy as the next Conservative Party leader. British paratroopers went on standby to fly to Macedonia to begin collecting arms from Albanian National Liberation Army rebels. **23.** Britain supplied a further 1,000 troops to 'Operational Essential Harvest' as part of the NATO peace keeping force in Macedonia. **24.** It was revealed that Edgar Griffin, a Conservative official who has been campaigning for Ian Duncan Smith, is the father of Nick Griffin, the leader of the far-right British National Party (BNP). Ken Livingstone won a legal case to force the Government to publish a report on its £13 billion plan to part-privatise the tube. **25.** Alan Milburn announced that the Government would change the law so that British NHS patients could obtain medical treatment in other EU member states. Tony Blair ordered a review of student tuition fees and loans following fears that it might deter school-leavers in lower income groups from going to university. **26.** 6 new cases of foot-and-mouth were confirmed in three days in Hexham, Northumberland. **28.** It was announced that the top civil servants were to receive a 50% pay rise, plus bonus payments to bring their salaries in line with the private sector. Street crime rose by 20% between January and July 2001 according to figures published by Scotland Yard. **30.** Government officials announced that health ministers were preparing guidelines for the primary care trusts to enable patients to receive treatment in other EU member states.

NORTHERN IRELAND AFFAIRS

SEPTEMBER 2000

20. A missile was fired at the M16 building in Vauxhall, London causing at least one explosion but minimal damage. It was thought to be the responsibility of the Real IRA although no group claimed responsibility. **21.** Police found part of a rocket-propelled grenade launcher in a park 300 yards from the MI6 building. **25.** Forty school children escaped injury when a gunman opened fire on their school bus in Miegh, South Armagh. **28.** The last inmates of Maze Prison were released. **29.** The Government announced that convicted IRA terrorists on the run in the Irish Republic and America will be allowed to return home to Northern Ireland and would qualify for immediate freedom under the Good Friday Agreement.

OCTOBER 2000

3. Ulster Unionist Party leader (David Trimble) came under increasing pressure to resign from the Northern Ireland power sharing Executive if the IRA did not relinquish their arms by Christmas. **9.** The BBC current affairs programme Panorama was granted the right to name the suspects in the Omagh bombing by the High Court. Relatives of some of the victims objected, fearing that the programme could prejudice any subsequent trial. **17.** Three men were arrested in connection with the Omagh bombing.

NOVEMBER 2000

5. Intelligence from the Royal Ulster Constabulary and Ireland's Garda Siochana showed that there were two Real IRA units operating in Britain, which initiated a tightening of security in the run-up to Christmas. **7.** The Government announced plans to provide £11 million of compensation to widows of RUC officers killed by the IRA. **11.** Security services intercepted a horsebox packed with explosives, thought to be heading for London. **12.** Police seized a bomb, believed to be the work of the Real IRA, being driven in a van eight miles from Enniskillen.

DECEMBER 2000

12. US President Bill Clinton began a visit to Northern Ireland with the objective of ending the political deadlocks, which developed within the power-sharing executive over issues including the decommissioning of weapons and policing reforms.

JANUARY 2001

1. The Fermanagh and South Tyrone MP Ken Maginnis announced that he would not be standing at the next election. **28.** David Trimble, the First Minster of the Northern Ireland Assembly, raised hopes in a television interview that the IRA were on the verge of decommissioning their weapons. **29.** The Belfast High Court ruled that David Trimble's ban on Sinn Féin ministers attending North-South ministerial councils was illegal as it was designed to put pressure on the IRA to decommis-

sion weapons. Mr Trimble lodged an appeal against the decision and insisted that the ban would remain in place.

FEBRUARY 2001

7. Unionist and Republican politicians voiced their concerns about the future of the peace process. Unionists stated that the process could not continue without the immediate decommissioning of IRA weapons, of which it saw no sign, while the leader of Sinn Féin, stated that the escalation of Loyalist violence was causing a collapse in confidence in the Good Friday agreement.

MARCH 2001

4. A taxi bomb exploded outside the BBC's London headquarters, injuring one man; the attack was believed to have been carried out by the Real IRA. **7.** The IRA issued a statement saying that it had entered into discussions with the decommissioning body, and that British Government 'must deliver on it obligations'. **30.** Michael McKevitt, the brother-in-law of IRA hunger striker Bobby Sands was charged in the Irish Republic with directing terrorism.

APRIL 2001

1. Sinn Féin Education Minister (Martin McGuinness) accused the Northern Ireland Secretary (John Reid) of dishonesty and putting the Good Friday Agreement in jeopardy after demanding an IRA surrender. **4.** The Cabinet Office Minister (Mo Mowlam) retracted an earlier comment to newspaper executives that Martin McGuinness was 'a murderer and a terrorist'.

MAY 2001

2. Martin McGuinness admitted to being second-in-command in Londonderry on Bloody Sunday. **4.** The European Court of Human Rights ordered the Government to pay compensation to the families of the IRA men killed by the SAS and the Royal Ulster Constabulary in the 1980s and 1990s. **7.** David Trimble told the UUP that he would resign as First Minister of the Northern Ireland Assembly on 1 July 2001 if there has been no progress from the IRA on decommissioning their weapons. **9.** An inquiry into the death of 14 civilians killed during the Bloody Sunday uprising in 1972 found that an MI5 agent, who claimed that the Northern Ireland Education Minister fired the first shot, which sparked the events, was a 'reliable operator'. **15.** The US Government declared the Real IRA a foreign terrorist organisation and moved to freeze the assets of any individual or group linked to the paramilitaries in the US.

JUNE 2001

4. The Ministry of Defence informed the second Bloody Sunday inquiry that 200 British soldiers would be at risk from dissident IRA squads if they were required to give evidence in Londonderry. **6.** During the general election the UUP won 5 seats remaining the largest party one seat ahead of Sinn Féin and 2 seats ahead of the SDLP. Sinn Féin became the largest single party on Belfast City Council. **18.** Riot police were mobilised to protect Catholic children going to school in north Belfast after clashes between rival gangs. **20.** Plastic bullets were fired and petrol bombs were thrown, injuring members of the RUC during sectarian rioting in North Belfast. **30.** David Trimble resigned his post as Northern Ireland First Minister. Reg Empey was nominated as caretaker, triggering a six-week period in which to resolve the decommissioning issue.

JULY 2001

1. The Northern Ireland Parades Commission banned the Orange Order's Drumcree March at Portadown for the third successive year. **8.** Party political talks attended by Tony Blair and Bertie Ahern (Irish Prime Minister) at Weston Park, Staffordshire failed to find a breakthrough over decommissioning. **10.** The Ulster Freedom Fighters withdrew their support from the Good Friday agreement. **11.** Around 55 officers were injured during rioting in Belfast, following celebrations by Orangemen to commemorate the 311th anniversary of the Battle of the Boyne. **13-14.** Political talks reconvened at Weston Park. The meeting ended without agreement. **22-27.** The British and Irish Governments spent a week preparing a final make or break non-negotiable deal to offer pro-agreement parties.

AUGUST 2001

1. The funeral of an 18 year-old Protestant boy killed by the Ulster Defence Association took place, his father, a paramedic, had been unable to revive him at the scene. **2.** Lord Saville, tribunal chairman of the 'Bloody Sunday' inquiry, upheld his request, that the soldiers who shot dead 13 Roman Catholic men and youths in a civil rights demonstration in 1972, must return to Londonderry to give evidence. **9.** John Reid suspended the devolved institutions for 24 hours. **11.** Devolution was restored, giving the parties a six-week deadline to agree a new deal. **13.** Three suspected Provisional IRA men were detained in Bogotá, on suspicion of training Colombian FARC guerrillas. **14.** The Provisional IRA withdrew its proposal on decommissioning their weapons six days after making the offer. **20.** The SDLP gave its support to the British Government's attempt to encourage Roman Catholics to join the proposed police service in Northern Ireland. **31.** The Northern Ireland Secretary ordered the Northern Ireland Police to review the Ulster Defence Association's cease-fire.

ACCIDENTS AND DISASTERS

SEPTEMBER 2000

4. 3 people were taken to hospital, one of them unconscious, when a Central line London Underground train broke down in a tunnel for two hours between Bank and Liverpool Street. **8.** 41 people, including 20 British holidaymakers, were injured in the USA when their tour bus crashed in Nevada. **15.** The Environment agency issued flood warnings to five English counties as an average month's rainfall fell in one day. The Meteorological Office reported that London had experienced 40 mm of rain between 5 a.m. and 5 p.m. **27.** More than 70 people were killed when a Greek ferry struck rocks in seas off the Aegean Island of Paros.

OCTOBER 2000

10. Serious flooding hit Kent and Sussex causing millions of pounds worth of damage and leaving many people homeless. **17.** 4 people died and 33 were injured when an express train travelling to Leeds derailed at Hatfield shortly after leaving Kings Cross station. **18.** Railtrack admitted that they knew about the faulty track, thought to have caused the Hatfield train crash, but had decided its repair was not a priority. Gerald Corbett, Chief Executive of Railtrack, later resigned. **26.** Two people were treated for shock after a train derailed at Virginia Water, Surrey; leaves on the line were thought to have caused the accident. **27.** A Royal Navy Merlin helicopter crashed into the sea off the coast of Raasay, near Skye, all five crewmembers were rescued. **28.** A tornado swept through Bognor Regis, West Sussex causing £5 million worth of damage. **29.** 5 people were killed when torrential rain and

90 mph winds caused flooding and massive disruption throughout the south of England and Wales. Continued bad weather caused flood waters to rise in the following days with Yorkshire, Shropshire and the West Country particularly badly effected. **31.** A Singapore Airlines jumbo jet bound for Los Angeles crashed on take-off from Taipei Airport in high winds, killing 95 passengers on board. It was later thought that it had taken off from the wrong runway and may have hit earthmoving equipment. The Italian registered tanker Ievoli Sun sank 11 miles off the coast of Alderney in the English Channel, prompting fears that her leaking cargo of highly toxic styrene posed a serious environmental threat.

NOVEMBER 2000

6. 27 people were airlifted to safety after three yachts were caught in storms off the Bay of Biscay. The death toll for the spate of storms and flooding which hit the British Isles reached 12, following an accident in Tunbridge Wells in which a tree fell on top of a car, killing the two occupants. **10.** Figures released showed a 140% increase in accidents involving police cars between 1998 and 1999. **11.** More than 150 people were killed, including one Briton, when a ski train caught fire in a tunnel in the Austrian Alps. **26.** The front three carriages of a Virgin train travelling from London Euston to Glasgow became derailed at Mossend South Junction, near Motherwell, causing minor injuries to a number of passengers. **30.** At least 60 people burned to death when a leaking oil pipeline caught fire engulfing the village of Ebute-Oko in Lagos.

DECEMBER 2000

2. A holiday jet flying from Birmingham to Paphos, Cyprus, came within 100ft of colliding with a US Airforce F15 jet over Northamptonshire. **3.** Typhoon Rumbia killed at least 24 people and injured many more when it struck the southern and central regions of the Philippines. **17.** The US State of Alabama suffered widespread devastation when it was hit by a band of tornadoes causing the deaths of 12 people in the town of Tuscaloosa and injuring many others throughout the state. **25.** 309 people died in a fire in an illegal discotheque in Luoyang, China.

JANUARY 2001

3. The prompt actions of a signalman prevented two trains from crashing with more than 400 passengers on board, when a signal failure allowed them to leave London's Victoria Station simultaneously. **13.** An earthquake measuring 7.6 on the Richter scale hit Central America causing widespread devastation throughout the region. 260 houses in Las Colinas near San Salvador, the capital of El Salvador, were buried under a mudslide, killing at least 349 people. **22.** The wildlife and marine animals in the Galapagos Islands region were put in serious danger after the oil tanker Jessica ran aground near the island of San Cristóbal, leaking 144,000 gallons of fuel oil. **26.** An earthquake measuring between 6.0 and 7.9 on the Richter scale hit the western India state of Gujarat and southern Pakistan causing widespread devastation. India's Defence Minister stated that it was anticipated that the death toll would rise to around 20,000.

FEBRUARY 2001

6. More than 50 people were injured and 32 needed hospital treatment when hydrochloric acid leaked into the ventilation systems of two factories in Staffordshire. **11.** The submarine USS Greeneville collided with and sank a Japanese fisheries training ship off the coast of Hawaii. The US coastguard rescued 26 people on board the ship while 9 remained missing. **28.** 10 people were killed and 33 seriously injured when a Land Rover careered off the M62 in Yorkshire down a railway embankment and into the path of an approaching express train in Selby, North Yorkshire. The express train was derailed but remained upright and continued to move forward, colliding with an oncoming coal train.

MARCH 2001

7. The inquiry into the Selby train crash has concluded that the rail industry could not have reasonably prevented the collisions. **12.** 9 people were injured when two rush-hour trains clipped each other at Hither Green, south east London when both tried to join the same track.

APRIL 2001

2. 27 British holiday makers died when their coach fell into a South African ravine after their driver pressed the wrong pedal.

MAY 2001

10. Around 100 people were killed during a stampede at a football match between two top African teams in Ghana. **22.** A South Atlantic storm hit the UK Overseas Territory Tristan da Cunha, wiping out its power supply and wrecking buildings. **25.** 23 people were killed, and around 300 injured at a wedding in Jerusalem when the third floor of a banqueting hall collapsed.

JUNE 2001

9. A 37 year-old man with a history of schizophrenia stabbed and killed 8 children at a Japanese primary school. **23.** Around 40 people died during an earthquake in Arequipa, Peru. 59 people were killed in Southern India when part of a bridge collapsed as three train carriages passed over it, and fell in to the river Kadalundi.

JULY 2001

22. A Briton was injured and 6 other people were held during a police raid on the Genoa Social Forum in Italy. The organisation had organised an anti-capitalist march during the G8 summit. **29.** 3 children were killed when their mother's boyfriend lost control of the car he was driving and plunged into a lake at the Blue Lagoon, a Bedfordshire picnic area.

AUGUST 2001

7. Two workmen were killed and others were injured during an explosion at a power station in Teeside. **20.** Amelia Ward, the 16 year-old daughter of a senior judge, died in a climbing accident during a school trip to South Africa. **26.** British school pupils were rescued from a Himalayan mountain after their group leader, an RAF officer, used a satellite positioning device to raise a distress signal, received by a military base 100 miles from their school.

ARTS AND THE MEDIA

SEPTEMBER 2000

5. The Millennium Dome received a further emergency payment from the Government of £47 million to avoid bankruptcy. **12.** The Japanese bid for the Millennium Dome, worth £105 million, was withdrawn, once again putting the future of the Dome in doubt. **14.** The BBC announced that Lorraine Heggessey was to take over as controller of BBC 1. Craig Phillips, from Liverpool, won the popular Channel Four game show *Big Brother*, following a television vote of 7.5 million people.

OCTOBER 2000

3. The BBC announced that it would be changing the *Nine O'Clock News* bulletin to a new 10 p.m. slot and moving its *Panorama* programme from Monday to Sunday despite misgivings by BBC news journalists and the Culture Secretary Chris Smith. **10.** A Michelangelo drawing of a woman in mourning, valued at £8 million, was discovered in the library of Castle Howard. **11.** An anonymous donor, who claimed to be on her deathbed, donated two rare miniature portraits to the Dulwich Art Gallery.

NOVEMBER 2000

16. English Heritage accused the trustees of the British Museum of 'dereliction of duty' when it was discovered that the new portico, constructed as a £100 million lottery-aided development of the Great Court, had been built using French limestone instead of Portland stone from Dorset. **19.** The Culture Secretary (Chris Smith) warned the governor of the BBC that action should be taken if viewing figures or programme quality were affected by the showing of nightly news bulletins on both BBC and ITV at ten o'clock. **20.** The Press Complaints Commission ruled that photos taken of Prince William whilst hiking in the South American jungle, which appeared in *OK!* magazine, were obtained as a result of 'persistent pursuit' and the publication was therefore guilty of 'harassment and breach of privacy'. The ratings war between the BBC and ITV was exacerbated when the final episode of the BBC's long running sitcom 'One Foot in the Grave' was beaten in the ratings by ITV's 'Who wants to be a Millionaire', when Judith Keppel won the million pound prize for the first time. **22.** Richard Desmond, the founder of Northern and Shell Media, bought Express Newspapers. **28.** The German photographer Wolfgang Tillmans won the Turner prize.

DECEMBER 2000

4. A record £2.9 million was paid by an anonymous bidder for the painting *My Naked Wife Watching Her Own Body* by the surrealist artist Salvador Dali at an auction at Sotheby's, London. **12.** It was announced in the Government's Communications White Paper that the Independent Television Commission, the Broadcasting Standards Commission and a number of other organisations would be merged into a new television and radio regulatory body called the Office of Communications (Ofcom). **14.** A newly discovered handwritten draft manuscript of the Circe episode of *Ulysses* by James Joyce, fetched over £1 million at Christie's in New York. **18.** An advertising poster for the Yves Saint Laurent perfume *Opium* featuring a naked image of the model Sophie Dahl, was banned by the Advertising Standards Authority for causing offence. **21.** Pierre-Yves Gerbeau, the Chief Executive of the Millennium Dome, annouced that the final lottery grant of £47 million awarded to the Dome in September was hoped to be returned as it had not been spent. **22.** Three masked men forced their way into Sweden's National Museum and stole two paintings by Renoir titled *Young Parisienne* and *Conversation* and a Rembrandt self portrait, valued in total at around £20 million. They later held the paintings to ransom.

JANUARY 2001

8. A Ph.D. student discovered documentation which revealed that Stonehenge had undergone considerable restoration to straighten and re-erect some of its stones between 1901 and 1964. **9.** Archaeologists excavating the site of a 2nd century villa in the City of London discovered a cache of 43 Roman gold coins (Aureii) which had been hidden beneath its floorboards. **10.** It was announced that

ITV would move its main nightly news bulletin back to the ten o'clock slot for three nights of the week, following a compromise deal with the Independent Television Commission. **11.** Tony Hall, the head of BBC News, was announced as the next executive director of the Royal Opera House, London. **13.** Six diary notebooks written by Rudyard Kipling were discovered in a desk at the Macmillan publishing house after lying undiscovered for nearly 75 years. **23.** The Whitbread Prize for book of the year went to Matthew Kneale for his historical novel *English Passengers*. **28.** A review of the Royal Shakespeare Company by its main funding body, the Arts Council, concluded that the company should concentrate on 'more and better' works of Shakespeare, which it said accounted for only half of the company's repertoire at that time.

FEBRUARY 2001

4. Greg Dyke the director-general of the BBC announced that 750 employees would be made redundant in the coming year. **6.** The magazine *Mad About Boys*, which was heavily criticised by the children's charity *Kidscape* for pushing children into grown up behaviour, was banned by Woolworths and placed under review by WH Smith. **12.** Liz Forgan was appointed chairman of the National Heritage Memorial Fund, the body which buys art and collections of historic importance for Britain. **15.** Figures published by the Public Lending Right showed that Catherine Cookson was the most popular author amongst library users for the 15th year.

MARCH 2001

3. Disney bought the rights to Winnie-the-Pooh books for £240 million in the most lucrative deal in British literary history. **8.** Dame Ninette de Valois, the founder of British ballet, died at the age of 102. **9.** Part of a panel from the Temple of Apollo at Bassae, a 400 BC Greek freeze on show in the British Museum, was stolen from the display. **16.** The television fundraiser Comic Relief raised more than £23 million on the night of its broadcast.

APRIL 2001

5. A lifesize bronze Roman arm, believed to be from a statue of the emperor Nero, was unearthed in the City of London. **6.** The skeleton of a Parisi tribal queen thought to be the predecessor of Boadicea was discovered in a Middle Iron Age burial ground in the village of Wetwang, near Driffield West Yorkshire. **23.** Michael Longley, the Northern Irish poet, was awarded The Queen's gold medal for poetry. **29.** Nelson Mandela, the former South African president, hosted a concert in Trafalgar Square in celebration of the freedom of South Africa.

MAY 2001

11. Tate Modern was voted the most popular art museum in the world, having received 5.2 million visitors in its first year. **24.** Adrian Noble, artistic director at The Royal Shakespeare Company, established a one-year postgraduate course, due to his concern that drama schools were failing to train actors in classical theatre in favour of television.

JUNE 2001

5. Kate Grenville won the Orange prize for Fiction for *The Idea of Perfection*. **6.** Mark Wallinger, the official British entrant at the Venice Biennale exhibition, caused controversy by flying the Union Jack flag in the colours of the Irish tricolour over his exhibition. A photograph album containing pictures of Alice Liddell, the inspiration for Lewis Carroll's children's book *Alice in Wonderland*, sold for £465,500 at auction. **25.** Marc Quinn, 37, won the

£25,000 Charles Wollaston prize for a marble sculpture of a one-armed woman. **26.** Monet's painting *Haystacks, Last Rays of the Sun* sold for £10 million at Sotheby's. Paintings by Gainsborough, including *The Belotto*, worth more than £2 million, were stolen from Russborough House, Co. Wicklow. The *Sherborne Missal*, an illuminated prayer book from the Middle Ages, worth £15 million was donated to the British Library.

JULY 2001

3. The City of London Sinfonia gained a £1 million sponsorship deal with Marsh & McLennan Companies. **4.** Prehistoric engravings dating 30,000 years ago were discovered in underground caves in the Dordogne, south-western France. **10** The drawing *The Horse and Rider* by Leonardo da Vinci sold for £8.14 million at Christie's in London. **11.** A drawing left undiscovered in a scrapbook in a library at Castle Howard, fetched £5.94 million at auction to a London dealer. **16.** The Culture Secretary (Tessa Jowell) approved the Arts Council of England plans to restructure the organisation despite objections from the Regional Arts Boards. **29.** Fans celebrated the centenary of the publication of the first episode of Conan Doyle's book, *The Hound of the Baskervilles*. Central Government gave a grant of £250 million to 13 national galleries and museums, most in London. The other regional areas received funds via local authorities at around £250 million divided between 2,000 museums.

AUGUST 2001

2. A sculpture, made of crushed animal bones, entitled *The Naked Christ*, on display in Shrewsbury Abbey, was criticised for being unsuitable for children. **5.** An old cornet, that Louis Armstrong learnt to play whilst at the Colored Waifs Home for Boys in New Orleans, was sold at auction on the Internet by Sotheby's. The mother of murdered toddler James Bulger and children's campaigners protested against a stage play *The Age of Consent* at the Edinburgh Festival Fringe about a child who was abducted and killed. **19.** Officials at the Department for Culture, Media and Sport confirmed that the Greek government had written to the Culture Secretary (Tessa Jowell) asking for the return of the 2,300 year old Elgin Marbles removed from the Acropolis by Lord Elgin in 1779. **22.** A 600 year old glass depiction of the face of Lady Godiva went on display in Coventry, West Midlands.

CRIMES AND LEGAL AFFAIRS

SEPTEMBER 2000

1. The head teacher of a school in Cardiff who was convicted of slapping a pupil won her appeal, but remained suspended from her post whilst new allegations that she mistreated pupils were investigated. **4.** Judges in the case of Siamese twins Jodie and Mary ruled that the twins should be separated against their parents' wishes. **12.** The British owner of the Thai guesthouse, where the Welsh backpacker Kirsty Jones was murdered, was arrested in connection with her death. **21.** Alan Milburn, the Health Secretary, confirmed that there would be a full public enquiry into the Harold Shipman murders. Serial rapist Nicholas Edwards was jailed for life after an unprecedented legal ruling that women he had already been cleared of raping could give evidence against him. Derek Hooper, a former special constable, was jailed for 18 years after being convicted of 40 child sex charges. The High Court ruled that Camelot were to be given a further chance to bid for the National Lottery license, stating that the decision to block them from the bidding process was unlawful and unfair. **22.** The Court of Appeal rejected attempts to prevent the separation of the Siamese twins known as Mary and Jodie. **25.** The Duchess of York's former aid, Jane Andrews, was remanded in custody after appearing before magistrates charged with the murder of her boyfriend, Tim Cressman. Police shot dead a former British mercenary, Kirk Davies, after he threatened a number of people around the town of Selby, North Yorkshire, with an air rifle. **26.** Lord Archer of Western-Super-Mare was charged with perjury and conspiracy to pervert the course of justice over allegations surrounding his libel case against the Daily Star. **29.** Police Constable Alan Paull was jailed for five years for raping a drunken colleague at a work party.

OCTOBER 2000

5. Police investigating the disappearance of a mother and her four children discovered three bodies in the shed behind their home in Cornwall and two buried in a field four miles away. All were strangled. **8.** Jennifer Cormack won damages of £345,000 after being wrongly diagnosed with cancer, which had resulted in her having to undergo 14 operations that included having both breasts removed, and a hysterectomy. Dame Elizabeth Butler-Sloss, head of the High Court's family division, ruled that doctors were allowed to withdraw artificial feeding from two patients who were in a state of 'living death', saying that the move would not infringe on their right to life. **14.** Police began an investigation into the deaths of more than 50 patients in the care of Ann David, a senior hospital intensive care specialist at Basildon hospital in Essex. Alan Milburn ordered an urgent enquiry into the abnormally high death rate amongst heart transplant patients at St George's Hospital, Tooting. **17.** The Enigma machine, stolen from Bletchley Park in June, was returned anonymously to the office of Jeremy Paxman. The Court of Appeal ruled that the body of James Hanratty, who was hanged in 1962 for the notorious A6 murder, should be exhumed in the interests of justice. **22.** Iain Hay Gordon began proceedings in the Court of Appeal in an attempt to get his 1953 conviction for murdering Patricia Curran quashed. **26.** Lord Woolfe, the Lord Chief Justice, ruled that Robert Thompson and Jon Venables, the killers of Jamie Bulger, should serve a minimum of eight years in detention. The ruling meant that the boys would be eligible for parole in February 2001.

NOVEMBER 2000

6. The Equal Opportunities Commission announced that it would back Jane Coker and Martha Osamor, who brought a case against the Lord Chancellor for appointing a friend, Garry Hart as his special adviser without first advertising the post. **7.** Robbers attempted to steal the 203-carat diamond, the *Millennium Star* from the Millennium Dome by smashing into the site on a JCB bulldozer. **9.** Robert Deadman, an ordained Roman Catholic priest known as Father James, was convicted of indecently assaulting four of his female parishioners. **11.** Following a challenge from three media groups, the Home Secretary, the Attorney General and the Official Solicitor backed the High Court in a move to preserve the ban on publicity in the media about the killers of Jamie Bulger. **13.** The High Court ruled that the killers of Jamie Bulger were to be given new identities upon their release to protect them from revenge attacks. **15.** The former butler to Princess Diana, Harold Brown, was arrested in connection with the alleged theft of a £500,000 wedding present to the Princess. Michael Abram, the man who broke into the home of George Harrison and repeatedly stabbed him,

was ordered to be held indefinitely in a secure hospital by Oxford Crown Court. Lord Jeffrey Archer of Western-Super-Mare appeared at Bow Street Magistrates' Court and was ordered to stand trial at the Central Criminal Court on 12 December 2000 accused of perverting the course of justice. **17.** A man from Derby was arrested in connection with the theft of the Enigma Machine, which was stolen from the Bletchley Park centre in April 2000. **24.** The record producer and recording artist Jonathan King was charged with the sexual assault of a number of boys in the late 1970s and early 1980s. **28.** Damilola Taylor, a ten-year-old Nigerian boy bled to death when he was attacked and stabbed in the leg on his way home from school in Peckham, London. The Netherlands became the first country to legalise euthanasia, by the passing of a bill that guaranteed doctors immunity from prosecution for mercy killings under a number of strict conditions.

DECEMBER 2000

4. The Crown Prosecution Service announced that two police marksmen who shot and killed a man they believed to be carrying a shot gun but who was in fact carrying a table leg, would not face criminal charges. **5.** Charges of child abuse against the former manager of Southampton Football Club, David Jones, were dropped when one of the four alleged victims refused to testify. Police renewed their search for the body of the Suzy Lamplugh, the estate agent from Fulham who went missing in 1986, looking specifically in the area around the former Norton Army Barracks in Worcestershire. **15.** The serial killer Harold Shipman refused to assist in police investigations into the deaths of a further 200 people. **21.** Dr Robert Ayling, a GP working in Kent, was found guilty of the indecent assault of 13 female patients and was sentenced to four years in prison. The Government ordered an inquiry into how Dr Ayling was allowed to continue to practice for two years after he was charged. Kurdish demonstrators took over two pods of the London Eye and threatened to set fire to themselves in protest against alleged human rights abuse in Turkish jails. **25.** Six Indian soldiers and three Kashmiri students were killed when a British Muslim suicide bomber blew up his car outside an Indian Army barracks in Srinagar, Kashmir. **29.** The cabin crew of a British Airways jumbo jet with 389 passengers on board, was attacked by a man during a flight from Gatwick to Nairobi. The man managed to disengage the auto-pilot causing the plane to nosedive before the crew and passengers overpowered him and the plane was landed safely.

JANUARY 2001

1. An Algerian man was stabbed and later died in what was thought to be a racially motivated attack outside a restaurant in Soho, London. **5.** The Government passed a dossier to the police and the Crown Prosecution Service which gave the names of 250 people who died in suspicious circumstances whilst under the medical care of the serial killer, Dr Harold Shipman. **8.** The High Court judge, Dame Elizabeth Butler Sloss, granted the killers of James Bulger, Jon Venables and Robert Thompson the right to lifelong anonymity via a ban on publicity concerning the new identities they would be given on release from prison. The ban applied to the media throughout England and Wales raising suspicions that their identities would eventually be revealed by foreign media. **15.** In a landmark case Steven Thoburn, a market trader, appeared in court accused of refusing to sell fruit in kilos and grams, as legally required by the amended Weights and Measures Act of 1985, introduced to bring Britain in line with the rest of the European Community. **16.** Home Office statistics revealed that violent crime increased in 2000 even though crime overall had fallen by 0.2%. **18.** The music publisher Boosey and Hawkes won its legal battle against Disney after claiming that Disney's payment for the rights to use Igor Stravinsky's *The Rite of Spring* in its animated film *Fantasia* did not extend to the film's release on video 52 years later. **31.** A Libyan intelligence service agent, Abdul Baset Ali al-Megrahi was sentenced to life imprisonment by a Scottish Court in the Netherlands for the Lockerbie bombing which killed 270 people. His alleged accomplice Al-Amin Khalifa Fhimah was acquitted.

FEBRUARY 2001

2. David Mulcahy was sentenced to life imprisonment for the murder of three women and the rape of 12 others after his accomplice John Duffy, who was convicted and imprisoned in 1998, gave evidence against him at the trial. **6.** Michael Stone, who was convicted for the murders of Lin and Megan Russell and the attempted murder of Josie Russell, won his case in the Court of Appeal which ruled that a key trial witness, Barry Thompson, had been a police informant and therefore his testimony was unreliable. The following day the court ruled that he should be re-tried. Roy Whitting, a 42-year-old mechanic, was charged with the murder of eight-year-old Sarah Payne, who went missing in July 2000 whilst playing with her brothers and sister in a field Kingston Gore, West Sussex. Her body was found 16 days later partially buried off the A29 near Pulborough. A gunman, identified as Robert Pickett from Indiana, USA, opened fire outside the White House whilst President George Bush Jnr was inside the building. He was eventually shot in the leg and overpowered by Secret Service agents. **13.** Judge Kenneth MacRae was criticised by children's charities after jailing members of the world's largest internet paedophile ring for a maximum of 30 months. **15.** Six Liverpool supporters were stabbed in clashes with rival fans before the UEFA Cup match against AS Roma. **16.** An appeal by the father of murdered toddler, Jamie Bulger, to block the early release of Jamie's killers was rejected by the High Court. **26.** Barry George, the man accused of murdering TV presenter Jill Dando, appeared at the Central Criminal Court for his opening hearing.

MARCH 2001

2. A second severed torso was pulled from a London waterway in less than two months, prompting fears that a serial killer might be at large. **3.** A car bomb exploded outside the BBC Television Centre in West London, injuring a London Underground worker. The bomb was thought to be the work of the dissident Irish terrorist group the Real IRA. **6.** Judith and Alan Kilshaw, the British couple who adopted American twin girls through an Internet agency, had their adoption annulled by an American court. **7.** Peter Noble was sentenced to 15 years in jail for killing six people in a car accident after drinking 13 pints of lager and two Bacardi Breezers. **13.** The Princess Royal was fined £400 for driving her Bentley at 93mph when she was late for an official engagement in August. **15.** A nurse at Wrexham Park Hospital in Slough was arrested after the deaths of four children on a paediatric ward. **21.** The remains of James Hanratty were exhumed in an effort to prove that he was not guilty of the murder of Michael Gregston on the A6 in 1961. He was hanged in April 1962.

APRIL 2001

3. DNA taken from the exhumed body of James Hanratty, the man hanged for the A6 murder in 1961, matched pieces

of evidence from the crime scene. Perry Wacker, the Dutch driver in whose lorry 58 illegal Chinese immigrants suffocated as they entered Dover, was jailed for 14 years. **9.** The trial of Leeds players Lee Bowyer and Jonathon Woodgate, accused of assaulting an Asian student, was halted following a prejudicial report in a tabloid newspaper. A date for retrial was later set. **14.** A bomb thought to be the work of the Real IRA exploded on the doorstep of a Royal Mail sorting office in Hendon, north-west London, no one was hurt in the blast. **23.** A 15-year-old schoolboy, who terrorised a community in Manchester with threats of murder and fire-bombings, was banned by Manchester Magistrates' from coming within a one-mile radius of the area for ten years. Anton Malloth, an 89 year old former nazi guard at Theresienstadt concentration camp, went on trial for the murder of hundreds of prisoners in Czechoslovakia. **26.** The preliminary hearing of David Shayler, former MI5 officer charged under the Official Secrets Act for passing information to *The Mail on Sunday* began at the High Court.

MAY 2001

2. The former chairman of Sotheby's and Christie's was charged with criminal collusion over commissions paid by clients during the 1990's in New York. **3.** Ronnie Biggs, the Great Train Robber, e-mailed Detective Chief Superintendent John Coles, head of the Flying Squad, to obtain documentation to allow him to return to the UK. **7.** Ronnie Biggs returned to Britain and was taken to Belmarsh prison over a warrant issued for his arrest for being unlawfully at large since his escape from Wandsworth Prison in 1965. **11.** The deaths of 466 patients of the serial killer Harold Shipman were to be investigated by an official public inquiry. **12.** The driver of the Land Rover involved in the Selby rail disaster was charged with causing the death of ten people by reckless driving. **15.** It was announced that supermarkets would be allowed to reduce the prices of medicines and vitamins after the Community Pharmacy Action Group, representing small pharmacies, withdrew its opposition to a High Court action brought by the Office of Fair Trading to end price fixing. **19.** Women police officers won the right in a legal test to refuse to walk the beat if it clashed with their childcare arrangements. **20.** Lord Philips of Worth Matravers, Master of the Rolls, called for a state no-fault compensation scheme for medical accidents to cut the cost of going to court. **23.** The family of Timothy Evans, who was wrongly hanged for the 10 Rillington Place murders in 1950, began a claim for compensation. **29.** Lord Archer of Western-Super-Mare, former Conservative Vice-Chairman, appeared at the Central Criminal Court, accused of forging his diary to provide a false alibi during a libel trial in 1987. **31.** A Shari'ah court in Saudi Arabia sentenced four British men to up to 500 lashes and up to two-and-a-half years each in jail for defying the Saudi prohibition laws.

JUNE 2001

4. Lord Archer's former secretary told an inquiry that she had faked a diary that gave the peer a false alibi for the evening when he allegedly consorted with a prostitute, the Peer later used it as evidence during a libel action against the *Daily Star* newspaper. **5.** Ian Brady, the Moors murderer, was denied the right to starve himself to death by a High Court Judge. **6.** The entertainer Michael Barrymore was arrested over suspected drug offences following the drowning of a guest in his swimming pool during an all-night party in March. A Belgian jury found two Catholic nuns guilty of war crimes for their part in the murder of 7,000 ethnic Tutsis in Rwanda. Richard Boeken was awarded £2.17 billion by a US court. Mr Boeken suffered from lung and brain cancer and previously smoked up to two packets of cigarettes per day. **10.** Timothy Mc Veigh, the Oklahoma City bomber, was executed in Indiana, USA. **11.** A blackmailer who failed in an attempt to extort £5 million from Tesco via a parcel bomb campaign was sentenced to 16 years imprisonment at Dorchester Crown Court. **18.** Two of the photographers who pursued Diana, Princess of Wales, on the night of her death in 1997 were charged under French privacy laws in connection with the accident. **20.** Mohammed Al-Fayed lost his High Court attempt to recover £500,000 legal costs from the backers who provided a fund for Neil Hamilton's unsuccessful 'cash for questions' libel trial. **22.** Robert Thompson and Jon Venables, both 18, were granted parole on life licence after serving eight years for the murder of toddler Jamie Bulger. **26.** Four teenagers were charged with the murder of Damilola Taylor, and remanded into local authority secure accommodation after appearing before West London Youth Court. **28.** Slobodan Milosevic, the former president of the Federal Republic of Yugoslavia was flown to the Hague to stand trial for 'crimes against humanity,' including mass murder and the deportation of Kosovo Albanians. Microsoft had the decision to break up the software company overruled by the US Court of Appeal.

JULY 2001

2. Barry George was sentenced to life imprisonment at the Central Criminal Court for the murder of TV presenter Jill Dando. **10.** The High Court ruled that internet service providers would not automatically face criminal sanction if they publish details about the new identities of the Jamie Bulger killers Jon Venables and Robert Thompson. **13.** Two British tourists, Joanne Lees and boyfriend Peter Falconio, were abducted by a man at gun-point. Joanne Lees escaped but her boyfriend was not found. **15.** A man brandishing a fake gun was shot dead by police in South London. **16.** A 14 year old boy became the first persistent offender to be tagged under a new Home Office funded computer system. **18.** A terminally ill man, who was suffering from multiple sclerosis and pneumonia began a legal action under the Human Rights Act to win the right to die at home. The Law Society announced plans to monitor incompetent solicitors whose performance repeatedly failed to meet a high professional standard. It was revealed that Derek Bennett, who was shot dead by police in South London, was a psychiatric patient at the Maudsley Hospital. **19.** Lord Archer of Western-Super-Mare began a four-year sentence for perjury at Belmarsh prison. **25.** Scotland Yard's Serious Fraud Office began an investigation into allegations that millions of pounds went missing from a fundraising campaign organised by Lord Archer to help Kurdish refugees. **26.** The Criminal Cases Review commission sent the case of a man hanged 74 years ago for the murder of his mother to the Court of Appeal, following a two-year investigation. It is the oldest case that the commission has referred since its formation in 1977.

AUGUST 2001

2. Police forces around the world were searching DNA databases to find a match to DNA samples believed to belong to the gunman who ambushed a British couple in the Australian outback. An international arrest warrant was issued to capture Alberto Fujimori, the former president of Peru, on charges of dereliction of duty. **10.** Neil Hamilton, the former Government minister, and his wife were arrested over an alleged rape. The couple was later released on bail. **13.** Neil and Christine Hamilton provided the police with an alibi for their whereabouts during the alleged rape claim. **14.** Nadine Milroy-Sloan,

the woman who claimed that she was sexually assaulted by Neil and Christine Hamilton, waived her rights to anonymity and discussed the case in a tabloid newspaper. **16.** Paul Burrell, 43, the former butler of Diana Princess of Wales, appeared in court accused of stealing thousands of personal possessions of the princess. **19.** A 26-year-old man was arrested in connection with the murder of a Kurdish refugee who was stabbed to death near Sighthill, Glasgow. He and an accomplice had been charged in the same day with the assault and robbery of a German tourist. **20.** Masked raiders stole computer hardware from the Express Newspapers halting production of later editions of the *Daily Express* and *Daily Star*. **24.** Ken Livingstone won the second round of his High Court case against the Government over its part-privatisation plans for the tube. **27.** The police dropped the case against Neil and Christine Hamilton who were accused of a serious sexual assault.

ECONOMIC AND BUSINESS AFFAIRS

SEPTEMBER 2000

1. The DIY retailer Wickes agreed to a £289 million hostile take-over bid by Focus Do-It-All. The market value of Manchester United Football Club fell by £25 million due to rows over the proposed abolition of transfer fees. **15.** The Chief Executive of the London Stock Exchange, Gavin Casey announced his resignation after its shareholders called on him to stand down. Ford announced that it would not pursue its £5 billion bid to take-over the South Korean car manufacturer Daewoo. **19.** Cadbury Schweppes expanded its drinks business when they acquired the Snapple Beverage Group for £1.03 billion. **19.** Official figures revealed that the number of pensioners living in households with incomes below half of the national average had risen by almost 100,000 since the last election. **26.** Car manufacturers Reliant announced that it would cease production of the Robin in December 2000.

OCTOBER 2000

3. A report by the United Nations Conference on Trade and Developments showed that Britain was the single most popular destination for inward investment into Europe and the biggest global investor last year. **31.** Honda suspended plans to build its new Super Mini in Great Britain blaming the weakness of the Euro against the pound and uncertainty over the pricing of cars, relocating the manufacture to Japan. Alliance and Leicester announced it would cut 1,500 jobs in a drive to reduce costs by £100 million by 2003.

NOVEMBER 2000

3. Welsh Water was sold to a consortium of businesses and local authorities for £2.4 billion under a plan for it to become a not-for-profit utility. **5.** The Director-General of the CBI, Digby Jones, criticised the Government's employment legislation, claiming that it had cost businesses more that £12.3 billion in red tape. **6** The European Commission announced that it would sue the American tobacco firms Philip Morris and R. J. Reynolds for their involvement in smuggling untaxed cigarettes into the EU. **20.** The Treasury raised £38 million pounds by selling broadband fixed-wireless access licences, which would allow Telecom companies to beam high-speed Internet data directly to homes using satellite technology. **21.** Nationwide Building Society pre-empted a suspected cut in base rates by reducing its variable mortgage rate by 0.2%. **27.** Casenove, the 177-year-old stock-broking partnership, announced that it would float with an estimated value of £1.5 billion. **30.** Royal Scottish Assurance, the mortgage endowment arm of the Royal Bank of Scotland, was fined a record £2 million because of failings in its mortgage endowment products.

DECEMBER 2000

6. The high street electrical retailer Dixons accepted a £1.62 billion take-over bid by Freeserve, the UK Internet service provider. **7.** Virgin Atlantic announced plans to create 1,700 jobs through expansion of staff at London's Gatwick Airport. Abbey National rejected an informal take-over bid by Lloyds TSB prompting suspicion that Lloyds would launch a hostile bid. **11.** The Competition Commission cut the powers of Ofgem, the electricity regulator, by stating a new 'good behaviour' licence condition imposed on the electricity market was unnecessary to protect the public interest. **12.** The car manufacturer Vauxhall announced that it would cease production at its Luton plant early in 2002 resulting in the loss of 6,500 jobs. **19.** Airbus Industrie announced the launch of its superjumbo, the A380, which is expected to bring 22,000 new jobs to the UK. **28.** A report in *The Times*, which stated that a group of brain tumour victims in the United States were planning to sue mobile phone companies such as Vodaphone and BT, caused their value to drop by £5 billion on the stock market. **29.** The Internet company Letsbuyit.com asked that dealing in its shares be suspended until it could restructure its finances.

JANUARY 2001

3. The US Federal Reserve cut interest rates by half a point to 6% in response to a risk of economic weakness. **8.** It was announced that Orange, the mobile phone company, would be floated on the stock market in London and Paris with an estimated value of £45 billion. **9.** The Post Office announced that it would be changing its name to Consignia and introducing a new logo at a cost of £2 million. **16.** Inflation was at the lowest levels since current records began in 1976 averaging 2.1% for the year 2000. **23.** Clara Furse was appointed as the new chief executive of the London Stock Exchange. **24.** GNER announced that if it won a 20 year contract to operate the South West Trains franchise, it would move Clapham Junction train station 500 yards to the east of its existing site in order to increase the number of lines to Waterloo and Victoria stations. **30.** Amazon.com, the internet retailer announced that it was to cut 1,300 jobs and close distribution centres in a major strategy rethink. **31.** Lloyds TSB offered an £18.7 billion conditional take-over bid for the Abbey National pre-empting the decision of the Office of Fair Trading as to whether such a merger would be a threat to customer choice.

FEBRUARY 2001

1. Britain's biggest steel manufacturer Corus announced 6,000 redundancies at its five main sites across the country and warned that further job cuts might be necessary. **6.** The International Monetary Fund suggested Britain and Europe were not ready to converge in the form of a single currency due their divergent economic cycles. It was stated that Britain's business cycle was more in line with that of the USA and that early adoption of the Euro would lead to higher inflation in Britain.

MARCH 2001

2. The Conservative Party treasurer (Lord Ashcroft) announced that he planned to raise £42 million (US$61 million) by selling shares on Wall Street. Lord Ashcroft gave more than £1 million to the Conservative Party last

year. Boeing, the American aircraft manufacturer joined forces with Britain's leading airlines in a bid to take over air traffic control. The FTSE 100 index dropped 50 points to its lowest level since February 1999, following a number of US profit warnings. **13.** Telecom giants Motorola and Cable and Wireless announced that they were to cut a total of 11,000 jobs across the world, including up to 2,700 in Britain. **29.** Marks and Spencer announced that they were cutting 4,400 jobs and planned to pull out of Europe and America in an attempt to boost the ailing profits.

APRIL 2001

10. Tesco announced that they were to create approximately 900 jobs in Scotland in the following six months. **23.** BPB, the UK building materials company, and four other construction firms were accused of price fixing by the European Commission. **26.** The International Monetary Fund warned policymakers around the world to respond 'rapidly and decisively to a weakening global economy' if they wanted to prevent recession. It was announced that Nasdaq, the US stock market, would become a public company in its own right with an estimated value of $2.5 billion. **27.** It was revealed that Matalan, the discount clothes chain, lost £350 million from its market capitalisation.

MAY 2001

3. The Royal & Sun Alliance made a £93 million loss on the sale of its Swinton chain of high street insurance brokers to MMA, the French mutual insurer. **4.** The Halifax building society and the Bank of Scotland agreed a £28 billion merger. **7.** The London Stock Exchange launched an inquiry into the share price of Shire Pharmaceuticals prior to the merger with BioChem Pharma. HSBC and Merrill Lynch launched a US$1 billion joint banking venture. **21.** Competition watchdogs in Britain and in the USA are set to investigate the US$4.95 billion acquisition of Clairol by Proctor and Gamble. **23.** The Westbourne Group, a Canadian plumbing business, acquired Woseley, the UK building products group, for £250 million. **29.** Vodafone, the mobile phone company, announced a £8.1 billion pre-tax loss. **31.** Guinness made 140 people redundant in Dundalk, Ireland; as part of their redundancy package they will each receive free alcohol for the next 10 years.

JUNE 2001

6. Carlton and Granada, the owners of ITV, signed a £50 million deal with Coca-Cola to sponsor their coverage of Premier League soccer. Safeway announced plans to create 12,000 new jobs in the UK. **9.** Virgin and Sprint, a leading US telecom group, have formed a joint mobile phone venture. **12.** Nokia, the mobile phone company, lost £22.5 billion of its market value after issuing a profit warning.

JULY 2001

2. Emap, the magazine and radio group, sold Primedia, its American Magazine business, for £366 million. It originally paid £950 million for the company in 1999. **4.** Marconi announced plans to cut 4,000 jobs worldwide, jobs in its eleven UK sites would also be affected. **10.** Hutchinson 3G became Britain's fifth mobile phones network operator after signing a £500 million deal with Motorola. The Trade and Industry Secretary (Patricia Hewitt) blocked the merger between Abbey National and Lloyds TSB as it would have reduced competition on the high street. **18.** JP Morgan Chase, the second largest US bank, announced a 61% reduction in profits, after writing off US$1 billion (£700 million) of investment in telecom companies. **25.** A survey for *Management Today* found that UK chief executives' pay had risen by 29% over the past two years. **26.** Dolphin Telecom, the provider of radio communications to British taxi firms and emergency services, filed for bankruptcy protection. **30.** The Department of Trade and Industry warned women against joining a bogus investment scheme operating in the UK, 'Women Empowering Women'.

AUGUST 2001

14. It was announced that thirteen of the UK's top 100 companies faced a shortfall in their pension schemes due to falling interest rates and lower return on equities. **19.** The publishing group Pearson launched 200 book titles on line via its new ePenguin venture. **20.** Fujitsu, the Japanese personal computer company, announced plans to make several hundred British workers redundant over the next 12 months. Cammell Laird shipyard announced the sacking of 117 workers at its Birkenhead and Tyneside yards. **21.** Stelios Haji-Ioannou, the founder of Easyjet airlines announced plans to diversify in to banking. **25.** Britannia, the in-house airline of Thompson Travel, announced plans to reduce its 3,500 British workforce by 500. **28.** CityReach, the computer data centre company, was placed in administration after its backers failed to find a trade buyer or additional finance. **30.** The European Central Bank cut interest rates by a quarter-point to 4.25%. A public inquiry into Equitable Life, which cut the value of almost a million pension funds by 16%, was announced.

ENVIRONMENT AND SCIENCE

SEPTEMBER 2000

8. Scientists from Nasa reported that the largest ever hole in the ozone layer has opened up over Antarctica and the southern tip of Latin America. The hole covered an area of 11 million square miles. **14.** A report funded by the Department of Health found that BSE could be spread by blood transfusions. **18.** British scientists unveiled plans to create an early warning system which would detect asteroids on a collision course with Earth. **19.** A report by the Government revealed that traces of pesticide were found in nearly half the fruit and vegetables sampled by Government inspectors in 1999. Scientists at Imperial College and Hammersmith Hospital discovered a natural protein involved in prostate cancer, which could be suppressed by the same family of drugs as the common pain-killer. **23.** It was revealed that up to 8 cows had contracted BSE since measures were introduced in 1996 to eradicate the disease. **24.** A report by the Cancer Research Campaign showed that lung cancer had overtaken breast cancer as the main cause of cancer deaths among women. **27.** Dozens of new species of plants, birds, reptiles and insects were discovered by a British-led expedition to a formerly closed part of Cambodia. **28.** Sir Robert May, the Government's Chief Scientific Adviser, reported that the level of plants and animals at risk of extinction was becoming critical, with one in four mammals and one in eight birds deemed seriously endangered.

OCTOBER 2000

5. The South African Medical Research Council announced that they would be conducting the first trials of an AIDS vaccine on humans in South Africa and America. **7.** Britain's first major refuge for red squirrels was opened at Thirlmere, in the Lake District, in a bid to save them from extinction. The red-bearded anotrichium, one of the world's rarest types of seaweed, was recorded in

British Waters for the first time in over 100 years. The discovery came during a project to map marine life off the north-west coast of Wales. **22.** Scientists discovered a method of screening embryos for fatal chromosomal defects that could slash the rate of failed pregnancies.

NOVEMBER 2000

5. Scientists from the International Council for the Exploration of the Sea met in Copenhagen to discuss the possibility of closing the North Sea to cod fishermen due to the dwindling numbers of remaining stock. **6.** A consortium of organisations including the British Trust for Ornithology and the RSPB are to conduct a Government backed research project into the dwindling numbers of certain British native birds, such as the house sparrow and starling. **8.** BNFL were fined £15,000 for discharging 5,000 gallons of bleach into the Irish Sea from its Wylfa Nuclear power station. **10.** The International Council for the Exploration of the Sea warned that the North Sea had been fished almost to exhaustion and immediate measures were needed to control the situation. **17.** The Government predicted that Britain would achieve the 23% reduction of the emission of gasses linked with global warming required by the Kyoto protocol. **20.** John Prescott revealed plans to reward people financially for buying or converting their cars to run on green fuels, such as liquid petroleum or natural gas.

DECEMBER 2000

4. The fossilised remains of the earliest known human ancestor, Millennium Man, were discovered in Kenya pre-dating previous discoveries by 1.5 million years. **19.** 40,000 people had to be evacuated from their homes when the volcano *Popocateptl* situated on the edge of Mexico City erupted twice. **26.** Following a period of panic when contact was lost for a period of 24 hours with the 15-year-old Mir space station, a British expert claimed that the station could crash into Earth with some pieces surviving re-entry if Russian mission control lost permanent radio contact with it. **27.** A ten-day-old baby white rhino born at Whipsnade Wild Animal Park made its first appearance in public. **29.** A red kite bird was spotted for the first time in 120 years in the centre of London.

JANUARY 2001

2. Health officials revealed that the UK's vaccination programme had virtually wiped out the brain disease Meningitis C. **3.** Scientists reported the results of investigations commissioned by the EU and the Swiss Government which showed that global warming had increased temperatures in the rocks and mud of the Alps by 1–2°C causing permafrost to melt and increasing the risk of mudslides and rockfalls throughout the Europe's alpine regions. **8.** The Ministry of Agriculture launched a scheme to halt the decline of the song thrush whose population had declined by 55% since 1970. **9.** A total lunar eclipse during which the moon appeared to turn dark red was clearly visible in most regions of the British Isles. **10.** Scientists in America announced they had created the world's first genetically modified monkey, which had received an extra gene from a jellyfish. They suggested that the baby rhesus monkey, which was named ANDi, could help to hasten the development of treatments for a range of diseases. Archaeologists and the Egyptian government called for urgent measures to be taken to prevent the Nile from eroding away hieroglyphics on the walls of some of Egypt's best know temples, including the temple at Karnak. **26.** Scientists from two biotechnology companies announced that they had mapped the complete genetic code of rice which they claim would allow its nutritional qualities and pest resistance to be enhanced.

FEBRUARY 2001

3. Researchers at University College London and the British Antarctic Survey announced that over the past eight years the Pine Island glacier, which covers 10% of the western Antarctic ice-sheet, had thinned by 33 feet and retreated inland by three miles. **11.** One of the world's rarest birds, the small blue macaw, was reported to have vanished from the wild after the last known specimen disappeared from Bahia in north eastern Brazil.

MARCH 2001

1. Scientists said that the freezing cold weather conditions had contributed to the spread of foot-and-mouth disease. Half of Britain's butterfly species have declined over the past 200 years, with nearly a third of the species suffering a 50% fall in numbers according to a survey by the Butterfly Conservation charity and the Centre for Hydrology. **3.** Research commissioned by the National Radiological Protection Board (NRPB), the Government radiation watchdog, officially established a link between high voltage power cables and cancer for the first time. **5.** Tony Blair announced a £100 million investment in wind, solar and wave power. **23.** The Met Office announced that official figures showed the last 12 months to have been the wettest since records began in 1766. **31.** The Government reported spending £2.6 million on research to create Genetically Modified fast-growing fish for human consumption.

APRIL 2001

4. It was announced that there had been 24 confirmed cases of tuberculosis centred around a Leicester secondary school. A screening programme for local children was immediately adopted. British scientists announced the discovery of a cluster of 'orphan' planets without a central star to orbit. Some astronomers disputed the suggestion that the new objects could be planets. **8.** Conservation groups asked the Government to add the willow tit, starling, lesser spotted woodpecker, marsh tit, yellow-hammer and lapwing to its list of birds in danger. **9.** It was announced that the Bronze Age timber circle knows as 'Seahenge' was to be reburied after heritage experts failed to find it a fixed address. Astronomers claimed that the earth needs more greenhouse gas emissions to prevent atmospheric cooling that could lead to the start of a new Ice Age. **22.** Scientists in the USA threatened to boycott all scientific journals that refused to back the creation of a free online public library of science.

MAY 2001

5. A draft report prepared for the Asian Development Bank found that a Chinese project to build up to nine dams along the Mekong River in Indo-China might pose a threat to people, wild life and water systems. **8.** A previously unknown species of predatory dinosaur, a cousin of Tyrannosaurus Rex was discovered on the Isle of Wight. **18.** The first test tube foals, Eezee and Quickzee, were born in Britain using an in-vitro fertilisation. **23.** A fruit tree in Worcester was discovered to grow both apples and pears. **26.** Doctor's devised a new heart bypass operation that could be carried out without opening up the patient's chest. Scientists created the first test tube eaglet via artificial insemination. **31.** Scientists discovered remains of a Paralititan Stromeri in Egypt, one of the biggest dinosaurs to have lived on earth.

JUNE 2001

2. Site engineers revealed that the ground underneath the Millennium Dome contained contaminated waste. **12.** The Port of London Health Authority issued a ban on collecting mussels, oysters, clams and cockles from the Essex side of the Thames estuary after dangerous toxins were found in them. **13.** A report by *Which* magazine found that improvements to the quality of British beaches had encouraged more UK holidaymakers to holiday in Britain. Officials in Brussels called for a reduction in North Sea cod and hake fishing in order to prevent further depletion of fish stocks.

JULY 2001

11. British Airways and other international Airlines agreed not to transport whale meat and blubber on their planes as part of a campaign to stop Norway resuming exports after a 15 year ban. **16.** An international team of workers, including 16 Britons, began a rescue operation to raise the Kursk submarine. Environmentalists feared that the salvage operation could cause the nuclear reactors on board to leak. **17.** The Government introduced strict rules to prevent developers from building on land that might be at risk from flood damage. **21.** The Department of Health was considering banning the re-use of surgical equipment for fear that it may spread CJD. **23.** Ministers from 180 countries agreed to a deal that will ratify the Kyoto treaty on climate change next year, the US did not take part. **30.** The UK water regulator the Office of Water Services (Ofwat) called for an improvement in service standards after it emerged that water companies had spent £700 million less on vital infrastructure work than they had agreed following a review in the year 2000.

AUGUST 2001

2. A report by the Food Standard agency claimed that BSE might have been present in sheep a decade ago. Red Kite birds nested in West Yorkshire and raised around eight chicks according to the Royal Society for the Protection of Birds. A red panda at a British wildlife park became the first in the world to give birth in captivity. **4.** Eight British women volunteered to be impregnated with cloned embryos as part of an attempt to produce the first human clone in a clinic in Rome. **13.** A 20 year-old British woman made a remarkable recovery after receiving a revolutionary drug treatment for CJD, the human form of BSE. **15.** Japanese scientists created a miniature 'microbull' sculpture that is seven thousandths of a millimetre high and the size of a single blood cell. Scientists hoped that that the technique could be adapted to make small machines to deliver drugs inside the human body. **19.** British and Colombian students have discovered a new bird species, the Chestnut-capped piha that lives in the Andes tropical rainforest.

SPORT

SEPTEMBER 2000

4. England defeated the West Indies to win the Wisden Trophy for the first time in 31 years. **12.** Gianluca Vialli was sacked as coach of Chelsea Football Club after alleged disagreements with players and management. **13.** Surrey became County Cricket Champions. **15.** The Games of the XXVII Olympiad were opened in Sydney with a spectacular four hour ceremony. Gary Thornhill was stripped of his British featherweight boxing title and banned for six months after testing positive for drugs. **16.** Britain's Jason Queally won Britain's first Olympic

630   The Year 2000–2001

gold medal in the 1km cycling time trial. Claudio Ranieri was appointed as Chelsea's new manager. **21.** Four times world champion motorbike rider Carl Fogarty announced his retirement. **23.** Steve Redgrave set an Olympic record by winning his fifth consecutive gold medal at the games as part of the coxless fours. A total of 12 world records were broken in Sydney as the world's top swimmers put on an unprecedented aquatic display of speed and agility. **25.** Mark Loram became the first Briton since 1992 to become the Speedway world champion.

OCTOBER 2000

1. The closing ceremony of the Sydney Olympics took place. Britain celebrated their best performance in the Olympics for 80 years with 28 medals. **7.** Kevin Keegan announced his resignation as manager of the national team after its defeat against Germany. **8.** Michael Schumacher led Ferrari to its first Formula 1 title in 21 years. **15.** In golf, Spain defeated South Africa to take the Dunhill Cup at St Andrews. **22.** Peter Taylor, the Leicester County manager, was appointed temporary manager of the England football team. **23.** Jaguar Racing's driver Johnny Herbert retired from Formula 1 after 12 years and 159 races. **31.** Sven-Göran Eriksson was appointed as the new manager of the England Football team amongst considerable controversy that the job should not have gone to a foreigner. An official report into cricket match-fixing by India's Central Bureau of Investigation alleged former England captain Alex Stewart accepted £5,000 for information on pitches and match conditions. He later denied the allegations.

NOVEMBER 2000

2. Garry Kasparov lost his title as the world's chess champion for the first time in 15 years to Vladimir Kramnik. **6.** Chris Hutchings was dismissed from his role as manager of Bradford City football club after only a dozen league matches. **12.** Lennox Lewis successfully defended his World Heavyweight Champion of the World title by defeating challenger David Tua of New Zealand over twelve rounds by a large points advantage. **18.** A last minute try by Dan Luger gave England the victory against world champions Australia in a Rugby Union match to win the Cook Cup. **21.** A number of players in the England Rugby Union squad went on strike in a pay dispute with the Rugby Football Union. **24.** The Spanish Paralympic team for the Sydney 2000 games were found to have cheated in a number of events, most markedly in basketball after a journalist posing as one of the athletes disclosed that the team consisted of 15 members who did not have mental or physical handicaps.

DECEMBER 2000

10. The five times Olympic gold medallist in rowing, Steve Redgrave, won the BBC Sports Personality of the Year award. The second prize went to the heptathlete Denise Lewis and third prize to paralympian Tanni Grey-Thompson. During trials for a round-the-world race the yachtsman Pete Goss and his team were forced to abandon their £4.5 million *Team Philips* catamaran due to high winds, 850 miles off the coast of Ireland. In tennis, Pat Cash ended John McEnroe's three-year reign as the Honda Challenge seniors champion with a victory at the Albert Hall, London. **11.** In cricket, England beat Pakistan in Karachi to win its first test match against them for 38 years. Murray Walker, the Formula One racing commentator announced that he would retire at the end of next season bringing his 52 year career to a close. **16.** An inquiry was launched when the featherweight boxer Paul Ingle collapsed at the end of a championship fight against

Mbulelo Botile and had to undergo emergency surgery to remove a blood clot from his brain. **18.** Silverstone Circuit secured a deal with the British Racing Drivers' Club to continue to host the British Grand Prix until 2015. **29.** Gayl King became the first woman to compete on equal terms with men in the World Darts Championships.

JANUARY 2001

9. Sven-Göran Eriksson, who was appointed in October 2000 to become the England Football team's new coach, left his job as the coach of the Italian football team Lazio. **15.** Michael Johnson, the only man to have won the 200 and 400 metre Olympic titles, announced that he would be retiring from athletics at the end of the season. **18.** Bruce Grobbelaar, the former Liverpool goalkeeper, faced a legal bill of £1.5 million when a Court of Appeal jury overturned his libel action victory against *The Sun*, following allegations of match fixing. **27.** Andrew Magee scored a hole-in-one on a par-four hole at a tournament in Scottsdale, Arizona in the United States. This had never been achieved since the formation of the US PGA tour and has only happened once during a European tournament. **27.** Jennifer Capriati, the teenage phenomenon who recently spent a number of years out of professional tennis competition, beat Martina Hingis to win the Australian Open, her first Grand Slam title.

FEBRUARY 2001

11. Ellen MacArthur became the fastest woman and the fastest Briton to circumnavigate the globe single-handedly when she arrived in Sables d'Olonne in her yacht *Kingfisher* at the end of the Vendée Globe yacht race.

MARCH 2001

1. Alan Street, the British figure skating champion, finished sixth at the World Junior Figure Skating Championships in Sofia, Bulgaria. It was the highest place achieved by a British skater at an international skating Union championship since 1998. Josh Hall finished ninth place in the Vendée Globe race and became the third British skipper to complete the race. **5.** International football players' salaries could match the top American baseball players under terms agreed by the European Commission and the international football authorities. The main beneficiaries would be leading players who now earned £50,000 a week in Premiership League football. **6.** Racing resumed at Lingfield race course after a seven-day suspension due to the foot-and-mouth disease outbreak. **9.** The Badminton Horse Trials was cancelled due to foot-and-mouth disease restrictions. **16.** Tottenham Hotspur sacked its manager George Graham. **24.** England defeated Finland 2–1 in their World Cup Qualifier at Anfield. **30.** British rower Jim Shekhdar completed his 8,000-mile voyage to become the first man to cross the Pacific Ocean non-stop and unaided.

APRIL 2001

7. Red Marauder, ridden by Richard Guest, won the Grand National after only two horses managed to finish the race. **22.** Lennox Lewis lost his heavyweight title after being knocked out in the fifth round by Hasim Rahman during their fight in South Africa. Edgar Davids, the Juventus Holland midfield player, tested positive for nandrolone, a banned steroid. Russian school boy Alexey Korobkin's cricketing performance at Dover College earned him an entry in Wisden, the cricketers' Almanack. **23.** Manchester United FC paid £19 million for Ruud van Nistelrooy, making him the most expensive player in British football. **25.** Michele Alboreto, the formula one racing driver, was killed whilst testing an Audi sports car in

Lausitzring, near Dresden. **30.** Teddy Sheringham won The Player of the Year award, and Steven Gerrard won The Young Player of the Year award at the Professional Footballers' Association (PFA) awards ceremony.

MAY 2001

5. Coventry City was relegated from the Premiership after 34 years in the First Division. **22.** Kathy Freeman, the Olympic 400 metres gold winner, won the Sports Woman of the Year Award at the Laureus World Sports Awards held in Monte Carlo. Sir Steve Redgrave, five times olympic gold medal winner, was awarded a lifetime achievement award. **24.** Lee Westwood was awarded the Vardon Trophy as the winner of the Order of Merit and as Europe's leading golfer. **26.** Lord Condon's report into match fixing in cricket was published. **6.** The English football team beat Greece to qualify for the world cup.

JUNE 2001

9. Galileo won the Vodafone Epsom Derby recording the second fastest time in the event's history. Jennifer Capriati won the French Open after winning the longest third set in the championship's history.

JULY 2001

2. Pete Sampras was beaten by a former junior Wimbledon champion Roger Federer, a 19-year-old from Switzerland. **4.** Tim Henman won a place in the semi-finals at Wimbledon. **5.** Helen Tew, 89, completed a double Atlantic crossing in a 26ft gaff-rigged cutter. **8.** Tim Henman was knocked out of Wimbledon men's semi-final by Goran Ivanišević. Venus Williams won her second singles title at Wimbledon. **9.** Goran Ivanišević, unseeded, won the men's Wimbledon final. Real Madrid FC broke the world record transfer fee by signing Zinedine Zidane from Juventus FC for £48 million. **26.** British swimmer Joanna Fargus won the bronze medal in the 200 metres backstroke at the World Swimming Championships in Fukuoka, Japan, bringing the British medal total to four. **29.** Michael Schumacher, the Formula 1 champion, escaped a serious injury when his Ferrari was rammed from behind by the Prost of Luciano Burti at more than 100 mph at the start of the German Grand Prix.

AUGUST 2001

9. Premier rugby player Julian White lost his court case to break his contract with Bristol and move to a different rugby club. **19.** Michael Schumacher won the Hungarian Grand Prix matching Alain Prost's record of 51 grand prix wins and four driver's world championships. **22.** Sir Geoff Hurst, the hat-trick hero of England's 1966 World Cup win over West Germany agreed to sell his commemorative medal to his former football club West Ham for £150,000. **25.** Mathew Pinsett and James Cracknell became the first sportsmen to win gold medals for both the coxless and coxed pairs at Lucerne, Switzerland. **31.** The England football team beat Germany 5–1 during World Cup qualifier. Footballer Michael Owen scored a hat-trick.

AFRICA

SEPTEMBER 2000

6. In Zimbabwe, an official forecast predicted that the 2001 tobacco crop would be at least 30 per cent below the 2000 harvest if the planned seizure of 3,270 farms went ahead. **9.** Maria Stevens, the widow of a white Zimbabwean farmer who was beaten and murdered by a gang of veterans, filed a US$400 million case against Robert Mugabe in New York. **10.** A British paratrooper was killed in Sierra Leone when airborne forces freed six captured British soldiers who had been hostage by the West Side Boys militia near Forodugu; 12 others were wounded in the attack, in which 25 members of the West Side Boys were killed. **11.** In the general election in Mauritius, the ruling coalition was defeated by the Mauritian Socialist Movement and the Mauritian Militant Movement, who won 54 of the 62 contested seats. **14.** In South Africa, the health committee of the ANC urged President Mbeki to acknowledge that HIV was the cause of AIDS; the Confederation of South African Trade Unions (COSATU) had previously urged him to do so. **17.** In Egypt, the flogging of prisoners was outlawed. **18.** In Côte d'Ivoire, President Gen. Robert Guëi survived an assassination attempt after rebels fought their way into the presidential palace. **20.** India announced it was to withdraw its troops from the UN Mission to Sierra Leone following demands from other countries for the Indian head of the peace-keeping force, Maj.-Gen. Vijay Jetley, to be replaced. In Zimbabwe, 2,500 squatters were evicted by police from nine white-owned farms. **26.** In Zimbabwe, almost 2,000 white farmers and black farm workers went on a law and order march in Karoi after a white farmer was brutally assaulted by a mob of squatters near the town.

OCTOBER 2000

1. The World Bank announced that Zimbabwe was to be listed among the world's poorest countries, following its failure to maintain its debt repayments. **3.** In Algeria, Islamic extremists killed 14 members of the same family in the village of Ouled Amrane.. **8.** In Côte d'Ivoire, the Supreme Court barred Alassane Ouattara, the leader of the main opposition party, and 14 other prospective candidates from standing in the presidential election on 22 October. **14–17.** In Nigeria, more than 100 people were killed in three days of ethnic violence in Lagos. **16–19.** In Zimbabwe, rioters fought with police in some of Harare's poorest townships after the price of bread rose 34 per cent and bus fares rose 20 per cent; troops were sent in to quell the riots. **17.** In South Africa, President Mbeki handed over responsibility for government policy on AIDS to a newly established committee following severe criticism of his views. **20–22.** An emergency Arab League summit was held in Cairo, Egypt, to discuss the security situation in Israel; £625 million in aid was pledged to the Palestinians. **24.** In Côte d'Ivoire, the government dissolved the electoral commission and declared that President Robert Guëi had been re-elected in the presidential election held on 22 October. **25.** In Zimbabwe, President Mugabe said that the national reconciliation policy that his government had officially followed since coming to power in 1980 was at an end, and that all whites who had fought in the former Rhodesian armed forces would be put on trial for genocide; however, parliamentary approval would be required to repeal the amnesty. **26.** Laurent Gbagbo was sworn in as president of Côte d'Ivoire after the National Electoral Commission declared that he had won the election with 59.36 per cent of the vote. It was estimated that about 155 people were killed in fighting as Christians, who had backed Laurent Gbagbo, fought Muslims, who had supported Alassane Ouattara, who had not been allowed to stand. **26.** In Zimbabwe, the MDC presented a parliamentary motion calling for the removal of the President, accusing him of gross misconduct and wilful violation of the constitution. **29.** In the Tanzanian general election, polling was cancelled in 16 out of 50 constituencies in Zanzibar; the opposition boycotted a rerun in the 16 constituencies on 6 December

NOVEMBER 2000

1. In Malawi, President Miluzi ordered the sale of 39 Mercedes-Benz limousines worth £1.72 million that had been bought for government ministers; the proceeds were to be put towards poverty reduction. **6.** In Ethiopia, Emperor Haile Selassie, the country's last emperor who was deposed in 1974 and died the following year, was reburied in Addis Ababa's Holy Trinity Cathedral. **9.** In Tanzania, the government of Zanzibar released 18 opposition supporters who had been held for three years on treason charges. **10.** In Sierra Leone, talks between the government and Revolutionary United Front (RUF) rebels began. On 14 November, the government and the rebels signed a 30-day cease-fire; the Royal Marines had carried out an amphibious landing near Freetown as part of an operation to deter the RUF from launching a new campaign. **10.** Zimbabwe's Supreme Court declared the government's land seizures illegal. **14.** In Swaziland, a two-day illegal national strike was held to demand democratic reforms. **15.** In Egypt, the legislative election was won by the ruling National Democratic Party, who won 388 of the 454 seats. **15.** President Taylor of Liberia accused the UK of fomenting the civil war in Sierra Leone and said that the flooding in the UK was God's punishment. **20.** In Guinea-Bissau, the former head of the military junta, Gen. Ansumane Mane, challenged President Kumba Yalla by declaring himself head of the army; troops loyal to the government drove him out of his military base on 23 November and shot him dead on 30 November. **27.** In Zimbabwe, the ruling Zanu-PF won a by-election in Marondera West; the MDC had abandoned its campaign after violent attacks by Zanu-PF supporters resulted in the death of one person and dozens injured. **30.** In Zimbabwe, the Supreme Court threw out a government decree withdrawing citizenship from those with British passports.

DECEMBER 2000

4-5. In Côte d'Ivoire, at least nine people were killed in violence between protestors and security forces in Abidjan. **7.** In the presidential election in Ghana, John Kufuor of the New Patriotic Party won 57.4 per cent of the vote; Vice President John Atta Mills of the ruling National Democratic Congress won 42.6 per cent. In Guinea, about 360 people were killed, more than 1,000 injured and thousands more fled their homes during fierce fighting in the town of Guékedou between rebels and government forces; on 11 December, government troops killed at least 150 rebels in Kissidougou. **10.** In Zimbabwe, where the High Court had been due to hear a case brought by the opposition Movement for Democratic Change contesting the legitimacy of the election of 38 Zanu-PF MPs during the general election in June 2000, President Mugabe issued a decree that allowed Zanu-PF MPs to retain their seats even if found guilty of electoral fraud. **12.** Ethiopia and Eritrea signed a peace treaty ending their two-year border dispute; it was agreed that an independent international commission would delineate the frontier. **13-23.** In Sudan, presidential and parliamentary elections were held over a ten-day period; President Omar Bashir was re-elected with 86 per cent of the vote. There was no voting in rebel-held areas of the south and the main opposition parties did not take part. **20.** In Zimbabwe, President Mugabe announced that the government had now completed its listing of white-owned land for compulsory acquisition; 2,540 white-owned farms had been listed, about 80 per cent of the land owned by white farmers.

JANUARY 2001

7. In Côte d'Ivoire, at least eight people died during a failed coup d'état. **10.** In Nigeria, Muslims burned down about 40 hotels and bars in Maiduguri in reaction to the lunar eclipse, which they blamed on sinners. **15.** The presidents of Kenya, Tanzania and Uganda announced the launch of a revived East African Community; the previous one collapsed 23 years ago. **16.** In the Democratic Republic of Congo, President Laurent Kabila was shot dead by one of his bodyguards; the government only admitted his death on 18 January after his son, Maj.-Gen. Joseph Kabila, had been proclaimed head of state. **25.** In Nigeria, President Olusegun Obasanjo dissolved the Cabinet on 24 January. **26.** Maj.-Gen. Joseph Kabila was sworn in as president of the Democratic Republic of Congo. **27.** In Tanzania, up to 32 people were killed and one police officer decapitated in the port and capital of Zanzibar when police opened fire on demonstrators from the main opposition party who were calling for a re-run of elections.

FEBRUARY 2001

1. In Tanzania, up to 100 people were feared dead after a police helicopter fired on civilians in two boats fleeing the violence on Zanzibar. **7.** In the Democratic Republic of Congo, President Joseph Kabila called for negotiations to end the civil war. **9.** In South Africa, an ANC MP, Andrew Feinstein, called on the government to answer allegations that senior officials had siphoned off millions of pounds in a 1999 arms deal. **16.** In Zimbabwe, Morgan Tsvangirai, the leader of the MDC, was charged with inciting the violent overthrow of the government. **24.** In the Democratic Republic of Congo, UN observers moved into position to monitor a withdrawal by Rwandan Armed Forces. **25.** In Cape Verde, Pedro Pires, the African Party for the Independence of Cape Verde (PAICV) candidate, won the second round of the presidential election by a margin of just 17 votes.

MARCH 2001

2. Former President Nelson Mandela accused the ANC of being as intolerant and corrupt as South Africa's white leaders during the apartheid years, saying that the party's reputation had been tarnished by a series of financial scandals and abuses of power. **7.** The UN Security Council voted unanimously to ban diamond exports from Liberia in punishment for its support of the rebel Revolutionary United Front in Sierra Leone; it also imposed an arms embargo. **12.** In Uganda, at least 12 civilians were killed and scores injured in pre-election clashes between members of the presidential protection unit and supporters of opposition candidates. **14.** In Uganda, President Yoweri Museveni was declared the winner of the Ugandan presidential election, gaining 69.3 per cent of the vote, but his main rival, Kizza Besigye, who got 27.8 per cent, said the vote had been rigged and demanded a new poll. **20.** The Foreign Affairs Minister, Stan Mudenge, rejected a decision by Commonwealth ministers to send an urgent mission to Harare to express concern at intimidation of the country's journalists and judiciary, saying the UK had irregularly sponsored it. **21.** In Zimbabwe, the Commercial Farmers' Union rejected a proposal to accept President Mugabe's land seizure plan, but reaffirmed its absolute commitment to land reform and a negotiated settlement with the government. **25.** In Burundi, more than 200 bodies were discovered in mass graves in a suburb of Bujumbura, the result of recent fighting between Hutu rebels and government troops. In Zimbabwe, the government announced that it had begun compensating white farmers whose land had been seized for improvements such as roads or buildings. **27.** In Somalia at least seven people were reported killed as gun battles erupted throughout the city between the forces of the transitional government and a rebel militia. **28.** In Kenya, President Moi dismissed three senior civil servants who had been appointed to fight corruption. **29.** UN troops began deploying in Congo to guard the 500 unarmed UN observers monitoring a cease-fire and a buffer zone between pro-government forces and rebels in the east of the country.

APRIL 2001

3. In Zimbabwe, parliament passed a series of measures to ban foreign funding of any political party and to tighten the regulations on the establishment of private radio and television stations. **6.** In Zambia, Tilenji Kaunda, the son of former president Kenneth Kaunda, was appointed leader of the opposition United National Independence Party. **11.** In Rwanda, the government ordered the arrest of former Prime Minister Pierre Céléstin Rwigema, who was accused of participating in the 1994 genocide. **17.** In Zimbabwe, President Mugabe insisted that he would stand for re-election. **18.** In Burundi, an attempted coup by junior army officers was put down by the army. **25.** In South Africa, Safety and Security Minister Steve Tshwete accused three senior members of the ruling ANC of plotting to kill President Mbeki. **25.** In Zimbabwe, pro-government mobs stormed at least 20 organisations linked to Harare's white community. **26.** In Zimbabwe, Morgan Tsvangirai, the leader of the opposition MDC, won an appeal that overturned his defeat in last year's parliamentary election. Lawyers for the winning candidate, Kenneth Manyonda of the ruling Zanu-PF, said that they would appeal. **27.** In the Democratic Republic of Congo, Ugandan troops found the bodies of six Red Cross workers near Bunia. **29.** President Yoweri Museveni of Uganda announced that the country would immediately withdraw its armed forces from the Democratic Republic of Congo.

MAY 2001

2. In Algeria, thousands of Berbers demonstrated in Algiers in protest at police repression and arabisation in the Kabyle region; around 80 people had been killed during several days of rioting preceding the march. **3.** In Zambia, more than 30 MPs signed a motion to impeach President Chiluba for abuse of power; the following day the president announced that he would not seek to amend the constitutional limit on a president serving more than two terms. **6.** In Zimbabwe, the trial began of MDC leader Morgan Tsvangirai on charges of treason. **7.** UN sanctions against Liberia came into force; the sanctions had been approved on 7 March, but the government had been given two months to end its support for RUF rebels in Sierra Leone. **10.** The British Council closed its offices in Zimbabwe after repeated threats of invasion by war veterans. **12.** In Somalia, 80 people died in fighting between government troops and militias battling for control of the port in Mogadishu. **15.** In Sierra Leone, government troops and rebels agreed to suspend hostilities and prepare to disarm; a cease-fire had been agreed in November 2000, but clashes had continued. **18.** In Zimbabwe, President Mugabe authorised arrests among the mobs that have invaded hundreds of white-owned businesses. **23.** In Tristan da Cunha, winds of up to 120 mph destroyed a community centre and the island's only pub; there were no casualties. **24.** In Zimbabwe, the Commercial Farmers' Union offered almost 2.5 million acres of land to poor blacks, together with free technical advice and £800,000 for seed and fertiliser. **28.** In the

Central African Republic, rebel soldiers attacked the home of President Ange-Félix Patasse in a failed coup attempt in which about 12 people were killed. **31.** More than a million voters in the former British protectorate of Somaliland voted in a referendum on independence from the rest of Somalia. In South Africa, the Truth and Reconciliation Commission, which attempted to settle grievances from the apartheid era, closed its investigations after five years of work.

JUNE 2001

4. In Zimbabwe, Chenjerai Hitler Hunzvi, the leader of the War Veterans' Association, died in Harare. He was given a state funeral on 8 June. **12.** In Zimbabwe, a black commercial farmer who had been an MDC candidate in the 2000 general election was ordered off his farm. **13.** The price of petrol rose by 74 per cent in Zimbabwe. The Zimbabwe Congress of Trade Unions threatened to call a general strike if the government refused to reverse the fuel price rise. **14.** In Algeria, up to half a million pro-democracy demonstrators marched on the presidential compound. **17.** In Algeria, Islamist guerrillas killed twenty soldiers in an ambush in the Chelf region. **20.** President Mugabe of Zimbabwe agreed to support a Commonwealth ministerial mission to investigate ways in which relations with the UK government could be repaired. **26.** In Swaziland, King Mswati III signed a decree that made any criticism of the king a criminal offence. **29.** The Zimbabwean government listed another 2,030 white-owned farms for seizure.

JULY 2001

3. In the Democratic Republic of Congo, nearly 300 people were killed in a witch-hunt around Aru near the Ugandan border; more than 80 suspects were arrested by the Ugandan armed forces. **4-5.** A general strike was held in Zimbabwe; more than half of the workforce stayed at home in defiance of the government. **5.** Zimbabwean Finance Minister Simba Makoni launched an international appeal for aid to prevent a famine. **12.** Kenyan President arap Moi urged his people to abstain from sex for two years to curb the spread of AIDS. **23.** In Burundi, an attempted coup was mounted in an effort to derail a peace deal intended to end eight years of civil war.

AUGUST 2001

2. In Zimbabwe, Agriculture Minister Joseph Made told delegates to the congress of the Commercial Farmers' Union that the government now intended to seize 21 million acres, rather than the 12.5 million acres it had previously claimed for resettlement**6.** In Zimbabwe, 22 white farmers were arrested on charges of public violence and assault after they responded to an appeal for help by a white landowner; they were granted bail on August 20. **9.** In the Comoros, the civilian administration was ousted in a military coup. **9-10.** In Zimbabwe, mobs of squatters attacked and looted 29 white-owned farms near Chinhoyi. **10.** In Swaziland, King Mswati III announced an extension of his powers after an opinion gathering exercise revealed that the majority of the population wanted an absolute monarchy. **11.** In Zimbabwe, about 300 white Zimbabwean women and children were evacuated from Doma after armed squatters ransacked farms in the district. **13.** In Algeria, 17 people were killed in an ambush by suspected Islamist rebels near Sidi M'hamed Benaouda. **18.** The Zimbabwean government refused to grant permission to the International Committee of the Red Cross to set up refugee camps for black farm labourers forced off the white-owned farms where they had worked. **23.** Gambia expelled the British Deputy High Commissioner, Bharat

Joshi, who had attended an opposition party meeting. **26.** The Zimbabwe Council of Churches issued a pastoral letter criticising the government for the breakdown of law and order. **29.** In Zimbabwe, thousands of acres of white-owned farmland were set ablaze by government supporters. **30.** Govan Mbeki, a veteran leader of the anti-apartheid struggle in South Africa and father of President, Thabo Mbeki, died aged 91.

THE AMERICAS

SEPTEMBER 2000

17. In Peru, President Alberto Fujimori announced that there would be a new presidential election in march 2001, at which he would not stand, after a secret video showed his most senior adviser, Vladimiro Montesinos, head of the National Intelligence Service (SIN) allegedly bribing an opposition politician. **18.** In the USA, an airline passenger was beaten and kicked to death by other passengers when he tried to break into the flight deck and attack the crew on a flight from Phoenix to Salt Lake City. **25.** In Chile, the trial of former President Gen. Pinochet was delayed to allow medical tests to be carried out to establish his mental health. **29.** In Bolivia, at least nine people died and up to 95 were injured in protests by farmers against plans to restrict the growth of coca, the raw material for cocaine.

OCTOBER 2000

18. The US Senate passed legislation easing its trade embargo on Cuba, by allowing the sale of American food and medicine to Cuba. **22.** In Canada, Prime Minister Jean Chrétien announced that there would be a general election on 27 November 2000. **27.** Argentina formally requested the extradition of Augusto Pinochet in connection with the 1974 assassination of a Chilean general in Buenos Aires. **27.** In the USA, the Microsoft Corporation called in the FBI to investigate hackers who were reported to have copied the source code blueprints of the latest version of Windows and Office products.

NOVEMBER 2000

7. In the USA, presidential and legislative elections took place. The outcome depended on Florida, whose 25 electoral college results would decide who became president, where the Republican candidate, George W. Bush, led by 1,784 votes from a total of almost six million cast in the state. As the winning margin was less than 0.5 per cent, Florida law demanded an automatic recount, which began the following day. Al Gore, the Democratic candidate, who had already conceded defeat, retracted his concession when the recount was announced. **9.** In the Florida recount, George W. Bush's lead fell from 1,784 votes to 225 after the results of the recounts in 65 of Florida's 67 counties had been declared; the Democrats indicated that they would not accept the results of the recount, citing several irregularities, among which was the rejection of 19,120 ballots in Palm Beach County because voters had selected more than one candidate on a ballot slip whose design was widely criticised. **11.** Republican presidential candidate George W. Bush initiated legal action to try to prevent a manual recount of votes in Florida's Volusia, Palm Beach, Broward and Miami-Dade counties. **14.** In Colombia, Revolutionary Armed Forces of Colombia (FARC) guerrillas suspended peace talks with the government, claiming that the authorities had not taken sufficient action against right-wing paramilitaries. **16.** President Clinton became the first US president to visit Vietnam since the victory of the Communist North over the US-backed South in 1975. **18.** In the US

presidential election, the count of absentee postal ballots added to the recounted results left George W. Bush with a 930-vote lead over Al Gore in Florida. **20.** President Alberto Fujimori of Peru submitted his resignation; the next day, the leader of Congress, Valentin Paniagua, was named to lead a caretaker government until elections scheduled for 8 April 2001. **22.** In Peru, Valentin Paniagua was sworn in and appointed Javier Pérez de Cuéllar, the former secretary-general of the UN, as prime minister; the Peruvian Congress rejected President Fujimori's resignation and dismissed him instead. Florida's Supreme Court ruled that the revised results of manual recounts which were being conducted in Volusia, Palm Beach, Broward and Miami-Dade counties would only be accepted if they were returned by 26 November. Miami-Dade county, the most populous in Florida, suspended its hand count, saying it could not complete it in time. Dick Cheney, the Republican vice-presidential candidate, suffered a minor heart attack. **23.** The last result was declared for the US Senate leaving the Democrats and Republicans with 50 seats each. The Florida Supreme Court denied Al Gore's request to order officials in Miami-Dade to reverse their decision to abandon their recount. **26.** In Haiti, Jean-Bertrand Aristide was elected president, securing 91.7% of the vote. George W. Bush was certified as the winner of the presidential election in Florida by a majority of 537 votes, giving him enough Electoral College votes to claim the presidency; the Democratic Party immediately challenged the certification. **28.** In Canada, the Liberal Party retained power in the legislative election, winning 173 seats; the main opposition party, the Canadian Alliance, won 66 seats.

DECEMBER 2000

1. Vicente Fox was inaugurated as President of Mexico. In Chile, Gen. Augusto Pinochet was place under house arrest after being charged by Judge Juan Guzmán with involvement in 55 murders and 18 kidnappings in the months after the coup against the socialist government of Salvador Allende in 1973. On 11 December, the Appeal Court ruled that the correct procedures had not been followed and ordered the release of Gen. Pinochet; on 20 December, the Supreme Court rejected an appeal by Judge Guzmán to overturn the Appeal Court's order. **4.** The US Supreme Court set aside the earlier decision of the Florida Supreme Court to extend a deadline for hand recounts at the request of the Democrats. On 8 December, the Florida Supreme Court upheld the Democrats' challenge and ordered a manual recount in Miami-Dade county. On 14 December, the US Supreme Court ruled that that there was no longer enough time to complete a recount in accordance with constitutional standards within the time available. **6.** In Florida, Democrat lawyers brought cases in Seminole and Martin counties, alleging that Republicans had illegally corrected about 25,000 absentee ballot applications. On 8 December, Circuit Court judges decided the corrections were in clear breach of electoral law, but ruled that discarding the votes was unacceptable. **11.** In the general election in Trinidad and Tobago, the ruling United National Congress won 19 of the 36 seats; the opposition People's National Movement won 16 seats. **13.** Governor George W. Bush became president-elect of the United States after Vice-President Al Gore conceded defeat. **15.** The Governor of Florida, Jeb Bush, established a bipartisan body to reform the Florida electoral system. **18.** In the USA, the 43rd Collegium of Electors met in 50 state capitals, giving George W. Bush 271 votes of the total of 538, one more than he needed to claim the presidency. **29.** In Colombia, Diego Turbay, the head of the congressional peace commission, was shot dead in an ambush in the province of Caqueta. Rebels from the Revolutionary Armed Forces of Colombia (FARC) were thought to be to blame for the attack

JANUARY 2001

15. A recount of disputed ballots in Miami-Dade county showed that George W. Bush would have gained an additional 251 votes and Al Gore 245; it had been thought that the county would have won Al Gore the presidency had the recount not been stopped. **18.** In Chile, doctors who examined Gen. Augusto Pinochet declared that he was suffering from mild vascular dementia, but might still be able to stand trial; he was served with an arrest order on murder and kidnapping charges on 31 January. **19.** The USA paid China US$28 million compensation for the damage done to the Chinese embassy in Belgrade embassy during the 1999 bombing campaign against Yugoslavia. **20.** George W. Bush was sworn in as the 43rd president of the USA in Washington DC. **22.** President Bush banned international agencies from using US funds to fund abortions abroad. **29.** President Bush announced the formation of the White House Office of Faith-Based and Community Initiatives, which would dispense billions of dollars of government funds to religious organisations for social welfare.

FEBRUARY 2001

3. In Ecuador, a state of emergency was imposed following a dispute with indigenous Indians over economic austerity measures imposed by the government that involved increases in fuel prices; it was lifted on 10 February. **7.** Jean-Bertrand Aristide was sworn in as president of Haiti. **9.** In Colombia, the Revolutionary Armed Forces guerrilla movement agreed to resume formal peace talks to try to end the 37-year civil war with the government at a meeting with President Pastrana. **14.** Ten Caribbean countries, nine of them former British colonies, signed an agreement to create a regional Supreme Court that would replace the Privy Chamber. **16.** The Supreme Court of Canada refused to extradite two Canadian citizens accused of murder to the USA, because Washington State, where the murders were committed, had the death penalty.

MARCH 2001

8. In the USA, the House of Representatives voted by 230 to 198 in favour of President Bush's proposed tax cuts. The Chilean Appeal Court voted by 2-1 to drop 57 counts of murder and 18 kidnapping charges against Gen. Augusto Pinochet, but ruled that he should still face trial for covering up the crimes after they took place; he was released on bail on 14 March. **12.** In Mexico, the leaders of the Zapatista movement met with President Fox to commence negotiations aimed at ending the seven-year revolt. **13.** The USA and Canada banned the import of all EU meat and livestock following the first case of foot and mouth disease in France. **19.** In Guyana, the ruling People's Progressive Party/Civil Alliance won the general election. **20.** The Florida Secretary of State, Katherine Harris, announced that punch card ballots would be replaced by an optical scanning system in future elections. **29.** President Bush announced that the USA would not ratify the 1997 Kyōto protocol, which aimed to reduce harmful emissions by 2010; world leaders condemned the decision.

APRIL 2001

5. The US Senate voted down President Bush's tax cutting proposals by 53 votes to 47. **12–16.** In the USA, there was

rioting in Cincinnati and a curfew was imposed after an unarmed black man was shot dead by police.

MAY 2001

16. The US State Department designated the Real IRA and the 32-County Sovereignty Movement as terrorist organisations. **18.** Canadian Foreign Minister John Manley called for his country to replace the Queen as its head of state. **24.** In the US Senate, Senator Jim Jeffords defected from the Republican party and became an independent; the Senate had been evenly divided between Republicans and Democrats, which had given the Republican Vice President Dick Cheney the casting vote. **29.** Four Islamic terrorists were convicted in New York of the bombing of two US embassies in Kenya and Tanzania in 1998 in which 224 people were killed.

JUNE 2001

4. In the Peruvian presidential election, Alejandro Toledo obtained 52 per cent of the vote, becoming the first Amerindian to be elected president. **7.** In Argentina, former President Carlos Menem was arrested and charged with involvement in illegal arms sales to Ecuador and Croatia while both countries were subject to international embargoes. **12.** In the USA, Mohamed Rashed Daoud al-Owhali, a Saudi Arabian, was jailed for life for the 1998 bombing of the US embassy in Kenya. **19.** In Canada, Prime Minister Jean Chrétien was accused of embarrassing his country after voicing his disapproval of knighthoods bestowed upon two British-Canadians who possessed dual citizenship; Canadian citizens were not permitted to receive honours.

JULY 2001

7-11. In Jamaica, 28 people died in violence that spread out from Kingston across the country; the entire army was mobilised to restore order. **9.** In Chile, the Court of Appeal suspended legal action against the former dictator Gen. Pinochet because of his deteriorating health. **30.** In Canada, the government approved the use of marijuana for medical purposes and announced the establishment of a government-run centre for cultivating the drug.

AUGUST 2001

1. The US House of Representatives voted by 265 – 162 to ban therapeutic cloning, which involved creating embryos to treat diseases. **6.** The president of Bolivia, Gen. Hugo Banzer, resigned after he was diagnosed as having cancer; vice-president Jorge Quiroga was sworn in as president the following day. **17.** The Cuban government announced that Niall Connolly, an IRA suspect accused by the Colombian army of training the FARC Marxist rebels, was Sinn Féin's Latin American representative; he had been arrested on 11 August together with two other suspected IRA members.

ASIA

SEPTEMBER 2000

3. Sri Lankan government forces launched an attack on Tamil Tiger rebels on the Jaffna peninsular. Government forces captured Chavakachcheri, the second largest town on the peninsular, on 18 September. **6.** In Afghanistan, the Taliban militia captured Taloqan, the political headquarters of the opposition Northern Alliance. In Indonesia, three UN workers were murdered by militiamen in Atambua, West Timor, when the offices of the UNHCR and International Organisation for Migration (IOM) were attacked. The following day, the UN and other aid agencies withdrew their staff to East Timor. **9.** In China, an explosion in the Xinjiang region which killed 60 people and injured more than 300 was believed to have been caused by Uygur separatists. **10.** In the Hong Kong legislative election, the Democratic Party remained the largest in the Legislative Council, but the pro-China Democratic Alliance for the betterment of Hong Kong gained seats. **14.** In Myanmar, Aung San Suu Kyi was freed after 12 days of house arrest. On 21 September, she was escorted home from Yangon's main railway station after attempting to leave the capital by train. **18.** President Kim Dae-jung of South Korea inaugurated the commencement of work on restoring road and railway links to North Korea. **21.** North Korea invited nine European countries, including the UK, to open full embassies in Pyongyang. **23.** In Indonesia, former President Suharto was examined by an independent medical team to determine his fitness to stand trial for corruption. **25.** The North and South Korean defence ministers met for the first time since the Korean War. In Nepal, at least 15 police officers were killed and more than 20 seriously injured when nearly 2,000 Maoist guerrillas attacked the district police station in Dolpa district; the rebels later broke into a local jail, releasing the prisoners, and attacked a local bank, stealing more than £300,000 in cash. **28.** In Indonesia, a court threw out a corruption case against former President Gen. Suharto after doctors had pronounced him unfit to stand trail. The following day, President Wahid called for the case against the former President to be reopened and accused judges of accepting bribes to dismiss the case. **29.** In India former Prime Minister P. V. Narasimha Rao was convicted of bribing MPs to support his Congress government during a confidence motion in 1993. On 12 November, he was sentenced to three years in jail, but was granted bail pending an appeal.

OCTOBER 2000

1. In China, several hundred protesters from the banned Falun gong sect forced the closure of Tiananmen Square on China's national day; on 10 November, the government described the Falun gong sect as an enemy of the nation, whose aim was to overthrow the socialist system. **2.** In Sri Lanka, a parliamentary candidate and 18 other people were killed when a bomb exploded during a meeting of the Sri Lanka Muslim Congress in Muttur. **3.** In Taiwan, Prime Minister Gen. Tang Fei resigned. **4.** India announced that it had agreed to purchase arms worth several billion pounds from Russia during a visit by President Putin. **7.** In Indonesia, at least 30 people died in clashes between security forces and independence activists in Irian Jaya province. **10.** In the Sri Lankan general election, the People's Alliance won 107 seats and the United National Party won 89 of the 225 seats. In Pakistan, Gen. Pervez Musharraf promised that provincial and general elections would be held by 2002. **11.** In the Philippines, Cardinal Sin, the Roman Catholic primate, demanded the resignation of President Joseph Estrada, who had been accused of receiving more than £5.3 million in payoffs from an illegal lottery; Vice-President Gloria Macapagal Arroyo resigned the following day. **13.** Ratnasiri Wickremanayake was sworn in as Prime Minister of Sri Lanka. **16.** In China, Abduhelil Abdulmejit, a Muslim separatist leader responsible for uprisings in Xinjiang province, was tortured to death by prison guards. **22.** In North Korea, a US delegation led by Madeleine Albright visited to assess if the country were serious about ending its isolation, during which President Kim Jong-il promised to halt the country's long-range missile programme. **23.** In Sri Lanka, the Trincomalee naval base was attacked by Tamil Tigers; six service personnel and 18 Tamil Tigers were killed and a transport ship was sunk. **28.** In Pakistan, 17 political parties formed a coalition, the Grand Democratic Alliance, with the aim of restoring democracy. **29.** In Afghanistan, Taliban leaders announced a ban on the cultivation of opium. **31.** In Taiwan, parliament tabled a motion to dismiss the government.

NOVEMBER 2000

3. The UK High Court ruled that hundreds of former inhabitants of the British Indian Ocean Territory who had been evicted by the British Government in the late 1960's to make way for a US airbase had been evicted illegally; the UK government announced that it would draft legislation to allow them to return. **6.** In the Philippines, a congressional committee passed a motion to commence impeachment proceedings against President Estrada. **19.** India ordered its security forces in Jammu and Kashmir state to suspend all operations against pro-independence guerrillas during the Muslim holy month of Ramadan; the cease-fire, which began on 27 November, was ignored by the United Jihad Council, a collection of 14 groups fighting Indian rule in Kashmir. **20.** In Japan, Prime Minister Yoshiro Mori survived a no-confidence motion when rebels in his party abandoned a plan to join the opposition and vote against him. **24.** In Cambodia, about 80 armed men attempted to stage a coup, which failed when eight of them were killed and 30 arrested. **30.** In Nepal, more than 150 Maoist terrorists blew up a police post in Kumal, killing 11 policemen and injuring six others.

DECEMBER 2000

7. In the Philippines, the trial of President Estrada opened; he faced charges of bribery, corruption, betrayal of public trust and culpable violation of the Constitution. **10.** The Pakistani army announced that the imprisoned former Prime Minister Nawaz Sharif was to be released to go into exile in Saudi Arabia. **12.** The UK and North Korea agreed to establish diplomatic relations. **20.** In Afghanistan, the ruling Taliban announced that it was closing the UN mission to the country in response to a UN Security Council arms embargo imposed the previous day in an attempt to force the surrender of the wanted Saudi terrorist Osama bin Laden. **21.** In Sri Lanka, Tamil Tiger rebels declared that a month-long cease-fire would begin on 25 December. The following day, government forces launched an attack that left at least 76 people from both sides died. **24.** In Indonesia, a series of bomb explosions in Christian churches killed 15 people; two men were arrested on 26 December in connection with the bombings. **25.** In India, a man from Birmingham, Mohammed Bilal, launched a suicide bomb attack at an army base in Srinagar, Kashmir, in which at least seven people were killed. **26—28.** In Nepal, four people died in clashes between protestors and police after rumours spread that a popular Indian actor, Hrithik Roshan, had made derogatory remarks about Nepal in a television interview. **30.** In the Philippines, a suspected Islamic extremist was arrested after at least 14 people died and almost 100 were wounded in a series of bomb blasts in Manila.

JANUARY 2001

2. In Cambodia, the National Assembly approved a law allowing the prosecution by a mixed UN-Cambodian court of Khmer Rouge leaders responsible for the deaths of an estimated 1.7 million people in slave labour camps and torture centres between 1975-9; the law was approved by the Senate on 15 January. **2.** Two Taiwanese ships made the first legal direct trip to Mainland China since 1949, when a ban on travel, post and communications was imposed. **3.** Indian troops launched an offensive against Muslim separatists in northern Kashmir, after the Hizbul Mujahidin ended the cease-fire that it had unilaterally declared 11 days before. **5.** An emergency meeting of the leaders of Kazakhstan, Uzbekistan, Kyrgyzstan and Tajikistan was held to co-ordinate efforts to counter Islamic terrorism in Central Asia sponsored by the Taliban regime in Afghanistan. **6.** In the general election in Thailand, the Thai Rak Thai party won the greatest number of seats in the Lower House; following re-runs in 62 constituencies on 29 January after evidence of malpractice was found in the original ballots, the Thai Rak Thai had won 248 seats. **8.** In India, The Maha Kumbh Mela (Great Pitcher Festival), a 12-yearly Hindu festival, began in Allahabad, Uttar Pradesh; on 24 January, the most auspicious day of the 42-day festival, more than 30 million Hindus bathed in the Ganges. In Pakistan, the military government announced that from 1 July 2001 all financial transactions would be conducted in accordance with Shari'ah law. **10.** In Myanmar, a UN special envoy announced that the pro-democracy leader Aung Suu Kyi had met members of the military junta to discuss national reconciliation. **11.** In Indonesia, six men suspected of murdering three UN aid workers in West Timor in September 2000 went on trial. **19.** In the Philippines, Vice President Gloria Macapagal Arroyo took over as president after Joseph Estrada was forced from office after the armed forces and police withdrew their support and most of the cabinet resigned. In Afghanistan, the Taliban government ordered three days of prayer for rain and snow to end a drought. **24.** In Singapore, Prime Minister Goh Chok Tong announced that he intended to hand over power in 2007 to Deputy Prime Minister Lee Hsien Loong. **27.** In Iran, a military court sentenced three Iranian intelligence agents to death and imposed life sentences on five others for the murders of dissidents in 1998. **29.** In Indonesia, about 10,000 protestors tried to storm parliament, demanding the resignation of President Wahid over corruption scandals; the following day, a parliamentary commission investigating two corruption scandals linked to the president concluded that he gave false testimony in one and probably had a role in the other.

FEBRUARY 2001

1. The Indonesian parliament formally censured President Abdurrahman Wahid over his alleged involvement in two financial corruption scandals; thousands of women marched to the presidential palace to call for the president's resignation. **4.** In Indonesia's Maluku province, more than 1,000 Christians from the islands of Kesui and Teor islands in Maluku province were forcibly converted to Islam and circumcised. **8.** Vietnam closed the Central Highlands region to foreigners and deployed troops to suppress protests by members of ethnic minority groups over the relocation to their region of lowland Vietnamese. **14.** In Afghanistan, the anti-Taliban United Front captured the town of Bamiyan in the Hazarajat region on 13 February. **20.** In the Philippines, President Gloria Arroyo announced that military operations against the Moro Islamic Liberation Front, the main Islamic separatist group, were to be suspended. **21.** In India, the Maha Kumbh Mela came to an end; more than 100 million Hindus were thought to have attended. **23.** In the Indonesian province of Central Kalimantan, around 200 people were killed following six days of violence by native Dayaks against migrants from the island of Madura; thousands of Maduran settlers fled the island. **24.** In Pakistan, police arrested more than 1,000 members of the

Islamic group Sipah-i-Sahaba before the planned execution on 28 February of one of its members for the murder of an Iranian diplomat. **26.** In Afghanistan, the Taliban ordered the destruction of all statues, claiming that they were classified as idols under Islamic law.

MARCH 2001

1. In Afghanistan, the Taliban militia said that they had begun to destroy all idols, including the two largest standing Buddhas in the world, despite appeals from the UN and several governments to save the statues. **11.** In Malaysia, five people died in ethnic fighting between Malays and ethnic Indians in Kuala Lumpur. **12-13.** In Indonesia, thousands of students besieged the presidential palace demanding the resignation of President Abdurrahman Wahid. **13.** In East Timor, two people died in violence in Viquequeto following the arrest of three men at a political rally on 8 March. **14.** In India, the president of the ruling Bharatiya Janata Party, Bangaru Laxman, resigned after he was secretly filmed accepting a bribe from journalists posing as arms dealers. The following day, the Minister of Defence, George Fernandes, resigned but denied any role in the arms bribery scandal. **18.** In Iran, the revolutionary court banned all activities by the Iran Freedom Movement, the main opposition party. **19.** Japan reduced its interest rate to zero per cent in a move to stave off recession. **27.** In the Philippines, the Moro Islamic Liberation Front agreed to a cease-fire and peace talks with the government. **28.** In China, preliminary census results showed that the population had risen to 1,270 million. **29.** In East Timor, the independence leader José Xanana Gusmão resigned from the National Council, the interim legislature, and said that he would not contest the planned presidential election.

APRIL 2001

1. A Chinese pilot was killed in a collision with a US EP-3 spy plane in international airspace 65 miles off the island of Hainan; the US Navy aircraft was forced to make an emergency landing on Hainan. The 24 crewmembers were held until 11 April when Adm. Joseph Prueher, the US ambassador to China, formally apologised for the incident. **2.** In Nepal, Maoist rebels killed 42 policemen in two attacks in Rukumkot and Maina Pokhari. **7.** In Nepal, at least 47 people including 29 policemen were killed when Maoist rebels bombed a police post in Dailekh district. **8.** In Iran, about 40 members of the liberal opposition were arrested and charged with plotting to overthrow the Islamic system. **12.** In China, at least 89 convicted people were executed in one day under the 'strike hard' campaign against organised crime. **17-19.** Clashes between border troops on the Bangladesh-India border led to the deaths of 18 soldiers. **19.** South Korean Foreign Minister Han Seung-soo warned that President Bush's hard-line policy towards North Korea was undermining efforts to forge closer ties between the two Koreas. In Pakistan, the Supreme Court ruled that the trial of former Prime Minister Benazir Bhutto on corruption charges had been rigged. **25.** In Cambodia, Prime Minister Hun Sen announced that there would be a referendum on whether to keep or cremate the remains of the Khmer Rouge. **26.** In Japan, Junichiro Koizumi was inaugurated as prime minister. In Pakistan, more than 500 people were arrested to prevent a pro-democracy rally in Karachi. **29.** In Singapore, an anti-government rally took place, the first since independence 35 years ago. **30.** In Indonesia, the House of Representatives voted by 363 to 52 to censure President Wahid over two corruption scandals.

MAY 2001

1. In the Philippines four people died and more than 30 were injured after an attempt was made to storm the presidential palace in Manila. In Indonesia, the House of Representatives censured President Abdurrahman Wahid for a second time. **4.** In Afghanistan, a mob attacked the Iranian consulate office in Herat after a bomb explosion inside a mosque killed at least eight worshippers, including an exiled Iranian Sunni Muslim dissident cleric; the consulate was closed the following day. **17.** In Iran, the transport minister and several junior ministers and members of parliament were killed in a plane crash. **18.** China rejected an offer by President Chen Shui-bian of Taiwan to hold discussions on bilateral relations during the APEC summit in October. **22.** In Afghanistan, the Taliban authorities announced that the Hindu minority would be compelled to wear an identity label on their clothing. **23.** India ended its unilateral six-month cease-fire in Kashmir, blaming continuing terrorist activity. **28.** The Indonesian Parliament voted to proceed with impeachment hearings against President Wahid despite an attempt by his supporters to storm the building. **29.** The Pakistani leader Gen. Pervez Musharraf accepted an invitation from Indian Prime Minister Atal Behari Vajpayee to discuss the Kashmir dispute in New Delhi.

JUNE 2001

1. In Nepal, King Birendra and Queen Aishwarya were killed by their son, Crown Prince Dipendra, when he opened fire with an automatic rifle in the Narayanhiti royal palace in Kathmandu; he killed 14 people before shooting himself. **2.** The funeral of the murdered Nepalese King and Queen took place. Crown Prince Dipendra, who was in a coma, was declared king. **3.** In Bangladesh, at least 10 people were killed and 20 injured when a bomb exploding during Mass in a church in Gopanlganj district. **4.** In Nepal, Prince Gyanendra was crowned as king following the death of King Dipendra. Riots broke out in Kathmandu as protestors blamed the new king and his son for the killings. In Afghanistan, the Taliban announced that foreign aid workers and journalists were to come under the jurisdiction of Islamic law and the religious police. **8.** In Iran, President Mohammed Khatami was re-elected with over 76 per cent of the vote. **12.** In Afghanistan, Taliban troops attacked the town of Yakowlang in the Hazarajat region of central Afghanistan, burning down every building, after recapturing it from United Front forces the previous day. **16.** In Afghanistan, the UN World Food Programme closed 130 bakeries after the Taliban banned women from working in them. **18.** In Thailand, Prime Minister Thaksin Shinawatra appeared in court and admitted having failed to declare more than £170 million. **20.** In Pakistan, the leader of the military government, Gen. Pervaiz Musharraf, assumed the presidency and formally dissolved parliament, which had been suspended since the 1999 coup.

JULY 2001

3. China returned the US spy plane that had been forced to land on 1 April following a collision with a Chinese warplane. **11.** In Sri Lanka, President Kumaratunga suspended parliament when her governing alliance lost its majority. **14–16.** In India, Prime Minister Atal Bihari Vajpayee met with the Pakistani Chief Executive Gen. Pervez Musharraf at a summit in Agra, but failed to agree a joint declaration. **19.** In Nepal, Prime Minister Girija Prasad Koirala resigned after demands for his removal by Maoist guerrillas who had been holding 71 policemen

hostage since 12 July. **21.** Thirty-one people were killed and 15 wounded in Kashmir when suspected guerrillas attacked a route along which thousands of Hindu pilgrims were trekking to a mountain shrine. The following day, at least 15 Hindus were massacred the village of Peddar. A decree issued by President Saparmurad Niyazov of Turkmenistan ordered that non-Turkmens would have to pay a dowry of US$50,000 to the state if they wished to marry a local woman. **23.** In Indonesia, the House of Representatives voted to oust President Abdurrahman Wahid and replace him with Vice-President Megawati Sukarnoputri; Wahid initially refused to accept his dismissal, locking himself inside the presidential palace, but fled the country on 26 July. **23.** In Nepal, the government and Maoist rebels announced a cease-fire and agreed to hold talks to end the five-year insurgency in which at least 1,600 people have died. **29.** In Japan, the Liberal Democrat-led ruling coalition won 72 of the 121 seats that were up for election the Upper House. **31.** The first British embassy was opened in North Korea.

AUGUST 2001

7. In the Philippines, the Moro Islamic Liberation Front signed a formal cease-fire with the government and agreed to begin negotiating a peace settlement. **9.** The Japanese Foreign Minister, Makiko Tanaka, announced that she would dock her own salary to atone for scandals in the foreign ministry prior to her taking office. **10.** In Indonesia, at least 30 civilians were found massacred in Aceh province; the Free Aceh Movement claimed that the military had committed the atrocity in revenge for an attack on a military post. **14.** In Pakistan, President Musharraf announced that legislative and provincial elections would take place between 1 and 11 October 2002. **17.** In Nepal, the Hindu practice of untouchability was outlawed. **21.** In Sri Lanka, Tamil Tiger rebels attacked a police camp in Ampara district, killing 17 police officers and wounding 18. **30.** East Timor held its first free general election; Fretilin, the independence movement, was expected to win a convincing victory. In Nepal, a government delegation met with Maoist rebels to attempt to begin a dialogue aimed at ending the Maoist insurgency.

AUSTRALASIA AND THE PACIFIC

SEPTEMBER 2000

11. At least eight people, including five policemen, were injured in Melbourne as about 2,000 anti-globalisation protesters blockaded the opening of the World Economic Forum.

OCTOBER 2000

15. In the Solomon Islands, the two militia groups, the Malaita Eagle Force and the Isatabu Freedom Movement, signed a peace deal intended to end a two-year ethnic war that had claimed 70 lives.

NOVEMBER 2000

2. In Fiji, rebel soldiers from the Counter Revolutionary Warfare Unit mutinied in Suva; the army put down the insurrection. **15.** In Fiji, interim Prime Minister Laisenia Qarase rejected a High Court ruling which had declared the interim government illegal and ordered the reinstatement of the previous Prime Minister, Mahendra Chaudhry.

MARCH 2001

1. In Fiji, the interim government was declared illegal and the president was ordered to step down in a court ruling by five international appeal judges, which found that the multi-racial 1997 constitution was still the supreme law of Fiji; the ruling stated that President Ratu Josefa Iloilo should reassemble MPs from the previous parliament, then relinquish power by 15 March. **14.** In Fiji, the president appointed Ratu Tevita Momoedonu to head a caretaker government to lead the country until fresh elections could be held and formally dismissed former Prime Minister Mahendra Chaudhry. **26.** Rebel soldiers in Papua New Guinea, who mutinied after the government announced plans to halve the size of the army, ended their 13-day rebellion after the government dropped the plans and offered an amnesty.

MAY 2001

8. In New Zealand, Prime Minister Helen Clark announced that the air force was to scrap all its combat and trainer aircraft and that the navy's only frigate would not be replaced.

JULY 2001

11. In Fiji, George Speight and 12 of his accomplices were ordered to stand trial for treason. **16.** George Speight was allowed to register as a candidate in the forthcoming general election.

AUGUST 2001

28. In Australia, 438 Afghan refugees who were rescued from a sinking raft by a Norwegian vessel demanded to be taken to the Australian territory of Christmas Island; they were refused permission to disembark, which caused a flurry of international protests.

EUROPE

SEPTEMBER 2000

8. The final report of the panel of three 'wise men' appointed by the EU to investigate Austria's human rights record urged the EU to end sanctions, as it had found no evidence that the Austrian government had breached the European Convention on Human Rights, and stated that Austria's treatment of ethnic minorities was better than many EU member states; the sanctions were lifted on 12 September. **11.** In Slovakia, an opposition-sponsored referendum which demanded an early legislative election failed when only about one-fifth of those eligible voted; the participation of at least 50 per cent of the electorate was required by the constitution to carry the demand. **13.** Spanish police arrested 19 suspected members of ETA, the armed Basque separatist group, and searched the offices of Herri Batasuna, ETA's legal political ally, in Bilbao and Pamplona. **15.** In France, the leader of the Basque terrorist organisation ETA, Ignacio Gracia Arregui, was arrested in Bidart. **20.** Yugoslav President Slobodan Milosević addressed Serb nationalists in the northern town of Berane during his first visit to Montenegro in four years, and accused the Montenegrin President Djukanović of selling out to the West. In Yugoslavia, an opposition rally in Belgrade was attended by more than 150,000 people. The Spanish government announced tougher measures against terrorism and street violence in the Basque country. **23.** In the Czech Republic, about 1,000 protestors demonstrated against the annual meeting of the IMF and World Bank and brought the centre of Prague to a standstill; on 26 September, around 10,000 anti-capitalist protestors attacked banks, department stores and fast-food outlets; 64 policeman and 20 demonstrators were injured. In Spain, almost 100,000 people demonstrated against the ETA killings in Donostia/San Sebastián. **24.** In France, a

referendum to reduce the length of the presidential term of office from seven years to five was passed with 73.2 per cent of those voting approving the plan; only 30.2 per cent of the electorate voted. In a referendum in Switzerland, 63.7 per cent of voters rejected a proposal to cut the number of foreigners living in the country from 20 per cent to 18 per cent. **25.** In Yugoslavia, at least 40,000 people gathered in Belgrade's central square to celebrate the defeat of President Milosević in the presidential election before the official results had been announced. **26.** In the first round of the Yugoslav presidential election, the official results gave Vojislav Koštunica 48.22 per cent and President Slobodan Milosević 40.23 per cent of the vote; candidates were required to gain over 50 per cent of the vote to win without a second round being required. Opposition parties, independent monitors and even one party in the ruling coalition had proclaimed Mr Koštunica the outright winner with 54 per cent of the vote; a second round was scheduled for 8 October. In the concurrent legislative election, the coalition of the Socialists, the United Yugoslav Left and the pro-Serb Socialist People's Party in Montenegro won 72 out of 138 seats in the lower house and 26 of 40 seats in the upper house. The elections were boycotted by more than 75 per cent of voters in Montenegro and 90 per cent in Kosovo. **27.** In France, President Chirac was put under pressure by his own party to reveal his role in an illegal party funding scandal, which concerned a videotape purporting to show a bribe being given in 1986 in Chirac's presence while he was mayor of Paris. **28.** In the Danish referendum on the adoption of the European single currency, 53.1 per cent of those who voted rejected the adoption of the Euro; the turnout was 88 per cent. Serbia's opposition threatened to bring the country to a halt by calling a general strike; amid controversy over who had won the presidential election. **29.** In Spain, riot police cleared blockades at the country's largest biggest fuel distribution centre after more than three weeks of protests over fuel prices.

OCTOBER 2000

2. In Serbia, a general strike began in protest at the official results of the Yugoslav presidential election. The Pope canonised 120 Chinese martyrs and apologised for errors committed by missionaries in China. **3.** In Switzerland, Finance Minister Kaspar Villiger revealed that the country had frozen £57 million from about 100 secret bank accounts linked to Slobodan Milosević. **4.** The Yugoslav presidential election result was annulled by the country's Supreme Court, citing irregularities in the conduct of the election; it recommended that fresh elections should be held in July 2001. In France, the Senate rejected a government attempt to bring the country into line with European laws on sexual equality by allowing women to work at night in manual and industrial employment. **5.** In Yugoslavia, President Milosević went into hiding after an estimated one million people took to the streets of Belgrade and stormed parliament and other government buildings; on the following day, he announced his resignation, saying that he had received official information that Vojislav Koštunica had won the election. **7.** Vojislav Koštunica was sworn in as president of Yugoslavia. In Luxembourg, Crown Prince Henri became Grand Duke after the formal abdication of his father, Jean. **8.** In Poland, Aleksander Kwaśniewski won a second term of office in the presidential election, winning 53.9 per cent of the vote. In Lithuania, the result of the general election was inconclusive, but on 12 October, a grouping of four centrist parties, the New Union, Lithuanian Liberal Union, Modern Christian Democrats and the Centre Union, announced that they were to form a coalition government. In Belgium, the far-right Vlaams Blok made significant advances in local elections, winning 20 seats in Antwerp's 55-member city council. **9.** In Spain, the chief prosecutor of the Supreme Court of Andalucia, Luís Portero, was murdered in Granada by the ETA. **10.** The Presidents of Russia, Belarus, Kazakhstan, Kyrgyzstan and Tajikistan signed a treaty establishing the Eurasian Economic Community. **12.** In France, the Defence Minister, Alain Richard, ordered the French Foreign Legion to accept female recruits. **13.** The Bosnian Muslim leader, Alija Izetbegović, resigned from the country's three-member presidency due to ill health; Halid Genjac replaced him as the representative of the Muslim community. **15.** In Slovenia, the centre-left Liberal Democrats won 34 of the 90 seats in the general election, becoming the largest party in the legislature. In Belarus, opposition parties boycotted the legislative election; only 54 of the 565 candidates were not supporters of President Lukashenko and the OSCE declared that the conduct of the election had not met normal democratic standards. **16.** In Yugoslavia, an agreement was reached between reformers and allies of ex-President Milošević to share power until a legislative election on 23 December. **24.** President Koštunica said that Slobodan Milošević would stand trial and acknowledged that the Yugoslav security forces had committed atrocities in Kosovo. The UN was to be allowed to reopen its office in Belgrade to prosecute those responsible for war crimes committed in the former Yugoslavia. The Italian parliament voted to abolish national service. **25.** At an informal Balkans summit in Skopje, President Rexhep Mejdani of Albania demanded that President Koštunica should denounce his predecessor, Slobodan Milošević, and hand him over to an international court; he also demanded that all Yugoslav officials involved in the oppression of Kosovo Albanians should be sacked and brought to trial. **29.** The pacifist leader Ibrahim Rugova claimed a landslide victory for his Democratic League of Kosovo over former Kosovo Liberation Army guerrillas in the province's first democratic elections. **30.** In Kosovo, the Democratic League of Kosovo won civic elections in 21 of 27 municipalities. The turnout was nearly 80 per cent. A car bomb in Madrid planted by ETA killed José Francisco Querol, a Supreme Court judge.

November 2000

2. In Serbia, democratic and human rights groups demanded the resignation of secret police chief Rade Marković, after a leaked document implicated the security agency in the assassination of journalist Slavko Curuvija in April 1999. **5.** In Azerbaijan, the incumbent New Azerbaijan party won the legislative election, securing about 70 per cent of the votes cast; foreign observers denounced the poll as unfair. **7.** The Roman Catholic Church in Germany announced that it would issue payments of about £1,500 per person in compensation to Second World War slave labourers. In France, following disclosures of an outbreak of bovine spongiform encephalopathy, (BSE), President Jacques Chirac called for an immediate ban on feed containing animal remains. **9.** In Germany, more than 200,000 people marched through Berlin to protest against neo-Nazi anti-Semitic and racist attacks. **11.** In the legislative election in Bosnia-Hercegovina, the multi-ethnic Social Democratic Party and the Muslim Party for Democratic Action emerged as the largest parties in the Muslim-Croat Federation; Serb nationalists remained in control of Republika Srpska. **16.** Yugoslavia announced the re-establishment of diplomatic relations with the USA, the UK, France and Germany. Russia announced that it would resume arms supplies to

Iran. **19.** In Azerbaijan, up to 15,000 people marched through Baku demanding a fresh election and the annulment of the legislative election on 5 November; demonstrations also took place in other towns. **20.** In Russia, President Putin announced that 2,600 soldiers had been killed in Chechnya since the fighting began in 1999; he criticised military standards, training and goals. **21.** In Spain, ETA terrorists assassinated Ernest Lluch, the former health minister, in Barcelona. On 23 November, nearly a million people demonstrated against ETA in Barcelona; Prime Minister José Maria Aznar was among the marchers. **23.** The European Court of Human Rights ruled that the Greek government had violated the human rights of former King Constantine when it seized his property after he was deposed; the Court ordered the Greek government to devise a compensation offer within six months. **23.** In Kosovo, British peacekeepers announced that they had arrested 10 suspected Kosovar Albanian guerrillas and seized a lorry packed with weapons. Xhemajl Mustafa, a senior political adviser to the political leader Ibrahim Rugova, was shot dead in Priština. **26.** In Romania, the primary round of the presidential election resulted in the Communist candidate, Ion Iliescu, winning 37 per cent of the vote and Corneliu Vadim Tudor, a nationalist, winning 28 per cent; the other four candidates were eliminated.

December 2000

5. The trial in the Netherlands of the two Libyans suspected of the Lockerbie bombing was adjourned until January 2001 to await documents from Syria, which the defence believed were crucial to its case. **6.** In Serbia, the Serbian Socialist Party selected former President Slobodan Milošević to head its list of candidates contesting the general election on 23 December. In France, about 60,000 people from throughout Europe demonstrated in Nice against globalisation and for of workers' rights. **7.** In Austria, an anti-EU umbrella organisation composed mainly of environmental organisations announced that it had collected almost double the 100,000 signatures needed to force a parliamentary debate and vote on membership of the EU. **8.** In Germany, the last remaining watchtower from the Berlin wall was demolished. **12.** At a UN conference on organised crime in Palermo, Italy, 142 nations signed the first legally binding UN convention on fighting organised crime. **15.** In Ukraine, the last functioning reactor at the Chernobyl nuclear plant was closed. **18.** In Kosovo, rebel Albanian separatists fired at US and Russian KFOR troops from within the five-kilometre buffer zone between Kosovo and Serbia. The KFOR troops had been destroying a road near Gornje Karačevo used by rebels to smuggle arms from Kosovo into the security zone. **19.** In Yugoslavia, President Vojislav Koštunica called on NATO to allow paramilitary forces to enter the border buffer zone to end a campaign by ethnic Albanian guerrillas in the Preševo valley. He asked for the buffer zone to be reduced by at least half. In the Netherlands, parliament passed legislation to permit homosexual couples to marry and adopt children. **19–22.** Turkish security forces stormed 20 jails in an attempt to end a two-month hunger strike by more than 1,100 prisoners, twenty-one prisoners were killed in the operation and many more wounded. **20.** In France, members of the National Assembly voted to postpone the legislative election that had been planned for March 2001 until after the presidential election due to be held in May 2001. **21.** Austria became the first EU country to impose a ban on German beef, a move that was approved by the European Commission. **24.** In Yugoslavia, the 18-party Democratic Opposition of Serbia (DOS) won 176 of the 250 seats in the general election; the Socialist Party of Serbia came second with 37 seats. **26.** The president of Moldova, Petru Lucinschi, announced the dissolution of parliament following its failure to elect his successor. In Russia, the old Soviet national anthem was officially restored, but was to remain wordless until new lyrics are agreed. **28.** In Romania, a left-wing minority government was appointed by parliament. **29.** In Montenegro, the government collapsed after the National Party withdrew from the ruling coalition.

JANUARY 2001

1. Greece formally adopted the Euro, becoming the 12th EU member state to do so. **2.** In Germany, women were given the right to join frontline units of the armed forces. **9.** Biljana Plavsić, a former president of the Republika Srpska, the Bosnian Serb entity in Bosnia-Hercegovina, surrendered herself to the UN War Crimes Commission in The Hague; on 11 January she pleaded not guilty to nine counts of genocide and crimes against humanity. **14.** In Portugal, Jorge Sampãio was re-elected president with 55.8 per cent of the vote. **18.** The Belgian government announced the decriminalisation of the use and possession of cannabis for personal consumption. Turkey recalled its ambassador from Paris in protest at a vote by the French parliament recognising massacres of Armenians by the Ottoman Empire in 1915 as genocide. **24.** In Russia, the Duma voted to impose limits on the immunity granted to all post-Soviet Russian presidents after leaving office and the Defence Ministry announced that it would reduce troop numbers in Chechnya in February. **26.** In Russia, President Putin warned that US plans for a missile defence shield and NATO proposals to expand eastward could seriously damage Russia's relationship with the West. **29.** In Germany, Defence Minister Rudolf Scharping announced that 59 military bases would be closed as part of a cost-cutting programme. Riots broke out in Zürich, Switzerland, in protest at the annual meeting of the World Economic Forum in Davos. **31.** In the Lockerbie trial at Camp Zeist, the Netherlands, Abdelbaset Ali Mohmed Al Megrahi was found guilty of the murder of 270 people and was told that he must serve at least 20 years in a Scottish prison. The other suspect, Al Amin Khalifa Fhimah, was found not guilty. In Turkey, a Kurdish True Path Party MP, Fevzi Sihanlioglu, died after being involved in a fight in the parliamentary chamber with fellow MPs. On 1 February, two MPs from the Nationalist Action Party who were charged with involuntary manslaughter said that they would give up their parliamentary immunity to face trial.

FEBRUARY 2001

1. The Vatican replaced its first 1929 constitution with a new basic law, incorporating amendments made since then and dropping all reference to the death penalty, which was abolished in 1969. **5.** Albanian separatists in the Preševo valley in southern Serbia launched a sustained attack against Yugoslav security forces. **6.** The Danish Cabinet announced that it would end its large subsidies to the Færøe Isles in four years' time if the inhabitants backed the plan of their Prime Minister, Anfinn Kallsberg, to seek full independence by 2012 in a referendum on the issue planned for 26 May. **8.** In Ukraine, the prosecutor general's office announced that President Leonid Kuchma had been questioned over allegations that he ordered the death of a journalist, George Gongadze, who had exposed government corruption. In Germany, former Chancellor Helmut Kohl agreed to pay a fine of about £100,000 in return for not facing further criminal investigation of breach of trust allegations. **12.** Ukraine and Russia agreed to reconnect the power grids of the two countries, create a

joint aerospace consortium and build a bridge connecting Russia to the Crimean peninsula. **16.** In Kosovo, a bus carrying Serb civilians was attacked, leaving seven people dead and 21 more injured near the town of Podujevo. **19.** In Russia, at least 20 Russian soldiers were killed and 20 wounded near Grozny, Chechnya. **22.** The Turkish government abandoned its currency control policy, causing the lira to fall by almost 30 per cent against the US dollar. **24.** In Yugoslavia, the former head of the secret police, Rade Marković, was arrested over the attempted assassination of a political opponent, Vuk Drasković, in October 1999. **25.** In the Moldovan general election, the Communist Party won 50.2 per cent of the vote.

MARCH 2001

4. In Switzerland, a referendum proposing the immediate commencement of negotiations to join the EU was rejected by 76.7 per cent of those who voted. Macedonia closed all border crossings with Kosovo after three soldiers were killed near a border village occupied by ethnic Albanian guerrillas. **5.** In Portugal, the Infrastructure Minister, Jorge Coelho, resigned, saying he accepted responsibility for the collapse of a road bridge over the river Douro near Entre-os-Rios in which at least 70 people died. **7.** In Bosnia-Hercegovina, Ante Jelavić, the Bosnian Croat member of the three-man collective presidency and other senior Bosnian Croat officials were sacked by Wolfgang Petritsch, the senior international administrator, after their party announced plans to break the alliance with the country's Muslims.
8. NATO acted to halt an insurrection by ethnic Albanians rebels on the Macedonian side of the border with Kosovo, capturing the main rebel headquarters in the Macedonian village of Tanusevci and allowing Yugoslav forces back into a border zone they had been forbidden to enter for two years. In France, the Basque separatist organisation ETA stole 1.5 tonnes of explosives from a warehouse near Grenoble. **12–30.** In Macedonia, the armed forces launched an offensive to drive out ethnic Albanian forces, who had occupied five villages near the Kosovan border. **22.** In Poland, President Aleksander Kwaśniewski vetoed a £7,000 million compensation payment to hundreds of thousands of people whose property had been seized by the Communists, saying that the economy could not afford it. **25.** Yugoslav forces re-entered much of the buffer zone bordering Kosovo with the agreement of NATO in an attempt to halt the activities of ethnic Albanian rebels in border regions of southern Serbia. **26–27.** In Germany, anti-nuclear protesters occupied sections of railway line to try to prevent a train full of nuclear waste from travelling to Dannenberg to be buried in a salt mine. **30.** In Spain, the Basque terrorist group ETA warned tourists to stay away from Spanish tourist resorts.

APRIL 2001

2. In Yugoslavia, former President Slobodan Milošević admitted that the Yugoslav government had secretly paid the cost of arming rebel Serbs in Croatia and Bosnia during the break-up of the former Yugoslavia. **4.** The Moldovan Parliament elected the Communist Party leader Vladimir Voronin as president. **5.** In Yugoslavia, Justice Minister Vladan Batić, declined to accept the arrest warrants for Slobodan Milošević brought from the International Tribunal for the Former Yugoslavia. **10.** In the Netherlands, the States General, the country's upper house, passed legislation by 46 to 28 to legalise euthanasia. **11.** In Turkey, hundreds of thousands of people protested in cities across the country to demand the resignation of Prime Minister Bülent Ecevit over his failure to control the country's economic crisis. **19.** The

Italian government approved plans to construct a bridge linking Sicily to the mainland. **22.** In Montenegro, the Democratic Party of Socialists and other pro-independence parties won 44 of the 77 seats in the general election. **24.** In France, Employment Minister Elisabeth Guigou announced a package of measures to bolster the rights of workers facing redundancy and to penalise companies suspected of laying them off to boost profits. **24.** The Yugoslav army charged 183 of its members with war crimes in the Kosovo conflict. **26.** In Ukraine, Prime Minister Viktor Yushchenko was dismissed by parliament. **29.** In Macedonia, eight members of the security forces were killed in an ambush by members of the ethnic Albanian National Liberation Army (NLA).

MAY 2001

3. In Macedonia, government forces attacked an ethnic Albanian village, ending their two-month cease-fire following the killing of 10 soldiers and police by the outlawed NLA. In Serbia, Slobodan Milošević was served with an arrest warrant issued by the International War Crimes Tribunal for the Former Yugoslavia. **6.** In Bosnia-Hercegovina, thousands of Bosnian Serb nationalists attacked Muslims and international officials, forcing the cancellation of a ceremony to mark the rebuilding of a mosque in Banja Luka. **8.** In Macedonia, it was announced that a coalition government of national unity was to be formed to avert the threat of civil war. **14.** In the Italian general election, the Centre-Right House of Liberty alliance won 368 seats in the 630-seat Chamber of Deputies and 177 seats of the 315 seats in the Senate. **16.** More than 7,000 Bosnian Croat soldiers who mutinied in support of separatists trying to carve out an ethnic Croat state returned to barracks following an agreement between nationalist generals and the central government. **21.** In Serbia, ethnic Albanian rebels agreed to disband, announcing that their aims would now be better served through political debate. **24.** The coalition government of Northern Cyprus collapsed amid disagreement over its stance on the future of the divided island. In Macedonia, the army and police launched an offensive against more than 10 rebel-held villages near Kumanovo. **28.** In the general election in Cyprus, the Communist Akel party won 34.7 per cent of the vote, making it the largest party.

JUNE 2001

5. Serbian Interior Minister Dušan Mihailović admitted the existence of three mass graves within Serbia containing the remains of Albanian Kosovars who were killed during the war in 1999. **8.** The Irish electorate voted against the ratification of the Treaty of Nice; only about 35 per cent of the electorate voted. **14.** President Boris Trajkovski made an official request for NATO help in disarming the NLA; the NLA had earlier made NATO involvement a prerequisite for disarmament. **15.** Macedonian political leaders held talks on concessions to ethnic Albanians in an attempt to halt an all-out war. **15-16.** In Sweden, 25,000 protestors demonstrated in Gothenburg against the EU summit that was taking place in the city; there was widespread violence and over 500 people were arrested. **17.** In the general election in Bulgaria, the National Movement for Simeon II won 43.4 per cent of the vote, obtaining 120 seats of the 240 seats. **22.** In Turkey, Virtue, the main opposition party, was ruled illegal by the country's highest court, which judged it to be a focal point for pro-Islamic and anti-secular activity. **22-24.** Macedonian forces ended a tenuous 11-day cease-fire and launched a three-day campaign against NLA positions in the village of Aracinovo until the NLA agreed to withdraw its forces. **25.** In the Macedonian capital Skopje, Slav

nationalists stormed parliament in protest against the government allowing NATO forces to escort NLA fighters from Aracinovo to safety. **28.** Yugoslavia extradited Slobodan Milošević to the UN tribunal in The Hague where he faced four charges of crimes against humanity and violations of the laws or customs of war for his responsibility for the conduct of the Kosovo campaign; further crimes committed in the Bosnian and Croatian wars were likely to be added. **30.** In Yugoslavia, Prime Minister Zoran Zizić and other ministers resigned in protest at the extradition of Milošević.

JULY 2001

1. In Austria, protestors attacked police and smashed cars and shop windows in a demonstration against a meeting of the World Economic Forum in Salzburg. **3.** In Cyprus, following the arrest of Marios Matsakis, an MP who had protested at the construction of a communications aerial in the RAF base at Akrotiri, more than 1,000 Greek Cypriots stormed the base and released him; 40 policemen and soldiers were injured in the attack. Former Yugoslav President Slobodan Milošević made his first appearance at his UN war crimes trial and refused to enter a plea on charges against humanity, saying that he did not recognise the authority of the court. **4.** In Bosnia-Hercegovina, the Prime Minister of the Republika Srpska, Mladen Ivanić, declared that the state was preparing to hand over the war crimes suspects Radovan Karadzić and Ratko Mladić to the UN War Crimes Tribunal for the Former Yugoslavia. **5.** In Macedonia, ethnic Albanian rebels and the Macedonian army signed separate cease-fire deals with NATO. **8.** In Croatia, four Cabinet ministers resigned in protest at the government's decision to hand over two generals accused of war crimes against Serb civilians in the mid-1990s. **9.** The Russian-appointed head of the Chechen administration, Mufti Akhmad Kadyrov, accused the Russian military of tormenting, humiliated and robbing people. **16.** The Russian President, Vladimir Putin, signed a friendship treaty with President Jiang Zemin of China. **17.** In Bulgaria the National Movement of the former King Simeon II of Bulgaria agreed to form a coalition government with the ethnic-Turkish Movement for Rights and Freedom. **24.** Macedonia closed its border with Kosovo after accusing peace envoys of siding with the country's ethnic Albanian minority in negotiations between the two sides. Demonstrators attacked the British and German embassies and UN offices in Skopje. A commission of Catholic and Jewish historians announced that it had suspended its study of the Church's role in the Holocaust because the Vatican had refused to release material from its archives. **25.** In Bulgaria, Simeon Saxe-Coburgotski, the former King Simeon II was appointed Prime Minister.

AUGUST 2001

6. In Macedonia, talks to end the conflict between the government and the NLA broke down after Macedonian hard-liners added new demands. **12.** Macedonian security forces shot dead five unarmed ethnic Albanian villagers and burnt at least a dozen houses in Ljuboten; the Interior Ministry claimed that the five killed were terrorists. **13.** In Macedonia, leaders of the Slav and Albanian parties signed an agreement aimed at tending the fighting and clearing the way for NATO troops to take up their positions within two weeks; the agreement accorded equal status to Christianity and Islam and made Albanian an official language. **15.** NATO authorised the deployment to Macedonia of troops for the Essential Harvest task force. **30.** In Macedonia, demonstrators tried to prevent deputies from entering the parliament building to debate the ratification of the peace agreement.

THE MIDDLE EAST

SEPTEMBER 2000

4. The first round of the Lebanese general election took place. Selim al-Hoss, the incumbent prime minister, conceded defeat when it became obvious that Rafik al-Hariri had won a large majority. **10.** The Palestinian Central Council decided to delay its declaration of Palestinian statehood, which it had promised for 13 September, for at least two months. **12.** Israeli Prime Minister Ehud Barak set out proposals, known as a civil revolution, which were designed to reduce the influence of religious leaders on daily life; the proposed changes included the introduction of civil marriage, allowing buses and El Al flights on the Sabbath and closing the religious affairs ministry. **18.** In Jordan, a military court sentenced six Islamic militants to death for plotting a bombing campaign against Jews and Christians during the Millennium celebrations at the start of the year. **23.** The US ambassador to Israel, Martin Indyk, was suspended pending an investigation into alleged security violations. **27.** In Israel, the Attorney General announced that there was insufficient evidence to prosecute former Prime Minister Binyamin Netanyahu on corruption charges. **28.** Violent unrest occurred in Jerusalem following a visit to the Temple Mount by Ariel Sharon, the opposition leader.

OCTOBER 2000

1. Palestinians protested throughout the West Bank and Gaza Strip; three Israeli soldiers and at least 28 Palestinians were killed and 700 people were reported wounded. There was also fighting between Jews and Arabs in major towns in Israel. **2.** Seven Israeli Arabs were killed in clashes inside Israel, the first to die in political clashes since 1976. **5.** An agreement aimed at ending the violence on the West Bank and Gaza was reached by the Israeli Prime Minister, Ehud Barak, and the leader of the Palestinian National Authority, Yasser Arafat, in talks hosted by Madeleine Albright in Paris. **7.** The Israeli air force bombed targets in Lebanon after Lebanese Hezbollah guerrillas captured three soldiers in a border raid. **8.** In the West Bank, Jewish settlers blocked roads and stoned Palestinian cars; in Tiberias, a crowd set fire to a mosque; the following day, thousands of Israeli Arabs demonstrated in Nazareth. **10.** In Yemen, a suicide bomb attack in Aden killed 17 US sailors dead and injured 35 others. **11.** Israeli helicopters launched rocket attacks on Yasser Arafat's compound in Gaza, a police station at Ramallah and a police academy in Jericho in revenge for the lynching of three Israeli soldiers in a police station in Ramallah. On 18 October, an Israeli undercover unit seized eight suspected members of the Palestinian mob that had lynched the Israeli soldiers; another two suspects were arrested on 25 June 2001. **12.** Oman cut diplomatic ties with Israel. **14.** A Saudi Arabian Airlines Boeing 777-200 carrying 90 passengers, of whom 40 were British, was seized by four terrorists on a flight from Jiddah to Heathrow and ordered to fly to Baghdād; the hostages were freed on the following day and flown back to Jiddah. The Iraqi authorities announced on 6 November that the hijackers had been granted political asylum. **16–17.** A crisis summit was hosted by the USA in Sharm el-Sheik, Egypt; an agreement was reached between the Israeli and Palestinian delegations in which both sides agreed to issue statements calling for an end to violence. **21.** Israel announced that it intended to suspend diplomatic contact with the Palestinian Authority because it had failed to keep to the agreed cease-fire. **23.** In Lebanon, President Gen. Lahoud appointed Rafiq al-Hariri as Prime Minister designate. **31.** On a state visit to Israel, Federal Chancellor Gerhard Schröder of Germany accidentally extinguished the eternal flame at the Yad Vashem Holocaust memorial in Jerusalem.

NOVEMBER 2000

5. In Iraq, the national airline, Iraqi Airways resumed domestic flights through the Western-imposed no-fly zones in defiance of the UN. **9.** A leading member of al-Fatah, the mainstream wing of the Palestine Liberation Organisation, Hussein Abayad, was killed in a helicopter rocket attack launched by Israel. The following day al-Fatah announced that it was at war with Israel. In Kuwait, four people were arrested on charges of planning terrorist attacks on US targets in the Gulf. **13.** Palestinian-ruled towns in the West Bank were cordoned off by the Israeli army following the killing of four Jewish settlers. **20.** Israeli helicopters attacked Palestinian targets in the Gaza Strip in retaliation for the bombing of a school bus, in which two teachers were killed. **21.** The Palestinian National Authority authorised its policemen to open fire in self-defence against Israeli forces in those areas that were under full Palestinian sovereignty. Egypt recalled its ambassador to Tel Aviv in protest at Israel's handling of the security situation. **22.** In Israel, two people were killed and about 55 were injured when a bus was bombed near Tel Aviv. **26.** At least four members of al-Fatah were killed in an ambush by an Israeli commando unit near the West Bank village of Habla. **26.** An Israeli soldier was killed and several were injured by a bomb planted by Hezbollah guerrillas near the Lebanese border; Israel responded with a bombing raid on three suspected Hezbollah positions in Lebanon. **30.** The PLO rejected an Israeli offer to negotiate a partial peace deal, in which Israel would hand over a further 10 per cent of the West Bank to connect the patches of autonomous territory and recognise Palestinian statehood, annexing some Jewish settlements in return, leaving the final status of Jerusalem and the return of Palestinian refugees to be decided within three years.

DECEMBER 2000

3. Israeli Prime Minister Ehud Barak warned President Bashar al-Assad of Syria that continued support for Hezbollah guerrillas would result in Israeli military strikes against Syrian targets. **4.** Israeli helicopters opened fire on buildings in Bethlehem to defend Rachel's Tomb, a Jewish shrine, against a Palestinian assault. **9.** In Israel, Prime Minister Ehud Barak resigned and was immediately adopted by the Labour Party's candidate for the forthcoming election. **19.** In Bahrain, a committee appointed by the Emir recommended the introduction of a bicameral parliament and suffrage for women. **23.** Israeli and Palestinian negotiators met President Clinton about peace talks in Washington. **28.** In Israel, two soldiers were killed when a bomb exploded at the Sufa border crossing to the Gaza Strip. Thirteen people were injured when two pipe bombs exploded on a bus in Tel Aviv.

JANUARY 2001

1. In Netanya, Israel, over 40 people were injured in a car bomb explosion. **8.** In Jerusalem, thousands demonstrated in protest at Prime Minister Barak's proposal to divide the Old City between Israel and the Palestinians. **16.** Palestinian police announced that six people suspected of collaborating with Israeli security forces had been executed and that a further 40 were under arrest. **17.** Gunmen in Gaza City shot the head of Palestinian television, Hisham Mekki, dead; the Al-Aqsa Martyrs' Brigade, a dissident faction of the al-Fatah party, claimed responsibility. **21—27.** Peace talks between Israel and the Palestinians opened in Taba, Egypt, but ended without a peace deal.

FEBRUARY 2001

6. In Israel, Ariel Sharon was elected prime minister winning 62.3 per cent of the vote. **7.** Prime Minister-elect Ariel Sharon declared Jerusalem to be the centre of the eternal and indivisible capital of the Jewish people. **14.** In Israel, a Palestinian bus driver drove into a bus queue of soldiers and commuters in Tel Aviv, killing eight people and injuring 20. **15.** In Bahrain, a referendum to approve a package of liberal reforms to create a partially elected parliament, an independent judiciary and to limit the powers of the Emir was approved by 98.4 per cent of voters; women were allowed to vote for the first time. **16.** In Iraq, the UK and the USA launched the biggest air raid on targets around Baghdad since operation Desert Fox in December 1998, damaging six new command-and-control facilities and involving at least 80 aircraft. An Israeli soldier was killed and three wounded in a cross-border rocket attack by Lebanese Hezbollah militants. **19.** Israeli and US soldiers began tests on the Patriot air-defence system.

MARCH 2001

4. In Israel, a suicide bomber blew himself up in Netanya, killing three people and wounding about 60. **5.** In Saudi Arabia, 35 people were crushed to death and a number of others injured at the annual Muslim pilgrimage, the Hajj, during the ritual stoning of pillars symbolising the devil near the holy city of Mecca (Al-Makkah). **8.** In Israel, Prime Minister Ariel Sharon announced an eight-party coalition government that was backed by 72 of the 120 MPs. **12.** In Kuwait, service personnel were killed and seven injured when a US Navy Hornet jet dropped a 500lb bomb on a group of military observers during a training mission. **27.** Two bombs exploded in Jerusalem; a suicide bomber was killed and 42 people were wounded in the attacks. **28.** The Israeli army bombed six bases of Force 17, Yasser Arafat's presidential guard, in response to three bombings, the third of which killed two teenagers. **31.** Israel jailed 600 reserve soldiers in an attempt to halt a growing rebellion against military service in the West Bank and Gaza Strip.

APRIL 2001

1. Israeli Special Forces seized six members of Yasser Arafat's Force 17 guard in Jilijiheh, a town in Palestinian-controlled territory. **7.** In Lebanon, a military court sentenced 12 former members of the South Lebanon Army to death for collaboration with Israel during its occupation of Lebanon. **4.** Israeli Foreign Minister Shimon Peres held formal talks with Palestinian negotiators in Athens. **15.** Israeli warplanes killed three soldiers and wounded six in a raid on a Syrian radar station in Lebanon; the attack was in retaliation for the earlier killing of an Israeli soldier by Hezbollah guerrillas. **16.** Israeli ships and helicopters fired missiles at bases of the Force 17 security unit in central Gaza, after Palestinian mortar bombs fell on the Israeli town of Sderot. **29.** In Yemen, President Ali Abdullah Saleh offered to exchange five Britons who had been convicted of terrorist offences in Yemen for the London-based Islamic cleric, Abu Hamza

al-Masri, whom the Yemeni authorities believed had ordered the attacks.

MAY 2001

6. Pope John Paul II became the first leader of the Roman Catholic Church to set foot inside a mosque when he entered the Great Ummayyid Mosque in Damascus together with the Mufti, Sheikh Ahmed Kuftaro. **18.** In Israel, five Israelis were killed in a Hamas suicide bomb attack in Netanya; Israel bombed a security headquarters in Nablus and fired rockets at targets in Ramallah, Gaza and Tulkarem in retaliation. **21.** Gen. Colin Powell, the US Secretary of State, urged the Israelis to use non-lethal responses to unarmed demonstrators and the Palestinians to prevent gunmen from firing on Israeli positions from Palestinian-controlled areas. **26.** The 56 member states of the Organisation of the Islamic Conference agreed to halt all political contact with Israel. **29.** Israeli and Palestinians security officials resumed talks in Ramallah.

JUNE 2001

1. In Israel, a Palestinian suicide bomber blew himself up in a crowd of teenagers outside a Tel Aviv disco killing 18 people and injuring more than 75; Yasser Arafat, the leader of the Palestinian National Authority, agreed to an immediate and unconditional cease-fire the following day. **4.** Iraq halted its official crude oil exports in an attempt to raise world oil prices. **5.** The family of a Palestinian man who was shot dead by Jews donated his organs to be transplanted to three Israelis. **11.** In Yemen, the USA closed its embassy in Aden, citing terrorist threats. **12.** Yasser Arafat accepted terms for a cease-fire with Israel after talks with the CIA director, George Tenet. **14.** In Lebanon, Syrian troops began to withdraw from strategic positions in Beirut.

JULY 2001

11. In Iraq, the Supreme Council for the Islamic Revolution in Iraq (SCIRI), a Shi'a Muslim dissident group backed by Iran, launched a rocket attack against government targets in Baghdad. **16.** In Israel, a suicide bomber blew himself up at a railway station in Binyamina, killing two people and injuring 11. Islamic Jihad claimed responsibility. **17.** Israeli helicopter gunships killed two senior Hamas members in Bethlehem. **20.** Israel launched artillery attacks on Hebron and two Christian districts of Bethlehem were shelled. **22.** In Yemen, four men were jailed for terms of between four and 15 years for a grenade attack on the British embassy in Sana'a' in October 2000. **27.** Israeli tanks shelled Palestinian security posts on the West Bank in retaliation for the shooting hours earlier of an Israeli teenager by Palestinian guerrillas. **30.** Two senior Hamas members were killed in an Israeli missile attack.

AUGUST 2001

5. A Palestinian opened fire on soldiers outside the largest army base in Tel Aviv, wounding 10 people. **7.** US combat aircraft bombed an Iraqi air defence site after being tracked by Iraqi artillery. **9.** In Jerusalem, a Palestinian suicide bomber blew himself up in a pizza restaurant in Jerusalem killing at least 15 people and injuring more than 100. Israeli fighter jets attacked the police station in the Palestinian-controlled West Bank city of Ramallah. **10.** British and US aircraft launched four raids on Iraqi air defence sites. Israeli troops and police seized key offices and buildings used by the PLO in Jerusalem. **14.** Israeli troops conducted a four-hour raid on the Palestinian-run West Bank town of Jenin, levelling the main police station with armoured bulldozers. US F16 jets bombed a mobile

Iraqi radar battery which had tracked NATO aircraft. **26.**
Three Israeli soldiers were killed by Palestinian comman-
dos in the Gaza Strip. The military responded with a wide-
scale air and land assault, destroying Palestinian security
headquarters in four towns. **28-30.** Israeli tanks occupied
Beit Jala, a Palestinian Christian town near Bethlehem to
silence gunfire directed at Jerusalem.

EUROPEAN UNION

SEPTEMBER 2000

5. The European Parliament approved plans to create an
EU Foreign Service, with its own embassies and training
academy, and co-ordinated representation in international organisation. **22.** Central banks of the Group of
Seven industrialised nations bought billions of euros on
foreign exchanges as fears grew that the currency's
performance was jeopardising economic growth.

OCTOBER 2000

6. The Council of Ministers agreed to extend the powers
of Europol, the European Police Office, to enable it to
investigate money-laundering stemming from all forms of
crime. **9.** The European Council agreed to the unconditional lifting of all sanctions against Yugoslavia. **13.** At the
European Council summit in Biarritz, agreement was
reached in principle to allow groups of member states that
wished to proceed to closer union to do so independently
of others. **17.** The Council of Ministers approved a
directive that will make illegal discrimination in the
workplace on the grounds of age, disability, religion or
sexual orientation and called for penalties against countries that had high levels of money laundering. **26.**
Yugoslavia was admitted to the EU's Stability Pact for
south eastern Europe.

NOVEMBER 2000

7. The European Commission announced that it was
launching legal action against Philip Morris, R. J.
Reynolds, Japan Tobacco and Nabisco Group for their
alleged involvement in smuggling cigarettes into the EU.
8. The annual Enlargement Strategy Paper praised all the
applicant countries except Turkey for meeting the
political requirements of EU membership. **15.** The
Court of Auditors refused to certify the 1999 EU budget.
It criticised the European Commission and the member
states for mismanagement of funds. The mistakes
amounted to between 5.5 and 7 per cent of the £60,000
million budget, but the majority were accumulated small
errors and incorrect expenditure, rather than fraud. **16.** A
German general, Lt.-Gen. Klaus Schuwirth, was
appointed the EU's Director of Military Staff, with the
task of creating a rapid reaction force of 60,000 by 2003.
24. Leaders of the EU and Albania, Bosnia-Hercegovina,
Croatia, Macedonia and Yugoslavia met at the EU-
Balkans summit in Zagreb; the EU offered £2.4 billion
in economic aid, duty-free access to EU markets and
eventual membership of the EU to the five Balkan states.

DECEMBER 2000

7-11. At the EU summit in Nice, a new EU treaty was
finalised which was intended to reform the EU prior to the
accession of new member states; the treaty would increase
qualified majority voting, limit the size of the Commission
and strengthen the powers of the Commission President.
15. The EU ordered drastic cuts in North Sea fishing
quotas. The UK's share of the cod quota was cut by 45 per
cent.

JANUARY 2001

24. The Economic and Monetary Affairs Commissioner,
Pedro Solbes, formally reprimanded Ireland for tax cuts
which were overheating the economy and causing higher
inflation. The EU and Norway agreed to ban cod fishing in
the North Sea for a two-and-a-half-month period from
mid-February until the end of April. **26.** The European
Court of Justice suspended the European Parliament's
decision to bar the French far-right leader Jean-Marie Le
Pen.

FEBRUARY 2001

12. The government of the Republic of Ireland was
reprimanded by the Commission for its lack of action in
controlling inflation; the UK was rebuked for allowing the
British economy to move into deficit.

MARCH 2001

2. The EU granted 48 of the poorest countries quota- and
tariff-free access to the EU market. **6.** The European
Commission suspended all livestock markets in the EU for
two weeks aimed at preventing the foot and mouth
epidemic in the UK from spreading. **30.** Gen. Gustav
Hägglund, the chief of the Finnish army, was chosen to
head the Military Committee. **31.** The EU declared that it
would ratify the Kyōto treaty regardless of the USA.

APRIL 2001

5. The Council of Ministers agreed to develop a European
satellite navigation system; the first satellites were due to
be launched by 2005. **26.** The EU suspended aid to
Slovakia after allegations of large-scale theft of EU funds
by the head of the Department of Foreign Assistance,
Roland Tóth, who was under investigation for fraud.

JUNE 2001

13. Agriculture and Fisheries Commissioner Franz
Fischler warned that further drastic cuts would need to
be made during 2001 to preserve fish stocks.

JULY 2001

18. Internal Market Commissioner Frits Bolkestein
declared that the UK would be brought before the
European Court of Justice if British customs staff did
not relax their rigid interpretation of EU guidelines on the
amount of alcohol and cigarettes which could be brought
into the UK.

AUGUST 2001

6. The European Commission launched a fraud enquiry
into compensation payments to British farmers following
a highly critical report by EU veterinary inspectors on the
government's handling of the foot and mouth epidemic.

INTERNATIONAL RELATIONS

SEPTEMBER 2000

5. The UN Millennium Summit opened in New York;
more than 150 presidents, prime ministers and rulers, the
largest gathering of world leaders in history, gathered for
the three-day meeting. **27.** The UN compensation
commission agreed that Iraq should pay £11 billion in
compensation to the Kuwaiti Petroleum Company for the
oil-well fires started by retreating Iraqi troops in the Gulf
War.

OCTOBER 2000

10. Ireland, Norway, Colombia, Singapore and Mauritius
won two-year terms on the UN Security Council. **25.** The

UN Secretary-General announced that Ruud Lubbers would be the next UN High Commissioner for Refugees.

NOVEMBER 2000

1. The UN General Assembly accepted Yugoslavia as a member; it had been suspended in 1992. **25.** The World Climate Change Conference ended in acrimony after a 12 day attempt to persuade world leaders to agree to legally binding reductions in greenhouse gases; Deputy Prime Minister John Prescott walked out after a British attempt to reach a compromise between the EU and the US positions was rejected. **30.** The IMF approved loans of nearly £425 million to Pakistan. The loan, for a period of ten months, was to prevent Pakistan from defaulting on its £26 billion debt in January.

DECEMBER 2000

9. Hans Hækkerup, the Danish Defence Minister, was named as the new head of the United Nations mission in Kosovo; he was to assume his new role in January 2000.

JANUARY 2001

14. The UN War Crimes Tribunal announced that Slobodan Milošević and four other former Serbian leaders should be arrested and surrendered to the tribunal to stand trial for human rights abuses against ethnic Albanians in Kosovo. **23.** A report issued by the International Labour Office declared that a third of the world's work force were unemployed or under-employed. **24.** The Chief Prosecutor of the UN War Crimes Tribunal, Carla Del Ponte, broke off talks with President Koštunica of Yugoslavia on 23 January after they failed to agree on the extradition of war criminals.

FEBRUARY 2001

22. The UN War Crimes Tribunal sentenced three Bosnian Serbs to between 12 and 28 years in prison for using rape and sexual slavery as a weapon of war during the 1992-1995 conflict. **26.** The UN War Crimes Tribunal jailed the former Vice-President of the Croatian Republic of Herceg-Bosna, the former self-declared Croat state within Bosnia-Herzegovina, Dario Kordić, for 25 years after finding him guilty of ordering the massacre of hundreds of Muslims in the Lasva Valley between 1991-1994. **27.** The annual UN human rights report stated that a million North Koreans had died of starvation and related diseases since 1995; North Korea was named as one of the three worst human rights abusers along with Cuba and Myanmar. UNICEF announced that it had airlifted more than 2,800 demobilised child soldiers away from the front lines in southern Sudan.

MARCH 2001

2. At a summit of the Organisation of African Unity in Libya, the heads of state and government of some 40 countries proclaimed the birth of the African Union, designed to unite Africa politically and economically; the formal birth of the union would effectively take place only when it had been ratified by at least 36 of the 53 member states. **20.** The Commonwealth Ministerial Action Group decided that the foreign ministers of Barbados, Australia and Nigeria should be sent to have talks with the Zimbabwean government. Zimbabwe said that it would not co-operate. **21.** NATO's decision-making North Atlantic Council unanimously called for the KFOR peacekeeping mission in Kosovo to be reinforced with additional troops.

APRIL 2001

22. At the Summit of the Americas in Québec, leaders of 34 countries signed plans to establish a free trade zone by 2005; the summit had been delayed by anti-globalisation protests.

MAY 2001

3. The USA was voted off the UN Human Rights Commission for the first time since 1947.

JUNE 2001

15. Uzbekistan became a member of the Shanghai Co-operation Organisation and together with the five original members, China, Russia, Kazakhstan, Kyrgyzstan and Tajikistan, signed the Shanghai pact, which aimed to combat ethnic and religious militancy, while promoting trade and investments. **29.** In a ruling upholding Turkey's decision in 1998 to dissolve the pro-Islamic Welfare Party, the European Court of Human Rights ruled that Islamic parties could be banned if they posed a threat to civil order and secular democracy. It justified its ruling on the basis that the Welfare Party had planned to institute Shari'ah law, which would have conflicted with the values embodied in the European convention on Human Rights.

JULY 2001

9. The OAU held its final summit before it was renamed the African Union; the summit was addressed by UN Secretary-General Kofi Annan, who told delegates to emulate the EU. **20.** A G8 summit was held in Genoa, Italy, which was accompanied by violent protests in which one demonstrator was shot dead and 184 people were injured; the summit agreed to a campaign to raise US$1 billion to combat AIDS and other diseases was begun. **23.** The UN climate treaty talks in Bonn agreed a compromise deal on the Kyōto Treaty, which was signed by all the participants except the USA. **25.** The USA rejected a proposed protocol strengthen the 1972 Biological Weapons Convention. All of the other 53 participating states had supported it.

AUGUST 2001

2. At the International War Crimes Tribunal for the Former Yugoslavia, Gen. Radislav Krstić, a senior Bosnian Serb officer, was convicted of genocide for the murder of more than 7,000 Muslims at Srebrenica and sentenced to 46 years imprisonment. **12-14.** At the South African Development Community summit in Blantyre, Malawi, a final communiqué was issued expressing concern at the situation in Zimbabwe. **22.** The NATO North Atlantic Council issued orders for troops to go to Macedonia to collect weapons handed over by the ethnic Albanian NLA.

Obituaries

Fletcher-Cooke, Sir Charles, Conservative MP for Darwen 1951–83; MEP 1977–79, aged 86 – *d*. 24 February 2001, *b*. 5 May 1914

Fock, Jeno, Prime Minister of Hungary 1967–75, aged 85 – *d*. 23 May 2001, *b*. 17 May 1916

Foster, Sir Richard, director of the National Museums and Galleries on Merseyside 1986–01, aged 59 – *d*. 8 March 2001, *b*. 3 October 1941

Francis, Mary, researcher and author, aged 76 – *d*. 30 September 2000, *b*. 17 June 1924

Fryd, Judy, CBE, founder of Mencap, aged 90 – *d*. 20 October 2000, *b*. 31 October 1909

Giedroyc, Jerzy, Polish publisher and editor, aged 94 – *d*. 14 September 2000, *b*. 27 July 1906

Gilmour, Dr Alan, CVO, CBE, director of the NSPCC 1979–89, aged 72 – *d*. 18 July 2001, *b*. 30 August 1928

Glasspole, Sir Florizel, GCMG, GCVO, Governor-General of Jamaica 1973–90, aged 91 – *d*. 25 November 2000, *b*. 25 September 1909

Gooding, Air Vice-Marshall Keith, CB, CBE, RAF Officer, aged 87 – *d*. 4 March 2001, *b*. 2 September 1913

Graham, Alastair, FRS, professor of Zoology, aged 94 – *d*. 12 December 2000, *b*. 6 November 1906

Green, The Revd Fred Pratt, MBE, Methodist minister, hymn writer and poet, aged 97 – *d*. 22 October 2000, *b*. 2 September 1903

Greenhill of Harrow, Lord, GCMG, OBE, Under Secretary of State, Foreign and Commonwealth Office and Head of the Diplomatic Service, 1969–73, aged 87 – *d*. 8 November 2000, *b*. 7 November 1913

Gross, Al, pioneer of mobile telecommunications, aged 82 – *d*. 21 December 2000, *b*. 22 February 1918

Grylls, Sir Michael, MP for Chertsey 1970–74; North West Surrey 1974–97 and free-marketer, aged 66 – *d*. 7 February 1934, *b*. 21 February 1934

Guiness, Lady, children's writer and artist, aged 86 – *d*. 18 October 2000, *b*. 16 October 1914

Hamilton, Liam, chief Justice of Ireland 1994–00, aged 81 – *d*. 29 November 2000, *b*. 30 December 1928

Hanley, Sir Michael, Director-General of MI5 1972–78, aged 82 – *d*. 1 January 2001, *b*. 24 February 1918

Hanna, William, American animator, aged 90 – *d*. 22 March 2001, *b*. 14 July 1910

Harmar-Nicholls, Lord, Conservative MP for Peterborough 1950–74; Member of the European Parliament 1979–84, aged 87 – *d*. 15 September 2000, *b*. 1 November 1912

Harris of Greenwich, Lord (John Henry), Labour Home Office minister, aged 71 – *d*. 1 April 2001, *b*. 5 April 1930

Hartwell, Lord, MBE, TD, proprietor of The Daily Telegraph 1954–85, aged 89 – *d*. 2 April 2001, *b*. 18 May 1911

Hastings, Professor Adrian, FBA, theologian and historian, aged 71 – *d*. 30 May 2001, *b*. 23 June 1929

Hattersley, Enid, Lord Mayor of Sheffield 1981–82, aged 96 – *d*. 17 May 2001, *b*. 19 September 2001

Hayr, Air Marshal Sir Kenneth, CBE, CB, KCB, KBE, New Zealand born holder of the Kuwait Liberation Order (1st Grade), aged 66 – *d*. (accidentally) 3 June 2001, *b*. 13 April 1935

Hearst, Randolph A., newspaper mogul, aged 85 – *d*. 18 December 2000, *b*. 2 December 1915

Helou, Charles, President of Lebanon 1964–70, aged 88 – *d*. 7 January 2001, *b*. 25 December 1912

Hewlett, William, co-founder of Hewlett-Packard, aged 87 – *d*. 12 January 2001, *b*. 20 May 1913

Hickman, John, CMG, ambassador to Chile 1982–87 and author, aged 73 – *d*. 23rd February 2001, *b*. 3rd July 1927

Hinds, Harvey, Labour Party Chief Whip in the Greater London Council 1967–86, aged 80 – *d*. 1 September 2000, *b*. 29 August 1920

Hinton, Milt, jazz double bassist, aged 90 – *d*. 19 December 2000, *b*. 23 June 1910

Hoddinott, Sir John, CBE, police chief constable of Hampshire 1988–99, aged 56 – *d*. 13 August 2001, *b*. 21 September 1944

Holder, Sir Paul, DFC, DSO, CB, FRS, pilot, aged 89 – *d*. 22 April 2001, *b*. 2 September 1912

Hollan-Martin, Lady, DBE, DL, Chairman of NSPCC 1969–87, aged 86 – *d*. 18 June 2001, *b*. 26 June 1914

Hooker, John Lee, American blues guitarist, aged 83 – *d*. 21 June 2001, *b*. 22 August 1920

Hoyle, Sir Fred, FRS, astronomer and writer, aged 86 – *d*. 20 August 2001, *b*. 24 June 1915

Hughes, The Right Revd John, CBE, Suffragan Bishop of Croydon 1956–77, *d*. 21 July 2001, *b*. 12 April 1908

Ingstad, Helge, Scandinavian writer and explorer, aged 101 – *d*. 29 March 2001, *b*. 30 December 1899

Jacob, Sir Jack, QC, senior Master of the Supreme Court, Queen's Bench Division 1975–80, aged 92 – *d*. 26 December 2000, *b*. 5 June 1908

Jamieson, Major David, VC, Officer who gained the VC for defending the bridgehead over the River Orne whilst wounded, aged 80 – *d*. 5 May 2001, *b*. 1 October 1920

Jeffrey, Betty, OAM, Australian nursing sister and war hero, aged 92 – *d*. 13 September 2000, *b*. 14 May 1908

Jennens, David, oarsman, aged 71 – *d*. 27 September 2000, *b*. 4 April 1929

John Howe, The Right Revd, Bishop of St Andrews, Dunkeld and Dunblane1955; 1969–82 and Secretary General of the Anglican Consultative Council, aged 80 – *d*. 26 April 2001, *b*. 14 July 1920

Johnson, Air Vice-Marshal Johnnie, CB, CBE, DSO and two bars, DFC, fighter pilot, aged 85 – *d*. 30 January 2001, *b*. 9 March 1915

José, Queen Marie, Queen of Italy for 27 days in May 1946, aged 94 – *d*. 27 January 2001, *b*. 4 August 1906

Ju-Yung, Chung, founder of Hyundai, aged 85 – *d*. 21March 2001, *b*. 25 November 1915

Kabila, Laurent, President of the Democratic Republic of Congo 1997–01, aged 61 – *d*. (shot dead) 16 January 2001, *b*. 27 November 1939

Kaujau, Konrad, forger of the 'Hitler Diaries', aged 62 – *d*. 12 September 2000, *b*. 27 June 1938

Kenneally, John, VC, Lance Corporal Irish Guard, aged 79 – *d*. 27 September 2000, *b*. 15 March 1921

Kenward, Betty, KBE, society columnist, aged 94 – *d*. 24 January 2001, *b*. 14 July 1906

Kilburn, Prof Tom, CBE, FRS, pioneer of the computer, aged 79 – *d*. 17 January 2001, *b*. 11 August 1921

King Birendra of Nepal, Bir Bikram Shah, Himalayan Monarch 1972–01, aged 55 – *d*. (Shot dead) 1 June 2001, *b*. 28 December 1945

King Dipendra of Nepal, Bir Bikram Shah Dev, Himalyan Monarch for 2 days in June 2001, aged 29 – *d*. (gunshot wounds) 4 June 2001, *b*. 27 June 1971

Knapp, Jimmy, general secretary, National Union of Railwaymen 1983–90, aged 60 – *d*. 13 August 2001, *b*. 29 September 1940

Kohl, Hannelore, wife of former German Chancellor, aged 68 – *d*. (suicide) 5 July 2001, *b*. 7 March 1933

Korda, Alberto, Cuban photographer, aged 72 – *d*. 25 May 2001, *b*. 14 September 1928

Kramer, Stanley, American film producer and director, aged 87 – *d*. 19 February 2001, *b*. 29 September 1913

Lang, Lieutenant-General Sir Derek, KCB, DSO, MC, GOC-IN-C, Scottish Infantry man, aged 87 – *d*. 7 April 2001, *b*. 7 October 1913

Lasdun, Sir Denys, CH, CBE, architect, aged 86 – *d*. 11 January 2001, *b*. 8 September 1914

Lawton, Sir Frederick, Lord Justice of Appeal 1972–76, aged 89 – *d*. 3 February 2001, *b*. 21 December 1911

Lees-Spalding, Rear-Admiral Tim, naval engineer, aged 81 – *d*. 20 July 2001, *b*. 16 June 1920

Lemmon, Jack, American actor, aged 76 – *d*. 27 June 2001, *b*. 8 February 1925

Lincoln, Frances, publisher, aged 55 – *d*. 26 February 2001, *b*. 20 March 1945

Longlord, Lord, Lord Privy Seal and Leader of the House of Lords 1964–68 and campaigner, aged 95 – *d*. 3 August 2001, *b*. 5 December 1905

Lord Cledwyn of Penrhos, Hughes, Labour Leader in the House of Lords 1982–92, aged 84 – *d*. 22 February 2001, *b*. 14 September 1916

Lord Cocks of Hartcliffe, Michael, Labour Chief Whip 1976–85, aged 71 – *d*. 26 March 2001, *b*. 19 August 1929

Lord Mackay of Ardbrecknish, Deputy Leader of the Opposition in the Lords 1998–01; Under Secretary at the Scottish Office 1982–87, aged 62 – *d*. 21 February 2001, *b*. 15 November 1938

Lord Onslow of Woking, Cranley Gordon Douglas, KCMG, Chairman of The 1922 Committee 1984–92 and former MP for Woking 1961–64, aged 74 – *d*. 13 March 2001, *b*. 8 June 1926

Ludlum, Robert, author, aged 73 – *d*. 12 March 2001, *b*. 25 May 1927

Macdonald, Vice-Admiral Sir Roderick, KBE, Nato Chief of Staff 1976–79, and artist, aged 79 – *d*. 19 January 2001, *b*. 25 February 1921

Mackworth-Young, Sir Robin, GCVO, librarian of Windsor Castle 1958–85, aged 80 – *d*. 5 December 2000, *b*. 12 February 1920

MacNeish, Richard, archaeologist, aged 82 – *d*. 16 January 2001, *b*. 29 April 1918

Madden, Adm. Sir Charles, GCB, Commander-in-Chief Home Fleet 1963–65, aged 38 – *d*. 12 April 2001, *b*. 10 August 1962

McTaggart, David, Chairman of Greenpeace 1979–91, aged 68 – *d*. 23 March 2001, *b*. 24 June 1932

Melville, Sir Ronald, KCB, Permanent Secretary to the Ministry of Aviation 1963–66, aged 89 – *d*. 4 June 2001, *b*. 9 March 1912

Mendoza, Maurice, CVO, MSM, conservationist, aged 79 – *d*. 11 October 2000, *b*. 1 May 1921

Miller, Canon Paul, Canon of Derby 1966–81 and Chaplin to the Queen 1981–83, aged 82 – *d*. 18 October 2000, *b*. 8 October 1918

Ming, General Duong Van, President of South Vietnam in 1995 for three days, aged 85 – *d*. 6 August 2001, *b*. 16 February 1916

Molloy, Lord William John, Labour MP for Ealing North, aged 82 – *d*. 26 May 2001, *b*. 26 October 1918

Morley, Eric, impresario, aged 82 – *d*. 9 November 2000, *b*. 26 September 1918

Morpurgo, Professor Jack, professor of American Literature, University of Leeds 1969–83, and author, aged 82 – *d*. 2 October 2000, *b*. 26 April 1918

Morrison, John, CBE, FBA, classicist, first President of Wolfson College, Cambridge 1966–80, aged 87 – *d*. 25 October 2000, *b*. 15 June 1913

Narayan, R. K., FRSL, Indian Novelist, aged 94 – *d*. 13 May 2001, *b*. 10 October 1906

Nunburnholme, Lord, 5th Baron Nunburnholme, aged 65 – *d*. 20 November 2000, *b*. 27 May 1935

O'Connor, Air Vice-Marshall Patrick, OBE, CB, RAF medical officer, *d*. 3 May 2001, *b*. 21 August 1914

O'Connor, Sir Patrick, Lord Justice of Appeal 1980–89, aged 86 – *d*. 3 May 2001, *b*. 29 December 1914

Olsen, Gary, actor, aged 42 – *d*. 13 September 2000, *b*. 3 November 1957

Pahlavi, Princess Leila, daughter of the Late Shah of Iran, aged 31 – *d*. (Drug overdose) 10 June 2001, *b*. Born around 1970

Palmer, Charles, OBE, Chairman of the British Olympic Association 1983–88, aged 71 – *d*. 17 August 2001, *b*. 15 April 1930

Pamphilj, Princess Orietta Doria, British custodian of European art, aged 78 – *d*. 19 November 2000, *b*. 22 April 1922

Peyrefitte, Roger, French author, aged 93 – *d*. 6 November 2000, *b*. 17 August 1907

Phipps, The Right Revd Simon, MC, Bishop of Lincoln 1974–86, aged 79 – *d*. 29 January 2001, *b*. 6 July 1921

Plowden, Lady Bridget, DBE, chair of the Central Advisory Council for Education (England); chair of the IBA 1975–80, aged 90 – *d*. 29 September 2000, *b*. 5 May 1910

Plowden, Lord, GBE, KCB, economic adviser 1947–53, aged 94 – *d*. 15 February 2001, *b*. 6 January 1907

Pontin, Sir Frederick William, KT, founder of Pontin's Holiday Camps, aged 93 – *d*. 2 October 2000, *b*. 24 October 1906

Porteous, Colonel Patrick, VC, war hero of the Dieppe raid, aged 82 – *d*. 9 October 2000, *b*. 1 January 1918

Prebble, John, OBE, writer and historian, aged 85 – *d*. 30 January 2001, *b*. 23 June 1915

Professor Christain, Jack, FRS, International Metallurgist, aged 74 – *d*. 27 February 2001, *b*. 9 April 1926

Queen Aiswarya of Nepal, Himalayan monarch, aged 51 – *d*. (shot dead) 1 June 2001, *b*. 7 November 1949

Quinn, Anthony, hollywood actor, aged 86 – *d*. 3 June 2001, *b*. 21 April 1915

Rabin, Leah, peace campaigner, wife of the assassinated former Israeli Prime Minister Yitzhak Rabin, aged 72 – *d*. 12 November 2000, *b*. 8 April 1928

Railton, Dame Ruth, OBE, DBE, founder and artistic director of the National Youth Orchestra 1948–65, aged 85 – *d*. 23 February 2001, *b*. 14 December 1915

Rajya Laxmi Devi Rana, Queen Aiswarya of Nepal, Himalayan Monarch, aged 51 – *d*. (shot dead) 1 June 2001, *b*. 7 November 1949

Rapaport, Rosemary, founder of the Purcell School and violinist, aged 83 – *d*. 8 June 2001, *b*. 29 March 1918

Raphael, Sarah, painter, aged 40 – *d*. 10 January 2001, *b*. 10 August 1960

Rawson, Michael, athlete, aged 66 – *d*. 25 October 2000, *b*. 26 May 1934

Read, General Sir Anthony, GCB, CBE, DSO, MC, quartermaster-General of the Army 1969–72, aged 87 – *d*. 22 September 2000, *b*. 10 September 1913

Reilly, Tommy, MBE, harmonica player, aged 81 – *d*. 25 September 2000, *b*. 21 August 1919

Ridley, Sir Harold, FRS, ophthalmic surgeon, aged 94 – *d*. 25 May 2001, *b*. 10 July 1906

Robards, Jason, actor, aged 78 – *d*. 26 December 2000, *b*. 26 July 1922

Roberts, The Rt Revd Edward, Bishop of Ely 1964–77, aged 93 – *d*. 29 June 2001, *b*. 18 April 1908

Rogers, William, United States Secretary of State 1968–73, aged 87 – *d*. 2 January 2001, *b*. 23 June 1913

Ross, Alan, OBE, editor of the London Magazine 1975–2001, aged 78 – *d*. 14 February 2001, *b*. 6 May 1922

Rotherham, Professor Leonard, CBS, FRS, Rotherham, aged 87 – *d*. 23 March 2001, *b*. 31 August 1913

Runciman, Sir Steven, CH, FBA, historian, aged 97 – *d*. 1 November 2000, *b*. 7 July 1903

Sage, Lorna, literary critic and scholar, aged 57 – *d*. 11 January 2001, *b*. 13 January 1943

Sampson, Nicos, Cypriot Newspaper publisher and President of Cyprus for eight days in July 1974, aged 66 – *d.* 9 May 2001, *b.* 16 December 1934

Sanger, Ruth, FRS, scientist, aged 82 – *d.* 4 June 2001, *b.* 6 June 1918

Sann, Son, Prime Minister of Cambodia 1967–68, aged 89 – *d.* 19 December 2000, *b.* 15 October 1911

Scatchard, Vice-Admiral Jack, CB, DSC and two bars, Naval officer Second-in-command Far East Fleet 1962–64, aged 90 – *d.* 22 June 2001, *b.* 5 September 1910

Schindler, Rabbi Alexander, leader of the America's Jewish Reform movement for 22 years, aged 75 – *d.* 15 November 2000, *b.* 4 October 1925

Sealy, Thodore, OJ, CBE, Jamaican born Editor of the 'Gleaner' newspaper, aged 91 – *d.* 18 June 2001, *b.* 6 November 1909

Secombe, Sir Harry, comedian and singer, aged 79 – *d.* 11 April 2001, *b.* 8 September 1921

Shackleton, Len, Sunderland and England footballer, aged 78 – *d.* 28 November 2000, *b.* 22 May 1922

Shepard, Mary, artist and illustrator, aged 90 – *d.* 4 September 2000, *b.* 25 December 1909

Shepherd, Lord, PC and Former Leader of The House of Lords 1974–76, aged 82 – *d.* 5 April 2001, *b.* 27 September 1918

Sieff of Brimpton, Lord Marcus Joseph, OBE, Chairman of Marks & Spencer 1972–84, aged 87 – *d.* 23 February 2001, *b.* 2 July 1913

Simmons, Jack, OBE, historian, aged 85 – *d.* 3 September 2000, *b.* 30 August 1915

Sims, Joan, actress, aged 71 – *d.* 28 June 2001, *b.* 9 May 1930

Sithole, The Revd Ndabaningi, African nationalist leader 1963–78, aged 80 – *d.* 12 December 2000, *b.* 31 July 1920

Southern, Sir Richard, FBA, historian, aged 88 – *d.* 6 February 2001, *b.* 8 February 1912

Speeding, Sir David, KCMG, CVO, OBE, M16 Chief 1994–99, aged 58 – *d.* 13 June 2001, *b.* 7 March 1943

Stakis, Sir Reo, Greek -born founder of Stakis Hotel, aged 88 – *d.* 28 August 2001, *b.* 13 March 1913

Stern, William T., CBE, botanical authority, aged 90 – *d.* 16 April 1911, *b.* 9 May 2001

Storr, Anthony, psychiatrist, aged 80 – *d.* 17 March 2001, *b.* 18 May 1920

Synnot, Admiral Sir Anthony, Commander of Defence Force Staff 1979–82, aged 79 – *d.* 4 July 2001, *b.* 5 January 1922

Talbot, Godfrey, LVO, OBE, broadcaster, aged 91 – *d.* 3 September 2000, *b.* 8 October 1908

Taylor, The Right Revd John, Bishop of Winchester 1975–85, aged 86 – *d.* 30 January 2001, *b.* 11 September 1914

Terrington, Lord, OBE, DSO, Conservative MP for Oxford 1959–66 and 1970–74; Parliamentary Secretary in the Ministry of Aviation 1961–62; Joint Under-Secretary of State at the Home Office 1962–64, aged 83 – *d.* 13 February 2001, *b.* 11 May 1917

Temple, The Rt Revd Frederick, Suffragan Bishop of Malmesbury 1973–83, aged 84 – *d.* 26 November 2000, *b.* 24 November 1916

Therond (with an accent over 'e'), Roger, Editor of Paris - Match 1976–99, aged 76 – *d.* 23 June 2001, *b.* 24 October 1924

Titov, Gherman, cosmonaut, aged 65 – *d.* 20 September 2000, *b.* 11 September 1935

Tjupurrula, Johnny Warrangkula, Aboriginal Artist, aged (around) 76 – *d.* 11 February 2001, *b.* born around 1925

Tonbridge, Lord Cowdrey of, cricketer, aged 67 – *d.* 4 December 2000, *b.* 24 December 1932

Trewby, Vice-Admiral Sir Allan, naval engineer, aged 84 – *d.* 23 July 2001, *b.* 8 July 1917

Trudeau, Pierre, Prime Minister of Canada 1968–79 and 1980–84, aged 80 – *d.* 28 September 2000, *b.* 18 October 1919

Tuke, Sir Anthony, Chairman of Barclays Bank 1973–81, aged 80 – *d.* 6 March 2001, *b.* 22 August 1920

Tyson, Alan, CBE, FBA, musicologist and psychoanalyst, aged 74 – *d.* 10 November 2000, *b.* 27 October 1926

Vanden Boeynants, Paul, Prime Minister of Belgium 1966–68; 1978–79, aged 81 – *d.* 9 January 2001, *b.* 22 May 1919

Venables, Bernard, MBE, angler and writer, aged 94 – *d.* 21 April 2001, *b.* 14 February 1907

Wakefield, Rev Gordon, Methodist minister and scholar, aged 79 – *d.* 11 September 2000, *b.* 15 January 1921

Walker, David, astronaut who made four shuttle flights including the 'Atlantis', aged 56 – *d.* 23 April 2001, *b.* 20 May 1944

Walker, General Sir Walter, KCB, CBE, DSO and two bars, fighting General, aged 89 – *d.* 12 August 2001, *b.* 11 November 1911

Warsaw, Baroness Ryder of, CMG; OBE, social worker, aged 77 – *d.* 2 November 2000, *b.* 3 July 1923

Watson, Colin, obituaries Editor of The Times 1956–82, aged 81 – *d.* 6 January 2001, *b.* 15 May 1919

Waugh, Auberon, journalist, aged 61 – *d.* 16 January 2001, *b.* 17 November 1939

Weir, Jack, General Secretary of the Presbyterian Church in Ireland 1964–85, aged 81 – *d.* 18 September 2000, *b.* 24 March 1919

Welch, David, CBE, former Chief Executive of the Royal Parks, aged 66 – *d.* 18 September 2000, *b.* 13 December 1933

Wilcox, Desmond, broadcaster, aged 69 – *d.* 6 September 2000, *b.* 21 May 1931

Williams, Michael, actor, aged 65 – *d.* 11 January 2001, *b.* 9 July 1935

Willimer, Professor Neil, FRS, biologist and author, aged 98 – *d.* 8 April 2001, *b.* 15 August 1902

Winning, Cardinal Thomas, Catholic Archbishop of Glasgow 1974–2001, aged 76 – *d.* 17 June 2001, *b.* 3 June 1925

Winstone, Howard, MBE, boxer, aged 61 – *d.* 30 September 2000, *b.* 15 April 1939

Wise, Audrey, MP, labour MP for Coventry South West 1974–79; Preston 1987–2000, aged 65 – *d.* 2 September 2000, *b.* 4 January 1935

Woodfield, Sir Philip, KCB, CBE, permanent Secretary to the Northern Ireland Office 1981–83, aged 77 – *d.* 17 September 2000, *b.* 30 August 1923

Woods, Donald, CBE, South African Editor and author, aged 67 – *d.* 19 August 2001, *b.* 15 December

Wright, Fred, FRSA, amateur archaeologist, aged 83 – *d.* 18 May 2001, *b.* 21 June 1918

Yates, Paula, television presenter, aged 40 – *d.* 17 September 2000, *b.* 24 April 1960

Young, Gavin, foreign correspondent and author, aged 72 – *d.* 18 January 2001, *b.* 24 April 1928

Ystradfellte, Baroness Brooke of, DBE, joint vice-chairman of the Conservative Party 1954–64; chairman of the Godolphin and Latymer School 1960–78, aged 92 – *d.* 1 September 2000, *b.* 14 January 1908

Index

Stop-Press

CHANGES SINCE PAGES WENT TO PRESS

LIFE PEERS
Died: Lord Shore of Stepney (peerage now extinct)

BARONETAGE AND KNIGHTAGE
Died: Sir James Gordon Reece

ORDERS OF CHIVALRY
The Most Eminent Order of the Indian Empire was instituted on 1 January 1878. Not 1868 as listed.

PARLIAMENT
SHADOW CABINET as at 14 September 2001
Leader of the Opposition, Iain Duncan Smith, MP
Deputy Leader and Shadow Secretary of State for Foreign and Commonwealth Affairs, Rt. Hon. Michael Ancram, QC, MP
Cabinet Office, Tim Collins, CBE, MP
Culture, Media and Sport, Tim Yeo, MP
Defence, Hon. Bernard Jenkin, MP
Education and Skills, Damian Green, MP
Environment, Food and Rural Affairs, Peter Ainsworth, MP
Foreign and Commonwealth Affairs, Rt. Hon Michael Ancram, QC, MP
Health, Dr Liam Fox, MP
Home Affairs, Oliver Letwin, MP
International Development, Mrs Caroline Spelman, MP
Law Officer, Bill Cash, MP
Leader of the House of Commons, Rt. Hon Eric Forth, MP
Leader of the House of Lords, Rt. Hon. Lord Strathclyde
Lord Chancellor's Department, Rt. Hon Lord Kingsland, QC, MP, TD, DL
Northern Ireland, Quentin Davies, MP
Scotland, Mrs Jackie Lait, MP
Trade and Industry, John Whittingdale, OBE, MP
Transport, Local Government and the Regions, Mrs Theresa May, MP
Transport, Eric Pickles, MP
Treasury, Rt. Hon Michael Howard, QC, MP
Wales, Nigel Evans, MP
Work and Pensions, David Willetts, MP
Whip (House of Commons), Rt. Hon David Maclean, MP
Whip (House of Lords), Rt. Hon. Lord Cope of Berkeley
Party Chairman, Rt. Hon. David Davis, MP

SOCIAL DEMOCRATIC AND UNIONIST PARTY
Leader, John Hume, MP, MEP stood down on the 17 September 2001

SOCIAL WELFARE
On the 20th September 2001 the total number of beds in NHS Hospitals stood at 135,794, an increase of 714 in the previous 12 months.

LOCAL GOVERNMENT
The election of the Lord Mayor of London 2001–2 took place on 1 October 2001. Michael Oliver was appointed and is due to take office on 9 November 2001.

EVENTS – SEPTEMBER 2001

BRITISH AFFAIRS
3. The 2,000th case of foot-and-mouth disease was diagnosed in Cumbria. Halifax's merger with the Bank of Scotland was approved by the High Court. **4.** British Airways announced 1,800 redundancies. Marconi, the telecoms company, announced 600 redundancies. The Rt. Revd John Saxbee, 55, was appointed Suffragan Bishop of Ludlow. Around 500 loyalist supporters were involved in riots in Belfast following the death of a loyalist teenager killed in a hit-and-run accident. Children attending the Holy Cross Primary School in Belfast were escorted to school under police guard due to continued sectarian clashes. **5.** New addresses number 9 and 11 were added to Downing Street. **11.** Hundreds of Britons were feared dead after two hijacked aeroplanes were flown into the twin towers of the World Trade Centre in New York. The Pentagon was also attacked by terrorists. **13.** Iain Duncan Smith became the new leader of the Conservative Party securing a 61 per cent majority. **14.** The Queen attended a remembrance service at St Paul's Cathedral for the victims of the terrorist attacks in New York and Washington. **16.** The Prime Minister announced that Britain would join the US in military strikes against the Taleban regime in Afghanistan, thought to be a base for the terrorists behind the attacks in the US. Virgin Atlantic made 1,200 staff redundant to cover losses on their transatlantic flights. **20.** The Deputy Prime Minister (John Prescott) was told by the Crown Prosecution Service (CPS), that he would not face prosecution over his scuffle with a Welsh farm worker during the general election campaign. **21.** The Foreign Secretary (Jack Straw) visited Iran to meet President Khatami, the first visit by a Foreign Secretary since the Iranian Revolution in 1979. Scotland Yard sent an extra 1,500 police to patrol the conurbations of Birmingham, Manchester and West Yorkshire to protect British Muslims against racist attacks. **22.** The dismembered body of a young boy was found floating in the River Thames. **24.** Jack Straw held surprise talks with the Palestinian leader Yassar Arafat at Amman airport after talks with King Abdullah of Jordan. **25.** All British hospitals were put on alert in case of chemical or biological terrorist attacks. The Prince of Wales visited farmers in the Lake District to discuss the continuing foot-and-mouth crisis.

WORLD
2. In the Seychelles, President France Albert René won a fifth term of office, securing 54 per cent of the vote. **6.** Zimbabwe agreed at a Commonwealth meeting in Nigeria to end all illegal occupations of white-owned farmland and return the country to the rule of law, in return for financial assistance. **9.** In Afghanistan, the United Front guerrilla commander Ahmed Shah Masood, the leader of the Northern Alliance, was mortally wounded by two Arab suicide bombers; he died of his injuries the following day. **10.** In Nigeria, at least 165 people died and about 1,000 were injured in clashes between Christian and Muslim youths in the city of Jos. **9.** In Norway, the general election resulted in losses for the governing Labour Party, who obtained only 43 of the 165 seats. In Belarus, President Alexander Lukashenko won a further term in office, winning 75 per cent of the vote. OSCE monitors

described the vote as neither free nor fair. **10.** The Southern African Development Community issued a sharp rebuke to Zimbabwe, citing the declining economy, the decline in the rule of law and instability. In Zimbabwe, the MDC won local and mayoral elections in Bulawayo. Laisenia Qarase was sworn in as the new prime minister of Fiji; he had been appointed interim prime minister following the 2000 coup. **11.** In the USA, two hijacked passenger airlines crashed into the twin towers of New York's World Trade Centre, causing both towers to collapse with the loss of thousands of lives. Minutes later, a third hijacked aircraft crashed into the Pentagon. A fourth, believed to be heading for the presidential retreat Camp David, crashed near Pittsburgh. The USA sealed its border and cleared its airspace of all but military aircraft. **12.** NATO declared that the terrorist suicide attacks on the USA were an assault on the entire alliance. The terrorist leader Osama bin Laden congratulated those responsible for the terrorist attacks in America, but denied involvement. **13.** President Bush announced that the USA was at war; senior government figures said that the response would be sophisticated, bloody and without mercy. The UN Security Council approved a unanimous resolution that recognised terrorism as a threat to international peace and security. NATO declared that it had collected more than two thirds of the declared NLA arsenal under the Macedonian peace plan. **14.** The FBI named nineteen men, including seven trained pilots, as being responsible for hijacking the four US airliners. The World Trade Organisation and China reached agreement on the terms of China's membership. **15.** President Bush called on the armed forces to prepare to crush the al-Qa'eda terrorist network run by Osama bin Laden who was based in Afghanistan. **16.** In Pakistan, Gen. Musharraf met religious figures, political party bosses and newspaper editors in an effort to justify his support for the USA. **23.** The Polish general election was won by the Coalition of the Alliance of the Democratic Left and the Union of Labour, who obtained 219 seats; the Solidarity Electoral Alliance, who had formed the previous government, failed to obtain the 7 per cent of the vote necessary to enter parliament. In France, following an election to the Senate, the state of the parties was RPR 83; PS 68; UDC 37; RI 35; RDE 16; PCF 16, Independents 65.

OBITUARIES – September 2001

Barnard, Christian, South African surgeon, 78, *d.* 2 September 2001, *b.* 8 November 1922

Bullus, Sir Eric, Wg Cdr., journalist and Conservative MP for Wembley North 1950–73; Parliamentary Private Secretary to the Minister of State for Overseas Trade 1953–56; Parliamentary Private Secretary to the Minister of Aviation 1960–62, Parliamentary Private Secretary to the Secretary of State for Defence 1962–64, 94, *d.* 31 August 2001, *b.* 20 November 1906

Fraser, Air Marshal the Rev Sir Paterson, KBE, CB, AFC, Inspector General RAF 1962–64, 94, *d.* 4 August 2001, *b.* 15 July 1907

Lord Cato, chairman of Morgan Grenfell 1973–87 and board member of News International 1969–96, 78, *d.* 3 September 2001, *b.* 14 January 1923

Lord Hamlyn, CBE, German born publisher of Spring and Hamlyn books 1960–87, philanthropist, 75, *d.* 31 August 2001, *b.* 12 February 1926

Lord Shaw of Stepney, PC, Secretary of State for Economic Affairs 1967–70, 77, *d.* 24 September 2001, *b.* 24 May 1924

Moore, Brian, sports broadcaster, 69, *d.* 1 September 2001, *b.* 28 February 1932

Peréz, Marcos, president of Venezuela 1952–58, 87, *d.* 20 September 2001, *b.* 1914

Sarell, Sir Roderick, KCMG, KCVO, ambassador to Libya 1964–69; and to Turkey 1969–73, 88, *d.* 15 August 2001, *b.* 23 January 1913

Stern, Issac, Ukrainian violinist, 81, *d.* 22 September 2001, *b.* 21 July 1920